CHEERS FOR THE COMPLETE BOOK OF THE OLYMPICS

1996 Edition

Sports Illustrated *presents* *THE*
COMPLETE
BOOK OF THE
SUMMER
OLYMPICS

DAVID WALLECHINSKY

Little, Brown and Company

Boston   New York   Toronto   London

TO ELIJAH AND AARON

First Edition

HC: 10 9 8 7 6 5 4 3 2 1
PB: 10 9 8 7 6 5 4 3 2

FG

Published simultaneously in Canada
by Little, Brown & Company (Canada) Limited

Printed in the United States of America

Library of Congress Cataloging-in-Publication Data

Wallechinsky, David.
  Sports Illustrated presents the complete book of the Summer Olympics / David Wallechinsky.—1996 ed., 1st ed.
      p. cm.
    Rev. ed. of: The complete book of the Olympics. 1992 ed. 1992.
      ISBN 0-316-92093-2(HC)—ISBN 0-316-92094-0(PB) (alk. paper)
    1. Olympics—History. 2. Olympics—Records.   I. Wallechinsky, David.   Complete book of the Olympics. II. Title.
    GV721.5.W25   1996
    796.48—dc20   95-46267

PHOTO CREDITS

Pages 6, 10, U.S.O.C.; 14, Inter-Sport Publicity; 15, Swiss Timing; 21, Reportagebild, AP/Wide World Photos; 23, Popperfoto; 24, 25, 27, U.S.O.C.; 32, AP/Wide World Photos; 36, 44, U.S.O.C.; 46, *Herald Weekly Times,* Ltd., Melbourne Pictures; 47, 48, AP/Wide World Photos; 49, Popperfoto; 52, 53, 54, U.S.O.C.; 61, Popperfoto; 63, AP/Wide World Photos; 64, UPI; 70, 71, Missouri Historical Society; 74, U.S.O.C.; 79, UPI; 80, Mark Shearman; 82, AP/Wide World Photos; 85, Popperfoto; 89, 90, U.S.O.C.; 95, Pelham Books; 96, Popperfoto; 97, Pressen Bild; 103, Eddie Keogh/TODAY NEWS-PAPER; 105, Pressebild-Agentur Schirner; 109, U.S.O.C., Pressen Bild; 110, AP/Wide World Photos; 112, J. Fairfax & Sons, Ltd.; 118, Pelham Books; 120, Toni Nett; 126, U.S.O.C.; 128, Reportagebild; 132 (left), University of Michigan Archives; 133, U.S.O.C., Brown Brothers; 135, UPI; 136, U.S.O.C.; 139, Courtesy of Erich Kamper; 143, Progress Publishers/Moscow; 145, 151, 168, 169 (left), U.S.O.C.; 169 (right), Courtesy of Bob Mathias; 173, Pressebild-Agentur Schirner; 174, 175, Pressen Bild; 181, 182, 189, 190, 191, U.S.O.C.; 194, AP/Wide World Photos; 199, Pressen Bild; 206, Agence France-Presse; 207 (left), Paul Chinn/*L.A. Herald Examiner;* 207 (right), Copyright Andrew Kent 85; 209, U.S.O.C.; 215, Keystone Press Agency; 217, Ken Geiger/*The Dallas Morning News;* 219, Canada's Sports Hall of Fame; 220, The Alice Coachman Track & Field Foundation; 226, U.S.O.C.; 230, Lia Manoliu; 234, U.S.O.C.; 236, Frederick Fliegner Publ.; 242 (left and upper right), Rick Clarkson/*Sports Illustrated,* Copyright Time Inc.; 242 (lower right), Szwarc Photo-Sport; 261, U.S.O.C.; 264, 268, AP/Wide World Photos; 270, Olympische Sports Bibliotek; 282 (upper left and right), U.S.O.C.; 282 (lower left), 283, AP/Wide World Photos; 295, Hungarian Olympic Committee; 297, David Wallechinsky; 300, AP/Wide World Photos; 302, 304, U.S.O.C.; 321, Gerry Cranham of Sporting Colour Library; 341, VMS Publications; 348, Reportagebild; 351, Michael Porte; 354, The Henning Library/International Swimming Hall of Fame; 356, Copyright Kishimoto/Live Action; 359, Pressen Bild; 391, Erik Betting/Pressehusel; 419, Melbourne *Herald and Weekly Times;* 495, U.S.O.C.; 499, Proteus Books, Ltd.; 530, Photo Kishimoto, Japan; 536, 547, U.S.O.C.; 557, Christo/Fairfax Photo Library; 583, Canada's Sports Hall of Fame; 613, Courtesy of The Academy of Motion Pictures Arts & Sciences; 615 (left), U.S.O.C.; 615 (right), UPI; 616, 621, U.S.O.C.; 623, Sportverlag Berlin; 624, Hungarian Olympic Committee; 633, Fizkultura Isdalesvo, Mosco; 654, The Henning Library/International Swimming Hall of Fame; 656, U.S.O.C.; 657, Reprinted by permission of Coward, McCann & Geoghegan, Inc., from *The Miracle Machine,* by Doug Gilbert, Copyright 1980 by P.L.T. Consultants, Ltd.; 685, AP/Wide World Photos; 694, Hulton-Deutsch Collection; 726, from the David Webster Collection; 733, Xinhua Photo; 734, David Woo/*The Dallas Morning News;* 737, U.S.O.C.; 760, from the David Webster Collection; 765, Progress Publishers; 789, Frederik Fliegner; 804, 811, AP/Wide World Photos; 816, Pressebild-Agentur Schirner; 838, Athanassios Tarassouleas.

CONTENTS

THE OLYMPIC GAMES

				COMPETITORS		NATIONS	
				Men	Women	REPRESENTED	EVENTS
I	1896	ATHENS, GREECE	April 6–15	245	0	14	43
II	1900	PARIS, FRANCE	May 20–October 28	1206	19	26	87
III	1904	ST. LOUIS, U.S.A.	July 1–November 23	681	6	13	94
—	1906	ATHENS, GREECE	April 22–May 2	877	7	20	78
IV	1908	LONDON, GREAT BRITAIN	April 27–October 31	1999	36	22	109
V	1912	STOCKHOLM, SWEDEN	May 5–July 22	2490	57	28	102
VI	1916	BERLIN, GERMANY	Cancelled because of war	—	—	—	—
VII	1920	ANTWERP, BELGIUM	April 20–September 12	2591	78	29	154
VIII	1924	PARIS, FRANCE	May 4–July 27	2956	136	44	126
IX	1928	AMSTERDAM, HOLLAND	May 17–August 12	2724	290	46	109
X	1932	LOS ANGELES, U.S.A.	July 30–August 14	1281	127	37	116
XI	1936	BERLIN, GERMANY	August 1–16	3738	328	49	129
XII	1940	TOKYO, JAPAN; HELSINKI, FIN-LAND	Cancelled because of war	—	—	—	—
XIII	1944	LONDON, GREAT BRITAIN	Cancelled because of war	—	—	—	—
XIV	1948	LONDON, GREAT BRITAIN	July 29–August 14	3714	385	59	136
XV	1952	HELSINKI, FINLAND	July 19–August 3	4407	518	69	149
XVI	1956	MELBOURNE, AUSTRALIA[1]	November 22–December 8	2958	384	72	151
XVII	1960	ROME, ITALY	August 25–September 11	4738	610	83	150
XVIII	1964	TOKYO, JAPAN	October 10–24	4457	683	93	163
XIX	1968	MEXICO CITY, MEXICO	October 12–27	4750	781	112	172
XX	1972	MUNICH, GERMANY	August 26–September 10	6065	1058	121	195
XXI	1976	MONTREAL, CANADA	July 17–August 1	4781	1247	92[2]	198
XXII	1980	MOSCOW, U.S.S.R.	July 19–August 3	4092	1125	80[3]	203
XXIII	1984	LOS ANGELES, U.S.A.	July 28–August 12	5230	1567	140	221
XXIV	1988	SEOUL, SOUTH KOREA	September 17–October 2	6279	2186	159[4]	237
XXV	1992	BARCELONA, SPAIN	July 24[5]–August 9	6659	2708	169	257
XXVI	1996	ATLANTA, U.S.A.	July 19–August 4				271
XXVII	2000	SYDNEY, AUSTRALIA	September 15–October 1				

[1]The equestrian events were held in Stockholm, Sweden, June 10–17, 1956.
[2]Some sources list this figure as 88. Cameroon, Egypt, Morocco, and Tunisia all boycotted the 1976 Olympics; however, athletes from each of these countries had already competed before the boycott was officially announced.
[3]Some sources list this figure as 81. Liberia entered seven athletes, but none of them competed.
[4]Some sources list this figure as 160. However, the delegation from Brunei, which marched in the Opening Ceremony, included one official, but no athletes.
[5]One soccer match, between Italy and the United States, took place on July 24, the day before the Opening Ceremony.

NATIONAL MEDAL TOTALS IN EACH OLYMPICS

The International Olympic Committee does not officially recognize national medal totals. However, these totals are frequently included in Official Reports, and during the Olympic Games, they are often displayed on huge screens in the Main Press Center and are updated on a continuous basis for the benefit of the press and the public.

The awarding of gold medals for first place, silver medals for second place, and bronze medals for third place began in 1904. In the charts for 1896 and 1900, G, S, and B are used to indicate first, second, and third. Precise totals by nation for 1896–1906 are difficult to determine because until 1908 athletes entered the Olympics as indi-

viduals rather than as selected members of a national team. In addition, athletes from different nations sometimes joined forces in team sports, including tennis doubles. In the following charts, combined teams are listed as "COM." However, the combined East and West German teams of 1956–1964 are presented in these charts as a single team, although in the rest of the book individuals from each nation are identified as East or West Germans. Koreans who in 1936 were forced to compete for Japan, Irish who competed for Great Britain, and so forth are listed in the following charts under the team for which they were officially entered.

1896 Athens

	G	S	B*
USA	11	7	1
GRE	10	17	22
GER	7	5	4
FRA	5	4	2
GBR	3	3	3
HUN	2	1	4
AUT	2	1	2
AUS	2	0	1
DEN	1	2	3
SWI	1	2	0
EGY	0	2	0
COM	1	1	1

*G = gold, S = silver, B = bronze.

1900 Paris

	G	S	B
FRA	26	39	30
USA	20	17	16
GBR	18	8	12
SWI	6	1	1
BEL	5	5	5

	G	S	B
GER	3	2	2
DEN	2	3	2
ITA	2	2	0
AUS	2	0	4
HUN	1	2	2
HOL	1	1	4
CUB	1	1	0
CAN	1	0	1
SWE	1	0	1
LUX	1	0	0
AUT	0	3	3
NOR	0	2	3
IND	0	2	0
BOH	0	1	2
COM	2	3	4

1904 St. Louis

	G	S	B
USA	78	84	82
GER	4	4	4
CAN	4	1	1
CUB	3	0	0
HUN	2	1	1
AUT	1	1	1
GBR	1	1	0

	G	S	B
GRE	1	0	1
SWI	1	0	2
FRA	0	1	0
COM	1	0	0

1906 Athens

	G	S	B
FRA	15	9	16
USA	12	6	5
GRE	8	13	12
GBR	8	11	5
ITA	7	6	3
SWI	5	6	4
GER	4	6	5
NOR	4	2	1
AUT	3	3	2
DEN	3	2	1
SWE	2	5	7
HUN	2	5	3
BEL	2	1	3
FIN	2	1	1
CAN	1	1	0
HOL	0	1	2

	G	S	B
AUS	0	0	3
BOH	0	0	2
COM	0	2	1

1908 London

	G	S	B
GBR	56	51	39
USA	23	12	12
SWE	8	6	11
FRA	5	5	9
GER	3	5	5
HUN	3	4	2
CAN	3	3	10
NOR	2	3	3
ITA	2	2	0
BEL	1	5	2
AUS	1	2	1
RUS	1	2	0
FIN	1	1	3
SAF	1	1	0
GRE	0	3	1
DEN	0	2	3
BOH	0	0	2
HOL	0	0	2
AUT	0	0	1
NZE	0	0	1

1912 Stockholm

	G	S	B
USA	25	18	20
SWE	23	24	17
GBR	10	15	16
FIN	9	8	9
FRA	7	4	3
GER	5	13	7
SAF	4	2	0
NOR	3	2	5
HUN	3	2	3
CAN	3	2	2
ITA	3	1	2
BEL	2	1	3
DEN	1	6	5
AUS	1	2	2
GRE	1	0	1
RUS	0	2	3
AUT	0	2	2
HOL	0	0	3
NZE	0	0	1
COM	1	0	0

1920 Antwerp

	G	S	B
USA	41	27	27
SWE	19	20	25
FIN	15	10	9
GBR	14	15	13
BEL	13	11	11
NOR	13	9	9
ITA	13	5	5
FRA	9	19	13
HOL	4	2	5
DEN	3	9	1
SAF	3	4	3
CAN	3	3	3
SWI	2	2	7
EST	1	2	0
BRA	1	1	1
AUS	0	2	1
JPN	0	2	0
SPA	0	2	0
GRE	0	1	0
LUX	0	1	0
CZE	0	0	2
NZE	0	0	1

1924 Paris

	G	S	B
USA	45	27	27
FIN	14	13	10
FRA	13	15	10
GBR	9	13	12
ITA	8	3	5
SWI	7	8	10
NOR	5	2	3
SWE	4	13	12
HOL	4	1	5
BEL	3	7	3
AUS	3	1	2
DEN	2	5	2
HUN	2	3	4
YUG	2	0	0
CZE	1	4	5
ARG	1	3	2
EST	1	1	4
SAF	1	1	1
URU	1	0	0
AUT	0	3	1
CAN	0	3	1
POL	0	1	1
HAI	0	0	1
JPN	0	0	1
NZE	0	0	1
POR	0	0	1
ROM	0	0	1

1928 Amsterdam

	G	S	B
USA	22	18	16
GER	10	7	14
FIN	8	8	9
SWE	7	6	12
ITA	7	5	7
SWI	7	4	4
FRA	6	10	5
HOL	6	9	4
HUN	4	5	0
CAN	4	4	7
GBR	3	10	7
ARG	3	3	1
DEN	3	1	2
CZE	2	5	2
JPN	2	2	1
EST	2	1	2
EGY	2	1	1
AUT	2	0	1
AUS	1	2	1
NOR	1	2	1
POL	1	1	3
YUG	1	1	3
SAF	1	0	2
IND	1	0	0
IRL	1	0	0
NZE	1	0	0
SPA	1	0	0
URU	1	0	0
BEL	0	1	2
CHI	0	1	0
HAI	0	1	0
PHI	0	0	1
POR	0	0	1

1932 Los Angeles

	G	S	B
USA	41	32	30
ITA	12	12	12
FRA	10	5	4
SWE	9	5	9
JPN	7	7	4
HUN	6	4	5
FIN	5	8	12
GBR	4	7	5
GER	3	12	5
AUS	3	1	1
ARG	3	1	0
CAN	2	5	8
HOL	2	5	0
POL	2	1	4
SAF	2	0	3
IRL	2	0	0
CZE	1	2	1
AUT	1	1	3
IND	1	0	0
DEN	0	3	3
MEX	0	2	0
LAT	0	1	0
NZE	0	1	0
SWI	0	1	0
PHI	0	0	3
SPA	0	0	1
URU	0	0	1

1936 Berlin

	G	S	B
GER	33	26	30
USA	24	20	12
HUN	10	1	5
ITA	8	9	5
FIN	7	6	6
FRA	7	6	6
SWE	6	5	5
JPN	6	4	8
HOL	6	4	7
GBR	4	7	3
AUT	4	6	3
CZE	3	5	0
ARG	2	2	3
EST	2	2	3
EGY	2	1	2
SWI	1	9	5
CAN	1	3	5
NOR	1	3	2
TUR	1	0	1
IND	1	0	0
NZE	1	0	0
POL	0	3	3
DEN	0	2	3
LAT	0	1	1
ROM	0	1	0
SAF	0	1	0
YUG	0	1	0
MEX	0	0	3
BEL	0	0	2
AUS	0	0	1
PHI	0	0	1
POR	0	0	1

1948 London

	G	S	B
USA	38	27	19
SWE	16	11	17
FRA	10	6	13
HUN	10	5	12
ITA	8	12	9
FIN	8	7	5
TUR	6	4	2
CZE	6	2	3
SWI	5	10	5
DEN	5	7	8
HOL	5	2	9

	G	S	B
GBR	3	14	6
ARG	3	3	1
AUS	2	6	5
BEL	2	2	3
EGY	2	2	1
MEX	2	1	2
SAF	2	1	1
NOR	1	3	3
JAM	1	2	0
AUT	1	0	3
IND	1	0	0
PER	1	0	0
YUG	0	2	0
CAN	0	1	2
POR	0	1	1
URU	0	1	1
CUB	0	1	0
SPA	0	1	0
TRI	0	1	0
SRL	0	1	0
KOR	0	0	2
PAN	0	0	2
BRA	0	0	1
IRN	0	0	1
POL	0	0	1
PUR	0	0	1
ARG	1	2	2
POL	1	2	1
CAN	1	2	0
YUG	1	2	0
ROM	1	1	2
BRA	1	0	2
NZE	1	0	2
IND	1	0	1
LUX	1	0	0
GER	0	7	17
HOL	0	5	0
IRN	0	3	4
CHI	0	2	0
AUT	0	1	1
LEB	0	1	1
IRL	0	1	0
MEX	0	1	0
SPA	0	1	0
KOR	0	0	2
URU	0	0	2
TRI	0	0	2
BUL	0	0	1
EGY	0	0	1
POR	0	0	1
VEN	0	0	1

1952 Helsinki

	G	S	B
USA	40	19	17
SOV	22	30	19
HUN	16	10	16
SWE	12	13	10
ITA	8	9	4
CZE	7	3	3
FRA	6	6	6
FIN	6	3	13
AUS	6	2	3
NOR	3	2	0
SWI	2	6	6
SAF	2	4	4
JAM	2	3	0
BEL	2	2	0
DEN	2	1	3
TUR	2	0	1
JPN	1	6	2
GBR	1	2	8

1956 Melbourne

	G	S	B
SOV	37	29	32
USA	32	25	17
AUS	13	8	14
HUN	9	10	7
ITA	8	8	9
SWE	8	5	6
GER	7	13	7
GBR	6	7	11
ROM	5	3	5
JPN	4	10	5
FRA	4	4	6
TUR	3	2	2
FIN	3	1	11
IRN	2	2	1
CAN	2	1	3
NZE	2	0	0
POL	1	4	4
CZE	1	4	1
BUL	1	3	1
DEN	1	2	1
IRL	1	1	3
NOR	1	0	2
MEX	1	0	1
BRA	1	0	0
IND	1	0	0
YUG	0	3	0
CHI	0	2	2
BEL	0	2	0
ARG	0	1	1
KOR	0	1	1
ICE	0	1	0
PAK	0	1	0
SAF	0	0	4
AUT	0	0	2
BAH	0	0	1
GRE	0	0	1
SWI	0	0	1
URU	0	0	1

1960 Rome

	G	S	B
SOV	43	29	31
USA	34	21	16
ITA	13	10	13
GER	12	19	11
AUS	8	8	6
TUR	7	2	0
HUN	6	8	7
JPN	4	7	7
POL	4	6	11
CZE	3	2	3
ROM	3	1	6
GBR	2	6	12
DEN	2	3	1
NZE	2	0	1
BUL	1	3	3
SWE	1	2	3
FIN	1	1	3
AUT	1	1	0
YUG	1	1	0
PAK	1	0	1
ETH	1	0	0
GRE	1	0	0
NOR	1	0	0
SWI	0	3	3
FRA	0	2	3
BEL	0	2	2
IRN	0	1	3
HOL	0	1	2
SAF	0	1	1
ARG	0	1	1
EGY	0	1	1
CAN	0	1	0
GHA	0	1	0
IND	0	1	0
MOR	0	1	0
POR	0	1	0
SIN	0	1	0
TAI	0	1	0
BRA	0	0	2
BWI	0	0	2
IRQ	0	0	1
MEX	0	0	1
SPA	0	0	1
VEN	0	0	1

1964 Tokyo

	G	S	B
USA	36	26	28
SOV	30	31	35
JPN	16	5	8
GER	10	22	8
ITA	10	10	7
HUN	10	7	5
POL	7	6	10
AUS	6	2	10
CZE	5	6	3
GBR	4	12	2
BUL	3	5	2
FIN	3	0	2
NZE	3	0	2
ROM	2	4	6
HOL	2	4	4
TUR	2	3	1
SWE	2	2	4
DEN	2	1	3
YUG	2	1	2
BEL	2	0	1
FRA	1	8	6
CAN	1	2	1
SWI	1	2	1
BAH	1	0	0
ETH	1	0	0

IND	1	0	0
KOR	0	2	1
TRI	0	1	2
TUN	0	1	1
ARG	0	1	0
CUB	0	1	0
PAK	0	1	0
PHI	0	1	0
IRN	0	0	2
BRA	0	0	1
GHA	0	0	1
IRL	0	0	1
KEN	0	0	1
MEX	0	0	1
NGR	0	0	1
URU	0	0	1

PAK	1	0	0
VEN	1	0	0
CUB	0	4	0
AUT	0	2	2
SWI	0	1	4
MON	0	1	3
BRA	0	1	2
BEL	0	1	1
KOR	0	1	1
UGA	0	1	1
CAM	0	1	0
JAM	0	1	0
ARG	0	0	2
GRE	0	0	1
IND	0	0	1
TAI	0	0	1

BEL	0	2	0
GRE	0	2	0
AUT	0	1	2
COL	0	1	2
ARG	0	1	0
KOR	0	1	0
LEB	0	1	0
MEX	0	1	0
MON	0	1	0
PAK	0	1	0
TUN	0	1	0
TUR	0	1	0
BRA	0	0	2
ETH	0	0	2
GHA	0	0	1
IND	0	0	1
JAM	0	0	1
NIG	0	0	1
NGR	0	0	1
SPA	0	0	1

MEX	1	0	1
TRI	1	0	0
CAN	0	5	6
BEL	0	3	3
HOL	0	2	3
POR	0	2	0
SPA	0	2	0
AUS	0	1	4
IRN	0	1	1
MON	0	1	0
VEN	0	1	0
BRA	0	0	2
AUT	0	0	1
BER	0	0	1
PAK	0	0	1
PUR	0	0	1
THA	0	0	1

1968 Mexico City

	G	S	B
USA	45	28	34
SOV	29	32	30
JPN	11	7	7
HUN	10	10	12
GDR	9	9	7
FRA	7	3	5
CZE	7	2	4
GER	5	11	10
AUS	5	7	5
GBR	5	5	3
POL	5	2	11
ROM	4	6	5
ITA	3	4	9
KEN	3	4	2
MEX	3	3	3
YUG	3	3	2
HOL	3	3	1
BUL	2	4	3
IRN	2	1	2
SWE	2	1	1
TUR	2	0	0
DEN	1	4	3
CAN	1	3	1
FIN	1	2	1
ETH	1	1	0
NOR	1	1	0
NZE	1	0	2
TUN	1	0	1

1972 Munich

	G	S	B
SOV	50	27	22
USA	33	31	30
GDR	20	23	23
GER	13	11	16
JPN	13	8	8
AUS	8	7	2
POL	7	5	9
HUN	6	13	16
BUL	6	10	5
ITA	5	3	10
SWE	4	6	6
GBR	4	5	9
ROM	3	6	7
FIN	3	1	4
CUB	3	1	4
HOL	3	1	1
FRA	2	4	7
CZE	2	4	2
KEN	2	3	4
YUG	2	1	2
NOR	2	1	1
PRK	1	1	3
NZE	1	1	1
UGA	1	1	0
DEN	1	0	0
SWI	0	3	0
CAN	0	2	3
IRN	0	2	1

1976 Montreal

	G	S	B
SOV	49	41	35
GDR	40	25	25
USA	34	35	25
GER	10	12	17
JPN	9	6	10
POL	7	6	13
BUL	6	9	7
CUB	6	4	3
ROM	4	9	14
HUN	4	5	13
FIN	4	2	0
SWE	4	1	0
GBR	3	5	5
ITA	2	7	4
FRA	2	3	4
YUG	2	3	3
CZE	2	2	4
NZE	2	1	1
KOR	1	1	4
SWI	1	1	2
JAM	1	1	0
NOR	1	1	0
PRK	1	1	0
DEN	1	0	2

1980 Moscow

	G	S	B
SOV	80	69	46
GDR	47	37	42
BUL	8	16	17
CUB	8	7	5
ITA	8	3	4
HUN	7	10	15
ROM	6	6	13
FRA	6	5	3
GBR	5	7	9
POL	3	14	15
SWE	3	3	6
FIN	3	1	4
CZE	2	3	9
YUG	2	3	4
AUS	2	2	5
DEN	2	1	2
BRA	2	0	2
ETH	2	0	2
SWI	2	0	0
SPA	1	3	2
AUT	1	2	1
GRE	1	0	2
BEL	1	0	0
IND	1	0	0
ZIM	1	0	0
PRK	0	3	2
MON	0	2	2

	G	S	B
TAN	0	2	0
MEX	0	1	3
HOL	0	1	2
IRL	0	1	1
UGA	0	1	0
VEN	0	1	0
JAM	0	0	3
GUY	0	0	1
LEB	0	0	1

1984 Los Angeles

	G	S	B
USA	83	61	30
ROM	20	16	17
GER	17	19	23
CHN	15	8	9
ITA	14	6	12
CAN	10	18	16
JPN	10	8	14
NZE	8	1	2
YUG	7	4	7
KOR	6	6	7
GBR	5	10	22
FRA	5	7	16
HOL	5	2	6
AUS	4	8	12
FIN	4	2	6
SWE	2	11	6
MEX	2	3	1
MOR	2	0	0
BRA	1	5	2
SPA	1	2	2
BEL	1	1	2
AUT	1	1	1
KEN	1	0	2
POR	1	0	2
PAK	1	0	0
SWI	0	4	4
DEN	0	3	3
JAM	0	1	2
NOR	0	1	2
GRE	0	1	1
NGR	0	1	1
PUR	0	1	1
COL	0	1	0
EGY	0	1	0
IRL	0	1	0
IVC	0	1	0
PER	0	1	0
SYR	0	1	0
THA	0	1	0
TUR	0	0	3
VEN	0	0	3
ALG	0	0	2
CAM	0	0	1
DOM	0	0	1
ICE	0	0	1
TAI	0	0	1
ZAM	0	0	1

1988 Seoul

	G	S	B
SOV	55	31	46
GDR	37	35	30
USA	36	31	27
KOR	12	10	11
GER	11	14	15
HUN	11	6	6
BUL	10	12	13
ROM	7	11	6
FRA	6	4	6
ITA	6	4	4
CHN	5	11	12
GBR	5	10	9
KEN	5	2	2
JPN	4	3	7
AUS	3	6	5
YUG	3	4	5
CZE	3	3	2
NZE	3	2	8
CAN	3	2	5
POL	2	5	9
NOR	2	3	0
HOL	2	2	5
DEN	2	1	1
BRA	1	2	3
FIN	1	1	2
SPA	1	1	2
TUR	1	1	0
MOR	1	0	2
AUT	1	0	0
POR	1	0	0
SUR	1	0	0
SWE	0	4	7
SWI	0	2	2
JAM	0	2	0
ARG	0	1	1
CHI	0	1	0
CRC	0	1	0
INA	0	1	0
IRN	0	1	0
NLA	0	1	0
PER	0	1	0
SEN	0	1	0
VIR	0	1	0
BEL	0	0	2
MEX	0	0	2
COL	0	0	1
DJI	0	0	1
GRE	0	0	1
MON	0	0	1
PAK	0	0	1
PHI	0	0	1
THA	0	0	1

1992 Barcelona

	G	S	B
SOV	45	38	28
USA	37	34	37
GER	33	21	28
CHN	16	22	16
CUB	14	6	11
SPA	13	7	2
KOR	12	5	12
HUN	11	12	7
FRA	8	5	16
AUS	7	9	11
ITA	6	5	8
CAN	6	5	7
GBR	5	3	12
ROM	4	6	8
CZE	4	2	1
PRK	4	0	5
JPN	3	8	11
BUL	3	7	6
POL	3	6	10
HOL	2	6	7
KEN	2	4	2
NOR	2	4	1
TUR	2	2	2
INA	2	2	1
BRA	2	1	0
GRE	2	0	0
SWE	1	7	4
NZE	1	4	5
FIN	1	2	2
DEN	1	1	4
MOR	1	1	2
IRL	1	1	0
ETH	1	0	2
ALG	1	0	1
EST	1	0	1
LIT	1	0	1
SWI	1	0	0
JAM	0	3	1
NGR	0	3	1
LAT	0	2	1
AUT	0	2	0
NAM	0	2	0
SAF	0	2	0
BEL	0	1	2
CRO	0	1	2
IRN	0	1	2
YUG	0	1	2
ISR	0	1	1
MEX	0	1	0
PER	0	1	0
TAI	0	1	0
MGL	0	0	2
SLO	0	0	2
ARG	0	0	1
BAH	0	0	1
COL	0	0	1
GHA	0	0	1
MAL	0	0	1
PAK	0	0	1
PHI	0	0	1
PUR	0	0	1
QAT	0	0	1
SUR	0	0	1
THA	0	0	1

A BRIEF HISTORY OF THE MODERN OLYMPICS

The ancient Olympic Games were held in Olympia, Greece, every four years from at least 776 B.C., until they were banned by Emperor Theodosius in 393 A.D. Originally there was only one race, a sprint, and the prize for the winner was an olive wreath. As time went on, other races were added, as were other sports, including boxing and wrestling. Among the more unusual events were the race in armor and the apene race, in which a chariot was pulled not by horses, but by two mules. Prizes became more elaborate, and there were even cases of bribery, corruption and boycotts.

Inspired by the original, uncorrupted Olympics, Baron Pierre de Coubertin of France conceived the modern Olympic Games. He proposed the idea publicly for the first time in 1892 and then spent the next three and a half years drumming up support. Interest was strongest in Greece, so it was decided to hold the first Olympics in Athens.

The **1896** Athens Games were funded by a gift from wealthy architect Georgios Averoff of one million drachma, and by the sale of souvenir stamps and medals. Although the quality of the athletes' performances was only mediocre, the Games were a huge success. The enthusiasm and good sportsmanship of the Greek spectators were rewarded when the highlight event, the marathon, was won by a Greek peasant, Spiridon Louis.

The second Olympic Games were held in de Coubertin's hometown of Paris in **1900,** but they turned out to be a failure. Reduced to a mere appendage to the World Exhibition of that year, the events of the Olympics were spread out over five months. Poor organization and poor attendance made things worse; some of the athletes were actually unaware that the meet they had taken part in was the Olympics.

De Coubertin had high hopes for the **1904** Games, which were scheduled for Chicago because Americans had shown such great enthusiasm for the first two Olympics. However, a dispute broke out between Chicago and St. Louis, which wanted the Games to be held as part of the Louisiana Purchase Exhibition. President Theodore Roosevelt eventually sided with St. Louis, and the Games were moved. This change proved to be an awful mistake, as the St. Louis organizers turned out to be even

less competent than the Paris organizers. Most European nations skipped the Games, and not even Baron de Coubertin bothered to attend. Events were spread out over four and a half months, and some included only U.S. athletes.

After two straight disasters the Olympic movement might have died had it not been for the Intercalated (or Interim) Games of **1906.** After the success of the 1896 Games, the Greeks had hoped to hold their own international games every four years between Olympics. However the proposed Games of 1898 had to be cancelled because of political and economic upheaval, and the 1902 Games weren't even considered. By 1906, though, the Greeks were ready to try again. Although de Coubertin opposed the Intercalated Games, they were quite successful and actually helped save the Olympic movement. These Games are considered unofficial by the International Olympic Committee (I.O.C.).

The **1908** Games had been planned for Rome, but the Italians backed out for financial reasons, and the Games were then awarded to London. Most of the events were held in Shepherd's Bush Stadium, which included a cycle track, a running track, a soccer field, a swimming pool, and a platform for wrestling and gymnastics. The London Games were basically well organized and produced the first comprehensive Official Report. There were, however, numerous disputes. The Russians tried to prevent the Finns from displaying the Finnish flag, and the English did the same to the Irish. The competitions were run entirely by the British, which led to protests over the rules by representatives of France, Canada, Italy, Sweden, and, especially, the United States. The bickering between Great Britain and its cheeky former colony was so acute that it almost put an end to the Olympics.

Fortunately, the **1912** Olympics were held in Stockholm. Well-organized, the Stockholm Games saw the first use of electronic timing devices and a public address system. The Swedes refused to allow boxing matches to be held in their country, which led the I.O.C. to pass a rule limiting the power of local organizing committees in future Olympics. The success of the 1912 Games helped the Olympic movement survive the interruption that came to be known as World War I. In ancient times, all wars were suspended to allow safe passage for Olympic athletes. In modern times, this truce has not been honored. Scheduled for Berlin, the **1916** Olympics were cancelled.

The **1920** Games were awarded to Antwerp, Belgium, as compensation for all the grief that had been inflicted on the Belgians during the war. The losers of World War I, Austria, Bulgaria, Germany, Hungary, and Turkey, were not allowed to participate. With little money available to run the Games, the 1920 Olympics were not very impressive and were not well documented. An Official Report does not exist for 1920—only a typed manuscript containing an incomplete listing of the results.

Much to the delight of Baron de Coubertin, Paris was given a second chance to host the Olympics in **1924,** which also saw the staging of the first Winter Olympics in Chamonix, France. The second Paris Games were well attended, with athletes from 44 nations taking part, as opposed to the previous record of 29. Competition was of a very high standard. However, the fanaticism of Parisian sports fans led to several outrages, including booing during the playing of national anthems of other countries and numerous incidents during the boxing and fencing tournaments. The French, who never had a very high opinion of their neighbors, were particularly irritated by the Americans, since the U.S. government had only recently criticized the French occupation of the Ruhr. During a rugby match between France and the United States, an American art student was severely caned by an incensed French spectator who had become annoyed by the loud U.S. "rooting."

In Europe and North America countless editorials were written calling for an end to the Olympics, but the next Games were held on schedule in Amsterdam in **1928**, with Germany taking part for the first time since 1912. The boxing tournament was once again disrupted by protests, but for the most part, the Amsterdam Games were a success. For the first time track and field events for women were included in the program, although women had previously taken part in tennis, golf, archery, figure skating, yachting, swimming, and fencing.

The **1932** Los Angeles Olympics faced two major obstacles: the Depression and the geographical isolation of California. Participation was the lowest since 1906, although the level of competition was excellent. Only three teams took part in the field hockey tournament, and football (soccer) had to be dropped completely. All of the male athletes lived in a makeshift Olympic Village in Baldwin Hills, while the women stayed in a hotel on Wilshire Boulevard. Although the United States was in the midst of Prohibition, an exception was made for the French and the Italians, who claimed that wine was an essential component of their diet. The 1932 Olympics saw the introduction of automatic timing and the photo-finish camera, as well as the first use of a victory platform for award ceremonies and the playing of national anthems to honor winners.

In 1931, when Berlin was chosen as the site for the **1936** Olympics, few people suspected that a mere two years would see the rise to power of Adolf Hitler and the Nazi Party. Jews in various countries asked for a boycott of the Berlin Olympics, and in the United States a boycott proposal was only narrowly defeated. An alternative People's Olympics was scheduled to take place in Barcelona, Spain, but it was cancelled at the last minute when the Spanish Civil War broke out the day before competition was set to begin. The 1936 Olympics are best remembered for Hitler's failed attempt to use them to prove his theories of Aryan superiority, but they are also noteworthy because they saw the introduction of the torch relay, in which a lighted torch is carried from Olympia to the site of the current Games. The 1936 Olympics were also the first to be shown on television. Twenty-five large TV screens were set up in theaters throughout Berlin, allowing locals to see the Games for free.

The **1940** Olympics were awarded to Japan—the Winter Games to Sapporo and the Summer Games to Tokyo—but when Japan invaded China and became caught up in a major war, the Olympics were taken away from the Japanese. The Winter Games, rescheduled for Garmisch-Partenkirchen, site of the 1936 Games, were cancelled less than five months before the planned starting date, when Germany invaded Poland to kick off World War II. The Summer Games, reawarded to Helsinki, were cancelled when Soviet troops invaded Finland.

After the war ended, London took on the unenviable task of staging the **1948** Olympics, the first in 12 years. There was much grumbling in England that the project was a waste of money, considering that Britain was still recovering from the war. However, the Games went off well, and interest among Londoners increased rapidly as the competitions progressed. Following the precedent set after World War I, the World War II losers, Germany and Japan, were not invited to participate. A minor incident developed when two swimmers from Northern Ireland were refused permission to compete for the team from Eire (Ireland). The 1948 Olympics also saw the first participation by Communist countries and, with this, the first defections of participants.

The U.S.S.R. joined the Olympics for the first time in Helsinki in **1952.** In the United Nations, the Ukraine and Byelorussia were both treated as independent nations, with full voting privileges. In the Olympics, on the other hand, the Ukraine and Byelorussia were considered part of the U.S.S.R., and Ukrainian and Byelorussian athletes were forced to represent the Soviet Union. Despite fears of a Cold War showdown, Soviet and American athletes in Helsinki were on their best behavior and actually got along quite well. In fact, the 1952 Games were so well run that some observers suggested that the Olympics be held permanently in Scandinavia.

In **1956** the Olympics were staged in the southern hemisphere for the first time. Melbourne, Australia, was so remote from most parts of the world that the number of competitors was the smallest since 1932. Australian quarantine laws caused the equestrian events to be held separately, in Stockholm. The Melbourne Games were stung by two boycotts. Egypt, Iraq, and Lebanon withdrew to protest the Israeli-led takeover of the Suez Canal, and Holland, Spain, and Switzerland boycotted to protest the Soviet invasion of Hungary. Actually, public pressure in Switzerland was so great that the Swiss Olympic Committee changed its mind and voted to participate after all, but by then it was too late to get the entire Swiss team to Australia in time. The I.O.C. scored a political coup by forcing West and East Germany to enter a combined team. This practice continued for the next two Olympics. The 1956 Olympics were also highlighted by an innovation in the Closing Ceremony. Following a suggestion by John Ian Wing, an Australian-born Chinese carpenter's apprentice, it was decided to let all the athletes march together instead of by nation, as a symbol of global unity.

The **1960** Olympics, held beneath the blazing summer sun of Rome, went off without major incident. Like Londoners in 1948, the Romans were fairly blasé at first, but got caught up in the excitement once the Games got going. Even the Pope became a spectator, as he watched the canoeing semifinals from a window of his summer residence. The Rome Olympics were the last in which South Africa was allowed to take part for 32 years, as the I.O.C. bowed to international pressure to punish the South African government for its racist policies.

In 1962 Indonesia hosted the Asian Games in Jakarta. When the Indonesian government refused to allow athletes from Israel and Taiwan to take part, the I.O.C. suspended the Indonesian Olympic Committee until it agreed to abide by the rules of the I.O.C. Indonesia withdrew its team from the **1964** Tokyo Olympics, as did North Korea. With that problem out of the way, the 1964 Olympics proceeded smoothly and efficiently.

The **1968** Mexico City Olympics are best known for the Black Power protests of the U.S. runners Tommie Smith and John Carlos. The year 1968 was a highly politicized one. China was in the throes of the Cultural Revolution, Czechoslovakia's burst of freedom was crushed by Soviet troops, the government of France was almost overthrown by student-led demonstrations, and civil rights and antiwar demonstrations were spreading across the United States. Mexico was by no means immune to such revolutionary activity. As the Olympics approached, 300,000 Mexican students and teachers were on strike. Ten days before the Olympics were scheduled to begin, government troops opened fire on several thousand unarmed students holding a rally in the Plaza de las Tres Culturas. Hundreds of young people were killed. The I.O.C. refused to take a stand on this, declaring that the incident was "an internal affair" which was "under control." Yet exactly two weeks later, when two black men made a silent, nonviolent protest, the I.O.C. was up in arms, condemning Smith and Carlos for their shocking, disrespectful behavior.

Two other controversies of 1968 were the introduction of sex tests for women athletes (first used at the Winter Games in Grenoble) and the altitude of Mexico City (7347 feet). The rarefied air led to numerous world records in races of short distances, but was disastrous to competitors engaged in endurance events, except those who had trained at high altitudes.

In **1972** the West Germans, hoping to erase embarrassing memories of the Nazi Games of 1936, staged the biggest Olympics yet, in Munich. However, the Olympic movement was permanently scarred on the morning of September 5, when eight Palestinian terrorists broke into the Olympic Village and made their way to the dormitory of the Israeli team. Two Israelis were killed immediately and another nine were taken hostage. The terrorists demanded the release of 200 prisoners from Israeli jails and safe passage for themselves out of Germany. They got as far as a military airport, where West German sharpshooters killed three of the terrorists. The battle that ensued left all nine Israeli hostages dead, as well as two more terrorists and one policeman. The Olympics were suspended for 34 hours, and a memorial service was held in the main stadium.

The **1976** Olympics, held in Montreal, were hit by a boycott of African nations led by Tanzania. The Africans had demanded expulsion of New Zealand because a rugby team from that nation had made a tour of South Africa. The I.O.C. claimed that controlling the travel of rugby teams was outside its authority since rugby isn't an Olympic sport, but the Africans, joined by Iraq and Guyana, held firm. Of the boycotting nations, only Tanzania stayed home completely, while the others traveled to Canada and didn't make their final decision until the last minute. Despite the absence of the Africans, the 1976 Olympics were filled with excellent competitions. However, poor planning and corruption caused the city of Montreal to suffer a major financial loss.

The **1980** Moscow Olympics were disrupted by another boycott, this one led by U.S. President Jimmy Carter, part of a package of actions to protest the Soviet invasion of Afghanistan. With his eyes on the upcoming presidential election and his pride on the line, Carter engaged in extensive arm-twisting to get other nations to support the boycott. Some governments, such as those of Great Britain and Australia, supported the boycott, but allowed the athletes to decide for themselves if they wanted to go to Moscow. No such freedom of choice was allowed U.S. athletes, as Carter threatened to revoke the passport of any athlete who tried to travel to the U.S.S.R.

Certain sports, such as yachting, equestrian events, field hockey, and men's swimming were hit particularly hard by the boycott. Yet the Games proceeded with much pomp and more world records than had been set in 1976. Security precautions were paranoically thorough, with track and field winners physically prevented from taking victory laps. Meanwhile, the Soviet spectators gave the worst impression of any host city since the Paris

Olympics of 1924. With traditional Olympic powers West Germany, Japan, and the United States missing, some Soviet fans took out their aggressions by booing and heckling the Poles and East Germans.

Not surprisingly, with the **1984** Olympics being held in Los Angeles, the government of the U.S.S.R. responded with a revenge boycott. Although the Soviets were noticeably unsuccessful in convincing other nations to join their action—more countries attended than ever before—those nations that did stay home accounted for 58% of the gold medals in 1976. Among the sports which lost most of their medal contenders were weightlifting, wrestling, gymnastics, women's swimming, football, handball, modern pentathlon and women's track and field. Nevertheless, the 1984 Games, the first since 1896 to be staged without government financing, were very successful. Good feelings prevailed to such an extent that at the Opening Ceremony the athletes broke ranks to join in spontaneous dancing, such celebration usually being reserved for the Closing Ceremony.

When the **1988** Olympics were awarded to Seoul, South Korea, grave concerns were raised about the ability of the organizers to run the Games in a nation which was not only ruled by an unpopular dictatorship but was in a state of permanent hostility with North Korea. The first half of the problem was solved when the South Korean government bowed to international pressure and held democratic elections. Attempts were made to appease the North Koreans by allowing them to stage several events, but in the end they boycotted the Olympics, taking Cuba, Ethiopia, and Nicaragua with them. Madagascar and the Seychelles also stayed away for reasons which are unclear, while Albania, acting independently, declared its fourth consecutive boycott—an Olympic record. Although tainted by steroid scandals and the assault on a referee by South Korean boxing officials, the Seoul Games were efficiently staged and the people of South Korea received high marks for their hospitality.

In the years following the Seoul Games, the world went through massive political changes. Apartheid was repealed in South Africa, allowing that nation to return to the Olympics. The Berlin Wall fell and West and East Germany were united. Communism collapsed in the Soviet Union, and the U.S.S.R. split into 15 separate countries. In **1992,** independent teams from Estonia and Latvia made their first appearance since 1936, and Lithuania fielded its first team since 1928. The remaining ex–Soviet republics competed at the Barcelona Games as the Unified Team, although individual winners were honored by the raising of the flag of their own republic. Even Albania, freed from Stalinist dictatorship, participated for the first time since 1972. Cuba, North Korea, and Ethiopia also ended their boycott streaks at two. In all, the 1992 Opening Ceremony was a festive occasion. The only controversy was what to do about Yugoslavia, which was the subject of United Nations sanctions because of its military aggression against Croatia and Bosnia-Herzegovina. At the last minute, it was decided that Yugoslavia would be banned from team sports, but that individual Yugoslav athletes could compete as "independent olympic participants." The star of the Games was the city of Barcelona itself, with its beautiful architecture and its cosmopolitan populace. The collective mood of the 1992 Olympics was one of guarded optimism that the Olympic movement had successfully survived a difficult two decades of political turmoil.

ISSUES

POLITICS IN THE OLYMPICS

There are only two places today where people from all parts of the world gather: the United Nations and the Olympics. The trouble with the United Nations is that two-thirds of the governments represented are ruled by dictators, royal families, and single parties that permit no opposition. Consequently, the people who represent these countries at the United Nations, far from being typical citizens, are generally the worst the country has to offer. Even those nations that aspire to democracy are represented by a most unrepresentative group: wealthy men and women, mostly men, who have gone to the right schools and know the right people.

Unlike U.N. delegates, Olympic athletes represent an almost complete economic cross-section of the world's population. In this book you will meet carpenters, farmers, housewives, teachers, psychiatrists, accountants, nurses, secretaries, and cartoonists, as well as the usual hordes of students, soldiers, and professional athletes. Some Olympians have been unemployed. Others came from families of sharecroppers, or from no families at all. Even lawyers, businessmen, and royalty have taken part in the Olympics.

This is not to say that the Olympics are any less political than the United Nations. However, contrary to popular belief, the politicization of the Olympics is not a recent phenomenon. From the very beginning the Olympics were exploited by the ruling classes of the nations in which they were held. In 1896 and 1906 the Greek royal family was highly visible at the Games, placing its box at the finish line and inserting itself into the festivities at the most exciting parts—the moment of victory and the award ceremonies. The British royal family did the same thing in 1908. In 1912 awards were handed out not only by King Gustav of Sweden, but by Czar Nicholas of Russia as well.

Staging the Olympics also helped the ruling classes by providing a distraction from serious political and economic problems. During the 1906 Intercalated Games in Athens, British and American tourists were shocked when a riot broke out in front of their hotel. Government troops attacked a political demonstration, killing three people and injuring 57. Meanwhile the Greek royal family was busy entertaining the English royal family at Olympic-related functions, including the competitions themselves.

Several days after Adolf Hitler and the Nazi Party seized control of Germany in March 1933, a delegation of German Olympic leaders met with Hitler and received his enthusiastic support for organizing the 1936 Olympics, which had been awarded to Berlin two years earlier. Hitler was so enthusiastic that he began to see the Games as a showcase for Nazi power and ideology. The president of the German Organizing Committee, Dr. Theodore Lewald, was a Christian, but, because one of his grandparents was Jewish, he was threatened with removal from his position. The international community was quick to show concern but slow to act. Only three months after the Nazi ascension to power, the International Olympic Committee met to consider moving the Games from Germany. Pressure was brought to bear on the Nazis to keep Dr. Lewald and to allow a couple of token Jewish athletes on the German team. But although the debate raged for over two years, the Nazis were allowed to stage the Olympics. In several countries, most notably in the United States, the debate shifted to whether the Games should be boycotted. In the end, nothing was done, and the Nazis were allowed their showcase, although the message of Aryan superiority fell flat when Jesse Owens and other African-American athletes were hailed as the stars of the Olympics by the German people themselves.

Despite this history, it is often stated that the "intrusion" of politics into the Olympics began in a serious manner with the black-gloved, clenched-fist salutes of U.S. sprinters Tommie Smith and John Carlos in Mexico City in 1968. Smith and Carlos staged their Black Power protest while "The Star-Spangled Banner" was being played during the medal ceremony for the 200-meter dash. They were immediately suspended by the I.O.C. and ordered to leave the Olympic Village by the

U.S.O.C. Yet they were hardly the first to make political gestures on the victory platform. During the 1936 Berlin Games, all German winners and several foreigners as well raised their right arms in the Nazi salute. Countless American athletes have placed their right hands over their hearts during the playing of their national anthem. Needless to say, none of these athletes was punished the way Smith and Carlos were.

The question then arises: If it was acceptable in 1936 to raise your right arm in the air with the open palm face down, and today it is acceptable to put your right hand over your heart, why was it *not* acceptable in 1968 to bow your head and raise your arm into the air with your gloved fist closed?

From the point of view of the I.O.C., the "crime" committed by Smith and Carlos was not that they had made a political statement, but that they had made the *wrong* political statement. Although Olympic *athletes* may be a representative group, I.O.C. members and other Olympic leaders are not. They are, in fact, very much like U.N. delegates. They have definite political beliefs. They support nationalism, and they support the ruling elites of the various nations of the world, no matter if they are Communist or capitalist. Thus it was perfectly all right in 1936 for German athletes to give the Nazi salute, because that salute was approved by the German government. And it is quite within the rules for U.S. athletes to put their hands over their hearts because that is a patriotic gesture which shows support for nationalism and the status quo.

It was *not* acceptable to the I.O.C. to have Smith and Carlos raise clenched fists because their gesture, rather than showing support for a recognized nation-state, showed support for an unrecognized political entity—African-Americans.

By 1972 it had become clear that because the Olympics commanded such massive international interest, they could be used to attract attention to a political cause. On September 5, the pro-Palestinian Black September group infiltrated the Olympic Village and eventually murdered eleven members of the Israeli team. The incident did not do much to advance the Palestinian cause, but it did force future Olympic organizers to turn the athletes' village and the competition venues into heavily secured armed camps.

Although the first boycotts of the modern Olympics took place in 1956, boycotting became a fad in 1976 when black African governments, led by Julius Nyerere of Tanzania, refused to allow their athletes to compete in the Montreal Games as a protest against apartheid in South Africa. Although their cause was a righteous one, it is difficult to view the African boycott with anything but cynicism considering that the boycotting governments were mostly dictatorships that did not tolerate dissent from their own citizens, much less support the concept of self-determination. In addition, the issue that triggered the boycott was tenuous at best. Nyerere demanded that the I.O.C. expel the team from New Zealand because a rugby team from that nation had toured South Africa. Rugby was not an Olympic sport and there was no connection between the New Zealand rugby team and any branch or twig of the Olympic movement.

Unfortunately, the success of the African boycott impressed at least one person: United States President Jimmy Carter. With the 1980 Olympics to be held in Moscow, Carter seized on a boycott as a way to punish the Soviet government for invading Afghanistan. Again the cause was a righteous one, but wouldn't it have been a more effective tactic to allow United States athletes to compete in Moscow and then ask them to display Afghani flags during the Parade of Nations? It went without saying that the Soviet Union would boycott the 1984 Los Angeles Olympics.

If ever there was an example of how the Olympics can have a *positive* effect on the political development of a country, it happened in 1988, when the Games were scheduled for Seoul. South Korea was ruled by a dictatorship that actually abdicated in favor of democratic elections in order to satisfy international opinion prior to the Olympics.

Perhaps it was this success that led almost half the members of the I.O.C. to vote to award the 2000 Olympics to China, which, in an age of spreading democracy, continues to forbid free speech and free elections, imprisons dissenters, and kills political demonstrators. Fortunately, cooler heads prevailed and Sydney defeated Beijing by two votes.

The Olympics will always reflect the politics of the world, from which they provide a temporary respite, and, because they are followed by a larger audience than any event in the world, they will always be a tempting forum for individuals and groups with a political agenda to promote.

AMATEURISM

Contrary to popular belief, the Ancient Greek athletes were not amateurs. Not only were they fully supported throughout their training, but even though a winner received only an olive wreath at the Games, back home he was amply rewarded and could become quite rich.

The concept of amateurism actually developed in nineteenth-century England as a means of preventing the working classes from competing against the aristocracy. The wealthy could take part in sports without worrying about having to make a living, and thus could pursue the ideal of amateurism. Everyone else had to give up training time in order to earn a living, or else take money for sports performances and become a professional, ineligible for competitions such as the Olympics.

Baron de Coubertin, although a member of the French aristocracy, was well aware of the inequities of the amateur system. His solution was to have wealthy people come forward as "patrons" to support worthy working-class athletes.

The qualifications for being an amateur have varied from decade to decade and from sport to sport. In the 1920s British sportsmen accused the Americans of circumventing the rules of amateurism by the awarding of athletic scholarships to universities (although even the ancient Greek medical colleges recruited athletes). As late as the 1930s physical education teachers and recreation directors were considered professional athletes and thus ineligible for the Olympics.

After the 1988 Games, the I.O.C. voted to declare all professionals eligible for the Olympics, subject to the approval of the international federations in charge of each sport. All but three federations eventually went along with the lifting of restrictions promoted by the I.O.C. Baseball and boxing continue to forbid professionals, while football (soccer) has agreed to allow each nation to include three professionals on their roster in addition to the professionals under the age of 23, against whom there is no prohibition. I believe the I.O.C. has made the right decision in opening the doors to professionals because Olympic events should be competitions among the best athletes in the world.

DRUGS

The use of performance-enhancing drugs and concoctions by Olympic athletes is nothing new. The winner of the 1904 marathon, Thomas Hicks, was administered multiple doses of strychnine and brandy *during* the race. Just before the running of the 1920 men's 100 meters, the U.S. sprint coach gave his soon-to-be-victorious team members a mixture of sherry and raw egg. In 1960, Danish cyclist Knut Jensen died during the Olympic road race as a result of ingesting amphetamines and nicotinyl tartrate.

It was not until 1967 that the Medical Commission of the International Olympic Committee began outlawing drugs. The following year, Hans-Gunnar Liljenvall, of the Swedish modern pentathlon team, was disqualified for using alcohol. Full-scale drug testing began in 1972. By this time the use of stimulants, sedatives, hormones, and steroids was so common that doctors and coaches were already coming up with masking agents to beat the tests and studying how close to competition an athlete could continue his or her drug program without risking a positive test result.

Although fewer athletes tested positive for drugs in 1988 than in 1984, it was in Seoul that the issue came to a head because one of those caught was Ben Johnson, the most visible hero of the Games (see p. 14). The subsequent investigation by the Canadian government into the use of banned substances by its athletes, as well as the revelations by athletes from East Germany and Czechoslovakia following the collapse of Communism in Eastern Europe, revealed that the use of steroids was widespread and extremely sophisticated.

According to current regulations there are six classes of banned substances and two banned methods. The doping classes are:

1. Stimulants, including amphetamines, cocaine, ephedrine, fencanfamine, mesocarbe, pemoline, phenylpropanolamine, strychnine, and excessive amounts of caffeine
2. Narcotic analgesics, including codeine, heroin, methadone, and morphine
3. Androgenic anabolic steroids, including clenbuterol, methenolone, nandrolone, stanozolol, and excessive levels of testosterone
4. Beta-blockers, including propranolol
5. Diuretics, including furosemide
6. Peptide hormones and analogues, including corticotrophin (ACTH) and growth hormone (HGH, somatotrophin).

The prohibited methods are:

1. Blood doping, in which athletes remove some of their blood, freeze it, and then, once their blood level has returned to normal, reinject it
2. The catch-all "pharmacological, chemical, and physical manipulation."

It is worth noting that alcohol and marijuana are not prohibited, although individual sports federations may set their own standards.

Most sports administer doping tests to at least the three medalists in each event. Some sports, most notably swimming, do not. When an athlete is chosen for doping control, he or she must produce a urine sample of at least 100 milliliters—not always an easy task after events that are seriously dehydrating. The urine sample is divided into two bottles. From this point on, the samples are labeled only by number. No one who tests the samples is aware of which athlete has produced which sample. If the "A" sample is positive, the athlete and his team are notified and are allowed to be present during the testing of the "B" sample. If the "B" sample also proves positive, the athlete is disqualified.

Drug testing at the Olympics is extremely reliable. The equipment is state of the art, and the technicians are highly competent. However, not all drug testing that affects the Olympics actually takes place *at* the Olympics. Testing is also conducted at international, regional, and national competitions around the world. In addition, many sports now conduct random, out-of-competition tests. The laboratories that analyze these various tests are not always up to Olympic standards. Some of them have more in common with the Los Angeles Police crime lab. Most athletes who test positive for banned substances dispute the results even if they are guilty. However, in some cases the results really are wrong. One case, from the Winter Games, suggests that testing procedures are not infallible. In 1991, Soviet ice dancer Marina Klimova tested positive for steroids at an unaccredited laboratory in Bulgaria. Klimova, a slim athlete who looked like, well, an ice dancer, seemed a highly unlikely suspect for steroid use. Sure enough, when her "B" sample was analyzed at an accredited lab in Germany, the result was negative and she was cleared. Although the first result was probably due to incompetence, it is possible that Klimova's urine sample had been tampered with by supporters of her rivals, who hoped to destabilize her psychologically just before the world championships. When a female ice dancer tests positive for steroids, it automatically raises suspicions about the competency of the testing procedures. But what if the incorrectly analyzed positive test had been that of a muscular shot putter or weightlifter? One wonders if he would have been treated as sympathetically as Klimova was before and after the testing of her "B" sample. The Butch Reynolds case (see page 32) illustrates some of the problems and complications in the field of drug testing.

46 Positive Drug Tests at the Summer Games

1968

Hans-Gunnar Liljenvall	SWE	modern pentathlon	alcohol

1972

Bakhaava Buidaa	MGL	judo—63 kg	caffeine
Miguel Coll	PUR	basketball	ephedrine
Rick DuMont	USA	swimming—400 free	ephedrine
Jaime Huelamo	SPA	cycling—road race	coramine
Walter Legel	AUT	weightlifting—67.5 kg	ephedrine
Mohamad Nasehi Ar Jomand	IRN	weightlifting—52 kg	ephedrine
Aad van den Hoek	HOL	cycling-team time trial	coramine

1976

Blagoi Blagoev	BUL	weightlifting—82.5 kg	anabolic steroids
Mark Cameron	USA	weightlifting—110 kg	anabolic steroids
Paul Cerutti	MON	shooting—trap	amphetamines
Valentin Hristov	BUL	weightlifting—110 kg	anabolic steroids
Dragomir Ciorosian	ROM	weightlifting—75 kg	fencanfamine
Phillip Grippaldi	USA	weightlifting—90 kg	anabolic steroids
Zbigniew Kaczmarek	POL	weightlifting—67.5 kg	anabolic steroids
Lorne Leibel	CAN	yachting—Tempest	phenylpropanolmine
Arne Norback	SWE	weightlifting—60 kg	anabolic steroids
Petř Pavlašek	CZE	weightlifting—110 kg	anabolic steroids
*Danuta Rosani	POL	track and field—shot put	anabolic steroids

1984

Serafin Grammatikopoulos	GRE	weightlifting—110+ kg	nandrolone
Vesteinn Hafsteinsson	ICE	track and field—discus	nandrolone
Tomas Johansson	SWE	Greco-Roman wrestling—heavy	methenolone
Stefan Laggner	AUT	weightlifting—110+ kg	nandrolone
Goran Petterson	SWE	weightlifting—110 kg	nandrolone
Eiji Shimomura	JPN	volleyball	testosterone
Mikiyasu Tanaka	JPN	volleyball	ephedrine
Ahmed Tarbi	ALG	weightlifting—56 kg	nandrolone
Mahmoud Tarha	LEB	weightlifting—52 kg	nandrolone
Gianpaolo Urlando	ITA	track and field—hammer	testosterone
Marti Vainio	FIN	track and field—10,000 meters	methenolone
*Anna Verouli	GRE	track and field—javelin	nandrolone

1988

Alidad	AFG	freestyle wrestling—62 kg	furosemide

*Women

Kerrith Brown	GBR	judo—71 kg	furosemide
Mitko Grablev	BUL	weightlifting—56 kg	furosemide
Angel Genchev	BUL	weightlifting—67.5 kg	furosemide
Ben Johnson	CAN	track and field—100 meters	stanozolol
Fernando Mariaca	SPA	weightlifting—67.5 kg	pemoline
Jorge Quesada	SPA	modern pentathlon	propranolol
Kalman Scengeri	HUN	weightlifting—75 kg	stanozolol
Andor Szanyi	HUN	weightlifting—100 kg	stanozolol
Alexander Watson	AUS	modern pentathlon	caffeine

1992

*Madina Biktagirova	SOV	track and field—marathon	norephedrine
*Bonnie Dasse	USA	track and field—shot put	clenbuterol
Jud Logan	USA	track and field—hammer	clenbuterol
*Nijole Medvedieva	LIT	track and field—long jump	mesocarde
*Wu Dan	CHN	volleyball	strychnine

*Women

There have also been five positive drug tests at the Winter Games.

GIGANTISM

One problem that is currently of great concern to the International Olympic Committee is what the I.O.C. calls "gigantism": in other words, that the Olympic Games have become too big. Specifically, according to the I.O.C., there are too many athletes and team officials who show up for the Games, putting an unnecessary burden on the organizing committee to provide them with housing, food, and transportation. Let us assume, for the sake of discussion, that the I.O.C.'s concerns are justified, that despite being given six years to prepare, the organizing committees cannot handle more than 15,000 participants. The question is How can the numbers be kept down? There are two basic solutions: (1) limit the number of entries in different sports and events by setting qualifying standards and/or hold regional qualifying tournaments; (2) eliminate certain events or entire sports.

The I.O.C. has already acted to limit entries while maintaining international diversity by allowing every nation to enter a total of six athletes in any of thirteen sports regardless of their ability to meet qualifying standards. This system seems to be working well, which is a good thing, because the second solution—eliminating events and sports—is much easier said than done.

For the public record, the I.O.C. has taken the position that sports will be added or axed according to their international popularity. If a sport is widely practiced on every continent, it stays; if it is only practiced in a small number of nations or its popularity is geographically limited, it goes. In reality there are other factors that are more important, namely, whether the sport looks good on television (especially U.S. television), and whether its proponents have power within the I.O.C. If international popularity were all that counted, canoeing and baseball would be eliminated, as would women's rowing, dressage, synchronized swimming, all yachting events except sailboarding, and the entire Winter Olympics. They would be replaced by squash and racquetball. Of course, that won't happen. Canoeing, like modern pentathlon, fencing, and equestrian events, is a well-established Olympic sport whose elimination would outrage certain countries. All of these threatened sports have made successful attempts to enliven their presentation in order to keep their place on the Olympic program.

And while the I.O.C. is complaining about gigantism, it is also adding to the program such sports as beach volleyball and, in the Winter Games, snowboarding and curling; none of which, if I am not mistaken, has a great deal of appeal in Africa or Asia. For the record, by the way, the only sports that have produced gold-medal winners from every continent are track and field, boxing, and swimming.

Frankly, I think the issue of gigantism is overstated. Sure, there are several sports and events that I could do without, but I recognize that large numbers of people like what I don't. If the I.O.C. and the organizing committees are concerned that the Olympic Village is too crowded, why not cut down the number of team officials and non-athletes? Athletes need coaches, but the roster of Olympic participants is bloated with bureaucrats and hangers-on.

ACKNOWLEDGMENTS

First of all I would like to thank my father, Irving Wallace, who introduced me to the world of the Olympics. In the course of my research I have encountered numerous people who have graciously helped me on my way, starting with C. Robert Paul, who made available to me the archives of the United States Olympic Committee. Mr. Paul was also kind enough to review my original manuscript in light of his long experience with the Olympic movement. I would also like to acknowledge the aid of David Kelly at the Library of Congress, Jan Foulstich and other members of the staff of Representative Anthony Beilenson, the staff of the library of Notre Dame University, Maynard Brichford and others at the University of Illinois, Champaign-Urbana, which houses the Avery Brundage Collection, Wayne Wilson and the staff of the Amateur Athletic Foundation library in Los Angeles, and Sandy Duncan of the British Olympic Association.

For this edition I would like to pay special thanks to Karel Wendl, Michelle Veillard, Patricia Eckert, and others at the Olympic Studies Center and the library of the International Olympic Committee, as well as to the Olympics research department of NBC television.

I am also indebted to Bill Mallon, Peter Diamond, John Lucas, and Harvey Abrams, who allowed me to enjoy and make use of their personal libraries. I would also like to thank the following people for their help in the research process: Cheryl Mick, Vicki Baker, Claudia Peirce, Wolf Lyberg, Pete Cava, Bob Bowman, Scott Davis, Ove Karlsson, Don Sayenga, Bill Plummer III, Dr. Dietrich Quanz, Dr. Uriel Simri, Miron Baramia, Jonathan Harley, C. Frank Zarnowski, Wally Wolf, and Dr. Jae Yoon Ryoo, as well as the numerous people who read the 1992 edition of this book and sent in corrections, updates, and new information, particularly Rubén Aguilera, Eric Aldin, Cris Freddi, Malcolm Heyworth, Richard Hymans, Joel Jeffries, Gareth Jones, Jeff Matlock, Helmut Mitterlehner, Martin Rix, Mort Tenner, Brian Woo, and Frans Woons.

Special acknowledgments are due to my wife, Flora Chavez, who helped when I needed it most; to my agent, Ed Victor, for his support and encouragement; and to Irv Goodman, who believed in the project from the start.

The author of this book may be reached by writing to:

Olympics
P.O. Box 49328
Los Angeles, California 90049
U.S.A.

I would particularly appreciate hearing from former Olympians willing to share their recollections.

THE CHARTS

SOURCES

It might seem to the casual reader that compiling the charts in this book was a simple task—just copy them from the Official Reports and fill in the blanks by consulting the International Olympic Committee. First of all, the Official Reports, particularly for 1896-1906 and 1920, are often terribly incomplete. Even as recently as 1948, the Official Report lists only the initial of each athlete's given name, not the name itself. As for the I.O.C., it has a beautiful library and a brilliantly staffed Olympic Studies Center. Unfortunately, the archives of the I.O.C. are devoted not to the study of the history of the Olympic Games but to the history of the I.O.C. and its members. One would think that an organization that has signed television contracts worth $3.5 billion with an American television network could launch a project to create an oral history of the Games by interviewing former Olympians around the world, or at least try to build an archive of newspaper, magazine, and video coverage of the competitions from sources in the various nations. Such is not the case.

There does exist a network of academics who study "Olympism" and the history of the Olympic movement. But the study of the competitions themselves is a less favored subject. When I began researching the first edition of this book in 1982, the archives of the United States Olympic Committee were housed in a converted meat locker. The U.S.O.C. archives were at least well organized. At that time, the archives of the British Olympic Association were stored in a shed with ivy growing through cracks in the wall. To this day, the archives of the International Olympic Committee are kept in an unused bomb shelter.

It has been left to individual, independent historians, most of them working in their spare time, to compile the records of the Olympic competitions and Olympic athletes. On December 5, 1991, seven of us gathered in the Duke of Clarence, a London pub, and founded the International Society of Olympic Historians. We now have two hundred members. I am indebted to the intrepid researchers of the I.S.O.H. from around the world for the full names of athletes from the early Olympics and for the correct spelling and accent marks in languages with which I was unfamiliar. The charts in this book are really the distillation of the work of dozens of Olympic enthusiasts. Those readers who are interested in joining the I.S.O.H. should write to:

International Society of Olympic Historians
303 Sutherland Court
Durham, NC 27712
USA

The primary sources for the information included in the charts are the Official Reports of the various Olympics. The man who has done the most to correct the inadequacies is the late Erich Kamper of Austria, author of *Enzyklopädie der Olympischen Spiele*. Wolf Lyberg of Sweden, in his unpublished work *The Athletes of the Games of the Olympiad 1896-1992*, has begun the task of compiling a complete roster of Olympic athletes. My search for correct spellings and accent marks has also led me to *Die Olympischen Spiele von 1896 bis 1980* by Volker Kluge of East Germany; *Starozytme i Nowozytne Igrazyska Olimpyskie* by Zbigniew Porada of Poland; *Meet the Bulgarian Olympians* by Kostadinov, Georgiev, and Kambourov; *Az Olimpiajátékokon Indult Magyar Versenyzök Névsora 1896–1980; Die Deutschen Sportler der Olympischen Spiele 1896 bis 1968;* and *Sveriges Deltagare i de Olympiska Spelen 1896–1952*. Many of the 1896 statistics are based on the research of Ture Widlund, who is also the author of *Weightlifting in the Olympic Games, 1896-1988*. For all of the early games (1896-1904) and the 1920 Games, I am particularly indebted to Bill Mallon of the United States, author of *A Statistical Summary of the 1904 Olympic Games* and *The Unofficial Report of the 1920 Olympics*; co-author, with Ian Buchanan, of *Quest for Gold: The Encyclopedia of American Olympians*; and co-author, with Erich Kamper, of the *Golden Book of the Olympics*. In fact, for readers who enjoy this book and want more statistics and facts, I enthusiastically recommend *The Golden Book of the Olympics*. Included in its pages are, among other things, the birth and death dates of every medalist, the medals each won, and records and medal charts for each sport and nation.

HOW TO READ THEM

year
location
number of competitors entered
number of nations represented
date of final
world record before Olympics began
world record holder

1952 Helsinki C: 66, N: 32, D: 7.27. WR: 2:20:42.2 (James Peters)

hours   minutes   seconds   tenths of seconds

Times: 2:20:42.2

Numbers in the charts indicate times unless otherwise noted. A dash symbol in the numbers column means that the information was not taken or is otherwise unavailable.

Whenever possible I have included an athlete's first and last names. If the first name was unavailable, I have included the first initial. If that was unavailable I have just included the surname. In cases where an athlete was commonly known by his middle name, I have included the initial of his first name as well as the middle name in full. If a female athlete competed under her maiden name, then married and took part in a second Olympics using her married name, I have included her maiden name in parentheses.

The 1906 Intercalated Games are considered unofficial by the I.O.C., but I have included them because of their historical importance.

In 1956, 1960, and 1964, West Germany (GER) and East Germany (GDR) entered combined teams. Nevertheless I have indicated which athletes were actually from each country because I thought it was interesting. For this edition, I have added to the nation an athlete represented the nation he or she would represent today. For example, "SOV/UKR" means the athlete competed for the Soviet Union but his homeland is now part of an independent Ukraine. "GBR/IRL" is a reminder that athletes from Ireland competed for Great Britain. Other examples are "YUG/CRO" (formerly Yugoslavia, now Croatia), colonies that are now independent (such as "FRA/ALG" for Algerians competing for France), and in the 1936 marathon, "JPN/KOR," Koreans competing for Japan. In team sports, "SOV" without a second national designation means the team combined athletes from more than one republic. In individual events, "SOV" without a second national designation means that the actual origin of the athlete is unclear, although in most of these cases they were probably from Russia. In 1992, 12 of the ex–Soviet republics competed as the Unified Team. But because winners were honored with the raising of the flag of their own republic, in the charts for 1992 I have indicated the specific republic for each athlete. In cases where athletes from more than one country competed for the same team, such as East and West Germany in 1956–1964 or in the early Olympics, I have used an ampersand rather than a slash. "GER&GDR" means a combined East and West German team. The designation "GBR[IRL]&GER," used in 1896 tennis doubles, indicates an Irish athlete representing Great Britain joining with a German athlete.

KEY TO ABBREVIATIONS

NATIONS

AFG	Afghanistan
ALG	Algeria
ARG	Argentina
ARM	Armenia
ASA	American Samoa
AUS	Australia
AUT	Austria
AZR	Azerbaijan
BAH	Bahamas
BAR	Barbados
BEL	Belgium
BER	Bermuda
BLR	Belarus
BOH	Bohemia
BRA	Brazil
BSH	Bosnia-Herzegovina
BUL	Bulgaria
BUR	Burma (Myanmar)
BWI	British West Indies (Jamaica and Trinidad)
CAM	Cameroon
CAN	Canada
CHI	Chile
CHN	China
COL	Colombia
CON	Congo
CRC	Costa Rica
CRO	Croatia
CUB	Cuba
CZE	Czechoslovakia
DEN	Denmark
DJI	Djibouti
DOM	Dominican Republic
EGY	Egypt
EST	Estonia
ETH	Ethiopia
FIN	Finland
FRA	France
GBR	Great Britain and Northern Ireland

GDR	East Germany (German Democratic Republic, 1956–1988)
GEO	Georgia
GER	Germany, West Germany (Federal Republic of Germany, 1952–1988)
GHA	Ghana
GRE	Greece
GUA	Guatemala
GUY	Guyana
HAI	Haiti
HKG	Hong Kong
HOL	Holland (Netherlands)
HUN	Hungary
ICE	Iceland
INA	Indonesia
IND	India
INT	International team
IRL	Ireland (Eire)
IRN	Iran
IRQ	Iraq
ISR	Israel
ITA	Italy
IVC	Ivory Coast
JAM	Jamaica
JPN	Japan
KAZ	Kazakhstan
KEN	Kenya
KOR	South Korea
KUW	Kuwait
KYR	Kyrgyzstan
LAT	Latvia
LEB	Lebanon
LIE	Liechtenstein
LIT	Lithuania
LUX	Luxembourg
MAC	Macedonia
MAD	Madagascar
MAL	Malaysia
MEX	Mexico
MGL	Mongolia
MLW	Malawi

MOL	Moldova
MON	Monaco
MOR	Morocco
MOZ	Mozambique
NAM	Namibia
NGR	Nigeria
NIG	Niger
NLA	Netherland Antilles
NOR	Norway
NZE	New Zealand
OMA	Oman
PAK	Pakistan
PAN	Panama
PAR	Paraguay
PER	Peru
PHI	Philippines
POL	Poland
POR	Portugal
PRK	North Korea (People's Republic of Korea)
PUR	Puerto Rico
QAT	Qatar
ROM	Romania
RUS	Russia
SAA	Saar
SAF	South Africa
SEN	Senegal
SEY	Seychelles
SIN	Singapore
SLE	Sierra Leone
SLO	Slovenia
SLV	Slovakia
SMR	San Marino
SOV	Soviet Union (Unified Team, 1992)
SPA	Spain
SRL	Sri Lanka (Ceylon)
SUD	Sudan
SUR	Suriname
SWE	Sweden
SWI	Switzerland
SYR	Syria
TAI	Taiwan
TAN	Tanzania
THA	Thailand
TJK	Tajikistan
TOG	Togo
TON	Tonga
TRI	Trinidad and Tobago
TRM	Turkmenistan
TUN	Tunisia
TUR	Turkey
UGA	Uganda
UKR	Ukraine

URU	Uruguay
USA	United States of America
UZB	Uzbekistan
VEN	Venezuela
VIR	U.S. Virgin Islands
YUG	Yugoslavia
ZAM	Zambia
ZIM	Zimbabwe

TERMS

A.A.A.	Amateur Athletic Association
A.A.U.	Amateur Athletic Union
AC	Also competed
C:	Number of competitors entered
D:	Date of final
Dec.	Won by judges' decision
DISC	Discus throw
DISQ	Disqualified
DNC	Did not compete in final
DNF	Did not finish
DNS	Did not start in final
e	Estimated
elim.	Eliminated
EOR	Equaled Olympic record
EWR	Equaled world record
F.I.N.A.	International Amateur Swimming Federation
F.I.T.A.	International Archery Federation
FT.	Feet
GA	Goals against
GF	Goals for
GRW	Greco-Roman wrestling
H	Hurdles
HAM	Hammer throw
HJ	High jump
I.A.A.F.	International Amateur Athletic Federation
IN.	Inches
I.O.C.	International Olympic Committee
JAV	Javelin throw
kg	Kilograms
km	Kilometers
KO	Knockout
L	Lost
LBS.	Pounds
LJ	Long jump (broad jump)
M	Meters
m.p.s.	Meters per second
N:	Number of nations represented
OR	Olympic record
PA	Points against
Pen.	Penalty

PF	Points for		T	Tied
PTS.	Points		TG	Touches given
PV	Pole vault		TR	Touches received
RA	Runs against		W	Won
Ret	Retired		w	Wind-aided
RF	Runs for		with	Withdrawn
RSC	Referee stopped contest		WB	World best
SLJ	Standing long jump		WO	Walkover
SP	Shot put		WR	World record
T:	Number of teams entered		YDS.	Yards

THE COMPLETE BOOK OF THE OLYMPICS

David Wallechinsky was introduced to the joys of the Olympics by his father, Irving Wallace, who took him to the Summer Games in Rome in 1960. Mr. Wallechinsky lives in the South of France with his wife and their two sons.

SUMMER
GAMES

TRACK AND FIELD

MEN

100 Meters	5000 Meters	3000-Meter Steeplechase	High Jump	Discus Throw
200 Meters	10,000 Meters	4 × 100-Meter Relay	Pole Vault	Hammer Throw
400 Meters	Marathon	4 × 400-Meter Relay	Long Jump	Javelin Throw
800 Meters	110-Meter Hurdles	20,000-Meter Walk	Triple Jump	Decathlon
1500 Meters	400-Meter Hurdles	50,000-Meter Walk	Shot Put	Discontinued Events

MEN

100 METERS

The 100-meter dash is run in lanes on a straightaway. Each lane is between 1.22 and 1.25 meters (4 feet and 4 feet 1¼ inches) wide. According to current rules, each runner is allowed one false start; a second false start results in disqualification. False starts are determined with the aid of pressure plates built into each runner's starting blocks. Although every finalist in the last three Olympics has been black, historically, the major division in this event has been not racial but linguistic. Since the modern Olympics were first held in 1896, 21 of 23 winners at 100 meters have been from English-speaking countries, as have 57 of the 69 medalists. In the following charts, the unofficial automatic times for 1952-1964, as compiled by Bob Sparks, have been included in parentheses. When a tailwind is measured at more than 2.0 meters per second (4.473 m.p.h.), times are not counted for record purposes. A runner is considered to have finished a race when his or her torso—from shoulder to waist—reaches the finish line. Heads, arms, legs, and feet do not count.

1896 Athens C: 15, N: 8, D: 4.10. WR: 10.8 (Luther Cary)

1. Thomas Burke	USA	12.0
2. Fritz Hofmann	GER	12.2e
3. Alajos Szokolyi	HUN/SLV	12.6e
4. Francis Lane	USA	12.6e
5. Alexandros Chalkokondilis	GRE	12.6e
DNS: Thomas Curtis (USA)		

The very first race of the modern Olympics was the opening heat of the 100-meter dash. It was won by Francis Lane of Princeton in the time of 12⅕ seconds. The European crowd was fascinated by the "crouch" start of the Americans, as Thomas Curtis and quarter-mile specialist Thomas Burke, both of Boston, won the other two qualifying heats. The first two finishers in each of the heats qualified for the final four days later, but Curtis chose not to start, preferring to save himself for the 110-meter hurdles, which was the next race. Burke, who had registered the fastest time (12.0) in the heats, equaled his time

in the final and defeated Hofmann by two meters. The other runners were bunched four meters further back. Although Hofmann was a champion sprinter, his athletic specialty was actually rope climbing. Thomas Burke, the first Olympic 100 meters champion, later became a lawyer and also wrote part-time for the *Boston Journal* and the *Boston Post*. He died on Valentine's Day, 1929, at the age of 53.

1900 Paris C: 20, N: 9, D: 7.14. WR: 10.8 (Luther Cary)

1. Frank Jarvis	USA	11.0
2. John Walter Tewksbury	USA	11.1
3. Stanley Rowley	AUS	11.2
DNF: Arthur Duffey (USA)		

The American runners had never competed before on a grass track, but this didn't prevent Jarvis of Princeton and Tewksbury of Pennsylvania from equaling the world record of 10.8 in the heats and semifinals, respectively. Despite these performances, the clear favorite was 5-foot 7-inch Arthur Duffey of Georgetown University, who had defeated both Jarvis and Tewksbury in London the previous week. As expected, Duffey burst into the lead and seemed well on his way to victory, when he suddenly began to wobble and fell to the ground at the 50-meter mark, the victim of a strained tendon in his left leg. Jarvis went on to win by about two feet. Duffey later told the press, "I do not know why my leg gave way. I felt a peculiar twitching after going twenty yards. I then seemed to lose control of it, and suddenly it gave out, throwing me on my face. But that is one of the fortunes of sport, and I cannot complain." In 1902 Duffey ran 100 yards in 9.6 seconds, setting a world record which stayed in the books for 24 years. Later he became a columnist for the *Boston Post*.

1904 St. Louis C: 13, N: 2, D: 9.3. WR: 10.8 (Luther Cary, Frank Jarvis, John Walter Tewksbury)

1. Charles "Archie" Hahn	USA	11.0
2. Nathaniel Cartmell	USA	11.2
3. William Hogenson	USA	11.2
4. Fay Moulton	USA	11.4
5. Frederick Heckwolf	USA	—
6. Lawson Robertson	USA	—

Archie Hahn, "The Milwaukee Meteor," had already won the 60-meter and 200-meter dashes when he settled down for the final of the 100. Running into a heavy wind, he shot out to a fast start, had a one-yard lead by the 20-meter mark, and held off the fast-finishing Louisville sprinter Nate Cartmell to win by almost two yards. Hahn was only 5-feet 5-inches tall and weighed about 130 pounds. He did not take up track until he was 19 years old. The following year, 1900, he was recruited by representatives of the University of Michigan, who saw him win a race at a county fair.

1906 Athens C: 42, N: 13, D: 4.27. WR: 10.8 (Luther Cary, Frank Jarvis, John Walter Tewksbury)

1. Charles "Archie" Hahn	USA	11.2
2. Fay Moulton	USA	11.3
3. Nigel Barker	AUS	11.3
4. William Eaton	USA	—
5. Lawson Robertson	USA	—
6. Knut Lindberg	SWE	—

William Eaton of Boston recorded the fastest time in the semifinals (11.2), but in the final Hahn, with a quick start, led the whole way and won by a yard. Back in the United States, Hahn studied law at Michigan, but never practiced his profession. Instead he devoted his life to coaching younger runners. His book *How to Sprint* is still considered a classic text.

1908 London C: 57, N: 16, D: 7.22. WR: 10.6 (Knut Lindberg)

1. Reginald Walker	SAF	10.8	EOR
2. James Rector	USA	10.9	
3. Robert Kerr	CAN	11.0	
4. Nathaniel Cartmell	USA	11.2	

In 1908 the excitement surrounding the 100-meter race rivaled that of the marathon. The tension was heightened by the fact that only the winner of each heat advanced to the next round. The favorites, James Rector, a University of Virginia student from Hot Springs, Arkansas, and Bobby Kerr, the Irish-born Canadian champion, did not disappoint their supporters in the opening heats. Rector was particularly impressive, tying the Olympic record of 10.8 seconds. He equaled this time in the semifinals, but so did Reggie Walker, a 19-year-old clerk from Durban. Walker had not been chosen for the South African team, but was sent to London as an afterthought by his fans in Natal. Arriving three weeks before the Olympics, he lost to Kerr in the final of the British A.A.A. championship. Nevertheless he caught the eye of the famous coach Sam Mussabini, who took the young man under his wing and spent the next couple of weeks working with him on his start. This last-minute training worked wonders. Running on the inside lane, Walker stormed into an early lead, gave way to Rector at the halfway point, and then was able to pull ahead once again to win by a "long yard," with Rector holding on to second by mere inches. The 5-foot 7-inch, 130-pound Walker, who had been pre-viously unknown to the general public, became an instant hero, as the crowd of 49,000 cheered wildly and threw their hats and programs into the air, while friends and officials competed for the right to carry the embarrassed South African on their shoulders. In the words of one U.S. newspaper, "The Englishmen were gratified to see the monotonous succession of American victories broken by a Britisher, even if he was a colonist."

1912 Stockholm C: 68, N: 22, D: 7.7. WR: 10.5 (Richard Rau)

1. Ralph Craig	USA	10.8
2. Alvah Meyer	USA	10.9
3. Donald Lippincott	USA	10.9
4. George Patching	SAF	11.0
5. Frank Belote	USA	11.0
DNS: Howard Drew (USA)		

Ralph Craig of the University of Michigan was considered the pre-Olympic favorite until he was beaten in the U.S trials by Howard Drew, a strong black student from Springfield, Massachusetts. In the first round in Stockholm, Donald Lippincott, the star of the University of Pennsylvania track team, set an Olympic record by winning his heat in 10.6 seconds. The semifinals were run with only the winner of each race advancing to the final. The Americans showed their strength by winning all five of the heats in which they were entered. Unfortunately, Drew strained a tendon just before the finish of his heat and, despite qualifying, was unable to start in the final.

The final was marred by seven false starts, the first three by Craig. After one false start, Craig and Lippincott raced all the way to the finish line. At the eighth try a clean break was made, with Patching taking the early lead. Craig caught him at the 60-meter mark and went on to win by two feet. Thirty-six years later, Craig, by then a wealthy 59-year-old industrial engineer, reappeared at the London Olympics as an alternate on the U.S. yachting team and was chosen to carry the United States' flag at the Opening Ceremony.

1920 Antwerp C: 61, N: 23, D: 8.16. WR: 10.5 (Richard Rau)

1. Charles Paddock	USA	10.8
2. Morris Kirksey	USA	10.9e
3. Harry Edward	GBR	10.9e
4. Jackson Scholz	USA	10.9e
5. Emile Ali-Khan	FRA	11.0e
6. Loren Murchison	USA	11.1e

Charley Paddock was born in Gainesville, Texas, on August 11, 1900. A sickly child, he weighed only 7½ pounds at the age of 7 months. His parents moved to Southern California for his health, eventually settling in Pasadena. The change of climate must have done the trick, because by age 15, Charley was a barrel-chested 170-pounder with big strong legs and a sprinter's body. He loved to run long distances, but his father convinced him to concentrate on the 100 yards and the 220 yards. Paddock came to international attention in 1919 when he won

Charley Paddock, Jackson Scholz, Loren Murchison, and Morris Kirksey spent anxious hours together before the final of the 100-meter dash in 1920. Six days later they teamed up to win the 4 × 100-meter relay.

both metric sprints at the Inter-Allied Games in Paris, with times of 10.8 and 21.6. Charley was a great crowd-pleaser, who delighted photographers with a flying finish in which he would leap at the tape from about 12 feet out, with his arms flung wide.

The semifinals of the Olympic championship were held in the early morning on Monday, August 16. The first heat was won by Guyanese-born Harry Edward and the second by Charley Paddock, both in 10.8. Scholz and Murchison had also run 10.8 in the earlier rounds. All four Americans qualified for the final and spent the next few hours together, waiting anxiously for their late afternoon race. The blond-haired Murchison kept muttering, half to himself, "I'm going to win. I've known it all along. . . . I can trim any sprinter who ever lived." The others tried to ignore him. Just before it was time to take the field, the four runners were approached by coach Lawson Robertson, who said, "What you fellows need to warm up is a glass of sherry and a raw egg." Murchison, Scholz, and Paddock were horrified by the suggestion, but when Stanford's Morris Kirksey agreed to try the drink, the others feared it would give him a psychological advantage to be the only one to follow the coach's advice, so they guzzled down the strange concoction as well.

Like many athletes, Charley Paddock followed a set of good-luck rituals. On the way to the starting line he would knock on "a friendly piece of wood." When called to his mark, he would put his hands far across the starting line and then draw them slowly back before the second call of "get set." Paddock was the last to stoop to his mark at the starting line of the 1920 100-meter final. The assistant starter, unaware of Charley's ritual, ordered him in French to pull back his hands, which he was actu-

Charley Paddock wins the 1920 100 meters with his famous "flying finish." Morris Kirksey (right) placed second and Jackson Scholz (left) fourth.

ally already in the process of doing. The starter then called out *"prêt,"* the French equivalent of "get set." Murchison misinterpreted the exchange and thought the runners had been ordered to stand up, so he was just beginning to relax and rise when the gun went off. He was left 10 yards behind. Kirksey took the early lead, but at the halfway mark Scholz had a two-foot advantage, with Edward in second. Then Kirksey surged ahead again, with Paddock at his shoulder. In the words of Charley Paddock: "Then I saw the thin white string stretched to the breaking point in front of me. I drove my spikes into the soft cinders and felt my foot give way as I sprang forward in a final jump for the tape. . . . There was nothing more I could do. My eyes closed as my chest hit the string and when I opened them, my feet were on the ground again and I was yards ahead of the field. I did not know if I had been in front when the string was broken. I dared not ask." In fact, Charley Paddock had won the race by 12 inches. "My dream had come true," he later wrote, "and I thrilled to the greatest moment I felt that I should ever know. . . . The real pleasure had been in the anticipation and in that single moment of glorious realization."

1924 Paris C: 82, N: 34, D: 7.7. WR: 10.2 (Charles Paddock)

1. Harold Abrahams	GBR	10.6	EOR
2. Jackson Scholz	USA	10.8	
3. Arthur Porritt	NZE	10.9	
4. Chester Bowman	USA	10.9	
5. Charles Paddock	USA	10.9	
6. Loren Murchison	USA	11.0	

The story of Harold Abrahams' victory in Paris in 1924 is well told in the beautiful film *Chariots of Fire*. Unfortunately, despite its claim of being "a true story," the film contains several factual distortions. Abrahams did not race around the great courtyard of Trinity College at Cambridge. (It was Lord Burghley who did that.) He did not look at the 100-meter contest as a chance to redeem himself after his failure in the 200, since the running of the 100 actually preceded the 200 in real life. Although Abrahams did feel himself an outsider because he was Jewish, a much more important motivating factor in his quest for victory was a desire to do better than his two older brothers, both of whom were well-known athletes and one of whom had represented Great Britain in the long jump at the 1906 and 1912 Olympics. Abrahams himself had competed in the 100 and 200 meters in Antwerp in 1920, but had been eliminated in the quarterfinals. In the year preceding the Paris Olympics, Abrahams came under the direction of Sam Mussabini, who had successfully coached Reggie Walker to victory in 1908. Among other things, Mussabini stressed to Abrahams the importance of the length and number of his strides. During practice sessions Abrahams would place pieces of paper on the track, to indicate where each stride should end. Then he would try to pick them up on his spikes as he ran. He always carried with him a piece

The real Harold Abrahams. Despite the film Chariots of Fire, Abrahams did not run around the courtyard at Trinity College, Cambridge. He did, however, win the 100-meter dash at the 1924 Olympics in Paris.

of string the length of his first stride. Before a race he would pull out the string, measure forward from the starting line, and make a mark on the track where his first step should land.

Abrahams was also a proficient long-jumper. One month before the Olympics he leaped 24 feet 2½ inches (7.38 meters) to set an English record, which lasted until 1956. For this reason he was chosen to represent Great Britain in the long jump as well as the 100, 200, and 4 × 100 relay. When an anonymous letter appeared in the *Daily Express*, criticizing the decision to enter Abrahams in the long jump, few people knew that the letter had been written by Harold Abrahams himself. He made his point and was excused from that event.

Despite his great feats, the 6-foot ½-inch, 175-pound Abrahams was considered a long shot in comparison to the U.S. team, which included defending champion Charley Paddock as well as Antwerp finalists Jackson Scholz and Loren Murchison. On June 18, 1921, Paddock had stunned the track world by running 110 yards (which is actually longer than 100 meters) in the unheard-of time of 10.2 seconds, a record that remained unbeaten for 29 years. Although the Americans were the favorites, it was Harold Abrahams, running faster than he had ever run before, who registered the fastest times in the early heats, tying the Olympic record (10.6) twice, in the quarterfinals and the semifinals, where he overcame an awful start. For the first time Abrahams realized that he had a chance to win the Olympic gold, and for the first time he began to feel the pressure. For the next 3¾ hours, as he waited for the final, he "felt like a condemned man feels just before going to the scaffold." As he went to his mark at 7:05 p.m. on July 7, Abrahams recalled Sam Mussabini's final words of advice: "Only think of two things—the report of the pistol and the tape. When you hear the one, just run like hell till you break the other." After a perfect start, the runners ran almost even for the first 40 or 50 meters, but then Abrahams began to move ahead, gaining with each stride until he crossed the tape with a two-foot victory.

Harold Abrahams is a perfect example of an athlete who peaks at exactly the right moment. After that day at the Stade Colombes in Paris, he never raced well again. The following year he injured his thigh while long-jumping and retired from competition forever. He once wrote, "I wonder if, in a sense, that was not another piece of good bad-luck. How many people find it almost impossible to retire at the right time. Would I have gone downhill, and tried to go on? That was the decision I never had to make; it was made for me. Rather painfully, but it was made." Abrahams went on to great success as a radio commentator, lawyer, writer, statistician, and president of the British Amateur Athletic Association. Arthur Porritt, who took the bronze medal even though he failed to win a single heat, had an even more distinguished career, culminating in a five-year term as Governor-General of New Zealand and 35 years as Surgeon to the British royal family. Until Abrahams' death in 1978, he and Porritt and their wives had dinner every year at 7:00 p.m. on July 7—the day and the hour of the 1924 100-meter final. As for Charley Paddock, he acted in a couple of Hollywood films, went into the newspaper business, and became active in local politics in Pasadena. During World War II he enlisted in the U.S. Marine Corps and died in a plane crash in Alaska on July 21, 1943.

1928 Amsterdam C: 81, N: 33, D: 7.30. WR: 10.2 (Charles Paddock)

1. Percy Williams	CAN	10.8
2. John "Jack" London	GBR	10.9
3. Georg Lammers	GER	10.9
4. Frank Wykoff	USA	11.0
5. Wilfred Legg	SAF	11.0
6. Robert McAllister	USA	11.0

Percy Williams was one of the most popular winners of the Amsterdam Games. Not considered a serious threat by the experts, the slim, almost frail-looking 20-year-old from Vancouver, British Columbia, caught the fancy of the crowd in the second round, when he tied the Olympic record of 10.6. This time was matched in both semifinals, first by Bob McAllister, "The Flying Cop" of New York City, who barely held off a slow-starting Williams, and then by Jack London, a Guyanese-born university student who was the first Briton to use starting blocks. As the six finalists lined up for the deciding race, the 126-pound Williams seemed an unlikely bet to become Olympic champion, particularly as he was standing beside the muscular 6-foot 2-inch, 200-pound London. After two false starts, by Legg and Wykoff (who had gained ten pounds on the boat ride from the United States), the runners were off. Williams took the lead immediately and kept it the entire way, holding off late rushes by London and Lammers to win by two feet. McAllister pulled a tendon 20 meters from the tape and finished last.

In the days before television, an unexpected winner like Williams could be famous and unrecognized at the same time. Only a few hours after his Olympic victory, Williams and a friend noticed a large crowd gathered in front of his hotel. "We joined the mob," Williams later recalled, "looking over their shoulders. I asked a person in front of me why they were there and he said, 'We're waiting for the Canadian runner Williams to come out of the hotel.' I didn't tell him who I was. I stood around waiting for him, too, and talking to some of the people—it was much more fun."

Upon his return to Canada, Williams, who also won the 200 meters, was greeted with an enthusiasm reminiscent of the ancient Greek Olympics. Crossing the continent by train with his mother, he stopped in Montreal, where he was presented with a gold watch. In Hamilton he received a silver tea service and in Winnipeg a bronze statue, a silver cup, and a golden retriever. When he finally reached Vancouver, a school holiday was declared, and he was met by tens of thousands of cheering fans. He was given a blue Graham-Paige sports car as well as $14,500 for his education.

1932 Los Angeles C: 32, N: 17, D: 8.1. WR: 10.2 (Charles Paddock, Ralph Metcalfe)

1. Thomas "Eddie" Tolan	USA	10.3	OR
2. Ralph Metcalfe	USA	10.3	OR
3. Arthur Jonath	GER	10.4	
4. George Simpson	USA	10.5	
5. Daniel Joubert	SAF	10.6	
6. Takayoshi Yoshioka	JPN	10.7	

Eddie Tolan was the third University of Michigan athlete to win the Olympic 100 meters gold medal, following in the tradition of Archie Hahn and Ralph Craig. The 5-foot 7-inch Tolan dominated U.S. sprinting from 1929 to 1931, but he was dethroned by Ralph Metcalfe of Marquette University in Milwaukee, who breezed undefeated through the 1932 season. At the U.S. Olympic trials Metcalfe beat Tolan in both sprints and went to Los

Angeles as the favorite. But in the second round it was Tolan who set an Olympic record of 10.4. In the final Yoshioka, an excellent starter, took the lead from the first step and held it for 40 meters, when he was caught by Tolan. Yoshioka faded at 60 meters, while Metcalfe began his famous finishing spurt. He pulled even with Tolan at 80 meters and the two ran neck and neck for the rest of the race, crossing the finish line in a near dead heat. Most of the spectators felt that there had been a tie or that Metcalfe had won. Several hours later, seven judges viewed a film of the race and determined that Tolan had *crossed* the line two inches ahead of Metcalfe. Current rules state that the first runner to *reach* the finish line is the winner. So close was the race that if the current rules had been in effect in 1932, Metcalfe would have been the winner.

There were also two also-rans who provoked interest in 1932. The first was Daniel Joubert, a white South African who spoke seven African dialects. Joubert arrived in Los Angeles in a somewhat weakened condition, having traveled 38 days to get there. Considering his ordeal, it was quite an achievement that he even made the final. The other was Liu Changchun, who marched in the opening day ceremony as the one and only representative of the 400,000,000 people of China. Liu finished last in his first round heat in both the 100 and 200. He also competed in both events at the Berlin Olympics four years later.

1936 Berlin C: 63, N: 30, D: 8.3. WR: 10.2 (Charles Paddock, Ralph Metcalfe, James "Jesse" Owens)

1. James "Jesse" Owens	USA	10.3
2. Ralph Metcalfe	USA	10.4
3. Martinus Osendarp	HOL	10.5
4. Frank Wykoff	USA	10.6
5. Erich Borchmeyer	GER	10.7
6. Lennart Strandberg	SWE	10.9

Jesse Owens assured himself a permanent place in sports history on May 25, 1935, when, while competing at the Big Ten championships at Ann Arbor, Michigan, he broke five world records and equaled a sixth in the space of 45 minutes. At 3:15 p.m. he won the 100-yard dash by five yards in 9.4 seconds to tie the world record. At 3:25 he long-jumped 26 feet 8¼ inches, breaking the existing world record by six inches. It was his only jump of the day, but it wasn't beaten for 25 years. At 3:45 he scored a ten-yard victory in the 220-yard dash, clocking 20.3 seconds and bettering the listed record by three-tenths of a second. He was also given credit for lowering the world record in the shorter 200-meter dash. At 4:00 p.m. he flew over the 220-yard low hurdles in 22.6, the first man to beat 23 seconds. En route he also established a record for the 200-meter hurdles. Despite these and other sensational performances, in the following year Owens lost three times to the great Alabama-born sprinter Eulace Peacock. And it wasn't until one week before the Olympic trials that Jesse was able to defeat Ralph Metcalfe.

But he peaked when he needed to, winning the 100, 200, and long jump at the trials, and he went to Berlin as the favorite in all three events.

Owens had little trouble living up to expectations. In the first round of the 100 meters he tied the Olympic record of 10.3. In the second round he ran a wind-aided 10.2. Jesse took it easy in the semifinals, winning his heat in 10.4 while Metcalfe won the other in 10.5. The final saw Owens take the lead from the first stride and pull out to a five-foot lead by the halfway mark. As usual Metcalfe started slowly and came on strong in the last 25 meters. He closed the gap, but was still a yard back when Owens broke the tape. Metcalfe, who was elected to the U.S. Congress 34 years later, picked up his second straight 100 meters silver medal, while Osendarp became the first Dutchman to win an individual track and field medal. Strandberg appeared to be a sure medalist, but he strained a tendon at the 80-meter mark and limped home in last place. Before the week was out, Jesse Owens had earned three more gold medals.

Nazi propaganda had portrayed Negroes as inferior, taunting the United States for relying on "black auxiliaries." Evidently, though, the message had little effect on the German masses, who considered Owens the hero of Berlin. Everywhere he went around town he was mobbed by fans seeking his autograph or photograph. They even shoved autograph books through his bedroom window in the Olympic Village while he tried to sleep.

Jesse Owens was born September 12, 1913, in Danville, Alabama, the son of sharecroppers and the grandson of slaves. By the age of 7 he was expected to pick 100 pounds of cotton a day. When he was 9 his family moved north to Cleveland, where Jesse pumped gas and delivered groceries. After he set national high school records in the long jump, the 100-yard dash, and the 220, he was recruited by 28 colleges, but chose to stay close to home at Ohio State. While a student there he worked as an elevator operator and, later, as a page in the state legislature. There is a famous myth that after Jesse won the 100 meters in Berlin he was snubbed by Adolf Hitler, who refused to meet Owens after he had personally congratulated three earlier gold medal winners. Actually, if such a snub did occur, the recipient was not Jesse Owens, but Cornelius Johnson and David Albritton, black Americans who had finished one-two in the high jump the previous day.

Owens *was* snubbed by a different world leader—Franklin Delano Roosevelt. Although Jesse received tickertape parades in New York City and Cleveland, the President not only failed to invite him to the White House, he never even sent a letter of congratulations. Owens was also snubbed by the Amateur Athletic Union, which suspended him for refusing to run in a Swedish meet, which he had never agreed to enter. The A.A.U. also bypassed him for the Sullivan award, which was presented to the best U.S. amateur athlete of the year. In 1935, the year that Jesse Owens set six world records, the award was given to a golfer named Lawson Little. In 1936, the year of

Owens' four gold medals, the award went to Glenn Morris, the Olympic decathlon champion.

After the Olympics Jesse worked as a paid campaigner for presidential candidate Alf Landon. When Landon lost to Roosevelt in a landslide, Owens took a $130-a-month job as a playground instructor in Cleveland. In an attempt to make ends meet, the hero of Berlin, "The Ebony Antelope," allowed promoters to stage exhibitions in which he raced against horses, dogs, and motorcycles. Tiring of this, he returned to his job as a playground instructor. Then he lent his name to a chain of cleaning stores which went bankrupt, leaving Owens $114,000 in debt. In the 1950s he finally achieved financial security when he opened a public relations firm and became a public speaker on behalf of various corporate sponsors. He developed a repertoire of five basic speeches including ones on religion, patriotism, and marketing for salesmen. In the words of writer William Oscar Johnson, Jesse Owens had become "a professional good example."

In 1968 Owens took the side of the U.S. Olympic Committee in its struggle with militant black athletes and two years later he wrote a book called *Blackthink,* which criticized racial militancy. However in 1972 he published another book, *I Have Changed,* retracting his earlier criticisms. After 35 years of pack-a-day cigarette smoking, Jesse Owens died of lung cancer in Tucson, Arizona, on March 31, 1980. Four years later a street in Berlin was renamed in his honor.

Would-be Olympic sprint champions might be interested to know the secret of Owens' success. In 1936 he told one London reporter, "I let my feet spend as little time on the ground as possible. From the air, fast down, and from the ground, fast up. My foot is only a fraction of the time on the track."

1948 London C: 66, N: 34, D: 7.31. WR: 10.2 (Charles Paddock, Ralph Metcalfe, James "Jesse" Owens, Harold Davis, Lloyd LaBeach, H. Norwood "Barney" Ewell)

1. Harrison Dillard	USA	10.3	EOR
2. H. Norwood "Barney" Ewell	USA	10.4	
3. Lloyd LaBeach	PAN	10.4	
4. Alastair McCorquodale	GBR	10.4	
5. Melvin Patton	USA	10.5	
6. Emmanuel McDonald Bailey	GBR	10.6	

Harrison Dillard was a 13-year-old schoolboy in Cleveland when he attended the huge parade in 1936 in honor of Jesse Owens. Later he met Owens, who took a liking to the young man and presented him with his first pair of running shoes. Dillard put those shoes to good use. By 1952 he had matched his hero's total of four Olympic victories. From May 31, 1947, through June 26, 1948, "Bones" Dillard, running mostly the hurdles, ran up an unprecedented string of 82 consecutive victories. The streak finally came to an end at the A.A.U. meet in Milwaukee when he tried to run four races in 67 minutes. First he lost the 100 meters to Barney Ewell and then he lost the 110-meter hurdles to Bill Porter. Nevertheless,

when the Olympic trials were held the following week in Evanston, Illinois, there seemed no surer gold medal bet than Harrison Dillard, the world record holder in the 110-meters hurdles. However, in the final he uncharacteristically hit the first hurdle, lost his stride, hit two more hurdles, and stopped at the seventh hurdle as the others raced ahead. Dillard's Olympic hopes seemed over. Fortunately he had qualified the day before as third man in the 100 meters. But Dillard would face stiff competition in London. First there was the prerace favorite, U.S.C.'s Mel Patton, who held the world record of 9.3 in the 100 yards. Then there was 30-year-old Barney Ewell, who had beaten Patton at the U.S. trials in the world record time of 10.2. And there was Patton's arch rival, Lloyd LaBeach, who had also run 100 meters in 10.2 and who went to London as the sole representative of his native country, Panama.

The three favorites and Dillard were joined in the Olympic final by two representatives of Great Britain, Mac Bailey of Trinidad, who, like Dillard, had been inspired by the feats of Jesse Owens, and Alastair McCorquodale, a burly Scot who had taken up running only a year earlier and who actually preferred rugby and cricket to track. After one false start, Dillard flashed into the lead and held it the entire way. Ewell caught him at the tape and, thinking he had won, danced around the field joyfully and embraced his opponents. But LaBeach told him, "Man, you no win; Bones win." LaBeach was right. When the photo-finish had been studied, it was announced that Dillard had won. Ewell graciously congratulated him on his good fortune, greatly impressing the crowd of 82,000 with his sportsmanship. LaBeach, whose parents were Jamaican, is the only Panamanian ever to have won an Olympic medal.

1952 Helsinki C: 72, N: 33, D: 7.21. WR: 10.1 (Lloyd LaBeach)

1. Lindy Remigino	USA	10.4	(10.79)
2. Herbert McKenley	JAM	10.4	(10.80)
3. Emmanuel McDonald Bailey	GBR	10.4	(10.83)
4. F. Dean Smith	USA	10.4	(10.84)
5. Vladimir Sukharyev	SOV	10.5	(10.88)
6. John Treloar	AUS	10.5	(10.91)

The 1952 100-meter final produced the closest finish in Olympic history and also one of the biggest sprint upsets. The title seemed pretty much up for grabs, particularly after the U.S. college champion, Jim Golliday, was injured and unable to participate in the Olympics. The position of favorite shifted to 31-year-old Mac Bailey and Arthur Bragg of Morgan State College. But Bragg pulled a muscle in the semifinals, which were won by Bailey and 30-year-old Herb McKenley, the 400-meter world record holder who had also entered the 100 as a means of practicing his start. With this race McKenley became the first—and only—man to qualify for a final in the 100 meters, 200 meters, and 400 meters. One of the surviving U.S. representatives was Texan Dean Smith, who later

The controversial finish of the 1952 100-meter dash. The straight white line down the middle is not the finish line, but a flash from a photographer's bulb. To see if Herb McKenley (Lane 2 from top) beat Lindy Remigino (Lane 3), take a piece of transparent lined paper and match one of the lines with the black line below the words "Omega Timer." Slowly move the paper to the left until it reaches one of the runners. Arms and legs don't count; only shoulders and torso.

became a stuntman in hundreds of television shows and films, including *Stagecoach* and *True Grit,* and doubled for Robert Redford three times in the early 1970s. The other was Lindy Remigino, a modest Manhattan College student from Hartford, Connecticut. Remigino must have been amazed to find himself a finalist in the Olympics. He had barely qualified for the U.S. Olympic tryouts by finishing fifth in the N.C.A.A. championship. Smith showed in front first, but Remigino had a clear lead at the halfway mark. He held on gamely for 90 meters, but was passed by McKenley just as they reached the tape.

"I was sure I had lost the race," said Remigino afterward. "I started my lean too early . . . and I saw Herb McKenley shoot past me. I was heartsick. I figured I had

blown it." Lindy walked over to the delighted Jamaican and offered his congratulations. But a photo-finish showed that Remigino's right shoulder had reached the finish line an inch ahead of McKenley's chest, and the judges ruled him the winner. When someone told Remigino the results before they had been flashed on the scoreboard, he was incredulous and was sure there had been a mistake. Finally he turned to McKenley and is reputed to have said, "Gosh, Herb, it looks as though I won the darn thing." The closeness of the finish is shown by the fact that Dean Smith was only 14 inches behind the winner, yet placed only fourth.

1956 Melbourne C: 65, N: 31, D: 11.24. WR: 10.1 (Lloyd LaBeach, Willie Williams, Ira Murchison, Leamon King)

1.	Bobby Joe Morrow	USA	10.5	(10.62)
2.	W. Thane Baker	USA	10.5	(10.77)
3.	Hector Hogan	AUS	10.6	(10.77)
4.	Ira Murchison	USA	10.6	(10.79)
5.	Manfred Germar	GER	10.7	(10.86)
6.	Michael Agostini	TRI	10.7	(10.88)

The Olympic record was tied in the second round by the favorites, 6-foot 1½-inch Bobby Morrow and 5-foot 4½-inch Ira Murchison. The same pair won the two semifinal heats with Morrow again running 10.3. The final was run into a nine-m.p.h. wind, which accounts for the slow times. Hec Hogan, the five-time Australian 100-yard champion from Queensland, took the early lead, but Morrow passed him after 50 meters and stormed to a decisive victory. Baker and Murchison caught Hogan with 25 yards to go, but Hogan churned out a final burst, and only a desperate lunge by Baker kept the Aussie from a silver medal. Morrow, a devout Christian from San Benito, Texas, never tried to anticipate the starters' gun with a rolling start because he considered it unsportsmanlike. A cotton and carrot farmer, he relied on getting 11 hours' sleep a night to keep up his strength. "Whatever success I have had," he said, "is due to being so perfectly relaxed that I can feel my jaw muscles wiggle." Bronze medalist Hogan died of leukemia at the age of 29 on September 2, 1960, the day after the 100-meter final at Rome.

1960 Rome C: 61, N: 45, D: 9.1. WR: 10.0 (Armin Hary, Harry Jerome)

1.	Armin Hary	GER	10.2	OR	(10.32)
2.	David Sime	USA	10.2		(10.35)
3.	Peter Radford	GBR	10.3		(10.42)
4.	Enrique Figuerola Camue	CUB	10.3		(10.44)
5.	Francis "Frank" Budd	USA	10.3		(10.46)
6.	O. Ray Norton	USA	10.4		(10.50)

On June 21, 1960, controversial Armin Hary, an office worker from Frankfurt, became the first man to be credited with 10.0 in the 100 meters. Running in Zurich, this fast-starting son of a coal miner in Quierschied, Saarland, actually achieved the time twice in one day. On the first occasion he was accused of "taking a flyer," or beating the gun, a tactic for which he was notorious. When the starter ordered the race rerun, Hary protested, but went ahead and ran another 10.0. Three and a half weeks later, on July 15, the son of a Pullman coach attendant, 19-year-old Harry Jerome of Vancouver, recorded the second official 10.0 at the Canadian Olympic trials at Saskatoon.

Despite the achievements of Hary and Jerome, most track aficionados were predicting victory for Ray Norton, who had swept both sprints at the U.S.A.-U.S.S.R. meet, the 1959 Pan American Games, and the 1960 U.S. Olympic trials. Another contender was Dave Sime, a medical student from Fair Lawn, New Jersey. Sime set a rather unusual world record when he ran 100 yards in 9.8 seconds while dressed in a baseball uniform. The previous record had been set by Jesse Owens in 1936.

In the second round in Rome, Armin Hary beat Dave Sime by a yard and set an Olympic record of 10.2. The first semifinal was won by Peter Radford, a Walsall schoolteacher who had spent three childhood years in a wheelchair because of a kidney disease. Harry Jerome had been in the lead when he pulled a muscle and couldn't finish. The second semi saw Armin Hary beat both Sime and Norton, who was running unusually tightly.

The start of the final was a tense affair. First Hary and Sime broke without a gun, but neither was penalized. The next try for a start was halted when Figuerola needed his starting block repaired. Then Hary beat the gun and was penalized. One more false start and he would be disqualified. But the usually volatile Hary kept his poise and at the next attempt got off to a fair and perfect start. By the end of the first stride he was already in the lead, and at the five-meter mark he led by a full meter. In the second half of the race, Sime stormed back from last place to make up over three meters, but Hary held on to win by a "long foot." Not only was Armin Hary the first winner of the Olympic 100 meters to come from a non-English-speaking country, he was also the first German male to win an Olympic gold medal in a track event.

In the end Hary proved that his amazing "blitz start" was legitimate. He contended, however, that there was more to it than quick reflexes. "More important to me," he said, "is the fact that I have learned, through relaxation, how to achieve full stride and smooth forward action very early in the race." He did, however, employ one "trick." Whenever the starter called "set," Hary would stay down until all the other runners were hanging heavily in the set position. Only then would he rise. Unsuspecting starters would invariably wait for him and then pull the trigger for the start, allowing Hary, in effect, to control the beginning of the race. Knowing that the anxious starter would pull the trigger as soon as he was set, Hary would rise, pause a moment, and then take off just as the gun was sounding. Hary's competitive career came to an abrupt halt shortly after the Olympics, when his knee was severely injured in an auto accident. In 1981 his name reappeared in the news when he was convicted of diverting Roman Catholic Church funds for use in a personal investment.

1964 Tokyo C: 73, N: 49, D: 10.15. WR: 10.0 (Armin Hary, Harry Jerome, Horacio Estevez)

1. Robert Hayes	USA	10.0	EWR	(10.05)
2. Enrique Figuerola Camue	CUB	10.2		(10.25)
3. Harry Jerome	CAN	10.2		(10.27)
4. Wieslaw Maniak	POL	10.4		(10.42)
5. Heinz Schumann	GER	10.4		(10.46)
6. Gaoussou Kone	IVC	10.4		(10.47)
6. Melvin Pender	USA	10.4		(10.47)
8. Thomas Robinson	BAH	10.5		(10.57)

This was one 100-meter final that was run exactly to form. Any doubts that Hayes had not recovered from a June leg injury were quickly dispelled when the burly, pigeon-toed Florida speedster demolished the field in the first semifinal in a wind-aided 9.9. Harry Jerome won the second semi, ahead of Kone, Figuerola, and Pender. Pender led most of the way but tore a rib muscle and had to be carried off the field on a stretcher. Advised by doctors to withdraw from the final, he ran anyway and spent the next three days in the hospital as a result. Hayes, who was the first person to run 100 yards in 9.1 and the first person to break 6.0 for 60 yards, entered the Olympics with a record of 48 straight finals victories at 100 yards and 100 meters. The start was delayed 10 minutes while the curb lane, Hayes' lane, was raked after having been chewed up by the start of the 20-kilometer walk. The big three, Hayes, Figuerola, and Jerome, had pulled away from the others by the 10-meter mark. Then Hayes unleashed his power, took a one-meter lead halfway, and pulled away to an awesome seven-foot victory. Both Figuerola, who became the first Cuban to win an Olympic track and field medal, and Jerome called it the best race they had run all year and had nothing but praise for the winner. After the Olympics, Bob Hayes became the first Olympic champion to make a successful transition to professional football. He played nine years for the Dallas Cowboys and was twice chosen All-Pro as a wide receiver. Hayes was so fast that opposing teams had to abandon their traditional man-to-man pass defenses and create the zone defenses that are the standard today. When he retired from football, Hayes plunged into alcoholism and drug use. In 1978 he was arrested by undercover narcotics agents and the following year he pleaded guilty to selling cocaine and methaqualone. In 15 years he went from the top of the Olympic podium to a cell in a Texas prison. He served ten months, drifted back to alcohol and drugs, and then underwent successful rehabilitation. In 1994, at the age of 51, Bob Hayes earned a degree in elementary education from Florida A&M University.

1968 Mexico City C: 64, N: 42, D: 10.14. WR: 9.9 (James Hines, Ronnie Ray Smith, Charles Greene)

1. James Hines	USA	9.95	WR
2. Lennox Miller	JAM	10.04	

3.	Charles Greene	USA	10.07
4.	Pablo Montes	CUB	10.14
5.	Roger Bambuck	FRA	10.16
6.	Melvin Pender	USA	10.17
7.	Harry Jerome	CAN	10.20
8.	Jean-Louis Ravelomanatsoa	MAD	10.28

The first accredited time of 9.9 seconds for 100 meters was registered at the A.A.U. championships in Sacramento, California, on June 20, 1968, by Jim Hines, the son of an Oakland construction worker. Hines had run a wind-aided 9.8 in a heat, then followed with his history-making run in the semifinal. However, in the final he was beaten by Charlie Greene, a graduate of the University of Nebraska. Previous to the Olympics, Hines and Greene had met in 12 finals, with Greene winning eight of them. However two of Hines' four victories had been the last two times they met, at the U.S. Olympic trials.

Competition was stiff in Mexico City. In the second round Heinz Erbstösser of East Germany had the distinction of being the first person to run 10.2 and not qualify for the semifinals. Greene clocked 10.0 in his first two heats, while Hines matched the time in the semis. Hermes Ramirez of Cuba also ran 10.0 in the second round, but was eliminated in the semis. The 1968 100 meters saw the first all-black final in Olympic history. Hines got off to what he later said was the best start of his career. However it was U.S. Army captain Mel Pender, now 30, who took the early lead. By 50 meters Hines and Greene had pulled even, and at 70 meters Hines shifted gears and pulled away to win by a meter. Greene, discouraged and suffering a cramp, was nipped at the tape by Lennox Miller, who represented U.S.C. in U.S. collegiate competition. Hines' electronically timed 9.95 was considered faster than the hand-timed world record of 9.9. Four days after his Olympic victory, Hines signed a contract with the Miami Dolphins football team. Another man who went into professional sports was Japan's Hideo Iijima, who made it to the semifinals in 1964 and 1968. As the fastest sprinter in Japanese history, Iijima attracted the attention of the Lotte Orions baseball team, who hired him to become a pinch-runner and base-stealer. The club insured Iijima's legs for 50 million yen. Unfortunately Iijima, though fast, hadn't played baseball since he was 12 and had no aptitude for getting a jump on a pitch or for sliding. After two years, during which he was caught stealing 17 of 40 times, he was finally dropped from the team.

1972 Munich C: 84, N: 55, D: 9.1. WR: 9.95 (James Hines)

1.	Valery Borzov	SOV/UKR	10.14
2.	Robert Taylor	USA	10.24
3.	Lennox Miller	JAM	10.33
4.	Aleksandr Kornelyuk	SOV/AZR	10.36
5.	Michael Fray	JAM	10.40
6.	Jobst Hirscht	GER	10.40
7.	Zenon Nowosz	POL	10.46

DNF: Hasely Crawford (TRI)

Valery Borzov was the clear favorite in 1972. The blond, blue-eyed Ukrainian was extremely consistent and had not been beaten in almost two years. However, Eddie Hart of Pittsburg, California, and Rey Robinson of Lakeland, Florida, had both been timed at 9.9 in the U.S. Olympic trials. Hart was considered the number-one threat to Borzov. The first round of 12 heats began at 11:09 a.m. on August 31. Borzov, Hart, and Robinson each won their heats. Vassilios Papageorgopoulous of Greece recorded the fastest time of the round, 10.24, a time that might have earned him a silver medal had he not suffered a groin injury that forced him to withdraw from the semifinals. The second round, the quarterfinals, was scheduled to commence at 4:15 p.m. As that time drew nearer, 1968 400-meter gold medalist Lee Evans noticed that Hart, Robinson, and the third U.S. sprinter, Robert Taylor, had not yet arrived at the stadium. When he couldn't find them at the warm-up track, Evans began to worry. Scheduled to run in the 4 × 400-meter relay later in the week, he raced at top speed from the stadium to the Olympic Village three quarters of a mile away in search of the missing Americans. But it was too late.

Two minutes earlier, Hart, Robinson, and Taylor, thinking the quarterfinals didn't begin until 7 p.m., had casually left their quarters to return to the stadium. Accompanied by their coach, Stan Wright, who had been working from an outdated 18-month-old preliminary schedule, the trio made their way to the bus stop at the Village gate. While waiting for the track stadium bus, they wandered into the doorway of the ABC-TV headquarters and began watching the television monitor. What they saw on the screen was several 100-meter runners lining up at the starting line. Robinson asked if this was a rerun of the first round. Told that it was a live transmission, Robinson realized with horror that he was watching the very heat in which he had been scheduled to run. Hart was entered in the second heat and Taylor in the third. The three athletes and their coach were pushed into a car and driven at breakneck speed to the stadium by ABC employee Bill Norris. It was too late for Robinson and Hart, but Taylor, who, like Jim Hines, had studied at Texas Southern, arrived just in time to slip off his sweats, put on his shoes, do a couple knee bends, and settle into the starting blocks. He finished second in the heat, a yard behind Borzov, which is exactly where he ended up 25 hours later, in the final. In that race, Borzov took the lead after 30 meters and was never headed. He even eased up at the end, throwing his arms wide in exultation five meters from the finish. A last-chance dive gained dental student Lennox Miller third place over Aleksandr Kornelyuk, the 5-foot 5-inch surprise from Azerbaijan. Oddly enough, Borzov almost missed the same quarterfinal heat that Hart and Robinson missed. First he was misinformed about the starting time of his heat. His coach convinced him to stay in the stadium. Borzov dozed off, and when he awoke his heat was being called. He raced to the track, but was stopped by a German official. Pushing aside the official, Borzov got to the line just in time to prepare his starting blocks.

Following the final, Borzov told reporters (in English) that he owed his success, "First and foremost to my country, secondly to my coach, Valentin Petrovsky, thirdly to all the people who helped me develop, and fourthly to myself." Borzov wasn't just toeing the party line. Listen to Petrovsky explain what went on at the Kiev Institute of Physical Culture, where Borzov was a graduate student: "We began with a search for the most up-to-date model of sprinting. We studied slow-motion films of leading world sprinters of past and present, figured out the push-off angle and the body incline at the breakaway and went deeply into a whole number of minor details. . . . For Borzov to be able to clock ten seconds flat over 100 meters, a whole team of scientists conducted research resembling the work of, say, car or aircraft designers. . . . When the mathematical equivalent of a runner was worked out and given a scientific basis, we began testing our calculations in practice. It was subtle work, which could be compared to the training of a ballerina." Such statements give the impression that Borzov was just a machine, but he was quite human. He once said, "I very often have the following urge: I suddenly feel on the street that I have to run. I absolutely have to run, dressed in a suit, wearing my hat and tie, not paying any attention to the passers-by. . . . Then convention gets the upper hand and I restrain myself." Borzov eventually married the famous gymnast Lyudmila Turischeva, who won even more gold medals than he did.

1976 Montreal C: 63, N: 40, D: 7.24. WR: 9.95 (James Hines)

1. Hasely Crawford	TRI	10.06
2. Donald Quarrie	JAM	10.07
3. Valery Borzov	SOV/UKR	10.14
4. Harvey Glance	USA	10.19
5. Guy Abrahams	PAN	10.25
6. John Jones	USA	10.27
7. Klaus-Dieter Kurrat	GDR	10.31
8. Peter Petrov	BUL	10.35

Several runners were given a strong chance to win, but the leading choices of track experts were Donald Quarrie, Silvio Leonard of Cienfuegos, Cuba, and Valery Borzov, who was aiming to become the first man to win two 100-meters gold medals (not counting Archie Hahn, whose second victory was in the Intercalated Games of 1906). In fact, Borzov was the first gold medalist even to attempt the feat since Percy Williams had been eliminated in the semifinals in 1932. The first of the leading contenders to fall by the wayside was the accident-prone Cuban Silvio Leonard. Leonard had won the 100 meters at the 1975 Pan American Games in Mexico City, but had pulled a muscle as he crossed the finish line. Hobbling forward in pain, he was unable to stop himself and fell into the ten-foot moat that surrounded

the track. Seriously injured, Leonard nonetheless regained his form in time for the Olympics. Ten days before the Games, however, he stepped on a cologne bottle during a bit of horseplay and cut his foot. He was eliminated in the quarterfinals.

Meanwhile, 6-foot 2¾-inch Hasely Crawford, a gear machinist from San Fernando, Trinidad, was breezing through his heats. In the quarterfinals he beat Borzov, and in the semis he defeated Quarrie. Crawford had been a finalist in Munich four years earlier but had stopped running after four or five strides, the victim of a hamstring pull and nervousness. He was still fighting his nerves in Montreal, but he wasn't the only one. In the staging room before the final Crawford ranted and raved and tried to intimidate his opponents. When he stared at Glance and Jones, who were only 19 and 18, respectively, their "eyes showed they were already defeated." Crawford later told reporters, "At the line I knew I could beat Borzov. I feared Don Quarrie." At the starting line, Crawford "shook a little bit," but got a good start anyway. Glance took the early lead. Quarrie caught him after 60 meters and passed him at 75 meters. Then Crawford flew past on the curb lane. He stumbled just before the finish, but held off the lunging Quarrie to win. Crawford kept running for another 150 meters, then stopped suddenly, as if the realization of his accomplishment had just hit him.

As Trinidad's first Olympic champion, Crawford received more than his share of honors. He was awarded the Trinity Cross, his picture appeared on two postage stamps, an airplane was named after him, and six different Calypso songs were written in his honor.

1980 Moscow C: 65, N: 40, D: 7.25. WR: 9.95 (James Hines)

1. Allan Wells	GBR	10.25
2. Silvio Leonard Tartabull	CUB	10.25
3. Peter Petrov	BUL	10.39
4. Aleksandr Aksinin	SOV/RUS	10.42
5. Osvaldo Lara Cañizares	CUB	10.43
6. Vladimir Muravyov	SOV/KAZ	10.44
7. Marian Woronin	POL	10.46
8. Hermann Panzo	FRA	10.49

Stanley Floyd of Albany, Georgia, won the U.S. Olympic trials and also recorded the best time of the year (10.07). But with U.S. athletes boycotted out of the Olympics the mantle of favorite fell to Silvio Leonard, who had successfully managed to steer clear of moats and cologne bottles. His most serious challengers were considered to be Marian Woronin, who predicted that he would win the gold medal in a time of 10.10, and Eugen Ray of East Germany. Aleksandr Aksinin recorded the fastest time of the first round—10.26. When the draw was announced for the second round, many eyebrows were raised. Of the nine first-round winners, four were thrown into the first heat, as was defending champion Hasely Crawford. On the other hand, heat number three saw

Aksinin unburdened by competition from other first-round winners. Aksinin won that heat in 10.29, a time that would have placed him seventh in the first heat. Heat number one was won by Allan Wells, a marine engineer from Edinburgh. His time of 10.11 pushed him to cofavorite with Leonard.

The final took place during the last round of the triple jump, an event of great interest to the Soviet crowd. Just as the starter called "set," a great roar went up for a jump made by local favorite Viktor Saneyev. The starter held the runners in their crouch, then shot the gun. Aksinin and Lara were off the fastest, with Leonard and Wells close behind. By 60 meters Lara had faded, and by 80 meters the race was between Leonard on the inside and Wells on the outside. Wells edged ahead, but Leonard drew even again. With seven meters to go the stocky Scot began an extreme lean which allowed his shoulder to cross the finish line two or three inches before Leonard's chest. Allan Wells had become Great Britain's first 100-meters winner since Harold Abrahams and Scotland's first track gold medalist since Eric Liddell. At 28 he was also the oldest winner of the 100 meters at that time. As a youngster Wells had enrolled in a Charles Atlas correspondence course in bodybuilding. His father was a blacksmith and his mother sewed nets for fishermen and worked as a hospital cleaner. Wells didn't turn from long-jumping to sprinting until 1976, at which time his personal best was only 10.9. Coached by his wife, Wells did not use starting blocks until 1980, when the International Amateur Athletic Federation (I.A.A.F.) required their use in international competitions.

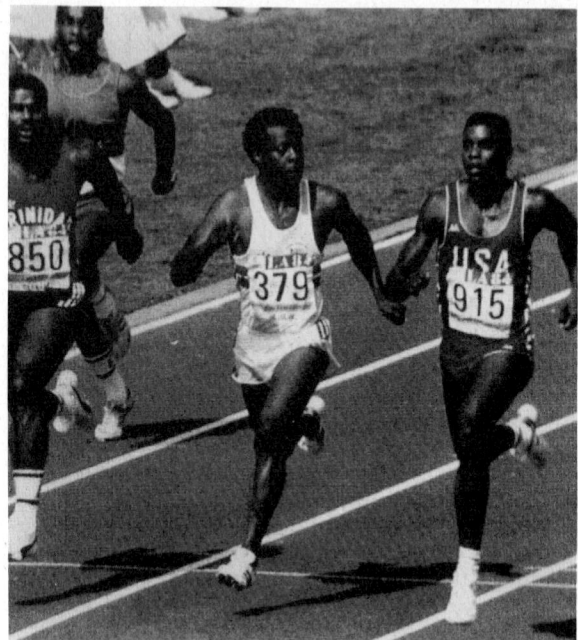

Hasely Crawford, Henry Ngoawe, and Michael McFarlane all divert their attention from the finish line as Carl Lewis (right) breezes past them to win the opening heat of the 1984 100 meters. Lewis went on to match Jesse Owens' four gold medals of 1936. Four years later, in Seoul, he became the first man to win the 100 meters twice.

1984 Los Angeles C: 82, N: 59, D: 8.4. WR: 9.93 (Calvin Smith)

1. F. Carlton Lewis	USA	9.99
2. Sam Graddy	USA	10.19
3. Benjamin Johnson	CAN	10.22
4. Ron Brown	USA	10.26
5. Michael McFarlane	GBR	10.27
6. Raymond Stewart	JAM	10.29
7. Donovan Reid	GBR	10.33
8. Tony Sharpe	CAN	10.35

The third son of two track coaches, Carl Lewis was born in Birmingham, Alabama, and raised in Willingboro, New Jersey. Small for his age and shy, Lewis began to grow so rapidly at the age of 15 (two and a half inches in one month), that he had to walk with crutches for three weeks while his body adjusted. Previously thought to be the least athletic member of his talented family, Lewis' achievements began to outstrip all around him. By 1981 he was ranked number one in the world in the 100-meter dash and in the long jump. In June of 1983, he won the 100, the 200, and the long jump at the U.S. national championships, the first person to do so since Malcolm Ford in 1886. Two months later, he earned three gold medals at the Helsinki world championships. The follow-

ing year he qualified for four events at the Los Angeles Olympics, giving him the opportunity to match Jesse Owens' four-gold-medal feat of 1936.

Lewis' first stop was the 100 meters, the event at which he was considered most vulnerable. As it turned out, he dominated the field. His second-round time of 10.04 was the best ever at a low-altitude Olympics. In the final, Graddy and Johnson were out fastest. Graddy still led at the 80-meter mark. "I thought, 'Hey, I'm going to win a gold medal,'" Graddy would later say. "Then I saw him out of the corner of my eye." Lewis, who was clocked at 28 m.p.h. at the finish, pulled away so strongly that his winning margin was a remarkable eight feet—the widest in Olympic history. Carl Lewis had won the first of his four gold medals.

1988 Seoul C: 102, N: 69, D: 9.24. WR: 9.83 (Benjamin Johnson)

1. F. Carlton Lewis	USA	9.92	OR
2. Linford Christie	GBR	9.97	
3. Calvin Smith	USA	9.99	
4. Dennis Mitchell	USA	10.04	
5. Robson Caetano da Silva	BRA	10.11	
6. Desai Williams	CAN	10.11	
7. Raymond Stewart	JAM	12.26	
DISQ (Drugs): Benjamin Johnson (CAN) 9.79			

Ben Johnson was born in Falmouth, Jamaica, on December 30, 1961. Small and shy, he began to stutter at the age of 12 as a result of constantly mimicking his older brother's stammer. When he was 14 he moved to Toronto with his mother and three of his five siblings. Like his future rival, Carl Lewis, Johnson experienced a rapid growth spurt when he was 15 years old. It was also at this time that Johnson came under the tutelage of sprint coach Charlie Francis, the man who would guide his running career for the next 11 years.

On August 29, 1980, Johnson took part in the Pan American Junior Championships in Sudbury, Ontario, finishing sixth with a time of 10.86. This seemingly unimportant race would, in retrospect, earn significance as the first encounter between Johnson and Lewis, who won the contest in 10.43. Johnson scored his first major international success two years later when he finished second at the 1982 Commonwealth Games. Two years after that he qualified for the 100-meter final at the Los Angeles Olympics. After purposely false-starting in an unsuccessful attempt to rattle Lewis, Johnson surprised track fans by earning the bronze medal behind Lewis and Sam Graddy.

In 1985, after seven consecutive losses, Johnson finally defeated Lewis. By 1986 there was no question that "Big Ben" had wrested the title of Fastest Man on Earth from "King Carl." By the time of their classic confrontation at the 1987 world championships in Rome, it was Johnson who had won their last four encounters. By that time, also, Johnson had developed a reputation as an incredibly fast starter who appeared to leap out of the blocks like a panther going after a kill or a guard dog attacking an intruder. In the Rome final he burst off the line with so much power that he almost fell over. After ten meters he was already in front by a full meter, a lead he would hold all the way to the finish line, which he reached in a mere 9.83 seconds, breaking the world record by a full tenth of a second. In less than ten seconds Ben Johnson had become an international celebrity. He would soon sign commercial endorsement contracts worth millions of dollars.

Meanwhile, Carl Lewis, who had equaled the world record of 9.93 only to finish second, was livid. Although he refused to name names, he made it clear that he thought Johnson was taking illegal, performance-enhancing drugs. Although many dismissed Lewis' charges as sour grapes, he was not alone in his suspicions. On the track circuit, Johnson's highly sculptured muscles and yellow-tinged eyes, two indications of steroid use, had earned Johnson the nickname "Benoid." However, as his coach, Charlie Francis, was quick to point out, Johnson had passed innumerable drug tests. In 1985 Johnson himself told Canada's *Athletics* magazine, "Drugs are both demeaning and despicable and when people are caught they should be thrown out of the sport for good. . . . I want to be the best on my own natural ability and no drugs will pass into my body."

As 1988 began, Johnson seemed to have a lock on the Olympic gold medal. But then disaster struck. In February, he pulled a hamstring muscle. In May, he reinjured his leg. In June, he broke away from Charlie Francis for the first time. However, a few weeks later they reconciled and Johnson returned to competition in time to win the Canadian Olympic trials. On August 17 in Zurich, the site of Johnson's first victory over Lewis three years earlier, the two met again for the first time since the Rome world championships. As usual, Johnson broke in front, but this time Lewis mowed him down to win with a time of 9.93 seconds. Calvin Smith was second at 9.97 and Johnson third at 10.00. Five days later in Cologne, Johnson was again beaten into third place, this time by Smith and Dennis Mitchell.

While Johnson retreated to Canada for a final month of training, Lewis was installed as the overwhelming favorite to become the first male sprinter to retain his Olympic title. Johnson dismissed this growing consensus. "When the gun go off," he said, "the race be over."

In Seoul, Lewis appeared to be in perfect form. He registered the fastest time in each of the first two rounds: 10.14 and 9.99. Johnson, meanwhile, caused a minor sensation in the second round. The rules stated that the top two finishers in each of the six heats would advance to the semifinals, as would the four fastest of the remaining runners. Johnson, misjudging the size of his lead, eased up long before the end, and dropped to third behind Linford Christie and Dennis Mitchell. Fortunately, Johnson's 10.17 allowed him to advance anyway.

The semifinals were held the following day, Saturday, at noon. Lewis won the first heat in 9.97. In the second, Johnson was called for a false start, a ruling that infuriated him. Still, he managed to control his anger and win the race in 10.03 despite running into a 1.2-meters-persecond head wind.

Less than an hour and a half later, the eight finalists met at the starting line. Carl Lewis was in lane 3, Ben Johnson in lane 6. They were separated by Linford Christie and Calvin Smith. By now Johnson's muscles were so highly developed that, as he waited for the sound of the starter's pistol, they seemed to be separate beings on the verge of exploding out of his skin. As expected, Johnson charged into the lead immediately.

On May 5, 1987, Carl Lewis' father had died of cancer. At the funeral, Carl had reached into his pocket and pulled out the gold medal he had earned for winning the 100 meters in 1984. He placed the medal in his father's hands and said, "I want you to have this because it was your favorite event." Noting his mother's surprise, he added, "Don't worry, I'll get another one."

Now, halfway through the 1988 final, he glanced to his right, saw Ben Johnson five feet ahead of him, and was convinced that he could catch him. At the 80-meter mark Lewis looked over again and discovered that he was still five feet behind. This time he knew the race was lost. "Damn," he thought. "Ben did it again. The bastard got away with it again. It's over, Dad." Just before the finish line, Johnson stared back at Lewis and thrust his right arm into the air, his index finger pointed to the sky. His time was an amazing 9.79.

Lewis, convinced that Johnson was on steroids, wanted to protest, but held his tongue. As he later wrote in his autobiography, *Inside Track,* "I didn't have the medal to replace the one I had given [my father], and that hurt. But I could still give something to my father by acting the way he had always wanted me to act, with class and dignity." He shook Johnson's hand and walked away, ignoring the taunts of a group of Canadian fans who chanted, "When the gun go off, the race be over."

Johnson accepted the accolades of the crowd, appeared live on Canadian television, and then went off to doping control where he required one and a half hours and several beers to produce a urine sample. Afterward he spent over an hour in a sauna, then celebrated by eating half of a cream cake given to him by his mother, dining with friends at an Italian restaurant, and visiting a disco.

Back in Canada, the population was in ecstasy. In the 12 Olympics prior to the boycotted Games of 1980 and 1984, Canada had averaged one gold medal per Olympics. Its last track-and-field gold had come in 1932. The

The finish of the 1988 100-meter dash—without Ben Johnson.

headline in the *Toronto Star* summed up the mood of the nation: "Ben Johnson—a national treasure."

Meanwhile, Johnson's urine sample was delivered to the Olympic Doping Control Center, numbered, and divided into two parts labeled "A" and "B." On Sunday, the testing center, not knowing whose urine they were examining, discovered that the "A" sample contained steroids. This information was passed on to Prince Alexandre de Merode of Belgium, the chairman of the I.O.C.'s medical commission. He matched the sample to a list of athletes' numbers and became the first person to learn that the guilty party was Ben Johnson. De Merode wrote a letter to the Canadian team, which was delivered at 1:45 a.m., Monday. At 7:00 a.m., Carol Anne Letheren, the Canadian *chef de mission,* informed Johnson of the positive test. Three hours later, with Canadian representatives in attendance, the "B" sample was tested and it too registered positive.

At 3:30 Tuesday morning, Letheren revisited Johnson to collect his gold medal. "We love you," she told him, "but you're guilty."

At 10:00 a.m., the I.O.C. called a press conference and issued the following statement: "The urine sample of Ben Johnson (Canada—Athletics—100 meters) collected on Saturday, 24th September 1988 was found to contain the metabolites of a banned substance namely stanozolol (anabolic steroid). . . . The I.O.C. Medical Commission recommends the following sanction: disqualification of this competitor from the Games of the XXIV Olympiad in Seoul. Of course, the gold medal has been withdrawn by the I.O.C."

Although Johnson was the 43rd Olympic athlete to be disqualified because of drugs since testing began in 1968, he was the first "big fish" to be caught. His disgrace was front-page news all over the world. Initially, Johnson denied having taken steroids. Charlie Francis claimed that Johnson was a victim of sabotage, that he had been given a spiked drink. Francis even hinted that agents of Carl Lewis had been responsible.

The Canadian government, to its great credit, wasted no time in ordering an investigation into the use of banned substances by Canadian athletes, including several of Johnson's sprinting teammates and a number of weightlifters who tested positive before the Games and were not allowed to travel to Seoul. The investigation, much of which was televised live, became known as the Dubin Inquiry in honor of the man in charge of the hearings, Charles Dubin, an associate chief justice of the Ontario Supreme Court.

Testifying before the Dubin Commission, Charlie Francis and Johnson's doctor, George (Jamie) Astaphan, revealed that the sprinter began taking steroids in November 1981 because Francis convinced him that everyone else was taking them and that if he didn't, he would be left behind. Over the next seven years, Johnson took the anabolic steroids Dianabol, stanozolol, and furazabol, as well as testosterone, diuretics, which he used as masking agents, and human growth hormone, which was made from human cadavers. Although Astaphan had once labeled a bottle of steroids "Do Not Take Within 28 Days of Competition," he apparently gave Johnson an injection only 26 days before the Olympic final. The Dubin Commission concluded that this injection contained Winstrol-V, a stanozolol compound used to fatten cattle before they are sent to market.

On June 12, 1989, Johnson himself appeared before the Dubin Commission. He admitted taking steroids and lying to the public when he said he hadn't. The following day, he was asked if he had any message for young athletes who had considered him their idol. With tears in his eyes, he replied, "I want to tell them to be honest and don't take drugs. It happened to me. I've been there. I know what it's like to cheat."

Three months later, the I.A.A.F., in a controversial decision, retroactively rescinded Johnson's 1987 world record even though he had passed the drug test in Rome. Johnson served out his standard two-year suspension and returned to competition in 1991. However, his times were not what they had been in his drug-augmented heyday. Johnson qualified for the 1992 Canadian Olympic team but was eliminated in the semifinals at the Olympics. Following a meet in Montreal on January 17, 1993, Johnson again tested positive for drugs—this time excessive levels of the male hormone testosterone—and he was banned for life. Although he had passed similar tests two days before and four days after the Montreal meet, Johnson chose not to appeal the ban.

The 1988 gold medal, which Johnson lost, did go to Carl Lewis after all, raising Lewis' career total to six golds and one silver.

1992 Barcelona C: 81, N: 66, D: 8.1. WR: 9.86 (F. Carlton Lewis)

1. Linford Christie	GBR	9.96
2. Frank Fredericks	NAM	10.02
3. Dennis Mitchell	USA	10.04
4. Bruny Surin	CAN	10.09
5. Leroy Burrell	USA	10.10
6. Olapade Adeniken	NGR	10.12
7. Raymond Stewart	JAM	10.22
8. Davidson Ezinwa	NGR	10.26

Ben Johnson was not the only Jamaican-born sprinter who tested positive for prohibited drugs at the 1988 Olympics. Linford Christie's doping test revealed traces of the banned stimulant pseudoephedrine. But because the amount was so small, Christie was not disqualified or otherwise punished. On August 25, 1991, Christie was one of the entrants in one of the greatest 100-meter races of all time—the world championship final in Tokyo. Carl Lewis won that race, setting a world record of 9.86. He was followed by Leroy Burrell at 9.88, Dennis Mitchell at 9.91, Christie at 9.92, Frank Fredericks at 9.95, and Raymond Stewart at 9.96—the first and only time that six runners have beaten ten seconds in one race. Christie was so discouraged by the result that he considered retiring.

Christie had a mixed reputation. On the one hand, he was reasonably popular with the public and was voted Britain's sexiest athlete in 1991. On the other hand, his defensive and hypersensitive demeanor earned him less respect with the press and with fellow athletes. As quartermiler Derek Redmond put it, Christie was "Britain's best-balanced athlete, because he has a chip on both shoulders."

Christie's Barcelona chances were improved when Lewis, winner of every major championship race since 1983, was weakened by a virus and placed only sixth at the U.S. Olympic trials, qualifying only for the 4 × 100-meter relay and the long jump.

Meanwhile, Christie, at age 32, was having his best season ever. His only loss was by 1/100 of a second to Olapade Adeniken. However, Christie still had to overcome former world record holder Leroy Burrell, who had beaten him ten straight times over the past three years. In the Olympic quarterfinals, Christie finally broke that streak, edging Burrell 10.07 to 10.08 in the last heat. The following day, running into a 1.2-meters-per-second headwind, Burrell beat Christie 9.97 to 10.00 in the first semifinal. The second semi was won by Fredericks in 10.17.

In the final, Burrell was charged with a false start even though he never left his blocks. Distressed, he was never a factor in the race. After a second delay, when Mitchell signaled that he was not ready, the runners finally took off. Haitian-born Bruny Surin grabbed the early lead and held it for 40 meters. Over the next 20 meters Christie caught first Fredericks and then Surin. By the 60-meter mark he was in first place and pulling away. Linford Christie is, by four years, the oldest man to win the Olympic 100 meters. Fredericks became the first black African to medal in the event, and, far from the hoopla and medal attention, Ray Stewart became the first man to run in three 100-meters finals.

200 METERS

The 200-meter race is one half lap—a sprint around a curve. Because the runners must stay in their lanes, there is a staggered start so that all runners end up covering the same distance. Like the 100 meters, the 200 meters has been dominated by runners from English-speaking countries. Anglophones have won 18 of 21 gold medals and a startling 54 of 63 total medals.

1896 not held

1900 Paris C: 15?, N: 7?, D: 7.22. WR (220 yards): 21.2 (Bernie Wefers)

1. John Walter Tewksbury	USA	22.2
2. Norman Pritchard	IND	22.8
3. Stanley Rowley	AUS	22.9
4. William Joseph Holland	USA	—

With this victory Tewksbury earned his fifth medal of the games. He had already won the 400-meter hurdles, finished second in the 60-meter and 100-meter sprints, and third in the 200-meter hurdles.

1904 St. Louis C: 7, N: 2, D: 8.31. WR (220 yards): 21.2 (Bernie Wefers)

1. Charles "Archie" Hahn	USA	21.6	OR
2. Nathaniel Cartmell	USA	21.9	
3. William Hogenson	USA	—	
4. Fay Moulton	USA	—	

Cartmell, Hogenson, and Moulton each false started once, which, according to the rules at that time, resulted in their being penalized two yards. Hahn took good advantage of his head start and led the entire way. Cartmell closed within one yard, but Hahn pulled away again and won by three yards. Commented Cartmell, "He's little, but he certainly can run."

1906 not held

1908 London C: 43, N: 14, D: 7.23. WR (220 yards): 21.2 (Bernie Wefers, Dan Kelly)

1. Robert Kerr	CAN	22.6
2. Robert Cloughen	USA	22.6
3. Nathaniel Cartmell	USA	22.7
4. George Hawkins	GBR	22.9

Bobby Kerr was born in Enniskillen, Ireland. When he was seven years old his family moved to Canada, settling in Hamilton, Ontario. As a teenager Kerr joined the International Harvester Fire Brigade, which prided itself on the speed of its members. Kerr represented Canada at the St. Louis Olympics in 1904 and had hoped to compete at Athens in 1906, but not enough money could be raised to pay his passage. He did make it to London, where, ten days before the Olympics, he swept both sprints at the British A.A.A. championships. At the 1908 Olympics he rebounded from the disappointment of finishing third in the 100 meters to win the 200 meters by less than a foot. The following year Kerr returned to Ireland and fulfilled his dream of representing the nation of his birth in an international meet. In 1928 he was the captain of the Canadian Olympic team, and in 1932 he was manager of the track and field division. Cloughen, the silver medalist, did not qualify for the U.S. team and was only able to compete because his parents paid his way.

1912 Stockholm C: 60, N: 19, D: 7.11. WR (220 yards): 21.2 (Bernie Wefers, Dan Kelly, Ralph Craig)

1. Ralph Craig	USA	21.7
2. Donald Lippincott	USA	21.8
3. William Applegarth	GBR	22.0
4. Richard Rau	GER	22.2
5. Charles Reidpath	USA	22.3
6. Donnell Young	USA	22.3

1920 Antwerp C: 48, N: 22, D: 8.20. WR (220 yards): 21.2 (Bernie Wefers, Dan Kelly, Ralph Craig, Howard Drew, William Applegarth)

1. Allen Woodring	USA	22.0
2. Charles Paddock	USA	22.0e
3. Harry Edward	GBR	22.1e
4. Loren Murchison	USA	22.2e
5. George Davidson	NZE	22.3e
6. Jack Oosterlaak	SAF	22.4e

Allen Woodring of Syracuse University had qualified for the U.S. team only as an alternate, but when George Massengale of Missouri was stiffened by an attack of rheumatism, Woodring was allowed to compete. In the final Paddock led from the start, but Woodring caught him at the 180-meter mark. Just as Paddock began the takeoff of his flying finish, Woodring flashed by him to steal the victory. The young New Yorker couldn't believe he had won and was sure that Paddock had graciously allowed him to finish first. Paddock finally convinced him that he had given his all and that the victory was legitimate.

1924 Paris C: 62, N: 32, D: 7.9. WR: 21.0 (Charles Paddock)

1. Jackson Scholz	USA	21.6	EOR
2. Charles Paddock	USA	21.7	
3. Eric Liddell	GBR	21.9	
4. George Hill	USA	22.0	
5. Bayes Norton	USA	22.0	
6. Harold Abrahams	GBR	22.3	

The day before the semifinals and final, Charley Paddock was convinced that he was over the hill and could never succeed the following day. His friend Douglas Fairbanks took him home, and together they dined and joked with Mary Pickford and Maurice Chevalier, who entertained them with imitations of Paavo Nurmi and Harold Abrahams, who had already won the 100 meters and who had beaten Charley in the first round of the 200 earlier that day. After dinner Fairbanks and Chevalier went for a walk while Mary Pickford gave Paddock an inspirational pep talk. She told him that his fate rested in his own hands. "If you believe in yourself," she said, "you will win tomorrow."

Paddock took her advice to heart, slept well, and awoke the next day refreshed and relaxed. He won his semifinal heat with ease, with Scholz winning the other semi. In the final Abrahams fell behind quickly while the others ran almost evenly. By the 120-meter mark Paddock had opened up a two-foot lead, but Scholz came on strong, reaching Paddock's shoulder with ten yards to go. In the final stride he moved ahead and won by less than a foot. Paddock pulled a ligament in his thigh in his final leap and collapsed to the ground beyond the finish line.

Scholz, who was born in St. Louis, later made his living as an author of "pulp" fiction, publishing 31 sports novels. Interest in Scholz was renewed with the release of the film *Chariots of Fire*, which took great liberties in its portrayal of him. There is one scene in the film in which Scholz, just before the start of the 400 meters, approaches Eric Liddell and hands him a piece of paper inscribed with a religious message. Scholz actually did no such thing—he wasn't even religious. This put him in a difficult situation. When *Chariots of Fire* became a hit, the 84-year-old Scholz, now living in Delray Beach, Florida, was inundated with mail from people requesting spiritual inspiration. "I'm afraid," he told reporters, "that my religious background was rather casual."

1928 Amsterdam C: 62, N: 30, D: 8.1. WR (track with curve): 20.6 (Roland Locke)

1. Percy Williams	CAN	21.8
2. Walter Rangeley	GBR	21.9
3. Helmuth Körnig	GER	21.9
4. Jackson Scholz	USA	21.9
5. John Fitzpatrick	CAN	22.1
6. Jakob Schüller	GER	22.2

The early rounds saw unusually stiff competition. In the quarterfinals Helmuth Körnig, pressed by Walter Rangeley of Salford, Lancashire, and Charlie Borah, the U.S. champion, equaled the Olympic record of 21.6. Since only two from each heat advanced to the semifinals, Borah was eliminated. The first semi saw the fall of Charley Paddock, who finished fifth behind Williams and Rangeley. The second semi was won by Körnig, with defending champion Scholz second. In the final Körnig led coming out of the turn, but with 50 meters to go he was passed by Williams and Rangeley. Williams, running his eighth race in four days, pulled away and won by almost a yard. A dead heat was declared for third place between Körnig and Scholz, and a rerun between the two was ordered. However, by the time this decision had been reached, Scholz had already broken training, so he forfeited the runoff. Subsequent examination of the photo-finish revealed that Körnig had actually won third place anyway.

1932 Los Angeles C: 25, N: 13, D: 8.3. WR: 20.6 (Roland Locke, James Carlton)

1. Thomas "Eddie" Tolan	USA	21.2	OR
2. George Simpson	USA	21.4	
3. Ralph Metcalfe	USA	21.5	
4. Arthur Jonath	GER	21.5	
5. Carlos Bianchi Luti	ARG	21.6	
6. William Walters	SAF	21.9	

One man who did not compete in the 1932 Olympics was James Carlton of Lismore, New South Wales, who had beaten George Simpson twice. On January 16, 1932, Carlton shocked the world by winning the Australian 220-yard championship in 20.6, around the curve of an oval track. Speculation on Carlton's chance for an Olympic gold medal was cut short when the 24-year-old became a monk and retired to a monastery. In the quarterfinals at Los Angeles the Olympic record of 21.6, which had first been set by Archie Hahn back in 1904, was broken in each of the four heats. In the first two heats it was lowered to 21.5 by Metcalfe, who had won the U.S. trials, and by Tolan, who had edged Metcalfe to win the 100

meters gold medal the day before. In the third heat Luti broke the record again, at 21.4, and in the fourth heat his time was matched by sportswriter Arthur Jonath. The following day the first heat of the semifinals was won by Metcalfe, with Simpson beside him. In the second semi, won by Jonath, Tolan was almost eliminated. Content to qualify for the final with a third-place finish, Tolan almost failed to notice the closing rush of Canadian Harold Wright, who closed within a foot but fell short.

Luti had the quickest start in the final, but as they came out of the turn Simpson of Ohio State was leading by almost a yard. Tolan, who chewed gum while he ran, surged ahead with 50 meters to go, stumbled just before the finish, and held on to win by five or six feet. When films of the race were viewed, it was discovered that Metcalfe had inadvertently been forced to dig his starting holes three or four feet behind the spot where they should have been, which deprived him of a silver medal. Metcalfe was offered a rerun by race officials, but he didn't want to jeopardize the U.S. medal sweep and so declined.

1936 Berlin C: 44, N: 22, D: 8.5. WR: 20.6 (Roland Locke, James Carlton)

1. James "Jesse" Owens	USA	20.7	OR
2. Matthew "Mack" Robinson	USA	21.1	
3. Martinus Osendarp	HOL	21.3	
4. Paul Hänni	SWI	21.6	
5. Lee Orr	CAN	21.6	
6. Wijnand van Beveren	HOL	21.9	

In the first round Jesse Owens set an Olympic record of 21.1 seconds, a time that he repeated in the second round and which was matched by Mack Robinson of Pasadena, California, in the semifinals. The final was run in a light rain, but this didn't prevent Owens from sprinting away from the field in record time. He led by almost two yards entering the straightaway and won by four yards to gain his third gold medal of the Berlin games. Silver medalist Robinson was something of a surprise. His high school coaches did not consider him athletic material and made his mother sign a statement absolving them of blame if his heart was damaged. Local businessmen paid his way to the U.S. Olympic trials. His younger brother, Jackie Robinson, gained fame with the Brooklyn Dodgers as the first black major league player in modern baseball history.

1948 London C: 50, N: 26, D: 8.3. WR: 20.6 (Roland Locke, James Carlton)

1. Melvin Patton	USA	21.1
2. H. Norwood "Barney" Ewell	USA	21.1
3. Lloyd LaBeach	PAN	21.2
4. Herbert McKenley	JAM	21.2
5. Clifford Bourland	USA	21.3
6. Leslie Laing	JAM	21.6

McKenley and Bourland looked strongest in the preliminaries, both of them clocking 21.3 in each of the first two rounds. They also won their respective semifinal heats. In the final, however, it was the favorites who came through fastest. Patton, intent on making up for his disappointing fifth place finish in the 100, pulled away coming out of the turn and led by almost two meters. Ewell closed fast, but Patton held him off with a final spurt to win by two feet.

1952 Helsinki C: 71, N: 35, D: 7.23. WR: 20.6 (Roland Locke, James Carlton, Andrew Stanfield)

1. Andrew Stanfield	USA	20.7	EOR	(20.81)
2. W. Thane Baker	USA	20.8		(20.97)
3. James Gathers	USA	20.8		(21.08)
4. Emmanuel McDonald Bailey	GBR	21.0		(21.14)
5. Leslie Laing	JAM	21.2		(21.45)
6. Gerardo Bönnhoff	ARG	21.3		(21.59)

Stanfield, a 6-foot 1-inch, 24-year-old from Jersey City, New Jersey, was the unanimous favorite. As expected, he and Mac Bailey won the semifinals. Bailey ran well on the turn in the final, and as they hit the straightaway he was almost even with Stanfield, but Stanfield pulled away with ease and won by a yard and a half. The official times appear to be incorrect, since Bailey actually finished quite close to Gathers.

1956 Melbourne C: 67, N: 32, D: 11.27. WR: 20.6 (Roland Locke, James Carlton, Andrew Stanfield, Bobby Joe Morrow, W. Thane Baker)

1. Bobby Joe Morrow	USA	20.6	OR	(20.75)
2. Andrew Stanfield	USA	20.7		(20.97)
3. W. Thane Baker	USA	20.9		(21.05)
4. Michael Agostini	TRI	21.1		(21.35)
5. Boris Tokaryev	SOV/RUS	21.2		(21.42)
6. José Telles da Conceição	BRA	21.3		(21.56)

Bobby Morrow, the winner of the 100, was the favorite to win the 200 and become the first man since Jesse Owens to achieve a double in the Olympic sprints. He appeared for the first round with his left thigh bandaged, having suffered a slight groin pull in the final of the 100. Fortunately he was able to breeze through the early heats with little competition while allowing his muscle to heal. Abdul Khaliq of Pakistan ran 21.1 in both of the first two rounds, but wore himself out and was eliminated in the semifinals, which were won by Baker (21.1) and Stanfield (21.2). One unexpected finalist was Telles da Conceição, who had won the bronze medal in the high jump at Helsinki four years earlier. Baker was so upset at receiving the outside lane in the final, just as he had at Helsinki, that he put his starting blocks in backwards, necessitating a delay while he readjusted them. At the halfway mark Stanfield led Morrow by a foot, but 20 meters later Morrow swept past the defending champion and won going away, with Stanfield and Baker completing the second straight sweep of the 200 for the United States. Of the 15 medals awarded between 1932 and 1956, 13 were won by the United States, which took the first two places in five straight Olympics.

1960 Rome C: 62, N: 47, D: 9.3. WR: 20.5 (Peter Radford, Stonewall Johnson, O. Ray Norton)

1. Livio Berruti	ITA	20.5	EWR	(20.62)
2. Lester Carney	USA	20.6		(20.69)
3. Abdoulaye Seye	FRA/SEN	20.7		(20.83)
4. Marian Foik	POL	20.8		(20.90)
5. Stonewall Johnson	USA	20.8		(20.93)
6. O. Ray Norton	USA	20.9		(21.09)

On May 28, 1960, Peter Radford set a world record of 20.5. His record was matched five weeks later at the U.S. Olympic trials by Stone Johnson of Dallas, Texas, and Ray Norton. In Rome, the first semifinal was won by Seye in 20.8. The second semi saw some bad seeding as the three world record holders were thrown together with local favorite Livio Berruti, with only three to qualify for the final. It was Radford who was left out, with Berruti, a chemistry student at the University of Padua, finishing first in the world record time of 20.5. The second semi was so hotly contested that last-place finisher, Paul Genevay of France, ran 21.0, good enough to take second place in the first semi.

The final saw one false start by Berruti and Johnson, although neither was charged. Berruti, always strong on the curve, hit the straight with a one-yard lead, which he held until the finish. Norton was placed second with 80 meters to go, but he faded. After crossing the line, both Berruti, who ran with dark glasses, and Carney (of Akron, Ohio) fell to the ground. Berruti's victory was met with enthusiastic cheering that went on for five minutes, and after the medal ceremony he was led to the V.I.P. box, where each Italian dignitary kissed him on both cheeks. Berruti was the first non–North American to win the 200 meters.

1964 Tokyo C: 57, N: 42, D: 10.17. WR: 20.2 (Henry Carr)

1. Henry Carr	USA	20.3	OR	(20.36)
2. O. Paul Drayton	USA	20.5		(20.58)
3. Edwin Roberts	TRI	20.6		(20.63)
4. Harry Jerome	CAN	20.8		(20.79)
5. Livio Berruti	ITA	20.8		(20.83)
6. Marian Foik	POL	20.8		(20.83)
7. Richard Stebbins	USA	20.8		(20.89)
8. Sergio Ottolina	ITA	20.9		(20.94)

This event went according to form. Drayton, a 25-year-old Army private, recorded the best series in the preliminaries (20.7, 20.9, and 20.5), but Carr, the world record holder, had paced himself well and turned it on in the final. Carr overtook Drayton quickly, led by a yard entering the stretch, and was able to extend his lead to win by over four feet. Carr had finished only fourth at the U.S. Olympic trials, but was given the nod by U.S. coaches over the third-place finisher, Bob Hayes.

1968 Mexico City C: 49, N: 36, D: 10.16. WR: 19.92 (John Carlos)

1. Tommie Smith	USA	19.83	WR
2. Peter Norman	AUS	20.06	
3. John Carlos	USA	20.10	

4.	Edwin Roberts	TRI	20.34
5.	Roger Bambuck	FRA	20.51
6.	Larry Questad	USA	20.62
7.	Michael Fray	JAM	20.63
8.	Joachim Eigenherr	GER	20.66

There seemed little question that the battle for the gold medal would be between Tommie Smith and John Carlos, both students at San Jose State College in California and both members of the Olympic Project for Human Rights, a group of athletes organized to protest the treatment of blacks in the United States. The 6-foot 3-inch, 180-pound Smith was an extraordinary runner who held 11 world records indoors and outdoors at distances up to 440 yards. He had also long-jumped 25 feet 11 inches (7.90 meters). Carlos, who grew up in Harlem, beat Smith for the first time (by three yards) at the U.S. Olympic trials and clocked a world record time of 19.7 seconds. His record was never officially recognized because he was wearing multipronged "brush spike" shoes which, at the time, were considered illegal. At 6 feet 4 inches and 198 pounds, Carlos was the largest competitor in the 1968 200 meters, 90 pounds heavier than José Astacio, who represented El Salvador.

In Mexico City Smith set the stage in the first round by tying the Olympic record of 20.3. But four heats later a surprise occurred when Peter Norman ran 20.2 to break the Olympic record. Norman, a 26-year-old physical education teacher and Salvation Army officer, had never beaten 20.5 until he arrived in Mexico. In the first heat of the second round Carlos slipped on the bend, but he regained his balance and won in 20.6. In the third heat Smith equaled Norman's earlier mark of 20.2. The semis were won by Carlos and Smith in 20.1, but Smith pulled an adductor muscle in his groin and limped off the field. "I was 80 percent certain I was out," he said, but he made it to the starting line of the final anyway. Coming out of the turn Carlos led by one and one-half yards, but then Smith turned on his "Tommie-jets," in a stunning display of speed reminiscent of Bob Hayes' 4 × 100-meter relay anchor leg in Tokyo. He passed his teammate with 60 meters to go and won so decisively that he was able to raise his arms in victory ten yards from the tape and smile and wave as he crossed the finish line. Carlos turned his head to watch Smith go by, allowing Norman, who had been in only sixth place entering the straight, to slip by on the other side and take the silver medal with a final lunge.

Smith's victory caused a sensation, but it was nothing compared to the sensation that he and Carlos caused at the victory ceremony. Mounting the dais barefooted, they wore civil rights buttons, as did Norman, who co-operated with Smith and Carlos in their protest. When "The Star-Spangled Banner" was played, Smith and Carlos bowed their heads and each raised one black-gloved hand in the Black Power salute. They later explained that their clenched fists symbolized black strength and unity and that their bare feet were a reminder of black poverty in the United States. They bowed their heads to express their belief that the words of freedom in the U.S. national anthem only applied to Americans with white skin. Carlos told reporters, "White America will only give us

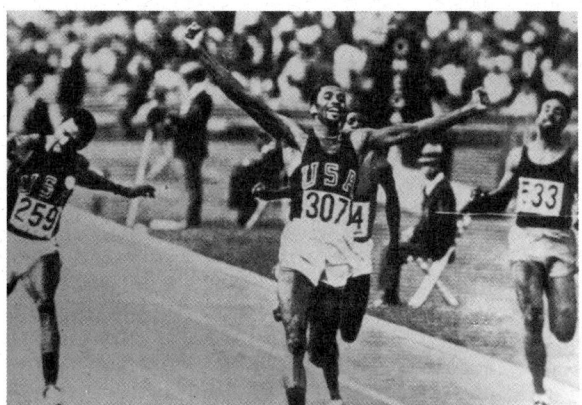

Tommie Smith won the 1968 200 meters in world record time. When he raised two clenched fists at the finish line to celebrate his victory he was hailed as a hero . . .

. . . but when he raised one clenched fist on the victory platform he was denounced by the I.O.C., suspended by the U.S. Olympic Committee, and ordered to leave Mexico within 48 hours.

credit for an Olympic victory. They'll say I'm an American, but if I did something bad, they'd say I was a Negro." Olympic officials were outraged. The International Olympic Committee made it known that Smith and Carlos should be punished, and the U.S. Olympic Committee responded quickly, suspending the two athletes and ordering them to leave the Olympic village.

The international response to the demonstration by Smith and Carlos was generally sympathetic, but back in the United States they were not so well received. Chicago sports columnist Brent Musburger spoke for the Establishment when he called them "black-skinned storm troopers." The two Olympic medalists found it difficult to make a living, and both their marriages broke up. Carlos' wife committed suicide. In 1972 Smith finally got a position as track coach at Oberlin College in Ohio. Six years later he moved to Santa Monica College in California. Carlos had an even tougher time—hustling, gambling, taking menial jobs. In 1977 he founded the John Carlos Youth Development Program in Los Angeles, which encouraged ghetto youth to become well educated. In February 1982, Carlos' Olympic experiences came full circle when he was hired by the Los Angeles Olympic Organizing Committee to promote the 1984 games and act as liaison with the black ghetto.

In retrospect, Smith and Carlos' gestures on the victory platform in Mexico City appear as eloquent expressions of nonviolent protest, while the reactions of the I.O.C. and the U.S.O.C. come off as knee-jerk traditionalism. Smith and Carlos made their point without interfering with anyone's free will. The same cannot be said of government-inspired boycotts or of the Black September guerrillas, whose attempt to stop the games was accompanied by murder. When Norman was asked why he had backed the Americans, he said that he supported human rights and opposed the "White Australia" immigration policy in his own country. John Carlos responded to criticisms that his political protest had tainted the games by pointing out that the Olympic movement was already highly political. "Why do you have to wear the uniform of your country?" he asked. "Why do they play national anthems? Why do we have to beat the Russians? Why do the East Germans want to beat the West Germans? Why can't everyone wear the same colors but wear numbers to tell them apart? What happened to the Olympic ideal of man against man?"

1972 Munich C: 57, N: 42, D: 9.4. WR: 19.83 (Tommie Smith)

1.	Valery Borzov	SOV/UKR	20.00
2.	Larry Black	USA	20.19
3.	Pietro Mennea	ITA	20.30
4.	Lawrence Burton	USA	20.37
5.	Charles Smith	USA	20.55
6.	Siegfried Schenke	GDR	20.56
7.	Martin Jellinghaus	GER	20.65
8.	Hans-Joachim Zenk	GDR	21.05

Borzov completely dominated the opposition to become the first non–North American to win the Olympic sprint double. He won his first two heats in 20.64 and 20.30 despite the fact that he turned around several times to check the position of the other runners. In the first heat of the semifinals he turned and spoke to Larry Burton as he passed him with 50 meters to go. Burton was a 6-foot 2-inch Purdue football player who had run in his first track meet only eight months earlier, and had competed in his first 220-yard race a mere four and a half months before the Olympics. The winner of the second semi was Larry Black, a Florida-born student of North Carolina Central. In the final, Black came out of the turn with a slight lead, but with 70 meters to go Borzov appeared to shift into overdrive, rocketing ahead to a clear two-meter lead. With five meters left, Borzov turned back for a final look at Black and the others, then crossed the line with arms flung high. Mennea edged past Burton at the 175-meter mark to take third. During the second round Mennea had entertained the crowd by stripping down to his jock strap while changing into his running shorts. Borzov refused to participate in the postrace interview, stating, with some justification, that he had been treated in an insulting manner by U.S. journalists after his victory in the 100.

Some people consider the athletes who finish fourth to be the big losers of the Olympics—so close to a medal, so far from glory. Not so Larry Burton. Burton returned to Purdue and earned All-American honors as a pass receiver. Prior to the Purdue–Notre Dame game in 1974, a reporter suggested to Notre Dame coach Ara Parseghian that Burton would have a tough time against Notre Dame's pass defenders. "I don't know about that," replied Parseghian. "There are only three people in the world who are faster than Larry Burton, and they are not in the Notre Dame defensive backfield." Burton played five years in the NFL and then devoted his life to helping troubled young people at Boys' Town, Nebraska, and in California.

1976 Montreal C: 45, N: 33, D: 7.26. WR: 19.83 (Tommie Smith)

1.	Donald Quarrie	JAM	20.22
2.	Millard Hampton	USA	20.29
3.	Dwayne Evans	USA	20.43
4.	Pietro Mennea	ITA	20.54
5.	Ruy da Silva	BRA	20.84
6.	Bogdan Grzejszczak	POL	20.91
7.	Colin Bradford	JAM	21.17
8.	Hasely Crawford	TRI	1:19.60

Donald Quarrie's Olympic career began back in 1968 when he was 17 years old. He made it to Mexico City but injured himself during training and was unable to compete. In 1971 he won the Pan American Games in 19.86, the second-fastest electronically timed 200 on record, but at the Olympics in Munich he pulled a hamstring muscle in the semifinals and had to be carried off the field on a stretcher. At Montreal he had already finished second to

Hasely Crawford in the 100 and was now the odds-on favorite to take the gold in the 200.

His challengers included one man who wanted to run but wasn't allowed to and another who didn't want to run but was forced to. James Gilkes of Guyana was the victor in the 1975 Pan American Games, but his government decided to boycott the Olympics. Gilkes appealed to the I.O.C. to let him compete under the Olympic flag, but his request was denied. Pietro Mennea, on the other hand, was so disappointed with his performance at the Italian championships in July that he decided not to compete in Montreal. Public reaction to his decision was so strong that he changed his mind. Also in the running were Millard Hampton of San Jose and 17-year-old high school student Dwayne Evans of Phoenix.

Quarrie had the lead coming out of the turn. Hampton made a run at him, but Quarrie held on to win by two feet. His long quest for an Olympic gold medal finally fulfilled, Don Quarrie is now honored by a statue in his hometown of Kingston, Jamaica.

The three medalists took the slowest victory lap on record. Forced to stop when they encountered the victory ceremony for the javelin, it was ten minutes before they completed their circuit of the track.

Hasely Crawford, whom the official report lists as not finishing, suffered a cramp after 50 meters and ended up on the ground, but a California track fan named Pitch Johnson noted that Crawford never actually left his lane until after he had jogged past the finish line, so he did finish the race, albeit in a rather unusual time.

An ecstatic Pietro Mennea pulls ahead of "The Beast" to win the 1980 200 meters.

1980 Moscow C: 57, N: 37, D: 7.28. WR: 19.72 (Pietro Mennea)

1. Pietro Mennea	ITA	20.19
2. Allan Wells	GBR	20.21
3. Donald Quarrie	JAM	20.29
4. Silvio Leonard Tartabull	CUB	20.30
5. Bernhard Hoff	GDR	20.50
6. Leszek Dunecki	POL	20.68
7. Marian Woronin	POL	20.81
8. Osvaldo Lara Cañizares	CUB	21.19

Like Donald Quarrie before him, Pietro Mennea of Barletta, Italy, had to wait until his third try to gain an Olympic gold medal. In 1979 at the World Student Games in Mexico City, Mennea had run 19.72 to break Tommie Smith's 11-year-old world record. But that same year, before a hometown crowd at the European Cup in Torino, Mennea had lost to Allan Wells. For this insult, the otherwise blameless Wells had become known as "The Beast" in Mennea's household. For the final of the 1980 Olympics, Mennea drew the outside lane, with "The Beast" just behind him in Lane 7. At the sound of the gun Wells tore out of the blocks at full speed and had made up the stagger after only 50 meters. Coming out of the turn he had a two-meter lead over Leonard, with Quarrie and Mennea close behind. But Mennea, as usual, shifted gears in the straight, closing the gap with

each stride until he moved ahead of Wells with less than ten meters to go. At the last moment Wells attempted the same final dip which had brought him victory in the 100, but this time he fell short. Quarrie's third-place finish, impressive as it was, was all the more remarkable considering he had been injured in an auto accident the previous year. Mennea, employed by the public relations department of Fiat, had received his doctorate in political science two weeks before the Olympics. He had been a candidate for local office for the Social Democratic Party, which supported the Moscow boycott, but 15 years of training and his belief in the Olympic ideal proved more important than the party line, and he decided to enter anyway.

1984 Los Angeles C: 76, N: 58, D: 8.8. WR: 19.72 (Pietro Mennea)

1. F. Carlton Lewis	USA	19.80	OR
2. Kirk Baptiste	USA	19.96	
3. Thomas Jefferson	USA	20.26	
4. João Batista da Silva	BRA	20.30	
5. Ralf Lübke	GER	20.51	
6. Jean-Jacques Boussemart	FRA	20.55	
7. Pietro Mennea	ITA	20.55	
8. Adeoye Mafe	GBR	20.85	

Carl Lewis, holder of the low-altitude world record with a 1983 time of 19.75, won his third gold medal by getting off to an unusually fast start. He came out of the curve with a two-meter lead and then held off the fast-finishing Kirk Baptiste to win by one and one-half meters. Considering that the race was run into the wind, Lewis' time was more impressive than Mennea's high-altitude world record of 19.72 or his own 19.75. Pietro Mennea, in seventh place, became the first runner to qualify for the final of the same event in four straight Olympics.

1988 Seoul C: 72, N: 59, D: 9.28. WR: 19.72 (Pietro Mennea)
1. Joseph DeLoach	USA	19.75	OR
2. F. Carlton Lewis	USA	19.79	
3. Robson Caetano da Silva	BRA	20.04	
4. Linford Christie	GBR	20.09	
5. Atlee Mahorn	CAN	20.39	
6. Gilles Quénéhervé	FRA	20.40	
7. Michael Rosswess	GBR	20.51	
8. Bruno Marie-Rose	FRA	20.58	

Carl Lewis suffered his first 200-meter defeat in two years when he was beaten 19.96-20.01 at the U.S. Olympic trials by his training partner, 21-year-old Joe DeLoach of Bay City, Texas. The two had first met when DeLoach, the youngest of 13 children, had asked Lewis for his autograph. In Seoul, Lewis led coming out of the turn. DeLoach drew even after 150 meters, then surged ahead 30 meters from the finish.

1992 Barcelona C: 79, N: 65, D: 8.6. WR: 19.72 (Pietro Mennea)
1. Michael Marsh	USA	20.01
2. Frank Fredericks	NAM	20.13
3. Michael Bates	USA	20.38
4. Robson Caetano da Silva	BRA	20.45
5. Olapade Adeniken	NGR	20.50
6. John Regis	GBR	20.55
7. Oluyemi Kayode	NGR	20.67
8. Marcus Adam	GBR	20.80

The overwhelming favorite in this event was world champion Michael Johnson of Texas. The first man to be ranked number one in both the 200 meters and 400 meters, Johnson had won 29 straight finals at the shorter distance until he was beaten by Frank Fredericks in Rome on June 9. Nineteen days later he came roaring back to win the U.S. Olympic trials in 19.79. But on July 13, Johnson contracted food poisoning after eating at a restaurant in Salamanca, Spain. He did not recover fully in time for the Olympics and was eliminated in the semifinals. Meanwhile, Mike Marsh was tearing up the track. In 1984 he had worked as a parking attendant at the Olympic fencing and volleyball venues. Eight years later he registered the fastest times in each of the first two rounds. In the semifinals he caused a sensation when he was clocked in 19.73—a mere 1/100 of a second shy of Pietro Mennea's 13-year-old world record. Because he didn't realize how fast he was running, Marsh actually eased up over the last 15 meters.

By the time of the final the following evening, Marsh was feeling the pressure of being expected to break the world record. Determined to remain relaxed in the final, he overdid it and got off to an awful start. Marsh immediately took the situation in hand and streaked to a clear victory. Marsh was the third straight 200-meter champion to be coached by Tom Tellez.

400 METERS

The 400 meters is a one-lap race run in lanes with a staggered start. Athletes from the United States have finished first 16 of the 22 times they have entered and have captured over half of the total medals.

1896 Athens C: 7, N: 4, D: 4.7. WR (440 yards): 48.5 (Henry Tindall, Edgar Bredin)
1. Thomas Burke	USA	54.2
2. Herbert Jamison	USA	55.2
3. Fritz Hofmann	GER	55.6
4. Charles Gmelin	GBR	55.6

The slow time was a result of the quality of the track rather than the quality of the contestants. The turns were so sharp that the runners had to slow down drastically to keep from falling. Burke, who won by over 13 meters, had previously beaten the world record holder Edgar Bredin. In 1896 Bredin, in the words of former 440-champion Montague Shearman, "voluntarily joined the professional ranks, a step which was received with great surprise, as he was a gentleman by birth and education."

1900 Paris C: 16, N: 7, D: 7.15. WR (440 yards): 48.5 (Henry Tindall, Edgar Bredin)
1. Maxwell "Maxey" Long	USA	49.4	OR
2. William Holland	USA	49.6	
3. Ernst Schultz	DEN	53.0	

DNS: Dixon Boardman (USA), Harry Lee (USA), William Moloney (USA)

Long was cheered heartily by the French spectators, who mistook his light-blue-and-white Columbia University uniform for that of the Racing Club of Paris. Boardman, Lee, and Moloney refused to compete in the final for religious reasons, since the race was run on a Sunday.

1904 St. Louis C: 13, N: 3, D: 8.29. WR (440 yards): 47.8 (Maxwell "Maxey" Long)
1. Harry Hillman	USA	49.2	OR
2. Frank Waller	USA	49.9	
3. Herman Groman	USA	50.0	
4. Joseph Fleming	USA	50.6	
5. Meyer Prinstein	USA	50.7	
6. George Poage	USA	50.8	

One can only imagine the chaos of this race, which the 13 entrants ran without lanes even though the course was only 1¼ laps long. Poage of Milwaukee was one of the first two black athletes to compete in the Olympics.

1906 Athens C: 25, N: 8, D: 4.29. WR (440 yards): 47.8 (Maxwell "Maxey" Long)
1. Paul Pilgrim	USA	53.2
2. Wyndham Halswelle	GBR	53.8
3. Nigel Barker	AUS	54.1
4. Harry Hillman	USA	—
5. Charles Bacon	USA	—
6. Fay Moulton	USA	—
7. William Anderson	GBR	—
8. M. Bellin du Coteau	FRA	—

Unknown Paul Pilgrim scored an upset victory in the 1906 400 meters. The next day he also won the 800 meters. He never again won a major race. Wyndham Halswelle (right), seen here finishing second, was the beneficiary two years later in the famous 400 meters controversy of 1908.

The victory of Pilgrim came as a complete surprise. This was the first time that the United States sent an official team. Pilgrim, a member of the New York Athletic Club, didn't make the team, but he paid his own way to Athens and was allowed to compete.

1908 London C: 36, N: 11, D: 7.25. WR (440 yards): 47.8 (Maxwell "Maxey" Long)
1. Wyndham Halswelle   GBR   50.0
DNS: William Robbins (USA), John Taylor (USA)
DISQ: John Carpenter (USA)

Few events in Olympic history have caused as much controversy as the final of the 1908 400 meters in London. The favorite was Lieutenant Wyndham Halswelle, a 26-year-old London-born Scot who had served in the Boer War. He had set an Olympic record of 48.4 in the semifinals. Halswelle was joined in the final by three Americans—John Taylor, William Robbins, and John Carpenter of Cornell. The British, afraid that the Americans would use team tactics, stationed officials every 20 yards around the track. Robbins charged to the front and built up a 12-yard lead by the halfway mark. Coming into the homestretch he was passed by Carpenter and Halswelle. Halswelle then attempted to go by Carpenter on the outside, but the American ran wide and kept Halswelle from taking the lead. British officials yelled "foul" and "no race" and broke the tape before Carpenter reached it. Taylor was physically pulled off the track by officials. British and American partisans argued and yelled at each other for a half hour before the track could be cleared. Carpenter was disqualified and the race was ordered rerun without him two days later, this time with strings laid out to divide the lanes. Robbins and Taylor refused to participate, however, and Halswelle was left to run the race alone. Halswelle was so disgusted by the incident that he quit sports and returned to his regiment. He was killed in World War I while fighting in France on March 31, 1915.

1912 Stockholm C: 49, N: 16, D: 7.13. WR (440 yards): 47.8 (Maxwell "Maxey" Long)
1. Charles Reidpath   USA   48.2   OR
2. Hanns Braun   GER   48.3
3. Edward Lindberg   USA   48.4
4. James "Ted" Meredith   USA   49.2
5. Carroll Haff   USA   49.5

The 400 meters was again the subject of controversy, this time occasioned by an incident at the beginning of the last heat of the semifinal round. Donnell Young of the United States jumped into the lead, but before the first curve the German champion, Hanns Braun, tried to cut in front of him. Young refused to allow this and rammed into Braun, throwing him to the outside. Young went on to win, but was disqualified. Young deserved to be disqualified; however, Braun's move was uncalled for and might have resulted in *his* disqualification had not Young responded so violently. The Swedish officials wisely decided that the final should be run in lanes. Braun took the lead at the halfway mark, but Charlie Reidpath of Syracuse passed him with 15 meters to go and won by two feet. Braun, who was killed in World War I, was much honored in Germany. A street in Berlin was named after him, as was an annual sportsfest in Munich.

1920 Antwerp C: 37, N: 16, D: 8.20. WR (440 yards): 47.4 (James "Ted" Meredith, Jesse Binga Dismond)
1. Bevil Rudd   SAF   49.6
2. Guy Butler   GBR   49.9e
3. Nils Engdahl   SWE   49.9e
4. Frank Shea   USA   49.9e
5. John Ainsworth-Davis   GBR   50.0e
6. Harry Davel   SAF   50.1e

Born in South Africa and educated at Oxford, Bevil Gordon D'Urban Rudd was an extremely popular winner who looked at running as a joyful experience. He was often seen smoking a pipe and drinking beer while watching the other athletes go through their strenuous exercises.

1924 Paris C: 60, N: 27, D: 7.11. WR (440 yards): 47.4 (James "Ted" Meredith, Jesse Binga Dismond)
1. Eric Liddell   GBR   47.6   OR
2. Horatio Fitch   USA   48.4
3. Guy Butler   GBR   48.6
4. David Johnson   CAN   48.8
5. John Coard Taylor   USA   56.0
DNF: Josef Imbach (SWI)

Eric Liddell was born on January 16, 1902, in Tientsin, China, where his father was a missionary. He grew up in Scotland from the age of five. His favorite sport was rugby, but he gave up a promising career in it in order to concentrate on running. He gained national attention in 1923 when he won both sprints at the A.A.A. championships. The following week his reputation was enhanced when he was knocked to the ground during a 440-yard race against England and Ireland. By the time he had regained his feet, Liddell was 20 yards behind the field.

The film Chariots of Fire *portrayed Eric Liddell as learning at the last minute that the final of his specialty, the 100-meter dash, would be held on a Sunday. Actually Liddell was informed of the schedule six months in advance and had plenty of time to adjust his training for the 200 and 400.*

Yet he was able to overtake every runner and win the race. Afterward he repeated his oft-spoken dictum, "I do not like to be beaten."

In the film *Chariots of Fire* Eric Liddell is portrayed as a devout Christian who learns, as he is boarding a ship en route to the Paris Olympics, that the heats of the 100-meter dash, his specialty, will be run on a Sunday. Because of his respect for the Sabbath, he refuses to run. Finally another member of the British team, a cinematic version of Lord Burghley, offers Liddell his spot in the 400 meters. This highly dramatized rendition of Liddell's Olympic experience bears only a slight resemblance to reality.

Liddell was in fact a devout Christian, and it is true that he withdrew from the 100 because he wouldn't run on a Sunday. He dropped out of the relays for the same reason. However, he did *not* find out the Olympic schedule at the last minute. In real life Liddell learned the schedule over six months in advance, and once he had

made his decision not to enter the 100, he was able to concentrate his training on the 200 and 400. As for Lord Burghley, he wasn't even entered in the 400 meters. Liddell did spend the Sunday of the 100-meter heats giving a sermon at a Scottish church in Paris, but he had doubts about his decision right up to the end, particularly as a result of criticism he received from certain quarters that he was being unpatriotic, since Scotland had few opportunities to win Olympic championships.

On July 9, Liddell finished third in the 200 meters, behind Jackson Scholz and Charley Paddock. The first two rounds of the 400 were held the next day, and Liddell qualified in respectable, but unspectacular times. The fastest race of the day was won by Imbach in 48.0. The first semifinal, held the morning of July 11, was won by Fitch in 47.8 and the second by Liddell in 48.2, an impressive performance by the "Flying Scot" considering that he had never before beaten the 49-second mark. The final, contested later in the day, was won by Liddell in an unorthodox and electrifying manner. Racing in the outside lane, Liddell took off as if he were running a short dash and passed the halfway mark in an extraordinary 22.2 seconds, only 0.3 seconds slower than he had run in the 200-meter final. Track experts considered this to be tactical foolishness, but Liddell was a man inspired. He actually increased his lead during the second half of the race and won by over five meters. His pace was so fast that two of his opponents, Imbach and Taylor, fell while trying to keep up. Taylor crawled and scrambled the last few yards to the finish line.

Eric Liddell returned to Scotland a hero of heroes and was paraded through the streets of Edinburgh. A year after his Olympic triumph, he returned to China to join his father in missionary work. Liddell made two more trips to Scotland, but he was back in China during World War II. He died of a brain tumor in a Japanese internment camp in Weifang, on February 21, 1945.

1928 Amsterdam C: 51, N: 20, D: 8.3. WR: 47.0 (Emerson Spencer)

1. Raymond Barbuti	USA	47.8
2. James Ball	CAN	48.0
3. Joachim Büchner	GER	48.2
4. John Rinkel	GBR	48.4
5. Werner "Harry" Storz	GER	48.8
6. Herman Phillips	USA	49.0

On May 12, 1928, Emerson Spencer set a world record of 47.0. But he failed to qualify for the Olympics except as a member of the relay team, because of a major misunderstanding at the U.S. final Olympic tryouts. Thinking he was running in a heat, he finished only fast enough to qualify for what he thought was the next round. Actually the race had been to decide the final places on the U.S. team and Spencer lost out.

The semifinals in Amsterdam were won by Ball and Büchner in 48.6. In the final Barbuti, a former captain of the Syracuse football team, started his finishing kick

James Ball (left) loses the 1928 400 meters to Ray Barbuti by committing the classic mistake of turning his head to check his position.

at the 300-meter mark even though he had been instructed to wait an extra 30 meters. Fortunately for Barbuti, James Ball of Winnipeg made the opposite mistake. Unaccustomed to running in lanes, Ball misjudged his position until the final straightaway and then unleashed a great finishing kick. As they approached the finish line, Ball had closed within a foot of Barbuti, but he turned to see where his opponent was just as Barbuti lunged for the tape. The plucky New Yorker fell to the ground, scraping his arm, leg, and side, but he had gained the victory. Afterward he told reporters, "I never noticed the other runners after the start. I heard them, but all I kept thinking was 'run, kid, run.' I don't remember anything of the last 100 meters except a mad desire to get to that tape."

1932 Los Angeles C: 27, N: 15, D: 8.5. WR (440 yards): 46.4 (Benjamin Eastman)

1. William Carr	USA	46.2	WR
2. Benjamin Eastman	USA	46.4	
3. Alexander Wilson	CAN	47.4	
4. William Walters	SAF	48.2	
5. James Gordon	USA	48.2	
6. George Golding	AUS	48.8	

Ben Eastman of Stanford University was considered king of the world at 400 and 800 meters, particularly after March 26, 1932, when he lowered his own world record at 440 yards (402.3 meters) by a full second in running the extraordinary time of 46.4. He ran 46.5 two months later and appeared to be a sure bet to win either the 400 or 800 at the Los Angeles Olympics. Then, seemingly from out of nowhere, came a new contender, University of Pennsylvania junior Bill Carr of Pine Bluff, Arkansas. At the U.S. intercollegiate championships at Berkeley on July 2, Carr came from behind to gain a shocking 440 victory over Eastman, 47.0 to 47.2. Two weeks later at the U.S. Olympic tryouts on Eastman's home track in Palo Alto, California, Carr again came from behind to defeat Eastman, 46.9 to 47.1.

Unfortunately, Eastman got caught up in a rivalry between his own coach, Dink Templeton of Stanford, and Carr's coach, Lawson Robertson of Pennsylvania, who had been chosen to coach the U.S. Olympic team. Obsessed with beating Robertson, Templeton convinced Eastman to skip the Olympic 800 meters, which was actually his best event, and concentrate on beating Carr at 400 meters.

At the 1932 Olympics Carr posted the fastest time in each of the first two rounds. Then he won the first semifinal in 47.2. Eastman won the second in 47.6. In the final Eastman held a slight edge through most of the race. Carr drew even with 80 meters to go and gradually pulled away to win by two yards. Whatever Dink Templeton thought of the race, Ben Eastman himself was an amiable loser. "Bill's just too fast for me," he said. "You don't need to sympathize. I know when I'm licked by a better runner." Unfortunately, Bill Carr's running career came to an abrupt halt on March 17, 1933, when he broke both ankles and fractured his pelvis in an automobile accident.

1936 Berlin C: 42, N: 25, D: 8.7. WR: 46.1 (Archie Williams)

1. Archie Williams	USA	46.5
2. Arthur Godfrey Brown	GBR	46.7
3. James LuValle	USA	46.8
4. William Roberts	GBR	46.8
5. William Fritz	CAN	47.8
6. John Loaring	CAN	48.2

Prior to the 1936 season, Archie Williams of Oakland, California, had never run a quarter mile faster than 49 seconds. However, in April 1936, he ran 47.4, in May 46.8, and on June 19, at the N.C.A.A. championships in Chicago, he clocked 46.5 for 440 yards around one turn, passing the 400-meter mark in 46.1 to break Bill Carr's world record. In the Olympic final Williams and fellow Californian James LuValle led the field entering the homestretch. But Godfrey Brown, three yards behind with 100 meters to go, staged a thrilling stretch drive, passed LuValle 40 meters from the tape, and closed in on the exhausted Williams. Brown had pulled within seven inches and was still coming strong when Williams breasted the tape before Brown could get any closer. The official times appear to have been inaccurate; the photo-finish camera yielded the following, more reliable results: Williams 46.66, Brown 46.68, LuValle 46.84, and Roberts 46.87. The day after Godfrey Brown won the 400 meters silver medal, his sister Audrey earned a silver medal of her own in the women's 4 × 100-meter relay. Godfrey added a gold medal to the family haul in the men's 4 × 400-meter relay. In 1939 Archie Williams earned a degree in mechanical engineering but, because he was black, he had to settle for a job digging ditches. Eventually he joined the Army Air Corps and trained pilots. When he retired from the military, he taught high school. James LuValle earned a doctorate in chemistry at Caltech and became director of the undergraduate chemistry labs at Stanford University. Since Godfrey Brown also taught school and became a headmaster, the 1936 400-meter medalists qualify as among the most academically accomplished in Olympic history.

1948 London C: 53, N: 28, D: 8.5. WR: 45.9 (Herbert McKenley)
WR (440 yards): 46.0 (Rudolf Harbig, Grover Klemmer, Herbert McKenley)

1. Arthur Wint	JAM	46.2	EOR
2. Herbert McKenley	JAM	46.4	
3. Malvin Whitfield	USA	46.9	
4. David Bolen	USA	47.2	
5. Morris Curotta	AUS	47.9	
6. George Guida	USA	50.2	

Jesse Abramson of the *New York Herald Tribune* had called Herb McKenley "the surest sure thing of the Games," but whenever anyone asked McKenley about it, he told them that his older teammate, 6-foot 4½-inch Arthur Wint, was really the man to beat. McKenley may not have actually believed that himself at the time, but it turned out that he was absolutely correct. Wint, a minister's son whose mother was a Scot, had joined the Royal Air Force during World War II. Staying on in England after the war, Wint was a 28-year-old medical student at the University of London at the time of the 1948 Olympics. Consequently, he was quite a local favorite among London sports fans.

Disappointed at having lost to Mal Whitfield at 800 meters, Wint was determined to finish ahead of the American at 400 meters. Although Wint had never lost to McKenley at 400 meters, he was prepared to settle for a silver medal behind his friend and rival, who seemed to be in prime condition. McKenley's usual tactics, or lack of them, consisted of running as fast as he could as soon as the starter's gun went off. Normally he could keep up his all-out pace for 350 meters and then coast through the final 50 meters.

True to form, McKenley went away at breakneck speed in the London final. Coming out of the final curve he was four yards ahead of Whitfield. But, McKenley, uncharacteristically, broke stride about 25 meters early and began to fade. Noticing the plight of his fellow Jamaican, Wint took off after him, closed the gap, caught McKenley with about 20 yards to go, and went on to win by two and a half yards.

Dave Bolen, who finished fourth, was later appointed U.S. ambassador to Botswana, Lesotho, and Swaziland, as well as East Germany.

1952 Helsinki C: 71, N: 35, D: 7.25. WR: 45.8 (V. George Rhoden)

1. V. George Rhoden	JAM	45.9	OR	(46.09)
2. Herbert McKenley	JAM	45.9	OR	(46.20)
3. Ollie Matson	USA	46.8		(46.94)
4. Karl-Friedrich Haas	GER	47.0		(47.22)
5. Arthur Wint	JAM	47.0		(47.24)
6. Malvin Whitfield	USA	47.1		(47.30)

In 1952 the track world had different expectations of Herb McKenley. The 30-year-old McKenley was considered a sure finalist but an unlikely medal winner. The favorite was George Rhoden, a 25-year-old from Kingston who had just graduated from Morgan State College in Baltimore. In the 1948 Olympics he had been eliminated in the semifinals, but by August of 1950 he had broken the 400-meter world record in 45.8.

Rhoden and McKenley were joined in the 1952 final by fellow Olympic veterans Arthur Wint and Mal Whitfield, who had already won the 800 meters, but was now fighting off a cold with Benzedrine. The other starters were University of San Francisco football star Ollie Matson, who later achieved success as a five-time All-Pro back in the National Football League, and Kaaro Haas, the only white finalist. McKenley had the sympathy of much of the crowd as a result of his photo-finish loss in the 100-meter final four days earlier.

The amazing thing about the 1952 400-meter final was that Wint and McKenley completely reversed the tactics that they had used in the 1948 final. McKenley, having learned from his experience four years earlier, began cautiously and saved his strength for the finish. Wint, on the other hand, for some reason unknown even to himself, took off at full speed and led by three yards at the 200-meter mark in 21.7—0.2 second faster than he had ever run the distance. Not surprisingly, Wint ran out of steam early and was passed by Rhoden, who entered the long final straightaway with a four-yard lead over McKenley. But then McKenley began to close the gap, pulling closer with every stride until he almost drew even. Rhoden recalled the moment after the race: "About 20 meters from home I heard the roar of the crowd and with split vision saw someone coming up. From someplace I summoned the necessary strength and held him off. I surely was glad to see that tape." Rhoden's margin of victory was about 18 inches.

1956 Melbourne C: 42, N: 23, D: 11.29. WR: 45.2 (Louis Jones)

1. Charles Jenkins	USA	46.7	(46.85)
2. Karl-Friedrich Haas	GER	46.8	(47.12)
3. Voitto Hellsten	FIN	47.0	(47.15)
3. Ardalion Ignatyev	SOV/RUS	47.0	(47.15)
5. Louis Jones	USA	48.1	(48.35)
6. Malcolm Spence	SAF	48.3	(48.40)

Lou Jones set a world record of 45.2 at the U.S. Olympic tryouts and went to Melbourne as the clear favorite. Ignatyev won the first semifinal in 46.8, with Jones coasting in third place to qualify for the final. The second semi was a hard-fought affair, won by the third-string U.S. runner, Charley Jenkins of Cambridge, Massachusetts. Jenkins had barely made the semifinal round by finishing third in his first- and second-round heats. The second semifinal was so fast that Kevan Gosper of Australia was eliminated even though he finished in 46.2 seconds.

Jones led the final for the first 300 meters. Coming out of the final turn he had expected to have a three- or four-meter lead and was psychologically unprepared when he realized that Ignatyev was right behind him. The Soviet runner took the lead with 60 yards to go, but then Jenkins launched a finishing kick, passed Ignatyev 25 yards from the finish, and broke the tape just ahead of Haas, who came from last place to second in the final 100 meters. The photo-finish was unable to separate Hellsten and Ignatyev, so they were both awarded third place. After the race Jenkins modestly told reporters, "Jones is still the champ. That 45.2 is it."

1960 Rome C: 54, N: 41, D: 9.6. WR: 45.2 (Louis Jones)

1. Otis Davis	USA	44.9	WR	(45.07)
2. Carl Kaufmann	GER	44.9	WR	(45.08)
3. Malcolm Spence	SAF	45.5		(45.60)
4. Milkha Singh	IND	45.6		(45.73)
5. Manfred Kinder	GER	45.9		(46.04)
6. Earl Young	USA	45.9		(46.07)

This was the first time since 1912 that the final was held on a different day than the semifinals. The improvement in times spoke well for the new procedure. Spence, who required nine painkilling injections before the final, took the early lead and was still in front at 200 meters, followed by Kaufmann, Milkha Singh, and Davis. Then Davis accelerated dramatically, covering the next 100 meters in 10.8 seconds and entering the final straight with a four-yard lead over Brooklyn-born Carl Kaufmann. Next it was Kaufmann's turn to stage a sensational sprint. He almost caught Davis, but the American leaned forward just in time, crossing the finish line ahead of the flying Kaufmann, who ended up sprawled on the track from exhaustion. The electronic timer gave Davis a victory of .01 second, both men being credited with a new world record.

Otis Davis was born in Tuscaloosa, Alabama. A basketball player at the University of Oregon, he didn't start running until he was 26 years old, two years before the Olympics. Like Charley Jenkins before him, Davis finished only third at the U.S. Olympic tryouts. Carl Kaufmann went on to become an operetta singer and actor.

1964 Tokyo C: 50, N: 33, D: 10.19. WR: 44.9 (Otis Davis, Carl Kaufmann, Adolph Plummer, Michael Larrabee)

1. Michael Larrabee	USA	45.1	(45.15)
2. Wendell Mottley	TRI	45.2	(45.24)
3. Andrzej Badeński	POL	45.6	(45.64)
4. Robbie Brightwell	GBR	45.7	(45.75)
5. Ulis Williams	USA	46.0	(46.01)
6. Timothy Graham	GBR	46.0	(46.08)
7. Peter Vassella	AUS	46.3	
8. Edwin Skinner	TRI	46.8	

His students laughed when Los Angeles high school mathematics teacher Mike Larrabee told them he was going to try out for the Olympics, but their laughter turned to excitement when they saw the times he was producing on the school track and at local meets. Larrabee had been a major contender in 1960, until he injured a tendon. Most observers thought Larrabee's track career was finished, but he returned in 1964 and qualified for the U.S. team at the age of 30. Sixth at the halfway mark of the final and fifth coming out of the final curve, Larrabee unleashed his patented finishing kick and churned past one runner after another. At last he caught Wendell Mottley of Yale ten meters from the finish and won by two feet. During a record-setting two-hour press conference following his victory, Larrabee told reporters, "I kept a copy of one story written about me that said I was too old. It's still on my wall. I think I'll take it down now." Larrabee was the first white winner of the 400 meters in 32 years.

1968 Mexico City C: 54, N: 35, D: 10.18. WR: 44.0 (Lee Evans)

1. Lee Evans	USA	43.86	WR
2. G. Lawrence James	USA	43.97	
3. Ronald Freeman	USA	44.41	
4. Amadou Gakou	SEN	45.01	
5. Martin Jellinghaus	GER	45.33	
6. Tegegne Bezabeh	ETH	45.42	

7. Andrzej Badeński   POL   45.42
8. Amos Omolo   UGA   47.61

A U.S. sweep seemed inevitable, considering that the top 12 400-meter runners in the world were all Americans. With each nation limited to only three entrants per event, several first-class U.S. runners had to be left behind. The big surprise was the success of the Africans, particularly Amadou Gakou of Senegal, who lowered his personal best from 46.7 to 45.0 and became the first black to hold the African 400-meter record.

Initially Lee Evans announced his intention to withdraw from the final after his friends John Carlos and Tommie Smith were expelled from the Olympic Village after their Black Power protest at the 200-meter victory ceremony. But Carlos and Smith personally convinced him to run and to win. Evans expected to have a five-yard lead when he reached the final straightaway. Instead he realized that Larry James was right behind him. "I felt faint. . . . Three steps from the finish, Larry dropped his head. I knew I had it then. . . . Larry ran three hundred ninety-five meters. I ran four hundred and one. That was the difference." The first seven finishers all bettered their pre-Olympic best times. Evans later served as coach to the national teams of Nigeria and Qatar.

1972 Munich C: 64, N: 49, D: 9.7. WR: 43.86 (Lee Evans)
1. Vincent Matthews   USA   44.66
2. Wayne Collett   USA   44.80
3. Julius Sang   KEN   44.92
4. Charles Asati   KEN   45.13
5. Horst-Rüdiger Schlöske   GER   45.31
6. Markku Kukkoaho   FIN   45.59
7. Karl Honz   GER   45.68
DNF: John Smith (USA)

Another U.S. sweep seemed to be a distinct possibility even though defending champion Lee Evans, hampered by a hamstring pull, had finished fourth at the U.S. Olympic trials and only qualified as a member of the 4 × 400 relay team. In his place was Vince Matthews, a New York City social worker who had just missed making the U.S. entry in 1968. U.S. officials and coaches were clearly disappointed that Evans hadn't qualified for the 400, and made Matthews feel extremely unwanted. The pre-Olympics favorites were Californians John Smith and Wayne Collett. In the final, Smith, running with an injured leg, pulled up lame after only 80 meters, but Collett and Matthews drove on. Matthews was somewhat shocked to find himself in the lead entering the final straight and still feeling strong. He held off Collett the rest of the way and won by four feet.

At the medal ceremony, Matthews and Collett showed little respect for the proceedings, talking and fidgeting during the playing of "The Star-Spangled Banner" rather than standing quietly at attention. The West German crowd booed them, and the International Olympic Committee, ignoring the U.S. Olympic Committee, banned the two runners from further competition. Matthews and Collett denied that their actions had constituted an organized protest. "If we did have any ideas about a demonstration," Matthews said, "we could have done a better job than that." Collett added, "I couldn't stand there and sing the words [to the national anthem] because I don't believe they're true. I wish they were. I think we have the potential to have a beautiful country, but I don't think we do."

Stepping down from the victory platform, Matthews had taken off his gold medal and twirled it around his finger, leading some people to believe that the medal meant little to him. In an article in the *New York Times*, Matthews responded to this criticism: "I took it off to tell them this was my medal. A lot of people had forgotten about me and given up on me. . . . Twenty years from now, I can look at this medal and say, 'I was the best quarter-miler in the world that day.' If you don't think that's important, you don't know what's inside an athlete's soul."

John Smith, the frustrated favorite, finally achieved Olympic satisfaction when he coached Steve Lewis and Danny Everett to gold and bronze in 1988. Lewis, who wasn't certain he had won until he and Smith watched a replay of the race on the stadium scoreboard, then turned to Smith and said, "That one is for you, Coach." In 1992 Smith coached two more gold-medal winners—Quincy Watts and Kevin Young.

1976 Montreal C: 44, N: 29, D: 7.29. WR: 43.86 (Lee Evans)
1. Alberto Juantorena Danger   CUB   44.26
2. Frederick Newhouse   USA   44.40
3. Herman Frazier   USA   44.95
4. Alfons Brijdenbach   BEL   45.04
5. Maxie Parks   USA   45.24
6. Richard Mitchell   AUS   45.40
7. David Jenkins   GBR   45.57
8. Jan Werner   POL   45.63

In 1972 Alberto Juantorena had been narrowly eliminated in the Olympic semifinals. He was unbeaten in 1973 and 1974, but before the 1975 season he underwent two operations on his foot. By the time of the Montreal Olympics he had emerged as the clear favorite at 400 meters. When he scored a surprising victory at 800 meters, it appeared that he had an excellent chance to become the first runner to score a 400/800 double since Paul Pilgrim in the Intercalated Games of 1906. Juantorena waltzed through the first two rounds, content to qualify without extending himself. After finishing his second-round heat, he kept on running, continuing through the tunnel and into the locker room without stopping. In the semifinals, Juantorena started poorly, then accelerated into first place and jogged home in 45.10, looking back at the other runners seven times on his way to the tape. Fred Newhouse, winner of the second semifinal in 44.89, sprinted into the lead in the final and was sure he was about to win the gold medal when Juantorena, the man with the nine-foot stride, appeared at his shoulder with 20 meters to go and moved right by him. Juantorena's winning time was a half-second faster than he had ever run before. The 6-foot 2-inch Cuban hero became the first man from a non-English-speaking country to win the 400 meters, although Juantorena himself actually spoke English quite well. Before the 1976 Olympics were over, Alberto Juantorena had run nine races and lost 11 pounds.

1980 Moscow C: 50, N: 32, D: 7.30. WR: 43.86 (Lee Evans)

1. Viktor Markin	SOV/RUS	44.60
2. Richard Mitchell	AUS	44.84
3. Frank Schaffer	GDR	44.87
4. Alberto Juantorena Danger	CUB	45.09
5. Alfons Brijdenbach	BEL	45.10
6. Michael Solomon	TRI	45.55
7. David Jenkins	GBR	45.56
8. Joseph Coombs	TRI	46.33

For the third straight time the 400 meters was won by the runner in lane 2. This time, though, the man in lane 2 was a complete outsider: a 23-year-old Siberian-born medical student named Viktor Markin. Markin gained the lead from Schaffer with 80 meters to go. Mitchell also finished strongly, moving from last to second in the final 100 meters. Although Juantorena was only a shadow of his former self, his fourth-place finish was actually quite an achievement considering that he was still recovering from an Achilles tendon operation. Markin's time, 0.73 second faster than his previous best, was the fastest 400 meters to be run in over two years. "I don't know my own limits," he said afterward. "Everything came to me so quickly in the final. . . . I finished like I was in a dream."

1984 Los Angeles C: 80, N: 57, D: 8.8. WR: 43.86 (Lee Evans)

1. Alonzo Babers	USA	44.27
2. Gabriel Tiacoh	IVC	44.54
3. Antonio McKay	USA	44.71
4. Darren Clark	AUS	44.75
5. Sunder Nix	USA	44.75
6. Sunday Uti	NGR	44.93
7. Innocent Egbunike	NGR	45.35

DNS: Bertland Cameron (JAM)

The battle on the track for the 400-meters title was preceded by a war of words between world champion Bert Cameron and U.S. Olympic trials winner Antonio McKay. Cameron had stated that the gold medal already had his name written on it. McKay responded by vowing, "I'm going to destroy Cameron." Cameron seemed unconcerned about McKay, for whom the Olympics would be his first international meet. But he was worried about Air Force second lieutenant Alonzo Babers, who had handed Cameron his only two defeats of the past two years. "He is so relaxed when he's running," Cameron would say of Babers on the eve of the Games. "Maybe McKay should be watching him instead of me."

The first round included one bizarre occurrence. Innocent Egbunike, one of the secondary favorites, thought he had prepared for any eventuality. But shortly after the start of the third heat, Egbunike, running in the inside lane, found himself cut off by Secundino Borabota of the small, impoverished West African nation of Equatorial Guinea. After yelling at Borabota for 100 meters, Egbunike finally squeezed by on the inside and went on to win the heat. After the race, Borabota, evidently unaware that 400-meter runners are supposed to stay in the same lane from start to finish, explained rather cryptically that an injury led him to switch lanes temporarily. "Lane one is a good lane," he added.

The quarterfinals saw some surprisingly fast times. McKay led 18-year-old Darren Clark 44.72 to 44.77 in the first heat, and Babers recorded 44.75 in the third. The following day, the first semifinal was won by Egbunike over Babers 45.16 to 45.17. But the real drama began in the second semi which pitted Cameron against McKay for the first time. After 100 meters Cameron was charging down the backstretch when he suddenly leaped into the air and grabbed his left thigh, the victim of a pulled hamstring muscle. Cameron's Olympics seemed over, but, remarkably, he took off again, having lost a good eight to ten meters to the field. Last at the halfway point and seventh with 100 meters to go, Cameron caught up in the homestretch, finishing fourth and earning a place in the final. Cameron's phenomenal performance overshadowed a great race by Gabriel Tiacoh, who set an African record of 44.64, with Sunday Uti placing second in 44.83 and McKay third at 44.92.

Of the eight finalists, all but Clark were U.S. collegians. Unfortunately, two days' rest did not heal Cameron's leg and he was forced to scratch from the final. Clark went out strongly and led the race all the way into the final straightaway. He thought the victory was his, but about 50 meters from the finish line, Tiacoh and Babers blew by him with Babers pulling away to win by 2½ meters. McKay just nipped Clark at the end for the bronze in what turned out to be the first 400-meter race in which six runners finished under 45 seconds. Babers' time of 44.27 was only one-hundredth of a second off Alberto Juantorena's sea-level best and was the fastest 400 meters in the world since Juantorena set that record at the 1976 Olympics. It was also .71 second better than Babers' pre-Olympic personal record. Tiacoh, who improved his own pre-Olympic best by .70 second, became the first representative of the Ivory Coast to win an Olympic medal. He died of viral meningitis eight years later, at the age of 28.

1988 Seoul C: 75, N: 55, D: 9.26. WR: 43.29 (Harry "Butch" Reynolds)

1. Steven Lewis	USA	43.87
2. Harry "Butch" Reynolds	USA	43.93
3. Danny Everett	USA	44.09
4. Darren Clark	AUS	44.55
5. Innocent Egbunike	NGR	44.72
6. Bertland Cameron	JAM	44.94
7. Ian Morris	TRI	44.95
8. Mohamed Al Malky	OMA	45.03

The U.S. Olympic trials were won by 24-year-old Butch Reynolds in a time of 43.93, with Danny Everett close behind in 43.98. It was the first time that the 44-second barrier had been broken since the 1968 Olympics. The third U.S. qualifier was Everett's U.C.L.A. teammate, 19-year-old Steve Lewis. As recently as May 1988, Lewis' personal record had been only 45.68, but in the semifinals of the trials he dropped it to 44.11. Four weeks later, on August 17, at the Weltklasse meet in Zurich, Reynolds shattered Lee Evans' 19-year-old world record, stopping the clock at 43.29 seconds.

Reynolds entered the Olympics as the overwhelming favorite, but Lewis recorded the fastest times in both of the first two rounds: 45.31 and 44.41. Lewis won the first semifinal in 44.35 and Reynolds the second in 44.33. The latter race saw the elimination of world champion Thomas Schönlebe of East Germany.

Everett led at the halfway point in the final, followed closely by Lewis. Reynolds, renowned for his powerful finishing kick, was sixth. With 100 meters to go, Lewis took the lead. Reynolds was still in only fifth place, a good 6 meters back. Then the world record holder made his move. But it was too late. He passed Everett 20 meters from the finish and had just caught Lewis when Lewis executed a perfect lean to snatch the victory. Lewis was the youngest male runner to win an individual gold medal since Reggie Walker took the 100 meters in 1908. Lewis was four days older than Walker had been. The Seoul final was the first race in history in which seven runners were clocked in under 45 seconds.

1992 Barcelona C: 68, N: 52, D: 8.5. WR: 43.29 (Harry "Butch" Reynolds)

1. Quincy Watts	USA	43.50	OR
2. Steven Lewis	USA	44.21	
3. Samson Kitur	KEN	44.24	
4. Ian Morris	TRI	44.25	
5. Roberto Hernández Prendes	CUB	44.52	
6. David Grindley	GBR	44.75	
7. Ibrahim Ismail	QAT	45.10	
8. Susumu Takano	JPN	45.18	

Because runners from the United States have dominated the 400 meters, the U.S. Olympic trials are often more nerve-wracking than the Olympics themselves. The procedure is simple. The best American quarter-milers face each other in head-to-head competition. The three fastest go to the Olympics. The next three qualify for the 4 × 400-meter relay team. The rest stay home. Clear and simple—except in 1992. The 1992 trials were held in New Orleans in late June. The defending Olympic champion, Steve Lewis, was there. The defending world champion, Antonio Pettigrew, was there. And the world record holder, Butch Reynolds? That's where things got complicated.

On August 12, 1990, Reynolds competed in Monte Carlo and tested positive for the steroid nandrolone. He was given an automatic two-year suspension. Like many athletes who fail doping tests, Butch Reynolds denied taking prohibited drugs and challenged the test results. But Reynolds' case appeared to have more merit than the average drug denial. Reynolds' lawyers contended that the urine samples from Monte Carlo had not been kept safe from tampering and that a circle around the number of a different sample on the paperwork from the drug-testing laboratory in Paris suggested that the positive result actually belonged to a German woman. On December 3, 1991, the executive board of The Athletic Congress (TAC), the governing body of track and field in the United States, recommended that Reynolds' suspension be lifted. Five months later, after five postponements, an I.A.A.F. arbitration panel curtly denied Reynolds' appeal and reminded the Americans that if Reynolds was allowed to race, anyone who ran against him would also be banned from international competition.

On May 28, a federal judge in Columbus, Ohio, ruled that Reynolds should be allowed to run in order to pick up a qualifying time for the Olympic trials. Reynolds ran twice and qualified—and the I.A.A.F. promptly banned the athletes who ran against him. Because of the I.A.A.F.'s "contamination" rule, the favorites in the 400 meters, Steve Lewis, Antonio Pettigrew, and veteran Danny Everett, joined the argument against Reynolds, stating that Reynolds' participation in the Olympic trials would cause them to be banned from the Olympics. On June 19, the day before the opening round of the 400 meters, an appellate judge in Ohio ruled against Reynolds and the issue appeared to be settled. But Reynolds' lawyers took the case to the U.S. Supreme Court and, on June 20, Justice John Paul Stevens ordered TAC to allow Reynolds to compete in the Olympic trials. Chaos reigned in New Orleans. The 400-meter heats were postponed two hours, then overnight, and then two more days. On June 23 the I.A.A.F. agreed to lift its contamination rule for the U.S. Olympic trials only. Reynolds responded by running 44.58, the fastest preliminary time ever. In the semifinals he ran 44.14, his best time since 1988. But in the final he faded to fifth place. Although he missed qualifying for the 400 meters, he did earn a spot as an alternate on the 4 × 400-meter relay team. On July 17, the U.S. Olympic Committee dropped Reynolds from its list of entrants. When the dust settled, the U.S. Olympic entry turned out to be Danny Everett, who won the final in 43.81, the second-fastest time in history, Steve Lewis, and 6-foot 3-inch Quincy Watts, who ran a powerful 43.97 in the semifinals only 16 months after switching from the sprints to the 400. In 1991 Watts had qualified for the world championships, but a throat infection led him to give up his spot at the last minute to Danny Everett.

In Barcelona the first two rounds went as expected, but the first semifinal saw one of the most moving moments in Olympic history, a reminder that behind the hype and the money and the controversies, the Olympics is really about human beings.

Starting in lane 5 was Derek Redmond of Great Britain, a talented runner whose 45.03 was the fastest time of the opening round and whose quarterfinal time of 45.02 was good enough to win his heat. But Redmond's running career had been frustrated by a constant battle against injury. He had already undergone five operations, one on his toe and four on his Achilles tendon, the latest in April. In 1988 Redmond had been forced to withdraw less than two minutes before his opening heat in Seoul and for four years he had agonized that he wasn't really an "Olympic athlete." Now, four years later, he was running well and felt confident that he could lower his personal record.

Like many athletes, Redmond sometimes forgot how much his parents had sacrificed to allow him to fulfill his athletic potential. But as Derek Redmond settled into his blocks in the Olympic semifinals, his thoughts went to his father and all the "time and money and care" he had devoted to see Redmond through all his injuries and to get him where he was. Silently, Derek Redmond dedicated the race to his father. "This one's for you, Dad," he told himself.

Redmond got off to a clean start and was running smoothly when suddenly, about 150 meters into the race, he heard a pop—his right hamstring had torn—and he fell to the ground. When he looked up he saw the other runners racing down the homestretch and across the finish line. When Redmond noticed the stretcher-bearers rushing toward him, he realized how important it was to him to finish the race and not end his Olympic experience on a stretcher. He jumped up and, despite the pain, he continued down lane 5. He couldn't run, he could only hop, so he hobbled forward.

Meanwhile up in the stands, Derek Redmond's father, Jim, watched heartbroken as his son fell, his dreams shattered. When the medics failed to arrive immediately, Jim Redmond, a father seeing his boy in pain, instinctively ran through the stands, past the security guards, and onto the field. By this time Derek had risen and started his slow journey to the finish line. When Jim reached him, he was in the far turn.

"You don't have to do this," said the father to the son.

"I've got to finish," replied the son.

"Okay," said the father. "We started your career together, so we're going to finish this race together."

Jim Redmond put one arm around Derek's shoulder, held his hand, and together they headed toward the homestretch. After a few steps Derek leaned against his father and began sobbing. A few steps from the finish line, Jim Redmond let go of his son and allowed him to finish the course on his own, while the crowd of 65,000 gave the young runner a standing ovation.

Prior to the Olympics, Derek Redmond had had a hostile relationship with team captain (and 100-meter gold medalist) Linford Christie, and the two had criti-

Derek Redmond is comforted by his father as he walks to the finish line in the semifinals of the 1992 400 meters.

cized each other publicly. But as Derek Redmond was walking to the bus after his race, he was approached by Christie. The two men embraced and cried together.

Almost overlooked in the drama of Redmond's ordeal was the result of the race itself, which was won by Steve Lewis. The second semi was won by Quincy Watts, with an Olympic record of 43.71. Watts did even better in the final, entering the homestretch with a huge lead and holding on to win by over five meters. His margin of victory was the largest since Eric Liddell's in 1924. Watts was the fifth African-American since 1956 to win the Olympic 400-meter championship after finishing only third at the U.S. Olympic trials.

There is a curious footnote about what happened to Quincy Watts after his sensational victory in Barcelona. As soon as the Olympics were over, he was forgotten by the American public. In Europe it was a different story. Nike chose Watts to star in a television commercial, shown in several countries, in which a Viking king offers to trade his "super-cushioned wife" for Watts' "super-cushioned Air MAX shoes." Watts takes one look at the massive Viking woman and sprints away at full speed while the super-cushioned wife bellows, "Quin-cy!" "Quin-cy!" became the European equivalent of such immortal U.S. advertising slogans as "Where's the beef?" and "Tastes great, less filling," transforming Watts into a continental celebrity.

800 METERS

The 800 meters is a two-lap race with a staggered start. The runners stay in lanes until the end of the first curve, at which point they are allowed to break to the inside.

1896 Athens C: 9, N: 6, D: 4.9. WR (880 yards): 1:53.4 (Charles Kirkpatrick)

1. Edwin Flack	AUS	2:11.0
2. Nándor Dáni	HUN	2:11.8e
3. Demitrios Golemis	GRE	2:28.0e

DNS: Albin Lermusiaux (FRA)

Teddy Flack was a 22-year-old accountant who took a month's holiday from his job with Price, Waterhouse and Company in London to travel to Athens and take part in the Olympics. Flack had a busy week. He also won the 1500 meters, took part in the marathon, and, on the very morning of the 800-meter final, played in the tennis tournament.

1900 Paris C: 18, N: 8, D: 7.16. WR (880 yards): 1:53.4 (Charles Kirkpatrick)

1. Alfred Tysoe	GBR	2:01.2
2. John Cregan	USA	2:01.8
3. David Hall	USA	2:03.0
4. Henri Deloge	FRA	—
5. Zoltán Speidl	HUN	—
6. John Bray	USA	—

David Hall won the first qualifying heat in 1:59.0, but was unable to repeat his time in the final, which was won by Alf Tysoe, who ran the last lap in 56.2 seconds. Tysoe was a farmhand from Skerton in Lancashire. He died of pleurisy at age 27, only one and a half years after his Olympic triumph.

1904 St. Louis C: 13, N: 3, D: 9.1. WR (880 yards): 1:53.4 (Charles Kirkpatrick)

1. James Lightbody	USA	1:56.0 OR
2. Howard Valentine	USA	1:56.3e
3. Emil Breitkreutz	USA	1:56.4e
4. George Underwood	USA	—
5. Johannes Runge	GER	—
6. William Frank Verner	USA	—

Lightbody ran most of the race in fifth place, then moved to the outside and passed the leaders to win by one and a half yards.

1906 Athens C: 23, N: 7, D: 4.30. WR (880 yards): 1:53.4 (Charles Kirkpatrick)

1. Paul Pilgrim	USA	2:01.5
2. James Lightbody	USA	2:01.6
3. Wyndham Halswelle	GBR	2:03.0
4. Reginald Percy Crabbe	GBR	—
5. Kristian Hellström	SWE	—
6. Charles Bacon	USA	—
7. Eli Burton Parsons	USA	—

DNF: Johannes Runge (GER)

Coming down the homestretch, Lightbody looked over his left shoulder to check the position of the other runners. Just then, Paul Pilgrim, the upset winner of the 400 meters the previous day, sped past him on the right to win by about two feet. Pilgrim never won a major race before or after the 1906 Games.

1908 London C: 39, N: 10, D: 7.21. WR (880 yards): 1:53.4 (Charles Kirkpatrick)

1. Melvin Sheppard	USA	1:52.8	WR
2. Emilio Lunghi	ITA	1:54.2	
3. Hanns Braun	GER	1:55.2	
4. Ödön Bodor	HUN	1:55.4e	
5. Theodore Just	GBR	1:56.4e	
6. John Halstead	USA		

DNF: Clarke Beard (USA), Ian Fairbairn-Crawford (GBR)

Fairbairn-Crawford raced into the lead and set a blistering pace, in the hope of wearing out 1500-meter winner Mel Sheppard for the benefit of Britain's number-one runner, Theodore Just. Fairbairn-Crawford opened a 15-yard gap after 200 meters and finished the first lap in 53 seconds. The British strategy failed, as Sheppard kept to his own pace, moved into the lead after 500 meters, and won by ten yards over the surprising Emilio Lunghi, who once won a long-distance road race in Genoa while carrying an open umbrella because it was raining. A second tape had been set up five yards four inches after the finish so that the winner's time could be measured at 880 yards. Sheppard slowed down so much that he needed 2.2 seconds to cover the extra distance, and thus missed breaking Kirkpatrick's 13-year-old half-mile world record.

1912 Stockholm C: 48, N: 15, D: 7.8. WR: 1:52.8 (Melvin Sheppard)

1. James "Ted" Meredith	USA	1:51.9	WR
2. Melvin Sheppard	USA	1:52.0	
3. Ira Davenport	USA	1:52.0	
4. Daniel Caldwell	USA	1:52.8e	
5. Melville Brock	CAN	1:53.0e	
6. Hanns Braun	GER	1:53.0e	
7. Clarence Edmundson	USA	—	
8. Herbert Putnam	USA	—	

Sheppard led from the start, passing the halfway mark in 52.4. Ted Meredith edged ahead in the final straightaway and won by about 18 inches, with the first four runners all breaking the world record. Meredith continued on to set a new 880-yard record of 1:52.5. According to the *New York Times,* "The excitement during the race was terrific, and was made more so by the terrible noise caused by thousands of throats yelling injunctions in every language to those in front to 'sit down.' "

1920 Antwerp C: 40, N: 17, D: 8.17. WR: 1:51.9 (James "Ted" Meredith)

1. Albert Hill	GBR	1:53.4
2. Earl Eby	USA	1:53.6
3. Bevil Rudd	SAF	1:54.0
4. Edgar Mountain	GBR	1:54.6
5. Donald Scott	USA	1:56.0
6. Albert Sprott	USA	1:56.4
7. Adriaan Paulen	HOL	1:56.4
8. Jean Esparbès	FRA	1:58.0

Albert Hill, a 31-year-old World War I veteran, won by about two meters an exciting race in which the lead changed hands numerous times. A notable instance of gentlemanly good sportsmanship was related by bronze medalist Bevil Rudd. When Earl Eby accidentally bumped into Rudd 300 meters from the finish, he turned to the South African and said, "Sorry, Bevil." Adriaan Paulen, who placed seventh, became a hero of the Dutch resistance during World War II and later served as president of the I.A.A.F.

1924 Paris C: 41, N: 21, D: 7.8. WR: 1:51.9 (James "Ted" Meredith)

1. Douglas Lowe	GBR	1:52.4
2. Paul Martin	SWI	1:52.5
3. Schuyler Enck	USA	1:52.9
4. Hyla "Henry" Stallard	GBR	1:53.0
5. William Richardson	USA	1:53.7
6. Ray Dodge	USA	1:54.2
7. John Watters	USA	1:54.8
8. Charles Hoff	NOR	1:56.7

The favorite, Henry Stallard, was suffering from an injured foot, but this didn't stop him from giving his all in the final and leading for the first 700 meters. Finally he was passed by Lowe and Martin, who engaged in a frantic battle, which Lowe won by about a yard. The final took place on Lowe's 22nd birthday. Charles Hoff, who finished in eighth place, was the reigning world record holder in the pole vault. Paul Martin competed in every Olympic 800 meters contest from 1920 through 1936, one of only two male runners (Pietro Mennea is the other) to take part in five Olympics.

1928 Amsterdam C: 54, N: 26, D: 7.31. WR: 1:50.6 (Séraphin Martin)

1. Douglas Lowe	GBR	1:51.8	OR
2. Erik Byléhn	SWE	1:52.8	
3. Hermann Engelhard	GER	1:53.2	
4. Philip Edwards	CAN	1:54.0	
5. Lloyd Hahn	USA	1:54.2	
6. Séraphin Martin	FRA	1:54.6	
7. Earl Fuller	USA	1:55.0	
8. Jean Keller	FRA	1:57.0	

The 1928 800 meters was an anxiously awaited contest among Germany's Dr. Otto Peltzer, who had broken Ted Meredith's 14-year-old world record in a classic showdown with Douglas Lowe in 1926, Lloyd Hahn, who had broken Peltzer's record, and Séra Martin, who had broken Hahn's record. Unfortunately, Peltzer became ill and was eliminated in the semifinals. As it turned out, the big confrontation was actually a rout, as defending champion Douglas Lowe swept past Hahn in the final curve and won by about eight yards. Following the Amsterdam Olympics, Peltzer received the following letter: "Dear Dr. Peltzer, The British halfmilers who have competed with you in the past feel duty bound to send you their deepest sympathy for the injury that prevented you from showing your best form in the Olympic Games. We realize what sadness this must have caused you, but we have to tell you that your sense of bitterness is fully shared not only by your compatriots, but also by all British sportsmen." The letter was signed, "Douglas Lowe."

1932 Los Angeles C: 19, N: 10, D: 8.2. WR: 1:50.0 (Benjamin Eastman)

1. Thomas Hampson	GBR	1:49.7	WR
2. Alexander Wilson	CAN	1:49.9	
3. Philip Edwards	CAN	1:51.5	
4. Edwin Genung	USA	1:51.7	
5. Edwin Turner	USA	1:52.5	
6. Charles Hornbostel	USA	1:52.7	
7. John Powell	GBR	1:53.1	
8. Séraphin Martin	FRA	1:53.6	

Missing from the competition was Ben Eastman, who had recorded 1:50.0 for 800 meters earlier in the year on his way to a time of 1:50.9 for 880 yards. Eastman had decided to concentrate on the 400 meters. Guyanese-born medical student Phil Edwards sprinted into the lead, covering the first lap in 52.3 seconds. Inevitably, he faded and was passed, first by Alex Wilson and then by 24-year-old schoolteacher Tommy Hampson, who had never before run faster than 1:52.4. Wilson and Hampson dueled stride for stride over the last 50 yards with Hampson just edging ahead to win by a foot.

Two days after his victory, Hampson recorded in his diary his impressions during the last half lap of the race: "Oh God help me—I'm tired. Oh Winnie [his fiancée], my darling, I cannot manage it. Yes I can, though, I beat Wilson two years ago. I beat Edwards twice two years ago. Oh damn this run—round the bend I can't see what's happening.

"We're in the straight. Oh God, let me get there—mustn't disappoint Winnie. Ah, goodbye Phil; now for Wilson. Wonder how far from the tape. I can't see. Caught him now for it. Harder, harder, harder—shall I do it? Yes, I will. Help me now, darling. I can't drop him; damn the man. At last, just in front—my shadow just ahead. Oh where is that tape? My legs won't take me there. What a row the crowd are making too! Ah, thank God, I felt it break, it must have been. Yes, here's Wilson, patting me: 'Well run, Tommy.' "

Hampson credited his victory to his love for his future wife. "I can truly say that but for her I would never have got where I am. A runner perhaps, for they can be made by diligence and hard work; a racer possibly, for they are born of experience in running; but a world beater must, like a great artist, be inspired—and what greater inspiration can anyone have than the love of such a beautiful, kind, gentle, sweet, good creature."

1936 Berlin C: 43, N: 24, D: 8.4. WR: 1:49.7 (Thomas Hampson)

1. John Woodruff	USA	1:52.9
2. Mario Lanzi	ITA	1:53.3
3. Philip Edwards	CAN	1:53.6
4. Kazimierz Kucharski	POL	1:53.8
5. Charles Hornbostel	USA	1:54.6

6. Harry Williamson	USA	1:55.8	
7. Juan Carlos Anderson	ARG	—	
8. Gerald Backhouse	AUS	—	

John Woodruff was a 21-year-old University of Pittsburgh freshman who came from a poor black family in South Connellsville, Pennsylvania. His time of 1:52.7 was the fastest of the qualifying rounds. As usual, Phil Edwards, now a doctor, stormed into the lead and led the field around the first lap. Meanwhile Woodruff was executing one of the most unusual tactics ever seen in the Olympics. Finding himself boxed in after 300 meters, Woodruff slowed down to the pace of a brisk walk and let all the other runners pass him. Then he moved way to the outside and sprinted past his opponents one by one until he found himself in the lead with one lap to go. Edwards regained the lead on the backstretch, but Woodruff took over again in the last curve. Mario Lanzi staged a great finishing drive, but Woodruff used his loping ten-foot stride to stave off the challenge and win by two yards. Phil Edwards won his fifth Olympic bronze medal.

1948 London C: 41, N: 24, D: 8.2. WR: 1:46.6 (Rudolf Harbig)

1. Malvin Whitfield	USA	1:49.2	OR
2. Arthur Wint	JAM	1:49.5	
3. Marcel Hansenne	FRA	1:49.8	
4. Herbert Barten	USA	1:50.1	
5. Ingvar Bengtsson	SWE	1:50.5	
6. Robert Chambers	USA	1:52.1	
7. Robert Chef d'Hôtel	FRA	1:53.0	
8. Niels Holst-Sörensen	DEN	1:53.4	

Chef d'Hôtel held the early lead, but at the end of the first lap 23-year-old Air Force sergeant Mal Whitfield jumped the field and pulled away. Arthur Wint made a late charge, but Whitfield held on to win by three yards. Between 1948 and 1954 Whitfield won 66 of 69 half-mile races. He was inspired to be an Olympic runner when he sneaked into the Los Angeles Coliseum during the 1932 Olympics.

1952 Helsinki C: 50, N: 32, D: 7.22. WR: 1:46.6 (Rudolf Harbig)

1. Malvin Whitfield	USA	1:49.2 EOR	(1:49.34)
2. Arthur Wint	JAM	1:49.4	(1:49.63)
3. Heinz Ulzheimer	GER	1:49.7	(1:49.78)
4. Gunnar Nielsen	DEN	1:49.7	(1:49.84)
5. Albert Webster	GBR	1:50.2	(1:50.47)
6. Günter Steines	GER	1:50.6	(1:50.81)
7. Reginald Pearman	USA	1:52.1	(1:52.31)
8. Lars-Eric Wolfbrandt	SWE	1:52.1	(1:52.38)

Between Olympics Mal Whitfield had worked as a tail-gunner during the Korean War, flying 27 bomber missions. But on July 22, 1952, he was back in the final of the Olympic 800 meters run, once again facing the challenge of Arthur Wint. The 32-year-old Wint led the field around the first lap, reaching 400 meters with Ulzheimer second and Whitfield third. On the backstretch, with 250 meters to go, Whitfield made his move and entered the

final curve in first place. Coming into the homestretch, Wint made a move of his own and gradually drew up to Whitfield's shoulder. But Whitfield had kept some extra strength in reserve and was able to pull away to a two-yard victory. Whitfield's time was exactly what it had been four years earlier, but Wint finished one yard closer.

1956 Melbourne C: 38, N: 24, D: 11.26. WR: 1:45.7 (Roger Moens)

1. Thomas Courtney	USA	1:47.7	OR	(1:47.75)
2. Derek Johnson	GBR	1:47.8		(1:47.88)
3. Audun Boysen	NOR	1:48.1		(1:48.25)
4. Arnold Sowell	USA	1:48.3		(1:48.41)
5. Michael Farrell	GBR	1:49.2		(1:49.29)
6. Lonnie Spurrier	USA	1:49.3		(1:49.38)
7. Emile Leva	BEL	1:51.8		(1:51.75)
8. Bill Butchart	AUS	1:52.5		

On August 3, 1955, Roger Moens of Belgium ran 1:45.7 to finally break Rudolf Harbig's 1939 world record. Unfortunately, Moens sustained a leg injury late in the 1956 season and was unable to compete in the Olympics. Nevertheless, the 800 meters final turned out to be the most dramatic race of the Melbourne Olympics. With Moens gone, the race shaped up to be the climactic chapter in the ongoing rivalry between Arnie Sowell of Pittsburgh and Tom Courtney of Livingston, New Jersey.

Sure enough, Courtney took the early lead, but Sowell quickly passed him and led the pack through the first lap and into the second. Toward the end of the backstretch, Courtney tried to pass Sowell, and the two ran shoulder to shoulder around the final curve. Emerging into the

Tom Courtney (153) edges Derek Johnson (137) in the 800 meters final of 1956, the most dramatic race of the Melbourne Olympics. Courtney exhausted himself so thoroughly that the award ceremony had to be delayed an extra hour until he recovered.

homestretch, the runners found themselves confronted by a stiff wind. Courtney moved ahead and then shifted to the third lane in order to avoid the chewed up inner lane. Noticing the sudden opening between the two Americans, Derek Johnson dashed between them and, with 60 yards to go, pushed into first place. It looked like a major upset in the making, but Courtney was not about to give up. Courtney later recalled, "I looked at the tape just 40 yards away and realized this was the only chance I would ever have to win the Olympics." Ignoring the pain throughout his body, Courtney fashioned one last sprint out of nothing but determination. Step by step he gained on Johnson and lunged across the finish line. In a delirium, he turned to Johnson and asked who had won. "Why you did, Tom," came the reply.

"It was a new kind of agony for me," Courtney recalled. "I had never run myself into such a state. My head was exploding, my stomach ripping and even the tips of my fingers ached. The only thing I could think was, 'If I live, I will never run again!' " The victory ceremony had to be delayed for an hour until he recovered. Twenty years later, Tom Courtney wrote about his years of competitive running: "It is a world that is gone now, but I still enjoy going out to a local track and taking a run and, with a half lap to go, I kind of savor the idea that I am re-running the last half lap of the best part of my life."

1960 Rome C: 51, N: 35, D: 9.2. WR: 1:45.7 (Roger Moens)

1. Peter Snell	NZE	1:46.3	OR	(1:46.48)
2. Roger Moens	BEL	1:46.5		(1:46.55)
3. George Kerr	BWI/JAM	1:47.1		(1:47.25)
4. Paul Schmidt	GER	1:47.6		(1:47.82)
5. Christian Wägli	SWI	1:48.1		(1:48.19)
6. Manfred Matuschewski	GDR	1:52.0		(1:52.21)

The 1960 800 meters was expected to be a great duel between 30-year-old world record holder Roger Moens and George Kerr of Jamaica. Kerr won the first semifinal, but the second semi produced a surprise when Moens was beaten by a little-known New Zealander from Opunake named Peter Snell, whose pre-Olympic best had been 1:49.2 for 880 yards. However, Moens had not really extended himself, so Snell was still not taken seriously. As expected, Christian Wägli took the lead in the final and held on for 700 meters, at which point Moens moved ahead. In the homestretch he looked back three times to check the position of the other runners, particularly George Kerr. Moens was still ahead 25 yards from the tape when Snell, realizing for the first time that he actually had a chance to win, charged ahead on the inside. "All I remember from that point is hurling every ounce of effort into the finish, and flinging myself forward," Snell wrote in his autobiography, *No Bugles, No Drums*. Like Tom Courtney four years earlier, Peter Snell had no idea in which place he had finished. Then a dejected Roger Moens approached him with congratulations. "Who won?" asked Snell. "You did," replied Moens.

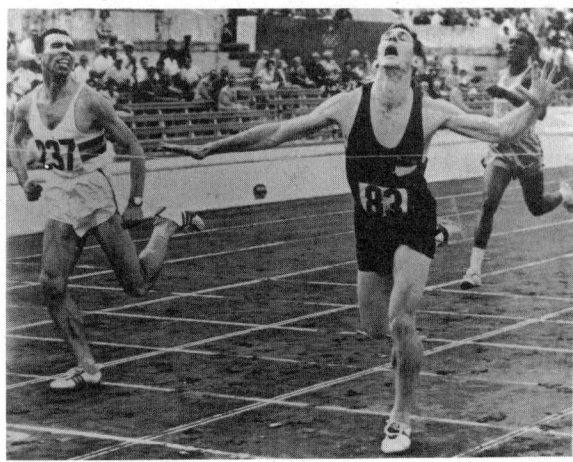

Peter Snell (right) scores a surprise victory over world record holder Roger Moens in the 1960 800 meters.

"It was a strange moment," Snell recalled. "What should I do now? Flashingly, I recalled films of past Olympics, and of champions who cavorted round the track, presumably letting their happy emotions run riot. But I felt in a semi-daze, partly from fatigue, partly from disbelief that this had actually happened to me." Snell did not take a victory lap. Instead he channeled his emotions into rooting for fellow New Zealander Murray Halberg, who won the next race on the schedule, the 5000 meters.

A word about one runner who never even made it to the starting line: Wym Essajas was the first person to represent the South American nation of Suriname at the Olympics. Unfortunately he was mistakenly told that the 800-meter heats would be held in the afternoon, so he spent the morning resting. When Essajas arrived at the stadium the heats were over, and he was forced to return to Suriname without having competed. It was eight years before Suriname sent another athlete to the Olympics.

1964 Tokyo C: 47, N: 32, D: 10.16. WR: 1:44.3 (Peter Snell)

1. Peter Snell	NZE	1:45.1	OR
2. William Crothers	CAN	1:45.6	
3. Wilson Kiprugut Chuma	KEN	1:45.9	
4. George Kerr	JAM	1:45.9	
5. Thomas Farrell	USA	1:46.6	
6. Jerome Siebert	USA	1:47.0	
7. Dieter Bogatzki	GER	1:47.2	
8. Jacques Pennewaert	BEL	1:50.5	

When Peter Snell arrived in Rome in 1960, no one had paid any attention, but four years later in Tokyo it was a completely different story. In one week in 1962 Snell had set world records of 3:54.4 for the mile and 1:44.3 for 800 meters. Now he was the favorite in both the 800 and 1500, although he didn't make his final decision to enter the 800 until the last minute. In the first round, Francis

Chatelet of France had the unfortunate experience of recording the fifth-fastest time of the round, and yet being eliminated because he finished fifth in his heat, with only the top four from each heat advancing to the semifinals. The final saw stocky Wilson Kiprugut lead the field for 550 meters. Then Snell swung outside, stormed around the leaders into first place, and pulled away to win by four yards. Kiprugut tripped on George Kerr's heel 50 yards from the finish, but still managed to gain a bronze medal, the first Olympic medal ever won by a Kenyan. Snell's winning time was the best on record since his own world record performance.

1968 Mexico City C: 41, N: 31, D: 10.15. WR: 1:44.3 (Peter Snell)

1. Ralph Doubell	AUS	1:44.3	EWR	(1:44.40)
2. Wilson Kiprugut Chuma	KEN	1:44.5		(1:44.57)
3. Thomas Farrell	USA	1:45.4		(1:45.46)
4. Walter Adams	GER	1:45.8		(1:45.83)
5. Josef Plachý	CZE	1:45.9		(1:45.99)
6. Dieter Fromm	GDR	1:46.2		(1:46.30)
7. Thomas Saisi	KEN	1:47.5		(1:47.59)
8. Benedict Cayenne	TRI	1:54.3		(1:54.40)

Following the usual Kenyan tactics, Kiprugut led the field from the start and still had a six-yard lead after 600 meters. Unheralded Ralph Doubell, who had nipped Kiprugut in the second semifinal, repeated his come-from-behind performance in the final. He passed Kiprugut 50 yards from the finish and won by a long yard. As soon as the race was over, Doubell asked Farrell what the world record was. Farrell pointed to the scoreboard and said, "That's it." The top four finishers all set personal records while Plachý equaled his.

1972 Munich C: 61, N: 46, D: 9.2. WR: 1:44.3 (Peter Snell, Ralph Doubell, David Wottle)

1. David Wottle	USA	1:45.9	(1:45.86)
2. Yevhen Arzhanov	SOV/UKR	1:45.9	(1:45.89)
3. Michael Boit	KEN	1:46.0	(1:46.01)
4. Franz-Josef Kemper	GER	1:46.5	(1:46.50)
5. Robert Ouko	KEN	1:46.5	(1:46.53)
6. Andrew Carter	GBR	1:46.6	(1:46.55)
7. Andrzej Kupczyk	POL	1:47.1	(1:47.10)
8. Dieter Fromm	GDR	1:48.0	(1:47.96)

At the U.S. Olympic tryouts, Dave Wottle of Canton, Ohio, had equaled the world record of 1:44.3, three seconds faster than he had ever run before. However, because of his lack of international experience and because he had suffered a recent attack of tendinitis, Wottle was not the favorite in Munich. This role fell rather naturally to Yevhen Arzhanov, who had not lost an 800-meter race in four years. As expected, the two Kenyans, Ouko and Boit, rushed into the early lead in the Olympic final, while Wottle ran in sixth place. Coming into the homestretch it looked like Arzhanov's race, and even Wottle, who had now begun his finishing kick, was only hoping for a medal. As the Kenyans faded, Wottle, who always wore an old golf cap while he ran,

saw his chance for second place. Then, 20 yards from the finish, he realized that Arzhanov had run out of steam and that the gold medal was still a possibility. Drawing on his last reserve of energy, Wottle caught and passed Arzhanov, who stumbled two meters short of the tape and fell onto the synthetic track. "It is very disappointing," Arzhanov later told the press, "to lose in the very last stride by the length of your nose."

Wottle was so shocked by his victory that he forgot to take off his cap during the playing of "The Star-Spangled Banner" at the medal ceremony. He didn't realize what he had done until a reporter asked him if he had been staging a protest. Although nobody back in the United States actually held it against him, Wottle, a member of the Air Force ROTC at Bowling Green University, was embarrassed to the point of tears and felt obliged to make a formal apology to the American people.

1976 Montreal C: 42, N: 31, D: 7.25. WR: 1:43.7 (Marcello Fiasconaro)

1. Alberto Juantorena Danger	CUB	1:43.50	WR
2. Ivo van Damme	BEL	1:43.86	
3. Richard Wohlhuter	USA	1:44.12	
4. Willi Wülbeck	GER	1:45.26	
5. Steven Ovett	GBR	1:45.44	
6. Luciano Susanj	YUG	1:45.75	
7. Sriram Singh	IND	1:45.77	
8. Carlo Grippo	ITA	1:48.39	

Alberto Juantorena went to the Montreal Olympics as the favorite at 400 meters, but somewhat of an unknown quantity at 800 meters. Although he had recorded 1:44.9 in April, the second fastest time of the year (to Rick Wohlhuter's 1:44.8), Juantorena had very little experience at the distance. In fact, his coach had tricked him into entering 800-meter races by telling him they would build his endurance for the 400. Wohlhuter himself dismissed the Cuban as a noncontender, assuming that he would not have the stamina to make it through three rounds of metric half-mile races. Wohlhuter could not have been more wrong. In the final, Juantorena moved ahead as the runners broke to the inside after running the first 300 meters in lanes. He passed the halfway mark in 50.9 seconds. Sriram Singh took the lead briefly, but Juantorena fought him off, easily beat back a challenge from Wohlhuter, and won decisively, to become the first 800 meters gold medalist from a non-English-speaking country. Conspicuously missing from the competition was Mike Boit of Kenya, who was forced to watch the meet from the stands after his nation's government joined the African boycott. Four weeks later Boit ran 1:43.90 and 1:43.57, leaving track fans to wonder what might have been. Silver medalist Ivo van Damme died in a car crash on December 29, 1976. He was only 22 years old.

Olympic history, of course, is not just made up of medalists, and some mention should be made of Wilnor Joseph of the notorious Haitian track and field team. Joseph finished the second heat of the first round in

2:15.26, a time so slow that it would not have qualified him for the 800 meters final in 1900, much less 1976.

1980 Moscow C: 41, N: 28, D: 7.26. WR: 1:42.33 (Sebastian Coe)

1. Stephen Ovett	GBR	1:45.40
2. Sebastian Coe	GBR	1:45.85
3. Nikolai Kirov	SOV/BLR	1:45.94
4. Agberto Guimaraes	BRA	1:46.20
5. Andreas Busse	GDR	1:46.81
6. Detlef Wagenknecht	GDR	1:46.91
7. Jose Marajo	FRA	1:47.26
8. David Warren	GBR	1:49.25

The final of the 1980 800 meters race was one of the most eagerly anticipated confrontations in Olympic history. Although there were six other runners in the race, the entire focus of sports fans around the world was on the two English world record holders, Sebastian Coe and Steve Ovett. The last time the two had met was at the 1978 European championships, where Ovett had beaten Coe at 800 meters, but both had lost to Olaf Beyer of East Germany. Since then Ovett and Coe had avoided each other like the plague, preferring to heat up their rivalry with increasingly faster times.

In 1979 Coe set the track world on its heels by breaking three world records in 41 days. On July 5 he ran 800 meters in 1:42.33 to lower Alberto Juantorena's world record by a full second. On July 17 Coe became the first person since Peter Snell to hold the records for both the 800 and the mile, when he ran the classic distance in 3:48.95. Then, on August 15, he covered 1500 meters in 3:32.03, to break Filbert Bayi's five-year-old mark.

The following year it was Steve Ovett's turn to enter the record books. On July 1, 1980, less than an hour after Coe set a new record for 1000 meters, Ovett gained great satisfaction by running a 3:48.8 mile to snatch the world record away from his rival. On July 15, nine days before the heats of the Olympic 800, Ovett beat a distinguished field of Olympic boycotters to win a 1500-meter race in 3:32.09, a time that rounded up to 3:32.1, the same as Coe's 3:32.03. The stage was definitely set for fireworks in the Olympics.

When Coe arrived in Moscow with the rest of the British team, he was met by an army of no less than 400 journalists, who assaulted him with a barrage of inane questions, such as, "Do you think you will win?" "How do you feel as a human being?" (this one from the representative of Tass, the Soviet news agency), and "How do you like Moscow?" (he had been there only a few hours). Ovett, on the other hand, slipped in two days before he was due to run and, following his usual procedure, refused to talk to the press, a wise decision considering Coe's experience.

The consensus of track experts was that Coe was the favorite at 800 meters, but that the 1500 was a toss-up. Ovett, on the other hand, had issued a public statement that the 800 was a toss-up, but that he was 90 percent sure he would win the 1500. The two did not meet in the heats and semifinals of the 800 meters, the first middle-distance race to be contested.

The first round was run without incident, but the semifinals saw the surprise elimination of Olaf Beyer. The three semifinal heats were won by Ovett, Nikolai Kirov, and Coe.

The final, run at 7:25 p.m. on July 26, turned out to be a strange, almost sluggish race. The first lap was covered in the unusually slow time of 54.3 with Guimaraes in the lead, Ovett badly boxed in, in sixth place, and Coe running last. Dave Warren jumped into the lead, but in the backstretch Kirov moved in front by three meters, while Ovett pushed his way into second place, throwing so many elbows that he verged on disqualification. Meanwhile Coe was floundering, wasting his time in outside lanes and evidently unsure of what tactics to follow. By the time he finally made his move, it was too late. Ovett shot past Kirov 70 meters from the finish and won by over three meters. Ironically, Ovett's winning time was exactly the same as his fifth-place time in Montreal four years earlier. Coe outsprinted Kirov for the silver medal, a prize that would earn a place of honor in most homes, but which for Sebastian Coe was a symbol of failure.

As usual, Ovett declined to attend the postrace press conference. However Coe did not. Sorrowfully, he told the world, "I chose this day of all days to run the worst race of my life. I cannot explain why. I suppose I must have compounded more cardinal sins of middle-distance running in 1½ minutes than I've done in a lifetime. What a race to choose." Fortunately for Coe, he still had a chance to redeem himself six days later. "I've got to come back and climb the mountain again," he said. "The 1500 was going to be a hard event anyway, but now it's going to be the big race of my life. I must win it."

1984 Los Angeles C: 69, N: 55, D: 8.6. WR: 1:41.73 (Sebastian Coe)

1. Joaquim Carvalho Cruz	BRA	1:43.00	OR
2. Sebastian Coe	GBR	1:43.64	
3. Earl Jones	USA	1:43.83	
4. Billy Konchellah	KEN	1:44:03	
5. Donato Sabia	ITA	1:44.53	
6. Edwin Koech	KEN	1:44.86	
7. Johnny Gray	USA	1:47.89	
8. Stephen Ovett	GBR	1:52.28	

Joaquim Cruz grew up in a poor neighborhood in Taguatinga, Brazil. Although his father worked from morning until night to support his wife and five children, it took a month's pay to produce enough extra to buy a pair of shoes for his only son. A few months after his father died in 1981, the 18-year-old Cruz, a reluctantly converted basketball player, set a world junior record of 1:44.3. His coach, Luiz de Oliveira, decided that if Cruz's potential was to be fulfilled, he would have to move north to the United States. So Cruz, de Oliveira, and de Oliveira's family went to live in Utah and then in Eugene, Oregon. By 1983 Cruz was ranked second in the world. The following year he entered the Olympics as a slight favorite over the veteran Sebastian Coe.

The young Brazilian was clearly in top form in Los Angeles. He won his first-round heat in 1:45.66, his quarterfinal heat in 1:44.84 and his semifinal in a personal best of 1:43.82. The other semi was won by Coe. In the final, Cruz positioned himself in second place and let Edwin Koech do the front-running, while Coe stayed right behind them. Coming out of the final turn, Cruz did a double-take at Coe behind him and then burst away from the other runners. Coe and Jones took off after him, but they never had a chance. Cruz's winning margin of five meters was the event's largest since 1928.

Sebastian Coe's silver medal was ample reward for a remarkable comeback. Only twelve months earlier, worn out by a prolonged debilitating illness, Coe had declared, "As far as the 800 meters goes, the game is up. . . . I have been obliged to walk away from an event which I did not believe I had fully explored." As for defending Olympic champion Steve Ovett, he had struggled to qualify for the final, lunging across the line to gain the last spot ahead of Omar Khalifa of Sudan. Ovett's semifinal time of 1:44.81 was his fastest 800 in six years. After the final, Ovett, who had been battling bronchitis, collapsed twice in the tunnel leading away from the track. Taken away on a stretcher, he spent the next two nights in a hospital, suffering from broncho-spasms, which he attributed to the legendary Los Angeles smog. Courageously, or, as he would later say, foolishly, Ovett returned to the track to compete in the 1500 meters.

1988 Seoul C: 70, N: 53, D: 9.26. WR: 1:41.73 (Sebastian Coe)

1.	Paul Ereng	KEN	1:43.45
2.	Joaquim Carvalho Cruz	BRA	1:43.90
3.	Saïd Aouita	MOR	1:44.06
4.	Peter Elliott	GBR	1:44.12
5.	Johnny Gray	USA	1:44.80
6.	José Luiz Barbosa	BRA	1:46.39
7.	Donato Sabia	ITA	1:48.03
8.	Nixon Kiprotich	KEN	1:49.55

In 1988 the 800 meters was blessed with a talent-rich field led by Saïd Aouita, who hadn't lost a flat race at any distance between 800 and 10,000 meters in over three years. Challenging the multitalented Moroccan were Commonwealth champion Steve Cram, the man who had beaten Aouita at 1500 meters more than 50 races ago on July 16, 1985, and Joaquim Cruz, the defending Olympic champion. The big three were expected to be pressed by the world championship silver and bronze medalists, Peter Elliott, a carpenter at a steelworks in Rotherham, South Yorkshire, and José Luiz Barbosa, who grew up in Três Lagoas in the jungles of western Brazil, and by Johnny Gray, who had recorded the fastest time of the year, 1:42.65, just one month before the Olympics. No one paid any attention to Paul Ereng. And why should they?

A converted quarter-miler, the 21-year-old Ereng did

not begin competing at 800 meters until 1988. Running for the University of Virginia, he won the N.C.A.A. title, then ran ten races in Europe, finishing first in only one. He was invited to the Kenyan Olympic trials only after someone sent Kenyan officials a newspaper article about Ereng's N.C.A.A. victory. In the absence of world champion Billy Konchellah, who was suffering a relapse of tuberculosis, the Kenyan trials were won by Nixon Kiprotich. Ereng, who led for most of the race, died at the end and barely held on for third place. He was the first member of the Turkana tribe to qualify for the Olympics.

Ereng still was not given serious consideration, even when he ran the fastest time of the opening round in Seoul (1:46.14). The quarterfinals saw the surprising elimination of Steve Cram. The semifinals were won by Ereng, in a personal record of 1:44.55, and Kiprotich in 1:44.71.

With two men in the final, the Brazilians planned a team race. Their strategy was to have Barbosa take out the first lap with a fast pace of between 49 and 50 seconds and try to disrupt Aouita by surging between 300 and 400 meters and 500 and 600, which was when they expected the Moroccan to accelerate. Then Cruz would take over in the backstretch and race to the tape.

The Kenyans had a similar plan, but with a twist. Kiprotich suggested that he set the early pace. Because he was better known, he reasoned, the others would not be expecting such a tactic and would be caught by surprise when Ereng made his move. Kiprotich did set a fast early pace (23.0 for 200 meters), so fast in fact that Ereng was horrified and almost yelled at him to stop. Barbosa moved ahead and led at the bell in 49.54, with Kiprotich second and Cruz third. Aouita was holding back in sixth place and Ereng in seventh.

The real scramble began in the backstraight. First Kiprotich regained the lead from Barbosa. Then Cruz shot by both of them with Elliott and Aouita close behind. Elliott tried to take the lead entering the final turn, but Cruz fought him off and reached the final straight looking like a winner. Meanwhile, though, Ereng was weaving his way between runners. While Elliott and Aouita engaged in a tough battle for second behind Cruz, Ereng slipped by both of them on the inside, then passed a shocked Cruz to win by 2 meters.

1992 Barcelona C: 59, N: 49, D: 8.5. WR: 1:41.73 (Sebastian Coe)

1.	William Tanui	KEN	1.43.66
2.	Nixon Kiprotich	KEN	1:43.70
3.	Johnny Gray	USA	1:43.97
4.	José Luiz Barbosa	BRA	1:45.06
5.	Andrea Benvenuti	ITA	1:45.23
6.	Curtis Robb	GBR	1:45.57
7.	Reda Abdenouz	ALG	1:48.34

DNF: Mark Everett (USA)

In the Olympic Village, Nixon Kiprotich dreamed that his teammate and friend, Air Force clerk William Tanui, would win the 800 meters final, and told him so. When the race was actually run, Johnny Gray burst into the lead and held it all the way into the homestretch. About 50 meters from the finish he was passed by Kiprotich and then, just at the end, both of them were passed by Tanui.

1500 METERS

The "metric mile," the 1500 meters race, is 1640 yards 1 foot 3 inches long and covers three and three-quarter laps. Twelve runners take part in the final. On the fortieth anniversary of the day he broke the four-minute mile, Roger Bannister, speaking to an audience that included thirteen other mile record setters, had this to say about the life of world-class milers: "Old men, they say, forget. It's true we forget the pain and the fatigue and lashing yourself to try harder next time and next, illness and injury, real and perhaps sometimes imagined, the castigations of the press and coaches—all these fade away, because memory is kind. We remember the good times, the sun on our backs, running through the beauty of the countryside, running thousands and thousands of miles. We remember laughter and friends. For us, no matter what life may bring, whatever subsequent shadows there may be, no one can strip us of these memories."

1896 Athens C: 8, N: 6, D: 4.7. WR (1 mile): 4:12.8 (Walter George)
1. Edwin Flack	AUS	4:33.2
2. Arthur Blake	USA	4:33.6e
3. Albin Lermusiaux	FRA	4.36.0e
4. Karl Galle	GER	4.39.0e
5. Angelos Phetsis	GRE	—
6. Demitrios Golemis	GRE	—

Flack outsprinted Blake in the final straightaway to win by about two meters. Two days later Flack also won the 800 meters race.

1900 Paris C: 9, N: 6, D: 7.15. WR: 4:10.4 (Albin Lermusiaux)
1. Charles Bennett	GBR	4:06.2	WR
2. Henri Deloge	FRA	4:06.6	
3. John Bray	USA	4:07.2	
4. Christian Christensen	DEN	—	
5. David Hall	USA	—	

Two of the leading contenders, John Cregan and Alex Grant of the United States, withdrew because the race was held on a Sunday. Bennett, a railway engine driver, celebrated his victory by going to the Folies Bergère.

1904 St. Louis C: 9, N: 3, D: 9.3. WR: 4:06.2 (Charles Bennett)
1. James Lightbody	USA	4:05.4	WR
2. William Frank Verner	USA	4:06.8	
3. Lacey Hearn	USA	—	
4. David Munson	USA	—	
5. Johannes Runge	GER	—	
6. Peter Deer	CAN	—	

7. Howard Valentine	USA	—
8. Harvey Cohn	USA	—

Lightbody moved into the lead at the end of the backstretch and won by six yards. The first three finishers were all members of the Chicago Athletic Association.

1906 Athens C: 20, N: 8, D: 4.30. WR: 4:05.4 (James Lightbody)
1. James Lightbody	USA	4.12.0
2. John McGough	GBR/IRL	4:12.6
3. Kristian Hellström	SWE	4:13.4
4. George Wheatley	AUS	—
5. James Sullivan	USA	—
6. George Bonhag	USA	—
AC: Reginald Percy Crabbe (GBR), Harvey Cohn (USA)		

1908 London C: 43, N: 15, D: 7.14. WR: 3:59.8 (Harold Wilson)
1. Melvin Sheppard	USA	4:03.4	OR
2. Harold Wilson	GBR	4:03.6	
3. Norman Hallows	GBR	4:04.0	
4. John Tait	CAN	4:06.8	
5. Ian Fairbairn-Crawford	GBR	4:07.6	
6. Joseph Deakin	GBR	4:07.9	
DNF: James Sullivan (USA), E. Victor Loney (GBR)			

Unfortunately, British officials decided to divide the 43 entrants into eight heats and allow only the winner of each heat to advance to the final. Because the runners were not seeded, this caused the elimination of several major contenders, most notably Emilio Lunghi, who clocked the second fastest time (4:03.8), but lost his heat to Norman Hallows, who ran 4:03.4. The final looked like a victory for the 5-foot 4-inch, 115-pound world record holder, Harold Wilson, until Mel Sheppard launched a sprint 100 yards from the tape, passed Wilson with 15 yards to go, and won by a yard and a half. For Sheppard, it was the first of his four Olympic gold medals. Ironically, Sheppard had applied to become a New York City policeman, but was rejected because he had a "weak heart."

1912 Stockholm C: 46, N: 14, D: 7.10. WR: 3:55.8 (Abel Kiviat)
1. Arnold Jackson	GBR	3:56.8	OR
2. Abel Kiviat	USA	3:56.9	
3. Norman Taber	USA	3:56.9	
4. John Paul Jones	USA	3:57.2	
5. Ernst Wide	SWE	3:57.6	
6. Philip Baker	GBR	3:59.6	
7. John Zander	SWE	4:02.0e	
8. Henri Arnaud	FRA	4:02.2e	

The United States entered a powerful team, including defending champion Mel Sheppard, 1500-meter world record holder Abel Kiviat, and mile world record holder John Paul Jones. Kiviat took the lead entering the final lap, followed by Taber and Jones, with Jackson and Sheppard close behind. Sheppard faded first. Entering the final straight it still looked like an American sweep, as Kiviat, Taber, and Jones raced almost shoulder to shoulder. Thirty meters from the finish Kiviat seemed assured of victory, when suddenly Arnold Jackson of

Great Britain burst by on the outside and won by almost two yards. The winner later gained greater fame as Arnold Nugent Strode-Jackson following his participation in World War I, during which he was wounded three times. In 1918, at the age of 27, he became the youngest acting brigadier general in the British army. As an athlete, Jackson was rather casual in his training, preferring golf, walking, and massages to the more vigorous and acceptable techniques of keeping in shape. As for Kiviat, 72 years later, at the age of 91, he participated in the 1984 torch relay, carrying the flame for one kilometer in New York City.

1920 Antwerp C: 29, N: 12, D: 8.19. WR: 3:54.7 (John Zander)

1. Albert Hill	GBR	4:01.8
2. Philip Baker	GBR	4:02.3e
3. Lawrence Shields	USA	4:03.0e
4. Vacláv Vohralík	CZE	4:04.6e
5. Sven Lundgren	SWE	4:06.3e
6. André Audinet	FRA	4:06.4e
7. Arturo Porro	ITA	4:06.6e
8. Joie Ray	USA	4:10.0e

The 31-year-old Hill completed his 800/1500 double with the help of Baker, who ran beside him for most of the final lap in order to "protect him from attacks." Baker later adopted his wife's maiden name and changed his name to Philip Noel-Baker. He served as a member of Parliament for 36 years and was awarded the 1959 Nobel Peace Prize in honor of his work in the pursuit of disarmament.

1924 Paris C: 40, N: 22, D: 7.10. WR: 3:52.6 (Paavo Nurmi)

1. Paavo Nurmi	FIN	3:53.6	OR
2. Wilhelm Schärer	SWI	3:55.0	
3. Hyla "Henry" Stallard	GBR	3:55.6	
4. Douglas Lowe	GBR	3:57.0	
5. Raymond Buker	USA	3:58.5	
6. Lloyd Hahn	USA	3:59.0	
7. Raymond Watson	USA	3:59.9	
8. Frej Liewendahl	FIN	4:00.3	

The crowd at the Stade Colombes Stadium rose to their feet to watch the thrilling race to the finish line, as Willy Schärer moved ahead in the last few strides to defeat the desperately struggling Henry Stallard, who collapsed to the ground and remained unconscious for a half hour. It had been an exciting battle—for second place. The race for first place had been no race at all, due to the presence of "The Phantom Finn," Paavo Nurmi.

Finnish Olympic officials had been extremely upset when the track and field schedule was announced and they learned that the final of the 1500 meters and the final of the 5000 meters would be separated by only a half hour, giving negligible time for recuperation to Nurmi, their star entrant in both events. A protest was filed, and the French organizers grudgingly agreed to expand the interval to 55 minutes. It still seemed an impossible feat to attempt, particularly after Nurmi injured both legs in

training. But the challenge simply made Nurmi more determined to succeed. On June 19, three weeks before the day of the two Olympic finals, Nurmi decided to simulate the task ahead of him. First he ran a 1500-meter race, setting a world record of 3:52.6. After a one-hour rest he returned to the track and ran 5000 meters, setting another world record of 14:28.2.

Needless to say, when the other runners lined up for the start of the Olympic 1500 final in Paris, they had little hope for the gold medal. Nurmi took off, stopwatch in hand, as usual, covering the first 400 meters in a blistering 58.0 designed to kill off the opposition. Ray Watson made the mistake of trying to keep up with the Finnish running machine, and paid for his folly by fading to a disappointing seventh place. As soon as Watson had dropped away, Nurmi consulted his stopwatch one last time, tossed it onto the infield, and sprinted away to a 40-meter lead. In order to save his strength for the 5000, he coasted the final 300 meters, picking up speed briefly just before the end to make sure the others didn't catch up. After he crossed the finish line, he ignored the cheers of the crowd, picked up his stopwatch and his sweater, and disappeared into the dressing room to rest up for his next race.

1928 Amsterdam C: 54, N: 26, D: 8.2. WR: 3:51.0 (Otto Peltzer)

1. Harry Larva	FIN	3:53.2	OR
2. Jules Ladoumègue	FRA	3:53.8	
3. Eino Purje-Borg	FIN	3:56.4	
4. Hans-Georg Wichmann	GER	3:56.8	
5. Cyril Ellis	GBR	3:57.6	
6. Paul Martin	SWI	3:58.4	
7. Helmut Krause	GER	3:59.0	
8. William Whyte	AUS	4:00.0	

Two hundred meters from the finish, Ladoumègue took the lead from Purje and appeared to be headed for victory. However he was passed 20 meters from the tape by "Harri" Larva, a goldsmith's engraver, who won by four yards. Larva was born to Swedish parents who lived in Turku, the hometown of Paavo Nurmi. He began training as a runner in 1924 after attending a post-Olympic race between Nurmi and Ritola. Ladoumègue, too, idolized Nurmi and kept a newspaper photo of the master underneath his bed. On the victory podium both Larva and Ladoumègue cried—the Finn from joy, the Frenchman from disappointment.

1932 Los Angeles C: 27, N: 15, D: 8.4. WR: 3:49.2 (Jules Ladoumègue)

1. Luigi Beccali	ITA	3:51.2	OR
2. John Cornes	GBR	3:52.6	
3. Philip Edwards	CAN	3:52.8	
4. Glenn Cunningham	USA	3:53.4	
5. Eric Ny	SWE	3:54.6	
6. Norwood Hallowell	USA	3:55.0	
7. John Lovelock	NZE	3:55.6	
8. Frank Crowley	USA	3:56.6	

Five months before the Los Angeles Games, world record holder Jules Ladoumègue was banned from competition by the French Athletics Federation after being charged with accepting payment for running in certain meets. The heated protests of French sports fans were to no avail. Still, the 1932 Olympic final was packed with splendid runners. The lead changed hands several times in the early going. Then, as the second lap came to a close, Glenn Cunningham, who was suffering a bad case of tonsilitis, burst ahead, followed by Phil Edwards. By the time the bell had rung to signal the final lap, Cunningham and Edwards had opened a 15-meter gap over the rest of the field. With 300 meters to go, John Cornes and 5-foot 6½-inch Luigi Beccali gave chase. In the backstretch Edwards passed Cunningham and took a five-yard lead. Beccali caught Cunningham at the head of the homestretch and then passed Edwards 100 yards from the finish. The young man from Milan won by six yards, breaking the tape by grabbing it in his hands and tearing it apart. At the medal ceremony Beccali gave the Fascist salute and became a national hero overnight. As a matter of fact, when he emerged from his cottage in the Olympic Village the next morning, he discovered that his Italian teammates had covered the walk from his bungalow with rugs from their own rooms and lined the path with wicker chairs adorned with flowers. Standing behind the chairs were his teammates, chanting, "Luigi, Luigi, Luigi." Beccali, choked with emotion, was speechless. He later emigrated to New York and went into the wine business.

1936 Berlin C: 44, N: 27, D: 8.6. WR: 3:48.8 (William Bonthron)

1. John Lovelock	NZE	3:47.8	WR
2. Glenn Cunningham	USA	3:48.4	
3. Luigi Beccali	ITA	3:49.2	
4. Archie San Romani	USA	3:50.0	
5. Philip Edwards	CAN	3:50.4	
6. John Cornes	GBR	3:51.4	
7. Miklós Szabó	HUN	3:53.0	
8. Robert Goix	FRA	3:53.8	

The 1936 1500-meter final promised to be one of the great races of all time and, unlike many athletic contests with great expectations, it lived up to its advance billing. Among the starters were six of the top seven finishers from the 1932 Olympics. The favorites were defending champion Luigi Beccali, one-mile world record holder Glenn Cunningham of Elkhart, Kansas, whose leg had been severely burned in a fire when he was eight years old, and Jack Lovelock of New Zealand, who had beaten Cunningham in "The Mile of the Century" at Princeton in 1935. Lovelock, a former Rhodes scholar at Oxford, was now a medical student who ran numerous tests on himself in order to determine the conditions necessary to achieve an optimum performance. He was particularly interested in learning how long he could sustain a final sprint, and this led to his development of a secret strategy to win at the Berlin Olympics.

When the great race finally began at 4:18 p.m., there was a good deal of jockeying for position. Cunningham took the lead at 400 meters, followed by Lovelock, who later dropped back to fourth place. Just before the bell, Eric Ny passed Cunningham. Then, 300 yards from the tape, Lovelock passed Cunningham and reached Ny's shoulder. Cunningham followed him. Then Lovelock paused and so did Cunningham, thinking the move had been a false alarm. But one second later Lovelock was off again, beginning the unusually long sprint that he had planned so carefully. Cunningham raced after him, but Lovelock was able to open up a lead of six yards. Cunningham tried to close the gap, but he could get no closer than four yards. Lovelock ran the final 400 meters in 56.8 seconds and the last 200 meters in 27.2, even though he slowed up in the last 20 yards, realizing that his victory was assured. Lovelock didn't believe in setting records, only in winning, but he broke the world record by a full second because that was what was required to defeat Cunningham.

In 1940 Jack Lovelock was thrown from a horse during a hunt and lay unconscious for an hour before he was discovered. He recovered, but suffered double vision and occasional dizziness for the rest of his life. He and his wife moved to New York, where Lovelock obtained a position as assistant director of physical medicine at the Hospital for Special Surgery. On December 28, 1949, eight days before his 40th birthday, Lovelock began having dizzy spells and telephoned his wife that he would be coming home early. He was standing on the southbound platform of the Church Street subway station in Brooklyn when he suddenly pitched forward onto the tracks. He was struck by an oncoming train and died instantly.

1948 London C: 37, N: 22, D: 8.6. WR: 3:43.0 (Günder Hägg, Lennart Strand)

1. Henry Eriksson	SWE	3:49.8
2. Lennart Strand	SWE	3:50.4
3. Willem Slijkhuis	HOL	3:50.4
4. Václav Čevona	CZE	3:51.2
5. Gösta Bergkvist	SWE	3:52.2
6. G. William Nankeville	GBR	3:52.6
7. Sándor Garay	HUN	3:52.8
8. Erik Jörgensen	DEN	3:52.8

The 1948 final was run on a rain-soaked track in the middle of a downpour. The two great Swedish runners Günder Hägg and Arne Andersson had been banned as professionals, but the Swedes still fielded the strongest team in Lennart Strand, Henry Eriksson, and Gösta Bergkvist. Marcel Hansenne of France led for 1000 meters, at which point the three Swedes, led by Eriksson, made their move. Coming out of the final turn, Eriksson, who had never beaten Strand, held a three-yard lead. Strand closed up to his shoulder and ran even for another 20 yards, but with 50 yards to go he realized that he couldn't pass his teammate. Looking behind him he saw Slijkhuis coming with a great rush on the inside. Determined to preserve second place, Strand veered to his left and bumped the Dutch runner off the track long enough to prevent him from passing. Eriksson was a fireman, Strand a linotype operator and pianist.

1952 Helsinki C: 52, N: 26, D: 7.26. WR: 3:43.0 (Günder Hägg, Lennart Strand, Werner Lueg)

1. Josef "Josy" Barthel	LUX	3:45.1	OR	(3:45.28)
2. Robert McMillen	USA	3:45.2		(3:45.39)
3. Werner Lueg	GER	3:45.4		(3:45.67)
4. Roger Bannister	GBR	3:46.0		(3:46.30)
5. Patrick El Mabrouk	FRA	3:46.0		(3:46.35)
6. Rolf Lamers	GER	3:46.8		(3:47.18)
7. Olle Åberg	SWE	3:47.0		(3:47.20)
8. Ingvar Ericsson	SWE	3:47.6		(3:47.70)

The 1952 1500 meters was up for grabs. If there were favorites they were probably Werner Lueg, who had tied the world record at the German championships on June 29, and Roger Bannister, whose greatest fame was yet to come. Bannister, a medical intern, had prepared himself very carefully for a competition that would include a heat and then a final two days later. Unfortunately, I.A.A.F. officials decided to add a semifinal round, which meant that the finalists would run three races in three days. This change of schedule greatly upset Bannister's plans. The semifinals were won by local favorite Denis Johansson in 3:49.8 and lightly regarded Josy Barthel, a small man from the small nation of Luxembourg, who finished in 3:50.4.

Audun Boysen of Norway was the first in front in the final, but he was soon passed by Rolf Lamers, who held the lead until the third lap, when he surrendered it to his teammate Werner Lueg. Coming into the backstretch, the action became frantic. Lueg fought off challenges from Olle Åberg, Patrick El Mabrouk, and Bannister. Lueg opened up a three-yard lead and held it around the final turn. However, almost unnoticed, two outsiders, Josy Barthel and Bob McMillen, had sprinted up from the very back of the field to within striking distance.

Fifty yards from the finish, Lueg began to tie up. With the crowd screaming wildly, first Barthel and then McMillen passed the German. Barthel could feel McMillen literally breathing down his back as the American inched closer with every stride until he was only one and a half feet behind. Let Josy Barthel tell the rest of the story: "Five meters to run, the victory is mine, and, just as I had always dreamed in secret, I raised my arms, I smiled and I crossed the finish line.

"Afterward, I didn't appreciate right away that I had won. For me, as for the public, it was a surprise. I sat down, without being excited, on a bench in the middle of the infield. Then, no longer able to contain my joy, I cried. My friend Audun Boysen asked me, '*Eh bien,* Josy, why are you crying? Are you ill?' It was only then that I truly understood. 'No,' I replied, 'I am crying because I won.' "

Six of the 12 finalists had run their best time ever, including Barthel, whose previous best had been 3:48.4,

Josy Barthel of Luxembourg wins the 1500 meters in 1952. "Just as I had always dreamed in secret," he later recalled. "I raised my arms, I smiled, and I crossed the finish line."

and McMillen, who had never bettered 3:49.3. On the victory platform, as he listened to the national anthem of Luxembourg being played for the first and only time in Olympic history, Josy Barthel cried again. Roger Bannister recalled, "He raised his hand to wipe away a tear. His great strength was overcome by the tide of joy. Then he turned the movement into a wave of gratitude to the crowd. . . . In the great joy of that single moment the agony of the previous week was quite forgotten. I had found new meaning in the Olympic words that the important thing was not the winning but the taking part—not the conquering but the fighting well."

1956 Melbourne C: 37, N: 22, D: 12.1. WR: 3:40.6 (István Rózsavölgyi)

1. Ron Delany	IRL	3:41.2	OR	(3:41.49)
2. Klaus Richtzenhain	GDR	3:42.0		(3:42.02)
3. John Landy	AUS	3:42.0		(3:42.03)
4. László Tábori	HUN	3:42.4		(3:42.55)
5. Brian Hewson	GBR	3:42.6		(3:42.69)
6. Stanislav Jungwirth	CZE	3:42.6		(3:42.80)
7. Neville Scott	NZE	3:42.8		(3:42.87)
8. Ian Boyd	GBR	3:43.0		(3:42.94)

May 6, 1954, stands as probably the greatest day in track and field history. Running in Oxford with the help of pace-setters Chris Brasher and Chris Chataway, Roger Bannister attempted to break the barrier of barriers—the four-minute mile. In his autobiography, appropriately entitled *The Four-Minute Mile*, Bannister recalled the final lap of that race: "I felt that the moment of a lifetime had come. . . . The world seemed to stand still, or did not exist. The only reality was the next two hundred yards of track under my feet. . . .

"I felt at that moment that it was my chance to do one thing supremely well. I drove on, impelled by a combination of fear and pride. The air I breathed filled me with the spirit of the track where I had run my first race. The noise in my ears was that of the faithful Oxford crowd. Their hope and encouragement gave me greater strength. I had now turned the last bend and there were only fifty yards more. . . .

"Those last few seconds seemed never-ending. The faint line of the finishing tape stood ahead as a haven of peace, after the struggle. The arms of the world were waiting to receive me if only I reached the tape without slackening my speed. If I faltered, there would be no arms to hold me and the world would be a cold, forbidding place, because I had been so close. I leapt at the tape like a man taking his last spring to save himself from the chasm that threatens to engulf him."

The track announcer that day was none other than Norris McWhirter, who later became world famous as the compiler, along with his brother Ross, of *The Guinness Book of World Records*. McWhirter milked the dramatic moment for all it was worth. "Ladies and gentlemen," he began, "here is the result of event number nine, the one mile. First, number forty-one, R. G. Bannister of the Amateur Athletic Association and formerly of Exeter and Merton Colleges, with a time which is a new meeting and track record and which, subject to ratification, will be a new English Native, British National, British All-Comers', European, British Empire and World's record. The time is THREE . . ." The rest of the announcement was lost in the roar of the crowd. In fact, Bannister's time was 3:59.4.

In the two and a half years between that day in Oxford and the Melbourne Olympics, Bannister had retired from competition, but nine other runners had broken the four-minute barrier. All ten were present in Melbourne for the running of the 1500 meters—six on the track (John Landy, Brian Hewson, László Tábori, Ron Delany, Gunnar Nielsen, and István Rózsavölgyi) and four in the stands (Bannister, Jim Bailey, Chris Chataway, and

Ron Delany leads the great mass finish of the 1956 1500 meters.

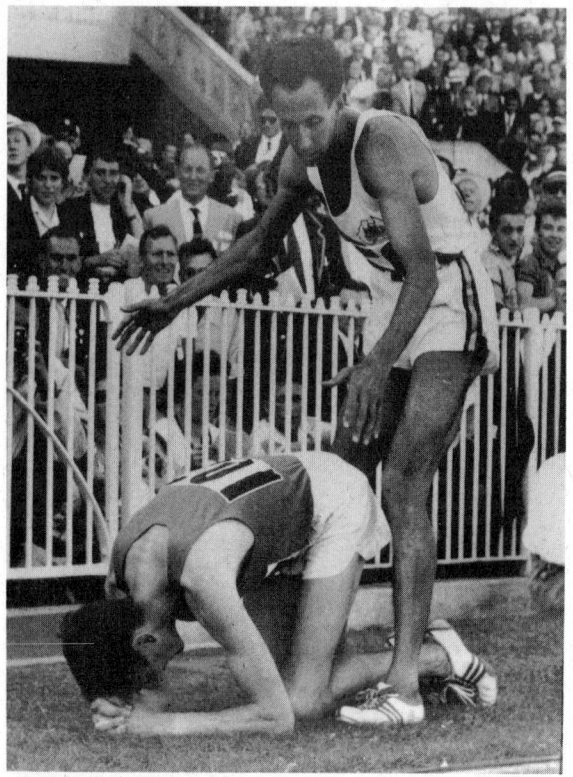

After the race, John Landy goes to the aid of Delany, whom he assumes to be doubled over in pain. Instead he discovers that Delany is deep in prayer.

Derek Ibbotson). Bannister presented to each of his successors a black silk tie with a monogram of a silver "4" and two gold "M"s within a gold laurel wreath.

The very first heat saw the elimination of several great runners, including Josy Barthel, István Rózsavölgyi, who had broken training during the Hungarian uprising against the U.S.S.R., Michel Jazy, who was to win a silver medal four years later in Rome, and an obscure Ethiopian named Mamo Wolde, who would gain fame *12* years later when he won the 1968 Olympic marathon.

The final turned out to be just as great a contest as had been expected. Before the race, the great sportsman John Landy, who once stopped in the middle of a race to help a fallen runner by the name of Ron Clarke, gave a pep talk to Ron Delany, the youngest of the four-minute milers, and told him, "I think you can win this one, Ron." The twelve finalists were so well matched that when they began the final lap, less than eight yards separated the leader from the man in last place. The official in charge of signaling the beginning of the final lap was so excited that he forgot to ring the bell. Hewson and Merv Lincoln of Australia were in the lead, but Lincoln, feeling a pain in his leg, began to fall back quickly. Mean-

while, Ron Delany was boxed in at tenth place. His coach at Villanova University, Jumbo Elliott, had always told him that if he was ever in a box just to relax. So Delany relaxed, even though there were only 300 yards left in the race.

Just then the runner in front of Delany, Gunnar Nielsen, realizing that he himself couldn't win the race, turned around and motioned Delany to pass him on the inside. Gradually Delany moved up; then, 120 meters from the finish, he burst out with all he had. The power of his sprint demoralized the other runners, and he was home free. He ran the last lap in 53.8, the last 200 meters in 25.6, and the final 100 meters in 12.9. He flew past the tiring Hewson and won by almost six yards, breasting the tape with his arms spread wide and a huge grin on his face. After crossing the finish, Delany fell to his knees. John Landy, thinking Delany was ill or injured, rushed up to help him, only to discover that the new Olympic champion was actually deep in prayer.

1960 Rome C:39, N: 25, D: 9.6. WR: 3:36.0 (Herbert Elliot)

1. Herbert Elliott	AUS	3:35.6	WR
2. Michel Jazy	FRA	3:38.4	
3. István Rózsavölgyi	HUN	3:39.2	
4. Dan Waern	SWE	3:40.0	
5. Zoltan Vamos	ROM	3:40.8	
6. Dyrol Burleson	USA	3:40.9	
7. Michel Bernard	FRA	3:41.5	
8. James Grelle	USA	3:45.0	

World record holder Herb Elliott of Perth was the clear favorite in 1960. After 950 meters he passed Michel Bernard and took off like a "scared bunny." To his opponents and to the 90,000 people in the stadium, Elliott appeared to be a sure winner, but Elliott himself refused to look behind him. Unaware that he had opened up an insurmountable 15-meter lead, he was sure that someone was close on his heels. When he reached the backstretch he saw his coach, Percy Cerutty, standing by the side of the track waving a white towel, which meant that a world record was achievable and that Elliott should give it all he had. Actually, the 66-year-old Cerutty had raced out of the stands and dashed across the protective moat that surrounded the track in order to signal his pupil. He was quickly grabbed by the police and hauled away, but his effort had been worth it. Elliott, still refusing to turn around and still thinking he might lose the gold medal, strained to the finish line and won by the amazing margin of 20 yards. His time of 3:35.6 was a new world record. Elliott, whose diet consisted mostly of raw, natural foods, celebrated by going out drinking. His most difficult concern for the remainder of the Olympics was protecting his kangaroo-hide track shoes, which were almost stolen on three separate occasions. Between 1954 and 1960, Herb Elliott won 44 consecutive races at 1500 meters or one mile before retiring from competition at the age of 22. Many years later Elliott paid tribute to Cerutty. "He challenged my totality. I came to realize that spirit, as much as or more than physical conditioning, had to be stored up before a race. I would avoid running on tracks because tracks were spiritually depleting. I never studied my opponents—they were an irrelevancy to me. Poetry, music, forests, ocean, solitude—they were what developed enormous spiritual strength." Of his early retirement he said, "Once I had satisfied myself . . . that my spirit *could* dominate my body, there was no reason to continue."

1964 Tokyo C: 43, N: 34, D: 10.21. WR: 3:35.6 (Herbert Elliott)

1. Peter Snell	NZE	3:38.1
2. Josef Odložil	CZE	3:39.6
3. John Davies	NZE	3:39.6
4. Alan Simpson	GBR	3:39.7
5. Dyrol Burleson	USA	3:40.0
6. Witold Baran	POL	3:40.3
7. Michel Bernard	FRA	3:41.2
8. John Whetton	GBR	3:42.4

Before the Tokyo Olympics, Peter Snell had never run a race at 1500 meters, although he had competed in many one-mile contests. Running his sixth race in eight days, Snell was boxed in at the bell when John Whetton stepped aside and let him through. Snell ran away from the field in the backstretch and won by 12 yards, to gain his third Olympic gold medal.

1968 Mexico City C:54, N: 37, D: 10.20. WR: 3:33.1 (James Ryun)

1. H. Kipchoge Keino	KEN	3:34.9	OR	(3:34.91)
2. James Ryun	USA	3:37.8		(3:37.89)
3. Bodo Tümmler	GER	3:39.0		(3:39.08)
4. Harald Norpoth	GER	3:42.5		(3:42.57)
5. John Whetton	GBR	3:43.8		(3:43.90)
6. Jacques Boxberger	FRA	3:46.6		(3:46.65)
7. Henryk Szordykowski	POL	3:46.6		(3:46.69)
8. Josef Odložil	CZE	3:48.6		(3:48.69)

Jim Ryun of Wichita, Kansas, went to the 1968 Olympics as the world record holder at 880 yards, 1500 meters, and the mile. He had not been beaten at 1500 or the mile in over three years. Yet his status as favorite was threatened by an attack of mononucleosis in June and by the fact that the Olympics were being held in the high altitude of Mexico City. For this reason, 28-year-old Kip Keino, an uncoached Nandi tribesman who had never defeated Ryun, was considered a serious contender. However Keino was having problems of his own. Recently he had been suffering violent stomach pains, which later turned out to be the result of a severe gall bladder infection. Ignoring the advice of doctors, Keino went ahead and entered not only the 1500, but also the 5000 and the 10,000. The 10,000 came first and Keino was running with the leaders with only two laps to go,

Mexico City, 1968: Kip Keino of Kenya scores the most decisive 1500 meters victory in Olympic history.

when he suddenly doubled up in pain and fell onto the infield. When the stretcher-bearers came to get him, he jumped back onto the track and, even though he had been disqualified, he finished the race. Four days later he took second place in the 5000 meters.

As if he hadn't run enough already, the day of the 1500 meters final he got caught in a traffic jam and jogged the last mile to the stadium. Keino was well aware that Jim Ryun possessed a devastating finishing kick, so he decided to try a dangerous gamble, hoping to neutralize Ryun's sprint by building up a huge lead. After fellow Kenyan Ben Jipcho set a torrid pace of 56.0 for the first 400 meters, Keino took over and pulled away from the pack, passing the 800-meter mark in a seemingly suicidal 1:55.3. Everyone waited for Keino to run out of steam but, remarkably, he never did. Ryun's famous kick was impressive, but he was unable to close within 12 yards of Keino and finally eased up in pain, as the Kenyan went on to win by 20 meters, the largest margin of victory in Olympic 1500 meters history. Keino improved his personal best by 1.8 seconds and lowered his own high-altitude world record by a phenomenal five seconds. That same day, back in Kenya, Kip Keino's wife gave birth to their third daughter, who was named Milka Olympia Chelagat in honor of her father's achievement. Keino and his wife, Phyllis, eventually established a children's home and raised dozens of orphaned and abandoned children.

1972 Munich C: 66, N: 46, D: 9.10. WR: 3:33.1 (James Ryun)

1. Pekka Vasala	FIN	3:36.3	(3:36.33)
2. H. Kipchoge Keino	KEN	3:36.8	(3:36.81)
3. Rodney Dixon	NZE	3:37.5	(3:37.46)
4. Michael Boit	KEN	3:38.4	(3:38.41)
5. Brendan Foster	GBR	3:39.0	(3:39.02)
6. Herman Mignon	BEL	3:39.1	(3:39.05)
7. Paul-Heinz Wellmann	GER	3:40.1	(3:40.08)
8. Vladimir Pantelei	SOV/UKR	3:40.2	(3:40.24)

Track aficionados awaited another showdown between defending champion Kip Keino and Jim Ryun, who had retired, returned to competition, had his ups and downs, and was now in top form once again. What no one expected was that their last confrontation as amateurs would come not in the Olympic final, but in the opening round. Entrants in the Olympics are seeded according to their previous times, so that leading contenders are separated in the opening heats. U.S. officials had submitted Ryun's superb time of 3:52.8 for the mile. However, somewhere along the line, this time was interpreted as being for 1500 meters, so the computer in charge of seeding treated Ryun as just another mediocre runner. Consequently, Ryun was thrown into the same first-round heat as top-seeded Kip Keino.

The fateful fourth heat, won easily by Keino, was to prove the end of Jim Ryun's amateur career. Caught in a box 550 meters from the finish, Ryun tried to squeeze his way between runners rather than pass on the outside. As

early leader Mohamed Younis of Pakistan faded on the inside lane, Vitus Ashaba of Uganda stepped to the outside to avoid him, and moved right into the space that Ryun was trying to fill. Ryun tripped on Ashaba's heel and fell back on Billy Fordjour of Ghana, sending both of them crashing to the ground. Ryun landed on the curb and Fordjour landed on Ryun, who came away with a bruised hip, a scraped knee, a sprained left ankle, and a contusion of his Adam's apple. Stunned, Ryun lay on the track for eight seconds before he got up and began chasing after the field. The sympathetic German crowd rooted him on, but he had lost at least 75 meters and it proved impossible for him to catch up. Ryun was in shock. "All I know is everything was going well," he said, "and I felt good, and the next thing I knew I was trying to figure out what happened."

Two days later, in the final, Kip Keino faced the challenge of Pekka Vasala, by no means an outsider, even though he was known in Finland as "Mr. Unpredictable." Vasala had competed in the Mexico City Games, but, struck down by "Montezuma's Revenge," he had finished last in his heat. Nevertheless, he had been quite moved by the opening ceremonies and vowed to himself that "someday, somewhere, I would accomplish something great."

In Munich, Keino made his move after 600 meters and Vasala followed close behind, dogging the former goatherder all the way until the homestretch, when he moved ahead to win by about three meters. Vasala had run the last 800 meters in the amazing time of 1:49.0. The surprise bronze medalist was Rod Dixon of New Zealand, who began sobbing when he realized that his dream of an Olympic medal had come true. Still weeping, he was ushered backstage for the urine test. After producing a meager sample, Dixon sheepishly asked the German official if it was enough. "For the gold medal, no," was the reply, "but for the bronze medal, it will do."

Dixon was not the only one to be moved to tears. Pekka Vasala recalled, "When I walked into the dressing room after the race . . . I realized in a second I had won. Somehow I had not fully understood it on the track. All became misty and I was crying uncontrollably. I had completely lost control of myself. I was still confused on the victory stand. It was not until I put the gold medal into my pocket and grabbed it in my fingers that I finally woke up."

1976 Montreal C: 42, N: 28, D: 7.31. WR: 3:32.2 (Filbert Bayi)

1. John Walker	NZE	3:39.17
2. Ivo van Damme	BEL	3:39.27
3. Paul-Heinz Wellmann	GER	3:39.33
4. Eamonn Coghlan	IRL	3:39.51
5. Frank Clement	GBR	3:39.65
6. Richard Wohlhuter	USA	3:40.64
7. David Moorcroft	GBR	3:40.94
8. Graham Crouch	AUS	3:41.80

In 1976, black African nations boycotted the Olympics because a rugby team from New Zealand had played a team from South Africa. Ironically, this prevented Tanzanian world record holder Filbert Bayi from competing, and handed over an almost sure gold medal to New Zealand, which was represented by John Walker, who held the world record for the mile. It was Walker who had pushed Bayi to his 1500 meters record at the 1974 Commonwealth Games, and the two friends had been looking forward to their Olympics showdown ever since. Without Bayi and Kenyan Mike Boit to set the pace, the Olympic final was a slow, almost dull race that came down to the final sprint. Walker passed Eamonn Coghlan in the backstretch and won by a meter. His winning time was the slowest in 20 years. When asked why he hadn't tried for a record even with Bayi missing, Walker replied, "Every record set in Montreal will eventually be broken and forgotten. The gold medal is the thing they can never take away from you." On February 17, 1985, running on his home track at Mount Smart Stadium in Auckland, John Walker became the first person to run 100 sub-four-minute miles, beating out Steve Scott of the United States by barely three months. Walker had first broken the four-minute barrier 11½ years earlier. On February 20, 1994, Eamonn Coghlan set a record of his own when, at age 41, he became the first person over the age of 40 to break the four-minute mile.

1980 Moscow C: 40, N: 29, D: 8.1. WR: 3:32.1 (Sebastian Coe, Stephen Ovett)

1.	Sebastian Coe	GBR	3:38.40
2.	Jürgen Straub	GDR	3:38.80
3.	Stephen Ovett	GBR	3:38.99
4.	Andreas Busse	GDR	3:40.17
5.	Vittorio Fontanella	ITA	3:40.37
6.	Josef Plachý	CZE	3:40.66
7.	José Marajo	FRA	3:41.48
8.	Stephen Cram	GBR	3:41.98

It certainly seemed to most observers that Steve Ovett entered the 1500 meters final with a tremendous advantage. Not only had he defeated Sebastian Coe at Coe's best distance, the 800, but Ovett had won 42 consecutive races at 1500 meters and one mile, going back to May 1977. In the semifinals Ovett had been so relaxed and in control that he actually gave a victory wave to the crowd before he had even taken the lead. Coe, on the other hand, had struggled through his first-round heat and had been hounded and mercilessly criticized by the British

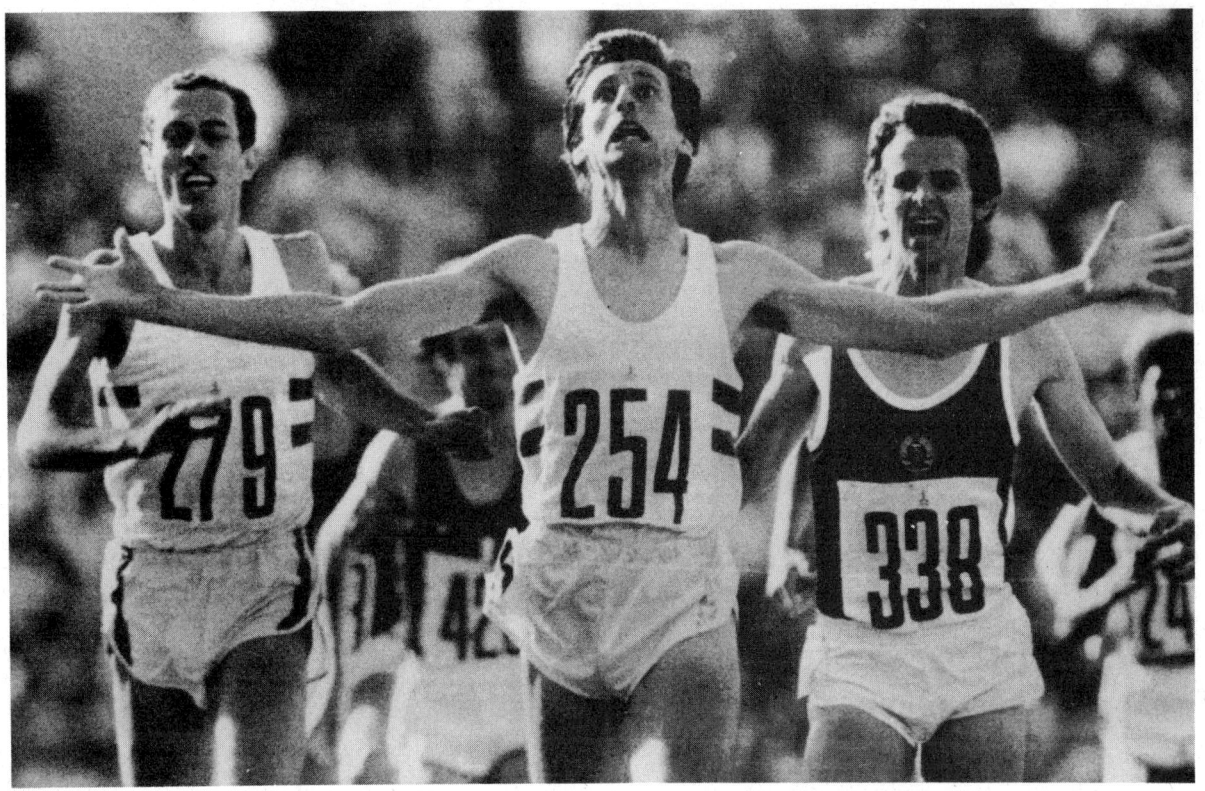

Sebastian Coe winning the 1500 meters in 1980 after his disappointing second-place finish in the 800.

press during the six days since the 800 meters final. As it turned out, however, Ovett's gold medal had taken away his competitive edge ever so slightly, while Coe had conquered his disappointment and depression, and couldn't wait to get out on the track to prove that he was a winner and not just a record-setter.

The withdrawal of Filbert Bayi, who had decided to concentrate on the 3000 meters steeplechase, left the race without a pace-setter, but before the first lap had ended it became clear that this was not going to be just a two-man race. Jürgen Straub took the lead at 400 meters, followed by Coe, who was determined to stay near the front and avoid the tactical errors he had committed in the 800. With 780 meters to go, Straub stepped up the pace, with Coe and Ovett close behind. It was just what Coe had hoped for: a long, open run to the finish.

With 200 meters to go, Straub was four meters ahead of Coe and six meters ahead of Ovett. Coming into the final curve, Coe unleashed his finishing kick, unaware that Ovett had chosen the exact same moment to make *his* move. Straub was not about to give in, but by the time they had hit the homestretch, Coe had taken the lead. A quick glance to each side to check the position of his opponents, and then, 80 meters from the finish line, Coe increased his speed again, crossing the finish line with a look of ecstatic relief that spoke far more than a thousand words. Straub, four meters back, held off Ovett for second place. Coe dropped to his knees and touched his forehead to the ground, seemingly unaware of the hearty congratulations being offered by Straub and Ovett. Coe had run the last lap in 52.2 seconds and the final 100 meters in 12.1.

Afterward, Coe and Ovett, who had been constantly portrayed by the press as bitter rivals, discussed the relief that they both felt and agreed to have a couple drinks together. On the victory stand, Coe looked up to the sky. When asked why he had done this, Coe replied, "Perhaps somebody, somewhere, loves me after all."

1984 Los Angeles C: 59, N: 40, D: 8.11. WR: 3:30.77 (Stephen Ovett)

1. Sebastian Coe	GBR	3:32.53	OR
2. Stephen Cram	GBR	3:33.40	
3. José Manuel Abascal Gómez	SPA	3:34.30	
4. Joseph Chesire	KEN	3:34.52	
5. Jim Spivey	USA	3:36.07	
6. Peter Wirz	SWI	3:36.97	
7. Andres Vera	SPA	3:37.02	
8. Omar Khalifa	SUD	3:37.11	

Following his Olympic victory in 1980, Sebastian Coe had been forced to call it quits for the rest of the season because of a back injury. He came back with a vengeance in 1981 and set four world records—in the 800, the 1000, and twice in the mile. However his 1982 season was a disappointing one, due apparently to an attack of glandular fever. Early in 1983 he seemed to have recovered, but as the season progressed, he found himself losing race after race. Finally, after withdrawing from the world championships, he checked into a hospital, where he underwent surgery for removal of a lymph node. It was discovered that Coe had been suffering from toxoplasmosis, a rare, sometimes fatal, protozoan infection. It looked like his championship days were over. As noted track writer Bob Hersh put it in an early Olympic preview article for *The Runner* magazine: "Based on 1983, I'd write Coe off completely."

It was to prove a premature obituary. After months of treatments and much time spent lying in hospital beds, Coe was released to resume training in December 1983. In the meantime his throne had been usurped by Steve Cram who had gone undefeated at 1500 meters in 1983 and had beaten Steve Scott, Saïd Aouita, and Steve Ovett in a tactical race at the world championships. Coe's comeback was treated with scorn by much of the British press, particularly after he was selected for the 1500 meters Olympic event even though he lost to Peter Elliott at the British Amateur Athletic Association championships in June in what had been billed as a showdown for the final spot on the team.

The Olympic 1500 developed into a battle of survivors. Saïd Aouita withdrew to concentrate on the less competitive 5000 meters. Former world record holder Sydney Maree withdrew due to a hamstring tear that failed to heal. World championship finalist Dragon Zdravković was sent home by Yugoslav officials for refusing to wear Adidas shoes. World record holder Steve Ovett had collapsed after the 800-meter final and spent two nights in the hospital. Yet there he was the next day on the starting line of heat 3 of the opening round. Ovett won the heat, but right behind him yet another contender fell by the wayside. Ten meters from the finish line, world championship finalist Pierre Delèze of Switzerland tripped on Ovett's heel and sprawled on the ground just short of his goal. The fourth heat was won by 800-meter gold medalist Joaquim Cruz, but the next day he pulled out of the semifinals because of a head cold.

Still, when the twelve finalists gathered barely 24 hours after the semifinals, the four leading favorites, Cram, Scott, Ovett, and Coe, were right there on the starting line. Ovett did seem doubtful, having required medical attention following the semifinals, and, although Coe had looked strong in winning the 800 silver, he, like Ovett, was about to run his seventh race in nine days.

Coe broke to the front, but quickly relinquished the lead to Omar Khalifa. Less than 600 meters from the start came the big surprise. For many years 1500-meter races in major championships had been run as kickers' races: three slow laps, followed by a final sprint. Steve Scott had decided to turn the 1984 Olympic final into "a true miler's race." In the backstretch of the second lap, he tore into the lead and forced the pace, testing the strength of the other runners. He passed the 800-meter mark in 1:56.81, followed more closely than he had hoped by Coe, Abascal, Khalifa, Cram, and Ovett.

The next runner to make a move was José Abascal. Knowing that he too would lose a kicker's finish, Abascal took the lead with about a lap and a quarter to go. Coe and Cram chased after him while Scott began to fade to an eventual tenth-place finish. Three hundred and fifty yards from the finish, Steve Ovett, running in fourth place, was overcome by the same chest pains he had experienced four days earlier. He stepped off the track and was taken away on a stretcher. Abascal sprinted down the backstretch, but he couldn't shake Coe and Cram. Coming into the final curve, Cram made his move, pulling up to Coe's shoulder. Coe glanced up quickly to see who was there, then began his own kick. They both sped by Abascal, racing hard around the turn. Coe entered the final straight with a four-foot lead which he extended to a six-meter winning margin.

Coe crossed the finish line with a smile on his face. Then he turned in the direction of the British press, made a defiant gesture, and shouted, "Who says I'm finished?!" He had run the final 200 meters in 26.1 seconds and the last 100 meters in 13.04. At the age of 27, Sebastian Coe had become the first male repeat winner of the Olympic 1500 meters (excepting James Lightbody's victory in the 1906 Intercalated Games).

1988 Seoul C: 59, N: 46, D: 10.1. WR: 3:29.46 (Saïd Aouita)

1. Peter Rono	KEN	3:35.96
2. Peter Elliott	GBR	3:36.15
3. Jens-Peter Herold	GDR	3:36.21
4. Stephen Cram	GBR	3:36.24
5. Steve Scott	USA	3:36.99
6. Han Kulker	HOL	3:37.08
7. S. Kipkoech Cheruiyot	KEN	3:37.94
8. Marcus O'Sullivan	IRL	3:38.39

On the eve of the Olympics, the favorites were world record holder Saïd Aouita; Steve Cram, who had recorded the fastest time of the year, 3:30.95, on August 19; and world champion Abdi Bile of Somalia. But Bile was forced to withdraw after sustaining a tibial stress fracture, and Aouita, also the victim of a leg injury, dropped out before the semifinals. Joaquim Cruz, the 800-meter silver medalist, also failed to appear for his semifinal heat. The finalists set out at a sluggish pace. With two laps to go, 5-foot 5¾-inch, 117-pound Peter Rono decided he had had enough. "The other guys were holding me up," he would later explain. He rushed into the lead. "I thought some of the fellows behind would follow me, but they didn't."

Most likely, the other fellows didn't take Rono seriously. After all, the undersized economics student at Mount St. Mary's College in Emmitsburg, Maryland, had no major victories to his credit. Besides, they were too busy watching Steve Cram. With half a lap to go, Rono led by two meters over Elliott, with Cram and Herold close behind. Elliott tried desperately to close the gap but could make little headway. Rono, who looked back 13 times in the final 200 meters, ran the last

800 meters in 1 minute 50 seconds. Afterward, Rono seemed as surprised as anyone by the result. "It was tougher to win the Kenyan trials," he said. At 21 years of age, he was the youngest 1500-meter medalist in Olympic history.

1992 Barcelona C: 50, N: 39, D: 8.8. WR: 3:29.46 (Saïd Aouita)

1. Fermín Cacho Ruiz	SPA	3:40.12
2. Rachid El Basir	MOR	3:40.62
3. Mohamed Ahmed Sulaiman	QAT	3:40.69
4. Joseph Chesire	KEN	3:41.12
5. Jonah Birir	KEN	3:41.27
6. Jens-Peter Herold	GER	3:41.53
7. Noureddine Morceli	ALG	3:41.70
8. Jim Spivey	USA	3:41.74

Few runners have dominated an event as thoroughly as Noureddine Morceli did the 1500 meters between 1990 and 1995. In 1991 he was undefeated at 1500 meters and one mile, crowning the season by winning the world championship by 15 meters. It seemed that nothing could stop him from winning Olympic gold except an injury. But early in 1992 Morceli did in fact injure his hip, reducing him to sudden, albeit temporary, vulnerability. He lost over six weeks' training, and on June 9 his 21-race winning streak was broken. On July 4, he lost again.

Nonetheless, Morceli did win the first semifinal in Barcelona. The second semi was won by Mohamed Sulaiman from the small Persian Gulf emirate of Qatar in 3:34.77—the fastest preliminary time in Olympic history. The most notable development was the complete shutout of British runners. The 1992 final would be only the second 1500-meter final since 1904 without a runner from Great Britain. (The first was in 1960.)

The final was run at a shockingly slow pace. Led by 34-year-old Joseph Chesire, the field completed the first 800 meters in 2:06.83, over one and three-quarters seconds slower than the women in their 1500-meter final. In the final backstretch Morceli was trapped in the pack, his every move marked by David Kibet of Kenya at his shoulder. When the real running started, he was unable to respond. Meanwhile local favorite Fermín Cacho of Agreda, Soria, had positioned himself behind Chesire, but found himself boxed in by Jens-Peter Herold on his right. Cacho's race plan was to begin his sprint with 150 meters to go, but about 50 meters before that suddenly, inexplicably, as they approached the final turn, Chesire drifted wide. Cacho reacted immediately, passed Chesire on the inside and, with a delirious crowd screaming his name, burst into a ten-meter lead. El Basir, moving from eighth to second in the final straightaway, closed the gap to four meters while Cacho, incredulous at the wonderful turn of events, looked back eight times in seeming disbelief before crossing the finish line. Although he ran the last lap in about 50.4 seconds, Cacho's winning time was the slowest since 1956. Cacho was the first Spanish runner to win a gold medal.

As for Morceli, he was so sickened by what had

happened that he "could not eat or sleep for a week." However, he recovered his form immediately. Four weeks later he ran 3:28.86 to break Saïd Aouita's seven-year-old world record. A year later he set a world record for the mile and he defended his world championship in both 1993 and 1995.

5000 METERS

A race of 12½ laps, the 5000 meters is 3 miles 188 yards 2 inches. Fifteen runners take part in the final.

1896–1908 not held

1912 Stockholm C: 31, N: 11, D: 7.10. WR: 15:01.2 (Arthur Robinson)
1. Johan "Hannes" Kolehmainen FIN 14:36.6 WR
2. Jean Bouin FRA 14:36.7
3. George Hutson GBR 15:07.6
4. George Bonhag USA 15:09.8
5. Tel Berna USA 15:10.0
6. Mauritz Karlsson SWE 15:18.6
7. Henry Scott USA —
8. Alex Decoteau CAN —

Hannes Kolehmainen, a vegetarian bricklayer from a running family, had already won the 10,000 meters two days earlier, and was taking part in his fourth long-distance race in four days. He and Jean Bouin pulled away from the other eight finalists after a couple of laps and ran the rest of the race with Bouin in front and Kolehmainen right behind him. Every time Kolehmainen tried to pass, Bouin would resist his challenge. On the final curve of the final lap, Kolehmainen tried again. Bouin swung wide, forcing the Finn back in line. When they reached the homestretch, Kolehmainen tried once more, finally reaching Bouin's shoulder 20 meters from the tape. Bouin veered into Kolehmainen, but his legs began to

buckle, and "Hannes the Mighty," as he became known, was able to win by a yard. Silver medalist Bouin and bronze medalist George Hutson were both killed in action in September 1914. Kolehmainen, on the other hand, moved to the United States and reappeared in Antwerp to win the 1920 marathon.

1920 Antwerp C: 37, N: 15, D: 8.17. WR: 14:36.6 (Johan "Hannes" Kolehmainen)
1. Joseph Guillemot FRA 14:55.6
2. Paavo Nurmi FIN 15:00.0
3. Eric Backman SWE 15:13.0
4. Teodor Koskenniemi FIN 15:17.0
5. Charles Blewitt GBR 15:19.0
6. William Seagrove GBR 15:21.0
7. Carlo Speroni ITA —
8. Alfred Nichols GBR —

This race, the first Olympic appearance by Paavo Nurmi, proved to be sweet, though temporary, revenge by the French for Kolehmainen's defeat of Bouin eight years earlier. Nurmi took the lead during the third lap and the 5-foot 3-inch Guillemot, whose heart was on the right side of his chest and who smoked a pack of cigarettes a day, followed him closely until the final backstretch. Then, 200 meters from the finish, Guillemot sprinted away to win by 30 yards.

1924 Paris C: 39, N: 22, D: 7.10. WR: 14:28.2 (Paavo Nurmi)
1. Paavo Nurmi FIN 14:31.2 OR
2. Vilho "Ville" Ritola FIN 14:31.4
3. Edvin Wide SWE 15:01.8
4. John Romig USA 15:12.4
5. Eino Seppälä FIN 15:18.4
6. Charles Clibbon GBR 15:29.0
7. Lucien Dolques FRA 15:33.0
8. Axel Eriksson SWE 15:38.0

Hannes Kolehmainen (left) passes Jean Bouin just before the finish of the 1912 5000 meters.

Paavo Nurmi checks his watch during the running of the 1924 5000 meters. He is followed by fellow Finn Ville Ritola.

A rare photo of Paavo Nurmi smiling. Between 1920 and 1928 he won nine gold medals and three silver.

Paavo Nurmi had hoped to defend his 10,000 meters championship in Paris and was very resentful when Ville Ritola returned from four years in the United States to break Nurmi's world record and bump him from the Finnish 10,000 meters entry. On July 6, Ritola had proved his worth by winning the 10,000 in world record time. Nurmi got his chance to face Ritola four days later in the 5000, a race that began less than an hour after Nurmi had won the 1500 meters. Taking advantage of Paavo's lack of rest, his opponents set a torrid pace, passing the 1000-meter mark in 2:46.4, the same pace as the 1972 Olympic final 48 years later. Unruffled, Nurmi stayed close and then took the lead at the halfway mark, followed by Ritola. For the last eight laps, Nurmi, refusing to look behind him, stayed two yards ahead of his rival. With 500 meters to go he checked his watch for the last time, threw it to the grass, and picked up the pace. Twenty yards from the tape Ritola tried to pass, but Nurmi increased his speed and won—by two yards.

1928 Amsterdam C: 36, N: 17, D: 8.3. WR: 14:28.2 (Paavo Nurmi)

1. Vilho "Ville" Ritola	FIN	14:38.0
2. Paavo Nurmi	FIN	14:40.0
3. Edvin Wide	SWE	14:41.2
4. Leo Lermond	USA	14:50.0
5. Ragnar Magnusson	SWE	14:59.6
6. Armas Kinnunen	FIN	15:02.0
7. Stepans Petkevics	LAT	—
8. Herbert "Johnny" Johnston	GBR	—

By 1928 it was a familiar sight to see Nurmi and Ritola pull away from the field, with only Edvin Wide able to

keep close. This time Ritola drew clear of Nurmi in the final curve and won by over 12 yards. Wide picked up his fourth bronze medal to go with his one silver. Ritola finished his Olympic career with five gold medals and three silver medals.

1932 Los Angeles C: 19, N: 12, D: 8.5. WR: 14:17.0 (Lauri Lehtinen)

1. Lauri Lehtinen	FIN	14:30.0	OR
2. Ralph Hill	USA	14:30.0	
3. Lauri Virtanen	FIN	14:44.0	
4. John Savidan	NZE	14:49.6	
5. Jean-Gunnar Lindgren	SWE	14:54.8	
6. Max Syring	GER	14:59.0	
7. James Burns	GBR	15:04.0	
8. Daniel Dean	USA	15:08.5	

This race produced the ugliest incident of the 1932 Olympics. Running in last place for the first mile, Ralph Hill of Oregon gradually moved his way up to third place behind the Finnish favorites, Lehtinen and Virtanen. Then, with the surprised American crowd wild with excitement, Hill passed Virtanen, who faded back. Over the last two laps Lehtinen tried desperately to shake the pesky Hill, but couldn't. Fifty yards from the finish, Hill moved to pass Lehtinen on the outside, but the world record holder swerved out to the third lane and blocked his path. Hill broke stride, dropped back, and attempted to pass on the inside. Lehtinen swerved back into lane one, again impeding Hill's progress. Forced to break stride again, Hill made one more move, but Lehtinen was able to beat him to the tape by about three inches. After a moment of stunned silence, the audience broke into a loud chorus of boos, which didn't end until announcer Bill Henry got on the public address system and said, "Please remember, folks, that these people are our guests." Although films of the race clearly showed that Lehtinen had interfered

Lauri Lehtinen interfered with Ralph Hill during the home stretch of the 1932 5000-meter run. However, Hill declined to file a protest.

with Hill, U.S. officials declined to lodge a protest. At the victory ceremony, a chagrined Lehtinen attempted to lift Hill onto the first-place platform, but Hill refused. He did allow Lehtinen to pin an enameled Finnish flag to his sweater as the crowd applauded in approval.

1936 Berlin C: 41, N: 23, D: 8.7. WR: 14:17.0 (Lauri Lehtinen)

1. Gunnar Höckert	FIN	14:22.2	OR
2. Lauri Lehtinen	FIN	14:25.8	
3. Henry Jonsson	SWE	14:29.0	
4. Kohei Murakoso	JPN	14:30.0	
5. Józef Noji	POL	14:33.4	
6. Ilmari Salminen	FIN	14:39.8	
7. Umberto Cerati	ITA	14:44.4	
8. Louis Zamperini	USA	14:46.8	

The 10,000 meters champion, Ilmari Salminen, lost his chance for a second medal when he tripped on Lehtinen with two laps to go and fell. At the same moment, Höckert made his move into the lead. Ahead by two yards at the bell, he sprinted away and won by 20 yards.

1948 London C: 33, N: 20, D: 8.2. WR: 13:58.2 (Günder Hägg)

1. Gaston Reiff	BEL	14:17.6	OR
2. Emil Zátopek	CZE	14:17.8	
3. Willem Slijkhuis	HOL	14:26.8	
4. Erik Ahldén	SWE	14:28.6	
5. Bertil Albertsson	SWE	14:39.0	
6. Curtis Stone	USA	14:39.4	
7. Vaino Koskela	FIN	14:41.0	
8. Vaino Makela	FIN	14:43.0	

Zátopek was perhaps a bit too tired from winning the 10,000 meters three days earlier, particularly after he had unnecessarily sprinted at the end of his 5000 heat. Trailing Reiff by 50 meters at the bell in the final, Zátopek thrilled the crowd by sprinting around the rain-soaked track and pulling closer and closer. Reiff thought that the applause he heard was for him, until someone on the infield called his attention to Zátopek's unexpected spurt. Reiff was able to pick up his own speed just enough to reach the finish one and a half meters ahead of the charging Czech. Reiff was the first Belgian to win a track and field gold medal.

1952 Helsinki C: 45, N: 24, D: 7.24. WR: 13:58.2 (Günder Hägg)

1. Emil Zátopek	CZE	14:06.6	OR	(14:06.72)
2. Alain Mimoun	FRA	14:07.4		(14:07.58)
3. Herbert Schade	GER	14:08.6		(14:08.80)
4. D. Gordon Pirie	GBR	14:18.0		(14:18.31)
5. Christopher Chataway	GBR	14:18.0		(14:18.38)
6. Leslie Perry	AUS	14:23.6		(14:23.16)
7. Ernö Béres	HUN	14:24.8		
8. Åke Andersson	SWE	14:26.0		

After he had won the 10,000 meters for the second time, Emil Zátopek was asked if it was true that he would also contest the 5000. "The marathon contest won't be for a long time yet, so I simply must do something until then," he replied. With five runners in each of the three heats

Emil Zátopek enters the homestretch of the 1952 5000 meters, followed by Alain Mimoun and Herbert Schade. An exhausted Chris Chataway has fallen after stepping on the curb.

qualifying for the final, Zátopek decided to enjoy himself during his heat. As the laps piled up, the multilingual Czech chatted amiably with the other runners, particularly after it had become clear who the five qualifiers would be. As they approached the bell lap, Zátopek, in the lead, slowed down, waited for Aleksandr Anoufriev of the U.S.S.R., and motioned for him to pass, acting like a traffic cop clearing an intersection. As he rounded the final turn, Zátopek noticed Bertil Albertsson of Sweden sprinting for the finish. Slowing down again, he hailed Albertsson as if he were hitching a ride and engaged him in conversation. The two ran the last straight together, with Zátopek giving way just before the finish. He also took a liking to fourth-place finisher Les Perry of Australia and later presented him with a gift of his training suit.

The final was, of course, a more serious affair. Yet Zátopek still took the time to speak to Herbert Schade before the start, advising him to hold back for the first 2000 meters and not waste his energy setting the pace. Schade ignored this advice and paid the price. The race itself was full of action, with the lead changing hands numerous times. As the laps wound down, it appeared that any of five runners could win: Zátopek, Schade, Mimoun, Chataway, or Pirie. At the bell, Zátopek was in first place, hard-pressed by Schade. In the backstretch, Chris Chataway, who later paced Roger Bannister and John Landy to the first two sub-four-minute miles, dashed into the lead, followed by Mimoun and Schade, leaving Zátopek in fourth place. Entering the final curve, Zátopek made his move, swinging wide into lane 3. Halfway through the bend, he was already in front again and pulling away. Entering the home straightaway, Chataway, exhausted, stepped on the curb and fell. He was able to regain his feet and stagger home, but by that time Zátopek had already gained a five-yard victory over Mimoun, who finished second to Zátopek for the third time in an Olympic final and improved his personal best by over 14 seconds.

Later in the afternoon, Emil Zátopek learned that his wife, Dana, had won a gold medal in the javelin throw. When asked if it was true that he was going to try for another win in the marathon, Zátopek replied, "At present, the score of the contest in the Zátopek family is 2–1. This result is too close. To restore some prestige I will try to improve on it—in the marathon race."

1956 Melbourne C: 23, N: 13, D: 11.28. WR: 13:36.8 (Gordon Pirie)

1. Volodymyr Kuts	SOV/UKR	13:39.6	OR	(13:39.86)
2. D. Gordon Pirie	GBR	13:50.6		(13:50.78)
3. G. Derek Ibbotson	GBR	13:54.4		(13:54.60)
4. Miklos Szabó II	HUN	14:03.4		(14:03.38)
5. Albert Thomas	AUS	14:04.6		(14:05.03)
6. László Tábori	HUN	14:09.8		(14:09.99)
7. Maiyoro Nyandika	KEN	14:19.0		(14:18.99)
8. Thyge Thögersen	DEN	14:21.0		(14:21.81)

After Kuts' decisive victory in the 10,000 five days earlier, it seemed a long shot that anyone would beat him in the 5000, although Gordon Pirie had defeated Kuts at this distance in world record time on June 9. In the Olympic final, Kuts went to the front immediately and was never headed, finishing 75 yards in front of Pirie and Ibbotson. Unfortunately for Kuts, the experimental training program which the Soviet coaches had imposed on him apparently took its toll. By 1960 he had suffered his first heart attack. His fourth heart attack killed him, on August 17, 1975, at the age of 48.

1960 Rome C: 48, N: 31, D: 9.2. WR: 13.35.0 (Volodymyr Kuts)

1. Murray Halberg	NZE	13:43.4	(13:43.76)
2. Hans Grodotzki	GDR	13:44.6	(13:45.01)
3. Kazimierz Zimny	POL	13:44.8	(13:45.09)
4. Friedrich Janke	GDR	13:46.8	(13:47.14)
5. David Power	AUS	13:51.8	(13:52.38)
6. Maiyoro Nyandika	KEN	13:52.8	(13:53.25)
7. Michel Bernard	FRA	14:04.2	(14:04.68)
8. Horst Flossbach	GER	14:06.6	(14:07.03)

When he was 17 years old, Murray Halberg was hit from behind in a crash tackle during a rugby match. He was left with a dislocated shoulder, ruptured veins and arteries, blood clots, and a paralyzed left arm. After two months in the hospital and two operations, he was released with a withered arm and shoulder. He had to relearn how to walk, run, dress himself, and feed himself. Prevented from competing in contact sports, Halberg concentrated on running. Six years after his accident, he represented New Zealand at the Melbourne Olympics and two years after that he broke the four-minute mile.

Back in the Olympics in 1960, Halberg and his coach, Arthur Lydiard, devised a radical strategy to win the 5000 meters, a strategy they had tried successfully at the 1958 Commonwealth Games. With three laps to go, at the stage

Murray Halberg, winner of the 5000 meters in 1960, collapses in the infield, still holding the tape that marked his victory.

in the race when runners usually gather their strength for the last lap sprint, Halberg suddenly pushed to the front of the pack and then darted away as if the finish line was just around the next curve. The tactic worked perfectly. His startled opponents were confused, and before Grodotzki was able to respond, Halberg had covered the tenth lap in 61.1 seconds and opened up a lead of 25 yards. He also ran the next lap as fast as he could, preventing Grodotzki from closing any ground. Then Halberg faced the grim task of completing the final lap even though he was totally exhausted. Checking behind himself frequently, he watched as Grodotzki gradually whittled his lead down to 15 yards, 12 yards, 10 yards. But then Halberg reached the finish line with eight yards to spare. He collapsed on his back on the infield, still holding the tape between his fingers. In his autobiography, *A Clean Pair of Heels,* Halberg recalled, "I had always imagined an Olympic champion was something more than a mere mortal, in fact, a god. Now I knew he was just a human being."

1964 Tokyo C: 48, N: 29, D: 10.18. WR: 13:35.0 (Volodymyr Kuts)

1. Robert Schul	USA	13.48.8
2. Harald Norpoth	GER	13:49.6
3. William Dellinger	USA	13:49.8
4. Michel Jazy	FRA	13:49.8
5. H. Kipchoge Keino	KEN	13:50.4
6. William Baillie	NZE	13:51.0
7. Nikolai Dutov	SOV/RUS	13:53.8
8. Thor Helland	NOR	13:57.0

Ron Clarke of Australia led the way for most of the race, but gave up the lead to Michel Jazy shortly before the 4000-meter mark. With one and a half laps to go, Bill Dellinger moved ahead, but just after the bell Jazy regained the lead and pulled ahead by ten yards, with Norpoth second and the favorite, Bob Schul, third. Two hundred meters from the finish, Jazy was sure that he would win. "I was beside myself with joy." Suddenly, in the course of only three strides, his legs turned to lead and "weighed a ton each." Meanwhile, Schul, known for his finishing kick, had begun sprinting in the backstretch. By the final curve he had cut Jazy's lead to five yards. Coming out of the turn, Schul saw Jazy look back and noticed his shoulders tighten. "I smiled inwardly," said Schul. "I knew I had him." Jazy's thoughts turned to Volodymyr Kuts' defeat of Gordon Pirie in 1956. "You are Pirie," he told himself. "You are dead." Desperately he

The varied emotions of the finish of the 1964 5000 meters. The joy of the winner, Bob Schul (center), the surprised thrill of silver medalist Harald Norpoth (left), and the agony and disappointment of Michel Jazy (third from left), who was in first place only 50 meters from the tape, but finished only fourth.

tried to draw an extra reserve of strength from his body, but there was nothing there. Schul passed the discouraged Frenchman 50 meters from the tape. Schul had run the last 300 meters in 38.7 seconds. Jazy was so drained that he wasn't even able to hold on to third place.

1968 Mexico City C: 37, N: 25, D: 10.17. WR: 13:16.6 (Ronald Clarke)

1. Mohamed Gammoudi	TUN	14:05.0	(14:05.01)
2. H. Kipchoge Keino	KEN	14:05.2	(14:05.16)
3. Naftali Temu	KEN	14:06.4	(14:06.41)
4. Juan Martínez	MEX	14:10.8	(14:10.76)
5. Ronald Clarke	AUS	14:12.4	(14:12.45)
6. Wohib Masresha	ETH	14:17.6	(14:17.70)
7. Nikolai Sviridov	SOV/RUS	14:18.4	(14:18.40)
8. Fikru Deguefu	ETH	14:19.0	(14:18.98)

Mohamed Gammoudi, a 29-year-old soldier, moved in front with two laps to go and, with great grit and determination, held off alternating challenges from Keino and Temu, finally winning by about four feet after running the last lap in 54.8 seconds. A Tunisian biography of Gammoudi claimed that a typical day's diet for the Olympic champion consisted of five yogurts, ten pieces of fruit, four cups of tea, two coffees, two pastries, large quantities of meat, fish, milk, and cheese, and as much parsley as he could eat. Gammoudi weighed 135 pounds.

1972 Munich C: 61, N: 35, D: 9.10. WR: 13:16.6 (Ronald Clarke)

1. Lasse Viren	FIN	13:26.4	OR	(13:26.42)
2. Mohamed Gammoudi	TUN	13:27.4		(13:27.33)
3. Ian Stewart	GBR	13:27.6		(13:27.61)
4. Steve Prefontaine	USA	13:28.4		(13:28.25)
5. Emiel Puttemans	BEL	13:30.8		(13:30.82)
6. Harald Norpoth	GER	13:32.6		(13:32.58)
7. Per Halle	NOR	13:34.4		(13:34.38)
8. Nikolai Sviridov	SOV/RUS	13:39.4		(13:39.31)

Before the competition, Steve Prefontaine had boldly warned that he would run the final mile in less than four minutes. Right on cue, Prefontaine took the lead with four laps to go and picked up the pace. Most of the field fell behind, but Viren and Gammoudi would not be shaken and were still shooting for the gold medal when the bell rang to signal the final lap. Viren led the way into the backstretch, was headed briefly by Gammoudi, but was back in the lead before the homestretch and couldn't be caught. Prefontaine faded and lost the bronze medal to the fast-finishing Ian Stewart. The last mile had been run in 4:01.2. Lasse Viren became the fourth runner to achieve a 5000/10,000 double, joining the ranks of Hannes Kolehmainen, Emil Zátopek, and Volodymyr Kuts. On May 30, 1975, Steve Prefontaine lost control of his sports car and was killed in a crash, at the age of 24.

1976 Montreal C: 36, N: 23, D: 7.30. WR: 13:13.0 (Emiel Puttemans)

1. Lasse Viren	FIN	13:24.76
2. Dick Quax	NZE	13:25.16
3. Klaus-Peter Hildenbrand	GER	13:25.38
4. Rodney Dixon	NZE	13:25.50
5. Brendan Foster	GBR	13:26.19
6. Willy Polleunis	BEL	13:26.99
7. Ian Stewart	GBR	13:27.65
8. Aniceto Silva Simoes	POR	13:29.38

Following his victory in the 10,000 meters, Lasse Viren was subjected to a double inquisition. First, members of the press grilled him about the practice of blood boosting. This unnatural, but, at that time, not illegal, procedure involves the extraction of a quart or more of blood from a runner before a major competition. This blood is frozen, while the runner's body rebuilds its blood to a normal level. Then, just before the race, the extracted blood is unfrozen and reinjected into the runner, increasing the body's hemoglobin level and oxygen-carrying capability, and thus providing the runner with greater endurance. Viren was accused of blood boosting because the procedure was first experimented with in Scandinavia, and because Viren only recorded his best performances in major competitions, particularly the Olympics. Viren always denied that he engaged in blood boosting and claimed that his training schedule was organized to peak at the Olympics, because only the Olympics really mattered to him.

The day before the 5000 meters final, Viren was called before the Technical Committee of the International Olympic Committee and asked to explain why he had carried his running shoes aloft while taking his victory lap following the 10,000 meters final. Accused of commercialism, the soft-spoken policeman said that he had removed his shoes because he had a blister. This seemed to satisfy the committee, which allowed him to continue competing.

The most notable performers in the 5000 heats were Brendan Foster, who set an Olympic record of 13:20.34 and Dieudonne Lamothe of Haiti, who led after the first lap, but finished five minutes after the other runners in his heat. His time, 18:50.07, was the slowest ever recorded in the Olympics.

In the final, most of the pace-setting was done by Viren and Foster, although the fourth kilometer saw Quax and Hildenbrand take their turns in front. With three laps to go, Viren picked up the pace, but at the start of the final lap there were still only five meters separating the first six runners. "At the bell," said Viren later, "I gave just one quick glance behind me and took in the situation in all its ghastliness. The wall at my heels was thick. . . . I had put in a couple of sixty-second laps and almost everybody was still chasing me, damn it! I was the fugitive now, and I realized I had to flee as if my life depended on it. . . . In the far turn I had the most frightening experience of my career. Some guy in black was forcing himself past me. It was Quax, whom I really hadn't reckoned very seriously. . . . I found my last gear, and it was just enough. The black shadow glided away from my eyes. The holy sanctuary of the finish line engulfed me—I had won!" Lasse Viren had earned his fourth gold medal and had become the first repeat winner of the 5000.

1980 Moscow C: 35, N: 22, D: 8.1. WR: 13:08.4 (Henry Rono)

1. Miruts Yifter	ETH	13:20.91
2. Suleiman Nyambui	TAN	13:21.60
3. Kaarlo Maaninka	FIN	13:22.00
4. Eamonn Coghlan	IRL	13:22.74
5. Markus Ryffel	SWI	13:23.03
6. Dietmar Millonig	AUT	13:23.25
7. John Treacy	IRL	13:23.62
8. Aleksandr Fedotkin	SOV/RUS	13:24.10

Miruts Yifter's quest for a gold medal at 5000 meters is a frustrating eight-year saga with a happy ending. Yifter first gained international attention in 1971 at a U.S.-Africa meet in North Carolina, when he sprinted to an apparent victory over Steve Prefontaine in the 5000 meters race, only to discover that he had miscounted the laps and quit running one lap too soon. The next day he made up for his mistake by defeating Frank Shorter at 10,000 meters. At the Munich Olympics in 1972, Yifter gained a bronze medal at 10,000 meters, but missed the start of his heat in the 5000 meters race. Typical of the mystery surrounding Yifter is the fact that there were three explanations for his failure to appear at the starting line. The first is that he was directed to the wrong check-in gate at the stadium and was refused admittance by German guards. The second is that he spent too long in the toilet before the race, and the third is that he left the bathroom in time but got lost on the way to the track. In interviews twelve years later, Yifter added a fourth, characteristically vague, explanation. He implied that he ran into problems with team officials and with the Ethiopian government because he came from Tigre Province, a region involved in a civil war against the ruling dictatorship. Whether the team trainer purposely misinformed him about the starting time of his heat or whether he feared the consequences of what would happen if he did race is still unclear. In 1976 Yifter was prevented from competing when Ethiopia boycotted the Olympics.

In Moscow, the 5-foot 4-inch, 117-pound father of six faced no such problems. For some strange reason, a semi-final round was added to the 5000 meters competition, despite the fact that the field of 35 was the smallest in 24 years. This didn't bother Yifter, who won his opening heat and finished second to teammate Yohannes Mohammed in the semifinals.

After 4000 meters of the final, the 12 finalists were still bunched within 12 meters. Ninety-nine-pound Mohammed Kedir led at the bell, as everyone waited for the infamous Yifter kick that had already brought victory in the 10,000 meters. However, in the backstretch Yifter was completely caught in a box, with Kedir in front of him, Eamonn Coghlan beside Kedir, and the pack behind him. Then, with less than 300 meters to go, Kedir turned around and asked Yifter if he was ready. A wave of the hand from the master and the selfless Kedir stepped aside. Yifter shot through on the inside as Coghlan watched in amazement. The rest was academic. Yifter ran the last 200 meters in 27.2 seconds to gain his

Miruts Yifter celebrates the culmination of his eight-year quest for a gold medal in the 5000 meters.

long-awaited 5000 meters gold medal. Kedir got tripped up by the pack, lost his shoe, and finished last. Coghlan lost the bronze medal to Kaarlo Maaninka, who came from a family of 23 children in Lapland.

Part of the mystery of Miruts Yifter is the question of his age, which was variously reported as 33, 35, 36, 37, or 42. When asked for a definitive answer, Yifter would only reply, "I don't count the years. Men may steal my chickens, men may steal my sheep. But no man can steal my age." Most likely he was 36.

1984 Los Angeles C: 56, N: 40, D: 8.11. WR: 13:00.41 (David Moorcroft)

1. Saïd Aouita	MOR	13:05.59	OR
2. Markus Ryffel	SWI	13:07.54	
3. Antonio Leitão	POR	13:09.20	
4. Timothy Hutchings	GBR	13:11.50	
5. Paul Kipkoech	KEN	13:14.40	
6. Charles Cheruiyot	KEN	13:18.41	
7. Doug Padilla	USA	13:23.56	
8. John Walker	NZE	13:24.46	

Despite the fact that the 5000 meters field was decimated by injuries, illness, boycott, and drug disqualification, the 1984 Olympic final was the fastest mass race ever at that distance. The favorite was Saïd Aouita by virtue of his June 13 performance of 13:04.78, second only to Dave Moorcroft's world record. Aouita did not disappoint, although it was the Portuguese runners Ezequiel Canario and Antonio Leitão who created the pace. Canario led for the first 1000 meters. When he couldn't push any harder, Leitão took over. One by one he burned away the other runners with successive 64-second laps until, with 500 meters to go, only Aouita and Markus Ryffel remained. With one half lap left, Aouita sprinted ahead. Ryffel tried to keep up, but gave up in the final turn and concentrated on protecting second place. Aouita ran the final lap in 55.08 despite taking time to wave to the crowd during the last 50 yards. Ryffel, Hutchings, Kipkoech, and Cheruiyot all bettered their personal records by at least five seconds. To celebrate the victory, King Hassan II of Morocco gave Aouita a villa in Casablanca. The Rabat-to-Casablanca express train was also renamed in his honor. Aouita was undefeated at 5000 meters from 1979 until June 20, 1989. He withdrew from the 1988 Olympic competittion because of injury.

1988 Seoul C: 56, N: 39, D: 10.1. WR: 12:58.39 (Saïd Aouita)

1. John Ngugi	KEN	13:11.70
2. Dieter Baumann	GER	13:15.52
3. Hansjörg Kunze	GDR	13:15.73
4. Domingos Castro	POR	13:16.09
5. Sydney Maree	USA	13:23.69
6. Jack Buckner	GBR	13:23.85
7. Stefano Mei	ITA	13:26.17
8. Yevgeny Ignatov	BUL	13:26.41

Just before the 1000-meter mark, three-time world cross-country champion John Ngugi, aware that he could not match the finishing kicks of the other runners, suddenly burst into the lead and ran away from the pack. Covering the next 800 meters in a startling 2:00.25, he opened up a huge gap of almost 50 meters. With four laps to go it became clear that Ngugi was not going to fall apart, so Domingos Castro reluctantly gave chase. He managed to close within about 25 meters, 1000 meters from the finish, but Ngugi, constantly looking back to check for challengers, loped steadily onward to win by 30 meters. The unfortunate Castro, who was passed by Baumann and Kunze in the last 50 meters and left without a medal, spent the next half hour sobbing inconsolably.

1992 Barcelona C: 56, N: 41, D: 8.8. WR: 12:58.39 (Saïd Aouita)
1. Dieter Baumann   GER   13:12.52
2. Paul Bitok   KEN   13:12.71
3. Fita Bayisa   ETH   13:13.03
4. Moulay Brahim Boutaïb MOR   13:13.27
5. Yobes Ondieki   KEN   13:17.50
6. Worku Bikila   ETH   13:23.52
7. Rob Denmark   GBR   13:27.76
8. Abel Antón Rodrigo   SPA   13:27.80

Dieter Baumann's pre-race strategy was simple: "Wait and see what the Kenyans will do." What the Kenyans did was very much to Baumann's liking. They set a decent pace without speeding up too early—perfect for a strong kicker like Baumann. Unfortunately for the 27-year-old from the small town of Blaustein, on the backstretch he found himself completely boxed in, surrounded by Bitok, Bayisa, Boutaïb, and Ondieki. On the final curve, as the Africans began sprinting, Baumann slipped out of the back of the box, swung wide and started picking off the leaders. He zipped right by Ondieki, then caught Boutaïb, wormed by Bayisa on the inside, cut back to the outside, passed Bitok 12 meters from the finish line, and won by one and a half meters. His time for the last 200 meters was 24.9 seconds.

10,000 METERS

A 25-lap race, the 10,000 meters is 6 miles 376 yards and 4 inches. Twenty runners take part in the final.

1896–1908 not held

1912 Stockholm C: 30, N: 13, D: 7.8, WR: 30:58.8 (Jean Bouin)
1. Johan "Hannes" Kolehmainen   FIN   31:20.8
2. Louis Tewanima   USA   32:06.6
3. Albin Stenroos   FIN   32:21.8
4. Joseph Keeper   CAN   32:36.2
5. Alfonso Orlando   ITA   33:31.2

Fifteen men qualified for the final but only 11 started. The hot sun and hard pace cut the field down further and only five finished. Twenty-two-year-old Hannes Kolehmainen

took the lead in the first lap and won the first of his four Olympic gold medals without being challenged. Silver medalist Louis Tewanima was a Hopi Indian.

1920 Antwerp C: 34, N: 17, D: 8.20. WR: 30:58.8 (Jean Bouin)
1. Paavo Nurmi   FIN   31:45.8
2. Joseph Guillemot   FRA   31:47.2
3. James Wilson   GBR   31:50.8
4. Augusto Maccario   ITA   32:02.0
5. James Hatton   GBR   32:14.0
6. Jean-Baptiste Manhès   FRA   32:26.0
7. Heikki Liimatainen   FIN   32:28.0
8. Frederick Faller   USA   32:38.0

Paavo Nurmi was born in Turku, Finland, on June 13, 1897, the son of a carpenter who died when Paavo was 12. He gained early success in Finland at 3000 meters, but caused his first sensation while serving in the army in the early summer of 1919. He entered a 20-kilometer march with full equipment. Running was allowed, so Nurmi ran the entire distance. Carrying a rifle, a cartridge belt, and an 11-pound sack of sand, he finished the course so quickly that some officials thought he must have discovered a shortcut.

In Antwerp Nurmi lost his first final, the 5000 meters, to Joseph Guillemot, but sought revenge three days later in the 10,000. This time he let James Wilson of Scotland do most of the pace-setting. Nurmi took the lead with two laps to go. Guillemot passed him in the backstretch of the final lap, but Nurmi sprinted back into the lead almost immediately and won by eight yards.

Although Paavo Nurmi's first Olympic victory was not his most difficult, it *was* his most unpleasant, since Guillemot almost vomited on him as soon as he crossed the finish line. The source of Guillemot's distress was a last-minute change in the starting time of the race. Guillemot had just finished a large lunch when he was informed that the race had been moved up from 5:30 p.m. to 2:15 p.m. at the request of the king of Belgium, who wished to appear at an art opening, leaving the Frenchman no time to digest his food.

1924 Paris C: 43, N: 17, D: 7.6. WR: 30:35.4 (Vilho "Ville" Ritola)
1. Vilho "Ville" Ritola   FIN   30:23.2   WR
2. Edvin Wide   SWE   30:55.2
3. Eero Berg   FIN   31:43.0
4. Väinö Sipilä   FIN   31:50.2
5. Ernest Harper   GBR   31:58.0
6. Halland Britton   GBR   32:06.0
7. Guillaume Tell   FRA   32:12.0
8. Earl Johnson   USA   32:17.0

For the first time, the 10,000 meters was run without heats. Ritola and Wide pulled away from the other 41 contestants after only two laps, but even Wide couldn't keep up with Ritola, who won by a half lap and broke his own world record by over 12 seconds. He continued on for another quarter lap before the officials were able to convince him that the race was over. Paavo Nurmi had been prevented from entering this race by Finnish officials, who felt he was entering too many events. Back in Finland after the games, Nurmi made his point by setting a world record of 30:06.2 that was to last for almost 13 years.

1928 Amsterdam C: 24, N: 12, D: 7.29. WR: 30:06.2 (Paavo Nurmi)

1. Paavo Nurmi	FIN	30:18.8	OR
2. Vilho "Ville" Ritola	FIN	30:19.4	
3. Edvin Wide	SWE	31:00.8	
4. Jean-Gunnar Lindgren	SWE	31:26.0	
5. Arthur Muggridge	GBR	31:31.8	
6. Ragnar Magnusson	SWE	31:37.2	
7. Toivo Loukola	FIN	31:39.0	
8. Kalle Matilainen	FIN	31:45.0	

Paavo Nurmi earned his ninth and last gold medal in the 10,000 meters flat race, the same event in which he had won his first gold medal. After nine laps only Ritola, Nurmi, and Wide were still in contention. During the 18th lap the Swede dropped back. Nurmi dogged Ritola for the remainder of the race, then passed him about 50 yards from the tape and won by two or three meters. Nurmi refused to be congratulated or photographed, and simply picked up his sweatsuit and walked off the track without a smile. The following week he gained two silver medals in the 5000 and the steeplechase.

Nurmi had planned to enter the 10,000 and the marathon in the 1932 Olympics, but was declared a professional by the International Amateur Athletic Federation and banned from competition. For a time Nurmi ran a construction business and then a men's clothing store, eventually gaining considerable financial security as a result of wise real estate investments. His last appearance on a track was a dramatic one. When the 1952 Olympics were held in Helsinki, Finland, the Opening Ceremony was staged in the Olympic Stadium, which was graced with a bronze statue of Nurmi in the front. After the athletes had paraded around the track and onto the infield, the audience awaited the arrival of the Olympic torch. When the final runner, whose name had not been announced, appeared from out of the tunnel bearing the torch aloft, the Finnish spectators broke into thunderous applause as they recognized the runner as none other than Paavo Nurmi, whose stride was unmistakable even though he was 55 years old. The athletes of the world broke rank and dashed to the side of the track to catch a glimpse of the legendary "Flying Finn," who bounded up the steps and passed the torch to 62-year-old Hannes Kolehmainen, who lit the Olympic flame.

Paavo Nurmi, who set 29 world records at distances ranging from 1500 meters to 20,000 meters, died on October 2, 1974. Six Finnish gold medal winners served as pallbearers at his funeral. Nurmi left the bulk of his estate to help the cause of heart research.

1932 Los Angeles C: 16, N: 11, D: 7.31. WR: 30:06.2 (Paavo Nurmi)

1. Janusz Kusociński	POL	30:11.4	OR
2. Volmari Iso-Hollo	FIN	30:12.6	
3. Lauri Virtanen	FIN	30:35.0	
4. John Savidan	NZE	31:09.0	
5. Max Syring	GER	31:35.0	
6. Jean-Gunnar Lindgren	SWE	31:37.0	
7. Juan Morales Rodriguez	MEX	32:03.0	
8. Calvin Bricker	CAN	—	

Kusociński and Iso-Hollo dueled at close quarters for 24 of 25 laps. Iso-Hollo led by one yard entering the final lap, but then Kusociński sprinted away to a big lead, before slowing to a jog and finishing with ten yards to spare. Seventh-place finisher Juan Morales Rodriguez was a Yaqui Indian who ran barefoot. Among the unplaced entrants was Adalberto Cardoso of Brazil, who got stranded in San Francisco and didn't arrive in Los Angeles until the day of the race.

1936 Berlin C: 30, N: 18, D: 8.2. WR: 30:06.2 (Paavo Nurmi)

1. Ilmari Salminen	FIN	30:15.4
2. Arvo Askola	FIN	30:15.6
3. Volmari Iso-Hollo	FIN	30:20.2
4. Kohei Murakoso	JPN	30:25.0
5. James Burns	GBR	30:58.2
6. Juan Carlos Zabala	ARG	31:22.0
7. Max Gebhardt	GER	31:29.6
8. Donald Lash	USA	31:39.4

Murakoso fought valiantly against the three Finns, who ran a team race that included a good deal of jostling every time one of them passed him. However Murakoso finally had to give in with one lap to go. Salminen, a 33-year-old army sergeant, jumped the others at the start of the last lap, but Askola regained the lead in the backstretch. Salminen caught him again coming out of the final turn and gradually inched ahead for a narrow victory.

1948 London C: 27, N: 15, D: 7.30. WR: 29:35.8 (Viljo Heino)

1. Emil Zátopek	CZE	29:59.6	OR
2. Alain Mimoun	FRA	30:47.4	
3. Bertil Albertsson	SWE	30:53.6	
4. Martin Stokken	NOR	30:58.6	
5. Severt Dennolf	SWE	31:05.0	
6. Abdallah ben Said	FRA	31:07.8	
7. Stanley Cox	GBR	31:08.0	
8. James Peters	GBR	31:16.0	

World record holder Viljo Heino was expected to receive a stiff challenge from Czech army lieutenant Emil Zátopek. As it turned out, it was the challenger who controlled the race. Moving in front during the tenth lap, Zátopek ground out the laps at a steady pace until both Heino and his teammate, Heinstrom, were forced to drop out from exhaustion. Eventually Zátopek lapped all but two runners and won by over 300 meters. The incompetent officials in charge of the race became confused by

Zátopek's performance and announced the start of the final circuit one lap too soon. Fortunately Zátopek knew better, although others didn't. When the race was over, it was announced that Dennolf of Sweden had finished fourth and Stokken of Norway fifth. The Norwegians protested, but the matter was settled quickly when Dennolf himself supported their case. Sixth place was awarded to Robert Everaert of Belgium, who had actually dropped out of the race over five laps before the finish. Everaert pointed out the mistake, but the judges refused to change their decision until a Belgian official intervened.

1952 Helsinki C: 33, N: 21, D: 7.20. WR: 29:02.6 (Emil Zátopek)

1. Emil Zátopek	CZE	29:17.0	OR
2. Alain Mimoun	FRA	29:32.8	
3. Aleksandr Anufriev	SOV/RUS	29:48.2	
4. Hannu Posti	FIN	29:51.4	
5. Frank Sando	GBR	29:51.8	
6. Valter Nyström	SWE	29:52.8	
7. D. Gordon Pirie	GBR	30:09.5	
8. Fred Norris	GBR	30:09.8	

The result was never in doubt as Zátopek wore out his opponents one by one, with Mimoun the last to go, four and a half laps from the finish. Zátopek won by about 100 yards to gain the first part of his unprecedented long-distance triple. Between 1948 and 1954 Emil Zátopek won 38 consecutive races at 10,000 meters. Fourteen years later, Zátopek presented his 1952 10,000-meter gold medal to the great Australian runner Ron Clarke, who had never won one.

1956 Melbourne C: 25, N: 15, D: 11.23. WR: 28:30.4 (Volodymyr Kuts)

1. Volodymyr Kuts	SOV/UKR	28:45.6	OR (28:45.59)
2. József Kovács	HUN	28:52.4	(28:52.36)
3. Allan Lawrence	AUS	28:53.6	(28:53.59)
4. Zdzislaw Kryszkowiak	POL	29:05.0	(29:05.41)
5. Kenneth Norris	GBR	29:21.6	
6. Ivan Chernyavsky	SOV/UKR	29:31.6	
7. David Power	AUS	29:49.2	
8. D. Gordon Pirie	GBR	29:49.6	

Volodymyr Kuts was a teenager when the Germans invaded his Ukrainian village in 1943. After the war, he joined the U.S.S.R. navy, and it was only then that he attracted the attention of Soviet coaches, who introduced him to competitive running at the age of 23.

Two months before the Melbourne Olympics, while running in Moscow, Kuts broke the world 10,000 meters record by over 12 seconds. By virtue of this performance, he was considered the favorite. But there were those who remembered that two months before that, Kuts had been beaten in England by Gordon Pirie at 5000 meters, and although he had never run the 10,000 faster than 29:17.2, Pirie was also given a good shot at the gold medal.

Kuts took off like a flash and completed the first of 25 laps in only 61.2 seconds. Slowing down only slightly, he had outdistanced everyone but Pirie by the seventh lap. Kuts ran the first half of the race so quickly that he passed the 5000-meter mark at 14:07.0, which almost equaled Emil Zátopek's Olympic record for that distance. And he still had another 5000 meters to run. Between laps 8 and 20, Kuts tried a variety of tactics to rid himself of the stubborn Pirie. Several times he sprinted out at a seemingly insane pace, only to have Pirie catch up each time. Alternatively, Kuts would slow down, move to the outside, and wave Pirie past him. But Pirie refused to bite, preferring to remain at Kuts' shoulder.

Suddenly, at the end of the 20th lap, Kuts stopped so abruptly that Pirie was forced to take the lead. Relieved of the pressure of having Pirie on his heels, Kuts rested for a half lap while he studied his adversary in front of him. Then, just as suddenly as he had slowed, Kuts burst past Pirie to take the lead for good. Pirie struggled to keep pace, but with four laps to go, he gave up, eventually dropping back to eighth place. Kovács and Lawrence finished strongly, but Kuts' victory was never in doubt.

Gordon Pirie and Volodymyr Kuts, still friendly despite their intense rivalry. In 1956 Kuts defeated Pirie in both the 10,000 meters and the 5000 meters.

1960 Rome C: 32, N: 20, D: 9.8. WR: 28:30.4 (Volodymyr Kuts)

1. Pyotr Bolotnikov	SOV/RUS	28:32.2	OR	(28:32.18)
2. Hans Grodotzki	GDR	28:37.0		(28:37.22)
3. David Power	AUS	28:38.2		(28:37.65)
4. Aleksei Desyachikov	SOV/RUS	28:39.6		(28:39.72)
5. Murray Halberg	NZE	28:48.6		(28:49.11)
6. Max Truex	USA	28:50.2		(28:50.34)
7. Zdzislaw Krzyszkowiak	POL	28:52.4		(28:52.75)
8. John Merriman	GBR	28:52.6		(28:52.89)

Dave Power tried to pull away with seven laps to go, but Bolotnikov, Grodotzki, and Desyachikov were able to stay with him. Seven hundred meters from the finish, Bolotnikov, a 30-year-old pupil of Volodymyr Kuts, left the others behind, running the last lap in 57.4 seconds and winning by 30 yards. Nine of the first ten finishers achieved personal records, including Power, who bettered his previous best time by 53.8 seconds.

1964 Tokyo C: 29, N: 17, D: 10.14. WR: 28:15.6 (Ronald Clarke)

1. William Mills	USA	28:24.4	OR
2. Mohamed Gammoudi	TUN	28:24.8	
3. Ronald Clarke	AUS	28:25.8	
4. Mamo Wolde	ETH	28:31.8	
5. Leonid Ivanov	SOV/KYR	28:53.2	
6. Kokichi Tsuburaya	JPN	28:59.4	
7. Murray Halberg	NZE	29:10.8	
8. Anthony Cook	AUS	29:15.8	

The 1964 10,000 meters produced one of the most electrifying upsets in Olympic history. Pregame predictions had the race as a tough battle among defending 5000-meter champion Murray Halberg, defending 10,000 meters champion Pyotr Bolotnikov, and the main favorite, world record holder Ron Clarke. By the halfway mark, Clarke, following a strategy of surging every other lap, had managed to eliminate from contention all but four runners: Mohamed Gammoudi and Mamo Wolde, who would both win gold medals four years later in Mexico City, local favorite Kokichi Tsuburaya, and Billy Mills, who had finished second at the U.S. Olympic trials. Tsuburaya was the first to lose contact; then, with two and a half laps to go, Wolde dropped away.

At this point, Ron Clarke appeared assured of victory, since neither Gammoudi nor Mills had ever broken 29 minutes. It was surely just a matter of time before Clarke would break away. They reached the final lap with Clarke and Mills running abreast and Gammoudi right behind. The track was cluttered with stragglers, and the three leaders were forced to thread their way through the congestion. It was "like a dash for a train in a peak-hour crowd," Clarke would later recall. In the backstretch Clarke found himself faced with a problem. In front of him was a straggler who wouldn't move aside to be passed. To his right was Mills. Clarke tapped Mills a couple times, but he wouldn't step aside either. So Clarke gave him a shove that sent the American unknown careening to the outside. Seeing his chance, Gammoudi, putting one hand on Clarke and the other on

Mohamed Gammoudi (second from left) pushes his way past Billy Mills (left) and Ron Clarke (right) during the spectacular last lap of the 1964 10,000 meters.

Mills, pushed his way to the front and opened a sudden ten-yard lead. Clarke took off after the Tunisian, while Mills appeared to be out of the running. By this time, the audience was already going wild with excitement.

Clarke gradually closed the gap, finally passing Gammoudi at the beginning of the homestretch. But Gammoudi wasn't finished. With a major upset within his grasp, he pulled up to Clarke's shoulder once again. Then came one of those rare moments that sports fans never forget. Billy Mills, fighting his way through still more stragglers, let loose a final sprint that sent Clarke and Gammoudi into shock and carried him across the finish line with a three-yard victory that left the crowd of 75,000 as exhausted as the runners. Mills was immediately surrounded by Japanese officials, one of whom asked him, "Who are you?"

During the two weeks that he had spent in the Olympic Village prior to the opening of the games, not one reporter had asked Billy Mills a single question. Now he was besieged by journalists from all over the world, all asking the same question: "Who is Billy Mills?" Humble and calm (after crying on the victory platform), Mills explained that he was seven sixteenths Sioux Indian, and had been born in Pine Ridge, South Dakota. Orphaned at 12, he had been sent to Haskell Institute, a school for Native Americans in Lawrence, Kansas. He had taken

Billy Mills crosses the finish line in the 1964 10,000 meters.

up running as training to become a boxer, but after losing a couple of fights, he had decided to stick to running. After attending the University of Kansas, he had joined the Marines and was now a motor pool officer at Camp Pendleton in California. His winning time in Tokyo was 46 seconds faster than his previous best (Gammoudi had improved his own personal record by 47 seconds). "I'm flabbergasted," said Mills. "I can't believe it. I suppose I was the only person who thought I had a chance."

In 1965 Billy Mills proved that his Olympic victory was no fluke by bettering Ron Clarke's six-mile world record by six seconds. That same year, he received an award that was to prove more meaningful to him than his gold medal—a ring made from Black Hills gold that was presented to him by the elders of the Oglala Sioux tribe. They also gave him warrior status, which he didn't have because he was a half-breed, and an Indian name: Loves His Country.

But there was one thing missing from Billy Mills' Olympic experience: because there were so many runners still finishing the race, he was not allowed to take a victory lap. Twenty years later, on a rainy day in 1984, Mills returned to the National Stadium in Tokyo along with his wife, Pat, U.S. filmmaker Bud Greenspan, and a film crew. Mills described what followed in the book *Tales of*

Gold, by Lewis Carlson and John Fogarty: "I knew what I wanted, and Pat knew what I was going to do. I went down onto the track and . . . went on around, taking that victory lap I so desperately needed. At the same time, in my mind, I was reliving the race. I could feel Clarke push me, and I could sense people in the stadium. Toward the end of my lap, I heard one person clapping; it was Pat, clapping for me. I started to cry. I needed that victory lap so badly, I started crying, and rather than let the group see me cry, I lifted my face up to the rain, walked up the track a way to get my composure, then finished my lap."

1968 Mexico City C: 37, N: 23, D: 10.13. WR: 27:39.4 (Ronald Clarke)

1. Naftali Temu	KEN	29:27.4	(29:27.40)
2. Mamo Wolde	ETH	29:28.0	(29:27.75)
3. Mohamed Gammoudi	TUN	29:34.2	
4. Juan Martinez	MEX	29:35.0	
5. Nikolai Sviridov	SOV/RUS	29:43.2	
6. Ronald Clarke	AUS	29:44.8	
7. Ronald Hill	GBR	29:53.2	
8. Wohib Masresha	ETH	29:57.0	

When the International Olympic Committee first announced that the 1968 Olympics would be held in Mexico City, there was much criticism that the competitions would be adversely affected by the high altitude. The I.O.C. denied that the altitude would make a difference, but they couldn't have been more wrong.

The 10,000 meters was the first track and field event to be decided. With six laps to go, two runners were carried away on stretchers. The first surprise came after 8900 meters, when Kip Keino dropped out, suffering stomach cramps as a result of a gall bladder infection. Although 11 different men had led over the first 8000 meters, with 800 meters left, the only runners still in contention were Wolde, Clarke, Temu, and Gammoudi. One and a half laps from the finish, Clarke finally lost contact. A 64.4-second 24th lap by Temu got rid of Gammoudi, but just after the bell Wolde shot past Temu and opened up a five-yard gap. However, Temu had the most strength left. He caught Wolde 50 meters from the finish line and won by four yards. The first five finishers were all from high-altitude countries or had lived in high-altitude areas of their nations. The first non-high-altitude runner to finish was Ron Clarke, who collapsed and was unconscious for ten minutes. Clarke, by the way, had previously endured physical suffering because of the Olympics. In 1956, when he was 19 years old, Clarke was chosen to be the final runner in the torch relay and to light the Olympic cauldron. He was badly burned by sparks and was rushed off for medical treatment while the ceremonies continued.

Temu, a 23-year-old Kisii tribesman, was resentful, as well he should have been, when he learned that his victory was being belittled because of the altitude. In 1966 he had attracted attention by finishing first at the Commonwealth Games in Jamaica. "Now tell me," he said after his win in Mexico City, "I beat that Clarke they were talking about in Jamaica, and tell me . . . were there mountains in Kingston?" Temu was the first Kenyan to earn an Olympic gold medal. The 1968 10,000 meters marked the first time that all three medals in an Olympic event had been won by Africans.

1972 Munich C: 50, N: 34, D: 8.31. WR: 27:39.4 (Ronald Clarke)

1.	Lasse Viren	FIN	27:38.4	WR	(27:38.35)
2.	Emiel Puttemans	BEL	27:39.6		(27:39.58)
3.	Miruts Yifter	ETH	27:41.0		(27:40.96)
4.	Mariano Haro Cisneros	SPA	27:48.2		(27:48.14)
5.	Frank Shorter	USA	27:51.4		(27:51.32)
6.	David Bedford	GBR	28:05.4		(28:05.44)
7.	Daniel Korica	YUG	28:15.2		(28:15.18)
8.	Abdelkader Zaddem	TUN	28:18.2		(28:18.17)

With 50 runners entered, qualifying heats were reinstituted for the first time since 1920. In the first heat, Dave Bedford and Emiel Puttemans pulled away from the field. After reaching 8000 meters in 22:16.2, Bedford turned to Puttemans and asked him if they should go for the world record. Puttemans declined. "But we're so close to the mark," said Bedford. Finally Puttemans convinced him that they should save themselves for the final, not to mention the 5000. The second heat saw the Olympic debut of Lasse Viren, a 23-year-old Finnish policeman from the small village of Myrskyla. Two and a half weeks earlier Viren had defeated Puttemans and Bedford in Stockholm, setting a two-mile world record of 8:14.0.

The third and last heat was highlighted by the appearance of Anilus Joseph of Haiti, who had evidently never taken part in a 10,000 meters race before. Joseph took off as if he was two laps from the finish line. He covered the first lap in 59.6 seconds, opening up a lead of 50 meters. He was still in first place after 800 meters, but then he ran out of steam, and by the 1000-meter mark he was in last place. By the eighth lap he had been lapped by

Lasse Viren, having fallen halfway through the final of the 1972 10,000 meters, briefly contemplates his fate before regaining his feet. Viren went on to win the first of his four gold medals and set a world record as well.

all the other runners and by the twelfth he had been lapped again. When the bell rang to signal the final lap for the leaders, Joseph thought that it meant that he too only had one more lap to go, so he began sprinting again. Informed by an official that even though all the other runners had finished, he still had another mile to run, Joseph finally dropped out. He wasn't seen again in the Olympics, but his performance was only a prelude to the unusual feats that would be accomplished by the Haitian track team four years later in Montreal.

The final, two days later, was a more serious race. Although Bedford set a pace not unlike that of Joseph's, he was able to sustain it for much longer. He was still in the lead after 4600 meters, when a surprising incident occurred behind him.

Running in fifth place, Lasse Viren, without being interfered with, stumbled and fell. Mohamed Gammoudi tripped on Viren and crashed to the ground. Gammoudi, stunned, was forced to give up a couple laps later, but Viren rose quickly and moved up to second place after only 230 meters.

Viren passed Bedford at the 6000-meter mark and Bedford began to fade soon after. Only Yifter, Haro, Puttemans, and Shorter were still in the hunt. The lead changed hands several times during the next few laps. Six hundred meters from the finish, Viren poured it on. Shorter fell back immediately, and Haro lost contact 100 meters later. Yifter fell away in the final backstretch. Puttemans tried desperately to keep up, but Viren had too much strength left and was able to pull away in the final straight to win by about six or seven yards. Viren's times for the last two laps were a remarkable 60.0 and 56.4. Lasse Viren had broken Ron Clarke's seven-year-old world record and won the first of his four gold medals.

1976 Montreal C: 41, N: 26, D: 7.26. WR: 27:30.8 (David Bedford)

1.	Lasse Viren	FIN	27:40.38
2.	Carlos Lopes	POR	27:45.17
3.	Brendan Foster	GBR	27:54.92
4.	Anthony Simmons	GBR	27:56.26
5.	Ilie Floroiu	ROM	27:59.93
6.	Mariano Haro Cisneros	SPA	28:00.28
7.	Marc Smet	BEL	28:02.80
8.	Bernard Ford	GBR	28:17.78

The final was a relatively simple race. Lopes took the lead after 3200 meters and eventually drew away from everyone but Viren, who passed him 450 meters from the finish and won easily by 30 meters.

However, the 1976 10,000 meters competition should not be left without making mention of Olmeus Charles of Haiti, whose performance in the opening heat was the ultimate expression of the Olympic ideal that what counts is not the winning, but the taking part. Charles completed the course in 42:00.11, the slowest time ever recorded in the Olympics, almost 14 minutes slower than Carlos Lopes, who won the heat, and over eight and one-half minutes slower than Chris McCubbins of Canada, who placed next to last. The entire schedule had to be held up while Charles plodded the final six laps alone. In 1972 and 1976 Haitian runners consistently finished in last place. At first reflection, one might feel sympathy for the Haitians. After all, Haiti is the poorest country in the Western Hemisphere, and malnutrition is widespread. However, there is no evidence that tryouts were actually held to determine the nation's best runners. Instead, "Baby Doc" Duvalier, the dictator of Haiti, simply chose his friends and other trusted soldiers, and rewarded them with a free trip to Canada. Unfortunately, none of them were athletes.

1980 Moscow C: 40, N: 26, D: 7.27. WR: 27:22.5 (Henry Rono)
1. Miruts Yifter   ETH   27:42.69
2. Kaarlo Maaninka   FIN   27:44.28
3. Mohammed Kedir   ETH   27:44.64
4. Tolossa Kotu   ETH   27:46.47
5. Lasse Viren   FIN   27:50.46
6. Jörg Peter   GDR   28:05.53
7. Werner Schildhauer   GDR   28:10.91
8. Enn Sellik   SOV/EST   28:13.72

The final resembled a dual meet between Ethiopia and Finland more than an international contest. The Ethiopians dominated the proceedings, changing the pace and the lead every few hundred meters. After lulling the pack into confusion for the first 5000 meters, they set off at a torrid clip until only Viren and Maaninka were left to challenge. In the 22nd lap Maaninka broke ahead, only to be passed by Kedir and Yifter. Then Viren took the lead, but Kedir moved ahead again just before the bell. Finally, the inevitable took place. With 300 meters left in the race, Miruts Yifter sprinted into the lead, covered the last 200 meters in 26.8 seconds, and won by ten meters. Viren faded to fifth, but Maaninka, who later admitted to blood boosting before the Olympics, finished strongly to prevent an Ethiopian sweep.

1984 Los Angeles C: 45, N: 33, D: 8.6. WR: 27:13.81 (Fernando Mamede)
1. Alberto Cova   ITA   27:47.54
2. Michael McLeod   GBR   28:06.22
3. Michael Musyoki   KEN   28:06.46
4. Salvatore Antibo   ITA   28:06.50
5. Christoph Herle   GER   28:08.21
6. Sosthenes Bitok   KEN   28:09.01
7. Yutaka Kanai   JPN   28:27.06
8. Stephen Jones   GBR   28:28.08
DISQ (Drugs): Martti Vainio (FIN) 27:51:10

In 1982, Alberto Cova won the European championships by outsprinting Werner Schildhauer of East Germany. In 1983, Cova won the world championships by outsprinting Schildhauer. In 1984, with Schildhauer missing because of the Soviet-bloc boycott, Cova's only competition was thought to be world record holder Fernando Mamede. But even Mamede was considered a doubtful challenger

because of his long record of becoming overcome by nerves at important meets. True to form, Mamede, after winning his qualifying heat, raced off the track halfway through the final.

While Mamede was disappearing into the tunnel, Nick Rose of Great Britain was making the first significant move of an otherwise slow race. He opened a ten-meter lead, but was quickly hauled in by Martti Vainio and Cova. Vainio then ran away from the field—except for Cova, who tracked him relentlessly for two and one-half miles. The result seemed inevitable. With 200 meters to go, Cova shot past the tall Finn and pulled away to a 25-meter victory. The second 5000 meters of the race had been run in 13:27.71. Vainio was subsequently disqualified when his drug test turned up traces of an anabolic steroid.

One admirable characteristic of the audience at the 1984 track events was their tendency to vigorously applaud last-place finishers. One such also-ran was Basil Kilani of Jordan, who finished the first preliminary heat in 30 minutes and 43.54 seconds, almost two and one-half minutes behind Fernando Mamede. The crowd probably would have given Kilani an even bigger ovation had they realized that their support had helped Kilani improve his personal record by a surprising 2 minutes and 50 seconds.

1988 Seoul C: 52, N: 35, D: 9.26. WR: 27:13.81 (Fernando Mamede)
1. Moulay Brahim Boutaïb MOR   27:21.46   OR
2. Salvatore Antibo   ITA   27:23.55
3. Kipkemboi Kimeli   KEN   27:25.16
4. Jean-Louis Prianon   FRA   27:36.43
5. Arturo Barrios Flores MEX   27:39.32
6. Hansjörg Kunze   GDR   27:39.35
7. Paul Arpin   FRA   27:39.36
8. Moses Tanui   KEN   27:47.23

Sicilian Salvatore Antibo rattled the field by running the first 800 meters in 2:07.4. Moses Tanui surged into the lead at the 2000-meter mark, carrying Kipkemboi Kimeli and Antibo with him. They were joined, three laps later, by Brahim Boutaïb, a former protege of Saïd Aouita, who had broken away from his mentor only a month before the Olympics. The rest of the runners were already out of the race, 40 meters back. Kimeli reached the halfway point in world record pace: 13:35.32. Boutaïb was on his heels. Tanui trailed by 10 meters with Antibo another 10 meters behind. One lap later Boutaïb made his move. By the end of the next lap he had opened up a 10-meter lead, which he gradually expanded to 40 meters by the bell. He slowed to a walk before the end, stopping completely just after the finish line in order to embrace Antibo, who passed Kimeli in the final straight to take the silver. At 21 years of age, Boutaïb was the youngest winner in the event's history. When asked "Where do you go from here?" he replied, "What can you ask a flower that is just blooming?"

1992 Barcelona C: 56, N: 38, D: 8.3. WR: 27:08.23 (Arturo Barrios Flores)

1. Khalid Skah	MOR	27:46.70
2. Richard Chelimo	KEN	27:47.72
3. Addis Abebe	ETH	28:00.07
4. Salvatore Antibo	ITA	28:11.39
5. Arturo Barrios Flores	MEX	28:17.79
6. Germán Silva Martínez	MEX	28:20.19
7. William Koech	KEN	28:25.18
8. Moses Tanui	KEN	28:27.11

Running is the purest of Olympic sports. There are no judges rating performances, crushing an athlete's dream with their personal prejudices. There is no sophisticated equipment, providing wealthy nations with an insurmountable advantage. Track champions come from rich families and poór families, warm regions and cold regions, superpower nations and tiny nations. In running races, each athlete covers the same distance and whoever crosses the finish line first is the winner. The results are simple and clear cut—usually. The 1992 men's 10,000-meter final was one of those rare races that was an exception to the rule.

By the 1990s the world of the 10,000 meters was dominated by East Africans and Moroccans with an occasional Italian or Mexican thrown in. In 1991, for example, eight of the eleven fastest runners in the world were from Kenya alone. But the Kenyans had a problem: a cocky Moroccan from Fez by the name of Khalid Skah. Skah, whose name in Arabic means "runaway," was a complete unknown when he shocked the Kenyans by winning the 1990 World Cross-Country Championship. He defended his title in 1991. By the time of the 1991 World Championships in Athletics, the Kenyans knew they had to take special measures to defeat Skah. The night before the 10,000 meters final Kenya's national coach, Mike Kosgei, devised a race plan that would send Moses Tanui

and Richard Chelimo out front with a blistering pace, while Thomas Osano stayed behind to badger Skah, covering his spurts, passing him, slowing his pace and generally keeping the Moroccan occupied. The plan worked perfectly as Tanui and Chelimo finished first and second while Skah had to settle for third. At the post-race press conference, an angry Skah brashly predicted that the 5000-meter final would be different because in that race Skah would have other Moroccan runners to support him. But Kenya won that one too. The pattern was repeated at the 1992 World Cross-Country Championship as Skah was beaten back into fourth place. Morocco simply did not have enough talent to execute a team strategy against the Kenyans.

The Olympic final did not begin until after 10 p.m., but the temperature was still 85 degrees Fahrenheit (29 degrees centigrade). After a suitably slow start considering the hot and humid conditions, Chelimo and fellow Kenyan William Koech began to force the pace. By the 3000-meter mark only eight runners were still in contention. By 5000 meters Barrios and Antibo had lost contact; by 6000 meters so had Tanui and Fita Bayisa of Ethiopia. On the sixteenth lap, Addis Abebe and Koech fell back, leaving only Chelimo and Skah to fight it out for the last 3600 meters. During the 20th lap Skah took the lead for the first time and slowed the pace. He continued to lead for about 800 meters. Then, with about 1400 meters to go, things got a bit strange.

Skah and Chelimo had already lapped one runner, Jon Halvorsen of Norway. On the backstretch of the 22nd lap they encountered a second runner ready to be lapped: 36-year-old Hammou Boutayeb of Morocco. Unlike Halvorsen, Boutayeb was a surprising person to find in next to last place. In 1990 he had recorded the third-fastest time of the year and in 1991 he had placed eighth at the world championships. As they drew closer to Boutayeb, Skah drifted wide, allowing Chelimo to retake the lead. As Boutayeb did not move out to let the leaders pass, they went around him. Boutayeb kept pace with Chelimo and Skah, then, on the next backstretch, he accelerated and cut in front of Chelimo, forcing the Kenyan to alter his stride. Chelimo was now sandwiched between the two Moroccans, with Skah so close behind him that he was clipping his heels. What had been a two-man race turned into a three-man race.

Chelimo regained the "lead," but with 700 meters to go, Boutayeb cut in front of him again. By now the crowd of 63,525 had become enraged, and whistles and boos rained down on the Moroccan pair. Fifty meters before the bell, with Chelimo back in front and Boutayeb running beside him, Carl Gustaf Tollemar, chairman of the I.A.A.F. technical committee, stepped onto the track and tried to grab Boutayeb, who evaded his grasp.

Two hundred meters from the finish line, Boutayeb dropped out, while Skah passed Chelimo and sprinted for home, running the last half lap in 26.0 seconds. Chelimo stuck with him for 140 meters, but then gave

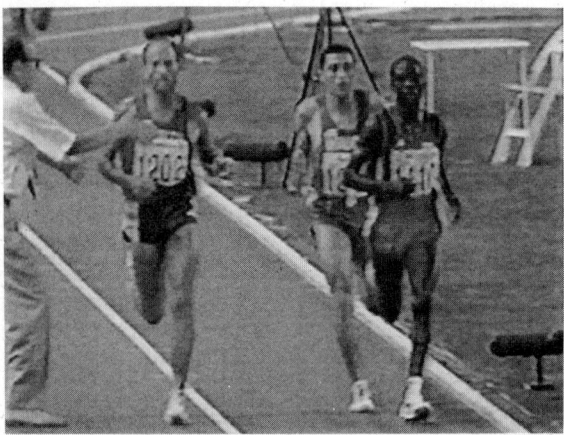

An Olympic official tries to stop Hammou Boutayeb during the controversial final laps of the 1992 10,000 meters.

way as Skah went on to win by about seven meters. Skah's victory lap was greeted by loud choruses of derision, not to mention soiled paper cups and other debris. Almost instantly the I.A.A.F. disqualified Skah and announced that Chelimo was the gold medal winner.

Skah was livid. He accused the Spanish race officials of being racists and thieves and even implied that unnamed U.S. officials had instigated his disqualification. He also had harsh words for Boutayeb, whom he accused of being "an animal, an imbecile" who didn't even know how to read or write. (Skah himself was the son of a professor of classical literature.) Skah's supporters maintained that he was an intellectual, a decent man who would never cheat or lie. "Why, he's a law student," said one U.S. television commentator, evidently unaware that most people consider lawyers and would-be lawyers *less* honest than most humans.

Perhaps it was Skah's lawyerly ambitions that helped him deal with some of the stickier aspects of the case. Chelimo claimed that Skah and Boutayeb had talked back and forth during the last three laps. At first Skah denied this. When video replays showed the two Moroccans exchanging words, Skah explained that he had been urging Boutayeb to go away and stop interfering. Skah also suggested that Boutayeb's actions were motivated by his fear of being humiliated as a result of being lapped by Skah, who was a member of a rival camp of runners in Morocco. He also postulated that Boutayeb might actually have been trying to help Chelimo. If Boutayeb was so proud, asked reporters, why did he fail to finish the race? The Moroccan team answer: because Skah had managed to convince him that he had been disqualified. In fact, Boutayeb was never disqualified. Boutayeb, for his part, had nothing to say to the press.

The Moroccan team immediately filed an appeal. Fourteen hours later an I.A.A.F. jury of appeal met to decide the case. Rule 143.2 of the I.A.A.F. handbook stated that "no competitor shall receive assistance during the progress of an event." Assistance was defined as including pacing by runners lapped or about to be lapped. The rulebook was specific about athletes who received assistance in field events—they should be cautioned after a first offense and debarred after a second—but no provision was made for penalties in running events. The jury of appeal, after viewing a videotape of the race, ruled that Chelimo's progress had not been physically impaired and voted unanimously to rescind the disqualification and reinstate Skah as the Olympic champion. Rule 143.2 was subsequently amended to include penalties for track athletes and for competitors who *give* assistance as well as those who receive it.

The Spanish crowd was not as forgiving as the I.A.A.F. They whistled and booed throughout the medal ceremony. It remains a mystery whether Boutayeb acted on his own on the spur of the moment or whether his actions were the result of a pre-race strategy concocted by the Moroccan team to gain revenge on the Kenyans. There seems little doubt though that Khalid Skah was simply the fastest man on the track that night. If Hammou Boutayeb had not been in the race, Skah still would have won.

MARATHON
(42,195 Meters—26 Miles 385 Yards)

The start and finish of the marathon may or may not take place within a stadium. The course should follow standard roads, although bicycle or footpaths are allowed. Refreshment stations must be provided every five kilometers. Competitors must not take refreshments between refreshment stations. However, water stations, to be used for drinking and sponging, must be provided between the refreshment stations. Any runner who receives outside assistance is automatically disqualified. An exception, added to the rules after 1984, allows a hands-on medical examination by designated medical personnel. If the official medical staff determines that an athlete is not fit to continue, the athlete must retire at once.

1896 Athens C: 17, N: 5, D: 4.10.
(40,000 Meters)

1.	Spiridon Louis	GRE	2:58:50
2.	Charilaos Vasilakos	GRE	3:06:03
3.	Gyula Kellner	HUN	3:09:35
4.	Ioannis Vrettos	GRE	—
5.	Elevtherios Papasimeon	GRE	—
6.	Demetrios Deligannis	GRE	—
7.	Evangelos Gerakakis	GRE	—
8.	Stamatios Massouris	GRE	—

The idea for a marathon race was inspired by the legend of Pheidippides, a professional runner who allegedly carried the news of the Greek victory over the Persians at the Battle of Marathon in 490 B.C. Upon his arrival in Athens, he called out, "Be joyful, we win!" and then dropped dead of exhaustion. Actually there is no evidence that this dramatic incident ever took place. The fifth century B.C. historian Herodotus, who thrived on such juicy tidbits, wrote about the Battle of Marathon, but made no mention of Pheidippides' feat. The story didn't appear in print until the second century A.D.— over 600 years after it was alleged to have occurred. The longest race to be included in the ancient Greek Olympics was only 4614 meters.

However, when meetings began to be held in 1894 to organize an international revival of the Olympics, Michel Bréal, a French linguist and historian, proposed that a long-distance race be included. He even offered to present a silver cup to the winner. Invoking the legend of Pheidippides, Bréal and Baron Pierre de Coubertin presented the idea to the Organizing Committee of the Athens Olympics. The Greeks, moved by the presumed historical importance associated with such a race, agreed immediately. Georgios Averoff, designer of the refurbished Panathenaic Stadium and the primary financial supporter of the Games, added an antique vase to the offer of Bréal's silver cup.

Before long, the marathon race had come to be considered the most important event of the upcoming games, and two preliminary races for Greeks were held along the proposed route from the Marathon Bridge to the stadium in Athens. The first race, on March 10, was won by Charilaos Vasilakos in 3:18:00. He was followed by Spiridon Belokas and Demetrios Deligannis. The second race was officially designated an Olympic trial and was contested by 38 runners. The winner was Ioannis Lavrentis, in 3:11:27. In fifth place was a young man of 24 years, from the village of Amarousion, named Spiridon Louis.

On the afternoon of Thursday, April 9, 17 runners were transported from Athens to an inn near the starting point of the race in Marathon. Among them were four foreigners, including the first three finishers in the 1500 meters: Edwin Flack, the London-based Australian accountant, who had won the 800 meters only a couple of hours earlier, Arthur Blake, and Albin Lermusiaux.

The next afternoon, the 17 entrants gathered on the Marathon Bridge and endured a preliminary speech by the starter, Major Papadiamantopoulos, who finally fired a gun to begin the race. There was much excitement among the Greek populace, and all along the route the runners were cheered by curious and enthusiastic peasants. Of the foreigners, only the Hungarian, Gyula Kellner, had ever run a race of such length, having qualified for the trip to Athens by running a 40-kilometer trial in Budapest. The other three set off relatively quickly and eventually paid for their inexperience. Lermusiaux set the early pace and soon built up a huge lead, which he carried past the halfway mark. At the village of Palini (Kharvati), the local people had built a triumphal arch. When Lermusiaux approached in first place, the villagers crowned him with a floral victor's wreath. By this time, Blake and four of the Greeks had already dropped out.

Shortly after Palini, there was an incline, and Lermusiaux began to stagger from exhaustion. A French companion, riding beside him on a bicycle, revived his countryman with an alcohol rubdown, but this delay allowed Flack to pass him and take the lead. Lermusiaux continued for some distance, but finally collapsed. Flack, who had never before run more than ten miles, had overextended himself in his attempt to catch Lermusiaux, and he too began to weave and sway four kilometers short of the stadium. Flack's companion, the British ambassador's butler, asked a nearby Greek to keep the Australian from falling over while he rushed off to get a wrap. The delirious Flack, thinking that he was being attacked, smashed the helpful Greek with his fist and knocked him to the ground. Flack was loaded into a carriage and driven to the dressing room at the stadium, where he was tended to by Prince Nicholas himself, and revived with a drink of egg and brandy.

As the race progressed, messengers were sent to the

Spiridon Louis, 1896.

stadium on horseback and bicycle to convey the identity of the leaders. The last news that the 100,000 spectators in and around the stadium heard was that Flack was in front, and their disappointment was great. Then Major Papadiamantopoulos entered the stadium on horseback and rushed to the royal box, where the king and queen and the rest of the royal family were anxiously awaiting the latest news. The word spread "with the rapidity of lightning," according to the Official Report of the Games. Shouts of *"Hellene! Hellene!"* ("A Greek! A Greek!") announced the joyous news that a Greek was in the lead. Then the Commissioner of Police appeared and formally announced what the growing roar of the crowd in the streets had already implied: the winner had arrived. At last, a small, dusty runner, Spiridon Louis, appeared at the marble entrance to the stadium. Prince George and Crown Prince Constantine rushed down to greet him and, one on each side, ran with him the rest of the way to the finish line, where Louis summoned enough energy to bow to the delighted King George. Louis was kissed and hugged and hauled off to the dressing room upon the shoulders of his admirers, while a collective ecstasy spread from the stadium throughout the city.

Seven minutes later, a second Greek, Charilaos Vasilakos, crossed the finish to be followed shortly by a third Greek, Spiridon Belokas. However, the fourth-place finisher, Gyula Kellner, raised a protest that Belokas had ridden part of the way in a carriage. Belokas admitted his deception, and was stripped of his awards, as well as his shirt, and thoroughly ostracized.

The story of Spiridon Louis is one of which legends are made. In fact, so many legends developed about Louis that it is difficult to sort out the truth. Was he a poor shepherd, a well-to-do farmer, a soldier, a post office messenger? Probably he was a shepherd who served in the army and became a messenger. A modest man, he appeared in the stadium the day after the race to accept his prize, but then returned quickly to his village, allowing journalists to invent whatever details they saw fit. Typical of the rumors that spread was that he had entered the race in hopes of convincing the king to grant clemency to his imprisoned brother—a romantic story that was deflated when it was learned that Louis didn't even have a brother. It is true that merchants throughout Athens tried to shower him with gifts, including watches, jewelry, wine, free haircuts, free clothing for life, free meals, free coffee for a year, monthly stipends, a shotgun, and a Singer sewing machine. Evidently, Louis graciously turned down all the offers except a horse and cart, which were needed to help transport water to his village.

Amazingly, Spiridon Louis managed to return to a relatively normal life. In 1936, however, he was rediscovered by the German Olympic Organizing Committee, which brought him to Berlin. There he presented a laurel wreath from the sacred grove at Olympia to Adolf Hitler. Louis died on March 27, 1940, but his name entered the Greek language in the expression *egine Louis*: "became Louis," or, ran quickly. More than any other single event, the victory of Spiridon Louis served as an inspiration to keep the Olympics going through the hard times that the movement faced over the next 12 years.

1900 Paris C: 13?, N: 5, D: 7.19.
(40,260 Meters)

1. Michel Théato	FRA/LUX	2:59:45
2. Emile Champion	FRA	3:04:17
3. Ernst Fast	SWE	3:37:14
4. Eugene Bessemar	FRA	4:00:43
5. Arthur Newton	USA	4:04:12
6. Richard Grant	USA	—
7. Ronald MacDonald	CAN	—

This unfortunate event was held in 102-degree Fahrenheit (39 degrees centigrade) heat. The course began in the Bois de Boulogne, followed the old city wall, and ended up back in the Bois. Only 7 of the runners were able to finish. Michel Théato, a 22-year-old baker's deliveryman, took the lead shortly after the halfway point and

never relinquished it. The details of this race are shrouded in myth. Apparently some members of the American contingent accused Théato of using the knowledge of Parisian streets that he had gained from his job to find shortcuts. There is no evidence to support this contention. In fact, one contemporary French account refers to Théato not as a baker's deliveryman, but as a "carpenter from Saint-Mandé."

1904 St. Louis C: 32, N: 5, D: 8.30.
(40,000 Meters)

1. Thomas Hicks	USA	3:28:53
2. Albert Corey	FRA	3:34:52
3. Arthur Newton	USA	3:47:33
4. Félix Carvajal de Soto	CUB	—
5. Demetrios Velouis	GRE	—
6. David Kneeland	USA	—
7. Henry Brawley	USA	—
8. Sidney Hatch	USA	—

The 1904 marathon ranks very high on the list of bizarre events in Olympic history. Among the more unusual entrants in the race was 5-foot-tall Félix Carvajal, a Cuban mail carrier, who raised the money for his trip to St. Louis by staging exhibitions in Havana. He took a boat to the United States and got as far as New Orleans, where he lost the rest of his savings in a crap game. After hitchhiking to St. Louis, he arrived on the starting line wearing heavy street shoes, long trousers, a long-sleeved shirt, and a beret. The start of the race was delayed while Martin Sheridan, the discus thrower, cut off Carvajal's pants at the knees. Also entered were the first two black Africans to participate in the Olympics: Lentauw and Yamasani, Zulu tribesmen who were in St. Louis as part of the Boer War exhibit at the Louisiana Purchase Exposition. Another foreign contestant was Albert Corey, a professional strikebreaker, who had arrived in Chicago in 1903 during a butchers' strike and stayed around, since there was never a shortage of business for him in the Windy City.

Among the American entrants were Sam Mellor, winner of the 1902 Boston Marathon; John Lordon, winner of the 1903 Boston Marathon; Michael Spring, winner of the 1904 Boston Marathon; Thomas Hicks, who had finished second at Boston in 1904; and Arthur Newton, who had finished fifth in Paris in 1900.

Unfortunately, the organizers of the race knew almost nothing about staging such an event. The course included seven hills and was run on dusty roads, made dustier by the many automobiles, which the judges, doctors, and journalists used to follow—and lead—the runners. The brutal nature of the contest was made worse by the fact that it was scheduled for the middle of the afternoon in 90-degree Fahrenheit (32 degrees centigrade) heat. In addition, the only water available to the runners was from a well located 12 miles from the stadium, where the race began and ended.

With all these obstacles in their path, it is not surpris-

The one and only Félix Carvajal. Financing his own trip from Cuba, he lost all his money in a crap game in New Orleans. He hitchhiked to St. Louis and arrived at the starting line wearing long pants and heavy shoes. The start of the race was delayed while a sympathetic U.S. athlete cut off Carvajal's pants at the knees.

Lentauw and Yamasani, the first black Africans to compete in the Olympics. They happened to be in St. Louis as part of the Boer War exhibit at the World's Fair and decided to enter the marathon race.

ing that only 14 of the 32 starters made it back to the finish line. John Lordon, for example, began vomiting after ten miles and had to withdraw. William Garcia of San Francisco was discovered lying unconscious by the side of the road. Sam Mellor, the leader at the halfway mark, finally gave up after 16 miles. Meanwhile, Lentauw lost a great deal of valuable time when he was chased off the course and through a cornfield by two large dogs. He still managed to finish ninth. The only runner who didn't seem bothered by all these catastrophes was Félix Carvajal, who stopped a number of times to chat with bystanders, discuss the progress of the race, and practice his English. He also quenched his thirst by snatching a couple of peaches from an official in one of the cars, and by raiding a farmer's orchard of some green apples. The latter detour caused him an attack of stomach cramps.

Back in the stadium, the spectators were unaware of all that had transpired, although the more knowledgeable sports fans may have wondered why three hours had passed without any of the runners showing up. Finally, after 3 hours and 13 minutes, Fred Lorz of New York appeared, and was immediately hailed as the winner. He had already been photographed with Alice Roosevelt, the daughter of the President of the United States, and was about to be awarded the gold medal, when it was discovered that he had actually stopped running after 9 miles, hitched a ride in a car for 11 miles, and then started running again. Lorz readily admitted his practical joke, but A.A.U. officials were not amused, and he was

slapped with a lifetime ban. However, he was reinstated well before the ban ran out and managed to win the Boston Marathon of 1905.

The real winner of the 1904 Olympic marathon was Thomas Hicks, an English-born brass worker from Cambridge, Massachusetts. If present-day rules had been enforced, however, he would have been disqualified. Second at the halfway point, Hicks found himself in front after Sam Mellor collapsed. Ten miles from the finish Hicks begged to be allowed to lie down, but his handlers wouldn't allow it, even though he had a lead of one and a half miles. Instead they administered to him an oral dose of strychnine sulfate mixed with raw egg white. A few miles later he was given more strychnine, as well as some brandy. He was also bathed with water made warm by being kept next to the boiler of the steam-powered automobile that accompanied him.

Hicks was forced to slow to a walk when faced with a final, steep hill two miles from the stadium, but a couple

Thomas Hicks, the winner of the St. Louis marathon, visibly under the influence of the strychnine and brandy that was administered to him during the course of the race.

more doses of strychnine and brandy revived him enough to win the race by six minutes. Needless to say, Hicks was in something of a stupor afterward. He had lost ten pounds during the afternoon, and gladly announced his retirement. When he had finally recovered, he told reporters, "I would rather have won this race than be President of the United States." The athletes who suffered through the 1904 marathon may have received some satisfaction when they learned that two of the officials in charge of patrolling the course were badly injured as well, when their brand-new car swerved to avoid one of the runners and careened down an embankment.

1906 Athens C: 53, N: 15, D: 5.1.
(41,860 Meters)

1. William Sherring	CAN	2:51:23.6
2. John Svanberg	SWE	2:58:20.8
3. William Frank	USA	3:00:46.8
4. Gustaf Törnros	SWE	3:01:00.0
5. John Alepous	GRE	3:09:25.4
6. George Blake	AUS	3:09:35.0
7. Constantinos Karvelas	GRE	3:15:54.0
8. André Roffi	FRA	3:17:49.8

There was great excitement in Athens when it was learned that another Olympic-style marathon would be held. Local merchants offered the winner a statue of Her-

mes, a loaf of bread every day for a year, three coffees a day for a year, free shaves for life, and a free lunch for six every Sunday for a year—but only if the winner was a Greek.

Billy Sherring of Hamilton, Ontario, had other ideas. Convinced he could win, he gathered his savings from his job as a railway brakeman, but they weren't enough to pay his way to Greece. A local athletic club raised an extra $75, but it still wasn't enough. In desperation, Sherring turned over the $75 to a friendly bartender, who bet the money on a horse named Cicely, who won and paid 6-1 odds. At last Billy Sherring was able to travel to Athens. He arrived two months early and took a job as a railway station porter, training every other day. On March 17, the Greeks staged a trial run that was won in 3:04:29.6. Sherring watched with pleasure, knowing that he had covered the same course, in secret, 20 minutes faster.

When the big day finally came, George Blake of Australia took the early lead. After four miles he was passed by William Frank of New York, who led for three miles before Blake regained the lead. Blake faded, however, and after 15 miles he was passed by Sherring and Frank. The two ran together for three more miles, at which point Sherring turned to Frank and said, "Well, goodbye, Billy." Then he took off and built up such a large lead that he was able to walk part of the way to the finish.

There was great disappointment in the Olympic Stadium when the news spread that the leader was not a Greek. However, when Sherring passed through the marble entrance, he was met by Prince George, who applauded him and ran with him around the track to the finish line, where Sherring bowed to the king, just as Spiridon Louis had done ten years earlier. Billy Sherring had weighed 135 pounds when he left Canada. By the morning of the race he was down to 112, and by the end of the race he had evaporated to 98 pounds. Sherring didn't receive all the goodies that had been offered a Greek winner, but he was presented with a three-foot statue of Athena and a young lamb. Back in Canada he did much better. The city of Hamilton gave him a purse of $5,000, while the city of Toronto chipped in $400.

One runner who was overlooked in 1906 was a 20-year-old Italian who developed stomach problems and dropped out after 24 kilometers. His name was Dorando Pietri. Before the decade was out, he would become a living legend.

1908 London C: 56, N: 16, D: 7.24.

1. John Hayes	USA	2:55:18.4	OR
2. Charles Hefferon	SAF	2:56:06.0	
3. Joseph Forshaw	USA	2:57:10.4	
4. Alton Welton	USA	2:59:44.4	
5. William Wood	CAN	3:01:44.0	
6. Frederick Simpson	CAN	3:04:28.2	
7. Harry Lawson	CAN	3:06:47.2	
8. John Svanberg	SWE	3:07:50.8	
DISQ: Dorando Pietri (ITA) 2:54:46.4			

July 24, 1908, dawned hot (by English standards) and muggy. The talk of the town was the bitter hostilities that had erupted between the British and the Americans following the controversial running of the 400 meters final the previous day. People had been looking forward to the marathon race with great anticipation, and a large crowd lined the 26-mile route from Windsor Castle to the Olympic Stadium in Shepherd's Bush. The race was scheduled to conclude with 385 yards around the stadium track, so that the finish line would be directly in front of the royal box of Queen Alexandra. As it happened, this random distance of 26 miles and 385 yards would later become the standardized length for marathon races.

The first 26 miles of the 1908 marathon were actually quite exciting, although they were quickly forgotten as a result of the extraordinary incidents that occurred during the final 385 yards. The British runners, under great pressure to perform well, started off at far too fast a clip and later paid the price of their folly. Thomas Jack of Scotland led for the first five miles, but quickly exhausted himself. Fred Lord and Jack Price took his place in front. Lord began to fade after ten miles. At the halfway mark at Ruislip, Price led by 200 yards. Charles Hefferon had moved into second place, followed by Lord and Dorando Pietri. The American entrants, at this point, were calmly running their own race, unruffled by the fast pace of the leaders.

Shortly after the 14-mile mark, Hefferon passed Price, who dropped out not long after. Lord also began to fade, eventually finishing 15th. The well-known Onondaga Indian Tom Longboat, of Toronto, who had been one of the favorites, came up to challenge, but he too fell back, slowing to a walk and then retiring completely.

By the 18-mile mark, it appeared that only Hefferon and Pietri (or Dorando, as he became better known) had a chance for the gold medal. Hefferon led by 3 minutes 18 seconds. By 20 miles he had built up a lead of 3 minutes 52 seconds, but then Dorando began to close the gap. Two miles from the stadium, the exhausted Hefferon made a crucial mistake. He accepted a drink of champagne and, within a mile, he had developed stomach cramps and become dizzy. Dorando also committed a major tactical blunder. Urged on by the well-meaning but overzealous crowd, he picked up his pace too early. Meanwhile, Americans John Hayes, Joseph Forshaw, and Alton Welton were drawing closer.

The spectators lining the route, having inadvertently damaged Dorando's chances for victory, now did the same to Hefferon. Hoping to boost his spirits, they slapped him on the back so many times that they sapped him of what little energy he had left. A mile from the entrance to the stadium, he was passed by Dorando.

The last report that had been received inside the stadium was that South Africa and Italy were in the lead. All eyes were on the entrance as Dorando Pietri, a small man from the small town of Carpi, near Modena, made his appearance. However, it immediately became obvious that something was wrong. Dorando appeared dazed and headed off in the wrong direction. Track officials rushed to his aid and pointed him the right way. But after going only a few yards, he collapsed on the track. The audience, which had never before seen or heard of Dorando, immediately became sympathetic. While many people screamed for the officials to help him, others, knowing that such aid would automatically disqualify the plucky Italian, called out to leave him alone. However, in the words of the official report, "It was impossible to leave him there, for it looked as if he might die in the very presence of the Queen . . ." Doctors and officials rushed to help him, and Dorando managed to struggle to his feet and plod on, only to fall again. And again and again. By this time, a second runner had arrived on the track. However, much to the horror of the spectators, he was not Charles Hefferon, a good man of the Empire, but an American, 5-foot 4-inch John Hayes, who had breezed past Hefferon 20 yards before the stadium grounds.

This was too much for the British officials. When Dorando started to collapse for a fifth time, just short of the finish, Jack Andrew, the head organizer of the race, caught him and carried him across the line. The Italian flag was immediately run up the victory pole, even as Hayes, still in good shape, crossed the finish himself. The Americans wasted no time in lodging a protest, and while Dorando, who had been carried away on a stretcher, lay seemingly on the verge of death, the protest was allowed and Hayes was declared the winner.

Remarkably, Dorando was back on his feet the next day, complaining that the British officials should have left him alone and that he could have finished without their assistance. However, photos of the incident make it quite clear that this was highly unlikely, and that the stretcher probably should have been called for the first time he fell. At any rate, Dorando showed up at the stadium the day after the race and was presented with a special gold cup by the Queen. Overnight he became an international celebrity. Even in the United States, songs were written about him, including one by Irving Berlin. Unfortunately, Berlin completely missed the point of what had happened, entitling his song "Dorando He'sa Gooda for Not" and portraying the courageous Italian as a "bigga de flop."

Somewhat lost in the excitement was the actual winner, John Hayes, a 22-year-old clerk at Bloomingdale's department store in New York City. Hayes, who had prepared for the big race by resting in bed for two days, had finished fifth in the 1906 Boston Marathon and third in 1907, before winning the 1907 Yonkers Marathon on Thanksgiving Day. Mr. Bloomingdale himself had taken a liking to Hayes, and ordered the construction of a cinder path on the roof of his store so that Hayes could train during his breaks. When Hayes was chosen for the Olympic team, Bloomingdale gave him a full vacation with pay, and when he won the gold medal, Hayes was promoted to manager of the sporting goods department.

Dorando Pietri collapses within sight of the finish of the 1908 marathon. This photo puts to rest Dorando's contention that he could have completed the course unaided if meddlesome British officials had not interfered with him.

But this job was not to last long. Dorando's sensational effort in London had set off a marathon craze that swept around the world. He and Hayes were offered very good money to turn professional. Both of them did, and they each built up a good deal of capital running scores of races over the next couple of years, far more than Hayes could have earned at Bloomingdale's or than Dorando could have earned back in Carpi. The most notable contests were two match races between Hayes and Dorando held in New York City on November 25, 1908, and March 15, 1909, both of which were won by the Italian. Between 1904 and 1911 Dorando competed in 128 long-distance races and won 88 of them. Dorando, whose opportunistic brother ran off with his fortune, lived out his life driving a taxi in Italy. He also received a stipend from the Italian government for scouting promising marathon runners.

1912 Stockholm C: 68, N: 19, D: 7.14. WB: 2:42:31.0 (Frederick "Harry" Barrett)
(40,200 Meters)

1. Kenneth McArthur	SAF	2:36:54.8
2. Christian Gitsham	SAF	2:37:52.0
3. Gaston Strobino	USA	2:38:42.4
4. Andrew Sockalexis	USA	2:42:07.9
5. James Duffy	CAN	2:42:18.8
6. Sigfrid "Sigge" Jacobsson	SWE	2:43:24.9
7. John Gallagher	USA	2:44:19.4
8. Joseph Erxleben	USA	2:45:47.4

Once again, the Olympic marathon was held on an oppressively hot day that caused half of the runners to retire before the finish. Tatu Kolehmainen, the older brother of Hannes, took the lead before three miles had been covered, and held it until just before the turnaround point, when he was passed by Gitsham. McArthur was third, followed by Fred Lord. After 17 miles, Gitsham and Kolehmainen were running together, with McArthur only a meter or two behind. Two or three miles later, Kolehmainen was forced to retire, and the two South Africans went on alone. Two miles from the stadium they reached a refreshment stand, and Gitsham stopped to take a drink of water. McArthur had said he would wait for his teammate, but instead he kept on going, opening up a lead that Gitsham was unable to close. McArthur was born at Dervock in County Antrim, Ireland, on February 10, 1880. The son of a farmer, he worked as a postman, often running his entire 15-mile daily round. He emigrated to South Africa in 1905 and became a policeman. After his Olympic victory, McArthur went back to Dervock, where thousands of people traveled from all over the countryside to honor him. Upon his return to South Africa, the town council of Potchefstroom presented him with a piece of land, and it was there that he died 48 years later.

The 1912 marathon was marred by a sad note. The 21-year-old Portuguese runner Francisco Lazaro collapsed from sunstroke and heart trouble toward the end of the race and was taken to a hospital, where he died the following day. He was the first of only two athletes to die as a result of their participation in the Olympics.

1920 Antwerp C: 48, N: 17, D: 8.22. WB: 2:36:06:6 (Alexis Ahlgren)
(42,750 Meters)

1. Johan "Hannes" Kolehmainen	FIN	2:32:35.8	WB
2. Jüri Lossmann	EST	2:32:48.6	
3. Valerio Arri	ITA	2:36:32.8	
4. Auguste Broos	BEL	2:39:25.8	
5. Juho Tuomikoski	FIN	2:40:18.8	
6. Sofus Rose	DEN	2:41:18.0	
7. Joseph Organ	USA	2:41:30.0	
8. Rudolf Hansen	DEN	2:41:39.4	

At last the Olympic marathon was contested on a cool day, and the runners responded with excellent times, particularly considering that the course was longer than ever before. Christian Gitsham took the early lead, but after 15 kilometers he was joined by Hannes Kolehmainen, who had returned from Brooklyn to compete for Finland. They reached the turnaround together, but after 27 kilometers, Kolehmainen moved ahead and began to draw away. Gitsham, suffering from foot trouble after one of his shoes tore open, retired after 35 kilometers. Meanwhile, Jüri Lossmann of Estonia closed the gap that separated him from the famous Finn, but Kolehmainen managed to hold on to his lead and win by 70 yards—the closest marathon finish in Olympic history.

In direct contrast to previous marathons, the runners finished in good health. Valerio Arri, the Italian champion, even celebrated his bronze medal by performing three cartwheels as soon as he crossed the finish line.

1924 Paris C: 58, N: 20, D: 7.13. WB: 2:32:35.8 (Johan "Hannes" Kolehmainen)

1. Albin Stenroos	FIN	2:41:22.6
2. Romeo Bertini	ITA	2:47:19.6
3. Clarence DeMar	USA	2:48:14.0
4. Lauri Halonen	FIN	2:49:47.4
5. Samuel Ferris	GBR	2:52:26.0
6. Miguel Plaza Reyes	CHI	2:52:54.0
7. M. Boughèra El Ouafi	FRA/ALG	2:54:19.6
8. Gustav Kinn	SWE	2:54:33.4

Albin Stenroos, a 35-year-old woodworker, had won a bronze medal in the 1912 10,000 meters race. However he did not run a single marathon between 1909 and May 18, 1924, when he placed second in the Finnish Olympic trial. In Paris, he passed G. Verger of France after 19½ kilometers, and steadily drew away to a huge lead, winning by almost six minutes. Silver medalist Romeo Bertini was 31 years old, while bronze medalist Clarence DeMar was 36. In 1930 DeMar won his seventh Boston Marathon at the age of 42. In the 1924 Olympics, 28 of the 58 starters failed to finish the course.

1928 Amsterdam C: 68, N: 23, D: 8.5. WB: 2:29:01.8 (Albert Michelsen)

1. M. Boughèra El Ouafi	FRA/ALG	2:32:57
2. Miguel Plaza Reyes	CHI	2:33:23
3. Martti Marttelin	FIN	2:35:02
4. Kanematsu Yamada	JPN	2:35:29
5. Joie Ray	USA	2:36:04
6. Seiichiro Tsuda	JPN	2:36:20
7. Yrjo Korholin-Koski	FIN	2:36:40
8. Samuel Ferris	GBR	2:37:41

M. Boughèra El Ouafi, 1928.

The lead changed several times during the first half of the race, with Joie Ray in first place at the turnaround. Shortly thereafter he was passed by Yamada and Tsuda. These three remained in front past 30 kilometers. By this time two outsiders, Algerian-born Boughèra El Ouafi and Miguel Plaza of Chile, had moved up to challenge. Plaza had evidently decided to run the race on El Ouafi's shoulder, just as he had four years earlier. Three kilometers short of the finish they had taken over second and third place, finally wearing down Yamada during the approach to the stadium. Both El Ouafi and Plaza finished strongly, with El Ouafi winning by about 150 meters. The victor was a former member of the French Colonial Army who had settled in Paris and was employed as an automobile mechanic. Twenty-eight years later, when another Algerian-born Frenchman, Alain Mimoun, won the Olympic marathon, journalists sought out El Ouafi and discovered him unemployed and living in poverty in Paris. French sportsmen got together a fund to help the forgotten hero of Amsterdam. However, three years later, on October 18, 1959, El Ouafi was shot to death while sitting in a café. He was 61 years old.

1932 Los Angeles C: 29, N: 15, D: 8.7. WB: 2:29:01.8 (Albert Michelsen)

1. Juan Carlos Zabala	ARG	2:31:36	OR
2. Samuel Ferris	GBR	2:31:55	
3. Armas Toivonen	FIN	2:32:12	
4. Duncan McLeod Wright	GBR	2:32:41	
5. Seiichiro Tsuda	JPN	2:35:42	
6. Kim Eun-bae	JPN/KOR	2:37:28	
7. Albert Michelsen	USA	2:39:38	
8. Oskar Heks	CZE	2:41:35	

Paavo Nurmi had been considered the favorite to win the 1932 marathon, until he was suspended by the I.A.A.F. one week before the race for accepting payments in excess of his expenses during an exhibition tour. Juan Carlos Zabala, a 20-year-old Argentinian, had set a world record at 30,000 meters in 1931. On June 25, 1932, the *Los Angeles Times* sponsored a marathon race over the Olympic course. Zabala built up an eight-and-a-half-minute lead in that race, but developed foot problems and was ordered to withdraw by his trainer. Albert Michelsen went on to win.

Zabala took the early lead in the Olympics. He was passed briefly by Margarito Baños of Mexico, but regained the lead and held it for over 30 kilometers. At the 31-kilometer mark, Lauri Virtanen, who had already finished third in the 10,000 and 5000, sprinted ahead suddenly and opened up a 300-meter gap. This shook up the field, and there was much jockeying for position. Duncan Wright, following a well-laid-out British plan, forged to the front after 20 miles (35.5 kilometers), and as Virtanen faded, he moved a full minute ahead of Zabala, with Toivonen another half-minute further back. By 37 kilometers, Virtanen had dropped out and Wright had begun to fade. Zabala moved back into the lead, and Sam Ferris,

taking over second place, took off after him. But he had waited too long. Zabala entered the Coliseum with a one-minute lead and was almost three quarters of the way around the track when Ferris appeared, followed closely by Toivonen and Wright. Thus, the crowd was treated to the rare spectacle of the first four finishers of the marathon being on the track at the same time. Zabala struggled across the finish line and then collapsed, whereas Ferris was still full of strength and probably would have won had the race continued for an extra half lap.

1936 Berlin C: 56, N: 27, D: 8.9. WB: 2:26:42.0 (Sohn Kee-chung)

1. Sohn Kee-chung	JPN/KOR	2:29:19.2	OR
2. Ernest Harper	GBR	2:31:23.2	
3. Nam Seung-yong	JPN/KOR	2:31:42.0	
4. Erkki Tamila	FIN	2:32:45.0	
5. Väinö Muinonen	FIN	2:33:46.0	
6. Johannes Coleman	SAF	2:36:17.0	
7. Donald Robertson	GBR	2:37:06.2	
8. Henry Gibson	SAF	2:38:04.0	

On November 3, 1935, Sohn Kee-chung of Korea set a world marathon record of 2:26:42.0. Because Korea was, at the time, occupied by Japanese forces, Sohn's hopes for competing in the Olympics depended on his ability to qualify for the Japanese team. This he accomplished, as did fellow Korean Nam Seung-yong. Both young men were forced to endure the further insult of adopting Japanese names. Sohn, a fervent nationalist, always signed his Korean name in Berlin, and whenever he was asked where he was from, he made it a point to explain that Korea was a separate nation which was currently a victim of Japanese imperialism.

Defending champion Juan Carlos Zabala had arrived in Berlin months in advance, and during his period of extended training had become a local favorite, particularly in the absence of a serious German threat in the marathon. As usual, Zabala tore into the lead and was 30 seconds in front at the four-kilometer mark. After 15 kilometers he was ahead by 1 minute and 40 seconds. He let the margin slip to 50 seconds at the turnaround, but pumped it back up to 90 seconds after 25 kilometers. For quite some time, Zabala had been followed by Sohn and 34-year-old Ernest Harper, who had been running together since the beginning. However, it came as a shock to Zabala when, after 28 kilometers, he was suddenly passed, first by Sohn and, ten meters later, by Harper. Zabala fell, got up, struggled on for four more kilometers, and then retired. Meanwhile, Sohn pulled away and won by over two minutes. Harper finished heroically, holding off the fast-closing Nam despite a bad blister that had filled one of his shoes with blood.

At the medal ceremony Sohn was forced to endure the humiliation of having his victory celebrated by the raising of the Japanese flag and by the playing of the Japanese national anthem. Both Sohn and Nam registered a silent protest by bowing their heads. Interviewed by the press afterwards, Sohn used the opportunity to educate the world about the plight of his nation. Few reporters were interested, and most seemed relieved when he turned to the race itself. "The human body can do so much," he said. "Then the heart and spirit must take over."

Back in Korea, however, Sohn was a national hero. One newspaper, *Dong-a-Ilbo,* published a wire-service photograph of Sohn on the victory platform—but with one alteration: they painted over the Japanese flag on his sweatshirt. The Japanese colonial government responded by jailing eight people connected with the paper and suspending its publication for nine months.

In 1948 Sohn was given the honor of carrying the South Korean flag in the Opening Ceremony of the London Olympics, the first to be attended by an independent Korea. Forty years later, in a moment that brought tears to an entire nation, Sohn Kee-chung entered the Seoul Olympic Stadium bearing the Olympic torch. The 76-year-old Sohn bounded around the track, leaping for joy and bursting with pride for himself and for his country.

1948 London C: 41, N: 21, D: 8.7. WB: 2:25:39.0 (Suh Yun-bok)
1. Delfo Cabrera   ARG   2:34:51.6
2. Thomas Richards   GBR   2:35:07.6
3. Etienne Gailly   BEL   2:35:33.6
4. Johannes Coleman   SAF   2:36:06.0
5. Eusebio Guiñez   ARG   2:36:36.0
6. Thomas Sidney Luyt   SAF   2:38:11.0
7. Gustav Ostling   SWE   2:38:40.6
8. John Systad   NOR   2:38:41.0

Twenty-five-year-old Etienne Gailly, running his first race longer than 32.5 kilometers, was in the lead by the ten-kilometer post and had opened up a 41-second gap by 25 kilometers, at which point he was followed by Guinez, Ostling, and Cabrera. The field then began to close in on him, and after 32.5 kilometers he was passed by Choi Yoon-chil of Korea. At 35 kilometers, Choi led by 28 seconds, with Delfo Cabrera, a 29-year-old fireman also running his first marathon, in second place. Gailly was third and Guinez fourth.

But Choi had used up all his energy and soon retired. Five thousand meters from Wembley Stadium, Cabrera led Gailly by five seconds. Tom Richards, a 38-year-old Welsh nurse, had moved into third place. Gailly gathered his strength and regained the lead. A half mile from the stadium, he led Cabrera by 50 yards and Richards by 100. The exhausted Belgian was the first to enter the stadium, but by now he was barely running. Spectators were immediately reminded of the ordeal endured by Dorando Pietri the last time the Olympics had been held in London. Gailly managed to stay on his feet, but before he had covered 100 yards of the track, he was passed by Cabrera and then by Richards. Gailly staggered on, almost collapsing 60 yards short of his goal. But he did finally cross the finish line and gain a well-earned bronze medal, much to the relief of the sympathetic crowd. In fourth place was 38-year-old Johannes Coleman, who had finished sixth in the last Olympics 12 years earlier.

Delfo Cabrera, 1948.

1952 Helsinki C: 66, N: 32, D: 7.27. WB: 2:20:42.2 (James Peters)
1. Emil Zátopek   CZE   2:23:03.2   OR
2. Reinaldo Gorno   ARG   2:25:35.0
3. Gustav Jansson   SWE   2:26:07.0
4. Choi Yoon-chil   KOR   2:26:36.0
5. Veikko Karvonen   FIN   2:26:41.8
6. Delfo Cabrera   ARG   2:26:42.4
7. József Dobronyi   HUN   2:28:04.8
8. Erkki Puolakka   FIN   2:29:35.0

Emil Zátopek was born in Koprivnice, Northern Moravia, on September 19, 1922, the exact same day that his wife, Dana, was born. He made his first appearance in the Olympics in 1948, finishing first in the 10,000 meters and second at 5000. Whenever he ran, his face was always contorted by a grimace, and his shoulders and body looked hunched with pain. Observers, on first viewing Zátopek, were sure that he was on the verge of collapse, but it turned out that that was just his style. Years later Zátopek was asked about this idiosyncrasy. He replied, "I was not talented enough to run and smile at the same time."

In 1952 Zátopek became the first runner since Hannes Kolehmainen to win both the 5000- and 10,000-meter races. But that wasn't enough for Zátopek. He decided to attempt an unprecedented triple by also competing in the marathon. The fact that he had never run a marathon before bothered him only slightly. He wasn't concerned about coming up with the necessary endurance, but it did worry him a bit that there might be pacing strategies with which he was not familiar. With this in mind, Zátopek decided to run along with the man whom he considered to be the favorite in the race—Jim Peters of Great Britain, who had run the fastest marathon in history only six weeks earlier. Zátopek took note of Peters' running number in the newspaper, and the next day he located Peters on the starting line and introduced himself.

Peters took off at what seemed to be an outlandish pace, but Zátopek, as well as Gustaf Jansson, kept contact with him. After 15 kilometers Zátopek and Jansson caught up with Peters, and the three ran together for a couple of miles. Then Zátopek turned to Peters and said, in English, "The pace? Is it good enough?" Peters, who had exhausted himself with his early running, pretended that he was still fresh, and replied, "Pace too slow." Zátopek mulled this over for a few moments and then said, "You say, 'too slow.' Are you sure the pace is too slow?" "Yes," came the reply. They continued on in silence for a short while, and then Zátopek zipped by Peters, taking Jansson with him.

They passed the turnaround together, with Peters ten seconds behind. Now Zátopek had to deal with Jansson. "He stopped at one feeding station," Zátopek later recalled, "and picked up a slice of lemon to suck. I was not so sure. I had never taken anything before in racing or training. But I thought, 'If he runs well, at the next feeding station I will take *two* lemons.' " Instead, Jansson began to fade. After 20 miles Peters developed a leg cramp and dropped out. By this time Zátopek had shaken off Jansson completely, and he was able to continue alone, chatting amiably with policemen, spectators, and cyclists along the route. He entered the stadium far ahead of the other runners. The huge crowd greeted him as the hero of the 1952 Games, chanting "Zá-to-pek, Zá-to-pek," as he completed the final lap. The Jamaican 4 × 400-meter relay team hoisted him on their shoulders and carried him around the field. Zátopek was already signing autographs by the time the next runner, the surprising Reinaldo Gorno, arrived. Zátopek greeted him at the finish line with a slice of orange.

Despite his convincing victory, Zátopek later said, "I was unable to walk for a whole week after that, so much

did the race take out of me. But it was the most pleasant exhaustion I have ever known."

Emil Zátopek also entered the Olympic marathon in 1956. But six weeks before the Games he had developed a hernia while trying to train with his wife on his shoulders. His doctors told him not to run for two months after his operation, but instead he resumed training the day after he left the hospital. Under the circumstances, his sixth-place finish could hardly be considered a failure.

Zátopek had been a member of the Czech army since 1944. His athletic successes gained him promotion to the rank of lieutenant-colonel, as well as a prominent position in the Communist Party. However, Emil Zátopek was not really a party man. In 1968 he signed the *2000 Words Manifesto,* which supported the establishment of freedom in Czechoslovakia. When Soviet tanks moved in and crushed the growing democratic movement in Czechoslovakia, Zátopek was expelled from both the army and the Communist Party. The only work he could find was a construction job, digging ditches and hauling sacks of cement for a geological survey team. Seven years later, the Ministry of Sport, taking advantage of his facility with languages, hired him as a "sports spy," translating sports periodicals in a search for tips from foreign coaches. He served in this capacity until his retirement in 1982.

Emil Zátopek has left an indelible impression on the world of sports that goes beyond his four gold medals and 18 world records. Unlike his predecessor Paavo Nurmi, Zátopek was greatly loved by his fellow competitors, as well as by all those who have had the good fortune to meet him personally.

1956 Melbourne C: 46, N: 23, D: 12.1. WB: 2:17:39.4 (James Peters)

1. Alain Mimoun	FRA	2:25:00
2. Franjo Mihalič	YUG	2:26:32
3. Veikko Karvonen	FIN	2:27:47
4. Lee Chang-hoon	KOR	2:28:45
5. Yoshiaki Kawashima	JPN	2:29:19
6. Emil Zátopek	CZE	2:29:34
7. Ivan Filin	SOV	2:30:27
8. Evert Nyberg	SWE	2:31:12

Thirty-five-year-old Algerian-born Alain Mimoun had made a habit of finishing second to Emil Zátopek—three times in the Olympics and twice in the European championships. But he was sure that December 1, 1956, would be his lucky day. Frenchmen had won the Olympic marathon in 1900, and then 28 years later in 1928. Now, 28 more years had passed. In addition, Mimoun was wearing what he considered to be the lucky number 13. As if these weren't enough good omens, he had just learned that he had become a father.

For the first time in Olympic history, there was a false start in the marathon. Mimoun stayed with the leading group for the first half of the race. Then he surged forward during an uphill segment before the turnaround. By the 25-kilometer mark he had opened a 50-second gap, and no one came close to him again. For the third time in a row, the Olympic marathon had been won by a converted track star competing in his first marathon.

At the finish line Mimoun waited for his old friend Emil Zátopek, who trotted home in a trance four and a half minutes later. "Emil," he asked, "why don't you congratulate me? I am an Olympic champion. It was I who won." Zátopek snapped out of his trance, took off his cap, saluted Mimoun, and then embraced him. "For me," Mimoun recalled, "that was better than the medal."

Surprisingly, Mimoun's marathon career had only just begun. He proceeded to win the French championship six times, the last in 1966, when he was 42 years old. At the age of 51, Mimoun completed the 26-mile, 385-yard race in a time of 2:34:36.2. In the 38 years after his Olympic triumph, 38 French sports centers were named in his honor.

1960 Rome C: 69, N: 35, D: 9.10. WB: 2:15:17.0 (Sergei Popov)

1. Abebe Bikila	ETH	2:15:16.2	WB
2. Rhadi Ben Abdesselem	MOR	2:15:41.6	
3. Barry Magee	NZE	2:17:18.2	
4. Konstantin Vorobyev	SOV/RUS	2:19:09.6	
5. Sergei Popov	SOV/RUS	2:19:18.8	
6. Thyge Tögersen	DEN	2:21:03.4	
7. Abebe Wakgira	ETH	2:21:10.0	
8. Bakir Benaissa	MOR	2:21:22.0	

The 1960 Olympic marathon was the first to be run at night, the first to start and end outside the stadium, and, as it turned out, the first to be won by a black African. After 18 kilometers, two men pulled away from the field: Rhadi Ben Abdesselem, who was one of the favorites, and barefooted Abebe Bikila, who was not. A member of the Ethiopian Imperial Bodyguard, the 28-year-old Abebe was running in his third marathon. The two ran side by side, mile after mile, never looking at each other, along a course lit by torches held by Italian soldiers, and lined by thousands of spectators who had to be restrained from interfering with the runners.

Reconnoitering the route some days earlier, Abebe and his Finnish coach, Onni Niskanen, had noticed that less than a mile from the finish line at the Arch of Constantine was the obelisk of Axum, which had been plundered from Ethiopia by Italian troops and hauled off to Rome. It seemed appropriate that the slight incline that followed the obelisk would be the proper place for Abebe to make his final move. Although none of the experts had even considered that the Ethiopian would still be in contention by that point, Abebe was sure that he would be. Right on schedule he pulled away from Rhadi, and his lead had increased to almost 200 yards by the time he breasted the tape. His final obstacle was a typical Roman driver, who had lurched his motor scooter onto the course 60 yards from the end.

1964 Tokyo C: 68, N: 35, D: 10.21. WB: 2:13:55.0 (B. Basil Heatley)

1. Abebe Bikila	ETH	2:12:11.2	WB
2. B. Basil Heatley	GBR	2:16:19.2	
3. Kokichi Tsuburaya	JPN	2:16:22.8	
4. Brian Kilby	GBR	2:17:02.4	
5. József Sütö	HUN	2:17:55.8	
6. Leonard "Buddy" Edelen	USA	2:18:12.4	
7. Aurele Vandendriessche	BEL	2:18:42.6	
8. Kenji Kimihara	JPN	2:19:49.0	

There was no clear-cut favorite in the 1964 marathon, with at least 15 runners in serious contention for the gold medal. Defending champion Abebe Bikila had undergone an appendectomy only 40 days before the race. The Australian Ron Clarke, running his fourth race in a week, rushed to an early lead, followed closely by Jim Hogan of Ireland. Abebe, running this time with shoes and socks, joined them before the seven-kilometer mark, and the three ran together for about half an hour. After 15 kilometers, Abebe, attempting to become the first person in history to win two Olympic marathons, began to apply pressure. By the turning point—Tobitakyu-machi, in Chofu city—Clarke had fallen behind and Abebe was five seconds ahead of Hogan. From 25 kilometers on, Abebe moved ahead steadily until, ten kilometers later, he led Hogan by two and a half minutes. Hogan slowed to a walk and then dropped out, leaving Kokichi Tsuburaya, who was running only the fourth marathon of his career, in second place.

When Abebe Bikila entered the stadium, he was greeted by 75,000 waving and cheering spectators. After crossing the finish line in the fastest marathon time ever recorded, Abebe entertained the crowd by doing stretching and bicycling exercises and generally looking like he was sorry the race had been so short. He told the press that he could have kept up the pace for another ten kilometers. At the medal ceremony later in the day, none of the Japanese officials knew the Ethiopian national anthem, so the band took the opportunity to play the Japanese anthem instead.

Tsuburaya was the second man to enter the stadium, followed ten yards later by Heatley. Despite the encouragement of the hometown crowd, Tsuburaya was exhausted, and when Heatley moved past him before the final curve, he was unable to respond. However, Tsuburaya's third-place finish brought him Japan's first track and field medal in 28 years, and he became a national hero.

Unfortunately, Kokichi Tsuburaya met a tragic end. A member of the Training School of the Japanese Ground Self-Defense Force, after the 1964 race he was ordered to stop seeing his fiancée and to begin training immediately for the 1968 Olympics. But in 1967 he suffered two injuries and was forced to spend three months in the hospital. The doctors declared him completely recovered, but when Tsuburaya started running again, he realized that his body had been irreversibly weakened and that he could not possibly win the next Olympic marathon. On January 9, 1968, two months after his release from the hospital and nine months before the Mexico City Olympics, Kokichi Tsuburaya ended his own life by cutting his right carotid artery with a razor blade. Beside him was a piece of paper on which he had written a single phrase: "Cannot run anymore."

Abebe Bikila also came up against tragedy. He entered the 1968 marathon, but had to withdraw after 17 kilometers because of a bone fracture in his leg. The following year he was driving his Volkswagen, a gift from the government following his second gold medal, when he crashed. He suffered a broken neck and a spinal cord injury that left him paralyzed below the waist. Confined to a wheelchair for the rest of his life, he died of a brain hemorrhage on October 25, 1973, at the age of 41.

1968 Mexico City C: 74, N: 41, D: 10.20. WB: 2:09:36.4 (Derek Clayton)

1. Mamo Wolde	ETH	2:20:26.4
2. Kenji Kimihara	JPN	2:23:31.0
3. Michael Ryan	NZE	2:23:45.0
4. Ismail Akcay	TUR	2:25:18.8
5. William Adcocks	GBR	2:25:33.0
6. Merawi Gebru	ETH	2:27:16.8
7. Derek Clayton	AUS	2:27:23.8
8. Timothy Johnston	GBR	2:28:04.4

Mamo Wolde had a long and unusual involvement in the Olympics. His first appearance was in Melbourne in 1956, where he had entered the 800 and 1500, and finished last in his heat in both events. He also ran the third leg for the Ethiopian 4 × 400 relay team, which finished last in its heat. He did not compete in 1960, but he was back in 1964. He failed to complete the marathon, but placed fourth in the 10,000. In 1968 he finished a close second to Naftali Temu in the 10,000, a week before the marathon. In the later race, Wolde and Temu let others set the pace without allowing the leaders to get too far ahead. Then, about the halfway mark, they picked up the pace considerably and left the others behind. Shortly after 30 kilometers Temu ran out of steam and began to drift back, eventually finishing 19th. This left Wolde with almost a two-minute lead at 35 kilometers. He went on to win as easily as Abebe Bikila had four years earlier. At the age of 36, he had finally come out from the shadow of his famous teammate and won an Olympic gold medal. More than one hour after Mamo Wolde, the final runner, John Akhwari of Tanzania, entered the stadium. He had injured his knee in a fall. Bloodied and bandaged, he struggled to the finish line. When asked why he had not quit despite the obvious pain he was feeling, Akhwari replied, "My country did not send me 7000 miles away to start the race. They sent me 7000 miles to finish it."

In mid-1992, Wolde was arrested, presumably for being on the wrong side of a political struggle. Three years later he was still being held without charge.

1972 Munich C: 69, N: 35, D: 9.10. WB: 2:08:33.6 (Derek Clayton)

1. Frank Shorter	USA	2:12:19.8
2. Karel Lismont	BEL	2:14:31.8
3. Mamo Wolde	ETH	2:15:08.4
4. Kenneth Moore	USA	2:15:39.8
5. Kenji Kimihara	JPN	2:16:27.0
6. Ronald Hill	GBR	2:16:30.6
7. Donald Macgregor	GBR	2:16:34.4
8. Jack Foster	NZE	2:16:56.2

Munich-born Yale graduate Frank Shorter, annoyed by the slow pace, took the lead before the 15-kilometer mark and pulled away steadily as the race progressed. He was never challenged. Quite naturally, he entered the stadium expecting to be greeted by cheers and applause. Instead, all he heard was whistling and booing, and he wondered what he had done wrong. Unbeknownst to Shorter, a hoaxer had appeared on the track a couple of minutes before him and run a full lap before being hustled away by security guards. The sounds of derision had been aimed at the hoaxer, not at Shorter. The silver

A perplexed Frank Shorter wonders why the spectators are booing as he circles the stadium on his way to victory in the 1972 Munich marathon.

medal went to previously undefeated Karel Lismont, and the bronze to Mamo Wolde, who ran his fastest marathon ever at the age of 40. Eighth-place finisher Jack Foster was also 40 years old. After the race, Shorter went back to his room and celebrated his victory by drinking three gins in the bathtub.

1976 Montreal C: 67, N: 35, D: 7.31. WB: 2:08:33.6 (Derek Clayton)

1. Waldemar Cierpinski	GDR	2:09:55.0	OR
2. Frank Shorter	USA	2:10:45.8	
3. Karel Lismont	BEL	2:11:12.6	
4. Donald Kardong	USA	2:11:15.8	
5. Lasse Viren	FIN	2:13:10.8	
6. Jerome Drayton	CAN	2:13:30.0	
7. Leonid Moseyev	SOV/RUS	2:13:33.4	
8. Franco Fava	ITA	2:14:24.8	

Defending champion Frank Shorter looked like the man to beat in 1976, although Lasse Viren was an unknown quantity. Viren had already run 30,000 meters during the last seven days, including victories in the 10,000 and, 24 hours before the marathon, in the 5000. This was his first marathon race. Bill Rodgers of the United States, who eventually finished 40th, guided the leading pack through the first ten kilometers, but the real action didn't begin until just before the 25-kilometer mark, when Shorter surged through the rain, leaving the others behind. Viren tried to keep up for 200 meters, but fell back. About four minutes later, Waldemar Cierpinski, a relatively unknown converted steeplechaser from East Germany, who had entered his first marathon on a whim in 1974, decided that Shorter wasn't really running so fast after all, and caught up with him.

"It was a wonderful feeling when I came alongside," Cierpinski later recalled. "I glanced at Shorter as I did so, and looked right into the eyes of the man who was my idol as a marathon runner. I knew all about him. And yet I could tell by the return glance that he didn't know much, if anything, about me. The psychological advantage was mine." In fact, for the entire race, Shorter thought Cierpinski was actually Carlos Lopes of Portugal. Cierpinski's coaches had told him to annoy Shorter by getting as close to his body as possible. This he did, until a couple shoves separated them. Shorter made periodic surges, but each time Cierpinski caught him. Then, after 34 kilometers, they disappeared from the sight of the crowds and the cameras during a short stretch through the campus of McGill University. When they emerged again, Cierpinski had taken the lead and begun to draw away. Shorter tried to close the gap, but couldn't.

Cierpinski entered the stadium just as the band had finished playing the East German national anthem to celebrate the victory of the women's 4 × 400-meter relay team. When he reached the finish line, Cierpinski noticed that the lap indicator read "1." Confused, he continued running for another lap and was surprised, when he crossed the finish again, to find Frank Shorter waiting to

Waldemar Cierpinski, winner of the marathon in both 1976 and 1980.

congratulate him. Cierpinski had bettered his personal best by two and one-half minutes.

Cierpinski's victory came as a shock even to his fellow countrymen. Back in the Olympic Village, the East German soccer team watched the race on television while waiting for their final match against Poland. Goalie Jürgen Croy later recalled, "We just sat there staring at each other, thinking that if this living example of mediocrity can lift himself up and win the marathon, and we don't beat Poland, we are never going to hear the end of it." They won.

1980 Moscow C: 74, N: 40, D: 8.1. WB: 2:08:33.6 (Derek Clayton)

1. Waldemar Cierpinski	GDR	2:11:03
2. Gerard Nijboer	HOL	2:11:20
3. Satymkul Dzhumanazarov	SOV/KYR	2:11:35
4. Vladimir Kotov	SOV/BLR	2:12:05
5. Leonid Moseyev	SOV/RUS	2:12:14
6. Rodolfo Gomez	MEX	2:12:39
7. Dereje Nedi	ETH	2:12:44
8. Massimo Magnani	ITA	2:13:12

Vladimir Kotov led for the first half of the race. After 24 kilometers, Lasse Viren, who had been running with the leaders, suddenly rushed off into the bushes with diarrhea. He dropped out three kilometers later. Rodolfo Gomez took advantage of Viren's indisposition to jump into the lead, quickly opening a 100-meter gap. At the 30-kilometer mark, he led by 23 seconds. However, five and a half kilometers later he was passed by Gerard Nijboer. Six hundred meters further along, Cierpinski passed them both, and was never headed. He ran the last 200 meters in 33.4 seconds and won by about 80 meters. As he crossed the finish line, there were five runners on the track, an Olympic record. Although he was only two days shy of his 30th birthday, Waldemar Cierpinski was still described by East German sources as a "sports student." After becoming the only person besides Abebe Bikila to win two Olympic marathons, he was elevated to "sports teacher."

1984 Los Angeles C: 107, N: 60, D: 8.12. WB: 2:08.18 (F. Robert de Castella)

1. Carlos Lopes	POR	2:09:21	OR
2. John Treacy	IRL	2:09:56	
3. Charles Spedding	GBR	2:09:58	
4. Takeshi Soh	JPN	2:10:55	
5. F. Robert de Castella	AUS	2:11:09	
6. Juma Ikangaa	TAN	2:11:10	
7. Joseph Nzau	KEN	2:11:28	
8. Djama Robleh	DJI	2:11:39	

The 1984 men's marathon was an eagerly awaited race with a talent-packed field that included seven different runners who had clocked times under 2 hours and 9 minutes. The leading favorites were world champion Rob de Castella, who had won all four marathons he had run in the last three and one-half years, and the reclusive Japanese star, Toshihiko Seko, whose last loss in 1979 had been followed by five victories. Among the other highly regarded entrants was Carlos Lopes, the 1976 Olympic silver medalist at 10,000 meters. Lopes had completed only one of three marathons he had attempted, but that was a two-second loss to de Castella in 1983.

Not surprisingly, the Olympic marathon was closely fought for the first half of the race. By the 25-kilometer mark, Juma Ikangaa, one of the sub-2:09 men, was heading a lead pack that still contained twelve runners. At the 20-mile mark, de Castella slowed down to grab a cup of water and looked up to discover himself 50 meters behind the pack. He was never able to close the gap. The lead pack was down to seven. A mile later, Seko lost contact. Then Charlie Spedding, a dark horse despite having won the Houston and London Marathons earlier in the year, forced the pace. The only ones who were able to stay with him were the 37-year-old Lopes and John Treacy, who was running his first marathon. Treacy had placed ninth in the 10,000-meter run six days earlier.

Then Lopes turned on the pressure, running the next five kilometers in 14 minutes 33 seconds, a remarkable achievement, considering he had just run 21½ hot and humid miles against the best marathon field ever assembled. Spedding and Treacy had no choice but to let him go. Lopes breezed ahead to win the gold medal. Treacy ran a 67-second last lap to earn the silver, while Spedding, whose dedication was so great that he had foresworn ale for an entire week before the race, happily settled for the bronze. De Castella finished fifth and Seko fourteenth.

World-class athletes often face unexpected obstacles on their way to the Olympics. Lopes, for example, was hit by a Mercedes-Benz while training only fifteen days before the Olympic marathon. "There goes the Olympics," Lopes thought, as he rolled over the hood and watched his elbow crash through the windshield. As luck would have it, his injuries were minor. The same could not be said of the unfortunate Richard Mbewa, the Tanzanian marathon alternate, who was shot to death while jogging on a golf course by a policeman who mistook him for a thief. And then there is the story of the 78th and last man to cross the finish line in the 1984 Olympic marathon: Dieudonne Lamothe of Haiti. When last heard from, Lamothe had competed in the 1976 5000-meter race, recording the slowest time in Olympic history, but insisting on finishing. While in Los Angeles in 1984, Lamothe did not speak to the press. However, after the fall of Haitian dictator Baby Doc Duvalier, Lamothe revealed that Haitian Olympic officials had threatened to kill him if he failed to finish. He did make it across the finish line—in 2 hours 52 minutes and 18 seconds, a much more respectable time than his 1976 performance. In 1988, under considerably less pressure, Lamothe placed 20th in 2:16:15.

1988 Seoul C: 118, N: 66, D: 10.2. WB: 2:06:50 (Belayneh Densimo)

1. Gelindo Bordin	ITA	2:10:32
2. Douglas Wakiihuri	KEN	2:10:47
3. Houssein Ahmed Saleh	DJI	2:10:59
4. Takeyuki Nakayama	JPN	2:11:05
5. Stephen Moneghetti	AUS	2:11:49
6. Charles Spedding	GBR	2:12:19
7. Juma Ikangaa	TAN	2:13:06
8. F. Robert de Castella	AUS	2:13:07

The 1988 men's marathon was run in humid weather along a route lined with 36,000 policemen. By the 25-kilometer mark Juma Ikangaa was leading a pack of 13. Four kilometers later the pace was forced by the 1986 European champion, Gelindo Bordin, who, back in April 1981, had been presumed dead after being hit from behind by a car while training in Verona.

By 30 kilometers the lead pack was down to Bordin; Nakayama, who had won two marathons on the Seoul course in 1985 and 1986; world champion Douglas Wakiihuri; the favorite, Ahmed Saleh, who had also triumphed on the Seoul course at the 1987 World Cup; Ikangaa; Charlie Spedding; and Toshihiko Seko, whose disappointing performance at the 1984 Olympics remained his only loss in nine years. After 31 kilometers Nakayama surged, causing Spedding and Seko to fall behind, the latter eventually finishing ninth. Spedding fought his way back over the next few kilometers, but 400 meters past the 35-kilometer mark, Saleh and Nakayama increased the pace, and Spedding and Ikangaa lost contact for good. Just short of 37 kilometers, Nakayama fell back as well.

With three miles left, the medals were to be decided among Saleh, Wakiihuri, and Bordin, the same three who had medaled at the 1987 world championships in Rome. In that race the then unknown Wakiihuri had run away from Saleh just before the 38-kilometer mark, while Bordin had come from behind to snatch the bronze from Steve Moneghetti.

Now, 13 months later, it was Saleh who broke away at 38 kilometers, gradually opening a lead of about 25 meters over Wakiihuri. Bordin, exhausted and suffering leg cramps, resigned himself to third place. In order to distract himself from worrying about Nakayama behind him, Bordin focused his attention on Wakiihuri's back. One and a half miles from the finish, Bordin suddenly realized, to his great surprise, that he was gaining on the Kenyan. At 40 kilometers he passed him and set his sights on Saleh, who was now in pain and looking back frequently. At 40.5 kilometers Saleh glanced over his left shoulder and didn't see Bordin. He looked over his right shoulder and there he was, with a smile on his face, only three meters behind.

Fifty meters later Bordin drove past Saleh and, another 250 meters on, so did Wakiihuri. Bordin went on to win the closest Olympic marathon in 68 years. As soon as he crossed the finish line he crossed himself, then knelt down and kissed the track. Approached by reporters, he described the last two kilometers as "a war" and commented that he was "too tired even to be happy."

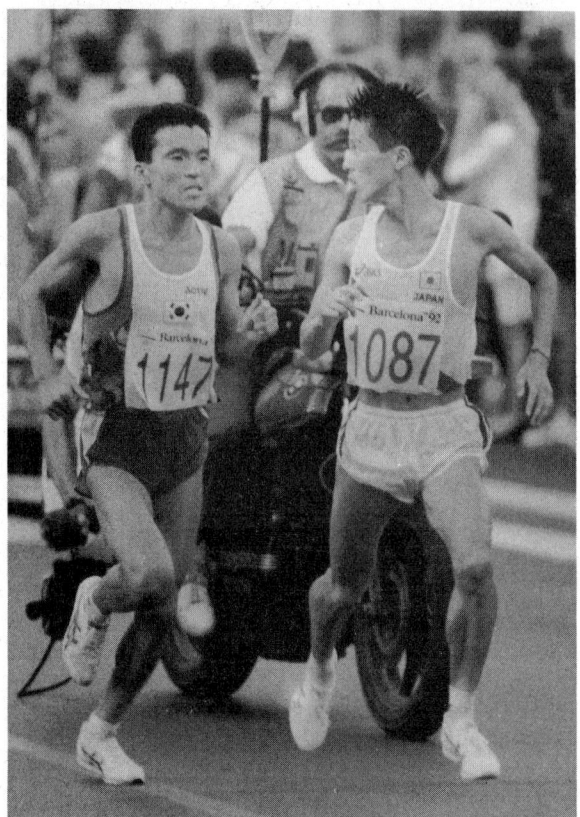

Koichi Morishita (right) looks over his shoulder in the final mile of the 1992 marathon and does not like what he sees.

1992 Barcelona C: 110, N: 72, D: 8.9. WB: 2:06:50 (Belayneh Densimo)

1. Hwang Young-cho	KOR	2:13:23
2. Koichi Morishita	JPN	2:13:45
3. Stephan Freigang	GER	2:14:00
4. Takeyuki Nakayama	JPN	2:14:02
5. Salvatore Bettiol	ITA	2:14:15
6. Salah Kokaich	MOR	2:14:25
7. Jan Huruk	POL	2:14:32
8. Hiromi Taniguchi	JPN	2:14:42

Although the race began at 6:30 p.m., for the third straight time the marathon was run in uncomfortably hot conditions. This time the demands on the runners were even more severe because, after 37½ kilometers, the course concluded with a brutal three-mile climb up Montjuïc to the Olympic Stadium. The field got off to a cautious start. After ten kilometers the first 50 runners were still bunched within 50 meters of each other, sharing water-soaked sponges, their rivalries forgotten before the common enemy: the course. At the halfway mark the lead pack still contained 30 men. It was Salvatore Bettiol who forced the pace after 23 kilometers, breaking up the pack at last. He was quickly hauled in, but by the 27-kilometer mark, three runners had pulled away: 24-year-old Koichi Morishita, who had recorded the fastest time of 1991, 22-year-old Hwang Young-cho, and Hwang's Korean teammate, Kim Wan-ki. Kim fell back seven kilometers later, eventually ending up in 28th place.

In 1936, Korean Sohn Kee-chung had won the Olympic marathon, but had been forced to endure the humiliation of competing for Japan, using a Japanese name. Now, 56 years later to the day, Hwang of Korea and Morishita of Japan were locked in a grim and dramatic struggle. Waiting in the stadium was Sohn himself, now 80 years old. For four kilometers, Hwang and Morishita ran side by side. Whenever one sped up, the other matched him. Then they reached the bottom of the awful Montjuïc hill. Still they pressed on, one surging, the other catching up. Finally, two kilometers from the stadium, Hwang accelerated, and Morishita, despite a noble effort, was unable to respond.

Hwang entered the stadium with a lead of over 100 meters. Although he was able to smile and wave to the crowd, as soon as he crossed the finish line, he collapsed. Hwang wanted to take a victory lap carrying the South Korean flag, but his legs could go no farther. He was carried away on a stretcher. Fortunately a quick massage revived him and he was able to return for the medal ceremony, the raising of the Korean flag and the playing of the South Korean national anthem. Hwang tried to telephone his mother back in Korea, but was unable to reach her because she spent the whole day in a temple, praying for him. When he returned to Seoul, Hwang met Sohn Kee-chung and placed his gold medal around the older man's neck. Sohn told Hwang, "Now I can die without any regrets." Hwang himself dismissed the political significance of his triumph over a Japanese runner and reminded his fellow Koreans that he had worn Japanese-made running shoes during his Olympic victory.

For the first time in Olympic history marathon runners were told that they would not be allowed to finish in the stadium unless they completed the course within a time limit, 2 hours 45 minutes, so as not to interfere with preparations for the Closing Ceremony 45 minutes later. Twenty-three runners failed to complete the course, including defending champion Gelindo Bordin. Eighty-four runners met the time limit, which was extended by two minutes, but three did not, and they were redirected to a nearby warm-up track. The next-to-last finisher was Hussain Haleen of the Maldive Islands. Although his time of 3:04:16 was not impressive, Haleen did gain the distinction of being the first Maldivian athlete in any sport to finish ahead of an athlete from another country. The last finisher was Pyambuu Tuul of Mongolia, whose time of 4:00:44 was the slowest in 84 years. But Tuul's achievement had a touch of drama of its own. A construction worker, he was blinded by an explosion in 1978. Twelve years later he was discovered by Richard Traum, founder of the Achilles Club, a New York–based organization that helped disabled athletes. Tuul, with the help of a guide, competed in the 1990 New York Marathon. Then, in January 1991, a cornea transplant restored sight in his right eye. One and a half years later he took part in—and finished—the Olympic Marathon, not to win but "to show that a man has many possibilities."

Far less inspirational is the story of the man who finished last at the 1988 Olympics (in a time of 3:14:02), Polin Belisle, who represented Belize. Although Belisle apparently did spend a few childhood years in Belize, he grew up and lived in Burbank, California. He convinced Belizean Olympic officials to let him compete in Seoul by sending them newspaper clippings that showed he had recorded an impressive time in the Long Beach Marathon. In fact there was no evidence that he had run any of the race except the beginning and the end. After 1988 he used his Olympic appearance to con people into donating money to support his "training." In 1992 he badgered the Belize Olympic Committee to send him to the Olympics again, but by this time the Belizeans were wise to him. So, armed with a Honduran birth certificate and more fake marathon results, he changed his name to Apolineria Belisle Gomez and won a place on the Olympic team of Honduras. But on the fifth day of the 1992 Olympics some Belizean athletes recognized Belisle's name on the entry list and told the president of the Belize Olympic Committee, who informed the president of the Honduras Olympic Committee, who kicked Belisle off the team. Not so easily discouraged, Belisle showed up on race day anyway, slipped into the first line of runners on the starting line and raced with the leaders for a mile before fading into the pack and disappearing. He was the first unauthorized athlete to compete in the Olympics since Madeline de Jesus of Puerto Rico took the place of her twin sister in the 1984 4 × 400-meter relay. Before that, the 1972 cycling road race was crashed by four members of the Irish Republican Army.

110-METER HURDLES

Contestants must clear ten hurdles, each of which is three feet six inches high. It is 45 feet to the first hurdle; the distance between hurdles is 30 feet; and it is 46 feet from the last hurdle to the finish. The United States has dominated this event. Competing in 22 Olympics (including 1906), U.S. hurdlers have won eighteen gold medals, fifteen silver, and fifteen bronze. No other nation has won more than five medals.

1896 Athens C: 7, N: 6, D: 4.10. WR (120 yards): 15.4 (Stephen Chase)
1. Thomas Curtis	USA	17.6
2. Grantley Goulding	GBR	17.6e

DNS: William Hoyt (USA) and Frantz Reichel (FRA)

Curtis won by about two inches.

1900 Paris C: 9, N: 3, D: 7.14. WR (120 yards): 15.2 (Alvin Kraenzlein)
1. Alvin Kraenzlein	USA	15.4	OR
2. John McLean	USA	15.5	
3. Frederick Moloney	USA	15.8	
4. Jean Lécuyer	FRA	—	
5. Norman Pritchard	IND	—	

Alvin Kraenzlein won the first of his four gold medals at the 1900 Games. Kraenzlein was responsible for introducing the leg-extended style to hurdling.

1904 St. Louis C: 8, N: 2, D: 9.3. WR (120 yards): 15.2 (Alvin Kraenzlein)
1. Frederick Schule	USA	16.0
2. Thaddeus Shideler	USA	16.3
3. Lesley Ashburner	USA	16.4
4. Frank Castleman	USA	—

Alvin Kraenzlein won four gold medals in three days at the 1900 Paris Olympics. His wins came in the 60-meter dash, the long jump, and the 110- and 200-meter hurdles.

1906 Athens C: 15, N: 8, D: 5.1. WR (120 yards): 15.2 (Alvin Kraenzlein)
1. Robert Leavitt   USA   16.2
2. Alfred Healey   GBR   16.2
3. Vincent Duncker   GER   16.3
4. Hugo Friend   USA   16.4
5. Henri Molinié   FRA   —
6. G. Issidonis   GRE   —

1908 London C: 25, N: 10, D: 7.25. WR (120 yards): 15.2 (Alvin Kraenzlein)
1. Forrest Smithson   USA   15.0   WR
2. John Garrels   USA   15.7
3. Arthur Shaw   USA   15.8
4. William Rand   USA   16.0

Smithson, of Portland, Oregon, shot into the lead before the first hurdle and won by five yards. There is an enduring anecdote that Smithson, while running the final, carried a Bible in one hand as a protest against Sunday competition. There is no evidence to support this otherwise admirable story. It is not mentioned in any contemporary newspaper accounts and none of Smithson's races were held on a Sunday. A much-reprinted photograph of Smithson clearing a hurdle while holding a Bible is clearly a posed shot not taken during competition.

1912 Stockholm C: 21, N: 9, D: 7.12. WR: 15.0 (Forrest Smithson)
1. Frederick Kelly   USA   15.1
2. James Wendell   USA   15.2
3. Martin Hawkins   USA   15.3
4. John Case   USA   15.3
5. Kenneth Powell   GBR   15.5
DNF: John Nicholson (USA)

1920 Antwerp C: 23, N: 14, D: 8.18. WR (120 yards): 14.4 (Earl Thomson)
1. Earl Thomson   CAN   14.8   WR
2. Harold Barron   USA   15.1e
3. Frederick Murray   USA   15.1e
4. Harry Wilson   NZE   15.2e
5. Walker Smith   USA   15.3e
6. Carl-Axel Christiernsson SWE 15.3e

Thomson was born in Saskatchewan, but grew up in Southern California from the age of eight. He represented Dartmouth in intercollegiate competition, but because he was still a Canadian citizen, he competed for Canada in the Olympics. Thomson, who survived a near-fatal rifle accident in 1914, took his hurdling very seriously, going so far as to tie his legs to the foot of his bed so that he wouldn't curl up and risk cramping. Thomson spent most of his life as a track coach, including 37 years as head coach of the Navy team at Annapolis. His Olympic time of 14.8 seconds was accepted as a world record even though his 14.4 for the slightly shorter distance of 120 yards was much more impressive.

1924 Paris C: 27, N: 15, D: 7.9. WR (120 yards): 14.4 (Earl Thomson)
1. Daniel Kinsey   USA   15.0
2. Sydney Atkinson   SAF   15.0
3. Sten Pettersson   SWE   15.4
4. Carl-Axel Christiernsson SWE 15.5
5. Karl Anderson   USA   15.8
DISQ: George Guthrie (USA)

Atkinson was in the lead as he and Kinsey rose to clear the last hurdle. However, the South African clipped the barrier with his rear foot and stumbled. He recovered well, but lost by inches. Guthrie finished third, but was disqualified for knocking over three hurdles.

1928 Amsterdam C: 41, N: 24, D: 8.1. WR (120 yards): 14.4 (Earl Thomson)

1. Sydney Atkinson	SAF	14.8
2. Stephen Anderson	USA	14.8
3. John Collier	USA	14.9
4. Leighton Dye	USA	14.9
5. George Weightman-Smith	SAF	15.0
6. Frederick Gaby	GBR	15.2

In the semifinals, Weightman-Smith set a metric world record of 14.6 seconds.

1932 Los Angeles C: 17, N: 10, D: 8.3. WR (120 yards): 14.2 (Percy Beard)

1. George Saling	USA	14.6
2. Percy Beard	USA	14.7
3. Donald Finlay	GBR	14.8
4. Jack Keller	USA	14.8
5. David Burghley	GBR	14.8
DISQ: Willi Welscher (GER)		

Jack Keller won the first semifinal in 14.5 and George Saling the second in 14.4. In the final, Keller showed in front first, but hit the fifth hurdle, allowing Beard to move ahead. However, Beard hit the sixth hurdle. Saling then caught up and took the lead. He tripped on the ninth hurdle, but held on to win by a yard. Welscher finished fourth, but was disqualified for knocking over four hurdles, a prohibition that is no longer in the rules. For the first time in Olympic history, the results of a final were changed after a film of the race had been viewed. Originally Keller had been placed third and awarded the bronze medal. When the revised results were announced, Keller sought out Finlay in the Olympic Village and handed over the medal.

1936 Berlin C: 31, N: 20, D: 8.6. WR: 14.1 (Forrest Towns)

1. Forrest Towns	USA	14.2
2. Donald Finlay	GBR	14.4
3. Frederick Pollard	USA	14.4
4. Håkan Lidman	SWE	14.4
5. John Thornton	GBR	14.7
6. Lawrence O'Connor	CAN	15.0

Forrest "Spec" Towns of Georgia equaled his own world record of 14.1 in the semifinals and then skimmed to a two-yard victory in the final. Towns became a hurdler by an unusual route. He had not competed in high school because his family was too poor to buy him track shoes. A couple years later a neighbor saw Towns high-jumping over a broomstick held by his father and brother. The neighbor told a local sportswriter, who wrote about the scene. Weems Baskin, the track coach at the University of Georgia, read the article, gave Towns a tryout and then a scholarship and then switched him to hurdling, an event Towns had never heard of. Three years later he was an Olympic champion.

1948 London C: 28, N: 18, D: 8.4. WR (120 yards): 13.6 (Harrison Dillard)

1. William Porter	USA	13.9	OR
2. Clyde Scott	USA	14.1	
3. Craig Dixon	USA	14.1	
4. Alberto Triulzi	ARG	14.6	
5. Peter Gardner	AUS	14.7	
6. Håkan Lidman	SWE	14.9	

The absence of world record holder Harrison Dillard, who was eliminated at the U.S. trials, did not prevent the U.S. from sweeping the medals so decisively that the final appeared to be two separate races.

1952 Helsinki C: 30, N: 20, D: 7.24. WR: 13.5 (Richard Attlesey)

1. Harrison Dillard	USA	13.7	OR	(13.91)
2. Jack Davis	USA	13.7		(14.00)
3. Arthur Barnard	USA	14.1		(14.40)
4. Yevhen Bulanchyk	SOV/UKR	14.5		(14.73)
5. Kenneth Doubleday	AUS	14.7		(14.82)
6. Raymond Weinberg	AUS	14.8		(15.15)

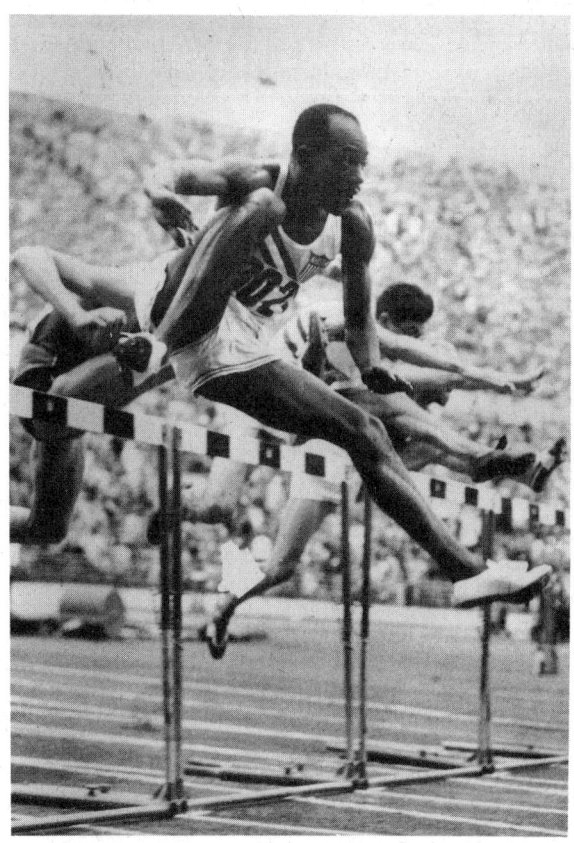

Harrison Dillard, the king of the high hurdles, failed to qualify in that event for the 1948 Olympics, but won the 100-meter dash instead. Four years later, in Helsinki, he finally earned his high hurdles gold medal.

Harrison Dillard began hurdling at the age of eight, running in an alley and using the springs from abandoned car seats as barriers. By 1948 Dillard was the unquestioned world champion of the high hurdles. However, he lost his stride in the U.S. Olympic trials and failed to finish. He did qualify in the 100-meter dash and went on to win the gold medal. Despite this unexpected triumph, he still wanted to earn an Olympic victory in the hurdles. Four years later, at the age of 29, Dillard got his chance. He was hard-pressed by Jack Davis, who knocked down the ninth hurdle, allowing Dillard to achieve the victory "on which I had set my heart." The usually calm Dillard jumped for joy and exclaimed, "Good things come to those who wait."

1956 Melbourne C: 24, N: 15, D: 11.26. WR: 13.4 (Jack Davis)
1. Lee Calhoun	USA	13.5 OR	(13.70)
2. Jack Davis	USA	13.5	(13.73)
3. Joel Shankle	USA	14.1	(14.25)
4. Martin Lauer	GER	14.5	(14.67)
5. Stanko Lorger	YUG	14.5	(14.68)
6. Boris Stolyarov	SOV	14.6	(14.71)

Once again, if each nation had not been limited to three entrants, the final would probably have been an all-American affair. Running into a 1.9-meters-per-second wind, Calhoun and Davis were even by the eighth hurdle. Using a lunge that he had learned from Davis, Calhoun got his shoulder across the finish line inches ahead. For the second straight time, Jack Davis had recorded the same time as the winner yet had been forced to settle for a silver medal.

1960 Rome C: 36, N: 21, D: 9.5. WR: 13.2 (Martin Lauer, Lee Calhoun)
1. Lee Calhoun	USA	13.8	(13.98)
2. Willie May	USA	13.8	(13.99)
3. Hayes Jones	USA	14.0	(14.17)
4. Martin Lauer	GER	14.0	(14.20)
5. Keith Gardner	JAM	14.4	(14.55)
6. Valentin Chistyakov	SOV/RUS	14.6	(14.71)

Lee Calhoun had to sit out the 1958 season after being suspended for receiving gifts on the television game show *Bride and Groom*. He was back in uniform in 1960, winning his second gold medal with the same lunge that he had used to win four years earlier, and United States hurdlers achieved their fourth consecutive sweep.

1964 Tokyo C: 37, N: 23, D: 10.18. WR: 13.2 (Martin Lauer, Lee Calhoun)
1. Hayes Jones	USA	13.6	(13.67)
2. H. Blaine Lindgren	USA	13.7	(13.74)
3. Anatoly Mikhailov	SOV/RUS	13.7	(13.78)
4. Eddy Ottoz	ITA	13.8	(13.84)
5. Gurbachan Randhawa Singh	IND	14.0	(14.09)
6. Marcel Duriez	FRA	14.0	(14.09)
7. Giovanni Cornacchia	ITA	14.1	(14.12)
8. Giorgio Mazza	ITA	14.1	(14.17)

A U.S. sweep was prevented when Willie Davenport, the surprise winner of the U.S. Olympic trials, succumbed to a leg injury and was eliminated in the semifinals. Jones and Lindgren ran evenly for almost the entire race, but Lindgren started his lean too early and was nipped at the tape.

1968 Mexico City C: 33, N: 23, D: 10.17. WR: 13.2 (Martin Lauer, Lee Calhoun, Earl McCullouch)
1. Willie Davenport	USA	13.33	EOR
2. Ervin Hall	USA	13.42	
3. Eddy Ottoz	ITA	13.46	
4. Leon Coleman	USA	13.67	
5. Werner Trzmiel	GER	13.68	
6. Bo Forssander	SWE	13.73	
7. Marcel Duriez	FRA	13.77	
8. Pierre Schoebel	FRA	14.02	

In 1968, 19 of the world's top 25 high hurdlers were from the United States. Since 1964, Willie Davenport had struggled through four years of injuries to gain another chance at an Olympic gold medal. He was so nervous before the start of the final that he almost fell while taking off his sweat pants, and he never even heard the starter say, "set." Yet "from the first step, the gun," he said, "I knew I had won the race. It was perhaps the only race I ever ran that way, but that first step was so perfect—right on the money. I coasted over the last three hurdles thinking, 'It's over, it's over.' " His official time of 13.3 equaled the Olympic record set by Erv Hall in the semifinals.

1972 Munich C: 39, N: 27, D: 9.7. WR: 13.2 (Martin Lauer, Lee Calhoun, Earl McCullouch, Willie Davenport); WR (120 yards): 13.0 (Rodney Milburn)
1. Rodney Milburn	USA	13.24	EWR
2. Guy Drut	FRA	13.34	
3. Thomas Hill	USA	13.48	
4. Willie Davenport	USA	13.50	
5. Frank Siebeck	GDR	13.71	
6. Leszek Wodzyński	POL	13.72	
7. Lubomir Nadenicek	CZE	13.76	
8. Petr Cech	CZE	13.86	

Rod Milburn almost pulled a Harrison Dillard in 1972. After going undefeated in 1971 and winning 27 consecutive finals, he hit two hurdles in the U.S. Olympic trials and barely qualified in third place. However, in Munich his superiority was absolute. He was first over the first hurdle and almost two meters in front by the sixth hurdle, winning by one meter over fast-closing Guy Drut.

1976 Montreal C: 23, N: 17, D: 7.28. WR: 13.0 (Guy Drut)
1. Guy Drut	FRA	13.30	
2. Alejandro Casañas Ramirez	CUB	13.33	
3. Willie Davenport	USA	13.38	
4. Charles Foster	USA	13.41	
5. Thomas Munkelt	GDR	13.44	
6. James Owens	USA	13.73	
7. Vyacheslav Kulebyakin	SOV/RUS	13.93	
8. Victor Myasnikov	SOV/RUS	13.94	

Early in 1975 Guy Drut predicted that he would win the Olympics in a time of 13.28. By 1976 he was under so much pressure from French sports fans that he was forced to train in secret. The son of a French father and an English mother, he was born in Oignies, on the same street as France's last male track and field medalist, Michel Jazy. Drut got off to a good start, took a slight lead after the third hurdle and held it the rest of the way. He was the first person from a non-English-speaking country to win the high hurdles. Drut was an excellent all-around athlete, whose other feats included pole-vaulting 17 feet ¾ inch, long-jumping 24 feet ½ inch, and high-jumping 6 feet 7 inches.

Thirty-three-year-old bronze medalist Willie Davenport was competing in his fourth Olympics. In 1980 he also took part in the Winter Olympics, placing twelfth in the four-man bobsled event.

1980 Moscow C: 22, N: 16, D: 7.27. WR: 13.00 (Renaldo Nehemiah)

1. Thomas Munkelt	GDR	13.39
2. Alejandro Casañas Ramirez	CUB	13.40
3. Aleksandr Puchkov	SOV/RUS	13.44
4. Andrei Prokofyev	SOV/RUS	13.49
5. Jan Pusty	POL	13.68
6. Arto Bryggare	FIN	13.76
7. Javier Moracho	SPA	13.78
8. Yuri Chervanyov	SOV/BLR	15.80

Renaldo Nehemiah, Dedy Cooper, and Greg Foster of the United States would have been favorites to finish at least first and second. Without them, the winning time was the slowest since 1964. Thomas Munkelt, a good-humored 27-year-old dental student, commented before the final, "I will drill through my opposition." He ended up winning by the skin of his teeth. Alejandro Casañas, having lost in 1976 by 0.03 second, experienced the frustration of coming even closer in 1980—0.01 second.

1984 Los Angeles C: 26, N: 17, D: 8.6. WR: 12.93 (Renaldo Nehemiah)

1. Roger Kingdom	USA	13.20	OR
2. Gregory Foster	USA	13.23	
3. Arto Bryggare	FIN	13.40	
4. Mark McKoy	CAN	13.45	
5. Anthony Campbell	USA	13.55	
6. Stephane Caristan	FRA	13.71	
7. Carlos Sala	SPA	13.80	
8. Jeff Glass	CAN	14.15	

When world record holder Renaldo Nehemiah gave up his eligibility to become a professional football player, the title of World's Best High Hurdler passed to Greg Foster. In the opening round, Foster equaled Rod Milburn's 12-year-old Olympic record of 13.24. In the first semifinal, the record was tied again, this time by fast-improving newcomer Roger Kingdom. Ten minutes later, Foster, running into the wind, clocked yet another 13.24.

In the final, Foster hesitated slightly after the gun,

thinking he had false-started. But he recovered quickly and moved into the lead by the second hurdle. About four meters from the finish, Foster, in lane 1, glanced to his right as Kingdom, in lane 8, pulled even and lunged for the tape. Kingdom thought he had finished second and didn't believe he had won until he watched a slow-motion replay of the finish on the huge video screen at the end of the stadium. Only then did he begin leaping up and down with joy.

1988 Seoul C: 41, N: 31, D: 9.28. WR: 12.93 (Renaldo Nehemiah)

1. Roger Kingdom	USA	12.98	OR
2. Colin Jackson	GBR	13.28	
3. Anthony Campbell	USA	13.38	
4. Vladimir Shishkin	SOV/RUS	13.51	
5. Jonathan Ridgeon	GBR	13.52	
6. Anthony Jarrett	GBR	13.54	
7. Mark McKoy	CAN	13.61	
8. Arthur Blake	USA	13.96	

On July 16, 1985, Roger Kingdom pulled his left hamstring muscle. As it was his first major injury, he did not take it seriously enough, and it failed to heal properly. The following year he injured it again. By 1987 he was no longer competing. When Greg Foster won the Rome world championships, Kingdom watched the race on television. He even had to listen to one of the TV commentators refer to him as "the forgotten man of the hurdles." However, when the 1988 season began, Kingdom was fully healed. He entered the Olympics undefeated with victories in 16 straight meets. Arthur Blake caught a flyer in the final. Kingdom started in third place, took the lead after the fourth hurdle, and powered to an impressive three-meter victory.

1992 Barcelona C: 39, N: 27, D: 8.3. WR: 12.92 (Roger Kingdom)

1. Mark McKoy	CAN	13.12
2. Michael "Tony" Dees	USA	13.24
3. Jack Pierce	USA	13.26
4. Anthony Jarrett	GBR	13.26
5. Florian Schwarthoff	GER	13.29
6. Emilio Valle	CUB	13.41
7. Colin Jackson	GBR	13.46
8. Hughie Teape	GBR	14.00

In 1988 Mark McKoy finished seventh in the high hurdles and then fled Seoul in the wake of the Ben Johnson scandal. Because Canadian team officials had expected him to make himself available for the 4 × 100-meter relay, he was suspended for two years. McKoy also admitted that he had taken steroids. In 1991 Welsh hurdler Colin Jackson invited McKoy and his family to move into his home in Rhoose, South Wales. Jackson and his coach, Malcolm Arnold, rekindled McKoy's enthusiasm for hurdling. The two friends agreed not to compete against each other until the Olympics. In the meantime Jackson established himself as the Barcelona favorite by defeating the U.S. champions Pierce and Dees.

In the opening round, Jackson ran a 13.10, the fastest

heat time in history. The final, however, belonged to McKoy, who led from start to finish. At age 30, he was the oldest winner in the event's history. He was also Canada's first gold medalist in track since 1928. Born in Guyana, McKoy lived in England, attended university in the United States, married a German, and, after the Olympics, became an Austrian citizen. But on the day he became an Olympic champion, Mark McKoy literally wrapped himself in the Canadian flag.

400-METER HURDLES

Contestants in this event must clear ten three-foot hurdles. The distance from the starting line to the first hurdle is 45 meters; the distance between hurdles is 35 meters; and the distance from the last hurdle to the finish line is 40 meters. Athletes from the United States have won this event 15 of the 19 times they have entered. The only time the winner came from a non-English-speaking country was when the United States boycotted the Olympics in 1980.

1896 not held

1900 Paris C: 5, N: 4, D: 7.15. WR (440 yards): 57.2 (Godfrey Shaw)
1. John Walter Tewksbury USA 57.6
2. Henri Tauzin FRA 58.3
3. George Orton CAN/USA 58.5
DNS: William Lewis (USA)

The results were a great disappointment to the French, since the Americans were unfamiliar with this event. This didn't prevent Tewksbury from easily defeating the previously unbeaten Tauzin. The "hurdles" were actually 30-foot-long telephone poles. A water jump was added just before the finish.

1904 St. Louis C: 4, N: 1, D: 8.31. WR (440 yards): 57.2 (Godfrey Shaw)
1. Harry Hillman USA 53.0
2. Frank Waller USA 53.2
3. George Poage USA 54.8e
4. George Varnell USA —

An oddity in the world of U.S. athletics, Harry Hillman was a 22-year-old bank teller who had never attended college. Writing in the September 1905 issue of *Physical Culture* magazine, Hillman advised aspiring hurdlers to avoid candy, pastries, tobacco, and meat, although he did recommend swallowing whole raw eggs, which he claimed were "excellent for the wind and stomach." He concluded by advising young men in the business world to take up athletics because it "gives one the needed virility demanded by modern business life." Hillman's time was not allowed as a world record because he tipped over one hurdle, and because the hurdles were only two feet six inches high anyway. George Poage was the first

black runner to win an Olympic medal. On April 24, 1909, Harry Hillman and Lawson Robertson set a world record of 11.0 seconds in the 100-yard three-legged race.

1906 not held

1908 London C: 15, N: 6, D: 7.22. WR (440 yards): 57.2 (Godfrey Shaw)
1. Charles Bacon USA 55.0 WR
2. Harry Hillman USA 55.3
3. Leonard Tremeer GBR 57.0
4. Leslie Burton GBR 58.0

Bacon won a close and exciting contest despite the fact that he went over a hurdle in the wrong lane midway through the race. When the judges measured the course he had taken, they discovered that he had actually run farther than if he had stayed in his own lane, so he was saved from disqualification.

1912 not held

1920 Antwerp C: 19, N: 9, D: 8.16. WR (440 yards): 54.2 (John Norton)
1. Frank Loomis USA 54.0 WR
2. John Norton USA 54.6e
3. August Desch USA 54.7e
4. Georges "Géo" André FRA 54.8e
5. Carl-Axel Christiernsson SWE 55.4e
6. Charles Daggs USA 55.7e

After the final, three American flags were raised and the European spectators watched with fascination as the U.S. team celebrated by chanting, "Rah rah rah, U-S-A. A-M-E-R-I-C-A. Loomis! Loomis! Loomis!" Fourth-place finisher Géo André had won a silver medal in the high jump in 1908.

1924 Paris C: 23, N: 13, D: 7.7. WR: 54.0 (Frank Loomis)
1. F. Morgan Taylor USA 52.6
2. Erik Vilén FIN 53.8 OR
3. Ivan Riley USA 54.1
4. Georges "Géo" André FRA 56.1
DISQ: Charles Brookins (USA), Frederick Blackett (GBR)

Taylor's world record time was not allowed because he knocked down one hurdle, thus violating the rules of the time. Brookins finished second, but was disqualified for running out of his lane and clearing a hurdle improperly. Consequently, it was Erik Vilén who was credited with an Olympic record, even though he finished only third. Géo André again made the final, this time at age 34—sixteen years after his first Olympic appearance. Even after his retirement from competition he continued to be a late achiever. Having served as a pilot during World War I, he was anxious to do his part again in World War II. Too old to be a fighter pilot, he joined the infantry and was killed by the Germans near Tunis on May 4, 1943. He was 53 years old.

F. Morgan Taylor, winner of the 1924 400-meter hurdles.

1928 Amsterdam C: 27, N: 16, D: 7.30. WR: 52.0 (F. Morgan Taylor)

1. David Burghley	GBR	53.4	OR
2. Frank Cuhel	USA	53.6	
3. F. Morgan Taylor	USA	53.6	
4. Sten Pettersson	SWE	53.8	
5. Thomas Livingston-Learmonth	GBR	54.2	
6. Luigi Facelli	ITA	55.8	

Lord David George Brownlow Cecil Burghley was one of the most popular winners of the 1928 Games. Heir to the Marquess of Exeter, he first appeared in the Olympics in 1924, when he was elminated in the first round of the 110-meter hurdles. In 1927, during his last year at Cambridge, he caused a sensation by running around the Great Court at Trinity College in the time it took the Trinity Clock to toll 12 o'clock. A completely distorted version of this event was presented in the film *Chariots of Fire*, in which the feat is credited to Harold Abrahams. For this reason, Lord Burghley, who was then 76 years old, reportedly refused to view the film. Actually, Lord Burghley was not the first person to accomplish the Great Court run. It had been done in the 1890s by Sir Walter Borley Fletcher, but in Sir Walter's time the clock took five more seconds to complete its toll.

Burghley was an extremely colorful character, who once set another unusual record by racing around the upper promenade deck of the ocean liner *Queen Mary* in 57 seconds, dressed in street clothes. Once he showed up for a meet in Antwerp but was denied admission at the main gate and told to circle the stadium and enter by the competitors' gate. Burghley took a few steps back, tightened his bowler hat on his head, got a firm grip on his attaché case, hurdled the four-foot fence, and dashed off before the astonished guards could react. Burghley is believed to be the first hurdler to place matchboxes on hurdles and practice knocking over the matchboxes with his lead foot without touching the hurdle. It is not true, despite his portrayal in *Chariots of Fire*, that he put glasses of champagne on the hurdles as well. In the words of his daughter, Lady Victoria Leatham, "He was never one to waste champagne." Burghley was elected to Parliament in 1931, but was granted a leave of absence to compete in the 1932 Olympics in Los Angeles. He later served as governor of Bermuda for three years, as well as president of the British Amateur Athletic Association for 40 years, president of the International Amateur Athletic Federation for 30 years, and as a member of the International Olympic Committee for 45 years. He was also chairman of the Organizing Committee of the 1948 Olympics.

1932 Los Angeles C: 18, N: 13, D: 8.1. WR: 52.0 (F. Morgan Taylor)

1. Robert Tisdall	IRL	51.7	
2. Glenn Hardin	USA	51.9	WR
3. F. Morgan Taylor	USA	52.0	
4. David Burghley	GBR	52.2	
5. Luigi Facelli	ITA	53.0	
6. Johan Kjell Areskoug	SWE	54.6	

Bob Tisdall, a well-known athlete while a student at Cambridge, had run the 400-meter hurdles only once when, in March 1932, he decided to try out for the Irish Olympic team. He quit his job in London and, with his wife, moved into a converted railway carriage in an orchard in Sussex, where he spent the next three months training, although he had no hurdles to practice with. He won a match race in early June and then, on June 18, finished first in the All-Ireland Championships in a time of 54.2 seconds. Less than a month later he was on his way to Los Angeles with the rest of the Irish team. Weakened by the two-week journey, he stayed in bed for 15 hours a day until the morning of his first-round heat. Full of energy, he qualified easily. In the semifinals, he surprised even himself by winning in 52.8, equaling the Olympic record that had been set by Glenn Hardin in the first semi. The final was only Tisdall's seventh race at the distance, and he faced not only Hardin, but former champions Morgan Taylor and Lord Burghley as well. Completely relaxed, Tisdall took the lead early and approached the last hurdle five yards ahead of the others.

"At that moment," Tisdall recalled, "I experienced a strange feeling of loneliness. . . . Everything was strangely quiet. . . . I began to wonder if the rest of the

Lord Burghley (center), winner of the 1928 400-meter hurdles, clears a barrier in classic style during a preliminary heat.

field had fallen over." He mistimed his leap, knocked over the barrier, and stumbled for five or six yards before regaining his balance. Hardin and Taylor closed fast, but Tisdall beat them to the tape in world record time. According to the rules of the day, which were not changed until 1938, his record was disallowed because he had failed to clear the final barrier. So Glenn Hardin entered the record books as world record holder even though he only finished second.

1936 Berlin C: 32, N: 20, D: 8.4. WR: 50.6 (Glenn Hardin)

1. Glenn Hardin	USA	52.4	
2. John Loaring	CAN	52.7	
3. Miguel White	PHI	52.8	
4. Joseph Patterson	USA	53.0	
5. Sylvio de Magalhães Padilha	BRA	54.0	
6. Christos Mantikas	GRE	54.2	

On July 26, 1934, while running in Stockholm, Glenn Hardin of Louisiana took a full second off the existing world record. His time of 50.6 was not beaten for more than 19 years. Following his second-place finish in the 1932 Olympics, Hardin never lost another race. In Berlin, he caught the fading Joe Patterson in the stretch and won by four yards.

1948 London C: 25, N: 17, D: 7.31. WR: 50.6 (Glenn Hardin)

1. Roy Cochran	USA	51.1	OR
2. Duncan White	SRL	51.8	
3. Rune Larsson	SWE	52.2	
4. Richard Ault	USA	52.4	
5. Yves Cros	FRA	53.3	
6. Ottavio Missoni	ITA	54.0	

1952 Helsinki C: 40, N: 24, D: 7.21. WR: 50.6 (Glenn Hardin)

1. Charles Moore	USA	50.8	OR	(51.06)
2. Yuri Lituyev	SOV	51.3		(51.57)
3. John Holland	NZE	52.2		(52.26)
4. Anatoly Yulin	SOV	52.8		(52.81)
5. Harold Whittle	GBR	53.1		(53.36)
6. Armando Filiput	ITA	54.4		(54.49)

Remarkably, the six finalists cleared the first five hurdles in unison. Then Moore, whose father had been an alternate on the 1924 U.S. Olympic team, pulled ahead. Lituyev drew even by the eighth hurdle, but Moore moved ahead again and won by four yards. Moore's near–world record time was quite extraordinary considering that the track had been soaked by rain. He also ran 50.8 in the second round.

1956 Melbourne C: 28, N: 13, D: 11.24. WR: 49.5 (Glenn Davis)

1. Glenn Davis	USA	50.1	EOR	(50.29)
2. Silas "Eddie" Southern	USA	50.8		(50.94)
3. Joshua Culbreath	USA	51.6		(51.74)
4. Yuri Lituyev	SOV	51.7		(51.91)
5. David Lean	AUS	51.8		(51.93)
6. Gerhardus Potgieter	SAF	56.0		

On June 29, at the U.S. Olympic trials, Glenn Davis set a world record of 49.5, pressed by Eddie Southern, who ran 49.7. In Melbourne Southern set an Olympic record of 50.1 in the semifinals, then set the pace in the final. Davis caught him midway and surged ahead at the seventh hurdle to win decisively. Potgieter was in third place when he hit the final hurdle and fell.

1960 Rome C: 34, N: 23, D: 9.2. WR: 49.2 (Glenn Davis)

1. Glenn Davis	USA	49.3	OR	(49.51)
2. Clifton Cushman	USA	49.6		(49.77)
3. Richard Howard	USA	49.7		(49.90)
4. Helmut Janz	GER	49.9		(50.05)
5. Jussi Rintamäki	FIN	50.8		(50.98)
6. Bruno Galliker	SWI	51.0		(51.11)

"Running scared," Glenn Davis ran off-stride until the seventh hurdle, when he regained his poise, passed Janz at the ninth hurdle and Howard at the tenth, to win by two meters. Silver medalist Cliff Cushman was lost in action in Vietnam in 1966. Bronze medalist Dick Howard died of a heroin overdose in 1967. They were 28 and 32 years old, respectively.

1964 Tokyo C: 39, N: 25, D: 10.16. WR: 49.1 (Warren "Rex" Cawley)

1. Warren "Rex" Cawley	USA	49.6
2. John Cooper	GBR	50.1
3. Salvatore Morale	ITA	50.1
4. Gary Knoke	AUS	50.4
5. James Luck	USA	50.5
6. Roberto Frinolli	ITA	50.7
7. Vasily Anisimov	SOV/UKR	51.1
8. Wilfried Geeroms	BEL	51.4

Rex Cawley ran off-stride until the sixth hurdle and was still three yards behind Frinolli at the eighth hurdle. Then the world record holder turned on his speed and pulled away to a clear victory. Silver medalist John Cooper was one of the 346 people who died in the famous Turkish Air Lines plane crash over France on March 3, 1974. He was 33 years old.

1968 Mexico City C: 30, N: 24, D: 10.15. WR: 48.8 (Geoffrey Vanderstock)

1. David Hemery	GBR	48.12	WR
2. Gerhard Hennige	GER	49.02	
3. John Sherwood	GBR	49.03	
4. Geoffrey Vanderstock	USA	49.07	
5. Vyacheslav Skomorokhov	SOV/UKR	49.12	
6. Ronald Whitney	USA	49.27	
7. Rainer Schubert	GER	49.30	
8. Roberto Frinolli	ITA	50.13	

The 1968 final had all the makings of a spectacular race. The favorites were world record holder Geoff Vanderstock, fellow American Ron Whitney, and David Hemery, who had beaten Vanderstock at the N.C.A.A. championships. Hemery, although born in England, had spent 10 of his 24 years in the United States. Other finalists included John Sherwood, whose wife, Sheila, had won a silver medal in the long jump the day before, Vyacheslav Skomorokhov, who was deaf, and 1964 finalist Roberto Frinolli, who had stripped down to his bikini-style black jock strap before the race, unaware that he was being shown live on U.S. television. Hemery was in lane 6, just inside Ron Whitney, the man he most feared because of his strong finishing kick.

Frinolli and Vanderstock were off quickest, but Hemery had taken the lead by the third hurdle. He passed the halfway mark in 23.3 and demoralized the rest of the field with an awesome display of speed in which he gained at least a yard between and over each of the next five hurdles. He crossed the finish line with an eight-yard lead, the largest winning margin since 1924. While millions of people around the world marveled at his extraordinary performance, Hemery himself wasn't even sure he had won. He had looked to his right at the end to check for Ron Whitney, but had failed to look to his left. It wasn't until he was approached by a BBC camera crew that his uncertainty was erased. At the victory ceremony, Hemery received his gold medal from David Burghley, who had won the same event 40 years earlier.

Final mention should be made of U.S. hurdler Boyd Gittins, who was eliminated at the U.S. Olympic semitrials when a pigeon dropping hit him in the eye and dislodged his contact lens just before the first hurdle. Fortunately, he won a runoff to qualify for the final Olympic trials, and then made the team. Unfortunately, a leg injury forced him to withdraw from his first-round heat.

1972 Munich C: 37, N: 25, D: 9.2. WR: 48.12 (David Hemery)

1. John Akii-Bua	UGA	47.82	WR
2. Ralph Mann	USA	48.51	
3. David Hemery	GBR	48.52	
4. James Seymour	USA	48.64	
5. Rainer Schubert	GER	49.65	
6. Yevgeny Gavrilenko	SOV/BLR	49.66	
7. Stavros Tziortzis	GRE	49.66	
8. Yuri Zorin	SOV/RUS	50.25	

The second semifinal was filled with misfortune. James Seymour and Australia's Gary Knoke, running in the two outside lanes, mistook the echo of the starter's gun for a second shot and thought a false start had been declared. Seymour, in lane 7, realized his mistake quickly enough to avoid disaster and win the heat anyway, but Knoke, in lane 8, was unable to recover, and finished last. As the runners cleared the tenth hurdle, East Germany's Christian Rudolph, in lane 1, stumbled and fell heavily into lane 2, right into the path of Dieter-Wolfgang Büttner of West Germany, who also fell. Neither man was able to finish. The judges decided not to order a rerun, since Büttner was only in fifth place at the time of the mishap.

In the final David Hemery actually set an even faster pace than he had in Mexico City, covering the first 200 meters in 22.8 seconds. Thus it came as quite a shock when he discovered that John Akii-Bua, running in lane 1, was right beside him with 100 meters to go. Akii-Bua surged ahead between the eighth and ninth hurdles and won by six meters. Despite the fact that he had just set a world record, Uganda's first gold medalist kept right on going over the next two flights of hurdles. Akii-Bua, who was also Uganda's decathlon champion, said that he was "scared to death" when he learned that he had drawn lane 1. "When you are in lane 1," he said, "you are always the loser. I couldn't sleep that night." Akii-Bua's father had eight wives and 43 children, 29 of whom were still alive in 1972. A police instructor, John Akii-Bua fled Uganda in 1979, following the overthrow of Idi Amin, and spent a month in a Kenyan jail before he was recognized and released. He eventually returned and in 1987 was arrested again for illegal possession of a submachine gun.

1976 Montreal C: 22, N: 16, D: 7.25. WR: 47.82 (John Akii-Bua)

1. Edwin Moses	USA	47.63	WR
2. Michael Shine	USA	48.69	
3. Yevgeny Gavrilenko	SOV/BLR	49.45	
4. Quentin Wheeler	USA	49.86	
5. José Carvalho	POR	49.94	
6. Yanko Bratanov	BUL	50.03	
7. Damaso Alfonso	CUB	50.19	
8. Alan Pascoe	GBR	51.29	

The African boycott prevented a potentially historic showdown. No matter how sympathetic one is to the movement to bring self-determination for blacks in South Africa, it is difficult to not be cynical when you realize that John Akii-Bua was not allowed to compete in Montreal because the leader of his nation's government, the notorious Idi Amin, was offended by human rights violations in another country.

With Akii-Bua gone and Alan Pascoe still recovering from a leg injury, the competition turned into a one-man show. Edwin Moses was a 20-year-old engineering and physics major at Atlanta's Moorhouse College, a school without a track and which he had entered with an academic rather than an athletic scholarship. Basically self-coached, Moses had entered only one 400-meter hurdles race before March 27, 1976. The Olympics was his first international meet. Moses wore down his last challenger, Yevgeny Gavrilenko, by the seventh hurdle and won by eight meters, the largest winning margin in the history of the event. Afterward, Moses said that his major regret was that training for the Olympics had interfered with his studies, allowing his grade-point average to dip to 3.57.

1980 Moscow C: 22, N: 19, D: 7.26. WR: 47.13 (Edwin Moses)

1. Volker Beck	GDR	48.70
2. Vasyl Arkhypenko	SOV/UKR	48.86
3. Gary Oakes	GBR	49.11
4. Mykola Vasilyev	SOV/UKR	49.34
5. Rok Kopitar	YUG	49.67
6. Horia Toboc	ROM	49.84
7. Franz Meier	SWI	50.00
8. Yanko Bratanov	BUL	56.35

The year 1980 saw a severely devalued competition as a result of the Jimmy Carter boycott. The preboycott favorite, Edwin Moses, set a world record of 47.13 on July 3, three weeks before the Olympics. The silver medal had been expected to be a toss-up among Harald Schmid of West Germany and James Walker and David Lee of the United States. In their absence, Volker Beck passed Arkhypenko on the run-in. His winning time was the slowest since 1964.

1984 Los Angeles C: 45, N: 30, D: 8.5. WR: 47.02 (Edwin Moses)

1. Edwin Moses	USA	47.75
2. Danny Harris	USA	48.13
3. Harald Schmid	GER	48.19
4. Sven Nylander	SWE	48.97
5. El Hadji Amadou Bâ	SEN	49.28
6. Tranel Hawkins	USA	49.42
7. Michel Zimmerman	BEL	50.69
8. Henry Amike	NGR	53.78

On August 26, 1977, Edwin Moses lost a race to Harald Schmid in Berlin. One week later in Düsseldorf he beat Schmid by 15 yards to begin an incredible winning streak that took him through 22 countries and extended, by the time of the 1984 Olympics, to 102 races including 89 finals. By this time the 48-second barrier had been broken 32 times: once by John Akii-Bua, once by Andre Phillips, three times by Harald Schmid, and 27 times by Edwin Moses, who also owned the nine fastest times ever recorded. Needless to say, Moses was a prohibitive favorite to win what should have been his third gold medal.

After being distracted at the starting line by the hundreds of cameras clicking away at him, Moses got off to a quick start and was never headed. Second place went to 18-year-old Danny Harris, who had not run his first 400-meter hurdle race until March 17, 1984. On June 4, 1987, it was Harris who finally ended Moses' finals winning streak at 107 by defeating him 47.56 to 47.69 in a race in Madrid. The streak had lasted nine years, nine months, and nine days.

1988 Seoul C: 37, N: 28, D: 9.25. WR: 47.02 (Edwin Moses)

1. Andre Phillips	USA	47.19	OR
2. El Hadji Amadou Bâ	SEN	47.23	
3. Edwin Moses	USA	47.56	
4. Kevin Young	USA	47.94	
5. Winthrop Graham	JAM	48.04	
6. Kriss Akabusi	GBR	48.69	
7. Harald Schmid	GER	48.76	
8. Edgar Itt	GER	48.78	

Following Danny Harris' defeat of Edwin Moses in Madrid, the next big 400-meter hurdles race came at the world championships in Rome on September 1, 1987. Moses won that contest, leaning across the finish line in 47.46 to beat Harris and Harald Schmid by a mere six inches.

At the 1988 U.S. Olympic trials, Moses won again, clocking 47.37 in the first race in which five runners went under 48 seconds. Andre Phillips was second in 47.58, with Danny Harris beaten back into fifth.

In Seoul the 29-year-old Phillips, who had lost over 20 times to the 33-year-old Moses without a single victory, chose a strategy which mirrored Moses' usual tactics—racing as hard as possible through three hurdles, then surging again at the seventh hurdle. Phillips reacted quickly to the gun and led by almost two meters after the third hurdle. Moses gradually closed the gap, then inched ahead as they reached the seventh barrier. Between the seventh and ninth hurdles, Phillips, following his plan perfectly, regained a clear lead. Moses faded, while Amadou Bâ came on with a rush, passing Moses and almost catching Phillips. Phillips' first thought after he realized he had won was not that he was the Olympic champion, but that he had beaten Moses. Both Phillips and Bâ ran the race of their lives, the former improving his personal record by .32, the latter by .80. Phillips' margin of victory was provided by the seven hundredths of a second he gained over Bâ between the gun and his first stride. Bâ earned Senegal's first Olympic medal, although in 1960, Abdoulaye Seye, another Senegalese, had won a bronze in the 200 meters while competing for France.

1992 Barcelona C: 47, N: 35, D: 8.6. WR: 47.02 (Edwin Moses)

1. Kevin Young	USA	46.78	WR
2. Winthrop Graham	JAM	47.66	
3. Kriss Akabusi	GBR	47.82	
4. Stéphane Diagana	FRA	48.13	
5. Niklas Wallenlind	SWE	48.63	
6. Oleg Tverdokhleb	UKR	48.63	
7. Stephane Caristan	FRA	48.86	
8. David Patrick	USA	49.26	

When Kevin Young arrived at the Olympic Village he taped to the walls of his room pieces of paper with the time "46.89" written on them. It was true that he was one of the favorites, having defeated world champion Samuel Matete of Zambia three times at the beginning of July. But breaking Edwin Moses' nine-year-old world record seemed a bit overly optimistic considering that Young's personal best was only 47.72—and that was set at the Olympic trials not of 1992, but of 1988. However, in the second semifinal (the first was won by Kriss Akabusi in 48.01), Young ran a 47.63. But he also suffered his first loss of the season because Winthrop Graham hit the finish line in 47.62. The big news of the second semi was that Matete, who placed third, was disqualified for knocking over the last hurdle—in the lane next to his.

In the final Young simply ran the race of his life. This is how his opponents described it:

Kriss Akabusi: "I thought I was running fast, but when Kevin came flying past me—and I mean flying—I thought, 'This guy means business.'"

Winthrop Graham: "It shocked me to come off the turn and see how far ahead Kevin was. I'd never had anybody be that far ahead of me going into the last stretch. It exhausted me right there."

David Patrick: "When I hit the line, I looked at the clock and thought, 'No wonder I'm so far behind.'"

Young smashed the last hurdle, but he was so far ahead that he was able to thrust his right arm into the air in triumph eight meters from the finish. "I always wanted to put my hand up at the end of a race," he said, "and I finally got my chance today."

3000-METER STEEPLECHASE

In the steeplechase, runners must negotiate a course of 28 hurdles and seven water jumps. The hurdles are three feet high and are solid, so that they cannot be knocked over. The tops of the hurdles are five inches wide, allowing the contestants to step on them. The water jump, which is preceded by a hedge, is 12 feet long, with a maximum depth of two feet three and one-half inches. Twelve runners take part in the final. The steeplechase event appears to have been introduced in Edinburgh in 1828, although the distance was not standardized at 3000 meters until 1920. It got its name from the fact that it was first run from the church steeple in one village to the church steeple in the next village.

1896 not held

1900 Paris C: 6, N: 6, D: 7.15.
(2500 Meters)

1. George Orton	CAN	7:34.4
2. Sidney Robinson	GBR	7:38.0
3. Jacques Chastanié	FRA	7:41.0
4. Arthur Newton	USA	—
5. Hermann Wraschtil	AUT	—
6. Franz Duhne	GER	—

1904 St. Louis C: 7, N: 2, D: 8.29.
(2590 Meters)

1. James Lightbody	USA	7:39.6
2. John Daly	GBR/IRL	7:40.6
3. Arthur Newton	USA	—
4. W. Frank Verner	USA	—

Lightbody came from behind to win the first of his three gold medals at St. Louis.

1906 not held

1908 London C: 24, N: 6, D: 7.18.
(3200 Meters)

1. Arthur Russell	GBR	10:47.8
2. Archie Robertson	GBR	10:48.4
3. John Eisele	USA	11:00.8
4. C. Guy Holdaway	GBR	—
5. Harold Sewell	GBR	—
6. William Galbraith	CAN	—

A rather unusual controversy developed during the heats, when some of the American runners showed up wearing white shorts, which were prohibited by A.A.A.

rules. They were finally allowed to compete after they had been provided with dark shorts. Russell and Robertson cleared the last hurdle together in the final, but Russell won by two yards in the run-in.

1912 not held

1920 Antwerp C: 16, N: 6, D: 8.20. WR: 9.49.8 (Josef Ternström)
1. Percy Hodge	GBR	10:00.4	OR
2. Patrick Flynn	USA	10:21.1e	
3. Ernesto Ambrosini	ITA	10:32.0e	
4. Gustaf Mattsson	SWE	10:32.1e	
5. Michael Devaney	USA	10:34.3e	
6. Albert Hulsebosch	USA	10:37.7e	
7. Lars Hedvall	SWE	10:42.2e	
8. Raymond Watson	USA	10:50.3e	

The 29-year-old Hodge won easily by 100 yards. Earlier in the year he had entered the A.A.A. steeplechase championship. In the second lap of that race, he was spiked and lost the heel of his shoe. Hodge stopped running, took off his shoe, readjusted and relaced it, and then took off again. He won by 60 yards. Hodge was a superb hurdler who gave exhibitions in which he cleared hurdles while carrying a tray, a bottle, and filled glasses without spilling a drop.

1924 Paris C: 21, N: 9, D: 7.9. WR: 9:33.4 (Paul Bontemps)
1. Vilho "Ville" Ritola	FIN	9:33.6	OR
2. Elias Katz	FIN	9:44.0	
3. Paul Bontemps	FRA	9:45.2	
4. E. Marvin Rick	USA	9:56.4	
5. Karl Ebb	FIN	9:57.6	
6. Evelyn Montague	GBR	9:58.0	
7. Michael Devaney	USA	10:01.0	
8. Albert Isola	FRA	10:14.8	

Paul Bontemps had run a 9:33.4 on June 9, 1924, but was unable to repeat his performance one month later at the Olympics, as Ville Ritola won by 75 meters. Silver medalist Elias Katz was murdered by Arab terrorists on December 24, 1947, while working as a film projectionist at a British army base near Gaza. Sixth-place finisher Evelyn Aubrey Montague is introduced in the film *Chariots of Fire* as a good friend of Harold Abrahams, whose acquaintance he makes when they both arrive at Cambridge as freshmen. In reality, Abrahams and Montague were rivals, since Montague attended not Cambridge, but Oxford.

1928 Amsterdam C: 22, N: 10, D: 8.4. WR: 9:33.4 (Paul Bontemps)
1. Toivo Loukola	FIN	9:21.8	WR
2. Paavo Nurmi	FIN	9:31.2	
3. Ove Andersen	FIN	9:35.6	
4. Nils Eklöf	SWE	9:38.0	
5. Henri Dartigues	FRA	9:40.0	
6. Lucien Duquesne	FRA	9:40.6	

7. Melvin Dalton	USA	—	
8. William Spencer	USA	—	

In the second heat of the qualifying round, Paavo Nurmi fell head over heels into the first water jump and had to be fished out by Lucien Duquesne. Nurmi repaid Duquesne's kindness by pacing him for the rest of the race, the two finishing together. The final marked the last Olympic appearances of Nurmi and Ville Ritola, both of whom were exhausted from their duel in the 5000 meters final the previous day. Ritola dropped out 600 yards short of the finish, but Nurmi held on grimly and placed second, 60 yards behind Toivo Loukola. Five years earlier Loukola had been declared unfit for military service because he had tuberculosis. He had then returned home and taken up running to restore his health.

1932 Los Angeles C: 15, N: 8, D: 8.6. WR: 9:08.4 (George Lermond)
(3460 Meters)
1. Volmari Iso-Hollo	FIN	10:33.4
2. Thomas Evenson	GBR	10:46.0
3. Joseph McCluskey	USA	10:46.2
4. Martti Matilainen	FIN	10:52.4
5. George Bailey	GBR	10:53.2
6. Glen Dawson	USA	10:58.0
7. Giuseppe Lippi	ITA	11:04.0
8. Walter Pritchard	USA	11:04.4

Volmari Iso-Hollo, a 25-year-old typesetter, crossed the finish line with a 40-yard lead, only to discover that there was no tape awaiting him and that the lap counter still read "1." He continued on for an extra lap and won by 75 yards. It was later determined that the lap checker, a substitute for the regular man, who was ill, had forgotten to change the lap count the first time the runners passed by. It didn't make any difference to Iso-Hollo, but the blunder had a profound effect on who won the silver medal. At the end of the regulation distance, McCluskey was in second place and Evenson in third. But during the extra lap Evenson passed McCluskey and beat him to the finish by two yards. When McCluskey pointed out to track officials what had happened, he was offered the opportunity of having the race re-run the next day. Quite exhausted, McCluskey declined, stating that anyway "a race has only one finish line."

1936 Berlin C: 28, N: 13, D: 8.8. WR: 9:08.2 (Harold Manning)
1. Volmari Iso-Hollo	FIN	9:03.8	WR
2. Kaarlo Tuominen	FIN	9:06.8	
3. Alfred Dompert	GER	9:07.2	
4. Martii Matilainen	FIN	9:09.0	
5. Harold Manning	USA	9:11.2	
6. Lars Larsson	SWE	9:16.6	
7. Woldemars Wihtols	LAT	9:18.8	
8. Glen Dawson	USA	9:21.2	

1948 London C: 26, N: 12, D: 8.5. WR: 8:59.6 (Erik Elmsater)
1. Thore Sjöstrand	SWE	9:04.6
2. Erik Elmsäter	SWE	9:08.2

3. Göte Hagström	SWE	9:11.3
4. Alex Guyodo	FRA	9:13.6
5. Pentti Siltaloppi	FIN	9:19.6
6. Petar Šegedin	YUG	9:20.4
7. H. Browning Ross	USA	9:23.2
8. Constantino Miranda Justo	SPA	9:25.0

The only runner given a chance of defeating the Swedes was the European champion, Raphael Pujazon of France. However, Pujazon developed a stomach cramp midway through the final and was forced to retire.

1952 Helsinki C: 35, N: 12, D: 7.25. WR: 8:48.6 (Vladimir Kazantsev)

1. Horace Ashenfelter	USA	8:45.4	WR	(8:45.68)
2. Vladimir Kazantsev	SOV/RUS	8:51.6		(8:51.52)
3. John Disley	GBR	8:51.8		(8:51.94)
4. Olavi Rinteenpää	FIN	8:55.2		(8:55.60)
5. Curt Söderberg	SWE	8:55.6		(8:55.87)
6. Günther Hesselmann	GER	8:55.8		(8:55.98)
7. Mikhail Saltykov	SOV	8:56.2		(8:56.47)
8. Helmut Gude	GER	9:01.4		(9:01.36)

Twenty-seven-year-old F.B.I. agent Horace Ashenfelter of Glen Ridge, New Jersey, caused something of a stir when he won his preliminary heat in 8:51.0. Not only was it the fastest time of the round, but Ashenfelter's previous best had been an undistinguished 9:06.4. Still, it seemed unlikely that Ashenfelter, who had trained at night, using park benches and a homemade bench as hurdles, could seriously challenge world record holder Vladimir Kazantsev. Mikhail Saltykov was the early leader in the final, but before the third lap had ended, Ashenfelter had moved ahead, followed closely by Kazantsev. They continued running together until the final lap. With half a lap to go, Kazantsev forged ahead, and it looked like the race was his. But Kazantsev stumbled slightly at the final water jump, while Ashenfelter breezed through without even breaking stride. Kazantsev had run out of energy, and Ashenfelter pulled away dramatically over the last 150 meters to win by almost 30 yards. Gleeful American sportswriters had a field day—it was the first time that an F.B.I. man had allowed himself to be followed by a Russian. Ashenfelter delighted the Finnish crowd by interrupting his victory lap to run 30 rows into the stands to kiss his wife.

1956 Melbourne C: 23, N: 13, D: 11.29. WR: 8:35.6 (Sándor Rozsnyói)

1. Christopher Brasher	GBR	8:41.2	OR	(8:41.35)
2. Sándor Rozsnyói	HUN	8:43.6		(8:43.68)
3. Ernst Larsen	NOR	8:44.0		(8:44.05)
4. Heinz Laufer	GER	8:44.4		(8:44.53)
5. Semyon Rzhischin	SOV/RUS	8:44.6		(8:44.58)
6. John Disley	GBR	8:44.6		(8:44.79)
7. Neil Robbins	AUS	8:50.0		(8:50.36)
8. Eric Shirley	GBR	8:57.0		

Larsen led until two laps from the finish, after which Rzhischin surged ahead. Entering the final curve, Rozsnyói made his move, with Larsen at his shoulder. As they approached the fourth-to-last hurdle, Rozsnyói swung wide to give himself room to clear. Chris Brasher, a 28-year-old oil company executive, saw his chance, elbowed his way between the two leaders, and sprinted away to an unexpected 15-yard victory. Twelve minutes later it was announced that Brasher had been disqualified for interfering with Larsen. However, Larsen made it clear that although he had been bumped, he considered the incident insignificant, and not worthy of disqualification. Rozsnyói, who was considerably more concerned about the fact that he hadn't heard from his wife or children since Soviet troops had invaded Hungary, also supported Brasher, as did Laufer, the potential bronze medalist. Three hours later, the Jury of Appeal voted unanimously to rescind the disqualification, giving Great Britain its first track and field gold medal since 1936.

1960 Rome C: 32, N: 20, D: 9.3. WR: 8.31.4 (Zdzislaw Krzyszkowiak)

1. Zdzislaw Krzyszkowiak	POL	8:34.2	OR	(8:34.30)
2. Nikolai Sokolov	SOV/RUS	8:36.4		(8:36.55)
3. Semyon Rzhischin	SOV/RUS	8:42.2		(8:42.34)
4. Gaston Roelants	BEL	8:47.6		(8:47.85)
5. Gunnar Tjörnebo	SWE	8:58.6		(8:58.87)

FBI agent Horace Ashenfelter surges past favorite Vladimir Kazantsev at the final water jump of the 1952 steeplechase.

6. Ludwig Müller	GER	9:01.6	(9:01.57)
7. Charles "Deacon" Jones	USA	9:18.2	(9:18.22)
8. Aleksei Konov	SOV/RUS	9:18.2	(9:18.23)

The three Soviet runners ran a team race, hoping to wear down Krzyszkowiak. It didn't work. The 31-year-old Polish world record holder glided past Sokolov on the final backstretch and won by 15 yards.

1964 Tokyo C: 29, N: 19, D: 10.17. WR: 8:29.6 (Gaston Roelants)

1. Gaston Roelants	BEL	8:30.8	OR
2. Maurice Herriott	GBR	8:32.4	
3. Ivan Bylyayev	SOV/UKR	8:33.8	
4. Manuel de Oliveira	POR	8:36.2	
5. George Young	USA	8:38.2	
6. Guy Texereau	FRA	8:38.6	
7. Adolfas Alekseunas	SOV/LIT	8:39.0	
8. Lars-Erik Gustafsson	SWE	8:41.8	

Ahead by five yards after the first lap, Gaston Roelants broke away from the field and led by 50 yards at the start of the bell lap. Maurice Herriott closed the gap rapidly, but fell ten yards short. Between 1961 and 1966 Roelants won 45 straight steeplechase finals. In 1977, at the age of 40, he was clocked in 8:41.5.

1968 Mexico City C: 37, N: 26, D: 10.16. WR: 8:24.2 (Jouko Kuha)

1. Amos Biwott	KEN	8:51.0	(8:51.02)
2. Benjamin Kogo	KEN	8:51.6	(8:51.56)
3. George Young	USA	8:51.8	(8:51.86)
4. Kerry O'Brien	AUS	8:52.0	(8:52.08)
5. Aleksandr Morozov	SOV/RUS	8:55.8	(8:55.61)
6. Mikhail Chelev	BUL	8:58.4	(8:58.41)
7. Gaston Roelants	BEL	8:59.4	(8:59.50)
8. Arne Risa	NOR	9:09.0	(9:08.98)

Amos Biwott's rise to Olympic glory was sudden and unexpected. Early in 1968 he had just finished fourth in the 10,000 meters in a provincial championship, when he noticed that the steeplechase was scheduled for two hours later and decided to "just have a go." He finished second and was selected to take part in the national championship. He won that, placed second to Ben Kogo in the East Africa Championships, and found himself on the Kenyan Olympic team.

The 20-year-old Biwott literally leaped to international prominence in the third and final elimination heat. Either unaware of or disdainful of accepted racing tactics and steeplechase techniques, Biwott sprinted to a 30-yard lead in the first half lap and led by 70 yards before the first lap had been completed. But what really made the crowd go wild was Biwott's bizarre method of clearing the water jump. Contradicting the teachings of every coach in the world, he would jump onto the hedge and then hop over the water, triple-jump-style, landing on dry ground with the same foot he used to take off. His hurdle style was also unique: he jumped over the barriers with his feet together. In the words of Joe Henderson of

Amos Biwott, defying accepted techniques, soars over the water barrier in the 1968 steeplechase.

Track and Field News, "He cleared the hurdles like he feared they had spikes imbedded on the top and leaped the water hazard as if he thought crocodiles were swimming in it." Despite his unorthodox approach, Biwott won his heat by 11.6 seconds.

Naturally, there was a great deal of curiosity as to how well Biwott would stand up in the final two days later against favorites Ben Kogo, Victor Kudinsky, and George Young. Surprisingly, Biwott started slowly, letting Kogo do most of the pace-setting. Unfortunately, Kudinsky withdrew with a hip injury during the second lap. With two laps to go, Gaston Roelants took the lead, while Biwott lingered in ninth place. By the start of the last lap, Kogo was back in the lead. Then, with 300 meters left, Young made his move, passing Kogo on the backstretch. Kogo fought him off, but out of nowhere came Amos Biwott. Kogo was still in front as they cleared the last hurdle, 60 meters from the finish, but Biwott loped right by him and won by three yards.

1972 Munich C: 49, N: 29, D: 9.4. WR: 8:21.98 (Kerry O'Brien)

1. H. Kipchoge Keino	KEN	8:23.6	OR	(8:23.64)
2. Benjamin Jipcho	KEN	8:24.6		(8:24.62)
3. Tapio Kantanen	FIN	8:24.8		(8:24.66)
4. Bronislaw Malinowski	POL	8:28.0		(8:27.92)
5. Dušan Moravčik	CZE	8:29.2		(8:29.06)
6. Amos Biwott	KEN	8:33.6		(8:33.48)
7. Romualdas Bite	SOV/LIT	8:34.6		(8:34.64)
8. Pekka Päivärinta	FIN	8:37.2		(8:37.17)

The second preliminary heat seemed to be cursed. Sergei Skrypka of the Soviet Union lost a shoe with six laps to go, but managed to stay with the leaders until the final water jump, when he slipped and fell headlong into the pond. World record holder Kerry O'Brien had similar bad luck, losing about 200 meters from the finish and smashing into the water jump barrier. In the fourth heat, Amos Biwott set an Olympic record of 8:23.8.

The final was won by Kip Keino, who outkicked his teammate Ben Jipcho. Keino had little steeplechase experience, having entered the race as a challenge. "I had a lot of fun jumping the hurdles," he said, although his lack of experience caused him to jump "like an animal. My style is not good." Anders Gärderud, who was eliminated in the heats, set a world record ten days after the Olympic final.

1976 Montreal C: 24, N: 16, D: 7.28. WR: 8:09.70 (Anders Gärderud)

1. Anders Gärderud	SWE	8:08.2	WR	(8:08.02)
2. Bronislaw Malinowski	POL	8:09.2		(8:09.11)
3. Frank Baumgartl	GDR	8:10.4		(8:10.36)
4. Tapio Kantanen	FIN	8:12.6		(8:12.60)
5. Michael Karst	GER	8:20.1		(8:20.14)
6. Euan Robertson	NZE	8:21.1		(8:21.08)
7. Dan Glans	SWE	8:21.5		(8:21.53)
8. Antonio Campos	SPA	8:22.7		(8:22.65)

The 1976 final was one of the greatest steeplechase races of all time. Antonio Campos led for almost half the race. Then Bronislaw Malinowski, who had issued a warning that he planned to run away from the field in order to make it difficult for "followers" like Anders Gärderud, took over and tried to pull away. But Gärderud and Frank Baumgartl stayed with him. With 300 meters to go, Gärderud, who previously had had trouble living up to expectations in major competitions, flew by Malinowski, with Baumgartl right behind him. Gärderud cleared the final water jump beautifully and opened a five-yard lead. However, the surprising Baumgartl closed the gap as they approached the final hurdle. Gärderud cleared perfectly again, but Baumgartl clipped the barrier with his trail knee and sprawled to the ground. Malinowski jumped over the human hurdle and beat the world record, but he couldn't catch Gärderud. Baumgartl, recalling Lasse Viren's fall in the 1972 10,000 meters, leaped to his feet and salvaged the bronze medal, improving his personal best by 7.2 seconds, despite his mishap.

Coming off the final hurdle of the 1976 steeplechase, Bronislaw Malinowski (724) is forced to add a human hurdle to the obstacles in his path as Anders Gärderud (812) streaks to victory.

1980 Moscow C: 31, N: 18, D: 7.31. WR: 8:05.4 (Henry Rono)

1. Bronislaw Malinowski	POL	8:09.7	(8:09.70)
2. Filbert Bayi	TAN	8:12.5	(8:12.48)
3. Eshetu Tura	ETH	8:13.6	(8:13.57)
4. Domingo Ramón	SPA	8:15.8	(8:15.74)
5. Francisco Sanchez	SPA	8:18.0	(8:17.93)
6. Giuseppe Gerbi	ITA	8:18.5	(8:18.47)
7. Boguslaw Mamiński	POL	8:19.5	(8:19.43)
8. Anatoly Dimov	SOV/RUS	8:19.8	(8:19.75)

No longer contemptuous of those who only follow during the early going, Bronislaw Malinowski was quite content to let Filbert Bayi set the pace in Moscow. Bayi, an air force mechanic from the Mbulu tribe, had little steeplechase experience, whereas Malinowski had been concentrating on the event for 13 years. The offspring of a Polish father and a Scottish mother, Malinowski had finished fourth in 1972 and second in 1976.

Bayi drove into the lead immediately and led by 35 meters with two laps to go, but about a half lap later he suddenly began to tire. Malinowski caught him on the backstretch and won easily, finally achieving his goal of an Olympic gold medal. When asked why he had followed such a suicidal race plan, Bayi replied, "Because it's fun. . . . It is fun to run as fast as one can until you are dead-tired." He was the first Tanzanian ever to win an Olympic medal. Unfortunately, Bronislaw Malinowski was killed in a car crash on September 26, 1981, near his hometown of Grudziadz. He was 30 years old.

1984 Los Angeles C: 35, N: 25, D: 8.10. WR: 8:05.4 (Henry Rono)

1. Julius Korir	KEN	8:11.80
2. Joseph Mahmoud	FRA	8:13.31
3. Brian Diemer	USA	8:14.06
4. Henry Marsh	USA	8:14.25
5. Colin Reitz	GBR	8:15.48
6. Domingo Ramón	SPA	8:17.27
7. Julius Kariuki	KEN	8:17.47
8. Pascal Debacker	FRA	8:21.51

After a slow first lap, Peter Renner of New Zealand moved to the front and set a hard pace for the first 2000 meters. With 500 meters to go, Washington State student Julius Korir took the lead. The pre-race favorite, Henry Marsh, moved into second shortly after the bell, positioning himself well for his famous finishing kick. But 220 meters from the finish line, Korir pulled away and scored a decisive victory. Mahmoud and Diemer passed Marsh in the stretch to gain the other medals. Marsh, suffering from a lingering virus, collapsed after the race and was taken away on a stretcher. Of the eight top finishers, all but Marsh and Ramón bettered their pre-Olympic personal records.

1988 Seoul C: 32, N: 24, D: 9.30. WR: 8:05.4 (Henry Rono)

1. Julius Kariuki	KEN	8:05.51	OR
2. Peter Koech	KEN	8:06.79	
3. Mark Rowland	GBR	8:07.96	
4. Alessandro Lambruschini	ITA	8:12.17	

5.	William Van Dijck	BEL	8:13.99
6.	Henry Marsh	USA	8:14.39
7.	Patrick Sang	KEN	8:15.22
8.	Boguslaw Mamiński	POL	8:15.97

Francesco Panetta of Italy won the 1987 world championship with an inspired piece of frontrunning. He tried the same strategy at the Olympics, but with considerably less success. Panetta held a slight lead for the first 2000 meters, but then began to struggle. Kariuki, finding himself in front, turned back toward Koech and asked him to take over. Koech whipped into the lead, taking his teammate with him. Panetta faded to a ninth-place finish. With 600 meters to go, Kariuki moved past Koech and opened a ten-meter lead. He eased up at the finish, unaware that he was so close to breaking Henry Rono's ten-year-old world record. Kariuki seemed unconcerned. At the post-race press conference he asked, "What did you say the time was? 8:05.51? Ah, truly not bad." On July 3, 1989, Rono's record finally was beaten: by Peter Koech in 8:05.35.

1992 Barcelona C: 32, N: 23, D: 8.7. WR: 8:05.35 (Peter Koech)

1.	Matthew Birir	KEN	8:08.84
2.	Patrick Sang	KEN	8:09.55
3.	William Mutwol	KEN	8:10.74
4.	Alessandro Lambruschini	ITA	8:15.52
5.	Steffen Brand	GER	8:16.60
6.	Tom Hanlon	GBR	8:18.14
7.	Brian Diemer	USA	8:18.77
8.	Azzeddine Brahmi	ALG	8:20.71

Since 1968 Kenyans have won every Olympic steeplechase they have entered (Kenya boycotted in 1976 and 1980). By 1992 their dominance was overwhelming: seven of the eight fastest runners of the year were Kenyan. They approached the Olympics in a matter-of-fact fashion. As Patrick Sang explained: "Before the race started, we discussed the way each of us runs, our strengths and weaknesses. As Mutwol is a cross-country and 5000-meter runner we decided that he should set a fast pace and lead the group. Birir is a 1500-meter runner and it was decided he should move to the front with four laps to go. That's all there was to it. Our aim was to run most of the race together and leave it to the one who was strongest at the end to come home first for Kenya." The only glitch in the Kenyan plan came after 1000 meters when Birir was clipped by Azzeddine Brahmi, tore his shoe, and fell to one knee. Although the mishap dropped him to ninth place, he was back to fourth within 100 meters and went on to win.

World champion Moses Kiptanui of Kenya missed the Olympics because of a knee injury and a strained tendon. "When the rest of the team went off to Barcelona I was injured," he explained later. "There was nothing I could do and I knew there were going to be no gold medals this year, so I decided to break some world records." Nine days after the Olympic final he broke the world record

for the unimpeded 3000 meters, and then, three days after that, he set a steeplechase world record of 8:02.08.

4 × 100-METER RELAY

The 4 × 100-meter relay is a one-lap race run in lanes with a staggered start. The first runner for each team begins in starting blocks; the second, third, and fourth runners use a running start. The baton, made of wood or metal, is between 11 inches (28 centimeters) and 11¾ inches (30 centimeters) long and between 4¾ inches (12 centimeters) and 5 inches (13 centimeters) in circumference. It must weigh at least 50 grams (1.76 ounces). The baton must be carried by hand. If the baton is dropped, the runner may go out of his or her lane to retrieve it as long as that does not lessen the distance covered. Baton exchanges must take place within a 20-meter (21.87-yard) passing zone. It is the position of the baton, not the position of the runners' hands or bodies, that determines whether a pass is successful. A pass out of zone results in immediate disqualification. In the following charts and for all relay charts, runners who took part in preliminary heats but not in the final are included in brackets.

This event has been dominated by the United States, which has won it 14 of 18 times. The only U.S. losses have been the result of disqualification (1912, 1960, and 1988) and boycott (1980). The United States has retained this edge by using raw speed to overcome mediocre passing.

1896–1908 not held

1912 Stockholm T: 8, N: 8, D: 7.9

1.	GBR	(David Jacobs, Henry Macintosh, Victor D'Arcy, William Applegarth)	42.4
2.	SWE	(Ivan Möller, Charles Luther, Ture Persson, Knut Lindberg)	42.6
DISQ:	GER	(Otto Röhr, Max Herrmann, Erwin Kern, Richard Rau)	

The U.S. team of Courtney, Belote, Wilson, and Cooke won the first semifinal in a time of 42.2, but was disqualified for passing out of the zone. The third semifinal was won by the German team, in 42.3; however they too were disqualified for passing out of the zone in the final, in which they finished second.

1920 Antwerp T: 13, N: 13, D: 8.22. WR: 42.3 (GER—Röhr, Herrmann, Kern, Rau)

1.	USA	(Charles Paddock, Jackson Scholz, Loren Murchison, Morris Kirksey)	42.2	WR
2.	FRA	(René Tirard, René Lorain, René Mourlon, Emile Ali-Khan)	42.5e	
3.	SWE	(Agne Holmström, William Petersson [Björneman], Sven Malm, Nils Sandström)	42.8e	
4.	GBR	(William Hill, Harold Abrahams, Victor D'Arcy, Denis Black)	43.0e	

| 5. | DEN | (Henri Thorsen, Fritiof Andersen, August Sörensen, Marinus Sörensen) | 43.3e | |
| 6. | LUX | (Jean Colbach, Paul Hammer, Jean Proess, Alex Servais) | 43.6e | |

1924 Paris T: 15, N: 15, D: 7.13. WR: 42.2 (USA—Paddock, Scholz, Murchison, Kirksey)

1.	USA	(Francis Hussey, Louis Clarke, Loren Murchison, Alfred Leconey)	41.0	EWR
2.	GBR	(Harold Abrahams, Walter Rangeley, Lancelot Royle, William Nichol)	41.2	
3.	HOL	(Jacob Boot, Henricus Broos, Jan de Vries, Marinus van den Berge)	41.8	
4.	HUN	(Ferenc Gerö, Lajos Kurunczy, László Muskát, Gusztáv Rózsahegyi)	42.0	
5.	FRA	(Maurice Degrelle, Albert Heise, René Mourlon, André Mourlon)	42.2	

DISQ: SWI (Karl Borner, Heinz Hemmi, Joseph Imbach, David Moriaud)

A wholesale assault on the world record began in the first heat of the first round, when Great Britain clocked 42.0. The Dutch team equaled this time in the next heat, but in the sixth heat the Americans ran away in 41.2. In the semifinal, the United States recorded a time of 41.0, and repeated this performance in the final. The most surprising aspect of the final was that the U.S. leadoff runner, Francis Hussey of Stuyvesant High School in New York City, beat 100-meter gold medalist Harold Abrahams by two yards.

1928 Amsterdam T: 13, N: 13, D: 8.5. WR: 41.0 (USA—Hussey, Clarke, Murchison, Leconey; Newark Athletic Club, USA—Bowman, Currie, Pappas, Cumming; Sports Club Eintracht, GER—Geerling, Wichmann, Metzner, Salz)

1.	USA	(Frank Wykoff, James Quinn, Charles Borah, Henry Russell)	41.0	EWR
2.	GER	(Georg Lammers, Richard Corts, Hubert Houben, Helmut Körnig)	41.2	
3.	GBR	(Cyril Gill, Edward Smouha, Walter Rangeley, Jack London)	41.8	
4.	FRA	(André Cerbonney, Gilbert Auvergne, Pierre Dufau, André Mourlon)	42.0	
5.	SWI	(Emmanuel Goldsmith, Willy Weibel, Willy Tschopp, Hans Niggl)	42.6	

DISQ: CAN (Ralph Adams, John Fitzpatrick, George Hester, Percy Williams)

1932 Los Angeles T: 8, N: 8, D: 8.7. WR: 40.8 (GER—Jonath, Corts, Houben, Körnig; Sports Club Charlottenburg, GER—Körnig, Grosser, Natan, Schloske; University of Southern California, USA—Delby, Mauer, Guyer, Wykoff)

1.	USA	(Robert Kiesel, Emmett Toppino, Hector Dyer, Frank Wykoff)	40.0	WR
2.	GER	(Helmut Körnig, Friedrich Hendrix, Erich Borchmeyer, Arthur Jonath)	40.9	
3.	ITA	(Giuseppe Castelli, Ruggero Maregatti, Gabriele Salviati, Edgardo Toetti)	41.2	
4.	CAN	(Percy Williams, James Brown, Harold Wright, Birchall Pearson)	41.3	

| 5. | JPN | (Takayoshi Yoshioka, Chuhei Nambu, Izuo Anno, Itaro Nakajima) | 41.3 | |
| 6. | GBR | (Donald Finlay, Stanley Fuller, Stanley Engelhart, Ernest Page) | 41.4 | |

The U.S. team set world records of 40.6 in the preliminaries and 40.0 in the final without having to use their leading sprinters, Eddie Tolan, Ralph Metcalfe, and George Simpson.

1936 Berlin T: 15, N: 15, D: 8.9. WR: 40.0 (USA—Kiesel, Toppino, Dyer, Wykoff)

1.	USA	(James "Jesse" Owens, Ralph Metcalfe, Foy Draper, Frank Wykoff)	39.8	WR
2.	ITA	(Orazio Mariani, Gianni Caldana, Elio Ragni, Tullio Gonnelli)	41.1	
3.	GER	(Wilhelm Leichum, Erich Borchmeyer, Erwin Gillmeister, Gerd Hornberger)	41.2	
4.	ARG	(Juan Lavenas, Antonio Sande, Carlos Hofmeister, Tomas Clifford Beswick)	42.2	
5.	CAN	(Samuel Richardson, Arthur Bruce Humber, Lee Orr, Howard McPhee)	42.7	

DISQ: HOL (Tjeerd Boersma, Wijnand van Beveren, Christiaan Berger, Martinus Osendarp)

The 4 × 100-meter relay was the focus of one of the uglier incidents of the 1936 Games, one that caused great embarrassment to the United States. For weeks it had been assumed that the U.S. team would consist of Sam Stoller, Marty Glickman, Frank Wykoff, and Foy Draper, and the foursome spent a good deal of time practicing their baton passing. On August 5, three days before the qualifying heats, Jesse Owens won the 200-meter dash, gaining his third gold medal. When asked if Owens would be added to the relay quartet, coach Lawson Robertson replied, "Owens has had enough glory and collected enough gold medals and oak trees to last him a while. We want to give the other boys a chance to enjoy the '*cérémonie protocolaire*.' Marty Glickman, Sam Stoller, and Frank Wykoff are assured places on the relay team. The fourth choice rests between Foy Draper and Ralph Metcalfe."

Two days later, however, Robertson announced that Owens would probably replace Glickman. Then, on the morning of the heats, the U.S. coaches informed both Glickman and Stoller that they were being dropped from the team and replaced by Owens and Metcalfe. What made the situation ugly was that Stoller and Glickman were the only Jews on the U.S. track team, and they returned to the United States as the only members of the squad who didn't compete. Robertson's excuse was that he feared the speed of the Dutch and German teams, and wanted to field the fastest foursome possible. Robertson's alleged fears turned out to be unfounded. If he had really been concerned about fielding the best teams possible, he should have paid more attention to the 4 × 400-meter relay team. In that event, Robertson bypassed medal winners Archie Williams,

James LuValle, and Glenn Hardin, and stuck with the original foursome, who promptly lost to the British by over 12 yards.

At any rate, the U.S. 4 × 100 team won easily by 15 yards, setting a world record that would last for 20 years. Frank Wykoff, running the anchor leg, won his third straight relay gold medal, setting a world record each time.

Fifty years after the Berlin Games, 68-year-old Marty Glickman visited the Olympic Stadium for the first time since he had been prevented from competing. Glickman blamed U.S. Olympic Committee president Avery Brundage for making the decision against him so as not to humiliate Adolf Hitler. Glickman described his visit in the *New York Times:* "I went down into the well of the stadium and walked along the backstretch of the track, the portion I should have run so many years before. I stopped and looked across to the far side where Hitler and his entourage had watched the Games. Fifty feet to the right was the section reserved for the athletes where I had watched the races. Suddenly a wave of rage overwhelmed me. I thought I was going to pass out. I began to scream every dirty curse word, every obscenity I knew. How could you no-good, dirty so-and-sos do this to an 18-year-old kid, to any young man who worked so hard to get there, you rotten S.O.B.s. . . . For 49 years that anger and frustration, that rage, had been inside me. . . . But being there, visualizing and reliving those moments, caused the eruption which had been gnawing at me for so long and which I thought I had expunged years ago."

1948 London T: 15, N: 15, D: 8.7. WR: 39.8 (USA—Owens, Metcalfe, Draper, Wykoff)

1.	USA	(Norwood "Barney" Ewell, Lorenzo Wright, Harrison Dillard, Melvin Patton)	40.6
2.	GBR	(John Archer, John Gregory, Alastair McCorquodale, Kenneth Jones)	41.3
3.	ITA	(Michele Tito, Enrico Perucconi, Antonio Siddi, Carlo Monti)	41.5
4.	HUN	(Ferenc Tima, László Bartha, György Csányi, Béla Goldoványi)	41.6
5.	CAN	(Don McFarlane, James O'Brien, Donald Pettie, Edward Haggis)	41.9
6.	HOL	(Jan Lammers, Johannes Meyer, Gabe Scholten, Jan Zwaan)	41.9

The U.S. team crossed the finish line six yards ahead of the British, but was disqualified when a judge claimed that the first pass, between Barney Ewell and Lorenzo Wright, had taken place beyond the legal zone. The Americans were dumbfounded and immediately lodged a formal protest. The medal ceremony was held anyway, but three days later a Jury of Appeal viewed films of the race and discovered that the pass had been perfectly legal, and that the track official had been in error. The disqualification was therefore rescinded.

1952 Helsinki T: 22, N: 22, D: 7.27. WR: 39.8 (USA—Owens, Metcalfe, Draper, Wykoff)

1.	USA	(F. Dean Smith, Harrison Dillard, Lindy Remigino, Andrew Stanfield)	40.1	(40.26)
2.	SOV	(Boris Tokaryev, Levan Kalyayev, Levan Sanadze, Vladimir Sukharyev)	40.3	(40.58)
3.	HUN	(László Zarándi, Géza Varasdi, György Csányi, Béla Goldoványi)	40.5	(40.83)
4.	GBR	(Emmanuel McDonald Bailey, William Jack, John Gregory, Brian Shenton)	40.6	(40.85)
5.	FRA	(Alain Porthault, Etienne Bally, Yves Camus, René Bonino)	40.9	(41.10)
6.	CZE	(František Brož, Jiři David, Miroslav Horčic, Zdenek Pospišil)	41.2	(41.41)

The United States and the U.S.S.R. were almost even after three legs, but Stanfield drew away from Sukharyev to win by two yards.

1956 Melbourne T: 18, N: 18, D: 12.1. WR: 39.8 (USA—Owens, Metcalfe, Draper, Wykoff)

1.	USA	(Ira Murchison, Leamon King, W. Thane Baker, Bobby Joe Morrow)	39.5 WR	(39.60)
2.	SOV	(Boris Tokaryev, Vladimir Sukharyev, Leonid Bartenyev, Yuri Konovalov)	39.8	(39.93)
3.	GER	(Lothar Knörzer, Leonhard Pohl, Heinz Fütterer, Manfred Germar)	40.3	(40.34)
4.	ITA	(Franco Galbiati, Giovanni Ghiselli, Luigi Gnocchi, Vincenzo Lombardo)	40.3	(40.43)
5.	GBR	(Kenneth Box, E. Roy Sandstrom, Brian Shenton, David Segal)	40.6	(40.74)
6.	POL	(Marian Foik, Janusz Jarzembowski, Edward Schmidt, Zenon Baranowski)	40.6	(40.75)

1960 Rome T: 19, N: 19, D: 9.8. WR: 39.5 (USA—Baker, King, Morrow, Murchison; GER—Steinbach, Lauer, Fütterer, Germar)

1.	GER	(Bernd Cullmann, Armin Hary, Walter Mahlendorf, Martin Lauer)	39.5 EWR	(39.66)
2.	SOV	(Gusman Kosanov, Leonid Bartenyev, Yuri Konovalov, Edvins Ozoliņs)	40.1	(40.24)
3.	GBR	(Peter Radford, David Jones, David Segal, J. Neville "Nick" Whitehead)	40.2	(40.32)
4.	ITA	(Armando Sardi, Pier Giorgio Cazzola, Salvatore Giannone, Livio Berruti)	40.2	(40.33)
5.	VEN	(S. Clive Bonas, Lloyd Murad, Emilio Romero, Rafael Romero)	40.7	(40.83)

DISQ: USA (Frank Budd, O. Ray Norton, Stonewall Johnson, David Sime)

The United States had won eight straight 4 × 100-meter relays, but in the opening round the West Germans served notice that they would be serious contenders when they equaled the world record of 39.5. Disaster struck the Americans in the final. Ray Norton, anxious to make up for his disappointing sixth-place finishes in the 100 and 200, took off too quickly on his second leg. Leadoff runner Frank Budd yelled at Norton, who came to almost a complete halt. But it was too late. He was already three yards beyond the twenty-meter passing zone. Norton didn't realize it at the time, and ran a strong leg anyway, moving the United States from fourth to second. Dave Sime's come-from-behind anchor leg brought the United States through the tape in first place, in world record time, but the disqualification gave the victory to the Germans, who equaled the world record again in the final.

1964 Tokyo T: 21, N: 21, D: 10.21. WR: 39.1 (USA—Jones, Budd, Frazier, Drayton)

1.	USA	(O. Paul Drayton, Gerald Ashworth, Richard Stebbins, Robert Hayes)	39.0 WR	(39.06)
2.	POL	(Andrzej Zieliński, Wieslaw Maniak, Marian Foik, Marian Dudziak)	39.3	(39.36)
3.	FRA	(Paul Genevay, Bernard Laidebeur, Claude Piquemal, Jocelyn Delecour)	39.3	(39.36)
4.	JAM	(Pablo McNeil, Patrick Robinson, Lynworth Headley, Dennis Johnson)	39.4	(39.49)
5.	SOV	(Edvins Ozoliņs, Boris Zubov, Gusman Kosanov, Boris Savchuk)	39.4	(39.50)
6.	VEN	(Arquimedes Herrera, Lloyd Murad, Rafael Romero, Hortensio Herrera Fucil)	39.5	(39.53)
7.	ITA	(Livio Berruti, Ennio Preatoni, Sergio Ottolina, Pasquale Giannattasio)	39.5	(39.54)
8.	GBR	(Peter Radford, Ronald Jones, Walter Campbell, Lynn Davies)	39.6	(39.69)

Poor baton passing put the United States in fifth place, three meters behind France, when Bob Hayes took over for the anchor leg. Hayes then unleashed one of the most awesome and breathtaking displays of sprinting ever seen. He swept into the lead after only 30 yards and crossed the finish line with a three-meter margin of victory. Observers disagreed as to Hayes' time for his flying-start 100-meter leg, but the slowest estimate was 8.9 seconds.

1968 Mexico City T: 19, N: 19, D: 10.20. WR: 38.6 (University of Southern California, USA/JAM—McCulloch, Kuller, Simpson, Miller)

1.	USA	(Charles Greene, Melvin Pender, Ronnie Ray Smith, James Hines)	38.24	WR
2.	CUB	(Hermes Ramírez, Juan Morales, Pablo Montes, Enrique Figuerola Camue)	38.40	
3.	FRA	(Gérard Fénouil, Jocelyn Delecour, Claude Piquemal, Roger Bambuck)	38.43	
4.	JAM	(Errol Stewart, Michael Fray, Clifton Forbes, Lennox Miller)	38.47	
5.	GDR	(Heinz Erbstösser, Hartmut Schelter, Peter Hasse, Harald Eggers)	38.66	
6.	GER	(Karl-Peter Schmidtke, Gerhard Wucherer, Gert Metz, Joachim Eigenherr)	38.76	
7.	ITA	(Sergio Ottolina, Ennio Preatoni, Angelo Sguazzero, Livio Berruti)	39.22	
8.	POL	(Wieslaw Maniak, Edward Romanowski, Zenon Nowosz, Marian Dudziak)	39.22	

With Charlie Greene running with heavily bandaged legs, the United States was beaten to the tape by Cuba in

both the opening round and the semifinals. Although Greene ran the final as if uninjured, mediocre baton passing left the United States in only third place when Jim Hines took over for the anchor leg. Five feet behind Enrique Figuerola at the exchange, Hines ripped into the lead after 30 yards and won by a yard. The Cubans mailed their silver medals to activist Stokely Carmichael as a symbol of support for U.S. blacks.

1972 Munich T: 27, N: 27, D: 9.10. WR: 38.24 (USA—Greene, Pender, R. R. Smith, Hines)

1.	USA	(Larry Black, Robert Taylor, Gerald Tinker, Edward Hart)	38.19	WR
2.	SOV	(Aleksandr Kornelyuk, Vladimir Lovetski, Juris Silovs, Valery Borzov)	38.50	
3.	GER	(Jobst Hirscht, Karlheinz Klotz, Gerhard Wucherer, Klaus Ehl)	38.79	
4.	CZE	(Jaroslav Matoušek, Juraj Demeč, Jiři Kynos, Ludvik Bohman)	38.82	
5.	GDR	(Manfred Kokot, Bernd Borth, Hans-Jürgen Bombach, Siegfried Schenke)	38.90	
6.	POL	(Stanislaw Wagner, Tadeusz Cuch, Jerzy Czerbniak, Zenon Nowosz)	39.03	
7.	FRA	(Patrick Bourbeillon, Jean-Pierre Gres, Gerard Fenouil, Bruno Cherrier)	39.14	
8.	ITA	(Vincenzo Guerini, Ennio Preatoni, Luigi Benedetti, Pietro Mennea)	39.14	

For the first time since 1932, the 4 × 100-meter relay was won by a team that did not include the 100-meter gold medalist. Eddie Hart, running the anchor leg for the United States, gained some degree of satisfaction after missing the start of his 100-meter quarterfinal heat.

1976 Montreal T: 20, N: 20, D: 7.31. WR: 38.19 (USA—Black, Taylor, Tinker, Hart)

1.	USA	(Harvey Glance, John Wesley Jones, Millard Hampton, Steven Riddick)	38.33
2.	GDR	(Manfred Kokot, Jörg Pfeifer, Klaus-Dieter Kurrat, Alexander Thieme)	38.66
3.	SOV	(Alexander Aksinin, Nikolai Kolesnikov, Juris Silovs, Valery Borzov)	38.78
4.	POL	(Andrzej Świerczyński, Marian Woronin, Bogdan Grzejszczak, Zenon Licznerski)	38.83
5.	CUB	(Francisco Gomez, Alejandro Casañas Ramírez, Hermes Ramírez, Silvio Leonard Tartabull)	39.01
6.	ITA	(Vincenzo Guerini, Luciano Caravani, Luigi Benedetti, Pietro Mennea)	39.08
7.	FRA	(Claude Amoureux, Joseph Arame, Lucien Sainte-Rose, Dominique Chauvelot)	39.16
8.	CAN	(Hugh Spooner, Marvin Nash, Albin Dukowski, Hugh Fraser)	39.47

1980 Moscow T: 16, N: 16, D: 9.1. WR: 38.03 (USA—Collins, Riddick, Wiley, Williams)

1.	SOV	(Vladimir Muravyov, Nikolai Sidorov, Aleksandr Aksinin, Andrei Prokofyev)	38.26

2. POL   (Krzysztof Zwoliński, Zenon Licznerski, Leszek   38.33
          Dunecki, Marian Woronin)
3. FRA   (Antoine Richard, Pascal Barré, Patrick Barré,   38.53
          Hermann Panzo)
4. GBR   (Michael McFarlane, Allan Wells, R. Cameron   38.62
          Sharp, Andrew McMaster)
5. GDR   (Sören Schlegel, Eugen Ray, Bernhard Hoff,   38.73
          Thomas Munkelt)
6. BUL   (Pavel Pavlov, Vladimir Ivanov, Ivailo   38.99
          Karaniotov, Peter Petrov)
7. NGR   (Hammed Adio, Kayode Elegbede, Samson   39.12
          Oyeledun, Peter Okodogbe)
8. BRA   (Milton Costa de Castro, Nelson Rocha Dos   39.54
          Santos, Katsuiko Nakaia, Altevir Araujo Filho)

The French team included 21-year-old twins, Pascal and Patrick Barré.

1984 Los Angeles T: 20, N: 20, D: 8.11. WR: 37.86 (USA—King, Gault, C. Smith, Lewis)
1. USA   (Sam Graddy, Ron Brown, Calvin Smith,   37.83   WR
          F. Carlton Lewis)
2. JAM   (Albert Lawrence, Gregory Meghoo, Don-   38.62
          ald Quarrie, Raymond Stewart, [Norman
          Edwards])
3. CAN   (Benjamin Johnson, Tony Sharpe, Desai   38.70
          Williams, Sterling Hinds)
4. ITA   (Antonio Ullo, Giovanni Bongiorni, Ste-   38.87
          fano Tilli, Pietro Mennea)
5. GER   (Jürgen Koffler, Peter Klein, Jürgen   38.99
          Evers, Ralf Lübke, [Christian Zirkelbach])
6. FRA   (Antoine Richard, Jean-Jacques Bousse-   39.10
          mart, Marc Gasparoni, Bruno Marie-
          Rose)
7. GBR   (Francis "Daley" Thompson, Donovan   39.13
          Reid, Michael McFarlane, Allan Wells)
8. BRA   (Arnaldo da Silva, Nelson Rocha Dos   39.40
          Santos, Katsuiko Nakaia, Paulo Correia,
          [Robson da Silva])

Running an 8.94 anchor leg, Carl Lewis won his fourth gold medal, as the U.S. team set the only track and field world record of the Los Angeles Games. The second-place Jamaican squad included 33-year-old Donald Quarrie, who brought his three-Olympic medal total to one gold, two silver and one bronze.

1988 Seoul T: 30, N: 30, D: 10.1. WR: 37.83 (USA—Graddy, Brown, Smith, Lewis)
1. SOV   (Viktor Bryzhin, Vladimir Krylov, Vladimir   38.19
          Muravyov, Vitaly Savin)
2. GBR   (Elliott Bunney, John Regis, Michael   38.28
          McFarlane, Linford Christie, [Clarence
          Callender])
3. FRA   (Bruno Marie-Rose, Daniel Sangouma,   38.40
          Gilles Quénéhervé, Max Morinière)
4. JAM   (Christopher Faulknor, Gregory Meghoo,   38.47
          Clive Wright, John Mair)
5. ITA   (Ezio Madonia, Sandro Floris,   38.54
          Pierfrancesco Pavoni, Stefano Tilli)

6. GER   (Fritz Heer, Christian Haas, Peter Klein,   38.55
          Dirk Schweisfurth)
7. CAN   (Desai Williams, Atlee Mahorn, Cyprian   38.93
          Enweani, Brian Morrison, [Andrew
          Mowatt])
8. HUN   (György Bakos, László Karaffa, István   39.19
          Tatár, Attila Kovács)

The favored U.S. team was disqualified in the opening round when Lee McNeill, who had finished eighth at the U.S. Olympic trials, failed to receive the pass from Calvin Smith until he was over five meters beyond the passing zone.

1992 Barcelona T: 26, N: 26, D: 8.8. WR: 37.50 (USA—Cason, Burrell, Mitchell, Lewis)
1. USA   (Mike Marsh, Leroy Burrell, Dennis Mitch-   37.40   WR
          ell, F. Carlton Lewis, [James Jett])
2. NGR   (Oluyemi Kayode, Chidi Imoh, Olapade   37.98
          Adeniken, Davidson Ezinwa, [Osmond
          Ezinwa])
3. CUB   (Andrés Simón Gómez, Joel Lamela   38.00
          Loaces, Joel Isasi González, Jorge Luis
          Aguilera Ruiz)
4. GBR   (Marcus Adam, Tony Jarrett, John Regis,   38.08
          Linford Christie, [Jason John])
5. SOV   (Pavel Galkin, Edvin Ivanov, Andrei   38.17
          Fedoriv, Vitaly Savin)
6. JPN   (Shinji Aoto, Hisatsugu Suzuki, Satoru   38.77
          Inoue, Tatsuo Sugimoto)
7. AUT   (Christoph Postinger, Thomas Renner,   39.30
          Andreas Berger, Franz Ratzenberger)
8. IVC   (Franck Waotta, Jean Olivier Zirignon,   39.31
          Gilles Bogui, Ouattara Lagazane)

When Carl Lewis finished only sixth in the 100 meters at the U.S. Olympic trials, his detractors claimed he was over the hill. Lewis said he had been suffering from a sinus infection that spread. Lewis was right. His sixth-place finish qualified him as only an alternate on the relay team, but when Mark Witherspoon ruptured an Achilles tendon in the semifinals of the 100 meters, Lewis was back where he wanted to be, anchoring the U.S. squad in the Olympic final. Unusually fine passing earned the United States its 15th world record in an Olympic 4 × 100-meter race and brought Carl Lewis his eighth gold medal.

4 × 400-METER RELAY

The 4 × 400-meter relay is begun in lanes from a staggered start with each runner covering one lap. The first runner remains in his or her lane. The second runner may cut to the inside after the first curve. The third and fourth runners, under the direction of an official, place themselves from lane 1 out, according to the order of their teams when the incoming runners are half a lap away. Even if the team order changes in the next 200 meters, the waiting runners must remain in their lanes. Incoming

In the 1992 4 × 100-meter relay, Davidson Ezinwa and Jorge Luis Aquilera are just as thrilled with their finishes as Carl Lewis is with his victory.

runners must stay in their lanes after passing the baton in order to avoid obstructing other teams. The construction of the baton and the length of the passing zones are the same as in the 4 × 100-meter relay.

1896–1906 not held

1908 London T: 7, N: 7, D: 7.25.
(Medley Relay: 200, 200, 400, 800)
1. USA (William Hamilton, Nathaniel Cartmell, John 3:29.4
       Taylor, Melvin Sheppard)
2. GER (Arthur Hoffman, Hans Eicke, Otto Trieloff, 3:32.4
       Hanns Braun)
3. HUN (Pal Simon, Frigyes Mezey-Wiesner, József 3:32.5
       Nagy, Ödön Bodor)

The U.S. team clocked 3:27.2 in the first round, but eased up in the final, winning by 25 yards. John Taylor, who ran the third leg, was the first black athlete to win an Olympic gold medal. He was just about to open up practice as a veterinarian, when he died of typhoid on December 2, 1908, at the age of 24.

1912 Stockholm T: 7, N: 7, D: 7.15. WR: 3:18.2 (USA—Schaaf, Sheppard, Gissing, Rosenberger)
1. USA (Melvin Sheppard, Edward Lindberg, 3:16.6 WR
       James "Ted" Meredith, Charles Reid-
       path)
2. FRA (Charles Lelong, Robert Schurrer, Pierre 3:20.7
       Failliot, Charles Poulenard)
3. GBR (George Nicol, Ernest Henley, James 3:23.2
       Tindal Soutter, Cyril Seedhouse)

Sheppard, running in his ninth race in ten days, also competed in the 800 meters, 1500 meters, and 400 meters. Meredith, running his eighth race, took part in the 800 and the 400.

1920 Antwerp T: 6, N: 6, D: 8.23. WR: 3:16.6 (USA—Sheppard, Lindberg, Meredith, Reidpath)
1. GBR (Cecil Griffiths, Robert Lindsay, John Ainsworth- 3:22.2
       Davis, Guy Butler)
2. SAF (Harry Davel, Clarence Oldfield, Jack Ooster- 3:23.0e
       laak, Bevil Rudd)

3. FRA (Georges "Géo" André, Gaston Fèry, Maurice 3:23.5e
Delvart, André Devaux)

4. USA (George Schiller, George Bretnall, James "Ted" 3:23.6e
Meredith, Frank Shea)

5. SWE (Sven Krokström, Sven Malm, Erik Sundblad, 3:24.3e
Nils Engdahl)

6. BEL (Jules Migeot, Auguste Corteyn, Omer Smet, 3:24.9e
François Morren)

1924 Paris T: 7, N: 7, D: 7.13. WR: 3:16.4 (American Legion, Pennsylvania, USA—Rodgers, Eby, Brown, Maxam)

1. USA Commodore Cochrane, Alan Helffrich, 3:16.0 WR
J. Oliver MacDonald, William Stevenson)

2. SWE (Artur Svensson, Erik Byléhn, Gustaf 3:17.0
Wejnarth, Nils Engdahl)

3. GBR (Edward Toms, George Renwick, Rich- 3:17.4
ard Ripley, Guy Butler)

4. CAN (Horace Aylwin, Allan Christie, David 3:22.8
Johnson, William Maynes)

5. FRA (Raymond Fritz, Gaston Fèry, Francis 3:23.4
Galtier, Barthélemy Favaudon)

6. ITA (Guido Cominotto, Alfredo Gargiullo, 3:28.0
Ennio Maffiolini, Luigi Facelli)

The British team was hampered by the absence of Eric Liddell, who was off preaching a sermon, it being a Sunday.

1928 Amsterdam T: 16, N: 16, D: 8.5. WR: 3:16.0 (USA—Cochrane, Helffrich, MacDonald, Stevenson)

1. USA (George Baird, Emerson "Bud" Spencer, 3:14.2 WR
Frederick Alderman, Raymond Barbuti)

2. GER (Otto Neumann, Richard Krebs, Werner 3:14.8
"Harry" Storz, Hermann Engelhard)

3. CAN (Alexander Wilson, Philip Edwards, Stan- 3:15.4
ley Glover, James Ball)

4. SWE (Björn Kugelberg, Bertil von Wachen- 3:15.8
feldt, Erik Byléhn, Sten Pettersson)

5. GBR (Roger Leigh-Wood, W. William Craner, 3:16.4
John Rinkel, Douglas Lowe)

6. FRA (Georges Krotoff, Joseph Jackson, 3:19.4
Georges Dupont, René Féger)

1932 Los Angeles T: 7, N: 7, D: 8.7. WR: 3:12.6 (Stanford University, USA—Shore, A. Hables, L. Hables, Eastman)

1. USA (Ivan Fuqua, Edgar Ablowich, Karl 3:08.2 WR
Warner, William Carr)

2. GBR (Crew Stoneley, Thomas Hampson, Da- 3:11.2
vid Burghley, Godfrey Rampling)

3. CAN (Raymond Lewis, James Ball, Philip Ed- 3:12.8
wards, Alexander Wilson)

4. GER (Joachim Büchner, Walter Nehb, Adolf 3:14.4
Metzner, Otto Peltzer)

5. JPN (Itaro Nakajima, Iwao Masuda, Seikan 3:14.6
Oki, Teiichi Nishi)

6. ITA (Giacomo Carlini, Giovanni Turba, Mario 3:17.8
De Negri, Luigi Facelli)

The U.S. team set a world record of 3:11.8 in the opening heat. In the final Bill Carr took off with a 12-yard lead. Godfrey Rampling closed the gap to six yards, at which point Carr pulled away and won by over 20 yards.

1936 Berlin T: 12, N: 12, D: 8.9. WR: 3:08.2 (USA—Fuqua, Ablowich, Warner, Carr)

1. GBR (Frederick Wolff, Godfrey Rampling, William 3:09.0
Roberts, Arthur Godfrey Brown)

2. USA (Harold Cagle, Robert Young, Edward O'Brien, 3:11.0
Alfred Fitch)

3. GER (Helmut Hamann, Friedrich von Stülpnagel, 3:11.8
Harry Voigt, Rudolf Harbig)

4. CAN (Marshall Limon, Philip Edwards, William Fritz, 3:11.8
John Loaring)

5. SWE (Sven Strömberg, Per Edfeldt, Olle Danielsson, 3:13.0
Bertil von Wachenfeldt)

6. HUN (Tibor Ribényi, Zoltán Zsitavi, József Vadas, 3:14.8
József Kovacs)

Compared to the Americans, the British team had an extremely casual view of training. As Godfrey Rampling once recalled, "I remember saying one day: 'Look here, chaps, we really ought to practice some baton-changing.' But we soon got bored and packed it in." But when Brown and Roberts finished second and fourth in the 400 meters, and the United States dropped Archie Williams and James LuValle, the gold and bronze medalists, from their relay squad, Rampling and his teammates suddenly realized, "We can beat these blighters."

Freddie Wolff was left over eight meters behind after the first leg, but Rampling ran a spectacular lap to make up the deficit and take a two-meter lead. Roberts expanded the lead to four meters and Brown pulled away to win by about 11 meters.

This race marked the only Olympic appearance of the great German runner Rudolf Harbig. Between August 1938 and September 1940, Harbig won 55 consecutive races at distances ranging from 50 meters to 1000 meters. On July 15, 1939, he ran 800 meters in 1:46.6, setting a world record that would last for 16 years. On August 12, he set a 400-meter world record of 46.0 that wasn't bettered until 1948. Harbig was killed fighting the Russians in World War II, on March 5, 1944.

1948 London T: 15, N: 15, D: 8.7. WR: 3:08.2 (USA—Fuqua, Ablowich, Warner, Carr)

1. USA (Arthur Harnden, Clifford Bourland, Roy Coch- 3:10.4
ran, Malvin Whitfield)

2. FRA (Jean Kerebel, François Schewetta, Robert 3:14.8
Chef d'Hôtel, Jacques Lunis)

3. SWE (Kurt Lundkvist, Lars Wolfbrandt, Folke Alnevik, 3:16.0
Rune Larsson)

4. FIN (Tauno Suvanto, Olli Talja, Runar Holmberg, 3:24.8
Bertil Storskrubb)

DNF: JAM (V. George Rhoden, Leslie Laing, Arthur Wint, Herbert McKenley), ITA (Giovanni Rocca, Ottavio Missoni, Luigi Paterlini, Antonio Siddi)

1952 Helsinki T: 18, N: 18, D: 7.27. WR: 3:08.2 (USA—Fuqua, Ablowich, Warner, Carr)

1. JAM (Arthur Wint, Leslie Laing, Her- 3:03.9 WR (3:04.04)
bert McKenley, V. George
Rhoden)

2. USA   (Ollie Matson, Gerald "Gene" 3:04.0   (3:04.21)
Cole, Charles Moore, Malvin
Whitfield)

3. GER   (Hans Geister, Günther Steines, 3:06.6   (3:06.78)
Heinz Ulzheimer, Karl-Friedrich
Haas)

4. CAN   (Douglas Clement, John Hutch- 3:09.3   (3:09.37)
ins, John Carroll, James Lavery)

5. GBR   (Leslie Lewis, Alan Dick, Ter- 3:10.0   (3:10.23)
ence Higgins, Nicholas Stacey)

6. FRA   (Jean-Pierre Goudeau, Robert 3:10.1   (3:10.33)
Bart, Jacques Degats, Jean-
Paul Martin du Gard)

In 1948, the Jamaican relay team had wanted more than anything to defeat the United States and win the gold medal. But Arthur Wint, running the third leg, had pulled a muscle and hobbled off the track in pain and anguish. Four years later the same four Jamaicans were back on the track, ready for another shot at their goal. Before the final began, Wint, Laing, McKenley, and Rhoden locked arms in a circle and said a prayer.

Wint ran the first leg and gave up a slight lead to Ollie Matson. Gerald Cole ran a tremendous second lap for the United States. When Herb McKenley took over for Jamaica, he was 12 yards behind 400-meter hurdles' champion Charley Moore. McKenley, competing in his fifth Olympic final without ever having won a gold medal, ran like a man inspired. Incredibly, he closed the gap and passed Moore in the last second, running a phenomenal 44.6 to Moore's far from shabby 46.3, and allowing 400-meter gold medalist George Rhoden to take off with a one-yard lead. Victory now seemed assured for the Jamaicans, since Mal Whitfield, the U.S. anchor man, had run a disappointing sixth in the 400-meter final. But Whitfield didn't give in, refusing to yield an inch the entire way. However, Rhoden, wearing the same vest that Wint had worn to run the first leg, also refused to let up, and managed to break the tape exactly one yard ahead of Whitfield. The 20-year-old world record, set at the Los Angeles Games, had been demolished by 4.3 seconds. That night, the Jamaican foursome celebrated in their quarters by drinking whisky with the Duke of Edinburgh, out of the only available vessel—a toothbrush tumbler.

1956 Melbourne T: 15, N: 15, D: 12.1. WR: 3:03.9 (JAM—Wint, Laing, McKenley, Rhoden)

1. USA   (Louis Jones, Jesse Mashburn, 3:04.8 (3:04.81)
Charles Jenkins, Thomas Courtney)

2. AUS   (Leon Gregory, David Lean, Graham 3:06.2 (3:06.19)
Gipson, Kevan Gosper)

3. GBR   (John Salisbury, Michael Wheeler, 3:07.2 (3:07.19)
F. Peter Higgins, Derek Johnson)

4. GER   (Jürgen Kühl, Walter Oberste, Man- 3:08.2 (3:08.27)
fred Pörschke, Karl-Friedrich Haas)

5. CAN   (Laird Sloan, Murray Cockburn, Doug- 3:10.2 (3:10.33)
las Clement, Terry Tobacco)

DISQ: JAM (Keith Gardner, George Kerr, Malcolm Spence, Melville Spence)

(Left to right) George Rhoden, Leslie Laing, Arthur Wint, and Herb McKenley failed to finish the 4 × 400-meter relay in 1948, when Wint pulled a muscle during the third leg. Four years later the same foursome fought back the challenge of the U.S. team to win the gold medal by one tenth of a second.

1960 Rome T: 19, N: 19, D: 9.8. WR: 3:03.9 (JAM—Wint, Laing, McKenley, Rhoden)

1. USA   (Jack Yerman, Earl Young, 3:02.2 WR (3:02.37)
Glenn Davis, Otis Davis)

2. GER   (Hans-Joachim Reske, Manfred 3:02.7   (3:02.84)
Kinder, Johannes Kaiser, Carl
Kaufmann)

3. BWI   (Malcolm Spence, James 3:04.0   (3:04.13)
Wedderburn, Keith Gardner,
George Kerr)

4. SAF   (Edward Jefferys, Edgar Davis, 3:05.0   (3:05.18)
Gordon Day, Malcolm Spence)

5. GBR   (H. Malcolm Yardley, Barry Jack- 3:08.3   (3:08.47)
son, John Wrighton, Robbie
Brightwell)

6. SWI   (René Weber, Ernst Zaugg, 3:09.4   (3:09.55)
Hansrüdi Bruder, Christian
Wägli)

Otis Davis began the anchor leg six yards ahead of Carl Kaufmann. Kaufmann closed the gap to one yard, but in the middle of the final curve, Davis accelerated and pulled away to win by four yards. In 1960, Jamaica, Trinidad, and Barbados competed as the British West Indies, also known as the West Indies Federation. Wedderburn was from Barbados; the rest of the relay team was from Jamaica.

1964 Tokyo T: 17, N: 17, D: 10.21. WR: 3:02.2 (USA—Yerman, Young, G. Davis, O. Davis)

1. USA (Ollan Cassell, Michael Larrabee, Ulis 3:00.7 WR Williams, Henry Carr)
2. GBR (Timothy Graham, Adrian Metcalfe, John 3:01.6 Cooper, Robbie Brightwell)
3. TRI (Edwin Skinner, Kent Bernard, Edwin 3:01.7 Roberts, Wendell Mottley)
4. JAM (Lawrence Kahn, Malcolm Spence, Melville Spence, George Kerr) 3:02.3
5. GER& (Jörg Jüttner, Hans-Ullrich Schulz, Johannes Schmitt, Manfred Kinder) 3:04.3
   GDR
6. POL (Marian Filipiuk, Ireneusz Kluczek, Stanislaw Swatowski, Andrzej Badeński) 3:05.3
7. SOV (Grigory Sverbetov, Victor Bychkov, Vasily Anisimov, Vadim Arkhipchuk) 3:05.9
8. FRA (Michel Hiblot, Bernard Martin, Germain Nelzy, Jean Pierre Boccardo) 3:07.4

1968 Mexico City T: 16, N: 16, D: 10.20. WR: 2:59.6 (USA—Frey, Evans, Smith, Lewis)

1. USA (Vincent Matthews, Ronald Freeman, G. Lawrence James, Lee Evans) 2:56.2 WR (2:56.16)
2. KEN (Daniel Rudisha, Matesi Munyoro Nyamau, Naftali Bon, Charles Asati) 2:59.6 (2:59.64)
3. GER (Helmar Müller, Manfred Kinder, Gerhard Hennige, Martin Jellinghaus) 3:00.5 (3:00.54)
4. POL (Jan Balachowski, Stanislaw Grędziński, Jan Werner, Andrzej Badeński) 3:00.5 (3:00.58)
5. GBR (Martin Winbolt-Lewis, Colin Campbell, David Hemery, John Sherwood) 3:01.2 (3:01.21)
6. TRI (George Simon, Euric Bobb, Benedict Cayenne, Edwin Roberts) 3:04.5 (3:04.52)
7. ITA (Sergio Ottolina, Giacomo Puosi, Furio Fusi, Sergio Bello) 3:04.6 (3:04.64)
8. FRA (Jean Nallet, Jacques Carette, Gilles Bertould, Jean Pierre Boccardo) 3:07.5 (3:07.51)

The final was really two separate races: the United States fighting for a world record and the other teams battling it out for second through eighth places. It was Ron Freeman's remarkable second leg that really did the trick for the Americans. His unofficial time of 43.2 is the fastest leg ever recorded in a 4 × 400-meter relay. Anchor man Lee Evans crossed the finish line 30 yards ahead of Charles Asati in second place.

1972 Munich T: 21, N: 21, D: 9.10. WR: 2:56.16 (USA—Matthews, Freeman, James, Evans)

1. KEN (Charles Asati, Hezakiah Nyamau, Robert Ouko, Julius Sang) 2:59.8 (2:59.83)
2. GBR (Martin Reynolds, Alan Pascoe, David Hemery, David Jenkins) 3:00.5 (3:00.46)
3. FRA (Gilles Bertould, Daniel Velasques, Francis Kerbiriou, Jacques Carette) 3:00.7 (3:00.65)
4. GER (Bernd Herrmann, Horst-Rüdiger Schlöske, Herrmann Köhler, Karl Honz) 3:00.9 (3:00.88)
5. POL (Jan Werner, Jan Balachowski, Zbigniew Jaremski, Andrzej Badeński) 3:01.1 (3:01.05)
6. FIN (Stig Lönnqvist, Ari Salin, Ossi Karttunen, Markku Kukkoaho) 3:01.1 (3:01.12)
7. SWE (Eric Carlgren, Anders Faager, Kent Öhman, Ulf Rönner) 3:02.6 (3:02.57)
8. TRI (Arthur Cooper, Pat Marshall, Charles Joseph, Edwin Roberts) 3:03.6 (3:03.58)

Ten days before the heats, each nation submitted a list of six names from which a team of four could be chosen. The names submitted by the United States were Vince Matthews, Wayne Collett, Lee Evans, John Smith, Maurice Peoples, and Tommie Turner. Unfortunately, Matthews and Collett were banned from further competition because of their behavior on the victory platform following the 400-meter final. Meanwhile, Smith had pulled a hamstring muscle and was unable to run. This left the United States without a full team, so they were forced to withdraw.

The final was an exciting race, with the hometown West Germans in first place most of the way. But Julius Sang, running a 43.5 anchor leg, passed the fading Karl Honz 75 meters from the finish and went on to give Kenya a three-meter victory.

The British anchor, David Jenkins, was sent to prison in 1987 after pleading guilty to charges related to the manufacture and smuggling of anabolic steroids.

1976 Montreal T: 16, N: 16, D: 7.31. WR: 2:56.16 (USA—Matthews, Freeman, James, Evans)

1. USA (Herman Frazier, Benjamin Brown, Frederick Newhouse, Maxie Parks) 2:58.65
2. POL (Ryszard Podlas, Jan Werner, Zbigniew Jaremski, Jerzy Pietrzyk) 3:01.43
3. GER (Franz-Peter Hofmeister, Lothar Krieg, Harald Schmid, Bernd Herrmann) 3:01.98
4. CAN (Ian Seale, Don Domansky, Leighton Hope, Brian Saunders) 3:02.64
5. JAM (Leighton Priestley, Donald Quarrie, Colin Bradford, Seymour Newman) 3:02.84
6. TRI (Michael Solomon, Horace Tuitt, Joseph Coombs, Charles Joseph) 3:03.46
7. CUB (Eddy Gutierrez, Damaso Alfonso, Carlos Alvarez, Alberto Juantorena Danger) 3:03.81
8. FIN (Hannu Mäkelä, Ossi Karttunen, Stig Lönnqvist, Markku Kukkoaho) 3:06.51

With the defending champions from Kenya boycotted out of the Olympics, the Americans were left unchallenged. The final was run during a hard rain. Also missing because of the African boycott was the team from Gambia, which included two runners with unusually colorful names: Bambo Fatty and Bannana Jarju.

1980 Moscow T: 24, N: 24, D: 8.1. WR: 2:56.16 (USA—Matthews. Freeman, James, Evans)

1. SOV (Remigijus Valiulis, Mikhail Linge, Nikolai Chernetsky, Viktor Markin, [Viktor Burakov]) 3:01.1 (3:01.08)
2. GDR (Klaus Thiele, Andreas Knebel, Frank Schaffer, Volker Beck) 3:01.3 (3:01.26)
3. ITA (Stefano Malinverni, Mauro Zuliani, Roberto Tozzi, Pietro Mennea) 3:04.3
4. FRA (Jacques Fellice, Robert Froissart, Didier Dubois, Francis Demarthon) 3:04.8
5. BRA (Paulo Roberto Correia, Antonio Dias Ferreira, Agberto Conceição Guimaraes, Geraldo José Pegado) 3:05.9
6. TRI (Joseph Coombs, Charles Joseph, Rafee Mohammed, Michael Solomon) 3:06.6
7. CZE (Josef Lomicky, Dusan Malovec, Frantisek Brecka, Karel Kolar) 3:07.0

DNF: GBR (Alan Bell, R. Terence Whitehead, Roderic Milne, Glendon Cohen)

With the top three teams—the United States, West Germany, and Kenya—absent because of the anti-Soviet boycott, this was a severely devalued contest. The Soviets, desperate for a victory, rested 400-meter champion Viktor Markin in the opening heat, then claimed that his replacement, Victor Burakov, had been injured, and brought Markin back for the final. They used the same trick to circumvent the anti-replacement rules in the women's 4 × 400 relay. The rejuvenated Markin fought off a surprisingly strong challenge from 400-meter hurdle gold medalist Volker Beck to gain a victory-at-any-cost for the U.S.S.R. The winning time was the slowest in 20 years. The slowest losing time since 1956 (3:25.0) was recorded by Sierra Leone.

1984 Los Angeles T: 25, N: 25, D: 8.11. WR: 2:56.16 (USA—Matthews, Freeman, James, Evans)

1. USA (Sunder Nix, Ray Armstead, Alonzo Babers, Antonio McKay, [Willie Smith, Walter McCoy]) 2:57.91
2. GBR (Kriss Akabusi, Gary Cook, Todd Bennett, Philip Brown) 2:59.13
3. NGR (Sunday Uti, Moses Ugbisie, Ulo Rotimi Peters, Innocent Egbunike) 2:59.32
4. AUS (Bruce Frayne, Darren Clark, Gary Minihan, Rick Mitchell, [Peter Van Mittenberg]) 2:59.70
5. ITA (Roberto Tozzi, Ernesto Nocco, Roberto Ribaud, Pietro Mennea, [Donato Sabia, Mauro Zuliani]) 3:01.44
6. BAR (Richard Louis, David Peltier, Clyde Edwards, Elvis Forde) 3:01.60
7. UGA (John Govile, Moses Kyeswa, Peter Rwamuhanda, Mike Okot) 3:02.09
8. CAN (Michael Sokolowski, Doug Hinds, Bryan Saunders, Tim Bethune) 3:02.82

The United States almost lost this one in the semifinals, when Walter McCoy took five steps in the wrong lane. A formal protest was rejected because his violation was unintentional and had not impeded the progress of any other runners. McCoy squeezed a lot of mileage out of his good fortune. In 1988 he received a neck injury in an elevator accident at a Holiday Inn in Tampa, Florida. He sued the hotel owners and the elevator manufacturer, claiming that the injury deprived him of a good shot at a second gold medal at the Seoul Olympics. In July 1994 a jury sided with McCoy and awarded him $900,000.

The final was hotly contested and marked the first time that four teams broke three minutes in a single race. Sunday Uti gave Nigeria the first lap lead, while Darren Clark's 43.86 leg put Australia ahead at the midway point. Then Alonzo Babers ran a 43.75 lap to put the U.S. in first place to stay.

1988 Seoul T: 22, N: 22, D: 10.1. WR: 2:56.16 (USA—Matthews, Freeman, James, Evans)

1. USA (Danny Everett, Steven Lewis, Kevin Robinzine, Harry "Butch" Reynolds, [Andrew Valmon, Antonio McKay]) 2:56.16 EWR
2. JAM (Howard Davis, Devon Morris, Winthrop Graham, Bertland Cameron, [Howard Burnett]) 3:00.30
3. GER (Norbert Dobeleit, Edgar Itt, Jörg Vaihinger, Ralf Lübke, [Mark Heinrich, Bodo Kühn]) 3:00.56
4. GDR (Jens Carlowitz, Mathias Schersing, Frank Möller, Thomas Schönlebe, [Michael Schimmer]) 3:01.13
5. GBR (Brian Whittle, Kriss Akabusi, Todd Bennett, Philip Brown, [Paul Harmsworth]) 3:02.00
6. AUS (Robert Ballard, Mark Garner, Miles Murphy, Darren Clark, [Leigh Miller]) 3:02.49
7. NGR (Sunday Uti, Moses Ugbisie, Henry Amike, Innocent Egbunike) 3:02.50
8. KEN (Tito Sawe, Lucas Sang, Paul Ereng, Simon Kipkemboi) 3:04.69

The U.S. team found that their real race was not against the other teams, but against the world record set in the 1968 Olympics. When Butch Reynolds crossed the finish line 40 meters clear of the rest of the field, the scoreboard clock stopped at 2:56.17, a frustrating one one-hundredth of a second short of the record. However, the official time turned out to be 2:56.16.

1992 Barcelona T: 24, N: 24, D: 8.8. WR: 2:56.16 (USA—Matthews, Freeman, James, Evans; USA—Everett, Lewis, Robinzane, Reynolds)

1. USA (Andrew Valmon, Quincy Watts, Michael Johnson, Steve Lewis, [Darnell Hall, Charles Jenkins]) 2:55.74 WR
2. CUB (Lázaro Martínez Despaigne, Héctor Herrera Ortiz, Norberto Téllez, Roberto Hernández Prendes) 2:59.51

3. GBR (Roger Black, David Grindley, Kriss 2:59.73
Akabusi, John Regis, [Mark Richard-
son, Duaine Ladejo])

4. BRA (Robson Caetano Da Silva, Edielson 3:01.61
Rocha Tenório, Sergio Matias De
Menezes, Sidney Telles De Souza,
[Eronilde Nunes de Araujo])

5. NGR (Udeme Ekpeyong, Emmanuel Okoli, 3:01.71
Hassan Bosso, Sunday Bada)

6. ITA (Alessandro Aimar, Marco Vaccari, 3:02.18
Fabio Grossi, Andrea Nuti)

7. TRI (Alvin Daniel, Patrick Delice, Neil De 3:03.31
Silva, Ian Morris)

DNF: KEN (Samson Kitur, Abednego Matilu, Simeon Kipkemboi,
Simon Kemboi, [David Kitur])

At the 1991 world championships Great Britain upset the
United States 2:57.53 to 2:57.57. Although there was
much bickering in the United States camp as to who
would run in the Olympic final, there was never any
doubt that the Americans would exact revenge. As in
1988, there were two races: the United States versus the
now 23-year-old world record and the battle for the other
medals. This time the Americans, with a 43.1 leg from
Quincy Watts and a 43.4 from Steve Lewis, won their
race. Thirty meters behind Lewis, the other race was won
by a gutsy Cuban squad when Roberto Hernández held
off John Regis by two meters.

20,000-METER WALK

In walking races, the contestants must keep at least one
foot in contact with the ground at all times. If a walker
loses contact with the ground, he or she receives a warning for "lifting." Another rule requires walkers to
straighten the leg at each step at the point of first contact
with the ground. If three judges give a walker warnings,
the third warning results in disqualification. The equivalent distance for 20,000 meters is 12.147 miles.

Official world records can be set only in walking races
contested on a track. Since Olympic walking events are
held on the road, winning times are not eligible for world
record consideration.

1896–1952 not held

1956 Melbourne C: 21, N: 10, D: 11.28. WR: 1:27:58.2 (Mikhail
Lavrov)

1.	Leonid Spirin	SOV/RUS	1:31:27.4
2.	Antanas Mikėnas	SOV/LIT	1:32:03.0
3.	Bruno Junk	SOV/EST	1:32:12.0
4.	John Ljunggren	SWE	1:32:24.0
5.	Stanley Vickers	GBR	1:32:34.2
6.	Donald Keane	AUS	1:33:52.0
7.	George Coleman	GBR	1:34:01.8
8.	Roland Hardy	GBR	1:34:40.4

So many disputes had developed over the judging of the
comparatively fast-paced 10,000-meter walk that it was
replaced by the less controversial 20,000-meter event.
Mikėnas, leading after 15 kilometers, received a warning,
and resigned himself to second place, urging on Spirin,
who had been placed only tenth at the halfway mark.

1960 Rome C: 36, N: 18, D: 9.2. WR: 1:27.05.0 (Volodymyr
Holubnychy)

1.	Volodymyr Holubnychy	SOV/UKR	1:34:07.2
2.	Noel Freeman	AUS	1:34:16.4
3.	Stanley Vickers	GBR	1:34:56.4
4.	Dieter Lindner	GDR	1:35:33.8
5.	Norman Read	NZE	1:36:59.0
6.	Lennart Back	SWE	1:37:17.0
7.	John Ljunggren	SWE	1:37:59.0
8.	Ladislav Moc	CZE	1:38:32.4

Holubnychy, a 24-year-old Ukrainian who eventually
competed in five Olympics, won the first of his four medals. Freeman, who apparently had not gone over the
course beforehand, misjudged his closing surge and fell
50 yards short of victory. In 1968 Freeman became something of a cause célèbre in Australia when he was omitted
from the national Olympic team despite the submission
of a 41,000-signature petition to the Australian Olympic
Federation.

1964 Tokyo C: 30, N: 15, D: 10.15. WR: 1:27:05.0 (Volodymyr
Holubnychy)

1.	Kenneth Matthews	GBR	1:29:34.0	OR
2.	Dieter Lindner	GDR	1:31:13.2	
3.	Volodymyr Holubnychy	SOV/UKR	1:31:59.4	
4.	Noel Freeman	AUS	1:32:06.8	
5.	Gennady Solodov	SOV/RUS	1:32:33.0	
6.	Ronald Zinn	USA	1:32:43.0	
7.	Boris Khrolovich	SOV	1:32:45.4	
8.	John Edgington	GBR	1:32:46.0	

Ken Matthews, an electrician at a power station near his
hometown of Sutton Coldfield, had collapsed and failed
to finish in 1960 after leading for eight kilometers. In
1964 he knew he would have a better chance of winning if
his wife, Sheila, could join him in Tokyo. His mates
agreed and collected £742 to send her along. Sure
enough, Matthews crossed the finish line far ahead of the
others. Sheila broke through stadium security, rushed
onto the track, and gave her hubby what was probably
the longest victory kiss in Olympic history. At the post-
race interview, Matthews said, "My legs hurt me at the
end of the race. They still do. But I wouldn't mind going
dancing now."

Sixth-place finisher Ron Zinn died in the Vietnam War
less than nine months later. He was 26 years old.

1968 Mexico City C: 33, N: 20, D: 10.14. WR: 1:27:05.0
(Volodymyr Holubnychy)

1.	Volodymyr Holubnychy	SOV/UKR	1:33:58.4
2.	José Pedraza Zuniga	MEX	1:34:00.0
3.	Nikolai Smaga	SOV/UKR	1:34:03.4

Ken Matthews celebrates his victory in the 1964 20,000-meter walk with his wife, Sheila.

4. Rudolph Haluza	USA	1:35:00.2
5. Gerhard Sperling	GDR	1:35:27.2
6. Otto Barch	SOV/UKR	1:36:16.8
7. Hans Reimann	GDR	1:36:31.4
8. Stefan Ingvarsson	SWE	1:36:43.4

After 85 minutes of hard walking, Volodymyr Holubnychy entered the stadium in first place, followed closely by teammate Nikolai Smaga. Then the 60,000-plus spectators went wild as a third walker appeared— José Pedraza, a 31-year-old Mexican soldier. Two hundred meters from the finish, Pedraza passed Smaga and set his sights on Holubnychy. Pedraza's style seemed far from legal, but it would have taken a suicidal judge to disqualify the determined Pedraza while the stadium echoed with chants of "May-hee-co" and "Pay-drah-

Volodymyr Holubnychy holds off a frantic finish of dubious legality by local favorite José Pedraza to win the 20,000-meter walk in Mexico City in 1968.

zah." An international incident was avoided when Holubnychy drew away slightly in the homestretch to win by a mere three yards.

1972 Munich C: 24, N: 12, D: 8.31. WR: 1:25:19.4 (Peter Frenkel, Hans Reimann)

1. Peter Frenkel	GDR	1:26:42.4	OR
2. Volodymyr Holubnychy	SOV/UKR	1:26:55.2	
3. Hans-Georg Reimann	GDR	1:27:16.6	
4. Gerhard Sperling	GDR	1:27:55.0	
5. Mykola Smaha	SOV/UKR	1:28:16.6	
6. V. Paul Nihill	GBR	1:28:44.4	
7. Jan Ornoch	POL	1:32:01.6	
8. Vittorio Visino	ITA	1:32:30.0	

Frenkel, Reimann, and Holubnychy were even after 15 kilometers, with the deaf walker, Gerhard Sperling, six seconds behind. Approaching the stadium, Holubnychy moved ahead, but Frenkel had the strongest finishing kick and was able to enter the stadium with a small but growing lead. Part of Frenkel's success was due to an amazing invention of East German sports scientists: an underground room with artificially thin air that simulated altitude training. Frenkel was described in East German press handouts as a "color designer and decorator."

1976 Montreal C: 38, N: 21, D: 7.23. WR: 1:24:45.0 (Bernd Kannenberg)

1. Daniel Bautista Rocha	MEX	1:24:40.6	OR
2. Hans-Georg Reimann	GDR	1:25:13.6	
3. Peter Frenkel	GDR	1:25:29.4	
4. Karl-Heinz Stadtmüller	GDR	1:26:50.6	
5. Raúl González Rodríguez	MEX	1:28:18.2	
6. Armando Zambaldo	ITA	1:28.25.2	
7. Volodymyr Holubnychy	SOV/UKR	1:29:24.6	
8. Vittorio Visini	ITA	1:29:31.6	

The contestants in the 1976 20-kilometer walk covered one of the widest age ranges in the Olympics. Eighteen-year-old Bengt Simonsen of Sweden finished 26th, while 48-year-old Alex Oakley of Canada placed 35th. The winner, Daniel Bautista, brought Mexico its first-ever track and field gold medal. He was so dehydrated at the end that he had to drink ten cans of soft drinks before he could produce enough urine for the drug test. Bautista's time was not accepted as a world record because it was set on the road rather than on a track.

1980 Moscow C: 34, N: 20, D: 7.24. WR: 1:20:06.8 (Daniel Bautista)

1. Maurizio Damilano	ITA	1:23:35.5	OR
2. Pyotr Pochinchuk	SOV/BLR	1:24:45.4	
3. Roland Wieser	GDR	1:25:58.2	
4. Yevgeny Yevsyukov	SOV/RUS	1:26:28.3	
5. José Marin	SPA	1:26:45.6	
6. Raúl González Rodríguez	MEX	1:27:48.6	
7. Bohdan Bulakowski	POL	1:28:36.3	
8. Karl-Heinz Stadtmüller	GDR	1:29:21.7	

In 1976 walk officials had been embarrassed by the publication of photographs which clearly showed gold medal winner Daniel Bautista with both feet off the ground during his final lap. In 1980 the officials decided to get tough. With less than 2500 meters to go, Bautista was in first place when he was suddenly disqualified and ordered off the course. This left Anatoly Solomin of the U.S.S.R. in front, but a few hundred meters later he too was disqualified. By the end of the race seven walkers had been ordered off by the judges, including three of the six leaders at the 15-kilometer mark. These crackdowns allowed Maurizio Damilano to win a surprise gold medal. His twin brother, Giorgio, finished 11th. Thipsamay Chanthaphone of Laos, celebrating his 19th birthday, crossed the finish line in 2:20:22.0—over a half hour after the other walkers, and 21½ minutes slower than any contestant since the event began in 1952. But, unlike Bautista and Solomin, he *did* finish.

1984 Los Angeles C: 38, N: 22, D: 8.3. WR: 1:18:39.9 (Ernesto Canto)

1. Ernesto Canto	MEX	1:23:13	OR
2. Raúl González Rodríguez	MEX	1:23:20	
3. Maurizio Damilano	ITA	1:23:26	
4. Guillaume Leblanc	CAN	1:24:29	
5. Carlo Mattioli	ITA	1:25:07	
6. José Marin	SPA	1:25:32	
7. Marco Evoniuk	USA	1:25:42	
8. Erling Andersen	NOR	1:25:54	

The Mexican population of Los Angeles is second only to that of Mexico City and it was out in force for the 20-kilometer walk, most of which was held on the streets surrounding the stadium. Guillaume Leblanc opened up an early lead, but by the halfway point, he had been passed by defending Olympic champion Maurizio Damilano and by world champion and world record holder Ernesto Canto. Damilano moved ahead by almost 40 meters in the next five kilometers, but was overhauled by Canto and González, who were enthusiastically rooted on by the home away from hometown crowd. The two Mexicans entered the stadium to tumultuous applause with Canto prevailing by 40 meters. For the first time in Olympic history, not one walker was disqualified for improper technique.

1988 Seoul C: 53, N: 28, D: 9.23. WR: 1:18:39.9 (Ernesto Canto)

1. Jozef Pribilinec	CZE/SLV	1:19:57	OR
2. Ronald Weigel	GDR	1:20:00	
3. Maurizio Damilano	ITA	1:20:14	
4. José Marin	SPA	1:20:34	
5. Roman Mrázek	CZE	1:20:43	
6. Mikhail Shchennikov	SOV/RUS	1:20:47	
7. Carlos Mercenario	MEX	1:20:53	
8. Axel Noack	GDR	1:21:14	

After 15 kilometers, Pribilinec, 50-kilometer world champion Weigel, and defending Olympic champion Ernesto Canto were eight seconds clear of the rest of the field. But then Canto was disqualified, just as he had been at

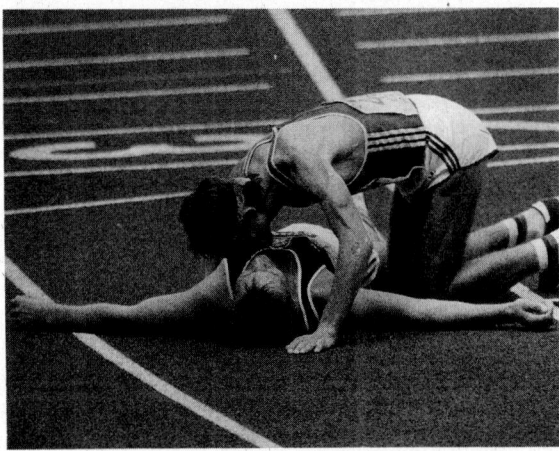

Jozef Pribilinec (bottom) defeated Ronald Weigel by three seconds in the 1988 20,000-meter walk. When Pribilinec proved too exhausted to respond to Weigel's congratulations, Weigel kissed his conqueror and silently walked away.

the 1987 world championships. Pribilinec entered the stadium less than ten meters ahead of Weigel but managed to extend his lead slightly on the track. After the finish, Pribilinec collapsed on his back. Weigel knelt over him and tried to extend his congratulations. But the Slovak winner was so exhausted that he was unable to respond. Silently, Weigel kissed Pribilinec and walked away.

1992 Barcelona C: 42, N: 23, D: 7.31. WR: 1:18:35.2 (Stefan Johansson)

1.	Daniel Plaza Montero	SPA	1:21.45
2.	Guillaume Leblanc	CAN	1:22.25
3.	Giovanni De Benedictis	ITA	1:23.11
4.	Maurizio Damilano	ITA	1:23.39
5.	Chen Shaoguo	CHN	1:24.06
6.	James McDonald	IRL	1:25.16
7.	Daniel García Córdova	MEX	1:25.35
8.	Sándor Urbanik	HUN	1:26.08

Daniel Plaza made his home in El Prat de Llobregat, ten kilometers from the Olympic Stadium. For the 26-year-old Plaza that was just a short walk away. At the 1991 world championships in Tokyo, Plaza had crossed the finish line in third place only to learn ten minutes later that he had been disqualified. This time, too, he received warnings from the judges but, spurred on by the enthusiasm of the hometown fans, he held his technique. Veteran Maurizio Damilano led the pack for the first half of the race and more, but shortly before the 15-kilometer checkpoint, Plaza, Leblanc, and Plaza's Catalan teammate, Valentí Massana, shifted gears and pulled away. By the time they reached the steep hill leading to the stadium, Plaza had broken free from the others. Only 800 meters from the stadium Massana was disqualified while in second place.

50,000-METER WALK

The rules for this punishing race are the same as those for the 20,000-meter walk. The equivalent distance of 50,000 meters is 31.068 miles.

1896–1928 not held

1932 Los Angeles C: 15, N: 10, D: 8.3. WR: 4:34:03.0 (Paul Sievert)

1.	Thomas Green	GBR	4:50:10
2.	Jánis Dalins	LAT	4:57:20
3.	Ugo Frigerio	ITA	4:59:06
4.	Karl Hähnel	GER	5:06:06
5.	Ettore Rivolta	ITA	5:07:39
6.	Paul Sievert	GER	5:16:41
7.	Henri Quintric	FRA	5:27:25
8.	Ernest Crosbie	USA	5:28:02

Tommy Green, a 38-year-old railway worker, took the lead seven miles from the finish and won easily. Ugo Frigerio added a bronze medal to the three golds he had won in 1920 and 1924. Green had to overcome considerable adversity to make it to the Olympics. Because he had rickets as a child, he was unable to walk until he was

five years old. At 12, he lied about his age and joined the army. A couple years later he was invalided out when a horse fell on him. Recalled to service in 1914, he was wounded three times in World War I and finally sent home again in 1917 after having been badly gassed while fighting in France. He did not enter his first walking contest until 1926, when he was 32 years old.

1936 Berlin C: 33, N: 16, D: 8.5. WR: 4:34:03.0 (Paul Sievert)

1.	H. Harold Whitlock	GBR	4:30:41.4	OR
2.	Arthur Schwab	SWI	4:32:09.2	
3.	Adalberts Bubenko	LAT	4:32:42.2	
4.	Jaroslav Štork	CZE	4:34:00.2	
5.	Edgar Bruun	NOR	4:34:53.2	
6.	Fritz Bleiweiss	GER	4:36:48.4	
7.	Karl Reiniger	SWI	4:40:45.0	
8.	Etienne Laisne	FRA	4:41:40.0	

Harry Whitlock, a 32-year-old auto mechanic, moved into first place after 33 kilometers. However, at the 38-kilometer mark, he began to vomit. His sickness continued for five kilometers, but he kept walking, recovered, and won by a wide margin. In 1952 Whitlock came out of retirement to compete in the Helsinki Olympics, where he finished 11th at the age of 48.

1948 London C: 23, N: 11, D: 7.31. WR: 4:34:03.0 (Paul Sievert)

1.	John Ljunggren	SWE	4:41:52
2.	Godel Gaston	SWI	4:48:17
3.	Terence "Tebbs" Lloyd-Johnson	GBR	4:48:31
4.	Edgar Bruun	NOR	4:53:18
5.	Harold Martineau	GBR	4:53:58
6.	Rune Bjurström	SWE	4:56:43
7.	Pierre Mazille	FRA	5:01:40
8.	Claude Hubert	FRA	5:03:12

Ljunggren led from start to finish and won easily. Bronze medalist Tebbs Lloyd-Johnson was 48 years old, the oldest person ever to win an Olympic track and field medal.

1952 Helsinki C: 31, N: 16, D: 7.21. WR: 4:31:21.6 (Antal Roka)

1.	Giuseppe Dordoni	ITA	4:28:07.8	OR
2.	Josef Doležal	CZE	4:30:17.8	
3.	Antal Róka	HUN	4:31:27.2	
4.	George Whitlock	GBR	4:32:21.0	
5.	Sergei Lobastov	SOV	4:32:34.2	
6.	Vladimir Ukhov	SOV	4:32:51.6	
7.	Dumitru Paraschivescu	ROM	4:41:05.2	
8.	Ionescu Baboie	ROM	4:41:52.8	

1956 Melbourne C: 21, N: 10, D: 11.24. WR: 4:21:07.0 (Ladislav Moc)

1.	Norman Read	NZE	4:30:42.8
2.	Yevgeny Maskinskov	SOV/RUS	4:32:57.0
3.	John Ljunggren	SWE	4:35:02.0
4.	Abdon Pamich	ITA	4:39:00.0
5.	Antal Róka	HUN	4:50:09.0
6.	Raymond Smith	AUS	4:56:08.0
7.	Adolf Weinacker	USA	5:00:16.0
8.	Albert Johnson	GBR	5:02:19.0

Norman Read celebrates his victory in the 1956 50,000-meter walk by resting his feet.

Norman Read moved from England to New Zealand in 1954. As the Melbourne Olympics approached, he wrote to the British A.A.A. asking for permission to represent Great Britain as a walker. He was rejected. At first he was rejected in New Zealand as well, but a strong showing in races in Australia and New Zealand paved his way. After receiving his naturalization papers he was ready to fulfill his dream. On the day of the 50,000-meter race Read got lost in the corridors of the stadium and didn't find his way to the track until the other runners were already standing on the starting line. Maskinskov led over most of the course, with Read two and a half minutes back after 30 kilometers. At 42 kilometers, however, Read caught the tiring Soviet walker and pulled away to a decisive victory. His unexpected win caused wild cheering in the stadium, and a whole section of the New Zealand contingent had to be restrained from streaming onto the track.

1960 Rome C: 39, N: 20, D: 9.7. WR: 4:16:08.6 (Sergei Lobastov)
1. Donald Thompson   GBR   4:25:30.0   OR
2. John Ljunggren   SWE   4:25:47.0
3. Abdon Pamich   ITA   4:27:55.4
4. Aleksandr Stcherbina SOV/UKR   4:31:44.0
5. Thomas Misson   GBR   4:33:03.0
6. Alexander Oakley   CAN   4:33:08.6
7. Giuseppe Dordoni   ITA   4:33:28.8
8. Zora Singh   IND   4:37:45.0

In 1956, Don Thompson had been in fifth place with only 5000 meters to go, when he collapsed and failed to finish. With this bad memory in mind, he decided to acclimatize himself well in advance. But it is not easy to simulate a hot and humid September day in Rome when you live in Cranford, Middlesex. Fortunately, Don Thompson was quite a resourceful person. Several times each week, the 5-foot 5½-inch fire insurance clerk hauled heaters, hot water, and boiling kettles into his bathroom, sealed the doors and windows, and did his exercises in steaming 100-degree Fahrenheit (38-degree centigrade) heat.

Sure enough, the race began in 87-degree Fahrenheit (30.5-degree centigrade) weather, but Don Thompson was ready. At the halfway point, he found himself in first place, following the disqualification of two of the leaders and the early overexertions of several others. Surprisingly, his only challenger was 1948 gold medalist John Ljunggren, who was two days shy of his 41st birthday. With 5000 meters to go, the two men were only one second apart. But then Thompson managed to pull away by 18 seconds over the next two kilometers, a lead that he was able to maintain the rest of the way.

1964 Tokyo C: 34, N: 19, D: 10.18. WR: 4:14:02.4 (Abdon Pamich)
1. Abdon Pamich   ITA   4:11:12.4   OR
2. V. Paul Nihill   GBR   4:11:31.2
3. Ingvar Pettersson   SWE   4:14:17.4
4. Burkhard Leuschke   GDR   4:15:26.8
5. Robert Gardiner   AUS   4:17:06.8
6. Christoph Höhne   GDR   4:17:41.6
7. Anatoly Vedyakov   SOV/RUS   4:19:56.0
8. Kurt Sakowski   GDR   4:20:31.0

The race resolved into a two-man battle between Pamich and Nihill. At the 38-kilometer mark, Pamich was overcome by nausea and forced to take a 15-second vomit break. He regained the lead quickly, however, and fought off Nihill's challenges for the remainder of the race.

1968 Mexico City C: 36, N: 18, D: 10.17. WR: 4:10:41.8 (Christoph Höhne)
1. Christoph Höhne   GDR   4:20:13.6
2. Antal Kiss   HUN   4:30:17.0
3. Larry Young   USA   4:31:55.4
4. Peter Selzer   GDR   4:33:09.8
5. Stig-Erik Lindberg SWE   4:34:05.0
6. Vittorio Visini   ITA   4:36:33.2
7. Bryan Eley   GBR   4:37:33.0
8. José Pedraza Zuniga MEX   4:37:52.0

Favorite Christoph Höhne drew away after passing the halfway mark, and won by an incredible ten-minute margin. Paul Nihill, who collapsed after 44 kilometers, suffered his only defeat in 86 races between December 1967 and June 1970. He finished ninth at the 1972 Olympics.

1972 Munich C: 36, N: 18, D: 9.3. WR: 3:52:44.6 (Bernd Kannenberg)
1. Bernd Kannenberg   GER   3:56:11.6   OR
2. Veniamin Soldatenko SOV/KAZ   3:58:24.0
3. Larry Young   USA   4:00:46.0
4. Otto Barch   SOV/KYR   4:01:35.4
5. Peter Selzer   GDR   4:04:05.4
6. Gerhard Weidner   GER   4:06:26.0
7. Vittorio Visini   ITA   4:08:31.4
8. Gabriel Hernandez   MEX   4:12:09.0

Kannenberg and Soldatenko walked together for 35 kilometers. Kannenberg, who had dropped out in the middle of the 20-kilometer race, noticed that Soldatenko was slow in taking his refreshments at the 35-kilometer food and drink stand, so he decided to pick up the pace. Soldatenko, worried because he had already received a warning, was unable to respond.

1976 not held

1980 Moscow C: 27, N: 14, D: 7.30. WR: 3:41:38.4 (Raúl González Rodríguez)

1. Hartwig Gauder	GDR	3:49:24	OR
2. Jorge Llopart Ribas	SPA	3:51:25	
3. Yevgeny Ivchenko	SOV/UKR	3:56:32	
4. Bengt Simonsen	SWE	3:57:08	
5. Vyacheslav Fursov	SOV/RUS	3:58:32	
6. José Marin	SPA	4:03:08	
7. Stanislaw Rola	POL	4:07:07	
8. Willi Sawall	AUS	4:08:25	

Gold medalist Hartwig Gauder was born in West Germany, but his family moved to East Germany in 1960. Forty-two-year-old bronze medalist Yevgeny Ivchenko had been credited with a controversial time of 3:37:36.0 on the Olympic course on May 23, 1980.

1984 Los Angeles C: 31, N: 16, D: 8.11. WR: 3:41:38.4 (Raúl González Rodríguez)

1. Raúl González Rodríguez	MEX	3:47:26	OR
2. Bo Gustafsson	SWE	3:53:19	
3. Alessandro Bellucci	ITA	3:53:45	
4. Reima Salonen	FIN	3:58:30	
5. Raffaello Ducceschi	ITA	3:59:26	
6. Carl Schueler	USA	3:59:46	
7. Jorge Llopart Ribas	SPA	4:03:09	
8. José Pinto	POR	4:04:42	

The popular 32-year-old veteran Raúl González, competing in his fourth Olympics, pushed the other walkers through a brutal early pace until the hot sun had worn out all of the leading challengers. Maurizio Damilano was the last to go, staying with González for 35 kilometers, before losing contact and then dropping out seven kilometers from the finish. Of the 31 starters, five were disqualified and nine more failed to complete the course.

1988 Seoul C: 42, N: 22, D: 9.30. WR: 3:41:38.4 (Raúl González Rodríguez)

1. Vyacheslav Ivanenko	SOV/RUS	3:38:29	OR
2. Ronald Weigel	GDR	3:38:56	
3. Hartwig Gauder	GDR	3:39:45	
4. Aleksandr Potashov	SOV/BLR	3:41:00	
5. José Marin	SPA	3:43:03	
6. Simon Baker	AUS	3:44:07	
7. Bo Gustafsson	SWE	3:44:49	
8. Raffaello Ducceschi	ITA	3:45:43	

Vyacheslav Ivanenko was a 22-year-old machine repairman at a textile factory when he watched a television program that said that walking was good therapy for a bad back. The 5-foot 4½-inch Ivanenko began walking the two and a half miles to work. Because he lived in Siberia, he walked fast. One day he was noticed by a coach, who began training him in earnest.

At the 20-kilometer mark in the Olympic contest, Hernan Andrade of Mexico led teammate Martin Bermudez by 14 seconds; the rest of the walkers were at least 32 seconds farther back. Ten minutes later Andrade was disqualified. Bermudez held a one-minute lead at the halfway point, but a group of five caught him in the 32nd kilometer and Bermudez eventually faded to fifteenth. The favorites, Gauder, Weigel, and Ivanenko, pulled away from Marin and Potashov, with Ivanenko holding a three-second lead after 40 kilometers. Ivanenko then pressed the pace, dropping first Gauder and then Weigel, who resigned himself to protecting second place after receiving his second warning for lifting.

1992 Barcelona C: 42, N: 20, D: 8.7. WR: 3:41:38.4 (Raúl González Rodríguez)

1. Andrei Perlov	RUS	3:50.13
2. Carlos Mercenario Carbajal	MEX	3:52.09
3. Ronald Weigel	GER	3:53.45
4. Valery Spitsyn	RUS	3:54.39
5. Roman Mrázek	CZE	3:55.21
6. Hartwig Gauder	GER	3:56.47
7. Valentin Kononen	FIN	3:57.21
8. Miguel Rodríguez López	MEX	3:58.26

In 1991 Andrei Perlov, a construction engineer from Novosibirsk, Siberia, had a frustrating year. First he was disqualified after finishing first at the World Walking Cup, then, at the World Championships in Athletics, he and teammate Aleksandr Potashov tried to deadheat by finishing arm in arm, but the judges ruled that Potashov had crossed the finish line first.

In Barcelona Potashov took the early lead, but was disqualified after 20 kilometers. Valentin Kononen took over and opened a 42-second gap at the 30-kilometer mark. By 35 kilometers he had been reeled in by Mercenario, Perlov, and Robert Korzeniowski of Poland and was soon left behind. At the 40-kilometer refreshment stand, without warning, Perlov shot ahead. Mercenario and Korzeniowski were unable to keep up with his pace. At the entrance to the stadium, Korzeniowski, in second place, was informed that he had been disqualified. In fact, he had received a record five warning cards, but it took a while for the recording system to catch up with him.

HIGH JUMP

In high jump competitions, the crossbar is four meters (13 feet 1½ inches) long. The runway leading to the crossbar must be at least 20 meters (65 feet 7½ inches) long and preferably at least 25 meters (82 feet) long. Each contestant may place one or two markers along the runway to assist in the timing of his or her run-up and takeoff. There is a time limit of 1½ minutes for each jump, although when there are only two or three competitors remaining, three minutes are allowed before each jump. A contestant may begin at any height and may pass at any height. Three successive misses results in elimination, even if the misses are at different heights. Touching the crossbar is acceptable as long as the bar does not fall. Current rules decide ties in the following manner:

1. The competitor with the fewest misses at the last cleared height wins. If there is still a tie, then:
2. The competitor with the fewest total misses wins. If there is still a tie, it is recorded as such, unless the tie is for first place. In that case:
3. Each competitor is given one extra jump. If there is still a tie, then the bar is raised or lowered until the tie is broken.

High-jumpers must take off from one foot. In April 1954, U.S. tumbler Dick Browning reportedly somersaulted over a bar set at 7 feet 6 inches (2.28 meters). In 1962 Gary Chamberlain did a back handspring with a back flip over a bar set at 7 feet 4 inches (2.23 meters). He landed on his feet.

1896 Athens C: 5, N: 3, D: 4.10. WR: 1.97, 6-5 ⅝ (Michael Sweeney)

			FT.-	
			M	IN.
1.	Ellery Clark	USA	1.81	5-11¼
2.	James Connolly	USA	1.65	5-5
2.	Robert Garrett	USA	1.65	5-5
4.	Henrik Sjöberg	SWE	1.60	5-3
5.	Fritz Hofmann	GER	1.55	5-1

Ellery Clark was a 22-year-old Harvard undergraduate who was granted a leave of absence for the Olympics because of his high grade point average.

1900 Paris C: 11, N: 7, D: 7.15. WR: 1.97, 6-5 ⅝ (Michael Sweeney)

			FT.-		
			M	IN.	
1.	Irving Baxter	USA	1.90	6-2¾	OR
2.	Patrick Leahy	GBR/IRL	1.78	5-10	
3.	Lajos Gönczy	HUN	1.75	5-8¾	
4.	Carl-Albert Andersen	NOR	1.70	5-7	
5.	Eric Lemming	SWE	1.70	5-7	
6.	Waldemar Steffen	GER	1.70	5-7	
7.	Louis Monnier	FRA	1.60	5-3	
8.	Tore Blom	SWE	1.50	4-11	

Two Americans, William Remington and Walter Carroll, refused to take part in the final because it was held on a Sunday. Silver medalist Pat Leahy had reportedly cleared 6 feet 4 inches at least six times back in Ireland, but in Paris he missed three times at 6 feet.

1904 St. Louis C: 6, N: 3, D: 8.29. WR: 1.97, 6-5 ⅝ (Michael Sweeney)

			FT.-	
			M	IN.
1.	Samuel Jones	USA	1.80	5-11
2.	Garrett Serviss	USA	1.77	5-9¾
3.	Paul Weinstein	GER	1.77	5-9¾
4.	Lajos Gönczy	HUN	1.75	5-9
5.	Emil Freymark	USA	—	
6.	Ervin Barker	USA	1.70	5-7

Lajos Gönczy had brought with him to the United States several bottles of potent Hungarian wine, which were confiscated by Hungarian team officials prior to the competition. Unable to clear even 5 feet 9¾ inches, Gönczy finished a disappointing fourth. Several days later, Gönczy took part in an unofficial handicap event and successfully cleared 6 feet 2 inches. When the other Hungarians rushed up to congratulate him, they smelled his breath and discovered that he had found the hidden bottles of wine.

1906 Athens C: 24, N: 10, D: 5.1. WR: 1.97, 6-5 ⅝ (Michael Sweeney)

			FT.-	
			M	IN.
1.	Cornelius "Con" Leahy	GBR/IRL	1.775	5-10
2.	Lajos Gönczy	HUN	1.75	5-8¾
3.	Themistoklis Diakidis	GRE	1.725	5-8
3.	Herbert Kerrigan	USA	1.725	5-8
5.	Gunnar Rönström	SWE	1.70	5-7
6.	H. Bjolgerud	NOR	1.67	5-5¾
6.	Bruno Söderström	SWE	1.67	5-5¾

Herbert Kerrigan had been the favorite, but he was injured when a huge wave hit the ship that carried the U.S. team to Athens.

1908 London C: 20, N: 10, D: 7.21. WR: 1.97, 6-5 ⅝ (Michael Sweeney)

			FT.-		
			M	IN.	
1.	Harry Porter	USA	1.905	6-3	OR
2.	Georges "Géo" André	FRA	1.88	6-2	
2.	Cornelius "Con" Leahy	GBR/IRL	1.88	6-2	
2.	István Somodi	HUN	1.88	6-2	
5.	Herbert Gidney	USA	1.855	6-1	
5.	Thomas Moffitt	USA	1.855	6-1	
7.	John Neil Patterson	USA	1.83	6-0	
8.	Edward Leader	GBR	1.77	5-9¾	
8.	Patrick Leahy	GBR/IRL	1.77	5-9¾	

Silver medalist Géo André had never before jumped higher than 1.79 meters (5 feet 10 inches). At the 1912 Olympics he took part in the decathlon. During World War I he was badly injured and taken prisoner. After escaping at his sixth try, he rejoined the fight as an aviator. At the 1920 Olympics he competed in the 400-meter hurdles and the 4 × 400-meter relay. In 1924, again entered in the hurdles, he was chosen to take the Athletes' Oath on behalf of all the athletes at the Paris Games.

1912 Stockholm C: 26, N: 9, D: 7.8. WR: 2.005, 6-7 (George Horine)

			FT.-	
		M	IN.	
1. Alma Richards	USA	1.93	6-4	OR
2. Hans Liesche	GER	1.91	6-3¼	
3. George Horine	USA	1.89	6-2¼	
4. Egon Erickson	USA	1.87	6-1½	
4. James Thorpe	USA	1.87	6-1½	
6. Harry Grumpelt	USA	1.85	6-0¾	
6. John Johnstone	USA	1.85	6-0¾	
8. Karl-Axel Kullerstrand	SWE	1.83	6-0	

Alma Richards was a tall, awkward-looking 22-year-old Mormon from Parowan, Utah. On the ship from New York to Stockholm, he became the butt of countless "country boob" jokes made by the other members of the U.S. team. In the final Olympic competition, Richards seemed to have quite a bit of trouble, missing as many jumps as he made. Yet when the bar was raised to 6 feet 3¼ inches, the only jumpers left were Richards, Hans Liesche of Germany, and the favorite, George Horine, inventor of what came to be known as the "western-roll" style of high-jumping. Liesche cleared smoothly on the first try, but Horine missed three times and was eliminated. Richards, however, cleared the bar on his third and final attempt.

The bar was then put up to 6 feet 4 inches. Alma Richards, scheduled to jump first, walked away from the high jump area to be by himself. He closed his eyes and bowed his head, and made a deal with God. "I told the Lord," he later wrote, "that if He would help me to win the high jump in the Olympic Games at Stockholm, I would do my best to be a good boy and set a good example." Without further hesitation, Richards, who had never before come close to jumping 6 feet 4 inches, dashed toward the bar and sailed over with almost two inches to spare. Liesche was completely unnerved. He failed twice. Then, just as he had composed himself for his final attempt, a gun went off to signal the start of a race. Liesche waited for the race to end and then composed himself once more. This time the band began to play. After nine minutes, a Swedish official approached him and asked him to hurry up. This was the final blow. Liesche ran at the bar, but missed completely. Alma Richards, transformed from a country bumpkin into a hero in the eyes of his teammates, went on to be a good boy for the rest of his life.

1920 Antwerp C: 23, N: 9, D: 8.17. WR: 2.01, 6-7¼ (Edward Beeson)

			FT.-	
		M	IN.	
1. Richmond Landon	USA	1.935	6-4	EOR
2. Harold Muller	USA	1.90	6-2¾	

3. Bo Ekelund	SWE	1.90	6-2¾
4. Walter Whalen	USA	1.85	6-0¾
5. John Murphy	USA	1.85	6-0¾
6. B. Howard Baker	GBR	1.85	6-0¾
7. Pierre Lewden	FRA	1.80	5-10¾
7. Einar Thulin	SWE	1.80	5-10¾

In his book *Un Champion à la Hauteur*, Pierre Lewden, who placed seventh, describes how shocked he was by an incident that occurred during Bo Ekelund's final attempt at 6 feet 4 inches. While Ekelund was racing down the runway, an American official walked over and picked up the marker belonging to Dick Landon, which happened to be only a couple inches away from Ekelund's marker. His concentration broken, but unable to stop himself, Ekelund hit the bar head-on and the competition was decided in Landon's favor.

1924 Paris C: 21, N: 15, D: 7.7. WR: 2.03, 6-8¼ (Harold Osborn)

			FT.-	
		M	IN.	
1. Harold Osborn	USA	1.98	6-6	OR
2. Leroy Brown	USA	1.95	6-4¾	
3. Pierre Lewden	FRA	1.92	6-3½	
4. Thomas Poor	USA	1.88	6-2	
5. Jenö Gáspár	HUN	1.88	6-2	
6. Helge Jansson	SWE	1.85	6-0¾	
7. Pierre Guilloux	FRA	1.85	6-0¾	
8. Sverre Helgesen	NOR	1.83	6-0	
8. Lawrence Roberts	SAF	1.83	6-0	

Harold Osborn cleared every height on his first attempt. Five days later he earned a second gold medal in the decathlon.

1928 Amsterdam C: 35, N: 17, D: 7.29. WR: 2.03, 6-8¼ (Harold Osborn)

			FT.-	
		M	IN.	
1. Robert King	USA	1.94	6-4½	
2. Benjamin Hedges	USA	1.91	6-3¼	
3. Claude Ménard	FRA	1.91	6-3¼	
4. Simeon Toribio	PHI	1.91	6-3¼	
5. Harold Osborn	USA	1.91	6-3¼	
6. Kazuo Kimura	JPN	1.88	6-2	
7. André Cherrier (FRA), Pierre Lewden (FRA), Charles McGinnis (USA), Mikio Oda (JPN)		1.88	6-2	

Places two through five were decided by a jump-off.

1932 Los Angeles C: 14, N: 10, D: 7.31. WR: 2.03, 6-8¼ (Harold Osborn)

			FT.-
		M	IN.
1. Duncan McNaughton	CAN	1.97	6-5½
2. Robert Van Osdel	USA	1.97	6-5½
3. Simeon Toribio	PHI	1.97	6-5½

			M	FT.-IN.	
4.	Cornelius Johnson	USA	1.97	6-5½	
5.	Ilmari Reinikka	FIN	1.94	6-4¼	
6.	Kazuo Kimura	JPN	1.94	6-4¼	
7.	Misao Ono	JPN	1.90	6-2¾	
7.	Jerzy Plawczyk	POL	1.90	6-2¾	

Bob Van Osdel and Duncan McNaughton were good friends and fellow students at the University of Southern California in Los Angeles. Van Osdel had qualified for the U.S. team, as expected, by clearing 6 feet 6⅝ inches at the U.S. trials. McNaughton, on the other hand, had to wage a one-man campaign to convince the Canadian Olympic Association to let him compete. Undeterred by their constant refusals, McNaughton waited until the Canadian team arrived in Los Angeles, and then badgered them in person until they finally relented.

Duncan McNaughton pestered the Canadian Olympic Association into letting him compete in the 1932 Olympics, since he lived in Los Angeles anyway. He went on to win the gold medal in the high jump.

Van Osdel, McNaughton, Toribio, and 18-year-old Los Angeles High School student Cornelius Johnson all cleared 6 feet 5½ inches, but they all missed at 6 feet 6¾ inches. Following the rules in force at the time, the bar was then raised, lowered, raised and lowered until the contest was decided. After Johnson and Toribio had been eliminated, Van Osdel, who had been informally coaching McNaughton ever since he had first arrived in Los Angeles from Vancouver two years earlier, approached his Canadian friend and advised him on improving his technique. He concluded, "Get your kick working and you will be over." That piece of advice and encouragement did the trick. McNaughton cleared the bar while Van Osdel missed.

If current tie-breaking rules had been used back in 1932, Van Osdel would have won the gold medal, Johnson the silver, and McNaughton the bronze.

1936 Berlin C: 40, N: 24, D: 8.2. WR: 2.07, 6-9¾ (Cornelius Johnson, David Albritton)

			M	FT.-IN.	
1.	Cornelius Johnson	USA	2.03	6-8	OR
2.	David Albritton	USA	2.00	6-6¾	
3.	Delos Thurber	USA	2.00	6-6¾	
4.	Kalevi Kotkas	FIN	2.00	6-6¾	
5.	Kimio Yada	JPN	1.97	6-5½	
6.	Yoshiro Asakuma	JPN	1.94	6-4¼	
6.	Lauri Kalima	FIN	1.94	6-4¼	
6.	Hiroshi Tanaka	JPN	1.94	6-4¼	
6.	Gustav Weinkötz	GER	1.94	6-4¼	

Johnson won the gold medal without a miss and didn't even take off his sweatsuit until the bar had reached 6 feet 6¾ inches. Places 2 through 4 were decided by a jump-off. Adolf Hitler had personally congratulated the winners of the first two events of the day, Germans and Finns, but he left the stadium before the ceremony honoring the three Americans. Both Johnson and Albritton were black. Fourth-place finisher Kotkas had finished seventh in the discus throw four years earlier.

1948 London C: 26, N: 16, D: 7.30. WR: 2.11, 6-11 (Lester Steers)

			M	FT.-IN.	
1.	John Winter	AUS	1.98	6-6	
2.	Björn Paulson	NOR	1.95	6-4¾	
3.	George Stanich	USA	1.95	6-4¾	
4.	Dwight Eddleman	USA	1.95	6-4¾	
5.	Georges Damitio	FRA	1.95	6-4¾	
6.	Arthur Jackes	CAN	1.90	6-2¾	
7.	Alan Paterson	GBR	1.90	6-2¾	
7.	Hans Wähli	SWI	1.90	6-2¾	

John Winter, a 23-year-old bank clerk from Perth, cleared 6 feet 6 inches on his first attempt. Then he watched in surprise as the remaining four jumpers, including two Americans who had had to clear 6 feet 7¼ inches just to make the team, failed three times each. For the first time in the Olympics, ties were decided according to fewer misses.

1952 Helsinki C: 36, N: 24, D: 7.20. WR: 2.11, 6-11 (Lester Steers)

			FT.-	
		M	IN.	
1. Walter Davis	USA	2.04	6-8½	OR
2. Kenneth Wiesner	USA	2.01	6-7	
3. José Telles da Conceição	BRA	1.98	6-6	
4. Gösta Svensson	SWE	1.98	6-6	
5. Ronald Pavitt	GBR	1.95	6-4¾	
6. Ion Söter	ROM	1.95	6-4¾	
7. Arnold Betton	USA	1.95	6-4¾	
8. Björn Gundersen	NOR	1.90	6-2¾	

The 6-foot 8-inch, 206-pound Davis was an All-American basketball player from Texas A. & M. Stricken by polio at the age of eight, he had been unable to walk for three years.

1956 Melbourne C: 28, N: 19, D: 11.23. WR: 2.15, 7-0½ (Charles Dumas)

			FT.-	
		M	IN.	
1. Charles Dumas	USA	2.12	6-11½	OR
2. Charles Porter	AUS	2.10	6-10¾	
3. Igor Kashkarov	SOV/RUS	2.08	6-9¾	
4. Stig Pettersson	SWE	2.06	6-9	
5. Kenneth Money	CAN	2.03	6-8	
6. Volodymyr Sytkin	SOV/UKR	2.00	6-6¾	
7. Phil Reavis	USA	2.00	6-6¾	
7. Colin Ridgeway	AUS	2.00	6-6¾	

When Les Steers jumped 6 feet 11 inches on June 14, 1941, it seemed that the magic 7-foot barrier would be cleared at any time. But it was 12 years before Walt Davis bettered Steer's record with a leap of 6 feet 11½ inches, and even he was unable to go that extra half-inch. It was as if the 7-foot mark was guarded by a protective aura. It is true that 7-foot jumps had been claimed, most notably by Davis in an exhibition, but the first official, in-competition 7-foot jump wasn't achieved until June 29, 1956, when 19-year-old Charley Dumas glided over at the U.S. Olympic trials. There was great interest in Dumas when he arrived in Melbourne, but some of that interest turned to hostility when it turned out that Dumas didn't believe in practicing or even training, other than a few stretching exercises each morning.

However, Dumas knew what he was up to. He won the gold medal with relative ease, despite the spirited challenge of local favorite Chilla Porter, who improved his personal best by two inches. Ken Money, who finished fifth, later became a space scientist and astronaut.

John Thomas (left) congratulates Robert Shavlakadze after the latter's upset victory in the 1960 high jump.

1960 Rome C: 32, N: 23, D: 9.1. WR: 2.23, 7-3¾ (John Thomas)

			FT.-	
		M	IN.	
1. Robert Shavlakadze	SOV/GEO	2.16	7-1	OR
2. Valery Brumel	SOV/UKR	2.16	7-1	
3. John Thomas	USA	2.14	7-0¼	
4. Viktor Bolshov	SOV/RUS	2.14	7-0¼	
5. Stig Pettersson	SWE	2.09	6-10¼	
6. Charles Dumas	USA	2.03	6-8	
7. Jiří Lansky	CZE	2.03	6-8	
7. Kjell-Åke Nilsson	SWE	2.03	6-8	
7. Theo Püll	GER	2.03	6-8	

American sportswriters boasted that the high jump was one gold medal that was "in the bag" for the United States. The U.S. team consisted of 17-year-old Joe Faust, who had cleared 7 feet, defending champion Charley Dumas, and the 6-foot 5-inch world record holder John Thomas, who had jumped 7 feet over 30 times and hadn't been defeated in two years. But Faust, hampered by an ankle injury, was unable to clear 6 feet 6¾ inches. And Dumas, plagued by a knee injury that American officials had tried to convince him was imaginary, bowed out at 6 feet 10¼ inches. This left Thomas to battle it out with three jumpers from the U.S.S.R.: Soviet champion Viktor Bolshov, 18-year-old Siberian-born Valery Brumel, who had suddenly improved three and a half inches in August to 7 feet 1½ inches, and Robert Shavlakadze, a mustachioed 27-year-old from Tbilisi, Georgia.

At 6 feet 11½ inches Thomas passed. Bolshov and Shavlakadze went over the bar on their first attempts, while Brumel missed twice before clearing. This height also saw the departure of Stig Pettersson. The bar was raised to 7 feet ¼ inch. Brumel and Bolshov missed, but Shavlakadze cleared with his first try, the first time he had ever jumped over 7 feet in competition. Thomas missed, but the second time around, he and the other two Soviet jumpers all cleared the bar.

The next height was 7 feet 1 inch. The only one to clear on the first attempt was Shavlakadze, who had now made seven straight successful jumps since missing his first try of the afternoon at 6 feet 6¾ inches. Brumel cleared on his second try, but Bolshov and Thomas missed all three times. For Robert Shavlakadze, this was the greatest day of his career. For Valery Brumel, it was just the beginning. As for John Thomas, he was disappointed, but proud that he had earned an Olympic medal. Consequently, it came as a shock to the mild-mannered teenager when the very same sportswriters and fans who had been singing his praises only a few days earlier turned on him and accused him of getting carried away with all the publicity that they themselves had spread.

"That was the first time I learned people didn't like me," Thomas later recalled. "They only like winners. They don't give credit to a man for trying. I was called a quitter, a man with no heart. It left me sick." Thomas had nightmares for months until he finally came to accept that American sports fans were fickle. "American spectators are frustrated athletes," he concluded. "In the champion, they see what they'd like to be. In the loser, they see what they actually are, and they treat him with scorn."

1964 Tokyo C: 29, N: 20, D: 10.21. WR: 2.28, 7-5¾ (Valery Brumel)

		M	FT.-IN.	
1. Valery Brumel	SOV/UKR	2.18	7-1¾	OR
2. John Thomas	USA	2.18	7-1¾	OR
3. John Rambo	USA	2.16	7-1	
4. Stig Pettersson	SWE	2.14	7-0¼	
5. Robert Shavlakadze	SOV/GEO	2.14	7-0¼	
6. Ralf Drecoll	GER	2.09	6-10¼	
6. Kjell-Åke Nilsson	SWE	2.09	6-10¼	
8. Edward Caruthers	USA	2.09	6-10¼	

By 1964 the pressure of great expectations had shifted from John Thomas to Valery Brumel, the current world record holder. And Brumel definitely felt that pressure. He lost to Shavlakadze at the 1964 U.S.S.R. championships, and arrived in Tokyo in somewhat of a crisis. Well below form, he worked out in secret so that his image of invincibility wouldn't be tarnished. When he cleared 6 feet 9¾ inches in practice, his coach lied to him and told him the bar had actually been two inches higher.

The Olympic qualifying round was held on October 20. Brumel missed twice at 6 feet 8 inches and was on the verge of not even making it to the final, when he got himself together and cleared the bar successfully, thus preventing a complete disaster.

The next day, for the final, Brumel was more composed. He made it through 6 feet 11½ inches without a miss, a feat matched only by Robert Shavlakadze. Pettersson, Rambo, and Thomas each cleared 6 feet 11½ inches with their second try. At 7 feet ¼ inch, only Rambo went over the first time, and only Pettersson made it the second time. The three medalists from 1960 were now each one miss from elimination. But all three literally rose to the challenge and sailed over without dislodging the bar. This seemed to be a turning point for Valery Brumel. With renewed confidence, he cleared 7 feet 1 inch on his first attempt. Thomas made it the second time around, and Rambo the third, while Pettersson and Shavlakadze failed at all three attempts. Rambo bowed out at 7 feet 1¾ inches, while Brumel and Thomas both succeeded with their first tries. However, neither man, by now good friends after four years of competition, was able to make it over 7 feet 2½ inches. Brumel and Thomas were both credited with the Olympic record, but Brumel was awarded first place because he had committed fewer misses.

On October 4, 1965, Valery Brumel was riding on the back of a motorcycle being driven by female motorcycle racing champion Tamara Golikova, when they skidded out of control. Although Golikova was unhurt, Brumel was smashed into a concrete pillar and suffered an open tibia fracture of his right leg. His right foot was hanging limply, barely connected to the rest of his body.

When Brumel had traveled to the United States to

The ecstasy of victory: Valery Brumel wins the 1964 high jump.

compete in a series of competitions against John Thomas, he had been shocked by the behavior of American crowds, which booed Thomas when he missed a jump or, worst of all, when he committed the sin of finishing second. But now that his own sporting career had come to a sudden end, Brumel learned that Soviet fans could be just as harsh. The newspapers lost interest in him, most of his friends drifted away, his wife, perhaps wondering what he had been doing whizzing around on the back of a motorcycle with Tamara Golikova in the first place, divorced him.

After his accident, Brumel received a telegram that read, "Sometimes a twist of fate seems to have been put there to test a man's strength of character. Don't admit defeat. I sincerely hope you come back to jump again." It was signed "John Thomas." Remarkably, Valery Brumel did jump again. Although he never made it back to international competition, in 1970 he actually cleared 6 feet 11¾ inches. He was also able to channel his energy into other directions, earning a doctorate in sports psychology and publishing a novel.

1968 Mexico City C: 39, N: 25, D: 10.20. WR: 2.28, 7-5¾ (Valery Brumel)

			M	FT.-IN.	
1.	Richard Fosbury	USA	2.24	7-4¼	OR
2.	Edward Caruthers	USA	2.22	7-3¼	
3.	Valentin Gavrilov	SOV/RUS	2.20	7-2½	
4.	Valery Skvortsov	SOV/RUS	2.16	7-1	
5.	Reynaldo Brown	USA	2.14	7-0¼	
6.	Giacomo Crosa	ITA	2.14	7-0¼	
7.	Günter Spielvogel	GER	2.14	7-0¼	
8.	Lawrie Peckham	AUS	2.12	6-11½	

The 1968 Olympics marked the international debut of Dick Fosbury and his celebrated "Fosbury Flop," which would soon revolutionize high-jumping. Fosbury's technique began by racing up to the bar at great speed and taking off with his left foot. But instead of swinging his right foot up and over the bar, as everyone else did, Fosbury would pivot his right leg back and approach head first with his back to the bar. While the coaches of the world, already exasperated by the steeplechase style of Amos Biwott, shook their heads in disbelief, the Mexico City audience was absolutely captivated by Fosbury. Fosbury cleared every height through 7 feet 3¼ inches without a miss and then achieved a personal record of 7 feet 4¼ inches to win the gold medal. By 1980, 13 of the 16 Olympic finalists were using the Fosbury Flop.

1972 Munich C: 40, N: 29, D: 9.10. WR: 2.29, 7-6 (Ni Chihchin, Patrick Matzdorf)

			M	FT.-IN.
1.	Jüri Tarmak	SOV/EST	2.23	7-3¾
2.	Stefan Junge	GDR	2.21	7-3
3.	Dwight Stones	USA	2.21	7-3
4.	Hermann Magerl	GER	2.18	7-1¾
5.	Ádám Szepesi	HUN	2.18	7-1¾
6.	John Beers	CAN	2.15	7-0½
6.	István Major	HUN	2.15	7-0½
8.	Rustam Akhmyetov	SOV/UKR	2.15	7-0½

1976 Montreal C: 36, N: 23, D: 7.31. WR: 2.31, 7-7 (Dwight Stones)

			M	FT.-IN.	
1.	Jacek Wszola	POL	2.25	7-4½	OR
2.	Gregory Joy	CAN	2.23	7-3¾	
3.	Dwight Stones	USA	2.21	7-3	
4.	Sergei Budalov	SOV	2.21	7-3	
5.	Serhei Senyukov	SOV/UKR	2.18	7-1¾	
6.	Rodolfo Bergamo	ITA	2.18	7-1¾	
7.	Rolf Beilschmidt	GDR	2.18	7-1¾	
8.	Jesper Torring	DEN	2.18	7-1¾	

In 1972 Dwight Stones had been one of the darlings of the Munich Games. A mere 18 years old, he had delighted the crowd with his exuberance. Four years later in Montreal, it was a completely different story. Now he was the world record holder and heavy favorite. But several days before the competition began, Stones launched a verbal attack against the French-Canadian organizers of the Games for failing to complete the stadium as planned. Of particular concern to Stones was the nonappearance of a retractable roof, which would have kept out the rain. Fear of rain was an obsession with Stones because his approach to the bar was unusually fast and sharp. Stones called the Olympic organizers "rude" for forcing the athletes to compete in an unfinished stadium. But by the time that his remarks had been translated into the local papers, he was being accused of calling all French Canadians "rude."

When Stones appeared on the track for the qualifying round, he was loudly booed. Whenever his name was announced, he was booed; whenever he began a jump he was booed; whenever he missed or made a jump he was booed. The situation degenerated rather badly when U.S. fans in the stadium retaliated by booing a French-Canadian high-jumper, Claude Ferragne.

The next day, Stones tried to make peace with the local crowd by wearing a shirt that bore on the back the slogan "I love French Canadians." Track officials made him take it off. Underneath he had on a 1972 Olympic shirt, which he was wearing because it had been made by a company with which he had a financial relationship. The officials made him take that one off too. By the time the bar had been raised to 7 feet 1¾ inches, a light rain had begun to fall. At 7 feet 3 inches, the rain had become heavy. Huge puddles formed in the high jump area. Stones, exasperated by the ineffectual attempts of the officials to clear the area, grabbed a squeegee and started mopping up the area himself. Other jumpers joined him, including surprise local favorite Greg Joy. For Stones it was a hopeless cause. Even the eventual winner, 19-year-old Jacek Wszola,

Dick Fosbury introduces the Fosbury Flop at the 1968 Olympics.

when asked later at what point he knew he would win, replied, "When it started to rain."

Four days later, in Philadelphia, Dwight Stones broke his own world record with a leap of 7 feet 7¼ inches.

1980 Moscow C: 30, N: 19, D: 8.1. WR: 2.35, 7-8½ (Jacek Wszola, Dietmar Mögenburg)

		FT.-		
		M	IN.	
1. Gerd Wessig	GDR	2.36	7-8¾	WR
2. Jacek Wszola	POL	2.31	7-7	
3. Jörg Freimuth	GDR	2.31	7-7	
4. Henry Lauterbach	GDR	2.29	7-6	
5. Roland Dalhäuser	SWI	2.24	7-4¼	
6. Vaso Komnenić	YUG	2.24	7-4¼	
7. Adrian Proteasa	ROM	2.21	7-3	
8. Aleksandr Grigoryev	SOV/RUS	2.21	7-3	

The anticipated showdown between co-world record holders Jacek Wszola and Dietmar Mögenburg was spoiled when West Germany joined the anti-Soviet boycott. As it turned out, however, neither of them held the world record anymore once the competition was over. Gerd Wessig, a 6-foot 7-inch 21-year-old cook from Schwerin, was one of the big surprises of the 1980 Olympics. He had qualified for the East German team only two weeks earlier when he won the national championship with what was then his personal record of 7 feet 6½ inches. In Moscow he improved by over two inches to become the first man to set a world record in the high jump in the Olympics. Oddly enough, Wessig was also the first jumper since 1896 to make a successful jump beyond the height that had won him the gold medal.

1984 Los Angeles C: 30, N: 20, D: 8.11. WR: 2.39, 7-10 (Zhu Jianhua)

		FT.-	
		M	IN.
1. Dietmar Mögenburg	GER	2.35	7-8½
2. Patrik Sjöberg	SWE	2.33	7-7¾
3. Zhu Jianhua	CHN	2.31	7-7
4. Dwight Stones	USA	2.31	7-7
5. Doug Nordquist	USA	2.29	7-6¼
6. Milton Ottey	CAN	2.29	7-6¼
7. Liu Yunpeng	CHN	2.29	7-6¼
8. Cai Shu	CHN	2.27	7-5¼

While the experts predicted the gold medal would go to world record holder Zhu Jianhua, with two-time bronze medalist Dwight Stones fighting it out for second place with Dietmar Mögenburg, *the* expert on the high jump knew better. That expert, loquacious Dwight Stones himself, picked the 6-foot 7-inch Mögenburg for the gold, Zhu for the silver and himself for the bronze. Had not 19-year-old Patrik Sjöberg equaled his personal record to take second, Stones' soothsaying would have been right on the mark. The most important factor, as Stones well knew, was that Mögenburg had a history of rising to the

occasion at important meets, while Zhu seemed to falter when the going got rough.

Two months earlier Zhu had defeated Mögenburg in West Germany by setting a world record of 7 feet 10 inches, but in Los Angeles Zhu's concentration was broken by an unexpected occurrence. After recording his first miss at 7-7¾, Zhu was just about to try again when 1500-meter finalist Steve Ovett walked off the track and collapsed on the apron of the high jump area. Startled officials prevented Zhu from going ahead with his jump until Ovett had been tended to. By this time Zhu had changed his mind and decided to pass. His final two attempts were taken at 7-8½ and he missed both. Meanwhile, Mögenburg cleared every height on the first try and gained the gold medal without a miss.

1988 Seoul C: 27, N: 18, D: 9.25. WR: 2.42, 7-11½ (Javier Sotomayor Sanabria)

		FT.-		
		M	IN.	
1. Hennady Avdeyenko	SOV/UKR	2.38	7-9¾	OR
2. Hollis Conway	USA	2.36	7-8¾	
3. Rudolf Povarnytsyn	SOV/UKR	2.36	7-8¾	
3. Patrik Sjöberg	SWE	2.36	7-8¾	
5. Clarence Saunders	BER	2.34	7-8	
6. Dietmar Mögenburg	GER	2.34	7-8	
7. Dalton Grant	GBR	2.31	7-7	
7. Igor Paklin	SOV/KYR	2.31	7-7	
7. Carlo Thränhardt	GER	2.31	7-7	

The 1988 high jump field included five former world record holders: Mögenburg, Zhu Jianhua (who failed to qualify for the final), Povarnytsyn, Paklin, and Sjöberg. None of them placed higher than third. Instead, the winner was 6-foot 7½-inch Hennady Avdeyenko, who made all five jumps he attempted through 7 feet 8¾ inches, and then cleared 7 feet 9¾ inches on his second try. Second place went to unheralded Hollis Conway, who, at 6 feet ¼ inch, was unusually short for a successful high jumper. Javier Sotomayor, kept out of the Olympics by the Cuban boycott, set a world record of 7 feet 11½ inches only 17 days before the Seoul final. On July 29, 1989, Sotomayor became the first person to clear 8 feet.

1992 Barcelona C: 43, N: 27, D: 8.2. WR: 2.44, 8-0 (Javier Sotomayor Sanabria)

		FT.-	
		M	IN.
1. Javier Sotomayor Sanabria	CUB	2.34	7-8
2. Patrik Sjöberg	SWE	2.34	7-8
3. Hollis Conway	USA	2.34	7-8
3. Timothy Forsythe	AUS	2.34	7-8
3. Artur Partyka	POL	2.34	7-8
6. Ralf Sonn	GER	2.31	7-7
7. Troy Kemp	BAH	2.31	7-7
8. Charles Austin	USA	2.28	7-5¾
8. Marino Drake Rodríguez	CUB	2.28	7-5¾
8. Dragutin Topić	YUG	2.28	7-5¾

It was a strange competition. Despite a high-quality field, the winning height was the lowest since 1976, and the last 20 attempts were all misses. Sotomayor earned the gold medal by being the only jumper to clear 7 feet 8 inches on his first try. The surprise medalist was 18-year-old Tim Forsythe from Thorpdale in Gippsland. Four years earlier Forsythe had been so uninterested in high jumping that when the Olympic final came on television he went outside and mowed the lawn.

POLE VAULT

Contestants may use a pole of any length and made of any material or combination of materials. They are given two minutes to make a vault, although when the competition is reduced to two or three competitors, the time limit is extended to four minutes. The runway must be at least 40 meters (131 feet 3 inches) long and, preferably, at least 45 meters (147 feet 8 inches) long. Each vaulter may place one or two markers along the runway to assist in the timing of the approach and takeoff. The vaulters plant their poles in a rigid box sunk level with the ground. The box is one meter long. It is 60 centimeters (1 foot 11½ inches) wide at the front and 15 centimeters (5¾ inches) wide at the stop board. The crossbar is 4.5 meters (14 feet 9¼ inches) long. As in the high jump, vaulters may touch the crossbar as long as they do not dislodge it. All other rules, including tie-breaking rules, are the same as those for the high jump.

Between 1896 and 1968 athletes from the United States won every Olympic pole vault competition (not including the unofficial games of 1906). At sixteen in a row, this remains the longest national winning streak in any event in any sport in Olympic history. The streak was finally broken, in controversial circumstances, in 1972.

1896 Athens C: 5, N: 2, D: 4.10. WR: 3.49, 11-5⅜ (Walter Rodenbaugh)

			FT.-	
			M	IN.
1.	William Welles Hoyt	USA	3.30	10-10
2.	Albert Tyler	USA	3.20	10-6
3.	Evangelos Damaskos	GRE	2.60	8-6¼
3.	Ioannis Theodoropoulos	GRE	2.60	8-6¼
3.	Vasilios Xydas	GRE	2.60	8-6¼

1900 Paris C: 8, N: 5, D: 7.15. WR: 3.62, 11-10½ (Raymond Clapp)

			FT.-		
			M	IN.	
1.	Irving Baxter	USA	3.30	10-10	EOR
2.	Michael Colket	USA	3.25	10-8	
3.	Carl-Albert Andersen	NOR	3.20	10-6	
4.	Louis Gontier	FRA	3.10	10-2	
4.	Jakab Kauser	HUN	3.10	10-2	
4.	Eric Lemming	SWE	3.10	10-2	
7.	Karl Gustaf Staaf	SWE	2.80	9-2¼	
8.	August Nilsson	SWE	2.60	8-6¼	

This event was marred by indecision on the part of the officials in charge. Three of the leading American entrants, Bascom Johnson, Charles Dvorak, and Daniel Horton, objected to the scheduling of the pole vault on a Sunday. Johnson and Dvorak showed up anyway, but were told that the event would be rescheduled, so they left. Then the officials changed their minds and went ahead with the contest without Johnson and Dvorak. In their absence, the pole vault was won by Irving Baxter, who was still on the field after winning the high jump. The next day Baxter finished second to Ray Ewry in the three standing jump events. A few days later, in order "to appease the indignant visitors from across the seas," a second pole vault contest was staged. This was won by Horton at 11 feet 3¾ inches with Dvorak second at 11 feet 1¾ inches.

1904 St. Louis C: 7, N: 2, D: 9.3. WR: 3.69, 12-1½ (Norman Dole)

			FT.-		
			M	IN.	
1.	Charles Dvorak	USA	3.50	11-5¾	OR
2.	Leroy Samse	USA	3.43	11-3	
3.	Louis Wilkins	USA	3.43	11-3	
4.	Ward McLanahan	USA	3.35	10-11¾	
5.	Claude Allen	USA	3.35	10-11¾	
6.	Walter Dray	USA	—	—	
7.	Paul Weinstein	GER	—	—	

1906 Athens C: 11, N: 8, D: 4.25. WR: 3.74, 12-3¼ (Fernand Gonder)

			FT.-	
			M	IN.
1.	Fernand Gonder	FRA	3.50	11-5¾
2.	Bruno Söderström	SWE	3.40	11-1¾
3.	Edward Glover	USA	3.35	10-11¾
4.	Theodoris Makris	GRE	3.25	10-8
5.	Heikki Ahlmann (Pennola) (FIN), Georgios Banikas (GRE), Otto Haug (NOR), I. Kiss (HUN), Stefanos Koudouriotis (GRE)		3.00	9-10

Gonder won first place by clearing 11 feet 5¾ inches with ease. When Glover attempted to clear the same height, an official crossed his path. Glover lost his balance and was injured. The Canadian vaulter, Ed Archibald, also had a tough time. His pole disappeared on a train ride through Italy. Olympic officials gave him some local models when he arrived in Athens, but when one of them broke and almost impaled him, he lost confidence and was unable to perform at his usual level.

1908 London C: 14, N: 7, D: 7.24. WR: 3.90, 12-9½ (Walter Dray)

			FT.-		
			M	IN.	
1.	Edward Cooke	USA	3.71	12-2	OR
1.	Alfred Gilbert	USA	3.71	12-2	OR
3.	Edward Archibald	CAN	3.58	11-9	

A.C. Gilbert earning a gold medal in the 1908 pole vault. He later achieved fame as the inventor of the Erector Set.

3. Charles Jacobs	USA	3.58	11-9	
3. Bruno Söderström	SWE	3.58	11-9	
6. Georgios Banikas	GRE	3.50	11-6	
6. Samuel Bellah	USA	3.50	11-6	
8. Károly Szathmáry	HUN	3.35	11-0	

Competition in the pole vault was severely disrupted by the sensational incidents surrounding the finish of the marathon. Gold medalist Alfred Gilbert worked his way through Yale as a magician. He is best known today as the inventor of the Erector Set, one of the most popular toys of all time.

1912 Stockholm C: 24, N: 11, D: 7.11. WR: 4.02, 13-2¼ (Marcus Wright)

			FT.-	
		M	IN.	
1. Harry Babcock	USA	3.95	12-11½	OR
2. Frank Nelson	USA	3.85	12-7½	
2. Marcus Wright	USA	3.85	12-7½	
4. William Hapenny	CAN	3.80	12-5½	
4. Frank Murphy	USA	3.80	12-5½	
4. Bertil Uggla	SWE	3.80	12-5½	
7. Samuel Bellah	USA	3.75	12-3½	
8. Frank Coyle (USA), Gordon Dukes (USA), William Fritz (USA)		3.65	11-11¾	

1920 Antwerp C: 16, N: 7, D: 8.20. WR: 4.02, 13-2¼ (Marcus Wright)

			FT.-	
		M	IN.	
1. Frank Foss	USA	4.09	13-5	WR
2. Henry Petersen	DEN	3.70	12-1½	
3. Edwin Myers	USA	3.60	11-9¾	
4. Edward Knourek	USA	3.60	11-9¾	
5. Ernfrid Rydberg	SWE	3.60	11-9¾	
6. Laurits Jörgensen	DEN	3.60	11-9¾	
7. Eldon Jenne	USA	3.60	11-9¾	
8. Georg Högström	SWE	3.50	11-6	

Foss' world record vault, made in the midst of wind and rain, excited the crowd more than any other event in the 1920 Games. His 15½-inch margin of victory was by far the largest in Olympic history.

1924 Paris C: 20, N: 13, D: 7.10. WR: 4.21, 13-9¾ (Charles Hoff)

			FT.-
		M	IN.
1. Lee Barnes	USA	3.95	12-11½
2. Glenn Graham	USA	3.95	12-11½
3. James Brooker	USA	3.90	12-9½
4. Henry Petersen	DEN	3.90	12-9½
5. Victor Pickard	CAN	3.80	12-5½
6. Ralph Spearow	USA	3.70	12-1½
7. Maurice Henrijean	BEL	3.66	12-0

Charles Hoff, the Norwegian world record holder, withdrew because of an injury. He did, however, take part in the 400- and 800-meter runs, finishing eighth in the latter. In Hoff's absence, the pole vault was won by 17-year-old Lee Barnes, a student at Hollywood High School in Los Angeles. In 1927 Barnes appeared in the film *College*, as a stand-in for Buster Keaton in a scene that required him to pole vault into a second-story window.

1928 Amsterdam C: 20, N: 13, D: 8.1. WR: 4.31, 14-1¾ (Lee Barnes)

			FT.-	
		M	IN.	
1. Sabin Carr	USA	4.20	13-9¼	OR
2. William Droegemuller	USA	4.10	13-5¼	
3. Charles McGinnis	USA	3.95	12-11½	
4. Victor Pickard	CAN	3.95	12-11½	
5. Lee Barnes	USA	3.95	12-11½	
6. Yonataro Nakazawa	JPN	3.90	12-9½	
7. Henry Lindblad	SWE	3.90	12-9½	
8. János Karlovits	HUN	3.80	12-5½	

Sabin Carr of Yale had become the first vaulter to clear 14 feet on May 27, 1927.

1932 Los Angeles C: 8, N: 4, D: 8.3. WR: 4.37, 14-4¼ (William Graber)

			FT.-	
		M	IN.	
1. William Miller	USA	4.31	14-1¾	OR
2. Shuhei Nishida	JPN	4.30	14-1¼	
3. George Jefferson	USA	4.20	13-9½	
4. William Graber	USA	4.15	13-7½	
5. Shizuo Mochizuki	JPN	4.00	13-1½	
6. Lucio de Castro	BRA	3.90	12-9½	
7. Peter Chlentzos	GRE	3.75	12-3½	

The 1932 competition was expected to provide a clean sweep for the United States, but no one had counted on the unexpected determination of Japan's Shuhei Nishida, who gained the support of the previously partisan crowd with his great performance and fine sportsmanship, sincerely congratulating Bill Miller when the latter broke the Olympic record. Nevertheless, most of the 80,000 American spectators breathed a sigh of relief when Miller avoided a vault-off by clearing 14 feet 1¾ inches on his third attempt.

1936 Berlin C: 30, N: 21, D: 8.5. WR: 4.43, 14-6½ (George Varoff)

		FT.-		
		M	IN.	
1. Earle Meadows	USA	4.35	14-3¼	OR
2. Shuhei Nishida	JPN	4.25	13-11¼	
3. Sueo Oe	JPN	4.25	13-11¼	
4. William Sefton	USA	4.25	13-11¼	
5. William Graber	USA	4.15	13-7¼	
6. Kiyoshi Adachi (JPN),		4.00	13-1½	

Sylvanus Apps (CAN), Péter Bácsalmási (HUN), Josef Haunzwickel (AUT), Danilo Innocenti (ITA), Jan Korejs (CZE), Bo Ljungberg (SWE), Alfred Proksch (AUT), Wilhelm Sznajder (POL), Frederick Webster (GBR), Viktor Zsuffka (HUN)

On July 4, 1936, George Varoff, a 22-year-old janitor from San Francisco, rose from obscurity to set a world record of 14 feet 6½ inches at the A.A.U. championships in Princeton, New Jersey. Sportswriters rushed in to get his story. They learned that he came from a poor family of Ukrainian immigrants; that he was a music major at Oregon University who played the string fiddle; that he hoped to land a good job in order to help his family. VAROFF TYPIFIES SPIRIT OF AMERICA read a typical headline. But the following week at the U.S. Olympic trials, Varoff bowed out at 14 feet 3 inches and failed to make the U.S. team. The press moved on to other stories.

The 1936 Olympic final was another dramatic duel between the Americans and the Japanese. It lasted into the night and finished in the eerie glow of floodlights. After it had been determined that Meadows had finished first

and Sefton fourth, Nishida and Oe refused to vault-off for second and third. Instead they decided by lot that Nishida would be placed second and Oe third. Back home in Japan, they brought their medals to a jeweler and had them cut in half lengthwise. Then they were fused back together so that each man had a medal that was half silver and half bronze.

1948 London C: 19, N: 10, D: 8.2. WR: 4.77, 15-7¾ (Cornelius Warmerdam)

		FT.-	
		M	IN.
1. O. Guinn Smith	USA	4.30	14-1¼
2. Erkki Kataja	FIN	4.20	13-9¼
3. Robert Richards	USA	4.20	13-9¼
4. Erling Kaas	NOR	4.10	13-5¼
5. Ragnar Lundberg	SWE	4.10	13-5¼
6. Richmond Morcom	USA	3.95	12-11½
7. Hugo Göllors	SWE	3.95	12-11½
7. Valto Olenius	FIN	3.95	12-11½

The period between the 1936 and 1948 Olympics was dominated by Cornelius "Dutch" Warmerdam, the first person to vault 15 feet. Between 1940 and his retirement in 1944, Warmerdam, using a bamboo pole, cleared 15 feet 43 times. No one else accomplished the height until 1951. In fact, when he retired, Warmerdam's best vault was nine inches higher than anyone else's. His world record of 15 feet 7¾ inches, set on May 23, 1942, wasn't broken until April 1957.

The 1948 Olympic final was concluded during a downpour. With ties now decided on the basis of fewer misses, Erkki Kataja was poised for victory if no one could clear 14 feet 1¼ inches. But Guinn Smith made it on his final try, and the U.S. pole vault winning streak was kept alive.

1952 Helsinki C: 25, N: 17, D: 7.22. WR: 4.77, 15-7¾ (Cornelius Warmerdam)

		FT.-		
		M	IN.	
1. Robert Richards	USA	4.55	14-11	OR
2. Donald Laz	USA	4.50	14-9	
3. Ragnar Lundberg	SWE	4.40	14-5¼	
4. Petro Denysenko	SOV/UKR	4.40	14-5¼	
5. Valto Olenius	FIN	4.30	14-1¼	
6. Bunkichi Sawada	JPN	4.20	13-9¼	
7. Vladimir Bražnik	SOV	4.20	13-9¼	
8. Viktor Knyazev	SOV	4.20	13-9¼	

The competition came down to a duel between Don Laz and "The Vaulting Vicar," Reverend Bob Richards, a theology professor in California. They both missed for the first time at 14 feet 9 inches and then cleared with their second attempts. When they both missed twice at 14 feet 11 inches, discussions began as to how a vault-off would be conducted. But Richards solved the problem quickly by clearing the bar on his third attempt. The year 1952 was the first time that the U.S.S.R. competed in the

Olympics, and many politicians, journalists, and athletes looked at the Olympics as a front-line battle in the Cold War. Bob Richards thought otherwise and was a major force in encouraging interaction and friendship between athletes from the United States and the U.S.S.R.

1956 Melbourne C: 19, N: 12, D: 11.26. WR: 4.77, 15-7¾ (Cornelius Warmerdam)

| | | | FT.- | |
		M	IN.	
1. Robert Richards	USA	4.56	14-11½	OR
2. Robert Gutowski	USA	4.53	14-10¼	
3. Georgios Roubanis	GRE	4.50	14-9	
4. George Mattos	USA	4.35	14-3¼	
5. Ragnar Lundberg	SWE	4.25	13-11¼	
6. Zenon Wazny	POL	4.25	13-11¼	
7. Eeles Landström	FIN	4.25	13-11¼	
8. Manfred Preussger	GDR	4.25	13-11¼	

The qualifying round almost saw a major upset when Bob Richards missed twice at the shockingly low height of 13 feet 1½ inches. He cleared on his third attempt and was in control for the rest of the contest. Gusty winds and a patchy runway hampered the quality of performance in the final. As it happened though, the wind actually helped Richards on his winning vault. After missing once at 14 feet 11½ inches, he hit the bar on his second attempt. Richards lay on his back for 30 seconds watching the bar bounce and quiver. "I was scared to change my position in the pit in case the slightest vibration brought it down," he explained. But the wind kept the bar in place and Richards became the only person to win two gold medals and three total medals in the pole vault.

It was silver medalist Bob Gutowski who finally broke Cornelius Warmerdam's world record with a vault of 15 feet 8¼ inches on April 27, 1957. Richards had predicted that Gutowski would someday be the first vaulter to break the 16-foot barrier. However, Bob Gutowski was killed in a car crash at the age of 25 on August 2, 1960.

The 1956 competition was also noteworthy because it saw the first appearance in the pole vault competition of the fiberglass pole, which would revolutionize pole vaulting. It was used by bronze medalist Georgios Roubanis, who improved his personal best by three and a half inches. The first Olympic athlete to use a fiberglass pole was Bob Mathias in the 1952 decathlon.

1960 Rome C: 30, N: 20, D: 9.7. WR: 4.80, 15-9¼ (Donald Bragg)

| | | | FT.- | |
		M	IN.	
1. Donald Bragg	USA	4.70	15-5	OR
2. Ronald Morris	USA	4.60	15-1	
3. Eeles Landström	FIN	4.55	14-11	
4. Rolando Cruz	PUR	4.55	14-11	
5. Günter Malcher	GDR	4.50	14-9	
6. Igor Petrenko	SOV/UKR	4.50	14-9	
6. Matti Sutinen	FIN	4.50	14-9	
8. Rudolf Tomášek	CZE	4.50	14-9	

Don "Tarzan" Bragg began the final competition cautiously, but gained confidence with each leap and finished strongly. After he had won, Bragg, whose dream it was to play Tarzan in the movies, delighted the crowd by celebrating with a Tarzan yell.

Silver medalist Ron Morris had failed to clear the qualifying height of 14 feet 5¼ inches. However, Olympic rules state that at least 12 men must compete in the final. Since only 10 had made the required height, the three vaulters with the next best records were added to the final. One of them was Morris. Bragg, by the way, never did get to play Tarzan, although he did come close. Shooting had already begun for *Tarzan and the Jewels of Opar* in 1964, and Bragg was in front of the cameras, happily swinging from vines, when a court order halted the production because of copyright infringement. Forced to become a salesman of drug supplies, Bragg later opened a boys' camp in New Jersey.

1964 Tokyo C: 32, N: 20, D: 10.17. WR: 5.28, 17-4 (Frederick Hansen)

| | | | FT.- | |
		M	IN.	
1. Frederick Hansen	USA	5.10	16-8¾	OR
2. Wolfgang Reinhardt	GER	5.05	16-6¾	
3. Klaus Lehnertz	GER	5.00	16-4¾	
4. Manfred Preussger	GDR	5.00	16-4¾	
5. Hennady Blyznetsov	SOV/UKR	4.95	16-2¾	
6. Rudolf Tomášek	CZE	4.90	16-0¾	
7. Pentti Nikula	FIN	4.90	16-0¾	
8. Billy Pemelton	USA	4.80	15-9	

The pole vault world record was broken 17 times between the Rome Olympics and the Tokyo Olympics, the last two times by Fred Hansen of Cuero, Texas. The 1964 final was a long, drawn-out competition that ended up lasting 8¾ hours. For the first eight hours, Hansen attempted only four vaults, all of them successful. When the bar was raised to 16 feet 6¾ inches, Hansen gambled by passing. Tomášek, Blyznetsov, Preussger, and Lehnertz all bowed out, but Wolfgang Reinhardt, who had beaten Hansen earlier in the year, cleared on his first try. The bar was moved up to 16 feet 8¾ inches and suddenly, after hours of boredom, the pole vault became a dramatic contest. Hansen and Reinhardt both missed twice. If Hansen missed again, the gold medal would go to Reinhardt and the United States would lose the pole vault for the first time ever (not including the 1906 Intercalated Games). "Please don't think I'm corny," Hansen later said, "but I was thinking what I could do for my country, not for myself." Hansen had the uprights moved back eight inches. Then he prepared himself at great length, raced down the runway, and cleared the bar by half a foot. Reinhardt had one more attempt, but he missed, and the competition was finally over.

Back in 11th place was John Pennel, a Tennessee farm boy who set or tied the world record seven times in 1963 alone but injured his back three weeks before the

With his final attempt, Fred Hansen clears 16 feet 8¾ inches to win the 1964 pole vault in Tokyo.

Olympics. Although Pennel made history on August 24, 1963, by becoming the first vaulter to clear 17 feet (landing in a sawdust pit), his personal highlight came earlier in the year at a meet in Warsaw, Poland. After winning the event before a crowd of almost 100,000 people, Pennel asked for the bar to be moved above the existing world record (it was later remeasured at equal to the record). Because the stadium had no lights, meet officials illuminated the runway with car headlights and the plant box with a photographer's spotlight. Pennel still couldn't see the crossbar and missed his first attempt. Then the stadium became brighter as the audience improvised torches by lighting seat cushions and rolled-up programs. They also encouraged Pennel by singing a Polish folk song. Pennel successfully cleared the world record height. As the fans continued singing, Pennel asked a Polish man who spoke English to translate the phrase that they kept repeating. It was "May he live a thousand years." "These people," Pennel later told John Ortega of the *Los Angeles Times*, "who were beautiful people who loved life and wanted to go crazy, but couldn't because of

the restrictions in Poland at the time, were all for me. It was like I had made their day. When he told me what they were singing, I just started crying. No amount of money or notoriety was worth that [experience]."

1968 Mexico City C: 23, N: 15, D: 10.16. WR: 5.41, 17-9 (Robert Seagren)

| | | | FT.- | |
		M	IN.	
1. Robert Seagren	USA	5.40	17-8½	OR
2. Claus Schiprowski	GER	5.40	17-8½	OR
3. Wolfgang Nordwig	GDR	5.40	17-8½	OR
4. Christos Papanicolaou	GRE	5.35	17-6½	
5. John Pennel	USA	5.35	17-6½	
6. Hennady Blyznetsov	SOV/UKR	5.30	17-4½	
7. Herve D'Encausse	FRA	5.25	17-2¾	
8. Heinfried Engel	GER	5.20	17-0¾	

Bob Seagren had set a world record of 17 feet 9 inches at the U.S. Olympic trials five weeks before the Olympics, but no one expected him to have an easy time of it in Mexico City, as the field was thick with great vaulters. Ignacio Sola of Spain cleared 17 feet 0¾ inch and only placed ninth. Herve D'Encausse cleared 17 feet 2¾ inches. This put him in first place, so he elected to pass the next height of 17 feet 4½ inches. He then watched in horror as the remaining six vaulters all made the height, dropping D'Encausse to seventh, which is where he finished.

At 17 feet 6½ inches, Seagren passed. This was thought to be a dangerous but shrewd gamble, comparable to Fred Hansen's pass four years earlier. Actually it was an error due to Seagren's unfamiliarity with the metric system. "If I'd known the metric system better," he later revealed, "I wouldn't have passed that high—5.35 meters doesn't sound as high as 17 feet 6½ inches." Ironically, Seagren's mistake may have won him the gold medal. At any rate, it was now Seagren's turn to sit on the sidelines and watch as the remaining four competitors all cleared the bar, dropping Seagren from first to fifth.

Next the bar was raised to 17 feet 8½ inches, only one half-inch below Seagren's new world record. Papanicolaou, Nordwig, Seagren, Pennel, and Schiprowski all missed their first attempts. If they continued to miss, the victory would go to Nordwig, since he had only missed once at lower heights. The second time around, Papanicolaou and Nordwig missed again, but Seagren cleared, to move into the lead again. Then John Pennel made a successful clearance, but his pole passed under the bar. The I.A.A.F. had just voted a new rule making such an occurrence legal, but they had also decreed that the rule wouldn't take effect until the following May. Too late for Pennel, who lost out on at least a bronze medal. Schiprowski, whose pre-Olympic best was only 17 feet, then cleared 17 feet 8½ inches, bettering his previous record for the fifth time in one day. Papanicolaou, who would later become the first person to vault 18 feet, and Pennel failed one last time, but Nordwig made it.

The bar then went up to 17 feet 10½ inches, but before Nordwig, Seagren, and Schiprowski could start vaulting, the competition was delayed while the victory ceremony for the 200 meters took place. This turned out to be a sensational event, as Tommie Smith and John Carlos staged their now famous Black Power protest, which was greeted by booing and whistling. This may have disturbed the concentration of the vaulters, but it didn't prevent each of them from making superb efforts at the world record height. None of them succeeded, however, so the medals were decided on the basis of fewer misses. Personal records had been set by five of the top six vaulters and eight of the top 11.

1972 Munich C: 21, N: 12, D: 9.2. WR: 5.63, 18-5¾ (Robert Seagren)

| | | | FT.- | |
		M	IN.	
1. Wolfgang Nordwig	GDR	5.50	18-0½	OR
2. Robert Seagren	USA	5.40	17-8½	
3. Jan Johnson	USA	5.35	17-6½	
4. Reinhard Kuretzky	GER	5.30	17-4½	
5. Bruce Simpson	CAN	5.20	17-0¾	
6. Volker Ohl	GER	5.20	17-0¾	
7. Hans Lagerqvist	SWE	5.20	17-0¾	
8. Francois Tracanelli	FRA	5.10	16-8¾	

The U.S. monopoly of the pole vault was finally broken in 1972, but only after a series of disruptive and disturbing events. On July 25, the Technical Committee of the International Amateur Athletic Federation announced that it was banning the new model of Cata-Poles, which was being used by most of the leading vaulters, including Olympic favorites Bob Seagren, Kjell Isaksson of Sweden, and Steve Smith of the United States. The original complaint, lodged by East Germany, was that the poles contained carbon fiber. Manufacturers of the poles pointed out that they didn't contain carbon fiber at all, while the vaulters referred to I.A.A.F. rules, which said that poles could be made of any material, anyway. The I.A.A.F. refused to withdraw the ban on the grounds that the new Cata-Poles "had not been available through normal supply channels" for at least 12 months prior to the Olympics. Once again it was pointed out that the I.A.A.F. rule book made no mention of such a requirement.

On August 27, four days before the competition was to begin, the I.A.A.F. reversed itself and lifted the ban. Relieved vaulters returned to practicing with their usual poles. Then, on August 30, the ban was reimposed. The night before the qualifying round, I.A.A.F. officials went to the athletes' rooms, confiscated all their poles, and took them off for inspection. Those vaulters who were found to be in possession of the now illegal poles were handed new ones, or rather, new old ones.

The qualifying round turned out to be a pretty sad affair. Only ten men were able to clear the qualifying height of 16 feet 8¾ inches, so four more who had only cleared 16 feet 4¾ inches were added for the final.

The vaulter who had benefited most by the ban of the new model Cata-Pole was Wolfgang Nordwig of East Germany, who had not adapted well to the new Cata-Pole and still used an old model. Nordwig, who kept out the noise of the stadium by stuffing his ears, missed once at 17 feet 4½ inches before clearing, which put him behind Seagren, who reached 17 feet 8½ inches without a miss. Nordwig made that height with his second attempt, while Seagren needed a third. This reversed their positions. At 17 feet 10½ inches, Nordwig went over the first time, but Seagren missed all three of his attempts. After his final miss, Seagren approached Adriaan Paulen, the I.A.A.F. official who had taken responsibility for the Cata-Pole ban, and thrust his pole into Paulen's lap. Seagren stated that Paulen had given him the unwanted pole and now he was returning it. Nordwig, a 29-year-old precision engineer, had the bar raised once more, and cleared 18 feet for the first time in his life.

1976 Montreal C: 27, N: 13, D: 7.26. WR: 5.70, 18-8¼ (David Roberts)

| | | | FT.- | |
		M	IN.	
1. Tadeusz Ślusarski	POL	5.50	18-0½	EOR
2. Antti Kalliomäki	FIN	5.50	18-0½	EOR
3. David Roberts	USA	5.50	18-0½	EOR
4. Patrick Abada	FRA	5.45	17-10½	
5. Wojciech Buciarski	POL	5.45	17-10½	
6. Earl Bell	USA	5.45	17-10½	
7. Jean-Michel Bellot	FRA	5.45	17-10½	
8. Itsuo Takanezawa	JPN	5.40	17-8½	

Pre-Olympic prognostications had the battle for the gold medal among Earl Bell, who had set a world record of 18 feet 7¼ inches on May 29, Dave Roberts, who had broken Bell's record on June 22, and Wladyslaw Kozakiewicz, known for his strong performances in important meets. Surprisingly, Kozakiewicz, hampered by injury, was unable to clear 17 feet 10½ inches. Since he had passed the previous three heights, he ended up in 11th place. Roberts, too, was playing a passing game. He didn't even start jumping until 17 feet 6¾ inches. He missed his first attempt, a miss that would later prove crucial, but cleared the second time. Then he passed the next two heights before sailing over 18 feet ½ inch with his first try.

When the bar was raised to 18 feet 2½ inches, there were still six vaulters left in the competition. Roberts, following a strategy he had prepared a month earlier, passed. His reasoning was that the contest would go on for quite some time and that fewer misses and fewer attempts might become crucial. He was absolutely right about that. But then two things happened that were unexpected. All five of the other remaining vaulters missed every one of their attempts at 18 feet 2½ inches, leaving

Roberts alone with the bar at 18 feet 4½ inches, and facing the other unexpected element—a strong and unpredictable headwind. He missed all three attempts and ended up in third place.

The silver medal went to surprising Antti Kalliomäki and the gold to Kozakiewicz's Polish teammate Tadeusz Ślusarski. Ślusarski had the same number of

Wladyslaw Kozakiewicz of Poland, winner of the 1980 Moscow pole vault, expresses his opinion of the Soviet crowd.

misses as Kalliomäki, but had made fewer attempts. As it turned out, if Dave Roberts hadn't missed his initial attempt at 17 feet 6¾ inches, he would have finished in first place.

1980 Moscow C: 19, N: 10, D: 7.30. WR: 5.77, 18-11 (Philippe Houvion)

			M	FT.-IN.	
1.	Wladyslaw Kozakiewicz	POL	5.78	18-11½	WR
2.	Tadeusz Ślusarski	POL	5.65	18-6½	
2.	Konstantin Volkov	SOV/RUS	5.65	18-6½	
4.	Philippe Houvion	FRA	5.65	18-6½	
5.	Jean-Michel Bellot	FRA	5.60	18-4½	
6.	Mariusz Klimczyk	POL	5.55	18-2½	
7.	Thierry Vigneron	FRA	5.45	17-10½	
8.	Sergei Kulibaba	SOV/KAZ	5.45	17-10½	

The year 1980 was a banner one for pole vaulting. For the first time ever, three different men set world records in the same season. Wladyslaw Kozakiewicz began the onslaught on May 11 when his jump of 18 feet 9¼ inches broke Dave Roberts' 1976 record. Three weeks later, on June 1, Thierry Vigneron vaulted 18 feet 10¼ inches. On June 29, he repeated this feat. On July 17, less than two weeks before the Olympic competition, Philippe Houvion set a new record of 18 feet 11 inches. The stage was set for a classic showdown, particularly with the addition of defending champion Tadeusz Ślusarski and local favorite Konstantin Volkov.

Unfortunately, the competition was marred by the incredibly boorish behavior of many of the Soviet fans, who whistled and jeered at the foreign vaulters, particularly the Poles. The 3000 Poles in the audience responded in kind whenever Volkov vaulted. Through it all, Wladyslaw Kozakiewicz seemed unperturbed. Indeed, he seemed to gain strength from the hostility of the Russians. He won the gold medal without a miss and punctuated his winning leap with an obscene gesture to the crowd. Then he had the bar raised, and set a world record on his second attempt, the first pole vault world record to be set in the Olympics since Frank Foss' in 1920. Afterward, Kozakiewicz ran into the stands and shook hands with his compatriots, while the Poles, surrounded by Soviet soldiers, sang "Poland Is Not Beaten. . . ." Subsequently, Kozakiewicz defected to West Germany.

1984 Los Angeles C: 19, N: 13, D: 8.8. WR: 5.90, 19-4¼ (Serhei Bubka)

			M	FT.-IN.	
1.	Pierre Quinon	FRA	5.75	18-10¼	
2.	Mike Tully	USA	5.65	18-6½	
3.	Earl Bell	USA	5.60	18-4½	
3.	Thierry Vigneron	FRA	5.60	18-4½	
5.	Kimmo Pallonen	FIN	5.45	17-10½	
6.	Doug Lytle	USA	5.40	17-8½	
7.	Felix Böhni	SWI	5.30	17-4½	
8.	Mauro Barella	ITA	5.30	17-4½	

The pre-boycott favorite, Ukrainian Serhei Bubka, set a world record of 19 feet 4¼ inches two weeks before the Olympics began. Nine days after the Olympic final Bubka was beaten at the Friendship Games by Soviet teammate Konstantin Volkov, but two weeks after that he set another world record of 19 feet 5¾ inches.

In the absence of the Soviets, the Los Angeles competition became a French-American confrontation with both teams fielding two 19-foot vaulters. By the time the bar reached 18 feet 4½ inches, only the four favorites remained, although none of them had taken more than two vaults. At this point, Bell and Vigneron cleared on their first attempts, while Quinon and Tully passed. The bar was raised two inches, and, while Bell and Vigneron watched, Quinon and Tully each missed. Quinon then elected to pass again, while Tully, after one more miss, cleared 18 feet 6½ inches on his final attempt to take the lead. At the next height, 18 feet 8¾ inches, Tully passed, Quinon cleared immediately, and Bell and Vigneron missed all three attempts, finishing in a tie for third.

With Quinon vaulting first, the bar was raised to 18 feet 10¼ inches. The young Frenchman with a reputation for inconsistency cleared on his first try. Although a clearance at this height would have put Tully in a tie for first, he elected to pass. Neither man was successful at 19 feet ¼ inch, and the competition was over.

1988 Seoul C: 21, N: 13, D: 9.28. WR: 6.06, 19-10½ (Serhei Bubka)

			FT.-	
		M	IN.	
1. Serhei Bubka	SOV/UKR	5.90	19-4¼	OR
2. Rodion Gataullin	SOV/UZB	5.85	19-2¼	
3. Grigory Yegorov	SOV/KAZ	5.80	19-0¼	
4. Earl Bell	USA	5.70	18-8¼	
5. Philippe Collet	FRA	5.70	18-8¼	
5. Thierry Vigneron	FRA	5.70	18-8¼	
7. István Bagyula	HUN	5.60	18-4½	
8. Philippe D'Encausse	FRA	5.60	18-4½	

Serhei Bubka was the sort of child who makes parents grow old fast. When he was three years old he tried to run away from home. When he was four he almost drowned in a barrel of water used for salting cabbage. He also fell out of a tree and was saved from serious injury only when his suspenders caught on a branch. When he finally started flying through the air at the end of a pole, it was almost a relief. Bubka burst on the international scene when, as a 19-year-old, he won an upset victory at the 1983 world championships. He completely dominated the event for the next five years, setting nine outdoor world records and winning another world championship in 1987 with only two vaults.

A minor revolt developed during the Olympic qualifying round. The leading vaulters objected to the fact that the bar used by the contestants in Group A was being raised at a rate different from the bar in Group B. The vaulters refused to continue the competition and the offi-

cials were forced to advance 15 of the 21 competitors into the final.

Bubka and his main rival, medical student Rodion Gataullin, did not begin vaulting in the final until the bar reached 18 feet 8¼ inches. Gataullin cleared on his first attempt, but Bubka needed two tries, and even then he grazed the bar on the way down. Yegorov cleared 19 feet ¼ inch, while Bubka and Gataullin passed. Then Gataullin cleared 19 feet 2¼ inches on his third attempt to take the lead, dropping Yegorov to second and Bubka to fourth behind Bell, who had already missed three times at 18 feet 10¼ inches. Yegorov went out at 19 feet 4¼ inches. Meanwhile Bubka missed twice at the same height. Suddenly, one of the surest favorites of the 1988 Games was one miss away from finishing out of the medals. Desperately nervous, Bubka sprinted down the runway, hurled himself into the air and cleared the bar by a huge margin—perhaps 7 or 8 inches. Gataullin made three attempts at 19 feet 6¼ inches, but was never close.

1992 Barcelona C: 34, N: 25, D: 8.7. WR: 6.11, 20-0½ (Serhei Bubka)

			FT.-	
		M	IN.	
1. Maksim Tarasov	RUS	5.80	19-0¼	
2. Igor Trandenkov	RUS	5.80	19-0¼	
3. Javier García Chico	SPA	5.75	18-10¼	
4. Kory Tarpenning	USA	5.75	18-10¼	
5. David Volz	USA	5.65	18-6½	
6. Asko Peltoniemi	FIN	5.60	18-4½	
7. Philippe Collet	FRA	5.55	18-2½	
8. Yevgeny Krasnov	ISR	5.40	17-8½	

Once again, Serhei Bubka was a big, big favorite. Since May 26, 1984, he had set 30 world records, 16 indoors and 14 outdoors, the latest on June 13, just eight weeks before the Olympic final. Among his many feats: first person to clear 6 meters (Paris; July 13, 1988), first person to clear 20 feet indoors (San Sebastian; March 15, 1991), and first person to clear 20 feet outdoors (Malmö, August 5, 1991). Along the way he had also won all three world championships, in 1983, 1987, and 1991.

In Barcelona, as in Seoul four years earlier, Bubka did not start vaulting until 18 feet 8¼ inches. With time running out on the clock, he went under the bar on his first attempt. On his second try he cleared easily, but his momentum did not take him far enough and he dislodged the crossbar on his way down. Now he was down to one last vault. Unsettled, he passed to gain more time. The situation was critical, but not unprecedented. In both the 1988 Olympics and the 1991 world championships he had been one miss away from finishing out of the medals, but pulled it out and won. The bar was raised to 18 feet 10¼ inches. Bubka decided that the windy conditions he had faced during his first two attempts required a softer pole. He switched poles—and while he was on the runway the wind died. Bubka's final try was an awkward one: he hit the bar with his shins on the way up.

The spectators, delirious because Spaniard Javier García was still in the running, unkindly booed and whistled at Bubka. His fellow vaulters—there were six still left in the competition—were stunned by the unexpected turn of events. It was 21-year-old Maksim Tarasov of Yaroslavl who came out on top, clearing 19 feet ¼ inch on his first try, while teammate Igor Trandenkov needed three attempts. In fact, Tarasov won the gold medal even though he made a grand total of only two clearances.

Trandenkov explained his mood this way: "I've got one weeping eye and one smiling one. My very good friend and teacher Serhei Bubka didn't achieve what he wanted, but his pupil took the silver."

So what did go wrong for Bubka? The swirling winds were definitely disruptive, but they affected everyone, and Bubka himself had handled worse conditions before. On his way out of the stadium Bubka conceded that maybe he had just been too nervous. Later he presented a more unusual theory, that his biorhythms were "unbelievably bad, the sort of situation that might occur once in a year." Other observers suggested a more prosaic explanation. As the star of the pole vault, Bubka was used to having meet organizers, hungry for a world record, allow him more than the usual two minutes to prepare for a vault. Before the final, U.S. vaulter Tim Bright approached the officials in charge of the competition and pointedly asked them not to show favoritism to Bubka. Forced to play by the same rules as everyone else, Bubka's first reaction had been, "To me it looked like the clock was running faster than usual."

Whatever the true cause of Bubka's Barcelona failure, it proved to be a mere glitch in his continued domination of the event. Twenty-three days after the Olympic final he set another world record and 13 days after that, yet another. In 1993 and 1995 he defended his world championship, becoming the only person to win the World Championship in Athletics every time it has been held.

LONG JUMP

The long jump runway must be at least 40 meters (131 feet 3 inches) long and, preferably, at least 45 meters (147 feet 8 inches) long. Each contestant may place one or two markers on the runway to assist with the timing of his or her run-up and takeoff. A valid jump must be made from behind the far edge of the takeoff board, which is eight inches (20 centimeters) wide and level to the ground. A plasticine indicator board abuts the takeoff board to help determine fouls. Somersaults are not allowed. There is a time limit of 1½ minutes per jump. Jumps are measured from the nearest impression made in the sand by any part of the jumper's body or limbs. Current competitions begin with a qualifying round, the results of which are not carried over to the final. In the final, each contestant is allowed three jumps. Then the first eight are allowed three more jumps. The long

jump has been dominated by U.S. athletes, who have won 20 of 23 times. The only U.S. losses have been by 2¼ inches, 1½ inches, and one boycott.

1896 Athens C: 9, N: 5, D: 4.7. WR: 7.21, 23-8 (J. J. Mooney)

			FT.-	
		M	IN.	
1. Ellery Clark	USA	6.35	20-10	
2. Robert Garrett	USA	6.00	19-8¼	
3. James Connolly	USA	5.84	19-2	
4. Alexandros Chalkokondilis	GRE	5.74	18-10	

Each man was allowed three jumps. Clark fouled the first two times. "It was little short of agony," he later wrote. "I shall never forget my feelings as I stood at the end of the path for my third—and last—try. Five thousand miles, I reflected, I had come; and was it to end in this? Three fouls, and then five thousand miles back again, with that for my memory of the games." Fortunately, his last jump was not only valid, but good enough to win.

1900 Paris C: 12, N: 6, D: 7.15. WR: 7.50, 24-7¼ (Meyer Prinstein)

			FT.-	
		M	IN.	
1. Alvin Kraenzlein	USA	7.18	23-6¾	OR
2. Meyer Prinstein	USA	7.17	23-6¼	
3. Patrick Leahy	GBR/IRL	6.95	22-9¾	
4. William Remington	USA	6.82	22-4½	
5. Albert Delannoy	FRA	6.75	22-1¾	
6. John McLean	USA	6.65	21-10	
7. Thaddeus McClain	USA	6.43	21-1¼	
8. Waldemar Steffen	GER	6.30	20-8	

Prinstein achieved his 23-foot 6¼-inch jump in the qualifying round, which, according to the rules of the time, counted in the final placings. The final was held on the next day, which was a Sunday. The official in charge of the Syracuse team prohibited Prinstein from competing on a Sunday even though Prinstein was Jewish. Kraenzlein did take part in the final and bettered Prinstein's mark by one centimeter. Peter O'Connor of Ireland was entered but did not compete. The following month he broke Prinstein's world record with a leap of 24 feet 7¾ inches. On August 5, 1901, he jumped 24 feet 11¾ inches to set a record that would last 20 years. In fact, O'Connor's jump remained an Irish national record until Carlos O'Connell broke it on June 2, 1990!

1904 St. Louis C: 10, N: 3, D: 9.1. WR: 7.61, 24-11¾ (Peter O'Connor)

			FT.-	
		M	IN.	
1. Meyer Prinstein	USA	7.34	24-1	OR
2. Daniel Frank	USA	6.89	22-7¼	
3. Robert Stangland	USA	6.88	22-7	
4. Fred Englehardt	USA	6.63	21-9	
5. George Van Cleaf	USA	—	—	
6. John Hagerman	USA	—	—	

Prinstein earned his well-deserved Olympic long jump championship after a four-year wait.

1906 Athens C: 27, N: 10, D: 4.27. WR: 7.61, 24-11¾ (Peter O'Connor)

			FT.-IN.	
		M	IN.	
1.	Meyer Prinstein	USA	7.20	23-7½
2.	Peter O'Connor	GBR/IRL	7.02	23-0½
3.	Hugo Friend	USA	6.96	22-10
4.	Hjalmar Mellander	SWE	6.58	21-7¼
5.	Sidney Abrahams	GBR	6.21	20-4½
6.	Thomas Cronan	USA	6.18	20-3½
7.	Gunnar Rönström	SWE	6.15	20-2¼
8.	István Somodi	HUN	6.05	19-10

Including the Intercalated Games of 1906, Meyer Prinstein won four gold medals and one silver in the long jump and triple jump.

1908 London C: 30, N: 9, D: 7.22. WR: 7.61, 24-11¾ (Peter O'Connor)

			FT.-IN.		
		M	IN.	
1.	Francis "Frank" Irons	USA	7.48	24-6½	OR
2.	Daniel Kelly	USA	7.09	23-3¼	
3.	Calvin Bricker	CAN	7.08	23-3	
4.	Edward Cooke	USA	6.97	22-10½	
5.	John Brennan	USA	6.86	22-6¼	
6.	Frank Mount Pleasant	USA	6.82	22-4½	
7.	Albert Weinstein	GER	6.77	22-2¾	
8.	Timothy Ahearne	GBR/IRL	6.72	22-0¾	

The victory of 5 foot 5½ inch Frank Irons came as quite a surprise since his pre-Olympic best was only 22 feet 7½ inches. Many British sports enthusiasts were disgusted by the exuberant displays of the Americans whenever a U.S. athlete won an event. One London paper described the American response to Irons' victory: "They were entertained then from the American stand by the singing of 'There'll be a hot time in the old town tonight,' by the fluttering of United States flags, and by the blowing of a new squeaking instrument of torture such as is employed at country fairs [probably a kazoo]. The Americans made themselves a nuisance and behaved in a manner which is happily quite foreign to the athletic grounds of England."

1912 Stockholm C: 32, N: 12, D: 7.13. WR: 7.61, 24-11¾ (Peter O'Connor)

			FT.-IN.		
		M	IN.	
1.	Albert Gutterson	USA	7.60	24-11¼	OR
2.	Calvin Bricker	CAN	7.21	23-8	
3.	Georg Åberg	SWE	7.18	23-6¾	
4.	Harry Worthington	USA	7.03	23-0¾	
5.	Eugene Leroy Mercer	USA	6.97	22-10½	
6.	Fred Allen	USA	6.94	22-9¼	
7.	James Thorpe	USA	6.89	22-7¼	
8.	Robert Pasemann	GER	6.82	22-4½	

Gutterson, of Andover, Vermont, settled the competition with his first jump, which was the best in the world since Peter O'Connor's record of 1901.

1920 Antwerp C: 29, N: 11, D: 8.18. WR: 7.61, 24-11¾ (Peter O'Connor)

			FT.-IN.	
		M	IN.	
1.	William Petersson (Björneman)	SWE	7.15	23-5½
2.	Carl Johnson	USA	7.095	23-3¼
3.	Erik Abrahamsson	SWE	7.08	23-2¾
4.	Robert "Dink" Templeton	USA	6.95	22-9¾
5.	Erling Aastad	NOR	6.885	22-7
6.	Rolf Franksson	SWE	6.73	22-1
7.	Solomon Butler	USA	6.60	21-8
8.	Einar Raeder	NOR	6.585	21-7¼

William Petersson, who later changed his last name to Björneman, was preparing to take his first jump when he noticed a silver coin lying on the runway. He picked it up and discovered that it was an American quarter. He put it in his left shoe for good luck and went on to win the gold medal. The favorite, Sol Butler, pulled a tendon on his first jump and had to withdraw. Fourth-place finisher Dink Templeton later became a famous track coach at Stanford University.

1924 Paris C: 34, N: 21, D: 7.8. WR: 7.69, 25-3 (Edward Gourdin)

			FT.-IN.	
		M	IN.	
1.	William DeHart Hubbard	USA	7.44	24-5
2.	Edward Gourdin	USA	7.27	23-10¼
3.	Sverre Hansen	NOR	7.26	23-10
4.	Vilho Tuulos	FIN	7.07	23-2½
5.	Louis Wilhelme	FRA	6.99	22-11¼
6.	C. Christopher Macintosh	GBR	6.92	22-8½
7.	Virgilio Tommasi	ITA	6.89	22-7¼
8.	Jacob Boot	HOL	6.86	22-6¼

A student at the University of Michigan, DeHart Hubbard was the first black athlete to win an individual Olympic gold medal. His performance, however, was overshadowed by that of Robert LeGendre the day before. LeGendre, who had failed to make the U.S. long jump team, set a world record of 25 feet 5¾ inches while competing in the pentathlon. In 1958, silver medalist Edward Gourdin became the first African-American member of the Massachusetts Supreme Court.

1928 Amsterdam C: 41, N: 23, D: 7.31. WR: 7.90, 25-11 (Edward Hamm)

			FT.-IN.		
		M	IN.	
1.	Edward Hamm	USA	7.73	25-4½	OR
2.	Silvio Cator	HAI	7.58	24-10½	
3.	Alfred Bates	USA	7.40	24-3½	
4.	Willi Meier	GER	7.39	24-3	
5.	Erich Köchermann	GER	7.35	24-1½	
6.	Hannes de Boer	HOL	7.32	24-0¼	
7.	Edward Gordon	USA	7.32	24-0¼	
8.	Erik Svensson	SWE	7.29	23-11	

William DeHart Hubbard became the first black athlete to win an Olympic gold medal in an individual event when he won the 1924 long jump in Paris.

Six weeks after the Olympic competition, silver medalist Silvio Cator became the first man to break the 26-foot barrier with a jump of 26 feet ¼ inch. Cator was also the captain of the Haitian soccer team. As it turned out, five different past and future gold medal winners took part in the 1928 long jump. In addition to Hamm, 1924 winner DeHart Hubbard finished 11th, 1932 winner Ed Gordon placed seventh, 1928 triple jump winner Mikio Oda tied with Hubbard for 11th, and 1932 triple jump winner Chuhei Nambu finished ninth.

1932 Los Angeles C: 12, N: 9, D: 8.2. WR: 7.98, 26-2¼ (Chuhei Nambu)

			M	FT.-IN.
1.	Edward Gordon	USA	7.64	25-0¾
2.	Charles Lambert Redd	USA	7.60	24-11¼
3.	Chuhei Nambu	JPN	7.45	24-5½
4.	Erik Svensson	SWE	7.41	24-3¾
5.	Richard Barber	USA	7.39	24-3
6.	Naoto Tajima	JPN	7.15	23-5½
7.	Hector Berra	ARG	6.66	21-10¼
8.	Clovis de Figueiredo Raposo	BRA	6.43	21-1¼

1936 Berlin C: 43, N: 27, D: 8.4. WR: 8.13, 26-8¼ (James "Jesse" Owens)

			M	FT.-IN.	
1.	James "Jesse" Owens	USA	8.06	26-5½	OR
2.	Carl Ludwig "Luz" Long	GER	7.87	25-10	
3.	Naoto Tajima	JPN	7.74	25-4¾	
4.	Wilhelm Leichum	GER	7.73	25-4½	
4.	Arturo Maffei	ITA	7.73	25-4½	
6.	Robert Clark	USA	7.67	25-2	
7.	John Brooks	USA	7.41	24-3¾	
8.	Robert Paul	FRA	7.34	24-1	

On May 25, 1935, Jesse Owens had jumped 26 feet 8¼ inches, setting a world record that would last for 25 years and 79 days. He seemed a sure bet to win the Olympic gold medal. But when he walked over to the long jump area, he was surprised to see a tall, blue-eyed, blond German taking practice jumps in the 26-foot range. Owens was fully aware of the Nazis' desire to prove their theory of "Aryan superiority" and he was also fully aware that Hitler and his followers had a particular distaste for Negroes. With this in mind, Jesse, still in his sweatsuit, took a practice run down the runway and into the pit. To his surprise, the officials in charge counted this as his first attempt of the qualifying round. Somewhat rattled, he fouled his second attempt. He was now one foul away from being eliminated from his best event.

At this point, Owens was approached by the tall, blue-eyed, blond German, who introduced himself, in English, as Luz Long.

"Glad to meet you," said Owens tentatively. "How are you?"

"I'm fine," replied Long. "The question is: How are *you?*"

"What do you mean?" asked Owens.

At the Berlin Olympics in 1936, German long-jumper Luz Long defied the Nazi ideology of racism and befriended his rival, Jesse Owens.

Owens, the son of sharecroppers, won four gold medals and returned home to a hero's welcome and a ticker-tape parade down Broadway.

"Something must be *eating* you," said Long, proud to display his knowledge of American slang. "You should be able to qualify with your eyes closed." For the next few minutes the black son of sharecroppers and the white model of Nazi manhood chatted. It turned out that Luz Long didn't believe in the theory of Aryan superiority

Jesse Owens' celebrity failed to earn him a living, and he was forced to make ends meet by racing against horses, dogs, and motorcycles. He eventually found his place as a "professional good example."

and the two joked about the fact that he looked the part anyway. Then Long made a suggestion. Since the qualifying distance was only 23 feet 5½ inches, why didn't Owens make a mark several inches before the takeoff board and jump from there to play it safe. Owens did just that. He took off one and a half feet before the board and qualified by just one centimeter.

The final was held that afternoon. Jesse Owens opened with an Olympic record of 25 feet 5½ inches and then followed with 25 feet 10 inches. In the fifth of six rounds, Luz Long brought the German crowd to life by matching Owens' jump exactly. Inspired by the challenge, Owens leaped 26 feet 3¾ inches. Then, with his final jump, he hit 26 feet 5½ inches, to clinch his second of four gold medals. The first person to congratulate Owens, in full view of Adolf Hitler, was Luz Long. "You can melt down all the medals and cups I have," Jesse Owens later wrote, "and they wouldn't be a plating on the 24-carat friendship I felt for Luz Long at that moment." Long was killed in the Battle of St. Pietro on July 14, 1943, but Owens continued to correspond with his family.

1948 London C: 21, N: 17, D: 7.31. WR: 8.13, 26-8¼ (James "Jesse" Owens)

			FT.-	
			M	IN.
1.	Willie Steele	USA	7.82	25-8
2.	Theodore Bruce	AUS	7.55	24-9¼
3.	Herbert Douglas	USA	7.54	24-9
4.	Lorenzo Wright	USA	7.45	24-5½
5.	Adegboyega Folaranmi Adedoyin	GBR/NGR	7.27	23-10¼
6.	Georges Damitio	FRA	7.07	23-2½
7.	Harold Whittle	GBR	7.03	23-0¾
8.	Felix Wurth	AUS	7.00	22-11¾

Fifth-place finisher Prince Adegboyega Folaranmi Adedoyin was a member of the royal family of the kingdom of Ijabu-Remo in Nigeria. A medical student at Queen's University in Belfast, he represented Great Britain, since Nigeria was not yet considered an independent nation.

1952 Helsinki C: 27, N: 19, D: 7.21. WR: 8.13, 26-8¼ (James "Jesse" Owens)

			FT.-	
			M	IN.
1.	Jerome Biffle	USA	7.57	24-10
2.	Meredith Gourdine	USA	7.53	24-8½
3.	Ödön Földessy	HUN	7.30	23-11½
4.	Ary Facanha de Sá	BRA	7.23	23-8¾
5.	Jorma Valtonen	FIN	7.16	23-6
6.	Leonid Grigoryev	SOV	7.14	23-5¼
7.	Karl-Erik Israelsson	SWE	7.10	23-3½
8.	Paul Faucher	FRA	7.02	23-0½

George Brown of U.C.L.A. had won 41 straight competitions before placing third at the U.S. Olympic trials. Yet he was still the heavy favorite to win in Helsinki. In the final, however, he fouled three times in a row and was eliminated. Gold medalist Jerome Biffle was an army private who came out of two years' retirement to compete. Neville Price of South Africa jumped 24 feet 1¾ inches in the qualifying round, but was unable to take part in the final because of an injury.

1956 Melbourne C: 32, N: 21, D: 11.24. WR: 8.13, 26-8¼ (James "Jesse" Owens)

			M	FT.-IN.
1.	Gregory Bell	USA	7.83	25-8¼
2.	John Bennett	USA	7.68	25-2½
3.	Jorma Valkama	FIN	7.48	24-6½
4.	Dmitri Bondarenko	SOV/UKR	7.44	24-5
5.	Karim Olowu	NGR	7.36	24-1¾
6.	Kazimierz Kropidlowski	POL	7.30	23-11½
7.	Neville Price	SAF	7.28	23-10¾
8.	Oleg Fyedoseyev	SOV/RUS	7.27	23-10¼

A short, loose runway and a strong fluctuating wind caused all entrants to perform well below their normal standards.

1960 Rome C: 49, N: 34, D: 9.2. WR: 8.21, 26-11¼ (Ralph Boston)

			M	FT.-IN.	
1.	Ralph Boston	USA	8.12	26-7¾	OR
2.	Irvin "Bo" Roberson	USA	8.11	26-7¼	
3.	Igor Ter-Ovanesyan	SOV/RUS	8.04	26-4½	
4.	Manfred Steinbach	GER	8.00	26-3	
5.	Jorma Valkama	FIN	7.69	25-2¾	
6.	Christian Collardot	FRA	7.68	25-2½	
7.	Henk Visser	HOL	7.66	25-1¾	
8.	Dmitri Bondarenko	SOV/UKR	7.58	24-10½	

On August 12, 1960, two weeks before the opening of the Rome Olympics, Ralph Boston finally broke Jesse Owens' 25-year-old world record with a leap of 26 feet 11¼ inches. He was expected to receive his stiffest challenge from Armenian Igor Ter-Ovanesyan, who had fouled out of the 1956 final and who would eventually go on to take part in five Olympics. Ter-Ovanesyan led at 25 feet 11

The three medalists in the 1960 long jump: (left to right) Bo Roberson, Ralph Boston, and Igor Ter-Ovanesyan.

inches after the first round of the final. Bo Roberson, whose pre-Olympic best had been 26 feet 0 inches, jumped 26 feet 4¼ inches in the second round to take the lead. However, the third round saw Boston's big jump of 26 feet 7¾ inches. There were no changes in position during the next two rounds, but the competition was far from over. With his last attempt, Ter-Ovanesyan leaped 26 feet 4½ inches to edge into second place. An exhausted Bo Roberson had considered passing, but now he had to give it one last try. He zoomed seven inches beyond his pre-Olympic record, but landed one centimeter short of a gold medal. This was the first meet in which four men jumped over 26 feet.

1964 Tokyo C: 32, N: 23, D: 10.18. WR: 8.34, 27-4¼ (Ralph Boston)

			M	FT.-IN.
1.	Lynn Davies	GBR	8.07	26-5¾
2.	Ralph Boston	USA	8.03	26-4¼
3.	Igor Ter-Ovanesyan	SOV/RUS	7.99	26-2¾
4.	Wariboko West	NGR	7.60	24-11¼
5.	Jean Cochard	FRA	7.44	24-5
6.	Luis Felipe Areta	SPA	7.34	24-1
7.	Mike Ahey	GHA	7.30	23-11½
8.	Andrzej Stalmach	POL	7.26	23-10

Lynn Davies, a physical education teacher from Nantymoel, Glamorganshire, in Wales, wasn't on anyone's list of potential winners in 1964. In fact, he barely made it into the final, qualifying with his last attempt. But the weather, cold, windy, and raining, was much more familiar to Davies than it was to the favorites, Ralph Boston and Igor Ter-Ovanesyan. "The Welsh gods must have been looking down on Tokyo that day," Davies later explained. "I'm convinced that had it been a warm, sunny day in Tokyo, I wouldn't have won the gold." The American and Soviet champions tried to convince the officials to reverse the running of the event, so that they would be jumping with the wind behind them instead of against them, but to no avail.

Ter-Ovanesyan took the first-round lead at 25 feet 6¼ inches. Boston moved ahead in the second round with a jump of 25 feet 9¼ inches. In the fourth round, he improved to 25 feet 10¼ inches. Entering the fifth round, Lynn Davies was in third place. "I remember thinking, this is it," he recalled. "I glanced up at the flag at the top of the stadium. Boston told me about this in New York, four months previously. 'If the flag drops,' he had said, 'it's a good indication that the wind is about to fade inside the stadium.' And as I looked up at it, it dropped dead." Davies took off down the runway immediately and hit the best jump of his career—26 feet 5¾ inches.

Ter-Ovanesyan followed with 26 feet 2¾ inches to move back into second place. The competition came down to Ralph Boston's final leap. Davies covered his face and peeked through his fingers. Boston's jump was long and Davies prepared himself for disappointment.

But the measurement showed Boston had missed by four centimeters, and Lynn Davies had become the first Welshman ever to win an Olympic gold medal in an individual event. Davies also competed in the 100 meters and the 4 × 100-meter relay.

1968 Mexico City C: 35, N: 22, D: 10.18. WR: 8.35, 27-4¾ (Ralph Boston, Igor Ter-Ovanesyan)

			FT.-		
		M	IN.	
1.	Robert Beamon	USA	8.90	29-2½	WR
2.	Klaus Beer	GDR	8.19	26-10½	
3.	Ralph Boston	USA	8.16	26-9¼	
4.	Igor Ter-Ovanesyan	SOV/RUS	8.12	26-7¾	
5.	Tõnu Lepik	SOV/EST	8.09	26-6½	
6.	Allen Crawley	AUS	8.02	26-3¾	
7.	Jacques Pani	FRA	7.97	26-1¾	
8.	Andrzej Stelmach	POL	7.94	26-0¾	

All three medalists from 1964, Lynn Davies, Ralph Boston, and Igor Ter-Ovanesyan, were back in 1968, and all three were in good enough shape to win the gold medal. However, none of them was the favorite. That distinction fell to Bob Beamon, a 6-foot 3-inch 22-year-old from South Jamaica in New York. In 1968 Beamon had won 22 of 23 meets, losing only once indoors. But Beamon was by no means a sure bet. Unlike the other leading contenders, he made no checkmarks on the side of the runway to help him with his stride, so he was unusually prone to fouling. In addition, he had been without the benefit of a regular coach since mid-April, when he had been suspended from the track team at the University of Texas at El Paso for refusing to compete against Brigham Young University, as a protest against the racial policies of the Mormon Church.

Beamon almost met disaster in the qualifying round. His first jump took off a full foot after the board and his second jump was also a foul. He was now one foul away from elimination. Remembering the Jesse Owens–Luz Long incident of 1936, Ralph Boston, who had been informally coaching Beamon, walked up to the nervous favorite and had a few words with him. He told Beamon to relax and to take off from a mark a few inches before the takeoff board. Like Jesse Owens 32 years earlier, Bob Beamon made a mark one foot up the runway, then raced down the path and qualified easily.

According to Dick Schaap's biography, *The Perfect Jump,* that night, the night before the most important final of his career, Bob Beamon did something he had never done before: he engaged in sexual intercourse the night before a major competition. At the moment of orgasm, he was suddenly overcome with the horrible feeling that he had blown it, that his chances for a gold medal and for the world record he had boldly predicted he would achieve had been thrown away right there in bed.

The following day was gloomy, with occasional rain, the kind of day that supposedly favored Lynn Davies.

There were 17 finalists ready to begin the competition at 3:40 p.m. Beamon's jumping order was fourth, Davies' 12th, Ter-Ovanesyan's 13th, and Ralph Boston's 17th. The first three jumpers fouled. Then it was Bob Beamon's turn. Boston called out to him, "Come on, make it a good one." For 20 seconds Beamon stood at the beginning of the runway, gathering his strength and telling himself, "Don't foul, don't foul." Then he tore down the runway (he was a 9.5 sprinter at 100 yards), hit the takeoff board perfectly, and sailed through the air at what seemed to be an uncommon elevation, estimated by observers to be between five and a half and six feet. He hit the sand so powerfully that he bounced back up and landed outside the pit.

"That's over 28 feet," Ralph Boston said to Lynn Davies. "With his first jump?" replied Davies. "No, it can't be." They trotted over to the pit to get a better look. Officials slid the marker of the sophisticated optical measuring device down its rail to the point where Beamon's feet had hit the sand. But before it got there, the marker fell off the end of the rail. An official turned to Beamon and murmured, "Fantastic. Fantastic." An old-fashioned steel tape was called for. A couple measurements were taken and then the result was flashed on

Bob Beamon stunned the sports world when he bettered the world long jump record by 21¾ inches with a leap of 29 feet 2½ inches, in 1968.

When he realized what he had accomplished, Beamon suffered a cataplectic seizure and fell to the ground in shock.

the electronic scoreboard: 8.90 meters. Beamon knew he had set a record, but being unfamiliar with the metric system, he didn't really understand how far he had jumped. He ran up to Ralph Boston, the man who had helped him so much, and embraced him. Boston then told Beamon, "Bob, you jumped 29 feet."

Beamon was stunned. "What do I do now?" he asked. "Ralph, I know you're gonna kick my ass."

"No, no," said Boston. "It's over for me. I can't jump that far."

"What about the Great Britain dude?" asked Beamon. "And what about the Russian?"

"The Russian," Igor Ter-Ovanesyan, had turned to Lynn Davies and said, "Compared to this jump, we are as children." Davies told Boston, "I can't go on. What is the point? We'll all look silly." Then he turned to Beamon and said, "You have destroyed this event."

By this time, Beamon's jump had been officially converted to 29 feet 2½ inches. Suddenly, Beamon realized what he had done. His legs gave in and he sank to the ground, experiencing what doctors would later describe as a "cataplectic seizure," an "atonic state of the somatic muscles which develops suddenly on the heels of emotional excitement." He was overcome with nausea and tears, and was helped to his feet by Boston and U.S.

teammate Charlie Mays, who supported him until he recovered from his dizziness.

The contest continued, but just as Ter-Ovanesyan began his first jump, the skies began pouring rain. Beamon took one more jump of 26 feet 4½ inches but then passed his last four opportunities. Boston, Ter-Ovanesyan, and Davies (who finished ninth), who had waited four years for another chance at Olympic victory, were dazed and unable to perform up to par. Klaus Beer of East Germany, on the other hand, had had no such grand expectations, and was able to take the silver medal by bettering his personal best by four inches. Lepik and Crawley also had their best jumps ever.

Beamon's 29-foot 2½-inch jump was hailed as the greatest athletic achievement of all time, although detractors criticized the suspicious Mexican wind readings which measured the exact legal maximum of 2.0 miles per second. In the 33 years since Jesse Owens' 1935 jump of 26 feet 8¼ inches, the world record had progressed eight and a half inches. In a matter of seconds, Beamon had added another 21¾ inches. Ironically—since Beamon completely bypassed the 28-foot barrier—the first 28-foot jump didn't take place until the 1980 Olympics. Beamon himself never again jumped farther than 26 feet 11½ inches.

1972 Munich C: 36, N: 25, D: 9.9. WR: 8.90, 29-2½ (Robert Beamon)

			FT.-	
			M	IN.
1. Randy Williams	USA		8.24	27-0½
2. Hans Baumgartner	GER		8.18	26-10
3. Clarence "Arnie" Robinson	USA		8.03	26-4¼
4. Joshua Owusu	GHA		8.01	26-3½
5. Preston Carrington	USA		7.99	26-2¾
6. Max Klauss	GDR		7.96	26-1½
7. Alan Lerwill	GBR		7.91	25-11½
8. Leonid Barkovsky	SOV/UKR		7.75	25-5¼

Nineteen-year-old Randy Williams, the youngest entrant, led the qualifying round with a jump of 27 feet 4¼ inches—over a foot farther than his pre-Olympic, non-wind-aided best. He was followed by Preston Carrington at 26 feet 11¾ inches, 7¾ inches better than *his* pre-Olympic record. Neither American was able to do as well in the final. Williams, who kept a good-luck teddy bear with him at all times, injured his leg warming up before the final, and wisely decided to put all his effort into his first leap, which turned out to be good enough for the gold medal.

1976 Montreal C: 33, N: 25, D: 7.29. WR: 8.90, 29-2½ (Robert Beamon)

			FT.-	
			M	IN.
1. Clarence "Arnie" Robinson	USA		8.35	27-4¾
2. Randy Williams	USA		8.11	26-7¼
3. Frank Wartenberg	GDR		8.02	26-3¾
4. Jacques Rousseau	FRA		8.00	26-3
5. João Carlos de Olivera	BRA		8.00	26-3
6. Nenad Stekić	YUG		7.89	25-10¾
7. Valery Pidluzhny	SOV/UKR		7.88	25-10¼
8. Hans Baumgartner	GER		7.82	25-8

For the third straight time, the long jump was won with a first round leap, and for the tenth time in 12 Olympics, it was won by a black American.

1980 Moscow C: 32, N: 24, D: 7.28. WR: 8.90, 29-2½ (Robert Beamon)

			FT.-	
			M	IN.
1. Lutz Dombrowski	GDR		8.54	28-0¼
2. Frank Paschek	GDR		8.21	26-11¼
3. Valery Pidluzhny	SOV/UKR		8.18	26-10
4. László Szalma	HUN		8.13	26-8¼
5. Stanislaw Jaskulka	POL		8.13	26-8¼
6. Viktor Belsky	SOV/BLR		8.10	26-7
7. Antonio Corgos	SPA		8.09	26-6½
8. Yordan Yanev	BUL		8.02	26-3¾

Before the Moscow Olympics, the longest jump other than Bob Beamon's had been 27 feet 11½ inches, by Larry Myricks of the United States. Myricks had qualified for the 1976 final, but fractured a bone in his foot and had to withdraw. In 1980, he was kept out again, this

time by the Jimmy Carter boycott. Without him, the long jump competition was dominated by Lutz Dombrowski, who put together a tremendous series that averaged 27 feet 3¼ inches. His fifth-round jump of 28 feet ¼ inch was the first ever in the 28-foot range. Something of a rebel, Dombrowski kept running away from the schools to which he had been assigned by the East German government in order to return home to his family, his girlfriend, and his soccer team. When he broke his left leg playing soccer in 1979, he finally gave in to the East German coaches, although he continued to insist that he preferred the triple jump to the long jump. In 1991 Dombrowski admitted that for eight years he had prepared secret reports on his teammates for the state security police.

1984 Los Angeles C: 31, N: 25, D: 8.6. WR: 8.90, 29-2½ (Robert Beamon)

			FT.-	
			M	IN.
1. F. Carlton Lewis	USA		8.54	28-0¼
2. Gary Honey	AUS		8.24	27-0½
3. Giovanni Evangelisti	ITA		8.24	27-0½
4. Larry Myricks	USA		8.16	26-9¼
5. Liu Yuhuang	CHN		7.99	26-2¾
6. Joey Wells	BAH		7.97	26-1¾
7. Junichi Usui	JPN		7.87	25-10
8. Kim Jong-il	KOR		7.81	25-7½

When Carl Lewis was seven years old his parents began a track club. Carl and his five-year-old sister, Carol, used the landing area in the long jump pit to build sand castles. As they grew older, Carl and Carol used the pit for more conventional purposes. By 1981, Carl Lewis was the world's leading long-jumper. After losing an indoor meet to Larry Myricks on February 28, 1981, Lewis won 36 straight competitions leading up to the Olympics, including 16 meets in which he leaped over 28 feet. Twice he reached 28 feet 10¼ inches, both times at low-altitude. Once, in 1982, he landed about thirty feet from the take-off board, but the jump was ruled a foul after a controversial judge's decision.

At the Los Angeles Olympics, Lewis secured the gold medal with a first-round leap into the wind that once again surpassed 28 feet. He took one more jump and then, with six races behind him and five more to go, he passed the last four rounds.

Meanwhile, the battle for second place continued hot and heavy. Giovanni Evangelisti took the first-round non-Lewis lead at 26 feet 6½ inches. In the third round he was passed by Gary Honey's personal record of 26 feet 10 inches. Evangelisti led off the final round with his first-ever jump over 27 feet. But Honey, next down the runway, matched him to the centimeter and won the silver medal by virtue of a better second jump.

Unfortunately, Carl Lewis' performance was met by boos by many in the crowd who resented his refusal to challenge Bob Beamon's record by taking four more jumps. These boorish "fans" seemed unappreciative of

Lewis' exacting Olympic schedule, and unaware that he had never taken a full complement of jumps at a meet in which he also competed in the sprints. It is also worth noting that the legendary Jesse Owens, to whom Lewis was often compared, took only one jump on the day he set his 1935 world record that would last for 25 years and, during his entire career, only twice did Owens take a full set of jumps.

At the 1984 Olympics, Carl Lewis' sister, Carol, placed ninth in the women's long jump.

1988 Seoul C: 41, N: 31, D: 9.26. WR: 8.90, 29-2½ (Robert Beamon)

			M	FT.- IN.
1.	F. Carlton Lewis	USA	8.72	28-7¼
2.	Michael Powell	USA	8.49	27-10¼
3.	Larry Myricks	USA	8.27	27-1½
4.	Giovanni Evangelisti	ITA	8.08w	26-6
5.	Antonio Corgos	SPA	8.03	26-4¼
6.	László Szalma	HUN	8.00	26-3
7.	Norbert Brige	FRA	7.97	26-1¾
8.	Leonid Voloshin	SOV/RUS	7.89	25-10¾

Carl Lewis went to the Olympics with a winning streak of 55 meets over seven and a half years. His latest victory came in a dramatic seesaw battle with longtime rival Larry Myricks at the U.S. Olympic trials. Lewis won that one 28 feet 9 inches (8.76 meters) to 28 feet 8¼ inches (8.74 meters). In Seoul, however, Lewis faced a tough assignment: the long jump final began only 55 minutes after he finished competing in the preliminaries of the 200-meter dash. Drawn to jump in the first position, Lewis appealed to the officials in charge of the event and was allowed to jump twelfth and last instead. He took the first-round lead with a leap of 27 feet 7 inches, then lengthened his lead with a wind-aided second jump of 28 feet.

After the third round, a new official arrived on the scene and ordered Lewis to begin jumping first instead of last. Lewis argued that if he had to comply, he should at least be allowed a 10-minute break. The Korean official refused, but then the long jump clock malfunctioned and Lewis got his break anyway. He responded with his winning leap of 28 feet 7¼ inches. Lewis, who registered the four longest jumps of the competition, became the first repeat winner in the history of the event (not including Meyer Prinstein's victory at the 1906 Intercalated Games).

1992 Barcelona C: 50, N: 37, D: 8.6. WR: 8.95, 29-4½ (Mike Powell)

			M	FT.- IN.
1.	F. Carlton Lewis	USA	8.67	28-5½
2.	Michael Powell	USA	8.64	28-4¼
3.	Joe Greene	USA	8.34	27-4
4.	Iván Pedroso Soler	CUB	8.11	26-7¼
5.	Jaime Jefferson Guilarte	CUB	8.08	26-6¼

6.	Konstantinos Koukodimos	GRE	8.04	26-4½
7.	Dmitri Bagryanov	RUS	7.98	26-2¼
8.	Huang Geng	CHN	7.87	25-10

The greatest duel in long jump history took place in Tokyo on the evening of August 30, 1991. By that time, Bob Beamon's Mexico City world record had stood for 22 years 316 days. But there was definitely a feeling in the air that something special was going to happen, that this could be the night. Carl Lewis had won 65 straight meets over a period of the last 10 years 170 days. But the 65th win had been a close call. At the U.S. National Championships on June 15, he had defeated 27-year-old Mike Powell by only one centimeter with his final jump. In the third round at the world championships in Tokyo, Lewis jumped a wind-aided 28 feet 11¾ inches. In the fourth round he stretched beyond Beamon's world record at 29 feet 2¾ inches, but that jump too was wind-aided. Then, in the fifth round, Powell, who had lost to Lewis 15 straight times over the past eight years, uncorked the jump everyone had been waiting for, a legal 29 feet 4½ inches. Lewis was stunned that the record he had sought for so long should fall to someone else, but he did not fold. Instead he responded with a jump of 29 feet 1¼ inches, his longest legal jump ever. In the final round he hit 29 feet exactly. Lewis had put together the greatest series in history, but it was Powell who had broken Beamon's record, ending Lewis' win streak.

The Olympic final a year later was not nearly so dramatic. Lewis, who had leaped 28 feet 5¾ inches to lead the qualifying round, went 28 feet 5½ inches with his first try in the final. Powell started poorly and then improved with each of his other four legal jumps. After hitting 28 feet in the fifth round, he prayed at the top of the runway and then took his final jump. It was his best of the evening, but he fell 1¼ inches short. Carl Lewis, who had become a vegetarian between Olympics, won his third straight long jump gold medal. He then offended many in the crowd by taking his victory lap in the outside lane while a 5000-meter semifinal was in progress.

TRIPLE JUMP

This used to be known as the hop, step, and jump, which accurately describes the event. The contestants land on the same foot with which they take off, take one step onto the other foot, and then jump. Other rules are the same as those for the long jump.

1896 Athens C: 7, N: 5, D: 4.6. WR: 15.25, 50-0½ (Daniel Shanahan)

			M	FT.- IN.
1.	James Connolly	USA	13.71	44-11¾
2.	Alexandre Tuffère	FRA	12.70	41-8
3.	Ioannis Persakis	GRE	12.565	41-3
4.	Alajos Szokolyi	HUN	11.26	36-11½
5.	Karl Schumann	GER	—	—

James Connolly of Boston became the first Olympic champion in 1527 years when he won the triple jump in 1896. He later became a well-known writer.

James Brendan Connolly came from a poor Irish-American family in South Boston, Massachusetts. He was a 27-year-old, self-educated undergraduate at Harvard when he read about the revival of the Olympic Games. As the national triple jump champion, he decided to go to Athens and take part. He asked permission for a leave of absence. When his dean refused, he dropped out and went anyway. Ten American athletes and one trainer spent 16½ days on a ship to Naples, where Connolly's wallet was stolen. Then they took the train to Athens, arriving at nine p.m. on April 5. According to Connolly, at 4 a.m. the following morning, they were awakened by a brass band and discovered, to their shock, that the competition was to begin that day rather than twelve days hence as they had expected. Apparently the Americans had forgotten that the Greek calendar differed from the American one.

At 2 p.m., on April 6, the first modern Olympic Games were officially opened. Connolly was the last to jump in the triple jump competition. After his second try he turned to the Englishman raking the pit and said, "They ought to tell how far each man jumps. Then a fellow won't be breaking his back when there's no need of it." The pit raker replied, "As far as the measurements go, there's nobody within a yard of you." James Connolly had become the first Olympic champion since the boxer Barasdates of Armenia in 369 A.D. Actually, Connolly had performed two hops and a jump rather than a hop, step, and jump, which followed the rules of the competition at the time.

Connolly later became a noted journalist and war correspondent, and also authored 25 novels and 200 short stories. He was once offered an honorary degree from Harvard, but refused it. Connolly died on January 20, 1957, at the age of 87.

1900 Paris C: 13, N: 6, D: 7.16. WR: 15.25, 50-0½ (Daniel Shanahan)

			M	FT.-IN.	
1.	Meyer Prinstein	USA	14.47	47-5¾	OR
2.	James Connolly	USA	13.97	45-10	
3.	Lewis Sheldon	USA	13.64	44-9	
4.	Patrick Leahy	GBR/IRL	—	—	
5.	Albert Delannoy	FRA	—	—	
6.	Alexandre Tuffère	FRA	—	—	

Prinstein made up for his disappointment at not being allowed to take part in the previous day's long jump final.

1904 St. Louis C: 7, N: 1, D: 9.1. WR: 5.25, 50-0½ (Daniel Shanahan)

			M	FT.-IN.
1.	Meyer Prinstein	USA	14.35	47-1
2.	Fred Englehardt	USA	13.90	45-7¼
3.	Robert Stangland	USA	13.36	43-10
4.	John Fuhler	USA	12.91	42-4½
5.	George Van Cleaf	USA	—	—
6.	John Hagerman	USA	—	—
7.	Samuel Jones	USA	—	—

Prinstein won with his sixth and final jump.

1906 Athens C: 21, N: 8, D: 4.30. WR: 15.25, 50-0½ (Daniel Shanahan)

			M	FT.-IN.
1.	Peter O'Connor	GBR/IRL	14.075	46-2¼
2.	Cornelius Leahy	GBR/IRL	13.98	45-10½
3.	Thomas Cronan	USA	13.70	44-11½
4.	Oscar Guttormsen	NOR	13.34	43-9¼
5.	Dimitrios Müller	GRE	13.125	43-0¾
6.	Francis Connolly	USA	12.75	41-10
7.	Vasilios Stournares	GRE	12.725	41-9
8.	Carl Pedersen	NOR	12.68	41-7¼

After his victory, O'Connor, who won with his final attempt, climbed the flagpole, pulled down the Union Jack of Great Britain, and replaced it with the green flag of Ireland.

1908 London C: 19, N: 7, D: 7.25. WR: 15.25, 50-0½ (Daniel Shanahan)

			FT.-	
		M	IN.	
1. Timothy Ahearne	GBR/IRL	14.92	48-11¼	OR
2. J. Garfield MacDonald	CAN	14.76	48-5¼	
3. Edvard Larsen	NOR	14.39	47-2¾	
4. Calvin Bricker	CAN	14.10	46-3	
5. Platt Adams	USA	14.07	46-2	
6. Frank Mount Pleasant	USA	13.97	45-10	
7. K. Fryksdal	SWE	13.65	44-9¼	
8. John Brennan	USA	13.59	44-7	

Ahearne won with his final jump.

1912 Stockholm C: 22, N: 9, D: 7.15. WR: 15.52, 50-11 (Daniel Ahearn)

			FT.-
		M	IN.
1. Gustaf Lindblom	SWE	14.76	48-5¼
2. Georg Åberg	SWE	14.51	47-7¼
3. Erik Almlöf	SWE	14.17	46-6
4. Erling Vinne	NOR	14.14	46-4¾
5. Platt Adams	USA	14.09	46-2¾
6. Edvard Larsen	NOR	14.06	46-1½
7. Hjalmar Olsson	SWE	14.01	45-11¾
8. Nils Fiksdal	NOR	13.96	45-9¾

1920 Antwerp C: 21, N: 8, D: 8.21. WR: 15.52, 50-11 (Daniel Ahearn)

			FT.-
		M	IN.
1. Vilho Tuulos	FIN	14.50	47-7
2. Folke Jansson	SWE	14.48	47-6
3. Erik Almlöf	SWE	14.27	46-9¾
4. Ivar Sahlin	SWE	14.17	46-6
5. Sherman Landers	USA	14.17	46-6
6. Daniel Ahearn	USA	14.08	46-2¼
7. Ossian Nylund	FIN	13.74	45-0½
8. Benjamin Howard Baker	GBR	13.67	44-10

1924 Paris C: 20, N: 12, D: 7.12. WR: 15.52, 50-11 (Daniel Ahearn)

			FT.-	
		M	IN.	
1. Anthony "Nick" Winter	AUS	15.525	50-11¼	WR
2. Luis Brunetto	ARG	15.425	50-7¼	
3. Vilho Tuulos	FIN	15.37	50-5	
4. Väinö Rainio	FIN	15.01	49-3	
5. Folke Jansson	SWE	14.97	49-1½	
6. Mikio Oda	JPN	14.35	47-1	
7. R. Earle Wilson	USA	14.235	46-8	
8. Ivar Sahlin	SWE	14.16	46-5½	

Nick Winter, a 29-year-old fireman, was the first Australian to compete in a field event. The triple jump was so little known in Australia that it was not included in the national championships until six years after Winter earned his gold medal. The son of the proprietor of a snooker salon, Winter specialized in odd events, such as backward cycling and the individual tug-of-war. In setting a world record with his final jump, Nick Winter improved on his pre-Olympic best by 14½ inches.

1928 Amsterdam C: 24, N: 13, D: 8.2. WR: 15.525, 50-11¼ (Anthony Winter)

			FT.-
		M	IN.
1. Mikio Oda	JPN	15.21	49-11
2. Levi Casey	USA	15.17	49-9¼
3. Vilho Tuulos	FIN	15.11	49-7
4. Chuhei Nambu	JPN	15.01	49-3
5. Toimi Tulikoura	FIN	14.70	48-2¾
6. Erkki Järvinen	FIN	14.65	48-0¾
7. Willem Peters	HOL	14.55	47-9
8. Väinö Rainio	FIN	14.41	47-3½

Mikio Oda of Japan was the first Asian to win an Olympic gold medal.

1932 Los Angeles C: 16, N: 12, D: 8.4. WR: 15.58, 51-1½ (Mikio Oda)

			FT.-	
		M	IN.	
1. Chuhei Nambu	JPN	15.72	51-7	WR
2. Eric Svensson	SWE	15.32	50-3¼	
3. Kenkichi Oshima	JPN	15.12	49-7¼	
4. Eamon Fitzgerald	IRL	15.01	49-3	
5. Willem Peters	HOL	14.93	48-11¾	
6. Sol Furth	USA	14.88	48-10	
7. Sidney Bowman	USA	14.87	48-9½	
8. Rolland Romero	USA	14.85	48-8¾	

Chuhei Nambu was the world record holder in the long jump, but a leg injury prevented him from placing better than third in Los Angeles. Two days later he entered the triple jump and finished first, achieving the rare distinction of holding the world record in both horizontal jump events.

1936 Berlin C: 31, N: 19, D: 8.6. WR: 15.78, 51-9¼ (Jim Metcalfe)

			FT.-	
		M	IN.	
1. Naoto Tajima	JPN	16.00	52-6	WR
2. Masao Harada	JPN	15.66	51-4½	
3. Jim Metcalfe	AUS	15.50	50-10¼	
4. Heinz Wöllner	GER	15.27	50-1¼	
5. Rolland Romero	USA	15.08	49-5¾	
6. Kenkichi Oshima	JPN	15.07	49-5½	
7. Erich Joch	GER	14.88	48-10	
8. Dudley Wilkins	USA	14.83	48-8	

Tajima duplicated Nambu's feat of winning the triple jump gold medal two days after he had earned a bronze medal in the long jump. Long jump silver medalist Luz Long placed tenth in the triple jump.

Chuhei Nambu, winner of the 1932 triple jump.

1948 London C: 29, N: 18, D: 8.3. WR: 16.00, 52-6 (Naoto Tajima)

			FT.-	
			M	IN.
1. Arne Åhman	SWE	15.40	50-6¼	
2. George Avery	AUS	15.36	50-4¾	
3. Ruhi Sarialp	TUR	15.02	49-3½	
4. Preben Larsen	DEN	14.83	48-8	
5. Geraldo de Oliveira	BRA	14.82	48-7½	
6. Valdemar Rautio	FIN	14.70	48-2¾	
7. Leslie McKnead	AUS	14.53	47-8	
8. Helio Coutinho de Silva	BRA	14.49	47-6½	

1952 Helsinki C: 35, N: 23, D: 7.23. WR: 16.01, 52-6½ (Ademar Ferreira da Silva)

			FT.-	
			M	IN.
1. Ademar Ferreira da Silva	BRA	16.22	53-2¾	WR
2. Leonid Sherbakov	SOV/RUS	15.98	52-5¼	
3. Arnoldo Devonish	VEN	15.52	50-11	
4. Walter Ashbaugh	USA	15.39	50-6	
5. Rune Nilsen	NOR	15.13	49-7¾	
6. Yoshio Iimuro	JPN	14.99	49-2¼	
7. Geraldo de Oliveira	BRA	14.95	49-0¾	
8. Roger Norman	SWE	14.89	48-10¼	

Da Silva put on an incredible show, breaking his old world record four times in six attempts in the final. Arnoldo Devonish was the first Venezuelan to win an Olympic medal.

1956 Melbourne C: 32, N: 20, D: 11.27. WR: 16.56, 54-4 (Ademar Ferreira da Silva)

			FT.-	
			M	IN.
1. Ademar Ferreira da Silva	BRA	16.35	53-7¾	OR
2. Vilhjálmur Einarsson	ICE	16.26	53-4¼	
3. Vitold Kreyer	SOV/RUS	16.02	52-6¾	
4. William Sharpe	USA	15.88	52-1¼	
5. Martin Rehák	CZE	15.85	52-0	
6. Leonid Sherbakov	SOV/RUS	15.80	51-10	
7. Koji Sakurai	JPN	15.73	51-7¼	
8. Teruji Kogake	JPN	15.64	51-3¾	

The second round of the final produced a tremendous shock, when a completely unknown Icelander, 22-year-old Vilhjálmur Einarsson, took the lead with a jump of 53 feet 4¼ inches, improving his personal record by 17 inches. Nevertheless, defending champion da Silva regained the lead in the fourth round and won his second gold medal. Afterward, reporters searched frantically to find an Icelandic interpreter, only to have Einarsson save them the trouble by explaining that he spoke English quite well, since he had just graduated from Dartmouth College, in New Hampshire. Einarsson was Iceland's first Olympic medal winner.

In 1958 Ademar Ferreira da Silva acted in the internationally acclaimed film *Black Orpheus*.

1960 Rome C: 39, N: 24, D: 9.6. WR: 17.03, 55-10½ (Józef Schmidt)

			FT.-	
			M	IN.
1. Józef Schmidt	POL	16.81	55-2	OR
2. Vladimir Goryayev	SOV/BLR	16.63	54-6¾	
3. Vitold Kreyer	SOV/RUS	16.43	53-11	
4. Ira Davis	USA	16.41	53-10¼	
5. Vilhjálmur Einarsson	ICE	16.37	53-8½	
6. Ryszard Malcherczyk	POL	16.01	52-6½	
7. Manfred Hinze	GDR	15.93	52-3¼	
8. Kari Rahkamo	FIN	15.84	51-11¾	

On August 5, 1960, Józef Schmidt had jumped 55 feet 10½ inches to become the first person to break both the 55-foot barrier and the 17-meter barrier, bettering the world record by 13 inches. In Rome, he won easily.

1964 Tokyo C: 34, N: 21, D: 10.16. WR: 17.03, 55-10½ (Józef Schmidt)

			FT.-	
			M	IN.
1. Józef Schmidt	POL	16.85	55-3½	OR
2. Oleg Fyedoseyev	SOV/RUS	16.58	54-4¾	
3. Viktor Kravchenko	SOV/RUS	16.57	54-4½	
4. Frederick Alsop	GBR	16.46	54-0	
5. Şerban Ciochină	ROM	16.23	53-3	
6. Manfred Hinze	GDR	16.15	53-0	
7. Georgi Stoikovski	BUL	16.10	52-10	
8. Hans-Jürgen Rückborn	GDR	16.09	52-9½	

Józef Schmidt had dominated the triple jump for six years. However, he underwent an operation to his knee less than two months before the Tokyo Games, and his condition was still in doubt. Competing in pain, needing an injection of novocaine, Schmidt jumped 54 feet 7½ inches in the second round of the final and then set an Olympic record of 55 feet 3½ inches with his last attempt.

1968 Mexico City C: 34, N: 24, D: 10.17. WR: 17.03, 55-10½ (Józef Schmidt)

			FT.-	
			M	IN.
1. Viktor Saneyev	SOV/GEO	17.39	57-0¾	WR
2. Nelson Prudêncio	BRA	17.27	56-8	
3. Giuseppe Gentile	ITA	17.22	56-6	
4. Arthur Walker	USA	17.12	56-2	
5. Nikolai Dudkin	SOV/BLR	17.09	56-1	
6. Philip May	AUS	17.02	55-10¼	
7. Józef Schmidt	POL	16.89	55-5	
8. Mamadou Mansour-Dia	SEN	16.73	54-10¾	

Giuseppe Gentile, a bearded 25-year-old law student who later played opposite Maria Callas in the film version of *Medea,* produced a stunning performance in the qualifying round when he leaped 56 feet 1¼ inches to break Józef Schmidt's eight-year-old world record. But this was just a prelude to the extraordinary events of the following day's final.

In the very first round, Gentile hit a whopping 56 feet 6 inches, 19 inches farther than his pre-Olympic best, and it seemed that he had surely put a lock on the gold medal. But in the second round, Nelson Prudêncio, who had never jumped beyond 53 feet 5¾ inches before Mexico City, leaped an ominous 55 feet 11¼ inches. In the third round it was the turn of Viktor Saneyev, a graduate of the Georgian Sub-Tropical Plant Cultivation Institute. The pre-Olympic favorite, Saneyev reached 56 feet 6½ inches to move ahead of Gentile by one centimeter.

In the fifth round, Nikolai Dudkin moved into third place with 56 feet 1 inch. Two jumps later, Prudêncio exploded with another world record of 56 feet 8 inches. With his last jump, Prudêncio again broke Schmidt's old record with a jump of 56 feet 3¼ inches. Saneyev, Art Walker, and Gentile each had one jump remaining. It was Saneyev who came up with the clutch performance, extending to 57 feet ¾ inch for yet another world record. Walker jumped 56 feet 2 inches, leaving Nikolai Dudkin in fifth place even though he had bettered the pre-Olympic world record. Gentile closed the amazing competition with his fourth foul in five jumps and had to settle for a bronze medal after twice setting a world record. The best jumps of Saneyev and Prudêncio were both accompanied by suspicious wind readings of exactly 2.0 m.p.s., which didn't affect the competition, but did affect their validity as world records, since 2.0

m.p.s. happened to be the maximum allowable wind speed.

1972 Munich C: 36, N: 28, D: 9.4. WR: 17.40, 57-1 (Pedro Perez Dueñas)

			FT.-	
			M	IN.
1. Viktor Saneyev	SOV/GEO	17.35	56-11¼
2. Jörg Drehmel	GDR	17.31	56-9½
3. Nelson Prudêncio	BRA	17.05	55-11¼
4. Carol Corbu	ROM	16.85	55-3½
5. John Craft	USA	16.83	55-2¾
6. Mamadou Mansour-Dia	SEN	16.83	55-2¾
7. Michal Joachimowski	POL	16.69	54-9¼
8. Kristen Flogstad	NOR	16.44	53-11¼

This was expected to be a dramatic showdown between defending champion Viktor Saneyev and his rival Jörg Drehmel, who had twice beaten Saneyev in important meets. But Saneyev belted out the third best jump of all time in the first round of the final, and Drehmel was unable to even come close until the fifth round. World record holder Pedro Perez withdrew in the middle of the qualifying round because of injury. Nelson Prudêncio's final jump was his best since the 1968 Olympic final.

1976 Montreal C: 25, N: 18, D: 7.30. WR: 17.89, 58-8½ (João Carlos de Oliveira)

			FT.-	
			M	IN.
1. Viktor Saneyev	SOV/GEO	17.29	56-8¾
2. James Butts	USA	17.18	56-4½
3. João Carlos de Oliveira	BRA	16.90	55-5½
4. Pedro Perez Dueñas	CUB	16.81	55-2
5. Tommy Haynes	USA	16.78	55-0¾
6. Wolfgang Kolmsee	GER	16.68	54-8¾
7. Eugeniusz Biskupski	POL	16.49	54-1¼
8. Carol Corbu	ROM	16.43	53-11

On October 15, 1975, João Carlos de Oliveira, competing at the Pan American Games in Mexico City, triple-jumped 58 feet 8½ inches to better Viktor Saneyev's world record by an incredible 17¾ inches. At the Montreal Olympics, de Oliveira led the qualifying round with a reserved jump of 55 feet 2 inches, followed by Saneyev at 55 feet ¼ inch. In the final, Perez took the first-round lead at 55 feet 2 inches, but Saneyev moved ahead in the third round with a jump of 55 feet 11¾ inches. In the fourth round, James Butts, aiming to become the first U.S. triple jump medalist in 48 years, leaped into the lead at 56 feet 4½ inches. However, Saneyev, ever the clutch performer, rebounded in the fifth round with a jump of 56 feet 8¾ inches, and that settled the issue. He joined standing jumper Ray Ewry, hammer thrower John Flanagan, and discus champion Al Oerter as the only track and field athletes to win three or more individual gold medals in the same event.

Viktor Saneyev won three gold medals in the triple jump, in 1968, 1972, and 1976, and came within 4½ inches of winning a fourth in 1980.

1980 Moscow C: 23, N: 19, D: 7.25. WR: 17.89, 58-8½ (João Carlos de Oliveira)

			M	FT.-IN.
1.	Jaak Uudmäe	SOV/EST	17.35	56-11¼
2.	Viktor Saneyev	SOV/GEO	17.24	56-6¾
3.	João Carlos de Oliveira	BRA	17.22	56-6
4.	Keith Connor	GBR	16.87	55-4¼
5.	Ian Campbell	AUS	16.72	54-10¼
6.	Atanas Chochev	BUL	16.56	54-4
7.	Béla Bakósi	HUN	16.47	54-0½
8.	Kenneth Lorraway	AUS	16.44	53-11¼

Unfortunately, this event was marred by ugly scenes: Soviet spectators whistling while de Oliveira jumped, and controversial officiating that caused leading non-Soviet contenders de Oliveira and Ian Campbell to be charged with nine fouls in 12 jumps. In the third round Campbell received a no-jump after allegedly dragging his trail leg during the step stage. He argued his case, but the pit was raked before impartial observers could arrive. The very next jump was the gold medal winner for 25-year-old Estonian Jaak Uudmäe. The final round was highlighted by a near world record by de Oliveira that was ruled a foul, and by 34-year-old Viktor Saneyev's noble attempt to match Al Oerter's feat of four consecutive gold medals. He landed four and a half inches short, but did manage to edge past de Oliveira for the silver medal. In January 1982, João Carlos de Oliveira was badly injured in an auto accident. After a nine-month battle to salvage his athletic career, his right leg was finally amputated below the knee.

1984 Los Angeles C: 28, N: 21, D: 8.4. WR: 17.89, 58-8½ (João Carlos de Oliveira)

			M	FT.-IN.
1.	Alfrederick Joyner	USA	17.26w	56-7½w
2.	Michael Conley	USA	17.18	56-4½
3.	Keith Connor	GBR	16.87	55-4¼
4.	Zou Zhenxian	CHN	16.83	55-2¾
5.	Peter Bouschen	GER	16.77	55-0¼
6.	William Banks	USA	16.75	54-11½
7.	Ajayi Agbebaku	NGR	16.67	54-8¼
8.	Eric McCalla	GBR	16.66	54-8

Mike Conley solidified his role of favorite by leading the qualifying round with a near Olympic record jump of 56 feet 11½ inches. The next morning, Conley's teammate Al Joyner was watching a television preview of the day's events when he saw pictures of Conley and the third U.S. triple-jumper, Willie Banks, come on the screen. "I thought they would show me too," Joyner would later recall, "but they didn't. So I wanted to go out and let everybody know who I was."

Joyner's first-round jump, aided by the only significant tailwind of the day, held up for the gold medal. He also recorded three of the four next best jumps as well. The first seven places were decided by the second round, although Conley almost pulled it out with a huge last-round leap that turned out to be a foul.

Joyner, of East St. Louis, Illinois, competed at the same time that his younger sister, Jackie, was taking part in the heptathlon. In fact, he passed his fourth-round turn in order to root her on during the last lap of the 800-meter run. On the way to the triple jump award ceremony he ran into Jackie coming off the platform after receiving her silver medal. Several days after the competition, while other athletes were nursing injured leg muscles, upset winner Al Joyner confided that he was suffering from sore *cheek* muscles—from smiling so much.

1988 Seoul C: 43, N: 31, D: 9.24. WR: 17.97, 58-11½ (William Banks)

			M	FT.-IN.	
1.	Khristo Markov	BUL	17.61	57-9¼	OR
2.	Igor Lapshin	SOV/BLR	17.52	57-5¾	
3.	Aleksandr Kovalenko	SOV/BLR	17.42	57-1¾	
4.	Oleg Protsenko	SOV/RUS	17.38	57-0¼	

5. Charles Simpkins	USA	17.29	56-8¾	
6. William Banks	USA	17.03	55-10½	
7. Ivan Slanař	CZE	16.75	54-11½	
8. Jacek Pastusiński	POL	16.72	54-10¼	

Markov's first-round attempt held up for the gold medal, but Lapshin gained the silver with his final try.

1992 Barcelona C: 47, N: 32, D: 8.3. WR: 17.97, 58-11½ (William Banks)

			FT.
		M	-IN.
1. Michael Conley	USA	18.17w	59-7¼w
2. Charles Simpkins	USA	17.60	57-9
3. Frank Rutherford	BAH	17.36	56-11½
4. Leonid Voloshin	RUS	17.32	56-10
5. Brian Wellman	BER	17.24	56-6¾
6. Yoelvis Quesada Fernández	CUB	17.18	56-4½
7. Aleksandr Kovalenko	RUS	17.06	55-11¾
8. Zou Sixin	CHN	17.00	55-9¼

After earning a silver medal in 1984, Mike Conley missed out on making the United States team in 1988 when judges at the Olympic trials ruled that his shorts grazed the sand four and a quarter inches before his feet. By 1992 Conley was taking no chances: he wore a formfitting bodysuit instead of loose shorts. Conley took the lead in the second round with a jump of 56 feet 10¼ inches. In the final round he leaped almost eight inches beyond Willy Banks' world record. But the wind gauge flashed 2.1 meters per second—the smallest possible amount above the legal limit. Conley's jump was the only wind-assisted measurement of the competition. Eight years earlier Conley had lost the gold medal when Al Joyner won with the only wind-assisted measurement of that competition. In Barcelona, Charlie Simpkins moved from fourth to second with his final jump.

SHOT PUT

A shot is a 16-pound ball made of iron or brass. It must be put rather than thrown and must not drop below the level of the contestant's shoulder. The shot circle is 2.135 meters (7 feet) in diameter. At the front of the circle is a wooden stop board 10 centimeters (4 inches) high. Contestants must not leave the circle until the shot lands. As with all throwing events, the twelve finalists are given three tries. The top eight are then given three more.

1896 Athens C: 7, N: 4, D: 4.7. WR: 14.32, 47-0 (George Gray)

		FT.-	
		M	IN.
1. Robert Garrett	USA	11.22	36-9¾
2. Miltiades Gouskos	GRE	11.20	36-9
3. Georgios Papasideris	GRE	10.36	34-0
4. Karl Schumann	GER	—	—

Garrett, who had placed first in the discus the day before, won the shot put with his first attempt.

1900 Paris C: 10, N: 6, D: 7.15. WR: 14.68, 48-2 (Dennis Horgan)

		FT.-		
		M	IN.	
1. Richard Sheldon	USA	14.10	46-3¼	OR
2. Josiah McCracken	USA	12.85	42-2	
3. Robert Garrett	USA	12.37	40-7	
4. Rezsö Crettier	HUN	12.05	39-6½	
5. Panagiotis Paraskevopoulos	GRE	11.52	37-9½	
6. Gustaf Söderström	SWE	11.18	36-8¼	

1904 St. Louis C: 8, N: 2, D: 8.31. WR: 14.68, 48-2 (Dennis Horgan)

		FT.-		
		M	IN.	
1. Ralph Rose	USA	14.81	48-7	WR
2. William Coe	USA	14.40	47-3	
3. Leon Feuerbach	USA	13.37	43-10½	
4. Martin Sheridan	USA	12.39	40-8	
5. Charles Chadwick	USA	—	—	
6. Albert Johnson	USA	—	—	
7. John Guiney	USA	—	—	

Ralph Rose was a 6-foot 6-inch, 235-pound giant from California. Before his Olympic career was over, he had won three gold medals, two silver, and one bronze. He died on October 16, 1913, at the age of 29. Nicolaos Georgantas of Greece was also entered in this event, but after his first two attempts were disallowed for throwing, he withdrew in disgust.

1906 Athens C: 18, N: 10, D: 4.27. WR: 15.09, 49-6 (Wesley Coe)

		FT.-	
		M	IN.
1. Martin Sheridan	USA	12.325	40-5¼
2. Mihály Dávid	HUN	11.83	38-9¾
3. Eric Lemming	SWE	11.26	36-11½
4. André Tison	FRA	11.02	36-2

Martin Sheridan was the star of the Intercalated Games, winning two gold medals and three silver medals. In 1908 he added two gold and a silver.

1908 London C: 26, N: 8, D: 7.16. WR: 15.12, 49-7½ (Ralph Rose)

		FT.-	
		M	IN.
1. Ralph Rose	USA	14.21	46-7½
2. Denis Horgan	GBR/IRL	13.62	44-8¼
3. John Garrels	USA	13.18	43-3
4. William Coe	USA	13.07	42-10½
5. Edward Barrett	GBR/IRL	12.89	42-3½
6. Marquis Horr	USA	12.82	42-1
7. Jalmari Sauli	FIN	12.58	41-3¼
8. Lee Talbott	USA	11.63	38-1¾

Denis Horgan was 37 years old and past his prime. His second-place performance was particularly noteworthy considering that he had almost been killed the year before. On duty as a New York City policeman, Horgan tried to break up a brawl and was severely attacked with

The winners of the 1912 shot put: (left to right) Patrick Mc-Donald (gold), Lawrence Whitney (bronze), and Ralph Rose (silver). Rose also won gold medals in 1904 and 1908.

sticks and shovels. After his surprising recovery, he was given a pension and allowed to return to Ireland.

1912 Stockholm C: 22, N: 14, D: 7.10. WR: 15.545, 51-0 (Ralph Rose)

			FT.-	
			M	IN.
1.	Patrick McDonald	USA	15.34	50-4	OR
2.	Ralph Rose	USA	15.25	50-0½
3.	Lawrence Whitney	USA	13.93	45-8½
4.	Elmer Niklander	FIN	13.65	44-9½
5.	George Philbrook	USA	13.13	43-1
6.	Imre Mudin	HUN	12.81	42-0½
7.	Einar Nilsson	SWE	12.62	41-5
8.	Patrick Quinn	GBR	12.53	41-1½

McDonald, another New York City policeman, surprised Rose in the fourth round of six by achieving the best put of his career.

1920 Antwerp C: 20, N: 10, D: 8:18. WR: 15.545, 51-0 (Ralph Rose)

			FT.-	
			M	IN.
1.	Frans "Ville" Pörhölä	FIN	14.81	48-7¼
2.	Elmer Niklander	FIN	14.155	46-5¼
3.	Harry Liversedge	USA	14.15	46-5¼
4.	Patrick McDonald	USA	14.08	46-3
5.	Einar Nilsson	SWE	13.87	45-6¼
6.	Harald Tammer	EST	13.605	44-7½
7.	George Bihlman	USA	13.575	44-6½
8.	Howard Cann	USA	13.52	44-4¼

1924 Paris C: 28, N: 15, D: 7.8. WR: 15.545, 51-0 (Ralph Rose)

			FT.-	
			M	IN.
1.	L. Clarence "Bud" Houser	USA	14.99	49-2¼
2.	Glenn Hartranft	USA	14.89	48-10¼
3.	Ralph Hills	USA	14.64	48-0½
4.	Hannes Torpo	FIN	14.45	47-5

5.	Norman Anderson	USA	14.29	46-10¾
6.	Elmer Niklander	FIN	14.26	49-9½
7.	Frans "Ville" Pörhölä	FIN	14.10	46-3¼
8.	Bertil Jansson	SWE	13.76	45-1¾

1928 Amsterdam C: 22, N: 14, D: 7.29. WR: 15.79, 51-9¾ (Emil Hirschfeld)

			FT.-	
			M	IN.
1.	John Kuck	USA	15.87	52-0¾	WR
2.	Herman Brix	USA	15.75	51-8¼
3.	Emil Hirschfeld	GER	15.72	51-7
4.	Eric Krenz	USA	14.99	49-2¼
5.	Armas Wahlstedt	FIN	14.69	48-2½
6.	Wilhelm Uebler	GER	14.69	48-2½
7.	Harlow Rothert	USA	14.68	48-2
8.	József Darányi	HUN	14.35	47-1

On May 6, 1928, Emil Hirschfeld finally broke Ralph Rose's 1909 world record. He was in good form in Amsterdam, but Kuck and Brix were superb. Kuck started his road to shot put gold when, at the age of four, he discovered a three-pound agate sphere and began throwing it around his yard. His practice shot turned out to be a 20,000-year-old Native American relic. Brix later changed his name to Bruce Bennett and became a well-known movie actor. Among his early roles was Tarzan in *The New Adventures of Tarzan* (1935). Although he appeared in such critically acclaimed features as *Mildred Pierce* (1945) and *The Treasure of Sierra Madre* (1948), he also acted in such clunkers as *The Alligator People* (1959) and *The Fiend of Dope Island* (1961).

1932 Los Angeles C: 15, N: 10, D: 7.31. WR: 16.05, 52-8 (Zygmont Heljasz)

			FT.-	
			M	IN.
1.	Leo Sexton	USA	16.00	52-6	OR
2.	Harlow Rothert	USA	15.67	51-5
3.	František Douda	CZE	15.61	51-2¾
4.	Emil Hirschfeld	GER	15.56	51-0¾
5.	Nelson Gray	USA	15.47	50-9¼
6.	Hans-Heinrich Sievert	GER	15.07	49-5½
7.	József Darányi	HUN	14.67	48-1¾
8.	Jules Noël	FRA	14.53	47-8

Leo Sexton was a 6-foot 4-inch insurance broker from New York. World record holder Zygmont Heljasz of Poland was able to place only ninth.

1936 Berlin C: 22, N: 14, D: 8.2. WR: 17.40, 57-1 (Jack Torrance)

			FT.-	
			M	IN.
1.	Hans Woellke	GER	16.20	53-1¾	OR
2.	Sulo Bärlund	FIN	16.12	52-10¾
3.	Gerhard Stöck	GER	15.66	51-4½
4.	Samuel Francis	USA	15.45	50-8¼
5.	Jack Torrance	USA	15.38	50-5½
6.	Dimitri Zaitz	USA	15.32	50-3¼
7.	František Douda	CZE	15.28	50-1¾
8.	Arnold Viiding	EST	15.23	49-11¾

Hans Woellke, a 25-year-old policeman, was the first German to win a track and field gold medal. Another policeman, 304-pound world record holder Jack Torrance of Baton Rouge, Louisiana, was out of shape and finished a disappointing fifth.

1948 London C: 24, N: 14, D: 8.3. WR: 17.68, 58-0⅜ (Charles Fonville)

			FT.-IN.	
1. Wilbur Thompson	USA	17.12	56-2	OR
2. F. James Delaney	USA	16.68	54-8¾	
3. James Fuchs	USA	16.42	53-10½	
4. Mieczyslaw Lomowski	POL	15.43	50-7½	
5. Gösta Arvidsson	SWE	15.37	50-5¼	
6. Yrjö Lehtilä	FIN	15.05	49-4½	
7. Pentti Jouppila	FIN	14.59	47-10½	
8. Cestmir Kalina	CZE	14.55	47-9	

The American putters were so strong that world record holder Charles Fonville failed to make the U.S. team. In London the Americans outdistanced the rest of the world by over three feet.

1952 Helsinki C: 20, N: 14, D: 7.21. WR: 17.95, 58-10½ (James Fuchs)

			FT.-IN.	
1. W. Parry O'Brien	USA	17.41	57-1½	OR
2. C. Darrow Hooper	USA	17.39	57-0¾	
3. James Fuchs	USA	17.06	55-11¾	
4. Otto Grigalka	SOV	16.78	55-0¾	
5. Roland Nilsson	SWE	16.55	53-3¾	
6. John Savidge	GBR	16.19	53-1½	
7. Georgi Fyodorov	SOV	16.06	52-8¼	
8. Per Stavem	NOR	16.02	52-6¾	

World record holder Jim Fuchs had won 88 consecutive meets when he was beaten at the 1951 A.A.U. championships by Parry O'Brien. At the 1952 U.S. Olympic trials, O'Brien was beaten by Darrow Hooper. It was his last loss for four years, during which time he won 116 straight meets. O'Brien and Hooper were almost the exact same size and weight. Their similarity also extended to their performances in the Olympics. O'Brien, who was two days older than Hooper, outputted him by only two centimeters. Parry O'Brien, a student at the University of Southern California, practiced at the Los Angeles Memorial Coliseum, site of the 1932 and 1984 Olympics, by sneaking over a fence late at night while no one was there. He revolutionized shot putting by introducing a new style in which he began with his back to the front of the throwing circle and then used every bit of momentum he could gather before he let go of the shot.

1956 Melbourne C: 14, N: 10, D: 11.28. WR: 19.25, 63-2 (W. Parry O'Brien)

			FT.-IN.	
1. W. Parry O'Brien	USA	18.57	60-11¼	OR
2. William Nieder	USA	18.18	59-7¾	

3. Jiři Skobla	CZE	17.65	57-11	
4. Kenneth Bantum	USA	17.48	57-4¼	
5. Boris Balyayev	SOV	16.96	55-7¾	
6. Erik Uddebom	SWE	16.65	54-7½	
7. Karlheinz Wegmann	GER	16.63	54-6¾	
8. Georgios Tsakanikas	GRE	16.56	54-4	

On May 8, 1954, two days after Roger Bannister broke the four-minute mile, Parry O'Brien became the first person to put the shot more than 60 feet, with a toss of 60 feet 5¼ inches. In Melbourne, at the 1956 Olympics, O'Brien overwhelmed the field, recording the five best puts of the competition. Even his worst put was beaten only by Bill Nieder's best. Parry O'Brien became the first reigning world record holder to win the shot put at the Olympics since 1908. Bronze medalist Jiři Skobla was the son of Jaroslav Skobla, who won the heavyweight weightlifting gold medal in 1932.

1960 Rome C: 24, N: 16, D: 8.31. WR: 20.06, 65-10 (William Nieder)

			FT.-IN.	
1. William Nieder	USA	19.68	64-6¾	OR
2. W. Parry O'Brien	USA	19.11	62-8½	
3. Dallas Long	USA	19.01	62-4½	
4. Viktor Lipsnis	SOV/UKR	17.90	58-8¾	
5. Michael Lindsay	GBR	17.80	58-4¾	
6. Alfred Sosgórnik	POL	17.57	57-7¾	
7. Dieter Urbach	GER	17.47	57-3¾	
8. Martyn Lucking	GBR	17.43	57-2¼	

Bill Nieder had failed to qualify for the U.S. team after finishing fourth in the Olympic trials. But a wrist injury suffered by Dave Davis, and a world record put by Nieder, convinced U.S. officials to make a rare replacement. In Rome, Nieder showed that they had made the right decision. Parry O'Brien led after four rounds, but in the fifth round, Nieder, recalling O'Brien's disparaging remark that he was a "cow pasture performer" who choked in important meets, let loose a monster toss that was almost two feet better than anything the defending champion was able to produce.

1964 Tokyo C: 22, N: 13, D: 10.17. WR: 20.68, 67-10 (Dallas Long)

			FT.-IN.	
1. Dallas Long	USA	20.33	66-8½	OR
2. James Randel Matson	USA	20.20	66-3¼	
3. Vilmos Varjú	HUN	19.39	63-7½	
4. W. Parry O'Brien	USA	19.20	63-0	
5. Zsigmond Nagy	HUN	18.88	61-11½	
6. Nikolai Karassev	SOV/RUS	18.86	61-10½	
7. Leslie Mills	NZE	18.52	60-9¼	
8. Adolfas Varanauskas	SOV/LIT	18.41	60-4¾	

Twenty-four-year-old Dallas Long, a 6-foot 4-inch, 260-pound dentist from Los Angeles, took the lead with a first-round toss of 64 feet 4 inches. In the third round, 19-

year-old Randy Matson of Pampa, Texas, moved ahead at 65 feet 2¾ inches. With his next throw he improved to 66 feet 3¼ inches, a new Olympic record. However, his record was short-lived. Two minutes later, Long countered with a put of 66 feet 8½ inches that held up for first place.

1968 Mexico City C: 19, N: 14, D: 10.14. WR: 21.78, 71-5½ (James Randel Matson)

			FT.-	
			M	IN.
1.	James Randel Matson	USA	20.54	67-4¾
2.	George Woods	USA	20.12	66-0¼
3.	Eduard Gushchin	SOV/RUS	20.09	65-11
4.	Dieter Hoffmann	GDR	20.00	65-7½
5.	David Maggard	USA	19.43	63-9
6.	Wladyslaw Komar	POL	19.28	63-3¼
7.	Uwe Grabe	GDR	19.03	62-5¼
8.	Heinfried Birlenbach	GER	18.80	61-8¼

Although he only placed third at the U.S. Olympic trials, 6-foot 6½-inch, 265-pound Randy Matson was still the overwhelming favorite by virtue of the fact that he had completely dominated the event over the previous four years. On May 8, 1965, he had demolished the world record with a put of 70 feet 7¼ inches, bettering the previous record by 2 feet 9¼ inches. By the time of the Mexico City Olympics, Matson had registered 23 of the 25 longest puts in history. He led the qualifying round with an Olympic record of 67 feet 10¼ inches. His first toss of the final was 67 feet 4¾ inches. No one else came close to that for the rest of the competition. U.S. shot putters finished first and second for the fifth straight time. Like many athletes during the Vietnam War period, Randy Matson was declared unfit for military service because of knee problems.

1972 Munich C: 29, N: 19, D: 9.9. WR: 21.78, 71-5½ (James Randel Matson)

			FT.-		
			M	IN.	
1.	Wladyslaw Komar	POL	21.18	69-6	OR
2.	George Woods	USA	21.17	69-5½	
3.	Hartmut Briesenick	GDR	21.14	69-4¼	
4.	Hans-Peter Gies	GDR	21.14	69-4¼	
5.	Allan Feuerbach	USA	21.01	68-11¼	
6.	Brian Oldfield	USA	20.91	68-7¼	
7.	Heinfried Birlenbach	GER	20.37	66-10	
8.	Vilmos Varjú	HUN	20.10	65-11½	

The 6-foot 5¼ inch, 276-pound Wladyslaw Komar had twice been kicked off the Polish team for "misbehavior," including once when he received a "life ban." However, he was back again in Munich for his third Olympics. Ninth in 1964, sixth in 1968, the 32-year-old Komar connected with the greatest put of his career in the first round of the 1972 final, bettering his previous best by seven and a quarter inches. Woods, Briesenick, and Gies all came very, very close, but each fell short by

inches. George Woods' last toss caused much controversy since it hit the marker that indicated Komar's best put. Many observers were quite surprised when it was measured at only 69 feet ¾ inch, and Woods himself believed that at the very least he deserved an extra put. But the officials in charge ruled it a valid toss and called an end to the competition. Films of the incident were inconclusive.

1976 Montreal C: 23, N: 18, D: 7.24. WR: 22.00, 72-2¼ (Aleksandr Baryshnikov)

			FT.-	
			M	IN.
1.	Udo Beyer	GDR	21.05	69-0¾
2.	Yevgeny Mironov	SOV/RUS	21.03	69-0
3.	Aleksandr Baryshnikov	SOV/RUS	21.00	68-10¾
4.	Allan Feuerbach	USA	20.55	67-5¼
5.	Hans-Peter Gies	GDR	20.47	67-2
6.	Geoffrey Capes	GBR	20.36	66-9¾
7.	George Woods	USA	20.26	66-5¾
8.	Hans Hoglund	SWE	20.17	66-2¼

Missing from the Olympics was the number-one shot putter in the world, Brian Oldfield, who owned the four longest unofficial puts in history, including one of 75 feet. Oldfield was a professional and thus ineligible to compete. The amateur record of 72 feet 2¼ inches was set by Aleksandr Baryshnikov on July 10. Baryshnikov looked good as gold when his one put of the qualifying round sailed 69 feet 11½ inches to break the Olympic record. Baryshnikov also took the lead in the first round of the final with a toss of 67 feet 4¼ inches. In the second round he was passed by Al Feuerbach's 67 feet 5 inches. Baryshnikov boomed back in front with a third-round 68 feet 10¾ inches. Then, in the fifth round, 20-year-old Udo Beyer, the youngest man in the competition, unleashed a put of 69 feet ¾ inch. Beyer had only been added to the East German team one week before the Olympics began. Yevgeny Mironov, who had been mired inconspicuously in sixth place, followed a few minutes later with 69 feet 0 inches, and the medals were decided. Most of the leading contenders fell several feet short of their best performances. Although the pressure of the Olympics may have been a contributing factor, most observers felt that the institution of steroid testing played a more important role.

1980 Moscow C: 16, N: 11, D: 7.30. WR: 22.15, 72-8 (Udo Beyer)

			FT.-		
			M	IN.	
1.	Volodymyr Kyselyov	SOV/UKR	21.35	70-0½	OR
2.	Aleksandr Baryshnikov	SOV/RUS	21.08	69-2	
3.	Udo Beyer	GDR	21.06	69-1¼	
4.	Reijo Ståhlberg	FIN	20.82	68-3¾	
5.	Geoffrey Capes	GBR	20.50	67-3¼	
6.	Hans-Jürgen Jacobi	GDR	20.32	66-8	
7.	Jaromir Vlk	CZE	20.24	66-5	
8.	Vladimir Milic	YUG	20.07	65-10¼	

Volodymyr Kyselyov was the only shot putter to achieve a personal best, ending Udo Beyer's string of 34 consecutive victories. In 1985 Kyselyov almost died as a result of past use of prohibited substances, specifically testosterone.

1984 Los Angeles C: 19, N: 13, D: 8.11. WR: 22.22, 72-10¾ (Udo Beyer)

			FT.-
		M	IN.
1. Alessandro Andrei	ITA	21.26	69-9
2. Michael Carter	USA	21.09	69-2½
3. Dave Laut	USA	20.97	68-9¾
4. Augie Wolf	USA	20.93	68-8
5. Werner Günthör	SWI	20.28	66-6½
6. Marco Montelatici	ITA	19.98	65-6¾
7. Sören Tallhem	SWE	19.81	65-0
8. Erik de Bruin	HOL	19.65	64-5¾

The quality of the 1984 shot put competition, already lessened by the Soviet-bloc boycott, was further diminished when the final was interrupted by no less than six medal award ceremonies. Michael Carter took the first-round lead with a put of 67 feet 8¼ inches. But 25-year-old Florence policeman Alessandro Andrei moved ahead with a second-round toss of 68 feet 9¾ inches. He improved by almost a foot with his next attempt. Carter improved as well, but still had to settle for the silver. Six days after the Olympic final, Carter was playing in his first professional football pre-season game, and six months later, he was taking part in the San Francisco 49ers' Super Bowl victory.

1988 Seoul C: 21, N: 17, D: 9.23. WR: 23.06, 75-8 (Ulf Timmermann)

			FT.-	
		M	IN.	
1. Ulf Timmermann	GDR	22.47	73-8¾	OR
2. E. Randolph Barnes	USA	22.39	73-5½	
3. Werner Günthör	SWI	21.99	72-1¾	
4. Udo Beyer	GDR	21.40	70-2½	
5. Remigius Machura	CZE	20.57	67-5¾	
6. Gert Weil	CHI	20.38	66-10¼	
7. Alessandro Andrei	ITA	20.36	66-9½	
8. Sergei Smirnov	SOV	20.36	66-9½	

World champion Werner Günthör set an Olympic record with an opening put of 70 feet 4½ inches. Later in the first round, Ulf Timmermann, who had broken the world record on May 22, took the lead at 72 feet 3 inches. Timmermann improved to 72 feet 8½ inches in the third round and to 73 feet 1½ inches in the fifth round. People began congratulating the East German, but Timmermann wisely noted that it was too early for a victory celebration. He breathed a little easier after Günthör failed to improve on his fifth-round best of 72 feet 1¾ inches. Then 22-year-old Randy Barnes, who was languishing in fourth place, uncorked a toss of 73 feet 5½ inches and suddenly the shot put circle was the site of high drama.

Two throwers later, Timmermann stepped up for the last put of the competition. Concentrating intensely, he shut out the outside world. "It was like I went into a tunnel," he later told *Track and Field News*. "Time became just a blur, a haze; throwing was just a reflex . . . I knew inside that this was my big chance; I could make my place in Olympic history." Timmermann heaved with everything he had—and managed to outdistance Barnes by a mere 3¼ inches.

On May 20, 1990, Randy Barnes broke Timmermann's world record, but two and a half months later he tested positive for anabolic steroids and was subsequently slapped with a two-year suspension.

1992 Barcelona C: 26, N: 18, D: 7.31. WR: 23.12, 75-10¼ (E. Randolph Barnes)

			FT.-
		M	IN.
1. Michael Stulce	USA	21.70	71-2½
2. James Doehring	USA	20.96	68-9¼
3. Vyacheslav Lykho	RUS	20.94	68-8½
4. Werner Günthör	SWI	20.91	68-7¼
5. Ulf Timmermann	GER	20.49	67-2¾
6. Klaus Bodenmüller	AUT	20.48	67-2¼
7. Dragen Perić	YUG	20.32	66-8
8. Aleksandr Klimenko	UKR	20.23	66-4½

The 1992 shot put competition may not have been the first in which all the medalists had taken prohibited drugs, but it was definitely the first in which all the medalists had actually served suspensions for taking prohibited drugs. Stulce tested positive for excessive testosterone on March 20, 1990, and was banned for two years. Doehring also tested positive for excessive testosterone in December 1990. He sat out 14 months until his ban was lifted because of procedural irregularities. However, Doehring had further drug problems. In December 1991, he pleaded guilty to possessing and conspiring to sell meth-amphetamine. Given a suspended sentence and probation, he left a halfway house a month before the U.S. Olympic trials. Lykho tested positive for stimulants in 1990 and served a three-month suspension.

In Barcelona, Stulce set three personal records, starting with a first-round heave of 70 feet 6¼ inches. He improved to 70 feet 9¾ inches in the second round and 71 feet 2½ inches in the fifth. The only drama came just before Stulce's winning throw, when double world champion Werner Günthör reached 71 feet 6 inches but fouled by touching beyond the ring with his fingers while trying to keep his balance. Stulce's margin of victory was the largest since 1900. At the 1993 world championships, Stulce again tested positive for testosterone as well as for mestanolone, a steroidlike substance.

DISCUS THROW

The men's discus weighs 2 kilograms (4 pounds 6.55 ounces) and has a diameter of 22 centimeters (8⅝ inches). The discus circle has a diameter of 2.5 meters (8 feet 2½ inches). The discus throw is the only track and field event in which a world record has never been set in the Olympics.

1896 Athens C: 9, N: 6, D: 4.6.

| | | | FT.- | |
		M	IN.	
1. Robert Garrett	USA	29.15	95-7½	
2. Panagiotis Paraskevopoulos	GRE	28.955	95-0	
3. Sotirios Versis	GRE	27.78	91-1¾	

Twenty-year-old Robert Garrett came from a wealthy Baltimore banking family. While a student at Princeton, he was shown a drawing of an ancient Greek discus. He ordered a facsimile made and tried practicing with it, but it proved too heavy and unwieldy and so he lost interest quickly. However, while strolling on the field in Athens, he chanced upon a similar object and was told that this was a real discus, which turned out to be much lighter than his American version. Encouraged, yet risking what he feared would be great embarrassment, he entered the Olympic discus contest. To the disappointment of the Greeks, he won the event with his final throw. Before the games were over, Garrett had won two events, placed second in two more, and third in yet another two.

1900 Paris C: 20, N: 8. D: 7.15. WR: 36.20, 118-9 (Charles Henneman)

| | | | FT.- | |
		M	IN.	
1. Rudolf (Rezsö) Bauer	HUN	36.04	118-3	OR
2. František Janda-Suk	BOH/CZE	35.25	115-7	
3. Richard Sheldon	USA	34.60	113-6	
4. Panagiotis Paraskevopoulos	GRE	34.04	111-8	
5. Rezsö Crettier	HUN	33.65	110-4	
6. Gustaf Söderström	SWE	33.30	109-3	
7. Robert Garrett	USA	33.07	108-5	
8. Eric Lemming	SWE	32.50	106-7	
8. Carl Winckler	DEN	32.50	106-7	

1904 St. Louis C: 6, N: 2, D: 9.3. WR: 40.71, 133-6½ (Martin Sheridan)

| | | | FT.- | |
		M	IN.	
1. Martin Sheridan	USA	39.28	128-10½	OR
2. Ralph Rose	USA	39.28	128-10½	
3. Nicolaos Georgantas	GRE	37.68	123-7½	
4. John Flanagan	USA	36.14	118-7	
5. John Biller	USA	—	—	
6. James Mitchell	USA	—	—	

Sheridan and Rose finished in a tie, so, for the only time in Olympic history, a throw-off was held to determine first place. Each man was given three throws. Sheridan won by about five feet.

1906 Athens C: 21, N: 9, D: 4.25. WR: 42.14, 138-3 (Martin Sheridan)

| | | | FT.- | |
		M	IN.	
1. Martin Sheridan	USA	41.46	136-0	
2. Nicolaos Georgantas	GRE	38.06	124-10	
3. Werner Järvinen	FIN	36.82	120-9	
4. Eric Lemming	SWE	35.62	116-10	
5. André Tison	FRA	34.81	114-2	

In 1906, Martin Sheridan competed in seven events. He won the discus and the shot put; finished second in the stone throw, the standing high jump, and standing long jump; and fourth in the Greek-style discus throw. He tried to take part in the pentathlon, but had to withdraw after the first event because of a knee injury.

1908 London C: 41, N: 11, D: 7.16. WR: 42.63, 139-10½ (Martin Sheridan)

| | | | FT.- | |
		M	IN.	
1. Martin Sheridan	USA	40.89	134-2	OR
2. Merritt Giffin	USA	40.70	133-6	
3. Marquis Horr	USA	39.44	129-5	
4. Werner Järvinen	FIN	39.42	129-4	
5. Arthur Dearborn	USA	38.52	126-4	
6. György Luntzer	HUN	38.34	125-9	
7. André Tison	FRA	38.30	125-8	
8. Wilbur Burroughs	USA	37.42	122-9	

Competing in the 1904, 1906, and 1908 Games, Irish-born policeman Martin Sheridan won five gold medals and four silver. He died of pneumonia on March 27, 1918, at the age of 37.

1912 Stockholm C: 40, N: 15, D: 7.12. WR: 47.58, 156-1 (James Duncan)

| | | | FT.- | |
		M	IN.	
1. Armas Taipale	FIN	45.21	148-3	OR
2. Richard Byrd	USA	42.32	138-10	
3. James Duncan	USA	42.28	138-8	
4. Elmer Niklander	FIN	42.09	138-1	
5. Hans Tronner	AUS	41.24	135-4	
6. Arlie Mucks	USA	40.93	134-3	
7. George Philbrook	USA	40.92	134-2½	
8. Emil Magnusson	SWE	39.91	130-11	

1920 Antwerp C: 16, N: 8, D: 8.22. WR: 47.58, 156-1 (James Duncan)

| | | | FT.- | |
		M	IN.	
1. Elmer Niklander	FIN	44.685	146-7	
2. Armas Taipale	FIN	44.19	145-0	
3. Augustus Pope	USA	42.13	138-2	
4. Edvin Zallhagen	SWE	41.07	134-9	
5. Kenneth Bartlett	USA	40.875	134-1	
6. Allan Eriksson	SWE	39.41	129-3	
7. Valther Jensen	DEN	38.23	125-5	
8. Frans "Ville" Pörhölä	FIN	38.19	125-3	

1924 Paris C: 32, N: 18, D: 7.13. WR: 47.58, 156-1 (James Duncan)

		FT.-		
		M	IN.	
1. L. Clarence "Bud" Houser	USA	46.15	151-4	OR
2. Vilho Niittymaa	FIN	44.95	147-5	
3. Thomas Lieb	USA	44.83	147-0	
4. Augustus Pope	USA	44.42	145-9	
5. Ketil Askildt	NOR	43.40	142-5	
6. Glenn Hartranft	USA	42.49	139-4	
7. Elmer Niklander	FIN	42.09	138-1	
8. Heikki Malmivirta	FIN	41.16	135-0	

Bud Houser also won the shot put five days later. He was the last athlete to achieve such a double in the Olympics.

1928 Amsterdam C: 34, N: 19, D: 8.1. WR: 48.20, 158-2 (L. Clarence "Bud" Houser)

		FT.-		
		M	IN.	
1. L. Clarence "Bud" Houser	USA	47.32	155-3	OR
2. L. Antero Kivi	FIN	47.23	154-11	
3. James Corson	USA	47.10	154-6	
4. Harald Stenerud	NOR	45.80	150-3	
5. John Anderson	USA	44.87	147-2	
6. Eino Kenttä	FIN	44.17	144-10	
7. Ernst Paulus	GER	44.15	144-9	
8. Johan Trandem	NOR	43.97	144-3	

1932 Los Angeles C: 18, N: 11, D: 8.3. WR: 51.73, 169-9 (Paul Jessup)

		FT.-		
		M	IN.	
1. John Anderson	USA	49.49	162-4	OR
2. Henri Jean Laborde	USA	48.47	159-0	
3. Paul Winter	FRA	47.85	156-11	
4. Jules Noël	FRA	47.74	156-7	
5. István Donogán	HUN	47.08	154-5	
6. Endre Madarász	HUN	46.52	152-7	
7. Kalevi Kotkas	FIN	45.87	150-5	
8. Paul Jessup	USA	45.25	148-5	

Two of the favorites, József Remecz of Hungary and Paul Jessup, the 6-foot 7-inch world record holder, failed to qualify for the final round of six. But the final competition was still hotly contested, as Anderson and Laborde traded the lead, with Anderson breaking the previous Olympic record four times in six throws. The Americans may have won the medals, but it was the fourth-place finisher, Jules Noël, who made the news. Because the 1932 Olympics were held in the United States during Prohibition, the French team had to receive special permission to import several thousand bottles of wine into the United States. The French successfully argued that although alcohol might be illegal in the United States, it was an essential part of the diet of many of the French athletes.

Evidently, Jules Noël was one of those athletes, as he caused the American track and field officials great con-sternation during the competition by making periodic visits to the dark tunnel that joined the field to the locker rooms. There he swigged champagne with his compatriots.

On his fourth attempt, Noël lofted a great throw that appeared to land just beyond the flag that marked Anderson's first-place effort. Unfortunately, every one of the officials in charge of the discus was, at that moment, distracted by the tense proceedings of the pole vault, taking place nearby, so none of them saw where Noël's discus had landed. Embarrassed by this blunder, they awarded Noël an extra throw in addition to the two that he still had coming. However, the Frenchman was unable to come up with another big throw and he was forced to return home without a medal.

1936 Berlin C: 31, N: 17, D: 8.5. WR: 53.10, 174-2 (Willy Schröder)

		FT.-		
		M	IN.	
1. W. Kenneth Carpenter	USA	50.48	165-7	OR
2. Gordon Dunn	USA	49.36	161-11	
3. Giorgio Oberweger	ITA	49.23	161-6	
4. Reidar Sörlie	NOR	48.77	160-0	
5. Willy Schröder	GER	47.93	157-3	
6. Nicolaos Syllas	GRE	47.75	156-7	
7. Gunnar Bergh	SWE	47.22	154-11	
8. Åke Hedvall	SWE	46.20	151-7	

The two favorites, Harald Andersson of Sweden and Willy Schröder of Germany, were unable to rise to the occasion. Andersson, hampered by injury, failed to qualify for the semifinals, while Schröder only made it to the final group of six by winning a throw-off against Bergh. Carpenter overhauled Dunn and Oberweger with his next to last attempt.

1948 London C: 28, N: 18, D: 8.2. WR: 54.93, 180-3 (Robert Fitch)

		FT.-		
		M	IN.	
1. Adolfo Consolini	ITA	52.78	173-2	OR
2. Giuseppe Tosi	ITA	51.78	169-10	
3. Fortune Gordien	USA	50.77	166-6	
4. Ivar Ramstad	NOR	49.21	161-5	
5. Ferenc Klics	HUN	48.21	158-2	
6. Veikko Nyqvist	FIN	47.33	155-3	
7. Nicolaos Syllas	GRE	47.25	155-0	
8. Stein Johnson	NOR	46.54	152-8	

Adolfo Consolini held the world record from October 1941 until June 1948. Two months after earning the Olympic gold medal, he regained the world record.

1952 Helsinki C: 32, N: 20, D: 7.22. WR: 56.97, 186-11 (Fortune Gordien)

		FT.-		
		M	IN.	
1. Sim Iness	USA	55.03	180-6	OR
2. Adolfo Consolini	ITA	53.78	176-5	

3. James Dillion	USA	53.28	174-10
4. Fortune Gordien	USA	52.66	172-9
5. Ferenc Klics	HUN	51.13	167-9
6. Otto Grigalka	SOV	50.71	166-4
7. Roland Nilsson	SWE	50.06	164-3
8. Giuseppe Tosi	ITA	49.03	160-10

Sim Iness of Tulare, California, bettered Consolini's Olympic record with all six of his throws in the final. Nicolaos Syllas of Greece, who had finished sixth in 1936, was still able to place ninth 16 years later.

1956 Melbourne C: 20, N: 15, D: 11.27. WR: 59.28, 194-6 (Fortune Gordien)

			FT.-	
		M	IN.	
1. Alfred Oerter	USA	56.36	184-11	OR
2. Fortune Gordien	USA	54.81	179-9	
3. Desmond Koch	USA	54.40	178-6	
4. Mark Pharaoh	GBR	54.27	178-0	
5. Otto Grigalka	SOV	52.37	171-9	
6. Adolfo Consolini	ITA	52.21	171-3	
7. Ferenc Klics	HUN	51.82	170-0	
8. Dako Radosević	YUG	51.69	169-7	

Twenty-year-old Al Oerter of West Babylon, New York, watched the favorites, Adolfo Consolini and Fortune Gordien, make their first-round throws. When his turn came, he felt "keyed up" and "inspired" and let loose the best throw of his career—184 feet 11 inches. No one else came within five feet as Oerter ended up with the three longest throws of the competition. On the victory rostrum he suddenly realized that he had actually won. His knees buckled and he almost fell. As it turned out, in the years to come Al Oerter would have plenty of opportunities to get used to standing on the gold medal platform at Olympic medal ceremonies.

1960 Rome C: 35, N: 22, D: 9.7. WR: 59.91, 196-6 (Edmund Piątkowski, Richard "Rink" Babka)

			FT.-	
		M	IN.	
1. Alfred Oerter	USA	59.18	194-2	OR
2. Richard "Rink" Babka	USA	58.02	190-4	
3. Richard Cochran	USA	57.16	187-6	
4. József Szécsényi	HUN	55.79	183-0	
5. Edmund Piątkowski	POL	55.12	180-10	
6. Viktor Kompaniyets	SOV/UKR	55.06	180-8	
7. Carmelo Rado	ITA	54.00	177-2	
8. Kim Bukhantsev	SOV/RUS	53.61	175-10	

In 1957 Al Oerter was involved in a near-fatal car crash, but he recovered fully and was back in shape before long. Then, at the U.S. Olympic trials, he suffered his first defeat in over two years when he lost to giant Rink Babka. Oerter was still considered a slight favorite at the Olympics, but he was definitely under great pressure. While warming up for the qualifying round, he casually threw the discus beyond the world record marker and then qualified with an Olympic record of 191 feet 8

inches. But the day of the final he was "so tense I could barely throw." Babka led off with a toss of 190 feet 4 inches. Oerter followed with 189 feet 1 inch, but couldn't get closer over the next three rounds. As Oerter prepared for his fifth throw, Babka told him that he seemed to be carrying his left arm too low as he spun. Oerter made the necessary adjustment and threw his discus 194 feet 2 inches—a personal record. He thanked Babka and wished him luck on his last throw, but Babka fell short and settled for the silver medal.

1964 Tokyo C: 28, N: 21, D: 10.15. WR: 64.54, 211-9 (Ludvik Daněk)

			FT.-	
		M	IN.	
1. Alfred Oerter	USA	61.00	200-1	OR
2. Ludvik Daněk	CZE	60.52	198-7	
3. David Weill	USA	59.49	195-2	
4. L. Jay Silvester	USA	59.09	193-10	
5. József Szécsényi	HUN	57.23	187-9	
6. Zenon Begier	POL	57.06	187-2	
7. Edmund Piątkowski	POL	55.81	183-1	
8. Vladimir Trusenev	SOV/RUS	54.78	179-9	

On May 18, 1962, Al Oerter became the first discus thrower to break officially the 200-foot barrier, with a throw of 200 feet 5 inches. Surprisingly, it was his first world record. It lasted only 17 days, when it was broken by Vladimir Trusenev. But 27 days later Oerter had the record back again.

In 1964, however, Oerter knew that he would be in for a real struggle if he wanted to win a third gold medal. Not only did he have to face current world record holder Ludvik Daněk, who had won 45 straight competitions, but he had also been suffering for quite some time from a chronic cervical disc injury, which caused him to wear a neck harness. As if that wasn't trouble enough, Oerter

Al Oerter, the only athlete ever to win the same Olympic track and field event four straight times. He earned four gold medals in the discus throw, in 1956, 1960, 1964, and 1968.

tore the cartilage in his lower ribs while practicing in Tokyo less than a week before the competition. Doctors advised him to rest for six weeks, but the day of the preliminary round, he showed up anyway, shot up with novocaine and wrapped with ice packs and tape. With his first throw Oerter set an Olympic record of 198 feet 8 inches.

Ludvik Daněk opened the final at 195 feet 11 inches. Before the competition, Al Oerter had told a fellow athlete, "If I don't do it on the first throw, I won't be able to do it at all." But his first attempt only went 189 feet 1 inch. After four rounds Oerter was in third place behind Daněk and David Weill. Then, with his fifth throw, Oerter gave it everything he had. While he doubled over in pain, his discus sailed 200 feet 1 inch to set another Olympic record and earn Oerter a third gold medal.

1968 Mexico City C: 27, N: 19, D: 10.15. WR: 68.40, 224-5 (L. Jay Silvester)

			M	FT.-IN.	
1.	Alfred Oerter	USA	64.78	212-6	OR
2.	Lothar Milde	GDR	63.08	206-11	
3.	Ludvik Daněk	CZE	62.92	206-5	
4.	Hartmut Losch	GDR	62.12	203-10	
5.	L. Jay Silvester	USA	61.78	202-8	
6.	Gary Carlsen	USA	59.46	195-1	
7.	Edmund Piątkowski	POL	59.40	194-10	
8.	Björn Rickard Bruch	SWE	59.28	194-6	

Jay Silvester, the 31-year-old world record holder, was the favorite in Mexico City. And yet, one couldn't help but wonder if Al Oerter might pull off one more miracle. Silvester dampened such speculations in the qualifying round by opening up with an Olympic record of 207 feet 10 inches, 16½ feet less than his own best, but several inches better than anything Oerter had ever done.

The final was delayed an hour because of rain, and this seemed to upset Silvester in particular. Lothar Milde took the first-round lead with a throw of 204 feet 10 inches and then improved to 206 feet 11 inches with his second attempt. The third round began with Oerter in fourth place, behind Milde, Losch, and Silvester. But, as if out of a fairy tale, the incomparable Oerter uncorked a throw of 212 feet 6 inches—five feet farther than he had ever thrown before. The rest of the finalists were demoralized, particularly Silvester, who fouled three times in a row. Oerter, meanwhile, added throws of 212 feet 5 inches and 210 feet 1 inch. Al Oerter had become the first track and field athlete to win four gold medals in the same event.

Oerter, after throwing the discus 33,000 times, didn't take part in the 1972 or 1976 Olympics, but then he came out of retirement to try out for the 1980 U.S. team. At the age of 43, he finished fourth at the U.S. Olympic trials, which were held after the anti-Soviet boycott had been declared. But who knows, if the top three had really been assured of going to Moscow instead of settling for

symbolic honors, Al Oerter, the ultimate clutch performer, just might have qualified after all.

1972 Munich C: 29, N: 19, D: 9.2. WR: 68.40, 224-5 (L. Jay Silvester, Björn Rickard Bruch)

			M	FT.-IN.
1.	Ludvik Daněk	CZE	64.40	211-3
2.	L. Jay Silvester	USA	63.50	208-4
3.	Björn Rickard Bruch	SWE	63.40	208-0
4.	John Powell	USA	62.82	206-1
5.	Géza Fejér	HUN	62.62	205-5
6.	Detlef Thorith	GDR	62.42	204-9
7.	Ferenc Tégla	HUN	60.60	198-10
8.	Tim Vollmer	USA	60.24	197-8

With Al Oerter gone, Ludvik Daněk and Jay Silvester, both 35 years old, could finally relax and get down to the business of winning a gold medal. They had previously met 24 times, with Daněk finishing ahead 12 times and Silvester 12 times. In Munich they also had to contend with high-strung but increasingly consistent Ricky Bruch.

Daněk led the qualifying round with an impressive throw of 211 feet. In the final, Géza Fejér took the first-round lead at 205 feet 1 inch. John Powell moved ahead in the second-round at 206 feet 1 inch, and then Silvester took over at the halfway mark with 208 feet 4 inches. With one round to go, the order was Silvester, Bruch, Powell, Fejér, and Daněk, who hadn't come within five feet of his qualifying toss. Since no Olympic discus contest had been won in the final round since 1896, it seemed a good bet that Jay Silvester was on the verge of victory. But Daněk, who had enlisted the aid of a psychologist to help him prepare for just such last-ditch situations, broke tradition and won with a final throw of 211 feet 3 inches.

1976 Montreal C: 30, N: 20, D: 7.25. WR: 70.86, 232-6 (Maurice "Mac" Wilkins)

			M	FT.-IN.
1.	Maurice "Mac" Wilkins	USA	67.50	221-5
2.	Wolfgang Schmidt	GDR	66.22	217-3
3.	John Powell	USA	65.70	215-7
4.	Norbert Thiede	GDR	64.30	210-11
5.	Siegfried Pachale	GDR	64.24	210-9
6.	Pentti Kahma	FIN	63.12	207-1
7.	Knut Hjeltnes	NOR	63.06	206-11
8.	L. Jay Silvester	USA	61.98	203-4

With his first and only throw of the preliminary round, Mac Wilkins, a 25-year-old schoolteacher from Oregon, set an Olympic record of 224 feet. The next day, his second-round throw of 221 feet 5 inches put a quick end to any doubt as to who would win the final. Wilkins was sharply criticized by the U.S. press for congratulating East German silver medalist Wolfgang Schmidt, with whom he had become quite friendly, while ignoring American bronze medalist John Powell, with whom he did not get along. The criticism seemed ironic in view of the concern that was simultaneously being expressed about excessive nationalism in the Olympics.

Beginning in 1982, Schmidt was imprisoned for 15 months for "antisocial behavior" because of his opposition to Communism and his friendships with Western athletes. He was unable to return to competition until 1988, after he was given permission to emigrate to West Germany. He placed fourth at the 1991 world championships.

1980 Moscow C: 18, N: 12, D: 7.28. WR: 71.16, 233-5 (Wolfgang Schmidt)

			FT.-
		M	IN.
1. Viktor Rashchupkin	SOV/RUS	66.64	218-8
2. Imrich Bugár	CZE/SLV	66.38	217-9
3. Luis Delis Fournier	CUB	66.32	217-7
4. Wolfgang Schmidt	GDR	65.64	215-4
5. Yuri Dumchev	SOV/RUS	65.58	215-2
6. Ihor Dugynets	SOV/UKR	64.04	210-1
7. Emil Vladimirov	BUL	63.18	207-3
8. Velko Velev	BUL	63.04	206-10

Conspicuously missing because of the anti-Soviet boycott were Knut Hjeltnes of Norway and Mac Wilkins, John Powell, and Ben Plucknett, each of whom had to throw over 223 feet just to make the U.S. team. With these leading contenders absent, Wolfgang Schmidt seemed a sure bet for the gold medal, but a foot injury upset his performance and he had to settle for fourth place. The first-round lead in the final went to Imrich Bugár at 213 feet 8 inches. The lead changed hands four more times before Rashchupkin moved from fourth place to first with his gold-medal-winning fourth-round throw. His pre-Olympic best had only been 216 feet 6 inches. The contest ended in controversy, as many observers felt that Luis Delis' final throw had been marked about a foot short, keeping him from a silver medal or maybe even a gold.

1984 Los Angeles C: 20, N: 14, D: 8.10. WR: 71.86, 235-9 (Yuri Dumchev)

			FT.-
		M	IN.
1. Rolf Danneberg	GER	66.60	218-6
2. Maurice "Mac" Wilkins	USA	66.30	217-6
3. John Powell	USA	65.46	214-9
4. Knut Hjeltnes	NOR	65.28	214-2
5. Arthur Burns	USA	64.98	213-2
6. Alwin Wagner	GER	64.72	212-4
7. Luciano Zerbini	ITA	63.50	208-4
8. Stefan Fernholm	SWE	63.22	207-5

With preboycott favorites Luis Delis and Imrich Bugár among the missing, a U.S. sweep seemed a distinct possibility. Olympic record holder Mac Wilkins took the early lead at 216 feet 5 inches, but in the fourth round, unheralded Rolf Danneberg, a bearded, 6-foot 6-inch unemployed schoolteacher, unleashed a toss of 218 feet 6 inches. Wilkins improved by a foot in the fifth round but could come no closer. The 31-year-old Danneberg, who

wore dark glasses while competing, was the least-expected track and field winner of the 1984 Olympics.

1988 Seoul C: 29, N: 20, D: 10.1. WR: 74.08, 243-0 (Jürgen Schult)

			FT.-	
		M	IN.	
1. Jürgen Schult	GDR	68.82	225-9	OR
2. Romas Ubartas	SOV/LIT	67.48	221-5	
3. Rolf Danneberg	GER	67.38	221-1	
4. Yuri Dumchev	SOV/RUS	66.42	217-11	
5. Maurice "Mac" Wilkins	USA	65.90	216-2	
6. Gejza Valent	CZE	65.80	215-10	
7. Knut Hjeltnes	NOR	64.94	213-1	
8. Alois Hannecker	GER	63.28	207-7	

World champion and world record holder Jürgen Schult earned the gold medal with his first throw. He also recorded the three next best throws of the competition. Dumchev held second place until the fifth round, when he was passed by Danneberg. But it was Lithuanian Ubartas who grabbed the silver medal with his final attempt.

1992 Barcelona C: 32, N: 24, D: 8.5. WR: 74.08, 243-0 (Jürgen Schult)

			FT.-
		M	IN.
1. Romas Ubartas	LIT	65.12	213-8
2. Jürgen Schult	GER	64.94	213-1
3. Roberto Moya Sandoval	CUB	64.12	210-4
4. Costel Grasu	ROM	62.86	206-3
5. Attila Horváth	HUN	62.82	206-1
6. Juan Martínez	CUB	62.64	205-7
7. Dmitri Kovtsun	UKR	62.04	203-6
8. Dmitri Shevchenko	RUS	61.78	202-8

Romas Ubartas led the qualifying round with a toss of 216 feet 9 inches. Jürgen Schult took the first-round lead in the final at 210 feet 10 inches. Ubartas moved ahead in round three with a throw of 211 feet 2 inches. The competition came to a head in the fifth round. First Schult hit 213 feet 1 inch, then Ubartas came right back with a throw of 213 feet 8 inches that held up for the win. The 6-foot 7½-inch, 270-pound Ubartas was Lithuania's first Olympic champion. He had refused to take part in the 1991 world championships rather than represent the Soviet Union, which then collapsed, allowing Lithuania to recapture its independence. Ubartas' stint as a national hero was short-lived—in 1993 he tested positive for anabolic steroids at the world championships in Stuttgart and was slapped with a four-year suspension.

HAMMER THROW

The hammer is a 16-pound metal sphere attached to a grip by means of a spring steel wire not longer than 3 feet 11¾ inches (121.5 centimeters). It is thrown from a circle with a diameter of 2.135 meters (7 feet). Most throwers spin around three or four times before releasing the implement. This potentially dangerous sport appears to have had it origins in the practice of sledgehammer throwing in 15th- and 16th-century England and Scotland.

1896 not held

1900 Paris C: 5, N: 2, D: 7.16. WR: 51.105, 167-8 (John Flanagan)

		M	FT.-IN.	
1.	John Flanagan	USA	49.73	163-1
2.	Thomas Truxtun Hare	USA	49.13	161-2
3.	Josiah McCracken	USA	42.46	139-4
4.	Eric Lemming	SWE	—	—
5.	Karl Gustaf Staaf	SWE	—	—

Irish-born John Flanagan emigrated to the United States in 1896 and became a policeman in New York City. Truxtun Hare was a four-time All-American football selection from the University of Pennsylvania.

1904 St. Louis C: 6, N: 1, D: 8.29. WR: 52.705, 172-11 (John Flanagan)

			M	FT.-IN.	
1.	John Flanagan	USA	51.23	168-1	OR
2.	John DeWitt	USA	50.26	164-11	
3.	Ralph Rose	USA	45.73	150-0	
4.	Charles Chadwick	USA	42.78	140-4	
5.	James Mitchel	USA	—	—	
6.	Albert Johnson	USA	—	—	

1906 not held

1908 London C: 18, N: 8, D: 7.14. WR: 53.35, 175-0 (Matthew McGrath)

			M	FT.-IN.	
1.	John Flanagan	USA	51.92	170-4	OR
2.	Matthew McGrath	USA	51.18	167-11	
3.	Cornelius Walsh	USA	48.51	159-1	
4.	Thomas Nicolson	GBR	48.09	157-9	
5.	Lee James Talbott	USA	47.86	157-0	
6.	Marquis Horr	USA	46.94	154-0	
7.	Simon Gillis	USA	45.58	149-6	
8.	Eric Lemming	SWE	43.06	141-3	

With his last attempt, Flanagan won his third straight hammer throw gold medal. On July 24, 1909, Flanagan threw the hammer 184 feet 4 inches to become the oldest world record breaker in the history of track and field. He was 41 years, 196 days old. He returned to Ireland in 1911 and lived there until his death in 1938.

1912 Stockholm C: 14, N: 4, D: 7.14. WR: 57.10, 187-4 (Matthew McGrath)

			M	FT.-IN.	
1.	Matthew McGrath	USA	54.74	179-7	OR
2.	Duncan Gillis	CAN	48.39	158-9	

			M	FT.-IN.
3.	Clarence Childs	USA	48.17	158-0
4.	Robert Olsson	SWE	46.50	152-7
5.	Carl Johan Lind	SWE	45.61	149-7
6.	Denis Carey	GBR	43.78	143-8
7.	Nils Linde	SWE	43.32	142-1
8.	Carl Jahnzon	SWE	42.58	139-8

Irish-American policeman Matt McGrath was truly in a class by himself in Stockholm. The *shortest* of his six throws—173 feet 4 inches—was almost 15 feet longer than anyone else's *longest* throw. McGrath's Olympic record held up for 24 years.

1920 Antwerp C: 12, N: 5, D: 8.18. WR: 57.77, 189-6 (Patrick Ryan)

			M	FT.-IN.
1.	Patrick Ryan	USA	52.875	173-5
2.	Carl Johan Lind	SWE	48.43	158-10
3.	Basil Bennet	USA	48.25	158-3
4.	Malcom Svensson	SWE	47.29	155-1
5.	Matthew McGrath	USA	46.67	153-1
6.	Thomas Nicolson	GBR	45.70	149-11
7.	Nils Linde	SWE	44.885	147-3
8.	James McEachern	USA	44.70	146-8

Pat Ryan emigrated from Ireland to New York in 1910. On August 17, 1913, he set a world record of 189 feet 6 inches that would last for 25 years. It remained as a U.S. record until 1953. In Antwerp, Ryan was unchallenged, particularly after Matt McGrath injured his knee and was forced to withdraw after only two throws.

1924 Paris C: 15, N: 10, D: 7.10. WR: 57.77, 189-6 (Patrick Ryan)

			M	FT.-IN.
1.	Frederick Tootell	USA	53.295	174-10
2.	Matthew McGrath	USA	50.84	166-9
3.	Malcolm Nokes	GBR	48.875	160-4
4.	Erik Eriksson	FIN	48.74	159-11
5.	Ossian Skiöld	SWE	45.285	148-7
6.	James McEachern	USA	45.225	148-4
7.	Carl Johan Lind	SWE	44.785	146-11
8.	John Murdock	CAN	42.48	139-4

Fred Tootell was the first American-born winner of the hammer throw. Silver medalist Matt McGrath was 45 years old.

1928 Amsterdam C: 16, N: 11, D: 7.30. WR: 57.77, 189-6 (Patrick Ryan)

			M	FT.-IN.
1.	Patrick O'Callaghan	IRL	51.39	168-7
2.	Ossian Skiöld	SWE	51.29	168-3
3.	Edmund Black	USA	49.03	160-10
4.	Armando Poggioli	ITA	48.37	158.8
5.	Donald Gwinn	USA	47.15	154-8
6.	Frank Connor	USA	46.75	153-4

7. Federico Kleger	ARG	46.60	152-11
8. Ricardo Bayer	CHI	46.34	152-0

Pat O'Callaghan, of Derrygallon in North Cork, had only been competing for 13 months when he won an Olympic gold medal with his next-to-last throw, improving his personal best by 20 inches.

1932 Los Angeles C: 14, N: 9, D: 8.1. WR: 57.77, 189-6 (Patrick Ryan)

		FT.-	
		M	IN.
1. Patrick O'Callaghan	IRL	53.92	176-11
2. Frans "Ville" Pörhölä	FIN	52.27	171-6
3. Peter Zaremba	USA	50.33	165-1
4. Ossian Skiöld	SWE	49.24	161-6
5. Grant McDougall	USA	49.12	161-2
6. Federico Kleger	ARG	48.33	158-7
7. Gunnar Jansson	SWE	47.79	156-9
8. Armando Poggioli	ITA	46.90	153-10

Ville Pörhölä, who had won the shot put gold medal 12 years earlier in Antwerp, led after five rounds. However, defending champion Dr. Pat O'Callaghan, who spent every free moment between throws filing down the spikes on his shoes, came through with a dramatic victory in his final attempt.

1936 Berlin C: 27, N: 16, D: 8.3. WR: 57.77, 189-6 (Patrick Ryan)

		FT.-		
		M	IN.	
1. Karl Hein	GER	56.49	185-4	OR
2. Erwin Blask	GER	55.04	180-7	
3. O. Fred Warngård	SWE	54.83	179-10	
4. Gustaf Alfons Koutonen	FIN	51.90	170-3	
5. William Rowe	USA	51.66	169-6	
6. Donald Favor	USA	51.01	167-4	
7. Bernhard Greulich	GER	50.61	166-0	
8. Koit Annamaa	EST	50.46	165-7	

Hein, a 28-year-old Hamburg carpenter, scored an upset victory with his final throw. All three medalists achieved personal records.

1948 London C: 24, N: 16, D: 7.31. WR: 59.02, 193-8 (Imre Németh)

		FT.-	
		M	IN.
1. Imre Németh	HUN	56.07	183-11
2. Ivan Gubijan	YUG	54.27	178-0
3. Robert Bennett	USA	53.73	176-3
4. Samuel Felton	USA	53.66	176-0
5. Lauri Tamminen	FIN	53.08	174-2
6. Bo Ericson	SWE	52.98	173-10
7. Teseo Taddia	ITA	51.74	169-9
8. Einar Söderqvist	SWE	51.48	168-11

Imre Németh, who broke Erwin Blask's ten-year-old world record two weeks before the Olympics began, weighed a mere 184 pounds.

1952 Helsinki C: 33, N: 18, D: 7.24. WR: 59.88, 196-5 (Imre Németh)

		FT.-		
		M	IN.	
1. József Csérmák	HUN	60.34	197-11	WR
2. Karl Storch	GER	58.86	193-1	
3. Imre Németh	HUN	57.74	189-5	
4. Jiři Dadák	CZE	56.80	186-4	
5. Mykola Redkin	SOV/UKR	56.55	185-6	
6. Karl Wolf	GER	56.49	185-4	
7. Sverre Strandli	NOR	56.36	184-11	
8. Georgi Dybenko	SOV	55.03	180-6	

Twenty-year-old József Csérmák, a pupil of defending champion Imre Németh, broke the 60-meter barrier for the first time with his third throw. Silver medalist Karl Storch, who had first cleared 190 feet in 1939, was 38 years old.

1956 Melbourne C: 22, N: 14, D: 11.24. WR: 68.54, 224-10 (Harold Connolly)

		FT.-		
		M	IN.	
1. Harold Connolly	USA	63.19	207-3	OR
2. Mikhail Krivonosov	SOV/BLR	63.03	206-9	
3. Anatoly Samotsvetov	SOV/RUS	62.56	205-3	
4. Albert Hall	USA	61.96	203-3	
5. József Csérmák	HUN	60.70	199-2	
6. Krešimir Račić	YUG	60.36	198-0	
7. Dmitri Yegorov	SOV	60.22	197-7	
8. Sverre Strandli	NOR	59.21	194-3	

For several months, Harold Connolly and Mikhail Krivonosov had been carrying on a long-distance duel between Boston and Minsk, breaking each other's most recent records. Krivonosov was a Belorussian who attracted the attention of athletic coaches during a hand-grenade throwing contest. In 1952 he had hoped to go to the Helsinki Olympics as a discus thrower, but finished only fourth in the U.S.S.R. trials and failed to make the team. Two days later he qualified in the hammer throw instead. In Helsinki he fouled twice, fell once, and failed to register a valid throw. Concentrating on the hammer from then on, Krivonosov set his first world record in 1954. His sixth record, 220 feet 10 inches, was made on October 22, 1956. Eleven days later, Harold Connolly, whose left arm was withered as a result of an accident at birth, broke Krivonosov's record by four feet. Three weeks later the two rivals met at the Melbourne Olympics.

The first-round lead went to Siberia's Anatoly Samotsvetov at 203 feet 9 inches. Krivonosov moved ahead in the second round with a throw of 206 feet 8 inches. His last three attempts were all fouls. Hal Connolly, wearing ballet shoes to improve his footing, finally won the contest with a fifth-round heave of 207 feet 3 inches.

What gained Connolly international attention was not his gold medal but his Olympic Village romance with Czechoslovakian discus champion Olga Fikotová. After a great deal of pressure, the Iron Curtain was drawn

The romance of U.S. hammer thrower Harold Connolly and Czechoslovakian discus thrower Olga Fikotová caused an international incident in 1956. They are seen here in the Olympic Village.

open long enough for Olga and Harold to wed. Forty thousand well-wishers attended their civil ceremony in Prague, which was followed by two more services, one Catholic and one Protestant. The couple then settled in the United States. Harold eventually took part in four Olympics and Olga in five. After they divorced in 1973, Harold married three-time Olympian Pat Daniels. What few people knew about Connolly, because he tried to keep it hidden, was that his left arm was four inches shorter than his right and was dysfunctional.

1960 Rome C: 28, N: 18, D: 9.3. WR: 70.33, 230-9 (Harold Connolly)

| | | | FT.- | |
		M	IN.	
1. Vasily Rudenkov	SOV/BLR	67.10	220-2	OR
2. Gyula Zsivótzky	HUN	65.79	215-10	
3. Tadeusz Rut	POL	65.64	215-4	
4. John Lawlor	IRL	64.95	213-1	
5. Olgierd Cieply	POL	64.57	211-10	
6. Zvonko Bezjak	YUG	64.21	210-7	
7. Anatoly Samotsvetov	SOV/RUS	63.60	208-8	
8. Harold Connolly	USA	63.58	208-7	

Harold Connolly broke his own world record only two weeks before the Olympics began but was troubled by injury and finished a disappointing eighth in Rome. Meanwhile, metal worker Vasily Rudenkov set an Olympic record of 219 feet 10 inches in the qualifying round and then led the final from start to finish.

1964 Tokyo C: 24, N: 13, D: 10.18. WR: 70.66, 231-10 (Harold Connolly)

| | | | FT.- | |
		M	IN.	
1. Romuald Klim	SOV/BLR	69.74	228-10	OR
2. Gyula Zsivótzky	HUN	69.09	226-8	
3. Uwe Beyer	GER	68.09	223-4	
4. Yuri Nikulin	SOV/RUS	67.69	222-1	
5. Yuri Bakarinov	SOV/RUS	66.72	218-11	
6. Harold Connolly	USA	66.65	218-8	
7. Edward Burke	USA	65.66	215-5	
8. Olgierd Cieply	POL	64.82	212-8	

Romuald Klim, a 31-year-old from Belarus, won with his fourth throw.

1968 Mexico City C: 22, N: 12, D: 10.17. WR: 73.76, 242-0 (Gyula Zsivótsky)

| | | | FT.- | |
		M	IN.	
1. Gyula Zsivótzky	HUN	73.36	240-8	OR
2. Romuald Klim	SOV/BLR	73.28	240-5	
3. Lázár Lovász	HUN	69.78	228-11	
4. Takeo Sugawara	JPN	69.78	228-11	
5. Sándor Eckschmidt	HUN	69.46	227-11	
6. Gennady Kondrashov	SOV/RUS	69.08	226-8	
7. Reinhard Theimer	GDR	68.84	225-10	
8. Helmut Baumann	GDR	68.26	223-11	

On September 4, 1965, Gyula Zsivótzky threw the hammer 241 feet 11 inches to better the world record by a shocking 8 feet 2 inches. Three years later he bumped the record up an extra inch, but at the Olympics he was not the favorite. Romuald Klim, unbeaten in three years, had defeated Zsivótzky nine straight times. Zsivótzky seemed to be held back by a psychological barrier whenever he faced Klim, but he received a big boost when he threw 247 feet 1 inch in practice one week before the competition began.

Klim's first throw of the final was 237 feet, but Zsivótzky, throwing immediately after Klim, gained further confidence by recording 237 feet 9 inches with his second throw. However, the third round saw Klim take the lead at 238 feet 11 inches, while Zsivótzky could only respond with 238 feet, two inches less than the Olympic record he had set in the qualifying round the previous day. In the fourth round of the final, Klim reached 240 feet 5 inches, while Zsivótzky fouled. However, the Hungarian put it together with his next-to-last throw and won with 240 feet 8 inches.

Takeo Sugawara, the smallest man in the competition at 5 feet 8½ inches and 185 pounds, tied with Lázár Lovász, but Lovász was awarded the bronze medal because his second-best throw was one foot longer than Sugawara's.

1972 Munich C: 31, N: 18, D: 9.7. WR: 76.40, 250-8 (Walter Schmidt)

			FT.-		
			M	IN.	
1. Anatoly Bondarchuk	SOV/UKR		75.50	247-8	OR
2. Jochen Sachse	GDR		74.96	245-11	
3. Vasily Khmelevski	SOV/RUS		74.04	242.11	
4. Uwe Beyer	GER		71.52	234-8	
5. Gyula Zsivótzky	HUN		71.38	234-2	
6. Sándor Eckschmidt	HUN		71.20	233-7	
7. Edwin Klein	GER		71.14	233-5	
8. Shigenobu Murofushi	JPN		70.88	232-6	

The favorite, 32-year-old Anatoly Bondarchuk, settled matters early in the final with an opening throw of 247 feet 8 inches. He claimed to have thrown the hammer 100,000 times in the previous 13 years.

1976 Montreal C: 20, N: 13, D: 7.28. WR: 79.30, 260-2 (Walter Schmidt)

			FT.-		
			M	IN.	
1. Yuri Syedykh	SOV/RUS		77.52	254-4	OR
2. Aleksei Spiridonov	SOV/RUS		76.08	249-7	
3. Anatoly Bondarchuk	SOV/UKR		75.48	247-8	
4. Karl-Hans Riehm	GER		75.46	247-7	
5. Walter Schmidt	GER		74.72	245-2	
6. Jochen Sachse	GDR		74.30	243-9	
7. Christopher Black	GBR		73.18	240-1	
8. Edwin Klein	GER		71.34	234-1	

On May 19, 1975, Karl-Hans Riehm had a truly remarkable day. Competing at Rehlingen, he bettered the previous world record with all six of his throws, his best of the day being 257 feet 6 inches. Three months later, he lost the record to Walter Schmidt, who was famous for achieving his best performances at minor meets. In Montreal, Riehm led the qualifying round at 244 feet 3 inches, but in the final, he and Schmidt had to take a backseat to the Soviet trio. Yuri Syedykh, a 21-year-old student of Anatoly Bondarchuk, won the competition with his second throw. Syedykh was introduced to the sport that would become his specialty in an unusual way. When he was 12 years old he chased a soccer ball onto a field, not realizing that hammer throwers were practicing nearby. He came very close to being decapitated by a flying hammer. He lingered—at a respectful distance—long enough to become fascinated, then returned every day until he was allowed to join in.

1980 Moscow C: 17, N: 12, D: 7.31. WR: 81.66, 267-11 (Sergei Litvinov)

			FT.-		
			M	IN.	
1. Yuri Syedykh	SOV/RUS		81.80	268-4	WR
2. Sergei Litvinov	SOV/RUS		80.64	264-7	
3. Jüri Tamm	SOV/EST		78.96	259-1	
4. Roland Steuk	GDR		77.54	254-5	
5. Detlef Gerstenberg	GDR		74.60	244-9	
6. Emannouil Dulgherov	BUL		74.04	242-11	
7. Gianpaulo Urlando	ITA		73.90	242-5	
8. Ireneusz Golda	POL		73.74	241-11	

Unfortunately missing because of the anti-Soviet boycott was Karl-Hans Riehm, who threw 265 feet 1 inch the day before the Olympic final. Riehm was the only man capable of threatening the Soviets, who dominated hammer throwing so thoroughly that three of their team members set world records during one nine-day period. On May 16, 1980, Syedykh took the record away from Riehm with a throw of 263 feet 8 inches. Then Jüri Tamm entered the circle and threw 263 feet 9 inches. Not to be outdone, Syedykh countered with 264 feet 7 inches. Eight days later, Sergei Litvinov beat them both with a new record of 267 feet 11 inches.

In Moscow, Syedykh opened the Olympic final with a world record of 268 feet 4 inches. Litvinov's first throw gained him the silver medal. He followed with five straight fouls.

1984 Los Angeles C: 23, N: 13, D: 8.6. WR: 86.34, 283-3 (Yuri Syedykh)

			FT.-		
			M	IN.	
1. Juha Tiainen	FIN		78.08	256-2	
2. Karl-Hans Riehm	GER		77.98	255-10	
3. Klaus Ploghaus	GER		76.68	251-7	
4. Orlando Bianchini	ITA		75.94	249-2	
5. William Green	USA		75.60	248-0	
6. Harri Huhtala	FIN		75.28	247-0	
7. Walter Ciofani	FRA		73.46	241-0	
8. Robert Weir	GBR		72.62	238-3	

DISQ (Drugs): Gianpaolo Urlando (ITA) 75.96 249-3

On July 3, 1984, Yuri Syedykh added 7 feet 3 inches to Sergei Litvinov's world record. Sadly, the Soviet boycott prevented these two great champions from battling it out at the Olympics. Juha Tiainen, the only one of the top twelve ranked hammer throwers present in Los Angeles, won with his third-round throw. Fourth-place finisher Urlando was disqualified when his doping test registered positive for testosterone.

1988 Seoul C: 30, N: 16, D: 9.26. WR: 86.74, 284-7 (Yuri Syedykh)

			FT.-		
			M	IN.	
1. Sergei Litvinov	SOV/RUS		84.80	278-2	OR
2. Yuri Syedykh	SOV/RUS		83.76	274-10	
3. Jüri Tamm	SOV/EST		81.16	266-3	
4. Ralf Haber	GDR		80.44	263-11	
5. Heinz Weis	GER		79.16	259-8	
6. Tibor Gécsek	HUN		78.36	257-1	
7. Imre Szitás	HUN		77.04	252-9	
8. Ivan Tanev	BUL		76.08	249-7	

The three medalists from 1980 returned to the victory platform in 1988. Two-time world champion Sergei

Litvinov settled the competition with a first-round heave of 278 feet 1 inch, then added a slightly longer throw in the fifth round.

1992 Barcelona C: 27, N: 19, D: 8.2. WR: 86.74, 284-7 (Yuri Syedykh)

| | | | FT.- |
		M	IN.
1. Andrei Abduvaliyev	TJK	82.54	270-9
2. Igor Astapkovich	BLR	81.96	268-11
3. Igor Nikulin	RUS	81.38	267-0
4. Tibor Gécsek	HUN	77.78	255-2
5. Jüri Tamm	EST	77.52	254-4
6. Heinz Weis	GER	76.90	252-3
7. Lance Deal	USA	76.84	252-1
8. Sean Carlin	AUS	76.16	249-10

DISQ (Drugs): Jud Logan (USA) 79.00, 259-2

Astapkovich and Abduvaliyev faced each other nine times in 1992. Astapkovich won eight of those encounters, but the ninth happened to be the Olympics. Astapkovich was leading when Abduvaliyev let fly his winner in the fourth round. Bronze medalist Igor Nikulin was the son of Yuri Nikulin, who placed fourth in 1964. The fourth-place finisher in 1992, Jud Logan, tested positive for the recently banned steroid substitute Clenbuterol and was disqualified.

JAVELIN THROW

A javelin must weigh a minimum of 800 grams (1 pound 12¼ ounces) and measure between 2.60 meters (8 feet 6¼ inches) and 2.70 meters (8 feet 10¼ inches). The shaft may be either wood or metal. In 1986, the balance point and grip of the men's javelin was moved up 10 cm. and the tail was made more narrow. These modifications were instituted in response to the increased frequency of dangerously long throws. For a throw to be considered valid the pointed metal head must break the turf. The javelin is thrown on the run and must be released above the shoulder. The runway is between 30 meters (98 feet 5 inches) and 36.5 meters (119 feet 9 inches) long. Each competitor may place one or two markers along the runway to assist in his or her run-up. Spinning around before throwing is illegal, since this technique could seriously discourage spectators from coming anywhere near the part of the stadium where the javelin competition is taking place.

1896–1906 not held

1908 London C: 16, N: 6, D: 7.17. WR: 54.40, 178-6 (Eric Lemming)

| | | | FT.- |
		M	IN.
1. Eric Lemming	SWE	54.825	179-10	WR
2. Arne Halse	NOR	50.57	165-11
3. Otto Nilsson	SWE	47.105	154-6
4. Aarne Salovaara	FIN	45.89	150-6
5. Armas Pesonen	FIN	45.18	148-3
6. Juho Halme	FIN	44.96	147-6
7. Jalmari Sauli	FIN	—	—

Eric Lemming, a 6-foot 3-inch, 26-year-old Stockholm policeman, had dominated javelin throwing since 1899.

1912 Stockholm C: 25, N: 7, D: 7.6. WR: 58.27, 191-2 (Eric Lemming)

| | | | FT.- |
		M	IN.
1. Eric Lemming	SWE	60.64	198-11	WR
2. Julius Juho Saaristo	FIN	58.66	192-5
3. Mór Kóczán	HUN	55.50	182-1
4. Juho Halme	FIN	54.65	179-3
5. Väinö Siikaniemi	FIN	52.43	172-0
6. Richard Åbrink	SWE	52.20	171-3
7. Arne Halse	NOR	51.98	170-6
8. Jonni Myyrä	FIN	51.32	168-4

Lemming received a standing ovation from the hometown crowd after he made the world's first 60-meter throw. Three days later, while competing in the now discontinued combined left- and right-hand event, Juho Saaristo set a world record of 200 feet 1 inch using his right hand.

1920 Antwerp C: 25, N: 12, D: 8.15. WR: 66.10, 216-10 (Jonni Myyrä)

| | | | FT.- |
		M	IN.
1. Jonni Myyrä	FIN	65.78	215-10	OR
2. Urho Peltonen	FIN	63.605	208-8
3. Paavo Johansson-Jaale	FIN	63.095	207-0
4. Julius Juho Saaristo	FIN	62.395	204-9
5. Aleksander Klumberg-Kolmpere	EST	62.39	204-8
6. Gunnar Lindström	SWE	60.52	198-7

Eric Lemming of Sweden dominated the javelin throw from 1899 until 1912.

7. Milton Angier	USA	59.275	194-5
8. Erik Blomqvist	SWE	58.18	190-10

1924 Paris C: 30, N: 13, D: 8.15. WR: 66.10, 216-10 (Jonni Myyrä)

			FT.-
		M	IN.
1. Jonni Myyrä	FIN	62.96	206-7
2. Gunnar Lindström	SWE	60.92	199-10
3. Eugene Oberst	USA	58.35	191-5
4. Yrjö Ekqvist	FIN	57.56	188-10
5. William Neufeld	USA	56.96	186-10
6. Erik Blomqvist	SWE	56.85	186-6
7. Urho Peltonen	FIN	55.66	182-7
8. Paavo Jaale-Johansson	FIN	55.10	180-9

The 32-year-old Myyrä successfully defended his title. However, he lost his world record two months later, when Lindström threw 218 feet 7 inches.

1928 Amsterdam C: 28, N: 18, D: 8.2. WR: 69.88, 229-3 (Eino Penttilä)

			FT.-	
		M	IN.	
1. Erik Lundkvist	SWE	66.60	218-6	OR
2. Béla Szepes	HUN	65.26	214-1	
3. Olav Sunde	NOR	63.97	209-10	
4. Paavo Liettu	FIN	63.86	209-6	
5. W. Bruno Schlokat	GER	63.40	208-0	
6. Eino Penttilä	FIN	63.20	207-4	
7. Stanley Lay	NZE	62.89	206-3	
8. Johannes Meimer	EST	61.46	201-8	

On October 8, 1927, Eino Penttilä recorded a throw of 229 feet 3 inches to improve the world record by an impressive 10 feet 8 inches. In Amsterdam, however, Penttilä suffered from overtraining, the pressure of high expectations, and a sore foot, and was only able to finish sixth. The winner, sign painter Erik Lundkvist, went on to set a world record of 232 feet 11 inches two weeks later.

1932 Los Angeles C: 13, N: 7, D: 8.4. WR: 74.02, 242-10 (Matti Järvinen)

			FT.-	
		M	IN.	
1. Matti Järvinen	FIN	72.71	238-6	OR
2. Matti Sippala	FIN	69.80	229-0	
3. Eino Penttilä	FIN	68.70	225-5	
4. Gottfried Weimann	GER	68.18	223-8	
5. Lee Bartlett	USA	64.46	211-6	
6. Kenneth Churchill	USA	63.24	207-6	
7. Malcolm Metcalf	USA	61.89	203-0	
8. Kohsaku Sumiyoshi	JPN	61.14	200-7	

Three sons of Finland's first gold medal winner, Verner Järvinen, took part in the 1932 Olympics, but only the youngest, Matti, won a gold medal. Matti's first five throws were the best of the competition, and all of them bettered the previous Olympic record. Matti didn't bother to take off the trousers of his track suit until the contest was over and it was time for photographs to be

Matti Järvinen pretending to throw the javelin following his victory in 1932. He competed with his sweat pants on and only took them off to pose for photographers.

taken. Between 1930 and 1936 Matti Järvinen broke the javelin world record ten times and became known as "Mr. Javelin."

1936 Berlin C: 28, N: 19, D: 8.6. WR: 77.23, 253-4 (Matti Järvinen)

			FT.-
		M	IN.
1. Gerhard Stöck	GER	71.84	235-8
2. Yrjö Nikkanen	FIN	70.77	232-2
3. Kaarlo Kalervo Toivonen	FIN	70.72	232-0
4. Lennart Attervall	SWE	69.20	227-0
5. Matti Järvinen	FIN	69.18	227-0
6. Alton Terry	USA	67.15	220-4
7. Eugeniusz Lokajski	POL	66.39	217-9
8. József Várszegi	HUN	65.30	214-3

Gerhard Stöck, who had finished third in the shot put four days earlier, was in fifth place after four rounds. It was then that Adolf Hitler arrived in the stadium. With the crowd chanting, "Stöck, Stöck, don't be a 'wet blanket,' go ahead and finally throw 70 meters," Stöck unleashed a throw of almost 72 meters that turned out to be sufficient for the gold medal. Matti Järvinen, suffering from a back injury, was only able to place fifth.

1948 London C: 22, N: 15, D: 8.4. WR: 78.70, 258-2 (Yrjö Nikkanen)

			FT.-
		M	IN.
1. Kai Tapio Rautavaara	FIN	69.77	228-10
2. Steve Seymour	USA	67.56	221-8

3. József Várszegi	HUN	67.03	219-11
4. Pauli Vesterinen	FIN	65.89	216-2
5. Odd Maehlum	NOR	65.32	214-3
6. Martin Biles	USA	65.17	213-9
7. Mirko Vujacic	YUG	64.89	212-10
8. Robert Likens	USA	64.51	211-7

Marty Biles led the qualifying round with a throw of 222 feet, which would have been good enough for a silver medal if he had been able to repeat it in the final. Gold medal winner Tapio Rautavaara later became a successful archer, folksinger, and actor. While posing for a photograph, he fell and hit his head on a concrete floor; he died on September 25, 1979, at the age of 64.

1952 Helsinki C: 26, N: 16, D: 7.23. WR: 78.70, 258-2 (Yrjö Nikkanen)

		FT.-	
		M	IN.
1. Cyrus Young	USA	73.78	242-1	OR
2. William Miller	USA	72.46	237-9
3. Toivo Hyytiäinen	FIN	71.89	235-10
4. Viktor Tsybulenko	SOV/UKR	71.72	234-4
5. Branko Dangubič	YUG	70.55	231-5
6. Vladimir Kuznetsov	SOV/RUS	70.37	230-10
7. Ragnar Ericzon	SWE	69.04	226-6
8. Soini Nikkinen	FIN	68.80	225-9

The two American medalists presented an unusual contrast. Cy Young, who celebrated his 24th birthday by winning the gold medal, was 6 feet 5 inches, while Bill Miller was only 5 feet 9 inches. When a third American, ninth-place finisher Bud Held, broke Yrjö Nikkanen's 15-year-old world record in 1953, it looked like the United States had found itself another specialty. However, the expected U.S. dominance did not materialize.

1956 Melbourne C: 21, N: 12, D: 26.11. WR: 83.66, 274-6 (Janusz Sidlo)

		FT.-	
		M	IN.
1. Egil Danielsen	NOR	85.71	281-2	WR
2. Janusz Sidlo	POL	79.98	262-5
3. Viktor Tsybulenko	SOV/UKR	79.50	260-10
4. Herbert Koschel	GER	74.68	245-0
5. Jan Kopyto	POL	74.28	243-8
6. Giovanni Lievore	ITA	72.88	239-1
7. Michel Macquet	FRA	71.84	235-8
8. Aleksandr Gorshkov	SOV	70.32	230-8

Cy Young led the qualifying round with a throw of 245 feet 3 inches. After three rounds of the final, Sidlo was in first place, followed by Tsybulenko and Koschel. For his fourth throw, Tsybulenko abandoned the wooden javelin he had been using and picked up a steel one that had been made in Sweden. He immediately improved his standing by almost 15 feet. Egil Danielsen, who had won 36 consecutive meets but was only in sixth place, asked Tsybulenko if he could borrow his steel javelin. He then let loose an enormous throw that broke the world record

and almost landed on the runway of the pole vault. Danielsen danced around, hugging and kissing everyone in the area of the javelin competition, while Tsybulenko was left to laugh, shake his head, and marvel at the result of his good sportsmanship.

1960 Rome C: 28, N: 18, D: 9.8. WR: 86.04, 282-3 (Albert Cantello)

		FT.-	
		M	IN.
1. Viktor Tsybulenko	SOV/UKR	84.64	277-8
2. Walter Krüger	GDR	79.36	260-4
3. Gergely Kulcsár	HUN	78.57	257-9
4. Väinö Kuisma	FIN	78.40	257-3
5. Willy Rasmussen	NOR	78.36	257-1
6. Knut Fredriksson	SWE	78.33	256-11
7. Zbigniew Radziwonowicz	POL	77.30	253-7
8. Janusz Sidlo	POL	76.46	250-10

In 1960 the javelin throw turned out to be a strange contest. The preliminary round was led by Janusz Sidlo at 279 feet 4 inches and Al Cantello at 261 feet 6 inches. If Sidlo and Cantello had been able to reproduce their form in the final, they would have finished first and third. Instead, they ended up eighth and tenth. The preliminary round also saw the elimination of defending champion Egil Danielsen and Bill Alley of the United States, who had a pending (and subsequently never ratified) world record of 283 feet 8 inches. The final was settled early with Viktor Tsybulenko's first-round throw of 277 feet 8 inches. Gusty winds and rain disrupted the competition from the second round on, and no one, Tsybulenko included, was able to do better than 257 feet 1 inch after that.

1964 Tokyo C: 25, L: 15, D: 10.14. WR: 91.72, 300-11 (Terje Pedersen)

		FT.-	
		M	IN.
1. Pauli Nevala	FIN	82.66	271-2
2. Gergely Kulcsár	HUN	82.32	270-1
3. Jānis Lūsis	SOV/LAT	80.57	264-4
4. Janusz Sidlo	POL	80.17	263-0
5. Urs von Wartburg	SWI	78.72	258-3
6. Jorma Kinnunen	FIN	76.94	252-5
7. Rolf Herings	GER	74.72	245-2
8. Vladimir Kuznetsov	SOV/RUS	74.26	243-8

On September 2, 1964, Terje Pedersen shocked the track and field world with a monster throw of 300 feet 11 inches that bettered his own world record by 15 feet 1 inch. Yet six weeks later in Tokyo, he could do no better than 236 feet 6 inches, and failed to qualify for the final. The 1964 Olympic competition, like the one in 1960, was marred by wind and rain. Janusz Sidlo had the best throw of the first round of the final at 263 feet. Jānis Lūsis took the lead in the second round with a throw of 264 feet 4 inches. But the real action took place in the fourth round. Ever-consistent Gergely Kulcsár reached 270 feet

1 inch, only to be topped by unheralded Pauli Nevala at 271 feet 2 inches. Von Wartburg's final throw appeared good enough for a silver medal, but was declared invalid on the grounds that it landed incorrectly, a ruling that raised many eyebrows.

Finnish Olympic officials had been criticized for wasting their money sending Nevala to Tokyo, particularly after he had failed to win the national championship. "Even if I'm not the Finnish champion," Nevala commented, "at least I've won the Olympics."

1968 Mexico City C: 27, N: 18, D: 10.16. WR: 91.98, 301-9 (Jānis Lūsis)

			FT.-	
		M	IN.	
1. Jānis Lūsis	SOV/LAT	90.10	295-7	OR
2. Jorma Kinnunen	FIN	88.58	290-7	
3. Gergely Kulcsár	HUN	87.06	285-7	
4. Wladislaw Nikiciuk	POL	85.70	281-2	
5. Manfred Stolle	GDR	84.42	277-0	
6. Åke Nilsson	SWE	83.48	273-11	
7. Janusz Sidlo	POL	80.58	264-4	
8. Urs von Wartburg	SWI	80.56	264-4	

A surprising thing happened in the 1968 javelin competition: for the first time since 1932, it was won by the favorite. The first-round lead went to 5-foot 9-inch, 165-pound Jorma Kinnunen. Popular Jānis Lūsis of Latvia, who was married to Elvira Ozolina, winner of the 1960 women's javelin, edged ahead by four centimeters in the second round. In the fourth round, Gergely Kulcsár moved in front with a personal and Olympic record of 285 feet 7 inches. And so the situation stood with one round remaining: Kulcsár in first, followed by Lūsis and Kinnunen. Lūsis calmly took his spear in hand and made his last attempt his best—295 feet 7 inches. He had one more moment of concern when Kinnunen also came up with a clutch performance, 290 feet 7 inches, but the Finn had to be content with second place. Janusz Sidlo, competing in his fifth Olympics, finished a creditable seventh. Kinnunen's son, Kimmo, placed fourth in 1992 after winning the 1991 world championship.

1972 Munich C: 23, N: 15, D: 9.3. WR: 93.80, 307-9 (Jānis Lūsis)

			FT.-	
		M	IN.	
1. Klaus Wolfermann	GER	90.48	296-10	OR
2. Jānis Lūsis	SOV/LAT	90.46	296-9	
3. William Schmidt	USA	84.42	277-0	
4. Hannu Siitonen	FIN	84.32	276-8	
5. Björn Grimnes	NOR	83.08	272-7	
6. Jorma Kinnunen	FIN	82.08	269-3	
7. Miklos Németh	HUN	81.98	268-11	
8. Fredrick Luke	USA	80.06	262-8	

Jānis Lūsis dominated javelin throwing between Olympics. In 1972 no one came within 17 feet of his performance of the year until one week before the Munich

Games, when Klaus Wolfermann hit 296 feet 7 inches. In the Olympic final, Lūsis had the first big throw—291 feet 7 inches in the first round. He improved to 293 feet 9 inches with his third attempt. Wolfermann, cheered on by the German crowd, picked up steam in the fourth round with a throw of 290 feet. Then, in the fifth round, he caused the spectators to roar with excitement when he exploded for a personal best of 296 feet 10 inches. However, Jānis Lūsis still had one attempt left, and many remembered his dramatic last-round victory four years earlier. Sure enough, Lūsis let loose a big one. Wolfermann and his supporters waited anxiously for the measurement. And then it came—296 feet 9 inches. The two-centimeter difference is the smallest unit of measurement used in javelin competitions. One more inch and Lūsis would have won on the basis of a longer second throw.

When Jānis Lūsis was a little boy, he had been forced to watch the execution of his father by German soldiers. Yet as a grown man, he bore no grudge against the German people, and later became good friends with Klaus Wolfermann, even vacationing with him in Bavaria.

1976 Montreal C: 23, N: 15, D: 7.25. WR: 94.08, 308-8 (Klaus Wolfermann)

			FT.-	
		M	IN.	
1. Miklos Németh	HUN	94.58	310-4	WR
2. Hannu Siitonen	FIN	87.92	288-5	
3. Gheorghe Megelea	ROM	87.16	285-11	
4. Pyotr Bielczyk	POL	86.50	283-9	
5. Sam Colson	USA	86.16	282-8	
6. Vasyl Yershov	SOV/UKR	85.26	279-9	
7. Seppo Hovinen	FIN	84.26	276-5	
8. Jānis Lūsis	SOV/LAT	80.26	263-4	

Miklos Németh was less than two years old when his father, Imre, won the gold medal for the hammer throw at the 1948 Olympics in London. His father pressed him to take up the hammer, but Miklos preferred the javelin, and by 1967 he was ranked second in the world. But he never performed well in major championships. In the 1968 Olympics an elbow injury kept Miklos from qualifying for the final. In 1972 he was one of the favorites, but finished a disappointing seventh. His father said he was too gentle. His critics said he was a choker. Miklos himself said, "It is not an easy thing in my country to be the son of an Olympic champion."

Then came Montreal. Now 29 years old and no longer a favorite, Miklos Németh was almost ignored as interest centered on the leading contenders, Hovinen, Siitonen, and Bielczyk. Németh was the tenth man up in the final, and with his first attempt he uncorked a beauty. He tried not to watch it, but kept looking back as the spear sailed on and on until it finally landed 310 feet 4 inches away from the throwing area. It was ten and a half feet farther than Németh had ever thrown before. It was also a new world record.

While Németh jumped for joy, the rest of the javelin throwers were absolutely demoralized. The remaining medals, it turned out, were also decided by first-round throws. Hovinen, who had led the qualifiers at 294 feet 6 inches, could do no better than 276 feet 5 inches. Nineteen-year-old Phil Olson of Canada, who had qualified with a throw of 287 feet 11 inches, finished 11th at 254 feet 11 inches. Németh was so excited that he had to pass the next two rounds. His winning margin was the widest in any field event in Olympic history (excluding the Intercalated Games of 1906). Imre and Miklos Németh are the only father-and-son combination ever to win track and field gold medals at the Olympics.

1980 Moscow C: 18, N: 11, D: 7.27. WR: 96.72, 317-4 (Ferenc Paragi)

			M	FT.-IN.
1.	Dainis Kūla	SOV/LAT	91.20	299-2
2.	Aleksandr Makarov	SOV/RUS	89.64	294-1
3.	Wolfgang Hanisch	GDR	86.72	284-6
4.	Heino Puuste	SOV/EST	86.10	282-6
5.	Antero Puranen	FIN	85.12	279-3
6.	Pentti Sinersaari	FIN	84.34	276-8
7.	Detlef Fuhrmann	GDR	83.50	273-11
8.	Miklos Németh	HUN	82.40	270-4

Only once since World War II has the leader of the qualifying round in the javelin gone on to victory, the exception being Klaus Wolfermann in 1972. Unfortunately for world record holder Ferenc Paragi, the jinx continued. After a preliminary throw of 291 feet 2 inches, his best in the final was only 260 feet 11 inches and he placed tenth. After two rounds, the leader was Wolfgang Hanisch, followed by Heino Puuste. The decisive moment came at the end of the third round. The last man to throw was Dainis Kūla, a 21-year-old Latvian. Having fouled on his first two attempts, Kūla needed not only a valid throw, but a big one, just to qualify for the extra three attempts accorded the top eight. To most observers, Kūla's third try appeared to land tail first and then bounce, which should have led to his immediate elimination. Instead, Soviet officials rushed out to measure it and announced a valid throw of 291 feet 7 inches. Taking advantage of his questionable reprieve, Kūla followed with an excellent, and perfectly legal, throw of 299 feet 2 inches that held up for the gold medal.

The U.S. team trials had been won by Rod Ewaliko at 291 feet, but Bruce Kennedy, who finished second, set what must be an Olympic record—and a most unfortunate one. A citizen of Zimbabwe, then known as Rhodesia, Kennedy had gone to Munich in 1972 as part of his nation's Olympic team. However, pressure from black African nations opposed to Rhodesia's white minority government prevented the Rhodesians from competing. In 1976 Kennedy was again selected to compete in the Olympics, but again Rhodesia was excluded. Meanwhile, Kennedy had moved to the United States and married an American. In 1977 he became a U.S. citizen. In 1980 he qualified for the U.S. team, but, for the third time, he was prevented from competing in the Olympics because of politics. Ironically, Zimbabwe, now ruled by its black majority, was readmitted into the Olympic movement and allowed to take part in the Moscow Games. In 1984 Bruce Kennedy, who by this time had earned a master's degree from Stanford University, finally made it inside an Olympic Stadium—as an usher.

1984 Los Angeles C: 28, N: 19, D: 8.5. WR: 104.80, 343-10 (Uwe Hohn)

			M	FT.-IN.
1.	Arto Härkönen	FIN	86.76	284-8
2.	David Ottley	GBR	85.74	281-3
3.	Kenth Eldebrink	SWE	83.72	274-8
4.	Wolfram Gambke	GER	82.46	270-6
5.	Masami Yoshida	JPN	81.98	268-11
6.	Einar Vihjalmsson	ICE	81.58	267-8
7.	A. Roald Bradstock	GBR	81.22	266-6
8.	Laslo Babits	CAN	80.68	264-8

On May 15, 1983, Tom Petranoff of the United States broke Ferenc Paragi's three-year-old world record by almost ten feet with a throw of 327 feet 2 inches (99.72 meters). At the world championships three months later, Petranoff was beaten by East Germany's Detlef Michel, with 1980 Olympic champion Dainis Kūla in third place. It seemed just a matter of time before Petranoff or Michel broke through the 100-meter barrier. However, on July 20, 1984, it was another East German, 22-year-old Uwe Hohn, who accomplished the feat. And Hohn, who also held the East German national record for throwing a 21-ounce grenade (328 feet 2 inches), did it in grand style with a massive throw of 343 feet 10 inches (104.80 meters)—the greatest world record improvement in javelin history.

With Hohn, Michel, and Kūla among the boycott missing, Petranoff found himself in the unusual and uncomfortable position of being the favorite in the most important meet of his career, the 1984 Olympics. Petranoff led the qualifying round with a throw of 282 feet, but like Ferenc Paragi four years earlier, he could do no better than tenth place in the final. David Ottley took the surprise early lead with a near-personal best of 281 feet 3 inches. But in the fourth round, Arto Härkönen, whose father was the coach of women's silver medalist Tiina Lillak, launched a throw of 284 feet 8 inches, to bring Finland its first javelin gold medal in twenty years.

1988 Seoul C: 38, N: 22, D: 9.25. WR: 87.66, 287-7 (Jan Železný)

			M	FT.-IN.
1.	Tapio Korjus	FIN	84.28	276-6
2.	Jan Železný	CZE	84.12	276-0

			FT.-		
3. Seppo Räty	FIN	83.26	273-2		
4. Klaus Tafelmeier	GER	82.72	271-5		
5. Viktor Yevsyukov	SOV/UKR	82.32	270-1		
6. Gerald Weiss	GDR	81.30	266-9		
7. Vladimir Ovchinnikov	SOV/RUS	79.12	259-7		
8. Dag Wennlund	SWE	78.30	256-11		

World record holder Jan Železný recorded the longest throw of the qualifying round at 281 feet 10 inches. In the final, Tapio Korjus took the first-round lead with a throw of 271 feet 5 inches. The second round was highlighted by throws of 270 feet 1 inch by both Železný and Viktor Yevsyukov. Seppo Räty, practically unknown when he won the 1987 world championship, moved ahead in the third round with a throw of 273 feet 2 inches. Meanwhile, Korjus passed his next two opportunities because of a cramp in his left leg. In his absence, Železný regained the lead by 8 inches. Korjus returned for the fifth round, but fouled. In the sixth and final round, Železný reached 276 feet to lengthen his lead. Korjus, in third place, was the final thrower of the competition. "This is all or nothing," he thought. "It was a good throw," he said of his last attempt. "You know it when you see only a dot against the sky." It landed 6 inches beyond Železný's mark to give Finland its seventh javelin gold.

1992 Barcelona C: 32, N: 21, D: 8.8. WR: 91.46, 300-1 (Stephen Backley)

			FT.-		
		M	IN.		
1. Jan Železný	CZE	89.66	294-2	OR	
2. Seppo Räty	FIN	86.60	284-1		
3. Stephen Backley	GBR	83.38	273-7		
4. Kimmo Kinnunen	FIN	82.62	271-1		
5. Sigurdur Einarsson	ICE	80.34	263-7		
6. Juha Laukkanen	FIN	79.20	259-10		
7. Michael Barnett	USA	78.64	258-0		
8. Andrei Shevchuk	RUS	77.74	255-1		

On July 4, Jan Železný obliterated the world record with a throw of 310 feet 10 inches. However, controversy immediately developed over whether Železný's Németh 2000 javelin, which had already been disallowed for the Olympics itself, was a legal implement. The issue was considered of such great significance in Finland that Finnish track officials took apart the Németh 2000 on live television to show that it contained graphite fiber and did not meet I.A.A.F. specifications. When the javelin area was laid out on the morning of the Olympic final, a marker was set at 310 feet 10 inches to indicate the world record. But less than an hour before the beginning of the competition, the marker was moved back to 300 feet 1 inch, the record set by Steve Backley on January 25. Far from being discouraged by this setback, Železný was inspired. Since his silver medal at the 1988 Olympics, he had not done well in major meets, failing to qualify for the final in the 1990 European Championships and the 1991 World Championships in Athletics. Now he had the added incentive of losing his world record. In fact,

Železný settled the matter with his first throw, breaking his own Olympic record by 12 feet 4 inches.

DECATHLON

The decathlon consists of ten events held over a two-day period. On the first day, the athletes take part in the 100-meter dash, long jump, shot put, high jump, and 400-meter run. On the second day they compete in the 110-meter hurdles, discus throw, pole vault, javelin throw, and 1500-meter run. Rules for these events are generally the same as for the equivalent individual events. Notable exceptions are that in the running events each contestant is allowed two false starts instead of one, and in the long jump and the three throwing events, each contestant is allowed only three attempts. Points are scored according to a set of tables approved by the International Amateur Athletic Federation. The tables currently in use were devised in 1962 and revised in 1971 and 1977 to take into account the advent of automatic electronic timing, with accuracy to $\frac{1}{100}$ second. They were further adjusted in 1985. The 1985 equivalent of each athlete's performance is included here for the purpose of historical comparison. If two contestants finish with the same point total, the tie is won by whichever competitor had a higher point total in the most separate events. If a tie still exists, the winner is the competitor who earned the most points for any single event.

Decathletes tend to show up later as movie actors. Jim Thorpe was an extra in several Westerns, Glenn Morris played Tarzan, Floyd Simmons was in *South Pacific,* Bob Mathias acted with Jayne Mansfield in *It Happened in Athens.* Rafer Johnson and C.K. Yang also appeared in movies. The 1976 gold medalist Bruce Jenner made his screen debut in *Can't Stop the Music,* one of the worst films ever made. Dennis Weaver, who became famous for his roles in the television series *Gunsmoke* and *McCloud,* placed sixth in the 1948 U.S. Olympic trials.

KEY TO ABBREVIATIONS

DISC = Discus throw
H = Hurdles
HAM = Hammer throw
HJ = High jump
JAV = Javelin throw
LJ = Long jump
M = Meters
PV = Pole vault
SP = Shot put

1896–1900 not held

1904 St. Louis C: 7, N: 2, D: 7.4.

		100 YDS	SP	HJ	800-YD WALK	HAM	PV	120-YD. H	56-LB. THROW	LJ	MILE	TOTAL POINTS
1. Thomas Kiely,	GBR/IRL	11.2	10.82	1.52	3:59.0	36.76	2.74	17.8	8.9 1	5.94	5:51.0	6036
2. Adam Gunn	USA	11.2e	12.21	1.65	4:13.0	31.40	2.97	17.9	7.2 2	5.53	5:45.0	5907
3. Thomas Truxtun Hare	USA	10.8	12.09	1.52	4:20.0	36.28	2.44	18.27	7.5 9	6.07	5:40.0	5813
4. John Holloway	GBR/IRL	10.9e	10.01	1.68	3:59.0	27.51	2.89	18.33	5.98	5.53	5:40.0 ·	5273
5. Ellery Clark	USA	11.0	10.26	1.62	4:11.0	29.11	DNF					2778
6. John Grieb	USA	11.2e	10.54	1.62	4:49.0	DNF						2199

This competition was known as the "All-Around Championship" and was noteworthy because all ten events were held on the same day. Offered a free trip if he would compete for Great Britain, 34-year-old Tom Kiely, of Ballyneal in County Tipperary, refused, paid his own way, and competed for Ireland. In 1899 Kiely had held the world record in the hammer throw for a period of 46 days.

1906–1908 not held

1912 Stockholm C: 29, N: 12, D: 7.13-15. WR: 7414 (James Austin Menaul)

		100 M	LJ	SP	HJ	400 M	DISC	110 H	PV	JAV	1500 M	TOTAL POINTS		1985 TABLES
1. James Thorpe	USA	11.2	6.79	12.89	1.87	52.2	36.98	15.6	3.25	45.70	4:40.1	8412	WR	6564
2. Hugo Wieslander	SWE	11.8	6.42	12.14	1.75	53.6	36.29	17.2	3.10	50.40	4:45.0	7724		5965
3. Charles Lomberg	SWE	11.8	6.87	11.67	1.80	55.0	35.35	17.6	3.2 5	41.83	5:12.2	7414		5721
4. Gösta Holmér	SWE	11.4	5.98	10.98	1.70	53.2	31.78	17.0	3. 20	46.28	4:41.9	7348		5748
5. James Donahue	USA	11.8	6.48	9.67	1.65	51.6	29.95	16.2	3.40	37.09	4:44.0	7083		5701
6. Eugene Leroy Mercer	USA	11.0	6.84	9.76	1.65	49.9	21.95	16.4	3.60	32.32	4:46.3	7075		5825
7. Woldemar Wickholm	FIN	11.5	5.95	11.09	1.60	52.3	29.78	17.0	3. 25	42.58	4:43.9	7059		5676
8. Erik Kugelberg	SWE	12.3	6.20	9.98	1.65	55.8	31.48	17.2	3. 00	45.67	4:43.5	6758		5346

James Francis Thorpe was born on May 28, 1888, on a farm near the town of Prague in what was then known as the Oklahoma Territory. His father was part Irish, part Sac and Fox Indian. His mother, who was part Potawatomie and Kickapoo Indian and part French, gave him the Indian name Wa-Tho-Huck, or "Bright Path." Jim's twin brother, Charles, died of pneumonia at the age of 10. His mother died when he was 12 and his father when he was 15. Educated at the government-run Indian schools of Haskell and Carlisle, Jim Thorpe did not become a noteworthy athlete until 1907. In the spring of that year he walked past the track area where the high jumpers were trying—and failing—to clear 5 feet 9 inches. Thorpe, dressed in work clothes, went over the bar on his first attempt, setting a school record.

He first came to national prominence as a football player. In 1911, tiny Carlisle upset Harvard 18-15, with Thorpe scoring all of Carlisle's points on four field goals and a touchdown. The following year against Army, he ran 92 yards for a touchdown, only to have the score nullified because of a penalty. On the next play, he ran 97 yards for a touchdown. Thorpe was chosen as an All-American halfback in both 1911 and 1912. An all-around athlete, he earned varsity letters in 11 different sports, and even won the 1912 intercollegiate ballroom dancing championship. He so excelled at track and field that he was chosen to represent the United States at the 1912 Olympics.

In Stockholm, Thorpe began by winning the pentathlon. The next day, while the other pentathletes were recuperating, Thorpe was back on the field taking fourth place in the high jump. He also finished seventh in the long jump. Finally, he took part in the decathlon, which was spread over three days because of the large number of entrants. Although he had never before competed in a decathlon, and had never thrown a javelin until two months earlier, he won easily. His performance was so impressive that it would have earned him a silver medal in the *1948* Olympics.

Besides his gold medals, Thorpe was awarded a jewel-encrusted chalice by Czar Nicholas of Russia, in honor of his victory in the decathlon, and a bronze bust of King Gustav V of Sweden for winning the pentathlon. When Gustav handed Jim the bust, he said, "Sir, you are the greatest athlete in the world." To which Thorpe replied shyly, "Thanks, King."

Back in the United States, Jim Thorpe had become a national hero. Honored with a ticker-tape parade down Broadway in New York City, Jim marveled at the experience. "I heard people yelling my name—and I couldn't realize how one fellow could have so many friends," he recalled.

Jim Thorpe led a ticker-tape parade in New York City following his victories in the decathlon and pentathlon in 1912. "I heard people yelling my name," he recalled, "and I couldn't realize how one fellow could have so many friends."

But in January 1913, Thorpe received a hard blow. It was revealed that in 1909 and 1910 he had earned $25 a week playing minor league baseball in North Carolina. Thus, by the strictest definition of the word, he had been a professional athlete and therefore ineligible to compete in the Olympics. Thorpe wrote a letter to James E. Sullivan, chairman of the Amateur Athletic Union, admitting what he had done but asking for leniency.

"I hope I will be partly excused by the fact that I was simply an Indian schoolboy and did not know all about such things," he wrote. "In fact, I did not know that I was doing wrong because I was doing what I knew several other college men had done except that they did not use their own names . . .

"I have received offers amounting to thousands of dollars since my victories last summer, but I have turned them all down because I did not care to make money from my athletic skill . . . I hope the Amateur Athletic Union and the people will not be too hard in judging me."

The "people" were not hard in judging Jim Thorpe, and generally rallied to his side. The A.A.U., on the other hand, was very hard in judging him. He was publicly vilified and his name was stricken from all record books. The American Olympic Committee issued a formal apology to the International Olympic Committee, which asked for the return of Thorpe's medals and trophies. The one bright spot in the whole unfortunate affair was that both Hugo Wieslander, who had finished second in the decathlon, and Ferdinand Bie, who had been runner-up in the pentathlon, refused to accept the trophies which the I.O.C. forwarded to them.

As soon as he had been declared a professional, Thorpe received offers to play major-league baseball. He signed with the New York Giants first, and played as well for the Cincinnati Reds until 1919. He also played professional football between 1915 and 1928. During the Depression, Jim Thorpe drifted from job to job. He was discovered wielding a pick and shovel at a construction site in Los Angeles, and when the 1932 Olympics came to town he was invited to sit with U.S. Vice-President Charles Curtis, who was also part Indian. Such high spots were few, however. He worked as an extra in Hollywood, mostly playing Indian chiefs, gave lectures, joined the Merchant Marine in 1945, and took a job as a bouncer in 1949.

In February 1950, a poll of sportswriters taken by the Associated Press voted Thorpe the greatest athlete of the first half of the century. The following year *Jim Thorpe—All-American,* a film based on his life and starring Burt Lancaster, was released. Yet two months later, when Jim was hospitalized with cancer of the lip, he was admitted as a charity case because he had no money. He had sold the film rights to his life to MGM in 1931 for $1500. When MGM sold the rights to Warner Bros., Thorpe thought he would be paid again, but he had failed to read the fine print. He died of a heart attack in Lomita, California, on March 28, 1953. Thorpe was buried in Mauch Chunk, Pennsylvania, a small town which agreed to change its name to Jim Thorpe in return for the right to have his body.

The movement to reinstate Jim Thorpe's records and trophies began in 1943, but met with no success during his lifetime. "Rules are like steam rollers," he once wrote. "There is nothing they won't do to flatten the man who stands in their way." It is interesting to note that Avery Brundage, who was President of the International Olympic Committee from 1952 to 1972, and who did nothing to help Jim Thorpe's cause, also took part in the 1912 pentathlon and decathlon, placing sixth in the former and failing to finish the latter. Not until October 13, 1982, did the I.O.C. finally lift the ban against Thorpe and allow his name to be returned to the record books. On January 18, 1983, his gold medals were presented to his children.

1920 Antwerp C: 23, N: 11, D: 8.20-21. WR: 7751 (James Thorpe)

		100 M	LJ	SP	HJ	400 M	110 H	DISC	PV	JAV	1500 M	TOTAL POINTS	1985 TABLES
1. Helge Lövland	NOR	12.0	6.28	11.19	1.65	54.8	16.2	37.34	3 .20	48.01	4:48.4	6803	5803
2. Brutus Hamilton	USA	11.4	6.325	11.61	1.60	55.0	17.3	36.14	3 .30	48.08	4:57.8	6771	5739
3. Bertil Ohlson	SWE	12.0	6.435	11.07	1.65	55.0	17.0	37.78	3.30	39.89	4:50.6	6580	5639
4. Gustaf Holmér	SWE	11.8	5.92	11.06	1.70	56.5	16.6	34.82	3. 20	47.62	5:01.6	6532	5551
5. Evert Nilsson	SWE	12.2	5.67	11.39	1.75	55.7	20.0	34.77	3.4 0	49.28	4:45.6	6433	5371
6. Valdemar Wickholm	FIN	11.6	6.12	11.44	1.60	52.8	16.8	32.30	3. 00	42.76	4:45.6	6405	5630
7. Eugene Vidal	USA	12.0	6.13	11.16	1.65	55.7	17.1	37.30	3.30	35.32	4:46.6	6358	5489
8. Axel-Erik Gyllenstolpe	SWE	12.0	6.35	10.69	1.65	55.8	16.8	33.65	2.90	49.31	5:01.4	6331	5482

Lövland passed Hamilton in the last event. His margin of victory was the equivalent of six seconds in the 1500 meters. In 1952 Brutus Hamilton served as coach of the U.S. Olympic track team.

1924 Paris C: 36, N: 22, D: 7.11-12. WR: 7482 (Aleksander Klumberg-Kolmpere)

		100 M	LJ	SP	HJ	400 M	110 H	DISC	PV	JAV	1500 M	TOTAL POINTS		1985 TABLES
1. Harold Osborn	USA	11.2	6.92	11.435	1.97	53.2	16.0	34.51	3.5 0	46.69	4:50.0	7711	WR	6476
2. Emerson Norton	USA	11.6	6.92	13.04	1.92	53.0	16.6	33.11	3.80	42.09	5:38.0	7351		6117
3. Aleksander Klumberg-Kolmpere	EST	11.6	6.96	12.27	1.75	54.4	17.6	3 6.795	3.30	57.70	5:16.0	7329		6056
4. Anton Huusari	FIN	12.0	6.16	12.025	1.70	53.4	16.6	33.15	3. 20	53.65	4:37.2	7005		5952
5. Edward Sutherland	SAF	11.6	6.67	10.865	1.80	56.0	16.6	30.83	3.30	51.015	5:19.0	6794		5928
6. Ernst Gerspach	SWI	11.4	6.46	10.355	1.70	53.4	16.8	33.91	3 .40	44.82	5:08.2	6744		5765
7. Helge Jansson	SWE	11.6	6.32	12.22	1.83	54.2	17.8	32.08	3.1 0	47.20	5:22.0	6656		5633
8. Harry Frieda	USA	11.6	5.94	11.01	1.60	54.0	19.0	35.095	3.4 0	54.90	5:02.6	6618		5541

Norton led after eight events, but fell off badly in the javelin, and barely finished the 1500 meters. Osborn, having already won a gold medal in the high jump on July 7, achieved a unique double.

1928 Amsterdam C: 38, N: 19, D: 8.3-4. WR: 7995 (Paavo Yrjölä)

		100 M	LJ	SP	HJ	400 M	110 H	DISC	PV	JAV	1500 M	TOTAL POINTS		1985 TABLES
1. Paavo Yrjölä	FIN	11.8	6.72	14.11	1.87	53.2	16.6	42.09	3.30	55.70	4:44.0	8053	WR	6607
2. Akilles Järvinen	FIN	11.2	6.87	13.64	1.75	51.4	15.6	36.95	3.30	55.58	4:52.4	7932		6645
3. John Kenneth Doherty	USA	11.6	6.61	11.85	1.80	52.0	15.8	38.72	3.3 0	56.56	4:54.0	7707		6428
4. James Stewart	USA	11.2	6.61	13.04	1.87	52.8	16.6	40.90	3.3 0	48.07	5:17.0	7624		6310
5. Thomas Churchill	USA	11.6	6.32	12.28	1.70	52.2	16.8	38.19	3 .60	50.93	4:55.0	7417		6165
6. Helge Jansson	SWE	11.4	6.85	13.59	1.87	53.2	16.6	36.83	3.3 0	41.73	5:27.0	7286		6111
7. Ludwig Vesely	AUT	11.6	6.73	12.58	1.70	52.2	15.8	35.46	3.20	47.44	4:47.0	7274		6224
8. Albert Andersson	SWE	12.0	6.30	12.19	1.75	54.0	15.8	36.64	3 .30	45.81	4:44.2	7109		6031

Yrjölä lived on a farm and trained alone, using equipment he fashioned himself out of local lumber.

1932 Los Angeles C. 14, N: 9, D: 8.5-6. WR: 8255 (Akilles [*] Järvinen)

			100 M	LJ	SP	HJ	400 M	110 H	DISC	PV	JAV	1500 M	TOTAL POINTS		1985 TABLES
1.	James Bausch	USA	11.7	6.95	15.32	1.70	54.2	16.2	44.58	4.00	61.91	5:17.0	8462	WR	6735
2.	Akilles Järvinen	FIN	11.1	7.00	13.11	1.75	50.6	15.7	36.80	3.60	61.00	4:47.0	8292		6879
3.	Wolrad Eberle	GER	11.4	6.77	13.22	1.65	50.8	16.7	41.34	3.50	57.49	4:34.4	8031		6661
4.	Wilson "Buster" Charles	USA	11.2	7.24	12.56	1.85	51.2	16.2	38.71	3.4 0	47.72	4:39.8	7985		6716
5.	Hans-Heinrich Sievert	GER	11.4	6.97	14.50	1.78	53.6	16.1	44.54	3.2 0	53.91	5:18.0	7941		6515
6.	Paavo Yrjölä	FIN	11.8	6.59	13.68	1.75	52.6	17.0	40.77	3.10	56.12	4:37.4	7688		6385
7.	Clyde Clifford Coffman	USA	11.3	6.77	11.86	1.70	51.8	17.8	34.40	4.0 0	48.88	4:48.0	7534		6265
8.	Robert Tisdall	IRL	11.3	6.60	12.58	1.65	49.0	15.5	33.31	3.2 0	45.26	4:34.4	7327		6398

Akilles Järvinen, older brother of javelin gold medalist Matti Järvinen, was the heavy favorite to win the decathlon. He did in fact break his own world record, but he was only able to place second. The upset winner was ex-University of Kansas football star Jim Bausch, whose entire decathlon career lasted less than 16 months. Fifth after the first day's events, Bausch took advantage of splendid performances in the discus and pole vault to build an insurmountable lead. Although Järvinen did win his second silver medal, had the 1985 tables been in use at the time he would have finished first in both 1928 and 1932.

1936 Berlin C: 28, N: 17, D: 8.7-8. WR: 7880 (Glenn Morris)

			100 M	LJ	SP	HJ	400 M	110 H	DISC	PV	JAV	1500 M	TOTAL POINTS		1985 TABLES
1.	Glenn Morris	USA	11.1	6.97	14.10	1.85	49.4	14.9	43.02	3.50	54.52	4:33.2	7900	WR	7254
2.	Robert Clark	USA	10.9	7.62	12.68	1.80	50.0	15.7	39.39	3.70	51.12	4:44.4	7601		7063
3.	Jack Parker	USA	11.4	7.35	13.52	1.80	53.3	15.0	39.11	3.50	56.46	5:07.8	7275		6760
4.	Erwin Huber	GER	11.5	6.89	12.70	1.70	52.3	15.8	35.46	3.80	56.45	4:35.2	7087		6588
5.	Reindert Brasser	HOL	11.6	6.69	13.49	1.90	51.5	16.2	39.45	3.4 0	55.75	5:06.0	7046		6570
6.	Armin Guhl	SWI	11.3	7.04	12.30	1.80	52.3	15.6	40.97	3.30	51.20	4:49.2	7033		6618
7.	Olle Bexell	SWE	11.6	6.68	13.54	1.75	54.9	16.0	38.83	3.70	57.07	4:40.4	7024		6558
8.	Helmut Bonnet	GER	11.6	6.66	13.45	1.75	53.7	16.2	39.16	3.60	58.15	4:54.0	6939		6489

A new set of tables was instituted in 1934, which accounts for the lower scores. Just before the running of the 1500 meters, it was announced that Glenn Morris, a 24-year-old automobile salesman from Colorado, needed to run 4:32.0 in order to set a new world record. This was 16 seconds faster than Morris, who was only competing in his third decathlon, had ever run. When he crossed the finish line in 4:33.2, there was much disappointment. But then it was discovered that an error had been made in computing his score, and that he had in fact broken the record after all. Morris's victory earned him an invitation to Hollywood, where he appeared in two bad films, *Tarzan's Revenge* and *Hold That Co-Ed*.

Glenn Morris was an automobile salesman when he won the Olympic decathlon in Berlin in 1936.

1948 London C: 35, N: 20, D: 8.5-6. WR: 7900 (Glenn Morris)

		100 M	LJ	SP	HJ	400 M	110 H	DISC	PV	JAV	1500 M	TOTAL POINTS	1985 TABLES
1. Robert Mathias	USA	11.2	6.615	13.04	1.86	51.7	15.7	44.00	3.50	50.32	5:11.0	7139	6628
2. Ignace Heinrich	FRA	11.3	6.895	12.85	1.86	51.6	15.6	40.94	3.20	40.98	4:43.8	6974	6559
3. Floyd Simmons	USA	11.2	6.725	12.80	1.86	51.9	15.2	32.73	3.40	51.99	4:58.0	6950	6531
4. C. Enrique Kistenmacher	ARG	10.9	7.08	12.67	1.70	50.5	16.3	41.11	3.20	45.06	4:49.6	6929	6542
5. Erik Peter Andersson	SWE	11.6	6.595	12.66	1.75	52.0	15.9	36.07	3.60	51.04	4:34.0	6877	6486
6. Peter Mullins	AUS	11.2	6.645	12.75	1.83	53.2	15.2	33.94	3.40	51.32	5:17.6	6739	6334
7. Per Axel Eriksson	SWE	11.9	6.80	11.96	1.80	52.5	16.2	34.91	3.30	56.70	4:35.8	6731	6382
8. Irving Mondschein	USA	11.3	6.810	12.74	1.83	51.6	16.6	38.74	3.50	36.81	4:49.8	6715	6357

Bob Mathias was only 17 years old when his track coach at Tulare High School in Central California suggested that he take up the decathlon. Mathias learned quickly, and less than three months later he had qualified for the U.S. Olympic team and was on his way to London. His inexperience led to one setback in the shot put. After lofting the 16-pound ball over 45 feet, he was surprised when an official raised the red flag that indicated a foul. The perplexed teenager was informed that he had left the throwing circle from the front, which was against the rules. Nobody had ever told Mathias about this particular rule, but there was nothing he could do about it. His best throw after that was only 42 feet 9¼ inches.

The next event was the high jump, and here Mathias almost met disaster, as he missed twice at the mediocre height of 5 feet 9 inches. Faced with virtual elimination, he ignored formal technique and threw himself over the bar with a jump that was clumsy, but successful. He went

Seventeen-year-old Bob Mathias was the youngest winner of a men's track and field gold medal in Olympic history.

After his victory in the 1948 decathlon, Mathias returned home to Tulare, California, for the small-town equivalent of a ticker-tape parade.

on to clear 6 feet 1¼ inches. After the first day's events, Mathias was in third place behind Enrique Kistenmacher and Ignace Heinrich.

The second day's competition began at 10 a.m., but bad weather and general confusion caused it to drag on into the night. The discus was Bob Mathias' specialty, and he connected with a good throw of about 145 feet. Unfortunately, the marker for his throw got knocked over. After a half hour search in the rain and gloom for the hole left by his discus, officials gave him credit for 144 feet 4 inches. Mathias' older brother, Gene, who had gained access to the field by flashing a bogus press pass, raced up to Bob and urged him to press the search. But Bob felt guilty about the delay he was causing, and so accepted his fate. The throw was good enough, however, to put him into first place. Because there were no infield lights, before the javelin throw began, cars were driven into the stadium and their headlights were turned on to illuminate the foul line. By the time he staggered across the finish line at the end of the 1500 meters, it was 10:35 p.m. and Bob Mathias had

become the youngest winner of a men's track and field event in the history of the Olympics. In the dressing room afterward, the exhausted teenager was asked how he intended to celebrate his victory. He replied, "I'll start shaving, I guess." In fact, he was so drained that he went right to sleep and had to be awakened to take part in the victory ceremony the next day.

Back home in Tulare, a small farming town of 12,000, the entire population had been on pins and needles waiting for the results from London. When the news came over the radio that Mathias had won, the town went wild. Factory whistles and fire sirens blared for 45 minutes, businesses closed down, and a spontaneous three-hour parade of cars clogged the downtown area and the nearby interstate highway. The local telegraph office had to stay open into the night as friends stood in line to send their congratulations to the hometown boy who had made good. When Mathias finally returned three weeks later, the excitement was so great that the airplane he was on had to delay its landing until the crowd could be cleared from around the runway.

Four days after Mathias' Olympic victory, 26-year-old Heino Lipp scored 7584 points in a meet in Tartu, Estonia. Between 1920 and 1936 Estonia had competed as an independent nation. However, Estonia lost its independence during World War II and was annexed by the Soviet Union. The U.S.S.R. chose not to compete in the 1948 Olympics and Lipp was left without a country. The U.S.S.R. did take part in the 1952 Olympics, but Lipp was considered a security risk and was forced to stay home again. After the fall of Communism in the Soviet Union, Estonia regained its independence and Estonia entered a separate team at the 1992 Olympics. When the Estonian team marched into the stadium at the Opening Ceremony for the first time in 56 years, the Estonian flag was proudly carried by 70-year-old Heino Lipp.

1952 Helsinki C: 28, N: 16, D: 7.25-26. WR: 7825 (Robert Mathias)

		100 M	LJ	SP	HJ	400 M	110 H	DISC	PV	JAV	1500 M	TOTAL POINTS		1985 TABLES
1. Robert Mathias	USA	10.9	6.98	15.30	1.90	50.2	14.7	46.89	4.00	59.21	4:50.8	7887	WR	7580
2. Milton Campbell	USA	10.7	6.74	13.89	1.85	50.9	14.5	40.50	3.30	54.54	5:07.2	6975		6948
3. Floyd Simmons	USA	11.5	7.06	13.18	1.92	51.1	15.0	37.77	3.60	54.69	4:53.4	6788		6903
4. Vladimir Volkov	SOV	11.4	7.09	12.62	1.75	51.2	15.8	38.04	3.80	56.68	4:33.2	6674		6868
5. Josef Hipp	GER	11.4	6.85	13.26	1.75	51.3	16.1	45.84	3.50	54.14	4:57.2	6449		6705
6. Göran Widenfeldt	SWE	11.4	6.76	11.61	1.94	51.3	16.1	39.53	3.50	49.36	4:38.6	6388		6661
7. Kjell Tånnander	SWE	11.4	6.90	12.97	1.85	52.6	15.8	39.30	3.50	52.79	4:57.2	6308		6607
8. Friedel Schirmer	GER	11.7	6.37	12.69	1.80	50.5	16.0	37.01	3.50	54.00	4:47.6	6118		6464

World records for this period get very confusing, since yet another new set of tables was devised in 1950 and revised a few days before the Olympics. It made little difference to Bob Mathias, who won by the largest margin in Olympic history. His only problem developed in the javelin, when his first two throws fell far short of his capabilities. Up in the stands, Jack Weiershauser, Mathias' track coach at Stanford, convinced a bunch of American rooters to chant, "Oh Bob, hey you, don't forget to follow through." Bob got the message, and followed through with a throw of 194 feet 3 inches.

1956 Melbourne C: 15, N: 8, D: 11.29-30. WR: 7985 (Rafer Johnson)

		100 M	LJ	SP	HJ	400 M	110 H	DISC	PV	JAV	1500 M	TOTAL POINTS		1985 TABLES
1. Milton Campbell	USA	10.8	7.33	14.76	1.89	48.8	14.0	44.98	3.40	57.08	4:50.6	7937	OR	7565
2. Rafer Johnson	USA	10.9	7.34	14.48	1.83	49.3	15.1	42.17	3.90	60.27	4:54.2	7587		7422
3. Vassily Kuznetsov	SOV/RUS	11.2	7.04	14.49	1.75	50.2	14.9	44.33	3.95	65.13	4:53.8	7465		7330
4. Uno Palu	SOV/EST	11.5	6.65	13.39	1.89	50.8	15.4	40.38	3.60	61.59	4:35.6	6930		7028
5. Martin Lauer	GER	11.1	6.83	12.86	1.83	48.2	14.7	39.38	3.10	50.66	4:43.8	6853		6910
6. Walter Meier	GDR	11.3	6.80	12.99	1.86	49.3	16.1	37.59	3.70	47.97	4:20.6	6773		6910
7. Torbjörn Lassenius	FIN	11.8	6.62	13.45	1.70	50.8	15.9	41.36	3.80	59.33	4:36.2	6565		6782
8. Yang Chuan-kwang	TAI	11.2	6.90	11.56	1.95	51.3	15.0	33.92	3.30	57.88	5:00.8	6521		6697

World record holder Rafer Johnson was hampered by injury, but even in full health he probably couldn't have beaten Milt Campbell in Melbourne. Campbell, a 22-year-old sailor from Plainfield, New Jersey, had hoped to qualify for the U.S. Olympic team as a hurdler, but only finished fourth in the final tryouts. "I was stunned," he said. "But then God seemed to reach into my heart and tell me he didn't want me to compete in the hurdles, but in the decathlon."

In the Olympics he led from start to finish. A time of 14.0 in the hurdles earned him 1124 points and assured him the victory. He lost his shot at a world record when he could do no better than 11 feet 1¾ inches in the pole vault, almost 20 inches below his best performance. But, paced and urged on by 11th-place finisher Ian Bruce of Australia, he ran the 1500 meters in 4:50.6 to gain the Olympic record.

1960 Rome C: 30, N: 20, D: 9.5-6. WR: 8683 (Rafer Johnson)

		100 M	LJ	SP	HJ	400 M	110 H	DISC	PV	JAV	1500 M	TOTAL POINTS		1985 TABLES
1. Rafer Johnson	USA	10.9	7.35	15.82	1.85	48.3	15.3	48.49	4.10	69.76	4:49.7	8392	OR	7901
2. Yang Chuan-kwang	TAI	10.7	7.46	13.33	1.90	48.1	14.6	39.83	4.30	68.22	4:48.5	8334		7820
3. Vassily Kuznetsov	SOV/RUS	11.1	6.96	14.46	1.75	50.2	15.0	50.52	3.90	71.20	4:53.8	7809		7527
4. Yuri Kutenko	SOV/UKR	11.4	6.93	13.97	1.80	51.1	15.6	45.63	4.20	71.44	4:44.2	7567		7401
5. Evert Kamerbeek	HOL	11.3	7.21	13.76	1.80	51.1	14.9	44.31	3.80	57.49	4:43.6	7236		7212
6. Franco Sar	ITA	11.4	6.69	13.89	1.80	51.3	14.7	49.58	3.80	55.74	4:49.2	7195		7140
7. Markus Kahma	FIN	11.5	6.93	14.55	1.75	50.5	15.9	44.93	3.60	60.50	4:22.8	7112		7161
8. Klaus Grogorenz	GDR	10.8	6.93	12.42	1.73	48.0	16.9	40.12	3.70	60.81	4:27.0	7032		7078

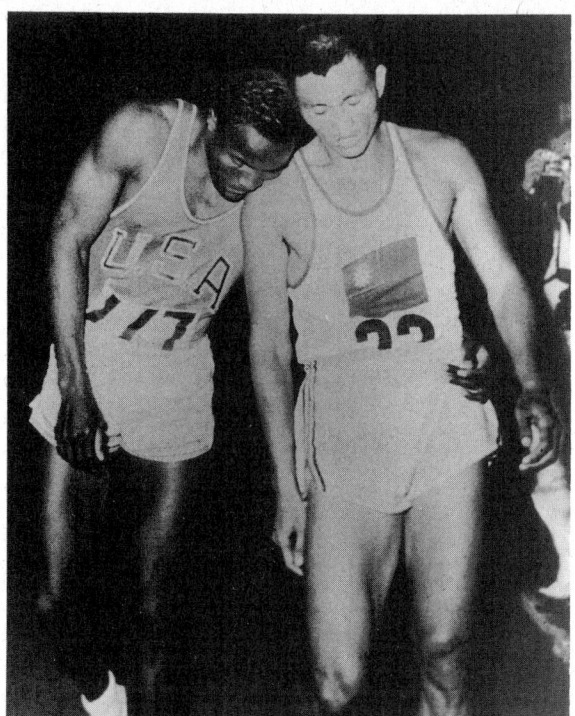

U.C.L.A. teammates Rafer Johnson (USA) and Yang Chuan-kwang (Taiwan) collapse against each other after completing the final event of the 1960 decathlon.

Rafer Johnson and Yang Chuan-kwang grew up in very different circumstances, yet they came together as fellow students at U.C.L.A., and then as friendly rivals at the Rome Olympics. Johnson was born in Hillsboro, Texas. In 1945, when Rafer was 11, his family moved to the small town of Kingsburg, California, less than 25 miles from Bob Mathias' hometown of Tulare. There they lived in a

boxcar for a year until things started looking up. Yang was a member of the Takasago ethnic group, which inhabited the island of Formosa long before the Chinese arrived. He visited the United States for a couple of months and decided to stay. At U.C.L.A. Johnson and Yang, now known as C.K. Yang, trained together, but in Rome Johnson represented the United States and Yang, Taiwan.

The first day of competition, interrupted by an 80-minute thunder shower, didn't end until 11 p.m. After five events, Johnson led Yang by only 55 points. They were back on the track again at 9 a.m. for the sixth event, the 110-meter hurdles, which was one of Johnson's specialties. But the poorly rested American hit the first hurdle badly and took 15.3 seconds to reach the finish line, far slower than his best of 13.9. He made up the lost points in the pole vault by achieving a personal record of 13 feet 5½ inches.

With only the 1500 meters left to run, Johnson led Yang by 67 points. This meant that if Yang, whose best time for the distance was 4:36.0, could beat Johnson by ten seconds, he would become Taiwan's first-ever gold medalist. Johnson's 1500 best was the 4:54.2 that he had recorded at the 1956 Olympics. The two very tired rivals took off at 9:15 p.m., with Yang in front and Johnson dogging him the entire way. Yang tried desperately to pull away in the final lap, but Johnson stuck close and earned the gold medal by finishing only six yards behind, in a career best of 4:49.7. Johnson and Yang wobbled on for a few yards and then fell against each other for support, while Italian fans chanted, "Give them both the gold medal." Yang was the first Taiwanese athlete to gain an Olympic medal.

Rafer Johnson later became an actor and television sportscaster before becoming involved in politics. On June 5, 1968, Johnson was walking through the kitchen in the Ambassador Hotel in Los Angeles with Robert Kennedy, when the Presidential candidate was shot and killed. In 1984, it was Johnson who was chosen to light the torch at the Opening Ceremony of the Los Angeles Olympics.

1964 Tokyo C: 22, N: 14, D: 10.19-20. WR: 8089 (Yang Chuan-kwang)

			100 M	LJ	SP	HJ	400 M	110 H	DISC	PV	JAV	1500 M	TOTAL POINTS	1985 TABLES
1.	Willi Holdorf	GER	10.7	7.00	14.95	1.84	48.2	15.0	46.05	4.20	57.37	4:34.3	7887	7726
2.	Rein Aun	SOV/EST	10.9	7.22	13.82	1.93	48.8	15.9	44.19	4.20	59.06	4:22.3	7842	7677
3.	Hans-Joachim Walde	GER	11.0	7.21	14.45	1.96	49.5	15.3	43.15	4.10	62.90	4:37.0	7809	7666
4.	Paul Herman	USA	11.2	6.97	13.89	1.87	49.2	15.2	44.15	4.35	63.35	4:25.4	7787	7651
5.	Yang Chuan-kwang	TAI	11.0	6.80	13.23	1.81	49.0	14.7	39.59	4.60	68.15	4:48.4	7650	7539
6.	Horst Beyer	GER	11.2	7.02	14.32	1.90	49.8	15.2	45.17	3.80	58.17	4:23.6	7647	7488
7.	Vassily Kuznetsov	SOV/RUS	10.9	6.98	14.06	1.70	49.5	14.9	43.81	4.40	67.87	5:02.5	7569	7454
8.	Mikhail Storozhenko	SOV/RUS	11.0	7.22	16.37	1.84	53.6	15.0	43.20	4.00	59.10	5:00.7	7464	7307

On April 28, 1963, Yang Chuan-kwang had severely disrupted the scoring of the decathlon by pole-vaulting 15 feet 10½ inches, which put him above the maximum height accounted for by the charts then in use. The new

charts, known as the 1962 tables, were not released until August 1964. They tended to equalize the ten events, and were particularly damaging to Yang, whose pole-vault best was suddenly worth 501 points less than it had been.

Using the old tables, Yang's best total of 1964 had been 485 points higher than anyone else's. With the new tables, he trailed both Holdorf and Beyer.

At the end of the first day in Tokyo, Holdorf led with 4090 points. He was followed by Walde with 4074 and Aun with 4067. After nine events, Holdorf led Walde by 60 points and Aun by 137. The 1500, however, was one of Aun's strong points. To win, Holdorf had to finish within 17 seconds of Aun, but his best time of the year was more than 30 seconds slower than Aun's. Holdorf's coach, Friedel Schirmer, purposely misled him, telling Holdorf that he had only 12 seconds to spare.

Aun finished in 4:22.3, while Holdorf pushed himself as hard as he could. Forty yards from the finish, he began to weave and appeared on the verge of collapse. But he struggled on until the end, crossing the finish with a time of 4:34.3—exactly 12 seconds slower than Aun. Then he collapsed. Aun tried to congratulate his fallen conqueror, but Holdorf was too dazed to comprehend. Eventually he was revived and shown the scoreboard that displayed his winning score.

1968 Mexico City C: 33, N: 20, D: 10.18-19. WR: 8319 (Kurt Bendlin)

		100 M	LJ	SP	HJ	400 M	110 H	DISC	PV	JAV	1500 M	TOTAL POINTS		1985 TABLES
1. William Toomey	USA	10.4	7.87	13.75	1.95	45.6	14.9	43.68	4.20	62.80	4:57.1	8193	OR	8158
2. Hans-Joachim Walde	GER	10.9	7.64	15.13	2.01	49.0	14.8	43.54	4.30	71.62	4:58.5	8111		8120
3. Kurt Bendlin	GER	10.7	7.56	14.74	1.80	48.3	15.0	46.78	4.60	75.42	5:09.8	8064		8096
4. Mykola Avilov	SOV/UKR	10.9	7.64	13.41	2.07	49.9	14.5	46.64	4.10	60.12	5:00.8	7909		7884
5. Joachim Kirst	GDR	10.5	7.61	16.43	1.98	50.2	15.6	46.89	4.15	57.02	5:20.1	7861		7791
6. Thomas Waddell	USA	11.3	7.47	14.45	2.01	51.2	15.3	43.73	4.50	63.70	5:04.5	7719		7694
7. Rick Sloan	USA	11.2	6.72	14.07	2.10	51.0	15.5	45.58	4.85	49.90	4:44.0	7692		7553
8. Steen Smidt-Jensen	DEN	10.9	7.17	13.03	1.95	50.2	14.9	41.07	4.85	46.80	4:41.3	7648		7507

"Behind every good decathlon man, there's a good doctor," Bill Toomey once declared, and he was an expert on the subject. Aside from the usual array of illnesses and pulled muscles, Toomey had suffered through hepatitis, mononucleosis, and a shattered kneecap on his way to an Olympic gold medal. A 29-year-old English teacher from California, Toomey faced his moment of truth in the pole vault. Leading after seven events, he suddenly found himself one miss away from elimination at the opening height of 11 feet 9¼ inches.

"I had done so many things wrong on my first two jumps," he later recalled, "I couldn't figure out how to correct anything. . . . Everything was closing in on me—the people in that huge arena, the people watching on televi-

sion back home, my whole life, all those years of working and waiting for this moment. If I missed, it would be like dying." Fortunately, Toomey didn't miss. "All the technique I had learned and practiced . . . had been forgotten in the fear and frustration I felt. I was like a beginner, clumsy and uncertain. But I had made that jump on sheer determination. I'm not even sure I needed my pole."

Toomey went on to clear 13 feet 9½ inches, his best ever in competition, and then managed to stave off the competition through the final two events.

Tom Waddell, who placed sixth, became a gay activist who organized the Gay Games to highlight the accomplishments of homosexual athletes. He died of AIDS on July 11, 1987, at the age of 49.

1972 Munich C: 33, N: 19, D: 9.7-8. WR: 8417 (William Toomey)

		100 M	LJ	SP	HJ	400 M	110 H	DISC	PV	JAV	1500 M	TOTAL POINTS		1985 TABLES
1. Mykola Avilov	SOV/UKR	11.00	7.68	14.36	2.12	48.45	14.31	46.98	4.55	61.66	4:22.8	8454	WR	8466
2. Leonid Lytvynenko	SOV/UKR	11.13	6.81	14.18	1.89	48.40	15.03	47.84	4.40	58.94	4:05.9	8035		7970
3. Ryszard Katus	POL	10.89	7.09	14.39	1.92	49.11	14.41	43.00	4.50	59.96	4:31.9	7984		7936
4. Jefferson Bennett	USA	10.73	7.26	12.82	1.86	46.25	15.58	36.58	4.80	57.48	4:12.2	7974		7920
5. Stefan Schreyer	GDR	10.82	7.44	15.02	1.92	49.51	15.00	45.08	4.40	50.42	4:48.2	7950		7907
6. Freddy Herbrand	BEL	11.00	7.30	13.91	2.04	49.78	14.87	47.12	4.40	50.42	4:27.1	7947		7897
7. Steen Smidt-Jensen	DEN	11.07	6.95	13.35	2.01	50.10	14.65	44.80	4.80	55.24	4:24.7	7947		7908
8. Tadeusz Janczenko	POL	10.64	7.28	14.45	2.04	49.10	16.89	45.26	4.50	63.80	5:01.5	7861		7791

The 1972 decathlon looked to be a wide-open affair, with at least four men considered leading contenders: two-time European champion Joachim Kirst of East Germany, Jeff Bannister of the United States, veteran

Lennart Hedmark of Sweden, and the fast-improving Ukrainian, Mykola Avilov of the U.S.S.R. Unfortunately, Hedmark, troubled by an injured foot, was forced to withdraw after three events. After five events,

Mykola Avilov, winner of the 1972 decathlon, achieved personal bests in eight of the ten events.

Kirst was in first place with 4364 points, followed by Avilov with 4345, and Tadeusz Janczenko and Ryszard Skowronek of Poland with 4266 and 4240, respectively.

The turning point came shortly after 9 a.m. the following morning, in the second heat of the high hurdles. Kirst hit the first hurdle, fell heavily at the next and pulled a muscle. Bannister, in the next lane, was thrown off stride, fell after the fourth hurdle, pushed over the next one, and was disqualified. Janczenko, forced to add the fallen Bannister to the obstacles in his path, was slowed down so much that it may have cost him a medal. Meanwhile, Avilov, unaware of the chaos behind him, finished first with a time of 14.31. In addition to all this, Skowronek had pulled a muscle in his heat and had to retire in the middle of the next event.

Avilov, who suddenly found himself with a huge lead, finished the day brilliantly, eventually recording personal records in seven of the ten decathlon events, and equaling his best in an eighth. A strong finish in the 1500 earned him a world record. Fellow Ukrainian Leonid Lytvynenko ran an even better 1500-meter race, enabling him to move from eighth place after nine events to second after ten.

The first to congratulate Avilov was the man whose record he had broken, Bill Toomey, on hand as a television commentator. Both Toomey and Avilov married Olympic medalists. Toomey wed 1964 long jump champion Mary Rand, and Avilov married Valentina Kozyr, winner of the bronze medal in the 1968 high jump.

1976 Montreal C: 28, N: 17, D: 7.29-30. WR: 8538 (Bruce Jenner)

		100 M	LJ	SP	HJ	400 M	110 H	DISC	PV	JAV	1500 M	TOTAL POINTS		1985 TABLES
1. Bruce Jenner	USA	10.94	7.22	15.35	2.03	47.51	14.84	50.04	4.80	68.52	4:12.6	8618	WR	8634
2. Guido Kratschmer	GER	10.66	7.39	14.74	2.03	48.19	14.58	45.70	4.60	66.32	4:29.1	8411		8416
3. Mykola Avilov	SOV/UKR	11.23	7.52	14.81	2.14	48.16	14.20	45.60	4.45	62.28	4:26.3	8369		8403
4. Raimo Pihl	SWE	10.93	6.99	15.55	2.00	47.97	15.81	44.30	4.4 0	77.34	4:28.8	8218		8216
5. Ryszard Skowronek	POL	11.02	7.26	13.74	1.91	47.91	14.75	45.34	4.80	62.22	4:29.9	8113		8099
6. Siegfried Stark	GDR	11.35	6.98	15.08	1.91	49.14	15.65	45.48	4.65	74.18	4:24.9	8048		8051
7. Leonid Lytvynenko	SOV/UKR	11.12	6.92	14.20	1.91	48.44	14.71	4 6.26	4.60	53.66	4:11.4	8025		7963
8. Lennart Hedmark	SWE	11.36	7.09	15.00	1.91	49.80	14.79	46.42	4.30	78.58	4:44.2	7974		8002

The 1976 decathlon was looked forward to as a classic duel between Mykola Avilov, the defending champion and holder of the automatically timed world record, and Bruce Jenner, tenth in Munich, but now the holder of the official, albeit hand-timed, world record. From the very first event, however, it was Jenner who was in control. Hoping to be within 200 points of the leaders, Kratschmer and Avilov, at the end of the first day, Jenner found himself only 35 points behind Kratschmer and

17 points behind Avilov. He went to bed completely confident of victory since the second day's events were his best.

By the time eight events had been completed, Jenner's victory was assured, and he began to cry as he realized that his goal was about to be achieved, and that his athletic career was about to come to an end. Encouraged by his wife, Chrystie, who had supported the young couple with her job as an air hostess, Jenner had totally

Bruce Jenner completes his world record performance in the 1976 decathlon.

immersed himself in the world of the decathlon. At night, he dreamed about the different events so often that Chrystie could tell which one he was unconsciously practicing. As Jenner rested on the infield in Montreal, his reverie was broken by Leonid Lytvynenko, who patted him on the shoulder and said, "Bruce, you going to be Olympic champion."

"Thanks," said Jenner.

Lytvynenko stared at Jenner for a few seconds, and then asked, "Bruce, you going to be a millionaire?"

Jenner just laughed.

Unlike most decathletes, who dread the 1500 meters, Jenner actually looked forward to it, and ran his final race full of strength, leaning forward as he crossed the finish line. The North American crowd roared with delight, but eventually Bruce made his way through the adulation, found Chrystie, and told her, "Congratulations. We did it together." When he left the stadium, he didn't even bother to take his vaulting poles with him, because he knew he wouldn't need them where he was going.

Bruce Jenner did become rich and famous, just as Lytvynenko had wondered, but his marriage didn't last. Since the media had constantly portrayed Bruce and Chrystie as the All-American couple, their divorce was a difficult one. Jenner later married Linda Thompson, former girlfriend of Elvis Presley.

1980 Moscow C: 21, N: 12, D: 7.25-26. WR: 8649 (Guido Kratschmer)

		100 M	LJ	SP	HJ	400 M	110 H	DISC	PV	JAV	1500 M	TOTAL POINTS	1985 TABLES
1. Francis "Daley" Thompson	GBR	10.62	8.00	15.18	2.08	48.01	14.47	42.24	4.70	64.16	4:39.9	8495	8522
2. Yuri Kutsenko	SOV/RUS	11.19	7.74	14.50	2.08	48.67	15.04	39. 86	4.90	68.08	4:22.6	8331	8369
3. Sergei Zhelanov	SOV/RUS	11.40	7.60	14.17	2.18	49.27	14.83	42.80	4.60	57.30	4:27.5	8315	8135
4. Georg Werthner	AUT	11.44	7.27	13.45	2.03	49.26	15.08	38.14	4.85	73.66	4:23.4	8050	8084
5. Josef Zeilbauer	AUT	11.29	7.14	15.31	2.03	50.91	14.80	44.00	4.50	64.86	4:30.6	8007	7989
6. Dariusz Ludwig	POL	11.35	7.51	13.32	2.08	50.55	15.38	45.82	4 .80	58.38	4:29.7	7978	7972
7. Atanas Andonov	BUL	11.38	6.86	15.59	2.00	50.36	14.83	47.62	4.70	53.54	4:29.2	7927	7887
8. Steffen Grummt	GDR	11.35	6.86	16.15	1.94	49.39	14.82	48.56	4 .30	55.24	4:30.2	7892	7840

In Montreal Daley Thompson had been the youngest entrant in the decathlon, finishing 18th at the age of 18. Four years later this gregarious offspring of a Nigerian father and a Scottish mother was expected to face a tough

battle for the gold medal against Guido Kratschmer of West Germany. When West Germany joined the Jimmy Carter boycott, Thompson broke training, so that he could compete against Kratschmer. He beat his rival in

May, and set a world record of 8622 in the process. Kratschmer responded with another world record of 8649 in June, but he would have been hard-pressed to beat Thompson in Moscow.

At the Olympics, Thompson was not seriously challenged. His nearest rival, Valery Kachanov of the U.S.S.R., pulled a calf muscle during the pole vault and had to withdraw while in second place. Thompson's world record pace was thwarted by rain on the second day, but the Soviet fans, who had been none too friendly to foreign athletes, gave Thompson a standing ovation anyway when he finished the 1500 meters.

1984 Los Angeles C: 26, N: 18, D: 8.8-9. WR: 8798 (Jürgen Hingsen)

		100 M	LJ	SP	HJ	400 M	110 H	DISC	PV	JAV	1500 M	TOTAL POINTS		1985 TABLES
1. Francis "Daley" Thompson	GBR	10.44	8.01	15.72	2.03	46.97	14.33	46.56	5.00	65.24	4:35.00	8798	EWR	8847
2. Jürgen Hingsen	GER	10.91	7.80	15.87	2.12	47.69	14.29	50.82	4.50	60.44	4:22.60	8673		8695
3. Siegfried Wentz	GER	10.99	7.11	15.87	2.09	47.78	14.35	46.60	4.50	67.68	4:33.96	8412		8416
4. Guido Kratschmer	GER	10.80	7.40	15.93	1.94	49.25	14.66	47.28	4.90	69.40	4:47.99	8326		8357
5. William Motti	FRA	11.28	7.45	14.42	2.06	48.13	14.71	50.92	4.50	63.76	4:35.15	8266		8278
6. John Crist	USA	11.33	6.98	14.05	2.06	48.45	15.01	46.18	4.80	61.88	4:23.78	8130		8115
7. Jim Wooding	USA	11.04	7.01	13.90	1.97	47.62	14.57	47.38	4.60	57.20	4:28.31	8091		8054
8. David Steen	CAN	11.20	7.41	12.57	2.03	48.09	15.39	44.04	4.80	56.92	4:17.70	8047		8034

In 1982, Jürgen Hingsen entered the European Championships as the world record holder. Daley Thompson beat him. In 1983, Jürgen Hingsen entered the world championships as the world record holder. Daley Thompson beat him. In 1984, Jürgen Hingsen entered the Olympics as the world record holder. Guess what?

This time the crucial moment in the meet came in the seventh event, the discus throw. While Thompson was flubbing his first two attempts, Hingsen hit a strong 166 feet 9 inches. If the defending Olympic champion couldn't improve with his final attempt, Hingsen would take the lead for the first time. Thompson, who relished moments such as these, threw 152 feet 9 inches to pick up 100 points and put himself back in front. During the next event, the pole vault, Hingsen became ill, performed well below standard, and the rest of the contest was a mere formality. Except that Daley Thompson still had a shot at Hingsen's world record. He needed to run the 1500 meters in 4:34.98, much slower than his personal best. However, the irreverent champion exasperated the crowd by easing off at the tape and finishing in 4:35.00. He then took a victory lap wearing a sweat shirt which read on the front: "THANKS AMERICA FOR A GOOD GAMES AND A GREAT TIME." On the back was another message: "BUT WHAT ABOUT THE TV COVERAGE," a reference to the myopic nationalism displayed by the U.S. television network that covered the Games.

In 1986, the I.A.A.F. announced that close examination of the electric phototimer revealed that Thompson had actually completed the 110-meter hurdles in 14.33 seconds rather than 14.34 seconds. One more point was added to his Olympic total, and he was given a belated share of the world record despite himself.

Daley Thompson (center), the 1980 decathlon champion, shows his delight after receiving his gold medal at the award ceremony.

1988 Seoul C: 39, N: 26, D: 9.28-29. WR: 8847 (Francis "Daley" Thompson)

		100 M	LJ	SP	HJ	400 M	110 H	DISC	PV	JAV	1500 M	TOTAL POINTS
1. Christian Schenk	GDR	11.25	7.43	15.48	2.27	48.90	15.13	49.28	4.70	61.32	4:28.95	8488
2. Torsten Voss	GDR	10.87	7.45	14.97	1.97	47.71	14.46	44.36	5.10	61.76	4:33.02	8399
3. David Steen	CAN	11.18	7.44	14.20	1.97	48.29	14.81	43.66	5.20	64.16	4:23.20	8328
4. Francis "Daley" Thompson	GBR	10.62	7.38	15.02	2.03	49.06	14.72	44.80	4.90	64.04	4:45.11	8306
5. Christian Plaziat	FRA	10.83	7.62	13.58	2.12	48.34	14.18	43.06	4.90	52.18	4:34.07	8272
6. Alain Blondel	FRA	11.02	7.43	12.92	1.97	47.44	14.40	41.20	5.20	57.46	4:16.64	8268
7. Timothy Bright	USA	11.18	7.05	14.12	2.06	49.34	14.39	41.68	5.70	61.60	4:51.20	8216
8. Robert de Wit	HOL	11.05	6.95	15.34	2.00	48.21	14.36	41.32	4.80	63.00	4:25.86	8189

The competition began on a startling note when, in the first heat of the 100 meters, Jürgen Hingsen was disqualified for committing three false starts. Christian Schenk, a 6-foot 7-inch medical student from Rostock, moved into the lead when he high jumped 7 feet 5¼ inches, using the archaic straddle technique. At the end of the first day, Schenk was in first place with 4470 points, Plaziat was second at 4375, Thompson third at 4332, and Voss fourth at 4299. Schenk's lead shrank to 25 points after the pole vault, but when Plaziat blew his javelin throw, Schenk found himself a solid 62 points ahead of Voss and 78 ahead of Thompson. The 23-year-old Schenk, who had won only one previous decathlon, had no trouble maintaining his lead in the final event. Dave Steen, in only eighth place after nine events, ran a strong 1500 meters to snatch the bronze medal from Thompson.

1992 Barcelona C: 36, N: 24, D: 8.5-6. WR: 8847 (Francis "Daley" Thompson) '

		100 M	LJ	SP	HJ	400 M	110 H	DISC	PV	JAV	1500 M	TOTAL POINTS
1. Robert Změlík	CZE	10.78	7.87	14.53	2.06	48.64	13.95	45.00	5.10	59.06	4.27.21	8611
2. Antonio Peñalver	SPA	11.09	7.54	16.50	2.06	49.66	14.58	49.68	4.90	58.64	4:38.02	8412
3. David Johnson	USA	11.16	7.33	15.28	2.00	49.76	14.76	49.12	5.10	62.86	4:36.62	8309
4. Dezsõ Szabó	HUN	11.09	7.42	13.73	1.97	48.24	14.86	39.22	5.30	59.14	4:19.96	8199
5. Robert Muzzio	USA	11.36	6.94	16.02	2.00	50.00	14.75	50.74	4.90	61.64	4:31.52	8195
6. Paul Meier	GER	10.75	7.54	15.34	2.15	48.33	15.22	42.14	4.60	55.44	4:38.21	8192
7. William Motti	FRA	11.42	7.13	15.44	2.12	50.44	15.02	50.58	4.70	67.50	4:48.89	8164
8. Ramil Ganiyev	UZB	10.97	7.49	14.35	2.12	49.30	14.78	45.08	4.90	54.70	4:42.20	8160

It was supposed to be the Dan and Dave show—at least according to the Reebok shoe company's $25 million advertising campaign. "Dan" was Dan O'Brien, the reigning world champion. "Dave" was Dave Johnson, who held the record for the highest second-day score. Dan was the favorite; Dave was the worthy contender. But at the United States Olympic trials, something went wrong. Dan O'Brien was on world record pace when he failed to clear his opening height of 15 feet 9 inches in the pole vault. Dave Johnson was left to carry the United States and Reebok flags in the decathlon. But he too almost ran aground in Barcelona. His first two shot put attempts were fouls. The red flag went up again on his final try when an official ruled that his foot had touched the top of the toe board. The head judge overruled the decision, but after that the Spanish crowd, rooting for Antonio Peñalver, jeered Johnson's every move. At the end of the first day, Paul Meier, a weak second-day decathlete, led with 4510 points, followed by Robert Změlík with 4435, and Peñalver with 4357. Johnson was back in ninth place and it was clear that something more

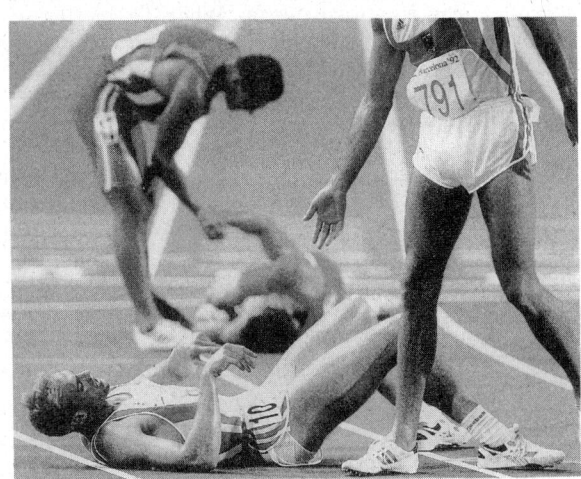

Competitors in the 1992 decathlon reach out to help each other after the tenth and final event.

than the heckling crowd was hurting him. It turned out that he was trying to keep secret the fact that he was suffering from the effects of a stress fracture in his right ankle.

Změlík took the lead after the first event of the second day, survived the discus, and then pulled away over the last three events. The good news for Reebok was that Změlík too was a Reebok man. As for Dan O'Brien, on September 5, one month after the Olympic final, he scored 8891 points at a meet in Talence, France, to break Daley Thompson's eight-year-old world record.

Discontinued Events

60 METERS

1900 Paris C: 10, N: 6, D: 7.15.
1. Alvin Kraenzlein	USA.	7.0	WR
2. John Walter Tewksbury	USA	7.1	
3. Stanley Rowley	AUS	7.2	
4. Edmund Minahan	USA	7.2	

1904 St. Louis C: 15, N: 3, D: 8.29. WR: 7.0 (Alvin Kraenzlein)
1. Charles "Archie" Hahn	USA	7.0	EWR
2. William Hogenson	USA	7.2	
3. Fay Moulton	USA	7.2	
4. Clyde Blair	USA	7.2	
5. Meyer Prinstein	USA	—	
6. Frank Castleman	USA	—	

Hahn won the first of his three gold medals at the St. Louis Games.

5 MILES (8047 METERS)

1906 Athens C: 28, N: 12, D: 4.25. WR: 24:33.4 (Alfred Shrubb)
1. Henry Hawtrey	GBR	26:11.8
2. Johan "John" Svanberg	SWE	26:19.4
3. Edward Dahl	SWE	26:26.2
4. George Bonhag	USA	—
5. Pericle Pagliani	ITA	—
6. George Blake	AUS	—

Hawtrey took the lead after two miles and pulled away to win by 50 yards. John Daly of Ireland finished third, but was disqualified for staggering in front of Dahl and impeding his progress.

1908 London C: 35, N: 14, D: 7.18. WR: 24:33.4 (Alfred Shrubb)
1. Emil Voigt	GBR	25:11.2
2. Edward Owen	GBR	25:24.0
3. Johan "John" Svanberg	SWE	25:37.2
4. Charles Hefferon	SAF	25:44.0
5. Arthur Robertson	GBR	26:13.0
6. Frederick Meadows	CAN	—
7. John Fitzgerald	CAN	—
8. Frederick Bellars	USA	—

Voigt, a 5-foot 5-inch vegetarian from Manchester, sprinted away in the final lap and won by 70 yards.

CROSS-COUNTRY, INDIVIDUAL

1912 Stockholm C: 46, N: 10, D: 7.15.
(ca. 12,000 Meters)
1. Johan "Hannes" Kolehmainen	FIN	45:11.6
2. Hjalmar Andersson	SWE	45:44.8
3. John Eke	SWE	46:37.6
4. Jalmari Eskola	FIN	46:54.8
5. Josef Ternström	SWE	47:07.1
6. Albin Stenroos	FIN	47:23.4
7. William Kyronen	FIN	47:32.0
8. Leonard Richardson	SAF	47:33.5

Hannes Kolehmainen won his third gold medal of the Stockholm Games, having already triumphed in the 5000 meters and 10,000 meters.

1920 Antwerp C: 47, N: 11, D: 8.23.
(ca. 8000 Meters)
1. Paavo Nurmi	FIN	27:15.0
2. Erik Backman	SWE	27:17.6
3. Heikki Liimatainen	FIN	27:37.4
4. James Wilson	GBR	27:45.2
5. A. Frank Hegarty	GBR	27:57.0
6. Teudor Koskenniemi	FIN	27:57.2
7. Julien van Campenhout	BEL	28:00.0
8. Gaston Heuet	FRA	28:10.0

Nurmi and Joseph Guillemot had split the 5000 and 10,000. The cross-country was to be the tie-breaker, but three kilometers from the finish Guillemot stepped in a hole, injured his ankle, and had to withdraw.

1924 Paris C: 38, N: 10, D: 7.12.
(ca. 10,000 Meters)
1. Paavo Nurmi	FIN	32:54.8
2. Vilho "Ville" Ritola	FIN	34:19.4
3. Earl Johnson	USA	35:21.0
4. Ernest Harper	GBR	35:45.4
5. Henri Lauvaux	FRA	36:44.8
6. Arthur Studenroth	USA	36:45.4
7. Carlo Martinenghi	ITA	37:01.0
8. August Fager	USA	37:40.2

This event proved to be an almost total disaster, which put an end to cross-country races in the Olympics. Thirty-eight runners started off in the afternoon of one of the hottest days in Parisian history. Only fifteen finished. The course was unusually difficult, including stone paths that were covered in knee-high thistles and weeds. The race was also run too close to an energy plant that was belching out poisonous fumes. The first

Paavo Nurmi leads the field during the running of the murderous 1924 cross-country race that put an end to cross-country as an Olympic event.

man to enter the stadium and cross the finish line was Paavo Nurmi. He appeared so fresh and untroubled that the spectators had no reason to suspect that anything was wrong. But as soon as the other runners started to arrive, the horrible situation began to unfold. One after another, strong athletes staggered onto the track. Aguilar of Spain collapsed, hit his head on a marker, and began bleeding. Sewell of Great Britain headed the wrong way. Pointed in the right direction, he collided with another runner. Both of them fell and failed to finish. Out on the roads there had been worse scenes of carnage, as various contestants were overcome by sunstroke and vomiting. Hours later, the Red Cross and Olympic officials were still searching the sides of the road for missing runners.

When the full extent of the tragedy became known, the remarkable performance of Paavo Nurmi was seen as even more impressive. Not only had the race taken place only two days after Nurmi had won the 1500 meters and the 5000 meters on the same day, but the very next day after the catastrophe, while most of the other cross-country runners were recuperating in bed or in the hospital, Nurmi was back again, winning another gold medal in the 3000 meters team race.

3000-METER TEAM RACE

1912 Stockholm T: 5, N: 5, D: 7.13.

	TEAM TOTALS	
1. USA	9	(1—Tel Berna 8:44.6, 3—Norman Taber 8:45.2, 5—George Bonhag 8:46.6)
2. SWE	13	(2—Thorild Ohlsson 8:44.6, 4—Ernst Wide 8:46.2, 7—Bror Fock 8:47.1)
3. GBR	23	(6—William Cottrill 8:46.8, 8—George Hutson 8:47.2, 9—Cyril Porter 8:48.0)

Finland was eliminated in the first-round heat by the well-balanced U.S. team, despite the fact that Hannes Kolehmainen set a world record of 8:36.9.

1920 Antwerp T: 6, N: 6, D: 8.22.

	TEAM TOTALS	
1. USA	10	(1—Horace Brown 8:45.4, 3—Arlie Schardt, 6—Ivan Dresser)
2. GBR	20	(5—Charles Blewitt, 7—Albert Hill, 8—William Seagrove)
3. SWE	24	(2—Erik Backman, 10—Sven Lundgren, 12—Edvin Wide)
4. FRA	30	(4—Armand Burtin, 11—Gaston Heuet, 15—Edmond Brossard)
5. ITA	36	(9—Ernesto Ambrosini, 13—Augusto Maccario, 14—Carlo Speroni)

For the team race, only the placings for the first three finishers from each country were counted.

1924 Paris T: 9, N: 9, D: 7.13.

	TEAM TOTALS	
1. FIN	8	(1—Paavo Nurmi 8:32.0, 2—Vilho "Ville" Ritola 8:40.6, 5—Elias Katz 8:45.4)
2. GBR	14	(3—Bernard Macdonald 8:44.0, 4—Herbert "Johnny" Johnston, 7—George Webber)
3. USA	25	(6—Edward Kirby 8:53.0, 8—William Cox, 11—Willard Tibbets)
4. FRA	31	(9—Paul Bontemps, 10—Armand Burtin, 12—Léonard Mascaux)

Paavo Nurmi, running his seventh race in six days, won his fifth gold medal.

3-MILE TEAM RACE (4828 METERS)

1908 London T: 6, N: 6, D: 7.15.

	TEAM TOTALS	
1. GBR	6	(1—Joseph Deakin 14:39.6, 2—Arthur Robertson, 14:41.0, 3—Wilfred Coales 14:41.6)
2. USA	19	(4—John Eisele 14:41.8, 6—George Bonhag 15:05.0, 9—Herbert Trube 15:11.0)
3. FRA	32	(8—Louis de Fleurac 15:08.4, 11—Joseph Dreher 15:40.0, 13—Paul Lizandier 16:03.0)

On July 14, Jean Bouin of France recorded the fastest time in the preliminary round, 14:53. As it happened to be the French national holiday, Bouin celebrated his victory by getting drunk on beer in the bars of Soho. He got into a fight and was arrested and thrown into jail. He was bailed out the next morning by team officials and put onto the starting line for the afternoon final. He started the race but was forced to withdraw. The incident failed to diminish Bouin's popularity back in France, and four years later he returned to the Olympics to win a silver medal in the 5000 meters.

5000-METER TEAM RACE

1900 Paris T: 2, N: 3, D: 7.22.

	TEAM TOTALS	
1. GBR/AUS	26	(1—Charles Bennett 15:20.0 WR, 2—John Rimmer 15:25.5, 6—Sidney Robinson, 7—Alfred Tysoe, 10—Stanley Rowley [AUS] DNF)
2. FRA	29	(3—Henri Deloge 15:32.0, 4—Gaston Ragueneau, 5—Jacques Chastanié, 8—André Castanet, 9—Michel Champoudry)

The United States team refused to take part because the race was held on a Sunday. Although only the first four finishers on each team counted for the team score, French officials insisted that each team start five runners, all of whom must finish. The British team was one man short, so they recruited Australian sprinter Stanley Rowley, who had already finished third in the 60-, 100-, and 200-meter races. Not accustomed to long distances, Rowley ran one lap and then slowed to a leisurely walk. After several more very slow laps, the French officials conceded the absurdity of the situation and allowed Rowley to retire.

4-MILE TEAM RACE (6437 METERS)

1904 St. Louis T: 2, N: 2, D: 9.3.

	TEAM TOTALS	
1. New York A.C.	27	(1—Arthur Newton 21:17.8, 5—George Underwood, 6—Paul Pilgrim, 7—Howard Valentine, 8—David Munson)
2. Chicago A.A.	28	(2—James Lightbody, 3—William Frank Verner, 4—Lacey Hearn, 9—Albert Corey [FRA], 10—Sidney Hatch)

CROSS-COUNTRY TEAM RACE

1912 Stockholm T: 6, N: 6, D: 7.15.
(ca. 12,000 Meters)

	TEAM TOTALS	
1. SWE	10	(2—Hjalmar Andersson 45:44.8, 3—John Eke 46:37.6, 5—Josef Ternström 47:07.1)
2. FIN	11	(1—Johan "Hannes" Kolehmainen 45:11.6, 4—Jalmari Eskola 46:54.8, 6—Albin Stenroos 47:23.4)
3. GBR	49	(15—Frederick Hibbins 49:18.2, 16—Ernest Glover 49:53.7, 18—Thomas Humphreys 50:28.0)
4. NOR	61	(19—Olav Hovdenak 50:40.8, 20—Parelius Finnerud 51:16.2, 22—Johannes Andersen 51:47.4)

5. DEN   63   (14—Lauritz Christiansen, 49:06.4, 23—Viggo Pedersen 53:00.8, 26—Carl Alfred Holmberg 54:24.9)

1920 Antwerp T: 7, N: 7, D: 8.23.
(ca. 8000 Meters)

	TEAM TOTALS	
1. FIN	10	(1—Paavo Nurmi 27:15.0, 3—Heikki Liimatainen 27:37.00, 6—Teodor Koskenniemi 27:57.2)
2. GBR	21	(4—James Wilson 27:45.2, 5—Frank Hegarty 27:57.0, 12—Arthur Nichols 28:20.0)
3. SWE	23	(2—Erik Backman 27:17.6, 10—Gustaf Mattsson 28:16.0, 11—Hilding Ekman 28:17.0)
4. USA	36	(9—Patrick Flynn 28:12.0, 13—Frederick Faller, 14—Max Bohland)
5. FRA	40	(8—Gaston Heuet 28:10.0, 15—Gustave Lauvaux, 17—Joseph Servella)
6. BEL	48	(7—Julien van Campenhout 28:00.0, 20—Henri Smets, 21—Aimée Proot)
7. DEN	55	(16—Albert Andersen, 19—Henrik Sorensen, 20—Jón Jónsson)

1924 Paris T: 7, N: 7, D: 7.12.
(ca. 10,000 Meters)

	TEAM TOTALS	
1. FIN	11	(1—Paavo Nurmi 32:54.8, 2—Vilho "Ville" Ritola 34:19.4, 8—Heikki Liimatainen 38:12.0)
2. USA	14	(3—Earl Johnson 35:21.0, 5—Arthur Studenroth 36:45.4, 6—August Fager 37:40.2)
3. FRA	20	(4—Henri Lauvaux 36:44.8, 7—Gaston Heuet 37:52.0, 9—Maurice Norland 41:38.6)

The same horrible race that was the individual cross-country also counted as the team race. In order for Finland to win, at least three men had to cross the finish line. Nurmi and Ritola finished easily, but Liimatainen, staggering along in the oppressive heat, halted 30 meters short of his goal. Delirious, he turned around and began staggering back the way he had come. The crowd shouted at him and he stopped. After standing for a while with his back to the finish line, he finally regained control of his senses, turned around, and walked across the finish. It took him two minutes to cover the last 30 meters. The British, Italian, Spanish, and Swedish teams failed to complete the course.

200-METER HURDLES

1900 Paris C: 8, N: 5, D: 7:16. WR: 23.6 (Alvin Kraenzlein)
1. Alvin Kraenzlein   USA   25.4
2. Norman Pritchard   IND   26.0
3. John Walter Tewksbury   USA   26.1e
4. Eugene Choisel   FRA   —

Kraenzlein won his fourth gold medal of the Paris Games.

1904 St. Louis C: 5, N: 1, D: 9.1. WR: 23.6 (Alvin Kraenzlein)
1. Harry Hillman   USA   24.6   OR
2. Frank Castleman   USA   24.9
3. George Poage   USA   25.2e
4. George Varnell   USA   —
5. Frederick Schule   USA   —

4000-METER STEEPLECHASE

1900 Paris C: 8, N: 5, D: 7.16.
1. John Thomas Rimmer   GBR   12:58.4
2. Charles Bennett   GBR   12:58.6
3. Sidney Robinson   GBR   12:58.8
4. Jacques Chastanié   FRA   —
5. George Orton   CAN   —
6. Franz Duhne   GER   —
AC: Alexander Grant (CAN), Thaddeus McClain (USA)

1500-METER WALK

1906 Athens C: 9, N: 6, D: 4:30.
1. George Bonhag   USA   7:12.6
2. Donald Linden   CAN   7:19.8
3. Konstantin Spetsiotis GRE   7:24.0
4. Georgios Saridakis   GRE   —
5. Charilaos Vasilakos   GRE   —
6. Alexandros Kouris   GRE   —
7. György Sztantics   HUN   —
DISQ: Richard Wilkinson (GBR), Eugen Spiegler (AUT)

Wilkinson and Spiegler finished first and second, but were disqualified for illegal technique. This left Bonhag with first place, although he too was disqualified by two of the four judges. The deciding vote in favor of Bonhag was cast by the president of the jury, Prince George. Bonhag had actually never entered a walking race before. Disappointed by his showings in the 5-mile run and the 1500-meter run in which he had finished fourth and sixth, Bonhag entered the 1500-meter walk hoping to make up for his previous failures. Vasilakos, who placed fifth, had finished second in the 1896 marathon.

3000-METER WALK

1906 Athens C: 8, N: 5, D: 5.1.
1. György Sztantics   HUN   15:13.2
2. Hermann Müller   GER   15:20.0
3. Georgios Saridakis   GRE   15:33.0
4. Pandelis Ektoros   GRE   —
5. I. Panagoulopoulos   GRE   —
DISQ: Richard Wilkinson (GBR), Eugen Spiegler (AUT), Konstantin Spetsiotis (GRE)

The day after the controversial 1500-meter walk, a second contest was held at 3000 meters. Once again Wilkin-

Musically minded crowd-pleaser Ugo Frigerio won a total of three walking gold medals in 1920 and 1924.

son and Spiegler moved to the front. Fifty meters from the finish, they both began to run and were again disqualified.

1908–1912 not held

1920 Antwerp C: 22, N: 12, D: 8.21. WR: 12:53.8 (Gunnar Rasmussen)

1. Ugo Frigerio	ITA	13:14.2	OR
2. George Parker	AUS	13:19.6e	
3. Richard Remer	USA	13:22.2e	
4. Cecil McMaster	SAF	13:23.6e	
5. Thomas Maroney	USA	13:25.0e	
6. Charles Dowson	GBR	13:28.0e	
7. William Hehir	GBR	13:29.8e	
8. William Roelker	USA	13:30.4e	

Ugo Frigerio was such a colorful character that his flamboyance often obscured the fact that he was a superb athlete who combined great speed with perfect style. While other walkers became nervous or annoyed when a judge got down on his hands and knees to scrutinize their style Frigerio seemed to enjoy the attention, and always made it a point to thank the judge when he was finished. Frigerio also enjoyed the attentions of the crowd, sometimes taking the time to exchange remarks with spectators, and even leading cheers for himself.

Just before the beginning of the 3000-meter walk, Frigerio approached the conductor of the band in the middle of the field and handed him several pages of sheet music which he requested to be played during the course of the race. Accompanied by the proper background music, Frigerio moved quickly to the front and led the entire race, pausing only once toward the end to admonish the band for not playing at the correct tempo. He won easily by 20 meters.

3500-METER WALK

1908 London C: 24, N: 9, D: 7.14.

1. George Larner	GBR	14:55.0
2. Ernest Webb	GBR	15:07.4
3. Harry Kerr	AUS/NZE	15:43.4
4. George Goulding	CAN	15:49.8
5. Edward Rowland	AUS	16:07.0
6. Charles Westergaard	DEN	17:21.8
7. Einar Rothman	SWE	17:50.0

Larner, a 33-year-old Brighton policeman, came out of retirement to take part in the Olympics. He won by 45 yards.

10,000-METER WALK

1912 Stockholm C: 22, N: 11, D: 7.11. WR: 45:15.6 (Ernest Webb)

1. George Goulding	CAN	46:28.4
2. Ernest Webb	GBR	46:50.4
3. Fernando Altimani	ITA	47:37.6
4. Aage Rasmussen	DEN	48:00.0

George Goulding, an English-born Canadian, had competed in the 1908 Olympics as both a walker and a runner, placing fourth in the 3500-meter walk and 22nd in the marathon. In 1912 he kept up such a rapid pace in the 10,000-meter walk that three of the ten finalists dropped out and another three were disqualified for lifting. After his victory, the laconic Canadian sent a telegram to his wife which read simply, "Won—George." Ernest Webb, who earned his third Olympic silver medal, was 40 years old.

1920 Antwerp C: 23, N: 13, D: 8.18. WR: 45:26.4 (Gunnar Rasmussen)

1. Ugo Frigerio	ITA	48:06.2
2. Joseph Pearman	USA	49:40.2e
3. Charles Gunn	GBR	49:43.9e
4. Cecil McMaster	SAF	50:04.0e
5. William Hehir	GBR	50:11.8e
6. Thomas Maroney	USA	50:24.4e
7. Jean Seghers	BEL	50:32.4e
8. Antoine Doyen	BEL	56:30.0e

Frigerio, as boisterous as ever, won by 250 meters to gain the first of his three gold medals.

1924 Paris C: 23, N: 13, D: 7.13. WR: 45:26.4 (Gunnar Rasmussen)

1. Ugo Frigerio	ITA	47:49.0
2. Gordon Goodwin	GBR	48:37.9
3. Cecil McMaster	SAF	49:08.0
4. Donato Pavesi	ITA	49:17.0
5. Arthur Tell Schwab	SWI	49:50.0
6. F. Ernest Clarke	GBR	49:59.2e
7. Armando Valente	ITA	—
8. Luigi Besatra	ITA	—

Frigerio's final gold medal was won by 200 meters.

1928–1936 not held

1948 London C: 19, N: 10, D: 8.7. WR: 42:39.6 (Verner Hardmo)

1. John Mikaelsson	SWE	45:13.2
2. Ingemar Johansson	SWE	45:43.8
3. Fritz Schwab	SWI	46:00.2
4. Charles Morris	GBR	46:04.0
5. Harold Churcher	GBR	46:28.0
6. Emile Maggi	FRA	47:02.8
7. Richard West	GBR	—
8. Giuseppe Dordoni	ITA	—

Mikaelsson set an Olympic record of 45:03.0 in the first round. The final saw the disqualification of the great Verner Hardmo, who set 29 ratified and unratified world records between 1943 and 1945, at distances ranging from 3000 meters to 10 miles.

1952 Helsinki C: 23, N: 12, D: 7.27. WR: 42:39.6 (Verner Hardmo)

1. John Mikaelsson	SWE	45:02.8 OR	(45:02.85)
2. Fritz Schwab	SWI	45:41.0	(45:41.03)
3. Bruno Junk	SOV/EST	45:41.0	(45:41.05)
4. Louis Chevalier	FRA	45:50.4	(45:50.28)
5. George Coleman	GBR	46:06.8	(46:06.69)
6. Ivan Yarmysh	SOV/UKR	46:07.0	(46:07.07)
7. Emile Maggi	FRA	46:08.0	(46:08.16)
8. Bruno Fait	ITA	46:25.6	

Mikaelsson was 38 years old when he won his second gold medal. Silver medalist Fritz Schwab was the son of Arthur Schwab, who won the 50-kilometer silver medal in 1936. Both Schwab and Junk began running 30 yards from the finish, making the judges, who had disqualified seven men in the heats and final, look foolish. The controversies which resulted from this race led Olympic officials to drop the 10,000 meters event and replace it with a 20,000 meters contest in 1956.

10-MILE WALK (16,093 METERS)

1908 London C: 25, N: 8, D: 7.17. WR: 1:14:45.0 (J. W. Raby)

1. George Larner	GBR	1:15:57.4
2. Ernest Webb	GBR	1:17:31.0
3. Edward Spencer	GBR	1:21:20.2
4. Frank Carter	GBR	1:21:20.2
5. Ernest Larner	GBR	1:24:26.2
6. William Palmer	GBR	—

DNF: Richard Harrison (GBR), Harry Kerr (NZE)

Larner broke the 11-year-old world's amateur record of 1:17:38.4 in winning his second gold medal in four days.

STANDING HIGH JUMP

1900 Paris C: 6, N: 3, D: 7.16. WR: 1.63, 5-4¼ (Raymond Ewry)

		FT.-	
		M	IN.
1. Raymond Ewry	USA	1.65	5-5	WR
2. Irving Baxter	USA	1.525	5-0
3. Lewis Sheldon	USA	1.50	4-11

Ray Ewry, a victim of childhood polio, won eight gold medals in the standing long jump events of 1900, 1904, and 1908, and two more in the Intercalated Games of 1906. He is seen here taking off in the standing high jump.

Ray Ewry won eight Olympic gold medals in 1900, 1904, and 1908, and added two more in the Intercalated Games of 1906. Yet he is almost unknown today because his unprecedented feats were performed in events that are no longer held. Born on October 18, 1873, in Lafayette, Indiana, Ewry contracted polio as a small boy. Confined to a wheelchair, it was thought that he might be paralyzed for life. However he began exercising on his own, and not only regained the use of his legs, but eventually grew up to be a superb athlete who specialized in the standing jumps. On July 16, 1900, Ewry won three gold medals in Paris, sweeping the standing high jump, the standing long jump, and the standing triple jump. He repeated his sweep in 1904. With the triple jump eliminated from the Games, he had to settle for double victories in 1906 and 1908. The standing jumps were dropped from the Olympics after 1912. Ewry also held the amateur record for the backward standing long jump—9 feet 3 inches. He died on September 27, 1937, at the age of 63.

1904 St. Louis C: 4, N: 1, D: 8.31. WR: 1.65, 5-5 (Raymond Ewry)

		FT.-	
		M	IN.
1. Raymond Ewry	USA	1.60	5-3
2. Joseph Stadler	USA	1.45	4-9
3. Lawson Robertson	USA	1.45	4-9
4. John Biller	USA	1.42	4-8

Joseph Stadler was the first black athlete to win an Olympic medal in a field event. He was awarded second place after a jump-off.

1906 Athens C: 10, N: 6, D: 5.1. WR: 1.65, 5-5 (Raymond Ewry)

		FT.-	
---	---	M	IN.
1. Raymond Ewry	USA	1.56	5-1¼
2. Léon Dupont	BEL	1.40	4-7
2. Lawson Robertson	USA	1.40	4-7
2. Martin Sheridan	USA	1.40	4-7
5. Lajos Gönczy	HUN	1.35	4-5
6. Konstantin Tsiklitiras	GRE	1.30	4-3¼
7. Themistoklis Diakidis	GRE	1.25	4-1¼
7. Paul Weinstein	GER	1.25	4-1¼

1908 London C: 22, N: 11, D: 7.23. WR: 1.65, 5-5 (Raymond Ewry)

		FT.-	
---	---	M	IN.
1. Raymond Ewry	USA	1.575	5-2
2. John Biller	USA	1.55	5-1
2. Konstantin Tsiklitiras	GRE	1.55	5-1
4. F. Leroy Holmes	USA	1.525	5-0
5. Platt Adams	USA	1.47	4-10
5. Georges "Géo" André	FRA	1.47	4-10
5. Alfred Motté	FRA	1.47	4-10

1912 Stockholm C: 16, N: 8, D: 7.13. WR: 1.65, 5-5 (Raymond Ewry)

		FT.-	
---	---	M	IN.
1. Platt Adams	USA	1.63	5-4¼
2. Benjamin Adams	USA	1.60	5-3
3. Konstantin Tsiklitiras	GRE	1.55	5-1
4. Richard Byrd	USA	1.50	4-11
4. Leo Goehring	USA	1.50	4-11
4. Evald Möller	SWE	1.50	4-11

Platt Adams was 27 years old. His brother Ben was 22. In 1980, Rune Almen of Sweden cleared 6 feet 2¾ inches in the standing high jump to set the current record in the event.

STANDING LONG JUMP

1900 Paris C: 7, N: 4, D: 7.16.

		FT.-	
---	---	M	IN.
1. Raymond Ewry	USA	3.21	10-6¼
2. Irving Baxter	USA	3.135	10-3¼
3. Emile Torcheboeuf	FRA	3.03	9-11¼
4. Lewis Sheldon	USA	3.02	9-10¾

1904 St. Louis C: 4, N: 1, D: 8.29.

		FT.-		
---	---	M	IN.	
1. Raymond Ewry	USA	3.476	11-4⅞	WR
2. Charles King	USA	3.28	10-9	
3. John Biller	USA	3.26	10-8¼	
4. Henry Field	USA	3.19	10-5½	

1906 Athens C: 30, N: 10, D: 4.27.

		FT.-	
---	---	M	IN.
1. Raymond Ewry	USA	3.30	10-10
2. Martin Sheridan	USA	3.095	10-1¾
3. Lawson Robertson	USA	3.05	10-0
4. Léon Dupont	BEL	2.975	9-9
5. Axel Ljung	SWE	2.955	9-8¼
6. Istzán Somodi	HUN	2.86	9-4½
7. Konstantin Tsiklitiras	GRE	2.84	9-3¾
8. Henri Jardin	FRA	2.83	9-3¼
8. Herbert Kerrigan	USA	2.83	9-3¼

1908 London C: 25, N: 11, D: 7.20.

		FT.-	
---	---	M	IN.
1. Raymond Ewry	USA	3.335	10-11¼
2. Konstantin Tsiklitiras	GRE	3.235	10-7¼
3. Martin Sheridan	USA	3.23	10-7
4. John Biller	USA	3.215	10-6½
5. Ragnar Ekberg	SWE	3.195	10-5¾
6. Platt Adams	USA	3.11	10-2½
6. F. LeRoy Holmes	USA	3.11	10-2½

1912 Stockholm C: 19, N: 8, D: 7.8.

		FT.-	
---	---	M	IN.
1. Konstantin Tsiklitiras	GRE	3.37	11-0¾
2. Platt Adams	USA	3.36	11-0¼
3. Benjamin Adams	USA	3.28	10-9
4. Gustaf Malmsten	SWE	3.20	10-6
5. Leo Goehring	USA	3.14	10-3½
6. Evald Möller	SWE	3.14	10-3½
7. András Baronyi	HUN	3.13	10-3¼
8. Richard Byrd	USA	3.12	10-2¾

In 1962 Johann Evandt of Norway performed a standing long jump of 11 feet 11¾ inches. The claims of professional jumpers are difficult to substantiate. Joe Darby of Great Britain was said to have jumped 12 feet 1½ inches on May 28, 1890, and W. Barker was reputed to have leaped 12 feet 6½ inches in May 1904.

STANDING TRIPLE JUMP

1900 Paris C: 10, N: 4, D: 7.16.

		FT.-	
---	---	M	IN.
1. Raymond Ewry	USA	10.58	34-8½
2. Irving Baxter	USA	9.95	32-7¾
3. Robert Garrett	USA	9.50	31-2
4. Lewis Sheldon	USA	9.45	31-0

1904 St. Louis C: 4, N: 1, D: 9.3.

		FT.-	
---	---	M	IN.
1. Raymond Ewry	USA	10.54	34-7¼
2. Charles King	USA	10.16	33-4
3. Joseph Stadler	USA	9.60	31-6
4. Garrett Serviss	USA	9.53	31-3¼

STONE THROW
(6.40 kg—14.08 lbs.)

1906 Athens C: 15, N: 8, D: 4.27.

		M	FT.-IN.
1. Nicolaos Georgantas	GRE	19.925	65-4½
2. Martin Sheridan	USA	19.035	62-5½
3. Mikhel Dorizas	GRE	18.585	60-11¾
4. Eric Lemming	SWE	18.21	59-9

The American favorite, James Mitchel, was unable to compete because he had suffered a dislocated shoulder when the ship carrying the U.S. team to Europe was hit by a large wave.

SHOT PUT (BOTH HANDS)

1912 Stockholm C: 7, N: 4, D: 7.11.

		M	TWO HANDS	FT.-IN.
1. Ralph Rose	USA	27.70	(15.23 + 12.47)	90-10½
2. Patrick McDonald	USA	27.53	(15.08 + 12.45)	90-4
3. Elmer Niklander	FIN	27.14	(14.71 + 12.43)	89-0½
4. Lawrence Whitney	USA	24.09	(13.48 + 10.61)	79-0½
5. Einar Nilsson	SWE	23.37	(12.52 + 10.85)	76-8¼
6. Paavo Aho	FIN	23.30	(12.72 + 10.58)	76-5½
7. Megerdich Megherian	TUR	19.78	(10.85 + 8.93)	64-10¾

The current world record for this event is 121 feet 6¼ inches, set by Al Feuerbach on August 24, 1974. He put 70 feet 1¾ inches with his right hand and 51 feet 5 inches with his left.

56-POUND WEIGHT THROW
(25.4 kg)

1904 St. Louis C: 6, N: 2, D: 9.1.

		M	FT.-IN.
1. Étienne Desmarteau	CAN	10.465	34-4
2. John Flanagan	USA	10.16	33-4
3. James Mitchel	USA	10.135	33-3
4. Charles Henneman	USA	9.18	30-1½
5. Charles Chadwick	USA	—	
6. Ralph Rose	USA	8.53	28-0e

Refused a leave of absence from his job as a Montreal policeman to compete in the St. Louis Games, Étienne Desmarteau went anyway and was fired. When it was learned that he had won a gold medal, his dismissal notice was conveniently lost. Unfortunately, Desmarteau, who was the first individual Olympic champion to represent Canada, died of typhoid the following year at the age of 32. A park was named in his honor.

1906–1912 not held

1920 Antwerp C: 12, N: 4, D: 8.21. WR: 12.36, 40-6¾ (Matthew McGrath)

		M	FT.-IN.	
1. Patrick McDonald	USA	11.265	36-11½	OR
2. Patrick Ryan	USA	10.965	35-11½	
3. Carl Johan Lind	SWE	10.255	33-7½	
4. Archie McDiarmid	CAN	10.12	33-2½	
5. Malcolm Svensson	SWE	9.455	31-0	
6. Petter Pettersson	FIN	9.375	30-9	
7. Edward Roberts	USA	9.36	30-8½	
8. Elmer Niklander	FIN	8.865	29-1	

McDonald is the oldest person ever to win an Olympic track and field gold medal. He was 42 years and 26 days old.

DISCUS (GREEK-STYLE)

1906 Athens C: 21, N: 9, D: 5.1.

		M	FT.-IN.
1. Verner Järvinen	FIN	35.17	115-4½
2. Nicolaos Georgantas	GRE	32.80	107-7
3. István Mudin	HUN	31.91	104-8½
4. Martin Sheridan	USA	31.50	103-4
5. G. Luntzer	HUN	30.26	99-3¼
6. E. Soucek	BOH/CZE	27.55	90-4½
7. M. Sustera	BOH/CZE	27.08	88-10

Contestants threw the discus from a pedestal that sloped forward, and they were required to follow a restricted set of movements. The discus had to be released from a standing position, with no spinning allowed. Verner Järvinen had four sons, three of whom competed in the 1932 Olympics.

1908 London C: 24, N: 9, D: 7.18.

		M	FT.-IN.	
1. Martin Sheridan	USA	38.00	124-8	OR
2. Marquis Horr	USA	37.33	122-5½	
3. Verner Järvinen	FIN	36.48	119-8¼	
4. Arthur Dearborn	USA	35.65	116-11½	
5. Mikhel Dorizas	GRE	33.35	109-4½	
6. Nicolaos Georgantas	GRE	33.20	108-11¼	
7. István Mudin	HUN	33.11	108-7½	
8. Wilbur Burroughs	USA	32.73	107-4¾	

DISCUS (BOTH HANDS)

1912 Stockholm C: 20, N: 6, D: 7.13.

		M	TWO HANDS	FT-IN
1. Armas Taipale	FIN	82.86	(44.68 + 38.18)	271-10
2. Elmer Niklander	FIN	77.96	(40.28 + 37.68)	255-9
3. Emil Magnusson	SWE	77.37	(40.58 + 36.79)	253-10
4. Einar Nilsson	SWE	71.40	(40.99 + 30.41)	234-3
5. James Duncan	USA	71.13	(39.78 + 31.35)	233-4½
6. Emil Muller	USA	69.56	(39.83 + 29.73)	229-2
7. Folke Fleetwood	SWE	68.22	(34.20 + 33.82)	223-10
8. Carl Johan Lind	SWE	68.02	(34.98 + 32.12)	223-2

Martin Sheridan earned five gold medals and four silver medals in 1904, 1906, and 1908. In this photo he is standing on the pedestal that was used for the Greek-style discus throw of 1908. Sheridan is also credited with shortening Félix Carvajal's pants at the starting line of the 1904 marathon.

The current record for this event, 324 feet 6 inches (178-0 + 146-6) was set by Hank Kraychir on March 24, 1984. This broke Fortune Gordien's 30-year-old record of 305 feet 10 inches.

JAVELIN (FREESTYLE)

1906 Athens C: 22, N: 7, D: 7.27. WR: 53.79, 176-5 (Eric Lemming)

			M	FT-IN.	
1.	Eric Lemming	SWE	53.90	176-10	WR
2.	Knut Lindberg	SWE	45.17	148-2	
3.	Bruno Söderström	SWE	44.92	147-4	
4.	Hjalmar Mellander	SWE	44.30	145-4	
5.	Verner Järvinen	FIN	44.25	145-2	
6.	A. Halse	NOR	43.60	143-0	
7.	C. Carlsrud	NOR	—	—	

1908 London C: 31, N: 9, D: 7.15. WR: 54.92, 180-2 (Eric Lemming)

			M	FT-IN.
1.	Eric Lemming	SWE	54.45	178-7½
2.	Mikhel Dorizas	GRE	51.36	168-6
3.	Arne Halse	NOR	49.73	163-1¾
4.	Charalambos Zouras	GRE	48.61	159-5¾
5.	Hugo Wieslander	SWE	47.55	156-0
6.	Armas Pesonen	FIN	46.04	151-0½
7.	Imre Mudin	HUN	45.95	150-9
8.	Jalmari Sauli	FIN	43.31	142-1

Since all of the successful throwers held the javelin in the middle, just as they did in the regular javelin event, the freestyle javelin was dropped from the Olympics.

JAVELIN (BOTH HANDS)

1912 Stockholm C: 14, N: 4, D: 7.9.

			M	TWO HANDS	FT-IN.
1.	Juho Julius Saaristo	FIN	109.42	(61.00 WR + 48.42)	359-0
2.	Väinö Siikaniemi	FIN	101.13	(54.09 + 47.04)	331-9½
3.	Urho Peltonen	FIN	100.24	(53.58 + 46.66)	328-10
4.	Eric Lemming	SWE	98.59	(58.33 + 40.26)	323-5½
5.	Arne Halse	NOR	96.92	(55.05 + 41.87)	318-0
6.	Richard Åbrink	SWE	93.12	(50.04 + 43.08)	305-6
7.	Daniel Johansen	NOR	92.82	(48.78 + 44.04)	304-6
8.	Otto Nilsson	SWE	88.90	(50.21 + 38.69)	291-8

When Finnish team officials realized that all three finalists were from Finland, they asked that the final round be canceled and that the preliminary results be allowed to stand. Swedish Olympic officials agreed with the request.

TRIATHLON

1904 St. Louis C: 118, N: 4, D: 7.2.

			PTS.	LJ	SP	100 YARDS
1.	Max Emmerich	USA	35.7	21-7	32-2¼	10.6
2.	John Grieb	USA	34.0	20-2¼	33-7	11.0
3.	William Merz	USA	32.95	19-10¾	31-1	10.8
4.	George Mayer	USA	32.4	18-1	36-7	11.4
5.	John Bissinger	USA	30.8	18-4¾	32-9½	11.4
6.	Phillip Kassel	USA	30.1	19-2¼	28-9½	11.2
7.	Christian Busch	GER	30.05	18-10¾	31-3½	11.6
8.	Fred Schmind	USA	30.0	19-4¾	30-2¼	11.6

This event was part of a combined gymnastics and track and field competition known as "turning" or "turnverein gymnastics."

PENTATHLON

Unlike the decathlon, the pentathlon was decided according to placement points. After the first three events, all but the top 12 athletes were eliminated. After the fourth event, only the top six could continue. Oddly enough, despite these rules, seven men competed in the final event in 1912, 1920, and 1924. In 1912, this was the result of a tie; in 1920, it was due to a controversy concerning the eligibility of Hugo Lahtinen; and in 1924 it was because of a mistake in computing the point total of Göran Unger. Ties in the final places were decided according to the decathlon tables.

1906 Athens C: 26, N: 10, D: 4.27.
(Standing Long Jump, Greek-Style Discus, Javelin, 192-Meter
Race, Greco-Roman Wrestling)

		SLJ	DISC	JAV	192M	GRW	PTS.
1. Hjalmar Mellander	SWE	7	5	5	4	3	24
2. István Mudin	HUN	6	1	9	8	1	25
3. Erik Lemming	SWE	15	2	1	7	4	29
4. Uno Häggman (Tuomela)	FIN	18	9	2	3	2	34
5. Lawson Robertson	USA	1	17	11	1	6	36
6. Knut Lindberg	SWE	16	11	3	2	5	37
7. Edward Archibald	CAN	10	13	4	6	—	—
8. Julius Wagner	GER	8	6	18	5	—	—

The events of the 1906 pentathlon were the same as those of the ancient Greek pentathlon.

1908 not held

1912 Stockholm C: 26, N: 11, D: 7.7.

		LJ	JAV	200M	DISC	1500M	TOTAL PTS.
1. James Thorpe	USA	7.07 (1)	46.71 (3)	22.9 (1)	35.75 (1)	4:44.8 (1)	7
2. Ferdinand Bie	NOR	6.85 (2)	46.45 (4)	23.5 (5)	31.79 (4)	5:07.8 (6)	21
3. James Donahue	USA	6.83 (3)	38.28 (10)	23.0 (2)	29.64 (11)	4:51.0 (3)	29
4. Frank Lukeman	CAN	6.45 (6)	36.02 (11)	23.2 (4)	33.76 (3)	5:00.2 (5)	29
5. James Austin Menaul	USA	6.40 (8)	35.85 (12)	23.0 (2)	31.38 (6)	4:49.6 (2)	30
6. Avery Brundage	USA	6.58 (4)	42.85 (7)	24.2 (11)	34.72 (2)	DNF (7)	31
7. Hugo Wieslander	SWE	6.27 (10)	49.56 (1)	24.1 (10)	30.74 (7)	4:51.1 (4)	32
8. Inge Lindholm	SWE	6.32 (9)	41.94 (8)	23.5 (5)	30.47 (8)	—	—

Thorpe and Bie clinched the gold and silver medals respectively before the 1500 meters was even run.

1920 Antwerp C: 19, N: 8, D: 8.6.

		LJ	JAV	200M	DISC	1500M	TOTAL PTS.
1. Eero Lehtonen	FIN	6.635 (2)	54.67 (2)	23.0 (1)	34.64 (7)	4:40.2 (2)	14
2. Everett Bradley	USA	6.61 (3)	49.16 (8)	23.0 (1)	36.78 (6)	5:10.0 (6)	24
3. Hugo Lahtinen	FIN	6.59 (4)	54.25 (3)	23.6 (5)	31.12 (13)	4:36.0 (1)	26
4. Robert LeGendre	USA	6.505 (5)	44.60 (11)	23.0 (1)	37.39 (4)	4:46.0 (5)	26
5. Helge Lövland	NOR	6.32 (7)	53.13 (4)	24.0 (10)	39.51 (2)	4:45.8 (4)	27
6. Brutus Hamilton	USA	6.86 (1)	48.36 (10)	23.4 (4)	37.13 (5)	5:12.8 (7)	27
7. Bertil Ohlson	SWE	6.27 (9)	43.68 (12)	23.6 (5)	39.80 (1)	4:42.8 (3)	30
8. Aleksander Klumberg-Kolmpere	EST	6.25 (10)	60.76 (1)	25.3 (15)	38.62 (3)	—	—

1924 Paris C: 31, N: 17, D: 7.7.

		LJ	JAV	200M	DISC	1500M	TOTAL PTS.
1. Eero Lehtonen	FIN	6.68 (7)	50.93 (4)	23.0 (1)	40.44 (1)	4:47.1 (1)	14
2. Elemér Somfay	HUN	6.77 (5)	52.07 (2)	23.4 (5)	37.76 (2)	4:48.4 (2)	16
3. Robert LeGendre	USA	7.765 (1)	48.04 (9)	23.0 (1)	36.76 (4)	4:52.6 (3)	18
4. Leo Leino	FIN	6.72 (6)	54.12 (1)	23.2 (4)	33.62 (8)	4:55.4 (4)	23
5. Morton Kaer	USA	6.96 (2)	50.20 (5)	23.0 (1)	32.70 (10)	5:38.6 (6)	24
6. Hugo Lahtinen	FIN	6.895 (3)	48.66 (7)	23.6 (7)	36.08 (5)	4:55.6 (5)	27
7. Brutus Hamilton	USA	6.83 (4)	48.96 (6)	24.4 (11)	37.70 (3)	—	—
8. Göran Unger	SWE	6.55 (8)	48.45 (8)	23.8 (8)	35.11 (6)	—	—

The highlight of this competition was the surprising world record of 25 feet 5¾ inches set in the long jump by Robert LeGendre of Georgetown University. First place was not decided until Lehtonen edged Somfay in the 1500 meters.

TRACK AND FIELD

WOMEN

100 METERS

1896–1924 not held

1928 Amsterdam C: 31, N: 13, D: 7.31. WR: 12.2 (Elizabeth Robinson)
1. Elizabeth Robinson   USA   12.2   EWR
2. Fanny Rosenfeld   CAN   12.3
3. Ethel Smith   CAN   12.3
4. Erna Steinberg   GER   12.4
DISQ: Myrtle Cook (CAN), Helene "Leni" Schmidt (GER)

This was the first women's track event to be contested in the Olympics, so the entrants were unusually nervous, as was the primarily male audience. The men found it particularly unsettling when the three Canadian finalists hugged and kissed each other before the race. First Cook and then Schmidt were disqualified for false-starting twice. The winner, Betty Robinson, was a 16-year-old high school student from Riverdale, Illinois. Robinson didn't know that she was a fast runner until one of her teachers saw her running for a bus and asked if he could time her running down the school corridor. The Olympics was only her fourth track meet of any kind. Three years after her victory she was badly injured in a plane crash, receiving a concussion, a broken leg, a crushed arm, and a severe cut across her forehead and eyelid. She was unconscious for seven weeks and was unable to walk normally for two years. However, she regained the use of her leg and returned to competitive running. Because she could not bend her leg fully at the knee, she could not assume the crouched starting position of a sprinter. She could, however, run in relays. In 1936, Betty Robinson won a second gold medal as a member of the U.S. 4 × 100-meter relay team.

1932 Los Angeles C: 20, N: 10, D: 8.2. WR: 11.9 (Tollien Schuurman)
1. Stanislawa Walasiewicz   POL   11.9   EWR
2. Hilda Strike   CAN   11.9
3. Wilhelmina Von Bremen   USA   12.0
4. Marie Dollinger   GER   12.2
5. Eileen Hiscock   GBR   12.3
6. Elizabeth Wilde   USA   12.3

Stanislawa Walasiewicz was born in Rypin, Poland, on April 3, 1911. When she was still an infant her family moved to the United States and settled in Cleveland, Ohio, where she grew up and became known as Stella Walsh. On May 30, 1930, she became the first woman to break the 11-second barrier for 100 yards. By 1932 U.S. track enthusiasts were looking forward to a gold medal from her in the Olympics. But Stella Walsh had a problem: as a result of the worldwide depression, her job with the New York Central Railroad had been eliminated. She was offered a position with the Cleveland Recreation Department, but taking it would have made her ineligible for the Olympics, since Olympic regulations at the time disqualified athletes who made their living from physical education or recreation. With no help forthcoming from her adopted country, Stella Walsh made a major decision in her life. Twenty-four hours before she was scheduled to take out U.S. naturalization papers, she accepted a job offer from the Polish consulate in New York and decided to compete for Poland.

Stella Walsh's performance in Los Angeles was no disappointment. Running with what the Canadian official report called "long man-like strides," Stella Walsh equaled Tollien Schuurman's two-month-old world record in every one of her three races. In the final she was hard-pressed by Hilda Strike, but managed to win by half a yard. While some U.S. observers pointed to the loss of Walsh to Poland as an example of the consequences of the lack of support for women's athletics in the U.S., there were also those who held a grudge against Walsh

What deep, dark secret prevented Stella Walsh from smiling even after she had won the gold medal in the 1932 100-meter dash?

Adolf Hitler made advances to Helen Stephens after her victory in the 1936 100 meters, but she turned him down.

herself, and she was not granted her naturalization papers until 1947.

1936 Berlin C: 30, N: 15, D: 8.4. WR: 11.6 (Helen Stephens)

1. Helen Stephens	USA	11.5w
2. Stanislawa Walasiewicz	POL	11.7
3. Käthe Krauss	GER	11.9
4. Marie Dollinger	GER	12.0
5. Annette Rogers	USA	12.2
6. Emmy Albus	GER	12.3

Helen Stephens was a 6-foot farm girl from Calloway County, Missouri, who loved to run. When she entered Fulton High School she was routinely timed in the 50-yard dash. Coach Burton Moore was astounded to discover that Stephens had run the race in 5.8 seconds, equaling the existing world record held by Betty Robinson. Moore taught Stephens the various events of track and field and then entered her in the 1935 national A.A.U. meet, which was being held in St. Louis. Wearing a borrowed sweatshirt and shoes, she won the shot put, set a world record in the 200 meters, and set another world record in the standing long jump. But the real sensation came when she beat Stella Walsh in the 50-yard dash, this time officially tying the world record. Walsh was outraged by such impudence and referred to Stephens as a "greenie from the sticks." When Stephens and Walsh met again in the Olympics in Berlin there was never any question as to who would take the gold medal. In the opening round Helen Stephens ran a wind-aided 11.4 to win her heat by ten yards. She ran wind-aided 11.5s in the semifinals and final, finishing the latter two yards ahead of Stella Walsh. After the race, Stephens was taken to meet Adolf Hitler in his private glass-enclosed box. "Hitler comes in and gives me the Nazi salute," she later recalled. "I gave him a good old Missouri handshake. Immediately Hitler goes for the jugular vein. He gets ahold of my fanny, and he begins to squeeze and pinch and hug me up, and he said, 'You're a true Aryan type. You should be running for Germany.' So after he gave me the once-over and a full massage, he asked me if I'd like to spend the weekend in Berchtesgaden." She declined.

After only two and a half years of competition, Helen Stephens retired from amateur athletics with an undefeated record in running events. For a while she made a living playing basketball and softball and then served as a marine during World War II. Later she worked until retirement for the Defense Mapping Agency Aerospace Center in St. Louis.

The rivalry between Helen Stephens and Stella Walsh had an ironic and long-delayed ending. After Stephens' victory in Berlin, a Polish journalist accused her of actually being a man, and German officials were forced to issue a statement that they had given her a sex check and that she had passed. Forty-four years later, on December 4, 1980, Stella Walsh went to a discount store in Cleveland to buy streamers for a reception for the Polish national basketball team. In the parking lot she got caught in the middle of a robbery attempt and was shot to death. When an autopsy was performed afterward, it turned out that although Helen Stephens may not have had male sexual organs, Stella Walsh did. All the while that Walsh had been setting 11 world records, winning 41 A.A.U. titles and two Olympic medals, she was, in fact, a man.

1948 London C: 38, N: 21, D: 8.2. WR: 11.5 (Helen Stephens)

1. Francina "Fanny" Blankers-Koen	HOL	11.9	
2. Dorothy Manley	GBR	12.2	
3. Shirley Strickland	AUS	12.2	
4. Viola Myers	CAN	12.3e	
5. Patricia Jones	CAN	12.3e	
6. Cynthia Thompson	JAM	12.4e	

Fanny Koen was 18 years old when she was chosen to join the Dutch team for the 1936 Olympics in Berlin. She tied for sixth place in the high jump and was part of the 4 × 100-meter relay team that finished fifth. The highlight of the games for her was when she got Jesse Owens' autograph. When the Olympics resumed after a 12-year

break, Fanny was the holder of six world records—in the 100 yards, the 80-meter hurdles, the high jump, the long jump, and in two relays. In the interim she had also married her coach, Jan Blankers, and given birth to two children. At 30 years of age she was thought by some to be too old to win the Olympic sprints, despite her string of records. She quieted her critics almost immediately by recording the best time of the opening round (12.0), in the 100-meter dash. She went on to win the final in the mud by three yards. Later in the week she also won gold medals in the 80-meter hurdles, the 200 meters, and the 4 × 100-meter relay. Of the nine women's track and field events included in the 1948 Olympics, Fanny Blankers-Koen won four of them. If she had entered the long jump she probably would have won that too, considering that the winning jump was 20 inches shorter than Fanny's world record. When she returned to Amsterdam she was driven through the crowded streets in an open carriage drawn by four gray horses. Her neighbors gave her a bicycle, "so she won't have to run so much."

1952 Helsinki C: 56, N: 27, D: 7.22. WR: 11.5 (Helen Stephens, Francina "Fanny" Blankers-Koen)

1. Marjorie Jackson	AUS	11.5	EWR	(11.67)
2. Daphne Hasenjager (Robb)	SAF	11.8		(12.05)
3. Shirley Strickland de la Hunty	AUS	11.9		(12.12)
4. Winsome Cripps	AUS	11.9		(12.16)
5. Maria Sander	GER	12.0		(12.27)
6. Mae Faggs	USA	12.1		(12.27)

Marjorie Jackson first gained international attention when she twice defeated Fanny Blankers-Koen in Australia in 1949. Jackson was used to competing on grass and digging her starting holes before the race. In order to prepare her for the Olympics, the people of her hometown of Lithgow built a cinder track, and her father made her a set of starting blocks. British fans, who had been looking forward to the playing of "God Save the Queen" following the victory by Jackson, whom they considered a British subject, were stunned when what they heard instead was "Advance Australia Fair." Back home in Australia, the residents of Lithgow welcomed her with a 250-pound cake to help her break training.

Studies of the film of the race have shown that Sander and Faggs actually tied for fifth place.

1956 Melbourne C: 34, N: 16, D: 11.26. WR: 11.3 (Shirley Strickland de la Hunty)

1. Elizabeth Cuthbert	AUS	11.5	(11.82)
2. Christa Stubnick	GDR	11.7	(11.92)
3. Marlene Matthews	AUS	11.7	(11.94)
4. Isabelle Daniels	USA	11.8	(11.98)
5. Giuseppina Leone	ITA	11.9	(12.07)
6. Heather Armitage	GBR	12.0	(12.10)

Eighteen-year-old Betty Cuthbert broke the Olympic record in the first round with an 11.4. In the semifinals she was beaten by Stubnick, but in the final she led from start

In 1948 Fanny Blankers-Koen won four of the nine women's track and field events.

to finish to win by five feet. Like Marjorie Jackson before her, Betty Cuthbert was as unassuming a heroine as one could hope for. In her autobiography, *Golden Girl,* Cuthbert wrote, "I broke the tape in 11.5s just like in any other race and there seemed nothing special about it. I couldn't realize then just what I had done and even later, when the telegrams, letters, honours, victory functions and the like started, I was too shy and self-conscious fully to appreciate it. . . . However, at the time, Mum must have realized what I had done because I looked up in the crowd just after the race was over and saw her crying her eyes out." Four days later Cuthbert won the 200-meter dash and then earned another gold medal as part of the Australian 4 × 100-meter relay team.

1960 Rome C: 31, N: 18, D: 9.2. WR: 11.3 (Shirley Strickland de la Hunty, Vira Krepkina)

1. Wilma Rudolph	USA	11.0w	(11.18)
2. Dorothy Hyman	GBR	11.3	(11.43)
3. Giuseppina Leone	ITA	11.3	(11.48)
4. Maria Itkina	SOV/RUS	11.4	(11.54)
5. Catherine Capdeville	FRA	11.5	(11.64)
6. Jennifer Smart	GBR	12.0	(11.72)

Wilma Rudolph was born in rural Tennessee on June 23, 1940, the 20th of her father's 22 children. She was born prematurely and weighed only 4½ pounds at birth. She suffered through polio, double pneumonia, and scarlet fever, which caused her to lose the use of her left leg. From the age of 6 she wore a brace. Her mother learned from doctors that rubbing her daughter's leg might help, so each day Wilma received four leg rubs from her brothers, sisters, and mother. Eventually she graduated from a brace to an orthopedic shoe and she joined her brothers playing basketball whenever she could. When Wilma was 11, her mother returned home one day to find her daughter playing basketball barefooted, having thrown away her corrective shoes. By the time she was 16, Rudolph had developed into a star runner and had qualified for the U.S. Olympic team. In Melbourne in 1956 she was eliminated in the first round of the 200 meters, but earned a bronze medal running the third leg of the U.S. 4 × 100-meter relay team. The same day that she returned from Australia to her hometown of Clarksville, Tennessee, she played for her high school's basketball team.

Four years later, the 5-foot 11-inch Rudolph, now a mother and a member of the Tennessee State University "Tigerbelles," went to the Rome Olympics as the favorite to succeed Betty Cuthbert as the world's fastest woman. She dominated the competition from the beginning. She actually fell asleep while waiting for her semifinal heat. Well-rested, she swept to a three-yard victory, equaling the world record of 11.3. She won the final by the same wide margin and was clocked in 11.0. However her time was not accepted as a world record because the wind was 2.752 meters per second—above the acceptable

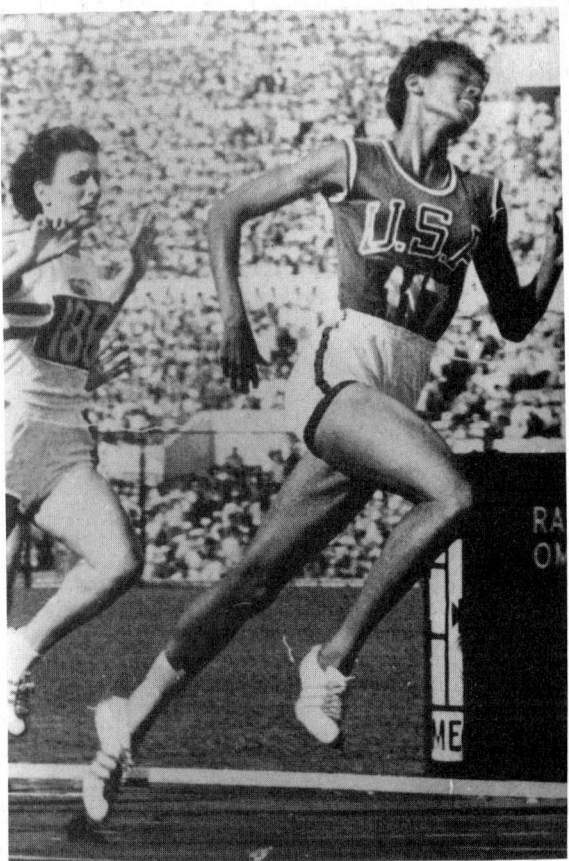

As a child in rural Tennessee, Wilma Rudolph suffered through polio, double pneumonia, and scarlet fever. Yet she grew up to win three gold medals in 1960, in the 100- and 200-meter dashes and the 4 × 100-meter relay.

limit of 2 meters per second. She went on to match Betty Cuthbert's triple gold by winning the 200 meters and the 4 × 100-meter relay.

1964 Tokyo C: 44, N: 27, D: 10.16. WR: 11.2 (Wilma Rudolph)

1. Wyomia Tyus	USA	11.4	(11.49)
2. Edith McGuire	USA	11.6	(11.62)
3. Ewa Klobukowska	POL	11.6	(11.64)
4. Marilyn White	USA	11.6	(11.67)
5. Miguelina Cobián	CUB	11.7	(11.72)
6. Marilyn Black	AUS	11.7	(11.73)
7. Halina Górecka	POL	11.8	(11.83)
8. Dorothy Hyman	GBR	11.9	(11.90)

Until the Olympics, 19-year-old Wyomia Tyus of Griffin, Georgia, had been overshadowed by her Tennessee State teammate Edith McGuire, whom she had never beaten. But in Tokyo, Tyus improved her personal best from 11.5 to 11.2 to equal Wilma Rudolph's world record in the second round. She won the final handily by two yards. Bronze medalist Klobukowska was later the subject of much controversy. On September 15, 1967, she was barred from international competition after she failed a sex chromosome test. Although she passed a visual examination she was subsequently stripped of all her records.

1968 Mexico City C: 41, N: 20, D: 10.15. WR: 11.1 (Irena Szewińska [Kirszenstein], Wyomia Tyus, Barbara Ferrell, Lyudmila Samotyosova, Margaret Bailes)

1. Wyomia Tyus	USA	11.08	WR
2. Barbara Ferrell	USA	11.15	
3. Irena Szewińska (Kirszenstein)	POL	11.19	
4. Raelene Boyle	AUS	11.20	
5. Margaret Bailes	USA	11.37	
6. Dianne Burge	AUS	11.44	
7. Chi Cheng	TAI	11.53	
8. Miguelina Cobián	CUB	11.61	

Competition was particularly stiff in 1968. In the first round, all three Americans, Tyus, Bailes, and Ferrell, equaled the Olympic record of 11.2. The second round saw Ferrell and Szewińska tie the world record of 11.1, while Wyomia Tyus ran a wind-aided 11.0. The semifinals, run in the rain, were won by Szewińska and Tyus, as co-world record holder Lyudmila Samotyosova was eliminated. The final matched four of the five world record holders. After false-starting, Tyus won a clear victory to become the first runner, male or female, to win an Olympic sprint title twice in a row.

1972 Munich C: 47, N: 33, D: 9.2. WR: 11.08 (Wyomia Tyus)

1. Renate Stecher	GDR	11.07	WR
2. Raelene Boyle	AUS	11.23	
3. Silvia Chivás	CUB	11.24	
4. Iris Davis	USA	11.32	
5. Annegret Richter	GER	11.38	
6. Alice Annum	GHA	11.41	
7. Barbara Ferrell	USA	11.45	
8. Eva Gleskova	CZE	12.48	

Although 17-year-old Silvia Chivás recorded the fastest times of the first two rounds (11.18 and 11.22), there was never any doubt that Stecher would win the gold.

1976 Montreal C: 39, N: 22, D: 7.25. WR: 10.8 (Renate Stecher, Annegret Richter); 11.04 (Inge Helten)

1. Annegret Richter	GER	11.08
2. Renate Stecher	GDR	11.13
3. Inge Helten	GER	11.17
4. Raelene Boyle	AUS	11.23
5. Evelyn Ashford	USA	11.24
6. Chandra Cheeseborough	USA	11.31
7. Andrea Lynch	GBR	11.32
8. Marlies Oelsner	GDR	11.34

Richter defeated Stecher 11.19 to 11.21 in heat number 6 of the first round. In the second round she ran an impressive 11.05. The next day she set a world record of 11.01 in

In 1968 Wyomia Tyus became the only woman to win the 100-meter dash twice.

the semifinals, before leading a German sweep in the final. Less than a yard separated the three medalists at the finish.

1980 Moscow C: 40, N: 25, D: 7.26. WR: 10.88 (Marlies Göhr [Oelsner])

1. Lyudmila Kondratyeva	SOV/RUS	11.06
2. Marlies Göhr (Oelsner)	GDR	11.07
3. Ingrid Auerswald	GDR	11.14
4. Linda Haglund	SWE	11.16

5. Romy Müller	GDR	11.16
6. Kathryn Smallwood	GBR	11.28
7. Chantal Rega	FRA	11.32
8. Heather Hunte	GBR	11.34

Haglund led at the halfway mark, but Kondratyeva and Göhr stormed by her after 60 meters. Göhr edged ahead with a few meters to go, but Kondratyeva came back and, despite pulling a hamstring muscle at the finish, won by the smallest margin imaginable.

1984 Los Angeles C: 46, N: 33, D: 8.5. WR: 10.79 (Evelyn Ashford)

1. Evelyn Ashford	USA	10.97	OR
2. Alice Brown	USA	11.13	
3. Merlene Ottey-Page	JAM	11.16	
4. Jeannette Bolden	USA	11.25	
5. Grace Jackson	JAM	11.39	
6. Angela Bailey	CAN	11.40	
7. Heather Oakes (Hunte)	GBR	11.43	
8. Angella Taylor	CAN	11.62	

In 1976, 19-year-old Evelyn Ashford competed at the Montreal Olympics, finishing fifth in the 100 meters. Three years later, back in Montreal, she gained international acclaim at the World Cup meet by defeating East German world record holder Marita Koch in the 200, 21.83 to 22.02, and then beating the 100-meter world record holder, Marlies Göhr, 11.06 to 11.17. Ashford seemed right on track to fulfill her dreams of Olympic glory—until Jimmy Carter announced that U.S. athletes would not be allowed to go to Moscow. When the boycott was made official, Ashford was competing in Canada. She and her coach and a teammate went to a bar, where Evelyn, completely out of character, "got sloppy drunk," stood up and fell on her face.

Ashford reset her goals for the 1983 inaugural world championships in Helsinki and for the 1984 Olympics. In June of 1983 she was beaten by Göhr in Los Angeles 11.39 to 11.53, but one week later, competing in Colorado, she set a world record of 10.79. Annoyed that her record was not properly respected because it was set at high altitude, Ashford vowed to prove herself by defeating Göhr in Helsinki. She recorded the fastest time in each of the three preliminary rounds, but in the final she pulled a hamstring muscle and fell to the ground while Göhr sped on to victory, followed closely by Marita Koch.

For all of her frustrations, Ashford still had the Los Angeles Olympics to look forward to. But as she warmed up for her semifinal heat at the U.S. trials on June 18, 1984, Ashford felt a twinge in her right hamstring muscle. Running very carefully, she qualified for the Olympic team, but, although she had hoped to win three gold medals at the Olympics, she withdrew from the 200 meters to protect her leg.

With Göhr boycotted out of the Olympics, only the very real threat of injury stood between Evelyn Ashford and her long-awaited goal of an Olympic title. In Los Angeles, her leg held up as she again recorded the fastest time in each of the three preliminary rounds. In the final, she took command at the midway point and won going away.

Over the years Evelyn Ashford had earned a reputation as a shy, somewhat unfriendly loner, who shunned the media and rarely expressed her emotions. "They should be bottled up inside," she would say. "You want it to come out on the track." But after crossing the finish line and hearing the track announcer say that she had broken the Olympic record, the years of frustration and anguish gave way to tearful relief. After collapsing into the arms of teammate Jeannette Bolden, she cried her way through her victory lap while she received a standing ovation.

"When I caught my first glimpse of the gold medal while I waited on the victory stand," she would later recall, "I was emotionally overcome. I couldn't believe it was over. I couldn't stop crying."

Actually it wasn't all over. Not quite. Evelyn Ashford was now the world record holder and the Olympic champion, but one more challenge remained: she wanted to beat Marlies Göhr. In fact, on August 16, Göhr won the Friendship Games meet with a time of 10.95, faster than Ashford's Olympic record. But the next day, in Berlin, Ashford clocked 10.92 and 10.94. Then, on August 22, the two met head-to-head in Zurich. Ashford overcame Göhr's fast start and final surge to gain the victory—and set a new world record of 10.76 in the process. When the time was announced, Göhr and East German teammate Ingrid Auerswald, gracious in defeat, each took one of Ashford's hands and raised it in the air. Finally, ten years after she had begun competing for the *boys'* track team at Roseville High School in California, Evelyn Ashford had proved that she was the fastest woman in the world.

1988 Seoul C: 64, N: 42, D: 9.25. WR: 10.49 (D. Florence Griffith Joyner)

1. D. Florence Griffith Joyner	USA	10.54w
2. Evelyn Ashford	USA	10.83
3. Heike Drechsler (Daute)	GDR	10.85
4. Grace Jackson	JAM	10.97
5. Gwendolyn Torrence	USA	10.97
6. Natalya Pomoshchnikova	SOV/RUS	11.00
7. Juliet Cuthbert	JAM	11.26
8. Anelia Vechernikova	BUL	11.49

Delorez Florence Griffith was born December 21, 1959. The seventh of eleven children, she grew up in Watts, a neighborhood in Los Angeles best known as the site of a black uprising in 1965. Griffith was always a bit eccentric. Once she was asked to leave a local shopping mall because she was wearing her pet boa constrictor like a muffler. But what really set her apart from her peers was her speed. She began racing at age 7 and continued to compete until 1979 when she was forced to drop out of college in order to help support her family.

Sprint coach Bob Kersee found Griffith working as a

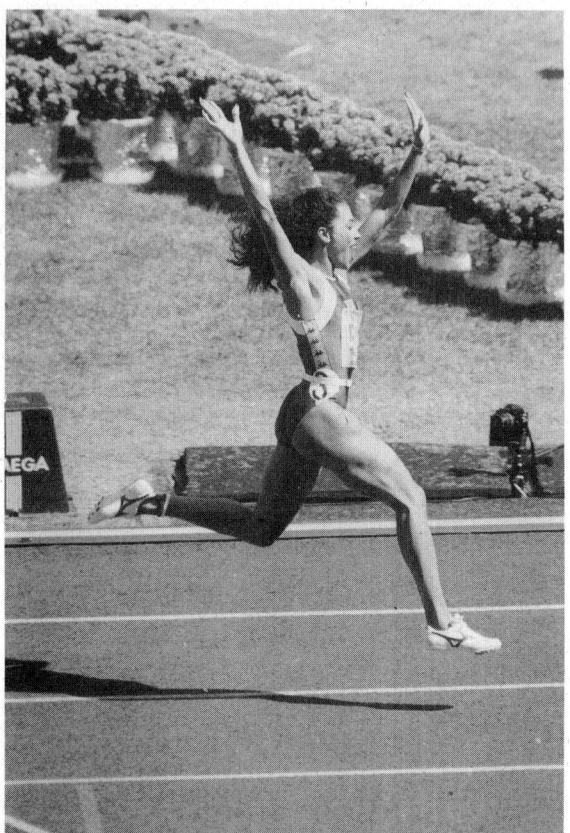

Florence Griffith Joyner won three gold medals and one silver in 1988 to go with the silver she won in 1984.

bank teller and helped her get financial aid so that she could attend U.C.L.A. Griffith first gained serious international attention when she placed fourth in the 200 meters at the 1983 world championships. The following year she earned a silver medal in the 200 at the Los Angeles Olympics, although her six-inch, wildly painted fingernails gained her more press than her running.

By 1986, Griffith, seemingly a perennial runner-up, was in semi-retirement, working in a bank again and also as a beautician. She returned to serious training in 1987 and finished second to Silke Gladisch of East Germany in that year's world championship 200. Her marriage to 1984 triple jump Olympic champion Al Joyner and her loss to Gladisch marked a turning point in her career. Now known as Florence Griffith Joyner, she became determined to end her string of second places. She obtained a videotape of Ben Johnson's explosive start in the world championship 100-meter final and watched it every day. After consulting with Johnson, she embarked on a vigorous weight-lifting program. She also incorporated endurance runs into her training and, along with her studies of Ben Johnson's start, she watched tapes of

Carl Lewis to analyze his form and his ability to run in a relaxed manner.

Griffith Joyner was still considered a 200-meter specialist, but on June 25, 1988, she ran a 10.89 100 in San Diego. Then, at the U.S. Olympic trials, exactly three weeks later, she achieved a stunning breakthrough. Running in a quarterfinal heat, she crossed the finish line in 10.49 seconds, obliterating Evelyn Ashford's 1984 world record of 10.76. In fact her time was faster than the automatically timed *men's* record in a wide range of nations, including Ireland, New Zealand, Norway, Iran, and Turkey. Griffith Joyner's shocking performance was not without controversy. Although the wind gauge next to the triple jump runway 30 feet away registered an unacceptable 4.3 meters per second, the gauge at the track registered exactly 0.0. Because gusty winds were sweeping through the stadium, it was assumed that the instrument had malfunctioned. But Omega Electronics defended their measuring device. In an official memo to the I.A.A.F., the company explained that a wind of 2.80 meters per second had blown across the track, but in a direction of 91 degrees perpendicular to the track. Subsequent analysis by Australian physicist Nicholas Linthorne has shown that the true wind reading was probably 5.5 meters per second or more. Nonetheless, Griffith Joyner's record stood. The next day she won the final in 10.61 with a legal wind of 1.2 meters per second.

Her spectacular times, coupled with her outrageous running suits, which she changed for each race, brought Florence Griffith Joyner overnight celebrity. She acquired yet another name: Flojo. Because of the wind controversy and because her record had been set at a domestic meet, the European sports press was still skeptical of Griffith Joyner's abilities. In Seoul, she put their doubts to rest. In the opening round she set an Olympic record of 10.88. Evelyn Ashford matched that time in the second round, but one heat later, Flojo ran a 10.62. She followed that with a wind-aided 10.70 in the semifinals.

In the final Griffith Joyner showed that her obsessive study of Ben Johnson's start was not wasted. Her reaction time of 0.131 seconds was not only the best in the race, it was faster than that of Johnson himself. Halfway through the race a smile began to spread across her face, and by the time she flashed across the finish line in a wind-aided 10.54, she was positively beaming. Behind her, Ashford edged Heike Drechsler for second place to become, at age 31, the oldest female sprint medalist in Olympic history. Anelia Vechernikova was even with Ashford at 80 meters, but pulled a muscle and hobbled in in last place.

Florence Griffith Joyner went on to win two more gold medals and one silver. Unfortunately, the disqualification of Ben Johnson left a cloud of suspicion over Flojo's performances as well. Skeptics pointed to her sudden improvement and her bulging muscles as evidence that she might be using steroids or human growth hormones. Griffith Joyner fueled this speculation by announcing her retirement on February 25, 1989, on the eve of the institution of mandatory random drug testing. However, the record clearly shows that Florence Griffith Joyner passed every drug test she ever took.

1992 Barcelona C: 54, N: 41, D: 8.1. WR: 10.49 (D. Florence Griffith Joyner)

1.	Gail Devers	USA	10.82
2.	Juliet Cuthbert	JAM	10.83
3.	Irina Privalova	RUS	10.84
4.	Gwendolyn Torrence	USA	10.86
5.	Merlene Ottey	JAM	10.88
6.	Anelia Nuneva (Vechernikova)	BUL	11.10
7.	Mary Onyali	NGR	11.15
8.	Liliana Allen Doll	CUB	11.19

When the Berlin Wall fell in 1989, no East German athlete was as well placed to take advantage of German reunification as sprinter Katrin Krabbe. She won both the 100 meters and 200 meters at the 1990 European championships and repeated the double at the 1991 world championships. She was voted the most popular female athlete in Germany, more popular even than Steffi Graf. Tall, blond, and beautiful, Krabbe was the perfect poster girl for newly unified Germany and she quickly signed endorsement contracts that made her rich. All was not rosy, however, for Katrin Krabbe. The tabloids dogged her wherever she went and the details of her romantic life were revealed as front-page gossip. When she returned to her hometown of Neubrandenburg in East Germany, she was greeted with hostility by some bitter neighbors for whom reunification had been a financial disaster. In addition, there was hostility between the athletes of what had been East and West Germany. The easterners produced far superior results, leading the westerners to accuse them of using prohibited drugs.

In January 1992, Katrin Krabbe and some of her East German teammates went to train in South Africa. Detractors accused them of fleeing Germany to escape drug testing. On January 24, a team of German medical officials flew down to South Africa and tested Krabbe and the others. The results were revealed on February 9: none of the women had tested positive, but the urine samples submitted by Krabbe, Grit Breuer, and Silke Möller all came from the same person. Six days later the German Track Federation charged the three women with tampering with a drug test and suspended them for four years. Because Krabbe was expected to be *the* German heroine of the upcoming Barcelona Olympics, the scandal was enormous. There was a flurry of appeals and hearings, and on April 4, the German Track Federation, much to the disgust of the rest of the world, revoked the suspensions, claiming that the urine samples might have been subject to outside tampering while they had been transferred from South Africa to the testing laboratory in Germany. On June 28 the I.A.A.F. arbitration panel cleared Krabbe's path to the Olympics on a technicality: the constitution of the German Track Federation did not

yet provide for random drug testing. Nevertheless, Krabbe did not take part in the Olympics. On July 2, she bowed out, claiming that the emotional ordeal of the past months had left her unable to perform at her usual standards. On July 21, Krabbe was given another test. This time the results showed traces of Clenbuterol, a steroid substitute. Krabbe never competed again.

With Katrin Krabbe out of the running, the role of favorite shifted to Gwen Torrence of Decatur, Georgia, who had finished second to Krabbe in both sprints at the 1991 world championships. Torrence's toughest challenge was expected to come from Merlene Ottey, who had been undefeated at 100 meters between the 1988 Olympics and the 1991 world championships, but who was known as "Ms. Bronze" because of a string of third-place finishes going back to the 200 meters at the 1980 Olympics and extending to both sprints at the 1984 Olympics, the 1987 world championships, and the 1991 world championships.

As it turned out, the most serious contenders were Juliet Cuthbert, who called herself a "Jamerican" because she grew up in Jamaica before moving to the United States with her mother when she was 16 years old, and Gail Devers, who had placed second behind Torrence at the United States Olympic trials. The story of Devers' travails the past four years almost defied belief. In June 1988 Devers began getting migraine headaches. She also experienced dizziness and temporary loss of sight in one eye. She managed to qualify for the Olympics in her speciality, the 100-meter hurdles, but in Seoul she was eliminated in the semifinals. At first it had been easy to assume that Devers' symptoms were the result of stress, but her condition continued to deteriorate. Unfortunately, it was two years before doctors finally came up with a correct diagnosis: Graves' disease. In order to control her hyperactive thyroid, Devers began radiation therapy on September 12, 1990. The therapy worked, but then she developed awful reactions to the radiation. She hemorrhaged blood clots, her weight fluctuated dramatically, and she experienced second-degree burns on her feet, which became infected and swollen. Incredibly, after missing 2½ years of training, Devers returned to competition and finished second in the 100-meter hurdles at the 1991 world championships.

The 100-meter final in Barcelona was the closest in Olympic history, even closer than the 1952 men's final. Devers and Privalova ran almost even most of the race, but Cuthbert, Torrence, and Ottey all came on at the end. It was impossible to tell who had won until slow-motion replays of the finish were shown in the stadium. Even then, one couldn't be sure. The official announcement finally gave the victory to Devers. Devers, Cuthbert, and Torrence had all set personal records, while Ottey ended up in fifth place even though she was less than one-tenth of a second behind the winner. Gail Devers was the third straight winner of the women's 100 meters to have attended UCLA.

Shut out of the medals, Gwen Torrence managed to spoil the event for the winners by publicly stating that two of the three medalists were drug users. At first she refused to name names. Then, under pressure from the media, she said she didn't mean Devers, which left Cuthbert and Privalova. The next day Cuthbert confronted Torrence, who told her she had meant Devers and Privalova. Finally Torrence made a public apology, but the damage had been done and Torrence came away more tainted than those she had accused.

200 METERS

1896–1936 not held

1948 London C: 33, N: 17, D: 8.6. WR: 23.6 (Stanislawa Walasiewicz)

1. Francina "Fanny" Blankers-Koen	HOL	24.4
2. Audrey Williamson	GBR	25.1
3. Audrey Patterson	USA	25.2
4. Shirley Strickland	AUS	25.2e
5. Margaret Walker	GBR	25.4e
6. Daphne Robb	SAF	25.5e

Fanny Blankers-Koen had already won two gold medals in the 100-meter dash and the 80-meter hurdles. Far from being exuberant about these accomplishments, she felt tremendous pressure to win a third gold medal and was close to a mental breakdown. Prior to the semifinals of the 200 meters she told her husband, Jan, that she wanted to withdraw. Jan tried to calm her down and gave her words of encouragement, but to no avail. In desperation he evoked memories of her parents and her two children, and she burst into tears. When she finally came out of her cry, she had recovered and was once again eager to run. She went out and won her heat by six yards, establishing an Olympic record of 24.3 seconds. The next day, running on a muddy track, she won the final by seven yards, the largest margin ever recorded in the women's 200 meters. In 1975, the photo finish of this race was discovered. It revealed that Strickland had actually finished ahead of Patterson.

1952 Helsinki C: 38, N: 21, D: 7.26. WR: 23.6 (Stanislawa Walasiewicz)

1. Marjorie Jackson	AUS	23.7	(23.89)
2. Bertha Brouwer	HOL	24.2	(24.25)
3. Nadezhda Khnykina	SOV/GEO	24.2	(24.37)
4. Winsome Cripps	AUS	24.2	(24.40)
5. Helga Klein	GER	24.6	(24.72)
6. Daphne Hasenjager (Robb)	SAF	24.6	(24.72)

One of the longest-lasting women's track and field world records ever was set by Stanislawa Walasiewicz on August 15, 1935, when she/he ran the 200 meters in 23.6 seconds. Almost 17 years later, Marjorie Jackson tied that record in the first round of the 1952 Helsinki Olympics, and in the first semifinal she ran a 23.4 to finally break it. In the

final she reached the tape four yards ahead of her nearest rival.

1956 Melbourne C: 27, N: 12, D: 11.30. WR: 23.2 (Elizabeth Cuthbert)

1. Elizabeth Cuthbert	AUS	23.4	EOR	(23.55)
2. Christa Stubnick	GDR	23.7		(23.89)
3. Marlene Matthews	AUS	23.8		(24.10)
4. Norma Croker	AUS	24.0		(24.22)
5. June Paul (Foulds)	GBR	24.3		(24.30)
6. Gisela Köhler	GDR	24.3		(24.68)

For the first and only time in Olympic history, the medalists in the two sprints (100 and 200 meters) finished in the exact same order.

1960 Rome C: 29, N: 17, D: 9.5. WR: 22.9 (Wilma Rudolph)

1. Wilma Rudolph	USA	24.0	(24.13)
2. Jutta Heine	GER	24.4	(24.58)
3. Dorothy Hyman	GBR	24.7	(24.82)
4. Maria Itkina	SOV/RUS	24.7	(24.85)
5. Barbara Janiszewska	POL	24.8	(24.96)
6. Giuseppina Leone	ITA	24.9	(25.01)

Wilma Rudolph dominated the event, setting an Olympic record of 23.2 in her opening heat. Silver medalist Jutta Heine was the daughter of a millionaire, while the father of bronze medalist Dorothy Hyman was a Yorkshire miner.

1964 Tokyo C: 29, N: 21, D: 10.19. WR: 22.9 (Wilma Rudolph, Margaret Burvill)

1. Edith McGuire	USA	23.0	OR	(23.05)
2. Irena Kirszenstein	POL	23.1		(23.13)
3. Marilyn Black	AUS	23.1		(23.18)
4. Una Morris	JAM	23.5		(23.58)
5. Lyudmila Samotyosova	SOV/RUS	23.5		(23.59)
6. Barbara Sobotta (Janiszewska)	POL	23.9		(23.97)
7. Janet Simpson	GBR	23.9		(23.98)
8. Daphne Arden	GBR	24.0		(24.01)

1968 Mexico City C: 36, N: 21, D: 10.18. WR: 22.7 (Irena Szewińska [Kirzenstein])

1. Irena Szewińska (Kirszenstein)	POL	22.58	WR
2. Raelene Boyle	AUS	22.74	
3. Jennifer Lamy	AUS	22.88	
4. Barbara Ferrell	USA	22.93	
5. Nicole Montandon	FRA	23.08	
6. Wyomia Tyus	USA	23.08	
7. Margaret Bailes	USA	23.18	
8. Jutta Stöck	GER	23.25	

Irena Kirszenstein was born in Leningrad to Jewish parents from Poland on May 24, 1946. Beginning in 1964 she competed in five Olympics, winning seven medals in five different events. As an 18-year-old at the 1964 Tokyo Olympics she finished second in the long jump and the 200 meters and ran the second leg on the Polish 4 × 100-meter relay team, which scored an upset victory. In 1967 she culminated a five-year courtship by marrying Janusz

Szewińsk, and when she arrived in Mexico City for the 1968 Olympics she was running under the name Irena Szewińska. She was disappointed in her first two events, failing to qualify for the final of the long jump and finishing third in the 100 meters, but in the final of the 200 meters she overcame a slow start to win in world record time.

Most people attribute the plethora of world records which were set in Mexico City to the altitude, but another factor was the unusual method that the Mexicans used for determining wind conditions. With the acceptable limit for world records set at a wind speed of 2 meters per second, the measurement during the women's 200 meters was exactly 2 m.p.s. The same recording of exactly 2.0 m.p.s. was registered when Bob Beamon made his famous 29-foot 2½-inch leap and when Nelson Prudencio and Viktor Saneyev set world records in the triple jump.

Eighth-place finisher Jutta Stöck was the daughter of 1936 javelin gold-medalist Gerhard Stöck.

1972 Munich C: 37, N: 27, D: 9.7. WR: 22.4 (Chi Cheng)

1. Renate Stecher	GDR	22.40	EWR
2. Raelene Boyle	AUS	22.45	
3. Irena Szewińska (Kirszenstein)	POL	22.74	
4. Ellen Stropahl	GDR	22.75	
5. Christina Heinich	GDR	22.89	
5. Annegret Kroniger	GER	22.89	
7. Alice Annum	GHA	22.99	
8. Rosie Allwood	JAM	23.11	

Between August 1970 and June 1974, Renate Stecher won 90 straight outdoor races at 100 meters and 200 meters.

1976 Montreal C: 36, N: 21, D: 7.28. WR: 22.21 (Irena Szewińska [Kirszenstein])

1. Bärbel Eckert	GDR	22.37	OR
2. Annegret Richter	GER	22.39	
3. Renate Stecher	GDR	22.47	
4. Carla Bodendorf	GDR	22.64	
5. Inge Helten	GER	22.68	
6. Tetyana Prorochenko	SOV/UKR	23.03	
7. Denise Robertson	AUS	23.05	
8. Chantal Rega	FRA	23.09	

The first shock came in the semifinals, when five-time sprint finalist Raelene Boyle was disqualified for false-starting twice. Boyle was furious and protested unsuccessfully. The electronic starting device had registered a clean start the first time, but the recall judge claimed that Boyle's head and shoulders had been moving. Unaware that she had actually been charged with a false start rather than a mere warning, Boyle was stunned when she was disqualified after her next false start. The real surprise was 21-year-old Bärbel Eckert, East Germany's third-string sprinter. In the quarterfinals she equaled her personal best of 22.85. She won her semifinal heat in 22.71 and then set an Olympic record to win the final.

1980 Moscow C: 35, N: 25, D: 7.30. WR: 21.71 (Marita Koch)

1. Bärbel Wöckel (Eckert)	GDR	22.03	OR
2. Natalya Bochina	SOV/RUS	22.19	
3. Merlene Ottey	JAM	22.20	
4. Romy Müller	GDR	22.47	
5. Kathryn Smallwood	GBR	22.61	
6. Beverley Goddard	GBR	22.72	
7. Denise Boyd (Robertson)	AUS	22.76	
8. Sonia Lannaman	GBR	22.80	

Defending champion Bärbel Eckert of Leipzig, now married, a mother, and renamed Wöckel, made it through to the final without winning a single heat. She finished second each time, once to Lyudmila Maslakova of the U.S.S.R., and twice to Merlene Ottey. Meanwhile, 18-year-old Natalya Bochina ran a 22.26 in the second round to break Wöckel's Olympic record. In the final, however, it was Wöckel who took the lead coming out of the turn and won going away. Missing from the competition were the two women who had clocked the fastest times in the world: Marita Koch, who chose to concentrate on the 400 meters, and Evelyn Ashford, who suffered the double blow of injury and boycott.

1984 Los Angeles C: 37, N: 28, D: 8.9. WR: 21.71 (Marita Koch)

1. Valerie Brisco-Hooks	USA	21.81	OR
2. D. Florence Griffith	USA	22.04	
3. Merlene Ottey-Page	JAM	22.09	
4. Kathryn Cook (Smallwood)	GBR	22.10	
5. Grace Jackson	JAM	22.20	
6. Randy Givens	USA	22.36	
7. Rose-Aimée Bacoul	FRA	22.78	
8. Liliane Gaschet	FRA	22.86	

In 1982, Valerie Brisco-Hooks was a retired runner, forty pounds overweight after giving birth to a baby boy. Encouraged by her family and her coach, she returned to the track the following year and found that childbirth and motherhood had actually increased her strength. In 1984, she seemed to come out of nowhere to make the U.S. team. Three days after winning the 400 meters, Brisco-Hooks, aided by the absence of East Germans Marita Koch and Marlies Göhr, overcame a mediocre start to become the first person to record a 200-400 double win in the Olympics.

1988 Seoul C: 59, N: 42, D: 9.29. WR: 21.71 (Marita Koch, Heike Drechsler)

1. D. Florence Griffith Joyner	USA	21.34	WR
2. Grace Jackson	JAM	21.72	
3. Heike Drechsler (Daute)	GDR	21.95	
4. Merlene Ottey	JAM	21.99	
5. Silke Möller (Gladisch)	GDR	22.09	
6. Gwendolyn Torrence	USA	22.17	
7. Maya Azarashvili	SOV/GEO	22.33	
8. Galina Malchugina	SOV/RUS	22.42	

Florence Griffith Joyner set an Olympic record of 21.76 in the quarterfinals. In the semifinals she ran a 21.56 to break the nine-year-old world record. The final, run 100 minutes later, was more of the same: Griffith Joyner pulled away in the second half of the race and leaped joyously across the finish line, stopping the clock in an almost unbelievable 21.34. Grace Jackson took almost a half second off her pre-Olympic best and came within one one-hundredth of a second of the pre-Olympic world record, yet found herself 4 meters behind Griffith Joyner at the finish.

1992 Barcelona C: 51, N: 40, D: 8.6. WR: 21.34 (D. Florence Griffith Joyner)

1. Gwendolyn Torrence	USA	21.81
2. Juliet Cuthbert	JAM	22.02
3. Merlene Ottey	JAM	22.09
4. Irina Privalova	RUS	22.19
5. Carlette Guidry	USA	22.30
6. Grace Jackson Small	JAM	22.58
7. Michelle Finn	USA	22.61
8. Galina Malchugina	RUS	22.63

Torrence ran 21.72 in the semifinals to better her personal best by .30 seconds. In the final she pulled away after hitting the final straight. Torrence also won medals in both relays, but her performance was tainted by the fact that her mouth ran even faster than her feet. After finishing out of the medals in the 100 meters, Torrence leveled unsupported accusations of drug use at her opponents (see page 196). At the press conference after the 200 meters, Juliet Cuthbert confronted Torrence, noting that when she spoke with her own mother after earning a silver medal in the 100, the elder Cuthbert immediately asked her daughter if it was true that she was taking drugs. Torrence appeared only mildly repentant and left the impression that she didn't understand the difference between being outspoken and being slanderous.

400 METERS

1896–1960 not held

1964 Tokyo C: 23, N: 17, D: 10.17. WR: 51.4 (Dan Shin-geum)

1. Elizabeth Cuthbert	AUS	52.0	OR	(52.01)
2. Ann Packer	GBR	52.2		(52.20)
3. Judith Amoore	AUS	53.4		
4. Antonia Munkácsi	HUN	54.4		
5. Maria Itkina	SOV/RUS	54.6		
6. Mathilda "Tilly" van der Zwaard	HOL	55.2		
7. Gertrud Schmidt	GDR	55.4		
8. Evelyne Lebret	FRA	55.5		

World record holder Dan Shin-geum of North Korea was barred from participating in the Olympics because of a dispute between the I.O.C. and the North Korean government. In her absence, the inaugural Olympic 400 meters was won by Betty Cuthbert, the remarkable Australian who had earned three gold medals eight years earlier in Melbourne. At the Rome Olympics in 1960 she was suffering from a hamstring pull and was forced to withdraw from competition after only one race. In

Tokyo she coasted through the opening round and the semifinals, satisfied to qualify for the final. Then, on October 16, she ran what she later called "the only perfect race I have ever run" to finish a long yard ahead of Ann Packer.

1968 Mexico City C: 29, N: 21. D: 10.16. WR: 51.2 (Dan Shin-geum)

1. Colette Besson	FRA	52.03	EOR
2. Lillian Board	GBR	52.12	
3. Natalya Pechenkina	SOV/RUS	52.25	
4. Janet Simpson	GBR	52.57	
5. Aurelia Penton	CUB	52.75	
6. Jarvis Scott	USA	52.79	
7. Helga Henning	GER	52.89	
8. Hermina Van Der Hoeven	HOL	53.02	

The victory of Colette Besson, a 22-year-old physical education teacher from Bordeaux, came as a complete surprise. Her best time previous to the Olympics was 53.8, but she was able to improve by 1.8 seconds when it counted. She passed the favorite, Lillian Board, just before the finish line and won by almost two feet. Although the harsher members of the British sports press were critical of Board for missing the gold medal, she was only 19 years old and seemed a good bet for the 1972 Olympics in Munich. She did make it to Munich, but the circumstances were tragic. In 1970 she developed cancer, complicated by peritonitis. She died in a Munich clinic 13 days after her 22nd birthday.

1972 Munich C: 49, N: 29, D: 9.7. WR: 51.0 (Marilyn Neufville, Monika Zehrt)

1. Monika Zehrt	GDR	51.08	OR
2. Rita Wilden (Jahn)	GER	51.21	
3. Kathy Hammond	USA	51.64	
4. Helga Seidler	GDR	51.86	
5. Mable Fergerson	USA	51.96	
6. Charlene Rendina	AUS	51.99	
7. Dagmar Käsling	GDR	52.19	
8. Györgyi Balogh	HUN	52.39	

Despite the absence of injured co-world record holder Marilyn Neufville of Jamaica, the competition was excellent. The Olympic record was broken by five different women before the final was run. However 19-year-old Monika Zehrt of Berlin seemed unaffected by the pressure of her opponents or by her role as favorite. She had taken the lead by the halfway mark and held off a late challenge by local favorite Rita Wilden to win by a meter.

1976 Montreal C: 38, N: 19, D: 7.29. WR: 49.75 (Irena Szewińska [Kirszenstein])

1. Irena Szewińska (Kirszenstein)	POL	49.28	WR
2. Christina Brehmer	GDR	50.51	
3. Ellen Streidt (Stropahl)	GDR	50.55	
4. Pirjo Häggman (Wilmi)	FIN	50.56	
5. Rosalyn Bryant	USA	50.65	
6. Sheila Ingram	USA	50.90	

| 7. Riita Salin | FIN | 50.98 |
| 8. Debra Sapenter | USA | 51.66 |

The amazing Irena Szewińska had already won Olympic medals in the 100 meters, 200 meters, long jump, and 4 × 100-meter relay when she switched to the 400 meters in 1973. The following year she became the first woman to break 50 seconds in what was only the second 400 meters race of her career. Early in 1976 her world record

Between 1964 and 1976 Irena Szewínska won seven medals in five different events. Here she acknowledges the applause of the crowd after winning the 400 meters in 1976.

was broken by Christina Brehmer. But later in the year Szewińska regained the record, and an Olympic showdown between the 18-year-old Brehmer and the 30-year-old Szewińska was eagerly awaited. Irena coasted through the first two rounds and then set an Olympic record of 50.48 in the semifinals. For the first 300 meters, the final was a close race, but then Szewińska pulled away dramatically to win by almost ten meters. Her total of seven medals (three gold, two silver, and two bronze) ranks her along with Shirley Strickland as one of the most successful female track and field athletes in Olympic history. Between 1974 and 1978 she won 34 straight 400-meter finals, until she was finally beaten by Marita Koch at the European championships. In 1980 Szewińska took part in the Moscow Olympics, but was eliminated in the semifinals when she pulled a muscle.

Pirjo Häggman, who finished fourth in Montreal, later became the first woman to be elected to the I.O.C.

1980 Moscow C: 38, N: 22, D: 7.28. WR: 48.60 (Marita Koch)

1. Marita Koch	GDR	48.88	OR
2. Jarmila Kratochvilová	CZE	49.46	
3. Christina Lathan (Brehmer)	GDR	49.66	
4. Irina Nazarova	SOV/RUS	50.07	
5. Nina Zyuskova	SOV/UKR	50.17	
6. Gabriele Löwe	GDR	51.33	
7. Pirjo Häggman	FIN	51.35	
8. Linsey MacDonald	GBR	52.40	

Marita Koch had been one of the favorites in 1976, but was forced to withdraw from her semifinal heat because of injury. In 1979 she became the first woman to break 22 seconds for 200 meters as well as the first woman to beat 49 seconds for 400 meters. In Moscow, using the same spikes she had used four years earlier in Montreal, Koch won a clear victory over Kratochvilová and Lathan, both of whom recorded personal bests. The race was the first in history in which three women broke the 50-second barrier.

1984 Los Angeles C: 28, N: 18, D: 8.6. WR: 47.99 (Jarmila Kratochvilová)

1. Valerie Brisco-Hooks	USA	48.83	OR
2. Chandra Cheeseborough	USA	49.05	
3. Kathryn Cook (Smallwood)	GBR	49.42	
4. Marita Payne	CAN	49.91	
5. Lillie Leatherwood	USA	50.25	
6. Ute Thimm	GER	50.37	
7. Charmaine Crooks	CAN	50.45	
8. Ruth Waithera	KEN	51.56	

At the U.S. trials, Cheeseborough had come from behind to defeat Brisco-Hooks, but in the Olympic final, competing only three miles from where her older brother had been shot to death by a stray bullet ten years earlier while jogging on a high school track, Brisco-Hooks held off Cheeseborough's finishing kick to win the first of her three gold medals.

Of the 28 women who took part in the 400-meter competition in 1984, the slowest was Zeina Mina who finished last in her heat with a time of 59.56. However, it is worth bearing in mind the difficulties which Mina faced training in her hometown—Beirut. Lebanon's leading heptathlete, Mina was unable to train for her specialty because shelling prevented her from reaching the stadium. So she ran on the beach, in the subway, anywhere she could find. For a year she didn't run on a track, until two weeks before the Olympics. Her performance in Los Angeles did not bother her. "It is wonderful here," she said, "away from the bombs."

1988 Seoul C: 46, N: 33, D: 9.26. WR: 47.60 (Marita Koch)
1. Olha Bryzhina	SOV/UKR	48.65	OR
2. Petra Müller	GDR	49.45	
3. Olga Nazarova	SOV/RUS	49.90	
4. Valerie Brisco	USA	50.16	
5. Diane Dixon	USA	50.72	
6. Denean Howard-Hill	USA	51.12	
7. Helga Arendt	GER	51.17	
8. Maree Holland	AUS	51.25	

Defending champion Valerie Brisco took the early lead. World champion Olha Bryzhina, fifth at the halfway mark, caught Brisco after 300 meters, opened up an 8-meter lead and won by 6 meters. Her husband, Viktor Bryzhin, also won a gold medal in the 4 × 100-meter relay. With the exception of Bryzhina and Müller, the times in the final were surprisingly slow. In the semis all three Americans had broken 50 seconds, while Olga Nazarova had clocked a 49.11. Unlike the men's 400-meter runners, the women were not allowed a day off between the semifinals and the final.

1992 Barcelona C: 41, N: 29, D: 8.5. WR: 47.60 (Marita Koch)
1. Marie-José Pérec	FRA	48.83
2. Olha Bryzhina	UKR	49.05
3. Ximena Restrepo Gaviria	COL	49.64
4. Olga Nazarova	RUS	49.69
5. Jillian Richardson-Briscoe	CAN	49.93
6. Rochelle Stevens	USA	50.11
7. Sandie Richards	JAM	50.19
8. Phylis Smith	GBR	50.87

Marie-José Pérec was born in Basse-Terre on the island of Guadeloupe in the Caribbean. She moved to Paris with her mother when she was 16 years old. Because of her natural ability, coaches practically forced her to become a sprinter. By 1988 she was representing France in the Olympics at 200 meters. She improved rapidly and in 1991 she won a clear victory in the 400 meters final at the world championships. Her athletic success, along with her model's body (5 feet 10¾ inches, 132 pounds, and long, long legs), catapulted her into major stardom in France. In the months leading up to the 1992 Olympics, the French media followed her every move, scrutinizing her training regimen, photographing her visit to her grandmother in Guadeloupe, even analyzing her opponents in greater detail than the press in their own countries. Despite this pressure, Pérec did not disappoint her followers. She was hard-pressed by defending champion Olha Bryzhina, who took an early lead and was still in front as the finalists entered the final straightaway. But then Pérec used her long, graceful strides to pull away and win by almost two meters.

Pérec's time of 48.83 was the first sub-49-second 400 to be run since 1988. At the post-race press conference, Pérec was asked if she thought she could someday break Marita Koch's world record of 47.60. She startled the audience by bluntly replying, "I think the world record is the race I ran today. I don't think that anyone has run under 49 seconds until now. To run this race today I didn't need any 'biological preparation.'" She thus accused of doping not only Marita Koch, but also five other runners, including Valerie Brisco annd Olha Bryzhina, who was sitting beside her. Bryzhina did not respond.

800 METERS

1896–1924 not held

1928 Amsterdam C: 25, N: 13, D: 8.2. WR: 2:19.6 (Karoline "Lina" Radke)
1. Karoline "Lina" Radke	GER	2:16.8	WR
2. Kinue Hitomi	JPN	2:17.6	
3. Inga Gentzel	SWE	2:18.8	
4. Jenny Thompson	CAN	2:21.4	
5. Fanny Rosenfeld	CAN	2:22.4	
6. Florence McDonald	USA	2:22.6	
7. Marie Dollinger	GER	2:23.0	
8. Gertruda Kilos	POL	2:28.0	

The 1928 women's 800-meter race touched off a major controversy in the athletic world. The competition itself was exciting enough. The three German finalists, Lina Radke, Marie Dollinger, and Elfriede Wever, ran a team race, with Dollinger and Wever wearing down the opposition and keeping a steady pace for Radke, who pulled away in the final 300 meters. Radke's winning time was a world record that lasted for sixteen years. After the race, several of the women collapsed in exhaustion and some had to be given aid. Antifeminists in the press and in the International Amateur Athletic Federation (I.A.A.F.) seized on their condition as evidence that women should be banned from running races of more than 200 meters. The London *Daily Mail* quoted doctors who said that women who took part in races of 800 meters and other such "feats of endurance" would "become old too soon." The president of the International Olympic Committee, Comte de Baillet-Latour, spoke out in favor of eliminating all women's sports from the Olympics and returning to the ancient Greek custom of an all-male competition. But there were those who supported women's athletics, and they pointed out that men frequently fainted after races just as women did. In fact, male rowers were *expected* to be nearly comatose at the finish of important races, such as those between Oxford and Cambridge or

Harvard and Yale. In retrospect, of course, the arguments of the antiwomen forces seem foolish and ridiculous, particularly in light of the inclusion of a women's marathon in the 1984 Olympics. What makes the story more of a tragedy than a comedy, however, is that the executive committee of the I.A.A.F. actually *did* ban races longer than 200 meters, and no women's race longer than ½ lap was run at the Olympics for another 32 years.

Some of the early women athletes were extremely versatile. Fifth-place finisher Fanny Rosenfeld, who worked in a Toronto chocolate factory, also took second in the 100 meters and first in the 4 × 100-meter relay. Silver medalist Kinue Hitomi was the world record holder in the 200 meters and the long jump. Since neither event was included in the Olympics program, she took part instead in the 100 meters and the 800 meters. At the third Women's World Games, held in Prague in 1930, Hitomi delighted the crowd by winning four medals: a gold in the long jump, a silver in the triathlon, and bronzes in the 60-meter dash and the discus. The following year Kinue Hitomi died of tuberculosis at the age of 23.

1932–1956 not held

1960 Rome C: 27, N: 15, D: 9.7. WR: 2:04.3 (Lyudmyla Shevtsova)

1. Lyudmyla Shevtsova	SOV/UKR	2:04.3	EWR	(2:04.50)
2. Brenda Jones	AUS	2:04.4		(2:04.58)
3. Ursula Donath	GDR	2:05.6		(2:05.73)
4. Vera Kummerfeldt	GER	2:05.9		(2:06.07)
5. Antje Gleichfeld	GER	2:06.5		(2:06.63)
6. Joy Jordan	GBR	2:07.8		(2:07.95)
7. Gizella Csoka	HUN	2:08.0		(2:08.11)
8. Beata Zbikowska	POL	2:11.8		(2:11.91)

Dixie Willis of Australia led the field for most of the race, but, with 150 meters to go, she suddenly threw her arms into the air and staggered off the track. Brenda Jones took the lead, but was passed by world record holder Lyudmyla Shevtsova just before the finish.

1964 Tokyo C: 23, N: 15, D: 10.20. WR: 1:58.0 (Dan Shin-geum)

1. Ann Packer	GBR	2:01.1	OR
2. Maryvonne Dupureur	FRA	2:01.9	
3. M. Ann Marise Chamberlain	NZE	2:02.8	
4. Zsuzsa Szabó	HUN	2:03.5	
5. Antje Gleichfeld	GER	2:03.9	
6. Laine Erik	SOV/EST	2:05.1	
7. Gerarda Kraan	HOL	2:05.8	
8. Anne Smith	GBR	2:05.8	

With unofficial world record holder Dan Shin-geum out because of politics and official world record holder (2:01.2) Dixie Willis out because of illness, the 800 meters looked like an open race. In the semifinals, Maryvonne Dupureur, a housewife and physical education teacher from Lille, set an Olympic record of 2:04.1. In the final Dupureur had a five-yard lead entering the

last straightaway, but Britain's Ann Packer, who had already won a silver medal in the 400 meters, turned on a fantastic finishing kick, passed Dupureur with 70 yards to go, and won by five yards. The 800 meters was not really Packer's race. She had finished fifth in her opening heat and third in her semifinal heat. She had considered skipping the final and going shopping instead, but when her fiancé, Robbie Brightwell, finished a disappointing fourth in the men's 400 meters, she decided to go all-out in his honor. "It was so easy, I could not believe I had won," she told reporters afterward. "I was thinking about him and not about myself, and so I wasn't nervous."

1968 Mexico City C: 24, N: 16, D: 10.19. WR: 1:58.0 (Dan Shin-geum)

1. Madeline Manning	USA	2:00.9	OR	(2:00.92)
2. Ileana Silai	ROM	2:02.5		(2:02.58)
3. Maria Gommers	HOL	2:02.6		(2:02.63)
4. Sheila Taylor	GBR	2:03.8		(2:03.81)
5. Doris Brown	USA	2:03.9		(2:03.98)
6. Patricia Lowe	GBR	2:04.2		(2:04.25)
7. Abigail Hoffman	CAN	2:06.8		(2:06.99)
8. Maryvonne Dupureur	FRA	2:08.2		(2:08.28)

The most shocking incident of the 1968 women's events occurred in the first semifinal heat, when the 20-year-old favorite, and official world record holder (2:00.5) Vera Nikolić of Yugoslavia, overcome by the pressure of being her nation's only hope for a track and field medal, dropped out after 300 meters and left the stadium. Rumors quickly spread that she had gone straight to a nearby bridge and was only prevented from committing suicide by her coach, who had followed her. That race was won by 20-year-old Madeline Manning, a Tennessee State "Tigerbelle" from Cleveland. Two days later, in the final, Manning took the early lead, then, spurred on by the garlicky perspiration of one of the other runners, she pulled away in the backstretch of the final lap and won by over ten meters.

1972 Munich C: 38, N: 26, D: 9.3. WR: 1:58.0 (Dan Shin-geum)

1. Hildegard Falck	GER	1:58.6	OR	(1:58.55)
2. Nijolė Sabaitė	SOV/LIT	1:58.7		(1:58.65)
3. Gunhild Hoffmeister	GDR	1:59.2		(1:59.19)
4. Svetla Zlateva	BUL	1:59.7		(1:59.72)
5. Vera Nikolić	YUG	2:00.0		(1:59.98)
6. Ileana Silai	ROM	2:00.0		(2:00.04)
7. Rosemary Stirling	GBR	2:00.2		(2:00.15)
8. Abigail Hoffman	CAN	2:00.2		(2:00.17)

The fireworks started in the second heat of the first round, when Svetla Zlateva slashed three seconds off her personal best to set an Olympic record of 1:58.9. Vera Nikolić finished close behind her in 1:59.6. Previous to this race, the only women to better two minutes had been Dan Shin-geum, Hildegard Falck, and Vasilena Amzina of Bulgaria, who had run a 1:59.9 a week before the Olympics began. In the fourth heat of the first round Amzina collided with Raisa Ruus of the U.S.S.R. and fell to the ground. She got up and finished the race with blood on her face, but she failed to qualify for the next round. The first semifinal was won by Lithuanian Nijolė Sabaitė and the second by local favorite Hildegard Falck, a 23-year-old schoolteacher. In the second semi, defending champion Madeline Manning was eliminated when she misjudged the finish line and was passed just before the real line by Rosemary Stirling. The final was a thrilling race. Falck, urged on by the partisan crowd, pulled away coming out of the last curve and held off a final burst by Sabaitė.

1976 Montreal C: 35, N: 20, D: 7.26. WR: 1:56.0 (Valentina Gerassimova)

1. Tatyana Kazankina	SOV/RUS	1:54.94	WR
2. Nikolina Shtereva	BUL	1:55.42	
3. Elfi Zinn	GDR	1:55.60	
4. Anita Weiss	GDR	1:55.74	
5. Svetlana Styrkina	SOV/BLR	1:56.44	
6. Svetla Zlateva	BUL	1:57.21	
7. Doris Gluth	GDR	1:58.99	
8. Mariana Suman	ROM	2:02.21	

The level of the competition was so high that world record holder Valentina Gerassimova, European champion Liliana Tomova of Bulgaria, Commonwealth champion Charlene Rendina of Australia, and 1968 Olympic champion Madeline Jackson (Manning) were all eliminated in the semifinals. Anita Weiss, who lowered the Olympic record by two seconds with a 1:56.53 in her semifinal heat, broke the world record in the final, but didn't even win a medal. Kazankina, a 1500-meter specialist who had been entered in the 800 meters as well on the final day for entries, moved from fifth place to first in the last 50 meters and slashed the world record by over a second.

1980 Moscow C: 28, N: 17, D: 7.27. WR: 1:54.85 (Nadiya Olizarenko)

1. Nadiya Olizarenko	SOV/UKR	1:53.43	WR
2. Olga Mineyeva	SOV/RUS	1:54.81	
3. Tatyana Providokhina	SOV/RUS	1:55.46	
4. Martina Kämpfert	GDR	1:56.21	
5. Hildegard Ullrich	GDR	1:57.20	
6. Jolanta Januchta	POL	1:58.25	
7. Nikolina Shtereva	BUL	1:58.71	
8. Gabriella Dorio	ITA	1:59.12	

For the first time in Olympic history, all three medals in a women's track event were won by athletes from the same nation. Olizarenko, a 26-year-old military office worker from Odessa, ran a spectacular race, leading from start to finish (a rarity at 800 meters) and clipping almost one and a half seconds from her own world record, set only six weeks earlier.

1984 Los Angeles C: 25, N: 20, D: 8.6. WR: 1:53.28 (Jarmila Kratochvilová)

1. Doina Melinte	ROM	1:57.60
2. Kimberly Gallagher	USA	1:58.63
3. Rafira Fita Lovin	ROM	1:58.83
4. Gabriella Dorio	ITA	1:59.05
5. Lorraine Baker	GBR	2:00.03
6. Ruth Wysocki	USA	2:00.34
7. Margrit Klinger	GER	2:00.65
8. Caroline O'Shea	IRL	2:00.77

Melinte, known for her fast times, but disappointing performances in important meets, took the lead from Dorio with about 225 meters to go and won by over five meters. Conspicuously missing because of the Soviet-bloc boycott was Czech world record holder Jarmila Kratochvilová, who had caused a sensation at the 1983 world championships by winning the 400- and 800-meter races, a most unusual double.

1988 Seoul C: 29, N: 20, D: 9.26. WR: 1:53.28 (Jarmila Kratochvilová)

1. Sigrun Wodars	GDR	1:56.10
2. Christine Wachtel	GDR	1:56.64
3. Kimberly Gallagher	USA	1:56.91
4. Slobodanka Čolović	YUG	1:57.50
5. Delisa Floyd	USA	1:57.80
6. Inna Yevseyeva	SOV/UKR	1:59.37
7. Teresa Zuñiga	SPA	1:59.82
8. Diane Edwards	GBR	2:00.77

The two Ws, Wodars and Wachtel, had a lot in common. They were both born in 1965, they were both 5 feet 5¼ inches tall, they ran for the same club and trained under the same coach, Walter Gladrow, and they both liked champagne, ice cream, and chocolate. Most important of all, they were both experts at running 800 meters. In 1987, Wachtel defeated Wodars four straight times, but in the biggest meet of the year, the world championships in Rome, Wodars came out on top.

In 1988, Wachtel was again dominant, finishing ahead of Wodars seven of eight times in the run-up to the Olympics. In Seoul, the two Ws took turns setting the pace. Wodars forged ahead in the final straightaway and went on to win by 5 meters. Unfortunately, the Cuban boycott prevented the participation of Ana Quirot, who had won all 13 of her 800-meter races in 1988, including victories over both Wodars and Wachtel. The entire Romanian squad also missed the Games; they were victims of blundering team officials who forgot to file their entry forms.

1992 Barcelona C: 36, N: 26, D: 8.3. WR: 1:53.28 (Jarmila Kratochvilová)

1. Ellen van Langen	HOL	1:55.54
2. Lilia Nurutdinova	RUS	1:55.99
3. Ana Fidelia Quirot Moret	CUB	1:56.80
4. Inna Yevseyeva	UKR	1:57.20
5. Maria de Lurdes Mutola	MOZ	1:57.49
6. Ella Kovacs	ROM	1:57.95
7. Joetta Clark	USA	1:58.06
8. Lyubov Gurina	RUS	1:58.13

It was widely assumed that the medals would be divided among the first four finishers at the 1991 world championships: Nurutdinova, Quirot, Kovacs, and Mutola. Few people outside of the Netherlands took it seriously when three weeks before the opening of the Olympics Ellen van Langen ran the fastest time of the year (1:55.63) and beat Nurutdinova and Kovacs in the process. A good race, but the 26-year-old van Langen had never before won a medal in a major championship.

Nurutdinova set a blistering pace, covering the first 400 meters in 55.72 seconds. Mutola was right beside her with Quirot third and van Langen back in sixth place. With 150 meters to go, Quirot began moving away from the curb to prepare herself for an attempt to pass Nurutdinova. Kovacs, now running behind Quirot, followed her. Seeing a gap, van Langen moved up on the inside. Into the homestretch Nurutdinova grappled to stay ahead, with van Langen at her heels. In her desperate effort, Nurutdinova veered to the outside. Again van Langen was quick to slip through the gap. She drew even with Nurutdinova with 50 meters to go and then pulled away to win by about three meters. The following year, at the 1993 world championships, Nurutdinova was banned after she tested positive for the "Ben Johnson steroid," Stanozolol.

1500 METERS

1896–1968 not held

1972 Munich C: 36, N: 21, D: 9.9. WR: 4:06.9 (Lyudmila Bragina)

1.	Lyudmila Bragina	SOV/RUS	4:01.4	WR	(4:01.38)
2.	Gunhild Hoffmeister	GDR	4:02.8		(4:02.83)
3.	Paola Cacchi	ITA	4:02.9		(4:02.85)
4.	Karin Burneleit	GDR	4:04.1		(4:04.11)
5.	Sheila Carey (Taylor)	GBR	4:04.8		(4:04.81)
6.	Ilja Keizer	HOL	4:05.1		(4:05.13)
7.	Tamara Pangelova	SOV/UKR	4:06.5		(4:06.45)
8.	Jennifer Orr	AUS	4:12.2		

Twenty-nine-year-old Lyudmila Bragina exploded onto the international scene six weeks before the Olympics when she chopped 2.7 seconds off Karin Burneleit's world record by running a 4:06.9 in a *heat* of the Soviet championships. A few weeks later she ran 3000 meters in 8:53.0, to better the world record at that distance by over 16 seconds. In the first heat of the first round of the 1500 meters at Munich, Bragina led from start to finish and broke her own world record in 4:06.47, carrying 17-year-old Glenda Reiser of Canada with her in 4:06.71. Three days later Bragina again broke the world record with a 4:05.07 in her semifinal heat. The semifinals saw 13 women better the pre-Olympic world record. In the final, Bragina moved to the front after two laps and pulled away to a 12-meter lead, which she held for the entire last lap. In a postrace interview, Bragina told reporters, "We shall be running 3 minutes 56 seconds before the next Olympics." She hit it right on the button, as 3:56.0 was exactly the world record at the time of the 1976 Olympics.

1976 Montreal C: 36, N: 19, D: 7.30. WR: 3:56.0 (Tatyana Kazankina)

1.	Tatyana Kazankina	SOV/RUS	4:05.48
2.	Gunhild Hoffmeister	GDR	4:06.02
3.	Ulrike Klapezynski	GDR	4:06.09
4.	Nikolina Shtereva	BUL	4:06.57
5.	Lyudmila Bragina	SOV/RUS	4:07.20
6.	Gabriella Dorio	ITA	4:07.27
7.	Ellen Wellmann	GER	4:07.91
8.	Janice Merrill	USA	4:08.54

Bragina's Munich world record went unbeaten until one month before the next Olympics, when Kazankina lowered it by 5.4 seconds. Track fans who had hoped for a new record in the Olympic final were disappointed, as the race turned into a tactical contest. With one lap to go, Bragina took the lead, but 200 meters later, with elbows flying, she was passed by the two East German training mates, Hoffmeister on the inside and Klapezynski on the outside. Meanwhile, Kazankina, who had already won the 800 meters gold medal, steered clear of the elbowing and moved up on the outside to take the lead with 50 meters to go. She won by three meters. Defending champion Lyudmila Bragina had to settle for fifth place, but her career was hardly over. A few days later, at a U.S.A. vs. U.S.S.R. meet, she ran the 3000 meters in 8:27.2, 18.3 seconds faster than the previous world record. This put her only 50 years behind the men's pace, something of a record in women's track events.

1980 Moscow C: 24, N: 14, D: 8.1. WR: 3:55.0 (Tatyana Kazankina)

1.	Tatyana Kazankina	SOV/RUS	3:56.6	OR	(3:56.56)
2.	Christiane Wartenberg	GDR	3:57.8		(3:57.71)
3.	Nadiya Olizarenko	SOV/UKR	3:59.6		(3:59.52)
4.	Gabriella Dorio	ITA	4:00.3		(4:00.30)
5.	Ulrike Bruns (Klapezynski)	GDR	4:00.7		(4:00.62)
6.	Lyubov Smolka	SOV/UKR	4:01.3		(4:01.25)
7.	Maricica Puică	ROM	4:01.3		(4:01.26)
8.	Ileana Silai	ROM	4:03.0		(4:02.98)

Covering the final 800 meters in 1:59.0, Kazankina took the lead with 600 meters to go and had left the other runners 20 meters behind by the time she reached the last curve. Twelve days later she lowered the world record to 3:52.47 and became the first woman to run 1500 meters faster than Paavo Nurmi. In September 1984, Kazankina received an 18-month suspension when the Soviet team manager refused to let her submit to a test for drugs following a 5000-meter race in Paris.

1984 Los Angeles C: 22, N: 15, D: 8.11. WR: 3:52.47 (Tatyana Kazankina)

1.	Gabriella Dorio	ITA	4:03.25
2.	Doina Melinte	ROM	4:03.76
3.	Maricica Puică	ROM	4:04.15
4.	Roswitha Gerdes	GER	4:04.41
5.	Christine Benning	GBR	4:04.70

6. Christina Boxer	GBR	4:05.53
7. Brit McRoberts	CAN	4:05.98
8. Ruth Wysocki	USA	4:08.92

At the 1983 world championships, the first five places had gone to Mary Decker, three Soviet runners, and Wendy Sly of Great Britain. With all five absent, the roles of favorites went to the two Romanians, Maricica Puică, who had won the 3000-meter gold 24 hours earlier, and Doina Melinte, who had been victorious in the 800 meters five days before the final of the 1500. But Gabriella Dorio had other ideas. Having suffered from taking the early lead in the 800, she held back in the 1500, allowing Chris Boxer to set a slow pace. Then, with 1½ laps to go, Dorio moved to the front, followed closely by Melinte. Melinte took the lead on the final lap and it looked like a repeat of the 800. But this time Dorio had saved an extra charge of energy for the finish. She regained the lead coming into the homestretch and could not be caught. Puică, who waited too long to make her final sprint, finished strongly to take the bronze. Among the many rewards that came Dorio's way as a result of her victory was an unusual one: her husband had promised her that if she won a gold medal he would give her a bath—in wine.

1988 Seoul C: 28, N: 19, D: 10.1. WR: 3:52.47 (Tatyana Kazankina)

1. Paula Ivan	ROM	3:53.96	OR
2. Laimutė Baikauskaite	SOV/LIT	4:00.24	
3. Tetyana Samolenko	SOV/UKR	4:00.30	
4. Christina Cahill (Boxer)	GBR	4:00.64	
5. Lynn Williams	CAN	4:00.86	
6. Andrea Hahmann	GDR	4:00.96	
7. Shireen Bailey	GBR	4:02.32	
8. Mary Slaney (Decker)	USA	4:02.49	

Until 1988, the career of 25-year-old Paula Ivan had been decent but undistinguished. Beginning in July of the Olympic year, she suddenly showed rapid and spectacular improvement. On August 17, she ran 3:56.22 for her third personal best in 6 weeks. Only Mary Slaney's 3:58.92 at the U.S. Olympic trials came within 4 seconds of Ivan's pre-Olympic time. In Seoul, 6 days before the 1500-meter final, Ivan thought she was about to win the gold medal at 3000 meters, when Tetyana Samolenko sprinted by her to steal the victory.

In order to neutralize Samolenko's kick, Ivan decided to try to run away from the field early in the 1500. Her strategy worked perfectly. She led by 3 meters after 400 meters, 10 meters after 800, and then seemed to increase her lead with each step for the remainder of the race, until she crossed the finish line with an unprecedented margin of victory of 40 meters. The battle for second was won by Lithuanian Laimutė Baikauskaite, who came from last place at the halfway mark to nip Samolenko in a photo finish.

1992 Barcelona C: 43. N: 31, D: 8.8. WR: 3:52.47 (Tatyana Kazankina)

1. Hassiba Boulmerka	ALG	3:55.30
2. Lyudmila Rogacheva	RUS	3:56.91
3. Qu Yunxia	CHN	3:57.08
4. Tetyana Dorovskikh (Samolenko)	UKR	3:57.92
5. Liu Li	CHN	4:00.20
6. Maite Zuñiga Dominguez	SPA	4:00.59
7. Malgorzata Rydz	POL	4:01.91
8. Yekaterina Podkopayeva	RUS	4:02.03

Since World War II, women's middle-distance running had been dominated by runners from Communist nations, with an occasional interruption by the likes of Ann Packer, Madeline Manning, and Mary Decker. In 1991 a new quarter was heard from when, in the same week that the Soviet Union collapsed, 23-year-old Hassiba Boulmerka of Algeria scored a stunning victory over Tetyana Dorovskikh and Lyudmila Rogacheva at the World Championship in Athletics. The men's 1500 had also been won by an Algerian, Noureddine Morceli. When Boulmerka and Morceli returned to Algiers they were driven through the streets while women showered them with flowers, candles, and wheat seeds, as they would at a wedding celebration. Overnight, Boulmerka was transformed not only into a national heroine but into a symbol for Arab women who wanted to break away from traditional Islamic restrictions. Heroine though she was for most Algerians, she was singled out for condemnation by one group: Islamic fundamentalists. In mosques across the country Boulmerka was denounced for "running with naked legs in front of thousands of men." In fact, Boulmerka herself was a devout Muslim. But her father had worked for many years as a truck driver in France and both he and his wife supported their daughter's educational and athletic pursuits. Distracted by the political situation in Algeria, Boulmerka retreated to a training camp in Germany for the weeks preceding the Olympics, and then showed up refreshed in Barcelona.

Rogacheva set a torrid pace in the final, covering the first 400 meters in 60.66 seconds. Applying relentless pressure, she burned away most of the field but was unable to shake Boulmerka. With a little more than 200 meters to go, Boulmerka drove past Rogacheva and cruised to victory. When she crossed the finish line Boulmerka screamed out, "Algérie! Algérie!" and pointed to the name of the nation on her jersey. The race was the first in which four women dipped below four minutes. It was such a fast race that nine of the top ten finishers (except 40-year-old Podkopayeva) set personal bests. Five of the runners—Boulmerka, Rogacheva, Qu, Zuñiga, and Maria Mutola in ninth place—improved their personal records by over four seconds.

If Hassiba Boulmerka was the star of 1992, it was the 19-year-old bronze medalist, Qu Yunxia, who would capture the headlines the following year. Trained by controversial coach Ma Junren, Qu, like the rest of "Ma's Detachment," ran 150 miles a week, ate soft-shell turtle soup, drank an elixir containing caterpillars, made frequent trips to the high altitude of the Qinghai-Tibet Plateau, and was forbidden to pursue romantic affairs until the age of 22. In 1993, Qu won the world championships 3000 meters and then, at the Chinese national championships, ran the 1500 meters in 3:50.46 to break Tatyana Kazankina's 13-year-old world record.

5000 METERS

This event will be held for the first time in 1996.

10,000 METERS

1896-1984 not held

1988 Seoul C: 34, N: 20, D: 9.30. WR: 30:13.74 (Ingrid Kristiansen)

1.	Olga Bondarenko	SOV/RUS	31:05.21	OR
2.	Elizabeth McColgan	GBR	31:08.44	
3.	Olena Zhupiyova	SOV/UKR	31:19.82	
4.	Kathrin Ullrich	GDR	31:29.27	
5.	Frances Larrieu Smith	USA	31:35.52	
6.	Lynn Jennings	USA	31:39.93	
7.	Wang Xiuting	CHN	31:40.23	
8.	Susan Lee	CAN	31:50.51	

Ingrid Kristiansen of Norway had dominated this event since 1985 when she set her first world record at 10,000 meters at the Bislett Games in Oslo. The following year, at the next Bislett Games, she ran a 30:13.74 to take an amazing 45.72 seconds off her own record. She also won the 1986 European championship and the 1987 world championship. But at the 1988 Bislett Games on July 2, she suffered her first defeat at 10,000 meters. At the 9000-meter mark Kristiansen experienced such a severe stomach cramp that she stopped running. She still managed to finish second, behind Scotland's Liz McColgan. A few days later, Kristiansen, who did not know that she was pregnant, suffered a miscarriage.

In Seoul, Kristiansen won the first qualifying heat, McColgan the second. The final began uneventfully. The early pace was set by Lyudmila Matveyeva of the Soviet Union and Lynn Nelson of the United States. Kristiansen moved in front after six laps, but then, at the end of the seventh lap, she suddenly stepped off the track—she had badly bruised the sole of her right foot in the preliminary round.

While Kristiansen was carried away on a stretcher, Kathrin Ullrich unexpectedly found herself in first place with a lead of 10 meters. She eventually increased the gap to 30 meters. McColgan finally hauled her in after 4800 meters, with Zhupiyova and Bondarenko close behind. Ullrich lost contact with the leaders after 7600 me-

ters and Zhupiyova fell back after 8800. That left only McColgan and Bondarenko in contention with three laps to go. The 5-foot ¾-inch, 91-pound Bondarenko patiently tracked McColgan until the middle of the last lap. Then she shot past her on the back straightaway, ran the final 200 meters in 31.2 seconds, and won by 20 meters. Bondarenko was one of the pioneers of the women's 10,000-meter run, having set world records at the distance in 1981 and 1984.

1992 Barcelona C: 48, N: 28, D: 8.7. WR: 30:13.74 (Ingrid Kristiansen)

1.	Derartu Tulu	ETH	31:06.02
2.	Elana Meyer	SAF	31:11.75
3.	Lynn Jennings	USA	31:19.89
4.	Zhong Huandi	CHN	31:21.08
5.	Elizabeth McColgan	GBR	31:26.11
6.	Wang Xiuting	CHN	31:28.06
7.	Uta Pippig	GER	31:36.45
8.	Judi St. Hilaire	USA	31:38.04

Liz McColgan won the 1991 world championships by grinding out one 75-second lap after another until she had worn out all of the other runners. The last to lose contact was Derartu Tulu, who drifted back to eighth place while McColgan went on to win by over 20 seconds. McColgan tried the same tactic at the Olympics, but in one year the world had caught up with her. After 5000 meters a large pack was still right behind her. At the 6100-meter mark, Elana Meyer moved outside to grab a sponge and then suddenly darted into the lead. McColgan did not respond and Meyer soon opened a ten-meter gap. It was Tulu who went after Meyer, eventually settling in at her shoulder. Soon the two of them had pulled 50 meters ahead of the rest of the runners. Lap after lap they continued, Meyer in front, Tulu just behind her to the right. Twice Meyer moved to the outside and invited Tulu to take the lead and set the pace. Tulu refused. At last, with 420 meters to go, she was ready. Effortlessly, Tulu moved into the lead and, covering the last lap in 65.9 seconds, went on to win by 30 meters. Tulu waited for Meyer at the finish line and then Tulu, the first black African woman to earn an Olympic medal, and Meyer, South Africa's first medalist since it was banned after the 1960 Games, set off hand in hand on a shared victory lap that seemed to symbolize hope for a new Africa. Tulu bettered her pre-Olympics personal best by 19.23 seconds, Meyer improved hers by 21.71 seconds, and Lynn Jennings, in third place, beat her pre-Olympics record by 20.04 seconds.

MARATHON

1896–1980 not held

The new Africa: Derartu Tulu and Elana Meyer, gold and silver medalists in the 1992 10,000 meters.

1984 Los Angeles C: 50, N: 28, D: 8.5. WB: 2:22:43 (Joan Benoit)

1. Joan Benoit	USA	2:24:52
2. Grete Waitz	NOR	2:26:18
3. Rosa Mota	POR	2:26:57
4. Ingrid Kristiansen	NOR	2:27:34
5. Lorraine Moller	NZE	2:28:34
6. Priscilla Welch	GBR	2:28:54
7. Lisa Martin	AUS	2:29:03
8. Sylvie Ruegger	CAN	2:29:09

The first woman to be officially timed in a marathon run was Violet Piercy of Great Britain who, on October 3, 1926, completed the Chiswick course in three hours forty minutes and twenty-two seconds. Her "record" stood, completely unchallenged, for 37 years until Merry Lepper of the U.S. ran a 3:37:07 on December 16, 1963. The three-hour barrier was first broken, and well-broken at that, on August 31, 1971, when Australia's Adrienne Beames clocked a 2:46:30. By 1981, Allison Roe of New Zealand had taken the record down to 2:25:29 (albeit on a short course). Then, on April 18, 1983, Joan Benoit of Freeport, Maine, smashed Roe's record, finishing the Boston Marathon in 2:22:43.

Although Benoit did not compete in another marathon until the U.S. Olympic trials 13 months later, her Boston feat qualified her as co-favorite with the popular Norwegian runner Grete Waitz. Waitz, a two-time Olympian at 1500 meters and a former marathon world record holder, was undefeated in the seven marathons she had completed and had beaten Benoit at various distances 10 of the 11 times they had met. She was also the victor at the 1983 world championships, finishing a full 3 minutes ahead of Marianne Dickerson in second place.

Favorites though they were, both Benoit and Waitz considered themselves blessed to make it to the Olympic starting line at all. Benoit had undergone arthroscopic surgery on her right knee only seventeen days before the U.S. Olympic trials, which she won anyway. Waitz woke up the morning before the Olympic marathon with a sore back that left her unable to run or even stand up straight. She spent the day crying with disappointment, but by racetime the next day the pain had disappeared.

As an event, the inaugural women's Olympic marathon was charged with emotion. The long struggle to achieve recognition for women's long-distance running had finally reached fruition and many spectators along the route were moved to tears as the women dashed by.

As a race, however, there wasn't much to it. Benoit, wearing a white painter's cap with the flap in back, moved ahead after only 14 minutes and pulled away at will, amazed that no one went with her.

As Waitz watched her disappear in the distance, she was convinced that Benoit had taken a reckless gamble and would eventually fade back to the pack. She never did. At 15 km., Benoit's lead was 51 seconds, by 25 km. it was 1 minute and 51 seconds. Waitz began to reel her in after 30 km., but by then it was too late. Meanwhile, Benoit had simply ploughed ahead, smiling only once when she spotted a banner of Bowdoin College, her alma mater. When she reached the Marina Freeway, a three-mile stretch where no spectators were allowed, Benoit chuckled to herself at the irony that this hunk of concrete had provided her with the peace and quiet she was used to during her training runs back home in Maine. "The one thing I'll tell my grandchildren," she later mused, "is that one time I ran alone on an L.A. freeway." One half mile from the stadium, she passed an enormous wall mural depicting her crossing of the finish line at the Boston Marathon.

As she approached the tunnel leading to the Coliseum track, she heard the crowd erupt and sensed the audience rise to its feet. In the tunnel, Benoit, a very private per-son, not comfortable with celebrity, told herself, "When you come out from underneath the tunnel, you're going to be a different person. Do you want to come out of the tunnel?" It was too late to turn back. "When I came into the stadium," she later recalled, "and saw all the colors and everything, I told myself, 'Listen, just look straight ahead, because if you don't you're probably going to faint.' " She ended up finishing 400 meters ahead of silver medalist Grete Waitz.

The race for the medals may have lacked suspense, but there was still high drama ahead. Twenty minutes after Joan Benoit entered the stadium, a ghostly figure emerged from the tunnel. It was 39-year-old Gabriele Andersen-Scheiss, an Idaho ski instructor, who had taken advantage of her dual citizenship to represent Switzerland. Suffering from heat prostration (but fortunately not heatstroke), she staggered forward, her left arm hanging limply, her right leg stiffened. It was as if Dorando Pietri had reappeared after 76 years. The audience gasped in horror, but when medical officers approached her, Andersen-Scheiss waved them off. As with Pietri in 1908, the crowd alternately cheered her on and begged for her to be stopped. Doctors accompanying her around the track noted that she was sweating profusely, a good sign, and let her proceed. For 5 minutes and 44 seconds she lurched along, occasionally stopping, blacking out on her feet, holding her head. Finally she fell across the finish line into the waiting arms of three medics. The records will show that Gabriele Andersen-Scheiss placed 37th.

Joan Benoit, first across the finish line in the 1984 inaugural women's marathon.

Gabriele Andersen-Scheiss, who gained unsought celebrity as a result of her staggering 5-minute 44-second final lap in the 1984 women's marathon.

Remarkably, she recovered rapidly and was released by medical personnel only two hours later to return to the Olympic Village and grab a bite to eat. Ten hours after her ordeal, Andersen-Scheiss was being interviewed on television. Two weeks later she was finishing fifth in a Utah "ride and tie" competition in which she ran twenty miles and rode a horse for eighteen. As a result of the controversy surrounding her condition during that final lap, the I.A.A.F. passed the "Scheiss rule," which allows athletes ro receive a hands-on medical examination without being subject to disqualification.

The travails of Gaby Andersen-Scheiss received a great deal of attention, but those of another runner received too little. Anne Audain of New Zealand, one of the secondary favorites, became ill after the 18th mile and began asking people the location of the nearest aid station. No one seemed to know, so she staggered on until she collapsed, as luck would have it, in front of two Los Angeles Fire Department paramedics who had stopped to watch the race. They carried her to their ambulance and drove her to a nearby hospital where she was treated for dehydration.

One more contestant worth noting was a late entrant, Leda Diaz de Cano of Honduras. De Cano fell behind immediately, trailing all of the other runners by 6½ minutes after only five kilometers. She was 27½ minutes behind at the 20-kilometer mark. Shortly thereafter, race officials, concerned less with the Olympic credo of taking part being more important than winning than they were with not interrupting the day's schedule at the track, convinced de Cano to leave the course and allow vehicular traffic to recapture the streets of Los Angeles.

1988 Seoul C: 69, N: 39, D: 9.23. WB: 2:21:06 (Ingrid Kristiansen)

1.	Rosa Mota	POR	2:25:40
2.	Lisa Martin	AUS	2:25:53
3.	Kathrin Dörre	GDR	2:26:21
4.	Tetyana Polovynska	SOV/UKR	2:27:05
5.	Zhao Youfeng	CHN	2:27:06
6.	Laura Fogli	ITA	2:27:49
7.	Daniele Kaber	LUX	2:29:23
8.	Maria Curatolo	ITA	2:30:14

In 1982, Rosa Mota was a 24-year-old middle-distance runner who was enjoying her sport, but whose career was going nowhere. At the European championships in Athens that year she finished twelfth at 3000 meters and then decided to enter the marathon as an experiment. Previously, she had never run more than 20 kilometers, even in practice. To everyone's surprise, including her own, she won. Two years later, she placed third in Los Angeles to become the first Portuguese woman ever to earn an Olympic medal.

By 1986, the 5-foot 1¾-inch, 97-pound Mota was not only winning every marathon she entered, she was winning big. She took the European championship by 4 minutes 14 seconds and the Tokyo Marathon by 4 minutes 39 seconds. In 1987, she won the Boston Marathon by 4

minutes 29 seconds and the world championship by a stunning 7 minutes 11 seconds. She tuned up for the Olympics by repeating at Boston in 1988, this time by 4 minutes 54 seconds.

Mota arrived in Seoul as the overwhelming favorite. She did not disappoint her fans. By the 30-kilometer mark the lead group had dwindled to Mota in front, with Martin, Dörre, and Polovynska close behind. At 32 kilometers, Mota motioned for the others to take their turn in the lead, but found no takers. Four kilometers later, Polovynska faded and the medal winners were decided, although who got what was still in doubt. About 2½ miles from the finish, Mota's coach and lover, José Pedroza, appeared on his bicycle and asked how she was feeling. When she replied that she was feeling fine, he advised her to follow their original plan: to take off when she reached the next hill, one of only a few bumps in an unusually flat course.

Immediately, Mota made her move. Martin, mesmerized and feeling "inert," failed to respond until it was too late. She pulled away from Dörre, but was unable to catch Mota, who went on to win by about 75 meters.

1992 Barcelona C: 47, N: 31, D: 8.1. WB: 2:21:06 (Ingrid Kristiansen)

1.	Valentina Yegorova	RUS	2:32:41
2.	Yuko Arimori	JPN	2:32:49
3.	Lorraine Moller	NZE	2:33:59
4.	Sachiko Yamashita	JPN	2:36:26
5.	Kathrin Dörre	GER	2:36:48
6.	Mun Gyong-ae	PRK	2:37:03
7.	Manuela Machado	POR	2:38:22
8.	Ramilia Burangulova	RUS	2:38:46

DISQ (Drugs): Madina Biktagirova (BLR) 2:35:39

When Valentina Yegorova qualified for the Olympics, all her neighbors in the small farming village of Iziderkino were thrilled. They couldn't wait to watch her on television. There was just one problem: no one in the village owned a television set. So all 1500 villagers chipped in and bought a single, 30-year-old black-and-white set that was placed at the entrance of the home of Yegorova's parents and faced out toward the street.

It was 84° Fahrenheit (29° centigrade) when Yegorova and 46 other marathoners set off at a cautious pace on a long, exposed course that culminated in a punishing climb of Montjuic to the Olympic Stadium. Lisa Ondieki (Martin) led the field through the first 20 kilometers. Then Madina Biktagirova made a break and pulled away by about 200 meters. She was reeled in by Manuela Machado, who was soon passed by Yegorova. By the 30-kilometer mark Yegorova had opened a lead of 54 seconds, but five kilometers later she found herself joined by Yuko Arimori. Over the final kilometers Yegorova repeatedly surged and Arimori repeatedly caught up to her. They raced up the hill and then, less than 300 meters from the stadium, Yegorova burst ahead and Arimori could not keep pace. Yegorova's margin of victory, barely 40 meters, was the slimmest in Olympic marathon history. Back in Iziderkino the villagers stayed up past midnight to watch Yegorova receive her gold medal—even if it was in black and white.

Biktagirova was disqualified after she tested positive for the stimulant norephedrine.

100-METER HURDLES

Women clear ten hurdles 2 feet 9 inches (.838 meters) high. It is 13 meters (14 yards 7¾ inches) from the start line to the first hurdle, 8½ meters (8 yards 2 feet 10⅝ inches) between hurdles, and 10½ meters (11 yards 5⅜ inches) from the last hurdle to the finish line.

1896–1928 not held

1932 Los Angeles C: 9, N: 6, D: 8.4. WR: 11.8 (Marjorie Clark)
(80 Meters)

1. Mildred "Babe" Didriksen	USA	11.7	WR
2. Evelyne Hall	USA	11.7	
3. Marjorie Clark	SAF	11.8	
4. Simone Schaller	USA	11.9	
5. Violet Webb	GBR	11.9	
6. Alda Wilson	CAN	12.0	

Babe Didriksen had already won a gold medal in the javelin throw when she began competition in the 80-meter hurdles. In her opening heat she tied the world record of 11.8 seconds. In the final she committed one false start and then broke the record, beating Evelyne Hall of Chicago by a mere two inches. Fourth-place finisher Simone Schaller of Pasadena, California, had taken up hurdling only three months earlier.

1936 Berlin C: 22, N: 11, D: 8.6. WR: 11.6 (Ruth Engelhard)
(80 Meters)

1. Trebisonda Valla	ITA	11.7
2. Anni Steuer	GER	11.7
3. Elizabeth Taylor	CAN	11.7
4. Claudia Testoni	ITA	11.7
5. Catharina ter Braake	HOL	11.8
6. Doris Eckert	GER	12.0

The finish was so close that the judges spent 30 minutes studying the photo-finish before they were able to sort out the places and announce the results. In the semifinals, Valla had run a wind-aided 11.6, which was recognized as an Olympic record but not a world record.

1948 London C: 21, N: 12, D: 8.4. WR: 11.0 (Francina "Fanny" Blankers-Koen)
(80 Meters)

1. Francina "Fanny" Blankers-Koen	HOL	11.2	OR
2. Maureen Gardner	GBR	11.2	
3. Shirley Strickland	AUS	11.3	
4. Yvette Monginou	FRA	11.8e	
5. Maria Oberbreyer	AUT	11.9e	
6. Libuše Lomská	CZE	11.9e	

Babe Didriksen qualified for all five individual women's track and field events in 1932, but was allowed to compete in only three of them. She won the javelin throw and the 80-meter hurdles and set a world record in the high jump, despite being placed second. She was later voted the greatest female athlete of the first half of the twentieth century.

Fanny Blankers-Koen had already won the 100-meter dash, but she was quite nervous about 19-year-old Maureen Gardner in the hurdles. She didn't meet her rival until the day of the opening heats, when Gardner showed up at the warmup track with her own set of hurdles. In the semifinals Gardner hit a hurdle and stumbled, barely qualifying in third place. But in the final it was Blankers-Koen who had a tough race. Left behind at the start, she caught Gardner at the fifth barrier, but hit the hurdle and lurched clumsily to the finish line. It was unclear who had won, and the first three finishers waited impatiently for the results. Suddenly the band struck up "God Save the King" and Fanny thought that meant she had lost. Actually the band was playing not because Maureen Gardner had won, but because the British royal family had just arrived at the stadium. Then the results appeared on the scoreboard, and Fanny Blankers-Koen had gained her second gold medal. The fact that she was a devoted mother and housewife and that Maureen Gardner was a ballet instructor did much to counter the pre–World War II masculine image of women athletes that had been established by Stella Walsh, Babe Didriksen, and Helen Stephens. Bronze medalist Shirley Strickland also finished third in the 100 meters, fourth in the 200, and second in the relay. Her official time of 11.4 is undoubtedly a mistake, since she was less than a meter behind the winner.

1952 Helsinki C: 33, N: 21, D: 7.24. WR: 11.0 (Francina "Fanny" Blankers-Koen)
(80 Meters)

1. Shirley Strickland de la Hunty	AUS	10.9	WR	(11.01)
2. Maria Golubnichaya	SOV/RUS	11.1		(11.24)
3. Maria Sander	GER	11.1		(11.38)
4. Anneliese Seonbuchner	GER	11.2		(11.46)
5. Jean Desforges	GBR	11.6		(11.75)

DNF: Francina "Fanny" Blankers-Koen (HOL)

Shirley Strickland, a 27-year-old teacher from Western Australia, equaled Fanny Blankers-Koen's world record in the first heat. The Dutch defending champion, suffering from a carbuncle on her leg, ran 11.2 and 11.3 to qualify for the final, while Strickland ran a wind-aided 10.8 in the semifinals. In the final, Blankers-Koen hit the first two hurdles and stopped running. Meanwhile, Shirley Strickland streaked to victory in world record time. Because there was a dispute as to which song to play for Australia's national anthem, the peacemaking Finnish hosts played *two* anthems: "God Save the Queen" and "Advance Australia Fair."

1956 Melbourne C: 22, N: 11, D: 11.28. WR: 10.6 (Kreszentia Gastl)
(80 Meters)

1. Shirley Strickland de la Hunty	AUS	10.7	OR	(10.96)
2. Gisela Köhler	GDR	10.9		(11.12)
3. Norma Thrower	AUS	11.0		(11.25)
4. Galina Bystrova	SOV/RUS	11.0		(11.25)
5. Maria Golubnichaya	SOV/RUS	11.3		(11.50)
6. Gloria Cooke	AUS	11.4		(11.60)

By 1956 Shirley Strickland had become a mother and was employed as an assistant lecturer in physics and mathematics at Perth Technical College. Her decisive two-yard victory in the 80-meter hurdles and her gold medal in the relay gave her a total of seven Olympic medals: three gold, one silver, three bronze.

1960 Rome C: 28, N: 17, D: 9.1. WR: 10.5 (Gisela Birkemeyer [Köhler])
(80 Meters)

1. Iryna Press	SOV/UKR	10.8	(10.93)
2. Carole Quinton	GBR	10.9	(10.99)
3. Gisela Birkemeyer (Köhler)	GDR	11.0	(11.13)
4. Mary Bignal	GBR	11.1	(11.22)
5. Galina Bystrova	SOV/RUS	11.2	(11.26)
6. Rimma Koschelyova	SOV/RUS	11.2	(11.28)

Iryna Press, the younger sister of shot put and discus champion Tamara Press, set an Olympic record of 10.6 in the semifinals before winning a clear start-to-finish victory in the final.

1964 Tokyo C: 27, N: 19, D: 10.19. WR: 10.5 (Gisela Birkemeyer [Köhler], Betty Moore, Karin Balzer, Iryna Press, Draga Stamejčić)
(80 Meters)

1. Karin Balzer	GDR	10.5w	(10.54w)
2. Teresa Ciepla-Wieczorek	POL	10.5	(10.55)
3. Pamela Kilborn	AUS	10.5	(10.56)
4. Iryna Press	SOV/UKR	10.6	(10.62)
5. Ikuko Yoda	JPN	10.7	(10.72)
6. Maria Piatkowska	POL	10.7	(10.76)
7. Draga Stamejčić	YUG	10.8	(10.86)
8. Rosie Bonds	USA	10.8	(10.88)

Hometown favorite Ikuko Yoda delighted the crowd with her unusual prerace routine, which included sweeping her lane up to the first hurdle, sucking a lemon, and dabbing cream behind her ears. She led until the third hurdle, but couldn't hold off the favorites. The three medalists finished within 12 inches of one another. Their world record time was disallowed because of a 2.23 meters per second wind. The competition was marred in the opening round when Canadian Marion Snider crashed into a hurdle and was carried away, unconscious, on a stretcher.

1968 Mexico City C: 32, N: 23, D: 10.18. WR: 10.2 (Vyera Korsakova)
(80 Meters)

1. Maureen Caird	AUS	10.39	OR
2. Pamela Kilborn	AUS	10.46	
3. Chi Cheng	TAI	10.51	
4. Patricia Van Wolvelaere	USA	10.60	
5. Karin Balzer	GDR	10.61	
6. Danuta Straszyńska	POL	10.66	
7. Elżbieta Zebrowska	POL	10.66	
8. Tatyana Talysheva	SOV/RUS	10.72	

When word spread from the U.S.S.R. that unknown Vyera Korsakova had broken Iryna Press's world record, many eyebrows were raised. Cynics doubted her time of 10.2 and said that it was just the Soviets' way of removing from the record books the names of the Press sisters, who had disappeared from competition following the institution of sex tests. Sure enough, Korsakova was eliminated in the semifinals after clocking only 10.6 and 10.8. Pam Kilborn had been undefeated since the Tokyo Olympics, but she suffered a slow start in the final and was unable to catch her 17-year-old teammate Maureen Caird. Chi Cheng, the first Asian woman in 40 years to win an Olympic track and field medal, was elected to the Taiwan parliament in 1981.

1972 Munich C: 25, N: 15, D: 9.8. WR: 12.5 (Anneliese Ehrhardt, Pamela Ryan [Kilborn])

1. Anneliese Ehrhardt	GDR	12.59	WR
2. Valeria Bufanu	ROM	12.84	
3. Karin Balzer	GDR	12.90	
4. Pamela Ryan (Kilborn)	AUS	12.98	

5.	Teresa Nowak	POL	13.17
6.	Danuta Straszyńska	POL	13.18
7.	Annerose Krumpholz	GDR	13.27
8.	Grażyna Rabsztyn	POL	13.44

Esther Shakhamorov had the potential of becoming Israel's first Olympic finalist, but she withdrew following the terrorist murder of Israeli athletes, including her coach, Amitzur Shapira. Anneliese Ehrhardt was never seriously challenged. The final was noteworthy for the success of the "older women," including 34-year-old Karin Balzer and 33-year-old Pam Ryan.

1976 Montreal C: 27, N: 15, D: 7.29. WR: 12.59 (Anneliese Ehrhardt)
1.	Johanna Schaller	GDR	12.77
2.	Tatiana Anisimova	SOV/RUS	12.78
3.	Natalya Lebedeva	SOV/RUS	12.80
4.	Gudrun Behrend	GDR	12.82
5.	Grażyna Rabsztyn	POL	12.96
6.	Esther Rot (Shakhamorov)	ISR	13.04
7.	Valeria Stefanescu	ROM	13.35
8.	Ileana Ongar	ITA	13.51

The semifinals saw an unusual incident. In the second heat, Lyubov Kononova of the U.S.S.R. stumbled and smashed into Valeria Stefanescu in the next lane. At first both women were disqualified, but fair play prevailed. Stefanescu was reinstated, and a rerun was ordered for the next day, 75 minutes before the final. This rerun allowed Stefanescu to replace injured defending champion Ehrhardt as the eighth finalist. The final was so close that only one and a half feet separated Schaller from fourth-place finisher Behrend. Esther Shakhamorov, now married and living then in Tarzana, California, at last succeeded in becoming Israel's first finalist.

1980 Moscow C: 20, N: 11, D: 7.28. WR: 12.36 (Grażyna Rabsztyn)
1.	Vera Komisova	SOV/RUS	12.56	OR
2.	Johanna Klier (Schaller)	GDR	12.63	
3.	Lucyna Langer	POL	12.65	
4.	Kerstin Claus	GDR	12.66	
5.	Grażyna Rabsztyn	POL	12.74	
6.	Irina Litovchenko	SOV	12.84	
7.	Bettine Gärtz	GDR	12.93	
8.	Zofia Bielczyk	POL	13.08	

Twenty-seven-year-old Vera Komisova was one of the surprise winners of the Moscow Games, as she improved her pre-Olympic best by .28 seconds, even greater than Schaller's 1976 Olympic improvement of .22.

1984 Los Angeles C: 22, N: 14, D: 8.10. WR: 12.36 (Grażyna Rabsztyn)
1.	Benita Fitzgerald-Brown	USA	12.84
2.	Shirley Strong	GBR	12.88
3.	Michele Chardonnet	FRA	13.06
3.	Kim Turner	USA	13.06
5.	Glynis Nunn	AUS	13.20

6.	Marie Noëlle-Savigny	FRA	13.28
7.	Ulrike Denk	GER	13.32
8.	Pamela Page	USA	13.40

In 1984 all of the leading contenders in the 100-meter hurdles came from boycotting nations, including the twelve women who registered the fastest times of the year.

Originally a dead-heat was announced for third place, but after viewing films of the race for 50 minutes, a Jury of Appeal awarded sole possession to Turner. Unfortunately, Chardonnet was not informed of this decision until she was standing in the award ceremony area. When her name was not announced, she was led away in tears. Three and a half months later, the I.A.A.F. reversed the decision of the Jury of Appeal and Chardonnet was awarded her bronze medal.

1988 Seoul C: 36, N: 24, D: 9.30. WR: 12.21 (Yordanka Donkova)
1.	Yordanka Donkova	BUL	12.38	OR
2.	Gloria Siebert	GDR	12.61	
3.	Claudia Zackiewicz	GER	12.75	
4.	Natalya Hryhoryeva	SOV/UKR	12.79	
5.	Florence Colle	FRA	12.98	
6.	Julie Rocheleau	CAN	12.99	
7.	Monique Ewanje-Épée	FRA	13.14	
8.	Cornelia Oschkenat	GDR	13.73	

In 1986, Yordanka Donkova broke the world record four times in 27 days. The following year she lost the record to teammate Ginka Zagorcheva and finished a disappointing fourth at the world championship in Rome. However, in 1988 she continued her pattern of excelling in even-numbered years. She regained the world record on August 20th and won all 15 finals that she entered, including the Olympics, which she led from start to finish. Her chief rivals both bowed out to injuries in Seoul—Zagorcheva failed to complete her opening-round heat and Cornelia Oschkenat pulled a hamstring in the final while running in third place.

1992 Barcelona C: 37, N: 23, D: 8.6. WR: 12.21 (Yordanka Donkova)
1.	Paraskevi "Voula" Patoulidou	GRE	12.64
2.	LaVonna Martin	USA	12.69
3.	Yordanka Donkova	BUL	12.70
4.	Lynda Tolbert	USA	12.75
5.	Gail Devers	USA	12.75
6.	Aliuska López	CUB	12.87
7.	Natalya Kolovanova	UKR	13.01
8.	Odalys Adams	CUB	13.57

This was expected to be a duel between world champion Lyudmila Narozhilenko of Russia, who had recorded the five fastest times of the year, and Gail Devers, who had finished second to Narozhilenko at the world championships and had already won the 100-meter dash in Barcelona. However, Narozhilenko pulled out of her semifinal heat after straining a hamstring. In the final, Devers moved in front by the fourth hurdle and seemed to be home free with only one hurdle left. But she came up to the final barrier too quickly, and just as she rose to clear it, she glanced briefly to her right. She hit the hurdle with her lead foot on the way up and lost her balance. As she scraped and scrambled toward the finish line, her lead vanished and she did well to place fifth despite her fall.

Meanwhile Tolbert, Martin, Patoulidou and Donkova finished almost in a line. The day before, Patoulidou, whose pre-Olympic personal best was only 12.96, had celebrated joyously because she had qualified for the final. Now she thought she had actually earned a bronze medal. When she saw the replay in the stadium she realized she had won the race. To say that Patoulidou's victory was a surprise would be a gross understatement. Previously her best performance had been a second-place in the Mediterranean Games. Patoulidou was the first Greek woman to qualify for a track final, the first Greek woman to win a medal in any sport (excluding the 1906 Intercalated Games), and the first Greek athlete of either sex to earn a gold medal in track and field since Konstantin Tsiklitiras won the standing long jump in 1912.

LaVonna Martin, who took the silver medal, had been suspended after testing positive for a banned diuretic. However, she was reinstated three months before the United States Olympic trials because her coach claimed that he had given her the drug without her knowledge. An even more creative excuse was the one given by Lyudmila Narozhilenko when she tested positive for steroids after a meet on February 13, 1993. Her husband, Nikolai, came forward and claimed that he had slipped steroids into her protein powder to punish her for initiating divorce proceedings against him after she fell in love with her manager.

400-METER HURDLES

Rules are the same as those for men except that the ten hurdles are 2 feet 6 inches (.762 meters) high.

1896–1980 not held

1984 Los Angeles C: 26, N: 20, D: 8.8. WR: 53.58 (Margarita Ponomaryova)

1. Nawal El Moutawakel	MOR	54.61	OR
2. Judi Brown	USA	55.20	
3. Cristina Cojocaru	ROM	55.41	
4. Pilavullakandi "P.T." Usha	IND	55.42	
5. Ann-Louise Skoglund	SWE	55.43	
6. Debra Flintoff	AUS	56.21	
7. Tuija Helander	FIN	56.55	
8. Sandra Farmer	JAM	57.15	

Nawal El Moutawakel, who led from start to finish and improved her personal best by .76 seconds, was the first woman from an Islamic nation to win an Olympic medal. She was also the first ever gold-medal winner from Mo-

rocco, a fact which did not go unnoticed in her hometown of Casablanca, where the 400-meter hurdle final was televised live at 2 a.m. After she crossed the finish line in first place and took her victory lap carrying a huge Moroccan flag, people poured into the streets of Casablanca to celebrate.

1988 Seoul C: 35, N: 25, D: 9.28. WR: 52.94 (Marina Stepanova)

1. Debra Flintoff-King	AUS	53.17	OR
2. Tatyana Ledovskaya	SOV/BLR	53.18	
3. Ellen Fiedler	GDR	53.63	
4. Sabine Busch	GDR	53.69	
5. Sally Gunnell	GBR	54.03	
6. Gudrun Abt	GER	54.04	
7. Tatyana Kurochkina	SOV/BLR	54.39	
8. LaTanya Sheffield	USA	55.32	

On the day that she and the rest of the Australian team left for Seoul, Debbie Flintoff-King attended the funeral of her sister, who had died of a heart attack three days earlier. In the semifinals, Flintoff-King edged Tatyana Ledovskaya 54.00 to 54.01. Halfway through the final she was in fifth place behind Ledovskaya, Fiedler, Kurochkina, and world champion Sabine Busch. By the eighth hurdle Fiedler was slightly in front of Ledovskaya, Busch had passed Kurochkina, and Flintoff-King was still fifth. Ledovskaya moved decisively into the lead over the ninth hurdle. As they cleared the tenth and final barrier, Flintoff-King caught Busch, but still trailed Fiedler and Ledovskaya, the latter by 0.24. She sprinted past the East German. Then, at the finish line, Ledovskaya failed to lean and Flintoff-King nipped her in the final stride.

1992 Barcelona C: 27, N: 18, D: 8.5. WR: 52.94 (Marina Stepanova)

1. Sally Gunnell	GBR	53.23
2. Sandra Farmer-Patrick	USA	53.69
3. Janeene Vickers	USA	54.31
4. Tatyana Ledovskaya	BLR	54.31
5. Vera Ordina	RUS	54.83
6. Margarita Ponomaryova	RUS	54.83
7. Deon Hemmings	JAM	55.58
DNF: Myrtle Bothma (SAF)		

Farmer-Patrick was leading when she had trouble with the seventh hurdle. Gunnell, a farmer's daughter from Chigwell, Essex, caught her at the beginning of the final straightaway, moved ahead at the ninth hurdle, and pulled away to win by three and a half meters.

4 × 100-METER RELAY

1896–1924 not held

1928 Amsterdam T: 8, N: 8, D: 8.5. WR (440 yards): 49.8 (GBR — Scovler, Haynes, Edwards, Thompson)

1. CAN	(Fanny Rosenfeld, Ethel Smith, Florence Bell, Myrtle Cook)	48.4	WR

2. USA (Mary Washburn, Jessie Cross, Loretta 48.8
McNeil, Elizabeth Robinson)
3. GER (Rosa Kellner, Helene "Leni" Schmidt, 49.0
Anni Holdmann, Helene "Leni" Junker)
4. FRA (Georgette Gagneux, Yvonne Plancke, 49.6
Marguerite Radideau, Lucienne Velu)
5. HOL (Mechelina Aengenendt, Maria Briejer, 49.8
Jeannette Hendrika Grooss, Elisabeth ter
Horst)
6. ITA (Luisa Bonfanti, Giannina Marchini, 53.6
Derna Polazzo, Vittorina Vivenza)

The relay victory was sweet revenge for the Canadian team, particularly for Fanny Rosenfeld, who had lost first place in the 100 meters on a disputed judges' decision, and for Myrtle Cook, who had cried by the side of the track for a half hour after being disqualified in the 100 meters final. Myrtle Cook and Fanny Rosenfeld both became sports editors for Canadian newspapers.

1932 Los Angeles T: 6, N: 6, D: 8.7. WR: 48.4 (CAN—Rosenfeld, Smith, Bell, Cook)

1. USA (Mary Carew, Evelyn Furtsch, Annette 46.9 WR
Rogers, Wilhelmina Von Bremen)
2. CAN (Mildred Frizzel, Lilian Palmer, Mary 47.0
Frizzel, Hilda Strike)
3. GBR (Eileen Hiscock, Gwendolina Porter, Vio- 47.6
let Webb, Nellie Halstead)
4. HOL (Johanna Dalmolen, Cornelia Aalten, 48.0
Elisabeth du Mee, Tollien Schurrman)
5. JPN (Mie Muraoka, Michi Nakanishi, Asa 48.9
Dogura, Sumiko Watanabe)
6. GER (Grete Heublein, Ellen Braumüller, Ottilie —
"Tilly" Fleischer, Marie Dollinger)

1936 Berlin T: 8, N: 8, D: 8.9. WR: 46.5 (GER—Albus, Krauss, Dollinger, Dörffeldt)

1. USA (Harriet Bland, Annette Rogers, Elizabeth 46.9
Robinson, Helen Stephens)
2. GBR (Eileen Hiscock, Violet Olney, Audrey 47.6
Brown, Barbara Burke)
3. CAN (Dorothy Brookshaw, Mildred Dolson, 47.8
Hilda Cameron, Aileen Meagher)
4. ITA (Lydia Bongiovanni, Trebisonda Valla, 48.7
Fernanda Bullano, Claudia Testoni)
5. HOL (Catharina ter Braake, Francina "Fanny" 48.8
Koen, Alida de Vries, Elisabeth Koning)
DISQ: GER (Emmy Albus, Käthe Krauss, Marie Dollinger, Ilse
Dörffeldt)

In the opening round the German team set a world record of 46.4 that was to remain unbroken for sixteen years. In the final they led by eight meters as Marie Dollinger prepared to make the final pass to Ilse Dörffeldt. However, as Adolf Hitler, King Boris of Bulgaria, and 100,000 others watched, Ilse Dörffeldt dropped the baton. The U.S. team, anchored by the heroic 1928 100 meters winner Betty Robinson and the 1936 100 meters winner Helen Stephens, took advantage of the German catastrophe and won by eight yards. Hitler

was so moved by the sight of Dörffeldt sobbing after the race that he called the four German women to his booth and comforted them.

1948 London T: 10, N: 10, D: 8.7. WR: 46.4 (GER—Albus, Krauss, Dollinger, Dörffeldt)

1. HOL (Xenia Stad-de Jong, Jeanette Witziers-Timmer, 47.5
Gerda van der Kade-Koudijs, Francina "Fanny"
Blankers-Koen)
2. AUS (Shirley Strickland, June Maston, Elizabeth 47.6
McKinnon, Joyce King)
3. CAN (Viola Myers, Nancy MacKay, Diane Foster, 47.8
Patricia Jones)
4. GBR (Dorothy Manley, Muriel Pletts, Margaret 48.0
Walker, Maureen Gardner)
5. DEN (Grete Lövsöe [Nielsen], Bente Bergendorff, 48.2
Birte Nielsen, Hildegard Nissen)
6. AUT (Grete Jenny, Elfi Steurer, Grete Pavlousek, 49.2
Maria Oberbreyer)

Fanny Blankers-Koen took over in fourth place, but was able to race through the field and catch Joyce King just before the finish. She thus became the only woman to win four track and field gold medals.

1952 Helsinki T: 15, N: 15, D: 7.27. WR: 46.4 (GER—Albus, Krauss, Dollinger, Dörffeldt)

1. USA (Mae Faggs, Barbara Jones, 45.9 WR (46.14)
Janet Moreau, Catherine Hardy)
2. GER (Ursula Knab, Maria Sander, 45.9 WR (46.18)
Helga Klein, Marga Petersen)
3. GBR (Sylvia Cheeseman, June 46.2 (46.41)
Foulds, Jean Desforges,
Heather Armitage)
4. SOV (Irina Turova, Yevgenya Setshe- 46.3 (46.42)
nova, Nadezhda Khnykina,
Vyera Kalashnikova)
5. AUS (Shirley Strickland de la Hunty, 46.6 (46.86)
Verna Johnson, Winsome
Cripps, Marjorie Jackson)
6. HOL (Grietje de Jongh, Bertha 47.8 (47.16)
Brouwer, Neeltje Büch, Wil-
helmina Lust)

The Australians set a world record of 46.1 in the very first heat. They led by one meter in the final at the last changeover. Winsome Cripps made a clean pass to Marjorie Jackson, winner of both sprints, but as Jackson took off, her hand hit Cripps's knee and the baton was jarred loose. Jackson caught it on a bounce and raced on, but the delay proved decisive. One of the four black women who made up the U.S. team was 15-year-old Barbara Jones of Chicago, who is the youngest person in Olympic history to win a gold medal in track and field.

1956 Melbourne T: 9, N: 9, D: 12.1. WR: 45.2 (SOV—Krepkina, Itkina, Kocheleva, Botchkaryova)

1. AUS (Shirley Strickland de la Hunty, 44.5 WR (44.65)
Norma Croker, Fleur Mellor,
Elizabeth Cuthbert)

The 1952 Australian, 4 × 100-meter relay team set a world record in their qualifying heat and were on their way to victory in the final when Winsome Cripps and Marjorie Jackson dropped the baton during the final changeover.

2. GBR	(Anne Pashley, Jean Scrivens, June Paul [Foulds], Heather Armitage)	44.7	(44.70)
3. USA	(Mae Faggs, Margaret Matthews, Wilma Rudolph, Isabelle Daniels)	44.9	(45.04)
4. SOV	(Vira Krepkina, Galina Reschikova, Maria Itkina, Irina Botchkaryova)	45.6	(45.81)
5. ITA	(Maria Musso, Letizia Bertoni, Maria Greppi, Giuseppina Leone)	45.7	(45.90)
6. GDR & GER	(Maria Sander, Christa Stubnick, Gisela Köhler, Barbara Mayer)	47.2	(47.29)

Pressed by the Germans, the Australian team set a world record of 44.9 in the opening heat. In the final, though, it was the British women who put on the pressure. Heather Armitage finished only half a yard behind Betty Cuthbert

(a closer margin than indicated by Great Britain's time of 44.7). Anne Pashley, who ran the opening leg for the British team, later gained renown as a mezzo-soprano.

1960 Rome T: 10, N: 10, D: 9.8. WR: 44.5 (AUS—Strickland de la Hunty, Croker, Mellor, Cuthbert)

1. USA	(Martha Hudson, Lucinda Williams, Barbara Jones, Wilma Rudolph)	44.5	(44.72)
2. GER	(Martha Langbein, Annie Biechl, Brunhilde Hendrix, Jutta Heine)	44.8	(45.00)
3. POL	(Teresa Wieczorek, Barbara Janiszewska, Celina Jesionowska, Halina Richter)	45.0	(45.19)
4. SOV	(Vira Krepkina, Valentina Maslovskaya, Maria Itkina, Iryna Press)	45.2	(45.39)
5. ITA	(Letizia Bertoni, Sandra Valenti, Piera Tizzoni, Giuseppina Leone)	45.6	(45.80)

DNF: GBR (Carole Quinton, Dorothy Hyman, Jennifer Smart, Mary Bignal)

Marie Dollinger was one of the two unfortunate German women who dropped their baton in 1936, during the changeover from the third runner to the fourth. Twenty-four years later she sat in the stands in Rome and watched tensely as her daughter, Brunhilde Hendrix, the third runner on the German team, prepared to pass the baton to Jutta Heine. Fortunately all went well, and the 1960 German team finished impressively in second place. The U.S. team from Tennessee State had a two-yard lead that was lost in a sloppy final pass. However Wilma Rudolph was able to regain the lead and cross the tape in first place for the ninth time in the Rome Games. The U.S. women had set a world record of 44.4 in the semifinals.

1964 Tokyo T: 15, N: 15, D: 10.21. WR: 44.3 (USA—White, Pollards, Brown, Rudolph)

1. POL	(Teresa Ciepla [Wieczorek], Irena Kirszenstein, Halina Górecka [Richter], Ewa Klobukowska)	43.6	(43.69)
2. USA	(Willye White, Wyomia Tyus, Marilyn White, Edith McGuire)	43.9	(43.92)
3. GBR	(Janet Simpson, Mary Rand [Bignal], Daphne Arden, Dorothy Hyman)	44.0	(44.09)
4. SOV	(Galina Gaide, Renata Lace, Lyudmila Samotysova, Galina Popova)	44.4	(44.44)
5. GER	(Karin Frisch, Erika Pollmann, Martha Pensberger [Langbein], Jutta Heine)	44.7	
6. AUS	(Dianne Bowering, Marilyn Black, Margaret Burvill, Joyce Bennett)	45.0	
7. HUN	(Erzsébet Bartos Heldt, Margit Nemeszházi Markó, Antónia Munkácsi, Ida Such)	45.2	
8. FRA	(Marlene Canguio, Daniele Gueneau, Michele Lurot, Denise Guenard)	46.1	

The Polish team was originally credited with a world record, but their names were later struck from the record books when Ewa Klobukowska became the first athlete to fail a sex test.

In 1964 Ewa Klobukowska won a bronze medal in the 100-meter dash and a gold in the 4 × 100-meter relay. Three years later she became the first athlete to fail a sex test.

1968 Mexico City T: 14, N: 14, D: 10.20. WR: 43.6 (SOV — Zharkova, Bukharina, Popkova, Samotysova)

1. USA	(Barbara Ferrell, Margaret Bailes, Mildrette Netter, Wyomia Tyus)	42.88	WR
2. CUB	(Marlene Elejarde, Fulgencia Romay, Violetta Quesada, Miguelina Cobián)	43.36	
3. SOV/RUS	(Lyudmila Zharkova, Galina Bukharina, Vyera Popkova, Lyudmila Samotysova)	43.41	

4. HOL	(Geertruida Hennipman, Mieke Sterk, Cornelia Bakker, Wilhelmina van den Berg)	43.44
5. AUS	(Jennifer Lamy, Joyce Bennett, Raelene Boyle, Dianne Burge)	43.50
6. GER	(Renate Meyer, Jutta Stöck, Rita Jahn, Ingrid Becker)	43.70
7. GBR	(Anita Neil, Maureen Tranter, Janet Simpson, Lillian Board)	43.78
8. FRA	(Michele Alayrangues, Gabrielle Meyer, Nicole Montandon, Silviane Telliez)	44.30

The American women set a world record of 43.4 in the first heat. This time was equaled, surprisingly, in the second heat by the unheralded Dutch team. In the final the U.S. team overcame mediocre baton-passing with rare speed to win by five yards and establish a new world record.

1972 Munich T: 15, N: 15, D: 9.10. WR: 42.88 (USA—Ferrell, Bailes, Netter, Tyus)

1. GER	(Christiane Krause, Ingrid Mickler [Becker], Annegret Richter, Heidemarie Rosendahl)	42.81	WR
2. GDR	(Evelyn Kaufer, Christina Heinich, Bärbel Struppert, Renate Stecher)	42.95	
3. CUB	(Marlene Elejarde, Carmen Valdes, Fulgencia Romay, Silvia Chivás)	43.36	
4. USA	(Martha Watson, Mattiline Render, Mildrette Netter, Iris Davis)	43.39	
5. SOV/RUS	(Marina Sidorova, Galina Bukharina, Lyudmila Zharkova, Nadezhda Besfamilnaya)	43.59	
6. AUS	(Maureen Caird, Raelene Boyle, Marion Hoffman, Penelope Gillies)	43.61	
7. GBR	(Andrea Lynch, Della Pascoe, Judith Vernon, Anita Neil)	43.71	
8. POL	(Helena Fliśnik, Barbara Bakulin, Urszula Jóźwik, Danuta Jędrejek)	44.20	

The East Germans had edged the West Germans in the European championships. Rematched in a poorly seeded opening heat, the East Germans again finished ahead, 42.88 to 42.97. In the final, however, long jump gold medalist Heide Rosendahl began the anchor leg with a one-meter advantage and raced flat-out to hold off Renate Stecher, who had won both the 100 meters and 200 meters earlier in the games.

1976 Montreal T: 10, N: 10, D: 7.31. WR: 42.50 (GDR—Maletzki, Stecher, Heinich, Eckert)

1. GDR	(Marlies Oelsner, Renate Stecher, Carla Bodendorf, Bärbel Eckert)	42.55	OR
2. GER	(Elvira Possekel, Inge Helten, Annegret Richter, Annegret Kroniger)	42.59	
3. SOV	(Tetyana Prorochenko, Lyudmila Maslakova [Zharkova], Nadezhda Besfamilnaya, Vera Anisimova)	43.09	

4. CAN   (Margaret Howe, Patty Loverock, Joanne   43.17
           McTaggart, Marjorie Bailey)
5. AUS   (Barbara Wilson, Deborah Wells, Denise   43.18
           Robertson, Raelene Boyle)
6. JAM   (Leleith Hodges, Rose Allwood, Carol   43.24
           Cummings, Jacqueline Pusey)
7. USA   (Martha Watson, Evelyn Ashford, Debra   43.35
           Armstrong, Chandra Cheeseborough)
8. GBR   (Wendy Clarke, Denise Ramsden,   43.79
           Sharon Colyear, Andrea Lynch)

The 200 meters champion, Bärbel Eckert, made up a one-meter deficit on the anchor leg to win by a foot. The East German victory brought Renate Stecher's Olympic medal total to six: three gold, two silver, and one bronze.

1980 Moscow T:8, N: 8, D: 8.1. WR: 41.85 (GDR—Müller, Wöckel [Eckert], Auerswald, Göhr [Oelsner])

1. GDR   (Romy Müller, Bärbel Wöckel   41.60   WR
           [Eckert], Ingrid Auerswald, Marlies
           Göhr [Oelsner])
2. SOV/RUS (Vera Komisova, Lyudmila Masla- 42.10
           kova [Zharkova], Vera Anisimova,
           Natalya Bochina)
3. GBR   (Heather Hunte, Kathryn Smallwood, 42.43
           Beverley Goddard, Sonia Lanna-
           man)
4. BUL   (Sofka Popova, Liliana Panayotova, 42.67
           Maria Shishkova, Galina Encheva)
5. FRA   (Veronique Grandrieux, Chantal   42.84
           Rega, Raymonde Naigre, Emma
           Sulter)
6. JAM   (Leleith Hodges, Jacqueline Pusey, 43.19
           Rosie Allwood, Merlene Ottey)
7. POL   (Lucyna Langer, Elżbieta Stachur- 43.59
           ska, Zofia Bielczyk, Grażyna
           Rabsztyn)

DNF: SWE (Linda Haglund, Lena Moller, Ann-Louise Skoglund, Helena Pihl)

Unusually poor baton passing failed to prevent the East Germans from winning by five meters and breaking their own world record.

1984 Los Angeles T: 11, N: 11, D: 8.11. WR: 41.53 (GDR—Gladisch, Koch, Auerswald, Göhr [Oelsner])

1. USA   (Alice Brown, Jeanette Bolden, Chandra 41.65
           Cheeseborough, Evelyn Ashford)
2. CAN   (Angela Bailey, Marita Payne, Angella 42.77
           Taylor, France Gareau)
3. GBR   (K. Simmone Jacobs, Kathryn Cook   43.11
           [Smallwood], Beverley Callender [God-
           dard], Heather Oakes [Hunte])
4. FRA   (Rose-Aimee Bacoul, Liliane Gaschet, 43.15
           Marie France Loval, Raymonde Naigre)
5. GER   (Edith Oker, Michaela Schabinger,   43.57
           Heide-Elke Gaugel, Ute Thimm)
6. BAH   (Eldece Clarke, Pauline Davis, Debbie 44.18
           Greene, Oralee Fowler)

7. TRI   (Janice Bernard, Gillian Forde, Ester 44.23
           Hope-Washington, Angela Williams)
8. JAM   (Juliette Cuthbert, Grace Jackson, Veron- 53.54
           ica Findlay, Merlene Ottey-Page, [Janet
           Burke])

1988 Seoul T: 19, N: 19, D: 10.1. WR: 41.37 (GDR—Gladisch, Reiger, Auerswald, Göhr [Oelsner])

1. USA   (Alice Brown, Sheila Echols, D. Florence 41.98
           Griffith Joyner, Evelyn Ashford [Dannette
           Young])
2. GDR   (Silke Möller [Gladisch], Kerstin Behrendt, 42.09
           Ingrid Lange [Auerswald], Marlies Göhr
           [Oelsner])
3. SOV/RUS (Lyudmila Kondratyeva, Galina   42.75
           Malchugina, Marina Zhirova, Natalya
           Pomoshchnikova)
4. GER   (Sabine Richter, Ulrike Sarvari, Andrea 42.76
           Thomas, Ute Thimm)
5. BUL   (Tzvetanka Ilieva, Valia Demireva,   43.02
           Nadezhda Georgieva, Yordanka Donkova)
6. POL   (Joanna Smolarek, Jolanta Janota, Ewa 43.93
           Pisiewicz, Agnieszka Siwek)
7. FRA   (Françoise Leroux, Muriel Leroy, Laurence 44.02
           Bily, Patricia Girard)

DNS: JAM (Ethlyn Tate, Grace Jackson, Juliet Cuthbert, Merlene Ottey, [Viviene Spence, Laurel Johnson])

In the semifinals, Evelyn Ashford, running the anchor leg, almost took off too quickly to receive the baton from Florence Griffith Joyner. In the final, Ashford overcompensated. Although Griffith Joyner reached her in first place, by the time Ashford achieved a tenuous grip on the baton, she trailed her rival of 12 years, Marlies Göhr, as well as Natalya Pomoshchnikova. Pomoshchnikova passed Göhr but then pulled a hamstring muscle 40 meters from the finish. She still managed to hobble across the line in third place. Meanwhile, Ashford was tearing up the track. She passed Göhr 20 meters before the finish and won by 1 meter to gain her third Olympic gold medal.

The Jamaican team qualified for the final but was forced to withdraw because of an injury to Merlene Ottey.

1992 Barcelona T: 14, N: 14, D: 8.8. WR: 41.37 (GDR—Gladisch, Reiger, Auerswald, Göhr [Oelsner])

1. USA   (Evelyn Ashford, Esther Jones, Carlette Guidry, 42.11
           Gwendolyn Torrence, [Michelle Finn])
2. RUS   (Olga Bogoslovskaya, Galina Malchugina, Ma- 42.16
           rina Trandenkova, Irina Privalova)
3. NGR   (Beatrice Utondu, Faith Idehen, Christy Opara- 42.81
           Thompson, Mary Onyali)
4. FRA   (Patricia Girard, Odiah Sidibe, Laurence Bily, 42.85
           Marie-José Pérec)
5. GER   (Andrea Philipp, Silke Knoll, Andrea Thomas, 43.12
           Sabine Günther)
6. AUS   (Melissa Moore, Melinda Gainsford, Kathleen 43.77
           Sambell, Kerry Johnson)

DNF: CUB (Eusebia Riquelme Terrazón, Aliuska López, Idalmis Bonne Rauseauk, Liliana Allen Doll); JAM (Michele Freeman, Juliet Cuthbert, Dahlia Duhaney, Merlene Ottey)

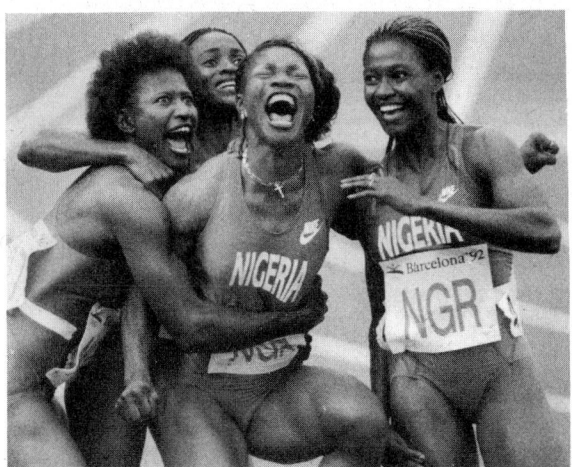

The Nigerian 4 × 100-meter relay team celebrates their bronze medal in 1992.

Torrence, the United States anchor, took the baton one meter behind Privalova, ran her down, and won by one-half meter. Ashford brought her career total to four gold medals and one silver. The Jamaican team, medal favorites, were thwarted again when Juliet Cuthbert pulled a hamstring mid-race.

4 × 400-METER RELAY

1896–1968 not held

1972 Munich T: 14, N: 14, D: 9.10. WR: 3:28.8 (GDR—Käsling, Seidler, Zehrt, Rohde)

1.	GDR	(Dagmar Käsling, Rita Kühne, Helga Seidler, Monika Zehrt)	3:23.0 WR	(3:22.95)
2.	USA	(Mable Fergerson, Madeline Manning, Cheryl Toussaint, Kathy Hammond)	3:25.2	(3:25.15)
3.	GER	(Anette Rückes, Inge Bödding, Hildegard Falck, Rita Wilden)	3:26.5	(3:26.51)
4.	FRA	(Martine Duvivier, Colette Besson, Bernadette Martin, Nicole Duclos)	3:27.5	(3:27.52)
5.	GBR	(Verona Bernard, Janet Simpson, Janette Roscoe, Rosemary Stirling)	3:28.7	(3:28.74)
6.	AUS	(Alison Rose-Edwards, Raelene Boyle, Cheryl Peasley, Charlene Rendina)	3:28.8	(3.28.84)
7.	FIN	(Marika Eklund, Pirjo Wilmi, Tuula Rautanen, Mona-Lisa Strandvall)	3:29.4	(3:29.44)
8.	SOV	(Lyubov Runtso, Olga Syrovatskaya, Natalya Chistyakova, Nadezhda Kolesnikova)	3:31.9	

1976 Montreal T: 11, D: 7.31. WR: 3:23.0 (GDR—Käsling, Seidler, Zehrt)

1.	GDR	(Doris Maletzki, Brigitte Rohde, Ellen Streidt, Christina Brehmer)	3:19.23 WR
2.	USA	(Debra Sapenter, Sheila Ingram, Pamela Jiles, Rosalyn Bryant)	3:22.81
3.	SOV	(Inta Klimoviča, Lyudmyla Aksenova, Natalya Sokolova, Nadezhda Ilyina)	3:24.24
4.	AUS	(Judith Canty, Verna Burnard, Charlene Rendina, Bethanie Nail)	3:25.56
5.	GER	(Claudia Steger, Dagmar Fuhrmann, Elke Barth, Rita Wilden)	3:25.71
6.	FIN	(Marika Lindholm, Pirjo Häggman [Wilmi], Mona-Lisa Pursiainen [Strandvall], Riita Salin)	3:25.87
7.	GBR	(Elizabeth Barnes, Gladys Taylor, Verona Elder [Bernard], Donna Murray)	3:28.01
8.	CAN	(Margaret Stride, Joyce Yakubowich, Rachelle Campbell, Yvonne Saunders)	3:28.91

The remarkable East German women won by almost 30 meters.

1980 Moscow T: 11, N: 11, D: 8.1. WR: 3:19.23 (GDR—Maletzki, Rohde, Streidt, Brehmer)

1.	SOV	(Tetyana Prorochenko, Tatyana Goistchik, Nina Zyuskova, Irina Nazarova, [Olga Mineyeva, Lyudmila Chernova])	3:20.2	(3:20.12)
2.	GDR	(Gabriele Löwe, Barbara Krug, Christina Lathan [Brehmer], Marita Koch)	3:20.4	(3:20.35)
3.	GBR	(Linsey MacDonald, Michelle Probert, Joslyn Hoyte-Smith, Donna Hartley [Murray], [Janine Macgregor])	3:27.5	
4.	ROM	(Iboia Korodi, Niculina Lazarciuc, Maria Samungi, Elena Tarita)	3:27.7	
5.	HUN	(Irén Orosz, Judit Forgacs, Éva Toth, Ilona Pal, [Ibolya Petrika])	3:27.9	
6.	POL	(Grażyna Oliszewska, Elżbieta Katolik-Skowrońska, Jolanta Januchta, Malgorzata Dunecka)	3:27.9	
7.	BEL	(Lea Alaerts, Regine Berg, Anne Michel, Rosine Wallez)	3:31.6	

DNF: BUL (Svobodka Damianova, Rossitza Stamenova, Milena Andonova, Bonka Dimova)

The defeat of the East German 4 × 400-meter relay team was a major upset, but it took an unusual set of circumstances to produce the result. Olympic rules at the time stated that the same athletes who ran in the heats had to run in the final, unless official certificates could be produced proving that they were medically unfit to run. The U.S.S.R. came up with two such certificates to replace Olga Mineyeva and Lyudmila Chernova with two fresh runners—Nina Zyuskova and Irina Nazarova, who had finished fifth and fourth respectively in the individual 400 meters event. At the beginning of the third leg, East Germany's Christina Lathan shot ahead of Zyuskova, but the Soviet runner pushed back in front as Lathan stepped on the curb and lost her rhythm. Nazarova took over with a lead of about 10 meters, but 400 meters champion Marita Koch slowly but surely closed the gap. As they entered the final straight it looked as if Koch would move ahead. However Nazarova, inspired by the wildly cheering hometown crowd of 100,000, managed to hold off Koch's challenge and win by one meter.

1984 Los Angeles T: 10, N: 10, D: 8.11. WR: 3:15.92 (GDR— Walther, Busch, Rübsam, Koch)

1. USA (Lillie Leatherwood, Sherri Howard, Valerie Brisco-Hooks, Chandra Cheeseborough, [Diane Dixon, Denean Howard])   3:18.29   OR
2. CAN (Charmaine Crooks, Jillian Richardson, Molly Killingbeck, Marita Payne, [Dana Wright])   3:21.21
3. GER (Heike Schulte-Mattler, Ute Thimm, Heide-Elke Gaugel, Gaby Bussmann, [Christina Sussiek, Nicole Leistenschneider])   3:22.98
4. GBR (Michelle Scutt [Probert], Helen Barnett, Gladys Taylor, Joslyn Hoyte-Smith)   3:25.51
5. JAM (Ilrey Oliver, Cynthia Green, Cathy Rattray, Grace Jackson, [Andrea Thomas])   3:27.51
6. ITA (Patrizia Lombardo, Cosetta Compana, Marisa Masullo, Erica Rossi, [Giuseppina Ciruli])   3:30.82
7. IND (M.D. Valsamma, Vandana Rao, Kurisingal "Shiny" Abraham, Pilavullakandi "P.T." Usha)   3:32.49

DNS: PUR (Evelyn Mathieu, Madeline de Jesus, Angelita Lind, Marie Lande Mathieu, [Margaret de Jesus])

Valerie Brisco-Hooks earned her third gold medal of the Los Angeles Games, while Chandra Cheeseborough won two gold medals in one hour, becoming the first woman to win golds in both Olympic relays. The Puerto Rican coach refused to let his team take part in the final when he discovered that the woman who ran the second leg for the Puerto Ricans in their qualifying heat was not team member Madeline de Jesus, but her twin sister Margaret. After being injured in the long jump, Madeline had asked her sister, who was in Los Angeles as a spectator, to take her place in the relay.

1988 Seoul T: 13, N: 13, D: 10.1. WR: 3:15.92 (GDR—Walther, Busch, Rübsam, Koch)

1. SOV (Tatyana Ledovskaya, Olga Nazarova, Mariya Pinihina, Olha Bryzhina, [Lyudmila Dzhigalova])   3:15.17   WR
2. USA (Denean Howard-Hill, Diane Dixon, Valerie Brisco, D. Florence Griffith Joyner, [Lillie Leatherwood, Sherri Howard])   3:15.51
3. GDR (Dagmar Neubauer [Rübsam], Kirsten Emmelmann, Sabine Busch, Petra Müller, [Grit Breuer])   3:18.29
4. GER (Ute Thimm, Helga Arendt, Andrea Thomas, Gudrun Abt, [Michaela Schabinger, Gisela Kinzel])   3:22.49
5. JAM (Sandi Richards, Andrea Thomas, Cathy Rattray-Williams, Sharon Powell, [Marcia Tate])   3:23.13
6. GBR (Linda Keough, Jennifer Stoute, Angela Piggford, Sally Gunnell, [Janet Smith])   3:26.89
7. FRA (Fabienne Ficher, Nathalie Simon, Nadine Debois, Evelyne Elien)   3:29.37

DNF: CAN (Charmaine Crooks, Molly Killingbeck, Marita Payne-Wiggins, Jillian Richardson, [Esmie Lawrence])

Running the third leg, Valerie Brisco of the United States cut a Soviet lead of about 8 meters down to 2. The anchor leg pitted 400-meter gold medalist Olha Bryzhina against Florence Griffith Joyner, who had won her third gold medal only 40 minutes earlier in the 4 × 100-meter relay. Griffith Joyner, who had never before run a 4 × 400-meter relay in an international meet, tucked in behind Bryzhina and chased the Soviet champion around the track. Although Griffith Joyner ran the fastest split of any of the U.S. runners, Bryzhina maintained her 2-meter lead all the way to the finish line.

1992 Barcelona T: 14, N: 14, D: 8.8. WR: 3:15.17 (SOV— Ledovskaya, Nazarova, Pinihina, Bryzhina)

1. SOV (Yelena Ruzina, Lyudmila Dzhigalova, Olga Nazarova, Olha Bryzhina, [Marina Shmonina, Lilia Nurutdinova])   3:20.20
2. USA (Natasha Kaiser, Gwendolyn Torrence, Jearl Miles, Rochelle Stevens, [Denean Hill, Dannette Young])   3:20.92
3. GBR (Phylis Smith, Sandra Douglas, Jennifer Stoute, Sally Gunnell)   3:24.23
4. CAN (Rosey Edeh, Charmaine Crooks, Camille Noel, Jillian Richardson, [Karen Clarke])   3:25.20
5. JAM (Catherine Scott, Cathy Rattray Williams, Juliet Campbell, Sandi Richards, [Claudine Williams])   3:25.68
6. GER (Uta Rohländer, Heike Meissner, Linda Kisabaka, Anja Rücker)   3:26.37
7. AUS (Catherine Freeman, Susan Andrews, Renee Poetschka, Michelle Lock)   3:26.42
8. POR (Marta Moreira, Lucrécia Jardim, Elsa Amaral, Eduarda Coelho)   3:36.85

Gwen Torrence brought the United States from third to first place on the second leg, giving Jearl Miles a lead of three meters. Olga Nazarova pulled almost even at the final exchange. Bryzhina tucked in behind Stevens for the first 250 meters of the last lap. She tried to pass her entering the final curve, found it difficult, waited, then shot by 60 meters from the finish to win by five meters. The following year, three of the six members of the team of ex-Soviets, Shmonina, Dzhigalova, and Nurutdinova, tested positive for steroids and were given suspensions.

10,000-METER WALK

1896-1988 not held

1992 Barcelona C: 44, N: 21, D: 8.3. WR: 41:30 (Kerry Junna-Saxby)
1. Chen Yueling	CHN	44:32
2. Yelena Nikolayeva	RUS	44:33
3. Li Chunxiu	CHN	44:41
4. Sari Essayah	FIN	45:08
5. Cui Yingzi	CHN	45:15
6. Madelein Svensson	SWE	45:17
7. Annarita Sidoti	ITA	45:23
8. Yelena Sayko	RUS	45:28

Chen entered the stadium with a 20-meter lead over Li. Twenty meters behind Li, Alina Ivanova of the Ukraine was beginning to make a move. Nikolayeva was thirty meters behind Ivanova. Ivanova raced past Li and Chen, provoking two quick red warning cards in the process. Chen tried to stay with her, but with 150 meters to go, Ivanova took off again. Her technique was so unacceptable that even the relatively uninitiated audience gasped as she skipped along the homestretch. Ivanova crossed the finish line first, but was disqualified. Chen, who held off a late surge by Nikolayeva, learned about her victory back in the locker room. Because the fourth walker across the line, Ileana Salvador of Italy, was also disqualified, Li had the strange experience of winning the bronze medal even though she was the fifth person to cross the finish line.

HIGH JUMP

1896–1924 not held

1928 Amsterdam C: 20, N: 9, D: 8.5. WR: 1.61, 5-3¼ (Carolina Gisolf)
		M	FT.-IN.
1. Ethel Catherwood	CAN	1.59	5-2½
2. Carolina Gisolf	HOL	1.56	5-1¼
3. Mildred Wiley	USA	1.56	5-1¼
4. Jean Shiley	USA	1.51	4-11½
5. Marjorie Clark	SAF	1.48	4-10¼
6. Helma Notte	GER	1.48	4-10¼
7. Inge Braumüller	GER	1.48	4-10¼
8. Catherine Maguire	USA	1.48	4-10¼

Ethel Catherwood, "The Saskatoon Lily," was a beautiful 18-year-old who became a favorite of the spectators and the photographers. During the three-hour competition she kept herself wrapped up in a big red blanket and didn't even take off her sweatsuit until the five-foot mark had been reached. Before each jump she would face the bar, smile and then go over. Her return to Saskatoon caused the largest celebration since the signing of the

Ethel Catherwood, "The Saskatoon Lily," won the 1928 high jump in Amsterdam.

1918 Armistice. She was presented with a $3000 education trust fund to be used to continue her piano studies. When asked about rumors that she had received offers to go to Hollywood, Catherwood replied, "I'd rather gulp poison than try my hand at motion pictures." However, she did move to the United States the following year, eventually settling in San Francisco.

1932 Los Angeles C: 10, N: 6, D: 8.7. WR: 1.62, 5-3¾ (Carolina Gisolf)
		M	FT.-IN.	
1. Jean Shiley	USA	1.657	5-5¼	WR
2. Mildred "Babe" Didriksen	USA	1.657	5-5¼	WR
3. Eva Dawes	CAN	1.60	5-3	
4. Carolina Gisolf	HOL	1.58	5-2¼	
5. Marjorie Clark	SAF	1.58	5-2¼	
6. Annette Rogers	USA	1.58	5-2¼	
7. Helma Notte	GER	1.55	5-1	
8. Yuriko Hirohashi	JPN	1.49	4-10½	

Jean Shiley and Babe Didriksen had tied for first place in the U.S. Olympic trials and they tied again in Los Angeles. Both women cleared 5 feet 5¼ inches but failed at 5 feet 6 inches. A jump-off was ordered, and both cleared a world record height of 5 feet 5¾ inches. At this point the judges intervened and declared that Didriksen's western-roll style caused her head to clear the bar before her body. This was deemed "diving" and ruled illegal. Deprived of her third gold medal, Babe was nonetheless given a share of the world record. Her jumping style was legalized not long afterward. Shiley wanted to try out for the U.S. team in 1936, but was declared ineligible because she had once worked as a swimming instructor.

1936 Berlin C: 17, N: 12, D: 8.7. WR: 1.67, 5-5¾ (Jean Shiley, Mildred "Babe" Didriksen)

		M	FT.-IN.
1. Ibolya Csák	HUN	1.60	5-3
2. Dorothy Odam	GBR	1.60	5-3
3. Elfriede Kaun	GER	1.60	5-3
4. Herman "Dora" Ratjen	GER	1.58	5-2¼
5. Marguerite Nicolas	FRA	1.58	5-2¼
6. Francina "Fanny" Blankers-Koen	HOL	1.55	5-1
6. Doris Carter	AUS	1.55	5-1
6. Annette Rogers	USA	1.55	5-1

Csák was awarded first place after clearing 1.62 meters in a jump-off. If the current tie-breaking rules had been in force, 16-year-old Dorothy Odam would have won the gold medal. The German high jump entry was riddled with controversy. Gretel Bergmann, a German Jew, won the Olympic trials with a jump of 1.64 meters, but two weeks before the opening of the Games, she was told by the German Olympic Committee that, because of her "mediocre performance," she would not be allowed to compete. Her place was not filled. Fourth-place finisher Dora Ratjen was barred from competition in 1938, when it was announced that she was a hermaphrodite, a rare sexual group for which international athletics has made no provisions. In 1966, Ratjen revealed that she was really *Herman* Ratjen and that she had been ordered to pose as a woman by officials of the Nazi Youth Movement.

1948 London C: 19, N: 10, D: 8.7. WR: 1.71, 5-7¼ (Francina "Fanny" Blankers-Koen)

		M	FT.-IN.	
1. Alice Coachman	USA	1.68	5-6	OR
2. Dorothy Tyler (Odam)	GBR	1.68	5-6	OR
3. Micheline Ostermeyer	FRA	1.61	5-3¼	
4. Vinton Beckett	CAN	1.58	5-2¼	
4. Doreen Dredge	CAN	1.58	5-2¼	
6. Bertha Crowther	GBR	1.58	5-2¼	
7. Ilse Steinegger	AUT	1.55	5-1	
8. Dora Gardner	GBR	1.55	5-1	

Once again, Dorothy Odam, now Dorothy Tyler, lost a tie despite having fewer misses than the winner. This time Alice Coachman of Albany, Georgia, was awarded first place because she cleared the final height on her first try, while Tyler required a second attempt. Coachman was the first black woman from any country to win an Olympic gold medal. When Coachman returned to Georgia, a motorcade in her honor was cheered by blacks and whites alike, but when she arrived at the Albany Municipal Auditorium for an official welcome, the audience was segregated and she was not allowed to speak. Four years later Coachman was chosen by Coca-Cola to become the first black female athlete to endorse an international consumer product. Bronze medalist Micheline Ostermeyer had already won the shot put and discus.

Alice Coachman, the first black woman from any country to earn an Olympic gold medal, shares the victory platform for the 1948 high jump with Dorothy Tyler and Micheline Ostermeyer.

1952 Helsinki C: 17, N: 10, D: 7.27. WR: 1.72, 5-7¾ (Sheila Lerwill)

		M	FT.-IN.
1. Esther Brand	SAF	1.67	5-5¾
2. Sheila Lerwill	GBR	1.65	5-5
3. Aleksandra Chudina	SOV/RUS	1.63	5-4¼
4. Thelma Hopkins	GBR	1.58	5-2¼
5. Olga Modrachová	CZE	1.58	5-2¼
6. Theodora Schenk-Solms	AUT	1.58	5-2¼
7. Nina Kossova	SOV	1.58	5-2¼
7. Dorothy Tyler (Odam)	GBR	1.58	5-2¼

1956 Melbourne C: 19, N: 12, D: 12.1. WR: 1.75, 5-8¾ (Iolanda Balaş)

		M	FT.IN.	
1. Mildred McDaniel	USA	1.76	5-9¼	WR
2. Thelma Hopkins	GBR	1.67	5-5¾	
2. Maria Pissaryeva	SOV/RUS	1.67	5-5¾	
4. Gunhild Larking	SWE	1.67	5-5¾	
5. Iolanda Balaş	ROM	1.67	5-5¾	
6. Michele Mason	AUS	1.67	5-5¾	
7. Mary Donaghy	NZE	1.67	5-5¾	
8. Hermina Geyser	SAF	1.64	5-4¼	
8. Jirina Voborilova	CZE	1.64	5-4½	

1960 Rome C: 23, N: 15, D: 9.8. WR: 1.86, 6-1¼ (Iolanda Balaş)

			M	FT.-IN.	
1.	Iolanda Balaş	ROM	1.85	6-0¾	OR
2.	Jaroslawa Jóźwiakowska	POL	1.71	5-7¼	
2.	Dorothy Shirley	GBR	1.71	5-7¼	
4.	Galina Dolya	SOV/RUS	1.71	5-7¼	
5.	Taisa Chenchyk	SOV/UKR	1.68	5-6	
6.	Helen Frith	AUS	1.65	5-5	
6.	Inga-Britt Lorentzon	SWE	1.65	5-5	
6.	Frances Slaap	GBR	1.65	5-5	

Few people have dominated an event as completely as Iolanda Balaş dominated the women's high jump. Following her fifth-place finish at the Melbourne Olympics, she won an incredible 140 consecutive competitions over the next ten and a half years. She set 14 world records and was the first woman to high-jump 6 feet. By the time a second woman, Michele Brown of Australia, had cleared that barrier, Balaş had done it in 46 different meets. On July 16, 1961, the 6-foot Balaş jumped 6 feet 3¼ inches, a height that wasn't beaten until September 4, 1971.

Iolanda Balaş completely dominated the high jump between 1957 and 1967, setting fourteen world records and winning two Olympic gold medals.

1964 Tokyo C: 27, N: 18, D: 10.15. WR: 1.91, 6-3¼ (Iolanda Balaş)

			M	FT.-IN.	
1.	Iolanda Balaş	ROM	1.90	6-2¾	OR
2.	Michele Brown (Mason)	AUS	1.80	5-11	
3.	Taisa Chenchyk	SOV/UKR	1.78	5-10	
4.	Aida Dos Santos	BRA	1.74	5-8½	
5.	Dianne Gerace	CAN	1.71	5-7¼	
6.	Frances Slaap	GBR	1.71	5-7¼	
7.	Olga Pluic	YUG	1.71	5-7¼	
8.	Eleanor Montgomery	USA	1.71	5-7¼	

1968 Mexico City C: 24, N: 14, D: 10.17. WR: 1.91, 6-3¼ (Iolanda Balaş)

			M	FT.-IN.
1.	Miloslava Rezková	CZE	1.82	5-11½
2.	Antonina Okorokova	SOV/RUS	1.80	5-10¾
3.	Valentyna Kozyr	SOV/UKR	1.80	5-10¾
4.	Jaroslava Valentová	CZE	1.78	5-10
5.	Rita Schmidt	GDR	1.78	5-10
6.	Maria Faithová	CZE	1.78	5-10
7.	Karin Schulze	GDR	1.76	5-9¼
8.	Ilona Gusenbauer	AUT	1.76	5-9¼

Eighteen-year-old Milena Rezková was a popular winner. Not only was she a complete outsider who had improved her personal best by 6 inches since the beginning of the year and who jumped 5 inches over her own height, but she was a Czech who won a dramatic showdown against two women from the U.S.S.R. Her victory was gained on her third and final try at 5 feet 11½ inches. Had Rezková missed, Okorokova would have won on the basis of fewer misses.

1972 Munich C: 40, N: 22, D: 9.4. WR: 1.92, 6-3½ (Ilona Gusenbauer)

			M	FT.-IN.	
1.	Ulrike Meyfarth	GER	1.92	6-3½	EWR
2.	Yordanka Blagoyeva	BUL	1.88	6-2	
3.	Ilona Gusenbauer	AUT	1.88	6-2	
4.	Barbara Inkpen	GBR	1.85	6-0¾	
5.	Rita Schmidt	GDR	1.85	6-0¾	
6.	Sara Simeoni	ITA	1.85	6-0¾	
7.	Rosemarie Witschas	GDR	1.85	6-0¾	
8.	Deborah Brill	CAN	1.82	5-11½	

If Rezková's win in Mexico City was considered an upset, then the victory of 16-year-old Ulrike Meyfarth in Munich was more like a fairy tale. The 6-foot ½-inch Köln-Rodenkirchen schoolgirl, who had only finished third in the West German trials, jumped 2¾ inches higher than her pre-Olympic best. Blagoyeva appeared to have cleared the bar on her last attempt at 6 feet 2¾ inches and was already starting to put her sweatsuit back on, when the bar fell and the judges ruled a miss. The admirably neutral German audience jeered the decision, which was, however, entirely in keeping with the rules of the competition. Gusenbauer looked the other way as Meyfarth equaled the world record that the Austrian had set exactly one year earlier to the day. Three weeks later, Blagoyeva raised the world record to 6 feet 4½ inches. Ulrike Meyfarth is the youngest person of either sex to win an individual track and field gold medal in the Olympics.

1976 Montreal C: 35, N: 23, D: 7.28. WR: 1.96, 6-5¼ (Rosemarie Ackermann [Witschas])

			M	FT.-IN.	
1.	Rosemarie Ackermann (Witschas)	GDR	1.93	6-4	OR
2.	Sara Simeoni	ITA	1.91	6-3¼	
3.	Yordanka Blagoyeva	BUL	1.91	6-3¼	
4.	Mária Mrachnová	CZE	1.89	6-2½	
5.	Joni Huntley	USA	1.89	6-2½	
6.	Tatyana Shlyahto	SOV/BLR	1.87	6-1½	
7.	Annette Tannander	SWE	1.87	6-1½	
8.	Cornelia Popa	ROM	1.87	6-1½	

The qualifying rounds saw the surprising early elimination of Ulrike Meyfarth, Rita Kirst (Schmidt), Debbie Brill of Canada, and Vera Bradacová of Czechoslovakia, all of whom had cleared 6 feet 3 inches previously. Although the competition was won by the favorite, Rosemarie Ackermann, the field had such depth that 18 women cleared 6 feet and 13 were still in the running after three hours. On August 26, 1977, Ackermann, a shop clerk from Cottbus, became the first woman to jump two meters—9½ inches over her own head.

1980 Moscow C: 20, N: 13, D: 7.26. WR: 2.01, 6-7 (Sara Simeoni)

			M	FT.-IN.	
1.	Sara Simeoni	ITA	1.97	6-5½	OR
2.	Urszula Kielan	POL	1.94	6-4¼	
3.	Jutta Kirst	GDR	1.94	6-4¼	
4.	Rosemarie Ackermann (Witschas)	GDR	1.91	6-3¼	
5.	Marina Sysoyeva	SOV/KYR	1.91	6-3¼	
6.	Christine Stanton	AUS	1.91	6-3¼	
7.	Andrea Reichstein	GDR	1.91	6-3¼	
8.	Cornelia Popa	ROM	1.88	6-2	

The ever-popular Sara Simeoni had switched to high-jumping at the age of 12 after being told that she couldn't be a ballet dancer because she was too tall and her feet were too big. She lost six out of seven meets to Rosemarie Ackermann between 1973 and 1977. Then she beat her in a dramatic showdown at the European championships in Prague in August 1978, and the tide turned. In Moscow Simeoni recorded her first miss at 1.94, but cleared on her second attempt to earn the gold medal. Fifth-place finisher Marina Sysoyeva jumped 6 feet 4 inches earlier in the year to set a women's world record for jumping higher than one's own height—10¼ inches.

1984 Los Angeles C: 29, N: 18, D: 8.10. WR: 2.07, 6-9½ (Lyudmila Andonova)

			M	FT.-IN.	
1.	Ulrike Meyfarth	GER	2.02	6-7½	OR
2.	Sara Simeoni	ITA	2.00	6-6¾	
3.	Joni Huntley	USA	1.97	6-5½	
4.	Maryse Ewanje-Épée	FRA	1.94	6-4¼	
5.	Deborah Brill	CAN	1.94	6-4¼	
6.	Vanessa Browne	AUS	1.94	6-4¼	
7.	Zheng Dazhen	CHN	1.91	6-3¼	
8.	D. Louise Ritter	USA	1.91	6-3¼	

Twelve years after becoming the youngest Olympic track and field champion ever, Ulrike Meyfarth earned her second gold medal to become the *oldest* person to win an Olympic high jump competition. The largest woman in the field, at 6 feet 2 inches and 154 pounds, Meyfarth also became the only track and field athlete besides Al Oerter and Irena Szewińska to win gold medals twelve years apart. Three of the top five places in 1984 belonged to women who had been finalists in Munich in 1972.

1988 Seoul C : 24, N: 15, D: 9.30. WR: 2.09, 6-10¼ (Stefka Kostadinova)

			M	FT.-IN.	
1.	D. Louise Ritter	USA	2.03	6-8	OR
2.	Stefka Kostadinova	BUL	2.01	6-7¼	
3.	Tamara Bykova	SOV/RUS	1.99	6-6¼	
4.	Olga Turchak	SOV/KAZ	1.96	6-5¼	
5.	Lyudmila Andonova	BUL	1.93	6-4	
5.	Galina Astafei	ROM	1.93	6-4	
7.	Christine Stanton	AUS	1.93	6-4	
8.	Diana Davies	GBR	1.90	6-2¾	
8.	Kim Hee-sun	KOR	1.90	6-2¾	

Between 1985 and 1987 Stefka Kostadinova of Plovdiv, Bulgaria, won 73 of 77 meets and set three world records, the last at the 1987 world championships. By the time of the Seoul Olympics, she had cleared 6 feet 8 inches at 29 different meets, compared to 10 times for all other jumpers combined. She also owned 11 of the top 12 jumps in history. Although she had lost twice in late June, she had also won 19 meets in 1988, so she entered the Olympic competition as the prohibitive favorite.

Favored for second place was 30-year-old Louise Ritter, who grew up in the tiny Texas town of Red Oak. Ritter's injury-riddled career had seen many disappointments, including eighth-place finishes at the 1984 Olympics and the 1987 world championships. However she had also earned a bronze medal at the 1983 world championships and handed Kostadinova two of her three defeats in 1987.

Kostadinova and Ritter both cleared seven heights without a miss to knock out the rest of their opponents. But then they both missed all three attempts at 6 feet 8 inches, forcing a sudden-death jump-off. Kostadinova missed a fourth time at 6–8 and it was Ritter's turn. The lanky Texan realized that this was probably her last chance for victory. "My hamstrings were about to fall off my legs," she would later explain in her thick drawl. Besides, she knew that Kostadinova was too good a competitor to miss again.

Ritter moved the start of her run-up back 1 foot, raced down the runway and leapt for all she was worth. She grazed the bar with her right thigh, but not hard enough to dislodge it, and the victory was hers.

1992 Barcelona C: 41, N: 26, D: 8.8. WR: 2.09, 6-10¼ (Stefka Kostadinova)

		M	FT.-IN.
1. Heike Henkel	GER	2.02	6-7½
2. Galina Astafei	ROM	2.00	6-6¾
3. Ioamnet Quintero Alvarez	CUB	1.97	6-5½
4. Stefka Kostadinova	BUL	1.94	6-4¼
5. Sigrid Kirchmann	AUT	1.94	6-4¼
6. Silvia Costa Acosta	CUB	1.94	6-4¼
7. Megumi Sato	JPN	1.91	6-3¼
8. Alison Inverarity	AUS	1.91	6-3¼

Competing in her third Olympics, world champion Heike Henkel did not begin jumping until 6 feet 3¼ inches (1.91 meters). At 6 feet 5¾ (1.97 meters) she faced unexpected problems. After missing twice, she cleared on her final attempt and seemed to regain confidence. Meanwhile, Galina Astafei, returning from a pregnancy sabbatical, cleared seven straight heights without a miss through 6 feet 6¾ inches (2 meters). At 6 feet 7½ inches (2.02 meters), Henkel went over on her first try while Astafei missed three times.

LONG JUMP

1896–1936 not held

1948 London C: 26, N: 13, D: 8.4. WR: 6.25, 20-6¼ (Francina "Fanny" Blankers-Koen)

		M	FT.-IN.
1. Olga Gyarmati	HUN	5.695	18-8¼
2. Noëmi Simonetto De Portela	ARG	5.60	18-4½
3. Ann-Britt Leyman	SWE	5.575	18-3¼
4. Gerda van der Kade-Koudijs	HOL	5.57	18-3¼
5. Neeltje Karelse	HOL	5.545	18-2¼
6. Kathleen Russell	JAM	5.495	18-0¼
7. Judy Canty	AUS	5.38	17-7¾
8. Yvonne Curtet-Chabot	FRA	5.35	17-6½

The importance of this competition was somewhat muted by the absence of world record holder Fanny Blankers-Koen, who was busy winning gold medals in four other events.

1952 Helsinki C: 34, N: 22, D: 7.23. WR: 6.25, 20-6¼ (Francina "Fanny" Blankers-Koen)

		M	FT.-IN.	
1. Yvette Williams	NZE	6.24	20-5¾	OR
2. Aleksandra Chudina	SOV/RUS	6.14	20-1¾	
3. Shirley Cawley	GBR	5.92	19-5¼	
4. Irmgard Schmelzer	GER	5.90	19-4¼	
5. Wilhelmina Lust	HOL	5.81	19-0¾	
6. Nina Tyurkina	SOV	5.81	19-0¾	
7. Mabel Landry	USA	5.75	18-10½	
8. Verna Johnson	AUS	5.74	18-10	

Twenty-three-year-old Yvette Williams led the qualifying rounds with a jump of 6.16 meters (20 feet 2½ inches). She faulted twice in the final and was one jump away from elimination. However, her third jump of 5.90

meters (19 feet 4¼ inches) was good enough to put her in the top six who qualified for three more jumps. Her fourth attempt was the winning one, and none of the leaders was able to improve after that. Williams also finished sixth in the shot put. However, the real award for versatility in field events went to Chudina, who took second in the long jump, second in the javelin, and third in the high jump.

1956 Melbourne C: 19, N: 11, D: 11.27. WR: 6.35, 20-10 (Elżbieta Krzesińska)

		M	FT.-IN.	
1. Elżbieta Krzesińska	POL	6.35	20-10	EWR
2. Willye White	USA	6.09	19-11¾	
3. Nadezhda Dvalischvili (Khnykina)	SOV/GEO	6.07	19-11	
4. Erika Fisch	GER	5.89	19-4	
5. Marthe Lambert	FRA	5.88	19-3½	
6. Valentina Schaprunova	SOV/RUS	5.85	19-2¼	
7. Beverly Weigel	NZE	5.85	19-2¼	
8. Nancy Borwick	AUS	5.82	19-1¼	

Krzesińska, a 21-year-old medical student, was in a class by herself. Seventeen-year-old Willye White, who was born in Money, Mississippi, was a surprise silver medalist. She read the New Testament between jumps and won second place with her final leap. She also competed in the next four Olympics, earning another silver medal as a member of the 1964 U.S. 4 × 100-meter relay team.

1960 Rome C: 30, N: 18, D: 8.31. WR: 6.40, 21-0 (Hildrun Claus)

		M	FT.-IN.	
1. Vira Krepkina	SOV/UKR	6.37	20-10¾	OR
2. Elżbieta Krzesińska	POL	6.27	20-7	
3. Hildrun Claus	GDR	6.21	20-4½	
4. Renate Junker	GER	6.19	20-3¾	
5. Lyudmyla Radchenko	SOV/UKR	6.16	20-2½	
6. Helga Hoffmann	GER	6.11	20-0½	
7. Johanna Bijleveld	HOL	6.11	20-0½	
8. Valentina Schaprunova	SOV/RUS	6.01	19-8¾	

Krepkina's victory came as a complete surprise, since she was better known as a sprinter. In fact, she was co-holder of the world record for 100 meters.

1964 Tokyo C: 31, N: 20, D: 10.14. WR: 6.70, 21-11¾ (Tatyana Schelkanova)

		M	FT.-IN.	
1. Mary Rand (Bignal)	GBR	6.76	22-2¼	WR
2. Irena Kirszenstein	POL	6.60	21-8	
3. Tatyana Schelkanova	SOV/RUS	6.42	21-0¾	
4. Ingrid Becker	GER	6.40	21-0	
5. Viorica Viscopoleanu	ROM	6.35	20-10	
6. Diana Yorgova	BUL	6.24	20-5¾	
7. Hildrun Laufer (Claus)	GDR	6.24	20-5¾	
8. Helga Hoffmann	GER	6.23	20-5¼	

In 1960 Mary Rand (then Mary Bignal) had been considered the favorite in the long jump, particularly after she had led the qualifying round with a personal best of 20 feet 9¼ inches. That jump would have won her a silver medal if she had been able to repeat it in the final. Instead she ran through twice and had to settle for ninth place with her third jump. She also finished fourth in the 80-meter hurdles the following day. Four years later in Tokyo, Mary Rand again had the best jump of the qualifying round—21 feet 4¾ inches. This time, though, everything went right in the final. Four of her six jumps were her best ever, and her whole series was so consistent that her worst leap would have earned her a silver medal. Her fifth jump registered 6.76 meters. Unfamiliar with the metric system, she raced back to her bag, pulled out the program, and learned that she had broken the world record. And this despite the fact that she had jumped into a 1.69 meters per second wind. Mary Rand was the first British woman to win an Olympic gold medal in track and field. Later in the week she also won a silver medal in the pentathlon and a bronze in the 4 × 100-meter relay. In 1967 she went to Mexico City and met her future second husband, the U.S. decathlon champion Bill Toomey.

The woman who finished sixth in 1964, Bulgarian Diana Yorgova, made the news several days later when she and Bulgarian gymnast Nikolai Prodanov held the first-ever Olympic wedding. The ceremony took place in the International Club of the Olympic Village in front of a huge Olympic flag and a photo of the Olympic flame. The couple honeymooned in Kyoto, but returned to Tokyo in time for the closing ceremonies.

1968 Mexico City C: 27, N: 19, D: 10.14. WR: 6.76, 22-2¼ (Mary Rand [Bignal])

		M	FT.-IN.	
1. Viorica Viscopoleanu	ROM	6.82	22-4½	WR
2. Sheila Sherwood	GBR	6.68	21-11	
3. Tatyana Talisheva	SOV/RUS	6.66	21-10¼	
4. Burghild Wieczorek	GDR	6.48	21-3¼	
5. Miroslawa Sarna	POL	6.47	21-2¾	
6. Ingrid Becker	GER	6.43	21-1¼	
7. Berit Berthelsen	NOR	6.40	21-0	
8. Heidemarie Rosendahl	GER	6.40	21-0	

Viscopoleanu recorded her winning jump on her first attempt of the final. The 29-year-old Romanian improved on her pre-Olympic personal best by no less than nine inches.

1972 Munich C: 33, N: 19, D: 8.31. WR: 6.84, 22-5¼ (Heidemarie Rosendahl)

		M	FT.-IN.
1. Heidemarie Rosendahl	GER	6.78	22-3
2. Diana Yorgova	BUL	6.77	22-2½
3. Eva Šuranová	CZE/SLV	6.67	21-10¾
4. Marcia Garbey	CUB	6.52	21-4¾
5. Heidi Schüller	GER	6.51	21-4¼
6. Meta Antenen	SWI	6.49	21-3½
7. Viorica Viscopoleanu	ROM	6.48	21-3¼
8. Margrit Olfert	GDR	6.46	21-2½

Heidemarie Rosendahl brought great joy to the crowd by becoming the first West German gold medal winner of the Munich Games. Her first leap of 6.78 meters appeared to be good enough for first place until the fourth round, when Diana Yorgova, the first Bulgarian to win a track and field medal, hit the best jump of her career. But it was one centimeter too short. Yorgova's last jump was also a long one, but was disallowed because her foot went over the board. Later in the Games Rosendahl picked up a silver medal in the pentathlon and another gold in the 4 × 100-meter relay.

1976 Montreal C: 30, N: 19, D: 7.23. WR: 6.99, 22-11¼ (Siegrun Siegl)

		M	FT.-IN.
1. Angela Voigt	GDR	6.72	22-0¾
2. Kathy McMillan	USA	6.66	21-10¼
3. Lidiya Alfeyeva	SOV/UKR	6.60	21-8
4. Siegrun Siegl	GDR	6.59	21-7½
5. Ildikó Szabo	HUN	6.59	21-7½
6. Jarmila Nygrýnová	CZE	6.54	21-5½
7. Heidemarie Wycisk	GDR	6.39	20-11¾
8. Elena Vintila	ROM	6.38	20-11¼

For the third straight time the women's long jump was won on a first-round jump. Angela Voigt had held the world record for ten days earlier in the year, but she had a reputation for doing poorly in important meets. The last jumper of the competition, 18-year-old Kathy McMillan of Raeford, North Carolina, finished with the longest leap of the day; however she had stepped an inch or so over the board, and a no-jump was declared.

1980 Moscow C: 19, N: 11, D: 7.31. WR: 7.09, 23-3¼ (Vilma Bardauskiene)

		M	FT.-IN.	
1. Tatyana Kolpakova	SOV/KYR	7.06	23-2	OR
2. Brigitte Wujak	GDR	7.04	23-1¼	
3. Tetyana Skachko	SOV/UKR	7.01	23-0	
4. Anna Wlodarczyk	POL	6.95	22-9¾	
5. Siegrun Siegl	GDR	6.87	22-6½	
6. Jarmila Nygrýnová	CZE	6.83	22-5	
7. Siegrid Heimann	GDR	6.71	22-0¼	
8. Lidiya Alfeyeva	SOV/UKR	6.71	22-0¼	

This was, without question, the most exciting women's Olympic long-jump contest ever. In 1978 Vilma Bardauskiene had become the first woman to break the 7-meter barrier, but two years later, hampered by injuries, she was unable to make the Soviet team. With one round to go Skachko was in first place as a result of her third round leap of 7.01 meters. She was followed by Wujak and Wlodarczyk, with 6.88 each, and Kolpakova with 6.87. Wlodarczyk's final jump of 6.95 put her into second place and had her crying for joy, but she and Skachko watched in horror as the situation changed dramatically in the next two minutes. First Kolpakova, third string on the U.S.S.R. team, jumped into first place with a 7.06—nine inches further than her pre-Olympic best. Then Wujak improved her personal best by 5½ inches to take the silver medal. Skachko, who had been in front for two hours, was forced to settle for a bronze medal, and

Wlodarczyk was left without any medal at all. At the postrace press conference, Kolpakova, a shy 20-year-old from Frunze in the Kirghiz Soviet Socialist Republic, summed up the competition by saying, "I think that one should always fight until the end, and my last attempt confirmed it."

1984 Los Angeles C: 23, N: 17, D: 8.9. WR: 7.43, 24-4½ (Anişoara Cuşmir-Stanciu)

			M	FT.-IN.
1. Anişoara Cuşmir-Stanciu	ROM		6.96	22-10
2. Valeria Ionescu	ROM		6.81	22-4¼
3. Susan Hearnshaw	GBR		6.80	22-3¾
4. Angela Thacker	USA		6.78	22-3
5. Jacqueline Joyner	USA		6.77	22-2½
6. Robyn Lorraway	AUS		6.67	21-10¾
7. Glynis Nunn	AUS		6.53	21-5¼
8. Shonel Ferguson	BAH		6.44	21-1½

The Soviet bloc boycott prevented the anticipated showdown between world record holder Anişoara Cuşmir-Stanciu and the rising East German star Heike Daute, who had upset Stanciu at the Helsinki world championships. At the Olympics Stanciu went ahead on her own, taking a first-round lead of 6.80 and sealing the victory in the fourth round.

1988 Seoul C: 30, N: 20, D: 9.29. WR: 7.52, 24-8¼ (Regina Cistjakova)

			M	FT.-IN.	
1. Jacqueline Joyner-Kersee	USA		7.40	24-3¼	OR
2. Heike Drechsler (Daute)	GDR		7.22	23-8¼	
3. Regina Cistjakova	SOV/LIT		7.11	23-4	
4. Olena Belevska	SOV/UKR		7.04	23-1¼	
5. Nicole Boegman	AUS		6.73	22-1	
6. Fiona May	GBR		6.62	21-8¾	
7. Agata Karczmarek	POL		6.60	21-7¾	
8. Sabine John	GDR		6.55	21-5¾	

This event pitted world record holder Regina Cistjakova against former world record holders Heike Drechsler and Jackie Joyner-Kersee. Drechsler, then known by her maiden name, Heike Daute, had won the 1983 world championship at the tender age of 18. She was ranked number one in the world four years in a row. Then her 27-meet winning streak was broken when she finished third at the 1987 world championships after injuring her knee on her fourth jump. The winner of that competition was Jackie Joyner-Kersee with a jump of 24 feet 1¾ inches (7.36 meters).

Five days before the Olympic final, Joyner-Kersee won a gold medal in the heptathlon, setting an Olympic long jump record of 23 feet 10½ inches (7.27 meters) in the process.

Cistjakova took the first-round lead with a leap of 7.11, but, hampered by injury, she was unable to improve after that. In the second round, Olena Belevska jumped 7.04 and Drechsler followed with a 7.06. She improved to 7.18 with her next jump, while Joyner-Kersee moved into sec-

ond at 7.16. In the fourth round, Drechsler improved again, this time to 7.22, while Joyner-Kersee fouled. As she prepared for her fifth jump, Joyner-Kersee noticed that her opponents were tiring and decided to go for one big one. Her husband and coach, Bob Kersee, called out to her, "You have a 7.40 in you." Concentrating on keeping her knees high and staying in the air as long as possible, Joyner-Kersee then won the competition with a jump of exactly 7.40 meters.

1992 Barcelona C: 35, N: 24, D: 8.7. WR: 7.52, 24-8¼ (Regina Cistjakova)

			M	FT.-IN.
1. Heike Drechsler	GER		7.14	23-5¼
2. Inessa Kravets	UKR		7.12	23-4½
3. Jacqueline Joyner-Kersee	USA		7.07	23-2½
4. Mirela Dulgheru	ROM		6.71	22-0¼
5. Irina Mushailova	RUS		6.68	21-11
6. Sharon Couch	USA		6.66	21-10¼
7. Sheila Echols	USA		6.62	21-8¾
8. Susen Tiedtke	GER		6.60	21-8
DISQ (Drugs): Nijole Medvedeva (LIT)			6.76	22-2¼

Jackie Joyner-Kersee defeated Heike Drechsler at the 1987 world championships, the 1988 Olympics, and the 1991 world championships. In Barcelona, Drechsler finally came out on top. Inessa Kravets, the world record holder in the triple jump, took the first-round lead with a leap of 7.12 meters. She and Joyner-Kersee never improved on their opening jumps. Drechsler moved into third place in the second round and then hit her winning jump in the fourth round.

TRIPLE JUMP

This event will be held for the first time in 1996.

SHOT PUT

The women's shot weighs 4 kilograms (8 pounds 14¾ ounces).

1896–1936 not held

1948 London C: 19, N: 12, D: 8.4. WR: 14.89, 48-10¼ (Tatyana Sevryukova)

			M	FT.-IN.
1. Micheline Ostermeyer	FRA		13.75	45-1½
2. Amelia Piccinini	ITA		13.09	42-11½
3. Ine Schäffer	AUT		13.08	42-11
4. Paulette Veste	FRA		12.985	42-7¼
5. Jaroslava Komárková	CZE		12.92	42-4¾
6. Anni Bruk	AUT		12.50	42-0¼
7. Maria Radosaljevic	YUG		12.355	40-6½
8. Bevis Reid	GBR		12.17	39-11¼

Three months before the Olympics, pianist Micheline Ostermeyer had graduated with high honors from the Paris Conservatory of Music. In London she used the hands that so delicately played the piano to win gold medals in both the shot put and discus. She also placed third in the high jump. Her success in track and field actually hurt her reputation as a concert pianist, and for a long time she was afraid to play Liszt because he was too *"sportif."*

1952 Helsinki C: 20, N: 13, D: 7.26. WR: 15.19, 49-10 (Galina Zybina)

			M	FT.-IN.	
1.	Galina Zybina	SOV/RUS	15.28	50-1¾	WR
2.	Marianne Werner	GER	14.57	47-9¾	
3.	Klavdia Tochenova	SOV/RUS	14.50	47-7	
4.	Tamara Tyshkevich	SOV/RUS	14.42	47-3¾	
5.	Gertrud Kille	GER	13.84	45-5	
6.	Yvette Williams	NZE	13.35	43-9¾	
7.	Maria Radosaljevic	YUG	13.30	43-7¾	
8.	Meeri Saari	FIN	13.02	42-8¾	

As a ten-year-old child, Galina Zybina had watched her mother and brother die of cold and starvation during World War II. She barely survived herself and entered adolescence thin and sickly. However, ten years after her ordeal, she proved to be one of the strongest women in the world. In Helsinki Zybina had the three longest throws of the competition and had already secured first place when she broke the world record on her final attempt. Werner moved from fourth to second on her final throw to prevent a Soviet sweep.

1956 Melbourne C: 18, N: 9, D: 11.30. WR: 16.76, 55-0 (Galina Zybina)

			M	FT.-IN.	
1.	Tamara Tyshkevich	SOV/RUS	16.59	54-5	OR
2.	Galina Zybina	SOV/RUS	16.53	54-2¾	
3.	Marianne Werner	GER	15.61	51-2¾	
4.	Zinaida Doynikova	SOV/RUS	15.54	51-0	
5.	Valerie Sloper	NZE	15.34	50-4	
6.	Earlene Brown	USA	15.12	49-7¼	
7.	Regina Branner	AUS	14.60	47-10¾	
8.	Nadya Kotlusek	YUG	14.56	47-9¼	

Zybina took the lead in the first round and appeared to be headed for a second gold medal. However, in the final round her 231-pound teammate, Tamara Tyshkevich, scored a dramatic victory by heaving the shot 2¼ inches further than Zybina's best. Los Angeles housewife Earlene Brown made a great impression on the Australians and became a local favorite. Arriving in Melbourne early, she took part in a regional meet and won. When a fan informed her that she had just broken the Victoria state record, Brown replied, "I'm sorry, honey. If I'd known I was going to do that I wouldn't have thrown it so far."

1960 Rome C: 18, N: 12, D: 9.2. WR: 17.78, 58-4 (Tamara Press)

			M	FT.-IN.	
1.	Tamara Press	SOV/UKR	17.32	56-10	OR
2.	Johanna Lüttge	GDR	16.61	54-6	
3.	Earlene Brown	USA	16.42	53-10½	
4.	Valerie Sloper	NZE	16.39	53-9¼	

The medalists in the 1956 shot put: (left to right) Marianne Werner, Tamara Tyshkevich, and Galina Zybina.

Tamara Press overwhelmed the opposition in the 1960 and 1964 shot put but disappeared from international competition when sex tests were introduced.

5.	Zinaida Doynikova	SOV/RUS	16.13	52-11
6.	Renate Garisch	GDR	15.94	52-3¾
7.	Galina Zybina	SOV/RUS	15.56	51-0¾
8.	Wilfriede Hoffmann	GDR	15.14	49-8¼

Between them, Tamara Press and her younger sister Iryna set 26 world records and won five Olympic gold medals and one silver. Unfortunately, when sex tests were instituted at international competitions, the careers of both Press sisters came to a sudden halt.

1964 Tokyo C: 16, N: 11, D: 10.20. WR: 18.55, 60-10½ (Tamara Press)

			M	FT.-IN.
1.	Tamara Press	SOV/UKR	18.14	59-6¼	OR
2.	Renate Garisch-Culmberger	GDR	17.61	57-9½
3.	Galina Zybina	SOV/RUS	17.45	57-3
4.	Valerie Young-Sloper	NZE	17.26	56-7½
5.	Margitta Helmboldt	GDR	16.91	55-5¾
6.	Iryna Press	SOV/UKR	16.71	54-10
7.	Nancy McCredie	CAN	15.89	52-1¾
8.	Ana Salagean	ROM	15.83	51-11¼

Tamara Press won the discus gold the day before the shot put. Zybina's bronze gave her a complete set of Olympic medals.

1968 Mexico City C: 14, N: 10, D: 10.20. WR: 18.87, 61-11 (Margitta Gummel [Helmboldt])

			M	FT.-IN.
1.	Margitta Gummel (Helmboldt)	GDR	19.61	64-4	WR
2.	Marita Lange	GDR	18.78	61-7½
3.	Nadezhda Chizhova	SOV/RUS	18.19	59-8¼
4.	Judit Bognar	HUN	17.78	58-4
5.	Renate Boy (Garisch-Culmberger)	GDR	17.72	58-1¾
6.	Ivanka Hristova	BUL	17.25	56-7¼
7.	Marlene Fuchs	GER	17.11	56-1¾
8.	Els Van Noorduyn	HOL	16.23	53-3

In the very first round Marita Lange heaved the shot 61 feet 7½ inches to improve her personal best by over a yard. Gummel broke the world record in the third round and then unleashed an amazing fifth-round toss of 64 feet 4 inches to better her own pre-Olympic world record by 29 inches.

1972 Munich C: 18, N: 11, D: 9.7. WR: 20.63, 67-8¼ (Nadezhda Chizhova)

			M	FT.-IN.
1.	Nadezhda Chizhova	SOV/RUS	21.03	69-0	WR
2.	Margitta Gummel (Helmboldt)	GDR	20.22	66-4¼
3.	Ivanka Hristova	BUL	19.35	63-6
4.	Esfir Dolzhenko	SOV/MOL	19.24	63-1½
5.	Marianne Adam	GDR	18.94	62-1¾
6.	Marita Lange	GDR	18.85	61-10¼
7.	Helena Fibingerová	CZE	18.81	61-8½
8.	Yelena Stoyanova	BUL	18.34	60-2

Siberian-born Nadezhda Chizhova put the championship out of reach on her first attempt with a world record of 69 feet.

1976 Montreal C: 13, N: 8, D: 7.31. WR: 21.89, 71-10 (Ivanka Hristova)

			M	FT.-IN.
1.	Ivanka Hristova	BUL	21.16	69-5¼	OR
2.	Nadezhda Chizhova	SOV/RUS	20.96	68-9¼
3.	Helena Fibingerová	CZE	20.67	67-9¾
4.	Marianne Adam	GDR	20.55	67-5¼
5.	Ilona Schoknecht	GDR	20.54	67-4¾
6.	Margitta Droese	GDR	19.79	64-11¼
7.	Eva Wilms	GER	19.29	63-3½
8.	Yelena Stoyanova	BUL	18.89	61-11¾

The 1976 shot put competition matched the world record holder against three former world record holders. Defending champion Chizhova led after the first round with a throw of 68 feet 4½ inches. In the second round Hristova hit 68 feet 6 inches, but Chizhova responded with 68 feet 9¼ inches. However, Chizhova slipped and injured her leg and was unable to come up with another serious throw. Her lead held up until the fifth round, when Hristova secured the victory with a new Olympic record of 69 feet 5¼ inches. Hristova's win culminated a steady rise in her career. In the 1964 Olympics she finished tenth. In 1968 she was sixth, and in 1972 she was third. Finally, at the age of 34, she won a gold medal, the first ever by a Bulgarian track and field athlete. Chizhova matched Galina Zybina's feat of earning a complete set of medals.

1980 Moscow C: 14, N: 8, D: 7.24. WR: 22.45, 73-8 (Ilona Slupianek [Schoknecht])

			M	FT.-IN.
1.	Ilona Slupianek (Schoknecht)	GDR	22.41	73-6¼	OR
2.	Svetlana Krachevskaya (Esfir Dolzhenko)	SOV/RUS	21.42	70-3½
3.	Margitta Pufe (Droese)	GDR	21.20	69-6¾
4.	Nunu Abashidze	SOV/UKR	21.15	69-4¾
5.	Verginia Vesselinova	BUL	20.72	67-11¾
6.	Elena Stoyanova	BUL	20.22	66-4¼
7.	Natalya Akhrimenko	SOV/RUS	19.74	64-9¼
8.	Ines Reichenbach	GDR	19.66	64-6

Slupianek was forced to sit out the 1979 season when she was caught taking steroids. In Moscow she put on an extraordinary performance, outclassing the opposition. The last to throw, she broke the Olympic record on her first attempt and then went over 70 feet on each of her five remaining throws. Her *worst* put, 70 feet 3½ inches, was equal to the *best* put of silver medalist Svetlana Krachevskaya.

1984 Los Angeles C: 13, N: 8, D: 8.3. WR: 22.53, 73-11 (Natalya Lisovskaya)

			M	FT.-IN.
1.	Claudia Losch	GER	20.48	67-2¼
2.	Mihaela Loghin	ROM	20.47	67-2
3.	Gael Martin	AUS	19.19	62-11½
4.	Judith Oakes	GBR	18.14	59-6¼
5.	Li Meisu	CHN	17.96	58-11¼
6.	Venissa Head	GBR	17.90	58-8¾

7. Carol Cady	USA	17.23	56-6½	
8. Florenta Craciunescu	ROM	17.23	56-6½	

Claudia Losch, a 24-year-old Bavarian optician, defeated a severely depleted field by edging Mihaela Loghin with her final throw.

1988 Seoul C: 25, N: 14, D: 10.1. WR: 22.63, 74-3 (Natalya Lisovskaya)

		M	FT.-IN.
1. Natalya Lisovskaya	SOV/RUS	22.24	72-11¾
2. Kathrin Neimke	GDR	21.07	69-1½
3. Li Meisu	CHN	21.06	69-1¼
4. Ines Müller	GDR	20.37	66-10
5. Claudia Losch	GER	20.27	66-6
6. Heike Hartwig	GDR	20.20	66-3¼
7. Natalya Akhrimenko	SOV/RUS	20.13	66-0½
8. Huang Zhihong	CHN	19.82	65-0¼

The 6-foot 2-inch, 218-pound Lisovskaya so dominated the competition that *any* of her six throws would have won the gold medal. The battle for the silver, on the other hand, was extremely close, as Neimke came from behind to edge Li by 1 centimeter with her final throw.

1992 Barcelona C: 18, N: 11, D: 8.7. WR: 22.63, 74-3 (Natalya Lisovskaya)

		M	FT.-IN.
1. Svetlana Krivelyova	RUS	21.06	69-1¼
2. Huang Zhihong	CHN	20.47	67-2
3. Kathrin Neimke	GER	19.78	65-2¾
4. Belsy Laza Muñoz	CUB	19.70	64-7¾
5. Zhou Tianhua	CHN	19.26	63-2¼
6. Svetlana Mitkova	BUL	19.23	63-1¼
7. Stephanie Storp	GER	19.10	62-8
8. Viktoriya Pavlysh	UKR	18.69	61-4

Krivelyova took the first round lead with a heave of 66 feet 8¾ inches (20.34 meters). In the third round Huang moved into first place at 67 feet 2 inches (20.47 meters). This was beyond Krivelyova's personal best and appeared to settle the question of who would win the gold medal. But in the fifth round Krivelyova, in a clutch performance, reached 68 feet 6½ inches (20.89 meters). She improved to 69 feet 1¼ inches in the final round to better her pre-Olympic best by 2 feet 3½ inches.

DISCUS THROW

The women's discus weighs 1 kilogram (2 pounds 3.27 ounces).

1896–1924 not held

1928 Amsterdam C: 21, N: 12, D: 7.31. WR: 39.18, 128-6 (Halina Konopacka)

		M	FT.-IN.	
1. Halina Konopacka	POL	39.62	129-11¾	WR
2. Lillian Copeland	USA	37.08	121-8	
3. Ruth Svedberg	SWE	35.92	117-10	

4. Emilie "Milly" Reuter	GER	35.86	117-8	
5. Grete Heublein	GER	35.56	116-8	
6. Liesl Perkaus	AUT	33.54	110-0½	
7. Maybelle Reichardt	USA	33.52	110-0	
8. Genowefa Kobielska	POL	32.72	107-4	

This was the first women's track and field event to be decided in the history of the Olympics.

1932 Los Angeles C: 9, N: 4, D: 8.2. WR: 42.43, 139-2½ (Jadwiga Wajs)

		M	FT.-IN.	
1. Lillian Copeland	USA	40.58	133-2	OR
2. Ruth Osburn	USA	40.12	131-7	
3. Jadwiga Wajs	POL	38.74	127-1	
4. Tilly Fleischer	GER	36.12	118-6	
5. Grete Heublein	GER	34.66	113-8	
6. Stanislawa Walasiewicz	POL	33.60	110-3	
7. Mitsue Ishizu	JPN	33.52	110-0	
8. Ellen Braumüller	GER	33.15	108-9	

Twenty-seven-year-old Lillian Copeland, a student at the nearby University of Southern California, won the contest on her final throw. She told reporters, "The only thing I could think of as I stood there waiting for my last throw of the day was Dr. O'Callaghan, who won the hammer throw [the previous day] on *his* last throw of the day."

1936 Berlin C: 19, N: 11, D: 8.4. WR: 48.31, 158-6 (Gisela Mauermayer)

		M	FT.-IN.	
1. Gisela Mauermayer	GER	47.63	156-3	OR
2. Jadwiga Wajs	POL	46.22	151-8	
3. Paula Mollenhauer	GER	39.80	130-7	
4. Ko Nakamura	JPN	38.24	125-5	
5. Hide Mineshima	JPN	37.35	122-6	
6. Birgit Lundström	SWE	35.92	117-10	
7. Anna Niesink	HOL	35.21	115-6	
8. Gertrude Wilhemsen	USA	34.43	112-11½	

Three weeks before the games began, Gisela Mauermayer heaved the discus 158 feet 6 inches to set a world record that would last for twelve years. Mauermayer was a modest 22-year-old, a 6-foot blonde, who was hailed in Germany as the perfect example of Aryan womanhood. She gave the Nazi salute on the victory stand and became a top-ranking member of the Nazi women's organization. During World War II she was a teacher in Munich. After the war she lost her job because of her high-profile Nazi involvement. Starting over at the Zoological Institute of Munich University she gained a doctor's degree by studying the social behavior of ants. Like Helen Stephens, another star of the 1936 games, Mauermayer eventually settled down as a librarian.

1948 London C: 21, N: 11, D: 7.30. WR: 48.31, 158-6 (Gisela Mauermayer)

		M	FT.-IN.
1. Micheline Ostermeyer	FRA	41.92	137-6
2. Edera Cordiale Gentile	ITA	41.17	135-0

The winners of the 1948 discus: Edera Cordiale Gentile (silver), Micheline Ostermeyer (gold), and Jacqueline Mazéas (bronze).

3. Jacqueline Mazéas	FRA	40.47	132-9	
4. Jadwiga Wajs-Marcinkiewicz	POL	39.30	128-11	
5. Charlotte "Lotte" Haidegger	AUT	38.81	127-3	
6. Anna Panhorst Niesink	HOL	38.74	127-1	
7. Majken Aberg	SWE	38.48	126-3	
8. Ingeborg Mello	ARG	38.44	126-1	

1952 Helsinki C: 20, N: 16, D: 7.20. WR: 53.37, 175-1 (Nina Dumbadze)

		M	FT.-IN.	
1. Nina Romaschkova	SOV/RUS	51.42	168-8	OR
2. Yelisaveta Bagryantseva	SOV/RUS	47.08	154-5	
3. Nina Dumbadze	SOV/GEO	46.29	151-10	
4. Toyoko Yoshino	JPN	43.81	143-8	
5. Charlotte "Lotte" Haidegger	AUT	43.49	142-8	
6. Lia Manoliu	ROM	42.65	139-11	
7. Ingeborg Pfuller	ARG	41.73	136-11	
8. Ilona Jozsa	HUN	41.61	136-6	

Romaschkova's margin of victory in Helsinki was extraordinary, particularly considering the presence of world record holder Nina Dumbadze. The following month Romaschkova broke Dumbadze's record, but on October 18, Dumbadze threw the discus 187 feet 1½ inches to set a world record that would last for almost eight years.

Olympic silver medalist Yelisaveta Bagryantseva was the mother of Irina Bagryantseva, who, under her married name, Nazarova, won a gold medal in the 4 × 400-meter relay in 1980.

1956 Melbourne C: 22, N: 12, D: 11.23. WR: 57.04, 187-1½ (Nina Dumbadze)

		M	FT.-IN.	
1. Olga Fikotová	CZE	53.69	176-1	OR
2. Irina Beglyakova	SOV/RUS	52.54	174-4	
3. Nina Ponomaryeva (Romaschkova)	SOV/RUS	52.02	170-8	
4. Earlene Brown	USA	51.35	168-5	
5. Albina Yelkina	SOV/UKR	48.20	158-2	
6. Isabel Ercilia Avellán	ARG	46.73	153-3	
7. Jiřina Voborilova	CZE	45.84	150-5	
8. Stepanka Mertová	CZE	45.78	150-2	

A former member of the Czechoslovakian national basketball team, Fikotová was taught by her first discus coach to regard the event as a dance step and was allowed to practice to the sounds of "The Blue Danube." In 1956, she gained great fame as a result of her Cold War-thawing romance with and marriage to U.S. hammer thrower Harold Connolly. The couple eventually settled in California, although they divorced in 1973. Olga took part in four more Olympics, finishing seventh in 1960, twelfth in 1964, sixth in 1968, and sixteenth in 1972. In 1972 Olga Connolly was elected by her teammates to carry the United States flag at the Opening Ceremony. The United States Olympic Committee, miffed by her outspoken opposition to United States involvement in the Vietnam War, tried to intervene, but Connolly was allowed to carry out the honor anyway.

1960 Rome C: 24, N: 15, D: 9.5, WR: 57.04, 187-1½ (Nina Dumbadze)

		M	FT.-IN.	
1. Nina Ponomaryeva (Romaschkova)	SOV/RUS	55.10	180-9	OR
2. Tamara Press	SOV/UKR	52.59	172-4	
3. Lia Manoliu	ROM	52.36	171-9	
4. Krimhild Hausmann	GER	51.47	168-10	
5. Yevgenya Kuznetsova	SOV/RUS	51.43	168-8	
6. Earlene Brown	USA	51.29	168-3	
7. Olga Connolly (Fikotová)	USA	50.95	167-2	
8. Jiřina Nemcova (Voborilova)	CZE	50.12	164-5	

The 1960 discus competition matched two former gold medal winners and two future gold medal winners. Ponomaryeva took the lead in the second round and won with the contest's three longest throws. A week later, Tamara Press set a world record of 57.15 meters (187 feet 6 inches).

1964 Tokyo C: 21, N: 15, D: 10.19. WR: 59.28, 194-5¾ (Tamara Press)

		M	FT.-IN.	
1. Tamara Press	SOV/UKR	57.27	187-10	OR
2. Ingrid Lotz	GDR	57.21	187-8	
3. Lia Manoliu	ROM	56.97	186-10	
4. Virzhinia Mikhailova	BUL	56.70	186-0	

5. Yevgenya Kuznetsova	SOV/RUS	55.17	181-0	
6. Jolán Kleiber	HUN	54.87	180-0	
7. Krimhild Limberg (Hausmann)	GER	53.81	176-6	
8. Olimpia Catarama	ROM	53.08	173-11	

After four rounds, world record holder Tamara Press was only in fourth place. Her fifth attempt, however, stretched two inches beyond Ingrid Lotz's first-round mark and gave Press the closest victory in Olympic discus history.

1968 Mexico City C: 15, N: 8, D: 10.18. WR: 62.54, 205-2¼ (Liesel Westermann)

		M	FT.-IN.	
1. Lia Manoliu	ROM	58.28	191-2	OR
2. Liesel Westermann	GER	57.76	189-6	
3. Jolán Kleiber	HUN	54.90	180-1	
4. Anita Otto	GDR	54.40	178-6	
5. Antonina Popova	SOV/RUS	53.42	175-3	
6. Olga Connolly (Fikotová)	USA	52.96	173-9	
7. Christine Speilberg	GDR	52.86	173-5	
8. Brigitte Berendonk	GER	52.80	173-3	

On November 5, 1967, while competing in Brazil, Liesel Westermann became the first woman to throw the discus over 200 feet, with a heave of 201 feet (61.26 meters). In Mexico City she was one of the three favorites, along with the East German Christine Speilberg and the Romanian Lia Manoliu, who was taking part in her fifth Olympics. In 1952 Manoliu had finished sixth, in 1956 ninth, in 1960 third, and in 1964 third again. Manoliu entered the competition in 1968 with a sore elbow, so she decided to put everything she had into her first throw. It went 191 feet 2 inches, good enough to take the lead after the first round. After that she fouled three times, passed once, and got off one poor throw. However, a rainstorm arrived during the second round, and the rest of the competi-

tition was severely impaired as the throwing circle became wetter and wetter. It turned out that Lia Manoliu's first toss held up to take first place, and the 36-year-old Manoliu became the oldest woman in Olympic history to win a track and field gold medal. She took part in one more Olympics in 1972, finishing ninth. No other female track and field athlete has taken part in six different Olympic Games.

1972 Munich C: 17, N: 10, D: 9.10. WR: 66.76, 219-0¼ (Faina Melnik)

		M	FT.-IN.	
1. Faina Melnik	SOV/UKR	66.62	218-7	OR
2. Argentina Menis	ROM	65.06	213-5	
3. Vassilka Stoyeva	BUL	64.34	211-1	
4. Tamara Danilova	SOV/RUS	62.86	206.3	
5. Liesel Westermann	GER	62.18	204-0	
6. Gabriele Hinzmann	GDR	61.72	202-6	
7. Carmen Ionescu	ROM	60.42	198-3	
8. Lyudmila Muraviova	SOV/RUS	59.00	193-7	

Argentina Menis, who wore makeup and false eyelashes while competing, led after three rounds, with world champion Faina Melnik struggling in fifth place. However, Melnik, who yelled at the top of her lungs with each throw, came within 5½ inches of her best ever on her fourth attempt. Menis gave one last mighty effort on her final try, nearly decapitating a marker judge with a throw of 212 feet 11 inches. Less than two weeks later Menis set a world record of 220 feet 10 inches.

1976 Montreal C: 15, N: 9, D: 7.29. WR: 70.50, 231-3½ (Faina Melnik)

		M	FT.-IN.	
1. Evelin Schlaak	GDR	69.00	226-4	OR
2. Maria Vergova	BUL	67.30	220-9	
3. Gabriele Hinzmann	GDR	66.84	219-3	
4. Faina Melnik	SOV/UKR	66.40	217-10	
5. Sabine Engel	GDR	65.88	216-2	
6. Argentina Menis	ROM	65.38	214-6	
7. Maria Betancourt	CUB	63.86	209-6	
8. Natalya Gorbachova	SOV/RUS	63.46	208-2	

Twenty-year-old Schlaak shocked the opposition with a 69-meter first throw that held up for the victory. It was originally announced that Faina Melnik had taken second place by virtue of her fifth-round toss of 225 feet 1 inch. However, the throw was later ruled illegal because Melnik had stepped in front of the circle twice before taking her shot. Danuta Rosani of Poland qualified for the final, but was disqualified after failing the test for anabolic steroids. She was the first Olympic track and field athlete to be disqualified for taking drugs.

1980 Moscow C: 17, N: 10, D: 8.1. WR: 71.80, 235-7 (Maria Petkova [Vergova])

		M	FT.-IN.	
1. Evelin Jahl (Schlaak)	GDR	69.96	229-6	OR
2. Maria Petkova (Vergova)	BUL	67.90	222-9	

Lia Manoliu, the first track and field athlete to take part in six Olympics, finally won a gold medal on her fifth attempt, in the 1968 discus throw.

3. Tatyana Lesovaya	SOV/KAZ	67.40	221-1	
4. Gisela Beyer	GDR	67.08	220-1	
5. Margitta Pufe (Droese)	GDR	66.12	216-11	
6. Florenţa Ţacu	ROM	64.38	211-2	
7. Galina Murashova	SOV/LIT	63.84	209-5	
8. Svetla Gunleva	BUL	63.14	207-1	

Now married and a first lieutenant in the army, Jahl had lost her world record to Petkova a few weeks before the games. However, in Moscow she posted the four longest throws of the competition after Petkova had taken the opening-round lead.

1984 Los Angeles C: 17, N: 14, D: 8.11. WR: 73.26, 240-4¼ (Galina Savinkova)

		M	FT.-IN.
1. Ria Stalman	HOL	65.36	214-5
2. Leslie Deniz	USA	64.86	212-9
3. Florenţa Craciunescu (Ţacu)	ROM	63.64	208-9
4. Ulla Lundholm	FIN	62.84	206-2
5. Margaret Ritchie	GBR	62.58	205-4
6. Ingra Manecke	GER	58.56	192-1
7. Venissa Head	GBR	58.18	190-10
8. Gael Martin	AUS	55.88	183-4

In a competition severely depleted by the Soviet-bloc boycott, Ria Stalman won a dramatic victory over her former Arizona State U. roommate, Leslie Deniz. Stalman took the lead with her first throw of 64.50, but was passed in the fifth round by Deniz's 64.86. But the 32-year-old Stalman was able to secure the gold medal with a final toss of 65.36. Stalman was subsequently caught trying to smuggle steroid tablets into the United States from Mexico.

1988 Seoul C: 22, N: 13, D: 9.29. WR: 76.80, 252-0 (Gabriele Reinsch)

		M	FT.-IN.	
1. Martina Hellmann	GDR	72.30	237-2½	OR
2. Diana Gansky	GDR	71.88	235-10	
3. Tzvetanka Hristova	BUL	69.74	228-10	
4. Svetla Mitkova	BUL	69.14	226-10	
5. Yellina Zveryova	SOV/BLR	68.94	226-2	
6. Zdeňka Šilhavá	CZE	67.84	222-7	
7. Gabriele Reinsch	GDR	67.26	220-8	
8. Hou Xuemei	CHN	65.94	216-4	

Gabriele Reinsch, whose pre-1988 best was 220 feet 5 inches (67.18 meters), added over 7 feet to Zdeňka Šilhavá's 1984 world record with a throw of 252 feet on July 9, 1988. At the Olympics two and a half months later, she needed all three attempts to make it out of the preliminary round, then placed a disappointing seventh in the final. Meanwhile, her teammate, two-time world champion Martina Hellmann, hit a 71.84 in the first round and extended to 72.30 with her fourth throw, to outdistance the third East German, Diana Gansky, whose fifth-round throw earned her the silver.

1992 Barcelona C: 28, N: 16, D: 8.3. WR: 76.80, 252-0 (Gabriele Reinsch)

		M	FT.-IN.
1. Maritza Marten García	CUB	70.06	229-10
2. Tzvetanka Khristova	BUL	67.78	222-4
3. Daniela Costian	AUS	66.24	217-4
4. Larissa Korotkevich	BLR	65.52	214-11
5. Olga Burova	RUS	64.02	210-0
6. Hilda Ramos Manez	CUB	63.80	209-4
7. Irina Yatchenko	BLR	63.74	209-1
8. Stefania Simova	BUL	63.42	208-1

Korotkevich led the qualifying round at 222 feet 10 inches (67.92 meters), but the favorite remained Ilke Wyludda of Germany. Wyludda had won 41 consecutive meets between 1988 and 1991, when she was upset at the world championships on the last throw by Tzvetanka Khristova. In the final, the early lead was taken by unheralded 28-year-old Maritza Marten of Havana. Kristova took over in the second round with a throw of 222 feet 4 inches. Through the fourth round, Khristova still led by 2 feet 10½ inches, with Marten in second, Korotkevich third, and Costian fourth. Wyludda, in ninth place, did not qualify for the final three throws. The medals were decided in the fifth round. First Costian reached 217 feet 4 inches to move into third place and then Marten hit 229 feet 10 inches to secure a decisive victory. Daniela Costian had a colorful history. In 1986 she was suspended for a drug violation. Returning to competition in 1988, she defected during the Balkan Games in Turkey and settled in Australia. In 1993 Khristova tested positive for steroids and was banned from competition.

JAVELIN THROW

The women's javelin must weigh a minimum of 600 grams (26.16 ounces) and measure between 2.20 meters (7 feet 2⅔ inches) and 2.30 meters (7 feet 6½ inches).

1896–1928 not held

1932 Los Angeles C: 8, N: 4, D: 7.31. WR: 46.75, 153-4½ (Nan Gindele)

		M	FT.-IN.	
1. Mildred "Babe" Didriksen	USA	43.68	143-4	OR
2. Ellen Braumüller	GER	43.49	142-8	
3. Ottilie "Tilly" Fleischer	GER	43.00	141-1	
4. Masako Shimpo	JPN	39.07	128-2	
5. Nan Gindele	USA	37.95	124-6	
6. Gloria Russell	USA	36.73	120-6	
7. Maria Uribe Jasso	MEX	33.66	110-5	
8. Mitsue Ishizu	JPN	30.81	101-1	

Born in Port Arthur, Texas, and raised in nearby Beaumont, Mildred "Babe" Didriksen* was already an all-

*Preferred family spelling

American basketball player when she gained sudden and dramatic national attention as a track and field star. On July 4, 1932, the women's A.A.U. championships, which also served as the Olympic trials, were held in Evanston, Illinois, on the campus of Northwestern University. Babe caused a sensation at the opening parade when she appeared as the entire team representing the Employers Casualty Insurance Company of Dallas, for whom she worked as an 85 w.p.m. typist. In the next three hours she took part in eight of the ten events and won six of them. She set world records in the 80-meter hurdles, the javelin, and the high jump, in which she tied with Jean Shiley. She also won the shot put, long jump, and baseball throw, and finished fourth in the discus. When the point totals were tallied, it was announced that Babe Didriksen had won the team title with 30 points. In second place with 22 points was the University of Illinois, which had sent a 22-woman contingent.

Olympic rules limited Babe to only three events, even though she had qualified for five, so she chose the three at which she had set world records. On the train across the country to the Los Angeles Olympics, the 21-year-old Babe irritated her fellow teammates by playing the harmonica, exercising in the aisles, and bragging about her numerous feats, which included earning a blue ribbon for sewing at the Texas State Fair. The same qualities that annoyed the athletes delighted reporters. Upon arrival in California, she told them, "I am out to beat everybody in sight, and that's just what I'm going to do." Her first event was the javelin, in which her first throw of 143 feet 4 inches was good enough for the gold medal even though the javelin slipped out of her hand. Before the Olympics were over she had recorded new world marks in the 80-meter hurdles and the high jump.

Overnight Babe Didriksen became a celebrity. But before the year was out she had been barred from amateur competition because she had allowed a photo of herself and an interview to be used in an automobile ad campaign. She tried her hand on the vaudeville circuit, telling jokes, shotputting, playing harmonica, and performing various athletic feats. For a time she toured as the only female and only nonbearded member of the House of David baseball team. She even pitched an inning against the Philadelphia Athletics during an exhibition game with the St. Louis Cardinals. After loading the bases with no outs, she got out of the inning on a double play and a fly ball to the outfield. Eventually she turned to golf, and it was there that she gained her greatest success. Encouraged by her 285-pound husband, wrestler George Zaharias, she became the greatest woman golfer in the world. During one 12-month period from 1946 to 1947, she won 14 straight tournaments and became the first American woman to win the British Amateur Open.

In 1953 Babe learned that she had cancer and was forced to undergo an emergency colostomy. Three and a half months after the surgery she was back on the circuit, finishing third in a minor tournament. The following year she won the U.S. Open by 12 strokes. But the cancer returned, and on September 17, 1956, Babe Didriksen, who had been voted the greatest female athlete of the half-century in an Associated Press poll, died at the age of 45.

1936 Berlin C: 14, N: 10, D: 8.2. WR: 46.75, 153-4½ (Nan Gindele)

		M	FT.-IN.	
1. Ottilie "Tilly" Fleischer	GER	45.18	148-3	OR
2. Luise Krüger	GER	43.29	142-8	
3. Maria Kwaśniewska	POL	41.80	137-2	
4. Hermine "Herma" Bauma	AUT	41.66	136-8	
5. Sadako Yamamoto	JPN	41.45	135-11	
6. Lydia Eberhardt	GER	41.37	135-8	
7. Gertrude Wilhelmsen	USA	37.35	122-6	
8. Gerda de Kock	HOL	36.93	121-2	

1948 London C: 15, N: 10, D: 7.31. WR: 50.32, 165-1 (Klavdia Mayuchaya)

		M	FT.-IN.	
1. Hermine "Herma" Bauma	AUT	45.57	149-6	OR
2. Kaisa Parviainen	FIN	43.79	143-8	
3. Lily Carlstedt	DEN	42.08	138-1	
4. Dorothy Dodson	USA	41.96	137-8	
5. Johanna Tenunissen Waalboer	HOL	40.92	134-3	
6. Johanna Koning	HOL	40.33	132-3	
7. Dana Ingrova	CZE	39.64	130-0	
8. Elly Dammers	HOL	38.23	125-5	

1952 Helsinki C: 19, N: 13, D: 7.24. WR: 53.41, 175-2¾ (Nina Smirnitskaya)

		M	FT.-IN.	
1. Dana Zátopková (Ingrova)	CZE	50.47	165-7	OR
2. Aleksandra Chudina	SOV/RUS	50.01	164-0	
3. Yelena Gorchakova	SOV/RUS	49.76	163-3	
4. Galina Zybina	SOV/RUS	48.35	158-7	
5. Lily Kelsby-Carlstedt	DEN	46.23	151-8	
6. Marlies Müller	GER	44.37	145-6	
7. Maria Ciach	POL	44.31	145-4½	
8. Jutta Kruger	GER	44.30	145.4	

Shortly before the competition began, Dana Zátopková's husband, Emil Zátopek, was awarded a gold medal for winning the 5000 meters. After the ceremony, she rushed up to him and said, "You've won! Splendid! Show me that medal." After examining it, she added, "I'll take it with me for luck." She put it in her bag and left. On her first throw she set an Olympic record and earned a gold medal of her own. That evening Emil claimed that he deserved partial credit for his wife's gold medal because he had inspired her. Naturally, Dana was quite offended and replied, "What? All right, go and inspire some other girl and see if she throws a javelin fifty meters."

The Zátopeks, Dana and Emil, heroes of the 1952 Helsinki Olympics.

1956 Melbourne C: 19, N: 12, D: 11.28. WR: 55.48, 182-0 (Nadezhda Konyayeva)

			M	FT.-IN.	
1.	Inese Jaunzeme	SOV/LAT	53.86	176-8	OR
2.	Marlene Ahrens	CHI	50.38	165-3	
3.	Nadiya Konyayeva	SOV/UKR	50.28	164-11½	
4.	Dana Zátopková (Ingrova)	CZE	49.83	163-5½	
5.	Ingrid Almqvist	SWE	49.74	163-2	
6.	Urszula Figwer	POL	48.16	158-0	
7.	Erszébeth Vig	HUN	48.07	157-8½	
8.	Karen Anderson	USA	48.00	157-5½	

1960 Rome C: 20, N: 14, D: 9.1. WR: 59.54, 195-4 (Elvira Ozolina)

			M	FT.-IN.	
1.	Elvira Ozoliņa	SOV/RUS	55.98	183-8	OR
2.	Dana Zátopková (Ingrova)	CZE	53.78	176-5	
3.	Birutė Kalėdienė	SOV/LIT	53.45	175-4	
4.	Vlasta Pesková	CZE	52.56	172-5	
5.	Urszula Figwer	POL	52.33	171-8	
6.	Anna Pazera	AUS	51.15	167-9	
7.	Susan Platt	GBR	51.01	167-4	
8.	Alevtina Shastitko	SOV/RUS	50.92	167-1	

Ozoliņa unleashed her winning throw at her first attempt. Zátopková was 18 days shy of her 38th birthday when she won her second Olympic medal. Not only was she the oldest woman in Olympic history to win a track and field medal, but two years earlier she had thrown the javelin 182 feet 10 inches to become the oldest female world record breaker.

In the third round, Susan Platt of Great Britain threw past the 177-foot mark. However she was so excited that she stepped over the line on her way to see where the spear had fallen. The judge immediately ruled a foul and Platt had to settle for seventh place.

1964 Tokyo C: 16, N: 10, D: 10.16. WR: 61.38, 201-4½ (Elvira Ozoliņa)

			M	FT.-IN.
1.	Mihaela Peneş	ROM	60.54	198-7
2.	Márta Rudas	HUN	58.27	191-2
3.	Yelena Gorchakova	SOV/RUS	57.06	187-2
4.	Birute Kalediene	SOV/LIT	56.31	184-8
5.	Elvira Ozoliņa	SOV/RUS	54.81	179-9
6.	Maria Diaconescu	ROM	53.71	176-2
7.	Hiroko Sato	JPN	52.48	172-2
8.	Anneliese Gerhards	GER	52.37	171-10

The 1964 javelin competition was full of surprises. On the very first throw of the qualification round, 31-year-old Yelena Gorchakova set a world record of 62.40 meters (204 feet 9 inches). This boosted her up to co-favorite along with defending champion Elvira Ozoliņa. However, when the final began a few hours later, it was 17-year-old high school student Mihaela Peneş of Bucharest who stunned the crowd with a throw of 198 feet 7 inches—17 feet further than she had ever thrown before. No one came close to her for the rest of the competition. Ozoliņa fouled on her last four attempts and had to settle for fifth place. She was so distressed by her performance that she went straight to the hairdresser at the Olympic Village and asked to have her head shaved. When the Japanese hairdresser refused, Ozoliņa took the clippers herself and removed a chunk of her long tresses. The hairdresser finished the job and Ozoliņa left the parlor bald, refusing a scarf to hide her shame. Ozoliņa was not the first Olympic athlete to react to defeat by having her head shaved, although she was the first woman. Four years earlier, in Rome, the entire Japanese wrestling team had had their heads shaved after an all-around poor showing.

1968 Mexico City C: 16, N: 11, D: 10.14. WR: 62.40, 204-8¾ (Yelena Gorchakova)

			M	FT.-IN.
1.	Angéla Németh	HUN	60.36	198-0
2.	Mihaela Peneş	ROM	59.92	196-7
3.	Eva Janko	AUT	58.04	190-5
4.	Márta Rudas	HUN	56.38	185-0
5.	Daniela Jaworska	POL	56.06	183-11
6.	Nataša Urbančič	YUG	55.42	181-10
7.	Ameli Koloska	GER	55.20	181-1
8.	Kaisa Launela	FIN	53.96	177-0

Elvira Ozoliņa, winner of the 1960 javelin throw, was so humiliated at finishing only fifth in 1964 that she shaved off all her hair and refused to wear a scarf to hide her shame.

1972 Munich C: 19, N: 10, D: 9.1. WR: 65.06, 213-5½ (Ruth Fuchs)

		M	FT.-IN.	
1. Ruth Fuchs	GDR	63.88	209-7	OR
2. Jacqueline Todten	GDR	62.54	205-2	
3. Kathryn Schmidt	USA	59.94	196-8	
4. Liutvian Mollova	BUL	59.36	194-9	
5. Nataša Urbančič	YUG	59.06	193-9	
6. Eva Janko	AUT	58.56	192-1	
7. Ewa Gryziecka	POL	57.00	187-0	
8. Svetlana Korolyova	SOV/RUS	56.36	184-11	

Yelena Gorchakova's 1964 qualifying toss of 204 feet 8¾ inches had been in the books as a world record for over seven and a half years when it was suddenly beaten twice in one day. On June 11, 1972, Ewa Gryziecka, competing in Bucharest, threw the javelin 205 feet 8 inches (62.70 meters). One half hour later, in Potsdam, East Germany, Ruth Fuchs began her domination of women's javelin with a throw of 213 feet 5½ inches (65.06 meters). Two and a half months later, at the Munich Olympics, Fuchs took the lead from Kate Schmidt in the second round,

improved in the fourth round, and broke the Olympic record in the fifth round. The competition ended on an exciting note when Urbančič's final throw almost skewered a wandering photographer.

1976 Montreal C: 15, N: 10, D: 7.24. WR: 69.12, 226-9¼ (Ruth Fuchs)

		M	FT.-IN.	
1. Ruth Fuchs	GDR	65.94	216-4	OR
2. Marion Becker	GER	64.70	212-3	
3. Kathryn Schmidt	USA	63.96	209-10	
4. Jacqueline Hein (Todten)	GDR	63.84	209-5	
5. Sabine Sebrowski	GDR	63.08	206-11	
6. Svetlana Babich (Korolyova)	SOV/RUS	59.42	194-11	
7. Nadezhda Yakubovich	SOV/BLR	59.16	194-1	
8. Karin Smith	USA	57.50	188-8	

Marion Becker reached the victory platform in Montreal after an unusual odyssey. Born in Hamburg in West Germany in 1950, she was nonetheless raised in East Germany. After marrying, she moved to Romania and represented Romania at the 1972 Olympics in Munich, finishing seventeenth. After the games, she stayed behind in West Germany and four years later competed for the nation of her birth in the 1976 Olympics. In the qualifying round she broke the Olympic record with a throw of 213 feet 8 inches (65.14 meters). However, in the competition proper, Ruth Fuchs knocked out her opposition with an opening throw of 216 feet 4 inches (65.94 meters).

1980 Moscow C: 21, N: 14, D: 7.25. WR: 70.08, 229-10 (Tatyana Biryulina)

		M	FT.-IN.	
1. María Colón Rueñes	CUB	68.40	224-5	OR
2. Saida Gunba	SOV/GEO	67.76	222-2	
3. Ute Hommola	GDR	66.56	218-4	
4. Ute Richter	GDR	66.54	218-4	
5. Ivanka Vancheva	BUL	66.38	217-9	
6. Tatyana Biryulina	SOV/UZB	65.08	213-6	
7. Eva Raduly-Zorgo	ROM	64.08	210-3	
8. Ruth Fuchs	GDR	63.94	209-9	

Ruth Fuchs continued to be the queen of javelin throwing all the way into 1980. On April 29 she set a world record of 69.96 meters (229 feet 6 inches) and she looked poised to become the first woman to break the 70-meter barrier. However, on July 12 a complete unknown, Tatyana Biryulina, improved her personal best by 27½ feet with a throw of 70.08. Less than two weeks later, at the Olympics, Biryulina could do no better than 65.08 and sixth place. In fact, the women with the four best pre-Olympic records all had disappointing performances. Fuchs, competing with a back injury, finished eighth, Raduly was seventh, and Tessa Sanderson, who had thrown 69.70, failed to qualify for the final. It was left to María Colón to win the competition on her first throw. She was the first Cuban woman to win an Olympic gold medal and the first non-white athlete of either sex to win an Olympic throwing event. From 1970 through 1980 Ruth Fuchs took part in 129 meets and won 113 of them, including 30 straight from 1972 to 1974. In 1994 Fuchs admitted that she had taken steroids for eight years, from 1972 until 1980.

1984 Los Angeles C: 24, N: 16, D: 8.6. WR: 74.73, 245-3 (Ilse "Tiina" Lillak)

		M	FT.-IN.	
1. Theresa "Tessa" Sanderson	GBR	69.56	228-2	OR
2. Ilse "Tiina" Lillak	FIN	69.00	226-4	
3. Fatima Whitbread	GBR	67.14	220-3	
4. Tuula Laaksalo	FIN	66.40	217-10	
5. Trine Solberg	NOR	64.52	211-8	
6. Ingrid Thyssen	GER	63.26	207-6	
7. Beate Peters	GER	62.34	204-6	
8. Karin Smith	USA	62.06	203-7	

Jamaican-born Tessa Sanderson, competing in her third Olympics, broke the Olympic record with her first throw. World record holder Tiina Lillak had won the 1983 world championship with a dramatic last round throw in front of an adoring hometown crowd. In Los Angeles her second round effort came within two feet of Sanderson's best, but she was forced to pass her last four chances because of a stress fracture of her right foot. Sanderson's record held up for the gold medal, while Fatima Whitbread, who had beaten Sanderson three times in a row after losing 21 of their first 22 confrontations, overhauled Laaksalo in the fifth round to secure the bronze. Sanderson was the first British athlete to win an Olympic throwing event.

1988 Seoul C: 29, N: 18, D: 9.26. WR: 80.00, 262-5 (Petra Felke)

		M	FT.-IN.	
1. Petra Felke	GDR	74.68	245-0	OR
2. Fatima Whitbread	GBR	70.32	230-8½	
3. Beate Koch	GDR	67.30	220-10	
4. Iryna Kostyuchenkova	SOV/UKR	67.00	219-10	
5. Silke Renk	GDR	66.38	217-9	
6. Natalya Yermolovich	SOV/BLR	64.84	212-9	
7. Donna Mayhew	USA	61.78	202-8	
8. Ingrid Thyssen	GER	60.76	199-4	

Between 1984 and the opening of the 1988 Olympics, Petra Felke won 69 of 76 meets. Her last three losses were all to Fatima Whitbread, who defeated her at the two most important meets—the 1986 European championships and the 1987 world championships. Eight days before the opening of the Seoul Games, Felke served notice that she was finally ready to win the big one when she became the first woman to throw a javelin 80 meters. In Seoul she delivered the three longest throws of the competitions. Whitbread secured the silver medal despite the fact that in the 12 preceding months she had experienced a trapped nerve in her throwing shoulder, a foot injury, a mouth infection, an abscess in her back, hamstring problems, glandular fever, and a car crash.

1992 Barcelona C: 25, N: 17, D: 8.1. WR: 80.00, 262-5 (Petra Felke)

		M	FT.-IN.
1. Silke Renk	GER	68.34	224-2
2. Natalya Shikolenko	BLR	68.26	223-11
3. Karen Forkel	GER	66.86	219-4
4. Theresa "Tessa" Sanderson	GBR	63.58	208-7
5. Trine Hattestad (Solberg)	NOR	63.54	208-5
6. Heli Rantanen	FIN	62.34	204-6
7. Petra Meier (Felke)	GER	59.02	193-8
8. Dulce García Gil	CUB	58.26	191-1

Shikolenko's first round throw of 223 feet 11 inches appeared to be good enough for the gold. But in the final round, Silke Renk, then in third place, extended the start of her run-up all the way back to lane 8 of the track and beat Shikolenko by 3 inches.

HEPTATHLON/PENTATHLON

In 1984 the five-event pentathlon was replaced by the seven-event heptathlon. On the first day, athletes compete in the 100-meter hurdles, the high jump, the shot put, and the 200-meter dash. On the second day, they conclude with the long jump, the javelin and the 800-meter run. Points are scored according to a set of tables approved by the International Amateur Athletic Federation.

1896–1960 not held

1964 Tokyo C: 20, N: 15, D: 10.16–17. WR: 5194 (Iryna Press)

		80M H	SP	HJ	LJ	200M	TOTAL	
1. Iryna Press	SOV/UKR	10.7	17.16	1.63	6.24	24.7	5246	WR
2. Mary Rand (Bignal)	GBR	10.9	11.05	1.72	6.55	24.2	5035	
3. Galina Bystrova	SOV/RUS	10.7	14.47	1.60	6.11	25.2	4956	
4. Mary Peters	GBR	11.0	14.48	1.60	5.60	25.4	4797	
5. Draga Stamejčič	YUG	10.9	12.73	1.54	6.19	25.2	4790	
6. Helga Hoffman	GER	11.2	10.67	1.60	6.44	25.0	4737	
7. Patricia Winslow	USA	12.0	13.04	1.63	5.90	24.6	4724	
8. Ingrid Becker	GER	11.6	11.62	1.60	6.17	24.6	4717	

Press's margin of victory was provided in the shot put, where she outpointed Rand 1173 to 789 with a throw of 56 feet 2½ inches, which was 16½ inches farther than she was able to throw in the shot put competition three days later.

1968 Mexico City C: 33, N: 24, D: 10.15–16. WR: 5246 (Iryna Press)

			80M H	SP	HJ	LJ	200M	TOTAL
1.	Ingrid Becker	GER	10.9	11.48	1.71	6.43	23.5	5098
2.	Elisabeth "Liese" Prokop	AUT	11.2	14.61	1.68	5.97	25.1	4966
3.	Annamária Tóth	HUN	10.9	12.68	1.59	6.12	23.8	4959
4.	Valentina Tikhomirova	SOV/RUS	11.2	14.12	1.65	5.99	24.9	4927
5.	Manon Bornholdt	GER	11.0	12.37	1.59	6.42	24.8	4890
6.	Patricia Winslow	USA	11.4	13.33	1.65	5.97	24.5	4877
7.	Ingeborg Bauer	GDR	11.4	13.00	1.59	6.22	24.5	4849
8.	Meta Antenen	SWI	10.7	11.06	1.62	6.30	24.9	4848

Heidemarie Rosendahl of West Germany was considered the pre-Games favorite, but she pulled a muscle while warming up and was unable to compete. Liese Prokop was the surprise leader after four events, but Ingrid Becker, competing in her third Olympics, ran the fastest 200 meters of the competition to take the gold medal.

1972 Munich C: 28, N: 18, D: 9.2–3. WR: 4775 (Burglinde Pollak)

			100M H	SP	HJ	LJ	200M	TOTAL	
1.	Mary Peters	GBR	13.29	16.29	1.82	5.98	24.08	4801	WR
2.	Heidemarie Rosendahl	GER	13.34	13.86	1.65	6.83	22.96	4791	
3.	Burglinde Pollak	GDR	13.53	16.04	1.76	6.21	23.93	4768	
4.	Christine Bodner	GDR	13.25	12.51	1.76	6.40	23.66	4671	
5.	Valentina Tikhomirova	SOV/RUS	13.77	14.64	1.74	6.15	24.25	4597	
6.	Nedialka Angelova	BUL	13.84	13.96	1.68	6.32	24.58	4496	
7.	Karen Mack	GER	14.45	14.10	1.76	6.11	24.72	4449	
8.	Ilona Bruzsenyák	HUN	13.65	12.48	1.65	6.29	24.35	4419	

In 1971, the 80-meter hurdles was replaced by the 100-meter hurdles, necessitating a change in the scoring tables and a reevaluation of the world record. Mary Peters, a 33-year-old English-born secretary from Belfast, Northern

The medalists in the 1972 pentathlon: (left to right) Heidemarie Rosendahl (silver), Mary Peters (gold), and Burglinde Pollak (bronze).

Ireland, finished fourth at Tokyo in 1964 and ninth in Mexico City in 1968. During the first day of competition in Munich she recorded personal bests in two of the three events—the 100-meter hurdles and the high jump. The high jump was a particularly magical moment for her, as the German crowd rooted her on and chanted her name despite the fact that she was competing against local favorite Heide Rosendahl, who had won the long jump two days earlier. At the end of the first day, Peters was 97 points ahead of Pollak and 301 points ahead of Rosendahl, who was in fifth place. But the two events of the second day, the long jump and the 200 meters, were Rosendahl's best and Peters' worst. Sure enough, Rosendahl jumped 22 feet 5 inches, 1 centimeter short of her world record. The 200 meters saw both women achieve personal bests. If Mary Peters had run one-tenth of a second slower she would have lost the gold medal. Afterward she told the press that she had become so exhausted in the last 50 meters of the 200 that her legs felt like jelly. In her autobiography, *Mary P.,* she revised her description and wrote that her legs felt like lead.

1976 Montreal C: 20, N: 13, D: 7.25–26. WR: 4932 (Burglinde Pollak)

		100M H	SP	HJ	LJ	200M	TOTAL
1. Siegrun Siegl	GDR	13.31	12.92	1.74	6.49	23.09	4745
2. Christine Laser (Bodner)	GDR	13.55	14.29	1.78	6.27	23.48	4745
3. Burglinde Pollak	GDR	13.30	16.25	1.64	6.30	23.64	4740
4. Lyudmila Popovskaya	SOV/RUS	13.33	15.02	1.74	6.19	24.10	4700
5. Nadiya Tkachenko	SOV/UKR	13.41	14.90	1.80	6.08	24.61	4669
6. Diane Jones	CAN	13.79	14.58	1.80	6.29	25.33	4582
7. Jane Frederick	USA	13.54	14.55	1.76	5.99	24.70	4566
8. Margit Papp	HUN	14.14	14.80	1.78	6.35	25.43	4535

Anyone who enjoys close finishes need look no further than the 1976 pentathlon. With four events finished and only the 200 meters to be run, the standings were as follows:

1. Tkachenko	3788		5. Laser	3757
2. Popovskaya	3772		6. Papp	3726
3. Pollak	3768		7. Siegl	3718
4. Jones	3764		8. Frederick	3693

All the leaders were matched against one another in the final heat. When the dust cleared 26 seconds later, officials and fans hurriedly consulted their scoring tables. It was discovered that Siegl, the world record holder in the long jump, and Laser, who had achieved personal records in the high jump and 200, had finished with the exact same point total, while Pollak was only five points behind. Siegl was finally awarded first place on the basis of having beaten Laser in three of the five events. Had Pollak run six one-hundredths of a second faster she would have won the gold medal. Instead she had to settle for her second straight bronze. While Siegl jumped from seventh to first in one event, Tkachenko had the misfortune of dropping from first to fifth in less than 25 seconds.

1980 Moscow C: 19, N: 12, D: 7.23-24. WR (with 800m): 4856
(Olga Kuragina)

		100M H	SP	HJ	LJ	800M	TOTAL	
1. Nadiya Tkachenko	SOV/UKR	13.29	16.84	1.84	6.73	2:05.2	5083	WR
2. Olga Rukavishnikova	SOV/RUS	13.66	14.09	1.88	6.79	2:04.8	4937	
3. Olga Kuragina	SOV/RUS	13.26	12.49	1.84	6.77	2:03.6	4875	
4. Ramona Neubert	GDR	13.93	13.68	1.77	6.63	2:07.7	4698	
5. Margit Papp	HUN	13.96	14.94	1.74	6.35	2:15.8	4562	
6. Burglinde Pollak	GDR	13.74	16.67	1.68	5.93	2:14.4	4553	
7. Valentina Dimitrova	BUL	14.39	15.65	1.74	5.91	2:15.5	4458	
8. Emilia Kunova	BUL	13.73	11.98	1.74	6.10	2:11.1	4431	

The 1980 pentathlon saw tremendous performances by all three Soviet athletes, each of whom broke the existing world record. Thirty-one-year-old Nadiya Tkachenko followed a long road to her gold medal. Ninth in Munich, fifth in Montreal, she won the European title in 1978 only to lose it after failing a test for anabolic steroids. Handed an 18-month suspension by the I.A.A.F., she was back in time for the 1980 Olympics. In Moscow she achieved personal bests in four of the five events and fell only three-quarters of an inch short of her lifetime record in the shot put. Rukavishnikova has the unusual distinction of setting the shortest-lived world record in history—two-fifths of a second. When she crossed the finish line of the 800 meters she became the world record holder in the pentathlon. But when Tkachenko finished right behind her, a new record was set.

1984 Los Angeles C: 23, N: 13, D: 8.3–4. WR: 6867 (Sabine Paetz)

		100M H	HJ	SP	200M	LJ	JT	800M	TOTAL	
1. Glynis Nunn	AUS	13.02	1.80	12.82	24.06	6.66	35.58	2:10.57	6390	OR
2. Jacqueline Joyner	USA	13.63	1.80	14.39	24.05	6.11	44.52	2:13.03	6385	
3. Sabine Everts	GER	13.54	1.89	12.49	24.05	6.71	32.62	2:09.05	6363	
4. Cindy Greiner	USA	13.71	1.83	13.36	24.40	6.15	40.86	2:11.75	6281	
5. Judith Simpson	GBR	13.07	1.86	13.86	24.95	6.33	33.64	2:13.01	6280	
6. Sabine Braun	GER	13.61	1.80	12.09	24.22	6.10	44.14	2:12.48	6236	
7. Tineke Hidding	HOL	13.70	1.74	13.48	24.12	6.35	33.94	2:12.84	6147	
8. Kim Hagger	GBR	13.39	1.86	12.29	24.72	6.37	35.42	2:18.44	6127	

With all of the leading medal contenders among the boycott missing, the first Olympic heptathlon became an open competition. After the four events of the first day, Simpson led with 3759 points. She was followed closely by Joyner at 3739, Nunn with 3731 and Everts with 3721. The first event of the second day, the long jump, turned out to be the turning point. This was Joyner's specialty. But after fouling her first two tries, she played it safe with her final jump, taking off over a foot before the takeoff board and registering only 20 feet ½ inch, 26 inches less than she would achieve in placing fifth in the long jump competition five days later. Meanwhile, Everts moved into first place, one point ahead of Nunn. However, Joyner took the lead for the first time following the javelin throw.

As Jackie Joyner struggled through the 800-meter run, she was rooted on by her brother Al, who was in the midst of winning the triple jump. When the race was over, coaches and officials rushed to their scoring tables booklets to compute the results. Initially, Glynis Nunn, a 24-year-old schoolteacher, thought she had lost by 3 points. In fact, she had improved her personal record by 108 points and won by 5 points. If Joyner had long-jumped 3 centimeters further or finished the 800 0.33 seconds faster, the victory would have been hers. Later in the Olympics Nunn placed seventh in the long jump and fifth in the 100-meter hurdles.

1988 Seoul C: 29, N: 19, D : 9.23-24. WR: 7215 (Jacqueline Joyner-Kersee)

		100M H	HJ	SP	200M	LJ	JT	800M	TOTAL	
1. Jacqueline Joyner-Kersee	USA	12.69	1.86	15.80	22.56	7.27	45.66	2:08.51	7291	WR
2. Sabine John (Paetz)	GDR	12.85	1.80	16.23	23.65	6.71	42.56	2:06.14	6897	
3. Anke Behmer	GDR	13.20	1.83	14.20	23.10	6.68	44.54	2:04.20	6858	
4. Natalya Shubenkova	SOV/RUS	13.51	1.74	14.76	23.93	6.32	47.46	2:07.90	6540	
5. Remigia Sablovskaitė	SOV/LIT	13.61	1.80	15.23	23.92	6.25	42.78	2:12.24	6456	
6. Ines Schulz	GDR	13.75	1.83	13.50	24.65	6.33	42.82	2:05.79	6411	
7. Jane Flemming	AUS	13.38	1.80	12.88	23.59	6.37	40.28	2:12.54	6351	
8. Cindy Greiner	USA	13.55	1.80	14.13	24.48	6.47	38.00	2:13.65	6297	

The baby girl born into the Joyner family on March 3, 1962, was named Jacqueline after the wife of U.S. President John Kennedy because, in the words of her grandmother, "Someday this girl will be the First Lady of something." How right she was. After finishing second in the 1984 Olympics, Jackie Joyner won all nine heptathlons that she entered over the next four years. She also married her coach, Bob Kersee, who told her that she couldn't use his name until she broke a world record. She became Jackie Joyner-Kersee in Moscow on July 7, 1986, when she became the first woman to break the 7000-point mark with a score of 7148. She set another world record 26 days later and another one at the U.S. Olympic trials in 1988.

By that time, Joyner-Kersee was so much better than all the other heptathletes that her husband had to create a new opponent for her: Wilhelmina World Record. In Seoul, Joyner-Kersee beat Wilhelmina again. Five days after the heptathlon, Joyner-Kersee earned a second gold medal in the long jump.

1992 Barcelona C: 32, N: 22, D: 8.1-2. WR: 7291 (Jacqueline Joyner-Kersee)

		100M H	HJ	SP	200M	LJ	JT	800M	TOTAL
1. Jacqueline Joyner-Kersee	USA	12.85	1.91	14.13	23.12	7.10	44.98	2:11.78	7044
2. Irina Belova	RUS	13.25	1.88	13.77	23.34	6.82	41.90	2:05.08	6845
3. Sabine Braun	GER	13.25	1.94	14.23	24.27	6.02	51.12	2:14.35	6649
4. Liliana Nastase	ROM	12.86	1.82	14.34	23.70	6.49	41.30	2:11.22	6619
5. Svetla Dimitrova	BUL	13.23	1.70	14.68	23.31	6.11	44.48	2:07.90	6464
6. Peggy Beer	GER	13.48	1.82	13.23	23.93	6.01	48.10	2:09.49	6434
7. Birgit Clarius	GER	14.10	1.82	15.33	24.86	6.13	45.14	2:08.83	6388
8. Urszula Wlodarczyk	POL	13.57	1.82	13.91	24.81	6.20	43.46	2:14.96	6333

Although there was some pre-Olympic talk that Sabine Braun—who won the 1991 world championship when Jackie Joyner-Kersee injured a hamstring mid-contest—might challenge Joyner-Kersee at the Olympics, it was not to be. Joyner-Kersee took the lead after the first event and never looked back. Her 7044 points was the sixth-highest total ever—the top five scores were also hers. Belova set personal records in five of the seven events and bettered her pre-Olympic total by 320 points. In 1994 Belova was suspended for four years after she tested positive for testosterone.

Discontinued Event

3000 METERS

1896–1980 not held

1984 Los Angeles C: 31, N: 21, D: 8.10. WR: 8:26.78 (Svetlana Ulmasova)

1. Maricica Puică	ROM	8:35.96	OR
2. Wendy Sly	GBR	8:39.47	
3. Lynn Williams	CAN	8:42.14	
4. Cindy Bremser	USA	8:42.78	
5. Cornelia Bürki	SWI	8:45.20	
6. Aurora Cunha	POR	8:46.37	
7. Zola Budd	GBR	8:48.80	
8. Joan Hansen	USA	8:51.53	

They called her "Little Mary Decker" when she first attracted international attention in 1973 by upsetting Olympic 800-meter silver medalist Nijolė Sabaitė at a U.S.A.-U.S.S.R. dual meet in Minsk. And why not? Five feet tall and weighing 86 pounds, the fawn-like Decker was only 14 years old at the time. She had discovered running at age 11, during a period when her life was in turmoil. Her family had just moved from New Jersey to California and her parents were on the road to divorce. Mary Decker threw herself into her new pursuit. During one seven-day period when she was 12 years old, she competed in a marathon (finishing with a time of 3:09), a 440, an 880, a mile race and a two-mile. The next day she was hospitalized for an emergency appendectomy.

In 1974, Decker again caused a minor sensation at a U.S.A.-U.S.S.R. dual meet, this time in Moscow. Running the anchor leg in a 4 × 800-meter relay, she was shoved off the indoor track by Latvian Sarmite Shtula. Decker responded by throwing her relay baton at Shtula. She retrieved the baton and continued the race, but at the finish line Decker again threw the baton at Shtula. Both teams were disqualified, and Decker was admonished for her unsportsmanlike behavior. However, no one in the United States had ever been condemned for

responding violently to blatant Soviet aggression, so she was quickly forgiven. Besides, she was still only 15 years old.

At this point, Mary Decker's career took a drastic downward turn. Her intense, some would say obsessive, devotion to running began to take its toll on her still-growing body. Her legs, in particular, began to give in to the strain, and for the next three years she went from doctor to doctor and treatment to treatment desperately trying to relieve her pain. In tears she watched the 1976 Olympics on television, as runners she had beaten two years earlier collected medals that should have been hers.

Then in 1977, she chanced to meet 1976 10,000-meter silver medalist Dick Quax, who immediately recognized her physical problems as Compartment Syndrome in which the sheaths of tissues surrounding muscles fail to expand with the muscles' growth. An operation on her calf relieved the pain. After surviving two automobile accidents and then another operation, her times began improving again.

In 1980 she set her first world record, running the mile in 4:21.7. She qualified easily for the U.S. Olympic team, but the anti-Soviet boycott prevented her from competing. Again she watched the Olympics on television. Then she flew to Europe where she was beaten at 1500 meters by Olympic champion Tatyana Kazankina and by Gabriella Dorio, who became the first Western woman to run the 1500 in less than four minutes. Despite increasing pain in her legs, Decker kept running until finally she had to be operated on to repair a partial tear of her Achilles' tendon. In 1981 she underwent a third operation on her shins and was forced to sit out the year.

The following year was her best yet. In June she set a 5000-meter world record of 15:08.26. On July 9, in Paris, she broke the mile record again with a time of 4:18.08. On the 14th, in Lausanne, she ran the 800 in 1:58.33. Two days later, after flying back to Eugene, Oregon, she set a 10,000-meter world record with a time of 31:35.3. 1983 would see further improvements. Until this time Decker was still considered unproven, because she had not beaten the Eastern Europeans who dominated women's middle-distance running. But then came Mary Decker's masterpieces. At the inaugural world championships in Helsinki she scored a thrilling start to finish victory in the 3000 meters, stunning 3-time Olympic champion Tatyana Kazankina, as well as world record holder Svetlana Ulmasova. Four days later, in the 1500 meters, she again led from the beginning. Entering the final curve she was passed and cut off by Zamira Zaitseva. Decker lost her momentum, but in the homestretch she came roaring back. After a heart-stopping stretch run she nipped Zaitseva at the finish to complete a spectacular double victory. Immediately, Decker became the early favorite for the 1984 Olympics, which would take place in her former hometown, Los Angeles.

Mary Decker returned to the United States as a national hero. Beautiful and strong, she had defeated the Soviets. She seemed to symbolize all that was good about the American character. Of course, track aficionados were all too aware of the dark side of Decker's personality. For example, there was the ugly incident that took place at the 1983 Millrose Games in New York. When Angelita Lind, a Puerto Rican runner about to be lapped, failed to move to the outside to let Decker pass, America's sweetheart shoved her to the ground and forged ahead. Decker's belated sensitivity to this incident would have tragic consequences 18 months later at the Olympics. In the meantime, all over the nation, all over the world in fact, young girls dreamed of becoming like Mary Decker.

One such hero-worshiper, half a world away, was a slight, shy South African teenager named Zola Budd, who kept a poster of Decker on the wall beside her bed. Like Decker, Budd was a precocious talent. When she first told her father that she was winning races at school, he thought that was nice, but when he watched her win one such race by a lap—in a three-lap race—he realized that he should take the situation more seriously and find her a coach. As Budd's times improved, word of her accomplishments began to trickle out to the outside world. In 1983, at the age of 17, the 5-foot, 82-pound Budd was ranked number one in the world at 5000 meters by *Track and Field News*. On January 5, 1984, Budd, who always competed barefooted, ran the distance in 15:01.83 to break Mary Decker's world record by over six seconds. Clearly Zola Budd was ready for international competition. However, South Africa had been banned by the I.A.A.F. in 1976 and had not been allowed in the Olympics since 1960. As long as Budd remained a South African citizen, her running career had no future.

But for Zola Budd, there was a loophole. Because her paternal grandfather was British, she could move to Great Britain and change her citizenship. On March 24, with all expenses paid by the *Daily Mail* newspaper, Zola and her parents arrived in England and set up residency in Guildford, Surrey. Less than two weeks later Zola Budd was granted British citizenship. The next four months would be enormously traumatic for the shy young girl. Accustomed to the quiet life on her farm in Bloemfontein in Orange Free State, she suddenly found herself the object of intense hostility—from other British runners, from the *Daily Mail*'s rivals and from the many opponents of South Africa's racial policies. She ran her first race in England on April 14, then withdrew from another to avoid confrontations with the left-wing local government. On April 25, she won a 1500-meter race, but crossed the finish line in tears after being taunted throughout the race by blacks displaying signs that read, "WHITE TRASH GO HOME." Amidst all this turmoil, she also had to qualify for the British team. This she did, by winning every race that she was required to. After one race, teammate Jane Furniss, who had initially harshly

criticized Budd, hugged her and gave her a kiss. At last, it seemed, Zola Budd would be allowed to get on with her running.

Back in the United States, Mary Decker had come up against another setback. In Helsinki she had been able to achieve her 1500/3000 double because the heats for the 1500 hadn't begun until after the final of the 3000. The Olympic schedule was different. The two events overlapped, making a double more difficult. The U.S. trials were set up with the same schedule as the Olympics, giving Decker an opportunity to try it out. She won the 3000, but was upset by Ruth Wysocki in the 1500. On July 11, 2½ weeks before the Games would begin, Decker announced that she would withdraw from the 1500 and compete only in the 3000, the same race that Zola Budd would be entering.

The scheduled Decker-Budd confrontation encouraged the U.S. media to indulge in an absolute orgy of pre-Olympic hype, much to the annoyance of both parties concerned. The problem was that all track fans knew that Budd was not really ready to compete at Decker's level, especially since Budd specialized at longer distances which were not yet a part of the Olympic program. Decker's real threat came not from Zola Budd, but from 34-year-old Maricica Puică. Although Puică had missed the Helsinki championships because of an injury sustained while playing basketball, her credentials were solid. Not only had she previously competed in the 1976 and 1980 Olympics, but she was the current world record holder in the mile and the reigning world cross-country champion. She had also recorded the fastest 3000-meter time of the pre-Olympic season: 8:33.57.

The qualifying heats of the Olympic 3000 were held on August 8. The first heat was won by Mary Decker, the second by Brigitte Kraus of West Germany, who had placed second behind Decker in the world championship 3000. In the third heat Budd led from the start but was passed in the run-in by Puică and Cindy Bremser. "It's unusual to run with a pack of people," commented Budd afterwards. "I'm happy to be running here, it's very nice."

The final was held two days later. The intense midday heat had cooled to a pleasant 75° Fahrenheit (24° centigrade) by race time. Decker took the early lead and set a fast pace, followed closely by Budd, Puică and Wendy Sly, although all of the runners were tightly packed. At the 1400-meter mark Joan Hansen tripped on Aurora Cunha's heel and fell. She recovered quickly and continued running. At 1600 meters, Sly moved up to challenge Decker along the backstretch, but Budd moved between them and took the lead entering the turn. As the pace accelerated, Budd, Decker, Sly and Puică began to pull away from the others.

Coming out of the turn Budd was in front, running on the outside edge of lane one. Decker, on the inside of the lane, maintained her position and pace. At about the 1700-meter mark, Decker hit one of Budd's legs, throwing Budd off balance just a bit. Five strides later, they

1. Disaster strikes the 1984 women's 3,000-meter run as gold-medal favorite Mary Decker steps on the barefooted heel of Zola Budd.

3. Zola Budd looks back to see her idol hit the infield in pain.

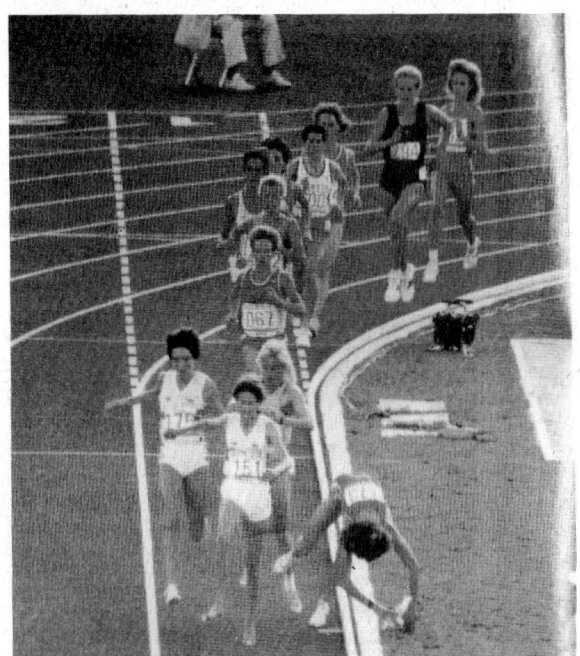

2. Decker falls to the ground as Budd tries to regain her balance, and the eventual winner, Maricica Puică (behind Budd), sidesteps Decker.

4. Mary Decker, too injured to continue, writhes in agony as the race goes on without her.

bumped again. This time Budd landed awkwardly, her left leg shooting out in search of balance. Decker, running straight and hard, tripped on Budd's right leg, her spikes cutting deeply into Budd's heel. Decker lost her balance and pitched forward onto the infield. Puică, running directly behind Decker, hurdled over her leg. Budd looked back to see her idol falling to the ground. As the runners zipped by, Mary Decker attempted to rise. But her hard landing had caused her to suffer a pulled left hip stabilizer muscle. "It was like I was tied to the ground," she would later explain. As the race continued, Decker was left writhing in agony, weeping in frustration.

The partisan crowd of over 85,000 was stunned. At first the stadium went silent. Then the booing began. Fifty-two years earlier, in the same stadium, a similar incident had occurred between a U.S. athlete and a foreign athlete during the running of the men's 5000-meter final at the 1932 Olympics. That time the track announcer, Bill Henry, had silenced the crowd by reminding them that "these people are our guests." In 1984 there was no Bill Henry to intervene. As the race continued, Zola Budd was met by booing at every turn. Bleeding, and in tears because of the crowd's reaction, she kept running, but her spirit was gone.

Five hundred meters from the finish, Sly and Puică passed Budd, entering the final lap with Sly in the lead. With 250 meters to go, Puică moved effortlessly ahead of Sly and went on to win by over fifteen meters. Budd, still in third only 200 meters from the finish, slowed to a jog and finished seventh.

In the tunnel leading away from the track, Mary Decker was being comforted by her fiancé, discus thrower Richard Slaney. As the other runners filed by, they offered their condolences. Budd approached Decker and said, "I'm sorry. I'm sorry. I'm sorry."

"Don't bother," replied Decker, "I don't want to talk to you."

As Budd stood crying, fifth place finisher Cornelia Bürki, a Swiss runner who was born in South Africa, came to Budd's defense. "It wasn't Zola's fault, Mary!" she said. "Not her fault."

"Yes, it was," Decker shot back. "I know it was. It was!"

Initially Budd was disqualified on the testimony of two track officials, both Americans. But upon reviewing videotapes of the incident from various angles, a jury of appeal voted unanimously to reinstate her. Decker, however, would not budge from her position that Zola Budd was at fault for cutting in before she had established a clear lead.

The controversy raged across the Atlantic Ocean. At first the U.S. media supported Decker, while the British press took Budd's side. The issue was so emotional that the comments of Maricica Puică, who was the closest witness to the incident, were quoted completely differently in the U.S. and Great Britain. American newspapers, without exception, limited their coverage of

Puică's remarks to "It was tough for me to decide [who was at fault]. I'm sorry for what happened to Mary. She is a fine competitor." In Great Britain, and the rest of the world, Puică was quoted as saying that Decker was at fault because Budd was in the lead and Decker tried to pass her on the inside, an assertion which Decker flatly denied.

As the public viewed repeated replays of the race, opinions on both sides of the Atlantic began to soften and almost everyone apologized. The truth is that neither Budd nor Decker was actually *at fault,* although both made mistakes. Budd should not have cut in so sharply. However such moves are not uncommon and are never cause for disqualification. Decker, for her part, should have known better than to bull forward like a tailgating commuter rushing home on a Friday evening. She could have given Budd a slight push, perhaps not quite as hard as the one she gave Angelita Lind at the Millrose Games. It is true that reaction to the Millrose incident might have haunted Decker. At her post-race press conference in Los Angeles, she said, "Looking back, I should have pushed her, but the headlines tomorrow would have read 'DECKER PUSHES ZOLA.' " Decker's other alternative was to do what she had done in Helsinki when she was cut off by Zaitseva in the last lap of the 1500: slow down and pass on the outside. In Los Angeles she even had the luxury of 1300 meters left in the race rather than 200.

Mary Decker did not run again in 1984. However, by 1985 she had recovered from her injuries and had a brilliant season, which she completed undefeated. Amongst her victories was a sensational mile race in Zurich in which she defeated both Puică and Budd, and stripped Puică of her world record to boot. Decker returned to the Olympics in 1988, placing tenth in the 3000 and eighth in the 1500.

If Decker's performance in Seoul was disappointing, at least she was able to compete. Zola Budd was not so lucky. She won the world cross-country championship in 1985 and 1986, then was forced to take time off because of injury. She returned to competition, but in April 1988, the I.A.A.F. recommended that the British Amateur Athletic Board suspend her from international athletics for at least twelve months because she *attended* a cross-country event in Brakpan, South Africa, even though she didn't compete in it. On the verge of emotional collapse, Budd gave up her Olympic dreams and returned to her family in South Africa. During her tumultuous four years in Great Britain, Zola Budd had steadfastly refused to comment on South Africa's racial policies, even though a simple statement against apartheid would have helped her personal cause immensely. Instead, she waited until 1989, when her racing career appeared to be finished, to issue an unequivocal denouncement of apartheid. After apartheid was dismantled, she represented South Africa at the 1992 Olympics and was eliminated in the heats of the 3000 meters.

1988 Seoul C: 35, N: 24, D: 9.25. WR: 8:22.62 (Tatyana Kazankina)

1. Tetyana Samolenko	SOV/UKR	8:26.53	OR
2. Paula Ivan	ROM	8:27.15	
3. Yvonne Murray	GBR	8:29.02	
4. Yelena Romanova	SOV/RUS	8:30.45	
5. Natalya Artemova	SOV/RUS	8:31.67	
6. Vicki Huber	USA	8:37.25	
7. Wendy Sly	GBR	8:37.70	
8. Lynn Williams	CAN	8:38.43	

Mary Slaney (Decker) rushed into the lead, taking the pack through a torrid world record pace for the first 1000 meters. She was still in front at the halfway mark, but, much to her disappointment, nine other runners were close behind her. Shortly before the 2000-meter mark, Vicki Huber swept by Slaney with Yvonne Murray, Paula Ivan, and the 27-year-old world champion, Tetyana Samolenko, right on her heels. With 450 meters to go, Murray made her move. Ivan and Samolenko followed easily. On the backstretch, about 200 meters from the finish, Ivan took the lead and tried to pull away. But Samolenko was not to be denied. Running a 59.4 last lap, she edged past a surprised Ivan 50 meters from the finish. Thanks in part to the pacesetting Americans, the final times were excellent. Samolenko, Ivan, Romanova, and Huber each improved their personal bests by over 9 seconds, Murray by over 8 seconds and Artemova by 7½.

On the darker side is the story of the South Korean record holder, Lim Chun-ae. A complete unknown from a poor rural family, Lim became a national hero in 1986 when, at the age of 17, she won three gold medals at the Asian Games. In June of 1987, word leaked out that Lim had been hospitalized for two weeks with a broken eardrum after her coach, Kim Pon-il, beat her as punishment for performing poorly in training. Kim was not punished, while Lim publicly accepted blame for her "accident." When the Olympics came to Seoul, Lim Chun-ae was chosen to be the final bearer of the Olympic torch. As the whole world watched, it was Lim who carried the torch around the track in the main stadium and handed it to the cauldron lighters. Six days later, Lim took part in her only individual event: the 3000 meters. Unfortunately, she finished fifteenth and last in her qualifying heat, crossing the finish line over fourteen seconds after the other runners were done. She immediately fell to the ground, buried her head between her legs, and wept. The following year, she retired from competition.

1992 Barcelona C: 33, N: 21, D: 8.2. WR: 8:22.62 (Tatyana Kazankina)

1. Yelena Romanova	RUS	8:46.04
2. Tetyana Dorovskikh (Samolenko)	UKR	8:46.85
3. Angela Chalmers	CAN	8:47.22
4. Sonia O'Sullivan	IRL	8:47.41
5. Patricia "PattiSue" Plumer	USA	8:48.29
6. Yelena Kopytova	RUS	8:49.55
7. Shelly Steely	USA	8:52.67
8. Yvonne Murray	GBR	8:55.85

Dorovskikh had won the 1987 world championships, the 1988 Olympics, and the 1991 world championships, but had done nothing outstanding in 1992. Still, the unusually slow pace of the final appeared to play right into the hands of Dorovskikh, who was known for her strong finishing kick. With 580 meters to go, Murray surged into the lead but was unable to shake the pack. At the beginning of the backstretch, O'Sullivan passed Murray, who was quickly left behind. Behind O'Sullivan came Romanova, Dorovskikh, Plumer, and Chambers. As the leaders entered the final straightaway, Romanova darted past O'Sullivan on the outside while Dorovskikh passed her on the inside. It was Romanova, rather than Dorovskikh, who had the most powerful kick, as she covered the last 200 meters in 28.6 seconds and pulled away to win by six meters.

One also-ran worth noting was Mirsada Buric of Bosnia-Herzegovina. Buric had trained in the rubble-strewn streets of Sarajevo in the midst of her nation's civil war. Twice she was shot at by snipers. At the beginning of June, she and other Muslim women and children were seized by Serb militiamen and held for 13 days during which her daily diet was one cup of tea and one slice of bread. When she was finally released in a prisoner exchange on June 13, all her sports equipment, including her track shoes, had been confiscated; the opening of the Olympics was only six weeks away. Buric and the rest of the Bosnian team managed to make it to Barcelona just six hours before the Opening Ceremony. Buric finished last in her heat, but for her merely making it to the starting line was a victory.

As for Dorovskikh, her career achievements were tainted when she tested positive for steroids in June 1993.

ARCHERY

MEN
Individual
Team
Discontinued Events

WOMEN
Individual
Team
Discontinued Events

Few Olympic sports have gone through as many rule changes in so short a time as archery did between 1984 and 1992. From 1972 to 1984, competitions consisted of two F.I.T.A. rounds. A F.I.T.A. round is 36 arrows shot at each of four distances: 90, 70, 50, and 30 meters. In 1988, all competitors took part in an opening F.I.T.A. round. The top twenty-four then moved on to the eighth final, where they shot nine arrows at each distance. The top eighteen in that round advanced to the quarterfinal. The top twelve in the quarterfinal advanced to the semifinal. The top eight in the semifinal qualified for the final. The scores were not cumulative. In the semifinal and final rounds the distances were reversed: 30, 50, 70, and 90 meters. Beginning in 1992, following a preliminary F.I.T.A. round, the top 32 archers moved on to single-elimination match play, with each match consisting of twelve arrows shot at 70 meters.

Archery targets are 122 centimeters (four feet) in diameter for the 90- and 70-meter distances, and 80 centimeters (2 feet 7½ inches) across for the 50- and 30-meter distances. The bulls-eye is 4.8 inches across on the larger target and 3.2 inches on the smaller. At 90 meters, this is the equivalent of shooting across a football field and hitting a grapefruit. Targets are divided into five colored rings: gold on the inside, then red, blue, black, and finally white on the outside. Each ring is divided in half. The inner gold zone is worth ten points, the outer gold nine points, on down to the outer white, which is worth one point. Modern bows are extremely complicated and are augmented by bowsights, bowmarks, foresights, and stabilizers.

MEN

INDIVIDUAL

1896–1968 not held

1972 Munich C: 55, N: 24, D: 9.10. WR: 2445 (John Williams)

			1st ROUND		2nd ROUND	TOTAL POINTS	
1.	John Williams	USA	1268	WR	1260	2528	WR
2.	Gunnar Jarvil	SWE	1229		1252	2481	
3.	Kyösti Laasonen	FIN	1213		1254	2467	
4.	Robert Cogniaux	BEL	1205		1240	2445	
5.	Edwin Eliason	USA	1193		1245	2438	
6.	Donald Jackson	CAN	1225		1212	2437	
7.	Viktor Sidorouk	SOV/UKR	1205		1222	2427	
8.	Arne Jacobsen	DEN	1188		1235	2423	

The reigning world champion, John Williams, was an 18-year-old army private from Cranesville, Pennsylvania, who spent 42 hours a week in training. In the first F.I.T.A. round he broke Arne Jacobsen's single round world record despite missing the target completely with one arrow.

1976 Montreal C: 37, N: 23, D: 7.30. WR: 2570 (Darrell Pace)

			1st ROUND	2nd ROUND	TOTAL POINTS	
1.	Darrell Pace	USA	1264	1307	2571	WR
2.	Hiroshi Michinaga	JPN	1226	1276	2502	
3.	Giancarlo Ferrari	ITA	1220	1275	2495	
4.	Richard McKinney	USA	1230	1241	2471	
5.	Vladimir Chendarov	SOV/RUS	1217	1250	2467	
6.	Willi Gabriel	GER	1203	1232	2435	
7.	David Mann	CAN	1190	1241	2431	
8.	Takanobu Nishi	JPN	1191	1231	2422	

1980 Moscow C: 38, N: 25, D: 8.2. WR (single round): 1341 (Darrell Pace)

			1st ROUND	2nd ROUND	TOTAL POINTS
1.	Tomi Poikolainen	FIN	1220	1235	2455
2.	Boris Isachenko	SOV/BLR	1217	1235	2452
3.	Giancarlo Ferrari	ITA	1215	1234	2449
4.	Mark Blenkarne	GBR	1224	1222	2446
5.	Béla Nagy	HUN	1225	1221	2446
6.	Vladimir Yesheyev	SOV/RUS	1222	1210	2432
7.	Kyösti Laasonen	FIN	1212	1207	2419
8.	Martinus Reniers	HOL	1205	1213	2418

1984 Los Angeles-Long Beach C: 62, N: 25, D: 8.11. WR: 1341
(Darrell Pace)

		1st ROUND	2nd ROUND	TOTAL POINTS	
1. Darrell Pace	USA	1317	1299	2616	OR
2. Richard McKinney	USA	1295	1269	2564	
3. Hiroshi Yamamoto	JPN	1276	1287	2563	
4. Takayoshi Matsushita	JPN	1264	1288	2552	
5. Tomi Poikolainen	FIN	1275	1263	2538	
6. Göran Bjerendal	SWE	1275	1247	2522	
7. Marnix Vervinck	BEL	1260	1259	2519	
8. Koo Ja-chung	KOR	1226	1274	2500	

Darrell Pace and Rick McKinney grew up 85 miles apart in Reading, Ohio, and Muncie, Indiana. Their rivalry began in 1973 when both were teenagers and Pace, at 16, won a place on the U.S. world championship team by finishing one point ahead of McKinney at the trials. In 1975, Pace won the next world championship and the following year added an Olympic victory. A discouraged McKinney decided to give himself one more year before retiring from competition. Relaxed and unpressured, McKinney won the 1977 world championship, with Pace slipping to fourth. However, Pace regained the title in 1979.

Pace and McKinney's most dramatic confrontation came at the 1983 world championship held at the Olympic site in Long Beach. Pace needed to fire all tens with his final three arrows to clinch another world championship. His first two arrows were bull's-eyes. But his final shot was so perfect that the arrow struck the nock of one of the first two arrows and glanced off into the nine ring.

McKinney, firing two targets away, heard Pace's arrow hit the nock and knew that if *he* could hit the ten ring with his final shot *he* would be the world champion. After many moments of quiet tension, McKinney released his bow and achieved his ten.

Ten months later, at the Los Angeles Olympics, there was no such drama, at least not for the gold medal. Pace took a 13-point lead after the first of four days and steadily widened the gap to win easily. McKinney, however, needed to fire a ten with his final arrow to secure second place. He did and the silver medal was his.

1988 Seoul C: 84, N: 34, D: 9.30. WR: 1341 (Darrell Pace)

		OPEN ROUND	8th FINAL	QUART. FINAL	SEMI-FINAL	GRAND FINAL	GRAND TOTAL
1. Jay Barrs	USA	1294 (3)	313 (13)	326 (4)	334 (2)	338 (1)	2605
2. Park Sung-soo	KOR	1303 (2)	322 (4)	324 (5)	329 (4)	336 (2)	2614
3. Vladimir Yesheyev	SOV/RUS	1304 (1)	313 (14)	320 (9)	328 (5)	335 (3)	2600
4. Chun In-soo	KOR	1284 (6)	326 (2)	323 (6)	334 (1)	331 (4)	2598
5. Martinus Reniers	HOL	1286 (5)	328 (1)	328 (2)	324 (8)	327 (5)	2593
6. Richard McKinney	USA	1288 (4)	321 (6)	327 (3)	332 (3)	324 (6)	2592
7. Pentti Vikström	FIN	1273 (13)	312 (15)	320 (10)	324 (7)	323 (7)	2552
8. Hiroshi Yamamoto	JPN	1271 (14)	316 (7)	318 (12)	324 (6)	321 (8)	2550

Twenty-six-year-old Jay Barrs, who listened to heavy metal music between rounds, gained his victory by picking up 2 points on Park during the final 18 arrows. Defending champion Darrell Pace finished ninth. In last place was Derrick Tenai, a security guard from the Solomon Islands, who had never seen a modern bow until he arrived in Seoul. In the open round, Tenai hit the target 89 times and missed 55 times. None of the other 83 contestants missed the target more than 5 times and 65 of them had no misses at all.

1992 Barcelona C: 75, N: 34, D: 8.3. WR: F.I.T.A. Round—1352 (Vladimir Yesheyev)

1. Sebastien Flute	FRA	
2. Chung Jae-hun	KOR	
3. Simon Terry	GBR	
4. Bertil Martinus Grov	NOR	
5. Jari Lipponen	FIN	
6. Hendra Setijawan	INA	
7. Jay Barrs	USA	
8. Vadim Shikarev	TJK	

Final: Flute 110-107 Chung
3rd Place: Terry 109-103 Grov

The 20-year-old European champion, Sebastien Flute, defeated all three South Korean archers on his way to the Olympic title. He and Chung were tied after nine arrows in the final, but Flute coolly scored 10, 9, and 10 with his last shots to earn a mild upset.

TEAM

In 1988, scores from the individual open round were used to determine the 16 teams that advanced to team play. The top 12 teams in a qualifying round then moved to the semifinals and the top eight in that round went on to the final. In each team round, each archer shot nine arrows at each of four distances. Beginning in 1992, the top 16 teams, based on scores from the individual open round, advanced to single-elimination match play. In match play each archer shoots nine arrows at 70 meters. Team members take turns shooting three arrows apiece.

1896–1984 not held

1988 Seoul T: 22, N: 22, D: 10.1. WR: 3948 (USA—McKinney, Barrs, Pace)

		OPEN ROUND	SEMI-FINAL	GRAND FINAL
1. KOR	(Chun In-soo, Lee Han-sup, Park Sung-soo)	3862 (1)	960 (6)	986 (1)
2. USA	(Jay Barrs, Richard McKinney, Darrell Pace)	3839 (2)	992 (1)	972 (2)
3. GBR	(Steven Hallard, Richard Priestman, Leroy Watson)	3733 (8)	965 (4)	968 (3)
4. FIN	(Ismo Falck, Tomi Poikolainen, Pentti Vikström)	3797 (4)	960 (7)	956 (4)
5. SOV	(Konstyantin Shkolny, Vladimir Yesheyev, Yuri Leontyev)	3799 (3)	976 (2)	949 (5)
6. JPN	(Terushi Furuhashi, Takayoshi Matsushita, Hiroshi Yamamoto)	3766 (5)	958 (8)	948 (6)
7. TAI	(Chiu Ping-kun, Hu Pei-wen, Yen Man-sung)	3693 (11)	968 (3)	937 (7)
8. SWE	(Gert Bjerendal, Göran Bjerendal, Mats Nordlander)	3759 (6)	964 (5)	925 (8)

The Koreans trailed the U.S. team by two points before surging ahead at the final distance of 90 meters.

1992 Barcelona T: 20, N: 20, D: 8.4. WR: F.I.T.A. Round—3963 (SOV—Zabrodsky, Shikarev, Yesheyev)
1. SPA (Juan Carlos Holgado Romero, Alfonso Menéndez Vallín, Antonio Vázquez Megido)
2. FIN (Ismo Falck, Jari Lipponen, Tomi Poikolainen)
3. GBR (Steven Hallard, Richard Priestman, Simon Terry)
4. FRA (Bruno Felipe,. Sebastien Flute, Michael Taupin)
5. KOR (Chung Jae-hun, Han Seung-hoon, Lim Hee-sik)
6. USA (Jay Barrs, Richard Johnson, Richard McKinney)
7. SOV (Vadim Shikarev, Vladimir Yesheyev, Stanislav Zabrodsky)
8. AUS (Simon Fairweather, Grant Greenham, Scott Hunter-Russell)
Final: SPA 238-236 FIN
3rd Place: GBR 233-231 FRA

The victory by the Spanish team was one of the biggest upsets of the Barcelona Games. In the individual competition, Vázquez had placed 29th, Menéndez 42nd, and Holgado 45th. Seeded tenth, they scored surprise victories over Denmark, the Unified Team, and Great Britain. In the final, Spain led by nine points after twenty arrows, and then held off a strong comeback by the Finns.

Discontinued Events

1900 Paris C: 68, N: 2, D: 5.28.
Au cordon doré—50 Meters

		PTS.
1. Henri Hérouin	FRA	31
2. Hubert van Innis	BEL	29
3. Emile Fisseux	FRA	28

Au chapelet—50 Meters
1. Eugène Mougin	FRA	—
2. Henri Helle	FRA	—
3. Emile Mercier	FRA	—

Au cordon doré—33 Meters
1. Hubert van Innis	BEL	—
2. Victor Thibaud	FRA	—
3. Charles Frédéric Petit	FRA	—

Au chapelet—33 Meters
1. Hubert van Innis	BEL	—
2. Victor Thibaud	FRA	—
3. Charles Frédéric Petit	FRA	—

Sur la perche à la herse
1. Emmanuel Foulon	FRA	—
2. Druart, Jr.	BEL	—
2. Auguste Serrurier	FRA	—

Sur la perche à la pyramide
1. Emile Grumiaux	FRA	—
2. Auguste Serrurier	FRA	—
3. Louis Glineux	BEL	—

1904 St. Louis C: 16, N: 1, D: 9.20.
Double York Round (100 Yards—80 Yards—60 Yards)

		PTS.
1. George Phillip Bryant	USA	820
2. Robert Williams	USA	819
3. William Thompson	USA	816
4. Wallace Bryant	USA	618
5. Benjamin Keys	USA	532
6. Ernest Frentz	USA	528
7. Homer Taylor	USA	506
8. Charles Woodruff	USA	487

1904 St. Louis C: 22, N: 1, D: 9.19.
Double American Round (60 Yards—50 Yards—40 Yards)

		PTS.
1. George Phillip Bryant	USA	1048
2. Robert Williams	USA	991
3. William Thompson	USA	949
4. Charles Woodruff	USA	907
5. William Clark	USA	880
6. Benjamin Keys	USA	840
7. Wallace Bryant	USA	818
8. Cyrus Dallin	USA	816

1904 St. Louis T: 4, N: 1, D: 9.21.
Team Round (60 Yards)

	PTS.
1. (Potomac Archers, Washington D.C.—William Thompson, Robert Williams, Louis Maxson, Galen Spencer)	1344
2. (Cincinnati Archers—Charles Woodruff, William Clark, Charles Hubbard, Samuel Duvall)	1341
3. (Boston Archers—George Phillip Bryant, Wallace Bryant, Cyrus Dallin, Henry Richardson)	1268
4. (Chicago Archers—Benjamin Keys, Homer Taylor, Edward Weston, Edward Bruce)	942

1908 London C: 27, N: 3, D: 7.18.
York Round (100 Yards—80 Yards—60 Yards)

		PTS.
1. William Dod	GBR	815
2. Reginald Brooks-King	GBR	768
3. Henry Richardson	USA	760
4. John Penrose	GBR	709
5. John Bridges	GBR	687
6. Harold James	GBR	652
7. Thomas Robinson	GBR	647
8. Hugh Nesham	GBR	643

Willy Dod was born into a family so wealthy that during his 87-year life span he never attended school, never worked, and never even married. In fact, he never attempted anything difficult until, in a burst of patriotic enthusiasm four weeks after the outbreak of World War I, he enlisted— at age 47—in the Sportsman's Battalion of the Royal Fusiliers and found himself serving as a private on the front lines in France. His zeal cooled rapidly and he managed a transfer to the navy as an administrative officer. Dod did not take up archery until he was 39 years old, but apparently it was in his blood: one of his ancestors, Sir Anthony Dod of Edge, commanded the victorious English archers at the Battle of Agincourt against the French in 1415. The Olympic competition was held over two days. Dod took a ten-point lead after the first day, during which action was delayed because of heavy rain, and then pulled away on the second day to take the title on his 41st birthday. When Dod's sister, Lottie, finished in second place in the women's archery contest, they became the first brother-sister medalists in Olympic history.

1908 London C: 17, N: 2, D: 7.20.
Continental Style (50 Meters)

		PTS.
1. Eugène Grisot	FRA	263
2. Louis Vernet	FRA	256
3. Gustave Cabaret	FRA	255
4. Charles Aubras	FRA	231
5. Charles Querviel	FRA	223
6. Albert Dauchez	FRA	222
7. L.A. Salingre	FRA	215
8. H. Berton	FRA	212

An unofficial entrant, R.O. Backhouse of Great Britain, finished second with a score of 260 and was awarded a certificate for special merit.

1920 Antwerp
Fixed Bird Target, Small Birds C: 6, N: 1, D: 8.3.

		PTS.
1. Edmond van Moer	BEL	11
2. Louis van de Perck	BEL	8
3. Joseph Hermans	BEL	6
4. Firmin Flamand	BEL	5
5. Edmond Cloetens	BEL	4
6. Auguste van de Verre	BEL	1

Fixed Bird Target, Large Birds
C: 6, N: 1, D: 8.3.

		PTS.
1. Edmond Cloetens	BEL	13
2. Louis van de Perck	BEL	11
3. Firmin Flamand	BEL	7
4. Edmond van Moer	BEL	6
5. Joseph Hermans	BEL	5
6. Auguste van de Verre	BEL	3

Fixed Bird Target, Small and Large Birds, Team T: 1, N: 1, D: 8.3.

	PTS.
1. BEL	25

(Louis van de Perck, Edmond Cloetens, Edmond van Moer, Firmin Flamand, Joseph Hermans, Auguste van de Verre)

Moving Bird Target
The top two finishers in each of the team events qualified for the individual final.

28 Meters: C: 24, N: 3, D: 8.5.

		PTS.
1. Hubert van Innis	BEL	144
2. Léonce Quentin	FRA	115

33 Meters: C: 16, N: 2, D: 8.5.

		PTS.
1. Hubert van Innis	BEL	139
2. Julien Brulé	FRA	94

50 Meters: C: 16, N: 2, D: 8.5.

		PTS.
1. Julien Brulé	FRA	134
2. Hubert van Innis	BEL	106

Van Innis outshot Brulé 404 to 380 in the qualifying round.

Moving Bird Target, Teams
28 Meters: T: 3, N: 3, D: 8.5.

	PTS.
1. HOL	3087

(Adrianus Theeuwes, Hendrikus van Bussel, Jan Packbiers, Adrianus van Merrienboer, Jan van Gestel, Theodorus Willems, Petrus de Brouwer, Johannes van Gastel)

	PTS.
2. BEL	2924

(Hubert van Innis, Alphonse Allaert, Edmond de Knibber, Louis Delcon, Jérome de Mayer, Louis van Beeck, Pierre van Thielt, Louis Fierens)

	PTS.
3. FRA	2328

(Léonce Quentin, Julien Brulé, Pascal Fauvel, Eugène Grisot, Eugène Richez, Paul Leroy, Artur Mabellon, Léon Epin)

33 Meters: T: 2, N: 2, D: 8.5.

	PTS.
1. BEL	2958

(Hubert van Innis, Alphonse Allaert, Edmond de Knibber, Louis Delcon, Jérome de Mayer, Louis van Beeck, Pierre van Thielt, Louis Fierens)

	PTS.
2. FRA	2586

(Léonce Quentin, Julien Brulé, Pascal Fauvel, Eugène Grisot, Eugène Richez, Paul Leroy, Artur Mabellon, Léon Epin)

50 Meters: T: 2, N: 2, D: 8.5.

	PTS.
1. BEL	2701

(Hubert van Innis, Alphonse Allaert, Edmond de Knibber, Louis Delcon, Jérome de Mayer, Louis van Beeck, Pierre van Thielt, Louis Fierens)

	PTS.
2. FRA	2493

(Léonce Quentin, Julien Brulé, Pascal Fauvel, Eugène Grisot, Eugène Richez, Paul Leroy, Artur Mabellon, Léon Epin)

WOMEN

Women's Olympic archery rules differ from men's only in that the distances are 70, 60, 50, and 30 meters.

INDIVIDUAL

1896–1968 not held

1972 Munich C: 40, N: 21, D: 9.10. WR: 2380 (Emma Gapchenko)

			1st ROUND	2nd ROUND	TOTAL POINTS	
1.	Doreen Wilber	USA	1198	1226	2424	WR
2.	Irena Szydlowska	POL	1224	1183	2407	
3.	Emma Gapchenko	SOV/RUS	1201	1202	2403	
4.	Keto Losaberidze	SOV/GEO	1195	1207	2402	
5.	Linda Myers	USA	1200	1185	2385	
6.	Maria Maczyńska	POL	1173	1198	2371	
7.	Kim Ho-gu	PRK	1195	1174	2369	
8.	Alla Peounova	SOV/UKR	1180	1184	2364	

Wilber was a 42-year-old housewife from Jefferson, Iowa.

1976 Montreal C: 27, N: 16, D: 7.30. WR: 2465 (Zebiniso Rustamova)

			1st ROUND	2nd ROUND	TOTAL POINTS	
1.	Luann Ryon	USA	1217	1282	2499	WR
2.	Valentyna Kovpan	SOV/UKR	1182	1278	2460	
3.	Zebiniso Rustamova	SOV/TJK	1202	1205	2407	
4.	Jang Sun-yong	PRK	1200	1205	2405	
5.	Lucille Lemay	CAN	1181	1220	2401	
6.	Jadwiga Wilejto	POL	1200	1195	2395	
7.	Linda Myers	USA	1180	1213	2393	
8.	Maria Urban	GER	1216	1160	2376	

Ryon, a 23-year-old student from Riverside, California, had never before competed in an international tournament.

1980 Moscow C: 29, N: 19, D: 8.2. WR (Single Round): 1321 (Natalya Butuzova)

			1st ROUND	2nd ROUND	TOTAL POINTS
1.	Keto Losaberidze	SOV/GEO	1257	1234	2491
2.	Natalya Butuzova	SOV/UZB	1251	1226	2477
3.	Päivi Meriluoto	FIN	1217	1232	2449
4.	Ždenka Padevetova	CZE	1206	1199	2405
5.	O Gwang-sun	PRK	1195	1206	2401
6.	Catherina Floris	HOL	1186	1196	2382
7.	Maria Szeliga	POL	1190	1175	2365
8.	Lotti Tschanz	SWI	1184	1162	2346

1984 Los Angeles-Long Beach C: 47, N: 24, D: 8.11. WR: 1325 (Lyudmila Arzhanikova)

			1st ROUND	2nd ROUND	TOTAL POINTS	
1.	Seo Hyang-soon	KOR	1275	1293	2568	OR
2.	Li Lingjuan	CHN	1279	1280	2559	
3.	Kim Jin-ho	KOR	1276	1279	2555	
4.	Hiroko Ishizu	JPN	1263	1261	2524	
5.	Päivi Meriluoto	FIN	1259	1250	2509	
6.	Manuela Dachner	GER	1260	1248	2508	
6.	Katrina King	USA	1265	1243	2508	
8.	Wu Yanan	CHN	1240	1253	2493	

Two-time world champion Kim Jin-ho was upset by 18-year-old Li Lingjuan and 17-year-old Seo Hyang-soon, the latter coming from behind to win on the final day of competition.

Finishing in 35th place was New Zealand's Neroli Fairhall, the first paraplegic athlete to take part in the Olympics. Paralyzed from the waist down following a motorbike accident, she competed while seated in a wheelchair.

1988 Seoul C: 62, N: 30, D: 9.30. WR: 1338 (Kim Soo-nyung)

			OPEN ROUND		8th FINAL		QUART. FINAL		SEMI-FINAL		GRAND FINAL		GRAND TOTAL
1.	Kim Soo-nyung	KOR	1331	(1)	331	(2)	337	(1)	340	(1)	344	(1)	2683
2.	Wang Hee-kyung	KOR	1298	(2)	320	(5)	330	(2)	332	(2)	332	(2)	2612
3.	Yun Young-sook	KOR	1296	(3)	328	(3)	326	(5)	326	(7)	327	(3)	2593
4.	Lyudmila Arzhanikova	SOV/RUS	1279	(6)	332	(1)	326	(6)	329	(5)	327	(4)	2593
5.	Jenny Sjöwall	SWE	1294	(4)	305	(16)	327	(4)	330	(3)	325	(5)	2581
6.	Claudia Kriz	GER	1250	(17)	311	(11)	322	(8)	326	(8)	318	(6)	2527
7.	Joanne Franks	GBR	1281	(5)	301	(18)	327	(3)	330	(4)	318	(7)	2557
8.	Tetyana Muntyan	SOV/UKR	1272	(7)	319	(6)	316	(12)	328	(6)	314	(8)	2549

The three Korean medalists were 17, 18, and 17 years old, respectively.

1992 Barcelona C: 61, N: 27, D: 8.2. WR: F.I.T.A. Round—1370 (Lee Eun-kyung)
1. Cho Youn-jeon   KOR
2. Kim Soo-nyung   KOR
3. Natalya Valeyeva   MOL

4. Wang Xiaozhu   CHN
5. Khatuna Kvrivichvili   GEO
6. Lai Fang-Mei   TAI
7. Alison Williamson   GBR
8. Denise Parker   USA
Final: Cho 112-105 Kim
3rd Place: Valeyeva 104-102 Wang

Cho set a world record of 1375 in the qualifying round. The previous record holder, Lee Eun-kyung, was defeated in the round of 16 by Wang of China. When asked how she calmed her nerves before competitions, Cho replied, "I take long walks at night through the cemetery."

TEAM

The rules for the women's team competition are the same as those for the men, with the exception that the women shoot at distances of 70, 60, 50, and 30 meters.

1896–1984 not held

1988 Seoul T: 15, N: 15, D: 10.1. WR: 3981 (KOR—Lee H.Y., Kim K.W., Kim S.N.)

		OPEN ROUND	SEMI-FINAL	GRAND FINAL
1. KOR	(Kim Soo-nyung, Wang Hee-kyung, Yun Young-sook)	3925 (1)	1000 (1)	982 (1)
2. INA	(Lilies Handayani, Nurfitriyana Saiman, Kusuma Wardhani)	3720 (5)	975 (4)	952 (2)
3. USA	(Debra Ochs, Denise Parker, Melanie Skillman)	3742 (4)	988 (2)	952 (3)
4. SOV	(Lyudmila Arzhanikova, Natalya Butuzova, Tetyana Muntyan)	3818 (2)	978 (3)	951 (4)
5. GBR	(Pauline Edwards, Joanne Franks, Cheryl Sutton)	3692 (7)	962 (5)	933 (5)
6. GER	(Doris Haas, Claudia Kriz, Christa Öckl)	3702 (6)	953 (6)	931 (6)
7. SWE	(Liselotte Andersson, Carina Jonsson, Jenny Sjöwall)	3662 (10)	949 (8)	930 (7)
8. FRA	(Marie-Josée Bazin, Nathalie Hibon, Catherine Pellen)	3653 (11)	950 (7)	898 (8)

The unheralded Indonesian team earned their nation's first-ever Olympic medals by defeating the U.S. in a shoot-out, 72-67. Said the Indonesian coach, Donald Pandiangan, "It is a silver, but for us it is more than one hundred gold medals, it is more than even a gold mine."

1992 Barcelona T: 17, N: 17, D: 8.1. WR: F.I.T.A. Round—4025 (KOR—Kim S.N., Wang H.K., Park M.K.)
1. KOR (Cho Youn-jeong, Kim Soo-nyung, Lee Eun-kyung)
2. CHN (Ma Xiangjun, Wang Hong, Wang Xiaozhu)
3. SOV (Lyudmila Arzhanikova, Khatuna Kvrivichvili, Natalya Valeyeva)
4. FRA (Severine Bonal, Christine Gabillard, Nathalie Hibon)
5. SWE (Liseiotte Djerf, Kristina Persson, Jenny Sjöwall)
6. TUR (Elif Ekşi, Natalia Çakir, Zehra Öktem)
7. PRK (Kim Jong-hwa, Li Myong-gum, Sin Song-hui)
8. USA (Sherry Block, Jennifer O'Donnell, Denise Parker)
Final: KOR 236-228 CHN
3rd Place: SOV 240-222 FRA

The South Korean women obliterated the world record in the qualifying round by scoring 4094 points. Still, they had to survive a tie-breaker against the Swedes in the quarterfinals before they recovered their composure to breeze though the semifinals and finals.

Discontinued Events

1904 St. Louis C: 6, N: 1, D: 9.19.
Double Columbia Round (50 Yards—40 Yards—30 Yards)

			PTS.
1. Lida Howell	USA	867
2. Emma Cooke	USA	630
3. Jessie Pollock	USA	630
4. Laura Woodruff	USA	547
5. Mabel Taylor	USA	243
6. Louise Taylor	USA	229

1904 St. Louis C: 6, N: 1, D: 9.20.
Double National Round (60 Yards—50 Yards)

			PTS.
1. Lida Howell	USA	620
2. Emma Cooke	USA	419
3. Jessie Pollock	USA	419
4. Laura Woodruff	USA	234
5. Mabel Taylor	USA	160
6. Louise Taylor	USA	159

1908 London C: 25, N: 1, D: 7.20.
National Round (60 Yards—50 Yards)

			PTS.
1. Sybil "Queenie" Newall	GBR	688
2. Charlotte "Lottie" Dod	GBR	642
3. Beatrice Hill-Lowe	GBR	618
4. Jessie Wadworth	GBR	605
5. G.W. Honnywill	GBR	587
6. S.H. Armitage	GBR	582
7. C. Foster	GBR	553
8. Lillian Wilson	GBR	534

Sybil "Queenie" Newall, winner of the 1908 women's archery competition.

Newall trailed Dod by ten points at the end of the first day but surged ahead on the second day. Fifty-three years old at the time of her victory, Newall remains the oldest female medalist in Olympic history.

Silver medalist "Lottie" Dod was an exceptional athlete. In 1887, at the age of 15, she won the first of five Wimbledon tennis championships. She was also a champion golfer and field hockey player. In 1894 she became one of the first women to attempt the Cresta Run at St. Moritz. She was also a fine skater who once played a cricket match on ice skates. The greatest female archer of the time, Alice Legh, did not take part in the Olympics. A week later, however, she defeated Queenie Newall by 151 points.

BADMINTON

MEN
Singles
Doubles

WOMEN
Singles
Doubles

MIXED
Doubles

Badminton is played on a court 44 feet (14.31 meters) long and across a net 5 feet 1 inch (1.55 meters) high at the post, which sags 1 inch at the center. The playing area is 17 feet (5.18 meters) wide for singles and 20 feet (6.1 meters) wide for doubles. Players use a racket to hit a leather-covered cork-tipped shuttlecock that is topped by 16 goose feathers taken from the same goose. Shuttles travel at speeds in excess of 150 m.p.h.—much faster than the other Olympic net sports: tennis, table tennis, and volleyball.

Men's games and women's doubles are played to 15 points; women's singles to 11. Points may be scored only by the server. If the score is tied at 13 (9 for women), the first player to reach 13 (or 9) has the option of "setting" the game to 5, meaning the first player to score 18, rather than 15, wins. If the score is tied at 14 (or 10 for women), the first player to reach 14 can set the game to 3, so that play continues to 17 (or 13 for women) instead of 15.

MEN

SINGLES

1896-1988 not held

1992 Barcelona C: 56, N: 32, D: 8.4.

			MATCHES		GAMES	
			W	L	W	L
1.	Allan Budi Kusuma	INA	6	0	12	0
2.	Ardy Wiranata	INA	4	1	8	3
3.	Thomas Stuer-Lauridsen	DEN	4	1	8	3
3.	Hermawan Susanto	INA	3	1	7	3
5.	Poul-Erik Høyer-Larsen	DEN	2	1	4	2
5.	Kim Hak-kyun	KOR	2	1	4	3
5.	Rashid Sidek	MAL	2	1	4	2
5.	Zhao Jianhua	CHN	2	1	5	2

Final: Kusuma—Wiranata 15-12, 18-13

The critical match of the early rounds came in the quarter-finals when world champion Zhao Jianhua staved off six match points but was finally beaten, 15-2, 14-17, 17-14, by Hermawan Susanto.

The final was an 84-minute marathon, which Kusuma won by earning 11 of the last 13 points. His victory came two hours after his girlfriend, Susi Susanti, won the women's title. Prior to the victories by Susanti and Kusuma, Indonesia, the fourth most populous nation in the world, had never earned a gold medal, despite taking part in the Olympics since 1952. Not surprisingly, the pair became national heroes and their return to Jakarta was cause for an enormous celebration that included a two-hour parade led by a car carrying a gigantic shuttlecock. Susanti and Kusuma were also awarded $500,000 each.

DOUBLES

1896-1988 not held

1992 Barcelona T: 30, N: 21, D: 8.4.

			MATCHES		GAMES	
			W	L	W	L
1.	KOR	(Kim Moon-soo, Park Joo-bong)	4	0	8	1
2.	INA	(Eddy Hartono, Rudy Gunawan)	3	1	6	2
3.	CHN	(Li Yongbo, Tian Bingyi)	3	1	6	5
3.	MAL	(Jalani Sidek, Rashid Sidek)	3	1	6	2
5.	DEN	(Jan Paulsen, Henrik Svarrer)	2	1	5	2
5.	INA	(Rexy Mainaky, Ricky Subagja)	2	1	4	2
5.	JPN	(Shuji Matsuno, Shinji Matsuura)	2	1	4	2
5.	KOR	(Lee Sang-bok, Shon Jin-hwan)	2	1	4	3

Final: Kim/Park—Hartono/Gunawan 15-11, 15-7

This tournament went completely according to form, with the favorites winning in every instance. There was a bit of controversy in the first round when China's Li Yongbo was almost disqualified for delaying the match when he twice gained several minutes of much-needed rest by slowly rewrapping the bandage on his injured ankle.

WOMEN

SINGLES

1896-1988 not held

1992 Barcelona C: 52, N: 27, D: 8.4.

			MATCHES		GAMES	
			W	L	W	L
1.	Susi Susanti	INA	5	0	10	1
2.	Bang Soo-hyun	KOR	4	1	9	3
3.	Huang Hua	CHN	3	1	6	2
3.	Tang Jiuhong	CHN	3	1	6	3
5.	Somhasurthai Jaroensiri	THA	3	1	6	4
5.	Sarwendah Kusumawardhani	INA	2	1	5	2
5.	Anna Lao	AUS	3	1	6	3
5.	Lee Heun-soon	KOR	2	1	5	2

Final: Susanti—Bang 5-11, 11-5, 11-3

Susanti crushed her first four opponents, outscoring them 88-22. In the final, the pressure of being Indonesia's first-ever gold-medal hope caused her to falter. However, she regained her composure midway through the second game and won with ease.

DOUBLES

1896-1988 not held

1992 Barcelona T: 29, N: 20, D: 8.4.

			MATCHES		GAMES	
			W	L	W	L
1.	KOR	(Hwang Hye-young, Chung So-young)	4	0	8	1
2.	CHN	(Guan Weizhen, Nong Qunhua)	3	1	7	3
3.	CHN	(Lin Yanfen, Yao Fen)	2	1	4	2
3.	KOR	(Gil Young-ah, Shim Eun-jung)	3	1	7	2
5.	AUS	(Rhonda Cator, Anna Lao)	2	1	4	2
5.	GBR	(Julie Bradbury, Gillian Clark)	2	1	4	3
5.	INA	(Aadijatmiko Finarsih, Lili Tampi)	2	1	4	2
5.	SWE	(Catrine Bengtsson, Maria Bengtsson)	2	1	4	3

Final: Hwang/Chung—Guan/Nong 18-16, 12-15, 15-13

The final, matching the two top-seeded pairs, lasted for almost two hours. With the score tied 10-10 in the deciding game, Guan scored a go-ahead point, only to have it disallowed because her racket crossed the net. Hwang and Chung then scored three straight points. Trailing 13-14, Guan served an ace, but was again penalized, this time for a foot fault. Finally, after fighting off four match points, Guan let one of Chung's serves fall—and it landed in giving the Koreans the victory.

MIXED

DOUBLES

This event will be held for the first time in 1996.

BASEBALL

BASEBALL TERMS

Balk—An illegal pitch when runners are on base, entitling all runners to advance one base.

Ball—A pitch that does not enter the strike zone and is not struck at by the batter.

Base on balls (walk)—An award of first base granted to a batter who, during his time at bat, receives four pitches outside the strike zone.

Bunt—A batted ball not swung at but intentionally met with the bat and tapped slowly within the infield.

Double play—A play by the defense in which two offensive players are put out as a result of continuous action.

Fielder's choice—The act of a fielder who handles a ground ball and instead of throwing to first base to put out the batter throws to another base in an attempt to put out a preceding runner.

Force play—A play in which a runner, because there is another runner trying to reach the base he has just occupied, can be put out by a defensive player who, while holding the ball, touches the base.

Foul ball—A batted ball that settles on foul territory. A foul ball that lands without being caught is ruled a strike, although a batter cannot strike out on a foul ball.

Foul territory—That part of the playing field outside the first- and third-base lines extending to the fence and upward.

Foul tip—A batted ball that goes directly from the bat to the catcher's hands and is legally caught. A foul tip is ruled a strike.

Illegal pitch—A pitch delivered to the batter when the pitcher does not have his pivot foot in contact with the pitcher's plate, or a pitch that is delivered before the batter is set.

Infield fly—A fair, high fly ball that can be caught by an infielder with ordinary effort. If an umpire calls out "Infield fly," the batter is automatically ruled out. The infield-fly rule is called to prevent the defensive team from purposely allowing the ball to drop and facilitating a force play on an advancing runner rather than the batter.

Pivot foot—The pitcher's foot in contact with the pitcher's plate as he delivers the pitch.

Safe—A declaration by the umpire that a runner is entitled to the base for which he is trying.

Squeeze play—A play by which a team with a runner on third base attempts to score that runner by means of a bunt.

Strike—A legal pitch that (a) is struck at by the batter and is missed; or (b) is not struck at, if any part of the ball passes through any part of the strike zone; or (c) is fouled by the batter when he has less than two strikes; or (d) is bunted foul; or (e) touches the batter as he strikes at it; or (f) touches the batter in the strike zone; or (g) becomes a foul tip.

Strike zone—That area over home plate the upper limit of which is a horizontal line at the midpoint between the top of the shoulders and the top of the uniform pants and the lower level of which is a line at the top of the knees. The strike zone is determined from the batter's stance as he prepares to swing at a pitched ball.

Triple play—A play by the defense in which three offensive players are put out as a result of continuous action.

Walk—See *base on balls*.

Wild pitch—A pitch so high, so low, or so wide of the plate that it cannot be handled by the catcher with ordinary effort.

Primary source: *Official Baseball Rules*, 1995.

A baseball field is composed of an infield and an outfield. The infield is dominated by four bases laid out in the shape of a diamond, with home plate at the bottom tip. The bases are 90 feet apart. Between the home plate and second base, 60 feet 6 inches from the plate, is the pitcher's mound, which is elevated, sloping down from 2 feet above the rest of the field.

Each team fields nine players at a time. Substitutions may be made at any time, but players who have been replaced may not return. Play is initiated when the pitcher throws the ball and the batter, who is waiting at home plate, tries to hit it with a bat. The offensive team attempts to score runs; the defensive team attempts to record outs. A run is scored when an offensive player proceeds, by various means, from home plate to first base to second base to third base and back to home plate again. An out can be recorded in several ways. The most common ways occur when (1) a batter hits the pitched ball and a defensive player catches it before it touches the ground, (2) the batter hits the ball on the ground and a fielder throws the ball to the first baseman who touches first base before the batter reaches first base, (3) the batter or a runner is touched by a fielder holding the ball while the batter or runner is between bases, (4) a runner is forced out at second base, third base, or home plate in the same manner that a batter is thrown out at first base, (5) the batter strikes out. When three outs are recorded, the teams change sides. When both sides have had a turn at bat, it is called an inning. A game lasts nine innings; if the teams are tied after nine innings, extra innings are played until one team is ahead at the end of an inning.

Olympic baseball differs from major league professional baseball in several minor ways:

(1) If one team is ahead by ten or more runs after seven or eight innings, a winner is declared without finishing the game.

(2) A designated hitter is used in all games.

(3) Non-wooden bats are allowed.

(4) Only one infielder at a time may visit the pitcher at the pitcher's mound, and only one such visit may be made during an inning.

BASEBALL

1992 Barcelona—L'Hospitalet T: 8, N: 8, D: 8.5.

			W	L	RF	RA
1.	CUB	(Luis Ulacia Álvarez, Alberto Hernández Pérez, Lazaro Vargas Álvarez, Omar Linares Izquierdo, Germán Mesa Fresneda, Juan Padilla Alfonso, Lourdes Gurriel Delgado, José Estrada González, Osvaldo Fernández Rodríguez, Orlando Hernández Pedroso, Giorge Díaz Loren, Omar Ajete Iglesias, Victor Mesa Martínez, Jorge Valdés Berriel, José Delgado Díez, Rolando Arrojo Ávila, Orestes Kindelan Olivares, Antonio Pacheco Masso, Juan Pérez Rondón, Ermidelio Urrutia Quiroga)	9	0	95	16
2.	TAI	(Lin Chao-Huang, Lin Kun-Han, Wang Kuang-Shih, Chen Wei-Chen, Huang Wen-Po, Wu Shih-Hsih, Chang Yaw-Teing, Liao Ming-Hsiung, Lo Kuo-Chong, Huang Chung-Yi, Lo Chen-Jung, Chen Chi-Hsin, Chiang Tai-Chuan, Pai Kun-Hong, Kuo Lee Chien-Fu, Ku Kuo-Chian, Tsai Ming-Hung, Chang Cheng-Hsien, Chang Wen-Chung, Jong Yeu-Jeng)	6	3	67	34
3.	JPN	(Koichi Oshima, Shigeki Wakabayashi, Masafumi Nishi, Koji Tokunaga, Akihiro Togo, Hirotami Kojima, Hiroki Kokubo, Hiroyuki Sakaguchi, Yasunori Takami, Yasuhiro Sato, Kento Sugiyama, Katsumi Watanabe, Kazutaka Nishiyama, Masahito Kohiyama, Tomohito Ito, Masonori Sugiura, Takashi Miwa, Shinichi Sato, Hiroshi Nakamoto, Shinichiro Kawabata)	6	3	70	23
4.	USA	(Anthony Garciaparra, Calvin Murray, Chris Wimmer, Craig Wilson, Jeffrey Hammonds, Michael Tucker, Billy Wallace, Jason Giambi, Phillip Nevin, William Adams, Ronald Villone, Jason Varitek, Christopher Roberts, Richard Greene, Ricky Helling, Robert Alkire, Daron Kirkreit, Darron Dreifort, Chad McConnell, Charles Johnson)	5	4	53	42
5.	PUR	(Abimael Rosario Marrero, Albert Bracero Chévere, Jorge Aranzamendi Torres, José Lorenzana Oquendo, Efrain Nieves Soto, Gualberto López Camacho, Luis Ramos Torres, Wilfredo Vélez León, Manuel Serrano, Ángel Morales Rodríguez, James Figueroa, Rafael Santiago Rivera, Jesús Feliciano Amadeo, José Mateo Rosario, Roberto López Ocasio, Efrain García Santiago, Orlando López Bobian, Helson Rodríguez Santiago, José Sepúlveda Pinto, Silvio Censale)	2	5	22	48
6.	DOM	(Féliz Nova, José Veras, Manuel Guzmán, Fabio Aquino, Roberto Casey García, Eugenio Váldez Cuevas, Rafelito Mercedes Díaz, Félix Tejada, Teófilo Peña Dilone, Alexis Peña, Fausto Peña Pichardo, Teodoro Novas, Cipriano Ventura, Juan Sánchez Fernández, Juan Viñas, Roque Solano, Silvestre Popoteur, Elías Olivo, Benjamín Heredia, José Santana)	2	5	23	60
7.	ITA	(Massimo Ciaramella, Guglielmo Trinci, Claudio Cecconi, Elio Gambuti, Marco Ubani, Maurizio De Sanctis, Francesco Petruzzelli, Fulvio Valle, Massimiliano Masin, Andrea Succi, Claudio Taglienti, Paolo Ceccaroli, Ruggero Bagialemani, Rolando Cretis, Alberto D'Auria, Roberto Bianchi, Leonardo Schianchi, Luigi Carrozza, Massimo Fochi, Massimo Melassi)	1	6	25	62
8.	SPA	(Manuel Martinez Carrasco, Jesús Lisarri Tomás, Juan Belza Jaurrieta, Antonio Salazar Calzado, Enrique Cortés Gallego, Miguel Pariente Álvarez, José Arza Laurenz, Javier Díez Serra, Juan Damborenea Garcia, Francisco Aristu Lozano, Luis León Anguiano, Felix Cano Riduejo, Juan Salmerón Agullo, Xavier Camps Quibus, José Pulido Aranda, Miguel Stella Pérez, Gabriel Valarezo Camps, José Becerra Puente, Xavier Civit Forner)	1	6	15	85

Final: CUB 11-1 TAI
3rd Place: JPN 8-3 USA

Baseball is the only sport to have been included as an exhibition or demonstration sport six times before finally achieving official medal status. Exhibition games were staged in Stockholm in 1912, in Berlin in 1936 (before a bewildered crowd of 90,000), and in Melbourne in 1956. Because the 1956 game was played in the main stadium while spectators filed in for a track and field session, it is thought that the late innings were seen by the largest live audience in baseball history—almost 114,000 people. In 1964, a team of United States college all-stars played a Japanese amateur all-star team in Tokyo. In 1984, when the Olympics were held in Los Angeles, a six-team tournament was organized. Cuba qualified, but joined the boycott led by the Soviet Union. Nicaragua, ruled by another Soviet-client regime, also qualified. So great was the excitement in Nicaragua about this achievement that the government resisted Soviet pressure to join the boycott and sent their team anyway. Japan won the tournament, defeating the United States 6-3 in the final. The 1988 tournament, this time including eight teams, was boycotted by Cuba again. The final saw a United States-Japan rematch, with the Americans coming out on top, 5-3.

After such a long buildup, the first official Olympic baseball tournament, held in Barcelona, was a major anticlimax because Olympic rules prohibited the use of professional players. This meant that only Communist Cuba was allowed to use their best players, while the other qualifying nations had to choose their squads from college or amateur ranks. The Cubans had won the previous 12 world championships in which they had participated, going back to 1969, and they were 64 and 1 in international tournaments played between 1986 and 1992. Not surprisingly, the Cubans swept through the Olympics as if they were, well, in another league. In nine games, they outscored their opponents 95-16. The Cuban *team* batting average was .404, their slugging percentage .646, and their team's earned run average 1.27. They trailed only once, when the United States scored five runs in the first inning. Even then, by the fourth inning the Cubans were back on top. So dull was the tournament from a competitive standpoint that of the 32 games played, only two were decided by one run and only one went into extra innings.

BASKETBALL

Olympic basketball matches are played on a court 28 meters (91 feet 10 inches) long and 15 meters (49 feet 2½ inches) wide. The object of the game is to dribble and pass the ball downcourt and shoot it into a netted basket 2.9 meters (10 feet) above the ground. The open ring or hoop into which the ball is shot is 45 centimeters (1 foot 5¾ inches) in diameter. A successful shot is worth two points. Extending in an arc 6.25 meters (20 feet 6 inches) from the basket is the three-point line. Any successful shot launched from beyond that line is worth three points. Free throws, awarded as a result of fouls, are taken from behind a line 5.8 meters (19 feet ¼ inch) from the endline. A successful free throw is worth one point.

Each team consists of five players. Substitutions may be made at any break in the play of the game. Substituted players may return at any time.

Olympic basketball matches are made up of two 20-minute halves. If the score is tied at the end of 40 minutes of play, a five-minute overtime period is played. Further overtime periods are added until the tie is broken. Tie games are not tolerated in basketball.

According to Olympic rules, the offensive team must take a shot within 30 seconds of gaining possession of the ball.

Personal fouls involve bodily contact with an opposing player. Common fouls include blocking the progress of an opponent, charging into an opponent, holding, pushing, and hand-checking. If a foul is committed on a player who is not in the act of shooting, the game resumes with a throw-in from out of bounds. If the foul is committed on a player who *is* in the act of shooting, if the goal is made, it counts and the fouled player is awarded one free throw. If the shot is unsuccessful, the shooter is awarded two free throws. If the shot was from beyond the three-point line and was unsuccessful the shooter is awarded three free throws. If a foul is committed by a player whose team is in possession of the ball, the opposing team is given possession with a throw-in from out of bounds. A technical foul is assessed when a player or coach acts in a violent or disrespectful manner. The opposing team is awarded two free throws and possession of the ball.

A player who commits five fouls must leave the game and may not return. Each team is allowed seven fouls per half. Each team foul after the seventh one is penalized by the awarding of two free throws to the opposing team even if the foul was not committed during the act of shooting.

One rule that newcomers to basketball find confusing is the three-second restriction. The restricted area on each end of the court begins at the endline, extending three meters (9 feet 10 inches) to each side of the basket, and extends to the free throw line. A player whose team has possession of the ball may not spend more than three seconds in the opposing team's restricted area. A violation of this rule is penalized by loss of possession of the ball.

Spectators familiar with basketball as played in the National Basketball Association (NBA) should be aware of certain differences in Olympic rules. Most notably, in Olympic basketball each team is allowed only two time-outs per half; balls bouncing on the rim after a shot may be touched; only a team's coach may call a time-out.

The 12 teams in an Olympic tournament play in two round-robin pools. The top four teams from each pool advance to direct-elimination quarterfinals, semifinals, and finals.

MEN

1896–1932 not held

1936 Berlin T: 21, N: 21, D: 8.14.

			W	L	PF	PA
1.	USA	(Ralph Bishop, Joe Fortenberry, Carl Knowles, Jack Ragland, Carl Shy, William Wheatley, Francis Johnson, Samuel Balter, John Gibbons, Frank Lubin, Arthur Mollner, Donald Piper, Duane Swanson, Willard Schmidt)	4	0	152	69
2.	CAN	(Gordon Aitchison, Jan Allison, Arthur Chapman, Charles Chapman, Douglas Peden, James Stewart, Malcolm Wiseman, Edward John Dawson, Irving Meretsky)	5	1	176	104
3.	MEX	(Carlos Borja Morca, Victor Hugo Borja Morca, Raúl Fernández Robert, Francisco Martinez Cordero, Jesus Olmos Moreni, Greer Skousen Spilsbury, Luis Ignacio de la Vega Leija, Rodolfo Choperno Irizarri, José Pamplona Lecuanda, Andrés Gómez Dominguez, Silvio Hernandez del Valle)	4	2	160	115

			W	L	PF	PA
4. POL	(Zdzislaw Filipkiewicz, Florian Grzechowiak, Jakub Kopowski, Edwaryst Lój, Andrzej Pluciński, Zenon Rózycki, Edward Szostak, Zdzislaw Kasprzak, Janusz Patrzykont, Pavel Stok)		1	4	119	180
5. PHI	(Charles Bork, Jacinto Cruz Ciria, Franco Marquicias, Primitivo Martinez, Jesús Marzan, Amador Obordo, Ambrosio Padilla, Bibiano Ouano, Fortunato Yamboa)		4	1	159	145
6. URU	(Gregorio Agos, Rodolfo Braseili, Leandro Gomez Harley, Alejo Gonzalez Roig, Victor Lato Jaimeu, Prudencio de Pena, Tabaré Quintans, Humberto Bernasconi, Carlos Gabin)		2	3	125	136
7. ITA	(Enrico Castelli, Galeazzo Dondi, Livio Franeschini, Emilio Giasetti, Gian Carlo Marinelli, Sergio Paganella, Egidio Premiani, Gino Basso)		3	2	160	129

Final: USA 19—8 CAN
3rd Place: MEX 26—12 POL
5th Place: PHI 33—23 URU

The first official Olympic basketball tournament was held outdoors in a tennis stadium on courts of clay and sand. Half the U.S. squad was made up of members of the winner of the U.S. trials—the team from Universal Studios. During the tournament, the International Basketball Federation passed a rule that banned all players who were taller than 6 feet 3 inches. The United States, which would have lost three of its players, objected, and the rule was withdrawn. The day of the final saw heavy rain, which turned the courts into mud. The players found it quite difficult to dribble on wet sand, which undoubtedly contributed to the low score. The United States led 15–4 at the half. Six-foot 8-inch center Joe Fortenberry of McPherson, Kansas, scored eight points to match the score of the entire Canadian team.

1948 London T: 23, N: 23, D: 8.13.

		W	L	PF	PA
1. USA	(Clifford Barker, Donald Barksdale, Ralph Beard, Lewis Beck, Vincent Boryla, Gordon Carpenter, Alexander Groza, Wallace Jones, Robert Kurland, Raymond Lumpp, Robert Pitts, Jesse Renick, Robert Robinson, Kenneth Rollins)	8	0	524	256
2. FRA	(André Barrais, Michel Bonnevie, André Buffière, René Chocat, René Dérency, Maurice Desaymonnet, André Even, Maurice Girardot, Fernand Guillou, Raymond Offner, Jacques Perrier, Yvan Quénin, Lucien Rebuffic, Pierre Thiolon)	5	2	331	281
3. BRA	(Zenny de Azevedo, João Francisco Bráz, Marcus Vinicius Dias, Alfonso Azevedo Évora, Ruy de Freitas, Alexandre Gemignani, Alberto Marson, Alfredo Rodrigues da Motta, Nilton Pacheco de Oliveira, Massinet Sorcinelli)	7	1	374	263
4. MEX	(Angel Acuna Lizaña, Isaac Alfaro Loza, Alberto Bienvenu Barajas, José de la Cruz Cabrera Gándara, Jorge Cardiel Gaitán, Rodolfo Diaz Mercado, Francisco Galinda Chávez, Jorge Gudiño Goya, Héctor Guerrero Delgado, Emilio López Enriquez, Ignacio Romo Porches, José Rojas Herrera, Fernando Rojas Herrera, José Santos de León)	5	2	314	264
5. URU	(Martin Acosta y Lara, Néstor Anton, Victorio Cieslinskas, Nelson Demarco, Miguel Diab, Abraham Eidlin, Eduardo Folle, Héctor Garcia Otero, Eduardo Gordon, Adesio Lombardo, Roberto Lovera, Gustavo Margariños, Carlos Rosselló, Héctor Ruiz)	5	3	369	301
6. CHI	(Eduardo Cordero Fernandez, Exequiel Figueroa Reyes, Juan Gallo Chinchilla, Roberto Hammer Casadio, Eduardo Kapstein Suckel, Manuel Ledesma Barraies, Victor Mahana Badrie, Luis Marmentini Gil, Andres Mitrovic Guic, Antonio Moreno Rodillo, Eduardo Parra Rojas, Hernán Raffo Abarca, Marcos Sanchez Carmona, Guillermo Verdugo Yanez)	4	4	391	301
7. CZE	(Karel Belohradsky, Cyril Benacek, Jiři Chlup, Jiři Drvota, Josef Ezr, Jozef Kalina, Jan Kozak, Vaclav Krasa, Zdenek Krenicky, Jozef Krepela, Ivan Mrazek, Jiři Siegel, Josef Toms, Ladislav Trpkos)	5	3	315	294
8. KOR	(Ahn Byung-suk, W. Bang, Chang Chin-ri, Chyo Joon-deuk, Kang Hyun-bong, Kim Shin-chung, Lee Yung-choon, Lee Hoon-sang, Oh Chul-soo)	3	5	364	279

Final: USA 65—21 FRA
3rd Place: BRA 52—47 MEX

The 1948 tournament had some unusual highlights: A British referee was knocked unconscious during a preliminary game between Chile and Iraq. A Chinese player dribbled between the legs of the 7-foot U.S. center, Bob Kurland, and followed through by scoring a basket. In the fiercely contested match for third place, da Motta of Brazil lost his pants and had to retire to the dressing room. Iraq lost by 100 points twice—to Korea and China (which finished eighteenth), and gave up an average of almost 104 points per game while scoring only 23.5. Ireland's offense was even less effective, averaging only 17 points a game. Meanwhile, the U.S. team survived an early 59–57 scare against Argentina and then breezed through the rest of its games. The halftime score in the final was 28–9. J. Llanusa Gobel of the Cuban team went on to become Minister of Education under Fidel Castro.

1952 Helsinki T: 23, N: 23, D:8.2.

			W	L	PF	PA
1.	USA	(Charles Hoag, William Hougland, Melvin Dean Kelley, Robert Kenney, Clyde Lovellette, Marcus Freiberger, Victor Wayne Glasgow, Frank McCabe, Daniel Pippin, Howard Williams, Ronald Bontemps, Robert Kurland, William Lienhard, John Keller)	8	0	562	406
2.	SOV	(Viktor Vlassov, Stepas Butautas, Joann Lõssov, Kazys Petkevičius, Nodar Dshordshikiya, Anatoly Konyev, Otar Korkiya, Ilmar Kullam, Yuri Ozerov, Aleksandr Moiseyev, Heino Kruus, Justinas Lagunavičius, Maigonis Valdmanis, Stasys Stonkus)	6	2	468	431
3.	URU	(Martin Acosta y Lara, Enrique Baliño, Victorio Cieslinskas, Héctor Costa, Nelson Demarco, Héctor Garcia Otero, Roberto Lovera, Adesio Lombardo, Tabaré Larre Borges, Sergio Matto, Wilfredo Pelaez, Carlos Rosselló)	5	3	486	471
4.	ARG	(Rubén Francisco Menini, Hugo Oscar del Vecchio, Leopoldo Contarbio, Raúl Pérez Varela, Juan Gazso, Roberto Viau, Ricardo Primitiva González, Juan Carlos Uder, Omar Monza, Rubén Pagliari, Rafael Lledo, Oscar Alberto Furlong, Alberto López, Ignacio Poletti)	5	3	600	523
5.	CHI	(Juan Gallo Chinchilla, Victor Mahana Badrie, Exequiel Figueroa Reyes, Eduardo Cordero Fernandez, Rufino Bernedo Zorzano, Alvaro Salvadores Salvi, Eric Maehn Godoy, Herman Ramos Muñoz, Hugo Fernandez Diaz, Orlando Silva Infante, Hernán Raffo Abarca, Pedro Araya Zabala, Juan Ostoic)	4	4	447	508
6.	BRA	(Zenny de Azevedo, Sebastião Gimenez, Ruy de Freitas, Mayr Facci, Raymundo Carvalho dos Santos, Angelo Bonfietti, João Francisco Bráz, Alfredo Rodrigues da Motta, Almir Nelson de Almeida, Mario Jorge da Fonseca Hermes, Thales Monteiro, José Luiz Santos Azevedo, Helio Marquez Pereira)				
7.	BUL	(Kiril Semov, Hristo Donchev, Vasil Manchenko, Peter Shishkov, Georgi Panov, Konstantin Totev, Anton Kuzov, Gencho Rashkov, Ivan Nikolov, Veselin Penkov, Konstantin Georgiev, Vladimir Slavov)	4	4	451	506
8.	FRA	(Bernard Planque, Robert Monclar, René Chocat, Jean Perniceni, Louis Devoti, Robert Guillin, Robert Crost, Jacques Dessemme, André Buffière, André Vacheresse, André Chavet, Jean-Paul Beugnot, Roger Haudegand, Jean-Pierre Salignon)	4	4	468	460

Final: USA 36—25 SOV
3rd Place: URU 68—59 ARG
5th Place: CHI 58—49 BRA
7th Place: BUL 58—44 FRA

Having been crushed by the United States 86–58, in the semifinal round, the Soviet team decided to freeze the ball in the final match. After ten minutes, the United States led 4–2. At halftime the score was still only 17–15. With five minutes to play, Clyde Lovellette scored a basket to give the United States a lead of 31–25. The next time the Americans got the ball, it was their turn to stall. One Soviet player became so exasperated that he sat down on the floor until his coach ordered him to stand up.

The tournament was enlivened by the participation of Uruguay. In the semifinal round, France had a 66–64 lead over the team from South America, which had been reduced to three players due to excessive fouling. With one minute to play, Uruguay tied the score, whereupon the American referee, Vincent Farrell, whistled a foul against Uruguay. The Uruguayan team rushed off the bench and abused Farrell for five minutes until he was finally able to communicate that the foul had occurred *after* the basket and that the 2 points had not been disallowed. France took the ball out of bounds and worked the ball to Jacques Dessemme, who scored an easy layup to win the game. At this point Uruguayan players and spectators attacked Farrell again. This time he was kicked in the groin and had to be carried from the court. Two Uruguayan players were banned from further competition. Three days later it was the U.S.S.R.'s turn to face the volatile Uruguayans. In the second half, three Soviet players had to receive first aid. The following day, the now exhausted Uruguayans faced their bitter rival, Argentina, in the match for third place. They mustered up enough energy for one more brawl with 25 people involved. So many fouls were called that Uruguay finished the game with only four players and Argentina with only three.

1956 Melbourne T: 15, N: 15, D: 12.1.

			W	L	PF	PA
1.	USA	(Carl Cain, William Hougland, K.C. Jones, William Russell, James Walsh, William Evans, Burdette Haldorson, Ronald Tomsic, Richard Boushka, Gilbert Ford, Robert Jeangerard, Charles Darling)	8	0	793	365
2.	SOV	(Valdis Muižnieks, Maigonis Valdmanis, Vladimir Torban, Stasys Stonkus, Kazys Petkevičius, Arkady Bochkaryov, Jānis Krūmiņš, Mikhail Semyonov, Algirdas Lauritenas, Yuri Ozerov, Viktor Zubkov, Mikhail Studenetsky)	5	3	574	524
3.	URU	(Carlos Blixen, Ramiro Cortes, Héctor Costa, Nelson Chelle, Nelson Demarco, Héctor Garcia Otero, Carlos González, Sergio Matto, Oscar Moglia, Raúl Mera, Ariel Olascoaga, Milton Scarón)	6	2	568	559
4.	FRA	(Roger Haudegand, Christian Baltzer, Robert Monclar, Roger Veyron, Gérard Sturla, Henri Rey, Roger Antoine, Henri Grange, Yves Gominon, Maurice Buffière, Andrè Schlupp, Jean-Paul Beugnot)	5	3	542	497
5.	BUL	(Atanas Atanasov, Vladimir Slavov, Ilia Mirchev, Victor Radev, Georgi Kunev, Vasil Manchenko, Georgi Panov, Konstantin Totev, Tsviatko Slavov, Lyubomir Panov, Nikola Ilov)	5	3	568	545
6.	BRA	(Zenny de Azevedo, Noel Marques Lisboa, Wlamir Marques, Angelo Bonfietti, Jamil Gedeão, Wilson Bombarda, Jorge Dortas Olivieri, Mayr Facci, Edson Bispo dos Santos, José Luiz Santos Azevedo, Fausto Sucena Rasga Filho, Amaury Antônio Passos)	3	4	500	535
7.	PHI	(Ramon Manulat, Ramon Campos, Carlos Badion, Loreto Carbonel, Martin Urra, Rafael Barretto, Leonardo Marquicias, Antonio Villamor, Mariano Tolentino, Carlos Loyzaga, Antonio Genato, Eduardo Lim)	4	4	534	599
8.	CHI	(Luis Salvadores, Juan Ostoic, Maximiliano Garafulic, Pedro Araya Zabala, Rufino Bernedo Zorzano, Victor Mahana Badrie, Orlando Silva Infante, Raul Urra, Hernán Raffo Abarca, Orlando Etcheverre-Garay, Juan Arrendondo, Rolando Etchepare)	2	5	490	518

Final: USA 89—55 SOV
3rd Place: URU 71—62 FRA
5th Place: BUL 64—52 BRA
7th Place: PHI 75—68 CHI

Led by Bill Russell and K.C. Jones, who later became great professional stars with the Boston Celtics, the team from the United States won all eight of its games by at least 30 points and scored over 100 points four times. Their average score was 99–46.

1960 Rome T: 16, N: 16, D: 9.10.

			W	L	PF	PA
1.	USA	(Jay Arnette, Walter Bellamy, Robert Boozer, Terry Dischinger, Jerry Lucas, Oscar Robertson, Adrian Smith, Burdette Haldorson, Darrall Imhoff, Allen Kelley, Lester Lane, Jerry West)	8	0	815	476
2.	SOV	(Yuri Korneyev, Jānis Krūmiņš, Guram Minaschvill, Valdis Muižnieks, Cēzars Ozers, Aleksandr Petrov, Mikhail Semyonov, Vladimir Ugrekhelidze, Maigonis Valdmanis, Albert Valtin, Gennady Volnov, Viktor Zubkov)	6	2	596	497
3.	BRA	(Edson Bispo dos Santos, Moyses Blas, Waldemar Blatkauskas, Zenny de Azevedo, Carmo de Souza, Carlos Domingos Massoni, Waldyr Geraldo Boccardo, Wlamir Marques, Amaury Antônio Passos, Fernando Pereira de Freitas, Antônio Salvador Sucar, Jatyr Eduardo Schall)	6	2	568	573
4.	ITA	(Augusto Giomo, Gabriele Vianello, Alessandro Riminucci, Gianfranco Lombardi, Gianfranco Pieri, Alessandro Gamba, Mario Alesini,	4	4	603	653

The 1960 U.S. team. Ten of its members went on to successful careers in professional basketball. Back row, L-R: Darrall Imhoff; Jerry Lucas; Walt Bellamy; Burdette Haldorson; Bob Boozer; Terry Dischinger; Oscar Robertson. Front row, L-R: Les Lane; Al Kelley; Adrian Smith; Jay Arnette; Dean Nesmith, Trainer. Kneeling, L-R: Warren Womble, Asst. Coach; Dutch Lonborg, Manager; Pete Newell, Coach.

Achille Canna, Antonio Calebotta, Paolo Vittori, Giovanni Gavagnin, Gianfranco Sardagna)

		W	L	PF	PA
5.	CZE (Jaroslav Tetiva, Josef Kinský, Zdeněk Bobrovský, Boris Lukašik, František Konvička, Zdeněk Konečný, Dušan Lukašik, Bohuslav Rylich, Jiři Baumruk, Vladimir Pištělák, Jiři Štastný, Bohumil Tomášek)	5	3	632	594
6.	YUG (Slobodan Gordič, Ivo Daneu, Sreten Dragojlovič, Josip Djerdja, Nemanja Djuric, Marjan Kandus, Radivoje Korač, Boris Kristančič, Miha Lokar, Miodrag Nikolič, Zvonimir Petricevič, Radovan Radovič)	4	4	582	603
7.	POL (Jerzy Piskun, Janusz Wichowski, Andrzej Pstrokoński, Andrzej Nartowski, Jerzy Mlynarczyk, Ryszard Olszewski, Krzysztof Sitkowski, Mieczyslaw Lopatka, Zbigniew Dregier, Bogdan Przywarski, Tadeusz Pacula, Dariusz Świerczewski)	4	4	582	653
8.	URU (Sergio Matto, Raul Mera, Nelson Chelle, Waldemar Rial, Washington Poyet, Carlos Blixen, Milton Scaron, Aldofo Lubnicki, Hector Costa, Danilo Coito, Edison Ciavattone, Manuel Gadea)	2	6	548	678

Final Round: USA 81—57 SOV
BRA 78—75 ITA
USA 112—81 ITA
SOV 64—62 BRA
SOV 78—70 ITA
USA 90—63 BRA

Ten members of the 1960 U.S. squad went on to play professionally in the National Basketball Association. The team was so strong that future Boston Celtic star John Havlicek qualified only as an alternate. Led by Jerry Lucas and Oscar Robertson, both of whom averaged 17 points a game, the Americans won every game by at least 24 points despite a much improved international field. The U.S. team averaged 102 points per game while giving up only 59.5. In the final match against Brazil, the United States built up a 41–14 lead after only 14 minutes and coasted for the rest of the game.

1964 Tokyo T: 16, N: 16, D: 10.23.

		W	L	PF	PA
1.	USA (James Barnes, William Bradley, Lawrence Brown, Joseph Caldwell, Mel Counts, Richard Davies, Walter Hazzard, Lucius Jackson, John McCaffrey, Jeffrey Mullins, Jerry Shipp, George Wilson)	9	0	704	434
2.	SOV (Valdis Muižnieks, Mykola Bahley, Armenak Alachachyan, Aleksandr Travin, Vyacheslav Khrynin, Jānis	8	1	674	544

Krūmiņš, Levan Mosechvili, Yuri Korneyev, Aleksandr Petrov, Gennady Voinov, Jaak Lipso, Juris Kalniņš)

		W	L	PF	PA
3.	BRA (Amaury Antônio Passos, Wlamir Marques, Ubiratan Pereira Maciel, Carlos Domingos Massoni, Friedrich Wilhelm Braun, Carmo de Souza, Jatyr Eduardo Schall, Edson Bispo dos Santos, Antônio Salvador Sucar, Victor Mirshawka, Sérgio de Toledo Machado, José Edvar Simões)	6	3	596	565
4.	PUR (William McCadney, Evelio Droz Ramos, Ruben Adorno Melendez, Teofilo Cruz Downs, Juan Vicens Sastre, Alberto Zamot Bula, Martin Anza Ortiz, Jaime Frontera Colley, Juan Ramon Baez Marino, Angel Garcia Lucas, Angel Cancel Acevedo, Thomas Gutierrez Ferrer)	5	4	595	592
5.	ITA (Augusto Giomo, Giusto Pellanera, Gianfranco Lombardi, Gianfranco Pieri, Gianfranco Bertini, Paolo Vittori, Gianfranco Sardagna, Ottorino Flaborea, Massimo Masini, Sauro Bufalini, Gabriele Vianello, Giovanni Gavagnin)	6	3	649	602
6.	POL (Janusz Wichowski, Andrzej Pstrokonski, Tadeusz Blauth, Andrzej Perka, Stanislaw Olejniczak, Krystian Czernichowski, Zbigniew Dregier, Kazimierz Frelkiewicz, Bogdan Liszko, Mieczyslaw Lopatka, Jerzy Piskun, Krzysztof Sitkowski)	5	4	608	596
7.	YUG (Slobodan Gordic, Radivoje Korač, Trajko Rajkovič, Dragan Kovacic, Dragoslav Ražnatuvič, Ivo Daneu, Zvonko Petricevic, Vital Eiselt, Vladimir Cvetkovič, Menamja Djuric, Miodrag Nikolic)	6	3	670	583
8.	URU (Washington Poyet, Walter Marquez, Julio Cesar Gomez, Luis Eduardo Koster, Edison Ciavattone, Alvaro Eduardo Roca, Sergio Pisano, Luis Agustin Garcia, Manuel Roberto Gadea, Ramiro Eduardo de Leon, Waldemar Jose Rial, Jorge Maya)	4	5	596	642

Final: USA 73—59 SOV
3rd Place: BRA 76—60 PUR
5th Place: ITA 79—59 POL
7th Place: YUG 78—55 URU

Once again the Americans went through the tournament undefeated. They were pressed only by the Yugoslavs, whom they beat 69–61. In the final, the U.S.S.R. led 16–13 after the first ten minutes, but the United States went on an 18–4 spurt and were never headed again. The Peruvian team sported four brothers, Ricardo, Enrique, Raul, and Luis Duarte.

1968 Mexico City T: 16, N: 16, D: 10.25.

			W	L	PF	PA
1.	USA	(John Clawson, Kenneth Spain, Joseph "Jo-Jo" White, Michael Barrett, Spencer Haywood, Charles Scott, William Hosket, Calvin Fowler, Michael Silliman, Glynn Saulters, James King, Donald Dee)	9	0	739	505
2.	YUG	(Aljoša Žorga, Radivoje Korač, Zoran Maroević, Trajko Rajković, Vladimir Cvetković, Dragoslav Ražnatović, Ivo Daneu, Krešimir Čosić, Damir Šolman, Nikola Plećas, Dragutin Čermak, Petar Skansi)	7	2	705	638
3.	SOV	(Anatoly Krikun, Modestas Paulauskas, Zurab Sakandelidze, Vadim Kapranov, Yuri Selikhov, Anatoly Polyvoda, Sergei Belov, Priit Tomson, Sergei Kovalenko, Gennady Volnov, Jaak Lipso, Vladimir Andreyev)	8	1	774	524
4.	BRA	(Sérgio de Toledo Machado, Wlamir Marques, Ubiratan Pereira Maciel, Celso Luiz Scarpini, Helio Rubens Garcia, Carmo de Souza, José Aparecido dos Santos, Luiz Claudio Menon, Antônio Salvador Sucar, José Edvar Simões, José Geraldo de Castro, Carlos Domingos Massoni)	6	3	677	563
5.	MEX	(Rafael Heredia Estrella, Arturo Guerrero, Fernando Tiscareño, Miguel Arellano, Antonio Ayala, Oscar Asiain, Luis Grajeda, Alejandro Guzman, Carlos Quintanar, Ricardo Pontvianne, John Hatch, Mañuel Raga)	7	2	641	580
6.	POL	(Grzegorz Korcz, Wlodzimierz Trams, Czeslaw Malec, Henryk Cegielski, Andrzej Kasprzak, Edward Jurkiewicz, Adam Niemiec, Bogdan Liszko, Mieczyslaw Lopatka, Kazimierz Frelkiewicz, Boleslaw Kwiatkowski, Andrzej Pasiorowski)	5	4	604	631
7.	SPA	(Juan Martinez, Vicente Ramos, Luis Santiago, Jesus Codina, Enrique Margall, Antonio Nava, Emiliano Rodriguez, Clifford Luyk, José Vela Sagi, Francisco Buscato, Lorenzo Alocen, Alfonso Martinez)	5	4	717	693
8.	ITA	(Carlo Recalcati, Giusto Pellanera, Gianfranco Lombardi, Enrico Bovone, Massimo Masini, Paolo	5	4	686	693

Vittori, Gabriele Vianello, Guido Gatti, Ottorino Flaborea, Sauro Fufalini, Massimo Cosmelli, Gianluigi Jessi)

Final: USA 65—50 YUG
3rd Place: SOV 70—53 BRA
5th Place: MEX 76—65 POL
7th Place: SPA 88—72 ITA

The best of the U.S. college players stayed away from the Olympic trials for various reasons. Notable absentees included Elvin Hayes, who had signed a professional contract, and Lew Alcindor (Kareem Abdul-Jabbar), who gave two reasons: not wanting to take time off from his studies and support for the threatened black boycott of the Olympics. But the U.S. team, although held to a 5-point victory by Puerto Rico, made it to the final by beating Brazil 75–63. In the other semifinal, Yugoslavia's captain, Ivo Daneu, sank two free throws with four seconds to play to upset the U.S.S.R. 63–62. At the end of the first half of the final, the Yugoslavs trailed the United States by only three points, 32–29. But at the beginning of the second half Spencer Haywood and Jo-Jo White went on a rampage, as the U.S. outscored Yugoslavia 22–3 to put the game out of reach. The vocal Mexican crowd, which had been rooting for the underdog Yugoslavs, was so impressed by the display of Haywood and White that they switched allegiance. The only incident of the tournament occurred when some photographers attempted to shoot pictures of the weeping Cuban team, which had just lost to Mexico by one point. The Cubans took out their frustrations by chasing the photographers across the court. There were no injuries.

1972 Munich T: 16, N: 16, D: 9.10.

			W	L	PF	PA
1.	SOV	(Anatoly Polyvoda, Modestas Paulauskas, Zurab Sakandelidze, Alshan Sharmukhamedov, Aleksandr Boloshev, Ivan Edeshko, Sergei Belov, Mishako Korkia, Ivan Dvorni, Gennady Volnov, Aleksandr Belov, Serhei Kovalenko)	9	0	757	590
2.	USA	(Kenneth Davis, Douglas Collins, Thomas Henderson, Michael Bantom, Robert Jones, Dwight Jones, James Forbes, James Brewer, Tommy Burleson, Thomas McMillen, Kevin Joyce, Ed Ratleff)	8	1	660	401
3.	CUB	(Juan Domecq, Roberto Herrera Tabio, Juan Roca, Pedro Chappé García, Jose Alvarez Pozo, Rafael Cãnizares Poey, Conrado Pérez Armenteros, Miguel Calderón Gómez, Tomás Herrera Martínez, Oscar Varona, Alejandro Urgellés Guibot, Franklin Standard)	7	2	687	577
4.	ITA	Ottorino Flaborea, Giuseppe	5	4	650	605

Aleksandr Belov, of the Soviet Union, scoring the winning layup against the U.S. in 1972 in the most controversial basketball game in Olympic history.

Brumatti, Giorgio Giomo, Mauro Cerioni, Massimo Masini, Renzo Bariviera, Marino Zanatta, Dino Meneghin, Pierluigi Marzorati, Luigi Serafini, Ivan Bisson, Giulio Jellini)

5.	YUG	(Ratko Tvrdič, Ljubodrag Simonovič, Vinko Jelovac, Zarko Knezevič, Miroljub Damnjanovič, Dragan Kapicić, Blagoje Georgievski, Krešimir Čosić, Damir Solman, Nikola Plecas, Dragutin Cermak, Milun Marovič)	7	2	734 617
6.	PUR	(Joe Hatton, Neftali Rivera, James Thordsen, Ruben Rodriguez, Eric William Baum, Hector Blondet, Earl Brown, Mariano Ortiz, Teofilo Cruz Downs, Raymond Dalmau, Ricardo Calzada)	6	3	743 683
7.	BRA	(Joseph Washington, Radvilas Gorauskas, Maciel Pereira Ubiratan, Sergio Francisco Garcia, Rubens Helio Garcia, Abdalla Marcos Leite, José Aparecido dos Santos, Luiz Claudio Menon,	3	5	625 642

Adilson de Nascimento, José Edivar Simões, José Geraldo de Castro, Carlos Domingos Massoni)

8.	CZE	(Petr Noviky, Zdenek Dousa, Jiři Konopasek, Jiři Pospisil, Zdenek Kos, Jiři Balastik, Jiři Zidek, Jiři Zednicek, Jan Bobrovsky, Kamil Brabenec, Jan Blazek, Jiři Ruzicka)	4	5	625 642

Final: SOV 51—50 USA
3rd Place: CUB 66—65 ITA
5th Place: YUG 86—70 PUR
7th Place: BRA 87—69 CZE

One of the greatest controversies in the history of international sports took place in Munich in the early morning hours of Sunday, September 10. The United States entered the final match with a record of 62 wins and no losses in Olympic basketball competition. The game began at 11:45 p.m., in order to accommodate U.S. television. One of the American team's strengths was speed, but the United States coach, Hank Iba, chose not to exploit it, ordering his squad to play at a more cautious and deliberate pace instead.

The U.S.S.R. scored first, led 26–21 at the half, and was ahead by eight points with 6:07 to play. But then the United States applied a full-court press and the Soviet team began to crumble. Nonetheless, with six seconds to play, the Soviets had the ball and clung to a one-point lead. Then Soviet star Sasha Belov inadvertently threw the ball toward Doug Collins of Illinois State. With three seconds left, Collins was fouled intentionally by Sako Sakandelidze. In fact, he was fouled so hard that he momentarily lost consciousness. Dazed, he mechanically followed his free throw routine—"three dribbles, a little spin, and then shoot"—and coolly sank two free throws to give the United States its first lead of the game, 50–49. The Soviet team in-bounded the ball, but two seconds later head referee Renato Righetto of Brazil noted a disturbance at the scorer's table and called an administrative time-out. The Soviet coach, Vladimir Kondrashkin, claimed that he had called for a time-out after Collins' first shot. Indeed, the time-out horn had gone off just as Collins released his second free throw attempt. According to the rules of the day, a coach calling for a time-out in a free throw situation could ask that the time-out begin before or after the first shot. Kondrashkin wanted his time-out *after* Collins' first shot. The German officials, in the excitement of the moment, apparently forgot about this option and, noting the Soviet players go to the line for Collins' first shot, thought that Kondrashkin had canceled his request, and so they failed to inform the referees of a time-out.

With one second on the clock, the U.S.S.R. was awarded a time-out. When play resumed, they in-bounded the ball and time ran out. The United States players began a joyous celebration.

But at this point Great Britain's R. William Jones, the

Secretary-General of the International Amateur Basketball Federation (F.I.B.A.), intervened and ordered the clock set back to three seconds, which was how much time remained on the clock when Kondrashkin originally tried to call time-out. Technically, Jones had no right to make any decisions, but he ruled F.I.B.A. with an iron hand, and hardly anyone dared to question his authority. Kondrashkin brought in Ivan Edeshko, who threw a long pass to Sasha Belov. Belov caught the pass perfectly, pushed past two defenders, and scored the winning basket. The United States filed a protest, which was heard by a five-man Jury of Appeal. Jones appointed Ferenc Hepp of Hungary to be chairman of the committee, and Hepp provided the deciding vote in favor of the U.S.S.R. He was joined by representatives of Poland and Cuba, while representatives of Italy and Puerto Rico voted to disallow Belov's basket. The U.S. team voted unanimously to refuse their silver medals. Coach Hank Iba felt doubly robbed. At two a.m., while he was signing the official protest, his pocket was picked and he lost $370.

The loss haunted many of the United States players for years to come, but others were able to put it in perspective. In 1992, Kenny Davis told *Sports Illustrated*, "I went back to my room and cried alone that night. But every time I get to feeling sorry for myself, I think of the Israeli kids who were killed at those Games. . . . Think of being in a helicopter with your hands tied behind your back and a hand grenade rolling toward you . . . and compare *that* to not getting a gold medal. If that final game is the worst injustice that ever happens to the guys on that team, we'll all come out of this life pretty good."

As for Sasha Belov, he died in mysterious circumstances on October 3, 1978. He was 26 years old.

1976 Montreal T: 12, N: 12, D: 7.27.

			W	L	PF	PA
1. USA	(Phil Ford, Steve Sheppard, Adrian Dantley, Walter Davis, William "Quinn" Buckner, Ernie Grunfeld, Kenneth Carr, Scott May, Michel Armstrong, Thomas La Garde, Philip Hubbard, Mitchell Kupchak)		7	0	584	500
2. YUG	(Blagoje Georgievski, Dragan Kicanović, Vinko Jelovać, Rajko Žižić, Željko Jerkov, Andro Knego, Zoran Slavnić, Krešimir Čošić, Damir Solman, Žarko Varajić, Dražen Dalipagić, Mirza Delibašić)		5	2	527	522
3. SOV	(Vladimir Arzamaskov, Aleksandr Salnikov, Valery Miloserdov, Alshan Sharmukhamedov, Andrei Makeev, Ivan Edeshko, Sergei Belov, Vladimir Tkachenko, Anatoly Myshkin, Mikhail Korkiya, Aleksandr Belov, Vladimir Zhigily)		6	1	732	535
4. CAN	(Alexander Devlin, Martin Riley,		4	3	595	611

Bill Robinson, John Cassidy, Derek Sankey, Robert Sharpe, Cameron Hall, James Russell, Robert Town, Romel Raffin, Lars Hansen, Phillip Tollestrup)

5. ITA	(Giulio Jellini, Carlo Recalcati, Luciano Vendemini, Fabrizio Della Fiori, Renzo Bariviera, Marino Zanatta, Dino Meneghin, Pierluigi Marzorati, Luigi Serafini, Ivan Bisson, Gianni Bertolotti)		5	2	526	491

UNITED STATES' BASKETBALL WINNING STREAK

1936

USA	52—28	EST
USA	56—23	PHI
USA	25—10	MEX
USA	19— 8	CAN

1948

USA	86—21	SWI
USA	53—28	CZE
USA	59—57	ARG
USA	66—28	EGY
USA	61—33	PER
USA	63—28	URU
USA	71—40	MEX
USA	65—21	FRA

1952

USA	66—48	HUN
USA	72—47	CZE
USA	57—44	URU
USA	86—58	SOV
USA	103—55	CHI
USA	57—53	BRA
USA	85—76	ARG
USA	36—25	SOV

1956

USA	98—40	JPN
USA	101—29	THA
USA	121—53	PHI
USA	84—44	BUL
USA	113—51	BRA
USA	85—55	SOV
USA	101—38	URU
USA	89—55	SOV

1960

USA	88—54	ITA
USA	125—66	JPN
USA	107—63	HUN
USA	104—42	YUG
USA	108—50	URU
USA	81—57	SOV
USA	112—81	ITA
USA	90—63	BRA

1964

USA	78—45	AUS
USA	77—51	FIN
USA	60—45	PER
USA	83—28	URU
USA	69—61	YUG
USA	86—53	BRA
USA	116—50	KOR
USA	62—42	PUR
USA	73—59	SOV

1968

USA	81—46	SPA
USA	93—36	SEN
USA	96—75	PHI
USA	73—58	YUG
USA	95—50	PAN
USA	100—61	ITA
USA	61—56	PUR
USA	75—63	BRA
USA	65—50	YUG

1972

USA	65—35	CZE
USA	81—55	AUS
USA	67—48	CUB
USA	61—54	BRA
USA	96—31	EGY
USA	72—56	SPA
USA	99—33	JPN
USA	68—38	ITA

6. CZE (Vladimir Ptaček, Petr Vojtech, Jiři   3 4 584 580
Konopašek, Justin Sedlak,
Stanislav Kropilak, Jaroslav Kantu-
rek, Zedenek Kos, Jiři Pospišil,
Vladimir Padrta, Kamil Brabeneč,
Zdenek Douša, Gustav Hraška)

7. CUB (Juan Domecq, Roberto Herrera   4 3 616 574
Tabio, Juan Roca, Pedro Alejandro
Ortiz Herrera, Rafael Cãnizares
Poey, Daniel Scott Brice, Angel
Padron, Tomás Herrera Martínez,
Oscar Varona, Alejandro Urgellés
Guibot, Felix Morales Alphonso)

8. AUS (Andrew Campbell, Ian Watson,   2 5 625 652
Robert Cadee, Anthony Barnett,
Edward Palubinskas, Andris
Blicavs, Michael Tucker, Perry
Crosswhite, Russell Simon, Peter
Walsh, John Maddock, Ray Tomlin-
son)

    Final: USA 95—74 YUG
    3rd Place: SOV 100—72 CAN
    5th Place: ITA 98—75 CZE
    7th Place: CUB 92—81 AUS

For four years the United States waited to gain revenge for their loss to the U.S.S.R., but their train was almost derailed by a young man from New York who also had something to prove. Butch Lee of Marquette University had been prevented from trying out for the U.S. team when his college coach, Al McGuire, sent another player to the tryouts instead. Lee returned to his birthplace of Puerto Rico and made the team there. Puerto Rico faced the United States in the second game of the Olympic tournament: Lee shot 15 of 18 from the field and scored 35 points, while his teammate Neftali Rivera added 26. But the gutsy Puerto Ricans fell one point short and lost 95–94. However, the U.S.–U.S.S.R. showdown was not to be. In the semifinals, an inspired Yugoslav team upset the Soviets 89–84. The final was no contest, as the Americans took an 8–0 lead and never looked back. High scorer in the tournament for the United States was Adrian Dantley of Notre Dame, who averaged 19.3 points a game.

1980 Moscow T: 12, N: 12, D: 7.30.

		W	L	PF	PA
1. YUG	(Andro Knego, Dragan Kicanović, Rajko Žižić, Mihovil Nakić-Vojnovic, Zeljko Jerkov, Branko Skroce, Zoran Slavnić, Krešimir Čošić, Ratko Radovanović, Duje Krstulović, Dražen Dalipagić, Mirze Delibašić)	9	0	920	768
2. ITA	(Romeo Sacchetti, Roberto Brunamonti, Michael Sylvester, Enrico Gilardi, Fabrizio Della Fiori, Marco Solfrini, Marco Bonamico, Dino	5	4	744	757

Meneghin, Renato Villalta, Renzo
Vecchiato, Pierluigi Marzorati,
Pietro Generali)

3. SOV (Stanislav Eremin, Valery Milo-   7 2 943 797
serdov, Sergei Tarakanov, Olek-
sander Salnikov, Andrei Lopatov,
Nikolai Deruguin, Sergei Belov,
Volodymyr Tkachenko, Anatoly
Myshkin, Sergejus Jovaiša, Oleksander Bilostinny, Vladimir Zhigily)

4. SPA (Wayne Brabender, José Luis   4 5 871 843
Llorente Gento, Candido-Antonio
Sibilio, José María Margall Tauler,
Manuel Flores, Fernando Romay
Pereiro, Luis-Miguel Santillana,
Juan Antonio Corbalán Alfocea,
Ignacio Solozábal Igartua, Juan
Domingo De La Cruz Fermanelli,
Juan Lopéz Iturriaga, Juan Antô-
nio San Epifanio Ruiz)

5. BRA (André Ernesto Stoffel, Luiz Gus-   4 4 745 712
tavo de Lage, José Carlos Saiani,
Milton Setrini, Wagner Machado
da Silva, Marcos Abdalla Leite,
Gilson Trindade de Jesus, Marcel
Ramon de Souza, Adilson de
Nascimento, Marcelo Vido, Oscar
Daniel Schmidt, Ricardo Cardoso
Guimaraes)

6. CUB (Jorge More Rojas, Ruperto   2 6 660 704
Herrera Tabio, Pedro Alejandro
Ortiz Herrara, Noangel Luaces Ro-
driguez, Generoso Marquez Saes,
Raul Dubois Cumbath, Pedro
Abreu Pascual, Miguel Calderón
Gómez, Tomás Herrera Martínez,
Daniel Scott Brice, Alejandro
Urgellés Guibot, Felix Morales Al-
phonso)

7. POL (Dariusz Zelig, Leszek Doliński,   5 3 709 656
Wojciech Rosinski, Eugeńiusz
Kijewski, Jerzy Bińkowski, Andrzej
Michalski, Ireneusz Mulak, Justyn
Weglorz, Mieczyslaw Mylarnski,
Zdzislaw Myrda, Ryszard Prostak,
Kryzstof Fikiel)

8. AUS (Melvyn Dalgleish, Gordon Mc-   6 2 641 596
Leod, Philip Smyth, Larry Seng-
stock, Peter Ali, Michael Tucker,
Stephan Berheny, Les Riddle, Ian
Davies, Peter Walsh, Danny
Morseu, Perry Crosswhite)

    Final: YUG 86—77 ITA
    3rd Place: SOV 117—94 SPA

The Yugoslavs were led by Dalipagić and Kicanović, who averaged 24.4 and 23.6 points per game respectively. Although the United States boycotted the 1980 Olympics, there was one American who earned a medal in Moscow. Mike Sylvester, a guard on the Italian team, was born and raised in the United States, but gained dual citizenship in 1977 after living in Italy for three years. The team from India brought back memories of the 1948 Iraqi squad, losing their eight matches by an average score of 65.5 to 116.

1984 Los Angeles-Inglewood T: 12, N: 12, D: 8.10.

			W	L	PF	PA
1.	USA	(Steve Alford, Leon Wood, Patrick Ewing, Vern Fleming, Alvin Robertson, Michael Jordan, Joseph Kleine, Jon Koncak, Wayman Tisdale, Chris Mullin, Samuel Perkins, Jeffrey Turner)	8	0	763	506
2.	SPA	(Fernando Arecega Aperte, José Manuel Beirán Lozano, Juan Antonio Corbalán Alfocea, Juan Domingo De La Cruz Fermanelli, Andres Jiménez Fernández, José Luis Llorente Gento, José Manuel López Iturriaga, José María Margall Tauler, Fernando Martin Espina, Fernando Romay Pereiro, Juan Antônio San Epifanio Ruiz, Ignacio Solozábal Igartua)	6	2	697	688
3.	YUG	(Dražen Petrović, Aleksandar Petrović, Nebojsa Zorkić, Rajko Žižić, Ivan Sunara, Emir Mutapcić, Saabit Hadžić, Andro Knego, Ratko Radovanović, Mihovil Nakić-Vojnovic, Dražen Dalipagić, Branko Vukicević)	7	1	716	604
4.	CAN	(Howard Kelsey, Tony Simms, I. Enrico Pasquale, Karl Tilleman, Gerald François Kazanowski, James Triano, John Hatch, Gord Herbert, Bill Wennington, Romel Raffin, Greg Wiltjer, Dan Meagher)	4	4	681	639
5.	ITA	(Carlo Caglieris, Roberto Premier, Marco Bonamico, Enrico Gilardi, Walter Magnifico, Roberto Brunamonti, Renato Villata, Dino Meneghin, Antonello Riva, Renzo Vecchiato, Pierluigi Marzorati, Romeo Sacchetti)	6	2	718	614
6.	URU	(Horacio Lopez, Luis Larrosa, Luis Pierri Barros, Hebert Nuñez Gonzalez, Wilfredo Ruiz Bruno, Horacio Perdomo Shaban, Carlos Peinado Stagnero, Julio Pereyra Mele, Alvaro Tito Moreno, Juan Mignone Crisera, Victor Frattini Bononi)	3	5	688	776
7.	AUS	(Andrew Campbell, Damian Keogh, Philip Smyth, Larry Sengstock, Mark Dalton, Wayne Carroll, Melvyn Dalgleish, Andrew Gaze, Ian Davies, Daniel Morseu, Bradley Dalton, Raymond Borner)	4	4	654	683
8.	GER	(Christoph Korner, Vladimir Kadlec, Uwe Brauer, Uwe Sauer, Ulrich Peters, Klaus Zander, Michael Pappert, Armin Sowa, Detlef Schrempf, Uwe Blab, Ingo Mendel, Christian Welp)	2	6	600	635

Final: USA 96—65 SPA
3rd Place: YUG 88—82 CAN
5th Place: ITA 111—102 URU
7th Place: AUS 83—78 GER

The powerful U.S. team breezed through the tournament, winning by an average of 32 points per game. Their only weak game was a 78–67 quarterfinal victory over West Germany. The well-balanced American squad included Michael Jordan, who averaged 17.1 points per game, Wayman Tisdale, who led the team in rebounding, Patrick Ewing, the tournament blocked-shot leader with 18, Leon Wood, the tournament assist leader with 63, and Alvin Robertson, who shot 65% from the field and registered 17 steals.

1988 Seoul T: 12, N: 12, D: 9.30.

			W	L	PF	PA
1.	SOV	(Aleksandr Volkov, Tiit Sokk, Sergei Tarakanov, Šarunas Marčulonis, Igors Miglinieks, Vadim Tikhonenko, Rimas Kurtinaitis, Arvydas Sabonis, Victor Pankracskin, Valdemaras Chomičius, Oleksander Bilostinny, Valery Goborov)	7	1	728	637
2.	YUG	(Dražen Petrović, Zdravko Radulović, Zoran Čutura, Toni Kukoč, Žarko Paspalj, Zelimir Obradović, Jurij Zdovc, Stojan Vranković, Vlade Divac, Franjo Arapović, Dino Radja, Danko Cvjetićanin)	6	2	717	603
3.	USA	(Mitchell Richmond, Charles D. Smith, Vernell Coles, Hersey Hawkins, Jeffrey Grayer, Charles E. Smith, Willie Anderson, Stacey Augmon, Daniel Majerle, Danny Manning, Herman Reid, David Robinson)	7	1	733	490
4.	AUS	(Darryl Pearce, Philip Smyth, Larry Sengstock, Damian Keogh, Wayne Carroll, Lucien Longley, Andrew Gaze, Mark Bradtke, Bradley Dalton, Andrew Vlahov, Raymond Borner)	4	4	625	651
5.	BRA	(Paulo Almeida, Jorge Guerra, Gerson Victalino, João Vianna, Rolando Ferreira, Ricardo Cardoso Guimarães, Maury Ponikwar De Souza, Marcel Ponikwar De Souza, Luiz Azevedo, Paulo Silva, Oscar Schmidt Bezerra, Israel Andrade)	5	3	905	808
6.	CAN	(Norman Clarke, David Turcotte, I. Enrico Pasquale, Karl Tilleman, Alan Kristmanson, James Triano,	3	5	738	747

Dwight Walton, John Hatch, Barry Mungar, Romel Raffin, Wayne Yearwood, Gerald François Kazanowski)

		W	L	PF	PA
7. PUR	(José Ortiz Rijos, Federico López, Raymond Gause, Vicente Ithier, Jerome Mincy, Roberto Rioos, Angel Cruz, Ramon Rivas, Mario Morales, Edgar De Léon Cruz, Francisco Leon, Ramon Ramos)	4	4	618	677
8. SPA	(Jordi Villacampa, José Luis Llorente Gento, José Biryukov, José María Margall Tauler, Andres Jiménez Fernández, Enrique Andreu, José António Montero, Fernando Arcega Aperte, Ignacio Solozábal Igartua, Ferran Martinez, Antônio Martin, Juan Antônio San Epifanio Ruiz)	4	4	741	701

Final: SOV 76–63 YUG
3rd Place: USA 78–49 AUS
5th Place: BRA 106–90 CAN
7th Place: PUR 93–92 SPA

The long-awaited Olympic rematch between the U.S. and the U.S.S.R. finally took place in the semifinal round at Seoul, 16 years after the controversial 1972 Munich final. This time the Soviets took a 10-point halftime lead, beat back every American challenge, and won 82–76. With this bit of history out of the way, the Soviets faced their arch rivals, the Yugoslavs, in the final, in what would be the sixth match between the two teams in six months.

Although the Yugoslavs had won four of the five previous encounters, including a 92–79 victory in the tournament's opening round, they had to have been haunted by memories of two earlier losses. In the semifinals of the 1986 world championships, Yugoslavia led by 9 points with 47 seconds left in the game. The Soviets then hit three straight three-point shots and went on to win by 1 point in overtime. In the 1988 European Olympic qualifying tournament, the Soviets overcame a 15-point second-half deficit to defeat the Yugoslavs 86–83.

In the Olympic final, Yugoslavia took a 24–12 lead. However the Soviets, led by Lithuanians Marčulonis, Sabonis, and Kurtinaitis, went on a 19–2 run and were never headed again.

In a preliminary-round loss to Spain, Brazil's Oscar Schmidt scored an Olympic record 55 points. Schmidt also *averaged* 42¼ points per game for the entire tournament.

1992 Barcelona T: 12, N: 12, D: 8.8.

Magic Johnson and Michael Jordan of the 1992 U.S. "Dream Team."

		W	L	PF	PA
1. USA	(Larry Bird, Earvin "Magic" Johnson, David Robinson, Patrick Ewing, Scottie Pippen, Michael Jordan, Clyde Drexler, Karl Malone, John Stockton, Christopher Mullin, Charles Barkley, Christian Laettner)	8	0	938	588
2. CRO	(Dražen Petrović, Velimir Perasović, Danko Cvjetićanin, Toni Kukoč, Vladan Alanović, Franjo Arapović, Zan Tabak, Stojko Vranković, Alan Gregov, Arijan Komazec, Dino Radja, Aramis Naglic)	6	2	681	656
3. LIT	(Valdemaras Chomičius, Aluydas Pazdrazdis, Arunas Visockas, Darius Dimavicius, Romanas Brazdauskis, Gintaras Krapikas, Rimas Kurtinaitis, Arvydas Sabonis, Arturas Karnisovas, Šarunas Marčulonis, Gintaras Einikis, Sergejus Jovaisa)	6	2	753	725
4. SOV	(Goundars Vetra, Sergei Bazarevich, Igor Miglinieks, Vladimir Gorin, Sergei Panov, Vadim Tikhonenko, Viktor Berezhnoi, Vitaly Nosov, Dmitri Sukharev, Elshad Gadashev, Aleksandr Volkov, Oleksandr Bilostinny)	5	3	660	606
5. BRA	(Paulo Villas Boas, Jorge Guerra, Gerson Victalino, João Viana, Ricardo Cardoso Guimarães, Maury Ponikwar De Souza, Marcel Ponikwar De Souza, Aristides Santos, Wilson Kuhn Minuci, Oscar Schmidt Bezerra, Israel Machado)	4	4	692	741
6. AUS	(Kevin Dorge, Michael McKay, Philip Smyth, Larry Sengstock, Damian Keogh, Leroy Loggins, Andrew Gaze, Shane Heal, Mark Bradtke, Lucien Longley, Andrew Vlahov, Raymond Borner)	4	4	686	663

7. GER (Gunther Behnke, Henrik Rödl, 3 5 620 710
Armin Andres, Stephan Baeck,
Arnd Neuhaus, Henning Harnisch,
Uwe Blab, Detlef Schrempf, Hans
Gnad, Kai Nurnberger, Jens
Kujawa, Michael Jackel)

8. PUR (José Ortiz Rijos, Federico López 3 5 692 737
Camacho, Raymond Gause Santi-
ago, Edwin Pellot Rosa, Jerome
Mincy Clark, James Carter, Javier
Colón Rodríguez, Ramon Rivas
Contreras, Mario Morales Micheo,
Edgar De León Cruz, Eddie
Casiano, Richard Soto)

Final: USA 117-85 CRO
3rd Place: LIT 82-78 SOV
5th Place: BRA 90-80 AUS
7th Place: GER 96-86 PUR

On April 17, 1989, the International Amateur Basketball Federation (F.I.B.A.) voted 56-13 to allow NBA players to participate in the Olympics. A myth soon developed that the United States, humiliated by the defeat of its college all-stars in 1988, had manipulated the vote to regain dominance in the Olympics. In fact, the United States was one of the 13 nations that voted *against* the proposal. USA Basketball, the organization in charge of international basketball in the United States, had two major objections to allowing American professionals in the Olympics: They feared that the presence of a dozen millionaires representing the United States would kill their fundraising efforts in support of women's and junior basketball, and they feared that the inevitable lopsided nature of the games would adversely effect television ratings. Other basketball powers, such as the Soviet Union and Yugoslavia, saw the situation differently. They were willing to concede the gold medal to the United States in exchange for allowing their own best players to play in the NBA and still remain eligible for the Olympics. Those nations that had little or no chance for a medal reasoned that as long as they were going to lose anyway, they would rather lose to the best.

And so was born the greatest basketball team ever assembled. Coached by Chuck Daly, the United States squad was captained by veterans Magic Johnson and Larry Bird, and included Michael Jordan, Charles Barkley, Patrick Ewing, and Karl Malone. It wasn't just hype when they gained their nickname the Dream Team. A lot of Americans whined that it was overkill to send the Dream Team to Barcelona, but in the rest of the world the decision was greeted with enormous enthusiasm, especially in Barcelona itself, home of one of Spain's leading professional teams.

Before they could play for the gold medal, the United States squad had to go through the formality of qualifying for the Olympics in the Tournament of the Americas. The Americans' first opponent was the team from Cuba.

For over thirty years, the governments of the United States and Cuba had treated each other as the bitterest of enemies. It soon became apparent that this enmity did not extend to the basketball court. The start of the game had to be delayed briefly—the Cubans asked if they could have their photographs taken with the U.S. players. The United States won 136-57, but the Cubans seemed content. This set the tone for the rest of the Tournament of the Americas as well as the Olympics. For opposing teams, playing against the NBA giants was a dream come true; it was something they would tell their grandchildren about.

The United States won the Olympic tournament as easily as expected. The Americans scored over 100 points in every game and averaged a record-setting 117¼ points. Their closest victories were over Croatia, 103-70 and 117-85. Charles Barkley (18.0) and Michael Jordan (14.9) led the team in scoring, Malone and Ewing in rebounds, and Scottie Pippen and Magic Johnson in assists. Jordan had a tournament high 37 steals.

If the final lacked drama, the bronze-medal match made up for it. Lithuanians had traditionally played a significant role in Soviet basketball. However, for 52 years Lithuania had been a reluctant member of the Soviet Union, and support for independence ran high. In 1988, the Soviet players posed for a team photo after winning the gold medal. After the session was over, the four Lithuanian members of the team gathered for their own "team" photo. Four years later, in Barcelona, those four players were back in the Olympics representing an independent Lithuania. Another four members of the 1988 Soviet team were also in Barcelona— playing for the Unified Team of ex-Soviet republics. One of the four, Igor Miglinieks, was actually from Latvia, but competed for the Unified Team rather than miss the Olympics.

In pool play the ex-Soviets overcame a 19-point deficit to beat Lithuania 92-80. The Lithuanian players were heartbroken by the loss, but a week later they were given a chance for revenge when Croatia, trailing by six points with 65 seconds to play in the semifinals, upset the ex-Soviets 75-74. This meant that Croatia earned the silver medal while Lithuania and the ex-Soviets battled for the final platform at the medal ceremony. This time Lithuania, led by Šarunas Marčulonis and Arvydas Sabonis with 29 and 27 points, led for most of the game, kept their poise, and won 82-78.

In the end, the inclusion of the Dream Team at the Olympics was a big success. Although they were so much better than the rest of the teams that Coach Daly never called a single time-out, their average margin of victory—43¾ points—was not as great as the U.S. team of 1956, nor did they double the scores of their opponents, as did the U.S. teams of 1936 and 1948.

WOMEN

1896–1972 not held

1976 Montreal T: 6, N: 6, D: 7.27.

			W	L	PF	PA
1.	SOV	(Angelė Rupšienė, Tatyana Zakharova, Raisa Kurvyakova, Olga Barisheva, Tatyana Ovechkina, Nadezhda Shuvayeva, Uljana Semjonova, Nadezhda Zakharova, Nelly Feriabnikova, Olga Sukharnova, Tamara Dauinene, Natalya Klimova)	5	0	504	346
2.	USA	(Cindy Brogdon, Susan Rojcewicz, Ann Meyers, Lusia Harris, Nancy Dunkle, Charlotte Lewis, Nancy Lieberman, Gail Marquis, Patricia Roberts, Mary Anne O'Connor, Patricia Head, Julienne Simpson)	3	2	415	417
3.	BUL	(Nadka Golcheva, Penka Metodieva, Petkana Makaveyeva, Snezhana Mihailova, Krassima Gyurova, Krassimira Bogdanova, Todorka Yordanova, Diana Dilova, Margarita Shturkelova, Maria Stoyanova, Girgina Skerlatova, Penka Stoyanova)	3	2	365	377
4.	CZE	(Ludmila Kraliková, Dana Ptačková, Pavla Davidová, Ludmila Chmeliková, Martina Balaštiková, Ivana Korinkova, Marta Pechová, Hana Doušová, Božena Miklošovičová)	2	3	351	359
5.	JPN	(Kazuko Kadoya, Kimi Wakitashiro, Mieko Fukui, Miyako Otsuka, Miho Matsuoka, Kazuyo Hayashida, Teruko Miyamoto, Keiko Namai, Reiko Aonuma, Sachiyo Yamamoto, Misako Satake)	2	3	405	400
6.	CAN	(Joyce Douthwright, Joanne Sargent, Anne Hurley, Christine Critelli, Beverly Bland, Coleen Dufresne, Sheila Strike, Sylvia Sweeney, Carol Turney, Donna Hobin, Angela Johnson, Beverly Barnes)	0	5	336	477

The Soviet women's basketball team had not lost a game for five years and was undefeated in international tournament competition since 1958. Not surprisingly, they won the Olympic gold medal with ease. High scorer for the Soviets was 6-foot 10½-inch, 284-pound Uljana Semjonova of Riga, who averaged 19.4 points and 12.4 rebounds a game, despite the fact that she spent more than half the time on the bench. The United States was awarded second place by virtue of its 95–79 victory over Bulgaria.

Just how big was Semjonova? United States' player

Uljana Semjonova guards 6-foot 3-inch Lucy Harris (with ball) in 1976.

Nancy Lieberman recalled one non-Olympic game in which 6-foot 8-inch Anne Donovan was assigned to guard the Latvian giant. "I'd have the ball on the point," said Lieberman, "and Anne would get position on Uljana. But I couldn't see Anne. I'd dribble the ball and yell, 'Anne, where are you?' and I'd hear this voice, 'I'm back here.'"

Ten years after the Montreal Olympics, Nancy Lieberman became the first woman to play in a men's professional league when she took the court for the Springfield, Mass., Fame of the United States Basketball League.

1980 Moscow T: 6, N: 6, D: 7.30.

			W	L	PF	PA
1.	SOV	(Angelė Rupšienė, Lyubov Sharmay, Vida Beseliene, Olga Korosteleva, Tatyana Ovechkina, Nadezhda Olkhova [Shuvayeva], Uljana Semjonova, Lyudmila Rogozina, Nelly Feriabnikova, Olga Sukharnova, Tatyana Nadyrova [Zakharova], Tatyana Ivinskaya)	6	0	657	389

2. BUL (Nadka Golcheva, Penka Meto- 4 2 513 509
dieva, Petkana Makaveeva, Sne-
zhana Mihailova, Vania Dermand-
zhieva, Krassimira Bogdanova, Angelina Mihailova, Diana Brainova
[Dilova], Evladia Zakatanova,
Kostadinka Radkova, Silvia Ger-
manova, Penka Stoyanova)

3. YUG (Vera Djurasković, Mersada 4 2 424 429
Becirspahić, Jelica Komnenović,
Mira Bjedov, Vukica Mitić, Sanja
Ozegović, Sofija Pekić, Marija
Tonković, Zorica Djurković, Vesna
Despotović, Biljana Majstorović,
Jasmina Perazić)

4. HUN (Éva Gulyás, Ágnes Németh, Ilona 2 4 409 475
Kovács, Györgyi Vertetics, Zsuzsa
Boksay, Ilona Lörincz, Katalin Szu-
chy, Magda Gulyás, Ildikó Gulyás,
Judit Medgyesi, Lenke Kiss,
Erzsébet Szentesi)

5. CUB (Leonor Borrell Hernandez, Nancy 1 4 346 403
Aties Sanchez, Barbara Becquer
Rivero, Maria Moret Hernandez,
Inocenta Corbea Aguirre, Caridad
Despaigne Savig, Matilde Charro
Mendoza, Maria de Los Santos
Iglesias, Sonia de La Paz Galan,
Virginia Perez Viart, Margarita
Skeet Quiñones, Vicenta Salom
Smith)

6. ITA (Chiara Guzzonato, Nunziata 0 5 308 452
Serradimigni, Roberta Faccin, Li-
dia Gorlin, Emanuela Silimbani,
Wanda Sandon, Bianca Rossi, An-
tonietta Baistrocchi, Marinella Dra-
ghetti, Rosanna Vergnano, Marian-
gela Piancastelli, Orietta Grossi)

Final: SOV 104—73 BUL
3rd Place: YUG 68—65 HUN

The U.S.S.R. had an even easier time than they had had in 1976, winning all their games by 31 points or more. Their average score was 109.5 to 65. Semjonova, now 27 years old, was high scorer in the tournament, with 21.8 points a game. She also averaged 12.5 rebounds. In fact, Semjonova and her 6-foot 3-inch teammate Olga Sukharnova pulled down more rebounds than the entire 12-woman Italian team.

1984 Los Angeles-Inglewood T: 6, N: 6, D: 8.7.

		W	L	PF	PA
1. USA	(Teresa Edwards, Lea Henry, Ly- nette Woodard, Anne Donovan, Cathy Boswell, Cheryl Miller, Ja- nice Lawrence, Cindy Noble, Kim Mulkey, Denise Curry, Pamela McGee, Carol Menken-Schaudt)	6	0	516	320
2. KOR	(Choi Aei-young, Kim Eun-sook, Lee Hyung-sook, Choi Kyung-hee,	4	2	347	387

Lee Mi-ja, Moon Kyung-ja, Kim
Hwa-soon, Jeong Myung-hee, Kim
Young-hee, Sung Jung-a, Park
Chan-sook)

3. CHN (Chen Yuefang, Li Xiaoqin, Ba 3 3 381 405
Yan, Song Xiaobo, Qui Chen,
Wang Jun, Xiu Lijuan, Zheng
Haixia, Cong Xuedi, Zhang Hui,
Liu Qing, Zhang Yueqin)

4. CAN (Lynn Polson, Tracie McAra, Anna 2 4 370 398
Pendergast, Debbie Huband,
Carol Jane Sealey, Alison Lang,
Bev Smith, Sylvia Sweeney, Candi
Clarkson-Lohr, Toni Kordic, An-
drea Blackwell, Misty Thomas)

5. AUS (Robyn Maher, Bronwyn Marshall, 1 4 267 317
Jennifer Cheesman, Patricia Cock-
rem, Donna Quinn, Patricia
Mickan, Julie Nykiel, Kathryn Fos-
ter, Marina Moffa, Karen Dalton,
Wendy Laidlaw, Susanna Geh)

5. YUG (Sanja Ozegović, Slavica Suka, 1 4 293 347
Jelica Komnenović, Zagorka Poce-
ković, Stojna Vangelovska, Slavica
Pecikoza, Sladjana Golić, Polona
Dornik, Biljana Majstorović, Jas-
mina Perazić, Gvetana Dekleva,
Marija Uzelać)

Final: USA 85—55 KOR
3rd Place: CHN 63—57 CAN

In 1982 the Soviet women's 24-year winning streak was finally broken by a U.S. team that beat them 85–83 in Budapest. The following year the Soviets came back to score a two-point victory of their own in the final of the world championships. The eagerly anticipated Olympic showdown between the two squads was prevented by the Soviet boycott.

The U.S. team cruised through the Olympic tournament, winning all of their games by 28 points or more. Cheryl Miller, averaging 16.5 points and 7 rebounds per game, led the team in scoring, rebounding, steals and assists. Another U.S. star, Lynette Woodard, later became the first female member of the Harlem Globetrotters.

As for the big U.S.–U.S.S.R. showdown, it finally took place two years later in Moscow, when the American women crushed the Soviets 83–60 in the finals of the Goodwill Games. Five weeks later, again in Moscow, the two teams met in the title match of the world championships, and again the U.S. won easily, 108–88.

1988 Seoul T: 8, N: 8, D: 9.29.

		W	L	PF	PA
1. USA	(Teresa Edwards, Mary Ethridge, Cynthia Brown, Anne Donovan, Teresa Weatherspoon, Bridgette Gordon, Vitora Bullett, Andrea Lloyd, Katrina McClain, Jennifer	5	0	461	392

Gillom, Cynthia Cooper, Suzanne McConnell)

2. YUG (Stojna Vangelovska, Mara Lakić, Žana Lelas, Eleonora Vild, Kornelija Kvesić, Danira Nakić, Sladjana Golić, Polona Dornik, Razija Mujanović, Vesna Bajkuša, Andjelija Arbutina, Bojana Milošević) — 3 2 326 344

3. SOV (Olga Yevkova, Irina Gerlits, Olesya Barel, Irina Sumnikova, Olga Buryakina, Olga Yakovleva, Irina Minkh, Aleksandra Leonova, Yelena Khudashova, Vitalija Tuomaite, Galina Savitskaya, Natalya Zasulskaya) — 3 2 364 343

4. AUS (Robyn Maher, Jennifer Cheesman, Michele Timms, Donna Brown, Patricia Mickan, Julie Nykiel, Debra Slimmon, Marina Moffa, Karen Dalton, Shelley Gorman, Maree White) — 2 3 287 321

5. BUL (Nina Khadzhiyankova, Larissa Spasova, Mariana Naydenova, Tzonka Vaysilova, Vania Dermendzhieva, Sonia Dragomirova, Radmila Vasileva, Kostadinka Radkova, Yevladiya Stefanova, Madlen Staneva, Polina Tzekova, Mariana Chobanova) — 3 2 400 393

6. CHN (Han Qingling, Ling Guang, Li Xiaoqin, Zhao Wei, Peng Ping, Zheng Haixia, Cong Xuedi, Xue Cuilan, Liu Qing, Xu Chunmei) — 2 3 371 411

7. KOR (Lee Keum-jin, Kim Mal-lyun, Choi Kyung-hee, Lee Hyung-sook, Park Chan-mi, Woo Eun-kyung, Chung Mi-kyung, Kim Hwa-soon, Kim Hye-youn, Park Chan-sook, Sung Jung-a, Cho Mun-joo) — 2 3 416 375

8. CZE (Svatava Kysilková, Alena Kašová, Eva Kalužáková, Ivana Nováková, Zuzana Hájková, Anna Janoštinová, Zora Brziakova, Hana Zarevúcka, Erika Dobrovičova, Eva Křížová, Irma Valová, Eva Berková) — 0 5 339 382

Final: USA 77–70 YUG
3rd Place: SOV 68–53 AUS
5th Place: BUL 102–74 CHN
7th Place: KOR 77–59 CZE

The victorious U.S. team was led by playmaker Teresa Edwards, who averaged 16.6 points a game, and her former University of Georgia teammate, Katrina McClain, who led the Americans in scoring (17.6 points a game) and rebounding (10.4 per game).

1992 Barcelona-Badalona T: 8, N: 8, D: 8.7.

			W	L	PF	PA
1. SOV	(Yelena Zhirko, Yelena Baranova, Irina Gerlits, Yelena Tornikidu, Yelena Shvaybovich, Marina Tkachenko, Irina Minkh, Yelena Khudashova, Irina Sumnikova, Elen Bunatyants, Natalya Zasulskaya, Svetlana Zaboluyeva)		4	1	399	361
2. CHN	(Cong Xuedi, Li Xin, Liu Jun, Wang Fang, Zheng Dongmei, He Jun, Peng Ping, Zhen Haixia, Zheng Xiulin, Li Dongmei, Liu Quing, Zhan Shuping)		3	2	380	372
3. USA	(Teresa Edwards, Daedra Charles, Clarissa Davis, Tammy Jackson, Teresa Weatherspoon, Vickie Orr, Victoria Bullett, Carolyn Jones, Katrina McClain, Medina Dixon, Cynthia Cooper, Suzanne McConnell)		4	1	479	334
4. CUB	(Leonor Borrel Hernández, Ana Hernández Álverez, Olga Vigil Gómez, Grisel Herrera Méndez, Biosoty Lagno Frometa, Judith Aguila Hernández, María León Molinet, Yamilet Martínez Calderón, Dalia Henry Hernández, Lissett Castillo Iglesias, Regla Hernández Buides, Milayda Enrique Parrado)		3	2	390	427
5. SPA	(Patrica Hernández Arencibia, Carolina Mújica Vallejo, Blanca Ares Torres, Pilar Alonso López, Mónica Pulgar Machado, Margarita Geuer Draeger, Almudena Vara Rivra, Ana Álvaro Bascuñana, Mónica Messa López, Marina Ferragut Castillo, Elisabeth Cebrián Scheurer, Catlota Castrejana Fernández)		3	2	332	376
6. CZE	(Iveta Bieliková, Martina Liptáková, Anna Janoštinová, Eva Nemcová, Andrea Chupíková, Eva Antalecová, Renata Hiráková, Adriana Chamajová, Erika Buriánová, Kamila Vodicková, Milena Razgova, Eva Berková)		1	4	315	363
7. BRA	(Hortência Marcari Oliva, Helen Santos Luz, Nadia Bento De Lima, Vania Souza, Maria Gonçalves, Janeth Santos Arcain, Adriana Santos, Marta Souza Sobral, Ruth Souza, Maria Bertolotti, Joycenara Batista, Simone Pontello)		2	3	385	398
8. ITA	(Elena Paparazzo, Monica Bastiani, Mara Fullin, Stefania Salvemini, Anna Costalunga, Francesca Rossi, Angela Arcangeli, Catarina Pollini, Stefania Stanzani, Silvia Todeschini, Giuseppina Tufano, Stefania Passaro)		0	5	353	402

Final: SOV 76–66 CHN

3rd Place: USA 88-74 CUB
5th Place: SPA 59-58 CZE
7th Place: BRA 86-83 ITA

Between 1982 and 1991 the United States' women won 42 straight games at international tournaments. However, at the Pan American Games in Havana the Americans were beaten by both Brazil and Cuba. Still, at the Barcelona Olympics the United States team looked unbeatable, crushing their three opponents in the qualifying pool by an average of 45.7 points. Meanwhile, the team from the former Soviet Union looked sluggish, even losing their opening game against Cuba 91-89. But in the semifinals, the ex-Soviets stunned the Americans 79-73. The other semifinal was won by the dark-horse team from China, who, surprisingly, overwhelmed the Cubans 109-70. In the final, China led 16-14 after six minutes. Then the ex-Soviets scored 16 points in a row and never relinquished the lead again. The victors were led by 6-foot 2½-inch power forward Natalya Zasulskaya, who averaged 17.4 points and 8.6 rebounds a game. She also led the tournament in fouls received with 7.2 per game. Zasulskaya was from Lithuania, but chose to continue playing with her teammates from the former Soviet republics so that she could take part in the Olympics.

BOXING

Light Flyweight—48 Kg
Flyweight—51 Kg
Bantamweight—54 Kg
Featherweight—57 Kg
Lightweight—60 Kg
Light Welterweight—63.5 Kg

Welterweight—67 Kg
Light Middleweight—71 Kg
Middleweight—75 Kg
Light Heavyweight—81 Kg
Heavyweight—91 Kg
Super Heavyweight—Unlimited Weight

KEY TO ABBREVIATIONS
Dec = Decision
KO = Knockout
Pts=Points
Ret = Retired
RSC = Referee stopped contest

Amateur boxing matches consist of three three-minute rounds with one-minute breaks between rounds. Olympic tournaments are single elimination and boxers are not seeded. For this reason it is possible—and indeed often happens—that the two best fighters in a division meet in their first match rather than in the final. Between 1904 and 1948, losing semifinalists faced off in a bronze medal fight; however, since 1952 both defeated semifinalists have been awarded bronze medals.

Several measures have been taken to protect the safety of the fighters, including the wearing of protective headgear. In addition, a boxer who has been knocked down or stunned may not resume fighting until the count of eight. Three eight counts in a round or four in a fight result in automatic defeat for the downed boxer. A single ten count is deemed a knockout, ending the fight. The referee is empowered to stop a contest if he believes a boxer is receiving excessive punishment or is otherwise in danger. Boxers must be as least 17 years old and no more than 32 years old. Although these age restrictions are a recent addition to the rules, in fact only one Olympic champion, Jackie Fields (1924 featherweight), has been younger than 17, and only one, Richard Gunn (1908 featherweight), has been older than 32.

Since 1960, Olympic bouts have been judged by five ringside judges. Like any judged sport, boxing is open to controversy. However no other sport has had anything approaching the tumultuous history of boxing, complete with attacks on referees and judges, sit-down strikes by boxers, and full-scale riots. These incidents peaked in the 1920s and returned in the 1980s. In the wake of several absurd decisions and outrageous scenes at the 1988 Seoul Games, the International Amateur Boxing Association (AIBA) instituted numerous reforms that were put in force in Barcelona in 1992. These included daily alcohol tests for all referees and judges, an attempt to keep referees and judges "out of reach"

of national associations and their officials, and a requirement that referees and judges not attend cocktail parties without the permission of the AIBA executive committee. The most visible reform related to the method of scoring. Prior to 1992 each judge voted for a winner based on his scoring of each round. The boxer who gained the vote of a majority of judges won the fight. (In 1984, whenever the judges split 3-2, the decision was referred to a five-member Jury of Appeals.) In 1992, however, AIBA introduced computerized scoring. Each judge was given a console. Whenever a boxer connected with a punch, the judge pushed a button corresponding to that boxer. If three of the five judges pushed their buttons within one second, the boxer automatically received a point. Whichever boxer registered the most points at the end of three rounds was declared the winner. Unfortunately, this system was not without its flaws. For example, in the words of a post-Olympic report issued by AIBA vice-president Emil Jetchev, it was discovered that "in some judges the eyesight was found to be poor," "judges have different motor reactions," "a certain degree of uncertainty and even fear is noticeable among judges in regard of electronics," and—imagine this—"there exist different criteria among the judges in assessing a bout." Because of these problems, there were several notable cases in Barcelona in which one boxer would batter his opponent throughout a round and yet receive no points, or in which all five judges would give the nod to one boxer, yet his opponent would win the fight. In fact, the AIBA was so embarrassed by the results of the Griffin-Lozano light-flyweight bout that they ceased to allow the public access to individual judge's scores and, to this day, the complete Barcelona results remain under lock and key.

Boxing remains one of the last Olympic sports in which professionals are not allowed to compete, although at least 75 Olympic boxers have gone on to become professional champions. This is probably a wise restriction, considering the dangers involved in potential mismatches. However, in practice this gives an unfair advantage to nations with Communist governments that don't allow professional boxing, and especially to Cuba, the only remaining Communist nation with a boxing tradition.

In the charts that follow, defeated quarterfinalists are listed as tied for fifth place, but defeated quarterfinalists who did not win a match are not included.

LIGHT FLYWEIGHT
(48 kg–106 lbs)

1896–1964 not held

1968 Mexico City C: 24, N: 24, D: 10.26.

			FINAL MATCH
1.	Francisco Rodríguez	VEN	Dec 3–2
2.	Jee Yong-ju	KOR	
3.	Harlan Marbley	USA	
3.	Hubert Skrzypczak	POL	
5.	Joseph Donovan (AUS), Hatha Karunaratne (SRL), Alberto Morales (MEX), Gabriel Ogun (NGR)		

After Rodríguez's victory was announced, few in the crowd could fail to be moved by the sight of the 23-year-old Venezuelan joyfully weeping into the national flag that his seconds had draped over his shoulders. Rodríguez is the only Venezuelan gold-medalist in Olympic history.

1972 Munich C: 31, N: 31, D: 9.10.

			FINAL MATCH
1.	György Gedó	HUN	Dec 5–0
2.	U-Gil Kim	PRK	
3.	Ralph Evans	GBR	
3.	Enrique Rodríguez	SPA	
5.	Rafael Carbonell (CUB), Chanyalew Haile (ETH), Vladimir Ivanov (SOV/RUS), James Odwori (UGA)		

1976 Montreal C: 27, N: 27, D: 7.31.

			FINAL MATCH
1.	Jorge Hernández	CUB	Dec 4–1
2.	Li Byong-uk	PRK	
3.	Orlando Maldonado	PUR	
3.	Payao Pooltarat	THA	
5.	György Gedó (HUN), Armando Guevara (VEN), Park Chan-lee (KOR), Hector Patri (ARG)		

Hernández was the reigning world amateur and Pan American champion. Eighteen-year-old bronze medalist Payao Pooltarat from Prachub Khirikhan was the first Thai athlete to win an Olympic medal. He accomplished this by outpointing defending champion Gedó in the quarterfinals.

1980 Moscow C: 22, N: 22, D: 8.2.

			FINAL MATCH
1.	Shamil Sabirov	SOV/RUS	Dec 3–2
2.	Hipólito Ramos	CUB	
3.	Ismail Hjuseinov	BUL	
3.	Li Byong-uk	PRK	
5.	György Gedó (HUN), Dietmar Geilich (GDR), Dumitru Şchiopu (ROM), Ahmed Siad (ALG)		

Gedó became the only boxer to compete in four Olympics.

1984 Los Angeles C: 24, N: 24, D: 8.11.

			FINAL MATCH
1.	Paul Gonzales	USA	Default
2.	Salvatore Todisco	ITA	
3.	José Marcelino Bolivar	VEN	
3.	Keith Mwila	ZAM	
5.	Mamoru Kuroiwa (JPN), John Lyon (GBR), Carlos Motta-Taracena (GUA), Rafael Ramos (PUR)		

It was less than four miles from Paul Gonzales' home in the Aliso Village housing project to the gold medal platform at the 1984 Olympics, but so rocky was the road he traveled to get there that they might as well have been a continent apart.

Growing up in what he called "a ghetto's ghetto," Gonzales saw his father walk out when he was 7, leaving his mother to raise 8 children on her own. By the time he was nine years old, Paul Gonzales had joined Primera Flats, one of 13 "major" gangs operating in his area. When he was 12 years old, he and his buddies were out cruising one night, when their '64 Chevy Impala stalled in an area controlled by a rival gang. Shots were fired through the car window and Gonzales was hit in the side of the head. Following a well-known local procedure, he washed his head in a lake at a nearby park and then had his cousin remove the remaining pieces of shot and glass with a pair of tweezers.

When he was 15, Gonzales was arrested on a murder charge. Fortunately he had a perfect alibi—he was boxing at the time—and his coach was a policeman. That policeman, Al Stankie, had convinced Gonzales to try his hands at boxing after seeing the 10-year-old in a street fight. At first Gonzales climbed into the gym through a back window, since it was located in the basement of the police station and he didn't want his fellow gang members to think he was a snitch.

As he began to take boxing more seriously, his friends would mock him because he stopped drinking, went home each night at 9 o'clock, and was up at 5 in the morning, running. But as he achieved more and more success, his friends became protective, making sure that he didn't stay out late or break training.

When he was 17, Gonzales missed 11 months of competition because of surgery to remove a bone spur from the back of his right hand. His first bout after the layoff was an upset victory over defending Olympic champion Shamil Sabirov.

At the Los Angeles Olympics, Gonzales blocked out the pressure and expectations of the wildly enthusiastic local crowd by imagining, as he entered the ring for each bout, that he was fighting in his opponent's hometown. His performances were impressive enough to earn him the Val Barker award for the best boxer at the Olympics.

He won his final match in a walkover, when his opponent, Salvatore Todisco, showed up with his hand in a cast, having broken his thumb in his semifinal bout. Gonzales himself had sustained a hairline stress fracture above his right wrist during his first round fight, requiring post-Olympic surgery and a cast of his own.

When he mounted the gold-medal platform, Paul Gonzales carried with him a United States flag in one hand and a Mexican flag in the other. He also carried with him the hopes and dreams of many disadvantaged youths, to whom he sent a message: "I won this gold medal, not just for myself or my mom or my coach, but for the kids like me who are always told, 'You're nothing.' The only way you're going to make it come true is by dreaming it, and when you dream something, you've got to turn it into reality. Because if you don't, you just die with your dreams."

Gonzales turned his Olympic dream into reality, but his dream of becoming a professional champion never materialized. In 1986 he broke a knuckle in a street fight and in 1987 he broke his ankle and injured his knee when he accidentally engaged the gear shift in his Corvette convertible and ran over his own leg. In 1988 he fractured his hip in a bicycle accident. Although he did not personally fulfill his potential as a professional, Gonzales paved the way for other low-weight boxers to earn the kind of money that had previously been reserved for heavier fighters.

1988 Seoul C: 34, N: 34, D: 10.1.

		FINAL MATCH
1. Ivailo Hristov [Ismail Hjuseinov]	BUL	Dec 5–0
2. Michael Carbajal	USA	
3. Róbert Isaszegi	HUN	
3. Leopoldo Serantes	PHI	
5. Aleksandr Makhmutov (SOV/RUS), Mahjoub M'Jirih (MOR), Robert Scott Olson (CAN), Chatchai Sasakul (THA)		

Ivailo Hristov, a 28-year-old sailor, used a quick left jab and clever counterpunching to earn his gold medal. However, he was aided by a secret weapon: his frequent changes of name. Few ringside observers in Seoul were aware that Hristov was the same fighter who won an Olympic bronze medal in 1980 using the name Ismail Hjuseinov, a world championship in 1982 as Ismail Mustafov, and a silver medal at the 1985 European championship as Ivajlo Marinov. The name changes were not meant to cause confusion or to put his opponents off their guard—Hristov, a member of Bulgaria's Turkish minority, was forced to change his name because of the Bulgarian government's attempt to crush all remnants of Turkish ethnic identity.

1992 Barcelona—Badalona C: 30, N: 30, D: 8.8.

		FINAL MATCH
1. Rogelio Marcelo García	CUB	Pts 24–10
2. Daniel Bojinov	BUL	
3. Jan Quast	GER	
3. Roel Velasco	PHI	
5. Valentin Barbu (ROM), Pál Lakatos (HUN), Rafael Lozano Muñoz (SPA), Rowan Williams (GBR)		

No boxer in the 1992 Olympic tournament except Félix Savón was considered more of a gold medal shoo-in than two-time world champion Eric Griffin of the United States. Griffin's only serious challenge was expected to come from Rogelio Marcelo, and Griffin had beaten him easily each of the five times they had met. But in his second fight in Barcelona, Griffin ran up against an opponent he couldn't beat—the new computerized scoring system. All five judges had Griffin outpointing hometown favorite Rafael Lozano—19-9, 18-9, 26-17, 8-5 and 10-9—but he lost the bout 5-6 because the judges didn't push the buttons of their consoles at the same time. In the closing seconds of the second round, Griffin landed a flurry of five hard blows to Lozano's head, leading the referee to step in and call a standing eight-count. Yet Griffin earned not a single point for the barrage. With Griffin out, Marcelo breezed to the gold medal. His closest match was an 11-3 quarterfinal victory over Lozano. Lozano was also involved in a bit of history in his opening match. His opponent, Fana Twala, was the first black athlete to officially represent South Africa. (The two Zulu runners who competed in the 1904 Marathon were independent entries.)

FLYWEIGHT
(51 kg–112½ lbs)

1896–1900 not held

1904 St. Louis C: 2, N: 1, D: 9.22.
(47.63 kg–105 lbs)

		FINAL MATCH
1. George Finnegan	USA	RSC 1
2. Miles Burke	USA	

For some unknown reason Burke was allowed to compete even though he was almost three pounds over the weight limit.

1906–1912 not held

1920 Antwerp C: 16, N: 9, D: 8.24.
(50.80 kg–112 lbs)

		FINAL MATCH
1. Frank DiGennara	USA	Dec
2. Anders Petersen	DEN	
3. William Cuthbertson	GBR	
4. Charles Albert	FRA	

5. Joseph Charpentier (BEL), Jean-Baptiste Rampignon (FRA), Nicolas Zegwaard (HOL), Peter Zivic (USA)

Seven and a half years later, DiGennara, fighting under the name Frankie Genaro, won the World Flyweight title by defeating Frenchy Belanger in Toronto.

1924 Paris C: 19, N: 13, D: 7.20.
(50.80 kg–112 lbs)

		FINAL MATCH
1. Fidel LaBarba	USA	Dec
2. James McKenzie	GBR	
3. Raymond Fee	USA	
4. Rinaldo Castellenghi	ITA	

5. Oscar Bergström (SWE), R. Biete-Berdes (SPA), John Mac-Gregor (CAN), Stephen Rennie (CAN)

LaBarba, an 18-year-old Los Angeles high school student, went on to a successful professional career. In 1925 he defeated Frankie Genaro for the American Flyweight title, and in 1927 he won the vacant World Flyweight title. He later worked as a screenwriter in Hollywood.

1928 Amsterdam C: 19, N: 19, D: 8.11.
(50.80 kg–112 lbs)

		FINAL MATCH
1. Antal Kocsis	HUN	Dec
2. Armand Appell	FRA	
3. Carlo Cavagnoli	ITA	
4. B. "Buddy" Lebanon	SAF	

5. Hubert Ausböck (GER), Barend "Ben" Bril (HOL), Alfred Gaona (MEX), Cuthbert Taylor (GBR)

In the first contest of the tournament, 16-year-old Hyman Miller of California appeared to have easily defeated Marcel Santos of Belgium. When the decision was announced in Santos' favor, Miller's confident smile turned to convulsive sobbing. The U.S. boxing team was so outraged that they requested permission to withdraw all their boxers from the Olympics. However the president of the U.S. Olympic Committee, Major-General Douglas MacArthur, refused permission, stating, "Americans never quit." The eventual winner, Antal Kocsis, was Hungary's first Olympic gold medalist in boxing. The following year he turned professional and emigrated to the United States.

1932 Los Angeles C: 12, N: 12, D: 8.13.
(50.80 kg–112 lbs)

		FINAL MATCH
1. István Énekes	HUN	Dec
2. Francisco Cabañas	MEX	
3. Louis Salica	USA	
4. Thomas Pardoe	GBR	

5. Edelweis Rodriguez (ITA), Werner Spannagel (GER)

1936 Berlin C: 25, N: 25, D: 8.15.
(50.80 kg–112 lbs)

		FINAL MATCH
1. Willi Kaiser	GER	Dec
2. Gavino Matta	ITA	
3. Louis Daniel Laurie	USA	
4. Alfredo Carlomagno	ARG	

5. Raoul Degryse (BEL), William Passmore (SAF), Edmund Sobkowiak (POL), Fidel Tricanico (URU)

1948 London C: 26, N: 26, D: 8.13.

		FINAL MATCH
1. Pascual Pérez	ARG	Dec
2. Spartaco Bandinelli	ITA	
3. Han Soo-ann	KOR	
4. František Majdloch	CZE	

5. Alex Bollaert (BEL), H.A.H. Corman (HOL), Luis Martinez Zapata (SPA), Frank Sodano (USA)

Pascual Pérez, a 22-year-old clerk in the Chamber of Deputies in Buenos Aires, faced his most difficult challenge *before* the fighting began. Pérez was unexpectedly disqualified for being overweight. However, it was later discovered that officials had confused him with his bantamweight teammate Arnoldo *Pares*.

1952 Helsinki C: 28, N: 28, D: 8.2.

		FINAL MATCH
1. Nathan Brooks	USA	Dec 3–0
2. Edgar Basel	GER	
3. Anatoly Bulakov	SOV/RUS	
3. William Toweel	SAF	

5. Thorbjorn Clausen (NOR), David Dower (GBR), Mircea Dobrescu (ROM), Han Soo-ann (KOR)

1956 Melbourne C: 19, N: 19, D: 12.1.

		FINAL MATCH
1. Terence Spinks	GBR	Dec
2. Mircea Dobrescu	ROM	
3. John Caldwell	IRL	
3. René Libeer	FRA	

5. Warner Batchelor (AUS), Ray Perez (USA), Vladimir Stolnikov (SOV), Kenji Yonekura (JPN)

1960 Rome C: 33, N: 33, D: 9.5.

			FINAL MATCH
1.	Gyula Török	HUN	Dec 3–2
2.	Sergei Sivko	SOV/RUS	
3.	Abdelmoneim Elguindi	EGY	
3.	Kiyoshi Tanabe	JPN	
5.	Humberto Barrera (USA), Miguel Botta (ARG), Mircea Dobrescu (ROM), Manfred Homberg (GER)		

1964 Tokyo C: 28, N: 28, D: 10.23.

			FINAL MATCH
1.	Fernando Atzori	ITA	Dec 4–1
2.	Artur Olech	POL	
3.	Robert Carmody	USA	
3.	Stanislav Sorokin	SOV/RUS	
5.	Otto Babiasch (GER), Choh Dong-kih (KOR), Constantin Ciucă (ROM), John McCafferty (IRL)		

After one minute and six seconds of the first round of his quarterfinal bout against Stanislav Sorokin, Korean boxer Choh Dong-kih was disqualified for holding his head too low. Unable to accept this verdict, Choh sat down in the middle of the ring and refused to leave. His sitdown strike continued for 51 minutes, until officials persuaded him to abandon his protest. Ironically, Sorokin was forced to withdraw before his next fight because of a cut that wasn't healing. The winner, Sardinian house-painter Fernando Atzori, fought the final with a black eye.

1968 Mexico City C: 26, N: 26, D: 10.26.

			FINAL MATCH
1.	Ricardo Delgado	MEX	Dec 5–0
2.	Artur Olech	POL	
3.	Servilio Oliveira	BRA	
3.	Leo Rwabwogo	UGA	
5.	Tibor Badari (HUN), Joseph Destimo (GHA), Tetsuaki Nakamura (JPN), Nicolai Novikov (SOV/RUS)		

Heriberto Cintron of Puerto Rico was standing in the ring waiting for his first-round bout with Polish policeman Artur Olech when he was suddenly disqualified for being younger than the minimum age of 17 years. He was, in fact, 16 years and one month old.

1972 Munich C: 37, N: 37, D: 9.10.

			FINAL MATCH
1.	Georgi Kostadinov	BUL	Dec 5–0
2.	Leo Rwabwogo	UGA	
3.	Leszek Blazyński	POL	
3.	Douglas Rodríguez	CUB	
5.	Neil McLaughlin (IRL), Calixto Perez (COL), You Chong-man (KOR), Boris Zoriktuev (SOV/RUS)		

Most Olympic boxers who went on to become world champions were also Olympic champions, or at least medalists.

But there is one boxing star who made little impression in his Olympic debut. As an underage 15-year-old representative of Puerto Rico, Wilfredo Gomez lost a 4–1 decision in the first round to Mohamed Selin of Egypt, who was in turn knocked out in his next fight. Less than five years later, on May 21, 1977, Gomez won the World Super Bantamweight championship and on March 9, 1979, he won the Junior Featherweight title. He added the WBC Featherweight title on May 19, 1985.

1976 Montreal C: 26, N: 26, D: 7.31.

			FINAL MATCH
1.	Leo Randolph	USA	Dec 3–2
2.	Ramón Duvalon	CUB	
3.	Leszek Blazyński	POL	
3.	David Torosyan	SOV/ARM	
5.	Ian Clyde (CAN), Jong Jo-ung (PRK), David Larmour (IRL), Alfrede Perez (VEN)		

Leo Randolph, an 18-year-old high school student from Tacoma, Washington, called his surprise victory "the best thing that happened to me since I became a Christian in 1969."

1980 Moscow C: 20, N: 20, D: 8.2.

			FINAL MATCH	
1.	Peter Lessov	BUL	RSC 2	2:08
2.	Viktor Myroshnychenko	SOV/UKR		
3.	Hugh Russell	IRL		
3.	János Váradi	HUN		
5.	Roman Gilberto (MEX), Daniel Radu (ROM), Henryk Średnicki (POL), Yo Ryon-sik (PRK)			

1984 Los Angeles C: 31, N: 31, D: 8.11.

			FINAL MATCH
1.	Steven McCrory	USA	Dec 4–1
2.	Redzep Redzepovski	YUG	
3.	Ibrahim Bilali	KEN	
3.	Eyup Can	TUR	
5.	Peter Ayesu (MLW), Jeffrey Fenech (AUS), Heo Yong-mo (KOR), Laureano Ramirez (DOM)		

Detroit's Steve McCrory, the younger brother of World Welterweight champion Milton McCrory, won a close decision over veteran Redzep Redzepovski, who complained, "As long as an American is standing on his feet for three rounds it is hard to get a decision over him."

1988 Seoul C: 44, N: 44, D: 10.2.

			FINAL MATCH
1.	Kim Kwang-sun	KOR	Dec 4–1
2.	Andreas Tews	GDR	
3.	Mario González	MEX	
3.	Timofei Skriabin	SOV/MOL	
5.	Benaissa Abed (ALG), Meluin Deleon (DOM), Alfred Amon Kotey (GHA), Serafim Todorov (BUL)		

In 1984, Kim Kwang-sun was favored to win the light flyweight division in Los Angeles. However, he was upset in his first-round bout by eventual gold-medal winner Paul Gonzales. Deeply depressed, Kim vowed that he would return to the Olympics and win a gold medal himself. For four years his mother went to a Buddhist temple every day and prayed for her son. In 1988, Kim, by then a flyweight, blasted his way through four opponents and into the final. There he faced European champion Andreas Tews, who had beaten him 3-2 at the 1987 World Cup. This time Kim dominated the last two rounds, bringing great joy to the highly partisan crowd.

1992 Barcelona—Badalona C: 31, N: 31, D: 8.9.

			FINAL MATCH
1. Choi Chol-su	PRK	Pts 12-2
2. Raúl González Sánchez	CUB	
3. Timothy Austin	USA	
3. István Kovács	HUN	
5. Héctor Ávila (DOM), Benjamin Mwangata (TAN), Robert Peden (AUS), David Serradas Suárez (VEN)		

The critical bout took place in the semifinals when world champion István Kovács faced Choi Chol-su, the man he had beaten 25-15 to win the 1991 title. This time it was Choi who came out on top, 10-5. In the round of 16 Choi had barely survived a late rush by Paul Ingle of Great Britain, winning 13-12. The North Korean had no such problems in the final, easily outgunning González.

BANTAMWEIGHT
(54 kg—119½ lbs)

1896–1900 not held

1904 St. Louis C: 2, N: 1, D: 9.22.
(52.16 kg–115 lbs)

			FINAL MATCH
1. Oliver Kirk	USA	RSC 3
2. George Finnegan	USA	

1906 not held

1908 London C: 6, N: 2, D: 10.27.
(52.62 kg–116 lbs)

			FINAL MATCH
1. Henry Thomas	GBR	Dec
2. John Condon	GBR	
3. William Webb	GBR	

1912 not held

1920 Antwerp C: 12, N: 7, D: 8.24.
(53.52 kg–118 lbs)

			FINAL MATCH
1. Clarence Walker	SAF	Dec
2. Chris Graham	CAN	
3. George McKenzie	GBR	
4. Henri Hébrants	BEL	
5. Edward Hartman (USA), Henri Ricard (FRA), Sam Vogel (USA)		

1924 Paris C: 21, N: 15, D: 7.20.
(53.52 kg–118 lbs)

			FINAL MATCH
1. William Smith	SAF	Dec
2. Salvatore Tripoli	USA	
3. Jean Ces	FRA	
4. Oscar Andrén	SWE	
5. Albert Barber (GBR), Antonio Sanchez Dietz (SPA), Jacques Lemouton (FRA), Benito Pertuzzo (ARG)		

Joe Lazarus of Cornell University had the unusual misfortune of knocking out his opponent, Oscar Andrén of Sweden, and yet being declared the loser. As Andrén was being revived, the referee, Maurice Siegel of France, announced that Lazarus was disqualified for striking the knockout punch while breaking from a clinch. Siegel later apologized to U.S. officials for his mistaken call and Andrén and the Swedish team manager urged Lazarus to file a protest. Moved by the Swedes' good sportsmanship, Lazarus declined, as did the U.S. officials.

1928 Amsterdam C: 18, N: 18, D: 8.11.
(53.52 kg–118 lbs)

			FINAL MATCH
1. Vittorio Tamagnini	ITA	Dec
2. John Daley	USA	
3. Harry Isaacs	SAF	
4. Edward Traynor	IRL	
5. John Garland (GBR), Vincent Glionna (CAN), Carmelo Robledo (ARG), János Széles (HUN)		

Controversy developed when Harry Isaacs was announced the winner of his semifinal bout with John Daley. In what the U.S. Official Report would refer to as "a demonstration never equalled in Olympic history," American supporters stormed the judges' table demanding that the decision be reversed. After several minutes, it was announced that one of the judges had transposed his figures for the two fighters. Daley was declared the victor. He moved on to the final while Isaacs went home certain that he had been robbed. It was, in the words of the London *Daily Express,* "an example of vacillation unprecedented in the history of a meeting of such worldwide scope."

In the final, Daley, perhaps rattled by his earlier experience, fought below his usual standard and Tamagnini was given a narrow victory. Again the Americans howled their disapproval. Complained one British reporter, "For more than two hours, there was little else save din and clatter, screeching and raving, and several skirmishes with the police. . . ." This time it was to no avail: the decision stood.

1932 Los Angeles C: 10, N: 10, D: 8.13.

			FINAL MATCH
1.	Horace Gwynne	CAN	Dec
2.	Hans Ziglarski	GER	
3.	José Villanueva	PHI	
4.	Joseph Lang	USA	
5.	Carlos Alberto Pereyra (ARG)		

Although he made his living as a jockey, Toronto's Lefty Gwynne started boxing when he was 4 years old. He and his 6-year-old brother put on exhibitions for British army troops in Wales. In Los Angeles Gwynne made no attempt to study the other fighters and didn't even bother to learn who his next opponent would be until he arrived at the arena. When Gwynne, now 19, returned to Toronto after winning the Olympic gold medal, the city honored him with a small reception and a gold watch. Gwynne, well aware of the realities of the Depression, immediately asked the mayor for a job. The mayor just laughed. Although Gwynne did fight professionally until 1939, there was little money for bantamweights and he was forced to supplement his income by working as a security guard at a Ford Motors auto plant.

1936 Berlin C: 24, N: 24, D: 8.15.
(53.52 kg–118 lbs)

			FINAL MATCH
1.	Ulderico Sergo	ITA	Dec
2.	Jack Wilson	USA	
3.	Fidel Ortiz	MEX	
4.	Stig Cederberg	SWE	
5.	Joseph Cornelis (BEL), Oscar Larrazabal (PHI), Alexander Hannan (SAF), Shunpei Haskioka (JPN)		

1948 London C: 30, N: 30, D: 8.13.

			FINAL MATCH
1.	Tibor Csik	HUN	Dec
2.	Giovanni Battista Zuddas	ITA	
3.	Juan Venegas	PUR	
4.	Alvaro Vicente Domenech	SPA	
5.	James Carruthers (AUS), Celestine Gonzalez Henriquez (CHI), Willie Lenihan (IRL), Albert Perera (SRL)		

Argentina's Arnoldo Pares, although innocent of any wrongdoing, was the center of much confusion and controversy. At the weigh-in he was found to be overweight. In a panic, his supporters cut off his hair, rubbed him down with a towel, scrubbed the soles of his feet, and blew the dust off the scales. He even wept for a few minutes which further reduced his weight. It was no use: he still couldn't make the limit. The Argentinians filed a protest, and

weights and measures experts were sent for. Sure enough, it turned out that the scales were inaccurate, and Pares was allowed to compete. In his first match the nearly bald Pares won a disputed decision over Vic Toweel of South Africa. Toweel didn't let this setback hurt his career. He turned professional and, less than two years later, won the World Bantamweight title, which he held for two and a half years before losing to Jimmy Carruthers of Australia, who happened to have been Arnoldo Pares' second opponent at the 1948 Olympics. Carruthers won that fight but sustained an eye injury that forced him to withdraw from his quarterfinal bout with Tibor Csik. The unusually lucky Csik was thus able to move on to the semifinals even though he had fought only one regular fight. (His first-round opponent had been disqualified.)

1952 Helsinki C: 23, N: 23, D: 8.2.

			FINAL MATCH
1.	Pentti Hämäläinen	FIN	Dec 2–1
2.	John McNally	IRL	
3.	Gennady Garbuzov	SOV/RUS	
3.	Kang Joon-ho	KOR	
5.	Vincenzo Dall'osso (ITA), František Majdloch (CZE), David Moore (USA), Helmuth Von Gravenitz (SAF)		

The victory of Hämäläinen, a 23-year-old typewriter mechanic from Kotka, was greeted with great enthusiasm by the local Finnish crowd, although the Irish felt they had gotten a raw deal. Nevertheless, Belfast's John McNally was the first Irishman to win an Olympic boxing medal.

1956 Melbourne C: 18, N: 18, D: 12.1.

			FINAL MATCH
1.	Wolfgang Behrendt	GDR	Dec
2.	Song Soon-chun	KOR	
3.	Claudio Barrientos	CHI	
3.	Frederick Gilroy	IRL	
5.	Eder Jofre (BRA), Owen Reilly (GBR), Mario Sitri (ITA), Carmelo Adolfo Tomaselli (ARG)		

Twenty-year-old Berlin machine-fitter Wolfgang Behrendt was the first Olympic champion from the German Democratic Republic (East Germany).

1960 Rome C: 33, N: 33, D: 9.5.

			FINAL MATCH
1.	Oleg Grigoryev	SOV/RUS	Dec
2.	Primo Zamparini	ITA	
3.	Brunon Bendig	POL	
3.	Oliver Taylor	AUS	
5.	Jerry Armstrong (USA), Fernandez Alfred Carbajo (SPA), Horst Rascher (GER), Myint Thein (BUR)		

In the third round of competition, Oleg Grigoryev won a much-disputed split decision over 17-year-old Frankie Taylor of Great Britain. Although a British protest was rejected, all three judges who voted for Grigoryev were fired, as were no less than half of the 30 referees and judges involved in the Olympic tournament.

1964 Tokyo C: 32, N: 32, D: 10.23.

			FINAL MATCH	
1.	Takao Sakurai	JPN	RSC 2	1:18
2.	Chung Shin-cho	KOR		
3.	Juan Fabila Mendoza	MEX		
3.	Washington Rodriguez	URU		
5.	Fermin Espinosa (CUB), Oleg Grigoryev (SOV/RUS), Nicolae Puiu (ROM), Karimu Young (NGR)			

The final contest was stopped after Sakurai had knocked down Chung four times in less than four and a half minutes. After a brief career as a professional, Sakurai opened a coffee shop in Tokyo called "The Medalist."

1968 Mexico City C: 39, N: 39, D: 10.26.

			FINAL MATCH	
1.	Valerian Sokolov	SOV/RUS	RSC 2	2:15
2.	Eridari Mukwanga	UGA		
3.	Chang Kyou-chull	KOR		
3.	Eiji Morioka	JPN		
5.	Roberto Cervantes (MEX), Michael Dowling (IRL), Samuel Mbugua (KEN), Horst Rascher (GER)			

1972 Munich C: 38, N: 38, D: 9.10.

			FINAL MATCH
1.	Orlando Martínez	CUB	Dec 5–0
2.	Alfonso Zamora	MEX	
3.	Ricardo Carreras	USA	
3.	George Turpin	GBR	
5.	Ferry Egberty Moniaga (INA), John Mwaura Nderu (KEN), Juan Francisco Rodriguez (SPA), Vassily Solomin (SOV/RUS)		

Martínez was the first Cuban to win an Olympic gold medal since Ramón Fonst, the fencer, in 1904.

1976 Montreal C: 24, N: 24, D: 7.31.

			FINAL MATCH
1.	Gu Yong-ju	PRK	Dec 5–0
2.	Charles Mooney	USA	
3.	Patrick Cowdell	GBR	
3.	Victor Rybakov	SOV/RUS	
5.	Stefan Förster (GDR), Reynaldo Fortaleza (PHI), Hwang Chul-soon (KOR), Veerachat Saturngrum (THA)		

1980 Moscow C: 33, N: 33, D: 8.2.

			FINAL MATCH
1.	Juan Hernández	CUB	Dec 5–0
2.	Bernardo José Pinango	VEN	
3.	Michael Anthony	GUY	
3.	Dumitru Cipere	ROM	
5.	Geral Issaick (TAN), Samson Khachatrian (SOV/ARM), John Sirakibbe (UGA), Daniel Zaragoza (MEX)		

Seventeen-year-old Hernández was the second youngest boxer at the Moscow Olympics. He stopped two African boxers before the fights had gone the distance, and he defeated his other three opponents with clear-cut decisions.

1984 Los Angeles C: 35, N: 35, D: 8.11.

			FINAL MATCH
1.	Maurizio Stecca	ITA	Dec 4–1
2.	Hector Lopez	MEX	
3.	Pedro Nolasco	DOM	
3.	Dale Walters	CAN	
5.	Pedro Ruben Decima (ARG), Ndaba Dube (ZIM), Moon Sung-kil (KOR), Robinson Pitalua Tamara (COL)		

1988 Seoul C: 48, N: 48, D: 10.1.

			FINAL MATCH
1.	Kennedy McKinney	USA	Dec 5–0
2.	Alexander Hristov	BUL	
3.	Phajol Moolsan	THA	
3.	Jorge Julio Rocha	COL	
5.	Nyamaa Altankhuyag (MGL), Aleksandr Artemyev (SOV/RUS), Katsuyuki Matsushima (JPN), Stephen Mwema (KEN)		

Since 1924, Olympic boxing tournaments have been plagued by riots and demonstrations of varying magnitude. In 1988, however, a new twist was added to the ringside ugliness when a referee was attacked, not by spectators, but by Korean boxing officials and security guards.

The incident was rooted in the 1984 Los Angeles Olympics, when the Korean team became upset by what they perceived as biased judging against their boxers. They were particularly incensed by the dubious victory of light welterweight Jerry Page of the U.S. over Kim Dong-kil. Four years later the wound was reopened when Korean light flyweight favorite Oh Kwang-soo was narrowly upset by Michael Carbajal of the U.S.

The day after the Carbajal-Oh fight, Korean bantamweight Byun Jong-il faced one of the division favorites, Alexander Hristov of Bulgaria. The fight was not a pretty one. There was much pushing, shoving, grabbing, and general brawling. Referee Keith Walker of New Zealand tried to control the bout, cautioning both boxers, but he focused his reprimands on Byun. After warning Byun three times to stop using his head as a battering ram, Walker ordered the judges to deduct a point from the Korean's score. Another head butt in the final round led to the deduction of a second point. As it turned out, those two points decided the outcome of the fight. Without the penalties Byun would have won the decision; instead, he lost 4–1.

As soon as the verdict was announced, Korean boxing trainer Lee Heung-soo charged into the ring and struck Keith Walker on the back. Other Koreans, apparently under the mistaken assumption that Walker had also refereed the Carbajal-Oh fight, followed suit. Within sec-

In 1964 South Korean flyweight Choh Dong-kih staged a 51-minute sitdown strike after being disqualified for holding his head too low.

In 1988 bantamweight Byun Jong-il beat his countryman's sitdown record by 16 minutes.

After the ring was cleared of unauthorized personnel and miscellaneous debris, Byun sat down in the middle of the ring and staged a silent protest. After 35 minutes he was given a chair. He finally left after 67 minutes, breaking the Olympic sit-in record of 51 minutes set in 1964 by Byun's countryman, flyweight Choh Dong-kih. Before leaving the arena, Byun returned to the ring and bowed to the remaining spectators.

Eventually, five Korean boxing officials were suspended, the president of the Korean Olympic Committee resigned, and the Korean government apologized to the government of New Zealand. Three days after the incident, Lee Heung-soo, the supposedly suspended trainer who had led the charge on Walker, was back in the arena shouting orders to his boxers from a ringside seat.

Hristov, who had slipped out of the stadium without harm, squeaked into the final by winning agonizingly close 3-2 decisions over Aleksandr Artemyev and Jorge Julio Rocha. The latter verdict led to bitter protests from the Colombian corner.

In the final, Hristov ran out of luck. Kennedy McKinney of Killeen, Texas, floored him with a left hook only 11 seconds into the fight. Although Hristov rose and completed the bout without going down again, McKinney was the clear winner.

One final note about a boxer who never made it to the starting gate: Eduard Paululum was scheduled to be the first-ever Olympic competitor from the small Pacific island nation of Vanuatu. Unfortunately, Paululum ate a large breakfast *before* the weigh-in and was disqualified for being 1 pound overweight.

1992 Barcelona—Badalona C: 31, N: 31, D: 8.8.

		FINAL MATCH
1. Joel Casamayor Johnson	CUB	Pts 14–8
2. Wayne McCullough	IRL	

onds the ring was filled with angry Koreans pummeling Walker. Walker's fellow referees came to his aid and held off his attackers until security personnel could escort him out of the arena. Unfortunately, some of the security guards also took part in the riot, one of them aiming a kick at Walker's head as he fled. Another guard, Yoon S. L., who took off his uniform jacket before going after Walker, was quoted as saying, "I acted instinctively for the love of my fatherland."

Walker went straight from the arena to his hotel, checked out and took the next flight to New Zealand. Earlier in the tournament, Walker had been criticized by Irish officials for *not* penalizing Korean welterweight Song Kyung-sup when he engaged in head butting.

Another victim of the Koreans' fury was Emil Jetchev, the Bulgarian president of the Referees' Committee of the International Amateur Boxing Association. When a Korean coach attempted to smash Jetchev on the head with a plastic box, a U.S. judge, Stan Hamilton, reached out and blunted the blow. Hamilton had to be treated for a badly cut hand.

3. Mohamed Achik   MOR
3. Li Gwang-sik   PRK
5. Roberto Jalnaiz (PHI), Remigio Molina Ferreyra (ARG), Sabo Mohammed (NGR), Serafim Todorov (BUL)

Between 1989 and 1991 the bantamweight division was dominated by Cuba's Enrique Carrion and Bulgaria's Serafim Todorov, and it was assumed that these two would be the favorites in Barcelona. However, when Carrion lost to Todorov at the 1991 world championships and was beaten twice by American Sergio Reyes, the Cubans replaced him with 21-year-old ex-featherweight Joel Casamayor. Todorov almost didn't make it to the Olympics either when the AIBA threatened to punish him for skipping the 1992 World Championships Challenge in order to fight in a pseudo-professional German club match. Another contender was Li Gwang-sik of North Korea, who had earned bronze medals at the 1989 and 1991 world championships. At the Barcelona Olympics, Li eliminated Reyes 15-8 and Todorov 16-15 before losing in the semifinals 21-16 to Wayne McCullough in what many observers considered the best fight of the Games. In the final, Casamayor took a 10-2 lead into the last round and then withstood an increasingly vigorous onslaught by the slow-starting McCullough. McCullough, a Protestant from Belfast, carried the Irish flag at the 1988 Seoul Games.

FEATHERWEIGHT

(57 kg–126 lbs)

1896–1900 not held

1904 St. Louis C: 3, N: 1, D: 9.22.
(56.70 kg–125 lbs)

		FINAL MATCH
1. Oliver Kirk	USA	Dec
2. Frank Haller	USA	
3. Fred Gilmore	USA	

Kirk is the only person to win two boxing titles at a single Olympics. The importance of his achievement is certainly muted by the fact that he fought only one bout in each division (Bantamweight and Featherweight).

1906 not held

1908 London C: 8, N: 2, D: 10.27.
(57.15 kg–126 lbs)

		FINAL MATCH
1. Richard Gunn	GBR	Dec
2. Charles Morris	GBR	
3. Hugh Roddin	GBR	
4. Thomas Ringer	GBR	

At 37, Gunn was the oldest fighter ever to win an Olympic championship. He had been British amateur champion from 1894 to 1896. Unfortunately, his superiority

At 37, 1908 Featherweight champion Richard Gunn was the oldest boxing gold medalist in Olympic history.

over other British featherweights was so pronounced that his entry in a tournament caused others to drop out. Consequently, amateur boxing authorities asked him to retire from competition and Gunn, ever the sportsman, agreed. He came out of retirement for the London Olympics and defeated one Frenchman and two Englishmen to win the gold medal. Then he retired again, having lost only one fight in 15 years.

1912 not held

1920 Antwerp C: 17, N: 9, D: 8.24.
(57.15 kg–126 lbs)

		FINAL MATCH
1. Paul Fritsch	FRA	Dec
2. Jean Gachet	FRA	
3. Edoardo Garzena	ITA	
4. Jack Zivic	USA	
5. Philippe Bovy (BEL), James Cater (GBR), Nicolaj Clausen (DEN), Paul Erdahl (NOR)		

1924 Paris C: 24, N: 17, D: 7.20.
(57.15 kg–126 lbs)

		FINAL MATCH
1. John Fields	USA	Dec
2. Joseph Salas	USA	

3. Pedro Quartucci ARG
4. Jean Devergnies BEL
5. Carlos Abarca-Gonzalez (CHI), Marcel Depont (FRA), Harry Dingley (GBR), Bruno Petrarca (ITA)

Jackie Fields and Joe Salas were best friends back home in Los Angeles. At 16, Fields, whose real name was Jacob Finkelstein, was the youngest boxer at the Paris Olympics. Salas later recalled, "We had to dress in the same room. When they knocked on the door to call us to the fight, we looked up at each other and started to cry and hugged. Ten minutes later we were beating the hell out of each other." After his victory over Salas in the final, Fields was so upset at having defeated his buddy that he went back to the dressing room and cried again. In 1929 Fields won the World Welterweight title. Fields and Salas died eight days apart in June 1987.

1928 Amsterdam C: 18, N: 18, D: 8.11.
(57.15 kg—126 lbs)

			FINAL MATCH
1.	Lambertus van Klaveren	HOL	Dec
2.	Victor Peralta	ARG	
3.	Harold Devine	USA	
4.	Lucien Biquet	BEL	
5.	George Boireau (FRA), Jan Górny (POL), Frederick Perry (GBR), Olavi Vakeva (FIN)		

There seemed little question in anyone's mind that Peralta had outclassed van Klaveren. Anyone, that is, except the judges who awarded the decision to the Dutch fighter. "It was as plain as a pike-staff which was the master," wrote the reporter for the London *Daily Telegraph*. A battle ensued between Argentinian spectators and Dutch police, and the commotion was still bubbling when the decision of the next match, the Lightweight championship, set off outrage among the Americans in the crowd. Bep van Klaveren, known as "The Dutch Windmill," is the only Dutch boxer ever to win an Olympic title.

1932 Los Angeles C: 10, N: 10, D: 8.13.
(57.15 kg—126 lbs)

			FINAL MATCH
1.	Carmelo Robledo	ARG	Dec
2.	Josef Schleinkofer	GER	
3.	Carl Carlsson	SWE	
4.	Gaspare Alessandri	ITA	
5.	John Hines (USA)		

1936 Berlin C: 25, N: 25, D: 8.15.
(57.15 kg—126 lbs)

			FINAL MATCH
1.	Oscar Casanovas	ARG	Dec
2.	Charles Catterall	SAF	

3. Josef Miner GER
4. Dezsö Frigyes HUN
5. Theodore Ernst Kara (USA), William Marquart (CAN), Aleksander Polus (POL), John Treadway (GBR)

1948 London C: 30, N: 30, D: 8.13.
(58 kg—128 lbs)

			FINAL MATCH
1.	Ernesto Formenti	ITA	Dec
2.	Dennis Shephard	SAF	
3.	Aleksy Antkiewicz	POL	
4.	Francisco Núñez	ARG	
5.	Edward Johnson (USA), Edward Kerschbaumer (AUT), Armand Savoie (CAN), Su Bung-nan (KOR)		

A new style in Olympic boxing protests was created following the announcement that American Eddie Johnson had been declared the winner over 33-year-old Basilio Alves of Uruguay in their second-round match. While the crowd booed for more than fifteen minutes, Alves' supporters hoisted him on their shoulders and stormed the table of the Jury of Appeal. In the semifinals, it was the turn of the Argentinians to protest. Upset over the loss of Núñez to Shephard, they grabbed Núñez, who had refused to leave the ring, lifted him to their shoulders, and attempted a Uruguayan charge toward the Jurors' table. Repulsed by a phalanx of twelve attendants, the Argentinians listened to speeches by two of their officials and were finally convinced to end their protest by an Argentinian member of the Jury of Appeal, Señor Oriani. The final saw Shephard enter the ring with six stitches over his right eye, the result of a cut that had been opened in four of his five preliminary bouts. He fought gamely but was finally worn down by Formenti in the final minute and a half.

Supporters of Uruguayan featherweight Basilio Alves storm the table of the Jury of Appeal following Alves' 1948 loss to American Eddie Johnson.

1952 Helsinki C: 30, N: 30, D: 8.2.

			FINAL MATCH
1.	Ján Zachara	CZE/SLV	Dec 2–1
2.	Sergio Caprari	ITA	
3.	Leonard Leisching	SAF	
3.	Joseph Ventaja	FRA	
5.	Edson Brown (USA), Leszek Drogosz (POL), János Erdei (HUN), Leonard Walters (CAN)		

1956 Melbourne C: 18, N: 18, D: 12.1.

			FINAL MATCH
1.	Vladimir Safronov	SOV/RUS	Dec
2.	Thomas Nicholls	GBR	
3.	Pentti Hämäläinen	FIN	
3.	Henryk Niedźwiedzki	POL	
5.	Andre De Sousa (FRA), Tristan Octavio Falfan (ARG), Shinetsu Suzuki (JPN), Jan Zachara (CZE)		

Safronov, an artist from Siberia, gained the U.S.S.R.'s first Olympic boxing title. He was added to the team at the last minute when Soviet champion Aleksandr Zasukhin injured his hand in training.

1960 Rome C: 31, N: 31, D: 9.5.

			FINAL MATCH
1.	Francesco Musso	ITA	Dec 4–1
2.	Jerzy Adamski	POL	
3.	Jorma Limmonen	FIN	
3.	William Meyers	SAF	
5.	Abel Bekker (ZIM), Ernest Chervet (SWI), Constantin Gheorghiu (ROM), Boris Nikanorov (SOV/RUS)		

In the first round of the tournament, Boris Nikanorov outpointed Nick Spanakos to become the first Soviet boxer ever to defeat an American.

1964 Tokyo C: 32, N: 32, D: 10.23.

			FINAL MATCH
1.	Stanislav Stepashkin	SOV/RUS	Dec 3–2
2.	Anthony Villanueva	PHI	
3.	Charles Brown	USA	
3.	Heinz Schulz	GDR	
5.	Constantin Crudu (ROM), José Duran Aguirre (MEX), Piotr Gutman (POL), Tun Tin (BUR)		

After all the hoopla and uproar that had gone on as a result of unpopular decisions in Olympic boxing, it was left to Spanish featherweight Valentin Loren to register the ultimate protest. Disqualified for repeated holding and open-glove hitting in the second round of his first fight, Loren turned on the Hungarian referee, György Sermer, and punched him in the face. This unfortunate indiscretion caused the Saragoza southpaw to receive a lifetime ban from international amateur boxing. Silver

Disqualified in his first fight in the 1964 Olympics, Spanish featherweight Valentin Loren takes out his frustration on the Hungarian referee.

medalist Anthony Villanueva was the son of José "Cely" Villanueva, who had won the Bantamweight bronze medal at the 1932 Olympics in Los Angeles. Anthony tried a brief career as a movie actor and then turned professional boxer. Stepashkin won his first four fights by knockout and technical knockout before gaining a split decision over Villanueva.

1968 Mexico City C: 28, N: 28, D: 10.26.

			FINAL MATCH
1.	Antonio Roldan	MEX	DISQ 2
2.	Albert Robinson	USA	
3.	Ivan Mihailov	BUL	
3.	Philip Waruinge	KEN	
5.	Miguel Garcia (ARG), Abdel Khallaf (EGY), Valery Plotnikov (SOV/RUS), Seyfi Tatar (TUR)		

The final match came to a sudden end when Robinson was disqualified for butting. Although the Mexican crowd was delighted with the victory, Roldan himself seemed apologetic. As the first disqualified finalist since Ingemar Johansson in 1952, Robinson was prevented from receiving his silver medal. After a protest by American officials, Robinson was finally awarded the medal after his return to the United States. In 1971 Robinson was injured while training and lapsed into a coma in which he remained until his death three years later.

1972 Munich C: 45, N: 45, D: 9.10.

			FINAL MATCH
1.	Boris Kuznetsov	SOV/RUS	Dec 3–2
2.	Philip Waruinge	KEN	
3.	András Botos	HUN	
3.	Clemente Rojas	COL	
5.	Kazuo Kobayashi (JPN), Jouko Lindberg (FIN), Gabriel Pometcu (ROM), Antonio Rubio (SPA)		

1976 Montreal C: 26, N: 26, D: 7.31.

			FINAL MATCH	
1.	Angel Herrera	CUB	KO 2	2:18
2.	Richard Nowakowski	GDR		
3.	Leszek Kosedowski	POL		
3.	Juan Paredes	MEX		

5. Davey Armstrong (USA), Choi Choon-gil (KOR), Gheorghe Ciochină (ROM), Bratislav Ristic (YUG)

1980 Moscow C: 35, N: 35, D: 8.2.

			FINAL MATCH
1.	Rudi Fink	GDR	Dec 4–1
2.	Adolfo Horta	CUB	
3.	Krzysztof Kosedowski	POL	
3.	Viktor Rybakov	SOV/RUS	

5. Tzacho Andreikovski (BUL), Sidnei Dalrovere (BRA), Winfred Kabunda (ZAM), Luis Pizarro (PUR)

1984 Los Angeles C: 36, N: 36, D: 8.11.

			FINAL MATCH
1.	Meldrick Taylor	USA	Dec 5–0
2.	Peter Konyegwachie	NGR	
3.	Targut Aykac	TUR	
3.	Omar Catari Peraza	VEN	

5. Mohamed Hegazy (EGY), Charles Lubulwa (UGA), Park Hyeong-oc (KOR), John Wanjau (KEN)

As a professional, Meldrick Taylor was involved in one of boxing's most memorable fights. On March 17, 1990, Taylor challenged Julio César Chávez for the WBC Super Lightweight championship. Both fighters were undefeated. After 11 rounds Taylor appeared to be ahead on points and needed only to survive the final round to win the title. Instead of sticking to his fight plan by staying close to Chávez, with one minute to go Taylor stepped back and stood up. Chávez quickly took advantage of Taylor's mistake, battering Taylor with all the strength he had left. With less than 15 seconds left in the fight, Taylor finally went down. He picked himself up at the count of six, but referee Richard Steele noted Taylor's lack of responsiveness, decided that Taylor had had enough, and stopped the fight—with two seconds remaining on the clock. A check of the judges' scorecards confirmed that if Taylor had been able to last two more seconds, he would have won the championship.

1988 Seoul C: 48, N: 48, D: 10.2.

			FINAL MATCH	
1.	Giovanni Parisi	ITA	RSC 1	1:41
2.	Daniel Dumitrescu	ROM		
3.	Abdelhak Achik	MOR		
3.	Lee Jae-hyuk	KOR		

5. Liu Dong (CHN), Tomasz Nowak (POL), Jacov Shmuel (ISR), Regilio Tuur (HOL)

An unusual incident occurred during the first-round match between Jamie Pagendam of Canada and Tserendorj Awarjargal of Mongolia. Pagendam, a 22-year-old crane operator from St. Catharines, Ontario, registered three knockdowns in the second round (including one standing eight-count). According to amateur rules, Pagendam should automatically have been declared the winner after the third knockdown. However, the referee, Marius Guiramo Lougbo of the Ivory Coast, lost count of the knockdowns and allowed the bout to continue. When Pagendam was himself floored in the third round, Lougbo stopped the fight and gave the victory to Awarjargal. A protest was filed and the decision was in fact overturned. However, because Pagendam's final knockdown was the result of a blow to his head, he received a 30-day medical suspension and was not allowed to advance in the tournament. Neither was Lougbo—he was suspended for the remainder of the Olympics.

1992 Barcelona—Badalona C: 31, N: 31, D: 8.9.

			FINAL MATCH
1.	Andreas Tews	GER	Pts 16–7
2.	Faustino Reyes López	SPA	
3.	Ramazi Paliani	GEO	
3.	Hocine Soltani	ALG	

5. Victoriano Damien Sosa (DOM), Daniel Dumitrescu (ROM), Park Duk-kyu (KOR), Eddy Suárez Edua (CUB)

At the 1988 Olympics Andreas Tews represented East Germany and won a silver medal in the flyweight division. In 1992 he represented a united Germany, moved up two divisions to featherweight, and earned a gold medal. And earn it he did, defeating world champion Kirkor Kirkorov of Bulgaria 9-5, world champion runner-up Park Duk-kyu 17-7, and, in the final, the hero of the local fans, 17-year-old Faustino Reyes. One loser who did not go quietly was the European champion, Paul Griffin. Griffin, Ireland's first European champion in 42 years, was eliminated in his first bout. After Zambia's Steven Chungu knocked him down twice in the second round, the ring doctor stopped the fight. Griffin was so outraged that he kicked his gumshield into the fourth row, engaged in abusive language, and had to be restrained from attacking the doctor. This outburst earned him a six-month suspension.

LIGHTWEIGHT

(60 kg–132 lbs)

1896–1900 not held

1904 St. Louis C: 8, N: 1, D: 9.22.
(61.24 kg–135½ lbs)

			FINAL MATCH
1.	Harry Spanger	USA	Dec
2.	James Eagan	USA	

3. Russell Van Horn   USA
4. Peter Sturholdt   USA

A well-known local boxer, Carroll Burton, entered the tournament and won his first match. However, it was then discovered that the victor was not Burton at all, but a man named Bollinger posing as Burton. Bollinger was disqualified and his opponent, Sturholdt, was advanced to the next round.

1906 not held

1908 London C: 12, N: 3, D: 10.27.
(63.50 kg–140 lbs)

		FINAL MATCH
1. Frederick Grace	GBR	Dec
2. M. Frederick Spiller	GBR	
3. Harry Johnson	GBR	
4. Harold Holmes (GBR), George Jessup (GBR), Matthew Wells (GBR)		

Early in the second round, the two finalists swung hard at each other. Both missed and fell on their faces.

1912 not held

1920 Antwerp C: 16, N: 10, D: 8.24.
(61.24 kg–135½ lbs)

		FINAL MATCH
1. Samuel Mosberg	USA	Dec
2. Gotfred Johansen	DEN	
3. Clarence Newton	CAN	
4. Richard Breland	SAF	
5. Frank Cassidy (USA), Frederick Grace (GBR), Julian van Muyzen (BEL), Johan Saeterhaug (NOR)		

Grace tried to defend his 12-year-old Olympic title at age 36, but lost a close quarterfinal decision to Mosberg. In the semifinals, Mosberg knocked out Breland in only 15 seconds.

1924 Paris C: 30, N: 22, D: 7.20.
(61.24 kg–135½ lbs)

		FINAL MATCH
1. Hans Nielsen	DEN	Dec
2. Alfredo Copello	ARG	
3. Frederick Boylstein	USA	
4. Jean Tholey	FRA	
5. Richard Breland (SAF), Alfred Genon (BEL), Haakon Hansen (NOR), Ben Rothwell (USA)		

1928 Amsterdam C: 24, N: 24, D: 8.11.
(61.24 kg–135½ lbs)

		FINAL MATCH
1. Carlo Orlandi	ITA	Dec
2. Stephen Michael Halaiko	USA	

3. Gunnar Berggren   SWE
4. Hans Nielsen   DEN
5. Dirk Baan (HOL), Cecil Bissett (ZIM), Pascual Bonfiglio (ARG), Jorge Diaz Hernandez (CHI)

1932 Los Angeles C: 13, N: 13, D: 8.13.
(61.24 kg–135½ lbs)

		FINAL MATCH
1. Lawrence Stevens	SAF	Dec
2. Thure Ahlqvist	SWE	
3. Nathan Bor	USA	
4. Mario Bianchini	ITA	
5. Frank Genovese (CAN), Franz Kartz (GER), Gaston Mayor (FRA)		

1936 Berlin C: 26, N: 26, D: 8.15.
(61.24 kg–135½ lbs)

		FINAL MATCH
1. Imre Harangi	HUN	Dec
2. Nikolai Stepulov	EST	
3. Erik Ågren	SWE	
4. Poul Kops	DEN	
5. Carlos Lillo (CHI), Lidoro Oliver (ARG), José Padilla (PHI), Andrew Scrivani (USA)		

Prior to the Olympics, Harangi was urged by doctors to retire from boxing and undergo an operation on his nose, which had been badly injured in previous fights. Harangi refused and went on to win the gold medal in Berlin. One unfortunate competitor was Thomas Hamilton-Brown of South Africa. In his opening-round match, he lost a split decision to Carlos Lillo of Chile. However, it was later discovered that one of the judges had mistakenly reversed his scores for the two boxers and that Hamilton-Brown was in fact the winner and thus eligible to move on to the next round. Unfortunately, Hamilton-Brown, who had had trouble making the weight limit, had softened the disappointment of his loss by going on an eating binge. By the time the South African manager found him it was after midnight and the boxer had already put on nearly five pounds. Desperately his trainer tried to boil him down, but it was no use. The next day Hamilton-Brown, still over the weight limit, was disqualified and Lillo was allowed to advance in his place.

1948 London C: 28, N: 28, D: 8.13.
(62 kg–135½ lbs)

		FINAL MATCH
1. Gerald Dreyer	SAF	Dec
2. Joseph Vissers	BEL	
3. Svend Wad	DEN	
4. Wallace Smith	USA	
5. Öivind Breiby (NOR), Edward Haddad (CAN), Maxie McCullagh (IRL), Ralf Benedito Zumbano (BRA)		

1952 Helsinki C: 27, N: 27, D: 8.2.

		FINAL MATCH
1. Aureliano Bolognesi	ITA	Dec 2–1
2. Aleksy Antkiewicz	POL	
3. Gheorghe Fiat	ROM	
3. Erkki Pakkanen	FIN	

5. Americo Bonetti (ARG), István Juhász (HUN), Vincente Matute (VEN), Frederick Reardon (GBR)

1956 Melbourne C: 18, N: 18, D: 12.1.

		FINAL MATCH
1. Richard McTaggart	GBR	Dec
2. Harry Kurschat	GER	
3. Anthony Byrne	IRL	
3. Anatoly Lagetko	SOV/RUS	

5. Edward Beattie (CAN), Zygmunt Milewski (POL), Louis Molina (USA), André Vairolatto (FRA)

McTaggart came from a family of 18 children in Dundee, Scotland. He competed in two more Olympics, losing both times to Polish boxers who went on to win the gold medal.

1960 Rome C: 34, N: 34, D: 9.5.

		FINAL MATCH
1. Kazimierz Paździor	POL	Dec 4–1
2. Sandro Lopopolo	ITA	
3. Abel Laudonio	ARG	
3. Richard McTaggart	GBR	

5. Velikton Barannikov (SOV/RUS), Harry Campbell (USA), Ferenc Kellner (HUN), Salah Shokweir (UAR)

Paździor, a 25-year-old blacksmith from Radom, used his experience of 175 fights to outpoint five straight opponents, although he had a tough time with McTaggart in the semifinals.

1964 Tokyo C: 34, N: 34, D: 10.23.

		FINAL MATCH
1. Józef Grudzień	POL	Dec
2. Velikton Barannikov	SOV/RUS	
3. Ronald Allan Harris	USA	
3. James McCourt	IRL	

5. Rodolfo Arpon (PHI), Domingo Barrera (SPA), János Kajdi (HUN), Stoyan Pilichev (BUL)

1968 Mexico City C: 37, N: 37, D: 10.26.

		FINAL MATCH
1. Ronald W. Harris	USA	Dec 5–0
2. Józef Grudzień	POL	
3. Calistrat Cutov	ROM	
3. Zvonimir Vujin	YUG	

5. Luis Minami (PER), Mohamed Muruli (UGA), Enzo Petriglia (ITA), Stoyan Pilichev (BUL)

1972 Munich C: 37, N: 37, D: 9.10.

		FINAL MATCH
1. Jan Szczepański	POL	Dec 5–0
2. László Orbán	HUN	
3. Samuel Mbugua	KEN	
3. Alfonso Pérez	COL	

5. Eraslan Doruk (TUR), Kim Tai-ho (KOR), Charles Nash (IRL), Sven Erik Paulsen (NOR)

The 32-year-old European champion, Szczepański, was almost upset in the round of 16 when he won the closest of split decisions over Chaidau Altankhuiag of Mongolia. He won his next two fights on a disqualification and a walkover. Then he took a close but unanimous decision from Orbán, the 1969 European champion.

1976 Montreal C: 23, N: 23, D: 7.31.

		FINAL MATCH
1. Howard Davis	USA	Dec 5–0
2. Simion Cutov	ROM	
3. Ace Rusevski	YUG	
3. Vassily Solomin	SOV/RUS	

5. András Botos (HUN), Yves Jeudy (HAI), Ove Lundby (SWE), Tsvetan Tsvetkov (BUL)

The year 1976 was a full one for Howard "John John" Davis. The father of a 2-year-old boy, Davis played guitar in a rock and soul group, having previously played drums for James Brown. In January he graduated from Glen Cove High School on Long Island. In February he turned 20. In July he went to Montreal with the intention of beating the favorite, European champion Simion Cutov. Two days before the start of the Olympics, Davis' mother, Catherine, died of a heart attack. Davis, deciding to honor his mother by winning the gold medal, was voted the Val Barker award for most outstanding boxer of the Olympics. Two of his five fights were stopped in the first round and the other three were won by unanimous decision.

1980 Moscow C: 29, N: 29, D: 8.2.

		FINAL MATCH	
1. Angel Herrera	CUB	RSC 3	0:13
2. Viktor Demyanenko	SOV/KAZ		
3. Kazimierz Adach	POL		
3. Richard Nowakowski	GDR		

5. Galsandorj Batbileg (MGL), George Gilbody (GBR), Yordan Lessov (BUL), Florin Livadaru (ROM)

Herrera, who had won the 1976 Olympic Featherweight title, moved up successfully to Lightweight four years later, winning four unanimous decisions on his way to the final.

1984 Los Angeles C: 40, N: 40, D: 8.11.

		FINAL MATCH	
1. Pernell Whitaker	USA	Ret 2	2:57
2. Luis Ortiz	PUR		

3. Chun Chil-sung   KOR
3. Martin Ndongo Ebanga   CAM
5. Leopoldo Cantancio (PHI), Reiner Gies (GER), José Antonio Hernando (SPA), Fahri Sumer (TUR)

Whitaker, of Norfolk, Va., like Herrera four years earlier, won four unanimous decisions on his way to the final. Ortiz's semifinal split decision victory over Ndongo Ebanga was roundly booed. In the final, Ortiz's handlers stopped the fight following a standing eight-count three seconds before the end of the second round. Whitaker went on to win the lightweight title of all three international professional federations, unifying the division in 1990 for the first time in 8 years. Later he won junior welterweight, welterweight, and junior middleweight titles as well. However, he said that winning these championships did not compare to winning an Olympic gold medal. "They placed that medal around my neck and played the national anthem. Nothing else I do in life will top that feeling. I came out of the ring and put that medal on my mother. After winning the gold medal, everything else is icing on the cake."

1988 Seoul C: 39, N: 39, D: 10.1.

		FINAL MATCH
1. Andreas Zuelow	GDR	Dec 5–0
2. George Cramne	SWE	
3. Romallis Ellis	USA	
3. Nerguy Enkhbat	MGL	
5. Mohamed Hegazy (EGY), Charles Kane (GBR), Kamal Marjonane (MOR), Emil Chuprenski (BUL)		

The key matchup of the tournament took place in the round of 16 when Andreas Zuelow, a technically pure boxer, faced Konstantin Tszu of the Soviet Union, who had knocked out his first two opponents in the first round. Two judges gave Zuelow the nod, two more gave the edge to Tszu, while the fifth judge, Abdul Hani of Iraq, scored the bout a draw. Olympic rules require each judge to designate a winner. Hani leaned toward Zuelow, who went on to win the gold medal with three straight unanimous decisions. George Cramne, who fought for Sweden, was born in Liberia.

1992 Barcelona—Badalona C: 29, N: 29, D: 8.8.

		FINAL MATCH
1. Oscar De La Hoya	USA	Pts 7–2
2. Marco Rudolph	GER	
3. Namjil Bayarsaikhan	MGL	
3. Hong Sung-sik	KOR	
5. Ronald Chávez (PHI), Julien Lorcy (FRA), Haji Matumla (TAN), Toncho Tonchev (BUL)		

Like 1984 light flyweight gold medalist Paul Gonzales, Oscar De La Hoya hailed from the East Los Angeles barrio. Both his father and his grandfather were boxers, and Oscar began his own career when he was seven years

old. By the age of 17 he had conquered the world at the Goodwill Games. Two months later De La Hoya's good life was shattered when his 38-year-old mother, Cecelia, died of breast cancer. Just before her death, he promised her that he would win an Olympic gold medal. It seemed like a reasonable goal until De La Hoya lost his first bout at the 1991 world championships. His conqueror, by a score of 17-13, was Marco Rudolph, a hotel restaurant charcutier from Cottbus in eastern Germany, who went on to win the world title. Despite this setback, De La Hoya continued to be regarded as a hero in East Los Angeles. One night he was surrounded on the street by five hoodlums with guns. They stole his wallet, which contained $150 in cash. Two hours later De La Hoya found the wallet on his front porch. When the thieves had opened it and discovered who they had robbed, they returned it. The $150 was still inside.

At the Barcelona Olympics De La Hoya breezed through his first three fights, celebrating each victory by kneeling and pointing skyward in honor of his mother. But in the semifinals he ran into Hong Sung-sik, a brawler whose style seemed more suited to a wrestling mat than a boxing ring. Both boxers were penalized three points for repeated infractions. The referee was so flustered that he forgot to disqualify Hong after his fourth warning and actually issued him a fifth warning. In the end De La Hoya escaped with an 11-10 win. In the final he faced a rematch with Marco Rudolph. Leading only 3-2 after two rounds, De La Hoya finally put the fight away when he floored Rudolph with 1:09 left in the third round. A gracious loser, Rudolph embraced De La Hoya as soon as the bout was over. At the victory ceremony De La Hoya carried the United States' flag in one hand and a Mexican flag in the other—the latter in honor of his Mexican-born mother. Back in Los Angeles De La Hoya fulfilled his vow to his mother by visiting her grave with the Olympic gold medal.

LIGHT WELTERWEIGHT
(63.5 kg—140 lbs)

1896–1948 not held

1952 Helsinki C: 28, N: 28, D: 8.2.

		FINAL MATCH
1. Charles Adkins	USA	Dec 2–1
2. Viktor Mednov	SOV/RUS	
3. Erkki Mallenius	FIN	
3. Bruno Visintin	ITA	
5. Terence Milligan (IRL), Jean Paternotte (BEL), Alexander Webster (SAF), René Weismann (FRA)		

The final saw the first-ever boxing match between fighters from the United States and the U.S.S.R. Adkins, a 20-year-old police administration student from Gary, Indiana, had had no trouble with his preliminary fights.

Mednov, on the other hand, entered the ring with stitches over both eyes, the result of a brutal second-round fight with Francisco Ambrus of Romania, which was finally stopped by a doctor due to injuries to both men. Fortunately for Mednov, his semifinal opponent, Erkki Mallenius, injured his hand and had to withdraw, allowing the Soviet boxer an extra day to heal. In the final bout Mednov fought gallantly, but was no match for Adkins' powerful two-handed hooking.

1956 Melbourne C: 22, N: 22, D: 12.1.

		FINAL MATCH
1. Vladimir Yengibaryan	SOV/ARM	Dec
2. Franco Nenci	ITA	
3. Constantin Dumitrescu	ROM	
3. Henry Loubscher	SAF	
5. Hwang Ei-kyung (KOR), Antonio Salvador Marcilla (ARG), Claude Saluden (FRA), Joseph Shaw (USA)		

1960 Rome C: 34, N: 34, D: 9.5.

		FINAL MATCH
1. Bohumil Nemeček	CZE	Dec 5–0
2. Clement "Ike" Quartey	GHA	
3. Quincey Daniels	USA	
3. Marian Kasprzyk	POL	
5. Piero Brandi (ITA), Sayed Elnahas (EGY), Kim Duck-bong (KOR), Vladimir Yengibaryan (SOV/ARM)		

The final matched two underdogs and was won by Bohumil Nemeček, a 22-year-old railway worker from Decin. Ike Quartey, however, gained distinction by becoming the first black African to win an Olympic medal.

1964 Tokyo C: 35, N: 35, D: 10.23.

		FINAL MATCH
1. Jerzy Kulej	POL	Dec 5–0
2. Yevgeny Frolov	SOV/RUS	
3. Eddie Blay	GHA	
3. Habib Galhia	TUN	
5. Felix Betancourt (CUB), Joao Henrique da Silva (BRA), Vladimir Kucera (CZE), Iosif Mihalic (ROM)		

1968 Mexico City C: 35, N: 35, D: 10.26.

		FINAL MATCH
1. Jerzy Kulej	POL	Dec 3–2
2. Enrique Regueiferos	CUB	
3. Arto Nilsson	FIN	
3. James Wallington	USA	
5. Yevgeny Frolov (SOV/RUS), Kim Sa-yong (KOR), Peter Stoichev (BUL), Peter Tiepold (GDR)		

Policeman Jerzy Kulej beat Enrique Requeiferos, a strong puncher eight years his junior, to win a rare repeat Olympic boxing title.

1972 Munich C: 32, N: 32, D: 9.10.

		FINAL MATCH
1. Ray Seales	USA	Dec 3–2
2. Angel Angelov	BUL	
3. Issaka Daborg	NIG	
3. Zvonimir Vujin	YUG	
5. Srisook Bantow (THA), Andres Molina (CUB), Graham Moughton (GBR), Kyoji Shinohara (JPN)		

The final between Angel Angelov and "Sugar Ray" Seales of Tacoma, Washington, was a surprisingly dull affair. Many observers felt that Sugar Ray's mother, who rooted him on enthusiastically from ringside, had shadow boxed a better fight than her son's. Seales turned professional and was reasonably successful until his career was ended by encroaching blindness.

1976 Montreal C: 32, N: 32, D: 7.31.

		FINAL MATCH
1. Ray Leonard	USA	Dec 5–0
2. Andrés Aldama	CUB	
3. Vladimir Kolev	BUL	
3. Kazimierz Szczerba	POL	
5. Ulrich Beyer (GDR), Calistrat Cutov (ROM), József Nagy (HUN), Luis Portillo (ARG)		

Ray Leonard, of Palmer Park, Maryland, made it two in a row for light welterweights nicknamed "Sugar Ray." He faced a tough customer in Andrés Aldama, who had stopped his first three opponents in the second round and knocked out Kolev in the semifinals. But Sugar Ray, wearing photos of his girlfriend and their 2-year-old son pinned to his socks, won a clear victory. He turned professional a few months later and won the World Welterweight championship on November 30, 1979. He lost the title to Roberto Duran on June 20, 1980, but regained it five months later. In 1982 he retired as a result of an eye injury. However, he returned to the ring in 1987 and scored a controversial victory over Marvin Hagler in a fight for the World Middleweight championship.

1980 Moscow C: 30, N: 30, D: 8.2.

		FINAL MATCH
1. Patrizio Oliva	ITA	Dec 4–1
2. Serik Konakbayev	SOV/KAZ	
3. José Aguilar	CUB	
3. Anthony Willis	GBR	
5. Farouk Chanchoun Jawad (IRQ), William Lyimo (TAN), José Angel Molina (PUR), Ace Rusevski (YUG)		

Bronze medalist Tony Willis followed in the great British tradition of middleweight Chris Finnegan and hurdler

David Hemery when he required three hours, an orange-ade, and a glass of water to produce enough urine to be used for a drug test. He passed.

1984 Los Angeles C: 32, N: 32, D: 8.11.

		FINAL MATCH
1. Jerry Page	USA	Dec 5–0
2. Dhawee Umponmaha	THA	
3. Mircea Fulger	ROM	
3. Mirko Puzović	YUG	
5. Lotfi Belkhir (TUN), Kim Dong-kil (KOR), Jorge Maisonet (PUR), Jean Pierre Mbereke (CAM)		

The light welterweight division was disrupted by controversy in 1984. In a preliminary bout, Jorge Maisonet of Puerto Rico was declared a split decision winner over Nigeria's Charles Nwokolo. While the crowd chanted references to animal excrement, Colonel J. Whyte Ukor, the president of the Nigerian Boxing Association, rushed towards the jury waving his walking stick. After striking at least one boxing official, he was restrained by his coaches and removed from the arena.

Two days later, eventual gold medal winner Jerry Page was awarded a 4–1 quarterfinal victory over South Korean medal favorite Kim Dong-kil, in a match that most ringside observers thought Page had lost. The Korean delegation was so enraged that they threatened to withdraw from the tournament, but they later admitted that the threat was primarily an attempt to call attention to a string of controversial pro-U.S. jury decisions.

Umponmaha's silver medal was the highest placing ever by a Thai Olympic athlete.

1988 Seoul C: 45, N: 45, D: 10.2.

		FINAL MATCH
1. Vyacheslav Yanovsky	SOV/BLR	Dec 5–0
2. Grahame Cheney	AUS	
3. Reiner Gies	GER	
3. Lars Myrberg	SWE	
5. Sodnomdar Jaa Altansukh (MGL), Todd Foster (USA), Antony Mwamba (ZAM), Humberto Rodriguez (MEX)		

Because there were so many entrants in the 1988 boxing tournament, two rings were used simultaneously until the quarterfinals. To avoid confusion, the end of a round was announced by a bell in ring A and a buzzer in ring B. The system did not work perfectly, leading to a bizarre incident in the round of 16 during the bout between Todd Foster of Great Falls, Montana, and Chun Jin-chul of South Korea.

The match was held in ring B. Just before the fight began, Foster's coaches reminded him to ignore the bell and listen only for "the horn." With 17 seconds left in round one, the bell sounded in ring A. In ring B Foster, Chun, and the Hungarian referee, Sandor Pajar, hesitated for a moment. Chun dropped his hands and took a step toward his corner. The referee called "Stop."

Foster, realizing that Chun and the referee had made a mistake, blasted Chun with a left hook that caught the Korean in his eye. Chun looked to his corner, then collapsed to the canvas, pretending to be knocked down in an attempt to have Foster disqualified for a late blow. Pajar began to count Chun out, but stopped at four and walked over to the judges for a consultation. Jury president Emil Jetchev called the bout a no-contest and ordered a rematch for the following day. An hour and a half later, Foster was sitting in the stands waiting to watch another American fight when he was told that, as a result of a U.S. protest, the rematch would take place in 45 minutes. Foster opened the second bout by charging after Chun and knocking him to the canvas only 6 seconds into the fight. In the final minute of the first round Chun pounded Foster's nose, splattering blood on both boxers. Round two began with the spilling of more Foster blood, but the American took charge, knocking out Chun with a left hook to the chin.

In his next bout, Foster lost a split decision to Grahame Cheney, who later became Australia's first-ever Olympic boxing finalist. In the final, Cheney fought gamely, but was no match for the experienced 31-year-old Yanovsky.

1992 Barcelona—Badalona C: 30, N: 30, D: 8.9.

		FINAL MATCH
1. Héctor Vinent Charon	CUB	Pts 11–1
2. Mark Leduc	CAN	
3. Leonard Doroftei	ROM	
3. Jyri Kjäll	FIN	
5. Laid Bouneb (ALG), Oleg Nikolayev (RUS), Peter Richardson (GBR), László Szücs (HUN)		

Vinent, a 20-year-old from Santiago de Cuba, was one of the most impressive fighters at the Barcelona Olympics, outpointing his five opponents by a combined score of 91 to 12. Leduc, a homosexual boxer from Toronto who once served 18 months in prison for armed robbery, had beaten Vinent two years earlier in Canada but was no match for him in Barcelona.

WELTERWEIGHT
(67 kg–148 lbs)

1896–1900 not held

1904 St. Louis C: 4, N: 1, D: 9.22.
(65.77 kg–145 lbs)

		FINAL MATCH
1. Albert Young	USA	Dec
2. Harry Spanger	USA	
3. Jack Eagan	USA	
3. Joseph Lydon	USA	

1906–1912 not held

1920 Antwerp C: 18, N: 11, D: 8.24.
(66.68 kg–147 lbs)

			FINAL MATCH
1.	Albert Schneider	CAN	Dec
2.	Alexander Ireland	GBR	
3.	Frederick Colberg	USA	
4.	William Clark	USA	
5.	Léon Gillet (FRA), Aage Steen (NOR), Trygve Stokstad (NOR), August Suhr (DEN)		

Bert Schneider of Canada was acutally a U.S. citizen. Born in Cleveland, his family moved to Montreal when he was 9 years old. Unaware that boxing was an Olympic sport, Schneider learned that he had been chosen for the Canadian team when he read it in a newspaper. His final bout with Ireland ended in a draw, so the referee ordered the two exhausted fighters to square off for an extra round. Schneider had the most energy left and earned the gold medal.

1924 Paris C: 29, N: 18, D: 7.20.
(66.68 kg–147 lbs)

			FINAL MATCH
1.	Jean Delarge	BEL	Dec
2.	Héctor Méndez	ARG	
3.	Douglas Lewis	CAN	
4.	Patrick Dwyer	IRL	
5.	Hugh Haggerty (USA), Roy Ingram (SAF), Alfons Mello (USA), Teodor Stauffer (SWI)		

The first two rounds of the final match were all Delarge's, as Méndez tried unsuccessfully to land his notorious knockout right. He finally caught the Belgian in the third round and pummeled him around the ring. But it was too late. Delarge wouldn't go down, and he had already built up a big enough lead to secure the victory. When the verdict was announced, pandemonium broke loose as thousands of Argentinians began chanting, "Méndez! Méndez! Méndez!" A furious Belgian rushed in among them and unfurled a Belgian flag, which led to further chaos. The demonstration went on for over fifteen minutes before order was restored. This incident was actually a mere anticlimax to what had occurred following a preliminary match three days earlier. On that day an English referee, T.H. Walker, disqualified an Italian boxer named Giuseppi Oldani for persistent holding of his opponent. Oldani fell to the floor, sobbing, while his supporters pelted Walker with sticks, coins, and walking stick knobs. This went on for almost an hour, until Walker was finally escorted from the arena by a contingent of British, American, and South African boxers, headed by the 265-pound wrestler Con O'Kelly.

1928 Amsterdam C: 22, N: 22, D: 8.11.
(66.68 kg–147 lbs)

			FINAL MATCH
1.	Edward Morgan	NZE	Dec
2.	Raúl Landini	ARG	
3.	Raymond Smillie	CAN	
4.	Robert Galataud	FRA	
5.	Cornelis Blommers (HOL), Romano Caneva (ITA), Johan Hellstrom (FIN), Kintaro Usuda (JPN)		

Twenty-two-year-old Ted Morgan was the first gold medalist to represent New Zealand.

1932 Los Angeles C: 16, N: 16, D: 8.13.
(66.68 kg–147 lbs)

			FINAL MATCH
1.	Edward Flynn	USA	Dec
2.	Erich Campe	GER	
3.	Bruno Ahlberg	FIN	
4.	David McCleave	GBR	
5.	Robert Barton (SAF), Luciano Fabbroni (ITA), Lucien Laplace (FRA), Carl Jensen (DEN)		

After the Olympics Flynn turned professional and fought just long enough to finance his way through dental school, eventually setting up practice in New Orleans.

1936 Berlin C: 25, N: 25, D: 8.15.
(66.68 kg–147 lbs)

			FINAL MATCH
1.	Sten Suvio	FIN	Dec
2.	Michael Murach	GER	
3.	Gerhard Petersen	DEN	
4.	Roger Tritz	FRA	
5.	Simplicio de Castro (PHI), Heinrich Dekkers (HOL), Imre Mándi (HUN), Raul Rodriguez (ARG)		

1948 London C: 26, N: 26, D: 8.13.

			FINAL MATCH
1.	Július Torma	CZE/SLV	Dec
2.	Horace Herring	USA	
3.	Alessandro D'Ottavio	ITA	
4.	Douglas Du Preez	SAF	
5.	William Boyce (AUS), Zygmunt Chychla (POL), Aurelio Cadabeda Diaz (SPA), Eladio Herrera (ARG)		

Before his second-round bout with Gerald Blackburn of Canada, Július Torma of Czechoslovakia attempted to shake hands with his opponent in the dressing room. When Blackburn refused, Torma became angry and decided to give the Canadian a lesson in the ring. This he did, with the referee stopping the fight in the second round. However, Torma's final left hook fractured a bone in his hand and it looked as if he might have to withdraw. Instead the 26-year-old Hungarian-born store clerk was able to hide his injury from his next three opponents, winning with careful defense and judicious use of his right hand.

1952 Helsinki C: 29, N: 29, D: 8.2.

			FINAL MATCH
1.	Zygmunt Chychla	POL	Dec 3–0
2.	Sergei Scherbakov	SOV/RUS	
3.	Günther Heidemann	GER	
3.	Victor Jörgensen	DEN	
5.	Nicholaas Linneman (HOL), Ronald Norris (IND), Július Torma (CZE), Franco Vescovi (ITA)		

1956 Melbourne C: 16, N: 16, D: 12.1.

			FINAL MATCH
1.	Nicolae Linca	ROM	Dec 3–2
2.	Frederick Tiedt	IRL	
3.	Nicholas Gargano	GBR	
3.	Kevin John Hogarth	AUS	
5.	Nicholas André (SAF), András Döri (HUN), Francisco Gelabert (ARG), Pearce Allen Lane (USA)		

Tiedt actually received more total points than Linca, but the Romanian was given the nod by three of the five judges. Romania has a strange history in Olympic boxing. Although nineteen different Romanian boxers have earned medals, Linca is the only one to have won a gold.

1960 Rome C: 33, N: 33, D: 9.5.

			FINAL MATCH
1.	Giovanni Benvenuti	ITA	Dec 4–1
2.	Yuri Radonyak	SOV/RUS	
3.	Leszek Drogosz	POL	
3.	James Lloyd	GBR	
5.	A. Phillip Baldwin (USA), Henry Loubscher (SAF), Shishman Mitsev (BUL), Andres Moreno Navarro (SPA)		

The European Light Middleweight champion, Benvenuti dropped down in weight class for the Olympics. He floored Radonyak toward the end of the first round, but the Soviet boxer came back strongly and was the aggressor in the final round. Benvenuti turned professional in 1961 and won the World Junior Middleweight title in 1965. On April 17, 1967, he defeated Emile Griffith for the World Middleweight championship, a title which he held for three of the next three and a half years.

1964 Tokyo C: 30, N: 30, D: 10.23.

			FINAL MATCH
1.	Marian Kasprzyk	POL	Dec 4–1
2.	Ričardas Tamulis	SOV/LIT	
3.	Silvano Bertini	ITA	
3.	Pertti Purhonen	FIN	
5.	Issaka Daborg (NIG), Kichijiro Hamada (JPN), Ernest Powell Mabwa (UGA), Michael Varley (GBR)		

1968 Mexico City C: 33, N: 33, D: 10.26.

			FINAL MATCH
1.	Manfred Wolke	GDR	Dec 4–1
2.	Joseph Bessala	CAM	
3.	Mario Guilloti	ARG	
3.	Volodymyr Musalimov	SOV/UKR	
5.	Armando Muniz (USA), Alfonso Ramirez Gutierrez (MEX), Celal Sandal (TUR), Victor Zilberman (ROM)		

1972 Munich C: 37, N: 37, D: 9.10.

			FINAL MATCH
1.	Emilio Correa	CUB	Dec 5–0
2.	János Kajdi	HUN	
3.	Dick "Tiger" Murunga	KEN	
3.	Jesse Valdez	USA	
5.	Maurice Hope (GBR), Anatoly Khohlov (SOV), Sergio Lozano (MEX), Günter Meier (GER)		

The final matched the 19-year-old Pan American champion, Emilio Correa, and the 32-year-old European titleholder, János Kajdi. The Cuban won a close but unanimous decision.

1976 Montreal C: 31, N: 31, D: 7.31.

			FINAL MATCH
1.	Jochen Bachfeld	GDR	Dec 3–2
2.	Pedro Gamarro	VEN	
3.	Reinhard Skricek	GER	
3.	Victor Zilberman	ROM	
5.	Clinton Jackson (USA), Michael McCallum (JAM), Carmen Rinke (CAN), Carlos Santos (PUR)		

Silver medalist Pedro Gamarro was the surprise of the tournament. In his third bout he stopped defending Olympic and world amateur champion Correa, and in the quarterfinals he defeated favorite Clinton Jackson on a split decision. The 21-year-old Venezuelan almost went all the way, but he lost a close split decision in the title match to 24-year-old Jochen Bachfeld.

1980 Moscow C: 29, N: 29, D: 8.2.

			FINAL MATCH
1.	Andrés Aldama	CUB	Dec 4–1
2.	John Mugabi	UGA	
3.	Karl-Heinz Krüger	GDR	
3.	Kazimierz Szczerba	POL	
5.	Memet Bogujević (YUG), Ionel Buduşan (ROM), Joseph Frost (GBR), Plamen Yankov (BUL)		

John Mugabi needed a total of only nine minutes to knock out his first three opponents. He got by Kazimierz Szczerba on a split decision but was defeated by Andrés Aldama, who had won the Light Welterweight silver medal four years earlier.

1984 Los Angeles C: 36, N: 36, D: 8.11.

		FINAL MATCH
1. Mark Breland	USA	Dec 5–0
2. An Young-su	KOR	
3. Luciano Bruno	ITA	
3. Joni Nyman	FIN	

5. Dwight Frazer (JAM), Vesa Koskela (SWE), Alexander Künzler (GER), Genaro Leon (MEX)

At 6 feet 2 inches, Brooklyn's Mark Breland, the most ballyhooed boxer at the Los Angeles Olympics, towered over his fellow welterweights. He also sported a 78-inch reach. Entering the tournament, Breland was the overwhelming favorite, having won the 1982 world amateur championship and having beaten everyone in his division including those from boycotting nations. His pre-Olympic record was 104 wins and 1 loss. As if all this wasn't intimidating enough to his opponents, Breland, who sparred with Tommy Hearns and with a professional karate champion, also received pre-fight advice from Muhammad Ali, Sugar Ray Robinson and Sugar Ray Leonard. A well-composed student of yoga, the 20-year-old Breland had already gained fame outside the world of boxing by starring in the 1983 film *The Lords of Discipline*.

1988 Seoul C: 44, N: 44, D: 10.1.

		FINAL MATCH	
1. Robert Wangila	KEN	KO 2	0:44
2. Laurent Boudouani	FRA		
3. Jan Dydak	POL		
3. Kenneth Gould	USA		

5. Adewale Adegbusi (NGR), Hristo Furnigov (BUL), Joni Nyman (FIN), Song Kyung-sup (KOR)

Wangila, a Nairobi brewery worker, was the first black African boxer to win an Olympic championship. This was also the first welterweight final to be decided by a knockout after 16 consecutive decisions. On July 22, 1994, Wangila lost a professional fight in Las Vegas to David Gonzales, walked back to the dressing room, and suddenly lapsed into a coma. He died 36 hours later. When his body was returned to Nairobi, fighting broke out between the police and local Moslems over what form of burial he should receive.

1992 Barcelona—Badalona C: 30, N: 30, D: 8.8.

		FINAL MATCH
1. Michael Carruth	IRL	Pts 13–10
2. Juan Hernández Sierra	CUB	
3. Aníbal Acevedo Santiago	PUR	
3. Arkhom Chenglai	THA	

5. Sören Antman (SWE), Vitalijus Karpačiauskas (LIT), Andreas Otto (GER), Francisc Vaştag (ROM)

The stereotypical Irishman loves a good fight, but until 1992 no boxer representing Ireland had ever won a gold medal. So it was a great day for the Irish on August 8, when not one but two Irish fighters made it to the finals in Barcelona—such a thing had never happened before. Despite the fact that it was the Cubans who had dominated the tournament, qualifying for five of the six finals being held that day, it was the Irish fans who filled the Joventut Pavilion with drum-beating, singing, and raucous celebration. The first Irish finalist, bantamweight Wayne McCullough, was thought to have the best chance of becoming Ireland's first Olympic champion in any sport since Ron Delany won the 1500 meters back in 1956. McCullough fought gamely, but was outpointed by Cuban Joel Casamayor. If McCullough couldn't defeat a Cuban opponent, what possible chance could Michael Carruth have? After all, Juan Hernández was the reigning world champion; Carruth wasn't even ranked in the top fifteen. Even the bookmakers in Ireland were giving 7-2 odds in favor of Hernández.

Carruth, an army corporal, came from a family of ten children in Greenhills, south Dublin, and was the last born of triplets. At the Seoul Olympics, fighting as a light welterweight, Carruth won one bout then lost his second. At the 1989 world championships he earned a bronze medal, losing 18-1 in the semifinals to Andreas Otto of Germany. At the Barcelona Olympics, three years later, Carruth faced Otto again, this time in the quarterfinals. When the fight was over the scoreboard read 6-6. In the event of a tie, the officials turn to the total punches registered by the five judges combined. This time Carruth came out on top, 35-22. By defeating Arkhom Chenglai 11-4 in the semis, he unexpectedly fought himself into the final against Hernández, who had overwhelmed his four opponents, stopping two of them in the second round and outpointing the other two 6-0 and 11-2.

Despite his long-shot status, Carruth had a couple things going for him. Because of a gymnastics injury, his right arm was more than two inches shorter than his left. Although he was right-handed, he was forced to fight as a southpaw, making him strong with both hands. Most important, in his corner he had something few other boxers had—a Cuban coach, Nicholas Cruz, not to mention a special trainer: his own father, Austin Carruth.

Sitting in the dressing room just before the final, Michael Carruth began to lose heart. It was hard for him to imagine defeating Hernández. Austin Carruth walked over and guessed what was going on. He pointed to his son's legs and said, "There's your ticket to the gold medal. That's the way you're going to win this fight—by using them." Michael closed his eyes, concentrated, and, as he later recalled, "miraculously, the self-doubt began to recede. I grabbed hold of Dad and the man nearly passed out on the spot with fright. 'Dad,' I told him, 'I'm going to win this fight. I'm going to bring the gold medal back with me to Dublin. Ronnie Delany's time is up.'"

In the first round Carruth successfully crowded the taller Hernández and came away with a 4-3 lead. In the second round, he was penalized three points for holding, but gained back a couple points as the round closed. The score was 8-8. Back in his corner Carruth suggested that he should "have a real go" at Hernández and try to back him into a corner. His father and Cruz bawled him out and told him to stick to his game plan of forcing Hernández to come to him and sneaking inside. They pointed across to the Cuban corner, where tempers were flaring and frustration and panic were starting to show. Sure enough, in the final three minutes, Hernández's impatience led to errors and Carruth was able to take the round, 5-2, and with it the fight and the Olympic championship. When the verdict was announced, the arena reverberated with the cheers of the Irish supporters. But the celebration in Barcelona was nothing compared to what went on back in Dublin. Carruth was instantly promoted to sergeant. Army helicopters flew over Carruth's house to salute his victory. And, most incredible of all, on the day of his return to Ireland, local pubs dropped the price of beer to that of 1956. For one day in 1992 a pint of Guinness could be bought for four pence.

LIGHT MIDDLEWEIGHT

(71 kg–156 lbs)

1896–1948 not held

1952 Helsinki C: 23, N: 23, D: 8.2.

			FINAL MATCH
1. László Papp	HUN	Dec 3–0
2. Theunis van Schalkwyk	SAF	
3. Eladio Herrera	ARG	
3. Boris Tishin	SOV/RUS	
5. Paulo de Jesus Cavalheiro (BRA), Guido Mazzinghi (ITA), Erich Schöppner (GER), Peter Stankov (BUL)		

Papp had a tough time with van Schalkwyk until the final round of their bout, when a right hook dropped the South African to his knees for an eight-count.

1956 Melbourne C: 14, N: 14, D: 12.1.

		FINAL MATCH
1. László Papp	HUN	Dec
2. José Torres	USA	
3. John McCormack	GBR	
3. Zbigniew Pietrzykowski	POL	
5. Ulrich Kienast (GER), Boris Nikolov (BUL), Franco Scisciani (ITA)		

In defeating Torres, the 30-year-old Papp became the first boxer to win three Olympic gold medals (he had won the Middleweight title in 1948). In 1965 Torres won the World Light Heavyweight professional title by knocking out Willie Pastrano. He later became commissioner of boxing for the State of New York.

László Papp, the first boxer to win three Olympic gold medals. He was Middleweight champion in 1948 and Light Middleweight champion in 1952 and 1956.

1960 Rome C: 23, N: 23, D: 9.5.

		FINAL MATCH
1. Wilbert McClure	USA	Dec 4–1
2. Carmelo Bossi	ITA	
3. William Fisher	GBR	
3. Boris Lagutin	SOV/RUS	
5. John Bukowski (AUS), Henryk Dempc (POL), Souleymane Diallo (FRA), Celedonio Lima (ARG)		

"Skeeter" McClure of Toledo, Ohio, survived two very close split decisions over Lima and Lagutin to qualify for the final. Against Bossi, he used his strong in-fighting abilities to wear down the aggressive Italian. McClure later became a professor at Northeastern University in Boston and president of his own counseling firm.

1964 Tokyo C: 25, N: 25, D: 10.23.

			FINAL MATCH
1.	Boris Lagutin	SOV/RUS	Dec 4–1
2.	Joseph Gonzales	FRA	
3.	Józef Grzesiak	POL	
3.	Nojim Maiyegun	NGR	
5.	Anthony Barber (AUS), Tom Bogs (DEN), Eddie Davies (GHA), Vasile Mirza (ROM)		

Boris Lagutin's path to the final included a victory by disqualification over José Chirino of Argentina, who was penalized for punching the referee, and a walkover in the quarterfinals. After two rounds with Gonzales, Lagutin had matters well in hand. But in the third round he decided to mix it up and received for his efforts a cut eye and a warning for pulling Gonzales. Maiyegun was the first Nigerian to win an Olympic medal.

1968 Mexico City C: 27, N: 27, D: 10.26.

			FINAL MATCH
1.	Boris Lagutin	SOV/RUS	Dec 5–0
2.	Rolando Garbey	CUB	
3.	John Baldwin	USA	
3.	Günther Meier	GER	
5.	Mario Benitez (URU), Eric Blake (GBR), David Jackson (UGA), Ianos Kovacs (ROM)		

The 30-year-old Lagutin outclassed all of his opponents to win his third straight medal. His final match with Garbey was an ugly, brawling contest, which led the crowd to boo and throw coins and burning newspapers at the Korean referee for failing to take action.

1972 Munich C: 33, N: 33, D: 9.10.

			FINAL MATCH
1.	Dieter Kottysch	GER	Dec 3–2
2.	Wieslaw Rudkowski	POL	
3.	Alan Minter	GBR	
3.	Peter Tiepold	GDR	
5.	Rolando Garbey (CUB), Loucif Hamani (ALG), Mohamed Majeri (TUN), Emeterio Villanueva (MEX)		

Kottysch eked out controversial split decisions over Minter and Rudkowski to take the gold medal. However, the most disputed verdict came in the opening round of the tournament when a battered and bleeding Valery Tregubov of the U.S.S.R. was declared the winner against Reggie Jones of the United States. The announcement was met by a quarter-hour of international catcalls, which continued throughout the next bout.

1976 Montreal C: 23, N: 23, D: 7.31.

			FINAL MATCH
1.	Jerzy Rybicki	POL	Dec 5–0
2.	Tadija Kacar	YUG	
3.	Rolando Garbey	CUB	
3.	Viktor Savchenko	SOV/UKR	
5.	Vasile Didea (ROM), Wilfredo Guzman (PUR), Kalevi Kosunen (FIN), Alfredo Lemus (VEN)		

1980 Moscow C: 23, N: 23, D: 8.2.

			FINAL MATCH
1.	Armando Martínez	CUB	Dec 4–1
2.	Aleksandr Koshkin	SOV/RUS	
3.	Ján Franek	CZE/SLV	
3.	Detlef Kästner	GDR	
5.	Francisco Carlos Jesus (BRA), Wilson Kaoma (ZAM), Leonidas Njunwa (TAN), Nicholas Colin Wilshire (GBR)		

1984 Los Angeles C: 34, N: 34, D: 8.11.

			FINAL MATCH
1.	Frank Tate	USA	Dec 5–0
2.	Shawn O'Sullivan	CAN	
3.	Christophe Tiozzo	FRA	
3.	Manfred Zielonka	GER	
5.	Israel Cole (SLE), Roderick Douglas (GBR), Christopher Kapopo (ZAM), Gnohere Sery (IVC)		

As expected, the final matched Frank Tate and Shawn O'Sullivan, who had split two previous fights with each other. What was not expected was that both boxers would reach the final as a result of unpopular decisions. Tate's came in his first bout against Lotfi Ayed, a Tunisian-born Swede. Despite being staggered and outpunched, Tate won a unanimous verdict.

Even more controversial was O'Sullivan's semifinal victory over Christophe Tiozzo. The judges voted 3–2 in Tiozzo's favor. However, new rules instituted before the 1984 Games required that all 3–2 decisions be submitted to a 5-man jury. If the jury voted 4–1 or 5–0 for the loser of the split decision, then the decision was reversed. The jury gave the nod to O'Sullivan, 4–1.

In the second round of the championship bout, Tate was twice given a standing eight-count. Nevertheless, four of the five judges awarded him the round. The announcement of Tate's victory by unanimous decision was met by a chorus of boos, but O'Sullivan, who was raised with the teachings of Henry David Thoreau, was philosophical. "It was an unfortunate decision," he told reporters. "I dearly wish things had gone different, but they didn't, and there's no gain in crying over spilled milk."

1988 Seoul C: 36, N: 36, D: 10.2.

			FINAL MATCH
1.	Park Si-hun	KOR	Dec 3–2
2.	Roy Jones	USA	

3. Raymond Downey   CAN
3. Richard Woodhall   GBR
5. Martin Kitel (SWE), Vincenzo Nardiello (ITA), Rey Rivera (PUR),
   Yevgeny Zaitsev (SOV/KAZ)

Probably no gold medalist in Olympic history has been less deserving of his prize than Park Si-hun, who benefited from five "hometown" decisions. Park's first bout, against Abdalla Ramadan of Sudan, was halted in the second round with Ramadan doubled over in pain and unable to continue following two illegal blows to the hip and kidney. The Australian referee, Ronald Mark Gregor, undoubtedly haunted by the attack on referee Keith Walker five days earlier, was hesitant to disqualify Park. Instead, he consulted the five judges, one of whom, Elmo Adolph of the U.S., told him that because Gregor had failed to caution Park after the low blows and because the fouls were not "flagrant," disqualification was inappropriate. Gregor ruled that the injured Ramadan had "retired" and declared Park the winner.

Park's second opponent was one of the favorites, Torsten Schmitz of East Germany. Most observers thought Schmitz had won the fight; however, Park was judged the victor in a narrow but unanimous decision. While the East Germans vented their fury, Park moved on to the quarterfinals and a bout with Vincenzo Nardiello of Acilia, Italy. Once again, it appeared to most observers that Park had been defeated. In fact, Nardiello was ahead on the cards of all five judges after the first two rounds. Two of the judges gave Nardiello the final round as well. However, the other three judges decided that Park had won the round by such a wide margin that they gave him the fight. When the verdict was announced, Nardiello fell to his knees and pounded the canvas. Then he charged out of the ring and began screaming at the jury. Italian team officials dragged him off to the dressing room. He raced back into the arena crying and screaming, only to be hauled back to his room.

Roy Jones, referee Aldo Leoni, and Park Si-hun react with shock at the announcement of the decision in the final of the 1988 Light Middleweight division.

In the semifinals, Park won another narrow but unanimous victory, defeating Ray Downey by the same margin by which he had beaten Schmitz. He was becoming known as "the unbeatable Park Si-hun." Now all that stood between Park and a gold medal was 19-year-old Roy Jones, Jr., of Pensacola, Florida. Jones had already alienated local fight fans and many others as well with his arrogant demeanor and showboating style. In the ring he emulated the theatrical ways of Muhammad Ali and Sugar Ray Leonard, dropping his guard and taunting his opponents, doing the Ali shuffle. Outside the ring, he gracelessly referred to one defeated opponent as "a bum." Nevertheless, Jones had also shown that he was a skillful boxer with unusually quick hands. He made it to the final without being seriously challenged. Three days before the gold-medal bout, Jones told reporters, "I know how tough it is to get a decision against a South Korean, but it doesn't matter. If they cheat me, that's OK. I'll know if I really won it." Still, to be on the safe side, Jones announced that he would be going for a knockout.

He didn't get the knockout, but he did pummel Park, dominating all three rounds. Compubox, a private company that kept track of punches thrown and connected for NBC, the U.S. television network, registered 86 hits for Jones and only 32 for Park. Incredibly, three of the five judges gave the victory to the Korean. Veteran ring observers of all nationalities, reporters, referees and fans agreed that it was the worst decision they had ever seen. The French sports newspaper *L'Equipe* summed up the consensus in blunt terms: "Scandalous. To vomit." The decision was so bad that Korean fans were embarrassed, telephoning local newspapers and television stations to complain. Even Park himself apologized to Jones, telling him, through an interpreter, "I am sorry. I lost the fight. I feel very bad." On the victory stand, Park raised Jones' arm in triumph.

So how could such an unjust decision have been made? There were accusations that officials of the Korea Amateur Boxing Federation had bribed or otherwise persuaded some of the judges as a payback for pro-U.S. decisions at the 1984 Olympics. *Sports Illustrated* reported that one judge, Hiouad Larbi of Morocco, told angry journalists, "The American won easily; so easily, in fact, that I was positive my four fellow judges would score the fight for the American by a wide margin. So I voted for the Korean to make the score only 4–1 for the American and not embarrass the host country." Unfortunately, the judges from Uruguay and Uganda did the same thing.

The Park-Jones affair, as well as numerous other dubious decisions, forced the International Boxing Federation to institute radical changes in scoring in 1989. Ringside computers are now used to allow the judges to push a button whenever a scoring punch is made. If a majority of the judges push the button simultaneously, a point is recorded on a scoreboard visible to all in the arena. The winner is known the instant a bout is over.

1992 Barcelona—Badalona C: 30, N: 30, D: 8.9.

			FINAL MATCH
1.	Juan Carlos Lemus García	CUB	Pts 6–1
2.	Orhan Delibas	HOL	
3.	György Mizsei	HUN	
3.	Robin Reid	GBR	
5.	Ole Klemetsen (NOR), Raul Marquez (USA), Fao Maselino (ASA), Igors Shaplavskis (LAT)		

World champion Lemus was never seriously challenged. He stopped one opponent in the first round and outpointed the other four by a combined score of 39 to 4. Runner-up Orhan Delibas was born in Turkey.

MIDDLEWEIGHT

(75 kg–165½ lbs)

1896–1900 not held

1904 St. Louis C: 2, N: 1, D: 9.22.
(71.67 kg–158 lbs)

			FINAL MATCH	
1.	Charles Mayer	USA	RSC 3	1:40
2.	Benjamin Spradley	USA		

1906 not held

1908 London C: 10, N: 3, D: 10.27.
(71.67 kg–158 lbs)

			FINAL MATCH
1.	John Douglas	GBR	Dec
2.	Reginald "Snowy" Baker	AUS	
3.	William Philo	GBR	
4.	Ruben Warnes	GBR	
5.	William Childs	GBR	

Douglas was a well-known cricketer, known as "Johnny Won't Hit Today" Douglas because of his defensive batting. Silver medalist Reginald "Snowy" Baker also took part in the springboard diving competition and the 4 × 200-meter freestyle relay at the 1908 Olympics. In fact, Baker was probably the greatest all-around athlete ever produced by Australia. He competed in twenty-nine different sports and represented Australia in international competition in five of them. He also knocked out Douglas in a rematch a few days after the Olympics. In later years, Baker starred in several silent films, most notably *The Fighting Breed* (1921), moved to Hollywood, and taught fencing, riding, and swimming to stars such as Greta Garbo and Douglas Fairbanks.

1912 not held

1920 Antwerp C: 17, N: 10, D: 8.24.
(72.57 kg–160 lbs)

			FINAL MATCH
1.	Henry Mallin	GBR	Dec
2.	Georges Prudhomme	CAN	
3.	Montgomery "Moe" Herscovitch	CAN	
4.	Hjalmar Strömme	NOR	
5.	William Bradley (SAF), Samuel Lagonia (USA), Martin Olsen (DEN), Marcel Rey-Golliet (FRA)		

1924 Paris C: 23, N: 14, D: 7.20.
(72.57 kg–160 lbs)

			FINAL MATCH
1.	Henry Mallin	GBR	Dec
2.	John Elliott	GBR	
3.	Joseph Beecken	BEL	
4.	Leslie Black	CAN	
5.	Roger Brousse (FRA), Daney (FRA), T. Harry Henning (CAN), James Murphy (IRL)		

Olympic boxing has a long and glorious history of protests, demonstrations, and general outrages. But of all the incidents and controversies, the real gold medal winner was the Brousse-Mallin Affair, which occurred in Paris in 1924. Harry Mallin, the defending champion,

"Unroasted human beef of Old England": Harry Mallin, the 1920 and 1924 Middleweight gold medalist.

was a 32-year-old London policeman. In the quarterfinals he faced 23-year-old Roger Brousse of France. As soon as the fight ended, Mallin approached the Belgian referee and displayed several well-defined teeth marks on his chest. The referee ignored him and proceeded to read out the verdict. Although most ringside observers gave the fight to Mallin, it was Brousse who won the decision, 2–1. The Italian judge and the Belgian referee voted for Brousse, while the South African judge sided with Mallin. Mallin, who had never lost a fight, left the ring without further comment. However, a protest was lodged by Mr. Söderland, a Swedish member of the International Boxing Association, and an inquiry was held. Examination of Mallin's chest revealed that he had most definitely been bitten, and quite robustly at that. In fact, in his previous bout Brousse had also been accused of biting his opponent, Manolo Gallardo of Argentina. Brousse's supporters claimed that he had an odd habit of snapping his jaw whenever he threw a punch. What had happened, they said, was that Mallin had ducked one of Brousse's punches and, coming back up, bumped his chest against Brousse's snapping mouth. The Jury of Appeal ruled that Brousse's bite had been unintentional, but disqualified him anyway. When this decision was announced at the Vélodrome d'Hiver the following evening, Brousse leapt to his feet and burst into tears. Immediately the hall became a scene of turmoil. Brousse was hoisted upon the shoulders of his loyal fans and paraded about the arena. Hundreds of demonstrators hooted and hollered and attempted to enter the ring. They were repulsed by the police. After about a half hour the commotion died down, but Brousse's supporters continued to launch attacks against the judges and referees for the rest of the evening.

The boxing finals were held the following night. The evening began with the announcement that two Italian boxers, flyweight Rinaldo Castellenghi and light heavyweight Carlo Saraudi, had withdrawn from their bronze-medal matches to protest the poor officiating. After the Mendez-Delarge welterweight final the arena was in an uproar, with hundreds of Argentinians expressing their outrage and anger vociferously. The confusion was added to when Mallin and Jack Elliot entered the ring, for the mere sight of Mallin set off the French spectators in their own chorus of catcalls. Not surprisingly, the two English middleweights had a hard time concentrating on their contest, which Mallin won in an uncharacteristically uninspired manner. The official report of the British Olympic Association included this account of the bout: "Mallin eventually won a close fight, but we are unable to give a more detailed description, owing to the fact that we were seated in the centre of a group of excited and gesticulating Frenchmen, who, not content with making themselves ridiculous . . . also refused to allow anyone in their proximity to get a view of the fight." The British press had a field day with the affair. "It was found necessary," said the *Daily Sketch,* "to substitute for a mere

boxer a man-eating expert named Brousse, whose passion for raw meat led him to attempt to bite off portions of his opponents' anatomies." Another reporter wrote, "Having got his teeth into a piece of Argentine meat during one of the earlier contests, M. Brousse decided to vary the menu by sampling some of the unroasted human beef of Old England." Less light-hearted observers called for an end to boxing, an end to the Olympics, and, at the very least, an end to the French. However, life did go on and so did boxing and so did the Olympics and so did the French.

1928 Amsterdam C: 17, N: 17, D: 8.11.
(72.57 kg–160 lbs)

			FINAL MATCH
1.	Piero Toscani	ITA	Dec
2.	Jan Heřmánek	CZE	
3.	Leonard Steyaert	BEL	
4.	Frederick Mallin	GBR	
5.	John Chase (IRL), Humberto Curi (ARG), Harry Henderson (USA), Oscar Kjällander (SWE)		

Wild scenes and alleged injustice hit the Middleweight division again in Amsterdam. In the final Heřmánek appeared to be the winner, but Toscani was awarded the gold medal. Heřmánek was hoisted on the shoulders of his countrymen and dumped at the feet of the judges, where he argued his case while the demonstration spread, erupting into violence in the back of the hall. While the light heavyweight finalists, Avendaño and Pistulla, prepared for their bout, Heřmánek's seconds tried to push him back into the ring. Finally the police intervened, and action *inside* the ring resumed.

1932 Los Angeles C: 10, N: 10, D: 8.13.
(72.57 kg–160 lbs)

			FINAL MATCH
1.	Carmen Barth	USA	Dec
2.	Amado Azar	ARG	
3.	Ernest Pierce	SAF	
4.	Roger Michelot	FRA	
5.	Hans Bernlöhr (GER)		

1936 Berlin C: 19, N: 19, D: 8.15.
(72.57 kg–160 lbs)

			FINAL MATCH
1.	Jean Despeaux	FRA	Dec
2.	Henry Tiller	NOR	
3.	Raúl Villarreal	ARG	
4.	Henryk Chmielewski	POL	
5.	Adolf Baumgarten (GER), James Atkinson (USA), Gerardus Dekkers (HOL), Josef Hrubes (CZE)		

1948 London C: 25, N: 25, D: 8.13.
(73 kg–161 lbs)

		FINAL MATCH	
1. László Papp	HUN	Dec	
2. John Wright	GBR		
3. Ivano Fontana	ITA		
4. Michael McKeon	IRL		
5. August Cavignac (BEL), Aime-Joseph Escudie (FRA), Dogomar Martinez (URU), Jan Schubart (HOL)			

This was the first milestone in László Papp's illustrious career. In 1952 he would go on to win the Light Middleweight gold medal and in 1956 he would successfully defend his title. The following year, at the age of 31, Papp gained permission from the Hungarian government to become the first boxer from a Communist country to fight professionally. He won the European Middleweight championship, but the Hungarian government refused to let him challenge for the world championship. He retired undefeated in 1965 and became a coach for the Hungarian Olympic team.

1952 Helsinki C: 23, N: 23, D: 8.2.

		FINAL MATCH	
1. Floyd Patterson	USA	KO 1	1:14
2. Vasile Țiță	ROM		
3. Boris Nikolov	BUL		
3. Stig Sjölin	SWE		
5. Leonardus Jansen (HOL), Anthony Madigan (AUS), Walter Sentimenti (ITA), Dieter Wemhöner (GER)			

Seventeen-year-old Floyd Patterson, who came from a family of 11 children in Brooklyn, breezed through his four bouts in the easiest manner imaginable. When the bell sounded at the start of the final, Patterson spun around in a circle, which earned him a warning from the Polish referee. A tremendous uppercut to Țiță's chin ended the contest after 74 seconds. Four years later Patterson knocked out Archie Moore to win the vacant World Heavyweight title and became the youngest heavyweight champion until Mike Tyson. In 1959 he lost the title to Ingemar Johansson; then, in 1960, he defeated Johansson to become the first boxer to regain the heavyweight championship.

1956 Melbourne C: 14, N: 14, D: 12.1.

		FINAL MATCH	
1. Gennady Shatkov	SOV/RUS	KO 1	
2. Rámon Tapia	CHI		
3. Gilbert Chapron	FRA		
3. Víctor Zalazar	ARG		
5. Giulio Rinaldi (ITA), Július Torma (CZE/SLV), Dieter Wemhöner (GER)			

1960 Rome C: 25, N: 25, 9.5.

		FINAL MATCH
1. Edward Crook	USA	Dec 3–2
2. Tadeusz Walasek	POL	
3. Vevgeny Feofanov	SOV/RUS	
3. Ion Monea	ROM	
5. Hans Buechi (SWI), Chang Lo-Pu (TAI), Luigi Napoleoni (ITA) Frederik Van Rooyen (SAF)		

The announcement of Crook's victory over Walasek was greeted by prolonged booing and whistling, which caused a delay in the awards ceremony.

1964 Tokyo C: 20, N: 20, D: 10.23.

		FINAL MATCH	
1. Valery Popenchenko	SOV/RUS	RSC 1	2:05
2. Emil Schulz	GER		
3. Franco Valle	ITA		
3. Tadeusz Walasek	POL		
5. Joe Darkey (GHA), Ahmed Hassan (EGY), Ion Monea (ROM), Guillermo Slinas (CHI)			

1968 Mexico City C: 22, N: 22, D: 10.26.

		FINAL MATCH
1. Christopher Finnegan	GBR	Dec 3–2
2. Aleksei Kiselyov	SOV/RUS	
3. Alfred Jones	USA	
3. Agustin Zaragoza	MEX	
5. Simeon Georgiev (BUL), Jan Hejdik (CZE), Mate Parlov (YUG), Wieslaw Rudkowski (POL)		

Chris Finnegan, a 24-year-old bricklayer from Iver, Buckinghamshire, almost didn't make it to the Olympics when

Outspoken Chris Finnegan, on his way to victory in the 1968 Middleweight division. His biggest challenge was producing a urine sample for the post-fight drug test.

an eye injury prevented him from taking part in the Amateur Boxing Association (ABA) championships that supposedly determined the Olympic team. He drowned his disappointment in a two-week drinking binge but was rescued by his trainer Dick Gunn, when Gunn helped secure a box-off for Finnegan based on Finnegan's excellent record. At the Mexico City Olympics, he survived two standing eight-counts in his semifinal bout against Al Jones of Detroit and was awarded an unpopular 4–1 decision. In the final Finnegan faced Aleksei Kiselyov, who had won the Light Heavyweight silver medal four years earlier. Kiselyov started strong, but was already tiring by the second round. The fight was close, but Finnegan thought he had won. "Then we were called to the centre of the ring for the announcement," he recalled in his autobiography *Finnegan: Self-Portrait of a Fighting Man.* "At first I couldn't cotton on to the jabber, but all of a sudden I heard the magic word which sounds the same in any language—FINNEGAN!" Three judges had voted 59–58 for Finnegan and two had voted 59–58 for Kiselyov. "I shall never be able to properly describe my feelings as I climbed up on that rostrum for the medal presentation," he went on. "The nearest I've felt to it was when walking down the aisle with my old woman after our wedding. . . . Only there was no gold medal at the end of that—only the golden rivet."

But Finnegan's most difficult challenge was still ahead: the urine test for drugs. As Finnegan put it: "Now if there's one thing I've never been able to do, it's have a piss while someone's watching me. I can never stand at those long urinals you get in gents' bogs, with all the other blokes having a quick squint." Sure enough, he was unable to produce. People turned on water faucets, whistled, whispered encouragement. He drank several glasses of water. Still nothing. Then he downed three or four pints of beer, but still without the desired result. After giving a television interview, Finnegan was hauled off to a local restaurant for a victory meal. Two Olympic officials tagged along with the necessary collection equipment. Finally, at 1:40 a.m., Finnegan jumped up and shouted, "Who wants some piss?" The officials followed him to the men's room, secured their sample, and returned to the lab. The test, of course, proved negative.

1972 Munich C: 22, N: 22, D: 9.10.

		FINAL MATCH	
1. Vyacheslav Lemechev	SOV/RUS	KO 1	2:17
2. Reima Virtanen	FIN		
3. Prince Amartey	GHA		
3. Marvin Johnson	USA		
5. Poul Knudsen (DEN), Nazif Kuran (TUR), Alejandro Montoya (CUB), Witold Stachurski (POL)			

Lemechev's performance was so impressive that only one of his five opponents lasted the full three rounds. In the semifinals he stopped Marvin Johnson in the second round to avenge an earlier loss in the Soviet Union. In

the final, Lemechev, a great counterpuncher, scored a sharp right cross over Virtanen's left lead that put the Finnish boxer out cold for a minute.

1976 Montreal C: 19, N: 19, D: 7.31.

		FINAL MATCH	
1. Michael Spinks	USA	RSC 3	1:54
2. Rufat Riskiyev	SOV/UZB		
3. Luis Martínez	CUB		
3. Alec Nastac	ROM		
5. Siraj Din (PAK), Fernando Martins (BRA), Ryszard Pasiewicz (POL), Dragomir Vujkovic (YUG)			

Twenty-year-old Michael Spinks of St. Louis won the gold medal even though he fought only two fights—his path to the title included one bye and two forfeits. Six months earlier Spinks had been beaten by Riskiyev in Tashkent, but in the third round of the final in Montreal, Spinks landed a tremendous blow to the Soviet boxer's stomach, causing Riskiyev to double up in pain and the referee to stop the contest. Spinks went on to great success as a professional boxer, gaining the WBA Light Heavyweight championship in 1981 and adding the WBC title in 1983. In 1985, he defeated Larry Holmes for the World Heavyweight championship.

1980 Moscow C: 19, N: 19, D. 8.2.

		FINAL MATCH	
1. José Gómez	CUB	Dec 4–1	
2. Viktor Savchenko	SOV/UKR		
3. Jerzy Rybicki	POL		
3. Valentin Silaghi	ROM		
5. Jang Bong-mun (PRK), Mark Kaylor (GBR), Peter Odhiambo (UGA), Manfred Trauten (GDR)			

Savchenko won his first four fights by technical knockouts, but Gómez, the favorite, was too much for him in the final.

1984 Los Angeles C: 27, N: 27, D: 8.11.

		FINAL MATCH	
1. Shin Joon-sup	KOR	Dec 3–2	
2. Virgil Hill	USA		
3. Aristides González	PUR		
3. Mohamed Zaoui	ALG		
5. Moses Mwaba (ZAM), Jeremiah Okorodudu (NGR), Damir Škaro (YUG), Pedro van Raamsdonk (HOL)			

Of the 38 fights involving U.S. boxers at the Los Angeles Olympics that went the full three rounds, 37 of them were decided in favor of the Americans. The only exception was the middleweight final in which Virgil Hill of North Dakota lost a very close decision to 23-year-old Shin Joon-sup, providing a cathartic happy ending for an otherwise frustrated and embittered Korean boxing squad. Four of Shin's five victories were by split decision.

1988 Seoul C: 33, N: 33, D: 10.1.

			FINAL MATCH
1.	Henry Maske	GDR	Dec 5–0
2.	Egerton Marcus	CAN	
3.	Chris Sande	KEN	
3.	Hussain Shah Syed	PAK	
5.	Zoltán Füzesy (HUN), Michele Mastrodonato (ITA), Sven Ottke (GER), Franco Wanyama (UGA)		

The most respected boxer in the middleweight division, Angel Espinoza of Cuba, was unable to compete because his government boycotted the Seoul Games. This put 6-foot 3½-inch Henry Maske into the role of favorite. Maske did not disappoint, registering unanimous decisions in each of his four fights. Maske's last victim, Guyana-born Egerton Marcus, fought the final with an injured right hand. Marcus' uncle, Charlie Arnos, represented Guyana in the 1968 Olympics. His mother was a boxer as well.

In a repeat of the 1972 men's 100-meter sprint snafu, the U.S. entrant, Anthony Hembrick, failed to show up on time for his opening bout when his coaches misread the day's schedule.

1992 Barcelona—Badalona C: 28, N: 28, D: 8.8.

			FINAL MATCH
1.	Ariel Hernández Ascuy	CUB	Pts 12–7
2.	Chris Byrd	USA	
3.	Chris Johnson	CAN	
3.	Lee Seung-bae	KOR	
5.	Ahmed Dine (ALG), Sven Ottke (GER), Albert Papilaya (INA), Stefan Trendafilov (BUL)		

Hernández and Byrd, whose father, Joe, was the United States' head coach, were far and away the class of the division. Hernández qualified for the final by outpointing his four opponents 47-9; Byrd outscored his four opponents 75-15. Both fighters were specialists in counterpunching. Unfortunately, this did not make for a thrilling final. The score was tied 4-4 after two rounds, but Hernández used his speed to pull out the victory in the final two minutes.

LIGHT HEAVYWEIGHT
(81 kg–179 lbs)

1896–1912 not held

1920 Antwerp C: 11, N: 6, D: 8.24.
(79.38 kg–175 lbs)

			FINAL MATCH
1.	Edward Eagan	USA	Dec
2.	Sverre Sörsdal	NOR	
3.	Harold Franks	GBR	
4.	Hugh Brown	GBR	
5.	Thomas Holdstock (SAF), Edwin Schell (USA)		

Eddie Eagan won the Light Heavyweight gold medal in 1920. Twelve years later, as a member of the winning four-man bobsled team, he became the only person to earn gold medals in both the Summer and Winter Games.

Eddie Eagan is the only person to have won a gold medal in both the Summer and Winter Olympics. Eagan grew up in a poor family in Denver, but made his way through Yale, Harvard Law School, and Oxford, became a successful lawyer, and married an automobile heiress. He lived his life according to the precepts of Frank Merriwell, the fictional hero of dime novels. In 1932, he wrote, "To this day I have never used tobacco, because Frank didn't. My first glass of wine, which I do not care for, was taken under social compulsion in Europe. Frank never drank." Twelve years after his boxing victory at the Antwerp Olympics, he reappeared as a member of the four-man bobsled team led by Billy Fiske that finished first at the Lake Placid Games.

1924 Paris C: 21, N: 15, D: 7.20.
(79.38 kg–175 lbs)

			FINAL MATCH
1.	Harry Mitchell	GBR	Dec
2.	Thyge Petersen	DEN	
3.	Sverre Sörsdal	NOR	
4.	Carlo Saraudi	ITA	
5.	John Courtis (GBR), Thomas Kirby (USA), George Mulholland (USA), Rossignon (FRA)		

1928 Amsterdam C: 16, N: 16, D: 8.11.
(79.38 kg–175 lbs)

			FINAL MATCH
1.	Víctor Avendaño	ARG	Dec
2.	Ernst Pistulla	GER	
3.	Karl Leendert Miljon	HOL	
4.	Donald McCorkindale	SAF	
5.	Donald Carrick (CAN), Alfred Jackson (GBR), Juozas Vinca (LIT), William Murphy (IRL)		

1932 Los Angeles C: 8, N: 8, D: 8.13.
(79.38 kg–175 lbs)

			FINAL MATCH
1.	David Carstens	SAF	Dec
2.	Gino Rossi	ITA	
3.	Peter Jörgensen	DEN	
4.	James Murphy	IRL	

1936 Berlin C: 22, N: 22, D: 8.15.
(79.38 kg–175 lbs)

			FINAL MATCH
1.	Roger Michelot	FRA	Dec
2.	Richard Vogt	GER	
3.	Francisco Risiglione	ARG	
4.	Sydney Leibbrandt	SAF	
5.	Thomas Griffin (GBR), František Havelka (CZE), Borge Holm (DEN), Johannes Koivunen (FIN)		

Michelot's most satisfying moment of the Berlin Games came when Adolf Hitler arrived during the medal ceremony and was obliged to remain standing during the playing of the "Marseillaise."

1948 London C: 24, N: 24, D: 8.13.
(80 kg–177 lbs)

			FINAL MATCH
1.	George Hunter	SAF	Dec
2.	Donald Scott	GBR	
3.	Maurio Cia	ARG	
4.	Adrian Holmes	AUS	
5.	Giacomo Di Segni (ITA), Hugh O'Hagan (IRL), Harri Siljander (FIN), Franciszek Szymura (POL)		

Before the match for third place, Maurio Cia had his broken right hand shot up with cocaine, then used it to knock down Adrian Holmes, who broke his ankle when he fell. Gold medalist George Hunter, a 21-year-old boilermaker, was awarded the Val Barker trophy for the best boxer of the Olympics.

1952 Helsinki C: 18, N: 18, D: 8.2.

			FINAL MATCH
1.	Norvel Lee	USA	Dec 3–0
2.	Antonio Pacenza	ARG	
3.	Anatoly Perov	SOV/RUS	
3.	Harri Siljander	FIN	
5.	Giovanni Battista Alfonsetti (ITA), Lucio Grotone (BRA), Tadeusz Grzelak (POL), Karl Kistner (GER)		

Norvel Lee went to Helsinki as a reserve heavyweight. Informed that he could compete as a light heavyweight if he made the weight limit, he lost twelve pounds and won the gold medal. An exception among boxers, Lee already had a master's degree, from Howard University. In 1948 Lee had been arrested in his hometown of Covington, Kentucky, for being one of the first blacks to sit in the all-white front section of a local bus.

1956 Melbourne C: 11, N: 11, D: 12.1.

			FINAL MATCH
1.	James Boyd	USA	Dec
2.	Gheorghe Negrea	ROM	
3.	Carlos Lucas	CHI	
3.	Romualdas Murauskas	SOV/LIT	
5.	Rodolfo Díaz (ARG), Anthony Madigan (AUS), Ottavio Panunzi (ITA), Andrzej Wojciechowski (POL)		

1960 Rome C: 19, N: 19, D: 9.5.

			FINAL MATCH
1.	Cassius Clay	USA	Dec 5–0
2.	Zbigniew Pietrzykowski	POL	
3.	Anthony Madigan	AUS	
3.	Giulio Saraudi	ITA	
5.	Gennady Shatkov (SOV/RUS), Rafael Gargiulo (ARG), Gheorghe Negrea (ROM), Petar Stankov (BUL)		

Long before Muhammad Ali became one of the most famous people in the world, he was Cassius Marcellus Clay, a brash and friendly 18-year-old who traveled to Rome from his hometown of Louisville, Kentucky, with hopes of winning a gold medal. Clay thrived in the atmosphere of the Olympic Village, garrulously introducing himself to people of all countries, joking with them, having his picture taken with them.

In the ring he was equally in his element. After stopping Yan Becaus of Belgium in the second round, he defeated the 1956 Olympic Middleweight champion, Gennady Shatkov, and the Australian Tony Madigan, by unanimous decisions. In the final he met the three-time European champion, Zbigniew Pietrzykowski, who was a veteran of 231 fights. Clay spent the first two rounds nimbly avoiding everything Pietrzykowski threw at him. Then in the last round he overwhelmed the Pole to earn a clear, unanimous decision.

At a press conference after the fight, a Soviet journalist asked Clay how he, as a Negro, felt about the fact that he wasn't allowed to eat at certain restaurants back home. Sensing an attempt to exploit him, Clay shot back, "Russian, we got qualified men working on that problem. We got the biggest and the prettiest cars. We get all the food we can eat. America is the greatest country in the world, and as far as places I can't eat

Cassius Clay, later Muhammad Ali (center), flanked by fellow 1960 gold medalists Edward Crook and Wilbert McClure.

goes, I got lots of places I can eat—more places I can than I can't."

And so Cassius Marcellus Clay achieved his goal of winning a gold medal. But the story of what happened to that medal tells volumes about the state of race relations in America at the beginning of the 1960s. Clay loved his medal. He slept with it, he ate with it, he wore it all the time. He wore it so much in fact that the gold began to wear off, revealing a common lead base. He returned to a hero's welcome in Louisville. The porch of his house was decorated with American flags, and his father had painted the steps red, white and blue. Cassius posed for photographers with his father—and his medal—while his father sang "The Star-Spangled Banner."

It wasn't long before Cassius turned professional and signed a contract with ten white Louisville millionaires, who agreed to sponsor his career. The millionaires gave him a slip of paper with all their phone numbers on it in case he ever needed help.

One day the mayor of Louisville asked Clay to come to his office so he could show off the gold medal to some visiting dignitaries. The mayor boasted to his visitors about the response Cassius had given to the Soviet reporter about the status of Negroes in the United States. The mayor told them, "Why, Cassius stood up tall, 'Look here, Commie . . . I'd rather live here in Louisville than in Africa cause at least I ain't fightin' off no snakes and alligators and livin' in mud huts.' He sho' told 'em! He's our own boy, Cassius, our next world champion."

By now Clay was sorry he had responded to the Soviet journalist the way he had. On the way home, he and a friend, Ronnie King, stopped at a whites-only restaurant and attempted to order two hamburgers and two vanilla milk shakes. They were refused service. "Miss," Clay told the waitress, "I'm Cassius Clay, the Olympic champion," and he showed off his gold medal with its red, white, and blue ribbons. The waitress turned to the owner of the restaurant, who boomed out, "I don't give a damn who he is! I done told you, we don't serve no niggers!" Several members of a white motorcycle gang happened to be in the restaurant and they rose and joined the owner by the counter. Ronnie King pulled out the paper with the names and numbers of Clay's millionaire sponsors and urged his friend to call them up for help. But Cassius just couldn't ask. In his book, *The Greatest,* Ali wrote, "I had earned my Gold Medal without their permission. It should mean something without their permission. I wanted that medallion to mean that I owned myself. And to call seemed to me to be exchanging one Owner for the Other."

Clay and Ronnie King left the restaurant. "Whatever illusions I'd built up in Rome as the All-American Boy were gone. My Olympic honeymoon was over." In the parking lot Clay was approached by one of the gang members, who ordered him to hand over his gold medal. Instead, he and Ronnie King raced off on their motor bikes, well aware that this gang had already seriously beaten several blacks who had been caught in white neighborhoods. Two of the gang leaders caught up with Clay and King at the Jefferson County Bridge on the Indiana border. A violent confrontation followed, which left the gang members bleeding and badly injured. When they left, Clay and King walked down to the river to wash the blood off their bodies and clothes. Ronnie King took the gold medal, cleaned it carefully, and hung it over his neck. It was the first time the medal had been away from Clay's chest. "For the first time," he wrote, "I saw it as it was. Ordinary, just an object." King put the gold medal back around Clay's neck, and the two friends walked back to the bridge. When they got to the middle of the bridge, Cassius Clay walked over to the side, pulled the gold medal off his chest, and threw it into the Ohio River. Later Ali wrote, "The medal was gone, but . . . I felt calmly relaxed, confident. My holiday as a White Hope was over. I felt a new, secret strength."

On February 25, 1964, Cassius Clay won the World Heavyweight championship by defeating Sonny Liston. He defended his title nine times over the next three years. Then he converted to Islam, announced that Cassius Clay was a slave name, and changed his name to Muhammad Ali. When he refused to be drafted during the Vietnam War, he was stripped of his title and didn't fight again for 3½ years. He won back the title on October 30, 1974, by knocking out George Foreman in Zaire. He defended his championship ten more times before losing to Leon Spinks on February 15, 1978. He regained the title from Spinks seven months later.

1964 Tokyo C: 19, N: 19, D: 10.23.

		FINAL MATCH
		Dec 3–2
1. Cosimo Pinto	ITA	
2. Aleksei Kiselyov	SOV/RUS	
3. Alexander Nikolov	BUL	
3. Zbigniew Pietrzykowski	POL	

5. Rafael Luis Gargiulo (ARG), Sayed Mersal (EGY), František Polacek (CZE), Jürgen Schlegel (GDR)

1968 Mexico City C: 18, N: 18, D: 10.26.

		FINAL MATCH
1. Danas Pozniakas	SOV/LIT	Default
2. Ion Monea	ROM	
3. Stanislaw Dragan	POL	
3. Georgi Stankov	BUL	

5. Fatai Ayinia (NGR), Walter Facchinetti (ITA), Bernard Malherbe (FRA), Jürgen Schlegel (GDR)

Monea suffered a broken nose in his semifinal victory over Dragan and was unable to compete in the final.

1972 Munich C: 28, N: 28, D: 9.10.

		FINAL MATCH	
1. Mate Parlov	YUG/CRO	RSC 2	2:39
2. Gilberto Carrillo	CUB		
3. Janusz Gortat	POL		
3. Isaac Ikhouria	NGR		

5. Nikolai Anfimov (SOV/RUS), Miguel Angel Cuello (ARG), Rudi Hornig (GER), Harald Skog (NOR)

Parlov blasted his way through the tournament, winning one walkover and stopping three of his other four opponents in the second round. Parlov turned professional in 1975 and three years later won the World Light Heavyweight title.

1976 Montreal C: 18, N: 18, D: 7.31.

		FINAL MATCH	
1. Leon Spinks	USA	RSC 3	1:09
2. Sixto Soria	CUB		
3. Costică Dafinoiu	ROM		
3. Janusz Gortat	POL		

5. Robert Burgess (BER), Wolfgang Gruber (GER), Ottomar Sachse (GDR), Juan Suárez (ARG)

Marine Corps Lance Corporal Leon Spinks stepped into the ring for his Olympic final immediately after his younger brother, Michael, had won the Middleweight championship. He faced knockout artist Sixto Soria, who had required only 9 minutes and 5 seconds to dispose of his first three opponents. However, the Cuban met his match in Spinks, who knocked him down in the first round and continued to batter him until the referee stopped the fight. A year and a half later Spinks defeated Muhammad Ali to win the World Heavyweight championship.

1980 Moscow C: 15, N: 15, D: 8.2.

		FINAL MATCH
1. Slobodan Kacar	YUG	Dec 4–1
2. Pawel Skrzeck	POL	
3. Herbert Bauch	GDR	
3. Ricardo Rojas	CUB	

5. Georgică Donici (ROM), David Kvachadze (SOV), Michael Madsen (DEN), Geoffrey Pike (AUS)

1984 Los Angeles C: 24, N: 24, D: 8.11.

		FINAL MATCH
1. Anton Josipović	YUG/BSH	Default
2. Kevin Barry	NZE	
3. Evander Holyfield	USA	
3. Mustapha Moussa	ALG	

5. Georgică Donici (ROM), Jean Paul Nanga (CAM), Syivaus Okello (KEN), Anthony Wilson (GBR)

Despite all of the uproar about pro-American judging at the Los Angeles Olympics, it was a U.S. boxer who was the victim of the most controversial decision of all. Evander Holyfield, who had defeated world amateur champion Ricky Womack to qualify for the U.S. team, had stopped his first three opponents and was on the verge of knocking out a fourth, when an unusual incident occurred. A few seconds before the end of the second round of his semifinal bout with Kevin Barry, Holyfield lashed out a right to the ribs and followed with a left hook that floored Barry for good. The referee, Gligorije Novicić of Yugoslavia, motioned Holyfield to a neutral corner, counted out Barry, then turned to Holyfield and disqualified him for throwing the left hook after Novicić had yelled, "Stop." Subsequent viewing of the videotapes of the fight confirmed the late hit, but also showed that Barry and Holyfield had previously thrown four late blows each.

When the decision was announced, Barry turned to Holyfield and said, "You won the fight fair and square." Then he took the American's hand and raised it in the air. The crowd went berserk, raining abuse and refuse on the Yugoslavian referee. The police had to be brought in to escort Novicić from the arena. Novicić had been scheduled to work one of the final bouts three days later, but was relieved of his obligation for security reasons.

What made the incident all the more shocking was the subsequent ruling that because Barry had been declared a knockout victim, amateur boxing regulations prevented him from fighting again for 28 days. This meant that the gold medal was awarded by default to the other semifinal winner, Anton Josipović, who, like referee Novicić, happened to hail from Yugoslavia.

At the medal ceremony, Josipović, a handsome 22-year-old literature student from Bosnia, endured loud booing. But after the playing of the Yugoslav national anthem, he reached down and pulled up a surprised Holyfield to join him on the gold-medal platform. Afterwards, he told reporters, "It is a great honor to win the gold medal in this city of light and sun. I would have liked to fight Holyfield, to show what I am capable of doing and to win the medal that way. I am a bit disappointed that the audience doesn't realize that this is not the way I wanted it. I took the opportunity to have Holyfield join me on the top step because I believe the Olympics are the spirit of friendliness and goodwill."

Holyfield went on to an extremely successful professional career, winning the World Heavyweight championship twice. Josipović became a sports journalist and established a friendship with Holyfield when he covered his fights.

1988 Seoul C: 26, N: 26, D: 10.2.

		FINAL MATCH
1. Andrew Maynard	USA	Dec 5–0
2. Nuramgomed Shanavazov	SOV/RUS	
3. Henryk Petrich	POL	
3. Damir Škaro	YUG/CRO	
5. Joseph Akhasamba (KEN), Ahmed Elnagar (EGY), Lajos Erös (HUN), Andrea Magi (ITA)		

The 12th of 14 children, Andrew Maynard grew up on the streets of Cheverly, Maryland. His mother died when he was 3 years old; his father, a truck driver, was frequently on the road. Maynard, who was once a marijuana dealer, was in and out of juvenile court for such charges as assault and breaking and entering. Finally, a judge told him that he would have to go to college, join the Army or go to jail. Maynard chose the Army. In the armed service, he became a cook and a boxer. He also married, became a father, and generally turned his life around. The Olympic final, a turgid affair that resembled two bears dancing, was not a fair representation of either boxer's talents. Maynard gave his gold medal to his father. "By winning the medal," he explained, "I was saying 'Forgive me for being a bad kid.' . . . Giving him that medal was the proudest moment of my life." Bronze medalist Damir Škaro set a curious record by losing to the eventual silver-medal winner for the third straight Olympics. In 1980 and 1984 he had competed as a middleweight.

1992 Barcelona—Badalona C: 26, N: 26, D: 8.9.

		FINAL MATCH
1. Torsten May	GER	Pts 8–3
2. Rostislav Zaulichnyi	UKR	
3. Wojciech Bartnik	POL	
3. Zoltán Béres	HUN	
5. Ángel Espinosa Capo (CUB), Montell Griffin (USA), Roland Raform (SEY), Stephen Wilson (GBR)		

Southpaw Torsten May was the surprise winner of the 1991 world championships but entered the Olympic tournament as the clear favorite. He won his first two matches easily but ran into major trouble in the quarterfinals. His opponent, Montell Griffin, was only 5 feet 7 inches tall—six inches shorter than May. The score was 1-1 after two rounds. However, less than a minute into the final round, Griffin opened a big cut over May's right eye, causing the taller German to bleed profusely. The referee, Osvaldo Bisbal of Argentina, stopped the fight,

but the ring doctor, Oscar Ramirez of Cuba, allowed the bout to continue. A minute later Bisbal issued a third warning to Griffin for "ducking"—leading with his head instead of his fists—which automatically added three points to May's score. The penalty proved decisive, as May eventually won 6-4.

The Americans were furious, but the rest of the world had little sympathy for Griffin, who had alienated boxing fans by showboating in the closing seconds of his previous fight. May's 8-6 semifinal victory over Wojciech Bartnik was roundly booed and jeered because May spent much of the match clinching in order to protect his cut eye.

The official records show that 26 light heavyweights competed in the 1992 Olympic tournament. In fact, 27 showed up in the arena. Ali Kazemi of Iran made it to the ring in time for his opening bout with Ashghar Muhammad of Pakistan. Unfortunately, he wasn't wearing any gloves. His handlers frantically searched for a pair, but he was disqualified after five minutes for not being ready on time.

HEAVYWEIGHT
(91 kg–200½ lbs)

1896–1980 not held

1984 Los Angeles C: 15, N: 15, D: 8.11.

		FINAL MATCH
1. Henry Tillman	USA	Dec 5–0
2. William deWit	CAN	
3. Angelo Musone	ITA	
3. Arnold Vanderlijde	HOL	
5. Håkan Brock (SWE), Dodovic Owiny (UGA), George Stefanopoulos (GRE), Tevita Taufoou (TON)		

Tillman, who learned to box while serving time for armed robbery, qualified for the U.S. team by twice defeating future World Heavyweight champion Mike Tyson. Tillman's semifinal victory was a controversial jury reversal decision over Angelo Musone, a decision that the Italian newspapers referred to as "hallucinatory" and "scandalous." In the final, Tillman upset deWit, who had beaten the American in their two previous encounters.

1988 Seoul C: 18, N: 18, D: 10.1.

		FINAL MATCH	
1. Raymond Mercer	USA	KO 1	2:16
2. Baik Hyan-man	KOR		
3. Andrzej Golota	POL		
3. Arnold Vanderlijde	HOL		
5. Gyula Alvics (HUN), Luigi Gaudiano (ITA), Maik Heydeck (GDR), Harold Obunga (KEN)			

World champion Félix Savón was conspicuously missing from the tournament because of Cuba's boycott of the Seoul Games. In Savon's absence, 27-year-old infantry-man Ray Mercer blasted his way through the tourna-ment. His four opponents, none of whom survived the full three rounds, lasted a total of 17 minutes 6 seconds. An oddity among boxers, Mercer did not take up the sport until he was 22, and only then because being a sparring partner for the camp champion meant that he wouldn't have to take part in a 30-day winter survival field exercise. In 1993 Mercer was involved in a bizarre incident. He was charged with offering an opponent, Jesse Ferguson, a $100,000 bribe *during* a fight on February 6 at Madison Square Garden. He was eventually acquitted of the charge.

1992 Barcelona—Badalona C: 23, N: 23, D: 8.8.

		FINAL MATCH
1. Félix Savón Fabre	CUB	Pts 14–1
2. David Izonritei	NGR	
3. David Tua	NZE	
3. Arnold Vanderlijde	HOL	
5. Paul Douglas (IRL), Kirk Johnson (CAN), Danell Nicholson (USA), Vojtěch Rückschloss (CZE)		

Three-time world champion Félix Savón had dominated the Heavyweight division since 1986. It was expected that his march to Olympic gold would be practically uncontested. However, in the quarterfinals he ran into an unexpected and unlikely obstacle: Chicago's Danell Nicholson, whose pre-Olympic international boxing ex-perience consisted of one fight. Nicholson, who had spent over 3½ years in prison for armed robbery, had only been back in the outside world for 14 months. Instead of cowering in terror like most of Savón's oppo-nents, Nicholson stood his ground and slugged it out. He shocked most observers by leading Savón 4-1 after the first round and 8-6 after the second. In the third round Savón finally took charge and pulled out a well-deserved 13-11 victory. In the semifinals Savón defeated 6 foot 6 inch Arnold Vanderlijde 23-3. It was the eighth time in eight tries that Vanderlijde had lost to Savón. The Dutchman did gain some consolation, however: he became the only boxer in Olympic history to earn three bronze medals.

SUPER HEAVYWEIGHT
(Over 91 kg—200½ lbs)

This division, which is the unlimited weight class, was known as Heavyweight from 1904 to 1980.

1896–1900 not held

1904 St. Louis C: 3, N: 1, D: 9.22.
(Over 71.67 kg–158 lbs)

		FINAL MATCH
1. Samuel Berger	USA	Dec
2. Charles Mayer	USA	
3. William Michaels	USA	

1906 not held

1908 London C: 6, N: 1, D: 10.27.
(Over 71.67 kg–158 lbs)

		FINAL MATCH
1. Albert Oldman	GBR	KO 1	2:00
2. Sydney Evans	GBR	
3. Frederick Parks	GBR	

Oldman knocked out I. Myrams of Manchester in less than a minute, received a bye in the semifinals and needed only two minutes to dispose of Evans.

1912 not held

1920 Antwerp C: 9, N: 7, D: 8.24.
(Over 79.38 kg–175 lbs)

		FINAL MATCH
1. Ronald Rawson	GBR	KO 2
2. Sören Petersen	DEN	
3. Xavier Eluere	FRA	
4. William Spengler	USA	

Rawson won all three of his fights by knockout.

1924 Paris C: 16, N: 11, D: 7.20.
(Over 79.38 kg–175 lbs)

		FINAL MATCH
1. Otto von Porat	NOR	Dec
2. Sören Petersen	DEN	
3. Alfredo Porzio	ARG	
4. Henk de Best	HOL	
5. Ricardo Bertazzolo (ITA), Arthur Clifton (GBR), Edward Greathouse (USA), Robert Larsen (DEN)		

The final was a popular battle that saw Petersen almost knocked out in the first round and von Porat almost put away in the second. The Norwegian rebounded in the final round to earn the victory.

1928 Amsterdam C: 10, N: 10, D: 8.11.
(Over 79.38 kg–175 lbs)

		FINAL MATCH
1. Arturo Rodríguez Jurado	ARG	RSC 1
2. Nils Ramm	SWE	
3. M. Jacob Michaelsen	DEN	
4. Sverre Sörsdal	NOR	
5. Sam Oliji (NZE)		

1932 Los Angeles C: 6, N: 6, D: 8.13.
(Over 79.38 kg–175 lbs)

			FINAL MATCH
1.	Santiago Lovell	ARG	Dec
2.	Luigi Rovati	ITA	
3.	Frederick Feary	USA	
4.	George Maughan	CAN	

1936 Berlin C: 17, N: 17, D: 8.15.
(Over 79.38 kg–175 lbs)

			FINAL MATCH
1.	Herbert Runge	GER	Dec
2.	Guillermo Lovell	ARG	
3.	Erling Nilsen	NOR	
4.	Ferenc Nagy	HUN	
5.	Jose Feans (URU), Vincent Stuart (GBR), Olle Tandberg (SWE), Ernest Toussaint (LUX)			

1948 London C: 17, N: 17, D: 8.13.
(Over 80 kg–176½ lbs)

			FINAL MATCH
1.	Rafael Iglesias	ARG	KO 2
2.	Gunnar Nilsson	SWE	
3.	John Arthur	SAF	
4.	Hans Müller	SWI	
5.	Uber Baccilieri (ITA), Adam Faul (CAN), Jack Gardner (GBR), E. Jay Lambert (USA),			

1952 Helsinki C: 22, N: 22, D: 8.2.
(Over 81 kg–179 lbs)

			FINAL MATCH
1.	H. Edward Sanders	USA	DISQ 2
2.	Ingemar Johansson	SWE	
3.	Ilkka Koski	FIN	
3.	Andries Nieman	SAF	
5.	Giacomo Di Segni (ITA), Edgar Hearn (GBR), Tomislav Krizmanic (YUG), Algirdas Schocikas (SOV/LIT)			

Evidently the punishment that Sanders inflicted on his first three opponents made a great impression on Ingemar Johansson, because the Swede spent all his time in the ring back-pedaling, without throwing a single punch. After receiving several warnings from the referee, he was finally disqualified for not "giving of his best." Because of the disqualification, he was not awarded his silver medal and he returned to Sweden in shame. As it happened, it was not Sanders but Johansson who went on to a successful professional career, knocking out Floyd Patterson on June 29, 1959, to win the World Heavyweight championship. Johansson later recalled, "At the moment of victory, at the summit of glory for a boxer, I could think of only one thing: 'It's over. Now I am able to go home with my head held high.'" Johansson was finally awarded his silver medal in 1982. Sanders died of a brain hemorrhage on December 12, 1954, after being knocked out in his ninth professional bout.

1956 Melbourne C: 11, N: 11, D: 12.1.
(Over 81 kg–179 lbs)

			FINAL MATCH	
1.	T. Peter Rademacher	USA	RSC 1	2:27
2.	Lev Mukhin	SOV/RUS		
3.	Daniel Bekker	SAF		
3.	Giacomo Bozzano	ITA		
5.	Thorner Åhsman (SWE)				

The final looked as if it would be a classic. Mukhin had beaten all three of his opponents by knockout or technical knockout, coming off the floor himself in two of the fights. Rademacher, a soldier from Yakima, Washington, never gave Mukhin a chance to make a third comeback. He knocked down the Soviet boxer in the first 50 seconds. Mukhin got up, but Rademacher flattened him twice more in the next 80 seconds, and the referee finally stopped the fight. Eight and a half months later, Rademacher became the first boxer to fight for the Heavyweight title in his first professional contest. Rademacher, who had never gone more than three rounds, sent champion Floyd Patterson to the canvas in the second round, but Patterson came back to win in round 6.

1960 Rome C: 17, N: 17, D: 9.5.
(Over 81 kg–179 lbs)

			FINAL MATCH	
1.	Franco De Piccoli	ITA	KO 1	1:30
2.	Daniel Bekker	SAF		
3.	Josef Nemec	CZE		
3.	Günter Siegmund	GDR		
5.	Andrei Abramov (SOV/RUS), Vasile Mariutan (ROM), Percy Price (USA), Obrad Sretenovic (YUG)				

1964 Tokyo C: 14, N: 14, D: 10.23.
(Over 81 kg–179 lbs)

			FINAL MATCH
1.	Joseph Frazier	USA	Dec 3–2
2.	Hans Huber	GER	
3.	Giuseppe Ros	ITA	
3.	Vadim Yemelyanov	SOV/RUS	
5.	Santiago Alberto Lovell (ARG), Vasile Mariutan (ROM), Athol McQueen (AUS)			

Philadelphia butcher's apprentice Joe Frazier was a last-minute substitute for 293-pound Buster Mathis, who had broken his knuckle. Frazier demolished his first three opponents and then won a much tamer split decision over Regensburg bus driver Hans Huber in the final, which Frazier fought with a broken right hand. In 1970 Frazier won the World Heavyweight championship, and in 1980 he was elected to the Boxing Hall of Fame.

1968 Mexico City C: 16, N: 16, D: 10.23.
(Over 81 kg–179 lbs)

		FINAL MATCH
1. George Foreman	USA	RSC 2
2. Jonas Čepulis	SOV/LIT	
3. Giorgio Bambini	ITA	
3. Joaquin Rocha	MEX	
5. Ion Alexe (ROM), Bernd Anders (GDR), Rudolfus Lubbers (HOL), Kiril Pandov (BUL)		

The relatively inexperienced Foreman, who had fought only 18 times before the Olympics, had little trouble winning the gold medal. After his final victory he paraded around the ring holding aloft a small U.S. flag. On January 22, 1973, Foreman knocked out Joe Frazier to win the World Heavyweight title. Foreman retired in 1977, became an active Christian, and opened a youth center in Humble, Texas. Then, in 1987, at the age of 38, Foreman began a comeback. Longtime ring observers scoffed or shook their heads sadly. It was the old story of the boxer who is addicted to the ring and to glory and who doesn't know when to quit. But Foreman's comeback was different. He took his time, and on November 5, 1994, he shocked the world by knocking out Michael Moorer in the 10th round and winning the WBA Heavyweight championship—at age 45.

1972 Munich C: 14, N: 14, D: 9.10.
(Over 81 kg–179 lbs)

		FINAL MATCH
1. Teófilo Stevenson Lorenzo	CUB	Default
2. Ion Alexe	ROM	
3. Peter Hussing	GER	
3. Hasse Thomsén	SWE	
5. Duane Bobick (USA), Jürgen Fanghänel (GDR), Carroll Morgan (CAN)		

Teófilo Stevenson, a handsome Jamaican-born 6-foot 3½-inch Cuban from Las Tunas, Oriente, was the most impressive Olympic boxer since Cassius Clay. After disposing of Poland's Ludwik Denderys in one round, he faced Duane Bobick of the U.S. Navy. In 1971 Bobick had beaten Stevenson in the semifinals of the Pan American Games. Now, at the Munich Olympics, Bobick wasn't too worried about Stevenson. "I know he's tall and strong," he told reporters, "but the last time all he had was a good jab—no right hand." Unbeknownst to Bobick, the Cuban had spent twelve months working on just that problem. Using a stinging left jab and a now powerful right hand, Stevenson plastered Bobick until the fight was stopped in the third round.

Stevenson's semifinal opponent was Peter Hussing of Germany. He lasted 4 minutes and 3 seconds. "I have never been hit so hard in all my 212 bouts," said the good-natured Hussing. "You just don't see his right hand. All of a sudden it is there—on your chin." The other semifinal matched Alexe of Romania and Thomsén

of Sweden, both of whom had been knocked out by Stevenson in previous tournaments. Some observers suggested that the *loser* should be forced to face Stevenson in the final.

In fact, neither of them did. Alexe won a unanimous decision over Thomsén, but showed up for the final with his hand in plaster, the result of a broken thumb. Although capitalist fight promoters drooled at the prospect, Stevenson refused to turn professional, stating that he was more interested in his studies and in revolution than he was in making a million dollars. In fact, he turned down an offer of $2,000,000. "Professional boxing treats a fighter like a commodity to be bought and sold and discarded when he is no longer of use," he said. "I wouldn't exchange my piece of Cuba for all the money they could give me."

1976 Montreal C: 15, N: 15, D: 7.31.
(Over 81 kg–179 lbs)

		FINAL MATCH	
1. Teófilo Stevenson Lorenzo	CUB	KO 3	2:35
2. Mircea Simion	ROM		
3. Clarence Hill	BER		
3. Johnny Tate	USA		
5. Peter Hussing (GER), Atanas Suvandzhiev (BUL)			

In the four years since the Munich Olympics, Stevenson had lost two fights—both to Igor Vysotsky of the U.S.S.R., who had knocked out the Cuban in Minsk three months before the 1976 Olympics. However, Vysotsky was unable to compete in Montreal because of eye injuries, and the road seemed clear for Stevenson to defend his title. He demolished his first three opponents in a record 7 minutes and 22 seconds. His last victim was Mircea Simion, who avoided Stevenson completely for the first two rounds. Although this same tactic had earned Ingemar Johansson a disqualification 24 years earlier, it seemed quite understandable in Simion's case. When Stevenson finally hit Simion in the third round, the Romanian's seconds immediately threw in the towel. Simion later defected to the United States. Clarence Hill's bronze made Bermuda (pop. 53,500) the smallest country ever to win a Summer Olympics medal.

1980 Moscow C: 14, N: 14, D: 8.2.
(Over 81 kg–179 lbs)

		FINAL MATCH
1. Teófilo Stevenson Lorenzo	CUB	Dec 4–1
2. Pyotr Zayev	SOV/RUS	
3. Jürgen Fanghänel	GDR	
3. István Levai	HUN	
5. Francesco Damiani (ITA), Grzegorz Skrzecz (POL), Peter Stoimenov (BUL)		

In the semifinals, Levai ran around the ring for three rounds, becoming the first Olympic boxer to go the distance against Stevenson. Stevenson, in turn, became the first boxer to win three Olympic gold medals in the same division. As late as 1986, he proved that he was still the best amateur boxer in the world by winning the world championship at age 34.

1984 Los Angeles C: 11, N: 11, D: 8.11.

		FINAL MATCH
1. Tyrell Biggs	USA	Dec 4–1
2. Francesco Damiani	ITA	
3. Hazis Salihu	YUG	
3. Robert Wells	GBR	
5. Peter Hussing (GER), Lennox Lewis (CAN)		

1988 Seoul C: 17, N: 17, D: 10.2.

		FINAL MATCH
1. Lennox Lewis	CAN	RSC 2 0:43
2. Riddick Bowe	USA	
3. Aleksandr Miroshnichenko	SOV/KAZ	
3. Janusz Zarenkiewicz	POL	
5. Petr Hrivnak (CZE), Ulli Kaden (GDR), Kim Yoo-hyun (KOR), Andreas Schneiders (GER)		

Lennox Lewis of Kitchener, Ontario, needed only 10 minutes 16 seconds to dispatch his three opponents. Most startling was his 34-second knockout of World Cup champion Ulli Kaden in the quarterfinals. Both Lewis and Bowe went on to successful professional careers, each of them claiming a share of the heavyweight championship.

One unfortunate boxer in Seoul was Mohamed Hammad of Sudan. When the bell rang to begin his opening round bout with South Korean Kim Yoo-hyun, Hammad took three steps forward and discovered that the fight was over and he was the loser. His coach, Abdellatif Mohamed Abbas, had literally thrown in the towel as a protest against an earlier decision in which South Korean light middleweight Park Si-hun had been declared the winner over Sudan's Abdallah Ramadan. Park had incapacitated Ramadan with an illegal kidney punch.

Another unusual highlight was the appearance of 5-foot 11-inch, 260-pound Ali Albaluchi of Kuwait. Clearly outclassed by the more athletically shaped Aleksandr Miroshnichenko, the good-natured Albaluchi took advantage of his moment in the spotlight to imitate Muhammad Ali. While Kuwaiti supporters chanted, "Ali, Ali," Albaluchi performed the rope-a-dope and the Ali Shuffle. He dropped his gloves, stuck out his chin and dared Miroshnichenko to hit him. Miroshnichenko won the fight easily, but it was Albaluchi who received the only standing ovation of the entire 429-match Seoul tournament.

1992 Barcelona—Badalona C: 17, N: 17, D: 8.9.

		FINAL MATCH
1. Roberto Balado Méndez	CUB	Pts 13–2
2. Igbeneghu Richard	NGR	
3. Brian Nielsen	DEN	
3. Svilen Russinov	BUL	
5. Larry Donald (USA), Wilhelm Fischer (GER), Peter Hrivnák (CZE), Gitas Juškevičius (LIT)		

Two-time world champion Roberto Balado outpointed his four opponents 54-9. In March he lost to American Larry Donald 16-14 in a fight held in Tampa, Florida, but in Barcelona, Balado outclassed Donald in the quarterfinals, 10-4.

THE VAL BARKER CUP

The Val Barker Cup, named in honor of the first General-Secretary of the International Amateur Boxing Association, is awarded to the boxer who displays the best style and technique.

1936	Louis Laurie	USA	flyweight	bronze
1948	George Hunter	SAF	light heavyweight	gold
1952	Norvel Lee	USA	light heavyweight	gold
1956	Richard McTaggart	GBR	lightweight	gold
1960	Giovanni Benvenuti	ITA	welterweight	gold
1964	Valery Popenchenko	SOV/RUS	middleweight	gold
1968	Philip Waruinge	KEN	featherweight	bronze
1972	Teófilo Stevenson	CUB	heavyweight	gold
1976	Howard Davis	USA	lightweight	gold
1980	Patrizio Oliva	ITA	light welterweight	gold
1984	Paul Gonzales	USA	light flyweight	gold
1988	Roy Jones	USA	light middleweight	silver
1992	Roberto Balado	CUB	super heavyweight	gold

CANOEING

MEN
Kayak Singles 500 Meters
Kayak Singles 1000 Meters
Kayak Pairs 500 Meters
Kayak Pairs 1000 Meters
Kayak Fours 1000 Meters
Canadian Singles 500 Meters
Canadian Singles 1000 Meters
Canadian Pairs 500 Meters
Canadian Pairs 1000 Meters
Kayak Slalom Singles
Canadian Slalom Singles
Canadian Slalom Pairs
Discontinued Events

WOMEN
Kayak Singles 500 Meters
Kayak Pairs 500 Meters
Kayak Fours 500 Meters
Kayak Slalom Singles

Olympic canoeing events are divided into two types, depending on the kind of paddle that is used. In *kayak* events, a paddle with a blade on each end is used. The canoeist alternately paddles one blade on the left side and the other on the right side. The paddle in *Canadian* canoeing has only one blade. The canoeist sits in a half-kneeling position, switching the blade from side to side.

One-person canoes and kayaks are about 5.18 meters (17 feet) long, two-person boats are about 6.4 meters (21 feet) long, and four-person kayaks are about 11 meters (36 feet) long. The lanes are nine meters (29 feet 6 inches) wide. The boats must stay in the middle of their lanes and are not allowed to come within five meters (16 feet 6 inches) of another boat, which keeps competitors from gaining an advantage by riding in the wake of the other boat. Each boat is allowed one false start. A second false start results in disqualification.

Canoeing contests begin with qualifying heats. The two or three winners of each heat advance directly to the semifinals, while the rest take part in a repêchage, or second-chance round (repêchage being the French word for "fishing again"). The three or four fastest participants in each repêchage race join the semifinals. Until 1984 the top six semifinalists took part in the final, while the other six took part in a *petit final* to determine seventh through twelfth places. In 1984 the final was expanded to nine participants and the *petit final* was eliminated.

MEN

KAYAK SINGLES 500 METERS

1896–1972 not held

1976 Montreal C: 18, N: 18, D: 7.30
1.	Vasile Dîba	ROM	1:46.41
2.	Zoltán Sztanity	HUN	1:46.95
3.	Rüdiger Helm	GDR	1:48.30
4.	Herminio Menéndez Rodriguez	SPA	1:48.40
5.	Grzegorz Śledziewski	POL	1:48.49
6.	Sergei Lizunov	SOV	1:49.21
7.	Oreste Perri	ITA	1:50.27
8.	Douglas Parnham	GBR	1:50.33

1980 Moscow C: 17, N: 17, D: 8.1.
1.	Vladimir Parfenovich	SOV/BLR	1:43.43
2.	John Sumegi	AUS	1:44.12
3.	Vasile Dîba	ROM	1:44.90
4.	Milan Janic	YUG/CRO	1:45.63
5.	Frank-Peter Bischof	GDR	1:45.97
6.	Anders Andersson	SWE	1:46.32
7.	Ian Ferguson	NZE	1:47.36
8.	Felix Masar	CZE	1:48.18

Parfenovich, a 21-year-old physical education instructor from Minsk, won three gold medals at the Moscow Olympics.

1984 Los Angeles–Lake Casitas C: 19, N: 19, D: 8.10.
1.	Ian Ferguson	NZE	1:47.84
2.	Lars-Erik Moberg	SWE	1:48.18
3.	Bernard Bregeon	FRA	1:48.41
4.	Vasile Dîba	ROM	1:48.77
5.	David Upson	GBR	1:49.32
6.	Daniele Scarpa	ITA	1:49.60
7.	Guillermo Del Riego Gordon	SPA	1:49.71
8.	Reiner Scholl	GER	1:49.89

A trained accountant, Ian Ferguson retired from kayaking after the Moscow Olympics and opened a business in Auckland repairing and distributing video-game machines. But when the New Zealand Sports Federation offered increased financial support to kayakers, Ferguson returned to the sport and won a silver medal at the 1983 world championships. The following year, at age 32, he won three gold medals at the Los Angeles Olympics.

1988 Seoul C: 18, N: 18, D: 9.30.
1. Zsolt Gyulay	HUN	1:44.82
2. Andreas Stähle	GDR	1:46.38
3. Paul MacDonald	NZE	1:46.46
4. Michael Herbert	USA	1:46.73
5. Karl Axel Sundqvist	SWE	1:46.76
6. Attila Szabó	CZE	1:47.38
7. Martin Hunter	AUS	1:47.66
8. Dirk Joestel	GER	1:47.91

1992 Barcelona-Castelldefels C: 28, N: 28, D: 8.7.
1. Mikko Kolehmainen	FIN	1:40.43
2. Zsolt Gyulay	HUN	1:40.64
3. Knut Holmann	NOR	1:40.71
4. Norman Bellingham	USA	1:40.84
5. Sergei Kalesnik	BLR	1:40.90
6. Roberto Liberato	SWI	1:41.98
7. Daniele Scarpa	ITA	1:42.00
8. Marin Popescu	ROM	1:42.24

The 27-year-old Kolehmainen won from behind after being placed only seventh at the halfway mark.

KAYAK SINGLES 1000 METERS

1896–1932 not held

1936 Berlin C: 15, N: 15, D: 8.8.
1. Gregor Hradetzky	AUT	4:22.9
2. Helmut Cämmerer	GER	4:25.6
3. Jacobus Kraaier	HOL	4:35.1
4. Ernest Riedel	USA	4:38.1
5. Joel Rahmqvist	SWE	4:39.5
6. Henri Eberhardt	FRA	4:41.2
7. Birger Johansson	FIN	4:42.2
8. Ivar Iversen	NOR	4:44.2

1948 London C: 15, N: 15, D: 8.12.
1. Gert Fredriksson	SWE	4:33.2
2. Johan Frederik Kobberup	DEN	4:39.9
3. Henri Eberhardt	FRA	4:41.4
4. Hans Martin Gulbrandsen	NOR	4:41.7
5. Willem Frederik van der Kroft	HOL	4:43.5
6. Harry Åkerfelt	FIN	4:44.2
7. Lubomir Vambera	CZE	4:44.3
8. Walter Piemann	AUT	4:50.3

In the first heat Fredriksson showed his superiority by casually lying in fourth place for the first 950 meters and then sprinting at the end to take first. The final was no contest, as Fredriksson attained the longest winning margin in any Olympic kayak final other than 10,000 meters.

Gert Fredriksson won six canoeing gold medals between 1948 and 1960.

1952 Helsinki C: 20, N: 20, D: 7.28.
1. Gert Fredriksson	SWE	4:07.9
2. Thorvald Strömberg	FIN	4:09.7
3. Louis Gantois	FRA	4:20.1
4. Willem Frederik van der Kroft	HOL	4:20.8
5. Meinrad Miltenberger	GER	4:21.6
6. Lubomir Vambera	CZE	4:24.0
7. Hendrik Verbrugghe	BEL	4:25.0
8. Lev Nikitin	SOV	4:26.2

Fredriksson started a long, sustained sprint from the halfway mark, which wore down his opponents and allowed him to turn the tables on Strömberg, who had beaten him the previous evening in the 10,000 meters.

1956 Melbourne C: 13, N: 13, D: 12.1.
1. Gert Fredriksson	SWE	4:12.8
2. Igor Pissarev	SOV/RUS	4:15.3
3. Lajos Kiss	HUN	4:16.2
4. Stefan Kaplaniak	POL	4:19.8
5. Louis Gantois	FRA	4:22.1
6. Ladislav Čepčianský	CZE	4:23.2
7. Villy Christiansen	DEN	4:25.2
8. Ernst Steinhauer	GER	4:25.5

Fredriksson earned his fifth individual Olympic gold medal.

1960 Rome C: 22, N: 22, D: 8.29.

1.	Erik Hansen	DEN	3:53.00
2.	Imre Szöllösi	HUN	3:54.02
3.	Gert Fredriksson	SWE	3:55.89
4.	Ibragim Khasanov	SOV/TJK	3:56.38
5.	Ronald Rhodes	GBR	4:01.15
6.	Rolf Olsen	NOR	4:02.31
7.	Wolfgang Lange	GDR	4:03.05
8.	Simo Kusimanen	FIN	4:03.66

1964 Tokyo C: 15, N: 15, D: 10.22.

1.	Rolf Peterson	SWE	3:57.13
2.	Mihály Hesz	HUN	3:57.28
3.	Aurel Vernescu	ROM	4:00.77
4.	Erich Suhrbier	GER	4:01.62
5.	Günther Pfaff	AUT	4:03.56
6.	Antonius Geurts	HOL	4:04.48
7.	Erik Hansen	DEN	4:04.72
8.	Alastair Wilson	GBR	4:05.80

Mihály Hesz and Aurel Vernescu, the reigning world champion, were the favorites, but were upset by Rolf Peterson, a 22-year-old student from Halmstead.

1968 Mexico City C: 20, N: 20, D: 10.25.

1.	Mihály Hesz	HUN	4:02.63
2.	Oleksander Shaparenko	SOV/UKR	4:03.58
3.	Erik Hansen	DEN	4:04.39
4.	Wladyslaw Szuszkiewicz	POL	4:06.36
5.	Rolf Peterson	SWE	4:07.86
6.	Václav Mára	CZE	4:09.35
7.	Andrei Contolenco	ROM	4:09.96
8.	Wolfgang Lange	GDR	4:10.03

Lying fifth at the halfway mark, Hesz waited to make his move until there were only 200 meters to go. In the last 100 meters he passed Hansen, the 1960 Olympic champion, and Shaparenko, the reigning world champion.

1972 Munich C: 24, N: 24, D: 9.9.

1.	Oleksander Shaparenko	SOV/UKR	3:48.06
2.	Rolf Peterson	SWE	3:49.38
3.	Géza Csapó	HUN	3:49.38
4.	Jean-Pierre Burny	BEL	3:50.29
5.	Ladislav Souček	CZE	3:51.05
6.	Joachim Mattern	GDR	3:51.94
7.	Erik Hansen	DEN	3:52.15
8.	Grzegorz Śledziewski	POL	3:53.22

1976 Montreal C: 19, N: 19, D: 7.31.

1.	Rüdiger Helm	GDR	3:48.20
2.	Géza Csapó	HUN	3:48.84
3.	Vasile Dîba	ROM	3:49.65
4.	Oreste Perri	ITA	3:51.13
5.	Oleksander Shaparenko	SOV/UKR	3:51.45
6.	Berndt Andersson	SWE	3:52.46
7.	Douglas Parnham	GBR	3:52.64
8.	Grzegorz Śledziewski	POL	3:54.29

In the opening heats Oreste Perri, the world champion, and Vasile Dîba were disqualified for using underweight boats. However, the decision was reversed when the judges announced that the super sensitive electronic scales had responded to a change in atmospheric pressure. Helm made his move in the last quarter of the race, passed Csapó, and shouted with joy as he stormed across the finish line. At 19, he was the youngest competitor in the event.

1980 Moscow C: 20, N: 20, D: 8.2.

1.	Rüdiger Helm	GDR	3:48.77
2.	Alain Lebas	FRA	3:50.20
3.	Ion Bîrlădeanu	ROM	3:50.49
4.	John Sumegi	AUS	3:50.63
5.	Oreste Perri	ITA	3:51.95
6.	Felix Masár	CZE	3:52.19
7.	Milan Janic	YUG/CRO	3:53.50
8.	Ian Ferguson	NZE	3:53.78

Two hours after this race, Helm joined his teammates in winning the Kayak Fours, to bring his Olympic medal total to five: three gold and two bronze.

1984 Los Angeles-Lake Casitas C: 19, N: 19, D: 8.11.

1.	Alan Thompson	NZE	3:45.73
2.	Milan Janić	YUG/CRO	3:46.88
3.	Gregory Barton	USA	3:47.38
4.	Kalle Sundqvist	SWE	3:48.69
5.	Peter Genders	AUS	3:49.11
6.	Philippe Boccara	FRA	3:49.38
7.	Vasile Dîba	ROM	3:51.61
8.	Stephen Jackson	GBR	3:52.25

1988 Seoul C: 19, N: 19, D: 10.1.

1.	Gregory Barton	USA	3:55.27
2.	Grant Davies	AUS	3:55.28
3.	André Wohllebe	GDR	3:55.55
4.	Dmitri Bankovsky	SOV/RUS	3:56.49
5.	Gunnar Olsson	SWE	3:56.84
6.	Alan Thompson	NZE	3:56.91
7.	Attila Szabó	CZE	3:57.52
8.	Morten Ivarsen	NOR	3:59.18

Greg Barton was a mechanical engineer who grew up in Homer, Michigan, a small town with more pigs than human beings. He was born with two club feet, a condition that was only aggravated by four operations. In Seoul, Barton and Davies crossed the finish line in a near dead heat. Barton was told by Korean officials that he had won. Then the scoreboard flashed the news that Davies was the victor. While the Australians celebrated and Barton prepared for the final of the 1000-meter pairs, the jury of the International Canoe Federation examined the finish line photo. A few minutes later they announced that Barton had won by .005 seconds—less than 1 centimeter. Greg Barton had become the first U.S. kayaker to win an Olympic gold medal. Davies was stoic. "If that's the biggest disappointment in my life," he said, "I can handle it."

1992 Barcelona-Castelldefels C: 26, N: 26, D: 8.8.

1. Clint Robinson	AUS	3:37.26
2. Knut Holmann	NOR	3:37.50
3. Gregory Barton	USA	3:37.93
4. Marin Popescu	ROM	3:38.37
5. Beniamino Bonomi	ITA	3:41.12
6. José Garcia	POR	3:41.60
7. Thor Nielsen	DEN	3:41.70
8. Renn Crichlow	CAN	3:43.46

Robinson, a 20-year-old from Maroochydore, Queensland, upset two-time world champion Knut Holmann by staying close to the Norwegian throughout the race and then surging ahead at the end. He pushed himself so hard that, for the first time in his life, his whole body went numb.

KAYAK PAIRS 500 METERS

1896–1972 not held

1976 Montreal T: 21, N: 21, D: 7.28.

1. Joachim Mattern, Bernd Olbricht	GDR	1:35.87
2. Serhei Nahorny, Vladimir Romanovsky	SOV	1:36.81
3. Larion Serghei, Policarp Malihin	ROM	1:37.43
4. José Seguin, Guillermo Del Riego Gordon	SPA	1:38.50
5. József Deme, János Rátkai	HUN	1:38.81
6. Hannu Kojo, Kari Markkanen	FIN	1:39.59
7. Anders Andersson, Lars Andersson	SWE	1:39.63
8. John Southwood, John Sumegi	AUS	1:39.77

1980 Moscow T: 18, N: 18, D: 8.1.

1. Vladimir Parfenovich, Serhei Chukhray	SOV	1:32.38
2. Herminio Menéndez Rodriguez, Guillermo Del Riego Gordon	SPA	1:33.65
3. Rüdiger Helm, Bernd Olbricht	GDR	1:34.00
4. Francis Hervieu, Alain Lebas	FRA	1:36.22
5. Barry Kelly, Robert Lee	AUS	1:36.45
6. Alexandru Giura, Ion Bîrlădeanu	ROM	1:36.96
7. Waldemar Merk, Zdzislaw Szubski	POL	1:37.20
8. László Szabó, Zoltán Romhányi	HUN	1:37.66

1984 Los Angeles-Lake Casitas T: 21, N: 21, D: 8.10.

1. Ian Ferguson, Paul MacDonald	NZE	1:34.21
2. Per-Inge Bengtsson, Lars-Erik Moberg	SWE	1:35.26
3. Hugh Fisher, Alwyn Morris	CAN	1:35.41
4. Daniele Scarpa, Francesco Uberti	ITA	1:35.50
5. Nicolae Feodosei, Angelin Velea	ROM	1:35.60
6. Francis Hervieu, Daniel Legras	FRA	1:36.40
7. Matthias Seack, Oliver Seack	GER	1:36.51
8. Andrew Sherriff, Jeremy West	GBR	1:36.73

1988 Seoul T: 22, N: 22, D: 9.30.

1. Ian Ferguson, Paul MacDonald	NZE	1:33.98
2. Ihor Nahayev, Viktor Denisov	SOV	1:34.15
3. Attila Ábrahám, Ferenc Csipes	HUN	1:34.32
4. Reiner Scholl, Thomas Pfrang	GER	1:34.40
5. Daniel Stoian, Angelin Velea	ROM	1:35.96
6. Maciej Frejmut, Wojciech Kurpiewski	POL	1:36.22

7. Kay Bluhm, André Wohllebe	GDR	1:36.49
8. Olney Kent, Terry White	USA	1:36.62

Ferguson and MacDonald opened a big lead and managed to lunge across the finish line before the field could catch them.

1992 Barcelona-Castelldefels T: 30, N: 30, D: 8.7.

1. Kay Bluhm, Torsten Gutsche	GER	1:28.27
2. Maciej Freimut, Wojciech Kurpiewski	POL	1:29.84
3. Antonio Rossi, Bruno Dreossi	ITA	1:30.00
4. Juan José Román Mangas, Juan Manuel Sánchez de Castro	SPA	1:30.93
5. Karl Sundqvist, Gunnar Olsson	SWE	1:31.48
6. Jesper Staal, Thor Nielsen	DEN	1:31.84
7. Ferenc Csipes, Zsolt Gyulay	HUN	1:32.34
8. Michael Harbold, Peter Newton	USA	1:33.02

Bluhm and Gutsche won the first of their two gold medals by recording the largest winning margin ever in a men's kayak 500 event. In 1988, Bluhm had earned a bronze medal as a member of East Germany's four-man team.

KAYAK PAIRS 1000 METERS

1896–1932 not held

1936 Berlin T: 12, N: 12, D: 8.8.

1. Adolf Kainz, Alfons Dorfner	AUT	4:03.8
2. Ewald Tilker, Fritz Bondroit	GER	4:08.9
3. Nicolaas Tates, Willem Frederik van der Kroft	HOL	4:12.2
4. František Brzák-Felix, Josef Dusil	CZE	4:15.2
5. Rudolf Vilim, Werner Klingelfuss	SWI	4:22.8
6. Edward Deir, Francis Willis	CAN	4:24.5
7. Werner Lovgreen, Axel Svendsen	DEN	4:26.6
DISQ: Sixten Jansson, Gunnar Lundqvist (SWE)		

1948 London T: 16, T: 16, D: 8.12.

1. Hans Berglund, Lennart Klingström	SWE	4:07.3
2. Ejvind Hansen, Bernhard Jensen	DEN	4:07.5
3. Thor Axelsson, Nils Björklof	FIN	4:08.7
4. Ivar Mathisen, Knut Östbye	NOR	4:09.1
5. Otto Kroutil, Miloš Pech	CZE	4:09.8
6. Cornelis Gravesteyn, Willem Pool	HOL	4:15.8
7. Gerald Covey, Henry Harper	CAN	4:56.8
DISQ: János Toldi, Gyula Andrási (HUN)		

Toldi and Andrási were disqualified for "hanging" in the wake of another canoe. It was thought by many that the ruling was a harsh one.

1952 Helsinki T: 19, N: 19, D: 7.28.

1. Kurt Wires, Yrjö Hietanen	FIN	3:51.1
2. Lars Glassér, Ingemar Hedberg	SWE	3:51.1
3. Max Raub, Herbert Wiedermann	AUT	3:51.4
4. Gustav Schmidt, Helmut Noller	GER	3:51.8
5. Ivar Mathisen, Knut Östbye	NOR	3:54.7
6. Maurice Graffen, Marcel Renaud	FRA	3:55.1

7. István Granek, János Kulcsár   HUN   3:55.1
8. Cornelis Koch, Abraham Klingers   HOL   3:55.8

Wires and Hietanen, who had already won the 10,000 meter pairs, were awarded a second set of gold medals only after a photo-finish had been studied.

1956 Melbourne T:15, N: 15, D: 7.28.
1. Michael Scheuer, Meinrad Miltenberger   GER   3:49.6
2. Mikhail Kaaleste, Anatoly Demitkov   SOV/RUS   3:51.4
3. Max Raub, Herbert Wiedermann   AUT   3:55.8
4. Mircea Anastasescu, Stavru Teodorov   ROM   3:56.1
5. Maurice Graffen, Michel Meyer   FRA   3:58.3
6. Henri Verbrugghe, Germain van de Moere   BEL   3:58.7
7. Walter Brown, Dennis Green   AUS   3:59.1
8. Miroslav Jemelka, Rudolph Klabouch   CZE   4:01.4

1960 Rome T: 23, N: 23, D: 8.29.
1. Gert Fredriksson, Sven-Olov Sjödelius   SWE   3:34.73
2. György Mészáros, András Szente   HUN   3:34.91
3. Stefan Kaplaniak, Wladislaw Zielinski   POL   3:37.34
4. Nikolas Rudzinskas, Ivan Holovachov   SOV   3:37.48
5. Kaj Schmidt, Vagn Schmidt   DEN   3:39.06
6. František Riha, František Vršovský   CZE   3:40.78
7. Rudolf Knuppe, Antonius Geurts   HOL   3:41.01
8. Wolfgang Lange, Dieter Krause   GDR   3:41.46

Fredriksson completed his Olympic career with six gold medals, one silver medal, and one bronze medal. Four years later in Tokyo he was the coach of the Swedish team.

1964 Tokyo T: 14, N: 14, D: 10.22.
1. Sven-Olov Sjödelius, Nils Gunnar Utterberg   SWE   3:38.54
2. Antonius Geurts, Paul Hoekstra   HOL   3:39.30
3. Heinz Büker, Holger Zander   GER   3:40.69
4. Haralambie Ivanov, Vasile Nicoară   ROM   3:41.12
5. György Mészáros, Imre Szöllösi   HUN   3:41.39
6. Cesare Beltrami, Cesare Zilioli   ITA   3:43.55
7. Erik Kalugin, Ibragim Khasanov   SOV   3:44.19
8. Gordan Jeffery, Adrian Powell   AUS   3:44.52

1968 Mexico City T: 20, N: 20, D: 10.25.
1. Oleksander Shaparenko, Volodymyr Morozov   SOV/UKR   3:37.54
2. Csaba Giczi, István Timár   HUN   3:38.44
3. Gerhard Seibold, Günther Pfaff   AUT   3:40.71
4. Paul Hoekstra, Antonius Geurts   HOL   3:41.36
5. Lars Andersson, Nils Gunnar Utterberg   SWE   3:41.99
6. Atanase Sciotnic, Aurel Vernescu   ROM   3:45.18
7. Jean-Pierre Burny, Herman Naegels   BEL   3:45.21
8. Cesare Beltrami, Cesare Zilioli   ITA   3:46.08

1972 Munich T: 25, N: 25, D: 9.9.
1. Nikolai Gorbachev, Viktor Kratasyuk   SOV   3:31.23
2. József Deme, János Rátkai   HUN   3:32.00
3. Wladyslaw Szuszkiewicz, Rafal Piszcz   POL   3:33.83
4. Reiner Kurth, Alexander Slatnow   GDR   3:34.16
5. Costel Coşnită, Vasile Simiocenco   ROM   3:35.66
6. Jean-Pierre Cordebois, Didier Niquet   FRA   3:36.51

7. Günther Pfaff, Helmut Hediger   AUT   3:36.61
8. Hans-Jürgen Riemenschneider, Horst Mattern   GER   3:38.67

1976 Montreal T: 24, N: 24, D: 7.31.
1. Serhei Nahorny, Vladimir Romanovsky   SOV   3:29.01
2. Joachim Mattern, Bernd Olbricht   GDR   3:29.33
3. Zoltán Bakó, István Szabó   HUN   3:30.36
4. Jean-Paul Hanquier, Alain Lebas   FRA   3:33.05
5. Guillermo Del Riego Gordon, José Seguin   SPA   3:33.16
6. Jean-Pierre Burny, Paul Hoekstra   BEL   3:33.86
7. Policarp Malihin, Larion Serghei   ROM   3:34.27
8. Steve King, Denis Barre   CAN   3:34.46

1980 Moscow T: 16, N: 16, D: 8.2.
1. Vladimir Parfenovich, Serhei Chukhray   SOV   3:26.72
2. István Szabó, István Joós   HUN   3:28.49
3. Luis Gregory Ramos Misioné, Herminio Menéndez Rodriguez   SPA   3:28.66
4. Alexandru Giura, Nicolae Ticu   ROM   3:28.94
5. Peter Hempel, Harry Nolte   GDR   3:31.02
6. José Marrero Rodriguez, Reynaldo Cunill Infante   CUB   3:31.12
7. Ron Stevens, Gert Lebbink   HOL   3:33.18
8. Alan Thompson, Geoffrey Walker   NZE   3:33.83

1984 Los Angeles-Lake Casitas T: 17, N: 17, D: 8.11.
1. Hugh Fisher, Alwyn Morris   CAN   3:24.22
2. Bernard Bregeon, Patrick Lefoulon   FRA   3:25.97
3. Barry Kelly, Grant Kenny   AUS   3:26.80
4. Olney Kent, Terry White   USA   3:27.01
5. Matthias Seack, Oliver Seack   GER   3:27.28
6. Daniele Scarpa, Francesco Uberti   ITA   3:27.46
7. Herminio Menéndez Rodriguez, Guillermo Del Riego Gordon   SPA   3:27.53
8. Bengt Andersson, Kalle Sundqvist   SWE   3:29.39

Alwyn Morris, a Mohawk Indian from the Caughawaga Reserve in Quebec, carried with him to the medal ceremony a decorated eagle feather to symbolize the sharing of his victory with the native people of North America. The feather had been presented to him by a California Indian group.

1988 Seoul T: 20, N: 20, D: 10.1.
1. Gregory Barton, Norman Bellingham   USA   3:32.42
2. Ian Ferguson, Paul MacDonald   NZE   3:32.71
3. Peter Foster, Kelvin Graham   AUS   3:33.76
4. Niels Ellwanger, Carsten Lömker   GER   3:34.63
5. Guido Behling, Torsten Krentz   GDR   3:35.44
6. Daniel Stoian, Angelin Velea   ROM   3:35.75
7. Anders Ohlsén, Hans Olsson   SWE   3:36.13
8. Svein Egil Solvang, Harald Amundsen   NOR   3:38.16

Pre-Olympic favorites Philippe Boccara and Pascal Boucherit of France were disqualified in the semifinals when they failed to make it to the starting line on time. Barton, the son of a pig farmer, and Bellingham, the son of a CIA agent, came from behind in the last 250 meters to nip Ferguson and MacDonald, who happened to have been Bellingham's mentors.

1992 Barcelona-Castelldefels T: 27, N: 27, D: 8.8.

1.	Kay Bluhm, Torsten Gutsche	GER	3:16.10
2.	Gunnar Olsson, Karl Sundqvist	SWE	3:17.70
3.	Grzegorz Kotowicz, Dariusz Bialkowski	POL	3:18.86
4.	Gregory Barton, Norman Bellingham	USA	3:19.26
5.	Paolo Luschi, Daniele Scarpa	ITA	3:20.34
6.	Krisztián Bártfai, András Rajna	HUN	3:20.71
7.	René Kučera, Petr Hruška	CZE	3:23.12
8.	Ian Ferguson, Paul MacDonald	NZE	3:26.84

Bluhm and Gutsche had won the event at the last three world championships. In the Olympic final they pulled out to a lead of almost three seconds at the halfway mark, continued to apply pressure over the next 250 meters, and held on for the victory.

KAYAK FOURS 1000 METERS

1896–1960 not held

1964 Tokyo T: 14, N: 14, D: 10.22.

1. SOV (Mykola Chuzhykov, Anatoly Grishin, Vyacheslav Ionov, Volodymyr Morozov) 3:14.67
2. GER (Günther Perleberg, Bernhard Schulze, Friedhelm Wentzke, Holger Zander) 3:15.39
3. ROM (Simion Cuciuc, Atanase Sciotnic, Mihai Turcaş, Aurel Vernescu) 3:15.51
4. HUN (Imre Kemecsey, György Mészáros, András Szente, Imre Szöllösi) 3:16.24
5. SWE (Rolf Peterson, Sven-Olov Sjödelius, Nils Gunnar Utterberg, Carl von Gerber) 3:17.47
6. ITA (Claudio Agnisetta, Cesare Beltrami, Angelo Pedroni, Cesare Zilioli) 3:19.32
7. HOL (Paul Hoekstra, Theodorus van Halteren, Guillaume Weijzen, Jan Wittenberg) 3:19.36
8. YUG (Dragan Desancić, Vladimir Ignjatijević, Aleksandar Kercov, Stanisa Radmanović) 3:19.79

1968 Mexico City T: 19, N: 19, D: 10.25.

1. NOR (Steinar Admundsen, Egil Söby, Tore Berger, Jan Johansen) 3:14.38
2. ROM (Anton Calenic, Dimitrie Ivanov, Haralambie Ivanov, Mihai Turcaş) 3:14.81
3. HUN (Csaba Giczi, Istvan Timár, Imre Szöllösi, István Csizmadia) 3:15.10
4. SWE (Per Larsson, Hans Nilsson, Tord Sahlén, Åke Sandin) 3:16.68
5. FIN (Karl-Gustav von Alfthan, Heikki Mäkelä, Jorma Lehtosalo, Ilkka Nummisto) 3:17.28
6. GDR (Joachim Wenzke, Klaus-Uwe Will, Erhard Riedrich, Klaus-Peter Ebeling) 3:18.03
7. AUT (Helmut Hediger, Kurt Lindlgruber, Günther Pfaff, Gerhard Seibold) 3:18.95
8. POL (Ewald Janusz, Ryszard Marchlik, Rafal Piszcz, Wladyslaw Zieliński) 3:22.10

Much credit for the Norwegians' upset victory went to their trainer, Stein Johnson, who had successfully coached track and field, skiing, and speed skating before trying his hand at canoeing. Johnson himself placed eighth in the 1948 discus throw.

1972 Munich T: 20, N: 20, D: 9.9.

1. SOV (Yuri Filatov, Yuri Stetsenko, Volodymyr Morozov, Valery Didenko) 3:14.02
2. ROM (Aurel Vernescu, Mihai Zafiu, Roman Vartolomeu, Atanase Sciotnic) 3:15.07
3. NOR (Egil Söby, Steinar Amundsen, Tore Berger, Jan Johansen) 3:15.27
4. ITA (Alberto Ughi, Pier Angelo Congiu, Mario Pedretti, Oreste Perri) 3:15.60
5. GER (Rudolf Blass, Eberhard Fischer, Rainer Hennes, Hans-Erich Pasch) 3:16.63
6. HUN (István Szabó, Peter Várhelyi, Zoltán Bakó, Csongor Vargha) 3:16.88
7. FIN (Kari Markkanen, Heikki Mäkelä, Ilkka Nummisto, Jorma Lehtosalo) 3:16.92
8. SWE (Lars Andersson, Nils Gunnar Utterberg, Per Larsson, Hans Nilsson) 3:17.39

1976 Montreal T: 20, N: 20, D: 7.31.

1. SOV (Serhei Chukhray, Aleksandr Degtyarev, Yuri Filatov, Volodymyr Morozov) 3:08.69
2. SPA (José María Esteban Celorrio, José Ramón López Diaz-Flor, Herminio Menéndez Rodriguez, Luis Gregorio Ramos Misioné) 3:08.95
3. GDR (Peter Bischof, Bernd Duvigneau, Rüdiger Helm, Jürgen Lehnert) 3:10.76
4. ROM (Nicuşor Eşanu, Vasile Simioncenco, Nicolae Simioncenco, Mihai Zafiu) 3:11.35
5. POL (Henryk Budzicz, Kazimierz Górecki, Grzegorz Koltan, Ryszard Oborski) 3:12.17
6. NOR (Morten Mörland, Einar Rasmussen, Olaf Söyland, Jostein Stige) 3:12.28
7. BUL (Ivan Manev, Bojidar Milenkov, Nikolai Nachev, Vasil Chilingirov) 3:12.94
8. HUN (József Deme, Csaba Giczi, János Rátkai, Zoltán Romhányi) 3:14.67

The Soviet team came from third place in the last 250 meters to nose out Spain, which had been the surprise winner of the 1975 world championship.

1980 Moscow T: 12, N; 12, D: 8.2.

1. GDR (Rüdiger Helm, Bernd Olbricht, Harald Marg, Bernd Duvigneau) 3:13.76
2. ROM (Mihai Zafiu, Vasile Dîba, Ion Geanta, Nicuşor Eşanu) 3:15.35
3. BUL (Borislav Borissov, Bozhidar Milenkov, Lazar Hristov, Ivan Manev) 3:15.46
4. POL (Ryszard Oborski, Grzegorz Koltan, Daniel Welna, Grzegorz Śledziewski) 3:16.33
5. HUN (József Deme, János Rátkai, József Kosztyán, Zoltán Sztaniti) 3:17.27
6. FRA (François Barouh, Patrick Berard, Philippe Boccara, Patrick Lefoulon) 3:17.60
7. SOV (Gennady Makhnev, Serhei Nahorny, Aleksandrs Avdejevs, Vladimir Tainikov) 3:19.83

8. AUS   (Barry Kelly, Robert Lee, Ken Vidler, Crosbie   3:19.87
        Baulch)

1984 Los Angeles-Lake Casitas T: 15, N: 15, D: 8.11.

1. NZE (Grant Bramwell, Ian Ferguson, Paul Mac- 3:02.28
       Donald, Alan Thompson)
2. SWE (Per-Inge Bengtsson, Tommy Karls, Lars-Erik 3:02.81
       Moberg, Thomas Ohlsson)
3. FRA (François Barouh, Philippe Boccara, Pascal 3:03.94
       Boucherit, Didier Vavasseur)
4. ROM (Ionel Constantin, Nicolae Fedosei, Ionel 3:04.39
       Letcaie, Angelin Velea)
5. GBR (Grayson Bourne, Andrew Sherriff, Kevin 3:04.59
       Smith, Jeremy West)
6. SPA (Ivan Gonzalez, Luis Gregorio Ramos Misioné, 3:04.71
       Juan José Roman, Juan Manuel Sanchez)
7. AUS (John Doak, Robert Doak, Raymond Martin, 3:06.02
       Scott Wooden)
8. GER (Bernd Hessel, Oliver Kegel, Dieter Schmidt, 3:06.47
       Reiner Scholl)

1988 Seoul T: 18, N: 18, D: 10.1.

1. HUN (Zsolt Gyulay, Ferenc Csipes, Sándor Hódosi, 3:00.20
       Attila Ábrahám)
2. SOV (Aleksandr Motuzenko, Serhei Kyrsanov, Ihor 3:01.40
       Nahayev, Viktor Denisov)
3. GDR (Kay Bluhm, André Wohllebe, Andreas Stähle, 3:02.37
       Hans-Jörg Bliesener)
4. AUS (Bryan Thomas, Steven Wood, Grant Kenny, 3:03.70
       Paul Gilmour)
5. POL Maciej Frejmut, Wojciech Kurpiewski, 3:04.73
       Grzegorz Krawców, Kazimierz Krzyżański)
6. GER (Gilbert Schneider, Reiner Scholl, Dirk Joestel, 3:05.43
       Thomas Reineck)
7. ITA (Beniamino Bonomi, Daniele Scarpa, Alessan- 3:05.97
       dro Pieri, Francesco Mandragona)
8. SWE (Per-Inge Bengtsson, Lars-Erik Moberg, Karl 3:06.03
       Axel Sundkvist, Bengt Andersson)

The Hungarians, seventh at the halfway point, blew away the field in the third quarter.

1992 Barcelona-Castelldefels T: 19, N: 19, D: 8.8.

1. GER (Oliver Kegel, Thomas Reineck, Mario Von 2:54.18
       Appen, André Wohllebe)
2. HUN (Attila Ábrahám, Ferenc Csipes, László Fidel, 2:54.82
       Zsolt Gyulay)
3. AUS (Ramon Andersson, Kelvin Graham, Ian 2:56.97
       Rowling, Steven Wood)
4. CZE (Róbert Erban, Juraj Kadnár, Attila Szabó, 2:57.06
       Jozef Turza)
5. ROM (Geza Magyar, Sorin Petcu, Romica Serban, 3:00.11
       Daniel Stoian)
6. POL (Maciej Freimut, Grzegorz Kaleta, Grzegorz 3:01.43
       Krawcow, Wojciech Kurpiewski)
7. SWE (Jonas Fager, Pablo Grate, Anders Ohlsén, 3:01.46
       Hans Olsson)
8. BUL (Petar Godev, Nikolay Georgiev, Milko Ka- 3:02.08
       zanov, Evlogiev Yordanov)

The Hungarians had won every world and Olympic championship since 1986. They were expected to repeat in Barcelona, especially since their main rivals, the Germans, had lost one of their key members, Detlef Holfmann, to a positive drug test (testosterone) two months before the Games began. However, the German team took the lead in the second quarter and never relinquished it.

CANADIAN SINGLES 500 METERS

1896–1972 not held

1976 Montreal C: 15, N: 15, D: 7.30.

1. Aleksandr Rogov	SOV/RUS	1:59.23
2. John Wood	CAN	1:59.58
3. Matija Ljubek	YUG/CRO	1:59.60
4. Borislav Ananiev	BUL	1:59.92
5. Wilfried Stephan	GDR	2:00.54
6. Károly Szegedi	HUN	2:01.12
7. Ivan Patzaichin	ROM	2:01.40
8. Ulrich Eicke	GER	2:02.30

John Wood thrilled the Canadian crowd of 5000 by leading from the start until the last few strokes, when he was overtaken by the favorite, Aleksandr Rogov.

1980 Moscow C: 11, N: 11, D: 8.1.

1. Serhei Postryekhin	SOV/UKR	1:53.37
2. Lyubomir Lyubenov	BUL	1:53.49
3. Olaf Heukrodt	GDR	1:54.38
4. Tamás Wichmann	HUN	1:54.58
5. Marek Lbik	POL	1:55.90
6. Timo Grönlund	FIN	1:55.94
7. Lipat Varabiev	ROM	1:56.80
8. Radomir Blazik	CZE	1:56.83

1984 Los Angeles-Lake Casitas C: 13, N: 13, D: 8.10.

1. Larry Cain	CAN	1:57.01
2. Henning Jakobsen	DEN	1:58.45
3. Costică Olaru	ROM	1:59.86
4. Philippe Renaud	FRA	1:59.95
5. Timo Grönlund	FIN	2:01.00
6. Kiyoto Inoue	JPN	2:01.79
7. Hartmut Faust	GER	2:01.86
8. Robert Rozanski	NOR	2:02.12

1988 Seoul C: 18, N: 18, D: 9.30.

1. Olaf Heukrodt	GDR	1:56.42
2. Mykhalo Slyvynsky	SOV/UKR	1:57.26
3. Martin Marinov	BUL	1:57.27
4. Attila Szabó	HUN	1:59.87
5. Jan Pinczura	POL	1:59.90
6. Aurel Macarencu	ROM	2:00.98
7. Narciso Suárez Amador	SPA	2:01.33
8. Petr Procházka	CZE	2:01.36

Five-time world champion Olaf Heukrodt of Magdeburg moved up from last place at the halfway mark. Heukrodt, who was married to world champion swimmer Birgit Meineke, would have been the clear favorite four years earlier in Los Angeles had not East Germany boycotted the 1984 Games.

1992 Barcelona-Castelldefels C: 19, N: 19, D: 8.7.

1.	Nikolay Bukhalov	BUL	1:51.15
2.	Mykhalo Slyvynsky	UKR	1:51.40
3.	Olaf Heukrodt	GER	1:53.00
4.	Slavomír Kňazovický	CZE	1:54.51
5.	Imre Pulai	HUN	1:54.86
6.	Stephen Giles	CAN	1:55.80
7.	Pascal Sylvoz	FRA	1:55.96
8.	Victor Partnoi	ROM	1:57.34

Slyvynsky had won the previous three world championships, but Bukhalov had bested him on the Olympic course in 1991.

CANADIAN SINGLES 1000 METERS

1896–1932 not held

1936 Berlin C: 6, N: 6, D: 8.8.

1.	Francis Amyot	CAN	5:32.1
2.	Bohuslav Karlik	CZE	5:36.9
3.	Erich Koschik	GER	5:39.0
4.	Otto Neumüller	AUT	5:47.0
5.	Joseph Hasenfus	USA	6:02.6
6.	Joseph Treinen	LUX	7:39.5

Amyot, who once saved three Ottawa Rough Riders football players from drowning, took an early lead but was passed by Karlik at the 750-meter mark. A 31-year-old veteran, Amyot refused to be rattled and continued stroking smoothly, until he had burst past Karlik with 50 meters to go. Amyot was Canada's only gold medal winner at the Berlin Olympics, thus embarrassing the Canadian Olympic Committee, which had refused to pay his way.

1948 London C: 6, N: 6, D: 8.12.

1.	Josef Holeček	CZE	5:42.0
2.	Douglas Bennett	CAN	5:53.3
3.	Robert Boutigny	FRA	5:55.9
4.	Ingemar Andersson	SWE	6:08.0
5.	Frank Havens	USA	6:14.3
6.	Henry Maidment	GBR	6:37.0

1952 Helsinki C: 10, N: 10, D: 7.28.

1.	Josef Holeček	CZE	4:56.3
2.	János Parti	HUN	5:03.6
3.	Olavi Ojanperä	FIN	5:08.5
4.	Frank Havens	USA	5:13:7
5.	Ingemar Andersson	SWE	5:15.0
6.	Ralf Berckhan	GER	5:22.8
7.	Jean Molle	FRA	5:24.1
8.	Vladimir Kotyrev	SOV	5:24.5

1956 Melbourne C: 9, N: 9, D: 12.1.

1.	Leon Rotman	ROM	5:05.3
2.	István Hernek	HUN	5:06.2
3.	Gennady Bukharin	SOV/RUS	5:12.7

4.	Karel Hradil	CZE	5:15.9
5.	Franz Johannsen	GER	5:18.6
6.	Verner Wettersten	SWE	5:28.0
7.	Bryan Harper	AUS	5:37.6
8.	George Bossy	CAN	5:39.4

1960 Rome C: 13, N: 13, D: 8.29.

1.	János Parti	HUN	4:33.93
2.	Aleksandr Silayev	SOV/RUS	4:34.41
3.	Leon Rotman	ROM	4:35.87
4.	Ove Emanuelsson	SWE	4:36.46
5.	Tibor Polakovič	CZE	4:39.28
6.	Detlef Lewe	GER	4:39.72
7.	Don Stringer	CAN	4:40.65
8.	Bogdan Ivanov	BUL	4:42.52

1964 Tokyo C: 11, N: 11, D: 10.22.

1.	Jürgen Eschert	GDR	4:35.14
2.	Andrei Igorov	ROM	4:37.89
3.	Yevgeny Penyayev	SOV/RUS	4:38.31
4.	András Törö	HUN	4:39.95
5.	Ove Emanuelsson	SWE	4:42.70
6.	Bogdan Ivanov	BUL	4:44.76
7.	Paul Stahl	CAN	5:04.79
8.	Dennis Van Valkenburgh	USA	5:12.55

1968 Mexico City C: 12, N: 12, D: 10.25.

1.	Tibor Tatai	HUN	4:36.14
2.	Detlef Lewe	GER	4:38.31
3.	Vitaly Galkov	SOV/RUS	4:40.42
4.	Jiří Čtvrtečka	CZE	4:40.74
5.	Boris Lyubenov	BUL	4:43.43
6.	Ove Emanuelsson	SWE	4:45.80
7.	Ivan Patzaichin	ROM	4:49.32
8.	Andreas Weigand	USA	4:50.42

Tibor Tatai made the Hungarian team only as a reserve, but he drove the other finalists to exhaustion and won decisively.

1972 Munich C: 13, N: 13, D: 9.9.

1.	Ivan Patzaichin	ROM	4:08.94
2.	Tamás Wichmann	HUN	4:12.42
3.	Detlef Lewe	GER	4:13.63
4.	Dirk Weise	GDR	4:14.38
5.	Vasyl Yurchenko	SOV/UKR	4:14.43
6.	Boris Lyubenov	BUL	4:14.65
7.	Jiří Čtvrtečka	CZE	4:14.98
8.	Roberto Altamirano	MEX	4:20.39

1976 Montreal C: 15, N: 15, D: 7.31.

1.	Matija Ljubek	YUG/CRO	4:09.51
2.	Vasyl Yurchenko	SOV/UKR	4:12.57
3.	Tamás Wichmann	HUN	4:14.11
4.	Borislav Ananiev	BUL	4:14.41
5.	Ivan Patzaichin	ROM	4:15.08
6.	Roland Iche	FRA	4:18.23
7.	Wilfried Stephan	GDR	4:22.43
8.	Ulrich Eicke	GER	4:22.77

Ljubek, a carpenter from Belisce, was the only finalist to paddle the second half of the race faster than the first. He was fourth at the halfway mark but won going away.

1980 Moscow C: 12, N: 12, D: 8.2.
1.	Lyubomir Lyubenov	BUL	4:12.38
2.	Serhei Postryekhin	SOV/UKR	4:13.53
3.	Eckhard Leue	GDR	4:15.02
4.	Libor Dvořák	CZE	4:15.25
5.	Lipat Varabiev	ROM	4:16.68
6.	Timo Grönlund	FIN	4:17.37
7.	Thomas Falk	SWE	4:20.66
8.	Matija Ljubek	YUG/CRO	4:22.40

1984 Los Angeles-Lake Casitas C: 11, N: 11, D: 8.11.
1.	Ulrich Eicke	GER	4:06.32
2.	Larry Cain	CAN	4:08.67
3.	Henning Jakobsen	DEN	4:09.51
4.	Timo Grönlund	FIN	4:15.58
5.	Costică Olaru	ROM	4:16.39
6.	Stephen Train	GBR	4:16.64
7.	Bruce Merritt	USA	4:18.17
8.	Kiyoto Inoue	JPN	4:18.72

1988 Seoul C: 15, N: 15, D: 10.1.
1.	Ivans Klemenjevs	SOV/LAT	4:12.78
2.	Jörg Schmidt	GDR	4:15.83
3.	Nikolay Bukhalov	BUL	4:18.94
4.	Larry Cain	CAN	4:20.70
5.	Aurel Macarencu	ROM	4:21.72
6.	Imre Pulai	HUN	4:21.86
7.	Petr Pales	CZE	4:22.14
8.	Ivan Šabjan	YUG	4:24.67

1992 Barcelona-Castelldefels C: 19, N: 19, D: 8.8.
1.	Nikolay Bukhalov	BUL	4:05.92
2.	Ivans Klementjevs	LAT	4:06.60
3.	György Zala	HUN	4:07.35
4.	Matthias Röder	GER	4:08.96
5.	Pascal Sylvoz	FRA	4:09.82
6.	Andrew Train	GBR	4:12.58
7.	Victor Partnoi	ROM	4:14.27
8.	Jan Bartůněk	CZE	4:15.25

Having defeated three-time world champion Mykhalo Slyvynsky in the 500-meter event the day before, Bukhalov did the same to the 1000-meter three-time world champion, Ivans Klementjevs. As with the 500, Bukhalov had bested Klementjevs at 1000 on the Olympic course in 1991. In the Olympic final Bukhalov led from start to finish, while Klementjevs moved up from fifth to second in the last 250 meters.

CANADIAN PAIRS 500 METERS

1896–1972 not held

1976 Montreal T: 15, N: 15, D: 7.30.
1.	Serhei Petrenko, Aleksandr Vinogradov	SOV	1:45.81
2.	Andrzej Gronowicz, Jerzy Opara	POL	1:47.77
3.	Tamás Buday, Oszkár Frey	HUN	1:48.35
4.	Gheorghe Danielov, Gheorghe Simionov	ROM	1:48.84
5.	Gerald Delacroix, Jean-François Millot	FRA	1:49.74
6.	Ivan Burchin, Krasimir Hristov	BUL	1:50.43
7.	Gregory Smith, John Wood	CAN	1:50.74
8.	Jiři Čtvrtecka, Tomáš Sach	CZE	1:50.85

1980 Moscow T: 10, N: 10, D: 8.1.
1.	László Foltán, István Vaskuti	HUN	1:43.39
2.	Petre Capusta, Ivan Patzaichin	ROM	1:44.12
3.	Borislav Ananiev, Nikolai Ilkov	BUL	1:44.83
4.	Jerzy Dunajski, Marek Wisla	POL	1:45.10
5.	Petr Kubiček, Jiři Vrdlovec	CZE	1:46.48
6.	Serhei Petrenko, Aleksandr Vinogradov	SOV	1:46.95
7.	Santos Magaz, Narcisco Suárez Amador	SPA	1:48.18
8.	Bernt Lindelof, Erik Zeidlitz	SWE	1:48.69

1984 Los Angeles-Lake Casitas T: 11, N: 11, D: 8.10.
1.	Matija Ljubek, Mirko Nišović	YUG/CRO	1:43.67
2.	Ivan Patzaichin, Toma Simionov	ROM	1:45.68
3.	Enrique Miguez Gómez, Narcisco Suárez Amador	SPA	1:47.71
4.	Didier Hoyer, Eric Renaud	FRA	1:47.72
5.	Steve Botting, Eric Smith	CAN	1:48.81
6.	Wolfram Faust, Ralf Wienand	GER	1:48.97
7.	Eric Jamieson, Andrew Train	GBR	1:49.59
8.	Shusei Fukuzato, Hiroyuki Izumi	JPN	1:50.22

Ljubek and Nišović won the gold with a devastating closing spurt that pushed them past the Romanians after 400 meters.

1988 Seoul T: 17, N: 17, D: 9.30.
1.	Viktor Reneisky, Nikolai Zhuravsky	SOV	1:41.77
2.	Marek Dopierala, Marek Lbik	POL	1:43.61
3.	Philippe Renaud, Joël Bettin	FRA	1:43.81
4.	Deyan Bonev, Petar Bozhilov	BUL	1:44.32
5.	Alexander Schuck, Thomas Zereske	GDR	1:44.36
6.	János Kis Sarusi, István Vaskuti	HUN	1:44.85
7.	Grigore Obreja, Gheorghe Andriev	ROM	1:45.84
8.	Christian Frederiksen, Arne Nielsson	DEN	1:45.90

Third-place finisher Philippe Renaud was the third member of his family to win a canoeing medal. His father, Marcel, earned a silver in the 10,000-meter Canadian pairs in 1956. In 1984, Philippe's brother, Eric, took a bronze in the 1000-meter Canadian pairs. In addition, his uncle, also named Marcel, placed fourth in the 1924 team pursuit cycling race.

1992 Barcelona-Castelldefels T: 15, N: 15, D: 8.7.
1.	Aleksandr Maseikov, Dmitri Dovgalenok	BLR	1:41.54
2.	Ulrich Papke, Ingo Spelly	GER	1:41.68
3.	Martin Marinov, Blagovest Stoyanov	BUL	1:41.94
4.	Gheorghe Andriev, Nicolae Juravschi (Nikolai Zhuravsky)	ROM	1:42.84
5.	Arne Nielsson, Christian Frederiksen	DEN	1:42.92

6. Didier Hoyer, Olivier Boivin	FRA	1:43.04
7. Attila Pálizs, György Kolonics	HUN	1:43.27
8. Jan Bartůněk, Waldemar Fibigr	CZE	1:44.70

The people of Romania and the people of Moldova are actually members of the same ethnic group and speak the same language. In 1988, Moldavan Nikolai Zhuravsky won two gold medals for the U.S.S.R. while teamed with Viktor Reneisky of Belarus. When the Soviet Union collapsed in 1991, Zhuravsky crossed the border, changed his name to Nicolae Juravschi, and obtained Romanian citizenship six weeks before the opening of the Barcelona Olympics. Teamed with Gheorghe Andriev, he managed to place fourth in both the C-2 500 and the C-2 1000—an impressive achievement, considering the pair had begun competing together only two weeks before the Olympics.

CANADIAN PAIRS 1000 METERS

1896–1932 not held

1936 Berlin T: 5, N: 5, D: 8.8.

1. Vladimir Syrovátka, Jan Brzák-Felix	CZE	4:50.1
2. Rupert Weinstabl, Karl Proisl	AUT	4:53.8
3. Frank Saker, Harvey Charters	CAN	4:56.7
4. Hans Wedemann, Heinrich Sack	GER	5:00.2
5. Clarence McNutt, Robert Graf	USA	5:14.0

1948 London T: 8, N: 8, D: 8.12.

1. Jan Brzák-Felix, Bohumil Kudrna	CZE	5:07.1
2. Stephen Lysak, Stephan Macknowski	USA	5:08.2
3. Georges Dransart, Georges Gandil	FRA	5:15.2
4. Douglas Bennett, Harry Poulton	CAN	5:20.7
5. Karl Molnar, Viktor Salmhofer	AUT	5:37.3
6. Gunnar Johansson, Verner Wettersten	SWE	5:44.9
7. John Symons, Henry Van Zwananberg	GBR	5:50.8
DNF: Hubert Coomans, Jean Dubois (BEL), man overboard		

Jan Brzák was one of the few gold medal winners at the Berlin Olympics who was able to retain his championship 12 years later in London. In 1955, when he was 43 years old, Brzák teamed with 46-year-old Bohuslav Karlik to paddle the 118 miles from Ceské Budějovice to Prague in 20 hours.

1952 Helsinki T: 11, N: 11, D: 7.28.

1. Bent Peder Rasch, Finn Haunstoft	DEN	4:38.3
2. Jan Brzák-Felix, Bohumil Kudrna	CZE	4:42.9
3. Egon Drews, Wilfried Soltau	GER	4:48.3
4. Georges Dransart, Armand Loreau	FRA	4:48.6
5. István Bodor, József Tuza	HUN	4:51.9
6. Kurt Liebhart, Englebert Lulla	AUT	4:55.8
7. John Haas, Frank Krick	USA	4:59.0
8. Arthur Johnson, Thomas Hodgson	CAN	5:01.4

1956 Melbourne T: 10, N: 10, D: 12.1.

1. Alexe Dumitru, Simion Ismailciuc	ROM	4:47.4
2. Pavel Kharine, Gratsian Botev	SOV/RUS	4:48.6
3. Károly Wieland, Ferenc Mohácsi	HUN	4:54.3

4. Georges Dransart, Marcel Renaud	FRA	4:57.7
5. William Jones, Thomas Ohman	AUS	5:03.0
6. Otto Schindler, Walter Waldner	AUT	5:04.4
7. William Collins, Bert Oldershaw	CAN	5:11.0
DISQ: Kai Sylvan, Gerner Christiansen (DEN)		

1960 Rome T: 11, N: 11, D: 8.29.

1. Leonid Geishtor, Sergei Makarenko	SOV	4:17.94
2. Aldo Dezi, Francesco La Macchia	ITA	4:20.77
3. Imre Farkas, András Törö	HUN	4:20.89
4. Igor Lipalit, Alexe Dumitru	ROM	4:22.36
5. Jiři Kodeš, Václav Vokal	CZE	4:27.66
6. Marin Gopov, Toma Sokolov	BUL	4:31.52
7. Willi Mehlberg, Werner Ulrich	GDR	4:31.68
8. Georges Turlier, Michel Picard	FRA	4:35.48

1964 Tokyo T: 12, N: 12, D: 10.22.

1. Andrey Khymych, Stepan Oschepkov	SOV	4:04.64
2. Jean Boudehen, Michel Chapuis	FRA	4:06.52
3. Peer Norrbohm Nielsen, John Sörensen	DEN	4:07.48
4. Antal Hajba, Árpád Soltesz	HUN	4:08.97
5. Igor Lipalit, Achim Sidorov	ROM	4:09.88
6. Klaus Böhle, Detlef Lewe	GER	4:13.18
7. Andor Ebert, Fred Heese	CAN	4:21.99
8. Miloslav Houzim, Rudolf Penkava	CZE	4:22.89

1968 Mexico City T: 12, N: 12, D: 10.25.

1. Ivan Patzaichin, Serghei Covaliov	ROM	4:07.18
2. Tamás Wichmann, Gyula Petrikovics	HUN	4:08.77
3. Naum Prokupets, Mikhail Zamotin	SOV	4:11.30
4. Juan Martinez, Felix Altamirano	MEX	4:15.24
5. Berndt Lindelöf, Erik Zeidltov	SWE	4:16.60
6. Jürgen Harpke, Helmut Wagner	GDR	4:22.53
7. Roland Kapf, Klaus Lewandowsky	GER	4:26.36
8. Ivan Vulov, Alexander Damianov	BUL	4:26.74

Ivan Patzaichin and Serghei Covaliov were fishermen from the village of Crisan-Mila, in the Danube delta. Silver medalist Tamás Wichmann was a chef.

1972 Munich T: 16, N: 16, D: 9.9.

1. Vladislavas Česiunas, Yuri Lobanov	SOV	3:52.60
2. Ivan Patzaichin, Serghei Covaliov	ROM	3:52.63
3. Fedia Damianov, Ivan Burchin	BUL	3:58.10
4. Hans-Peter Hoffmann, Hermann Glaser	GER	3:59.24
5. Miklós Darvas, Péter Povázsay	HUN	4:00.42
6. Roland Muhlen, Andreas Weigand	USA	4:01.28
7. Dirk Weise, Dieter Lichtenberg	GDR	4:01.50
8. Berndt Lindelöf, Eric Zeidlitz	SWE	4:01.60

Česiunas and Lobanov took an early lead, but at the 700-meter mark Patzaichin and Covaliov mounted a furious challenge that brought them to the finish line only three one-hundredths of a second too late.

1976 Montreal T: 15, N: 15, D: 7.31.

1. Serhei Petrenko, Aleksandr Vinogradov	SOV	3:52.76
2. Gheorghe Danielov, Gheorghe Simionov	ROM	3:54.28
3. Tamás Buday, Oszkár Frey	HUN	3:55.66
4. Jerzy Opara, Andrzej Gronowicz	POL	3:59.56

5. Detlef Bothe, Hans-Jürgen Tode — GDR — 4:00.37
6. Jiří Čtvrtečka, Tomáš Sach — CZE — 4:01.48
7. Ivan Burchin, Krasimir Hristov — BUL — 4:02.44
8. Hermann Glaser, Heinz Lucke — GER — 4:03.86

1980 Moscow T: 11, N: 11, D: 8.2.
1. Ivan Patzaichin, Toma Simionov — ROM — 3:47.65
2. Olaf Heukrodt, Uwe Madeja — GDR — 3:49.93
3. Vasyl Yurchenko, Yuri Lobanov — SOV — 3:51.28
4. Matija Ljubek, Mirko Nišović — YUG/CRO — 3:51.30
5. Jiří Vrdlovec, Petr Kubiček — CZE — 3:52.50
6. Marek Dopiérala, Jan Pinczura — POL — 3:53.01
7. Raiko Kurmadzhiev, Kamen Kutzev — BUL — 3:53.89
8. Tamás Buday, Oszkár Frey — HUN — 3:54.31

1984 Los Angeles-Lake Casitas T: 10, N: 10, D: 8.11.
1. Ivan Patzaichin, Toma Simionov — ROM — 3:40.60
2. Matija Ljubek, Mirko Nišović — YUG/CRO — 3:41.56
3. Didier Hoyer, Eric Renaud — FRA — 3:48.01
4. Wolfram Faust, Ralf Wienand — GER — 3:52.69
5. John Plankenhorn, Rodney McClain — USA — 3:52.72
6. Enrique Miguez Gómez, Narcisco Suárez Amador — SPA — 3:56.92
7. Steve Botting, Eric Smith — CAN — 3:56.99
8. Arturo Ferrer, Victor Velasco — MEX — 3:57.49

Thirty-four-year-old Ivan Patzaichin closed out his Olympic career with four gold medals and three silvers.

1988 Seoul T: 17, N: 17, D: 10.1.
1. Victor Reneisky, Nikolai Zhuravsky — SOV — 3:48.36
2. Olaf Heukrodt, Ingo Spelly — GDR — 3:51.44
3. Marek Dopierala, Marek Lbik — POL — 3:54.33
4. Christian Frederiksen, Arne Nielsson — DEN — 3:54.94
5. Hartmut Faust, Wolfram Faust — GER — 3:55.62
6. Grigore Obreja, Gheorghe Andriev — ROM — 3:56.56
7. Gábor Takács, Gusztáv Leikep — HUN — 4:04.18
8. Pascal Sylvoz, Didier Hoyer — FRA — 4:04.75

1992 Barcelona-Castelldefels T: 14, N: 14, D: 8.8.
1. Ulrich Papke, Ingo Spelly — GER — 3:37.42
2. Arne Nielsson, Christian Frederiksen — DEN — 3:39.26
3. Didier Hoyer, Olivier Boivin — FRA — 3:39.51
4. Gheorghe Andriev, Nicolae Juravschi (Nicolai Zhuravsky) — ROM — 3:39.88
5. Attila Pálizs, György Kolonics — HUN — 3:42.86
6. Martin Marinov, Blagovest Stoyanov — BUL — 3:43.97
7. Larry Cain, David Frost — CAN — 3:46.21
8. Aleksei Igrayev, Aleksandr Gromovich — SOV — 3:53.90

Papke and Spelly, defending two-time world champions, fought off a mid-race challenge from Nielsson and Frederiksen and won going away.

WHITE-WATER (SLALOM)

This unusual sport requires the canoeist to paddle down an obstacle course in much the same manner as the slalom races in skiing. Courses are 340 meters long and include 25 gates, of which at least six must be negotiated upstream. The last gate is 25 meters from the finish line. In 1972 the course was 600 meters long and included 30 gates. A 5-point penalty is assessed if the canoeist negotiates the gate but touches one of the two gate poles. A 50-point penalty is assessed if the canoeist (1) pushes the gate intentionally, (2) crosses the gate line upside down, (3) negotiates a gate in the wrong direction, (4) misses a gate, (5) touches a gate during a failed negotiation, (6) crosses a gate underwater. Each penalty point equals one second. Each competitor runs the course twice, with only the better run, as defined by both time and penalty points, counting.

KAYAK SLALOM SINGLES

1896–1968 not held

1972 Munich-Augsburg C: 37, N: 15, D: 8.28.

		TIME	PENALTIES	PTS
1. Siegbert Horn	GDR	4:18.56	10	268.56
2. Norbert Sattler	AUT	4:20.76	10	270.76
3. Harald Gimpel	GDR	4:17.95	20	277.95
4. Ulrich Peters	GER	4:12.82	30	282.82

The exotic sport of slalom, or white-water, canoeing was included in the 1972 Olympics and dominated by the East Germans, who had constructed an exact copy of the West German course that was used for the Olympics.

5. Alfred Baum	GER	4:18:01	30	288.01
6. Marian Havlíček	CZE	4:09.56	40	289.56
7. Eric Evans	USA	4:25.34	30	296.34
8. Jürgen Bremer	GDR	4:23.15	40	303.15

The West Germans spent 17 million marks ($4 million) constructing an artificial river at Augsburg for the competition, and they hoped to gain several medals at the Olympics. However, a year before the Munich games, the East Germans came over, studied the facilities at Augsburg, and built an exact replica back home. In 1972 East Germany won all four canoe slalom events. Their first winner was Siegbert Horn, a 22-year-old army sergeant from Leipzig. Horn keeled over in the first run and finished 17th. But the second time he paddled a smooth race and, although his time was only the eighth best, he picked up so few penalty points that he won anyway.

1976–1988 not held

1992 Barcelona-Seu d'Urgell C: 44, N: 21, D: 8.2.

		TIME	PENALTIES	PTS
1. Pierpaolo Ferrazzi	ITA	1:46.89	0	106.89
2. Sylvain Curinier	FRA	1:47.06	0	107.06
3. Jochen Lettmann	GER	1:48.52	0	108.52
4. Richard Fox	GBR	1:48.85	0	108.85
5. Laurent Brissaud	FRA	1:49.37	0	109.37
6. Marjan Štrukelj	SLO	1:50.11	0	110.11
7. Melvyn Jones	GBR	1:50.40	0	110.40
8. Ian Wiley	IRL	1:50.45	0	110.45

Ferrazzi, who trained full-time as a member of a government-sponsored canoe club, placed only 17th in the first run, which was won by Jochen Lettmann.

CANADIAN SLALOM SINGLES

1896–1968 not held

1972 Munich-Augsburg C: 22, N: 9, D: 7.28.

		TIME	PENALTIES	PTS
1. Reinhard Eiben	GDR	4:45.84	30	315.84
2. Reinhold Kauder	GER	5:07.89	20	327.89

3. James McEwan	USA	4:55.95	40	335.95
4. Jochen Förster	GDR	4:44.42	70	354.42
5. Wolfgang Peters	GER	4:46.25	70	356.25
6. Jürgen Köhler	GDR	5:12.88	60	372.88
7. Karel Tresnak	CZE	5:15.07	70	385.07
8. Petr Sodomka	CZE	5:01.11	90	391.11

The victory of Reinhard Eiben, a 20-year-old industrial blacksmith from Zwickau, came as a complete surprise. He had placed 13th at the 1971 world championships and only sixth in the East German championships. However, at the Olympics he recorded the best score in both rounds to finish well ahead of the favorite, Reinhold Kauder.

1976–1988 not held

1992 Barcelona-Seu d'Urgell C: 31, N: 15, D: 8.1.

		TIME	PENALTIES	PTS
1. Lukáš Pollert	CZE	1:53.69	0	113.69
2. Gareth Marriott	GBR	1:51.48	5	116.48
3. Jacky Avril	FRA	1:57.18	0	117.18
4. Jon Lugbill	USA	1:53.62	5	118.62
5. Renato De Monti	ITA	1:59.02	0	119.02
6. Martin Lang	GER	1:59.19	0	119.19
7. Emmanuel Brugvin	FRA	1:54.19	5	119.19
8. Juraj Ontko	CZE	2:00.23	0	120.23

Jon Lugbill competed in his first world championship at the age of 15 and dominated the sport of Canadian white-water canoeing for over a decade. He won his first world championship in 1979 and his fifth in 1989. Unfortunately, during his entire reign, white-water canoeing was not an Olympic sport. When it was finally reintroduced in 1992, Lugbill was already 31 years old. Still, he came within inches of winning a gold medal, brushing gate 23 with his shoulder on his first run. The five-second penalty turned out to be the difference between first and fourth place.

CANADIAN SLALOM PAIRS

1896–1968 not held

1972 Munich-Augsburg T: 20, N: 9, D: 8.30.

		TIME	PENALTIES	PTS
1. Walter Hofmann, Rolf-Dieter Amend	GDR	4:30.68	40	310.68
2. Hans Otto Schumacher, Wilhelm Baues	GER	4:51.90	20	311.90
3. Jean-Louis Olry, Jean-Claude Olry	FRA	5:05.10	10	315.10
4. Jürgen Kretschmer, Klaus Trummer	GDR	4:59.57	30	329.57
5. Jan Frączek, Ryszard Seruga	POL	5:26.21	40	366.21
6. Janez Andrijasić, Peter Guzelj	YUG	5:18.01	50	368.01
7. Michael Reimann, Olaf Fricke	GER	5:01.86	70	371.86
8. Heimo Müllneritsch, Helmar Steindl	AUT	5:05.14	70	375.14

1976–1988 not held

1992 Barcelona-Seu d'Urgell T: 17, N: 8, D: 8.2.

		TIME	PENALTIES	PTS
1. Scott Strausbaugh, Joe Jacobi	USA	2:02.41	0	122.41
2. Miroslav Šimek, Jiří Rohan	CZE	1:59.25	5	124.25
3. Franck Adisson, Wilfrid Forgues	FRA	2:04.38	0	124.38
4. James McEwan, Jacob "Lecky" Haller	USA	2:08.05	0	128.05
5. Ueli Matti, Peter Matti	SWI	2:03.55	5	128.55
6. Pavel Štercl, Petr Štercl	CZE	2:10.42	0	130.42
7. Jan Petříček, Tomaš Petříček	CZE	2:06.86	5	131.86
8. Thierry Saidi, Emmanuel Delrey	FRA	2:07.29	5	132.29

Strausbaugh and Jacobi were the only pair to paddle penalty-free on both runs. They led after the first run but needed to improve their time on the second run to stay ahead of Šimek and Rohan. Jamie McEwan of the fourth-place United States team had earned a bronze medal the last time canoe slalom races were included in the Olympics—20 years earlier. McEwan was the only Munich slalom veteran to compete at the Barcelona Games.

Discontinued Events

KAYAK SINGLES 10,000 METERS

1936 Berlin C: 15, N: 15, D: 8.7.
1. Ernst Krebs	GER	46:01.6
2. Fritz Landertinger	AUT	46:17.7
3. Ernest Riedl	USA	47.23.9
4. Jacobus van Tongeren	HOL	47:31.0
5. Evert Johansson	FIN	47:35.5
6. František Brzák-Felix	CZE	47:36.8
7. Bruno Lips	SWI	48:01.2
8. Sasso Sant	ITA	49:20.0

1948 London C: 13, N: 13, D: 8.11.
1. Gert Fredriksson	SWE	50:47.7
2. Kurt Wires	FIN	51:18.2
3. Eivind Skabo	NOR	51:35.4
4. Knud Ditlevsen	DEN	51:54.2
5. Henri Eberhardt	FRA	52:09.0
6. Jochem Bobeldijk	HOL	52:13.2
7. Czeslaw Sobieraj	POL	52:51.0
8. Alfred Corbiaux	BEL	53:23.5

1952 Helsinki C: 17, N: 17, D: 7.27.
1. Thorvald Strömberg	FIN	47:22.8
2. Gert Fredriksson	SWE	47:34.1
3. Michael Scheuer	GER	47:54.4
4. Ejvind Hansen	DEN	47:58.8
5. Hans Martin Gulbrandsen	NOR	48:12.9
6. Miloš Pech	CZE	48:25.8
7. Ivan Sotnikov	SOV	48:36.8
8. Jochem Bobeldijk	HOL	49:36.2

Fredriksson spent most of the race hanging in the wake of Strömberg's bow, but when he finally made his move, the 21-year-old Finnish fisherman had saved enough for a spurt of his own and pulled away to victory.

1956 Melbourne C: 11, N: 11, D: 11.30.
1. Gert Fredriksson	SWE	47:43.4
2. Ferenc Hatlaczky	HUN	47:53.3
3. Michael Scheuer	GER	48:00.3
4. Thorvald Strömberg	FIN	48:15.8
5. Igor Pissaryev	SOV/RUS	49:58.2
6. Ladislav Čepciansky	CZE	50:08.2
7. Svend Fromming	DEN	50:10.0
8. Knut Östbye	NOR	51:28.2

FOLDING KAYAK SINGLES 10,000 METERS

1936 Berlin C: 13, N: 13, D: 8.7.
1. Gregor Hradetzky	AUT	50:01.2
2. Henri Eberhardt	FRA	50:04.2
3. Xaver Hörmann	GER	50:06.5
4. Lennart Dozzi	SWE	51:23.8
5. František Svoboda	CZE	51:52.5
6. Hans Mooser	SWE	52:43.8
7. Frans Nordberg	FIN	52:45.8
8. George Lawton	GBR	52:50.0

KAYAK PAIRS 10,000 METERS

1936 Berlin T: 12, N: 12, D: 8.7.
1. Paul Wevers, Ludwig Landen	GER	41:45.0
2. Viktor Kalisch, Karl Steinhuber	AUT	42:05.4
3. Tage Falhborg, Helge Larsson	SWE	43:06.1
4. Werner Lövgreen, Axel Svendsen	DEN	44:39.8
5. Hendrik Starreveld, Gerardus Siderius	HOL	45:12.5
6. Werner Zimmermann, Othmar Bach	SWI	45:14.6
7. William Gaehler, William Lofgren	USA	45:15.4
8. Zdenek Cernicky, Jaroslav Humpal	CZE	46:05.4

1948 London T: 15, N: 15, D: 8.11.
1. Gunnar Åkerlund, Hans Wetterström   SWE   46:09.4
2. Ivar Mathisen, Knut Östbye   NOR   46:44.8
3. Thor Axelsson, Nils Björklof   FIN   46:48.2
4. Alfred Christensen, Finn Rasmussen   DEN   47:17.5
5. Gyula Andrási, János Urányi   HUN   47:33.1
6. Cornelius Koch, Hendrik Stroo   HOL   47:35.6
7. Ludvik Klima, Oldrich Lomecky   CZE   48:14.9
8. Hilaire Deprez, Jozef Massy   BEL   48.23.1

1952 Helsinki T: 18, N: 18, D: 7.27.
1. Kurt Wires, Yrjö Hietanen   FIN   44:21.3
2. Gunnar Åkerlund, Hans Wetterström   SWE   44:21.7
3. Ferenc Varga, József Gurovits   HUN   44:26.6
4. Max Raub, Herbert Wiedermann   AUT   44:29.1
5. Ivar Mathiesen, Knut Östbye   NOR   45:04.7
6. Karl-Heinz Schäfer, Meinrad Miltenberger   GER   45:15.2
7. Rudolf Klabouch, Bedřich Dvořák   CZE   45:39.6
8. Ingvard Norregaard, Svend Fromming   DEN   45:59.6

Although Wires and Hietanen led from start to finish, they won by only half a meter.

1956 Melbourne T:12, N: 12, D: 11.30.
1. János Urányi, László Fábián   HUN   43:37.0
2. Fritz Briel, Theo Kleine   GER   43:40.6
3. Dennis Green, Walter Brown   AUS   43:43.2
4. Hans Wetterström, Carl-Axel Sundin   SWE   44:06.7
5. Yevhen Yatsynenko, Sergei Klimov   SOV   45:49.3
6. Miloslav Jemelka, Rudolf Klabouch   CZE   46:13.1
7. Yrjö Hietanen, Simo Kuismanen   FIN   46:40.4
8. Brian Bullivant, Raymond Blick   GBR   47:03.7

FOLDING KAYAK PAIRS 10,000 METERS

1936 Berlin T: 13, N: 13, D: 8.7.
1. Sven Johansson, Eric Bladström   SWE   45:48.9
2. Willi Horn, Erich Hanisch   GER   45:49.2
3. Pieter Wijdekop, Cornelis Wijdekop   HOL   46:12.4
4. Adolf Kainz, Alfons Dorfner   AUT   46:26.1
5. Otokar Kouba, Ludvik Klima   CZE   47:46.2
6. Eugen Knoblauch, Emil Bottlang   SWI   47:54.4
7. John Lysak, James O'Rourke   USA   49:46.0
8. Armand Pagnoulle, Charles Pasquier   BEL   49:57.1

KAYAK SINGLES RELAY 4 × 500 METERS

1960 Rome T: 18, N: 18, D: 8.29.
1. GDR/GER   (Paul Lange, Günter Perleberg,   7:39.43
Friedhelm Wentzke, Dieter Krause)
2. HUN   (Imre Szöllösi, Imre Kemecsey, András   7:44.02
Szente, György Mészáros)
3. DEN   (Helmuth Sörensen, Arne Höyer, Erling   7:46.09
Jessen, Erik Hansen)
4. POL   (Stefan Kaplaniak, Wladislaw Zieliński,   7:49.93
Ryszard Skwarski, Ryszard Marchlik)

5. SOV   (Igor Pissaryev, Anatoly Kononyenko,   7:50.72
Fedir Lyakhovsky, Volodymyr Natalukha)
6. ROM   (Mircea Anastasescu, Aurel Vernescu,   7:53.00
Ion Sideri, Stavru Teodorov)

CANADIAN SINGLES 10,000 METERS

1948 London C: 5, N: 5, D: 8.11.
1. František Čapek   CZE   1:02:05.2
2. Frank Havens   USA   1:02:40.4
3. Norman Lane   CAN   1:04:35.3
4. Raymond Argentin   FRA   1:06:44.2
5. Ingemar Andersson   SWE   1:07:27.1

Čapek, a 33-year-old bank clerk from Prague, used a "crooked" canoe which curved at the keel, allowing him to paddle on one side and not waste energy maintaining a straight course.

1952 Helsinki C: 10, N: 10, D: 7.27.
1. Frank Havens   USA   57:41.1
2. Gábor Novák   HUN   57:49.2
3. Alfréd Jindra   CZE   57:53.1
4. Bengt Backlund   SWE   59:02.8
5. Norman Lane   CAN   59:26.4
6. Jarl Fagerström   FIN   59:45.9
7. Franz Johannsen   GER   1:00.26.5
8. Robert Boutigny   FRA   1:01.15.2

Jindra led most of the way, but Havens, a 28-year-old auto insurance adjuster from Arlington, Virginia, overtook him on the home stretch of the last lap and won by about 18 yards.

1956 Melbourne C: 9, N: 9, D: 11.30.
1. Leon Rotman   ROM   56:41.0
2. János Parti   HUN   57:11.0
3. Gennady Bukharin   SOV/RUS   57:14.5
4. Jiři Vokněr   CZE   57:44.5
5. Franz Johannsen   GER   58:50.1
6. Verner Wettersten   SWE   59:24.7
7. Donald Stringer   CAN   59:57.5
8. Frank Havens   USA   1:01:23.6

CANADIAN PAIRS 10,000 METERS

1936 Berlin T: 5, N: 5, D: 8.7.
1. Václav Mottl, Ždenek Škrdlant   CZE   50:35.5
2. Frank Saker, Harvey Charters   CAN   51:15.8
3. Rupert Weinstabl, Karl Proisl   AUT   51:28.0
4. Walter Schuur, Christian Holzenberg   GER   52:35.6
5. Joseph Hasenfus, Walter Hasenfus   USA   57:06.2

1948 London T: 6, N: 6, D: 8.11.
1. Stephen Lysak, Stephan Macknowski   USA   55:55.4
2. Václav Havel, Jiři Pecka   CZE   57:38.5
3. Georges Dransart, Georges Gandil   FRA   58:00.8
4. Karl Molnar, Viktor Salmhofer   AUT   58:59.3

5. Bert Oldershaw, William Stevenson   CAN   59:48.4
6. Gunnar Johansson, Verner Wettersten   SWE   1:03:34.4

Stephen Lysak, age 26, and Stephen Macknowski, age 33, of Yonkers, New York, using a homemade mahogany canoe, took the lead after only five strokes and went on to win by an enormous margin.

1952 Helsinki T: 9, N: 9, D: 7.27.
1. Georges Turlier, Jean Laudet   FRA   54:08.3
2. Kenneth Lane, Donald Hawgood   CAN   54:09.9
3. Egon Drews, Wilfried Soltau   GER   54:28.1
4. Valentin Orischenko, Nikolai Perevozchikov   SOV   54:36.6
5. John Haas, Frank Krick   USA   54:42.5
6. Bohuslav Karlík, Oldřich Lomecky   CZE   55:10.9
7. Ernö Söptei, Róbert Söptei   HUN   55:35.3
8. Rune Blomqvist, Harry Lindbeck   SWE   55:41.3

With only 200 meters to go, Turlier and Laudet trailed Lane and Hawgood by half a boatlength. Turlier, exhausted, called out to his partner, "That's enough, we've already got the silver. That's not bad, let it go, I can't go on!" Laudet responded, "Shut up! We can beat them; the line is right there!" The French pair increased their speed and swept past the surprised Canadians just before the finish.

1956 Melbourne T: 10, N: 10, D: 11.30.
1. Pavel Kharin, Gratsian Botev   SOV/RUS   54:02.4
2. Georges Dransart, Marcel Renaud   FRA   54:48.3
3. Imre Farkas, József Hunics   HUN   55:15.6
4. Egon Drews, Wilfried Soltau   GER   55:21.1
5. Alexe Dumitru, Simion Ismailciuc   ROM   55:51.1
6. Aksel Dunn, Finn Haunstoft   DEN   55:54.3
7. William Jones, Thomas Ohman   AUS   56:18.6
8. Otto Schindler, Walter Waldner   AUT   56:48.7

WOMEN

KAYAK SINGLES 500 METERS

1896–1936 not held

1948 London C: 10, N: 10, D: 8.12.
1. Karen Hoff   DEN   2:31.9
2. Alida van der Anker-Doedens   HOL   2:32.8
3. Fritzi Schwingl   AUT   2:32.9
4. Klára Bánfalvi   HUN   2:33.8
5. Ružena Koštalová   CZE   2:38.2
6. Sylvi Saimo   FIN   2:38.4
7. Anna van Marcke   BEL   2:43.4
8. C. Vautrin   FRA   2:44.4

1952 Helsinki C: 13, N: 13, D: 7.28.
1. Sylvi Saimo   FIN   2:18.4
2. Gertrude Liebhart   AUT   2:18.8
3. Nina Savina   SOV/RUS   2:21.6
4. Alida van der Anker-Doedens   HOL   2:22.3
5. Bodil Svendsen   DEN   2:22.7
6. Cecília Hartmann   HUN   2:23.0
7. Marta Kroutilová   CZE   2:23.8
8. Josefa Köster   GER   2:25.9

1956 Melbourne C: 10, N: 10, D: 12.1.
1. Yelizaveta Dementyeva   SOV/RUS   2:18.9
2. Therese Zenz   GER   2:19.6
3. Tove Soby   DEN   2:22.3
4. Cecília Berkes (Hartmann)   HUN   2:23.5
5. Edith Cochrane   AUS   2:23.8
6. Daniela Walkowiak   POL   2:24.1
7. Patricia Moody   GBR   2:25.3
8. Eva Marion   FRA   2:27.9

Dementyeva false-started once, then spurted into the lead and held on to win by six feet. Zenz had competed at the 1952 Helsinki Olympics as a representative of the then independent nation of Saar.

1960 Rome C: 13, N: 13, D: 8.29.
1. Antonina Seredina   SOV/RUS   2:08.08
2. Therese Zenz   GER   2:08.22
3. Daniela Walkowiak   POL   2:10.46
4. Annemarie Werner-Hansen   DEN   2:13.88
5. Klára Fried-Bánfalvi   HUN   2:14.02
6. Else Marie Lindmark   SWE   2:14.17
7. Alberta Zanardi   ITA   2:14.31
8. Eva Kutova   CZE   2:15.30

1964 Tokyo C: 13, N: 13, D: 10.22.
1. Lyudmila Khvedosyuk   SOV/RUS   2:12.87
2. Hilde Lauer   ROM   2:15.35
3. Marcia Jones   USA   2:15.68
4. Elke Felten   GER   2:15.94
5. Else Marie Ljungdahl (Lindmark)   SWE   2:16.00
6. Hanneliese Spitz   AUT   2:16.11
7. Daniela Pilecka   POL   2:17.52
8. Mária Roka   HUN   2:17.85

1968 Mexico City C: 13, N: 13, D: 10.25.
1. Lyudmila Pinayeva (Khvedosyuk)   SOV/RUS   2:11.09
2. Renate Breuer   GER   2:12.71
3. Viorica Dumitru   ROM   2:13.22
4. Marcia Smoke (Jones)   USA   2:14.68
5. Ivona Vávrová   CZE   2:14.78
6. Anita Nüssner   GDR   2:16.02
7. Ingmärie Svensson   SWE   2:16.04
8. Mieke Jaapies   HOL   2:18.38

In the middle of the race the ninth finalist, Anna Pfeffer of Hungary, spun over in the water and was rescued by a special emergency craft following the kayakists. One and a half hours later she was back in action, winning a silver medal in the kayak pairs.

1972 Munich C: 15, N: 15, D: 9.5.

1. Yulia Ryabchynska	SOV/UKR	2:03.17
2. Mieke Jaapies	HOL	2:04.03
3. Anna Pfeffer	HUN	2:05.50
4. Irene Pepinghege	GER	2:06.55
5. Bettina Müller	GDR	2:06.85
6. Maria Nichiforov	ROM	2:07.13
7. Kate Olsen	DEN	2:07.16
8. Ingmárie Svensson	SWE	2:07.61

Four months after winning her gold medal, Ryabchynska, exhausted and flushed after a winter training session, fell into the cold water of Lake Paleostomi in Soviet Georgia and died as a result of abrupt cooling. Every spring, in Moscow, an international competition is held in her honor.

1976 Montreal C: 15, N: 15, D: 7.30.

1. Carola Zirzow	GDR	2:01.05
2. Tatiana Korshunova	SOV/RUS	2:03.07
3. Klára Rajnai	HUN	2:05.01
4. Ewa Kamińska	POL	2:05.16
5. Maria Mihoreanu	ROM	2:05.40
6. Anastazie Hajná	CZE	2:06.72
7. Julie Leach	USA	2:06.92
8. Irene Peppinghege	GER	2:07.80

East German boat designers spent a month in Montreal studying the layout of the Olympic course. Then they went home and constructed special fiberglass canoes and kayaks that curved inward when placed in the water, becoming longer and faster. Using one of these kayaks, Carola Zirzow, a 5-foot 10-inch, 21-year-old student of physiotherapy, overcame a poor start to take first place.

1980 Moscow C: 11, N: 11, D: 8.1.

1. Birgit Fischer	GDR	1:57.96
2. Vania Gesheva	BUL	1:59.48
3. Antonina Melnikova	SOV/BLR	1:59.66
4. Maria Ştefan (Mihoreanu)	ROM	2:00.90
5. Ewa Eichler	POL	2:01.23
6. Agneta Andersson	SWE	2:01.33
7. Katalin Povázsán	HUN	2:01.52
8. Beatrice Knopf	FRA	2:02.91

1984 Los Angeles-Lake Casitas C: 11, N: 11, D: 8.10.

1. Agneta Andersson	SWE	1:58.72
2. Barbara Schüttpelz	GER	1:59.93
3. Annemiek Derckx	HOL	2:00.11
4. Tecla Marinescu	ROM	2:00.12
5. Beatrice Basson	FRA	2:01.21
6. Sheila Conover	USA	2:02.38
7. Lucie Guay	CAN	2:02.49
8. Elizabeth Blencowe	AUS	2:02.63

1988 Seoul C: 15, N: 15, D: 9.30.

1. Vania Gesheva	BUL	1:55.19
2. Birgit Schmidt (Fischer)	GDR	1:55.31
3. Izabella Dylewska	POL	1:57.38
4. Rita Köbán	HUN	1:57.58
5. Yvonne Brandstrup Knudsen	DEN	1:58.80
6. Traci Phillips	USA	2:00.81
7. Galina Savenko	SOV/RUS	2:00.88
8. Agneta Andersson	SWE	2:01.00

In 1980, Birgit Schmidt, then 18 years old, defeated Vania Gesheva to become the youngest-ever winner of an Olympic canoeing event. If East Germany had not boycotted the 1984 Games, she would have been favored to win all three women's kayak events, just as she did in the world championships of 1981, 1982, 1983, 1985, and 1987. She took off 1986 to have a baby. Schmidt was the overwhelming favorite again in Seoul but was upset in the final by the fast-finishing Gesheva.

1992 Barcelona-Castelldefels C: 16, N: 16, D: 8.7.

1. Birgit Schmidt (Fischer)	GER	1:51.60
2. Rita Köbán	HUN	1:51.96
3. Izabella Dylewska	POL	1:52.36
4. Josefa Idem	ITA	1:52.78
5. Ursula Profanter	AUT	1:53.17
6. Sabine Goetschy	FRA	1:53.53
7. Caroline Brunet	CAN	1:54.82
8. Sanda Toma	ROM	1:54.84

The amazing Birgit Schmidt retired from competition between Olympics but continued to train. At the age of 30, she earned her fourth gold medal—twelve years after her first Olympic victory in Moscow.

KAYAK PAIRS 500 METERS

1896–1956 not held

1960 Rome T: 11, N: 11, D: 8.29.

1. Maria Chubina, Antonina Seredina	SOV/RUS	1:54.76
2. Therese Zenz, Ingrid Hartmann	GER	1:56.66
3. Klára Fried-Bánfalvi, Vilma Egresi	HUN	1:58.22
4. Daniela Walkowiak, Janina Mendalska	POL	1:59.03
5. Annemarie Werner-Hansen, Birgit Jensen	DEN	2:01.36
6. Maria Szekeli, Elena Lipalit	ROM	2:01.68
7. Gabriella Cotta Ramusino, Luciana Guindani	ITA	2:02.47
8. Eva Kutova, Eva Kolinska	CZE	2:02.76

1964 Tokyo T: 10, N: 10, D: 10.22.

1. Roswitha Esser, Annemarie Zimmermann	GER	1:56.95
2. Francine Fox, Gloriane Perrier	USA	1:59.16
3. Hilde Lauer, Cornelia Sideri	ROM	2:00.25
4. Nina Gruzintseva, Antonina Seredina	SOV/RUS	2:00.69
5. Birthe Hansen, Annemarie Werner-Hansen	DEN	2:00.88
6. Else-Marie Ljungdahl (Lindmark), Eva-Britt Sisth	SWE	2:02.24
7. Katalin Benkö, Mária Roka	HUN	2:03.67
8. Izabella Antonowicz, Daniela Pilecka	POL	2:04.31

Silver medalist Francine Fox was only 15 years old, while her partner, Glorianne Perrier, was 20 years older.

1968 Mexico City T: 11, N: 11, D: 10.25.

1.	Roswitha Esser, Annemarie Zimmermann	GER	1:56.44
2.	Anna Pfeffer, Katalin Rozsnyói	HUN	1:58.60
3.	Lyudmila Pinayeva (Khvedosyuk), Antonina Seredina	SOV/RUS	1:58.61
4.	Valentina Serghei, Viorica Dumitru	ROM	1:59.17
5.	Anita Kobuss, Karin Haftenberger	GDR	2:00.18
6.	Mieke Jaapies, Tjeertje Bergers-Duif	HOL	2:02.02
7.	Sperry Rademaker, Marcia Smoke (Jones)	USA	2:02.97
8.	Lesley Oliver, Barbara Mean	GBR	2:03.70

1972 Munich T: 12, N: 12, D: 9.9.

1.	Lyudmila Pinayeva (Khvedosyuk), Kateryna Nahirna-Kuryshko	SOV	1:53.50
2.	Ilse Kaschube, Petra Grabowski	GDR	1:54.30
3.	Maria Nichiforov, Viorica Dumitru	ROM	1:55.01
4.	Anna Pfeffer, Katalin Hollósy	HUN	1:55.12
5.	Roswitha Esser, Renate Breuer	GER	1:55.64
6.	Izabella Antonowicz-Szuszkiewicz, Ewa Grajkowska	POL	1:57.45
7.	Mieke Jaapies, Maria van der Holst	HOL	1:58.11
8.	Natasha Petrova, Petrana Koleva	BUL	1:59.40

1976 Montreal T: 14, N: 14, D: 7.30.

1.	Nina Gopova, Galina Kreft	SOV/RUS	1:51.15
2.	Anna Pfeffer, Klára Rajnai	HUN	1:51.69
3.	Bärbel Köster, Carola Zirzow	GDR	1:51.81
4.	Nastasia Nichitov, Agafia Orlov	ROM	1:53.77
5.	Barbara Lewe-Pohlmann, Heiderose Wallbaum	GER	1:53.86
6.	Maria Kazanecka, Katarzyna Kulczak	POL	1:55.05
7.	Maria Mincheva, Natasha Yanakieva	BUL	1:55.95
8.	Anne Dodge, Susan Holloway	CAN	1:56.75

1980 Moscow T: 12, N: 12, D: 8.1.

1.	Carsta Genäuss, Martina Bischof	GDR	1:43.88
2.	Galina Alexeyeva (Kreft), Nina Trofimova (Gopova)	SOV/RUS	1:46.91
3.	Éva Rakusz, Mária Zakariás	HUN	1:47.95
4.	Elisabeta Băbeanu, Agafia Buhaev	ROM	1:48.04
5.	Agneta Andersson, Karin Olsson	SWE	1:49.27
6.	Anne-Marie Loriot, Valerie Leclerc	FRA	1:49.48
7.	Ewa Eichler, Ewa Wojtaszek	POL	1:51.31
8.	Frances Wetherall, Lesley Smither	GBR	1:52.76

Genäuss and Bischof achieved the most decisive victory ever in women's Olympic canoeing.

1984 Los Angeles-Lake Casitas T: 10, N: 10, D: 8.10.

1.	Agneta Andersson, Anna Olsson	SWE	1:45.25
2.	Alexandra Barre, Susan Holloway	CAN	1:47.13
3.	Josefa Idem, Barbara Schüttpelz	GER	1:47.32
4.	Agafia Constantin (Buhaev), Nastasia Ionescu	ROM	1:47.56
5.	Shirley Dery, Leslie Klein	USA	1:49.51
6.	Bernadette Hettich, Cathérine Mathevon	FRA	1:51.40
7.	Kari Ofstad, Anne Wahl	NOR	1:51.61
8.	A. Lucy Perrett, Lesley Smither	GBR	1:51.73

Silver medalist Sue Holloway had represented Canada in Nordic skiing in 1976.

1988 Seoul T: 15, N: 15, D: 9.30.

1.	Birgit Schmidt (Fischer), Anke Nothnagel	GDR	1:43.46
2.	Vania Gesheva, Diana Paliiska	BUL	1:44.06
3.	Annemiek Derckx, Annemarie Cox	HOL	1:46.00
4.	Erika Mészáros, Éva Rakusz	HUN	1:46.58
5.	Irina Salomykova, Irina Khmelevskaya	SOV/RUS	1:47.68
6.	Anna Olsson, Agneta Andersson	SWE	1:48.39
7.	Sheila Conover, Cathy Marino-Geers	USA	1:50.33
8.	Barbara Olmsted, Sheila Taylor	CAN	1:51.03

One and a half hours after being upset in the singles final, Birgit Schmidt teamed with Anke Nothnagel to win a gold medal in the pairs.

1992 Barcelona-Castelldefels T: 18, N: 18, D: 8.7.

1.	Ramona Portwich, Anke von Seck (Nothnagel)	GER	1:40.29
2.	Susanne Gunnarsson (Wiberg), Agneta Andersson	SWE	1:40.41
3.	Rita Köbán, Éva Dónusz	HUN	1:40.81
4.	Sanda Toma, Carmen Simion	ROM	1:42.12
5.	Alison Herst, Klari MacAskill	CAN	1:42.14
6.	Izabella Dylewska, Elżbieta Urbanczyk	POL	1:42.44
7.	Zhao Xiaoli, Ning Menghua	CHN	1:42.46
8.	Jeanette Brandstrup Knudsen, Yvonne Brandstrup Knudsen	DEN	1:43.98

KAYAK FOURS 500 METERS

1896–1980 not held

1984 Los Angeles-Lake Casitas T: 7, N: 7, D: 8.11.

1.	ROM	(Agafia Constantin [Buhaev], Nastasia Ionescu, Tecla Marinescu, Maria Ştefan [Mihoreanu])	1:38.34
2.	SWE	(Agneta Andersson, Anna Olsson, Eva Karlsson, Susanne Wiberg)	1:38.87
3.	CAN	(Alexandra Barre, Lucie Guay, Susan Holloway, Barbara Olmsted)	1:39.40
4.	USA	(Sheila Conover, Shirley Dery, Leslie Klein, Ann Turner)	1:40.49
5.	GER	(Josefa Idem, Regina Schmidt, Barbara Schüttpelz, Judith Skolnik)	1:42.68
6.	NOR	(Wenche Legraid, Kari Ofstad, Ingeborg Rasmussen, Anne Wahl)	1:42.97
7.	GBR	(Janine Lawler, A. Lucy Perrett, Lesley Smither, Deborah Watson)	1:46.30

1988 Seoul T: 13, N: 13, D: 10.1.

1.	GDR	(Birgit Schmidt [Fischer], Anke Nothnagel, Ramona Portwich, Heike Singer)	1:40.78
2.	HUN	(Erika Géczi, Erika Mészáros, Éva Rakusz, Rita Köbán)	1:41.88
3.	BUL	(Vania Gesheva, Diana Paliiska, Ogniana Petkova, Borislava Ivanova)	1:42.63
4.	SOV	(Irina Salomykova, Irina Khmelevskaya, Alexandra Apanovich, Nadezhda Kovalevich)	1:44.26

5. GER (Josefa Idem, Claudia Österheld, Andrea 1:45.62
Martin, Ruth Domgörgen)
6. SWE (Anna Olsson, Agneta Andersson, Susanne 1:45.67
Wiberg, Liselotte Olsson)
7. DEN (Yvonne Brandstrup Knudsen, Susanne 1:47.10
Sanggaard Petersen, Jeanette Brandstrup
Knudsen, Birgitte Lynning Froberg)
8. POL (Bozena Ksiazek, Jolanta Lukaszewicz, 1:47.40
Elżbieta Urbanczyk, Katarzyna Weiss)

1992 Barcelona-Castelldefels T: 16, N: 16, D: 8.8.
1. HUN (Éva Dónusz, Kinga Czigány, Rita Köbán, 1:38.32
Erika Mészáros)
2. GER (Katrin Borchert, Ramona Portwich, Birgit 1:38.47
Schmidt [Fischer], Anke von Seck
[Nothnagel])
3. SWE (Agneta Andersson, Maria Haglund, Anna 1:39.79
Olsson, Susanne Rosenqvist)
4. ROM (Viorica Iordache, Claudia Nicula, Carmen 1:41.02
Simion, Sanda Toma)
5. CHN (Ning Menghua, Wang Jing, Wen Yanfang, 1:41.12
Zhao Xiaoli)
6. CAN (Caroline Brunet, Alison Herst, Klari MacAskill, 1:42.28
Kevyn Stafford)
7. USA (Sheila Conover, Alexandra Harbold, Cathy 1:43.00
Marino, Traci Phillips)
8. AUS (Denise Cooper, Lynda Lehmann, Gayle 1:43.88
Mayes, Anna Wood)

The Hungarians finally defeated the Germans after four years of finishing second behind them in every major competition. Gold medal winner Erika Mészáros was the daughter of György Mészáros, who had won a silver in the 1960 kayak pairs 1000 meters. With this race Birgit Fischer raised her Olympic medal total to six—four gold and two silver—while Anke von Seck won her first silver to go with her three golds.

KAYAK SLALOM SINGLES

1896–1968 not held

1972 Munich-Augsburg C: 22, N: 10, D: 8.30.

			TIME	PENALTIES	PTS
1.	Angelika Bahmann	GDR	5:04.50	60	364.50
2.	Gisela Grothaus	GER	5:38.15	60	398.15
3.	Magdalena Wunderlich	GER	5:40.50	60	400.50
4.	Maria Ćwiertniewicz	POL	5:42.30	90	432.30
5.	Kunegunda Godawska	POL	6:21.05	60	441.05
6.	Victoria Brown	GBR	5:53.71	90	443.71
7.	Ulrike Deppe	GER	6:06.44	90	456.44
8.	Bohumila Kapplova	CZE	6:00.16	100	460.16

1976–1988 not held

1992 Barcelona-Seu d'Urgell C: 36, N: 13, D: 8.1.

			TIME	PENALTIES	PTS
1.	Elisabeth Micheler	GER	2:06.41	0	126.41
2.	Danielle Woodward	AUS	2:08.27	0	128.27
3.	Dana Chladek	USA	2:06.75	5	131.75
4.	Eva Roth	GER	2:07.29	5	132.29
5.	Marianne Agulhon	FRA	2:12.89	0	132.89
6.	Kordula Striepecke	GER	2:09.49	5	134.49
7.	Zdenka Grossmannová	CZE	2:10.79	5	135.79
8.	Joanne Woods	CAN	2:08.06	10	138.06

The defending world champion, Micheler, was born and raised in Augsburg, site of the 1972 Olympic white-water competition. Silver medalist Woodward was a detective with Australia's federal police. Gilda Montenegro of Costa Rica accumulated 470 penalty points on her first run, then spent most of the second run upside-down before giving up with 11 gates to go.

CYCLING

MEN
1000-Meter Match Sprint
1000-Meter Time Trial
4000-Meter Individual Pursuit
4000-Meter Team Pursuit
Points Race
Road Time Trial
Road Race
Cross-Country Race
Discontinued Events

WOMEN
1000-Meter Match Sprint
4000-Meter Individual Pursuit
Points Race
Road Time Trial
Road Race
Cross-Country Race

Traditionally there have been two types of Olympic cycling contests: those held on a track, and those held on the road. In 1996 a third type of cycling will be added to the program: mountain bike, or cross-country, racing. Another major change for 1996 will be the inclusion of professional cyclists for the first time. Considering the great popularity of professional cycling in Europe, this is expected to lead to tremendously increased interest in the Olympic competition.

The world records listed in the following charts are for outdoor tracks only.

MEN
1000-METER MATCH SPRINT

The individual match sprint, or scratch, is a tactical, and sometimes violent, race. For the first 800 meters the cyclists circle the track, carefully maneuvering for position, usually trying to avoid taking the lead so that they can take advantage of the slipstream created by the leader. Then they sprint for the finish line. Times are usually taken only for the final 200 meters.

Current rules provide for a qualifying round to be held as a time trial over 200 meters with a flying start. The racers are then seeded based on their times, and a tournament begins. Winners of the opening races advance to a round of 16; losers compete in a repêchage round. There is also a repêchage round for the losers in the round of 16.

Since 1928 separate races have been held to determine first place and third place. Since 1976 all four defeated quarterfinalists have raced off for places 5 through 8.

1896 Athens C: 4, N: 3, D: 4.11.
(2000 Meters)
1. Paul Masson   FRA   4:58.2
2. Stamatios Nikolopoulos   GRE   5:00.2
3. Léon Flameng   FRA   —
4. Joseph Rosemeyer   GER   —

1900 Paris C: 26, N: 5, D: 9.13.
(2000 Meters)
1. Georges Taillandier   FRA   2:52.0 (last 200 meters 13.0)
2. Fernand Sanz   FRA   —
3. John Henry Lake   USA   —

1904 not held

1906 Athens C: 26, N: 9, D: 4.23.
1. Francesco Verri   ITA   1:42.2
2. Herbert Bouffler   GBR   —
3. Eugène Debougnie   BEL   —

1908 London C: 40, N: 9, D: 7.16.

The final was declared void because the time limit was exceeded. The finalists were: 1. Maurice Schilles (FRA), 2. Benjamin Jones (GBR). DNF: Victor Johnson (GBR) and Clarence Kingsbury (GBR).

Johnson suffered a punctured tire shortly after the start. The other three crawled around the track, carefully jockeying for position. At the beginning of the last bank, Kingsbury also punctured. Then the remaining two raced to the finish line, with Schilles winning by inches. However, the time limit of 1 minute 45 seconds had been exceeded, so the race was declared void. Much to the surprise of most of those present, the judges of the National Cyclists' Union refused to allow the race to be rerun.

1912 not held

1920 Antwerp C: 37, N: 11, D: 8.10.
1. Mouritius "Maurice" Peeters   HOL   13.0 (last 200 meters)
2. Horace "Tiny" Johnson   GBR   —
3. Harry Ryan   GBR   —

Peeters defeated Johnson by inches with Ryan three lengths behind. At age 38, Peeters was the oldest cycling gold medalist in Olympic history. Four years later he won a bronze in the tandem event to become the sport's oldest medalist.

1924 Paris C: 31, N: 17, D: 7.27.
1. Lucien Michard   FRA   12.8 (last 200 meters)
2. Jacob Meijer   HOL   —
3. Jean Cugnot   FRA   —

1928 Amsterdam C: 18, N: 18, D: 8.7.
1. Roger Beaufrand   FRA   13.2 (last 200 meters)
2. Antoine Mazairac   HOL   —
3. Willy Falck-Hansen   DEN
4. Hans Bernhardt   GER
5. Jerzy Koszutski (POL), Antonio Malvassi (ARG), Jack Standen (AUS), Yves van Massenhove (BEL)

1932 Los Angeles C: 9, N: 9, D: 8.3.

		1ST RACE	2ND RACE	3RD RACE
1. Jacobus van Egmond	HOL	—	12.6	12.6
2. Louis Chaillot	FRA	12.5	—	—
3. Bruno Pellizzari	ITA			
4. Edgar "Dunc" Gray	AUS			

5. Ernest Chambers (GBR), Willy Gervin (DEN), Leo Marchiori (CAN), Robert Thomas (USA)

Beginning in 1932, it was necessary to win two out of three races. Louis Chaillot won the first race of the final by inches. But Jacobus van Egmond set the pace in the second, leading all the way to the finish. He then won the tie-breaker by a foot. Dunc Gray withdrew from the bronze-medal race in order to save himself for the time trial the same evening.

1936 Berlin C: 20, N: 20, D: 8.7.

		1ST RACE	2ND RACE
1. Toni Merkens	GER	11.8	11.8
2. Arie van Vliet	HOL	—	—
3. Louis Chaillot	FRA		
4. Benedetto Pola	ITA		

5. Henri Collard (BEL), Edgar "Dunc" Gray (AUS), Carl Magnussen (DEN), Werner Wagelin (SWI)

As Arie van Vliet began to overtake Toni Merkens in the first race of the final, the German swerved to his right and blatantly interfered with his rival. No foul was called, and a disconcerted van Vliet lost the second race as well. The Dutch team protested. In a bizarre twist, cycling officials decided not to disqualify Merkens, but to fine him 100 marks instead. The next day, van Vliet returned to win the 1000-meter time trial. Merkens died toward the end of World War II after being wounded while fighting the Russians.

1948 London C: 23, N: 23, D: 8.9.

		1ST RACE	2ND RACE
1. Mario Ghella	ITA	12.2	12.0
2. Reginald Harris	GBR	—	—
3. Axel Schandorff	DEN		
4. Charles Bazzano	AUS		

5. John Heid (USA), Hernan Masanes Gimeno (CHI), Luis Rocca (URU), Emile Van de Velde (BEL)

Reg Harris, the reigning world sprint champion, was struck from the British team a few days before the Olympics because he insisted on staying in his hometown of Manchester instead of training with the rest of the team in London. After a public outcry, Harris was reinstated, but not until he had won a ride-off against his tandem partner, Alan Bannister. In the final he faced 20-year-old Mario Ghella, a student from Turin. In the first race, Ghella caught Harris in a moment of inattention with 350 meters to go, slipped inside of him, and won easily. In the second race, Ghella fought off three challenges from Harris to earn a dramatic and emotional victory.

1952 Helsinki C: 27, N: 27, D: 7.31.
1. Enzo Sacchi   ITA   12.0
2. Lionel Cox   AUS   —
3. Werner Potzernheim   GER
4. Cyril Peacock (GBR), Raymond Robinson (SAF), Béla Szekeres (HUN)

1956 Melbourne C: 19, N: 19, D: 12.6. WR: 11.0 (Arie van Vliet)

		1ST RACE	2ND RACE
1. Michel Rousseau	FRA	11.4	11.4
2. Guglielmo Presenti	ITA	—	—
3. Richard Ploog	AUS		
4. Warren Johnston	NZE		

5. Jack Disney (USA), Ladislav Fouček (CZE), Boris Romanov (SOV), Thomas Shardelow (SAF)

1960 Rome C: 30, N: 18, D: 8.29. WR: 10.8 (Antonio Maspes)

		1ST RACE	2ND RACE
1. Sante Gaiardoni	ITA	11.1	11.5
2. Leo Sterckx	BEL	—	—
3. Valentino Gasparella	ITA		
4. Ronald Baensch	AUS		

5. Anesio Argenton (BRA) Lloyd Binch (GBR), Antoine Pellegrina (FRA), August Rieke (GER)

For the third straight time, the Olympic sprint championship was won by the reigning world champion. The 5-foot 6-inch, 174-pound Gaiardoni had already won the 1000-meter time trial when he swept through the sprint competition without being seriously challenged.

1964 Tokyo C: 39, N: 22, D: 10.19. WR: 10.8 (Antonio Maspes)

		1ST RACE	2ND RACE
1. Giovanni Pettenella	ITA	13.85	13.69
2. Sergio Bianchetto	ITA	—	—
3. Daniel Morelon	FRA		
4. Pierre Trentin	FRA		

5. Willi Fuggerer (GER), Patrick Sercú (BEL), Mario Vanegas Jimenez (COL), Zbyslaw Zajac (POL)

In the semifinals Pettenella and Trentin set an Olympic record by standing still for 21 minutes 57 seconds.

1968 Mexico City C: 46, N: 27, D: 19.10. WR: 10.61 (Omar Pkhakadze)

		1ST RACE	2ND RACE
1. Daniel Morelon	FRA	11.27	10.68
2. Giordano Turrini	ITA	—	—
3. Pierre Trentin	FRA		
4. Omar Pkhakadze	SOV/GEO		
5. Jürgen Barth (GER), Johannes Jansen (HOL), Leijn Loevesijn (HOL), Dino Verzini (ITA)			

The tactical highlight of the competition came in the first race of the quarterfinal contest between Dino Verzini and Omar Pkhakadze. The first time out they stood and watched each other until a restart was ordered. The second attempt saw them both stop again, with Pkhakadze slipping off the banking and causing both of them to slide into the infield. The next restart, the two cyclists stopped for 4 minutes 47 seconds before continuing. This time they made it all the way to the finish with Verzini in the lead. However, Pkhakadze won the next two races and advanced to the semifinals, where he lost two out of three to Daniel Morelon, the eventual gold medalist. Morelon was a police officer from Bourg-en-Bresse, northeast of Lyon.

1972 Munich C: 51, N: 29, D: 9.2. WR: 10.61 (Omar Pkhakadze)

		1ST RACE	2ND RACE
1. Daniel Morelon	FRA	11.69	11.25
2. John Nicholson	AUS	—	—
3. Omar Pkhakadze	SOV/GEO		
4. Klaas Balk	HOL		
5. Niels Fredborg (DEN), Hans-Jürgen Geschke (GDR), Massimo Marino (ITA), Peter van Doorn (HOL)			

1976 Montreal C: 25, N: 25, D: 7.24. WR: 10.61 (Omar Pkhakadze)

		1ST RACE	2ND RACE	3RD RACE
1. Anton Tkáč	CZE/SLV	10.78	—	11.17
2. Daniel Morelon	FRA	—	11.58	—
3. Hans-Jürgen Geschke	GDR			
4. Dieter Berkmann	GER			
5. Serhei Kravtsov	SOV/UKR			
6. Yoshika Cho	JPN			
7. Niels Fredborg	DEN			
8. Giorgio Rossi	ITA			

This was the first time that Olympic cycling events were held indoors. The Czechoslovakian team got off to a bad start at the Montreal Olympics when all of their wheels and spare tires were inadvertently picked up by garbage collectors and fed into a trash compactor. The final was held the day before the 32nd birthday of Daniel Morelon, the sentimental as well as the betting favorite. But Anton Tkáč, a pipe fitter from Bratislava, jumped early in the tie-breaker, took a five-length lead, and was too strong to be caught. In the first race Tkáč had crossed the finish line at almost 42 miles per hour. Morelon's second-place finish earned him his fifth Olympic medal: two golds, one silver, and one bronze in the sprint, and one more gold in the tandem.

1980 Moscow C: 15, N: 15, D: 7.26. WR: 10.61 (Omar Pkhakadze)

		1ST RACE	2ND RACE	3RD RACE
1. Lutz Hesslich	GDR	11.40	—	12.01
2. Yave Cahard	FRA	—	10.86	—
3. Sergei Kopylov	SOV/RUS			
4. Anton Tkáč	CZE/SLV			
5. Henrik Salee	DEN			
6. Heinz Isler	SWI			
7. Kenrick Tucker	AUS			
8. Octavio Dazzan	ITA			

1984 Los Angeles-Carson C: 33, N: 25, D: 8.3. WR: 10.249 (Sergei Kopylov)

		1ST RACE	2ND RACE
1. Mark Gorski	USA	10.49	10.95
2. Nelson Vails	USA	—	—
3. Tsutomu Sakamoto	JPN		
4. Philippe Vernet	FRA		
5. Gerhard Scheller	GER		
6. Marcelo Alexandre	ARG		
7. Kenrick Tucker	AUS		
8. Fredy Schmidtke	GER		

With the winners of the last four world championships, Lutz Hesslich and Sergei Kopylov, boycotted out of the Olympics, the final became an all-American contest.

In 1981, Nelson Vails, the youngest of ten children and a father himself since age 15, was living in Harlem, working eight hours a day as a bicycle messenger in Manhattan and training two hours a night in New York City's Central Park. In 1981, Mark Gorski had given up on cycling following a bad spill that left him with a broken collarbone and a severe concussion. Gorski returned to racing and, in 1983, defeated Kopylov three times. He had also defeated the fast-improving Vails three times before their Olympic encounter. After making it four in a row for the gold medal, Gorski took his 13-month-old son, Alexander, along with him on his victory lap.

1988 Seoul C: 25, N: 25, D: 9.24. WR: 10.118 (Michael Hübner)

		1ST RACE	2ND RACE
1. Lutz Hesslich	GDR	13.98	11.82
2. Nikolai Kovsh	SOV/RUS	—	—
3. Gary Neiwand	AUS		
4. Edward Alexander	GBR		
5. Vratislav Šuster	CZE		
6. Erik Schoefs	BEL		
7. Frank Weber	GER		
8. Maxwell Cheesman	TRI		

In the last three world championships, all three medals had gone to East Germans. In the Olympics, however, each nation is allowed only one entrant. Thus it came as no surprise that Hesslich, having defeated his friend and rival Michael Hübner to qualify for the East German team, was not seriously challenged in Seoul.

1992 Barcelona C: 23, N: 23, D: 7.31. WR: 10.118 (Michael Hübner)

			1ST RACE	2ND RACE
1.	Jens Fiedler	GER	10.995	10.778
2.	Gary Neiwand	AUS	—	—
3.	Curt Harnett	CAN	10.930	11.120
4.	Roberto Chiappa	ITA	—	—
5.	Ken Carpenter	USA	11.648	—
6.	José Lovito Morales	ARG	—	—
7.	Nikolai Kovsh	RUS	—	—
8.	José Moreno Periñán	SPA	—	—

Gary Neiwand and Jens Fiedler battle for the lead in the 1992 match sprint.

Once again the Olympic competition suffered from the fact that the two leading sprinters, 1989 and 1990 world champion Bill Huck and 1991 world champion Jens Fiedler, were both from Germany and each nation was only allowed one entrant. It was the 22-year-old Fiedler who won the right to compete. Everything went according to form in Barcelona. The four cyclists who recorded the fastest times in the qualifying time trial placed in the same order in the end; of the eight match-ups to be decided by the best two out of three races, none required a third race. However, the final itself was full of drama. It took a photo-finish camera to decide the winner of the first race. The photo showed that Fiedler had held off Neiwand's come-from-behind effort by about two inches. In the second race, when Fiedler tried to move ahead in the middle of the race, Neiwand moved up the banking, forcing Fiedler to the outside of the track. With one 250-meter lap to go, Fiedler cut in front, forcing Neiwand to backpedal and drop back four lengths. Neiwand fought back furiously and crossed the line first. After a five-minute delay it was announced that Neiwand had been "declassed for dangerous riding" and that Fiedler was the winner. Despite their bitter struggle, Fiedler immediately consoled the distraught Neiwand and the two embraced on the infield.

1000-METER TIME TRIAL

In the time trial, the competitors take turns racing against the clock from a standing start.

1896–1924 not held

1928 Amsterdam C: 14, N: 14, D: 8.7.
1.	Willy Falck Hansen	DEN	1:14.4
2.	Gerard Bosch van Drakestein	HOL	1:15.2
3.	Edgar "Dunc" Gray	AUS	1:15.6
4.	Octave Dayen	FRA	1:16.0
5.	Kurt Einsiedel	GER	1:17.2
6.	Edward Kerridge	GBR	1:18.0
6.	Józef Lange	POL	1:18.0
8.	Jean Aerts	BEL	1:18.6

The bronze medalist, Dunc Gray, had never ridden in a time trial before the Olympics.

1932 Los Angeles C: 9, N: 9, D: 8.1.
1.	Edgar "Dunc" Gray	AUS	1:13.0	OR
2.	Jacobus van Egmond	HOL	1:13.3	
3.	Charles Rampelberg	FRA	1:13.4	
4.	Luigi Consonni	ITA	1:14.7	
4.	William Harvell	GBR	1:14.7	
6.	Lewis Rush	CAN	1:15.6	
7.	Harald Christensen	DEN	1:16.0	
8.	Bernard Mammes	USA	1:18.0	

1936 Berlin C: 19, N: 19, D: 8.8.
1. Arie van Vliet	HOL	1:12.0	OR
2. Pierre Georget	FRA	1:12.8	
3. Rudolf Karsch	GER	1:13.2	
4. Benedetto Pola	ITA	1:13.6	
5. László Orczán	HUN	1:14.0	
5. Arne Pedersen	DEN	1:14.0	
7. Raymond Hicks	GBR	1:14.8	
8. George Giles	NZE	1:15.0	

1948 London C: 21, N: 21, D: 8.11. WR: 1:10.0 (F. Battesini)
1. Jacques Dupont	FRA	1:13.5
2. Pierre Nihant	BEL	1:14.5
3. Thomas Godwin	GBR	1:15.0
4. Hans Fluckiger	SWI	1:15.3
5. Axel Schandorff	DEN	1:15.5
6. Sidney Patterson	AUS	1:15.7
7. John Heid	USA	1:16.2
8. Walter Freitag	AUT	1:16.8

1952 Helsinki C: 27, N: 27, D: 7.31. WR: 1:09.8 (Reginald Harris)
1. Russell Mockridge	AUS	1:11.1	OR
2. Marino Morettini	ITA	1:12.7	
3. Raymond Robinson	SAF	1:13.0	
4. Clodomiro Cortoni	ARG	1:13.2	
5. Donald McKellow	GBR	1:13.3	
6. Ib Vagn Hansen	DEN	1:14.4	
6. Ion Ioniță	ROM	1:14.4	
8. Johannes Hijzelendoorn	HOL	1:14.5	

Russell Mockridge believed that cycling was somewhat boring, but he felt compelled to keep returning to it because it was clearly something that he was very good at. Mockridge worked as a journalist but quit his job. He studied art but dropped out. After competing in the road race at the 1948 London Olympics and winning two gold medals at the 1950 British Empire Games, Mockridge told the press, "I feel there is a lot more to this life than riding a bicycle," and announced that he was giving up cycling to become a minister in the Church of England. A few months later he changed his mind again and returned to competitive cycling.

Mockridge seemed assured a place on the 1952 Australian Olympic team until he refused to sign a statement that he would refrain from turning professional for two years. While the controversy over his participation was reaching the floor of Parliament, Mockridge was racing in Europe. A month before the Olympics he became the first amateur to win the Paris Open Grand Prix. Back in Australia, Mockridge's hometown of Geelong worked out a face-saving compromise with the Australian Olympic Federation by which the agreement was limited to one year.

Mockridge arrived in Helsinki four days before he was scheduled to compete. On July 31 he won the gold medal for the time trial and then teamed with Lionel Cox to win a second gold medal in the tandem. Six years later Mockridge was in Melbourne, competing in the 140-mile Tour of Gippsland. Three miles after the start, Mockridge

and five other cyclists, followed in a car by Mockridge's wife and 3-year-old daughter, were crossing an intersection when a bus came up on the right and struck Mockridge, killing him instantly. He was 30 years old.

1956 Melbourne C: 22, N: 22, D: 12.6. WR: 1:08.6 (Reginald Harris)
1. Leandro Faggin	ITA	1:09.8	OR
2. Ladislav Fouček	CZE	1:11.4	
3. Alfred Swift	SAF	1:11.6	
4. Warren Scarfe	AUS	1:12.1	
5. Alan Danson	GBR	1:12.3	
5. Boris Savostin	SOV	1:12.3	
5. Louis Serra	URU	1:12.3	
8. Warwick Dalton	NZE	1:12.6	

1960 Rome C: 25, N: 25, D: 8.26. WR: 1:07.5 (Sante Gaiardoni)
1. Sante Gaiardoni	ITA	1:07.27	WR
2. Dieter Gieseler	GER	1:08.75	
3. Rostislav Vargashkin	SOV/RUS	1:08.86	
4. Pieter van der Touw	HOL	1:09.20	
5. Ian Chapman	AUS	1:09.55	
6. Anesio Argenton	BRA	1:09.96	
7. Jean Govaerts	BEL	1:10.23	
8. Josef Helbling	SWI	1:10.42	

1964 Tokyo C: 27, N: 27, D: 10.16. WR: 1:07.27 (Sante Gaiardoni)
1. Patrick Sercu	BEL	1:09.59
2. Giovanni Pettenella	ITA	1:10.09
3. Pierre Trentin	FRA	1:10.42
4. Pieter van der Touw	HOL	1:10.68
5. Jiří Pecka	CZE	1:10.70
6. Lothar Claesges	GER	1:10.86
7. Waclaw Latocha	POL	1:11.12
8. Roger Gibbon	TRI	1:11.19

1968 Mexico City C: 32, N: 32, D: 10.17. WR: 1:04.61 (Gianni Sartori)
1. Pierre Trentin	FRA	1:03.91	WR
2. Niels Fredborg	DEN	1:04.61	
3. Janusz Kierzkowski	POL	1:04.63	
4. Gianni Sartori	ITA	1:04.65	
5. Roger Gibbon	TRI	1:04.66	
6. Leijn Loevesijn	HOL	1:04.84	
7. Jocelyn Lovell	CAN	1:05.18	
8. Serhei Kravtsov	SOV/UKR	1:05.21	

Trentin won three medals in Mexico City: a gold in the time trial, a gold in the tandem, and a bronze in the sprint.

1972 Munich C: 32, N: 32, D: 8.31. WR: 1:03.91 (Pierre Trentin)
1. Niels Fredborg	DEN	1:06.44
2. Daniel Clark	AUS	1:06.87
3. Jürgen Schütze	GDR	1:07.02
4. Karl Köther	GER	1:07.21
5. Janusz Kierzkowski	POL	1:07.22
6. Dimo Angelov	BUL	1:07.55
7. Christian Brunner	SWI	1:07.71
8. Eduard Rapp	SOV/RUS	1:07.73

1976 Montreal C: 30, N: 30, D: 7.20. WR: 1:03.91 (Pierre Trentin)
1. Klaus-Jürgen Grünke   GDR   1:05.927
2. Michel Vaarten   BEL   1:07.516
3. Niels Fredborg   DEN   1:07.617
4. Janusz Kierzkowski   POL   1:07.660
5. Eric Vermeulen   FRA   1:07.846
6. Hans Michalsky   GER   1:07.878
7. Harald Bundli   NOR   1:08.093
8. Walter Baeni   SWE   1:08.112

One of the favorites, Eduard Rapp of the U.S.S.R. was eliminated due to an unfortunate incident. He started before the gun and, assuming he would be ordered to restart, he stopped racing. But the officials ruled his start to be legal, and he was disqualified for stopping.

1980 Moscow C: 18, N: 18, D: 7.22. WR: 1:04.225 (José Ruchansky)
1. Lothar Thoms   GDR   1:02.955   OR
2. Aleksandr Panfilov   SOV/UZB   1:04.845
3. David Weller   JAM   1:05.241
4. Guido Bontempi   ITA   1:05.478
5. Yave Cahard   FRA   1:05.584
6. Heinz Isler   SWI   1:06.273
7. Petr Kocek   CZE   1:06.368
8. Bjarne Carl Sorensen   DEN   1:07.422

Thom's time was recognized as a world indoor record.

1984 Los Angeles-Carson C: 25, N: 25, D: 7.30. WR: 1:02.547 (Maic Malchow)
1. Fredy Schmidtke   GER   1:06.10
2. Curtis Harnett   CAN   1:06.44
3. Fabrice Colas   FRA   1:06.65
4. Gene Samuel   TRI   1:06.69
5. Craig Adair   NZE   1:06.96
6. David Weller   JAM   1:07.24
7. Marcelo Alexandre   ARG   1:07.29
8. Rory O'Reilly   USA   1:07.39

1988 Seoul C: 30, N: 30, D: 9.20. WR: 1:02.091 (Maic Malchow)
1. Oleksandr Kyrychenko   SOV/UKR   1:04.499
2. Martin Vinnicombe   AUS   1:04.784
3. Robert Lechner   GER   1:05.114
4. Kurt Kenneth Ropke   DEN   1:05.168
5. Bernardo Gonzalez   SPA   1:05.281
6. Maic Malchow   GDR   1:05.393
7. Anthony Graham   NZE   1:05.744
8. Frédéric Magné   FRA   1:06.142

Kyrychenko's rear tire began to deflate with one lap to go. By the time he crossed the finish line, half the air was gone. According to the rules of the competition, Kyrychenko could have demanded a restart, but his coach, Boris Vasilyev (a bronze medalist in the 1960 tandem), refused, reasoning that Kyrychenko would be too exhausted to improve his time. Soviet team officials were furious and let it be known that Vasilyev could begin looking for a new job. When the last rider, the favorite, Martin Vinnicombe, crossed the finish line without bet-tering Kyrychenko's time, Vasilyev tearfully embraced Kyrychenko and thanked him for saving his job.

1992 Barcelona C: 32, N: 32, D: 7.27. WR: 1:02.091 (Maic Malchow)
1. José Manuel Moreno Periñán   SPA   1:03.342
2. Shane Kelly   AUS   1:04.288
3. Erin Hartwell   USA   1:04.753
4. Jens Glücklich   GER   1:04.798
5. Adler Capelli   ITA   1:05.065
6. Frederic Lancien   FRA   1:05.157
7. Jon Andrews   NZE   1:05.240
8. Gene Samuel   TRI   1:05.485

José Manuel Moreno was the defending world champion and very familiar with the Olympic Velodrome. But the Spanish team decided to take no chances in securing their nation's first gold medal of the Barcelona Games. Moreno warmed up at a track a few kilometers away and was then airlifted by helicopter to the Velodrome just in time for his ride.

4000-METER INDIVIDUAL PURSUIT

In pursuit races, two cyclists or teams of cyclists start off on opposite sides of the track. If one cyclist, or team, catches the other, the race is over. Otherwise, the winner is the first one to cross the finish line. Two cyclists or teams take part in the race for first place and two in the race for third. For this reason, the times for third through eighth place are often faster than those for first and second. Places five through eight are determined by times recorded in the quarterfinals or distance covered before being overtaken. Prior to the 1992 Olympics, official world records could not be set unless there were no other competitors on the track.

1896–1960 not held

1964 Tokyo C: 24, N: 24, D: 10.17. WR: 4:51.20 (Van Looy)
1. Jiří Daler   CZE   5:04.75
2. Giorgio Ursi   ITA   5:05.96
3. Preben Isaksson   DEN   5:01.90
4. Tiemen Groen   HOL   5:04.21
5. Lucjan Józefowicz (POL), Stanislav Moskvin (SOV/RUS), Hugh Porter (GBR), Lothar Spiegelberg (GER)

1968 Mexico City C: 28, N: 28, D: 10.18. WR: 4:45.94 (Jiří Daler)
1. Daniel Rebillard   FRA   4:41.71
2. Mogens Frey Jensen   DEN   4:42.43
3. Xaver Kurmann   SWI   4:39.42
4. John Bylsma   AUS   4:41.60
5. Cipriano Chamello (ITA), Paul Crapez (BEL), Rupert Kratzer (GER), Radamés Treviño (MEX)

Jensen set a world record of 4:37.54 in the quarterfinals to defeat the favorite, Chamello. Rebillard went to Mexico City as the fourth man in the team pursuit, but he performed so well in practice that he was given the French place in the individual pursuit.

1972 Munich C: 28, N: 28, D: 9.1. WR: 4:37.54 (Mogens Frey Jensen)

1. Knut Knudsen   NOR   4:45.74
2. Xaver Kurmann   SWI   4:51.96
3. Hans Lutz   GER   4:50.80
4. John Christopher Bylsma   AUS   4:54.93
5. Carlos Miguel Alvarez (ARG), Luciano Borgognoi (ITA), Luis Diaz (COL), Roy Schuiten (HOL)

Knut Knudsen was such an outsider that he didn't even get nervous until the final. Using wheels lent to him by the Danish team, the 21-year-old welder from Levanger took the lead from Kurmann after the fourth of 14 laps and pulled away to win comfortably.

1976 Montreal C: 28, N: 28, D: 7.22. WR: 4:37.54 (Mogens Frey Jensen)

1. Gregor Braun   GER   4:47.61
2. Herman Ponsteen   HOL   4:49.72
3. Thomas Huschke   GDR   4:52.71
4. Vladimir Osokin   SOV/RUS   4:57.34
5. Jan Georg Iversen (NOR), Michal Klasa (CZE), Orfeo Pizzoferrato (ITA), Garry Sutton (AUS)

The crucial match-up occurred in the semifinals, when the 20-year-old Braun upset Osokin by 0.17 seconds, as both men recorded personal bests.

1980 Moscow C: 14, N: 14, D: 7.24. WR: 4:34.66 (Uwe Unterwalder)

1. Robert Dill-Bundi   SWI   4:35.66
2. Alain Bondue   FRA   4:42.96
3. Hans-Henrik Örsted   DEN   4:36.54
4. Harald Wolf   GDR   4:37.58
5. Pierangelo Bincoletto (ITA), Vladimir Osokin (SOV/RUS), Martin Penc (CZE), Sean Yates (GBR)

In the semifinals Robert Dill-Bundi set a world record of 4:32.29. After his victory in the final he got off his bike and kissed the track.

1984 Los Angeles-Carson C: 33, N: 21, D: 8.1. WR: 4:32.29 (Robert Dill-Bundi)

1. Steve Hegg   USA   4:39.35
2. Rolf Gölz   GER   4:43.82
3. Leonard Harvey Nitz   USA   4:44.03
4. Dean Woods   AUS   4:44.08
5. Jörgen Pedersen   DEN
6. Jelle Nijdam   HOL
7. Robert Pascal   FRA
8. Michael Grenda   AUS

Former U.S. downhill ski champion Steve Hegg stunned his fellow cyclists by posting an opening round qualifying time that was almost 11 seconds faster than that of any of the other 32 riders. Considered a dark horse for a medal, the 20-year-old Hegg powered his way into the final against the more experienced Gölz. The night before the gold medal race, Hegg, who began cycling after reading that his hero, Jean-Claude Killy, cycled, dreamt that he

had skied the greatest run of his life. The next day he scored a decisive victory when Gölz, unnerved by the enthusiastic pro-U.S. crowd and by the bizarre space-age bicycles being used by the U.S. team, pushed the pace too quickly and was unable to withstand Hegg's finishing rush. After the race, Gölz bitterly told Hegg, "You wouldn't have beaten me in Germany." To which Hegg replied, "I really don't care—this is Los Angeles."

As it turned out, it wasn't just the hometown crowd and the advanced technology that gave Hegg an extra edge. Less than a week before the competition, Hegg, bronze medalist Leonard Harvey Nitz, and six other members of the U.S. cycling team, encouraged by their coach, Eddie Borysewicz, had taken advantage of the dubious practice called blood boosting.

Blood boosting, which first became an Olympic issue as a result of long-distance runner Lasse Viren's successes in 1976 (see p. 57), is a procedure whereby blood is extracted from an athlete's body and frozen while the athlete's blood returns to a normal level. Then, before an important competition, it is reinjected, increasing the athlete's hemoglobin level and endurance. Borysewicz, who had also experimented with giving his cyclists caffeine suppositories, seemed to approach the issue with the same nonchalance that allowed U.S. track coach Lawson Robertson to suggest to his sprinters that they drink warm sherry and a raw egg before the 1920 100-meter final (see p. 5).

Ethically questionable to begin with, blood boosting was given an uglier twist by the U.S. cyclists. Because it was too late to remove and freeze their own blood, the eight U.S. team members went to a nearby motel and injected other people's blood, some of them relatives, some of them not. The two U.S. points racers, Mark Whitehead and Danny Van Haute, both became ill. Match sprinter Nelson Vails seemed to think the procedure was required of team members and was standing in line waiting for his transfusion when team doctor Thomas Dickson informed him that it was optional and discouraged him from going ahead with it. A relieved Vails left immediately. Blood boosting was finally banned in 1985.

In 1988, Steve Hegg was chosen to represent the U.S. in the team pursuit. However, one week before the Games began, he was kicked off the team when he tested positive for excessive caffeine.

1988 Seoul C: 22, N: 22, D: 9.22. WR: 4:31.160 (Gintautas Umaras)

1. Gintautas Umaras   SOV/LIT   4:32.00   OR
2. Dean Woods   AUS   4:35.00
3. Bernd Dittert   GDR   4:34.17
4. Colin Sturgess   GBR   4:34.90
5. Ryszard Dawidowicz   POL   4:39.44
6. Peter Clausen   DEN   4:42.62
7. Gary Anderson   NZE   4:42.82
8. Ivan Beltrami   ITA   Overtaken

In the final, Woods rushed out to an early lead. However, Umaras, the 25-year-old world champion from Klaipeda,

Lithuania, caught him just after the halfway point and went on to an easy victory.

1992 Barcelona C: 29, N: 29, D: 7.29. WR: 4:31.16 (Gintautas Umaras)
1.	Christopher Boardman	GBR	
2.	Jens Lehmann	GER	Overtaken
3.	Gary Anderson	NZE	4:31.061
4.	Mark Kingsland	AUS	4:32.716
5.	Philippe Ermenault	FRA	4:28.838
6.	Cedric Mathy	BEL	4:33.942
7.	Adolfo Alperi Plaza	SPA	4:34.760
8.	Ivan Beltrami	ITA	4:36.541

Boardman caused a sensation when he appeared with his revolutionary bike, described as an "advanced composite monocoque with minimum-drag aerodynamic cross-sections, formed with unidirectional and stitched high-strength carbon fibre in an epoxy resin matrix." Designed by Mike Burrows and built by Lotus, the bike weighed less than 20 pounds. In the preliminary rounds Boardman recorded world records of 4:27.357 and 4:24.496, demoralizing the rest of the field even before the semifinals. In the final he lapped world champion Jens Lehmann, an unprecedented achievement in an Olympic final. Lehmann, with the graciousness typical of athletes from East Germany, dismissed talk about Boardman's bike, insisting that he had been beaten by the rider not the bike. Boardman earned Britain's first cycling gold medal since 1920.

4000-METER TEAM PURSUIT

The official time is that of the third rider on each team. Riders who took part in preliminary rounds but not in the finals are included in brackets.

1896–1906 not held

1908 London T:5, N: 5, D: 7.17.
(1810.5 Meters)
1.	GBR	(Leonard Meredith, Benjamin Jones, Ernest Payne, Clarence Kingsbury)	2:18.6
2.	GER	(Hermann Martens, Bruno Götze, Karl Neumer, Richard Katzer)	2:28.6
3.	CAN	(William Morton, Walter Andrews, Frederick McCarthy, William Anderson)	2:29.6
4.	HOL	(Johannes van Spengen, Antonie Gerrits, Dorotheus Nijland, Gerard Bosch van Drakestein)	2:44.0

1912 not held

1920 Antwerp T: 8, N: 8, D: 8.11.
1.	ITA	(Franco Giorgetti, Ruggero Ferrario, Arnaldo Carli, Primo Magnani)	5:14.2
2.	GBR	(Albert White, Horace "Tiny" Johnson, William Stewart, Cyril Alden)	—
3.	SAF	(James Walker, William Smith, Henry Kaltenbrun, Harry Goosen)	—
4.	BEL	(Albert de Bunné, Charles van Doorslaer, Gustave Deschryver, Jean Janssens)	

The British team actually finished first, but a protest of interference was allowed and Italy was awarded first place.

1924 Paris T: 10, N: 10, D: 7.27.
1.	ITA	(Angelo De Martino, Alfredo Dinale, Aleardo Menegazzi, Francesco Zucchetti)	5:15.0
2.	POL	(Józef Lange, Jan Lazarski, Tomasz Stankiewicz, Franciszek Szymczyk)	—
3.	BEL	(Léonard Daghelinckx, Henri Hoevenaers, Fernand Saive, Jean van den Bosch)	—
4.	FRA	(Lucien Choury, Joseph Vuillemin, René Hournon, Marcel Renaud)	—

The French team set an Olympic record of 5:11.4 in the heats.

1928 Amsterdam T: 12, N: 12, D: 8.7.
1.	ITA	(Luigi Tasselli, Giacomo Gaioni, Cesare Facciani, Mario Lusiani)	5:01.8	OR
2.	HOL	(Adriaan Braspenninx, Jacobus Maas, Johannes Pijnenburg, Piet van der Horst)	5:06.2	
3.	GBR	(Frederick Wyld, Leonard Wyld, Percy Wyld, M. George Southall)	—	
4.	FRA	(André Aumerle, Octave Dayen, René Brossy, André Trantoul)	—	

5. BEL (August Meuleman, Yves van Massenhove, A. Muylle, Jean van Buggenhout), CAN (L.R. Elder, James Davies, A. Houting, William Peden), GER (Josef Steger, Anton Joksch, Kurt Einsiedel, Hans Dornebach), POL (Józef Lange, Artur Reul, Jan Zybert, Józef Oksiutycz)

The British team set an Olympic record of 5:11.2 in the quarter finals. Three of the four British riders were the Wyld brothers from Derby: Frank, Leonard, and Percy.

1932 Los Angeles T: 5, N: 5, D: 8.3.
1.	ITA	(Marco Cimatti, Paolo Pedretti, Alberto Ghilardi, Nino Bosari)	4:53.0
2.	FRA	(Amédée Fournier, René Legrèves, Henri Mouillefarine, Paul Chocque)	4:55.7
3.	GBR	(Ernest Johnson, William Harvell, Frank Southall, Charles Holland)	4:56.0
4.	CAN	(Lewis Rush, Glen Robbins, Russell Hunt, Francis Elliott)	6:04.0

The Italian team set an Olympic record of 4:52.9 in the heats.

1936 Berlin T: 13, N: 13, D: 8.8.
1.	FRA	(Robert Charpentier, Jean Goujan, Guy Lapébie, Roger Le Nizerhy)	4:45.0
2.	ITA	(Bianco Bianchi, Mario Gentili, Armando Latini, Severino Rigoni)	4:51.0
3.	GBR	(Harold Hill, Ernest Johnson, Charles King, Ernest Mills)	4:53.6
4.	GER	(Erich Arndt, Heinz Hasselberg, Heiner Hoffman, Karl Klöckner)	4:55.0

The French team set an Olympic record of 4:41.8 in the heats.

1948 London T: 15, N: 15, D: 8.9.
1. FRA   (Charles Coste, Serge Blusson, Ferdinand   4:57.8
     Decanali, Pierre Adam)
2. ITA   (Arnaldo Benfenati, Guido Bernardi, Anselmo   5:36.7
     Citterio, Rino Pucci)
3. GBR   (R. Alan Geldard, Thomas Godwin, David   4:55.8
     Ricketts, Wilfred Waters)
4. URU   (Atilio François, Juan De Armas, Luis De Los   5:04.4
     Santos, W. Bernatsky)
5. AUS (Sidney Patterson, Jim Nestor, Jack Hoobin, Russell Mockridge), BEL (Joseph DeBeukelaere, Maurice Blomme, Lionel van Brabant, Raphael Glorieux), DEN (Max Jorgensen, Borge Gissel, Borge Mortensen, Benny Schnoor), SWI (Walter Bucher, Gaston Gerosa, Eugen Kamber, Hans Pfenninger)

1952 Helsinki T: 22, N: 22, D: 7.29.
1. ITA   (Marino Morettini, Guido Messina, Mino De   4:46.1
     Rossi, Loris Campana)
2. SAF   (Thomas Shardelow, Alfred Swift, Robert   4:53.6
     Fowler, George Estman)
3. GBR   (Ronald Stretton, Alan Newton, George New-   4:51.5
     berry, Donald Burgess)
4. FRA   (Henri Andrieux, Pierre Michel, Jean-Marie   4:51.9
     Joubert, Claude Brugerolles)
5. BEL (Gabriel Glorieux, José Pauwels, Robert Raymond, Paul de Paepe), DEN (Knud Andersen, Edvard Preben Lundgren-Kristensen, Jean Hansen, Bent Jorgensen), HOL (Johannes Plantaz, Adrianus Voorting, Daniël de Groot, Jules Maenen), SWI (Hans Pfenninger, Heini Müller, Max Wirth, Oscar von Büren)

1956 Melbourne T: 16, N: 16, D: 12.4.
1. ITA   (Leandro Faggin, Valentino Gasparella,   4:37.4   OR
     Antonio Domenicali, Franco Gandini,
     [Valentino Pizzali])
2. FRA   (Michel   Vermeulin,   Jean-Claude   4:39.4
     Lecante, René Bianchi, Jean Graczyk)
3. GBR   (Donald Burgess, Michael Gambrill,   4:42.4
     John Geddes, Thomas Simpson)
4. SAF   (Alfred Swift, Robert Fowler, Charles   4:43.8
     Jonker, Anne-Jan Hettema)
5. BEL (André Bar, Gustave de Smet, François de Wagheneire, Guillaume Van Tongerloo), CZE (Jaroslav Cihlar, Jiři Opavsky, Jiři Nouza, František Jursa), NZE (Warwick Dalton, Donald Eagle, Leonard Kent, Neil Ritchie), SOV (Viktor Iline, Vladimir Mitine, Rodislav Tchijikov, Edouard Goussev)

Great Britain won its sixth straight bronze medal in the team pursuit. One member of the British team, Thomas Simpson, later became the only cyclist to die during the Tour de France.

1960 Rome T: 19, N: 19, D: 8.29.
1. ITA   (Luigi Arienti, Franco Testa, Mario Vallotto,   4:30.90
     Marino Vigna)
2. GDR   (Siegfried Köhler, Peter Gröning, Manfred   4:35.78
     Klieme, Bernd Barleben)
3. SOV   (Stanislav Moskvin, Viktor Romanov, Leonid   4:34.05
     Kolumbet, Arnold Belgardt)
4. FRA   (Marcel Delattre, Jacques Suire, Guy Claud,   4:35.72
     Michel Nedelec)

5. ARG (Alberto Trillo, Ernesto Contreras, Héctor Acosta, Juan Brotto), CZE (Slavoy Cerny, Ferdinand Duchon, Jan Chlistovsky, Josef Volf), DEN (John Lundgren, Leif Larsen, Jens Sorensen, Kurt Stein), HOL (Jacob Oudkerk, Theodorus Nikkessen, Hendrix Nijdam, Petrus van der Lans)

The Italian team set an Olympic record of 4:28.88 in the semifinals.

1964 Tokyo T: 18, N: 18, D: 10.21. WR: 4:26.60 (West Germany)
1. GER   (Lothar Claesges, Karlheinz Henrichs, Karl   4:35.67
     Link, Ernst Streng)
2. ITA   (Luigi Roncaglia, Vincenzo Mantovani, Carlo   4:35.74
     Rancati, Franco Testa)
3. HOL   (Gerard Koel, Hendrik Cornelissen, Jacob   4:38.99
     Oudkerk, Cornelis Schuuring)
4. AUS   (Kevin Brislin, Robert Baird, Victor Browne,   4:39.42
     Hendrikus Vogels)
5. ARG (Carlos Alvarez, Ernesto Contreras, Juan Alberto Merlos, Alberto Trillo), CZE (Jiři Daller, Antonin Kritz, Jiři Pecka, František Rezac), DEN (Bent Kurt Hansen, Preben Isaksson, Alf Johansen, Kurt Vid Stein), SOV (Dzintars Lacis, Leonid Kolumbet, Stanislav Moskvin, Sergei Terechenkov)

The world champion German team broke the Italian pursuit monopoly in dramatic fashion. The two teams raced evenly for the last quarter of the contest. The finish was so close that it took ten minutes to determine the winner, despite the use of electronic timing devices.

1968 Mexico City T: 20, N: 20, D: 10.21. WR: 4:20.64 (Italy)
1. DEN   (Gunnar Asmussen, Per Pedersen Lyngemark,   4:22.44
     Reno Olsen, Mogens Frey Jensen)
2. GER   (Udo Hempel, Karl Link, Karlheinz Henrichs,   4:18.94
     Jürgen Kissner)
3. ITA   (Lorenzo Bosisio, Cipriano Chemello, Luigi   4:18.35
     Roncaglia, Giorgio Morbiato)
4. SOV   (Dzintars Lacis, Stanislav Moskvin, Vladimir   4:33.39
     Kuznyetsov, Mikhail Kolyuschev)
5. BEL (Ernest Bens, Ronny Vanmarcke, Willy Debosscher, Paul Crapez), CZE (Jiři Daler, Pavel Kondr, Milan Puzrla, František Rezac), FRA (Bernard Darmet, Daniel Rebillard, Jack Mourioux, Alain Van Lancker), POL (Wojciech Matusiak, Janusz Kierzkowski, Waclaw Latocha, Rajmund Zieliński)

In the qualifying round the West Germans set a world record of 4:19.90, which was broken quickly by the Italians at 4:16.10. In the first semifinal the Germans took back the record by beating the Italians 4:15.76 to 4:16.21. The final saw the exhausted West Germans hold on to finish first. But with one lap to go, Jürgen Kissner touched his teammate Karlheinz Henrichs on the back. East German officials, bitter because West German team member Kissner was a defector from the east, protested that the "touch" had been an illegal shove. Their protest was upheld, and West Germany was disqualified. At first it was announced that Italy would receive the silver medal and the U.S.S.R. the bronze, but a post-Olympic decision allowed the West Germans to retain second place.

1972 Munich T: 22, N: 22, D: 9.4.
1. GER (Jürgen Colombo, Günter Haritz, Udo 4:22.14 Hempel, Günther Schumacher)
2. GDR (Thomas Huschke, Heinz Richter, Herbert 4:25.25 Richter, Uwe Unterwalder)
3. GBR (Michael Bennett, Ian Hallam, Ronald Keeble, 4:23.78 William Moore)
4. POL (Bernard Kreçzyński, Pawel Kaczorowski, Ja- 4:26.06 nusz Kierzkowski, Mieczyslaw Nowicki)
5. BUL (Nikifor Petrov, Plamen Timchev, Dimo Angelov, Ivan Stanoyev), HOL (Ad Dekkers, Gerard Kamper, Herman Ponsteen, Roy Schuiten), SOV (Viktor Bykov, Vladimir Kuznetsov, Anatoly Stepanenko, Aleksandr Yudin), SWI (Martin Steger, Xaver Kurmann, René Savary, Christian Brunner)

The dramatic confrontation between the two German teams turned out to be a one-sided affair, as the West Germans took an early lead and were up by 3.82 seconds with 1000 meters to go.

1976 Montreal T:16, N: 16, D: 7.24.
1. GER (Gregor Braun, Hans Lutz, Günther 4:21.06 Schumacher, Peter Vonhof)
2. SOV/ (Vladimir Osokin, Aleksandr Perov, Vitaly Pe- 4:27.15 RUS trakov, Viktor Sokolov)
3. GBR (Ian Banbury, Michael Bennett, Robin Croker, 4:22.41 Ian Hallam)
4. GDR (Norbert Dürpisch, Thomas Huschke, Uwe 4:22.75 Unterwalder, Matthias Wiegand)
5. CZE (Zdenek Dohnal, Michal Klasa, Petr Koček, Jiři Pokorny), HOL (Gerrit Mohlmann, Peter Nieuwenhuis, Herman Ponsteen, Gerrit Slot), ITA (Sandro Callari, Cesare Cipollini, Rino de Candido, Giuseppe Saronni), POL (Jan Jankiewicz, Czeslaw Lang, Krzysztof Sujka, Zbigniew Szczepkowski)

The world champion West German team filled their tires with helium instead of air because it was lighter. They also arrived in Montreal with one-piece silk racing suits, which they were not allowed to use because of the unfair aerodynamic advantage it would have given them.

1980 Moscow C: 13, N: 13, D: 7.26.
1. SOV (Viktor Manakov, Valery Movchan, Vladimir 4:15.70 Osokin, Vitaly Petrakov, [Aleksandr Krasnov])
2. GDR (Gerald Mortag, Uwe Unterwalder, Matthias 4:19.67 Wiegand, Volker Winkler)
3. CZE (Teodor Černý, Martin Penc, Jiři Pokorný, Igor Over Sláma) took
4. ITA (Pierangelo Bincoletto, Guido Bontempi, Ivano Maffei, Silvestro Milani)
5. AUS (Colin Fitzgerald, Kevin Nichols, Kelvin Poole, Garry Sutton), FRA (Alain Bondue, Philippe Chevalier, Pascal Poisson, Jean-Marc Rebiere), GBR (Anthony Doyle, Malcolm Elliott, Glen Mitchell, Sean Yates), SWI (Robert Dill-Bundi, Urs Freuler, Hans Kaenel, Hans Ledermann)

The Soviet team set a world best of 4:14.64 in the quarterfinals, achieving a speed of 56.55 kilometers per hour.

1984 Los Angeles-Carson C: 14, N: 14, D: 8.3.
1. AUS (Michael Grenda, Kevin Nichols, Michael 4:25.99 Turtur, Dean Woods)
2. USA (David Grylls, Steve Hegg, R. Patrick Mc- 4:29.85 Donough, Leonard Harvey Nitz, [Brent Emery])
3. GER (Reinhard Alber, Rolf Gölz, Roland Günther, 4:25.60 Michael Marx)
4. ITA (Roberto Amadio, Massimo Brunelli, Maurizio 4:26.90 Colombo, Silvio Martinello)
5. DEN (Dan Frost, Michael Marcussen, Jörgen 4:25.16 Pedersen, Brian Holm Sörensen)
6. FRA (Didier Garcia, Eric Louvel, Pascal Potie, Rob- 4:30.28 ert Pascal)
7. SWI (Daniel Huwyler, Hans Ledermann, Hansrüdi 4:30.47 Märki, Jörg Müller)
8. BEL (Rudi Ceyssens, Roger Ilegems, Peter Roes, 4:31.53 Joseph Smeets)

In the final, the toe strap of U.S. team member Dave Grylls came loose almost immediately, forcing the Americans to complete the race with only three riders. The Australians took an early lead, allowed the Americans to pull close by the halfway mark, and then drew away for a clear victory.

1988 Seoul T: 19, N: 19, D: 9.24. WR: 4:17.710 (CZE—Soukup, Buchta, Cerny, Trčka)
1. SOV (Vyacheslav Yekimov, Artūras Kasputis, 4:13.31 OR Dmitri Nelyubin, Gintautas Umaras)
2. GDR (Steffen Blochwitz, Roland Hennig, Dirk 4:14.09 Meier, Carsten Wolf, [Uwe Preissier])
3. AUS (Brett Dutton, Wayne McCarney, Ste- 4:16.02 phen McGlede, Dean Woods, [Scott McGrory])
4. FRA (Hervé Dagorne, Pascal Lino, Didier 4:22.23 Pasgrimaud, Pascal Potie)
5. CZE (Svatopluk Buchta, Zbynek Fiala, Pavel 4:19.05 Soukup, Aleš Trčka, [Pavel Tesař])
6. ITA (Ivan Beltrami, Gianpaolo Grisandi, Da- 4:20.90 vid Solari, Fabrizio Trezzi, [Fabio Baldato])
7. POL (Ryszard Dawidowicz, Joachim Halup- 4:22.50 czok, Andrzej Sikorski, Marian Turowski)
8. DEN (Peter Clausen, Dan Frost, Jimmi 4:25.30 Madsen, Lars Olsen, [Ken Frost])

Four different teams beat the world record in the qualifying round, with the Soviets leading the way in 4:16.10. In the quarterfinals they lowered their time to 4:14.22, then set a third record in the final. The East Germans almost edged the Soviets for the gold. They trailed by only three tenths of a second with half a lap to go and were closing fast when two of their riders, Wolf and Hennig, misjudged the finish line and sat up in their seats.

1992 Barcelona T: 20, N: 20, D: 7.31. WR: 4:16.100 (SOV— Yekimov, Kasputis, Nelyubin, Umaras)
1. GER (Guido Fulst, Michael Glöckner, Jens 4:08.791 OR Lehmann, Stefan Steinweg, [Andreas Walzer])

2. AUS (Brett Aitken, Stephen McGlede, Shaun 4:10.218
O'Brien, Stuart O'Grady)
3. DEN (Ken Frost, Klaus Kynde Nielsen, Jimmi 4:15.860
Madsen, Jan Petersen, [Dan Frost,
Michael Sandstod])
4. ITA (Ivan Beltrami, Rossano Brasi, Ivan 4:18.291
Cerioli, Fabrizio Trezzi, [Giovanni Lom-
bardi])
5. GBR (Christopher Boardman, Paul Jennings, 4:14.350
Bryan Steel, Glen Sword)
6. SOV (Valery Baturo, Aleksandr Gonchenkov, 4:16.685
Dmitri Nelyubin, Roman Saprykin, [Niko-
lai Kuznetzov])
7. NZE (Gary Anderson, Nigel Donnelly, Carlos Over-
Marryatt, Stuart Williams, [Glenn taken
McLeay])
8. CZE (Svatopluk Buchta, Rudolf Juřický, Jan Over-
Panáček, Pavel Tesař) taken

The Australians set a world best of 4:11.245 in the qualifying round, but the Germans twice lowered that time with
a 4:10.980 in overtaking New Zealand in the quarterfinals, and a 4:10.446 while defeating Denmark in the
semis. They broke quickly in the final and the Australian
team was unable to reel them in.

POINTS RACE

The points race is full of action but difficult to follow. In
1996 it will be run over a distance of 40 kilometers. The
race ends when one rider completes the course. The winner is chosen from among those cyclists who are on the
same lap as the first finisher. Points are awarded for
sprints that take place every two kilometers—basically
20 races within the race. The winner of a sprint earns five
points, second place three points, third place two points,
and fourth place one point. Double points are awarded
for the final sprint. A rider who has been lapped is not
eligible to gain points; a rider who has been lapped twice
is eliminated.

1896–1980 not held

1984 Los Angeles-Carson C: 43, N: 25, D: 8.3.
50 KM

			LAPS DOWN	POINTS
1.	Roger Ilegems	BEL	0	37
2.	Uwe Messerschmidt	GER	0	15
3.	José Manuel Youshimatz	MEX	1	29
4.	Jörg Müller	SWI	1	23
5.	Juan Esteban Curuchet	ARG	1	20
6.	Glenn Clarke	AUS	1	13
7.	Brian Fowler	NZE	1	12
8.	Derk van Egmond	HOL	2	56

Roger Ilegems, Belgium's only gold-medal winner of the
Los Angeles Games, moved into the lead after 110 laps.
World champion and heavy favorite Michael Marcussen
of Denmark was relegated to ninth place.

1988 Seoul C: 34, N: 34, D: 9.24.
50 KM

			LAPS DOWN	POINTS
1.	Dan Frost	DEN	0	38
2.	Leo Peelen	HOL	0	26
3.	Marat Ganeyev	SOV/RUS	1	46
4.	Robert Burns	AUS	1	20
5.	Juan Esteban Curuchet	ARG	1	18
6.	Uwe Messerschmidt	GER	2	28
7.	Pascal Lino	FRA	2	21
8.	Frankie Andreu	USA	2	21

1992 Barcelona C: 38, N: 38, D: 7.31.
50 KM

			LAPS DOWN	POINTS
1.	Giovanni Lombardi	ITA	0	44
2.	Leon van Bon	HOL	0	43
3.	Cedric Mathy	BEL	0	41
4.	Glenn McLeay	NZE	0	30
5.	Lubor Tesař	CZE	0	30
6.	Eric Magnin	FRA	0	24
7.	Guido Fulst	GER	0	24
8.	Andreas Aeschbach	SWI	0	23

The final was an excellent race, averaging more than 49
kilometers per hour. The pace was so fast that no one
could break away and gain a lap on the field. With only
the last double-point sprint left, van Bon led with 41
points, followed by Lombardi with 38, and Mathy with
31. The crowd was on its feet and cheering as the riders
began the final lap. Mathy, in the middle, appeared well-
placed to win the sprint, van Bon was prepared to protect
second place on the outside, while Lombardi was caught
in a box. Suddenly, McLeay challenged van Bon on the
outside, a gap opened, and in a split second Lombardi
zipped through. Van Bon raised his arms in victory and
the Dutch fans celebrated. But the videotape showed
that the order of finish was Mathy (10 points), Lombardi
(6 points), McLeay (4 points), and van Bon (2 points).
Lombardi had won the gold medal by one point.

ROAD TIME TRIAL

This is a race on the road against the clock. Riders start
at one-and-a-half-minute intervals. The men's course
may vary from 45 to 55 kilometers. The riders begin on a
launching ramp, where they are held by a race official
and then released. The same official holds and releases
all entrants.

This event will be held for the first time in 1996.

ROAD RACE

The traditional road race, also known as the in-line road race, begins with a mass start. The first rider across the finish line is the winner. Current rules require repeated circuits of a course 12 to 18 kilometers long. The total distance of the men's race must be between 210 and 240 kilometers. In 1996 any rider who falls 15 minutes behind the lead pack will be ordered to leave the course.

1896 Athens C: 7, N: 3, D: 4.12.
87 KM
1. Aristidis Konstantinidis   GRE   3:21:10.
2. August Goedrich   GER   3:31:14.
3. Edward Battel   GBR   —

The cyclists raced from Athens to Marathon, where they signed their names, and then rode back again on the same road. Battel was a servant at the British Embassy in Athens. Some British residents tried to prevent him from entering the race because, according to them, as he was not a "gentleman" he could not be an amateur.

1900–1904 not held

1906 Athens C: 24, N: 9, D: 5.1.
84 KM
1. Fernand Vast   FRA   2:41:28.0
2. Maurice Bardonneau   FRA   2:41:28.4
3. Edmond Luguet   FRA   2:41:28.6
4. Prospère Verschelden-Romeo   BEL   —
5. Ad. Böhm   GER   —
6. I. Petritsas   GRE   —
7. Carl Andreasen   DEN   —
8. Otto Meixner   AUT   —

1908 not held

1912 Stockholm C: 123, N: 16, D: 7.7.
320 KM
1. Rudolph "Okey" Lewis   SAF   10:42:39.0
2. Frederick Grubb   GBR   10:51:24.2
3. Carl Schutte   USA   10:52:38.8
4. Leon Meredith   GBR   11:00:02.6
5. Frank Brown   CAN   11:01:00.0
6. Antti Raita   FIN   11:02:20.3
7. Eric Friborg   SWE   11:04:17.0
8. Ragnar Malm   SWE   11:08:14.5

This grueling 199-mile race around Lake Mälar began at 2:00 a.m. The competitors were sent out on the course at two-minute intervals over the next four hours. "Okey" Lewis of South Africa began at an unusually fast pace and held an 11½-minute lead at the 120 km control station. He increased this lead to 17 minutes at 200 km and held on for the last 4¼ hours to win by 8¾ minutes. While racing in Germany, Lewis got caught up in World War I. He was wounded several times and incarcerated in prison camps. He returned to Johannesburg after the war in very poor health, but survived until 1933.

There was one terrible accident at the beginning of the race. A few hundred meters after the start, Karl Landsberg of Sweden was hit by a motor-wagon and dragged along for some distance before the wagon stopped.

1920 Antwerp C: 46, N: 12, D: 8.13.
175 KM
1. Harry Stenqvist   SWE   4:40:01.8
2. Henry Kaltenbrun   SAF   4:41:26.6
3. Fernand Canteloube   FRA   4:42:54.4
4. Jean Janssens   BEL   4:44:20.6
5. Albert de Bunné   BEL   4:45:23.4
6. Georges Detreille   FRA   4:46:13.4
7. Ragnar Malm   SWE   4:46:22.0
8. Piet Ikelaar   HOL   4:46:54.0

The course was intersected by six railway crossings which might be closed at any time. Timekeepers were posted at each crossing to record any delays. At first it appeared that Kaltenbrun had won, and his victory was acknowledged by triumphant music in the stadium. However, it was later learned that Stenqvist had been held up for four minutes at a railway crossing, and the subtraction from his time put him into first place.

1924 Paris C: 72, N: 22, D: 7.23.
188 KM
1. Armand Blanchonnet   FRA   6:20:48.0
2. Henri Hoevenaers   BEL   6:30:27.0
3. René Hamel   FRA   6:30:51.6
4. Gunnar Sköld   SWE   6:33:36.2
5. Albert Blattmann   SWE   6:34:09.0
6. Alphonse Pardondry   BEL   6:35:57.0
7. Eric Bohlin   SWE   6:36:12.4
8. Georges Wambst   FRA   6:38:34.4

1928 Amsterdam C: 63, N: 21, D: 8.7.
168 KM
1. Henry Hansen   DEN   4:47:18
2. Frank Southall   GBR   4:55:06
3. Gösta Carlsson   SWE   5:00:17
4. Allegro Grandi   ITA   5:02:05
5. John Lauterwasser   GBR   5:02:57
6. Gottlieb Amstein   SWI   5:04:48
7. Leo Nielsen   DEN   5:05:37
8. André Aumerle   FRA   5:07:12

1932 Los Angeles C: 33, N: 11, D: 8.4.
100 KM
1. Attilio Pavesi   ITA   2:28:05.6
2. Guglielmo Segato   ITA   2:29:21.4
3. Bernhard Britz   SWE   2:29:45.2
4. Giuseppe Olmo   ITA   2:29:48.2
5. Frode Sörensen   DEN   2:30:11.2.
6. Frank Southall   GBR   2:30:16.2
7. Giovanni Cazzulani   ITA   2:31:07.2
8. Sven Hoglund   SWE   2:31:29.4

1936 Berlin C: 100, N: 29, D: 8.10.
100 KM

1.	Robert Charpentier	FRA	2:33:05.0
2.	Guy Lapébie	FRA	2:33:05.2
3.	Ernst Nievergelt	SWI	2:33.05.8
4.	Fritz Scheller	GER	2:33:06.0
4.	Charles Holland	GBR	2:33:06.0
4.	Robert Dorgebray	FRA	2:33:06.0
7.	Pierino Favalli	ITA	2:33:06.2
8.	Auguste Garrebeek	BEL	2:33:06.6
8.	Armand Putzeys	BEL	2:33:06.6
8.	Talat Tuncalp	TUR	2:33:06.6

For the first time, all the competitors started together rather than at intervals. This, coupled with the narrow road, led to numerous accidents and injuries during the last five kilometers. Charpentier had already won a gold medal in the team pursuit two days earlier.

1948 London C: 101, N: 29, D: 8.13.
194.63 KM

1.	José Beyaert	FRA	5:18:12.6
2.	Gerardus Petrus Voorting	HOL	5:18:16.2
3.	Lode Wouters	BEL	5:18:16.2
4.	Léon Delathouwer	BEL	5:18:16.2
5.	Nils Johansson	SWE	5:18:16.2
6.	Robert Maitland	GBR	5:18:16.2
7.	Jack Hoobin	AUS	5:18:18.2
8.	Gordon Thomas	GBR	5:18:18.2

Beyaert, a 22-year-old shoemaker from Lens, sprinted ahead with half a mile to go and won by 8 lengths.

1952 Helsinki C: 112, N: 30, D: 8.2.
190.4 KM

1.	André Noyelle	BEL	5:06:03.4
2.	Robert Grondelaers	BEL	5:06:51.2
3.	Edi Ziegler	GER	5:07:47.5
4.	Lucien Victor	BEL	5:07:52.0
5.	Dino Bruni	ITA	5:10:54.0
6.	Vincenzo Zucconelli	ITA	5:11:16.5
7.	Gianni Ghidini	ITA	5:11:16.8
8.	Oscar Zeissner	GER	5:11:18.5

1956 Melbourne C: 88, N: 28, D: 12.7.
187.73 KM

1.	Ercole Baldini	ITA	5:21:17
2.	Arnaud Geyre	FRA	5:23:16
3.	Alan Jackson	GBR	5:23:16
4.	Horst Tüller	GDR	5:23:16
5.	Gustav-Adolf Schur	GDR	5:23:16
6.	Arthur Stanley Brittain	GBR	5:23:40
7.	Arnaldo Pambianco	ITA	5:23:40
8.	Maurice Moucheraud	FRA	5:23:40

The year 1956 was known as "Baldini's Year," because the 23-year-old Italian won the world championship in the 4000-meter pursuit, set a world record for the one-hour time trial, and won the Olympic road race by a full mile. His victory was protested by the French and Brit-

ish, who charged that in the later stages of the race he had been protected from the hot sun by the Olympic film unit van that rode alongside him. The protest was rejected. The start of the race was delayed fifteen minutes when it was discovered that two "unauthorized" Irish bicyclists, butcher Tom Gerrard and carpenter Paul Fitzgerald, were in the middle of the 88 starters. After they were removed, they joined 200 supporters in passing out Irish nationalist literature.

1960 Rome C: 148, N: 42, D: 8.30.
175.38 KM

1.	Viktor Kapitonov	SOV/RUS	4:20:37
2.	Livio Trapé	ITA	4:20:37
3.	Willy van den Berghen	BEL	4:20:57
4.	Yuri Melikhov	SOV/RUS	4:20:57
5.	Ion Cosma	ROM	4:20:57
6.	Stanislaw Gazda	POL	4:20:57
7.	Benoni Beheyt	BEL	4:20:57
8.	Janez Zirovnik	YUG	4:20:57

Kapitonov sprinted to the finish line to defeat Trapé by inches, only to discover that he still had one more 14½-km lap to go. Twenty-four-minutes later, the scene was repeated but this time Kapitonov's victory was official. Kapitonov later joined the editorial board of *Theory and Practice of Physical Culture* magazine and became the manager of the U.S.S.R. cycling team.

1964 Tokyo C: 132, N: 35, D: 10.22.
194.83 KM

1.	Mario Zanin	ITA	4:39:51.63
2.	Kjell Åkerström Rodian	DEN	4:39:51.65
3.	Walter Godefroot	BEL	4:39:51.74
4.	Raymond Bilney	AUS	4:39:51.74
5.	José Lopez Rodriguez	SPA	4:39:51.74
6.	Wilfried Peffgen	GER	4:39:51.74

Viktor Kapitonov (left) edges Livio Trapé at the finish line of the 1960 road race, only to discover that he still has one more 14½-kilometer lap to go. Twenty-four minutes later, Kapitonov defeated Trapé again.

7. Gösta Pettersson	SWE	4:39:51.74
8. Delmo Delmastro	ARG	4:39:51.74

A spectacular finish saw Zanin, a mechanic from Treviso, emerge from the pack with 20 meters to go and win by a wheel. Sture Pettersson of Sweden finished only sixteen-hundredths of a second behind Zanin, yet he ended up in 51st place.

1968 Mexico City C: 144, N: 44, D: 10.23.
196.2 KM

1. Pierfranco Vianelli	ITA	4:41:25.24
2. Leif Mortensen	DEN	4:42:49.71
3. Gösta Pettersson	SWE	4:43:15.24
4. Stephan Abrahamian	FRA	4:43:36.54
5. Marinus Pijnen	HOL	4:43:36.81
6. Jean-Pierre Monsère	BEL	4:43:51.77
7. Tomas Pettersson	SWE	4:43:58.11
8. Giovanni Bramucci	ITA	4:43:58.19

1972 Munich C: 163, N: 48, D: 9.7.
182.4 KM

1. Hennie Kuiper	HOL	4:14.37
2. Keven Clyde Sefton	AUS	4:15:04
3. Bruce Biddle	NZE	4:15:04
4. Philip Bayton	GBR	4:15:07
5. Philip Edwards	GBR	4:15.13
6. Wilfried Trott	GER	4:15:13
7. Francesco Moser	ITA	4:15:13
8. Miguel Samaca	COL	4:15:21

DISQ (Drugs): Jaime Huelamo (SPA) 4:15:04

The four Dutch contestants rode a team race with Cees Priem and Fedor den Hertog protecting Kuiper and fighting off challengers. Freddy Maertens was so frustrated by Priem's dogged persistence in sticking to his wheel that he tried to hit Priem in the face. Said Priem, "We worked for Hennie because he is one of the nicest blokes around." Four Irish Republican Army cyclists joined the race to protest the fact that the Irish Cycling Federation competed against cyclists from Northern Ireland. One of them tried to run Irish Olympian Noel Taggart into a ditch. The 4 IRA cyclists were arrested but later released without charge.

Third-place finisher Jaime Huelamo was disqualified after he failed a test for drugs.

1976 Montreal C: 134, N: 40, D: 7.26.
175 KM

1. Bernt Johansson	SWE	4:46:52
2. Giuseppe Martinelli	ITA	4:47:23
3. Mieczyslaw Nowicki	POL	4:47:23
4. Alfons de Wolf	BEL	4:47:23
5. Nikolai Gorelov	SOV/RUS	4:47:23
6. George Mount	USA	4:47:23
7. Jean René Bernaudeau	FRA	4:47:23
8. Vittorio Algeri	ITA	4:47:23

Peter Thaler of Germany crossed the finish line in second place, but was demoted to ninth because he had interfered with Martinelli in the final sprint.

1980 Moscow C: 112, N: 32, D: 7.28.
189 KM

1. Sergei Sukhoruchenkov	SOV/RUS	4:48:28.9
2. Czeslaw Lang	POL	4:51:26.9
3. Yuri Barinov	SOV	4:51:29.9
4. Thomas Barth	GDR	4:56:12.9
5. Tadeusz Wojtas	POL	4:56:12.9
6. Anatoly Yarkin	SOV	4:56:54.9
7. Adri van der Poel	HOL	4:56:54.9
8. Christian Faure	FRA	4:56:54.9

Sukhoruchenkov pulled away with 20 miles to go and won by the largest Olympics margin since 1928.

1984 Los Angeles-Mission Viejo C: 135, N: 43, D: 7.29.
190.2 KM

1. Alexi Grewal	USA	4:59:57
2. Steve Bauer	CAN	4:59:57
3. Dag Otto Lauritzen	NOR	5:00:18
4. Morten Saether	NOR	5:00:18
5. Davis Phinney	USA	5:01:16
6. Thurlow Rogers	USA	5:01:16
7. Bojan Ropret	YUG	5:01:16
8. Nestor Mora	COL	5:01:16

The son of a Sikh father from India and a British mother of German descent, Alexi Grewal was considered too temperamental and too much of a loner to be an effective member of the U.S. team. Two places on the team were to be decided by the combined results of three trials; the other two were to be filled by the team coaches. Since U.S. head coach Eddie Borysewicz was definitely *not* a fan of Grewal's, the 23-year-old naturalized U.S. citizen had no choice but to make it as one of the two automatic qualifiers. He succeeded, but his troubles were not yet over. Ten days before the Olympic road race, Grewal won a 92-mile contest in Colorado, but his post-race doping test turned up positive for phenyethylamine, apparently caused by a Chinese herbal tablet which he had casually popped before the race. The U.S. Cycling Federation immediately slapped him with a 30-day suspension and dropped him from the Olympic team.

Grewal appealed the ruling by pointing out that he regularly took albuterol, a legal drug, for asthma, and that the doping test had not been sophisticated enough to distinguish between the asthma drug and the herbal pill. On the Monday before the Sunday Olympic race, Grewal was reinstated.

In Los Angeles, with a crowd of 300,000 lining the route, Grewal broke away from the pack 20 kilometers from the finish and opened up a 24-second lead after 11 of 12 laps. With 10 kilometers to go he appeared exhausted and began to wobble and weave. Steve Bauer of Fenwick, Ontario, passed him. Grewal faced a moment of panic and confusion, then regained his self-control and caught Bauer. The two raced the final lap together. After almost 5 hours of riding, the gold medal was to be decided by a sprint, which was Bauer's specialty. Bauer made his jump 100 meters from the finish, but Grewal zipped by with less than 50 meters to go and won by little more than a bike length.

Bronze medalist Dag Otto Lauritzen took up cycling in 1981 to rehabilitate his knee after suffering an injury while parachute jumping.

1988 Seoul C: 136, N: 54, D: 9.27.
196.8 KM

1.	Olaf Ludwig	GDR	4:32:22
2.	Bernd Gröne	GER	4:32:25
3.	Christian Henn	GER	4:32:46
4.	Robert Mionske	USA	4:32:46
5.	Djamolidin Abdoujaparov	SOV/UZB	4:32:46
6.	Edward Salas	AUS	4:32:46
7.	Roberto Pelliconi	ITA	4:32:46
8.	Graeme Miller	NZE	4:32:46

The unusually flat course laid out by the Seoul organizers was good news for talented sprinter Olaf Ludwig of Gera-Thieschity. Eight years earlier, in Moscow, Ludwig had taken a silver in the team time trial and finished thirty-second in the road race. In Seoul he placed fourteenth in the points race three days before winning the road race.

A sidelight of note: by finishing ninth, 21-year-old Emili Perez became the highest placed athlete in Olympic history in any sport from the minuscule European nation of Andorra (pop. 50,000).

1992 Barcelona-Sant Sadurní d'Anoia C: 154, N: 59, D: 8.2.
194 KM

1.	Fabio Casartelli	ITA	4:35.21
2.	Hendrik Dekker	HOL	4:35.22
3.	Dainis Ozols	LAT	4:35.24
4.	Erik Zabel	GER	4:35.56
5.	Lauri Aus	EST	4:35.56
6.	Andrzej Sypykowski	POL	4:35.56
7.	Sylvain Bolay	FRA	4:35.56
8.	Arvis Piziks	LAT	4:35.56

Casartelli, the third man on the three-man Italian team, led the decisive break at the end of the penultimate lap. Only Dekker came with him, although Ozols joined them as the bell rang for the final lap. Two hundred and fifty meters from the finish, the 21-year-old from Como sprinted away to a clear victory. On July 18, 1995, Casartelli was competing in his first Tour de France when he lost control on a fast, steep, descending curve in the Pyrénées Mountains. Helmetless, he flew headfirst into a concrete pylon. Although doctors were on the scene within ten seconds, Casartelli's life could not be saved.

CROSS-COUNTRY RACE

The cross-country, or mountain bike, race is run on forest roads, fields, earth, and gravel paths. Paved and tarred roads cannot exceed 15% of the total route. There is a mass start and the first rider across the finish line is the winner. All dangerous obstacles are preceded by warning signs 30 meters in advance.

This event will be held for the first time in 1996.

Discontinued Events
ONE-LAP RACE

1896 Athens C: 8, N: 5, D: 4.11.
(333.33 Meters)

1.	Paul Masson	FRA	24.0
2.	Stamatios Nikolopoulos	GRE	26.0
3.	Adolf Schmal	AUT	26.0
4.	Edward Battel	GBR	26.2
5.	Theodor Flameng	GER	27.0
5.	Frank Keeping	GBR	27.0
5.	Theodor Leupold	GER	27.0
8.	Joseph Rosemeyer	GER	27.2

Nikolopoulos was awarded second place after defeating Schmal in a race-off 25.4 to 26.6.

1900–1904 not held

1906 Athens C: 24, N: 9, D: 4.23.
(333.33 Meters)

1.	Francesco Verri	ITA	22.8
2.	Herbert Crowther	GBR	23.2
3.	Menjou	FRA	23.2
4.	Emile Demangel	FRA	23.2
5.	Eugène Debougnie	BEL	23.6
6.	F. Della Ferrera	ITA	23.8
7.	A. Verdesopoulos	GRE	23.8
8.	Herbert Bouffler (GBR), Bruno Götze (GER), Max Götze (GER), T. John Matthews (GBR) 24.2		

Crowther was awarded second place after winning a race-off. His time was 22.8, while Menjou clocked 23.2 and Demangel 23.6.

1908 London C: 46, N: 9, D: 7.15.
(603.49 Meters)

1.	Victor Johnson	GBR	51.2
2.	Emile Demangel	FRA	—
3.	Karl Neumer	GER	—
4.	Daniel Flynn	GBR	—

In 1909 Johnson recorded a time of 28.0 seconds for a quarter mile from a standing start. This was recognized as a world record for 21 years until stricter standards for records were enforced.

5000-METER TRACK RACE

1906 Athens C: 26, N: 9, D: 4.23.
1. Francesco Verri ITA 7:28.6
2. Herbert Crowther GBR —
3. Fernand Vast FRA —
AC: Emile Demangel (FRA), Max Götze (GER)

1908 London C: 42, N; 8, D: 7.18.
1. Benjamin Jones   GBR   8:36.2
2. Maurice Schilles   FRA   —
3. André Auffray   FRA   —
4. Emile Maréchal   FRA   —
5. Clarence Kingsbury   GBR   —
6. Johannes van Spengen   HOL   —
7. Gerard Bosch van Drakestein HOL   —

In the final of the 1000-meter sprint, Schilles beat Jones by inches. However, the race was declared void because the time limit was exceeded. Two days later in the 5000 meters it was Jones who held off Schilles' finishing sprint to win by 6 inches. Jones was a coal miner from Wigan.

10 KM TRACK RACE

1896 Athens C: 6, N: 4, D: 4.11.
1. Paul Masson   FRA   17:54.2
2. Léon Flameng   FRA   17:54.8
3. Adolf Schmal   AUT   —
4. Joseph Rosemeyer GER   —
DNF: Georgios Kolettis (GRE), Aristidis Konstantinidis (GRE)

20 KM TRACK RACE

1906 Athens C: 24, N: 9, D: 4.23.
1. William Pett   GBR   29:00.0
2. Maurice Bardonneau   FRA   29:30.0
3. Fernand Vast   FRA   29:32.0
4. Hans Holly   AUT   —
5. Eduard Dannenberg   GER   —
AC: Ad. Böhm (GER), Edmond Luguet (FRA)

Billy Pett did not begin cycling until he was 20 years old. His training was hampered by the fact that he worked 11 hours a day in the wine cellars at Harrods. He was 32 when he earned his gold medal in Athens.

1908 London C: 44, N: 11, D: 7.14.
1. Clarence Kingsbury   GBR   34:13.6
2. Benjamin Jones   GBR   —
3. Joseph Werbrouck   BEL   —
4. Louis Weintz   USA   —

Kingsbury, of Portsmouth, won by 3 inches. From the Olympics, Kingsbury went to the world championships in Leipzig, Germany. After triumphing there he returned home to a hero's welcome attended by tens of thousands of people.

50 KM TRACK RACE

1920 Antwerp C: 31, N: 10, D: 8.11.
1. Henry George   BEL   1:16:43.2
2. Cyril Alden   GBR   —

3. Piet Ikelaar   HOL   —
4. Ruggero Ferrario   ITA   —
5. Herbert MacDonald   CAN   —
6. Franco Giorgetti   ITA   —
7. William Smith   SAF   —

Eyewitnesses said that Ikelaar actually finished second. The Jury of Appeal eventually agreed, but refused to reverse the judges' verdict, since it had already been announced.

1924 Paris C: 36, N: 16, D: 7.27.
1. Jacobus Willems   HOL   1:18:24.0
2. Cyril Alden   GBR   —
3. Frederick Wyld   GBR   —
4. Angelo De Martino   ITA   —
5. Józef Lange   POL   —
6. Alfredo Dinale   ITA   —

100 KM TRACK RACE

1896 Athens C; 9, N: 5, D: 4.8.
1. Léon Flameng   FRA   3:08:19.2
2. Georgios Kolettis GRE   —

The race required 300 circuits of the track. Once, when Kolettis' bike needed repair, Flameng stopped and waited for him. Flameng fell towards the end of the race, but still won by six or seven laps. He raced with a French flag tied around his leg.

1908 London C: 43, N: 11, D: 7.16.
1. Charles Bartlett   GBR   2:41:48.6
2. Charles Denny   GBR   —
3. Octave Lapize   FRA   —
4. William Pett   GBR   —
5. Pierre Teixier   FRA   —
6. Walter Andrews   CAN   —
7. D.C. Robertson   GBR   —
8. Sydney Bailey   GBR   —

This was considered the most important cycling contest of the 1908 Olympics, and there were so many entrants that qualifying heats had to be run to cut down the field. In the second of these heats, a bad accident occurred when Harry Venn, a walking official, walked right onto the track and collided with Coeckelberg of Belgium. Coeckelberg fell to the ground and was cut on the thigh and head, but he managed to finish the race, qualifying for the final as a consequence of his having led much of the way. The final was contested on a wet track with rain still falling when the race began. After 70 kilometers Bartlett fell and was forced to mount a new bike. He lost a lap but caught up with one lap to go. By this time the race had come down to Octave Lapize of France and three representatives of Great Britain, Bartlett, Charles Denny, and Billy Pett. The four were moving around at a crawl when Bartlett suddenly darted to the inside, took the lead, and sprinted home to win by almost a length.

12-HOUR RACE

1896 Athens C: 7, N: 4, D: 4.13.

		KM
1. Adolf Schmal	AUT	295.3
2. Frank Keeping	GBR	294.946

DNF: Georgios Paraskevopoulos (GRE), Konstantinos Konstantinou (GRE), Loverdos (GRE), Tryfiatis (GRE), Josef Welzenbacher (GER)

2000-METER TANDEM

1906 Athens T: 6, N: 4, D: 4.23.
1. GBR   (T. John Matthews, Arthur Rushen)   2:15.0
2. GER   (Max Götze, Bruno Götze)   —
3. GER   (Eduard Dannenberg, Otto Küpferling)   —

Matthews and Rushen upset the Götze brothers, winning by 20 yards.

1908 London T: 17, N: 7, D: 7.15.
1. FRA   (Maurice Schilles, André Auffray)   3:07.6
2. GBR   (Frederick Hamlin, Horace "Tiny" Johnson)   —
3. GBR   (Colin Brooks, Walter Isaacs)   —

Schilles and Auffray had never ridden together before the first round of this contest.

1912 not held

1920 Antwerp T: 11, N: 6, D: 8.11.
1. GBR   (Harry Ryan, Thomas Lance)   2:49.2
2. SAF   (James Walker, William Smith)   —
3. HOL   (Frans de Vreng, Piet Ikelaar)   —
4. GBR   (William Stewart, Cyril Alden)   —

Ryan and Lance covered the last 200 meters in 11.2 seconds to win by a length.

1924 Paris T: 5, N: 5, D: 7.27.
1. FRA.   (Lucien Choury, Jean Cugnot)   12.6 (last 200 meters)
2. DEN   (Willy Falck Hansen, Edmund Hansen)   —
3. HOL   (Gerard Bosch van Drakestein, Mouritius "Maurice" Peeters)   —

1928 Amsterdam T: 7, N: 7, D: 8.7.
1. HOL   (Bernhard Leene, Daniel van Dijk)   11.8
2. GBR   (John Sibbitt, Ernest Chambers)   —
3. GER   (Karl Köther, Hans Bernhardt)   —
4. ITA   (Francesco Malatesta, Adolf Corsi)   —

1932 Los Angeles T: 5, N: 5, D: 8.3.

		1ST RACE	2ND RACE
1. FRA	(Maurice Perrin, Louis Chaillot)	12.3	12.0
2. GBR	(Ernest Chambers, Stanley Chambers)		—
3. DEN	(Willy Gervin, Harald Christensen)		
4. HOL	(Bernhard Leene, Jacobus van Egmond)		

1936 Berlin T: 11, N: 11, D: 8.8.

		1ST RACE	2ND RACE
1. GER	(Ernst Ihbe, Carl Lorenz)	11.0	11.0
2. HOL	(Bernhard Leene, Hendrik Ooms)	—	—
3. FRA	(Pierre Georget, Georges Maton)		
4. ITA	(Carlo Legutti, Bruno Loatti)		

5. BEL (François Cools, Roger Pirotte), DEN (Heino Dissing, Bjorn Stièler), GBR (Ernest Chambers, John Sibbitt), USA (William Logan, Albert Sellinger)

1948 London T: 10, N: 10, D: 8.11.

		1ST RACE	2ND RACE	3RD RACE
1. ITA	(Ferdinando Teruzzi, Renato Perona)	—	11.3	11.6
2. GBR	(Reginald Harris, Alan Bannister)	11.1	—	—
3. FRA	(René Faye, Georges Dron)			
4. SWI	(Jean Roth, Max Aeberli)			

5. BEL (Louis van Schill, Roger de Pauw), DEN (Hans Andersen, Evan Klamer), HOL (Nicolaas Buchly, Martinus van Gelder), USA (Marvin Thompson, Alfred Stiller)

In a thrilling finish, held in the dark, Teruzzi and Perona won the tie-breaker by a mere six inches.

1952 Helsinki T: 14, N: 14, D: 7.31.
1. AUS   (Lionel Cox, Russell Mockridge)   11.0
2. SAF   (Raymond Robinson, Thomas Shardelow)   —
3. ITA   (Antonio Maspes, Cesare Pinarello)
4. FRA   (Franck Le Normand, Robert Vidal)
5. DEN (Jens Eriksen, Olaf Holmstrup), GBR (Leslie Wilson, Alan Bannister), HUN (István Schillerwein, Imre Furmen), NZE (Colin Dickinson, Clarence Simpson)

1956 Melbourne T: 10, N: 10, D: 6.12.
1. AUS   (Ian Browne, Anthony Marchant)   10.8
2. CZE   (Ladislav Fouček, Václav Machek)   —
3. ITA   (Giuseppe Ogna, Cesare Pinarello)
4. GBR   (Peter Brotherton, Eric Thompson)
5. FRA (Robert Vidal, André Gruchet), NZE (Richard Johnston, Warren Johnston), SAF (Thomas Shardelow, Raymond Robinson), USA (James Rossi, Donald Ferguson)

Browne and Marchant were surprise winners. They finished last in their first-round heat and lost the repêchage to Czechoslovakia. However, in another repêchage, the Germans and Soviets crashed, leaving the Soviet riders unable to restart. In need of opponents for the German pair, the officials turned to the already-eliminated Australians and Americans. Browne and Marchant won the race, scored two more unexpected victories in the quarterfinals and semifinals, and then upset Fouček and Machek in the final.

1960 Rome T: 12, N: 12, D: 8.27.

		1ST RACE	2ND RACE
1. ITA	(Giuseppe Beghetto, Sergio Bianchetto)	10.7	10.8
2. GDR	(Jürgen Simon, Lothar Stäber)	—	—
3. SOV/RUS	(Boris Vasilyev, Vladimir Leonov)		

4. HOL   (Marinus Paul, Melis Gerritsen)
5. CZE (Juraj Miklusica, Dusan Skvarenina), FRA (Roland Surrugue, Michael Scob), GBR (David Handley, Eric Thompson), USA (Jack Hartman, David Sharp)

1964 Tokyo T: 13, N: 13, D: 10.20.

		1ST RACE	2ND RACE	3RD RACE
1. ITA	(Angelo Damiano, Sergio Bianchetto)	—	10.85	10.75
2. SOV	(Imant Bodnieks, Viktor Logunov)	10.80	—	—
3. GER	(Willi Fuggerer, Klaus Kobusch)			
4. HOL	(Arie de Graaf, Peiter van der Touw)			

5. AUS (Ian Browne, Daryl Perkins), CZE (Karel Paar, Karel Stark), DEN (Niels Fredborg, Per Jorgensen), HUN (Richárd Bicskey, Ferenc Habony)

1968 Mexico City T: 14, N: 14, D: 10.21.

		1ST RACE	2ND RACE
1. FRA	(Daniel Morelon, Pierre Trentin)	10.03	9.83
2. HOL	(Johannes Jansen, Leijn Loevesijn)	—	—
3. BEL	(Daniel Goens, Robert van Lancker)		
4. ITA	(Walter Gorini, Luigi Borghetti)		

5. CZE (Ivan Kucirek, Milos Jelinek), GDR (Werner Otto, Jürgen Geschke), GER (Klaus Kobusch, Martin Stenzel), SOV (Igor Tselovalnikov, Imant Bodnieks)

1972 Munich T: 14, N: 14, D: 9.3.

		1st RACE	2ND RACE	3RD RACE
1. SOV/ UKR	(Volodymyr Semenets, Ihor Tselovalnykov)	—	10.52	10.60
2. GDR	(Jürgen Geschke, Werner Otto)	10.68	—	—
3. POL	(Andrzej Bek, Benedykt Kocot)			
4. FRA	(Daniel Morelon, Pierre Trentin)			

5. BEL (Manu Snellinx, Noel Scetaert), CZE (Ivan Kucirek, Vladimir Popelka), GER (Jürgen Barth, Rainer Müller), HOL (Klaas Balk, Peter van Doorn)

TEAM TIME TRIAL

Until 1960 the results of the individual road race were used to determine the team winner. However, starting with the 1960 Rome Olympics a separate team event was held in which four cyclists from each team race against the clock, riding together in a line and periodically changing positions as in the team pursuit. The official time was that of the third rider for each team.

1912 Stockholm T: 15, N: 14, D: 7.7.
320 KM

		COMBINED TIME
1. SWE	(Eric Friborg, Ragnar Malm, Axel Persson, Algot Lönn)	44:35:33.6
2. GBR/England	(Frederick Grubb, Leon Meredith, Charles Moss, William Hammond)	44:44:39.2

3. USA	(Carl Schutte, Alvin Loftes, Albert Krushel, Walter Martin)	44:47:55.5
4. GBR/Scotland	(John Wilson, Robert Thompson, John Miller, David Stevensen)	46:29:55.1
5. FIN	(Antti Raita, Vilho Tilkanen, Johan Kankonnen, Hjalmar Väre)	46:34:03.5
6. GER	(Franz Lemnitz, Rudolf Baier, Oswald Rathmann, Georg Warsow)	46:35:16.1
7. AUT	(Robert Rammer, Adolf Kofler, Rudolf Kramer, Josef Hellensteiner)	46:57:26.4
8. DEN	(Olaf Meyland Smith, Charles Hansen, Johannes Reinwald, Hans Olsen)	47:16:07.0

1920 Antwerp T:11, N: 11, D: 8.13.
175 KM

		COMBINED TIME
1. FRA	(Fernand Canteloube, Georges Detreille, Achille Souchard, Marcel Gobillot)	19:16:43.4
2. SWE	(Harry Stenqvist, Ragnar Malm, Axel Person, Sigfrid Lundberg)	19:23:10.0
3. BEL	(Jean Janssens, Albert de Bunné, André Vercruysse, Albert Wyckmans)	19:28:44.4
4. DEN	(Christian Johansen, Arnold Lundgren, Kristian Frisch, Ahrensborg Claussen)	19:52:32.2
5. ITA	(Federico Gay, Pietro Bestetti, Camillo Arduino, Dante Ghindani)	20:26:44.0
6. HOL	(Piet Ikelaar, Nico de Jong, Arie van der Stel, Pieter Kloppenburg)	20:28:39.2
7. USA	(Ernest Kockler, August Nogara, James Freeman, John Otto)	21:32:36.6
8. NOR	(Helge Flateby, Paul Henricksen, Olaf Nygaard, Thorstein Stryken)	21:35:11.8

1924 Paris T: 16, N: 16, D: 7.23.
188 KM

		COMBINED TIME
1. FRA	(Armand Blanchonnet, René Hamel, Georges Wambst)	19:30:14.0
2. BEL	(Henri Hoevenaers, Alphonse Parfondry, Jean van den Bosch)	19:46:55.4
3. SWE	(Gunnar Sköld, Erik Bohlin, Ragnar Malm)	19:59:41.6
4. SWI	(Albert Blattmann, Otto Lehner, Georg Antenen)	20:11:15.0
5. ITA	(Ardito Bresciani, Antonio Negrini, Nello Ciaccheri)	20:19:59.2
6. HOL	(Cornelis Heeren, Jan Maas, Phillippus Hendrik Innemee)	20:37:27.8

1928 Amsterdam T: 15, N: 15, D: 8.7.
168 KM

		COMBINED TIME
1. DEN	(Henry Hansen, Leo Nielsen, Orla Jörgensen)	15:09:14.0
2. GBR	(Frank Southall, John Lauterwasser, John Middleton)	15:14:49.0

3. SWE (Gösta Carlsson, Erik Jansson, E. Georg Johnsson) 15:27:49.0

4. ITA (Allegro Grandi, Michele Orecchia, Ambrogio Beretta) 15:33:12.0

5. BEL (Jean Aerts, Pierre Houdé, Joseph Lowagie) 15:33:50.0

6. SWI (Gottlieb Amstein, Jakob Caironi, Tütel Wanzenried) 15:35:21.0

7. FRA (André Aumerle, Louis Bessière, Octave Dayen) 15:38:20.0

8. ARG (Cosme Saavedra, Francisco Bonvehi, José López) 15:42:55.0

1932 Los Angeles T: 8, N: 8, D: 8.4.
100 KM

		COMBINED TIME
1. ITA	(Attilio Pavesi, Guglielmo Segato, Giuseppe Olmo)	7:27:15.2
2. DEN	(Frode Sörensen, Leo Nielsen, Henry Hansen)	7:38:50.2
3. SWE	(Bernhard Britz, Sven Höglund, A. Arne Berg)	7:39:12.6
4. GBR	(Frank Southall, Charles Holland, Stanley Butler)	7:44:53.0
5. FRA	(Paul Chocque, Amédée Fournier, Henri Mouillefarine)	7:46:31.8
6. USA	(Henry O'Brien, Frank Connell, Otto Luedeke)	7:51:55.6
7. CAN	(Frances Elliott, James Jackson, Francis Robbins)	8:01:38.0
8. GER	(Hubert Ebner, Werner Lange-Wittich, Julius Maus)	8:21:21.2

1936 Berlin T: 22, N: 22, D: 8.10.
100 KM

		COMBINED TIME
1. FRA	(Robert Charpentier, Guy Lapébie, Robert Dorgebray)	7:39:16.2
2. SWI	(Ernst Nievergelt, Edgar Buchwalder, Kurt Ott)	7:39:20.4
3. BEL	(Auguste Garrebeek, Armand Putzeys, Francois Vandermette)	7:39:21.0
4. ITA	(Pierino Favalli, Glauco Servadei, Corrado Ardizzoni)	7:39:22.0
5. AUT	(Virgilius Altmann, Hans Höfner, Hans Schnalek)	7:39:24.0

1948 London T: 25, N: 25, D: 8.13.
194.63 KM

		COMBINED TIME
1. BEL	(Lode Wouters, Léon Delathouwer, Eugène van Roosbroeck)	15:58:17.4
2. GBR	(Robert Maitland, Gordon Thomas, C.S. Ian Scott)	16:03:31.6
3. FRA	(José Beyaert, Alain Moineau, Jacques Dupont)	16:08:19.4

4. ITA (Alfo Ferrari, Silvio Pedroni, Franco Fanti) 16:13:05.2

5. SWE (Nils Johansson, Harry Snell, Åke Olivestedt) 16:20:26.6

6. SWI (Jakob Schenk, Jean Brun, Walter Reiser) 16:23:04.2

7. ARG (Ceferino Perone, Dante Benvenuti, Miguel Sevillano) 16:39:46.2

1952 Helsinki T: 27, N: 27, D: 8.2.
190.4 KM

		COMBINED TIME
1. BEL	(André Noyelle, Robert Grondelaers, Lucien Victor)	15:20:46.6
2. ITA	(Dino Bruni, Vincenzo Zucconelli, Gianni Ghidini)	15:33:27.3
3. FRA	(Jacques Anquetil, Alfred Tonello, Claude Rover)	15:38:58.1
4. SWE	(Yngve Lundh, Stig Mårtensson, Allan Carlsson)	15:41:34.3
5. GER	(Edi Ziegler, Oskar Zeissner, Paul Maue)	15:43:50.5
6. DEN	(Hans Andersen, Jörgen Rasmussen, Poul Östergaard)	15:48:02.0
7. LUX	(André Moes, Roger Ludwig, Nicolas Morn)	15:49:04.0
8. HOL	(Arend Van't Hof, Johannes Planatz, Adrianus Voorting)	15:52:22.7

Jacques Anquetil of the French team went on to win the Tour de France five times.

1956 Melbourne T: 20, N: 20, D: 12.7.
187.73 KM

		PTS.
1. FRA	(2—Arnaud Geyre, 8—Maurice Moucheraud, 12—Michel Vermeulin)	22
2. GBR	(3—Alan Jackson, 6—Arthur Stanley Brittain, 14—William Holmes)	23
3. GDR& GER	(4—Horst Tüller, 5—Gustav-Adolf Schur, 18—Reinhold Pommer)	27
4. ITA	(1—Ercole Baldini, 7—Arnaldo Pambianco, 28—Dino Bruni)	36
5. SWE	(10—Lars Nordwall, 17—Karl-Ivan Andersson, 20—Roland Ströhm)	47
6. SOV	(15—Anatoly Cherepovich, 16—Mykola Kolumbet, 32—Viktor Kapitonov)	63
7. BEL	(23—Norbert Verougstraete, 24—Gustave De Smet, 42—François van den Bosch)	89
8. COL	(13—Ramon Hoyos Vallejo, 39—Pablo Hurtada Castañeda 40—Jaime Villegas)	92

In 1956 the placings in the team road race were determined not by combined times, but by adding together the individual placings of the team members. Great Britain lost its chances for a gold medal when Billy Holmes crashed into a photographer who had stepped onto the course. Holmes was injured, but worse still, was delayed two and a half minutes while he changed a wheel. Holmes caught up with the leaders eleven miles later, but had he finished one second earlier, Britain would have taken first place.

1960 Rome T: 32, N: 32, D: 8.26.
100 KM

1.	ITA	(Antonio Bailetti, Ottavio Cogilati, Giacomo Fornoni, Livio Trapé)	2:14:33.53
2.	GDR	(Gustav-Adolf Schur, Egon Adler, Erich Hagen, Günter-Lörke)	2:16:56.31
3.	SOV/RUS	(Viktor Kapitonov, Yevgeny Klevzov, Yuri Melikhov, Aleksei Petrov)	2:18:41:67
4.	HOL	(Johannes Hugens, Cornelis Lotz, Albert Sluis, Pieter van Kreuningen)	2:19:15.71
5.	SWE	(Owe Adamson, Gunnar Göransson, Oswald Johansson, Gösta Pettersson)	2:19:36.37
6.	ROM	(Ion Cosma, Gabriel Moiceanu, Aurel Şelaru, Ludovic Zanoni)	2:20:18.91
7.	FRA	(Henri Duez, François Hamon, Roland Lacombe, Jacques Simon)	2:20:36.38
8.	SPA	(Ignacio Astigarraga Uriarte, Juan Sanchez Camero, José Momene Campo, Ramon Saez Marzo)	2:21:34:59

This race, which was run in 93-degree heat, was marred by the death of Danish cyclist Knut Jensen, who collapsed from sunstroke and suffered a fractured skull. It was later determined that before the race Jensen had taken Ronicol, a blood circulation stimulant. Jensen was the first person to die in Olympic competition since the 1912 marathon.

1964 Tokyo T: 33, N: 33, D: 10.14.
109.89 KM

1.	HOL	(Evert Dolman, Gerben Karstens, Johannes Pieterse, Hubertus Zoet)	2:26:31.19
2.	ITA	(Severino Andreoli, Luciano Dalla Bona, Pietro Guerra, Ferrucio Manza)	2:26:55.39
3.	SWE	(Sven Hamrin, Erik Pettersson, Gösta Pettersson, Sture Pettersson)	2:27:11.52
4.	ARG	(Héctor Acosta, Roberto Breppe, Delmo Delmastro, Rubén Placanica)	2:27:58.55
5.	SOV/RUS	(Yuri Melikhov, Anatoly Olizarenko, Aleksei Petrov, Gaynan Saidkhuschin)	2:28:26.48
6.	FRA	(Marcel-Ernest Bidault, Georges Chappe, André Desvages, Jean-Claude Wuillemin)	2:28:52.74
7.	DEN	(Flemming Hansen, Henning Petersen, Ole Pedersen, Ole Ritter)	2:29:10.33
8.	SPA	(José Goyeneche, José Lopez, Mariano Diaz, Luis Santamarina)	2:30:55.26

1968 Mexico City T: 30, N: 30, D: 10.15.
104 KM

1.	HOL	(Fedor den Hertog, Jan Krekels, Marinus Pijnen, Gerardes Zoetemelk)	2:07:49.06
2.	SWE	(Erik Pettersson, Gösta Pettersson, Sture Pettersson, Tomas Pettersson)	2:09:26.60
3.	ITA	(Giovanni Bramucci, Vittorio Marcelli, Mauro Simonetti, Pierfranco Vianelli)	2:10:18.74
4.	DEN	(Verner Blaudzun, Jörgen Emil Hansen, Ole Hojlund Pederson, Leif Martensen)	2:12:41.41

In 1968 the four Pettersson brothers of Sweden joined forces to win silver medals in the cycling team time trial.

5.	NOR	(Thorleif Andresen, Ornulf Andresen, Tore Milsett, Leif Yli)	2:14:32.85
6.	POL	(Jan Magiera, Zenon Czechowski, Marian Kegel, Andrzej Blawdzin)	2:14:40.98
7.	ARG	(Juan Merlos, Carlos Alvarez, Roberto Breppe, Ernesto Contreras)	2:15:34.24
8.	GER	(Burkhard Ebert, Jürgen Tschan, Ortwin Czarnowski, Dieter Koslar)	2:15:37.25

The four Swedish silver medalists were all brothers. They won the world championship in 1967, 1968, and 1969. Three of them subsequently changed their last names from Pettersson to that of their home village, Fåglum.

1972 Munich T: 35, N: 35, D: 9.6.
100 KM

1.	SOV/RUS	(Boris Shukhov, Valery Yardy, Gennady Komnatov, Valery Likhachov)	2:11:17.8
2.	POL	(Lucjan Lis, Edward Barcik, Stanislaw Szozda, Ryszard Szurkowski)	2:11:47.5
3.	BEL	(Ludo Delcroix, Gustaaf Hermans, Gustaaf Van Cauter, Louis Verreydt)	2:12:36.7
4.	NOR	(Thorleif Andresen, Arve Haugen, Knut Knudsen, Magne Orre)	2:13:20.7
5.	SWE	(Lennart Fagerlund, Tord Filipsson, Leif Hansson, Sven-Åke Nilsson)	2:13:36.9
6.	HUN	(Tibor Decreceni, Imre Géra, József Peterman, András Takács)	2:14:18.8
7.	SWI	(Gilbert Bischoff, Bruno Hubschmid, Roland Schaer, Ulrich Sutter)	2:14:33.6
8.	ITA	(Osvaldo Castellan, Pasqualino Moretti, Francesco Moser, Giovanni Tonoli)	2:14:36.2

DISQ (Drugs): HOL (Fedor den Hertog, Hennie Kuiper, Cees Priem, Aad van den Hoek) 2:12:27.1

The Dutch team was disqualified after it was determined that one of their members, Aad van den Hoek, had taken

Coramine, a drug which was permitted by the International Cyclists' Union but forbidden by the International Olympic Committee. It was decided that the Belgian team would not be awarded bronze medals because its members had not been tested for drugs.

1976 Montreal T: 28, N: 28, D: 7.18.
100 KM

1.	SOV	(Anatoly Chukanov, Valery Chaplygin, Vladimir Kaminsky, Aavo Pikkuus)	2:08:53.
2.	POL	(Tadeusz Mytnik, Mieczyslaw Nowicki, Stanislaw Szozda, Ryszard Szurkowski)	2:09:13.
3.	DEN	(Verner Blaudzun, Gert Frank, Jörgen Hansen, Törgen Lund)	2:12:20.
4.	GER	(Hans-Peter Jakst, Olaf Paltian, Friedrich von Löffelholz, Peter Weibel)	2:12:35.
5.	CZE	(Petr Buchaček, Petr Matoušek, Milan Puzrla, Vladimir Vondraček)	2:12:56.
6.	GBR	(Paul Carbutt, Philip Griffiths, M. Dudley Hayton, F. William Nickson)	2:13:10.
7.	SWE	(Tord Filipsson, Bernt Johansson, Sven-Åke Nilsson, Tommy Prim)	2:13:13.
8.	NOR	(Stein Bråthen, Geir Digerud, Arne Klavenes, Magne Orre)	2:13:17.

1980 Moscow T: 23, N: 23, D: 7.20.
101 KM

1.	SOV	(Yuri Kashirin, Oleg Logvin, Sergei Shelpakov, Anatoly Yarkin)	2:01:21.7
2.	GDR	(Falk Boden, Bernd Drogan, Olaf Ludwig, Hans-Joachim Hartnick)	2:02:53.2
3.	CZE	(Michal Klasa, Vlastibor Konečný, Alipi Kostadinov, Jiří Škoda)	2:02:53.9
4.	POL	(Stefan Ciekanski, Jan Jankiewicz, Czeslaw Lang, Witold Plutecki)	2:04:13.8
5.	ITA	(Mauro De Pellegrin, Gianni Giacomini, Ivano Maffei, Alberto Minetti)	2:04:36.2
6.	BUL	(Borislav Assenov, Venelin Houbenov, Yordan Penchev, Nencho Staikov)	2:05:55.2
7.	FIN	(Harry Hannus, Kari Puisto, Patrick Wackstrom, Sixten Wackstrom)	2:05:58.2
8.	YUG	(Bruno Bilic, Vinko Poloncic, Bojan Ropret, Bojan Udović)	2:07:12.0

1984 Los Angeles T: 26, N: 26, D: 8.5.
100 KM

1.	ITA	(Marcello Bartalini, Marco Giovannetti, Eros Poli, Claudio Vandelli)	1:58.28
2.	SWI	(Alfred Achermann, Richard Trinkler, Laurent Vial, Benno Wiss)	2:02:38
3.	USA	(Ronald Kiefel, Roy Knickman, Davis Phinney, Andrew Weaver)	2:02:46
4.	HOL	(Johan Alberts, Erik Breukink, Martinus Ducrot, Gert Jakobs)	2:02:57
5.	SWE	(Bengt Asplund, Per Christiansson, Magnus Knutsson, Håkan Larsson)	2:04:46
6.	FRA	(Jean François Bernard, Philippe Bouvatier, Thierry Marie, Denis Prlizzari)	2:05:07
7.	DEN	(John Carlsen, Kim Jolin Eriksen, Lars Erik Jensen, Sören Liholt)	2:05:31

8.	GBR	(Steven Poulter, Keith Reynolds, Peter Sanders, Darryl Webster)	2:05:51

The Soviet Union surely would have been the gold medal favorite had their team not been prevented by their government from competing. The U.S.S.R. had won the last three Olympic team time trials as well as the 1983 world championship. However, as it turned out, they would have been hard-pressed to defeat the amazing Italians who, equipped with revolutionary spokeless carbon fiber disc wheels, completed the course in the fastest time ever recorded, despite losing 20 seconds while changing a wheel. Their winning margin of 4 minutes 10 seconds was unheard of at international-level competition.

The site of the race was one of the dullest venues in Olympic history—a 15½ mile concrete stretch of the Artesia Freeway between the Harbor Freeway and the Santa Ana Freeway. During the medal ceremony, the winning teams enjoyed the rare privilege of seeing their national flags raised in front of the Regal Plastic Company and a freeway exit sign for Avalon Blvd.

1988 Seoul T: 31, N: 31, D: 9.18.

1.	GDR	(Uwe Ampler, Mario Kummer, Maik Landsmann, Jan Schur)	1:57:47.7
2.	POL	(Joachim Halupczok, Zenon Jaskula, Marek Leśniewski, Andrzej Sypytkowski)	1:57:54.2
3.	SWE	(Björn Johansson, Jan Karlsson, Michel Lafis, Anders Jarl)	1:59:47.3
4.	FRA	(Laurent Bezault, Eric Heulot, Pascal Lance, Thierry Laurent)	1:59:49.8
5.	ITA	(Roberto Maggioni, Eros Poli, Mario Scirea, Flavio Vanzella)	1:59:58.3
6.	GER	(Ernst Christl, Bernd Gröne, Rajmund Lehnert, Remig Stumpf)	2:00:06.3
7.	SOV	(Vassily Zhdanov, Viktor Klimov, Asyat Saitov, Igor Sumnikov)	2:00:27.0
8.	CZE	(Vladimír Hruza, Vladimír Kinst, Milan Křen, Jozef Regec)	2:00:57.1

1992 Barcelona T: 30, N: 30, D: 7.26.

1.	GER	(Bernd Dittert, Christian Meyer, Uwe Peschel, Michael Rich)	2:01:39
2.	ITA	(Flavio Anastasia, Luca Colombo, Gianfranco Contri, Andrea Peron)	2:02:39
3.	FRA	(Hervé Boussard, Didier Faivre-Pierret, Philippe Gaumont, Jean-Louis Harel)	2:05:25
4.	SOV	(Igor Dzyuba, Oleg Galkin, Igor Pastukhovich, Igor Patenko)	2:05:34
5.	SPA	(Miguel Fernández Fernández, Álvaro González Gladeano, Eleuterio Mancebo Herrero, David Plaza Romero)	2:06:11
6.	POL	(Grzegorz Piwowarski, Andrzej Sypytkowski, Dariusz Baranowski, Marek Leśniewski)	2:06:34
7.	SWI	(Thomas Boutellier, Roland Meier, Beat Meister, Theodor Rinderknecht)	2:06:35
8.	CZE	(Jaroslav Bílek, Miroslav Lipták, Pavel Padrnos, František Trkal)	2:06:44

WOMEN

1000-METER MATCH SPRINT

1896–1984 not held

1988 Seoul C: 12, N: 12, D: 9.24. WR: 11.383 (Isabelle Gautheron)

		1ST RACE	2ND RACE	3RD RACE
1. Erika Salumäe	SOV/EST	—	12.00	12.58
2. Christa Luding-Rothenburger	GDR	11.68	—	—
3. Connie Young	USA			
4. Isabelle Gautheron	FRA			
5. Julie Speight	AUS			
6. Zhou Suying	CHN			
7. Louise Jones	GBR			
8. Yang Hsiu-Chen	TAI			

In 1984 Christa Rothenburger of Dresden won a gold medal in the 500-meter speed skating event in Sarajevo. In 1988, in Calgary, she missed another gold in the 500 by two one-hundredths of a second, but came back three days later to win the 1000-meter event. Eight years earlier, her coach, Ernst Luding, had persuaded her to take up cycling in the off-season. When she saw her first match sprint race she was terrified. "I was convinced that as soon as I tried to ride I would undoubtedly topple right over." Rothenburger learned quickly. But when asked to be allowed to enter competitions, East German sports officials turned her down and told her to stick to skating. She went over their heads and petitioned the president of East Germany's sports federation, Manfred Ewald, who gave her permission. At the 1986 world championships, her first international competition, she upset Estonian Erika Salumäe for the gold medal. Although Salumäe turned the tables in 1987, Rothenburger, who married Luding after Calgary, was on target to become the first person to win medals in the Winter and Summer Olympics in the same year.

In Seoul Luding-Rothenburger ensured her place in sports history by defeating Gautheron in the semifinals. She won the first race of the final and it looked like she might match Eddie Eagan's feat of winning Olympic championships in both winter and summer sports. But Salumäe outmaneuvered her twice in a row and Luding-Rothenburger ended up instead like Jacob Tullin: gold in winter, silver in summer.

1992 Barcelona C: 12, N: 12, D: 7.31. WR: 11.101 (Galina Yenyukhina)

		1ST RACE	2ND RACE	3RD RACE
1. Erika Salumäe	EST	—	12.667	12.244
2. Annett Neumann	GER	12.776	—	—
3. Ingrid Haringa	HOL	12.402	12.410	—
4. Felicia Ballanger	FRA	—	—	—
5. Galina Yenyukhina	RUS	12.575		
6. Tanya Dubnicoff	CAN	—		
7. Mika Kuroki	JPN	—		
8. Wang Yang	CHN	—		

As a member of the Soviet team, Erika Salumäe won the inaugural women's sprint in Seoul. When she returned to the Estonian capital of Tallinn, where she had been raised in an orphanage, she was welcomed as a hero. At the victory parade in her honor, one sign read OUR OWN TEAM IN BARCELONA IN 1992. Once upon a time, Estonia did have its own Olympic team, competing as an independent nation between 1920 and 1936 and winning 23 medals, 7 gold, 6 silver, and 10 bronze, most of them in wrestling and weightlifting. Then, in 1940, the Soviet Union annexed Estonia and those Estonian athletes who took part in the Olympics did so under the banner of the U.S.S.R. In 1988, at the time of Salumäe's victory parade, the idea of a separate Estonian Olympic team seemed a fantasy. But miracles do happen. Between Olympics, the Soviet Union disintegrated, Estonia declared its independence, and on July 25, 1992, Erika Salumäe and 36 other Estonian athletes marched behind the Estonian flag at the Opening Ceremony in Barcelona.

Salumäe faced stiff competition on the track. Although she had won the 1989 world championship, the political and economic chaos in her country made it difficult for her to train properly. One of her "rivals," Connie Paraskevin-Young, who had won the world championship in 1990 (not to mention 1982, 1983, and 1984), arranged for Salumäe to train once a year in the United States, but in the run-up to the Olympics, Salumäe was further handicapped by a back injury. Besides Paraskevin-Young, another favorite was Ingrid Haringa, a policewoman and ex-speed skater who switched to cycling and surprised everyone by winning the 1991 world championship only five months after taking up the sport. It was Haringa who set the standard in the qualification round with a time of 11.419. Salumäe and Paraskevin-Young recorded only the sixth and seventh best times in a field of twelve. The next round consisted of four heats with the winner of each heat advancing to the quarterfinals and the rest fighting it out in a *repêchage* round. Haringa and Salumäe went through, but Paraskevin-Young, although she finished first in her heat, was disqualified for interfering with Felicia Ballanger. The American was then eliminated by Annett Neumann after her own protest against the German rider was denied.

In the quarterfinals, Salumäe needed a tie-breaker to defeat world record holder Galina Yenyukhina. She had less trouble with Ballanger in the semifinals. The other semifinal, between Haringa and Neumann, turned out to be a dramatic struggle. Haringa won the first race but was disqualified in the second for passing too low on the inside. The winner of the next race would go on to the final. With a little over a lap to go, Haringa fell and a re-race was ordered. This time Neumann crashed. She almost fell again in the third try, but came from behind to win at last. Neumann also won the first race in the final, but Salumäe then took two in a row for the gold medal. It was an emotional moment at the award ceremony when the Estonian flag was raised at the Olympics for the first time in 56 years. Unfortunately, it was raised upside down. This blunder on the part of the Spanish officials failed to dampen Salumäe's enthusiasm. "The next time," she noted with a smile, "they will get it right."

3000-METER INDIVIDUAL PURSUIT

1896-1988 not held

1992 Barcelona C: 17, N: 17, D: 7.31. WR: 3:38.190 (Jeannie Longo)

1. Petra Rossner	GER	3:41.753
2. Kathryn Watt	AUS	3:43.438
3. Rebecca Twigg	USA	3:52.429
4. Hanne Malmberg	DEN	3:53.516
5. Jeannie Longo Ciprelli	FRA	3:46.547
6. Svetlana Samokhvalova	RUS	3:47.444
7. Tea Vikstedt-Nyman	FIN	3:48.918
8. Leontien van Moorsel	HOL	3:49.795

During the 1980s, before the women's pursuit was included in the Olympics, the event was dominated by two riders: Rebecca Twigg of the United States and Jeannie Longo of France. Twigg won the world championship in 1982, 1984, 1985, and 1987; Longo in 1986, 1988, and 1989. Then they both retired. But when the news came that the pursuit was being added to the Olympic program in Barcelona, both Twigg and Longo returned to the track. They faced each other prematurely—in the quarterfinals. Twigg led by 0.306 seconds with 750 meters to go. Gradually, Longo closed the gap, moving ahead by 0.110 with only one lap remaining. With a half lap to go Longo's lead was down to 0.009. Twigg barely edged ahead to win 3:46.508 to 3:46.549—a difference of four one-hundredths of a second. Twigg was no match for Kathy Watt in the semifinals, but she did earn a bronze medal as the faster semifinal loser. In the final, Watt tried to shake the defending world champion, Petra Rossner, by rocketing off the mark and building a lead of 2.323 seconds. But Rossner ignored her, kept to her own pace, took the lead with 2½ laps to go, and won going away.

POINTS RACE

The rules for the women's points race are the same as those for the men's except that the distance is 24 kilometers.

This event will be held for the first time in 1996.

ROAD TIME TRIAL

The rules for the women's road time trial are the same as those for the men's except that the course is between 25 and 35 kilometers long.

This event will be held for the first time in 1996.

ROAD RACE

1896–1980 not held

1984 Los Angeles-Mission Viejo C: 45, N; 16, D: 7.29.
79.2 KM

1. Connie Carpenter-Phinney	USA	2:11:14
2. Rebecca Twigg	USA	2:11:14
3. Sandra Schumacher	GER	2:11:14
4. Unni Larsen	NOR	2:11:14
5. Maria Canins	ITA	2:11:14
6. Jeannie Longo	FRA	2:12:35
7. Helle Sörensen	DEN	2:13:28
8. Ute Enzenauer	GER	2:13:28

At the age of 14, Connie Carpenter had competed at the 1972 Winter Olympics in Sapporo, finishing seventh in the 1500-meter speed skating event. An ankle injury forced her to switch to cycling four years later. She gave up the sport for rowing, but returned to the track in 1981, dominating U.S. women's cycling until the arrival of another early achiever, Rebecca Twigg of Seattle, Wash. Twigg's early achievements were not athletic, but academic. After completing 8th grade, the 14-year-old Twigg skipped four years of secondary schooling and went straight to the University of Washington, where she studied biology.

In 1982, when she was 19, Twigg beat Carpenter to become the world pursuit champion. She did not defend her championship, preferring to concentrate on road racing, since that would be the only women's cycling event

Connie Carpenter-Phinney (foreground) edges ahead of Rebecca Twigg in the last second of the 1984 women's road race.

contested at the Los Angeles Olympics. In her absence, Carpenter took the world pursuit title despite competing less than two months after breaking her arm.

In the Olympic road race, six women broke away at the mid-point. With 800 meters to go, Jeannie Longo clashed wheels with Maria Canins, causing her rear derailleur to break and her chain to come off. The remaining five prepared for the final sprint. Canins took off first, 500 meters from the finish. Schumacher, a 17-year-old surprise, was the next to make her move. With 200 meters to go it was the turn of Carpenter and Twigg. Twigg seemed to have a decisive lead at the 100-meter mark and Carpenter thought she had lost the gold as late as the 50-meter mark. But she sped on, caught Twigg a mere three meters from the finish line and, using a technique which she had practiced every day for a month, she threw her bike forward and won by less than half a wheel.

Carpenter's husband, Davis Phinney, who had taught her the bike-throw move, also competed at the 1984 Olympics, finishing fifth in the men's road race and earning a bronze medal in the team time trial.

1988 Seoul C: 53, N: 23, D: 9.26.
82 KM

1. Monique Knol	HOL	2:00:52
2. Jutta Niehaus	GER	2:00:52
3. Laima Zilporite	SOV/LIT	2:00:52
4. Genevieve Brunet	CAN	2:00:52
5. Valentyna Yevpak	SOV/UKR	2:00:52
6. Maria Blower	GBR	2:00:52
7. Marie Höljer	SWE	2:00:52
8. Inga Benedict	USA	2:00:52

Until the very end, this was a dull race inspired by a dull course. The only attempt at a break came from Inga Benedict with about 5 kilometers to go. But she was hauled in by the heavy favorite, Jeannie Longo, who took the pack with her. Longo, still recovering from a hip fracture and bruise, eventually finished twenty-first. As they neared the finish line, 45 of the 53 starters were still in a pack. With 400 meters to go, 24-year-old substitute teacher Monique Knol, as she put it, "saw a little hole—

schwoook—I went away and that was it. I sprinted by myself."

1992 Barcelona-Sant Sadurní.d'Anoia C: 57, N: 26, D: 7.26.
81 KM

1. Kathryn Watt	AUS	2:04.42
2. Jeannie Longo Ciprelli	FRA	2:05.02
3. Monique Knol	HOL	2:05.03
4. Natalya Kyschuk	UKR	2:05.03
5. Monica Valvik	NOR	2:05.03
6. Jeanne Golay	USA	2:05.03
7. Kathleen Shannon	AUS	2:05.03
8. Luzia Zberg	SWI	2:05.03

Three kilometers from the finish line Jeannie Longo, four-time world champion, three-time winner of the women's Tour de France, pulled away from the pack, took a lead of 100 meters, and never looked behind her. Attacking for the rest of the race, she crossed the finish line one second ahead of defending champion Monique Knol and 29 other riders. It was a classic, gutsy performance by Longo, who had finally earned the one prize that was missing from her trophy collection: an Olympic gold medal. The French team raised their arms in triumph. There was only one problem: the real winner, 5-foot ½-inch (1.54 meters) Kathy Watt, had already crossed the finish line 20 seconds earlier. With one ten-mile circuit to go, Watt slipped away from the main pack while another rider was coming back, and many riders didn't see her go. Watt took off after the two leaders, Maria Turcotto of Italy and Marie Purvis of Great Britain, and rode right past them without hesitating. She opened a 38-second lead and won handily. Like Longo, Watt, a 27-year-old from the small town of Warragul, did not know what place she was in. She was so dizzy when she crossed the finish that when she looked up and saw two riders nearby, she thought she had finished third. (The other two had failed to finish and were waiting for teammates.)

CROSS-COUNTRY RACE

This event will be held for the first time in 1996.

DIVING

MEN
Springboard
Platform
Discontinued Event

WOMEN
Springboard
Platform

Diving Terms

Positions

Straight—body remains straight
Pike—body bent at the waist with legs straight
Tuck—body bent at the knees and hips with the knees held together against the chest
Free—a combination of positions used in twisting dives

Categories

Forward—body facing forward and dive made forward
Backward—back to the water, rotating away from the board
Reverse—facing forward, rotating back toward the board
Inward—back to the water, rotating back toward the board
Forward with a twist—body facing forward and twisting in the air
Armstand—the diver begins with a steady handstand on the edge of the board (used in the platform event only)

MEN

SPRINGBOARD DIVING

This event is performed from a springboard three meters (9 feet 10 inches) above the water. The easiest dive, with a coefficient of 1.4, is a simple forward dive in the tuck position. The most difficult, with a coefficient of 3.6, is the back 1½ somersault with 4½ twists free. The scores of the seven judges are multiplied by a coefficient that is determined by the degree of difficulty of the attempted dive. Olympic competitions begin with a preliminary round. Between 1968 and 1992 the top twelve divers then advanced to the final, which in 1992 consisted of 11 dives—five required and six voluntary. In 1996 a new system will be used: the top 18 divers in the preliminary will advance to a semifinal. The top 12 semifinalists will go on to the final. Scores in the semifinal will be added to scores in the final to determine the winners. The semifinal in the men's springboard will comprise five dives with a total degree of difficulty not to exceed 9.5. The final will comprise six dives with unlimited degree of difficulty.

1896–1906 not held

1908 London C: 23, N: 8, D: 7.18.

			PTS.
1.	Albert Zürner	GER	85.5
2.	Kurt Behrens	GER	85.3
3.	George Gaidzik	USA	80.8
3.	Gottlob Walz	GER	80.8

1912 Stockholm C: 18, N: 7, D: 7.9.

			ORDINALS	PTS.
1.	Paul Günther	GER	6	79.23
2.	Hans Luber	GER	9	76.78
3.	Kurt Behrens	GER	22	73.73
4.	Albert Zürner	GER	23	73.33
5.	Robert Zimmerman	CAN	24	72.54
6.	Herbert Pott	GBR	28	71.45
7.	John Jansson	SWE	32	69.64
8.	George Gaidzik	USA	36	68.01

1920 Antwerp C: 14, N: 9, D: 8.27.

			ORDINALS	PTS.
1.	Louis Kuehn	USA	6	675.4
2.	Clarence Pinkston	USA	11	655.3
3.	Louis Balbach	USA	15	649.5
4.	Gustaf Blomgren	SWE	19	587.05
5.	Gunnar Ekstrand	SWE	27	559.25
6.	Johan Jansson	SWE	27	544.75

1924 Paris C: 17, N: 9, D: 7.17.

			ORDINALS	PTS.
1.	Albert White	USA	7	696.4
2.	Ulise "Pete" Desjardins	USA	8	693.2
3.	Clarence Pinkston	USA	15	653.0
4.	Edmund Lindmark	SWE	22	599.1
5.	Richmond Eve	AUS	26	564.3
6.	Adolf Hellqvist	SWE	30	544.9
7.	Kurt Sjöberg	SWE	34	538.3
8.	Hendrik Hemsing	HOL	39	490.8

A recent graduate of Stanford University, 29-year-old Albert White was the first diver in Olympic history to win both the springboard and platform events.

1928 Amsterdam C: 24, N: 15, D: 8.8.

			ORDINALS	PTS.
1.	Ulise "Pete" Desjardins	USA	5	185.04
2.	Michael Galitzen (Mickey Riley)	USA	14	174.06
3.	Farid Simaika	EGY	13	172.46
4.	Harold Smith	USA	18	168.96

Pete Desjardins (center), who won both diving events in 1928, with Al White and Johnny Weissmuller.

5. Arthur Mund	GER	29.5	154.72
6. Ewald Riebschläger	GER	31	153.86
7. Heinz Plumanns	GER	32.5	150.18
8. Alfred Phillips	CAN	37	149.48

Born in Canada, and raised from the age of 10 in Miami Beach, 5-foot 3-inch Pete Desjardins was a graduate of Stanford University. In Amsterdam, Desjardins received tens for two of his dives, a half gainer and a gainer 1½. He later turned professional and was billed as "The Little Bronze Statue from the Land of Real Estate, Grapefruits and Alligators."

Galitzen was awarded the silver medal over Simaika, even though he had more ordinals, because three of the five judges ranked him higher than Simaika.

1932 Los Angeles C: 13, N: 7, D: 8.8.

		PTS.
1. Michael Galitzen (Mickey Riley)	USA	161.38
2. Harold Smith	USA	158.54

3. Richard Degener	USA	151.82
4. Alfred Phillips	CAN	134.64
5. Leo Esser	GER	134.30
6. Kazuo Kobayashi	JPN	133.76
7. Emile Poussard	FRA	128.66
8. Tetsutaro Namae	JPN	125.18

1936 Berlin C: 24, N: 15, D: 8.11.

		PTS.
1. Richard Degener	USA	163.57
2. Marshall Wayne	USA	159.56
3. Albert Greene	USA	146.29
4. Tsuneo Shibahara	JPN	144.92
5. Erhard Weiss	GER	141.24
6. Leo Esser	GER	137.99
7. Winfried Marauhn	GER	134.61
8. Tomio Koyanagi	JPN	133.07

Dick Degener's margin of victory was provided by an almost perfect full twist with a one and a half somersault. He was awarded a score of 19.55. Wayne attempted the same dive but earned only 15.54 points.

1948 London C: 26, N: 15, D: 8.3.

		PTS.
1. Bruce Harlan	USA	163.64
2. Miller Anderson	USA	157.29
3. Samuel Lee	USA	145.52
4. Joaquin Capilla Pérez	MEX	141.79
5. Raymond Mulinghausen	FRA	126.55
6. Svante Johansson	SWE	120.20
7. Kamal Hassan	EGY	119.90
8. Thomas Christiansen	DEN	114.59

Miller Anderson culminated a long comeback in London by earning the first of two silver medals. A highly decorated pilot in the army air corps during World War II, Anderson was shot down over Italy. His leg was almost torn off by the plane's tail. He spent a month in a German hospital until it was captured by United States troops. An operation at a United States Army hospital left him with silver plates attached to his left thigh bone. After a four-year absence, Anderson returned to competition in 1946. In 1966 he died of a heart attack, at the age of 42. Gold medalist Bruce Harlan also died young. On June 21, 1959, when he was 33 years old, Harlan took part in an exhibition in Fairfield, Connecticut. Following the performance, Harlan was helping dismantle the scaffolding of the diving tower when he fell 27 feet to his death.

1952 Helsinki C: 36, N: 20, D: 7.28.

		PTS.
1. David "Skippy" Browning	USA	205.29
2. Miller Anderson	USA	199.84
3. Robert Clotworthy	USA	184.92
4. Joaquin Capilla Pérez	MEX	178.33
5. Roman Brener	SOV	165.63
6. Milton Busin	BRA	155.91

7. Anthony Turner	GBR	151.90
8. Aleksei Zigalov	SOV/RUS	151.31

The divers were somewhat distracted by the presence of too many people near the board, including a photographer in a frogman outfit who actually stationed himself *in* the pool. After his victory, Skippy Browning was arrested for shinnying up a flag pole in Helsinki and trying to steal an Olympic flag. A navy jet pilot, Browning was killed in a crash in Kansas on March 14, 1956. He was 23 years old.

1956 Melbourne C: 24, N: 19, D: 8.29.

		PTS.
1. Robert Clotworthy	USA	159.56
2. Donald Harper	USA	156.23
3. Joaquin Capilla Pérez	MEX	150.69
4. Glen Whitten	USA	148.55
5. Gennady Udalov	SOV	140.64
6. Roman Brener	SOV	139.14
7. Gunther Mund	CHI	137.53
8. József Gerlach	HUN	136.08

1960 Rome C: 32, N: 19, D: 8.29.

		PTS.
1. Gary Tobian	USA	170.00
2. Samuel Hall	USA	167.08
3. Juan Botella	MEX	162.30
4. Alvaro Gaxiola	MEX	150.42
5. Ernest Meissner	CAN	144.07
6. Lamberto Mari	ITA	143.97
7. Toshio Yamano	JPN	140.46
8. Hans-Dieter Pophal	GDR	133.95

After the preliminary round, one judge, a Soviet woman, was replaced for being overly nationalistic in her scoring. Silver medalist Sam Hall gained dubious international fame in December 1986, when he was arrested as a freelance spy in Nicaragua. Hall, who once served in the Ohio House of Representatives, described himself as a "self-employed military advisor and counterterrorist." He was subsequently released by the Nicaraguan government, who declared him a victim of mental illness.

1964 Tokyo C: 27, N: 16, D: 10.14.

		PTS.
1. Kenneth Sitzberger	USA	159.90
2. Francis Gorman	USA	157.63
3. Larry Andreasen	USA	143.77
4. Hans-Dieter Pophal	GDR	142.58
5. Göran Lundqvist	SWE	138.65
6. Boris Polulyakh	SOV/GEO	138.64
7. Mikhail Safonov	SOV/RUS	134.00
8. Vladimir Vasin	SOV/RUS	133.48

Navy Lieutenant Frank Gorman actually outscored Ken Sitzberger on nine of his ten dives. But he missed badly with his ninth round back, two-and-a-half somersault tuck, and lost 11.20 points. In 1988, toward the end of the Seoul Olympics, 1964 bronze medalist Larry An-

dreasen, then 42 years old, dived 160 feet from the center of the Gerald Desmond Bridge in Long Beach, California. Andreasen was under the mistaken impression that he was breaking the record for the highest dive. In fact, the record was 174 feet 8 inches. He survived the dive uninjured, but was arrested.

1968 Mexico City C: 28, N: 16, D: 10.20.

		PTS.
1. Bernard Wrightson	USA	170.15
2. Klaus Dibiasi	ITA	159.74
3. James Henry	USA	158.09
4. Luis Niño de Rivera	MEX	155.71
5. Franco Giorgio Cagnotto	ITA	155.70
6. Keith Russell	USA	151.75
7. Tord Anderson	SWE	151.50
8. Donald Wagstaff	AUS	150.18

Bernie Wrightson moved up from third place to first with his last three dives.

1972 Munich C: 32, N: 16, D: 8.30.

		PTS.
1. Vladimir Vasin	SOV/RUS	594.09
2. Franco Giorgio Cagnotto	ITA	591.63
3. Craig Lincoln	USA	577.29
4. Klaus Dibiasi	ITA	559.05
5. Michael Finneran	USA	557.34
6. Vyacheslav Strahov	SOV/RUS	556.20
7. Falk Hoffmann	GDR	544.95
8. Norbert Huda	GER	524.16

The U.S. string of eleven straight springboard victories was finally broken. The next to last dive was the decisive one. Cagnotto missed and was awarded only 48.72 points, while Vasin recorded 75.60 points, the highest score of the competition. Vasin finished eighth in 1964 and eleventh in 1968.

1976 Montreal C: 30, N: 16, D: 7.22.

		PTS.
1. Philip Boggs	USA	619.05
2. Franco Giorgio Cagnotto	ITA	570.48
3. Aleksandr Kosenkov	SOV/BLR	567.24
4. Falk Hoffmann	GDR	553.53
5. Robert Cragg	USA	548.19
6. Gregory Louganis	USA	528.96
7. Carlos Giron	MEX	523.59
8. Klaus Dibiasi	ITA	516.18

1980 Moscow C: 24, N: 16, D: 7.23.

		PTS.
1. Aleksandr Portnov	SOV/BLR	905.025
2. Carlos Giron	MEX	892.140
3. Franco Giorgio Cagnotto	ITA	871.500
4. Falk Hoffmann	GDR	858.510
5. Aleksandr Kosenkov	SOV/BLR	855.120
6. Christopher Snode	GBR	844.470
7. Vyacheslav Troshin	SOV/RUS	820.050
8. Ricardo Camacho	SPA	749.340

Aleksandr Portnov's victory was clouded by controversy. Distracted by the noise of the crowd watching the final of the men's 100-meter butterfly, Portnov turned a two-and-a-half backward somersault into a belly flop. He immediately protested and was awarded a re-dive, which he hit beautifully. Giron, Cagnotto, and Hoffman objected, claiming that they had been subjected to similar distractions. Hoffman was particularly annoyed, since his later claim that one of his dives had been disrupted by a photographer's flash was denied. The medal ceremony was delayed for two days until a final decision was announced by the International Amateur Swimming Federation (F.I.N.A). In Mexico City demonstrations were held outside the Soviet embassy to protest the ruling.

1984 Los Angeles C: 30, N: 19, D: 8.8.
1. Gregory Louganis   USA   754.41
2. Tan Liangde   CHN   662.31
3. Ronald Merriott   USA   661.32
4. Li Hongping   CHN   646.35
5. Christopher Snode   GBR   609.51
6. Piero Italiani   ITA   578.94
7. Albin Killat   GER   569.52
8. Stephen Foley   AUS   561.93

Of Samoan and northern European ancestry, Greg Louganis was given up for adoption by his 15-year-old parents. Like so many future Olympic champions, Louganis suffered through a difficult childhood. Taunted by his classmates in El Cajon, California, he was called "retarded" because he was dyslexic, and "nigger" because he had dark skin. He began smoking tobacco when he was 9 years old and marijuana when he was 12. When he turned 13, he kicked his adoptive mother in the chest, injuring her. His parents turned him over to the police. As a teenager Louganis depended so heavily on alcohol that he considered himself an alcoholic. But Louganis survived these hard times by escaping into the world of diving. He was so good that he qualified for the Montreal Olympics at the age of 16. He finished sixth in the springboard event and second in the platform. Favored to win two gold medals at the 1980 Olympics, he was shut out by the U.S. boycott, but accomplished the feat instead at the 1982 world championships. In 1984 he performed brilliantly despite the heavy pressure of being the overwhelming favorite. His winning margin of over 94 points was unprecedented in Olympic history.

1988 Seoul C: 35, N: 23, D: 9.20.

		PTS.
1. Gregory Louganis	USA	730.80
2. Tan Liangde	CHN	704.88
3. Li Deliang	CHN	665.28
4. Albin Killat	GER	661.47
5. Mark Bradshaw	USA	642.99
6. Jorge Mondragón Vázquez	MEX	616.02
7. Jesús Mena	MEX	598.77
8. Edwin Jongejans	HOL	588.33

Greg Louganis hits his head on the board during the 1988 springboard diving competition.

Greg Louganis won 19 consecutive international springboard competitions between 1982 and 1987. Then, in 1988, he was beaten twice by Tan Liangde, who had been studying videotapes of Louganis for 6 years. In Seoul, Louganis was leading the preliminary round when he stepped onto the board for his ninth dive, a reverse two and a half somersault in the pike position. The defending Olympic champion leapt into the air, but failed to push out far enough. When he came down, he hit his head on the board and fell clumsily into the water. It was not Louganis' first confrontation with diving danger. Once, in 1976, he hit the bottom of the platform and ended up with two black eyes and a bloody nose. In 1979 in Tbilisi in Soviet Georgia he hit the top of the platform and was knocked unconscious. He had to be rescued from the pool. He woke up 20 minutes later surrounded by doctors. In 1981 he broke his collarbone when he hit the bottom of a pool. In 1984 he became disoriented during a platform dive in New Zealand and landed on his back. In 1987, at the U.S. Indoor Championship, in an incident eerily similar to the one in Seoul, he came within an inch or two of hitting the springboard on a reverse one and a half in the layout position.

In Seoul, Louganis climbed out of the pool unassisted. Four temporary sutures were applied to his head and, incredibly, 35 minutes later he was back on the board ready for his next dive: another reverse somersault. He scored 87.12 points, the highest score by any diver in the preliminaries. After qualifying for the final with his last dive, he was taken to the hospital where the sutures were replaced by five mattress stitches and a waterproof patch.

The next day, despite great pressure from Tan, Louganis hit all 11 of his dives—including the one he had botched in the preliminaries—and earned his third gold medal.

One week later Louganis won another gold medal in the platform event. As he came out of the water, an international television audience watched as he sobbed in the arms of his coach, Ron O'Brien, who whispered to him words unheard. Most people assumed that Louganis was crying because he had won a close contest with the final dive of his career. Although this was a contributing factor to the release of Louganis' emotion, there was much more to the story.

What O'Brien had said to Louganis in those touching moments was, "Nobody will ever know what we've been through." For over six years this was true. But in 1995 Louganis went public with the full story. Six months before the Olympics Louganis learned that he had tested HIV-positive and that he might already have AIDS. By the time he got to Seoul, he was taking the drug AZT every four hours and was frightened that teammates might hear the alarm that woke him in the middle of each night so that he wouldn't miss a dose. When a fellow diver asked about the pills he popped all day long, Louganis told him they were aspirins for a sore shoulder. Only Ron O'Brien and a handful of others knew that Louganis was HIV-positive. When Louganis hit his head on his ninth dive of the springboard prelims, he felt blood on his head and was horrified that he might have bled in the pool, possibly infecting other divers. He later learned that the water would have diluted his blood enough to keep it from being dangerous. But he did risk contaminating two other people. Ron O'Brien, who was aware that Louganis was HIV-positive, wiped away a trickle of blood on Louganis' neck so that his Chinese rivals wouldn't see it and gain confidence. Dr. Jim Puffer, who treated Louganis' wound and sewed the sutures, did not know about Louganis' condition. Both O'Brien and Puffer later took AIDS tests that proved negative.

1992 Barcelona C: 32, N: 22, D: 7.29.

			PTS.
1.	Mark Lenzi	USA	676.53
2.	Tan Liangde	CHN	645.57
3.	Dmitri Sautin	RUS	627.78
4.	Michael Murphy	AUS	611.97
5.	Kent Ferguson	USA	609.12
6.	Jorge Mondragón Vázquez	MEX	604.14
7.	Edwin Jongejans	HOL	581.40
8.	Valery Statsenko	UKR	577.92

Mark Lenzi of Federicksburg, Virginia, didn't begin diving until, at the age of 16, he watched Greg Louganis performing on television at the 1984 Olympics. Until that time Lenzi had been a wrestler. Seven years later he became the first person to earn over 100 points on a single dive when he earned 101.85 points for a reverse 3½ somersault tuck at the 1991 United States Indoor Championship.

In the Barcelona final, Albin Killat of Germany held a slight lead over Tan Liangde and Lenzi. But then Killat slipped as he began his seventh dive, belly-flopping a forward 3½ somersault pike. Instantly, he dropped from first place to last (he ended up tenth), and Lenzi sprang into the lead. By day's end Lenzi had earned the three highest scores of the competition, leaving Tan with his third consecutive silver medal.

PLATFORM DIVING

This event is staged from a rigid platform ten meters (32 feet 9¾ inches) above the water. In 1996 the semifinalists will perform four dives with a total degree of difficulty not to exceed 7.6. The finalists will perform six dives with unlimited degree of difficulty.

1896–1900 not held

1904 St. Louis C: 5, N: 2, D: 9.7.

			PTS.
1.	George Sheldon	USA	12.66
2.	Georg Hoffmann	GER	11.66
3.	Alfred Braunschweiger	GER	11.33
3.	Frank Kehoe	USA	11.33
5.	Otto Hooff	GER	—

The German team protested Sheldon's victory, but their protest was rejected by James Sullivan, the U.S. official in charge. Kehoe and Braunschweiger tied, and a dive-off was ordered. Braunschweiger refused to take part, so Kehoe was awarded third place. Most Olympic historians credit Braunschweiger with a share of third anyway. Apparently the Americans and Germans disagreed as to what constituted a proper dive. The Americans felt that the manner in which a diver hit the water was important, while the Germans, who attempted more difficult dives but tended to land on their stomachs and chests, contended that landings didn't matter.

1906 Athens C: 24, N: 8, D: 4.26.

			PTS.
1.	Gottlob Walz	GER	156.0
2.	Georg Hoffmann	GER	150.2
3.	Otto Satzinger	AUT	147.4
4.	Albert Zürner	GER	144.6
5.	Gordan Melville Clarke	GBR	144.0
6.	Hjalmar Johansson	SWE	143.4
7.	Robert Andersson	SWE	142.2
8.	Fritz Nicolai	GER	138.0

1908 London C: 23, N: 6, D: 7.24.

			PTS.
1.	Hjalmar Johansson	SWE	83.75
2.	Karl Malmström	SWE	78.73
3.	Arvid Spångberg	SWE	74.00
4.	Robert Andersson	SWE	68.30
5.	George Gaidzik	USA	56.30

1912 Stockholm D: 21, N: 6, D: 7.15.

			ORDINALS	PTS.
1.	Erik Adlerz	SWE	7	73.94
2.	Albert Zürner	GER	10	72.60
3.	Gustaf Blomgren	SWE	16	69.56
4.	Hjalmar Johansson	SWE	22	67.80
5.	George Yvon	GBR	22	67.66
6.	Harald Arbin	SWE	31	62.62
7.	Albin Carlsson	SWE	32	63.16
8.	Toivo Aro	FIN	40	57.05

1920 Antwerp C: 15, N: 7, D: 8.29.

			ORDINALS	PTS.
1.	Clarence Pinkston	USA	7	503.3
2.	Erik Adlerz	SWE	10	495.4
3.	Harry Prieste	USA	16	468.66
4.	Gustaf Blomgren	SWE	23	453.8
5.	Yngve Johnson	SWE	27	441.8
6.	Louis Balbach	USA	28	424.0
7.	Adolfo Wellisch	BRA	29	423.8

1924 Paris C: 20, N: 10, D: 7.20.

			ORDINALS	PTS.
1.	Albert White	USA	9	97.46
2.	David Fall	USA	11.5	97.30
3.	Clarence Pinkston	USA	16.5	94.60
4.	Erik Adlerz	SWE	19	93.78
5.	Eugène Lenormand	FRA	24	87.54
6.	Helge Öberg	SWE	31	85.80
7.	Svend Palle Sorensen	DEN	36	80.92
8.	Adolf Hellqvist	SWE	37.5	80.64

1928 Amsterdam C: 24, N: 12, D: 8.11.

			ORDINALS	PTS.
1.	Ulise "Pete" Desjardins	USA	6	98.74
2.	Farid Simaika	EGY	9	99.58
3.	Michael Galitzen (Mickey Riley)	USA	15	92.34
4.	Walter Colbath	USA	21	87.78
5.	Ewald Riebschläger	GER	27	82.44
6.	Karl Schumm	GER	28	80.54
7.	Alfred Phillips	CAN	35	77.26
8.	Albert Reginald Knight	GBR	41	72.22

Simaika was originally announced as the winner, and the Egyptian national anthem was played. Then it was declared that a mistake had been made, that ordinals (place-figures), not total points, determined the winner. Consequently, Desjardins was given his second gold medal. In fact, only one of the five judges ranked Simaika ahead of Desjardins. Simaika and Desjardins later gave diving exhibitions together in Europe. In March 1942, Simaika became a United States citizen. He joined the United States Army Air Corps as a pilot and was shot down over New Guinea.

1932 Los Angeles C: 8, N: 5, D: 8.13.

			PTS.
1.	Harold "Dutch" Smith	USA	124.80
2.	Michael Galitzen (Mickey Riley)	USA	124.28
3.	Frank Kurtz	USA	121.98
4.	Josef Staudinger	AUT	103.44
5.	Carlos Curiel	MEX	83.82
6.	Jesús Flores Albo	MEX	77.94
7.	Alfred Phillips	CAN	77.10
8.	Hidekatsu Ishida	JPN	75.92

1936 Berlin C: 26, N: 15, D: 8.15.

			PTS.
1.	Marshall Wayne	USA	113.58
2.	Elbert Root	USA	110.60
3.	Hermann Stork	GER	110.31
4.	Erhard Weiss	GER	110.15
5.	Frank Kurtz	USA	108.61
6.	Tsuneo Shibahara	JPN	107.40
7.	Siegfried Viebahn	GER	105.00
8.	Tomio Koyanagi	JPN	94.54

1948 London C: 25, N: 15, D: 8.5.

			PTS.
1.	Samuel Lee	USA	130.05
2.	Bruce Harlan	USA	122.30
3.	Joaquin Capilla Pérez	MEX	113.52
4.	Lennart Brunnhage	SWE	108.62
5.	Peter Heatly	GBR	105.29
6.	Thomas Christiansen	DEN	105.22
7.	Raymond Mulinghausen	FRA	103.01
8.	George Athans	CAN	100.91

Sammy Lee was a 28-year-old Korean-American army doctor. For his last dive he chose a forward three and a half somersault. Once, when performing a similar dive, he had mistaken the sky for the water and pulled out too soon. Now with the Olympic title on the line, he was afraid he would repeat the mistake. "I dove, hit the water, felt numb and tingling and decided: 'I did a belly flop.'" When he popped out of the water he discovered that, far from belly-flopping, his dive had been rated almost perfect. "I just walked on water out of that pool," he later recalled. Lee was the first male Asian-American Olympic medalist.

1952 Helsinki C: 31, N: 17, D: 8.1.

			PTS.
1.	Samuel Lee	USA	156.28
2.	Joaquin Capilla Pérez	MEX	145.21
3.	Günther Haase	GER	141.31
4.	John McCormack	USA	138.74
5.	Alberto Capilla Pérez	MEX	136.44
6.	Rodolfo Perea	MEX	128.28
7.	Aleksandr Bakatin	SOV	126.86
8.	Roman Brener	SOV	126.31

Sammy Lee celebrated his 32nd birthday by winning his second gold medal.

1956 Melbourne C: 22, N: 10, D: 12.6.

			PTS.
1.	Joaquin Capilla Pérez	MEX	152.44
2.	Gary Tobian	USA	152.41
3.	Richard Connor	USA	149.79
4.	József Gerlach	HUN	149.25
5.	Roman Brener	SOV	142.95
6.	William Farrell	USA	139.12
7.	Ferenc Siák	HUN	138.83
8.	Mikhail Chachba	SOV	134.51

Third in 1948 and second in 1952, Capilla, a 27-year-old architect, completed his set of platform diving medals by executing a superb forward one and a half somersault with a double twist on his final dive. The highest-scored dive of the competition, it gave Capilla a 0.03 point edge over Tobian. The U.S. team lodged a protest against the Soviet and Hungarian judges, but F.I.N.A. Secretary Bertil Sallfors rejected the complaint, explaining, "There can be no protests against the judges." Soviet judge Eva Bozd-Morskaya had given Gary Tobian an average score of 6.35, while his average overall score had been 7.3. On the other hand, she had scored Mikhail Chachba 7.38, while *his* overall average had been 6.37. This incident led to a change in the rules which allowed individual judges to be eliminated because of incompetence.

1960 Rome C: 28, N: 18, D: 9.2.

			PTS.
1. Robert Webster	USA		165.56
2. Gary Tobian	USA		165.25
3. Brian Phelps	GBR		157.13
4. Roberto Madrigal Garcia	MEX		152.86
5. Rolf Sperling	GDR		151.83
6. Gennady Galkin	SOV/RUS		141.69
7. Fritz Enskat	GER		138.86
8. Anatoly Sysoyev	SOV/RUS		135.59

Webster moved from third place to first with his last three dives.

1964 Tokyo C: 30, N: 16, D: 10.18.

			PTS.
1. Robert Webster	USA		148.58
2. Klaus Dibiasi	ITA		147.54
3. Thomas Gompf	USA		146.57
4. Roberto Madrigal Garcia	MEX		144.27
5. Viktor Palagin	SOV/RUS		143.77
6. Brian Phelps	GBR		143.18
7. Rolf Sperling	GDR		142.24
8. Toshio Otsubo	JPN		142.05

This time Webster was only in sixth place with three dives to go, but still managed to withstand the pressure and successfully defend his championship.

1968 Mexico City C: 35, N: 17, D: 10.26.

			PTS.
1. Klaus Dibiasi	ITA		164.18
2. Alvaro Gaxiola	MEX		154.49
3. Edwin Young	USA		153.93
4. Keith Russell	USA		152.34
5. José Robinson	MEX		143.62
6. Lothar Matthes	GDR		141.75
7. Luis Niño de Rivera	MEX		141.16
8. Franco Giorgio Cagnotto	ITA		138.89

Coached by his father, Carlo, who had finished tenth in the 1936 Olympics, Klaus Dibiasi of Bolzano practiced between 130 and 150 dives a day, six days a week. In Mexico City, Dibiasi began his amazing Olympic winning

Klaus Dibiasi won an unprecedented three consecutive gold medals in the platform diving competitions of 1968, 1972, and 1976. He also earned a silver medal in 1964.

streak by becoming the first Italian ever to win a gold medal in a swimming or diving event.

1972 Munich C: 35, N: 18, D: 9.4.

			PTS.
1. Klaus Dibiasi	ITA		504.12
2. Richard Rydze	USA		480.75
3. Franco Giorgio Cagnotto	ITA		475.83
4. Lothar Matthes	GDR		465.75
5. David Ambartsumyan	SOV/ARM	463.56
6. Richard Early	USA		462.45
7. Vladimir Kapirulin	SOV/RUS		459.21
8. Carlos Giron	MEX		442.41

1976 Montreal C: 25, N: 14 D: 7.27.

			PTS.
1. Klaus Dibiasi	ITA		600.51
2. Gregory Louganis	USA		576.99
3. Vladimir Aleynik	SOV/BLR		548.61
4. Kent Vosler	USA		544.14
5. Patrick Moore	USA		538.17
6. Falk Hoffmann	GDR		531.60
7. David Ambartsumyan	SOV/ARM	516.21
8. Carlos Giron	MEX		513.93

Seventeen-year-old Soviet diver Sergei Nemtsanov finished a diappointing ninth, and then caused something of a sensation when he disappeared mysteriously from the Olympic Village. Soviet officials charged that he had been abducted. When he showed up again, the Western press claimed that Nemtsanov had left the Village voluntarily, but that the Soviets had tracked him down and hauled him back against his will.

1980 Moscow C: 23, N: 14, D: 7.28.

			PTS.
1.	Falk Hoffmann	GDR	835.650
2.	Vladimir Aleynik	SOV/BLR	819.705
3.	David Ambartsumyan	SOV/ARM	817.440
4.	Carlos Giron	MEX	809.805
5.	Dieter Waskow	GDR	802.800
6.	Thomas Knuths	GDR	783.975
7.	Sergei Nemtsanov	SOV/RUS	775.860
8.	Niki Sajkovic	AUT	725.145

1984 Los Angeles C: 26, N: 18, D: 8.12.

			PTS.
1.	Gregory Louganis	USA	710.91
2.	Bruce Kimball	USA	643.50
3.	Li Kongzheng	CHN	638.28
4.	Tong Hui	CHN	604.77
5.	Albin Killat	GER	551.97
6.	Dieter Dörr	GER	536.07
7.	Christopher Snode	GBR	524.40
8.	David Bedard	CAN	518.13

As Greg Louganis stood 33 feet above the water, preparing for his final dive, he told himself, "No matter what I do, my mother is still going to love me." He then executed a near-perfect reverse tuck to become the first platform diver to score over 700 points and the first male since 1928 to win both the springboard and platform competitions.

Bruce Kimball overtook Li Kongzheng with his final dive to win the silver medal. In 1981 Kimball was struck head-on by a drunken driver. Every bone in his face was broken, his skull was fractured, his left leg broken, the ligaments in his knee torn, his liver was lacerated, and his spleen had to be removed. When he returned to diving nine months later, he earned the nickname "The Comeback Kid." On August 1, 1988, two weeks before the U.S. Olympic diving trials, Kimball, himself drunk, plowed into a crowd of teenagers while driving 75 miles per hour, killing two boys and injuring six others. Despite the tragedy, Kimball took part in the trials but failed to make the team. He subsequently pleaded guilty to vehicular manslaughter and was sentenced to 17 years in prison. He was released on November 24, 1993, after serving less than five.

1988 Seoul C: 26, N: 15, D: 9.27.

			PTS.
1.	Gregory Louganis	USA	638.61
2.	Xiong Ni	CHN	637.47
3.	Jesús Mena	MEX	594.39
4.	Georgy Chogovadze	SOV/GEO	585.96
5.	Jan Hempel	GDR	583.77
6.	Li Kongzheng	CHN	543.81
7.	Steffen Haage	GDR	541.02
8.	Vladimir Timoshinin	SOV/RUS	534.66

Greg Louganis, hoping to become the first male diver to win both the springboard and platform events twice in a row, found himself in an unusually close battle with 14-year-old Xiong Ni. The difference in their scores was never more than 10 points. With one dive remaining,

Xiong led by exactly three points. His final dive was a brilliantly executed inward three and a half somersault in the tuck position. With a degree of difficulty of 3.2, it earned him 82.56 points. This meant that Louganis needed to score 85.56 points on *his* last dive, a reverse three and a half somersault in the tuck position, also known as the "Dive of Death" because it had proved fatal to two divers. Louganis performed it beautifully, although his entry was less than perfect. However, the high degree of difficulty, 3.4, allowed him to score 86.70 points and squeeze out a narrow, highly emotional victory. And just how young was Xiong Ni? After one dive he came out of the water with blood on his face. At first it was thought that he had injured himself. But it turned out that all he had suffered was a broken pimple.

1992 Barcelona C: 23, N: 14, D: 8.4.

			PTS.
1.	Sun Shuwei	CHN	677.31
2.	Scott Donie	USA	633.63
3.	Xiong Ni	CHN	600.15
4.	Jan Hempel	GER	574.17
5.	Robert Morgan	GBR	568.59
6.	Dmitri Sautin	RUS	565.95
7.	Michael Kühne	GER	558.54
8.	Keita Kaneto	JPN	529.14

Tiny Sun Shuwei of Jieyang in Guangdong Province burst onto the international scene when he won the 1990 Asian Games at the age of 14. The following year he won the world championships. Less than three months before the Olympics, at the Dive Canada meet, Sun set a world record for the most points earned on a single dive: he was awarded perfect tens on a reverse 3 1/2 somersault tuck for a total score of 102.00 points. Standing 5 feet 1 inch (1.55 m) and weighing 99 pounds (45 kg), Sun took the lead in the fourth round of the Olympic final and won easily.

Discontinued Event

PLAIN HIGH DIVING

The plain high dive was just that—nothing fancy, no twists or somersaults.

1912 Stockholm C: 30, N: 8, D: 7.11.

			ORDINALS	PTS.
1.	Erik Adlerz	SWE	7	40.0
2.	Hjalmar Johansson	SWE	12	39.3
3.	John Jansson	SWE	12	39.1
4.	Viktor Crondahl	SWE	22	37.1
5.	Tovio Aro	FIN	26	36.5
6.	Axel Runström	SWE	26	36.0
7.	Ernst Brandsten	SWE	28	36.2

DNF: Paul Günther (GER)

1920 Antwerp C: 22, N: 11, D: 8.25.

		ORDINALS	PTS.
1. Arvid Wallman	SWE	7	183.5
2. Nils Skoglund	SWE	8	183.0
3. John Jansson	SWE	16	175.0
4. Erik Adlerz	SWE	19	173.0
5. Yrjö Valkama	FIN	23	167.5
6. Herold Jansson	DEN	27	159.0
7. Fernand Sauvage	BEL	34	148.5
8. Adolpho Wellish	BRA	37	153.0

Silver medalist Nils Skoglund was 14 years old.

1924 Paris C: 25, N: 10, D: 7.15.

		ORDINALS	PTS.
1. Richmond Eve	AUS	13.5	160.0
2. John Jansson	SWE	14.5	157.0
3. Harold Clarke	GBR	15.5	158.0
4. Ben Trash	USA	23.5	145.0
5. Raymond Vincent	FRA	26.5	144.0
6. Ulise "Pete" Desjardins	USA	28	141.0
7. Albert Reginald Knight	GBR	31	137.0
8. Arvid Wallman	SWE	31	136.0

WOMEN

SPRINGBOARD DIVING

This event is performed from a springboard three meters above the water. Prior to 1996 each finalist made five compulsory dives and five voluntary dives. In 1996 the semifinal will comprise five dives with a total degree of difficulty not to exceed 9.5. The 12 finalists will take five more dives with no limit on the degree of difficulty.

1896–1912 not held

1920 Antwerp C; 4, N: 1, D: 8.29.

		ORDINALS	PTS.
1. Aileen Riggin	USA	9	539.9
2. Helen Wainwright	USA	9	534.8
3. Thelma Payne	USA	12	534.1
4. Aileen Allen	USA	20	489.9

Tiny Aileen Riggin of Newport, Rhode Island, was only 14 years old when she won her Olympic gold medal. At 4 feet 7 inches and 65 pounds, she was the smallest athlete at the 1920 Olympics. Silver medalist Helen Wainwright was also 14 years old. In 1922 Riggin was the subject of the first underwater and slow-motion swimming films. She returned to the Olympics in 1924 and won a silver medal for springboard diving and a bronze in the 100-meter backstroke. Later she turned professional, played the part of a slave dancer in the 1933 film *Roman Scandals,* and starred in Billy Rose's first Aquacade. She also

Aileen Riggin and Helen Wainwright were both 14 years old when they earned the gold and silver medals in the 1920 springboard diving contest.

became one of America's first women sportswriters and, at the age of 82, she set nine national age-group swim records. At the age of 86 she won six age-group titles at the World Masters Swimming Championships.

1924 Paris C: 17, N: 7, D: 7.18.

		ORDINALS	PTS.
1. Elizabeth Becker	USA	8	474.5
2. Aileen Riggin	USA	12	460.4
3. Caroline Fletcher	USA	16	436.4
4. Eva Ollivier	SWE	20	412.6
5. Signe Johanson	SWE	21	412.6
6. Klara Bornett	AUT	28	370.2

1928 Amsterdam C: 10, N; 4, D: 8.9.

		ORDINALS	PTS.
1. Helen Meany	USA	6	78.62
2. Dorothy Poynton	USA	13	75.62
3. Georgia Coleman	USA	14	73.38
4. Ilse Meudtner	GER	22	67.42

5.	Margret Borgs	GER	26	65.16
6.	Lini Söhnchen	GER	34	63.28
7.	Geertruida Klapwijk	HOL	35	60.98
8.	A.I.M. van Leeuwen	HOL	35	59.82

1932 Los Angeles C: 8, N: 6, D: 8.10.

			PTS.
1.	Georgia Coleman	USA	87.52
2.	Katherine Rawls	USA	82.56
3.	Jane Fauntz	USA	82.12
4.	Olga Jordan	GER	77.60
5.	Doris Ogilvie	CAN	77.00
6.	Magdalene Epply	AUT	63.70
7.	Etsuo Kamakura	JPN	60.78
8.	Ingrid Larsen	DEN	57.26

Georgia Coleman, the first woman to do a two and a half forward somersault, completed her Olympic career with four medals: one gold, two silver, and one bronze. She died in 1941 at the age of 29. In 1932 the system of ordinals (place-figures) was dropped and total points became the determining factor in deciding places.

1936 Berlin C: 16, N: 9, D: 8.12.

			PTS.
1.	Marjorie Gestring	USA	89.27
2.	Katherine Rawls	USA	88.35
3.	Dorothy Poynton Hill	USA	82.36
4.	Gerda Daumerlang	GER	78.27
5.	Olga Jentsch-Jordan	GER	77.98
6.	Masayo Osawa	JPN	73.94
7.	Suse Heinze	GER	71.49
8.	Fusako Kono	JPN	70.27

Gold medalist Marjorie Gestring of Los Angeles was only 13 years and 9 months old. She remains the youngest person in Olympic history to win an individual gold medal in any sport. Katy Rawls repeated her silver medal and, two days later, added a bronze medal as a member of the U.S. freestyle relay team.

1948 London C: 16, N: 8, D: 8.3.

			PTS.
1.	Victoria Draves	USA	108.74
2.	Zoe Ann Olsen	USA	108.23
3.	Patricia Elsener	USA	101.30
4.	Nicole Pellissard	FRA	100.38
5.	Gudrun Grömer	AUT	93.30
6.	Edna Child	GBR	91.63
7.	Madeleine Moreau	FRA	89.43
8.	Jacoba Heck	HOL	87.61

Vicki Draves had a Filipino father and an English mother, but she was born and raised in San Francisco. She did not begin diving until she was 16 years old. The first ever Asian-American Olympic medalist, Draves faced racial discrimination early in her career. Her first swim club required that she drop her father's name and use her mother's maiden name, Taylor, instead. Silver medalist Zoe Ann Olsen married baseball star Jackie Jensen before the next Olympics.

1952 Helsinki C: 15, N: 7, D: 7.30.

			PTS.
1.	Patricia McCormick	USA	147.30
2.	Madeleine Moreau	FRA	139.34
3.	Zoe Ann Jensen-Olsen	USA	127.57
4.	Ninel Krutova	SOV/RUS	116.86
5.	Charmain Welsh	GBR	116.38
6.	Lyubov Shigalova	SOV	113.83
7.	Nicole Pellissard	FRA	111.98
8.	Phyllis Long	GBR	108.82

Pat McCormick of Long Beach, California, won the first of her four gold medals. Mady Moreau became the first non-American woman to win a springboard medal after six straight U.S. sweeps.

1956 Melbourne C: 17, N: 8, D: 12.4.

			PTS.
1.	Patricia McCormick	USA	142.36
2.	Jeanne Stunyo	USA	125.89
3.	Irene MacDonald	CAN	121.40
4.	Barbara Gilders	USA	120.76
5.	Valentina Chumicheva	SOV	118.50
6.	Phyllis Long	GBR	107.61
7.	Nicole Darrigrand (Pellissard)	FRA	106.32
8.	Kanoko Tsutani	JPN	103.12

Eight months before the Melbourne Olympics, Pat McCormick gave birth to a baby boy. She had continued training throughout her pregnancy and swam a half-mile a day up until two days before childbirth. In 1956 she repeated her double gold medal performance of 1952.

1960 Rome C; 16, N: 10, D: 8.27.

			PTS.
1.	Ingrid Krämer	GDR	155.81
2.	Paula Jean Pope (Myers)	USA	141.24
3.	Elizabeth Ferris	GBR	139.09
4.	Mary "Patsy" Willard	USA	137.82
5.	Ninel Krutova	SOV/RUS	136.11
6.	Irene MacDonald	CAN	134.69
7.	Phyllis Long	GBR	129.63
8.	Dorothea DuPon	HOL	123.35

The U.S. string of eight consecutive springboard victories was finally broken by 17-year-old Ingrid Krämer of Dresden. The Rome Games were the fourth straight Olympics at which both diving events were won by the same woman.

1964 Tokyo C: 21, N: 9, D: 10.12.

			PTS.
1.	Ingrid Engel-Krämer	GDR	145.00
2.	Jeanne Collier	USA	138.36
3.	Mary "Patsy" Willard	USA	138.18
4.	Sue Gossick	USA	129.70
5.	Tamara Fyedosova	SOV/RUS	126.33

6.	Yelena Anokhina	SOV/RUS	125.60
7.	Kanoko Mabuchi	JPN	125.28
8.	Angelika Hilbert	GER	123.27

Ingrid Engel-Krämer took over the lead from Patsy Willard on her seventh dive and went on to win her third gold medal.

1968 Mexico City C: 22, N: 15, D: 10.18

			PTS.
1.	Sue Gossick	USA	150.77
2.	Tamara Pogosheva (Fyedosova)	SOV/RUS	145.30
3.	Keala O'Sullivan	USA	145.23
4.	Maxine "Micki" King	USA	137.38
5.	Ingrid Gulbin (Engel-Krämer)	GDR	135.82
6.	Vyera Baklanova	SOV/RUS	132.31
7.	Beverly Boys	CAN	130.31
8.	Yelena Anokhina	SOV/RUS	129.17

Twenty-year-old Sue Gossick of Tarzana, California, didn't move into the lead until the ninth round. Pogosheva, leading after seven dives, missed her eighth dive badly, but earned the highest score of the competition with her final attempt, to jump back from fourth place to second. In fifth place was the one and only Ingrid Krämer, competing in her third Olympics, each under a different name.

1972 Munich C: 30, N: 18, D: 8.28

			PTS.
1.	Maxine "Micki" King	USA	450.03
2.	Ulrika Knape	SWE	434.19
3.	Marina Janicke	GDR	430.92
4.	Janet Ely	USA	420.99
5.	Beverly Boys	CAN	418.89
6.	Agneta Henriksson	SWE	417.48
7.	Cynthia Potter	USA	413.58
8.	Elzbieta Wierniuk	POL	408.36

In Mexico City Micki King of Pontiac, Michigan, had been in first place after eight dives. But during her ninth dive, a reverse one and a half layout, she hit the board and broke her left forearm. She completed her final dive, but dropped to fourth place. Four years later in Munich, King, now a 28-year-old air force captain, took the lead from Ulrika Knape with her eighth dive and this time steered clear of the diving board to win the gold medal. Her final dive, a reverse one and a half somersault with one and a half twists, was the same dive she had attempted four years earlier with a broken arm. After her victory she had to submit to a drug test. However it took King two hours to produce a urine sample. By that time everyone but the doctors had gone home, so she returned alone to the Olympic Village and had a chocolate drink. Three Australian weightlifters told her "a gold medalist shouldn't be drinking chocolate" and shared with her a bottle of wine.

1976 Montreal C: 27, N: 15, D: 7.20.

			PTS.
1.	Jennifer Chandler	USA	506.19
2.	Christa Köhler	GDR	469.41
3.	Cynthia Potter	USA	466.83
4.	Heidi Ramlow	GDR	462.15
5.	Karin Guthke	GDR	459.81
6.	Olga Dmitrieva	SOV/RUS	432.24
7.	Irina Kalinina	SOV/RUS	417.99
8.	Barbara Nejman	USA	365.07

1980 Moscow C: 24, N: 13, D: 7.21.

			PTS.
1.	Irina Kalinina	SOV/RUS	725.910
2.	Martina Proeber	GDR	698.895
3.	Karin Guthke	GDR	685.245
4.	Zhanna Tsyrulnikova	SOV/UKR	673.665
5.	Martina Jäschke	GDR	668.115
6.	Valerie McFarlane	AUS	651.045
7.	Irina Sidorova	SOV/BLR	650.265
8.	Lourdes Gonzalez	CUB	640.005

1984 Los Angeles C: 24, N: 18, D: 8.6.

			PTS.
1.	Sylvie Bernier	CAN	530.70
2.	Kelly McCormick	USA	527.46
3.	Christina Seufert	USA	517.62
4.	Li Yihua	CHN	506.52
5.	Li Qiaoxian	CHN	487.68
6.	Elsa Tenorio	MEX	463.56
7.	Lesley Smith	ZIM	451.89
8.	Debbie Fuller	CAN	450.99

The women's springboard event had been billed as a showdown between the Americans and the Chinese, but a consistent performance by 20-year-old Sylvie Bernier of Ste. Foy, Quebec, gave her the victory. Bernier, who had a history of caving in in pressure situations, solved her problem by completely ignoring the standings throughout the competition. She even drowned out the public-address announcer by listening to the soundtrack from the movie "Flashdance" between dives. It wasn't until she had completed her final dive that her coach informed her the gold medal would be hers unless Kelly McCormick, daughter of four-time Olympic champion Pat McCormick, scored over 70 points on her last dive. McCormick's dive was an excellent one, but earned her only 67.20 points.

1988 Seoul C: 27, N: 19, D: 9.25.

			PTS.
1.	Gao Min	CHN	580.23
2.	Li Qing	CHN	534.33
3.	Kelly McCormick	USA	533.19
4.	Irina Lashko	SOV/RUS	526.65
5.	Marina Babkova	SOV/RUS	506.43
6.	Wendy Lucero	USA	498.81
7.	Brita Baldus	GDR	479.19
8.	Daphne Jongejans	HOL	465.45

In 1988, world champion Gao Min of Zigong in Sichuan Province became the first female diver to score over 600 points in a springboard competition. In Seoul, the 18-year-old Gao took the lead with her sixth dive, finished with the three highest scores of the day, and achieved the most decisive women's diving victory since Pat McCormick's in 1956. When she first began diving, as a child, Gao was troubled by stiff arches that made it difficult to point her toes in the manner preferred by diving judges. Her teammates said she had "hoe feet." In desperation she supplemented her toe stretching exercises by tying the tips of her feet to the end of her bed whenever she went to sleep.

1992 Barcelona C: 29, N: 20, D: 8.3.

			PTS.
1.	Gao Min	CHN	572.40
2.	Irina Lashko	RUS	514.14
3.	Brita Baldus	GER	503.07
4.	Heidemarie Bártová	CZE	491.49
5.	Julie Ovenhouse	USA	477.84
6.	Vera Ilyna	RUS	470.67
7.	Simona Koch	GER	468.96
8.	Mary DePiero	CAN	449.49

Competing in pain because of shoulder injuries, Gao moved ahead in the sixth round and pulled away to win by an even larger margin than she had four years earlier. This was the first time in the history of the event that divers from the United States had competed but failed to win a medal.

PLATFORM DIVING

This event is performed from a static board ten meters above the water. Prior to 1996 each finalist attempted four compulsory dives and four voluntary dives. In 1996, semifinalists will perform four dives, with a total degree of difficulty not to exceed 7.6. The 12 finalists will perform five more dives with no limit on degree of difficulty.

1896–1908 not held

1912 Stockholm C: 14, N; 3, D: 7.13.

			ORDINALS	PTS.
1.	Margareta Johanson	SWE	5	39.9
2.	Lisa Regnell	SWE	11	36.0
3.	Isobel White	GBR	17	34.0
4.	Elsa Regnell	SWE	20	33.2
5.	Ellen Eklund	SWE	22	31.9
6.	Elsa Andersson	SWE	25	31.3
7.	Selma Andersson	SWE	36	27.3
8.	Thora Larsson	SWE	39	26.8

Seventeen-year-old Greta Johanson was the unanimous choice of the five judges.

1920 Antwerp C: 15, N: 6, D: 8.28.

			ORDINALS	PTS.
1.	Stefanie Clausen	DEN	6	173.0
2.	B. Eileen Armstrong	GBR	10	166.0
3.	Eva Olliwer	SWE	11	166.0
4.	Isobel White	GBR	18	158.5
5.	Aileen Riggin	USA	20	157.0
6.	Betty Grimes	USA	30	133.5

1924 Paris C: 11, N: 6, D: 7.20.

			ORDINALS	PTS.
1.	Caroline Smith	USA	10.5	33.2
2.	Elizabeth Becker	USA	11	33.4
3.	Hjördis Töpel	SWE	15.5	32.8
4.	Edith Bechmann-Nielsen	DEN	17.5	31.6
5.	Helen Meany	USA	22	29.6
6.	Isobel White	GBR	28.5	28.0

National prejudice reared its ugly head in the judging of the women's high dive. The Danish judge gave first place to Bechmann-Nielsen of Denmark. The Swedish judge voted for Töpel of Sweden, and the American judge registered a three-way tie for first among the three Americans. The British judge voted for Smith and the French judge for Becker.

1928 Amsterdam C: 17, N; 8, D: 8.11.

			ORDINALS	PTS.
1.	Elizabeth Becker Pinkston	USA	9	31.6
2.	Georgia Coleman	USA	10.5	30.6
3.	Lala Sjöquist	SWE	13.5	29.2
4.	Mietje Baron	HOL	21	27.2
5.	Greta Onnela	FIN	25	26.0
6.	Hanni Rehborn	GER	26	25.6

Elizabeth Becker Pinkston balanced her 1924 springboard gold with first place in the platform diving four years later. Between Olympics she had married Clarence Pinkston, whom she had met when both were members of the 1924 U.S. diving team in Paris. Husband and wife eventually won seven Olympic medals between them.

1932 Los Angeles C: 7, N: 5, D: 8.12.

			PTS.
1.	Dorothy Poynton	USA	40.26
2.	Georgia Coleman	USA	35.56
3.	Marion Roper	USA	35.22
4.	Lala Sjöquist	SWE	34.52
5.	Ingrid Larsen	DEN	31.96
6.	Etsuko Kamakuru	JPN	31.36
7.	Magdalene Epply	AUS	26.76

1936 Berlin C: 22, N: 10, D: 8.13.

			PTS.
1.	Dorothy Poynton Hill	USA	33.93
2.	Velma Dunn	USA	33.63
3.	Käthe Köhler	GER	33.43
4.	Reiko Osawa	JPN	32.53
5.	Cornelia Gilissen	USA	30.47
6.	Fusako Kono	JPN	30.24

7. Jean Gilbert GBR 30.16
8. Anne Ehseheidt GER 29.90

Stylish Dorothy Poynton Hill, competing in her third Olympics at the age of 21, gained her fourth medal. She won two gold medals in the platform and a silver and bronze in the springboard.

1948 London C: 15, N: 9, D: 8.6.

		PTS.
1. Victoria Draves	USA	68.87
2. Patricia Elsener	USA	66.28
3. Birte Christoffersen	DEN	66.04
4. Ali Staudinger	AUT	64.59
5. Juno Stover	USA	62.63
6. Nicole Pellissard	FRA	61.07
7. Eva Petersen	SWE	59.86
8. Inge Beeken-Gregersen	DEN	59.54

Vicki Draves became the first female diver to win two gold medals in one Olympics.

1952 Helsinki C: 15, N: 8, D: 8.2

		PTS.
1. Patricia McCormick	USA	79.37
2. Paula Jean Myers	USA	71.63

PAT McCORMICK (U.S.A)
Olympic Springboard and
Highboard Diving Champion

In 1952 and 1956 Pat McCormick swept both the springboard and platform diving competitions.

		PTS.
3. Juno Irwin (Stover)	USA	70.49
4. Nicole Pellissard	FRA	66.89
5. Phyllis Long	GBR	63.19
6. Tatyana Vereina	SOV	61.09
7. Diana Spencer	GBR	60.76
8. Eugenia Bogdanovskaya	SOV	57.50

This was the second of Pat McCormick's four gold medals. Bronze medalist Juno Irwin was three and a half months' pregnant with her second child.

1956 Melbourne C: 18, N: 10, D: 12.7.

		PTS.
1. Patricia McCormick	USA	84.85
2. Juno Irwin (Stover)	USA	81.64
3. Paula Jean Myers	USA	81.58
4. Nicole Darrigrand (Pellissard)	FRA	78.80
5. Tatyana Karakashyants-Vereina	SOV	76.95
6. Lyubov Shigalova	SOV	76.40
7. Phyllis Long	GBR	76.15
8. Birte Hansson	SWE	75.21

Pat McCormick moved ahead of Juno Irwin after the sixth of seven dives to win her fourth gold medal. McCormick was a 26-year-old mother of one, Irwin a 28-year-old mother of three.

1960 Rome C: 18, N: 12, D: 8.30.

		PTS.
1. Ingrid Krämer	GDR	91.28
2. Paula Jean Pope (Myers)	USA	88.94
3. Ninel Krutova	SOV/RUS	86.99
4. Juno Irwin (Stover)	USA	83.59
5. Raisa Gorokhovskaya	SOV/UKR	83.03
6. Norma Thomas	GBR	82.21
7. Nicole Darrigrand (Pellissard)	FRA	81.18
8. Phyllis Long	GBR	80.98

Krämer clinched her diving double with a final one and a half forward somersault with a double twist that turned out to be the highest-scoring dive of the competition. Paula Jean Pope, a 25-year-old mother of two, won her third straight platform medal.

1964 Tokyo C: 24, N: 11, D: 10.15.

		PTS.
1. Lesley Bush	USA	99.80
2. Ingrid Engel-Krämer	GDR	98.45
3. Galina Alekseyeva	SOV/RUS	97.60
4. Linda Cooper	USA	96.30
5. Christine Lanzke	GDR	92.92
6. Ingeborg Pertmayr	AUT	92.70
7. Natalya Kuznetsova	SOV/RUS	90.91
8. Barbara Talmage	USA	89.60

Seventeen-year-old Lesley Bush of Princeton, New Jersey, took the lead after the first dive and was never headed. Asked afterward how she felt when she realized she was in first place and might upset Ingrid Krämer's attempt to match Pat McCormick's four gold medals, Bush replied, "It was sort of scary, but gee, gosh, it was great."

1968 Mexico City C: 24, N: 15, D: 10.23.

		PTS.
1. Milena Duchková	CZE	109.59
2. Natalya Lobanova (Kuznetsova)	SOV/RUS	105.14
3. Ann Peterson	USA	101.11
4. Beverly Boys	CAN	97.97
5. Boguslawa Pietkiewicz	POL	95.28
6. Regina Krause	GER	93.08
6. Keiko Ohsaki	JPN	93.08
8. Nancy Robertson	CAN	90.66

Duchková overcame Lobanova with her last two dives, much to the delight of the crowd, which favored the 16-year-old Czechoslovakian because she was small and because her nation was occupied by Soviet troops.

1972 Munich C: 27, N: 17, D: 9.2.

		PTS.
1. Ulrika Knape	SWE	390.00
2. Milena Duchková	CZE	370.92
3. Marina Janicke	GDR	360.54
4. Janet Ely	USA	352.68
5. Maxine "Micki" King	USA	346.38
6. Sylvia Fiedler	GDR	341.67
7. Nancy Robertson	CAN	334.02
8. Ingeborg Pertmayr	AUT	321.03

Knape took the lead from Duchková after the sixth of eight dives and then earned the gold medal with a final dive that received the highest score of the competition.

1976 Montreal C: 25, N: 12, D: 7.25.

		PTS.
1. Elena Vaytsekhovskaya	SOV/RUS	406.59
2. Ulrika Knape	SWE	402.60
3. Deborah Wilson	USA	401.00
4. Irina Kalinina	SOV/RUS	398.67
5. Cindy Shatto	CAN	389.50
6. Teri York	CAN	378.39
7. Melissa Briley	USA	376.86
8. Heidi Ramlow	GDR	365.64

Eighteen-year-old Elena Vaytsekhovskaya jumped from fifth place to first with her fifth dive, a superbly executed backward two and a half somersault, piked.

1980 Moscow C: 17, N: 11, D: 7.26.

		PTS.
1. Martina Jäschke	GDR	596.250
2. Servard Emirzyan	SOV/ARM	576.465
3. Liana Tsotadze	SOV/GEO	575.925
4. Ramona Wenzel	GDR	542.070
5. Yelena Matyushenko	SOV/RUS	540.180
6. Elsa Tenorio	MEX	539.445
7. Valerie McFarlane	AUS	499.785
8. Ildikó Kelemen	HUN	476.535

In fourth place after the preliminaries, Jäschke swept into first place on the fifth dive of the final round.

1984 Los Angeles C: 21, N: 14, D: 8.10.

		PTS.
1. Zhou Jihong	CHN	435.51
2. Michele Mitchell	USA	431.19
3. Wendy Wyland	USA	422.07
4. Chen Xiaoxia	CHN	419.76
5. Valerie Beddoe	AUS	388.56
6. Debbie Fuller	CAN	371.49
7. Elsa Tenorio	MEX	360.45
8. Guadalupe Canseco	MEX	352.89

At five-feet, one-inch and weighing 92 pounds, 19-year-old Zhou Jihong of Hubei Province was unusually small for a diver. She also differed from her competitors in the choice of music she listened to on her headphones between dives. While the others received inspiration from upbeat popular songs, Zhou relaxed with piano concertos. This tactic seemed to help her avoid the last-minute choking for which Chinese divers had become famous.

1988 Seoul C: 20, N: 14, D: 9.18.

		PTS.
1. Xu Yanmei	CHN	445.20
2. Michele Mitchell	USA	436.95
3. Wendy Lian Williams	USA	400.44
4. Angela Stasiulevich	SOV/BLR	386.22
5. Chen Xiaodan	CHN	384.15
6. Yelena Miroshina	SOV/RUS	381.93
7. Kamilla Gamme	NOR	366.45
8. Silke Abicht	GDR	350.61

After seven dives, the 17-year-old favorite, Xu Yanmei, led Michele Mitchell by only .27 of a point. For her final dive, Xu earned mostly 8s for a back 2½ pike for a total of 68.73 points. Mitchell, next to dive, missed slightly on the entry of her forward 3½ tuck and was awarded 7.5s for 60.75 points. The last diver was 14-year-old Chen Xiaodan, who had led the preliminary round, but who now stood firmly in third place, a formidable 83.82 points away from a gold medal. But Chen had scored 81.18 on her last dive and decided to forego caution and instead try "to win the whole meet." However, she went way too far over on a back 3½ tuck and almost landed on her stomach. Scores ranging from 1.5 to 3.0 left her with 22.77 points and fifth place. The ecstatic beneficiary of Chen's mistake was Wendy Lian Williams. Williams had been in last place after three dives and only fifth place after seven.

1992 Barcelona C: 28, N: 17, D: 7.27.

		PTS.
1. Fu Mingxia	CHN	461.43
2. Yelena Miroshina	RUS	411.63
3. Mary Ellen Clark	USA	401.91
4. Zhu Jinhong	CHN	400.56
5. Inga Afonina	UKR	398.43

6. María Alcalá Izguerra	MEX	394.35
7. Ellen Owen	USA	392.10
8. Verónica Ribot De Canales	ARG	384.03

When Fu Mingxia was 9 years old she was plucked from her home in Wuhan and taken 600 miles away to a diving school in Beijing. There she practiced seven days a week. To correct her posture and her bulging knees she was made to sit upright on a chair with her legs stretched out on a bench in front of her. Then an adult would sit on her knees and urge her to endure the excruciating pain. She was allowed to see her parents twice a year. When asked at the Barcelona Olympics what kind of work her parents did, she didn't know. She won the 1990 Goodwill Games title 12 days before her twelfth birthday, and the 1991 world championship at the age of 12½. The International Amateur Swimming Federation responded to Fu's success by passing a rule that required Olympic divers to be at least 14 years old in the Olympic year. Fu was able to compete because she turned 14 twenty days after the Olympic platform final. In that competition she moved ahead of her rivals with her third dive and then pulled away to the most decisive women's platform victory in sixty years.

On December 18, 1995, silver medalist Yelena Miroshina committed suicide by jumping out of a fifth-floor window in Moscow. She was 21 years old.

EQUESTRIAN

Three-Day Event, Individual
Three-Day Event, Team
Jumping, Individual
Jumping (Prix des Nations), Team
Dressage, Individual
Dressage, Team
Discontinued Events

As with many Olympic sports, equestrian regulations require a minimum age limit for participants: 18 years old for the three-day and jumping events, 16 years old for the dressage. A lesser known fact is that the horses, too, must be of a certain age: at least seven years old. They must also have an official passport approved by the International Equestrian Federation.

THREE-DAY EVENT, INDIVIDUAL

The three-day event consists of three parts: dressage, endurance, and show jumping. The dressage and jumping portions follow the same basic rules and scoring as the regular dressage and jumping events. The endurance phase is a long-distance obstacle run broken into four sections. Phase A, short road and tracks, is ridden at about 9 miles per hour and is basically a warm-up. Phase B, steeplechase, is run on a course between 3,105 and 3,450 meters long and includes eight to ten brush fences.

Optimum speed is considered to be about 26 miles per hour. Phase C, long road and tracks, is a longer version of phase A. Phase D, cross-country, is the most critical test. The course is between 6,840 and 7,980 meters long. It includes jumping obstacles made of logs, banks, ditches, stone walls, and water. Optimum speed is considered to be about 21 miles per hour. In the steeplechase and cross-country phases, a first disobedience at a jump incurs a 20-point penalty; a second disobedience at the same jump incurs a 40-point penalty; a third disobedience at the same obstacle results in elimination. A fall is penalized by 60 points; a second fall by elimination. Penalty points are also assessed for exceeding the optimum time limit. It used to be possible to score bonus points by beating the time limit, but this rule was changed prior to the 1976 Olympics.

1896–1908 not held

1912 Stockholm C: 27, N: 7, D: 7.17.

			HORSE	PTS.
1.	Axel Nordlander	SWE	Lady Artist	46.59
2.	Friedrich von Rochow	GER	Idealist	46.42
3.	Jean Cariou	FRA	Cocotte	46.32
4.	Nils Adlercreutz	SWE	Atout	46.31
5.	Ernst Casparsson	SWE	Irmelin	46.16
5.	Richard Graf von Schaesberg-Tannheim	GER	Grundsee	46.16
7.	Benjamin Lear	USA	Poppy	45.91
8.	Eduard von Lütcken	GER	Blue Boy	45.90

1920 Antwerp C: 25, N: 8, D: 9.10.

			HORSE	PTS.
1.	Graf Helmer Mörner	SWE	Germania	1775.00
2.	Åge Lundström	SWE	Ysra	1738.75
3.	Ettore Caffaratti	ITA	Caniche	1733.75
4.	Roger Moeremans d'Emaus	BEL	Sweet Girl	1652.50
5.	Garibaldi Spighi	ITA	Otello	1647.50
6.	Harry Chamberlin	USA	Nigra	1568.75
7.	William West	USA	Black Boy	1558.75
8.	Georg von Braun	SWE	Diana	1543.75

The competition consisted of jumping, a 20-kilometer course, and a 50-kilometer course, but no dressage.

1924 Paris C: 44, N: 13, D: 7, 26.

			HORSE	DRESSAGE	ENDURANCE	JUMPING	TOTAL PTS.
1.	Adolph van der Voort van Zijp	HOL	Silver Piece	174.0	1402.0	400.0	1976.0
2.	Frode Kirkebjerg	DEN	Meteor	164.0	1409.5	280.0	1853.5
3.	Sloan Doak	USA	Pathfinder	156.0	1369.5	320.0	1845.5
4.	Charles Pahud de Mortanges	HOL	Johnny Walker	174.0	1334.0	320.0	1828.0
5.	Claës König	SWE	Bojar	166.0	1284.0	280.0	1730.0
6.	Beaudouin de Brabandère	BEL	Modestie	138.0	1190.5	400.0	1728.5
6.	Edward de Fonblanque	GBR	Copper	133.0	1275.5	320.0	1728.5
8.	Frank Carr	USA	Proctor	154.0	1333.0	240.0	1727.0

1928 Amsterdam C: 46, N: 17, D: 8.11.

			HORSE	DRESSAGE	ENDURANCE	JUMPING	TOTAL PTS.
1.	Charles Pahud de Mortanges	HOL	Marcroix	237.82	1432.0	300.0	1969.82
2.	Gerard de Kruyff	HOL	Va-t-en	251.26	1416.0	300.0	1967.26
3.	Bruno Neumann	GER	Ilja	208.42	1436.0	300.0	1944.42
4.	Adolph van der Voort van Zijp	HOL	Silver Piece	224.60	1404.0	300.0	1928.60
5.	Hans Olof von Essen	FIN	El Kaid	180.64	1444.0	300.0	1924.64
6.	Bjart Ording	NOR	And Over	200.98	1412.0	300.0	1912.98
7.	Nils Kettner	SWE	Caesar	197.66	1404.0	300.0	1901.66
8.	Arthur Quist	NOR	Hidalgo	221.14	1404.0	270.0	1895.14

1932 Los Angeles C: 14, N: 5, D: 8.13.

			HORSE	DRESSAGE	ENDURANCE	JUMPING	TOTAL PTS.
1.	Charles Pahud de Mortanges	HOL	Marcroix	311.833	− 58.0	−40.00	1813.833
2.	Earl Thomson	USA	Jenny Camp	300.000	− 29.0	−60.00	1811.000
3.	Clarence von Rosen	SWE	Sunnyside Maid	310.666	− 58.5	−42.75	1809.416
4.	Harry Chamberlin	USA	Pleasant Smiles	340.333	−192.5	−60.00	1687.833
5.	Ernst Hallberg	SWE	Marokan	290.333	−171.0	−40.00	1679.333
6.	Karel Johan Schummelketel	HOL	Duiveltje	267.500	−195.0	−58.00	1614.000
7.	Morishige Yamamoto	JPN	Kingo	257.333	−207.5	−40.25	1609.583
8.	Edwin Argo	USA	Honolulu Tomboy	333.000	−392.5	− 0.75	1539.250

Lieutenant Pahud de Mortanges completed his Olympic career with four gold medals and one silver.

1936 Berlin C: 50, N: 19, D: 8.16.

			HORSE	DRESSAGE	ENDURANCE	JUMPING	TOTAL PTS.
1.	Ludwig Stubbendorff	GER	Nurmi	− 96.7	+69	−10	− 37.7
2.	Earl Thomson	USA	Jenny Camp	−127.9	+38	−10	− 99.9
3.	Hans Mathiesen-Lunding	DEN	Jason	−134.2	+42	−10	−102.2
4.	Vincens Grandjean	DEN	Grey Friar	−115.9	+11	0	−104.9
5.	Agoston Endrödy	HUN	Pandur	−134.7	+39	−10	−105.7
6.	Rudolf Lippert	GER	Fasan	−118.6	+27	−20	−111.6
7.	Alec Scott	GBR	Bob Clive	−152.3	+45	−10	−117.3
8.	Mario Mylius	SWI	Saphir	−122.0	+57	−20	−145.0

The course was so difficult that three horses met their deaths and only 27 of the 50 entrants finished the competition.

1948 London C: 45, N: 16, D: 8.10.

			HORSE	DRESSAGE	ENDURANCE	JUMPING	TOTAL PTS.
1.	Bernard Chevallier	FRA	Aiglonne	−104	+108	0	+ 4
2.	Frank Henry	USA	Swing Low	−117	+ 96	0	−21
3.	Robert Selfelt	SWE	Claque	−109	+ 84	0	−25
4.	Charles Anderson	USA	Reno Palisade	−111	+ 96	−11.5	−26.5
5.	Joaquin Nogueras Marquez	SPA	Epsom	−128	+ 87	0	−41
6.	Erik Carlsen	DEN	Ezja	−113	+ 69	0	−44
7.	Aecio Morrot Coelho	BRA	Guapo	−114	+ 72	−10	−52
8.	Fernando Marques Caveleiro	POR	Satari	−135	+ 90	−10	−55
8.	Fabio Mangilli	ITA	Guerriero da Capestrano	− 85	+ 72	−42	−55

1952 Helsinki C: 59, N: 21, D: 8.2.

			HORSE	DRESSAGE	ENDURANCE	JUMPING	TOTAL PTS.
1.	Hans von Blixen-Finecke, Jr.	SWE	Jubal	−123.33	+105	−10	−28.33
2.	Guy Lefrant	FRA	Verdun	−119.50	+ 75	−10	−54.50
3.	Wilhelm Büsing	GER	Hutbertus	−103.50	+ 48	0	−55.50
4.	Pedro Mercado	ARG	Mandinga	−130.80	+ 78	−10	−62.80
5.	Klaus Wagner	GER	Dachs	−109.66	+ 54	−10	−65.66
6.	Piero D'Inzeo	ITA	Pagoro	−118.80	+ 52	0	−66.80
7.	Albert Hill	GBR	Stella	−126.33	+ 69	−10	−67.33
8.	Olof Stahre	SWE	Komet	−108.66	+ 81	−41.75	−69.41

Blixen-Finecke's father won a bronze medal in the 1912 dressage.

1956 Stockholm C: 57, N: 19, D: 6.14.

			HORSE	DRESSAGE	ENDURANCE	JUMPING	TOTAL PTS.
1.	Petrus Kastenman	SWE	Iluster	−116.40	+69.87	−20	− 66.53
2.	August Lütke-Westhues	GER	Trux von Kamax	−129.60	+64.73	−20	− 84.87
3.	Francis Weldon	GBR	Kilbarry	−103.20	+37.72	−20	− 85.48
4.	Lev Baklychkine	SOV/RUS	Guimnast	−119.20	+42.55	−20	− 96.65
5.	Genko Rashkov	BUL	Euphoria	−146.00	+44.77	−10	−111.23
6.	A. Laurence Rook	GBR	Wild Venture	−101.60	− 4.29	−13.75	−119.64
7.	Giancarlo Gutierrez	ITA	Wiston	−138.80	+12.37	−10	−136.43
8.	Juan Martín Merbilháa	ARG	Gitana I	−150.00	+23.54	−10	−136.46

1960 Rome C: 73, N: 19, D: 9.10.

			HORSE	DRESSAGE	ENDURANCE	JUMPING	TOTAL PTS.
1.	Lawrence Morgan	AUS	Salad Days	−106.00	+128.4	−15.25	+ 7.15
2.	Neale Lavis	AUS	Mirrabooka	−124.50	+108.0	0	−16.50
3.	Anton Bühler	SWI	Gay Spark	− 89.01	+ 50.8	−13	−51.21
4.	Michael Bullen	GBR	Cottage Romance	−129.00	+ 66.4	0	−62.60
5.	Saibattal Mursalimov	SOV/KYR	Satrap	− 79.00	+ 46.0	−30.75	−63.75
6.	Jack Le Goff	FRA	Image	−108.51	+ 55.6	−20	−72.91
7.	Lev Baklychkine	SOV/RUS	Bazis	−103.50	+ 58.4	−20.25	−85.35
8.	Marian Babirecki	POL	Volt	−127.00	+ 61.6	−20	−85.40

The endurance course was unnecessarily dangerous, and two horses were killed. The Italian organizers seemed unprepared for such disasters. The Danish horse Rolf II had to wait two and a half hours for the arrival of a veterinarian, and the Romanian horse Mures II, driven across the finish line despite a fatal injury, lay dead for hours before he was finally removed. Only 35 of the 73 entrants completed the competition.

1964 Tokyo C: 48, N: 12, D: 10.19.

			HORSE	DRESSAGE	ENDURANCE	JUMPING	TOTAL PTS.
1.	Mauro Checcoli	ITA	Surbean	−54.00	+118.4	0	+64.40
2.	Carlos Moratorio	ARG	Chalan	−42.00	+ 98.4	0	+56.40
3.	Fritz Ligges	GER	Donkosak	−32.00	+ 91.2	−10	+49.20
4.	Michael Page	USA	Grasshopper	−43.00	+ 90.4	0	+47.40
5.	Anthony Cameron	IRL	Black Salmon	−70.67	+117.2	0	+46.53
6.	Horst Karsten	GER	Condora	−49.00	+ 95.6	−10	+36.60
7.	J. William Roycroft	AUS	Eldorado	−65.00	+ 97.2	0	+32.20
8.	Richard Meade	GBR	Barberry	−52.67	+118.4	−36	+29.73

Mauro Checcoli, a 21-year-old student from Bologna, won the gold medal, but it was the 33rd-place finisher who made equestrian history. Helen Dupont of the United States became the first woman to compete in the Olympic three-day event.

1968 Mexico City C: 49, N: 13, D: 10.21.

			HORSE	DRESSAGE	ENDURANCE	JUMPING	TOTAL PTS
1.	Jean-Jacques Guyon	FRA	Pitou	− 73.01	+44.4	−10.25	−38.86
2.	Derek Allhusen	GBR	Lochinvar	− 85.01	+44.4	0	−41.61
3.	Michael Page	USA	Foster	−107.51	+59.2	− 4	−52.31
4.	Richard Meade	GBR	Cornishman V	− 97.01	+54.8	−22.25	−64.46
5.	Reuben Jones	GBR	The Poacher	− 68.51	+ 4.4	− 5.75	−69.86
6.	James Wofford	USA	Kilkenny	−101.51	+71.2	−43.75	−74.06
7.	Juliet Jobling-Purser	IRL	Jenny	− 72.51	+ 5.6	− 1	−79.11
8.	Wayne Roycroft	AUS	Zhivago	−103.50	+21.2	−12.75	−95.05

Two more horses were killed during the endurance competition. This time they died of exhaustion.

1972 Munich C: 73, N: 19, D: 9.1.

			HORSE	DRESSAGE	ENDURANCE	JUMPING	TOTAL PTS.
1.	Richard Meade	GBR	Laurieston	−50.6	+108.4	0	+57.73
2.	Alessandro Argenton	ITA	Woodland	−48.6	+ 92.0	0	+43.33
3.	Jan Jönsson	SWE	Sarajevo	−50.3	+ 90.0	0	+39.67
4.	Mary Gordon-Watson	GBR	Cornishman V	−51.3	+ 81.6	0	+30.27
5.	Kevin Freeman	USA	Good Mixture	−51.3	+ 91.2	−10	+29.87
6.	J. William Roycroft	AUS	Warrathoola	−36.0	+ 65.6	0	+29.60
7.	Richard Sands	AUS	Depeche	−64.3	+ 99.2	−10	+24.87
8.	Bruce Davidson	USA	Plain Sailing	−40.3	+ 74.8	−10	+24.47

1976 Montreal C: 49, N: 13, D: 7.25.

			HORSE	DRESSAGE	ENDURANCE	JUMPING	TOTAL PTS.
1.	Edmund Coffin	USA	Bally-Cor	− 64.59	− 50.4	0	−114.99
2.	J. Michael Plumb	USA	Better & Better	− 66.25	− 49.6	−10	−125.85
3.	Karl Schultz	GER	Madrigal	− 46.25	− 63.2	−20	−129.45
4.	Richard Meade	GBR	Jacob Jones	− 73.75	− 57.6	−10	−141.35
5.	Wayne Roycroft	AUS	Laurenson	− 80.84	− 97.2	0	−178.04
6.	Gerard Sinnott	IRL	Croghan	−101.25	− 77.6	0	−178.85
7.	Jean Valat	FRA	Vampire	− 92.50	− 95.2	0	−187.70
8.	Yuri Salnikov	SOV/RUS	Rumpel	− 86.66	−102.8	0	−189.46

1980 Moscow C: 28, N: 7, D: 7.27.

		HORSE	DRESSAGE	ENDURANCE	JUMPING	TOTAL PTS.
1. Euro Federico Roman	ITA	Rossinan	−54.4	− 49.2	− 5	−108.6
2. Aleksandr Blinov	SOV/KYR	Galzun	−64.4	− 56.4	0	−120.8
3. Yuri Salnikov	SOV/RUS	Pintset	−53.0	− 93.6	− 5	−151.6
4. Valery Volkov	SOV/RUS	Tskheti	−54.0	−125.6	− 5	−184.6
5. Tzvetan Donchev	BUL	Medisson	−66.4	−114.4	− 5	−185.8
6. Miroslaw Sziapka	POL	Erywan	−52.4	−184.4	− 5	−241.8
7. Anna Casagrande	ITA	Daleye	−61.2	−190.0	−15	−266.2
8. Mauro Roman	ITA	Dourakine 4	−63.4	−218.0	0	−281.4

The equestrian events were badly hit by the anti-Soviet boycott, and an alternative competition was held in August at Fontainebleau, France, with 42 riders representing 14 nations. The winner was Nils Haagensen of Denmark, with Americans James Wofford and Torrance Watkins finishing second and third.

1984 Los Angeles-Arcadia C: 48, N: 15, D: 8.3.

		HORSE	DRESSAGE	ENDURANCE	JUMPING	TOTAL
1. Mark Todd	NZE	Charisma	−51.6	.0	0	−51.6
2. Karen Stives	USA	Ben Arthur	−49.2	.0	−5	−54.2
3. Virginia Holgate	GBR	Priceless	−56.4	− .4	0	−56.8
4. Torrance Watkins Fleischmann	USA	Finvarra	−57.6	− 2.8	0	−60.4
5. Pascal Morvillers	FRA	Gulliver "B"	−52.6	−10.4	0	−63.0
6. Lucinda Green	GBR	Regal Realm	−63.8	.0	0	−63.8
7. Marina Sciocchetti	ITA	Master Hunt	−67.0	.0	0	−67.0
8. Mauro Checcoli	ITA	Spey Cast Boy	−60.4	− 1.6	−5	−67.0

Thirty-three-year-old Karen Stives, the final rider of the competition, entered the arena knowing that her ride would decide both the individual and team gold medals. If she cleared all 12 obstacles without a fault, she would come away with both golds. If she dislodged the rail of one fence, she would lose the individual gold to Mark Todd, but she would still secure first place for the U.S. team. If she knocked down two fences the team gold would be won by Great Britain. As the capacity crowd watched nervously, Stives successfully guided Ben Arthur over the first ten obstacles. But then, at the next to last obstacle—a triple jump—the horse nicked the top of the middle fence, sending the pole to the ground. Stives and Ben Arthur recovered to complete the course without incident.

Mark Todd was a 28-year-old dairy farmer who sold most of his herd to finance his Olympic quest.

1988 Seoul C: 50, N: 16, D: 9.22.

		HORSE	DRESSAGE	ENDURANCE	JUMPING	GRAND TOTAL
1. Mark Todd	NZE	Charisma	−37.6	.0	− 5	−42.6
2. Ian Stark	GBR	Sir Wattie	−50.0	− 2.8	0	−52.8
3. Virginia Leng (Holgate)	GBR	Master Craftsman	−43.2	− 8.8	−10	−62.0
4. Claus Erhorn	GER	Justyn Tyme	−39.6	−16.0	− 6.75	−62.35
5. Judith "Tinks" Pottinger	NZE	Volunteer	−65.8	.0	0	−65.8
6. Matthias Baumann	GER	Shamrock	−50.6	−13.2	− 5	−68.8
7. Jean Teulère	FRA	Mohican V	−57.6	− 6.4	− 5	−69.0
8. Andrew Hoy	AUS	Kiwi	−57.0	−32.0	0	−89.0

Todd and Charisma led the field in both the dressage and endurance stages, then knocked over just one fence to become only the second repeat winners of the three-day event. Todd later wrote a 112-page biography of Charisma.

1992 Barcelona C: 82, N: 25, D: 7.30.

			DRESSAGE	ENDURANCE	JUMPING	GRAND TOTAL
		HORSE	DRESSAGE	ENDURANCE	JUMPING	TOTAL
1.	Matthew Ryan	AUS	Kibah Tic Toc	−57.8	− 7.2	−5	−70.0
2.	Herbert Blöcker	GER	Feine Dame	−52.2	−27.6	−1.5	−81.3
3.	Blyth Tait	NZE	Messiah	−78.8	− 8.8	0	−87.6
4.	Vicky Latta	NZE	Chief	−58.0	−24.8	−5	−87.8
5.	Andrew Hoy	AUS	Kiwi	−58.8	−25.6	−5	−89.4
6.	Karen Dixon (Straker)	GBR	Get Smart	−44.6	−42.8	−5	−92.4
7.	Luis Álvarez Cervera	SPA	Mr. Chrisalis	−65.0	−37.2	0	−102.2
8.	Karin Donckers	BEL	Britt	−75.4	−24.0	−5	−104.4

Unheralded Matt Ryan held a lead of 5.4 points over Andrew Nicholson of New Zealand after the endurance test but was considered suspect at show jumping after knocking over five fences while qualifying for the Olympics at the prestigious Badminton event. He had no such problems in Barcelona and came away with the gold medal. The same could not be said of Nicholson, who dislodged nine fences, incurred 45 penalty points—the most of any competitor—and finished in 16th place. Blyth Tait staged a remarkable comeback: placed only 69th after the dressage test, he performed so well the rest of the way that he was able to salvage the bronze medal.

THREE-DAY EVENT, TEAM

According to current rules, each team has four members, but the scores of only the top three finishers are counted.

1896–1908 not held

1912 Stockholm T: 7, N: 7, D: 7.17.

		HORSE	TOTAL PTS.
1.	SWE		139.06
	Axel Nordlander	Lady Artist	46.59
	Nils Adlercreutz	Atout	46.31
	Ernst Casparsson	Irmelin	46.16
2.	GER		138.48
	Friedrich von Rochow	Idealist	46.42
	Richard Graf von Schaesberg-Tannheim	Grundsee	46.16
	Eduard von Lütcken	Blue Boy	45.90
3.	USA		137.33
	Benjamin Lear	Poppy	45.91
	John Montgomery	Deceive	45.88
	Guy Henry	Chiswell	45.54
4.	FRA		136.77
	Jean Cariou	Cocotte	46.32
	Bernard Meyer	Allons-y	45.30
	Seigner	Dignité	45.15

1920 Antwerp T: 6, N: 6, D: 9.10.

		HORSE	TOTAL PTS.
1.	SWE		5057.50
	Graf Helmer Mörner	Germania	1775.00
	Åge Lundström	Yrsa	1738.75
	Georg von Braun	Diana	1543.75
2.	ITA		4735.00
	Ettore Caffaratti	Caniche	1733.75
	Garibaldi Spighi	Otello	1647.50
	Giulio Cacciandra	Facetto	1353.75
3.	BEL		4560.00
	Roger Moeremans d'Emaus	Sweet Girl	1652.50
	Oswald Lints	Martha	1515.00
	Jules Bonvalet	Weppelghem	1392.50
4.	USA		4477.50
	Harry Chamberlin	Nigra	1568.75
	William West	Black Boy	1558.75
	John Barry	Raven	1350.00

1924 Paris T: 10, N: 10, D: 7.26.

		HORSE	TOTAL PTS.
1.	HOL		5297.5
	Adolph van der Voort van Zijp	Silver Piece	1976.0
	Charles Pahud de Mortanges	Johnny Walker	1828.0
	Gerard de Kruyff	Addio	1493.5
2.	SWE		4743.5
	Claës König	Bojar	1730.0
	Carl Torsten Sylvan	Amita	1678.0
	Gustaf Hagelin	Varius	1335.5
3.	ITA		4512.5
	Alberto Lombardi	Pimplo	1572.0
	Alessandro Alvisi	Capiligio	1536.0
	Emanuele di Pralormo	Mount Felix	1404.5

	HORSE	TOTAL PTS.
4. SWI		4338.5
Hans Bühler	Mikosch	1477.5
Charles Stoffel	Kreuzritter	1466.0
Werner Fehr	Prahihans	1395.0
5. BEL		4233.5
Beaudouin de Brabandère	Modestie	1728.5
Jules Bonvalet	Weppelghem	1428.0
Joseph Fallon	Le Divorce	1077.0
6. GBR		4064.5
Edward de Fonblanque	Copper	1728.5
Keith Hervey	Wild Gal	1354.0
Alec Tod	White Surrey	982.0
7. POL		3571.5
Karol Rómmel	Krechowiak	1648.5
Kazimierz Szosland	Helusia	961.5
Kazimierz Rostowo-Suski	Lady	958.5

1928 Amsterdam T: 14, N: 14, D: 8.11.

	HORSE	TOTAL PTS.
1. HOL		5865.68
Charles Pahud de Mortanges	Marcroix	1969.82
Gerard de Kruyff	Va-t-en	1967.26
Adolph van der Voort van Zijp	Silver Piece	1928.60
2. NOR		5395.68
Bjart Ording	And Over	1912.98
Arthur Quist	Hidalgo	1895.14
Eugen Johansen	Baby	1587.56
3. POL		5067.92
Michal Antoniewicz	Moja Mita	1822.50
Józef Trenkwald	Lwi Pazur	1645.20
Karol Rómmel	Doneuse	1600.22

1932 Los Angeles T: 4, N: 4, D: 8.13.

	HORSE	TOTAL PTS.
1. USA		5038.083
Earl Thomson	Jenny Champ	1811.000
Harry Chamberlin	Plesant Smiles	1687.833
Edwin Argo	Honolulu Tomboy	1539.250
2. HOL		4689.083
Charles Pahud de Mortanges	Marcroix	1813.833
Karel Johan Schummelketel	Duiveltje	1614.500
Aernout van Lennep	Henk	1260.750

1936 Berlin T: 14, N: 14, D: 8.16.

	HORSE	TOTAL PTS.
1. GER		– 676.65
Ludwig Stubbendorff	Nurmi	– 37.70
Rudolf Lippert	Fasan	– 111.60
Konrad Freiherr von Wangenheim	Kurfürst	– 527.35
2. POL		– 991.70
Henryk Rojcewicz	Arlekin III	– 253.00
Zdzislaw Kawecki	Bambino	– 300.70
Seweryn Kulesza	Tosca	– 438.00
3. GBR		– 9195.50
Alec Scott	Bob Clive	– 117.30
Edward Howard-Vyse	Blue Steel	– 324.00
Richard Fanshawe	Bowie Knife	– 8754.20
4. CZE		–18952.70
Václav Procházka	Harlekyn	– 324.30
Josef Dobes	Leskov	– 497.70
Otomar Bureš	Mirko	–18130.70

Lieutenant Konrad Freiherr von Wangenheim was one of the German heroes of the Berlin Games. During the

A leading German hero of the 1936 Berlin Olympics, Konrad von Wangenheim broke his collarbone during the steeple-chase portion of the equestrian three-day event. The next day he was thrown from his horse a second time, but completed the competition, enabling the German team to win the gold medal.

steeplechase portion of the endurance run, his horse, Kurfürst, stumbled at the fourth obstacle, a hurdle and pond, throwing the 26-year-old von Wangenheim to the ground and breaking his collarbone. Knowing that the German team would be disqualified if he failed to finish, von Wangenheim remounted and negotiated the remaining 32 obstacles without a fault. But the jumping competition still remained. The next day von Wangenheim appeared in the stadium with his arm in a sling. Just before he mounted Kurfürst, the sling was removed and his arm was tightly bound. However, at one of the early obstacles, a double jump, Kurfürst rushed ahead and von Wangenheim was forced to pull the reins with both hands. The horse reared up, fell backward, and landed on von Wangenheim, who managed to crawl out from underneath. Kurfürst lay still and was thought to be dead, but suddenly jumped back up. Von Wangenheim remounted and again completed the course without another fault. The stadium crowd of 100,000 gave von Wangenheim a prolonged standing ovation, as Germany won the gold medal. The German team had spent 18 months practicing full-time on a replica of the Olympic course that had been built on a private estate.

The unusually enormous number of penalty points accumulated by Lieutenant Bureš of Czechoslovakia was a result of his taking 2 hours 46 minutes and 36 seconds to complete the eight-kilometer cross-country course, for which the time limit was 17 minutes 46 seconds.

1948 London T: 14, N: 14, D: 8.12.

	HORSE		TOTAL PTS.
1. USA			−161.50
Frank Henry	Swing Low	− 21.00	
Charles Anderson	Reno Palisade	− 26.50	
Earl Thomson	Reno Rhythm	−114.00	
2. SWE			−165.00
Robert Selfelt	Claque	− 25.00	
Olof Stahre	Komet	− 70.00	
Sigurd Svensson	Dust	− 70.00	
3. MEX			−305.25
Humberto Mariles Cortés	Parral	− 61.75	
Raúl Campero	Tarahumara	−120.50	
Joaquin Solano Chagoya	Malinche	−123.00	
4. SWI			−404.50
Alfred Blaser	Mahmud	− 59.25	
Anton Bühler	Amour Amour	− 95.00	
Pierre Musy	Französin	−250.25	
5. SPA			−422.50
Joaquin Nogueras Marquez	Epsom	− 41.00	
Fernando Gazapo de Sarraga	Vivian	−179.25	
Santiago Martinez Larraz	Fogoso	−202.25	

1952 Helsinki T: 19, N: 19, D: 8.2.

	HORSE		TOTAL PTS.
1. SWE			−221.94
Hans von Blixen-Finecke, Jr.	Jubal	− 28.33	
Olof Stahre	Komet	− 69.41	
Karl Folke Frölén	Fair	−124.20	
2. GER			−235.49
Wilhelm Büsing	Hubertus	− 55.50	
Klaus Wagner	Dachs	− 65.66	
Otto Rothe	Trux von Kamax	−114.33	
3. USA			−587.16
Charles Hough	Cassivellannus	− 70.66	
Walter Staley	Craigwood Park	−168.50	
John Wofford	Benny Grimes	−348.00	
4. POR			−618.00
Fernando Marques Cavaleiro	Caudel	−183.00	
António Pereira de Almeida	Florentina	−216.20	
Joaquim Miguel Duarte Silva	Faial	−218.80	
5. DEN			−828.86
Hans Anderson	Tom	−222.20	
Otto Acthon	Sirdar	−267.66	
Aage Rybaeck-Nielsen	Sahara	−339.00	
6. IRL			−953.52
Henry Freeman-Jackson	Cuchulain	−268.66	
Ian Dudgeon	Hope	−269.20	
Mark Darley	Emily Little	−415.66	

1956 Stockholm T: 19, N: 19, D: 6.14.

	HORSE		TOTAL PTS.
1. GBR			− 355.48
Francis Weldon	Kilbarry	− 85.48	
A. Laurence Rook	Wild Venture	−119.64	
Albert Hill	Countryman III	−150.36	
2. GER			− 475.91
August Lütke-Westhues	Trux von Kamax	− 84.87	
Otto Rothe	Sissi	−158.04	
Klaus Wagner	PrinzeB	−233.00	
3. CAN			− 572.72
John Rumble	Cilroy	−162.53	
James Elder	Colleen	−193.69	
Brian Herbinson	Tara	−216.50	
4. AUS			− 619.98
Brian Crago	Radar	−147.42	
Wyatt Thompson	Brown Sugar	−155.06	
Ernest Barker	Dandy	−317.50	
5. ITA			− 691.14
Giancarlo Gutierrez	Wiston	−136.43	
Adriano Capuzzo	Tuft of Heather	−139.41	
Giuseppe Molinari	Uccello	−415.30	

	HORSE	TOTAL PTS.
6. ARG		− 724.18
Juan Martín Merbilháa	Gitana I	−136.46
Eduardo Cano	Why	−242.01
Carlos de la Serna	Fanion	−345.71
7. SOV		−1112.33
Lev Baklychkine	Guimnast	− 96.65
Nikolai Chelenkov	Satrap	−297.68
Valerian Kouibychev	Perekop	−718.00
8. SWI		−1360.90
Emil-Otto Gmür	Romeo	−378.51
Roland Perret	Erlfried	−405.18
Samuel Koechlin	Goya	−577.21

1960 Rome T: 18, N: 18, D: 9.10.

	HORSE	TOTAL PTS.
1. AUS		−128.18
Lawrence Morgan	Salad Days	+ 7.15
Neale Lavis	Mirrabooka	− 16.50
J. William Roycroft	Our Solo	−118.83
2. SWI		−386.02
Anton Bühler	Gay Spark	− 51.21
Hans Schwarzen- bach	Burn Trout	−131.45
Rudolf Günthardt	Atbara	−203.36
3. FRA		−515.71
Jack Le Goff	Image	− 72.91
Guy Lefrant	Nicias	−208.50
Jean Raymond Le Roy	Gardem	−234.30
4. GBR		−516.21
Michael Bullen	Cottage Romance	− 62.60
Albert Hill	Wild Venture	−215.60
Francis Weldon	Samuel Johnson	−238.01
5. ITA		−528.21
Lucio Tasca	Rahin	−125.80
Ludovico Nava	Arcidosso	−161.91
Giovanni Grignolo	Court Hill	−240.50
6. IRL		−674.00
Edward Harty	Harlequin	−112.30
Anthony Cameron	Sonnet	−251.55
Ian Dudgeon	Corrigneagh	−310.15

Suffering from a concussion and a broken collarbone as a result of a fall during the endurance test, 45-year-old Bill Roycroft insisted on leaving his hospital bed to compete in the jumping test, thus ensuring that the gold medal would go to Australia. Over the next 16 years, three of Roycroft's sons represented Australia in the Olympics. He himself competed four more times.

1964 Tokyo T: 12, N: 12, D:10.19.

	HORSE	TOTAL PTS.
1. ITA		+ 85.80
Mauro Checcoli	Surbean	+ 64.40

Paolo Angioni	King	+ 17.87	
Giuseppe Ravano	Royal Love	+ 3.53	
2. USA			+ 65.86
Michael Page	Grasshopper	+ 47.40	
Kevin Freeman	Gallopade	+ 17.13	
J. Michael Plumb	Bold Minstrel	+ 1.33	
3. GER&GDR			+ 56.73
Fritz Ligges	Donkosak	+ 49.20	
Horst Karsten	Condora	+ 36.60	
Gerhard Schulz	Balza X	− 29.07	
4. IRL			+ 42.86
Anthony Cameron	Black Salmon	+ 46.53	
Thomas Brennan	Kilkenny	+ 1.13	
John Harty	San Michele	− 4.80	
5. SOV/RUS			− 19.63
German Gazyumov	Gran	+ 23.47	
Boris Konkov	Rumb	− 10.97	
Pavel Deyev	Satrap	− 32.13	
6. ARG			− 34.80
Carlos Moratorio	Chalan	+ 56.40	
Elvio Flores	Legitima	− 2.73	
Juan Gesualdi	Morrina	− 88.47	
7. AUS			− 67.27
J. William Roycroft	Eldorado	+ 32.20	
Brien Cobcroft	Stony Crossing	+ 8.40	
John Kelly	Brigalow	−107.87	
8. FRA			−133.87
Jack Le Goff	Leopard	− 37.87	
Jean de Croutte de St. Martin	Mon Clos	− 38.47	
Hughes Landon	Laurier	− 57.53	

1968 Mexico City T: 12, N: 12, D: 10.21.

	HORSE	TOTAL PTS.
1. GBR		−175.93
Derek Allhusen	Lochinvar	− 41.61
Richard Meade	Cornishman V	− 64.46
Reuben Jones	The Poacher	− 69.86
2. USA		−245.87
Michael Page	Foster	− 52.31
James Wofford	Kilkenny	− 74.06
J. Michael Plumb	Plain Sailing	−119.50
3. AUS		−331.26
Wayne Roycroft	Zhivago	− 95.05
Brien Cobcroft	Depeche	−108.76
J. William Roycroft	Warrathoola	−127.55
4. FRA		−505.83
Jean-Jacques Guyon	Pitou	− 38.86
André Le Goupil	Olivette B	−107.26
Jean Sarrazin	Joburg	−359.71
5. GER		−518.22
Horst Karsten	Adagio	−102.96
Jochen Mehrdorf	Lapiz Lazuli	−199.41
Klaus Wagner	Abdulla	−215.85
6. MEX		−631.56
Ernesto Del Castillo	Coficioso	−170.60
Ramon Mejia	Centinela	−182.90
Evaristo Avalos	Ludmilla II	−278.06

7. GDR			−690.72
Karl-Heinz Fuhrmann	Saturn	−218.25	
Uwe Plank	Kranich	−231.01	
Helmut Hartmann	Ingwer	−241.46	
8. CAN			−787.68
Robin Hahn	Taffy	− 95.41	
Norman Elder	Questionnaire	−332.46	
Barry Sonshine	Durlas Eile	−359.81	

Australia's bronze medalist team included the father-son combination of Bill and Wayne Roycroft. The Roycrofts repeated their performance in 1976, when father Bill was 61 years old. Two more of Bill Roycroft's sons competed in the Olympics: Clarke in 1972 and Barry in 1976 and 1988. Wayne's wife, Vicki, took part in 1984 and 1988.

1972 Munich T: 18, N: 18, D: 9.1.

	HORSE		TOTAL PTS.
1. GBR			+ 95.53
Richard Meade	Laurieston	+ 57.73	
Mary Gordon Watson	Cornishman V	+ 30.27	
Bridget Parker	Cornish Gold	+ 7.53	
2. USA			+ 10.81
Kevin Freeman	Good Mixture	+ 29.87	
Bruce Davidson	Plain Sailing	+ 24.47	
J. Michael Plumb	Free and Easy	− 43.53	
3. GER			− 18.00
Harry Klugmann	Christopher Rob	+ 8.00	
Ludwig Goessing	Chikago	− 0.40	
Karl Schultz	Pisco	− 25.60	
4. AUS			− 27.86
J. William Roycroft	Warrathoola	+ 29.60	
Richard Sands	Depeche	+ 24.87	
Brian Schrapel	Wakool	− 82.33	
5. GDR			−127.93
Rudolf Beerbohm	Ingolf	+ 3.80	
Jens Niehls	Big-Ben	− 60.00	
Joachim Brohmann	Uranio	− 71.73	
6. SWI			−156.43
Paul Hürlimann	Grand Times	− 11.03	
Anton Bühler	Wukari	− 19.87	
Alfred Schwarzen-bach	Big Boy	−125.53	
7. SOV			−190.06
Sergei Mukhin	Reisfeder	− 0.13	
Valentin Gorelkin	Rok	− 34.93	
Vladimir Lanugin	Zimar	−155.00	
8. ITA			−203.58
Alessandro Argenton	Woodland	− 43.33	
Dino Costantini	Lord Jim	− 98.18	
Mario Turner	Forgotten Fred	−148.73	

Many Olympic gold-medal winners have exploited their success by pursuing movie careers. Almost all of these athletes-turned-actors have been human. One exception is Cornishman V, who helped two different riders to Olympic victory, in 1968 and 1972. He later appeared in *Dead Cert* (1974), based on a Dick Francis novel, and *International Velvet* (1978).

1976 Montreal T: 12, N: 12, D: 7.25.

	HORSE		TOTAL PTS.
1. USA			−441.00
Edmund Coffin	Bally-Cor	−114.99	
J. Michael Plumb	Better & Better	−125.85	
Bruce Davidson	Irish-Cap	−200.16	
2. GER			−584.60
Karl Schultz	Madrigal	−129.45	
Herbert Blöcker	Albrant	−213.15	
Helmut Rethemeier	Pauline	−242.00	
3. AUS			−599.54
Wayne Roycroft	Laurenson	−178.04	
Mervyn Bennett	Regal Reign	−206.04	
J. William Roycroft	Version	−215.46	
4. ITA			−682.24
Euro Federico Roman	Shamrock	−194.14	
Mario Turner	Tempest Blisland	−213.19	
Alessandro Argenton	Woodland	−274.91	
5. SOV			−721.55
Yuri Salnikov	Rumpel	−189.46	
Valery Dvorianinov	Zeila	−218.25	
Viktor Kalinin	Araks	−313.84	
6. CAN			−808.81
Juliet Graham	Sumatra	−202.69	
Cathy Wedge	City Fella	−286.76	
Robin Hahn	L'Esprit	−319.36	

1980 Moscow T: 7, N: 7, D: 7.27.

	HORSE		TOTAL PTS.
1. SOV			− 457.00
Aleksandr Blinov	Galzun	−120.80	
Yuri Salnikov	Pintset	−151.60	
Valery Volkov	Tskheti	−184.60	
2. ITA			− 656.20
Euro Federico Roman	Rossinan	−108.60	
Anna Casagrande	Daleye	−266.20	
Mauro Roman	Dourakine 4	−281.40	
3. MEX			−1172.85
Manuel Mendivil Yocupicio	Remember	−319.75	
David Barcena Rios	Bombon	−362.50	
José Luis Perez Soto	Quelite	−490.60	
4. HUN			−1603.40
László Cseresnyes	Fapipa	−436.20	
István Grozner	Biboros	−498.60	
Zoltán Horvath	Lamour	−668.60	

The substitute three-day event, held in August at Fountainbleau, was won by France, with West Germany second and Australia third.

1984 Los Angeles-Arcadia T: 11, N: 11, D: 8.3.

	HORSE		TOTAL PTS.
1. USA			−186.00
Karen Stives	Ben Arthur	− 54.20	
Torrance Watkins Fleischmann	Finvarra	− 60.40	
J. Michael Plumb	Blue Stone	− 71.40	

		HORSE	TOTAL PTS.
2.	GBR		−189.20
	Virginia Holgate	Priceless	− 56.80
	Lucinda Green	Regal Realm	− 63.80
	Ian Stark	Oxford Blue	− 68.60
3.	GER		−234.00
	Dietmar Hogrefe	Foliant	− 74.40
	Bettina Overesch	Peacetime	− 79.60
	Claus Erhorn	Fair Lady	− 80.00
4.	FRA		−236.00
	Pascal Morvillers	Gulliver "B"	− 63.00
	Marie Christine Duroy	Harley	− 85.40
	Armand Bigot	Jacquou Du Bois	− 87.60
5.	AUS		−258.40
	Andrew Hoy	Davey	− 80.00
	Mervyn Bennett	Regal Reign	− 87.40
	Vicki Roycroft	Looking Ahead	− 91.00
6.	NZE		−280.00
	Mark Todd	Charisma	− 51.60
	Mary Hamilton	Whist	− 98.00
	Andrew Nicholson	Kahlua	−130.40
7.	ITA		−280.70
	Mauro Checcoli	Spey Cast Boy	− 67.00
	Marina Sciocchetti	Master Hunt	− 67.00
	Bartolo Ambrosione	Brick	−146.70
8.	SWE		−339.85
	Jan Jonsson	Isolde	− 86.40
	Göran Breisner	Bobalong	− 99.65
	Christian Persson	Joel	−153.80

1988 Seoul T: 10, N: 10, D: 9.22.

		HORSE	TOTAL PTS.
1.	GER		−225.95
	Claus Erhorn	Justyn Thyme	− 62.35
	Matthias Baumann	Shamrock	− 68.80
	Thies Kaspareit	Sherry	− 94.80
2.	GBR		−256.80
	Ian Stark	Sir Wattie	− 52.80
	Virginia Leng (Holgate)	Master Craftsman	− 62.00
	Karen Straker	Get Smart	−142.00
3.	NZE		−271.20
	Mark Todd	Charisma	− 42.60
	Judith "Tinks" Pottinger	Volunteer	− 65.80
	Andrew Bennie	Grayshott	−162.80
4.	POL		−389.60
	Boguslaw Jarecki	Niewiaza	−111.40
	Krzystof Rogowski	Alkierz	−114.80
	Jerzy Rafalak	Dzwinograd	−163.40
5.	AUS		−457.60
	Andrew Hoy	Kiwi	− 89.00
	Scott Keach	Trade Commissioner	−176.60
	David Green	Shannagh	−192.00
6.	FRA		−498.80
	Jean Teulère	Mohican V	− 69.00
	Vincent Berthet	Jet Crub	−202.20
	Pascal Morvillers	Frangin III	−227.60

		HORSE	
7.	KOR		−740.15
	Choi Myung-jin	Snuffler	−130.55
	Park Dong-joo	Aqaba Legend	−227.00
	Park So-woon	Moisson d'Avril	−382.60

1992 Barcelona T: 18, N: 18, D: 7.30.

		HORSE	TOTAL PTS.
1.	AUS		−288.6
	Matthew Ryan	Kibah Tic Toc	− 70.0
	Andrew Hoy	Kiwi	− 89.4
	Gillian Rolton	Peppermint Grove	−129.2
2.	NZE		−290.8
	Blyth Tait	Messiah	− 87.6
	Vicky Latta	Chief	− 87.8
	Andrew Nicholson	Spinning Rhombus	−115.4
3.	GER		−300.3
	Herbert Blöcker	Feine Dame	− 81.3
	Ralf Ehrenbrink	Kildare	−108.4
	Cord Mysegaes	Ricardo	−110.4
4.	BEL		−333.05
	Karin Donckers	Britt	−104.4
	Jef Desmedt	Dolleman	−108.4
	Willy Sneyers	Drum	−120.25
5.	SPA		−388.8
	Luis Álvarez Cervera	Mr. Chrisalis	−102.2
	Santiago De La Rocha Mille	Kinvarra B'92	−122.4
	Fernando Villalón Gómez	Clever Night	−164.2
6.	GBR		−406.6
	Karen Dixon (Straker)	Get Smart	− 92.4
	Mary Thomson	King William	−105.4
	Richard Walker	Jacana	−208.8
7.	JPN		−434.8
	Yoshihiko Kowata	Hellatdawn	−135.8
	Eiki Miyazaki	Mystery Cargo	−137.8
	Kojiro Goto	Retalic	−161.2
8.	IRL		−445.8
	Eric Smiley	Enterprise	−140.4
	Mairead Curran	Watercolour	−149.4
	Melanie Duff	Rathlin Roe	−156.0

New Zealand led Australia by 32.8 points after the endurance test and seemed a lock for the gold medals. Indeed, with Andrew Nicholson on Spinning Rhombus left to jump for New Zealand and Matt Ryan on Kibah Tic Toc left for Australia, the Kiwis had actually lengthened their lead to 37.8 points. But Nicholson had a disastrous round, knocking over nine obstacles worth 45 points. This meant that if Ryan could clear all but one jump, Australia would earn an unexpected victory. Despite the pressure, Ryan and Kibah Tic Toc cleared all but the last obstacle.

JUMPING, INDIVIDUAL

Each horse and rider jumps three qualifying rounds. Competitors who finish in the top half of the qualifying rounds advance to final course A. The top 20 (and those tied for 20th) in that round qualify for final course B. The results are determined by adding the scores from both rounds. Ties for the medal places are decided by a jump-off over six of the obstacles used in course B. If a tie still exists, the competitor with the fastest time in the jump-off is declared the winner. Course A must be between 600 and 800 meters long and include 12 to 15 obstacles and a water jump. The obstacles may vary from 1.4 meters (4 feet 7 inches) to 1.6 meters (5 feet 3 inches) in height. Course B must be between 500 and 600 meters long. It must be different from course A and must include ten obstacles varying in height from 1.4 meters to 1.7 meters (5 feet 7 inches). Course A must include three double jumps or one double and one triple; course B must include one double and one triple, with a water jump being optional.

Faults are assessed for disobedience at an obstacle and backtracking. First disobedience at an obstacle is penalized by 3 faults; second disobedience by 6 faults; third disobedience results in disqualification. If an obstacle is knocked down or the horse's hoof touches the white border of a water jump, 4 faults are assessed. A fall by either horse or rider is penalized by 8 faults; a second fall results in elimination. Riders exceeding the time limit are penalized a quarter of a point per second or part of a second.

1896 not held

1900 Paris C: 45, N: 5, D: 5.29.

		HORSE	
1. Aimé Haegeman	BEL	Benton II	2:16.0
2. Georges van de Poele	BEL	Windsor Squire	2:17.6
3. Louis de Champsavin	FRA	Terpsichore	2:26.0

1904–1908 not held

1912 Stockholm C: 31, N: 8, D: 7.16.

		HORSE	FAULTS	JUMP-OFF
1. Jean Cariou	FRA	Mignon	4	5
2. Rabod Wilhelm von Kröcher	GER	Dohna	4	7
3. Emanuel de Blommaert de Soye	BEL	Clonmore	5	
4. Herbert Scott	GBR	Shamrock	6	
5. Sigismund Freyer	GER	Ultimus	7	
6. Wilhelm Graf von Hohenau	GER	Pretty Girl	9	
6. Nils Adlercreutz	SWE	Ilex	9	
6. Ernst Casparsson	SWE	Kiriki	9	

1920 Antwerp C: 25, N: 6, D: 7.12.

		HORSE	FAULTS
1. Tommaso Lequio di Assaba	ITA	Trebecco	2
2. Alessandro Valerio	ITA	Cento	3
3. Carl-Gustaf Lewenhaupt	SWE	Mon Coeur	4
4. Paul Michelet	NOR	Ravn	5
5. Ferdinand de la Serna	BEL	Arsinoe	6
5. Lars von Stockenström	SWE	Reward	6
7. Henry Allen	USA	Don	7
7. Santorre de Rossi Santa Rosa	ITA	Neruccio	7
7. Roger Moeremans d'Emaus	BEL	Sweet Girl	7

1924 Paris C: 43, N: 11, D: 7.27.

		HORSE	FAULTS	
1. Alphonse Gemuseus	SWI	Lucette	6	
2. Tommaso Lequio di Assaba	ITA	Trebecco	8.75	
3. Adam Królikiewicz	POL	Picador	10	
4. Philip Bowden-Smith	GBR	Billy Boy	10.5	
5. António Borges de Almeida	POR	Reginald	12	2:28.8
6. Åke Thelning	SWE	Loke	12	2:30.4
7. Axel Ståhle	SWE	Cecil	12.25	
8. Nicolas Leroy	BEL	Vif Argent	14.75	

1928 Amsterdam C: 46, N: 16, D: 8.12.

		HORSE	FAULTS	1ST JUMP-OFF	2ND JUMP-OFF
1. František Ventura	CZE/SLV	Eliot	0	0	0
2. Pierre Bertran de Balanda	FRA	Papillon	0	0	2
3. Charley Kuhn	SWI	Pepita	0	0	4
4. Kazimierz Gzowski	POL	Mylord	0	2	1:33.0
5. José Navarro Morenés	SPA	Zapatazo	0	2	1:36.0
6. Karl Hansen	SWE	Gerold	0	2	1:39.0
7. Francisco Fourquet	ITA	Joe Aleshire	0	DISQ.	
8. Alphonse Gemuseus	SWI	Lucette	2		

1932 Los Angeles C: 11, N: 4, D: 8.14.

		HORSE	FAULTS
1. Takeichi Nishi	JPN	Uranus	8
2. Harry Chamberlin	USA	Show Girl	12
3. Clarence von Rosen, Jr.	SWE	Empire	16
4. William Bradford	USA	Joe Aleshire	24
5. Ernst Hallberg	SWE	Kornett	50.5

An extremely wealthy man, Takeichi Nishi was a lieutenant in the Japanese army when he won his gold medal. Promoted to colonel toward the end of World War II, he was made commander of a tank battalion on Iwo Jima. During the fierce fighting on that island, some of the U.S. officers learned that Nishi was on the island and hoped to meet him. They never got a chance. Nishi, who had many American friends, including Will Rogers, Mary Pickford, and Douglas Fairbanks, refused to surrender and instead joined a mass Japanese suicide.

1936 Berlin C: 54, N: 18, D: 8.16.

			HORSE	FAULTS	JUMP-OFF	
1.	Kurt Hasse	GER	Tora	4	4	59.2
2.	Henri Rang	ROM	Delfis	4	4	1:12.8
3.	József Platthy	HUN	Sello	8	0	1:02.6
4.	Georges van der Meersch	BEL	Ibrahim	8	0	1:09.0
5.	Carl Raguse	USA	Dakota	8	4	
6.	José Beltrão	POR	Biscuit	12		
6.	Xavier Bizard	FRA	Bagatelle	12		
6.	Johan Jacob Greter	HOL	Ernica	12		
6.	Maurice Gudin de Vallerin	FRA	Ecuyère	12		
6.	Cevat Koula	TUR	Sapkin	12		

1948 London C: 44, N: 15, D: 8.14.

			HORSE	FAULTS	JUMP-OFF	
1.	Humberto Mariles Cortés	MEX	Arete	6.25		
2.	Rubén Uriza	MEX	Harvey	8	0	
3.	Jean François d'Orgeix	FRA	Sucre de Pomme	8	4	38.9
4.	Franklin Wing	USA	Democrat	8	4	40.1
5.	Jaime García Cruz	SPA	Bizarro	12		
5.	Eric Sörensen	SWE	Blatunga	12		
7.	Max Fresson	FRA	Decametre	16		
7.	Henry Llewellyn	GBR	Foxhunter	16		
7.	Henry Nicoll	GBR	Kilgeddin	16		

General Mariles won the title in dramatic fashion. The last rider to enter the arena, he needed to incur fewer than eight faults to win the gold medal. This he did, clearing every obstacle but the water jump and losing 2¼ points for being eight seconds overtime. On the night of August 14, 1964, the 51-year-old Mariles was driving home from a party in his honor in Mexico City when another motorist attempted to force him off the road. At the next traffic light Mariles pulled out a gun and shot the man. He was sent to prison, but later released by presidential pardon. In 1972 he was arrested in Paris for drug-smuggling, but died in prison before coming to trial.

1952 Helsinki C: 51, N: 20, D: 8.3.

			HORSE	FAULTS	JUMP-OFF	
1.	Pierre Jonquères d'Oriola	FRA	Ali Baba	8	0	
2.	Oscar Cristi	CHI	Bambi	8	4	
3.	Fritz Thiedemann	GER	Meteor	8	8	38.5
4.	Eloi Massey Oliveira de Menezes	BRA	Bigua	8	8	45.0
5.	Wilfred White	GBR	Nizefella	8	12	
6.	Humberto Mariles Cortés	MEX	Petrolero	8.75		
7.	Cesar Mendoza	CHI	Pillan	12		3:08.8
8.	Argentino Molinuevo	ARG	Discutido	12		3:13.0

On July 24 d'Oriola watched as his young cousin, Christian d'Oriola, was awarded the gold medal in foil fencing. Throughout the tournament Christian had worn a white cap for good luck. Pierre asked if he could wear the cap now that Christian no longer needed it. Christian handed it over and ten days later Pierre too earned a gold medal.

1956 Stockholm C: 66, N: 24, D: 6.16.

			HORSE	FAULTS
1.	Hans-Günter Winkler	GER	Haila	4
2.	Raimondo D'Inzeo	ITA	Merano	8
3.	Piero D'Inzeo	ITA	Uruguay	11
4.	Fritz Thiedemann	GER	Meteor	12
4.	Wilfred White	GBR	Nizefella	12
6.	Pierre Jonquères d'Oriola	FRA	Voulette	15
7.	Henrique Callado	POR	Martingil	16
8.	Carlos Delía	ARG	Discutido	19

1960 Rome C: 60, N: 23, D: 9.7.

			HORSE	FAULTS
1.	Raimondo D'Inzeo	ITA	Posillipo	12
2.	Piero D'Inzeo	ITA	The Rock	16
3.	David Broome	GBR	Sunslave	23
4.	George Morris	USA	Simjon	24
5.	Hans-Günter Winkler	GER	Halla	25
6.	Fritz Thiedemann	GER	Meteor	25.5
7.	Naldo Dasso	ARG	Final	28
7.	Bernard de Fombelle	FRA	Buffalo	28
7.	Hugh Wiley	USA	Master William	28

1964 Tokyo C: 46, N: 17, D: 10.24.

			HORSE	FAULTS	JUMP-OFF
1.	Pierre Jonquères d'Oriola	FRA	Lutteur	9	
2.	Hermann Schridde	GER	Dozent	13.75	
3.	Peter Robeson	GBR	Firecrest	16	0
4.	Thomas Fahey	AUS	Bonvale	16	8
5.	Joaquim Miguel Duarte Silva	POR	Jeune France	20	
5.	Nelson Pessoa Filho	BRA	Huipil	20	
7.	Frank Chapot	USA	San Lucas	20.5	
8.	Kurt Jarasinski	GER	Torro	22.25	

1968 Mexico City C: 41, N: 15, D: 10.23.

			HORSE	FAULTS	JUMP-OFF	
1.	William Steinkraus	USA	Snowbound	4		
2.	Marion Coakes	GBR	Stroller	8		
3.	David Broome	GBR	Mister Softee	12	0	35.3
4.	Frank Chapot	USA	San Lucas	12	0	36.8
5.	Hans-Günter Winkler	GER	Enigk	12	0	37.5
6.	James Elder	CAN	The Immigrant	12	0	39.2
7.	Monika Bachmann	SWI	Erbach	16		
7.	Piero D'Inzeo	ITA	Fidux	16		
7.	Argentino Moliñuevo	ARG	Don Gustavo	16		
7.	Alwin Schockemöhle	GER	Donal Rex	16		

1972 Munich C: 56, N: 22, D: 9.3.

		HORSE	FAULTS	JUMP-OFF
1. Graziano Mancinelli	ITA	Ambassador	8	0
2. Ann Moore	GBR	Psalm	8	3
3. Neal Shapiro	USA	Sloopy	8	8
4. James Day	CAN	Steelmaster	8.75	
4. Hugo Simon	AUT	Lavendel	8.75	
4. Hartwig Steenken	GER	Simona	8.75	
7. Jean-Marcel Rozier	FRA	Sans Souci	12	
8. Alfonso Segovia	SPA	Tic Tac	16	
8. Fritz Ligges	GER	Robin	16	

For a long time Mancinelli was a rider for the Milan horse-dealing company of Fratelli Rivolta. Consequently he was considered a professional, and many observers were surprised when he was included as a member of the Italian team in Tokyo in 1964. Banned from the team the day before the competition was to begin, he was reinstated at the last minute. The ruling turned in his favor when it was revealed that he was the adopted son of one of the Rivolta brothers—part of the family and therefore not a professional. Eight years later in Munich, Mancinelli rode a perfect round in the jump-off to earn the individual gold medal.

1976 Montreal C: 48, N: 20, D: 7.27.

		HORSE	FAULTS	JUMP-OFF
1. Alwin Schockemöhle	GER	Warwick Rex	0	
2. Michel Vaillancourt	CAN	Branch County	12	4
3. François Mathy	BEL	Gai Luron	12	8
4. Deborah Johnsey	GBR	Moxy	12	15.25
5. Frank Chapot	USA	Viscount	16	
5. Guy Creighton	AUS	Mr. Dennis	16	
5. Marcel Rozier	FRA	Bayard de Maupas	16	
5. Hugo Simon	AUT	Lavendel	16	

A 39-year-old factory owner, Alwin Schockemöhle was the first rider to complete the Olympic competition without a fault since František Ventura in 1928.

1980 Moscow C: 14, N: 7, D: 8.3.

		HORSE	FAULTS	JUMP-OFF	
1. Jan Kowalczyk	POL	Artemor	8		
2. Nikolai Korolkov	SOV/RUS	Espadron	9.5		
3. Joaquin Perez Heras	MEX	Alymony	12	4	43.23
4. Oswaldo Mendez Herbruger	GUA	Pampa	12	4	43.59
5. Viktor Pohanovsky	SOV/UKR	Topky	15.5		
6. Wieslaw Hartman	POL	Norton	16		
7. Barnabas Hevesi	HUN	Bohem	24		
8. Marian Kozicki	POL	Bremen	24.5		

The Rotterdam Show Jumping Festival for Olympic boycotters was won by Hugo Simon of Austria, with John Whitaker of Great Britain second and Melanie Smith of the United States third.

1984 Los Angeles-Arcadia C: 51, N: 21, D: 8.12.

			HORSE	FAULTS	JUMP-OFF
1.	Joe Fargis	USA	Touch of Class	4	0
2.	Conrad Homfeld	USA	Abdullah	4	8
3.	Heidi Robbiani	SWI	Jessica V	8	0
4.	Mario Deslauriers	CAN	Aramis	8	4
5.	Bruno Candrian	SWI	Slygof	8	8
6.	Luis Alvarez Cervera	SPA	Jexico De Park	8.5	
7.	Frédéric Cottier	FRA	Flambeau C	12	
7.	Paul Schockemöhle	GER	Deister	12	
7.	Melanie Smith	USA	Calypso	12	

Joe Fargis and Conrad Homfeld were companions and business partners who owned a breeding stable in Petersburg, Virginia. Fargis would have won the gold medal without a jump-off had not he and Touch of Class knocked down the final rail in the second round. This was their only fault in six rounds of Olympic competition.

1988 Seoul C: 74, N: 24, D: 10.2.

			HORSE	FAULTS	JUMP-OFF	
1.	Pierre Durand	FRA	Jappeloup	1.25		
2.	Greg Best	USA	Gem Twist	4	4	45.70
3.	Karsten Huck	GER	Nepomuk	4	4	54.75
4.	David Broome	GBR	Countryman	8		
4.	Anne Kursinski	USA	Starman	8		
6.	Jaime Azcarraga	MEX	Chin Chin	8		
7.	Joe Fargis (USA)—Mill Pearl, Marcus Fuchs (SWI)—Shandor II, Thomas Fuchs (SWI)—Diners Dollar Girl, Jos Lansink (HOL)—Felix, Nicholas Skelton (GBR)—Apollo, Franke Sloothaak (GER)—Walzerkönig, Johannes Tops (HOL)—Doreen				12		

In 1984, France lost its chance for bronze in the team jumping competition when Pierre Durand fell. Four years later in Seoul, Durand, a 33-year-old bankruptcy administrator from Libourne, near Bordeaux, was given a chance to redeem himself. If he could ride a clear round, the bronze would go to the French. If he made even one mistake, the Canadians would take part in the medal ceremony. This time the team of Durand and Jappeloup was faultless. Four days later, in the individual final, it was Karsten Huck who needed a perfect round to win. But he and Nepomuk knocked down the next-to-last fence and the victory went to Durand.

1992 Barcelona C: 87, N: 30, D: 8.9.

			HORSE	FAULTS
1.	Ludger Beerbaum	GER	Classic Touch	0
2.	Piet Raymakers	HOL	Ratina Z	0.25

3.	Norman Dello Joio	USA	Irish	4.75
4.	Hervé Godignon	FRA	Quidam De Revel	6.25
5.	Jan Tops	HOL	Top Gun	8.25
6.	Maria Gretzer	SWE	Marcoville	10.25
7.	Ludo Philippaerts	BEL	Darco	12.25
8.	Merethe Jensen	DEN	Maxime	12.75

Piet Raymakers rode clear on both final courses, but incurred a quarter-point penalty when he exceeded the time limit on course B by 0.66 seconds. This fraction of a second kept Raymakers from a jump-off for the gold medal when the final rider, Ludger Beerbaum, also jumped clear, but beat the limit by over six seconds.

JUMPING (PRIX DES NATIONS), TEAM

The team jumping final consists of two rounds contested on the same course. The course must be between 600 and 800 meters long and include 12 to 15 obstacles and a water jump. Ties for medal placings are decided by a jump-off over a course of 350 to 450 meters with six obstacles. If a tie still exists, the faster team is declared the winner. Each team consists of three or four riders and horses, but only the best three scores in each round are used to determine the team score. Thus, a rider's score may count in one round but not in the other. Beginning in 1992, only those team members whose scores counted in at least one round were awarded medals.

1896–1908 not held

1912 Stockholm T: 6, N: 6, D: 7.17.

		HORSE	FAULTS	TOTAL PTS.
1.	SWE			25
	Carl-Gustaf Lewenhaupt	Medusa	2	
	Gustaf Kilman	Gatan	10	
	Hans von Rosen	Lord Iron	13	
2.	FRA			32
	Michel d'Astafort	Amazone	5	
	Jean Cariou	Mignon	8	
	Bernard Meyer	Allons-y	19	
3.	GER			40
	Sigismund Freyer	Ultimus	9	
	Wilhelm Graf von Hohenau	Pretty Girl	13	
	Ernst-Hubertus Deloch	Hubertus	18	
4.	USA			43
	John Montgomery	Deceive	10	
	Guy Henry	Chiswell	16	
	Benjamin Lear	Poppy	17	
5.	RUS			50
	Aleksandr Rodzianko	Eros	14	
	Michel Plechkov	Yvette	18	
	Alexis Selikhov	Tugela	18	

	HORSE	FAULTS	TOTAL PTS.
6. BEL			60
Emanuel de Blommaert de Soye	Clonmore	2	
Gaston de Trannoy	Capricieux	28	
Paul Convert	La Sioute	30	

1920 Antwerp T: 5, N: 5, D: 9.12.

	HORSE	FAULTS	TOTAL PTS.
1. SWE			14.00
Claes König	Tresor	2	
Daniel Norling	Eros II	6	
Hans von Rosen	Poor Boy	6	
2. BEL			16.25
Henri Laame	Biscuit	2.75	
André Coumans	Lisette	5.25	
Herman de Gaiffier d'Herstroy	Miss	8.25	
3. ITA			18.75
Ettore Caffaratti	Tradittore	1.50	
Alessandro Alvisi	Raggio di Sole	6.25	
Giulio Cacciandra	Fortunello	11	
4. FRA			34.75
Auguste de Laissardière	Othello	7.50	
Henri Horment	Dignité	13.25	
Théophile Carbon	Incas	14	
5. USA			42.00
Harry Chamberlin	Nigra	9	
Karl Greenwald	Moses	12	
Vincent Erwin	Joffre	21	

1924 Paris T: 11, N: 11, D: 7.27.

	HORSE	FAULTS	TOTAL PTS.
1. SWE			42.25
Åke Thelning	Loke	12.00	
Axel Ståhle	Cecil	12.25	
Åge Lundström	Anvers	18.00	
2. SWI			50.00
Alphonse Gemuseus	Lucette	6.00	
Werner Stüber	Glrandole	20.00	
Hans Bühler	Sailor Boy	24.00	
3. POR			53.00
António Borges de Almeida	Reginald	12.00	
Hélder de Souza Martins	Avro	19.00	
José Mousinho de Albuquerque	Hetrugo	22.00	
4. BEL			57.00
Nicolas Leroy	Vif Argent	14.75	
Jacques Misonne	Torino	19.50	
Gaston Mesmaekers	As de Pique	22.75	
5. ITA			57.50
Tommaso Lequio di Assaba	Trebecco	8.75	
Leone Valle	Struffo	20.00	
Alessandro Alvisi	Grey Fox	28.75	

	HORSE	FAULTS	TOTAL PTS.
6. POL			58.50
Adam Królikiewicz	Picador	10.00	
Karol Rómmel	Faworyt	18.00	
Zdzislaw Dziadulski	Zefer	30.50	
7. GBR			65.75
Philip Bowden-Smith	Billy Boy	10.50	
Capel Brunker	—	25.50	
Geoffrey Brooke	—	29.75	
8. SPA			73.75
José Alvarez de las Asturias Bohorques y Goyeneche (de los Trujillos)	—	18.00	
Nemesio Martinez Hombre	—	22.00	
José Navarro Morenés	—	33.75	

1928 Amsterdam T: 15, N: 15, D: 8.12.

	HORSE	FAULTS	TOTAL PTS.
1. SPA			4
José Navarro Morenés	Zapatazo	0	
José Alvarez de las Asturias Bohorques y Goyeneche (de los Trujilos)	Zalamero	2	
Julio García Fernández	Revistada	2	
2. POL			8
Kazimierz Gzowski	Mylord	0	
Kazimierz Szosland	Ali	2	
Michal Antoniewicz	Readgleadt	6	
3. SWE			10
Karl Hansen	Gerold	0	
Carl Björnstierna	Kornett	2	
Ernst Hallberg	Loke	8	
4. FRA			12
Pierre Bertran de Balanda	Papillon	0	
Jacques Couderc de Fonlongue	Vangerville	4	
Pierre Clavé	Le Trouvere	8	
4. ITA			12
Francesco Forquet	Capineca	0	
Alessandro Bettoni-Cazzago	Aladino	6	
Tommaso Lequio di Assaba	Trebecco	6	
4. POR			12
Luiz Ivens Ferraz	Marco Visconti	4	
Henrique de Sousa Martins	Avro	4	
José Mousinho de Albuquerque	Hebraico	4	
7. GER			14
Eduard Krüger	Donauwelle	2	
Richard Sahla	Correggio	4	
Carl Friedrich Freiherr von Langen-Parow	Falkner	8	
8. SWI			18
Charles Kuhn	Pepita	0	
Alphonse Gemuseus	Lucette	2	
Pierre de Muralt	Notas	16	

1932 Los Angeles T: 3, N: 3, D: 8.14.

No nation completed the course with three riders.

1936 Berlin: T: 18, N: 18, D: 8.16.

	HORSE	FAULTS	TOTAL PTS.
1. GER			44.00
Kurt Hasse	Tora	4.00	
Marten von Barnekow	Nordland	20.00	
Heinz Brandt	Alchimist	20.00	
2. HOL			51.50
Johan Jacob Greter	Ernica	12.00	
Jan Adrianus de Bruine	Trixie	15.00	
Henri Louis van Schaik	Santa Bell	24.50	
3. POR			56.00
José Beltrão	Biscuit	12.00	
Luis Marquéz do Funchal	Merle Blanc	20.00	
Luiz Mena e Silva	Faussette	24.00	
4. USA			72.50
Carl Raguse	Dakota	8.00	
William Bradford	Don	27.00	
Cornelius Jadwin	Ugly	37.50	
5. SWI			74.50
Arnold Mettler	Durmitor	15.00	
Jürg Fehr	Corona	29.00	
Max Iklé	Exile	30.50	
6. JPN			75.00
Manabu Iwahashi	Falaise	15.25	
Takeichi Nishi	Uranus	20.75	
Hirotsugu Inanami	Asafuji	39.00	
7. FRA			75.25
Xavier Bizard	Bagatelle	12.00	
Maurice Gudin de Vallerin	Ecuyère	12.00	
Jean de Tilière	Adriano	51.25	

1948 London T: 14, N: 14; D: 8.14.

	HORSE	FAULTS	TOTAL PTS.
1. MEX			34.25
Humberto Mariles Cortés	Arete	6.25	
Rubén Uriza	Harvey	8.00	
Alberto Valdes	Chihuchoc	20.00	
2. SPA			56.50
Jaime García Cruz	Bizarro	12.00	
José Navarro Morenés	Quorum	20.00	
Marcelino Gavilán y Ponce de León	Forajido	24.50	
3. GBR			67.00
Henry Llewellyn	Foxhunter	16.00	
Henry Nicoll	Kilgeddin	16.00	
Arthur Carr	Monty	35.00	

The course was so difficult that only three of the 14 teams managed to finish intact.

1952 Helsinki T: 15, N: 15, D: 8.3.

	HORSE	FAULTS	TOTAL PTS.
1. GBR			40.75
Wilfred White	Nizefella	8.00	
Douglas Stewart	Aherlow	16.00	
Henry Llewellyn	Foxhunter	16.75	
2. CHI			45.75
Oscar Cristi	Bambi	8.00	
Cesar Mendoza	Pillan	12.00	
Ricardo Echeverria	Lindo Peal	25.75	
3. USA			52.25
William Steinkraus	Hollandia	13.25	
Arthur John McCashin	Miss Budweiser	16.00	
John Russell	Democrat	23.00	
4. BRA			56.50
Eloi Massey Oliveira de Menezes	Bigua	8.00	
Renyldo Guimaraes Ferreira	Bibelot	20.50	
Alvaro Dias de Toledo	Eldorado	28.00	
5. FRA			59.00
Pierre Jonquères d'Oriola	Ali Baba	8.00	
Bertran Pernot du Breuil	Tourbillon	20.00	
Jean-François d'Orgeix	Arlequin D.	31.00	
6. GER			60.00
Fritz Thiedemann	Meteor	8.00	
Georg Höltig	Fink	20.00	
Hans-Hermann Evers	Baden	32.00	
7. ARG			60.75
Sergio Dellacha	Santa Fe	12.00	
Argentino Molinuevo	Discutido	12.00	
Julio Sagasta	Don Juan	36.75	
8. POR			64.00
João Craveiro Lopes	Raso	20.00	
Henrique Alves Calado	Caramulo	20.00	
José Alves Carvalhosa	Mondina	24.00	

It was the last event of the last day of the Helsinki Olympics. The British team had failed to win a single event in any sport and were on the verge of being shut out of the gold for the first time since 1904—before the days of official national teams. In the first round of the team jumping final, the British trio of Wilf White, Duggie Stewart, and Harry Llewellyn had picked up 28.75 faults, including 16.75 by Llewellyn alone, and they were buried back in fifth place. But both White and Stewart knocked over only one fence each and Britain was back in the game. If Llewellyn and his horse, Foxhunter, could complete the course with no more than one mistake, they would save the day for their nation. In fact, they rode a completely clear round and Great Britain had its gold medal. The dramatic nature of the final ride created a national hero: Foxhunter. White and Stewart received a little bit of credit and Llewellyn a bit more, but it was the horse who became a media star. He was inundated with fan letters and gifts, and when a rumor spread that Foxhunter had learned to sign his own name, Llewellyn was flooded with requests for Foxhunter's autograph. After Foxhunter died, his skeleton was preserved by the Royal College of Veterinary Surgeons.

1956 Stockholm T: 20, N: 20, D: 6.16.

	HORSE	FAULTS	TOTAL PTS.
1. GER			40.00
Hans-Günter Winkler	Halla	4.00	
Fritz Thiedemann	Meteor	12.00	
Alfons Lütke-Westhues	Ala	24.00	
2. ITA			66.00
Raimondo D'Inzeo	Merano	8.00	
Piero D'Inzeo	Uruguay	11.00	
Salvatore Oppes	Pagoro	47.00	
3. GBR			69.00
Wilfred White	Nizefella	12.00	
Patricia Smythe	Flanagan	21.00	
Peter Robeson	Scorchin	36.00	
4. ARG			99.50
Carlos Delía	Discutido	19.00	
Pedro Mayorga	Coriolano	32.00	
Naldo Dasso	Ramito	48.50	
5. USA			104.50
Hugh Wiley	Trail Guide	24.00	
William Steinkraus	Night Owl	28.00	
Frank Chapot	Belair	52.25	
6. SPA			117.25
Carlos López Quesada	Tapatio	27.75	
Francisco Goyoaga	Fahnenkönig	28.00	
Carlos Figueroa Castillejo	Gracieux	61.50	
7. IRL			131.25
Kevin Barry	Ballyneety	35.00	
William Ringrose	Liffey Vale	44.00	
Patrick Kiernan	Ballynonty	52.25	
8. FRA			154.50
Pierre Jonquères d'Oriola	Voulette	15.00	
Bernard Jevardat de Fombelle	Doria	52.75	
Georges Calmon	Virtuoso	86.75	

1960 Rome T: 18, N: 18, 9.11.

	HORSE	FAULTS	TOTAL PTS.
1. GER			46.50
Hans-Günter Winkler	Halla	13.25	
Fritz Thiedemann	Meteor	16.00	
Alwin Schockemöhle	Ferdl	17.25	
2. USA			66.00
Frank Chapot	Trail Guide	20.00	
William Steinkraus	Ksar d'Esprit	21.50	
George Morris	Sinjon	24.50	

	HORSE	FAULTS	TOTAL PTS.
3. ITA			80.50
Raimondo D'Inzeo	Posillipo	8.00	
Piero D'Inzeo	The Rock	32.00	
Antonio Oppes	The Scholar	40.50	
4. EGY			135.50
Gamal Harres	Nefertiti	24.00	
Mohammed Zaki	Artos	48.00	
Alwi Gazi	Mabrouk	63.50	
5. FRA			168.75
Bernard Jevardat de Fombelle	Buffalo	32.50	
Max Fresson	Grand Veneur	50.25	
Pierre Jonquères d'Oriola	Eclaire au Chocolat	86.00	
6. ROM			175.00
Vasile Pinciu	Barsan	41.50	
Virgil Bărbuceanu	Robot	57.75	
Gheorghe Langa	Rubin	75.75	

1964 Tokyo T: 14, N: 14, D: 10.24.

	HORSE	FAULTS	TOTAL PTS.
1. GER			68.50
Hermann Schridde	Dozent	13.75	
Kurt Jarasinski	Torro	22.25	
Hans-Günter Winkler	Fidelitas	32.50	
2. FRA			77.75
Pierre Jonquères d'Oriola	Lutteur	9.00	
Janou Lefebvre	Kenavo D	32.00	
Guy Lefrant	Monsieur de Littry	36.75	
3. ITA			88.50
Piero D'Inzeo	Sunbeam	24.50	
Raimondo D'Inzeo	Posillipo	28.00	
Graziano Mancinelli	Rockette	36.00	
4. GBR			97.25
Peter Robeson	Firecrest	16.00	
David Broome	Jacopo	37.00	
David Barker	North Flight	44.25	
5. ARG			101.00
Jorge Canaves	Confinado	29.50	
Hugo Arrambide	Chimbote	34.25	
Carlos Delia	Popin	37.25	
6. USA			107.00
Frank Chapot	San Lucas	20.50	
Kathyrn Kusner	Untouchable	29.75	
Mary Mairs	Tomboy	56.75	
7. AUS			109.00
Thomas Fahey	Bonvale	16.00	
Bridget MacIntyre	Coronation	39.50	
Kevin Bacon	Ocean Foam	53.50	
8. SPA			118.75
Fernando Goyoaga Caamano	Kif-Kif B.	35.00	
Enrique Martinez de Vallejo	Eolo IV	40.00	
Antonio Queipo de Llano	Infernal	43.75	

1968 Mexico City T: 15, N: 15, D: 10.27.

	HORSE	FAULTS	TOTAL PTS.
1. CAN			102.75
James Elder	The Immigrant	27.25	
James Day	Canadian Club	36.00	
Thomas Gayford	Big Dee	39.50	
2. FRA			110.50
Janou Lefebvre	Rocket	29.75	
Marcel Rozier	Quo vadis	33.50	
Pierre Jonquères d'Oriola	Nagir	47.25	
3. GER			117.25
Alwin Schockemöhle	Donald Rex	18.75	
Hans-Günter Winkler	Enigk	28.25	
Hermann Schridde	Dozent	70.25	
4. USA			117.50
Frank Chapot	San Lucas	25.00	
Kathryn Kusner	Untouchable	44.50	
Mary Chapot	White Lightning	48.00	
5. ITA			129.25
Raimondo D'Inzeo	Bellevue	24.25	
Piero D'Inzeo	Fidux	47.50	
Graziano Mancinelli	Donerailo	57.50	
6. SWI			136.75
Paul Weier	Satan	36.75	
Monica Bachmann	Erbach	49.50	
Arthur Blickenstorfer	Marianka	50.50	
7. BRA			138.00
Nelson Pessoa	Pass-Op	38.75	
Lucia Faria	Rush du Camp	44.75	
José Reynoso	Cantal	54.50	
8. GBR			159.50
David Broome	Mr. Softee	20.00	
R. Harvey Smith	Madison Time	45.00	
Marion Coakes	Stroller	94.50	

1972 Munich T: 17, N: 17, D: 9.11.

	HORSE	FAULTS	TOTAL PTS.
1. GER			32.00
Fritz Ligges	Robin	8.00	
Gerhard Wiltfang	Askan	12.00	
Hartwig Steenken	Simona	12.00	
Hans-Günter Winkler	Torphy	16.00	
2. USA			32.25
William Steinkraus	Main Spring	4.00	
Neal Shapiro	Sloopy	8.25	
Kathryn Kusner	Fleet Apple	32.00	
Frank Chapot	White Lightning	36.00	
3. ITA			48.00
Vittorio Orlandi	Fulmer Feather	8.00	
Raimondo D'Inzeo	Fiorello II	12.00	
Graziano Mancinelli	Ambassador	28.00	
Piero D'Inzeo	Easter Light	135.25	
4. GBR			51.00
Michael Saywell	Hideaway	16.00	
R. Harvey Smith	Summertime	20.00	
David Broome	Manhaton VI	20.00	
Ann Moore	Psalm	32.00	

	HORSE	FAULTS	TOTAL PTS.
5. SWI			61.25
Monica Weier	Erbach	17.75	
Paul Weier	Wulf	20.00	
Max Hauri	Haiti	23.50	
Hermann von Siebenthal	Royal Havana	135.25	
6. CAN			64.00
James Elder	Houdini	8.00	
James Day	Happy Fellow	24.00	
Terrance Miller	Le Dauphin	35.00	
Ian Millar	Shoeman	44.00	
7. SPA			66.00
Alfonso Segovia	Tic Tac	19.00	
Enrique Martinez Vallejo	Val de Loire	19.00	
Luis Alvarez Cervera	Acorn	28.00	
Duque de Aveyro	Sunday Beau	115.25	
8. ARG			121.00
Hugo Arrambide	Camalote	27.00	
Roberto Tagle	Simple	46.00	
Jorge Llambi	Okey Amigo	48.00	
Argentino Molinuevo	Abracadabra	135.25	

Beginning in 1972, team totals were determined by adding the three best scores for each round rather than the three best scores for both rounds combined.

1976 Montreal T: 14, N: 14, D: 8.1.

	HORSE	FAULTS	TOTAL PTS.
1. FRA			40.00
Hubert Parot	Rivage	12.00	
Marcel Rozier	Bayard de Maupas	12.00	
Marc Roguet	Belle de Mars	24.00	
Michel Roche	Un Espoir	32.00	
2. GER			44.00
Alwin Schockemöhle	Warwik Rex	12.00	
Hans-Günter Winkler	Torphy	16.00	
Sönke Sönksen	Kwepe	20.00	
Paul Schockemöhle	Agent	24.00	
3. BEL			63.00
Eric Wauters	Gute Sitte	15.00	
François Mathy	Gai Luron	20.00	
Edgar Gupper	Le Champion	28.00	
Stanny van Paeschen	Porsche	36.00	
4. USA			64.00
Frank Chapot	Viscount	16.00	
Robert Ridland	South Side	20.00	
William Brown	Sandsablaze	28.00	
Michael Matz	Grande	40.00	
5. CAN			64.50
James Day	Sympatico	20.00	
Michel Vaillancourt	Branch County	20.50	
Ian Millar	Countdown	27.50	
James Elder	Raffles II	36.00	
6. SPA			71.00
Luis Alvarez-Cervera	Acorne	16.00	
Alfonso Segovia	Val de Loire	23.00	
José Rosillo	Agamenon	36.00	
Eduardo Amoros	Limited Edition	39.00	

	HORSE	FAULTS	TOTAL PTS.
7. GBR			76.00
Deborah Johnsey	Moxy	24.00	
Rowland Fernyhough	Bouncer	31.00	
Peter Robeson	Law Court	32.00	
Graham Fletcher	Hideaway	36.00	
8. MEX			76.25
Fernando Hernandez	Fascination	24.00	
Fernando Senderos	Jet Run	24.00	
Luis Razo	Pueblo	28.50	
Carlos Aguirre	Consejero	38.25	

1980 Moscow T: 6, N: 6, D: 7.29.

	HORSE	FAULTS	TOTAL PTS.
1. SOV			20.25
Vyacheslav Chukanov	Gepatit	4.00	
Viktor Pohanovsky	Topky	8.25	
Viktor Asmayev	Reis	11.25	
Nikolai Korolkov	Espadron	12.00	
2. POL			56.00
Jan Kowalczyk	Artemor	12.00	
Wieslaw Hartman	Norton	24.00	
Marian Kozicki	Bremen	37.50	
Janusz Bobik	Szampan	40.00	
3. MEX			59.75
Joaquin Perez Heras	Alymony	12.00	
Alberto Valdes Lacarra	Lady Mirka	20.75	
Gerardo Tazzer Valencia	Caribe	31.75	
Jesus Gomez Portugal	Massacre	35.25	
4. HUN			124.00
Barnabás Hevesy	Bohem	28.00	
Ferenc Krucsó	Vadrozsa	32.00	
József Varró	Gambrinusz	97.75	
András Balogi	Artemis	101.75	
5. ROM			150.50
Alexandru Bozan	Prejmer	43.75	
Dania Popescu	Sonor	53.00	
Dumitru Velicu	Fudul	73.75	
Ioan Popa	Licurici	95.50	
6. BUL			159.50
Nikola Dimitrov	Vals	46.75	
Dimitar Ghenov	Makbet	56.00	
Boris Pavlov	Monblan	60.75	
Hristo Katchov	Povdo	73.00	

The surprise winners of the Rotterdam Show Jumping Festival were the Canadians. Great Britain was second and Austria was third.

1984 Los Angeles-Arcadia T: 15, N: 15, D: 8.7.

	HORSE	FAULTS	TOTAL PTS.
1. USA			12.00
Joe Fargis	Touch of Class	0	
Conrad Homfeld	Abdullah	8.00	
Leslie Burr	Albany	12.00	
Melanie Smith	Calypso	with.	

	HORSE	FAULTS	TOTAL PTS.
2. GBR			36.75
Michael Whitaker	Overton Amanda	8.00	
John Whitaker	Ryans Son	20.75	
Steven Smith	Shining Example	27.00	
Timothy Grubb	Linky	28.25	
3. GER			39.25
Paul Schockemöhle	Deister	8.00	
Peter Luther	Livius	12.00	
Franke Sloothaak	Farmer	19.25	
Fritz Ligges	Ramzes	29.00	
4. CAN			40.00
Ian Millar	Big Ben	12.00	
Hugh Graham	Elrond	16.00	
James Elder	Shawline	20.00	
Mario Deslauriers	Aramis	24.50	
5. SWI			41.00
Heidi Robbiani	Jessica V	5.00	
Bruno Candrian	Slygof	12.00	
Philippe Guerdat	Pybalia	32.00	
Willi Melliger	Van Gogh	32.00	
6. FRA			49.75
Philippe Rozier	Jiva	20.00	
Frédéric Cottier	Flambeau C	20.00	
Eric Navet	J'T'Adore	21.75	
Pierre Durand	Jappeloup	elim.	
7. SPA			52.00
Alberto Honrubia	Kaoua	8.00	
Luis Alvarez Cervera	Jexico De Park	11.00	
Rutherford Latham	Idaho E	33.00	
Luis Astolfi	Feinschnitt "Z"	56.50	
8. ITA			75.25
Giorgio Nuti	Impedoumi	16.00	
Filippo Moyersoen	Adam II	16.00	
Graziano Mancinelli	Ideal De La Haye	20.00	
Bruno Scolari	Joyau D'Or	39.25	

1988 Seoul T: 16, N: 16, D: 9.28.

	HORSE	FAULTS	TOTAL PTS.
1. GER			17.25
Ludger Beerbaum	The Freak	4.25	
Wolfgang Brinkmann	Pedro	10.00	
Dirk Hafemeister	Orchidee	12.00	
Franke Sloothaak	Walzerkönig	with.	
2. USA			20.50
Joe Fargis	Mill Pearl	4.25	
Greg Best	Gem Twist	8.00	
Lisa Jacquin	For the Moment	8.25	
Anne Kursinski	Starman	16.00	
3. FRA			27.50
Pierre Durand	Jappeloup	5.00	
Michel Robert	Pequignet La Fayette	10.00	
Frédéric Cottier	Flambeau	16.00	
Hubert Bourdy	Morgat	16.50	
4. CAN			28.75
Ian Millar	Big Ben	8.00	
Mario Deslauriers	Box Car Willie	12.00	
Lisa Carlsen	Kahlua	16.00	
Laura Tidball-Balisky	Lavendel	22.75	

5. HOL		32.25
Wout-Jan van der Schans	Treffer	8.25
Robbertus Ehrens	Sunrise	12.00
Johannes Tops	Doreen	16.00
Jos Lansink	Felix	20.00
6. GBR		40.00
Nicholas Skelton	Apollo	12.00
David Broome	Countryman	16.00
Malcolm Pyrah	Anglezarke	16.00
Joseph Turi	Vital	20.00
7. SWI		44.25
Markus Fuchs	Shandor II	12.00
Thomas Fuchs	Diners Dollar Girl	12.25
Philippe Guerdat	Lanciano II	20.00
Walter Gabathuler	Jogger	36.25
8. BRA		75.00
Christina Johannpeter	Société	25.50
André Johannpeter	Heartbreaker	27.50
Vitor Teixeira	Going	30.50
Paulo Stewart	Platon	42.00
8. SPA		75.00
Alfredo Fernández Duran	Kaoua	21.00
Pedro Sanchez Aleman	Nuit Des Tourell	28.25
Juan Garcia Trevijano	Tirol	32.75
Luis Alvarez Cervera	Mirage Mexicain	45.00

1992 Barcelona T: 19, N: 19, D: 8.4.

	HORSE	FAULTS	TOTAL PTS.
1. HOL			12.00
Jos Lansink	Egano	0	
Piet Raymakers	Ratina Z	4.00	
Jan Tops	Top Gun	8.00	
2. AUT			16.75
Thomas Frühmann	Genius	0	
Hugo Simon	Apricot D	4.00	
Jörg Münzner	Graf Grande	12.75	
3. FRA			24.75
Hervé Godignon	Quidam De Revel	4.75	
Hubert Bourdy	Razzia Du P	12.00	
Eric Navet	Quito De Baussy	16.00	
Michel Robert	Nonix	20.25	
4. SPA			25.50
Luis Astolfi	Fino B'92	4.00	
Luis Álvarez Cervero	Let's Go B'92	5.50	
Enrique Sarasola Marulanda	Minstrel	16.00	
5. SWI			28.00
Lesley McNaught-Mändli	Pirol B	8.00	
Thomas Fuchs	Dylano	8.00	
Markus Fuchs	Shandor II	12.00	
5. USA			28.00
Michael Matz	Heisman	4.00	
Lisa Jacquin	For the Moment	8.00	
Norman Dello Joio	Irish	20.00	
Anne Kursinski	Cannonball	elim.	

7. GBR		28.75
John Whitaker	Milton	4.00
Michael Whitaker	Monsanta	8.00
Timothy Grubb	Denizen	17.00
Nick Skelton	Dollar Girl	elim.
8. SWE		37.00
Peter Eriksson	Moritz	0
Maria Gretzer	Marcoville	13.00
Ulrika Hedin	Lipton	24.00

The one-two finish by the Dutch and Austrian teams came as a shock. Neither country had ever earned medals in this event before and Austria's best Olympic performance prior to Barcelona was 11th, in 1976.

DRESSAGE, INDIVIDUAL

Until knitting is added to the Olympic program, dressage will remain the least action-packed of Olympic events. The object of dressage is to demonstrate the horse's responsiveness to the rider's commands by taking the horse through a series of prearranged movements. The closest human-only equivalent is the compulsory figures in figure skating—which were eliminated after 1988 because they were too boring. Five judges grade each movement in dressage on a scale of 0 to 10. The horses canter, trot, and perform four varieties of walking. In addition to the movements, the judges award four "collective" marks, worth up to 20 points each, for freedom and regularity of the paces, the "impulsion" of the horse, the submission of the horse, and the form and position of the rider. The scores of the five judges are added to determine the final score for each rider. The team event is used as the qualifying competition for the individual event. In 1996 the top 20 competitors in the team event will participate in the individual final, although only three riders per nation are allowed to advance. The top 12 in the initial phase of the individual final will then advance to a final of freestyle dressage, which is performed to music. This will be the first appearance of freestyle dressage in the Olympics.

1896–1908 not held

1912 Stockholm C: 21, N: 8, D: 7.15.

			HORSE	PTS.
1. Carl Bonde		SWE	Emperor	15
2. Gustaf-Adolf Boltenstern, Sr.		SWE	Neptun	21
3. Hans von Blixen-Finecke, Sr.		SWE	Maggie	32
4. Friedrich von Oesterley		GER	Condor	36
5. Carl Rosenblad		SWE	Miss Hastings	43
6. Oskar af Ström		SWE	Irish Lass	47
7. Felix Burkner		GER	King	51
8. Carl Kruckenberg		SWE	Kartusch	51

1920 Antwerp C: 17, N: 5, D: 9.9.

		HORSE	PTS.
1. Janne Lundblad	SWE	Uno	27.9375
2. Bertil Sandström	SWE	Sabel	26.3125
— Gustaf-Adolf Boltenstern, Sr.	SWE	Iron	26.1875
3. Hans von Rosen	SWE	Running Sister	25.125
4. Wilhelm von Essen	SWE	Nomeg	24.875
5. Hédoin de Maillé de la Tour Landry	FRA	Chéri Biribi	23.9375
6. Michel Artola	FRA	Plumard	23.4375
7. Gaston de Trannoy	BEL	Bouton d'Or	23.125
8. Balthazar Falkenberg	NOR	Hjördis	22.375

Colonel Boltenstern, on Iron, finished in third place, but was disqualified for practicing in the ring before the competition began.

1924 Paris C: 24, N: 9, D: 7.25.

		HORSE	PTS.
1. Ernst Linder	SWE	Piccolomini	276.4
2. Bertil Sandström	SWE	Sabel	275.8
3. Xavier Lesage	FRA	Plumard	265.8
4. Wilhelm von Essen	SWE	Zobel	260.0
5. Victor Ankarcrona	SWE	Corona	256.5
6. Emanuel Thiel	CZE	Ex	256.2
7. Robert Wallon	FRA	Magister	243.2
7. Hans von der Weid	SWI	Uhlard	243.2

1928 Amsterdam C: 29, N: 12, D: 8.11.

		HORSE	PTS.
1. Carl Friedrich Freiherr von Langen-Parow	GER	Draufgänger	237.42
2. Charles Marion	FRA	Linon	231.00
3. Ragnar Ohlson	SWE	Gunstling	229.78
4. Janne Lundblad	SWE	Blackmar	226.70
5. Emanuel Thiel	CZE	Loki	225.96
6. Hermann Linkenbach	GER	Gimpel	224.26
7. Robert Wallon	FRA	Clough-banck	224.08
8. Jan van Reede	HOL	Hans	220.70

1932 Los Angeles C: 10, N: 4, D: 8.10.

		HORSE	POINTS	ORDI-NALS
1. Xavier Lesage	FRA	Taine	343.75	6
2. Charles Marion	FRA	Linon	305.42	14
3. Hiram Tuttle	USA	Olympic	300.50	14
4. Thomas Byström	SWE	Guliver	293.50	16
5. André Jousseaume	FRA	Sorelta	290.42	17
6. Isaac Kitts	USA	American Lady	282.08	17
7. Alvin Moore	USA	Water Pat	276.33	20
8. Gustaf-Adolf Boltenstern, Jr.	SWE	Ingo	277.83	21

Bertil Sandström of Sweden came in second but was relegated to last place for encouraging his horse, Kreta, by making clicking noises. He claimed that the noises were actually made by a creaking saddle, but the Jury of Appeal was not convinced. Moore was awarded seventh place, ahead of Boltenstern, because places were determined not by total points but by the rankings of the judges, using a system of ordinals such as is used in figure skating.

1936 Berlin C: 29, N: 11, D: 8.13.

		HORSE	PTS.
1. Heinz Pollay	GER	Kronos	1760.0
2. Friedrich Gerhard	GER	Absinth	1745.5
3. Alois Podhajsky	AUT	Nero	1721.5
4. Gregor Adlercreutz	SWE	Teresina	1675.0
5. André Jousseaume	FRA	Favorite	1642.5
6. Gérard de Ballore	FRA	Debaucheur	1634.0
7. Peder Jensen	DEN	His Ex	1596.0
8. Pierre Versteegh	HOL	Ad Astra	1579.0

1948 London C: 19, N: 9, D: 8.9.

		HORSE	PTS.
1. Hans Moser	SWI	Hummer	492.5
2. André Jousseaume	FRA	Harpagon	480.0
3. Gustaf-Adolf Boltenstern, Jr.	SWE	Trumf	477.5
4. Robert Borg	USA	Klingson	473.5
5. Henri Saint Cyr	SWE	Djimm	444.5
— Gehnäll Persson	SWE	—	444.0
6. Jean Saint Fort Paillard	FRA	Sous les Ceps	439.5
7. Alois Podhajsky	AUT	Teja	437.5
8. Earl Thomson	USA	Pancraft	421.0

The absurdity of the rules governing Olympic dressage reached its pinnacle in 1948, when sixth-place finisher Gehnäll Persson was disqualified when it was discovered that he was only a noncommissioned officer and thus ineligible to compete.

1952 Helsinki C: 27, N: 10, D: 7.29.

		HORSE	PTS.
1. Henri Saint Cyr	SWE	Master Rufus	561.0
2. Lis Hartel	DEN	Jubilee	541.5
3. André Jousseaume	FRA	Harpagon	541.0
4. Gustaf-Adolf Boltenstern, Jr.	SWE	Krest	531.0
5. Gottfried Trachsel	SWI	Kursus	531.0
6. Henri Chammartin	SWI	Wohler	529.5
7. Gustav Fischer	SWI	Soliman	518.5
7. Heinz Pollay	GER	Adular	518.5

Between 1948 and 1952 dressage competition underwent a radical change. Not only were noncommissioned officers allowed to enter in 1952, so were other enlisted men. And not only were enlisted men allowed to enter, so were men who were civilians. And not only were men who were civilians allowed to enter, but for the first time in Olympic equestrian history, four women were allowed to compete against men. One of those women was Lis Hartel of Denmark. In 1944 Lis Hartel, a 23-year-old pregnant mother, was one of Denmark's leading riders. Then, one morning in September, she awoke with a headache and a strange stiffness in her neck. A few days later paralysis began spreading throughout her body—she had become a victim of polio. But Lis Hartel was determined to regain her

In 1952 Lis Hartel of Denmark won a silver medal in the individual dressage event only eight years after being stricken with polio. Paralyzed below the knees, she had to be helped on and off her horse.

health. First she learned to lift her arm, then she regained the use of her thigh muscles. Then she gave birth to a healthy daughter. Soon she was crawling, and eight months after the attack, she was able to walk a bit by using crutches. Her friends hailed her recovery, but she was not finished. She insisted on mounting a horse. Reactivating the muscles necessary to keep from falling was so exhausting that she had to rest for two weeks before she tried a second time. Slowly but surely, Lis Hartel improved until, three years after her polio attack, she was able to compete in the Scandinavian riding championship, finishing second in the women's dressage. She remained paralyzed below the knees, but learned to do without those muscles. In 1952 she was chosen to represent Denmark in the Olympics, and she responded by earning the silver medal, even though she had to be helped on and off her horse. When gold medalist Henri Saint Cyr helped her up onto the victory platform for the medal presentation, it was one of the most emotional moments in Olympic history. Four years later, in Stockholm, she won another silver medal.

1956 Stockholm C: 36, N: 17, D: 6.16.

			HORSE	PTS.
1. Henri Saint Cyr	SWE		Juli	860
2. Lis Hartel	DEN		Jubilee	850
3. Liselott Linsenhoff	GER		Adular	832
4. Gehnäll Persson	SWE		Knaust	821
5. André Jousseaume	FRA		Harpagon	814
6. Gottfried Trachsel	SWI		Kursus	807
7. Gustaf-Adolf Bolterstern, Jr.	SWE		Krest	794
8. Henri Chammartin	SWI		Woehler	789

The judging caused something of a scandal. The German judge, General Berger, ranked the three German riders first, second, and third and the Swedish judge, General Colliander, ranked the three Swedish riders first, second, and third. First-place finisher Henri Saint Cyr completed his harvest of four gold medals. The fifth-place finisher, 61-year-old André Jousseaume, was competing in his fifth Olympics. Between 1932 and 1952 he won two gold medals, two silver, and one bronze.

1960 Rome C: 17, N: 10, D: 9.6.

		HORSE	PTS.
1. Sergei Filatov	SOV/RUS	Absent	2144
2. Gustav Fischer	SWI	Wald	2087
3. Josef Neckermann	GER	Asbach	2082
4. Henri Saint Cyr	SWE	L'Etoile	2064
5. Ivan Kalita	SOV/RUS	Korbey	2007
6. Patricia Galvin	USA	Rath Patrick	995
7. Rosemarie Springer	GER	Doublette	985
8. Henri Chammartin	SWI	Wolfdietrich	978

Finishing in 16th place was Kroum Lekarski of Bulgaria, whose first Olympic appearance had been in the three-day event in 1924.

1964 Tokyo C: 22, N: 9, D:10.23.

		HORSE	PTS.
1. Henri Chammartin	SWI	Woermann	1504
2. Harry Boldt	GER	Remus	1503
3. Sergei Filatov	SOV/RUS	Absent	1486
4. Gustav Fischer	SWI	Wald	1485
5. Josef Neckermann	GER	Antoinette	1429
6. Reiner Klimke	GER	Dux	1404
7. Marianne Gossweiler	SWI	Stephan	802
8. Patricia Galvin de la Tour d'Auvergne	USA	Rath Patrick	783

1968 Mexico City C: 26, N; 9, D: 10.25.

		HORSE	PTS.
1. Ivan Kizimov	SOV/RUS	Ikhor	1572
2. Josef Neckermann	GER	Mariano	1546
3. Reiner Klimke	GER	Dux	1537
4. Ivan Kalita	SOV/RUS	Absent	1519
5. Horst Köhler	GDR	Neuschnee	1475
6. Yelena Petushkova	SOV/RUS	Pepei	1471
7. Gustav Fischer	SWI	Wald	1465
8. Liselott Linsenhoff	GER	Piaff	855

1972 Munich C: 33, N: 13, D: 9.7.

		HORSE	PTS.
1. Liselott Linsenhoff	GER	Piaff	1229
2. Yelena Petushkova	SOV/RUS	Pepel	1185
3. Josef Neckermann	GER	Venetia	1177
4. Ivan Kizimov	SOV/RUS	Ikhor	1159
5. Ulla Håkansson	SWE	Ajax	1126
6. Ivan Kalita	SOV/RUS	Tarif	1130
7. Karin Schlueter	GER	Liostroa	1113
8. Maud Von Rosen	SWE	Lucky Boy	1088

Twenty-one of the 33 riders were women, including Liselott Linsenhoff, the first female individual gold medalist. Second-place finisher Petushkova was a professor of biology at the University of Moscow and was, for some time, married to high-jumper Valery Brumel.

1976 Montreal C: 27, N: 11, D: 7.30.

		HORSE	PTS.
1. Christine Stückelberger	SWI	Granat	1486
2. Harry Boldt	GER	Woycek	1435
3. Reiner Klimke	GER	Mehmed	1395
4. Gabriela Grillo	GER	Ultimo	1257
5. Dorothy Morkis	USA	Monaco	1249
6. Viktor Ugryumov	SOV/BLR	Said	1247
7. Christilot Boylen	CAN	Gaspano	1217
8. Ulla Petersen	DEN	Chigwell	1192

1980 Moscow C: 14, N: 6, D: 8.1.

		HORSE	PTS.
1. Elisabeth Theurer	AUT	Mon Cherie	1370
2. Yuri Kovshov	SOV/UZB	Igrok	1300
3. Viktor Ugryumov	SOV/BLR	Shkval	1234
4. Vira Misevych	SOV/UKR	Plot	1231
5. Kyra Kyrklund	FIN	Piccolo	1121
6. Anghelache Donescu	ROM	Dor	960
7. Georgi Gadzhev	BUL	Vnimatelen	881
8. Svetoslav Ivanov	BUL	Aleko	850

Theurer was the only leading dressage rider to enter the Olympics. All the rest took part in the Dressage Festival the following week, which was won by Christine Stückelberger.

1984 Los Angeles-Arcadia C: 43, N: 18, D: 8.10.

		HORSE	PTS.
1. Reiner Klimke	GER	Ahlerich	1504
2. Anne Grethe Jensen	DEN	Marzog	1442
3. Otto Hofer	SWI	Limandus	1364
4. Ingamay Bylund	SWE	Aleks	1332
5. Herbert Krug	GER	Muscadeur	1323
6. Christopher Bartle	GBR	Wily Trout	1279
6. Uwe Sauer	GER	Montevideo	1279
8. Annemarie Sanders-Keyzer	HOL	Amon	1271

Dr. Reiner Klimke, a 48-year-old lawyer from Münster, won his first individual gold medal to bring his Olympic total to 5 golds and 2 bronzes. In 1988, he was awarded another gold in the team competition.

1988 Seoul C: 55, N: 18, D: 9.27.

		HORSE	PTS.
1. Nicole Uphoff	GER	Rembrandt	1521
2. Margit Otto-Crépin	FRA	Corlandus	1462
3. Christine Stückelberger	SWI	Gauguin De Lully	1417
4. Cynthia Ishoy	CAN	Dynasty	1401
5. Kyra Kyrklund	FIN	Matador	1393
6. Monica Theodorescu	GER	Ganimedes	1385
7. Otto Hofer	SWI	Andiamo	1383
8. Ann-Kathrin Linsenhoff	GER	Courage	1374

This was the first time all three dressage medals were won by women.

1992 Barcelona C: 48, N: 18, D: 8.5.

		HORSE	PTS.
1. Nicole Uphoff	GER	Rembrandt	1626
2. Isabell Werth	GER	Gigolo	1551
3. Nikolaus "Klaus" Balkenhol	GER	Goldstern	1515
4. Anky van Grunsven	HOL	Olympic Bonfire	1447
5. Kyra Kyrklund	FIN	Edinburgh	1428
6. Carol Lavell	USA	Gifted	1408
7. Pia Laus	ITA	Adrett	1389
8. Elisabeth Max-Theurer	AUT	Liechtenstein	1380

Monica Theodorescu of Germany placed fourth in the qualifying round on Grunox but was left out of the individual final because the three riders ahead of her were also from Germany. Rembrandt became the first horse to win the dressage title twice. Bronze medalist Klaus Balkenhol was a 52-year-old policeman from Düsseldorf.

DRESSAGE, TEAM

Each team may enter four riders and horses, but only the scores of the top three finishers for each team are counted. In case of a tie, the team whose third rider had the highest score is declared the winner. Every time Germany has entered this event, their team has won a medal: 8 gold, 2 silver, 1 bronze.

1896–1924 not held

1928 Amsterdam T: 8, N: 8, D: 8.11.

	HORSE		TOTAL PTS.
1. GER			669.72
Carl Friedrich Freiherr von Langen-Parow	Draufgänger	237.42	
Hermann Linkenbach	Gimpel	224.26	
Eugen Freiherr von Lotzbeck	Caracalla	208.04	
2. SWE			650.86
Ragnar Ohlson	Gunstling	229.78	
Janne Lundblad	Blackmar	226.70	
Carl Bonde	Ingo	194.38	
3. HOL			642.96
Jan van Reede	Hans	220.70	
Pierre Versteegh	His Excellence	216.44	
Gérard Le Heux	Valerine	205.82	

4. FRA			642.18
Charles Marion	Linon	231.00	
Robert Wallon	Cloughbank	224.08	
Pierre Danloux	Rempart	187.10	
5. CZE			637.94
Emanuel Thiel	Loki	225.96	
Otto Schöniger	Ex	210.28	
Jaroslav Hauf	Elegant	201.70	
6. AUT			600.40
Arthur von Pongracz	Turridu	204.28	
Wilhelm Jaich	Graf	204.16	
Gustav Grachegg	Daniel	191.96	
7. SWI			569.08
Adolphe Mercier	Queen-Mary	203.34	
Otto Frank	Solon	190.62	
Werner Stuber	Ulhard	175.12	
8. BEL			499.70
Oscar Lints	Rira-t-elle	185.86	
Henri Laame	Belga	167.70	
René Delrue	Dreypuss	146.14	

1932 Los Angeles T: 3, N: 3, D: 8.10.

	HORSE		TOTAL PTS.
1. FRA			2818.75
Xavier Lesage	Taine	1031.25	
Charles Marion	Linon	916.25	
André Jousseaume	Sorelta	871.25	
2. SWE			2678.00
Bertil Sandström	Kreta	964.00	
Thomas Byström	Gulliver	880.50	
Gustaf-Adolf Boltenstern, Jr.	Ingo	833.50	
3. USA			2576.75
Hiram Tuttle	Olympic	901.50	
Isaac Kitts	American Lady	846.25	
Alvin Moore	Water Pat	829.00	

1936 Berlin T: 9, N: 9, D: 8.13.

	HORSE		TOTAL PTS.
1. GER			5074.0
Heinz Pollay	Kronos	1760.0	
Friedrich Gerhard	Absinth	1745.5	
Hermann von Oppeln-Bronikowski	Gimpel	1568.5	
2. FRA			4846.0
André Jousseaume	Favorite	1642.5	
Gerard de Ballore	Debaucheur	1634.0	
Daniel Gillois	Nicolas	1569.5	
3. SWE			4660.5
Gregor Adlercreutz	Teresina	1675.0	
Sven Colliander	Kal	1530.5	
Folke Sandström	Pergoia	1455.0	
4. AUT			4627.5
Alois Podhajsky	Nero	1721.5	
Albert Dolleschall	Infant	1476.0	
Arthur von Pongracz	Georgine	1430.0	

5. HOL			4382.0
Pierre Versteegh	Ad Astra	1579.0	
Gérard Le Heux	Zonnetje	1422.0	
Daniel Camerling-Helmolt	Wodan	1381.0	
6. HUN			4090.0
Gusztáv von Pados	Ficsur	1424.0	
László von Magasházy	Tucsok	1415.5	
Pál Kerméry	Csintaian	1250.5	
7. NOR			4050.5
Arthur Quist	Jaspis	1438.0	
Eugene Johansen	Sorte Mand	1388.0	
Bjorn Bjornseth	Invictus	1224.5	
8. CZE			4026.0
Frantisek Jandl	Nestor	1453.0	
Matej Pechmann	Ideal	1319.0	
Otto Schöniger	Helios	1254.0	

The oldest competitor at the Berlin Olympics was 72-year-old General Arthur von Pongracz, of Austria's fourth-place team. Von Pongracz made his Olympic debut in Paris in 1924, when he was a mere youngster of 60.

1948 London T: 5, N: 5, D: 8.9.

	HORSE		TOTAL PTS.
— SWE			1366.0
Gustav-Adolf Boltenstern, Jr.	Trumf	477.5	
Henri Saint Cyr	Djimm	444.5	
Gehnäll Persson	—	444.0	
1. FRA			1269.0
André Jousseaume	Harpagon	480.0	
Jean Saint Fort Paillard	Sous les Ceps	439.5	
Maurice Buret	Saint Ouen	349.5	
2. USA			1256.0
Robert Borg	Klingson	473.5	
Earl Thomson	Pancraft	421.0	
Frank Henry	Reno Overdo	361.5	
3. POR			1182.0
Fernando Pais da Silva	Matamas	411.0	
Franciso Valadas	Feitico	405.0	
Luiz Mena e Silva	Fascinante	366.0	
4. ARG			1005.5
Justo Iturralde	Pajarito	397.0	
Humberto Terzano	Bienvenido	327.0	
Oscar Goulú	Grillo	281.5	

In the middle of the competition, Commandant Hector of France, the Secretary General of the International Equestrian Federation, suddenly pointed to Gehnäll Persson, who had been entered as an officer, and said, "This man is not an officer. He is riding in the cap of a sergeant." Initially the Swedish team was allowed to keep their gold medals, but eight months later they were formally disqualified and forced to turn over the medals to the French team.

1952 Helsinki T: 8, N: 8, D: 7.29.

	HORSE		TOTAL PTS.
1. SWE			1597.5
Henri Saint Cyr	Master Rufus	561.0	
Gustaf-Adolf Boltenstern, Jr.	Krest	531.0	
Gehnäll Persson	Knaust	505.5	
2. SWI			1579.0
Gottfried Trachsel	Krusus	531.0	
Henri Chammartin	Wohler	529.5	
Gustav Fischer	Solimon	518.5	
3. GER			1501.0
Heinz Pollay	Adular	518.5	
Ida von Nagel	Afrika	503.0	
Fritz Thiedemann	Chronist	479.5	
4. FRA			1423.5
André Jousseaume	Harpagon	541.0	
Jean Peiterin de Saint André	Vol au vent	479.0	
Jean Saint Ford Paillard	Tapir	403.5	
5. CHI			1340.5
José Larrain	Rey de Oros	473.5	
Hector Clavel	Frontalera	452.0	
Ernesto Silva	Viareggio	415.0	
6. USA			1253.5
Robert Borg	Bill Biddle	492.0	
Marjorie Haines	The Flying Dutchman	446.0	
Hartmann Pauly	Reno Overde	315.5	
7. SOV			1205.5
Vladimir Raspopov	Imeninnik	433.5	
Vassily Tihonov	Pevec	395.0	
Nikolai Sitko	Cesar	377.0	
8. POR			1196.5
Antonio Reymão Nogueira	Napeiro	428.4	
Francisco Valadas Júnior	Feitico	422.0	
Fernando Paisda Silva	Matamas	346.0	

1956 Stockholm T: 8, N: 8, D: 6.16.

	HORSE		TOTAL PTS.
1. SWE			2475.0
Henri Saint Cyr	Juli	860.0	
Gehnäll Persson	Knaust	821.0	
Gustaf-Adolf Boltenstern, Jr.	Krest	794.0	
2. GER			2346.0
Liselott Linsenhoff	Adular	832.0	
Hannelore Weygand	Perkunos	785.0	
Anneliese Küppers	Afrika	729.0	
3. SWI			2346.0
Gottfried Trachsel	Kursus	807.0	
Henri Chammartin	Wohler	789.0	
Gustav Fischer	Vasello	750.0	
4. SOV			2170.0
Sergei Filatov	Ingas	744.0	
Aleksandr Vtorov	Repertoir	726.0	
Nikolai Sitko	Skatschek	700.0	
5. DEN			2167.0
Lis Hartel	Jubilee	850.0	
Hermann Zobel	Monty	673.0	
Inger Lemvigh-Müller	Bel Ami	644.0	

6. FRA			2016.0
André Jousseaume	Harpagon	814.0	
Jean-Albert Brau	Vol d'Amour	648.0	
Jean Salmon	Kipling	554.0	
7. NOR			1912.5
Else Christophersen	Diva	739.0	
Anne Lise Kielland	Clary	601.5	
Bodil Russ	Corona	572.0	
8. ROM			1862.0
Gheorghe Teodorescu	Palatin	721.0	
Nicolae Mihalcea	Mihnea	625.0	
Niculae Marcoci	Corvin	516.0	

1960 not held

1964 Tokyo T: 6, N: 6, D: 10.23.

	HORSE		TOTAL PTS.
1. GER			2558.0
Harry Boldt	Remus	889.0	
Reiner Klimke	Dux	837.0	
Josef Neckermann	Antoinette	832.0	
2. SWI			2526.0
Henri Chammartin	Wormann	870.0	
Gustav Fischer	Wald	854.0	
Marianne Gossweiler	Stepan	802.0	
3. SOV/RUS			2311.0
Sergei Filatov	Absent	847.0	
Ivan Kizimov	Ikhor	758.0	
Ivan Kalita	Moar	706.0	
4. USA			2130.0
Patricia Galvin de la Tour d'Auvergne	Rath Patrick	783.0	
Anne Newberry	Forstrat	707.0	
Karen McIntosh	Malteser	640.0	
5. SWE			2068.0
William Hamilton	Delicado	777.0	
Hans Wikne	Gaspari	753.0	
Bengt Ljungquist	Karat	538.0	
6. JPN			1779.5
Kikuko Inoue	Katsunobori	648.0	
Nagahira Okabe	Seiha	589.5	
Yoritsune Matsudaira	Hamachidori	542.0	

1968 Mexico City T: 8, N: 8, D: 10.24.

	HORSE		TOTAL PTS.
1. GER			2699
Josef Neckermann	Mariano	948	
Reiner Klimke	Dux	896	
Liselott Linsenhoff	Piaff	855	
2. SOV/RUS			2657
Ivan Kizimov	Ikhor	908	
Ivan Kalita	Absent	879	
Yelena Petushkova	Pepel	870	

3. SWI 2547
Gustav Fischer — Wald — 866
Henri Chammartin — Wolfdietrich — 845
Marianne Gossweiler — Stephan — 836
4. GDR 2357
Horst Köhler — Neuschnee — 875
Gerhard Brockmüller — Tristah — 789
Wolfgang Müller — Marios — 693
5. GBR 2332
Domini Lawrence — San Fernando — 793
H. Lorna Johnstone — El Guapo — 777
Johanna Hall — Conversano Caprice — 762
6. CHI 2015
Guillermo Squella — Colchaguino — 693
Antonio Piraino — Ciclon — 672
Patricio Escudero — Prete — 650
7. CAN 2012
Inez Fischer-Credo — Marius — 732
Christilot Hanson — Bonheur — 677
Zoltan Sztehlo — Virtuose — 603
8. USA 1919
Kyra Downton — Cadet — 657
Edith Master — Helios — 646
Donnan Plumb — Attache — 616

1972 Munich T: 10, N: 10, D: 9.7.

	HORSE	TOTAL PTS.
1. SOV/RUS		5095
Yelena Petushkova	Pepel	1747
Ivan Kizimov	Ikhor	1701
Ivan Kalita	Tarif	1647
2. GER		5083
Liselott Linsenhoff	Piaff	1763
Josef Neckermann	Venetia	1706
Karin Schlüter	Lisotro	1614
3. SWE		4849
Ulla Håkansson	Ajax	1649
Ninna Swaab	Casanova	1622
Maud Von Rosen	Lucky Boy	1578
4. DEN		4606
Aksel Mikkelsen	Talisman	1597
Ulla Petersen	Chigwell	1534
Charlotte Ingemann	Souliman	1475
5. GDR		4552
Gerhard Brockmüller	Marios	1545
Wolfgang Müller	Semafor	1521
Horst Köhler	Imanuel	1486
6. CAN		4418
Christilot Hanson	Armagnac III	1615
Cynthia Neal	Bonne Annee	1424
Lorraine Stubbs	Venezuela	1379
7. SWI		4383
Christine Stückelberger	Granat	1528
Hermann Duer	Sod	1466
Marita Aeschbacher	Charlamp	1389
8. HOL		4309
Annie van Doorne	Pericles	1480

Friederie Benedictus — Turista — 1420
John Swaab — Maharadscha — 1409

1976 Montreal T: 8, N: 8, D: 7.29.

	HORSE	TOTAL PTS.
1. GER		5155
Harry Boldt	Woycey	1863
Reiner Klimke	Mehmed	1751
Gabriela Grillo	Ultimo	1541
2. SWI		4684
Christine Stückelberger	Granat	1869
Ulrich Lehmann	Widin	1425
Doris Ramseier	Roch	1390
3. USA		4647
Hilda Gurney	Keen	1607
Dorothy Morkis	Monaco	1559
Edith Master	Dahlwitz	1481
4. SOV		4542
Viktor Ugryumov	Said	1597
Ivan Kalita	Tarif	1520
Ivan Kizimov	Rebus	1425
5. CAN		4538
Christilot Boylen	Gaspano	1590
Lorraine Stubbs	True North	1549
Barbara Stracey	Jungherr II	1399
6. DEN		4448
Ulla Petersen	Chigwell	1552
Tonny Jensen	Fox	1521
Niels Haagensen	Lowenstern	1375
7. HOL		4380
Jo Rutten	Banjo	1533
Louky Van Olphen	Aleric	1449
Marjolyn Greeve	Lucky Boy	1398
8. GBR		4076
Sarah Whitmore	Junker	1375
A. Jennifer Loriston-Clarke	Kadett	1375
Diana Mason	Special Ed	1326

1980 Moscow T: 4, N: 4, D: 7.31.

	HORSE	TOTAL PTS.
1. SOV		4383
Yuri Kovshov	Igrok	1588
Viktor Ugryumov	Shkval	1541
Vira Misevych	Plot	1254
2. BUL		3580
Peter Mandazhiev	Stchibor	1244
Svetoslav Ivanov	Aleko	1190
Georgi Gadjev	Vnimatelen	1146
3. ROM		3346
Anghelache Donescu	Dor	1255
Dumitru Veliku	Decebal	1076
Petre Roşca	Derbist	1015
4. POL		2945
Józef Zagor	Hellios	1061
Elżbieta Morciniec	Sum	954
Wanda Waśowska	Damask	930

The Goodwood Dressage Festival, held as an alternative to the Olympics, was won by West Germany, with Switzerland second and Denmark third.

1984 Los Angeles-Arcadia T: 12, N: 12, D: 8.9.

	HORSE		TOTAL PTS.
1. GER			4955
Reiner Klimke	Ahlerich	1797	
Uwe Sauer	Montevideo	1582	
Herbert Krug	Muscadeur	1576	
2. SWI			4673
Otto Hofer	Limandus	1609	
Christine Stückelberger	Tansanit	1606	
Amy-Cathérine de Bary	Aintree	1458	
3. SWE			4630
Ulla Håkanson	Flamingo	1589	
Ingamay Bylund	Aleks	1582	
Louise Nathhorst	Inferno	1459	
4. HOL			4586
Annemarie Sanders-Keyzer	Amon	1591	
Tineke Bartels de Vrie	Duco	1539	
Jo Rutten	Ampere	1456	
5. DEN			4574
Anne Grethe Jensen	Marzog	1701	
Torben Ulsö Olsen	Patricia	1496	
Marie-Louise Castenskiöld	Stradivarius	1377	
6. USA			4559
Hilda Gurney	Keen	1530	
Sandy Pflueger-Clarke	Marco Polo	1516	
Robert Dover	Romantico	1513	
7. CAN			4503
Christilot Boylen	Anklang	1540	
Bonny Chesson	Satchmo	1496	
Eva-Maria Pracht	Little Joe	1467	
8. GBR			4463
Christopher Bartle	Wily Trout	1547	
Jane Bartle-Wilson	Pinocchio	1489	
Jennie Loriston-Clarke	Prince Consort	1427	

1988 Seoul T: 12, N: 12, D: 9.25.

	HORSE		TOTAL PTS.
1. GER			4302
Nicole Uphoff	Rembrandt	1458	
Monica Theodorescu	Ganimedes	1433	
Ann-Kathrin Linsenhoff	Courage	1411	
2. SWI			4164
Christine Stückelberger	Gauguin De Lully	1430	
Otto Hofer	Andiamo	1392	
Daniel Ramseier	Random	1342	
3. CAN			3969
Cynthia Ishoy	Dynasty	1363	
Ashley Nicoll	Reipo	1308	
Gina Smith	Malte	1298	

4. SOV			3926
Nina Menkova	Dixon	1395	
Olha Klymko	Buket	1272	
Yuri Kovshov	Barin	1259	
5. HOL			3903
Ellen Bontje	Petit Prince	1312	
Annemarie Sanders-Keyzer	Amon	1303	
Tineke Bartels	Olympic	1288	
6. FIN			3883
Kyra Kyrklund	Matador	1416	
Tuulikki Sohlberg	Pakistan	1242	
Jennifer Eriksson	My Way	1225	
6. USA			3883
Robert Dover	Federleicht	1327	
Jessica Ransehousen	Orpheus	1308	
Belinda Baudin	Christopher	1248	
8. FRA			3832
Margit Otto-Crépin	Corlandus	1455	
Dominique D'Esme	Hopal Fleury Hn	1219	
Philippe Limousin	Iris de la Fosse	1158	

1992 Barcelona T: 11, N: 11, D: 8.2.

	HORSE		TOTAL PTS.
1. GER			5224
Nicole Uphoff	Rembrandt	1768	
Isabell Werth	Gigolo	1762	
Nikolaus "Klaus" Balkenhol	Goldstern	1694	
2. HOL			4742
Anky Van Grunsven	Olympic Bonfire	1631	
Ellen Bontje	Olympic Larius	1577	
Tineke Bartels de Vrie	Olympic Courage	1534	
3. USA			4643
Carol Lavell	Gifted	1629	
Charlotte Bredahl	Monsieur	1507	
Robert Dover	Lectron	1507	
4. SWE			4537
Tinne Wilhelmsson	Caprice	1522	
Ann Behrenfors	Leroy	1514	
Annica Westerberg	Taktik	1501	
5. DEN			4533
Anne van Olst	Chevalier	1542	
Anne Greth Törnblad (Jensen)	Ravel	1540	
Lene Hoberg	Bayard	1451	
6. SWI			4524
Otto Hofer	Renzo	1548	
Ruth Hunkeler	Afghadi	1498	
Doris Ramseier	Renatus	1478	
7. GBR			4522
Carl Hester	Giorgione	1523	
Emile Faurie	Virtu	1513	
Laura Fry	Quarryman	1486	
8. ITA			4491
Pia Laus	Adrett	1571	
Paolo Margi	Destino Di Acci	1481	
Daria Fantoni Camilla	Sonny Boy	1439	

Discontinued Events

HIGH JUMP

1900 Paris C: 18, N: 5, D: 6.2.

			HORSE	M
1.	Dominique Maximien Gardéres	FRA	Canela	1.85
1.	Gian Giorgio Trissino	ITA	Oreste	1.85
3.	Georges van de Poele	BEL	Ludlow	1.70
4.	Gian Giorgio Trissino	ITA	Melopo	1.70

The current record for the equestrian high jump is 2.47 meters, set in 1949 by Alberto Larraguibel of Chile on Huaso.

LONG JUMP

1900 Paris C: 17, N: 5, D: 5.31.

			HORSE	M
1.	Constant van Langhendonck	BEL	Extra Dry	6.10
2.	Gian Giorgio Trissino	ITA	Oreste	5.70
3.	de Bellegarde	FRA	Tolla	5.30
4.	Louis Napoléon Murat	FRA	Bayard	—

The current record for the equestrian long jump is 8.40 meters, set in 1975 by André Ferreira of South Africa on Something.

FIGURE RIDING, INDIVIDUAL

1920 Antwerp C: 18, N: 3, D: 9.11.

			PTS.
1.	Bouckaert	BEL	30.5
2.	Field	FRA	29.5
3.	Finet	BEL	29.0
4.	van Ranst	BEL	28.0
5.	van Schauwbroeck	BEL	27.25
6.	van Cauwenberg	BEL	26.666
7.	Salins	FRA	26.333
8.	des logis Claes	BEL	26.163

FIGURE RIDING, TEAMS

1920 Antwerp T: 3, N: 3, D: 9.11.

			PTS.
1.	BEL	(Bouckaert, Finet, van Ranst)	87.5
2.	FRA	(Field, Salins, Cauchy)	81.083
3.	SWE	(Karl Green, Anders Mårtensson, Oskar Nilsson)	59.416

This event was open only to army officers. It included several acrobatic moves such as jumping on and off a horse and standing on a horse, as well as jumping *over* horses.

FENCING

MEN	WOMEN
Foil, Individual	Foil, Individual
Foil, Team	Foil, Team
Épée, Individual	Épée, Individual
Épée, Team	Épée, Team
Sabre, Individual	
Sabre, Team	
Discontinued Events	

Some Common Fencing Terms

Balestra—A short jump toward the opponent

Barrage—A fence-off, used to decide ties

En garde position—The position taken before combat begins. Standing sideways, with the rear arm curled up for balance, the fencer tries to present the smallest possible target area to the opponent.

Flèche—A short run toward the opponent

Lunge—An attack that includes the extension of the front leg

Parry—A blocking of an opponent's thrust

Piste—The dueling surface. For foil events it is two meters (6 feet 7 inches) wide and 14 meters (46 feet) long. For épée and sabre events it is the same width, but the length is 18 meters (59 feet). The en garde lines are two meters (6 feet 7 inches) from the center line.

Reprise—An attack that follows a recovery from an opponent's lunge

Riposte—The offensive action that follows a parry

Thrust—An attack with a quick extension of the sword blade but without foot movement

The three swords used in fencing competitions are the foil, the épée, and the sabre.

The *foil* has a flexible rectangular blade and a blunt point. Touches must be made with the point on the trunk of the body, between the collar and the hipbones.

The *épée* has a rigid triangular blade with a point that is covered by a cone with barbed points. Touches may be made on any part of the body.

The *sabre* is a flexible triangular blade with a blunt point. Both the point and the cutting edges can be used to score touches, which must be made on the body, above the waist, including the head and arms.

In all events, a wire is attached to the sword. This wire runs through the fencer's outfit to a scoring box. When contact is made on the opponent's body a light flashes on and a buzzer sounds to record a hit.

Over the years Olympic fencing tournaments have used a variety of formats incorporating both round-robin pools and double-elimination rounds. According to the rules currently in force a tournament begins with pool competition. The majority of the competitors advance to a straight elimination round. When 32 fencers are left, they begin a double-elimination round. A fencer who loses a bout is relegated to the repêchage half of the elimination round. Four fencers from the direct elimination and four from the repêchage advance to direct elimination to decide the top eight places.

In pool competition a match is won by the first fencer to score five hits (or touches). In the elimination round, if the score is tied at four, the fencers continue to six. The first fencer to reach five twice (like sets in tennis) wins the match. If neither fencer makes five hits within the time limit, the score is moved to 5-5 and the first fencer to score a hit wins.

Traditionally in team competition each team had five members. The first team to record nine victories won. If the contest ended at a tie (8-8), the team with the most touches was declared the winner. In 1996 a new format will be used. Each team will have three members. The first two fencers (one from each team) fence for four minutes or until one of them scores five touches. The next pair takes over for four minutes or until one team reaches ten points. This continues until one side reaches 45 points or until the end of regulation time. If the teams are tied at the end of regulation time, an additional minute of fencing is allowed. The first team to score a touch wins. Before the final minute, the referee flips a coin to determine the winner should no touch be made in the additional minute.

MEN

FOIL, INDIVIDUAL

1896 Athens C: 8, N: 2, D: 4.7.

		W	L	TG	TR
1. Eugène-Henri Gravelotte	FRA	4	0	12	7
2. Henri Callot	FRA	3	1	11	7

3. Perikles Pierrakos-Mavromichalis	GRE	2	1	7	4	
3. Athanasios Vouros	GRE	2	1	5	4	
5. Henri de Laborde	FRA	1	2	5	7	
5. Konstantinos Komnios-Milliotis	GRE	1	2	5	4	
7. Georgios Balakakis	GRE	0	3	3	9	
7. Ioannis Poulos	GRE	0	3	3	9	

Gravelotte, France's first Olympic champion, was a medical student. He defeated his friend Callot 3-2 in the final. That evening he celebrated his triumph by drinking a glass of retzina at the Acropolis.

1900 Paris C: 54, N: 3, D: 5.21.

		W	L
1. Emile Coste	FRA	6	1
2. Henri Masson	FRA	5	2
3. Marcel Jacques Boulenger	FRA	4	3
4. Debax	FRA	4	3
5. Pierre d'Hugues	FRA	3	4
6. Sénat	FRA	3	4
7. Georges Dillon-Kavanagh	FRA	2	5
8. Rudolf Brosch	AUT	1	6

1904 St. Louis C: 9, N: 3, D: 9.7.

		W	L
1. Ramón Fonst	CUB	3	0
2. Albertson Van Zo Post	USA	2	1
3. Charles Tatham	USA	1	2
4. Gustav Casmir	GER	0	3

1906 Athens C: 37, N: 12, D: 4.28.

1. Georges Dillon-Kavanagh	FRA
2. Gustav Casmir	GER
3. Pierre d'Hugues	FRA
4. Martin Harden	AUT
5. Simon Okker	HOL
6. Federico Cesarano	ITA

1908 not held

1912 Stockholm C: 104, N: 16, D: 7.8.

		W	L	TG	TR
1. Nedo Nadi	ITA	7	0	35	8
2. Pietro Speciale	ITA	5	2	29	24
3. Richard Verderber	AUT	4	3	27	25
4. László Berti	HUN	4	3	23	25
5. Edoardo Alajmo	ITA	4	3	27	26
6. Edgar Seligman	GBR	3	4	23	29
7. Béla Bekessy	HUN	1	6	20	34
8. Robert Montgomerie	GBR	0	7	22	35

Nadi was a mere 18 years old when he won his first Olympic gold medal. The French team boycotted the competition after their proposal to include the upper arm as an attackable surface was rejected.

1920 Antwerp C: 56, N: 10, D: 8.18.

		W	L	TR
1. Nedo Nadi	ITA	10	1	
2. Philippe Cattiau	FRA	9	2	14

3. Roger Ducret	FRA	9	2	19
4. André Labatut	FRA	7	4	
5. Aldo Nadi	ITA	6	5	19
6. Fernand de Montigny	BEL	6	5	27
7. Oreste Puliti	ITA	5	6	
8. Ivan Osiier	DEN	4	7	

Nadi's performance at Antwerp was nothing short of spectacular, as he won an unprecedented and unequaled five gold medals. Not only did he win both the individual

Nedo Nadi won gold medals in five of the six fencing events of 1920.

foil and sabre, but he was also the leader of the winning Italian teams in the foil, épée, and sabre. His record in the individual foil tournament was 22-2. However, he almost didn't win because his second loss was to Ducret in the final round. Ducret, in his memoirs, described what happened next: "I was the Olympic champion: I struggled to contain the joy that was overflowing in my heart. I thanked destiny for having given me this marvelous form and, in the Olympic period, this day of invincibility, the kind that fencers rarely encounter in their lives. Meanwhile, Nedo Nadi was crying in his corner. All that remained for me was one match against the last place of the pool [Pietro Speciale of Italy, who was 0-10 in the final]. A final formality that didn't worry me in the least. Crossing swords with this adversary was like stretching my legs. I had, without effort, touched him a dozen times in a row. I could beat him with my eyes closed. I attacked immediately—too hastily perhaps, because I missed. I was touched. Bah! Not important. I aimed again, with a casual assurance. This thrust was well parried; I received the riposte without making a counterriposte: 2-0. It was starting to go badly. Alas! Having believed the contest won, I had relaxed my pace to such a degree that I was unable to regain my rhythm. I no longer understood anything. I lost completely the flow and the match and the title, all at the same time." But Ducret had learned his lesson. Four years later in Paris he would win his gold medal at last by keeping his concentration when he needed it most.

1924 Paris C: 49, N: 17, D: 7.4.

		W	L	TG	TR
1. Roger Ducret	FRA	6	0	30	14
2. Philippe Cattiau	FRA	5	1	29	11
3. Maurice van Damme	BEL	4	2	23	16
4. Jacques Coutrot	FRA	3	3	18	25
5. Roberto Larraz	ARG	2	4	21	25
6. Ivan Osiier	DEN	1	5	14	27
7. Balthazar de Beuckelaer	BEL	0	6	13	30

DNS: Edgar Seligman (GBR)

In the absence of the Italians, who had withdrawn following an incident during the team foil, the individual competition was dominated by the French. Particularly formidable was Philippe Cattiau, who whipped through the tournament with an outstanding record of 23 wins and one loss and 119 touches given, as opposed to only 54 received. Unfortunately, his only loss was in the final pool to 26-year-old Roger Ducret, who beat Cattiau five touches to four to win the gold medal. Ducret had suffered six defeats (against 13 wins) on his way to the final.

1928 Amsterdam C: 54, N: 23, D: 8.1.

						BARRAGE			
		W	L	TG	TR	W	L	TG	TR
1. Lucien Gaudin	FRA	9	2	49	24	2	0	10	5
2. Erwin Casmir	GER	9	2	49	33	1	1	6	8
3. Giulio Gaudini	ITA	9	2	53	34	0	2	7	10

4. Oreste Puliti	ITA	8	3	51	27
5. Philippe Cattiau	FRA	7	4	43	32
6. Raymond Bru	BEL	7	4	42	41
7. Ugo Pignotti	ITA	4	7	40	48
8. Fritz August Gazzera	GER	4	7	37	49

Lucien Gaudin and Oreste Puliti entered the finals undefeated, but Puliti lost to Gaudin, Erwin Casmir, and Raymond Bru. In the final Casmir beat Gaudin 5–4, but in the barrage Gaudin was the victor, 5–1. However Gaudin still needed to face Gaudini. With the score tied 2–2, Gaudini grazed Gaudin's fencing jacket. The referee called out, "No touch." The Italians were furious and began protesting vehemently. Gaudin removed his mask, walked over to the jury, and calmly announced, "I was touched." Gaudini was awarded the point and then earned another. However, Gaudin then scored three times in a row to win 5-4. Gaudin was 41 years old.

1932 Los Angeles C: 26, N: 12, D: 8.5.

		W	L	TG	TR
1. Gustavo Marzi	ITA	9	0	45	17
2. Joseph Levis	USA	6	3	38	35
3. Giulio Gaudini	ITA	5	4	34	27
4. Gioacchino Guaragna	ITA	5	4	37	33
5. Erwin Casmir	GER	5	4	36	34
6. John Emrys Lloyd	GBR	5	4	36	34
7. Roberto Larraz	ARG	3	6	33	31
8. René Bougnol	FRA	3	6	28	41

Twenty-three-year-old Gustavo Marzi completed the tournament with a record of 21–2.

1936 Berlin C: 62, N: 22, D: 8.6.

		W	L	TG	TR
1. Giulio Gaudini	ITA	7	0	35	20
2. Edward Gardère	FRA	6	1	33	25
3. Giorgio Bocchino	ITA	4	3	28	22
4. Erwin Casmir	GER	4	3	31	29
5. Gioacchino Guaragna	ITA	3	4	30	28
6. Raymond Bru	BEL	3	4	25	31
7. André Gardère	FRA	1	6	23	32
8. Georges de Bourguignon	BEL	0	7	17	35

Between 1928 and 1936 the 6-foot 3½-inch Gaudini won three gold medals, four silver, and two bronze. The 1936 foil was his only individual gold.

1948 London C: 63, N: 25, D: 8.4.

		W	L	TG	TR
1. Jehan Buhan	FRA	7	0	35	14
2. Christian d'Oriola	FRA	5	2	29	18
3. Lajos Maszlay	HUN	4	3	25	22
4. John Emrys Lloyd	GBR	4	3	23	29
5. René Bougnol	FRA	3	4	28	26
6. Manlio Di Rosa	ITA	3	4	22	27
7. Paul Valcke	BEL	1	6	23	31
8. Ivan Ruben	DEN	1	6	15	33

The 36-year-old Buhan had gone to London to compete in the épée and was only entered in the foil at the last minute. Runner-up d'Oriola had surprised the fencing world in 1947 by winning the world championship in Lisbon at the tender age of 18. Buhan finished the tournament with a record of 24–1.

1952 Helsinki C: 61, N: 25, D: 7.24.

		W	L	TG	TR
1. Christian d'Oriola	FRA	8	0	40	12
2. Edoardo Mangiarotti	ITA	6	2		21
3. Manlio Di Rosa	ITA	5	3		22
4. Jacques Lataste	FRA	4	4		31
5. Jehan Buhan	FRA	4	4	29	33
6. Mahmoud Younes	EGY	4	4	27	33
7. Salah Dessouki	EGY	2	6		35
8. Giancarlo Bergamini	ITA	2	6		36

All three medalists were left-handed.

Christian d'Oriola won four gold medals and two silver medals in foil fencing between 1948 and 1956.

1956 Melbourne C: 32, N: 14, D: 11.26.

						BARRAGE			
		W	L	TG	TR	W	L	TG	TR
1. Christian d'Oriola	FRA	6	1	33	17				
2. Giancarlo Bergamini	ITA	5	2	33	26	1	0	5	4
3. Antonio Spallino	ITA	5	2	30	21	0	1	4	5
4. Allan Jay	GBR	4	3	29	26				
5. József Gyuricza	HUN	3	4	21	25				
6. Claude Netter	FRA	3	4	19	30				
7. Mark Midler	SOV/RUS	2	5	19	30				
8. Raymond Paul	GBR	0	7	15	35				

D'Oriola was a 27-year-old law student when he became the first man since Nedo Nadi to win two individual foil gold medals. D'Oriola, a native of Perpignan, had some trouble adapting to the new electric foil, but he solved it quite well in time for the Melbourne Olympics.

1960 Rome C: 78, N: 31, D: 8.30.

						BARRAGE			
		W	L	TG	TR	W	L	TG	TR
1. Viktor Zhdanovich	SOV/RUS	7	0	35	20				
2. Yuri Sissikin	SOV/RUS	4	2	27	21				
3. Albert Axelrod	USA	3	3	23	24	2	0	10	7
4. Witold Woyda	POL	3	3	24	23	1	1	9	7
5. Mark Midler	SOV/RUS	3	4	28	25	0	2	5	10
6. Roger Closset	FRA	2	2	14	16				
7. Henry Hoskyns	GBR	2	5	21	33				
8. Christian d'Oriola	FRA	1	6	22	32				

A 22-year-old student teacher from Leningrad, Zhdanovich was the first Soviet fencer to win a gold medal. As such, he became a hero and was known in the newspapers as "Viktor the Victor."

1964 Tokyo C: 55, N: 21, D: 10.14.

		W	L	TG	TR
1. Egon Franke	POL	3	0	15	9
2. Jean-Claude Magnan	FRA	2	2	14	10
3. Daniel Revenu	FRA	1	3	12	11
4. Roland Losert	AUT	0	3	4	15
5. Jenö Kamuti	HUN				
6. Tim Gerresheim	GER				
7. Henry Hoskyns	GBR				
7. Sándor Szabó	HUN				

Egon Franke, a 29-year-old technical administrator from the small town of Gliwice, was an unexpected and popular winner.

1968 Mexico City C: 64, N: 25, D: 10.16.

						BARRAGE			
		W	L	TG	TR	W	L	TG	TR
1. Ionel Drimbă	ROM	4	1	22	15				
2. Jenö Kamuti	HUN	3	2	19	14	1	0	5	4
3. Daniel Revenu	FRA	3	2	22	17	0	1	4	5
4. Christian Noël	FRA	2	3	14	18				
5. Jean-Claude Magnan	FRA	2	3	18	22				
6. Mihai Tiu	ROM	1	4	14	23				
7. Tănase Mureşan	ROM								
7. German Sveshnikov	SOV/RUS								

Ion Drimbă, a 26-year-old physical training instructor, went through the tournament with a record of 19–2. Two years later he defected to the West and retired from competition.

1972 Munich C: 58, N: 26, D: 8.30.

			W	L	TG	TR
1.	Witold Woyda	POL	5	0	25	7
2.	Jenö Kamuti	HUN	4	1	23	19
3.	Christian Noël	FRA	2	3	17	18
4.	Mihai Tiu	ROM	2	3	17	20
5.	Vladimir Denissov	SOV/RUS	2	3	17	21
6.	Marek Dabrowski	POL	0	5	10	25

Thirty-three-year-old Witold Woyda qualified for the final with a modest record of 14–6, but then he completely dominated his last five opponents to take the gold medal.

1976 Montreal C: 56, N: 23, D: 7.21.

							BARRAGE			
			W	L	TG	TR	W	L	TG	TR
1.	Fabio Dal Zotto	ITA	4	1	24	15	1	0	5	1
2.	Aleksandr Romankov	SOV/BLR	4	1	21	13	0	1	1	5
3.	Bernard Talvard	FRA	3	2	19	21				
4.	Vasyl Stankovych	SOV/UKR	2	3	19	18				
5.	Frédéric Pietruszka	FRA	2	3	13	19				
6.	Gregory Benkö	AUS	0	5	15	25				
7.	Vladimir Denissov	SOV								
7.	Christian Noël	FRA								

Dal Zotto, a student from Venice, celebrated his 19th birthday three days before the competition began.

1980 Moscow C: 37, N: 16, D: 7.23.

							BARRAGE			
			W	L	TG	TR	W	L	TG	TR
1.	Volodymyr Smirnov	SOV/UKR	4	1	24	16	1	1	9	5
2.	Pascal Jolyot	FRA	4	1	24	17	1	1	5	5
3.	Aleksandr Romankov	SOV/BLR	4	1	22	15	1	1	5	9
4.	Sabirzhan Ruziyev	SOV/UZB	2	3	20	19				
5.	Lech Koziejowski	POL	1	4	15	21				
6.	Petru Kuki	ROM	0	5	8	25				
7.	Frédéric Pietruszka	FRA								
7.	István Szelei	HUN								

Two years after winning the Olympic gold medal, Smirnov was defending his world championship in Rome when the foil of his opponent, Matthias Behr of West Germany, snapped, pierced Smirnov's mask, penetrated his eyeball and entered his brain. The 28-year-old Soviet fencer died nine days later.

1984 Los Angeles-Long Beach C: 58, N: 26, D: 8.2.

1.	Mauro Numa	ITA
2.	Matthias Behr	GER
3.	Stefano Cerioni	ITA
4.	Frédéric Pietruszka	FRA
5.	Andrea Borella	ITA
6.	Mathias Gey	GER

7.	Philippe Omnès	FRA
8.	Thierry Soumagne	BEL

Final: Numa 10–9 Behr
3rd Place: Cerioni 10–5 Pietruszka

Mauro Numa may have won the gold medal, but his victory did not come easily. In his quarterfinal bout with Philippe Omnès, Numa trailed 6–8 with one minute left and then scored four straight touches in 49 seconds to win 10–8. In his semifinal match, he trailed Stefano Cerioni 1–6 before coming from behind to win 11–9. In the final against Matthias Behr, Numa was behind 3–7 with one minute to go. Again he scored four straight touches. Then Behr moved ahead 8–7. Numa was back with two quick scores. However, with two seconds remaining, Behr evened the count, sending the contest into sudden-death overtime. Within seconds Numa finally secured the win. Among the boycott missing was five-time world champion Aleksandr Romankov, who had won the last two world championships.

1988 Seoul C: 68, N: 29, D: 9.21.

1.	Stefano Cerioni	ITA
2.	Udo Wagner	GDR
3.	Aleksandr Romankov	SOV/BLR
4.	Ulrich Schreck	GER
5.	Zsolt Érsek	HUN
6.	Mauro Numa	ITA
7.	Jens Howe	GDR
8.	Mathias Gey	GER

Final: Cerioni 10-7 Wagner
3rd Place: Romankov 10-8 Schreck

Cerioni's victory capped a successful comeback following a 15-month suspension. During the 1986 world championships, the volatile Spanish-born fencer had offended tournament officials by screaming wildly and making obscene gestures.

1992 Barcelona C: 59, N: 25, D: 7.31.

1.	Philippe Omnès	FRA
2.	Sergei Golubitsky	UKR
3.	Elvis Gregory Gil	CUB
4.	Udo Wagner	GER
5.	Andrea Borella	ITA
6.	Marian Sypniewski	POL
7.	Guillermo Bétancourt Scull	CUB
8.	Joachim Wendt	AUT

Final: Omnès—Golubitsky 6-5, 3-5, 5-2
3rd Place: Gregory—Wagner 5-3, 2-5, 5-3

The 31-year-old Omnès had won the world championship in 1990 but was considered past his prime by the time of the Barcelona Olympics. He lost to Borella, but qualified for the final eight through repêchage. In the semifinals Omnès defeated Wagner 5-3, 5-6, 5-3, and Golubitsky, who had also come through the repêchage round, beat Gregory 3-5, 5-2, 5-1.

FOIL, TEAM

Current rules allow each team to have five members, four of whom take part in each contest. Each contest consists of 16 matches, with each member of a team fencing against each other member of the opposing team. Ties are decided by total touches. Very often a contest will end as soon as one team has clinched the victory.

1896–1900 not held

1904 St. Louis T: 2, N: 2, D: 9.8.

		WON
1. CUB/USA	(Ramón Fonst—CUB, Manuel Diaz—CUB, Albertson Van Zo Post—USA)	7
2. USA	(Charles Tatham, Fitzhugh Townsend, Arthur Fox)	2

1906–1912 not held

1920 Antwerp T: 8, N: 8, D: 8.17.

		WON	LOST	MATCHES W	L
1. ITA	(Baldo Baldi, Tommaso Constantino, Aldo Nadi, Nedo Nadi, Abelardo Olivier, Oreste Puliti, Pietro Speciale, Rodolfo Terlizzi)	4	0	50	14
2. FRA	(Lionel Bony de Castellane, Gaston Amson, Phillippe Cattiau, Roger Ducret, André Labatut, Georges Trombert, Marcel Perrot, Lucien Gaudin)	3	1	45	19
3. USA	(Henry Breckinridge, Francis Honeycutt, Arthur Lyon, Harold Rayner, Robert Sears)	2	2	22	42
4. DEN	(Ivan Osiier, Georg Hegner, Ejnar Levison, Poul Rasmussen, Kay Schröder)	1	3	26	38
5. GBR	(Edgar Seligman, Richard Willoughby, Philip Doyne, Robert Montgomerie, H. Evan James, Cecil Kershaw)	0	4	17	47
6. BEL	(Marcel Berré, Charles Crahay, Marcel Cuypers, Fernand de Montigny, Emile de Schepper, Robert Hennet, Leon Tom, Charles Pape)				
6. CZE	(Josef Javůrek, Antony Mikala, Vilém Tvrzský, František Dvořák)				
6. HOL	(Wouter Brouwer, Raphael "Felix" Vigeveno, Salomon Zeldenrust, Andrianus de Jong, Jan van der Wiel)				

Italy defeated France 9-7 in the decisive match-up of the final pool.

1924 Paris T: 12, N: 12, D: 6.30.

		WON	LOST	MATCHES W	L
1. FRA	(Lucien Gaudin, Philippe Cattiau, Jacques Coutrot, Roger Ducret, Henri Jobier, André Labatut, Guy de Luget, Joseph Peroteaux)	3	0	31	6
2. BEL	(Désiré Beaurain, Charles Crahay, Fernand de Montigny, Maurice van Damme, Marcel Bérré, Albert de Roocker)	2	1	12	20
3. HUN	(László Berti, Sándor Posta, Zoltán Schenker, Ödön Tersztyánszky, István Licteneckert)	1	2	9	23
4. ITA	(Oreste Puliti, Giorgio Pessina, Valentino Argento, Giorgio Chiavacci, Giulio Gaudini, Aldo Boni, Luigi Cuomo, Dante Carniel)	0	3	1	4
5. ARG	(F. C. Bollini, Carmelo Camet, Horacio Casco, C. Guerrico, Roberto Larraz, Luis Lucchetti, Antonio Santamarina, J. N. Sosa)				

When the French and Italian teams met in the final pool at the Vélodrome d'Hiver, it was assumed that the winner would go on to take the gold medal. France took a 3–1 lead. In the fifth assault, Lucien Gaudin and Aldo Boni were tied at four touches each when the jury awarded a decisive, and questionable, fifth touch to Gaudin. Boni was incensed and launched a verbal attack against Kovács, the Hungarian judge. Kovács approached the Jury of Appeal and demanded an apology, whereupon Boni denied everything. Kovács then produced a witness, the Italian-born Hungarian fencing master Italo Santelli, who reluctantly supported Kovács' allegations of abusive language. The Italian team withdrew in protest, singing the Fascist hymn as they left, and their remaining matches were declared forfeited. Lost in the excitement was a brilliant performance by Gaudin, who scored 22 victories without a defeat and recorded 110 touches while receiving only 21.

However, the affair was not over. Back in Italy, the Italian foil team issued a statement which accused Santelli of testifying against them because he feared the Italians would defeat the Hungarian team, which he had coached. When he heard about this insult, Santelli, who was over 60 years old, challenged Adolfo Contronei, the Italian captain, to a real duel. Government permission was obtained to fight the duel, but before the two men could meet, Santelli's 27-year-old son, Giorgio, invoked the *code duello* and demanded that he fight in his father's place. In the small town of Abazzia near the Hungarian border, Giorgio and Contronei met and fought with heavy sabres. After two minutes the younger Santelli slashed Contronei deeply on the side of the head, drawing blood. Doctors rushed in and halted the duel. Giorgio Santelli later moved to the United States, where he became the coach of the U.S. team. He taught fencing to 8,000 people and spent over 100,000 hours with a sword in his hand, but he never again engaged in a real duel.

1928 Amsterdam T: 16, N: 16, D: 7.30.

				MATCHES	
		WON	LOST	W	L
1. ITA	(Ugo Pignotti, Oreste Puliti, Giulio Gaudini, Giorgio Pessina, Giorgio Chiavacci, Gioacchino Guaragna)	3	0	34	14
2. FRA	(Lucien Gaudin, Philippe Cattiau, Roger Ducret, An-	2	1	23	25

dré Labatut, Raymond Flacher, André Gaboriaud)

		WON	LOST	W	L
3. ARG	(Roberto Larraz, Raúl Anganuzzi, Luis Lucchetti, Héctor Lucchetti, Carmelo Camet)	1	2	23	25
4. BEL	(Max Janlet, Pierre Pecher, Raymond Bru, Albert de Roocker, Jean Verbrugghe, Charles Crahay)	0	3	16	32
5. HUN	(Ödön Tersztyánszky, György Rozgonyi, György Piller, József Rády, Gusztáv Kálniczky, Péter Toth)				
5. USA	(George Calnan, René Peroy, Joseph Levis, Harold Rayner, Henry Breckinridge, Dernell Every)				

In Amsterdam the Italians gained their revenge against the French with a 10–6 victory. The Italian team was led by Chiavacci, who finished the tournament with 22 wins and two losses, and Gaudini, who was 30–2, including four straight victories against the French.

1932 Los Angeles T: 6, N: 6, D: 8.1.

				MATCHES		BARRAGE		MATCHES	
		WON	LOST	W	L	WON	LOST	W	L
1. FRA	(Philippe Cattiau, Edward Gardère, René Lemoine, René Bondoux, Jean Piot, René Bougnol)	2	1	26	22	2	0	19	13
2. ITA	(Giulio Gaudini, Gustavo Marzi, Ugo Pignotti, Giorgio Pessina, Gioacchino Guaranga, Rodolfo Terlizzi)	2	1	31	17	1	1	17	9
3. USA	(George Calnan, Joseph Levis, Hugh Allesandroni, Dernell Every, Richard Steere, Frank Righeimer)	2	1	22	26	0	2	6	20
4. DEN	(Axel Bloch, Erik Kofoed-Hansen, Aage Leidersdorff, Ivan Osiier)	0	3	17	31				

Italy and France tied in the barrage, 8–8, but France was awarded the victory on fewer touches received, 58–62.

1936 Berlin T: 18, N: 18, D: 8.4.

				MATCHES	
		WON	LOST	W	L
1. ITA	(Giulio Gaudini, Gioacchino Guaranga, Gustavo Marzi, Giorgio Bocchino, Manlio Di Rosa, Ciro Verratti)	3	0	38	7

		WON	LOST	W	L
2. FRA	(Jacques Coutrot, André Gardère, René Lemoine, René Bougnol, Edward Gardère, René Bondoux)	2	1	27	18
3. GER	(Siegfried Lerdon, August Heim, Julius Eisenecker, Erwin Casmir, Stefan Rosenbauer, Otto Adam)	1	2	13	33
4. AUT	(Hans Lion, Roman Fischer, Hans Schönbaumsfeld, Ernst Baylon, Josef Losert, Karl Sudrich)	0	3	13	33
5. BEL	(Georges de Bourguignon, André van de Werve de Vorselaer, Henri Paternoster, Raymond Bru, Heremans, Paul Valcke)				
5. USA	(Joseph Levis, Hugh Alessandroni, John Potter, John Hurd, Warren Dow, William Pecora)				
7. ARG	(Roberto Larraz, Héctor Luchetti, Angel Gorordo Palacios, Luis Luccheti, Rodolfo Valenzuela, Manuel Torrente)				
7. HUN	(Jószef Hatszeghy Hatz, Lajos Maszlay, Aladár Gerevich, Béla Bay, Ottó Hatszeghy Hatz, Antal Zirczy)				

France was the slight favorite, but the Italians breezed through the tournament with 104 wins and 19 losses. Verratti was 23–1 and Marzi 18–1. The deciding match with France was halted when Italy achieved an unbeatable 9–4 advantage.

1948 London T: 16, N: 16, D: 7.31.

		MATCHES			
		WON	LOST	W	L
1. FRA	(André Bonin, René Bougnol, Jehan Buhan, Jacques Lataste, Christian d'Oriola, Adrian Rommel)	3	0	28	18
2. ITA	(Renzo Nostini, Manlio Di Rosa, Edoardo Mangiarotti, Giuliano Nostini, Giorgio Pellini, Saverio Ragno)	2	1	28	15
3. BEL	(Georges de Bourguignon, Henry Paternoster, Edouard Yves, Raymond Bru, André van de Werwe de Vorsslaer, Paul Valcke)	1	2	19	27
4. USA	(Daniel Bukantz, Dean Cetrulo, Dernell Every, Silvio Giolito, Nathaniel Lubell, Austin Prokop)	0	3	14	29
5. ARG	(José Rodriguez, Fulvio Galimi, Manuel Torrente, Félix Galimi)				

5. EGY	(Osman Abdelhafiz, Salah Dessouki, Mahmoud Younes, Mohamed Zulficar, Hassan Hosni Tawfik, Mahmoud Abdin)
5. GBR	(R. René Paul, Albert Smith, Harold Cooke, John Emrys Lloyd, Pierre Turquet, Ulrich Wendon)
5. HUN	(Béla Bay, Aladár Gerevich, Jószef Hatszeghy Hatz, Lajos Maszlay, Pál Dunay, Endre Palócz)

An incident marred the semifinal round. Dissatisfied with a call by the president of the judges, the Argentine team gave three cheers for their opponents, the Belgians, and withdrew in protest. A more pleasant kind of event took place in the semifinal match between Great Britain and the United States. Harry Cooke of Britain was trailing Dean Cetrulo 3–4, when the two men collided. Cooke's mask smashed into his face, cutting his nose. The American team immediately administered first aid to their opponent. After a rest Cooke returned to action and rallied to win 5–4. Prior to their deciding match against the Italians, the French team found themselves in a different situation. They were exhausted and unable to find proper French nourishment. English cuisine was making them ill—in fact, an hour before the match, Bougnol was so sick he had to be replaced by Lataste. Fifteen minutes before they were due to enter the piste, French team member Jehan Buhan, who happened to be a wine merchant, managed to obtain a case of good French vintage. Revived, the French jumped out to a 6-3 lead. But the Italians came from behind to win five of the last seven fights. However, France won anyway on fewer touches received, 60–62.

1952 Helsinki T: 15, N: 15, D: 7.22.

		MATCHES			
		WON	LOST	W	L
1. FRA	(Jehan Buhan, Christian d'Oriola, Adrian Rommel, Claude Netter, Jacques Noël, Jacques Lataste)	3	0	35	11
2. ITA	(Giancarlo Bergamini, Antonio Spallino, Manlio Di Rosa, Giorgio Pellini, Renzo Nostini, Edoardo Mangiarotti)	2	1	34	12
3. HUN	(Endre Tilli, Aladár Gúrevich, Endre Palócz, Lajos Maszlay, Tibor Berczelly, József Sákovics)	1	2	16	31
4. EGY	(Salah Dessouki, Mohamed Ali Riad, Osman Abdelhafiz, Mahmoud Younes, Mohamed Zulficar, Hassan Hosni Tawfik)	0	3	8	39

5. ARG (Fulvio Galimi, José Rodriguez, Eduardo Sastre, Félix Galimi, Santiago Massini)

5. BEL (Pierre van Houdt, André Verhalle, Alex Bourgeois, Paul Valcke, Edouard Yves, Gustave Balister)

As usual, France and Italy dominated all other countries, entering their final showdown with match records of 54–9 and 55–6, respectively. Christian d'Oriola was the star of the tournament, winning ten matches without a loss. In the deciding confrontation he swept all four Italians by the scores of 5–0, 5–0, 5–1, and 5–2, leading the French team to an 8–6 victory.

1956 Melbourne T: 9, N: 9, D: 11.23.

		WON	LOST	MATCHES W	L
1. ITA	(Edoardo Mangiarotti, Giancarlo Bergamini, Antonio Spallino, Luigi Carpaneda, Manlio Di Rosa, Vittorio Lucarelli)	3	0	26	22
2. FRA	(Christian d'Oriola, Bernard Baudoux, Claude Netter, Jacques Lataste, Roger Closset, René Coicaud)	2	1	28	20
3. HUN	(József Gyuricza, József Sákovics, Mihály Fülöp, Endre Tilli, Lajos Somodi, Sr., József Marosi)	1	2	22	24
4. USA	(Albert Axelrod, Daniel Bukantz, Harold Goldsmith, Byron Kreiger, Nathaniel Lubell, Sewall Shurtz)	0	3	18	28
5. GBR	(R. René Paul, Henry Hoskyns, Raymond Paul, Allan Jay, Arnold Ralph Cooperman)				
5. SOV	(Yuri Rudov, Yuri Ossipov, Mark Midler, Aleksandr Ovsyankin, Viktor Zhdanovich, Yuri Ivanov)				

Once again the championship was between France and Italy, and once again d'Oriola swept the Italians, receiving only seven hits in four assaults. This time, though, Italy's team was better balanced. Going into the last bout, Italy led 8–7, but because the touches were even at 57, whoever won the last bout, which matched Spallino and Netter, would win the gold medal. Netter took an early lead, but Spallino came from behind to tie 4–4 and then win the championship for Italy on the final touch.

1960 Rome T: 16, N: 16, D: 9.2.
1. SOV/ (Viktor Zhdanovich, Mark Midler, Yuri Sissikin, German
   RUS Sveshnikov, Yuri Rudov)
2. ITA (Alberto Pellegrino, Luigi Carpaneda, Mario Curletto, Aldo Aureggio, Edoardo Mangiarotti)
3. GER (Jürgen Brecht, Tim Gerresheim, Eberhard Mehl, Jürgen Theuerkauff)
4. HUN (Ferenc Czvikovsky, Jenö Kamuti, Mihály Fülöp, László Kamuti, József Gyuricza, József Sákovics)
5. FRA (Jacky Courtillat, Jean-Claude Magnan, Guy Barrabino, Claude Netter, Christian d'Oriola)
5. GBR (Henry Hoskyns, Allan Jay, Arnold Ralph Cooperman, R. Angus McKenzie, Raymond Paul)
5. POL (Egon Franke, Ryszard Parulski, Janusz Różycki, Ryszard Kunze, Witold Woyda)
5. USA (Eugene Glazer, Harold Goldsmith, Joseph Paletta, Albert Axelrod, Daniel Bukantz)
Final: SOV 9–4 ITA
3rd Place: Ger 9–5 HUN

The Soviet Union became the first team since 1904 to break the Franco-Italian monopoly of the team foil event. In the final, Zhdanovich and Midler provided seven of the nine Soviet wins.

1964 Tokyo T: 16, N: 16, D: 10.16.
1. SOV/ (German Sveshnikov, Yuri Sissikin, Mark Midler, Viktor
   RUS Zhdanovich, Yuri Sharov)
2. POL (Zbigniew Skrudlik, Witold Wyoda, Egon Franke, Ryszard Parulski, Janusz Rózycki)
3. FRA (Daniel Revenu, Jacky Courtillat, Pierre Rodocanachi, Christian Nöel, Jean-Claude Magnan)
4. JPN (Kazuhiko Tabuchi, Fujio Shimizu, Kazuo Mano, Heizaburo Okawa, Sosuke Toda)
5. GER (Jürgen Brecht, Dieter Wellmann, Eberhard Mehl, Tim Gerresheim, Jürgen Theuerkauff)
6. ROM (Tănase Mureşan, Ionel Drimbă, Iuliu Falb, Ştefan Haukler, Atilla Csipler)
7. HUN (Jenö Kamuti, László Kamuti, József Gyuricza, Sándor Szabó, Béla Gyarmati)
7. ITA (Gianguido Milanesi, Pasquale La Ragione, Arcangelo Pinelli, Nicola Granieri)
Final: SOV 9–7 POL
3rd Place: FRA 9–4 JPN
5th Place: GER 8(60)–8(57)ROM

1968 Mexico City T: 17, N: 17, D: 10.19.
1. FRA (Daniel Revenu, Gilles Berolatti, Christian Nöel, Jean-Claude Magnan, Jacques Dimont)
2. SOV (German Sveshnikov, Yuri Sharov, Vasyl Stankovych, Viktor Putyatin, Yuri Sissikin)
3. POL (Witold Woyda, Ryszard Parulski, Egon Franke, Zbigniew Skrudlik, Adam Lisewski)
4. ROM (Ionel Drimbă, Mihai Tiu, Ştefan Haukler, Tănase Mureşan, Iuliu Falb)
5. HUN (Sándor Szabó, Jenö Kamuti, László Kamuti, Gábor Füredi, Attila May)
6. GER (Jürgen Theuerkauff, Friedrich Wessel, Tim Gerresheim, Jürgen Brecht, Dieter Wellmann)

7. ITA   (Pasquale La Ragione, Alfredo Del Francia, Nicola Granieri, Arcangelo Pinelli, Michelle Maffei)
7. JPN   (Masaya Fukuda, Heizaburo Ohkawa, Fujio Shimizu, Kazuhiko Wakasugi, Kazuo Mano)
   Final: FRA 9–6 SOV
   3rd Place: POL 9–3 ROM
   5th Place: HUN 9–4 GER

1972 Munich T: 13, N: 13, D: 9.2.
1. POL   (Lech Koziejowski, Witold Woyda, Marek Dabrowski, Jerzy Kaczmarek, Arkadiusz Godel)
2. SOV   (Vasyl Stankovych, Viktor Putyatin, Leonid Romanov, Anatoly Koteshev, Vladimir Denissov)
3. FRA   (Daniel Revenu, Bernard Talvard, Gilles Berolatti, Jean-Claude Magnan, Christian Nöel)
4. HUN   (Sándor Szabó, Csaba Fenyvesi, László Kamuti, István Marton, Jenö Kamuti)
5. GER   (Klaus Reichert, Friedrich Wessel, Harald Hein, Dieter Wellmann, Erk Sens-Gorius)
6. JPN   (Shiro Maruyama, Masaya Fukuda, Hiroshi Nakajima, Kiyoshi Uehara, Ichiro Serizawa)
7. CUB   (Evelio Gonzalez, Eduardo Jhons, Jesus Gil, Enrique Salvat, Jorge Garbey)
7. ROM   (Iuliu Falb, Ştefan Haukler, Mihai Tiu, Tănase Mureşan, Aurel Ştefan)
   Final: POL 9–5 SOV
   3rd Place: FRA 9–7 HUN
   5th Place: GER 9–7 JPN

Poland secured the gold medal despite an early loss to Germany. In the same round, the U.S.S.R. was defeated by Japan. The match for first place was highlighted by Woyda's sweep of the four Soviet fencers. The French had been the favorites, but they lost in the semifinals, 9–6, to the Soviet Union.

1976 Montreal T: 14, N: 14, D: 7.24.
1. GER   (Harald Hein, Thomas Bach, Erk Sens-Gorius, Klaus Reichert, Matthias Behr)
2. ITA   (Fabio Dal Zotto, Attilio Calatroni, Carlo Montano, Stefano Simoncelli, Giovan Battista Coletti)
3. FRA   (Daniel Revenu, Christian Nöel, Didier Flament, Bernard Talvard, Frédéric Pietruszka)
4. SOV   (Sabirzhan Ruziyev, Aleksandr Romankov, Vladimir Denissov, Vasyl Stankovych)
5. POL   (Leszek Martewicz, Lech Koziejowski, Ziemowit Wojciechowski, Arkadiusz Godel, Marek Dabrowski)
6. GBR   (Geoffrey Grimmett, Barry Paul, Robert Bruniges, Graham Paul, Nicholas Bell)
7. HUN   (József Komatits, Csaba Fenyvesi, Lajos Somodi, Jr., Jenö Kamuti, Sándor Erdös)
7. USA   (Martin Lang, Edward Ballinger, Edward Wright, Edward Donofrio, Brooke Mackler)
   Final: GER 9–6 ITA
   3rd Place: FRA 9–4 SOV
   5th Place: POL 9–1 GBR

1980 Moscow T: 9, N: 9, D: 7.26.
1. FRA   (Didier Flament, Pascal Jolyot, Frédéric Pietruszka, Philippe Bonnin, Bruno Boscherie)

2. SOV   (Aleksandr Romankov, Volodymyr Smirnov, Ashot Karagyan, Vladimir Lapitsky, Sabirzhan Ruziyev)
3. POL   (Boguslaw Zych, Adam Robak, Marian Sypniewski, Lech Koziejowski)
4. GDR   (Siegmar Gutzeit, Hartmuth Behrens, Adrian Germanus, Klaus Kotzmann, Klaus Haertter)
5. ROM   (Petru Kuki, Mihai Tiu, Sorin Roca, Tudor Petruş)
6. HUN   (István Szelei, Ernö Kolczonay, András Papp, László Demény, Jenö Pap)
7. CUB   (Efigenio Favier, Guillermo Betancourt, Heriberto Gonzalez, Pedro Hernandez)
8. GBR   (John Llewellyn, Steven Paul, Robert Bruniges, Pierre Harper, Neal Mallett)
   Final: FRA 8(68)–8(60)SOV
   3rd Place: POL 9–5 GDR
   5th Place: ROM 9–7 HUN

In the semifinals, Soviet world champion Vladimir Lapitsky was accidentally run through the chest when his Polish opponent's foil broke his leather protective clothing. The sword severed a blood vessel but missed his heart. France's victory marked their 13th team foil medal in 14 Olympics.

1984 Los Angeles-Long Beach T: 14, N: 14, D: 8.7.
1. ITA   (Mauro Numa, Andrea Borella, Stefano Cerioni, Angelo Scuri, Andrea Cipressa)
2. GER   (Matthias Behr, Mathias Gey, Harald Hein, Frank Beck, Klaus Reichert)
3. FRA   (Philippe Omnès, Patrick Groc, Frédéric Pietruszka, Pascal Jolyot, Marc Cerboni)
4. AUT   (Joachim Wendt, Dieter Kotlowski, Georg Somloi, Robert Blaschka, Georg Loisel)
5. USA   (Michael Marx, Gregory Massialas, Peter Lewison, Mark Smith, Michael McCahey)
6. GBR   (William Gosbee, Pierre Harper, Nicholas Bell, Robert Bruniges, Graham Paul)
7. CHN   (Chu Shisheng, Cui Yining, Yu Yifeng, Wang Wei, Zhang Jian)
8. BEL   (Thierry Soumagne, Peter Joos, Stefan Joos, Stephane Ganeff)
   Final: ITA 8–7 GER
   3rd Place: FRA 9–3 AUT
   5th Place: USA 9–6 GBR
   7th Place: CHN 9–0 BEL (forfeit)

1988 Seoul T: 16, N: 16, D: 9.27.
1. SOV   (Vladimir Aptsiauri, Anvar Ibragimov, Boris Koretsky, Ilgar Mamedov, Aleksandr Romankov)
2. GER   (Matthias Behr, Thomas Endres, Mathias Gey, Ulrich Schreck, Thorsten Weidner)
3. HUN   (István Busa, Zsolt Érsek, Róbert Gátai, Pál Szekeres, István Szelei)
4. GDR   (Aris Enkelmann, Adrian Germanus, Jens Gusek, Jens Howe, Udo Wagner)
5. POL   (Leszek Bandach, Waldemar Ciesielczyk, Piotr Kielpikowski, Marian Sypniewski, Boguslaw Zych)
6. FRA   (Laurent Bel, Patrick Groc, Youssef Hocine, Patrice Lhotellier, Philippe Omnès)

7. ITA   (Andrea Borella, Stefano Cerioni, Federico Cervi, Andrea Cipressa, Mauro Numa)
8. CHN   (Lao Shaopei, Liu Yunhong, Ye Chong, Zhang Zhicheng)
Final: SOV 9–5 GER
3rd Place: HUN 9–5 GDR
5th Place: POL 8(60)–8(53) FRA
7th Place: ITA 9–4 CHN

The underdog Soviet team received its stiffest challenge from the Hungarians in the semifinals. Both sides won eight matches, but the U.S.S.R. won on touches, 57–51.

1992 Barcelona T: 12, N: 12, D: 8.5.
1. GER   (Alexander Koch, Ulrich Schreck, Thorsten Weidner, Udo Wagner, Ingo Weissenborn)
2. CUB   (Guillermo Bétancourt Scull, Tulio Díaz Babier, Hermenegildo García Marturell, Óscar García Pérez, Elvis Gregory Gil)
3. POL   (Piotr Kielpikowski, Adam Krzesiński, Marian Sypniewski, Cezary Siess, Ryszard Sobczak)
4. HUN   (István Busa, Zsolt Érsek, Róbert Gátai, Róbert Kiss, Zsolt Németh)
5. SOV   (Dmitri Shevchenko, Sergei Golubitsky, Vyacheslav Grigoryev, Anvar Ibragimov, Ilgar Mamedov)
6. ITA   (Marco Arpino, Andrea Borella, Stefano Cerioni, Mauro Numa, Alessandro Puccini)
7. FRA   (Patrick Groc, Youssef Hocine, Olivier Lambert, Patrice Lhotellier, Philippe Omnès)
8. KOR   (Kim Young-ho, Kim Seung-pyo, Lee Ho-sung, Lee Seung-yong, You Bong-hyung)
Final: GER 8(65)-8(53) CUB
3rd Place: POL 9-4 HUN
5th Place: SOV 9-5 ITA
7th Place: FRA 9-2 KOR

At the 1991 world championships, the Cuban team shocked the fencing world by defeating Germany 9-6 in the final. In the quarterfinals at the Olympics they survived a close 8(59)-8(53) victory over South Korea. In the final the Cubans took a 7-3 lead, but the Germans fought back and won on touches.

ÉPÉE, INDIVIDUAL

1896 not held

1900 Paris C: 101, N: 4, D: 6.14.
1. Ramón Fonst   CUB
2. Louis Perrée   FRA
3. Léon Sée   FRA
4. Georges de la Falaise FRA
5. Camet   FRA
6. Edmond Wallace   FRA
7. Gaston Alibert   FRA
8. Leon Thiebaut   FRA

Ramón Fonst was only 16 years old when he won the Olympic championship. His teacher, Albert Ayot, won the competition for masters.

1904 St. Louis C: 5, N: 3, D: 9.7.
1. Ramón Fonst   CUB
2. Charles Tatham   USA
3. Albertson Van Zo Post USA
4. Gustav Casmir   GER
5. Fitzhugh Townsend   USA

Not only did Fonst achieve a rare double victory in winning both the foil and épée, but he is also the only repeat winner in the individual épée.

1906 Athens C: 29, N: 10, D: 4.28.
1. Georges de la Falaise   FRA
2. Georges Dillon-Kavanagh   FRA
3. Alexander van Blijenburgh HOL
4. Raphael Vigeveno   HOL
5. Emil Schön   GER
6. Maurits Jacob van Löben Sels   HOL

1908 London C: 84, N: 13, D: 7.24

			W	L	T	BARRAGE W	BARRAGE L
1.	Gaston Alibert	FRA	5	0	2		
2.	Alexandre Lippmann	FRA	4	2	1	2	0
3.	Eugène Olivier	FRA	4	3	0	1	1
4.	Robert Montgomerie	GBR	4	1	2	0	2
5.	Paul Anspach	BEL	2	5	0		
5.	Cecil Haig	GBR	2	5	0		
5.	Alfred Labouchère	HOL	2	3	2		
8.	Martin Holt	GBR	1	5	1		

Gaston Alibert, winner of the 1908 épée fencing event.

Gaston Alibert completed the tournament with 21 wins, no losses, and two double hits, or ties. Two other contestants worth noting were Alfred Labouchère, who attracted quite a bit of attention because he was 6 feet 9 inches tall and Ivan Osiier, a 19-year-old from Denmark. Osiier ultimately competed in seven Olympics, making his first and final appearances in London—40 years apart. Along the way he qualified for nine finals, achieving his greatest success in 1912, when he won the individual épée silver medal. His wife, Ellen, was the first female Olympic fencing champion.

1912 Stockholm C: 112, N: 16, D: 7.13.

		W	L	T
1. Paul Anspach	BEL	6	1	0
2. Ivan Osiier	DEN	5	2	0
3. Philippe Le Hardy de Beaulieu	BEL	4	2	1
4. Victor Boin	BEL	4	2	1
5. Einar Sörensen	SWE	3	4	0
6. Edgar Seligman	GBR	2	4	1
7. Léon Tom	BEL	1	6	0
8. Martin Holt	GBR	0	4	3

The Italian Fencing Federation proposed that the length of the épée blade be extended to 94 cm. When this was rejected, the Italians refused to participate. Between 1908 and 1920 Paul Anspach won a total of four medals: two gold, one silver, and one bronze.

1920 Antwerp C: 80, N: 13, D: 8.23.

		WON
1. Armand Massard	FRA	9
2. Alexandre Lippmann	FRA	7
3. Gustave Buchard	FRA	6
4. Ernest Gevers	BEL	6
5. Georges Casanova	FRA	5
6. Antonio Mascarenhas de Menezes	POR	5
6. Emile Moreau	FRA	5
6. Abelardo Olivier	ITA	5

Massard later served as president of the French Olympic Committee.

1924 Paris C: 67, N: 18, D: 7.11.

		WON	LOST	1st BAR-RAGE W	1st BAR-RAGE L	2nd BAR-RAGE W	2nd BAR-RAGE L
1. Charles Delporte	BEL	8	3				
2. Roger Ducret	FRA	7	4	2	1	1	0
3. Nils Hellsten	SWE	7	4	2	1	0	1
4. Emile Cornereau	FRA	7	4	1	2	1	0
5. Armand Massard	FRA	7	4	1	2	0	1
6. Virgilio Mantegazza	ITA	6	5				
7. Gustave Buchard	FRA	5	6				
7. Léon Tom	BEL	5	6				

1928 Amsterdam C: 59, N: 22, D: 8.7.

		W	L	T	TG	TR	EXTRA FINAL W	EXTRA FINAL L	EXTRA FINAL TG	EXTRA FINAL TR
1. Lucien Gaudin	FRA	8	0	1	18	5	2	0	20	12
2. Georges Buchard	FRA	7	2	0	15	8	1	1	19	21
3. George Calnan	USA	6	3	0	14	9	1	1	21	19
4. Léon Tom	BEL	6	2	1	15	9	0	2	12	20
5. Nils Hellsten	SWE	5	4	0	12	13				
6. Charles Delporte	BEL	4	5	0	11	13				
7. Charles Debeur	BEL	3	6	0	10	15				
8. S. Cicurel	EGY	3	6	0	10	15				

Gaudin's record for the tournament was an impressive 34 wins and five losses, as he became the only fencer besides Ramón Fonst to win both the foil and épée.

1932 Los Angeles C: 28, N: 12, D: 8.9.

		W	L	T	TG	TR
1. Giancarlo Cornaggia-Medici	ITA	8	1	2	31	18
2. Georges Buchard	FRA	8	3	0	27	17
3. Carlo Agostoni	ITA	7	3	1	30	17
4. Saverio Ragno	ITA	7	4	0	27	20
5. Bernard Schmetz	FRA	7	4	0	26	22
6. Philippe Cattiau	FRA	6	5	0	23	22
7. George Calnan	USA	6	5	0	22	22
8. Balthazar de Beuckelaer	BEL	4	7	0	19	25

1936 Berlin C: 68, N: 26, D: 8.11.

		W	L	T	TG	TR
1. Franco Riccardi	ITA	5	1	3	25	18
2. Saverio Ragno	ITA	6	3	0	24	15
3. Giancarlo Cornaggia-Medici	ITA	6	3	0	22	16
4. Hans Drakenberg	SWE	4	3	2	20	20
5. Charles Debeur	BEL	4	4	1	21	21
6. Henrique da Silveira	POR	4	5	0	18	19
7. Raymond Stasse	BEL	3	4	2	21	21
8. Ian Campbell-Gray	GBR	3	4	2	18	24

Riccardi's total record was 24 wins, three losses, and four ties. In the quarterfinal pool, defending champion Cornaggia-Medici demonstrated his acute awareness of distance. Perplexed by the call of two straight double hits, he insisted that his opponent's blade was the wrong length. Measurements showed that it was in fact a half-inch too long.

1948 London C: 66, N: 25, D: 8.9.

		W	L	TG	TR	BARRAGE TG	BARRAGE TR
1. Luigi Cantone	ITA	7	2	24	15		
2. Oswald Zappelli	SWI	5	4	20	17	3	0
3. Edoardo Mangiarotti	ITA	5	4	20	17	0	3
4. Henri Guérin	FRA	5	4	20	19		
5. Jean Radoux	BEL	5	4	19	20		
6. Henri Lepage	FRA	4	5	19	20		
7. Carlo Agostoni	ITA	4	5	22	21		
8. Emile Gretsch	LUX	3	6	16	22		

Thirty-one-year-old Luigi Cantone was allowed to compete at the last minute after Dario Mangiarotti injured his foot and had to withdraw. In the final pool, which took five and a half hours, Cantone lost his first two bouts to Carlo Agostoni and Edoardo Mangiarotti. Then he won seven straight to take first place without a barrage.

1952 Helsinki C: 76, N: 29, D: 7.28.

		W	L	TR
1. Edoardo Mangiarotti	ITA	7	2	12
2. Dario Mangiarotti	ITA	6	3	16
3. Oswald Zappelli	SWI	6	3	18
4. Léon Buck	LUX	6	3	19
5. József Sákovics	HUN	5	4	17
6. Carlo Pavesi	ITA	4	5	21
7. Per Carleson	SWE	3	6	20
8. Carl Forsell	SWE	3	6	23

Milanese fencing master Giuseppe Mangiarotti began giving his sons lessons when they turned eight years old. Although both were right-handed, Giuseppe converted the younger boy, Edoardo, into a left-hander because he considered it an advantage in competition. When he was 11, Edoardo won the Italian junior foil title. But Giuseppe had been Italian professional épée champion 17 times, so when Edoardo turned 15 his father started training him with that weapon. At age 17, Edoardo was a member of the Italian épée team that won the gold medal at Berlin. By 1960 Edoardo had won 13 Olympic medals: four gold and one silver in team épée, one gold and two bronze in individual épée, one gold and three silver in team foil, and one silver in individual foil. His older brother, Dario, gained one gold and two silver.

1956 Melbourne C: 40, N: 17, D: 11.30.

						1st BARRAGE				2nd BARRAGE			
		W	L	TG	TR	W	L	TG	TR	W	L	TG	TR
1. Carlo Pavesi	ITA	5	2	29	20	1	1	9	7	2	0	10	5
2. Giuseppe Delfino	ITA	5	2	30	27	1	1	7	7	1	1	10	8
3. Edoardo Mangiarotti	ITA	5	2	30	17	1	1	7	9	0	2	3	10
4. Richard Pew	USA	4	3	25	28								
5. Lajos Balthazár	HUN	4	3	30	29								
6. René Queyroux	FRA	3	4	29	25								
7. Per Carleson	SWE	2	5	22	29								
8. Rolf Wiik	FIN	0	7	15	35								

Giuseppe Delfino came within one touch of winning the gold, but lost 5–4 to Richard Pew and was forced into the barrage.

1960 Rome C: 79, N: 32, D: 9.6.

						BARRAGE	
		W	L	TG	TR	TG	TR
1. Giuseppe Delfino	ITA	5	2	39	32	5	2
2. Allan Jay	GBR	5	2	39	23	2	5
3. Bruno Habārovs	SOV/LAT	4	3	32	23	8	7
4. József Sákovics	HUN	4	3	30	31	7	8
5. Roger Achten	BEL	3	4	31	30		
6. Yves Dreyfus	FRA	3	4	30	30		
7. Armand Mouyal	FRA	3	4	25	30		
8. Giovanni Breda	ITA	1	6	19	34		

The 38-year-old Delfino utilized a rather unusual style to achieve his long-awaited gold medal. Rather than waste his energy going for a five-touch victory, he would content himself with a tie until time ran out. Then he would concentrate on, and usually win, the single sudden-death over-time hit. This tactic defeated Allan Jay in the final pool to force the barrage.

1964 Tokyo C: 65, N: 25, D: 10.19.

						BARRAGE			
		W	L	TG	TR	W	L	TG	TR
1. Hryhory Kryss	SOV/UKR	2	1	12	11	1	0	5	2
2. Henry Hoskyns	GBR	2	1	15	12	0	1	2	5

		W	L	TG	TR	W	L	T	TG	TR
3. Guram Kostava	SOV/GEO	1	2	12	12	1	0		5	0
4. Gianluigi Saccaro	ITA	1	2	10	14	0	1		0	5
5. Bogdan Gonsior	POL									
6. Claude Bourquard	FRA									
7. Orvar Lindwall	SWE									
8. Franz Rompza	GER									

In the final pool Kryss, a 23-year-old soldier from Kiev, defeated Hoskyns in a bout that saw four straight double (or simultaneous) hits. Hoskyns was a 33-year-old Somerset fruit farmer.

1968 Mexico City C; 73, N: 28, D: 10.22.

						BARRAGE				
		W	L	TG	TR	W	L	T	TG	TR
1. Gyözö Kulcsár	HUN	4	1	24	14	2	0	0	10	5
2. Hryhory Kryss	SOV/UKR	4	1	25	19	0	1	1	8	10
3. Gianluigi Saccaro	ITA	4	1	21	19	0	1	1	7	10
4. Viktor Modzalevsky	SOV/RUS	2	3	20	23					
5. Herbert Polzhuber	AUT	1	4	17	24					
6. Jean-Pierre Allemand	FRA	0	5	17	25					
7. Peter Loetscher	SWI									
7. Henryk Nielaba	POL									

The hero of Hungary's team épée victory four years earlier in Tokyo, Kulcsár completed the 1968 individual tournament with 17 wins and only one loss.

1972 Munich C: 72, N: 28, D: 9.6.

		W	L	TG	TR
1. Csaba Fenyvesi	HUN	4	1	25	10
2. Jacques la Degaillerie	FRA	3	2	23	19
3. Gyözö Kulcsár	HUN	3	2	20	19
4. Anton Pongratz	ROM	3	2	19	20
5. Rolf Edling	SWE	1	4	15	22
6. Jacques Brodin	FRA	0	5	13	25

Two of the three medals went to fencers from Budapest. Csaba Fenyvesi was a 29-year-old physician, Gyözö Kulcsár a 31-year-old engineer.

1976 Montreal C: 64, N: 25, D: 7.23.

						BARRAGE			
		W	L	TG	TR	W	L	TG	TR
1. Alexander Pusch	GER	3	2	22	18	2	0	10	7
2. Jürgen Hehn	GER	3	2	18	20	1	1	9	7
3. Gyözö Kulcsár	HUN	3	2	22	19	0	2	5	10
4. Istvan Osztrics	HUN	2	3	18	19				
5. Jerzy Janikowski	POL	2	3	20	21				
6. Rolf Edling	SWE	2	3	18	21				
7. Csaba Fenyvesi	HUN								
7. Göran Floodström	SWE								

In the barrage Pusch defeated Hehn, 5–4, in a seesaw battle, and then scored the last two touches to beat Kulcsár 5–3. Pusch was only 21 years old.

1980 Moscow C: 42, N: 16, D: 7.28.

		W	L	TG	TR
1. Johan Harmenberg	SWE	4	1	22	21
2. Ernö Kolczonay	HUN	3	2	23	19

		W	L	TG	TR
3. Philippe Riboud	FRA	3	2	20	17
4. Rolf Edling	SWE	3	2	18	16
5. Aleksandr Mozhayev	SOV/RUS	1	4	18	22
6. Ioan Popa	ROM	1	4	18	24
7. Jaroslav Jurka	CZE				
7. Boris Lukomsky	SOV/RUS				

1984 Los Angeles-Long Beach C: 63, N: 26, D: 8.8.
1. Philippe Boisse — FRA
2. Björne Väggö — SWE
3. Philippe Riboud — FRA
4. Stefano Bellone — ITA
5. Michael Poffet — SWI
6. Elmar Borrmann — GER
7. Alexander Pusch — GER
8. Volker Fischer — GER
Final: Boisse 10–5 Väggö
3rd Place: Riboud 10–7 Bellone

Björne Väggö, ranked only 44th in the world, registered four straight upsets to qualify for the gold medal match, defeating World Cup champion Olivier Lenglet, World Cup runner-up Angelo Mazzoni, world champion Elmar Borrmann and World University Games champion Stefano Bellone. In the final, however, he was no match for 29-year-old Paris radiologist Philippe Boisse, who had survived a tight 12–11 semifinal bout against teammate Philippe Riboud, with whom he fenced twice a week.

1988 Seoul C: 79, N: 32, D: 9.24.
1. Arnd Schmitt — GER
2. Philippe Riboud — FRA
3. Andrei Shuvalov — SOV/RUS
4. Sandro Cuomo — ITA
5. Torsten Kühnemund — GDR
6. Jerri Bergström — SWE
7. Martin Brill — NZE
8. Vladimir Reznitšenko — SOV/EST
Final: Schmitt 10–9 Riboud
3rd Place: Shuvalov 10–8 Cuomo

Andrei Shuvalov compiled a record of 16 wins and only one loss before being tipped 10–9 in the semifinals by 23-year-old dental student Arnd Schmitt. In the final, Schmitt defeated two-time world champion Philippe Riboud by the same score.

1992 Barcelona C: 70, N: 30, D: 8.1.
1. Éric Srecki — FRA
2. Pavel Kolobkov — RUS
3. Jean-Michel Henry — FRA
4. Kaido Kaaberma — EST
5. Elmar Borrmann — GER
6. Angelo Mazzoni — ITA
7. Mauricio Rivas Nieto — COL
8. Iván Kovács — HUN
Final: Srecki—Kolobkov 6-5, 5-2
3rd Place: Henry—Kaaberma 2-5, 5-2, 5-3

Éric Srecki, a 28-year-old bank employee, had a reputation as a consistently high-level performer who could never quite make it to the medal podium. At the last three world championships he had finished fourth, seventh, and fifth. In Barcelona he survived the repêchage by beating defending world champion Andrei Shavalov of Russia 5-3, 5-2. In the semifinals he encountered Kaido Kaaberma, who had earlier defeated him 5-3, 3-5, 6-5. This time Srecki came out on top 5-2, 5-3. In the final he spotted Kolobkov a 1-3 lead and then outscored him 10-4 to take the gold medal.

ÉPÉE, TEAM

1896–1904 not held

1906 Athens T: 6, N: 6, D 4.28.
1. FRA (Pierre d'Hugues, Georges Dillon-Kavanagh, Mohr, Georges de la Falaise)
2. GBR (William Desborough, Cosmo Duff Gordon, Charles Newton Robinson, Edgar Seligman)
3. BEL (Constant Cloquet, Fernand de Montigny, Edmond Crahay, Philippe Le Hardy de Beaulieu)

In the first round Germany was due to meet Great Britain. However, a misunderstanding of the schedule found the Germans asleep at their hotel at the time the match was to start. Quickly roused, the Germans rushed to the fencing grounds and were easily beaten, 9–2. The final resulted in a tie. The rematch was held immediately; France won, 9–6.

1908 London T: 9, N: 9, D: 7.23.
1. FRA (Gaston Alibert, Bernard Gravier, Alexandre Lippmann, Eugène Olivier, Henri-Georges Berger, Charles Collignon, Jean Stern)
2. GBR (Edgar Amphlett, C. Leaf Daniell, Cecil Haig, Robert Montgomerie, Martin Holt, Edgar Seligman)
3. BEL (Paul Anspach, Fernand Bosmans, Fernand de Montigny, François Rom, Victor Willems, Désiré Beaurain, Ferdinand Feyerick)
4. ITA (Marcello Bertinetti, Giuseppe Mangiarotti, Riccardo Nowak, Abelardo Olivier)
Final: FRA 9–7 BEL
Pool for 2nd: GBR 9–8 DEN; GBR 9–5 BEL

1912 Stockholm T: 11, N: 11, D: 7.10.

		W	L	TR
1. BEL	(Paul Anspach, Henri Anspach, Robert Hennet, Fernand de Montigny, Jacques Ochs, François Rom, Gaston Salmon, Victor Willems)	3	0	
2. GBR	(Edgar Seligman, Edgar Amphlett, Robert Montgomerie, John Blake, Percival Davson, Arthur Everitt, Sydney Martineau, Martin Holt)	1	2	28
3. HOL	(Adrianus de Jong, Willem Hubert van Blijenburgh, Jetze Doorman, Leonardus Salomonson, George van Rossem)	1	2	30
4. SWE	(Einar Sörensen, Gustaf Lindblom, Pontus von Rosen, Louis Sparre, Georg Branting)	1	2	32

1920 Antwerp T: 11, N: 11, D: 8.21.

					MATCHES	
		WON	LOST	TIED	W	L
1. ITA	(Nedo Nadi, Aldo Nadi, Abelardo Olivier, Tullio Bozza, Giovanni Canova, Andrea Marrazi, Dino Urbani, Antonio Allocchio, Tommaso Constantino, Paolo Thaon di Revel)	5	0	0	41	22
2. BEL	(Ernest Gevers, Paul Anspach, Félix Goblet d'Alviella, Victor Boin, Joseph de Craecker, Léon Tom, Philippe Le Hardy de Beaulieu)	4	1	0	39	34
3. FRA	(Armand Massard, Alexandre Lippmann, Gustave Buchard, Georges Trombert, S. Casanova, Gaston Amson, Emile Moreau)	2	2	1	39	31
4. POR	(Antonio Mascarenhas de Menezes, Jorge Paiva, Rui Mayer, João Sassetti, Henrique da Silveira, Frederico Paredes, Manuel Queiroz)	2	2	1	30	35

			WON	LOST	W	L
5.	SWI	(Henri Jacquet, Léopold Montagnier, Franz Wilhelm, Frédéric Fitting, Eugène Empeyta, Louis de Tribolet, John Albaret, Edouard Fitting)	1	4	0	33	41
6.	USA	(William Russell, Ray Dutcher, Henry Breckinridge, Arthur Lyon, Robert Sears, Harold Rayner)	0	5	0	19	38
7.	GBR	(John Blake, G.M. Burt, Martin Holt, Robert Montgomerie, Barry Notley, Edgar Seligman)					
7.	HOL	(Adrianus de Jong, Willem Hubert van Blijenburgh, George van Rossem, Salomon Zeldenrust, Henri Wijnoldij-Daniëls, Jetze Doorman)					

Two competitors worth noting were Nedo Nadi of Italy and Victor Boin of Belgium. Nadi, who won five gold medals in foil and sabre, was not as well known as an épéeist. His father, Beppe, considered the épée to be an "undisciplined" weapon and forbade the use of it in his *salle*. So Nedo would sneak out to enjoy the taboo sword. His insubordination paid off with a team épée gold medal in 1920. Boin's silver medal as part of the Belgian team was his third Olympic medal. His first two, however, were earned not in fencing but in water polo: a silver in 1908 and a bronze in 1912. Boin also enjoyed swimming, skating, flying, ice hockey, and motorcycle racing. He was founder of the International Association of Sports Journalists and President of the Belgian Olympic Committee.

1924 Paris T: 16, N: 16, D: 7.9.

			WON	LOST	MATCHES W	L
1.	FRA	(Lucien Gaudin, Georges Buchard, Roger Ducret, André Labatut, Lionel Liottel, Alexandre Lippmann, Georges Tainturier)	3	0	29	16
2.	BEL	(Paul Anspach, Joseph de Craecker, Charles Delporte, Fernand de Montigny, Ernest Gevers, Léon Tom)	2	1	24	22
3.	ITA	(Giulio Basletta, Marcello Bertinetti, Giovanni Canova, Vincenzo Cuccia, Virgilio Mantegazza, Oreste Moricca)	1	2	21	26
4.	POR	(Antonio Mascarenhas de Menezes, Jorge Paiva, Paulo d'Eca Leal, Rui	0	3	18	28

Mayer, Henrique da Silveira, Mário de Noronha, Frederico Paredes, Antonio Pinto Leite)

5.	SPA	(José Delgado y Hernandez de Tejada, Félix de Pomes Soler, Diego Diez de Rivera y Figueroa, Fernando García Bilbao, Diego García-Montoro, Jesus López-Lara-Mallor, Carlos Miguel de los Reyes, Miguel Zabalza de la Fuente)				
5.	USA	(Henry Breckinridge, George Breed, George Calnan, Arthur Lyon, Allen Millner, William Russell, Leon Shore, Donald Waldhaus)				

1928 Amsterdam T: 18, N: 18, D: 8.5.

			WON	LOST	MATCHES W	L
1.	ITA	(Carlo Agostoni, Marcello Bertinetti, Giancarlo Cornaggia Medici, Renzo Minoli, Giulio Basletta, Franco Riccardi)	3	0	28	19
2.	FRA	(Armand Massard, Georges Buchard, Gaston Amson, Emile Cornic, Bernard Schmetz, René Barbier)	2	1	24	22
3.	POR	(Paulo d'Eca Leal, Mário de Noronha, Jorge Paiva, João Sassetti, Frederico Paredes, Henrique de Silveira)	1	2	21	26

			WON	LOST	MATCHES W	L
4.	BEL	(Emile Barbier, Balthazar de Beuckalaer, Charles Delporte, Charles Debeur, Léon Tom, Georges Dambois)	0	3	20	26
5.	CZE	(Martin Harden, Josef Jungmann, František Kriz, Jan Tille, Miroslav Beznovska, Jan Çernohorský)				
5.	HOL	(Laurens Kuypers, Adrianus de Jong, Henri Wijnoldij Daniëls, William Driebergen, Alfred Labouchère, Karel van den Brandeler)				
5.	SPA	(José Delgado y Hernandez de Tejada, Diego García Montoro, Diego Diez de Rivera y Figueroa, Félix de Pomes Soler, Fidel Gonzalez Badia)				
5.	USA	(Arthur Lyon, George Calnan, Allen Milner, Harold Rayner, Henry Breckinridge, Edward Barnett)				

1932 Los Angeles T: 7, N: 7, D: 8.7.

			WON	LOST	MATCHES W	L
1.	FRA	(Philippe Cattiau, Georges Buchard, Bernard Schmetz, Jean Piot, Fernand Jourdant, Georges Tainturier)	3	0	30.5	17.5
2.	ITA	(Carlo Agostoni, Giancarlo Cornaggia-Medici, Renzo Minoli, Franco Riccardi, Saverio Ragno)	2	1	27.5	20.5
3.	USA	(George Calnan, Gustave Heiss, Frank Righeimer, Tracy Jaeckel, Curtis Shears, Miguel de Capriles)	1	2	20.5	22.5
4.	BEL	(Raoul Henkaert, André Poplimont, Max Janlet, Balthazar de Beuckelaer, Albert Mund)	0	3	12.5	30.5

1936 Berlin T: 21, N: 21, D: 8.8.

			WON	LOST	MATCHES W	L
1.	ITA	(Saverio Ragno, Alfredo Pezzana, Giancarlo Cornaggia-Medici, Edoardo Mangiarotti, Franco Riccardi, Giancarlo Brusati)	3	0	26	41
2.	SWE	(Hans Granfelt, Sven Thofelt, Gösta Almgren, Gustaf Dyrssen, Hans Drakenberg, Birger Cederin)	2	1	21	22
3.	FRA	(Michel Pécheux, Bernard Schmetz, Georges Buchard, Henri Dulieux, Paul Wormser, Philippe Cattiau)	1	2	21	23
4.	GER	(Siegfried Lerdon, Joseph Uhlmann, Hans Esser, Eugen Geiwitz, Ernst Röthig, Otto Schröder)	0	3	11	23
5.	BEL	(Raymond Stasse, T'Sas, Charles Debeur, de Monceau, Plumier, Heim)				
5.	POL	(Jerzy Staszewicz, Teodor Zaczyk, Rajmund Karwicki, Roman Kantor, Kazimierz Szempliński, Antoni Franz)				
5.	POR	(Henrique de Silveira, Paulo d'Eca Leal, Antonio Mascarenhas de Menezes, Sasseti, Carinhas)				
5.	USA	(Frank Righeimer, Thomas Sands, Tracy Jaeckel, Gustave Heiss, Miguel de Capriles, Andrew Boyd)				

Two members of the Swedish team, Gustaf Dyrssen and Sven Thofelt, had previously won gold medals in modern pentathlon. Both men went on to serve as members of the International Olympic Committee.

1948 London T: 21, N: 21, D: 8.6.

			WON	LOST	MATCHES W	L
1.	FRA	(Henri Guérin, Henri Lepage, Marcel Desprets, Michel Pécheux, Edouard Artigas, Maurice Huet)	3	0	31	10
2.	ITA	(Luigi Cantone, Antonio Mandruzzato, Dario Mangiarotti, Edoardo Mangiarotti, Fiorenzo Marini, Carlo Agostoni)	2	1	25	21
3.	SWE	(Per Carleson, Frank Cervell, Carl Forssel, Bengt Ljungquist, Sven Thofelt, H. Arne Tollbom)	1	2	18	26
4.	DEN	(Mogens Lüchow, Erik Andersen, Ib Benjamin Nielsen, René Dybkaer, Jacob Lyng, Kenneth Flindt)	0	3	12	29
5.	BEL	(Raymond Stasse, L. Hauben, Raymond Bru, Jean Radoux, Raoul Henkaert, Charles Debeur)				

5. HUN (Imre Hennyey, Pál Dunay, Béla Rerrich, Béla Mikla, Lajos Balthazár, Béla Bay)

5. LUX (Fernand Leischen, Paul Anen, Emile Gretsch, Gustav Lamesch, Einy Putz)

5. SWI (François Thiebaud, René Lips, Jean Hauert, Oswald Zappelli, Otto Rufenacht, Michel Chamay)

France qualified for the final pool despite being upset 10–5 in the semifinal pool by Belgium. The French team was led by Michel Pécheux, a last-minute addition, who was 11–0 in the final pool and 23–3 total.

1952 Helsinki T: 19, N: 19, D: 7.26.

		WON	LOST	MATCHES W	L
1. ITA	(Dario Mangiarotti, Edoardo Mangiarotti, Franco Bertinetti, Carlo Pavesi, Giuseppe Delfino, Roberto Battaglia)	3	0	32	11
2. SWE	(Bengt Ljundquist, Berndt-Otto Rehbinder, Sven Fahlman, Per Carleson, Carl Forssell, Lennart Magnusson)	2	1	26	17
3. SWI	(Otto Rüfenacht, Paul Meister, Oswald Zappelli, Paul Barth, Willy Fitting, Mario Valota)	1	2	18	24
4. LUX	(Emile Gretsch, Fernand Leischen, Paul Anen, Léon Buck)	0	3	9	33
5. DEN	(Raimondo Carnera, Erik Swane-Lund, René Dybkaer, Mogens Lüchow, Ib Benjamin Nielsen, Jacob Lyng)				
5. HUN	(Lajos Balthazár, Barnabás Berzsenyi, Béla Rerrich, József Sákovics, Imre Hennyey)				

The 1952 Olympics saw the downfall of defending champion France, eliminated in the second round after losses to Luxembourg and Hungary. Italy defeated Sweden 8–5 in the deciding match, despite the efforts of Bengt Ljundquist, who beat all four Italians.

1956 Melbourne T: 11, N: 11, D: 11.28.

		WON	LOST	MATCHES W	L
1. ITA	(Giuseppe Delfino, Alberto Pellegrino, Edoardo Mangiarotti, Carlo Pavesi, Giorgio Anglesio, Franco Bertinetti)	3	0	34	10

2. HUN	(József Sákovics, Béla Rerrich, Lajos Balthazár, Ambrus Nagy, József Marosi, Barnabás Berzsenyi)	2	1	22	22
3. FRA	(Armand Mouyal, Claude Nigon, Daniel Dagallier, Yves Dreyfus, René Queyroux)	1	2	17	27
4. GBR	(R. René Paul, Michael Howard, Henry Hoskyns, Allan Jay)	0	3	15	29
5. BEL	(François Dehez, Roger Achten, Ghislain Delaunois, Marcel Vanderauwera, Jacques Debeur)				
5. SOV	(Arnold Chernushevich, Valentin Chernikov, Lev Saitchuk, Revas Tsirekidze, Iosas Oudras)				

1960 Rome T: 21, N: 21, D: 9.9.
1. ITA (Giuseppe Delfino, Alberto Pellegrino, Carlo Pavesi, Edoardo Mangiarotti, Fiorenzo Marini, Gianluigi Saccaro)
2. GBR (Allan Jay, Michael Howard, John Pelling, Henry Hoskyns, Raymond Harrison, Michael Alexander)
3. SOV (Guram Kostava, Bruno Habãrovs, Arnold Chernushevich, Valentin Chernikov, Aleksandr Pavlovsky)
4. HUN (József Marosi, Tamás Gábor, István Kausz, József Sákovics, Árpád Bárány)
5. GER (Paul Gnaier, Fritz Zimmerman, Dieter Fänger, Georg Neuber, Helmut Anschütz, Walter Kostner)
5. LUX (Roger Theisen, Edouard Schmit, Robert Schiel, Rodolphe Kugeler, Edmond Gutenkauff)
5. SWE (Hans Lagerwall, Göran Abrahamsson, Ling Vannerus, Berndt Rehbinder, Carl-Wilhem Engdahl, Orvar Lindwall)
5. SWI (Hans Baessler, Amez Droz, Paul Meister, Charles Ribordy, Claudio Polledri, Michel Steininger)
Final: ITA 9–5 GBR
3rd Place: SOV 9–5 HUN

The Italian squad included the last three individual épée champions: Mangiarotti (1952), Pavesi (1956), and Delfino (1960), as well as 21-year-old Gianluigi Saccaro, who fenced with a patch over his injured right eye. In Italy's semifinal match against the U.S.S.R., the usually subdued Delfino found himself trailing Chernikov 4–1 with 13 seconds left. He then scored three hits in 12 seconds to force an overtime bout, which he also won.

1964 Tokyo T: 18, N: 18, D: 10.21.
1. HUN (Gyözö Kulcsár, Zoltán Nemere, Támás Gábor, István Kausz, Árpád Bárány)
2. ITA (Gianluigi Saccaro, Giovanni Battista Breda, Gianfranco Paolucci, Giuseppe Delfino, Alberto Pellegrino)
3. FRA (Claude Brodin, Yves Dreyfus, Claude Bourquard, Jack Guittet, Jacques Brodin)
4. SWE (Ivar Genesjö, Orvar Lindwall, Hans Lagerwall, Göran Abrahamsson, Carl-Wilhem Engdahl)

5. POL   (Henryk Nielaba, Mikolaj Pomarnacki, Bogdan Gonsior, Bogdan Andrzejewski, Jerzy Pawlowski)

6. GER   (Franz Rompza, Max Geuter, Volkmar Würtz, Paul Gnaier, Haakon Stein)

7. SOV   (Bruno Habărovs, Guram Kostava, Yuri Smolyakov, Hryhory Kryss, Aleksei Nikanchikov)

7. SWI   (Claudio Polledri, Paul Meister, Walter Bar, Jean Gontier, Michel Steininger)

    Final: HUN 8–3 ITA
    3rd Place: FRA 8(64)–8(59) SWE
    5th Place: POL 8(66)–8(62) GER

Hungary broke the 44-year Italian-French domination of team épée, as Gyözö Kulcsár won all 20 of his bouts.

1968 Mexico City T: 20, N: 20, D: 10.25.

1. HUN   (Csaba Fenyvesi, Zoltán Nemere, Pál Schmitt, Gyözö Kulcsár, Pál Nagy)

2. SOV   (Hryhory Kryss, Iosyf Vitebsky, Aleksei Nikanchikov, Yuri Smolyakov, Viktor Modzelevsky)

3. POL   (Bohdan Andrzejewicz, Michal Butkiewicz, Bohdan Gonsior, Henryk Nielaba, Kazimierz Barburski)

4. GER   (Dieter Jung, Franz Rompza, Fritz Zimmerman, Max Geuter, Paul Gnaier)

5. GDR   (Bernd Uhlig, Klaus Dumke, Harry Fiedler, Hans-Peter Schulze)

6. ITA   (Gianfranco Paolucci, Claudio Francesconi, Giovanni Battista Breda, Gianluigi Saccaro, Antonio Albanese)

7. FRA   (François Jeanne, Claude Bourquard, Yves Boissier, Jacques Ladegaillerie, Jean-Pierre Allemand)

7. GBR   (Nicholas Halsted, E. Owen Bourne, Henry Hoskyns, W. Ralph Johnson, Peter Jacobs)

    Final: HUN 7–4 SOV
    3rd Place: POL 9–6 GER
    5th Place: GDR 9–6 ITA

For the first time in 56 years, Italy failed to finish among the top three.

1972 Munich T: 20, N: 20, D: 9.9.

1. HUN   (Istvan Osztrics, Sándor Erdös, Csaba Fenyvesi, Pál Schmitt, Gyözö Kulcsár)

2. SWI   (Peter Löetscher, Christian Kauter, Guy Evéquoz, Daniel Giger, François Suchanecki)

3. SOV   (Georgi Zažitski, Hryhory Kryss, Viktor Modzelevsky, Igor Valetov, Serhei Paramonov)

4. FRA   (François Jeanne, Jacques Brodin, Pierre Marchand, Jean-Pierre Allemand, Jacques La Degaillerie)

5. ROM   (Constantin Dutu, Costică Bărăgan, Anton Pongratz, Alexandru Istrate, Nicolae Iorgu)

6. POL   (Bohdan Andrzejewski, Jerzy Janikowski, Henryk Nielaba, Kazimierz Barburski, Bohdan Gonsior)

7. NOR   (Jan von Koss, Jeppe Normann, Ole Morch, Claus Morch)

7. SWE   (Hans Wieselgren, Carl Von Essen, Orvar Joensson, Rolf Edling, Per Sundberg)

    Final: HUN 8–4 SWI
    3rd Place: SOV 9–4 FRA
    5th Place: ROM 9–3 POL

1976 Montreal T: 19, N: 19, D: 7.29.

1. SWE   (Hans Jacobson, Orvar Jonsson, Carl Von Essen, Leif Högström, Göran Flodström, Rolf Edling)

2. GER   (Alexander Pusch, Jürgen Hehn, Hanns Jana, Reinhold Behr, Volker Fischer)

3. SWI   (Jean-Blaise Evéquoz, Michel Poffet, Daniel Giger, Christian Kauter, François Suchanecki)

4. HUN   (Csaba Fenyvesi, Sándor Erdös, István Osztrics, Pál Schmitt, Gyözö Kulcsár)

5. SOV   (Aleksandr Abushakhmetov, Viktor Modzelevsky, Vasyl Stankovych, Aleksandr Bykov, Boris Lukomski)

6. ROM   (Ioan Popa, Anton Pongratz, Nicolae Iorgu, Paul Szabo)

7. ITA   (John Pezza, Nicola Granieri, Fabio Dal Zotto, Marcello Bertinetti, Giovan Battista Coletti)

7. NOR   (Nils Koppang, Jeppe Normann, Kjell Otto Moe, Bård Vonen, Ole Morch)

    Final: SWE 8–5 GER
    3rd Place: SWI 9–3 HUN
    5th Place: SOV 9–2 ROM

The world champion Swedish team received a setback in the first bout of the final match, when Göran Flodström was knocked out. Carl Von Essen was brought in as a replacement and won two crucial bouts, including one against Alexander Pusch, which took place while Flodström was being carried out on a stretcher.

1980 Moscow T: 11, N: 11, D: 7.31.

1. FRA   (Philippe Riboud, Patrick Picot, Hubert Gardas, Michel Salesse, Philippe Boisse)

2. POL   (Piotr Jablkowski, Andrzej Lis, Mariusz Strzalka, Ludomir Chronowski, Leszek Swornowski)

3. SOV   (Boris Lukomsky, Aleksandr Abushakhmetov, Volodymyr Smirnov, Ashot Karagan, Aleksandr Mozhayev)

4. ROM   (Ioan Popa, Octavian Zidaru, Anton Pongratz, Costică Bărăgan, Petru Kuki)

5. SWE   (Johan Harmenberg, Rolf Edling, Leif Högström, Göran Malkar, Hans Jacobsen)

6. CZE   (Jaroslav Jurka, Jaromír Holub, Jiři Douba, Jiři Adam, Oldřich Kubišta)

7. GBR   (Steven Paul, John Llewellyn, Neal Mallett, Robert Bruniges)

8. HUN   (Ernö Kolczonay, István Osztrics, Laszlo Petö, Jenö Pap, Péter Takács)

    Final: FRA 8–4 POL
    3rd Place: SOV 9–5 ROM
    5th Place: SWE 9–2 CZE
    7th Place: GBR 16–0 HUN (forfeit)

Led by Philippe Riboud's 16–2 effort, France pulled off a major upset and won the team épée gold medal for the first time in 32 years.

1984 Los Angeles-Long Beach T: 16, N: 16, D: 8.11.

1. GER   (Elmar Borrmann, Volker Fischer, Gerhard Heer, Rafael Nickel, Alexander Pusch)

2. FRA   (Philippe Boisse, Jean-Michel Henry, Olivier Lenglet, Philippe Riboud, Michel Salesse)

3. ITA   (Stefano Bellone, Sandro Cuomo, Cosimo Ferro, Roberto Manzi, Angelo Mazzoni)

4. CAN (Jacques Cardyn, Jean-Marc Chouinard, Alain Cote, Michel Dessureault, Daniel Perreault)
5. SWE (Jerri Bergström, Greger Forslöw, Kent Hjerpe, Jonas Rosén, Björne Väggö)
6. CHN (Cui Yining, Pang Jin, Zhao Lizhong, Zong Xiangqing)
7. KOR (Bong-Man Kim, Sung-Moon Kim, Il-Hee Lee, Kyung-Seung Min, Nam-Jin Yoon)
8. GBR (W. Ralph Johnson, John Llewellyn, Neal Mallett, Steven Paul, Jonathan Stanbury)
Final: GER 8–5 FRA
3rd Place: ITA 8–2 CAN
5th Place: SWE 8–6 CHN
7th Place: KOR 8(69)–8(62) GBR

1988 Seoul T: 18, N: 18, D: 9.30.
1. FRA (Frédéric Delpla, Jean-Michel Henry, Olivier Lenglet, Philippe Riboud, Éric Srecki)
2. GER (Elmar Borrmann, Volker Fischer, Thomas Gerull, Alexander Pusch, Arnd Schmitt)
3. SOV (Andrei Shuvalov, Pavel Kolobkov, Vladimir Reznitšenko, Mykhalo Tyshko, Igor Tikhomirov)
4. ITA (Stefano Bellone, Andrea Bermond Das Ambrois, Sandro Cuomo, Angelo Mazzoni, Stefano Pantano)
5. SWI (Patrice Gaille, André Kuhn, Zsolt Madarasz, Gérald Pfefferle, Michel Poffet)
6. HUN (Laszlo Fabian, Ferenc Hegédus, Ernö Kolczonay, Szabolcs Pásztor, Zoltán Székely)
7. KOR (Cho Hee-jae, Lee Il-hee, Lee Sang-ki, Yang Dal-sik, Yoon Nam-jin)
8. SWE (Johan Bergdahl, Jerri Bergström, Otto Drakenberg, Ulf Sandegren, Péter Vánky)
Final: FRA 8-3 GER
3rd Place: SOV 8(65)–8(63) ITA
5th Place: SWI 8–4 HUN
7th Place: KOR 8(64)–8(60) SWE

In a rematch of the 1984 final, France was led by Lenglet (4–0) and Henry (3–0).

1992 Barcelona T: 12, N: 12, D: 8.6.
1. GER (Elmar Borrmann, Robert Felisiak, Uwe Proske, Vladimir Resnitschenko [Reznitšenko], Arnd Schmitt)
2. HUN (Iván Kovács, Krisztián Kulcsár, Ferenc Hegedüs, Ernö Kolczonay, Gabor Totola)
3. SOV (Andrei Shuvalov, Pavel Kolobkov, Sergei Kravchuk, Sergei Kostarev, Valery Zakharevich)
4. FRA (Éric Srecki, Jean-Michel Henry, Olivier Lenglet, Jean-François Di Martino, Robert Leroux)
5. ITA (Sandro Cuomo, Angelo Mazzoni, Stefano Pantano, Maurizio Randazzo, Sandro Resegotti)
6. SPA (Fernando De La Peño Olivas, Ángel Fernández García, César Gonzalez Llorens, Raúl Maroto López, Manuel Pereira Senabre)
7. CAN (Jean-Marc Chouinard, Alain Coté, Allan Francis, Bogdan Nowosielski, Laurie Shong)
8. SWE (Mats Ahlgren, Jerri Bergström, Tomas Lundblad, Ulf Sandegren, Péter Vánky)
Final: GER 8-4 HUN

3rd Place: SOV 8(70)-8(66) FRA
5th Place: ITA 8(67)-8(66) SPA
7th Place: CAN 9-5 SWE

Days before the competition was to begin the five members of the épée team of the ex-Soviet Union threatened to boycott unless they were paid the bonuses of about $1500 each that they had been promised for winning the 1991 world championship. A tentative agreement was reached, but the squad performed below expectations, losing 8-7 to Germany in the semifinals. One of the German team members was Vladimir Resnitschenko, who had earned a bronze medal in Seoul as a member of the Soviet team. Resnitschenko, a Russian from Estonia, gained German citizenship just in time to compete in Barcelona. Hungary defeated Germany 9-5 in pool play, but in the final the Germans dominated the Hungarians, outtouching them 59-44.

SABRE, INDIVIDUAL

1896 Athens C: 5, N: 3, D: 4.9.

			W	L	TG	TR
1.	Ioannis Georgiadis	GRE	4	0	12	6
2.	Telemachos Karakalos	GRE	3	1	11	5
3.	Holger Nielsen	DEN	2	2	10	9
4.	Adolf Schmal	AUT	1	3	7	11
5.	Georgios Iatridis	GRE	0	4	3	12

1900 Paris C: 32, N: 10, D: 6.25.
1. Georges de la Falaise FRA
2. Léon Thiébaut FRA
3. Siegfried Flesch AUT
4. Ámon von Gregurich HUN
5. Gyula von Iványi HUN
6. de Boissière FRA
7. Heinrich Terner AUT
8. Camillo Müller AUT

1904 St. Louis C: 5, N: 2, D: 9.8.

						BARRAGE	
			W	L	TG	W	L
1.	Manuel Diaz	CUB	3	0	21		
2.	William Grebe	USA	2	1	20	1	0
3.	Albertson Van Zo Post	USA	2	1	18	0	1
4.	Theodore Carstens	USA	1	2			
5.	Arthur Fox	USA	0	4			

1906 Athens C: 29, N: 8, D: 4.28.
1. Ioannis Georgiadis GRE
2. Gustav Casmir GER
3. Federico Cesarano ITA
4. Georges de la Falaise FRA
5. Ervin Mészáros HUN
6. Jëno Apáthy HUN

1908 London C: 76, N: 11, D: 7.24.

		W	L	T	W	L
					BARRAGE	
1. Jenö Fuchs	HUN	6	0	1	1	0
2. Béla Zulavszky	HUN	6	1	0	0	1
3. Vilém Goppold von Lobsdorf	BOH/CZE	4	2	1		
4. Jenö Szántay	HUN	3	3	1		
5. Péter Tóth	HUN	3	4	0		
6. Lajos Werkner	HUN	2	5	0		
7. Jetze Doorman	HOL	1	5	1		
7. Georges de la Falaise	FRA	1	6	0		

Dr. Jenö Fuchs, the winner of four sabre gold medals in 1908 and 1912, recorded 22 wins, two losses, and one draw in the individual competition. Fuchs was also active in rowing and bobsledding.

1912 Stockholm C: 40, N: 9, D: 8.23.

		W	L	TG	TR
1. Jenö Fuchs	HUN	6	1	18	10
2. Béla Békéssy	HUN	5	2	17	11
3. Ervin Mészáros	HUN	5	2	17	12
4. Zoltán Schenker	HUN	4	3	17	13
5. Nedo Nadi	ITA	4	3	16	17
6. Péter Tóth	HUN	2	5	12	17
7. Lajos Werkner	HUN	1	6	13	19
8. Dezsö Földes	HUN	1	6	9	20

1920 Antwerp C: 42, N: 9, D: 8.26.

		W	L	TR
1. Nedo Nadi	ITA	11	0	
2. Aldo Nadi	ITA	9	2	
3. Adrianus de Jong	HOL	6	5	19
4. Oreste Puliti	ITA	6	5	19
5. Jan van der Wiel	HOL	6	5	22
6. Léon Tom	BEL	5	6	24
7. Robert Hennet	BEL	5	6	24
8. Robin Dalglish	GBR	5	6	27

The only break in Hungary's incredible 56-year domination of individual sabre occurred in 1920. Having been on the losing side of World War I, Hungary was not invited to the Antwerp Olympics.

1924 Paris C: 47, N: 15, D: 7.18.

		W	L	TG	TR	W	L	TG	TR
						BARRAGE			
1. Sándor Posta	HUN	5	2	26	20	2	0	8	1
2. Roger Ducret	FRA	5	2	22	18	1	1	4	7
3. János Garay	HUN	5	2	23	20	0	2	4	8
4. Zóltán Schenker	HUN	4	3	24	21	1	0	4	3
5. Adrianus de Jong	HOL	4	3	24	21	0	1	3	4
6. Ivan Osiier	DEN	2	5	15	24	1	0	4	2
7. Georges Conraux	FRA	2	5	23	22	0	1	2	4
8. Héctor Casco	ARG	1	6	16	27				

The Italians, led by Oreste Puliti, had already defeated the Hungarians to win the team sabre title, and another showdown seemed certain in the individual championship as four Italians and three Hungarians were among the twelve who qualified for the final round. The final matches began with the Official Jury of Appeal ordering the four Italians—Puliti, Bertinetti, Bini, and Sarrocchi—to fight off against each other. As expected, Puliti beat the other three with ease. But the judges were not satisfied. Led by Kovács, the Hungarian judge, they maintained that the other three had thrown their matches against Puliti in order to increase his chances for a gold medal.

Outraged by these accusations, Puliti threatened to cane Judge Kovács. Puliti was disqualified, and Bertinetti, Bini, and Sarrocchi walked out in protest. Two days later Puliti and Kovács ran into each other at a music hall and renewed their argument. When Kovács haughtily told Puliti that he couldn't understand the furious fencer because he didn't speak Italian, Puliti hit the Hungarian in the face and said that Kovács surely couldn't fail to understand that. The two men were pulled apart, but further words were exchanged and a formal duel was proposed.

Four months later Puliti and Kovács met again, at Nagykanizsa on the Yugoslav-Hungarian border. This time they were accompanied by seconds, swords, and spectators. After slashing away at each other for an hour, the two were finally separated by spectators, who had become concerned about the wounds which both men had received. Their honor restored, Puliti and Kovács shook hands and made up.

As for the Olympic competition, it was won by Sándor Posta in a three-way fence-off against fellow Hungarian János Garay and the French champion Roger Ducret, who left the 1924 Olympics with three gold medals and two silver.

1928 Amsterdam C: 44, N: 17, D: 8.11.

		W	L	TG	TR	TG	TR
						BARRAGE	
1. Ödön Tersztyánszky	HUN	9	2	51	33	5	2
2. Attila Petschauer	HUN	9	2	52	28	2	5
3. Bino Bini	ITA	8	3	49	32		
4. Gustavo Marzi	ITA	8	3	49	34		
5. Sándor Gombos	HUN	8	3	49	38		
6. Erwin Casmir	GER	6	5	44	32		
7. Arturo De Vecchi	ITA	5	6	44	36		
8. Roger Ducret	FRA	5	6	42	47		

Lieutenant Colonel Tersztyánszky died in an auto accident outside Budapest ten months after winning his gold medal. He was 40 years old.

1932 Los Angeles C: 25, N: 12, D: 8.13.

		W	L	TG	TR
1. György Piller (Jekelfalussy)	HUN	8	1	42	19
2. Giulio Gaudini	ITA	7	2	39	28
3. Endre Kabos	HUN	5	4	36	29
4. Erwin Casmir	GER	5	4	32	30
5. Attila Petschauer	HUN	5	4	37	32
6. John Huffman	USA	5	4	38	35
7. Ivan Osiier	DEN	4	5	32	35
8. Arturo De Vecchi	ITA	3	6	27	36

Colonel Piller completed the tournament with a record of 19–2.

1936 Berlin C: 71, N: 26, D: 8.15.

		W	L	TG	TR
1. Endre Kabos	HUN	7	1	37	20
2. Gustavo Marzi	ITA	6	2	35	22
3. Aladár Gerevich	HUN	6	2	37	26
4. László Rajcsányi	HUN	5	3	34	25
5. Vincenzo Pinton	ITA	5	3	32	28
6. Giulio Gaudini	ITA	3	5	27	28
7. Antoni Sobik	POL	2	6	22	34
8. Josef Losert	AUT	2	6	20	36

As a student, Kabos received a fencing outfit as a birthday gift from his godfather. He hid it in his wardrobe, but his friends came across it and teased him. The next day he enrolled in a fencing club to spite them. At the Berlin Olympics Kabos compiled a record of 24–1 to win the gold medal. Kabos was killed during World War II when the Budapest Margaret Bridge blew up, the day before his 38th birthday.

1948 London C: 60, N: 24, D: 8.13.

		W	L	TG	TR
1. Aladár Gerevich	HUN	7	0	35	18
2. Vincenzo Pinton	ITA	5	2	32	23
3. Pál Kovács	HUN	5	2	33	24
4. Jacques Lefèvre	FRA	4	3	27	26
5. George Worth	USA	2	5	26	27
6. Gastone Darè	ITA	2	5	25	30
7. Tibor Nyilas	USA	2	5	20	31
8. Antonio Oliva Haro	MEX	1	6	15	34

Aladár Gerevich competed in six Olympics between 1932 and 1960 (when he was 50 years old). He won seven gold medals, one silver, and two bronze. In winning his only

Aladár Gerevich (left) won seven gold medals, one silver, and two bronze between 1932 and 1960 (when he was 50 years old). Pál Kovács (right) earned six gold medals and one bronze between 1936 and 1960.

individual gold medal Gerevich scored 19 victories against only one defeat.

1952 Helsinki C: 66, N: 26, D: 8.1.

		W	L	TR
1. Pál Kovács	HUN	8	0	19
2. Aladár Gerevich	HUN	7	1	16
3. Tibor Berczelly	HUN	5	3	22
4. Gastone Darè	ITA	5	3	27
5. Werner Plattner	AUT	4	4	34
6. Jacques Lefèvre	FRA	3	5	25
7. Vincenzo Pinton	ITA	2	6	32
8. Heinz Lechner	AUT	2	6	35

Kovács was the third straight Hungarian to win the sabre gold after winning the bronze in the previous Olympics. Kovács was 40 years old and had first won the world sabre championship fifteen years earlier. In the final pool he needed one last victory to clinch the gold medal. Trailing Pinton 4–2, he scored three hits in the final minute to secure the championship with an undefeated record of 19–0. A mechanic, Kovács ultimately earned six Olympic gold medals.

1956 Melbourne C: 35, N: 17, D: 12.5.

						BARRAGE	
		W	L	TG	TR	TG	TR
1. Rudolf Kárpáti	HUN	6	1	32	19		
2. Jerzy Pawlowski	POL	5	2	30	22		
3. Lev Kuznetsov	SOV/RUS	4	3	29	24	5	2
4. Jacques Lefèvre	FRA	4	3	27	25	2	5
5. Aladár Gerevich	HUN	3	4	30	31		
6. Wojciech Zablocki	POL	2	5	17	29		
7. Pál Kovács	HUN	2	5	25	30		
8. Luigi Narduzzi	ITA	2	5	21	31		

The 36-year-old Kárpáti, eventual winner of six Olympic gold medals, earned his first individual championship by putting together 18 victories against only one loss (to Pawlowski). Kárpáti believed that his love of music contributed to his skills as a fencer, since both are based on rhythm and timing.

1960 Rome C: 70, N: 29, D: 9.8.

						BARRAGE			
		W	L	TG	TR	W	L	TG	TR
1. Rudolf Kárpáti	HUN	5	2	31	25				
2. Zoltán Horváth	HUN	4	3	29	26	2	1	14	8
3. Wladimiro Calarese	ITA	4	3	31	29	2	1	13	12
4. Claude Arabo	FRA	4	3	31	29	2	1	11	12
5. Wojciech Zablocki	POL	4	3	27	26	0	3	9	15
6. Jerzy Pawlowski	POL	3	4	28	28				
7. David Tyshler	SOV/RUS	2	5	24	29				
8. Yakov Rylsky	SOV/RUS	2	5	21	32				

Following the quarterfinal round, the French team lodged a protest against Kárpáti, claiming the defending champion had purposely lost to Rohonyi of Romania in order to ensure that he, instead of Lefèvre of France, would advance to the next round. The protest was overruled. In the semifinals Kárpáti's loss to Arabo allowed the Frenchman to qualify for the final without a barrage. This time no protest was filed.

1964 Tokyo C: 52, N: 21, D: 10.20.

		W	L	TG	TR	BARRAGE TG	TR
1. Tibor Pézsa	HUN	2	1	13	13	5	2
2. Claude Arabo	FRA	2	1	14	9	2	5
3. Umyar Mavlikhanov	SOV/RUS	1	2	9	13	5	3
4. Yakov Rylsky	SOV/RUS	1	2	11	12	3	5
5. Emil Ochyra	POL						
6. Marcel Parent	FRA						
7. Walter Köstner	GER						
8. Dieter Wellmann	GER						

Pézsa won despite a relatively unimpressive overall record of 12 wins and seven losses.

1968 Mexico City C: 40, N: 16, D: 10.17.

		W	L	TG	TR	BARRAGE TG	TR
1. Jerzy Pawlowski	POL	4	1	22	18	5	4
2. Mark Rakita	SOV/RUS	4	1	24	16	4	5
3. Tibor Pézsa	HUN	3	2	20	16		
4. Vladimir Nazlymov	SOV/RUS	3	2	21	17		
5. Rolando Rigoli	ITA	1	4	11	21		
6. Józef Nowara	POL	0	5	15	25		
7. Umyar Mavlikhanov	SOV/RUS						
8. Serge Panizza	FRA						

In June, Pawlowski, a 35-year-old major in the Polish army, received his master's degree in law, having written his dissertation on "A Critique of Hayek's Neo-Liberal Conception of Liberty and Law." In the final pool Pawlowski defeated world champion Mark Rakita 5–4. Then he beat him again by the same score in the barrage, to achieve a final win-loss total of 16-2. Pawlowski became interested in fencing at age 16 when he saw films of the 1948 London Olympics. He was world sabre champion three times (in 1957, 1965, 1966) and runner-up four times. In his military pursuits, Pawlowski was considered a protégé of General Wojciech Jaruzelski, who later became Premier of Poland. In 1981 Pawlowski was asked by the Polish government to become a spy. When he refused, he was charged with *being* a spy and sentenced to twenty-five years in prison. His name was also removed from all Polish books about the Olympics.

1972 Munich C: 54, N: 23, D: 8.31.

		W	L	TG	TR
1. Viktor Sidyak	SOV/RUS	4	1	23	15
2. Péter Maróth	HUN	3	2	21	20
3. Vladimir Nazlymov	SOV/RUS	3	2	21	21
4. Michele Maffei	ITA	3	2	20	21
5. Regis Bonissent	FRA	1	4	19	22
6. Tamás Kovács	HUN	1	4	17	22

Maffei, Kovács, and Sidiak each entered the final pool with records of 17–3, but Sidiak, emitting a growl each time he scored a hit, prevailed.

1976 Montreal C: 46, N: 18, D: 7.22.

		W	L	TG	TR
1. Viktor Krovopuskov	SOV/RUS	5	0	25	14
2. Vladimir Nazlymov	SOV/RUS	4	1	23	18
3. Viktor Sidyak	SOV/RUS	3	2	22	20
4. Ioan Popa	ROM	2	3	22	20
5. Mario Montano	ITA	1	4	16	21
6. Michele Maffei	ITA	0	5	13	25
7. Francisco de La Torre	CUB				
7. Imre Gedóvári	HUN				

1980 Moscow C: 30, N: 12, D: 7.25.

		W	L	TG	TR	BARRAGE TG	TR
1. Viktor Krovopuskov	SOV/RUS	4	1	24	17	5	3
2. Mikhail Burtsev	SOV/RUS	4	1	23	18	3	5
3. Imre Gedovari	HUN	3	2	23	21		
4. Vassil Etropolski	BUL	2	3	17	23		
5. Hristo Etropolski	BUL	1	4	19	21		
6. Michele Maffei	ITA	1	4	15	21		
7. Ferdinando Meglio	ITA						
7. Vladimir Nazlymov	SOV/RUS						

Burtsev beat Krovopuskov in the final pool, 5–4, but Krovopuskov turned the tables in the barrage to become the third repeat winner in individual sabre.

1984 Los Angeles-Long Beach C: 33, N: 14, D: 8.4.

1. Jean-François Lamour	FRA
2. Marco Marin	ITA
3. Peter Westbrook	USA
4. Hervé Granger-Veyron	FRA
5. Pierre Guichot	FRA
6. Marin Mustață	ROM
7. Giovanni Scalzo	ITA
8. Ioan Popa	ROM

Final: Lamour 12–11 Marin
3rd Place: Westbrook 10–5 Granger-Veyron

The sabre competition was severely depleted by the Soviet-bloc boycott. However, Lamour's performance was nonetheless impressive, as he won all 19 of his bouts.

1988 Seoul C: 40, N: 18, D: 9.23.

1. Jean-François Lamour	FRA
2. Janusz Olech	POL
3. Giovanni Scalzo	ITA
4. Philippe Delrieu	FRA
5. György Nébald	HUN
6. Heorgy Pohosov	SOV/UKR
7. Felix Becker	GER
8. Jürgen Nolte	GER

Final: Lamour 10–4 Olech
3rd Place: Scalzo 10–2 Delrieu

When Lamour first competed in the Olympics in 1980, he was the only member of the 16-man French squad to go home without a medal. He finished twenty-first. When he was crowned Olympic champion in 1984, many French fencing aficionados scorned his victory over a boycott-depleted field and spoke of him winning a medal not of gold, but of chocolate. Lamour silenced his critics by winning the 1987 world championships and then repeating his Olympic triumph in Seoul.

1992 Barcelona C: 44, N: 19, D: 8.2.
1. Bence Szabó   HUN
2. Marco Marin   ITA
3. Jean-François Lamour   FRA
4. Giovanni Scalzo   ITA
5. Antonio García Hernández   SPA
6. Ferdinando Meglio   ITA
7. Robert Kościelniakowski   POL
8. Jürgen Nolte   GER
     Final: Szabó—Marin 5-1, 5-1
     3rd Place: Lamour—Scalzo 3-5, 6-5, 5-1

Both Szabó and Marin reached the final with semifinal victories over opponents who had beaten them earlier in the tournament. Szabó had lost to Scalzo 6-4, 6-5, but came back in the semis to win 5-3, 3-5, 6-4. Marin's defeat of Lamour was even sweeter. They had faced each other in the 1984 final with Marin coming back from a 9-5 deficit, only to lose 12-11. In Barcelona, Lamour, at age 36, was trying for a third gold medal. In the elimination round he beat Marin 6-4, 5-2, but in the semifinals Marin prevailed, 6-4, 5-3. The final was never close. Szabó was the first fencer from Hungary to win the individual sabre since the Hungarian dynasty of 1908 to 1964.

SABRE, TEAM

1896–1904 not held

1906 Athens T: 4, N: 4, D: 4.28.
1. GER   (Gustav Casmir, Jacob Erckrath de Bary, August Petri, Emil Schön)
2. GRE   (Jean Georgiadis, Menelaos Sakorraphos, Ch. Zorbas, Triantaphylos Kordogiannis)
3. HOL   (James van Carnbee, Johannes Osten, George van Rossem, Maurits van Löben Sels)
4. HUN   (Péter Tóth, Jëno Apáthy, Ervin Mészáros, Bela Nagy)

1908 London T: 8, N: 8, D: 7.23.
1. HUN   (Jeno Fuchs, Oszkár Gerde, Péter Tóth, Lajos Werkner, Dezsö Földes)
2. ITA   (Riccardo Nowak, Alessandro Pirzio-Biroli, Abelardo Olivier, Marcello Bertinetti, Sante Ceccherini)
3. BOH/   (Vilém Goppold von Lobsdorf, Jaroslav Tuček, Vlastimil
   CZE   Lada-Sázavsky, Otakar Lada, Bedřich Schejbal)
4. FRA   (Georges de la Falaise, Bernard de Lesseps, Marc Perrodon, Jean Joseph Renaud)
     Final: HUN 9-7 BOH

Péter Tóth of the Hungarian team became involved in a fight with a fellow student at age 15 and was challenged

to a duel. After consultation with their classmates, the boys decided to postpone the duel until after final examinations. In the meantime Tóth enrolled in a fencing school and became so proficient that when final exams were over his opponent decided to drop the matter. Eleven years later Tóth won the first of his team sabre gold medals. Dr. Dezsö Földes, another member of the Hungarian team, emigrated to the United States in 1912 and set up a clinic for the poor in Cleveland.

Jean Joseph Renaud of the French team wrote more than sixty novels and several plays. However, he was best known as the organizer and director of several hundred illegal private duels. He justified his role in these clandestine encounters by explaining that "generally both parties are so nervous that nobody gets hurt, the offended hero soothes his honor, and everyone goes away happy."

In 1908, second place was contested by a pool of those teams which had lost to Hungary. Bohemia refused to take part, so Italy defeated Germany for second place.

1912 Stockholm T: 11, N: 11, D: 7.15.
1. HUN   (Jenö Fuchs, László Berti, Ervin Mészáros, Dezsö Földes, Oszkár Gerde, Zoltán Schenker, Péter Tóth, Lajos Werkner)
2. AUT   (Richard Verderber, Otto Herschmann, Rudolf Cvetko, Friedrich Golling, Andreas Suttner, Albert Bogen, Reinhold Trampler)
3. HOL   (Willem van Blijenburgh, George van Rossem, Adrianus de Jong, Jetze Doorman, Dirk Scalongne, Hendrik de Iongh)
4. BOH/   (Vilém Goppold von Lobsdorf, Otakar Svorčík, Josef
   CZE   Javůrek, František Kříž, Zdeněk Bárta, Josef Pfeiffer, Bedřich Schejbal, Josef Čipera)
5. BEL   —
5. GBR   (Edward Brookfield, Harry Butterworth, Archibald Corble, Douglas Godree, Alfred Keene, William Marsh, Alfred Martin, Alfred Syson, Charles Vander Byl)
5. GER   —
5. RUS   —

Otto Herschmann of the second-place Austrian team had previously won a bronze medal in the 1896 100-meter freestyle swimming event. At the time of the 1912 Games, Herschmann was president of the Austrian Olympic Committee, making him the only sitting national Olympic committee president to win an Olympic medal. Herschmann died at the Nazi concentration camp of Izbica in Poland on June 14, 1942.

1920 Antwerp T: 8, N: 8, D: 8.26.

		MATCHES			
		WON	LOST	W	L
1. ITA	(Nedo Nadi, Aldo Nadi, Oreste Puliti, Baldo Baldi, Francesco Gargano, Giorgio Santelli, Dino Urbani)	7	0	76	20
2. FRA	(Georges Trombert, J. A. Margraff, Marc Perrodon, Henri de Saint Germain)	6	1	53	42

	WON	LOST	MATCHES W	L
3. HOL (Jan van der Wiel, Adrianus de Jong, Jetze Doorman, William van Blijenburgh, Louis Delaunoij, Salomon Zeldenrust, Henri Wijnoldij-Daniëls)	5	2	51	45
4. BEL (Robert Hennet, Pierre Calle, Alexis Simonson, Léon Tom, Robert Feyerick, Charles Delporte, Harry Dombeeck)	4	3	47	47
5. USA (Edwin Fulinwidder, Arthur Lyon, Joseph Brooks Parker, John Dimond, Frederick Cunningham, Claiborne Walker, C. Bradford Fraley, Roscoe Bowman)	3	4	37	58
6. DEN (Ivan Osiier, Poul Rasmussen, Ejnar Levison, Aage Berntsen, Verner Bonde)	2	5	39	55
7. GBR (Alfred Ridley-Martin, William Marsh, William Hammond, Cecil Kershaw, Ronald Campbell, Robin Dalglish, Herbert Huntingdon)	1	6	30	50
8. CZE (Josef Javůrek, Otakar Svorčík, František Dvořák, Antony Mikala, Josef Jungmann)	0	7	16	32

1924 Paris T: 14, N: 14, D: 7.15.

	WON	LOST	MATCHES W	L
1. ITA (Renato Anselmi, Guido Balzarini, Marcello Bertinetti, Bino Bini, Vincenzo Cuccia, Oreste Moricca, Oreste Puliti, Giulio Sarrocchi)	3	0	28	20
2. HUN (László Berti, János Garay, Sándor Pósta, Jozsef Rády, Zoltán Schenker, Laszlo Széchy, Ödön Tersztyánszky, Jenö Uhlyárik)	2	1	33	15
3. HOL (Adrianus de Jong, Jetze Doorman, Hendrik Scherpenhuizen, Jan van der Wiel, Maarten van Dulm, Henri Wijnoldij-Daniëls)	1	2	18	30
4. CZE (František Dvořák, Alexander Bárta, Josef Jungmann, Luděk Oppl, Otakar Svorčík)	0	3	17	31
5. ARG (Carmelo Camet, Horacio Casco, C. Guerrico, Carmelo Merlo, Pedro Nazar Anchorena, Antonio Ponce				

Costa, Roberto Sola, Santiago Torres Blanco)

5. FRA (Georges Conraux, Henri de Saint-Germain, Jean Jannekeyn, Louis Lifschitz, Jean Margraff, Marc Perrodon, Maurice Taillandier, Georges Trombert)

The crucial match between Italy and Hungary ended in an 8–8 tie, but Italy won by four touches, 46 to 50. Puliti was the star of the tournament, winning 26 of 28 bouts and scoring 110 touches while receiving only 39.

1928 Amsterdam T: 12, N: 12, D: 8.9.

	WON	LOST	MATCHES W	L
1. HUN (Ödön Tersztyánszky, Sándor Gombos, Attila Petschauèr, János Garay, József Rády, Gyula Glykais)	2	0	23	9
2. ITA (Bino Bini, Renato Anselmi, Gustavo Marzi, Oreste Puliti, Emilio Salafia, Giulio Sarrocchi)	1	1	21	11
3. POL (Adam Papée, Tadeusz Friedrich, Kazimierz Laskowski, Wladyslaw Segda, Aleksander Malecki, Jerzy Zabielski)	1	1	11	21
4. GER (Erwin Casmir, Heinrich Moos, Hans Halberstadt, Hans Thomson)	0	2	9	23
5. FRA (René Fristeau, Roger Ducret, Jean Lacroix, Maurice Taillandier, Jean Piot, Paul Oziol de Pignol)				
5. HOL (Cornelis Ekkart, Hendrik Hagens, Maarten van Dulm, Jan van der Wiel, Adrianus de Jong, Henri Wijnoldij-Daniëls)				
7. BEL (Joseph Stordeur, Marcel Cuypers, Jacques Kesteloot, Edouard Yves, Gaston Kaanen)				
7. TUR (Muhiddin Turhan Okyayyüz, Ergun Fouad, Nami Demir Yayak, Enver Balkan)				

Hungary defeated Italy 9–7 in the decisive match. The Hungarian team was led by the high-strung 23-year-old Attila Petschauèr of Budapest, who won all 20 of his bouts. While fighting in the Ukraine in 1943, Petschauèr was tortured to death by anti-Semitic Hungarian army officers. Another Jewish member of the Hungarian team, János Garay, died in a Nazi concentration camp.

1932 Los Angeles T: 6, N: 6, D: 8.11.

		WON	LOST	MATCHES W	L
1. HUN	(György Piller, Endre Kabos, Attila Petschauer, Ernö Nagy, Gyula Glykais, Aladár Gerevich)	3	0	31	6
2. ITA	(Renato Anselmi, Arturo De Vecchi, Emilio Salafia, Ugo Pignotti, Gustavo Marzi, Giulio Guadini)	2	1	20	14
3. POL	(Adam Papée, Tadeusz Friedrich, Wladyslaw Segda, Leszek Lubicz-Nyzz, Wladyslaw Doborowolski, Marian Suski)	1	2	10	26
4. USA	(Peter Bruder, John Huffman, Norman Armitage, Nikolas Muray, Harold van Buskirk, Ralph Faulkner)	0	3	15	30

Hungary won 56 bouts and lost only nine.

1936 Berlin T: 21, N: 21, D: 8.13.

		WON	LOST	MATCHES W	L
1. HUN	(Tibor Berczelly, László Rajcsányi, Pál Kovács, Aladár Gerevich, Imre Rajczy, Endre Kabos)	3	0	32	10
2. ITA	(Vincenzo Pinton, Giulio Gaudini, Aldo Masciotta, Gustavo Marzi, Aldo Montano, Athos Tanzini)	2	1	25	17
3. GER	(Richard Wahl, Julius Eisenecker, Erwin Casmir, August Heim, Hans Esser, Hans Jörger)	1	2	14	25
4. POL	(Antoni Sobik, Wladyslaw Sagda, Wladyslaw Dobrowolski, Adam Papée, Marian Suski, Teodor Zaczyk)	0	3	10	29
5. AUT	(Josef Losert, Hugo Weczerek, Karl Sudrich, Hubert Loisel, Karl Hanisch, Karl Kaschka)				
5. FRA	(Marcel Faure, Maurice Gramain, Edward Gardere, Jean Piot, Roger Barisien, André Gardere)				
5. HOL	(Ate Faber, Antonius Montfoort, Franciscus Mosman, Franciscus van Wieringen, Jacob Schriever)				
5. USA	(Peter Bruder, Miguel de Capriles, Bela de Nagy, John Huffman, Samuel Stewart, Norman Armitage)				

The Hungarians won their first seven matches by scores of 13–3 or better, and then defeated Italy 9–6 to win the gold medal. Their final bout total was 106 wins and 16 losses. Leading Hungarian scorers were Berczelly (24–3), Kovács (21–2), Rajcsányi (20–4) and Gerevich (17–2).

1948 London T: 17, N: 17, D: 8.11.

		WON	LOST	MATCHES W	L
1. HUN	(Tibor Berczelly, Rudolf Kárpáti, Aladár Gerevich, Pál Kovács, László Rajcsányi, Bertalan Papp)	3	0	29	13
2. ITA	(Gastone Darè, Carlo Turcato, Vincenzo Pinton, Mauro Racca, Aldo Montano, Renzo Nostini)	2	1	24	24
3. USA	(Norman Armitage, George Worth, Tibor Nyilas, Dean Cetrulo, Miguel de Capriles, James Flynn)	1	2	24	23
4. BEL	(Robert Bayot, Georges de Bourguignon, Ferdinand Jassogne, Eugène Laermans, Marcel Nys, Edouard Yves)	0	3	12	29
5. ARG	(Manuel Aguero, José Luis D'Andrea Mohr, Edgardo Pomini, Jorge Cermesoni, Francesco Huergo, Daniel Sande)				
5. FRA	(Jean-François Tournon, Jacques Parent, Maurice Gramain, Jacques Lefèvre, Jean Levavasseur, Georges Levèque)				
5. HOL	(Henricus ter Weer, Antoon Hoevers, Willem van den Berg, Franciscus Mosman, Ludovicus Kuijpers)				
5. POL	(Antoni Sobik, Boleslaw Banas, Teodor Zaczyk, Jerzy Wójcik, Jan Nawrocki)				

Berczelly had a 15–2 record, including four straight victories in the final 10–6 defeat of Italy. Hungary's total for the tournament was 65 wins and 20 losses.

1952 Helsinki T: 19, N: 19, D: 7.30.

		WON	LOST	MATCHES W	L
1. HUN	(Bertalan Papp, László Rajcsányi, Rudolf Kárpáti, Aladár Gerevich, Pál Kovács, Tibor Berczelly)	3	0	34	13

		WON	LOST	MATCHES W	L
2. ITA	(Vincenzo Pinton, Mauro Racca, Roberto Ferrari, Gastone Darè, Renzo Nostini, Giorgio Pellini)	2	1	32	15
3. FRA	(Jacques Lefèvre, Jean Laroyenne, Maurice Piot, Jean Levavasseur, Bernard Morel, Jean-François Tournon)	1	2	14	32
4. USA	(Norman Armitage, Miguel de Capriles, Tibor Nyilas, Alex Treves, George Worth, Allan Kwartler)	0	3	13	33
5. AUT	(Werner Plattner, Heinz Putzl, Hubert Loisel, Heinz Lechner, Paul Kerb)				
5. BEL	(Marcel Vanderauwera, Gustave Balister, François Heyvaert, Robert Bayot, Georges de Bourguignon, Edouard Yves)				
5. GBR	(Roger Tredgold, Olgierd Porebski, Robert Anderson, William Maurice Beatley, Ulrich Wendon)				
5. POL	(Jerzy Twardokens, Leszek Suski, Jerzy Pawlowski, Wojciech Zablocki, Zygmunt Pawlas)				

Great tension built up in the final contest as Hungary's string of 35 victories and four Olympic gold medals appeared in jeopardy when Italy took a 7–5 lead. Then Berczelly beat Nostini 5–0 and Kárpáti beat Ferrari 5–0 to even the match at 7–7. Gerevich, who had lost his other three bouts against the Italians, recovered to defeat Enzo Pinton 5–3 and give Hungary an insurmountable lead of 8–7, with a 14-touch advantage. Hungary's tournament totals were 111 wins and 25 losses.

1956 Melbourne T: 8, N: 8, D: 12.3.

		WON	LOST	MATCHES W	L
1. HUN	(Attila Keresztes, Pál Kovács, Rudolf Kárpáti, Aladár Gerevich, Jenö Hámori, Dániel Magay)	3	0	30	15
2. POL	(Jerzy Pawlowski, Wojciech Zablocki, Marek Kuszewski, Zygmunt Pawlas, Ryszard Zub, Andrzej Piatkowski)	2	1	23	22
3. SOV	(Lev Kuznetsov, Yakov Rylsky, Yevhen Cherepovsky, David Tyshler, Leonid Bogdanov)	1	2	22	25

				MATCHES	
4. FRA	(Claude Gamot, Jacques Lefèvre, Bernard Morel, Jacques Roulot)	0	3	17	30
5. ITA	(Roberto Ferrari, Domenico Pace, Mario Ravagnan, Giuseppe Comini, Luigi Narduzzi, Gastone Daré)				

By 1956 the sabre contests were the only ones not using electronic scoring, which was finally introduced in 1992. Tensions were high during the match between Hungary and the U.S.S.R., since the Soviets had just invaded Hungary. The Hungarians were victorious, 9–7. After the Olympics Keresztes, Hámori, and Magay defected to the West. Keresztes and Hámori fenced for the United States in the 1964 Olympics.

1960 Rome T: 16, N: 16, D: 9.10.
1. HUN (Zoltán Horváth, Rudolf Kárpáti, Tamás Mendelényi, Pál Kovács, Gábor Delneky, Aladár Gerevich)
2. POL (Andrzej Piatkowski, Emil Ochyra, Wojciech Zablocki, Jerzy Pawlowski, Ryszard Zub, Marek Kuszewski)
3. ITA (Wladimiro Calarese, Gianpaolo Calanchini, Pierluigi Chicca, Mario Ravagnan, Roberto Ferrari)

HUNGARY'S TEAM SABRE WINNING STREAK

1924			1948			1960		
14	HOL	2	9	EGY	3	9	BEL	3
11	CZE	5	15	ARG	1	9	ROM	3
			12	POL	3	9	ITA	6
1928			10	USA	6	9	POL	7
14	USA	2	9	BEL	1			
13	GBR	3	10	ITA	6	**1964**		
12	GER	4				9	ARG	2
12	FRA	4	**1952**			9	ROM	0
14	POL	2	15	POR	1			
9	ITA	7	15	SAA	1			
11	DEN	1	9	DEN	0			
			13	FRA	3			
1932			13	BEL	3			
14	MEX	2	12	AUT	4			
13	USA	3	13	FRA	3			
9	ITA	2	13	USA	3			
9	POL	1	8	ITA	7			
1936			**1956**					
16	DEN	0	9	USA	1			
14	URU	2	12	FRA	4			
15	GER	1	9	SOV	4			
15	HOL	1	9	POL	4			
14	USA	2						
13	GER	3						
10	POL	1						
9	ITA	6						

4. USA (Allan Kwartler, George Worth, Michael D'Asaro, Alfonso Morales, Tibor Nyilas, R. Richard Dyer)
5. FRA (Marcel Parent, Claude Gamot, Jacques Lefèvre, Jacques Roulot, Claude Arabo)
5. GER (Dieter Lohr, Jürgen Theuerkauff, Wilfried Wohler, Peter von Krockov, Walter Köstner)
5. ROM (Dumitru Mustaţă, Cornel Pelmuş, Ion Szanto, Ladislau Rohony, Eméric Arus)
5. SOV (Yevhen Cherepovsky, Umyar Mavlikhanov, Nugzar Asatiani, David Tyshler, Yakov Rylsky)
Final: HUN 9–7 POL
3rd Place: ITA 9–6 USA

In the match for first place, Poland took a 3–0 lead. Then Hungary won five in a row, but Poland came back to tie it, 6–6. Finally Kárpáti beat Pawlowski 5–3 to secure the gold medal. Gerevich, 50 years old, won his sixth straight team sabre gold medal.

1964 Tokyo T: 13, N: 13, D: 10.23.
1. SOV (Yakov Rylsky, Nugzar Asatiani, Mark Rakita, Umyar Mavlikhanov, Boris Melnikov)
2. ITA (Wladimiro Calarese, Cesare Salvadori, Gianpaolo Calanchini, Pierluigi Chicca, Mario Ravagnan)
3. POL (Emil Ochyra, Jerzy Pawlowski, Ryszard Zub, Andrzej Piatkowski, Wojciech Zablocki)
4. FRA (Jean Ramez, Jacques Lefèvre, Claude Arabo, Marcel Parent, Robert Fraisse)
5. HUN (Péter Bakonyi, Miklós Meszéna, Attila Kovács, Zoltan Horvath, Tibor Pézsa)
6. GER (Dieter Wellmann, Klaus Allissat, Walter Köstner, Jürgen Theuerkauff, Percy Borucki)
7. ROM (Attila Csipler, Octavian Vintilă, Tănase Mureşan, Ionel Drimbă)
7. USA (Alfonso Morales, Robert Blum, Eugene [Jenö] Hamori, Attila Keresztes, Thomas Orley)
Final: SOV 9–6 ITA
3rd Place: POL 8(60)–8(59) FRA
5th Place: HUN 9–3 GER

In the semifinals Hungary's winning streak was finally stopped at 46 when they were upset by Italy, 9–7. It was Italy that had handed the Hungarians their last defeat 40 years earlier in Paris.

1968 Mexico City T: 12, N: 12, D: 10.21.
1. SOV/ (Vladimir Nazlymov, Eduard Vinokurov, Viktor Sidyak,
   RUS   Mark Rakita, Umyar Mavlikhanov)
2. ITA (Wladimiro Calarese, Cesare Salvadori, Michele Maffei, Pierluigi Chicca, Rolando Rigoli)
3. HUN (Tamás Kóvács, Miklós Meszéna, Janos Kalmar, Péter Bakonyi, Tibor Pézsa)
4. FRA (Marcel Parent, Claude Arabo, Bernard Vallée, Serge Panizza, Jean Ramez)
5. POL (Jerzy Pawlowski, Józef Nowara, Franciszek Sobczak, Zygmunt Kawecki, Emil Ochyra)
6. USA (Alex Orban, Alfonso Morales, Anthony Keane, Robert Blum, Thomas Balla)

7. GBR (Alexander Leckie, Rodney Craig, David Acfield, Richard Oldcorn)
7. GER (Percy Borucki, Walter Köstner, Paul Wischeidt, Klaus Allisat, Volker Duschner)
Final: SOV 9–7 ITA
3rd Place: HUN 9–5 FRA
5th Place: POL 9–5 USA

1972 Munich T: 13, N: 13, D: 9.4.
1. ITA (Michele Maffei, Mario Aldo Montano, Cesare Salvadori, Mario Tullio Montano, Rolando Rigoli)
2. SOV/ (Mark Rakita, Eduard Vinokurov, Viktor Bazhenov, Viktor
   RUS   Sidyak, Vladimir Nazlymov)
3. HUN (Pál Gerevich, Támás Kovács, Péter Marót, Tibor Pézsa, Péter Bakonyi)
4. ROM (Dan Irimiciuc, Iosif Budahazi, Gheorghe Culcea, Constantin Nicolae, Octavian Vintilă)
5. POL (Józef Nowara, Krzysztof Grzegorek, Zygmunt Kawecki, Jerzy Pawlowski, Janusz Majewski)
6. CUB (Hilario Hipolito, Guzman Salazar, Francisco de la Torre, Manuel Ortiz, Manuel Suarez)
7. FRA (Regis Bonissent, Bernard Dumont, Bernard Vallee, Philippe Bena, Serge Panizza)
7. GER (Walter Convents, Volker Duschner, Knut Höhne, Dieter Wellmann, Paul Wischeidt)
Final: ITA 9–5 SOV
3rd Place: HUN 8–7 ROM
5th Place: POL 9–5 CUB

Maffei defeated all four Soviet fencers in the final, but it was Aldo Montano who won the decisive bout with Vinokurov, 5–1. Montano had previously been warned by the officials not to remove his mask before a decision had been announced. When he scored the winning hit the 205-pound Montano leaped up and down while his team manager and his cousin (and teammate), Tullio Montano, desperately held on to his helmet until the official call was made.

1976 Montreal T: 13, N: 13, D: 7.27.
1. SOV/ (Eduard Vinokurov, Viktor Krovopuskov, Mikhail Burtsev,
   RUS   Viktor Sidyak, Vladimir Nazlymov)
2. ITA (Mario Aldo Montano, Michele Maffei, Angelo Arcidiacono, Tommaso Montano, Mario Tullio Montano)
3. ROM (Dan Irimiciuc, Ioan Popa, Marin Mustaţă, Corneliu Marin, Alexandru Nilca)
4. HUN (Péter Marót, Tamás Kovács, Imre Gedövari, Ferenc Hammang, Csaba Körmöczi)
5. CUB (Manuel Ortiz, Francisco de La Torre, Guzman Salazar, Ramon Hernandez, Lazaro Mora)
6. POL (Leszek Jablonowski, Sylwester Królikowski, Jacek Bierkowski, Józef Nowara)
7. USA (Paul Apostol, Peter Westbrook, Stephen Kaplan, Thomas Losonczy, Alex Orban)
7. FRA (Philippe Bena, Regis Bonnissent, Bernard Dumont, Didier Flament, Patrick Quivrin)
Final: SOV 9–4 ITA
3rd Place: ROM 9–4 HUN
5th Place: CUB 9–6 POL

1980 Moscow T: 8, N: 8, D: 7.29.
1. SOV (Mikhail Burtsev, Viktor Krovopuskov, Viktor Sidyak, Vladimir Nazlymov, Nikolai Alyokhin)
2. ITA (Michele Maffei, Mario Aldo Montano, Marco Romano, Ferdinando Meglio)
3. HUN (Imre Gedövari, Rudolf Nebald, Pál Gerevich, Ferenc Hammang, György Nebald)
4. POL (Tadeusz Pigula, Leszek Jablonowski, Jacek Bierkowski, Andrzej Kostrzewa)
5. ROM (Ioan Pop, Marin Mustaţă, Corneliu Marin, Ion Pantelimonescu, Alexandru Nilca)
6. GDR (Rüdiger Müller, Hendrik Jung, Peter Ulbrich, Frank-Eberhard Höltje, Gerd May)
7. CUB (Manuel Ortiz, Jesus Ortiz, Jose Laverdecia, Guzman Salazar)
8. BUL (Hristo Etropolski, Nikolai Marincheshki, Vassil Etropolski, Georgi Chomakov, Marin Ivanov)
   Final: SOV 9–2 ITA
   3rd Place: HUN 9–6 POL
   5th Place: ROM 9–6 GDR

1984 Los Angeles-Long Beach T: 8, N: 8, D: 8.9.
1. ITA (Marco Marin, Gianfranco Dalla Barba, Giovanni Scalzo, Ferdinando Meglio, Angelo Arcidiacono)
2. FRA (Jean-François Lamour, Pierre Guichot, Hervé Granger Veyron, Philippe Delrieu, Franck Ducheix)
3. ROM (Marin Mustaţă, Ioan Pop, Alexandru Chiculita, Corneliu Marin, Vilmos Szabo)
4. GER (Dieter Schneider, Jürgen Nolte, Freddy Scholz, Jörg Stratmann, Jörg Volkmann)
5. CHN (Wang Ruiji, Chen Jinchu, Yang Shisheng, Liu Guozhen, Liu Yunhong)
6. USA (Peter Westbrook, Steve Mormando, Phillip Reilly, Joel Glucksman, Michael Lofton)
   Final: ITA 9–3 FRA
   3rd Place: ROM 8–7 GER
   5th Place: CHN 9–7 USA

1988 Seoul T: 11, N: 11, D: 9.29.
1. HUN (Imre Bujdosó, László Csongrádi, Imre Gedóvári, György Nébald, Bence Szabó)
2. SOV (Andrei Alshan, Mikhail Burtsev, Sergei Koryazhkin, Serhei Mindyrhasov, Heorgy Pohosov)
3. ITA (Massimo Cavaliere, Gianfranco Dalla Barba, Marco Marin, Ferdinando Meglio, Giovanni Scalzo)
4. FRA (Philippe Delrieu, Franck Ducheix, Hervé Granger Veyron, Pierre Guichot, Jean-François Lamour)
5. POL (Marek Gniewkowski, Robert Kościelniakowski, Andrzej Kostrzewa, Janusz Olech, Tadeusz Pigula)
6. GER (Felix Becker, Jörg Kempenich, Jürgen Nolte, Dieter Schneider, Stephan Thoennessen)
7. USA (Robert Cottingham, Paul Friedberg, Michael Lofton, George Mormando, Peter Westbrook)
8. BUL (Hristo Etropolski, Vassil Etropolski, Nikolai Marincheshki, Nikolai Mateyev, Georgi Chomakov)
   Final: HUN 8(67)–8(64) SOV
   3rd Place: ITA 8(64)–8(63) FRA
   5th Place: POL 9–4 GER

The glory years of Hungarian team sabre ended in 1964 and the mantle passed to the Soviets who have, since then, qualified for every Olympic final except the boycotted Games of Los Angeles. Prior to the 1988 Olympics, the Soviets had won three straight world championships. In Seoul the Hungarians survived with a 3-touch victory over Poland in the quarterfinals. The U.S.S.R. took a 7-3 lead in the final, but Hungary fought back with four victories in a row and went on to win another 3-touch squeaker.

If the Hungarian triumph was a throwback to the 1950s, what happened in the bronze medal match brought back memories of the 1920s. Trailing 2-6, the French team protested the officiating. A violent argument ensued and the French stalked off the piste, threatening to withdraw. After 30 minutes they were lured back. They rallied to tie the Italians 8-8, but lost by 1 touch.

1992 Barcelona T: 12, N: 12, D: 8.7.
1. SOV (Grigory Kiriyenko, Aleksandr Shirshov, Vadim Guttsayt, Stanislav Pozdniakov, Heorgy Pohosov)
2. HUN (Péter Abay, Imre Bujdosó, Csaba Kóves, György Nébald, Bence Szabó)
3. FRA (Franck Ducheix, Jean-Philippe Daurelle, Hervé Granger-Veyron, Pierre Guichot, Jean-François Lamour)
4. ROM (Alexandru Chiculita, Victor Gaureanu, Daniel Grigore, Florin Lupeica, Vilmos Szabo)
5. GER (Felix Becker, Jörg Kempenich, Jürgen Nolte, Jacek Huchwajda, Steffen Wiesinger)
6. POL (Marek Gniewkowski, Norbert Jaskot, Jarsolaw Kisiel, Robert Kościelniakowski, Janusz Olech)
7. CHN (Jia Guihua, Ning Xiankui, Yang Zhen, Jiang Yefei, Zheng Zhaokang)
8. ITA (Marco Marin, Ferdinando Meglio, Giovanni Scalzo, Giovanni Sirovich, Tonhi Terenzi)
   Final: SOV 9–5 HUN
   3rd Place: FRA 9–4 ROM
   5th Place: GER 9–6 POL
   7th Place: CHN 9–7 ITA

Discontinued Events
MASTERS FOIL FENCING

1896 Athens C: 2, N: 2, D: 4.7.

		TG	TR
1. Leon Pyrgos	GRE	3	1
2. Jean Perronnet	FRA	1	3

Pyrgos, although a professional, was the first Greek winner of the modern Olympic Games.

1900 Paris C: 64, N: 7, D: 5.22.

			W	L	BARRAGE W	L
1.	Lucien Mérignac	FRA	6	1	1	0
2.	Alphonse Kirchhoffer	FRA	6	1	0	1
3.	Jean-Baptiste Mimiague	FRA	4	3	1	0
4.	Antonio Conte	ITA	4	3	0	1
5.	Jules Rossignol	FRA	3	4		
6.	Leopold Ramus	FRA	2	5		
7.	Italo Santelli	ITA	0	7		
8.	Adolphe Rouleau	FRA	3	4		

Rouleau was placed last in the final pool because he withdrew from his bout with Mimiague "under the pretext of a sore thumb."

MASTERS ÉPÉE FENCING

1900 Paris C: 54, N: 3?, D: 6.14.
1. Albert Ayat — FRA
2. Emile Bougnol — FRA
3. Henri Laurent — FRA
4. Hippolyte-Jacques Hyvernaud — FRA
5. Damotte — FRA
6. Brassart — FRA
7. Lezard — FRA
8. Jourdant — FRA

1904 not held

1906 Athens C: 3, N: 3, D: 4.28.
1. Cyril Verbrugge — BEL
2. Carlo Gandini — ITA
3. Ioannis Raïssis — GRE

ÉPÉE FOR AMATEURS AND MASTERS

1900 Paris C: 8, N: 2, D: 6.15.
1. Albert Ayat — FRA
2. Ramón Fonst — CUB
3. Léon Sée — FRA
4. Georges de la Falaise — FRA
5. Emile Bougnol — FRA
5. Hippolyte-Jacques Hyvernaud — FRA
5. Henri Laurent — FRA
5. Louis Perrée — FRA

This event brought together the first four finishers in the amateur and masters tournaments. Ayat won without receiving a hit and was awarded a prize of 3000 francs.

MASTERS SABRE FENCING

1900 Paris C: 44, N: 10, D: 6.27.

			W	L
1.	Antonio Conte	ITA	7	0
2.	Italo Santelli	ITA	6	1

3.	Milan Neralić	AUT	4	3
4.	François Delibes	BEL	3	4
5.	Michaux	FRA	3	4
6.	Xavier Anchetti	FRA	2	5
7.	Zacharov	RUS	2	5
8.	Hébrant	BEL	1	6

1904 not held

1906 Athens C: 5, N: 5, D: 4.28.
1. Cyril Verbrugge — BEL
2. Ioannis Raïssis — GRE
3. Carlo Gandini — ITA

THREE-CORNERED SABRE

1906 Athens C: 22, N: 6, D: 4.28.
1. Gustav Casmir — GER
2. George van Rossem — HOL
3. Péter Tóth — HUN
4. Emil Schön — GER
5. Jëno Apáthy — HUN
6. Ernst Königsgarten — AUT

SINGLE STICKS

1904 St. Louis C: 3, N: 1, D: 9.10.

			TG
1.	Albertson Van Zo Post	USA	11
2.	William Scott O'Connor	USA	8
3.	William Grebe	USA	2

WOMEN

FOIL, INDIVIDUAL

1896–1920 not held

1924 Paris C: 25, N: 9, D: 7.4.

			W	L	TG	TR
1.	Ellen Osiier	DEN	5	0	25	14
2.	Gladys Davies	GBR	4	1	23	16
3.	Grete Heckscher	DEN	3	2	22	16
4.	Muriel Freeman	GBR	2	3	17	20
5.	Yutha Barding	DEN	1	4	20	22
6.	Gizella Tary	HUN	0	5	6	25

The first female Olympic fencing champion was 33-year-old Ellen Ottilia Osiier, who won all 16 of her bouts. She scored 80 touches and received only 34.

1928 Amsterdam C: 27, N: 11, D: 8.1.

		W	L	TG	TR
1. Helene Mayer	GER	7	0	35	9
2. Muriel Freeman	GBR	6	1	32	19
3. Olga Oelkers	GER	4	3	25	27
4. Erna Sondheim	GER	3	4	22	29
5. Gladys Daniell	GBR	2	5	23	27
6. Jenny Addams	BEL	2	5	23	30
6. Margit Dany	HUN	2	5	23	30
8. Johanna de Boer	HOL	2	5	23	33

A German Jew, 17-year-old Helene Mayer swept through the tournament with surprising ease, winning 18 bouts and losing two.

1932 Los Angeles C: 17, N: 11, D: 8.3.

		W	L	TG	TR	BARRAGE TG	BARRAGE TR
1. Ellen Preis	AUT	8	1	44	27	5	3
2. Heather "Judy" Guinness	GBR	8	1	43	19	3	5
3. Erna Bogáthy Bogen	HUN	7	2	38	30		
4. Jenny Addams	BEL	6	3	37	29		
5. Helene Mayer	GER	5	4	38	27		
6. Johanna de Boer	HOL	5	4	30	35		
7. Gerda Munck	DEN	2	7	29	39		
8. Marion Lloyd	USA	2	7	26	42		
8. Grete Olsen	DEN	2	7	31	42		

Preis won by defeating Guinness 5–3 in both the final pool and the barrage. During the barrage, Heather Guinness pointed out to the officials two touches against her which the officials had failed to acknowledge. This act of fair play proved to be the margin of victory. Preis eventually competed in five Olympics. Bronze medalist Erna Bogen was the daughter of Albert Bogen, who won a silver medal in team sabre in 1912. She later married seven-time sabre gold medalist Aladár Gerevich. Their son, Pál, earned two bronze medals in team sabre in 1972 and 1980.

1936 Berlin C: 41, N: 17, D: 8.5.

		W	L	TG	TR
1. Ilona Elek	HUN	6	1	33	17
2. Helene Mayer	GER	5	2	33	19
3. Ellen Preis	AUT	5	2	32	20
4. Hedwig Hass	GER	5	2	30	23
5. Karen Lachmann	DEN	3	4	23	24
6. Jenny Addams	BEL	2	5	18	28
7. Ilona Vargha	HUN	2	5	17	31
8. Elisabeth Grasser	AUT	0	7	11	35

In 1932 Helene Mayer left her family behind in Königstein, Germany, and moved to the United States, where she taught German at Mills College in Oakland, California. Under pressure from the U.S., the Nazis invited her back to compete in the Olympics. The Nazis rationalized their leniency toward her by stating that although she was Jewish, she had two "Aryan" grandparents. Also competing at Berlin were the defending

The award ceremony for the 1936 women's foil: (left to right) Ellen Preis (bronze), Ilona Elek (gold), and German Jew Helene Mayer (silver).

Olympic champion, Ellen Preis and the European champion, Ilona Elek, who was also Jewish. In the final pool, Elek defeated Mayer 5–4 and Preis 5–3, losing only to Hedwig Hass. On the victory platform Helene Mayer pleased the large German crowd by giving a "Heil Hitler" salute.

1948 London C: 39, N: 15, D: 8.2.

		W	L	TG	TR
1. Ilona Elek	HUN	6	1	31	15
2. Karen Lachmann	DEN	5	2	24	11
3. Ellen Müller-Preis	AUT	5	2	24	16
4. Maria Cerra	USA	5	2	23	16
5. Fritzi Filz	AUT	4	3	20	21
6. Margit Elek	HUN	1	6	10	26
7. Velleda Cessari	ITA	1	6	15	27
8. Mary Glen Haig	GBR	1	6	10	27

Ilona Elek's retention of her Olympic title after a 12-year interlude was a tremendous achievement in itself. But the manner in which she won added to the drama. In her next-to-last bout she trailed Maria Cerra 2–0 before scoring four straight hits. Then, with the winner earning the gold medal, she defeated Karen Lachmann 4–2 as well.

1952 Helsinki C: 37, N: 15, D: 7.27.

		W	L	TR	BARRAGE W	BARRAGE L	BARRAGE TG	BARRAGE TR
1. Irene Camber	ITA	5	2	22	1	0	4	3
2. Ilona Elek	HUN	5	2	21	0	1	3	4
3. Karen Lachmann	DEN	4	3	22	3	0	12	4
4. Janice Lee York	USA	4	3	25	2	1	8	7
5. Maxine Mitchell	USA	4	3	23	1	2	9	8
6. Renée Garilhe	FRA	4	3	24	0	3	2	12
7. Lylian Lecomte-Guyonneau	FRA	1	6	30				
8. Magdolna Kovács-Nyári	HUN	1	6	32				

The 45-year-old Elek appeared well on her way to her third gold medal when she won her first 20 bouts, including five in the final pool. But then she lost to Mitchell and then to Camber, 4–3. Forced into a barrage, she was again defeated by Camber, 4–3.

1956 Melbourne C: 23, N: 11, D: 11.29.

			W	L	TG	TR	BARRAGE TG	BARRAGE TR
1.	Gillian Sheen	GBR	6	1	26	20	4	2
2.	Olga Orban	ROM	6	1	27	17	2	4
3.	Renée Garilhe	FRA	5	2	26	14		
4.	Janice Lee Romary (York)	USA	4	3	23	21		
5.	Kate Delbarre	FRA	3	4	20	25		
6.	Karen Lachmann	DEN	2	5	17	20		
7.	Ellen Müller-Preis	AUT	1	6	20	25		
8.	Bruna Colombetti	ITA	1	6	14	27		

Sheen, a 28-year-old London dental surgeon, barely qualified for the final by defeating world champion Lydia Domolki of Hungary in a barrage to finish fourth in her semifinal pool. She lost 4–2 to Orban, but won the rest of her bouts to force a barrage. This time she defeated the Romanian, 4–2. Sheen remains the only British fencer ever to win a gold medal.

1960 Rome C: 56, N: 24, D: 9.1.

			W	L	TG	TR	BARRAGE TG	BARRAGE TR	BARRAGE W	BARRAGE L
1.	Heidi Schmid	GER	6	1	26	13				
2.	Valentina Rastvorova	SOV/RUS	5	2	24	12				
3.	Maria Vicol	ROM	4	3	23	18	2	0	8	5
4.	Galina Gorokhova	SOV/RUS	4	3	22	19	1	1	7	6
5.	Olga Szabó-Orban	ROM	4	3	20	20	0	2	4	8
5.	Elżbieta Pawlas	POL	2	5	14	24				
7.	Maria del Pilar Roldan	MEX	2	5	13	25				
8.	Waltraut Ebert	AUT	1	6	14	27				

Heidi Schmid was a left-handed 21-year-old music teacher from Augsburg. She scored 18 wins against only two losses, one of which occurred after she had clinched the championship.

1964 Tokyo C: 39, N: 17, D: 10.15.

			W	L	TG	TR	BARRAGE W	BARRAGE L	BARRAGE TG	BARRAGE TR
1.	Ildikó Ujlaki-Rejtö	HUN	2	1	10	5	2	0	8	1
2.	Helga Mees	GER	2	1	8	9	1	1	4	6
3.	Antonella Ragno	ITA	2	1	9	7	0	2	3	8
4.	Galina Gorokhova	SOV/RUS	0	3	6	12				
5.	Katalin Juhász	HUN								
6.	Giovanna Masciotta	ITA								
7.	Bruna Colombetti	ITA								
7.	Catherine Rousselet	FRA								

Ildikó Ujlaki-Rejtö was born deaf on May 11, 1937. When she began fencing at age 14 her coaches communicated

their instructions on pieces of paper. A factory worker, she faced Helga Mees, a 27-year-old secretary from Saarbrücken, for the championship. Mees had already beaten Ujlaki-Rejtö twice, in the first round and in the final round, but in the barrage the Hungarian won, 4–0.

1968 Mexico City C: 38, N: 16, D: 10.20.

			W	L	TG	TR
1.	Yelena Novikova	SOV/BLR	4	1	19	11
2.	Maria del Pilar Roldan	MEX	3	2	17	14
3.	Ildikó Ujlaki-Rejtö	HUN	3	2	14	16
4.	Brigitte Gapais	FRA	2	3	15	15
5.	Kerstin Palm	SWE	2	3	17	17
6.	Galina Gorokhova	SOV/RUS	1	4	10	19
7.	Giovanna Masciotta	ITA				
7.	Heidi Schmid	GER				

Novikova, a tall 21-year-old student teacher, compiled a record of 15 wins and two losses. Silver medalist Roldan, a mother of two, came out of retirement to compete in the Olympics before a hometown crowd.

1972 Munich C: 44, N: 20, D: 9.3.

			W	L	TG	TR
1.	Antonella Ragno-Lonzi	ITA	4	1	19	13
2.	Ildikó Bóbis	HUN	3	2	17	14
3.	Galina Gorokhova	SOV/RUS	3	2	16	14
4.	Marie-Chantal Demaille	FRA	3	2	14	16
5.	Yelena Belova (Novikova)	SOV/BLR	2	3	15	13
6.	Kerstin Palm	SWE	0	5	9	20

1976 Montreal C: 48, N: 20, D: 7.24.

			W	L	TG	TR	BARRAGE TG	BARRAGE TR
1.	Ildikó Schwarczenberger	HUN	4	1	21	15	5	4
2.	Maria Consolata Collino	ITA	4	1	24	12	4	5
3.	Yelena Belova (Novikova)	SOV/BLR	3	2	21	19		
4.	Brigitte Dumont-Gapais	FRA	2	3	17	17		
5.	Cornelia Hanisch	GER	1	4	13	22		
6.	Ildikó Bóbis	HUN	1	4	13	24		
7.	Valentina Sidorova	SOV/RUS						
7.	Ecaterina Stahl (Iencic)	ROM						

The reigning world champion, Ecaterina Stahl, ran up a 15–2 record before being eliminated in the prefinal round by Ildikó Schwarczenberger. The final pool turned into an exciting three-way affair. Collino defeated Schwarczenberger 5–1, which appeared to end the Hungarian's chance for a gold medal. Then Yelena Belova beat Collino on the last hit to put Schwarczenberger back into a tie for first place. In her final match, Belova faced Ildikó Bóbis, who had lost all of her other final pool matches. A win would put her into a triple barrage. However, Bóbis summoned all her skill and defeated Belova 5–4. Inspired by her teammate's effort, Schwarczenberger won the final hit against Collino to take the championship.

1980 Moscow C: 33, N: 14, D: 7.24.

		W	L	TG	TR
1. Pascale Trinquet	FRA	4	1	21	16
2. Magda Maros	HUN	3	2	23	17
3. Barbara Wysoczańska	POL	3	2	19	18
4. Ecaterina Stahl (Iencic)	ROM	2	3	19	21
5. Brigitte Latrille-Gaudin	FRA	2	3	20	22
6. Dorina Vaccaroni	ITA	1	4	14	22
7. Katarina Loksova	CZE				
7. Delfina Skapska	POL				

1984 Los Angeles-Long Beach C: 42, N: 18, D: 8.3.
1. Luan Jujie — CHN
2. Cornelia Hanisch — GER
3. Dorina Vaccaroni — ITA
4. Elisabeta Guzganu — ROM
5. Véronique Brouquier — FRA
6. Laurence Modaine — FRA
7. Sabine Bischoff — GER
8. Brigitte Gaudin (Latrille) — FRA
   Final: Luan 8–3 Hanisch
   3rd Place: Vaccaroni 8–5 Guzganu

Luan, a 25-year-old from Nanjing, finished the tournament with a record of 17 wins and 2 losses. Hanisch had entered the final at 16–1.

1988 Seoul C: 45, N: 19, D: 9.22.
1. Anja Fichtel — GER
2. Sabine Bau — GER
3. Zita-Eva Funkenhauser — GER
4. Zsuzsanna Jánosi — HUN
5. Tatyana Sadovskaya — SOV/RUS
6. Gertrúd Stefanek — HUN
7. Sun Hongyun — CHN
8. Yelena Glikina — SOV/RUS
   Final: Fichtel 8–5 Bau
   3rd Place: Funkenhauser 8–7 Jánosi

The final was a rematch of the 1986 world championship, in which then-18-year-old Fichtel defeated Bau 8–3. Kerstin Palm of Sweden, who finished twenty-ninth, became the first woman in any sport to compete in seven Olympics. Her first appearance was in 1964.

1992 Barcelona C: 46, N: 19, D: 7.30.
1. Giovanna Trillini — ITA
2. Wang Huifeng — CHN
3. Tatyana Sadovskaya — RUS
4. Laurence Modaine — FRA
5. Margherita Zalaffi — ITA
6. Reka Szabó — ROM
7. Sabine Bau — GER
8. Fiona McIntosh — GBR
   Final: Trillini—Wang 5–6, 5–3, 6–5
   3rd Place: Sadovskaya—Modaine 5–1, 1–5, 5–3

The 1992 tournament was unusually competitive. All four semifinalists qualified through repêchage. Trillini, although the defending world champion, lost four of her

first nine bouts. In the semis, Wang defeated Modaine 5–0, 2–5, 5–3 and Trillini outlasted Sadovskaya 5–2, 3–5, 5–3. In the third match of the final Trillini led 3–1 with only 24 seconds remaining. But Wang was able to score twice and force a deciding point. However, it was Trillini who struck first to win the dramatic marathon.

FOIL, TEAM

1896–1956 not held

1960 Rome T: 12, N: 12, D: 9.3.
1. SOV (Tatyana Petrenko, Valentina Rastvorova, Lyudmila Shishova, Valentina Prudskova, Aleksandra Zabelina, Galina Gorokhova)
2. HUN (Györgyi Szekely, Ildikó Ujlaki-Reijtö, Magdolna Kovács-Nyári, Katalin Juhász, Lidia Dömölky)
3. ITA (Irene Camber, Velleda Cesari, Antonella Ragno, Bruna Colombetti, Claudia Pasini)
4. GER (Heidi Schmid, Helga Mees, Helga Stroh, Helmi Höhle, Gudrun Theuerkauff, Rosemarie Weiss)
5. FRA (Monique Leroux, Regine Veronnet, Françoise Mailliard, Renée Garilhe, Kate Delbarre)
5. HOL (Nina Kleyweg, Daniel Van Rossem, Helena Kokkes, Elisa Botbjil)
5. POL (Elżbieta Pawlas, Silwia Julito, Barbara Orzechowska, Genowefa Migas, Wanda Kaczmarczyk)
5. ROM (Ecaterina Lazar, Eugenia Mateianu, Olga Szabó-Orban, Maria Vicol)
   Final: SOV 9–3 HUN
   3rd Place: ITA 9–2 GER

The Soviets received their only scare in the quarterfinals, when they had to rally from a 3–8 deficit to defeat France by two touches. Their final win-loss total was 48–21.

1964 Tokyo T: 10, N: 10, D: 10.17.
1. HUN (Ildikó Ujlaki-Rejtö, Katalin Juhász-Nagy, Lidia Sákovics-Dömölky, Judit Mendelényi-Ágoston, Paula Földessy Marosi)
2. SOV (Galina Gorokhova, Valentina Prudskova, Tatyana Samusenko [Petrenko], Lyudmila Shishova, Valentina Rastvorova)
3. GER (Heidi Schmid, Helga Mees, Rosemarie Scherberger, Gudrun Theuerkauff)
4. ITA (Antonella Ragno, Giovanna Masciotta, Irene Camber, Natalina Sanguineti, Bruna Colombetti)
5. ROM (Olga Szabó-Orban, Ileana Gyulai, Ana Derşidan, Maria Vicol, Ecaterina Iencic)
6. FRA (Catherine Rousselet, Marie-Chantal Depetris, Brigitte Gapais, Annick Level, Colette Revenu)
   Final: HUN 9–7 SOV
   3rd Place: GER 9–5 ITA
   5th Place: ROM 9–6 FRA

1968 Mexico City T: 10, N: 10, D: 10.24.
1. SOV (Aleksandra Zabelina, Yelena Novikova, Galina Gorokhova, Tatyana Samusenko [Petrenko], Svetlana Tširkova)

2. HUN (Ildikó Bóbis, Lidia Sákovics, Ildikó Ujlaki-Rejtö, Mária Gulácsy, Paula Földessy-Marosi)
3. ROM (Ecaterina Stahl [Iencic], Ileana Drimbă [Gyulai], Olga Szabó-Orban, Maria Vicol, Ana Ene-Derşidan)
4. FRA (Cathérine Ceretti, Brigitte Gapais, Marie-Chantal Depetris, Claudette Herbster, Annick Level)
5. GER (Heidi Schmid, Helga Koch, Gudrun Theuerkauff, Monika Pulch, Helga Volz-Mees)
6. ITA (Antonella Ragno, Giulia Lorenzoni, Giovanna Masciotta, Bruna Colombetti, Silvana Sconciafurno)
Final: SOV 9–3 HUN
3rd Place: ROM 8(47)–8(45)FRA
5th Place: GER 8–7 ITA

1972 Munich T: 11, N: 11, D: 9.8.
1. SOV (Yelena Belova [Novikova], Alexandra Zabelina, Tatyana Samusenko [Petrenko], Galina Gorokhova, Svetlana Tširkova)
2. HUN (Ildikó Ságiné-Rejtö [Ujlaki-Rejtö], Ildikó Schwarczenberger [Tordasi], Ildikó Matuscakné-Ronay, Maria Szolnoki, Ildikó Bóbis)
3. ROM (Ileana Gyulai, Ana Pascu [Ene-Derşidan], Ecaterina Stahl [Iencic], Olga Szabó-Orban)
4. ITA (Antonella Ragno-Lonzi, Giulia Lorenzoni, Reka Der Cipriani, Maria Consolata Collino, Giuseppina Bersani)
5. GER (Gudrun Theuerkauff, Irmela Broniecki, Karin Giesselmann, Monika Pulch, Erika Bethmann)
6. FRA (Marie-Chantal Demaille, Catherine Ceretti, Claudie Josland, Brigitte Dumont-Gapais)
7. POL (Halina Balon, Krystyna Urbánska-Machnicka, Jolanta Bebel-Rzymowska, Kamila Skladanowska, Elżbieta Franke)
7. USA (Ruth White, Natalia Clovis, Tanya Adamovich, Harriet King, Ann O'Donnell)
Final: SOV 9–5 HUN
3rd Place: ROM 9–7 ITA
5th Place: GER 8–7 FRA

The Soviet team compiled a record of 52 wins and 20 losses. They were led by Belova (17–3) and Zabelina (14–4).

1976 Montreal T: 13, N: 13, D: 7.28.
1. SOV (Yelena Belova [Novikova], Olga Kniazeva, Valentina Sidorova, Nailya Gilyazova, Valentina Nikonova)
2. FRA (Brigitte Latrille, Brigitte Dumont-Gapais, Christine Muzio, Véronique Trinquet, Claudie Josland)
3. HUN (Ildikó Schwarczenberger [Tordasi], Edit Kovács, Magda Maros, Ildikó Ságiné-Rejtö [Ujlaki-Rejtö], Ildikó Bóbis)
4. GER (Karin Rutz, Cornelia Hanisch, Ute Kircheis, Brigitte Oertel, Jutta Höhne)
5. ITA (Maria Consolata Collino, Giulia Lorenzoni, Doriana Pigliapoco, Susanna Batazzi, Carola Mangiarotti)
6. POL (Jolanta Bebel-Rzymowska, Barbara Wysoczańska, Kamilla Mazurowska-Skladanowska, Krystyna Urbańska-Machnicka, Grażyna Staszak-Makowska)
7. GBR (Wendy Agar, Susan Wrigglesworth, Hilary Cawthorne, Clare Halsted, Susan Green)

7. ROM (Ileana Jenei [Gyulai, Drimbă], Marcela Moldovan, Ecaterina Stahl [Iencic], Ana Pascu [Ene-Derşidan], Magdalena Bartos)
Final: SOV 9–2 FRA
3rd Place: HUN 9–4 GER
5th Place: ITA 9–7 POL

The U.S.S.R. won almost without competition, with 50 wins and only 13 losses. Belova was 13–0 and Kniazeva 11–2. The final victory came on Belova's 29th birthday.

1980 Moscow T: 9, N: 9, D: 7.27.
1. FRA (Brigitte Latrille-Gaudin, Pascale Trinquet, Isabelle Boeri-Bégard, Véronique Brouquier, Christine Muzio)
2. SOV (Valentina Sidorova, Nailya Gilyazova, Yelena Belova [Novikova], Irina Ushakova, Larissa Tsagarayeva)
3. HUN (Ildikó Schwarczenberger [Tordasi], Magda Maros, Gertrud Stefanek, Zsuzsa Szöcz, Edit Kovács)
4. POL (Delfina Skapska, Agnieszka Dubrawska, Jolanta Królikowska, Barbara Wysoczańska, Kamila Mazurowska-Skladanowska)
5. ITA (Dorina Vaccaroni, Anna Rita Sparaciari, Susanna Batazzi, Carola Mangiarotti, Clara Mochi)
6. CUB (Margarita Rodriguez Vargas, Marlene Font Kindelan, Maria Garcia Pascau, Clara Alfonso Freire, Mercedes del Risco Randich)
7. GBR (Susan Wrigglesworth, Ann Brannon, Wendy Grant, Linda Martin, Hilary Cawthorne)
8. GDR (Mandy Niklaus, Gabriele Janke, Sabine Hertrampf, Beate Schubert, Marion Schulze)
Final: FRA 9–6 SOV
3rd Place: HUN 9–7 POL
5th Place: ITA 9–6 CUB

1984 Los Angeles-Long Beach T: 10, N: 10, D: 8.7.
1. GER (Christiane Weber, Cornelia Hanisch, Sabine Bischoff, Zita-Eva Funkenhauser, Ute Wessel)
2. ROM (Aurora Dan, Monica Koszto-Veber, Rozalia Oros, Marcela Zsak [Moldovan], Elisabeta Guzganu)
3. FRA (Laurence Modaine, Pascale Trinquet-Hachin, Brigitte Gaudin [Latrille], Véronique Brouquier, Anne Meygret)
4. ITA (Dorina Vaccaroni, Clara Mochi, Margherita Zalaffi, Lucia Traversa, Carola Cicconetti)
5. CHN (Luan Jujie, Zhu Qingyuan, Li Huahua, Wu Qiuhua)
6. USA (Vincent Bradford, Sharon Monplaisir, Susan Badders, Debra Waples, Jana Angelakis)
7. GBR (Ann Brannon, Linda Martin, Fiona McIntosh, Elizabeth Thurley, Katie Arup)
8. JPN (Mieko Miyahara, Azusa Oikawa, Miyuki Maekawa, Tomoko Oka)
Final: GER 9–5 ROM
3rd Place: FRA 9–7 ITA
5th Place: CHN 9–5 USA

The decisive contest was the semifinal matchup between West Germany and Italy. Both sides registered eight wins, but in the final bout, Zita Funkenhauser managed three hits in her loss to Lucia Traversa, giving the West Germans a one touch advantage.

1988 Seoul T: 12, N: 12, D: 9.28.
1. GER (Sabine Bau, Anja Fichtel, Zita-Eva Funkenhauser, Anette Klug, Christiane Weber)
2. ITA (Francesca Bortolozzi, Annapia Gandolfi, Lucia Traversa, Dorina Vaccaroni, Margherita Zalaffi)
3. HUN (Zsuzsanna Jánosi, Edit Kovács, Gertrúd Stefanek, Zsuzsa Szöcs, Katalin Tuschák)
4. SOV/ (Yelena Glikina, Yelena Grishina, Tatyana Sadovskaya,
   RUS Marina Soboleva, Olga Voshchakina)
5. CHN (Li Huahua, Luan Jujie, Sun Hongyun, Xiao Aihua, Zhu Qingyuan)
6. USA (Caitlin Bilodeau, Elaine Cheris, Sharon Monplaisir, Mary O'Neill)
7. FRA (Brigitte Gaudin [Latrille], Gisèle Meygret, Laurence Modaine, Nathalie Pallet, Isabelle Spennato)
8. KOR (Kim Jin-soon, Shin Sung-ja, Tak Jung-im, Yoon Jung-sook)
   Final: GER 9–4 ITA
   3rd Place: HUN 9–2 SOV
   5th Place: CHN 8(61)–8(60) USA
   7th Place: FRA 9–4 KOR

The West Germans whipped their five opponents, registering 45 wins against only 15 losses. Weber was 14–1 and Fichtel 12–2.

1992 Barcelona T: 12, N: 12, D: 8.4.
1. ITA (Diana Bianchedi, Francesca Bortolozzi, Giovanna Trillini, Dorina Vaccaroni, Margherita Zalaffi)
2. GER (Sabine Bau, Annette Dobmeier, Anja Fichtel-Mauritz, Zita-Eva Funkenhauser, Monika Weber-Koszto [Koszto-Veber]
3. ROM (Laura Badea, Roxana Dumitrescu, Claudia Grigorescu, Reka Szabo, Elisabeta Tufan [Gunganzu])
4. RUS (Yelena Glikina, Yelena Grishina, Tatyana Sadovskaya, Olga Velichko, Olga Voshchakina)
5. FRA (Camille Couzi, Gisèle Meygret, Laurence Modaine, Julie-Anne Gross, Isabelle Spennato)
6. CHN (E Jie, Liang Jun, Wang Huifeng, Xiao Aihua, Ye Lin)
7. HUN (Gabriella Lantos, Ildikó Mincza, Zsuzsanna Némethné-Jánosi, Ildikó Pusztai, Gertrúd Stefanek)
8. POL (Katarzyne Felusiak, Monika Maciejewska, Anna Sobczak, Barbara Szewczyk, Agnieszka Szuchnicka)
   Final: ITA 9–6 GER
   3rd Place: ROM 8(60)–8(55) RUS
   5th Place: FRA 9–5 CHN
   7th Place: HUN 9–7 POL

The Italians dominated the tournament, winning 45 matches and losing only 13. Bianchedi was 15–0 and Zalaffi 15–1.

ÉPÉE, INDIVIDUAL

This event will be held for the first time in 1996.

ÉPÉE, TEAM

This event will be held for the first time in 1996.

FIELD HOCKEY

Field hockey is played on a field, or pitch, of artificial turf 100 yards long and 60 yards wide. There are eleven players on a team, including a goalie. Using sticks that are flat on one side and curved on the other, each team hits and dribbles the ball down the field and tries to shoot it past the goalie into a goal that is 7 feet high and 12 feet wide. The ball is small—slightly larger than a baseball. Only the flat side of the stick may be used to strike the ball. The sticks are between 36 and 38 inches long. Except for the goalie, players may not touch the ball with their hands or their bodies. Matches are divided into two 35-minute halves. If play is suspended to deal with an injury, the missed time is added to the end of the second half. If the score is tied after 90 minutes, a 30-minute overtime period, divided into two halves, is played. In pool play ties after 120 minutes are allowed to stand, but once the elimination rounds begin, ties are decided by penalty-stroke shootouts. Penalty strokes are taken from seven yards out; the ball may be pushed or flicked, but not hit. The goalie may not move his feet until the ball has been played.

Many of the rules of field hockey are similar to those of soccer. For example, an offside rule is enforced. If a player crosses the line 25 yards from the opponent's goal, either the ball or two defenders must be between the player and the goal. There are certain rules that are specific to field hockey. All shots on goal must be taken within the striking circle, which extends in a semicircle 16 yards from the goal. Players are not allowed to shield the ball from an opponent with their bodies or with their sticks. Another novel aspect of field hockey is the bully, which is the equivalent of a face-off in ice hockey. The ball is placed on the ground between two players, one from each team. Each player taps the ground with his stick once. Then the players tap sticks together three times and go for the ball.

Penalties can be called for (1) striking the ball with the rounded side of the stick, (2) taking part in the play while not holding a stick, (3) kicking, throwing, or otherwise propelling the ball without the stick, (4) wielding the stick in a dangerous manner or aiming the ball at an opponent, (5) interfering with an opponent's stick, (6) kicking, tripping, shoving, or striking an opponent, (7) obstructing play by running between an opponent and the ball or placing one's body or stick between an opponent and the ball. Generally these infractions are penalized by awarding a free hit to the opposing team. However, if the infraction is committed by a defender within the striking circle, the attacking team is awarded a penalty corner or a penalty stroke. A penalty corner is also awarded for a deliberate offense inside the 25-yard line or if the defensive team intentionally plays the ball over the goal line. In a penalty corner the ball is placed on the goal line ten yards from the nearest goal post. One attacking player hits the ball to a teammate standing just outside the striking circle line. All other players on both teams must wait beyond the striking circle or out of bounds and may not move until the ball is struck. Intentional fouls preventing a goal or illegal positioning on penalty corners are penalized by awarding the attacking team a penalty stroke.

Currently, Olympic field hockey tournaments begin with preliminary pool play. The top two teams in each of the two pools advance to the semifinals, while the other teams play off for the remaining places.

MEN

1896–1908 not held

1908 London T: 6, N: 3, D:.10.31.

			W	L	T	PF	PA
1.	GBR	England (Harvey Wood, Harry Freeman, Louis Baillon, John Robinson, Edgar Page, Alan Noble, Percy Rees, Gerald Logan, Stanley Shoveller, Reginald Pridmore, Eric Green)	3	0	0	24	3
2.	GBR	Ireland (Edward Holmes, Henry Brown, Walter Peterson, William Graham, Walter Campbell, Henry Murphy, Charles Power, Richard Gregg, Edward Allman-Smith, Frank Robinson, Robert Kennedy)	1	1	0	4	9
3.	GBR	Scotland (John Burt, Hugh Neilson, Charles Foulkes, Hew Fraser, Alexander Burt, Andrew Dennistoun, Norman Stevenson, Iain Laing, James Harper-Orr, Hugh Walker, William Orchardson)	1	1	0	5	6

3. GBR Wales (W. Bruce Turnbull, Edward Richards, Llewellyn Evans, Charles Shephard, Richard Lyne, Frederick Connah, Frederick Gordon Phillips, Arthur Law, Philip Turnbull, James Ralph Williams, William Pallott)

W	L	T	PF	PA
0	1	0	1	3

Final: ENG 8–1 IRL

1912 not held

1920 Antwerp T: 4, N: 4, D: 9.5.

	W	L	T	PF	PA
1. GBR	3	0	0	17	2

1. GBR (Harry Haslam, John Bennett, Charles Atkin, Harold Cooke, Eric Crockford, Cyril Wilkinson, William Smith, George McGrath, John McBryan, Stanley Shoveller, Reginald "Rex" Crummack, Arthur Leighton, Harold Cassels, C. Sholto Marcon)

2. DEN (Andreas Rasmussen, Hans Christian Herlak, Frans Faber, Erik Husted, Henning Holst, Hans Jörgen Hansen, Hans Adolf Bjerrum, Thorvald Eigenbrod, Svend Blach, Steen Due, Ejvind Blach, Paul Metz)

2	1	0	15	8

3. BEL (Charles Delelienne, Maurice van den Bemden, Raoul Daufresne de la Chevalerie, René Strauwen, Fernand de Montigny, Adolphe Goemaere, Pierre Chibert, Andre Becquet, Raymond Keppens, Pierre Valcke, Jean van Nerom, Robert Gevers, Louis Diercxens, Charles Gniette)

1	2	0	6	19

4. FRA (Paul Haranger, Robert Lelong, Pierre Estrabant, Georges Breuille, Jacques Morise, Edmond Loriol, Désiré Guard, Roland Bedel, André Bounal, Gaston Rogot, Pierre Rollin)

0	3	0	3	12

1924 not held

1928 Amsterdam T: 9, N: 9, D: 5.26.

	W	L	T	PF	PA
1. IND	5	0	0	29	0

1. IND (Richard Allen, Leslie Hammond, Michael Rocque, Sayed Yusuf, Broome Eric Pinniger, Rex Norris, William Cullen, Frederic Seaman, Dhyan Chand, George Marthins, Maurice Gateley, Jaipal Singh, Shaukat Ali, Feroze Khan)

2. HOL (Adrian Katte, Reindert de Waal, Albert Tresling, Jan Ankerman, Emile Duson, Johannes Brand, August Kop, Gerrit Jannink, Paulus van de Rovaert, Robert van der Veen, Hendrik Visser t'Hooft)

3	1	0	8	5

3. GER (Georg Brunner, Heinz Wöltje, Werner Proft, Erich Zander, Theodor Haag, Werner Freyberg, Herbert Kemmer, Herbert Hobein, Bruno Boche, Herbert Müller, Friedrich Horn, Erwin Franzkowiak, Hans Haussmann, Karl-Heinz Irmer, Aribert Heymann, Kurt Haverbeck, Rolf Wollner, Gerd Strantzen, Heinz Förstendorf)

3	1	0	11	3

4. BEL (Etienne Soubre, Johnny van der Straeten, Corneille Wellens Lambert Adelot, Claude Baudoux, Adolphe Goemaere, An

3	2	0	8	12

Dhyan Chand, star of the Indian field hockey team from 1928 to 1936, later became coach of the national team.

dré Seeldrayers, Charles Delheid, Louis Diercxens, Yvon Baudoux, Charles Koning, Freddy Cattoir, Louis de Deken, Emile Vercken, Auguste Goditiabois, Georges Grosjean, René Mallieux)

Final: IND 3–0 HOL
3rd Place: GER 3–0 BEL

The first Indian hockey clubs were formed in Calcutta in 1885. In 1926 India played its initial international matches against New Zealand. But it was the 1928 Olympics in Amsterdam that established India as the world's number-one power in field hockey. Led by 22-year-old Dhyan Chand, an army captain from Uttar Pradesh, the Indians whipped through the tournament without giving up a single goal. Chand eventually won three Olympic gold medals and later became coach of the Indian national team.

1932 Los Angeles T: 3, N: 3, D: 8.11.

		W	L	T	PF	PA
1. IND	(Richard Allen, Arthur Hind, Carlyle Tapsell, Leslie Hammond, Masud Minhas, Broome Eric Pinniger, Lal Shah Bokhari, Richard Carr, Gurmit Singh Kullar, Dhyan Chand, Roop Singh, Sayed Mohammed Jaffar, Muhammed Aslam, Frank Brewin, William Sullivan)	2	0	0	35	2
2. JPN	(Shumkichi Hamada, Akio Sohda, Sadayoshi Kobayashi, Katsumi Shibata, Yoshio Sakai, Eiichi Nakamura, Haruhiko Kon, Hiroshi Nagata, Kenichi Konishi, Toshio Usami, Junzo Inohara)	1	1	0	10	13
3. USA	(Harold Brewster, Samuel Ewing, Leonard O'Brien, Henry Greer, James Gentle, Horace Disston, Lawrence Knapp, Charles Shaeffer, Amos Deacon, William Boddington, David McMullin, Frederick Wolters, Roy Coffin)	0	2	0	3	33

Interest in hockey spread rapidly throughout India following the Olympic triumph of 1928. When it came time to raise money to send a team to the Los Angeles Olympics, a journalist representing the Indian Hockey Federation approached Mahatma Gandhi and asked him to issue an appeal to the masses. Gandhi's only reply was, "What's hockey?" Nevertheless, an Indian team did make it to Los Angeles, paying its way by playing exhibition matches in Europe on the way home. The Indians had no problems with the competition, defeating Japan, 11–1, and the United States, 24–1. In the latter game, which

had the highest score ever achieved in an international match, Roop Singh scored twelve goals and Dhyan Chand seven.

1936 Berlin T: 11, N: 11, D: 8.15.

		W	L	T	PF	PA
1. IND	(Richard Allen, Carlyle Tapsell, Mohomed Hussain, Baboo Narsoo Nimal, Earnest Cullen, Joseph Galibardy, Shabban Shahab-ud-Din, Ali Iqtidar Shah Dara, Dhyan Chand, Roop Singh, Sayed Mohammed Jaffar, Cyril Michie, Paul Peter Fernandes, Joseph Phillip, Garewal Gurcharan Singh, Ahsan Mohomed Khan, Ahmed Sher Khan, Lionel Emmett, Mirza Nasir-ud-Din Masood)	5	0	0	38	1
2. GER	(Karl Dröse, Herbert Kemmer, Erich Zander, Alfred Gerdes, Erwin Keller, Heinrich Schmalix, Harald Huffmann, Werner Hamel, Kurt Weiss, Hans Scherbart, Fritz Messner, Tito Warnholtz, Detlef Okrent, Hermann Auf der Heide, Heinrich Peter, Carl Menke, Heinz Raack, Paul Mehlitz, Ludwig Beisiegel, Karl Ruck, Erich Cuntz, Werner Kubitzki)	3	1	0	14	9
3. HOL	(Jan de Looper, Reindert de Waal, Max Westerkamp, Hendrik de Looper, Rudolf van der Haar, Antoine van Lierop, Pieter Gunning, Henri Schnitger, Ernst Willem van den Berg, Agathon de Roos, René Sparenberg, Carl Haybroek)	3	1	1	13	10
4. FRA	(Raymond Tixier, Guy Chevalier, Paul Imbault, Claude Graveraux, Félix Grimonprez, François Verger, Paul Sartorius, Anatole Vologe, Joseph Goubert, Claude Soulé, Claude Roques, Etienne Guibal, Michel Verkindere, Marcel Lachmann, Guy Hénon, Emmanuel Gonat, Jean Rouget, Charles Imbault, Robert Rousse)	2	3	0	7	19

Final: IND 8–1 GER
3rd Place: HOL 4–3 FRA

As a British colony, India was forced to march behind the flag of Great Britain. But in the dressing room before their final match against Germany, the Indian team saluted the tricolor flag of the Indian National Congress. The Germans fought hard and trailed only 1–0 at halftime. But the Indians wore them down after the break, winning 8–1, with Dhyan Chand scoring six goals while playing barefoot.

1948 London T: 13, N: 13, D: 8.13.

		W	L	T	PF	PA
1. IND	(Leo Pinto, Trilochan Singh, Randhir Singh Gentle, Keshava Datt, Amir Kumar, Maxie Vaz, Kishan Lal, Kunwar Digvijai Singh, Grahanandan Singh, Patrick Jansen, Lawrie Fernandes, Ranganandhan Francis, Akhtar Hussain, Leslie Claudius, Jaswant Rajput, Reginald Rodrigues, Latifur Rehman, Balbir Singh, Walter D'Souza, Gerry Glacken)	5	0	0	25	2
2. GBR	(David Brodie, George Sime, William Lindsay, Michael Walford, Frank Reynolds, F. Robin Lindsay, John Peake, W. Neil White, Robert Adlard, Norman Borrett, William Griffiths, Ronald Davies)	3	1	1	21	4
3. HOL	(Antonius Richter, Henri Derckx, Johan Drijver, Jenne Langhout, Hermanus Loggere, Edouard Tiel, Willem van Heel, Andries Boerstra, Pieter Bromberg, Jan Kruize, Rius Esser, Henricus Bouwman)	4	2	1	17	11
4. PAK	(Mohamad Anwar Beg Moghal, Mohamad Niaz Khan, Mohamad Abdul Razzao, Hamid Ullah Khan Burki, Abdul Ghafoor Khan, Shah-Rukh Shahzada, Ahmed Masud, M. Shaikh, Iqtidar Ali Shah Dara, Abdul Aziz, Rhamat Ullah Shaikh, Sayed Mohamed Saleem, Khurrum Shahzada, Mohamed Khawaja Taki, Mukhtar Bhatti, Abdul Hamid, Mohamad D'Mello, Abdul Qayyum Khan, Azziz-ur-Rahman Khan, Mohmood Ul Hassan)	4	2	1	25	7

Final: IND 4–0 GBR
3rd Place: HOL 1–1 PAK
3rd Place Replay: HOL 4–1 PAK

Ever since India first appeared on the international field hockey scene, Great Britain had studiously avoided playing the Indian team, apparently afraid of the embarrassment of losing to one of its colonies. However in 1948 India gained not only its independence from Britain, but also a chance to face its former mentor in what had now become the Indian national sport. The match for first place turned out to be no contest, as Great Britain, which had advanced to the final without giving up a goal, was itself shut out, 4–0.

1952 Helsinki T: 12, N: 12, D: 7.24.

		W	L	T	PF	PA
1. IND	(Ranganandhan Francis, Dharam Singh, Randhir Singh Gentle, Leslie Claudius, Keshava Datt, Govind Perumal, Raghbir Lal, Kunwar Digvijai Singh, Balbir Singh, Udham Singh, Muniswarmy Rajagopal, Chinadorai Deshmutu, Meldric St. Clair Daluz, Grahanandan Singh)	3	0	0	13	2
2. HOL	(Laurentz Mulder, Henri Derckx, Johan Drijver, Julius Ancion, Hermanus Loggere, Edouard Tiel, Willem van Heel, Rius Esser, Jan Hendrik Kruize, Andries Boerstra, Leonard Wery, Andries Dirk)	2	1	0	3	6
3. GBR	(Graham Dadds, Roger Midgley, Denys Carnill, John Cockett, Dennis Eagan, Anthony Robinson, Anthony Nunn, Robin Fletcher, Richard Norris, John Conroy, John Taylor, Derek Day, Neil Nugent)	2	1	0	4	4
4. PAK	(Abdul Waheed Qazl, Mohamad Niaz Khan, Asghar Ali Khan, Jack Britto, Manzoor Hussain Atif, Habib Ali Kiddi, Mahmudal Hassan, Abdul Hamid, Abdul Aziz Mallick, Habibur Rehman, Latifur Rehman, Abdul Latif Mir, Safdor Bahul, Mohamad Rafique Khan, Fazar Ur Rehman, Abdul Qayyum Khan, Azmat)	1	2	0	7	3

Final: IND 6–1 HOL
3rd Place: GBR 2–1 PAK

Nine of India's 13 goals were scored by Balbir Singh, a police inspector from Punjab.

1956 Melbourne T: 12, N: 12, D: 12.6.

		W	L	T	PF	PA
1. IND	(Shankar Laxman, Bakshish Singh, Randhir Singh Gentle, Leslie Claudius, Amir Kumar, Govind Perumal, Raghbir Lal, Gurdev Singh, Balbir Singh, Udham Singh, Raghbir Singh Bhola, Charles Stephen, Ranganandhan Francis, Balkrishnan Singh, Amit Singh Bakshi, Kaushik Haripal, Hardyal Singh)	5	0	0	38	0
2. PAK	(Zakir Hussain, Munir Ahmad Dar, Manzoor Hussain Atif, Ghulam Rasul, Anwar Ahmad Khan, Hussain Mussarat, Noor Alam, Abdul Hamid, Habibur	3	1	1	10	4

Rehman, Nasir Ahmad, Mutih Ullah, Latifur Rehman Akhtar Hussain, Habib Ali Kiddi)

			W	L	T	PF	PA
3.	GER	(Alfred Lücker, Helmut Nonn, Günther Brennecke, Werner Delmes, Eberhard Ferstl, Hugo Dollheiser, Heinz Radzikowski, Wolfgang Nonn, Hugo Budinger, Werner Rosenbaum, Günther Ullerich)	2	1	2	8	6
4.	GBR	(David Archer, John Strover, Denys Carnill, John Cockett, Francis Davis, Anthony Robinson, Frederick Hugh Scott, Neil Forster, David Thomas, John Conroy, Michael Doughty, Steven Johnson, Colin Dale, Geoffrey Cutter)	2	2	2	9	10
5.	AUS	(Louis Hailey, Alan Barblett, Desmond Spackman, Kevin Carton, Keith Leeson, Dennis Kemp, Raymond Whiteside, Ian Dick, Melville Pearce, Eric Pearce, Gordon Pearce, Maurice Foley)	2	2	0	6	5
6.	NZE	(David Goldsmith, Brian Johnston, Reginald Johansson, John Tynan, Murray Loudon, John Abrams, Archie Currie, Noel Hobson, Guy McGregor, Bruce Turner, Ivan Armstrong, Phillip Bygrave, William Schaefer)	1	2	0	8	10

Final: IND 1–0 PAK
3rd Place: GER 3–1 GBR

India began confidently with victories of 14–0 over Afghanistan and 16–0 over the United States. However they barely got by a roughhouse German team, 1–0, in the semifinal, and they won the final by the same score on a short corner hit by Gentle midway through the second half.

1960 Rome T: 16, N: 16, D: 9.9.

			W	L	T	PF	PA
1.	PAK	(Abdul Rashid, Bashir Ahmad, Manzoor Hussain Atif, Ghulam Rasul, Anwar Ahmad Khan, Habib Ali Kiddi, Noor Alam, Abdul Hamid, Abdul Waheed, Nasir Ahmad, Mutih Ullah, Mushtaq Ahmad, Munir Ahmad Dar, Khurshid Aslam)	6	0	0	25	1
2.	IND	(Shankar Laxman, Prithipal Singh, Jaman Lal Sharma, Leslie Claudius, Joseph Antic, Mohinder Lal, Joginder Singh, John Peter, Jaswant Singh, Udham Singh, Raghbir Singh Bhola. Charanjit Singh, Govind Savant)	5	1	0	19	2
3.	SPA	(Pedro Amat Fontanals, Francisco Caballer Soteras, Juan Angel Calzado de Castro, José Colomer Rivas, Carlos Del Coso Iglesias, José Antonio Dinarés Massagué, Eduardo Dualde Santos de Lamadrid, Joaquin Dualde Santos · de Lamadrid, Rafael Egusquiza Basterra, Ignacio Macaya Santos de Lamadrid, Pedro Murúa Leguizamón, Pedro Roig Junyent, Luis María Usoz Quintana, Narciso Ventalló Surralles)	4	1	1	11	4
4.	GBR	(Harold Cahill, John Neill, Denys Carnill, Charles Jones, F. Howard Davis, Neil Livingstone, Ian Taylor, John Hindle, Stuart Mayes, Frederick Hugh Scott, Derek Miller, Peter Croft, John Bell, Christopher Saunders-Griffiths, Patrick Austen)	3	2	1	7	5
5.	NZE	(William Schaefer, John Abrams, Ian Kerr, Bruce Turner, John Cullen, John Ross Gillespie, Anthony Hayde, Guy McGregor, Noel Hobson, Mervyn McKinnon, Phillip Bygrave, James Barclay, Kelvin Percy, Murray Mathieson)	4	3	1	10	9
6.	AUS	(Louis Hailey, William Spackman, Mervyn Crossman, John McBryde, Kevin Carton, Julian Pearce, Gordon Pearce, Michael Craig, Raymond Evans, Eric Pearce, Donald Currie, Phillip Pritchard, Graham Wood, Errol Bill, Barry Malcolm)	4	3	2	16	10
7.	GER	(Wolfgang End, Helmut Nonn, Günther Ullerich, Dieter Krause, Werner Delmes, Eberhard Ferstl, Klaus Woller, Carsten Keller, Hugo Budinger, Norbert Schuler, Herbert Winters, Christian Buchting, Willi Brendel, Klaus Greinert)	2	3	0	11	4
7.	KEN	(George Saudi, Anthony Vaz, Sohal Avtar Singh, Jagnandan Singh, Deol Surjeet Singh, Silvester Fernandes, Edgar Fernandes, Hilary Fernandes, Panaser Surjeet Singh, Sandhu Pritan Singh, John Simonian, Gurarian Kirpal Singh, Egbert Fernandes, Aloysius Mendonca, Krishan Aggarwal, Sehmi Cursarah Singh)	2	2	2	11	5

Final: PAK 1–0 IND
3rd Place: SPA 2–1 GBR

INDIA'S FIELD HOCKEY WINNING STREAK

1928			1948			1960		
IND	6–0	AUS	IND	8–0	AUS	IND	10–0	DEN
IND	9–0	BEL	IND	9–1	ARG	IND	4–1	HOL
IND	5–0	DEN	IND	2–0	SPA	IND	3–0	NZE
IND	5–0	SWI	IND	2–1	HOL	IND	1–0	AUS
IND	3–0	HOL	IND	4–0	GBR	IND	1–0	GER

1932			1952		
IND	11–1	JPN	IND	4–0	AUS
IND	24–1	USA	IND	3–1	GBR
			IND	6–1	HOL

1936			1956		
IND	4–0	HUN	IND	14–0	AFG
IND	7–0	USA	IND	16–0	USA
IND	9–0	JPN	IND	6–0	SIN
IND	10–0	FRA	IND	1–0	GER
IND	8–1	GER	IND	1–0	PAK

The early rounds saw some surprising incidents. In the quarterfinal contest between Germany and Pakistan, the score was tied 1–1 with only a few minutes to play. A penalty was called against Ullerich of Germany for illegally blocking a shot with his hand. The referee, Asselmann of Belgium, ordered a bully, or face-off. When a bully is called, two players, one from each team, touch sticks three times and then go after the ball. Ullerich bullied off for the Germans, but only touched sticks twice. The referee caught him and ordered the bully repeated. Again Ullerich struck before the third touch. This time the referee awarded a goal to Pakistan, a goal which gave Pakistan a 2–1 victory. The next day a consolation match was held between France and Belgium. With the score 0–0 and the French attacking, an Italian traffic policeman, on duty just outside the field, blew his whistle. The Belgians thought it was an umpire's whistle and stopped playing, whereupon the French team knocked the ball into the net for what proved to be the only goal of the game. Meanwhile India was forced into double overtime in the quarterfinals before they were able to defeat Australia, 1–0. But that was nothing compared to the Great Britain–Kenya match that followed. That contest went into six overtimes before Saunders of Great Britain scored to give the British a 2–1 victory after 127 minutes of play. The semifinals were tense contests, with both Pakistan and India scoring early and holding on for 1–0 wins over Spain and Great Britain, respectively. Entering the final, India had a cumulative Olympic record of 30 wins and no losses, their teams having scored 197 goals while allowing only eight. Unintimidated, the Pakistanis attacked aggressively from the beginning. After 12 min-

utes Nasir Ahmad of Pakistan pushed a goal into the corner of the net. Despite vigorous play on both sides, that was the only score of the match. The Pakistanis were ecstatic, and most observers were thrilled to have seen such a hard-fought match. But back in India the loss to Pakistan was considered a national tragedy, and plans were immediately made to regain the Olympic title in Tokyo in 1964.

1964 Tokyo T: 15, N: 15, D: 10.23.

		W	L	T	PF	PA
1. IND	(Shankar Laxman, Prithipal Singh, Dharam Singh, Mohinder Lal, Charanjit Singh, Gurbux Singh, Joginder Singh, John Peter, Harbinder Singh, Kaushik Haripal, Darshan Singh, Jagjit Singh, Bandu Patil, Udham Singh, Ali Sayeed)	7	0	2	22	5
2. PAK	(Abdul Hamid, Munir Ahmad Dar, Manzoor Hussain Atif, Saeed Anwar, Anwar Ahmad Khan, Muhammad Rashid, Khalid Mahmood, Zaka-ud-Din, Muhammad Afzal Manna, Mohammad Asad Malik, Mutih Ullah, Tariq Niazi, Zafar Hayat, Khurshid Azam, Khizar Nawaz, Tariq Aziz)	7	1	0	20	4
3. AUS	(Paul Dearing, Donald McWatters, Brian Glencross, John McBryde, Julian Pearce, Graham Wood, Robin Hodder, Raymond Evans, Eric Pearce, Patrick Nilan, Donald Smart, Antony Waters, Mervyn Crossman, Desmond Piper)	5	3	0	20	10
4. SPA	(Carlos Del Coso Iglesias, José Colomer Rivas, Julio Solaun Garteizgogeascoa, Juan Angel Calzado de Castro, José Antonio Dinarés Massagué, Narciso Ventalló Surralles, Ignacio Macaya Santos de Lamadrid, Jaime Amat Fontanals, Eduardo Dualde Santos de Lamadrid, Jorge Vidal Mitjans, Jaime Echevarria Arteche, Luis María Usoz Quintana, Pedro Amat Fontanals, Francisco Amat Fontanals)	4	2	3	18	9
5. GDR	(Rainer Stephan, Axel Thieme, Klaus Vetter, Horst Brennecke, Klaus Bahner, Horst Dahmlos, Reiner Hanschke, Rolf Westphal, Lothar Lippert, Dieter Ehrlich, Adolf Krause, Karl-Heinz Freiberger)	4	0	5	17	5
6. KEN	(John Simonian, Anthony Querobino Vaz, Avtar Singh	4	3	1	10	13

Soñal, Surjeet Singh Panesar, Silvester Fernandes, Leo Fernandes, Edgar Simon Fernandes, Egbert Carmo Fernandes, Amar Singh Mangat, Aloysius Mendonca, Saude André George, Krishan Kumar Aggarwal, Tejparkash Singh Brar, Reynold D'Souza, Santokh Singh Matharu)

		W	L	T	PF	PA
7.	HOL (Joost Boks, Jacob Leemhius, Jan van Gooswilligen, Johan Fokker, Franciscus Fiolet, Theodorus Terlingen, Theo van Vroonhoven, Arie Leendert de Keyzer, Guillaume Zweerts, Jacob Voigt, Nicolaas Spits, Jan Veentjer, John Elffers, Leendert Krol, Jan van Hooft, Johan Mijnarends, Eric van Rossem, Charles Coster van Voorhout)	4	3	1	21	7
7.	JPN (Hiroshi Miwa, Tsuneya Yuzaki, Akio Takashima, Katsuhiro Yuzaki, Tetsuya Wakabayashi, Toshihiko Yamaoka, Kenji Takizawa, Shigeo Kadku, Hiroshi Tanaka, Michio Okabe, Seiji Kihara, Junichi Yamaguchi, Kunio Iwahashi)	3	4	0	7	11

Final: IND 1–0 PAK
3rd Place: AUS 3–2 SPA
5th Place: GDR 3–0 KEN

India struggled through to the final, surviving 1–1 ties with Germany and Spain. Pakistan, on the other hand, won seven straight matches. However, in the deciding contest, with five minutes gone in the second half, Munir Ahmad Dar of Pakistan was penalized for stopping a shot with his foot. Mohinder Lal converted the penalty shot for the only goal of the game.

1968 Mexico City T: 16, N: 16, D: 10.26.

		W	L	T	PF	PA
1.	PAK (Zakir Hussain, Tanvir Ahmad Dar, Tariq Aziz, Saeed Anwar, Riaz Ahmed, Gulrez Akhtar, Khalid Mahmood Hussain, Mohammad Ashfaq, Abdul Rashid, Mohammad Asad Malik, Jahangir Ahmad Butt, Riaz-ud-Din, Tariq Niazi)	9	0	0	26	5
2.	AUS (Paul Dearing, James Mason, Brian Glencross, Gordon Pearce, Julian Pearce, Robert Haigh, Donald Martin, Raymond Evans, Ronald Riley, Patrick Nilan, Donald Smart, Desmond Piper, Eric Pearce, Frederick Quinn)	5	3	1	15	8
3.	IND (Rajendra Absolem Christy,	7	2	0	23	7

Gurbux Singh, Prithipal Singh, Balbir Singh II, Ajitpal Singh, Krishnamurtay Perumal, Balbir Singh III, Balbir Singh I, Harbinder Singh, Inamur Rehman, Inder Singh, Munir Sait, Harmik Singh, Jagjit Singh, John Peter, Tarsem Singh, Gurbaksh Singh)

		W	L	T	PF	PA
4.	GER (Wolfgang Rott, Günter Krauss, Utz Aichinger, Dirk Michel, Klaus Greinert, Ulrich Vos, Michael Krause, Norbert Schuler, Fritz Schmidt, Carsten Keller, Ulrich Sloma, Wolfgang Müller, Eckart Suhl, Friedrich-Wilhelm Josten, Jürgen Wein, Detlef Kittstein, Wolfgang Baumgart, Hermann End)	5	3	1	16	8
5.	HOL (Joost Boks, Theodorus Terlingen, Heiko Locker van Staveren, Charles de Lanoy Meijer, Johan Fokker, John Elffers, Frans Spits, Otto Boudewijn ter Haar, Charles Thole, Petrus Weemers, Arie de Keyzer, Aernout Brederode, Ewaldus Kist, Sebo Onno Ebbens, Theo van Vroonhoven, Gerardus Hijikema, Edo Buma)	6	3	0	15	12
6.	SPA (Carlos Del Coso Iglesias, Antonio Nogues, Julio Solaun Garteizgogeascoa, Francisco Fábregas Bosch, José Antonio Dinarés Massagué, Juan Amat Fontanals, Juan Quintana Bosch, José Salles Salva, Francisco Amat Fontanals, Pedro Amat Fontanals, Agustín Masana, José Colomer Rivas, Jorge Fábregas, Narciso Ventalló Surralles, Rafael Camina, Jorge Vidal Mitjans, Juan José Alvear Calleja)	3	3	3	9	7
7.	NZE (Ross McPherson, Roger Capey, Alan Patterson, Keith Thomson, Selwyn Maister, John Anslow, Bruce Judge, John Christensen, Alan McIntyre, Barry Maister, Jan Borren, Edwin Salmon, John Hicks)	3	1	4	9	7
8.	KEN (John Simonian, Kirpal Bhardwaj, Avtar Singh Sohal, Harvinder Marwa, Surjeet Singh Panesar, Silvester Fernandes, Leo Fernandes, Santokh Singh Matharu, Davinder Deegan, Hilary Fernandes, Aloysius Mendonca, Mohamed Malik, Egbert Fernandes, Reynold Pereira)	4	3	1	12	8

Final: PAK 2–1 AUS
3rd Place: IND 2–1 GER
5th Place: HOL 1–0 SPA
7th Place: NZE 2–0 KEN

With the score tied 0–0 after 55 minutes in a preliminary match between India and Japan, a penalty stroke was awarded to India. The Japanese were so upset that they laid down their sticks and walked off the field, forfeiting the game. Earlier, India had lost to New Zealand, 2–1—the first time that India had given up more than one goal in an Olympic match. They lost their semifinal match to Australia by the same score. In the final, the winning goal was scored by Mohammad Asad Malik after 56 minutes of play.

The Australian team included three brothers: Eric, Gordan, and Julian Pearce. A fourth Pearce brother, Mel, represented Australia in 1956.

1972 Munich T: 16, N: 16, D: 9.10.

			W	L	T	PF	PA
1.	GER	(Wolfgang Rott, Michael Peter, Dieter Freise, Michael Krause, Eduard Thelen, Horst Dröse, Carsten Keller, Ulrich Klaes, Wolfgang Baumgart, Uli Vos, Peter Trump, Peter Kraus, Werner Kaessmann, Wolfgang Strödter, Detlef Kittstein, Rainer Seifert, Eckart Suhl, Fritz Schmidt)	8	1	0	21	5
2.	PAK	(Saleem Sherwani, Akhtarul Islam, Munawaruz Zaman, Saeed Anwar, Rasool Akhtar, Fazalur Rehman, Mudassar Asghar, Islahud Din, Abdul Rashid, Mohammad Asad Malik, Mohammad Shahnaz, Riaz Ahmed, Iftikhar Ahmed, Muhammad Zahid, Jahangir Ahmad Butt)	6	2	1	19	7
3.	IND	(Manuel Frederick, Mukhbain Singh, Kindo Michael, Krishnamurtay Perumal, Ajitpal Singh, Harmik Singh, Ganesh Mollerapoovayya, Harbinder Singh, Kulwant Singh, Ashok Kumar, Harcharan Singh, Govin Bilimogaputtaswamy, Virinder Singh, Cornelius Charles)	6	1	2	27	11
4.	HOL	(Andre Bolhuis, Thijs Kaanders, Coen Kranenberg, Thies Kruize, Maarten Sikking, Frans Spits, Nico Spits, Bart Taminiau, Charles Thole, Piet Weemers, Jeroen Zweerts, Wouter Leefers, Flip van Lidth de Jeude, Paul Litjens, Marinus Dijkerman, Irving van Nes)	5	3	1	21	14
5.	AUS	(Brian Glencross, Robert Haigh, Richard Charlesworth, Paul Dearing, Thomas Colder, James Mason, Terry McAskell, Patrick Nilan, Desmond Piper, Ronald Riley, Donald Smart, Gregory Browning, Robert Andrew, Graham Reid, Ronald Wilson, Wayne Hammond)					
6.	GBR	(D. Austin Savage, Paul Svehlik, Tony Ekins, Keith Sinclair, Bernard Cotton, N. Rui Saldanha, Richard Oliver, Michael Crowe, Michael Corby, Peter Marsh, John French, Dennis Hay, Terence Gregg, Peter Mills, Sheikh Mahmood Ahmad, Graham Evans, Christopher Langhorne)	5	3	1	18	12
7.	SPA	(Luis Alberto Carrera, Jorge Fábregas Bosch, Francisco Segura Ruda, Juan Amat Fontanals, Francisco Fábregas Bosch, José Salles Salva, José Alusitza García, José Borrell, Francisco Amat Fontanals, Ramon Quintana Bosch, Juan Arbós Perarnau, Juan Quintana Bosch, Luis Towse Roura, Jorge Camina Borda, Antonio Nogues Dalmases, Agustin Churruca Otero)	3	2	4	11	11
8.	MAL	(Khairuddin Bin Zainal, Belavantheran Francis, Sri Shanmuganathan Naganathy, Poh-meng Phang, Choon-hin Wong, Balasingam Singaram, Siow-ming Yang, Franco D'Cruz, Mahendran Murugesan, Harnahal Sewa Singh, Pathmarajah Ramalingam, Omar Razali Yeop, Sayed Samàt, Sulaiman Saibot, Brian Santa Maria)	4	4	1	11	11

Final: GER 1–0 PAK
3rd Place: IND 2–1 HOL
5th Place: AUS 2–1 GBR
7th Place: SPA 2–1 MAL

The final was a bitter and violent contest, with Michael Krause of Germany scoring the only goal of the game from a penalty corner with ten minutes to play. The Pakistani team and their supporters in the stands were so angry at the officiating that they stormed the judges' table and poured water on René Frank, President of the International Hockey Federation. At the medal ceremony, several of the Pakistani players refused to face the German flag during the playing of the German national anthem. All 11 Pakistani finalists were banned for life by the International Olympic Committee, but reinstated in time for the 1976 Olympics.

AUS row stats: 5, 2, 2, 22, 10

1976 Montreal T: 11, N: 11, D: 7.30.

		W	L	T	PF	PA
1.	NZE (Paul Ackerley, Jeff Archibald, Thur Borren, Alan Chesney, John Christensen, Greg Dayman, Tony Ineson, Alan McIntyre, Barry Maister, Selwyn Maister, Trevor Manning, Arthur Parkin, Mohan Patel, Ramesh Patel)	3	1	2	9	9
2.	AUS (Robert Haigh, Richard Charlesworth, David Bell, Gregory Browning, Ian Cooke, Barry Dancer, Douglas Golder, Wayne Hammond, James Irvine, Malcolm Poole, Robert Proctor, Graham Reid, Ronald Riley, Trevor Smith, Terry Walsh)	4	3	0	16	8
3.	PAK (Saleem Sherwani, Manzoor Hassan, Munawar-Uz-Zaman, Saleem Nazim, Rasool Akhtar, Iftikhar Syed, Islahuddin, Manzoor Hussain, Abdul Rashid, Shanaz Sheikh, Samiulah Khan, Qamar Zia, Arshad Mahmood, Arshad Ali Chaudry, Mudassar Asghar, Haneef Khan)	4	1	1	20	11
4.	HOL (Maarten Sikking, Andre Bolhuis, Tim Steens, Geert van Eijk, Theodoor Doyer, Coen Kranenburg, Rob Toft, Wouter Leefers, Hans Jorritsma, Hans Kruize, Jan Albers, Paul Litjens, Imbert Jebbink, Ron Steens, Bart Taminiau, Wouter Kan)	5	2	0	14	8
5.	GER (Wolfgang Rott, Klaus Ludwiczak, Michael Peter, Dieter Freise, Fritz Schmidt, Michael Krause, Horst Dröse, Werner Kaessmann, Uli Vos, Peter Caninenberg, Peter Trump, Hans Montag, Wolfgang Strödter, Heiner Dopp, Rainer Seifert, Ralf Lauruschkat)	3	2	1	22	13
6.	SPA (Luis Alberto Carrera, Juan Amat Fontanals, Jaime Arbós Serra, Juan Arbós Perarnau, Ricardo Cabot Durán, Juan Colomer, Francisco Codina, Agustin Churruca Otero, Francisco Fábregas Bosch, Jorge Fábregas Bosch, Agustin Masana, Juan Pellón Fernández, Ramon Quintana Bosch, José Salles Salva, Francisco Segura Ruda, Luis Towse Roura)	2	2	2	12	17
7.	IND (Ajitpal Singh, Vaduvelu Phillips, Baldev Singh, Ashok	4	3	0	16	12
	Diwan, Bilimogga Govinda, Ashok Singh, Varinder Singh, Harcharan Singh, Mohinder Singh, Aslam Sher Khan, Syed Ali, Birbhadur Chattri, Chand Singh, Ajit Singh, Surjit Singh, Vasudevan Baskaran)					
8.	MAL (Khairuddin Bin Zainal, Azraai Mohammed Zain, Sri Shanmuganathan Naganathy, Francis Anthonysamy, Kok-ming Lam, Mohindar Singh Amar, Choon-hin Wong, Balasingam Singaram, Palanisamy Nallasamy, Rama Krishnan Rengasamy, Mahendran Murugesan, Avtar Gill Singh, Antony D'Cruz, Fook-loke Poon, Pathmarajah Ramalingam, Soon-kooi Ow)	2	5	0	4	11

Final: NZE 1–0 AUS
3rd Place: PAK 3–2 HOL
5th Place: GER 9–1 SPA
7th Place: IND 2–0 MAL

New Zealand didn't exactly overwhelm their opposition; in fact, they didn't even outscore them. But they scored when it counted, including a penalty shot by Tony Ineson early in the second half that gave them a 1–0 victory over Australia in the final.

1980 Moscow T: 6, N: 6, D: 7.26.

		W	L	T	PF	PA
1.	IND (Allan Schofield, Chettri Bir Bhadur, Dung Dung Sylvanus, Rajinder Singh, Davinder Singh, Gurmail Singh, Ravinder Pal Singh, Baskaran Vasudevan, Somaya Maneypandemuttana, Maharaj Krishon Kaushik, Charanjit Kumar, Mervyn Fernandis, Amarjit Rana Singh, Shahid Mohamed, Zafar Iqbal, Surinder Singh)	4	0	2	43	9
2.	SPA (José Miguel García Messeguer, Juan Amat Fontanals, Santiago Malgosa Morera, Rafael Garralda Garre, Francisco Fábregas Bosch, Juan Luis Coghen Alberdingk, Ricardo Cabot Durán, Jaime Arbós Serra, Carlos Roca Portolés, Juan Pellón Fernández, Miguel De Paz Pla, Miguel Chaves Sánchez, Juan Arbós Perarnau, Javier Cabot Durán, Paulino Monsalve Ballesteros, Jaime Zumalacárregui Benítez)	4	1	1	36	7

		W	L	T	PF	PA
3. SOV	(Vladimir Pleshakov, Vyacheslav Lampeyev, Leonid Pavlovsky, Sos Airapetyan, Farit Zigangirov, Valery Belyakov, Sergei Klevtsov, Oleg Zagorodnev, Aleksandr Gusev, Sergei Pleshakov, Mikhail Nichepurenko, Minneula Azizov, Aleksandr Sytchev, Aleksandr Myasnikov, Viktor Deputatov, Aleksandr Goncharov)	4	2	0	32	12
4. POL	(Zygfryd Józefiak, Andrzej Mikina, Krystian Bąk, Wlodzimierz Stanislawski, Leszek Hensler, Jan Sitek, Jerzy Wybieralski, Leszek Tórz, Zbigniew Rachwalski, Henryk Horwat, Andrzej Myśliwiec, Leszek Andrzejczak, Jan Mielniczak, Mariusz Kubiak, Adan Dolatowski, Krysztof Glodowski)	2	3	1	20	17
5. CUB	(Angel Mora Parra, Severo Frometa Conte, Bernabe Izquierdo Martinez, Edgardo Vazquez Marquez, Hector Pedroso Garcia, Manuel Varela Perez, Raul Garcia Cabrera, Jorge Mico Gutierrez, Rudolfo Delgado Orbañez, Lazaro Hernández Rangel, Juan Blanco Peñalver, Juan Caballero Perez, Roberto Ramirez Hernandez, Angel Fontane Escobar, Ricardo Campos Hernandez, Juan Rios Alvarez)	2	4	0	11	43
6. TAN	(Leopold Gracias, Benedict Mendes, Soter Da Silva, Abraham Sykes, Yusuf Manwar, Jaypal Singh, Mohamed Manji, Rajabu Rajab, Jasbir Virdee, Islam Islam, Stephen D'Silva, Frederick Furtado, Taherali Hassanali, Anoop Mukundan, Patrick Toto, Julius Peter)	0	6	0	4	58

Final: IND 4–3 SPA
3rd Place: SOV 2–1 POL
5th Place: CUB 4–1 TAN

The 1980 field hockey tournament was decimated by the boycott. Of the 11 teams that competed in Montreal in 1976, only Spain and India were represented in Moscow. Cuba and Tanzania were added to fill the field even though they had little experience with the sport. It was like old times for India, trouncing Tanzania 18–0 and Cuba 13–0. However, they had a tougher match with Poland, salvaging a 2–2 tie when Mervyn Fernandis scored a goal with five seconds to play. India also scraped through with a 2–2 tie against Spain. The two teams met again in the final. India took a 3–0 lead and held on to win, 4–3, despite the fact that Juan Amat of Spain scored three goals in twelve minutes.

1984 Los Angeles-Monterey Park T: 12, N: 12, D: 8.11.

		W	L	T	PF	PA
1. PAK	(Ghulam Moinuddin, Qasim Zia, Nasir Ali, Abdul Rashid, Ayaz Mahmood, Naeem Akhtar, Kaleemullah, Manzoor Hussain, Hassan Sardar, Haneef Khan, Khalid Hameed, Shahid Ali Khan, Tauqeer Dar, Ishtiaq Ahmed, Salleem Sherwani, Mushtaq Ahmad)	4	0	3	19	8
2. GER	(Christian Bassemir, Tobias Frank, Horst-Ulrich Hänel, Carsten Fischer, Karl-Joachim Hürter, Eckhard Schmidt-Opper, Reinhard Krull, Michael Peter, Stefan Blöcher, Andreas Keller, Thomas Reck, Markku Slawyk, Thomas Gunst, Heiner Dopp, Volker Fried, Dirk Brinkmann)	4	2	1	14	6
3. GBR	(Ian Taylor, Stephen Martin, Paul Barber, Robert Cattrall, Jonathan Potter, Richard Dodds, William McConnell, Norman "Billy" Hughes, David Westcott, Richard Leman, Stephen Batchelor, Sean Kerly, James Duthie, Kulbir Bhaura, Mark Precious)	5	1	1	13	8
4. AUS	(Richard Charlesworth, James Irvine, Colin Batch, David Bell, Adrian Berce, Grant Boyce, Craig Davies, Peter Haselhurst, Treva King, Terry Leece, Grant Mitton, Michael Nobbs, Nigel Patmore, Trevor Smith, Neil Snowden, Terry Walsh)	5	2	0	19	8
5. IND	(Romeo James, Manohar Topno, Vineet Kumar Sharma, Somaya Maneypandemuttana, Joaquimmartin Carvaho, Rajinder Singh, Charanjit Kumar, Mervyn Fernandis, Hardeep Singh, Shahid Mohamed, Zafar Iqbal, Nila Komol Singh, Iqbaljit Grewal, Ravinder Pal Singh, Marcellusmark Gomes, Jaladudin Syed)	5	1	1	20	11
6. HOL	(Petrus Hermans, Arno den Hartog, Cees Jan Diepeveen, Henricus Pierik, Theodoor Doyer, Thomas van't Hek, Peter van Asbeck, Willem van Asbeck, Hans Kruize, Ties Kruize, Ronaldus Steens, Jan Hidde Kruize, Alexander Bos, Roderik	4	2	1	18	14

Bouwman, René Klaassen, Maarten van Grimbergen)

| 7. | NZE | (Jeffrey Archibald, Husmukh Bhikha, Christopher Brown, George Carnoutsos, Peter Daji, Laurence Gallen, Stuart Grimshaw, Trevor Laurence, Grant McLeod, Brent Miskimmin, Peter Miskimmin, Arthur Parkin, Ramesh Patel, Robin Wilson, Maurice Marquet, Graham Sligo) | 2 | 3 | 2 | 11 | 11 |
| 8. | SPA | (José Agut Bonsfills, Javier Cabot Durán, Juan Arbós Perarnau, Andres Goméz Rodriquez, Juan Carlos Peon Melon, Jaime Arbós Serra, Ricardo Cabot Durán, Juan Malgosa Paloma, Carlos Roca Portolés, Mariano Bordas Mon, Ignacio Cobos Vidal, Jorge Oliva Izquierdo, Miguel De Paz Pal, Ignacio Escudé Torrente, Santiago Malgosa Morera) | 2 | 5 | 0 | 11 | 13 |

Final: PAK 2–1 GER
3rd Place: GBR 3–2 AUS
5th Place: IND 5–2 HOL
7th Place: NZE 1–0 SPA

Australia, unbeaten in two years and the winner of five straight international tournaments, seemed well on their way to their first Olympic championship when they were beaten 1–0 by a rough Pakistani team in a stunning semi-final upset.

"PAKISTAN AVENGES MUNICH" read a banner hoisted in the stands as play began in the final match, a reference to the ugly 1972 final between Pakistan and West Germany. This time, in the blistering heat at East Los Angeles College, it was the Asian champions who prevailed. For the first time in Olympic history, the gold medal was decided in overtime, as Kaleemullah scored his only goal of the tournament in the twelfth minute.

In the bronze medal match, the demoralized Australians were upset again, this time by a surprising British team which had qualified for the Olympic tournament only as a result of the Soviet withdrawal.

1988 Seoul T: 12, N: 12, D: 10.1.

			W	L	T	PF	PA
1.	GBR	(Ian Taylor, David Faulkner, Paul Barber, Jonathan Potter, Richard Dodds, Martyn Grimley, Stephen Batchelor, Richard Leman, James Kirkwood, Kulbir Bhaura, Sean Kerly, Robert Clift, Imran Sherwani, Russell Garcia, Veryan Pappin, Stephen Martin)	5	1	1	18	8
2.	GER	(Christian Schliemann, Tobias Frank, Horst-Ulrich Hänel, Carsten Fischer, Andreas Mollandin, Ekkhard Schmidt-Opper, Dirk Brinkmann, Heiner Dopp, Stefan Blöcher, Andreas Keller, Thomas Reck, Thomas Brinkmann, Hanns-Henning Fastrich, Michael Hilgers, Volker Fried, Michael Metz)	5	1	1	16	7
3.	HOL	(Prank Leistra, Marc Benninga, Cees Jan Diepeveen, Maurits Crucg, Rene Klaassen, Hendrik Jan Kooijman, Marc Delissen, Jacques Brinkman, Gerrit Jan Schlatmann, Tim Steens, Floris Jan Bove Lander, Patrick Faber, Ronald Jansen, Jan Hidde Kruize, Erik Parlevliet, Taco van den Honert)	4	2	1	15	9
4.	AUS	(Craig Davies, Colin Batch, John Bestall, Warren Birmingham, Richard Charlesworth, Andrew Deane, Michael York, Mark Hager, Jay Stacy, Neil Hawgood, Peter Noel, Graham Reid, Roger Smith, Neil Snowden, David Wansbrough, Ken Wark)	5	2	0	22	8
5.	PAK	(Mansoor Ahmed, Nasir Ali, Qazi Mohib-Ur-Rehman, Aamir-Zafar, Ishtiaq Ahmed, Naeem Akhtar, Muhammad Qamar Ibrahim, Shahbaz Ahmed, Tariq Sheikh, Zahid Sharif, Khalid Hamid, Khalid Bashir, Naeem Amjad, Tahir Zaman, Musaddiq Hussain)	5	2	0	18	9
6.	IND	(Rawat Rajinder Singh, Pargat Singh, Ashok Kumar, Mohinder-Pal Singh, Somaya Maneypandemuttana, Vivek Singh, Sujit Kumar, Subramani Baladadalaiash, Shahid Mohamed, Sebastian Jude Felix, Balwinder Singh, Mervyn Fernandis, Thoiba Singh, Gundeep Kumar, Jagbir Singh, Patterson Markphilip)	3	3	1	16	15
7.	SOV	(Vladimir Pleshakov, Viktor Deputatov, Igor Yulchiyev, Sos Airapetyan, Vladimir Antakov, Vyacheslav Chechenov, Igor Atanov, Sergei Chakvorostov, Sergei Pleshakov, Mikhail Nichepurenko, Aleksandr Domashev, Igor Davydov, Aleksandr Myasnikov, Yevgeny Nechayev, Mikhail Bukatin)	3	3	1	9	12

		W	L	T	PF	PA
8. ARG	(Otto Schmitt, Alejandro Siri, Miguel Altube, Marcelo Mascheroni, Marcelo Garraffo, Edgardo Pailos, Alejandro Doherty, Aldo Ayala, Carlos Geneyro, Gabriel Minadeo, Alejandro Verga, Fernando Ferrara, Emanuel Roggero, Franco Nicola, Martín Sordelli, Mariano Silva)	2	5	0	15	22

Final: GBR 3–1 GER
3rd Place: HOL 2–1 AUS
5th Place: PAK 2–1 IND
7th Place: SOV 4–1 ARG

As in 1984, the favored Australians swept through the preliminary round undefeated, only to be beaten in the semifinals. This time Great Britain spoiled the Australians' tournament when Sean Kerly broke a 2–2 tie with 1:22 to play. In the final, Britain faced West Germany, who had defeated them 2–1 in the preliminary round. But the Germans were frustrated by Britain's superb defensive play. Imran Sherwani, a newsagent from Stoke-on-Trent, scored two of Great Britain's three goals.

1992 Barcelona-Terrassa T: 12, N: 12, D: 8.8.

		W	L	T	GF	GA
1. GER	(Michael Knauth, Christopher Reitz, Jan Peter Tewes, Carsten Fischer, Christian Blunck, Stefan Saliger, Michael Metz, Christian Mayerhöfer, Sven Meinhardt, Andreas Keller, Michael Hilgers, Andreas Becker, Stefan Tewes, Klaus Michler, Volker Fried, Oliver Kurtz)	6	0	1	20	6
2. AUS	(Warren Birmingham, David Wansbrough, John Bestall, Lee Bodimeade, Ashley Carey, Stephen Davies, Damon Diletti, Lachlan Dreher, Lachlan Elmer, Michael Evans, Gregory Corbitt, Paul Lewis, Graham Reid, Jay Stacey, Kenneth Wark, Michael York)	5	1	1	24	6
3. PAK	(Shahid Ali Khan, Rana Mujahid Ali, Khalid Bashsir, Anjum Saeed, Farhat Hassan Khan, Khawaja Muhammad Junaid, Muhammad Qamar Ibrahim, Tahir Zaman, Muhammad Asif Akhlaq, Shahbaz Ahmed, Wasim Feroze, Mansoor Ahmed, Muhammad Ikhlaq, Muhammad Khalid, Musaddiq Hussain, Muhammad Shahbaz)	6	1	0	25	11
4. HOL	(Frank Leistra, Harrie Kwinten, Cees-Jan Diepeveen, Pieter	4	3	0	25	17

van Ede, Bastiaan Poortenaar, Wouter van Pelt, Marc Delissen, Jacques Brinkman, Gisj Weterings, Stephan Veen, Floris Jan Bovelander, Hendrik Kooijman, Bart Looije, Maarten van Grimbergen, Leo Klein Gebbnick, Taco van den Honert)

		W	L	T	GF	GA
5. SPA	(Santiago Grau Viola, Ignacio Escudé Torrente, Joaquín Malgosa Morera, Miguel Ortego Fernández, Juantxo Garcia-Mauriño, Jaime Amat Durán, Jordi Avilés Cortés, Pere Jufresa Lluch, Jose Iglesias Bilbao, Xavi Escudé Torrente, Xavi Arnau Creus, Victor Pujol Sala, Juan Dinares Quera, David Freixa Paloma, Pablo Usoz Ciriza, Ramon Jufresa Lluch)	5	2	0	19	12
6. GBR	(Sean Rowlands, Stephen Martin, Paul Bolland, Simon Nicklin, Jonathan Potter, Jason Laslett, Robert Hill, Stephen Batchelor, Russell Garcia, John Shaw, Robert Thompson, Sean Kerly, Robert Clift, Jason Lee, Donald Williams)	4	3	0	11	14
7. IND	(Cheppudira Poonacha, Jagdev Rai, Harpreet Singh, Sukhjit Singh, Shaqeel Ahmed, Mukesh Nandanoori, Sebastian Jude Felix, Singh Jagbir Singh, Pillay Dhanraj Pillay, Didar Singh, Ashish Ballal, Pargat Powar, Ravi Nayakar, Darryl D'Souza, Lakra Ajit)	3	4	0	7	12
8. NZE	(Peter Daji, Brett Leaver, David Grundy, Scott Hobson, D. Grant McLeod, Peter Miskimmin, Paresh Patel, David Penfold, John Radovonich, Craig Russ, Gregory Russ, Umesh Parag, James Smith, Anthony Thornton, Scott Anderson, Ian Woodley)	1	6	0	11	18

Final: GER 2–1 AUS
3rd Place: PAK 4–3 HOL
5th Place: SPA 2–1 GBR
7th Place: IND 3–2 NZE

Germany qualified for the final by winning a difficult semifinal against Pakistan. Carsten Fischer, a medical doctor, scored from a penalty corner in the 13th minute of overtime to give the Germans a 2–1 victory. In the final, Germany faced Australia. The two teams had drawn 1–1 in pool play. The Germans were known for their methodical play, but they startled the Australians by attacking from the start and were rewarded when insurance broker Michael Hilgers scored after only 90 seconds. Hilgers added a second goal in the 59th minute. Gregory Corbitt brought Australia back to 2–1 with four minutes to play, but it was too little, too late. German midfielder Andreas Keller came from a remarkable hockey family. His grandfather Erwin earned a silver medal in 1936 and his father, Carsten, represented Germany in three Olympics and was a member of the 1972 gold-medal-winning squad. Andreas himself won silver in 1984 and 1988 before picking up his own gold. As if that weren't enough, Andreas' girlfriend, Anke Wild, earned a silver medal as a member of the 1992 German women's team.

The match for third place was an unusually exciting contest. With 15 minutes to play Holland held a seemingly safe 2–0 lead. But Pakistan scored four goals in the next 13 minutes. Although the Dutch scored once more, the bronze medal went to Pakistan, 4–3.

WOMEN

1896–1976 not held

1980 Moscow T: 6, N: 6, D: 7.31.

			W	L	T	PF	PA
1.	ZIM	(Sarah English, Ann Mary Grant, Brenda Phillips, Patricia McKillop, Sonia Robertson, Patricia Davies, Maureen George, Linda Watson, Susan Huggett, Gillian Cowley, Elizabeth Chase, Sandra Chick, Helen Volk, Christine Prinsloo, Arlene Boxhall, Anthea Stewart)	3	0	2	13	4
2.	CZE	(Jarmila Kralicková, Berta Hruba, Iveta Sranková, Lenka Vymazalová, Jirina Krizová, Jirina Kadlecová, Jirina Čermaková, Marta Urbanová, Kveta Petricková, Marie Sykorová, Ida Hubacková, Milada Blazková, Jana Lahodová, Alena Kyselicová, Jirina Hajková, Viera Podhanyiová)	3	1	1	10	5
3.	SOV	(Galina Inzhuvatova, Nelli Gorbyatkova, Valentina Zazdravnykh, Nadezhda Ovechkina, Natella Krasnikova, Natalya Bykova, Lidiya Glubokova, Galina Vyuzhanina, Natalya Buzunova, Lyailya Akhmerova, Nadezhda Filipova, Yelena Guryeva, Tatyana Yembakhtova, Tatyana Shvyganova, Alina Kham, Lyudmila Frolova)					
4.	IND	(Margaret Toscano, Sudha Chaudhry, Gangotri Bhandari, Rekha Mundphan, Rupa Kumari Saini, Varsha Soni, Eliza Nelson, Prem Maya Sonir, Naazleen Madraswalla, Selma D'Silva, Lorraine Fernandes, Harpreet Gill, Balwinder Kaur Bhatia, Geeta Sareen, Nisha Sharma, Hutoxi Bagli)	2	2	1	9	6
5.	AUT	(Patricia Lorenz, Sabine Blemenschütz, Elisabeth Pistauer, Andrea Kozma, Brigitta Pecanka, Brigette Kindler, Friederike Stern, Regina Lorenz, Eleonore Pecanka, Ilse Stipanovsky, Andrea Porsch, Erika Csar, Dorit Ganster, Ulrike Kleinhansl, Eva Cambal, Jana Cejpek)	2	3	0	6	11
6.	POL	(Malgorzata Gajewska, Bogumila Pajor, Jolanta Sekulak, Jolanta Błędowska, Lucyna Matuszna, Danuta Stanislawska, Wieslawa Rylko, Lidia Zgajewska, Maria Kornek, Malgorzata Lipska, Halina Koldras, Lucyna Siejka, Dorota Bielska, Dorota Załęczna, Michalina Plekaniec, Jadwiga Koldras)	0	5	0	0	18

When five of the six nations scheduled to compete in the inaugural women's field hockey tournament withdrew as part of the Jimmy Carter boycott, it set the stage for a true Cinderella story. As white-ruled Rhodesia, Zimbabwe had been banned from the Olympics, but when the black majority took power, the ban was lifted. Desperate to fill the field, the Soviet Union and the International Olympic Committee contacted Zimbabwe five weeks before the start of the Games and offered to subsidize the sending of a team, the members of which were not selected until the weekend before the Olympics opened. Ironically, the team that represented Zimbabwe was all white. They were held to ties by Czechoslovakia and India, but they were the only team to avoid defeat. A 4–1 victory over Austria assured them of gold medals.

1984 Los Angeles-Monterey Park T: 6, N: 6, D: 8.10.

			W	L	T	PF	PA
1.	HOL	(Bernadette de Beus, Alette Pos, Margriet Zegers, Laurien Willemse, Marjolein Eysvogel, Josephine Boekhorst, Carina Benninga, Alexandra le Poole, Francisca Hillen, Marieke van Doorn, Sophie von Weiler, Aletta van Manen, Irene	4	0	1	14	6

		W	L	T	PF	PA
	Hendriks, Elisabeth Sevens, Martine Ohr, Anneloes Nieuwenhuizen)					
2. GER	(Ursula Thielemann, Elke Drüll, Beate Deininger, Christina Moser, Hella Roth, Dagmar Breiken, Birgit Hagen, Birgit Hahn, Gabriele Appel, Andrea Lietz-Weiermann, Corinna Lingnau, Martina Koch, Gabriela Schley, Patricia Ott, Susanne Schmid, Sigrid Landgraf)	2	1	2	9	9
3. USA	(Gwen Cheeseman, Beth Anders, Kathleen McGahey, Anita Miller, Regina Buggy, Christine Larson-Mason, Beth Beglin, Marcella Place, Julie Staver, Diane Moyer, Sheryl Johnson, Charlene Morett, Karen Shelton, Brenda Stauffler, Leslie Milne, Judy Strong)	2	2	1	9	7
4. AUS	(Kym Ireland, Liane Tooth, Pamela Glossop, Susan Watkins, Lorraine Hillas, Robyn Leggatt, Sandra Pisani, Penny Gray, Robyn Holmes, Sharon Buchanan, Marian Aylmore, Colleen Pearce, Loretta Dorman, Julene Sunderland, Trisha Heberle, Evelyn Botfield)	2	2	1	9	7
5. CAN	(Laurie Lambert, Sharon Creelman, Jean Major, Laura Branchaud, Lynne Beecroft, Shelley Andrews, Darlene Stoyka, Phyllis Ellis, Karen Hewlett, Diane Virjee, Terry Wheatley, Lisa Bauer, Sheila Forshaw, Sharon Bayes, Zoe Mackinnon, Nancy Charlton)	2	2	1	9	11
6. NZE	(Lesley Murdoch, Barbara Tilden, Mary Clinton, Susan McLeish, Isobel Thomson, Sandra Mackie, Jillian Smith, Jane Goulding, Robyn Blackman, Jan Martin, Harina Kohere, Jennifer McDonald, Shirley Haig, Catherine Thompson, Lesley Elliott, Christine Arthur)	0	5	0	2	12

The Australian women entered the final match of the round-robin tournament with a clear understanding of what they needed to accomplish. If they could beat the heavily favored Dutch team by two goals, they would earn gold medals. If they won by one goal or tied, they would finish second. If they lost by one goal they would win bronze medals, and if they lost by three goals, they would finish out of the money. The Dutch won 2–0, which meant that Australia and the U.S. completed the tournament with identical records. Although the Australians had defeated the Americans 3–1, tournament rules stated that the bronze medals would be decided by a penalty stroke shoot-off, which took place 15 minutes after the last match. The U.S. won easily, 10–5.

1988 Seoul T: 8, N: 8, D: 9.30.

		W	L	T	PF	PA
1. AUS	(Kathleen Partridge, Elspeth Clement, Liane Tooth, Loretta Dorman, Lorraine Hillas, Michelle Capes, Sandra Pisani, Deborah Bowman, Lee Capes, Kim Small, Sally Carbon, Jacqueline Pereira, Tracey Belbin, Rechelle Hawkes, Sharon Patmore, Maree Fish)	3	0	2	12	8
2. KOR	(Kim Mi-sun, Han Ok-kyung, Chang Eun-jung, Han Keum-sil, Choi Choon-ok, Kim Soon-duk, Chung Sang-hyun, Jin Won-sim, Hwang Keum-sook, Cho Ki-hyang, Seo Kwang-mi, Park Soon-ja, Kim Young-sook, Seo Hyo-sun, Lim Kye-sook, Chung Eun-kyung)	3	1	1	13	9
3. HOL	(Bernadette de Beus, Yvonne Buter, Willemien Aardenburg, Laurien Willemse, Marjolein Bolhuis, Elisabeth "Lisanne" Lejeune, Carina Benninga, Annemieke Fokke, Ingrid Wolff, Marieke van Doorn, Sophie von Weiler, Aletta van Manen, Noor Holsboer, Helen van der Ben, Martine Ohr, Anneloes Nieuwenhuizen)	4	1	0	14	6
4. GBR	(Jillian Atkins, Wendy Banks, Gillian Brown, Karen Brown, Mary Nevill, Julie Cook, Victoria Dixon, Wendy Fraser, Barbara Hambly, Caroline Jordan, Violet McBride, Moira Macleod, Caroline Brewer, Jane Sixsmith, Kate Parker, Alison Ramsey)	1	3	1	5	11
5. GER	(Susanne Schmid, Carola Hoffmann, Heike Gehrmann, Dagmar Bremer, Gabriele Uhlenbruck, Viola Grahl, Bettina Blumenberg, Gabriele Appel, Martina Hallmen, Christine Ferneck, Silke Wehrmeister, Caren Jungjohann, Eva Hegener, Susanne Wollschläger, Gabriela Schowe)	3	2	0	9	9
6. CAN	(Sharon Bayes, Wendy Baker, Deb Covey, Lisa Lyn, Laura Branchaud, Sandra Levy, Kathryn Johnson, Shona Schleppe, Michelle Conn, Liz Czenczek,	1	3	1	8	11

Sheila Forshaw, Nancy Charlton, Sara Ballantyne, Sharon Creelman)

		W	L	T	GF	GA
7.	ARG (Laura Mulhall, Cecilia Colombo, Marisa López, Alejandra Tucat, Victoria Carbó, Fabiana Ricchezza, Gabriela Liz, Gabriela Sánchez, Moira Brinnand, Marcela Hussey, Alejandra Palma, Verónica Bengochea, Alina Vergara, Gabriela Pazos, Andrea Fioroni)	2	3	0	6	7
8.	USA (Patricia Shea, Yolanda Hightower, Mary Koboldt, Marcia Pankratz, Cheryl Van Kuren, Diane Bracalente, Elizabeth Beglin, Marcell Von Schottenstein, Sandra Vander-Heyden, Tracey Fuchs, Sheryl Johnson, Sandra Costigan, Christy Morgan, Barbara Marois, Megan Donnelly, Donna Lee)	0	4	1	6	12

Final: AUS 2–0 KOR
3rd Place: HOL 3–1 GBR
5th Place: GER 4–2 CAN
7th Place: ARG 3–1 USA

When Australia defeated the Netherlands 3–2 in the semifinals, it marked the first time in 8 years that the Dutch had failed to reach the final of an international tournament. Australia and South Korea played an exciting 5–5 draw to close the preliminary round. Australia tightened its defense for the final and successfully choked off the fast-paced offense of the Korean "Red Bees." Five minutes into the second half, Australian captain Debbie Bowman scored on a penalty stroke. Lee Capes added an insurance goal in the 58th minute.

1992 Barcelona-Terrassa T: 8, N: 8, D: 8.7.

		W	L	T	GF	GA
1.	SPA (María González Laguillo, Natalia Dorado Gómez, Virginia Ramírez Merino, María del Carmen Barea Cobos, Silvia Manrique Pérez, Nagore Gabellanes Marieta, María Rodríguez Suárez, Sonia Barrio Gutiérrez, Elisabeth Maragall Verge, Teresa Motos Iceta, Maider Telleria Goñi, Mercedes Coghen Alberdingo, Núria Olivé Vancells, Ana Maiques Dern, María Martínez De Murguía)	4	0	1	9	5
2.	GER (Susanne Wollschläger, Bianca Weiss, Tanja Dickenscheid, Susanne Müller, Nadine Ernsting-Krienke, Simone Thomaschinski, Irina Kuhnt, Anke Wild, Franziska Hentschel, Kristina Peters, Eva Hagenbäumer, Britta Becker, Caren Jungjohann, Christine Ferneck, Heike Lätzsch, Katrin Kauschke)	3	1	1	10	5
3.	GBR (Joanne Thompson, Helen Morgan, Lisa Bayliss, Karen Brown, Mary Nevill, Gillian Atkins, Vickey Dixon, Wendy Fraser, Sandra Lister, Jane Sixsmith, Alison Ramsay, Jackie McWilliams, Tammy Miller, Mandy Nicholls, Kathryn Johnson, Susan Fraser)	3	2	0	12	10
4.	KOR (You Jae-sook, Han Gum-shil, Chang Eun-jung, Lee Seon-young, Lee Kui-joo, Son Jeong-im, Ro Young-mi, Kim Kyung-ae, Lee Eun-kyung, Jang Dong-sook, Kwon Chang-sook, Yang Hea-sook, Lee Kyoung-hei, Koo Mun-young, Lim Gae-sook, Jin Deok-sah)	2	3	0	12	9
5.	AUS (Kathleen Partridge, Christine Dobson, Liane Tooth, Alyson Annan, Juliet Haslam, Michelle Hager, Alison Peek, Lisa Powell, Lisa Naughton, Katie Starre, Sally Carbon-Bell, Jacqueline Pereira, Tracey Belbin, Rechelle Hawkes, Sharon Buchana, Deborah Sullivan [Bowman])	3	2	0	9	3
6.	HOL (Jacqueline Toxopeus, Carina Bleeker, Caroline van Nieuwenhuyze-Leenders, Annemieke Fokke, Cécile Vinke, Jeannette Lewin, Carina Benninga, Daniëlle Koenen, Ingrid Wolff, Mieketine Wouters, Martine Ohr, Florentine Steenberghe, Noor Holsboer, Helen Lejeune-van de Ben, Wietske de Ruiter, Carole Thate)	3	2	0	6	5
7.	CAN (Deborah Whitten, Deb Covey, Rochelle Low, Tara Croxford, Sandra Levy, Sue Reid, Heather Jones, Candy Thomson, Bernadette Bowyer, Michelle Conn, Laurelee Kopeck, Joel Brough, Milena Gaiga, Sherri Field, Sharon Creelman)	1	4	0	3	10
8.	NZE (Elaine Jensen, Mary Clinton, Tina Bell, Christine Arthur, Shane Collins, Sapphire Cooper, Kylie Foy, Sue Duggan, Susan Furmage, Trudy Kilkolly, Anna Lawrence, Kieren O'Grady, Amanda Smith, Robyn Toomey, Kate Trolove)	0	5	0	3	17

Final: SPA 2–1 GER
3rd Place: GBR 4–3 KOR

5th Place: AUS 2–0 HOL
7th Place: CAN 2–0 NZE

The victory of the Spanish women's field hockey team was one of the least likely of the Barcelona Games. Spain had no tradition to speak of in the sport and although they had performed credibly in recent years, they were basically a fifth-place team. But they took advantage of their status as the host country by training continuously on the Olympic pitches at Terrassa for over five months prior to the Games. In pool play they came from behind to tie Germany 2–2, beat Canada 2–1, and then qualified for the semifinals by shocking the defending champions, Australia, 1–0 on a fourth-minute penalty corner by Silvia Manrique. In the semis they defeated South Korea when María Barea converted a penalty corner with two minutes left in overtime. The final was a rematch with Germany. Spain scored first as Barea smashed in a penalty corner in the eighth minute. High-scoring Franziska Hentschel evened the match four minutes later, but there were no more goals during regulation play. Thirteen minutes into overtime, Eli Maragall, the niece of the president of the Barcelona Olympic Organizing Committee, made a spectacular dive to deflect the ball into the net and earn the Spanish team its unexpected championship.

FOOTBALL (SOCCER)

Football, also known as soccer, is played on a field 105 meters (114 yards, 2 feet, 5 inches) long and 68 meters (74 yards, 1 foot, 1 inch) wide. Olympic matches must be played on natural turf. There are 11 players on each team including a goalie. Only two substitutions are allowed per match or three if the goalie is one of the players replaced. Substituted players may not return. The object of football is to move the ball down the field by dribbling and passing and to kick or head the ball into the goal. Except for the throw-ins, after the ball goes out of bounds, only the goalie may touch the ball with his hands or arms and even the goalie may use his hands only within the penalty area, which extends 16.47 meters (18 yards) in front of the goal and is 40 meters (44 yards) wide.

A player is considered offside if he is in the opponent's half of the field with less than two opposing players (including the goalie) between him and the goal at the time that the ball is kicked or headed. This infraction leads to an indirect kick for the opposing team. A goal may not be scored on an indirect kick. A direct kick, which can result in a goal, is awarded for such fouls as tripping, holding, or kicking an opponent, charging an opponent from behind in a dangerous manner, or touching the ball with the hand or arm. When direct kick fouls occur within the penalty area, a penalty kick is awarded. The ball is placed 11 meters (36 feet 1 inch) in front of the net and a player is given a free shot against the goalie, who may not move his feet until the ball is kicked. When the ball crosses the endline after being touched last by a defending player the attacking team is awarded a corner kick.

Football matches consist of two 45-minutes halves. If play is suspended because of injury, the time lost is added to the end of each half. In the qualifying round of pool play, ties are allowed to stand. In the elimination rounds, if the score is tied after 90 minutes, a 30-minute overtime period, divided into two halves, is played. However, Olympic rules actually provide for sudden-death overtime. The first team to score in overtime is declared the winner. If the score is still tied after 120 minutes of play, the match is decided by a penalty shoot-out, five against five. If the shoot-out is tied, each team shoots once until the tie is broken.

Soccer is the most widely played sport in the world, and Olympic soccer has had trouble dealing with the immense popularity of the professional leagues. The growth of professional soccer after World War II meant that the best players were not eligible to compete in the Olympics—unless they lived in Communist countries. Beginning in 1952, Olympic tournaments featured the best players from the Communist nations defeating amateurs from the real soccer powers of Western Europe and South America. In 1984 some professional players were allowed to take part in the Olympics, but for European and South American teams, it was only those professionals who had not yet played in the World Cup—the quadrennial championship of soccer. In 1992, all professionals were considered eligible, provided they were less than 23 years old. This rule was still in force for the regional qualifying tournaments that determined the 16 teams to take part in the 1996 Olympics (except that players may turn 23 in the year of the Olympics). For the Olympic tournament itself, each qualifying team may add to its squad three professionals regardless of age.

Women's football will be included in the Olympics for the first time in 1996. The rules are the same as those for the men's tournament except that only eight teams will qualify for the Olympics and players must turn 16 years old in the Olympic year.

1896 not held

1900 Paris T: 3, N: 3, D: 9.23.

			W	L	PF	PA
1.	GBR	(Upton Park Football Club—J.H. Jones, Claude Buckenham, William Gosling, Alfred Chalk, J.E. Barridge, William Quash, R.R. Turner, F.G. Spackman, J. Nicholas, James Zealley, A. Haslam)	1	0	4	0
2.	FRA	(Union des sociétés françaises de sports athlétiques—Lucien Huteau, Louis Bach, Pierre Allemane, Virgile Gaillard, Alfred Bloch, Maurice Macaire, Eugène Fraysse, Georges Garnier, Lambert, Grandjean, Fernand Canelle, Duparc, Gaston Peltier)	1	1	7	8
3.	BEL& GBR	Marcel Leboutte, R. Kelecom, Ernest Moreau, Alphonse Renier, Gustave Pelgrims, E. Neefs, Eric Thornton [GBR], Albert Delbecque, W. Spanoghe, van Heuckelum, Lucien Londot)	0	1	4	7

1904 St. Louis T: 3, N: 2, D: 11.23.

			W	L	T	PF	PA
1.	CAN	(Galt Football Club—Ernest Linton, George Ducker, John Gourley, John Fraser, Albert Johnson, Robert Lane, Tom Taylor, Frederick Steep, Alexander Hall, Gordon McDonald, William Twaits)	2	0	0	11	0

			W	L	T	PF	PA
2.	USA	(Christian Brothers College— Louis Menges, Joseph Lydon, Thomas January, John January, Charles January, Peter Ratican, Warren Brittingham, Alexander Cudmore, Charles Bartliff, Oscar Brockmeyer, Raymond Lawler)	1	1	1	2	7
3.	USA	(St. Rose Parish School—Frank Frost, George Cooke, Henry Jameson, Joseph Brady, Martin Dooling, Dierkes, Cormic Cosgrove, O'Connell, Claude Jameson, Harry Tate, Thomas Cooke, Johnson)	0	2	1	0	6

The St. Rose team managed to put one ball into the net. Unfortunately, it was into the goal they were defending.

1906 Athens T: 4, N: 2, D: 4.24.

			W	L	PF	PA
1.	DEN	(Viggo Andersen, Peter Petersen, Charles Buchwald, Parmo Ferslew, Stefan Rasmussen, Aage Andersen, Oscar Nielsen-Nörland, Carl Frederick Petersen, Holger Fredriksen, August Lindgreen, Henry Rambusch, Hjalmar Heerup, Axel Hansen)	2	0	14	1
2.	INT	Smyrna (Edwin Charnaud, Zareck Couyoumdzian, Edouard Giraud, Jacques Giraud, Henri Joly, Percy de la Fontaine, Donald Whittal, Albert Whittal, Godfrey Whittal, Harold Whittal, Edward Whittal)	1	1	4	5
3.	GRE	Thessaloniki Music Club (Georgios Vaporis, Nicolaos Pindos, Andonios Tegon, Nicolaos Pentzikis, Ioannis Kyrou, Georgis Sotiriadis, Vasilios Zarkadis, Dimitrios Mikhitsopoulos, Andonios Karangonidis, Ioannis Saridakis, Ioannis Abbot)	1	1	6	3

The team from Smyrna was an international one, including players from Great Britain, France, and Greece. The five British players were all members of the Whittal family. Albert, Edward, and Godfrey were the sons of Edward Whittal; Donald and Harold were the sons of Edward's brother, Easton.

1908 London T: 6, N: 5, D: 10.24.

			W	L	PF	PA
1.	GBR	(Horace Bailey, Walter Corbett, Herbert Smith, Kenneth Hunt, Frederick Chapman, Robert Hawkes, Arthur Berry, Vivian Woodward, Henry Stapley, Clyde Purnell, Harold Hardman)	3	0	18	1
2.	DEN	(Ludvig Drescher, Charles Buchwald, Harald Hansen, Harald Bohr,	2	1	26	3

			W	L	PF	PA
		Kristian Middelboe, Nils Middelboe, Oscar Nielsen-Nörland, August Lindgren, Sophus Nielsen, Vilhelm Wolffhagen, Björn Rasmussen, P. Marius Andersen, Johannes Gandil)				
3.	HOL	(Reinier Beeuwkes, Karel Heijting, Louis Otten, Johannes Sol, Johannes de Korver, Emil Mundt, Jan-Herman Welcker, Everardus Snethlage, Gerard Reeman, Jan Thomée, Georges de Bruyn Kops, Johannes Kok)	1	1	2	4
4.	SWE	(Oskar Bengtsson, Ake Fjästad, Teodor Malm, Sven Olsson, Hans Lindman, Olof Ohlsson, Sune Almkvist, Gustaf Bergström, Sven Ohlsson, Karl Ansén, Nils Andersson, Valter Lidén, Arvid Fagrell, Karl Gustafsson)	0	2	1	14

Final: GBR 2–0 DEN
3rd Place: HOL 2–0 SWE

France entered two teams, both of which were thrashed by Denmark. In the 17–1 defeat of the French "B" team, Sophus Nielsen of Denmark scored 10 goals.

1912 Stockholm T: 11, N: 11, D: 7.4.

			W	L	PF	PA
1.	GBR	(Ronald Brebner, Thomas Burn, Arthur Knight, Douglas McWhirter, Henry Littlewort, Joseph Dines, Arthur Berry, Vivian Woodward, Harold Walden, Gordon Hoare, Ivan Sharpe, Edward Hanney, E. Gordon Wright, Harold Stamper)	3	0	15	2
2.	DEN	(Sophus Hansen, Nils Middelboe, Harald Hansen, Charles Buchwald, Emil Jörgensen, Poul Berth, Oscar Nielsen-Nörland, Axel Thufason, Anton Olsen, Sophus Nielsen, Vilhelm Wolffhagen, Hjalmar Christoffersen, Aksel Petersen, Ivar Seidelin-Nielsen, Poul Nielsen)	2	1	13	5
3.	HOL	(Marius Jan Göbel, David Wijnveldt, Pieter Bouman, Gerardus Fortgens, Constant Feith, Nicolaas de Wolf, Dirk Lotsy, Johannes Boutmy, Jan van Breda Kolff, Henri de Groot, Caesar ten Cate, Jan van der Sluis, Jan Vos, Jan Bouvy, Johannes de Korver)	3	1	17	8
4.	FIN	(August Syrjäläinen, Jalmari Holopainen, Gösta Löfgren, Kurt Lund, Eino Soinio, Viljo Lietola, Lauri Tanner, Bror Wiberg, Jarl Öhman, Artturi Nyyssönen, Algoth Niska, Ragnar Wickström, Kaarlo Soinio)	2	2	5	16
5.	HUN	(Gáspár Borbás, Imre Schlosser, Mihály Pataky, Sándor Bodnár, Béla Sebestyén, Antal Vágó-Weisz, Jenö	2	1	6	8

Károly, Gyula Biró, Imre Payer, Gyula Rumbold, László Domonkos, Kálmán Szury, Zoltán Blum, Miklóz Ferete)

			W	L	PF	PA
5.	AUT	(Alois Müller, Leopold Neubauer, Johann Studnicka, Robert Merz, Ludwig Hussak, Robert Cimera, Karl Braunsteiner, Josef Brandstetter, Bernhard Graubard, Ladislavs Kurpiel, Otto Noll, Gustav Blana, Franz Weber)	3	2	12	8
7.	GER	(Julius Hirsch, Eugen Kipp, Willi Worpitzky, Adolf Jäger, Karl Wegele, Hermann Bosch, Max Breunig, Georg Krogmann, Ernst Hollstein, Helmut Röpnack, Adolf Weber, Gottfried Fuchs, Hans Reese, Walter Hempel, Karl Burger, Josef Glaser, Camillo Ugi, Karl Uhle, Fritz Förderer, Emil Oberle)	1	2	18	8
7.	ITA	(Edoardo Mariani, Enrico Sardi, Felice Berardo, Franco Bontadini, Enea Zuffi, Pietro Leone, Giuseppe Milano, Carlo Demarchi, Renzo De Vecchi, Angelo Binaschi, Piero Campelli, Luigi Barbesiono, Modesto Valle)	1	2	4	8

Final: GBR 4–2 DEN
3rd Place: HOL 9–0 FIN

Great Britain was leading 2–1 in the final when Buchwald of Denmark was injured and had to be helped from the field. Denmark was forced to continue with only ten players, and Britain quickly capitalized by scoring two goals in three minutes. The Danes then adjusted to playing shorthanded, but it was too late and they lost, 4–2. In a consolation match against Russia, Gottfried Fuchs of Germany scored ten goals to match Sophus Nielsen's feat of four years earlier. Eleven of Britain's 15 tournament goals were scored by Harold Walden, who later became a popular music-hall comedian in West Yorkshire.

1920 Antwerp T: 14, N: 14, D: 9.2.

			W	L	PF	PA
1.	BEL	(Jan de Bie, Armand Swartenbroeks, Oscar Verbeeck, Joseph Musch, Emile Hanse, André Fierens, Louis van Hege, Henri Larnoe, Mathieu Bragard, Robert Coppée, Désiré Bastin, Félix Balyu, Fernand Nisot, Georges Hebdin)	3	0	8	1
—	CZE	(Rudolf Klapka, Antonín Hojer, Miroslav Pospíšil, Karel Steiner, František Kolenatý, Karel Pešek-Kaďa, Antonín Perner, Emil Seifert, Josef Sedlášek, Antonín Janda, Václav Pilát, Jan Vaník, Ota Mazal, Jan Plaček	3	1	15	3
2.	SPA	(Ricardo Zamora Martínez, Pedro Vallana Jeanguenat, Mariano Arrate Esnaola, José Samitier Vilalta, José Maria Belaustequigoita Landaluca, Agustin Sancho Agustina, Ramón Equizábal Berroa, Félix Sesúmaga Segura, Patricio Arabolaza Aramburu, Rafael "Pichichi" Moreno Aranzadi, Domingo Gómez-Acedo Villanueva, Juan Artola Letamendíe, Francisco Pagazaurtundúa González, Louis Otero Sánchez-Encinas, Joaquin Vázquez-González, Ramón "Moncho" Gil Fegueiros, Sabino Bilbao Libano, Silverio Izaguirre)	4	1	9	5
3.	HOL	(Richard MacNeill, Henri Dénis, Bernard Verweij, Leonard Bosschart, Frederik Kuipers, Hermanus Steeman, Oscar van Rappard, Jan van Dort, Bernardus Groosjohan, Herman van Heijden, Jacob Bulder, Johannes de Natris, Evert Bulder, Adriánus Bieshaar)	2	2	9	10
4.	ITA	(Piero Campelli, Giovanni Giacone, Antonio Bruna, Renzo de Vecchi, Virginio Rosetta, Grazzo de Nardo, Ettore Reynaudi, Mario Meneghetti, Giuseppe Parodi, Luigi Burlando, Rinaldo Roggero, Giustiniano Marucco, Pio Ferraris, Giuseppe Forlivesi, Cesare Lovati, Enrico Sardi, Adolfo Baloncieri, Emilio Badini, Guglielmo Brezzi, Aristodemo Emilio Santamaria Alevildo de Marchi)	2	2	5	7
5.	NOR	(Rolf Aas, Arne Andersen, Gunnar Andersen, Otto Aulie, Einar Gundersen, Asbjorn Hansen, Johnny Helgesen, Per Holm, John Johnsen, Ellef Mohn, Michael Paulson, Per Skou, Rolf Semb Thorstvedt, Sigurd Wathne, Einar Wilhelms, Adolf Wold)	1	2	4	7
5.	SWE	(Rune Bergström, Albin Dahl, Karl Gustafsson, Fritjof Hillén, Herbert Carlsson, Valdus Lund, Bertil Nordenskjöld, Albert Olsson, Mauritz Sandberg, Ragnar Wicksell, Robert Zander, Albert Öijermark)	1	2	14	7

2nd Place: SPA 3–1 HOL

The final matched the home team, Belgium, against the Czechoslovakians, who had outscored their opponents 15–1, on their way to the final. A partisan crowd of 40,000 watched with pleasure as Belgium took a 2–0 lead. But after several controversial calls, the Czech team had had enough and walked off the field en masse in protest six minutes before the end of the first half. This threw the tournament into chaos. With Czechoslovakia disqualified, a playoff for second place was ordered. But

France, which had lost to Czechoslovakia in the semifinals, refused to participate since many of the leading French players had already gone home. Eventually Spain defeated Sweden and Italy to qualify for the second-place match against Holland.

1924 Paris T: 22, N: 22, D: 6.9.

			W	L	T	PF	PA
1.	URU	(Andrés Mazali, José Nasazzi, Pedro Arispe, José Leandro Andrade, José Vidal, Alfredo Ghierra, Santos Urdinarán, Hector Scarone, Pedro Petrone, Pedro Céa, Angel Romano, Umberto Tomasina, José Naya, Alfredo Zibechi, Antonio Urdinaran)	5	0	0	20	2
2.	SWI	(Hans Pulver, Adolphe Reymond, Rudolf Ramseyer, August Oberhauser, Paul Schmiedlin, Aron Pollitz, Karl Ehrenbolger, Robert Pache, Walter Dietrich, Max Abegglen, Paul Fässler, Felix Bédouret, Adolphe Mengotti, Paul Sturzenegger, Edmond Kramer)	4	1	1	15	6
3.	SWE	(Sigfrid Lindberg, Axel Alfredsson, Fritjof Hillén, Gunnar Holmberg, Sven Friberg, Harry Sundberg, Evert Lundqvist, Sven Rydell, Per Kaufeldt, Tore Keller, Rudolf Kock, Gustaf Carlson, Charles Brommesson, Thorsten Svensson, Albin Dahl, Konrad Hirsch, Sven Lindqvist, Sten Mellgren)	3	1	1	18	5
4.	HOL	(Gejus van der Meulen, Henri Dénis, Hendrik Vermetten, Albert Oosthoek, Gerardus Krom, Gerardus Horstén, Johannes de Natris, Gerrit Visser, André Lefèvre, Ocker Formenoy, Marinus Sigmond, Bernard Verweij, Johannes Tetzner, Evert van Linge, Klaas Jan Breeuwer, Bernardus Groosjohan, Cornelius Pijl, Albert Snouck-Hurgronje, Johannes ter Beek)	2	2	1	11	7
5.	EGY	(Abaza Sayed Fahmy, Abdel Hamid Moharren, Abdel Kader Mohammed, Ali Fahmi El Hassani, Mohammed El Mahdwy, Mahmoud Fouad, Ibrahim Yaghen, Abdel Salam Hamdy, Hussein Hegazi, Rizkalla Henein, Housny Khalil, Ismail El Sayed, Ismail Mahmoud Hooda, Ahmed Mansour Hooda, Marey Mahmoud, Moktar Mahmoud, Osman Gamil, Ali Mohamed Riad, Mohammed Rouston, Salim Ahmed, Shawky Riad, Kamel Taha)	1	1	0	3	5
5.	FRA	(Henri Bard, Jean Batmale, Edouard Baumann, Pierre Bonnardel, Jean Boyer, Jacques Canthelou, Pierre Chayriguès, Pierre Chesnau, Maurice Cottenet, Edouard Crut, Jules Dewaquez, Marcel Domergue, René Dufour, Raymond Dubly, Ernest Gravier, Ernest Gross, Léon Huot, Gérard Isbecque, Albert Jourda, Antoine Parachini, Albert Renier, Paul Nicolas)	1	1	0	8	5
5.	IRL	(Tom Aungier, Billy Cowzer, W. Ernest Crawford, Charlie Dowdall, Robert Duncan, Jimmy Dykes, John Farrell, Jimmy Ghent, Dennis Hannon, Tommy Healy, Frank Heaney, Joe Kendrick, Bertie Kerr, Pat Lee, Jack McCarthy, Alec McKay, Tom Muldoon, Tom Murphy, Jim Murray, Paddy O'Reilly, Sam Robinson, Bob Thomas)	1	1	0	2	2
5.	ITA	(Giuseppe Aliberti, Mario Ardissone, Giuseppe Baldi, Adolpho Baloncieri, Ottavio Barbieri, Antonio Bruna, Luigi Burlando, Giampiero Combi, Leopoldo Conti, Giuseppe Della Valle, Giovanni De Pra, Renzo De Vecchi, Antonio Fayenz, Antonio Janni, Virgilio Levratto, Mario Magnozzi, Martin, Feliciano Monti, Virgilio Rosetta, Severino Rosso)	2	1	0	4	2

Final: URU 3–0 SWI
3rd Place: SWE 1–1 HOL
SWE 3–1 HOL

The tournament opened with an upset as Italy defeated one of the favorites, Spain, 1–0, on a goal that was actually kicked through the net by the Spanish captain, Vallana. The Uruguayan team caught the fancy of the crowd with its 2–1 come-from-behind win over Holland in the semifinals. Holland lodged a protest, but it was denied. Then, when a Dutch referee was assigned to the final, it was Uruguay's turn to protest. Their protest was accepted, and the Dutch official was replaced by a Frenchman. The stadium was packed with 60,000 people for the final match and another 5000 were left outside, causing a crush that led to several injuries. The Swiss struggled vigorously but were unable to stop the

Uruguayans, who led 1–0 at the break before winning 3–0.

1928 Amsterdam T: 17, N: 17, D: 6.13.

		W	L	T	PF	PA
1. URU	(Andres Mazáli, José Nasazzi, Pedro Arispe, José Leandro Andrade, Lorenzo Fernández, Juan Piriz, Alvaro Gestido, Santos Urdináran, Hector Castro, Pedro Petrone, Pedro Céa, Antonio Campolo, Adhemar Canavesi, Juan Arremón, René Borjas, Hector Scarone, Roberto Figueroa)	4	0	1	12	5
2. ARG	(Angel Bossio, Fernando Paternoster, Ludovico Bidoglio, Juan Evaristo, Luis Monti, Segundo Medici, Raimundo Orsi, Enrique Gainzarain, Manuel Ferreyra, Domingo Tarasconi, Adolfo Carricaberry, Feliciano Angel Perducca, Octavio Díaz, Roberto Cherro, Rodolfo Orlandini, Saúl Calandra)	3	1	1	25	8
3. ITA	(Giampiero Combi, Delfo Bellini, Umberto Caligaris, Alfredo Pitto, Fulvio Bernardini, Pietro Genovesi, Adolfo Baloncieri, Elvio Banchero, Angelo Schiavio, Mario Magnozzi, Virgilio Levratto, Giovanni De Prà, Virginio Rosetta, Silvio Pietroboni, Antonio Janni, Enrico Rivolta, Gino Rossetti)	3	1	1	25	11
4. EGY	(Abdell Salam Hamdi, Sayed Fahmi Abaza, Mohammed Ahmad Shemais, Gaber Yacout El-Soury, Ali Fahmi El-Hassani, Abdel Halim Younis Hassan, Ismail El-Said Hooda, Aly Mohamed Riad, Ismail Mahmoud Hooda, Moosa Hassan Moussa El-Ezam, Mohamed Gamil El-Zubeir, Mohamed Ali Rostam, Mohamed Salem, Mohamed Ezzel Din Gamal, Mahmoud Mokhtar Refaee, Ali Mahmoud Soliman)	2	2	0	12	19
5. BEL	(Jan de Bie, S.J.M. Verhulst, Henri Bierna, Georges Despae, Louis Versyp, H.M.J. de Deken, August Ruyssevelt, Jean Diddens, Jacques Moeschal, Raymond Braine, Gerard de Vos, Pierre Braine, Bernard Voorhoof, Florimond van Halme, Gustave Boesman, Jules Lavigne, Nicolaas Hoydonckx, Jean Caudron)	1	1	0	8	9
5. GER	(Ernst Albrecht, Albert Beier, Ludwig Hofmann, Richard Hofmann, Josef Hornauer, Hans Kalb, Georg Knöpfle, Ludwig Leinberger, Josef Pöttinger, Heinrich Stuhlfauth, Henrich Weber)	1	1	0	5	4
5. POR	(Antonio Fernandes Roquete, Carlos Alves, Jorge Gomes Vieira, Raul Soares Figueiredo, Augusto Silva, Césarde Matos Rodrigues, Valdemar Mota Fonseca, José Manuel Soares Louro, Victor Marcolino da Silva, Armando Martins, José Manuel Martins, C. Santos Nunes, O. Maia Vasques de Carvalho, A.J. João, A. Ramos, J. Conçalves Tavares, R. Ornellas, Joãodos Santos, L. dos Santos)	1	1	0	3	3
5. SPA	(J. M. Yermo Solaegui, Martin Marculeta Barberia, Luis Regueiro Pagola, Jacinto Quinococes López, José María Jauregui Lagunas, Luis Iruretagoyena Ayestaran, Antonio Mariscal Ibeuba, Trino Arizcorreta Sein, Francisco Gamborena Hernandorena, Amadeo Labarta Rey, Pedro Vallana Jeanaguenat, Ciriaco Errasti Suinaga, Domingo de Zaldua Anabitarte, José Legarreta Abaitua, Antero Gonzáles de Audicana Inchaurraga, M. Sagarzazu Martinez, Ignacio Alcorta y Hermoso, J. Errazquin Aumas, J. Izaguirre Goena, A. Villaverde Llanos, Francisco Bienzobas Ocariz, Robustiano Bilbao, Echevarria)	1	1	1	9	9

Final: URU 1–1 ARG
URU 2–1 ARG
3rd Place: ITA 11–3 EGY

The first final ended in a draw and had to be replayed.

1932 Los Angeles not held

1936 Berlin T: 16, N: 16, D: 8.15.

		W	L	PF	PA
1. ITA	(Bruno Venturini, Alfredo Foni, Pietro Rava, Giuseppe Baldo, Achille Piccini, Ugo Locatelli, Annibale Frossi, Libero Marchini, Sergio Bertoni, Carlo Biagi, Francesco Gabriotti, Luigi Scarabello, Giulio Cappelli, Alfonso Negro)	4	0	13	2

			W	L	PF	PA
2. AUT	(Eduard Kainberger, Ernst Künz, Martin Kargl, Anton Krenn, Karl Wahlmüller, Max Hofmeister, Walter Werginz, Adolf Laudon, Klement Steinmetz, Karl Kainberger, Franz Fuchsberger, Franz Mandi, Josef Kitzmüller)		2	1	7	4
3. NOR	(Henry Johansen, Nils Eriksen, Öivind Holmsen, Frithjof Ulleberg, Jörgen Juve, Rolf Holmberg, Magdalon Monsen, Reidar Kvammen, Alf Martinsen, Odd Frantzen, Arne Brustad, Fredrik Horn, Sverre Hansen, Magnar Isaksen)		3	1	10	4
4. POL	(Spirydion Albanski, Wladyslaw Szczepaniak, Antoni Galecki, Wilhelm Góra, Franciszek Cebulak, Ewald Dytko, Walerian Kisielinski, Michal Matyas, Teodor Peterek, Hubert God, Gerhard Wdarz, Henryk Martyna, Józef Kotlarczyk, Jan Wasiewicz, Ryszard Piec, Walenty Musielak, Fryc Scherfke)		2	2	11	10
5. GBR	(Hadyn Hill, Guy Holmes, Robert Fulton, John Gardiner, Bernard Joy, Daniel Pettit, James Crawford, Joseph Kyle, John Dodds, Maurice Edelston, Lester Finch)		1	1	6	5
5. GER	(Hans Jakob, Reinhold Münzenberg, Heinz Ditgens, Rudolf Gramlich, Ludwig Goldbrunner, Robert Bernard, Ernst Lehner, Otto Siffling, August Lenz, Adolf Urban, Wilhelm Simetsreiter)		1	1	9	2
5. JPN	(Rihei Sano, Sekiji Suzuki, Teizo Takeuchi, Matoo Tatsuhara, Oita, Yoshuku Kin, Matsunaga Ukon, Taigo Kawamoto, Takeshi Kamo, Shogo Kamo, Koichi Teneda)		1	1	3	10
5. PER	(Juan Valdivieso, Arturo Fernandez, Victor Lavalle, Carlos Tovar, Segundo Castillo, Orestes Jordan, Adelfo Magallanes, Jorge Alcade, Teodoro Fernandez, Alejandro Villanueva, José Morales)		1	0	7	3

Final: ITA 2–1 AUT
3rd Place: NOR 3–2 POL

The stature of Olympic soccer, already weakened by the introduction of the World Cup in 1930 and the exclusion of the sport from the 1932 Olympic Games, received another blow when the 1936 tournament was marred by unruly incidents. First came the match between Italy and the United States, in which two Americans were injured. When the German referee, Weingartner, ordered Achille Piccini of Italy to leave the game, he refused to go. Several Italian players surrounded Weingartner, pinned his arms to his sides, and covered his mouth with their hands. The game continued with Piccini still in the lineup, and Italy won 1–0.

This unfortunate affair was nothing compared to what took place five days later, during the quarterfinal contest between Peru and Austria. Austria led 2–0 at the interval, but Peru tied the game with two goals in the last 15 minutes. A 15-minute overtime period was then played without further scoring, so a second overtime was ordered. By this time the small but vocal group of Peruvian spectators had become frantic with emotion. What followed depends on which continent is telling the story. Evidently, some Peruvian fans rushed onto the field while the game was still in progress and actually attacked one of the Austrian players. The Peruvian team took advantage of the chaos to score two quick goals and win the game, 4–2. Austria protested immediately, and a Jury of Appeal, composed of five European men, ordered the match replayed two days later. The jury also decreed that the game be played behind locked doors with no spectators allowed. The Peruvians refused to show up, and the entire Peruvian Olympic contingent withdrew from the games, as did the Colombians, who supported their South American neighbors. Back in Lima, Peruvian demonstrators threw stones at the German consulate, while Peru's president, Oscar Benavides, denounced "the crafty Berlin decision." When German diplomats appealed to Benavides and pointed out that the decision had been made not by Germans but by officials of F.I.F.A., the International Football Federation, the president changed his position and blamed the demonstrations on Communists.

Meanwhile, back in Berlin, a bitterly contested final was fought between Italy and Austria. The first 45-minute half ended without a score. Midway in the second half, Annibale Frossi, Italy's right wing, scored the first goal of the game. Eleven minutes later Karl Kainberger, Austria's inside left, tied the score and the match went into overtime. A quick goal by Frossi proved decisive, and Italy won the gold medal, 2–1.

1948 London T: 18, N: 18, D: 8.13.

			W	L	PF	PA
1. SWE	(Torsten Lindberg, Knut Nordahl, Erik Nilsson, Birger Rosengren, Bertil Nordahl, Sune Andersson, Kjell Rosén, Gunnar Gren, Gunnar Nordahl, Henry Carlsson, Nils Liedholm, Börje Leander)		4	0	22	3
2. YUG	(Ljubomir Lovric, Miroslav Brozovic, Branislav Stanovic, Zlatko Čajkovski, Miodrag Jovanovic, Zvonko Cimermančic, Rajko Mitić, Stjepan Bobek, Željko Čajkovski, Bernard Vukas, Franjo Šoštaric, Prvoslav Mihajlovic, Fränjo Wolfl, Kosta Tomašević)		3	1	13	6
3. DEN	(Ejgil Nielsen, Viggo Jensen, Knud Börge Overgaard, Axel Pilmark, Dion Örnvoid, Ivan Jensen, Jo-		3	1	15	11

hannes Plöger, Knud Lundberg, Carl Aage Praest, John Hansen, Jörgen Sörensen, Holger Seebach, Karl Aage Hansen)

4.	GBR	(Ronald Simpson, Charles "Jack" Neale, Andrew Carmichael, John Roderick Hardisty, Eric Lee, Eric Fright, J. Alan Boyd, Andrew Aitken, Harold McIlvenny, John Rawlings, William Amor, Kevin McAlinden, George Manning, James McColl, Douglas McBain, Frank Donovan, Thomas Hopper, Denis Kelleher, Frederick Peter Kippax)	2	2	9	11
5.	FRA	(Gaston Rouxel, Robert Krug, Bernard Bienvue, René Persillon, Marcel Colau, Georges Robert, Jean Heckel, Antoine Strappe, René Hebinger, Jacques Paluch, René Courbin)	1	1	2	2
5.	ITA	(Giuseppe Casari, Guglielmo Giovannini, Adone Stellin, Tommaso Maestrelli, Maino Neri, Giacomo Mari, Emilio Cavigioli, Angelo Turconi, Francesco Pernigo, Valerio Cassani, Emilio Caprile)	1	1	12	5
5.	KOR	(Hong Duk-yung, Pak Kyoo-chung, Pak Dai-chong, Choi Soon-gon, Kim Kyoo-whan, Min Byung-dai, Woo Zung-whan, Bai Chong-hoo, Chung Nam-sik, Kim Yong-sik, Chung Kook-chin)	1	1	5	13
5.	TUR	(Cihat Arman, Murat Alyuz, Vedu Tosuncuk, Naim Ozhaya, Bülent Eken, Hüseyin Saygun, Fikret Kercan, Erol Keskin, Gündüz Kilic, Lefter Andonyadis, Sükrü Gülesin)	1	1	5	3

Final: SWE 3–1 YUG
3rd Place: DEN 5–3 GBR

An unusual play from the 1948 football (soccer) tournament. Henry Carlsson of Sweden scores a goal against Denmark that is caught by his teammate Gunnar Nordahl, who had dashed into the opposing goal too avoid an offside call.

By 1948 the best players of Western Europe and South America were turning professional, and Olympic soccer began to be dominated by the state-sponsored "amateur" teams of Eastern Europe. Sweden was the last non-Communist team to win an unboycotted Olympic football tournament until 1992. Their team included three brothers, Gunnar, Bertil, and Knut Nordahl, as well as three firemen, including Gunnar Nordahl.

1952 Helsinki T: 25, N: 25, D: 8.2.

			W	L	T	PF	PA
1.	HUN	(Gyula Grosics, Jenö Buzánszky, Mihály Lantos, József Bozsik, Gyula Lóránt, József Zakariás, Nándor Hidegkuti, Sándor Kocsis, Péter Palotás, Ferenc Puskás, Zoltán Czibor, Jenö Dalnoki, Imre Kovács, László Budai II, Lajos Csordás)	5	0	0	20	2
2.	YUG	(Vladimir Beara, Branislav Stankovič, Tomislav Crnkovič, Zlatko Čajkovski, Ivan Horvat, Vujadin Boškov, Tihomir Ognjanov, Rajko Mitič, Bernard Vukas, Stjepan Bobek, Branko Zebec)	4	1	1	26	13
3.	SWE	(Karl Svensson, Lennart Samuelsson, Erik Nilsson, Olof Ahlund, Bengt Gustavsson, Gösta Lindh, Sylve Bengtsson, Gösta Löfgren, Ingvar Rydell, Yngve Brodd, Gösta Sandberg, Holger Hansson)	3	1	0	9	8
4.	GER	(Rudolf Schönbeck, Hans Eberle, Herbert Jäger, Kurt Sommerlatt, Herbert Schäfer, Alfred Post, Ludwig Hinterstocker, Georg Stollenwerk, Hans Zeitler, Willi Schröder, Kurt Ehrmann, Erich Gleixner, Matthias Mauritz, Karl Klug)	2	2	0	8	8
5.	AUT	(Fritz Nikolai, Walter Kollmann, Anton Krammar, Anton Wolf, Josef Walter, Robert Fendler, Hermann Hochleitner, Franz Feldinger, Erich Stumpf, Herbert Grohs, Otto Gollnhuber)	1	1	0	5	6
5.	BRA	(Carlos Martins Cavalheiro, Mauro Torres Homen Rodrigues, Waldir Villas Boas, Alves "Zozimo" Calazans, Adesio Alves Machado, Edison Campos Martins, Larry Pinto de Faria, Milton Pessanha, Edvaldo "Vava" Neto, Humberto Barbosa Tozzi, Jansen Moreira)	2	1	0	9	6
5.	DEN	(Jorgen Johansen, Poul Erik Petersen, Svend Nielsen, Erik Terkelsen, Poul Andersen,	2	1	0	7	6

		W	L	T	PF	PA
	Steen Blicher, Jorgen Hansen, Poul Eyvind Petersen, Jens Hansen, Knud Lundberg, Holger Seebach)					
5. TUR	(Erdoğan Akin, Nekdet Sentürk, Ridvan Bolatli, Mustafa Ertan, Basri Dirimilili, Erküment Güder, Vasif Cetinel, Tekin Bilge, Yalçin Çaka, Muzaffer Tokac, Makit Gürdal)	1	1	0	3	8

Final: HUN 2–0 YUG
3rd Place: SWE 2–0 GER

Entering the Olympics for the first time, the Soviet Union expected to win the gold medal, but in the second round they were beaten by Yugoslavia. This was such a humiliating shock that the match was not mentioned in the Soviet press until after the death of dictator Josef Stalin the following year.

1956 Melbourne T: 11, N: 11, D: 12.8.

		W	L	T	PF	PA
1. SOV	(Lev Yashin, Anatoly Bashashkin, Mikhail Ogonikov, Boris Kuznetsov, Igor Netto, Anatoly Maslyonkin, Boris Tatushin, Anatoly Issayev, Nikita Simonyan, Sergei Salnikov, Anatoly Ilyin, Vadym Tyshchenko, Aleksei Paramonov, Eduard Streltsov, Valentin Ivanov, Vladimir Ryshkin, Yosif Betsa, Boris Razinsky)	4	0	1	9	2
2. YUG	(Petar Radenkovic, Mladen Koščak, Nikola Radovič, Ivan Šantek, Ljubisa Spajič, Dobroslav Krstič, Dragoslav Šekularac, Zlatko Papec, Sava Antič, Todor Veselinovič, Muhamed Mujič, Blagoje Vidinic, Ibrahim Biogradič, Luka Lipošinovič)	2	1	0	13	3
3. BUL	(Yosif Yosilov, Kiril Rakarov, Nikola Kovatschev, Stefan Stefanov, Manol Manolov, Gavril Stojanov, Dimiter Milanov, Georgy Dimitrov, Panayot Panayotov, Ivan Kolev, Todor Diyev, Georgy Naydenov, Miltscho Goranov, Krum Yanev)	2	1	0	10	3
4. IND	(Narayan Subramaniam, Syed Khaja Aziz, Shaikh Abdul Lateef, Mohamed Kempiah, Noor Muhamed, Ahmed Husain, Mohamed Kannayan, Neville Stephen D'Souza, Krishna Chandra Pal, Nikhil Kumar Nunday, Krishna Swamy	1	2	0	10	3

Kittu, T. Abdul Rahman, Muhamed Abdus Salam, Pradip Kuma Banerjee, Tulsidas Balaram, Peter Ramaswamy Thangaraj, Samar Banerjee)

		W	L	T	PF	PA
5. AUS	(Ronald Lord, Robert Bignell, John Pettigrew, George Arthur, William Sander, Bruce Morrow, Francis Loughran, Jack Lennard, Graham McMillan, Edward Smith, Alwyn Warren)	1	1	0	4	4
5. GBR	(Harry Sharratt, Donald Stoker, Leslie Thomas Farrer, Lawrence Topp, Stanley Prince, Herbert Dodkins, James Lewis, John Roderick Hardisty, John Laybourne, George Bromilow, Charles Twissell)	1	1	0	10	6

Final: SOV 1–0 YUG
3rd Place: BUL 3–0 IND

The winning goal was headed in early in the second half by Anatoly Ilyin. The Soviet victory was preserved when a goal by Yugoslavia's Zlatko Papec was disallowed because of an offside infraction. Of the 18 men on the Soviet squad, only Ukrainian Vadym Tyshchenko was not from Russia.

1960 Rome T: 16, N: 16, D: 9.10.

		W	L	T	PF	PA
1. YUG	(Blagoje Vidinič, Novak Roganovič, Fahrudin Jusufi, Zeljko Perušič, Vladimir Durkovič, Ante Žanetič, Andrija Ankovič, Zeljko Matuš, Milan Galič, Tomislav Knez, Borivoje Kostič, Milutin Soskič, Velimir Sombolac, Aleksandar Kozlina, Silvester Takač, Dusan Maravič)	3	0	2	17	7
2. DEN	(Henry From, Poul Andersen, Poul Jensen, Bent Hansen, Hans Nielsen, Flemming Nielsen, Poul Pedersen, Tommy Troelsen, Harald Nielsen, Henning Enoksen, Jörn Sörensen, John Danielsen)	4	1	0	11	7
3. HUN	(Gábor Török, Zoltán Dudás, Jenö Dalnoki, Ernö Solymosi, Pál Várhidi, Ferenc Kovács, Imre Sátori, János Göröcs, Flórián Albert, Pál Orosz, János Dunai, Lajos Faragó, Dezsö Novák, Oszkár Vilezsál, Gyula Rákosi, László Pál, Tibor Pál)	4	1	0	17	6
4. ITA	(Luciano Alfieri, Tarcisio Burgnich, Mario Trebbi, Paride Tumburus, Sandro Salvadore, Giovanni Trappatoni, Giancarlo Cella, Giovanni Rivera, Ugo Tomeazzi, Giacomo Bulgarelli, Giorgio Rossano, Orazio Ran-	2	1	2	11	7

cati, Giorgio Ferrini, Giovanni Fanello, Gilberto Noletti, Luciano Magistrelli)
Final: YUG 3–1 DEN
3rd Place: HUN 2–1 ITA

Three-time runner-up Yugoslavia shocked Denmark when their captain, Milan Galič, scored a goal from 30 meters out in the first minute of play. Ten minutes later, Zeljko Matuš made it 2–0 and it looked like a rout might be in the making. However, late in the first half, Galič was ejected for insulting a referee, and Yugoslavia played the rest of the game with only ten players. Nevertheless, they held on to their lead and prevailed 3–1. It is worth noting that Yugoslavia tied with Bulgaria in their preliminary pool and qualified for the semifinals only because they won a coin toss.

1964 Tokyo T: 14, N: 14, D: 10.23.

		W	L	T	PF	PA
1. HUN	(Antal Szentmihályi, Dezsö Novák, Kálmán Ihász, Gusztáv Szepesi, Árpád Orban, Ferenc Nógrádi, János Farkas, Tibor Csernai, Ferenc Bene, Imre Komora, Sándor Katona, József Gelei, Károly Polotai, Zoltán Varga)	5	0	0	22	6
2. CZE	(František Schmucker, Anton Urban, Karel Zdenek Pičman, Josef Vojta, Vladimir Weiss, Jan Geleta, Jan Brumovsky, Ivan Mráz, Karel Lichtnégl, Vojtech Masny, František Valošek, Anton Svajlen, Karel Knesl, Stefan Matlak, Karel Nepomucky, František Knebort, Ludevit Cvetler)	5	1	0	19	5
3. GDR	(Hans Jürgen Heinsch, Peter Rock, Manfred Geisler, Herbert Pankau, Manfred Walter, Gerhard Körner, Hermann Stöcker, Otto Frässdorf, Henning Frenzel, Jürgen Nöldner, Eberhard Vogel, Horst Weigang, Klaus Urbanczyk, Bernd Bauchspiess, Klaus-Dieter Seehaus, Werner Unger, Wolfgang Barthels, Klaus Lisiewicz, Dieter Engelhardt)	4	1	1	12	4
4. EGY	(Reda Ahmed, Yaken Zaki, Amin Elisnawi, Mohamed Kotb, Raafat Attia, Mohamed Abdelat Elsherbini, Seddik Mohamed, Ibrahim Riad, Mohamed Badawi, Nabil Nosseir, K. Aly Etman, F. Aly Korshed, Darwish Amin, Rifaat Elfanagili, Ahmed Moust Gad, Kalil Shahin, Mahmoud Hassan, Taha Ismail, Farouk Mahmoud)	2	3	1	18	16
5. GHA	(Dodoo-Ankrah, Samuel Okai, Emmanuel Oblitey, Sam Acquah, Addo-Odametey, Emmanuel Nkansah, Gyau Agyemang, Wilberforce Mfum, Edward Aggrey Fynn, Edward Acquah, Kofi Pare)	1	1	1	5	8
5. JPN	(Kenzo Yokoyama, Hiroshi Katayama, Yoshitada Yamaguchi, Ryozo Suzuki, Aritatsu Ogi, Mitsuo Kamata, Saburo Kawabuchi, Shigeo Yaegashi, Kunishige Kamamoto, Teruki Miyamoto, Masashi Watanabe)	1	2	0	5	9
5. ROM	(Ilie Datcu, Ilie Greavu, Bujor Hălmăgeanu, Emil Petru, Ion Nunweiler, Niculae Georgescu, Ion Pircălab, Gheorge Constantin, Ion Ionescu, Dan Coe, Carol Crăinicheanu)	2	1	0	5	4
5. YUG	(Ivan Curkovic, Mirsad Fazlagić, Svetozar Vujović, Rudolf Belin, Milan Cop, Jovan Miladinović, Spasoje Samardzic, Slaven Zambata, Ivan Osim, Lazar Radovič, Dragan Dzajič)	1	2	0	8	8

Final: HUN 2–1 CZE
3rd Place: GDR 3–1 EGY

Most of the fireworks took place before the tournament even started. Beginning in 1952, so many nations began applying to compete in the Olympics that pre-Olympic soccer tournaments had to be held to decide the 16 Olympic teams. On May 24, 1964, one such qualifying match took place in Lima between Peru and Argentina. Argentina led 1–0, but with two minutes to play Peru scored to tie the game. However, the Uruguayan referee, Angel Eduardo Payos, nullified the goal because of rough play by the Peruvians. While the crowd of 45,000 booed its disapproval, two spectators leaped onto the field and attacked the referee. They were quickly arrested, which angered the crowd even more. Then Payos ordered the game suspended, claiming, with obvious justification, that police protection on the field was inadequate. The incensed crowd surged onto the field while the police hustled Payos and the players to safety. Some spectators began breaking windows and before long mounted police appeared and began herding the rioters toward the exits, many of which were, unfortunately, locked. Tear-gas grenades were fired by the police, while the Peruvian soccer fans responded by throwing stones and bottles and setting part of the stadium on fire. The fighting spilled into the streets of Lima, and before the night was out, 328 people had been killed and over 500 injured. Most of those killed had been trampled to death, but at least four persons were shot by police bullets. The Peruvian government declared a national "state of siege" and suspended the constitution. Meanwhile, demonstrators marched to the

National Palace demanding an end to police brutality and the declaration of a tie in the match with Argentina. Neither demand was met. Argentina, by the way, went to Tokyo but lost both of their games.

When the Olympic tournament finally commenced, two of the 16 qualifying teams were missing. North Korea dropped out following a dispute with the I.O.C. Italy, the only Western European team to qualify for the Tokyo tournament, withdrew following accusations that several of its players were actually professionals. This charge was fairly hard to deny considering that three members of the Italian Olympic team were also members of the Inter-Milan team, which was the reigning European Cup champion. In fact, Sandro Mazzola scored two of the goals that defeated Real Madrid in the Cup final.

The Olympic tournament itself was not very impressive, particularly after all that had preceded it. However, the final between Hungary and Czechoslovakia was an exciting match. Hungary's first goal, scored at the beginning of the second half, was actually put through the net by Josef Vojta of Czechoslovakia, who inadvertently deflected a Hungarian pass past his own goalie. Thirteen minutes later, Hungarian center forward Ferenc Bene outran the Czech defense and blasted in a second goal, which proved to be decisive.

1968 Mexico City T: 16, N: 16, D: 10.26.

		W	L	T	PF	PA
1. HUN	(Károly Fatér, Dezsö Novák, Lajos Dunai, Miklós Páncsics, Iván Menczel, Lajos Szüca, Laszló Fazekas, Antal Dunai, László Nagy, Ernö Noskó, István Juhász, Lajos Kocsis, István Básti, László Keglovich, István Sárközi)	5	0	1	18	3
2. BUL	(Stoyan Yordanov, Atanas Gerov, Georgi Hristakiev, Milko Gaidarski, Kiril Ivkov, Ivailo Georgiev, Tsvetan Veselinov, Yevgeny Yanchovski, Peter Zhekov, Atanas Hristov, Asparuh Nikodimov, Kiril Stankov, Todor Krustev, Mihail Gionin, Yancho Dimitrov, Georgi Tsetkov, Ivan Zafirov, Georgi Vasilev)	3	1	2	16	10
3. JPN	(Kenzo Yokoyama, Hiroshi Katayama, Yoshitada Yamaguchi, Mitsuo Kamata, Takaji Mori, Aritátsu Ogi, Teruki Miyamoto, Masashi Watanabe, Kunishige Kamamoto, Ikuo Matsumoto, Ryuichi Sugiyama, Masakatsu Miyamoto, Yasuyuki Kuwahara, Shigeo Yaegashi)	3	3	0	10	9
4. MEX	(Javier Vargas, Juan Mañuel Alejándrez, Héctor Sanabria, Mario Pérez, Luis Regueiro, Luis Estrada, Vicente Pereda, Cesáreo Victorino, Javier Sánchez Galindo, Ignacio Basaguren, Albino Morales, Humberto Medina, Héctor Pulido, Elias Muñoz, Fernando Bustos)	3	3	0	10	9
5. FRA	(Jean Lempereur, Freddy Zix, Michel Verhoeve, Gilbert Plante, Jean-Michel Larque, Jean Louis Hodoul, Daniel Perrigaud, Daniel Hortaville, Marc Case, Gerard Hallet, Henri Ribul)	2	2	0	9	8
5. GUA	(Alberto Lopez, Llijon Leon, Roberto Camposeco, Hugo Montoya, Armando Melgar, Jorge Roldan, Hugo Torres, Carlos Valdez, Hugo Pena, David Stokes, Julio Garcia)	2	2	0	6	4
5. ISR	(Haim Levin, Menacham Bello, Zvi Rosen, Shaia Shwager, Shmuel Rosenthal, Rachamim Talbi, Giora Shpigal, Jehoshua Faygenbaum, Mordechai Shpiegler, Itzhak Druker, George Borba)	2	1	1	9	7
5. SPA	(Pedro Mora Marine, Gregorio Benito Rubio, Francisco Espildora Muñoz, Miguel Ochoa Vaca, Isidro Sala Puigvedal, Juan Asensi Ripoll, Rafael Jaen Rodríguez, Juan Fernández Vilella, José Garzon Fito, José Grande Cereijo, Fernando Ortuno Blasco)	2	1	1	4	2

Final: HUN 4–1 BUL
3rd Place: JPN 2–0 MEX

Morocco qualified for the final tournament, but refused to participate against Israel. They were replaced by Ghana. The Ghana-Israel game, won by Israel 5–3, disintegrated into brawling, which continued back at the Olympic Village. A match between Czechoslovakia and Guatemala was also disrupted by fighting. The final pitted defending champion Hungary against Bulgaria, which qualified only after their tied quarterfinal game with Israel was decided by the toss of a coin. Bulgaria scored first on a header by Dimitrov, but four minutes before the end of the first half, Menczel of Hungary evened the score. A minute later Dunai of Hungary put in another goal. At this point the situation deteriorated drastically. Referee Diego De Leo, an Italian-born naturalized Mexican, ejected Dimitrov for rough play. Seconds later another Bulgarian, Kiril Ivkov, was thrown out. An angry teammate, Atanas Hristov, kicked the ball toward the referee, and he too was ejected. The Mexican crowd was none too pleased with the actions of Mr. De Leo. Having already disrupted the third-place game by throwing cushions onto the field, they used the same tactic to show their disapproval and cause delay in the final. The ejections effectively ended the contest, as Bulgaria was forced to play the second half with only eight players. Juhász of Hungary was eventually banished as well, but the Hungarians still outnumbered the Bulgarians 10–8 and won easily, 4–1.

1972 Munich T: 16, N: 16, D: 9.10.

			W	L	T	PF	PA
1.	POL	(Hubert Kostka, Zbigniew Gut, Jerzy Gorgon, Zygmunt Anczok, Leslaw Cmikiewicz, Zygmunt Maszczyk, Jerzy Kraska, Kazimierz Deyna, Zygfryd Szoltysik, Wlodzimierz Lubanski, Robert Gadocha, Ryszard Szymczak, Antoni Szymanowski, Marian Ostafinski, Grzegorz Lato, Joachim Marx, Kazimierz Kmiecik)	6	0	1	21	5
2.	HUN	(István Géczi, Péter Vépi, Miklós Páncsics, Péter Juhász, Lajos Szücs, Mihály Kozma, Antal Dunai, Lajos Kü, Béla Váradi, Ede Dunai, László Bálint, Lajos Kocsis, Kálmán Tóth, Jozsef Kovács, László Branikovits, Csaba Vidáts, Ádám Rothermel)	5	1	1	18	5
3.	GDR	(Jürgen Croy, Manfred Zapf, Konrad Weise, Bernd Bransch, Jürgen Pommerenke, Jürgen Sparwasser, Hans-Jürgen Kreische, Joachim Streich, Wolfgang Seguin, Peter Ducke, Frank Ganzera, Lothar Kurbjuweit, Eberhard Vogel, Ralf Schulenberg, Reinhard Häfner, Harald Irmscher, Siegmar Wätzlich)	4	2	1	23	9
3.	SOV	(Oleh Blokhin, Murtaz Khurtsilava, Yuri Istomin, Vladimir Kaplichnyi, Viktor Kolotov, Yevgeny Lovchev, Sergei Olshansky, Yevhen Rudakov, Vyacheslav Semenov, Gennady Yevryuzhikhin, Oganes Zanazanyan, Andrei Yakubik, Arkady Andriasyan)	5	1	1	17	6
5.	DEN	(Mogens Therkilosen, Flemming Ahlberg, Svend Andersen, Per Rontved, Jorgen Rasmussen, Jack Hansen, Kresten Nygaard, Allan Simonsen, Max Rasmussen, Arvo Heino Hansen, Keld Bak, Leif Prinzlau, Hans Ewald Hansen)	3	2	1	11	10
5.	GER	(Hans Jürgen Bradler, Heiner Baltes, Reiner Hollmann, Egon Schmitt, Friedhelm Häbermann, Jürgen Kalb, Hermann Bitz, Ulrich Hoeness, Ottmar Hitzfeld, Bernd Nickel, Klaus Wunder, Ronald Worm, Rudi Seliger)	3	2	1	17	8
5.	MEX	(Jesus Rico, José Luis Trejo, Juan Alvarez, Enrique Martin Del Campo, Alejandro Hernandez, Fernando Blanco, Manuel Manzo, Daniel Razo, Leonardo Cuellar, Horacio Sanchez, Alejandro Peña, Alfredo Hernandez)	2	3	1	4	14
5.	MOR	(Mohamed Hazzaz, Mohamed Elfilali, Boujamaa Benkhrif, Abdallah Tazi, Ahmed Faras, Mohamed Merzaq, Ahmed Belkorchi, Larbi Ihardane, Khalifa Elbakhti, Abdelali Zahraoui, Mustapha Yaghcha, Ghazouani Mouhoub, Ahmed Najah, Atati Zouita Mohamed, Abdelfattah Jafri)	1	4	1	7	14

Final: POL 2–1 HUN
3rd Place: GDR 2–2 SOV

Hungary entered the final having lost only one of their last 21 Olympic matches going back to 1960. The game was played in torrential rain and near gale-force wind. Hungary led 1–0 at the interval, but when the teams switched sides for the second half Poland took advantage of having the wind at their backs and scored two goals to gain the victory.

1976 Montreal T: 13, N: 13, D: 7.31.

			W	L	T	PF	PA
1.	GDR	(Jürgen Croy, Gerd Weber, Hans-Jürgen Dörner, Konrad Weise, Lothar Kurbjuweit, Reinhard Lauck, Gert Heidler, Reinhard Häfner, Hans-Jürgen Riediger, Bernd Bransch, Martin Hoffmann, Gerd Kische, Wolfram Löwe, Hartmut Schade, Dieter Riedel, Hans-Ullrich Grapenthin, Wilfried Gröbner)	4	0	1	10	2
2.	POL	(Jan Tomaszewski, Antoni Szymanowski, Jerzy Gorgoń, Wojciech Rudy, Wladyslaw Zmuda, Zygmunt Maszczyk, Grzegorz Lato, Henryk Kasperczak, Kazimierz Deyna, Andrzej Szarmach, Kazimierz Kmiecik, Piotr Mowlik, Henryk Wawrowski, Henryk Wieczorek, Leslaw Ćmikiewicz, Jan Beniger, Roman Ogaza)	3	1	1	11	5
3.	SOV	(Vladimir Astapovsky, Anatoly Konkov, Viktor Matvyinko, Mykhalo Fomenko, Stefan Reshko, Volodymyr Troshkin, David	4	1	0	10	4

		W	L	T	PF	PA
	Kipiani, Volodymyr Onyshenko, Viktor Kolotov, Volodymyr Veremiyev, Oleh Blokhin, Leonid Buryak, Vladimir Feodorov, Aleksandr Minayev, Viktor Zvyagintsev, Leonid Nazarenko, Aleksandr Prokhorov)					
4. BRA	(Carlos Gallo, Rosemiro Corrêa de Souza, Roberto Franqueira, Edino Nazareth Filho, Léovegildo Lins Gama, Alberto Marques, Mario Emiliano, João Batista da Silva, Eudes Medeiros, Erivelto Martins, João dos Santos, Mauro de Campos, Julio da Silva Gurjol, Francisco Fraga da Silva, Jarbas Tomazoli Nunes, Edval da Costa, José Pessanha)	2	2	1	6	6
5. FRA	(Jean-Claude Larrieu, Henri Orlandini, Patrick Battiston, Claude Chazottes, Francis Meynieu, Michel Pottier, Alexandre Strassievitch, Henri Zambelli, Michel Couge, Jean Fernandez, Michel Platini, Francisco Rubio, Loic Amisse, Bruno Baronchelli, Eric Pecout, Olivier Rouyer, Jean Marc Schaer)	2	2	1	9	7
5. IRN	(Mansour Rashidi, Hassan Nazari, Andranik Eskandarian, Bijan Zolfagharnasab, Parviz Qelichkhani, Ali Parvin, Nasrollah Abdollahi, Nasser Nouraii, Hassan Rowshan, Ali-reza Khorshidi, Hassan Nayebagha, Gholam Mazloomi, Hessem Mirfakhali, Ghafoor Jahani, Ali-Reza Azizi, Nasser Hejazi)	1	2	0	4	5
5. ISR	(Itzhak Vissoker, Abrahm Lev, Yaron Oz, Haim Bar, Moshe Shani, Itzak Peretz, Itzhak Shum, Elimeleh Leventhal, Rifaat Tourk, Gideon Damti, Josef Sorynow, Meir Nimni, Oded Nachness, Avraham Cohen, Joshua Gal, Ehud Ben-Tovim, Alon Ben-Dor)	0	1	3	4	7
5. PRK	(Jin In-Chol, Kim Gwangsok, Kim Il-nam, Kim Myong-song, Ma Jong-u, Pak Jong-hun, An Se-uk, Hong Song-nam, Cha Jong-sok, Kim Sung-gyu, Yang Song-guk, An Gil-wan, Li Hi-yon, Myong Dong-chan, Pak Kyong-won)	1	2	0	3	9

Final: GDR 3–1 POL
3rd Place: SOV 2–0 BRA

Again the Olympic soccer final was played in heavy rain, and again it was dominated by the professional amateurs of Eastern Europe, including ten members of Poland's 1974 World Cup team. In the final match, East Germany scored two goals in the first 15 minutes and scored again with six minutes to play to secure the gold medal.

1980 Moscow T: 16, N: 16, D: 8.2.

		W	L	T	PF	PA
1. CZE	(Stanislav Seman, Luděk Macela, Josef Mazura, Libor Radimec, Zdeněk Rygel, Petr Němec, Ladislav Vizek, Jan Berger, Jindřich Svoboda, Lubos Pokluda, Werner Lička, Rostislav Václavíček, Jaroslav Netolicka, Oldřich Rott, František Štambacher, František Kunzo)	4	0	2	10	1
2. GDR	(Bodo Rudwaleit, Artur Ullrich, Lothar Hause, Frank Uhlig, Frank Baum, Rüdiger Schnuphase, Frank Terletzki, Wolfgang Steinbach, Jürgen Bähringer, Werner Peter, Dieter Kühn, Norbert Trieloff, Matthias Liebers, Bernd Jakubowski, Wolf-Rüdiger Netz, Matthias Müller)	4	1	1	12	2
3. SOV	(Rinat Dasayev, Tengiz Sulakvelidze, Aleksandr Chivadze, Vagiz Khidiyatullin, Oleg Romantsev, Sergei Shavlo, Sergei Andreyev, Volodymyr Bezsonov, Yuri Gavrilov, Fyodor Cherenkov, Valery Gazzayev, Vladimir Pilguy, Serhei Baltacha, Sergei Nikulin, Khoren Oganesyan, Aleksandr Prokopenko, Revaz Chelebadze)	5	1	0	10	3
4. YUG	(Dragan Pantelić, Nikica Cukrov, Ivan Gudelj, Milos Hrstic, Milan Jovin, Nikica Klincarski, Miso Krstiçević, Dzevad Secerbegović, Vladimir Matijević, Dušan Pestić, Tomislav Ivković, Boro Primorać, Srebrenko Repcić, Milos Sestić, Zlatko Vujović, Zoran Vujović)	3	2	1	9	7
5. ALG	(Mourad Ahara, Mahmoud Guendouz, Bouzid Mahiduz, Chaabane Merzekane, Mohamed Kheddis, Rabah Madjer, Ali Fergani, Tadj Bensaoula, Lakhdar Belloumi, Salah Assad, Mohamed Rahmani, Salah Larbes, Djamel Menad, Abderrahmane Derquaz, Hocine Yahi, Mohamed Quamar Ghrib)	1	2	1	4	4
5. CUB	(Jose Reinoso, Miguel Lopez, Raimundo Frometa, Luis Sán-	2	2	0	3	12

chez, Luis Dreke, Roberto Espinosa, Andres Roldan, Amado Povea, Dagoberto Lara, Ramon Núñez, Calixto Martinez, Roberto Pereira, Jorge Masso, Fermin Madera, Carlos Loredo, Luis Hernandez)

5. IRQ (Abdul Fatah Jassim, Adnan Derchal Hutar, Jamal Ali Hamza, Saad Jassih Mohammed, Hassan Farhan Hassoun, Alaa Ahmed Khdhayir, Adil Khohayrr Hafidh, Falah Hassan Jasim, Hadi Ahmed Basheer, Hussain Saeed Muhammed, Thamir Assoufi Elias, Ibrahim Ali Kadhum, Wathiq Aswad Muhyi, Nazar Asmraf Salman, Ali Kadhum Nasir, Kadom Shibib Abdulsada) 1 1 2 4 5

5. KUW (Ahmad Al-Tarabulsi, Naeem Sa'ad Mubarak, Mahoub Mubarak, Jamal Alqabendi, Walid Al-Jasem Mubarak, Sa'ad Al-Houti, Fathi Marzouq, Jasem Sultan, Mujayed Alhaddad, Hamad Bohamad, Youssef Al-Suwayed, Ahmad Hasan, Humoud Al-Shemmari, Sami Alhashash, Faisal Al-Dakhil, Abdulnabi Alkhadi) 1 1 2 4 5

Final: CZE 1–0 GDR
3rd Place: SOV 2–0 YUG

Seven of the 16 qualifying teams withdrew as part of the anti-Soviet boycott and were replaced by lesser teams. The only goal of the final was scored by a substitute, Jindřich Svoboda, who entered the game with 19 minutes to play and put in a header six minutes later. For the third straight time, the Olympic final was played in a rainstorm.

1984 Los Angeles-Pasadena T: 16, N: 16, D: 8.11.

		W	L	T	PF	PA
1. FRA	(Albert Rust, William Ayache, Michel Bibard, Dominique Bijotat, François Brisson, Patrick Cubaynes, Patrice Garande, Philippe Jeannol, Guy Lacombe, Jean-Claude Lemoult, Jean-Philippe Rohr, Didier Sénac, Jean-Christoph Thouvenel, José Touré, Daniel Xuereb, Jean-Louis Zanon)	4	0	2	13	6
2. BRA	(Gilmar Rinaldi, Ronaldo Silva, Jorge Luiz Brum, Mauro Galvão, Ademir Roque Kaeser, André Luiz Ferreira, Paulo Santos, Carlos "Dunga" Verri, João Leiehardt Neto, Augilmar Ol-	5	1	0	9	5

iveira, Silvio Paiva, Luiz Carlos Winck, Davi Cortez Silva, Antonio José Gil, Francisco "Chicão" Vidal, Milton Cruz)

		W	L	T	PF	PA
3. YUG	(Ivan Pudar, Vlado Capljić, Mirsad Baljić, Srecko Katanec, Marko Elsner, Ljubomir Radanović, Admir Smajić, Nenad Gracan, Milko Djurovski, Mehmed Bazdarević, Borislav Cvetković, Tomislav Ivković, Jovica Nikolić, Stjepan Deverić, Branko Miljus, Dragan Stojković, Mitar Mrkela)	5	1	0	16	10
4. ITA	(Franco Tancredi, Riccardo Ferri, Filippo Galli, Sebastiano Nela, Roberto Tricella, Pietro Vierchowod, Salvatore Bagni, Franco Baresi, Sergio Battistini, Antonio Sabato, Beniamino Vignola, Walter Zenga, Pietro Fanna, Daniele Massaro, Massimo Briaschi, Maurizio Iorio, Aldo Serena)	3	3	0	5	5
5. CAN	(Tino Lettieri, Bob Lenarduzzi, Bruce Wilson, Terry Moore, Ian Bridge, Randy Ragan, David Norman, Gerry Gray, Ken Garraway, Dale Mitchell, Mike Sweeney, Igor Vrablic, Paul James, John Catliff)	1	2	1	5	4
5. CHI	(Edwardo Fournier, Daniel Ahumada, Luis Mosquera, Alex Martinez, Leonel Contreras, Alejandro Hisis, Alfredo Núñez, Jaime Vera, Fernando Santis, Sergio Marchant, Juvenal Olmos, Carlos Ramos, Jaime Baeza, Marco Figueroa)	1	1	2	2	2
5. EGY	(Adel Elmaamour, Ali El Sayed Gadallah, Rabie Yassen, Mahmoud Saleh, Ibrahim Youssif, Yehia Sedky, Mostafa Ismail, Shawki Gharib, Magdy Abdelghani, Mahmoud Elkhatib, Emad Soleman, Taher Abouzied, Badreldin Hamed, Mohamad Helmy, Omar Elzeer, Alaa Morsy, Nagy Salem)	1	2	1	5	5
5. GER	(Bernd Franke, Manfred Bockenfeld, Roland Dickgiesser, Dieter Bast, Bernd Wehmeyer, Guido Buchwald, Jürgen Groh, Rudolf Bommer, Dieter Schatzschneider, Andreas Brehme, Frank Mill, Alfred Schoen, Peter Lux, Uwe Rahn, Christian Schreier)	2	2	0	10	6

Final: FRA 2–0 BRA
3rd Place: YUG 2–1 ITA

For the first time, professional football players were allowed to take part in an Olympic tournament. In the case of European and South American teams, only those professionals who had not yet competed in World Cup competition were considered eligible. This, plus the absence of all of the 1980 medalists, due to the Soviet-bloc boycott, led to a lively and wide-open competition.

The final, played before a crowd of 101,799, was won by the French on two second-half goals, a header by François Brisson, ten minutes into the half and a follow shot by Daniel Xuereb less than eight minutes later.

1988 Seoul T: 16, N: 16, D: 10.1.

		W	L	T	PF	PA
1. SOV	(Dmitri Kharin, Gela Ketashvili, Igor Sklyarov, Oleksei Cherednyk, Arvidas Janonis, Yevgeny Kuznetsov, Igor Ponomarev, Aleksandr Borodyuk, Igor Dobrovolsky, Volodymyr Lyuty, Yevgeny Yakovenko, Sergei Fokin, Volodymyr Tatarchuk, Oleksei Mykhaylychenko, Viktor Losev, Sergei Gorlukovich, Yuri Savichev, Arminas Narbekovas)	5	0	1	14	6
2. BRA	(Claudio Taffarel, Jorge "Jorginho" Campos, João Santos Batista, Ricardo Raimundo, Ademir Roque Kaeser, Geovani Silva, Edmar dos Santos, Hamilton "Careca II" de Souza, Romário de Souza Faria, José Araujo, André Cruz, Luiz Winck, Aloisio Alves, Milton de Souza Filho, José Ferreira Neto, Sergio Luiz, Jorge "Andrade" da Silva, José "Bebeto" Gama de Oliveira)	5	1	0	12	4
3. GER	(Oliver Reck, Michael Schulz, Armin Görtz, Wolfgang Funkel, Thomas Hörster, Olaf Janssen, Rudi Bommer, Holger Fach, Jürgen Klinsmann, Wolfram Wuttke, Frank Mill, Uwe Kamps, Roland Grahammer, Thomas Hässler, Christian Schreier, Fritz Walter, Ralf Sievers, Gerhard Kleppinger, Karlheinz Riedle)	4	2	0	16	4
4. ITA	(Stefano Tacconi, Roberto Cravero, Andrea Carnevale, Luigi De Agostini, Ciro Ferrara, Mauro Tassotti, Angelo Colombo, Luca Pellegrini, Massimo Brambati, Stefano Carobbi, Massimo Crippa, Giuliano Giuliani, Antonio Virdis, Ruggiero Rizzitelli, Roberto Galla, Giuseppe Iachini, Stefano Desideri, Massimo Mauro, Alberigo Evani)	3	3	0	11	13
5. ARG	(Luis Islas, Rubén Aguero, Mauro Aires, Carlos Alfaro Moreno, Claudio Cabrera, Jorge Comas, Hernán Díaz, Nestor Fabri, Daniel Hernández, Néstor Lorenzo, Fabián Candelarich, Mario Lucca, Carlos Mayor, Pedro Monzón, Hugo Pérez, Alejandro Ruidiaz, Alejandro Russo, Dario Siviski)	1	2	1	4	5
5. AUS	(Jeffrey Olver, Gary Van Egmond, Graham Jennings, Charlie Yankos, Robert Dunn, Paul Wade, Frank Farina, Mike Petersen, Graham Arnold, John Kosmina, Oscar Crino, Alan Davidson, Andrew Koczka, Vlado Bozinoski, Robert Slater, David Mitchell, Scott Ollerenshaw, Michael Gibson)	2	2	0	2	6
5. SWE	(Sven Andersson, Sulo Vattovaara, Peter Lönn, Göran Arnberg, Roland Nilsson, Jonas Thern, Leif Engqvist, Michael Andersson, Joakim Nilsson, Anders Limpár, Håkan Lindman, Bengt Nilsson, Martin Dahlin, Hans Eskilsson, Jan Hellström, Roger Ljung, Lars Eriksson, Ola Svensson, Anders Palmer, Stefan Rehn)	2	1	1	7	5
5. ZAM	(David Chabala, Peter Mwanza, Edmon Mumba, Samuel Chomba, James Chitalu, Derby Makinka, Johnson Bwalya, Charles Musonda, Beston Chambeshi, Webster Chikabala, Lucky Msiska, Kalusha Bwalya, Manfred Chabinga, Ashols Melu, Richard Mwanza, Pearson Mwanza, Wisdom Mumba Chansa, Stone Nyirenda, Eston Mulenga)	2	1	1	10	6

Final: SOV 2–1 BRA
3rd Place: GER 3–0 ITA

The highlight of the preliminary round was the shocking 4–0 trouncing of Italy by unheralded Zambia. Both Brazil and the Soviet Union advanced to the final with come-from-behind overtime victories. The Soviets scored two goals in extra time to beat Italy, while the Brazilians defeated West Germany in a penalty kick shoot-out. Brazil's Romário de Souza, the leading scorer in the tournament with seven, scored the first goal of the final in the 30th minute. Eleven minutes into the second half, Igor

Dobrovolsky evened the match with a penalty kick. The decisive goal—the result of a fast-breaking counterattack—was struck in the 14th minute of overtime by substitute Yuri Savichev of Moscow.

1992 Barcelona T: 16, N: 16, D: 8.8.

			W	L	T	PF	PA
1.	SPA	(Albert Ferrer Llopis, Mikel Lasa Goicoechea, Roberto Solozábel Villanueva, Juan López Martínez, David Villabona Etxaleku, José Amavisca Garate, Luis "Enrique" Martínez Garcia, Josep Guardiola Sala, Abelardo Fernández Antuña, Antonio Jiménez Sistachs, Gabriel Vidal Nova, Francisco Soler Atencis, Miguel Hernández Sánchez, Rafael Berges Marín, Antonio Pinilla Miranda, Francisco "Kiko" Narváez, Alfonso Pérez Muñoz)	6	0	0	14	2
2.	POL	(Aleksander Klak, Marcin Jalocha, Tomasz Lapiński, Marek Kozmiński, Tomasz Waldoch, Dariusz Gesior, Piotr Swierczewski, Dariusz Adamczuk, Grzegorz Mielcarski, Jerzy Brzeczek, Andrzej Juskowiak, Ryszard Staniek, Marek Bajor, Andrzej Kobylański, Miroslaw Waligora, Dariusz Kosela, Wojciech Kowalczyk)	4	1	1	17	6
3.	GHA	(Anthony Mensah, Frank Amankwah, Isaac Asare, Mohammed Gargo, Joachin Acheampong, Alex Nyarko, Oli Rahman, Nii Lamptey, Kwame Ayew, Shamo Quaye, Samuel Kumah, Osei Kuffuor, Sammi Adjei, Mohammed Kalilu, Bernard Aryee, Simon Addo, Maxwell Konadu, Yaw Preko, Mamood Amadu, Ibrahim Dossey)	3	1	2	9	6
4.	AUS	(John Filan, Milan Blagojevic, Dominic Longo, Ned Zelic, Shaun Murphy, Anthony Vidmar, Paul Okon, Zlatko Arambasic, George Slifkas, John Markovski, Damian Mori, Carl Veart, Steve Refenes, Tony Popovic, David Seal, Gary Hasler, Stephen Corica, Bradley Maloney, Mark Bosnich)	2	3	1	8	12
5.	ITA	(Francesco Antonioli, Mauro Bonomi, Giuseppe Favalli, Luca Luzardi, Salvatore Matrecano, Stefano Rossini, Rufo Verga, Demetrio Albertini, Dino Baggio, Eugenio Corini, Dario Marcolin, Gianluca Sordo, Renato Buso, Pasquale Rocco, Alessandro Melli, Roberto Muzzi)	2	2	0	3	5
5.	PAR	(Ruben Ruiz Díaz, Andrés Duarte Villamayor, Juan Jara Martínez, Celso Ayala Gavilán, Carlos Gamarra Pavón, Francisco Ferreiro Romero, Hugo Sosa Franco, Arsenio Benítez Zarza, Gustavo Neffa Rodríguez, Julio Yegros Torres, Juan Marecos Talavera, Ricardo Sanabria Acuña, Guido Alvarenga Torales, Francisco Arce Rolón, Harles Bourdier Molinas, Mauro Caballero López, Jorge Campos Valázquez)	1	1	2	5	5
5.	QAT	(Ahmad Saleh, Hamad Al-Attev, Rashid Suwaid, Zamel Al-Kuwari, A-Nasser Al-Obaidly, Waleed Maayof, Mubarak Nooralla, Jumah Johar, Mahmoud Souf, Fahad Al Kuwari, Adel Al-Mulla, Yousuf Mahmoud, Waleed Ibrahim, Abdulla Alabdulla, Mohd Al-Mohannadi, Rashid Al Kuwari, A-Aziz Jaloof, Khalid Al-Waheebi)	1	2	1	2	5
5.	SWE	(Jan Ekholm, Magnus Johansson, Joachim Björklund, Filip Apelstav, Niclas Alexandersson, Håkan Mild, Patrik Andersson, Stefan Landberg, Christer Fursth, Jonny Rödlund, Tomas Brolin, Jesper Jansson, Björn Lilius, Pascal Simpson, Niklas Gudmundsson, Jonas Axeldahl)	1	1	2	6	3

Final: SPA 3–2 POL
3rd Place: GHA 1–0 AUS

Prior to hosting the 1992 Games, Spain had taken part in 16 summer Olympics and won a grand total of four gold medals. In Barcelona, they earned 13. None was as dramatic and as satisfying as the final one—in the soccer tournament. The Spanish team cruised through to the finals without giving up a single goal in five matches. Their shutout streak came to an end at the close of the first half of the final when Wojciech Kowalczyk put Poland in the lead, 1-0. The Poles were still on top 15 minutes into the second half when Juan Carlos, the king of Spain, arrived in the stadium with his family. Four minutes later Abelardo Fernández tied the score with a header off a free kick by Josep Guardiola. Six minutes after that, Francisco Narváez, known as Kiko or Quico, put Spain into the lead. But Poland wasn't about to fold before 95,000 screaming Spanish fans. In the 76th minute, Ryszard Staniek tied the score again. It looked like the match would go into overtime. With 72 seconds left in regulation, Spain was awarded a corner kick. There was a flurry of activity in front of the goal. Luis Enrique took a shot that was blocked and rebounded to Kiko, who blasted the ball into the upper left corner of the net.

The entire Spanish team fell back on defense and 52 seconds later the game was over.

WOMEN

This event will be held for the first time in 1996.

GYMNASTICS

MEN
All-Around
Horizontal Bar
Parallel Bars
Long Horse Vault
Side Horse (Pommeled Horse)

Rings
Floor Exercises
Team Combined Exercises
Discontinued Events

There are three stages to Olympic gymnastics competitions: the team competition, followed by the individual All-Around competition, and finally the individual apparatus finals. Each team enters six gymnasts, and each gymnast performs twice on each apparatus: once doing compulsory exercises and once optional exercises. The 1996 Olympics will be the last in which compulsory exercises are included. Each team is allowed to drop its lowest score on each apparatus; the scores of the remaining five gymnasts are added to determine the team score for each apparatus. Gymnasts who are not part of a six-person national squad take part in the team competition because the team competition also serves as the qualifying round for both the individual all-around competition and the apparatus finals.

The 36 gymnasts with the highest scores in the team competition advance to the all-around final. However, no more than three gymnasts per nation may compete in the all-around final. Prior to the break-up of the Soviet Union this restriction led to some awkward situations in which leading medal contenders were dropped to make room for lesser gymnasts.

The top eight scorers for each apparatus in the team competition qualify for the apparatus finals, although no more than two gymnasts per nation may compete in the final for any apparatus. Until 1992, scores from the team competition were carried over to the all-around and apparatus finals. For the Barcelona Games the rules were changed: the gymnasts now start again at zero.

Each routine is scored by six judges on a scale from zero to ten with ten being the best possible score. The highest and lowest marks are dropped and the four remaining marks are added to determine the gymnast's score.

Current rules require that male gymnasts be at least 16 years old in the year of the Olympics and that female gymnasts turn at least 15 in the Olympic year. Following the 1996 Olympics, the minimum age for women will also be 16.

MEN

ALL-AROUND

HB	= Horizontal bar
PB	= Parallel bars
LHV	= Long horse vault
SH	= Side horse (pommeled horse)
R	= Rings
FE	= Floor exercises
SHV	= Side horse vault
CLSV	= Combined long and side horse vaults
100	= 100-yard run
SP	= Shot put
LJ	= Long jump
RC	= Rope climb
CLHJ	= Combined long and high jump
PV	= Pole vault
H	= Heaving a 50-kilogram stone

1896 not held

1900 Paris C: 134, N: 6?, D: 7.30.
Events: HB, PB, LHV, SH, R, FE, LJ, RC, CLHJ, PV, H

			PTS.
1.	Gustave Sandras	FRA	302
2.	Nöel Bas	FRA	295
3.	Lucien Démanet	FRA	293
4.	Pierre Payssé	FRA	290
4.	Jules Rolland	FRA	290
6.	Gustave Fabry	FRA	283
7.	Joseph Martinez	FRA/ALG	277
8.	Marcel Lalu	FRA	275
8.	Mauvezain	FRA	275

Silver medalist Bas was an opera singer.

1904 St. Louis C: 119, N: 4, D: 7.2.

			PB	HB	CLSV	FT.-IN. LJ	SP	TIME 100	TOTAL PTS.
1.	Julius Lenhart	AUT	14.40	14.60	14.00	18-0	28-6	12.0	69.80
2.	Wilhelm Weber	GER	14.17	13.93	13.50	18-1	30-1	12.0	69.10
3.	Adolf Spinnler	SWI	14.53	14.53	14.43	16-2¼	29-7	12.4	67.99
4.	Ernest Mohr	GER	12.90	13.00	13.00	18-8¼	30-0	11.4	67.90
5.	Otto Wiegand	GER	14.20	13.12	13.50	17-6	30-4¾	12.0	67.82
6.	Otto Steffen	USA	12.80	14.10	12.63	18-1	30-9½	12.0	67.03
7.	Hugo Peitsch	GER	14.03	14.30	13.23	16-10¾	27-4¾	12.0	66.66
8.	John Bissinger	USA	13.10	12.37	12.10	18-4¾	32-9½	11.4	66.57

1906 Athens C: 37, N: 8, D: 5.1.
Events: HB, PB, LHV, R, CLHJ

			PTS.
1.	Pierre Payssé	FRA	97
2.	Alberto Braglia	ITA	95
3.	Georges Charmoille	FRA	94
4.	Carl Ohms	GER	93
5.	Vitaliano Masotti	ITA	92
6.	Pissié	FRA	91

7. Nicolaos Aliprantis (GRE), Béla Erody (HUN), Mario Gubiani (ITA), Bohumil Hunzatko (BOH/CZE), Joseph Krämer (GER), Daniel Lavielle (FRA), Carl Schwartz (GER), Wilhelm Weber (GER)—90

1906 Athens C: 17, N: 6, D: 5.1.
Events: HB, PB, LHV, SH, R, CLHJ

			PTS.
1.	Pierre Payssé	FRA	116
2.	Alberto Braglia	ITA	115
3.	Georges Charmoille	FRA	113
4.	Carl Ohms	GER	112
5.	Vitaliano Masotti	ITA	111
6.	Béla Erody	HUN	110
6.	Mario Gubiani	ITA	110
6.	Pissié	FRA	110
6.	Wilhelm Weber	GER	110

This event combined the results of the five apparatuses in the previous event with the results of one more apparatus: the side or pommeled horse.

1908 London C: 97, N: 12, D: 7.15.
Events: HB, PB, SH, R, RC

			PTS.
1.	Alberto Braglia	ITA	317.0
2.	S.Walter Tysal	GBR	312.0
3.	Louis Ségura	FRA	297.0
4.	Curt Steuernagel	GER	273.5
5.	Friedrich Wolf	GER	267.0
6.	Samuel Hodgetts	GBR	266.0
7.	Marcel Lalu	FRA	258.75
8.	Robert Diaz	FRA	258.5

1912 Stockholm C: 44, N: 9, D: 7.12.

			HB	PB	R	SH	TOTAL PTS.
1.	Alberto Braglia	ITA	32.75	34.75	31.75	35.75	135.0
2.	Louis Ségura	FRA	30.0	35.75	32.25	34.5	132.5
3.	Adolfo Tunesi	ITA	30.25	35.0	30.5	35.75	131.5
4.	Guido Boni	ITA	29.75	35.25	28.25	34.75	128.0
4.	Giorgio Zampori	ITA	29.0	35.0	30.75	33.25	128.0
6.	Pietro Bianchi	ITA	29.5	33.75	30.75	33.75	127.75
7.	Marcel Lalu	FRA	29.25	35.5	30.5	31.75	127.0
7.	Marco Torrès	FRA	30.25	35.0	31.0	30.75	127.0

1920 Antwerp C: 25, N: 7, D: 8.25.
Events: HB, PB, SH, R, FE

			PTS.
1.	Giorgio Zampori	ITA	88.35
2.	Marco Torrès	FRA	87.62
3.	Jean Gounot	FRA	87.45
4.	Félicien Kempeneers	BEL	86.25
5.	Georges Thurnherr	FRA	86.00
6.	Laurent Grech	FRA	85.65
7.	Luigi Maiocco	ITA	85.38
8.	Luigi Costigliolo	ITA	84.90

1924 Paris C: 72, N: 9, D: 7.20.

			HB		PB		LHV		SH		R		SHV		RC		TOTAL PTS.
1.	Leon Štukelj	YUG/SLO	19.73	(1)	20.40	(20)	9.91	(4)	19.37	(10)	21.33	(4)	9.6	(17)	10.0	(10)	110.34
2.	Robert Pražak	CZE	18.73	(9)	21.61	(2)	9.73	(9)	18.97	(13)	21.483	(2)	9.8	(8)	10.0	(13)	110.323
3.	Bedřich Supčik	CZE	17.86	(16)	21.26	(8)	9.33	(15)	17.53	(24)	21.12	(5)	9.83	(6)	10.0	(1)	106.93
4.	Ferdinando Mandrini	ITA	18.12	(14)	20.21	(24)	9.75	(7)	16.06	(30)	20.943	(8)	8.73	(21)	10.0	(18)	105.583
5.	Miroslav Klinger	CZE	16.47	(26)	21.13	(10)	9.75	(7)	19.67	(7)	20.73	(11)	9.75	(12)	8.0	(21)	105.5
6.	Ladislav Vácha	CZE	14.7	(39)	21.31	(6)	9.7	(10)	18.33	(17)	21.43	(3)	9.83	(6)	10.0	(4)	105.3
7.	August Güttinger	SWI	18.886	(8)	21.63	(1)	9.08	(17)	19.6	(8)	17.57	(37)	8.41	(29)	10.0	(3)	105.176
8.	Jean Gounot	FRA	19.043	(6)	20.15	(25)	9.0	(18)	17.3	(27)	19.73	(19)	9.93	(2)	10.0	(6)	105.153

Štukelj, a lawyer from Novo Mesto, eventually won three gold medals, one silver, and two bronze in his Olympic career, including a silver in the rings in 1936, when he was 37 years old. In 1992, when he was 93 years old, Štukelj attended the Opening Ceremony of the Barcelona Olympics and watched as athletes from Slovenia marched behind their own flag for the first time.

1928 Amsterdam C: 88, N: 11, D: 8.10.

		HB		PB		LHV		SH		R		TOTAL PTS.
1. Georges Miez	SWI	57.5	(1)	49.75	(30)	28.25	(4)	57.75	(2)	54.25	(8)	247.5
2. Hermann Hänggi	SWI	56.5	(4)	54.25	(3)	27.125	(18)	59.25	(1)	49.5	(36)	246.625
3. Leon Štukelj	YUG/SLO	53.75	(21)	53.5	(7)	26.625	(28)	53.25	(12)	57.75	(1)	244.875
4. Romeo Neri	ITA	57.0	(2)	53.0	(12)	27.25	(16)	51.5	(19)	56.0	(4)	244.75
5. Josip Primožič	YUG/SLO	56.0	(6)	55.5	(2)	28.25	(4)	51.75	(18)	52.5	(18)	244.0
6. Mauri Nybёrg-Noroma	FIN	54.0	(16)	53.5	(7)	26.75	(26)	54.5	(7)	55.0	(5)	243.75
6. Heikki Savolainen	FIN	54.5	(13)	51.75	(17)	27.25	(16)	56.5	(3)	53.75	(12)	243.75
8. Eugen Mack	SWI	56.75	(3)	51.0	(21)	28.75	(1)	54.25	(9)	52.5	(18)	243.25

At the Amsterdam Games, 23-year-old Georges Miez won three gold medals and one silver. Between 1924 and 1936 his Olympic total was four gold, three silver, and one bronze.

1932 Los Angeles C: 24, N: 5, D: 8.12.

		HB		PB		LHV		SH		R		TOTAL PTS.
1. Romeo Neri	ITA	28.9	(2)	28.1	(3)	27.525	(3)	28.0	(4)	28.0	(3)	140.625
2. István Pelle	HUN	29.15	(1)	27.9	(6)	24.675	(9)	24.85	(11)	28.35	(1)	134.925
3. Heikki Savolainen	FIN	27.25	(7)	28.4	(1)	22.925	(15)	28.35	(3)	27.65	(5)	134.575
4. Mario Lertora	ITA	28.2	(3)	27.25	(8)	27.25	(4)	23.35	(14)	28.35	(1)	134.4
5. Savino Guglielmetti	ITA	28.2	(3)	28.4	(1)	28.325	(1)	22.6	(16)	26.85	(6)	134.375
6. Frank Haubold	USA	26.9	(10)	28.0	(4)	25.725	(7)	28.45	(1)	23.45	(16)	132.525
7. Oreste Capuzzo	ITA	27.5	(6)	27.3	(7)	23.7	(10)	26.15	(9)	27.8	(4)	132.45
8. Frederick Meyer	USA	27.1	(9)	26.45	(14)	27.55	(2)	28.4	(2)	22.15	(19)	131.65

1936 Berlin C: 111, N: 14, D: 8.11.

		HB		PB		LHV		SH		R		FE		TOTAL PTS.
1. Alfred Schwarzmann	GER	19.233	(3)	18.967	(3)	19.2	(1)	19.0	(7)	18.534	(4)	18.166	(10)	113.1
2. Eugen Mack	SWI	18.9	(9)	18.834	(5)	18.967	(2)	19.167	(2)	18.0	(13)	18.466	(3)	112.334
3. Konrad Frey	GER	19.267	(2)	19.067	(1)	17.666	(20)	19.333	(1)	17.733	(18)	18.466	(3)	111.532
4. Alois Hudec	CZE	18.834	(10)	18.966	(4)	17.867	(18)	17.966	(26)	19.433	(1)	18.133	(11)	111.199
5. Martti Uosikkinen	FIN	19.0	(7)	18.433	(11)	18.3	(6)	19.066	(4)	17.634	(22)	18.267	(8)	110.7
5. Michael Reusch	SWI	18.566	(18)	19.034	(2)	18.266	(7)	19.0	(7)	18.434	(6)	17.4	(22)	110.7
7. Matthias Volz	GER	18.8	(11)	17.033	(38)	18.467	(3)	18.766	(10)	18.667	(3)	18.366	(5)	110.099
8. Willi Stadel	GER	18.7	(14)	18.133	(18)	18.033	(14)	18.887	(9)	16.966	(36)	18.3	(6)	108.999

1948 London C: 123, N: 16, D: 8.13.

		HB		PB		LHV		SH		R		FE		TOTAL PTS.
1. Veikko Huhtanen	FIN	39.2	(3)	39.3	(2)	38.4	(6)	38.7	(1)	37.8	(11)	36.3	(34)	229.7
2. Walter Lehmann	SWI	39.4	(12)	39.0	(5)	38.1	(8)	37.6	(11)	38.4	(4)	36.5	(29)	229.0
3. Paavo Aaltonen	FIN	38.4	(12)	38.8	(7)	39.1	(1)	38.7	(1)	37.3	(17)	36.5	(29)	228.8
4. Josef Stalder	SWI	39.7	(1)	39.1	(3)	36.9	(33)	37.7	(8)	38.3	(5)	37.0	(16)	228.7
5. Christian Kipfer	SWE	38.6	(9)	39.1	(3)	37.9	(14)	37.2	(14)	37.8	(11)	36.5	(29)	227.1
6. Emil Studer	SWI	38.8	(4)	37.8	(21)	38.0	(10)	37.7	(8)	38.3	(5)	36.0	(41)	226.6
7. Zdenek Ružicka	CZE	37.9	(17)	38.8	(7)	36.6	(46)	36.3	(30)	38.5	(3)	38.1	(3)	226.2
8. Kalevi Laitinen	FIN	38.1	(14)	38.1	(16)	38.0	(10)	36.9	(19)	37.4	(16)	37.15	(13)	225.65

1952 Helsinki C: 185, N: 29, D: 7.21.

		HB		PB		LHV		SH		R		FE		TOTAL PTS.
1. Viktor Chukarin	SOV/UKR	19.4	(5)	19.6	(2)	19.2	(1)	19.5	(1)	19.55	(2)	18.45	(29)	115.7
2. Grant Shaginyan	SOV/ARM	19.05	(14)	19.35	(4)	18.5	(35)	19.4	(2)	19.75	(1)	18.9	(8)	114.95
3. Josef Stalder	SWI	19.5	(2)	19.5	(3)	18.8	(13)	19.2	(5)	19.1	(11)	18.65	(19)	114.75
4. Valentin Muratov	SOV/RUS	19.2	(9)	19.25	(8)	18.7	(19)	18.3	(32)	19.35	(5)	18.85	(11)	113.65
5. Hans Eugster	SWI	19.15	(11)	19.65	(1)	18.95	(5)	18.55	(25)	19.4	(3)	17.7	(66)	113.4
6. Vladimir Belyakov	SOV/RUS	18.8	(23)	19.25	(8)	18.5	(35)	19.1	(7)	18.95	(14)	18.75	(14)	113.35
6. Yevgeny Korolkov	SOV/RUS	18.8	(23)	19.3	(5)	18.4	(44)	19.4	(2)	19.15	(7)	18.3	(35)	113.35
8. Jean Tschabold	SWI	19.35	(6)	19.3	(5)	18.7	(19)	19.05	(8)	18.75	(23)	18.15	(41)	113.3

Chukarin, a Ukrainian who had spent four years in a concentration camp during World War II, earned six medals at Helsinki—four gold and two silver.

1956 Melbourne C: 63, N: 18, D: 12.6.

		HB		PB		LHV		SH		R		FE		TOTAL PTS.
1. Viktor Chukarin	SOV/UKR	19.25	(4)	19.2	(1)	18.6	(7)	19.1	(3)	19.0	(7)	19.1	(2)	114.25
2. Takashi Ono	JPN	19.6	(1)	19.1	(3)	18.5	(16)	19.2	(2)	19.05	(5)	18.75	(8)	114.2
3. Yuri Tytov	SOV/UKR	19.4	(2)	18.85	(8)	18.75	(3)	19.0	(5)	18.85	(10)	18.95	(5)	113.8
4. Masao Takemoto	JPN	19.3	(3)	19.1	(3)	18.65	(6)	18.9	(7)	19.1	(3)	18.5	(16)	113.55
5. Valentin Muratov	SOV/RUS	18.6	(25)	18.7	(16)	18.85	(1)	18.8	(9)	19.15	(2)	19.2	(1)	113.3
6. Helmut Bantz	GER	19.15	(6)	18.8	(13)	18.85	(1)	18.75	(12)	18.6	(18)	18.75	(8)	112.9
7. Albert Azaryan	SOV/ARM	18.95	(8)	19.0	(5)	18.55	(11)	18.75	(12)	19.35	(1)	17.95	(40)	112.55
8. Borys Shakhlin	SOV/UKR	18.75	(13)	18.85	(8)	18.7	(4)	19.25	(1)	18.7	(15)	18.25	(28)	112.5

Chukarin, by then a 35-year-old teacher, added to his medal collection three gold, one silver, and one bronze at Melbourne, for a remarkable total of 11 Olympic medals.

1960 Rome C: 130, N: 23, D: 9.7.

		HB		PB		LHV		SH		R		FE		TOTAL PTS.
1. Borys Shakhlin	SOV/UKR	19.55	(2)	19.4	(1)	19.2	(3)	19.35	(1)	19.5	(2)	18.95	(7)	115.95
2. Takashi Ono	JPN	19.6	(1)	19.4	(1)	19.3	(1)	19.15	(4)	19.45	(3)	19.0	(4)	115.9
3. Yuri Tytov	SOV/UKR	19.5	(4)	19.2	(6)	19.0	(5)	19.2	(3)	19.45	(3)	19.25	(2)	115.6
4. Shuji Tsurumi	JPN	19.25	(8)	19.15	(8)	19.0	(5)	19.1	(6)	19.2	(9)	18.85	(13)	114.55
5. Yukio Endo	JPN	19.45	(6)	19.2	(6)	19.05	(4)	18.85	(10)	19.0	(12)	18.9	(10)	114.45
5. Masao Takemoto	JPN	19.55	(2)	19.25	(4)	19.0	(5)	18.6	(26)	19.25	(8)	18.8	(14)	114.45
7. Nobuyuki Aihara	JPN	19.0	(13)	19.25	(4)	18.85	(9)	18.6	(26)	19.4	(5)	19.3	(1)	114.4
8. Miroslav Cerar	YUG/SLO	19.5	(4)	19.15	(8)	18.75	(13)	19.05	(7)	19.05	(11)	18.75	(17)	114.25

Borys Shakhlin, a Ukrainian from the small town of Ishin, won four gold medals, two silver, and one bronze at the Rome Games to add to the two gold medals he had won at Melbourne four years earlier.

1964 Tokyo C: 130, N: 30, D: 10.20.

		HB		PB		LHV		SH		R		FE		TOTAL PTS.
1. Yukio Endo	JPN	19.4	(3)	19.55	(1)	19.4	(3)	18.7	(16)	19.5	(1)	19.4	(1)	115.95
2. Viktor Lisitsky	SOV/RUS	19.25	(6)	19.5	(2)	19.5	(1)	18.75	(13)	19.1	(9)	19.3	(2)	115.4
2. Borys Shakhlin	SOV/UKR	19.55	(1)	19.25	(9)	19.35	(4)	18.9	(7)	19.4	(2)	18.95	(14)	115.4
2. Shuji Tsurumi	JPN	18.9	(21)	19.5	(2)	19.3	(6)	19.25	(3)	19.35	(5)	19.1	(9)	115.4
5. Franco Menichelli	ITA	19.25	(6)	19.3	(6)	19.05	(24)	18.8	(10)	19.45	(2)	19.3	(2)	115.15
6. Haruhiro Yamashita	JPN	19.25	(6)	19.3	(6)	19.5	(1)	19.15	(4)	18.75	(21)	19.15	(7)	115.1
7. Miroslav Cerar	YUG/SLO	19.3	(5)	19.5	(2)	19.1	(19)	19.45	(1)	19.05	(12)	18.65	(30)	115.05
8. Takuji Hayata	JPN	19.1	(12)	19.15	(10)	19.15	(16)	18.9	(7)	19.45	(2)	19.15	(7)	114.9

1968 Mexico City C: 117, N: 28, D: 10.24.

		HB		PB		LHV		SH		R		FE		TOTAL PTS.
1.	Sawao Kato	JPN	19.45 (3)	19.35 (3)		18.9 (5)		19.0 (8)		19.55 (1)		19.65 (1)		115.9
2.	Mikhail Voronin	SOV/RUS	19.5 (1)	19.45 (2)		19.0 (2)		19.2 (2)		19.45 (3)		19.25 (4)		115.85
3.	Akinori Nakayama	JPN	19.5 (1)	19.55 (1)		18.85 (7)		18.85 (12)		19.5 (2)		19.4 (2)		115.65
4.	Eizo Kenmotsu	JPN	19.35 (5)	19.25 (5)		18.95 (4)		19.1 (4)		19.0 (7)		19.25 (4)		114.9
5.	Takeshi Kato	JPN	19.1 (11)	19.3 (4)		19.05 (1)		18.65 (21)		19.4 (4)		19.35 (3)		114.85
6.	Sergei Diomidov	SOV/RUS	19.3 (6)	18.9 (23)		18.9 (5)		19.0 (8)		19.05 (6)		18.95 (9)		114.1
7.	Vladimir Klimenko	SOV/RUS	19.1 (11)	19.25 (5)		18.85 (7)		19.1 (4)		18.9 (9)		18.75 (13)		113.95
8.	Yukio Endo	JPN	19.25 (7)	19.15 (9)		19.0 (2)		18.4 (26)		18.95 (8)		18.8 (11)		113.55

1972 Munich C: 113, N: 26, D: 8.30.

		HB		PB		LHV		SH		R		FE		TOTAL PTS.
1.	Sawao Kato	JPN	19.525 (2)	19.275 (1)		19.0 (2)		18.9 (3)		19.15 (4)		18.8 (6)		114.65
2.	Eizo Kenmotsu	JPN	19.3 (3)	19.1 (4)		19.0 (2)		19.15 (1)		19.05 (5)		18.975 (3)		114.575
3.	Akinori Nakayama	JPN	19.275 (4)	19.275 (1)		18.75 (7)		18.75 (7)		19.25 (1)		19.025 (1)		114.325
4.	Nikolai Andrianov	SOV/RUS	19.25 (5)	18.925 (6)		19.35 (1)		18.7 (8)		19.0 (6)		18.975 (3)		114.2
5.	Shigeru Kasamatsu	JPN	19.25 (5)	18.825 (10)		18.625 (10)		19.075 (2)		18.9 (7)		19.025 (1)		113.7
6.	Viktor Klimenko	SOV/RUS	18.755 (18)	19.275 (1)		18.8 (6)		18.875 (4)		18.7 (13)		18.675 (9)		113.075
6.	Klaus Köste	GDR	18.975 (11)	19.1 (4)		18.875 (4)		18.4 (17)		18.85 (9)		18.875 (5)		113.075
8.	Mitsuo Tsukahara	JPN	19.675 (1)	18.625 (15)		18.35 (22)		18.15 (20)		19.225 (2)		18.75 (8)		112.775

The 5-foot 3-inch, 125-pound Kato became the third repeat winner of the men's All-Around championship, joining Alberto Braglia of Italy (1908 and 1912) and Viktor Chukarin of the Soviet Union (1952 and 1956).

Sawao Kato won eight gold medals between 1968 and 1976.

1976 Montreal C: 90, N: 20, D: 7.21.

		HB		PB		LHV		SH		R		FE		TOTAL PTS.
1.	Nikolai Andrianov	SOV/RUS	19.3	(4)	19.4	(2)	19.475	(1)	19.425	(3)	19.6	(1)	19.45	(1)	116.65
2.	Sawao Kato	JPN	19.5	(2)	19.475	(1)	19.1	(8)	19.3	(5)	19.075	(6)	19.2	(3)	115.65
3.	Mitsuo Tsukahara	JPN	19.525	(1)	19.375	(3)	19.45	(2)	19.2	(7)	19.0	(9)	19.025	(7)	115.575
4.	Aleksandr Dityatin	SOV/RUS	19.0	(11)	19.05	(5)	19.275	(6)	19.35	(4)	19.5	(2)	19.35	(2)	115.525
5.	Hiroshi Kajiyama	JPN	19.225	(7)	19.325	(4)	19.325	(5)	19.275	(6)	19.2	(3)	19.075	(6)	115.425
6.	Andrzej Szajna	POL	19.1	(9)	19.05	(5)	19.35	(4)	18.95	(10)	19.075	(6)	19.1	(5)	114.625
7.	Michael Nikolay	GDR	19.2	(8)	18.725	(12)	18.725	(21)	19.575	(2)	18.8	(16)	18.575	(16)	113.6
8.	Imre Molnár	HUN	18.875	(16)	18.875	(9)	19.375	(3)	19.2	(7)	18.7	(19)	18.55	(17)	113.575

The 5-foot 5½-inch Andrianov, who had collected a complete set of medals in 1972, added seven more in Montreal—four gold, two silver, and one bronze.

1980 Moscow C: 65, N: 14, D: 7.24.

		HB		PB		LHV		SH		R		FE		TOTAL PTS.
1.	Aleksandr Dityatin	SOV/RUS	19.8	(2)	19.7	(2)	19.875	(1)	19.8	(3)	19.875	(1)	19.6	(3)	118.65
2.	Nikolai Andrianov	SOV/RUS	19.725	(3)	19.6	(4)	19.8	(2)	19.7	(4)	19.725	(3)	19.675	(1)	118.225
3.	Stoyan Deltchev	BUL	19.825	(1)	19.675	(3)	19.725	(5)	19.65	(6)	19.775	(2)	19.35	(6)	118.0
4.	Aleksandr Tkachyov	SOV/RUS	19.525	(4)	19.775	(1)	19.75	(4)	19.675	(5)	19.675	(6)	19.3	(8)	117.7
5.	Roland Brückner	GDR	19.075	(17)	19.45	(5)	19.775	(3)	19.625	(7)	19.725	(3)	19.65	(2)	117.3
6.	Michael Nikolay	GDR	19.475	(6)	19.35	(7)	19.575	(11)	19.875	(2)	19.525	(8)	18.95	(13)	116.75
7.	Lutz Hoffmann	GDR	19.4	(9)	19.05	(11)	19.7	(6)	19.125	(14)	19.425	(10)	19.325	(7)	116.025
8.	Jiři Tabák	CZE	19.225	(11)	18.975	(15)	19.675	(7)	18.675	(22)	19.6	(7)	19.525	(4)	115.675

Handsome Aleksandr Dityatin became the first person to win eight medals in one Olympic celebration. He gained three gold, four silver, and one bronze. Dityatin also became the first male gymnast to receive a ten in an Olympic competition, with his longhorse vault. Four more tens were awarded in rapid succession to Stoyan Deltchev on the rings, Aleksandr Tkachyov on the horizontal bar, and Zoltán Magyar and Michael Nikolay on the side horse. Meanwhile, Nikolai Andrianov added two gold, two silver, and one bronze to his collection for a grand career total of 15 Olympics medals—seven gold, five silver, and three bronze.

1984 Los Angeles C: 71, N: 19, D: 8.2.

		HB		PB		LHV		SH		R		FE		TOTAL PTS.
1.	Koji Gushiken	JPN	19.9	(3)	19.8	(3)	19.875	(1)	19.525	(10)	19.85	(2)	19.75	(3)	118.7
2.	Peter Vidmar	USA	19.95	(2)	19.8	(3)	19.725	(4)	19.85	(2)	19.75	(4)	19.6	(8)	118.675
3.	Li Ning	CHN	19.6	(9)	19.675	(7)	19.775	(3)	19.9	(1)	19.8	(3)	19.825	(1)	118.575
4.	Tong Fei	CHN	19.975	(1)	19.625	(8)	19.725	(4)	19.75	(4)	19.75	(4)	19.725	(5)	118.55
5.	Mitchell Gaylord	USA	19.625	(8)	19.85	(1)	19.825	(2)	19.775	(3)	19.875	(1)	19.575	(9)	118.525
6.	Bart Conner	USA	19.8	(4)	19.8	(3)	19.625	(10)	19.675	(5)	19.675	(9)	19.775	(2)	118.35
7.	Xu Zhiqiang	CHN	19.6	(9)	19.775	(6)	19.725	(4)	19.65	(6)	19.725	(6)	19.75	(3)	118.225
8.	Nobuyuki Kajitani	JPN	19.225	(22)	19.825	(2)	19.7	(7)	19.625	(7)	19.7	(7)	19.3	(17)	117.375

Twenty-seven-year-old Koji Gushiken, placed only fifth after the preliminaries, came from behind to edge Peter Vidmar in the closest Olympic All-Around competition in sixty years. "I'm neither a Christian nor a Buddhist," Gushiken later said, reflecting on the medal ceremony, "and suddenly I felt the existence of God. It was clear-cut and exceedingly beautiful."

Among the boycott missing was world champion and pre-boycott favorite Dmitri Bilozerchev of the U.S.S.R.

1988 Seoul C: 89, N: 23, D: 9.22.

		HB		PB		LHV		SH		R		FE		TOTAL PTS.
1. Vladimir Artemov	SOV/RUS	19.95	(1)	19.975	(1)	19.775	(2)	19.775	(8)	19.8	(4)	19.85	(1)	119.125
2. Valery Lyukin	SOV/KAZ	19.925	(2)	19.9	(2)	19.7	(3)	19.875	(2)	19.875	(2)	19.8	(4)	119.025
3. Dmitri Bilozerchev	SOV/RUS	19.575	(13)	19.9	(2)	19.8	(1)	19.95	(1)	19.975	(1)	19.775	(5)	118.975
4. Sven Tippelt	GDR	19.4	(23)	19.65	(7)	19.675	(4)	19.8	(5)	19.875	(2)	19.6	(14)	118.0
5. Marius Gherman	ROM	19.75	(5)	19.65	(7)	19.55	(10)	19.7	(10)	19.525	(17)	19.65	(12)	117.825
6. Kalofer Hristozov	BUL	19.55	(14)	19.725	(5)	19.3	(24)	19.675	(13)	19.8	(4)	19.7	(8)	117.75
6. Wang Chongsheng	CHN	19.775	(4)	19.5	(24)	19.65	(5)	19.7	(10)	19.625	(14)	19.5	(21)	117.75
8. Györg...														
8. György Guczoghy	HUN	19.425	(19)	19.625	(12)	19.525	(13)	19.8	(5)	19.775	(7)	19.525	(19)	117.675
8. Yukio Iketani	JPN	19.625	(10)	19.65	(7)	19.475	(14)	19.55	(18)	19.525	(17)	19.85	(1)	117.675

Dmitri Bilozerchev caused a sensation in 1983 when he became world champion at the tender age of 16. The following year he was kept out of the Olympics by the Soviet boycott, but he did win the Friendship Games for athletes from boycotting nations. In 1985 he won the European championships and seemed on target to defend his world title when his career was suddenly derailed. Bilozerchev, on unauthorized leave from training camp, drank too much champagne and, only ten days after receiving his driver's license, borrowed his father's car and went driving in a rainstorm. On the slippery Moscow streets he turned in front of a truck and lost control. His left leg was shattered into more than 40 pieces. He was injured so badly that amputation was seriously considered.

Abandoned by the Soviet sports community, Bilozerchev was determined to regain his world-class form. Unfortunately he renewed his training too early. Overcompensating for his still tender left leg, he injured his *right* leg and required surgery on his ankle in December 1986. Despite these setbacks, Bilozerchev managed to return to competition in time to win the 1987 world championship. Still only 21 years old, he was installed as the favorite for the 1988 Olympics. Bilozerchev performed brilliantly in Seoul. But at Olympic-level gymnastics it is necessary to make no mistakes. Bilozerchev made a big one. While performing on the horizontal bar, normally his best apparatus, he veered off center on a one-armed giant swing, lost his momentum, and landed on the bar. The resulting half-point penalty cost him the gold medal.

Ready to take advantage of Bilozerchev's lapse was teammate Vladimir Artemov. Back home in the Soviet Union Artemov was known as "The Permanent Runner-Up" and "Always Second." Indeed he had made a career of finishing second: at the 1984 Friendship Games, the 1985 World Championships, and the 1986 Goodwill Games. He had placed third at the 1987 World Championships. In Seoul, however, Artemov was not to be denied.

Bilozerchev went on to win two gold medals in the apparatus finals. But in August 1989, he and teammate Vladimir Gogoladze were expelled from the Soviet team for going on a two-day drinking binge and for having "a corrupting influence on other members of the team."

1992 Barcelona C: 93, N: 25, D: 7.31.

		HB		PB		LHV		SH		R		FE		TOTAL PTS.
1. Vitaly Scherbo	BLR	9.775	(5)	9.8	(2)	9.8	(2)	9.875	(1)	9.9	(1)	9.875	(1)	59.025
2. Grigory Misyutin	UKR	9.9	(1)	9.8	(2)	9.825	(1)	9.775	(7)	9.8	(2)	9.825	(2)	58.925
3. Valery Belenky	AZR	9.775	(5)	9.825	(1)	9.575	(15)	9.85	(3)	9.775	(4)	9.825	(2)	58.625
4. Andreas Wecker	GER	9.85	(2)	9.7	(6)	9.55	(19)	9.85	(3)	9.8	(2)	9.7	(8)	58.45
5. Li Xiaoshuang	CHN	9.6	(13)	9.65	(9)	9.625	(8)	9.75	(8)	9.7	(5)	9.825	(2)	58.15
6. Guo Linyao	CHN	9.65	(11)	9.675	(7)	9.55	(19)	9.8	(5)	9.6	(12)	9.65	(12)	57.925
7. Marius Gherman	ROM	9.7	(9)	9.675	(7)	9.725	(4)	9.675	(16)	9.4	(27)	9.525	(26)	57.7
8. Lee Joo-hyung	KOR	9.8	(3)	9.575	(20)	9.6	(11)	9.625	(23)	9.475	(20)	9.6	(17)	57.675

Two months before the Olympics, Igor Korobchinsky, the son of a Ukrainian coal miner, won the European championship and looked to be the favorite to repeat the win in Barcelona. He placed fifth out of 93 in the team competition in which the top 36 gymnasts advanced to the individual final. Unfortunately for Korobchinsky, three of the four gymnasts ahead of him were also from the Unified Team of the ex–Soviet Union and only three competitors per nation were allowed to advance. So, while James May of Great Britain, who qualified in 49th place, took part in the individual All-Around competition, Korobchinsky had to watch from the sidelines. What he saw was a superb and consistent performance by his teammate, 20-year-old Vitaly Scherbo of Minsk. Two days later Scherbo won four straight apparatus finals to become the first gymnast in history to earn six gold medals in one Olympics.

HORIZONTAL BAR

1896 Athens C: 15, N: 4, D: 4.9.
1. Hermann Weingärtner   GER
2. Alfred Flatow   GER
3. Aristophoulos Petmetsas   GRE
4. Conrad Böcker   GER
5. Karl Schumann   GER

1900 not held

1904 St. Louis C: 9, N: 1, D: 10.28.

			PTS.
1.	Anton Heida	USA	40
1.	Edward Hennig	USA	40
3.	George Eyser	USA	39

1908–1920 not held

1924 Paris C: 72, N: 9, D: 7.20.

			PTS.
1.	Leon Štukelj	YUG/SLO	19.73
2.	Jean Gutweniger	SWI	19.236
3.	André Higelin	FRA	19.163
4.	Antoine Rebetez	SWI	19.053
4.	Georges Miez	SWI	19.053
6.	Jean Gounot	FRA	19.043
7.	François Gangloff	FRA	18.933
8.	August Güttinger	SWI	18.886

1928 Amsterdam C: 86, N: 11, D: 8.10.

			PTS.
1.	Georges Miez	SWI	19.17
2.	Romeo Neri	ITA	19.00
3.	Eugen Mack	SWI	18.92
4.	Hermann Hänggi	SWI	18.83
4.	Vittorio Lucchetti	ITA	18.83
6.	Josip Primožič	YUG/SLO	18.67
7.	Hans Grieder	SWI	18.58
7.	August Güttinger	FRA	18.58

1932 Los Angeles C: 12, N: 6, D: 8.11.

			PTS.
1.	Dallas Bixler	USA	18.33
2.	Heikki Savolainen	FIN	18.07
3.	Einari Teräsvirta	FIN	18.07

4.	Veikko Pakarinen	FIN	17.27
4.	István Pelle	HUN	17.27
6.	Michael Schuler	USA	15.57
7.	Miklós Péter	HUN	15.13
8.	Mahito Haga	JPN	12.47

Savolainen and Teräsvirta tied for second. While the judges discussed a method for deciding which one should get the silver medal, the two Finns talked it out and agreed that Savolainen should receive the silver and Teräsvirta the bronze. The judges abided by their decision.

1936 Berlin C: 111, N: 14, D: 8.11.

			PTS.
1.	Aleksanteri Saarvala	FIN	19.367
2.	Konrad Frey	GER	19.267
3.	Alfred Schwarzmann	GER	19.233
4.	Innozenz Stangl	GER	19.167
5.	Heikki Savolainen	FIN	19.133
6.	Veikko Pakarinen	FIN	19.067
7.	Martti Uosikkinen	FIN	19.00
8.	Walter Steffens	GER	18.966

1948 London C: 123, N: 16, D: 8.13.

			PTS.
1.	Josef Stalder	SWI	19.85
2.	Walter Lehmann	SWI	19.70
3.	Veikko Huhtanen	FIN	19.60
4.	Raymond Dot	FRA	19.40
4.	Aleksanteri Saarvala	FIN	19.40
4.	Lajos Sántha	HUN	19.40
4.	Emil Studer	SWI	19.40
8.	Einari Teräsvirta	FIN	19.35

1952 Helsinki C: 185, N: 29, D: 7.21.

			PTS.
1.	Jack Günthard	SWI	19.55
2.	Alfred Schwarzmann	GER	19.50
2.	Josef Stalder	SWI	19.50
4.	Heikki Savolainen	FIN	19.45
5.	Viktor Chukarin	SOV/UKR	19.40
6.	Jean Tschabold	SWI	19.35
7.	Helmut Bantz	GER	19.25
7.	Melchior Thalmann	SWI	19.25

1956 Melbourne C: 63, N: 18, D: 12.6.

			PTS.
1.	Takashi Ono	JPN	19.60
2.	Yuri Tytov	SOV/UKR	19.40
3.	Masao Takemoto	JPN	19.30
4.	Pavel Stolbov	SOV/RUS	19.25
4.	Viktor Chukarin	SOV/UKR	19.25
6.	Helmut Bantz	GER	19.15
7.	John Beckner	USA	19.00
8.	Albert Azaryan	SOV/ARM	18.95

1960 Rome C: 130, N: 28, D: 9.10.

			PTS.
1.	Takashi Ono	JPN	19.60
2.	Masao Takemoto	JPN	19.525

3. Borys Shakhlin — SOV/UKR — 19.475
4. Yukio Endo — JPN — 19.425
5. Miroslav Cerar — YUG/SLO — 19.40
5. Yuri Tytov — SOV/UKR — 19.40

1964 Tokyo C: 130, N: 24, D: 10.23.

			PTS.
1.	Borys Shakhlin	SOV/UKR	19.625
2.	Yuri Tytov	SOV/UKR	19.550
3.	Miroslav Cerar	YUG/SLO	19.50
4.	Viktor Lisitsky	SOV/RUS	19.325
5.	Yukio Endo	JPN	19.050
6.	Takashi Ono	JPN	19.00

1968 Mexico City C: 115, N: 27, D: 10.26.

			PTS.
1.	Akinori Nakayama	JPN	19.55
1.	Mikhail Voronin	SOV/RUS	19.55
3.	Eizo Kenmotsu	JPN	19.375
4.	Klaus Köste	GDR	19.225
5.	Sergei Diomidov	SOV/RUS	19.15
6.	Yukio Endo	JPN	19.025

1972 Munich C: 113, N: 26, D: 9.1.

			PTS.
1.	Mitsuo Tsukahara	JPN	19.725
2.	Sawao Kato	JPN	19.525
3.	Shigeru Kasamatsu	JPN	19.45
4.	Eizo Kenmotsu	JPN	19.35
5.	Akinori Nakayama	JPN	19.225
6.	Nikolai Andrianov	SOV/RUS	19.10

1976 Montreal C: 90, N: 20, D: 7.23.

			PTS.
1.	Mitsuo Tsukahara	JPN	19.675
2.	Eizo Kenmotsu	JPN	19.50
3.	Henry Boërio	FRA	19.475
3.	Eberhard Gienger	GER	19.475
5.	Gennady Kryssin	SOV/RUS	19.25
6.	Ferenc Donáth	HUN	19.20

1980 Moscow C: 65, N: 14, D: 7.25.

			PTS.
1.	Stoyan Deltchev	BUL	19.825
2.	Alexandr Dityatin	SOV/RUS	19.75
3.	Nikolai Andrianov	SOV/RUS	19.675
4.	Ralf-Peter Hemmann	GDR	19.525
4.	Michael Nikolay	GDR	19.525
6.	Sergio Suarez Aime	CUB	19.45

1984 Los Angeles C: 71, N: 19, D: 8.4.

			PTS.
1.	Shinji Morisue	JPN	20.00
2.	Tong Fei	CHN	19.975
3.	Koji Gushiken	JPN	19.95
4.	Timothy Daggett	USA	19.85
4.	Lou Yun	CHN	19.85
4.	Peter Vidmar	USA	19.85
7.	Marco Piatti	SWI	19.80
8.	Daniel Wunderlin	SWI	19.675

1988 Seoul C: 89, N: 23, D: 9.24.

			PTS.
1.	Vladimir Artemov	SOV/RUS	19.90
1.	Valery Lyukin	SOV/KAZ	19.90
3.	Holger Behrendt	GDR	19.80
3.	Marius Gherman	ROM	19.80
5.	Wang Chongsheng	CHN	19.775
6.	Xu Zhiqiang	CHN	19.70
7.	Curtis Hibbert	CAN	19.675
8.	Andreas Wecker	GDR	19.50

1992 Barcelona C: 93, N: 25, D: 8.2.

			PTS.
1.	Trent Dimas	USA	9.875
2.	Grigory Misyutin	UKR	9.837
2.	Andreas Wecker	GER	9.837
4.	Guo Linyao	CHN	9.812
5.	Valery Belenky	AZR	9.787
5.	Yoshiaki Hatakeda	JPN	9.787
5.	Daisuke Nishikawa	JPN	9.787
8.	Li Jing	CHN	6.425

Twenty-one-year-old Trent Dimas was a highly unlikely Olympic champion. He had never qualified for an apparatus final in an international event and even in Barcelona he only placed sixth in the qualifying round. The performer before Dimas in the final, Li Jing, fell off the bar, and the judges' confusion as to how to score his routine caused an unexpected delay. As Dimas stood waiting for his turn, he was so nervous he was afraid he might fall over. But once he began, everything went right—for 30 seconds Trent Dimas performed the best routine of his life, culminating with a triple-back-somersault dismount and a perfect landing that he held for several seconds to make sure the judges were quite clear that he had hit it. The judges got the message. Dimas was the first American gymnast to win a gold medal in a non-boycotted Olympics since Dallas Bixler won the same event in 1932. He was also only the second Olympic champion ever who was a native of the state of New Mexico. The first was Cathy Carr, who won the 100-meter breaststroke in 1972.

As for silver medalist Andreas Wecker, it took him 30 seconds to earn his medal, but five hours to produce a urine sample for drug testing.

PARALLEL BARS

1896 Athens C: 18, N: 4, D: 4.10.
1. Alfred Flatow — GER
2. Louis Zutter — SWI
3. Hermann Weingärtner — GER

One of Germany's first gold-medal winners, Alfred Flatow perished in the Nazi concentration camp at Theresienstadt in 1942.

1900 not held

1904 St. Louis C: ?, N: 1, D: 10.28.

		PTS.
1. George Eyser	USA	44
2. Anton Heida	USA	43
3. John Duha	USA	40

Eyser also won a gold in the long horse vault, two silvers in the pommeled horse and combined competitions, and a bronze in the horizontal bar. His gymnastic feats were all the more impressive considering that his left leg was made of wood. His leg had been amputated after he was run over by a train.

1908–1920 not held

1924 Paris C: 72, N: 9, D: 7.20.

		PTS.
1. August Güttinger	SWI	21.63
2. Robert Pražak	CZE	21.61
3. Giorgio Zampori	ITA	21.45
4. Josef Wilhelm	SWI	21.40
5. Mario Lertora	ITA	21.33
6. Ladislav Vácha	CZE	21.31
7. Jaroslav Kos	CZE	21.28
8. Jean Gutweniger	SWI	21.26
8. Bedrich Supčik	CZE	21.26

1928 Amsterdam C: 85, N: 11, D: 8.10.

		PTS.
1. Ladislav Vácha	CZE	18.83
2. Josip Primožič	YUG/SLO	18.50
3. Hermann Hänggi	SWI	18.08
4. Jan Gajdoš	CZE	17.92
4. André Lemoine	FRA	17.92
4. Bedrich Supčik	CZE	17.92
7. Mario Lertora (ITA), Mauri Nyberg-Noroma (FIN), Leon Štukelj (YUG/SLO), Melchior Wetzel (SWI)		17.83

1932 Los Angeles C: 15, N: 6, D: 8.12.

		PTS.
1. Romeo Neri	ITA	18.97
2. István Pelle	HUN	18.60
3. Heikki Savolainen	FIN	18.27
4. Mauri Nyberg-Noroma	FIN	17.80
5. Mario Lertora	ITA	17.53
6. Alfred Jochim	USA	17.47
7. József Hegedüs	HUN	17.30
7. Miklós Péter	HUN	17.30

1936 Berlin C: 111, N: 14, D: 8.11.

		PTS.
1. Konrad Frey	GER	19.067
2. Michael Reusch	SWI	19.034
3. Alfred Schwarzmann	GER	18.967
4. Alois Hudec	CZE	18.966
5. Eugen Mack	SWI	18.834
6. Walter Bach	SWI	18.733
7. Heikki Savolainen	FIN	18.633
8. Eduard "Edi" Steinemann	SWI	18.500

1948 London C: 123, N: 16, D: 8.13.

		PTS.
1. Michael Reusch	SWI	19.75
2. Veikko Huhtanen	FIN	19.65
3. Christian Kipfer	SWI	19.55
3. Josef Stalder	SWI	19.55
5. Walter Lehmann	SWI	19.50
6. Heikki Savolainen	FIN	19.45
7. Paavo Aaltonen	FIN	19.40
7. Zdenek Ružička	CZE	19.40

1952 Helsinki C: 185, N: 29, D: 7.21.

		PTS.
1. Hans Eugster	SWI	19.65
2. Viktor Chukarin	SOV/UKR	19.60
3. Josef Stalder	SWI	19.50
4. Grant Shaginyan	SOV/ARM	19.35
5. Ferdinand Daniš	CZE	19.30
5. Yevgeny Korolkov	SOV/RUS	19.30
5. Jean Tschalbold	SWI	19.30
8. Vladimir Belyakov	SOV/RUS	19.25
8. Valentin Muratov	SOV/RUS	19.25

1956 Melbourne C: 63, N: 18, D: 12.6.

		PTS.
1. Viktor Chukarin	SOV/UKR	19.20
2. Masami Kubota	JPN	19.15
3. Takashi Ono	JPN	19.10
3. Masao Takemoto	JPN	19.10
5. Albert Azaryan	SOV/ARM	19.00
6. Nobuyuki Aihara	JPN	18.90
6. Bengt Lindfors	FIN	18.90
8. Onni Lappalainen (FIN), Olavi Leimuvirta (FIN), Borys Shakhlin (SOV/UKR), Shinsaku Tsukawai (JPN), Yuri Tytov (SOV/UKR)		18.85

1960 Rome C: 130, N: 28, D: 9.10.

		PTS.
1. Borys Shakhlin	SOV/UKR	19.40
2. Giovanni Carminucci	ITA	19.375
3. Takashi Ono	JPN	19.35
4. Nobuyuki Aihara	JPN	19.275
5. Yuri Tytov	SOV/UKR	19.20
6. Masao Takemoto	JPN	19.125

1964 Tokyo C: 130, N: 29, D: 10.23.

		PTS.
1. Yukio Endo	JPN	19.675
2. Shuji Tsurumi	JPN	19.45
3. Franco Menichelli	ITA	19.35
4. Sergei Diomidov	SOV/UZB	19.225
5. Viktor Lisitsky	SOV/RUS	19.20
6. Miroslav Cerar	YUG/SLO	18.45

1968 Mexico City C: 117, N: 28, D: 10.26.

		PTS.
1. Akinori Nakayama	JPN	19.475
2. Mikhail Voronin	SOV/RUS	19.425

3. Vladimir Klimenko   SOV/RUS   19.225
4. Takeshi Kato   JPN   19.20
5. Eizo Kenmotsu   JPN   19.175
6. Václav Kubička   CZE   18.95

1972 Munich C: 113, N: 26, D: 9.1.

			PTS.
1.	Sawao Kato	JPN	19.475
2.	Shigeru Kasamatsu	JPN	19.375
3.	Eizo Kenmotsu	JPN	19.25
4.	Viktor Klimenko	SOV/RUS	19.125
5.	Akinori Nakayama	JPN	18.875
6.	Nikolai Andrianov	SOV/RUS	17.975

1976 Montreal C: 90, N: 20, D: 7.23.

			PTS.
1.	Sawao Kato	JPN	19.675
2.	Nikolai Andrianov	SOV/RUS	19.50
3.	Mitsuo Tsukahara	JPN	19.475
4.	Bernd Jäger	GDR	19.20
5.	Miloslav Netušil	CZE	19.125
6.	Andrzej Szajna	POL	18.95

1980 Moscow C: 65, N: 14, D: 7.25.

			PTS.
1.	Aleksandr Tkachyov	SOV/RUS	19.775
2.	Aleksandr Dityatin	SOV/RUS	19.75
3.	Roland Brückner	GDR	19.65
4.	Michael Nikolay	GDR	19.60
5.	Stoyan Deltchev	BUL	19.575
6.	Roberto Leon Richards-Aguiar	CUB	19.50

1984 Los Angeles C: 71, N: 19, D: 8.4.

			PTS.
1.	Bart Conner	USA	19.95
2.	Nobuyuki Kajitani	JPN	19.925
3.	Mitchell Gaylord	USA	19.85
4.	Tong Fei	CHN	19.825
5.	Koji Gushiken	JPN	19.80
6.	Li Ning	CHN	19.775
7.	Jürgen Geiger	GER	19.60
7.	Daniel Winkler	GER	19.60

1988 Seoul C: 89, N: 23, D: 9.24.

			PTS.
1.	Vladimir Artemov	SOV/RUS	19.925
2.	Valery Lyukin	SOV/KAZ	19.90
3.	Sven Tippelt	GDR	19.75
4.	Kalofer Hristozov	BUL	19.725
5.	Marius Gherman	ROM	19.70
6.	Curtis Hibbert	CAN	19.675
7.	Sylvio Kroll	GDR	19.625
8.	Boris Preti	ITA	19.60

1992 Barcelona C: 93, N: 25, D: 8.2.

			PTS.
1.	Vitaly Scherbo	BLR	9.90
2.	Li Jing	CHN	9.812
3.	Guo Linyao	CHN	9.80

3. Igor Korobchinsky   UKR   9.80
3. Masayuki Matsunaga   JPN   9.80
6. Jair Lynch   USA   9.712
7. Andreas Wecker   GER   9.612
8. Daisuke Nishikawa   JPN   9.575

Li Jing was the favorite, but he didn't stick his double-pike dismount whereas Scherbo did. Because of the restriction of two finalists per nation, Jair Lynch made it to the final even though he placed only 16th in the qualifying round.

LONG HORSE VAULT

1896 Athens C: 15, N: 4, D: 4.9.
1. Carl Schuhmann   GER
2. Louis Zutter   SWI
3. Hermann Weingärtner GER

1900 not held

1904 St. Louis C: ?, N: 1, D: 10.28.

			PTS.
1.	George Eyser	USA	36
1.	Anton Heida	USA	36
3.	William Merz	USA	31

1908–1920 not held

1924 Paris C: 70, N: 9, D: 7.20.

			PTS.
1.	Frank Kriz	USA	9.98
2.	Jan Koutny	CZE	9.97
3.	Bohumil Mořkovsky	CZE	9.93
4.	Leon Štukelj	YUG/SLO	9.91
5.	Max Wandrer	USA	9.85
6.	Ivan Porenta	YUG/SLO	9.76
7.	Miroslav Klinger	CZE	9.75
7.	Ferdinando Mandrini	ITA	9.75

1928 Amsterdam C: 85, N: 11, D: 8.10.

			PTS.
1.	Eugen Mack	SWI	9.58
2.	Emanuel Löffler	CZE	9.50
3.	Stane Derganc	YUG/SLO	9.46
4.	Georges Miez	SWI	9.42
4.	Josip Primožič	YUG/SLO	9.42
6.	Georges Leroux	FRA	9.33
7.	August Güttinger	SWI	9.28
7.	Ivan Porenta	YUG/SLO	9.28
7.	Herman Witzig	USA	9.28

1932 Los Angeles C: 10, N: 4, D: 8.10.

			PTS.
1.	Savino Guglielmetti	ITA	18.03
2.	Alfred Jochim	USA	17.77
3.	Edward Carmichael	USA	17.53
4.	Einari Teräsvirta	FIN	17.53
5.	Marcel Gleyre	USA	17.46
6.	István Pelle	HUN	17.13

7. Miklós Péter   HUN   16.97
8. Mario Lertora   ITA   16.40

1936 Berlin C: 110, N: 14, D: 8.11.

			PTS.
1.	Alfred Schwarzmann	GER	19.20
2.	Eugen Mack	SWI	18.967
3.	Matthias Volz	GER	18.467
4.	Walter Bach	SWI	18.40
5.	Walter Beck	SWI	18.367
6.	Martti Uosikkinen	FIN	18.30
7.	Michael Reusch	SWI	18.266
8.	Georges Miez	SWI	18.234
8.	Josef Walter	SWI	18.234

1948 London C: 123, N: 16, D: 8.13.

			PTS.
1.	Paavo Aaltonen	FIN	19.55
2.	Olavi Rove	FIN	19.50
3.	János Mogyorósi-Klencs	HUN	19.25
3.	Ferenc Pataki	HUN	19.25
3.	Leo Sotornik	CZE	19.25
6.	Veikko Huhtanen	FIN	19.20
7.	Einari Teräsvirta	FIN	19.15
8.	Walter Lehmann	SWI	19.05
8.	Sulo Salmi	FIN	19.05

1952 Helsinki C: 185, N: 29, D: 7.21.

			PTS.
1.	Viktor Chukarin	SOV/UKR	19.20
2.	Masao Takemoto	JPN	19.15
3.	Takashi Ono	JPN	19.10
3.	Tadao Uesako	JPN	19.10
5.	Hans Eugster	SWI	18.95
5.	Theo Wied	GER	18.95
7.	Iosef Berdiyev	SOV/RUS	18.90
7.	Ernst Fivian	SWI	18.90

1956 Melbourne C: 63, N: 18, D: 12.6.

			PTS.
1.	Helmut Bantz	GER	18.85
1.	Valentin Muratov	SOV/RUS	18.85
3.	Yuri Tytov	SOV/UKR	18.75
4.	Borys Shakhlin	SOV/UKR	18.70
4.	Theo Wied	GER	18.70
6.	Masao Takemoto	JPN	18.65
7.	John Beckner (USA), Jakob Kiefer (GER), Robert Klein (GER), Viktor Chukarin (SOV)		18.60

1960 Rome C: 130, N: 28, D: 9.10.

			PTS.
1.	Takashi Ono	JPN	19.35
1.	Borys Shakhlin	SOV/UKR	19.35
3.	Vladimir Portnoy	SOV/RUS	19.225
4.	Yuri Tytov	SOV/UKR	19.20
5.	Yukio Endo	JPN	19.175
6.	Shuji Tsurumi	JPN	19.15

1964 Tokyo C: 130, N: 29, D: 10.23.

			PTS.
1.	Haruhiro Yamashita	JPN	19.60
2.	Viktor Lisitsky	SOV/RUS	19.325
3.	Hannu Rantakari	FIN	19.30
4.	Shuji Tsurumi	JPN	19.225
5.	Borys Shakhlin	SOV/UKR	19.20
6.	Yukio Endo	JPN	19.075

Yamashita executed a handspring in a piked position, a vault that became known as a "yamashita." One of the judges, Dr. Widmer of Switzerland, was so impressed that he gave Yamashita a ten—the highest mark possible.

1968 Mexico City C: 116, N: 28, D: 10.26.

			PTS.
1.	Mikhail Voronin	SOV/RUS	19.00
2.	Yukio Endo	JPN	18.95
3.	Sergei Diomidov	SOV/RUS	18.925
4.	Takeshi Kato	JPN	18.775
5.	Akinori Nakayama	JPN	18.725
6.	Eizo Kenmotsu	JPN	18.65

1972 Munich C: 113, N: 26, D: 9.1.

			PTS.
1.	Klaus Köste	GDR	18.85
2.	Viktor Klimenko	SOV/RUS	18.825
3.	Nikolai Andrianov	SOV/RUS	18.80
4.	Sawao Kato	JPN	18.55
4.	Eizo Kenmotsu	JPN	18.55
6.	Peter Rohner	SWI	18.525

Performing a yamashita and a forward somersault, the 5-foot 4½-inch Köste won East Germany's first gold medal in men's gymnastics.

1976 Montreal C: 90, N: 20, D: 7.23.

			PTS.
1.	Nikolai Andrianov	SOV/RUS	19.45
2.	Mitsuo Tsukahara	JPN	19.375
3.	Hiroshi Kajiyama	JPN	19.275
4.	Dănut Grecu	ROM	19.20
5.	Zoltán Magyar	HUN	19.15
5.	Imre Molnár	HUN	19.15

1980 Moscow C: 65, N: 14, D: 7.25.

			PTS.
1.	Nikolai Andrianov	SOV/RUS	19.825
2.	Aleksandr Dityatin	SOV/RUS	19.80
3.	Roland Brückner	GDR	19.775
4.	Ralf-Peter Hemmann	GDR	19.75
5.	Stoyan Deltchev	BUL	19.70
6.	Jiři Tabák	CZE	19.525

1984 Los Angeles C: 71, N: 19, D: 8.4.

1.	Lou Yun	CHN	19.95
2.	Mitchell Gaylord	USA	19.825
2.	Koji Gushiken	JPN	19.825
2.	Li Ning	CHN	19.825

2. Shinji Morisue   JPN   19.825
6. James Hartung   USA   19.80
7. Warren Long   CAN   19.70
8. Daniel Wunderlin   SWI   19.625

1988 Seoul C: 89, N: 23, D: 9.24.

		PTS.
1. Lou Yun	CHN	19.875
2. Sylvio Kroll	GDR	19.862
3. Park Jong-hoon	KOR	19.775
4. Dian Kolev	BUL	19.737
5. Holger Behrendt	GDR	19.65
6. Sergei Kharkov	SOV/RUS	19.60
7. Yukio Iketani	JPN	19.525
8. Vladimir Gogoladze	SOV/GEO	19.512

1992 Barcelona C: 93, N: 25, D: 8.2.

		PTS.
1. Vitaly Scherbo	BLR	9.856
2. Grigory Misyutin	UKR	9.781
3. Yoo Ok-ryul	KOR	9.762
4. Li Xiaoshuang	CHN	9.731
5. Zoltán Supola	HUN	9.674
6. Sylvio Kroll	GER	9.662
7. Szilveszter Csollány	HUN	9.524
8. Yutaka Aihara	JPN	9.45

SIDE HORSE (POMMELED HORSE)

1896 Athens C: 15, N: 4, D: 4.9.
1. Louis Zutter   SWI
2. Hermann Weingärtner   GER

1900 not held

1904 St. Louis C: 9, N: 1, D: 10.28.

		PTS.
1. Anton Heida	USA	42
2. George Eyser	USA	33
3. William Merz	USA	29

1908–1920 not held

1924 Paris C: 70, N: 9, D: 7.20.

		PTS.
1. Josef Wilhelm	SWI	21.23
2. Jean Gutweniger	SWI	21.13
3. Antoine Rebetez	SWI	20.73
4. Carl Widmer	SWI	20.50
5. Giuseppe Paris	ITA	20.10
6. Stane Derganc	YUG/SLO	19.93
7. Miroslav Klinger	CZE	19.67
8. August Güttinger	SWI	19.60

1928 Amsterdam C: 87, N: 11, D: 8.10.

		PTS.
1. Hermann Hänggi	SWI	19.75
2. Georges Miez	SWI	19.25
3. Heikki Savolainen	FIN	18.83

4. Eduard "Edi" Steinemann   SWI   18.67
5. August Güttinger   SWI   18.58
6. Georges Leroux   FRA   18.25
7. Mauri Nyberg-Noroma   FIN   18.17
7. Melchior Wetzel   SWI   18.17

1932 Los Angeles C: 10, N: 5, D: 8.11.

		PTS.
1. István Pelle	HUN	19.07
2. Omero Bonoli	ITA	18.87
3. Frank Haubold	USA	18.57
4. Frank Cumiskey	USA	18.23
5. Péter Boros	HUN	17.57
6. Alfred Jochim	USA	17.07
7. Heikki Savolainen	FIN	17.00
8. Veikko Pakarinen	FIN	16.63

1936 Berlin C: 110, N: 14, D: 8.11.

		PTS.
1. Konrad Frey	GER	19.333
2. Eugen Mack	SWI	19.167
3. Albert Bachmann	SWI	19.067
4. Martti Uosikkinen	FIN	19.066
5. Walter Steffens	GER	19.033
5. Walter Bach	SWI	19.033
7. Michael Reusch	SWI	19.00
7. Alfred Schwarzmann	GER	19.00

1948 London C: 123, N: 16, D: 8.13.

		PTS.
1. Paavo Aaltonen	FIN	19.35
1. Veikko Huhtanen	FIN	19.35
1. Heikki Savolainen	FIN	19.35
4. Luigi Zanetti	ITA	19.15
5. Guido Figone	ITA	19.10
6. Frank Cumiskey	USA	18.95
7. Michael Reusch	SWI	18.90
8. Aleksanteri Saarvala	FIN	18.85
8. Josef Stalder	SWI	18.85
8. Emil Studer	SWI	18.85

Between 1928 and 1952 Heikki Savolainen of Joensuu won two gold medals, one silver, and six bronze. When he received his last medal, as a member of the third-place Finnish team in Helsinki, Savolainen was 44 years old.

1952 Helsinki C: 185, N: 29, D: 7.21.

		PTS.
1. Viktor Chukarin	SOV/UKR	19.50
2. Yevgeny Korolkov	SOV/RUS	19.40
2. Grant Shaginyan	SOV/ARM	19.40
4. Mikhail Perelman	SOV/RUS	19.30
5. Josef Stalder	SWI	19.20
6. Hans Sauter	AUT	19.15
7. Vladimir Belyakov	SOV/RUS	19.10
8. Jean Tschabold	SWI	19.05

1956 Melbourne C: 63, N: 18, D: 12.6.

		PTS.
1. Borys Shakhlin	SOV/UKR	19.25
2. Takashi Ono	JPN	19.20
3. Viktor Chukarin	SOV/UKR	19.10
4. Josef Škvor	CZE	19.05
5. Yuri Tytov	SOV/UKR	19.00
6. Jaroslav Bim	CZE	18.95
7. Pavel Stolbov	SOV/RUS	18.90
7. Masao Takemoto	JPN	18.90

1960 Rome C: 130, N: 28, D: 9.10.

		PTS.
1. Eugen Ekman	FIN	19.375
1. Borys Shakhlin	SOV/UKR	19.375
3. Shuji Tsurumi	JPN	19.15
4. Takashi Mitsukuri	JPN	19.125
5. Yuri Tytov	SOV/UKR	18.95
6. Takashi Ono	JPN	18.525

1964 Tokyo C: 130, N: 29, D: 10.22.

		PTS.
1. Miroslav Cerar	YUG/SLO	19.525
2. Shuji Tsurumi	JPN	19.325
3. Yuri Tsapenko	SOV/RUS	19.20
4. Haruhiro Yamashita	JPN	19.075
5. Harald Wigaard	NOR	18.925
6. Takashi Mitsukuri	JPN	18.65

1968 Mexico City C: 114, N: 27, D: 10.26.

		PTS.
1. Miroslav Cerar	YUG/SLO	19.325
2. Olli Eino Laiho	FIN	19.225
3. Mikhail Voronin	SOV/RUS	19.20
4. Wilhelm Kubica	POL	19.15
5. Eizo Kenmotsu	JPN	19.05
6. Viktor Klimenko	SOV/RUS	18.95

1972 Munich C: 113, N: 26, D: 9.1.

		PTS.
1. Viktor Klimenko	SOV/RUS	19.125
2. Sawao Kato	JPN	19.00
3. Eizo Kenmotsu	JPN	18.95
4. Shigeru Kasamatsu	JPN	18.925
5. Mikhail Voronin	SOV/RUS	18.875
6. Wilhelm Kubica	POL	18.75

1976 Montreal C: 90, N: 20, D: 7.23.

		PTS.
1. Zoltán Magyar	HUN	19.70
2. Eizo Kenmotsu	JPN	19.575
3. Nikolai Andrianov	SOV/RUS	19.525
3. Michael Nikolay	GDR	19.525
5. Sawao Kato	JPN	19.40
6. Aleksandr Dityatin	SOV/RUS	19.35

1980 Moscow C: 65, N: 14, D: 7.25.

		PTS.
1. Zoltán Magyar	HUN	19.925
2. Aleksandr Dityatin	SOV/RUS	19.80

		PTS.
3. Michael Nikolay	GDR	19.775
4. Roland Brückner	GDR	19.725
5. Aleksandr Tkachyov	SOV/RUS	19.475
6. Ferenc Donáth	HUN	19.40

1984 Los Angeles C: 71, N: 19, D: 8.4.

		PTS.
1. Li Ning	CHN	19.95
1. Peter Vidmar	USA	19.95
3. Timothy Daggett	USA	19.825
4. Tong Fei	CHN	19.75
5. Jean-Luc Cairon	FRA	19.70
6. Nobuyuki Kajitani	JPN	19.625
7. Benno Gross	GER	19.525
8. Josef Zellweger	SWI	19.50

1988 Seoul C: 89, N: 23, D: 9.24.

		PTS.
1. Dmitri Bilozerchev	SOV/RUS	19.95
1. Zsolt Borkai	HUN	19.95
1. Lubomir Geraskov	BUL	19.95
4. Koichi Mizushima	JPN	19.90
5. Valery Lyukin	SOV/KAZ	19.875
6. Daisuke Nishikawa	JPN	19.85
7. Sven Tippelt	GDR	19.80
8. Sylvio Kroll	GDR	19.775

1992 Barcelona C: 93, N: 25, D: 8.2.

		PTS.
1. Pae Gil-su	PRK	9.925
1. Vitaly Scherbo	BLR	9.925
3. Andreas Wecker	GER	9.887
4. Guo Linyao	CHN	9.875
5. M. Chris Waller	USA	9.825
6. Yoshiaki Hatakeda	JPN	9.775
7. Li Jing	CHN	9.25
7. Valery Belenky	AZR	9.25

Pae's unusually long set amazed gymnastics fans, but three of the six judges gave Scherbo a higher mark, and the two ended up in a tie for first place. It was the fifth time that the pommels gold was shared and the third time in a row.

RINGS

1896 Athens C: 8, N: 3, D: 4.9.

1. Ioannis Mitropoulos	GRE
2. Hermann Weingärtner	GER
3. Petros Persakis	GRE
4. —	
5. Carl Schuhmann	GER

1900 not held

1904 St. Louis C: 10, N: 1, D: 10.28.

		PTS.
1. Hermann Glass	USA	45
2. William Merz	USA	35
3. Emil Voigt	USA	32

1908–1920 not held

1924 Paris C: 70, N: 9, D: 7.20.

			PTS.
1.	Francesco Martino	ITA	21.553
2.	Robert Pražak	CZE	21.483
3.	Ladislav Vácha	CZE	21.43
4.	Leon Štukelj	YUG/SLO	21.33
5.	Bedřich Supčik	CZE	21.12
6.	Bohumil Mořkovsky	CZE	21.083
7.	Jan Koutny	CZE	21.053
8.	Ferdinando Mandrini	ITA	20.943

1928 Amsterdam C: 87, N: 11, D: 8.10.

			PTS.
1.	Leon Štukelj	YUG/SLO	19.25
2.	Ladislav Vácha	CZE	19.17
3.	Emanuel Löffler	CZE	18.83
4.	Romeo Neri	ITA	18.67
5.	Mauri Nyberg-Noroma	FIN	18.33
6.	Bedřich Supčik	CZE	18.25
7.	Paul Krempel	USA	18.17
8.	Jan Gajdoš	CZE	18.08
8.	Georges Miez	SWI	18.08
8.	Armand Solbach	FRA	18.08

1932 Los Angeles C: 14, N: 6, D: 8.12.

			PTS.
1.	George Gulack	USA	18.97
2.	William Denton	USA	18.60
3.	Giovanni Lattuada	ITA	18.50
4.	Richard Bishop	USA	18.47
5.	Oreste Capuzzo	ITA	18.27
6.	Franco Tognini	ITA	18.03
7.	Heikki Savolainen	FIN	17.70
8.	Toshihiko Sasano	JPN	17.47

1936 Berlin C: 111, N: 14, D: 8.11.

			PTS.
1.	Alois Hudec	CZE	19.433
2.	Leon Štukelj	YUG/SLO	18.867
3.	Matthias Volz	GER	18.667
4.	Alfred Schwarzmann	GER	18.534
5.	Franz Beckert	GER	18.533
6.	Michael Reusch	SWI	18.434
7.	Jaroslav Kollinger	CZE	18.433
8.	Heikki Savolainen	FIN	18.40

1948 London C: 123, N: 16, D: 8.13.

			PTS.
1.	Karl Frei	SWI	19.80
2.	Michael Reusch	SWI	19.55
3.	Zdenek Ružička	CZE	19.25
4.	Walter Lehmann	SWI	19.20
5.	Josef Stalder	SWI	19.15
5.	Emil Studer	SWI	19.15

7.	Vladimir Karas	CZE	19.10
8.	Heikki Savolainen	FIN	19.05

1952 Helsinki C: 185, N: 29, D: 7.21.

			PTS
1.	Grant Shaginyan	SOV/ARM	19.75
2.	Viktor Chukarin	SOV/UKR	19.55
3.	Hans Eugster	SWI	19.40
3.	Dmytro Leonkin	SOV/UKR	19.40
5.	Valentin Muratov	SOV/RUS	19.35
6.	Masao Takemoto	JPN	19.20
7.	Attia Ali Alizaky (EGY),		19.15
	Ferenc Kemény (HUN),		
	Yevgeny Korolkov (SOV/RUS),		
	Berndt Lindfors (FIN)		

1956 Melbourne C: 63, N: 18, D: 12.6.

			PTS.
1.	Albert Azaryan	SOV/ARM	19.35
2.	Valentin Muratov	SOV/RUS	19.15
3.	Masami Kubota	JPN	19.10
3.	Masao Takemoto	JPN	19.10
5.	Nobuyuki Aihara	JPN	19.05
5.	Takashi Ono	JPN	19.05
7.	Viktor Chukarin	SOV/UKR	19.00
7.	Shinsaku Tsukawaki	JPN	19.00

Albert Azaryan was a blacksmith who didn't take up gymnastics until he was 16 years old. He was the inventor of the Olympic cross, a variation of the iron cross, in which the gymnast twists sideways while maintaining a cross position. Most new moves in gymnastics are developed after extensive planning, experimentation, and practice. That was not the case with the Olympic cross. Azaryan was competing at the 1953 U.S.S.R. championships. The Armenian team felt they were being underscored by the Russian judges. When the Armenian coach demanded an explanation, he was told that his gymnasts were not holding their crosses for the required three seconds. When Azaryan's turn came, he lowered into the cross position, turned to the judge on one side and asked, "Is this long enough?" Then he turned to the judge on the other side and asked the same question. Then he twisted sideways into what is now called an Olympic cross and asked one of the judges behind him, "Is this long enough?" Finally he twisted in the other direction and repeated his question to the other rear judge. The judges were not amused and awarded him a score of only 9.30. However, the Olympic cross had been born.

1960 Rome C: 130, N: 28, D: 9.10.

			PTS.
1.	Albert Azaryan	SOV/ARM	19.725
2.	Borys Shakhlin	SOV/UKR	19.50
3.	Velik Kapsazov	BUL	19.425
3.	Takashi Ono	JPN	19.425
5.	Nobuyuki Aihara	JPN	19.40
6.	Yuri Tytov	SOV/UKR	19.275

1964 Tokyo C: 130, N: 29, D: 10.22.

		PTS.
1. Takuji Haytta	JPN	19.475
2. Franco Menichelli	ITA	19.425
3. Borys Shakhlin	SOV/UKR	19.40
4. Viktor Leontyev	SOV/RUS	19.35
5. Shuji Tsurumi	JPN	19.275
6. Yukio Endo	JPN	19.25

1968 Mexico City C: 117, N: 28, D: 10.26.

		PTS.
1. Akinori Nakayama	JPN	19.45
2. Mikhail Voronin	SOV/RUS	19.325
3. Sawao Kato	JPN	19.225
4. Mitsuo Tsukahara	JPN	19.125
5. Takeshi Kato	JPN	19.05
6. Sergei Diomidov	SOV/RUS	18.975

1972 Munich C: 113, N: 26, D: 9.1.

		PTS.
1. Akinori Nakayama	JPN	19.35
2. Mikhail Voronin	SOV/RUS	19.275
3. Mitsuo Tsukahara	JPN	19.225
4. Sawao Kato	JPN	19.15
5. Eizo Kenmotsu	JPN	18.95
5. Klaus Köste	GDR	18.95

1976 Montreal C: 90, N: 20, D: 7.23.

		PTS.
1. Nikolai Andrianov	SOV/RUS	19.65
2. Aleksandr Dityatin	SOV/RUS	19.55
3. Dănut Grecu	ROM	19.50
4. Ferenc Dónath	HUN	19.20
5. Eizo Kenmotsu	JPN	19.175
6. Sawao Kato	JPN	19.125

1980 Moscow C: 65, N: 14, D: 7.25.

		PTS.
1. Aleksandr Dityatin	SOV/RUS	19.875
2. Aleksandr Tkachyov	SOV/RUS	19.725
3. Jiři Tabak	CZE	19.60
4. Roland Brückner	GDR	19.575
5. Stoyan Deltchev	BUL	19.475
6. Dănut Grecu	ROM	10.85

1984 Los Angeles C: 71, N: 19, D: 8.4.

		PTS.
1. Koji Gushiken	JPN	19.85
1. Li Ning	CHN	19.85
3. Mitchell Gaylord	USA	19.825
4. Tong Fei	CHN	19.75
4. Peter Vidmar	USA	19.75
6. Kyoji Yamawaki	JPN	19.725
7. Emilian Nicula	ROM	19.50
8. Josef Zellweger	SWI	19.375

1988 Seoul C: 89, N: 23, D: 9.24.

		PTS.
1. Holger Behrendt	GDR	19.925
1. Dmitri Bilozerchev	SOV/RUS	19.925
3. Sven Tippelt	GDR	19.875
4. Kalofer Hristozov	BUL	19.825
4. Valery Lyukin	SOV/KAZ	19.825
6. Juri Chechi	ITA	19.80
7. Lou Yun	CHN	19.80
8. György Guczoghy	HUN	19.70

1992 Barcelona C: 93, N: 25, D: 8.2.

		PTS.
1. Vitaly Scherbo	BLR	9.937
2. Li Jing	CHN	9.875
3. Li Xiaoshuang	CHN	9.862
3. Andreas Wecker	GER	9.862
5. Valery Belenky	AZR	9.825
6. Szilveszter Csollány	HUN	9.80
7. Yukio Iketani	JPN	9.762
8. Kalofer Hristozov	BUL	9.75

FLOOR EXERCISES

1896–1928 not held

Vitaly Scherbo won four gold medals in one day in 1992.

1932 Los Angeles C: 25, N: 6, D: 8.8.

			PTS.
1.	István Pelle	HUN	9.60
2.	Georges Miez	SWI	9.47
3.	Mario Lertora	ITA	9.23
4.	Frank Haubold	USA	9.00
4.	Romeo Neri	ITA	9.00
6.	Heikki Savolainen	FIN	8.97
7.	Alfred Jochim	USA	8.80
7.	Martti Uosikkinen	FIN	8.80

1936 Berlin C: 110, N: 14, D: 8.11.

			PTS.
1.	Georges Miez	SWI	18.666
2.	Josef Walter	SWI	18.50
3.	Konrad Frey	GER	18.466
3.	Eugen Mack	SWI	18.466
5.	Matthias Volz	GER	18.366
6.	Willi Stadel	GER	18.30
6.	Walter Steffens	GER	18.30
8.	Martti Uosikkinen	FIN	18.267

1948 London C: 123, N: 16, D: 8.13.

			PTS.
1.	Ferenc Pataki	HUN	19.35
2.	János Mogyorósi-Klencs	HUN	19.20
3.	Zdenek Ružička	CZE	19.05
4.	Raymond Dot	FRA	18.90
5.	Elkana Grönne	DEN	18.825
6.	Pavel Benetka	CZE	18.80
6.	Leo Sotornik	CZE	18.80
8.	Vladimir Karas	CZE	18.10

As a teenager in Budapest, Ferenc Pataki wanted to become an actor. His first role was a walk-on part in which he performed some acrobatic moves. His skill was immediately noticed and he was rerouted into gymnastics.

1952 Helsinki C: 185, N: 29, D: 7.21.

			PTS.
1.	K. William Thoresson	SWE	19.25
2.	Jerzy Jokiel	POL	19.15
2.	Tadao Uesako	JPN	19.15
4.	Takashi Ono	JPN	19.05
5.	Onni Lappalainen	FIN	19.00
6.	Kalevi Laitinen	FIN	18.95
6.	Anders Lindh	SWE	18.95
8.	Ferdinand Daniš	CZE	18.90
8.	Grant Shanginyan	SOV/ARM	18.90
8.	Robert Stout	USA	18.90

1956 Melbourne C: 63, N: 18, D: 12.6.

			PTS.
1.	Valentin Muratov	SOV/RUS	19.20
2.	Nobuyuki Aihara	JPN	19.10
2.	Viktor Chukarin	SOV/UKR	19.10
2.	K. William Thoresson	SWE	19.10
5.	Yuri Tytov	SOV/UKR	18.95
6.	Ferdinand Daniš	CZE	18.80
6.	Mintscho Todorov	BUL	18.80

8.	Helmut Bantz	GER	18.75
8.	Takashi Ono	JPN	18.75

1960 Rome C: 130, N: 28, D: 9.10.

			PTS.
1.	Nobuyuki Aihara	JPN	19.45
2.	Yuri Tytov	SOV/UKR	19.325
3.	Franco Menichelli	ITA	19.275
4.	Takashi Mitsukuri	JPN	19.20
4.	Takashi Ono	JPN	19.20
6.	Jaroslav Štastny	CZE	19.05

1964 Tokyo C: 130, N: 29, D: 10.22.

			PTS.
1.	Franco Menichelli	ITA	19.45
2.	Yukio Endo	JPN	19.35
2.	Viktor Lisitsky	SOV/RUS	19.35
4.	Viktor Leontyev	SOV/RUS	19.20
5.	Takashi Mitsukuri	JPN	19.10
6.	Yuri Tsapenko	SOV/RUS	18.85

1968 Mexico City C: 117, N: 28, D: 10.26.

			PTS.
1.	Sawao Kato	JPN	19.475
2.	Akinori Nakayama	JPN	19.40
3.	Takeshi Kato	JPN	19.275
4.	Mitsuo Tsukuhara	JPN	19.05
5.	Valery Karasyov	SOV/RUS	18.95
6.	Eizo Kenmotsu	JPN	18.925

1972 Munich C: 113, N: 26, D: 9.1.

			PTS.
1.	Nikolai Andrianov	SOV/RUS	19.175
2.	Akinori Nakayama	JPN	19.125
3.	Shigeru Kasamatsu	JPN	19.025
4.	Eizo Kenmotsu	JPN	18.925
5.	Klaus Köste	GDR	18.825
6.	Sawao Kato	JPN	18.75

1976 Montreal C: 90, N: 20, D: 7.23.

			PTS.
1.	Nikolai Andrianov	SOV/RUS	19.45
2.	Vladimir Marchenko	SOV/RUS	19.425
3.	Peter Kormann	USA	19.30
4.	Roland Brückner	GDR	19.275
5.	Sawao Kato	JPN	19.25
6.	Eizo Kenmotsu	JPN	19.10

1980 Moscow C: 65, N: 14, D: 7.25.

			PTS.
1.	Roland Brückner	GDR	19.75
2.	Nikolai Andrianov	SOV/RUS	19.725
3.	Aleksandr Dityatin	SOV/RUS	19.70
4.	Jiři Tabák	CZE	19.675
5.	Péter Kovács	HUN	19.425
6.	Lutz Hoffmann	GDR	18.725

1984 Los Angeles C: 71, N: 19, D: 8.4.

		PTS.
1. Li Ning	CHN	19.925
2. Lou Yun	CHN	19.775
3. Koji Sotomura	JPN	19.70
3. Philippe Vatuone	FRA	19.70
5. Bart Conner	USA	19.675
6. Valerian Pintea	ROM	19.60
7. Peter Vidmar	USA	19.55
8. Koji Gushiken	JPN	19.45

Li Ning, a good-natured crowd-pleaser, went home with more medals than any other athlete at the Los Angeles Olympics: 3 gold, 2 silver and 1 bronze. When he retired in 1989, he opened a sportswear factory and became a successful entrepreneur.

1988 Seoul C: 89, N: 23, D: 9.24.

		PTS.
1. Sergei Kharkov	SOV/RUS	19.925
2. Vladimir Artemov	SOV/RUS	19.90
3. Yukio Iketani	JPN	19.85
3. Lou Yun	CHN	19.85
5. Li Ning	CHN	19.80
6. Boris Preti	ITA	19.775
7. Kalofer Hristozov	BUL	19.75
8. Curtis Hibbert	CAN	19.525

1992 Barcelona C: 93, N: 25, D: 8.2.

		PTS.
1. Li Xiaoshuang	CHN	9.925
2. Yukio Iketani	JPN	9.787
2. Grigory Misyutin	UKR	9.787
4. Yoo Ok-ryul	KOR	9.775
5. Yutaka Aihara	JPN	9.737
6. Vitaly Scherbo	BLR	9.712
7. Andreas Wecker	GER	9.687
8. Li Chunyang	CHN	9.387

Since the previous Olympics this event had been dominated by Igor Korobchinsky and Vitaly Scherbo. Korobchinsky won at the 1989 European Championships, the 1989 World Championships, the 1991 World Championships, and the Individual Event World Championships in April 1992. Scherbo won at the 1990 European Championships, the 1990 World Cup, and the 1992 European Championships in May. However, in Barcelona Korobchinsky failed to make it to the finals despite placing fourth in the qualifying round; two of the three gymnasts ahead of him were also from the Unified Team of ex–Soviet republics. Scherbo did qualify for the final but was penalized one-tenth of a point when he stepped out of bounds on his mount. In the end it was 18-year-old Li Xiaoshuang of Wuchang who earned the gold medal by dazzling the judges with his backward triple salto tucked.

TEAM COMBINED EXERCISES

According to current rules, each nation's final score is determined by combining the scores of the top five performers on each apparatus.

1896–1900 not held

1904 St. Louis T: 13, N: 2, D: 7.2.

	TOTAL PTS.
1. Turngemeinde Philadelphia	374.43
Julius Lenhart 69.80 (1), Philipp Kassel 64.56 (11), Anton Heida 62.72 (17), Max Hess 59.29 (31), Ernst Reckeweg 56.15 (46), John Grieb 55.21 (50)	
2. New York Turnverein	356.37
Otto Steffen 67.03 (6), John Bissinger 66.57 (8), Emil Beyer 59.70 (30), Max Wolf 57.85 (33), Julian Schmitz 54.58 (56), Arthur Rosenkampf 48.34 (87)	
3. Central Turnverein Chicago	349.69
George Mayer 61.66 (21), John Duha 61.02 (24), Edward Siegler 59.03 (32), Philipp Schuster 55.44 (49), Robert Mayack 54.53 (57), Charles Krause 53.01 (66)	
4. Concordia Turnverein St. Louis	344.01
William Merz 65.25 (10), Georges Stapf 61.97 (20), John Dellert 57.41 (35), Emil Voigt 54.33 (59), George Eyser 52.10 (70), Hyacinth Meyland 48.52 (86)	
5. South St. Louis Turnverein	338.65
Charles Umbs 63.39 (16), Andy Neu 61.21 (23), William Tritschler 54.73 (54), Christian Deubler 54.63 (55), Edward Tritschler 53.16 (65), John Leichinger 50.00 (81)	
6. Norwegischer Turnverein Brooklyn	334.00
Ragnar Berg 60.24 (28), Charles Sörum 57.40 (36), Oliver Olsen 57.27 (38), Harry Hansen 55.00 (51), Oluf Landnes 53.64 (72), Bergin Nilsen 50.45 (80)	

1906 Athens T: 6, N: 5, D: 4.22.

		TOTAL PTS.
1. NOR	(Carl Albert Andersen, Oskar Bye, Conrad Carlsrud, Harald Eriksen, Osvald Falk, Christian Fjeringen, Yngvar Fredriksen, Karl Johan Haagensen, Harald Halvorsen, Peter Hol, Andreas Hagelund, Eugene Ingebretsen, Mathias Jespersen, Finn Münster, Fridtjof Olsen, Carl Alfred Pedersen, Rasmus Pettersen, Thorleif Pettersen, Thorleif Rohn, Johan Stumpf)	19.00
2. DEN	(Carl Andersen, Halvor Birch, H. Bukdahl, Kaj Gnudtzmann, Knud Holm, Erik Klem, Harald Klem, R. Kraft, Edvard Larsen, J. Lorentzen, Robert Madsen, Carl Manicus-Hansen, Oluf Olsen, Christian Petersen, Hans Pedersen, Niels Petersen, Viktor Rasmussen, Marius Skram-Jensen, Marius Thuesen)	18.00
3. ITA	Pistoia (Manlio Pastorini, Spartaco Nerozzi, Federico Bertinotti, Vitaliano Masotti, Raffaello	16.71

Gianoni, Quintilio Mazzoncini, Azeglio Innocenti, Filiberto Innocenti, Ciro Civinini, Maurizio Masetti)

			TOTAL PTS.
4.	ITA	Roma (Cesare Tifi, Dante Aloisi, Enrico Brignoli, Pierino Caccialupi, Guido Colavini, Romeo Gianotti, Mario Gubiani, Venceslao Rossi, Romolo Tuzzi, Amadeo Zinzi)	16.60
5.	GER	(O. Franke, Cassius Hermes, Fritz Hofmann, Julius Keyl, Bruno Mahler, Carl Ohms, Wilhelm Weber, Otto Wiegand)	16.25
6.	HUN	(Béla Dáner, Arpád Erdös, Béla Erödi, Frigyes Gráf, Gyula Kakas, Nándor Kovács, Kálmán Szabó, Vilmos Szücs)	14.45

1908 London T: 8, N: 8, D: 7.18.

			TOTAL PTS.
1.	SWE	(Gösta Åsbrink, Per Bertilsson, Andreas Cervin, Hjalmar Cedercrona, Rudolf Degermark, Carl Folcker, Sven Forssman, Erik Granfelt, Carl Hårleman, Nils Hellsten, Gunnar Höjer, Arvid Holmberg, Carl Holmberg, Osvald Holmberg, Hugo Jahnke, John Jarlén, Harald Johnsson, Rolf Johnsson, Nils Kantzow, Sven Landberg, Olle Lanner, Axel Jung, Osvald Moberg, Carl Martin Norberg, Erik Norberg, Thor Norberg, Axel Norling, Daniel Norling, Gösta Olsson, Leonard Peterson, Sven Rosen, Gustav Rosenqvist, Axel Sjöblom, Birger Sörvik, Haakon Sorvik, Karl Johan Svensson [Sarland], Gustaf Vinqvist, Nils Widforss)	438
2.	NOR	(Carl Albert Andersen, Hermann Bolme, Trygve Böyesen, Oscar Bye, Conrad Carlsrud, Sverre Gröner, Harald Halvorsen, Harald Hansen, Peter Hol, Eugene Ingebretsen, Ole Iversen, Mathias Jespersen, Sigge Johannessen, Nicolai Kiaer, Karl Klaeth, Thor Larsen, Rolf Lefdahl, Hans Lem, Anders Moen, Frithjof Olsen, Carl Alfred Pedersen, Paul Pedersen, Sigvard Sivertsen, Johannes Skrataas, Harald Smedvik, Andreas Strand, Olaf Syvertsen, Thomas Thorstensen)	425
3.	FIN	(Eino Forsström, Otto Granström, Johan Kemp, Jivari Kyykoski, Heikki Lehmusto, John Lindroth, Yrjö Linko, Edvard Linna, Matti Markanen, Kaarlo Mikkolainen, Veli Nieminen, Kaarlo Kustaa Paasia, Arvi Pohjanpää, Aarne Pohjonen, Eino Railio, Heikki Riipinen, Arno Saarinen, Einari Verner Sahlstein, Arne Salovaara, Kaarlo Sandelin, Elias Sipilä, Viktor Smeds, Kaarlo Soinio, Kurt Enoch Stenberg, Väinö Tiiri, Magnus Wegelius)	405
4.	DEN	(Carl Andersen, Hans Bredmose, Jens Chiewitz, Arvor Hansen, Christian Hansen, Ingvardt Hansen, Einar Hermann, Knud Holm, Paul Holm, Oluf Husted Nielsen, Charles Jensen, Gorm Jensen, Hendrik Johansen, Harald Klem, Robert Madsen, Viggo Meulengracht Madsen, Lucas Nielsen, Oluf	378

Olsen, Niels Petersen, Nicolaj Philipsen, Heini Rasmussen, Victor Rasmussen, Marius Thuesen, Niels Turin Nielsen)

5.	FRA	(L. Bogart, A. Borizée, H. de Breyne, N. Constant, C. A. Courtois, L. Delattre, A. Delecluse, L. Delecluse, G. Demarle, J. Derou, Charles Desmarcheliers, Claude Desmarcheliers, E. Dharaney, G. Donnet, E. Duhamel, A. Duponchel, Paul Durin, A. Eggremont, G. Guiot, L. Hennebic, H. Hubert, D. Hudels, E. Labitte, L. Léstienne, R. Lis, V. Magnier, G. Nys, J. Parent, L. Pappe, V. Polidori, G. Pottier, A. Pinoy, L. Sandray, E. Schmoll, E. Steffe, E. Vercruysse, H. Vergin, E. Vicogne, J. Walmée, G. Warlouzer)	319
6.	ITA	(Alfredo Accorsi, Nemo Agodi, Umberto Agliorini, Adriano Andreani, Vincenzo Blo, Flaminio Bottoni, Bruto Buozzi, Giovanni Bonati, Pietro Borsetti, Adamo Borzani, Gastone Calabresi, Carlo Celada, Tito Collevati, Antonio Cotechini, Guido Cristofori, Stanislao Dichiara, Giovanni Gasperini, A. Marchi, Carlo Marchiandi, Ettore Massari, Roberto Nardini, Gaetano Preti, Decio Pavani, Gino Ravenna, Massimo Ridolfi, Gustavo Taddia, Giannetto Termanini, Ugo Savonuzzi, Gioacchino Vaccari)	316
7.	HOL	(C.L.J. Becker, M. Biel, J. de Boer, R.J.C. Blom, J. Bolt, E. Brouwer, C. van Daalen, J.H. Flemer, G.C. Göckel, J. Goudeket, Dirk Janssen, J.J. Kiefl, S. Köngins, Herman van Leeuwen, A. Mok, A. d'Oliviera, J.J. Posthumus, J.H.A.G. Schmitt, J. Slier, J.J. Stikkelman, H.J.F. Thijssen, G.J. Wesling)	297
8.	GBR	(P.A. Baker, W.F. Barrett, R. Bonney, J.H. Catley, M. Clay, E. Clough, J. Cotterell, W. Cowy, G.C. Cullen, F. Denby, Herbert Drury, W. Fitt, H. Gill, A.S. Harley, A.E. Hawkins, William Hoare, J.A. Horridge, H.J. Huskinson, J.W. Jones, E. Justice, N.J. Keighly, R. Laycock, R. McGaw, J. McPhail, W. Manning, W.G. Merrifield, C.J. Oldaker, G. Parrott, E. Parsons, E.F. Richardson, J. Robertson, George Ross, D. Scott, J.E.F. Simpson, W.R. Skeeles, J. Speight, H. Stell, C.V. Suderman, William Titt, Charles Vigurs, E. Walton, H. Waterman, E.A. Watkins, John Whitaker, F. Whitehead)	196

1912 Stockholm T: 5, N: 5, D: 7.11.

			TOTAL PTS.
1.	ITA	(Guido Boni, Giuseppe Domenichelli, Luciano Savorini, Guido Romano, Angelo Zorzi, Giorgio Zampori, Giovanni Mangiante, Lorenzo Mangiante, Adolfo Tunesi, Pietro Bianchi, Paolo Salvi, Alberto Braglia, Alfredo Gollini, Serafino Mazzarocchi, Francesco Loi, Carlo Fregosi)	265.75
2.	HUN	(Lajos Aradi-Kmetykó, József Berkes-Bittenbinder, Imre Erdödy, Samu Fóti, Imre	227.25

			TOTAL PTS.
	Gellért, Gyözö Halmos-Haberfeld, Ottó Helmich, István Herczeg, József Keresztessy, János Korponai-Krizmanich, Elemér Pászty, Árpád Pétery, Jenö Réti-Rittich, Ferenc Szücs, Ödön Téry, Géza Tuli)		
3.	GBR	(Albert Betts, Harold Dickason, Samuel Hodgetts, Alfred Messenger, Edward Pepper, Charles Vigurs, Samuel Walker, John Whitaker, Sidney Cross, Bernard Franklin, Edward Potts, Reginald Potts, George Ross, Henry Oberholzer, Charles Simmons, Arthur Southern, Ronald McLean, Charles Luck, Herbert Drury, William MacKune, William Titt, William Cowhig, Leonard Hanson)	184.50
4.	LUX	(Nicolas Adam, Charles Behm, André Bordang, Jean-Pierre Frantzen, François Hentges, Pierre Hentges, Michal Hemmerling, Jean-Baptiste Horn, Nicolas Kanivé, Emile Knepper, Nicolas Kummer, Marcel Langsam, Emile Lanners, Jean-Pierre Thommes, François Wagner, Antoine Wehrer, Ferdinand Wirtz, Joseph Zuang, Maurice Palgen)	179.75
5.	GER	(Walter Engelmann, Adolf Seebass, Alfred Staats, Hans Roth, Arno Glockauer, Alexander Sperling, Kurt Reichenbach, Rudolf Körner, Erwin Buder, Wilhelm Brülle, Heinrich Pahner, Johannes Reuschle, Walter Jesinghaus, Eberhard Sorge, Karl Richter, Erich Worm, Karl Jordan, Hans Werner)	162.00

1920 Antwerp T: 5, N: 5, D: 8.24.

			TOTAL PTS.
1.	ITA	(Arnaldo Andreoli, Ettore Bellotto, Pietro Bianchi, Fernando Bonatti, Luigi Cambiaso, Luigi Contessi, Carlo Costigliolo, Luigi Costigliolo, Giuseppe Domenichelli, Roberto Ferrari, Carlo Fregosi, Romualdo Ghiglione, Ambrogio Levati, Francesco Loi, Vittorio Lucchetti, Luigi Maiocco, Ferdinando Mandrini, Lorenzo Mangiante, Antonio Marovelli, Michele Mastromarino, Giuseppe Paris, Manlio Pastorini, Ezio Roselli, Paolo Salvi, Giovanni Battista Tubino, Giorgio Zampori, Angelo Zorzi)	359.855
2.	BEL	(Eugenius Auwerkerken, Théophile Bauer, François Claessens, Auguste Cootmans, François Gibens, Albert Haepers, Dominique Jacobs, Félicien Kempeneers, Jules Labéeu, Hubert Lafortune, Auguste Landrieu, Charles Lannie, Constant Loriot, Nicolas Maerloos, Ferdinand Minnaert, Louis Stoop, Jean van Guysse, Alphonse van Mele, François Verboven, Jean Verboven, Julien Verdonck, Joseph Verstraeten, Georges Vivex, Julianus Wagemans)	346.765

			TOTAL PTS.
3.	FRA	(Emile Bouchès, Paul Joseph Durin, Paulin Lemaire, Georges Berger, Léon Delsarte, Georges Duvant, Louis Kempe, Lucien Démanet, Auguste Hoël, René Boulanger, Fernand Fauconnier, Albert Hersoy, Georges Lagouge, Ernest Lepinasse, Jules Pirard, Julien Wartelle, Paul Wartelle, Emile Martel, Georges Thurnherr, Alfred Buyenne, Eugène Pollet, Eugène Cordonnier, Arthur Hermann, André Higelin, Marco Torrès, François Walker)	340.100
4.	CZE	(Josef Bochníček, Ladislav Bubeníček, Josef Čada, Stanislav Indruch, Miroslav Klinger, Josef Malý, Zdenek Opočensky, Josef Pagáč, František Pecháček, Robert Pražák, Josef Stolař, Svatopluk Svoboda, Ladislav Vácha, František Vaněček, Jaroslav Velda, Václav Wirt)	305.255
5.	GBR	(S. Andrew, Albert Betts, A.E. Cocksedge, J. Cotterell, William Cowhig, Sydney Cross, H.S. Dawswell, J.E. Dingley, S. Domville, H.W. Doncaster, R.E. Edgecombe, W. Edwards, Henry Finchett, Bernard Wallis Franklin, J. Harris, Samuel Hodgetts, Stanley Leigh, G. Masters, Ronald McLean, O. Morris, E.P. Ness, A.E. Page, A.O. Pinner, E. Pugh, H.W. Taylor, J.A. Walker, R.H. Zandell)	299.115

1924 Paris T: 9, N: 9, D: 7.20.

			TOTAL PTS.
1.	ITA	(Fernando Mandrini 105.583 [4], Mario Letora 103.619 [10], Vittorio Lucchetti 102.803 [12], Francesco Martino 101.529 [16], Luigi Cambiaso 101.320 [17], Giuseppe Paris 101.169 [18], Giorgio Zampori 96.549 [26], Luigi Maiocco 92.486 [33])	839.058
2.	FRA	(Jean Gounot 105.153 [8], Léon Delsarte 104.739 [9], Albert Séquin 102.326 [15], Eugène Cordonnier 99.906 [21], François Gangloff 98.796 [23], Arthur Hermann 95.716 [27], André Higelin 92.133 [34], Joseph Huber 88.119 [39])	820.528
3.	SWI	(August Güttinger 105.176 [7], Jean Gutweniger 102.342 [14], Hans Grieder 99.646 [22], Georges Miez 98.796 [24], Josef Wilhelm 97.096 [25], Otto Pfister 95.746 [28], Carl Widmer 94.936 [32], Antoine Rebetez 89.583 [38])	816.661
4.	YUG	(Leon Štukelj 110.340 [1], Ivan Porenta 100.172 [20], Stane Zilič 95.523 [29], Stane Derganc 95.293 [30], Miha Osvald 91.066 [36], Slavko Hlastan 81.248 [44], Rastko Poljšak 77.665 [45], Josip Primožič 77.393 [47])	762.101
5.	USA	(Frank Kriz 100.293 [19], Alfred Jochim 95.090 [31], John Pearson 89.852 [37], Frank Safanda 86.953 [41], Curtis Rottman 82.946 [42], Rudolph Novak 77.593 [46],	715.117

Max Wandrer 76.320 [48], John Mais 72.770 [53])

		TOTAL PTS.
6. GBR	(Stanley Leigh 91.266 [35], Harold Brown 87.059 [40], Henry Finchett 81.710 [43], Frank Hawkins 73.796 [49], Thomas Hopkins 72.350 [54], Edward Leigh 69.200 [55], Samuel Humphreys 64.656 [64], Albert Spencer 64.253 [65])	637.790
7. FIN	(Jaakko Kunnas 73.473 [51], Otto Suhonen 72.843 [52], Akseli Roine 66.503 [56], Aarne Roine 65.46 [59], Mikko Hamalainen 65.23, Karonen 65.18 [63], Evert Kerttula 62.863 [66], Edward "Eetu" Kostamo 50.443 [70])	521.998
8. LUX	(C. Quaino 73.569 [50], T. Jeitz 65.98 [57], E. Munhofen 65.556 [58], Mathias Erang 65.356 [60], A. Neumann 65.196 [62], J. Palzer 61.563 [67], P. Tolar 58.713 [68], M. Weishaupt 58.596 [69])	514.529

1928 Amsterdam T: 11, N: 11, D: 8.10.

		TOTAL PTS.
1. SWI	(Georges Miez 247.500 [1], Hermann Hänggi 246.625 [2], Eugen Mack 243.250 [8], Melchior Wetzel 240.875 [12], Eduard "Edi" Steinemann 237.875 [15], August Güttinger 237.750 [16], Hans Grieder 234.125 [18], Otto Pfister 230.875 [24])	1718.625
2. CZE	(Ladislav Vácha 242.875 [9], Emanuel Löffler 242.500 [10], Jan Gajdoš 240.625 [13], Josef Effenberger 238.875 [14], Bedřich Šupčík 233.250 [20], Václav Vesely 227.625 [28], Jan Koutny 225.250 [31], Ladislav Tikal 217.750 [37])	1712.25
3. YUG	(Leon Štukelj 244.875 [3], Josip Primožič 244.000 [5], Anton Malej 228.875 [25], Eduard Antonijevič 228.000 [26], Boris Gregorka 221.000 [33], Ivan Porenta 220.250 [34], Stane Derganc 211.875 [43], Dragutin Ciotti 210.000 [45])	1648.75
4. FRA	(Armand Solbach 241.625 [11], Georges Leroux 235.750 [17], André Lemoine 232.000 [22], Jean Larrouy 226.500 [29], Étienne Schmitt 219.125 [35], Jean Gounot 216.750 [39], Antoine Chatelain 202.375 [54], Alfred Kraus 100.25 [DNF])	1620.75
5. FIN	(Heikki Savolainen 243.750 [6], Mauri Nyberg-Noroma 243.750 [6], Martti Uosikkinen 231.875 [23], Jaakko Kunnas 217.500 [38], Urho Korhonen 209.875 [46], Rafael Ylönen 188.750 [61], Kaiku Kinos 185.375 [62], Birger Stenman 179.750 [66])	1609.25
6. ITA	(Romeo Neri 244.750 [4], Mario Lertora 233.375 [19], Vittorio Lucchetti 228.000 [26], Fernando Mandrini 226.250 [30], Giuseppe Lupi 224.000 [32], Mario Tambini 212.500 [41], Giuseppe Paris 203.250 [53], Ezio Roselli 192.625 [58])	1599.125
7. USA	(Alfred Jochim 218.250 [36], Glenn Berry 212.750 [40], Frank Kriz 211.625 [44], Frank	1519.125

Haubold 209.375 [47], Harold Newhart 209.375 [47], John Pearson 208.75 [50], Herman Witzig 206.250 [51], Paul Krempel 203.625 [52])

8. HOL	(E.H. Melkman 199.500 [56], P.J. van Dam 199.375 [59], M. Jacobs 199.000 [60], I. Wijnschenk 182.625 [64], W.B. Pouw 182.125 [65], Klaas Boot 169.000 [71], J.F. van der Vinden 169.000 [71], Hugo Licher 143.500 [85])	1364.875

1932 Los Angeles T: 5, N: 5, D: 8.10.

		TOTAL PTS.
1. ITA	(Romeo Neri 140.625 [1], Mario Lertora 134.400 [4], Savino Guglielmetti 134.375 [5], Oreste Capuzzo 132.450 [7])	541.850
2. USA	(Frank Haubold 132.525 [6], Frederick Meyer 131.650 [8], Alfred Jochim 129.075 [11], Frank Cumiskey 129.025 [12])	522.275
3. FIN	(Heikki Savolainen 134.575 [3], Mauri Nyberg-Noroma 129.800 [10], Veikko Pakarinen 122.700 [14], Einari Teräsvirta 122.700 [14])	509.995
4. HUN	(István Pelle 134.925 [2], Miklós Péter 119.200 [17], Péter Boros 105.775 [20], József Hegedüs 105.750 [21])	465.650
5. JPN	(Toshihiko Sasano 108.475 [19], Shigeo Honma 103.100 [22], Takashi Kondo 101.925 [23], Yoshitaki Takeda 88.500 [24])	402.000

1936 Berlin T: 14, N: 14, D: 8.11.

		TOTAL PTS.
1. GER	(Alfred Schwarzmann 113.100 [1], Konrad Frey 111.532 [3], Matthias Volz 110.099 [7], Willi Stadel 108.999 [8], Franz Beckert 107.200 [15], Walter Steffens 106.500 [17])	657.430
2. SWI	(Eugen Mack 112.334 [2], Michael Reusch 110.700 [5], Eduard "Edi" Steinemann 108.633 [10], Walter Bach 108.299 [11], Albert Bachmann 107.502 [13], Georges Miez 107.334 [14])	654.802
3. FIN	(Martti Uosikkinen 110.700 [5], Heikki Savolainen 108.766 [9], Mauri Nyberg-Noroma 106.801 [16], Aleksanteri Saarvala 105.235 [19], Esa Seeste 103.934 [24], Veikko Pakarinen 103.032 [28])	638.468
4. CZE	(Alois Hudec 111.199 [4], Jaroslav Kollinger 104.733 [23], Jan Sládek 103.399 [26], Jan Gajdoš 103.065 [27], Vratislav Petraček 101.966 [34], Jindřich Tintera 101.401 [38])	625.763
5. ITA	(Savino Guglielmetti 107.699 [12], Oreste Capuzzo 102.500 [30], Egidio Armelloni 101.601 [36], Danilo Fioravanti 101.467 [37], Franco Tognini 101.266 [39], Nicolo Tronci 100.600 [41])	615.133
6. YUG	(Konrad Gralc 103.632 [25], Josip Primožič 102.367 [31], Leon Štukelj 102.300 [32],	598.366

Miroslav Forte 99.200 [46], Jože Vadnov 95.934 [56], Janoz Pristov 94.933 [61])

		TOTAL PTS.
7. HUN	(István Pelle 105.566 [18], Lajos Tóth 101.867 [35], Miklós Péter 99.034 [47], Gábor Kecskeméti 97.766 [51], István Sárkány 94.565 [64], Jósef Sarlós 93.132 [71])	591.930
8. FRA	(Armand Walter 98.933 [49], Armand Solbach 97.633 [52], Lucien Masset 97.233 [53], Robert Herold 96.168 [55], Antoine Schildwein 95.633 [59], Maurice Rousseau 94.666 [62])	580.266

1948 London T: 16, N: 16, D: 8.13.

		TOTAL PTS.
1. FIN	(Veikko Huhtanen 229.70 [1], Paavo Aaltonen 228.80 [3], Kalevi Laitinen 225.65 [8], Olavi Rove 225.20 [10], Einari Teräsvirta 225.00 [12], Heikki Savolainen 223.95 [14])	1358.30
2. SWI	(Walter Lehmann 229.00 [2], Josef Stalder 228.70 [4], Christian Kipfer 227.10 [5], Emil Studer 226.60 [6], Robert Lucy 223.30 [15], Michael Reusch 222.00 [18])	1356.70
3. HUN	(Lajos Tóth 225.20 [10], Lajos Sántha 224.30 [13], László Baranyai 222.40 [16], Ferenc Pataki 221.30 [19], János Mogyorósi-Klencs 218.95 [27], Ferenc Varköi 218.70 [29])	1330.85
4. FRA	(Raymond Dot 220.80 [20], Michel Mathiot 220.40 [22], Lucien Masset 219.95 [24], André Weingand 219.80 [25], Antoine Schlindwein 216.50 [34], Alphonse Anger 216.40 [35])	1313.85
5. ITA	(Guido Figone 225.30 [9], Luigi Zanetti 219.00 [26], Savino Guglielmetti 217.20 [32], Domenico Grosso 214.10 [40], Quinto Vadi 214.00 [42], Danilo Fioravanti 210.70 [51])	1300.30
6. CZE	(Zdenek Ružička 226.20 [7], Pavel Benetka 220.30 [23], Miroslav Málek 212.90 [47], Vladimir Karas 212.20 [48], Leo Sotornik 210.80 [50], František Wirth 209.70 [52])	1292.10
7. USA	(Edward Scrobe 213.90 [44], Vincent D'Autorio 211.30 [49], William Roetzheim 209.10 [53], Joseph Kotys 208.50 [55], Frank Cumiskey 205.15 [62], Raymond Sorensen 204.55 [63])	1252.50
8. DEN	(Paul Jessen 214.30 [38], Tage Gronne 213.50 [45], Freddy Jensen 208.35 [56], Arnold Thomsen 206.25 [58], Wilhelm Moller 201.75 [68], Poul Jensen 201.25 [70])	1245.40

1952 Helsinki T: 29, N: 29, D: 7.21.

		TOTAL PTS.
1. SOV	(Viktor Chukarin 115.70 [1], Grant Shaginyan 114.95 [2], Valentin Muratov	574.40

113.65 [4], Yevgeny Korolkov 113.35 [6], Vladimir Belyakov 113.35 [6], Iosif Berdiyev 113.10 [10], Mikhail Perelman 112.50 [11], Dmytro Leonkin 103.75 [78])

		TOTAL PTS.
2. SWI	(Josef Stalder 114.75 [3], Hans Eugster 113.40 [5], Jean Tschabold 113.30 [8], Jack Günthard 111.60 [17], Melchior Thalmann 110.75 [25], Ernst Gebendinger 109.75 [39], Hans Schwarzentruber 108.40 [52], Ernst Fivian 107.95 [55])	567.50
3. FIN	(Onni Lappalainen 111.85 [14], Berndt Lindfors 111.45 [19], Paavo Aaltonen 111.40 [20], Kaino Lempinen 110.60 [28], Heikki Savolainen 110.45 [29], Kalevi Laitinen 110.10 [35], Kalevi Viskari 109.80 [38], Olavi Rove 109.45 [42])	564.20
4. GER	Helmut Bantz 113.25 [9], Adalbert Dickhut 110.85 [24], Theo Wied 110.70 [26], Alfred Schwarzmann 110.65 [27], Hans Pfann 110.20 [33], Erich Wied 109.70 [40], Friedel Overwien 108.65 [48], Jakob Kiefer 91.70 [150])	561.20
5. JPN	(Takashi Ono 112.20 [12], Tadao Uesako 111.65 [15], Masao Takemoto 111.65 [15], Akitomo Kaneko 111.30 [21], Tetsumi Nabeya 110.10 [35])	556.90
6. HUN	(Lajos Santha 111.50 [18], Ferenc Pataki 110.90 [23], József Fekete 108.90 [46], Karoly Kocsis 108.65 [48], Ferenc Kemény 108.40 [52], Sándor Rétl 107.75 [57], Lajos Tóth 107.45 [58], János Mogyorósi-Klencs 106.80 [61])	555.80
7. CZE	(Ferdinand Daniš 112.00 [13], Zdenek Ružička 110.40 [30], Josef Svoboda 110.05 [37], Lee Sotornik 109.50 [41], Josef Škvor 109.10 [44], Jindřich Mikulec 108.95 [45], Vladimir Kejř 108.15 [54], Miloslav Kolejka 106.70 [63])	555.55
8. USA	(Edward Scrobe 110.40 [30], Robert Stout 110.15 [34], William Roetzheim 107.05 [59], Donald Holder 103.50 [80], John Beckner 103.40 [81], Charles Simms 102.40 [89], Walter Blattmann 102.35 [90], Vincent D'Antorio 101.20 [100])	543.15

1956 Melbourne T: 7, N: 7, D: 12.6.

		TOTAL PTS.
1. SOV	(Viktor Chukarin 114.25 [1], Yuri Tytov 113.80 [3], Valentin Muratov 113.30 [5], Albert Azaryan 112.55 [7], Borys Shakhlin 112.50 [8], Pavel Stolbov 111.75 [14])	568.25
2. JPN	(Takashi Ono 114.20 [2], Masao Takemoto 113.55 [4], Masami Kubota 112.50 [8], Nobuyuki Aihara 112.45 [10], Shinsaku Tsukawaki 112.20 [12], Akira Kono 111.55 [16])	566.40
3. FIN	(Kalevi Suoniemi 112.35 [11], Berndt Lindfors 111.60 [15], Martti Mansikka 110.60 [20], Onni Lappalainen 110.45 [22], Olavi	555.95

Leimuvirta 109.35 [27], Raimo Heinonen 108.10 [37])

4. CZE (Ferdinand Daniš 111.90 [13], Josef Škvor 110.85 [18], Vladimir Kejř 110.30 [23], Zdenek Ružička 109.65 [26], Jaroslav Mikoška 109.35 [27], Jaroslav Bim 108.25 [26]) — 554.10

5. GER (Helmut Bantz 112.90 [6], Robert Klein 110.60 [20], Theo Wied 109.90 [25], Hans Pfann 109.15 [29], Erich Wied 107.50 [29], Jakob Kiefer 107.45 [42]) — 552.45

6. USA (John Beckner 111.00 [17], Jose Armando Vega 108.45 [31], Charles Simms 108.40 [32], Richard Beckner 108.30 [35], Abraham Grossfeld 107.75 [39], William Tom 107.35 [43]) — 547.50

7. AUS (Brian Blackburn 91.40 [58], Graham Bond 96.40 [54], David Gourlay 95.90 [55], John Lees 93.05 [56], Alexander Punton 85.75 [59], Bruce Sharp 92.95 [57]) — 477.15

1960 Rome T: 20, N: 20, D: 9.7.

			TOTAL PTS.
1.	JPN	(Takashi Ono 115.90 [2], Shuji Tsurumi 114.55 [4], Yukio Endo 114.45 [5], Masao Takemoto 114.45 [5], Takashi Mitsukuri 114.10 [9])	575.20
2.	SOV	(Borys Shakhlin 115.95 [1], Yuri Tytov 115.60 [3], Albert Azaryan 113.35 [11], Vladimir Portnoy 113.30 [12], Nikolai Miligulo 113.05 [13], Valery Kerdemelidi 111.95 [17])	572.70
3.	ITA	(Franco Menichelli 113.80 [10], Giovanni Carminucci 112.30 [14], Angelo Vicardi 110.90 [24], Pasquale Carminucci 110.40 [31], Orlando Polmonari 109.95 [38], Gianfranco Marzolla 109.05 [50])	559.05
4.	CZE	(Ferdinand Daniš 112.10 [15], Jaroslav Štastny 111.50 [18], Jaroslav Bim 111.00 [23], Pavel Gajdoš 110.60 [28], Josef Trmal 110.25 [33], Ladislav Pazdera 108.85 [54])	557.15
5.	USA	(Larry Banner 111.05 [21], John Beckner 110.85 [25], Donald Tonry 110.75 [27], Abraham Grossfeld 110.05 [36], Fred Orlofsky 109.45 [44], Garland O'Quinn 109.00 [53])	555.20
6.	FIN	(Otto Kestola 112.00 [16], Eugen Ekman 110.45 [30], Olavi Leimuvirta 110.25 [33], Kauko Heikkinen 109.85 [40], Raimo Heinonen 109.60 [42], Sakkari Olkkonnen 109.40 [45])	554.45
7.	GDR& GER	(Günter Lyhs 110.80 [26], Siegfried Fülle 110.60 [28], Erwin Koppe 109.05 [50], Günter Nachtigall 108.75 [59], Karlheinz Friedrich 108.00 [67], Philipp Fürst 106.65 [76])	553.35
8.	SWI	(Ernst Fivian 111.05 [21], Max Benker 110.00 [37], Fritz Feuz 109.85 [40], André Brullmann 109.15 [47], Hans Schwarzentruber 109.15 [47], Edy Thomi 108.35 [63])	551.45

Masao Takemoto, a member of the Japanese team, had won a total of two silver medals and three bronze in 1952 and 1956, but he didn't win a gold medal until 1960, when he was 40 years old. He is the oldest gymnast in Olympic history to win a gold medal. In 1960 he also gained another silver medal on the horizontal bar.

1964 Tokyo T: 18, N: 18, D: 10.20.

			TOTAL PTS.
1.	JPN	(Yukio Endo 115.95 [1], Shuji Tsurumi 115.40 [2], Haruhiro Yamashita 115.10 [6], Takuji Hayata 114.90 [8], Takashi Mitsukuri 114.80 [9], Takashi Ono 114.40 [11])	577.95
2.	SOV	(Borys Shakhlin 115.40 [2], Viktor Lisitsky 115.40 [2], Viktor Leontyev 114.50 [10], Yuri Tsapenko 114.40 [11], Yuri Tytov 114.35 [13], Sergei Diomidov 114.20 [14])	575.45
3.	GER& GDR	(Siegfried Fülle 114.10 [15], Klaus Köste 112.75 [18], Erwin Koppe 112.45 [19], Peter Weber 112.35 [21], Philipp Fürst 112.35 [24], Günter Lyhs 111.70 [29])	565.10
4.	ITA	(Franco Menichelli 115.15 [5], Luigi Cimnaghi 112.35 [21], Giovanni Carminucci 111.80 [27], Pasquale Carminucci 110.70 [42], Angelo Vicardi 109.40 [63], Bruno Franceschetti 108.70 [75])	560.90
5.	POL	(Mikolaj Kubica 113.20 [16], Aleksander Rokosa 111.95 [25], Wilhelm Kubica 111.10 [35], Alfred Kucharczyk 111.05 [37], Jan Jankowicz 110.60 [45], Andrzej Konopka 108.70 [75])	559.50
6.	CZE	(Bohumil Mudřik 111.50 [30], Ladislav Pazdera 110.70 [42], Václav Kubička 110.65 [44], Přemysl Krbec 110.60 [45], Karel Klečka 110.35 [52], Pavel Gajdoš 101.75 [106])	558.15
7.	USA	(Makoto Sakamoto 112.40 [20], Russell Mitchell 111.20 [32], Ronald Barak 110.95 [39], Larry Banner 110.05 [55], Gregor Weiss 109.90 [59], Arthur Shurlock 109.10 [68])	556.95
8.	FIN	(Eino Laiho 111.85 [26], Eugen Ekman 111.15 [34], Raimo Heinonen 110.95 [39], Hannu Rantakara 110.50 [48], Otto Kestola 109.95 [58], Kauko Heikkinen 109.35 [64])	556.20

1968 Mexico City T: 16, N: 16, D: 10.24.

			TOTAL PTS.
1.	JPN	(Sawao Kato 115.90 [1], Akinori Nakayama 115.65 [3], Eizo Kenmotsu 114.90 [4], Takeshi Kato 114.85 [5], Yukio Endo 113.55 [8], Misuo Tsukahara 111.50 [18])	575.90
2.	SOV	(Mikhail Voronin 115.85 [2], Sergei Diomidov 114.10 [6], Viktor Klimenko 113.95 [7], Valery Karasyov 113.25 [10], Viktor Lisitsky 112.60 [14], Valery Ilyinykh 111.90 [15])	571.10
3.	GDR	(Matthias Brehme 112.85 [12], Klaus Köste 111.85 [16], Siegfried Fülle 111.10 [21],	557.15

		TOTAL PTS.
	Peter Weber 110.15 [26], Gerhard Dietrich 109.70 [34], Günter Beier 108.20 [51])	
4. CZE	(Václav Kubička 111.30 [19], Jiří Fejtek 111.20 [20], František Bocko 111.00 [22], Bohumil Mudřik 109.95 [28], Miloslav Netusil 109.40 [37], Václav Skoumal 109.30 [38])	557.10
5. POL	(Wilhelm Kubica 113.15 [11], Mikolaj Kubica 112.80 [13], Sylwester Kubica 109.80 [31], Andrzej Gonera 109.25 [39], Aleksander Rokosa 108.85 [44], Jerzy Kruza 108.15 [53])	555.40
6. YUG	(Miroslav Cerar 113.30 [9], Janez Brodnik 110.75 [23], Milenko Kersnič 109.85 [30], Milko Vratič 108.90 [42], Damir Anić 105.80 [75], Martin Šrot 104.80 [84])	550.75
7. USA	(David Thor 110.60 [24], Fred Roethlisberger 109.70 [34], Stephen Hug 109.60 [36], Stephen Cohen 108.75 [46], Sidney Freudenstein 108.00 [57], Kanati Allen 105.45 [80])	548.90
8. GER	(Heinz Häussler 108.80 [45], Helmut Tepasse 108.35 [50], Heiko Reinemer 108.20 [51], Hermann Hopfner 108.10 [55], Erich Hess 107.75 [60])	548.35

1972 Munich T: 16, N: 16, D: 8.29.

		TOTAL PTS.
1. JPN	(Sawao Kato 115.10 [1], Eizo Kenmotsu 114.75 [2], Shigeru Kasamatsu 114.40 [3], Akinori Nakayama 114.25 [4], Mitsuo Tsukahara 112.25 [11], Teruichi Okamura 111.20 [14])	571.25
2. SOV	(Nikolai Andrianov 113.80 [5], Mikhail Voronin 112.95 [7], Viktor Klimenko 112.65 [8], Eduard Mikhaelyan 112.50 [9], Aleksandr Maleyev 110.70 [18], Vladimir Shukin 110.20 [20])	564.05
3. GDR	(Klaus Köste 113.25 [6], Matthias Brehme 112.45 [10], Wolfgang Thüne 112.15 [12], Wolfgang Klotz 111.05 [16], Reinhard Rychly 109.95 [21], Jürgen Paeke 109.35 [28])	559.70
4. POL	(Mikolaj Kubica 111.25 [13], Andrzej Szajna 111.15 [15], Sylwester Kubica 110.75 [16], Wilhelm Kubica 109.90 [22], Mieczyslaw Strzalka 106.45 [47], Jerzy Kruza 106.35 [49])	551.70
5. GER	(Eberhard Gienger 109.75 [23], Walter Mössinger 109.70 [24], Günter Spies 108.70 [30], Bernd Effing 107.75 [37], Reinhard Ritter 106.80 [43], Heinz Häussler 106.25 [51])	546.40
6. PRK	(Li Song-sob 110.75 [16], Kim Song-yu 109.45 [25], Kim Song-il 108.25 [32], Shin Heung-do 107.75 [37], Ho Yun-hang 106.45 [47], Jo Jong-ryol 106.15 [53])	545.05
7. ROM	(Petre Mihăiuc 109.30 [29], Dănut Grecu	538.90

108.10 [33], Gheorghe Păunescu 107.25 [41], Mircea Gheorghiu 105.00 [62], Nicolae Oprescu 104.60 [66], Constantin Petrescu 103.70 [73])

8. HUN	(Imre Molnár 110.55 [19], Zoltán Magyar 108.70 [30], István Kiss 106.65 [45], Béla Herczeg 105.60 [56], Antal Kisteleki 105.30 [61], István Bérczi 104.95 [63])	538.60

1976 Montreal T: 12, N: 12, D: 7.20.

		TOTAL PTS.
1. JPN	(Sawao Kato 115.90 [2], Mitsuo Tsukahara 115.75 [3], Hiroshi Kajiyama 115.25 [5], Eizo Kenmotsu 115.15 [6], Hisato Igarashi 113.55 [15], Shun Fujimoto 84.55 [89])	576.85
2. SOV	(Nikolai Andrianov 116.50 [1], Aleksandr Dityatin 115.15 [6], Gennady Kryssin 114.25 [8], Vladimir Marchenko 113.85 [11], Vladimir Tikhonov 112.15 [23])	576.45
3. GDR	(Lutz Mack 113.00 [17], Bernd Jäger 112.95 [18], Michael Nikolay 112.90 [19], Roland Brückner 112.00 [24], Wolfgang Klotz 111.95 [25], Rainer Hanschke 111.50 [28])	564.65
4. HUN	(Zoltán Magyar 114.25 [8], Imre Molnár 113.65 [13], Ferenc Donáth 113.60 [14], Béla Laufer 111.60 [26], Árpád Farkas 109.65 [40], Imre Bánrévi 109.15 [48])	564.45
5. GER	(Eberhard Gienger 113.30 [16], Volker Rohrwick 112.20 [22], Edgar Jorek 111.25 [29], Werner Steinmetz 110.30 [34], Reinhard Dietze 108.80 [53], Reinhard Ritter 107.75 [61])	557.40
6. ROM	Dănut Grecu 114.10 [10], Nicolae Oprescu 110.30 [34], Sorin Cepoi 109.95 [36], Ionel Checicheş 109.85 [37], Mihai Borş 109.75 [38], Ştefan Gal 109.15 [48])	557.30
7. USA	(Wayne Young 111.55 [27], Kurt Thomas 111.05 [30], Peter Kormann 110.75 [31], Thomas Beach 110.55 [32], Marshall Avener 109.45 [43], Bart Conner 109.35 [46])	556.10
8. SWI	(Robert Bretscher 112.35 [21], Ueli Bachmann 109.60 [41], Philippe Gaille 109.40 [44], Bernhard Locher 108.30 [55], Peter Rohner 108.25 [56], Armin Vock 81.45 [90])	550.60

The entire team competition came down to the horizontal bar routine of the Japanese star Mitsuo Tsukahara. A score above 9.5 would give Japan first place, while a score below 9.5 would turn over the gold medal to the U.S.S.R. Tsukahara came through in superb fashion and earned a 9.9 to ensure the fifth straight Japanese team victory.

Another hero of the Japanese gymnastics team was Shun Fujimoto. Fujimoto broke his leg at the knee while finishing his floor exercises routine. Not wanting to cause concern among his coaches or fellow team members during the tense competition with the Soviets, Fujimoto kept his injury to himself and went ahead with his side horse performance, earning a 9.5. Next up were the rings. Fujimoto completed a successful routine (9.7) and then faced a difficult moment—the dismount. Landing on his feet, he compounded his injury by dislocating his knee. The pain was intense: "My whole blood was boiling at my stomach." Fujimoto finally submitted himself to medical inspection and was convinced to withdraw from the remainder of the competition. Asked years later if he would have gone ahead on the rings if he had known how much pain he would experience, Fujimoto replied without hesitation: "No."

1980 Moscow T: 9, N: 9, D: 7.22.

			TOTAL PTS.
1.	SOV	(Aleksandr Dityatin 118.40 [1], Nikolai Andrianov 118.15 [2], Eduard Azaryan 117.40 [4], Aleksandr Tkachyov 117.40 [4], Bohdan Makuts 116.95 [6], Vladimir Markelov 116.40 [9]	598.60
2.	GDR	(Roland Brückner 116.90 [7], Michael Nikolay 116.50 [8], Lutz Hoffmann 115.75 [13], Ralf-Peter Hemmann 115.70 [14], Andreas Bronst 114.85 [15], Lutz Mack 114.00 [20])	581.15
3.	HUN	(Ferenc Donáth 115.90 [11], Zoltán Magyar 115.85 [12], Péter Kovács 114.70 [18], György Guczoghy 113.85 [21], István Vamos 113.10 [27], Zoltán Kelemen 112.70 [33])	575.00
4.	ROM	(Dănut Grecu 114.85 [15], Kurt Szilier 114.80 [17], Aurelian Georgescu 113.75 [22], Sorin Cepoi 113.55 [25], Nicolae Oprescu 112.95 [28], Romulus Bucuroiu 112.75 [32])	572.30
5.	BUL	(Stoyan Delchev 117.50 [3], Dancho Yordanov 113.75 [22], Plamen Petkov 113.50 [26], Roumen Petkov 112.50 [34], Ognyan Bangiev 112.05 [39], Yanko Radanchev 111.60 [42])	571.55
6.	CZE	(Jiří Tabák 115.95 [10], Rudolf Babiak 114.10 [19], Dan Zoulík 113.70 [24], Miroslav Kučeřik 112.10 [38], Jan Migdau 111.95 [40], Jozef Konečný 111.35 [43])	569.80
7.	CUB	(Sergio Suarez Aime 112.50 [34], Roberto Leon Richards-Aguiar 112.45 [36], Miguel Arroyo 112.15 [37], Enrique Bravo 111.75 [41], Mario Castro 111.15 [46], Jorge Roche 83.40 [65])	563.20
8.	FRA	(Michel Boutard 112.95 [28], Willi Moy 112.85 [30], Henry Boerio 111.35 [43], Joel Suty 111.25 [45], Yves Boquel 108.65 [59], Marc Touchais 108.10 [62])	559.20

1984 Los Angeles T: 9, N: 9, D: 7.31.

			TOTAL PTS.
1.	USA	Peter Vidmar 118.55 [1], Bart Conner 118.30 [4], Mitchell Gaylord 118.15 [6], Timothy Daggett 117.85 [8], James Hartung 117.75 [9], Scott Johnson 116.60 [16]	591.40
2.	CHN	Li Ning 118.45 [2], Tong Fei 118.40 [3], Xu Zhiqiang 118.15 [6], Lou Yun 117.65 [10], Li Xiaoping 116.85 [12], Li Yuejiu 116.70 [15]	590.80
3.	JPN	Koji Gushiken 118.20 [5], Nobuyuki Kajitani 116.95 [11], Noritoshi Hirata 116.80 [13], Shinji Morisue 116.60 [16], Koji Sotomura 116.05 [25], Kyoji Yamawaki 115.65 [29]	586.70
4.	GER	Jürgen Geiger 116.75 [14], Daniel Winkler 116.40 [18], Andreas Japtok 116.20 [21], Benno Gross 116.05 [25], Volker Rohrwick 115.45 [32], Bernhard Simmelbauer 115.25 [36]	582.10
5.	SWI	Josef Zellweger 116.40 [18], Markus Lehmann 116.30 [20], Daniel Wunderlin 116.10 [22], Marco Piatti 115.95 [27], Bruno Cavelti 114.60 [43], Urs Meister 113.25 [59]	579.95
6.	FRA	Jean-Luc Cairon 116.10 [22], Joël Suty 115.50 [31], Philippe Vatuone 115.45 [32], Laurent Barbieri 115.30 [34], Jacques Def 114.85 [41], Michel Boutard 113.25 [59]	578.25
7.	CAN	Philippe Chartrand 115.75 [28], Brad Peters 115.15 [37], Warren Long 115.05 [38], Daniel Gaudet 114.60 [43], Frank Nutzenberger 114.30 [49], Allan Reddon 114.05 [51]	577.15
8.	KOR	Chang Tae-eun 115.30 [34], Han Chung-sik 115.05 [38], Lee Jeoung-sik 114.70 [42], Ju Young-sam 113.95 [52], Nam Seoung-gu 113.75 [56], Chae Kwang-suk 113.50 [57]	574.95

Competing at Pauley Pavilion on the campus of UCLA, the home arena for three of the six Americans (Vidmar, Gaylord and Daggett), the U.S. team scored an emotional upset victory over the world champion Chinese.

1988 Seoul T: 12, N: 12, D: 9.20.

			TOTAL PTS.
1.	SOV	(Vladimir Artemov 118.95 [1], Valery Lyukin 118.85 [2], Dmitri Bilozerchev 118.45 [3], Sergei Kharkov 118.40 [4], Vladimir Gogoladze 117.70 [6], Vladimir Novikov 117.50 [11])	593.35
2.	GDR	(Sylvio Kroll 117.85 [5], Sven Tippelt 117.60 [9], Ralf Büchner 117.20 [15], Holger Behrendt 116.95 [19], Ulf Hoffman 116.40 [29], Andreas Wecker 116.30 [30])	588.45
3.	JPN	(Yukio Iketani 117.65 [8], Koichi Mizushima 117.45 [12], Daisuke Nishikawa 117.25 [13], Toshiharu Sato 116.65 [26], Hiroyuki Konishi 115.80 [37], Takahiro Yamada 115.40 [43])	585.60
4.	CHN	(Wang Chongsheng 117.20 [15], Lou Yun 117.10 [17], Xu Zhiqiang 117.00 [18], Li Chunyang 116.15 [32], Guo Linxian 115.35 [45], Li Ning 114.95 [50])	585.25
5.	BUL	(Kalofer Hristozov 117.70 [6], Lubomir Geraskov 116.75 [21], Dimitar Taskov 116.75 [21], Dian Kolev 116.30 [30], Stoycho	585.10

		TOTAL PTS.
	Gochev 115.95 [36], Petar Georgiev 115.60 [39])	
6. HUN	(György Guczoghy 117.25 [13], Csaba Fajkusz 116.75 [21], Zsolt Horváth 115.50 [41], Zsolt Borkai 115.40 [43], Jenö Paprika 114.70 [55], Balázs Tóth 77.05 [89])	582.30
7. ROM	(Marius Gherman 117.55 [10], Marius Eugen Toba 116.75 [21], Nicolae Bejenaru 115.30 [46], Adrian Sandu 115.15 [48], Marian Rizan 114.85 [51], Valerian Pintea 105.55 [87])	581.70
8. ITA	(Boris Preti 116.90 [20], Juri Chechi 116.55 [27], Paolo Bucci 115.70 [38], Riccardo Trapella 114.75 [53], Gabriele Sala 114.25 [61], Vittorio Allievi 112.65 [78])	579.00

1992 Barcelona T: 12, N: 12, D: 7.29.

		TOTAL PTS.
1. SOV	(Vitaly Scherbo 117.875 [1], Valery Belenky 117.500 [2], Grigory Misyutin 116.975 [3], Igor Korobchinsky 116.500 [5], Aleksei Voropayev 115.125 [16], Rustam Charipov 114.950 [22])	585.450
2. CHN	(Li Xiaoshuang 116.450 [6], Li Chunyang 115.925 [7], Guo Linyao 115.900 [8], Li Jing 114.950 [22], Li Dashuang 114.875 [24], Li Ge 114.875 [24])	580.375
3. JPN	(Yukio Iketani 115.450 [9], Yoshiaki Hatakeda 115.300 [10], Takashi Chinen 115.275 [13], Daisuke Nishikawa 115.100 [17], Yutaka Aihara 114.975 [21], Masayuki Matsunaga 114.325 [35])	578.250
4. GER	(Andreas Wecker 116.875 [4], Sylvio Kroll 114.850 [26], Oliver Walther 114.425 [31], Ralf Büchner 114.400 [33], Sven Tippelt 113.775 [41], Mario Franke 113.175 [50])	575.575
5. ITA	(Boris Preti 115.275 [13], Paolo Bucci 115.100 [17], Ruggero Rossato 114.175 [37], Gabriele Sala 113.075 [53], Gianmatteo Centazzo 112.125 [66], Alexandro Viligiardi 111.850 [71])	571.750
6. USA	(M. Chris Waller 114.800 [27], John Roethlisberger 114.200 [36], Scott Keswick 113.725 [43], Trent Dimas 113.675 [44], Dominick Minicucci 112.950 [56], Jair Lynch 112.775 [60])	571.725
7. ROM	(Marius Gherman 115.300 [10], Marian Rizan 114.725 [28], Adrian-Francisc Gal 113.325 [47], Nicolae Bejenaru 113.150 [51], Nicu Stroia 112.925 [57], Adrian Sandu 113.850 [59])	571.150
8. KOR	(Yoo Ok-ryul 115.025 [19], Lee Joo-hyung 114.375 [34], Han Yoon-soo 113.825 [40], Jung Jin-soo 113.625 [45], Han Kwang-ho 112.350 [64], Yeo Hong-chul 110.525 [81])	570.850

Discontinued Events

COMBINED COMPETITION (3 EVENTS)

1904 St. Louis C: 119, N: 3, D: 7.2.

Events: PB, HB, CLSV

			PTS.
1.	Adolf Spinnler	SWI	43.49
2.	Julius Lenhart	AUT	43.00
3.	Wilhelm Weber	GER	41.60
4.	Hugo Peitsch	GER	41.56
5.	Otto Wiegand	GER	40.82
6.	Otto Steffen	USA	39.53

COMBINED COMPETITION (4 EVENTS)

1904 St. Louis C: 10, N: 1, D: 10.28.

Events: PB, HB, SH, LHV

			PTS.
1.	Anton Heida	USA	161
2.	George Eyser	USA	152
3.	William Merz	USA	135
4.	John Duha	USA	—
5.	Edward Hennig	USA	—

ROPE CLIMBING

1896 Athens C: 5, N: 4, D: 4.10.

1.	Nikolaos Andriakopoulos	GRE	23.4
2.	Thomas Xenakis	GRE	—
3.	Fritz Hofmann	GER	DNF
4.	Viggo Jensen	DEN	DNF
5.	Launceston Elliot	GBR	DNF

1904 St. Louis C: ?, N: 1, D: 10.28.

1.	George Eyser	USA	7.0
2.	Charles Krause	USA	7.8
3.	Emil Voigt	USA	9.8

1906 Athens C: 17, N: 4, D: 4.25.

1.	Georgios Aliprantis	GRE	11.4
2.	Béla Erody	HUN	13.8
3.	Konstantinos Kozanitas	GRE	13.8
4.	G. Georgantopoulos	ITA	14.0
5.	Nicolaos Aliprantis	GRE	14.2
6.	K. Pantzopoulos	GRE	14.8
7.	G. Koemzopoulos	GRE	15.2
8.	P. Pavlides	GRE	15.6

1908–1920 not held

1924 Paris C: 70, N: 9, D: 7.20.
1. Bedřich Supčik   CZE   7.2
2. Albert Séguin   FRA   7.4
3. August Güttinger   SWI   7.8
3. Ladislav Vácha   CZE   7.8
5. Stane Žilič   YUG   8.0
6. Jean Gounot   FRA   8.4
6. Arthur Hermann   FRA   8.4
6. Frank Kriz   USA   8.4
6. Ivan Porenta   YUG   8.4

Supčik was Czechoslovakia's first Olympic champion.

1928 not held

1932 Los Angeles C: 5, N: 2, D: 8.10.
1. Raymond Bass   USA   6.7
2. William Galbraith   USA   6.8
3. Thomas Connelly   USA   7.0
4. Miklós Péter   HUN   11.5
5. Péter Boros   HUN   11.6

CLUB SWINGING

1904 St. Louis C: 9, N: 1, D: 10.28.
                    PTS.
1. Edward Hennig   USA   13.0
2. Emil Voigt   USA   9.0
3. Ralph Wilson   USA   5.0

Hennig remained active in club swinging and won the American championship as late as 1951, when he was 71 years old.

1906–1928 not held

1932 Los Angeles C: 4, N: 2, D: 8.9.
                    PTS.
1. George Roth   USA   8.97
2. Philip Erenberg   USA   8.90
3. William Kuhlmeier   USA   8.63
4. Francisco Alvarez   MEX   8.47

Unemployed and nearly starving in the midst of the Great Depression, Roth, who once went 15 days without eating, would go to the Olympic Village each day, collect some food, and sneak it home to his wife and baby girl in East Hollywood. He competed with one of his daughter's booties stuffed inside his own shoe for good luck. After receiving his gold medal before 60,000 cheering spectators, Roth walked out of the stadium and hitchhiked home.

SIDEHORSE VAULT

1924 Paris C: 70, N: 9, D: 7.20.
                    PTS.
1. Albert Séguin   FRA   10.00
2. François Gangloff   FRA   9.93

2. Jean Gounot   FRA   9.93
4. Slavko Hlastan   YUG   9.86
5. Stane Derganc   YUG   9.85
6. Bedřich Supčik   CZE   9.83
6. Ladislav Vácha   CZE   9.83
8. Eugene Cordonnier (FRA), Mathias Erang (LUX), Frank Kriz (USA), Robert Pražak (CZE)   9.80

TUMBLING

1932 Los Angeles C: 4, N: 2, D: 8.10.
                    PTS.
1. Rowland Wolfe   USA   18.90
2. Edward Gross   USA   18.67
3. William Hermann   USA   18.37
4. István Pelle   HUN   15.43

PARALLEL BARS—TEAM

1896 Athens T: 3, N: 2, D: 4.9.
1. GER   (Conrad Böcker, Alfred Flatow, Gustav Felix Flatow, Georg Hilmar, Fritz Manteuffel, Karl Neukirch, Richard Röstel, Gustav Schuft, Carl Schuhmann, Hermann Weingärtner)
2. GRE   (Panhellenic Club of Athens—Sotirios Athanasopoulos, Nicolaos Andriakopoulos, Petros Persakis, Thomas Yenakis)
3. GRE   (National Gymnastic Club of Athens—Ioannis Chrysaphis, Ioannis Mitropoulos, Dimitrios Loundras, Philippos Karvelas)

Loundras of the National Gymnastic Club was 10 years old.

HORIZONTAL BAR—TEAM

1896 Athens T: 1, N: 1, D: 4.9.
1. GER   (Conrad Böcker, Alfred Flatow, Gustav Felix Flatow, Georg Hilmar, Fritz Manteuffel, Karl Neukirch, Richard Röstel, Gustav Schuft, Carl Schuhmann, Hermann Weingärtner)

FREE EXERCISES AND APPARATUS—TEAM

1912 Stockholm T: 5, N: 5, D: 7.10.

                    TOTAL PTS.
1. NOR   (Isak Abrahamsen, Hans Beyer, Hartmann Björnson, Alfred Engelsen, Bjarne Johnsen, Sigurd Jörgensen, Knud Knudsen, Alf Lie, Rolf Lie, Tor Lund, Petter Martinsen, Per Mathiesen, Jacob Opdahl, Nils Opdahl, Bjarne Pettersen, Frithjof Saelen, Öistein Schirmer, Georg Selenius, Sigvard Sivertsen, Robert   114.25

		TOTAL PTS.
	Sjursen, Einar Ström, Gabriel Thorstensen, Thomas Torstensen, Nils Voss)	
2. FIN	(Kaarlo Ekholm, Eino Forsström, Ero Hyvarinen, Mikko Hyvärinen, Ilmari Keinänen, Hjalmari Kivenheimo, Karl Fredrick Lund, Arvid Rydman, Eino Saastamoinen, Aarne Salovaara, Heikki Sammallahti, Hannes Sirola, Klaus Uno Suomela, Lauri Tanner, Väino Tiiri, Kaarlo Vähämäki, Kaarlo Vasama, Tauno Ilmoniemi, Aarne Pelkonen, Ilmari Pernaja)	109.25
3. DEN	(Aksel Andersen, Hjalmar Andersen, Halvor Birch, Herman Grimmelmann, Aage Hansen, Arvor Hansen, Christian Hansen, Charles Jensen, Poul Jörgensen, Hjalmar Johansen, Poul Krebs, Viggo Madsen, Lucas Nielsen, Richard Nordström, Oluf Olsen, Steen Olsen, Carl Pedersen, Christian Petersen, Niels Petersen, Christian Svendsen)	106.25
4. GER	(Walter Engelmann, Adolf Seebass, Alfred Staats, Hans Roth, Arno Glockauer, Alexander Sperling, Kurt Reichenbach, Rudolf Körner, Erwin Buder, Wilhelm Brülle, Heinrich Pahner, Johannes Reuschle, Walter Jesinghaus, Eberhard Sorge, Karl Richter, Erich Worm, Karl Jordan, Hans Werner)	84.25
5. LUX	(Nicolas Adam, Charles Behm, André Bordang, Jean-Pierre Frantzen, François Hentges, Pierre Hentges, Michel Hemmerling, Jean-Baptiste Horn, Nicolas Kanivé, Emile Knepper, Nicolas Kummer, Marcel Langsam, Emile Lanners, Jean-Pierre Thommes, François Wagner, Antoine Wehrer, Ferdinand Wirtz, Joseph Zuang, Maurice Palgen)	81.50

1920 Antwerp T: 2, N: 2, D: 8.27.

		TOTAL PTS.
1. DEN	(Georg Albertsen, Carl Andersen, Viggo Dibbern, Aage Frandsen, Hugo Helsten, Harry Holm, Herold Jansson, Robert Johnsen, Christian Juhl, Vilhelm Lange, Svend Meulengracht Madsen, Peder Marcussen, Peder Moller, Niels Turin Nielsen, Steen Olsen, Christian Pedersen, Stig Ronne, Harry Sorensen, Christian Thomas, Knud Vermehren)	51.35
2. NOR	(Alf Aaning, Karl Aas, Jorgen Andersen, Gustav Bayer, Jorgen Bjornstad, Asbjorn Bodahl, Eilert Bohm, Trygue Boyesen, Ingolf Davidsen, Haakon Endreson, Jacob Erstad, Harald Faerstad, Hermann Helgesen, Petter Hol, Otto Johannessen, Anker Johansen, Steen Kristoffersen, Henrik Nielsen, Jacob Opdahl, Arthur Rydstrom, Frithjof Saelen, Bjorn Skjaerpe, Wilhelm Steffensen, Olav Sundal, Reidar Tonsberg, Lauritz Wigand-Larsen)	48.55

SWEDISH SYSTEM—TEAM

1912 Stockholm T: 3, N: 3, D: 7.8.

		TOTAL PTS.
1. SWE	(Per Daniel Bertilsson, Carl-Ehrenfried Carlberg, Nils Daniel Granfelt, Curt Hartzell, Osward Holmberg, Anders Hylander, Axel Janse, Anders Boo Kullberg, Sven Landberg, Per Nilsson, Benkt Rudolf Norelius, Axel Norling, Sven Rosén, Nils Silfverskiöld, Carl Silfverstrand, John Sörensson, Yngve Stiernspetz, Carl Erik Svensson, Karl Johan Svensson [Sarland], Knut Torell, Edvard Wennerholm, Claës Wersäll, David Wiman, Daniel Norling)	937.46
2. DEN	(Sören Christensen, Ingvald Eriksen, Georg Falche, Thorkild Garp, Hans Trier Hansen, Johannes Hansen, Rasmus Hansen, Jens Kristian Jensen, Sören Alfred Jensen, Valdemar Jensen, Karl Kirk, Jens Kirkegaard, Olav Kjems, Carl Otto Larsen, Jens Peter Laursen, Marius Lefevre, Poul Sörensen Mark, Ejnar Olsen, Hans Pedersen, Hans Ejlert Pedersen, Aksel Sörensen, Martin Hansen Thau, Sören Thorborg, Kristen Möller Vadgaard, Peder Villemoes, Johannes Larsen Vinther, Olaf Pedersen, Peder Larsen Pedersen)	898.84
3. NOR	(Arthur Amundsen, Jorgen Andersen, Trygve Boyesen, Georg Brustad, Conrad Christensen, Oscar Engelstad, Marius Eriksen, Axel Henry Hansen, Peter Hol, Eugene Ingebretsen, Olof Ingebretsen, Olof Jacobsen, Thor Jensen, Erling Jenssen, Frithjof Olsen, Oscar Olstad, Edvin Paulsen, Carl Alfred Pedersen, Paul Pedersen, Realf Robach, Sigurd Smeby, Torleif Torkildsen)	857.21

1920 Antwerp T: 3, N: 3, D: 8.26.

		TOTAL PTS.
1. SWE	(Fausto Acke, Albert Andersson, Arvid Andersson, Helge Bäckander, Bengt Bengtsson, Fabion Biörck, Carl-Erik Charpentier, Sture Ericsson, Konrad Granström, Helge Gustafson, Åke Häger, Ture Hedman, Sven Johnson, Sven-Olof Jonsson, Karl Lindahl, Edmund Lindmark, Bengt Mohrberg, Frans Persson, Klas Särner, Curt Sjöberg, Gunnar Söderlindh, John Sörenson, Erik Svensen, Gösta Törner)	1363.833
2. DEN	(Johannes Birk, Frede Hansen, Frederik Hansen, Kristian Hansen, Hans Hovgaard Jakobsen, Aage Jorgensen, Alfred Jorgensen [Frökjaer], Alfred Jorgensen [Ollerup], Arne Jorgensen, Knud Kirkelokke, Jens Lambaek, Kristian Larsen, Kristian Madsen, Niels Erik Nielsen, Niels Kristian Nielsen, Dynes Pedersen, Hans Pedersen, Johannes Pedersen, P. Dorf Pedersen, Rasmus Rasmus-	1324.833

sen, Hans Christian Sorensen, Hans Laurids Sorensen, Soren Sorensen, Georg Vest, Aage Walther)

3. BEL (Paul Arets, Léon Bronckart, Léopold Clabots, Jean-Baptist Claessens, Léon Darrien, Lucien Dehoux, Ernest Deleu, Emile Duboisson, Er-nest Dureuil, Joseph Fiems, Marcel Hansen, Louis Henin, Omer Hoffman, Félix Logiest, Charles Marschaelcke, René Paenhuysen, Arnold Pierret, René Pinchart, Gaspard Pirotte, Augustien Pluys, Léopold Son, Edouard Taeymans, Pierre Thiriar, Henri Verhavert) 1094.000

GYMNASTICS

WOMEN

ALL-AROUND

HV = Horse vault
AB = Asymmetrical (uneven) bars
BB = Balance beam
FE = Floor exercises

1896–1948 not held

1952 Helsinki C: 134, N: 18, D: 7.23.

		HV		AB		BB		FE		TOTAL PTS.
1. Maria Horokhovska	SOV/UKR	19.19	(2)	19.26	(2)	19.13	(2)	19.2	(2)	76.78
2. Nina Bocharova	SOV/UKR	19.03	(6)	18.99	(4)	19.22	(1)	18.7	(10)	75.94
3. Margit Korondi	HUN	18.4	(22)	19.4	(1)	19.02	(3)	19.0	(3)	75.82
4. Galina Minaicheva	SOV/RUS	19.16	(3)	18.89	(8)	18.66	(10)	18.96	(6)	75.67
5. Galina Urbanovich	SOV/RUS	19.1	(5)	18.62	(12)	18.93	(5)	18.99	(4)	75.64
6. Ágnes Keleti	HUN	18.1	(41)	19.16	(3)	18.96	(4)	19.36	(1)	75.58
7. Pelageya Danilova	SOV/RUS	18.62	(12)	18.99	(7)	18.76	(9)	18.6	(11)	75.03
8. Galina Shamrai	SOV/UZB	18.93	(7)	18.39	(23)	18.79	(8)	18.86	(8)	74.97

1956 Melbourne C: 65, N: 15, D: 12.5.

		HV		AB		BB		FE		TOTAL PTS.
1. Larysa Latynina	SOV/UKR	18.833	(1)	18.833	(2)	18.533	(4)	18.733	(1)	74.933
2. Ágnes Keleti	HUN	18.133	(23)	18.966	(1)	18.8	(1)	18.733	(1)	74.633
3. Sofia Muratova	SOV/RUS	18.666	(5)	18.8	(3)	18.433	(10)	18.566	(4)	74.466
4. Elena Leuştean	ROM	18.633	(6)	18.533	(10)	18.5	(6)	18.7	(3)	74.366
4. Olga Tass	HUN	18.733	(3)	18.633	(6)	18.466	(7)	18.533	(7)	74.366
6. Tamara Manina	SOV/RUS	18.8	(2)	18.333	(16)	18.633	(2)	18.466	(9)	74.233
7. Eva Bosáková (Věchtová)	CZE	18.166	(22)	18.733	(4)	18.633	(2)	18.566	(4)	74.1
8. Helena Rakoczy	POL	18.5	(7)	18.7	(5)	18.133	(16)	18.366	(14)	73.7

The 1956 competition was dominated by 35-year-old Ágnes Keleti and 21-year-old Larysa Latynina. Keleti captured gold medals on three of the four apparatuses, but a lapse on the vault lost her the All-Around title to Latynina, a Ukrainian from Kherson. In 1952 and 1956 Keleti won a total of ten Olympic medals: five gold, three silver, and two bronze. After the games she decided not to return to Hungary. Instead she stayed in Australia and eventually settled in Israel.

1960 Rome C: 124, N: 27, D: 9.8.

		HV		AB		BB		FE		TOTAL PTS.
1. Larysa Latynina	SOV/UKR	18.966	(3)	19.433	(2)	19.066	(3)	19.566	(1)	77.031
2. Sofia Muratova	SOV/RUS	19.032	(2)	19.299	(3)	19.132	(2)	19.233	(4)	76.696
3. Polina Astakhova	SOV/UKR	18.766	(4)	19.633	(1)	18.233	(28)	19.532	(2)	76.164
4. Marharyta Nikolayeva	SOV/UKR	19.1	(1)	18.799	(20)	18.966	(4)	18.966	(15)	75.831
5. Sonia Iovan	ROM	18.732	(6)	19.266	(4)	18.6	(11)	19.199	(5)	75.797
6. Keiko Ikeda (Tanaka)	JPN	18.432	(18)	19.266	(4)	18.932	(5)	19.066	(12)	75.696
7. Lidiya Ivanova (Kalinina)	SOV/RUS	18.566	(8)	19.053	(7)	18.699	(8)	19.133	(7)	75.431
8. Vera Čáslavská	CZE	18.699	(7)	18.733	(21)	18.766	(6)	19.1	(9)	75.298

1964 Tokyo C: 86, N: 24, D: 10.21.

		HV		AB		BB		FE		TOTAL PTS.
1. Vera Čáslavská	CZE	19.5	(1)	19.432	(1)	19.366	(1)	19.266	(3)	77.564
2. Larysa Latynina	SOV/UKR	19.166	(5)	19.133	(4)	19.233	(3)	19.466	(1)	76.998
3. Polina Astakhova	SOV/UKR	19.032	(7)	19.333	(2)	19.2	(5)	19.4	(2)	76.965
4. Birgit Radochla	GDR	19.366	(2)	18.933	(13)	18.933	(9)	19.199	(5)	76.431
5. Hana Ružičková	CZE	18.866	(18)	19.033	(7)	19.232	(4)	18.966	(10)	76.097
6. Keiko Ikeda (Tanaka)	JPN	18.999	(9)	18.766	(16)	19.166	(6)	19.1	(7)	76.031
7. Toshiko Aihara (Shirasu)	JPN	19.233	(3)	19.099	(5)	18.599	(29)	19.066	(8)	75.997
8. Yelena Volchetskaya	SOV/BLR	19.233	(3)	18.633	(24)	18.966	(7)	18.933	(13)	75.765

Latynina collected six more Olympic medals to bring her career total to an unprecedented 18: nine gold, five sil-

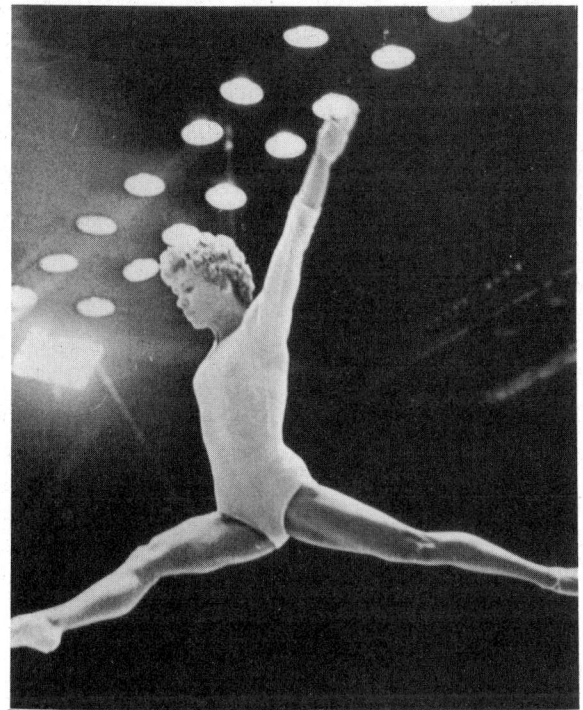

Between 1956 and 1964, gymnast Larysa Latynina won 18 medals (nine gold, five silver, and four bronze), more than any athlete in Olympic history.

ver, and four bronze. But in Tokyo she lost the All-Around title to a new star, Vera Čáslavská, a 22-year-old secretary from Prague.

1968 Mexico City C: 101, N: 24, D: 10.23.

		HV		AB		BB		FE		TOTAL PTS.
1. Vera Čáslavská	CZE	19.75	(1)	19.5	(1)	19.45	(2)	19.55	(2)	78.25
2. Zinaida Voronina	SOV/RUS	19.4	(5)	19.25	(4)	18.8	(15)	19.4	(4)	76.85
3. Natalya Kuchinskaya	SOV/RUS	19.45	(3)	18.1	(37)	19.6	(15)	19.6	(1)	76.75
4. Larissa Petrik	SOV/BLR	19.2	(8)	18.95	(11)	19.0	(5)	19.55	(2)	76.7
4. Erika Zuchold	GDR	19.65	(2)	19.05	(6)	19.0	(5)	19.0	(8)	76.7
6. Karin Janz	GDR	19.2	(8)	19.3	(2)	19.05	(4)	19.0	(8)	76.55
7. Olga Karasyova	SOV/RUS	19.15	(10)	19.0	(7)	18.7	(18)	19.15	(5)	76.0
7. Bohumila Řimnácová	CZE	18.7	(24)	19.3	(2)	18.85	(10)	19.15	(5)	76.0

The undisputed heroine of the Mexico City Olympics was defending All-Around champion Vera Čáslavská. In April 1968, Čáslavská had signed the "Manifesto of 2000 Words," which rejected Soviet involvement in Czechoslovakia. On August 21, she was at a training camp in Moravia when Soviet tanks rolled into Prague. Warned by friends that she was in danger of arrest, Čáslavská fled to the small town of Šumperk in the Jeseníky Mountains. With the Olympics only two months away, Čáslavská was in hiding, keeping in shape by swinging from tree limbs and practicing her floor exercise in a meadow. After three weeks, the government consented to let her join the rest of the Czechoslovak team in Mexico.

After one of Čáslavská's performances on the balance beam received a 9.6, the audience spent ten minutes booing, howling, and chanting "Ver-a, Ver-a," until finally her mark was upped to 9.8. The last performer in the final event, Čáslavská thrilled her admirers by performing her floor exercise to the tune of "The Mexican Hat Dance." She eventually earned four gold medals and two silver to add to the three gold and two silver she had won four years earlier in Tokyo. In the floor exercises she shared first place with Larissa Petrik of the Soviet Union, which meant that the two women stood together on the top platform at the medal ceremony and listened first to Czechoslovakia's national anthem and then to the U.S.S.R.'s. Political observers noted that Čáslavská bowed her head and turned away during the playing of the Soviet anthem. Twenty-four hours later Čáslavská topped off her week by marrying Czechoslovak 1500-meter champion Josef Odlozil. After a civil ceremony at the Czechoslovakian ambassador's house, the happy couple pushed their way through a mob of 10,000 people to get to the altar of the Roman Catholic church in Xocalo Square. The couple divorced in 1992. After the fall of the Communist government in 1989, Čáslavská was appointed president of Czechoslovakia's national Olympic committee.

1972 Munich C: 118, N: 23, D: 8.30.

		HV		AB		BB		FE		TOTAL PTS.
1. Lyudmila Turischeva	SOV/RUS	19.3	(1)	19.275	(3)	18.8	(5)	19.65	(1)	77.025
2. Karin Janz	GDR	19.275	(2)	19.475	(1)	18.825	(4)	19.3	(3)	76.875
3. Tamara Lazakovich	SOV/BLR	19.0	(6)	19.225	(4)	19.325	(1)	19.3	(3)	76.85
4. Erika Zuchold	GDR	19.275	(2)	19.30	(2)	18.8	(5)	19.075	(6)	76.45
5. Lyubov Burda	SOV/RUS	19.075	(5)	18.875	(8)	18.675	(8)	19.15	(5)	75.775
6. Angelika Hellmann	GDR	18.925	(7)	19.15	(5)	18.425	(14)	19.05	(7)	75.55
7. Olga Korbut	SOV/BLR	19.175	(4)	17.15	(35)	19.3	(2)	19.475	(2)	75.1
8. Elvira Saadi	SOV/UZB	18.8	(9)	18.7	(15)	18.625	(10)	18.95	(9)	75.075

Vera Čáslavská had played a major role in popularizing women's gymnastics, but the real turning point came at the 1972 Munich Olympics. The All-Around championship was won by 19-year-old world champion Lyudmila Turischeva, and the silver medal went to Karin Janz of Berlin, who also took first place on the horse vault and the uneven parallel bars. But it was neither of these capable young women who focused the attention of the world on gymnastics. Instead it was the seventh-place finisher,

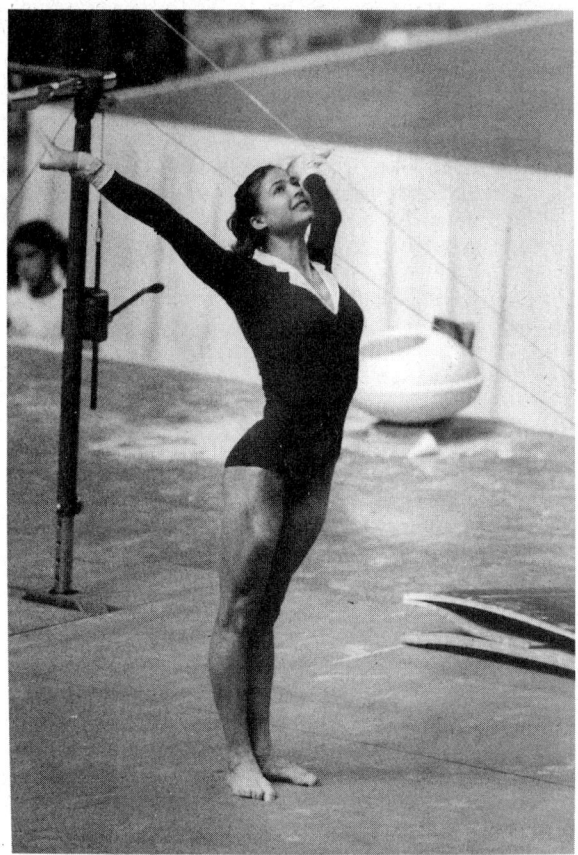

Lyudmila Turischeva won the 1972 All-Around championship, but received little attention from the Western press, which was more interested in her less accomplished but more charismatic teammate . . .

. . . Olga Korbut, the Munchkin of Munich.

a 4-foot 11-inch, 85-pound 17-year-old from Grodno in Belarus—Olga Korbut.

Korbut was trained by the eccentric and sometimes physically abusive Renald Knysh, who kept a card file on all the young married couples in Grodno, particularly those whom he thought might produce future gymnasts. During the team competition Korbut caught the public's eye with a spectacular routine on the uneven parallel bars. By the end of the day it looked as if she had a good chance of pulling an upset and depriving Turischeva of the All-Around championship. This was the first time Korbut had competed in a major international event and she was unprepared for her sudden popularity. The crowd chanted "Olga" and people asked for her autograph. "It was amazing," she later recalled in her 1992 autobiography, *My Story*. "One day, I was nobody, and the next day, I was a *star*. It was almost more than I could take in." Two days later the individual final began and halfway through, Korbut moved into first place. But then disaster struck.

The crowd watched in silence as she started her performance on the uneven bars. She scuffed her feet on the mat as she mounted, then slipped off the bars during a later move; finally, she missed a simple kip to remount. The judges gave her a 7.5, and she was effectively eliminated from the race for All-Around champion. She returned to her seat to weep with disappointment.

Twenty hours later Olga Korbut was back in the arena to compete for the championships on the four individual apparatuses. With hundreds of millions of people all over the world watching, Olga regained her form, finished second to Karin Janz on the uneven parallel bars, and won the gold medal for both the balance beam and the floor exercises. Even in the United States, with its widespread antipathy to the U.S.S.R, little Olga Korbut's dramatic cycle of success, failure, and success captured the national imagination. However, because the Soviet team was kept completely isolated, Olga herself was unaware of how popular she had become outside the arena itself. She would find out soon enough. When she returned to the Olympic Village she discovered that her room was filled with flowers, letters, and telegrams. The messages were in Russian, English, German, French, and Japanese. When she went for a walk in Munich, public buses stopped so that the riders could get out and ask for her autograph. When she went shopping for gifts to bring back to her family, she found it impossible to spend any money because all the shopkeepers insisted that she take whatever she wanted free of charge. Finally she had to buy a wig and a wide-brimmed hat to wear as a disguise in order to gain a bit of peace. When she returned home to Grodno she received so much fan mail—20,000 letters in one year—that the post office had to assign a special clerk to sort out her mail.

1976 Montreal C: 86, N: 18, D: 7.21.

		HV		AB		BB		FE		TOTAL PTS.
1. Nadia Comăneci	ROM	19.625	(4)	20.0	(1)	19.95	(1)	19.7	(3)	79.275
2. Nelli Kim	SOV/KAZ	19.85	(1)	19.725	(2)	19.3	(5)	19.8	(2)	78.675
3. Lyudmila Turischeva	SOV/RUS	19.75	(2)	19.575	(9)	19.475	(3)	19.825	(1)	78.625
4. Teodora Ungureanu	ROM	19.425	(7)	19.8	(2)	19.7	(2)	19.45	(5)	78.375
5. Olga Korbut	SOV/BLR	19.525	(6)	19.8	(2)	19.325	(4)	19.375	(6)	78.025
6. Gitta Escher	GDR	19.65	(3)	19.625	(8)	19.125	(7)	19.35	(8)	77.75
7. Márta Egervári	HUN	19.6	(5)	19.775	(4)	18.725	(10)	19.225	(9)	77.325
8. Marion Kische	GDR	19.325	(10)	19.7	(6)	18.55	(14)	19.375	(6)	76.95

Soviet women's gymnastics went through a period of turmoil and crisis between 1972 and 1976. Olga Korbut never did defeat Lyudmila Turischeva, and it must have been confusing, at the very least, to the Soviet champion to realize that no matter how successful she was, she could never achieve Olga's popularity. When the Soviet team made an exhibition tour of the United States, the leader of the group was Lyudmila Turischeva and the highlighted performer was their up-and-coming star Nelli Kim. But Americans showed little interest in Turischeva and Kim; instead they turned out by the thousands to see Olga Korbut, the Munchkin of Munich. It didn't take long for Olga to realize that huge profits were being made on her popularity, and she became more demanding of rewards for herself.

Back home, however, where heroes were measured by the number of medals they won and by their willingness to follow orders and be team players, Olga Korbut had become a thorn in the side of the Soviet bureaucracy. The situation was also hard on Turischeva, who had always toed the party line and yet was forced to play second fiddle to an inferior gymnast. In his book *The Big Red Machine*, Yuri Brodkin tells of the shock and betrayal experienced by Turischeva when, two days before the opening of the Montreal Olympics, the Soviet Training Council decided to remove her from her role of team captain and give the designation to Olga Korbut instead.

However, the real threat to the competitive success of the Soviet team came not from internal dissension, but from a 4-foot 11-inch Romanian named Nadia Comăneci. Born in Onesti, Moldova, Nadia had been trained as a gymnast since the age of 6. In 1975 she dethroned her idol, five-time European champion Turischeva. At Montreal she was considered a slight favorite to take the All-Around championship even though she was only 14 years old. During the team competition she made Olympic history by receiving the first perfect scores of ten for her performances on the uneven bars and the balance beam. Before the Olympics were over, Nadia had been awarded seven 10s, while Nelli Kim had earned two perfect scores for her vault and floor exercise. Despite their superb performances, Korbut and Turischeva were left with tears of disappointment. Turischeva, in fact, won four medals, to bring her Olympic totals to four gold, two silver, and three bronze.

Nadia Comăneci didn't have the charisma of Olga Korbut, but she was an incredible athlete who was absolutely unafraid of dangerous moves and seemingly oblivious to the millions of people watching her. The most difficult part of the Olympics for Nadia were the obligatory press conferences. Many journalists seemed to forget her age. When one asked what her greatest wish was, she replied, "I want to go home." When another asked if she had plans for retirement, Nadia reminded him, "I'm only 14."

In an attempt to lessen the dominance of the nations strongest in gymnastics, a ruling had been passed prior to the Olympics that only three gymnasts from each country could compete in the final round of 36. The absurdity of this decision was shown when Elvira Saadi, who had achieved the seventh highest score during the individual competitions, was eliminated because she was the fourth-best Soviet performer, while Monique Bolleboom of Holland was allowed to continue even though she ranked 62nd out of 86. Not surprisingly, Bolleboom finished last in the final round.

As for Olga Korbut, she married a famous Byelorussian singer and settled down as a housewife. Soviet sports officials punished her for her independent ways by not informing her of the frequent invitations she received to visit the United States and other Western nations. In 1986 she was still in Grodno when the meltdown at the Chernobyl nuclear power plant sent radioactive clouds over her hometown. When she finally did get permission to go to the United States, she brought with her several hundred blood samples of victims of the Chernobyl disaster. She eventually moved to Atlanta and set up a foundation to help the Chernobyl victims.

1980 Moscow C: 62, N: 16, D: 7.24.

		HV		AB		BB		FE		TOTAL PTS.
1. Yelena Davydova	SOV/RUS	19.8	(1)	19.80	(3)	19.7	(5)	19.85	(3)	79.15
2. Nadia Comăneci	ROM	19.675	(4)	19.725	(6)	19.8	(1)	19.875	(1)	79.075
2. Maxi Gnauck	GDR	19.625	(5)	19.925	(1)	19.65	(6)	19.875	(1)	79.075
4. Natalya Shaposhnikova	SOV/RUS	19.8	(1)	19.775	(4)	19.775	(3)	19.675	(6)	79.025
5. Nelli Kim	SOV/BLR	19.525	(10)	19.725	(6)	19.8	(1)	19.375	(13)	78.425
6. Emilia Eberle	ROM	19.4	(14)	19.85	(2)	19.3	(11)	19.85	(3)	78.4
7. Rodica Dunka	ROM	19.6	(6)	19.35	(14)	19.75	(4)	19.65	(7)	78.35
8. Steffi Kräker	GDR	19.725	(3)	19.775	(4)	19.175	(12)	19.525	(10)	78.2

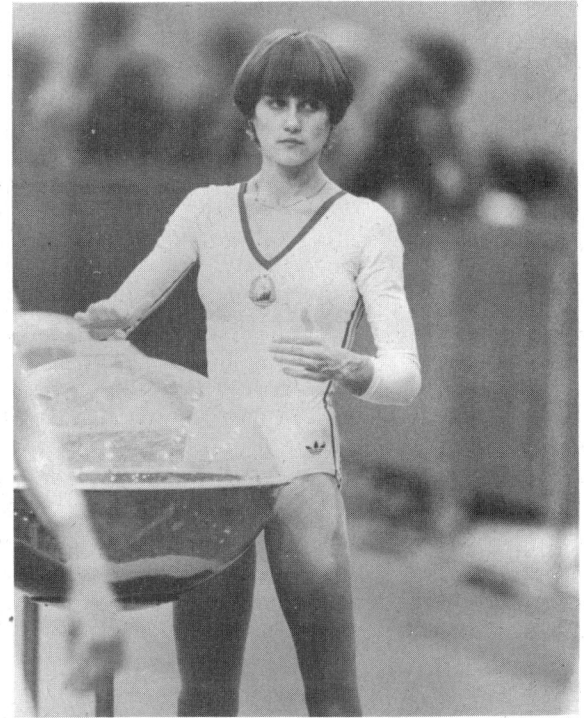

Nadia Comăneci, a veteran of 18 at the Moscow Olympics in 1980.

The favorite in 1980 was defending world champion Yelena Mukhina of the U.S.S.R. However, sixteen days before the opening of the Moscow Olympics, Mukhina was practicing her floor exercise when she missed a one-and-a-half-turn salto with a 540-degree twist and broke her spine. Mukhina was paralyzed from the neck down. She was unable even to speak for six months.

In Mukhina's absence the contest for All-Around champion came down to the final apparatus. If Nadia Comăneci could score 9.95 on the balance beam, she would win outright. If she scored 9.9 she would share the gold medal with a surprising 18-year-old: 4-foot 10-inch Yelena Davydova. Since Nadia had previously been awarded a 9.9 and a 10 on the balance beam, it was quite possible that she could earn the higher mark. With the arena in complete silence, she went through her routine magnificently with only the slightest flaw following a forward flip with a half-twist. It seemed as if she had made it. But her score was not forthcoming. For 28 minutes the judges argued. Finally Nadia's score was flashed on the computer: 9.85, thanks to 9.8s awarded by the judges from Poland and the U.S.S.R. The next day Nadia took first place in the beam and the floor exercise events, giving her an Olympic total of five gold medals, three silver, and one bronze. Nineteen-eighty marked the first time that Soviet gymnasts failed to earn at least two of the medals in the All-Around event.

On the night of November 27, 1989, Nadia Comăneci, the youngest-ever recipient of the Hero of Socialist Labor Award, defected from Romania, slipping across the border to Hungary on foot. After contacting the U.S. embassy in Vienna, she made her way to America accompanied by Romanian émigré Constantin Panait, a Florida roofer. Her long-time fans in the West were thrilled by Comăneci's escape to freedom, but her relationship with her public quickly soured when it was revealed that she planned to live with Panait, even though he was married and the father of four children. Comăneci and Panait were soon separated, and she claimed he had held her hostage for three months. Free for the first time in her life,

Comăneci blossomed. She picked up numerous commercial endorsements, began performing again after a six-year lapse, and married fellow Olympic champion Bart Conner.

1984 Los Angeles C: 65, N: 16, D: 8.3.

		HV		AB		BB		FE		TOTAL PTS.
1.	Mary Lou Retton	USA	19.95	(1)	19.7	(4)	19.6	(3)	19.925	(1)	79.175
2.	Ecaterina Szabó	ROM	19.85	(2)	19.5	(8)	19.85	(1)	19.925	(1)	79.125
3.	Simona Păuca	ROM	19.625	(6)	19.575	(6)	19.85	(1)	19.625	(5)	78.675
4.	Julianne McNamara	USA	19.725	(3)	19.95	(1)	19.075	(13)	19.65	(4)	78.4
5.	Laura Cutina	ROM	19.7	(4)	19.725	(3)	19.125	(11)	19.75	(3)	78.3
6.	Ma Yanhong	CHN	19.3	(15)	19.95	(.1)	19.55	(4)	19.05	(13)	77.85
7.	Zhou Ping	CHN	19.525	(7)	19.4	(9)	19.175	(10)	19.375	(8)	77.775
8.	Chen Yongyan	CHN	19.525	(7)	19.275	(11)	19.5	(5)	19.425	(7)	77.725

Ever since Olga Korbut had melted American hearts in 1972, U.S. sports fans had wondered when a home-grown female gymnastics star would emerge. Considering that no American woman had ever won an individual Olympics gymnastics medal, the prospects did not look bright. However, the Soviet boycott of 1984 opened the door—and in walked a 16-year-old from Fairmont, West Virginia, named Mary Lou Retton. At 4 feet 8¾ inches and weighing 94 pounds, the powerful Italian-American represented a new breed of female gymnast—more muscular and athletic.

Retton had never taken part in a major international tournament before the Olympics, having missed the 1983 world championships because of a wrist injury. She almost missed the Olympics as well when she incurred a knee injury less than six weeks before the Games began. Torn cartilage removed during arthroscopic surgery saved the day.

In Los Angeles the battle for the All-Around gold medal developed into a tight contest between Retton and the Romanian champion Kati Szabó. With two rotations to go, Szabó led by .15 of a point. But Retton rose to the occasion, earning 10s for the floor exercise and the vault, and ensuring her place in sports history books, as well as in the pantheon of U.S. cultural heroes. Aspiring gymnasts should take heart from the story of Retton's first competition when she was still a little girl. Like so many little girls around the world, Mary Lou watched Nadia Comăneci score her history-making 10s in 1976. Retton noticed that the scoreboard, unprepared for Comăneci's perfection, had registered "1.0" rather than "10.0." After performing on the first apparatus in her first meet (the uneven bars), 8-year-old Mary Lou Retton jumped with joy when the scoreboard flashed "1.0." Alas, it really was a 1.0. However, she refused to give up on gymnastics until her 1.0s turned to genuine 10.0s.

1988 Seoul C: 90, N: 23, D: 9.23.

		HV		AB		BB		FE		TOTAL PTS.
1.	Yelena Shushunova	SOV/RUS	20.0	(1)	19.862	(4)	19.85	(1)	19.95	(1)	79.662
2.	Daniela Silivaş	ROM	19.85	(3)	20.0	(1)	19.837	(2)	19.95	(1)	79.637
3.	Svetlana Boginskaya	SOV/BLR	19.887	(2)	19.862	(4)	19.837	(2)	19.812	(4)	79.4
4.	Gabriela Potorac	ROM	19.687	(7)	19.737	(7)	19.837	(2)	19.775	(7)	79.037
5.	Natalija Lascenova	SOV/LAT	19.725	(5)	19.662	(14)	19.687	(6)	19.8	(5)	78.875
6.	Aurelia Dobre	ROM	19.612	(11)	19.762	(6)	19.787	(5)	19.65	(14)	78.812
7.	Dörte Thümmler	GDR	19.7	(6)	19.925	(2)	19.325	(19)	19.85	(3)	78.8
8.	Dagmar Kersten	GDR	19.8	(4)	19.887	(3)	19.325	(19)	19.762	(9)	78.775

With two apparatuses left in the final, Silivaş led Shushunova by the slim margin of .025 of a point. The deficiencies in gymnastics judging quickly became apparent. Shushunova performed a flawless floor exercise and was awarded a perfect 10.0. Silivaş followed her onto the mat and gave an even better performance. But because Shushunova had already received the highest possible score, Silivaş had to settle for a tie despite her superiority. This meant that the competition came down to the

final apparatus: the vault. Silivaş hopped slightly on landing. Although Soviet judge Nelli Kim gave her a scandalously low 9.8, Silivaş' total score was 9.95. Still, this left the door open for Shushunova. Like Mary Lou Retton four years earlier, if she could achieve a 10.0, she would win the All-Around title. Shushunova's vault, a full-twisting Yurchenko, was high and perfect and the gold was hers. However, like Los Angeles silver-medalist Kati Szabó, Silivaş came back two days later to win three of the four apparatus finals, while Shushunova, like Retton, won none.

Women's gymnastics is a breeding ground for media stars: Olga Korbut, Nadia Comăneci, Mary Lou Retton. Next in line for megastardom was the 1987 world champion, Aurelia Dobre of Romania. Besides being the best female gymnast in the world, she was charming, graceful and unusually beautiful. Only 14 years old at the time she won the world championship, Dobre was on track to become a bigger celebrity than her predecessors. But a knee injury forced her to submit to three operations, and the pressure to produce a winner led her coaches to ignore the advice of doctors and make her resume training before she was fully recovered. In Seoul she was already only a shadow of her former self. She placed sixth in the All-Around competition, went home without an individual medal and was ignored by the television cameras of the world. Three years later, however, Aurelia Dobre did earn a place in sports history when she became the first Olympic athlete to appear nude in Playboy magazine—even if it was only in the Dutch edition.

1992 Barcelona C: 92, N: 24, D: 7.30.

		HV		AB		BB		FE		TOTAL PTS.
1. Tatyana Gutsu	UKR	9.95	(5)	9.95	(1)	9.912	(2)	9.925	(3)	39.737
2. Shannon Miller	USA	9.975	(1)	9.925	(2)	9.925	(1)	9.9	(7)	39.725
3. Lavinia Miloşovici	ROM	9.975	(1)	9.9	(4)	9.85	(9)	9.962	(1)	39.687
4. Cristina Bontaş	ROM	9.95	(5)	9.862	(11)	9.9	(5)	9.962	(1)	39.674
5. Svetlana Boginskaya	BLR	9.962	(3)	9.887	(7)	9.912	(2)	9.912	(4)	39.673
6. Gina Gogean	ROM	9.95	(5)	9.862	(11)	9.9	(5)	9.912	(4)	39.624
7. Tatyana Lysenko	UKR	9.962	(3)	9.9	(4)	9.875	(7)	9.8	(18)	39.537
8. Henrietta Ónodi	HUN	9.95	(5)	9.875	(10)	9.712	(20)	9.912	(4)	39.449

In the press, the women's individual All-Around was billed as a showdown between 1989 world champion Svetlana Boginskaya of Belarus and 1991 world champion Kim Zmeskal of the United States. Gymnastics aficionados knew better—not since Lyudmila Turischeva in 1972 had a world champion gone on to win at the Olympics. Tatyana Gutsu of Odessa, on the other hand, was peaking at the right time. The 15-year-old with white hair won the European Championship only two months before the Olympic competition. But in Barcelona, Gutsu fell off the beam during the team optionals and it looked like her chance for gold was finished. Although she qualified in ninth place, only three gymnasts from each country were allowed to advance to the final, and three of the eight ahead of Gutsu were also from the Unified Team of ex–Soviet republics. Not to worry—Unified Team officials announced that 15-year-old Roza Galiyeva of Uzbekistan had conveniently aggravated a knee injury, and overnight Gutsu was back in the hunt.

With three rotations completed in the final and only one to go, Gutsu and Lavinia Miloşovici were tied for first place with 29.787 points. Boginskaya was third with 29.761, and Shannon Miller, who looked so much like Gutsu that the two could have been sisters, was fourth with 29.750. The advantage was with Gutsu and Miller because they would perform on the high-scoring side horse while Miloşovici was on the bars and Boginskaya on the beam. Sure enough, it came down to the vaulters. Miller hit a beautiful Yurchenko-full and earned a 9.975. This meant that Gutsu, performing a full-twisting Yurchenko, needed a 9.39 to beat her. She hopped after landing her first vault and received a 9.25. And so, as in 1984 and 1988, the gold medal came down to one gymnast having to hit her vault. On her second attempt, Gutsu stuck her landing and was rewarded with a 9.5. By placing second, Shannon Miller became the first female United States gymnast to earn a silver medal in a non-boycotted Olympics.

Tatyana Gutsu added a silver on the uneven bars and a bronze for floor exercises, but for the fourth straight time the winner of the All-Around championship failed to earn a single gold in the apparatus finals.

SIDE HORSE VAULT

1896–1948 not held

1952 Helsinki C: 134, N: 18, D: 7.23.

		PTS.
1. Yekaterina Kalinchuk	SOV/RUS	19.20
2. Maria Horokhovska	SOV/UKR	19.19
3. Galina Minaicheva	SOV/RUS	19.16
4. Medeya Dzchugeli	SOV/GEO	19.13
5. Galina Urbanovich	SOV/RUS	19.10
6. Nina Bocharova	SOV/UKR	19.03
7. Karin Lindberg	SWE	18.79
7. Helena Rakoczy	POL	18.79

1956 Melbourne C: 65, N: 15, D: 12.5.

		PTS.
1. Larysa Latynina	SOV/UKR	18.833
2. Tamara Manina	SOV/RUS	18.80
3. Ann-Sofi Colling-Pettersson	SWE	18.733
3. Olga Tass	HUN	18.733
5. Sofia Muratova	SOV/RUS	18.666
6. Elena Leuştean	ROM	18.633
7. Natalia Kot	POL	18.50
7. Helena Rakoczy	POL	18.50

1960 Rome C: 124, N: 27, D: 9.9.

		PTS.
1. Marharyta Nikolayeva	SOV/UKR	19.316
2. Sofia Muratova	SOV/RUS	19.049
3. Larysa Latynina	SOV/UKR	19.016
4. Adolfina Tačová	CZE	18.783
5. Sonia Iovan	ROM	18.766
6. Polina Astakhova	SOV/UKR	18.716

1964 Tokyo C: 82, N: 23, D: 10.22.

		PTS.
1. Vera Čáslavská	CZE	19.483
2. Larysa Latynina	SOV/UKR	19.283
2. Birgit Radochla	GDR	19.283
4. Toshiko Aihara (Shirasu)	JPN	19.282
5. Yelena Volchetskaya	SOV/BLR	19.149
6. Ute Starke	GDR	19.116

1968 Mexico City C: 101, N: 24, D: 10.25.

		PTS.
1. Vera Čáslavská	CZE	19.775
2. Erika Zuchold	GDR	19.625
3. Zinaida Voronina	SOV/RUS	19.50
4. Maria Krajčirová	CZE	19.475
5. Natalya Kutschinskaya	SOV/RUS	19.375
6. Miroslava Skleničková	CZE	19.325

1972 Munich C: 118, N: 23, D: 8.31.

		PTS.
1. Karin Janz	GDR	19.525
2. Erika Zuchold	GDR	19.275
3. Lyudmila Turischeva	SOV/RUS	19.25
4. Lyubov Burda	SOV/RUS	19.225
5. Olga Korbut	SOV/BLR	19.175
6. Tamara Lazakovich	SOV/BLR	19.05

1976 Montreal C: 86, N: 18, D: 7.22.

		PTS.
1. Nelli Kim	SOV/KAZ	19.80
2. Carola Dombeck	GDR	19.65
2. Lyudmila Turischeva	SOV/RUS	19.65
4. Nadia Comăneci	ROM	19.625
5. Gitta Escher	GDR	19.55
6. Márta Egervári	HUN	19.45

1980 Moscow C: 62, N: 16, D: 7.25.

		PTS.
1. Natalya Shaposhnikova	SOV/RUS	19.725
2. Steffi Kräker	GDR	19.675
3. Melita Rühn	ROM	19.65
4. Yelena Davydova	SOV/RUS	19.575
5. Nadia Comăneci	ROM	19.35
6. Maxi Gnauck	GDR	19.30

1984 Los Angeles C: 65, N: 16, D: 8.5.

		PTS.
1. Ecaterina Szabó	ROM	19.875
2. Mary Lou Retton	USA	19.85
3. Lavinia Agache	ROM	19.75

4. Tracee Talavera	USA	19.70
5. Zhou Ping	CHN	19.50
6. Kelly Brown	CAN	19.425
6. Brigitta Lehmann	GER	19.425
8. Chen Yongyan	CHN	19.30

Two nights after finishing second to Mary Lou Retton in the All-Around competition, Kati Szabó reestablished her dominance by winning three of the four apparatus finals. Szabó went home with 4 gold medals and 1 silver, a better haul than even Carl Lewis.

1988 Seoul C: 90, N: 23, D: 9.25.

		PTS.
1. Svetlana Boginskaya	SOV/BLR	19.905
2. Gabriela Potorac	ROM	19.83
3. Daniela Silivaş	ROM	19.818
4. Boriana Stoyanova	BUL	19.78
5. Brandy Johnson	USA	19.774
6. Dagmar Kersten	GDR	19.756
7. Wang Xiaoyan	CHN	19.73
8. Yelena Shushunova	SOV/RUS	19.712

Shushunova, who had dominated the event for three years, led after the preliminaries with a score of 10.0. However she muffed both vaults in the final, finishing her second attempt by landing on her knees.

1992 Barcelona C: 92, N: 24, D: 8.1.

		PTS.
1. Lavinia Miloşovici	ROM	9.925
1. Henrietta Ónodi	HUN	9.925
3. Tatyana Lysenko	UKR	9.912
4. Svetlana Boginskaya	BLR	9.899
5. Gina Gogean	ROM	9.893
6. Shannon Miller	USA	9.837
7. Eva Rueda Bravo	SPA	9.787
8. Kim Zmeskal	USA	9.593

ASYMMETRICAL (UNEVEN) BARS

1896–1948 not held

1952 Helsinki C: 134, N: 18, D: 7.23.

		PTS.
1. Margit Korondi	HUN	19.40
2. Maria Horokhovska	SOV/UKR	19.26
3. Ágnes Keleti	HUN	19.16
4. Nina Bocharova	SOV/UKR	18.99
4. Pelageya Danilova	SOV/RUS	18.99
6. Edit Perényi-Weckinger	HUN	18.96
7. Galina Shamrai	SOV/UZB	18.93
8. Galina Minaicheva	SOV/RUS	18.89

1956 Melbourne C: 65, N: 15, D: 12.5.

		PTS.
1. Ágnes Keleti	HUN	18.966
2. Larysa Latynina	SOV/UKR	18.833
3. Sofia Muratova	SOV/RUS	18.80
4. Eva Bosáková (Věchtová)	CZE	18.733

5. Helena Rakoczy   POL   18.70
6. Aliz Kertész   HUN   18.633
6. Olga Tass   HUN   18.633
8. Natalia Kot   POL   18.60

1960 Rome C: 124, N: 27, D: 9.9.

			PTS.
1.	Polina Astakhova	SOV/UKR	19.616
2.	Larysa Latynina	SOV/UKR	19.416
3.	Tamara Lyukhina	SOV/RUS	19.399
4.	Sofia Muratova	SOV/RUS	19.382
5.	Keiko Ikeda (Tanaka)	JPN	19.333
6.	Sonia Iovan	ROM	19.099

The audience was so upset by the low scoring of Ikeda's final routine that they booed for ten minutes until Astakhova stepped up for her turn.

1964 Tokyo C: 82, N: 23, D: 10.22.

			PTS.
1.	Polina Astakhova	SOV/UKR	19.332
2.	Katalin Makray	HUN	19.216
3.	Larysa Latynina	SOV/UKR	19.199
4.	Toshiko Aihara (Shirasu)	JPN	18.782
5.	Vera Čáslavská	CZE	18.416
6.	Tamara Zamotailova (Lyukhina)	SOV/RUS	17.833

1968 Mexico City C: 101, N: 24, D: 10.25

			PTS.
1.	Vera Čáslavská	CZE	19.65
2.	Karin Janz	GDR	19.50
3.	Zinaida Voronina	SOV/RUS	19.425
4.	Bohumila Řimnácová	CZE	19.35
5.	Erika Zuchold	GDR	19.325
6.	Miroslava Skleničková	CZE	18.20

1972 Munich C: 118, N: 23, D: 8.31.

			PTS.
1.	Karin Janz	GDR	19.675
2.	Olga Korbut	SOV/BLR	19.45
2.	Erika Zuchold	GDR	19.45
4.	Lyudmila Turischeva	SOV/RUS	19.425
5.	Ilona Békési	HUN	19.275
6.	Angelika Hellmann	GDR	19.20

1976 Montreal C: 86, N: 18, D: 7.22.

			PTS.
1.	Nadia Comăneci	ROM	20.00
2.	Teodora Ungureanu	ROM	19.80
3.	Márta Egervári	HUN	19.775
4.	Marion Kische	GDR	19.75
5.	Olga Korbut	SOV/BLR	19.30
6.	Nelli Kim	SOV/KAZ	19.225

1980 Moscow C: 62, N: 16, D: 7.25.

			PTS.
1.	Maxi Gnauck	GDR	19.875
2.	Emilia Eberle	ROM	19.85
3.	Maria Filatova	SOV/RUS	19.775
3.	Steffi Kräker	GDR	19.775

3. Melita Rühn   ROM   19.775
6. Nelli Kim   SOV/BLR 19.725

1984 Los Angeles C: 65, N: 16, D: 8.5.

			PTS.
1.	Ma Yanhong	CHN	19.95
1.	Julianne McNamara	USA	19.95
3.	Mary Lou Retton	USA	19.80
4.	Miháela Stănulet	ROM	19.65
5.	Romi Kessler	SWI	19.425
6.	Zhou Ping	CHN	19.35
7.	Noriko Mochizuki	JPN	19.325
8.	Lavinia Agache	ROM	19.15

1988 Seoul C: 90, N: 23, D: 9.25.

			PTS.
1.	Daniela Silivaş	ROM	20.00
2.	Dagmar Kersten	GDR	19.987
3.	Yelena Shushunova	SOV/RUS	19.962
4.	Dörte Thümmler	GDR	19.90
5.	Svetlana Boginskaya	SOV/BLR	19.899
6.	Iveta Poloková	CZE	19.837
7.	Aurelia Dobre	ROM	19.824
8.	Phoebe Mills	USA	19.787

1992 Barcelona C: 92, N: 24, D: 8.1.

			PTS.
1.	Lu Li	CHN	10.000
2.	Tatyana Gutsu	UKR	9.975
3.	Shannon Miller	USA	9.962
4.	Kim Gwang-suk	PRK	9.912
4.	Lavinia Miloşovici	ROM	9.912
4.	Mirela Paşca	ROM	9.912
7.	Cristina Fraguas Sánchez	SPA	9.900
8.	Li Li	CHN	9.887

Lu Li, a 15-year-old from Changsha, in Hunan Province, stood only 4 feet 5½ inches (1.36 m) and weighed only 66 pounds (30 kg). She qualified for the final with only the sixth best score and then hit a perfect routine to earn tens from all six judges.

BALANCE BEAM

1896–1948 not held

1952 Helsinki C: 134, N: 18, D: 7.23.

			PTS.
1.	Nina Bocharova	SOV/UKR	19.22
2.	Maria Horokhovska	SOV/UKR	19.13
3.	Margit Korondi	HUN	19.02
4.	Ágnes Keleti	HUN	18.96
5.	Galina Urbanovich	SOV/RUS	18.93
6.	Tsvetana Stancheva	BUL	18.86
6.	Olga Tass	HUN	18.86
8.	Galina Shamrai	SOV/UZB	18.79

1956 Melbourne C: 65, N: 15, D: 12.5.

			PTS.
1.	Ágnes Keleti	HUN	18.80
2.	Eva Bosáková (Věchtová)	CZE	18.633
2.	Tamara Manina	SOV/RUS	18.633
4.	Larysa Latynina	SOV/UKR	18.533
4.	Anna Marejkova	CZE	18.533
6.	Elena Leuştean	ROM	18.50
7.	Margit Korondi	HUN	18.466
7.	Olga Tass	HUN	18.466
7.	Lyudmila Yegorova	SOV/RUS	18.466

1960 Rome C: 124, N: 27, D: 9.9.

			PTS.
1.	Eva Bosáková (Věchtová)	CZE	19.283
2.	Larysa Latynina	SOV/UKR	19.233
3.	Sofia Muratova	SOV/RUS	19.232
4.	Marharyta Nikolayeva	SOV/UKR	19.183
5.	Keiko Ikeda (Tanaka)	JPN	19.132
6.	Vera Čáslavská	CZE	19.083

1964 Tokyo C: 83, N: 24, D: 10.23.

			PTS.
1.	Vera Čáslavská	CZE	19.449
2.	Tamara Manina	SOV/RUS	19.399
3.	Larysa Latynina	SOV/UKR	19.382
4.	Polina Astakhova	SOV/UKR	19.366
5.	Hana Ružčková	CZE	19.349
6.	Keiko Ikeda (Tanaka)	JPN	19.216

1968 Mexico City C: 101, N: 24, D: 10.25.

			PTS.
1.	Natalya Kuchinskaya	SOV/RUS	19.65
2.	Vera Čáslavská	CZE	19.575
3.	Larissa Petrik	SOV/BLR	19.25
4.	Karin Janz	GDR	19.225
4.	Linda Metheny	USA	19.225
6.	Erika Zuchold	GDR	19.15

1972 Munich c: 118, N: 23, D: 8.31.

			PTS.
1.	Olga Korbut	SOV/BLR	19.40
2.	Tamara Lazakovich	SOV/BLR	19.375
3.	Karin Janz	GDR	18.975
4.	Mónika Császár	HUN	18.925
5.	Lyudmila Turischeva	SOV/RUS	18.80
6.	Erika Zuchold	GDR	18.70

1976 Montreal C: 86, N: 18, D: 7.22.

			PTS.
1.	Nadia Comăneci	ROM	19.95
2.	Olga Korbut	SOV/BLR	19.725
3.	Teodora Ungureanu	ROM	19.70
4.	Lyudmila Turischeva	SOV/RUS	19.475
5.	Angelika Hellmann	GDR	19.45
6.	Gitta Escher	GDR	19.275

1980 Moscow C: 62, N: 16, D: 7.25.

			PTS.
1.	Nadia Comăneci	ROM	19.80
2.	Yelena Davydova	SOV/RUS	19.75
3.	Natalya Shaposhnikova	SOV/RUS	19.725
4.	Maxi Gnauck	GDR	19.70
5.	Radka Zemanová	CZE	19.65
6.	Emilia Eberle	ROM	19.40

1984 Los Angeles C: 65, N: 16, D: 8.5.

			PTS.
1.	Simona Păuca	ROM	19.80
1.	Ecaterina Szabó	ROM	19.80
3.	Kathy Johnson	USA	19.65
4.	Mary Lou Retton	USA	19.55
5.	Ma Yanhong	CHN	19.45
6.	Romi Kessler	SWI	19.35
7.	Chen Yongyan	CHN	19.20
7.	Anja Wilhelm	GER	19.20

1988 Seoul C: 90, N: 23, D: 9.25.

			PTS.
1.	Daniela Silivaş	ROM	19.924
2.	Yelena Shushunova	SOV/RUS	19.875
3.	Phoebe Mills	USA	19.837
3.	Gabriela Potorac	ROM	19.837
5.	Svetlana Boginskaya	SOV/BLR	19.787
6.	Diana Dudeva	BUL	19.724
7.	Kelly Garrison-Steves	USA	19.649
8.	Ulrike Klotz	GDR	18.125

Phoebe Mills of Northfield, Illinois, became the first female gymnast from the U.S. to win an individual medal at an unboycotted Olympics.

1992 Barcelona C: 92, N: 24, D: 8.1.

			PTS.
1.	Tatyana Lysenko	UKR	9.975
2.	Lu Li	CHN	9.912
2.	Shannon Miller	USA	9.912
4.	Cristina Bontaş	ROM	9.875
5.	Svetlana Boginskaya	BLR	9.862
6.	Elizabeth Okino	USA	9.837
7.	Yang Bo	CHN	9.300
8.	Lavinia Miloşovici	ROM	9.262

Lysenko, a 17-year-old from Kherson, became the first non-Romanian to win this event in 20 years.

FLOOR EXERCISES

1896–1948 not held

1952 Helsinki C: 134, N: 18, D: 7.23.

			PTS.
1.	Ágnes Keleti	HUN	19.36
2.	Maria Horokhovska	SOV/UKR	19.20
3.	Margit Korondi	HUN	19.00
4.	Erzsébet Gulyás	HUN	18.99
4.	Galina Urbanovich	SOV/RUS	18.99

6. Galina Minaicheva   SOV/RUS   18.96
7. Olga Tass   HUN   18.89
8. Galina Shamrai   SOV/UZB   18.86

1956 Melbourne C: 65, N: 15, D: 12.5.

			PTS.
1.	Ágnes Keleti	HUN	18.733
1.	Larysa Latynina	SOV/UKR	18.733
3.	Elena Leuştean	ROM	18.70
4.	Eva Bosáková (Věchtová)	CZE	18.566
4.	Sofia Muratova	SOV/RUS	18.566
4.	Keiko Tanaka	JPN	18.566
7.	Olga Tass	HUN	18.533
8.	Doris Hedberg	SWE	18.50

1960 Rome C: 124, N: 27, D: 9.9.

			PTS.
1.	Larysa Latynina	SOV/UKR	19.583
2.	Polina Astakhova	SOV/UKR	19.532
3.	Tamara Lyukhina	SOV/RUS	19.449
4.	Eva Bosáková (Věchtová)	CZE	19.383
5.	Sofia Muratova	SOV/RUS	19.349
6.	Sonia Iovan	ROM	19.232

1964 Tokyo C: 83, N: 24, D: 23.10.

			PTS.
1.	Larysa Latynina	SOV/UKR	19.599
2.	Polina Astakhova	SOV/UKR	19.50
3.	Anikó Jánosi-Ducza	HUN	19.30
4.	Birgit Radochla	GDR	19.299
5.	Ingrid Föst	GDR	19.266
6.	Vera Čáslavská	CZE	19.099

1968 Mexico City C: 101, N: 24, D: 10.20.

			PTS.
1.	Vera Čáslavská	CZE	19.675
1.	Larissa Petrik	SOV/BLR	19.675
3.	Natalya Kuchinskaya	SOV/RUS	19.65
4.	Zinaida Voronina	SOV/RUS	19.55
5.	Olga Karasyova	SOV/RUS	19.325
5.	Bohumila Řimnácová	CZE	19.325

1972 Munich C: 118, N: 23, D: 10.25.

			PTS.
1.	Olga Korbut	SOV/BLR	19.575
2.	Lyudmila Turischeva	SOV/RUS	19.55
3.	Tamara Lazakovich	SOV/BLR	19.45
4.	Karin Janz	GDR	19.40
5.	Lyubov Burda	SOV/RUS	19.10
5.	Angelika Hellmann	GDR	19.10

1976 Montreal C: 86, N: 18, D: 7.22.

			PTS.
1.	Nelli Kim	SOV/KAZ	19.85
2.	Lyudmila Turischeva	SOV/RUS	19.825
3.	Nadia Comăneci	ROM	19.75
4.	Anna Pohludková	CZE	19.575
5.	Marion Kische	GDR	19.475
6.	Gitta Escher	GDR	19.45

1980 Moscow C: 62, N: 16, D: 7.25.

			PTS.
1.	Nadia Comăneci	ROM	19.875
1.	Nelli Kim	SOV/BLR	19.875
3.	Maxi Gnauck	GDR	19.825
3.	Natalya Shaposhnikova	SOV/RUS	19.825
5.	Emilia Eberle	ROM	19.75
6.	Jana Labáková	CZE	19.725

1984 Los Angeles C: 65, N: 16, D: 8.5.

			PTS.
1.	Ecaterina Szabó	ROM	19.975
2.	Julianne McNamara	USA	19.95
3.	Mary Lou Retton	USA	19.775
4.	Zhou Qiurui	CHN	19.625
5.	Romi Kessler	SWI	19.575
6.	Ma Yanhong	CHN	19.45
7.	Maiko Morio	JPN	19.375
8.	Laura Cutina	ROM	19.15

When Ecaterina Szabó stepped up for her final Olympic routine, a power outage plunged the arena into darkness. When the lights were restored eight minutes later, the scoreboard showed that Szabó's closest rival, Julianne McNamara, had been awarded a 10 for her performance. This meant that Szabó would need a 10 as well to assure herself sole possession of first place. Unfazed by the delay or the pressure, she earned her 10 and, with it, her fourth gold medal.

1988 Seoul C: 90, N: 23, D: 9.25.

			PTS.
1.	Daniela Silivaş	ROM	19.937
2.	Svetlana Boginskaya	SOV/BLR	19.887
3.	Diana Dudeva	BUL	19.85
4.	Deliana Vodenicharova	BUL	19.837
5.	Beáta Storczer	HUN	19.675
6.	Phoebe Mills	USA	19.662
7.	Yelena Shushunova	SOV/RUS	19.575
8.	Dörte Thümmler	GDR	19.525

Silivaş returned home from Seoul with three gold medals and two silver. Dudeva became the first Bulgarian woman to win an Olympic gymnastics medal.

1992 Barcelona C: 92, N: 24, D: 8.1.

			PTS.
1.	Lavinia Miloşovici	ROM	10.000
2.	Henrietta Ónodi	HUN	9.950
3.	Cristina Bontaş	ROM	9.912
3.	Tatyana Gutsu	UKR	9.912
3.	Shannon Miller	USA	9.912
6.	Kim Zmeskal	USA	9.900
7.	Oksana Chusovitina	UZB	9.812
8.	Sylvia Mitova	BUL	9.400

Svetlana Boginskaya finished in a tie for first place in the qualifying round, but officials of the Unified Team replaced her in the final with world champion Oksana Chusovitina.

TEAM COMBINED EXERCISES

According to current rules, each nation's final score is determined by combining the scores of the top five performers on each apparatus.

1896–1924 not held

1928 Amsterdam T: 5, N: 5, D: 8.10.

			TOTAL PTS.
1.	HOL	(Petronella van Randwijk, Jacomina van den Berg, Anna Polak, Helena Nordheim, Alida van den Bos, Hendrika van Rumt, Anna van der Vegt, Elka de Levie, Jacoba Stelma, Estella Agsteribbe)	316.75
2.	ITA	(Bianca Ambrosetti, Lavinia Gianoni, Luigina Perversi, Diana Pizzavini, Luigina Giavotti, Luisa Tanzini, Carolina Tronconi, Ines Vercesi, Rita Vittadini, Virginia Giorgi, Germana Malabarba, Clara Marangoni)	289.00
3.	GBR	(Margaret Hartley, Edith Carrie Pickles, Annie Broadbent, Amy Jagger, Ada Smith, Lucy Desmond, Doris Woods, Jessie Kite, Isabel "Queenie" Judd, Marjorie "Midge" Moreman, Ethel Seymour, Hilda Smith)	258.25
4.	HUN	(Mária Hámos, Aranka Hennyei, Anna Kael, Margit Pályi, Erzsébet Rudas, Nandorné Szeiler, Ilona Szöllösi, Judit Tóth, Rudolfné Herpich, Irén Hennyey, Margit Kövessy, Irén Rudas)	256.50
5.	FRA	(Honorine Delescluse, Louise Delescluse, R. Oger, Georgette Meulebrouck, Mathilde Bataille, Galuelle Dhont, Valentine Héméryck, Jeanne Vanoverloop, Paulette Houteer, Berthe Verstraete, Geneviève Vankiersbilck, Antonie Straeteman)	247.50

Four of the ten members of the Dutch team were Jewish. Helena Nordheim died in a Nazi gas chamber at Sobibor on July 2, 1943, along with her husband and 10-year-old daughter; Anna Polak and her 6-year-old daughter died July 23, 1943, also at Sobibor; Estella Agsterribe lost her life in a gas chamber at Auschwitz on September 17, 1943, along with her 6-year-old daughter and 2-year-old son. Alternate Judikje Simons also died with her son and daughter at Sobibor. The only Jewish member of the team to survive World War II was Elka de Levi.

1932 not held

1936 Berlin T: 8, N: 8, D: 8.12.

			TOTAL PTS.
1.	GER	(Trudi Meyer 67.55 [1], Erna Bürger 67.45 [2], Käthe Sohnemann 67.05 [3], Isolde Frölian 65.75 [8], Anita Bärwirth 65.45 [9], Paula Pöhlsen 65.00 [12], Friedel Iby 63.75 [17], Julie Schmitt 62.10 [27])	506.50
2.	CZE	(Vlasta Foltová 66.45 [5], Vlasta Dekanová	503.60

65.95 [6], Zdenka Veřmiřovska 65.90 [7], Matylda Pálfyová 64.10 [16], Anna Hřebřinová 62.70 [21], Božena Dobešová 62.65 [22], Marie Vetrovská 60.25 [28], Marie Bajerová 59.35 [45])

			TOTAL PTS.
3.	HUN	(Margit Csillik 65.30 [11], Judit Tóth 64.70 [13], Margit Sándor-Nagy 64.55 [15], Gabriella Mészáros 63.05 [19], Eszter Voit 62.90 [20], Olga Törös 61.90 [30], Ilona Madary 61.25 [33], Margit Kalocsai 59.85 [41])	499.00
4.	YUG	(Dušica Radivojević 62.30 [25], Lidica Rupnik 62.25 [26], Marta Pustišek 62.00 [28], Olga Rajkovič 62.00 [28], Drogana Djordjevič 61.20 [34], Angelina Kopurenko 60.75 [35], Katarina Hribar 60.60 [36], Maja Veršec 58.65 [46])	485.60
5.	USA	(Consetta Caruccio 66.85 [4], Jennie Caputo 65.45 [9], Irma Haubold 62.45 [23], Margaret Duff 60.50 [37], Ada Lunardoni 60.25 [38], Adelaide Meyer 56.55 [50], Mary Wright 55.10 [54], Marie Kibler 5.75 [injured])	471.60
6.	POL	(Klara Sierońska 64.65 [14], Marta Majowska 63.15 [18], Matylda Osadnik 62.45 [23], Wislawa Noskiewicz 61.40 [32], Janina Skirlińska 60.20 [40], Alina Cichecka 59.70 [44], Julia Wojciechowska 57.87 [47], Stefania Krupowa 56.95 [49])	470.30
7.	ITA	(Ebore Canella 61.75 [31], Clara Bimbocci 59.75 [42], Elda Cividino 59.75 [42], Carmela Toso 57.60 [48], Pina Cipriotto 55.35 [52], Anny Avanzini 55.20 [53], Vittoria Avanzini 54.75 [55], Gianna Guaita 51.40 [59])	442.05
8.	GBR	(Mary Heaton 56.15 [51], Mary Kelly 53.70 [56], Lilian Ridgewell 53.00 [57], Doris Blake 52.45 [58], Brenda Crowe 49.00 [60], Clarice Hanson 49.00 [60], Marion Wharton 46.95 [62], Edna Gross 43.84 [63])	408.30

1948 London T: 11, N: 11, D: 8.14.

			TOTAL PTS.
1.	CZE	(Zdenka Honsová 54.85 [1], Miloslava Misáková 53.40 [4], Vera Ružičkova 53.00 [7], Božena Srncová 52.95 [8], Milena Mullerová 52.50 [10], Zdenka Veřmiřovská 50.00 [23], Olga Silhanová 49.95 [24], Marie Kovářová 49.60 [26])	445.45
2.	HUN	(Edit Perényi-Weckinger 54.25 [2], Mária Kova 53.40 [4], Irén Kárpáti-Karcsics 53.26 [6], Erzsébet Gulyás-Köteles 52.25 [12], Erzsébet Balázs 52.10 [13], Olga Tass 51.45 [15], Anna Fehér 49.15 [28], Margit Sandor-Nagy 39.10 [74])	440.55
3.	USA	(Helen Schifano 51.70 [14], Clara Schroth 51.05 [17], Meta Elste 50.90 [18], Marian Barone 50.30 [19], Ladislava Bakanic 50.10 [20], Consetta Lenz [Caruccio] 49.10 [29], Anita Simonis 47.80 [39], Dorothy Dalton 47.65 [41])	422.63
4.	SWE	(Karin Lindberg 52.70 [9], Kerstin Bohman 51.40 [16], Ingrid Sandahl 51.00 [18], Göta	417.95

Pettersson 50.10 [21], Gunnel Johansson 49.10 [29], Märta Andersson 49.05 [30], E. Ingrid Andersson 47.10 [47], Stina Haage 39.10 [74])

			TOTAL PTS.
5.	HOL	(Jacoba Tonneman 52.50 [10], Helena Gerrietsen 49.50 [27], Jacoba Wijnands 47.25 [44], Johanna Ros 45.75 [54], Anna van Geene 45.45 [57], Klassje Post 44.80 [62], Geertruida Heil-Bonnet 42.55 [67], Barendina Meijer-Haantjes 38.30 [78])	408.35
6.	AUT	(Gertrude Fesl 51.05 [17], Gretchen Hehenberger 50.00 [23], Gertrude Kolar 48.65 [36], Edeltraud Schramm 45.10 [60], Erika Enzenhofer 38.95 [76])	405.45
7.	YUG	(Vida Gerbeč 49.00 [34], Dragan Djordjevič 47.60 [42], Rusa Vojsk 47.20 [45], Draginja Djipalovič 47.15 [46], Tanja Žutič 45.25 [58], Dragica Basletič 42.70 [66], Zlatica Mijatovič 40.35 [72], Noda Cerne 24.70 [88])	397.90
8.	ITA	(Laura Micheli 53.65 [3], Elena Santoni 47.55 [43], Licia Macchini 46.30 [52], Wanda Nuti 45.75 [54], Liliana Torriani 45.10 [60], Renata Bianchi 43.25 [65], Norma Icardi 40.70 [70], Luciana Pezzoni 28.20 [85])	394.20

In gymnastics, as in other sports in which scoring is dependent on subjective judging, controversies and partisan decisions are commonplace. But a special level of incompetence was displayed by one of the judges in the 1948 women's gymnastics competition when, scoring on a scale of one through ten, she awarded one gymnast a 13.1. The major benefactors of the strange scoring standards of 1948 were the Czechoslovakians, who won the gold medal under dramatic circumstances. Shortly after the Czech team arrived in London, one of its members, 22-year-old Eliska Misáková, was taken ill and confined to an iron lung. The day of her team's appearance at the Olympics, she died of infantile paralysis. The Czech team, which included her older sister, Miloslava, went ahead with its performance and was awarded first place. When the Czech flag was raised for the medal ceremony, it was bordered with a black ribbon. After the Olympics, Marie Provaznikova, the leader of the Czech women's team and the president of the Women's Technical Commission, refused to return to Czechoslovakia because "there is no freedom of speech, of the press or of assembly." She was the first Olympic participant to defect, although hardly the last.

1952 Helsinki T: 18, N: 18, D: 7.24.

			TOTAL PTS.
1.	SOV	(Maria Horokhovska 76.78 [1], Nina Bocharova 75.94 [2], Galina Minaicheva 75.67 [4], Galina Urbanovich 75.64 [5], Pelageya Danilova 75.03 [7], Galina Shamrai 74.97 [8], Yekaterina Kalinchuk 73.91 [13])	527.03
2.	HUN	(Margit Korondi 75.82 [3], Agnes Keleti 75.58 [6], Edit Perényi-Weckinger 74.77 [10], Olga	520.96

Tass 74.71 [11], Erzsébet Gulyás 74.61 [12], Mária Zalai-Kövi 73.87 [15], Andrea Bodó 71.67 [28], Irén Daruházi-Karcscics 70.87 [40])

			TOTAL PTS.
3.	CZE	(Eva Věchtová 73.87 [14], Alena Chadimová 72.25 [20], Jana Rabasová 72.13 [21], Božena Srncová 72.08 [22], Hana Bobková 71.52 [31], Matylda Šinová 71.47 [33], Vera Vančurová 71.38 [34], Alena Reichová 70.40 [47])	503.32
4.	SWE	(Karin Lindberg 73.13 [17], Gun Röring 72.07 [23], Evy Berggren 71.07 [36], Göta Pettersson 70.97 [37], Ann-Sofi Colling-Pettersson 70.71 [44], Ingrid Sandahl 69.68 [57], Hjördis Nordin 69.28 [65], Vanja Blomberg 67.84 [83])	501.83
5.	GER	(Irma Walther 71.95 [24], Hanna Grages 71.77 [26], Elisabeth Ostermeier 70.91 [38], Wolfgard Voss 70.00 [53], Inge Sedlmaier 69.83 [54], Lydia Zeitlhofer 69.57 [60], Brigitte Kiesier 67.98 [80], Hilde Koop 63.40 [118])	495.20
6.	ITA	(Lidia Pitteri 71.60 [30], Miranda Cicognani 71.50 [32], Licia Macchini 71.24 [35], Liliana Scaricabarozzi 70.81 [41], Grazia Bozzo 70.77 [42], Luciana Reali 70.62 [45], Elisabetta Durelli 70.39 [48], Renata Bianchi 69.76 [55])	494.74
7.	BUL	(Tsvetana Stancheva 73.67 [16], Ivanka Doldzheva 72.81 [18], Saltirka Turpova 72.30 [19], Vasilka Stancheva 71.64 [29], Raina Grigorova 70.18 [49], Yordanka Yovkova 66.37 [98], Stoyanka Angelova 64.85 [110], Penka Prisadashka 62.91 [122])	493.77
8.	POL	(Stefania Świerzy 71.68 [27], Stefania Reindlowa 70.91 [38], Helena Rakoczy 70.74 [43], Zofia Kowalczyk 69.20 [67], Honorata Marcińczak 68.85 [69], Barbara Wilk-Slizowska 68.14 [76], Dorota Horzonek, 67.57 [86], Ursula Lukomska 62.90 [123])	483.72

1956 Melbourne T: 9, N: 9, D: 12.7.

			TOTAL PTS.
1.	SOV	(Larysa Latynina 74.933 [1], Sofia Muratova 74.466 [3], Tamara Manina 74.233 [6], Lyudmila Yegorova 73.533 [10], Polina Astakhova 72.700 [17], Lidiya Kalinina 72.033 [21])	444.800
2.	HUN	(Ágnes Keleti 74.633 [2], Olga Tass 74.366 [4], Margit Korondi 73.333 [12], Andrea Bodó 72.900 [14], Erzsébet Gulyás-Köteles 72.200 [18], Aliz Kertész 63.400 [61])	443.500
3.	ROM	(Elena Leuştean 74.366 [4], Sonia Iovan 72.900 [14], Georgeta Hurmuzache 72.733 [16], Emilia Vătăşoiu 72.100 [20], Elena Mărgărit 72.033 [21], Elena Săcalici 71.433 [30])	438.200
4.	POL	(Helena Rakoczy 73.700 [8], Natalia Kot 73.633 [9], Danuta Nowak-Stachow 71.800 [25], Dorota Jokiel 71.666 [27], Barbara Ślizowska 70.533 [45], Lidia Szczerbińska 70.300 [47])	436.500

		TOTAL PTS.
5. CZE	(Eva Bosáková [Věchtová] 74.100 [7], Hana Marejková 73.500 [11], Matylda Šínová 71.800 [25], Vera Drazdiková 71.333 [32], Alena Reichová 70.866 [39], Miroslava Brdičková 70.833 [40])	435.356
6. JPN	(Keiko Tanaka 73.100 [13], Mitsuka Ikeda 71.900 [23], Kazuko Sogabe 71.833 [24], Shizuko Sakashita 71.500 [29], Kyoko Kubota 71.133 [34], Suzuko Seki 71.000 [35])	433.653
7. ITA	(Miranda Cicognani 71.600 [28], Luciana Reali 70.933 [37], Rosella Cicognani 70.766 [42], Elisa Calsi 70.733 [43], Elena Lagorara 70.700 [44], Luciana Lagorara 69.700 [50])	428.654
8. SWE	(Ann-Sofi Colling-Pettersson 71.40 [31], Eva Rönström 70.933 [37], Doris Hedberg 70.466 [46], Karin Lindberg 70.033 [48], Evy Berggren 69.966 [49], Maude Karlén 68.80 [53])	428.600

1960 Rome T: 17, N: 17, D: 9.8.

		TOTAL PTS
1. SOV	(Larysa Latynina 77.031 [1], Sofia Muratova 76,696 [2], Polina Astakhova 76.164 [3], Marharyta Nikolayeva 75.831 [4], Lidiya Ivanova [Kalinina] 75.431 [7], Tamara Lyukhina 66.664 [89])	382.320
2. CZE	(Vera Čáslavská 75.298 [8], Eva Bosáková [Věchtová] 75.197 [10], Ludmila Svédová 74.565 [13], Adolfina Tačová 74.564 [14], Matylda Matoušková [Šínová] 73.265 [26], Hana Ruzickova 72.732 [33])	373.323
3. ROM	(Sonia Iovan 75.797 [5], Elena Leuştean 74.865 [11], Emilia Liţă [Vătăşoiu] 74.264 [16], Atanasia Ionescu 73.564 [21], Uta Poreceau 73.197 [27], Elena Niculescu [Mărgărit] 70.563 [67])	372.053
4. JPN	(Keiko Ikeda [Tanaka] 75.696 [6], Kiyoko Ono 75.398 [15], Kimiko Tsukada 73.398 [22], Toshiko Shirasu 73.298 [24], Ginko Abukawa 72.311 [43], Kazuko Sogabe 17.598 [56])	371.422
5. POL	(Natalia Kot 74.864 [12], Danuta Stachow 73.930 [17], Barbara Eustachiewicz 73.298 [24], Eryka Madra 72.764 [32], Gizela Niedurna 72.647 [37], Brygida Dziuba 71.898 [52])	368.620
6. GDR	(Ingrid Föst 75.265 [9], Roselore Sonntag 72.964 [29], Ute Starke 72.798 [31], Gretel Schiener 72.697 [34], Renate Schneider 72.029 [48], Karin Boldermann 71.298 [59])	367.754
7. HUN	(Judit Füle 73.831 [19], Anikó Jánosi-Ducza 73.398 [22], Klára Förstner 72.697 [34], Katalin Müller 72.530 [38], Olga Tass 72.397 [40], Mária Bencsik 72.030 [46])	367.054
8. BUL	(Raina Grigorova 73.898 [18], Ivanka Doldzheva 72.332 [42], Saltirka Turpova 72.064 [45], Tsvetana Rangelova 71.996 [49],	364.920

Elisaveta Mileva 71.964 [50], Stanka Pavlova 71.697 [54])

1964 Tokyo T: 10, N: 10, D: 10.21.

		TOTAL PTS.
1. SOV	(Larysa Latynina 76.998 [2], Polina Astakhova 76.965 [3], Yelena Volchetskaya 75.765 [8], Tamara Zamotailova [Lyukhina] 75.398 [13], Tamara Manina 75.397 [14], Lyudmila Gromova 74.398 [30])	380.890
2. CZE	(Vera Čáslavská 77.564 [1], Hana Ružičková 76.097 [5], Jaroslava Sedlačková 75.598 [11], Adolfina Tkačiková [Tačová] 75.331 [19], Mária Krajčirová 74.898 [21], Jana Posnerová 74.765 [23])	379.989
3. JPN	(Keiko Ikeda [Tanaka] 76.031 [6], Toshiko Aihara [Shirasu] 75.997 [7], Kiyoko Ono 75.665 [9], Taniko Nakamura 75.198 [19], Ginko Chiba [Abukawa] 74.665 [24], Hiroko Tsuji 74.597 [25])	377.889
4. GER& GDR	(Birgit Radochla 76.431 [4], Ute Starke 75.632 [10], Ingrid Föst 75.465 [12], Karin Mannewitz 74.363 [31], Christel Felgner 74.014 [35], Barbara Stolz 73.430 [44])	376.038
5. HUN	(Anikó Janosi-Ducza 75.33 [16], Katalin Makray 75.330 [18], Mária Tressel 74.932 [21], Gyöngyi Kovacs-Mák 74.597 [26], Katalin Müller 74.565 [27], Márta Erdösi-Talnai 74.231 [32])	375.455
6. ROM	(Sonia Iovan 75.397 [14], Elena Popescu-Leuştean 75.130 [20], Elena Ceampelea 73.831 [37], Atanasia Ionescu 73.698 [41], Emilia Liţă [Vătăşoiu] 72.995 [48], Cristina Doboşan 72.497 [54])	371.984
7. POL	(Gerda Brylka 74.563 [28], Malgorzata Wilczek 74.563 [28], Elzbieta Apostolska 73.831 [37], Dorota Miller 73.465 [43], Gizela Niedurny 72.365 [56], Barbara Eustachiewicz 72.197 [58])	371.287
8. SWE	(Anna Marie Lundquist 73.798 [39], Laila Egman 73.764 [40], Ewa Rydell 73.599 [42], Ulla Lindstrom 72.898 [50], Anne-Marie Lambert 72.796 [52], Gercla Lindahl 72.763 [53])	367.888

1968 Mexico City T: 14, N: 14, D: 10.23.

		TOTAL PTS.
1. SOV	(Zinaida Voronina 76.85 [2], Natalya Kuchinskaya 76.75 [3], Larissa Petrik 76.70 [4], Olga Karasyova 76.00 [7], Lyudmila Turischeva 74.50 [24], Lyubov Burda 74.20 [25])	382.85
2. CZE	(Vera Čáslavská 78.25 [1], Bohumila Řimnácová 76.00 [7], Miroslava Skleničková 75.85 [9], Máriana Krajčirová 75.85 [9], Hana Lišková 75.65 [11], Jana Kubičková [Posnerová] 75.05 [15])	382.20
3. GDR	(Erika Zuchold 76.70 [4], Karin Janz 76.55 [6], Maritta Bauerschmidt 75.45 [12], Ute Starke	379.10

74.65 [22], Marianne Noack 74.10 [27], Magdalena Schmidt 73.95 [29])

4. JPN (Kazue Hanyu 75.30 [13], Miyuki Matsuhisa 74.90 [17], Taniko Mitsukuri 74.85 [18], Chieko Oda 74.80 [19], Mitsuko Kandori 74.65 [22], Kayoko Hashiguchi 73.15 [33]) — 375.45

5. HUN (Ágnes Bánfai 75.10 [14], Anikó Jánosi-Ducza 74.80 [19], Katalin Schmitt-Makray 74.15 [26], Márta Erdösi-Tolnai 72.45 [35], Katalin Száll-Müller 72.15 [37], Ilona Békési 71.85 [38]) — 369.80

6. USA (Cathy Rigby 74.95 [16], Linda Metheny 74.00 [28], Joyce Tanac 73.65 [30], Kathy Gleason 73.60 [31], Colleen Mulvihill 73.05 [34], Wendy Cluff 71.80 [39]) — 369.75

7. FRA (Evelyne Letourneur 74.80 [19], Jacqueline Brisepierre 72.45 [35], Mireille Cayre 71.75 [40], Françoise Nourry 70.75 [46], Dominique Lauvard 70.15 [57], Nicole Bourdiau 69.05 [69]) — 361.75

8. BUL (Maria Karashka 73.30 [32], Vania Marinova 71.30 [44], Veselina Pasheva 70.45 [51], Neli Stoyanova 70.45 [51], Raina Atanasova 69.60 [65]) — 355.10

1972 Munich T: 19, N: 19, D: 9.28.

TOTAL PTS.

1. SOV (Lyudmila Turischeva 76.85 [1], Olga Korbut 76.70 [3], Tamara Lazakovich 76.40 [4], Lyubov Burda 75.35 [6], Elvira Saadi 74.65 [8], Antonina Koshel 73.00 [20]) — 380.50

2. GDR (Karin Janz 76.85 [1], Erika Zuchold 76.00 [5], Angelika Hellmann 75.30 [7], Irene Abel 73.75 [13], Christine Schmitt 73.70 [14], Richarda Schmeisser 73.20 [17]) — 376.55

3. HUN (Ilona Békési 74.40 [9], Mónika Császár 73.85 [12], Krisztina Medveczky 73.60 [15], Anikó Kéry 73.40 [16], Márta Kelemen 73.00 [20], Zsuzsanna Nagy 71.45 [41]) — 368.25

4. USA (Cathy Rigby 74.25 [10], Kimberly Chace 73.05 [18], Roxanne Pierce 72.55 [25], Linda Metheny 72.50 [26], Joan Moore 72.50 [26], Nancy Thies 71.95 [35]) — 365.90

5. CZE (Mariana Némethová [Krajčirová] 74.00 [11], Zdena Dornáková 72.90 [23], Sona Brázdová 72.80 [24], Zdena Bujnáčková 72.50 [26], Hana Lišková 72.05 [33], Marcela Váchová 71.95 [35]) — 365.00

6. ROM (Elena Ceampelea 73.05 [18], Alina Goreac 72.25 [30], Anca Grigoraş 72.10 [31], Elisabeta Turcu 71.20 [44], Paula Ion 71.10 [46], Marcela Păunescu 70.50 [55]) — 360.70

7. JPN (Miyuki Matsuhisa 72.50 [26], Takato Hasegawa 72.00 [34], Eiko Hirashima 71.95 [35], Kayoko Saka 71.80 [40], Kazue Hanyu 71.30 [43], Toshiko Miyamoto 70.000 [60]) — 359.75

8. GER (Uta Schorn 72.10 [31], Jutta Oltersdorf 71.95 [35], Andrea Niederheide 71.10 [46], Angelika Kern 70.95 [48], Ulrike Weyh 70.85 [50], Ingrid Santer 68.85 [76]) — 357.95

1976 Montreal T: 12, N: 12, D: 7.19.

TOTAL PTS.

1. SOV (Nelli Kim 78.25 [2], Lyudmila Turischeva 78.25 [2], Olga Korbut 77.95 [5], Elvira Saadi 77.45 [7], Maria Filatova 77.05 [9], Svetlana Grozdova 77.05 [9]) — 466.00

2. ROM (Nadia Comăneci 79.05 [1], Teodora Ungureanu 78.05 [4], Mariana Constantin 76.75 [14], Anca Grigoraş 76.70 [15], Gabriela Truşcă 76.10 [18], Georgeta Gabor 75.70 [21]) — 462.35

3. GDR (Gitta Escher 77.60 [6], Marion Kische 77.20 [8], Kerstin Gerschau 77.00 [12], Angelika Hellmann 76.90 [13], Steffi Kräker 75.70 [21], Carola Dombeck 74.90 [33]) — 459.30

4. HUN (Márta Egervári 77.05 [9], Kriszta Medveczky 76.15 [17], Margit Tóth 76.05 [19], Éva Ovári 75.40 [25], Mária Lövei 75.15 [20], Márta Kelemen 74.65 [34]) — 454.45

5. CZE (Anna Pohludková 76.40 [16], Ingrid Holkovičova 75.60 [23], Jana Knopová 75.10 [28], Eva Porádková 75.05 [29], Drahomira Smoliková 75.05 [29], Alena Černáková 74.55 [40]) — 451.75

6. USA (Kimberly Chace 75.45 [24], Debra Willcox 75.05 [29], Leslie Wolfsberger 74.65 [34], Colleen Casey 74.50 [41], Carrie Englert 74.40 [42], Doris Howard 74.15 [46]) — 448.20

7. GER (Andrea Bieger 75.95 [20], Petra Kurbjuweit 74.60 [36], Jutta Oltersdorf 74.60 [36], Traudi Schubert 73.60 [55], Uta Schorn 73.55 [56], Beate Renschler 73.25 [59]) — 445.55

8. JPN (Satoko Okazaki 75.30 [26], Miyuki Hironaki 75.00 [32], Nobue Yamazaki 73.85 [50], Chieko Kikkawa 73.65 [53], Sakiko Nozawa 73.45 [57], Kyoko Mano 72.80 [65]) — 444.05

1980 Moscow T: 8, N: 8, D: 7.23.

TOTAL PTS.

1. SOV (Natalya Shaposhnikova 79.15 [2], Yelena Davydova 79.00 [5], Nelli Kim 78.95 [6], Maria Filatova 78.80 [7], Stella Zakharova 78.75 [8], Yelena Naimushina 78.40 [12]) — 394.90

2. ROM (Emilia Eberle 79.10 [3], Nadia Comăneci 79.05 [4], Rodica Dunca 78.50 [10], Melita Rühn 78.30 [13], Cristina Grigoraş 78.00 [15], Dumitrita Turner 77.25 [22]) — 393.50

3. GDR (Maxi Gnauck 79.35 [1], Katharina Rensch 78.55 [9], Steffi Kräker 78.50 [10], Birgit Süss 77.90 [17], Silvia Hindorff 77.35 [21], Karola Sube 77.20 [23]) — 392.55

4. CZE (Eva Marečková 78.05 [14], Jana Labáková 77.85 [18], Katarina Šarišská 77.55 [19], Dana Brydlová 77.05 [26], Anita Sauerová 76.05 [33], Radke Zemanova 76.05 [33]) — 388.80

5. HUN (Erika Csányi 77.50 [29], Erika Flander 77.20 [23], Márta Egervári 76.50 [27], Lenke Almási — 384.30

76.25 [29], Éva Óvári 76.25 [29], Erzsébet Hanti 75.35 [37])

		TOTAL PTS.
6. BUL	(Silvia Topalova 77.20 [23], Galina Marinova 76.50 [27], Krassimira Toneva 76.25 [29], Kamelia Eftimova 75.60 [35], Dimitrinka Filipova 75.50 [36], Antoaneta Rahneva 74.35 [41])	382.10
7. POL	(Lucja Matraszek-Chydzińska 76.15 [32], Malgorzata Majza 75.20 [38], Anita Jokiel 74.95 [39], Wieslawa Zelaskowska 74.30 [42], Agata Jaroszek 73.65 [43], Katarzyna Snopko 73.45 [45])	376.25
8. PRK	(Choe Jong-sil 74.85 [40], Sin Myong-ok 72.50 [45], Kang Myong-suk 72.35 [48], Kim Chun-son 71.40 [52], Choe Myong-hui 71.20 [54], Lo Ok-sil 70.50 [59])	364.05

1984 Los Angeles T: 16, N: 16, D: 8.1.

		TOTAL PTS.
1. ROM	(Ecaterina Szabó 78.12 [2], Laura Cutina 78.40 [3], Simona Păuca 78.05 [7], Cristina Grigoraş 77.90 [8], Miháela Stănulet 77.70 [10], Lavinia Agache 77.60 [11])	392.02
2. USA	(Mary Lou Retton 79.05 [1], Julianne McNamara 78.40 [3], Kathy Johnson 78.10 [6], Michelle Dusserre 77.55 [12], Tracee Talavera 77.10 [16], Pamela Bileck 76.80 [17])	391.20
3. CHN	(Ma Yanhong 78.20 [5], Wu Jiani 77.75 [9], Chen Yongyan 77.35 [13], Zhou Ping 77.35 [13], Zhou Qiurui 76.50 [19], Huang Qun 76.30 [21])	388.60
4. GER	(Elke Heine 76.55 [18], Anja Wilhelm 76.45 [20], Astrid Beckers 75.25 [29], Angela Golz 74.85 [31], Brigitta Lehmann 74.85 [31], Heike Schwarm 74.85 [31])	379.15
5. CAN	(Andrea Thomas 75.85 [23], Bonnie Wittmeier 75.85 [23], Anita Botnen 75.55 [27], Gigi Zosa 75.40 [28], Jessica Tudos 74.75 [36], Kelly Brown 73.50 [50])	378.90
6. JPN	(Maiko Morio 75.90 [22], Noriko Mochizuki 75.70 [26], Tokie Kawase 74.85 [31], Chihiro Oyagi 74.85 [31], Ayami Yukimori 73.90 [45], Sae Watanabe 73.75 [47])	376.75
7. GBR	(Natalie Davies 75.05 [30], Amanda Harrison 74.55 [38], Kathleen Williams 74.45 [39], Hayley Price 74.05 [43], Lisa Young 74.05 [43], Sally Larner 73.60 [48])	373.85
8. SWI	(Romi Kessler 77.35 [13], Susi Latanzio 74.40 [41], Natalie Seiler 74.15 [42], Monika Beer 73.20 [51], Bettina Ernst 73.20 [51], Marisa Jervella 72.55 [58])	373.50

As the winners of eight consecutive Olympic titles, the Soviet women's team would have been the overwhelming favorites in Los Angeles had they not been prevented from competing by their government's boycott.

1988 Seoul T: 12, N: 12, D: 9.21.

		TOTAL PTS.
1. SOV	(Yelena Shushunova 79.675 [1], Svetlana Boginskaya 79.40 [3], Natalija Lascenova 78.90 [5], Svetlana Baitova 78.425 [13], Yelena Shevchenko 78.35 [14], Olha Strazheva 68.175 [85])	395.475
2. ROM	(Daniela Silivaş 79.575 [2], Gabriela Potorac 78.925 [4], Aurelia Dobre 78.615 [6], Celestina Popa 78.575 [10], Eugenia Golea 77.875 [18], Camelia Voinea 77.775 [22])	394.125
3. GDR	(Dagmar Kersten 78.65 [8], Dörte Thümmler 78.55 [11], Ulrike Klotz 78.275 [16], Gabriele Fähnrich 77.625 [25], Betti Schieferdecker 77.45 [30], Martina Jentsch 38.25 [87])	390.875
4. USA	(Phoebe Mills 78.675 [6], Brandy Johnson 78.55 [11], Kelly Garrison-Steves 77.825 [21], Theresa Spivey 77.45 [30], Chelle Stack 77.40 [32], Melissa Marlowe 76.85 [46])	390.575
5. BUL	(Diana Dudeva 78.65 [8], Deliana Vodenicharova 78.325 [15], Boriana Stoyanova 77.95 [17], Ivelina Raikova 77.85 [20], Maria Kartalova 77.25 [35], Khrabrina Khrabova 76.025 [62])	390.550
6. CHN	(Chen Cuiting 77.875 [18], Fan Di 77.475 [28], Wang Wenjing 77.40 [32], Wang Huiying 77.35 [34], Ma Ying 77.025 [41], Wang Xiaoyan 76.925 [44])	388.400
7. CZE	(Iveta Poloková 77.65 [23], Hana Řičná 77.175 [38], Alena Dřevjaná 76.975 [43], Ivona Krmelová 76.725 [49], Martina Velisková 76.60 [52], Jana Vejrková 76.175 [58])	386.150
8. HUN	(Eszter Óváry 77.50 [26], Andréa Ladányi 77.25 [35], Beáta Storczer 77.25 [35], Zsuzsanna Csisztu 76.775 [47], Zsuzsanna Miskó 76.275 [56], Ágnes Miskó 38.15 [88])	385.625

The Soviet women overcame the embarrassment of losing the 1987 World Championships to the Romanians by easily continuing their Olympic undefeated streak.

Although the race for gold and silver was uneventful, controversy emerged in the battle for bronze when the East Germans found themselves facing unexpectedly stiff challenges from the U.S. and Bulgaria. The problem arose during the compulsory round while the American women were performing on the uneven bars. It was the responsibility of the U.S. alternate, Rhonda Faehn, to remove the springboard that competing gymnasts used to mount the bars. After Kelly Garrison-Steves had mounted, Faehn took hold of the springboard. But instead of climbing down from the podium, the competition platform, to the bench, she withdrew to the edge of the podium and watched Garrison-Steves go through her routine.

Ellen Berger, the East German president of the technical committee of the International Gymnastics Federation, immediately pointed out that Faehn's presence on the podium was an infraction of the rules and imposed a penalty of five tenths of a point. To apply this rarely enforced rule was petty, but technically correct. Unfortunately, as it turned out, the deduction cost the U.S. the bronze medal—they lost it to the East Germans by three tenths of a point.

U.S. coach Béla Karolyi was furious. He referred to Berger as a "cow" and called the ruling against the U.S. "a Communist plot."

International politics undoubtedly influenced the controversial decision; however, the ruling probably involved another factor of a more personal nature. Four years earlier at the Los Angeles Olympics, Béla Karolyi had jumped the press barricade to embrace his pupil, Mary Lou Retton. Ellen Berger, who was the head of the technical committee at that meet as well, reminded Karolyi that he was not a member of the U.S. coaching squad and was not allowed to be on the competition floor. She warned U.S. team officials that if Karolyi appeared on the floor again, she would enforce the rules and deduct three-tenths of a point from Retton's score. When U.S. head coach Don Peters told Karolyi of Berger's threat, he replied, "She doesn't have the guts to do it here with 10,000 screaming Americans."

Karolyi, who had been observed practicing his jump over the barricade the night before the competition, hopped over again on the night after he had been warned, when Retton completed the vault that won her the All-Around gold medal. Karolyi was right about Berger: she didn't penalize Retton three-tenths of a point, a penalty that would have cost her the gold medal, not in front of 10,000 screaming Americans. But four years later, Berger got her revenge on Karolyi and six young women were the victims.

1992 Barcelona T: 12, N: 12, D: 7.28.

			TOTAL PTS.
1.	SOV	(Svetlana Boginskaya 79.287 [2], Tatyana Lysenko 79.122 [5], Rozalya Galiyeva 78.886 [8], Tatyana Gutsu 78.848 [9], Yelena Grudneva 78.411 [22], Oksana Chusovitina 78.111 [30])	395.666
2.	ROM	(Cristina Bontaş 79.211 [3], Lavinia Miloşovici 79.198 [4], Gina Gogean 78.886 [7], Vanda Hădărean 78.761 [11], Maria Neculişă 78.623 [17], Mirela Paşca 78.585 [19])	395.079
3.	USA	(Shannon Miller 79.311 [1], Elizabeth Okino 78.998 [6], Kim Zmeskal 78.749 [12], Kerri Strug 78.735 [14], Dominique Dawes 78.360 [26], Wendy Bruce 78.161 [28])	394.704
4.	CHN	(Yang Bo 78.737 [13], Lu Li 78.734 [15], Li Yifang 78.598 [18], Li Li 78.536 [20], He Xuemei 78.198 [27], Zhang Xia 77.773 [35])	392.941
5.	SPA	(Cristina Fraguas Sánchez 78.436 [21], Sonia Fraguas Sánchez 78.147 [29], Alicia Fernández 78.062 [31], Eva Rueda Bravo 78.035 [32], Ruth Rollán Gonzealez 77.397 [42], Silvia Martínez Albalat 77.111 [49])	391.428
6.	HUN	(Henrietta Ónodi 78.698 [16], Andrea Molnár 78.386 [23], Bernadette Balázs 76.898 [54], Kinga Horváth 76.836 [55], Ildikó Balog 75.624 [81], Krisztina Molnár 67.859 [89])	388.602
7.	AUS	(Lisa Read 77.935 [33], Monique Allen 77.548 [39], Kylie Shadbolt 77.196 [46], Jane Warrilow 77.049 [51], Julie-Anne Monico 76.360 [68], Brooke Gysen 76.311 [69])	387.502
8.	FRA	(Marie Angeline Colson 77.661 [36], Virginie Machado 77.611 [37], Chloe Maigre 77.284 [43], Karine Boucher 76.573 [62], Karine Charlier 76.148 [71], Jenny Rolland 75.422 [84])	386.052

The Barcelona Olympics marked the tenth and final time that the republics of the former Soviet Union would compete as one team. Despite a spirited challenge from the Romanians, they kept their winning streak alive, earning their tenth straight set of gold medals.

RHYTHMIC ALL-AROUND

In rhythmic gymnastics, thin young women perform 60- to 90-second routines using various accessories: hoop, rope, clubs, ball, and ribbon. Only four of the five accessories are chosen for each Olympic competition. Each routine is scored by ten judges, five for composition and five for execution. Acrobatic feats, such as cartwheels, flips, and handsprings, are not allowed. The accessories, or apparatus as they are known officially, may be any color except gold, silver, and bronze. The All-Around competition begins with a qualifying round. The 20 best gymnasts take part in a semifinal round. The ten best gymnasts in the semifinals advance to the final. Scores are not carried forward from round to round. Competitors must be at least 15 years old. Their dress is strictly regulated. Gymnasts must wear leotards of nontransparent material without decoration or trim. The cut of the leotard must not go beyond the fold of the crotch, the neckline in the back cannot extend beyond the center point between the shoulder blades, and the neckline of the front must be "proper."

In the team competition, all five apparatuses are used. Each team consists of three or four gymnasts. Two gymnasts from each team perform with each apparatus.

1896–1980 not held

1984 Los Angeles C: 33, N: 20, D: 8.11.

			HOOP		BALL		CLUBS		RIBBON		TOTAL PTS.
1.	Lori Fung	CAN	14.525	(3)	14.425	(4)	14.6	(2)	14.4	(2)	57.95
2.	Doina Stăiculescu	ROM	14.55	(1)	14.7	(1)	14.725	(1)	13.925	(9)	57.90

		HOOP		BALL		CLUBS		RIBBON		TOTAL PTS.
3. Regina Weber	GER	14.55	(1)	14.425	(4)	14.35	(5)	14.375	(3)	57.70
4. Alina Drăgan	ROM	14.475	(4)	14.5	(2)	14.525	(3)	13.875	(11)	57.375
5. Milena Reljin	YUG	14.175	(10)	14.375	(6)	14.275	(7)	14.425	(1)	57.25
6. Marta Canton	SPA	14.275	(7)	14.2	(9)	14.35	(5)	14.125	(4)	56.95
7. Giulia Staccioli	ITA	14.45	(5)	14.25	(8)	14.25	(8)	13.825	(14)	56.775
8. Hiroko Yamasaki	JPN	14.3	(6)	14.35	(7)	14.175	(10)	13.85	(12)	56.675

There were few winners at the 1984 Olympics more unexpected than 21-year-old Lori Fung of Vancouver, Canada. Even with the absence of the boycotting nations, in particular the Bulgarians, Fung was a rank outsider, having finished 23rd at the 1983 World Championships. However, in the interim, she had studied hard in Romania with gold medal favorite Doina Stăiculescu. In Los Angeles, while others were dropping their balls, or having their ribbons disrupted by unpredictable currents from the air conditioning system, or suffering the exposure of their bra straps (an automatic deduction), Fung performed smoothly and went home with the gold medal.

1988 Seoul C: 35, N: 21, D: 9.30.

		HOOP		ROPE		CLUBS		RIBBON		TOTAL PTS.
1. Marina Lobach	SOV/BLR	15.0	(1)	15.0	(1)	15.0	(1)	15.0	(1)	60.00
2. Adriana Dunavska	BUL	15.0	(1)	15.0	(1)	14.95	(2)	15.0	(1)	59.95
3. Oleksandra Tymoshenko	SOV/UKR	15.0	(1)	15.0	(1)	14.875	(3)	15.0	(1)	59.875
4. Bianka Panova	BUL	15.0	(1)	15.0	(1)	14.775	(4)	14.95	(4)	59.725
5. María Isabel Lloret	SPA	14.725	(5)	14.75	(5)	14.7	(6)	14.725	(6)	58.90
6. Andrea Sinkó	HUN	14.65	(7)	14.75	(5)	14.725	(5)	14.65	(8)	58.775
7. Teresa Folga	POL	14.55	(10)	14.675	(9)	14.6	(13)	14.8	(5)	58.625
8. Diana Schmiemann	GER	14.6	(8)	14.65	(11)	14.7	(6)	14.65	(8)	58.60

Lobach, who had never before placed higher than fourth in a major international competition, was awarded a perfect score for each of her four routines in both the preliminary and the final. Nevertheless, she almost lost the gold medal when she came within one second of exceeding the time limit during her clubs performance. Fortunately, her pianist, Anatoly Vekshin, began playing faster at the end of the routine and Lobach finished just as the gong sounded.

Seventh-place finisher Teresa Folga of Kraków won the Miss Olympic Village beauty contest. In the words of the *Korea Herald*, Folga "outshined other contestants with her beautiful hair, slim and attractive body and eloquent conversation skills." She had been voted a similar prize by journalists attending the 1987 rhythmic world championships.

1992 Barcelona C: 43, N: 25, D: 8.8.

		HOOP		ROPE		CLUBS		BALL		TOTAL PTS.
1. Oleksandra Tymoshenko	UKR	14.812	(1)	14.85	(1)	14.85	(1)	14.525	(2)	59.037
2. Carolina Pascual Gracia	SPA	14.5	(3)	14.45	(2)	14.562	(2)	14.587	(1)	58.100
3. Oksana Skaldina	UKR	14.587	(2)	14.325	(4)	14.487	(3)	14.512	(3)	57.912
4. Carmen Acedo Jorge	SPA	14.337	(4)	14.262	(6)	14.275	(5)	14.35	(4)	57.225
5. Maria Petrova	BUL	14.225	(6)	14.312	(5)	14.325	(4)	14.225	(6)	57.087
6. Irina Deleanu	ROM	13.8	(12)	14.387	(3)	14.262	(6)	14.162	(7)	56.612
7. Joanna Bodak	POL	14.112	(7)	14.0	(9)	14.25	(7)	14.112	(8)	56.475
8. Lenk Oulehlová	CZE	14.0	(9)	14.175	(7)	13.862	(10)	14.1	(9)	56.137

Rhythmic gymnastics has a reputation as one of the joke sports of the Olympics, included in the program to please a limited constituency. The International Gymnastics Federation did not help matters when they approved an unusually ridiculous format for the 1992 Games. Rather than choosing the gymnasts with the highest scores in the qualifying round to advance to the final, they decided that the six best would qualify for the final, along with the top 12 for each apparatus. Because the medals were decided on the basis of total score with all four apparatus, this meant that nine of the 17 finalists were performing with only one to three apparatus and had no chance to win.

Tymoshenko, although Ukrainian, was born and raised in Omsk, in Siberia. The competition had more than its share of controversy. Skaldina, convinced that Pascual had beaten her out for the silver medal only because the judges were trying to please the Spanish hosts, refused to acknowledge her rival at the medal ceremony. But Skaldina, although the defending world champion, was lucky to be at the Olympics at all. On June 8, she placed only fifth at the European Championships (won by Maria Petrova) and, with only two entrants allowed for each nation, it appeared that she would lose her spot to the up-and-coming Siberian Oksana Kostina. Three and a half months after the Olympics, Kostina won the world championships, but on February 11, 1993, she was killed in a car crash. She was 17 years old.

As for European champion Petrova, she would have placed fourth at the Olympics, but while she was performing with her hoop, her zipper broke and the back of her leotard popped open. Naturally she was penalized two-tenths of a point, which dropped her back to fifth place.

RHYTHMIC TEAM

This event will be held for the first time in 1996.

Discontinued Event
TEAM EXERCISE WITH PORTABLE APPARATUS

1952 Helsinki T: 16, N: 16, D: 7.24.

			TOTAL PTS.
1.	SWE	(Karin Lindberg, Gun Röring, Evy Berggren, Göta Pettersson, Ann-Sofi Colling-Pettersson, Ingrid Sandahl, Hjördis Nordin, Vanja Blomberg)	74.2
2.	SOV	(Maria Horokhovska, Nina Bocharova, Galina Minaicheva, Galina Urbanovich, Pelageya Danilova, Galina Shamrai, Medeya Dzchugeli, Yekaterina Kalinchuk)	73.0
3.	HUN	(Margit Korondi, Ágnes Keleti, Edit Perényi-Weckinger, Olga Tass, Erzsébet Gulyás, Mária Zalai-Kövi, Andrea Bodó, Irén Daruházi-Karcscics)	71.6

			TOTAL PTS.
4.	GER	(Irma Walther, Hanna Grages, Elisabeth Ostermeier, Wolfgard Voss, Inge Sedelmeier, Lydia Zeitlhofer, Brigitte Kiesler, Hilde Koop)	71.2
5.	FIN	(Raili Tuominen, Vappu Salonen, Arja Lehtinen, Raili Hoviniemi, Pirkko Vilppunen, Maila Nisula, Pirkko Pyykönen, Raija Simola)	70.6
6.	CZE	(Eva Vechtová, Alena Chadimová, Jana Rabasová, Boẑena Srncová, Hana Bobková, Matylda Ŝinová, Vera Vančurová, Alena Reichová)	70.0
6.	HOL	(Helena Gerrietsen, Huiberdina Krul van der Nolk van Gogh, Johanna Cox-Ladru, Catharina Selbach, Jacoba Kampen, Johanna Ros, Bertha Selbach, Anna Simon)	70.0
8.	YUG	(Sonja Roẑman, Tanja Ẑutić, Anka Drinic, Nada Spasic, Milica Roẑman, Ada Smolnikar, Marija Ivandekič, Tereza Kočiš)	69.2

1956 Melbourne T: 9, N: 9, D: 12.7.

			TOTAL PTS.
1.	HUN	(Ágnes Keleti, Margit Korondi, Olga Tass, Andrea Bodó, Aliz Kertész, Erzsébet Gulyás-Köteles)	75.2
2.	SWE	(Ann-Sofi Colling-Pettersson, Karin Lindberg, Eva Rönström, Evy Berggren, Doris Hedberg, Maude Karlén)	74.2
3.	POL	(Helena Rakoczy, Natalia Kot, Dorota Jokiel, Danuta Nowak-Stachow, Barbara Ślizowska, Lidia Szczerbińska)	74.0
3.	SOV	(Tamara Manina, Larysa Latynina, Sofia Muratova, Lidiya Kalinina, Polina Astakhova, Lyudmila Yegorova)	74.0
5.	ROM	(Georgeta Hurmuzache, Sonia Iovan, Elena Leuştean, Elena Mărgărit, Elena Săcălici, Emilia Vătăşoiu)	73.4
6.	JPN	(Mitsuka Ikeda, Keiko Tanaka, Kazuko Sogabe, Kyoko Kubota, Suzuko Seki, Shizuko Sakashita)	73.2
7.	CZE	(Eva Bosáková, [Vechtová], Hana Marejková, Matylda Ŝinová, Vera Drazdiková, Alena Reichová, Miraslava Brdičková)	73.0
8.	ITA	(Miranda Cicognani, Luciana Reali, Rosella Cicognani, Elisa Calsi, Elena Lagorara, Luciana Lagorara)	72.8

TEAM HANDBALL

Team handball is an exciting, fast-paced sport that deserves greater popularity. It is a hybrid of basketball and soccer: the ball is moved down the court by passing and dribbling, as in basketball, but instead of being shot into a basket, it is thrown past a goalie and into a goal, as in soccer. There are seven players on a team. Besides goalies, the most common positions are big shooters (usually tall and good jumpers, like forwards in basketball), middle backcourt players (playmakers who direct the offense), wings (smaller, faster players who shoot from difficult angles), and circle runners (large and aggressive players who set screens and picks for other shooters as well as shooting themselves).

Unlike basketball, a player may take three steps before and after dribbling, but he or she may not hold the ball for more than three seconds without dribbling or passing.

A handball court is 40 meters (131 feet 2 inches) long and 20 meters (65 feet 7 inches) wide. The goals are three meters (9 feet 10 inches) wide and two meters (6 feet 7 inches) high. The goal area extends six meters (19 feet 8 inches) from the goal. No player other than the goalie may enter the goal area. However, a player may take off outside the goal area and leap toward the goal as long as he releases a shot before landing. Clearly, this is a sport made to order for American basketball players. Fortunately for the rest of the world, Americans have not yet discovered team handball and the cumulative record of United States men's teams in the Olympics is a dismal 2 wins, 22 losses, and 1 tie.

Penalty throws, usually awarded when a player is fouled in the act of shooting, are taken from 7 meters (22 feet 9 inches) out, with only the goalie between the shooter and the goal.

Games are divided into two 30-minute halves. In preliminary matches, ties are allowed to stand. Beginning with the semifinals, a ten-minute overtime period is played. If the game is still tied, the teams play for ten more minutes. If the score is still tied, the match is decided by penalty throws.

MEN

1896–1932 not held

1936 Berlin T: 6, N: 6, D: 8.14.

			W	L	PF	PA
1.	GER	(Heinz Körvers, Arthur Knautz, Willy Bandholz, Hans Keiter, Wilhelm Brinkmann, Georg Dascher, Erich Hermann, Hans Theilig, Helmut Berthold, Alfred Klingler, Fritz Fromm, Carl Kreutzberg, Heinrich Keimig, Wilhelm Müller, Kurt Dossin, Rudolf Stahl, Hermann Hansen, Fritz Spengler, Edgar Reinhardt, Günther Ortmann, Wilhelm Baumann, Helmuth Braselmann)	5	0	96	19
2.	AUT	(Alois Schnabel, Franz Bartl, Johann Tauscher, Otto Licha, Emil Juracka, Leopold Wohlrab, Jaroslav Volak, Alfred Schmalzer, Ludwig Schubert, Ferdinand Kiefler, Anton Perwein, Fritz Maurer, Franz Brunner, Fritz Wurmböck, Siegfried Purner, Hans Zehetner, Hans Houschka, Franz Bistricky, Franz Berghammer, Walter Reisp, Josef Krejci, Siegfried Powolny)	4	1	60	29
3.	SWI	(Willy Gysi, Robert Studer, Erich Schmitt, Rolf Faes, Erland Herkenrath, Burkhard Gantenbein, Werner Meyer, Max Streib, Georg Mischon, Ernst Hufschmid, Eugen Seiterle, Edy Schmid, Max Blösch, Werner Scheurmann, Willy Schäfer, Willy Hufschmid, Rudolf Wirz)	2	3	33	52
4.	HUN	(Antal Ujváry, János Koppány, István Serényi, Lajos Kutasi, Frigyes Rakosi, Lörinc Galgóczy, Ferenc Cziráki, Gyula Takács, Miklós Fodor, Endre Salgó, Sándor Cséffai, Tibor Máté, Antal Benda, Imre Páli, Ferenc Velkei, Sándor Szomori)	1	4	25	64
5.	ROM	(Ştefan Zoller, Carol Haffer, Ludovic Haffer, Bruno Holtzträger, Ştefan Höchsmann, Robert Speck, Gheorghe Hertog, Frederic Halmen, Wilhelm Kirschmer, Wilhelm Heidel, Günter Schörsten, Peter Fasci, Ion Zikeli, Vilhelm Zaharias, Stadter Herman)	1	2	19	27
6.	USA	(Henry Oehler, Charles Dauner, Alfred Roseco, Herbert Carl Oehmichen, Edmund Schallenberg, William Ahlemeyer, Gerald Yantz, Joe Kaylor, Willy Renz, Walter Bowden,	0	3	6	46

Fred Leinweber, Edward John Hagen, Otto Oehler, Philip Schupp)
Final: GER 10–6 AUT
3rd Place: SWI 10–5 HUN
5th Place: ROM 10–3 USA

Field handball was invented in Germany, so when the Germans were given the opportunity to add one sport to the 1936 Olympics, they chose handball. In 1936 the game was played outdoors with 11 men on a side. Not surprisingly, Germany dominated the tournament, defeating the United States 29–1, Hungary 22–0 and 19–6, and Switzerland 16–6. Austria put up the best fight, trailing only 8–6 with five minutes to play.

1948–1968 not held

1972 Munich T: 16, N: 16, D: 9.11.

		W	L	T	PF	PA
1. YUG	(Abaz Arslanagić, Zoran Živković, Miroslav Pribanić, Hrvoje Horvat, Djoko Lavrnić, Zdravko Miljak, Slobodan Mišković, Branislav Pokrajać, Nebojša Popović, Milan Lazarević, Milorad Karalić, Albin Vidović, Zdenko Zorbo, Petar Fajdrić)	7	0	0	140	105
2. CZE	(Ivan Satrapa, Vladimir Jarý, Jiři Kavan, Vladimir Haber, Jindřich Krepindl, Ladislav Beneš, Vincent Lafko, František Bruna, Petr Pospišil, Jaroslav Konecny, Pavel Mikes, Jaroslav Škarvan, František Králik, Andrej Lubósik, Zdenek Skara, Arnošt Limčik)	3	3	1	114	99
3. ROM	(Cornel Penu, Gavril Kicsid, Valentin Samungi, Ştefan Birtalan, Cristian Gatu, Roland Gunesch, Simion Schöbel, Gheorghe Gruia, Constantin Tudosie, Alexandru Dincă, Werner Stöckl, Dan Marin, Ghiță Licu, Radu Voina, Adrian Cosma)	6	1	0	111	92
4. GDR	(Reiner Frieske, Peter Randt, Klaus Langhoff, Reiner Ganschow, Wolfgang Lakenmacher, Rainer Würdig, Jürgen Hildebrandt, Udo Röhrig, Wolfgang Böhme, Harry Zörnack, Josef Rose, Siegfried Voigt, Klaus Weiss, Rainer Zimmerman, Horst Jankhöfer, Peter Larisch)	5	2	0	103	85
5. SOV	(Nikolai Semenov, Mykhalo Ischenko, Aleksander Panov, Vladimir Maksimov, Valentin Kulev, Vassily Ilyin, Anatoly Shevchenko, Yuri Klimov, Mikhail Lutsenko, Oleksander Reza-	3	1	3	91	84
	nov, Valery Gassi, Albert Oganezov, Yuri Lahutyn, Ivan Ussatiy, Yan Vilson)					
6. GER	(Klaus Kater, Uwe Rathjen, Herwig Ahrendsen, Wolfgang Braun, Peter Bucher, Diethard Finkelmann, Klaus Lange, Herbert Lübking, Heiner Möller, Hans-Peter Neuhaus, Herbert Rogge, Herbert Wehnert, Hans-Jürgen Bode, Jochen Feldhoff, Josef Karrer, Klaus Westebbe)	2	4	1	98	106
7. SWE	(Sten Olsson, Frank Ström, Björn Andersson, Dan Eriksson, Lennart Eriksson, Johan Fischerström, Benny Johansson, Jan Jonsson, Michael Koch, Thomas Persson, Goeran Hard, Af Segerstad, Bertil Söderberg)	2	2	3	93	92
8. HUN	(József Horváth, Sándor Kaló, Károly Vass, István Varga, István Szabó, István Marosi, Sándor Vass, Lajos Simó, János Adorján, Sándor Takács, János Stiller, László Szabó)	2	5	0	126	119

Final: YUG 21–16 CZE
3rd Place: ROM 19–16 GDR
5th Place: SOV 17–16 GER
7th Place: SWE 19–18 HUN

With the Olympics back in Germany, team handball was returned to the schedule, but this time there were seven men on a side and the matches were played indoors. The decisive match was the second-round contest between Yugoslavia and world champion Romania. With 15 minutes to play, Milan Lazarević scored to give Yugoslavia a 10–9 lead. Four minutes later Djoko Lavrnić scored again, and Yugoslavia had the first two-goal lead of the game. They built their lead to 14–11 and survived two late goals to win, 14–13. The final against Czechoslovakia was anticlimatic; Yugoslavia led 12–5 at halftime and 18–8 with 13 minutes to play.

1976 Montreal T: 11, N: 11, D: 7.28.

		W	L	T	PF	PA
1. SOV	Mykhalo Ishchenko, Anatoly Fedyukin, Vladimir Maksimov, Serhei Kushniryuk, Vassily Ilyin, Vladimir Kravzov, Yuri Klimov, Yuri Lahutyn, Aleksandr Anpilogov, Yevgeny Chernyshov, Valery Gassy, Mykola Tomyn, Yuri Kidyayev, Oleksander Rezanov)	5	1	0	130	92
2. ROM	(Cornel Penu, Gavril Kicsid, Cristian Gatu, Cezar Drăgănită, Radu Voina, Roland Gunesch, Alexandru Fölker, Ştefan Birtalan, Adrian Cosma, Constantin Tudosie, Nicolae Munteanu,	3	1	1	106	90

	W	L	T	PF	PA
Werner Stöckl, Mircea Grabovschi, Ghiță Licu)					
3. POL (Andrzej Szymczak, Piotr Cieśla, Zdzislaw Antczak, Zygfryd Kuchta, Jerzy Klempel, Janusz Brzozowski, Ryszard Przbysz, Jerzy Melcer, Andrzej Sokolowski, Jan Gmyrek, Henryk Rozmiarek, Alfred Kaluźiński, Wlodzimierz Zieliński, Mieczyslaw Wojczak)	4	1	0	101	89
4. GER (Manfred Hofmann, Jürgen Hahn, Günter Böttcher, Kurt Klühspies, Peter Kleibrink, Walter Oepen, Horst Spengler, Gerd Becker, Bernhard Busch, Joachim Deckarm, Rudolf Rauer, Arno Ehret, Heiner Brand, Peter Jaschke)	4	2	0	115	97
5. YUG (Abaz Arslanagić, Vlado Bojović, Ždravko Radjennović, Milorad Karalić, Radisav Pavicević, Žvonimir Serdarusić, Hrvoje Horvat, Branislav Pokrajać, Radivoj Krivokapić, Predrag Timko, Ždravko Miljak, Ždenko Žorko, Nebojsa Popović, Željko Nims)	5	1	0	131	112
6. HUN (Béla Bartalos, Ferenc Buday, Péter Kovács, István Varga, Mihály Süvöltös, István Szilágyi, József Kenyeres, László Janovszki, Károly Vass, Ernö Gubányi, Zsolt Kontra, Gábor Veröci)	2	3	0	111	103
7. CZE (Jan Packa, František Sulc, Ivan Satrapa, Vladimir Jary, Jiři Kavan, Stefan Katusak, Vladimir Haber, Jindrich Krepindl, Jiři Hanzl, Jaroslav Papiernik, Jozef Dobrotka, Bohumil Cepak, Jiři Liska, Pavel Mikes)	2	2	1	110	103
8. DEN (Kay Jorgensen, Palle Jensen, Anders Dahl-Nielsen, Lars Bock, Jorgen Frandsen, Claus From, Thomas Pazyj, Bent Larsen, Soren Andersen, Morten Christensen, Henrik Jacobsgaard, Johnny Pechnik, Thor Munkager, Jesper Petersen)	2	4	0	113	127

Final: SOV 19–15 ROM
3rd Place: POL 21–18 GER
5th Place: YUG 21–19 HUN
7th Place: CZE 25–21 DEN

Again Romania entered the Olympics as defending world champions and again they were unable to win the tournament. They survived the preliminary pool undefeated to qualify for the final. The other pool was won by the Soviet Union despite a 20–18 loss to Yugoslavia,

A typical scene from a team handball match.

which was unlucky to finish fifth considering they lost only one match—to West Germany, 18–17. The U.S.S.R. took control of the final early, led 10–6 at halftime, and was never behind.

1980 Moscow T: 12, N: 12, D: 7.30.

	W	L	T	PF	PA
1. GDR (Siegfried Voigt, Günter Dreibrodt, Peter Rost, Klaus Gruner, Hans-Georg Beyer, Dietmar Schmidt, Hartmut Krüger, Lothar Döring, Ernst Gerlach, Frank-Michael Wahl, Ingolf Wiegert, Wieland Schmidt, Rainer Höft, Hans-Georg Jaunich)	5	0	1	131	114
2. SOV (Mykhalo Ishchenko, Viktor Makhorin, Serhei Kushniryuk, Aleksandr Karshakevich, Vladimir Kravzov, Vladimir Belov, Anatoly Fedyukin, Aleksandr Anpilogov, Yevgeny Chernyshov, Aleksei Zhuk, Mykola Tomyn, Yuri Kidyayev, Vladimir Repyev, Voldemaras Novickis)	4	2	0	156	98
3. ROM (Nicolae Munteanu, Marian Dumitru, Iosif Boroș, Maricel Voinea, Vasile Stîngă, Radu	5	1	0	139	106

Voina, Cezar Drăgăniţa, Cornel
Durău, Ştefan Birtalan, Alexandru Fölker, Neculai Vasilca, Lu-
cian Vasilache, Adrian Cosma,
Claudiu Ionescu)

4. HUN (Béla Bartalos, László Szabó, 3 1 2 114 108
Péter Kovács, Sándor Vass,
János Fodor, István Szilágyi,
József Kenyeres, László Jánov-
szki, Ambrus Lele, Ernö Gubá-
nyi, Zsolt Kontra, Alpár Jegen-
yés, Árpád Pál, Miklós Kovác-
sics)

5. SPA (José Pagoaga, Juan Cabanas, 3 2 1 126 129
Juan Maria Albisu, Vicente Cala-
buig, Juan de la Puente, Leon
López, José Novoa, Juan Uria,
Agustin Milian, Francisco Lo-
pez, Eugenio Serrano, Gregorio
López, Juan de Miguel, Juan
Munoz)

6. YUG (Zlatan Arnautović, Momir Rnić, 4 2 0 156 116
Enver Koso, Drago Jovović,
Stjepan Obran, Jasmin Mrkonja,
Peter Mahne, Pavle Jurina,
Goran Nerić, Jovica Cvetković,
Velibor Nenadić, Adnan Dizdar,
Mile Isaković, Jovica Elezović)

7. POL (Andrzej Kącki, Zbigniew Gaw- 3 2 1 146 119
lik, Piotr Czaczka, Marek Panas,
Jerzy Klempel, Janusz Brz-
ozowski, Zbigniew Tluczyński,
Grzegorz Kosma, Daniel
Waszkiewicz, Ryszard Jedliń-
ski, Henryk Rozmiarek, Alfred
Kaluziński, Jerzy Garpiel, Mieczyslaw Wojczak)

8. SWI (Edi Wickli, Ernst Zuellig, Robert 2 4 0 132 121
Jehle, Roland Brand, Max
Schaer, Peter Haag, Walter
Müller, Rudolf Weber, Hans
Huber, Konrad Affolter, Hans-
peter Lutz, Ugo Jametti, Peter
Jehle, Martin Ott)

Final: GDR 23–22 SOV
3rd Place: ROM 20–18 HUN
5th Place: SPA 24–23 YUG
7th Place: POL 23–22 SWI

The final was a particularly exciting match, as neither
team ever led by more than two goals. As the clock ran
down, East Germany led 20–19, but Aleksandr
Anpilogov of the U.S.S.R. made a penalty shot with 22
seconds to play and the game went into overtime.
Anpilogov also scored the first goal of the ten-minute
extra period, but the Soviet Union was held scoreless for
the next eight and a half minutes while the Germans
took a 23–21 lead. Anpilogov scored the final goal of the
game with 51 seconds left to play. East Germany's last
point was put in by 23-year-old Hans-Georg Beyer,

whose older brother, Udo, was winning the bronze
medal in the shot put at the exact same time. Two days
later, their sister, Gisela, finished fourth in the discus.
Last-place finisher Kuwait had a tough tournament, including losses of 44–10 to Yugoslavia and 38–11 to the
U.S.S.R.

1984 Los Angeles-Inglewood T: 12, N: 12, D: 8.11.

		W	L	T	PF	PA
1. YUG	(Zlatan Arnautović, Momir Rnić, Veselin Vuković, Milan Kalina, Jovica Elezović, Zdravko Zovko, Branko Strbać, Pavle Jurina, Veselin Vujović, Slobodan Kuzmanovski, Mirko Basić, Dragan Mladenović, Zdravko Radjenović, Mile Isaković)	5	0	1	141	93
2. GER	(Andreas Thiel, Arnulf Meffle, Rüdiger Neitzel, Martin Schwalb, Dirk Rauin, Michael Paul, Thomas Happe, Erhard Wunderlich, Thomas Springel, Klaus Wöller, Jochen Fraatz, Siegfried Roch, Ulrich Roth, Uwe Schwenker, Michael Roth)	5	1	0	131	113
3. ROM	(Nicolae Munteanu, Marian Dumitru, Iosif Boroş, Maricel Voinea, Vasile Stîngă, Gheorghe Dogarescu, Gheorghe Covaciu, Cornel Durău, Alexandru Fölker, Neculai Vasilca, Alexandru Buligan, Vasile Oprea, Mircea Bedivan, Adrian Simion)	5	1	0	143	110
4. DEN	(Mogens Jeppesen, Jens Erik Roepstorff, Anders Dahl-Nielsen, Erik Veje Rasmussen, Keld Nielsen, Klaus Sletting Jensen, Morten Stig Christensen, Carsten Haurum, Hans Henrik Hattesen, Jörgen Gluver, Peter Michael Fenger, Poul Sörensen, Michael Strom, Per Skaarup)	4	2	0	134	122
5. SWE	(Claes Hellgren, Per Öberg, Danny Augustsson, Göran Bengtsson, Christer Magnusson, Per Carlén, Pär Jilsén, Lennarth Ebbinge, Björn Jilsén, Mats Lindau, Sten Sjögren, Rolf Hertzberg, Peter Olofsson, Mats Olsson)	4	2	0	145	134
6. ICE	(Einar Thorvardson, Thorglis Mathiesen, Thorbergur Adalsteinsson, Bjarni Gudmundsson, Jakob Sigurdsson, Sigurdur Gunnarsson, Atli Hilmarsson, Gudmundur Gudmundsson, Kristjan Arason, Thörbjorn Jensson, Jens Einarsson, Sigurdur Sveinsson, Brynjar Kvaran,	3	2	1	126	122

			W	L	T	PF	PA
	Alfred Gíslason, J. Steinar Birgisson)						
7.	SWI	(Martin Ott, Martin Glaser, Jürgen Baetschmann, Peter Weber, Max Schaer, Heinz Karrer, Roland Gassmann, René Barth, Norwin Platzer, Peter Hürlimann, Uwe Mall, Peter Jehle, Max Delhees, Markus Braun)	3	3	0	101	119
8.	SPA	(Pedro Garcia, Juan Javier Cabanas, Juan Munoz, Javier Reino, Juan de la Puente, Cecilio Alonso, Juan Novoa, Juan Uria, Julian Ruiz, Eugenio Serrano, Lorenzo Rico, Rafael Lopez, Jaime Puig, Juan de Miguel)	2	4	0	122	124

Final: YUG 18–17 GER
3rd Place: ROM 23–19 DEN
5th Place: SWE 26–24 ICE
7th Place: SWI 18–17 SPA

West Germany was admitted to the Olympic tournament only after four of the qualifying teams withdrew as part of the Soviet-bloc boycott. Yet the Germans were able to complete their preliminary pool undefeated and advance to the final. There they met the Yugoslavs, who had survived an early 22–22 tie against Iceland and then beaten Romania 19–18 in a crucial matchup of the pre-Olympic favorites. The West Germans never held a lead after the first 12 minutes of the final, but they still clung to a 15–15 tie with 6 minutes remaining. Then Yugoslavia scored three unanswered goals and held on to win 18–17. Yugoslav coach Branislav Pokrajać was one of the players on the 1972 team that won Yugoslavia's other Olympic championship.

1988 Seoul T: 12, N: 12, D: 10.1.

			W	L	T	PF	PA
1.	SOV	(Andrei Lavrov, Aleksandr Tuchkin, Aleksandr Rymanov, Aleksandr Karshakevich, Yuri Nesterov, Georgy Sviridenko, Andrei Tyumentsev, Mikhail Vasilyev, Yuri Shevtsov, Vyacheslav Atavin, Voldemaras Novickis, Igor Chumak, Konstantin Sharovarov)	6	0	0	162	107
2.	KOR	(Yoon Tae-il, Kim Jae-hwan, Sin Young-suk, Park Do-hun, Park Young-dae, Koh Suk-chang, Roh Hyun-suk, Oh Young-ki, Choi Suk-jae, Kang Jae-won, Lee Sang-hyo, Lim Jin-suk)	4	2	0	152	149
3.	YUG	(Momir Rnić, Žlatko Saracević, Iztok Puč, Goran Perkovać, Irfan Smajlagić, Žlatko Portner,	4	1	1	143	132

			W	L	T	PF	PA
	Veselin Vujović, Jozef Holpert, Mirko Basić, Alvaro Nacinović, Slobodan Kuzmanovski, Ermin Velić)						
4.	HUN	(László Hoffmann, József Bordás, Péter Kovács, Mihály Kovács, János Fodor, László Marosi, Mihály Iváncsik, Jacob Sibalin, László Szabó, Géza Tóth, Ottó Csicsai, Imre Bíró, János Gyurka, Tibor Oross)	3	3	0	125	120
5.	SWE	(Mats Olsson, Peder Järphag, Magnus Wislander, Johan Eklund, Ola Lindgren, Per Carlén, Erik Hajas, Per Carlsson, Björn Jilsén, Pär Jilsén, Sten Sjögren, Mats Fransson, Steffan Olsson, Claes Hellgren)	4	2	0	133	109
6.	CZE	(Michal Barda, Josef Škandík, Miroslav Bajgar, Libor Sovadina, Jiří Kotrč, Milan Brestovanský, Milan Folta, František Štika, Tomáš Bártek, Zdeněk Vaněk, Petr Baumruk, Karel Jindřichovský, Jan Novák, Peter Mesiarik)	3	3	0	127	130
7.	GDR	(Peter Hofmann, Stephan Hauck, Peter Pysall, Frank-Michael Wahl, Holger Winselmann, Bernd Metzke, Andreas Neitzel, Rüdiger Borchardt, Jens Fiedler, Mike Fuhrig, Matthias Hahn, Wieland Schmidt, Holger Schneider)	4	2	0	140	129
8.	ICE	(Einar Þorvardarson, Thorgilsóttar Mathiesen, Jakob Sigurdsson, Bjarki Sigurdsson, Karl Thráinsson, Sigurdur Gunnarsson, Alfred Gíslason, Gudmundur Gudmundsson, Páll Ólafsson, Kristján Arason, Geir Sveinsson, Brynjar Kvaran, Sigurdur Sveinsson, Atli Hilmarsson, Gudmundur Hrafnkelsson)	2	3	1	125	133

Final: SOV 32–25 KOR
3rd Place: YUG 27–23 HUN
5th Place: SWE 27–18 CZE
7th Place: GDR 31–29 ICE

The Soviet team, whose players averaged almost 6 feet 4 inches, swept through the tournament. Their closest match was a 22–18 victory over Sweden.

1992 Barcelona T: 12, N: 12, D: 8.8.

			W	L	T	PF	PA
1.	SOV	(Andrei Lavrov, Igor Chumak, Igor Vassiliyev, Yuri Gavrilov, Andrei Barbashinsky, Sergei Bebeshko, Valery Gopin, Vasily	7	0	0	166	137

Kudinov, Mikhail Yakimovich, Oleg Grebnev, Oleg Kiselyev, Talant Duishebayev)

2.	SWE	(Mats Olsson, Tomas Svensson, Magnus Wislander, Ola Lindgren, Per Carlén, Erik Hajas, Magnus Cato, Axel Sjöblad, Robert Andersson, Pierre Thorsson, Steffan Olsson, Magnus Andersson, Robert Hedin, Anders Bäckegren, Patrik Liljestrand, Tommy Suoraniemi)	6	1	0	165	130
3.	FRA	(Philippe Medard, Frederic Perez, Pascal Mahe, Philippe Debureau, Frederic Volle, Denis Lathoud, Eric Quintin, Philippe Gardent, Thierry Perreux, Laurent Munier, Jackson Richardson, Stéphane Stoecklin, Denis Tristant, Jean Luc Thiebaut, Alain Portes, Gael Monthurel)	5	2	0	157	143
4.	ICE	(Gunnar Andresson, Gudmundur Hrafnkelsson, Bergsveinn Bergsveinsson, Birgir Sigurdsson, Jakob Sigurdsson, Vladimar Grimsson, Gunnar Gunnarsson, Sigurdur Bjarnason, Konrad Olavsson, Hedinn Gilsson, Geir Sveinsson, Einar Sigurdsson, Julius Jonasson)	3	3	1	140	146
5.	SPA	(Jaume Fort Mauri, Lorenzo Rico Díaz, Javier Cabanas López, Juan Muñoz Melo, Ricardo Marín Marín, Mateo Garralda Larumbe, Ignacio Urdangarin Liebaert, Enric Masip Borràs, Juan Alemany Marín, Aitor Etxaburu Castro, Luis García López, Aleix Franch Alfós, Fernando Bolea Alonso, Ánegel Hermida García, David Barrufet Bofill, Alberto Urdiales Márquez)	4	2	0	133	119
6.	KOR	(Choi Suk-jai, Lee Ki-ho, Cho Bum-yun, Park Do-hun, Lim Jinsuk, Cho Young-shin, Back Sang-suh, Cho Chi-hyo, Lee Sun-soon, Kang Jae-won, Moon Byung-wook, Shim Jae-hong, Lee Kyu-chang, Jung Kangwook, Youn Kyung-shin)	3	3	0	135	153
7.	HUN	(János Szatmári, Imre Bíró, Attila Borsos, László Sótonyi, László Marosi, Mihály Iváncsik, Jacob Sibalin, Igor Zubjuk, József Éles, Ferenc Füzesi, Richárd Mezei, Attila Horváth, Ottó Csicsai, Sándor Györffy,	3	3	0	125	127

Istaván Csoknyai)

8.	ROM	(Alexandru Buligan, Gabriel Toacsen, Valentin Zaharia, Marian Dumitru, Alexandru Dedu, Robert Licu, Ioan Prisacaru, Dumitru Berbece, Ion Mocanu, Adi Popovici, Gheorghe-Titel Raduta, Maricel Voinea, Ionel Radu, Costica Neagu, Mitica Bontaş)	1	4	1	126	138

Final: SOV 22–20 SWE
3rd Place: FRA 24–20 ICE
5th Place: SPA 36–21 KOR
7th Place: HUN 23–19 ROM

The final was a tight match all the way. Eight and a half minutes into the second half, Sweden led 14–12. Then the aggressive man-to-man defense of the ex–Soviet Union took its toll, holding the Swedes to only one goal over the next nine minutes and moving ahead 17–15. Still, the defending world champions refused to fold. With three and a half minutes to play, Erik Hajas scored on a fast break and the ex-Soviet's lead was cut to 20–19. However, Sweden was unable to come up with another goal until four seconds before the end and the game ended at 22–20.

WOMEN

1896–1972 not held

1976 Montreal T: 6, N: 6, D: 7.28.

			W	L	T	PF	PA
1.	SOV	(Natalya Sherstyuk, Rafiga Shabanova, Lyubov Berezhnaya, Zinaida Turchyna, Tetyana Makarets, Mariya Litoshenko, Lyudmyla Bobrus, Tetyana Hluschenko, Lyudmila Shubina, Halyna Zakharova, Aldona Česaityte, Nina Lobova, Lyudmyla Panchuk, Larysa Karlova)	5	0	0	92	40
2.	GDR	(Hannelore Zober, Gabriele Badorek, Evelyn Matz, Roswitha Krause, Christina Rost, Petra Uhlig, Christina Voss, Liane Michaelis, Silvia Siefert, Marion Tietz, Kristina Richter, Eva Paskuy, Waltraud Kretzschmar, Hannelore Burosch)	3	1	1	89	47
3.	HUN	(Ágota Bujdosó, Márta Magyeri, Borbála Tóth-Harsányi, Katalin Laki, Amália Sterbinszky, Ilona Nagy, Klára Csík, Rozália Lelkes, Mária Vadász, Erzsébet	3	1	1	85	55

		W	L	T	PF	PA
	Németh, Éva Angyal, Mária Berzsenyi, Marianna Nagy, Zsuzsanna Kezi)					
4. ROM	(Elisabeta Ionescu, Rozalia Şoş, Simona Arghir, Georgeta Lacusta, Doina Furcoi, Niculina Sasu, Cristina Petrovici, Constantina Pitigoi, Doina Cojocaru, Magdalena Mikloş, Maria Bosi, Viorica Ionică, Maria Lackovics, Iuliana Hobincu)	2	3	0	73	83
5. JPN	(Shoko Wada, Hiroko Kosahara, Natsue Shimada, Terumi Kurata, Mikiko Kato, Hitomi Matsushita, Emiko Yamashita, Kuriko Komori, Eiko Kawada, Mihoko Hozumi, Nanami Kino, Tokuko Kubo)	1	4	0	72	115
6. CAN	(Danielle Chenard, Louise Hurtubise, Denise Lemaire, Francine Boulay-Parizeau, Joanes Rail, Nicole Genier, Lucie Balthazar, Hélène Tetreault, Manon Charette, Monique Prud'-Homme, Louise Beaumont, Mariette Houle, Nicole Robert, Johanne Valois)	0	5	0	35	106

1980 Moscow T: 6, N: 6, D: 7.29.

		W	L	T	PF	PA
1. SOV	(Natalya Tymoshkina [Sherstyuk], Larysa Karlova, Iryna Palchykova, Zinaida Turchyna, Tetyana Kocherhina [Makarets], Lyudmyla Poradnyk [Bobrus], Larissa Savkina, Aldona Nenėnienė [Česaityte], Yulia Safina, Olha Zubaryeva, Valentyna Lutayeva, Lyubov Odynokova [Berezhnaya], Sigita Strečen)	5	0	0	99	52
2. YUG	(Ana Titlić, Slavica Jeremić, Zorica Vojinovic, Radmila Drljaca, Katica Iles, Mirjana Ognjenović, Svetlana Anastasovski, Rada Savić, Svetlana Kitić, Mirjana Djurica, Biserka Višnjić, Vesna Radović, Jasna Merdan, Vesna Milosević)	3	1	1	107	67
3. GDR	(Hannelore Zober, Katrin Krüger, Evelyn Matz, Roswitha Krause, Christina Rost, Petra Uhlig, Claudia Wunderlich, Sabine Röther, Kornelia Kunisch, Marion Tietz, Kristina Richter, Waltraud Kretzschmar, Birgit Heinecke, Renate Rudolph)	3	1	1	91	58
4. HUN	(Mária Berzsenyi, Erzsébet Csajbok [Németh], Rozália Lelkes, Éva Csulik, Amália Sterbinszky,	1	3	1	65	74

		W	L	T	PF	PA
	Klára Csik, Marianna Nagy, Ilona Mihályka, Mária Vadász, Erzsébet Balogh, Eva Angyal, Györgyi Ori, Piroska Budai, Klára Bonyhádi)					
5. CZE	(Mária Končeková, Elena Boledovičová, Daniela Nováková, Katerina Lamrichová, Alena Horalová, Jolana Nemethová, Viola Pavlasová, Piroska Polačekova, Jana Kutková, Věra Datinská, Milena Foltýnová, Elena Brezanyová, Petra Kominková)	1	3	1	65	78
6. CON	(Madeleine Mitsotso, Pascaline Bobeka, Angelik Abebame, Nicole Oba, Henriette Koula, Solange Koulinka, Isabelle Azanga, Micheline Okemba, Viviane Okoula, Germaine Djimbi, Yolande Kada-Gango, Lopez-Pemba, Julienne Malaki, Yvonne Makouala)	0	5	0	46	159

The U.S.S.R. faced its only threat against Hungary when they led 12–11 with just five minutes to play. The Soviets then scored four straight goals and won, 16–12. Roswitha Krause of the bronze-medal-winning East German team had won a silver medal in the freestyle swimming relay 12 years earlier in Mexico City.

1984 Los Angeles-Fullerton T: 6, N: 6, D: 8.9.

		W	L	T	PF	PA
1. YUG	(Jasna Ptujeć, Mirjana Ognjenović, Zorica Pavicević, Ljubinka Janković, Svetlana Anastasovski, Svetlana Dasić-Kitić, Emilija Ercić, Alenka Cuderman, Svetlana Mugosa, Mirjana Djurica, Biserka Višnjić, Slavica Djukić, Jasna Kolar-Merdan, Ljijana Mugosa, Dragica Djurić)	5	0	0	143	102
2. KOR	(Son Mi-na, Kim Kyung-soon, Lee Soon-ei, Jeong Hyoi-soon, Kim Mi-sook, Han Hwa-soon, Kim Ok-hwa, Kim Choon-yei, Jeung Soon-bok, Yoon Byung-soon, Lee Young-ja, Sung Kyung-hwa, Youn Soo-kyung)	3	1	1	125	119
3. CHN	(Wu Xingjiang, He Jianping, Zhu Juefeng, Zhang Weihong, Gao Xiumin, Wang Linwei, Liu Liping, Zhang Peijun, Sun Xiulan, Liu Yumei, Li Lan, Wang Mingxing, Chen Zhen)	2	2	1	112	115
4. GER	(Elke Blumauer, Maike Becker, Corinna Kunze, Silvia Schmitt, Roswitha Mroczynski, Sabine	2	3	0	91	100

Erbs, Dagmar Stelberg, Kerstin Jönsson, Astrid Hühn, Petra Platen, Claudia Sturm, Sabrina Koschella, Vanadis Putzke)

		W	L	T	PF	PA
4. USA	(Pamela Boyd, Carol Lindsey, Reita Clanton, Sherry Winn, Theresa Contos, Carmen Forest, Sandra De La Riva, Janice Trombly, Mary Phyllis Dwight, Cynthia Stinger, Melinda Hale, Leora "Sam" Jones, Penelope Stone)	2	3	0	114	123
6. AUT	(Ulrike Huber, Ulrike Popp, Martina Neubauer, Karin Prokop, Susanne Unger, Milena Gschiessl-Foltýnová, Maria Sykora, Silvia Steinbauer, Karin Hillinger, Elisabeth Zehetner, Gabriele Gebauer, Vesna Radović, Teresa Zielewicz, Gudrun Neunteufel, Monika Unger)	0	5	0	91	117

Yugoslavia was seriously challenged only in their opening match when they defeated West Germany 20–19 after Mirjana Djurica converted a penalty with 1:06 to play. During the Yugoslavs' 33–20 drubbing of the U.S., 27-year-old Jasna Kolar-Merdan scored an Olympic record 17 goals.

1988 Seoul-Suwon T: 8, N: 8, D: 9.29.

		W	L	T	PF	PA
1. KOR	(Song Ji-hyun, Han Hyun-sook, Kim Choon-rye, Kim Myung-soon, Lee Ki-soon, Kim Hyun-mee, Kim Mi-sook, Suk Min-hee, Son Mi-na, Lim Mi-kyung, Kim Kyung-soon, Sung Kyung-hwa)	4	1	0	120	106
2. NOR	(Vibeke Johnsen, Cathrine Svendsen, Heidi Sundal, Hanne Hegh, Susann Goksor, Hanne Hogness, Karin Singstao, Trine Haltvik, Berit Digre, Ingrid Steen, Karin Pettersen, Annette Skotvoll, Kristin Midthun, Marte Eliasson, Kjerstin Andersen)	3	1	1	115	91
3. SOV	(Natalya Matryuk, Larysa Karlova, Svitlana Mankova, Zinaida Turchyna, Olha Semenova, Maryna Bazhanova, Natalya Morskova, Tetyana Horb, Yevhenia Tovstohan, Natalya Rusnachenko, Olena Nemashkalo, Tatyana Dzhandzhgava, Natalya Anissimova, Elina Guseva, Natalya Lapitskaya)	3	1	1	112	85
4. YUG	(Mirjana Krstić, Slavica Rincić, Dragana Pesić, Svetlana Obucina, Zita Galić, Ljubinka Janković, Svetlana Micić, Ljijana	2	3	0	88	96

Marković, Mirjana Djurica, Natasa Kolega, Slavica Djukić, Ljijana Mugosa, Svetlana Mugosa, Deanka Stojanović, Dragica Djurić)

		W	L	T	PF	PA
5. CZE	(Anna Hradská, Irena Tomašovičová, Daniela Trandžíková, Marie Šmídová, Gabriela Sabadošová, Julia Kolečániová, Zuzana Budayová, Alena Damitšová, Petra Lupačová, Mária Ďurišinová, Monika Hejtmánková, Lenka Pospíšilová, Jana Stašová, Bozena Mazgutova, Marta Pösová)	4	1	0	141	102
6. CHN	(Zhang Hong, He Jianping, Zhang Weihong, Wang Mingxing, Chen Zhen, Li Lirong, Li Jie, Sun Xiulan, Xue Jinhua, Dai Jianfen, Wang Tao, Lu Guanghong)	2	3	0	128	106
7. USA	(Kathy Callaghan, Amy Gamble, Margaret Gallagher, Sherry Winn, Karyn Palgut, Portia Lack, Sandra De La Riva, Kim Clarke, Cynthia Stinger, Angie Raynor, Leora Jones, Carol Peterka, Penelope Stone, Laura Coenen)	1	4	0	104	123
8. IVC	(Elisabeth Kouassi, Wandou Guehi, Koko Elleingand, Emilie Djoman, Zomou Awa, Alimata Douamba, Mahoula Kramo, Clementinea Ble, Adjoua Ndri, Doumbia Bah, Julienne Vodoungbo, Hortense Konan, Gouna Irie, Brigitte Guigui)	0	5	0	65	164

The Korean women, who had finished eleventh at the 1986 world championships, clinched their gold medal with a stunning, emotion-charged 21–19 upset of the U.S.S.R.

1992 Barcelona T: 8, N: 8, D: 8.8.

		W	L	T	PF	PA
1. KOR	(Moon Hyang-ja, Jang Ri-ra, Nam Eun-young, Lee Ho-youn, Lee Mi-young, Hong Jeong-ho, Lim O-kyung, Min Hye-sook, Park Jeong-lim, Oh Sung-ok, Kim Hwa-sook, Park Kap-sook, Cha Jae-kyung)	4	0	1	136	107
2. NOR	(Annette Skotvoll, Tonje Sagstuen, Hanne Hogness, Heidi Sundal, Cathrine Svendsen, Susann Goksor, Siri Eftedal, Ingrid Steen, Karin Pettersen, Kristine Duvholt, Heidi Tjugum, Mona Dahle, Hege Froseth, Henriette Henriksen)	3	2	0	100	111

		W	L	T	PF	PA
3. SOV	(Svetlana Bogdanova, Natalya Deryugina, Galina Onoprienko, Maryna Bazhanova, Natalya Morskova, Lyudmila Gudz, Sveltana Pryakhina, Galina Borzenkova, Tetyana Horb, Tatyana Dzhandzhgava, Elina Guseva, Natalya Anissimova, Larissa Kiseleva)	4	1	0	124	100
4. GER	(Sabine Adamik, Andrea Stolletz, Bianka Urbanke, Birgit Wagner, Kerstin Mühlner, Carola · Ciszewski, Silvia Schmitt, Andrea Bölk, Michaela Erler, Sybille Gruner, Anja Krüger, Silke Fittinger, Eike Bram, Elena Leonte, Rita Köster, Gabriele Palme)	2	3	0	131	111
5. AUT	(Natali Rusnatchenko, Marianna Racz, Jadranka Jez, Kerstin Jönsson, Karin Prokop, Edith Matei, Nicole Peissl, Liliana Topea, Jasna Kolar, Stanka Bozovic, Iris Morhammer, Barbara Strass, Slavic Djukic, Teresa Zurowski)	2	1	1	90	79
6. USA	(Laurie Fellner, Angie Raynor, Patricia Neder, Laura Coenen, Karyn Palgut, Portia Lack, Sharon Cain, Kim Clarke, Dannette Leininger, Cynthia Stinger, Leora Jones, Carol Peterka, Barbara Schnaf)	1	3	0	72	102
7. SPA	(Montserrat Marín Lopez, María Sanchez Bravo, Amaia Ugartemendia Sagarzazu, Esperanza Tercero Rolando, Paloma Arranz Santamarta, Mercedes Fuertes Valmaña, Karmele Makazaga Urrutia, Cristina Gómez Arquer, Begoña Sánchez Santos, Raquel Vizcaíno Torre, Dolores Ruiz De Assín Jordá, Blanca Martín-Calero, Rita Hernández Martin, Montserrat Puche Díaz)	1	3	0	76	85
8. NGR	(Chinyere Diribe, Immaculate Nwawu, Agustina Nkechi Abi, Bridget Yamala, Eunice Idausa, Mary Jane Soronnadi, Mary Nwachukwu, Justina Anyiam, Auta Olivia Sana, Angela Ajodo, Chiaka Ihebom, Mary Ihedioha, Ngozi Opara, Justina Akpuluo, Victoria Umunna)	0	4	0	73	107

Final: KOR 28–21 NOR
3rd Place: SOV 24–20 GER
5th Place: AUT 26–17 USA
7th Place: SPA 26–17 NGR

Norway was an unlikely finalist. Although they placed second in Seoul, they were admitted to the 1992 Olympic tournament only as a replacement for Yugoslavia, which was banned by the I.O.C. at the last minute. In their first match in Barcelona, the Norwegians were crushed 27–16 by defending champion South Korea. Still, they managed to qualify for the semifinals, where they upset the team from the former Soviet Union 24–23 when Siri Eftedal scored with three seconds to play. The other semi was won by the Koreans 26–25 over Germany. Midway through the first half of the final, Norway was leading 7–5 when the momentum shifted completely. Over the next 15 minutes, South Korea outscored Norway 11–1 to take a 16–8 halftime lead. The Koreans allowed the Norwegians only two more goals in the first 12½ minutes of the second half and Norway was never able to cut the deficit to less than five points.

JUDO

MEN	WOMEN
Extra-Lightweight—60 kg	Extra-Lightweight—48 kg
Half-Lightweight—65 kg	Half-Lightweight—52 kg
Lightweight—71 kg	Lightweight—56 kg
Half-Middleweight—78 kg	Half-Middleweight—61 kg
Middleweight—86 kg	Middleweight—66 kg
Half-Heavyweight—95 kg	Half-Heavyweight—72 kg
Heavyweight—over 95 kg	Heavyweight—over 72 kg
Discontinued Event	

JUDO TERMS

Scoring

Ippon	Full Point
Waza-ari	Almost ippon
Yuko	Almost waza-ari
Koka	Almost yuko

Penalties

Hansokumake (= ippon)	Disqualification
Keikoku (= waza-ari)	Warning
Chui (= yuko)	Caution
Shido (= koka)	Note

Throws

Ashi-guruma	Leg wheel
Harai goshi	Sweeping hip throw
Kochiki-taoshi	Leg grab shoulder throw
Ko-soto-gake	Minor outer hook
Ko-soto-gari	Minor outer reap
Kouchi-gari	Minor inner reap
Morote-gari	Double wheel leg grab
O-soto-gari	Major outer reaping throw
O-uchi-gari	Major inner reaping throw
Sasae-tsuri-komi-ashi	Pull throw foot sweep
Tai-otoshi	Body drop
Tani-otoshi	Valley drop throw
Tomoe-nage	Whirl throw
Uchi-mata	Inner thigh throw

Holds

Juji-gatame	Arm lock
Kami-shiho-gatame	Upper four quarters hold
Kesa-gatame	Sash hold
Kuzure-kami-shiho-gatame	Variant on upper four quarters hold
Yoko-shiho-gatame	Side four quarters hold

Other Terms

Awasewaza	Ippon by two waza-ari
Katsu	A system of resuscitation
Kinsa	Slight superiority or close decision
Shime-waza	Strangulation or choking techniques
Yusei-gachi	Win by superiority scores or officials' decision

Judo matches are held on rectangular mats called tatamis. The contest area is 9 to 10 meters (29 feet 6 inches to 32 feet 10 inches) square.

A judo match is won by a score of "ippon" which ends the match. A match which goes to full term without an ippon is decided by lesser scores. In the case of a tie, the majority decision of the referee and the two judges awards the match to the competitor who has displayed superiority.

Ippon can be scored by a clean, forceful throw; by holding the opponent mainly on his back for 30 seconds, under control, but not necessarily immobile; or by submission to a strangle, a choke or a lock applied against the elbow. Waza-ari is scored by a throw not quite good enough for ippon or by a 25-second hold-down. Yuko and koka can be scored for inferior throws or by 20- and 10-second hold-downs respectively. A second waza-ari in a match counts as ippon, but any amount of yukos is inferior to one waza-ari and any amount of kokas is inferior to one yuko.

In 1964 preliminary matches lasted ten minutes and final matches 15 minutes. In 1972 and 1976, the matches were six and ten minutes, and in 1980 and 1984 five and seven minutes. Since 1988, all matches have lasted five minutes. Olympic judo competitions are divided into two direct-elimination pools. The winner of each pool advances to the final. All those who lost to the pool winner take part in a repêchage. The winners of the two repêchage pools are awarded bronze medals.

The word *judo* in Japanese means "gentleness" or "giving way."

MEN

EXTRA-LIGHTWEIGHT
(60 kg–132.25 lbs)

1896–1976 not held

1980 Moscow C: 29, N: 29, D: 8.1.

			FINAL MATCH	
1.	Thierry Rey	FRA	Ko-soto-gari	7:00
2.	Rafael Rodríguez Carbenell	CUB		
3.	Aramby Yemizh	SOV/RUS		
3.	Tibor Kincses	HUN		
5.	John Holliday	GBR		
5.	Pavel Petrikov	CZE		
7.	Samir Elnajjar	SYR		
7.	Reino Fagerlund	FIN		

1984 Los Angeles C: 27, N: 27, D: 8.4.

			FINAL MATCH	
1.	Shinji Hosokawa	JPN	Yoko-shiho-gatame	1:09
2.	Kim Jae-yup	KOR		
3.	Neil Eckersley	GBR		
3.	Edward Liddie	USA		
5.	Guy Delvingt	FRA		
5.	Felice Mariani	ITA		

Hosokawa needed only 23 seconds to take Kim to the mat in the final.

1988 Seoul C: 37, N: 37, D: 9.25.

			FINAL MATCH	
1.	Kim Jae-yup	KOR	Shido	5:00
2.	Kevin Asano	USA		
3.	Shinji Hosokowa	JPN		
3.	Amiran Totikashvili	SOV/GEO		
5.	Patrick Roux	FRA		
5.	Sheu Tsay-chwan	TAI		

Three years after losing to Hosokawa at the Los Angeles Olympics, Kim won the 1987 world championship by throwing Hosokawa after just 27 seconds. It was expected that the two would meet again in the Seoul final, but in the semifinals Hosokawa lost a controversial split decision to Kevin Asano. Kim thrilled the hometown crowd by showing up for the medal ceremony wearing not a sports suit but a traditional Korean outfit.

To qualify for the Olympic Games, Kim needed to lose 13 pounds in 20 days. He did this by limiting himself to one meal a day: a bowl of porridge with raw fish slices.

Kim, who was recovering from an injury to his backbone, had actually lost the Korean Olympic trials to Yun Hyun. However, the Korea Judo Association chose Kim as its representative anyway. After his victory in Seoul, Kim told the press, "I apologize to Yun and his mother. My gold medal is won together by them and me." In honor of his Olympic championship, Kim (unlike Yun and his mother) was rewarded with a lifetime pension of $16,600 a year by Korea's National Sports Promotion Foundation.

1992 Barcelona C: 43, N: 43, D: 8.2.

			FINAL MATCH	
1.	Nazim Guseynov	AZR	Sasae-tsuri-komi-ashi	5:00
2.	Yoon Hyun	KOR		
3.	Tadanori Koshino	JPN		
3.	Richard Trautmann	GER		

5.	Philippe Pradayrol	FRA
5.	József Wágner	HUN
7.	Dashgombo Battulga	MGL
7.	Willis García García	VEN

HALF-LIGHTWEIGHT
(65 kg—143 lbs)

1896–1976 not held

1980 Moscow C: 29, N: 29, D: 7.31.

			FINAL MATCH	
1.	Nikolai Solodukhin	SOV/RUS	Shido	7:00
2.	Tsendying Damdin	MGL		
3.	Iliyan Nedkov	BUL		
3.	Janusz Pawlowski	POL		
5.	Yves Delvingt	FRA		
5.	Torsten Reissmann	GDR		
7.	Wolfgang Biedron	SWE		
7.	Jaroslav Kriz	CZE		

Damdin spent most of the final backpedaling and was finally charged with a shido that proved decisive.

1984 Los Angeles C: 34, N: 34, D: 8.5.

			FINAL MATCH	
1.	Yoshiyuki Matsuoka	JPN	Seoi-nage	7:00
2.	Hwang Jung-oh	KOR		
3.	Marc Alexandre	FRA		
3.	Josef Reiter	AUT		
5.	Stephen Gawthorpe	GBR		
5.	Sandro Rosati	ITA		

1988 Seoul C: 42, N: 42, D: 9.26.

			FINAL MATCH	
1.	Lee Kyung-keun	KOR	Yusei-gachi	5:00
2.	Janusz Pawlowski	POL		
3.	Bruno Carabetta	FRA		
3.	Yosuke Yamamoto	JPN		
5.	Tamás Bujkó	HUN		
5.	Brent Cooper	NZE		

Like all members of the Korean judo team, Lee's training included periodic midnight visits to a cemetery, where he was forced to sit alone for an hour before being returned to his dormitory to watch videotapes of his potential opponents. Lee's path to the gold medal included a controversial semifinal split decision over Bruno Carabetta.

1992 Barcelona C: 46, N: 46, D: 8.1.

			FINAL MATCH	
1.	Rogerio Sampaio Cardoso	BRA	O-soto-gari	5:00
2.	József Csák	HUN		
3.	Israel Hernández Planas	CUB		
3.	Udo Quellmalz	GER		
5.	Philip Laats	BEL		
5.	Francisco Lorenzo Aparicio	SPA		
7.	Kim Sang-moon	KOR		
7.	Kenji Maruyama	JPN		

LIGHTWEIGHT
(71 kg—156.5 lbs)

1896–1960 not held

1964 Tokyo C: 25, N: 18, D: 10.20
(68 kg—150 lbs)

			FINAL MATCH	
1.	Takehide Nakatani	JPN	Awasewaza	1:15
2.	Eric Hänni	SWI		
3.	Aron Bogolubovs	SOV/LAT		
3.	Oleg Stepanov	SOV/RUS		
5.	Chang Won-ku (TAI), Paul Maruyama (USA),			
	Park Chung-sam (KOR), Gerhard Zotter (AUT)			

1968 not held

1972 Munich C: 29, N: 29, D: 9.4.
(63 kg—139 lbs)

			FINAL MATCH	
1.	Takao Kawaguchi	JPN	Kami-shiho-gatame	0:39
3.	Kim Yong-ik	PRK		
3.	Jean-Jacques Mounier	FRA		
5.	Wolfram Koppen	GER		
5.	Hector Rodriguez Torres	CUB		
7.	Cheng Chi-hsiang	TAI		
7.	Ferenc Szabó	HUN		

DISQ (Drugs): Bakhaavaa Buidaa (MGL)

Buidaa lost a silver medal when he became the first person in judo history to fail a drug test. He tested positive for excess caffeine. Buidaa was so unschooled in judo tradition that he wrapped his belt around his waist only once instead of twice.

1976 Montreal C: 32, N: 32, D: 7.26.
(63 kg—139 lbs)

			FINAL MATCH	
1.	Hector Rodriguez Torres	CUB	Uchi-mata	10:00
2.	Chang Eun-kyung	KOR		
3.	Felice Mariani	ITA		
3.	József Tuncsik	HUN		
5.	Erich Pointner	AUT		
5.	Marian Standowicz	POL		
7.	Brad Farrow	CAN		
7.	José Pinto Gomes	POR		

Surprisingly, two-time world champion Yoshiharu Minami was eliminated in his first match by Yves Delvingt of France. The final was a rugged contest, which was interrupted at one point to allow Rodriguez's ribs to be wrapped up by a doctor. Rodriguez told reporters that he began practicing judo to protect himself from his six older brothers.

1980 Moscow C: 30, N: 30, D: 7.30.

			FINAL MATCH	
1.	Ezio Gamba	ITA	Yusei-gachi	7:00
2.	A. Neil Adams	GBR		
3.	Ravdan Davaadalai	MGL		
3.	Karl-Heinz Lehmann	GDR		
5.	Edward Alksnin	POL		
5.	Christian Dyot	FRA		
7.	Kim Byong-gun	PRK		
7.	Michael Picken	AUS		

European champion Neil Adams needed less than four minutes to defeat his first three opponents, but in the final he lost a unanimous decision to his 21-year-old nemesis, Ezio Gamba. Gamba was the only Italian judoka to resist the anti-Soviet boycott. He took a leave of absence from the army and traveled to Moscow on his own.

1984 Los Angeles C: 30, N: 30, D: 8.6.

			FINAL MATCH	
1.	Ahn Byeong-keun	KOR	Seoi-nage	7:00
2.	Ezio Gamba	ITA		
3.	Kerrith Brown	GBR		
3.	Luis Onmura	BRA		
5.	Glenn Beauchamp	CAN		
5.	Hidetoshi Nakanishi	JPN		

Defending Olympic champion Ezio Gamba needed only 4 minutes and 1 second to demolish his first four opponents, but he ran out of steam in the final and was beaten by Ahn Byeong-keun. Earlier, Ahn had defeated world champion Hidetoshi Nakanishi, who had suffered a broken rib in his opening match.

1988 Seoul C: 41, N: 41, D: 9.27.

			FINAL MATCH	
1.	Marc Alexandre	FRA	Kouchi-gari	5:00
2.	Sven Loll	GDR		
3.	Michael Swain	USA		
3.	Georgy Tenadze	SOV/GEO		
5.	Bertalan Hajtós	HUN		
5.	Steffen Stranz	GER		

DISQ (Drugs): Kerrith Brown (GBR)

Alexandre scored by knocking down Loll at 3:55 with a well-timed foot hook. Initially Kerrith Brown of Great Britain was awarded a bronze medal by virtue of his repêchage victory over world champion Michael Swain. However, he tested positive for Furosemide, a proscribed diuretic. When asked how he felt about backing into a bronze medal, Swain was philosophical. "I didn't want to win it this way," he said, "but I can always lie to my grandchildren."

1992 Barcelona C: 44, N: 44, D: 7.31.

			FINAL MATCH	
1.	Toshihiko Koga	JPN	Yusei-gachi	5:00
2.	Bertalan Hajtós	HUN		
3.	Chung Hoon	KOR		
3.	Shay Oren Smadga	ISR		
5.	Bruno Carabetta	FRA		
5.	Stefan Dott	GER		
7.	Wieslaw Blach	POL		
7.	Khaliun Boldbaatar	MGL		

Hajtós qualified for the final with four straight ippons, but in the final he lost to two-time world champion Toshihiko Koga in a decision that shocked and outraged the crowd.

HALF-MIDDLEWEIGHT
(78 kg–172 lbs)

1896–1968 not held

1972 Munich C: 29, N: 29, D: 9.3.
(70 kg–154 lbs)

		FINAL MATCH
1. Toyokazu Nomura	JPN	Seoi-nage 0:27
2. Antoni Zajkowski	POL	
3. Dietmar Hötger	GDR	
3. Anatoly Novikov	SOV/UKR	
5. Engelbert Doerbandt	GER	
5. Antal Hetényi	HUN	
7. Wang Jong-she	TAI	
7. Reto Zinsli	SWI	

Nomura disposed of his five opponents in a total of ten minutes and 49 seconds.

1976 Montreal C: 29, N; 29, D: 7.29.
(70 kg–154 lbs)

		FINAL MATCH
1. Vladimir Nevzorov	SOV/RUS	Tai-otoshi 10.00
2. Koji Kuramoto	JPN	
3. Marian Talaj	POL	
3. Patrick Vial	FRA	
5. Lee Chang-sun	KOR	
5. Vaccinuf Morrison	GBR	
7. Juan Carlos Rodriguez	SPA	
7. John Van Hoek	AUS	

1980 Moscow C: 29, N: 29, D: 7.29.

		FINAL MATCH
1. Shota Khabareli	SOV/GEO	Ouchi-gari 7:00
2. Juan Ferrer La Hera	CUB	
3. Harald Heinke	GDR	
3. Bernard Tchoullyan	FRA	
5. Mircea Fratica	ROM	
5. Ignacio Sanz Paz	SPA	
7. Georgi Petrov	BUL	
7. Slavko Sikiric	YUG	

Noticeably missing because of the anti-Soviet boycott was four-time world champion Shozo Fuji of Japan.

1984 Los Angeles C: 38, N: 38, D: 8.7.

		FINAL MATCH
1. Frank Wieneke	GER	Seoi-nage 4:04
2. A. Neil Adams	GBR	
3. Mircea Fratiçă	ROM	
3. Michel Nowak	FRA	
5. Filip Lesčak	YUG	
5. Hiromitsu Takano	JPN	

Wieneke's sudden victory over Adams was a shocking upset. At the 3:50 mark, Adams glanced at the clock and thought, "Three minutes to go and you're Olympic champion." Wieneke launched a weak right-handed attack, which Adams easily repelled. But then Wieneke noticed Adams relax momentarily, so he quickly executed a left shoulder throw. The former world champion was down on the mat and the contest was over. It was the first time in his entire career that Adams had lost a match by ippon.

1988 Seoul C: 41, N: 41, D: 9.28.

		FINAL MATCH
1. Waldemar Legień	POL	Seoi-nage 4:44
2. Frank Wieneke	GER	
3. Torsten Bréchôt	GDR	
3. Bashir Varayev	SOV/RUS	
5. Kevin Doherty	CAN	
5. Pascal Tayot	FRA	

Wieneke was defeated by the same shoulder throw that he had used to win four years earlier.

1992 Barcelona C: 42, N: 42, D: 7.30.

		FINAL MATCH
1. Hidehiko Yoshida	JPN	Uchi-mata 3:35
2. Jason Morris	USA	
3. Bertrand Damaisin	FRA	
3. Kim Byung-joo	KOR	
5. Lars Adolfsson	SWE	
5. Johan Laats	BEL	
7. Alexandru Ciupe	ROM	
7. Bashir Varayev	RUS	

Yoshida defeated all six of his opponents by ippon. The total time for all his matches was 16 minutes and 21 seconds.

MIDDLEWEIGHT
(86 kg–189.5 lbs)

1896–1960 not held

1964 Tokyo C: 25, N: 20, D: 10.21.
(80 kg–176 lbs)

		FINAL MATCH
1. Isao Okano	JPN	Yoko-shiho-gatame 1:36
2. Wolfgang Hofmann	GER	
3. James Bregman	USA	
3. Kim Eui-tae	KOR	
5. Lionel Grossain (FRA), Rodolfo Pérez (ARG), Lhoffei Shiozawa (BRA), Petrus Snijders (HOL)		

In the quarterfinal match between Okano and Grossain, the referee failed to notice that Grossain had been rendered unconscious by shime-waza. When the Japanese coach called his attention to the Frenchman's condition, Okano revived his opponent through the use of katsu. In his book *Vital Judo*, Okano described his state of mind during major competitions: "By . . . the second or third bout of the tournament, the athlete becomes conscious of an imaginary membrane separating him from all outside things, including the spectators. . . . Surrounded by that imaginary membrane, I found my mind alert and cool. I was like an animal standing alone. Voices and shouts from the crowd had no effect on me. Winning and losing were the only important things.

"When I reached the semifinal or final stage, a tension of an entirely different kind welled up inside me. I was entirely enclosed in a veil of transparency; I felt that I could see through everything. The opponent was nothing but a physical object. The sense of doing battle with myself became clearer in my mind. I sensed a unity with all of the spectators. When I won . . . the world seemed to belong to me, and the single moment of intensely concentrated meaning is unforgettable."

1968 not held

1972 Munich C: 35, N: 35, D: 9.2.
(80 kg–176 lbs)

		FINAL MATCH	
1. Shinobu Sekine	JPN	Yusei-gachi	10:00
2. Oh Seung-lip	KOR		
3. Jean-Paul Coché	FRA		
3. Brian Jacks	GBR		
5. Guram Gogalauri	SOV/GEO		
5. Lutz Lischka	AUT		
7. Gerd Egger	GER		
7. Petr Jaekl	CZE		

Sekine, the All-Japan open category champion, actually lost to Oh in the preliminary pool. But he was able to fight his way into the final through repêchage, or second-chance matches, and won by a split decision, to the great relief of all the Japanese who were present.

1976 Montreal C: 32, N:32, D: 7.28.
(80 kg–176 lbs)

		FINAL MATCH	
1. Isamu Sonoda	JPN	O-uchi-gari	10:00
2. Valery Dvoynikov	SOV/UKR		
3. Slavko Obadov	YUG		
3. Park Young-chul	KOR		
5. José Luis Frutos	SPA		
5. Fred Marhenke	GER		
7. Paul Buganey	AUS		
7. Suheyl Yesilnur	TUR		

Policeman Isamu Sonoda upset three-time world champion Shozo Fuji in the All-Japan championships, which served as Japan's Olympic qualifying tournament.

1980 Moscow C: 27, N: 27, D: 7.28.

		FINAL MATCH	
1. Jürg Röthlisberger	SWI	Harai-goshi	7:00
2. Isaac Azcuy Oliva	CUB		

3. Aleksandrs Jackevičs	SOV/LAT	
3. Detlef Ultsch	GDR	
5. Walter Carmona	BRA	
5. Bertil Ström	SWE	
7. Peter Donnelly	GBR	
7. Henri-Richard Lobe	CAM	

The final was twice delayed mid-contest because of a controversy concerning the size of Röthlisberger's jacket. After a five-minute argument, the referee ordered Röthlisberger to change his jacket. He did so and the fight resumed. But the referee stopped the contest again, declaring that the second jacket was also unacceptable. Röthlisberger changed back into his original jacket, which had miraculously transformed into the proper size, and the match continued.

1984 Los Angeles C: 29, N: 29, D: 8.8.

		FINAL MATCH	
1. Peter Seisenbacher	AUT	Ashi-guruma	2:26
2. Robert Berland	USA		
3. Walter Carmona	BRA		
3. Seiki Nose	JPN		
5. Fabien Canu	FRA		
5. Densign White	GBR		

Seisenbacher, a 24-year-old goldsmith, was the first Austrian ever to win a major judo championship. He dispatched his five opponents in an elapsed time of 11 minutes and 5 seconds.

1988 Seoul C: 36, N: 36, D: 9.29.

		FINAL MATCH	
1. Peter Seisenbacher	AUT	Yusei-gachi	5:00
2. Vladimir Shestakov	SOV/RUS		
3. Akinobu Osako	JPN		
3. Ben Spijkers	HOL		
5. Fabien Canu	FRA		
5. Densign White	GBR		

At age 28, Seisenbacher became the first judoka in Olympic history to retain his title. A curious incident occurred in the repêchage rounds. After Ben Spijkers defeated Densign White, the two longtime rivals embraced and left the mat arm in arm. This was a breach of the strict protocols of judo and the judges ordered them to return for a more formal farewell. Spijkers and White bowed properly—and again walked off arm in arm. This time the officials waived the rules, to the delight of the crowd.

1992 Barcelona C: 33, N: 33, D: 7.29.

		FINAL MATCH	
1. Waldemar Legień	POL	Uchi-mata	5:00
2. Pascal Tayot	FRA		
3. Nicolas Gill	CAN		
3. Hirotaka Okada	JPN		
5. Adrian Croitoru	ROM		
5. Axel Lobenstein	GER		
7. Daniel Kistler	SWI		
7. Yang Jong-ock	KOR		

Legień moved up in weight class and won his second gold medal. He got off to a quick start in Barcelona, defeating Michael Oduor of Kenya in 8 seconds and Yahya Mufarrich of Bulgaria in 12. But that was slow work compared to the record set by Cuba's Andrés Franco. In the second round Franco dispatched Illus Isako of Zaire with morote-gari in only 3 seconds.

HALF-HEAVYWEIGHT

(95 kg–209 lbs)

1896–1968 not held

1972 Munich C: 30, N: 30, D: 9.1.
(93 kg–205 lbs)

		FINAL MATCH	
1. Shota Chochoshvili	SOV/GEO	Yushi-gachi	10:00
2. David Starbrook	GBR		
3. Paul Barth	GER		
3. Chiaki Ishii	BRA		
5. Helmut Howiller	GDR		
5. James Wooley	USA		
7. Pierre Albertini	FRA		
7. Terry Farnsworth	CAN		

Two-time world champion Fumio Sasahara of Hokkaido, Japan, was unexpectedly thrown and defeated by 22-year-old Shota Chochoshvili of Tbilisi, Georgia. Chochoshvili then lost a split decision to Dave Starbrook, the operator of a newspaper, tobacco, and sweet shop in Hackney. The two met again in the finals, and this time Chochoshvili prevailed with a unanimous decision.

1976 Montreal C: 35, N: 35, D: 7.27.
(93 kg–205 lbs)

		FINAL MATCH	
1. Kazuhiro Ninomiya	JPN	Keikoku	10:00
2. Ramaz Kharshiladze	SOV/GEO		
3. Jürg Röthlisberger	SWI		
3. David Starbrook	GBR		
5. Jeaki Cho	KOR		
5. Dietmar Lorenz	GDR		
7. An Ung-nam	PRK		
7. Abdoulaye Djiba	SEN		

Ninomiya, who won three of his four preliminary fights in one minute or less, had to lose over 25 pounds to make the weight limit.

1980 Moscow C: 23, N: 23, D: 7.27.

		FINAL MATCH	
1. Robert Van de Walle	BEL	Tani-otoshi	7:00
2. Tengiz Khubuluri	SOV/GEO		
3. Dietmar Lorenz	GDR		
3. Henk Numan	HOL		
5. István Szepesi	HUN		
5. R. José Tornes Bastardo	CUB		
7. Daniel Radu	ROM		
7. Jean-Luc Rouge	FRA		

1984 Los Angeles C: 22, N: 22, D: 8.9.

		FINAL MATCH	
1. Ha Hyoung-zoo	KOR	Yusei-gachi	7:00
2. Douglas Vieira	BRA		
3. Bjarni Fridriksson	ICE		
3. Günter Neureuther	GER		
5. Yuri Fazi	ITA		
5. Joseph Meli	CAN		

1988 Seoul C: 21, N: 21, D: 9.30.

		FINAL MATCH	
1. Aurélio Miguel	BRA	Chui	5:00
2. Marc Meiling	GER		
3. Dennis Stewart	GBR		
3. Robert van de Walle	BEL		
5. Jacek Beutler	POL		
5. Jiří Sosna	CZE		

Incredibly, Miguel won all five of his matches without scoring a single point. He gained two victories by judges' decision and three, including the final, when his opponents were penalized for excessive passivity. Nineteen-eighty Olympic champion Robert van de Walle earned a bronze in 1988 at the age of 34.

1992 Barcelona C: 34, N: 34, D: 7.28.

		FINAL MATCH	
1. Antal Kovács	HUN	Uchi-mata	5:00
2. Raymond Stevens	GBR		
3. Theo Meijer	HOL		
3. Dmitri Sergeyev	RUS		
5. Pawel Nastula	POL		
5. Indrek Pertelson	EST		
7. Yasuhiro Kai	JPN		
7. Robert van de Walle	BEL		

The 20-year-old Kovács was a suprising and gracious winner. "I was lucky," he told reporters after defeating Stevens. "I have a partner back home who is very similar in his build and style."

HEAVYWEIGHT

(Over 95 kg–209 lbs)

1896–1960 not held

1964 Tokyo C: 15, N: 13, D: 10.22.
(Over 80 kg–176 lbs)

		FINAL MATCH	
1. Isao Inokuma	JPN	Kinsa	15.00
2. A. Douglas Rogers	CAN		
3. Parnaoz Chikviladze	SOV/GEO		
3. Anzor Kiknadze	SOV/GEO		
5. Kim Jong-dal	KOR		

Inokuma and Rogers were used to practicing together in Japan, so the final was a relatively quiet affair. The referee, Charles Palmer of Great Britain, became so annoyed by their passivity that he threatened to disqualify both men and deprive them of medals. The lightest entrant in the heavyweight division, Inokuma weighed only 192 pounds, compared to Rogers' 260 pounds.

1968 not held

1972 Munich C: 21, N: 21, D: 8.31.
(Over 93 kg–205 lbs)

			FINAL MATCH	
1.	Willem Ruska	HOL	Harai-goshi	1:43
2.	Klaus Glahn	GER		
3.	Motoki Nishimura	JPN		
3.	Givi Onashvili	SOV/GEO		
5.	Jean-Claude Brondani	FRA		
5.	Douglas Nelson	USA		
7.	Tijive Bankassou	MOR		
7.	M'Bagnik Mebodj	SEN		

1976 Montreal C: 20, N: 20, D: 7.26.
(Over 93 kg–205 lbs)

			FINAL MATCH	
1.	Serhei Novikov	SOV/UKR	O-soto-gari	1:19
2.	Günther Neureuther	GER		
3.	Allen Coage	USA		
3.	Sumio Endo	JPN		
5.	Gunsem Jalaa	MGL		
5.	Keith Remfry	GBR		
7.	Abdoulaye Kote	SEN		
7.	Radomir Kovačević	YUG		

Because there was no seeding system, the two favorites, Sumio Endo and Serhei Novikov, met in the very first round. It was a dull match without any scoring, won by Novikov by decision. A most unusual sight was the repêchage match between the 5-foot 6½-inch, 259-pound Sumio Endo and 7-foot 0-inch, 350-pound Pak Jong-gil of North Korea. Endo, the defending world champion, was the victor.

1980 Moscow C: 18, N: 18, D: 7.27.

			FINAL MATCH	
1.	Angelo Parisi	FRA	Ippon	6:14
2.	Dimitur Zapryanov	BUL		
3.	Radomir Kovačević	YUG		
3.	Vladimir Kocman	CZE		
5.	Kim Myong-gyu	PRK		
5.	Paul Radburn	GBR		
7.	Wojciech Reszko	POL		

Born in Italy, Parisi was a former member of the British team who married a Frenchwoman and changed citizenship. Because of the anti-Soviet boycott, neither of the two Japanese world champions, Sumio Endo and Yasuhiro Yamashita, could compete.

1984 Los Angeles C: 16, N: 16, D: 8.10.

			FINAL MATCH	
1.	Hitoshi Saito	JPN	Shido	7:00
2.	Angelo Parisi	FRA		
3.	Mark Berger	CAN		

3.	Cho Yong-chul	KOR		
5.	Radomir Kovačević	YUG		
5.	Douglas Nelson	USA		

The 320-pound Saito made quick work of his first three opponents. Mark Berger lasted 17 seconds, Isidore Silas of Cameroon 29 seconds, and Radomir Kovačević 44 seconds. In the final, Parisi held firm, so firm in fact that he was penalized once too often for inactivity, and lost the match.

1988 Seoul C: 26, N: 26, D: 10.1.

			FINAL MATCH	
1.	Hitoshi Saito	JPN	Keikoku	5:00
2.	Henry Stöhr	GDR		
3.	Cho Yong-chul	KOR		
3.	Grigory Verichev	SOV/RUS		
5.	István Dubovsky	HUN		
5.	Dimitar Zaprianov	BUL		

Saito, down to a trim 315 pounds, won his second Olympic championship by incurring only two warnings for inactivity to Stöhr's three.

1992 Barcelona C: 28, N: 28, D: 7.27.

			FINAL MATCH	
1.	David Khakhaleishvili	GEO	Tani-otoshi	1:04
2.	Naoya Ogawa	JPN		
3.	Imre Csösz	HUN		
3.	David Douillet	FRA		
5.	Frank Moreno García	CUB		
5.	Harry van Barneveld	BEL		
7.	Damon Keeve	USA		
7.	Ernesto Pérez Lobo	SPA		

The 1989 world champion, Naoya Ogawa, tore through his first four opponents in 7 minutes 53 seconds. In the final, however, it was Ogawa who was thrown twice in the first minute.

Discontinued Event

OPEN

1964 Tokyo C: 9, N: 9, D: 10.23.

			FINAL MATCH	
1.	Antonius Geesink	HOL	Kesa-gatame	9:22
2.	Akio Kaminaga	JPN		
3.	Theodore Boronovskis	AUS		
3.	Klaus Glahn	GER		

Geesink's victory was a shocking blow to the Japanese, even though he was two-time world champion and the clear favorite. In 1961 the 6-foot 6-inch, 267-pound judo instructor from Utrecht had become the first non-Japanese to win a world championship. Geesink won his semifinal fight with Boronovskis in only 12 seconds. Although he failed to gain the gold medal, Kaminaga set an Olympic speed record that would last for 28 years when he threw Thomas Ong of the Philippines in four seconds in the repêchage round. Ten minutes earlier, Ong had been thrown in six seconds by John Ryan of Ireland.

1968 not held

1972 Munich C: 29, N: 29, D: 9.9.

		FINAL MATCH	
1. Willem Ruska	HOL	Yoko-shiho-gatame	3:58
2. Vitaly Kusnetzov	SOV/RUS		
3. Jean-Claude Brondani	FRA		
3. Angelo Parisi	GBR		
5. Klaus Glahn	GER		
5. Alfred Douglas Rogers	CAN		
7. Tijini Benkassou	MOR		
7. Chiaki Ishii	BRA		

Having previously swept to victory in the heavyweight class, Ruska became the only person ever to win two Olympic gold medals in judo in the same year. In the open division, Ruska lost an early unanimous decision to Kusnetzov, but was able to pin him when they met again in the final.

1976 Montreal C: 30, N: 30, D: 7.31.

		FINAL MATCH	
1. Haruki Uemura	JPN	Kuzure-kami-shiho-gatame	7:28
2. Keith Remfry	GBR		
3. Jeaki Cho	KOR		
3. Shota Chochoshvili	SOV/GEO		
5. Jorge Portelli	ARG		
5. Jean-Luc Rouge	FRA		
7. Gunther Neureuther	GER		
7. Pak Jong-gil	PRK		

1980 Moscow C: 21, N: 21, D: 8.2.

		FINAL MATCH	
1. Dietmar Lorenz	GDR	Yushi-gachi	7:00
2. Angelo Parisi	FRA		
3. Arthur Mapp	GBR		
3. András Ozsvár	HUN		
5. Serhei Novikov	SOV/UKR		
5. Dambajan Tsend-Auish	MGL		
7. Pavelj Dragoi	ROM		

Lorenz, a car mechanic and army officer, had the rare distinction of being a sixth Dan red-and-white belt judoka. At 5 feet 11 inches, he was also the shortest entrant in the open category.

1984 Los Angeles C: 15, N: 15, D: 8.11.

		FINAL MATCH	
1. Yasuhiro Yamashita	JPN	Yoko-shiho-gatame	1:05
2. Mohamed Ali Rashwan	EGY		
3. Mihai Cioc	ROM		
3. Arthur Schnabel	GER		
5. Laurent del Colombo	FRA		
5. Xu Guoqing	CHN		

Yasuhiro Yamashita prepares to throw Hitoshi Saito in the 1984 All-Japan Judo championship. Three and a half months later, they both won gold medals at the Los Angeles Olympics.

In October of 1977, Yasuhiro Yamashita lost by decision in the final of the Japanese Student Championships. Furious with himself for not fighting "like a warrior," he vowed never to allow such a lapse to occur again. In the next seven years Yamashita would suffer not a single loss, including 194 matches at national and international-level competition. All but five of his victories were by ippon. Included in that unbeaten string were four world championship titles. But one goal, his greatest goal, had eluded him—an Olympic gold medal.

When Japan joined the U.S.-led boycott of the 1980 Moscow Olympics, Yamashita appeared on national television pleading, with tears in his eyes, for a reversal of that decision. A week later Yamashita was held to a draw by Sumio Endo, who fell on top of Yamashita's left leg, breaking his ankle.

By the time 1984 rolled around, all this was forgotten and Yamashita seemed as sure a bet for a gold medal as anyone in Los Angeles. But in his second match, a victory over Arthur Schnabel, Yamashita tore a muscle in his right calf, causing him great pain and forcing him to walk with a limp. His next opponent, Laurent del Colombo, attacked Yamashita's right leg and scored a throw for Koka. Ten seconds later del Colombo was flat on his back with the 5-foot 11-inch, 280-pound Yamashita on top of him. The match was quickly over.

In the final, Yamashita, described by one disgruntled ·opponent as "a refrigerator with a head on top," faced Mohamed Ali Rashwan, a 28-year-old building contractor from Alexandria. Yamashita scored a quick and easy victory, and was immediately overcome by his emotions. So sore was his leg that Rashwan had to help him onto the top step at the medal ceremony.

Afterwards, Rashwan told reporters, "I did not attack his right side because this is against my principles. I would not want to win this way." Rashwan was applauded for his good sportsmanship and news of his deed spread far and wide. On September 26, 1985, Rashwan was awarded the Fair Play Trophy by the International Committee for Fair Play. However, this inspiring tale of the true Olympic spirit has an odd twist to it. Videotapes of the Olympic final clearly show that Rashwan *did* try to attack Yamashita's injured leg. In fact, it was his first move, a mere ten seconds after the match began.

WOMEN

Women's matches last for four minutes.

EXTRA-LIGHTWEIGHT
(48 kg–106 lbs)

1896-1988 not held

1992 Barcelona C: 22, N: 22, D: 8.2.

			FINAL MATCH
1. Cécile Nowak	FRA		Kochiki-taoshi 4:00
2. Ryoko Tamura	JPN		
3. Amarilis Savón Carmenaty	CUB		
3. Hülya Şenyurt	TUR		
5. Karen Briggs	GBR		
5. Salima Souakri	ALG		
7. Yolanda Soler Grajera	SPA		
7. María Villapol Blanco	VEN		

The division was dominated by Cécile Nowak and Karen Briggs, who had met in the final of the 1991 world championship and the last three European championships, with Nowak winning each time. It was assumed that the two would meet again in the Olympic final, but in her semifinal bout against 16-year-old Ryoko Tamura,

Briggs dislocated her shoulder and ended up without a medal.

HALF-LIGHTWEIGHT
(52 kg–114.61 lbs)

1896-1988 not held

1992 Barcelona C: 25, N: 25, D: 8.1.

			FINAL MATCH
1. Almudena Muñoz Martinez	SPA		Tani-otoshi 4:00
2. Noriko Mizoguchi	JPN		
3. Li Zhongyun	CHN		
3. Sharon Rendle	GBR		
5. Jessica Gal	HOL		
5. Alessandra Giungi	ITA		
7. Claudia Mariani Ambrueso	ARG		
7. Paula Saldanha	POR		

Muñoz was the beneficiary of a series of "hometown" decisions that pleased the Spanish crowd but shocked judo aficionados. Particularly surprising was the result of her third-round match against tournament favorite Sharon Rendle. The referee declared Rendle the winner, but the judges overruled the decision, leaving even Muñoz with a look of surprise on her face.

LIGHTWEIGHT
(56 kg–123 lbs)

1896-1988 not held

1992 Barcelona C: 23, N: 23, D: 7.31.

			FINAL MATCH
1. Míriam Blasco Soto	SPA		Ko-soto-gake 4:00
2. Nicola Fairbrother	GBR		
3. Driulis González Morales	CUB		
3. Chiyori Tateno	JPN		
5. Kate Donahoo	USA		
5. Nicole Flagothier	BEL		
7. Catherine Arnaud	FRA		
7. María Gontowicz Szalas	POL		

Twenty-eight-year-old Míriam Blasco was the defending world champion. A popular figure in Spain, when she appeared the enthusiastic audience loudly chanted her name. Two minutes into the final she earned a yuko on a counterattack and then survived a near-strangulation when the referee called a break.

HALF-MIDDLEWEIGHT
(61 kg–134.5 lbs)

1896-1988 not held

1992 Barcelona C: 29, N: 29, D: 7.30.

			FINAL MATCH	
1. Catherine Fleury	FRA		Yusei-gachi	4:00
2. Yael Arad	ISR			
3. Yelena Petrova	RUS			
3. Zhang Di	CHN			
5. Frauke Eickoff	GER			
5. Koo Hyun-sook	KOR			
7. Xiomara Griffith Mahon	VEN			
7. Begoña Gómez Martín	SPA			

In the semifinals, world champion Frauke Eickoff faced Yael Arad, who was attempting to become Israel's first Olympic medalist. Two minutes and twenty-one seconds into the bout the referee signaled an ippon, ending the fight. Eickoff leaped to her feet, her arms raised in victory. Then the referee pointed to Arad, indicating that it was she who had scored. Twenty years after eleven members of the Israeli Olympic team had been killed by terrorists, Arad, a native-born Israeli, had earned her nation's first medal.

In the final, Arad faced Catherine Fleury, who had won the European and world championships in 1989, but had not made it to a major final since. The contest ended without a single point being scored. The two judges split and the referee gave the nod to Fleury.

MIDDLEWEIGHT

(66 kg–145.5 lbs)

1896-1988 not held

1992 Barcelona C: 21, N: 21, D: 7.29.

		FINAL MATCH	
1. Odalys Reve Jiménez	CUB	Uchi-mata	4:00
2. Emanuela Pierantozzi	ITA		
3. Kate Howey	GBR		
3. Heidi Rakels	BEL		
5. Claire Lecat	FRA		
5. Alexandra Schreiber	GER		
7. Grace Jividen	USA		
7. Laura Martinel Acuña	ARG		

Two-time world champion Emanuela Pierantozzi needed only seven seconds to defeat Alexandra Schreiber in the semifinals. In the final she faced Odalys Reve, whom she had beaten in the 1991 world championship final. However, in the Olympic final it was Reve who dominated the match. When asked afterward to describe the bout, she replied, "The final was very fast—so fast I can't remember what happened."

HALF-HEAVYWEIGHT

(72 kg–158.5 lbs)

1896-1988 not held

1992 Barcelona C: 22, N: 22, D: 7.28.

		FINAL MATCH	
1. Kim Mi-jung	KOR	Yusei-gachi	4:00
2. Yoko Tanabe	JPN		
3. Irene de Kok	HOL		
3. Laetitia Meignan	FRA		
5. Josie Horton	GBR		
5. Regina Schüttenhelm	GER		
7. Kåtarina Hakansson	SWE		
7. Katarzyna Juszczak	POL		

Kim, the defending world champion, won her first bout in five seconds and her second in ten seconds. Her four victories leading to the final took a total of only six minutes.

HEAVYWEIGHT

(Over 72 kg–158.5 lbs)

1896-1988 not held

1992 Barcelona C: 21, N: 21, D: 7.27.

		FINAL MATCH	
1. Zhuang Xiaoyan	CHN	Kami-shiho-gatame	2:42
2. Estela Rodriguez Villanueva	CUB		
3. Natalina Lupino	FRA		
3. Yoko Sakaue	JPN		
5. Beata Maksymow	POL		
5. Claudia Weber	GER		
7. Svetlana Gundarenko	RUS		
7. Éva Gránicz	HUN		

Zhuang won four of her five bouts using kami-shiho-gatame.

MODERN PENTATHLON

Individual
Discontinued Event

One of the highlights of the ancient Olympics for over 900 years was the pentathlon, in which athletes would run a short distance, jump, throw a javelin, throw a discus, and wrestle. Baron Pierre de Coubertin, the founder of the modern Olympics, created the modern pentathlon and managed to get it included in the Olympic program for 1912.

The basic premise behind the modern pentathlon is that a soldier is ordered to deliver a message. He starts out on the back of an unfamiliar horse, but is forced to dismount and fight a duel with swords. He escapes, but is trapped and has to shoot his way out with a pistol. Then he swims across a river, and finally he finishes his assignment by running 4000 meters through the woods.

In 1912, from 1924 to 1980, and in 1988, the modern pentathlon competition was held over a period of five days with one event each day. In 1920, 1984, and 1992 it lasted four days. Faced with the sport's elimination from the Olympic program, the International Modern Pentathlon Union has radically altered the format for 1996 by scheduling all five events in one day. In addition, the team competition has been eliminated and each nation will be limited to two entries.

Between 1912 and 1952 the scoring was based on an athlete's placing in each of the five events. Since 1956, the modern pentathlon has been scored like the decathlon, with a set of charts assigning a point total to each performance.

According to current regulations, the pentathletes begin by firing 20 shots with an air pistol at a target 10 meters away. A bull's-eye earns ten points. A total score of 172 out of 200 points is worth 1000 pentathlon points.

Every target point above or below is worth plus or minus 12 pentathlon points.

In the fencing competition the athletes use épée swords. Each athlete fences for one touch against every other athlete. If no touch is made within one minute, both fencers are credited with a loss. A total score of 70 percent victories is equal to 1000 pentathlon points.

The swimming event is a freestyle race over 300 meters. A time of 3 minutes 54 seconds is worth 1000 pentathlon points. For every half second above or below that time four points are subtracted or added.

The riding portion of the contest is a show-jumping competition with horses picked by lot twenty minutes before the competition begins. The track can be between 350 and 450 meters long and must include twelve obstacles including one double and one triple. Competitors begin with 1100 points and lose 30 points for a knockdown, 40 points for refusal to jump, 60 points for falling off, and 3 points per second for being over the time limit.

The competition concludes with a 4000-meter cross-country run. A time of 14 minutes 15 seconds earns 1000 pentathlon points. Every second above or below this time subtracts or adds three points to the score. Happily, a handicapped start system, used in 1984 and 1988, will be revived in 1996. The runners' starting order is based on their total score for the first four events. The leader starts first; the others start sometime later, with three points equaling a one-second delay.

INDIVIDUAL

1896–1908 not held

1912 Stockholm C: 32, N: 10, D: 7.12.

		SHOOTING	SWIMMING	FENCING	RIDING	RUNNING	TOTAL
1. Gösta Lilliehöök	SWE	3	10	5	4	5	27
2. Gösta Åsbrink	SWE	1	4	15	7	1	28
3. Georg de Laval	SWE	2	3	10	3	12	30
4. Åke Grönhagen	SWE	18	5	1	1	10	35
5. George Patton	USA	21	7	4	6	3	41
6. Sidney Stranne	SWE	11	9	3	8	11	42
7. Karl Mannström	SWE	14	14	16	2	9	55
8. Edmund Bernhardt	AUT	26	2	6	12	14	60

The fifth-place finisher was a 26-year-old army lieutenant, George S. Patton, Jr. who later went on to considerable fame as a general during World War II. Ironically,

Patton might have won the event had he not been such a poor marksman, placing a mediocre 21st in a field of 32 in the shooting competition. Patton claimed that he was penalized for missing the target completely when in fact the bullet had gone through a previously-made hole. If he had been been able to prove his case, he would have won the gold medal. However, there is no evidence at all to support his contention.

If Lilliehöök had taken five more seconds to finish the 4000-meter cross-country run, he would have lost the gold medal.

1920 Antwerp C: 23, N: 8, D: 8.27.

		SHOOTING	SWIMMING	FENCING	RIDING	RUNNING	TOTAL
1. Gustaf Dyrssen	SWE	6	2	2	6	2	18
2. Erik de Laval	SWE	1	13	5	1	3	23
3. Gösta Runö	SWE	4	1	16	5	1	27
4. Bengt Uggla	SWE	13	5	10	13	5	46
5. Marius Christensen	DEN	12	7	3	7	18	47
6. Harold Rayner	USA	5	12	13	14	4	48
7. Emil Hagelberg	FIN	10	3	21	9	8	51
8. Robert Sears	USA	3	8	9	11	20	51

1924 Paris C: 38, N: 11, D: 7.17.

		SHOOTING	SWIMMING	FENCING	RIDING	RUNNING	TOTAL
1. Bo Lindman	SWE	9	1	3	4	1	18
2. Gustaf Dyrssen	SWE	20	4	1	3	11.5	39.5
3. Bertil Uggla	SWE	7	21	5	5	7	45
4. Ivan Duranthon	FRA	4	18	17.5	11	4	54.5
5. Harry Avellan	FIN	17	6	17.5	1	14	55.5
6. Helge Jensen	DEN	2	19	11.5	9.5	19	61
7. George Vokins	GBR	24	11	10	8	11.5	64.5
8. Christiaan Tonnet	HOL	22	12	13.5	16	2	65.5

1928 Amsterdam C: 37, N: 14, D: 8.4.

		SHOOTING	SWIMMING	FENCING	RUNNING	RIDING	TOTAL
1. Sven Thofelt	SWE	6	2	4	21	14	47
2. Bo Lindman	SWE	15	5	22	3	5	50
3. Helmuth Kahl	GER	10	9	2	19	12	52
4. Ingvar Berg	SWE	3	11	36	7	1	58
5. Heinz Hax	GER	1	15	21	20	2	59
6. David Turquand-Young	GBR	24	7	15	9	10	65
7. Hermann Hölter	GER	16	8	11	21	13	69
7. Christiaan Tonnet	HOL	8	24	27	6	4	69

Thofelt later won medals in team épée fencing in 1936 and, 20 years after his modern pentathlon gold, in 1948.

1932 Los Angeles C: 25, N: 10, D: 8.6.

		RIDING	FENCING	SHOOTING	SWIMMING	RUNNING	TOTAL
1. Johan Oxenstierna	SWE	4	14	2	5	7	32
2. Bo Lindman	SWE	1	2.5	19	9	4	35.5
3. Richard Mayo	USA	2	4.5	1	14	17	38.5
4. Sven Thofelt	SWE	15	1	9	1	13	39
5. Willy Remer	GER	12	10	4	13	8	47
6. Conrad Miersch	GER	10	10	5	17	6	48
7. Elemér Somfay	HUN	20	4.5	6	12	10	52.5
8. Charles Digby Legard	GBR	6	18	10	18	1	53

After taking a few practice shots in the woods just before the competition was to begin, Oxenstierna was confronted by an angry policeman who threatened to arrest him. Since the competition was about to begin, the police officer agreed to wait. He watched Oxenstierna shoot, realized he was not a criminal, and let him go.

1936 Berlin C: 42, N: 16, D: 8.6.

			RIDING	FENCING	SHOOTING	SWIMMING	RUNNING	TOTAL
1.	Gotthardt Handrick	GER	2.5	2	4	9	14	31.5
2.	Charles Leonard	USA	15	10	1	6	7.5	39.5
3.	Silvano Abba	ITA	1	15.5	10	14	5	45.5
4.	Sven Thofelt	SWE	8.5	5.5	6	3	24	47
5.	Nándor Orbán	HUN	4	12.5	21	2	16	55.5
6.	Hermann Lemp	GER	31	3.5	11	1	21	67.5
7.	Alfred Starbird	USA	8.5	8.5	23	20	7.5	67.5
8.	Rezsö Bartha	HUN	27	12.5	3	12	22	76.5

In the pistol-shooting portion of the competition, Lieutenant Charles Leonard of St. Petersburg, Florida, became the first person in the history of the event to achieve a perfect score of 200.

1948 London C: 45, N: 16, D: 8.4.

			RIDING	FENCING	SHOOTING	SWIMMING	RUNNING	TOTAL
1.	William "Willie" Grut	SWE	1	1	5	1	8	16
2.	George Moore	USA	2	3	21	17	4	47
3.	Gösta Gärdin	SWE	6	17	10	11	5	49
4.	Lauri Vilkko	FIN	17	38	4	3	2	64
5.	Olavi Larkas	FIN	26	3	7	19	16	71
6.	Bruno Riem	SWI	19	9	1	36	9	74
7.	Fritz Hegner	SWI	24	13	3	7	29	79
8.	Richard Gruenther	USA	13	12	14	24	19	81

Captain William Grut, a 33-year-old artillery officer, accomplished the most decisive victory in the history of the modern pentathlon, finishing first in three of the five events. Six months earlier, at the Winter Olympics in St. Moritz, Grut had finished second in a demonstration event called the "winter pentathlon," consisting of downhill skiing, cross-country skiing, shooting, fencing, and an equestrian course.

1952 Helsinki C: 51, N: 19, D: 7.25.

			RIDING	FENCING	SHOOTING	SWIMMING	RUNNING	TOTAL
1.	Lars Hall	SWE	1	7	15	1	8	32
2.	Gábor Benedek	HUN	8	2	9	18	2	39
3.	István Szondy	HUN	3	4	12	5	17	41
4.	Igor Novikov	SOV/ARM	24	13	4	4	10	55
5.	Frederick Denman	USA	9	11	6	17	19	62
5.	Olavi Mannonen	FIN	2	37	10	9	4	62
7.	Lauri Vilkko	FIN	1	8	38	11	5	63
8.	W. Thad McArthur	USA	29	3	23	12	1	68

Twenty-five-year-old Lars Hall was the first nonmilitary winner of the modern pentathlon. A carpenter from

Lars Hall, the only repeat winner of the modern pentathlon (1952 and 1956).

Gothenburg, Hall had two lucky breaks. The horse that he drew for the equestrian competition was discovered to be lame. The horse that he was assigned as a substitute turned out to be the best horse in Finland, and Hall's only challenge was to keep from falling off as the horse raced through the course. Two days later, Hall arrived 20 minutes late for the pistol-shooting, but was saved from disqualification due to a Soviet protest that was still being sorted out.

1956 Melbourne C: 40, N: 16, D: 11.28.

		RIDING	FENCING	SHOOTING	SWIMMING	RUNNING	TOTAL
1. Lars Hall	SWE	1035 (4)	889 (4)	720(24)	1030 (2)	1159 (8)	4833
2. Olavi Mannonen	FIN	997.5 (5)	815 (8)	880 (5)	920(15)	1162 (7)	4774
3. Väinö Korhonen	FIN	885 (9)	963 (2)	880 (5)	905(16)	1117(12)	4750
4. Igor Novikov	SOV/ARM	802.5(14)	815 (8)	920 (2)	935 (6)	1192 (4)	4714
5. George Lambert	USA	1070 (1)	667(17)	900 (4)	975 (7)	1081(15)	4693
6. Gábor Benedek	HUN	860 (11)	889 (4)	920 (2)	855(18)	1126(10)	4650
7. William André	USA	887.5 (5)	889 (4)	860 (8)	870(17)	1123(11)	4629
8. Aleksandr Tarassov	SOV/RUS	810 (13)	778(10)	880 (5)	825(21)	1186 (5)	4479

1960 Rome C: 60, N: 23, D: 8.31.

		RIDING	FENCING	SHOOTING	SWIMMING	RUNNING	TOTAL
1. Ferenc Németh	HUN	1009(31)	977 (2)	880(10)	990 (6)	1168 (7)	5024
2. Imre Nagy	HUN	1048(19)	1000 (1)	840(23)	935(18)	1165 (8)	4988
3. Robert Beck	USA	1039(24)	977 (2)	940 (3)	1010 (4)	1015(24)	4981
4. András Balczó	HUN	1037(20)	885 (6)	760(36)	1075 (1)	1216 (2)	4973
5. Igor Novikov	SOV/ARM	982(33)	839 (9)	860(15)	1035 (2)	1246 (1)	4962
6. Nikolai Tatarinov	SOV/RUS	1138 (5)	747(19)	820(27)	885(28)	1168 (6)	4758
7. Stanislaw Przybylski	POL	1111(13)	747(20)	860(16)	815(39)	1198 (3)	4731
8. Jack Daniels	USA	1024(27)	793(12)	900 (6)	1015 (3)	985(26)	4717

1964 Tokyo C: 37, N: 15, D: 10.15.

		RIDING	FENCING	SHOOTING	SWIMMING	RUNNING	TOTAL
1. Ferenc Török	HUN	1070(15)	1000 (1)	960(10)	960(23)	1126 (5)	5116
2. Igor Novikov	SOV/ARM	1040(26)	856 (5)	1020 (3)	1055 (5)	1096 (6)	5067
3. Albert Mokeyev	SOV/RUS	970(33)	748(15)	1060 (1)	1045 (7)	1216 (1)	5039
4. Peter Macken	AUS	1070(19)	640(21)	1020 (4)	1035 (8)	1132 (3)	4897
5. Viktor Mineyev	SOV/AZR	1040(24)	820 (9)	960(13)	1050 (6)	1024(15)	4894
6. James Moore	USA	1070(16)	676(20)	960(12)	990(15)	1195 (2)	4891
7. Imre Nagy	HUN	1040(30)	892 (2)	960 (9)	940(28)	1042(11)	4874
8. Bo-Herman Jansson	SWE	1100 (3)	748(16)	780(28)	1075 (1)	1057(10)	4760

1968 Mexico City C: 48, N: 18, D: 10.17.

		RIDING	FENCING	SHOOTING	SWIMMING	RUNNING	TOTAL
1. Björn Ferm	SWE	1100 (5)	885 (8)	934(11)	1075 (2)	970 (5)	4964
2. András Balczó	HUN	1010(22)	931 (6)	934(12)	1054 (5)	1024 (2)	4953
3. Pavlo Lednyov	SOV/UKR	1070 (8)	839(15)	934 (9)	1060 (4)	892(16)	4795
4. Karl-Heinz Kutschke	GDR	1070(10)	632(41)	846(26)	1126 (1)	1090 (1)	4764
5. Borys Onyshchenko	SOV/UKR	995(28)	885 (8)	912(15)	1054 (5)	910(13)	4756
6. Raoul Gueguen	FRA	1040(14)	954 (5)	912(13)	1000(10)	850(20)	4756
7. István Moná	HUN	1010(20)	1040 (2)	868(22)	943(23)	847(22)	4714
8. Jeremy Fox	GBR	1010(21)	862(12)	890(18)	1006 (9)	895(15)	4663

DISQ (Drugs): Hans-Gunnar Liljenvall (SWE) 4664

Ferm, a 24-year-old economics student, kept busy during the 12-hour fencing competition by reading detective stories. When it came down to the final cross-country run, he needed to beat 14 minutes 30 seconds to win the gold medal. Ferm struggled through the unfamiliar rarefied air and crossed the finish line with only four seconds to spare. An ugly incident had marred the riding event.

Hans-Jürgen Todt of West Germany drew a beautiful but stubborn horse named Ranchero, which balked three times at one of the obstacles. After completing the course, Todt, disconsolate at seeing his years of training gone to waste because of bad luck, attacked the horse and had to be pulled away by his teammates.

1972 Munich C: 59, N: 21, D: 8.31.

		RIDING	FENCING	SHOOTING	SWIMMING	RUNNING	TOTAL
1. András Balczó	HUN	1060(17)	1057 (2)	956(12)	1060(25)	1279 (3)	5412
2. Borys Onyshchenko	SOV/UKR	945(42)	1076 (1)	1066 (2)	1128(11)	1120(21)	5335
3. Pavlo Lednyov	SOV/UKR	1060(14)	1019 (3)	1022 (4)	1092(18)	1135(14)	5328
4. Jeremy "Jim" Fox	GBR	1100 (2)	1019 (3)	868(22)	1024(32)	1300 (1)	5311
5. Vladimir Shmelyov	SOV/RUS	920(47)	962 (7)	1022 (5)	1176 (6)	1222 (6)	5302
6. Björn Ferm	SWE	1100 (4)	943(10)	978 (7)	1112(13)	1150(10)	5283
7. Heiner Thade	GER	1065(12)	962 (7)	956(13)	1012(37)	1150 (9)	5145
8. Risto Hurme	FIN	950(40)	981 (5)	1044 (3)	1068(24)	1051(33)	5094

Five-time world champion András Balczó finally won an Olympic individual gold medal at the age of 34. Tied for third place after four events, Balczó, a typewriter mechanic, set off on the cross-country course at a terrific pace and staggered home a winner. Quite an uproar developed when it was discovered through drug tests that 14 pentathletes had taken the tranquilizers Valium and Librium before going out on the shooting range. These drugs were banned by the International Modern Pentathlon Union, but were considered acceptable by the International Olympic Committee. For this reason no disqualifications were made.

1976 Montreal C: 47, N: 15, D: 7.22.

		RIDING	FENCING	SHOOTING	SWIMMING	RUNNING	TOTAL
1. Janusz Pyciak-Peciak	POL	1066(23)	928 (5)	1044 (3)	1164(17)	1318 (3)	5520
2. Pavlo Lednyov	SOV/UKR	1032(32)	1096 (1)	1022 (6)	1092(30)	1243(10)	5485
3. Jan Bártu	CZE	1100 (1)	976 (3)	1044 (5)	1184(13)	1162(22)	5466
4. Daniele Masala	ITA	1090(14)	832(13)	1066 (2)	1244 (2)	1201(17)	5433
5. Adrian Parker	GBR	1100 (1)	712(30)	868(29)	1240 (7)	1378 (1)	5298
6. John Fitzgerald	USA	1036(25)	952 (4)	1000 (9)	1232 (8)	1066(42)	5286
7. Jorn Steffensen	DEN	1100 (1)	856 (9)	1044 (4)	1068(38)	1213(14)	5281
8. Boris Mosolov	SOV/RUS	1036(25)	856 (9)	934(20)	1212 (9)	1162(22)	5200

Pyciak-Peciak was only in fifth place after four events, but he ran a strong 4000 meters and finished with 12 seconds to spare in 12:29.70.

1980 Moscow C: 43, N: 19, D: 7.24.

		RIDING	FENCING	SHOOTING	SWIMMING	RUNNING	TOTAL
1. Anatoly Starostin	SOV/RUS	1068(13)	1000 (4)	1110 (2)	1216(10)	1174 (8)	5568
2. Tamás Szombathelyi	HUN	1100 (2)	1026 (2)	1088 (3)	1144(24)	1144(11)	5502
3. Pavlo Lednyov	SOV/UKR	1026(21)	1026 (2)	1022(15)	1104(31)	1204 (4)	5382
4. Svante Rasmuson	SWE	936(40)	922 (7)	1000(17)	1332 (2)	1183 (6)	5373
5. Tibor Maracskó	HUN	980(32)	964 (6)	956(27)	1208(12)	1171 (9)	5279
6. Janusz Pyciak-Peciak	POL	1070(12)	844(13)	978(25)	1172(14)	1204 (5)	5268
7. Lennart Pettersson	SWE	1050(18)	922 (7)	1088 (6)	1156(19)	1027(32)	5243
8. Milan Kadlec	CZE	1084 (8)	792(20)	1088 (4)	1088(34)	1177 (7)	5229

Following his victory at the 1986 world championships, Starostin was one of 15 pentathletes who failed a doping test for sedatives and were banned from competition for 30 months.

1984 Los Angeles-Irvine C: 52, N: 18, D: 8.1.

		RIDING	FENCING	SWIMMING	SHOOTING	RUNNING	TOTAL
1. Daniele Masala	ITA	1100 (1)	956 (4)	1300 (8)	978(10)	1135(20)	5469
2. Svante Rasmuson	SWE	1070(13)	1022 (2)	1304 (4)	912(24)	1148(16)	5456
3. Carlo Massullo	ITA	1100 (2)	758(27)	1220(20)	1066 (2)	1262 (2)	5406
4. Richard Phelps	GBR	1100 (3)	912 (5)	1304 (5)	780(43)	1295 (1)	5391
5. Michael Storm	USA	1040(23)	868(12)	1288 (9)	1088 (1)	1041(30)	5325
6. Paul Four	FRA	1040(20)	978 (3)	1204(21)	1066 (2)	999(35)	5287
7. Ivar Sisniega	MEX	1070 (9)	912 (5)	1320 (2)	780(43)	1200 (7)	5282
8. Jorge Quesada	SPA	1060(16)	890 (9)	1172(25)	1000 (8)	1159(14)	5281

The 1984 Olympics saw two important changes in the organization of the modern pentathlon competition. First, the event was compressed into four days instead of five. In order to discourage the pentathletes from taking sedatives and beta-blockers to steady their nerves before shooting, the shooting portion of the competition was moved to the morning of the final day, five hours before the cross country run.

The second change was instituted to create a more dramatic finish. Instead of starting the runners in random order, the leader after four events, in this case Daniele Masala, started first. The other runners were given a handicap time depending on how many points behind they were, with 3 points equaling one second. Thus Svante Rasmuson had to wait 8⅔ seconds before he started and Paul Four 15⅓ seconds. By the time Carlo Massullo hit the course in fifth place, Masala had been running 1 minute 10⅔ seconds. The new method meant that even though the scoring was the same, the first person across the finish line was actually the winner.

The finish was indeed a dramatic one. Rasmuson caught Masala with 100 meters to go and appeared headed for victory. But 20 meters from the finish, the exhausted Swedish medical student stumbled on the soft dirt after rounding the final sharp left turn. Rasmuson staggered into a potted plant which was being used to brighten up the course boundary, and Masala ran by to take the gold medal.

"Have you ever been so tired you can't even control your body?" Rasmuson asked later. Then he added, "I hate soft dirt."

1988 Seoul C: 65, N: 26, D: 9.22.

		RIDING	FENCING	SWIMMING	SHOOTING	RUNNING	TOTAL
1. János Martinek	HUN	1066 (6)	990 (2)	1264(15)	868(45)	1216 (6)	5404
2. Carlo Massullo	ITA	1010(19)	881(13)	1204(32)	1044 (8)	1240 (4)	5379
3. Vakhtang Yagorashvili	SOV/GEO	980(24)	915 (8)	1344 (2)	978(16)	1150(19)	5367
4. Attila Mizsér	HUN	1010(20)	847(18)	1196(33)	934(26)	1294 (1)	5281
5. Christophe Ruer	FRA	968(28)	779(30)	1348 (1)	934(29)	1213 (7)	5242
6. Richard Phelps	GBR	964(29)	898(11)	1304 (8)	868(47)	1195(11)	5229
7. László Fábián	HUN	876(47)	1051 (1)	1304 (8)	802(53)	1168(17)	5201
8. Joël Bouzou	FRA	1004(22)	983 (3)	1172(37)	868(46)	1171(16)	5198

In 1988, thanks to improved drug-testing procedures, the competition was able to revert to its traditional five-day format. Martinek began the cross-country course 9⅔ seconds after Yagorashvili, passed him at the halfway mark and pulled away to a convincing victory, finishing 9 seconds ahead of Massullo.

1992 Barcelona C: 66, N: 30, D: 7.29.

		FENCING	SWIMMING	SHOOTING	RUNNING	RIDING	TOTAL
1. Arkadiusz Skrzypaszek	POL	1000 (2)	1252(21)	1120(11)	1147(23)	1040(13)	5559
2. Attila Mizsér	HUN	898 (7)	1208(40)	1135 (7)	1213 (9)	992(27)	5446
3. Eduard Zenovka	RUS	830(21)	1300 (7)	1240 (1)	1255 (3)	736(56)	5361
4. Anatoly Starostin	RUS	864(13)	1236(32)	1120 (9)	1117(31)	1010(22)	5347
5. Roberto Bomprezzi	ITA	847(16)	1148(56)	1105(12)	1216 (8)	1010(24)	5326
6. Håkan Norebrink	SWE	847(17)	1272(14)	1030(37)	1072(39)	1100 (3)	5321
7. Marian Gheorghe	ROM	878 (8)	1252(22)	955(50)	1108(35)	1100 (1)	5293
8. Graham Brookhouse	GBR	762(44)	1304 (6)	1015(40)	1141(24)	1070 (5)	5292

Between Olympics the International Modern Pentathlon Union decided that, since the riding portion of the sport was so volatile it often caused leading contenders to be knocked out of serious contention on the first day, it would be more dramatic if the riding test was the final event rather than the first. As an attempt to attract media attention, this experiment (which had been tried once before in 1928) failed. After Barcelona, the Union voted to return to the handicapped start system that had been used successfully in 1984 and 1988. However, the 1992 format did in fact produce a dramatic shift on the final day.

After four events Eduard Zenovka led world champion Arkadiusz Skrzypaszek by 106 points. But the 23-year-old Zenovka had a history of falling off horses and landing on his head. Indeed, he had already lost two major titles this way. Sure enough, having already chalked up 120 penalty points over the first nine obstacles, his horse stumbled at the tenth obstacle, dumping Zenovka, who lost his riding helmet and then breached the rules by heading on to the next obstacle before remembering to retrieve it. He fell again at the triple jump, although this time he kept his helmet on and doffed it to the VIP box after he remounted. Zenovka also lost 124 points when he exceeded the time limit of 1 minute 43 seconds by over a minute. By this time, he was lucky to hold on for a bronze medal.

Zenovka's sports misfortunes were nothing compared to the tragedy that would strike him on February 11, 1993. That night he was involved in a car crash that killed his passenger, world champion rhythmic gymnast Oksana Kostina. Zenovka, who was critically injured in the incident, was charged with drunken driving.

Discontinued Event
TEAM

1952 Helsinki T: 15, N: 15, D: 7.25.

		RIDING	FENCING	SHOOTING	SWIMMING	RUNNING	TOTAL
1. HUN	Gábor Benedek István Szondy Aladár Kovácsi	21 (2)	16 (1)	45 (4)	46 (5)	38 (3)	166
2. SWE	Lars Hall Torsten Lindqvist Claes Egnell	18 (1)	16 (1)	68 (8)	29 (2)	51 (6)	182
3. FIN	Olavi Mannonen Lauri Vilkko Olavi Rokka	38 (4)	90(10)	30 (1)	27 (1)	28 (1)	213
4. USA	Frederick Denman W. Thad McArthur Guy Troy	27 (3)	50 (5)	41 (2)	49 (6)	48 (4)	215
5. SOV	Igor Novikov Pavel Rakityansky Aleksandr Dehayev	76 (6)	69 (6)	81(11)	37 (4)	30 (2)	293
6. BRA	Eduardo Leal Medeiros Aloysio Alves Borges Eric Tinoco Marques	94(11)	42 (3)	70 (9)	34 (3)	73 (9)	313
7. CHI	Nilo Floody Buxton Hernán Fuentes Besoain Luis Carmona Barrales	77 (7)	42 (3)	42 (3)	90(11)	81(11)	336
8. ARG	Luis Riera Carlos Velázquez Jorge Cáceres Monie	53(15)	98(12)	52 (5)	75 (9)	77(10)	355

1956 Melbourne T: 12, N: 12, D: 11.28.

		RIDING	FENCING	SHOOTING	SWIMMING	RUNNING	TOTAL
1. SOV	Igor Novikov Aleksandr Tarassov Ivan Deryuhin	2457.5 (3)	2194 (2)	2850 (1)	2880 (1)	3579 (1)	13690.5
2. USA	George Lambert William André Jack Daniels	3020 (1)	2008 (4)	2560 (2)	2780 (2)	3114 (5)	13482
3. FIN	Olavi Mannonen Väinö Korhonen Berndt Katter	2512.5 (2)	2008 (4)	2520 (4)	2755 (3)	3390 (3)	13185.5
4. HUN	Gábor Benedek János Bódy Antal Moldrich	1727.5 (4)	2566 (1)	2460 (5)	2660 (4)	3141 (4)	12554.5
5. MEX	José Pérez Mier Antonio Almada Félix David Romero Vargas	1700 (5)	2008 (4)	2560 (2)	2640 (5)	2073 (8)	10981
6. ROM	Cornel Vena Dumitru Tintea Victor Teodorescu	1160 (8)	2194 (2)	2160 (6)	2195 (8)	2904 (6)	10613
7. GBR	Donald Cobley Thomas Hudson George Norman	335 (11)	1574 (7)	1340 (8)	2560 (6)	3417 (2)	9226

8. AUS	Neville Sayers						
	Sven Coomer	1060 (9)	1264 (8)	2040 (7)	2220 (7)	2241 (7)	8825
	George Nicoll						

1960 Rome T: 17, N: 17, D: 8.31.

		RIDING	FENCING	SHOOTING	SWIMMING	RUNNING	TOTAL
1. HUN	Ferenc Németh						
	Imre Nagy	3094 (5)	2740 (1)	2480 (6)	3000 (1)	3549 (2)	14863
	András Balczó						
2. SOV	Igor Novikov						
	Nikolai Tatarinov	3087 (6)	2326 (5)	2460 (7)	2845 (4)	3591 (1)	14309
	Hanno Selg						
3. USA	Robert Beck						
	Jack Daniels	3228 (4)	2402 (3)	2580 (2)	3000 (2)	2982 (7)	14192
	George Lambert						
4. FIN	Kurt Lindeman						
	Berndt Katter	2929(13)	2480 (2)	2580 (3)	2705 (7)	3171 (5)	13865
	Eero Lohi						
5. POL	Stanislaw Przybylski						
	Kazimierz Paszkiewicz	3315 (3)	1804(11)	2660 (1)	2535(12)	3432 (3)	13746
	Kazimierz Mazur						
6. SWE	Per-Erik Ritzén						
	Sture Ericson	3078 (8)	2352 (4)	2360 (9)	2585(11)	2841(10)	13216
	Björn Thofelt						
7. GBR	Patrick Harvey						
	Donald Cobley	3060 (9)	1700(15)	2400 (8)	2670 (8)	3273 (4)	13103
	Peter Little						
8. MEX	Antonio Almada Félix						
	Sergio Escobedo	3393 (1)	2184 (6)	2540 (4)	2625 (9)	2103(16)	12845
	José Pérez Mier						

1964 Tokyo T: 11, N: 11, D: 10.15.

		RIDING	FENCING	SHOOTING	SWIMMING	RUNNING	TOTAL
1. SOV	Igor Novikov						
	Albert Mokeyev	3050(11)	2385 (3)	3040 (1)	3150 (2)	3336 (1)	14961
	Viktor Mineyev						
2. USA	James Moore						
	David Kirkwood	3240 (3)	2262 (4)	2640 (5)	2915 (6)	3132 (3)	14189
	Paul Pesthy						
3. HUN	Ferenc Török						
	Imre Nagy	3150 (8)	2590 (1)	2380 (9)	2885 (7)	3168 (2)	14173
	Otto Török						
4. SWE	Bo-Herman Jansson						
	Rolf Junefelt	3240 (4)	2057 (6)	2460 (8)	3200 (1)	3099 (4)	14056
	Hans-Gunnar Liljenwall						
5. AUS	Peter Macken						
	Donald McMiken	3210 (5)	1770 (7)	2880 (2)	2990 (4)	2853 (6)	13703
	Duncan Page						
6. GER & GDR	Wolfgang Gödicke						
	Uwe Adler	3130 (9)	1729 (8)	2800 (4)	2955 (5)	2985 (5)	13599
	Elmar Frings						
7. FIN	Jorma Hotanen						
	Keijo Vanhala	3120(10)	2221 (5)	2560 (6)	2885 (8)	2754 (9)	13540
	Kari Kaaja						
8. JPN	Yoshihide Fukutome						
	Shigeaki Uchino	3210 (6)	1524(10)	2860 (3)	2865 (9)	2943 (6)	13402
	Shigeki Mino						

1968 Mexico City T: 15, N: 15, D: 10.17.

		RIDING	FENCING	SHOOTING	SWIMMING	RUNNING	TOTAL
1. HUN	András Balczó István Móna Ferenc Török	2940 (5)	3130 (1)	2714 (1)	2877 (6)	2664 (4)	14325
2. SOV	Pavlo Lednyov Borys Onyshchenko Stasys Šaparnis	3135 (1)	2558 (2)	2648 (5)	3141 (1)	2766 (2)	14248
3. FRA	Raoul Gueguen Lucien Guiguet Jean-Pierre Giudicelli	2855 (8)	2168(11)	2626 (6)	2931 (4)	2709 (3)	13289
4. USA	James Moore Robert Beck M. Thomas Lough	3030 (2)	2324 (7)	2670 (4)	2844 (7)	2412 (9)	13280
5. FIN	Seppo Aho Martti Ketelä Jorma Hotanen	2890 (6)	2558 (2)	2384(13)	2799 (8)	2607 (5)	13238
6. GDR	Karl-Heinz Kutschke Jörg Tscherner Wolfgang Lüderitz	2485(12)	2194(10)	2626 (6)	3093 (2)	2769 (1)	13167
7. JPN	Toshio Fukui Yuso Makihira Katsuaki Tashiro	2980 (4)	2428 (5)	2428 (9)	2796 (9)	2451 (6)	13083
8. GBR	Jeremy Fox Barry Lillywhite Robert Phelps	2790 (9)	2324 (9)	2670 (2)	2952 (3)	2157(11)	12893

DISQ (Drugs): SWE (Björn Ferm, Hans-Gunnar Liljenvall, Hans Jacobson) 14188

The Swedish team finished third with 14,188 points, but was disqualified when one of its members, Hans-Gunnar Liljenvall, failed the drug test for alcohol. It was a common practice for pentathletes to steady their nerves with a bit of alcohol before the shooting contest, but Liljenvall, who finished eighth individually, was found to have a blood alcohol concentration well above the acceptable limit, despite the fact that he claimed he had only drunk two beers.

1972 Munich T: 19, N: 19, D: 8.31.

		RIDING	FENCING	SHOOTING	SWIMMING	RUNNING	TOTAL
1. SOV	Borys Onyshchenko Pavlo Lednyov Vladimir Shmelyov	2925(13)	3060 (1)	3110 (1)	3396 (2)	3477 (2)	15968
2. HUN	András Balczó Zsigmond Villányi Pál Bakó	2975(10)	2820 (2)	2736 (2)	3280 (5)	3537 (1)	15348
3. FIN	Risto Hurme Veikko Salminen Martti Ketelä	3010 (6)	2580 (4)	2670 (3)	3300 (3)	3252 (9)	14812
4. USA	Charles Richards John Fitzgerald Scott Taylor	3115 (3)	2280(10)	2450(10)	3564 (1)	3393 (5)	14802
5. SWE	Björn Ferm Bo-Herman Jansson Hans-Gunnar Liljenvall	3125 (2)	2640 (3)	2428(11)	3236 (7)	3279 (8)	14708
6. GER	Heiner Thade Walter Esser Hole Rössler	3010 (7)	2520 (7)	2626 (4)	3232 (8)	3294 (7)	14682

		RIDING	FENCING	SHOOTING	SWIMMING	RUNNING	TOTAL
7. FRA	Michel Gueguen Jean-Pierre Giudicelli Raoul Gueguen	2990 (8)	2320 (9)	2538 (8)	3252 (6)	3459 (3)	14559
8. POL	Ryszard Wach Janusz Pyciak-Peciak Stanislaw Skwira	2955(11)	2420 (8)	2362(13)	3296 (4)	3252(10)	14285

1976 Montreal T: 14, N: 14, D: 7.22.

		RIDING	FENCING	SHOOTING	SWIMMING	RUNNING	TOTAL
1. GBR	Adrian Parker Robert "Danny" Nightin- gale Jeremy "Jim" Fox	3212 (3)	2256 (8)	2648 (8)	3492 (5)	3951 (1)	15559
2. CZE	Jan Bártu Bohumil Starnovsky Jiři Adam	2962(10)	2783 (1)	3000 (1)	3400 (8)	3306(12)	15451
3. HUN	Tamás Kancsal Tibor Maracskó Szvetiszláv Sasics	2772(12)	2773 (2)	2758 (5)	3528 (4)	3564 (5)	15395
4. POL	Janusz Pyciak-Peciak Krzysztof Trybusiewicz Zbigniew Pacelt	3170 (6)	2132(11)	2912 (3)	3544 (3)	3585 (2)	15343
5. USA	John Fitzgerald Michael Burley Robert Nieman	3140 (7)	2535 (4)	2296(12)	3768 (1)	3546 (7)	15285
6. ITA	Daniele Masala Pier Paolo Cristofori Mario Medda	3194 (4)	2256 (8)	2670 (6)	3428 (7)	3483 (8)	15031
7. FIN	Risto Hurme Jussi Pelli Heikki Hulkkonen	2794(11)	2597 (3)	2802 (4)	3228(10)	3579 (3)	15000
8. SWE	Hans Lager Bengt Lager Gunnar Jacobson	3268 (1)	2318 (7)	2340(11)	3468 (6)	3552 (6)	14946

In 1976 the noble sport of modern pentathlon was wracked by controversy. First of all, Captain Orben Greenwald, a member of the U.S. team, was prevented from competing when his team manager, Lieutenant-Colonel Donald Johnson of the U.S. Modern Pentathlon Training Center, courtmartialed him for insubordination. Although the charge was thrown out as soon as an investigation was begun, Greenwald was refused accreditation when he arrived in Montreal.

The real shock came on the second day of competition, during the fencing tournament. The favored Soviet team was fencing against the team from Great Britain, when the British pentathletes noticed something odd about the defending silver medalist, Army Major Borys Onyshchenko. In his fight against Adrian Parker, the automatic light registered a hit for the Ukrainian even though he didn't appear to have touched his opponent. Veteran Jeremy Fox was next to be drawn against Onyshchenko. When he too lost a hit without being touched, it became obvious that something was wrong with Onyshchenko's épée. The weapon was taken away

to be examined by the Jury of Appeal. Onyshchenko continued with a different sword, but an hour or so later the news came that he had been disqualified.

Evidently Onyshchenko, desperate for victory in his final international competition, had wired his sword with a well-hidden push-button circuit breaker which enabled him to register a hit whenever he wanted. It is unknown how long Onyshchenko had been using this trick, but his fencing scores, which were already high, had showed a marked upward surge beginning in 1970. He was spirited away from the Olympic Village almost immediately and was never seen outside the U.S.S.R. again. He was forever after known as Borys Dis-Onyshchenko.

Onyshchenko's disqualification eliminated the Soviets from the team competition, leaving an open field. After four events the British team was in fifth place, 547 points behind Czechoslovakia. But running was their specialty, and Parker, the first runner of the day, inspired the others to victory by completing the 4000-meter course in 12 minutes 9 seconds, the fastest time ever recorded in Olympic competition. Strong performances by Nightingale and Fox assured Britain of the unexpected victory.

1980 Moscow T: 12, N: 12, D: 7.24.

		RIDING	FENCING	SHOOTING	SWIMMING	RUNNING	TOTAL
1. SOV	Anatoly Starostin Pavlo Lednyov Yevgeny Lipeyev	3194 (2)	2896 (2)	2956(7)	3552 (4)	3528 (1)	16126
2. HUN	Tamás Szombathelyi Tibor Maracskó László Horváth	3088 (5)	3042 (1)	3000(6)	3428 (9)	3354 (4)	15912
3. SWE	Svante Rasmuson Lennart Pettersson George Horvath	3022 (8)	2714 (3)	3220(1)	3640 (1)	3249 (7)	15845
4. POL	Janusz Pyciak-Peciak Jan Olesiński Marek Bajan	3208 (1)	2506 (5)	2846(8)	3576 (3)	3498 (2)	15634
5. FRA	Paul Four Joel Bouzou Alani Cortes	3070 (6)	2600 (4)	3088(3)	3464 (8)	3123(10)	15345
6. CZE	Milan Kadlec Jan Bártu Bohumil Starnovsky	3154 (3)	2298 (8)	3044(5)	3504 (5)	3339 (6)	15339
7. FIN	Heikki Hulkkonen Jussi Pelli Pekka Santanen	2851(11)	2480 (6)	3132(2)	3384(10)	3240 (8)	15087
8. GBR	Robert Nightingale Peter Whiteside Nigel Clark	2946(10)	2246(10)	2824(9)	3584 (2)	3462 (3)	15062

1984 Los Angeles-Irvine T: 17, N: 17, D: 8.1.

		RIDING	FENCING	SWIMMING	SHOOTING	RUNNING	TOTAL
1. ITA	Daniele Masala Carlo Massullo Pierpaolo Cristofori	3240 (1)	2560 (4)	3716 (4)	2912 (4)	3632(1)	16066
2. USA	Michael Storm Robert Gregory Losey Dean Glenesk	3188 (2)	2604 (3)	3700 (6)	2802 (7)	3274(8)	15568
3. FRA	Paul Four Didier Boube Joel Bouzou	2994 (9)	2626 (2)	3484(11)	3044 (1)	3417(7)	15565
4. SWI	Andy Jung Peter Steinmann Peter Minder	3090 (5)	2516 (5)	3564(10)	2956 (2)	3217(9)	15343
5. MEX	Ivar Sisniega Alejandro Yrizar Marcelo Hoyo	3056 (7)	2450 (7)	3704 (5)	2648 (9)	3425(6)	15283
6. GER	Achim Bellmann Michael Rehbein Christian Sandow	3058 (6)	2494 (6)	3736 (3)	2296(14)	3444(5)	15028
7. GBR	Richard Phelps Michael Mumford Stephen Sowerby	2605(15)	2362 (9)	3764 (2)	2626(10)	3537(2)	14894
8. SPA	Jorge Quesada Eduardo Burguete Federico Galera	3106 (4)	2208(11)	3568 (9)	2516(12)	3493(4)	14891

1988 Seoul T: 19, N: 19, D: 9.22.

			RIDING	FENCING	SWIMMING	SHOOTING	RUNNING	TOTAL
1.	HUN	János Martinek Attila Mizsér László Fábián	2952 (5)	2888 (1)	3764 (4)	2604(14)	3678 (1)	15886
2.	ITA	Carlo Massullo Daniele Masala Gianluca Tiberti	2998 (3)	2392 (8)	3732 (8)	3110 (1)	3339 (7)	15571
3.	GBR	Richard Phelps Dominic Mahony Graham Brookhouse	2986 (4)	2439 (7)	3764 (4)	2604(14)	3483 (3)	15276
4.	FRA	Christophe Ruer Joël Bouzou Bruno Genard	2884 (6)	2473 (6)	3780 (3)	2714(11)	3417 (4)	15268
5.	SOV	Vakhtang Yagorashvili German Yuferov Anatoly Avdeyev	2376(14)	2735 (2)	3992 (1)	2802 (7)	3309 (8)	15214
6.	CZE	Milan Kadlec Tomáš Fleissner Jiří Prokopius	3050 (2)	2361 (9)	3508(14)	2758 (9)	3366 (6)	15043
7.	SWI	Peter Steinmann Andy Jung Peter Burger	2832 (8)	2541 (5)	3616(13)	2472(17)	3402 (5)	14863
8.	MEX	Ivar Sisniega Alejandro Yrizar Marcelo Hoyo	2730(11)	2361 (9)	3648(11)	2560(16)	3486 (2)	14785

1992 Barcelona T: 17, N: 17, D: 7.29.

			FENCING	SWIMMING	SHOOTING	RUNNING	RIDING	TOTAL
1.	POL	Maciej Czyżowicz Akradiusz Skrzypaszek Dariusz Goździak	2575 (2)	3632(16)	3420 (1)	3369 (8)	3022 (2)	16018
2.	RUS	Anatoly Starostin Dmitri Svatkovsky Eduard Zenovka	2490 (7)	3760 (4)	3345 (2)	3573 (2)	2756 (8)	15924
3.	ITA	Gianluca Tiberti Carlo Massullo Roberto Bomprezzi	2388 (12)	3640 (13)	3330 (3)	3252 (9)	3150 (1)	15760
4.	USA	Rob Stull James Haley J. Michael Gostigian	2507 (5)	3812 (1)	3195 (5)	3240 (10)	2895 (6)	15649
5.	HUN	László Fábián Attila Kis Kálnoki Attila Mizsér	2796 (1)	3696 (9)	3000 (11)	3489 (5)	2590 (13)	15571
6.	GBR	Graham Brookhouse Richard Phelps Dominic Mahony	2490 (7)	3756 (5)	2835 (14)	3480 (6)	3010 (3)	15571
7.	FRA	Joel Bouzou Christophe Ruer Sebastien Deleigne	2388 (11)	3704 (6)	3120 (8)	3546 (3)	2683 (11)	15441
8.	SWE	Per-Olov Danielsson Håkan Norebrink Per Nyqvist	2422 (10)	3668 (10)	3105 (10)	3237 (11)	2996 (4)	15428

The same disastrous ride that dropped Eduard Zenovka from first to third in the individual event allowed Poland to upset the Russians in the team event.

ROWING

MEN	WOMEN
MEN	*WOMEN*
Single Sculls	Single Sculls
Double Sculls	Double Sculls
Quadruple Sculls	Quadruple Sculls
Pair-Oared Shell Without Coxswain	Four-Oared Shell Without Coxswain
Four-Oared Shell Without Coxswain	Eight-Oared Shell With Coxswain
Eight-Oared Shell With Coxswain	Lightweight: Double Sculls
Lightweight: Double Sculls	Discontinued Events
Lightweight: Four-Oared Shell Without Cox-swain	
Discontinued Events	

There are two kinds of rowing events. In sculling events, each rower pulls two oars. In sweep events, each rower pulls one oar. In races in which a coxswain calls the strokes for the rower, the coxswain must weigh at least 50 kg (110½ lbs) for men's races and 45 kg (99¼ lbs) for women's races. If the coxswain is underweight, up to 5 kg of dead weight may be added to the boat. In 1996, lightweight events will be included in the Olympics for the first time. Men in lightweight events may weigh no more than 72.5 kg (160 lbs), women no more than 59 kg (130 lbs). In men's races, lightweight crews must average no more than 70 kg (154.3 lbs); in women's races, the average must be no more than 57 kg (125.7 lbs).

Since 1964 rowing contests have begun with qualifying tests. The eight fastest qualifiers advance directly to the semifinals, while the rest take part in a repêchage, or second-chance round (repêchage being the French word for "fishing again"). The four fastest participants in the repêchage races join the semifinals. The top six semifinalists take part in the final, while the other six take part in a "petit-final," to determine 7th through 12th places.

In 1900 the course was 1750 meters long, in 1904 3218 meters (2 miles), in 1908 2414 meters (1.5 miles), and in 1948, 1883 meters. In 1906 the courses varied. In all other years, including 1996, all races have been 2000 meters long.

MEN

SINGLE SCULLS

1896 not held

1900 Paris C: 10, N: 2, D: 8.26.
1. Henri Barrelet   FRA   7:35.6
2. André Gaudin   FRA   7:41.6

3. Saint George Ashe   GBR   8:15.6
4. Robert d'Heilly   FRA   8:16.0
DNF: Louis Prével (FRA)

1904 St. Louis C: 4, N: 1, D: 7.30.
1. Frank Greer   USA   10:08.5
2. James Juvenal   USA   —
3. Constance Titus   USA   —
4. David Dulfield   USA   —

1906 Athens C: 2, N: 1, D: ?.
1. Gaston Delaplane   FRA   5:53.4
2. Joseph Larran   FRA   6:07.2

1908 London-Henley-on-Thames C: 9, N: 6, D: 7.31.
1. Henry Blackstaffe   GBR   9:26.0
2. Alexander McCulloch   GBR   —
3. Bernhard von Gaza   GER   —
3. Károly Levitzky   HUN   —

The 40-year-old Blackstaffe, who worked as a butcher, was twice the age of McCulloch, his opponent in the final. Yet he was able to finish more strongly and win by one and a quarter lengths.

1912 Stockholm C: 13, N: 11, D: 7.19.
1. William Kinnear   GBR   7:47.6
2. Polydore Veirman   BEL   7:56.0
3. Everard Butler   CAN   —
3. Mihkel Kuusik   RUS/EST   —

1920 Antwerp-Vilvoorde C: 10, N: 10, D: 8.29.
1. John Kelly, Sr.   USA   7:35.0
2. Jack Beresford   GBR   7:36.0
3. D. Clarence Hadfield d'Arcy   NZE
4. Frits Eyken   HOL

Philadelphia bricklayer Jack Kelly, who once won 126 straight races, was barred from competing in London's famous Diamond Sculls race at Henley because the Vesper Boat Club, of which he was a member, had been

Jack Kelly, father of Princess Grace of Monaco, won three rowing gold medals in 1920 and 1924.

accused of professionalism. Kelly got his revenge a few weeks later in the Olympics, when he defeated the Diamond Sculls winner, Jack Beresford, in the final. The two men were so exhausted after the race that they were unable to shake hands. Nevertheless, Kelly managed to recover sufficiently to win a second gold medal in the double sculls 30 minutes later. Kelly had two illustrious offspring. His son John, Jr., who competed in four Olympics himself, brought his father great joy when he won the Diamond Sculls at Henley in 1947 and 1949. His daughter was Grace Kelly, the famous film actress who later became Princess of Monaco.

1924 Paris C: 8, N: 8, D: 7.17.
1. Jack Beresford	GBR	7:49.2
2. William Garrett Gilmore	USA	7:54.0
3. Josef Schneider	SWI	8:01.1
DNF: Arthur Bull (AUS)		

In 1924 the system of repêchage was introduced, in which the second-place finishers in the preliminary heats were allowed a row-off for a place in the final. This was a break for Beresford, who lost to Gilmore in the opening round. Qualifying through the repêchage, Beresford turned the tables on Gilmore in the final and won by two and a half lengths. Despite his defeat, Gilmore had fond memories of the race. "During the last 200 meters," he later wrote, "when the sun seemed to get hotter with every stroke and I was making a supreme effort to grasp victory, a kindly breeze swept across the Seine, carrying a strong but pleasant scent from a perfumery which was not within sight. It was truly so strong that it first gagged me, but in a moment I was rowing on as if in a flowing river of the perfume itself."

1928 Amsterdam-Sloten C: 15, N: 15, D: 8.10.
1. Henry Pearce	AUS	7:11.0
2. Kenneth Myers	USA	7:20.8
3. Theodore Collet	GBR	7:29.8
4. Lambertus Gunther	HOL	7:31.6

5. Joseph Wright	CAN	
6. Josef Straka	CZE	
7. Edouard Candeveau	SWI	
8. Victor Saurin	FRA	

"Bobby" Pearce, a third-generation sculling champion from Sydney, faced an unexpected challenge in the middle of his quarterfinal race against Victor Saurin when a family of ducks passed single-file in front of his boat. Pearce let them pass and then sculled to a popular victory. He had hoped that his Olympic win would allow him to row in the Diamond Sculls at Henley, but he was refused admission because he was a carpenter. Back in Sydney he was unable to find work due to the Depression. When Lord Dewar, the Canadian whisky manufacturer, learned of Pearce's plight, he offered him a job as a salesman. This new position made Pearce eligible for Henley, since he was no longer a laborer. In 1931 he went to London and won the Diamond Sculls by six lengths. Although he moved to Hamilton, Ontario, in Canada, Pearce represented Australia again in 1932 and won a second gold medal.

1932 Los Angeles-Long Beach C: 5, N: 5, D: 8.13.
1. Henry Pearce	AUS	7:44.4
2. William Miller	USA	7:45.2
3. Guillermo Douglas	URU	8:13.6
4. Leslie Southwood	GBR	8:33.6

1936 Berlin-Grünau C: 20, N: 20, D: 8.14.
1. Gustav Schäfer	GER	8:21.5
2. Josef Hasenöhrl	AUT	8:25.8
3. Daniel Barrow	USA	8:28.0
4. Charles Campbell	CAN	8:35.0
5. Ernst Rufli	SWI	8:38.9
6. Pascual José Giorgio	ARG	8:57.5
7. Roger Verey	POL	
7. Humphrey Lloyd Warren	GBR	

The Olympic final was Schäfer's 51st consecutive victory.

1948 London-Henley-on-Thames C: 14, N: 14, D: 8.9.
1. Mervyn Wood	AUS	7:24.4
2. Eduardo Risso	URU	7:38.2
3. Romolo Catasta	ITA	7:51.4
4. Tranquilo Cappozzo	ARG	
4. John Kelly, Jr.	USA	
4. Jean Sepheriades	FRA	
7. Anthony Rowe	GBR	

The unusually handsome Wood was dubbed "The Cary Grant of Scullers" by U.S. journalists. A policeman who specialized in fingerprint analysis, Wood celebrated his victory by smoking his pipe for the first time in five months.

1952 Helsinki C: 18, N: 18, D: 7.23.
1. Yuri Tyukalov	SOV/RUS	8:12.8
2. Mervyn Wood	AUS	8:14.5
3. Teodor Kocerka	POL	8:19.4
4. T. Anthony Fox	GBR	8:22.5
5. Ian Stephen	SAF	8:31.4

1956 Melbourne-Ballarat C: 12, N: 12, D: 11.27.
1. Vyacheslav Ivanov   SOV/RUS   8:02.5
2. Stuart Mackenzie   AUS   8:07.7
3. John Kelly, Jr.   USA   8:11.8
4. Teodor Kocerka   POL   8:12.9

Mackenzie, who made his living as a chicken-sexer, seemed to have the race well in hand, but Ivanov made a sensational spurt with 200 meters to go and won going away. Eighteen-year-old Ivanov was so thrilled when he was presented with the gold medal that he jumped up and down with joy—and dropped the medal into Lake Wendouree. He immediately dived to the bottom of the water, but came back up empty-handed. After the games were over he was given a replacement medal by the I.O.C. He earned two more gold medals in 1960 and 1964. In 1959 Mackenzie became the first person to win both the single and double sculls at Henley.

1960 Rome-Lake Albano C: 13, N: 13, D: 9.3.
1. Vyacheslav Ivanov   SOV/RUS   7:13.96
2. Achim Hill   GDR   7:20.21
3. Teodor Kocerka   POL   7:21.26
4. James Hill   NZE   7:23.98
5. Harry Parker   USA   7:29.26
6. Savino Rebek   ITA   7:31.09

1964 Tokyo C: 13, N: 13, D: 10.15.
1. Vyacheslav Ivanov   SOV/RUS   8:22.51
2. Achim Hill   GDR   8:26.24
3. Gottfried Kottmann   SWI   8:29.68
4. Alberto Demiddi   ARG   8:31.51
5. Murray Watkinson   NZE   8:35.57
6. Donald Spero   USA   8:37.53
7. Robert Groen   HOL
8. Leif Gotfredsen   CAN

Ivanov staged another one of his famous finishing bursts, gaining 11 seconds on Hill in the last 500 meters. Actually he made such a tremendous effort that he blacked out before the finish line. In his book, *Winds of Olympic Lakes,* Ivanov wrote, "I don't remember how long it was before consciousness gradually returned. . . . I mustered the last ounce of my strength, raised my head and couldn't believe it: there was clear water ahead of me and nobody in front of me in those last 50 meters to the finish. I wondered whether it was a case of delirium and that I was having hallucinations. . . . I managed to find an extra bit of strength, picked up the oars and crossed the line first."

1968 Mexico City-Xochimilco C: 17, N: 17, D: 10.19.
1. Henri Jan Wienese   HOL   7:47.80
2. Jochen Meissner   GER   7:52.00
3. Alberto Demiddi   ARG   7:57.19
4. John Van Blom   USA   8:00.51
5. Achim Hill   GDR   8:06.09
6. Kenneth Dwan   GBR   8:13.76

7. Zdzsislaw Bromek   POL
8. Niels Secher   DEN

1972 Munich-Oberschleissheim C: 18, N: 18, D: 9.2.
1. Yuri Malishev   SOV/RUS   7:10.12
2. Alberto Demiddi   ARG   7:11.53
3. Wolfgang Güldenpfennig   GDR   7:14.45
4. Udo Hild   GER   7:20.81
5. James Dietz   USA   7:24.81
6. Melchior Bürgin   SWI   7:31.99
7. John Drea   IRL
8. Yordan Vulchev   BUL

1976 Montreal C: 15, N: 15, D: 7.25.
1. Pertti Karppinen   FIN   7:29.03
2. Peter Michael Kolbe   GER   7:31.67
3. Joachim Dreifke   GDR   7:38.03
4. Sean Drea   IRL   7:42.53
5. Mykhalo Dovgan   SOV/UKR   7:57.39
6. Ricardo Ibarra   ARG   8:03.05
7. James Dietz   USA
8. Edward Hale   AUS

Karppinen, a 6-foot 7-inch fireman from Parsio, won Finland's first rowing gold medal by coming from behind to upset world champion Kolbe and co-favorite Dreifke.

1980 Moscow C: 14, N: 14, D: 7.27.
1. Pertti Karppinen   FIN   7:09.61
2. Vassily Yakusha   SOV/BLR   7:11.66
3. Peter Kersten   GDR   7:14.88
4. Vladek Lacina   CZE   7:17.57
5. Hans Svensson   SWE   7:19.38
6. Hugh Matheson   GBR   7:20.28
7. Bernard Destraz   SWI
8. Konstantinos Kontomanolis   GRE

1984 Los Angeles-Lake Casitas C: 16, N: 16, D: 8.5.
1. Pertti Karppinen   FIN   7:00.24
2. Peter Michael Kolbe   GER   7:02.19
3. Robert Mills   CAN   7:10.38
4. John Biglow   USA   7:12.00
5. Ricardo Ibarra   ARG   7:14.59
6. Konstantinos Kontomanolis   GRE   7:17.03
7. Gary Reid   NZE
8. Raimund Haberl   AUT

Kolbe, now a ball-bearing salesman in Norway and the winner of four world championships, took the early lead. But Karppinen, as usual, came from behind, caught Kolbe after 1750 meters and then powered ahead in the last 25 meters to match Vyacheslav Ivanov's record of three single sculls gold medals.

1988 Seoul C: 22, N: 22, D: 9.24.
1. Thomas Lange   GDR   6:49.86
2. Peter Michael Kolbe   GER   6:54.77
3. Eric Verdonk   NZE   6:58.66
4. Hamish McGlashan   AUS   7:01.43
5. Kajetan Broniewski   POL   7:03.67

6. Andrew Sudduth   USA   7:11.45
7. Pertti Karpinnen   FIN
8. Jüri Jaanson   SOV/EST

Lange, a 24-year-old medical student from Halle, was the defending world champion. He overhauled Kolbe at 1300 meters and pulled away to win by a wide margin. Kolbe earned his third silver medal at age 35.

1992 Barcelona-Banyoles C: 22, N: 22, D: 8.1.
1. Thomas Lange   GER 6:51.40
2. Václav Chalupa   CZE 6:52.93
3. Kajetan Broniewski   POL 6:56.82
4. Eric Verdonk   NZE 6:57.45
5. Jüri Jaanson   EST 7:12.92
6. Sergio Fernández González   ARG 7:15.53
7. Joaquín Gómez Gurza   MEX
8. Harald Faderbauer   AUT

Lange followed up his 1988 Olympic victory by winning the world championship in 1989 and 1991. He missed the 1990 world championship after his father, a high-ranking member of the Communist Party, committed suicide following the collapse of Communism in East Germany.

DOUBLE SCULLS

1896–1900 not held

1904 St. Louis T: 3, N: 1, D: 7.30.
1. USA   (Atalanta Boat Club, New York—John   10.03.2
        Mulcahy, William Varley)
2. USA   (Ravenswood Boat Club, Long Island—John   —
        Hoben, James McLoughlin)
3. USA   (Independent Rowing Club, New Orleans—   —
        John Wells, Joseph Ravanack)

1906–1912 not held

1920 Antwerp-Vilvoorde T: 5, N: 5, D: 8.29.
1. USA   (John Kelly, Sr., Paul Costello)   7:09.0
2. ITA   (Erminio Dones, Pietro Annoni)   7:19.0
3. FRA   (Alfred Plé, Gaston Giran)   7:21.0

1924 Paris T: 5, N: 5, D: 7.17.
1. USA   (Paul Costello, John Kelly, Sr.)   6:34.0
2. FRA   (Marc Detton, Jean-Pierre Stock)   6:38.0
3. SWI   (Rudolf Bosshard, Heinrich Thoma)   —
4. BRA   (Edumundo Castello-Branco,   —
        Carlos Castello-Branco)

1928 Amsterdam-Sloten T: 10, N: 10, D: 7.17.
1. USA   (Paul Costello, Charles McIlvaine)   6:41.4
2. CAN   (Joseph Wright, Jack Guest)   6:51.0
3. AUT   (Leo Losert, Viktor Flessl)   6:48.8
4. GER   (Horst Hoeck, Gerhard Voigt)   6:48.2
5. HOL   (Henri Cox, Constant Pieterse)   6:52.8
6. SWI   (Rudolf Bosshard, Maurice Rieder)   6:53.4

Costello won his third straight double sculls gold medal with relative ease. He and McIlvaine were never seriously challenged and won the final against Wright and Guest by five lengths.

1932 Los Angeles-Long Beach T: 5, N: 5, D: 8.13.
1. USA   (Kenneth Myers, William Garrett Gilmore)   7:17.4
2. GER   (Herbert Buhtz, Gerhard Boetzelen)   7:22.8
3. CAN   (Charles Pratt, Noël de Mille)   7:27.6
4. ITA   (Orfeo Paroli, Mario Moretti)   7:49.2

Veteran Olympians Myers and Gilmore were 36 and 37 years old, respectively.

1936 Berlin-Grünau T: 12, N: 12, D: 8.14.
1. GBR   (Jack Beresford, Leslie Southwood)   7:20.8
2. GER   (Willy Kaidel, Joachim Pirsch)   7:26.2
3. POL   (Roger Verey, Jersy Ustupski)   7:36.2
4. FRA   (André Giriat, Robert Jacquet)   7:42.3
5. USA   (John Houser, William Dugan)   7:44.8
6. AUS   (William Dixon, Herbert Turner)   7:45.1

A few weeks before the Olympics, British coach Eric Phelps, who was also coaching the German scullers, advised Beresford and Southwood to use a lighter boat and to follow the same training regimen he had devised for the Germans. He also warned his countrymen that Kaidel and Pirsch would launch their final sprint at the 1800-meter mark. Beresford and Southwood ordered a new, lighter boat, but the boat disappeared on its way to Berlin. It was finally located in a railway siding in Hamburg and transported to the anxious British pair.

Beresford and Southwood were beaten by Kaidel and Pirsch in the first round, but qualified for the final through repêchage. In the first match-up, Southwood observed that the Germans were able to gain a stroke at the start because the starter, Victor de Bisschop of Belgium, could not see around the large megaphone he was using. In the final the Brits employed a bit of gamesmanship themselves. First they deliberately false-started. Then they caused a further delay by taking off their sweaters. Then, instead of waiting for the starter, they watched Kaidel and Pirsch and took off when they did. The Germans led from the start, but the British pair caught them at 1800 meters, rowed neck and neck for 100 meters, and then pulled away to win by two and a half lengths.

The 37-year-old Beresford was competing in his fifth Olympic Games. Each time he won a medal: in 1920 a silver in the single sculls; in 1924 a gold in the same event; in 1928 a silver in the eights; in 1932 a gold in the coxswainless fours; and finally, in 1936, this third gold, in the double sculls. Considering that he and Southwood won the Double Sculls Challenge Cup at Henley in 1939, it is quite possible that Beresford would have won a sixth medal had not World War II intervened. His father, Julius, won a silver medal in the coxed fours in 1912.

1948 London-Henley-on-Thames T: 15, N: 15, D: 8.9.
1. GBR (Richard Burnell, Bertie Bushnell) 6:51.3
2. DEN (Ebbe Parsner, Aage Larsen) 6.55.3
3. URU (William Jones, Juan Rodriguez) 7:12.4

Bushnell and Burnell were competing on their home course at Henley. Burnell's father, Charles, won a gold medal in the eights race in 1908, also at Henley.

1952 Helsinki T: 16, N: 16, D: 7.23.
1. ARG (Tranquilo Cappozzo, Eduardo Guerrero) 7:32.2
2. SOV/UKR (Heorhi Zhylin, Ihor Yemchuk) 7:38.3
3. URU (Miguel Seijas, Juan Rodriguez) 7:43.7
4. FRA (Jacques Maillet, Achille Giovannoni) 7:46.8
5. CZE (Antonín Malinković, Jiři Vykoukal) 7:53.8
6. AUS (John Rogers, Murray Riley), BEL (Robert George, Joseph Van Stichel), ITA (Silvio Bergamini, Lodovico Sommaruga)

1956 Melbourne-Ballarat T: 8, N: 8, D: 11.27.
1. SOV/RUS (Aleksandr Berkutov, Yuri Tyukalov) 7:24.0
2. USA (Bernard Paul Costello, James Gardiner) 7:32.2
3. AUS (Murray Riley, Mervyn Wood) 7:37.4
4. GER (Thomas Schneider, Kurt Hipper) 7:41.7

1960 Rome-Lake Albano T: 16, N: 16, D: 9.3.
1. CZE (Václav Kozák, Pavel Schmidt) 6:47.50
2. SOV/RUS (Aleksandr Berkutov, Yuri Tyukalov) 6:50.49
3. SWI (Ernst Hürlimann, Rolf Larcher) 6:50.59
4. FRA (René Duhamel, Bernard Monnereau) 6:52.22
5. HOL (Peter Bakker, Jacobus Rentmeester) 6:53.86
6. BEL (Gérard Higny, Jean Lemaire) 6:56:40

Václav Kozák was a 23-year-old noncommissioned officer. His partner was 30-year-old Pavel Schmidt, a psychiatrist from Bratislava.

1964 Tokyo T: 13, N: 13, D: 10.15.
1. SOV/RUS (Oleg Tyurin, Boris Dubrovsky) 7:10.66
2. USA (Seymour Cromwell, James Storm) 7:13.16
3. CZE (Vladimir Andrs, Pavel Hofmann) 7:14.23
4. SWI (Melchior Bürgin, Martin Studach) 7:24.97
5. GER (Helmut Lebert, Josef Steffes-Mies) 7:30.03
6. FRA (René Duhamel, Bernard Monnereau) 7:41.80
7. GBR (Arnold Cook, Peter Webb)
8. HOL (Max Alwin, Peter Bots)

1968 Mexico City-Xochimilco T: 13, N: 13, D: 10.19.
1. SOV/ RUS (Anatoly Sass, Aleksandr Timoshinin) 6:51.82
2. HOL (Leendert Frans van Dis, Henricus Droog) 6:52.80
3. USA (William Maher, John Nunn) 6:54.21
4. BUL (Atanas Schelev, Yordan Valtschev) 6:58.48
5. GDR (Hans-Ulrich Schmied, Manfred Haake) 7:04.92
6. GER (Wolfgang Glock, Udo Hild) 7:12.20
7. BRA (Harri Klein, Edgard Gijsen)
8. ROM (Alexandru Aposteanu, Octavian Pavelescu)

1972 Munich-Oberschleissheim T: 18, N: 18, D: 9.2.
1. SOV/ RUS (Aleksandr Timoshinin, Gennady Korshikov) 7:01.77
2. NOR (Frank Hansen, Svein Thögersen) 7:02.58
3. GDR (Joachim Böhmer, Hans-Ulrich Schmied) 7:05.55
4. DEN (Niels Secher, Jörgen Engelbrecht) 7:14.19
5. GBR (Timothy Crooks, Patrick Delafield) 7:16.29
6. CZE (Josef Straka, Vladek Lacina) 7:17.60
7. HOL (Jan Bruyn, Paul Veenemans)
8. SWI (Hans Ruckstuhl, Ulrich Isler)

Timoshinin and Korshikov took the lead shortly before the halfway mark and held on to win in the closest double sculls finish in Olympic history.

1976 Montreal T: 13, N: 13, D: 7.25.
1. NOR (Frank Hansen, Alf Hansen) 7:13.20
2. GBR (Christopher Baillieu, Michael Hart) 7:15.26
3. GDR (Hans-Ulrich Schmied, Jürgen Bertow) 7:17.45
4. SOV/RUS (Yevgeny Barbakov, Gennady Korshikov) 7:18.87
5. GER (Peter Becker, Gerhard Kroschewski) 7:22.15
6. FRA (Jean-Noël Ribot, Jean-Michel Izart) 7:50.18
7. ITA (Umberto Ragazzi, Silvio Ferrini)
8. USA (William Belden, Lawrence Klecatsky)

Two years after Frank Hansen won the silver medal in the double sculls at the Munich Olympics, he asked his younger brother, Alf, to become his new partner. Together they took first place at the 1975 world championships and then went on to win the Olympics the following year. Frank, 30, was an electrician; Alf, 28, worked for the telephone company.

1980 Moscow T: 9, N: 9, D: 7.27.
1. GDR (Joachim Dreifke, Klaus Kröppelien) 6:24.33
2. YUG (Zoran Pancic, Milorad Stanulov) 6:26.34
3. CZE (Zdeněk Pecka, Václav Vochoska) 6:29.07
4. GBR (R. James Clark, Christopher Baillieu) 6:31.13
5. SOV (Aleksandr Fomchenko, Yevgeny Duleyev) 6:35.34
6. POL (Wieslaw Kujda, Piotr Tobolski) 6:39.66
7. SPA (José Ramon Oyarzabal, José Luis Corta)
8. FRA (Marc Boudoux, Didier Gallet)

1984 Los Angeles-Lake Casitas T: 11, N: 11, D: 8.5.
1. USA (Bradley Lewis, Paul Enquist) 6:36.87
2. BEL (Pierre-Marie Deloof, Dirk Crois) 6:38.19
3. YUG (Zoran Pančič, Milorad Stanulov) 6:39.59
4. GER (Andreas Schmelz, Georg Agrikola) 6:40.41
5. ITA (Francesco Esposito, Ruggero Verroca) 6:44.29
6. CAN (Tim Storm, Peter MacGowan) 6:46.68
7. AUT (Wilfried Auerbach, Thomas Linemayr)
8. FIN (Reina Karppinen, Aarne Lindroos)

Starting in last place, Lewis and Enquist passed Deloof and Crois 300 meters from the finish and pulled away for a clear victory.

1988 Seoul C: 17, N: 17, D: 9.24.
1. HOL (Ronald Florijn, Nicolaas Rienks) 6:21.13
2. SWI (Beat Schwerzmann, Ueli Bodenmann) 6:22.59

3. SOV   (Oleksander Marchenko, Vassily Yakusha)   6:22.87
4. GER   (Christian Händle, Ralf Thienel)   6:24.97
5. GDR   (Uwe Mund, Uwe Heppner)   6:26.20
6. DEN   (Per Henrik Stisen Rasmussen, Bjarne Eltang)   6:26.98
7. SPA   (José Manuel Bermudez, Manuel Vera)
8. BUL   (Vassil Radev, Danail Yordanov)

Florijn and Rienks fashioned a startling upset by rowing a powerful middle 1000 meters and then holding off the equally surprising Swiss.

1992 Barcelona-Banyoles C: 19, N: 19, D: 8.1.
1. AUS   (Stephen Hawkins, Peter Antonie)   6:17.32
2. AUT   (Arnold Jonke, Christoph Zerbst)   6:18.42
3. HOL   (Henk-Jan Zwolle, Nicolaas Rienks)   6:22.82
4. EST   (Priit Tasane, Roman Lutochkin)   6:23.34
5. POL   (Andrzej Marszalek, Andrzej Krzepiński)   6:24.32
6. SPA   (Miguel Álvarez Villar, José Merín Hierro)   6:26.96
7. CAN   (Donald Dickison, Todd Hallett)
8. GER   (Jens Köppen, Christian Händle)

Antonie and Hawkins were by far the lightest pair in the competition, and Hawkins, at 75 kg (165 lbs.) was the lightest of all. They took the lead from the Dutch in the second quarter of the final and fought off a late challenge from the Austrians to earn a surprise victory.

QUADRUPLE SCULLS

1896–1972 not held

1976 Montreal T: 11, N: 11, D: 7.25.
1. GDR   (Wolfgang Güldenpfennig, Rüdiger Reiche, Karl-Heinz Bussert, Michael Wolfgramm)   6:18.65
2. SOV   (Yevgeny Duleyev, Yuri Yakomov, Aivars Lazdenieks, Vytautas Butkus)   6:19.89
3. CZE   (Jaroslav Helebrand, Václav Vochoska, Ždeněk Pecka, Vladek Lacina)   6:21.77
4. GER   (Norbert Kothe, Helmut Krause, Michael Gentsch, Helmut Wolber)   6:24.81
5. BUL   (Yordan Vulchev, Mincho Nikolov, Hristo Zhelev, Eftim Gerzilov)   6:32.04
6. USA   (Peter Cortes, Kenneth Foote, Neil Halleen, John van Blom)   6:34.33
7. FRA   (Roland Weill, Roland Thibaut, Patrick Morineau, Charles Imbert)
8. SWI   (Hans Ruckstuhl, Denis Oswald, Jürg Weitnauer, Reto Wyss)

Martin Winter of the East German team had to undergo an emergency appendectomy and was replaced at the last minute by Bussert. The sudden change caused the team some problems in the opening round, and they lost to the U.S.S.R. But by the final they were all straightened out and won a hard-fought race. Winter finally won his gold medal in 1980.

1980 Moscow T: 12, N: 12, D: 7.27.
1. GDR   (Frank Dundr, Karsten Bunk, Uwe Heppner, Martin Winter)   5:49.81

2. SOV   (Yuri Shapochka, Yevgeny Barbakov, Valery Kleshnev, Mykola Dovhan)   5:51.47
3. BUL   (Mincho Nikolov, Lubomir Petrov, Ivo Roussev, Bogdan Dobrev)   5:52.38
4. FRA   (Christian Marquis, Jean Raymond Peltier, Charles Imbert, Roland Weill)   5:53.45
5. SPA   (Juan Solano, Jesus Gonzalez, Manuel Vera, Julio Oliver)   6:01.19
6. YUG   (Milan Arezina, Darko Zibar, Dragan Obradovič, Nikola Stefanovič)   6:10.76
7. POL   (Andrzej Skowroński, Zbigniew Andruszkiewicz, Ryszard Burak, Stanislaw Wierzbicki)
8. HOL   (Victor Schheffers, Jeroen Vervoort, Rob Robbers, Ronald Vervoort)

1984 Los Angeles-Lake Casitas T: 10, N: 10, D: 8.5.
1. GER   (Albert Hedderich, Raimund Hörmann, Dieter Wiedenmann, Michael Dürsch)   5:57.55
2. AUS   (Paul Reedy, Gary Gullock, Timothy McLaren, Anthony Lovrich)   5:57.98
3. CAN   (Doug Hamilton, Mike Hughes, Phil Monckton, Bruce Ford)   5:59.07
4. ITA   (Piero Poli, Renato Gaeta, Antonio Dell'Aquila, Stefano Lari)   6:00.94
5. FRA   (Marc Boudoux, Serge Fornara, Pascal Body, Pascal Dubosquelle)   6:01.35
6. SPA   (Luis Oliver, Jesus Gonzalez, Manuel Vera, Julio Oliver)   6:04.99
7. USA   (Curtis Fleming, Gregg Montesi, Ridgely Johnson, Bruce Beall)
8. NOR   (Pal Sandli, Espen Thorsen, Vetle Vinje, Ivan Enstad)

Six weeks before the 1980 Olympics, the West German crew, prevented by the anti-Soviet boycott from taking part in the Games themselves, defeated the East German crew that went on to win in Moscow. The West Germans, a pipefitter, a butcher, a bank clerk and a machinist, stayed together for four more years and, in Los Angeles in 1984, staged a furious come-from-behind sprint to defeat the Australians in a photo-finish.

1988 Seoul T: 13, N: 13, D: 9.25.
1. ITA   (Piero Poli, Gianluca Farina, Davide Tizzano, Agostino Abbagnale)   5:53.37
2. NOR   (Lars Bjonness, Vetle Vinje, Rolf Bernt Thorsen, Alf Hansen)   5:55.08
3. GDR   (Steffen Bogs, Steffen Zühlke, Heiko Habermann, Jens Köppen)   5:56.13
4. SOV   (Pavlo Krupko, Oleksander Zaskalko, Sergei Kiniakin, Yuri Zelikovich)   5:57.18
5. AUS   (Richard Powell, Brenton Terrell, Paul Reedy, Peter Antonie)   5:59.15
6. GER   (Christoph Galandi, Oliver Grüner, Georg Agrikola, Andreas Reinke)   5:59.59
7. POL   (Slawomir Cieślakowski, Andrzej Krzepiński, Miroslaw Mruk, Tomasz Świątek)
8. HOL   (Robbert Bakker, Hans Kelderman, Juergen Nelis, Hermanus Van der Eerenbeemt)

Alf Hansen, the Norwegian stroke, had won gold in the double sculls in 1976. He added a silver in the quadruple twelve years later at age 40. During the celebration by the Italians, team member Davide Tizzano was thrown into the water and lost his gold medal in the muddy bottom of the Han River. A Korean diver, working as a security guard at the regatta course, retrieved it after a 50-minute search.

1992 Barcelona-Banyoles T: 15, N: 15, D: 8.2.
1. GER (Andre Willms, Andreas Hajek, Stephan Volkert, Michael Steinbach) — 5:45.17
2. NOR (Lars Bjønness, Rolf Bernt Thorsen, Kjetil Undset, Per Albert Saetersdal) — 5:47.09
3. ITA (Gianluca Farina, Rossano Galtarossa, Alessandro Corona, Filippo Soffici) — 5:47.33
4. SWI (Ueli Bodenmann, Alexander Ruckstuhl, Beat Schwerzmann, Marc-Sven Nater) — 5:47.39
5. HOL (Hans Kelderman, Ronald Florijn, Koos Maasdijk, Rutger Arisz) — 5:48.92
6. FRA (Fiorenzo Di Giovanni, Fabrice LeClerc, Yves Lamarque, Samuel Barathay) — 5:54.80
7. SOV (Valery Dosenko, Sergei Kinyakin, Nikolai Chuprina, Girts Vilks)
8. USA (Kier Pearson, John Riley, Robert Kaehler, John "Chip" McKibben)

The Germans gained a decisive victory, but it was the Norwegians who won the admiration of the spectators by using a wooden boat and wooden oars while everyone else used molded glass fiber reinforced with carbon fiber and bonded with epoxy resin.

PAIR-OARED SHELL WITHOUT COXSWAIN

1896–1900 not held

1904 St. Louis T: 3, N: 1, D: 7.30.
1. USA (Seawanhaka Boat Club, Brooklyn, New York—Robert Farnam, Joseph Ryan) — 10:57.0
2. USA (Atalanta Boat Club, New York—John Mulcahy, William Varley) — —
3. USA (Western Rowing Club, St. Louis, Missouri—John Joachim, Joseph Buerger) — —

1906 not held

1908 London-Henley-on-Thames T: 4, N: 3, D: 7.31.
1. GBR (John Fenning, Gordon Thomson) — 9:41.0
2. GBR (George Fairbairn, Philip Verdon) — —
3. CAN (F.B. Toms, Norwey Jackes) — —
3. GER (Martin Stahnke, Willy Düskow) — —

Fenning and Thomson won by two and a half lengths.

1912–1920 not held

1924 Paris T: 3, N: 3, D: 7.17.
1. HOL (Antonie Beijnen, Wilhelm Rösingh) — 8:19.4
2. FRA (Maurice Bouton, Georges Piot) — 8:21.6
DNS: GBR (Gordon Killick, Charles Southgate)

1928 Amsterdam-Sloten T:8, N: 8, D: 8.10.
1. GER (Bruno Müller, Kurt Moschter) — 7:06.4
2. GBR (Terence O'Brien, Robert Archibald Nisbet) — 7:08.6
3. USA (Paul McDowell, John Schmitt) — 7:20.4
4. ITA (Romeo Sisti, Nino Bolzoni) — 7:24.4
5. SWI (Alois Reinhard, Wilhelm Müller) — 7:29.1
6. HOL (Carel van Wankum, Hendrik van Suylekom) — 7:30.2

1932 Los Angeles-Long Beach T: 6, N: 6, D: 8.13.
1. GBR (Hugh Edwards, Lewis Clive) — 8:00.0
2. NZE (Cyril Stiles, Frederick Thompson) — 8:02.4
3. POL (Henryk Budziński, Janusz Mikolajczak) — 8:08.2
4. HOL (Godfried Röel, Pieter Roelofsen) — 8:08.4
5. FRA (Fernand Vandernotte, Marcel Vandernotte)

Hugh "Jumbo" Edwards won two gold medals in one day, following up his victory in the coxless pairs with another in the coxless fours. During World War II Edwards used his rowing ability to save his life. While serving as a squadron leader with the Royal Air Force's Coastal Command in 1943, he was forced to ditch his plane in the Atlantic Ocean. He rowed a dinghy four miles through a minefield to safety. He was the only member of the plane's crew to survive. Edwards' Olympic partner, Lewis Clive, was killed in the Spanish Civil War on August 2, 1938, at the age of 27.

1936 Berlin-Grünau T: 13, N: 13, D: 8.14.
1. GER (Willi Eichhorn, Hugo Strauss) — 8:16.1
2. DEN (Richard Olsen, Harry Larsen) — 8:19.2
3. ARG (Horacio Podestá, Julio Curatella) — 8:23.0
4. HUN (Károly Györy, Tibor Mamusich) — 8:25.7
5. SWI (Wilhelm Klopfer, Karl Müller) — 8:33.0
6. POL (Ryszard Borzuchowski, Edward Kobyliński) — 8:41.9

1948 London-Henley-on-Thames T: 12, N: 12, D: 8.6.
1. GBR (John Wilson, William Laurie) — 7:21.1
2. SWI (Hans Kalt, Josef Kalt) — 7:23.9
3. ITA (Felice Fanetti, Bruno Boni) — 7:31.5

Jack Wilson and Ran Laurie were best friends who joined the Colonial Service and were sent to the Sudan. Returning to London on leave in 1938, they entered the Henley Regatta and took first place. Then they went back to the Sudan and didn't touch an oar for ten years. In May 1948 they returned to Britain on another leave and decided to take up rowing again. After six weeks' training they entered the Henley Regatta and won again. This gained them an invitation to represent Great Britain at the Olympics, and they were granted six months' leave to prepare. Rowing on their favorite course at Henley, "the Desert Rats," as they were known, took the lead after 1150 meters and fought off a late challenge from the Kalt brothers to secure the gold medal.

1952 Helsinki T: 16, N: 16, D: 7.23.
1.	USA	(Charles Logg, Thomas Price)	8:20.7
2.	BEL	(Michel Knuysen, Robert Baetens)	8:23.5
3.	SWI	(Kurt Schmid, Hans Kalt)	8:32.7
4.	GBR	(David Callender, Christopher Davidge)	8:37.4
5.	FRA	(Jean-Pierre Souche, René Guissart)	8:48.8

Logg and Price, of Rutgers University, were the Cinderella pair of 1952. Neither man had sat in a pair-oared shell until two months before the Olympics, and the 19-year-old Price had only started rowing in January.

1956 Melbourne-Ballarat T: 9, N: 9, D: 11.27.
1.	USA	(James Fifer, Duvall Hecht)	7:55.4
2.	SOV/RUS	(Igor Buldakov, Viktor Ivanov)	8:03.9
3.	AUT	(Alfred Sageder, Josef Kloimstein)	8.11.8
4.	AUS	(Peter Adrian Raper, Maurice Grace)	8:22.2

1960 Rome-Lake Albano T: 18, N: 18, D: 9.3.
1.	SOV/RUS	(Valentin Boreyko, Oleg Golovanov)	7:02.01
2.	AUT	(Alfred Sageder, Josef Kloimstein)	7:03.69
3.	FIN	(Veli Lehtelä, Toimi Pitkänen)	7:03.80
4.	GDR	(Jochen Neuling, Heinz Weigel)	7:08.81
5.	USA	(Ted Frost, Robert Rogers)	7:17.08
6.	YUG	(Nikola Čupin, Antun Ivankovic)	7:20.91

1964 Tokyo T: 14, N: 14, D: 10.15.
1.	CAN	(George Hungerford, Roger Jackson)	7:32.94
2.	HOL	(Steven Blaisse, Ernst Venemans)	7:33.40
3.	GER	(Michael Schwan, Wolfgang Hottenrott)	7:38.63
4.	GBR	(James Lee Nicholson, Stewart Farquharson)	7:42.00
5.	DEN	(Peter Fich Christiansen, Hans Jórgen Boye)	7:48.13
6.	FIN	(Toimi Pitkänen, Veli Lehtelä)	8:05.74
7.	SWI	(Peter Bolliger, Nicolas Gobet)	
8.	POL	(Czeslaw Nawrot, Alfons Ślusarski)	

Sent to Tokyo as reserves for the Canadian eights team, Hungerford and Jackson were allowed to enter the coxless pairs as compensation. Given only six weeks to get used to each other, they had their first race together ever in the opening round of the Olympics. To compound their problems, Hungerford had not yet recovered from an attack of mononucleosis. In the final they stroked to a one-and-a-half-length lead at the 1500-meter mark and hung on desperately to win Canada's only victory of the 1964 Olympics. Hungerford and Jackson were considered such long shots that no Canadian journalists were present for their race. The two young men celebrated their victory by drinking seven Cokes each. The shell that they used had been loaned to them by the University of Washington; it was the same shell that had been used by Fifer and Hecht when they won the gold medal in 1956.

1968 Mexico City-Xochimilco T: 18, N: 18, D: 10.19.
1.	GDR	(Jörg Lucke, Hans-Jürgen Bothe)	7:26.56
2.	USA	(Lawrence Hough, Philip "Tony" Johnson)	7:26.71

3.	DEN	(Peter Christiansen, Ib Ivan Larsen)	7:31.84
4.	AUT	(Dieter Ebner, Dieter Losert)	7:41.80
5.	SWI	(Fred Rüssli, Werner Zwimpfer)	7:46.79
6.	HOL	(Roelof Luynenburg, Rudolf Stokvis)	—
7.	AUS	(David Ramage, Paul Guest)	
8.	POL	(Alfons Ślusarski, Jerzy Broniec)	

An exciting nip-and-tuck battle saw the favored team of Hough and Johnson take the lead with 500 meters to go, only to have Lucke and Bothe pass them in the last ten meters.

1972 Munich-Oberscheissheim T: 20, N: 20, D: 9.2.
1.	GDR	(Siegfried Brietzke, Wolfgang Mager)	6:53.16
2.	SWI	(Heinrich Fischer, Alfred Bachmann)	6:57.06
3.	HOL	(Roelof Luynenburg, Rudolf Stokvis)	6:58.70
4.	CZE	(Lubomir Zapletal, Petr Lakomy)	6:58.77
5.	POL	(Alfons Ślusarski, Jerzy Broniec)	7:02.74
6.	ROM	(Ilie Oantă, Dumitru Grumezescu)	7:42.90
7.	GER	(Erwin Haas, Lutz Ulbricht)	
8.	SOV/RUS	(Vladimir Polyakov, Nikolai Vasiliev)	

In 1968 a comedian named Heinz Quermann appealed over radio and TV for tall young people in East Germany to register with the rowing section of the Leipzig Sports Club. Among the respondents were two 16-year-olds, Siegfried Brietzke and Wolfgang Mager. When they began to achieve competitive success they became known as the "Quermann pair."

1976 Montreal T: 15, N: 15, D: 7.25.
1.	GDR	(Jörg Landvoigt, Bernd Landvoigt)	7:23.31
2.	USA	(Calvin Coffey, Michael Staines)	7:26.73
3.	GER	(Peter Vanroye, Thomas Strauss)	7:30.03
4.	YUG	(Žlatko Celent, Duško Mrduljas)	7:34.17
5.	BUL	(Valentin Stoyev, Georgi Georgiev)	7:37.42
6.	CZE	(Miroslav Knapek, Vojtech Časka)	7:51.06
7.	SOV/EST	(Gennadi Kinko, Tiit Helmja)	
8.	FIN	(Leo Ahonen, Kari Hanska)	

The Landvoigt twins were 25-year-old steelworkers from Potsdam. The U.S. team, besides being the only American rowers to win medals at Montreal, were also noteworthy for their unusual combination of names—Coffey and Staines.

1980 Moscow T: 15, N: 15, D: 7.27.
1.	GDR	(Bernd Landvoigt, Jörg Landvoigt)	6:48.01
2.	SOV/RUS	(Yuri Pimenov, Nikolai Pimenov)	6:50.50
3.	GBR	(A. Charles Wiggin, Malcolm Carmichael)	6:51.47
4.	ROM	(Constantin Postoiu, Valer Toma)	6:53.49
5.	CZE	(Miroslav Vrastil, Miroslav Knapek)	7:01.54
6.	SWE	(Anders Larson, Anders Wilgotson)	7:02.52
7.	IRL	(Patrick Gannon, William Ryan)	
8.	FRA	(Jean-Claude Roussel, Dominique Lecointe)	

The medal ceremony presented a bizarre sight, as the gold-medal-winning Landvoigt twins stood beside the silver-medal-winning Pimenov twins.

1984 Los Angeles-Lake Casitas T: 14, N: 14, D: 8.5.
1.	ROM	(Petru Iosub, Valer Toma)	6:45.39
2.	SPA	(Fernando Climent Huerta, Luis María Lasúrtegui Berridi)	6:48.47
3.	NOR	(Hans Magnus Grepperud, Sverre Loken)	6:51.81
4.	GER	(Thomas Möllenkamp, Axel Wöstmann)	6:52.53
5.	ITA	(Marco Romano, Pasquale Aiese)	6:55.88
6.	USA	(David De Ruff, John Strotbeck)	6:58.46
7.	HOL	(Sjoerd Hoekstra, Joost Adema)	
8.	BRA	(Ronaldo Carvalho, Ricardo Carvalho)	

1988 Seoul T: 18, N: 18, D: 9.24.
1.	GBR	(Andrew Holmes, Steven Redgrave)	6:36.84
2.	ROM	(Dragoş Neagu, Dănut Dobre)	6:38.06
3.	YUG/SLO	(Bojan Preşeren, Sadik Mujkić)	6:41.01
4.	BEL	(Alain Lewuillon, Wim Van Belleghem)	6:45.47
5.	GDR	(Carl Ertel, Uwe Gasch)	6:48.86
6.	SOV/BLR	(Igor Zyborenko, Valery Vyrvich)	6:51.11
7.	GER	(Frank Dietrich, Michael Twittmann)	
8.	FRA	(Lavrent Lacasa, Alex Perahia)	

Holmes and Redgrave had already earned gold medals in the coxed fours in 1984. In Seoul they led from start to finish to win the coxless pairs. Twenty-three hours later they placed third in the coxed pairs.

1992 Barcelona-Banyoles T: 18, N: 18, D: 8.1.
1.	GBR	(Steven Redgrave, Matthew Pinsent)	6:27.72
2.	GER	(Peter Höltzenbein, Colin von Ettingshausen)	6:32.68
3.	SLO	(Iztok Čop, Denis Žvegelj)	6:33.43
4.	FRA	(Michel Andrieux, Jean Christophe Rolland)	6:36.34
5.	BEL	(Jaak van Driessche, Luc Goiris)	6:38.20
6.	USA	(Peter Sharis, John Pescatore)	6:39.23
7.	NOR	(Snorre Lorgen, Sverke Lorgen)	
8.	HOL	(Sjors van Iwaarden, Kai Compagner)	

Steve Redgrave became only the third British athlete—and the first in 72 years—to earn gold medals in three consecutive Olympics. The other two were water polo players Paul Radmilovic and Charles Smith.

FOUR-OARED SHELL WITHOUT COXSWAIN

1896-1900 not held

1904 St. Louis T: 3, N: 1, D: 7.30.
1.	USA	(Century Boat Club, St. Louis—George Dietz, August Erker, Albert Nasse, Arthur Stockhoff)	9:05.8
2.	USA	(Mound City Rowing Club, St. Louis—Charles Aman, Michael Begley, Martin Fromanack, Frederick Suerig)	—
3.	USA	(Western Rowing Club, St. Louis—Gustav Voerg, John Freitag, Louis Helm, Frank Dummerth)	—

1906 not held

1908 London-Henley-on-Thames T: 4, N: 3, D: 7.31.
1.	GBR	(Magdalen College Boat Club, Oxford—R. Collier Cudmore, J. Angus Gillan, Duncan McKinnon, John Somers-Smith)	8:34.0
2.	GBR	(Leander Club—Philip Filleul, Harold Barker, John Fenning, Gordon Thomson)	—
3.	CAN	(Toronto Argonauts—Gordon Balfour, Becher Gale, Charles Riddy, Geoffrey Taylor)	
3.	HOL	(Amstel Amsterdam—Hermanus Höfte, Albertus Wielsma, Johan Burk, Bernardus Croon)	

Two members of the Magdalen team, Somers-Smith and McKinnon, were killed in action during World War I.

1912–1920 not held

1924 Paris T: 4, N: 4, D: 7.17.
1.	GBR	(Charles Eley, James Macnabb, Robert Morrison, Terence Sanders)	7:08.6
2.	CAN	(Colin Finlayson, Archibald Black, George Mackay, William Wood)	7:18.0
3.	SWI	(Emile Albrecht, Alfred Probst, Eugen Sigg-Bächthold, Hans Walter)	—
4.	FRA	(Théo Cremnitz, Jean Camuset, Henri Bonzano, Albert Bonzano)	—

All four members of the British crew attended Eton and Trinity College, Cambridge.

1928 Amsterdam-Sloten T: 6, N: 6, D: 8.10.
1.	GBR	(John Lander, Michael Warriner, Richard Beesly, Edward Bevan)	6:36.0
2.	USA	(Charles Karle, William Miller, George Heales, Ernest Bayer)	6:37.0
3.	ITA	(Cesare Rossi, Pietro Freschi, Umberto Bonadè, Paolo Gennari)	6:37.6
4.	GER	(Henry Zänker, Wolfgang Goedecke, Günther Roll, Werner Zschieke)	DNS

The semifinal race between Great Britain and Germany saw a dramatic finish. The Germans led by half a length with 50 meters to go, when Zschieke, their stroke, suddenly collapsed and fell forward on his oars. His teammates stopped rowing and watched the British crew shoot past to victory. In the final, the British team, which was from Trinity College, Cambridge, trailed the U.S. crew for almost the entire race, caught them with 20 yards to go and spurted ahead to a half-length win.

1932 Los Angeles-Long Beach T: 5, N: 5, D: 8.13.
1.	GBR	(John "Felix" Badcock, Hugh Edwards, Jack Beresford, Rowland George)	6:58.2
2.	GER	(Karl Aletter, Ernst Gaber, Walter Flinsch, Hans Maier)	7:03.0
3.	ITA	(Antonio Ghiardello, Francesco Cossu, Giliante D'Este, Antonio Provenzani)	7:04.0
4.	USA	(John McCosker, George Mattson, Thomas Pierie, Edgar Johnson)	7:14.2

1936 Berlin-Grünau T: 9, N: 9, D: 8.14.
1. GER (Rudolf Eckstein, Anton Rom, Martin Karl, Wilhelm Menne) 7:01.8
2. GBR (Thomas Bristow, Alan Barrett, Peter Jackson, John Duncan Sturrock) 7:06.5
3. SWI (Hermann Betschart, Hans Homberger, Alex Homberger, Karl Schmid) 7:10.6
4. ITA (Antonio Ghiardello, Luigi Luscardo, Aldo Pellizzoni, Francesco Pittaluga) 7:12.4
5. AUT (Rudolf Höpfler, Camillo Winkler, Wilhelm Pichler, Johann Binder) 7:20.5
6. DEN (Knud Olsen, Keld Karise, Björn Dröyer, Boye Emil Jensen) 7:26.3

1948 London-Henley-on-Thames T: 10, N: 10, D: 8.9.
1. ITA (Giuseppe Moioli, Elio Morille, Giovanni Invernizzi, Franco Faggi) 6:39.0
2. DEN (Helge Halkjaer, Aksel Bonde Hansen, Helge Schröder, Ib Storm Larsen) 6:43.5
3. USA (Frederick John Kingsbury, Stuart Griffing, Gregory Gates, Robert Perew) 6:47.7
4. GBR (Peter Kirkpatrick, Hedley Rushmere, Thomas Christie, Anthony Butcher) —
5. HOL (Henrik van Suylekom, Sietze Haarsma, Johannes Dekker, Johannes van den Berg) —
6. SAF (Edward Ramsay, Anthony Ikin, David Mayberry, Charles Kietzman) —

1952 Helsinki T: 17, N: 17, D: 7.23.
1. YUG/ CRO (Duje Bonačič, Velimir Valenta, Mate Trojanovič, Petar Šegvič) 7:16.0
2. FRA (Pierre Blondiaux, Jacques Guissart, Marc Bouissou, Roger Gautier) 7:18.9
3. FIN (Veikko Lommi, Kauko Wahlsten, Oiva Lommi, Lauri Nevalainen) 7:23.3
4. GBR (Harry Almond, John Jones, James Crowden, George Cadbury) 7:25.2
5. POL (Edward Schwarzer, Zbigniew Schwarzer, Henryk Jagodziński, Zbigniew Żarnowiecki) 7:28.2

1956 Melbourne-Ballarat T: 12, N: 12, D: 11.27.
1. CAN (Archibald McKinnon, Lorne Loomer, Walter D'Hondt, Donald Arnold) 7:08.8
2. USA (John Welchli, John McKinlay, Arthur McKinlay, James McIntosh) 7:18.4
3. FRA (René Guissart, Yves Delacour, Gaston Mercier, Guy Guillabert) 7:20.9
4. ITA (Giuseppe Moioli, Attilio Cantoni, Giovanni Zucchi, Abbondio Marcelli) 7:22.5

The Canadian crew consisted of four small-town boys from the University of British Columbia, three of whom had only been rowing for a year. In the final they were so nervous that they almost missed the water with their first stroke and were left behind. However, they were able to catch up by the halfway mark and pull away to a five-length victory. The four Canadians returned to the Olympics four years later in Rome and won silver medals as part of the eights crew.

1960 Rome-Lake Albano T: 16, N: 16, D: 9.3.
1. USA (Arthur Ayrault, Ted Nash, John Sayre, Richard Wailes) 6:26.26
2. ITA (Tullio Baraglia, Renato Bosatta, Giancarlo Crosta, Giuseppe Galante) 6:28.78
3. SOV/ RUS (Igor Akhremchik, Yuri Bachurov, Valentin Morkoykin, Anatoly Tarabrin) 6:29.62
4. CZE (Jindřich Blažek, Miroslav Jiska, René Libal, Jaroslav Starosta) 6:34.30
5. GBR (J. Michael Beresford, Christopher Davidge, Colin Porter, John Vigurs) 6:36.18
6. SWI (Paul Kölliker, Gottfried Kottmann, Kurt Schmid, Rolf Streuli) 6:38.81

1964 Tokyo T: 14, N: 14, D: 10.15.
1. DEN (John Hansen, Björn Haslöv, Erik Petersen, Kurt Helmudt) 6:59.30
2. GBR (John Michael Russell, Hugh Arthur Wardell-Yerburgh, William Barry, John James) 7:00.47
3. USA (Geoffrey Picard, Richard Lyon, Theodore Mittet, Theodore Nash) 7:01.37
4. HOL (Sjoerd Wartena, Jaap Enters, Herman Boelen, Spike Castelein) 7:09.98
5. ITA (Romano Sgheiz, Fulvio Balatti, Giovanni Zucchi, Luciano Sgheiz) 7:10.05
6. GER (Günter Schrörs, Horst Effertz, Albrecht Müller, Manfred Misselhorn) 7:10.33
7. SOV/LIT (Tselestinas Yutsis, Eugenius Levitskas, Ionas Mateyunas, Pavilas Liutkaitis)
8. AUT (Dieter Ebner, Horst Kuttelwascher, Dieter Losert, Manfred Kraushar)

1968 Mexico City-Xochimilco T: 11, N: 11, D: 10.19.
1. GDR (Frank Forberger, Dieter Grahn, Frank Rüle, Dieter Schubert) 6:39.18
2. HUN (Zoltán Melis, György Sarlós, József Csermely, Antal Melis) 6:41.64
3. ITA (Renato Bosatta, Tullio Baraglia, Pier Angelo Conti Manzini, Abramo Albini) 6:44.01
4. SWI (Roland Altenburger, Nicolas Noël Gobet, Franz Rentsch, Alfred Meister) 6:45.78
5. USA (Peter Raymond, Raymond Wright, Charles Hamlin, Lawrence Terry) 6:47.70
6. GER (Thomas Hitzbleck, Manfred Weinreich, Volkhart Buchter, Jochen Heck) 7:08.22
7. ROM (Pavel Cichi, Dumitru Ivanov, Emanoil Stratan, Anton Chirlacopschi)
8. MEX (Roberto Retolaza, Arcadio Padilla, Jesus Toscano, David Trejo)

1972 Munich-Oberschleissheim T: 20, N: 20, D: 9.2.
1. GDR (Frank Forberger, Frank Rüle, Dieter Grahn, Dieter Schubert) 6:24.27
2. NZE (Dick Tonks, Dudley Storey, Ross Collinge, Noel Mills) 6:25.64
3. GER (Joachim Ehrig, Peter Funnekötter, Franz Held, Wolfgang Plottke) 6:28.41
4. SOV/ RUS (Anatoly Tkachuk, Igor Kashurov, Aleksandr Motin, Vitaly Sapronov) 6:31.92

5. ROM (Emeric Tuşa, Adalbert Agh, Mihai Naumencu, 6:35.60
        Francisc Papp)
6. DEN (Willy Poulsen, Peter Fich Christiansen, Egon 6:37.28
        Peterson, Rolf Andersen)
7. GBR (Frederick Smallbone, Leonard Robertson, R.
        James Clark, William Mason)
8. BUL (Biser Boyadzhiev, Borislav Vasilev, Nikolai
        Kolev, Metodi Halvadzhiiski)

Forberger, Rüle, Grahn, and Schubert had been rowing together for 11 years. In winning their second Olympic title, the Dresden four completed six years of unbeaten rowing in which they also won two world championships and two European championships. The lead changed hands six times in their exciting final race with the crew from New Zealand.

1976 Montreal T: 15, N: 15, D: 7.25.
1. GDR (Siegfried Brietzke, Andreas Decker, Stefan 6:37.42
        Semmler, Wolfgang Mager)
2. NOR (Ole Nafstad, Arne Bergodd, Finn Tveter, Rolf 6:41.22
        Andreassen)
3. SOV (Raul Arnemann, Nikolai Kuznetsov, Valery 6:42.52
        Dolinin, Anushavan Gasan-Dzhalalov)
4. NZE (Bob Murphy, Grant McAuley, Des Lock, 6:43.23
        David Lindstrom)
5. CAN (Brian Dick, Philip Monckton, Andrew van 6:46.11
        Ruyven, Ian Gordon)
6. GER (Bernhard Foelkel, Klaus Roloff, Wolfgang 6:47.44
        Horak, Johann Gabriel Konertz)
7. BUL (Dimiter Vulov, Dimiter Yanakiev, Todor Mrun-
        kov, Rumen Hristov)
8. USA (Tony Brooks, James Moroney, Gary Pian-
        tedosi, Hugh Stevenson)

1980 Moscow T: 11, N: 11, D: 7.27.
1. GDR (Jürgen Thiele, Andreas Decker, Stefan 6:08.17
        Semmler, Siegfried Brietzke)
2. SOV/ (Aleksei Kamkin, Valery Dolinin, Aleksandr 6:11.81
   RUS Kulagin, Vitaly Yeliseyev)
3. GBR (John Beattie, Ian McNuff, David Townsend, 6:16.58
        Martin Cross)
4. CZE (Vojtěch Caska, Jiři Prudil, Josef Neštický, 6:18.63
        Lubomir Zapletal)
5. ROM (Daniel Voiculescu, Carolică Ilieş, Petru Iosub, 6:19.45
        Nicolae Simion)
6. SWI (Jürg Weitnauer, Bruno Saile, Hans-Konrad 6:26.46
        Trümpler, Stefan Netzle)
7. FRA (Jean-Pierre Bremer, Nicolas Lourdaux, Ber-
        nard Bruand, Dominique Basset)
8. POL (Miroslaw Jarzembowski, Mariusz Trzciński,
        Henryk Trzciński, Marek Niedzialkowski)

Siegfried Brietzke became the fourth of five rowers to win gold medals in three different Olympics, joining company with Paul Costello, Jack Beresford, and Vyacheslav Ivanov. Their number was joined in 1992 by Steve Redgrave. In 1980 the East Germans dominated rowing so thoroughly that they won 11 of 14 finals. Every one of their 54 oarsmen and women went home with a medal.

1984 Los Angeles-Lake Casitas T: 10, N: 10, D: 8.5.
1. NZE (Leslie O'Connell, Shane O'Brien, Conrad 6:03.48
        Robertson, Keith Trask)
2. USA (David Clark, Jonathan Smith, Philip Stekl, 6:06.10
        Alan Forney)
3. DEN (Michael Jessen, Lars Nielsen, Per Rasmus- 6:07.72
        sen, Erik Christiansen)
4. GER (Norbert Kesslau, Volker Grabow, Jörg Puttlitz, 6:09.27
        Guido Grabow)
5. SWI (Bruno Saile, Jürg Weitnauer, Hans-Konrad 6:09.50
        Trümpler, Stefan Netzle)
6. SWE (Anders Wilgotson, Hans Svensson, Lars-Ake 6:11.71
        Lindqvist, Anders Larson)
7. CAN (Tim Turner, Ted Gibson, David Johnson,
        Stephen Beatty)
8. AUS (David Doyle, James Lowe, Dunçan Fisher,
        John Bentley)

1988 Seoul T: 15, N: 15, D: 9.25.
1. GDR (Roland Schröder, Thomas Greiner, Ralf 6:03.11
        Brudel, Olaf Förster)
2. USA (Raoul Rodriguez, Thomas Bohrer, David 6:05.53
        Krmpotich, Richard Kennelly)
3. GER (Norbert Kesslau, Volker Grabow, Jörg 6:06.22
        Puttlitz, Guido Grabow)
4. GBR (Mark Buckingham, Stephen Peel, Simon 6:06.74
        Berrisford, Peter Mulkerrins)
5. ITA (Sergio Caropreso, Carlo Gaddi, Pasquale 6:09.55
        Marigliano, Valter Molea)
6. SOV/ (Ivan Vysotsky, Sergei Smirnov, Yuri 11:03.77
   RUS Pimenov, Nikolai Pimenov)
7. NZE (Campbell Clayton-Greene, Geoffrey Cot-
        ter, William Coventry, Neil Gibson)
8. FRA (Pascal Bahuaud, Dominique Lecointe,
        Jean Jacques Martigne, Olivier Pons)

The unusual time registered by the Soviet team was a result of one of their seats breaking in the middle of the race.

1992 Barcelona-Banyoles T: 14, N: 14, D: 8.2.
1. AUS (Andrew Cooper, Michael McKay, Nicholas 5:55.04
        Green, James Tomkins)
2. USA (William Burden, Jeffrey McLaughlin, 5:56.68
        Thomas Bohrer, Patrick Manning)
3. SLO (Janez Klemenčič, Sašo Mirjanič, Milan 5:58.24
        Janša, Sadik Mujkič)
4. GER (Armin Weyrauch, Matthias Ungemach, 5:58.39
        Dirk Balster, Markus Vogt)
5. HOL (Bart Peters, Niels van der Zwan, Jaap 5:59.14
        Krijtenburg, Sven Schwarz)
6. NZE (Scott Brownlee, Christopher White, Patrick 6:02.13
        Peoples, Campbell Clayton-Greene)
7. GBR (Salih Hassan, John Garrett, Gavin Stewart,
        Richard Stanhope)
8. ITA (Luca Sartori, Rocco Pecoraro, Carmine La
        Mura, Riccardo Dei Rossi)

Known as the "Oarsome Foursome," the Australian crew from Melbourne burst on the scene when they won the 1990 world championship. In the Olympic final they

Andrew Cooper of the victorious coxless four team pays the price of fame during a 1992 parade in honor of Australia's medalists.

built up a two-and-a-half-second lead with 500 meters to go and then hung on for the victory.

EIGHT-OARED SHELL WITH COXSWAIN

1896 not held

1900 Paris T: 4, N: 4, D: 8.26.

1.	USA	(Vesper Boat Club, Philadelphia—Louis Abell, Harry Debaecke, William Carr, John Exley, John Geiger, Edward Hedley, James Juvenal, Roscoe Lockwood, Edward Marsh)	6:09.8
2.	BEL	(Royal Club Nautique de Gand—Marcel van Crombrugghe, Maurice Hemelsoet, Oscar de Cock, Maurice Verdonck, Prospère Bruggeman, Oscar de Somville, Frank Odberg, Jules de Bisschop, Alfred Vanlandeghem)	6:13.8

3.	HOL	(Minerva, Amsterdam—Walter Thijssen, Ruurd Leegstra, Johannes van Dijk, Henricus Tromp, Hendrik Offerhaus, Roelof Klein, François Brandt, Walter Middleberg, Hermanus Brockmann)	6:23.0
4.	GER	(Germania, Hamburg—Oscar Gossler, Walther Katzenstein, Ernst Ascan Jencquel, Theodor Alphons Lauezzari, Waldemar Tietgens, Arthur Warncke, Edgar Katzenstein, Gustav Gossler, Alexander Gleichmann von Oven)	6:33.0

1904 St. Louis T: 2, N: 2, D: 7.30.

1.	USA	(Vesper Boat Club, Philadelphia—Louis Abell, Joseph Dempsey, Michael Gleason, Frank Schell, James Flanigan, Charles Armstrong, Harry Lott, Frederick Cresser, John Exley)	7:50.0
2.	CAN	(Argonaut Rowing Club, Toronto—Joseph Wright, Donald MacKenzie, William Wadsworth, George Strange, Philip Boyd, George Reiffenstein, William Rice, Arthur Bailey, Thomas Loudon)	—

1906 not held

1908 London-Henley-on-Thames T: 6, N: 5, D: 7.31.

1.	GBR	(Leander Club—Albert Gladstone, Frederick Kelly, Banner Johnstone, Guy Nickalls, Charles Burnell, Ronald Sanderson, Raymond Etherington-Smith, Henry Bucknall, Gilchrist Maclagan)	7:52.0
2.	BEL	(Royal Club Nautique de Gand—Oscar Taelman, Marcel Morimont, Rémy Orban, Georges Mijs, François Vergucht, Polydore Veirman, Oscar de Somville, Rodolphe Poma, Alfred Vanlandeghem)	—
3.	CAN	(Argonaut Rowing Club, Toronto—Irvine Robertson, George Wright, Julius Thomson, Walter Lewis, Gordon Bruce Balfour, Becher Gale, Charles Riddy, Geoffrey Taylor, Douglas Kertland)	—
3.	GBR	(Cambridge University Boating Club—Frank Jerwood, Eric Powell, Oswald Carver, Edward Williams, Henry Goldsmith, Harold Kitching, John Burn, Douglas Stuart, Richard Boyle)	—

The Leander eight won by two lengths.

1912 Stockholm T: 11, N: 7, D: 7.19.

1.	GBR	(Leander Club—Edgar Burgess, Sidney Swann, Leslie Wormwald, Ewart Horsfall, J. Angus Gillan, Arthur Garton, Alister Kirby, Philip Fleming, Henry Wells)	6:15.0
2.	GBR	(New College, Oxford—William Fison, William Parker, Thomas Gillespie, Beaufort Burdekin, Frederick Pitman, Arthur Wiggins, Charles Littlejohn, Robert Bourne, John Walker)	6.19.0
3.	GER	(Berliner Ruder-Gesellschaft—Otto Liebing, Max Bröske, Max Vetter, Willi Bartholomä, Fritz	

Bartholomä, Werner Dehn, Rudolf Reichelt, Hans Mathiä, Kurt Runge)

Sidney Swann of the Leander crew was the only one of the 18 finalists who had not attended Oxford University.

1920 Antwerp-Vilvoorde T: 8, N: 8, D: 8.30.
1. USA	(Virgil Jacomini, Edwin Graves, William Jordan, Edward Moore, Allen Sanborn, Donald Johnston, Vincent Gallagher, Clyde King, Sherman Clark)	6:05.0
2. GBR	(Ewart Horsfall, Guy Oliver Nickalls, Richard Lucas, Walter James, John Campbell, Sebastian Earl, Ralph Shove, Sidney Swann, Robin Johnstone)	6:05.8
3. NOR	(Theodor Nag, Conrad Olsen, Adolf Nilsen, Håkon Ellingsen, Thore Michelsen, Arne Mortensen, Karl Nag, Tollef Tollefsen, Thoralf Hagen)	
4. FRA	(Albert Diebold, Charles Hahn, Frédéric Grossmann, Robert Fleig, Henri Barbenès, Frédéric Fleig, Charles Schlewer, Emile Ruhlmann, Emile Barberolle)	

The winning crew represented the U.S. Naval Academy. They trailed from the start and caught the British crew from the Leander Club 50 meters from the finish. Regatta officials first awarded the bronze medals to the Swiss team because they had recorded the third fastest time in the preliminary heats when they lost to Great Britain. But after a protest, it was decided that the semifinal losers, Norway and France, should row off for third place; however, this race was never held. Most Olympic historians credit Norway with third place, since their semifinal time was faster than that of France.

1924 Paris T: 10, N: 10, D: 7.17.
1. USA	(Leonard Carpenter, Howard Kingsbury, Daniel Lindley, John Miller, James Rockefeller, Frederick Sheffield, Benjamin Spock, Alfred Wilson, Laurence Stoddard)	6:33.4
2. CAN	(Arthur Bell, Robert Hunter, William Langford, Harold Little, John Smith, Warren Snyder, Norman Taylor, William Wallace, Ivor Campbell)	6:49.0
3. ITA	(Antonio Cattalinich, Francesco Cattalinich, Simeon Cattalinch, Giuseppe Crivelli, Latino Galasso, Pietro Ivanov, Bruno Sorich, Carlo Toniatti, Vittorio Gliubich)	
4. GBR	(Reginald Bare, Edward Chandler, H.C. Debenham, Hugh Dulley, Stephen Ian Fairbairn, A.F. Long, H.L. Morphy, Charles Rew, J.S. Godwin)	

Bill Havens was a member of the Yale University team that won the right to represent the United States. However, he chose not to make the trip to Paris because his wife was expecting their first child. That child, a boy named Frank, was born five days after the closing of the 1924 Olympics. Twenty-eight years later, the Havens family finally got their Olympic gold medal when Frank won the 10,000 meters Canadian canoeing singles event in Helsinki.

One Yale crew member who did compete in 1924 and win was a gangly 6-foot 4-inch junior named Ben Spock. After graduating from medical school, Spock became a pediatrician. In 1945 he finished writing a book called *The Common Sense Book of Baby and Child Care*, which eventually sold over 25 million copies and gained its author international fame as "Dr. Spock, the baby expert." In 1972 he was the presidential candidate of the People's Party.

1928 Amsterdam-Sloten T: 11, N: 11, D: 8.10.
1. USA	(Marvin Stalder, John Brinck, Francis Frederick, William Thompson, William Dally, James Workman, Hubert Caldwell, Peter Donlon, Donald Blessing)	6:03.2
2. GBR	(James Hamilton, Guy Oliver Nickalls, John "Felix" Badcock, Donald Gollan, Harold Lane, Gordon Killick, Jack Beresford, Harold West, Arthur Sulley)	6:05.6
3. CAN	(Frederick Hedges, Frank Fiddes, John Hand, Herbert Richardson, Jack Murdock, Athol Meech, Edgar Norris, William Ross, John Donnelly)	
4. POL	(Otto Gordzialkowski, Stanislaw Urban, Andrzej Soltan, Marian Wodziański, Janusz Ślązak, Waclaw Michalski, Jósef Laszewski, Henryk Niezabitowski, Jerzy Skolimowski)	
5. GER	(Karl Aletter, Ernst Gaber, Willi Reichert, Erwin Hoffstätter, Hermann Herbold, Gustav Maier, Robert Huber, Hans Maier, Fritz Bauer)	
6. ITA	(Medardo Lamberti, Arturo Moroni, Vittore Stocchi, Guglielmo Carubbi, Amilcare Canevari, Medardo Galli, Giulio Lamberti, Benedetto Borella, Angelo Polledri)	

The United States was represented by the crew from the University of California at Berkeley. *New York Times* correspondent Wythe Williams described the work of coxswain Don Blessing as "one of the greatest performances of demonical howling ever heard on a terrestrial planet. . . . He gave the impression of a terrier suddenly gone mad. But such language and what a vocabulary! . . . One closed his eyes and waited for the crack of a cruel whip across the backs of the galley slaves." After they had won the Olympic championship, the galley slaves, following custom, grabbed their tormentor and threw him into the middle of Sloten Canal.

1932 Los Angeles-Long Beach T: 8, N: 8, D: 8.13.
1. USA	(Edwin Salisbury, James Blair, Duncan Gregg, David Dunlap, Burton Jastram, Charles Chandler, Harold Tower, Winslow Hall, Norris Graham)	6:37.6
2. ITA	(Vittorio Cioni, Mario Balleri, Renato Bracci, Dino Barsotti, Roberto Vestrini, Guglielmo Del Bimbo, Enrico Garzelli, Renato Barbieri, Cesare Milani)	6:37.8

3. CAN (Earl Eastwood, Joseph Harris, Stanley   6:40.4
Stanyar, Harry Fry, Cedric Liddell, William
Thoburn, Donald Boal, Albert Taylor, George
MacDonald)

4. GBR (Lewis Luxton, Donald McCowen, Harold   6:40.8
Rickett, Charles Sergell, William Sambell,
Thomas Askwith, Kenneth Payne, David Haig-
Thomas, John Ranking)

The U.S. team from the University of California and the
Italian team from the University of Pisa staged a dramatic battle, which the Californians won by a foot with
their very last stroke.

1936 Berlin-Grünau T: 14, N: 14, D: 8.14.

1. USA (Herbert Morris, Charles Day, Gordon Adam,   6:25.4
John White, James McMillin, George Hunt,
Joseph Rantz, Donald Hume, Robert Moch)

2. ITA (Guglielmo Del Bimbo, Dino Barsotti, Oreste   6:26.0
Grossi, Enzo Bartolini, Mario Checcacci,
Dante Secchi, Ottorino Quaglierini, Enrico
Garzelli, Cesare Milani)

3. GER (Alfred Rieck, Helmut Radach, Hans Kuschke,   6:26.4
Heinz Kaufmann, Gerd Völs, Werner Löckle,
Hans-Joachim Hannemann, Herbert Schmidt,
Wilhelm Mahlow)

4. GBR (Annesley Kingsford, Thomas Askwith,   6:30.1
McAlister Pender Lonnon, Desmond
Kingsford, John Cherry, John Couchman,
Hugh Mason, William Laurie, John Duckworth)

5. HUN (Pál Domonkos, Sándor Korompay, Hugo   6:30.3
Ballya, Imre Kapossy, Antal Szendey, Gábor
Alapy, Frigyes Hollósi-Jung, László Szabó,
Ervin Kereszthy)

6. SWI (Werner Schweizer, Fritz Feldmann, Rudolf   6:35.8
Homberger, Oskar Neuenschwander, Her-
mann Betschart, Hans Homberger, Alex
Homberger, Karl Schmid, Rolf Spring)

An exciting blanket finish was won by the crew of the
University of Washington, which moved up from fifth
place at the halfway mark.

1948 London-Henley-on-Thames T: 12, N: 12, D: 8.9.

1. USA (Ian Turner, David Turner, James Hardy,   5:56.7
George Ahlgren, Lloyd Butler, David Brown,
Justus Smith, John Stack, Ralph Purchase)

2. GBR (Christopher Barton, Michael Lepage, Guy   6:06.9
Richardson, Ernest Paul Bircher, Paul Massey,
Charles Brian Lloyd, David Meyrick, Alfred
Mellows, Jack Dearlove)

3. NOR (Kristoffer Lepsøe, Torstein Kråkenes, Hans   6:10.3
Egil Hansen, Halfdan Gran Olsen, Harald
Kråkenes, Leif Naess, Thor Pedersen, Carl
Henrik Monssen, Sigurd Monssen)

The victorious University of California at Berkeley crew
had barely qualified for the Olympics, winning the U.S.
tryouts by a mere one-tenth second over the University of
Washington. But when they got to London they discov-

ered that their most difficult challenge was behind them,
as they won all three of their races by at least ten seconds.

1952 Helsinki T: 14, N: 14, D: 7.23.

1. USA (Franklin Shakespeare, William Fields, James   6:25.9
Dunbar, Richard Murphy, Robert Detweiler,
Henry Proctor, Wayne Frye, Edward Stevens,
Charles Manring)

2. SOV (Yevgeny Brago, Vladimir Rodimushkin, Alek-   6:31.2
sei Komarov, Igor Borisov, Slava Amiragov,
Leonid Gissen, Yevgeny Samsonov, Vladimir
Krukov, Igor Polyakov)

3. AUS (Robert Tinning, Ernest Chapman, Nimrood   6:33.1
Greenwood, Mervyn Finlay, Edward Pain,
Phillip Cayzer, Thomas Chessel, David Ander-
son, Geoffrey Williamson)

4. GBR (David Macklin, Alastair MacLeod, Nicholas   6:34.8
Clack, Roger Sharpley, Edward Worlidge,
Charles Lloyd, William Windham, David
Jennens, John Hinde)

5. GER (Anton Reinartz, Michael Reinartz, Roland   6:42.8
Freiloff, Heinz Zünkler, Peter Betz, Stefan
Reinartz, Hans Betz, Toni Siebenhaar, Her-
mann Zander)

The winning crew was from the U.S. Naval Academy.

1956 Melbourne-Ballarat T: 10, N: 10, D: 11.27.

1. USA (Thomas Charlton, David Wight, John Cooke,   6:35.2
Donald Beer, Caldwell Esselstyn, Charles
Grimes, Richard Wailes, Robert Morey, William
Becklean)

2. CAN (Philip Kueber, Richard McClure, Robert Wil-   6:37.1
son, David Helliwell, Donald Pretty, William
McKerlich, Douglas McDonald, Lawrence
West, Carlton Ogawa)

3. AUS (Michael Aikman, David Boykett, Angus Ben-   6:39.2
field, James Howden, Garth Manton, Walter
Howell, Adrian Monger, Bryan Doyle, Harold
Hewitt)

4. SWE (Olof Larsson, Lennart Andersson, Kjell   6:48.1
Hansson, Rune Ivar Andersson, Sture Lennart
Hanson, Gösta Eriksson, Ivar Aronsson, Sven
Gunnarsson, Bertil Göransson)

The United States, represented by the Yale crew, finished third to Australia and Canada in the opening
round, but qualified for the semifinal through repêchage.
No Olympic eights had ever been won by a team that
lost its opening race, but the Yale crew broke this tradition to give the United States its eighth straight win in
the event.

1960 Rome-Lake Albano T: 14, N: 14, D: 9.3.

1. GER (Klaus Bittner, Karl-Heinz Hopp, Hans Lenk,   5:57.18
Manfred Ruiffs, Frank Schepke, Kraft
Schepke, Walter Schröder, Karl-Heinrich von
Groddeck, Willi Padge)

2. CAN (Donald Arnold, Walter D'Hondt, Nelson Kuhn,   6:01.52
John Lecky, Lorne Loomer, Archibald Mc-

Kinnon, William McKerlich, Glen Mervyn, Sohen Biln)

3. CZE (Bohumil Janoušek, Jan Jindra, Jiří Lundak, Stanislav Lusk, Václav Pavkovič, Ludek Pojezny, Jan Švéda, Josef Ventus, Miroslav Koniček)   6:04.84

4. FRA (Christian Puibaraud, Jean Bellet, Emile Clerc, Jean Ledoux, Gaston Mercier, Bernard Meynadier, Joseph Moroni, Michel Viaud, Alain Bouffard)   6:06.57

5. USA (Joseph Baldwin, Peter Bos, Mark Moore, Lyman Perry, Warren Sweetser, Gayle Thompson, Robert Wilson, Howard Winfree, William Long)   6:08.06

6. ITA (Paolo Amorini, Vasco Cantarello, Giancarlo Casalini, Luigi Prato, Vincenzo Prina, Mazzareno Simonato, Luigi Spozio, Armido Torri, Giuseppe Pira)   6:12.73

The U.S. winning streak was finally broken by a combined crew from Ratzeburg and Ditmarsia Kiel rowing clubs. The Germans led from the start and were never headed.

1964 Tokyo T: 14, N: 14, D: 10.15.

1. USA (Joseph Amlong, Thomas Amlong, Harold Budd, Emory Clark, Stanley Cwiklinski, Hugh Foley, William Knecht, William Stowe, Robert Zimonyi)   6:18.23

2. GER (Klaus Aeffke, Klaus Bittner, Karl-Heinrich von Groddeck, Hans-Jürgen Wallbrecht, Klaus Behrens, Jürgen Schröder, Jürgen Plagemann, Horst Meyer, Thomas Ahrens)   6:23.29

3. CZE (Petr Čermák, Jiň Lundak, Jan Mrvik, Julius Toček, Josef Ventus, Ludek Pojezny, Bohumil Janoušek, Richard Novy, Miroslav Koniček)   6:25.11

4. YUG (Boris Klavora, Jadran Barut, Joža Berc, Vjekoslav Skalak, Marko Mandič, Alojz Colja, Pavajo Martič, Lucijan Kelva, Zdenko Balaš)   6:27.15

5. SOV (Juozas Jagelavičius, Yuri Suslin, Piatras Karla, Vytautas Briedis, Volodymyr Sterlyk, Zigmas Jukna, Antanas Bogdanavičius, Rischard Voitkevich, Yuri Lorentson)   6:30.69

6. ITA (Dario Giani, Sergio Tagliapetra, Gianpietro Gilardi, Francesco Glorioso, Pietro Polti, Giuseppe Schiavon, Orlando Savarin, Sereno Brunello, Ivo Stefanoni)   6:42.78

7. FRA (André Fevret, Pierre Maddaloni, André Sloth, Joseph Moroni, Robert Dumontois, Jean Pierre Grimaud, Bernard Meynadier, Michel Viaud, Alain Bouffard)

8. AUS (David Ramage, David Boykett, Terence Davies, Robert Lachel, Paul Guest, Martin Tomanovits, Brian Vear, Graeme McCall, Kevin Wickham)

The Vesper Club of Philadelphia, the first noncollegiate eight to represent the United States in 60 years, scored a one-and-a-quarter-length upset victory over the crew from Ratzeburg, Germany. The Vesper coxswain was

Bob Zimonyi, a 46-year-old accountant who had defected after being a member of the 1956 Hungarian squad. Zimonyi's first Olympic appearance had been in the coxed fours of 1948.

1968 Mexico City-Xochimilco T: 12, N: 12, D: 10.19.

1. GER (Horst Meyer, Dirk Schreyer, Rüdiger Henning, Wolfgang Hottenrott, Lutz Ulbricht, Egbert Hirschfelder, Jörg Siebert, Nikolaus "Nico" Ott, Günther Tiersch)   6:07.00

2. AUS (Alfred Duval, Michael Morgan, Joseph Fazio, Peter Dickson, David Dougals, John Ranch, Gary Pearce, Robert Shirlaw, Alan Grover)   6:07.98

3. SOV (Zigmas Jukna, Antanas Bogdanavičius, Volodymyr Sterlyk, Juozas Jagelavičius, Aleksandr Martyshkin, Vytautas Briedis, Valentyn Kravchuk, Viktor Suslin, Yuri Lorentson)   6:09.11

4. NZE (Alan Webster, Wybo Veldman, Alistair Dryden, John Hunter, Mark Brownlee, John Gibbons, Thomas Just, Gilbert Cawood, Robert Page)   6:10.43

5. CZE (Vladimir Jánoš, Zdenék Kuba, Oldřich Svojanovský, Karel Kolesa, Pavel Svojanovský, Jan Walisch, Otakar Mareček, Petr Čermák, Jiří Pták)   6:12:17

6. USA (Stephen Brooks, Curtis Canning, Andrew Larkin, Scott Steketee, Franklin Hobbs, Jacques Fiechter, Cleve Livingston, David Higgins, Paul Hoffman)   6:14.34

7. GDR (Günter Bergau, Klaus-Dieter Bähr, Claus Wilke, Peter Gorny, Reinhard Zerfowski, Peter Hein, Manfred Schneider, Peter Prompe, Karl-Heinz Danielowski)   6:14.91

8. HOL (Maarten Kloosterman, Pieter Bon, Eric Nieche, Jaap Reesink, Gerard van Enst, Jan Steinhauser, Izak Wesdrop, Jan van Laarhoven, Arthur Koning)

The victorious Ratzeburg crew used a shell that was 75 pounds lighter than the shells of the other teams.

1972 Munich-Oberschleissheim T: 15, N: 15, D: 9.2.

1. NZE (Tony Hurt, Wybo Veldman, Dick Joyce, John Hunter, Lindsay Wilson, Athol Earl, Trevor Coker, Gary Robertson, Simon Dickie)   6:08.94

2. USA (Lawrence Terry, Fritz Hobbs, Peter Raymond, Timothy Mickelson, Eugene Clapp, William Hobbs, Cleve Livingston, Michael Livingston, Paul Hoffman)   6:11.61

3. GDR (Hans-Joachim Borzym, Jörg Landvoigt, Harold Dimke, Manfred Schneider, Hartmut Schreiber, Manfred Schmorde, Bernd Landvoigt, Heinrich Mederow, Dietmar Schwarz)   6:11.67

4. SOV (Aleksandr Riazankin, Viktor Dementiev, Sergei Koliaskin, Aleksandr Shitov, Valery Bissarnov, Boris Vorobiev, Vladimir Savelov, Aleksandr Martyshkin, Viktor Mikheyev)   6:14.48

5. GER (Reinhard Wendemuth, Frithjof Henckel, Norbert Kindlmann, Wolfgang Hottenrott, Hans-   6:14.91

Ulrich Buchholz, Günter Petermann, Bernd Truschinski, Winfried Ringwald, Manfred Klein)

6: POL (Jerzy Ulczyński, Marian Siejkowski, Krzysztof 6:29.35
Marek, Jan Mlodzikowski, Grzegorz Stellak, Marian Drążdżewski, Ryszard Gilo, Slawomir Maciejowski, Ryszard Kubiak)

7. HUN (Zoltán Melis, András Pályi, Antal Gelley, Béla Zsitnik, László Romvári, Péter Kokas, Imre Dávid, Ágoston Bányai, Robert Oelschleger)

8. AUS (John Clark, Michael Morgan, Bryan Curtin, Richard Curtin, Robert Paver, Kerry Jelbart, Gary Pearce, Malcolm Shaw, Alan Grover)

The New Zealand team raised the $45,000 needed to support their training and trip to Munich by holding a series of bingo games, as well as a raffle for a "dream kitchen."

1976 Montreal T: 13, N: 13, D: 7.25.
1. GDR (Bernd Baumgart, Gottfried Döhn, Werner 5:58.29
Klatt, Hans-Joachim Lück, Dieter Wendisch, Roland Kostulski, Ulrich Karnatz, Karl-Heinz Prudöhl, Karl Heinz Danielowski)

2. GBR (Richard Lester, John Yallop, Timothy Crooks, 6:00.82
Hugh Matheson, David Maxwell, R. James Clark, Frederick Smallbone, Leonard Robertson, Patrick Sweeney)

3. NZE (Ivan Sutherland, Trevor Coker, Peter Dignan, 6:03.51
Lindsay Wilson, Athol Earl, Dave Rodger, Alex Mclean, Tony Hurt, Simon Dickie)

4. GER (Reinhard Wendemuth, Bernd Truschinski, 6:06.15
Frank Schütze, Frithjof Henckel, Wolfram Thiem, Volker Sauer, Otmar Kaufhold, Wolf-Dieter Oschlies, Helmut Latz)

5. AUS (Islay Lee, Ian Clubb, Timothy Conrad, Robert 6:09.75
Paver, Gary Eubergang, Athol MacDonald, Peter Shakespear, Brian Richardson, Stuart Carter)

6. CZE (Pavel Konvička, Vaclav Mls, Josef Plaminek, 6:14.29
Josef Pokorny, Karel Mejta, Josef Nesticky, Lubomir Zapletal, Miroslav Vrastil, Jiři Pták)

7. SOV (Aleksandr Shitov, Antanas Chikotas, Vassily Potapov, Aleksandr Plyushkin, Anatoly Nemtyrev, Igor Konnov, Anatoly Ivanov, Vladimir Vasilyev, Vladimir Zharov)

8. CAN (Edgar Smith, Dirk Gidney, George Tintor, James Henniger, Patrick Croskerry, Melvin La Forme, Ronald Burak, Alexander Manson, Robert Choquette)

The East German team included a butcher, a plumber, a gardener, a mechanic, and a student.

1980 Moscow T: 9, N: 9, D: 7.27.
1. GDR (Bernd Krauss, Hans-Peter Koppe, Ulrich 5:49.05
Kons, Jörg Friedrich, Jens Doberschütz, Ulrich Karnatz, Uwe Dühring, Bernd Höing, Klaus-Dieter Ludwig)

2. GBR (Duncan McDougall, Allan Whitwell, J. Henry 5:51.92
Clay, Christopher Mahoney, Andrew Justice,

John Pritchard, Malcolm McGowan, Richard Stanhope, Colin Moynihan)

3. SOV (Viktor Kokoshyn, Andrei Tyshchenko, Jonas 5:52.66
Pinskus, Jonas Normantas, Andrei Lugin, Oleksander Mantsevych, Igor Maistrenko, Hrigory Dmytrienko, Oleksander Tkachenko)

4. CZE (Pavel Pevný, Lubomir Janko, Ctirad 5:53.75
Jungmann, Karel Neffe, Karel Mejta, Dušan Vičik, Milan Doleček, Milan Kyselý, Jiři Pták)

5. AUS (Islay Lee, Stephen Handley, William 5:56.74
Dankbaar, Andrew Withers, Timothy Willoughby, James Lowe, Timothy Young, Brian Richardson, David England)

6. BUL (Dimitur Yanakiev, Todor Mrunkov, Bozhidar 6:04.05
Rogelov, Ivan Botev, Yani Ignatóv, Mikhail Petrov, Petur Patzev, Vesselin Shterev, Ventzislav Kunchev)

7. HUN (Ferenc Kiss, Péter Tóvári, Róbert Sass, Attila Strochmayer, András Kormos, Zoltán Sztárcsevics, Kálmán Toronyi, László Kiss, Miklós Bálint)

8. CUB (Wenceslao Borroto, Ismael Same, Juan Alfonso, Juan Bueno, Francisco Mora, Hermenegildo Palacio, Jorge Alvarez, Antonio Riano, Enrique Carrillo)

1984 Los Angeles-Lake Casitas T: 7, N: 7, D: 8.5.
1. CAN (Patrick Turner, Kevin Neufeld, Mark Evans, 5:41.32
Grant Main, Paul Steele, J. Michael Evans, Dean Crawford, Blair Horn, Brian McMahon)

2. USA (Walter Lubsen, Andrew Sudduth, John 5:41.74
Terwilliger, Christopher Penny, Thomas Darling, Earl Borchelt, Charles Clapp, Bruce Ibbetson, Robert Jaugstetter)

3. AUS (Craig Muller, Clyde Hefer, Sam Patten, Timothy Willoughby, Ian Edmunds, James Battersby, Ion Popa, Steve Evans, Gavin Thredgold) 5:43.40

4. NZE (Nigel Atherfold, David Rodger, Roger White-Parsons, George Keys, Gregory Johnston, Christopher White, Andrew Stevenson, Michael Stanley, Andrew Hay) 5:44.14

5. GBR (Duncan McDougal, Christopher Mahoney, Salih Hassan, Clive Roberts, David Adam Clift, John Pritchard, Malcolm McGowan, Allan Whitwell, Colin Moynihan) 5:47.01

6. FRA (Alain Duprat, Dominique Lecointe, Thierry Louvet, Patrick Vibert-Vichet, Jacques Taborski, Jean-Jacques Martigne, Olivier Pons, Bernard Chevalier, Jean-Pierre Huguet-Balent) 5:49.52

7. CHI (Mario Castro, Carlos Neyra, Zibor Llanos, Giorgio Vallebuona, Alejandro Rojas, Victor Contreras, Rodolfo Pereira, Marcelo Rojas, Rodrigo Abasolo) 6:07:03

A bizarre incident enlivened the eights competition. One hundred meters after the start of the repêchage, the oarlock gate of the number 6 rower on the French crew broke and he lost his oar. This was not unusual in itself, but upon examination it was discovered that the gate had been intentionally filed down so that it would snap under pressure. A similar act of sabotage had occurred two weeks earlier at the junior championships in Sweden. That time the victims had been a U.S. women's crew. In Los Angeles, the French were allowed to participate in the final along with the six qualifiers. Thus all seven of the original entrants went on to the final despite having to endure two preliminary races and a repêchage.

The final had been expected to be a hot contest among New Zealand, the U.S. and Australia. But the Canadians led from start to finish, holding off a late sprint by the Americans. At the 1984 Olympics, each of the eight men's rowing titles was won by a different nation.

1988 Seoul T: 10, N: 10, D: 9.25.
1. GER   (Thomas Möllenkamp, Matthias Mellinghaus,   5:46.05
     Eckhardt Schultz, Ansgar Wessling, Armin
     Eichholz, Thomas Domian, Wolfgang Maen-
     nig, Bahne Rabe, Manfred Klein)
2. SOV   (Veniamin But, Mykhalo Komarov, Vassily   5:48.01
     Tikhanov, Aleksandr Dumchev, Pavlo Hurkov-
     sky, Viktor Diduk, Viktor Omelyanovych, An-
     drei Vassilyev, Aleksandr Lukyanov)
3. USA   (Michael Teti, John Smith, Ted Patton, John   5:48.26
     Rusher, Peter Nordell, Jeff McLaughlin, Doug
     Burden, John Pescatore, Seth Bauer)
4. GBR   (Richard Stanhope, Anton Obholzer, Peter   5:51.59
     Beaumont, Gavin Stewart, Terence Dillon,
     Salih Hassan, Stephen Turner, Nicholas Bur-
     fitt, Simon Jeffries)
5. AUS   (James Galloway, Hamish McGlashan, An-   5:53.73
     drew Cooper, Michael Mckay, Mark Doyle,
     James Tomkins, Ion Popa, Stephen Evans,
     Dale Caterson)
6. CAN   (Don Telfer, Kevin Neufeld, Jason Dorland,   5:54.26
     Andrew Crosby, Paul Steele, Gerald Main,
     Jamie Schaffer, John Wallace, Robert Mc-
     Mahon)
7. ITA   (Antonio Baldacci, Ettore Bulgarelli, Piero
     Carletto, Giuseppe Di Palo, Renato Gaeta,
     Dino Lucchetta, Giovanni Suarez, Annibale
     Venier, Franco Zucchi)
8. BUL   (Rumen Aleksiev, Emil Bondev, Yuri
     Dyulgurov, Ivo Gulov, Dimitar Kamburski,
     Ventzislav Kanchev, Ivan Stanev, Dimitar
     Tonchev, Nikola Zlatanov)

1992 Barcelona-Banyoles T: 14, N: 14, D: 8.2.
1. CAN   (John Wallace, Bruce Robertson, Michael   5:29.53
     Forgeron, Darren Barber, Robert Marland,
     Michael Rascher, Andrew Crosby, Derek Por-
     ter, Terrence Paul)
2. ROM   (Ioan Vizitiu, Dănut Dobre, Claudiu Marin,   5:29.67
     Iulica Ruican, Viorel Talapan, Vasile Nastase,
     Valentin Robu, Vasile Mastacan, Marin
     Gheorghe)
3. GER   (Frank Richter, Thorsten Streppelhoff, Detlef   5:31.00
     Kirchhoff, Armin Eichholz, Bahne Rabe, Hans

     Sennewald, Ansgar Wessling, Roland Baar,
     Manfred Klein)
4. USA   (Michael Teti, Christian Sahs, James Munn,   5:33.18
     Jeffrey Klepacki, Robert Shepherd, Malcolm
     Baker, Richard Kennelly, John Parker, Michael
     Moore)
5. AUS   (Simon Spriggs, Peter Murphy, Wayne   5:33.72
     Diplock, Jaime Fernandez, Ben Dodwell, Sam
     Patten, Boden Hanson, Robert Scott, David
     Colvin)
6. GBR   (Martin Cross, Tim Foster, Richard Phelps, Jim   5:39.92
     Walker, Ben Hunt Davis, Stephen Turner,
     Rupert Obholzer, Johnathan Singfield, Adrian
     Ellison)
7. DEN   (Jens Pørneki, Jens Tramm, Thomas Larsen,
     Lars Christensen, Carsten Hassing, Jesper
     Thusgaard Kristiansen, Martin Hansen, Kent
     Skovsager, Stephen Masters)
8. SAF   (Martin Walsh, Rogan Clarke, Grant Hillary,
     Andrew Gordon-Brown, Erich Mauff, Timothy
     Lahner, Robin McCall, Ivan Pentz, Andrew
     Lonmon-Davis)

Germany had won all three world championships since the last Olympics, but it was the Canadians and the surprising Romanians who fought for the gold medal. Romania took the early lead, but Canada edged ahead by the halfway mark and held on to win by less than a foot in the closest rowing final in Olympic history. Spain's coxswain, 11-year-old Carlos Front, was the youngest competitor in the Summer Games since 1900.

LIGHTWEIGHT: DOUBLE SCULLS

This event will be held for the first time in 1996.

LIGHTWEIGHT: FOUR-OARED SHELL WITHOUT COXSWAIN

This event will be held for the first time in 1996.

Discontinued Events
PAIR-OARED SHELL WITH COXSWAIN

1900 Paris T: 6, N: 3, D: 8.26.
1. HOL&   (Minerva, Amsterdam—François Antoine   7:34.2
   FRA   Brandt, Roelof Klein, Hermanus Brockmann)
2. FRA   (Société Nautique de la Marne—Louis Marti-   7:34.4
     net, Waleff, coxswain unknown)
3. FRA   (Rowing Club Castillon—Carlos Deltour, An-   7:57.2
     toine Védrenne, Paoli)

4. FRA (Cercle Nautique de Reims—Mathieu, Ferlin, 8:01.0
coxswain unknown)

Brockmann was coxswain for the Dutch crew in the opening heat, which they lost to the Société Nautique de la Marne. It was decided that Brockmann was too heavy, so he was replaced in the final by a small French boy whose name is unknown. This boy, who appears to have been under 10 years old and may have been as young as 7, is presumed to be the youngest competitor in Olympic history.

1904 not held

1906 Athens T: 8, N: 5, D: 4.26.
(1000 Meters)
1. ITA (Bucintoro, Venice—Enrico Bruna, Emilio Fontanella, Giorgio Cesana) 4:23.0
2. ITA (Barion, Bari—Luigi Diana, Francesco Civera, Emilio Cesarana) 4:30.0
3. FRA (Société Nautique de la Basse Seine, Paris— Gaston Delaplane, Charles Delaporte, Marcel Frebourg) —
4. FRA (Société Nautique de Bayonne—Adolphe Bernard, Joseph Halcet, Jean-Baptiste Mathieu) —
5. BEL& (Club Nautique—Max Orban, Rémy Orban, GRE Th. Psiliakos)

1906 Athens T: 7, N: 5, D: 4.26.
(1609 Meters)
1. ITA (Bucintoro, Venice—Enrico Bruna, Emilio Fontanella, Giorgio Cesana) 7:32.4
2. BEL& (Société Nautique de Gand—Max Orban, 8:00.0
GRE Rémy Orban, Th. Psiliakos)
3. FRA (Société Nautique de Bayonne—Adolphe Bernard, Joseph Halcet, Jean-Baptiste Mathieu) 8:08.6
4. DEN (Hannibal Ostergaard, Henning Rasmussen, Axel Steinthal)

Psiliakos was a young Greek who offered to cox for the Belgian pair.

1908–1912 not held

1920 Antwerp-Vilvoorde T: 4, N: 4, D: 8.29.
1. ITA (Ercole Olgeni, Giovanni Scatturin, Guido De 7:56.0
Filip)
2. FRA (Gabriel Poix, Maurice Bouton, Ernest Barberolle) 7:57.0
3. SWI (Edouard Candeveau, Alfred Felber, Paul —
Piaget)

1924 Paris T: 5, N: 5, D: 7.17.
1. SWI (Edouard Candeveau, Alfred Felber, Emile 8:39.0
Lachapelle)
2. ITA (Ercole Olgeni, Giovanni Scatturin, Gino Sopracordevole) 8:39.1

3. USA (Leon Butler, Harold Wilson, Edward Jennings) —
4. FRA (Eugène Constant, Raymond Talleux, Marcel Lepan) —

The final was, by all accounts, a thrilling race, and was won by the Swiss by only two feet.

1928 Amsterdam-Sloten T: 6, N: 6, D: 8.10.
1. SWI (Hans Schöchlin, Karl Schöchlin, Hans 7:42.6
Bourquin)
2. FRA (Armand Marcelle, Edouard Marcelle, Henri 7:48.4
Préaux)
3. BEL (Léon Flament, François de Coninck, Georges Anthony)
4. ITA (Renzo Vestrini, Roberto Vestrini, Cesare Milani)

1932 Los Angeles-Long Beach T: 4, N: 4, D: 8.13.
1. USA (Joseph Schauers, Charles Kieffer, Edward 8:25.8
Jennings)
2. POL (Jerzy Braun, Janusz Ślązak, Jerzy Skolimowski) 8:31.2
3. FRA (Anselme Brusa, André Giriat, Pierre Brunet) 8:41.2
4. BRA (José Ramalho, Estevam Strata, Francisco 8:53.2
Bricio)

1936 Berlin-Grünau T: 12, N: 12, D: 8.14.
1. GER (Gerhard Gustmann, Herbert Adamski, Dieter 8:36.9
Arend)
2. ITA (Almiro Bergamo, Guido Santin, Luciano 8:49.7
Negrini)
3. FRA (Georges Tapie, Marceau Fourcade, Noël 8:54.0
Vandernotte)
4. DEN (Raymond Larsen, Carl Berner, Aage Jensen) 8:55.8
5. SWI (Georges Gschwind, Hans Appenzeller, Rolf 9:10.9
Spring)
6. YUG (Ivo Fabris, Elko Mrduljaš, Line Ljubičič) 9:19.4

1948 London-Henley-on-Thames T: 9, N: 9, D: 8.9.
1. DEN (Finn Pedersen, Tage Henriksen, Carl-Ebbe 8:00.5
Andersen)
2. ITA (Giovanni Steffe, Aldo Tarlao, Alberto Radi) 8:12.2
3. HUN (Antal Szendey, Béla Zsitnik, Róbert Zimonyi) 8:25.2
4. FRA (Ampelio Sartor, Aristide Sartor, René Crezen)
4. YUG (Veljko Ristic, Milan Horvatin, Dragutin Djordjevič)

1952 Helsinki T: 15, N: 15, D: 7.23.
1. FRA (Raymond Salles, Gaston Mercier, Bernard 8:28.6
Malivoire)
2. GER (Heinz-Joachim Manchen, Helmut Heinhold, 8:32.1
Helmut Noll)
3. DEN (Svend Pedersen, Poul Svendsen, Jörgen 8:34.9
Frandsen)
4. ITA (Giuseppe Ramani, Aldo Tarlao, Luciano Marion) 8:38.4
5. FIN (Veijo Mikkolainen, Toimi Pitkänen, Erkki 8:40.8
Lyijynen)

The French coxswain, Bernard Malivoire, was 14 years old.

1956 Melbourne-Ballarat T: 8, N: 8, D: 11.27.
1. USA (Arthur Ayrault, Conn Findlay, A. Kurt Seiffert) 8:26.1
2. GER (Karl-Heinrich von Groddeck, Horst Arndt, Rainer Borkowsky) 8:29.2
3. SOV (Ihor Yemchuk, Heorhi Zhylin, Vladimir Petrov) 8:31.0
4. POL (Henryk Jagodziński, Zbigniew Szwarcer, Berthold Mainka) 8:31.5

1960 Rome-Lake Albano T: 18, N: 18, D: 9.3.
1. GER (Bernhard Knubel, Heinz Renneberg, Klaus Zerta) 7:29.14
2. SOV (Antanas Băgdanavičius, Zigmas Jukna, Igor Rudakov) 7:30.17
3. USA (Richard Draeger, Conn Findlay, H. Kent Mitchell) 7:34.58
4. DEN (Jens Behrendt Jensen, Knud Nielsen, Sven Lysholt Hansen) 7:39.20
5. ITA (Giancarlo Piretta, Renzo Ostino, Vincenzo Bruno) 7:40.92
6. ROM (Ştefan Kureska, Gheorghe Riffelt, Mircea Roger) 7:49.57

German coxswain Klaus Zerta was 13 years old. Except for the unknown coxswain in 1900, Zerta is the youngest male in Olympic history to win a gold medal.

1964 Tokyo T: 16, N: 16, D: 15.
1. USA (Edward Ferry, Conn Findlay, H. Kent Mitchell) 8:21.23
2. FRA (Jacques Morel, Georges Morel, Jean-Claude Darouy) 8:23.15
3. HOL (Jan Bos, Herman Rouwé, Frederik Hartsuiker) 8:23.42
4. SOV/ RUS (Nikolai Safronov, Leonid Rakovschik, Igor Rudakov) 8:24.85
5. CZE (Václav Chalupa, Jiři Palko, Zdenek Mejstřik) 8:36.21
6. POL (Kazimierz Maskręcki, Marian Siejkowski, Stanislaw Kozera) 8:40.00
7. GDR (Günter Bergau, Peter Gorny, Karl-Heinz Danielowski)
8. AUT (Alfred Sageder, Josef Kloimstein, Peter Salzbacher)

1968 Mexico City-Xochimilco T: 18, N: 18, D: 10.19.
1. ITA (Primo Baran, Renzo Sambo, Bruno Cipolla) 8:04.81
2. HOL (Herman Suselbeek, Hadriaan van Nes, Roderick Rijnders) 8:06.80
3. DEN (Jörn Krab, Harry Jörgensen, Preben Krab) 8:08.07
4. GDR (Helmut Wollmann, Wolfgang Gunkel, Klaus-Dieter Neubert) 8:08.22
5. USA (William Hobbs, Richard Edmunds, Stewart MacDonald) 8:12.60
6. GER (Bernhard Hiesinger, Rolf Hartung, Lutz Benter) 8:41.51
7. SWI (Urs Frankhauser, Urs Bitterli, Beat Wirz)
8. BUL (Georgi Atanasov, Georgi Nikolov, Veselin Stayevski)

1972 Munich-Oberschleissheim T: 21, N: 21, D: 9.2.
1. GDR (Wolfgang Gunkel, Jörg Lucke, Klaus-Dieter Neubert) 7:17.25
2. CZE (Oldřich Svojanovský, Pavel Svojanovský, Vladimir Petřiček) 7:19.57
3. ROM (Ştefan Tudor, Petre Ceapura, Ladislau Lovrenschi) 7:21.36
4. GER (Heinz Mussmann, Bernd Krause, Stefan Kuhnke) 7:21.52
5. SOV/ RUS (Vladimir Yeshinov, Nikolai Ivanov, Yuri Lorentson) 7:24.44
6. POL (Wojciech Repsz, Wieslaw Dlugosz, Jacek Rylski) 7:28.92
7. NOR (Rolf Andreassen, Arne Bergodd, Thor Egil Olsen)
8. GBR (David Maxwell, Michael Hart, Alan Inns)

1976 Montreal T: 17, N: 17, D: 7.25.
1. GDR (Harald Jährling, Friedrich-Wilhelm Ulrich, Georg Spohr) 7:58.99
2. SOV/ RUS (Dmitri Bekhterev, Yuri Shurkalov, Yuri Lorentson) 8:01.82
3. CZE (Oldřich Svojanovský, Pavel Svojanovský, Ludvik Vebr) 8:03.82
4. BUL (Rumen Hristov, Tsvetan Petkov, Tosho Kishev) 8:11.27
5. ITA (Primo Baran, Annibale Venier, Franco Venturnin) 8:15.97
6. POL (Ryszard Stadniuk, Grzegorz Stellak, Ryszard Kubiak) 8:23.02
7. GBR (A. Neil Christie, James Macleod, David Webb)
8. GER (Winfried Ringwald, Klaus Jaeger, Holger Hocke)

1980 Moscow T: 11, N: 11, D: 7.20.
1. GDR (Harald Jährling, Friedrich-Wilhelm Ulrich, Georg Spohr) 7:02.54
2. SOV (Viktor Pereverzev, Gennady Kryuchkin, Aleksandr Lukyanov) 7:03.35
3. YUG/ CRO (Dusko Mrduljas, Zlatko Celent, Josip Reic) 7:04.92
4. ROM (Petre Ceapura, Gabriel Bularda, Ladislau Lovrenschi) 7:07.17
5. BUL (Tsvetan Petkov, Rumen Hristov, Tosho Kishev) 7:09.21
6. CZE (Josef Plaminek, Milan Škopek, Oldřich Hejdušek) 7:09.41
7. ITA (Antonio Dell'Aquila, Giuseppe Abbagnale, Giuseppe Di Capua)
8. FRA (Serge Fornara, Herve Bourqvel, Jean-Pierre Huguet-Balenx)

1984 Los Angeles-Lake Casitas T: 12, N: 12, D: 8.5.
1. ITA (Carmine Abbagnale, Giuseppe Abbagnale, Giuseppe Di Capua) 7:05.99
2. ROM (Dimitrie Popescu, Vasile Tomoiagă, Dumitru Răducanu) 7:11.21
3. USA (Kevin Still, Robert Espeseth, Douglas Herland) 7:12.81

4. BRA   (Valter Hime Soares, Angelo Rosio Neto, Nilton   7:17.07
         Silva Alonco)

5. CAN   (Harold Backer, Tony Zasada, Ian Barkley)   7:18.98

6. GER   (Hermann Gress, Dieter Göpfert, Rudolf Zieg-   7:25.16
         ler)

7. YUG   (Dario Vidosević, Zlatko Celent, Mirko Ivancić)

8. GBR   (Adrian Genziani, William Lang, Alan Inns)

The coxswain for the bronze-medal-winning U.S. team was 32-year-old Doug Herland, who stood 4 feet 9 inches tall and weighed 103 pounds. Herland was born with broken hips, broken ribs and a broken collarbone as a result of osteogenesis imperfecta—brittle bone disease. He broke bones twice a year for the first eight years of his life. Herland discovered rowing at Pacific Lutheran U. in Tacoma, Washington, where he earned a degree in social psychology. He went on to a career in social work, counseling handicapped and mentally retarded children, and establishing a rowing team for the disabled in Michigan.

The coxswain for the 11th place Belgian pair was the youngest competitor at the 1984 Olympics, 12-year-old Philippe Cuelenaere.

1988 Seoul T: 14, N: 14, D: 9.25.

1. ITA   (Carmine Abbagnale, Giuseppe Abbagnale,   6:58.79
         Giuseppe Di Capua)

2. GDR   (Mario Streit, Detlef Kirchhoff, René Rensch)   7:00.63

3. GBR   (Andrew Holmes, Steven Redgrave, Patrick   7:01.95
         Sweeney)

4. ROM   (Dimitrie Popescu, Vasile Tomoiagă, Ladislau   7:02.60
         Lovrenchi)

5. BUL   (Emil Groitzov, Atanas Andreyev, Stefan   7:03.04
         Stoykov)

6. SOV/ (Andrei Korikov, Roman Kazantsev, Andrei   7:06.07
   RUS   Lipsky)

7. CZE   (Jan Kabrhel, Jiří Ptak, Milan Škopek)

8. YUG   (Roman Ambrozić, Milan Janša, Sašo Mirjanič)

The Abbagnale brothers of Pompeii parlayed a furious start into their second Olympic championship. Their younger brother, Agostino, a member of the Italian quadruple sculls team, also went home with a gold medal.

1992 Barcelona-Banyoles T: 16, N: 16, D: 8.2.

1. GBR   (Jonathon Searle, Greg Searle, Garry Herbert)   6:49.83

2. ITA   (Carmine Abbagnale, Giuseppe Abbagnale,   6:50.98
         Giuseppe Di Capua)

3. ROM   (Dimitrie Popescu, Nicolaie Taga, Dumitru   6:51.58
         Răducanu)

4. GER   (Thomas Woddow, Michael Peter, Peter   6:56.98
         Thiede)

5. CUB   (Ismael Carbonell Same, Arnaldo Rodríguez   6:58.26
         Silva, Roberto Ojeda González)

6. FRA   (Patrick Berthou, Laurent Lacasa, Emmanuel   7:03.01
         Bunoz)

7. POL   (Piotr Basta, Tomasz Mruczkowski, Bartosz
         Sroga)

8. USA   (Aaron Pollock, John Moore, Stephen
         Shellans)

The Abbagnale brothers had won seven world championships and two Olympic championships and they had not been beaten since 1986. The Searle brothers, on the other hand, although respected rowers, had only taken up the coxed pairs in April 1992. But it was the Searles who recorded the fastest times in both the preliminary round and the semifinals. In the final the Abbagnales followed their usual strategy of setting a blistering pace. They led by almost four seconds at the halfway mark. The Searles, lying in third place, picked up speed with 750 meters to go and passed the stunned Italians in the final hundred meters. Greg Searle later admitted to a "pang of guilt" when he looked over at the Italians and saw that they looked "suddenly very old . . . I could tell how devastated they were and utterly gutted." The Abbagnales and Di Capua rowed over and offered their congratulations, and Greg Searle "was very touched by their graciousness and chivalry."

FOUR-OARED SHELL WITH COXSWAIN

1900 Paris T: 8, N: 4, D: 8.26, 8.29.

First Final

1. FRA   (Cercle de l'Aviron de Roubaix—Emile Del-   7:11.0
         chambre, Jean Cau, Henri Bouchaert, Henri
         Hazebrouck, Charlot)

2. FRA   (Union Nautique de Lyon—Charles Perrin,   7:18.0
         Daniel Soubeyran, Emile Wegelin, Georges
         Lumpp, coxswain unknown)

3. GER   (R.C. Favorite Harmonia, Hamburg—Hugo   7:18.2
         Rüster, Wilhelm Carstens, Julius Körner, Adolf
         Möller, Gustav Moths, Max Ammermann)

Second Final

1. GER   (Germania Rowing Club, Hamburg—Oscar   5:59.0
         Gossler, Walther Katzenstein, Waldemar
         Tietgens, Gustav Gossler, Carl Gossler)

2. HOL   (Minerva Amsterdam—Gerhard Lotsy,   6:33.0
         Coenraad Hiebendaal, Paulus Jan Lotsy, Jo-
         hannes Terwogt, Hermanus Brockmann)

3. GER   (Ludwigshafener R.V.—Carl Lehle, Ernst   6:35.0
         Feller, Hermann Wilker, Otto Fickeisen, Franz
         Kröwerath)

Incompetence on the part of regatta officials resulted in the unusual development of two separate finals in the 1900 Olympics in this event. At first it was declared that the winners of three heats would qualify for the final as would the second-place finisher in heat 3, which included four of the eight entrants. When it was discovered that the losers in heats 2 and 3 had recorded faster times than the winner of heat 1, the officials announced that an extra qualifying heat would have to be run. However, they were unable to notify all of the crews, so the extra heat was cancelled. It was then decided that the three heat winners would be joined in the final by the three fastest losers. But since the course was laid out for only four boats, the heat winners protested and refused to participate in the final. So the first final was run off with only Roubaix of the original qualifiers in the water. The result was obviously ridiculous, so a second final was announced for the three heat winners. Participants in both finals were awarded prizes.

1904 not held

1906 Athens T: 8, N: 6, D: 4.24.
1. ITA (Bucintoro, Venice—Enrico Bruna, Emilio Fontanella, Riccardo Jandinoni, Giorgio Cesana, Giuseppe Poli) 8:13.0
2. FRA (Société Nautique de la Basse Seine, Paris—Gaston Delaplane, Charles Delaporte, Léon Delignières, Paul Echard, Marcel Frebourg) —
3. FRA (Société Nautique de Bayonne—Adolphe Bernard, Joseph Halcet, Jean-Baptiste Laporte, Pierre Sourbe, Jean-Baptiste Mathieu) —
4. DEN Knud Bay, Emanuel Saugmann, Frederick Bielefeldt, Henning Rasmussen, Hannibal Ostergaard —
5. GRE (N. Viaguinis, J. Kountouris, P. Nomikos, G. Tsakonas, Ch. Brisimitzakis) —
6. GRE (N. Zamanos, G. Georgitseas, N. Bertos, P. Saousopoulos, D. Rediadis) —
7. INT (Donald Whittal, N. Petroppulos, P. Pavlidis, J. Gounaris, N. Mardelis) —
DNF: GRE (Ch. Liambeis, Ch. Rangos, M. Sakorrafos, G. Bouboulis, K. Athanasiadis)

1908 not held

1912 Stockholm T: 11, N: 9, D: 7.19.
1. GER (Ludwigshafener R.V.—Albert Arnheiter, Otto Fickeisen, Rudolf Fickeisen, Hermann Wilker, Otto Maier) 6:59.4
2. GBR (Thames Rowing Club—Julius Beresford, Karl Vernon, Charles Rought, Bruce Logan, Geoffrey Carr) —
3. DEN (Polytehnic Roklub—Erik Bisgaard, Rasmus Peter Frandsen, Magnus Simonsen, Poul Thymann, Eigil Clemmensen) —
3. NOR (Christiana Roklub—Henry Larsen, Matias Torstensen, Theodor Klem, Håkon Tönsager, Ejnar Tönsager) —

1920 Antwerp-Vilvoorde T: 8, N: 8, D: 8.29.
1. SWI (Willy Brüderlin, Max Rudolf, Paul Rudolf, Hans Walter, Paul Staub) 6:54.0
2. USA (Kenneth Myers, Carl Otto Klose, Franz Federschmidt, Erich Federschmidt, Sherman Clark) 6:58.0
3. NOR (Birger Var, Theodor Klem, Henry Larsen, Per Gulbrandsen, Thoralf Hagen) —

1924 Paris T: 10, N: 10, D: 7.17.
1. SWI (Emile Albrecht, Alfred Probst, Eugen Sigg-Bächthold, Hans Walter, Emile Lachapelle) 7:18.4
2. FRA (Eugène Constant, Louis Gressier, Georges Lecointe, Raymond Talleux, Marcel Lepan) 7:21.6

3. USA (Robert Gerhardt, Sidney Jelinek, Edward Mitchell, Henry Welsford, John Kennedy) 7:23.0
4. ITA (Renato Berninzone, Marcello Casanova, Gastone Cerato, Jean Cipollina, Massimo Ballestrero) —
DNF: HOL (Johannes Brandsma, Jacob Brandsma, Dirk Fortuin, Jean van Silfhout, Louis Dekker)

1928 Amsterdam-Sloten T: 11, N: 11, D: 8.10.
1. ITA (Valerio Peretin, Giliante D'Este, Nicolo Vittori, Giovanni Delise, Renato Petronio) 6:47.8
2. SWI (Ernst Haas, Joseph Meyer, Otto Bucher, Karl Schwegler, Fritz Bösch) 7:03.4
3. POL (Franciszek Bronikowski, Edmund Jankowski, Leon Birkholc, Bernard Ormanowski, Bdeslaw Drewek) 7:12.8
4. GER (Karl Golzo, Hans Nickel, Karl Hoffmann, Werner Kleine, Alfred Krohn) 7:26.4
5. BEL (Maurice Delplanck, Théo Wambeke, Alphonse Dewette, Charles van Son, Jean Bauwens) 7:30.2

1932 Los Angeles-Long Beach T: 7, N: 7, D: 8.13.
1. GER (Hans Eller, Horst Hoeck, Walter Meyer, Joachim Spremberg, Karl-Heinz Neumann) 7:19.0
2. ITA (Bruno Vattovaz, Giovanni Plazzer, Riccardo Divora, Bruno Parovel, Giovanni Scherl) 7:19.2
3. POL (Jerzy Braun, Janusz Ślązak, Stanislaw Urban, Edward Kobyliński, Jerzy Skolimowski) 7:26.8
4. NZE (Noel Pope, Somers Cox, Charles Saunders, John Solomon, Delmont Gullery) 7:32.6

A spectacular finish saw the Germans win by a mere one foot.

1936 Berlin-Grünau T: 16, N: 16, D: 8.14.
1. GER (Hans Maier, Walter Volle, Ernst Gaber, Paul Söllner, Fritz Bauer) 7:16.2
2. SWI (Hermann Betschart, Hans Homberger, Alex Homberger, Karl Schmid, Rolf Spring) 7:24.3
3. FRA (Fernand Vandernotte, Marcel Vandernotte, Marcel Cosmat, Marcel Chauvigné, Noël Vandernotte) 7:33.3
4. HOL (Martinus Schoorl, Hotse Sjoerd Bartlema, John Regout, Simon de Wit, Gerard Hallie) 7:34.7
5. HUN (Miklós Mihók, Vilmos Éden, Ákos Inotay, Alajos Szilassy-Szymiczek, László Molnár) 7:35.6
6. DEN (Hans Mikkelsen, Ibsen Sörensen, Flemming Jensen, Svend Aage Sörensen, Aage Jensen) 7:40.4

Coxswain for the French bronze medalists was 12-year-old Noël Vandernotte, whose father, Fernand, and uncle, Marcel, were also members of the crew. Noël also coxed for the pair-oared shell.

1948 London-Henley-on-Thames T: 16, N: 16, D: 8.9.
1. USA (Warren Westlund, Robert Martin, Robert Will, Gordon Giovanelli, Allen Morgan) 6:50.3
2. SWI (Rudolf Reichling, Erich Schriever, Emile Knecht, Pierre Stebler, André Moccand) 6:53.3

3. DEN (Erik Larsen, Börge Nielsen, Henry Larsen, 6:58.6
Harry Knudsen, Jörgen Ib Olsen)
4. FRA (Jean Pieddeloup, René Lotti, Gaston Maquat,
Jean-Pierre Souche, Marcel Boigegrain); HUN
(Miklós Zágon, Lajos Nagy, Béla Nyilasi, Tibor
Nádas, Róbert Zimonyi); ITA (Reginaldo
Polloni, Francesco Gotti, Renato Macario,
Riccardo Cerutti, Dominico Cambieri)

1952 Helsinki T: 17, N: 17, D: 7.23.
1. CZE (Karel Mejta, Jiři Havlis, Jan Jindra, Stanislav 7:33.4
Lusk, Miroslav Koranda)
2. SWI (Enrico Bianchi, Karl Weidmann, Heinrich 7:36.5
Scheller, Emile Ess, Walter Leiser)
3. USA (Carl Lovested, Alvin Ulbrickson, Richard 7:37.0
Wahlström, Matthew Leanderson, Albert
Rossi)
4. GBR (Roderick Macmillan, Graham Fisk, Laurence 7:41.2
Guest, Peter de Giles, Paul Massey)
5. FIN (Kurt Grönholm, Paul Stråhlman, Birger Karls- 7:43.8
son, Karl-Erik Johansson, Antero Tukiainen)

1956 Melbourne-Ballarat T: 10, N: 10, D: 11.27.
1. ITA (Alberto Winkler, Romano Sgheiz, Angelo 7:19.4
Vanzin, Franco Trincavelli, Ivo Stefanoni)
2. SWE (Olof Larsson, Gösta Eriksson, Ivar Aronsson, 7:22.4
Sven Ever Gunnarsson, Bertil Göransson)
3. FIN (Kauko Hänninen, Reino Poutanen, Veli 7:30.9
Lehtelä, Toimi Pitkänen, Matti Niemi)
4. AUS (Gordon Cowey, Kevin McMahon, Reginald 7:31.1
Libbis, Ian Allen, John Jenkinson)

1960 Rome-Lake Albano T: 21, N: 21, D: 9.3.
1. GER (Gerd Cintl, Horst Effertz, Klaus Rieckemann, 6:39.12
Jürgen Litz, Michael Obst)
2. FRA (Robert Dumontois, Claude Martin, Jacques 6:41.62
Morel, Guy Nosbaum, Jean-Claude Klein)
3. ITA (Fulvio Balatti, Romano Sgheiz, Franco 6:43.72
Trincavelli, Giovanni Zucchi, Ivo Stefanoni)
4. SOV/ (Oleg Aleksandrov, Igor Khokhlov, Boris 6:45.67
RUS Fyodorov, Valentin Zanin, Igor Rudakov)
5. AUS (Graeme Allen, Maxwell Annett, John Hudson, 6:45.80
Roland Waddington, Lionel Robberds)
6. HUN (Tibor Bedekovics, Csaba Kovács, László 6:51.65
Munteán, Pál Wágner, Gyula Lengyel)

1964 Tokyo T: 16, N: 16, D: 10.15.
1. GER (Peter Neusel, Bernhard Britting, Joachim 7:00.44
Werner, Egbert Hirschfelder, Jürgen Oelke)
2. ITA (Renato Bosatta, Emilio Trivini, Giuseppe 7:02.84
Galante, Franco De Pedrina, Giovanni
Spinola)
3. HOL (Alex Mullink, Jan van de Graaf, Frederick van 7:06.46
de Graaf, Robert van de Graaf, Marius
Klumperbeek)
4. FRA (Yves Fraisse, Claude Pache, Gérard 7:13.92
Jacquesson, Michel Dumas, Jean Claude
Darouy)
5. SOV/ (Anatoly Tkatchuk, Vitaly Kurdchenko, Boris 7:16.05
RUS Kuzmin, Anatoly Luzgin, Vladimir Yevseyev)

6. POL (Szczepan Grajczyk, Marian Leszczyński, 7:28.15
Ryszard Lubicki, Andrzej Nowaczyk, Jerzy
Pawlowski)
7. USA (Paul Gunderson, Harry Pollock, Thomas Pollock, James Tew, Edward Washburn)
8. NZE (Darien Boswell, Alistair Dryden, Peter Masfen,
Robert Page, Dudley Storey)

1968 Mexico City-Xochimilco T: 13, N: 13, D: 10.19.
1. NZE (Richard Joyce, Dudley Storey, Ross Hounsell 6:45.62
Collinge, Warren Cole, Simon Dickie)
2. GDR (Peter Kremtz, Roland Göhler, Manfred 6:48.20
Gelpke, Klaus Jakob, Dieter Semetzky)
3. SWI (Denis Oswald, Hugo Waser, Peter Bolliger, 6:49.04
Jakob Grob, Gottlieb Fröhlich)
4. ITA (Romano Sgheiz, Emilio Trivini, Giuseppe 6:49.54
Galante, Luciano Sgheiz, Mariano Gottifredi)
5. USA (Luther Jones, William Purdy, Anthony Martin, 6:51.41
Aspinwall Gardner Cadwalader, John Har-
tigan)
6. SOV (Anatoly Mentyrev, Nikolai Surov, Oleksei 7:00.00
Myschyn, Arkady Kudinov, Viktor Mikheyev)
7. ROM (Reinhold Batschi, Petre Ceapura, Ştefan Tudor, Francisc Papp, Ladislau Lovrenchi)
8. ARG (Hugo Aberastegui, José Robledo, Juan
Gómez, Guillermo Segurado, Rolando Loca-
telli)

The winning New Zealand crew had never competed together before the Olympics.

1972 Munich-Oberschleissheim T: 14, N: 14, D; 9.2.
1. GER (Peter Berger, Hans-Johann Färber, Gerhard 6:31.85
Auer, Alois Bierl, Uwe Benter)
2. GDR (Dietrich Zander, Reinhard Gust, Eckhard 6:33.30
Martens, Rolf Jobst, Klaus-Dieter Ludwig)
3. CZE (Otakar Mareček, Karel Neffe, Vladimir Jánoš, 6:35.64
František Provaznik, Vladimir Petřiček)
4. SOV (Volodymyr Sterlyk, Vladimir Soloviev, Alek- 6:37.71
sandr Lyubaturov, Yuri Shamayev, Igor
Rudakov)
5. USA (David Sawyer, Charles Ruthford, Chad Ru- 6:41.86
dolph, Michael Vespoli, Stewart MacDonald)
6. NZE (Warren Cole, Chris Nilsson, John Clark, David 6:42.55
Linstrom, Peter Lindsay)
7. HOL (Wim Grothuis, Evert Kroes, Jan Woudenberg,
Johan ter Haar, Cornelis de Korver)
8. SWI (Hanspeter Leuthi, Urs Frankhauser, Franz
Rentsch, Denis Oswald, Rolf Stadelmann)

1976 Montreal T: 14, N: 14, D: 7.25.
1. SOV/ (Vladimir Yeshinov, Nikolai Ivanov, Mikhail 6:40.22
RUS Kuznetsov, Aleksandr Klepikov, Aleksandr
Lukianov)
2. GDR (Andreas Schulz, Rüdiger Kunze, Walter 6:42.70
Diessner, Ullrich Diessner, Johannes Thomas)
3. GER (Hans-Johann Färber, Ralph Kubail, Siegfried 6:46.96
Fricke, Peter Niehusen, Hartmut Wenzel)
4. CZE (Otakar Mareček, Karel Neffe, Milan 6:50.15
Suchopar, Vladimir Jánoš, Vladimir Petřiček)

5. BUL   (Luchezar Boichev, Nasko Minchev, Ivan   6:52.88
Botev, Kiril Kirchev, Nenko Dobrev)

6. NZE   (Viv Haar, Danny Keane, Tim Logan, Ian   7:00.17
Boserio, David Simmons)

7. IRL   (Michael Ryan, James Muldoon, Willyam
Ryan, Christy O'Brien, Liam Redmond)

8. POL   (Jerzy Broniec, Adam Tomasiak, Jerzy
Ulczyński, Ryszard Burak, Wlodzimierz
Chmielewski)

1980 Moscow T: 12, N: 12, D: 7.27.

1. GDR   (Dieter Wendisch, Ullrich Diessner, Walter   6:14.51
Diessner, Gottfried Döhn, Andreas Gregor)

2. SOV/   (Artūrs Garonskis, Dimants Krišjānis, Dzintars   6:19.05
   LAT   Krišjānis, Džoržs Tikmers, Juris Bērziņš)

3. POL   (Grzegorz Stellak, Adam Tomasiak, Grzegorz   6:22.52
Nowak, Ryszard Stadniuk, Ryszard Kubiak)

4. SPA   (Manuel Bermudez, Isidro Martin, Salvador   6:26.23
Verges, Luis Marie Lasurtegui, Javier Sabria)

5. BUL   (Hristo Aleksandrov, Vilhem Germanov,   6:28.13
Georgi Petkov, Stoyan Stoyanov, Nenko
Dobrev)

6. SWI   (Daniel Homberger, Peter Rahn, Roland   6:30.26
Stocker, Peter Stocker, Karl Graf)

7. GBR   (Leonard Robertson, Gordon Rankine, Colin
Seymour, John Roberts, Alan Inns)

8. BRA   (Laildo Machado, Wandir Kuntze, Walter
Soares, Henrique Johann, Manoel Novo)

1984 Los Angeles-Lake Casitas T: 8, N: 8, D: 8.5.

1. GBR   (Martin Cross, Richard Budgett, Andrew   6:18.64
Holmes, Steven Redgrave, Adrian Ellison)

2. USA   (Thomas Kiefer, Gregory Springer, Michael   6:20.28
Bach, Edward Ives, John Stillings)

3. NZE   (Kevin Lawton, Donald Symon, Barrie Mab-   6:23.68
bott, Ross Tong, Brett Hollister)

4. ITA   (Giovanni Sergi Sergas, Giovanni Suarez,   6:26.44
Gino Iseppi, Giuseppe Carando, Siro Meli)

5. CAN   (David Ross, Tim Christian, Richard Doey,   6:28.78
Nick Toulmin, Paul Tessier)

6. GER   (Heribert Karches, Georg Konermann, Wolf-   6:34.23
ram Theim, Wolfgang Maennig, Manfred Klein)

7. BRA   (Andre Berezin, Luiz Santos, Denis Marinho,
Laildo Machado, Manoel Novo)

8. JPN   (Satoru Miyoshi, Tadashi Abe, Shunsuke
Kawamoto, Hideaki Maeguchi, Akihiro Koike)

1988 Seoul T: 14, N: 14, D: 9.24.

1. GDR   (Frank Klawonn, Bernd Eichwurzel, Bernd   6:10.74
Niesecke, Karsten Schmeling, Hendrik Reiher)

2. ROM   (Dimitrie Popescu, Ioan Snep, Valentin Robu,   6:13.58
Vasile Tomoiagă, Ladislau Lovrenchi)

3. NZE   (George Keys, Ina Wright, Gregory Johnston,   6:15.78
Christopher White, Andrew Bird)

4. GBR   (D. Adam Clift, John Maxey, John Garrett,   6:18.08
Martin Cross, H. Vaughan Thomas)

5. USA   (John Terwilliger, Christopher Huntington,   6:18.47
Tom Darling, John Walters, Mark Zembsch)

6. YUG   (Sead Marušić, Lazo Pivač, Zlatko Celent,   6:23.28
Vladimir Banjanac, Dario Varga)

7. GER   (Roland Baar, Wolfgang Klapheck, Christoph
Korte, Andreas Lütkefeis, Martin Ruppel)

8. CZE   (Milan Doleček, Oldřich Hejdušek, Petr Hlídek,
Dušan Macháček, Michal Subrt)

1992 Barcelona-Banyoles T: 12, N: 12, D: 8.1.

1. ROM   (Viorel Talapan, Iulica Ruican, Dimitrie   5:59.37
Popescu, Nicolaie Taga, Dumitru Răducanu)

2. GER   (Uwe Kellner, Ralf Brudel, Thoralf Peters,   6:00.34
Karsten Finger, Hendrik Reiher)

3. POL   (Jacek Streich, Wojciech Jankowski, Tomasz   6:03.27
Tomiak, Maciej Lasicki, Michal Cieslak)

4. USA   (James Neil, Teo Bielefeld, Michael Hall, John   6:06.03
Rusher, Timothy Evans)

5. FRA   (Yannick Schulte, Philippe Lot, Daniel Fauche,   6:06.82
Jean Paul Vergnes, Jean Pierre Huguet-
Balent)

6. SOV   (Veniamin But, Igor Bortnitsky, Vladimir Ro-   6:12.13
manishin, Gennady Kryuchkin, Pyotr Petrinich)

7. CRO   (Sead Marušić, Marko Banović, Ninoslav
Saraga, Aleksandar Fabijanić, Goran Puljko)

8. CHN   (Feng Feng, Sun Senlin, Huang Xiaoping, Xu
Wuling, Li Jianxin)

SIX-MAN NAVAL ROWING BOATS

1906 Athens T: 4, N: 2, D: 4.24
(2000 Meters)

1. ITA   (Varese—Giuseppe Russo, P. Toio, R.   10:45.0
Taormina, G. Tarantino, E. Bellotti, Angelo
Formaciari, Giovanni Battista Tanio)

2. GRE   (Spetsai—D. Balourdos, S. Vessalas, N.   —
Dekavalas, D. Dais, N. Karsouvas, P.
Kipraios, K. Misonginis)

3. GRE   (Hydra—D. Grous, P. Lomvardos, G.   —
Maroulis, D. Souranis, N. Photinakis, Diony-
sius Khristeas, P. Mexis)

4. GRE   (Psara)   —

SEVENTEEN-MAN NAVAL ROWING BOATS

1906 Athens T: 5, N: 2, D: 4.24.
(3000 Meters)

1. GRE   (Poros—I. Georgas, K. Tsirigotakis, I.   16:35.0
Agrimis, K. Kephalas, D. Kakousis, I. Pilouris,
P. Karrgiozis, D. Piaditis, E. Laphiotis, I.
Mikhas, M. Mouratis, M. Sokos, A. Drivas, A.
Milonas, I. Kaisarevs, I. Loukas, P. Velliotis)

2. GRE   (Hydra—P. Ptemeas, I. Dolas, Ioannis   17:09.6
Gripaios, Ioannis Tsirakis, Evangelos
Khaldeos, K. Niotis, K. Papayiannoulis, N.
Steryiou, S. Lemonis, I. Papapanayiotou,
Evangelos Kanakaris, G. Nikoloutsos, X.
Stellas, S. Diomataras, M. Katsoulis, I.
Phasilis, I. Milakas)

3. ITA   (Varese—G. Cingottu, F. Pieraccini, G. Pizzo,   —
Augusto Graffigna, L. Frediani, Alberto

Ruggia, F. Mennella, S. Messina, Antonio Mautrere, Ezio Germignani, Angelo Sartini, Sebastiano Randazzo, Angelo Buoni, A. Nordio, P. Oddone, G. Zanino, E. Rossi)
4. GRE (Psara) —
5. GRE (Spetzia) —

FOUR-OARED INRIGGERS WITH COXSWAIN

1912 Stockholm T: 6, N: 4, D: 7.18.
1. DEN (Ejlert Allert, Jörgen Hansen, Carl Möller, Carl   7:47.0
Petersen, Poul Hartmann)
2. SWE (Ture Rosvall, William Bruhn-Möller, Conrad   7:56.2
Brunkman, Herman Dahlbäck, Wilhelm Wilkens)
3. NOR (Claus Hoyer, Reidar Holter, Magnus Herseth,   —
Frithjof Olstad, Olaf Bjornstad)

WOMEN

All women's races are rowed on a 2000-meter course. Before 1988, they were rowed at 1000 meters.

SINGLE SCULLS

1896–1972 not held

1976 Montreal C: 11, N: 11, D: 7.24.
1. Christine Scheiblich GDR 4:05.56
2. Joan Lind USA 4:06.21
3. Yelena Antonova SOV/RUS 4:10.24
4. Rositsa Spasova BUL 4:10.86
5. Ingrid Munneke HOL 4:18.71
6. Mariann Ambrus HUN 4:22.59
7. Annick Anthoine FRA
8. Christel Agrikola GER

1980 Moscow C: 11, N: 11, D: 7.26.
1. Sanda Toma ROM 3:40.69
2. Antonina Makhina SOV/RUS 3:41.65
3. Martina Schröter GDR 3:43.54
4. Rositsa Spasova BUL 3:47.22
5. Beryl Mitchell GBR 3:49.71
6. Beata Dziadura POL 3:51.45
7. Frances Cryan IRL
8. Mariann Ambrus HUN

1984 Los Angeles-Lake Casitas C: 16, N: 16, D: 8.4.
1. Valeria Răcilă ROM 3:40.68
2. Charlotte Geer USA 3:43.89
3. Ann Haesebrouck BEL 3:45.72
4. Andrea Schreiner CAN 3:45.97
5. Lise Marianne Justesen DEN 3:47.79

6. Beryl Mitchell GBR 3:51.20
7. Stephanie Foster NZE
8. Jos Compaan HOL

1988 Seoul C: 13, N: 13, D: 9.25.
1. GDR Jutta Behrendt 7:47.19
2. USA Anne Marden 7:50.28
3. BUL Magdalena Georgieva 7:53.65
4. HOL Harriet van Ettekoven 7:57.29
5. ROM Marioara Popescu 7:59.44
6. DEN Inger Pors 7:59.77
7. GRE Antonia Svaier
8. SOV/UKR Natalya Kvasha

Defending world champion Magdalena Georgieva pushed to a 2.86-second lead at the 1500-meter mark, but then blew up and faded to third, leaving the victory to 1986 world champion Jutta Behrendt of Berlin.

1992 Barcelona-Banyoles C: 15, N: 15, D: 8.2.
1. ROM Elisabeta Lipa (Oleniuc) 7:25.54
2. BEL Annelies Bredael 7:26.64
3. CAN Silken Laumann 7:28.85
4. USA Anne Marden 7:29.84
5. SWE Maria Brandin 7:37.55
6. FRA Corine Le Moal 7:41.85
7. GRE Antonia Svaier
8. HOL Irene Eijs

Having won the 1991 world championship by over three seconds, 27-year-old Silken Laumann of Mississauga, Ontario, was considered the overwhelming favorite for Barcelona. But on May 16, 1992, 73 days before she was scheduled to race for the first time at the Olympics, Laumann was the victim of a horrific accident. In a poorly supervised warm-up area in Essen, Germany, her shell was rammed by the shell of the German coxless pair, Peter Höltzenbein and Colin von Ettingshausen. A piece of wood ripped through Laumann's lower right leg, fracturing the bone, cutting the muscles in her calf and causing extensive nerve and tissue damage. The wound was so gruesome that both Höltzenbein and Ettingshausen, after helping to save Laumann, fainted.

Doctors told Laumann she would need at least six months to recover. But Laumann insisted that she wanted to compete at the Olympics. Her goal was to finish ahead of at least one other rower. Miraculously, after five operations, she made it to Barcelona, although she walked with a cane and was advised to avoid standing up for more than fifteen minutes at a time.

With Laumann out of contention, the favorite's mantle fell to Elisabeta Lipa, who made her living working for the Romanian version of the CIA. Lipa did not disappoint, leading from start to finish and earning her fifth Olympic medal (two gold, two silver, one bronze).

Meanwhile, Laumann was performing new miracles every couple of days. First she finished second in her qualifying heat behind Anne Marden. Then she won her semifinal race. In the final, Laumann held on to third place for three quarters of the race. Then she was passed by Marden, but Laumann pulled ahead of her again in the last 100 meters to earn a bronze medal.

DOUBLE SCULLS

1896–1972 not held

1976 Montreal T: 10, N: 10, D: 7.24.
1.	BUL	(Svetla Otsetova, Zdravka Yordanova)	3:44.36
2.	GDR	(Sabine Jahn, Petra Boesler)	3:47.86
3.	SOV/ LIT	(Leonora Kaminskaitė, Genovaitė Ramoš-kienė)	3:49.93
4.	NOR	(Solfrid Johansen, Ingunn Brechan)	3:52.18
5.	USA	(Jan Palchikoff, Diane Braceland)	3:58.25
6.	CAN	(Cheryl Howard, Beverley Cameron)	4:06.23
7.	HOL	(Andrea Vissers, Hellie Klaasee)	
8.	CZE	(Miluse Neffova, Zuzana Prokesova)	

1980 Moscow T: 7, N: 7, D: 7.26.
1.	SOV	(Yelena Khloptseva, Larissa Popova [Aleksandrova])	3:16.27
2.	GDR	(Cornelia Linse, Heidi Westphal)	3:17.63
3.	ROM	(Olga Homeghi, Valeria Răcilă-Roşca)	3:18.91
4.	BUL	(Svetla Otsetova, Zdravka Yordanova)	3:23.14
5.	POL	(Hanna Jarkiewicz, Janina Klucznik)	3:27.25
6.	HUN	(Ilona Bata, Klara Pétervári-Langhoffer)	3:35.70

1984 Los Angeles-Lake Casitas T: 8, N: 8, D: 8.4.
1.	ROM	(Marioara Popescu, Elisabeta Oleniuc)	3:26.75
2.	HOL	(Greet Hellemans, Nicolette Hellemans)	3:29.13
3.	CAN	(Daniele Laumann, Silken Laumann)	3:29.82
4.	SWE	(Carina Gustavsson, Marie Carlsson)	3:30.79
5.	NOR	(Haldis Lenes, Solfrid Johansen)	3:32.09
6.	USA	(Cathleen Thaxton, Julia Geer)	3:32.33
7.	AUT	(Ingeborg Niedermayer, Vera Sommerbauer)	
8.	GBR	(Nonie Ray, Sally Bloomfield)	

1988 Seoul T: 10, N: 10, D: 9.24.
1.	GDR	(Birgit Peter, Martina Schröter)	7:00.48
2.	ROM	(Elisabeta Lipa [Oleniuc], Veronica Cogeanu)	7:04.36
3.	BUL	(Violeta Ninova, Stefka Madina)	7:06.03
4.	SOV	(Marina Zhukova, Marya Omelyanovych)	7:12.67
5.	CHN	(Guo Mei, Cao Mianying)	7:18.69
6.	USA	(Monica Havelka, Cathy Tippett)	7:21.28
7.	CAN	(Silken Laumann, Kay Worthington)	
8.	SWE	(Maria Brandin, Carina Gustafsson)	

1992 Barcelona-Banyoles T: 13, N: 13, D: 8.1.
1.	GER	(Kerstin Köppen, Kathrin Boron)	6:49.00
2.	ROM	(Veronica Cochelea [Cogeanu], Elisabeta Lipa [Oleniuc])	6:51.47
3.	CHN	(Gu Xiaoli, Lu Huali)	6:55.16
4.	NZE	(Philippa Baker, Brenda Lawson)	6:56.81
5.	GBR	(Annabel Eyres, Alison Gill)	7:06.62
6.	SOV	(Sariya Zakirova, Inna Frolova)	7:09.45
7.	BUL	(Daniela Oronova, Galina Kamenova)	
8.	AUS	(Jennifer Luff, Gillian Campbell)	

QUADRUPLE SCULLS

1896–1984 not held

1988 Seoul T: 10, N: 10, D: 9.25.
1.	GDR	(Kerstin Förster, Kristina Mundt, Beate Schramm, Jana Sorgers)	6:21.06
2.	SOV	(Iryna Kalimbet, Svitlana Mazy, Inna Frolova, Antonina Dumcheva)	6:23.47
3.	ROM	(Anişoara Bălan, Anişoara Minea, Veronica Cogeanu, Elisabeta Lipa [Oleniuc])	6:23.81
4.	BUL	(Pavlina Hristova, Galia Anohrieva, Iskra Velinova, Krassimira Tocheva)	6:24.10
5.	CZE	(Hana Krejčová, Ľubica Kurhajcová, Blanka Mikysková, Irena Soukupová)	6:41.86
6.	BEL	(Marie-Anne Vandermoere, Ann Haesebrouck, Lucia Focque, Annelies Bredael)	6:43.79
7.	HOL	(Jos Compaan, Marjan Pentenga, Nicolette Wessel, Marijke Zeekant)	
8.	HUN	(Erika Bertényi, Ildikó Cserey, Anikó Kapócs, Katalin Sarlós)	

1992 Barcelona-Banyoles T: 9, N: 9, D: 8.2.
1.	GER	(Kerstin Müller, Sybille Schmidt, Birgit Peter, Kristina Mundt)	6:20.18
2.	ROM	(Constanţa Pipotă, Doina Ignat, Veronica Cochelea [Cogeanu], Anişoara Dobre Bălan)	6:24.34
3.	SOV	(Yekaterina Khodatovich, Antonina Zelikovich, Tatyana Ustyuzhanina, Yelena Khloptseva)	6:25.07
4.	HOL	(Laurien Vermulst, Marjan Pentenga, Anita Meiland, Harriet van Ettekoven)	6:32.40
5.	USA	(Kristine Karlson, Alison Townley, Serena Eddy-Moulton, Michelle Knox-Zaloom)	6:32.65
6.	CZE	Ľubica Novotníková [Kurhajcová], Michaela Burešova, Hana Kafková, Irena Soukupová)	6:35.99
7.	CHN	(Feng Lili, Yang Hong, Lu Huali, Gu Xiaoli)	
8.	DEN	(Berit Christoffersen, Lene Pedersen, Trine Hansen, Ulla Hansen)	

FOUR-OARED SHELL WITHOUT COXSWAIN

1896–1988 not held

1992 Barcelona-Banyoles T: 9, N: 9, D: 8.1.
1.	CAN	(Kirsten Barnes, Brenda Taylor, Jessica Monroe, Kay Worthington)	6:30.85
2.	USA	(Shelagh Donohoe, Cynthia Eckert, Amy Fuller, Carol Freeney)	6:31.86
3.	GER	(Antje Frank, Gabriele Mehl, Birte Siech, Annette Hohn)	6:32.34
4.	CHN	(Liu Xirong, He Yanwen, Cao Mianying, Zhou Shouying)	6:32.50
5.	ROM	(Vicotria Lepădatu, Iulia Bobeică, Adriana Bazon [Chelariu], Maria Păduraru)	6:37.24
6.	AUS	(Jodie Dobson, Emmelia Snook, Megan Still, Kate Slatter)	6:41.72
7.	FRA	(Fréderique Heligon, Chantal Lafon, Christine Jullien, Hélène Cortin)	
8.	GBR	(Alison Barnett, Kim Thomas, Suzanne Kirk, Gillian Lindsay)	

EIGHT-OARED SHELL WITH COXSWAIN

1896–1972 not held

1976 Montreal T: 8, N: 8, D: 7.24.
1. GDR (Viola Goretzki, Christiane Knetsch, Ilona   3:33.32
   Richter, Brigitte Ahrenholz, Monika Kallies,
   Henrietta Ebert, Helma Lehmann, Irina Müller,
   Marina Wilke)
2. SOV (Lyubov Talalayeva, Nadezhda Roshchina,   3:36.17
   Klavdia Koženkova, Elena Zubko, Olha
   Kolkova, Nelli Tarakanova, Nadiya Rozhon,
   Olha Huzenko, Olha Pukhovska)
3. USA (Jacqueli Zoch, Anita DeFrantz, Carie Graves,   3:38.68
   Marion Greig, Anne Warner, Peggy McCarthy,
   Carol Brown, Gail Ricketson, Lynn Silliman)
4. CAN (Carol Eastmore, Rhonda Ross, Nancy Hig-   3:39.52
   gins, Mazina DeLure, Susan Antoft, Wendy
   Pullan, Christine Neuland, Gail Cort, Illoana
   Smith)
5. GER (Waltraud Roick, Erika Endriss, Monika   3:41.06
   Zipplies, Birgit Kiesow, Hiltrud Gürtler, Isolde
   Eisele, Marianne Weber, Eva Dick, Ingrid
   Huhn-Wagner)
6. ROM (Elena Oprea, Florica Petcu, Filigonia Tol,   3:44.79
   Aurelia Marinescu, Georgeta Militaru, Iuliana
   Munteanu, Elena Avram, Marioara Constantin,
   Aneta Matei)
7. POL (Anna Brandysiewicz, Boguslawa Kozlowska,
   Barbara Wenta-Wojciechowska, Danuta
   Konkalec, Róża Data, Mieczyslawa Franczyk,
   Maria Stadnicka, Aleksandra Kaczyńska,
   Dorota Zdanowska)
8. HOL (Karin Abma, Joke Dierdorf, Barbara Dejong,
   Annette Schortingshuis, Marleen Van Ry, Ma-
   ria Kusters, Liesbeth Pascal, Loes Schutte,
   Evelien Koogie)

In 1986, Anita DeFrantz of the 1976 third-place U.S. team became the first black woman to be selected for membership on the International Olympic Committee.

1980 Moscow T: 6, N: 6, D: 7.26.
1. GDR (Martina Boesler, Kersten Neisser, Christiane   3:03.32
   Köpke [Knetsch], Birgit Schütz, Gabriele Kühn
   [Lohs], Ilona Richter, Marita Sandig, Karin
   Metze, Marina Wilke)
2. SOV (Olha Pyvovarova, Nina Umanets, Nadiya   3:04.29
   Pryshchepa, Valentina Zhulina, Tetyana Stetsenko, Olena Tereshyna, Nina Preobrazhen-
   ska, Mariya Pazyun, Nina Frolova)
3. ROM (Angelica Aposteanu, Marlena Zagoni   3:05.63
   [Predescu], Rodica Frintu, Florica Bucur,
   Rodica Puşcatu, Ana Iliuta, Maria Constan-
   tinescu, Elena Bondar, Elena Dobritoiu)
4. BUL (Daniela Stavreva, Stefka Koleva, Todorka   3:10.03
   Vassileva, Snezhka Hristeva, Roumiana Kostova, Veneta Karamandtzukova, Mariana

Mincheva, Valentina Aleksandrova, Stanka
Georgieva)
5. GBR (Gillian Hodges, Joanna Toch, Penelope   3:13.85
   Sweet, Linda Clark, Elizabeth Paton, Rose-
   mary Clugston, Nicola Boyes, Beverly Jones,
   Pauline Wright)

1984 Los Angeles-Lake Casitas T: 6, N: 6, D: 8.4.
1. USA (Shyril O'Steen, Harriet Metcalf, Carol Bower,   2:59.80
   Carie Graves, Jeanne Flanagan, Kristine
   Norelius, Kristen Thorsness, Kathryn Keeler,
   Betsy Beard)
2. ROM (Doina Balan, Marioara Trasca, Aurora Plesca,   3:00.87
   Aneta Mihaly, Adriana Chelariu, Mihaela
   Armasescu, Camelia Diaconescu, Lucia
   Sauca, Viorica Ioja)
3. HOL (Nicolette Hellemans, Lynda Cornet, Harriet   3:02.92
   van Ettekoven, Greet Hellemans, Marieke van
   Drogenbroek, Anne Marie Quist, Catharina
   Neelissen, Willemien Vaandrager, Martha
   Laurijsen)
4. CAN (Christine Clarke, Lisa Robertson, Kathey   3:03.64
   Lichty, Carol Colgan, Cathy Lund, Kay Wor-
   thington, Gail Cort, Joan Gillingham, Lesleh
   Anderson-Herweck)
5. GBR (Alexa Forbes, Katherine McNicol, Kathryn   3:04.51
   Holroyd, Belinda Holmes, Sarah Hunter-Jones,
   Astrid Ayling, Ann Callaway, Gillian Hodges,
   Susan Bailey)
6. GER (Elke Riesenkönig, Claudia Hornung, Iris   3:09.92
   Völkner, Ellen Becker, Sabine Hinkelmann,
   Heike Neu, Kerstin Rehders, Angelika Beblo,
   Heidrun Barth)

1988 Seoul T: 7, N: 7, D: 9.25.
1. GDR (Annegret Strauch, Judith Zeidler, Kathrin   6:15.17
   Haacker, Ute Wild, Anja Kluge, Beatrix
   Schröer, Ramona Balthasar, Uta Stange, Da-
   niela Neunast)
2. ROM (Doina Bălan, Marioara Trasca, Veronica   6:17.44
   Necula, Herta Anitas, Adriana Bazon
   [Chelariu], Mihaela Armasescu, Rodica Arba
   [Puşcatu], Olga Homeghi, Ecaterina Oancia)
3. CHN (Zhou Xiuhua, Zhang Yali, He Yanwen, Han   6:21.83
   Yaqin, Zhang Xianghua, Zhou Shouying, Yang
   Xiao, Hu Yadong, Li Ronghua)
4. SOV (Margarita Teselko, Marina Znak, Nadezhda   6:22.35
   Sugako, Sandra Brazauskaitė, Olena Puk-
   hayeva, Sariya Zakirova, Natalya Fedorenko,
   Lidiya Averyanova, Aouchra Gudeliunaitė)
5. BUL (Teodora Zareva, Violeta Zareva, Neviana   6:25.02
   Ivanova, Olia Stoichkova, Todorka Vassileva,
   Rita Todorova, Mariana Stoyanova, Daniela
   Oronova, Greta Georgieva)
6. USA (Juliet Thompson, Christine Campbell, Abigail   6:26.66
   Peck, Margaret Mallery, Susan Broome,
   Stephanie Maxwell, Anna Seaton, Alison
   Townley, Elizabeth Beard)
7. GER (Ingeburg Althoff, Meike Holländer, Elke
   Markwort, Gabriele Mehl, Kerstin Peters,

Cerstin Petersmann, Katrin Petersmann, Kerstin Rehders, Ana Schäfer)

1992 Barcelona-Banyoles T: 8, N: 8, D: 8.2.
1. CAN (Kirsten Barnes, Brenda Taylor, Megan Delehanty, Shannon Crawford, Marnie McBean, Kay Worthington, Jessica Monroe, Kathleen Heddle, Lesley Thompson) — 6:02.62
2. ROM (Doina Snep [Bălan], Doina Robu, Ioana Olteanue, Viorica Lepădatu, Iulia Bobeică, Viorica Neculai, Andriana Bazon [Chelariu], Maria Păduraru, Elena Georgescu) — 6:06.26
3. GER (Annegret Strauch, Sylvia Dördelmann, Kathrin Haacker, Dana Pyritz, Cerstin Petersmann, Ute Wagner [Stange], Christiane Harzendorf, Judith Zeidler, Daniela Neunast) — 6:07.80
4. SOV (Svetlana Fil, Marina Znak, Irina Gribko, Sarmīte Stone, Marina Suprun, Natalya Stasyuk, Natalya Grigoryeva, Yekaterina Kotko, Yelena Medvedeva) — 6:09.68
5. CHN (Lin Zhiai, Ma Linqin, Pei Jiayun, He Yanwen, Liu Xirong, Liang Xiling, Cao Mianying, Zhou Shouying, Li Ronghua) — 6:12.08
6. USA (Tina Brown, Shannon Day, Betsy McCagg, Mary McCagg, Sarah Gengler, Tracy Rude, Kelley Jones, Diana Olson, Yasmin Farooq) — 6:12.25
7. GBR (Fiona Freckleton, Philippa Cross, Dorothy Blackie, Susan Smith, Kate Grose, Rachel Hirst, Kareen Marwick, Kathrine Brownlow, Alison Paterson)
8. CZE (Lenka Zavadilová, Eliška Jandová, Renata Beránková, Martina Šefčíková, Sabina Telenská, Michaela Vávrová, Hana Žáková, Hana Dariusová, Lenka Kováčová)

LIGHTWEIGHT: DOUBLE SCULLS

This event will be held for the first time in 1996.

Discontinued Events

QUADRUPLE SCULLS WITH COXSWAIN

1976 Montreal T: 9, N: 9, D: 7.19.
1. GDR (Anke Borchmann, Jutta Lau, Viola Poley, Roswietha Zobelt, Liane Weigelt) — 3:29.99
2. SOV (Anna Kondrachina, Mira Bryunina, Larissa Aleksandrova, Galina Yermolayeva, Nadezhda Chernyshova) — 3:32.49
3. ROM (Ioana Tudoran, Maria Micşa, Felicia Afrăsiloaia, Elisabeta Lazăr, Elena Giurcă) — 3:32.76
4. BUL (Iskra Velinova, Verka Aleksieva, Troyanka Vasileva, Svetla Gincheva, Stanka Georgieva) — 3:34.13

5. CZE (Anna Marešová, Marie Bartaková, Jarmila Patková, Hana Kavková, Alena Svobodová) — 3:42.53
6. DEN (Kirsten Thomsen, Else Maersk-Kristensen, Judith Andersen, Karen Nielsen, Kirsten Plum-Jensen) — 3:46.99
7. USA (Karen McCloskey, Lisa Hansen, Elizabet Hills, Claudia Schneider, Irene Moreno)
8. HUN (Ilona Bata, Kamilla Kosztolányi, Valéria Gyimesi, Ágnes Szijj, Erzsébet Nagy)

1980 Moscow T: 7, N: 7, D: 7.26.
1. GDR (Sybille Reinhardt, Jutta Ploch, Jutta Lau, Roswietha Zobelt, Liane Buhr [Weigelt]) — 3:15.32
2. SOV (Antonina Pustovit, Yelena Matievskaya, Olga Vasilchenko, Nadezhda Lyubimova, Nina Cheremisina) — 3:15.73
3. BUL (Mariana Serbezova, Roumeliana Boneva, Dolores Nakova, Ani Bakova, Stanka Georgieva) — 3:16.10
4. ROM (Marta Macoviciuc, Aneta Mihaly, Sofia Banovici, Mariana Zaharia, Elena Giurcă) — 3:16.82
5. POL (Boguslawa Tomasiak, Mariola Abrahamczyk, Maria Kobylińska, Aleksandra Kaczyńska, Maria Dzieża) — 3:20.95
6. HOL (Ineke Donkervoort, Lily Meeuwisse, Greet Hellemans, Jos Compaan, Monique Pronk) — 3:22.64

1984 Los Angeles-Lake Casitas T: 7, N: 7, D: 8.4.
1. ROM (Maricica Tăran, Anişoara Sorohan, Ioana Badea, Sofia Corban [Banovici], Ecaterina Oancia) — 3:14.11
2. USA (Anne Marden, Lisa Rohde, Joan Lind, Virginia Gilder, Kelly Rickon) — 3:15.57
3. DEN (Hanne Eriksen, Birgitte Hanel, Charlotte Koefoed, Bodil Steen Rasmussen, Jette Hejli Sörensen) — 3:16.02
4. GER (Anne Dickmann, Regina Kleine-Kuhlmann, Ute Kumitz, Sabine Reuter, Kathrien Plückhahn) — 3:16.81
5. FRA (Evelyne Imbert, Lydie Dubedat, Christine Gosse, Helene Ledoux, Patricia Couturier) — 3:17.87
6. ITA (Raffaella Memo, Alessandra Borio, Donata Minorati, Antonella Corazza, Roberta Del Core) — 3:21.48

PAIR-OARED SHELL WITHOUT COXSWAIN

1896–1972 not held

1976 Montreal T: 11, N: 11, D: 7.24.
1. BUL (Siika Kelbecheva, Stoyanka Gruicheva) — 4:01.22
2. GDR (Angelika Noack, Sabine Dähne) — 4:01.64
3. GER (Edith Eckbauer, Thea Einöder) — 4:02.35
4. SOV/UKR (Nataliya Horodilova, Anna Karnaushenko) — 4:03.27
5. CAN (Tricia Smith, Elisabeth Craig) — 4:08.09
6. ROM (Marlena Predescu, Marinela Maxim) — 4:15:44
7. USA (Susan Morgan, Laura Staines)
8. POL (Anna Karbowiak, Malgorzata Kowalska)

1980 Moscow T: 6, N: 6, D: 7.26.

1.	GDR	(Ute Steindorf, Cornelia Klier)	3:30.49
2.	POL	(Malgorzata Dluzewska, Czeslawa Kościań-ska)	3:30.95
3.	BUL	(Siika Barbulova [Kelbecheva], Stoyanka Kurbatova [Gruicheva])	3:32.39
4.	ROM	(Florica Dospinescu [Petcu], Elena Oprea)	3:35.14
5.	SOV	(Larissa Zavarzina, Galina Stepanova)	4:12.53

Despite the fact that there were only six entrants, regatta officials insisted that two elimination heats and a repêchage be run in order to trim the field in the final to five.

1984 Los Angeles-Lake Casitas T: 6, N: 6, D: 8.4.

1.	ROM	(Rodica Arba [Puşcatu], Elena Horvat)	3:32.60
2.	CAN	(Elizabeth Craig, Tricia Smith)	3:36.06
3.	GER	(Ellen Becker, Iris Völkner)	3:40.50
4.	HOL	(Harriet van Ettekoven, Lynda Cornet)	3:44.01
5.	USA	(Barbara Kirch, Chari Towne)	3:44.35
6.	GBR	(Katerine Panter, Ruth Howe)	3:48.53

1988 Seoul T: 10, N: 10, D: 9.24.

1.	ROM	(Rodica Arba [Puşcatu], Olga Homeghi)	7:28.13
2.	BUL	(Radka Stoyanova, Lalka Berberova)	7:31.95
3.	NZE	(Nicola Payne, Lynley Hannen)	7:35.68
4.	GDR	(Kerstin Spittler, Katrin Schröder)	7:40.47
5.	SOV	(Sarmīte Stone, Marina Smorodina)	7:53.19
6.	USA	(Barbara Kirch, Mara Keggi)	7:56.27
7.	CAN	(Jennifer-Kirsten Barnes, Sarah Ann Ogilvie)	
8.	GBR	(Alison Bonner, Kim Thomas)	

Arba and Homeghi were the overwhelming favorites, having won 40 straight races since 1986, including two world championships. In addition, they both had extensive Olympic experience. Arba, besides being the defending champion in the pairs, had won a bronze medal in the eights in 1980. Homeghi too took home a bronze in 1980 and a gold in 1984; hers were in the double sculls and coxed fours. In Seoul they were unchallenged in the pairs. Twenty-four hours later they both added silvers to their medal haul as part of the Romanian eights crew.

1992 Barcelona-Banyoles T: 13, N: 13, D: 8.1.

1.	CAN	(Marnie McBean, Kathleen Heddle)	7:06.22
2.	GER	(Stefani Werremeier, Ingeburg Schwerzmann [Althoff])	7:07.96
3.	USA	(Anna Seaton, Stephanie Pierson)	7:08.11
4.	FRA	(Christine Gosse, Isabelle Danjou)	7:08.70
5.	GBR	(Joanne Turvey, Miriam Batten)	7:17.28
6.	BUL	(Violeta Zareva, Teodora Zareva)	7:32.67
7.	ROM	(Doina Snep [Bălan], Doina Robu)	
8.	UKR	(Anna Motrechko, Yelena Ronzhina)	

Marnie McBean was 16 years old when she was inspired by the performances of Canadian rowers at the 1984 Olympics. She took her first step in the sport by looking up Rowing in the Toronto phone directory and then calling a local club. Her partner, Kathleen Heddle, didn't start rowing until age 18, when she was recruited by a coach while she was a student at the University of British Columbia, in 1983.

FOUR-OARED SHELL WITH COXSWAIN

1976 Montreal T: 8, N: 8, D: 7.24.

1.	GDR	(Karin Metze, Bianka Schwede, Gabriele Lohs, Andrea Kurth, Sabine Hess)	3:45.08
2.	BUL	(Ginka Gyurova, Liliana Vaseva, Reni Yordanova, Mariika Modeva, Kapka Georgieva)	3:48.24
3.	SOV/ RUS	(Nadezhda Sevostyanova, Lyudmila Krokhina, Galina Mishenina, Anna Pasokha, Lidiya Krylova)	3:49.38
4.	ROM	(Elena Oprea, Florica Petcu, Filigonia Tol, Aurelia Marinescu, Aneta Matei)	3:51.17
5.	HOL	(Liesbeth Vosmaer-De Bruin, Hette Borrias, Myrian van Rooyen, Ans Gravesteyn, Monique Pronk)	3:54.36
6.	USA	(Pamela Behrens, Catherine Menges, Nancy Storrs, Julia Geer, Mary Kellogg)	3:56.50
7.	CAN	(Linda Schaumleffel, Dolores Young, Monica Draeger, Joy Fera, Barbara Mutch)	
8.	GBR	(Gillian Webb, Pauline Bird, Clare Grove, Diana Bishop, Pauline Wright)	

1980 Moscow T: 6, N: 6, D: 7.26.

1.	GDR	(Ramona Kapheim, Silvia Fröhlich, Angelika Noack, Romy Saalfeld, Kirsten Wenzel)	3:19.27
2.	BUL	(Ginka Gyurova, Mariika Modeva, Rita Todorova, Iskra Velinova, Nadezhda Filipova)	3:20.75
3.	SOV/ RUS	(Mariya Fadeyeva, Galina Sovetnikova, Marina Studneva, Svetlana Semyonova, Nina Cheremisina)	3:20.92
4.	ROM	(Georgeta Maşca [Militaru], Florica Szilaghy, Maria Tănasa, Valeria Cătescu, Aneta Matei)	3:22.08
5.	AUS	(Anne Chirnside, Verna Westwood, Pamela Westendorf, Sally Harding, Susanne Palfreyman)	3:26.37

1984 Los Angeles-Lake Casitas T: 9, N: 9, D: 8.4.

1.	ROM	(Florica Lavric, Maria Fricioiu, Chira Apostol, Olga Bularda [Homeghi], Viorica Ioja)	3:19.30
2.	CAN	(Marilyn Brain, Angie Schneider, Barbara Armbrust, Jane Tregunno, Lesley Thompson)	3:21.55
3.	AUS	(Robyn Grey-Gardner, Karen Brancourt, Susan Chapman, Margot Foster, Susan Lee)	3:23.29
4.	USA	(Abigail Peck, Patricia Spratlen, Janet Harville, Elizabeth Miles, Valerie McClain-Ward)	3:23.58
5.	HOL	(Marieke van Drogenbroek, Anne Marie Quist, Catharina Neelissen, Willemien Vaandrager, Martha Laurijsen)	3:23.97
6.	GER	(Heike Neu, Sabine Hinkelmann, Kerstin Rehders, Angelika Beblo, Heidrun Barth)	3:29.03
7.	GBR	(Teresa Millar, Jean Genchi, Joanna Toch, Kathryn Ball, Kathryn Talbot)	
8.	CHN	(Huang Meixia, Yang Xiao, Shi Meiping, Chen Changfeng, Zhang Liming)	

1988 Seoul T: 10, N: 10, D: 9.24.

1. GDR (Martina Walther, Gerlinde Doberschütz, 6:56.00
Carola Hornig, Birte Siech, Sylvia Rose)
2. CHN (Zhang Xianghua, Hu Yadong, Yang Xiao, 6:58.78
Zhou Shouying, Li Ronghua)
3. ROM (Marioara Traşča, Veronica Necula, Herta 7:01.13
Anitas, Doina Bălan, Ecaterina Oancia)
4. BUL (Teodora Zareva, Violeta Zareva, Miglena 7:02.27
Mihaleva, Svetla Durchova, Greta Georgieva)
5. USA (Jennifer Corbet, Sarah Gengler, Elizabeth 7:09.12
Bradley, Cynthia Eckert, Kimberly Santiago)
6. GBR (Fiona Johnston, Katherine Grose, Joanne 7:10.80
Gough, Susan Smith, Alison Norrish)
7. CAN (Heather Clarke, Tricia Smith, Lesley Thompson, E. Jane Tregunno, Jennifer Walinga)
8. POL (Grażyna Blad, Elżbieta Jankowska, Zyta
Jarka, Elwira Lorenz, Czeslawa Szczepińska)

SHOOTING

MEN	WOMEN
Rapid-Fire Pistol	Sport Pistol
Free Pistol	Air Pistol
Air Pistol	Small Bore Rifle, Three Positions
Small-Bore Rifle, Prone	Air Rifle
Small-Bore Rifle, Three Positions	Double Trap
Air Rifle	
Moving Target	
Trap	
Double Trap	
Skeet	
Discontinued Events	

International shooting competitions have employed a wide variety of tie-breaking rules, including shoot-offs (designated by slash lines in the following charts) and by the positions of the bullets on the target. Current practice in case of ties is to award the victory to whichever shooter recorded the highest score in the final series. Ties for medal spots are decided by shootout.

Every few years someone conquers a target and achieves a perfect score. At this point the officials of the International Shooting Union alter the target by decreasing the size of the bull's-eye and the rings. It is for this reason that the world records for various events sometimes go down instead of up.

Sexual integration of Olympic shooting began in 1968. In 1984, however, some of the events were divided into separate men's and women's competitions. In 1996 the sexes will be completely segregated once again.

Another major change was instituted in 1988. For the first time, a final round was created in which the leading scorers from the preliminary round shoot off against each other while standing on the firing line at the same time. Scores in the final are added to the preliminary scores to determine the winner.

MEN

RAPID-FIRE PISTOL

Since 1948 the rapid-fire pistol event has consisted of two 30-shot courses at five silhouettes 25 meters away. The shooter, using a .22 caliber pistol, has eight seconds to fire at each of the five targets. Then the targets reappear

and he has six seconds to fire. Finally he must attempt shots at each of the targets within four seconds. This set of 15 shots is repeated four times. In 1992 the top eight in the preliminary round advanced to the semifinal round, and the top four in the semis advanced to the finals. In the final, two sets of five shots are taken with a four-second time limit.

1896 Athens C: 4, N: 3, D: 4.11.

			PTS.
1.	Ioannis Phrangoudis	GRE	344
2.	Georgios Orphanidis	GRE	249
3.	Holger Nielsen	DEN	—
DNF: Sidney Merlin (GBR)			

1900 Paris C: ?, N: ?, D: 8.4.

			PTS.
1.	Maurice Larrouy	FRA	58
2.	Léon Moreaux	FRA	57
3.	Eugène Balme	FRA	57
4.	Paul Moreau	FRA	57
5.	Paul Probst	SWI	57
6.	Joseph Labbé	FRA	57

1904 not held

1906 Athens C: 28, N: 8, D: 4.26.

			PTS.
1.	Maurice Lecoq	FRA	258
2.	Léon Moreaux	FRA	249
3.	Aristides Rangavis	GRE	244
4.	Louis Richardet	SWI	241
5.	Johan Hübner von Holst	SWE	239
6.	Cesare Liverziani	ITA	238
7.	Hermann Martin	FRA	236
8.	Thephtsakis	GRE	235

1908 London C: 43, N: 7, D: 7.11.

			PTS.
1.	Paul van Asbroeck	BEL	490
2.	Réginald Storms	BEL	487
3.	James Gorman	USA	485
4.	Charles Axtell	USA	480
5.	Jesse Wallingford	GBR	467
6.	André Barbillat	FRA	466
7.	Walter Ellicot	GBR	458
8.	Ira Calkins	USA	457

1912 Stockholm C: 42, N: 10, D: 6.29.

			PTS.
1.	Alfred Lane	USA	287
2.	Paul Palén	SWE	286
3.	Johan Hübner von Holst	SWE	283
3.	John Dietz	USA	283
5.	Curt Törnmark	SWE	280
6.	Eric Carlberg	SWE	278
7.	Georg de Laval	SWE	277
8.	Walter Winans	USA	276

1920 Antwerp-Beverloo C: 38, N: 14, D: 8.3.

			PTS.
1.	Guilherme Paraense	BRA	274
2.	Raymond Bracken	USA	272
3.	Fritz Zulauf	SWI	269

1924 Paris C: 55, N: 17, D: 6.28.

			PTS.
1.	Henry Bailey	USA	18
2.	Wilhelm Carlberg	SWE	18
3.	Lennart Hannelius	FIN	18
4.	Lorenzo Amaya	ARG	18
5.	Matías Osinaldi	ARG	18
6.	André de Castelbajac	FRA	18
7.	Unio Sarlin	FIN	18
8.	Einar Liberg	NOR	18

The 1924 match consisted of three series of six shots at six silhouettes in ten seconds. Eight of the 55 competitors achieved perfect scores and, according to the rules of the day, shot off another round of six shots, but this time within eight seconds. All eight shooters had perfect scores, so a second shoot-off string was ordered. This time three of the shooters missed. The third round saw Osinaldi fall by the wayside, the fourth round Amaya, and the fifth round Hannelius. Bailey and Carlberg had now each hit 48 straight targets. A sixth shoot-off was called, and again the two men had perfect scores. Bailey, a 31-year-old gunnery sergeant in the U.S. Marine Corps, fired first in the seventh shoot-off. After calling for the silhouettes, he attempted to fire his first shot. But his .22 autoloader malfunctioned and the cartridge stuck in the breech. Rather than give up, Bailey coolly pulled the spent case out with his fingers, closed the breech, and got off five shots in what remained of his eight seconds. All five shots hit their tar-

gets. Carlberg, who had already won three gold medals, three silver, and one bronze since the 1906 games, was either unnerved or gracious, for he missed two of his next six shots and Bailey won the match.

1928 not held

1932 Los Angeles C: 18, N: 7, D: 8.12.

			PTS.
1.	Renzo Morigi	ITA	36
2.	Heinz Hax	GER	36
3.	Domenico Matteucci	ITA	36
4.	Walter Boninsegni	ITA	35
4.	José Gonzalez Delgado	SPA	35
4.	Arturo Villanueva	MEX	35

The first three series of six shots were shot at eight seconds each. Those with perfect scores took another six shots in six seconds. The eleven survivors shot again at four seconds. Six men were still perfect and shot another round in three seconds. Boninsegni, Delgado, and Villanueva each missed once, leaving Hax, Morigi, and Matteucci still in the contest. The next round required shooting six shots at six turning silhouettes in two seconds. Major Morigi amazed the crowd, which consisted mostly of Los Angeles policemen, by hitting all six targets, the last one after it had already started to turn away.

1936 Berlin C: 53, N: 22, D: 8.7.

			PTS.
1.	Cornelius van Oyen	GER	30/6
2.	Heinz Hax	GER	30/5
3.	Torsten Ullman	SWE	30/4/4
4.	Angelos Papadimas	GRE	30/4/1
5.	Helge Meuller	SWE	30/3
6.	Walter Boninsegni	ITA	29/6/3
7.	Kazimierz Suchorzewski	POL	29/6/1
8.	Haralds Marwe	LAT	29/3

1948 London C: 59, N: 22, D: 8.4. WR: 570 (Carlos Enrique Diaz Sáenz Valiente)

			PTS.	
1.	Károly Takács	HUN	580	WR
2.	Carlos Enrique Díaz Sáenz Valiente	ARG	571	
3.	Sven Lundqvist	SWE	569	
4.	Torsten Ullman	SWE	564	
5.	Leonard Ravilo	FIN	563/36	
6.	Väinö Heusala	FIN	563/34	
7.	Lajos Borzsonyi	HUN	562	
8.	Buhring Anderson	NOR	559	

Károly Takács was a member of the Hungarian world champion pistol shooting team in 1938 when, while serving as a sergeant in the army, a grenade exploded in his right hand—his pistol hand—and shattered it completely. Undaunted, Takács taught himself to shoot with

Károly Takács was a champion shooter when his right hand, his pistol hand, was shattered by a grenade. Ten years later, in 1948, Takács won his first Olympic gold medal—using his left hand.

his left hand, and ten years later, at the age of 38, he won an Olympic gold medal.

1952 Helsinki C: 53, N: 28, D: 7.28. WR: 582 (Huelet Benner)

		PTS.	
1. Károly Takács	HUN	579	
2. Szilárd Kun	HUN	578	
3. Gheorghe Lichiardopol	ROM	578	
4. Carlos Enrique Díaz Sáenz Valiente	ARG	577	
5. Pentti Linnosvuo	FIN	577	
6. Panait Calcai	ROM	575	
7. William McMillan	USA	575	
8. Vassily Frolov	SOV	573	

1956 Melbourne C: 35, N: 22, D: 12.5. WR: 589 (Carlos Enrique Diaz Sáenz Valiente)

		PTS.	
1. Stefan Petrescu	ROM	587	OR
2. Yevgeny Cherkasov	SOV/RUS	585	
3. Gheorghe Lichiardopol	ROM	581	
4. Pentti Linnosvuo	FIN	581	
5. Oscar Cervo	ARG	580	
6. Szilárd Kun	HUN	578	
7. Kalle Sievänen	FIN	576	
8. Károly Takács	HUN	575	

1960 Rome C: 57, N: 35, D: 9.9. WR: 592 (Aleksandr Kropotin, Aleksandr Zabelin)

		PTS.	
1. William McMillan	USA	587/147	EOR
2. Pentti Linnosvuo	FIN	587/139	EOR
3. Aleksandr Zabelin	SOV/RUS	587/135	EOR
4. Hansrüdi Schneider	SWI	586	
5. Stefan Petrescu	ROM	585	
6. Gavril Maghiar	ROM	583	
7. Czeslaw Zając	POL	582	
8. Jiři Hrnecek	CZE	582	

1964 Tokyo C: 53, N: 34, D: 10.19. WR: 595 (Aleksandr Kropotin)

		PTS.	
1. Pentti Linnosvuo	FIN	592	OR
2. Ion Tripşa	ROM	591	
3. Lubomir Nacovsky	CZE	590	
4. Hans Albrecht	SWI	590	
5. Szilárd Kun	HUN	589	
6. Marcel Roşca	ROM	588	
7. Igor Bakalov	SOV/RUS	588	
8. Kanji Kubo	JPN	587	

Pentti Linnosvuo became only the second shooter to win gold medals in both the rapid-fire and free pistol events. Alfred Lane won both in the same year (1912), while Linnosvuo's victories were eight years apart.

Two different participants in this event were inspired to defect following the Games. First Bela Gabor, who finished 23rd, sought asylum at the West German Embassy rather than return to his native Hungary. Then 53rd place finisher Ma Chin-shan, a retired army officer from Taiwan, took refuge in the Ginza office of the General Council of Chinese Merchants of Tokyo, requesting that he be allowed to return to mainland China to live with his parents whom he had not seen since World War II. To this day, Ma remains the only Olympic athlete to defect *to* a Communist country.

1968 Mexico City C: 56, N: 34, D: 10.23. WR: 596 (Virgil Atanasiu)

		PTS.	
1. Józef Zapędzki	POL	593	OR
2. Marcel Roşca	ROM	591/147	
3. Renart Suleimanov	SOV/RUS	591/146/148	
4. Christian Düring	GDR	591/146/147	
5. Erich Masurat	GER	590	
6. Gerhard Dommrich	GDR	589	
7. Lubomir Nacovsky	CZE	588	
8. Giovanni Liverzani	ITA	588	

1972 Munich C: 62, N: 38, D: 9.1. WR: 598 (Giovanni Liverzani)

		PTS.	
1. Józef Zapędzki	POL	595	OR
2. Ladislav Falta	CZE	594	
3. Victor Torshin	SOV/RUS	593	
4. Paul Buser	SWI	592	
5. Jaime Gonzalez	SPA	592	
6. Giovanni Liverzani	ITA	591	

7. Dencho Denev	BUL	590
8. Gerhard Petritsch	AUT	590

The 43-year-old Zapędzki was a major in the Polish army when he won his second gold medal. After the competition he visited nearby Dachau and laid a wreath at the grave of his father, who had been killed by the Nazis thirty years earlier.

1976 Montreal C: 48, N: 30, D: 7.23. WR: 598 (Giovanni Liverzani)

		PTS.	
1. Norbert Klaar	GDR	597	OR
2. Jürgen Wiefel	GDR	596	
3. Roberto Ferraris	ITA	595	
4. Afanasijs Kuzmins	SOV/LAT	595	
5. Corneliu Ion	ROM	595	
6. Erwin Glock	GER	594	
7. Gerhard Petritsch	AUT	594	
8. Marin Stan	ROM	594	

Bill McMillan of the United States, competing in his sixth Olympics, scored only one point below his gold-medal-winning performance of 1960. However, the quality of marksmanship had improved so much in 16 years that he was able to finish in only a tie for 16th place in 1976. The winner, Norbert Klaar, was a 26-year-old car mechanic from the small industrial town of Wittenberge on the river Elbe. He shot a perfect 300 in the second course.

1980 Moscow C: 40, N: 26, D: 7.25. WR: 598 (Giovanni Liverzani, Corneliu Ion)

		PTS.
1. Corneliu Ion	ROM	596/148/147/148
2. Jürgen Wiefel	GDR	596/148/147/147
3. Gerhard Petritsch	AUT	596/146
4. Vladas Turla	SOV/LIT	595
5. Roberto Ferraris	ITA	595
6. Afanasijs Kuzmins	SOV/LAT	595
7. Marin Stan	ROM	595
8. Rafael Rodriguez	CUB	594

1984 Los Angeles-Chino C: 55, N: 31, D: 8.2. WR: 599 (Igor Puzyrev)

		PTS.
1. Takeo Kamachi	JPN	595
2. Corneliu Ion	ROM	593
3. Rauno Bies	FIN	591/146
4. Delival Nobre	BRA	591/141
5. Yang Choong-yull	KOR	590
6. Alfred Radke	GER	590
7. Park Jong-gil	KOR	590
8. Bernardo Tobar Ante	COL	590

Competing in his fourth Olympics, Takeo Kamachi finally won a medal at the age of 48.

1988 Seoul C: 32, N: 23, D: 9.23. WR: 697 (Ralf Schumann)

		PTS.	
1. Afanasijs Kuzmins	SOV/LAT	698	WR
2. Ralf Schumann	GDR	696	

3. Zoltán Kovács	HUN	693
4. Alberto Sevieri	ITA	693
5. Adam Kaczmarek	POL	691
6. Bernardo Tobar Ante	COL	690
7. John McNally	USA	690
8. Dirk Köhler	GER	689

When he was 22 years old, Afanasijs Kuzmins had a dream that he had won an Olympic gold medal. As a result, he kept going in the sport until his dream came true—19 years later. Kuzmins shot a 598 in the qualifying round to lead by 1 point, then achieved a perfect score in the final.

1992 Barcelona-Mollet del Vallès C: 30, N: 23, D: 7.30. WR: 891 (Ralf Schumann)

		PTS.
1. Ralf Schumann	GER	885
2. Afanasijs Kuzmins	LAT	882/97
3. Vladimir Vokhmyanin	KAZ	882/96
4. Krzysztof Kucharczyk	POL	880
5. John McNally	USA	781
6. Miroslav Ignatyuk	UKR	779
7. Adam Kaczmarek	POL	778
8. Bernardo Tobar Ante	COL	776

Since 1986 Ralf Schumann had earned a medal in all 30 of his starts. Twenty-one times he finished first, four times second, and five times third. He was the defending world champion and the world record holder. But because he was upset in Seoul by Afanasijs Kuzmins, he was still missing an Olympic gold medal. In Barcelona he took a three-point lead in the qualifying round and held it through the semifinal and final.

FREE PISTOL

The free pistol event is a leisurely affair in which the shooter has two and a half hours in which to fire 60 shots at a target 50 meters (55 yards) away. The 10-ring, or bull's-eye, of the target is only two inches in diameter. The final consists of 10 shots with 75 seconds for each shot.

1896 Athens C: 5, N: 3, D: 4.11.

		PTS.
1. Sumner Paine	USA	442
2. Holger Nielsen	DEN	285
3. Ioannis Phrangoudis	GRE	—
4. Leonidas Morakis	GRE	—
5. Georgios Orphanidis	GRE	—

Sumner Paine was working in Paris when his brother John showed up as part of the Boston Athletic Association team that was on its way to the Olympic Games. John convinced his brother to join him, so the two, not knowing the events or conditions, loaded up with eight guns and 3500 rounds of ammunition (they used only 96) and took the next train to Athens.

1900 Paris C: 20, N: 4, D: 8.1.

			PTS.
1.	Conrad Karl Röderer	SWI	503
2.	Achille Paroche	FRA	466
3.	Konrad Stäheli	SWI	453
4.	Louis Richardet	SWI	448
5.	Louis Duffoy	FRA	442
6.	Gerardus van Haan	HOL	437
7.	Friedrich Luthi	SWI	435
7.	Léon Moreau	FRA	435

1904 not held

1906 Athens C: 21, N: 8, D: 4.23.

			PTS.
1.	Georgios Orphanidis	GRE	221
2.	Jean Fouconnier	FRA	219
3.	Aristides Rangavis	GRE	218
4.	Konrad Stäheli	SWI	206
5.	Konstantinos Skarlotos	GRE	206
6.	Maurice Lecoq	FRA	205
7.	Ludwig Ternajgo	AUT	199
8.	Cesare Liverziani	ITA	199

1908 not held

1912 Stockholm C: 54, N: 12, D: 7.2.

			PTS.
1.	Alfred Lane	USA	499
2.	Peter Dolfen	USA	474
3.	Charles Stewart	GBR	470
4.	Georg de Laval	SWE	470
5.	Erik Boström	SWE	468
6.	Horatio Poulter	GBR	461
7.	Henry Sears	USA	459
8.	Nikolai Panin (Kolomenkin)	RUS	457

Alfred Lane of New York City was only 20 years old when he went to Stockholm and won three gold medals. Eight years later in Antwerp he added two more gold medals and one bronze. Eighth-place finisher Kolomenkin, a ten-time Russian pistol champion, was also a well-known figure skater who had won a gold medal in the special figures event of 1908.

1920 Antwerp-Beverloo C: 36, N: 13, D: 8.2.

			PTS.
1.	Karl Frederick	USA	496
2.	Afranio da Costa	BRA	489
3.	Alfred Lane	USA	481
4.	Lauritz Larsen	DEN	475
5.	Niels Larsen	DEN	470
6.	Anders Wilhelm Andersson	SWE	467
7.	Paul van Asbroek	BEL	466
8.	Iason Sappas	GRE	464

Da Costa used a new Colt .22 that had been loaned to the Brazilian team by the U.S. team, and ammunition given to him by Alfred Lane.

1924–1932 not held

1936 Berlin C: 43, N: 19, D: 8.7. WR: 547 (Torsten Ullman)

			PTS.	
1.	Torsten Ullman	SWE	559	WR
2.	Erich Krempel	GER	544	
3.	Charles Juchault des Jammonières	FRA	540	
4.	Marcel Bonin	FRA	538	
5.	Tapio Vartiovaara	FIN	537	
6.	Elliott Jones	USA	536	
7.	Georges Stathis	GRE	532	
8.	Aatto Nuora	FIN	532	

Earlier in the day Ullman had won a bronze medal in the rapid-fire pistol event.

1948 London C: 50, N: 22, D: 8.2. WR: 559 (Torsten Ullman)

			PTS.
1.	Edwin Vasquez Cam	PER	545
2.	Rudolf Schnyder	SWI	539/60/21
3.	Torsten Ullman	SWE	539/60/16
4.	Huelet Benner	USA	539/58
5.	Beat Rhyner	SWI	536
6.	Angel León de Gozalo	SPA	534
7.	Ambrus Balogh	HUN	532
8.	Marcel La Fortune	BEL	530

Vasquez is the only Peruvian ever to win an Olympic gold medal.

1952 Helsinki C: 48, N: 28, D: 7.25. WR: 559 (Torsten Ullman)

			PTS.	
1.	Huelet Benner	USA	553	OR
2.	Angel León de Gozalo	SPA	550	
3.	Ambrus Balogh	HUN	549	
4.	Konstantin Martazov	SOV	546	
4.	Lev Vainshtein	SOV/RUS	546	
6.	Torsten Ullman	SWE	543	
7.	Klaus Lahti	FIN	541	
8.	Beat Rhyner	SWI	539	

1956 Melbourne C: 33, N: 22, D: 11.30. WR: 566 (Anton Yasinsky)

			PTS.	
1.	Pentti Linnosvuo	FIN	556/26	OR
2.	Makhmud Umarov	SOV/RUS	556/24	OR
3.	Offutt Pinion	USA	551	
4.	Choji Hosaka	JPN	550/24	
5.	Anton Yasinsky	SOV	550/20	
6.	Torsten Ullman	SWE	549	
7.	Åke Lindblom	SWE	542	
8.	Leonard Tolhurst	AUS	541	

1960 Rome C: 67, N: 40, D: 9.6. WR: 566 (Anton Yasinsky)

			PTS.	
1.	Aleksei Gushchin	SOV/RUS	560	OR
2.	Makhmud Umarov	SOV/RUS	552/26	
3.	Yoshihisa Yoshikawa	JPN	552/20	
4.	Torsten Ullman	SWE	550	
5.	Stanislaw Romik	POL	548	
6.	Alfred Späni	SWI	546	

7. Vladimir Kudrna	CZE	545	
8. Horst Kadner	GDR	544	

Fourth-place finisher Ullman was now 52 years old.

1964 Tokyo C: 52, N: 42, D: 10.18. WR: 566 (Anton Yasinsky)

		PTS.	
1. Väinö Markkanen	FIN	560	EOR
2. Franklin Green	USA	557	
3. Yoshihisa Yoshikawa	JPN	554/26	
4. Johann Garreis	GDR	554/24	
5. Anthony Chivers	GBR	552	
6. Antonio Vita Segura	PER	550	
7. Leif Larsson	SWE	549	
8. Thomas Smith	USA	548	

1968 Mexico City C: 69, N: 42, D: 10.18. WR: 566 (Anton Yasinsky)

		PTS.	
1. Grigory Kossykh	SOV/RUS	562/30	OR
2. Heinz Mertel	GER	562/26	OR
3. Harald Vollmar	GDR	560	
4. Arnold Vitarbo	USA	559	
5. Pawel Malek	POL	556	
6. Helmut Artelt	GDR	555	
7. Nelson Onate	CUB	555	
8. Neagu Bratu	ROM	554	

1972 Munich C: 59, N: 37, D: 8.28. WR: 572 (Grigory Kossykh)

		PTS.	
1. Ragnar Skanåker	SWE	567	OR
2. Dan Iuga	ROM	562	
3. Rudolf Dollinger	AUT	560	
4. Rajmund Stachurski	POL	559	
5. Harald Vollmar	GDR	558	
6. Hynek Hromada	CZE	556	
7. Kornel Marosvari	HUN	555	
8. Grigory Kossykh	SOV/RUS	555	

1976 Montreal C: 47, N: 32, D: 7.18. WR: 572 (Grigory Kossykh, Harald Vollmar)

		PTS.	
1. Uwe Potteck	GDR	573	WR
2. Harald Vollmar	GDR	567	
3. Rudolf Dollinger	AUT	562	
4. Heinz Mertel	GER	560	
5. Ragnar Skanåker	SWE	559	
6. Vincenzo Tondo	ITA	559	
7. Grigory Kossykh	SOV/RUS	559	
8. Dencho Denev	BUL	557	

1980 Moscow C: 33, N: 19, D: 7.20. WR: 577 (Moritz Minder, Paavo Palokangas)

		PTS.	
1. Aleksandr Melentyev	SOV/KYR	581	WR
2. Harald Vollmar	GDR	568	
3. Ljubcho Diakov	BUL	565	
4. Soh Gil-san	PRK	565	
5. Seppo Saarenpää	FIN	565	
6. Sergei Pyzhyanov	SOV/RUS	564	

7. Ragnar Skanåker	SWE	563	
8. Paavo Palokangas	FIN	561	

1984 Los Angeles-Chino C: 56, N: 38, D: 7.29. WR: 581 (Aleksandr Melentyev)

		PTS.	
1. Xu Haifeng	CHN	566	
2. Ragnar Skanåker	SWE	565	
3. Wang Yifu	CHN	564	
4. Jürgen Hartmann	GER	560	
5. Vincenzo Tondo	ITA	560	
6. Philippe Cola	FRA	559	
7. Hector De Lima Carrillo	VEN	558	
8. Paavo Palokangas	FIN	558	

To Xu Haifeng, a former "barefoot doctor" and chemical fertilizer salesman, went the honor of not only being the first gold-medal winner of the 1984 Olympics, but also of becoming the first representative of China to win an Olympic medal. He defeated 50-year-old Ragnar Skanåker, who added a silver medal to the gold he had won twelve years earlier.

1988 Seoul C: 43, N: 31, D: 9.18. WR: 666 (Igor Basinsky)

		PTS.	
1. Sorin Babii	ROM	660	
2. Ragnar Skanåker	SWE	657	
3. Igor Basinsky	SOV/BLR	657	
4. Taniu Kiryakov	BUL	656	
5. Gernot Eder	GDR	654	
6. Gyula Karácsony	HUN	654	
7. Arndt Kaspar	GER	651	
8. Wang Yifu	CHN	651	

Babii trailed Basinsky by 4 points following the preliminary round, with 54-year-old Skanåker another 2 points back in fourth place. Basinsky seemed rattled in the final and scored only 87 points to Babii's 94 and Skanåker's 93. Skanåker was more than twice as old as the other top five finishers.

1992 Barcelona-Mollet del Vallès C: 44, N: 29, D: 7.26. WR: 671 (Sergei Pyzhyanov)

		PTS.	
1. Konstantin Lukashik	BLR	658	
2. Wang Yifu	CHN	657/92	
3. Ragnar Skanåker	SWE	657/91	
4. Darius Young	USA	655	
5. Sorin Babii	ROM	653	
6. István Ágh	HUN	652/91	
7. Xu Haifeng	CHN	652/87	
8. Taniu Kiryakov	BUL	618	

The final was a tight contest. Taniu Kiryakov, who had won a gold medal in the air pistol event in 1988, scored a 567 in the qualifying round, as did 16-year-old Konstantin Lukashik of Grodno. One shot behind were 54-year-old Darius Young and 58-year-old Ragnar Skanåker, followed by the two Chinese shooters, Wang Yifu and 1984 Olympic champion Xu Haifeng with 565.

Xu and Kiryakov were the first to fall from contention. After his sixth shot, an 8, dropped him four points off the pace, Kiryakov slammed his pistol against the rest, altering the sight. Unable to shoot properly afterward, he stalked off the range. Meanwhile, Skanåker caught Lukashik after the first shot, moved ahead with his third and led by two points midway through the ten-shot final. Lukashik pulled even again with his sixth shot. With four shots to go, Wang, Young, and 1988 Olympic champion Sorin Babii were all just two points behind the leaders. Lukashik inched one point ahead of Skanåker in the ninth round. With one shot remaining, the score stood: Lukashik—649, Skanåker—648, and Wang—648. A ten would have won the match for any of them. However, all three scored nines, with Wang gaining the silver medal because of his higher total in the final.

AIR PISTOL

Competition in the qualification round consists of 60 shots at a distance of 10 meters with a time limit of 2 hours and 15 minutes. The top eight shooters take part in a 10-shot final series. The bull's-eye has a diameter of 11.5 mm (.45 in).

1896-1984 not held

1988 Seoul C: 44, N: 29, D: 9.24. WR: 692.3 (Igor Basinsky)

			PTS.
1.	Taniu Kiryakov	BUL	687.9
2.	Erich Buljung	USA	687.9
3.	Xu Haifeng	CHN	684.5
4.	Sorin Babii	ROM	683.3
5.	Igor Basinsky	SOV/BLR	683.2
6.	Miroslav Ružička	CZE	681.4
7.	Jerzy Pietrzak	POL	678.3
8.	Boris Kokorev	SOV/RUS	677.3

U.S. Army shooting instructor Erich Buljung equaled the 60-shot world record of 590 in the preliminary round. In the 10-shot final, however, his 5-point lead gradually evaporated until Kiryakov trailed by only 0.7 points after nine shots. On the final shot Kiryakov outscored Buljung 9.8 to 9.1 to finish in a tie. The Bulgarian was awarded the gold medal on the basis of his higher point total in the final round.

1992 Barcelona-Mollet del Vallès C: 45, N: 30, D: 7.28. WR: 695.1 (Sergei Pyzhyanov)

			PTS.
1.	Wang Yifu	CHN	684.8
2.	Sergei Pyzhyanov	RUS	684.1/100.1
3.	Sorin Babii	ROM	684.1/98.1
4.	Xu Haifeng	CHN	681.5
5.	Sakari Paasonen	FIN	680.1/98
6.	Jerzy Pietrzak	POL	680.1/93

| 7. | Taniu Kiryakov | BUL | 679.7 |
| 8. | Robert Di Donna | ITA | 678.5 |

Babii set an Olympic record of 586 in the qualifying round. He was followed by Wang at 585 and Pyzhyanov at 584. The Romanian led by 1.7 points after six rounds in the final, but then he began to falter. With one shot remaining, Wang crept to within one-tenth of a point of Babii: 675.2 to 675.1. Babii fired first and scored only 8.9 points. Wang, normally a quick shooter himself, was about to fire when he heard the surprised reaction to Babii's shot. Wang peeked at the score and lowered his gun. For years Wang had lived with the reputation of being a poor performer at major competitions. In the words of Xie Bian of *China Sports* magazine, "His repeated failures hung over his head, turning him from an easygoing man into a somewhat melancholy one." Wang raised his pistol, but again lowered it. "You must overcome yourself," he told himself, "this is the chance of a lifetime." With exquisite concentration, he aimed again and finally fired. His 9.7 earned him the gold medal. Pyzhyanov, meanwhile, scored 9.9 to tie Babii and gain the silver medal due to his higher point total in the final.

Wang Yifu's wife, Zhang Qiuping, finished tenth in the women's small-bore rifle, three positions event.

SMALL-BORE RIFLE, PRONE

The small-bore rifle, prone match is shot at a distance of 50 meters with a .22 rimfire rifle. Originally the 10-ring bull's-eye was .89 inches in diameter. When high scores became too common, it was scaled down in 1958 to .487 inches. Currently, the diameter is 10.4 mm (.409 inches)—smaller than a dime. The shooter must keep his wrist at least six inches above the ground. He is given one hour and 45 minutes in which to take 60 shots and is also allowed 15 sighting shots, which can only be taken between the strings of ten record shots. The final consists of 10 shots with a time limit of 45 seconds per shot.

1896–1906 not held

1908 London C: 19, N: 5, D: 7.11.

			PTS.
1.	Arthur Carnell	GBR	387
2.	Harold Humby	GBR	386
3.	George Barnes	GBR	385
4.	Michael Matthews	GBR	384
5.	Edward Amoore	GBR	383
6.	William Pimm	GBR	379
7.	Albert Taylor	GBR	376
8.	Harold Hawkins	GBR	374

In his book *British Olympians*, Ian Buchanan relates the story of the unfortunate Philip Plater of Great Britain. The rules of the competition limited each nation to 12 entries. When the entry form of George Barnes was misplaced, Plater was entered in his place. Barnes' entry form was subsequently found, but on the day of the match, confusion reigned. Thinking that only 11 British shooters had fired, Plater was allowed to start even though there were only 30 minutes remaining. Plater set a world record of 391 and was initially recognized as the Olympic champion. Then it was discovered that all 12 members of the official British team had shot before Plater. Several days later Plater was declared an illegal entrant and his performance was expunged from the records.

1912 Stockholm C: 41, N: 9, D: 7.4.

			PTS.
1.	Frederick Hird	USA	194
2.	William Milne	GBR	193
3.	Harold Burt	GBR	192
4.	Edward Lessimore	GBR	192
5.	Francis Kemp	GBR	190
6.	Robert Murray	GBR	190
7.	William Leushner	USA	189
8.	Erik Bostrom	SWE	189

1920 not held

1924 Paris C: 66, N: 19, D: 6.23.

			PTS.	
1.	Pierre Coquelin de Lisle	FRA	398	WR
2.	Marcus Dinwiddie	USA	396	
3.	Josias Hartmann	SWI	394	
4.	Erik Saetter-Lassen	DEN	393	
4.	Anders Peter Nielsen	DEN	393	
4.	Johannes Theslöf	FIN	393	
7.	Viktor Knutsson	SWE	392	
7.	Jakob Reich	SWI	392	

Silver medalist Marcus Dinwiddie was a 17-year-old schoolboy from Washington, D.C. His record score of 396 out of 400 held up for most of the match, until the 23-year-old Coquelin de Lisle hit a sensational set of 100, 100, 99, and 99. Following his victory, Coquelin de Lisle sent the following succinct cable to his mother: "Am Olympic champion. World record beaten. Will arrive Tuesday morning."

1928 not held

1932 Los Angeles C: 26, N: 9, D: 8.13.

			PTS.
1.	Bertil Rönnmark	SWE	294/296
2.	Gustavo Huet	MEX	294/290
3.	Zoltán Hradetzky-Soós	HUN	293
4.	Mario Zorzi	ITA	293
5.	Gustaf Andersson	SWE	292
5.	William Harding	USA	292
5.	Karl Larsson	SWE	292
5.	Francisco Real	POR	292

Antonius Limberkovits of Hungary fired one bull's-eye which he had unfortunately aimed at the wrong target.

He called out his mistake to the officials, who ruled the shot a complete miss. Had he not made this error and had he not been so honest, Limberkovits would have won the gold medal.

1936 Berlin C: 66, N: 25, D: 8.8.

			PTS.	
1.	Willy Rögeberg	NOR	300	WR
2.	Ralph Berzsenyi	HUN	296	
3.	Wladyslaw Karaś	POL	296	
4.	Martin Gison	PHI	296	
5.	José Trindade Mello	BRA	296	
6.	Jacques Mazoyer	FRA	296	
7.	Gustavo Huet	MEX	296	
8.	Bertil Rönnmark	SWE	295	

The 30-year-old Rögeberg fired the first perfect score ever recorded in international competition. Fourth-place finisher Gison was captured by the Japanese during World War II and forced to take part in the infamous Bataan death march. He survived and was able to compete in the 1948 Olympics in London.

1948 London C: 71, N: 26, D: 8.3.

			PTS.	
1.	Arthur Cook	USA	599/43	WR
2.	Walter Tomsen	USA	599/42	WR
3.	Jonas Jonsson	SWE	597/44	
4.	Halvor Kongsjorden	NOR	597/39	
5.	Thore Skredegaard	NOR	597/39	
6.	Enrique Baldwin Ponte	PER	596/39	
7.	Jaako Ravila	FIN	596/39	
8.	Willy Rögeberg	NOR	596/37	

Cook and Tomsen each missed the 10-ring only once in 60 shots, but Cook was awarded first place because he had fired one shot more than Tomsen within the ⅜-inch inner bull's-eye.

1952 Helsinki C: 58, N: 32, D: 7.29. WR: 400 (T. Manttari)

			PTS.	
1.	Iosif Sîrbu	ROM	400/33	EWR
2.	Boris Andreyev	SOV/RUS	400/28	EWR
3.	Arthur Jackson	USA	399/28	
4.	Gilmour Boa	CAN	399/28	
5.	Erich Spörer	GER	399/25	
6.	Otto Horber	SWI	398/29	
7.	Veikko Leskinen	FIN	398/28	
8.	Severino Moreira	BRA	398/22	

Sîrbu was Romania's first Olympic champion.

1956 Melbourne C: 44, N: 25, D: 12.5. WR: 598 (Gilmour Boa)

			PTS.
1.	Gerald Ouellette	CAN	600
2.	Vassily Borissov	SOV/RUS	599
3.	Gilmour Boa	CAN	598
4.	Otakar Horinek	CZE	598
5.	Iosif Sârbu	ROM	598
6.	Sándor Krebs	HUN	598

7. Erling Kongshaug   NOR   598
8. Severino Moreira   BRA   597

After he had done poorly in the three-position small-bore event, Ouellette and his teammate Gilmour Boa decided that they should both use Boa's rifle for the prone competition, even though this meant that they both had to shoot within the same two-and-a-half-hour time limit. Boa went first and, coached by Ouellette, matched his world record of 598. Then, with half the time remaining, it was Ouellette's turn. Coached by Boa, who encouraged the Windsor, Ontario, tool designer to take two breaks to ease the pressure, Ouellette shot 60 straight bull's-eyes for a perfect score. Unfortunately, his score was not accepted as a world record because the Australian officials had set the targets one and a half meters too close. Ouellette's second appearance in the Olympics didn't come until 12 years later, when he finished sixth in the three-position event in Mexico City.

Gerald Ouellette shot 60 straight bull's-eyes to win the 1956 small-bore rifle, prone event.

1960 Rome C: 85, N: 46, D: 9.10. WR: 595 (János Holup)

			PTS.
1.	Peter Kohnke	GER	590
2.	James Hill	USA	589
3.	Enrico Forcella Pelliccioni	VEN	587
4.	Vassily Borissov	SOV/RUS	586
5.	Arthur Skinner	GBR	586
6.	Yukio Inokuma	JPN	586
7.	Daniel Puckel	USA	585
8.	Marcel Koen	BUL	585

Eighteen-year-old Peter Kohnke of Bremervörde was the youngest of the 85 entrants in the prone event.

1964 Tokyo C: 73, N: 43, D: 10.16. WR: 595 (János Holup, Rudolf Bortz)

			PTS.	
1.	László Hammerl	HUN	597	WR
2.	Lones Wigger	USA	597	WR
3.	Tommy Pool	USA	596	
4.	Gilmour Boa	CAN	595	
5.	Nicolae Rotaru	ROM	595	
6.	Akihiro Rinzaki	JPN	594	
7.	Karl Wenk	GER	594	
8.	Traian Cogut	ROM	593	

László Hammerl was a 22-year-old medical student from Budapest. He was awarded the victory on the basis of a tie-breaking rule which stated that whoever had the highest score in the final string of ten shots was the winner.

1968 Mexico City C: 86, N: 45, D: 10.19. WR: 598 (David Boyd, Alfons Meyer)

			PTS.	
1.	Jan Kurka	CZE	598	EWR
2.	László Hammerl	HUN	598	EWR
3.	Ian Ballinger	NZE	597	
4.	Nicolae Rotaru	ROM	597	
5.	John Palin	GBR	596	
6.	Jean Loret	FRA	596	
7.	Bjorn Bakken	NOR	595	
8.	Gary Anderson	USA	595	

This time Hammerl lost the gold medal because of the same tie-breaking rule from which he had benefitted four years earlier. Eulalia Rolińska of Poland and Gladys de Seminario of Peru had the distinction of being the first women to compete in Olympic shooting. They finished 22nd and 31st, respectively.

1972 Munich C: 101, N: 59, D: 8.28. WR: 598 (David Boyd, Alfons Meyer, Jan Kurka, László Hammerl, Peter Gorewski, Wolfram Waibel, Manfred Fiess, Esa Kervinen)

			PTS.	
1.	Li Ho-jun	PRK	599	WR
2.	Victor Auer	USA	598	
3.	Nicolae Rotaru	ROM	598	
4.	Giuseppe de Chirico	ITA	597	
5.	Jiři Vogler	CZE	597	

6. Jaime Santiago	PUR	597
7. Lones Wigger	USA	597
8. László Hammerl	HUN	597

After his victory, Li was asked by reporters to what he attributed his brilliant performance. He replied, "I thought I was shooting at my enemies. Our Prime Minister, Kim-Il Sung, told us prior to our departure to shoot as if we were fighting our enemies. And that's exactly what I did." This attitude was considered to be unsportsmanlike, and so a second press conference was called at which Li claimed he had been misquoted. Second-place finisher Vic Auer was a North Hollywood TV scriptwriter who had written for *Death Valley Days, Gunsmoke,* and *Bonanza.*

1976 Montreal C: 76, N: 49, D: 7.19. WR: 599 (Li Ho-jun, Karel Bulan, Mircea Ilca)

		PTS.	
1. Karlheinz Smieszek	GER	599	EWR
2. Ulrich Lind	GER	597	
3. Gennady Lushchikov	SOV/RUS	595	
4. Anton Müller	SWI	595	
5. Walter Frescura	ITA	594	
6. Arne Sörensen	CAN	593	
7. Henning Clausen	DEN	593	
8. Desanka Pesut	YUG	592	

Smieszek, a 27-year-old insurance agent, was a surprise winner who had never before won a major shooting title.

1980 Moscow C: 56, N: 33, D: 7.21. WR: 599 (Li Ho-jun, Karel Bulan, Mircea Ilca, Karlheinz Smieszek, Alister Allan, Lones Wigger)

		PTS.	
1. Károly Varga	HUN	599	EWR
2. Hellfried Heilfort	GDR	599	EWR
3. Petur Zapianov	BUL	598	
4. Krzysztof Stefaniak	POL	598	
5. Timo Hagmaan	FIN	597	
6. Aleksandr Mastianin	SOV	597	
7. Nonka Matova	BUL	597	
8. Walter Frescura	ITA	597	

Varga broke his shooting hand playing soccer two days before the competition and had to wear a bandage while he shot. After winning the gold medal he explained that the injury had actually helped him, because it forced him to squeeze the trigger more delicately.

1984 Los Angeles-Chino C: 71, N: 46, D: 7.30. WR: 600 (Alister Allan, Ernest VandeZande, Edward Etzel, Donald Durbin)

		PTS.	
1. Edward Etzel	USA	599	EOR
2. Michel Bury	FRA	596	
3. Michael Sullivan	GBR	596	
4. Alister Allan	GBR	595	
5. Francesco Nanni	SMR	594	
6. Hans Strand	SWE	594	

7. John Duus	NOR	594
8. Ulrich Lind	GER	593

Ed Etzel of Morgantown, West Virginia, completed his 60 shots in only 40 minutes and was the first of the 71 shooters to finish. Francesco Nanni's fifth place finish made him the most successful Olympic athlete ever from the tiny nation of San Marino (pop. 22,000).

1988 Seoul C: 55, N: 33, D: 9.19. WR: 704.9 (Petr Kůrka)

		PTS.
1. Miroslav Varga	CZE	703.9
2. Cha Young-chul	KOR	702.8
3. Attila Záhonyi	HUN	701.9
4. Pavel Soukeník	CZE	701.2
5. Alister Allan	GBR	700.9
6. Xu Xiaoguang	CHN	700.6
7. Bernd Rücker	GER	700.5
8. Michael Ashcroft	CAN	698.5

Varga required only 28 minutes to achieve a perfect score of 600 in the qualifying round. His speed turned out to be well advised, as a thunderstorm swept in a few minutes later, darkening the sky and impairing the vision of the remaining shooters. In the final, Cha drew within 0.2 points with two shots remaining, but Varga shot a pair of 10.6s to hold him off. Cha's closing in on Varga caused great excitement among the Korean spectators, who clapped and cheered after each of Cha's shots even though other shooters were still firing. This was an unprecedented breach of etiquette on the part of the crowd.

1992 Barcelona-Mollet del Vallès C: 52, N: 34, D: 7.29. WR: 703.5 (Jens Harskov)

		PTS.
1. Lee Eun-chul	KOR	702.5
2. Harald Stenvaag	NOR	701.4
3. Stevan Pletikosić	YUG	701.1/104.1
4. Hubert Bichler	GER	701.1/103.1
5. Michel Bury	FRA	700.0
6. Juha Hirvi	FIN	699.5/102.5
7. Peter Gabrielsson	SWE	699.5/102.5
8. Grachya Petikyan	ARM	699.2

Bichler led the qualifying round with a score of 598, but all of the other seven finalists were only one point back, at 597. Lee passed Bichler in the sixth round and held his lead to the end. Bichler, in second place with one shot remaining, fell to fourth after missing the ten-ring for the second straight time. Stenvaag, on the other hand, went from sixth place halfway through the final to second at the end.

SMALL-BORE RIFLE, THREE POSITIONS

In the small-bore rifle, three-position event, each entrant shoots 40 shots prone, 40 kneeling, and 40 standing, with a .22 rifle at a target 50 meters away. The target is the same as that used in the prone event. The time limits are 1 hour 15 minutes for the prone round, 1 hour 45 minutes standing and 1 hour 30 minutes kneeling. In the final the top eight qualifiers take ten shots in the standing position. The time limit is 75 seconds per shot.

1896–1948 not held

1952 Helsinki C: 44, N: 25, D: 7.29. WR: 1167 (K. Steigelmann)

		PRONE		KNEELING		STANDING	TOTAL PTS.
1. Erling Kongshaug	NOR	397		387		380	1164/53
2. Vilho Ylönen	FIN	397		394	WR	373	1164/53
3. Boris Andreyev	SOV/RUS	400	WR	387		376	1163
4. Ernst Huber	SWI	397		390		375	1162
5. Pyotr Avilov	SOV	395		385		382	1162
6. Iosif Sârbu	ROM	400	WR	383		378	1161
7. Uno Berg	SWE	396		388		374	1158
8. Veikko Leskinen	FIN	398		390		369	1157

1956 Melbourne C: 44, N: 28, D: 12.4. WR: 1176 (Ole Jensen)

		PRONE		KNEELING	STANDING	TOTAL PTS.	
1. Anatoly Bogdanov	SOV/RUS	396		392	384	1172	OR
2. Otakar Hořinek	CZE	393		395	384	1172	OR
3. Nils Johan Sundberg	SWE	397		396	374	1167	
4. Vassily Borrisov	SOV/RUS	395		391	377	1163	
5. Vilho Ylönen	FIN	394		386	381	1161	
6. Gilmour Boa	CAN	400	WR	391	368	1159	
7. Iosif Sârbu	ROM	397		392	368	1157	
8. Anders Kvissbérg	SWE	394		389	373	1156	

1960 Rome C: 75, N: 40, D: 9.8. WR: 1149 (Klaus Zähringer)

		PRONE	KNEELING	STANDING	TOTAL PTS.	
1. Viktor Shamburkin	SOV/RUS	394	386	369	1149	EWR
2. Marat Niyazov	SOV/TRM	384	388	373	1145	
3. Klaus Zähringer	GER	394	381	364	1139	
4. Dušan Houdek	CZE	387	386	366	1139	
5. Jerzy Nowicki	POL	394	378	365	1137	
6. Esa Kervinen	FIN	392	381	364	1137	
7. Daniel Puckel	USA	390	385	361	1137	
8. János Holup	HUN	394	384	356	1134	

1964 Tokyo C: 75, N: 40, D: 9.8. WR: 1157 (Gary Anderson)

		PRONE	KNEELING	STANDING	TOTAL PTS.	
1. Lones Wigger	USA	398	394	372	1164	WR
2. Velichko Velichkov	BUL	396	384	372	1152	
3. László Hammerl	HUN	397	387	367	1151	
4. Harry Köcher	GDR	394	389	365	1148	
5. Jerzy Nowicki	POL	396	389	362	1147	
6. Tommy Pool	USA	393	392	362	1147	
7. Ion Olarescu	ROM	393	391	360	1144	
8. Kurt Müller	SWI	390	386	367	1143	

U.S. Army Captain Lones Wigger of Carter, Montana, had never shot before a large crowd before. Teammate

Gary Anderson advised him not to be afraid of the crowd but to feel a part of it. Wigger set a world record in the prone event, but lost on a tie-breaker. Four days later he set another world record in the three-position event, but this time he finished 12 points ahead of his nearest opponent. Eight years later, at the Munich Olympics, Wigger won another gold medal in the 300-meter free rifle event.

1968 Mexico City C: 62, N: 35, D: 10.21. WR: 1165 (Gary Anderson)

		PRONE	STANDING	KNEELING		TOTAL PTS.
1. Bernd Klingner	GER	394	367	396	WR	1157
2. John Writer	USA	395	370	391		1156
3. Viktor Parkhimovich	SOV/BLR	395	366	393		1154
4. John Foster	USA	394	369	390		1153
5. José Gonzales	MEX	397	376	379		1152
6. Gerald Ouellette	CAN	396	364	391		1151
7. Peter Kohnke	GER	395	368	388		1151
8. Kurt Müller	SWI	390	373	388		1151

1972 Munich C: 69, N: 41, D: 8.30. WR: 1165 (Gary Anderson, Oleg Lapkin)

		PRONE	STANDING		KNEELING	TOTAL PTS.	
1. John Writer	USA	395	381	WR	390	1166	WR
2. Lanny Bassham	USA	390	375		392	1157	
3. Werner Lippoldt	GDR	393	372		388	1153	
4. Petr Kovařik	CZE	397	368		388	1153	
5. Vladimir Agishev	SOV/RUS	392	369		391	1152	
6. Andrzej Sieledcow	POL	395	369		387	1151	
7. Gottfried Kustermann	GER	397	364		388	1149	
8. Nicolae Rotaru	ROM	397	361		390	1148	

1976 Montreal C: 57, N: 35, D: 7.21. WR: 1167 (Lones Wigger)

		PRONE	STANDING	KNEELING	TOTAL PTS.
1. Lanny Bassham	USA	397	373	392	1162
2. Margaret Murdock	USA	398	376	388	1162
3. Werner Seibold	GER	397	377	386	1160
4. Srecko Pejović	YUG	391	379	386	1156
5. Sven Johansson	SWE	394	367	391	1152
6. Li Ho-jun	PRK	390	373	389	1152
7. Zdravko Milutinović	YUG	394	394	389	1152
8. Aleksandr Mitrofanov	SOV/RUS	394	369	388	1151

After finishing second in 1972, Lanny Bassham, a soldier from Fort Worth, Texas, became convinced that his technical skill had to be supplemented by mental training. He went to the Montreal Olympics as the favorite. His U.S. teammate was Margaret Murdock, a 33-year-old nurse from Topeka, Kansas. In 1970 Murdock had won the standing event at the world championships while she was four months' pregnant. At the 1976 Olympics, Bassham and Murdock finished in a tie at 1162. Bassham was awarded the gold medal because he had scored three 100s to Murdock's two. Bassham felt that the tie-breaker was a silly rule, and at the medal ceremony he pulled Murdock up to the first-place platform and they stood together for the playing of the U.S. national anthem. Murdock was probably less upset about the tie-breaking rule, since it was the same rule that had allowed her to gain a place on the U.S. team when she and John Writer finished with the same scores at the U.S. tryouts. Bassham later started a mental management business to help people become better shooters and make more money. Murdock was the first woman to win an Olympic shooting medal.

1980 Moscow C: 39, N: 21, D: 7.23. WR: 1172 (Nonka Matova)

		PRONE	STANDING	KNEELING	TOTAL PTS.	
1. Viktor Vlasov	SOV/RUS	398	378	397	1173	WR
2. Bernd Hartstein	GDR	399	374	393	1166	
3. Sven Johansson	SWE	398	379	388	1165	
4. Mauri Röppänen	FIN	397	379	388	1164	
4. Aleksandr Mitrofanov	SOV/RUS	397	378	389	1164	
6. Nonka Matova	BUL	396	377	390	1163	
7. Hellfried Heilfort	GDR	394	378	390	1162	
8. Eugeniusz Pędzisz	POL	397	368	391	1156	

1984 Los Angeles-Chino C: 51, N: 29, D: 8.1. WR: 1173 (Viktor Vlasov, Vladimir Lvov)

		PRONE	STANDING	KNEELING	TOTAL PTS.	
1. Malcolm Cooper	GBR	397	381	395	1173	EWR
2. Daniel Nipkow	SWI	396	381	386	1163	
3. Alister Allan	GBR	392	378	392	1162	
4. Kurt Hillenbrand	GER	396	369	389	1154	
5. Bo Arne Lilja	DEN	394	375	384	1153	
6. Glenn Dubis	USA	396	368	387	1151	
7. Jean-Pierre Amat	FRA	393	375	382	1150	
7. Peter Heinz	GER	394	375	381	1150	

1988 Seoul C: 47, N: 25, D: 9.22. WR: 1283.4 (Petr Kůrka)

		PRONE	STANDING	KNEELING	FINAL	TOTAL PTS.
1. Malcolm Cooper	GBR	400 EWR	387	393	99.3	1279.3
2. Alister Allan	GBR	399	386	396	94.6	1275.6
3. Kirill Ivanov	SOV/RUS	399	382	392	102.0	1275.0
4. Klaus Jorn Christensen	DEN	399	387	391	96.6	1273.6
5. Glenn Dubis	USA	400 EWR	386	388	99.5	1273.5
6. Grachya Petikyan	SOV/ARM	394	387	392	99.2	1272.2
7. Harald Stenvaag	NOR	395	389	389	98.7	1271.7
8. Goran Maksimović	YUG	399	383	391	98.5	1271.5

One week before the competition began, a clumsy technician from the BBC knocked over Cooper's rifle and cracked the stock. Fortunately the defending Olympic champion was able to repair it with the help of a Soviet gunsmith.

1992 Barcelona-Mollet del Vallès C: 42, N: 24, D: 7.31. WR: 1276.7 (Rajmond Debevec)

		PRONE	STANDING	KNEELING	FINAL	TOTAL PTS.
1. Grachya Petikyan	ARM	399	383	387	98.4	1267.4
2. Robert Foth	USA	395	386	388	97.6	1266.6
3. Ryohei Koba	JPN	393	387	391	94.9	1265.9
4. Juha Hirvi	FIN	398	384	390	92.8	1264.8
5. Harald Stenvaag	NOR	397	381	388	98.6	1264.6
6. Rajmond Debevec	SLO	394	387	386	95.6	1262.6
7. Peter Gabrielsson	SWE	398	379	391	93.1	1261.1
8. Zsolt Vári	HUN	398	379	387	94.6	1258.6

Hirvi led the qualifying round at 1172. He was followed by Koba at 1171, and Petikyan and Foth at 1169. But Hirvi put himself out of contention with the first shot of the final when he scored only 5.0 points. The lead changed hands eight times in the final, with Petikyan taking over for the first time after the seventh shot. With one shot remaining, the score could hardly have been closer: Foth—1257.4, Petikyan—1257.3, and Koba—1257.1. It was Petikyan who came through in the end, scoring a 10.1 to Foth's 9.2 and Koba's 8.8. The sacrifices of Olympic athletes know no limits. After the competition was over, Koba revealed to the press that during his final weeks of training he had given up not only alcohol but karaoke singing as well.

AIR RIFLE

In the qualifying round 60 shots are taken at a distance of 10 meters. The center ring is 1 millimeter across. The final consists of 10 shots with a 75-second time limit per shot.

1896–1980 not held

1984 Los Angeles-Chino C: 52, N: 35, D: 8.3. WR: 590 (Harald Stenvaag)

		PTS.
1. Philippe Héberle	FRA	589
2. Andreas Kronthaler	AUT	587
3. Barry Dagger	GBR	587
4. Nicolas Berthelot	FRA	585
5. Peter Heinz	GER	583
5. John Rost	USA	583
7. Harald Stenvaag	NOR	582
7. Itzchak Yonassi	ISR	582

Defending world champion Philippe Héberle, a 21-year-old fire fighter from Belfort, was also two-time crossbow world champion. During a pre-Olympic tournament at the Olympic site in Chino in April 1984, Héberle was impressed by the stifling heat. Back home in France he simulated the Olympic conditions by employing a large gas heater to raise the temperature at his practice site. When the French shooting team returned to Los Angeles they decided to avoid the Olympic villages, which were far from the shooting venue. Instead, they rented nine motor homes and set up shop in a campground where they used fishing rods and crossbows to satisfy their taste for fish, rabbits, and ducks.

1988 Seoul C: 46, N: 29, D: 9.20. WR: 699.1 (Tapio Saeynevirta)

		PTS.
1. Goran Maksimović	YUG	695.6
2. Nicolas Berthelot	FRA	694.2
3. Johann Riederer	GER	694.0
4. Robert Foth	USA	692.5
5. Harald Stenvaag	NOR	692.0
6. Attila Záhonyi	HUN	691.4
7. An Byung-kyun	KOR	690.7
8. Andreas Wolfram	GDR	689.8

1992 Barcelona-Mollet del Vallès C: 44, N: 28, D: 7.27. WR: 699.4 (Rajmond Debevec)

		PTS.
1. Yuri Fedkin	RUS	695.3
2. Franck Badiou	FRA	691.9
3. Johann Riederer	GER	691.7
4. Jean-Pierre Amat	FRA	691.6
5. Goran Maksimović	YUG	690.6
6. Thomas Farnik	AUT	690.2
7. Robert Foth	USA	689.4
8. Chae Keun-bae	KOR	687.8

MOVING TARGET

Between 1972 and 1988 the moving target or running boar event consisted of 60 shots at 50 meters. The target, a life-size reproduction of a wild boar with a two-inch 10-ring, crossed a ten-meter gap. The boar did 30 fast runs at two and a half seconds and 30 slow runs at five seconds. In 1988 the four best shooters in the qualification round took 10 more shots in the final at fast-run speed. Beginning in 1992 the moving target event has been shot with a .177-caliber air rifle at 10 meters. In addition, the boar was replaced by a regular target. In the slow run the target is exposed for 5 seconds; in the fast run it is exposed for 2.5 seconds. The final consists of ten shots at the fast speed. Ties in the qualifying round are decided by the number of tens shot. Ties for medal positions are decided by a second ten-shot run. Only six shooters compete in the final. This is the only event in which telescopic sights are allowed.

1896 not held

1900 Paris C: ?, N: 3, D: 7.17.

		PTS.
1. Louis Debray	FRA	20
2. Pierre Nivet	FRA	20
3. Georges de Lambert	FRA	19
4. Gabriel Veyre	FRA	19
5. André de Schlumberger	FRA	19
6. Paul Desart	FRA	19

1904–1968 not held

1972 Munich C: 28, N: 16, D: 9.1. WR: 566 (Göete Gåård)

		PTS.	
1. Yakiv Zhelez-nyak	SOV/UKR	569	WR
2. Helmut Bellingrodt	COL	565	
3. John Kynoch	GBR	562	
4. Valery Postoianov	SOV/RUS	560	
5. Christoph-Michael Zeisner	GER	554	
6. Göete Gåård	SWE	553	
7. Günther Danne	GER	551	
8. Karl-Axel Karlsson	SWE	551	

1976 Montreal C: 27, N: 16, D: 7.23. WR: 577 (Helmut Bellingrodt, Valery Postoianov)

		PTS.	
1. Aleksandr Gazov	SOV/BLR	579	WR
2. Aleksandr Kedyarov	SOV/BLR	576	
3. Jerzy Greszkiewicz	POL	571	
4. Thomas Pfeffer	GDR	571	
5. Wolfgang Hamberger	GER	567	
6. Helmut Bellingrodt	COL	567	
7. Karl Karlsson	SWE	565	
8. Louis Theimer	USA	564	

1980 Moscow C: 19, N: 11, D: 7.24. WR: 581 (Thomas Pfeffer)

		PTS.	
1. Igor Sokolov	SOV/RUS	589	WR
2. Thomas Pfeffer	GDR	589	
3. Aleksandr Gazov	SOV/BLR	587	
4. András Doleschall	HUN	584	
5. Tibor Bodnár	HUN	584	
6. Jorma Lievonen	FIN	584	
7. Giovanni Mezzani	ITA	582	
8. Hans-Jürgen Helbig	GDR	579	

1984 Los Angeles-Chino C: 23, N: 15, D: 7.31. WR: 595 (Igor Sokolov)

		PTS.
1. Li Yuwei	CHN	587
2. Helmut Bellingrodt	COL	584
3. Huang Shiping	CHN	581
4. Uwe Schröder	GER	581
5. David Lee	CAN	580
6. Kenneth Skoglund	NOR	576
7. Jorma Lievonen	FIN	576
8. Ezio Cini	ITA	576

1988 Seoul C: 23, N: 16, D: 9.23. WR: 691 (Sergei Lusov, Nikolai Lapin)

		PTS.
1. Tor Heiestad	NOR	689
2. Huang Shiping	CHN	687
3. Hennady Avramenko	SOV/UKR	686
4. Ján Kermiet	CZE	679
5. András Doleschall	HUN	588
6. Attila Solti	HUN	588
7. Thomas Pfeffer	GDR	587
8. Christian Stützinger	GER	586

Heiestad was a 26-year-old farm mechanic from Oslo.

1992 Barcelona-Mollet del Vallès C: 24, N: 15, D: 8.1. WR: 679 (Luboš Račanský)

		PTS.
1. Michael Jakosits	GER	673
2. Anatoly Asrabayev	RUS	672
3. Luboš Račanský	CZE	670
4. Andrei Vasilyev	BLR	667/91
5. József Sike	HUN	667/91
6. Jens Zimmermann	GER	667/89
7. Kim Man-chol	PRK	573
8. Su Qingquan	CHN	573

TRAP

In the trap or clay pigeon event, clay saucers four and a third inches in diameter are flung into the air at various angles. The shooter is allowed two shots with a .12-gauge shotgun at each saucer (or bird). According to current rules, after 150 targets, the top 24 shooters advance to a semifinal round and fire at 50 more targets. The 6 best semifinalists shoot 25 targets in the final.

1896 not held

1900 Paris C: 51, N: 4, D: 7.15.

		PTS.
1. Roger de Barbarin	FRA	17
2. René Guyot	FRA	17
3. Justinien de Clary	FRA	17
4. Cesar Bettex	FRA	16
5. Hilaret	FRA	15
6. Edouard Geynet	FRA	13
7. Sidney Merlin	GBR	12
8. André de Schonen	FRA	12

1904 St. Louis not held

1906 Athens C: 12, N: 4, D: 4.26.
Single Shot

		PTS.
1. Gerald Merlin	GBR	24
2. Ioannis Peridis	GRE	24
3. Sidney Merlin	GBR	23
4. Maurice Faure	FRA	22
5. Thanopoulos	GRE	16

		PTS.
6. I. Delpopoulos	GRE	14
7. Sándor Török	HUN	12
8. D. P. Petropoulos	GRE	7

Merlin defeated Peridis on the fourth shot of a sudden-death shoot-out.

1906 Athens C: 10, N: 4, D: 4.26.
Double Shot

		PTS.
1. Sidney Merlin	GBR	15
2. Anastasios Metaxas	GRE	13
3. Gerald Merlin	GBR	12
4. Ioannis Theophilakis	GRE	11
5. Maurice Faure	FRA	9
6. Jean Fouconnier	FRA	8
6. K. Tanopoulos	GRE	8
6. Sándor Török	HUN	8

Sidney and Gerald Merlin were cousins who were born in Greece and lived in Athens.

1908 London C: 61, N: 8, D: 8.11.

		PTS.
1. Walter Ewing	CAN	72
2. George Beattie	CAN	60
3. Alexander Maunder	GBR	57
3. Anastasios Metaxas	GRE	57
5. Charles Palmer	GBR	55
5. Arthur Westover	CAN	55
7. Mylie Fletcher	CAN	53
7. Richard Hutton	GBR/IRL	53
7. F. W. Moore	GBR	53
7. Willem Wilson	HOL	53

1912 Stockholm C: 61, N: 11, D: 7.2.

		PTS.
1. James Graham	USA	96
2. Alfred Göldel	GER	94
3. Harry Blau	RUS	91
4. Harold Humby	GBR	88
4. Anastasios Metaxas	GRE	88
4. Albert Preuss	GER	88
4. Gustaf Adolf Schnitt	FIN	88
4. Freiherr von Zeidlitz und Leipe	GER	88

1920 Antwerp-Beverloo C: 53, N: 9, D: 7.24.

		PTS.
1. Mark Arie	USA	95
2. Frank Troeh	USA	93
3. Frank Wright	USA	87
4. Frederick Plum	USA	87
5. Horace Bonser	USA	87
6. Robert Montgomery	CAN	86
7. Johannes Nordahl-Lunde	NOR	85
7. Henri Quevsin	BEL	85

1924 Paris C: 44, N: 14, D: 7.8.

		PTS.	
1. Gyula Halasy	HUN	98/8	OR
2. Konrad Huber	FIN	98/7	OR

		PTS.
3. Frank Hughes	USA	97
4. James Montgomery	CAN	97
5. Louis d'Heur	BEL	96/8
6. George Beattie	CAN	96/7
6. Samuel Sharman	USA	96/7
6. Samuel Vance	CAN	96/7

1928–1948 not held

1952 Helsinki C: 40, N: 22, D: 7.26.

		PTS.
1. George Généreux	CAN	192
2. Knut Holmqvist	SWE	191
3. Hans Liljedahl	SWE	190
4. František Čapek	CZE	188
5. Konrad Huber	FIN	188
6. Ioannis Koutsis	GRE	187
7. Galliano Rossini	ITA	187
8. Italo Bellini	ITA	186

George Généreux, of Saskatoon, Saskatchewan, was only 17 years old when he won the Olympic championship. Holmqvist needed to score a perfect 25 on his last round to tie Généreux, but he missed his next to last shot.

1956 Melbourne C: 32, N: 18, D: 12.1.

		PTS.	
1. Galliano Rossini	ITA	195	OR
2. Adam Smelczyński	POL	190	
3. Alessandro Ciceri	ITA	188/24	
4. Nikolai Mogilevsky	SOV	188/23	
5. Yuri Nikandrov	SOV/UKR	188/22	
6. František Čapek	CZE	187	
7. Knut Holmqvist	SWE	178	
8. Hans Liljedahl	SWE	177	

1960 Rome C: 51, N: 28, D: 10.1.

		PTS.
1. Ion Dumitrescu	ROM	192
2. Galliano Rossini	ITA	191
3. Sergei Kalinin	SOV/RUS	190
4. James Clark	USA	188
5. Hans Aasnes	NOR	185
5. Joseph Wheater	GBR	185
7. Adam Smelczyński	POL	184
8. Claude Foussier	FRA	183
8. Karni Singh	IND	183

1964 Tokyo-Tokorozawa C: 51, N: 28, D: 10.17.

		PTS.	
1. Ennio Mattarelli	ITA	198	OR
2. Pavels Senitčevs	SOV/LAT	194/25	
3. William Morris	USA	194/24	
4. Galliano Rossini	ITA	194/23	
5. Ion Dumitrescu	ROM	193	
5. Mario Lira	CHI	193	
7. John Braithwaite	GBR	192	
8. Joachim Marscheider	GDR	191	

1968 Mexico City C: 59, N: 34, D: 10.19. WR: 198 (Ennio Mattarelli)

		PTS.	
1. John "Bob" Braithwaite	GBR	198	EWR
2. Thomas Garrigus	USA	196/25/25	
3. Kurt Czekalla	GDR	196/25/23	
4. Pavels Senitčevs	SOV/LAT	196/22	
5. Pierre Candelo	FRA	195	
6. Adam Smelczyński	POL	195	
7. Aleksandr Alipov	SOV/RUS	195	
8. John Primrose	CAN	194	

The 43-year-old Braithwaite missed two of his first 13 shots, but then hit the last 187 in a row. A veterinary surgeon from Preston, near Liverpool, Bob Braithwaite took up clay pigeon shooting because he could no longer stand to shoot real birds and animals and see them suffer.

1972 Munich C: 57, N: 33, D: 8.29. WR: 198 (Ennio Mattarelli, John Braithwaite, Silvano Basagni)

		PTS.	
1. Angelo Scalzone	ITA	199	WR
2. Michel Carrega	FRA	198	
3. Silvano Basagni	ITA	195	
4. Burckhardt Hoppe	GDR	193	
5. Johnny Påhlsson	SWE	193	
6. James Poindexter	USA	192	
7. John Primrose	CAN	192	
8. Marcos Olsen	BRA	191	

1976 Montreal C: 44, N: 29, D: 7.20. WR: 199 (Angelo Scalzone, Michel Carrega)

		PTS.
1. Donald Haldeman	USA	190
2. Armando da Silva Marques	POR	189
3. Ubaldesco Baldi	ITA	189
4. Burckhardt Hoppe	GDR	186
5. Aleksandr Androshkin	SOV/RUS	185
6. Adam Smelczyński	POL	183
7. John Primrose	CAN	183
8. Bernard Blondeau	FRA	182

The low scores were due to poor weather conditions. In a sport where contestants are known to calm their nerves with alcohol or tranquilizers, it came as a shock when 65-year-old Paul Cerutti of Monaco was disqualified after it was found that he had been taking amphetamines. The stimulants did him little good anyway. He finished 43rd out of a field of 44.

1980 Moscow C: 34, N: 22, D: 7.22. WR: 199 (Angelo Scalzone, Michel Carrega)

		PTS.
1. Luciano Giovannetti	ITA	198
2. Rustam Yambulatov	SOV/UZB	196/24/25
3. Jörg Damme	GDR	196/24/24
4. Josef Hojny	CZE	196/23
5. Eladio Vallduvi	SPA	195
6. Aleksandr Asanov	SOV/KAZ	195

7. Silvano Basagni	ITA	194
8. Burckhardt Hoppe	GDR	192

The 34-year-old Giovannetti celebrated his victory by tossing his cap into the air and shooting a hole through it.

1984 Los Angeles-Chino C: 70, N: 42, D: 7.31. WR: 200 (Daniel Carlisle)

		PTS.
1. Luciano Giovannetti	ITA	192/24
2. Francisco Boza	PER	192/23
3. Daniel Carlisle	USA	192/22
4. Timo Nieminen	FIN	191
5. Michel Carrega	FRA	190
6. Eli Ellis	AUS	190
7. Terry Rumbel	AUS	189
8. Johnny Pahlsson	SWE	189

Giovannetti, a gun-shop owner from Pistoia, finished strongly to become the first repeat winner in Olympic trap shooting. On May 22, 1990, bronze medalist Dan Carlisle broke an obscure world record by shooting down 3,172 clay targets in one hour.

1988 Seoul C: 49, N: 28, D: 9.20. WR: 224 (Miroslav Bednařík)

		PTS.
1. Dmytro Monakov	SOV/UKR	222/8
2. Miroslav Bednařík	CZE	222/7
3. Franz Peeters	BEL	219/16
4. Francisco Boza	PER	219/15
5. Bean van Limbeek	HOL	219/7
6. Kazumi Watanabe	JPN	216
7. Urmas Saaliste	SOV/EST	194
8. Arimatti Nummela	FIN	194

Monakov, the defending world champion, and Bednařík, the 1986 world champion, both completed the semifinals with a score of 197 and then shot perfect rounds in the final. This necessitated a sudden-death shoot-off. But first Monakov and Bednařík had to wait for the three-way shoot-off for third place. When their turn came, Monakov and Bednařík both hit their first seven shots, but the Czechoslovak missed his eighth bird, and when Monakov made his, the contest was over. Less than a year later, Bednařík was killed in a motorcycle accident. He was 24 years old.

1992 Barcelona-Mollet del Vallès C: 54, N: 36, D: 8.2. WR: 224 (Jörg Damme)

		PTS.
1. Petr Hrdlička	CZE	219/1
2. Kazumi Watanabe	JPN	219/0
3. Marco Venturini	ITA	218/23/9
4. Jörg Damme	GER	218/23/8
5. Pavel Kubec	CZE	218/22
6. Jay Waldron	USA	217
7. José Bladas Torras	SPA	194/25
8. Zhang Bing	CHN	194/24

Hrdlička won the match when Watanabe missed the first shot of the shoot-out. The shoot-out for third place, on the other hand, wasn't decided until the ninth target.

DOUBLE TRAP

This event will be held for the first time in 1996.

SKEET

Skeet shooting is similar to trap shooting in that the shooter, using a .12-gauge shotgun, fires at a flung four-and-a-third-inch clay saucer. However, in the skeet match, the shooter moves around to eight different stations and is sometimes thrown two "birds" at a time. The birds may be thrown up to three seconds after they are called. Whereas trap birds are sent out from ground level, in skeet they are released from two towers, one high, one low. In 1968, 1972, 1980, and 1984, ties for medal positions were decided by shoot-offs while ties for other positions were decided by scores in the final round. In 1976 all ties were decided by the countback rule. Current rules use the score in the final as the tie-breaker.

1896–1964 not held

1968 Mexico City C: 52, N: 30, D: 10.22. WR: 198 (J. Faber, Konrad Wirnhier)

		PTS.	
1. Yevgeny Petrov	SOV/RUS	198/25	EWR
2. Romano Garagnani	ITA	198/24/25	EWR
3. Konrad Wirnhier	GER	198/24/23	EWR
4. Yuri Tsuranov	SOV/RUS	196	
5. Pedro Gianella	PER	194	
6. Nicolas Atalah	CHI	194	
7. Jorge Jottar	CHI	194	
8. Panagiotis Xanthakos	GRE	194	

1972 Munich C: 63, N: 37, D: 9.2. WR: 200 (Yevgeny Petrov, Yuri Tsuranov)

		PTS.
1. Konrad Wirnhier	GER	195/25
2. Yevgeny Petrov	SOV/RUS	195/24
3. Michael Buchheim	GDR	195/23
4. Joseph Neville	GBR	194
5. Roberto Castrillo Garcia	CUB	194
6. Klaus Reschke	GDR	193
7. Elie Penot	FRA	193
8. Paschalis Georgiou	GRE	192

World champion Yuri Tsuranov of the U.S.S.R. was so upset by a judge's call against him that he walked off the field. The jury decided to penalize him three birds for leaving, but permitted him to continue the round. He ended up three points shy of a tie for first place and finished ninth instead.

1976 Montreal C: 68, N: 41, D: 7.24. WR: 200 (Yevgeny Petrov, Yuri Tsuranov, Jariel Zhgentii, Hans Kjeld Rasmussen, Wieslaw Gawlikowski)

		PTS.	
1. Josef Panaček	CZE	198	EOR
2. Eric Swinkels	HOL	198	EOR
3. Wieslaw Gawlikowski	POL	196	
4. Klaus Reschke	GDR	196	
5. Franz Schitzhofer	AUT	195	
6. Edgardo Zachrisson	GUA	194	
7. Juan Avalos	SPA	194	
8. Jean Petitpied	FRA	194	

1980 Moscow C: 46, N: 25, D: 7.26. WR: 199 (Joseph Clemmons)

		PTS.
1. Hans Kjeld Rasmussen	DEN	196/25/25
2. Lars-Göran Carlsson	SWE	196/25/24
3. Roberto Castrillo Garcia	CUB	196/25/23
4. Pavel Pulda	CZE	196/24
5. Celso Giardini	ITA	196/24
6. Guillermo Torres	CUB	195
7. Francisco Perez	SPA	195
8. Ari Westergard	FIN	195

Because too many perfect scores had been achieved, the rules were changed to make the match speedier and more difficult.

1984 Los Angeles-Chino C: 69, N: 41, D: 8.4. WR: 200 (Matthew Dryke, Jan Hula)

		PTS.	
1. Matthew Dryke	USA	198	EOR
2. Ole Riber Rasmussen	DEN	196/25	
3. Luca Scribani Rossi	ITA	196/23	
4. Johannes Pierik	HOL	194	
5. Anders Berglind	SWE	194	
6. Norbert Hofmann	GER	194	
7. Jorge Molina	COL	194	
8. Ian Hale	AUS	193	

As a teenager, Matt Dryke performed as a trick shooter, shooting through washers and shooting speed skeet while riding a unicycle. Although he never gave up trick and fancy shooting, he also became involved in competitive shooting, entering the Olympics as the world record holder and prohibitive favorite. Spurred on by an enthusiastic crowd which unnerved other competitors, Dryke did not disappoint his supporters. In 1989 Dryke received a two-year suspension when he tested positive for cocaine.

1988 Seoul C: 52, N: 31, D: 9.24. WR: 224 (Matthew Dryke, Luca Scribani Rossi, Ole Riber Rasmussen)

		PTS.
1. Axel Wegner	GDR	222
2. Alfonso de Iruarrizaga	CHI	221
3. Jorge Guardiola Hay	SPA	220/24
4. Daniel Carlisle	USA	220/23
5. Zhang Weigang	CHN	219
6. Jürgen Raabe	GDR	219

7. Luca Scribani Rossi   ITA   196
8. Firmo Emilio Roberti   ARG   196

Guardiola was awarded the bronze medal by virtue of his higher score over Carlisle in the final.

1992 Barcelona-Mollet del Vallès C: 60, N: 38, D: 7.28. WR: 225 (Hennie Dompeling, Axel Wegner)

			PTS.
1.	Zhang Shan	CHN	223
2.	Juan Giha Yarur	PER	222/24/3
3.	Bruno Rossetti	ITA	222/24/2/10
4.	Ioan Toman	ROM	222/24/2/9
5.	José Mariá Colorado González	SPA	222/23
6.	Matthew Dryke	USA	221
7.	Luca Scribani Rossi	ITA	197/24
8.	Erik Swinkels	HOL	197/23

Zhang Shan, a 24-year-old from Nanchong, in Sichuan province, caused a sensation when she became the first female shooter to win a mixed competition at the Olympics. Unfortunately, the International Shooting Union had already decided to bar women from future skeet competitions, so Zhang will not be allowed to defend her title in Atlanta.

Discontinued Events

RAPID-FIRE PISTOL TEAMS

1920 Antwerp-Beverloo T: 9, N: 9, D: 8.3.
(30 Meters)

			TOTAL PTS.
1.	USA	(Louis Harant, Alfred Lane, Karl Frederick, James Snook, Michael Kelly)	1310
2.	GRE	(Alexandros Theophilakis, Ioannis Theophilakis, Georgios Moraitinis, Alexandros Vrasivanopoulos, Iason Sappas)	1285
3.	SWI	(Fritz Zulauf, Joseph Jehle, Gustave Amoudruz, Hans Egli, Domenico Giambonini)	1270
4.	BRA	(Guilherme Paraense, Afrânio da Costa, Sebastião Wolf, Dario Barbosa, Fernando Soledade)	1261
5.	FRA	(Joseph Pecchia, Maujean, Léon Johnson, Emile Boitout, André Regaud)	1239
6.	SPA	(José Bento López, Luis Calvet Sandoz, Antônio Bonilla Sanmartin, Antônio Vasquez de Aldana, José Maria Miró Trepat)	1224
7.	BEL	(Paul van Asbroek, Norbert van Molle, Philippe Cammaerts, Robert Andrieux, Bastin, de Coster)	1221
8.	POR	(Herminio Rebelo, Antônio Dos Santos, Antônio Soares Ferreira Damiao, Antônio da Silva Martins, Dario Cannas)	1184

FREE PISTOL TEAMS

1920 Antwerp-Beverloo T: 13, N: 13, D: 8.2.
(50 Meters)

			TOTAL PTS.
1.	USA	(Karl Frederick, Alfred Lane, James Snook, Michael Kelly, Raymond Bracken)	2372
2.	SWE	(Anders Andersson, Casimir Reuterskiöld, Gunnar Gabrielsson, Sigvard Hultcrantz, Anders Johnson)	2289
3.	BRA	(Afrânio da Costa, Guilherme Paraense, Sebastião Wolf, Dario Barbosa, Fernando Soledade)	2264
4.	GRE	(Iason Sappas, Ioannis Theophilakis, Alexandros Theophilakis, Georgios Moraitinis, Alexandros Vrasivanopoulos)	2240
5.	BEL	(Paul van Asbroek, Conrad Adriansens, Arthur Balbaert, Joseph Haesaerts, François Heyens)	2229
6.	FRA	(Joseph Pecchia, Maujean, Léon Johnson, Emile Boitout, André Regaud)	2225
7.	ITA	(Riccardo Ticchi, Alfredo Galli, Roberto Preda, Giancarlo Boriani, Raffaele Frasca)	2224
8.	DEN	(Niels Larsen, Lars Jörgen Madsen, Otto Plantener, Carl Pedersen, Jens Andersen)	2159

Dr. James H. Snook of the gold-medal-winning U.S. team gained national notoriety in June of 1929 after he was arrested for first-degree murder. Snook, then a 48-year-old professor of veterinary medicine at Ohio State University, confessed to killing his 25-year-old mistress, Theora Hix, by beating her with a hammer following an overly violent sexual act that took place in a car parked at the local rifle range. He was put to death in an electric chair eight months later.

MILITARY REVOLVER

1896 Athens C: 16, N: 3, D: 4.10.
(25 Meters)

			PTS.
1.	John Paine	USA	442
2.	Sumner Paine	USA	380
3.	Nikolaos Dorakis	GRE	205
4.	Ioannis Phrangoudis	GRE	—
5.	Holger Nielsen	DEN	—

The Paine brothers set a precedent for family involvement in the Olympics by taking first and second.

1900–1904 not held

1906 Athens C: 31, N: 9, D: 4.24.
(20 Meters)

			PTS.
1.	Louis Richardet	SWI	253
2.	Alexandros Theophilakis	GRE	250
3.	Georgios Skotadis	GRE	240
4.	Konrad Stäheli	SWI	240
5.	Léon Moreaux	FRA	239

6. Ludwig Ternajgo	AUT	235	
7. M. Triantaphilades	GRE	235	
8. Anastasios Metaxas	GRE	233	

1906 Athens C: 31, N: 9, D: 4.23.
(20 Meters—Model 1873–74)

			PTS.
1. Jean Fouconnier	FRA	219	
2. Raoul de Boigne	FRA	216	
3. Hermann Martin	FRA	215	
4. Maurice Lecoq	FRA	211	
5. Ludwig Ternajgo	AUT	208	
6. Aristides Rangavis	GRE	201	
7. Louis Richardet	SWI	199	
8. A. Hronis	GRE	198	

This contest required the use of a Gras-type revolver first made in France in 1873.

MILITARY REVOLVER TEAMS

1900 Paris T: 4, N: 4, D: 8.1.
(50 Meters)

			TOTAL PTS.
1. SWI	(Conrad Karl Röderer, Konrad Stäheli, Louis Richardet, Friedrich Lüthi, Paul Probst)		2271
2. FRA	(Achille Paroche, Louis Duffoy, Léon Moreaux, Trinité, Maurice Lecoq)		2203
3. HOL	(Gerardus van Haan, Henrik Sillem, Antonius Bouwens, Solko van den Bergh, Anthony Sweus)		1876
4. BEL	(Rooman, Théves, Victor Robert, Eichorn, Lebègue)		1823

1904–1906 not held

1908 London T: 7, N: 7, D: 7.11.
(50 Yards)

			TOTAL PTS.
1. USA	(James Gorman, Ira Calkins, John Dietz, Charles Axtell)		1914
2. BEL	(Paul van Asbroek, Réginald Storms, Charles Paumier du Verger, René Englebert)		1863
3. GBR	(Jesse Wallingford, Geoffrey Coles, Henry Lynch-Staunton, Walter Ellicot)		1817
4. FRA	(André Barbillat, André Regaud, Léon Moreaux, Jean Depassis)		1750
5. SWE	(Wilhelm Carlberg, Eric Carlberg, Johan Hübner von Holst, Frans Albert Schartau)		1732
6. HOL	(Jacob van der Kop, Gerard van den Bergh, Jan Johannes de Blécourt, Petrus ten Bruggencate)		1632
7. GRE	(Frangiskos Mavromatis, Alexandros Theophilakis, Ioannis Theophilakis, Georgios Orphanidis)		1576

1912 Stockholm T: 7, N: 7, D: 6.29.
(30 Meters)

			TOTAL PTS.
1. SWE	(Wilhelm Carlberg, Eric Carlberg, Johan Hübner von Holst, Paul Palén)		1145
2. RUS	(Amos de Kasch, Nikolai de Melnitsky, Pavel de Voyloshnikov, Georgi de Panteleymonov)		1091/118
3. GBR	(Hugh Durant, Albert Kempster, Charles Stewart, Horatio Poulter)		1107/117
4. USA	(Alfred Lane, Reginald Sayre, Walter Winans, John Dietz)		1097/117
5. GRE	(Konstantinos Skarlatos, Ioannis Theophilakis, Frangiskos Mavromatis, Georgios Petropoulos)		1057
6. FRA	(Edmond Sandoz, Charles de Jaubert, Georges de Crequi-Montfort de Courtivron, Maurice Faure)		1041
7. GER	(Bernhard Wandollek, Gerhard Bock, Georg Meyer, Heinrich Hoffmann)		890

1912 Stockholm T: 5, N: 5, D: 7.2.
(50 Meters)

			TOTAL PTS.
1. USA	(Alfred Lane, Henry Sears, Peter Dolfen, John Dietz)		1916
2. SWE	(Georg de Laval, Eric Carlberg, Wilhelm Carlberg, Erik Boström)		1849
3. GBR	(Horatio Poulter, Hugh Durant, Albert Kempster, Charles Stewart)		1804
4. RUS	(Nikolai Panin [Kolomenkin], Grigory de Schesterikov, Pavel de Voyloshnikov, Nikolai de Melnitsky)		1801
5. GRE	(Frangiskos Mavromatis, Ioannis Theophilakis, Konstantinos Skarlatos, Alexandros Theophilakis)		1731

DUELING PISTOL

1906 Athens C: 24, N: 7, D: 4.24.
(20 Meters)

		PTS.
1. Léon Moreaux	FRA	242
2. Cesare Liverziani	ITA	233
3. Maurice Lecoq	FRA	231
4. Konstantinos Skarlatos	GRE	221
5. Ludwig Ternajgo	AUT	218
6. Frangiskos Mavromatis	GRE	214

The participants in the two dueling pistol events of 1906 shot at dummies dressed in frock coats.

1906 Athens C: 22, N: 7, D: 4.25.
(25 Meters)

		BULL'S-EYE/PTS.
1. Konstantinos Skarlatos	GRE	29/133
2. Johann Hubner von Holst	SWE	27/115
3. Wilhelm Carlberg	SWE	26/115

4. Gerald Merlin	GBR	26/103
5. Sándor Török	HUN	25/104
6. Léon Moreaux	FRA	23/104
7. Sidney Merlin	GBR	23/103
7. Ludwig Ternajgo	AUT	23/103

FREE RIFLE

1896 Athens C: 42, N: 7, D: 4.9.
(200 Meters)

		PTS.
1. Pantelis Karasevdas	GRE	2320
2. Paulos Pavlidis	GRE	1978
3. Nikolaos Trikoupes	GRE	1713
4. Anastasios Metaxas	GRE	1701
5. Georgios Orphanidis	GRE	1698
6. Viggo Jensen	DEN	1640
7. Georgios Diamantis	GRE	1456
8. A. Baumann	SWI	1294

1900–1904 not held

1906 Athens C: 25, N: 5, D: 4.28.
(300 Meters, Any Position)

		PTS.
1. Marcel Meyer de Stadelhofen	SWI	243
2. Konrad Stäheli	SWI	238
3. Léon Moreaux	FRA	234
4. Gudbrand Skatteboe	NOR	230
5. Albert Helgerud	NOR	230
6. Julius Braathe	NOR	224
7. Raoul de Boigne	FRA	224
8. Jean Fouconnier	FRA	223

1908 London C: 49, N: 8, D: 7.11.
(1000 Yards)

		PTS.
1. Joshua "Jerry" Millner	GBR/IRL	98
2. Kellogg Kennon Casey	USA	93
3. Maurice Blood	GBR	92
4. Richard Barnett	GBR	92
5. Thomas "Ted" Ranken	GBR	92
6. Thomas Caldwell	GBR	91
7. John Sellars	GBR	91
8. S. Harry Kerr	CAN	91

The target for this long-range event was six feet by ten feet, with a 36-inch bull's-eye. Colonel Millner was 58 or 59 years old.

FREE RIFLE, THREE POSITIONS

This event required 120 shots from 300 meters at a 39-inch target with a bull's-eye less than four inches in diameter. In other words, it was like shooting a bullet through an apple three football fields away.

1896 Athens C: 20, N: 3, D: 4.12.

		TOTAL PTS.
1. Georgios Orphanidis	GRE	1583
2. Ioannis Phrangoudis	GRE	1312
3. Viggo Jensen	DEN	1305
4. Anastasios Metaxas	GRE	1102
5. Pantelis Karasevdas	GRE	1039

1900–1904 not held

1906 Athens C: 20, N: 4, D: 4.28. WR: 1004 (Charles Paumier de Verger)

		PRONE	KNEELING	STANDING	TOTAL PTS.
1. Gudbrand Skatteboe	NOR	339	310	324	973
2. Konrad Stäheli	SWI	328	340	278	946
3. Jean Reich	SWI	327	320	289	936
4. Louis Richardet	SWI	332	338	265	935
5. Léon Moreaux	FRA	322	317	293	932
6. Marcel Meyer de Stadelhofen	SWI	306	324	296	926
7. Julius Braathe	NOR	319	292	310	921
8. Maurice Lecoq	FRA	309	305	300	914

1908 London C: 51, N: 10, D: 7.11. WR: 1004 (Charles Paumier de Verger)

		PRONE	KNEELING	STANDING	TOTAL PTS.
1. Albert Helgerud	NOR	340	292	277	909
2. Harry Simon	USA	365	294	228	887
3. Ole Saether	NOR	327	284	272	883
4. Gustav Adolf Sjöberg	SWE	338	285	251	874
5. Janne Gustafsson	SWE	324	283	265	872
6. Julius Braathe	NOR	303	291	257	851
7. Axel Jansson	SWE	312	296	235	843
8. Léon Johnson	FRA	303	282	250	835

1912 Stockholm C: 84, N: 9, D: 7.2. WR: 1078 (Konrad Stäheli)

		PRONE	KNEELING	STANDING	TOTAL PTS.
1. Paul Colas	FRA	362	342	283	987
2. Lars Jörgen Madsen	DEN	330	333	318	981
3. Niels Larsen	DEN	355	334	318	962
4. Carl Hugo Johansson	SWE	341	326	292	959
5. Gudbrand Skatteboe	NOR	343	308	305	956
6. Bernhard Larsson	SWE	341	339	274	954
7. Albert Helgerud	NOR	354	317	281	952
8. Tonnes Björkman	SWE	340	322	285	947

1920 Antwerp-Beverloo C: 70, N: 14, D: 7.31. WR: 1078 (Konrad Stäheli)

		PRONE	KNEELING	STANDING	TOTAL PTS.
1. Morris Fisher	USA	347	361	288	996
2. Niels Larsen	DEN	328	341	320	989
3. Östen Östensen	NOR	347	324	309	980
4. Carl Osburn	USA	353	347	280	980
5. Gudbrand Skatteboe	NOR	351	330	294	975
5. Lloyd Spooner	USA	341	328	306	975
7. Mauritz Eriksson	SWE	349	333	294	974
7. Voitto Kolho	FIN	357	316	301	974

Sergeant Morris Fisher, who played the violin for relaxation, found himself too nervous to take the first shot in the standing position. After 20 minutes of standing at the firing line, aiming but not taking a shot, his coach ordered him to shoot even if he missed the target. Fisher shot wide but within the scoring rings, and then went on to win the match.

1924 Paris C: 73, N: 19, D: 6.27.
(600 Meters)

		PTS.
1. Morris Fisher	USA	95
2. Carl Osburn	USA	95
3. Niels Larsen	DEN	93
4. Walter Stokes	USA	92
5. Ludovic Augustin	HAI	91
6. Albert Courquin	FRA	90
6. Ludovic Valborge	HAI	90
8. Carl Hugo Johansson	SWE	88

Fisher earned two gold medals in 1924 to go with the three he had won in 1920.

1928–1936 not held

1948 London C: 46, N: 13, D: 8.6. WR: 1124 (E. Kivistik)

		PRONE	KNEELING	STANDING	TOTAL PTS.
1. Emil Grünig	SWI	390	375	355	1120
2. Pauli Janhonen	FIN	387	376	351	1114
3. Willy Rögeberg	NOR	382	373	357	1112
4. Kurt Johansson	SWE	383	374	347	1104
5. Kullervo Leskinen	FIN	389	368	346	1103
6. Olavi Elo	FIN	379	359	357	1095
7. Halvor Kongsjorden	NOR	384	373	336	1093
8. Holger Erbén	SWE	380	367	344	1091

1952 Helsinki C: 32, N: 18, D: 7.27. WR: 1124 (E. Kivistik)

		PRONE	KNEELING		STANDING	TOTAL PTS.	
1. Anatoly Bogdanov	SOV/RUS	388	376		359	1123	OR
2. Robert Bürchler	SWI	389	381	WR	350	1120	
3. Lev Vainshtein	SOV/RUS	378	376		355	1109	
4. August Hollenstein	SWI	384	370		354	1108	
5. Vilho Ylönen	FIN	379	377		351	1107	
6. Robert Sandager	USA	384	371		349	1104	
7. Holger Erbén	SWE	347	376		379	1102	
8. Walther Fröstell	SWE	335	375		389	1099	

1956 Melbourne C: 20, N: 14, D: 12.1. WR: 1143 (Anatoly Bogdanov)

		PRONE		KNEELING	STANDING	TOTAL PTS	
1. Vassily Borissov	SOV/RUS	396	WR	383	359	1138	OR
2. Allan Erdman	SOV/RUS	392		385	360	1137	
3. Vilho Ylönen	FIN	387		382	359	1128	
4. Jorma Taitto	FIN	392		379	349	1120	
5. Constantin Antonescu	ROM	386		374	341	1101	
6. Nils Johan Sundberg	SWE	384		367	343	1094	
7. Anders Kvissberg	SWE	389		362	342	1093	
8. James Smith	USA	381		368	333	1082	

1960 Rome C: 39, N: 22, D: 9.5. WR: 1145 (Anatoly Bogdanov)

		PRONE	KNEELING	STANDING	TOTAL PTS.
1. Hubert Hammerer	AUT	390	379	360	1129
2. Hans Spillman	SWI	397	377	353	1127
3. Vassily Borissov	SOV/RUS	383	381	363	1127
4. Vilho Ylönen	FIN	389	381	356	1126
5. Moissey Itkis	SOV/UKR	380	379	365	1124
6. Vladimir Stiborik	CZE	383	380	360	1123
7. John Foster	USA	380	384	357	1121
8. Sandor Krebs	HUN	386	373	359	1118

1964 Tokyo C: 30, N: 18, D: 10.15. WR: 1150 (August Hollenstein)

		PRONE	KNEELING	STANDING	TOTAL PTS.	
1. Gary Anderson	USA	382	384	377	1153	WR
2. Shota Kveliashvili	SOV/GEO	389	389	366	1144	
3. Martin Gunnarsson	USA	389	380	367	1136	
4. Aleksandr Gerasimenok	SOV/LAT	396	376	363	1135	
5. August Hollenstein	SWI	382	381	372	1135	
6. Esa Kervinen	FIN	392	383	358	1133	
7. Kurt Müller	SWI	392	385	354	1121	
8. Harry Köcher	GDR	392	378	360	1130	

Gary Anderson was a theological student from Axtell, Nebraska.

1968 Mexico City C: 30, N: 16, D: 10.23. WR: 1156 (Gary Anderson)

		PRONE		KNEELING	STANDING	TOTAL PTS.	
1. Gary Anderson	USA	394		389	374	1157	WR
2. Vladimir Kornev	SOV/RUS	398	WR	384	369	1151	
3. Kurt Müller	SWI	395		379	374	1148	
4. Shota Kveliashvili	SOV/GEO	394		383	365	1142	

5. Erwin Vogt	SWI	398 WR	384	358	1140
6. Hartmut Sommer	GER	389	384	358	1140
7. John Foster	USA	386	386	368	1140
8. Péter Sándor	HUN	394	376	368	1138

Anderson, by now a 29-year-old army lieutenant and Presbyterian minister, told reporters that he intended to keep up his involvement in shooting "because I think it's important for a minister to be actively involved in what people are doing." He later became executive director of the National Rifle Association.

1972 Munich C: 33, N: 20, D: 9.2. WR: 1157 (Gary Anderson)

		PRONE	KNEELING	STANDING	TOTAL PTS.
1. Lones Wigger	USA	394	382	379 WR	1155
2. Borys Melnyk	SOV/UKR	394	387	374	1155
3. Lajos Papp	HUN	394	391	364	1149
4. Uto Wunderlich	GDR	393	388	368	1149
5. Karel Bulan	CZE	394	382	370	1146
6. Jaakko Minkkinen	FIN	396	386	364	1146
7. Lanny Bassham	USA	389	387	368	1144
8. Valentin Kornev	SOV/RUS	391	387	365	1143

FREE RIFLE TEAMS

1906 Athens T: 4, N: 4, D: 4.28.
(300 Meters)

			TOTAL PTS.
1. SWI	(Konrad Stäheli, Jean Reich, Louis Richardet, Marcel Meyer de Stadelhofen, Alfred Grutter)		4617
2. NOR	(Gudbrand Skattebøe, Albert Helgerud, Julius Braathe, Johann Möller, O. Holm)		4534
3. FRA	(Jean Fouconnier, Léon Moreaux, Maurice Faure, Raoul de Boigne, Maurice Lecoq)		4511

1908 London T: 9, N: 9, D: 7.11.
(300 Meters)

			TOTAL PTS.
1. NOR	(Albert Helgerud, Ole Saether, Gudbrand Skattebøe, Olaf Saether, Einar Liberg, Julius Braathe)		5055
2. SWE	(G. Adolf Jonsson, Per-Olof Árvidsson, Axel Jansson, Gustav Adolf Sjöberg, Claes Rundberg, Janne Gustafsson)		4711
3. FRA	(Léon Johnson, Eugène Balme, André Parmentier, Albert Courquin, Maurice Lecoq, Raoul de Boigne)		4652
4. DEN	(Niels Andersen, Lars Jörgen Madsen, Ole Olsen, Kristian Christensen, Christian Petersen, Hans Kristian Schultz)		4543
5. BEL	(Charles Paumier du Verger, Paul van Asbroek, Ernest Ista, Henri Sauveur, Joseph Geens, Edouard Poty)		4509
6. GBR	(Jesse Wallingford, Harold Hawkins, Charles Churcher, Thomas Raddall, John Bostock, Robert Brown)		4355
7. HOL	(Gerard van den Bergh, Cornelis Brosch, Cornelis van Altenburg, Willem de Gee, Uilke Vuurman, Pieter Brussaard)		4130
8. FIN	(Frans Nassling, Gustaf Nyman, Heikki Huttunen, Voitto Kolko, Emil Nassling, Huvi Tuiskunen)		3962

1912 Stockholm T: 7, N: 7, D: 7.4.
(300 Meters)

			TOTAL PTS.
1. SWE	(Mauritz Eriksson, Carl Hugo Johansson, Erik Blomqvist, Carl Björkman, Bernhard Larsson, G. Adolf Jonsson)		5655
2. NOR	(Gudbrand Skattebøe, Ole Saether, Östen Östensen, Albert Helgerud, Olaf Saether, Einar Liberg)		5605
3. DEN	(Ole Olsen, Lars Jörgen Madsen, Niels Larsen, Lauritz Larsen, Niels Andersen, Jens Madsen Haislund)		5529
4. FRA	(Paul Colas, Louis Percy, Léon Johnson, Pierre Gentil, Raoul de Boigne, Auguste Marion)		5471
5. FIN	(Voitto Kolho, Heikki Huttunen, Gustaf Richard Nyman, Emil Holm, Huvi Tuiskunen, Vilho Vauhkonen)		5323
6. SAF	(George Harvey, Robert Bodley, Robert Patterson, Andrew Smith, Ernest Keeley, George Whelan)		4897

7. RUS   Paul de Waldaine, Theothan de Lebedoff,   4892
          Alexander de Tillo, Constantin de Kalinine,
          Dimitri de Kouskoff, Paul de Lesche)

1920 Antwerp-Beverloo T: 14, N: 14, D: 7.31.
(300 Meters)

		TOTAL PTS.
1. USA	(Morris Fisher, Carl Osburn, Lloyd Spooner, Willis Lee, Dennis Fenton)	4876
2. NOR	(Östen Östensen, Gudbrand Skatteboe, Albert Helgerud, Olaf Sletten, Otto Olsen)	4748
3. SWI	(Fritz Kuchen, Gustave Amoudruz, Schneeberger, Fahrner, Siegenthaler)	4698
4. FIN	(Voitto Kolho, Vilho Vauhkonen, Kalle Lappalainen, Veli Nieminen, Magnus Wegelius)	4668
5. DEN	(Niels Larsen, Lars Jörgen Madsen, Peter Petersen, Niels Laursen, Anton Andersen)	4644
6. SWE	(Mauritz Eriksson, Carl Hugo Johansson, Erik Blomqvist, Viktor Knutsson, Leon Lagerlöf)	4591
7. FRA	(Achille Paroche, Georges Roes, André Parmentier, Paul Colas, Albert Regnier)	4487
8. HOL	(Gerard van den Bergh, Antonius Bouwens, Pieter Brussaard, Herman Bouwens, Cornelis van Dalen)	4383

1924 Paris T: 18, N: 18, D: 6.27.
(400 + 600 + 800 Meters)

		TOTAL PTS.
1. USA	(Morris Fisher, Walter Stokes, Joseph Crockett, Raymond "Chan" Coulter, Sidney Hinds)	676
2. FRA	(Emile Rumeau, Albert Courquin, Pierre Hardy, Georges Roes, Paul Colas)	646
3. HAI	(Ludovic Augustin, Astrel Rolland, Ludovic Valborge, Destin Destine, Eloi Metullus)	646
4. SWI	(Jakob Reich, Arnold Rösli, Willy Schnyder, C. Stucheli, Albert Tröndle)	635
5. FIN	(Aarne Valkama, Vilho Nieminen, Voitto Kolho, Heikki Huttunen, Johannes Theslöf)	628
6. DEN	(Niels Larsen, Lars Jörgen Madsen, Anders Nielsen, Erik Saetter-Lassen, Peter Geltzer)	626
7. SWE	(Carl Hugo Johansson, Ivar Wester, Mauritz Eriksson, Olle Ericsson, Gustaf Anderson)	623
8. NOR	(Ludvig Larsen, Olaf Johansson, Willy Rogeberg, Halvard Angaard, Otto Olsen)	594

France defeated Haiti in the shoot-off for second place. Lieutenant Sidney Hinds shot a perfect 50 for the U.S. team, a performance that was all the more remarkable considering that he was accidentally shot in the foot in the middle of the competition, when the Belgian rifleman beside him knocked his rifle to the ground in the midst of an argument with an official.

MILITARY RIFLE

1900 Paris C: 30, N: 6, D: 8.5.
(300 Meters, Three Positions)

		PRONE	KNEELING	STANDING	TOTAL PTS.
1. Emil Kellenberger	SWI	324	314	292	930
2. Anders Peter Nielsen	DEN	330	314	277	921
3. Paul van Asbroek	BEL	329	289	299	917
3. Ole Östmo	NOR	312	308	297	917
5. Lars Jörgen Madsen	DEN	301	299	305	905
6. Charles Paumier du Verger	BEL	302	297	298	897
7. Achille Paroche	FRA	332	287	268	887
8. Franz Böckli	SWI	289	300	294	883

(300 Meters, Standing)

		PTS.
1. Lars Jörgen Madsen	DEN	305
2. Ole Östmo	NOR	299
3. Charles Paumier du Verger	BEL	298
4. Paul van Asbroek	BEL	297
5. Franz Böckli	SWI	294
6. Emil Kellenberger	SWI	292
7. Jules Bury	BEL	282
7. Alfred Grütter	SWI	282

(300 Meters, Kneeling)

		PTS.
1. Konrad Stäheli	SWI	324
2. Emil Kellenberger	SWI	314
2. Anders Peter Nielsen	DEN	314
4. Paul van Asbroek	BEL	308
5. Maximiliaan Ravenswaaij	HOL	306
6. Uilke Vuurman	HOL	303
7. Franz Böckli	SWI	300
8. Lars Jörgen Madsen	DEN	299

(300 Meters, Prone)

			PTS.
1.	Achille Paroche	FRA	332
2.	Anders Peter Nielsen	DEN	330
3.	Ole Östmo	NOR	329
4.	Léon Moreaux	FRA	325
5.	Emil Kellenberger	SWI	324
6.	Henrik Sillem	HOL	317
7.	Auguste Cavadini	FRA	316
8.	Paul van Asbroek	BEL	312
8.	Uilke Vuurman	HOL	312

1904 not held

1906 Athens C: 31, N: 8, D: 4.24.
(200 Meters, Standing or Kneeling)

			PTS.
1.	Léon Moreaux	FRA	187
2.	Louis Richardet	SWI	187
3.	Jean Reich	SWI	183
4.	Johann Möller	NOR	175
5.	Maurice Faure	FRA	173
6.	Gerald Merlin	GBR	169
7.	Sidney Merlin	GBR	166
8.	Georgios Orphanidis	GRE	165

1906 Athens C: 46, N: 11, D: 4.23.
(300 Meters, Standing or Kneeling)

			PTS.
1.	Louis Richardet	SWI	238
2.	Jean Reich	SWI	234
3.	Raoul de Boigne	FRA	232
4.	Léon Moreaux	FRA	231
5.	Maurice Lecoq	FRA	224
6.	Julius Braathe	NOR	223
7.	Marcel Meyer de Stadelhofen	SWI	222
8.	Gudbrand Skatteboe	NOR	221

1908 not held

1912 Stockholm C: 91, N: 12, D: 7.1.
(300 Meters)

			PTS.
1.	Sándor Prokopp	HUN	97
2.	Carl Osburn	USA	95
3.	Embret Skogen	NOR	95
4.	Nicolaos Levidis	GRE	95
5.	Nils Romander	SWE	94
6.	Arthur Fulton	GBR	92
7.	Rezsö Velez	HUN	92
8.	Carl Flodström	SWE	91

1912 Stockholm C: 85, N: 12, D: 7.1.
(600 Meters, Any Position)

			PTS.
1.	Paul Colas	FRA	94
2.	Carl Osburn	USA	94
3.	John Jackson	USA	93
4.	Allan Briggs	USA	93

5.	Phillip Plater	GBR	90
6.	Verner Jernström	SWE	88
7.	Harcourt Ommundsen	GBR	88
8.	Charles Burdette	USA	87

1920 Antwerp-Beverloo T: 49, N: 12, D: 7.29–30.
(300 Meters, Prone)

			PTS.
1.	Otto Olsen	NOR	60
2.	Léon Johnson	FRA	59/58
3.	Fritz Kuchen	SWI	59/57
4.	Vilho Vauhkonen	FIN	59/56
5.	Achille Paroche	FRA	59/56
6.	Erik Blomqvist	SWE	58
6.	Mauritz Eriksson	SWE	58
6.	Albert Helgerud	NOR	58
6.	Carl Hugo Johansson	SWE	58
6.	Olaf Sletten	NOR	58
6.	Lloyd Spooner	USA	58

1920 Antwerp-Beverloo C: 48, N: 12, D: 7.29–30.
(300 Meters, Standing)

			PTS.
1.	Carl Osburn	USA	56
2.	Lars Jörgen Madsen	DEN	55
3.	Lawrence Nuesslein	USA	54/56
4.	Erik Saetter-Lassen	DEN	54/52
5.	Joseph Janssens	BEL	54/47
6.	Riccardo Ticchi	ITA	54/44
7.	Anders Peter Nielsen	DEN	53
7.	Anders Petersen	DEN	53
7.	Lloyd Spooner	USA	53

1920 Antwerp-Beverloo C: 46, N: 11, D: 7.29–30.
(600 Meters, Prone)

			PTS.
1.	Carl Hugo Johansson	SWE	59/58
2.	Mauritz Eriksson	SWE	59/56/6
3.	Lloyd Spooner	USA	59/56/5
4.	Ioannis Theophilakis	GRE	59/55
5.	Erik Blomqvist	SWE	58
5.	Joseph Jackson	USA	58
5.	Olaf Sletten	NOR	58
8.	Poul Gerlow	DEN	57
8.	Joseph Lawless	USA	57
8.	Erik Ohlsson	SWE	57

MILITARY RIFLE TEAMS

1900 Paris T: 6, N: 6, D: 8.5.
(300 Meters)

			TOTAL PTS.
1.	SWI	(Emil Kellenberger, Franz Böckli, Konrad Stäheli, Louis Richardet, Alfred Grütter)	4399
2.	NOR	(Ole Östmo, Hellmer Hermandsen, Tom Seeberg, Ole Saether, Olaf Frydenlund)	4290
3.	FRA	(Achille Paroche, Léon Moreaux, Auguste Cavadini, Maurice Lecoq, René Thomas)	4278

4.	DEN	(Anders Peter Nielsen, Lars Jörgen Madsen, Viggo Jensen, Laurids Worslund Jensen-Kjaer, Axel Kristensen)	4265
5.	HOL	(Maximiliaan Ravenswaaij, Uilke Vuurman, Henrik Sillem, Antonius Bouwens, Solko van den Bergh)	4221
6.	BEL	(Paul van Asbroek, Charles Paumier du Verger, Jules Bury, Edouard Myin, Joseph Baras)	4166

1904–1906 not held

1908 London T: 8, N: 8, D: 7.11.
(200 + 500 + 600 + 800 + 900 + 1000 Yards)

			TOTAL PTS.
1.	USA	(William Leushner, William Martin, Charles Winder, Kellogg Kennon Casey, Albert Eastman, Charles Benedict)	2531
2.	GBR	(Harcourt Ommundsen, Fleetwood Varley, Arthur Fulton, Philip Richardson, William Padgett, John Martin)	2497
3.	CAN	(William Smith, Charles Crowe, Bruce Williams, Dugald McInnis, William Eastcott, S. Harry Kerr)	2439
4.	FRA	(Raoul de Boigne, Albert Courquin, Eugène Balme, Daniel Merillon, Léon Hecht, André Parmentier)	2227
5.	SWE	(Claes Rundberg, Ossian Jörgensen, Janne Gustafsson, Per-Olof Arvidsson, Axel Jansson, Gustaf Adolf Jonsson)	2213
6.	NOR	(Ole Saether, Einar Liberg, Gudbrand Skatteboe, Albert Helgerud, Mathias Glomnes, Jörgen Bruu)	2192
7.	GRE	(Ioannis Theophilakis, Frangiskos Mavromatis, Alexandros Theophilakis, Georgios Orphanidis, Mathias Triantaphilades, Devkalion Rediadis)	1999
8.	DEN	(Niels Andersen, Kristian Christensen, Lauritz Jensen, Niels Larsen, J. H. Jensen, Ole Olsen)	1909

The Russians had sent word that they were going to enter a team, but when they finally arrived the competition was long over. It turned out that Russia was still operating on the Julian calendar, whereas the rest of the world was using the Gregorian calendar; the two calendars were 12 days apart.

1912 Stockholm T: 10, N: 10, D: 6.29.
(200 + 400 + 500 + 600 Meters)

			TOTAL PTS.
1.	USA	(Charles Burdette, Allan Briggs, Harry Adams, John Jackson, Carl Osburn, Warren Sprout)	1687
2.	GBR	(Harcourt Ommundsen, Henry Burr, Edward Skilton, James Reid, Edward Parnell, Arthur Fulton)	1602
3.	SWE	(Mauritz Eriksson, Verner Jernström, Carl Björkman, Tönnes Björkman, Bernhard Larsson, Carl Hugo Johansson)	1570

4.	SAF	(George Harvey, Robert Bodley, Andrew Smith, Ernest Keeley, Charles Jeffreys, Robert Patterson)	
5.	FRA	(Louis Percy, Paul Colas, Raoul de Boigne, Pierre Gentil, Léon Johnson, Maxime Lardin)	1515
6.	NOR	(Ole Christian Degnäs, Arne Sunde, Ole Jensen, Hans Nordvik, Olav Husby, Mathias Glomnes)	1473
7.	GRE	(Frangiskos Mavromatis, Alexandros Theophilakis, Ioannis Theophilakis, Nicolaos Levidis, Iakovos Theophilas, Spiridon Mostras)	1445
8.	DEN	(Niels Andersen, Lars Jörgen Madsen, Rasmus Friis, Hans Schultz, Niels Larsen, Jens Hajslund)	1419

1920 Antwerp-Beverloo T: 15, N: 15, D: 7.29.
(300 Meters, Standing)

			TOTAL PTS.
1.	DEN	(Erik Saetter-Lassen, Lars Jörgen Madsen, Anders Petersen, Anders Peter Nielsen, Niels Larsen)	266
2.	USA	(Carl Osburn, Lawrence Nuesslein, Lloyd Spooner, Willis Lee, Thomas Brown)	255
3.	SWE	(Olle Ericsson, Walfrid Hellman, Mauritz Eriksson, Carl Hugo Johansson, Leonard Lagerlöf)	255
4.	ITA	(Riccardo Ticchi, Camillo Isnardi, Luigi Favretti, Giancarlo Boriani, Sem De Ranieri)	251
5.	FRA	(Léon Johnson, Achille Paroche, Emile Rumeau, André Parmentier, Georges Roes)	249
6.	NOR	(Östen Östensen, Otto Olsen, Olaf Sletten, Albert Helgerud, Gudbrand Skatteboe)	242
7.	FIN	(Kalle Lapalainen, Vilho Vauhkonen, Karl Magnus Wegelius, Voitto Kolho, Nestor Toivonen)	235
8.	SWI	(Fritz Kuchen, Albert Tröndle, Arnold Rösli, Walter Lienhard, Caspar Widmer)	234

1920 Antwerp-Beverloo T: 15, N: 15, D: 7.29.
(300 Meters, Prone)

			TOTAL PTS.
1.	USA	(Carl Osburn, Lloyd Spooner, Morris Fisher, Willis Lee, Joseph Jackson)	289
2.	FRA	(Léon Johnson, Achille Paroche, Emile Rumeau, André Parmentier, Georges Roes)	283
3.	FIN	(Vilho Vauhkonen, Kalle Lappalainen, Heikki Veli Nieminen, Karl Magnus Wegelius, Voitto Kolho)	281
4.	SWI	(Fritz Kuchen, Albert Tröndle, Arnold Rösli, Walter Lienhard, Caspar Widmer)	281
5.	SWE	(Carl Hugo Johansson, Mauritz Eriksson, Erik Blomqvist, Thure Holmberg, Verner Jernström)	281
6.	NOR	(Östen Östensen, Otto Olsen, Olaf Stetten, Albert Helgerud, Jacob Onsrud)	280
7.	SPA	(José Bento López, Antônio Bonilla Sanmartin, Domingo Rodriguez Somoza, Luis Calvet Sandoz, Antônio Moreira Montero)	278
8.	SAF	(Robert Bodley, David Smith, George Paxton, Frederick Morgan, John Lishman)	276

1920 Antwerp-Beverloo T: 14, N: 14, D: 7.29–30, 8.2.
(600 Meters, Prone)

			TOTAL PTS.
1.	USA	(Dennis Fenton, Willis Lee, Lloyd Spooner, Ollie Schriver, Joseph Jackson)	287/283/284
2.	SAF	(Robert Bodley, Ferdinand Buchanan, George Harvey, Frederick Morgan, David Smith)	287/283/279
3.	SWE	(Carl Hugo Johansson, Mauritz Eriksson, Erik Blomqvist, Erik Ohlsson, Gustaf Adolf Jonsson)	287/275
4.	NOR	(Otto Olsen, Östen Östensen, Albert Helgerud, Olaf Sletten, Jacob Onsrud)	282
5.	FRA	(Léon Johnson, Achille Paroche, Emile Rumeau, André Parmentier, Georges Roes)	280
6.	SWI	(Fritz Kuchen, Albert Tröndle, Arnold Rösli, Walter Lienhard, Caspar Widmer)	279
7.	GRE	(Andreas Vichos, Ioannis Theophilakis, Alexandros Theophilakis, Konstantinos Kephalas, Emmanuel Peristerakis)	270
8.	FIN	(Heikki Veli Nieminen, Voitto Kolho, Vilho Vauhkonen, Karl Magnus Wegelius, Kalle Lapalainen)	268

1920 Antwerp-Beverloo T: 14, N: 14, D: 7.29.
(300 + 600 Meters, Prone)

			TOTAL PTS.
1.	USA	(Joseph Jackson, Willis Lee, Ollie Schriver, Lloyd Spooner, Carl Osburn)	573
2.	NOR	(Otto Olsen, Östen Östensen, Albert Helgerud, Olaf Sletten, Jacob Onsrud)	565
3.	SWI	(Schneeberger, Joseph Jehle, Weibel, Fritz Kuchen, Eugen Addor)	563
4.	FRA	(Léon Johnson, Achille Paroche, Emile Rumeau, André Parmentier, Georges Roes)	563
5.	SAF	(David Smith, Robert Bodley, Ferdinand Buchanan, George Harvey, Frederick Morgan)	560
6.	SWE	(Erik Blomqvist, Carl Hugo Johansson, Gustaf Adolf Jonsson, Mauritz Eriksson, Bror Andreasson)	558
7.	GRE	(Alexandros Theophilakis, Ioannis Theophilakis, Konstantinos Kephalas, Vassilios Xylinakis, Emmanuel Peristerakis)	553
8.	CZE	(Rudolf Jelen, Josef Sucharda, Vaclav Kindl, Josef Linert, Antonín Brych)	536

SMALL-BORE RIFLE

1908 London C: 22, N: 5, D: 7.11.
(25 Yards, Moving Target)

			PTS.
1.	John Fleming	GBR	24
2.	Michael Matthews	GBR	24
3.	William Marsden	GBR	24
4.	Edward Newitt	GBR	24
5.	Phillip Plater	GBR	22
6.	William Pimm	GBR	21
7.	William Milne	GBR	21
8.	Otto von Rosen	SWE	18

(25 Yards, Disappearing Target)

			PTS.
1.	William Styles	GBR	45
2.	Harold Hawkins	GBR	45
3.	Edward Amoore	GBR	45
4.	William Milne	GBR	45
5.	John Milne	GBR	45
6.	Arthur Wilde	GBR	45
7.	Wilhelm Carlberg	SWE	45
8.	Harold Humby	GBR	45

1912 Stockholm C: 36, N: 8, D. 7.5.
(25 Meters, Disappearing Target)

			PTS.
1.	Wilhelm Carlberg	SWE	242
2.	Johan Hübner von Holst	SWE	233
3.	Gustaf Ericsson	SWE	231
4.	Joseph Pepé	GBR	231
5.	Robert Murray	GBR	228
6.	Axel Gyllenkrok	SWE	227
7.	William Pimm	GBR	225
8.	Frederick Hird	USA	221

1920 Antwerp-Beverloo C: 50, N: 10, D: 8.2.
(50 Meters, Standing)

			PTS.
1.	Lawrence Nuesslein	USA	391
2.	Arthur Rothrock	USA	386
3.	Dennis Fenton	USA	385

SMALL-BORE RIFLE TEAMS

1908 London T: 3, N: 3, D: 7.11.
(50 + 100 Yards)

			TOTAL PTS.
1.	GBR	(Michael Matthews, Harold Humby, William Pimm, Edward Amoore)	771
2.	SWE	(Wilhelm Carlberg, Eric Carlberg, Johan Hübner von Holst, Frans Albert Schartau)	737
3.	FRA	(Paul Colas, André Regaud, Léon Lecuyer, Henri Bonnéfoy)	710

1912 Stockholm T: 4, N: 4, D: 7.5.
(25 Meters)

			TOTAL PTS.
1.	SWE	(Johan Hübner von Holst, Eric Carlberg, Wilhelm Carlberg, Gustaf Boivie)	925
2.	GBR	(William Pimm, Joseph Pepé, William Milne, William Styles)	917
3.	USA	(Frederick Hird, Warren Sprout, Neil McDonnell, William Leushner)	881
4.	GRE	(Ioannis Theophilakis, Frangiskos Mavromatis, Nicolaos Levidis, Iakovos Theophilas)	716

1912 Stockholm T: 6, N: 6, D: 7.3.
(50 Meters)

			TOTAL PTS.
1. GBR	(William Pimm, Edward Lessimore, Joseph Pepé, Robert Murray)		762
2. SWE	(Arthur Nordenswan, Eric Carlberg, Ruben Örtegren, Wilhelm Carlberg)		748
3. USA	(Warren Sprout, William Leushner, Frederick Hird, Carl Osburn)		744
4. FRA	(Léon Johnson, Pierre Gentil, André Regaud, Maxime Lardin)		714
5. DEN	(Paul Gerlow, Lars Jörgen Madsen, Frants Nielsen, Hans Petter Denver)		708
5. GRE	(Ioannis Theophilakis, Iakovos Theophilas, Frangiskos Mavromatis, Nicolaos Levidis)		708

1920 Antwerp-Beverloo T: 10, N: 10, D: 8.2.
(50 Meters)

		TOTAL PTS.
1. USA	(Lawrence Nuesslein, Arthur Rothrock, Dennis Fenton, Willis Lee, Ollie Schriver)	1899
2. SWE	(Sigvard Hultcrantz, Erik Ohlsson, Leonard Lagerlöf, Olle Ericsson, Ragnar Stare)	1873
3. NOR	(Anton Olsen, Albert Helgerud, Sigvart Johansen, Olaf Sletten, Östen Östensen)	1866
4. DEN	(Lars Jörgen Madsen, Erik Saetter-Lassen, Anders Peter Nielsen, Otto Wegener, Christian Möller)	1862
5. FRA	(Léon Johnson, Achille Paroche, Emile Rumeau, André Parmentier, Georges Roes)	1847
6. BEL	(Paul van Asbroek, Norbert van Molle, Phillippe Cammaerts, Victor Robert, Louis Andrieu)	1785
7. ITA	(Alfredo Galli, Raffaele Frasca, Peppy Campus, Franco Micheli, Riccardo Ticchi)	1777
8. SAF	(John Lishman, Frederick Morgan, George Harvey, Robert Bodley, George Paxton)	1755

RUNNING DEER SHOOTING, SINGLE SHOT

1908 London C: 15, N: 4, D: 7.11.

		PTS.
1. Oscar Swahn	SWE	25
2. Thomas "Ted" Ranken	GBR	24
3. Alexander Rogers	GBR	24
4. Maurice Blood	GBR	23
5. Albert Kempster	GBR	22
6. William Lane-Joynt	GBR	21
7. Walter Winans	USA	21
8. James Cowan	GBR	21

In 1908, Oscar Swahn was already 60 years old when he won his *first* Olympic gold medal, taking a total of two gold and one bronze. In 1912 he won one gold and one bronze, and in Antwerp, in 1920, at the age of 72, he won his first silver medal as part of the Swedish double-shot running deer team. He died in 1927.

1912 Stockholm C: 34, N: 7, D: 7.1.

		PTS.
1. Alfred Swahn	SWE	41/20
2. Åke Lundeberg	SWE	41/17
3. Nestori Toivonen	FIN	41/11
4. Karl Larsson	SWE	39
5. Oscar Swahn	SWE	39
6. Sven Arvid Lindskog	SWE	39
7. Heinrich Elbogen	AUT	38
8. Adolf Ture Cederström	SWE	37

Although Oscar Swahn was able to finish only fifth in Stockholm, his 32-year-old son Alfred earned the gold medal after a three-way shoot-off. Alfred's Olympic career was even more successful than his father's. Between 1908 and 1924 he won nine medals—three gold, three silver, and three bronze.

1920 Antwerp-Beverloo C: 22, N: 4, D: 7.27.

		PTS.
1. Otto Olsen	NOR	43
2. Alfred Swahn	SWE	41/20
3. Harald Natvig	NOR	41/19
4. Yrjö Kolho	FIN	40
5. Toivo Tikkanen	FIN	40
6. Frederic Landelius	SWE	39
7. Laurence Nuesslein	USA	38
8. Oscar Swahn	SWE	37

1924 Paris C: 32, N: 8, D: 7.3.

		PTS.
1. John Boles	USA	40
2. Cyril Mackworth-Praed	GBR	39
3. Otto Olsen	NOR	39
4. Otto Hultberg	SWE	39
5. Martti Liuttula	FIN	37
6. Alfred Swahn	SWE	37
7. Einar Liberg	NOR	36
8. Harold Natvig	NOR	36

Twenty-eight years after he earned three medals at the Paris Games, Cyril Mackworth-Praed took part in the Olympics for a second time, placing eleventh in the trap event at Helsinki at the age of 60. Mackworth-Praed was a noted ornithologist who spent 40 years compiling his six-volume *African Handbook of Birds*.

TEAM RUNNING DEER SHOOTING, SINGLE-SHOT

1908 London T: 2, N: 2, D: 7.11.

		TOTAL PTS.
1. SWE	(Alfred Swahn, Arvid Knöppel, Oscar Swahn, Ernst Rosell)	86
2. GBR	(Charles Nix, William Lane-Joynt, Walter Ellicot, Thomas "Ted" Ranken)	85

1912 Stockholm T: 5, N: 5, D: 7.4.

		TOTAL PTS.
1. SWE	(Alfred Swahn, Oscar Swahn, Åke Lundeberg, Per-Olof Arvidsson)	151
2. USA	(W. Neil McDonnell, Walter Winans, William Leushner, William Libbey)	132
3. FIN	(Axel Fredrik Londen, Nestori Toivonen, Toivo Väänänen, Ernst Rosenqvist)	123
4. AUT	(Adolf Michel, Eberhard Steinböck, Peter Paternelli, Heinrich Ellbogen)	115
5. RUS	(Harry Blau, Basil de Skrotsky, Dmitri de Barkov, Aleksandr de Dobryansky)	108

1920 Antwerp-Beverloo T: 4, N: 4, D: 7.26.

		TOTAL PTS.
1. NOR	(Harald Natvig, Otto Olsen, Ole Andreas Lilloe-Olsen, Einar Liberg, Hans Nordvik)	178
2. FIN	(Toivo Tikkanen, Nestor Toivonen, Karl Magnus Wegelius, Kalle Lapalainen, Yrjö Kolho)	159
3. USA	(Thomas Brown, Lawrence Nuesslein, Lloyd Spooner, Carl Osburn, Willis Lee)	158
4. SWE	(Alfred Swahn, Per Kinde, Bengt Lagercrantz, Oscar Swahn, Karl Larsson)	153

1924 Paris T: 6, N: 6, D: 7.3.

		TOTAL PTS.
1. NOR	(Ole Andreas Lilloe-Olsen, Einar Liberg, Harald Natvig, Otto Olsen)	160
2. SWE	(Alfred Swahn, Fredrik Landelius, Otto Hultberg, G. Mauritz Johansson)	154
3. USA	(John Boles, Walter Stokes, Raymond "Chan" Coulter, Dennis Fenton)	148
4. GBR	(Cyril Mackworth-Praed, Alexander Rogers, John Faunthorpe, John O'Leary)	136
5. FIN	(Karl Magnus Wegelius, Martti Liuttula, Jalo Urho Autonen, Robert Tikkanen)	130
6. HUN	(Gusztáv Szomjas, Rezsö Velez, Elemér Takács, László Szomjas)	97

RUNNING DEER SHOOTING, DOUBLE-SHOT

1908 London C: 15, N: 4, D: 7.11.

		PTS.
1. Walter Winans	USA	46/44
2. Thomas "Ted" Ranken	GBR	46/41
3. Oscar Swahn	SWE	38
4. Maurice Blood	GBR	34
5. Albert Kempster	GBR	34
6. Walter Ellicot	GBR	33
7. Alexander Rogers	GBR	33
8. Ernst Rosell	SWE	33

1912 Stockholm C: 20, N: 6, D: 7.3.

		PTS.
1. Åke Lundeberg	SWE	79
2. Edvard Benedicks	SWE	74
3. Oscar Swahn	SWE	72
4. Alfred Swahn	SWE	68
5. Per Olof Arvidsson	SWE	68
6. Sven Arvid Lindskog	SWE	67
7. Erik Sökjer-Petersén	SWE	65
8. Emil Lindewald	SWE	64

1920 Antwerp-Beverloo C: 23, N: 4, D: 7.27.

		PTS.
1. Ole Andreas Lilloe-Olsen	NOR	82
2. Fredrik Landelius	SWE	77
3. Einar Liberg	NOR	71

1924 Paris C: 31, N: 8, D: 7.3.

		PTS.
1. Ole Andreas Lilloe-Olsen	NOR	76
2. Cyril Mackworth-Praed	GBR	72
3. Alfred Swahn	SWE	72
4. Fredrik Landelius	SWE	70
5. Einar Liberg	NOR	70
6. Robert Tikkanen	FIN	69
7. John Boles	USA	64
8. Karl Magnus Wegelius	FIN	64

TEAM RUNNING DEER SHOOTING, DOUBLE-SHOT

1920 Antwerp-Beverloo T: 4, N: 4, D: 7.26.

		TOTAL PTS.
1. NOR	(Ole Andreas Lilloe-Olsen, Thorstein Johansen, Harald Natvig, Hans Nordvik, Einar Liberg)	343
2. SWE	(Fredrik Landelius, Alfred Swahn, Oscar Swahn, Bengt Lagercrantz, Edvard Benedicks)	336
3. FIN	(Toivo Tikkanen, Karl Magnus Wegelius, Nestor Toivonen, Yrjö Kolho, Vilho Vauhkonen)	285
4. USA	(Lloyd Spooner, Willis Lee, Lawrence Nuesslein, Carl Osburn, Thomas Brown)	282

1924 Paris T: 6, N: 6, D: 7.3.

		TOTAL PTS.
1. GBR	(Cyril Mackworth-Praed, Allen Whitty, Herbert Perry, Philip Neame)	263
2. NOR	(Ole Andreas Lilloe-Olsen, Otto Olsen, Harald Natvig, Einar Liberg)	262
3. SWE	(Alfred Swahn, G. Mauritz Johansson, Fredrik Landelius, Axel Ekblom)	250
4. FIN	(Karl Magnus Wegelius, Jalo Urho Autonen, Martti Liuttula, Robert Tikkanen)	239
5. USA	(Raymond "Chan" Coulter, Walter Stokes, John Boles, Dennis Fenton)	233

6. CZE (Miloslav Hlavác, Josef Sucharda, Rudolf 204
Jelen, Josef Hosa)

Philip Neame of the British team is the only person to be awarded the Victoria Cross and win an Olympic gold medal.

RUNNING DEER SHOOTING, SINGLE- AND DOUBLE-SHOT

1952 Helsinki C: 14, N: 7, D: 7.29. WR: 398 (Rolf Bergersen)

			PTS.	
1.	John Larsen	NOR	413	WR
2.	Per Olof Sköldberg	SWE	409	
3.	Tauno Mäki	FIN	407	
4.	Rolf Bergersen	NOR	399	
5.	B. Thorleif Kockgård	SWE	397	
6.	Yrjö Miettinen	FIN	392	
7.	Petr Nikolayev	SOV	385	
8.	Vladimir Sevryugin	SOV	383	

1956 Melbourne C: 11, N: 6, D: 12.4.

			PTS.	
1.	Vitaly Romanenko	SOV/UKR	441	OR
2.	Per Olof Sköldberg	SWE	432	
3.	Vladimir Sevryugin	SOV	429	
4.	Miklós Kovács	HUN	417	
5.	Miklós Kocsis	HUN	416	
6.	Rolf Bergersen	NOR	409	
7.	Benkt Austrin	SWE	405	
8.	John Larsen	NOR	390	

TRAP (CLAY PIGEON) SHOOTING TEAMS

1908 London T: 4, N: 3, D: 7.11.

			TOTAL PTS.
1.	GBR	(Alexander Maunder, James Pike, Charles Palmer, John Postans, Frank Moore, Philip Easte)	407
2.	CAN	(Walter Ewing, George Beattie, Arthur Westover, Mylie Fletcher, George Vivian, Donald McMackon)	405
3.	GBR	(George Whitaker, Gerald Skinner, John Butt, William Morris, Harold Creasey, Richard Hutton)	372
4.	HOL	(Willem Wilson, Franciscus von Voorst tot Voorst, Cornelis Viroly, Eduardus von Voorst tot Voorst, Reindert de Favauge)	174

1912 Stockholm T: 6, N: 6, D: 7.1.

			TOTAL PTS.
1.	USA	(Charles Billings, Ralph Spotts, John Hendrickson, James Graham, Edward Gleason, Frank Hall)	532

2.	GBR	(John Butt, William Grosvenor, Harold Humby, Alexander Maunder, Charles Palmer, George Whitaker)	511
3.	GER	(Erich Graf von Bernstorff, Freiherr von Zeidlitz und Leipe, Horst Goeldel, Albert Preuss, Erland Koch, Alfred Goeldel)	510
4.	SWE	(Carl Wollert, Alfred Swahn, Johann Ekman, Hjalmar Frisell, Åke Lundeberg, Victor Wallenberg)	243
5.	FIN	(Edvard Bacher, Karl Fazer, Robert Huber, Gustaf Adolf Schnitt, Emil Johannes Collan, Axel Fredrik Londen)	233
6.	FRA	(Henri de Castex, Georges de Crequi-Montfort de Courtivan, Edouard Creuzè de Lesser, André Fleury, Charles Jaubert, René Texier)	90

1920 Antwerp-Beverloo T: 8, N: 8, D: 7.23.

			TOTAL PTS.
1.	USA	(Mark Arie, Frank Troeh, Horace Bonser, Forest McNeir, Frank Wright, Jay Clark)	547
2.	BEL	(Albert Bosquet, Joseph Cogels, Emile Dupont, Henri Quersin, Louis van Tilt, Edouard Fesinger)	503
3.	SWE	(Erik Lundqvist, Per Kinde, Fredrik Landelius, Alfred Swahn, Karl Richter, Erik Sökjer-Petersén)	500
4.	GBR	(Harold Humby, William Grosvenor, W. Ellicot, George Whitaker, Ernest Pocock, Charles Palmer)	488
5.	CAN	(George Beattie, Samuel Vance, William Hamilton, Robert Montgomery, James Oliver, William McLaren)	474
6.	HOL	(Reindert de Favauge, Gerard van der Vliet, M. Pieter Waller, Emile Jurgens, Frits Jurgens, Eduardus van Voorst tot Voorst)	222
7.	FRA	(André Fleury, Marcel Lafite, Henri de Castex, Augustin Berjat, René Texier, Jan de Lareinty-Tholozau)	210
7.	NOR	(Oluf Wesmann-Kjaer, Johannes Nordal-Lunde, Harald Natvig, Thorstein Johansen, Hans Nordvik, Ole Andreas Lilloe-Olsen)	210

1924 Paris T: 12, N: 12, D: 7.7.

			TOTAL PTS.
1.	USA	(Frank Hughes, Samuel Sharman, William Silkworth, Frederick Etchen)	363
2.	CAN	(George Beattie, James Montgomery, Samuel Vance, John Black, Samuel Newton, William Barnes)	360
3.	FIN	(Konrad Huber, Robert Huber, Werner Ekman, Robert Tikkanen)	360
4.	SWE	(Erik Lundqvist, Fredrik Landelius, Alfred Swahn, Magnus Hallman)	354
5.	BEL	(Albert Bosquet, Louis d'Heur, Emile Dupont, Jacques Mouton)	354
6.	AUT	(Heinrich Bartosch, August Baumgartner, Hans Schödl, Erich Zoigner)	347

7. NOR (Ole Andreas Lilloe-Olsen, Oluf Wesmann-Kjaer, Eivind Holmsen, Martin Steenersen)   336

8. GBR (John O'Leary, Enoch Jenkins, Herbert Larsen, Cyril Mackworth-Praed)   328

LIVE PIGEON SHOOTING

1900 Paris C: 52, N: 7?, D: 6.27.

		BIRDS KILLED
1. Léon de Lunden	BEL	21
2. Maurice Faure	FRA	20
3. Donald Mackintosh	AUS	18
3. Crittenden Robinson	USA	18
5. J. Pederzoli	ITA	15
6. C. Béthune	FRA	14
7. J. Banwell	GBR	12
8. Paul de Lunden	BEL	11

This disgusting event marked the only time in Olympic history when animals were killed on purpose.

WOMEN

SPORT PISTOL

The sport pistol competition is fired at a distance of 25 meters. The qualifying round is divided into two 30-shot stages: precision and rapid-fire. Six minutes are allowed for the precision stage. In the rapid-fire stage shots are taken at a turning target. The bull's-eye in the precision stage is 5 centimeters (1.97 inches) across. The rapid-fire bull's-eye is 10 centimeters (4 inches) across. The final consists of 10 rapid-fire shots.

1896–1980 not held

1984 Los Angeles-Chino C: 30, N: 21, D: 7.29. WR: 592 (G. Korsun)

		PTS.
1. Linda Thom	CAN	585/198
2. Ruby Fox	USA	585/197
3. Patricia Dench	AUS	583/196
4. Liu Haiying	CHN	583/195
5. Kristina Fries	SWE	581
6. Wen Zhifang	CHN	578
7. Debora Srour	BRA	578
8. Maria Macovei	ROM	577

Linda Thom was a 40-year-old chef and caterer from Ottawa.

1988 Seoul C: 35, N: 24, D: 9.19. WR: 695 (Nino Salukvadze)

		PTS.
1. Nino Salukvadze	SOV/GEO	690
2. Tomoko Hasegawa	JPN	686
3. Jasna Šekarić	YUG	686
4. Lieselotte Breker	GER	685
5. Ágnes Ferencz	HUN	685
6. Kristina Fries	SWE	685
7. Evelyne Manchon	FRA	684
8. Marina Dobrancheva	SOV/RUS	682

Nineteen-year-old Nino Salukvadze of Soviet Georgia also won a silver medal in the air pistol event.

1992 Barcelona-Mollet del Vallès C: 41, N: 29, D: 7.27. WR: 693 (Nino Salukvadze)

		PTS.
1. Marina Logvinenko (Dobrancheva)	RUS	684
2. Li Duihong	CHN	680
3. Dorzhsuren Munkhbayar	MGL	679
4. Mirela Skoko	CRO	677
5. Nino Salukvadze	GEO	676
6. Jasna Šekarić	YUG	676
7. Lynne-Marie Freh	AUS	675
8. Julita Macur	POL	674

Silver medalist Li Duihong had been one of the favorites in 1988 until she tested positive for drugs and was slapped with a two-year suspension. Li's older sister, Li Shuanghong, placed ninth in the air pistol event.

AIR PISTOL

Forty shots are taken from a distance of 10 meters with a time limit of 90 minutes. The bull's-eye has a diameter of 11.5 millimeters (.45 inches). The top eight qualifiers take part in a 10-shot final with 75 seconds per shot.

1896–1984 not held

1988 Seoul C: 37, N: 26, D: 9.21. WR: 489 (Jasna Šekarić)

		PTS.	
1. Jasna Šekarić	YUG	489.5	WR
2. Nino Salukvadze	SOV/GEO	487.9	
3. Marina Dobrancheva	SOV/RUS	485.2	
4. Anne Goffin	BEL	480.2	
5. Anke Völker	GDR	479.3	
6. Liu Haiying	CHN	476.9	
7. Lieselotte Breker	GER	476.0	
8. Christine Strahalm	AUT	472.6	

Salukvadze, who had won the sport pistol championship 2 days earlier, set a world record of 390 in the preliminary round. However, this left her only one point up on defending world champion Jasna Šekarić, who outshot her on seven of the first eight shots of the final to set a world record of her own. The battle for the bronze medal looked like it would be a tight contest between Breker and Dobrancheva. However, when the final began,

Breker failed to get off her first shot before the time limit elapsed. She was forced to take a zero for the shot, which put her out of the running.

1992 Barcelona-Mollet del Vallès C: 47, N: 31, D: 8.1. WR: 492.4 (Lieselotte Breker)

			PTS.
1. Marina Logvinenko (Dobrancheva)	RUS	486.4/99.4
2. Jasna Šekarić	YUG	486.4/97.4
3. Maria Grozdeva	BUL	481.6
4. Wang Lina	CHN	479.7
5. Cris Kajd	SWE	478.9
6. Mariá Fernández Julián	SPA	478.5
7. Daniela Dumitraşcu	ROM	478.1
8. Miroslawa Sagun	POL	477.8

Defending Olympic champion Jasna Šekarić took a two-point lead into the final and was still ahead by .8 points after the ninth of ten rounds. However, in the final round, Logvinenko, who had won the sport pistol event five days earlier, outshot Šekarić 10.6 to 9.8. This left the two shooters with the exact same score, but because Logvinenko had a higher score in the final, the Rostov-on-Don native earned her second gold medal.

SMALL-BORE RIFLE, THREE POSITIONS

The rules are the same as for the men's competition with the exception that 20 shots, rather than 40, are taken at each position. Also, there is no time limit for each position, but rather an overall time limit of 2 hours 30 minutes.

1896–1980 not held

1984 Los Angeles-Chino C: 27, N: 17, D: 8.2. WR: 592 (Marlies Helbig)

		PRONE	STAND-ING	KNEEL-ING	TOTAL
1. Wu Xiaoxuan	CHN	197	187	197	581
2. Ulrike Holmer	GER	197	191	190	578
3. Wanda Jewell	USA	194	189	195	578
4. Gloria Parmentier	USA	199	187	190	576
5. Anne Grethe Jeppesen	NOR	196	190	188	574
6. Jin Dongxiang	CHN	193	183	195	571
7. Biserka Vrbek	YUG	196	181	192	569
8. Mirjana Jovović	YUG/BSH	196	182	191	569

Wu, who also won a bronze medal in the air rifle event, told reporters the secret of her success at the Olympics: "I just concentrated on the music of our national anthem and shot."

1988 Seoul C: 37, N: 21, D: 9.21. WR: 691.6 (Vessela Lecheva)

		PRONE	STAND-ING	KNEEL-ING	FINAL	TOTAL
1. Sylvia Sperber	GER	200	193	197	95.6	685.6
2. Vessela Lecheva	BUL	199	192	192	100.2	683.2
3. Valentina Cherkasova	SOV/RUS	198	193	195	95.4	681.4
4. Katja Klepp	GDR	199	187	198	96.5	680.5
5. Sharon Bowes	CAN	196	194	194	96.5	680.5
6. Anna Malukhina	SOV/RUS	198	191	196	93.4	678.4
7. Launi Meili	USA	197	190	195	94.5	676.5
8. Anita Karlsson	SWE	198	193	192	93.4	676.4

After finishing eleventh in the air rifle event in 1984, Sylvia Sperber retired from the sport even though she was only 19 years old. She returned to competition three years later. In 1988 she equaled the world record in the air rifle, took a silver in that event at Seoul, and then, three days later, earned a gold in the three-position competition.

1992 Barcelona-Mollet del Vallès C: 36, N: 21, D: 7.30. WR: 684.9 (Vessela Lecheva)

		PRONE	STAND-ING	KNEEL-ING	FINAL	TOTAL
1. Launi Meili	USA	200	194	193	97.3	684.3
2. Nonka Matova	BUL	200	190	194	98.7	682.7
3. Malgorzata Ksiazkiewicz	POL	195	191	199	96.5	681.5
4. Éva Fórián	HUN	199	189	194	97.5	679.5
5. Suzana Skoko	CRO	196	191	193	98.7	678.7
6. Vessela Lecheva	BUL	199	187	195	97.0	678.0
7. Sharon Bowes	CAN	198	189	193	93.6	673.6
8. Eva Joó	HUN	198	191	191	93.6	673.6

In 1988 Launi Meili entered the final of the air rifle event tied for first place. Then she succumbed to nerves and dropped to seventh place. Four years later in Barcelona Meili took a two-point lead into the final of the small-bore event. This time despite her nervousness, she shot a solid final round and earned the gold medal.

AIR RIFLE

The shooters have 90 minutes to fire 40 shots at a target 10 meters away. The bull's-eye is only .5 millimeters (.02 inches) in diameter. The eight finalists take 10 more shots with a time limit of 75 seconds per shot.

1896–1980 not held

1984 Los Angeles-Chino C: 33, N: 20, D: 7.31. WR: 395 (Anna Malukhina, Marlies Helbig)

		PTS.
1. Pat Spurgin	USA	393
2. Edith Gufler	ITA	391
3. Wu Xiaoxuan	CHN	389
4. Sharon Bowes	CAN	388
5. Yvette Courault	FRA	386
6. Gisela Sailer	GER	385
7. Siri Landsem	NOR	384
8. Sirpa Ylonen	FIN	383

Just before the competition began, a friend gave Pat Spurgin the following advice: "Just be like a duck." After winning the gold medal, the surprisingly poised 18-year-old from Billings, Montana, explained that to be like a duck meant, "Sit still on the surface, but paddle like hell underneath."

1988 Seoul C: 45, N: 29, D: 9.18. WR: 504.0 (Vessela Lecheva)

			PTS.
1.	Irina Shilova	SOV/BLR	498.5
2.	Sylvia Sperber	GER	497.5
3.	Anna Malukhina	SOV/RUS	495.8
4.	Zhang Qiuping	CHN	494.7
5.	Pirjo Peltola	FIN	493.6
6.	Launi Meili	USA	493.3
7.	Sharon Bowes	CAN	493.1
8.	Gabriele Bühlmann	SWI	493.0

The favorite in this event, the first to be decided at the Seoul Olympics, was world champion, world record holder, and two-time Female Shooter of the Year, Vessela Lecheva of Bulgaria. Lecheva was the focus of heavy media attention in South Korea, where she was considered unusually beautiful. Unnerved by the pressure of celebrity, she finished in a tie for seventeenth place. A few minutes later, a Korean shooting official found Lecheva wailing and beating her head against a restroom wall. Three days later she came from behind to earn a silver medal in the three-position event.

1992 Barcelona-Mollet del Vallès C: 45, N: 28, D: 7.26. WR: 500.8 (Valentina Cherkasova)

			PTS.
1.	Yeo Kab-soon	KOR	498.2
2.	Vessela Lecheva	BUL	495.3
3.	Aranka Binder	YUG	495.1
4.	Dagmar Bílková	CZE	494.9
5.	Valentina Cherkasova	SOV/RUS	494.6
6.	Lee Eun-ju	KOR	492.6
7.	Éva Fórián	HUN	492.4
8.	Mirjana Horvat (Jovović)	BSH	491.6

The first gold medal of the 1992 Olympics was won by an unknown 18-year-old, Yeo Kab-soon, who was competing in her first international match. An extra level of tension was added to the final when Binder of Yugoslavia and Horvat of Bosnia were placed next to each other on the firing line. The two had been roommates when both competed for Yugoslavia, but now they represented two nations at war. After the competition ended, they embraced, but Binder declined to take part in the postcompetition medalists' press conference.

DOUBLE TRAP

This event will be held for the first time in 1996.

SOFTBALL

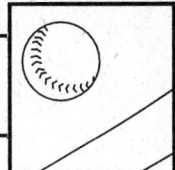

The rules of women's fast-pitch softball are basically the same as those of baseball. There are, however, several important differences:

1) Baseball: pitchers throw overhand
   Softball: pitchers throw underhand
2) Baseball: the ball weighs 9¼ ounces
   Softball: the ball, although larger in circumference, weighs between 6¼ and 7 ounces
3) Baseball: the pitcher's mound is 60 feet 6 inches from home plate
   Softball: the pitcher's mound is 40 feet from home plate
4) Baseball: the bases are 90 feet from each other
   Softball: the bases are 60 feet from each other
5) Baseball: the infield is covered in grass
   Softball: the infield is covered in dirt
6) Baseball: the outfield fences are well over 200 feet from home plate
   Softball: the outfield fences are 200 feet from home plate
7) Baseball: a designated hitter may be used for the pitcher only
   Softball: a designated hitter may replace any player
8) Baseball: regulation play lasts 9 innings
   Softball: regulation play lasts 7 innings

This event will be held for the first time in 1996.

SWIMMING

MEN
50-Meter Freestyle
100-Meter Freestyle
200-Meter Freestyle
400-Meter Freestyle
1500-Meter Freestyle
100-Meter Backstroke
200-Meter Backstroke
100-Meter Breaststroke
200-Meter Breaststroke
100-Meter Butterfly
200-Meter Butterfly

200-Meter Individual Medley
400-Meter Individual Medley
4 × 100-Meter Freestyle Relay
4 × 200-Meter Freestyle Relay
4 × 100-Meter Medley Relay
Discontinued Events

Olympic pools must be 50 meters long. Olympic swimming competitions begin with a preliminary round. The swimmers with the eight fastest times advance to the final while the next eight fastest qualify for the B final to determine places 9 through 16. The swimmer with the fastest qualifying time is assigned lane 4, the second-fastest lane 5, the third-fastest lane 3, the fourth-fastest lane 6, and so on until the slowest finalist, who is assigned lane 8.

The false-start rule in swimming is a bit odd. The first false start in a race is excused and the violator is not noted. However, anyone who commits a false start after the first one is immediately disqualified even if the first false start was committed by someone else. The International Federation of Amateur Swimming (F.I.N.A.) also employs a rather questionable procedure for drug testing. Unlike most other sports, all medalists are not required to be tested. Instead, the subjects for testing are picked at random. At the 1992 Olympics, two of the top four finishers were tested and one of the next four. This rule led to controversy when it was revealed that certain Chinese women swimmers, who appeared to be taking banned substances, were not tested. Under pressure from coaches and the media, the federation agreed—in the middle of the meet—to require testing of gold medalists. After the Barcelona Olympics, F.I.N.A. returned to its policy of random testing.

MEN

50-METER FREESTYLE

In freestyle events swimmers may use any style whatsoever. Some part of the swimmer must touch the wall at the end of each lap of the pool before heading back the other way; some part of the swimmer must also touch the wall at the finish.

1896–1900 not held

1904 St. Louis C: 9, N: 2, D: 9.6.
(50 Yards—45.72 Meters)

				SWIM-OFF
1.	Zoltán Halmay	HUN	28.2	28.0
2.	J. Scott Leary	USA	28.2	28.6
3.	Charles Daniels	USA	—	
4.	David Gaul	USA	—	
5.	Leo Goodwin	USA	—	
6.	Raymond Thorne	USA	—	

Halmay defeated Leary by a foot. However, the U.S. judge declared that Leary had won. A brawl broke out and went on for some time. Finally it was decided to call the race a dead heat and to have the two men swim again. After two false starts, Halmay was off quickly and won easily.

1906–1984 not held

1988 Seoul C: 71, N: 44, D: 9.24. WR: 22.23 (Thomas Jager)

1.	Matthew Biondi	USA	22.14	WR
2.	Thomas Jager	USA	22.36	
3.	Gennady Prigoda	SOV/RUS	22.71	
4.	Dano Halsall	SWI	22.83	
5.	Stefan Volery	SWI	22.84	
6.	Vladimir Tkashenko	SOV/UKR	22.88	
7.	Frank Henter	GER	23.03	
8.	Andrew Baildon	AUS	23.15	

Prior to the Olympics, friendly rivals Tom Jager and Matt Biondi had faced each other 14 times at 50 meters. Jager, a psychology graduate from U.C.L.A., had won 10 of those confrontations, including the ones at the 1986 world championships and the 1988 Olympic trials. In fact, Biondi hadn't beaten Jager in two years. However, Biondi entered the final on a roll. Although his personal best in competition was a 22.33 set in 1986, he had beaten that time 50 times at the U.S. Olympic training camp. And in Seoul he had already won five medals, including three gold. In the final, Biondi was able to keep up with Jager's typically fast start and then power his way to the finish in world record time.

Peter Williams, a South African competing in the United States for the University of Indiana, was not allowed to take part in the Games. In April, Williams had clocked a 22.18 in a time trial without competitors. His time was not allowed as a world record, not because it was achieved outside of competition, but because Williams was a citizen of South Africa. Steve Crocker also did not compete, due to the rule limiting each nation to two entrants. Crocker's time of 22.65 at the U.S. trials, had he been given the opportunity to repeat it in Seoul, would have been good enough for the bronze medal. On the other hand, so would Dano Halsall's Olympic preliminary time of 22.61 or Gennady Prigoda's of 22.57.

1992 Barcelona C: 75, N: 51, D: 7.30. WR: 21.81 (Thomas Jager)

1. Aleksandr Popov	RUS	21.91	OR
2. Matthew Biondi	USA	22.09	
3. Thomas Jager	USA	22.30	
4. Christophe Kalfayan	FRA	22.50	
4. Peter Williams	SAF	22.50	
6. Mark Foster	GBR	22.52	
7. Gennady Prigoda	RUS	22.54	
8. Nils Rudolph	GER	22.73	

In the run-up to the Barcelona Olympics, it was widely assumed that this race would be a battle between two close friends: 26-year-old Matt Biondi and 27-year-old Tom Jager. Between the two of them, Biondi and Jager had recorded 23 of the 24 fastest times in history. One or the other of them had held the world record for the past 6½ years, with Jager having set the current record on March 24, 1990. Biondi was the defending Olympic champion. That was the way it looked the day the Olympics began. But by the morning of the 50-meter final, the outlook appeared completely different. Two days earlier, 20-year-old Aleksandr Popov had won the 100-meter freestyle, leaving a stunned Biondi back in fifth place. On May 30, the fast-improving Popov had set a European record in the 50 free of 22.31. Exactly two months later he led the qualifying round with a time of 22.21, just ahead of Biondi's 22.32. In the final Popov got off to a quick start and was never headed.

100-METER FREESTYLE

1896 Athens C: 10, N: 4, D: 4.11.

1. Alfréd Hajós (Guttmann)	HUN	1:22.2	OR
2. Otto Herschmann	AUT	1:22.8	

The first Olympic swimming contests were held outdoors in open water, in and around the Bay of Zea at Phaleron, near Piraeus, and were watched by 40,000 people on the shore. The weather had turned unusually cold, and on the morning of the competition the temperature in the water dropped to 55 degrees Fahrenheit (13 degrees centigrade). The eventual winner of two of the three races, the 100 meters and the 1200 meters, was Alfréd Hajós, an 18-year-old from Budapest. Hajós recalled the experience of climbing into the water from the boat that had carried the 13 swimmers to the starting point: "The icy water almost cut into our stomachs. Until 70 meters it was a neck-and-neck race, but then I got my second wind and won the competition. My time wasn't anything to brag about."

Hajós was 13 years old when he felt compelled to become a good swimmer after his father drowned in the Danube River. In 1895 he won the 100-meter title at the unofficial European championships in Vienna. In 1902 he was a member of the first Hungarian national football team. Hajós went on to become a successful architect, winning a prize in the architectural division of the Olympic Art Contest in 1924. He was born Alfréd Guttmann, but, following the fashion among Eastern European Jews of the time, he competed under a pseudonym. Later he legally changed his name to Hajós.

1900 not held

1904 St. Louis C: 8 or 9, N: 2, D: 9.5.
(100 yards)

1. Zoltán Halmay	HUN	1:02.8
2. Charles Daniels	USA	—
3. J. Scott Leary	USA	—
4. Francis Gailey	USA	—
5. David Hammond	USA	—
6. Leo Goodwin	USA	—

Including the Intercalated Games of 1906, in which he won one gold medal and one silver, Halmay earned a total of nine Olympic medals: three gold, five silver, and one bronze.

1906 Athens C: 9, N: 5, D: 4.24. WR: 1:05.8 (Zoltán Halmay)

1. Charles Daniels	USA	1:13.4
2. Zoltán Halmay	HUN	1:14.2
3. Cecil Healy	AUS	—
4. Paul Radmilovic	GBR	—
5. John Derbyshire	GBR	—
6. Hjalmar Johansson	SWE	—

1908 London C: 34, N: 12, D: 7.20. WR: 1:05.8 (Zoltán Halmay)

1. Charles Daniels	USA	1:05.6	WR
2. Zoltán Halmay	HUN	1:06.2	
3. Harald Julin	SWE	1:08.0	
4. Leslie Rich	USA	—	

In 1908, 23-year-old Charles Daniels of New York City closed out his Olympic career, having won five gold medals, one silver, and two bronze, including the Intercalated Games of 1906.

1912 Stockholm C: 34, N: 12, D: 7.10. WR: 1:02.4 (Kurt Bretting)

1. Duke Paoa Kahanamoku	USA	1:03.4
2. Cecil Healy	AUS	1:04.6
3. Kenneth Huszagh	USA	1:05.6
4. Kurt Bretting	GER	1:05.8
5. Walter Ramme	GER	1:06.4

DNS: William Longworth (AUS)

Duke Paoa Kahinu Makoe Hulikohoa Kahanamoku was born on August 24, 1890, in the palace of Princess Ruth in Honolulu. At the time of his birth, Queen Victoria's son, the Duke of Edinburgh, was visiting Hawaii, so Kahanamoku's father named his own new son Duke in honor of the occasion. In Stockholm Kahanamoku impressed the European spectators with his powerful, smooth stroking, and quickly became one of the most popular figures at the Games. His first-round time of 1:02.6 was more than two seconds faster than any of the other swimmers. He won his second round heat in a lei-

Duke Kahanamoku, winner of the 1912 and 1920 100-meter freestyle. He also finished second in 1924 at the age of 33.

surely 1:03.8, the fastest time of the round. Because of a misunderstanding, the three U.S. representatives, Kahanamoku, Kenneth Huszagh, and Perry McGillivray, failed to show up for the semifinals on Sunday evening July 7. Holding the final without them seemed absurd, so the three were allowed to take part in an extra heat on Tuesday, with the stipulation that to qualify for the final the winner would have to beat the time of William Longworth, who had finished third in the first heat in 1:06.2. If this happened, then the second-place finisher in the special heat would also advance to the final. Not wanting to take any chances, Duke Kahanamoku equaled Kurt Bretting's world record of 1:02.4, allowing Huszagh to qualify as well. In the final, the following day, Kahanamoku took the time to look back and survey the field at the halfway mark. Noting that he had a comfortable lead, he eased up a bit and still won by two yards.

1920 Antwerp C: 31, N: 15, D: 8.24/8.29. WR: 1:01.4 (Duke Paoa Kahanamoku)

First Final

1. Duke Paoa Kahanamoku	USA	1:00.4	WR
2. Pua Kela Kealoha	USA	1:02.2	
3. William Harris	USA	1:03.2	
4. William Herald	AUS	—	

DISQ: Norman Ross (USA) 1:03.8

Second Final

1. Duke Paoa Kahanamoku	USA	1:01.4
2. Pua Kela Kealoha	USA	1:02.6
3. William Harris	USA	1:03.0
4. William Herald	AUS	1:03.8

Kahanamoku equaled his own world record of 1:01.4 in the semifinals, and then set a new record of 1:00.4 in the final, to celebrate his 30th birthday. However, Herald claimed that he had been fouled by Ross. Ross was disqualified and the race was ordered reswum. The order of the finish was exactly the same the second time, except that Ross, who had won the 1500-meter championship the day after the first 100-meter final, didn't take part.

Kahanamoku eventually competed in four Olympics, winning three gold medals and two silver. Later he appeared in minor roles in 28 Hollywood films. He also played a major role in introducing the sport of surfing around the world. One day in June 1925, Kahanamoku was relaxing on the beach in Newport Beach, California, when a luxury yacht capsized, killing 17 people. The death toll would have been higher, but Duke used his surfboard to save the lives of eight of the yacht's passengers.

1924 Paris C: 30, N: 15, D: 7.20. WR: 57.4 (P. "Johnny" Weissmuller)

1. P. "Johnny" Weissmuller	USA	59.0	OR
2. Duke Paoa Kahanamoku	USA	1:01.4	
3. Samuel Kahanamoku	USA	1:01.8	
4. Arne Borg	SWE	1:02.0	
5. Katsuo Takaishi	JPN	1:03.0	
6. Orvar Trolle (SWE)			

Johnny Weissmuller was born to German Swabian parents in what is now Romania on June 2, 1904. His family emigrated to the United States in 1908. His father worked as a coal miner before moving to Chicago, where he died of tuberculosis before his son had started on the path to fame and fortune. On July 9, 1922, Johnny made swimming history by becoming the first person to swim 100 meters in less than one minute. On February 17, 1924, he lowered his time from 58.6 to 57.4, establishing a world record that would last for ten years. At the start of the 100-meter final at the Paris Olympics, Weissmuller found himself with 34-year-old defending champion Duke Kahanamoku on one side of him and Duke's 19-year-old brother, Sam, on the other side. Weissmuller was worried that the two Hawaiians had planned to swim a team race against him, but as they stood above the water Duke turned to him and said, "Johnny, good luck. The most important thing in this race is to get the American flag up there three times. Let's do it." And they did, with Weissmuller starting quickly and winning easily. That day he also won a gold medal in the 4 × 200-meter relay and a bronze medal in water polo. Two days earlier he had won the 400-meter freestyle. Johnny Weissmuller was one of the most popular participants at the 1924 Olympics, delighting the tough Parisian crowd not only with his superb swimming, but also with a comedy diving act, which he put on several times between races with his partner, Stubby Kruger. After Weissmuller's 100 meters victory, the crowd of 7000 stood and called for him for two or three minutes, until it was announced that he would appear again later in the afternoon.

1928 Amsterdam C: 30, N: 17, D: 8.11. WR: 57.4 (P. "Johnny" Weissmuller)

1. P. "Johnny" Weissmuller	USA	58.6	OR
2. István Bárány	HUN	59.8	
3. Katsuo Takaishi	JPN	1:00.0	
4. George Kojac	USA	1:00.8	
5. Walter Laufer	USA	1:01.0	
6. Walter Spence	CAN	1:01.4	
7. Alberto Zorilla	ARG	1:01.6	

Coming out of the midrace turn in the 100 meters final at Amsterdam, Weissmuller inadvertently gulped a mouthful of water and almost blacked out. He lost two yards, but regained his composure and went on to win the fourth of his five Olympic gold medals. A couple of years later Weissmuller was training for the 1932 Olympics, when he got an offer of $500 a week to work for the BVD Underwear Company, advertising swimsuits. Out in Hollywood one of his BVD photos was noticed, and he was invited to try out for the part of Tarzan. Needless to say, he got the part, and in 1932 Weissmuller made his film debut in *Tarzan, the Ape Man*. The first of four Olympic medalists to play the part of Tarzan in the movies (the others being Buster Crabbe, Herman Brix, and Glenn Morris), Weissmuller acted in 11 more Tarzan films in the next 16 years.

Johnny Weissmuller won five gold medals in 1924 and 1928 and then gained international fame as Tarzan.

Another activity he engaged in more than once was getting married, which he did five times.

In 1959 Johnny Weissmuller was taking part in a celebrity golf tournament in Havana during a period in which Fidel Castro's guerrilla troops were doing battle with the soldiers of the Batista government. Weissmuller was on his way to the golf course with some friends and a couple of bodyguards, when rebel soldiers suddenly appeared out of the bushes and surrounded their car. The guerrillas disarmed the guards and pointed their rifles at the decadent Yankee imperialists. But Weissmuller had the proper solution to an otherwise difficult situation. Slowly raising himself to his full height, he beat his chest with his fists and let out an enormous yell. After a moment of stunned silence, the revolutionaries broke into smiles of delight and began calling out, "Tarzan! Tarzan! *Bienvenido!* Welcome to Cuba!" Dropping their weapons, they crowded around Johnny, shaking his hand and asking for his autograph. After a few minutes Weissmuller and his party were not only not kidnapped, but they were actually given a rebel escort to the golf course.

1932 Los Angeles C: 22, N: 10, D: 8.7. WR: 57.4 (P. "Johnny" Weissmuller)

1. Yasuji Miyazaki	JPN	58.2
2. Tatsugo Kawaishi	JPN	58.6

3. Albert Schwartz	USA	58.8
4. Manuella Kalili	USA	59.2
5. Zenjiro Takahashi	JPN	59.2
6. Ramond Thompson	USA	59.5

The 1932 men's swimming contests were highlighted by the fantastic performances of the Japanese, who stunned the Americans by winning the relay and by taking first and second in four of the five individual events. The first of these victories was recorded by 15-year-old Yasuji Miyazaki, who brought his schoolbooks with him to Los Angeles so that he wouldn't fall too far behind in his studies. Miyazaki had set an Olympic record of 58.0 in the semifinals.

1936 Berlin C: 45, N: 23, D: 8.9. WR: 56.4 (Peter Fick)

1. Ferenc Csík	HUN	57.6
2. Masanori Yusa	JPN	57.9
3. Shigeo Arai	JPN	58.0
4. Masaharu Taguchi	JPN	58.1
5. Helmut Fischer	GER	59.3
6. Peter Fick	USA	59.7
7. Arthur Lindegren	USA	59.9

Between 1912 and 1944 there were only three world record holders for the 100-meter freestyle: Duke Kahanamoku (1912–1922), Johnny Weissmuller (1922–1934), and Peter Fick (1934–1944). After the first round it appeared that the final would be a contest between Fick and the three Japanese, Taguchi recording the fastest time of 57.5 (an Olympic record), followed by Fick's 57.6. The semifinals were won by Taguchi and Yusa in 57.9 and 57.5, respectively, with Fick looking unusually off form. However, the final provided a major upset. While the Japanese and Americans raced against each other, a 22-year-old Hungarian medical student named Ferenc Csík sneaked up in the outside lane to win the race in his fastest time ever. Although there was no question of who had finished first, there was a good deal of controversy regarding the remaining places. Photos of the finish led observers to believe that the actual order was 2—Taguchi, 3—Yusa, 4—Fick, 5—Arai, 6—Fischer, 7—Lindegren.

Dr. Csík died in an air raid on March 29, 1945, while administering first aid to a wounded man.

1948 London C: 41, N: 20, D: 7.31. WR: 55.4 (Alan Ford)

1. Walter Ris	USA	57.3	OR
2. Alan Ford	USA	57.8	
3. Géza Kádas	HUN	58.1	
4. Keith Carter	USA	58.3	
4. Alexandre Jany	FRA	58.3	
6. Per-Olof Olsson	SWE	59.3	
7. Zoltán Szilárd	HUN	59.6	
8. Taha El Gamal	EGY	1:00.5	

Alex Jany led at the 50-meter turn, but he was passed in the next 25 meters by Ford, Kádas, and Ris. In the last ten meters Wally Ris of Iowa surged past the others to take first place. On March 18, 1944, Alan Ford had made history by becoming the first person to swim 100 yards in less than 50 seconds.

1952 Helsinki C: 61, N: 33, D: 7.27. WR: 55.4 (Alan Ford)

1. Clarke Scholes	USA	57.4
2. Hiroshi Suzuki	JPN	57.4
3. Göran Larsson	SWE	58.2
4. Toru Goto	JPN	58.5
5. Géza Kádas	HUN	58.6
6. Rex Aubrey	AUS	58.7
7. Aldo Eminente	FRA	58.7
8. Ronald Gora	USA	58.8

Scholes set an Olympic record of 57.1 in his preliminary heat.

1956 Melbourne C: 34, N: 19, D: 11.30. WR: 54.8 (Richard Cleveland)

1. Jon Henricks	AUS	55.4	OR
2. John Devitt	AUS	55.8	
3. Gary Chapman	AUS	56.7	
4. Logan Reid Patterson	USA	57.2	
5. Richard Hanley	USA	57.6	
6. William Woolsey	USA	57.6	
7. Atsushi Tani	JPN	58.0	
8. Aldo Eminente	FRA	58.1	

Jon Henricks was the first favorite to win the 100-meter freestyle since Johnny Weissmuller. His victory in the final was his 56th win at that distance in 57 starts over a three-year period. When asked the secret of his success, Henricks, who was as feisty as his good friend and fellow Olympic champion Dawn Fraser, once replied, "You see that goddamn pool there—well, if you want to get to the top of it, dive in and start swimming. You do that for three, four or five years, and every time you stop swimming your coach bawls you out. . . . You get a crazy ear disease from these tropical waters, but you've still got to keep on swimming. You get your head shaved to make you look like a zombie so that you will cut down water resistance, and you shave your legs for the same reason. You get invitations to a party and you write back regretting you are unable to attend owing to a prior engagement. That's a lie, of course, the only prior engagement is at the pool, going up and down, up and down, then up and down again. You finish going up and down and it's time to do some weightlifting—or maybe go to sleep while your coach goes out playing golf or fishing."

1960 Rome C: 51, N: 34, D: 8.26. WR: 54.6 (John Devitt)

1. John Devitt	AUS	55.2	OR
2. Lance Larson	USA	55.2	OR
3. Manuel Dos Santos	BRA	55.4	
4. R. Bruce Hunter	USA	55.6	
5. Gyula Dobai	HUN	56.3	
6. Richard Pound	CAN	56.3	
7. Aubrey Burer	SAF	56.3	
8. Per-Ola Lindberg	SWE	57.1	

Lance Larson, in lane four, appears to touch first at the finish of the 1960 100-meter freestyle. Yet John Devitt, in lane three, was awarded the gold medal.

In 1964 Don Schollander became the first swimmer to earn four gold medals at one Olympics.

Two leading contenders were absent from the final. An emergency appendectomy six days before the U.S. trials prevented Jeff Farrell from qualifying as one of the three American representatives, and defending champion Jon Henricks was eliminated in the semifinals as a result of intestinal problems developed on the way from Australia to Rome.

Dos Santos led the final at the turn, but Larson and Devitt passed him at 70 meters and finished in a near dead heat. Devitt congratulated Larson and left the pool in disappointment. Confusion developed, however, when the judges met to discuss their verdict. Of the three judges assigned the task of determining who had finished first, two voted for Devitt and one for Larson. However the second-place judges also voted 2-1 for Devitt. In other words, of the six judges involved, three thought Devitt had won and three thought Larson had won. When the electronic timers were consulted, it turned out that Larson had registered 55.1 seconds and Devitt 55.2. The unofficial electronic timer also showed Larson winning—by four inches, 55.10 to 55.16. Despite this evidence, the chief judge, Hans Runströmer of Germany, who did not have any say in the matter according to the official rules, ordered Larson's time changed to 55.2 and gave the decision to Devitt. Four years of protests failed to change the result.

1964 Tokyo C: 66, N: 33, D: 10.12. WR: 52.9 (Alain Gottvalles)

1. Donald Schollander	USA	53.4	OR
2. Robert McGregor	GBR	53.5	
3. Hans-Joachim Klein	GER	54.0	
4. Gary Ilman	USA	54.0	
5. Alain Gottvalles	FRA	54.2	
6. Michael Austin	USA	54.5	
7. Gyula Dobai	HUN	54.9	
8. Uwe Jacobsen	GER	56.1	

The fastest times of the qualifying rounds, 54.0 and 53.9, were recorded by Gary Ilman, with Don Schollander close behind at 54.3 and 54.0. In the final, however, Ilman ran into a wave just after the turn and momentarily lost his concentration. Schollander finished strongly, passed McGregor in the last five meters, and won by about six inches. Schollander, who was born in Charlotte, North Carolina, and raised in Lake Oswego, Oregon, was trained by George Haines in Santa Clara, California. Before the Tokyo Games were over, the 18-year-old Schollander had become the first swimmer to win four gold medals at one Olympics.

A minor controversy developed over the awarding of the bronze medal. The judges were split as to whether Ilman or Klein had finished third. Both were clocked in the same time. The Japanese had thoughtfully provided electronic timers for the swimming events and, even though they were not used officially, they were consulted by the judges. It turned out that Ilman and Klein had stopped the clock at the exact same hundredth of a second, but that Klein had finished one one-thousandth of a second sooner. After 35 minutes of consultation, the judges decided that even if the electronic timing was unofficial, it had provided sufficient cause to award third place to Klein.

1968 Mexico City C: 64, N: 35, D: 10.19. WR: 52.6 (Kenneth Walsh, Zachary Zorn)

1. Michael Wenden	AUS	52.2	WR
2. Kenneth Walsh	USA	52.8	
3. Mark Spitz	USA	53.0	
4. Robert McGregor	GBR	53.5	
5. Leonid Ilyichov	SOV/RUS	53.8	
6. Georgi Kulikov	SOV/LAT	53.8	
7. Luis Nicolao	ARG	53.9	
8. Zachary Zorn	USA	53.9	

Zac Zorn had equaled Ken Walsh's world record at the U.S. Olympic trials, and the Americans went to Mexico City as heavy favorites. But they hadn't counted on 18-year-old Michael Wenden of Liverpool, New South Wales. Wenden had arrived in Mexico City hoping to qualify for the final, but when he clocked 53.0 in a trial meet, he began to think he had a shot at the bronze medal. Wenden's heat time of 53.6 was seven-tenths of a second faster than anyone else's, and his semifinal time of 52.9 was a half-second better than the rest. In the final, Zac Zorn, weakened by a week-long illness, went all-out for the first 50 meters and reached the turn almost a full body length ahead of the other swimmers. But he had exhausted himself, and eventually faded to last place. Wenden, on the other hand, swam the race of his life to score the most decisive 100-meter victory in 40 years.

1972 Munich C: 48, N: 30, D: 9.3. WR: 51.47 (Mark Spitz)

1. Mark Spitz	USA	51.22	WR
2. Jerry Heidenreich	USA	51.65	
3. Vladimir Bure	SOV/RUS	51.77	
4. John Murphy	USA	52.08	
5. Michael Wenden	AUS	52.41	
6. Igor Grivennikov	SOV/RUS	52.44	
7. Michel Rousseau	FRA	52.90	
8. Klaus Steinbach	GER	52.92	

Mark Spitz had three goals at the Munich Games. The first was to prove himself better than Don Schollander by becoming the first swimmer to win five gold medals in one Olympics. The second was to become the first athlete in any sport to win six gold medals in one Olympics. The third goal was to go one better and win seven gold medals. It was this final goal that Mark Spitz was having doubts about on September 1. He had already won five gold medals. A sixth gold medal seemed assured, since the final race of the Olympics, the medley relay, looked to be a certain U.S. victory. But about the 100-meter freestyle, Spitz was not so certain. Jerry Heidenreich had been swimming very well lately and had to be considered a serious threat. Spitz's father, Arnold, had constantly stressed to his son from an early age the motto "Swimming isn't everything, winning is." For Mark Spitz, it would have been better to enter four events and win all four than to enter seven events and win only six.

When he heard rumors that Spitz was thinking of withdrawing from the 100 freestyle, Spitz's coach, Sherm Chavoor, who was in Munich as the coach of the U.S. women's team, rushed over to see his student. Chavoor successfully convinced Spitz that he would be perceived as "chicken" if he avoided a confrontation with Heidenreich. Finding this an unacceptable option, Spitz decided against withdrawing.

The heats were swum on the morning of September 2, and the semifinals seven hours later. In both races Spitz held back and finished behind defending champion Michael Wenden and slower than Jerry Heidenreich. In the final the following night, Spitz surprised Heidenreich

In 1968 and 1972 Mark Spitz earned nine gold medals, one silver, and one bronze, including a record seven gold medals in 1972.

when he departed from his usual tactics by going out at full speed rather than saving his strength for the second lap, as he usually did. Spitz reached the turn with a clear lead. With 15 yards to go, Spitz suddenly lost his rhythm, but he pulled himself together and reached the wall a half-stroke ahead of the onrushing Heidenreich.

1976 Montreal C: 41, N: 28, D: 7.25. WR: 50.59 (James Montgomery)

1. James Montgomery	USA	49.99	WR
2. Jack Babashoff	USA	50.81	
3. Peter Nocke	GER	51.31	
4. Klaus Steinbach	GER	51.68	
5. Marcello Guarducci	ITA	51.70	
6. Joe Bottom	USA	51.79	
7. Vladimir Bure	SOV/RUS	52.03	
8. Andrei Krylov	SOV/RUS	52.15	

Jim Montgomery won his semifinal heat in 50.39 to break his own world record. In the final he not only set another record, but he also became the first person to break the 50-second barrier for 100 meters. Three weeks later in Philadelphia, Jonty Skinner brought the record down to 49.44. Skinner was not allowed to compete in the Olympics because he was from South Africa. He later became a coach at the University of Alabama.

1980 Moscow C: 39, N: 27, D: 7.27. WR: 49.44 (Jonty Skinner)

1. Jörg Woithe	GDR	50.40	
2. Per Holmertz	SWE	50.91	
3. Per Johansson	SWE	51.29	
4. Sergei Kopliakov	SOV/BLR	51.34	
5. Raffaele Franceschi	ITA	51.69	
6. Serhei Krasyuk	SOV/UKR	51.80	
7. René Ecuyer	FRA	52.01	
8. Graeme Brewer	AUS	52.22	

Woithe recorded his best time ever, 50.21, in the semifinals. Three days after the boycotted Olympic final, the U.S. Outdoor National was won in 50.19 by Rowdy Gaines, who had twice clocked 49.61. Chris Cavanaugh was second in 50.26.

1984 Los Angeles C: 68, N: 44, D: 7.31. WR: 49.36 (Ambrose "Rowdy" Gaines)

1. Ambrose "Rowdy" Gaines	USA	49.80	OR
2. Mark Stockwell	AUS	50.24	
3. Per Johansson	SWE	50.31	
4. Michael Heath	USA	50.41	
5. Dano Halsall	SWI	50.50	
6. Stephan Caron	FRA	50.70	
6. Alberto Mestre Sosa	VEN	50.70	
8. Dirk Korthals	GER	50.93	

In 1980, Rowdy Gaines, then at the peak of his career, had been expected to win four gold medals. His dreams of triumph and glory were shattered by the U.S. boycott. He decided to stick it out until 1984 and qualified for the 100-meter freestyle by finishing second to Mike Heath at the U.S. trials. This time Gaines felt much less confident of victory. He even prepared a loser's speech in which he would graciously praise those swimmers who had beaten him. In the afternoon, between the qualifying heats and the final, a nervous Gaines tried to relax by watching "The Newlywed Game" and Woody Woodpecker cartoons on television. Only a talk with fellow swimmer Tracy Caulkins calmed him down temporarily.

But standing on the starting block before the race, Gaines, who, at 25, was older than 66 of his 67 rivals in Los Angeles, was trembling like a leaf. However, he still had the presence of mind to recall some important advice from his coach, Richard Quick. Quick had noticed that the starter for the men's swimming events, Frank Silvestri of Panama, was very quick to pull the trigger, so quick in fact that the U.S. team had protested against him at the 1983 Pan-American Games.

With this in mind, Gaines was ready for Silvestri and was first off the blocks, while leading contenders Mark Stockwell and Mike Heath were left behind. Gaines main-

tained his lead for the entire race, earning the first of his three gold medals. The Australians filed an official protest, but it was disallowed.

1988 Seoul C: 77, N: 51, D: 9.22. WR: 48.42 (Matthew Biondi)

1. Matthew Biondi	USA	48.63	OR
2. Christopher Jacobs	USA	49.08	
3. Stephan Caron	FRA	49.62	
4. Gennady Prigoda	SOV/RUS	49.75	
5. Yuri Bashkatov	SOV/MOL	50.08	
6. Andrew Baildon	AUS	50.23	
7. Per Johansson	SWE	50.35	
8. Tommy Werner	SWE	50.54	

Six-foot-six-inch Matt Biondi had already recorded the 10 fastest 100-meter times in history, so his victory in Seoul was not surprising. Still, it was his first gold medal in an individual event and made up for his disappointment in losing the 100-meter butterfly by one one-hundredth of a second. When he climbed out of the Olympic pool after his victory, Biondi fulfilled a commercial contract by announcing to the TV cameras, "I'm going to Disneyland." And then, "I'm going to Disney World." The I.O.C. ordered NBC-TV to destroy the tape of Biondi's statement, which they did quickly. Silver medalist Chris Jacobs was a former cocaine and alcohol addict who gave up drugs and drink two years before the Games.

1992 Barcelona C: 75, N: 52, D: 7.28. WR: 48.42 (Matthew Biondi)

1. Aleksandr Popov	RUS	49.02	
2. Gustavo Borges	BRA	49.43	
3. Stephan Caron	FRA	49.50	
4. Jon Olsen	USA	49.51	
5. Matthew Biondi	USA	49.53	
6. Tommy Werner	SWE	49.63	
7. Christian-Alexander Tröger	GER	49.84	
8. Gennady Prigoda	RUS	50.25	

Aleksandr Popov was a backstroker when coach Gennady Touretsky converted him to freestyle, using underwater tapes of Matt Biondi for training. In the Olympics Popov, who had won the 1991 European championship in 49.18, would face the real Matt Biondi. At the time, Biondi had recorded nine of the ten fastest times in history and he hadn't lost a major race at 100 meters in eight years. He hadn't gone below 49 seconds since 1988, but he had won the United States trials in 49.17.

In Barcelona it was Popov who led the qualifying round at 49.27. In the final Biondi turned first, followed by Prigoda and Borges, while Popov held back in sixth place. Then Popov cut loose with a superb back 50—the first sub-25-second back 50 in history (24.99)—and won a clear victory. The race for second place was not so clear. Gustavo Borges, a 19-year-old student at the University of Michigan, appeared to touch second, but his name did not appear on the scoreboard because the touch pad in his lane malfunctioned. Officials studied a videotape of the finish and concluded that Borges had placed fourth.

A disappointed Borges was sitting crying by the warm-up pool when he was informed that he was actually second—the officials had mistakenly studied Biondi's finish, not that of Borges.

The results of the final left little doubt that the 100 free is a tall man's race. Three of the top five finishers—Borges, Caron, and Biondi—were 6 feet 7 inches tall, while Popov was 6 feet 6 inches and Olsen 6 feet 4 inches. Tommy Werner, in sixth place, was a mere 6 feet 3½ inches, which was no doubt his undoing.

Way, way back in the pack in the qualifying round, Ahmed Imthiyaz became the first athlete from the Maldive Islands not to finish last at the Olympics when he finished next to last in the first heat. Unfortunately, the swimmer he beat was also from the Maldive Islands.

200-METER FREESTYLE

1896 not held

1900 Paris C: 26, N: 9, D: 8.12. WR (220 yards): 2:38.2 (Frederick Lane)

1. Frederick Lane	AUS	2:25.2	OR
2. Zoltán Halmay	HUN	2:31.4	
3. Karl Ruberl	AUT	2:32.0	
4. Robert Crawshaw	GBR	2:45.6	
5. Maurice Hochepied	FRA	2:53.0	
6. F. Stapleton	GBR	2:55.0	

The unusually fast times were due to the fact that the 1900 swimming races were held in the River Seine and swum *with* the current. Freddie Lane was unusually small for a swimmer: 5 feet 6 inches tall (1.68 m) and 133 pounds (60 kg). In honor of his victories in Paris, Lane was awarded a 50-pound bronze statue of a horse and an equally large bronze of Jean François Millet's *The Gleaners*. Lane managed to haul the statues back to Australia where he displayed them in his home until they were destroyed by a fire in 1968 when he was 88 years old. Two years after his Olympic triumphs, on July 24, 1902, Lane became the first person to swim 100 yards in one minute.

1904 St. Louis C: 4, N: 2, D: 9.6 WR (220 yards): 2:28.6 (Frederick Lane)

(220 Yards)

1. Charles Daniels	USA	2:44.2	
2. Francis Gailey	USA	2:46.0	
3. Emil Rausch	GER	2:56.0	
4. Edgar Adams	USA	—	

1906–1964 not held

1968 Mexico City C: 57, N: 27, D: 10.24. WR: 1:54.3 (Donald Schollander)

1. Michael Wenden	AUS	1:55.2	OR
2. Donald Schollander	USA	1:55.8	
3. John Nelson	USA	1:58.1	
4. Ralph Hutton	CAN	1:58.6	
5. Alain Mosconi	FRA	1:59.1	
6. Robert Windle	AUS	2:00.9	
7. Semyon Belits-Geiman	SOV/RUS	2:01.5	

DNS: Stephen Rerych (USA)

Michael Wenden won his second gold medal, while Don Schollander added a silver to his five golds. Both swimmers were stretched to the limit by their high-altitude ordeal. Schollander had to be given oxygen while Wenden actually lost consciousness in the pool and almost drowned. He was saved by teammate Robert Windle. Afterward Schollander announced his retirement, telling reporters, "I'm finished with water—in fact I may not take a bath or a shower for another two years." As for Wenden, he returned to Australia a hero and had to face the shock of suddenly being a public person. His advice to future gold medalists? "Seek advice about an appropriate business manager and maintain close contact with a psychologist."

1972 Munich C: 46, N: 31, D: 8.29. WR: 1:53.5 (Mark Spitz)

1. Mark Spitz	USA	1:52.78	WR
2. Steven Genter	USA	1:53.73	
3. Werner Lampe	GER	1:53.99	
4. Michael Wenden	AUS	1:54.40	
5. Frederick Tyler	USA	1:54.96	
6. Klaus Steinbach	GER	1:55.65	
7. Vladimir Bure	SOV/RUS	1:57.24	
8. Ralph Hutton	CAN	1:57.56	

Spitz trailed Genter with 50 meters to go, but came from behind to win his third gold medal in two days. Genter's performance was remarkable for the fact that he underwent surgery in Munich for a partially collapsed lung and had been released from the hospital only the day before the race. On the victory platform Spitz waved his shoes at the crowd and the cameras. Called before an I.O.C. committee, he successfully convinced them that he had been motivated by exuberance rather than commercialism.

1976 Montreal C: 55, N: 33, D: 7.19. WR: 1:50.32 (Bruce Furniss)

1. Bruce Furniss	USA	1:50.29	WR
2. John Naber	USA	1:50.50	
3. Jim Montgomery	USA	1:50.58	
4. Andrei Krylov	SOV/RUS	1:50.73	
5. Klaus Steinbach	GER	1:51.09	
6. Peter Nocke	GER	1:51.71	
7. Gordon Downie	GBR	1:52.78	
8. Andrei Bogdanov	SOV/RUS	1:53.33	

Furniss moved ahead in the last 50 meters to edge Naber, who had won the 100-meter backstroke an hour earlier.

1980 Moscow C: 42, N: 25, D: 7.21. WR: 1:49.16 (Ambrose "Rowdy" Gaines)

1. Sergei Kopliakov	SOV/BLR	1:49.81	OR
2. Andrei Krylov	SOV/RUS	1:50.76	
3. Graeme Brewer	AUS	1:51.60	
4. Jörg Woithe	GDR	1:51.86	

5. Ron McKeon	AUS	1:52.60	
6. Paolo Revelli	ITA	1:52.76	
7. Thomas Lejdström	SWE	1:52.94	
8. Fabrizio Rampazzo	ITA	1:53.25	

On August 1, the U.S. Outdoor National was won by Rowdy Gaines in 1:50.02.

1984 Los Angeles C: 56, N: 36, D: 7.29. WR: 1:47.55 (Michael Gross)

1. Michael Gross	GER	1:47.44	WR
2. Michael Heath	USA	1:49.10	
3. Thomas Fahrner	GER	1:49.69	
4. Jeffrey Float	USA	1:50.18	
5. Alberto Mestre Sosa	VEN	1:50.23	
6. Frank Drost	HOL	1:51.62	
7. Marco Dell'Uomo	ITA	1:52.20	
8. Peter Dale	AUS	1:53.84	

Standing 6 feet 7 inches and with a "wingspan" of 6 feet 11 inches, Michael Gross of Offenbach gained the nickname "The Albatross." In the 200-meter freestyle, Gross overwhelmed his opposition, winning by two bodylengths (two very long bodylengths) and becoming the first West German ever to win an Olympic swimming title.

1988 Seoul C: 63, N: 41, D: 9.19. WR: 1:47.44 (Michael Gross)

1. Duncan Armstrong	AUS	1:47.25	WR
2. Anders Holmertz	SWE	1:47.89	
3. Matthew Biondi	USA	1:47.99	
4. Artur Wojdat	POL	1:48.40	
5. Michael Gross	GER	1:48.59	
6. Steffen Zesner	GDR	1:48.77	
7. Troy Dalbey	USA	1:48.86	
8. Thomas Fahrner	GER	1:49.19	

A talent-rich field lined up for the final. Michael Gross was the world record holder at 200 meters, the defending Olympic champion, and the two-time defending world champion. Matt Biondi, the world record holder in the 100-meter freestyle, had clocked the fastest non-Gross time of the year. Artur Wojdat, the world record holder in the 400-meter freestyle, had registered the best time of the preliminaries: 1:48.02. Anders Holmertz, although barely qualifying for the Olympic final, had swum the fastest time of 1987 in winning the European championship.

Few people paid any attention to Duncan Armstrong of Brisbane. More should have, though—his qualifying time of 1:48.66 bettered his two-year-old pre-Olympic best by 1.3 seconds. Armstrong, who was ranked forty-sixth in the world at the time, appeared to be peaking at the right time.

Armstrong was coached by Lawrie Laurence, who had coached Jon Sieben to an upset victory over Michael Gross in the 200-meter butterfly at the 1984 Olympics. Following the preliminaries of the Seoul 200-meter freestyle, Lawrence devised a special strategy for Armstrong in the final. He was assigned to lane 6 (as Sieben had been four years earlier) with Biondi beside him in lane 5. Because Biondi could be counted on to lead for the first 150 meters, Lawrence advised Armstrong to conserve energy by swimming as close to Biondi's lane as possible, drafting in the wake of the powerful American. Armstrong followed the strategy to perfection. As he explained later, "I just sucked into his trough and body-surfed the first 100 meters." Placed third at the final turn, he passed Holmertz and then slingshotted away from Biondi with 25 meters to go. His time of 1:47.25 ended Michael Gross' 5-year reign as world record holder.

1992 Barcelona C: 55, N: 39, D: 7.26. WR: 1:46.69 (Giorgio Lamberti)

1. Yevgeny Sadovyi	RUS	1:46.70	OR
2. Anders Holmertz	SWE	1:46.86	
3. Antti Kasvio	FIN	1:47.63	
4. Artur Wojdat	POL	1:48.24	
5. Vladimir Pyshnenko	RUS	1:48.32	
6. Joseph Hudepohl	USA	1:48.36	
7. Steffen Zesner	GER	1:48.84	
8. Douglas Gjertsen	USA	1:50.57	

Laid low by flu, world champion and world record holder Giorgio Lamberti failed to qualify for the Italian team except in the 100 free. Lightly regarded at 200 meters prior to the Olympics, Yevgeny Sadovyi of Volgograd almost broke Lamberti's world record in the qualifying round when he swam a 1:46.74. In the final he came even closer, winning the first of his three gold medals, while Holmertz picked up his second straight silver medal. Antti Kasvio, in third place, became the first Finnish swimmer to earn an Olympic medal.

400-METER FREESTYLE

1896 Athens C: 3, N: 2, D: 4.11.
(500 Meters)

1. Paul Neumann	AUT	8:12.6
2. Antonios Pepanos	GRE	9:57.6
3. Eustathios Choraphas	GRE	—

1900 not held

1904 St. Louis C: 4, N: 2, D: 9.7. WR(440 yards): 5:22.2
(440 Yards)

1. Charles Daniels	USA	6:16.2
2. Francis Gailey	USA	6:22.0
3. Otto Wahle	AUT	6:39.0
4. Leo Goodwin	USA	—

1906 Athens C: 12, N: 5, D: 4.26. WR(440 yards): 5:19.0

1. Otto Scheff	AUT	6:23.8
2. Henry Taylor	GBR	6:24.4
3. John Arthur Jarvis	GBR	6:27.2
4. Alajos Bruckner	HUN	—
5. Paul Radmilovic	GBR	—
6. Cecil Healy	AUS	—

1908 London C: 25, N: 10, D: 7.16. WR(440 yards): 5:19.0
1. Henry Taylor   GBR   5:36.8
2. Francis Beaurepaire   AUS   5:44.2
3. Otto Scheff   AUT   5:46.0
4. William Foster   GBR   —

Henry Taylor, a cotton mill worker from Oldham, Lancashire, won the first of his three gold medals at the London Games. Including the Intercalated Games of 1906 and the Olympics of 1912 and 1920, Taylor earned a total of four gold medals, one silver, and three bronze. This race also marked the first appearance of "Frank" Beaurepaire, who was still winning Olympic medals in 1924 at the age of 33. Beaurepaire missed the 1912 Olympics when he was suspended for professionalism. His crime? As part of his job as a physical education teacher, he lectured on swimming and lifesaving.

1912 Stockholm C: 26, N: 13, D: 7.14. WR: 5:23.0 (Frank Beaurepaire)
1. George Hodgson   CAN   5:24.4   OR
2. John Hatfield   GBR   5:25.8
3. Harold Hardwick   AUS   5:31.2
4. Cecil Healy   AUS   5:37.8
5. Béla Las-Torres   HUN   5:42.0

Hodgson had won the 1500 meters four days earlier. Bronze medalist Harold Hardwick was a multitalented athlete who won the Australian professional heavyweight boxing championship in 1915.

1920 Antwerp C: 22, N: 11, D: 8.28. WR: 5:14.6 (Norman Ross)
1. Norman Ross   USA   5:26.8
2. Ludy Langer   USA   5:29.0
3. George Vernot   CAN   5:29.6
4. Fred Kahele   USA   —
DNF: Francis Beaurepaire (AUS)

Twenty-four-year-old Norman Ross also won gold medals in the 1500-meter freestyle and in the 4 × 200-meter relay. He later achieved success as a radio music announcer.

1924 Paris C: 23, N: 13, D: 7.18. WR: 4:54.7 (Arne Borg)
1. P. "Johnny" Weissmuller   USA   5:04.2   OR
2. Arne Borg   SWE   5:05.6
3. Andrew "Boy" Charlton   AUS   5:06.6
4. Åke Borg   SWE   5:26.0
5. John Hatfield   GBR   5:32.0
6. Lester Smith (USA)

This was a thrilling race in which no more than five feet separated Weissmuller and Borg at any time. At 100 meters, Borg led by six inches. At the halfway mark, it was Weissmuller by nine inches, and at 300 meters, Borg touched first by three inches. Weissmuller finally drew away 20 meters from the finish and won by four feet.

Arne and Åke Borg were twin brothers.

1928 Amsterdam C: 26, N: 17, D: 8.9. WR: 4:50.3 (Arne Borg)
1. Alberto Zorrilla   ARG   5:01.6   OR
2. Andrew "Boy" Charlton AUS   5:03.6
3. Arne Borg   SWE   5:04.6
4. Clarence "Buster" Crabbe   USA   5:05.4
5. Austin Clapp   USA   5:16.0
6. Raymond Ruddy   USA   5:25.0

Charlton and Borg were so intent on their personal duel that they failed to notice Zorrilla creep up in the outside lane and move ahead in the last 50 meters. In 1931, Zorrilla won the European ballroom dancing championship.

1932 Los Angeles C: 19, N: 10, D: 8.10. WR: 4:47.0 (Jean Taris)
1. Clarence "Buster" Crabbe   USA   4:48.4   OR
2. Jean Taris   FRA   4:48.5
3. Tsutomu Oyokota   JPN   4:52.3
4. Takashi Yokoyama   JPN   4:52.5
5. Noboru Sugimoto   JPN   4:56.1
6. Andrew "Boy" Charlton AUS   4:58.6

Takashi Yokoyama set Olympic records of 4:53.2 and 4:51.4 in the opening round and the semifinals, but the final turned out to be a duel between world record holder

Buster Crabbe came from behind to win the 1932 400-meter freestyle by one tenth of a second, in a thrilling finish. He attracted the attention of Hollywood producers, who later cast him as Tarzan, Buck Rogers, and Flash Gordon.

Jean Taris and local favorite Buster Crabbe. Taris sprinted to an early lead and reached the halfway mark two lengths ahead. By 300 meters, Crabbe had cut the gap to one length. He continued to edge closer, finally drawing even 25 meters from the finish. The excitement was so great that swimmers and ushers rushed over from all parts of the stadium, while Johnny Weissmuller, sitting in the front row, leaped a fence to get a closer view of the finish. Crabbe touched the wall inches ahead of Taris. "That one-tenth of a second changed my life," Crabbe later recalled. "It was then that [the Hollywood producers] discovered latent histrionic abilities in me." Crabbe went on to great fame as an actor; he was best known for his roles as Tarzan, Buck Rogers, and Flash Gordon. He died on April 23, 1983, at the age of 75.

1936 Berlin C: 34, N: 16, D: 8.12. WR: 4:38.7 (Jack Medica)
1. Jack Medica   USA   4:44.5   OR
2. Shumpei Uto   JPN   4:45.6
3. Shozo Makino   JPN   4:48.1
4. Ralph Flanagan   USA   4:52.7
5. Hiroshi Negami   JPN   4:53.6
6. Jean Taris   FRA   4:53.8
7. Robert Leivers   GBR   5:00.9

Jack Medica of Seattle staged a thrilling last-lap spurt to overtake Uto ten meters from the finish.

1948 London C: 41, N: 21, D: 8.4. WR: 4:35.2 (Alexandre Jany)
1. William Smith   USA   4:41.0   OR
2. James McLane   USA   4:43.4
3. John Marshall   AUS   4:47.4
4. Géza Kádas   HUN   4:49.4
5. György Mitró   HUN   4:49.9
6. Alexandre Jany   FRA   4:51.4
7. Jack Hale   GBR   4:55.9
8. Alfredo Yantorno   ARG   4:58.7

Bill Smith had been stricken with typhoid when he was six years old, and took up swimming to rebuild his body.

1952 Helsinki C: 51, N: 29, D: 7.30. WR: 4:26.9 (John Marshall)
1. Jean Boiteux   FRA   4:30.7   OR
2. Ford Konno   USA   4:31.3
3. Per-Olof Östrand   SWE   4:35.2
4. Peter Duncan   SAF   4:37.9
5. John Wardrop   GBR   4:39.9
6. Wayne Moore   USA   4:40.1
7. James McLane   USA   4:40.3
8. Hironashin Furuhashi JPN   4:42.1

Boiteux held off a late challenge from Ford Konno to win a surprise gold medal. As soon as he touched the wall, an older Frenchman in a beret rushed forward, leaped fully clothed into the water, and embraced the new champion. Reporters gathered around to find out who he was. "Coach?" "Manager?" they asked in various languages. Beaming with pride and overcome with emotion, the man in the beret held his arms up and uttered one word: "Papa!"

Jean Boiteux, winner of the 1952 400-meter freestyle, helps his proud father out of the pool after the latter leaped in to congratulate his son.

1956 Melbourne C: 32, N: 19, D: 12.4. WR: 4:26.7 (Ford Konno)
1. I. Murray Rose   AUS   4:27.3   OR
2. Tsuyoshi Yamanaka   JPN   4:30.4
3. George Breen   USA   4:32.5
4. Kevin O'Halloran   AUS   4:32.9
5. Hans Zierold   GDR   4:34.6
6. Garry Winram   AUS   4:34.9
7. Koji Nonoshita   JPN   4:38.2
8. Angelo Romani   ITA   4:41.7

Murray Rose was a 17-year-old vegetarian who became known as "The Seaweed Streak." Since his diet could not be provided for in the Olympic Village, Rose's parents moved him out and took care of his nutrition. His three gold medals at the Melbourne Games made a lot of Australians think twice about their diet.

1960 Rome C: 40, N: 25, D: 8.31. WR(440 yards): 4:15.9 (John Konrads)
1. I. Murray Rose   AUS   4:18.3   OR
2. Tsuyoshi Yamanaka   JPN   4:21.4
3. John Konrads   AUS   4:21.8
4. Ian Black   GBR   4:21.8
5. Alan Somers   USA   4:22.0
6. Murray McLachlan   SAF   4:26.3
7. Eugene Lenz   USA   4:26.8
8. Makoto Fukui   JPN   4:29.6

By 1960, both Murray Rose and Tsuyoshi Yamanaka had moved to Los Angeles and become students at the University of Southern California. In Rome, Alan Somers set an Olympic record of 4:19.2 in the qualifying round, but was unable to reproduce his time in the final. Although four years had passed since the last Olympics, Rose and Yamanaka repeated their one-two finish, with the exact same distance separating them.

1964 Tokyo C: 49, N: 27, D: 10.15. WR: 4:12.7 (Donald Schollander)

1. Donald Schollander	USA	4:12.2	WR
2. Frank Wiegand	GDR	4:14.9	
3. Allan Wood	AUS	4:15.1	
4. Roy Saari	USA	4:16.7	
5. John Nelson	USA	4:16.9	
6. Tsuyoshi Yamanaka	JPN	4:19.1	
7. Russell Phegan	AUS	4:20.2	
8. Semyon Belits-Geiman	SOV/RUS	4:21.4	

Schollander swam the last 100 meters in 1:01.7 to win his third gold medal.

1968 Mexico City C: 37, N: 20, D: 10.23. WR: 4:06.5 (Ralph Hutton)

1. Michael Burton	USA	4:09.0	OR
2. Ralph Hutton	CAN	4:11.7	
3. Alain Mosconi	FRA	4:13.3	
4. Gregory Brough	AUS	4:15.9	
5. Graham White	AUS	4:16.7	
6. John Nelson	USA	4:17.2	
7. Hans-Joachim Fassnacht	GER	4:18.1	
8. Brent Berk	USA	4:26.0	

The day before the qualifying heats, Mike Burton woke up feeling nauseated; later he fainted in an elevator in the Olympic Village. The next day he "took it easy" and qualified in 4:19.3. He took charge of the final before the halfway mark and won going away, covering the last 100 meters in 1:01.6.

1972 Munich C: 43, N: 28, D: 9.1. WR: 4:00.11 (Kurt Krumpholz)

— Rick DeMont	USA	4:00.26	
1. Bradford Cooper	AUS	4:00.27	OR
2. Steven Genter	USA	4:01.94	
3. Tom McBreen	USA	4:02.64	
4. Graham Windeatt	AUS	4:02.93	
5. Brian Brinkley	GBR	4:06.69	
6. Bengt Gingsjö	SWE	4:06.75	
7. Werner Lampe	GER	4:06.97	

Rick DeMont was a 16-year-old from San Rafael, California. Allergic to wheat and fur, he had been taking medication for asthma since he was four years old. When DeMont qualified for the U.S. Olympic team, he was asked to fill out a standard medical form in which he listed all medications that he took. The team physicians of most other nations took this information from their athletes, found out the component parts of the various drugs from the *Physician's Desk Reference (PDR)* or similar works, and compared them to the list of banned drugs issued by the I.O.C. for the 1972 Olympics. If any forbidden drugs were being used, the physicians came up with acceptable substitutes for their athletes. Unfortunately the U.S. team physicians were not so well organized. Evidently they never even looked at the forms. Instead, they just told the athletes not to take any drugs within 48 hours of competing without first clearing it with a doctor.

The night before the 400 meters competition, Rick De-

Sixteen-year-old Rick DeMont (center) finished first in the 1972 400-meter freestyle, but was disqualified for taking an asthma drug he didn't know was on the prohibited list.

Mont woke up wheezing between 1 a.m. and 2 a.m., and took a tablet of Marax, unaware that it contained the banned drug ephedrine. At 8 a.m. he took another tablet. He swam his heat at about noon and qualified easily. Since his prescription said to take one tablet every six hours, he might have taken one more dose of Marax later in the day. The final began at 6:40 p.m. DeMont started slowly, saving his strength. In last place after 100 meters and sixth after 200, he picked up speed in the second half of the race. Swimming the last 100 meters in 58.22 seconds, he defeated Cooper by one-hundredth of a second, the smallest margin possible. After the race, DeMont, along with the other two medalists, was taken away for dope testing. At the awards ceremony there was no indication of any problem.

Two days later, on Sunday, DeMont, who was the world record holder at 1500 meters, took part in the preliminary round of that event, qualifying without being pressed. The next morning, however, he was informed that he had failed the drug test after the 400 meters and therefore would not be allowed to take part in the final of the 1500 meters. A distraught DeMont watched from the stands.

Over the next couple of days, hearings were held, affidavits were filed, and confusion reigned. At one point, DeMont's pharmacist in California received a call from a U.S. doctor in Munich asking him, among other things, what Marax contained. Apparently, not one U.S. team physician had bothered to take a copy of the *PDR* to Germany. The I.O.C. ordered DeMont disqualified and issued a stern reprimand to the U.S. officials in charge. Put on the defensive, team physicians tried to blame the swimming coaches, DeMont's family doctor, even the teenager himself. Yet DeMont had made no attempt to hide the fact that he took Marax. He didn't even know it was forbidden. When team officials had entered his room at the Olympic Village on Sunday to confiscate his drugs, the bottle of Marax was sitting in plain view.

By 1976 U.S. swim officials had learned their lesson. Before the Montreal Olympics, the 51 members of the U.S. team were questioned carefully about their medications, and it was learned that 16 of them were unknowingly using banned drugs. Substitutes were found for those 16, but all of this was far too late to help Rick DeMont, who had become the first American since Jim Thorpe to be forced to return his gold medal.

1976 Montreal C: 47, N: 29, D: 7.22. WR: 3:53.08 (Brian Goodell)

1. Brian Goodell	USA	3:51.93	WR
2. Tim Shaw	USA	3:52.54	
3. Volodymyr Raskatov	SOV/UKR	3:55.76	
4. Djan Madruga Garrido	BRA	3:57.18	
5. Stephen Holland	AUS	3:57.59	
6. Sándor Nagy	HUN	3:57.81	
7. Vladimir Mikheyev	SOV/RUS	4:00.79	
8. Stephen Badger	CAN	4:02.83	

Brian Goodell had already won the 1500 meters gold medal two days earlier. United States dominance in the 400-meter freestyle was so great that Volodymyr Raskatov's pre-Olympic European record of 3:58.02 would not have qualified him for the final at the U.S. trials. Silver medalist Tim Shaw also won a silver medal in water polo in 1984.

1980 Moscow C: 28, N: 16, D: 7.24. WR: 3:50.49 (Peter Szmidt)

1. Vladimir Salnikov	SOV/RUS	3:51.31	OR
2. Andrei Krylov	SOV/RUS	3:53.24	
3. Ivar Stukolkin	SOV/EST	3:53.95	
4. Djan Madruga Garrido	BRA	3:54.15	
5. Daniel Machek	CZE	3:55.66	
6. Sándor Nagy	HUN	3:56.83	
7. Max Metzker	AUS	3:56.87	
8. Ronald McKeon	AUS	3:57.00	

Twenty-year-old Vladimir Salnikov of Leningrad was one of several Soviet swimmers who had been training in the United States when President Jimmy Carter made his first speech threatening a boycott of the Moscow Olympics unless Soviet troops pulled out of Afghanistan. However, Soviet coach Sergei Vaitsekhovsky was quick to thank American swimmers and coaches for the subsequent Soviet successes at the Olympics. "The Americans," he explained, "surprised us by not keeping any of their training secrets from us, which means there must still be some decent people left in the world."

Peter Szmidt of Canada set a world record of 3:50.49 in the 400 meters just before the Moscow Games began. At the U.S. Outdoor National on July 31, Mike Bruner finished first in 3:52.19, followed by Brian Goodell in 3:52.99.

1984 Los Angeles C: 36, N: 25, D: 8.2. WR: 3:48.32 (Vladimir Salnikov)

1. George DiCarlo	USA	3:51.23	OR
2. John Mykkanen	USA	3:51.49	
3. Justin Lemberg	AUS	3:51.79	
4. Stefan Pfeiffer	GER	3:52.91	
5. Franck Iacono	FRA	3:54.58	
6. Darjan Petric	YUG	3:54.88	
7. Marco Dell'Uomo	ITA	3:55.44	
8. Ronald McKeon	AUS	3:55.48	

In the absence of world record holder and defending Olympic champion Vladimir Salnikov, the gold medal was won by 21-year-old George DiCarlo, who led from the start and held on to break Salnikov's Olympic record. But the real stir in the 400-meter freestyle came a few minutes later. For the 1984 Games a consolation final had been added to determine places 9 through 16. It was here that Thomas Fahrner of West Germany saw a chance to redeem himself for the blunder he had committed in the preliminary round. Hoping to qualify just fast enough to gain an outside lane for the final, Fahrner took it easy and found himself shut out completely with only the ninth fastest qualifying time. In the consolation race, Fahrner gave it everything he had, bettering his personal best by almost two seconds and breaking DiCarlo's short-lived Olympic record with a time of 3:50.91.

1988 Seoul C: 49, N: 33., D: 9.23. WR: 3:47.38 (Artur Wojdat)

1. Uwe Dassler	GDR	3:46.95	WR
2. Duncan Armstrong	AUS	3:47.15	

Uwe Dassler, winner of the 1988 400-meter freestyle.

3. Artur Wojdat	POL	3:47.34
4. Matthew Cetlinski	USA	3:48.09
5. Mariusz Podkościelny	POL	3:48.59
6. Stefan Pfeiffer	GER	3:49.96
7. Kevin Boyd	GBR	3:50.16
8. Anders Holmertz	SWE	3:51.04

All eight finalists had to break Thomas Fahrner's Olympic record just to qualify for the final. Holmertz took the early lead with Cetlinski and Wojdat close behind, Dassler in fourth, and Armstrong last. There were no changes in position for the first 200 meters. At 225 meters Cetlinski passed Holmertz and stayed in front until the 350 mark. Then he was caught by Wojdat, who sprinted home to break his own world record. Wojdat finished third. He was no match for the incredible closing rushes of Dassler and Armstrong, who swam the last 100 meters in 55.55 and 55.02, respectively. Dassler beat Armstrong by 1 foot with Wojdat another foot behind. Dassler improved his personal record by 2 seconds; Armstrong bettered his pre-Olympic best by 5 seconds.

1992 Barcelona C: 46, N: 31, D: 7.29. WR: 3:46.47 (Kieren Perkins)

1. Yevgeny Sadovyi	RUS	3:45.00	WR
2. Kieren Perkins	AUS	3:45.16	
3. Anders Holmertz	SWE	3:46.77	
4. Artur Wojdat	POL	3:48.10	
5. Ian Brown	AUS	3:48.79	
6. Sebastian Wiese	GER	3:49.06	
7. Stefan Pfeiffer	GER	3:49.75	
8. Danyon Loader	NZE	3:49.97	

Just as he had four years earlier in Seoul, Anders Holmertz took the early lead and was still on world record pace after 300 meters. But as fast as he was going, Holmertz was never much more than a meter ahead of either Yevgeny Sadovyi or Kieren Perkins. Sadovyi had already won two golds in the 200-meter freestyle and the 4 × 200-meter relay. Perkins had broken Uwe Dassler's world record at the Australian Olympic trials in April. The two passed Holmertz almost in tandem, with Sadovyi holding his edge the whole way as both he and Perkins swam the last 100 meters in 54.62 seconds to blast Perkins' world record. All of the finalists set personal bests except Wojdat and Pfeiffer. Sadovyi beat his by 4 seconds. Almost as thrilling for Sadovyi as his victory was the fact that after the race he was interviewed for Russian television by his idol, Vladimir Salnikov, whom he had never met.

This was the first time in 80 years that swimmers from the United States had competed but failed to qualify for the final.

1500-METER FREESTYLE

1896 Athens C: 9, N: 4, D: 4.11.
(1200 Meters)

1. Alfréd Hajós	HUN	18:22.2
2. Ioannis Andreou	GRE	21:03.4
3. Eustathios Choraphas	GRE	—

The competitors had to battle not only each other, but also horribly cold weather and 12-foot waves. Alfréd Hajós, the eventual winner, gave the following graphic description of the race:

"Three small boats took us out to the open sea, which was quite rough. My body had been smeared with a half-inch-thick layer of grease, for I was more cunning after the 100 meters event, and tried to protect myself against the cold. We jumped into the water at the start of a pistol, and from that point on the boats left the competitors to the mercy of the waves, rushing back to the finish line, to inform the jury of the successful start.

"I must say that I shivered from the thought of what would happen if I got a cramp from the cold water. My will to live completely overcame my desire to win. I cut through the water with a powerful determination and only became calm when the boats came back in my direction, and began to fish out the numbed competitors who were giving up the struggle. At that time I was already at the mouth of the bay. The roar of the crowd increased . . . I won ahead of the others with a big lead."

Alfréd Hajós survived 55-degree Fahrenheit water and 12-foot waves to win the 1200-meter freestyle in 1896. He later recalled, "My will to live completely overcame my desire to win."

1900 Paris C: 16, N: 6, D: 8.12.
(1000 Meters)

1. John Arthur Jarvis   GBR   13:40.2
2. Otto Wahle   AUT   14:53.6
3. Zoltán Halmay   HUN   15:16.4
4. Max Hainle   GER   15:22.6
5. Louis Martin   FRA   16:34.4
6. Leuillieux   FRA   16:53.2

1904 St. Louis C: 7, N: 4, D: 9.6. WR: 24:36.2
(1 Mile—1609.34 Meters)

1. Emil Rausch   GER   27:18.2
2. Géza Kiss   HUN   28:28.2
3. Francis Gailey   USA   28:54.0
4. Otto Wahle   AUT   —

DNF: Edgar Adams (USA), Louis deBreda Handley (USA), John Meyers (USA)

1906 Athens C: 24, N: 10, D: 4.24.

1. Henry Taylor   GBR   28:28.0
2. John Arthur Jarvis   GBR   30:07.6
3. Otto Scheff   AUT   30:53.4
4. Max Pape   GER   32:34.6
5. Emil Rausch   GER   32:40.6
6. Ernst Bahnmeyer   GER   33:29.4
7. Oskar Schiele   GER   33:52.4
8. Leopold Mayer   AUT   34:41.0

1908 London C: 19, N: 8, D: 7.25.

1. Henry Taylor   GBR   22:48.4   WR
2. Thomas Battersby   GBR   22:51.2
3. Francis Beaurepaire   AUS   22:56.2

DNF: Otto Scheff (AUT)

Battersby led from the start and wasn't overtaken by Taylor until less than 200 meters remained. Taylor's time was the first internationally acknowledged world record for the 1500-meter freestyle. An English swimmer with the unusually appropriate name of L. Moist was eliminated in the semifinals.

1912 Stockholm C: 19, N: 11, D: 7.10. WR: 22:48.4 (Henry Taylor)

1. George Hodgson   CAN   22:00.0   WR
2. John Hatfield   GBR   22:39.0
3. Harold Hardwick   AUS   23:15.4

DNF: Malcolm Champion (NZE), Béla Las-Torres (HUN)

Until the 1984 Games, George Hodgson of Montreal was the only Canadian to win an Olympic swimming championship. In the first round he set a world record of 22:23.0. He bettered this time in the final, setting a 1000-meter world record of 14:37.0 on the way. After completing 1500 meters, he continued on to swim the mile, setting three world records in one race. Four days later, he also won the 400-meter race. His 1500-meter record lasted for 11 years.

1920 Antwerp C: 23, N: 12, D: 8.25. WR: 22:00.0 (George Hodgson)

1. Norman Ross   USA   22:23.2
2. George Vernot   CAN   22:36.4e
3. Francis Beaurepaire   AUS   23:04.0e
4. Fred Kahele   USA   23:59.1e
5. Eugene Bolden   USA   24:04.3e

Ross allowed Vernot to set the early pace, then took charge midway and went on to win by 12 meters.

1924 Paris C: 22, N: 12, D: 7.15. WR: 21:15.0 (Arne Borg)

1. Andrew "Boy" Charlton   AUS   20:06.6   WR
2. Arne Borg   SWE   20:41.4
3. Francis Beaurepaire   AUS   21:48.4
4. John Hatfield   GBR   21:55.6
5. Katsuo Takaishi   JPN   22:10.4
6. Åke Borg (SWE)

The son of a bank manager in Manly, Boy Charlton became an Australian cultural icon when, at the age of 16, he defeated the great Swedish swimmer, Arne Borg, in a heavily publicized 440-yard race in Sydney in early 1924. Borg added to the sensation of Charlton's victory by rowing his conqueror the length of the pool in a dinghy and hailing him as a champion. A few months later, Charlton sailed for Paris, accompanied by his coach, a local war veteran named Tom Adrian, as well as the rest of the Australian team. Unfortunately, Adrian suffered from what was then known as shell shock and what is now known as post-traumatic stress syndrome. As the steamer headed west, Adrian became increasingly moody. Finally he threw himself overboard. He was fished out safely, but he was never the same again, and there was great apprehension that Charlton's performance would be adversely affected. Instead, the teenager seemed more determined than ever, winning his preliminary heat in 21:20.8. Arne Borg, "The Swedish Sturgeon," came right back in the next heat to break his own world record in a time of 21:11.4. However, in the final, it was Charlton who prevailed, bettering Borg's two-day-old record by over a minute.

1928 Amsterdam C: 19, N: 13, D: 8.6. WR: 19:07.2 (Arne Borg)

1. Arne Borg   SWE   19:51.8   OR
2. Andrew "Boy" Charlton   AUS   20:02.6
3. Clarence "Buster" Crabbe   USA   20:28.8
4. Raymond Ruddy   USA   21:05.0
5. Alberto Zorrilla   ARG   21:23.8
6. Garnet Ault   CAN   21:46.0

Arne Borg led from start to finish to win his only Olympic gold medal. Borg was an extremely popular athlete in Sweden and abroad. Once he was called up for military service, but ignored the notice in order to take a tour of Spain. Imprisoned upon his return to Sweden, he received so many gifts of food and wine during his incarceration that he gained 17 pounds before he was finally released. Between 1921 and 1929, Borg set 32 world records at distances from 300 yards to one mile. His 1500 meters world record of 19:07.2, set in Bologna on September 2, 1927, remained unbroken for almost 11 years. He set the record despite having just lost four teeth in a water polo match against France.

1932 Los Angeles C: 15, N: 8, D: 8.13. WR: 19.07.2 (Arne Borg)
1. Kusuo Kitamura   JPN   19:12.4   OR
2. Shozo Makino   JPN   19:14.1
3. James Cristy   USA   19:39.5
4. Noel Philip Ryan   AUS   19:45.1
5. Clarence "Buster" Crabbe USA 20:02.7
6. Jean Taris   FRA   20:09.7

Fourteen-year-old Kusuo Kitamura pulled away from his 17-year-old teammate, Shozo Makino, in the final 300 meters. Kitamura, the youngest male ever to win an Olympic gold medal in an individual event in any sport, grew up to become the Japanese representative to the International Labor Organization.

1936 Berlin C: 21, N: 10, D: 8.15. WR: 19.07.2 (Arne Borg)
1. Noboru Terada   JPN   19:13.7
2. Jack Medica   USA   19:34.0
3. Shumpei Uto   JPN   19:34.5
4. Sunao Ishiharada   JPN   19:48.5
5. Ralph Flanagan   USA   19:54.8
6. Robert Leivers   GBR   19:57.4
7. Heinz Arendt   GER   19:59.0

Terada took the lead at the gun and drew away slowly but steadily to win by 25 meters.

1948 London C: 39, N: 21, D: 8.7. WR: 18:58.8 (Tomikatsu Amano)
1. James McLane   USA   19:18.5
2. John Marshall   AUS   19:31.3
3. György Mitró   HUN   19:43.2
4. György Csordás   HUN   19:54.2
5. Marjan Stipetič   YUG   20:10.7
6. Forbes Norris   USA   20:18.8
7. Donald Bland   GBR   20:19.8
8. William Heusner   USA   20:45.4

Seventeen-year-old Jimmy McLane studied the technique of rival John Marshall and discovered that Marshall stayed close to the lane line on his breathing side. Swimming in the next lane, McLane took advantage of this quirk on each lap that found him on Marshall's right side. McLane swam as close to Marshall as he could and kept exactly one body length ahead of him so that the splashing from his powerful kick distracted the Australian. After the Olympics, the two became teammates at Yale.

1952 Helsinki C: 37, N: 22, D: 8.2. WR: 18:19.0 (Hironashin Furuhashi)
1. Ford Konno   USA   18:30.3   OR
2. Shiro Hashizume   JPN   18:41.4
3. Tetsuo Okamoto   BRA   18:51.3

4. James McLane   USA   18:51.5
5. Joseph Bernardo   FRA   18:59.1
6. Yasuo Kitamura   JPN   19:00.4
7. Peter Duncan   SAF   19:12.1
8. John Marshall   AUS   19:53.4

Ford Konno of Hawaii caught up with Hashizume after 1200 meters and pulled away to a decisive victory, covering the last 100 meters in 1:11.7.

1956 Melbourne C: 20, N: 11, D: 12.7. WR: 17:59.5 (I. Murray Rose)
1. I. Murray Rose   AUS   17:58.9
2. Tsuyoshi Yamanaka   JPN   18:00.3
3. George Breen   USA   18:08.2
4. Murray Garretty   AUS   18:26.5
5. William Slater   CAN   18:38.1
6. Jean Boiteux   FRA   18:38.3
6. Yukiyoshi Aoki   JPN   18:38.3
8. Garry Winram   AUS   19:06.2

George Breen set a world record of 17:52.9 in the third heat of the qualifying round. After 800 meters in the final, he, Rose, and Yamanaka were neck and neck. Then Rose began to surge ahead. He had built up a six-meter lead with only 100 meters to go, when Yamanaka began to sprint. He drew to within a yard of Rose, while the Australian crowd screamed at their young hero until he was finally alerted to the danger behind him. One last push earned Rose his third gold medal.

1960 Rome C: 30, N: 19, D: 9.3. WR: 17:11.0 (John Konrads)
1. John Konrads   AUS   17:19.6   OR
2. I. Murray Rose   AUS   17:21.7
3. George Breen   USA   17:30.6
4. Tsuyoshi Yamanaka   JPN   17:34.7
5. József Katona   HUN   17:43.7
6. Murray McLachlan   SAF   17:44.9
7. Alan Somers   USA   18:02.8
8. Richard Campion   GBR   18:22.7

John Konrads' family fled Latvia in 1944, when John was two years old. They wanted to emigrate to the United States, but were rejected because their family was too large. Instead, they settled in Australia. John started swimming as therapy after being hospitalized with a minor case of polio. In Rome, Konrads swam stroke for stroke with George Breen for 1050 meters before drawing away. Konrads' sister, Ilsa, won a silver medal in the 4 × 100-meter freestyle relay.

1964 Tokyo C: 31, N: 21, D: 10.17. WR: 16:58.7 (Roy Saari)
1. Robert Windle   AUS   17:01.7   OR
2. John Nelson   USA   17:03.0
3. Allan Wood   AUS   17:07.7
4. William Farley   USA   17:18.2
5. Russell Phegan   AUS   17:22.4
6. Sueaki Sasaki   JPN   17:25.3
7. Roy Saari   USA   17:29.2
8. József Katona   HUN   17:30.8

Noticeably absent was Murray Rose, who had been refused a place on the Australian team because he wouldn't return home for the Australian National Championships in February, unaware that they also served as Olympic tryouts. Rose presented his own version of a tryout on August 2, when he set a world record of 17:01.8. This embarrassed the officials of the Australian Swimming Union, but they refused to make an exception to the rules they had laid down. In Tokyo, Windle opened a 12-meter lead at the halfway mark and held on for the victory.

1968 Mexico City C: 21, N: 16, D: 10.26. WR: 16:08.5 (Michael Burton)

1. Michael Burton	USA	16:38.9	OR
2. John Kinsella	USA	16:57.3	
3. Gregory Brough	AUS	17:04.7	
4. Graham White	AUS	17:08.0	
5. Ralph Hutton	CAN	17:15.6	
6. Guillermo Echevarria	MEX	17:36.4	
7. Juan Alanis	MEX	17:46.6	
8. John Nelson	USA	18:05.1	

1972 Munich C: 42, N: 30, D: 9.4. WR: 15:52.91 (Rick DeMont)

1. Michael Burton	USA	15:52.58	WR
2. Graham Windeatt	AUS	15:58.48	
3. Douglas Northway	USA	16:09.25	
4. Bengt Gingsjö	SWE	16:16.01	
5. Graham White	AUS	16:17.22	
6. Mark Treffers	NZE	16:18.84	
7. Bradford Cooper	AUS	16:30.49	
8. Guillermo Garcia	MEX	16:36.03	

Burton led for the first 600 meters, then Windeatt took over. By the 1200-meter mark, Burton was back in the lead for good, and dipped just below Rick DeMont's world record to win the third gold medal of his career.

1976 Montreal C: 31, N: 20, D: 7.20. WR: 15:06.66 (Brian Goodell)

1. Brian Goodell	USA	15:02.40	WR
2. Bobby Hackett	USA	15:03.91	
3. Stephen Holland	AUS	15:04.66	
4. Djan Madruga Garrido	BRA	15:19.84	
5. Vladimir Salnikov	SOV/RUS	15:29.45	
6. Max Metzker	AUS	15:31.53	
7. Paul Hartloff	USA	15:32.08	
8. Zoltán Wladár	HUN	15:45.97	

The 1976 1500 meters final quickly evolved into a three-man race, with all three medalists ultimately breaking the world record. Bobby Hackett of Yonkers, New York, took the early lead and held it for 950 meters, at which point he was passed by Steve Holland. Holland was still in front after 1300 meters, but then Brian Goodell of Mission Viejo, California, stormed past both Hackett and Holland, taking the lead 150 meters from the finish and pulling away with a time of 57.73 seconds over the last 100 meters.

1980 Moscow C: 18, N: 11, D: 7.22. WR: 15:02.40 (Brian Goodell)

1. Vladimir Salnikov	SOV/RUS	14:58.27	WR
2. Aleksandr Chayev	SOV/RUS	15:14.30	
3. Max Metzker	AUS	15:14.49	
4. Rainer Strohbach	GDR	15:15.29	
5. Borut Petric	YUG	15:21.78	
6. Rafael Escalas	SPA	15:21.88	
7. Zoltán Wladár	HUN	15:26.70	
8. Eduard Petrov	SOV/UKR	15:28.24	

Vladimir Salnikov won three gold medals at the 1980 Olympics, but the big one was in the 1500 meters. In the final, on July 22, Salnikov became the first swimmer to break the 15-minute barrier, a feat that had been eagerly anticipated since Brian Goodell came within two and a half seconds at the previous Olympics.

1984 Los Angeles C: 27, N: 19, D: 8.4. WR: 14:54.76 (Vladimir Salnikov)

1. Michael O'Brien	USA	15:05.20
2. George DiCarlo	USA	15:10.59
3. Stefan Pfeiffer	GER	15:12.11
4. Rainer Henkel	GER	15:20.03
5. Franck Iacono	FRA	15:26.96
6. Stefano Grandi	ITA	15:28.58
7. David Shemilt	CAN	15:31.28
8. Wayne Shillington	AUS	15:38.18

Mike O'Brien, a 6-foot 6-inch 18-year-old, took the lead from DiCarlo after 600 meters and pulled away for an unchallenged victory. At the Friendship Games in Moscow three weeks later, Vladimir Salnikov took first place with a time of 15:03.51.

1988 Seoul C: 35, N: 22, D: 9.25. WR: 14:54.76 (Vladimir Salnikov)

1. Vladimir Salnikov	SOV/RUS	15:00.40
2. Stefan Pfeiffer	GER	15:02.69
3. Uwe Dassler	GDR	15:06.15
4. Matthew Cetlinski	USA	15:14.76
5. Mariusz Podkościelny	POL	15:14.76
6. Rainer Henkel	GER	15:18.19
7. Kevin Boyd	GBR	15:21.16
8. Darjan Petric	YUG	15:37.12

Between 1977 and 1986 Vladimir Salnikov won 61 consecutive finals at 1500 meters. He broke the 15-minute mark four times. No one else did it even once. Then, at the 1986 world championships, Salnikov finished fourth. The following year, at the European championships, he failed to qualify for the final. It appeared that he was over the hill and ready for retirement. But Salnikov refused to give up. Trained by his wife, Marina, he mounted a comeback aimed at regaining his Olympic title in Seoul. The coaches of the Soviet team were dubious and refused to select him as a member of the national team. However, the Soviet Minister of Sport intervened and announced that if Vladimir Salnikov thought he deserved to represent the U.S.S.R. in the 1988 Olympics, then the coaches must find a place for him. Still, Salnikov was not considered a serious medal contender. *Time* magazine summed up the consensus: "Salnikov's long day as the world's freestyle champion has passed. He can expect nothing more in Seoul than to see the last of his records fall in front of him."

But in the preliminary round, Salnikov served notice that he was still a threat. His qualifying time of 15:07.83 was second only to that of Matt Cetlinski. In the final, Cetlinski, in lane 4, took the early lead. Salnikov, beside him in lane 5, stayed close behind him in second place. Then, after 675 meters, Salnikov surged ahead, extending his lead steadily until the final 100 meters when Stefan Pfeiffer managed to close the gap somewhat. Salnikov became only the third swimmer to win Olympic gold medals eight years apart. The others were Duke Kahanamohu and Dawn Fraser. At 28, Salnikov was also the oldest Olympic swimming champion in 56 years.

At 11:30 that night, after all the photos and interviews and ceremonies and congratulations were over, Vladimir Salnikov walked into the cafeteria at the athletes' village, hoping to grab a late snack. There were about 250 or 300 athletes and coaches in the room, representing a wide variety of nations and sports. As word spread that Salnikov had entered, the athletes and coaches spontaneously stopped eating, rose, and gave him a standing ovation.

1992 Barcelona C: 30, N: 24, D: 7.31. WR: 14:48.40 (Kieren Perkins)

1. Kieren Perkins	AUS	14:43.48	WR
2. Glen Housman	AUS	14:55.29	
3. Jörg Hoffmann	GER	15:02.29	
4. Stefan Pfeiffer	GER	15:04.28	
5. Ian Wilson	GBR	15:13.35	
6. Igor Majcen	SLO	15:19.12	
7. Lawrence Frostad	USA	15:19.41	
8. Viktor Andreyev	RUS	15:33.94	

When Kieren Perkins was nine years old he ran through a sliding glass door while playing with his brother. His left calf was badly slashed and he needed 86 stitches. His doctor prescribed swimming to help heal the muscle. In 1990, when Perkins was only 16 years old, he became the third person to break 15 minutes. The following year, at the world championships in Perth, he pushed Jörg Hoffman to a world record of 14:50.36, touching only .22 seconds later. On April 5, 1992, at the Australian Olympic trials, Perkins broke that record with a time of 14:48.40. In the Olympic final, Perkins ripped through the first 100 meters in 55.30 seconds and the first 400 meters in 3:51.59. He pulled away steadily and won by over 20 meters, setting another world record in the process.

100-METER BACKSTROKE

Swimmers begin backstroke races in the water, facing the starting wall, with both hands holding starting grips. Their feet, including the toes, must be submerged. Swimmers may remain completely submerged for the first 15 meters of a race. After that, some part of the swimmer must be above the surface of the water, except during turns. Swimmers must swim on their backs, but they are permitted to rotate up to, but not including, 90 degrees from horizontal. Before 1991, backstrokers had to touch the wall with their hands during turns. Now it is possible to do a flip turn. During turns, a swimmer may turn his or her shoulders to the vertical. Once the body has left the position on the back, no kick or arm pull can be made that is independent of the continuous turning action. The swimmer must touch the wall with some part of the body and must return to a position on the back upon leaving the wall.

1896–1900 not held

1904 St. Louis C: 6, N: 2, D: 9.6.
(100 Yards)

1. Walter Brack	GER	1:16.8
2. Georg Hoffmann	GER	—
3. Georg Zacharias	GER	—
4. William Orthwein	USA	—

AC: David Hammond (USA), Edwin Swatek (USA)

1906 not held

1908 London C: 21, N: 11, D: 7.17. WR: 1:25.0

1. Arno Bieberstein	GER	1:24.6	WR
2. Ludvig Dam	DEN	1:26.6	
3. Herbert Haresnape	GBR	1:27.0	
4. Gustav Aurisch	GER	—	

1912 Stockholm C: 18, N: 7, D: 7.14. WR: 1:15.6 (Otto Fahr)

1. Harry Hebner	USA	1:21.2
2. Otto Fahr	GER	1:22.4
3. Paul Kellner	GER	1:24.0
4. András Baronyi	HUN	1:25.2
5. Otto Gross	GER	1:25.8

Hebner set an Olympic record of 1:20.8 in the semifinals.

1920 Antwerp C: 13, N: 6, D: 8.23. WR: 1:15.6 (Otto Fahr)

1. Warren Paoa Kealoha	USA	1:15.2
2. Ray Kegeris	USA	1:16.8
3. Gérard Blitz	BEL	1:19.0
4. Percy McGillivray	USA	1:19.4
5. Harold Kruger	USA	—

Seventeen-year-old Warren Kealoha set a world record of 1:14.8 in the preliminary round.

1924 Paris C: 20, N: 11, D: 7.8. WR: 1:12.4 (Warren Kealoha)

1. Warren Paoa Kealoha	USA	1:13.2	OR
2. Paul Wyatt	USA	1:15.4	
3. Károly Bartha	HUN	1:17.8	
4. Gérard Blitz	BEL	1:19.6	
5. Austin Rawlinson	GBR	1:20.0	
6. Giyo Saito (JPN)			

1928 Amsterdam C: 19, N: 12, D: 8.9. WR: 1:09.0 (George Kojac)
1. George Kojac   USA   1:08.2   WR
2. Walter Laufer   USA   1:10.0
3. Paul Wyatt   USA   1:12.0
4. Toshio Irie   JPN   1:13.6
5. Ernst Küppers   GER   1:13.8
6. John Besford   GBR   1:15.4

1932 Los Angeles C: 16, N: 9, D: 8.12. WR: 1:08.2 (George Kojac)
1. Masaji Kiyokawa   JPN   1:08.6
2. Toshio Irie   JPN   1:09.8
3. Kentaro Kawatsu   JPN   1:10.0
4. Robert Zehr   USA   1:10.9
5. Ernst Küppers   GER   1:11.3
6. Robert Kerber   USA   1:12.8

1936 Berlin C: 30, N: 17, D: 8.14. WR: 1:04.8 (Adolf Kiefer)
1. Adolf Kiefer   USA   1:05.9   OR
2. Albert Vandeweghe   USA   1:07.7
3. Masaji Kiyokawa   JPN   1:08.4
4. Taylor Drysdale   USA   1:09.4
5. Kiichi Yoshida   JPN   1:09.7
6. Yasuhiko Kojima   JPN   1:10.4
7. Percival Oliver   AUS   1:10.7

1948 London C: 39, N: 24, D: 8.6. WR: 1:04.0 (Allen Stack)
1. Allen Stack   USA   1:06.4
2. Robert Cowell   USA   1:06.5
3. Georges Vallerey   FRA   1:07.8
4. Mario Chaves   ARG   1:09.0
5. Clemente Mejia Avila   MEX   1:09.0
6. Johannes Wild   SAF   1:09.1
7. W. John Brockway   GBR   1:09.2
8. Albert Kinnear   GBR   1:09.6

1952 Helsinki C: 38, N: 25, D: 8.1. WR: 1:03.6 (Allen Stack)
1. Yoshinobu Oyakawa   USA   1:05.4   OR
2. Gilbert Bozon   FRA   1:06.2
3. Jack Taylor   USA   1:06.4
4. Allen Stack   USA   1:07.6
5. Pedro Galvao   ARG   1:07.7
6. Robert Wardrop   GBR   1:07.8
7. Boris Škanata   YUG   1:08.1
8. Nicolaas Meiring   SAF   1:08.3

1956 Melbourne C: 25, N: 14, D: 12.6. WR: 1:02.1 (Gilbert Bozon)
1. David Theile   AUS   1:02.2   OR
2. John Monckton   AUS   1:03.2
3. Frank McKinney   USA   1:04.5
4. Robert Christophe   FRA   1:04.9
5. John Hayres   AUS   1:05.0
6. Graham Sykes   GBR   1:05.6
7. Albert Wiggins   USA   1:05.8
8. Yoshinobu Oyakawa   USA   1:06.9

1960 Rome C: 37, N: 27, D: 8.31. WR(110 yards): 1:01.5 (John Monckton)
1. David Theile   AUS   1:01.9   OR
2. Frank McKinney   USA   1:02.1

3. Robert Bennett   USA   1:02.3
4. Robert Christophe   FRA   1:03.2
5. Leonid Barbier   SOV/UKR   1:03.5
6. Wolfgang Wagner   GDR   1:03.5
7. John Monckton   AUS   1:04.1
8. Veiko Siimar   SOV/EST   1:04.6

After the 1956 Olympics, David Theile of Brisbane dropped out of swimming for two years so that he could concentrate on his medical studies. Yet he was able to come back better than ever to defend his championship. John Monckton was even with Theile at 50 meters but misjudged the turn and hit the wall with his head.

1964 not held

1968 Mexico City C: 37, N: 26, D: 10.22. WR: 58.4 (Roland Matthes)
1. Roland Matthes   GDR   58.7   OR
2. Charles Hickcox   USA   1:00.2
3. Ronald Mills   USA   1:00.5
4. Larry Barbiere   USA   1:01.1
5. James Shaw   CAN   1:01.4
6. Bob Schoutsen   HOL   1:01.8
7. Reinhard Blechert   GER   1:01.9
8. Franco Del Campo   ITA   1:02.0

Roland Matthes of Erfurt, Thuringia, was 16 years old when he set his first backstroke world record on September 11, 1967. In the next six years he would break records in the 100-meter and 200-meter backstroke 16 times. He also won four Olympic gold medals, two silver, and two bronze. In 1978 Matthes married Olympic champion Kornelia Ender. Their first child, Franziska, was born later that year, the product of parents who, between them, had earned eight gold medals, six silver medals, and two bronze. The couple was later divorced.

1972 Munich C: 39, N: 27, D: 8.29. WR: 56.3 (Roland Matthes)
1. Roland Matthes   GDR   56.58   OR
2. Michael Stamm   USA   57.70
3. John Murphy   USA   58.35
4. Mitchell Ivey   USA   58.48
5. Igor Grivennikov   SOV/RUS   59.50
6. Lutz Wanja   GDR   59.80
7. Jürgen Krüger   GDR   59.93
8. Tadashi Honda   JPN   1:00.41

1976 Montreal C: 41, N: 29, D: 7.19. WR: 56.30 (Roland Matthes)
1. John Naber   USA   55.49   WR
2. Peter Rocca   USA   56.34
3. Roland Matthes   GDR   57.22
4. Carlos Berrocal   PUR   57.28
5. Lutz Wanja   GDR   57.49
6. Bob Jackson   USA   57.69
7. Mark Kerry   AUS   57.94
8. Mark Tonelli   AUS   58.42

When John Naber was 9 years old he visited Olympia, in Greece, and told his parents that someday he would become an Olympic champion. Eleven years later, now 6 feet 6 inches tall and 195 pounds, Naber fulfilled his vow. In 1974 he had ended Roland Matthes' seven-year winning streak. Matthes was still the holder of the world record, but an appendectomy six weeks before the 1976 Olympics hurt his chances for defending his title. Naber set a world record of 56.19 in the semifinals and then set another one 24 hours later to win the first of his four gold medals.

1980 Moscow C: 33, N: 23, D: 7.21. WR: 55.49 (John Naber)

1.	Bengt Baron	SWE	56.33
2.	Viktor Kuznetsov	SOV/RUS	56.99
3.	Volodymyr Dolhov	SOV/UKR	57.63
4.	Miloslav Rolko	CZE	57.74
5.	Sándor Wladár	HUN	57.84
6.	Fred Eefting	HOL	57.95
7.	Mark Tonelli	AUS	57.98
8.	Gary Abraham	GBR	58.38

The victory of 18-year-old Bengt Baron of Finspång, Sweden, was so unexpected that even he was stunned. "I just can't understand how I did it," he told reporters afterward. His pre-Olympic best had been 57.77. Silver medalist Viktor Kuznetsov served a suspension after testing positive for steroids in 1978. Ten days after the Olympic final, the U.S. Outdoor National championship was won by Peter Rocca in a time of 56.64, with Bob Jackson second at 56.78.

1984 Los Angeles C: 45, N: 31, D: 8.3. WR: 55.19 (Richard Carey)

1.	Richard Carey	USA	55.79
2.	David Wilson	USA	56.35
3.	Mike West	CAN	56.49
4.	Gary Hurring	NZE	56.90
5.	Mark Kerry	AUS	57.18
6.	Bengt Baron	SWE	57.34
7.	Donald "Sandy" Goss	CAN	57.46
8.	Hans Kroes	HOL	58.07

Rick Carey won the second of his three gold medals. This time he pleased his critics by smiling and celebrating his victory despite his disappointment at not setting a world record. Three weeks later, the Friendship Games were won by Vladimir Shemetov in a time of 55.88.

1988 Seoul C: 52, N: 38, D: 9.24. WR: 54.91 (David Berkoff)

1.	Daichi Suzuki	JPN	55.05
2.	David Berkoff	USA	55.18
3.	Igor Polyansky	SOV/RUS	55.20
4.	Sergei Zabolotnov	SOV/UZB	55.37
5.	Mark Tewksbury	CAN	56.09
6.	Frank Baltrusch	GDR	56.10
7.	Frank Hoffmeister	GER	56.19
8.	Sean Murphy	CAN	56.32

On March 15, 1988, Rick Carey's 4½-year-old world record finally fell to Igor Polyansky, who swam 55.17 in Tallinn, Estonia. Polyansky dropped the record to 55.16 the following night and then to 55.00 four months later in Moscow. But on August 13, David Berkoff, competing in the U.S. Olympic trials, broke Polyansky's record twice: 54.95 in the prelims and 54.91 in the final. Berkoff, a Harvard senior from Willow Grove, Pennsylvania, caused a sensation with his submarine start. Using a dolphin kick borrowed from the butterfly stroke, Berkoff swam 32 kicks underwater, exploding to the surface after 35 meters. Berkoff was not the first to use the technique, but he was the first world-class backstroker to stay under for so long.

In the preliminaries at Seoul, Berkoff swam a 54.51 to set the sixth world record in less than six and a half months. In the final, however, Berkoff got off to a slow start. After 30 meters, Berkoff, Suzuki, and Polyansky were all still underwater. When Berkoff popped up last, 5 meters later, he was in first place, but not by nearly the margin he had expected. Suzuki, who had been practicing the submerged start daily for seven years (three years longer than Berkoff) caught Berkoff with 10 meters to go and won by about 10 inches. Suzuki had placed eleventh at the 1984 Olympics and competed only once a year at the international level. He appeared truly stunned by his victory. After the medal ceremony he told reporters, "I did not expect to win the gold medal. I can't believe it's true, yet I find myself in this interview."

F.I.N.A. banned the submarine start immediately after the Seoul Olympics, ruling that any backstroker still underwater after 10 meters would be disqualified. This ruling was later amended to 15 meters.

1992 Barcelona C: 52, N: 37, D: 7.30. WR: 53.93 (Jeffrey Rouse)

1.	Mark Tewksbury	CAN	53.98	OR
2.	Jeffrey Rouse	USA	54.04	
3.	David Berkoff	USA	54.78	
4.	Martín López-Zubero Purcell	SPA	54.96	
5.	Vladimir Selkov	RUS	55.49	
6.	Franck Schott	FRA	55.72	
7.	Rodolfo Falcón Cabrera	CUB	55.76	
8.	Dirk Richter	GER	56.26	

At the 1991 world championships, Jeff Rouse beat Mark Tewksbury by .06 seconds. At the Olympics, Tewksbury came from behind to turn the tables by the exact same slim margin. Before the Olympics, the Canadian had never swum faster than 55.19.

200-METER BACKSTROKE

1896 not held

1900 Paris C: 36, N: 5, D: 8.12.

1.	Ernst Hoppenberg	GER	2:47.0
2.	Karl Ruberl	AUT	2:56.0
3.	Johannes Drost	HOL	3:01.0
4.	Johannes Bleomen	HOL	3:02.2
5.	Thomas Burgess	FRA	3:12.6
6.	de Romand	FRA	3:38.0

1904–1960 not held

1964 Tokyo C: 34, N: 21, D: 10.13. WR: 2:10.9 (Thomas Stock)
1. Jed Graef	USA	2:10.3	WR
2. Gary Dilley	USA	2:10.5	
3. Robert Bennett	USA	2:13.1	
4. Shigeo Fukushima	JPN	2:13.2	
5. Ernst-Joachim Küppers	GER	2:15.7	
6. Viktor Mazanov	SOV/RUS	2:15.9	
7. Ralph Hutton	CAN	2:15.9	
8. Peter Reynolds	AUS	2:16.6	

1968 Mexico City C: 30, N: 21, D: 10.25. WR: 2:07.5 (Roland Matthes)
1. Roland Matthes	GDR	2:09.6	OR
2. Mitchell Ivey	USA	2:10.6	
3. Jack Horsley	USA	2:10.9	
4. Gary Hall	USA	2:12.6	
5. Santiago Esteva	SPA	2:12.9	
6. Leonid Dobrosskokin	SOV/RUS	2:15.4	
7. Joachim Rother	GDR	2:15.8	
8. Franco Del Campo	ITA	2:16.5	

1972 Munich C: 36, N: 25, D: 9.2. WR: 2:02.8 (Roland Matthes)
1. Roland Matthes	GDR	2:02.82	EWR
2. Michael Stamm	USA	2:04.09	
3. Mitchell Ivey	USA	2:04.33	
4. Bradford Cooper	AUS	2:06.59	
5. Alexander "Tim" McKee	USA	2:07.29	
6. Lothar Noack	GDR	2:08.67	
7. Zoltán Verrasztó	HUN	2:10.09	
8. Jean-Paul Berjeaud	FRA	2:11.77	

1976 Montreal C: 33, N: 23, D: 7.24. WR: 2:00.64 (John Naber)
1. John Naber	USA	1:59.19	WR
2. Peter Rocca	USA	2:00.55	
3. Dan Harrigan	USA	2:01.35	
4. Mark Tonelli	AUS	2:03.17	
5. Mark Kerry	AUS	2:04.07	
6. Miloslav Rolko	CZE	2:05.81	
7. Robert Rudolf	HUN	2:07.30	
8. Zoltán Verrasztó	HUN	2:08.23	

With this race, John Naber won his fourth gold medal and became the first backstroker to break the two-minute barrier for 200 meters.

1980 Moscow C: 25, N: 16, D: 7.26. WR: 1:59.19 (John Naber)
1. Sándor Wladár	HUN	2:01.93
2. Zoltán Verrasztó	HUN	2:02.40
3. Mark Kerry	AUS	2:03.14
4. Vladimir Shemetov	SOV/RUS	2:03.48
5. Fred Eefting	HOL	2:03.92
6. Michael Söderlund	SWE	2:04.10
7. Douglas Campbell	GBR	2:04.23
8. Paul Moorfoot	AUS	2:06.15

Three days after the Moscow final, Steve Barnicoat won the U.S. Outdoor National in 2:01.06. Second place went to Peter Rocca in 2:01.34.

1984 Los Angeles C: 34, N: 25, D: 7.31. WR: 1:58.86 (Richard Carey)
1. Richard Carey	USA	2:00.23
2. Frédéric Delcourt	FRA	2:01.75
3. Cameron Henning	CAN	2:02.37
4. Ricardo Prado	BRA	2:03.05
5. Gary Hurring	NZE	2:03.10
6. Nicolai Klapkarek	GER	2:03.95
7. Ricardo Aldabe	SPA	2:04.53
8. David Orbell	AUS	2:04.61

After setting an Olympic record of 1:58.99 in the prelims, Rick Carey of Mt. Kisco, New York, an extremely self-critical perfectionist, assumed that he would be able to break his own world record in the final. He won the race, but fell far short of the record. Afterwards he expressed nothing but disappointment, anger and dejection. He ignored the cheers of the crowd and the congratulations of his opponents. At the medal ceremony he hung his head and again ignored the audience, pausing only once on the way out to kiss his mother. This behavior led to such a torrent of harsh criticism from the U.S. press that Carey felt compelled to issue a formal apology which concluded, "I found it very difficult to smile when my performance didn't live up to my expectations. By not breaking the world record I felt I had not only let myself down, but also the crowd. . . . But, please, don't get the impression that I didn't appreciate winning. What everyone saw was purely an emotional reaction—or over-reaction—to Rick Carey's imperfection." Ironically, at the Friendship Games in Moscow three weeks later, Carey's world record was broken by Sergei Zabolotnov in a time of 1:58.41.

1988 Seoul C: 44, N: 32, D: 9.22. WR: 1:58.14 (Igor Polyansky)
1. Igor Polyansky	SOV/RUS	1:59.37
2. Frank Baltrusch	GDR	1:59.60
3. Paul Kingsman	NZE	2:00.48
4. Sergei Zabolotnov	SOV/UZB	2:00.52
5. Dirk Richter	GDR	2:01.67
6. Jens-Peter Berndt	GER	2:01.84
7. Daniel Veatch	USA	2:02.26
8. Rogerio Romero	BRA	2:02.28

Polyansky hailed from Novosibirsk in western Siberia, where his mother was a librarian and his father worked in a meat factory. He had dominated this event since 1985, losing only once to Zabolotnov at the 1987 European championships. In Seoul, Polyansky, Zabolotnov, and Baltrusch swam first, second, and third for the first 150 meters. Then Zabolotnov faded and Baltrusch came on with a rush, but Polyansky held on for the victory.

1992 Barcelona C: 44, N: 34, D: 7.28. WR: 1:56.57 (Martín López-Zubero Purcell)
1. Martín López-Zubero Purcell	SPA	1:58.47	OR
2. Vladimir Selkov	RUS	1:58.87	
3. Stefano Battistelli	ITA	1:59.40	
4. Hajime Itoi	JPN	1:59.52	

5. William "Trippi" Schwenk	USA	1:59.73	
6. Tino Weber	GER	1:59.78	
7. Tamás Deutsch	HUN	2:00.06	
8. Stefaan Maene	BEL	2:00.91	

Martín López-Zubero was born in Jacksonville, Florida, raised in Jacksonville, Florida, attended the University of Florida, and won the United States Summer National Championship. But at the Olympics he competed for Spain because his father was Spanish. Martín's older brother, David, who was also born and raised in the United States, won Spain's first swimming medal when he placed third in the 100-meter butterfly in 1980. As expected, Vladimir Selkov set the early pace, while López-Zubero conserved his energy in fifth place for the first half of the race. Hajime Itoi led briefly at 150 meters, then faded. López-Zubero passed Selkov 25 meters from the finish and won going away.

100-METER BREASTSTROKE

The most rigidly defined of swimming strokes, the breaststroke requires swimmers to follow several rules:

1. All leg and arm movements must be made simultaneously. Alternating movements are not allowed.

2. Both shoulders must be kept in line with the water.

3. The hands must be pushed forward together and from the breast, and must be brought back on or under the surface of the water. They must not be brought back beyond the line of the hips.

4. Only the backward and out frog-leg kick is allowed.

5. At turns and at the finish, both hands must touch the wall simultaneously.

6. Except for the start and the first stroke and kick after each turn, a part of the head must break the surface of the water during each stroke and kick cycle.

The breaststroke has always been the most controversial stroke because of ongoing arguments as to what constitutes legal or illegal technique. In the early 1930s some U.S. swimmers discovered a "loophole" in the rules then in force and began bringing their arms back *above* the surface of the water, which saved precious time and energy. In 1952, this new technique, known as the butterfly, was officially recognized as the fourth Olympic swimming style and given its own set of competitions, separate from the breaststroke.

Classical breaststroke enthusiasts, rid at last of the upstart butterfly stroke, were not allowed even a moment to breathe a sigh of relief, thanks to the Japanese, who discovered another loophole—underwater swimming. Swimming *below* the surface of the water turned out to be faster than swimming on the surface, so in 1956 underwater swimming was banned from breaststroke competitions.

1896–1964 not held

1968 Mexico City C: 39, N: 24, D: 10.19. WR: 1:06.2 (Nikolai Pankin)

1. Donald McKenzie	USA	1:07.7	OR
2. Vladimir Kosinsky	SOV/RUS	1:08.0	
3. Nikolai Pankin	SOV/RUS	1:08.0	
4. José Sylvio Fiolo	BRA	1:08.1	
5. Yevhen Mykhaylov	SOV/UKR	1:08.4	
6. Ian O'Brien	AUS	1:08.6	
7. Alberto Forelli	ARG	1:08.7	
8. Egon Henninger	GDR	1:09.7	

1972 Munich C: 44, N: 31, D: 8.30. WR: 1:05.8 (Nikolai Pankin)

1. Nobutaka Taguchi	JPN	1:04.94	WR
2. Thomas Bruce	USA	1:05.43	
3. John Hencken	USA	1:05.61	
4. Mark Chatfield	USA	1:06.01	
5. Walter Kusch	GER	1:06.23	
6. José Sylvio Fiolo	BRA	1:06.24	
7. Nikolai Pankin	SOV/RUS	1:06.36	
8. David Wilkie	GBR	1:06.52	

In the first semifinal John Hencken set a world record of 1:05.68. Less than ten minutes later, Nobutaka Taguchi broke that record with a time of 1:05.13 in the second semifinal. The following evening, in the final, Taguchi overtook Tom Bruce in the last 25 meters and set yet another world record.

1976 Montreal C: 32, N: 22, D: 7.20. WR: 1:03.88 (John Hencken)

1. John Hencken	USA	1:03.11	WR
2. David Wilkie	GBR	1:03.43	
3. Arvydas Juozaitis	SOV/LIT	1:04.23	
4. Graham Smith	CAN	1:04.26	
5. Giorgio Lalle	ITA	1:04.37	
6. Walter Kusch	GER	1:04.38	
7. Duncan Goodhew	GBR	1:04.66	
8. Chris Woo	USA	1:05.13	

John Hencken, a 22-year-old graduate of Stanford University with a degree in electrical engineering, equaled his own world record of 1:03.88 in the preliminary round, and broke it with a time of 1:03.62 in the semifinals. Hardpressed by David Wilkie in the final, he set another record of 1:03.11.

1980 Moscow C: 26, N: 20, D: 7.22. WR: 1:02.86 (Gerald Mörken)

1. Duncan Goodhew	GBR	1:03.44
2. Arsens Miskarovs	SOV/LAT	1:03.82
3. Peter Evans	AUS	1:03.96
4. Aleksandr Fedorovsky	SOV/RUS	1:04.00
5. János Dzvonyár	HUN	1:04.67
6. Lindsay Spencer	AUS	1:05.04
7. Pablo Restrepo	COL	1:05.91

DISQ: Albán Vermes (HUN)

Jeered at by his schoolmates as an adolescent because a fall from a tree at age ten had left him bald, and also because he was dyslexic, Duncan Goodhew vowed that he would become an Olympic champion. Although his stepfather, a retired air vice-marshal, refused to attend

Mocked by his schoolmates because an accident left him bald and because he was dyslexic, Duncan Goodhew fought back by winning a gold medal in the 1980 100-meter breaststroke.

the Games because his government opposed British participation, Goodhew's mother was in the audience to watch her son's dream come true. Despite all the noise in the stadium, Goodhew "seemed to hear her voice above all the others."

At the U.S. Outdoor National a week later, Steve Lundquist clocked 1:02.88 and Bill Barrett 1:02.93. The world record of 1:02.86 had been set by Gerald Mörken of West Germany in 1977.

1984 Los Angeles C: 52, N: 37, D: 7.29. WR: 1:02.13 (John Moffet)

1. Steve Lundquist	USA	1:01.65	WR
2. Victor Davis	CAN	1:01.99	
3. Peter Evans	AUS	1:02.97	
4. Adrian Moorhouse	GBR	1:03.25	
5. John Moffet	USA	1:03.29	
6. Brett Stocks	AUS	1:03.49	
7. Gerald Mörken	GER	1:03.95	
8. Raffaele Avagnano	ITA	1:04.11	

At the U.S. Olympic trials on June 25, John Moffet had defeated Steve Lundquist for the first time, and taken away his world record for good measure. Competing in the Olympics five weeks later, Moffet led all qualifiers with an Olympic record of 1:02.16. Unfortunately, pushing off the wall at the 50-meter turn, Moffet badly tore a muscle in his right thigh. As the seriousness of his injury became apparent, doctors injected his leg with xylocaine and taped his thigh. But his chances for Olympic victory were fading fast. In the ready room before the final, Moffet took Lundquist aside and said, "If something goes haywire with my leg, win the gold for the U.S.A." Lundquist did just that, fighting off a determined challenge from Victor Davis and regaining his world record.

1988 Seoul C: 61, N: 45, D: 9.19. WR: 1:01.65 (Steve Lundquist)

1. Adrian Moorhouse	GBR		1:02.04
2. Károly Güttler	HUN		1:02.05
3. Dmitri Volkov	SOV/RUS		1:02.20
4. Victor Davis	CAN		1:02.38
5. Tamás Debnár	HUN		1:02.50
6. Richard Schroeder	USA		1:02.55
7. Gianni Minervini	ITA		1:02.93
8. Christian Poswiat	GDR		1:03.43

When he was 12 years old, Adrian Moorhouse of Bingley, Yorkshire, watched on television as David Wilkie won a gold medal in the 200-meter breaststroke. Moorhouse thought to himself, "I want one of those."

Eight years later at the Los Angeles Olympics swimming aficionados thought that he had a very good chance of winning "one of those" in the 100-meter event. However, he finished a disappointing fourth and went home to England without a medal. While he was still in Los Angeles he received a telegram from his former Sunday school teacher, Geoff Carter. It read, "Very bad luck, all proud of you. There will be a next time." Moorhouse kept the telegram and four years later took it with him to Seoul. This time he entered the competition as the clear favorite, having recorded the fastest time in the world in 1986, 1987, and pre-Olympic 1988.

In the preliminaries, Moorhouse was the fastest qualifier, with a time of 1:02.19. In the final, Dmitri Volkov turned first, with Moorhouse 1.3 seconds back in sixth place. Moorhouse expected Volkov to die by the 75-meter mark. When he didn't, Moorhouse realized for the first time that "maybe the Olympics mean something to him too." In fact, Volkov was, in his own words, "washed out" by the 75-meter mark, but he managed to stay in front for another 15 meters.

When Moorhouse reached the finish, he wasn't sure whether he had beaten Volkov for the gold. He hadn't even noticed Károly Güttler two lanes away. When he looked back at the scoreboard, Moorhouse discovered that he had edged out Güttler by only one one-hundredth of a second. As elated as he was, Moorhouse cringed with guilt for having "stolen" the gold from Güttler. Actually, the Hungarian, who was not considered a medal contender, was ecstatic at having earned an unexpected silver.

After the medal ceremony, Moorhouse tucked the four-year-old telegram from his Sunday school teacher into the box that contained his gold medal.

1992 Barcelona C: 59, N: 45, D: 7.26. WR: 1:01.29 (Norbert Rózsa)

1. Nelson Diebel	USA	1:01.50	OR
2. Norbert Rózsa	HUN	1:01.68	
3. Philip Rogers	AUS	1:01.76	
4. Akira Hayashi	JPN	1:01.86	
5. Vassily Ivanov	RUS	1:01.87	
6. Dmitri Volkov	RUS	1:02.07	
7. Nicholas Gillingham	GBR	1:02.32	
8. Adrian Moorhouse	GBR	1:02.33	

After his parents separated when he was 12 years old, Nelson Diebel, who was already a hyperactive child, spent several years getting into trouble. He drank alcohol, smoked marijuana, partied excessively, got into fights, and was thrown out of schools. He was, in his own words, "a rebel without a clue." Fortunately, at the Peddie School, a private high school in Hightstown, New Jersey, he was coached by Chris Martin, who turned Diebel into a serious swimmer. When he was 17 years old, Diebel placed an impressive and very encouraging fifth at the 1988 United States Olympic trials. Three days later Diebel tried to dive into the Peddie pool from the railing above the stands, twenty feet above the pool. He slipped and landed on concrete. He broke the fall with his hands and broke his wrists. Reasonably under control four years later, he won the 1992 United States Olympic trials in a time of 1:01.40. The favorite in the Olympics was Norbert Rózsa, the world champion and world record holder. However, Rózsa did not appear to be in top form in Barcelona. He barely qualified for the final, edging fellow Hungarian Károly Güttler by .03 seconds. In the final, Volkov and Ivanov led at the turn, with Diebel, Rózsa, and Rogers close behind. Immediately, the Russians began to fade while the others maintained their positions all the way to the finish.

200-METER BREASTSTROKE

1896–1906 not held

1908 London C: 27, N: 10, D: 7.18.

1. Frederick Holman	GBR	3:09.2	WR
2. William Robinson	GBR	3:12.8	
3. Pontus Hanson	SWE	3:14.6	
4. Ödön Toldi	HUN	3:15.2	

Twenty-five meters from the finish, the 25-year-old Holman overtook Robinson, who was 38 years old.

1912 Stockholm C: 24, N: 11, D: 7.10. WR: 3:00.8 (Felicien Coubert)

1. Walter Bathe	GER	3:01.8	OR
2. Wilhelm Lützow	GER	3:05.0	
3. Kurt Mahlisch	GER	3:08.0	
4. Percy Courtman	GBR	3:08.8	
DNF: Thor Henning (SWE)			

1920 Antwerp C: 24, N: 11, D: 8.29. WR: 2:56.6 (Percy Courtman)

1. Håkan Malmroth	SWE	3:04.4
2. Thor Henning	SWE	3:09.2
3. Arvo Aaltonen	FIN	3:12.2
4. Jack Howell	USA	—
5. Ivan Stedman	AUS	—
DNF: Per Cederblom (SWE)		

1924 Paris C: 28, N: 16, D: 7.17. WR: 2:50.4 (Erich Rademacher)

1. Robert Skelton	USA	2:56.6
2. Joseph de Combe	BEL	2:59.2
3. William Kirschbaum	USA	3:01.0
4. Bengt Linders	SWE	3:02.2
5. Robert Wyss	SWI	3:05.6
6. Thor Henning (SWE)		

Skelton set an Olympic record of 2:56.0 in the opening round.

1928 Amsterdam C: 21, N: 13, D: 8.8. WR: 2:48.0 (Erich Rademacher)

1. Yoshiyuki Tsuruta	JPN	2:48.8	OR
2. Erich Rademacher	GER	2:50.6	
3. Teofilo Yldefonzo	PHI	2:56.4	
4. Erwin Sietas	GER	2:56.6	
5. Eric Harling	SWE	2:56.8	
6. Walter Spence	CAN	2:57.2	

1932 Los Angeles C: 18, N: 11, D: 8:13. WR: 2:44.0 (Leonard Spence)

1. Yoshiyuki Tsuruta	JPN	2:45.4
2. Reizo Koike	JPN	2:46.6
3. Teofilo Yldefonzo	PHI	2:47.1
4. Erwin Sietas	GER	2:48.0
5. Jikirum Adjaluddin	PHI	2:49.2
6. Shigeo Nakagawa	JPN	2:52.8

Koike defeated Tsuruta 2:44.9 to 2:45.4 in the first semifinal. The defending champion repeated his time exactly in the final, but this time it was good enough to win.

1936 Berlin C: 25, N: 11, D: 8.15. WR: 2:37.2 (Jack Kasley)

1. Tetsuo Hamuro	JPN	2:41.5	OR
2. Erwin Sietas	GER	2:42.9	

3. Reizo Koike   JPN   2:44.2
4. John Herbert Higgins   USA   2:45.2
5. Saburo Ito   JPN   2:47.6
6. Joachim Balke   GER   2:47.8
7. Teofilo Yldefonzo   PHI   2:51.1

1948 London C: 32, N: 20, D: 8.7. WR: 2:30.0 (Joseph Verdeur)
1. Joseph Verdeur   USA   2:39.3   OR
2. Keith Carter   USA   2:40.2
3. Robert Sohl   USA   2:43.9
4. John Davies   AUS   2:43.7
5. Anton "Tone" Cerer   YUG   2:46.1
6. Willy Otto Jordan   BRA   2:46.4
7. Ahmed Kandil   EGY   2:47.5
8. Bjorn Bontê   HOL   2:47.6

The first seven finishers all used the butterfly stroke. The judges awarded Bob Sohl the bronze medal even though his official time was slower than that of Davies.

1952 Helsinki C: 40, N: 27, D: 8.2. WR: 2:27.3 (Herbert Klein)
1. John Davies   AUS   2:34.4   OR
2. Bowen Stassforth   USA   2:34.7
3. Herbert Klein   GER   2:35.9
4. Nobuyasu Hirayama   JPN   2:37.4
5. Takayoshi Kajikawa   JPN   2:38.6
6. Jiro Nagasawa   JPN   2:39.1
7. Maurice Lusien   FRA   2:39.8
8. Ludevit Komadel   CZE   2:40.1

John Davies believed, contrary to popular theory at the time, that the key to winning was to swim even lap times rather than go all out at the beginning or save energy for a finishing burst. Four years earlier he had lost out on a bronze medal when the lane judges overruled the timers. In Helsinki, he would take no chances. Two and a half seconds behind after 100 meters, Davies patiently held his pace. He passed the fading Klein and then just outtouched Stassforth. Davies later graduated from UCLA, became a United States citizen and an entertainment lawyer, and was appointed a United States district judge. In 1993, forty years after his Olympic celebrity, Davies was in the news again when he presided over the trial of Los Angeles police officers Laurence Powell and Stacey Koon in the case of the videotaped beating of Rodney King. Coincidentally, one of the witnesses in the trial was another gold medalist, 1964 shot putter Dallas Long.

1956 Melbourne C: 21, N: 17, D: 12.6. WR: 2:31.0 (Masaru Furukawa)
1. Masaru Furukawa   JPN   2:34.7   OR
2. Masahiro Yoshimura   JPN   2:36.7
3. Kharis Yunichev   SOV/RUS   2:36.8
4. Terry Gathercole   AUS   2:38.7
5. Ihor Zasyeda   SOV/UKR   2:39.0
6. Knud Gleie   DEN   2:40.0
7. Manuel Sanguily   CUB   2:42.0
DISQ: Hughes Broussard (FRA)

For the first time, the butterfly stroke and the breaststroke were separated into two different events. Differences in interpretation of what was a breaststroke and what wasn't led to six disqualifications. The most controversial was the ousting of Herbert Klein of Germany, who won the second heat. He was accused of using a scissors kick and of dipping his right shoulder. Furukawa was one of the least visible Olympic champions, since his unusual technique kept him underwater 75 percent of the time.

1960 Rome C: 42, N: 30, D: 8.30. WR: 2:36.5 (Terry Gathercole)
1. William Mulliken   USA   2:37.4
2. Yoshihiko Osaki   JPN   2:38.0
3. Wieger Mensonides   HOL   2:39.7
4. Egon Henninger   GDR   2:40.1
5. Roberto Lazzari   ITA   2:40.1
6. Terry Gathercole   AUS   2:40.2
7. Andrezj Klopotowski   POL   2:41.2
8. Paul Hait   USA   2:41.4

The slower times in 1960 were the result of the banning of underwater swimming in 1957, five months after Masaru Furukawa's Olympic victory. Bill Mulliken's win was considered a major upset, since his pre-Olympic best had been 2:40.9. In the semifinals he set an Olympic record of 2:37.2.

1964 Tokyo C: 33, N: 20, D: 10.15. WR: 2:28.2 (Chester Jastremski)
1. Ian O'Brien   AUS   2:27.8   WR
2. Heorhy Prokopenko   SOV/UKR   2:28.2
3. Chester Jastremski   USA   2:29.6
4. Aleksandr Tutakayev   SOV/GEO   2:31.0
5. Egon Henninger   GDR   2:31.1
6. Osamu Tsurumine   JPN   2:33.6
7. Wayne Anderson   USA   2:35.0
8. Vladimir Kosinsky   SOV/RUS   2:38.1

Seventeen-year-old Ian O'Brien didn't catch Prokopenko until five meters from the finish. In winning, he improved his personal best by more than 4 seconds.

1968 Mexico City C: 36, N: 23, D: 10.22. WR: 2:27.4 (Vladimir Kosinsky)
1. Felipe Múñoz   MEX   2:28.7
2. Vladimir Kosinsky   SOV/RUS   2:29.2
3. Brian Job   USA   2:29.9
4. Nikolai Pankin   SOV/RUS   2:30.3
5. Yevhen Mykhaylov   SOV/UKR   2:32.8
6. Egon Henninger   GDR   2:33.2
7. Philip Long   USA   2:33.6
8. Osamu Tsurumine   JPN   2:34.9

The 1968 Olympics was ten days old and the host country had yet to win a gold medal when 17-year-old Felipe "Pepe" Múñoz stood at the edge of the pool before the start of the final of the 200-meter breaststroke. He was also known as "Tibio" (lukewarm) because his father was from Aguascalientes (hot waters) and his mother from Río Frío (cold river). Múñoz was not the favorite, that role falling to world record holder Vladimir Kosinsky, but there was hope that the Mexican would gain a medal, and since he *had* registered the fastest time of the heats (2:31.1), maybe, just maybe, a miracle might happen.

At the halfway mark Múñoz was in fourth place behind Kosinsky, Henninger, and Job. But then, in the most dramatic fashion possible, Múñoz began to gain on the leaders. Coming off the final turn, with 50 meters to go, he was only inches behind Kosinsky. The excitement in the stadium reached a fever pitch as 8000 cheering Mexicans voiced the hopes of the hundreds of thousands more who were watching on television. Twenty-five meters from the finish Múñoz caught Kosinsky, and in the last few meters he moved ahead, touching the wall a half-second ahead of the Soviet champion. Before he could make a move of his own, Múñoz was hoisted out of the pool and carried, dripping wet and in tears, around the arena. His American coach, Ron Johnson, was thrown into the pool despite the fact that his broken hand was encased in plaster.

1972 Munich C: 40, N: 27, D: 9.2. WR: 2:22.79 (John Hencken)
1. John Hencken   USA   2:21.55   WR
2. David Wilkie   GBR   2:23.67
3. Nobutaka Taguchi JPN   2:23.88
4. Richard Colella   USA   2:24.28
5. Felipe Muñoz   MEX   2:26.44
6. Walter Kusch   GER   2:26.55
7. Igor Cherdakov   SOV   2:27.15
8. Klaus Katzur   GDR   2:27.44

Hencken's superiority was never in doubt, as he led from start to finish.

1976 Montreal C: 26, N: 18, D: 7.24. WR: 2:18.21 (John Hencken)
1. David Wilkie   GBR   2:15.11   WR
2. John Hencken   USA   2:17.26
3. Richard Colella   USA   2:19.20
4. Graham Smith   CAN   2:19.42
5. Charles Keating   USA   2:20.79
6. Arvydas Juozaitis   SOV/LIT   2:21.87
7. Nikolai Pankin   SOV/RUS   2:22.21
8. Walter Kusch   GER   2:22.36

In 1976, 12 of the 13 men's swimming events were won by swimmers from the United States. The only exception was the 200-meter breaststroke. In that race, double world champion David Wilkie of Scotland became the first British male to win an Olympic swimming title in 68 years.

1980 Moscow C: 19, N: 14, D: 7.26. WR: 2:15.11 (David Wilkie)
1. Robertas Žulpa   SOV/LIT   2:15.85
2. Albán Vermes   HUN   2:16.93
3. Arsens Miskarovs   SOV/LAT   2:17.28
4. Gennady Utenkov   SOV/RUS   2:19.64
5. Lindsay Spencer   AUS   2:19.68

6. Duncan Goodhew   GBR   2:20.92
7. Peter Berggren   SWE   2:21.65
8. Jörg Walter   GDR   2:22.39

1984 Los Angeles C: 47, N: 35, D: 8.2. WR: 2:14.58 (Victor Davis)
1. Victor Davis   CAN   2:13.34   WR
2. Glenn Beringen   AUS   2:15.79
3. Etienne Dagon   SWI   2:17.41
4. Richard Schroeder   USA   2:18.03
5. Ken Fitzpatrick   CAN   2:18.86
6. Pablo Restrepo   COL   2:18.96
7. Alexandre Yokochi   POR   2:20.69
DISQ: Marco Del Prete (ITA)

World-record holder Victor Davis took command before the 50-meter turn, kept a clear lead throughout the race, and then poured it on in the final 50 meters to set another world record and win by the largest margin in an Olympic breaststroke final in 60 years. Victor Davis died on Nov. 13, 1989, after being struck by a car following an altercation outside a bar. He was 25 years old. His ashes were scattered at sea along with a quart of water from lane 5 of the University of Southern California pool, where he had won his Olympic gold medal.

1988 Seoul C: 54, N: 40, D: 9.23. WR: 2:13.34 (Victor Davis)
1. József Szabó   HUN   2:13.52
2. Nicholas Gillingham GBR   2:14.12
3. Sergio Lopez   SPA   2:15.21
4. Michael Barrowman   USA   2:15.45
5. Valery Lozyk   SOV/UKR   2:16.16
6. Vadim Alekseyev   SOV/KAZ   2:16.70
7. Jonathan Cleveland   CAN   2:17.10
8. Péter Szabó   HUN   2:17.12

The two Szabós (not related) and Barrowman all practiced the new "wave-action" breaststroke taught by Hungarian coach József Nagy.

1992 Barcelona C: 54, N: 41, D: 7.29. WR: 2:10.60 (Michael Barrowman)
1. Michael Barrowman   USA   2:10.16   WR
2. Norbert Rózsa   HUN   2:11.23
3. Nicholas Gillingham GBR   2:11.29
4. Sergio López Miró   SPA   2:13.29
5. Károly Güttler   HUN   2:13.32
6. Philip Rogers   AUS   2:13.59
7. Kenji Watanabe   JPN   2:14.70
8. Akira Hayashi   JPN   2:15.11

There were no surprises in this race. Mike Barrowman had dominated the event since the last Olympics and owned the five fastest times in history. He led from start to finish and set his sixth world record. All the finalists except López and Güttler set personal bests. When Barrowman returned to his home in Potomac, Maryland, his neighbors had painted the front lawn gold.

100-METER BUTTERFLY

As in the breaststroke, butterfly swimmers must keep their shoulders in line with the surface of the water, they must move their arms and legs simultaneously, and they must not swim underwater, except for the first stroke after the start and after each turn. Unlike the breaststroke, butterfly rules allow swimmers to bring back their arms over the water and to kick their legs and feet up and down, as long as the movement of left and right arms or legs is simultaneous.

1896–1964 not held

1968 Mexico City C: 47, N: 23, D: 10.21. WR: 55.6 (Mark Spitz)
1. Douglas Russell   USA   55.9   OR
2. Mark Spitz   USA   56.4
3. Ross Wales   USA   57.2
4. Volodymyr Nemshilov   SOV/UKR   58.1
5. Satoshi Maruya   JPN   58.6
6. Yuri Suzdaltsev   SOV/RUS   58.8
7. Lutz Stoklasa   GER   58.9
8. Robert Cusack   AUS   59.8

Mark Spitz and Doug Russell had raced against each other many times in the 100-meter butterfly, and the result was always the same: Russell would take the early lead and then Spitz would finish strongly to win. In Mexico City, though, the two Californians separately and secretly decided to reverse their tactics. This allowed Russell to come from behind and defeat Spitz for the first time.

1972 Munich C: 39, N: 26, D: 8.31. WR: 54.56 (Mark Spitz)
1. Mark Spitz   USA   54.27   WR
2. Bruce Robertson   CAN   55.56
3. Jerry Heidenreich   USA   55.74
4. Roland Matthes   GDR   55.87
5. David Edgar   USA   56.11
6. Byron MacDonald   CAN   57.27
7. Hartmut Flöckner   GDR   57.40
8. Neil Rogers   AUS   57.90

Spitz won his fourth gold medal of the Munich Games.

1976 Montreal C: 43, N: 29, D: 7.21. WR: 54.27 (Mark Spitz)
1. Matt Vogel   USA   54.35
2. Joe Bottom   USA   54.50
3. Gary Hall   USA   54.65
4. Roger Pyttel   GDR   55.09
5. Roland Matthes   GDR   55.11
6. Clay Evans   CAN   55.81
7. Hideaki Hara   JPN   56.34
8. Neil Rogers   AUS   56.57

1980 Moscow C: 34, N: 29, D: 7.23. WR: 54.15 (Pär Arvidsson)
1. Pär Arvidsson   SWE   54.92
2. Roger Pyttel   GDR   54.94
3. David López-Zubero Purcell SPA   55.13
4. Kees Vervoorn   HOL   55.25
5. Yevgeny Seredin   SOV/RUS   55.35
6. Gary Abraham   GBR   55.42
7. Xavier Savin   FRA   55.66
8. Aleksei Markovsky   SOV/RUS   55.70

On August 2, William Paulus won the U.S. Outdoor National championship in 54.34. Second was Matt Gribble in 54.51. On July 22, in Canada, West Germany's Michael Gross recorded a 54.69.

1984 Los Angeles C: 53, N: 39, D: 7.30. WR: 53:38 (P. Pablo Morales)
1. Michael Gross   GER   53.08   WR
2. P. Pablo Morales   USA   53.23
3. Glenn Buchanan   AUS   53.85
4. Rafael Vidal Castro   VEN   54.27
5. Andrew Jameson   GBR   54.28
6. Anthony Mosse   NZE   54.93
7. Andreas Behrend   GER   54.95
8. Bengt Baron   SWE   55.14

In a race that was so fast that the top six finishers all set national records, Michael Gross rocketed past Pablo Morales ten meters from the finish to win his second gold medal and set his second world record of the 1984 Olympics.

1988 Seoul C: 51, N: 36, D: 9.21. WR: 52.84 (P. Pablo Morales)
1. Anthony Nesty   SUR   53.00   OR
2. Matthew Biondi   USA   53.01
3. Andrew Jameson   GBR   53.30
4. Jonathan Sieben   AUS   53.33
5. Michael Gross   GER   53.44
6. Jay Mortenson   USA   54.07
7. Thomas Ponting   CAN   54.09
8. Vadym Yaroshchuk   SOV/UKR   54.60

Favorite Matt Biondi led from the start. Ten meters from the finish, he was still in first place by 2 feet. But as he neared the touch pad, he was caught between strokes and elected to kick in the last few feet instead of taking an extra stroke. However, he was farther away than he thought and his miscalculation allowed 20-year-old Anthony Nesty of Suriname to slip by and win by less than an inch.

The top five finishers all set personal records. Nesty had placed fifth at the 1986 world championships and had the fourth best time of 1987. Still, his victory was a shocker. Suriname, a small tropical nation (population: 380,000) on the east coast of South America, had never before produced an Olympic medalist. Suriname had only one Olympic-size pool, so Nesty, who was born in Trinidad, had gone to live and train in the United States and to study at the University of Florida.

Nesty, a retiring sort, returned to Suriname a hero. After leaving the airport, his motorcade was stopped by a crowd of people in Onverwacht who insisted on giving him $3000. The government chipped in with a larger sum. In addition, the local stadium was renamed for him and a stamp was issued in his honor, as were gold and silver commemorative coins. Anthony Nesty was also the first black swimmer to win an Olympic medal.

As for Biondi, he was left to ponder his narrow loss. After the race he mused, "One one-hundredth of a second—what if I had grown my fingernails longer?" Biondi successfully channeled his anger and disappointment and went on to win five gold medals.

1992 Barcelona C: 69, N: 48, D: 7.27. WR: 52.84 (P. Pablo Morales)
1. P. Pablo Morales   USA   53.32
2. Rafal Szukala   POL   53.35
3. Anthony Nesty   SUR   53.41
4. Pavel Khnykin   UKR   53.81
5. Melvin Stewart   USA   54.04
6. Marcel Gery   CAN   54.18
7. Martín López-Zubéro Purcell   SPA   54.19
8. Vladislav Kulikov   RUS   54.26

In 1984, Pablo Morales went to the Olympics as the world record holder and the favorite to win a gold medal. He did swim fast enough to break his world record, but Michael Gross swam even faster. Morales earned a gold medal in the medley relay, two silvers in the 100-meter butterfly and the 200-meter individual medley, and he finished fourth in the 200-meter butterfly. Not a bad haul for a 19-year-old, but he didn't go home with the individual golds that were expected of him. On June 23, 1986, Morales won back the world record and by 1988 he was again the butterfly favorite for the Olympics. But at the United States Olympic trials, with only two Americans qualifying for each event, Morales placed third in both butterfly finals. When the Olympic 100-meter butterfly final came on television, Morales couldn't bring himself to watch it and left the room. He retired from swimming and entered law school at Cornell University.

In the summer of 1991, Morales' mother, Blanca, died of cancer. In November, Morales returned to competitive swimming, after a three-and-a-half-year absence. In March he won the U.S. Olympic trials, and as his 1986 mark of 52.84 had not been beaten, he was the reigning world record holder for the third straight Olympics. Morales led the qualifying round with a time of 53.59, with Rafal Szukala close behind at 53.60. In the final, Morales was slow to leave the starting platform, but by the turn he was leading Pavel Khnykin by three-tenths of a second. In the closing meters, Szukala, sixth at the turn, rapidly closed in on Morales, but it was the 27-year-old American who touched first.

During the playing of the United States national anthem at the medal ceremony, Morales thought of his mother and how, when he was a boy, the two of them used to watch Bud Greenspan's Olympic documentaries on television. They told stories of courage and triumph over adversity. "When I was up on the victory stand," Morales told reporters, "I was thinking that my mother would want to be here to experience this, and I know

that she was with me in spirit. This was my time at last."

200-METER BUTTERFLY

1896–1952 not held

1956 Melbourne C: 19, N: 14, D: 12.1. WR: 2:16.7 (William Yorzyk)
1. William Yorzyk   USA   2:19.3   OR
2. Takashi Ishimoto   JPN   2:23.8
3. György Tumpek   HUN   2:23.9
4. Jack Nelson   USA   2:26.6
5. John Marshall   AUS   2:27.2
6. Eulalio Rios Aleman   MEX   2:27.3
7. Brian Wilkinson   AUS   2:29.7
8. Alexandru Popescu   ROM   2:31.0

1960 Rome C: 34, N: 23, D: 9.2. WR: 2:13.2 (Michael Troy)
1. Michael Troy   USA   2:12.8   WR
2. Neville Hayes   AUS   2:14.6
3. J. David Gillanders   USA   2:15.3
4. Federico Dennerlein   ITA   2:16.0
5. Haruo Yoshimuta   JPN   2:18.3
6. Kevin Berry   AUS   2:18.5
7. Valentin Kuzmin   SOV/RUS   2:18.9
8. Kenzo Izutsu   JPN   2:19.4

1964 Tokyo C: 32, N: 19, D: 10.18. WR: 2:06.9 (Kevin Berry)
1. Kevin Berry   AUS   2:06.6   WR
2. Carl Robie   USA   2:07.5
3. Fred Schmidt   USA   2:09.3
4. Philip Riker   USA   2:11.0
5. Valentin Kuzmin   SOV/RUS   2:11.3
6. Yoshinori Kadonaga   JPN   2:12.6
7. Brett Hill   AUS   2:12.8
8. Daniel Sherry   CAN   2:14.6

Even though Kevin Berry held the world record in the 200-meter butterfly, he still had to earn a living. In 1964 he was working as a dishwasher at the Angus Steak House in Sydney when a reception was held there to honor Australia's Olympic team. Berry washed dishes, changed his clothes, attended the luncheon, and then went to the back of the restaurant and returned to his dishwashing. In the Tokyo final, Berry overtook Robie after 130 meters and broke his own world record.

1968 Mexico City C: 29, N: 18, D: 10.24. WR: 2:05.7 (Mark Spitz)
1. Carl Robie   USA   2:08.7
2. Martin Woodroffe   GBR   2:09.0
3. John Ferris   USA   2:09.3
4. Valentin Kuzmin   SOV/RUS   2:10.6
5. Peter Feil   SWE   2:10.9
6. Folkert Meeuw   GER   2:11.5
7. Viktor Sharygin   SOV/RUS   2:11.9
8. Mark Spitz   USA   2:13.5

Having won five gold medals at the 1967 Pan American Games, Mark Spitz brashly predicted that he would win six golds at the 1968 Olympics in Mexico City. Instead, he fell far short of his expectations. He did gain two gold medals, but they were in relays rather than individual events. After finishing third in the 100-meter freestyle, he placed second in his specialty, the 100-meter butterfly, thus losing his place on the medley relay team to the winner, Douglas Russell. Spitz's last appearance of the 1968 Olympics was in the 200-meter butterfly, in which he was the world record holder. Along with John Ferris, Spitz managed to lead the qualifiers in 2:10.6. But in the final it was clear that his confidence had been shattered. Exhausted by a long week of races, he was never in contention and finished far back in last place.

Carl Robie, on the other hand, was in tip-top shape. Four years earlier he had been the favorite, but was beaten by Kevin Berry. In Mexico City, with the attention on Spitz, Robie was able to relax and hold off a late challenge from Martin Woodroffe to gain the victory.

1972 Munich C: 29, N: 20, D: 8.28. WR: 2:01.53 (Mark Spitz)

1. Mark Spitz	USA	2:00.70	WR
2. Gary Hall	USA	2:02.86	
3. Robin Backhaus	USA	2:03.23	
4. Jorgé Delgado Panchama	ECU	2:04.60	
5. Hans Fassnacht	GER	2:04.69	
6. András Hargitay	HUN	2:04.69	
7. Hartmut Flöckner	GDR	2:05.34	
8. Folkert Meeuw	GER	2:05.57	

It seemed only fitting that Mark Spitz's first race of the 1972 Olympics should be the same one as his last race at the 1968 Games—the 200-meter butterfly. Here was a chance for Spitz to redeem himself immediately for his disappointing performances four years earlier. Not surprisingly Spitz was more than a bit nervous as he stood on the starting block before the final, but once he was in the water his victory was never in doubt. Afterward he leaped out of the water with his arms held high. The four-year psychological burden had been lifted, and Mark Spitz was on his way to becoming the first person in history to win seven gold medals in one Olympics.

1976 Montreal C: 38, N: 25, D: 7.18 WR: 1:59.63 (Roger Pyttel)

1. Mike Bruner	USA	1:59.23	WR
2. Steven Gregg	USA	1:59.54	
3. Bill Forrester	USA	1:59.96	
4. Roger Pyttel	GDR	2:00.02	
5. Michael Kraus	GER	2:00.46	
6. Brian Brinkley	GBR	2:01.49	
7. Jorgé Delgado Panchama	ECU	2:01.95	
8. Aleksandr Manachinsky	SOV/UKR	2:04.61	

1980 Moscow C: 25, N: 19, D: 7.20. WR: 1:59.23 (Mike Bruner)

1. Serhei Fesenko	SOV/UKR	1:59:76
2. Philip Hubble	GBR	2:01.20
3. Roger Pyttel	GDR	2:01.39
4. Peter Morris	GBR	2:02.27
5. Mikhail Gorelik	SOV/RUS	2:02.44
6. Kees Vervoorn	HOL	2:02.52

7. Pär Arvidsson	SWE	2:02.61
8. Stephen Poulter	GBR	2:02.93

This was one event in which the boycotting Americans were sorely missed. In 1972 and 1976 U.S. swimmers had swept all three medals, and they probably could have done it again in 1980. At the U.S. Outdoor National on July 30, Craig Beardsley of Harrington Park, New Jersey, set a world record of 1:58.21 in his qualifying heat. He won the final in 1:58.46, followed by Mike Bruner in 1:59.13 and Bill Forrester in 1:59.40. Eighth-place finisher Steve Gregg clocked 2:00.98—faster than the silver medal winner in Moscow ten days earlier.

1984 Los Angeles C: 35, N: 28, D: 8.3. WR: 1:57.05 (Michael Gross)

1. Jonathon Sieben	AUS	1:57.04	WR
2. Michael Gross	GER	1:57.40	
3. Rafael Vidal Castro	VEN	1:57.51	
4. P. Pablo Morales	USA	1:57.75	
5. Anthony Mosse	NZE	1:58.75	
6. Thomas Ponting	CAN	1:59.37	
7. Peter Ward	CAN	2:00.39	
8. Patrick Kennedy	USA	2:01.03	

With two gold medals already under his belt, Michael Gross entered his best event, the 200-meter butterfly, as the clear favorite. He expected stiff challenges from Pablo Morales and Rafael Vidal and that's exactly what he got. But over in lane 6, something completely unexpected happened. Seventeen-year-old Jon Sieben, from the Brisbane suburb of Coorparoo, seventh at the halfway mark and fourth with 50 meters to go, shot past the favorites to out-touch Gross and gain the victory, the world record, and one of the most surprising upsets in Olympic swimming history. Sieben's time of 1:57.04 was over four seconds faster than his pre-Olympic best of 2:01.17.

The rabidly pro-U.S. crowd gave Sieben a standing ovation, and the outcome was so delightful that the defeated favorites expressed pleasure more than disappointment. Gross, who had refused to appear before reporters following his two gold-medal races, and whose disdain for pomp and press had earned him the nickname "The American" in West Germany, sat beside Sieben after the 200 butterfly preferring to praise the young Australian rather than talk about himself.

1988 Seoul C: 40, N: 29, D: 9.24. WR: 1:56.24 (Michael Gross)

1. Michael Gross	GER	1:56.94	OR
2. Benny Nielsen	DEN	1:58.24	
3. Anthony Mosse	NZE	1:58.28	
4. Thomas Ponting	CAN	1:58.91	
5. Melvin Stewart	USA	1:59.19	
6. David Wilson	AUS	1:59.20	
7. Jon Kelly	CAN	1:59.48	
8. Anthony Nesty	SUR	2:00.80	

Michael Gross had dominated this event since 1981, winning two world championships, four European championships, and setting four world records. The only stain on his record was his unexpected loss to Jon Sieben at the 1984 Olympics. In Seoul, Gross placed fifth in the two events he had won in Los Angeles: the 200-meter free-style and the 100-meter butterfly. But in the 200 fly, he lived up to the expectations, leading from start to finish and winning by a body length.

1992 Barcelona C: 46, N: 32, D: 7.30. WR: 1:55.69 (Melvin Stewart)

1. Melvin Stewart	USA	1:56.26	OR
2. Danyon Loader	NZE	1:57.93	
3. Franck Esposito	FRA	1:58.51	
4. Rafal Szukala	POL	1:58.89	
5. Keiichi Kawanaka	JPN	1:58.97	
6. Denis Pankratov	RUS	1:58.98	
7. Robert Pinter	ROM	1:59.34	
8. Martin Roberts	AUS	1:59.64	

"Disneyland with a halo" was the way Melvin Stewart described the place where he grew up: Heritage USA, the Christian theme park created by television evangelist Jim Bakker and his wife, Tammy Faye. His father was the athletic director at the Heritage Academy and Melvin himself once worked as a bellhop in the park hotel. Since the 1988 Olympics, Stewart had dominated the 200-meter butterfly, setting a world record at the 1991 world championships and winning every other meet of importance. In Barcelona, Stewart lived up to expectations, leading from start to finish. Dan Loader, on the other hand, was on nobody's list of favorites but improved his pre-Olympic personal best by 3.36 seconds to earn the silver medal.

200-METER INDIVIDUAL MEDLEY

In individual medley races the order of strokes is butter-fly, backstroke, breaststroke, and freestyle.

1896–1964 not held

1968 Mexico City C: 46, N: 27, D: 10.20. WR: 2.10.6 (Charles Hickcox)

1. Charles Hickcox	USA	2:12.0	OR
2. Gregory Buckingham	USA	2:13.0	
3. John Ferris	USA	2:13.3	
4. Juan Bello	PER	2:13.7	
5. George Smith	CAN	2:15.9	
6. John Gilchrist	CAN	2:16.6	
7. Michael Holthaus	GER	2:16.8	
8. Péter Lázár	HUN	2:18.3	

Hickcox won the first of his three gold medals.

1972 Munich C: 39, N: 26, D: 9.3. WR: 2:09.3 (Gunnar Larsson, Gary Hall)

1. Gunnar Larsson	SWE	2:07.17	WR
2. Alexander "Tim" McKee	USA	2:08.37	
3. Steven Furniss	USA	2:08.45	
4. Gary Hall	USA	2:08.49	
5. András Hargitay	HUN	2:09.66	
6. Mikhail Suharev	SOV/RUS	2:11.78	
7. Juan Bello	PER	2:11.87	
8. Hans Ljungberg	SWE	2:13.56	

Larsson and McKee duplicated their one-two finish in the 400-meter individual medley, as the first four finishers all broke the world record.

1976–1980 not held

1984 Los Angeles C: 45, N: 34, D: 8.4. WR: 2:02.45 (Alex Baumann)

1. Alex Baumann	CAN	2:01.42	WR
2. P. Pablo Morales	USA	2:03.05	
3. Neil Cochran	GBR	2:04.38	
4. Robin Brew	GBR	2:04.52	
5. Steve Lundquist	USA	2:04.91	
6. Andrew Phillips	JAM	2:05.60	
7. Nicolai Klapkarek	GER	2:05.88	
8. Ralf Diegel	GER	2:06.66	

Baumann won his second gold medal of the Los Angeles Games, setting a world record, as he had in the 400 individual medley five days earlier. The victor at the Friendship Games, with a time of 2:02.51, was Jens-Peter Berndt of East Germany, who defected to the U.S. less than five months later and competed for West Germany in 1988.

1988 Seoul C: 56, N: 35, D: 9.25. WR: 2:00.56 (Tamás Darnyi)

1. Tamás Darnyi	HUN	2:00.17	WR
2. Patrick Kühl	GDR	2:01.61	
3. Vadym Yaroshchuk	SOV/UKR	2:02.40	
4. Mikhail Zubkov	SOV/RUS	2:02.92	
5. Peter Bermel	GER	2:03.81	
6. Robert Bruce	AUS	2:04.34	
7. Raik Hannemann	GDR	2:04.82	
8. Gary Anderson	CAN	2:06.35	

When Tamás Darnyi was 15 years old, he lost the vision in his left eye after being hit by an icy snowball during some horseplay three years earlier. He underwent seven operations to repair a detached retina. Although the surgery did not restore his sight, it did give him sensitivity to light. Beginning in 1985 Darnyi won every major title in both individual medal events. In Seoul, the 21-year-old Budapest native was in third place after 150 meters. Then, as expected, he pulled away with a 27.73 freestyle leg to win his second gold medal and set his second world record.

1992 Barcelona C: 56, N: 41, D: 7.31. WR: 1:59.36 (Tamás Darnyi)

1. Tamás Darnyi	HUN	2:00.76
2. Gregory Burgess	USA	2:00.97
3. Attila Czene	HUN	2:01.00
4. Jani Sievinen	FIN	2:01.28
5. Christian Gessner	GER	2:01.97
6. Ronald Karnaugh	USA	2:02.18

| 7. Matthew Dunn | AUS | 2:02.79 |
| 8. Gary Anderson | CAN | 2:04.30 |

Tamás Darnyi had not lost an individual medley race since 1984 and he was not about to start at the Olympics. Fourth after 150 meters, he swam a 27.53 freestyle leg to earn his fourth gold medal.

The second-fastest time of the pre-Olympic season had been recorded by Ron Karnaugh of Maplewood, New Jersey, the son of a retired truck driver. Because Karnaugh's family couldn't afford to travel to Barcelona, the 23,000 people of Maplewood raised the funds to send them. During the Parade of Nations at the Opening Ceremony, Ron's father, Peter, caught his eye and took his photograph. On the way back to his seat, Peter Karnaugh was stricken by a heart attack and died. Six days later Ron swam in the Olympic final. He led after 50 meters, held on to third place until the final leg, and then faded to sixth.

400-METER INDIVIDUAL MEDLEY

1896–1960 not held

1964 Tokyo C: 30, N: 18, D: 10.14. WR: 4:48.6 (Richard Roth)
1. Richard Roth	USA	4:45.4	WR
2. Roy Saari	USA	4:47.1	
3. Gerhard Hetz	GER	4:51.0	
4. Carl Robie	USA	4:51.4	
5. John Gilchrist	CAN	4:57.6	
6. Johannes Jiskoot	HOL	5:01.9	
7. György Kosztolánczy	HUN	5:01.9	
8. Terry Buck	AUS	5:03.0	

Three days before the competition, world record holder Dick Roth was stricken with an acute attack of appendicitis. Japanese doctors recommended an immediate operation, but Roth refused. Since he also refused to take drugs, they packed him in ice instead. Willing the pain to subside temporarily, the 17-year-old Californian took the lead 70 meters from the finish and won the final in world record time.

1968 Mexico City C: 35, N: 22, D: 10.23. WR: 4:39.0 (Charles Hickcox)
1. Charles Hickcox	USA	4:48.4
2. Gary Hall	USA	4:48.7
3. Michael Holthaus	GER	4:51.4
4. Gregory Buckingham	USA	4:51.4
5. John Gilchrist	CAN	4:56.7
6. Reinhard Merkel	GER	4:59.8
7. Andrei Dunayev	SOV/RUS	5:00.3
8. Rafael Hernandez	MEX	5:04.3

Hickcox and Hall swam side by side, almost neck and neck for the entire race.

1972 Munich C: 32, N: 24, D: 8.30. WR: 4:30.81 (Gary Hall)
1. Gunnar Larsson	SWE	4:31.98	OR
2. Alexander "Tim" McKee	USA	4:31.98	OR
3. András Hargitay	HUN	4:32.70	

4. Steven Furniss	USA	4:35.44
5. Gary Hall	USA	4:37.38
6. Bengt Gingsjö	SWE	4:37.96
7. Graham Windeatt	AUS	4:40.39
8. Wolfram Sperling	GDR	4:40.66

Both Larsson and McKee were credited with the Olympic record, but Larsson was declared the winner by two one-thousandths of a second, 4:31.981 to 4:31.983. Bronze medalist András Hargitay had almost drowned in the Danube River at the age of nine. "After that," he recalled, "my mother ordered me to learn how to swim, and this is what's come of it."

1976 Montreal C: 31, N: 22, D: 7.25. WR: 4:26.00 (Zóltan Verrasztó)
1. Rod Strachan	USA	4:23.68	WR
2. Alexander "Tim" McKee	USA	4:24.62	
3. Andrei Smirnov	SOV/RUS	4:26.90	
4. András Hargitay	HUN	4:27.13	
5. Graham Smith	CAN	4:28.64	
6. Steven Furniss	USA	4:29.23	
7. Andrew Ritchie	CAN	4:29.87	
8. Hans-Joachim Geisler	GER	4:34.95	

1980 Moscow C: 23, N: 17, D: 7.27. WR: 4:20.05 (Jesse Vassallo)
1. Oleksander Sydorenko	SOV/UKR	4:22.89	OR
2. Serhei Fesenko	SOV/UKR	4:23.43	
3. Zoltán Verrasztó	HUN	4:24.24	
4. András Hargitay	HUN	4:24.48	
5. Djan Madruga Garrido	BRA	4:26.81	
6. Miloslav Rolko	CZE	4:26.99	
7. Leszek Górski	POL	4:28.89	
8. Daniel Machek	CZE	4:29.86	

Three days after the Olympic final, the U.S. Outdoor National was won by world record holder Jesse Vassallo in 4:21.51.

1984 Los Angeles C: 23, N: 19, D: 7.30. WR: 4:17.53 (Alex Baumann)
1. Alex Baumann	CAN	4:17.41	WR
2. Ricardo Prado	BRA	4:18.45	
3. Robert Woodhouse	AUS	4:20.50	
4. Jesus "Jesse" Vassallo	USA	4:21.46	
5. Maurizio Divano	ITA	4:22.76	
6. Jeffrey Kostoff	USA	4:23.28	
7. Stephen Poulter	GBR	4:25.80	
8. Giovanni Franceschi	ITA	4:26.05	

Born in Prague, 4-year-old Alex Baumann was in New Zealand with his family when Soviet tanks rolled into Czechoslovakia in 1968. Baumann's parents refused to return to their homeland, eventually settling instead in Sudbury, Ontario. Proud to be a Canadian, Baumann appeared at the Olympics sporting a maple-leaf tattoo (and a diamond-stud earring)—and earned Canada's first swimming gold medal since 1912. Baumann was unable to meet with reporters after the race because he required almost two hours to produce a urine sample for the drug-testing. In the middle of his third beer, medical officials discovered that he was under age and forced him to switch to soft drinks.

In Moscow three weeks later, Jens-Peter Berndt of East Germany clocked 4:18.29 to win at the Friendship Games.

1988 Seoul C: 34, N: 24, D: 9.21. WR: 4:15.42 (Tamás Darnyi)
1. Tamás Darnyi   HUN   4:14.75   WR
2. David Wharton   USA   4:17.36
3. Stefano Battistelli   ITA   4:18.01
4. József Szabó   HUN   4:18.15
5. Patrick Kühl   GDR   4:18.44
6. Jens-Peter Berndt   GER   4:21.71
7. Luca Sacchi   ITA   4:23.23
8. Peter Bermel   GER   4:24.02

This race was billed as a showdown between world record holder Tamás Darnyi, who was blind in one eye, and former world record holder David Wharton, who was born severely hearing-impaired. However, Darnyi built such a large lead during the backstroke leg that the second half of the contest was anticlimactic.

1992 Barcelona C: 32, N: 25, D: 7.27. WR: 4:12.36 (Tamás Darnyi)
1. Tamás Darnyi   HUN   4:14.23   OR
2. Eric Namesnik   USA   4:15.57
3. Luca Sacchi   ITA   4:16.34
4. David Wharton   USA   4:17.26
5. Christian Gessner   GER   4:17.88
6. Patrick Kühl   GER   4:19.66
7. Sergei Marinyuk   MOL   4:22.93
8. Takahiro Fujimoto   JPN   4:23.86

Namesnik led after 200 meters, but Darnyi, unbeaten in eight years, forged ahead at the end of the breaststroke leg and pulled away to a clear victory.

4 × 100-METER FREESTYLE RELAY

Swimmers who took part in preliminary rounds of relays but not in the final are listed in brackets.

1896–1960 not held

1964 Tokyo T: 13, N: 13, D: 10.14. WR: 3:36. 1 (USA—Clark, McDonough, Ilman, Townsend)
1. USA   (Stephen Clark, Michael Austin,   3:32.2   WR
              Gary Ilman, Donald Schollander,
              [Lary Schulhof])
2. GER&GDR   (Horst Löffler, Frank Wiegand,   3:37.2
              Uwe Jacobsen, Hans-Joachim
              Klein)
3. AUS   (David Dickson, Peter Doak, John 3:39.1
              Ryan, Robert Windle)
4. JPN   (Kunihiro Iwasaki, Tadaharu Goto, 3:40.5
              Tatsuo Fujimoto, Yukiaki Okabe,
              [Katsuki Ishihara])
5. SWE   (Bengt-Olof Nordvall, E. Lester   3:40.7
              Eriksson, Jan Lundin, Per-Ola
              Lindberg)

6. SOV/RUS   (Viktor   Mazanov,   Vladimir   3:42.1
              Shuvalov, Viktor Semchenkov,
              Yuri Sumtsov, [Vladimir Berezin])
7. GBR   (Robert Lord, John Martin-Dye,   3:42.6
              Peter Kendrew, Robert McGregor)
DISQ: FRA (Alain Gottvalles, Gerard Gropaiz, Pierre Canavese, Jean Curtillet, [Robert Christophe])

Steve Clark had failed to qualify for the U.S. team in any individual events, but he made up for it by winning three gold medals in the relays. His lead-off leg in the 4 × 100-meter freestyle relay equaled Alain Gottvalles' 100-meter world record of 52.9 seconds and also earned him the right to swim the freestyle leg of the medley relay.

1968 Mexico City T: 16, N: 16, D: 10.17. WR: 3:32.5 (USA—Zorn, Rerych, Walsh, Schollander)
1. USA   (Zachary Zorn, Stephen Rerych, Mark   3:31.7   WR
          Spitz, Kenneth Walsh, [William Johnson,
          David Johnson, Michael Wall, Donald
          Schollander])
2. SOV   (Semyon Belits-Geiman, Viktor Mazanov, 3:34.2
          Georgi Kulikov, Leonid Ilyichev, [Sergei
          Gusev])
3. AUS   (Gregory Rogers, Robert Windle, Robert 3:34.7
          Cusack, Michael Wenden)
4. GBR   (Michael Turner, David Hembrow, Robert 3:38.4
          McGregor, Anthony Jarvis)
5. GDR   (Frank Wiegand, Udo Poser, Horst-   3:38.8
          Günther Gregor, Lothar Gericke)
6. GER   (Wolfgang Kremer, Olaf von Schilling, 3:39.0
          Peter Schorning, Hans Fassnacht)
7. CAN   (Glen Finch, George Smith, Ralph Hut- 3:39.2
          ton, John Gilchrist)
8. JPN   (Kunihiro Iwasaki, Masayuki Ohsawa,   3:41.5
          Satoru Nakano, Teruhiko Kitani)

1972 Munich T: 13, N: 13, D: 8.28. WR: 3:28.8 (USA, Los Angeles Swim Club—Havens, Weston, Frawley, Heckl)
1. USA   (David Edgar, John Murphy, Jerry   3:26.42   WR
          Heidenreich, Mark Spitz, [David Fair-
          bank, Gary Conelly])
2. SOV   (Vladimir Bure, Viktor Mazanov, Viktor 3:29.72
          Aboimov, Igor Grivennikov, [Georgy
          Kulikov])
3. GDR   (Roland Matthes, Wilfried Hartung, Pe- 3:32.42
          ter Bruch, Lutz Unger, [Udo Poser])
4. BRA   (Ruy Aquino Oliveira, Paulo Zanetti,   3:33.14
          Paulo Becskehazy, José Diaz-Aranha)
5. CAN   (Bruce Robertson, Brian Phillips, Timo-3:33.20
          thy Bach, Robert Kasting)
6. GER   (Klaus Steinbach, Werner Lampe,   3:33.90
          Rainer Jacob, Hans Fassnacht, [Ger-
          hard Schiller, Hans-Günther Vosseler,
          Kersten Meier])
7. FRA   (Gilles Vigne, Alain Mosconi, Alain   3:34.13
          Hermitte, Michel Rousseau)
8. SPA   (Jorge Comas, Antonio Culebras, En-   3:38.21
          rique Melo, José Pujol)

The U.S. "reserve" team of Dave Fairbank, Gary Conelly, Jerry Heidenreich, and Dave Edgar clocked 3:28.84 in the qualifying round to equal the world record. Six hours later, in the final, Fairbank and Conelly were replaced by John Murphy and Mark Spitz, and a new world record was set. It was Spitz's second gold medal of the evening.

1976–1980 not held

1984 Los Angeles T: 23, N: 23, D: 8.2. WR: 3:19.26 (USA—Cavanaugh, Leamy, McCagg, Gaines)

1. USA	(Christopher Cavanaugh, Michael Heath, Matthew Biondi, Ambrose "Rowdy" Gaines, [Thomas Jager, Robin Leamy])	3:19.03	WR
2. AUS	(Gregory Fasala, Neil Brooks, Michael Delany, Mark Stockwell)	3:19.68	
3. SWE	(Thomas Lejdström, Bengt Baron, Mikael Örn, Per Johansson, [Richard Milton, Michael Söderlund])	3:22.69	
4. GER	(Dirk Korthals, Andreas Schmidt, Alexander Schowtka, Michael Gross, [Nicolai Klapkarek])	3:22.98	
5. GBR	(David Lowe, Roland Lee, Paul Easter, Richard Burrell)	3:23.61	
6. FRA	(Stephan Caron, Laurent Neuville, Dominique Bataille, Bruno Lesaffre)	3:24.63	
7. CAN	(David Churchill, Blair Hicken, Alex Baumann, Donald "Sandy" Goss, [Levente Mady])	3:24.70	
8. ITA	(Marcello Guarducci, Marco Colombo, Metello Savino, Fabrizio Rampazzo, [Raffaele Franceschi])	3:24.97	

1988 Seoul T: 22, N: 22, D: 9.23. WR: 3:17.08 (USA—McCadam, Heath, Wallace, Biondi)

1. USA	(Christopher Jacobs, Troy Dalbey, Thomas Jager, Matthew Biondi, [Brent Lang, Douglas Gjertsen, Shaun Jordan])	3:16.53	WR
2. SOV	(Gennady Prigoda, Yuri Bashkatov, Nikolai Yevseyev, Vladimir Tkachenko, [Raimundas Mažuolis, Aleksei Borislavsky])	3:18.33	
3. GDR	(Dirk Richter, Thomas Flemming, Lars Hinneburg, Steffen Zesner)	3:19.82	
4. FRA	(Stephan Caron, Christophe Kalfayan, Laurent Neuville, Bruno Gutzeit)	3:20.02	
5. SWE	(Per Johansson, Tommy Werner, Joakim Holmquist, Göran Titus, [Richard Milton])	3:21.07	
6. GER	(Michael Gross, Thomas Fahrner, Björn Zikarsky, Peter Sitt)	3:21.65	
7. GBR	(Michael Fibbens, Mark Foster, Roland Lee, Andrew Jameson, [Torsten Wiegel])	3:21.71	
8. ITA	(Roberto Gleria, Giorgio Lamberti, Fabrizio Rampazzo, Andrea Ceccarini)	3:22.93	

As usual, the U.S. won this event with a world record. This time the U.S.S.R., by placing their fastest swimmers first, managed to keep pace with the Americans for 300 meters. But as soon as anchor Matt Biondi hit the water the race ceased to be close. Biondi, already credited with the seven fastest relay splits in history, swam a 47.81 to earn the third of his five gold medals.

1992 Barcelona T: 18, N: 18, D: 7.29.92. WR: 3:16.53 (USA—Jacobs, Dalbey, Jager, Biondi)

1. USA	(Joseph Hudepohl, Matthew Biondi, Thomas Jager, Jon Olsen, [Shaun Jordan, Joel Thomas])	3:16.74
2. SOV	(Pavel Khnykin, Gennady Prigoda, Yuri Bashkatov, Aleksandr Popov, [Vladimir Pyshnenko, Veniamin Tayanovich])	3:17.56
3. GER	(Christian-Alexander Tröger, Dirk Richter, Steffen Zesner, Mark Pinger, [Andreas Szigat, Bengt Zikarsky])	3:17.90
4. FRA	(Christophe Kalfayan, Franck Schott, Frederic Lefevre, Stephan Caron, [Ludovic Depickere, Bruno Gutzeit])	3:19.16
5. SWE	(Tommy Werner, Håkan Karlsson, Fredrik Letzler, Anders Holmertz, [Göran Titus])	3:20.10
6. BRA	(José Souza-Junior, Gustavo Borges, Emmanuel Fortes Nascimento, Cristiano Michelena)	3:20.99
7. GBR	(Roland Lee, Mark Foster, Michael Fibbens, Paul Howe)	3:21.75
8. AUS	(Christopher Fydler, Andrew Baildon, Thomas Stachewicz, Darren Lange)	3:22.04

The United States continued its streak of winning this event every time it has been held, but for the first time the Americans failed to break the world record. Matt Biondi moved the United States from fourth place to first on the second leg. Tom Jager held the lead, and then Jon Olsen fended off Aleksandr Popov's 47.83 final leg.

4 × 200-METER FREESTYLE RELAY

1896–1904 not held

1906 Athens T: 6, N: 6, D: 4.26.
(4 × 250 Meters)

1. HUN	(József Ónody, Henrik Hajós, Geza Kiss, Zoltán Halmay)	16:52.4
2. GER	(Ernst Bahnmeyer, Oskar Schiele, Emil Rausch, Max Pape)	17:16.2
3. GBR	(William Henry, John Derbyshire, Henry Taylor, John Arthur Jarvis)	—
4. USA	(Frank Bornamann, Joseph Spencer, Maquard Schwartz, Charles Daniels)	—
5. SWE	(Harald Julin, Robert Andersson, Charles Norelius, Hjalmar Johansson)	—
DNF: AUT	(Edmund Bernhardt, Leopold Mayer, Simon Orlik, Otto Scheff)	

Forty-seven-year-old William Henry of the British team is the oldest person ever to have won a swimming medal.

1908 London T: 6, N: 6, D: 7.24.
1. GBR (John Derbyshire, Paul Radmilo- 10:55.6 WR
vic, William Foster, Henry Taylor)
2. HUN (József Munk, Imre Zachár, Béla 10:59.0
Las-Torres, Zoltán Halmay)
3. USA (Harry Hebner, Leo Goodwin, 11:02.8
Charles Daniels, Leslie Rich)
4. AUS&NZE (Francis Beaurepaire, Fred Spring- —
field, Reginald "Snowy" Baker,
Theodore Tartakover)

The Hungarians seemed to have the race well in hand, when Halmay suddenly began to lose consciousness during the last 50 meters. He struggled to the finish line, but had to be hauled from the pool before he drowned. William Foster, at age 18 years 2 weeks, remains Great Britain's youngest gold medalist in any sport.

1912 Stockholm T: 5, N: 5, D: 7.15. WR: 10:55.6 (GBR—
Derbyshire, Radmilovic, Foster, Taylor)
1. AUS&NZE (Cecil Healy, Malcolm Champion, 10:11.6 WR
Leslie Boardman, Harold Hard-
wick)
2. USA (Kenneth Huszagh, Harry Hebner, 10:20.0
Perry McGillivray, Duke Paoa Kahanamoku)
3. GBR (William Foster, Thomas Batters- 10:28.2
by, John Hatfield, Henry Taylor)
4. GER (Oskar Schiele, Georg Kunisch, 10:37.0
Kurt Bretting, Max Ritter)

1920 Antwerp T: 7, N: 7, D: 8.29. WR: 10:11.6 (AUS&NZE—
Healy, Champion, Boardman, Hardwick)
1. USA (Perry McGillivray, Pua Kela Kealoha, 10:04.4 WR
Norman Ross, Duke Paoa Kahana-
moku)
2. AUS (Henry Hay, William Herald, Ivan Sted- 10:25.4
man, Francis Beaurepaire, [Keith Kirk-
land])
3. GBR (Leslie Savage, Edward Percival Peter, 10:37.2
Henry Taylor, Harold Annison)
4. SWE (Robert Andersson, Frans Möller, Orvar 10:50.2
Trolle, Arne Borg)
5. ITA (Mario Massa, Agostino Frassinetti, An- —
tonio Quarantotto, Gilio Bisagno)

1924 Paris T: 13, N: 13, D: 7.20. WR: 10:04.4 (USA—McGillivary,
Kealoha, Ross, Kahanamoku)
1. USA (J. Wallace O'Connor, Harrison 9:53.4 WR
Glancy, Ralph Breyer, P. "Johnny"
Weissmuller, [Richard Howell])
2. AUS (Maurice Christie, Ernest Henry, Fran- 10:02.2
cis Beaurepaire, Andrew "Boy" Charl-
ton, [Ivan Stedman])

3. SWE (Georg Werner, Orvar Trolle, Åke Borg, 10:06.8
Arne Borg, [Thor Henning, Gösta
Persson])
4. JPN (Torahiko Miyahata, Katsuo Takaishi, 10:15.2
Kazuo Noda, Kazuo Onoda)
5. GBR (John Thomson, Albert Dicken, Harold 10:29.4
Annison, Edward Percival Peter, [Leslie
Savage])
6. FRA (Guy Middleton, Henri Padou, Edouard
Vanzeveren, Emile Zeibig)

1928 Amsterdam T: 13, N: 13, D: 8.11. WR: 9:53.4 (USA—
O'Conner, Glancy, Breyer, Weissmuller)
1. USA (Austin Clapp, Walter Laufer, George 9:36.2 WR
Kojac, P. "Johnny" Weissmuller, [Paul
Samson, David Young])
2. JPN (Hiroshi Yoneyama, Nobuo Arai, 9.41.4
Tokuhei Sada, Katsuo Takaishi)
3. CAN (F. Munroe Bourne, James Thompson, 9:47.8
Garnet Ault, Walter Spence)
4. HUN (András Wanié, Rezsö Wanié, Géza 9:57.0
Sziagritz-Tarródy, István Bárány)
5. SWE (Aulo Gustafsson, Sven Pettersson, 10:01.8
Eskil Lundahl, Arne Borg)
6. GBR (Reginald Sutton, Joseph Whiteside, 10:15.8
Edward Percival Peter, Albert Dicken)
7. SPA (José González Espuglas, Estanislao —
Artal Garriga, Ramon Artigas Rigual,
Francisco Segala Torres)

Johnny Weissmuller completed his Olympic career by winning his fifth gold medal.

1932 Los Angeles T: 7, N: 7, D: 8.9. WR: 9:36.2 (USA—Clapp,
Laufer, Kojac, Weissmuller)
1. JPN (Yasuji Miyazaki, Masonori Yusa, 8:58.4 WR
Takashi Yokoyama, Hisakichi Toyoda)
2. USA (Frank Booth, George Fissler, Marola 9:10.5
Kalili, Manuella Kalili)
3. HUN (András Wanié, László Szabados, 9:31.4
András Székely, István Bárány)
4. CAN (George Larson, George Burrows, Wal- 9:36.3
ter Spence, F. Munro Bourne)
5. GBR (Joseph Whiteside, Robert Leivers, 9:45.8
Martyn Ffrench-Williams, Reginald Sutton)
6. ARG (Carlos Kennedy, Leopoldo Tahier, Ro- 10:13.1
berto Peper, Alfredo Rocca)
7. BRA (Manoel Lourenço Silva, Isaac Dos 10:36.5
Santos Moraes, Manoel Rocha Villar,
Benevenuto Martins Nunes)

1936 Berlin T: 18, N: 18, D: 8.11. WR: 8:52.2 (JPN—Yusa,
Makino, Isharada, Negami)
1. JPN (Masanori Yusa, Shigeo Sugiura, Masa- 8:51.5 WR
haru Taguchi, Shigeo Arai)
2. USA (Ralph Flanagan, John Macionis, Paul 9:03.0
Wolf, Jack Medica, [Ralph Gilman,
Charles Hutter])

3. HUN (Árpád Lengyel, Oszkár Abay-Nemes, 9:12.3
Ödön Gróf, Ferenc Csík)

4. FRA (Alfred Nakache, Christian Talli, René 9:18.2
Cavalero, Jean Taris)

5. GER (Werner Plath, Wolfgang Heimlich, Her- 9:19.0
mann Heibel, Helmut Fischer)

6. GBR (Martyn Ffrench-Williams, Romund Gabri- 9:21.5
elsen, Robert Leivers, Norman Wain-
wright)

7. CAN (F. Munroe Bourne, Robert Hamerton, 9:27.5
Robert Hooper, Robert Pirie)

8. SWE (Björn Borg, Sten Olov Bolldén, Sven 9:37.5
Petterson, Gunnar Werner)

1948 London T: 14, N: 14, D: 8.3. WR: 8:51.5 (JPN—Yusa,
Sugiura, Taguchi, Arai)

1. USA (Walter Ris, James McLane, Wallace 8:46.0 WR
Wolf, William Smith, [Robert Gibe, William Dudley, Edwin Gilbert, Eugene Rog-
ers])

2. HUN (Elemér Szathmáry, György Mitró, Imre 8:48.4
Nyéki, Géza Kádas)

3. FRA (Joseph Bernardo, Henri Padou, René 9:08.0
Cornu, Alexandre Jany)

4. SWE (Martin Lundén, Per-Olof Östrand, Olle 9:09.1
Johansson, Per-Olof Olsson)

5. YUG (Vanja Illič, Čiril Pelhan, Ivan Puhar, 9:14.0
Branko Vidovič)

6. ARG (Horacio White, José Durañona, Juan 9:19.2
Garay, Alfredo Yantorno, [Antonio Can-
ton])

7. MEX (Ramon Bravo Prieto, Angel Maldonado 9:20.2
Campos, Apolonio Diaz Castillo, Alberto
Isaac Ahumada)

8. BRA Sergio Alencar Rodrigues, Willy Jordan, 9:31.0
Rof Kestener Egon, Aram Boghossian)

1952 Helsinki T: 17, N: 17, D: 7.29, WR: 8:29.4 (USA, Yale
University—Moore, McLane, Sheff, Thoman)

1. USA (Wayne Moore, William Woolsey, Ford 8:31.1 OR
Konno, James McLane, [Wallace Wolf,
Donald Sheff, Frank Dooley, Burwell
Jones])

2. JPN (Hiroshi Suzuki, Yoshihiro Hamaguchi, 8:33.5
Toru Goto, Teijiro Tanikawa)

3. FRA (Joseph Bernardo, Aldo Eminente, Alex- 8:45.9
andre Jany, Jean Boiteux)

4. SWE (Lars Svanteson, Göran Larsson, Per- 8:46.8
Olof Östrand, Olle Johansson, [Rolf
Olander])

5. HUN (László Gyöngyösi, György Csordás, 8:52.6
Géza Kádas, Imre Nyéki, [Gusztáv
Kettesi])

6. GBR (Frank Botham, Ronald Burns, Thomas 8:52.9
Welsh, John Wardrop)

7. SAF (Graham Johnston, Dennis Ford, John 8:55.1
Durr, Peter Duncan)

8. ARG (Federico Zwanck, Marcelo Trabucco, 8:56.9
Pedro Galvao, Alfredo Yantorno)

Knowing that they would lose under normal circumstances, the Japanese reversed the usual order of their
swimmers, putting the fastest man first and the slowest
last. They did build up a big lead, but Ford Konno closed
the gap and Jimmy McLane pulled away in the final 100
meters.

1956 Melbourne T: 11, N: 11, D: 12.3. WR: 8:24.5 (SOV—Nikitin,
Strushanov, Nikolayev, Sorokin)

1. AUS (Kevin O'Halloran, John Devitt, I. Mur- 8:23.6 WR
ray Rose, Jon Henricks, [Gary Chap-
man, Graham Hamilton, Murray Gar-
retty])

2. USA (Richard Hanley, George Breen, Wil- 8:31.5
liam Woolsey, Ford Konno, [Perry
Jecku, Richard Tanabe])

3. SOV (Vitaly Sorokin, Vladimir Strushanov, 8:34.7
Gennady Nikolayev, Boris Nikitin)

4. JPN (Manabu Koga, Atsushi Tani, Koji 8:36.6
Nonoshita, Tsuyoshi Yamanaka)

5. GER&GDR (Hans Köhler, Hans-Joachim Reich, 8:43.4
Hans Zierold, Horst Bleeker)

6. GBR (Kenneth Williams, Ronald Roberts, 8:45.2
Neil McKecknie, John Wardrop)

7. ITA (Federico Dennerlein, Paolo Galletti, 8:46.2
Guido Elmi, Anthony Romani)

8. SAF (William Steuart, Anthony Briscoe, 8:49.5
Dennis Ford, Peter Duncan)

1960 Rome T: 15, N: 15, D: 9.1. WR(880 yards): 8:16.6 (AUS—
Henricks, Dickson, Konrads, Rose)

1. USA (George Harrison, Richard Blick, Mi- 8:10.2 WR
chael Troy, F. Jeffrey Farrell, [William
Darnton, Thomas Winters, Stephen
Clark])

2. JPN (Makoto Fukui, Hiroshi Ishii, Tsuyoshi 8:13.2
Yamanaka, Tatsuo Fujimoto)

3. AUS (David Dickson, John Devitt, I. Murray 8:13.8
Rose, John Konrads, [John Rigby,
Allan Wood])

4. GBR (Hamilton Milton, John Martin-Dye, 8:28.1
Richard Campion, Ian Black)

5. FIN (Ilkka Suvanto, Kari Haavisto, Stig- 8:29.7
Olof Grenner, Harri Käyhkö)

6. SWE (Sven-Göran Johansson, Lars-Erik 8:31.0
Bengtsson, Bengt Nordvall, Per-Ola
Lindberg, [Almsted Bengt])

7. GER&GDR (Frank Wiegand, Gerhard Hetz, Hans 8:31.8
Zierold, Hans Klein)

8. SOV (Igor Lushkovski, Gennady Nikolayev, 8:32.2
Vitaly Sorokin, Boris Nikitin, [Sergei
Tovstoplet])

1964 Tokyo T: 15, N: 15, D: 10.18. WR: 8:01.8 (USA—Mettler,
Wall, Lyons, Schollander)

1. USA (Stephen Clark, Roy Saari, Gary Ilman, 7:52.1 WR
Donald Schollander, [William Mettler,
David Lyons, Michael Wall, Robert
Townsend])

2. GDR&GER (Horst-Günther Gregor, Gerhard Hetz, 7:59.3
Frank Wiegand, Hans-Joachim Klein)

3. JPN (Makoto Fukui, Kunihiro Iwasaki, 8:03.8
Toshio Shoji, Yukiaki Okabe)

4. AUS (David Dickson, Allan Wood, Peter 8:05.5
Doak, Robert Windle, [John Konrads,
John Ryan])

5. SWE (Mats Svensson, E. Lester Eriksson, 8:08.0
Hans Rosendahl, Jan Lundin)

6. FRA (Jean-Pascal Curtillet, Pierre Cana- 8:08.7
vese, Francis Luyce, Alain Gottvalles)

7. SOV/RUS (Semyon Belits-Geiman, Vladimir Bere- 8:15.1
zin, Aleksandr Paramonov, Yevgeny
Novikov)

8. ITA (Sergio De Gregorio, Bruno Bianchi, 8:18.1
Giovanni Orlando, Pietro Bascaini)

With this race Steve Clark earned his third gold medal,
and Don Schollander became the first swimmer in Olympic history to win four gold medals in one Olympics.

1968 Mexico City T: 16, N: 16, D: 10.21 WR: 7:52.1 (USA—Clark,
Saari, Ilman, Schollander; USA, Santa Clara Swim Club—Ilman,
Spitz, Wall, Schollander)

1. USA (John Nelson, Stephen Rerych, Mark Spitz, 7:52.33
Donald Schollander, [William Johnson, David
Johnson, Andrew Strenk, Michael Wall])

2. AUS (Gregory Rogers, Graham White, Robert 7:53.77
Windle, Michael Wenden)

3. SOV (Vladimir Bure, Semyon Belits-Geiman, Georgi 8:01.66
Kulikov, Leonid Ilyichev)

4. CAN (George Smith, Ronald Jacks, John Gilchrist, 8:03.22
Ralph Hutton)

5. FRA (Michel Rousseau, Gerard Letast, Francis 8:03.77
Luyce, Alain Mosconi)

6. GER (Hans Fassnacht, Olaf von Schilling, Volkert 8:04.33
Meeuw, Wolfgang Kremer)

7. GDR (Frank Weigand, Horst-Günter Gregor, Alfred 8:06.00
Müller, Jochen Herbst)

8. SWE (Hans Ljungberg, Karl Larson, Sven Ferm, Erik 8:12.11
Eriksson)

1972 Munich T: 14, N: 14, D: 8.31. WR: 7:43.3 (USA—Spitz,
Heidenreich, Tyler, McBreen)

1. USA (John Kinsella, Frederick Tyler, Steven 7:35.78 WR
Genter, Mark Spitz, [Gary Conelly,
Thomas McBreen, Michael Burton])

2. GER (Klaus Steinbach, Werner Lampe, 7:41.69
Hans-Günter Vosseler, Hans-Joachim
Fassnacht, [Gerhard Schiller, Folkert
Meeuw])

3. SOV (Igor Grivennikov, Viktor Mazanov, 7:45.76
Georgi Kulikov, Vladimir Bure, [Viktor
Aboimov, Aleksandr Samsonov])

4. SWE (Bengt Gingsjö, Hans Ljungberg, 7:47.37
Anders Bellbring, Gunnar Larsson)

5. AUS (Michael Wenden, Graham Windeatt, 7:48.66
Robert Nay, Bradford Cooper, [Robert
Featherstone, Graham White])

6. GDR (Wilfried Hartung, Peter Bruch, Udo 7:49.11
Poser, Lutz Unger, [Roger Pyttel])

7. CAN (Bruce Robertson, Brian Phillips, Ian 7:53.61
MacKenzie, Ralph Hutton, [Dean
Buckboro])

8. GBR (Brian Brinkley, John Mills, Michael 7:55.59
Bailey, Colin Cunningham)

One hour after winning the 100-meter butterfly, Mark
Spitz was back in the water to swim the anchor leg for the
4 × 200-meter freestyle relay team. Steve Genter's third
leg of 1:52.72 gave the U.S. a big lead. Spitz took over
from there to gain his fifth gold medal and fifth world
record in four days.

1976 Montreal T: 18, N: 18, D: 7.21. WR: 7:30.54 (USA, Long
Beach Swim Club—Favero, Shaw, S. Furniss, B. Furniss)

1. USA (Michael Bruner, Bruce Furniss, John 7:23.22 WR
Naber, James Montgomery, [Douglas
Northway, Timothy Shaw])

2. SOV (Volodymyr Raskatov, Andrei 7:27.97
Bogdanov, Sergei Kopliakov, Andrei
Krylov, [Andrei Smirnov, Vladimir
Mikheyev])

3. GBR (Alan McClatchey, David Dunne, Gor- 7:32.11
don Downie, Brian Brinkley)

4. GER (Klaus Steinbach, Peter Nocke, Werner 7:32.27
Lampe, Hans-Joachim Geisler [An-
dreas Schmidt])

5. GDR (Roger Pyttel, Wilfried Hartung, Rainer 7:38.92
Strohbach, Frank Pfütze)

6. HOL (Abdul Ressand, René van der Kuil, 7:42.56
André in Het Veld, Henk Elzerman)

7. SWE (Pär Arvidsson, Peter Petterson, 7:42.84
Anders Bellbring, Bengt Gingsjö)

8. ITA (Marcello Guarducci, Roberto 7:43.39
Pangaro, Paolo Barelli, Paolo Revelli)

The U.S. team of Doug Northway, Tim Shaw, Mike
Bruner, and Bruce Furniss set a world record of 7:30.33
in the qualifying round. That night, Northway and Shaw
were replaced by John Naber and Jim Montgomery, and
another world record was set.

1980 Moscow T: 13, N: 13, D: 7.23. WR: 7:20.82 (USA—B.
Furniss, Forrester, Hackett, Gaines)

1. SOV (Sergei Kopliakov, Vladimir Salnikov, Ivar Stu- 7:23.50
kolkin, Andrei Krylov, [Sergei Rusin, Sergei
Krasyuk, Yuri Presekin])

2. GDR (Frank Pfütze, Jörg Woithe, Detlev Grabs, 7:28.60
Rainer Strohbach)

3. BRA (Jorge Lutz Fernandes, Marcus Laborne 7:29.30
Mattioli, Cyro Marques, Djan Madruga
Garrido)

4. SWE (Michael Söderlund, Pelle Wikström, Per-Alvar 7:30.10
Magnusson, Thomas Lejdström, [Anders
Rutkvist, Per-Ola Quist])

5. ITA (Paolo Revelli, Raffaele Franceschi, Andrea 7:30.37
Ceccarini, Fabrizio Rampazzo, [Federic
Silvestri])

6. GBR   (Douglas Campbell, Philip Hubble, T. Martin   7:30.81
        Smith, Andrew Astbury, [Mark Taylor, Kevin
        Lee])

7. AUS   (Graeme Brewer, Mark Tonelli, Mark Kerry,   7:30.82
        Ron McKeon, [Max Metzker])

8. FRA   (Fabien Noel, Mark Lazzaro, Dominique Petit,   7:36.08
        Paskal Laget)

1984 Los Angeles T: 14, N: 14, D: 7.30. WR: 7:20.40 (GER—
Fahrner, Schmidt, Schwotka, Gross)

1. USA   (Michael Heath, David Larson, Jeffrey   7:15.69   WR
        Float, L. Bruce Hayes, [Geoffrey
        Gamberino, Richard Saeger])

2. GER   (Thomas Fahrner, Dirk Korthals, Alexan-   7:15.73
        der Schowtka, Michael Gross, [Rainer
        Henkel])

3. GBR   (Neil Cochran, Paul Easter, Paul Howe,   7:24.78
        Andrew Astbury)

4. AUS   (Peter Dale, Justin Lemberg, Ronald   7:25.63
        McKeon, Graeme Brewer, [Thomas
        Stachewicz])

5. CAN   (Donald "Sandy" Goss, Wayne Kelly,   7:26.51
        Peter Szmidt, Alex Baumann, [Benoit
        Clement])

6. SWE   (Michael Söderlund, Tommy Werner,   7:26.53
        Anders Holmertz, Thomas Lejdström,
        [Mikael Orn])

7. HOL   (Hans Kroes, Peter Drost, Edsard   7:26.72
        Schlingemann, Frank Drost)

8. FRA   (Stephan Caron, Dominique Bataille,   7:30.16
        Michel Pou, Pierre Andraca)

The 1984 gold medal for prescience goes to sportswriter Craig Neff of *Sports Illustrated* who predicted in the magazine's souvenir program: "In what should be a heartstopping 4 × 200 free relay, the West Germans will likely lose their world record and the gold medal to the U.S.—but just barely."

The world record went quickly in the qualifying round when the U.S. "B" team of Geoffrey Gamberino, David Larson, Bruce Hayes and Richard Saeger swam a 7:18.87. In the final, Gamberino and Saeger were replaced by Mike Heath and Jeff Float. Normally the U.S. coaches would have had Heath swim the anchor leg, since he was the fastest man on the team. But the presence of Michael Gross as the West German anchor called for a change of strategy. It was decided to swim Heath first and build up as big a lead as possible before Gross hit the water. The unenviable task of fighting off the brilliant German swimmer was given to 21-year-old Bruce Hayes, an experienced anchor man. This was the only event for which Hayes had qualified, so much of his training concentrated on practicing his finishing touch.

Swimming the third leg for the U.S. was Jeff Float, who had lost 80% of his hearing in his right ear and 60% in his left ear when he contracted viral meningitis at the age of 13 months. So great was the roar of the crowd during the final as Float lengthened the U.S. lead against

Alexander Schowtka that, for the first time in his life, he heard the crowd cheering him on. When Float touched the wall at the end of his leg, he handed over to Hayes a three-yard lead. But Gross went out so powerfully that he caught Hayes after only 50 meters, and passed him after 100. Hayes was shocked that Gross had appeared by his side so quickly, but he didn't panic. Instead he kept the pressure on. Gross came out of the final turn with a two-foot lead, but then Hayes began gaining on the world record holder. As they reached for the wall it was impossible to to tell who had won. All eyes turned to the scoreboard. Almost immediately, the number "1" appeared next to "USA," setting off a wildly emotional celebration.

Michael Gross, whose 1:46.89 split was the fastest ever recorded, was, as always, as gracious in defeat as in victory. "I just ran out of gas," he said. "That was a really hot race. It was an honorable defeat."

1988 Seoul T: 16, N: 16, D: 9.21. WR: 7:13.10 (GER—Sitt, Henkel, Fahrner, Gross)

1. USA   (Troy Dalbey, Matthew Cetlinski, Doug-   7:12.51   WR
        las Gjertsen, Matthew Biondi, [Craig
        Oppel, Daniel Jorgensen])

2. GDR   (Uwe Dassler, Sven Lodziewski,   7:13.68
        Thomas Flemming, Steffen Zesner,
        [Lars Hinneburg])

3. GER   (Erik Hochstein, Thomas Fahrner,   7:14.35
        Rainer Henkel, Michael Gross, [Peter
        Sitt, Stefan Pfeiffer])

4. AUS   (Thomas Stachewicz, Ian Brown, Jason   7:15.23
        Plummer, Duncan Armstrong, [Martin
        Roberts])

5. ITA   (Roberto Gleria, Giorgio Lamberti, Mas-   7:16.00
        simo Trevisan, Valerio Giambalvo,
        [Fabrizio Rampazzo])

6. SWE   (Anders Holmertz, Tommy Werner, Mi-   7:19.10
        chael Söderlund, Christer Wallin, [Hen-
        rik Jangvall])

7. FRA   (Michel Pou, Franck Iacono, Olivier   7:24.69
        Fougeroud, Ludovic Depickere, [Ste-
        phan Caron, Laurent Neuville])

8. CAN   (Turlough O'Hare, Donald "Sandy"   7:24.91
        Goss, Donald Haddow, Gary Vander-
        meulen, [Darren Ward])

The United States entered this race in the unaccustomed role of underdog to the world record-holding West Germans and the world champion East Germans. Anders Holmertz put Sweden in the lead after the first leg. At the halfway mark, Italy was in front, thanks to a powerful swim by Giorgio Lamberti. At that point East Germany was in second place, West Germany in fourth, and the U.S. in fifth. Thomas Flemming gave the GDR a body-length lead over the U.S. with one lap to go. Then Matt Biondi took over. Two hours earlier he had missed a gold medal in the 100-meter butterfly by one one-hundredth of a second and now he was tired of losing. He passed

Steffen Zesner after 75 meters, recorded the fastest relay split in history (1:46.44), and won by a bodylength.

The following night, U.S. team member Troy Dalbey caused a scandal when he stole a 65-pound decorative lion's mask from a hotel bar. He was arrested along with teammate Doug Gjertsen, but both swimmers were subsequently released after they apologized to the Korean people.

1992 Barcelona T: 18, N: 18, D: 7.27. WR: 7:12.51 (USA—Dalbey, Cetlinski, Gjertsen, Biondi)

1.	RUS	(Dmitri Lepikov, Vladimir Pyshnenko, Veniamin Tayanovich, Yevgeny Sadovyi, [Aleksei Kudryavtsev, Yuri Mukhin])	7:11.95	WR
2.	SWE	(Christer Wallin, Anders Holmertz, Tommy Werner, Lars Frölander)	7:15.51	
3.	USA	(Joseph Hudepohl, Melvin Stewart, Jon Olsen, Douglas Gjertsen, [Scott Jaffe, Daniel Jorgenson])	7:16.23	
4.	GER	(Peter Sitt, Steffen Zesner, Andreas Szigat, Stefan Pfeiffer, [Christian Tröger])	7:16.58	
5.	ITA	(Roberto Gleria, Giorgio Lamberti, Massimo Trevisan, Stefano Battistelli, [Emanuele Idini, Piermaria Siciliano])	7:18.10	
6.	GBR	(Paul Palmer, Steven Mellor, Stephen Akers, Paul Howe)	7:22.57	
7.	BRA	(Gustavo Borges, Emmanuel Fortes Nascimento, Teofilo Laborne Ferreira, Cristiano Michelena)	7:24.03	

DISQ: AUS (Ian Brown, Deane Pieters, Kieren Perkins, Duncan Armstrong, [Martin Roberts])

The United States' winning streak in the 4×200 was finally stopped at seven. The well-prepared Russian team passed the Swedes during the third leg, allowing Yevgeny Sadovyi an easy race to the finish to pick up the second of his three gold medals.

4 × 100-METER MEDLEY RELAY

In medley relays, the order of strokes is backstroke, breaststroke, butterfly, and freestyle.

1896–1956 not held

1960 Rome T: 18, N: 18, D: 9.1. WR: 4:09.2 (USA, Indianapolis Athletic Club—McKinney, Jastremski, Troy, Sintz)

1.	USA	(Frank McKinney, Paul Hait, Lance Larson, F. Jeffrey Farrell, [Robert Bennett, David Gillanders, Stephen Clark])	4:05.4	WR
2.	AUS	(David Theile, Terry Gathercole, Neville Hayes, Geoffrey Shipton, [Julian Carroll, William Burton, Kevin Berry])	4:12.0	
3.	JPN	(Kazuo Tomita, Koichi Hirakida, Yoshihiko Osaki, Keigo Shimizu, [Kazuo Watanabe, Katsuki Ishikara])	4:12.2	

4.	CAN	(Robert Wheaton, Steve Rabinovitch, Cameron Grout, Richard Pound)	4:16.8
5.	SOV	(Leonid Barbier, Leonid Kolesnikov, Grigory Kiselyov, Igor Lushkovski)	4:16.8
6.	ITA	(Guiseppe Avellone, Roberto Lazzari, Federico Dennerlein, Bruno Bianchi)	4:17.2
7.	GBR	(Graham Sykes, Christopher Walkden, Ian Black, Stanley Clarke)	4:17.6
8.	HOL	(Johannes Jiskoot, Wieger Mensonides, Gerrit Korteweg, Ronald Kroon)	4:18.2

The U.S. "reserve" team of Bob Bennett, Paul Hait, Dave Gillanders, and Steve Clark set a world record of 4:08.2 in the qualifying round. Only Hait also took part in the final, in which a new U.S. team set another world record.

1964 Tokyo T: 14, N: 14, D: 10.16. WR: 4:00.1 (USA—McGeagh, Craig, Richardson, Clark)

1.	USA	(Harold Thompson Mann, William Craig, Fred Schmidt, Stephen Clark, [Richard McGeagh, Virgi Luken, Walter Richardson, Robert Bennett])	3:58.4	WR
2.	GDR&GER	(Ernst-Joachim Küppers, Egon Henninger, Horst-Günther Gregor, Hans-Joachim Klein)	4:01.6	
3.	AUS	(Peter Reynolds, Ian O'Brien, Kevin Berry, David Dickson, [Peter Tonkin])	4:02.3	
4.	SOV	(Viktor Mazanov, Heorhy Prokopenko, Valentin Kuzmin, Vladimir Schuvalov, [Aleksandr Tutakayev, Viktor Semchenkov])	4:04.2	
5.	JPN	(Shigeo Fukushima, Kenji Ishikawa, Isao Nakajima, Yukiaki Okabe)	4:06.6	
6.	HUN	(József Csikány, Ferenc Lenkei, József Gurrich, Gyula Dobai)	4:08.5	
7.	ITA	(Chiaffredo Rora, Gian Corrado Gross, Giampiero Fossati, Pietro Boscaini)	4:10.3	
8.	GBR	(Geoffrey Thwaites, Neil Nicholson, Brian Jenkins, Robert McGregor)	4:11.4	

Backstroker Thompson Mann led off for the United States with a world record of 59.6, the first time that the one minute barrier had ever been broken for the 100-meter backstroke. The German and Soviet teams caught up by the halfway mark, but Fred Schmidt put the victory away for the United States with a 56.8 butterfly leg, and Steve Clark sealed it with a 52.4 anchor.

1968 Mexico City T: 18, N: 18, D: 10.26. WR: 3:56.5 (GDR—Matthes, Henninger, Gregor, Wiegand)

| 1. | USA | (Charles Hickcox, Donald McKenzie, Douglas Russell, Kenneth Walsh, [Ronald Mills, Chester Jastremski, Carl Robie, Donald Schollander]) | 3:54.9 | WR |
| 2. | GDR | (Roland Matthes, Egon Henninger, Horst-Günther Gregor, Frank Wiegand) | 3:57.5 | |

3. SOV (Yuri Hromak, Vladimir Kossinsky, 4:00.7
Volodymyr Nemshilov, Leonid Ilyichev,
[Viktor Mazanov, Nikolai Pankin, Yuri
Suzdatsev, Sergei Gusev])

4. AUS (Karl Byrom, Ian O'Brien, Robert Cusack, 4:00.8
Michael Wenden)

5. JPN (Yasuo Tanaka, Nobutaka Taguchi, 4:01.8
Satoshi Maruya, Kunihiro Iwasaki)

6. GER (Reinhard Blechert, Gregor Betz, Lutz 4:05.4
Stoklasa, Wolfgang Kremer)

7. CAN (James Shaw, William Mahony, Toomas 4:07.3
Arusoo, John Gilchrist)

8. SPA (Santiago Esteva, José Duran, Arturo 4;08.8
Lang, José Chicoy)

Roland Matthes opened with a backstroke world record
of 58.0, but Doug Russell's butterfly leg put the United
States in the lead to stay.

1972 Munich T: 17, N: 17, D: 9.4. WR: 3:50.4 (USA—Campbell,
Dahlberg, Spitz, Heidenreich)

1. USA (Michael Stamm, Thomas Bruce, Mark 3:48.16 WR
Spitz, Jerry Heidenreich, [Mitchell Ivey,
John Hencken, Gary Hall, David Fair-
bank])

2. GDR (Roland Matthes, Klaus Katzur, 3:52.12
Hartmut Flöckner, Lutz Unger)

3. CAN (Eric Fish, William Mahony, Bruce Rob- 3:52.26
ertson, Robert Kasting, [William Ken-
nedy])

4. SOV/ (Igor Grivennikov, Nikolai Pankin, Viktor 3:53.26
RUS Sharygin, Vladimir Bure, [Viktor
Stulikov, Viktor Aboimov])

5. BRA (Romulo Duncan Arantes, José Sylvio 3:57.89
Fiolo, Sergio Waismann, José Roberto
Diñiz-Aranha)

6. JPN (Tadashi Honda, Nobutaka Taguchi, 3:58.23
Yasuhiro Komazaki, Jiro Sasaki)

7. GBR (Colin Cunningham, David Wilkie, John 3:58.82
Mills, Malcolm Windeatt)

8. HUN (László Cseh, Sándor Szabó, István 3:59.07
Szentirmay, Attila Császári, [András
Hargitay])

Once again, Roland Matthes opened with a world record
performance, but then the Americans took over, as Mark
Spitz, swimming the butterfly leg, won his seventh gold
medal.

1976 Montreal T: 14, N: 14, D: 7.22. WR: 3:48.16 (USA—Stamm,
Bruce, Spitz, Heidenreich)

1. USA (John Naber, John Hencken, Matt Vo- 3:42.22 WR
gel, Jim Montgomery, [Peter Rocca,
Christopher Woo, Joseph Bottom, Jack
Babashoff])

2. CAN (Stephen Pickell, Graham Smith, Clay 3:45.94
Evans, Gary MacDonald, [Bruce Rob-
ertson])

3. GER (Klaus Steinbach, Walter Kusch, Mi- 3:47.29
chael Kraus, Peter Nocke, [Peter Lang,
Dirk Braunleder])

4. GBR (James Carter, David Wilkie, John 3:49.56
Mills, Brian Brinkley, [Gary Abraham,
Duncan Goodhew, Kevin Burns])

5. SOV (Igor Omelchenko, Arvydas Juozaitis, 3:49.90
Yevgeny Seredin, Andrei Krylov, [Niko-
lai Pankin, Andrei Bogdanov])

6. AUS (Mark Kerry, Paul Jarvie, Neil Rogers, 3:51.54
Peter Coughlan)

7. ITA (Enrico Bisso, Giorgio Lalle, Paolo 3:52.92
Barelli, Marcello Guarducci)

8. JPN (Tadashi Honda, Nobutaka Taguchi, 3:54.74
Hideaki Hara, Tsuyoshi Yanagidate)

In the qualifying round, Americans Peter Rocca, Chris
Woo, Joe Bottom, and Jack Babashoff set a world record
of 3:47.28. The 1976 U.S. team was so strong that they
were able to field a completely different foursome in the
final and set yet another world record.

1980 Moscow T: 11, N: 11, D: 7.24. WR: 3:42.22 (USA—Naber,
Hencken, Vogel, Montgomery)

1. AUS (Mark Kerry, Peter Evans, Mark Tonelli, Neil 3:45.70
Brooks, [Glen Patching])

2. SOV (Viktor Kuznetsov, Arsens Miskarovs, Yevgeny 3:45.92
Seredin, Sergei Kopliakov, [Vladimir Shmetov,
Aleksandr Fedorovsky, Aleksei Markovsky,
Sergei Krasyuk])

3. GBR (Gary Abraham, Duncan Goodhew, David 3:47.71
Lowe, T. Martin Smith, [Paul Marshall, Mark
Taylor])

4. GDR (Dietmar Göhring, Jörg Walter, Roger Pyttel, 3:48.25
Jörg Woithe, [Frank Kühn])

5. FRA (Frédéric Delcourt, Olivier Borios, Xavier 3;49.19
Savin, René Ecuyer)

6. HUN (Sándor Wladár, Janos Dzvonyar, Zoltán 3:50.29
Verrasztó, Gábor Mészáros)

7. HOL (Fred Eefting, Albert Boonstra, Kees Vervoorn, 3:51.81
Cees Jan Winkel)

8. BRA (Romulo Duncan Arantes, Sergio Pinto 3:53.23
Ribeiro, Claudo Mamede Kestener, Jorge Luiz
Fernandes, [Ciro Marques Delgado])

Australian anchorman Neil Brooks swam a stirring 49.86
to overtake 200-meter freestyle gold medalist Sergei Kopliakov and give Australia an upset victory. While most
teams choose aggressive-sounding names for a nickname—like the Mean Machine or the Fearsome Foursome—the Australian 4 × 100-meter medley relay team
christened themselves the Quietly Confident Quartet.

1984 Los Angeles T: 21, N: 21, D: 8.4. WR: 3:40.42 (USA—
Carey, Lundquist, Gribble, Gaines)

1. USA (Richard Carey, Steve Lundquist, P. 3:39.30 WR
Pablo Morales, Ambrose "Rowdy"
Gaines, [David Wilson, Richard
Schroeder, Michael Heath, Thomas
Jager])

2. CAN (Mike West, Victor Davis, Thomas 3:43.23
Ponting, Donald "Sandy" Goss)

3. AUS (Mark Kerry, Peter Evans, Glenn Bu- 3:43.25
chanan, Mark Stockwell, [Jonathon
Sieben, Neil Brooks])
4. GER (Stefan Peter, Gerald Mörken, Michael 3:44.26
Gross, Dirk Korthals, [Andreas
Behrend, Alexander Schowtka])
5. SWE (Bengt Baron, Peter Berggren, Thomas 3:47.13
Lejdström, Per Johansson, [Michael
Söderlund, Peter Berggren])
6. GBR (Neil Harper, Adrian Moorhouse, An- 3:47.39
drew Jameson, Richard Burrell, [David
Lowe])
7. SWI (Patrick Ferland, Etienne Dagon, 3:47.93
Theophile David, Dano Halsall)
DISQ: JPN (Daichi Suzuki, Shigehiro Takahashi, Taihei Saka, Hiro-
shi Sakamoto)

Rick Carey opened with an Olympic backstroke record
of 55.41 and the rest of the race was never close.

1988 Seoul T: 25, N: 25, D: 9.25. WR: 3:38.28 (USA—Carey,
Moffet, Morales, Biondi)
1. USA (David Berkoff, Richard Schroeder, 3:36.93 WR
Matthew Biondi, Christopher Jacobs,
[Jay Mortenson, Thomas Jager])
2. CAN (Mark Tewksbury, Victor Davis, 3:39.28
Thomas Ponting, Donald "Sandy"
Goss)
3. SOV (Igor Polyansky, Dmitri Volkov, Vadym 3:39.96
Yaroshchuk, Gennady Prigoda, [Sergei
Zabolotnov, Valery Lozik, Konstantin
Petrov, Nikolai Yevseyev])
4. GER (Frank Hoffmeister, Alexander Mayer, 3:42.98
Michael Gross, Björn Zikarsky, [Mark
Warnecke])
5. JPN (Daichi Suzuki, Hironobu Nagahata, 3:44.36
Hiroshi Miura, Shigeo Ogata)
6. AUS (Carl Wilson, Ian Mcadam, Jonathon 3:45.85
Sieben, Andrew Baildon)
7. HOL (Hans Kroes, Ronald Dekker, Frank 3:46.85
Drost, Patrick Dybiona)
DISQ: GBR (Neil Harper, Adrian Moorhouse, Andrew Jameson,
Mark Foster, [Gary Binfield, Roland Lee])

David Berkoff opened with a sizzling 54.56 backstroke
leg and the U.S. never looked back. Matt Biondi left
Seoul with five gold medals, one silver, and one bronze.
The West German team celebrated the end of the meet
by walking to the blocks dressed in lederhosen. At the
1986 world championships they had appeared in togas
made of bedsheets.

1992 Barcelona T: 23, N: 23, D: 7.31. WR: 3:36.93 (USA—
Berkoff, Schroeder, Biondi, Jacobs)
1. USA (Jeffrey Rouse, Nelson Diebel, P. Pablo 3:36.93 EWR
Morales, Jon Olsen, [David Berkoff,
Hans Dersch, Melvin Stewart, Matthew
Biondi])
2. SOV (Vladimir Selkov, Vasily Ivanov, Pavel
Khnykin, Aleksandr Popov, [Vladislav

Kulikov, Dmitri Volkov, Vladimir 3:38.56
Pyshnenko])
3. CAN (Mark Tewksbury, Jonathan Cleveland, 3:39.66
Marcel Gery, Stephen Clarke, [Thomas
Ponting])
4. GER (Tino Weber, Mark Warnecke, Christian 3:40.19
Keller, Mark Pinger, [Bengt Zikarsky])
5. FRA (Franck Schott, Stephane Vossart, 3:40.51
Bruno Gutzeit, Stephan Caron, [Franck
Esposito, Christophe Kalfayan])
6. HUN (Tamás Deutsch, Norbert Rózsa, Péter 3:42.03
Horváth, Béla Szabados)
7. AUS (Thomas Stachewicz, Philip Rogers, 3:42.65
Jonathon Sieben, Christopher Fydler)
8. JPN (Hajime Itoi, Akira Hayashi, Keiichi 3:43.25
Kawanaka, Tsutomu Nakano)

A day after he was outtouched by Mark Tewksbury in
the 100-meter backstroke final, Jeff Rouse led off with a
world record of 53.86 seconds. The United States extended its win streak in this event to eight in a row. By
swimming in the preliminary round, Matt Biondi earned
a gold medal, bringing his career medal total to eleven: 8
gold, 2 silver, 1 bronze.

Discontinued Events

100-METER FREESTYLE FOR SAILORS

1896 Athens C: 3, N: 1, D: 4.11.
1. Ioannis Malokinis   GRE   2:20.4
2. Spiridon Chasapis   GRE   —
3. Dimitrios Drivas   GRE   —

This rather specialized event was limited to members of
the Greek navy.

880-YARD FREESTYLE

1904 St. Louis C: 6, N: 4, D: 9.7.
1. Emil Rausch   GER   13:11.4
2. Francis Gailey   USA   13.23.4
3. Géza Kiss   HUN   —
4. Edgar Adams   USA   —
AC: Jamison Handy (USA), Otto Wahle (AUT)

4000-METER FREESTYLE

1900 Paris C: 29, N: 7, D: 8.19.
1. John Arthur Jarvis   GBR   58:24.0
2. Zoltán Halmay   HUN   1:08:55.4
3. Louis Martin   FRA   1:13:08.4
4. Thomas Burgess   FRA   1:15:07.6

5. Eduard Meijer	HOL	1:16:37.2	
6. Fabio Mainoni	ITA	1:18:25.4	

400-METER BREASTSTROKE

1904 St. Louis C: 4, N: 2, D: 9.7.
(440 Yards—402.33 Meters)

1. Georg Zacharias	GER	7:23.6
2. Walter Brack	GER	—
3. H. Jamison Handy	USA	—
4. Jörg Hoffmann	GER	—

Jam Handy later became known as swimming's most prolific inventor. He was the first person to paint lines on the bottom of a pool to help swimmers keep to a straight course, the first swimmer to use alternating armstrokes in the backstroke, and the first person to use modern breathing techniques. At the age of 80, he was still able to swim more laps than his age.

1906–1908 not held

1912 Stockholm C: 17, N: 10, D: 7.12.

1. Walter Bathe	GER	6:29.6	OR
2. Thor Henning	SWE	6:35.6	
3. Percy Courtman	GBR	6:36.4	
4. Kurt Malisch	GER	6:37.0	
DNF: Willy Lützow (GER)			

The appropriately named Walter Bathe won without being seriously threatened.

1920 Antwerp C: 20, N: 10, D: 8.25.

1. Håkan Malmroth	SWE	6:31.8
2. Thor Henning	SWE	6:45.2
3. Arvo Aaltonen	FIN	6:48.0
4. Jack Howell	USA	6:51.0
5. Per Cederblom	SWE	—

200-METER TEAM SWIMMING

1900 Paris T: 4, N: 2, D: 8.12.

1. GER	(1—Ernst Hoppenberg 2:35.0, 2—Max Hainle 2:36.0, 4—Max Schöne, 6—Julius Frey, 19—Herbert von Petersdorff)	32
2. FRA	(Tritons Lillois—Maurice Hochepied, Verbecke, Cadet, Bertrand, Victor Hochepied)	51
3. FRA	(Pupilles de Neptune, Lille—Jean Leuillieux, Louis Martin, Houben, Tartara, Désiré Merchez)	61
4. FRA	(Libellule de Paris—members unknown)	65

This was not a relay, but a team race in which 20 men were entered. Each team was assigned points according to the places in which its individual members finished. Von Petersdorff did not actually take part and so was awarded a tie for last place. A British team had also been entered, but was misinformed as to the starting time and arrived after the race was over.

4 × 50-YARD FREESTYLE RELAY

1904 St. Louis T: 4, N: 1, D: 9.7.

1. USA	(New York Athletic Club # 1—Joseph Ruddy, Leo Goodwin, Louis Handle, Charles Daniels)	2:04.6
2. USA	(Chicago Athletic Club—David Hammond, William Tuttle, Hugo Goetz, Raymond Thorne)	—
3. USA	(Missouri Athletic Club—Amadee Reyburn, Gwynne Evans, Marquard Schwartz, William Orthwein)	—
4. USA	(New York Athletic Club #2—Edgar Adams, David Bratton, George Van Cleaf, David Hesser)	—

A German team lined up to start the race, but the Americans objected, claiming that the race was for clubs only and that the German swimmers were not all from the same club. Not surprisingly, the U.S. officials in charge ruled in favor of the Americans.

OBSTACLE RACE

1900 Paris C: 12, N: 5, D: 8.12.

1. Frederick Lane	AUS	2:38.4
2. Otto Wahle	AUT	2:40.0
3. Peter Kemp	GBR	2:47.4
4. Karl Ruberl	AUT	2:51.2
5. F. Stapleton	GBR	2:55.0
6. William Henry	GBR	2:58.0

This quaint event required the participants to struggle past three sets of obstacles. First they had to climb over a pole, then they had to scramble over a row of boats, and finally they had to swim *under* another row of boats. Freddie Lane grew up around boats in Sydney's harbor and put this experience to good use in the obstacle race. Rather than clamber over the middle of the boats, he crossed them at the stern, where the going was smoother. Lane was probably better known for his victory in the unimpeded 200-meter freestyle.

UNDERWATER SWIMMING

1900 Paris C: 10, N: 4, D: 8.12.

		M	TIME	PTS.
1. Charles de Vendeville	FRA	60	1:08.4	188.4
2. André Six	FRA	60	1:05.4	185.4
3. Peder Lykkeberg	DEN	28.50	1:30.0	147.0
4. de Romand	FRA	47.50	50.2	145.0
5. Tisserand	FRA	30.75	48.0	109.5
6. Hans Aniol	GER	36.95	30.0	103.9

Two points were awarded for each meter swum and one point for each second that the swimmer was able to stay under water.

PLUNGE FOR DISTANCE

1904 St. Louis C: 5, N: 1, D: 9.5.

		M	FT.-IN.
1. William Dickey	USA	19.05	62-6
2. Edgar Adams	USA	17.53	57-6
3. Leo Goodwin	USA	17.37	57-0
4. Newman Samuels	USA	16.76	55-0
5. Charles Pyrah	USA	14.02	46-0

In the plunge for distance, the contestants began with a standing dive, then remained motionless for 60 seconds or until their heads broke the surface of the water, whichever came first. Then the length of their dives was measured. Charles Pyrah held the U.S. record at 63 feet, but was "completely out of form" according to the local newspapers. It was most unfortunate that the great British plungers John Arthur Jarvis and W. Taylor did not make the trip to St. Louis. Jarvis won the 1904 Amateur Swimming Association plunging championship with a plunge of 75 feet 4 inches, while Taylor was the national record holder at 78 feet 9 inches. In 1930 Arthur Beaumont plunged 85 feet 10 inches. The A.S.A. championship was discontinued after 1946.

SWIMMING

WOMEN

50-METER FREESTYLE

1896–1984 not held

1988 Seoul C: 50, N: 33, D: 9.25. WR: 24.98 (Yang Wenyi)

1. Kristin Otto	GDR	25.49	OR
2. Yang Wenyi	CHN	25.64	
3. Katrin Meissner	GDR	25.71	
3. Jill Sterkel	USA	25.71	
5. Leigh Ann Fetter	USA	25.78	
6. Tamara Costache	ROM	25.80	
7. Catherine Plewinski	FRA	25.90	
8. Karen Van Wirdum	AUS	26.01	

At the 1982 world championships, 6-foot 1-inch Kristin Otto of Leipzig won three gold medals. At the 1986 world championships she won four gold medals and at the 1987 European championships she won five. Incredibly, Otto was able to improve on her record by earning an unprecedented six golds in Seoul. Her final victory, and the one that was least expected, came in the 50-meter freestyle. Otto, who had been expected to win three to five gold medals four years earlier, until East Germany announced its boycott of the Los Angeles Games, was unanimously voted the outstanding competitor of the 1988 Olympics by an I.O.C. panel. East German documents declassified in 1994 revealed that Otto had been put on a steady diet of prohibited drugs, notably testosterone, throughout her career.

Jill Sterkel, who tied for third place, became the first female swimmer to win medals 12 years apart. In 1976 she had earned a gold as a member of the U.S. freestyle relay team.

1992 Barcelona C: 50, N: 35, D: 7.31. WR: 24.98 (Yang Wenyi)

1. Yang Wenyi	CHN	24.79	WR
2. Zhuang Yong	CHN	25.08	
3. Angelina Martino	USA	25.23	
4. Catherine Plewinski	FRA	25.36	
5. Jennifer Thompson	USA	25.37	
6. Natalya Meshcheryakova	MOL	25.47	
7. Simone Osygus	GER	25.74	
8. Inge de Bruijn	HOL	25.84	

For four years after Yang Wenyi set her world record, on April 11, 1988, she did not live up to expectations. The favorite at the 1988 Olympics, she finished second to Kristin Otto. At the 1989 Pan Pacific Championships, she was second to Jenny Thompson. At the 1991 world championships, she dropped to fourth place. In the qualifying round at the 1992 Olympics, she dropped even further to sixth place. But in the final that evening, the 5-foot 10-inch Yang was first into the water, held her lead to the end, and broke her world record. All of the finalists except Thompson and Osygus beat or tied their personal bests.

100-METER FREESTYLE

1896–1908 not held

1912 Stockholm C: 27, N: 8, D: 7.2. WR: 1:20.6 (Daisy Curwen)

1. Sarah "Fanny" Durack	AUS	1:22.2
2. Wilhelmina Wylie	AUS	1:25.4
3. Jennie Fletcher	GBR	1:27.0
4. Margarete "Grete" Rosenberg	GER	1:27.4
5. Annie Speirs	GBR	1:27.4
DNS: Daisy Curwen (GBR)		

Fanny Durack's biggest struggle came before the Olympics. The men who were in charge of naming the Australian team thought it an absurd waste of time and money to send women to Stockholm. Eventually the New South Wales Ladies' Amateur Swimming Association voted to let Durack and her friend and rival, Mina Wylie, go, but only if they paid their own way. A fund was raised to send Durack, and Wylie's family and friends covered her expenses. In the fourth heat of the second round, Durack swam a 1:19.8 to break Daisy Curwen's world record. In the semifinals she defeated Curwen herself, who then went straight to the hospital for an emergency appendectomy. Durack led the final from start to finish and won easily despite running into the side wall of the pool. At

The medalists in the first women's swimming contest, the 1912 100-meter freestyle: Fanny Durack, Mina Wylie, and Jennie Fletcher.

one time Fanny Durack held every world record in women's swimming, from 100 yards to one mile. Bronze medalist Jennie Fletcher came from a poor family in Leicester. She worked 72 hours a week at a textile factory and had little free time to train.

1920 Antwerp C: 16, N: 9, D: 8.25. WR: 1:16.2 (Sarah "Fanny" Durack)

1. Ethelda Bleibtrey	USA	1:13.6	WR
2. Irene Guest	USA	1:17.0	
3. Frances Schroth	USA	1:17.2	
4. Constance Jeans	GBR	1:22.8	
5. Violet Walrond	NZE	—	
6. Jane Gylling	SWE	—	
DNF: Charlotte Boyle (USA)			

Bleibtrey broke the world record in the third heat with a time of 1:14.4, then broke the record again in winning the final. Eventually she won all three swimming events at Antwerp. The year before the Antwerp Olympics, Bleibtrey caused a sensation in New York when she was arrested for "nude swimming"—she had removed her stockings before entering the ocean. In later years, she was a co-founder of the United States Olympians Association.

1924 Paris C: 16, N: 7, D: 7.20. WR: 1:12.8 (Gertrude Ederle)

1. Ethel Lackie	USA	1:12.4
2. Mariechen Wehselau	USA	1:12.8
3. Gertrude Ederle	USA	1:14.2
4. Constance Jeans	GBR	1:15.4
5. Irene Tanner	GBR	1:20.8
6. Maria Vierdag (HOL)		

The U.S. sweep was particularly impressive considering the absurd restrictions imposed on the female swimmers by the U.S. Olympic Committee. American officials, concerned about protecting their teenaged swimmers from the immoral temptations of Paris, housed the young ladies way outside the city and forced them to spend five to six hours a day traveling to and from the Olympic pool. In the first heat, Mariechen Wehselau of Honolulu set a world record of 1:12.2. Lackie and Ederle won the next two heats in 1:12.8 and 1:12.6. In the final race, Wehselau held a two-yard lead at the 50-meter turn, with Ederle second and Lackie third. But 17-year-old Ethel Lackie of Chicago put on a fantastic spurt in the last 25 meters to edge Wehselau for first place.

Two years later Gertrude Ederle, the 19-year-old daughter of a New York City butcher, carved herself a permanent place in the history books with a swimming feat that shocked the world. Just after seven a.m. on the morning of August 6, 1926, she set off from France in an attempt to become the first woman to swim the English Channel. That day, the London *Daily News* ran an editorial which haughtily announced, "Even the most uncompromising champion of the rights and capacities of women must admit that in contests of physical skill, speed and endurance they must remain forever the weaker sex." Such overblown male chauvinism was buried in an avalanche of feminist joy when Ederle reached the English coast at Kingsdown in a time of 14 hours 31 minutes—almost two hours faster than the *men's* record for the Channel swim.

Ederle returned home to a tickertape parade attended by an estimated 2,000,000 people. A slew of personal appearances followed, but this period involved a series of setbacks. By 1933 she had suffered a nervous breakdown, become deaf as a result of her Channel swim, and received a serious back injury that forced her to wear a cast for four and a half years. Not one to wallow in self-pity, Ederle went right ahead with her life and eventually began teaching swimming to deaf children.

1928 Amsterdam C: 24, N: 11, D: 8.11. WR: 1:10.0 (Ethel Lackie)

1. Albina Osipowich	USA	1:11.0	OR
2. Eleanor Garatti	USA	1:11.4	
3. Margaret Joyce Cooper	GBR	1:13.6	
4. Jean McDowell	GBR	1:13.6	
5. Susan Laird	USA	1:14.6	
6. Charlotte Lehmann	GER	1:15.2	

1932 Los Angeles C: 20, N: 10, D: 8.8. WR: 1:06.6 (Helene Madison)

1. Helene Madison	USA	1:06.8	OR
2. Willemijntje den Ouden	HOL	1:07.8	
3. Eleanor Saville (Garatti)	USA	1:09.3	
4. Josephine McKim	USA	1:09.3	
5. Frances Bult	AUS	1:09.9	
6. Jennie Maakal	SAF	1:10.8	

If ever there was a sure bet for a gold medal, it was 5-foot 10½-inch, 154-pound Helene Madison, a 19-year-old from Seattle, Washington, who was invariably referred to by the press as "shapely." During a 16½-month period in 1930–31, Madison broke all 16 world records for the distances between 100 yards and 1 mile. However, the results of the semifinals in Los Angeles raised serious doubts as to whether she could actually win the final. The first semifinal was won by 14-year-old Willy den Ouden in the surprisingly fast time of 1:07.6. In the second semi, Helene Madison went all out for the first 50 meters and then huffed home to win in 1:09.9, a time that would have placed her only fifth in the first semi. The American coaches advised Madison to change her tactics and save herself for the second half of the final race. This proved to be advice well worth taking, as Madison forged to a full-length lead between 50 and 75 meters before bumping into the lane divider. A final burst of speed provided her with a comfortable margin of victory.

Joyce Cooper of Great Britain was most unlucky to be drawn in the first semifinal. Her times of 1:09.0 and 1:09.2 would have been good enough for third place in the final.

After the Olympics it appeared that Helene Madison was headed for a very glamorous life, but things didn't work out that way. In 1933 she played a minor role in the film *The Warrior's Husband*. Then she tried to earn a living as a nightclub entertainer, a swimming instructor, and a department store clerk. In 1935 she became a probationary nurse at a Seattle hospital, but she failed to earn a registered nurse's certificate. She was also frustrated in her personal life. Married and divorced three times, she was living alone with her Siamese cat when she died of cancer in 1970 at the age of 56.

1936 Berlin C: 33, N: 14, D: 8.10. WR: 1:04.6 (Willemijntje den Ouden)

1. Hendrika "Rie" Mastenbroek	HOL	1:05.9	OR
2. Jeannette Campbell	ARG	1:06.4	
3. Gisela Arendt	GER	1:06.6	
4. Willemijntje den Ouden	HOL	1:07.6	
5. Catherina Wagner	HOL	1:08.1	
6. Olive McKean	USA	1:08.4	
7. Katherine Rawls	USA	1:08.7	

Six months before the Berlin Games, Willy den Ouden swam a phenomenal 1:04.6, setting a world record that would last for 20 years. But in the preliminary rounds of the Olympics, it was her 17-year-old teammate, Rie Mastenbroek, who recorded the fastest times. In the final Mastenbroek was fifth at the 50-meter turn and was still behind Arendt and Campbell (whose parents were Scottish) with only ten meters to go. But her furious finishing strokes gave her a dramatic victory. Over the next five days Mastenbroek won two more gold medals and one silver medal.

1948 London C: 34, N: 14, D: 8.2. WR: 1:04.6 (Willemijntje den Ouden)

1. Greta Andersen	DEN	1:06.3
2. Ann Curtis	USA	1:06.5
3. Marie-Louise Vaessen	HOL	1:07.6
4. Karen-Margrete Harup	DEN	1:08.1
5. Ingegärd Fredin	SWE	1:08.4
6. Irma Schumacher	HOL	1:08.4
7. Elisabeth Ahlgren	SWE	1:08.8
8. Fritze Carstensen	DEN	1:09.1

Greta Andersen later became a professional and swam the English Channel six times, culminating in an England-to-France record of 13 hours 14 minutes, which she set in 1964 at the age of 36.

1952 Helsinki C: 41, N: 19, D: 7.28. WR: 1:04.6 (Willemijntje den Ouden)

1. Katalin Szöke	HUN	1:06.8
2. Johanna Termeulen	HOL	1:07.0
3. Judit Temes	HUN	1:07.1
4. Joan Harrison	SAF	1:07.1
5. Joan Alderson	USA	1:07.1
6. Irma Heijting-Schuhmacher	HOL	1:07.3
7. Marilee Stepan	USA	1:08.0
8. Angela Barnwell	GBR	1:08.6

The 1952 100-meter freestyle race saw a thrilling finish in which the lead changed hands three times in the last ten meters and the first six women finished within two feet of each other. Judit Temes, who had set an Olympic record of 1:05.5 in the first round, pushed to the front after 90 meters, but then Joan Harrison moved ahead. The South African swimmer had the unfortunate experience of finishing out of the medals despite the fact that she appeared to be in first place with only five meters to go. The eventual winner, 16-year-old Katalin Szöke, had been well-known in Hungary for quite some time. Her mother had introduced her to swimming when she was only six months old, and she became known as "Kati, the World's First Waterproof Baby." She was able to stay afloat unaided before she was two years old. Szöke's husband, Kalman Markovits, was a member of Hungary's gold medal water polo team in 1952 and 1956.

1956 Melbourne C: 35, N: 16, D: 12.1 WR: 1:02.4 (Lorraine Crapp)

1. Dawn Fraser	AUS	1:02.0	WR
2. Lorraine Crapp	AUS	1:02.3	
3. Faith Leech	AUS	1:05.1	
4. Joan Rosazza	USA	1:05.2	
5. Virginia Grant	CAN	1:05.4	
6. Shelley Mann	USA	1:05.6	
7. Marrion Roe	NZE	1:05.6	
8. Natalie Myburgh	SAF	1:05.8	

Dawn Fraser was the youngest of eight children born to working-class parents in Balmain, an industrial suburb of Sydney. On February 21, 1956, Fraser broke Willy den Ouden's 20-year-old world record and upset Lorraine Crapp to win the Australian championship in a time of 1:04.5. Dawn was not that impressed by her feat and told reporters that she could do a lot better. At the time some people may have considered Fraser to be excessively cocky, but it turned out that she was absolutely right. In fact, the quality of women's freestyle swimming was going through a period of rapid change. In the next eight months the 100 meters record was lowered five more times, twice by Cockie Gastelaars of the Netherlands, once more by Dawn Fraser, and, finally, twice in the month of October by Lorraine Crapp.

Controversial Dawn Fraser won a total of four gold medals and four silver medals in 1956, 1960, and 1964.

With Gastelaars out of the Games because of the Dutch Olympic boycott, there was no question that the battle for the gold medal would be between Crapp and Fraser. In the first heat of the first round, Crapp swam a 1:03.4 to lower the Olympic record by over two seconds. In the fifth heat Fraser lowered it further with a 1:02.4. The two Australian teenagers then won their semifinal races, Fraser in 1:03.0 and Crapp in 1:03.1. The day before the women's final, the Australian men had scored a sweep in the 100-meter freestyle, and with Faith Leech recording the third fastest time in each of the first two rounds, it looked as if the Australian women might match the accomplishments of their male counterparts.

The night before the race Dawn Fraser went to bed early, prayed for the strength to win, and then thought through the race, particularly the turn, before she finally dropped off to sleep. Before long she was stricken by a nightmare, which she later described quite graphically in her autobiography, *Below the Surface*. "The gun went off," she began, "but I had honey on my feet and it was hard to pull them away from the starting block. I finally fought free and dived high. . . . It seemed a long time before I hit the water, and the water wasn't water; it was spaghetti. I fought with it and kept going up and down in the one place, like a yo-yo. The spaghetti strands tangled and tied my feet, and I was swimming with my arms alone. Of course I fouled up the turn and took a few mouthfuls, and I woke up gasping and fighting in a sea of spaghetti."

She must have been somewhat relieved the next day to discover that the pool was in fact filled with water, although she was still incredibly nervous, since she had never before swum in an international meet. Fraser and Crapp pulled away from the others after only 25 meters. Fraser completed the turn first, but Crapp caught up with her with 25 meters to go; the two reached the finish without knowing which one had won. They were so far ahead of the others that they were able to turn around and watch their teammate, Faith Leech, win the battle for third place. After her victory was announced, Dawn Fraser borrowed a ladder from a TV crew and climbed into the stands to share tears of joy with her parents, and to savor a moment which they had all dedicated to Dawn's dead brother, Don, who had introduced her to swimming when she was a child. Starting with that day in Melbourne, Dawn Fraser was the world record holder at 100 meters for the next 15 years.

1960 Rome C: 32, N: 19, D: 8.29. WR(110 yards). 1:00.2 (Dawn Fraser)

1. Dawn Fraser	AUS	1:01.2	OR
2. S. Christine Von Saltza	USA	1:02.8	
3. Natalie Steward	GBR	1:03.1	
4. Carolyn Wood	USA	1:03.4	
5. Csilla Dobai-Madarász	HUN	1:03.6	
6. Erica Terpstra	HOL	1:04.3	
7. Cockie Gastelaars	HOL	1:04.7	
8. Marie Stewart	CAN	1:05.5	

Undefeated at 100 meters since the last Olympics, Dawn Fraser made news by becoming the first woman to defend an Olympic swimming title. But she made bigger news the following day with her defiance of Australian officials. Thinking she had the day off, she had stayed up late, celebrating. In the morning a routine meeting of the Australian women's swim team turned into a violent argument, which didn't end until Fraser had smacked teammate Jan Andrew in the face with a pillow. Fraser spent the rest of the morning shopping for a wedding dress (which she didn't use) and sightseeing in Rome. She returned to the Olympic Village in time for lunch and had just finished a big plate of spaghetti when Roger Pegram, the manager of the Australian swimming team, approached her and ordered her to get dressed so that she could swim the butterfly leg of the medley relay qualifying heat. Stating that she was stuffed and unprepared, Fraser refused to swim and returned to her room for a nap. Eventually Alva Colquhoun volunteered to take her place, but for the remainder of their stay in Rome, the Australian women punished Fraser by "sending her to Coventry." In others words, they refused to speak a single word to her or to each other as long as Fraser was in the room.

1964 Tokyo C: 44, N: 22, D: 10.13. WR: 58.9 (Dawn Fraser)

1. Dawn Fraser	AUS	59.5	OR
2. Sharon Stouder	USA	59.9	
3. Kathleen Ellis	USA	1:00.8	
4. Erica Terpstra	HOL	1:01.8	
5. Marion Lay	CAN	1:02.2	
6. Csilla Dobai-Madarász	HUN	1:02.4	
7. Ann Hagberg	SWE	1:02.5	
8. Lynette Bell	AUS	1:02.7	

On October 27, 1962, Dawn Fraser, swimming in Melbourne, became the first woman to break the one-minute barrier for 100 meters when she covered the longer distance of 110 yards in 59.9 seconds. By February 29, 1964, she had cut her time down to 58.9, and it was almost eight years before anyone would do better. But in March, tragedy struck. She was driving home from a football social with three passengers, her mother, her sister, and a friend, when her car skidded and crashed into a parked truck. Her mother was killed, her sister was knocked unconscious, and Dawn herself spent six weeks with her neck in plaster because of a chipped vertebra.

Seven months later Dawn Fraser was, remarkably, back in form for the Olympics. By this time she was 27 years old, an old-timer by swimming standards who was known to her teammates as "Granny." She had by no means lost her rebellious spirit, however. Ordered by team officials to skip the opening-day ceremonies, she sneaked in anyway and enjoyed the parade and festivities. She tied her own Olympic record of 1:00.6 (set in the 1960 relay) in the first round and then swam a 59.9 in the semifinals. Entering the final she was sure that her only serious challenger would be 15-year-old Sharon Stouder of Glendora, California. Fraser took the lead immediately, but Stouder swam a tremendous race and caught her at the 70-meter mark. Fraser was not to be denied, though, and she called on an extra reserve of strength to pull away once again. Stouder's time of 59.9 made her the first woman other than Dawn Fraser to break one minute. Later Fraser committed the final indiscretion of her career, when she led a middle-of-the-night raid to steal a "souvenir" flag from the Emperor's palace. She was arrested, but the charges were dropped and the Emperor gave her the flags as a gift. However, the Australian Swimming Union slapped her with a ten-year suspension which was lifted after four years. The escapade in no way detracted from her status as a national heroine, since most Australians were less interested in her out-of-the-pool antics than they were in the fact that she had become the first Olympic swimmer of either sex to win the same event three times. In 1990, Fraser was elected to the parliament of New South Wales.

1968 Mexico City C: 57, N: 27, D: 10.19. WR: 58.9 (Dawn Fraser)
1.	Jan Henne	USA	1:00.0
2.	Susan Pedersen	USA	1:00.3
3.	Linda Gustavson	USA	1:00.3
4.	Marion Lay	CAN	1:00.5
5.	Martina Grunert	GDR	1:01.0
6.	Alexandra Jackson	GBR	1:01.0
7.	Mirjana Segrt	YUG	1:01.5
8.	Judit Turóczy	HUN	1:01.6

1972 Munich C: 46, N: 23, D: 8.29. WR: 58.5 (Shane Gould)
1.	Sandra Neilson	USA	58.59	OR
2.	Shirley Babashoff	USA	59.02	
3.	Shane Gould	AUS	59.06	
4.	Gabriele Wetzko	GDR	59.21	
5.	Heidemarie Reineck	GER	59.73	
6.	Andrea Eife	GDR	59.91	

7.	Magdolna Patoh	HUN	1:00.02
8.	Enith Brigitha	HOL	1:00.09

Following the Australian sweeps of 1956, the number of entrants per nation per event was reduced from three to two. This restriction was dropped after 1960, then reinstated after the U.S. sweeps of 1968. It was dropped again in 1976, but reinstated once more in 1984 as a result of the East German sweeps of 1976 and 1980. In 1972 the Australian favorite, Shane Gould, lost her first freestyle race in two years when she was beaten by two Southern California high school students, Sandy Neilson and Shirley Babashoff. Neilson led all the way, but Babashoff had to come from seventh place at the turn to nip Gould for the silver. The one-two victory gave confidence to the U.S. swimmers, who had been wearing T-shirts that read, "All that glitters is not Gould."

1976 Montreal C: 45, N: 25, D: 7.19. WR: 55.73 (Kornelia Ender)
1.	Kornelia Ender	GDR	55.65	WR
2.	Petra Priemer	GDR	56.49	
3.	Enith Brigitha	HOL	56.65	
4.	Kim Peyton	USA	56.81	
5.	Shirley Babashoff	USA	56.95	
6.	Claudia Hempel	GDR	56.99	
7.	Jill Sterkel	USA	57.06	
8.	Jutta Weber	GER	57.26	

At Munich in 1972, the East German women swimmers failed to win a single gold medal, yet four years later in Montreal they were able to finish first in 11 of 13 events. This extraordinary transformation actually began at the 1973 world swimming championships in Belgrade, Yugoslavia, where the East German women appeared wearing

Little Franziska Matthes, with her parents, Kornelia Ender and Roland Matthes, who between them won 16 swimming medals in 1968, 1972, and 1976. The couple later divorced.

the latest model of their skin-tight, semi-see-through Lycra suits. Some people began to raise a protest, until it was revealed that the suits had actually been invented and manufactured in *West* Germany. By 1976 the Americans in particular were also accusing the East German women of appearing too muscular and masculine, of being shot up with anabolic steroids, and of being "all work and no play" types, who would be unable ever to bear children.

Although there is no doubt that steroids and other drugs were being used by virtually all East German women swimmers, whether they knew it or not, East Germany's success also depended on the enormous emphasis that country placed on legitimate sports science. While U.S. and Soviet scientists were busy conquering space and designing weapons systems, the East Germans were studying athletes—taking blood tests and muscle biopsies, checking oxygen levels, and testing for nutritional needs. The scandalous "Belgrade suits" of 1973 soon became commonplace throughout the world. Likewise, the East Germans were years ahead in studies of such things as lactic acid buildup during training.

At the age of 13, Kornelia Ender of Bitterfeld won three silver medals at the 1972 Olympics. The following year, in East Berlin, she broke Shane Gould's world record in the 100-meter freestyle. In the three years preceding the 1976 Olympics, Ender broke the world record for that event nine times. Two months before the Montreal Games, the 5-foot 10-inch, 154-pound Ender announced her engagement to backstroker Roland Matthes. She set her tenth 100 meters world record in the Olympic final, her second gold medal of the Games. After the Olympics were over Kornelia Ender was reunited with her grandmother, who had left East Germany in 1961 and moved to Kansas. After the fall of the Berlin Wall, in 1989, Ender revealed that during her competitive career, she was given frequent injections without being told what they contained.

1980 Moscow C: 30, N: 22, D: 7.21. WR: 55.41 (Barbara Krause)

1. Barbara Krause	GDR	54.79	WR
2. Caren Metschuck	GDR	55.16	
3. Ines Diers	GDR	55.65	
4. Olga Klevakina	SOV/RUS	57.40	
5. Cornelia van Bentum	HOL	57.63	
6. Natalya Strunnikova	SOV/RUS	57.83	
7. Guylaine Berger	FRA	57.88	
8. Agneta Eriksson	SWE	57.90	

In 1980 the East German women duplicated their 1976 feat of winning 11 of 13 events. But this time, with the U.S. and Canada out of the Games, they were able to take 15 other medals as well, which meant that they *averaged* two out of three medals per event.

Like Kornelia Ender, Barbara Krause was introduced to swimming as therapy for orthopedic problems. One of East Germany's leading swimmers in 1976, she was forced to sit out the Montreal Games because of illness.

As she followed the competition from her sickbed, she made the decision to continue swimming for four more years so that she could take part in the 1980 Olympics. With only 30 starters in the 100-meter freestyle, the smallest field since 1932, it was decided to skip the semifinals and simply allow the swimmers with the eight fastest times in the heats to qualify directly for the final, a practice which has since been institutionalized. Barbara Krause won the third heat in 54.98 to lower her own world record and to become the first woman to break the 55-second barrier. In the final she was hard-pressed by her East German teammates, but she led all the way and set yet another world record.

1984 Los Angeles C: 45, N: 30, D: 7.29. WR: 54.79 (Barbara Krause)

1. Nancy Hogshead	USA	55.92
1. Carrie Steinseifer	USA	55.92
3. Annemarie Verstappen	HOL	56.08
4. Cornelia van Bentum	HOL	56.43
5. Michele Pearson	AUS	56.83
6. June Croft	GBR	56.90
7. Susanne Schuster	GER	57.11
8. Angela Russel	AUS	58.09

In 1972, when Gunnar Larsson and Tim McKee were both timed at 4:31.98 in the final of the men's 400-meter individual medley, the timing was taken to thousandths of a second and Larsson was declared the winner. Because of possible technical problems, it was decided that hundredths of a second would have to do in the future. So, in 1984, when Hogshead and Steinseifer registered the same time in the 100-meter freestyle, a dead-heat was declared and each was awarded a gold medal, the first double gold medal in Olympic swimming history. Nancy Hogshead eventually left Los Angeles with three gold medals and one silver. Conspicuously missing from the competition were Kristin Otto and Birgit Meineke of East Germany, who had clocked 55.75 and 55.79 respectively at the Friendship Games on August 19.

1988 Seoul C: 57, N: 35, D: 9.19. WR: 54.73 (Kristin Otto)

1. Kristin Otto	GDR	54.93
2. Zhuang Yong	CHN	55.47
3. Catherine Plewinski	FRA	55.49
4. Manuela Stellmach	GDR	55.52
5. Silvia Poll Ahrens	CRC	55.90
6. Karin Brienesse	HOL	56.15
7. Dara Torres	USA	56.25
8. Cornelia van Bentum	HOL	56.54

Twenty-two-year-old Kristin Otto won the first of her six gold medals.

1992 Barcelona C: 48, N: 34, D: 7.26. WR: 54.48 (Jennifer Thompson)

1. Zhuang Yong	CHN	54.64	OR
2. Jennifer Thompson	USA	54.84	

3. Franziska van Almsick	GER	54.94	
4. Nicole Haislett	USA	55.19	
5. Catherine Plewinski	FRA	55.72	
6. Le Jingyi	CHN	55.89	
7. Simone Osygus	GER	55.93	
8. Karin Brienesse	HOL	56.59	

On March 1, 1992, Jenny Thompson, swimming in the qualifying round of the United States Olympic trials, broke Kristin Otto's world record by a quarter of a second. She was the first non–East German to set a world record in the 100-meter freestyle in 20 years. In the qualifying round at the Olympics, she set an Olympic record of 54.69. But in the final it was not Thompson but Seoul silver medalist Zhuang Yong who led from start to finish. Zhuang immediately became the focus of a growing suspicion that the Chinese women swimmers were taking steroids and other prohibited substances. With her deep voice, heavy muscles, and bad acne, she fit the profile of a steroid user. Opposing coaches were particularly upset when Zhuang was not tested for drugs after her victory. F.I.N.A.'s policy was to test randomly only two of the top four finishers, whereas other sports tested all medalists.

200-METER FREESTYLE

1896–1964 not held

1968 Mexico City C: 39, N: 23, D: 10.22. WR: 2:06.7 (Deborah Meyer)

1. Deborah Meyer	USA	2:10.5	OR
2. Jan Henne	USA	2:11.0	
3. Jane Barkman	USA	2:11.2	
4. Gabriele Wetzko	GDR	2:12.3	
5. Mirjana Segrt	YUG	2:13.3	
6. Claude Mandonnaud	FRA	2:14.9	
7. Lynette Bell	AUS	2:15.1	
8. Olga Kozicova	CZE	2:16.0	

This was Debbie Meyer's second gold medal of the 1968 Olympics.

1972 Munich C: 33, N: 17, D: 9.1. WR: 2:05.21 (Shirley Babashoff)

1. Shane Gould	AUS	2:03.56	WR
2. Shirley Babashoff	USA	2:04.33	
3. Keena Rothhammer	USA	2:04.92	
4. Ann Marshall	USA	2:05.45	
5. Andrea Eife	GDR	2:06.27	
6. Hansje Bunschoten	HOL	2:08.40	
7. Anke Rijnders	HOL	2:09.41	
8. Karin Tuelling	GDR	2:11.70	

Between July 1971 and January 1972, Shane Gould set world records in all five internationally recognized freestyle distances: the 100, 200, 400, 800, and 1500 meters. In the 1972 Olympics, the 15-year-old phenomenon swam 12 races in eight days, logging 4200 meters of competitive swimming. In the 200 meters final Gould built up

a large lead in the first 100 meters. World record holder Shirley Babashoff almost cut the gap in half, but could get no further. Shane Gould closed out the Munich Olympics with three gold medals, one silver, and one bronze. A year later, tired of the sacrifices required of a champion swimmer, Gould announced her retirement at the age of 16.

1976 Montreal C: 40, N: 22, D: 7.22. WR: 1:59.78 (Kornelia Ender)

1. Kornelia Ender	GDR	1:59.26	WR
2. Shirley Babashoff	USA	2:01.22	
3. Enith Brigitha	HOL	2:01.40	
4. Annelies Maas	HOL	2:02.56	
5. Gail Amundrud	CAN	2:03.32	
6. Jennifer Hooker	USA	2:04.20	
7. Claudia Hempel	GDR	2:04.61	
8. Irina Vlasova	SOV/RUS	2;05.63	

Kornelia Ender equaled her own world record to win the 100-meter butterfly, then returned to face Shirley Babashoff in the very next race, the 200-meter freestyle. Babashoff had defeated Ender in the 200 at the 1975 world championships, but Ender had chopped almost three seconds off her time in the following year. Babashoff took the early lead and held it for the first 100 meters, but Ender moved ahead over the next length of the pool and won going away to earn her second gold medal in 27 minutes. She thus became the first female swimmer to win four gold medals at one Olympics.

1980 Moscow C: 22, N; 14, D: 7.24. WR: 1.58.23 (Cynthia Woodhead)

1. Barbara Krause	GDR	1:58.33	OR
2. Ines Diers	GDR	1:59.64	
3. Carmela Schmidt	GDR	2:01.44	
4. Olga Klevakina	SOV/RUS	2:02.29	
5. Reggie de Jong	HOL	2:02.76	
6. June Croft	GBR	2:03.15	
7. Natalya Strunnikova	SOV/RUS	2:03.74	
8. Irina Aksyonova	SOV/RUS	2:04.00	

Krause staged a phenomenal comeback to win her second gold medal. Trailing Ines Diers by over a second after 150 meters, she swam the last 50 meters in 28.47 to win by a comfortable margin. Eight days later, world record holder Cynthia Woodhead won the U.S. Outdoor National championship in 1:59.44.

1984 Los Angeles C: 36, N: 25, D: 7.30. WR: 1:57.75 (Kristin Otto)

1. Mary Wayte	USA	1:59.23	
2. Cynthia Woodhead	USA	1:59.50	
3. Annemarie Verstappen	HOL	1:59.69	
4. Michele Pearson	AUS	1:59.79	
5. Cornelia van Bentum	HOL	2:00.59	
6. June Croft	GBR	2:00.64	
7. Ina Beyermann	GER	2:01.89	
8. Anna McVann	AUS	2:02.87	

On May 23, at the East German trials, Kristin Otto had set a world record of 1:57.75. She was followed by Birgit Meineke in 1:58.75.

1988 Seoul C: 44, N: 29, D: 9.21. WR: 1:57.55 (Heike Friedrich)
1. Heike Friedrich	GDR	1:57.65	OR
2. Silvia Poll Ahrens	CRC	1:58.67	
3. Manuela Stellmach	GDR	1:59.01	
4. Mary Wayte	USA	1:59.04	
5. Natalya Trefilova	SOV/RUS	1:59.24	
6. Mitzi Kremer	USA	2:00.23	
7. Stephanie Ortwig	GER	2:00.73	
8. Cecile Prunier	FRA	2:02.88	

The prohibitive favorite, world champion and world record holder Heike Friedrich, let Wayte and Kremer set the pace for the first half of the race, then stormed ahead for an easy bodylength victory over Silvia Poll, Costa Rica's first Olympic medalist. The 6-foot 3½-inch, blonde-haired Poll was the daughter of German-born parents who had moved to Costa Rica from Nicaragua when she was 8 years old.

1992 Barcelona C: 37, N: 26, D: 7.27. WR: 1:57.55 (Heike Friedrich)
1. Nicole Haislett	USA	1:57.90
2. Franziska van Almsick	GER	1:58.00
3. Kerstin Kielgass	GER	1:59.67
4. Catherine Plewinski	FRA	1:59.88
5. L. Liliana Dobrescu	ROM	2:00.48
6. Suzu Chiba	JPN	2:00.64
7. Olha Kirichenko	UKR	2:00.90
8. Lu Bin	CHN	2:02.10

The final was a straight duel between 19-year-old Nicole Haislett of St. Petersburg, Florida, and 14-year-old Franziska van Almsick, who had led the qualifying round with a time of 1:57.90. In the final, van Almsick went out very fast for the first 50 meters, then calmed down without letting up pressure. Haislett, swimming beside her, noticed that the inexperienced German girl was swimming right next to the lane line. Haislett moved into her wake and saved precious energy drafting off her for much of the race. Haislett pulled even with van Almsick ten meters from the finish and then edged ahead to win by about six inches.

400-METER FREESTYLE

1896–1912 not held

1920 Antwerp C: 16, N: 7, D: 8.28. WR (300 meters): 4:43.6
(300 Meters)
1. Ethelda Bleibtrey	USA	4:34.0	WR
2. Margaret Woodbridge	USA	4:42.8	
3. Frances Schroth	USA	4:52.0	
4. Constance Jeans	GBR	4:52.4	
5. Eleanor Uhl	USA	—	
6. Jane Gylling	SWE	—	
7. Violet Walrond	NZE	—	

Bleibtrey set a world record of 4:41.4 in her preliminary heat and then set another record in the final. Between August 23 and August 29, Bleibtrey swam in five races in three events and broke the world record in every one.

1924 Paris C: 18, N: 8, D: 7.15. WR: 5:53.2 (Gertrude Ederle)
1. Martha Norelius	USA	6:02.2	OR
2. Helen Wainwright	USA	6:03.8	
3. Gertrude Ederle	USA	6:04.8	
4. Doris Molesworth	GBR	6:25.4	
DNF: Gwitha Shand (NZE)			
6. Irene Tanner (GBR)			

Fifteen-year-old, Stockholm-born Martha Norelius pulled away from Wainwright and Ederle in the final 15 meters. In the 1924 Olympics five swimmers took part in each final, while sixth place was awarded to the non-finalist who recorded the fastest time in the semifinals.

1928 Amsterdam C: 14, N: 9, D: 8.6. WR: 5:49.6 (Martha Norelius)
1. Martha Norelius	USA	5:42.8	WR
2. Maria Braun	HOL	5:57.8	
3. Josephine McKim	USA	6:00.2	
4. Sarah Stewart	GBR	6:07.0	
5. Frederica van der Goes	SAF	6:07.2	
6. Irene Tanner	GBR	6:11.6	

Norelius swam a 5:45.4 opening heat to break her own world record, and defended her title by winning the final easily, again in world record time. Norelius dominated women's swimming from 1922 to 1929. She later married Canada's 1928 double sculls silver medalist, Joe Wright.

1932 Los Angeles C: 14, N: 9, D: 8.13. WR: 5:31.0 (Helene Madison)
1. Helene Madison	USA	5:28.5	WR
2. Lenore Kight	USA	5:28.6	
3. Jennie Maakal	SAF	5:47.3	
4. Margaret Joyce Cooper	GBR	5:49.7	
5. Yvonne Godard	FRA	5:54.4	
6. Norene Forbes	USA	6:06.0	

Helene Madison and Lenore Kight pulled away from the others immediately and went through most of the race with Madison one foot ahead. Kight moved into the lead at 325 meters, but Madison drew even at the final turn. In the end, Madison was able to touch the last wall inches ahead of Kight and thus win her third gold medal.

1936 Berlin C: 20, N: 10, D: 8.15. WR: 5:16.0 (Willemijntje den Ouden)
1. Hendrika "Rie" Mastenbroek	HOL	5:26.4	OR
2. Ragnhild Hveger	DEN	5:27.5	
3. Lenore Wingard (Kight)	USA	5:29.0	
4. Mary Lou Petty	USA	5:32.2	
5. Piedade Coutinho Azevedo	BRA	5:35.2	
6. Kazue Koijma	JPN	5:43.1	
7. Grete Frederiksen	DEN	5:45.0	
8. Catharine Wagner	HOL	5:46.0	

Fifteen-year-old Ragnhild Hveger led throughout the race, but Rie Mastenbroek fought back in the final 25 meters to gain a one-meter victory and win her third gold medal. Between 1936 and 1942 Hveger broke 42 individual world records. From 1938 until 1953 she was the official world record holder in the 200, 400, 800, and 1500 meters. She retired in 1945, but came back in 1952 to finish fifth in the 400 in the Helsinki Olympics at the age of 31. Rie Mastenbroek, who won three gold medals and one silver, had a most difficult post-Olympic life. After a disastrous first marriage ended, she worked 14 hours a day as a cleaning woman to support her children. In 1972 she told *Sports Illustrated,* "I am forgotten. No one remembers who I was. . . . Sometimes I think, 'Oh, dear, oh, dear, how good I must have been, how really *good*!' "

1948 London C: 19, N: 11, D: 8.7. WR: 5:00.1 (Ragnhild Hveger)
1. Ann Curtis	USA	5:17.8	OR
2. Karen-Margrete Harup	DEN	5:21.2	
3. Catherine Gibson	GBR	5:22.5	
4. Fernande Caroen	BEL	5:25.3	
5. Brenda Helser	USA	5:26.0	
6. Piedade Silva Tavares	BRA	5:29.4	
7. Fritze Carstensen	DEN	5:29.4	
8. Nancy Lees	USA	5:32.9	

1952 Helsinki C: 34, N: 17, D: 8.2. WR: 5:00.1 (Ragnhild Hveger)
1. Valéria Gyenge	HUN	5:12.1	OR
2. Éva Novák	HUN	5:13.7	
3. Evelyn Kawamoto	USA	5:14.6	
4. Carolyn Green	USA	5:16.5	
5. Ragnhild Andersen-Hveger	DEN	5:16.9	
6. Éva Székely	HUN	5:17.9	
7. Anna Maria Schultz	ARG	5:24.0	
8. Greta Andersen	DEN	5:27.0	

Ragnhild Hveger's 1940 world record was still in the books when, as Ragnhild Andersen-Hveger, she prepared for the start of the 1952 Olympic 400 meters final, the same event in which she had won a silver medal 16 years earlier. In Helsinki she led for the first 275 meters, but couldn't keep up the pace.

1956 Melbourne C: 26, N: 13, D: 12.7. WR: 4:47.2 (Lorraine Crapp)
1. Lorraine Crapp	AUS	4:54.6	OR
2. Dawn Fraser	AUS	5:02.5	
3. Sylvia Ruuska	USA	5:07.1	
4. Marley Shriver	USA	5:12.9	
5. Rypszima Székely	HUN	5:14.2	
6. Sandra Morgan	AUS	5:14.3	
7. Héda Frost	FRA	5:15.4	
8. Valéria Gyenge	HUN	5:21.0	

On August 25, 1956, 17-year-old Lorraine Crapp became the first woman to swim 400 meters in less than five minutes when she broke Ragnhild Hveger's 16-year-old world record with a time of 4:50.8. In that same race she also bettered the world records for 200 meters, 220 yards, and 440 yards. Two and a half months later at the Olympics, Dawn Fraser kept up with her teammate for 100 meters, but then Crapp drew clear to win by almost eight seconds.

1960 Rome C: 22, N: 13, D: 9.1. WR: 4:44.5 (S. Christine Von Saltza)
1. S. Christine Von Saltza	USA	4:50.6	OR
2. Jane Cederqvist	SWE	4:53.9	
3. Catharina Lagerberg	HOL	4:56.9	
4. Ilsa Konrads	AUS	4:57.9	
5. Dawn Fraser	AUS	4:58.5	
6. A. Nancy Rae	GBR	4:59.7	
7. Cornelia Schimmel	HOL	5:02.3	
8. Bibbi Segerstrom	SWE	5:02.4	

Sixteen-year-old Chris Von Saltza moved quickly into the lead, built up a five-second gap after 300 meters, and was too far ahead to be affected by the late surge of Jane Cederqvist. Von Saltza had won the first of her three gold medals. Third- and fourth-place finishers Lagerberg and Konrads were the world record holders at 800 meters and 1500 meters, respectively, neither of which was an Olympic distance at the time.

1964 Tokyo C: 30, N: 16, D: 10.18. WR: 4:39.5 (Marilyn Ramenofsky)
1. Virginia Duenkel	USA	4:43.3	OR
2. Marilyn Ramenofsky	USA	4:44.6	
3. Terri Stickles	USA	4:47.2	
4. Dawn Fraser	AUS	4:47.6	
5. Jane Hughes	CAN	4:50.9	
6. Elizabeth Long	GBR	4:52.0	
7. Kim Herford	AUS	4:52.9	
8. Gun Lilja	SWE	4:53.0	

Seventeen-year-old Ginny Duenkel of West Orange, New Jersey, also won a bronze medal in the 100-meter backstroke. In the 400-meter freestyle she took the lead after 175 meters and pulled away, slowly but steadily.

1968 Mexico City C: 30, N: 17, D: 10.20. WR: 4:24.5 (Debbie Meyer)
1. Debbie Meyer	USA	4:31.8	OR
2. Linda Gustavson	USA	4:35.5	
3. Karen Moras	AUS	4:37.0	
4. Pamela Kruse	USA	4:37.2	
5. Gabriele Wetzko	GDR	4:40.2	
6. Maria Teresa Ramirez	MEX	4:42.2	
7. Angela Coughlan	CAN	4:51.9	
8. Ingrid Morris	SWE	4:53.8	

At the U.S. Olympic trials, 16-year-old Debbie Meyer set world records in the 200, 400, and 800. The rarefied air of Mexico City prevented her from duplicating that feat, but she did win all three races, starting with the 400 meters.

1972 Munich C: 29, N: 17, D: 8.30. WR: 4:21.2 (Shane Gould)

1. Shane Gould	AUS	4:19.04	WR
2. Novella Calligaris	ITA	4:22.44	
3. Gudrun Wegner	GDR	4:23.11	
4. Shirley Babashoff	USA	4:23.59	
5. Jenny Wylie	USA	4:24.07	
6. Keena Rothhammer	USA	4:24.22	
7. Hansje Bunschoten	HOL	4:29.70	
8. Anke Rijnders	HOL	4:31.51	

Shane Gould came back from her loss in the 100 meters the previous day to win her second gold medal.

1976 Montreal C: 34, N: 22, D: 7.20. WR: 4:11.69 (Barbara Krause)

1. Petra Thümer	GDR	4:09.89	WR
2. Shirley Babashoff	USA	4:10.46	
3. Shannon Smith	CAN	4:14.60	
4. Rebecca Perrott	NZE	4:14.76	
5. Kathy Heddy	USA	4:15.50	
6. Brenda Borgh	USA	4:17.43	
7. Annelies Maas	HOL	4:17.44	
8. Sabine Kahle	GDR	4:20.42	

On June 3, 1976, Barbara Krause broke Shirley Babashoff's world record by over three seconds. However, two weeks later she suffered an attack of angina and had to be dropped from the East German squad. Fifteen-year-old Petra Thümer, who had finished second to Krause in the East German championships, rose to the occasion at the Olympics. She built up most of her lead during the second 100 meters and then fought off Babashoff's attempts to close the gap. Thümer's time would have won her a silver medal in the 1968 *men's* 400-meter race and a gold in 1964.

1980 Moscow C: 19, N: 12, D: 7.22. WR: 4:06.28 (Tracey Wickham)

1. Ines Diers	GDR	4:08.76	OR
2. Petra Schneider	GDR	4:09.16	
3. Carmela Schmidt	GDR	4:10.86	
4. Michelle Ford	AUS	4:11.65	
5. Irina Aksyonova	SOV/RUS	4:14.40	
6. Annelies Maas	HOL	4:15.79	
7. Reggie de Jong	HOL	4:15.95	
8. Olga Klevakina	SOV/RUS	4:19.18	

This was one race that was definitely affected by the anti-Soviet boycott. Missing was world record holder Tracey Wickham of Australia as well as Kim Linehan and Cynthia "Sippy" Woodhead of the United States, who clocked 4:07.77 and 4:08.17, respectively, at the U.S. national championships on July 31. In their absence, the East Germans had a field day. Petra Schneider led for over 300 meters, but 16-year-old Ines Diers finished strongly to win. Before the Moscow Games were over Diers had won five medals: two gold, two silver and one bronze.

1984 Los Angeles C: 25, N: 17, D: 7.31. WR: 4:06.28 (Tracey Wickham)

1. Tiffany Cohen	USA	4:07.10	OR
2. Sarah Hardcastle	GBR	4:10.27	
3. June Croft	GBR	4:11.49	
4. Kimberly Linehan	USA	4:12.26	
5. Anna McVann	AUS	4:13.95	
6. Jolande van der Meer	HOL	4:16.05	
7. Birgit Kowalczik	GER	4:16.33	
8. Julie Daigneault	CAN	4:16.41	

Eighteen-year-old Tiffany Cohen led from start to finish and won by five meters, registering the fastest women's 400-meter time since Tracey Wickham set her world record in 1978. The Friendship Games event in Moscow three weeks later was won by East Germany's Astrid Strauss with a time of 4:07.66.

1988 Seoul C: 30, N: 21, D: 9.22. WR: 4:05.45 (Janet Evans)

1. Janet Evans	USA	4:03.85	WR
2. Heike Friedrich	GDR	4:05.94	
3. Anke Möhring	GDR	4:06.62	
4. Tami Bruce	USA	4:08.16	
5. Janelle Elford	AUS	4:10.64	
6. Isabelle Arnould	BEL	4:11.73	
7. Stephanie Ortwig	GER	4:13.05	
8. Natalya Trefilova	SOV/RUS	4:13.92	

When Heike Friedrich was only 15 years old, she won five gold medals at the 1985 European championships. The following year she added four golds at the world championships. By the time of the 1988 Olympics, she was still undefeated in major international competition, having won 13 consecutive finals. She added a fourteenth victory in Seoul when she finished first in the 200-meter freestyle. But the following night she finally met her match in Janet Evans, a 17-year-old student at appropriately named El Dorado High School in Placentia, California.

Despite her small size and unorthodox windmill stroke, Evans was a natural-born swimmer. She was swimming laps at the age of two, literally before she was out of diapers. By the time she was 3 years old she had already mastered the butterfly and breaststroke. During her early years of competition other swimmers snickered and laughed at her diminutive stature, but the laughter stopped in 1987 when, at the age of 15, the 95-pound Evans broke the world record at 800 meters and 1500 meters, the 1500 record having stood the onslaught of larger swimmers for over seven and a half years and the 800 for almost nine. On December 20, 1987, she eclipsed Tracey Wickham's nine-year-old record at 400 meters.

In the Olympic final Evans took the early lead, but Friedrich and East German teammate Anke Möhring, both strong finishers, stayed right by her shoulder. Friedrich, who had planned to win the race with a world record of 4:05, pushed the pace in the third 100, leaving Möhring behind. But Evans refused to be passed. However, with 100 meters to go, her lead was down to 1 foot.

Then, surprisingly, it was Evans who pulled away in the final two laps by swimming the second half of the race faster than she had the first half. It was the first "negative split" of her career and it earned her the second of her three gold medals.

1992 Barcelona C: 33, N: 24, D: 7.28. WR: 4:03.85 (Janet Evans)

1. Dagmar Hase	GER	4:07.18	
2. Janet Evans	USA	4:07.37	
3. Hayley Lewis	AUS	4:11.22	
4. Erika Hansen	USA	4:11.50	
5. Kerstin Kielgass	GER	4:11.52	
6. Isabelle Arnould	BEL	4:13.75	
7. Malin Nilsson	SWE	4:14.10	
8. Suzu Chiba	JPN	4:15.71	

Janet Evans entered the Olympics with a six-year win streak covering 18 national and international meets. Dagmar Hase, on the other hand, was a backstroke specialist who entered the 400-meter freestyle at the German Olympics trials in May because it was held after her other races were already completed. She won in a personal best of 4:12.60. The Olympics would be the first major meet at which she swam the 400 free. In her mind, Hase conceded the gold medal to Evans, but thought herself capable of a silver or bronze. Evans set a hard pace, hoping to burn off the rest of the field, but Hase was able to keep within striking distance. By 300 meters, Evans had managed to stretch her lead to a body length. Hase crept closer, executed an excellent final turn, and then powered ahead over the last lap. She caught Evans with 15 or 20 meters to go and won by a foot.

800-METER FREESTYLE

1896–1964 not held

1968 Mexico City C: 26, N: 16, D: 10.24. WR: 9.10.4 (Deborah Meyer)

1. Deborah Meyer	USA	9:24.0	OR
2. Pamela Kruse	USA	9:35.7	
3. Maria Teresa Ramirez	MEX	9:38.5	
4. Karen Moras	AUS	9:38.6	
5. Patricia Caretto	USA	9:51.3	
6. Angela Coughlan	CAN	9:56.4	
7. Denise Langford	AUS	9:56.7	
8. Laura Vaca	MEX	10.02.5	

Debbie Meyer was never really challenged as she became the first swimmer to win three individual gold medals in one Olympics. The only excitement of the race came when 15-year-old Maria Teresa Ramirez came from behind to nip Karen Moras for the bronze medal, bringing joy to the Mexican crowd.

1972 Munich C: 36, N: 19, D: 9.3. WR: 8:53.83 (Jo Harshberger)

1. Keena Rothhammer	USA	8:53.68	WR
2. Shane Gould	AUS	8:56.39	
3. Novella Calligaris	ITA	8:57.46	

4. Ann Simmons	USA	8:57.62	
5. Gudrun Wegner	GDR	8:58.89	
6. Jo Harshberger	USA	9:01.21	
7. Hansje Bunschoten	HOL	9:16.69	
8. Narelle Moras	AUS	9:19.06	

Calligaris led for 500 meters, but then Rothhammer, fourth at the halfway mark, took the lead and pulled away.

1976 Montreal C: 19, N: 11, D: 7.25. WR: 8:39.63 (Shirley Babashoff)

1. Petra Thümer	GDR	8:37.14	WR
2. Shirley Babashoff	USA	8:37.59	
3. Wendy Weinberg	USA	8:42.60	
4. Rosemary Milgate	AUS	8:47.21	
5. Nicole Kramer	USA	8:47.33	
6. Shannon Smith	CAN	8:48.15	
7. Regina Jäger	GDR	8:50.40	
8. Jennifer Turrall	AUS	8:52.88	

On June 4, 1976, Petra Thümer set a world record of 8:40.68, but 17 days later Shirley Babashoff bettered that time by a second. This was Babashoff's last chance for an individual gold medal so she withdrew from the 400-meter individual medley in order to save her strength for her long-distance showdown with Thümer, who had beaten her at 400 meters five days earlier. Shannon Smith led for 300 meters, but then Thümer took over. Babashoff trailed right behind her, but every time she drew closer, Thümer would draw away again. In the end Thümer had her second world record and Babashoff had her sixth Olympic silver medal.

1980 Moscow C: 14, N: 9, D: 7.27. WR: 8:24.62 (Tracey Wickham)

1. Michelle Ford	AUS	8:28.90	OR
2. Ines Diers	GDR	8:32.55	
3. Heike Dähne	GDR	8:33.48	
4. Irina Aksyonova	SOV/RUS	8:38.05	
5. Oksana Komissarova	SOV/RUS	8:42.04	
6. Pascale Verbauwen	BEL	8:44.84	
7. Ines Geissler	GDR	8:45.28	
8. Yelena Ivanova	SOV/UKR	8:46.45	

Eighteen-year-old Michelle Ford took the lead after 250 meters and pulled away to break the East German gold medal monopoly. Missing were world record holder Tracey Wickham of Australia and U.S. champion Kim Linehan whose best time was 8:24.70 and who clocked an 8:27.86 two days after the Olympic final.

1984 Los Angeles C: 20, N: 14, D: 8.3. WR: 8:24.62 (Tracey Wickham)

1. Tiffany Cohen	USA	8:24.95	OR
2. Michele Richardson	USA	8:30.73	
3. Sarah Hardcastle	GBR	8:32.60	
4. Anna McVann	AUS	8:37.94	
5. Carla Lasi	ITA	8:42.45	
6. Jolande van der Meer	HOL	8:42.86	
7. Monica Olmi	ITA	8:47.32	
8. Karen Ward	CAN	8:48.12	

Challenged only by the memory of Tracey Wickham's six-year-old world record, Tiffany Cohen added the 800 gold to the one she had won in the 400 three days earlier.

1988 Seoul C: 27, N: 19, D: 9.24. WR: 8:17.12 (Janet Evans)

1. Janet Evans	USA	8:20.20 OR
2. Astrid Strauss	GDR	8:22.09
3. Julie McDonald	AUS	8:22.93
4. Anke Möhring	GDR	8:23.09
5. Tami Bruce	USA	8:30.86
6. Janelle Elford	AUS	8:30.94
7. Isabelle Arnould	BEL	8:37.47
8. Antoaneta Strumenlieva	BUL	8:41.05

As they stood on the blocks waiting for the start of the final, Janet Evans and her East German rivals presented an odd sight. Astrid Strauss measured 6 feet 1½ inches and weighed 181 pounds. Teammate Anke Möhring was 5 feet 11¼ inches and 152 pounds. Between them stood the favorite, Evans, 5 feet 5¼ inches and a mere 101 pounds. Her main challengers were thought to be Möhring, the former world record holder, and Julie McDonald, the fastest qualifier and the last person to beat Evans, a year earlier in Brisbane. However, it was Strauss who gave Evans the best run for her money, improving her personal best by 4.43 seconds. But even she was 10 feet behind at the finish, as Janet Evans won the last of her three Seoul gold medals.

1992 Barcelona C: 25, N: 18, D: 7.30. WR: 8:16.22 (Janet Evans)

1. Janet Evans	USA	8:25.52
2. Hayley Lewis	AUS	8:30.34
3. Jana Henke	GER	8:30.99
4. Philippa Langrell	NZE	8:35.57
5. Irene Dalby	NOR	8:37.12
6. Olga Šplíchalová	CZE	8:37.66
7. Erika Hansen	USA	8:39.25
8. Isabelle Arnould	BEL	8:41.86

Janet Evans had not lost an 800-meter race in five years. Although her time was slower than in the last Olympics, her margin of victory was larger. She led from start to finish and won by eight meters.

100-METER BACKSTROKE

1896–1920 not held

1924 Paris C: 10, N: 5, D: 7.20. WR: 1:22.4 (Sybil Bauer)

1. Sybil Bauer	USA	1:23.2 OR
2. Phyllis Harding	GBR	1:27.4
3. Aileen Riggin	USA	1:28.2
4. Florence Chambers	USA	1:30.8
5. Jarmila Müllerová	CZE	1:31.2
6. Ellen King (GBR)		

Sybil Bauer of Chicago was the world record holder in all women's backstroke events when she completely outclassed her opposition at the Paris Olympics. She was still

undefeated when she died of intestinal cancer on January 31, 1927, at the age of 23. Bronze medalist Aileen Riggin became the first person to win medals in both swimming and diving.

1928 Amsterdam C: 12, N: 7, D: 8.11 WR: 1:22.0 (Willy van den Turk)

1. Maria Braun	HOL	1:22.0
2. Ellen King	GBR	1:22.2
3. Margaret Joyce Cooper	GBR	1:22.8
4. Marion Gilman	USA	1:24.2
5. Eleanor Holm	USA	1:24.4
5. Lisa Lindstrom	USA	1:24.4
7. Elizabeth Stockley	NZE	1:25.8

Ellen King of Scotland equaled the world record in the first heat. In the second heat, 17-year-old local favorite Sis Braun broke the world record with a time of 1:21.6.

1932 Los Angeles C: 12, N. 7, D: 8.11. WR: 1:18.2 (Eleanor Holm)

1. Eleanor Holm	USA	1:19.4
2. Philomena "Bonny" Mealing	AUS	1:21.3
3. Elizabeth Valerie Davies	GBR	1:22.5
4. Phyllis Harding	GBR	1:22.6
5. Joan McSheehy	USA	1:23.2
6. Margaret Joyce Cooper	GBR	1:23.4
DNS: Maria Philipsen-Braun (HOL)		

Eighteen-year-old Eleanor Holm, the daughter of a Brooklyn fire captain, inched ahead after 25 meters, held off the challenge of Bonny Mealing, and pulled away in the last 25 meters. Holm had set an Olympic record of 1:18.3 in her qualifying heat.

1936 Berlin C: 21, N: 12, D: 8.13. WR: 1:15.8 (Hendrika "Rie" Mastenbroek)

1. Dina "Nida" Senff	HOL	1:18.9
2. Hendrika "Rie" Mastenbroek	HOL	1:19.2
3. Alice Bridges	USA	1:19.4
4. Edith Motridge	USA	1:19.6
5. Tove Bruunström	DEN	1:20.4
6. Lorna Frampton	GBR	1:20.6
7. Phyllis Harding	GBR	1:21.5

Life had been very full for Eleanor Holm between Olympics. While in Hollywood she had met singer and orchestra leader Art Jarrett, who was a fellow alumnus of Erasmus Hall High School back in Brooklyn. Five months later, on September 2, 1933, they were married in Beverly Hills. For the next three years Holm led a very active social life and joined her husband singing in nightclubs. But she always kept in shape. In 1935 she set a world record for the 100-meter backstroke, and in 1936 she also broke the record for 200 meters. On February 27, 1936, her 100-meter record was broken by Rie Mastenbroek. However, when Eleanor Holm boarded the S.S. *Manhattan* on July 15 for the nine-day voyage to Germany, along with about 350 other members of the U.S. Olympic team, she was still the favorite to defend her championship, and there was little hint of the outra-

Eleanor Holm won the 100-meter backstroke in 1932 and was on her way to defend her title in Berlin in 1936 when she was derailed by a major scandal.

geous scandal that was about to bring an abrupt end to her amateur career.

Now on her way to her third Olympics, married and used to a flashy and independent life-style, Eleanor did not take too well to the third-class accommodations and strict regulations that had been arranged by the Ameri-

can Olympic Committee. She felt more comfortable in the first-class section, which happened to be where the American officials were staying, as well as the press. On Friday, July 17, Mr. Maybaum of the United States Lines, which owned the S.S. *Manhattan,* invited Eleanor to attend a party he was throwing that night in the A-deck bar and lounge. She was the only team member invited. Quick to accept, she stayed up until six a.m., matching drinks with the sportswriters. She had to be helped back to her cabin.

The next day there was much joking and wisecracking among the non-Olympic first-class passengers about the "training techniques" of the U.S. team. Embarrassed U.S. Olympic officials issued Holm a warning, but she was defiant and continued to drink in public off and on for the next few days. When advised by friends to moderate her behavior, she reminded them that she was "free, white, and 22."

On July 23, while the ship made a prolonged stopover in Cherbourg, France, with the passengers confined to ship, Holm attended an afternoon and evening champagne party. At about ten-thirty p.m. the official team chaperone, Ada Taylor Sackett, discovered Eleanor staggering along the deck, accompanied by a young man. After returning to her cabin, which she shared with two other swimmers, Holm stuck her head out the porthole and began shouting obscenities. Her roommates, Olive McKean and Mary Lou Petty, pulled her back inside and convinced her to go to sleep. At midnight Mrs. Sackett returned with the team doctor, J. Hubert Lawson, and the ship's doctor. Dr. Lawson found Holm "in a deep slumber which approached a state of coma." His diagnosis: "Acute alcoholism." The physical examination failed to awaken her. Members of the American Olympic Committee met to discuss the charges against Holm, which also included shooting craps. (She never denied the charges and later boasted that she had won "a couple hundred dollars" just before the final party.)

At six a.m. team manager Herbert Holm (no relation) woke Eleanor and informed her that the American Olympic Committee had voted to remove her from the team. She went to the stateroom of Avery Brundage, president of the A.O.C., and pleaded her case through a crack in the door. It was to no avail. More than half of the U.S. team members signed a petition asking for Eleanor's reinstatement and the press split was about the same.

The news of Eleanor Holm's expulsion caused a sensation when the S.S. *Manhattan* docked in Hamburg, particularly when word began to spread about the details of the case. When her final appeal was denied, Holm lashed back at the American officials, pointing out that they had held cocktail parties every night and that they had ignored the athletes. Joseph Goebbels' Nazi propaganda periodical, *Der Angriff,* took the side of the A.O.C., editorializing, "She probably didn't believe they could disqualify her, but she thought wrong. It wasn't herself who mattered. It was the others—and discipline. For that no sacrifice is too great, no matter how many tears are shed."

Eleanor Holm didn't get to participate in the 1936 Olympics, but that didn't prevent her from having a good time in Berlin. The Nazis quickly forgave her lack of discipline and entertained her as a special visitor. "I had such fun!" she told *Sports Illustrated* 36 years later. "I enjoyed the parties, the *Heil Hitlers,* the uniforms, the flags. . . . Göring was fun. He had a good personality. So did the one with the club foot [Goebbels]. Göring gave me a sterling-silver swastika. I had a mold made of it and I put a diamond Star of David in the middle." Holm issued a public challenge to whoever won the Olympic championship to face her in a swim-off, but when the day came for the final of the women's 100-meter backstroke, Eleanor Holm, who hadn't been beaten in seven years, was sitting in the stands instead of swimming in the pool.

As it happened, the competition, although it did not get as much press attention as all that had preceded it, was not without its own element of sensation. Sixteen-year-old Nida Senff surprised the experts by recording the fastest preliminary times, 1:16.6. and 1:17.1. In the final she was away quickly and had opened up a two-meter lead by the halfway mark. But she missed touching the wall and had to go back. This dropped her to sixth place out of seven, but she sped on, regained the lead with 20 meters to go, and won with a very little bit to spare. She might have lost anyway had not world record holder Rie Mastenbroek become entangled in the lane ropes. Of the four events which Mastenbroek entered in 1936, this was the only one she didn't win.

As for Eleanor Holm, she became more popular than ever. In 1938 she divorced Art Jarrett and also acted in her only film, co-starring as Jane in *Tarzan's Revenge* with 1936 decathlon champion Glenn Morris. The following year she married impresario Billy Rose. The pair divorced in 1954 following a spicy case, which became known as "The War of the Roses" and which was filled with titillating accusations of sexual "misbehavior" on both sides. She later became an interior decorator and retired to Miami Beach.

1948 London C: 24, N: 16, D: 8.5. WR: 1:10.9 (Cornelia Kint)
1. Karen-Margrete Harup   DEN   1:14.4   OR
2. Suzanne Zimmerman   USA   1:16.0
3. Judith Davies   AUS   1:16.7
4. Ilona Novák   HUN   1:18.4
5. Hendrika van der Horst   HOL   1:18.8
6. Dirkje van Ekris   HOL   1:18.9
7. Muriel Mellon   USA   1:19.0
8. Greta Galliard   HOL   1:19.1

Eliminated in the semifinals was French swimmer and journalist Monique Berlioux who later became Director of the International Olympic Committee.

1952 Helsinki C: 20, N: 14, D: 7.31. WR: 1:10.9 (Cornelia Kint)
1. Joan Harrison   SAF   1:14.3
2. Geertje Wielema   HOL   1:14.5
3. Jean Stewart   NZE   1:15.8
4. Johanna de Korte   HOL   1:15.8
5. Barbara Stark   USA   1:16.2
6. Gertrud Herrbruck   GER   1:18.0
7. Margaret McDowell   GBR   1:18.4
DISQ: Hendrika van der Horst (HOL)

Joan Harrison's upset victory was so unexpected that Alex Bulley, the South African team manager, fainted from excitement when he realized she had won. Wielema set an Olympic record of 1:13.8 in her opening heat.

1956 Melbourne C: 23, N: 14, D: 12.5. WR: 1:10.9 (Cornelia Kint)
1. Judith Grinham   GBR   1:12.9   OR
2. Carin Cone   USA   1:12.9
3. Margaret Edwards   GBR   1:13.1
4. Helga Schmidt   GER   1:13.4
5. Maureen Murphy   USA   1:14.1
6. Julie Hoyle   GBR   1:14.3
7. Sara Barber   CAN   1:14.3
8. Gerganyia Beckitt   AUS   1:14.7

Seventeen-year-old Judy Grinham got off to a bad start and was only fifth at the turn. She caught Cone with ten meters left and just outtouched her.

1960 Rome C: 30, N: 19, D: 9.3. WR: 1:09.2 (Lynn Burke)
1. Lynn Burke   USA   1:09.3   OR
2. Natalie Steward   GBR   1:10.8
3. Satoko Tanaka   JPN   1:11.4
4. Laura Ranwell   SAF   1:11.4
5. Rosy Piacentini   FRA   1:11.4
6. Sylvia Lewis   GBR   1:11.8
7. Maria van Velsen   HOL   1:12.1
8. Nadine Delache   FRA   1:12.4

On September 22, 1939, Holland's Cor Kint swam a 1:15.0 to slash two seconds off the world record. Kint's time remained unapproachable for almost 21 years, until the summer of 1960. On July 10, Ria van Velsen equaled Kint's record. A week later Lynn Burke finally broke it. At the U.S. Olympic trials in August she set two more world records.

1964 Tokyo C: 31, N: 17, D: 10.14. WR: 1:08.3 (Virginia Duenkel)
1. Cathy Ferguson   USA   1:07.7   WR
2. Christine Caron   FRA   1:07.9
3. Virginia Duenkel   USA   1:08.0
4. Satoko Tanaka   JPN   1:08.6
5. Nina Harmar   USA   1:09.4
6. Linda Ludgrove   GBR   1:09.5
7. Eileen Weir   CAN   1:09.8
8. Jill Norfolk   GBR   1:11.2

The 1964 final matched six past and present world record holders at various backstroke distances: Caron, Duenkel, Tanaka, Ferguson, Ludgrove, and Norfolk. Sixteen-year-old Kiki Caron had set a 100 meters world record of

1:08.6 on June 14, but that was broken by Ginny Duenkel on September 28. In the Olympic final, however, it was 16-year-old 200 meters record holder Cathy Ferguson who edged ahead just before the finish to gain her second world record and her first gold medal.

1968 Mexico City C: 40, N: 23, D: 10.23. WR: 1:06.4 (Karen Muir)

1. Kaye Hall	USA	1:06.2	WR
2. Elaine Tanner	CAN	1:06.7	
3. Jane Swagerty	USA	1:08.1	
4. Kendis Moore	USA	1:08.3	
5. Andrea Gyarmati	HUN	1:09.1	
6. Lynette Watson	AUS	1:09.1	
7. Sylvie Canet	FRA	1:09.3	
8. Glenda Stirling	NZE	1:10.6	

Sixteen-year-old world record holder Karen Muir was excluded from Olympic competition because she was from South Africa, which has been banned from the Olympics since 1964 because of its government's racial policies. In Muir's absence, the favorite was 17-year-old Elaine Tanner of Vancouver, who had the fastest times of the qualifying rounds, setting Olympic records of 1:07.6 and 1:07.4 in the heats and semifinals. But as Canada's main gold medal hope, she carried a heavy burden. "Usually, before a race," she explained afterward, "you're concentrating on strategy, the other swimmers, the race. But at Mexico all I could think about was the twenty million people who were expecting me to win." Another finalist was 17-year-old Kaye Hall of Tacoma, Washington, who had been beaten by Tanner several times and as recently as the semifinals the previous day. Tanner and Hall swam neck and neck for 50 meters. but Hall surged ahead at the turn, and even though Tanner produced her best time ever, she couldn't catch the inspired American teenager.

1972 Munich C: 37, N: 21, D: 9.2. WR: 1:05.6 (Karen Muir)

1. Melissa Belote	USA	1:05.78	OR
2. Andrea Gyarmati	HUN	1:06:26	
3. Susan Atwood	USA	1:06.34	
4. Karen Moe	USA	1:06.69	
5. Wendy Cook	CAN	1:06.70	
6. Enith Brigitha	HOL	1:06.82	
7. Christine Herbst	GDR	1:07.27	
8. Silke Pielen	GER	1:07.36	

This was the first of Melissa Belote's three gold medals. She had orginally turned to the backstroke because it was the only stroke that kept the chlorine out of her eyes. Belote attributed her fine performance in Munich to the fact that she felt relaxed and unpressured since she was not expected to win.

1976 Montreal C: 34, N: 21, D: 7.21. WR: 1:01.51 (Ulrike Richter)

1. Ulrike Richter	GDR	1:01.83	OR
2. Birgit Treiber	GDR	1:03.41	
3. Nancy Garapick	CAN	1:03.71	
4. Wendy Hogg-Cook	CAN	1:03.93	
5. Cheryl Gibson	CAN	1:05.16	
6. Nadiya Stavko	SOV/UKR	1:05.19	
7. Antje Stille	GDR	1:05.30	
8. Diane Edelijn	HOL	1:05.53	

The order of finish for the first four places was exactly the same as it had been a year earlier at the 1975 world championships in Cali, Colombia. Seventeen-year-old Ulrike Richter had broken the 100 meters world record nine times in the three years preceding the Montreal Olympics.

1980 Moscow C: 26, N: 18, D: 7.23. WR: 1:01.51 (Ulrike Richter)

1. Rica Reinisch	GDR	1:00.86	WR
2. Ina Kleber	GDR	1:02.07	
3. Petra Riedel	GDR	1:02.64	
4. Carmen Bunaciu	ROM	1:03.81	
5. Carine Verbauwen	BEL	1:03.82	
6. Larissa Gorchakova	SOV/RUS	1:03.87	
7. Monique Bosga	HOL	1:04.47	
8. Manuela Carosi	ITA	1:05.10	

Fifteen-year-old Rica Reinisch had quite a successful week at the Moscow Olympics. First she equaled Ulrike Richter's four-year-old 100-meter backstroke world record of 1:01.51 while swimming the opening leg for East Germany's victorious medley relay team. Two days later she broke Richter's record by clocking 1:01.50 in her elimination heat. In the final, 24 hours later, Reinisch took the lead early on the way to her third world record. Four days later, in the 200-meter backstroke final, she earned her third gold medal and her fourth world record.

1984 Los Angeles C: 31, N: 21, D: 7.31. WR: 1:00.86 (Rica Reinisch)

1. Theresa Andrews	USA	1:02.55	
2. Betsy Mitchell	USA	1:02.63	
3. Jolanda de Rover	HOL	1:02.91	
4. Carmen Bunaciu	ROM	1:03.21	
5. Aneta Patrascoiu	ROM	1:03.29	
6. Svenja Schlicht	GER	1:03.46	
7. Beverley Rose	GBR	1:04.16	
8. Carmel Clark	NZE	1:04.47	

On August 24, at the Friendship Games in Moscow, East Germany's Ina Kleber set a world record of 1:00.59. At the East German Olympic trials, Kristin Otto had clocked her best time of the year, 1:01.13.

1988 Seoul C: 41, N: 30, D: 9.22. WR: 1:00.59 (Ina Kleber)

1. Kristin Otto	GDR	1:00.89
2. Krisztina Egerszegi	HUN	1:01.56
3. Cornelia Sirch	GDR	1:01.57
4. Betsy Mitchell	USA	1:02.71
5. Beth Barr	USA	1:02.78
6. Silvia Poll Ahrens	CRC	1:03.34
7. Nicole Livingstone	AUS	1:04.15
8. Marion Aizpors	GER	1:04.19

Kristin Otto won the second of her six gold medals and, an hour later, earned her third in the 4 × 100-meter freestyle relay. One curiosity of note occurred among the lower-ranked swimmers. Olympic rules provided for a "B" final to be swum by the ninth through sixteenth fastest qualifiers. Manuela Carosi of Italy and Karen Lord of Australia tied for sixteenth place and were forced to swim off for the final spot in the "B" final. Again they finished in a dead heat and had to return to the water for a second swimoff. They were exactly even at 50 meters, but Carosi finally won, 1:04.62 to 1:04.75. To her credit, Carosi finished third in the "B" final, her fourth race of the day, with her best time yet: 1:03.80.

1992 Barcelona C: 45, N: 31, D: 7.28. WR: 1:00.31 (Krisztina Egerszegi)
1. Krisztina Egerszegi   HUN   1:00.68   OR
2. Tünde Szabó   HUN   1:01.14
3. Lea Loveless   USA   1:01.43
4. Nicole Stevenson (Livingstone)   AUS   1:01.78
5. Elizabeth "Janie" Wagstaff   USA   1:01.81
6. Joanne Meehan   AUS   1:02.07
7. Nina Zhivanevskaya   UKR   1:02.36
8. Yoko Koikawa   JPN   1:03.23

Egerszegi set an Olympic record of 1:00.85 in her qualifying heat and then broke the record again in the final to win the second of her three gold medals in Barcelona.

200-METER BACKSTROKE

1896–1964 not held

1968 Mexico City C: 30, N: 19, D: 10.25. WR: 2:23.8 (Karen Muir)
1. Lillian "Pokey" Watson   USA   2:24.8   OR
2. Elaine Tanner   CAN   2:27.4
3. Kaye Hall   USA   2:28.9
4. Lynette Watson   AUS   2:29.5
5. Wendy Burrell   GBR   2:32.3
6. Zdenka Gasparac   YUG   2:33.5
7. Maria Corominas   SPA   2:33.9
8. Bendicte Duprez   FRA   2:36.6

1972 Munich C: 37, N: 20, D: 9.4. WR: 2:20.64 (Melissa Belote)
1. Melissa Belote   USA   2:19.19   WR
2. Susan Atwood   USA   2:20.38
3. Donna Gurr   CAN   2:23.22
4. Annegret Kober   GER   2:23.35
5. Christine Herbst   GDR   2:23.44
6. Enith Brigitha   HOL   2:23.70
7. Deborah Palmer   AUS   2:24.65
8. Leslie Cliff   CAN   2:25.80

Melissa Belote swam a 2:20.58 in the heats to break her own world record. She broke it again in the final eight hours later to win her third gold medal in three days.

1976 Montreal C: 31, N: 18, D: 7.25. WR: 2:12.47 (Birgit Treiber)
1. Ulrike Richter   GDR   2:13.43   OR
2. Birgit Treiber   GDR   2:14.97
3. Nancy Garapick   CAN   2:15.60

4. Nadiya Stavko   SOV/UKR   2:16.28
5. Melissa Belote   USA   2:17.27
6. Antje Stille   GDR   2:17.55
7. Klavdia Studennikova   SOV/UKR   2:17.74
8. Wendy Hogg-Cook   CAN   2:17.95

The 200-meter backstroke had seen five different world record holders in the two and a half years prior to the Montreal Olympics: Belote, Richter, Garapick, Treiber, and Stille. All five started in the Olympic final. As it turned out, there was little drama; Ulrike Richter led from start to finish to gain her third gold medal.

1980 Moscow C: 21, N: 13, D: 7.27. WR: 2:11.95 (Linda Jezek)
1. Rica Reinisch   GDR   2:11.77   WR
2. Cornelia Polit   GDR   2:13.75
3. Birgit Treiber   GDR   2:14.14
4. Carmen Bunaciu   ROM   2:15.20
5. Yolande van der Straeten   BEL   2:15.58
6. Carine Verbauwen   BEL   2:16.66
7. Lisa Forrest   AUS   2:16.75
8. Larissa Gorchakova   SOV/RUS   2:17.72

Reinisch improved her personal best from 2:15.59 in only eight weeks.

1984 Los Angeles C: 27, N: 18, D: 8.4. WR: 2:09.91 (Cornelia Sirch)
1. Jolanda de Rover   HOL   2:12.38
2. Amy White   USA   2:13.04
3. Aneta Patrascoiu   ROM   2:13.29
4. Georgina Parkes   AUS   2:14.37
5. Tori Trees   USA   2:15.73
6. Svenja Schlicht   GER   2:15.93
7. Carmen Bunaciu   ROM   2:16.15
8. Carmel Clark   NZE   2:17.89

At the Friendship Games, three weeks after the Olympics, Kathrin Zimmermann of East Germany recorded a time of 2:12.56.

1988 Seoul C: 32, N: 23, D: 9.25. WR: 2:08.60 (Betsy Mitchell)
1. Krisztina Egerszegi   HUN   2:09.29   OR
2. Kathrin Zimmerman   GDR   2:10.61
3. Cornelia Sirch   GDR   2:11.45
4. Cynthia "Beth" Barr   USA   2:12.39
5. Nicole Livingstone   AUS   2:13.43
6. Andrea Hayes   USA   2:15.02
7. Jolanda de Rover   HOL   2:15.17
8. Svenja Schlicht   GER   2:15.94

Two-time world champion Cornelia Sirch led the qualifying round with an Olympic record of 2:10.46. But 14-year-old Krisztina Egerszegi, emboldened by her silver medal in the 100-meter backstroke, felt for the first time that she was capable of beating the East Germans. This despite the fact that, at 99 pounds, the Budapest native was *42* pounds lighter than any of her opponents in the final. Sirch took the early lead with Egerszegi right beside her. After the turn at 100 meters, Egerszegi suddenly sprinted ahead and continued to pull away for the remainder of the race. Discouraged, Sirch was also passed by teammate Kathrin Zimmerman, who had to beat her four-year-old personal best to do it.

1992 Barcelona C: 43, N: 30, D: 7.31. WR: 2:06.62 (Krisztina Egerszegi)

1. Krisztina Egerszegi	HUN	2:07.06	OR
2. Dagmar Hase	GER	2:09.46	
3. Nicole Stevenson (Livingstone)	AUS	2:10.20	
4. Lea Loveless	USA	2:11.54	
5. Anna Simcic	NZE	2:11.99	
6. Tünde Szabó	HUN	2:12.94	
7. Sylvia Poll Ahrens	CRC	2:12.97	
8. Leigh Habler	AUS	2:13.68	

Krisztina Egerszegi, by now a seasoned 17-year-old, swam the second-fastest time in history, 2:07.34, in the qualifying round to break her own Olympic record. In the final she took the early lead and won by four meters to earn her third gold medal of the 1992 Games. This brought her career total to 4 golds and 1 silver, all in individual events.

100-METER BREASTSTROKE

1896–1964 not held

1968 Mexico City C: 33, N: 20, D: 10.19. WR: 1:14.2 (Catie Ball)

1. Djurdjica Bjedov	YUG/CRO	1:15.8	OR
2. Halina Prozumenshchykova	SOV/UKR	1:15.9	
3. Sharon Wichman	USA	1:16.1	
4. Uta Frommater	GER	1:16.2	
5. Catie Ball	USA	1:16.7	
6. Kyoe Nakagawa	JPN	1:17.0	
7. Svetlana Babanina	SOV/RUS	1:17.2	
8. Ana Norbis	URU	1:17.3	

Catie Ball of Jacksonville, Florida, set her fifth 100-meter breaststroke world record seven weeks before the opening of the 1968 Olympics. But in Mexico City she succumbed to a viral infection and lost ten pounds. She competed anyway, but could finish only fifth. Twenty-one-year-old Djurdjica Bjedov is the only representative of Yugoslavia ever to have won an Olympic swimming championship. Previous to the Olympics her main claim to fame had been finishing third in a 200-meter heat at the 1966 European championships.

1972 Munich C: 40, N: 23, D: 9.2. WR: 1:14.2 (Catie Ball)

1. Catherine Carr	USA	1:13.58	WR
2. Halina Stepanova (Prozumenshchykova)	SOV/UKR	1:14.99	
3. Beverley Whitfield	AUS	1:15.73	
4. Ágnes Kiss-Kaczander	HUN	1:16.26	
5. Judy Melick	USA	1:17.16	
5. Verena Eberle	GER	1:17.16	
7. Britt-Marie Smedh	SWE	1:17.19	
8. Dorothy Harrison	GBR	1:17.49	

1976 Montreal C: 38, N: 23, D: 7.24. WR: 1:11.93 (Carola Nitschke)

1. Hannelore Anke	GDR	1:11.16
2. Lyubov Rusanova	SOV/RUS	1:13.04
3. Marina Koshevaia	SOV/RUS	1:13.30
4. Carola Nitschke	GDR	1:13.33
5. Gabriele Askamp	GER	1:14.15
6. Maryna Yurchenya	SOV/UKR	1:14.17
7. Margaret Kelly	GBR	1:14.20
8. Karla Linke	GDR	1:14.21

In the fifth heat of the opening round, 18-year-old Hannelore Anke of Aue set a new world record of 1:11.11. Nine hours later in the semifinals, she lowered the record to 1:10.86. In the final, two nights later, Anke's slowest performance of the Games was good enough for an easy gold medal.

1980 Moscow C: 25, N: 19, D: 7.26. WR: 1:10.20 (Ute Geweniger)

1. Ute Geweniger	GDR	1:10.22
2. Elvira Vasilkova	SOV/RUS	1:10.41
3. Susanne Nielsson	DEN	1:11.16
4. Margaret Kelly	GBR	1:11.48
5. Eva-Marie Håkansson	SWE	1:11.72
6. Susannah Brownsdon	GBR	1:12.11
7. Lina Kačiušytė	SOV/LIT	1:12.21
8. Monica Bonon	ITA	1:12.51

Sixteen-year-old Ute Geweniger clocked a 1:10.11 in the fourth heat to break her own world record. In the final she was only fifth at the turn. Three days later, Tracy Caulkins set a U.S. record of 1:10.40.

1984 Los Angeles C: 30, N: 21, D: 8.2. WR: 1:08.51 (Ute Geweniger)

1. Petra van Staveren	HOL	1:09.88	OR
2. Anne Ottenbrite	CAN	1:10.69	
3. Cathérine Poirot	FRA	1:10.70	
4. Tracy Caulkins	USA	1:10.88	
5. Eva-Marie Håkansson	SWE	1:11.14	
6. Hiroko Nagasaki	JPN	1:11.33	
7. Susan Rapp	USA	1:11.45	
8. Jean Hill	GBR	1:11.82	

Three weeks after the Olympic final, 15-year-old Sylvia Gerasch of East Germany set a world record of 1:08.29 at the Friendship Games. Second place went to fellow East German Ute Geweniger in 1:08.59, and third to Larissa Belokon of the Soviet Union in 1:09.63.

1988 Seoul C: 42, N: 27, D: 9.23. WR: 1:07.91 (Silke Hörner)

1. Tania Dangalakova (Bogomilova)	BUL	1:07.95	OR
2. Antoaneta Frenkeva	BUL	1:08.74	
3. Silke Hörner	GDR	1:08.83	
4. Allison Higson	CAN	1:08.86	
5. Yelena Volkova	SOV/RUS	1:09.24	
6. Tracey McFarlane	USA	1:09.60	
7. Huang Xiaomin	CHN	1:10.53	
8. Annett Rex	GDR	1:10.67	

In 1987 Tania Dangalakova, the reigning European champion in the 200-meter breaststroke, made a move not uncommon among 23-year-old female swimmers: she put aside her competitive career to have a baby. But the following year she did something highly unusual: she staged a successful comeback. In the preliminary round she set an Olympic record of 1:08.35. This time was matched two heats later by the overwhelming favorite, Silke Hörner. Hörner, the world record holder at 100 meters, had won the 200-meter gold medal with a world record two days earlier. In the 100-meter final Hörner swam the first 50 meters in 31.58, faster than world record pace. Dangalakova was right behind her. Prior to her pregnancy, Dangalakova had had a reputation for swimming a fast first half and then dying badly for the remainder of the race. In fact that is exactly what she did in the 200-meter final. This time, however, it was Hörner who struggled to the finish line while Dangalakova took the lead at 80 meters and went on to become Bulgaria's first Olympic swimming champion. She was so overcome by emotion after her victory that she collapsed in tears and was unable to speak to the press.

1992 Barcelona C: 43, N: 31, D: 7.29. WR: 1:07.91 (Silke Hörner)
1. Yelena Rudkovskaya   BLR   1:08.00
2. N. Anita Nall   USA   1:08.17
3. Samantha Riley   AUS   1:09.25
4. Guylaine Cloutier   CAN   1:09.71
5. Jana Dörries   GER   1:09.77
6. Gabriella Csépe   HUN   1:10.19
7. Manuela Dalla Valle   ITA   1:10.39
8. Daniela Brendel   GER   1:11.05

The 19-year-old daughter of a Minsk trolley car driver, Rudkovskaya led from start to finish. The first name of silver medalist Anita Nall is really Nadia. While baby Anita was emerging from her mother's womb, her father and the obstetrician were watching Nadia Comǎneci earn perfect tens on television at the 1976 Olympics.

200-METER BREASTSTROKE

1896–1920 not held

1924 C: 15, N: 8, D: 7.18. WR: 3:20.4 (Irene Gilbert)
1. Lucy Morton   GBR   3:33.2   OR
2. Agnes Geraghty   USA   3:34.0
3. Gladys Carson   GBR   3:35.4
4. Vivan Pettersson   SWE   3:37.6
5. Irene Gilbert   GBR   3:38.0
6. Laury Koster   LUX   3:39.2
7. Hjördis Töpel   SWE   3:47.6

The first qualifying heat was won by Marie Baron of Holland in 3:22.6, with Agnes Geraghty second in 3:27.6. Baron was disqualified, however, for making a faulty turn. Geraghty led the final for 150 meters, but she couldn't withstand the surprising closing rush of 26-year-old Lucy Morton.

1928 Amsterdam C: 21, N: 12, D: 8.9. WR: 3:11.2 (Lotte Mühe)
1. Hildegard Schrader   GER   3:12.6
2. Mietje "Marie" Baron   HOL   3:15.2
3. Lotte Mühe   GER   3:17.6
4. Else Jacobsen   DEN   3:19.0
5. Margaret Hoffman   USA   3:19.2
6. Brita Hazelius   SWE   3:23.0

Lotte Mühe broke Marie Baron's world record on July 15, but three weeks later in Amsterdam it was her teammate, 18-year-old Hilde Schrader, who was in control. Her opening heat time of 3:11.6 bettered the Olympic record by 16 seconds. In the semifinals Schrader equaled Mühe's world record. The final was her slowest race, but with good reason: the straps of her bathing suit broke. She was able to finish, but after the race she had to stay in the water until her suit could be fixed.

1932 Los Angeles C: 11, N: 7, D: 8.9. WR: 3:03.4 (Else Jacobsen)
1. Clare Dennis   AUS   3:06.3   OR
2. Hideko Maehata   JPN   3:06.4
3. Else Jacobsen   DEN   3:07.1
4. Margery Hinton   GBR   3:11.7
5. Margaret Hoffman   USA   3:11.8
6. Anne Govednik   USA   3:16.0
7. Jane Cadwell   USA   3:18.2

On August 6, Clare Dennis, a 16-year-old from Sydney, set an Olympic record of 3:08.2 in winning her preliminary heat. After the race, she was approached by the American swimmer Buster Crabbe. Crabbe advised her to begin the final by taking three strokes underwater before surfacing after her dive. He also urged her to demoralize her opponents by touching first at each turn. Three days later, Dennis followed Crabbe's instructions to the letter. Mere inches separated Dennis and Jacobsen for the first 175 meters. Jacobsen wilted slightly at the end, enabling the fast-finishing Maehata to beat her by a foot for second place.

1936 Berlin C: 23, N: 12, D: 8.11. WR: 3:00.4 (Hideko Maehata)
1. Hideko Maehata   JPN   3:03.6
2. Martha Geneger   GER   3:04.2
3. Inge Sörensen   DEN   3:07.8
4. Johanna "Hanni" Hölzner   GER   3:09.5
5. Johanna Waalberg   HOL   3:09.5
6. Doris Storey   GBR   3:09.7
7. Jeannette Kastein   HOL   3:12.8

The year 1936 saw the first Olympic appearance of the controversial butterfly stroke, in which the swimmer recovers her arms above the water rather than under. The first woman to try the stroke in the Olympics was Lenk of Brazil who was eliminated in the semifinals. Silver medalist Martha Geneger was 14 years old, while bronze medalist Inge Sörensen was only 12 years and 24 days old.

Sörensen is the youngest athlete ever to win an Olympic medal in an individual event. By contrast, Hideko Maehata, who set an Olympic record of 3:01.9 in her preliminary heat, was an elderly 22. Maehata brought a small piece of paper with a prayer on it to the starting platform. She read it one last time before the final and then ate it.

1948 London C: 22, N: 14, D: 8.3. WR: 2:49.2 (Petronella van Vliet)
1. Petronella van Vliet   HOL   2:57.2
2. Beatrice Lyons   AUS   2:57.7
3. Éva Novák   HUN   3:00.2
4. Éva Székely   HUN   3:02.5
5. Adriana de Groot   HOL   3:06.2
6. Elizabeth Church   GBR   3:06.1
7. Antonia Hom   HOL   3:07.5
8. Jytte Hansen   DEN   3:08.1

De Groot was awarded fifth place despite the fact that her official time was slower than that of Church.

1952 Helsinki C: 34, N: 19, D: 7.29. WR: 2:48.5 (Éva Novák)
1. Éva Székely   HUN   2:51.7   OR
2. Éva Novák   HUN   2:54.4
3. Helen "Elenor" Gordon   GBR   2:57.6
4. Klára Killermann   HUN   2:57.6
5. Jytte Hansen   DEN   2:57.8
6. Maria Havrysh   SOV/UKR   2:58.9
7. Ulla-Britt Eklund   SWE   3:01.8
8. Petronella Garritsen   HOL   3:02.1

Like 100-meter freestyle winner Katalin Szöke, 25-year-old Éva Székely was married to a member of the 1952 champion Hungarian water polo team. Husband Dezsö Gyarmati also won water polo gold medals in 1956 and 1964. In 1972, their daughter Andrea earned medals in the backstroke and butterfly. Székely was the first female butterfly stroker to win a gold medal. Following the 1952 Olympics, the breaststroke and butterfly were separated into two different events.

1956 Melbourne C: 14, N: 10, D: 11.30. WR: 2:46.4 (Adelaide den Haan)
1. Ursula Happe   GER   2:53.1   OR
2. Éva Székely   HUN   2:54.8
3. Eva-Maria ten Elsen   GDR   2:55.1
4. Vinka Jeričevič   YUG   2:55.8
5. Klára Killermann   HUN   2:56.1
6. Helen "Elenor" Gordon   GBR   2:56.1
7. Mary Sears   USA   2:57.2
8. Christine Gosden   GBR   2:59.2

World record holder Ada den Haan was unable to compete because the Netherlands withdrew from the 1956 Games to protest the Soviet invasion of Hungary.

1960 Rome C: 29, N: 19, D: 9.27. WR: 2:50.2 (Wiltrud Urselmann)
1. Anita Lonsbrough   GBR   2:49.5   WR
2. Wiltrud Urselmann   GER   2:50.0

3. Barbara Göbel   GDR   2:53.6
4. Adelaide den Haan   HOL   2:54.4
5. Margareta Kok   HOL   2:54.6
6. Anne Warner   USA   2:55.4
7. Patty Kempner   USA   2:55.5
8. Dorrit Kristensen   DEN   2:55.7

In 1957 underwater stroking was banned from breaststroke competitions, which explains why the world record was slower in 1960 than it was in 1956. Nineteen-year-old Anita Lonsbrough, a clerk for the Huddersfield Corporation in Yorkshire, faced a problem not uncommon to amateur athletes in Great Britain. Far from being appreciative of the free publicity that her swimming exploits brought them, her employers actually docked her wages whenever she took time off for training. Her victory in Rome was the result of iron nerves and perfect tactics. She trailed Urselmann by two seconds at the half-way mark, then she gradually closed the gap, catching the tiring German with 25 meters to go. Urselmann surprised Lonsbrough with a final spurt, but Lonsbrough held on for the victory.

1964 Tokyo C: 26, N: 15, D: 10.12. WR: 2:45.4 (Halyna Prozumenshchykova)
1. Halyna Prozumenshchykova   SOV/UKR   2:46.4   OR
2. Claudia Kolb   USA   2:47.6
3. Svetlana Babanina   SOV/RUS   2:48.6
4. Stella Mitchell   GBR   2:49.0
5. Jill Slattery   GBR   2:49.6
6. Bärbel Grimmer   GDR   2:51.0
7. Klena Bimolt   HOL   2:51.3
8. Ursula Küper   GDR   2:53.9

Prozumenshchykova, a 15-year-old schoolgirl from Sevastopol, let Babanina set the pace for 100 meters and then surged ahead to win the U.S.S.R.'s first gold medal in swimming.

1968 Mexico City C: 21, N: 20, D: 10.23. WR: 2:38.5 (Catie Ball)
1. Sharon Wichman   USA   2:44.4   OR
2. Djurdjica Bjedov   YUG/CRO   2:46.4
3. Halyna Prozumenshchykova   SOV/UKR   2:47.0
4. Alla Grebennikova   SOV/RUS   2:47.1
5. Cathy Jamison   USA   2:48.4
6. Svetlana Babanina   SOV/RUS   2:48.4
7. Chieno Shibata   JPN   2:51.5
8. Ana Norbis   URU   2:51.9

Prozumenshchykova was leading after 175 meters when she suddenly ran out of energy and barely hung on for third place. She had to be administered oxygen as soon as the race was over. Sharon Wichman's victory meant that the gold medals in the first ten Olympic women's 200-meter breaststroke competitions had been won by swimmers from eight different nations.

1972 Munich C: 39, N: 22, D: 8.29. WR: 2:38.5 (Catie Ball)
1. Beverley Whitfield   AUS   2:41.71   OR
2. Dana Schoenfield   USA   2:42.05

3. Halyna Stepanova (Prozumenshchykova)	SOV/UKR	2:42.36	
4. Claudia Clevenger	USA	2:42.88	
5. Petra Nows	GER	2:43.41	
6. Ágnes Kiss-Kaczander	HUN	2:43.41	
7. Lyudmila Porubaiko	SOV/RUS	2:44.48	
8. Éva Kiss	HUN	2:45.12	

As usual, Halyna Prozumenshchykova took the early lead and eventually opened a four-meter gap. But just as she had done four years earlier, the Soviet swimmer, now Halyna Stepanova, "died" in the final 50 meters and faded to third place. Meanwhile, 18-year-old Bev Whitfield, in last place after 50 meters and fourth place after 150 meters, sprinted home to pass Stepanova and stave off a final challenge from Schoenfield. As she climbed out of the pool, Whitfield called out to her teammates, "For once I kept my cool. This is the greatest feeling in the world."

1976 Montreal C: 38, N: 21, D: 7.21. WR: 2:34.99 (Karla Linke)

1. Marina Koshevaia	SOV/RUS	2:33.35	WR
2. Maryna Yurchenya	SOV/UKR	2:36.08	
3. Lyubov Rusanova	SOV/RUS	2:36.22	
4. Hannelore Anke	GDR	2:36.49	
5. Karla Linke	GDR	2:36.97	
6. Carola Nitschke	GDR	2:38.27	
7. Margaret Kelly	GBR	2:38.37	
8. Deborah Rudd	GBR	2:39.01	

Koshevaia moved up from fifth to first during the third 50 meters and then pulled away to the most decisive women's breaststroke victory in Olympic history.

1980 Moscow C: 25, N: 19, D: 7.23. WR: 2:28.36 (Lina Kačiušytė)

1. Lina Kačiušytė	SOV/LIT	2:29.54	OR
2. Svetlana Varganova	SOV/RUS	2:29.61	
3. Yulia Bogdanova	SOV/RUS	2:32.39	
4. Susanne Nielsson	DEN	2:32.75	
5. Irena Fleissnerová	CZE	2:33.23	
6. Ute Geweniger	GDR	2:34.34	
7. Bettina Löbel	GDR	2:34.51	
8. Sylvia Rinka	GDR	2:35.38	

Svetlana Varganova led for almost the entire race while Lithuanian Lina Kačiušytė improved from last place at 50 meters to fourth place at the halfway mark and second place two and a half seconds behind Varganova, with 50 meters to go. An impressive finishing spurt earned 17-year-old Kačiušytė the gold medal.

1984 Los Angeles C: 23, N: 16, D: 7.30. WR: 2:28.36 (Lina Kačiušytė)

1. Anne Ottenbrite	CAN	2:30.38
2. Susan Rapp	USA	2:31.15
3. Ingrid Lempereur	BEL	2:31.40
4. Hiroko Nagasaki	JPN	2:32.93
5. Sharon Kellett	AUS	2:33.60
6. Ute Hasse	GER	2:33.82
7. Susannah Brownsdon	GBR	2:35.07
8. Kimberly Rhodenbaugh	USA	2:35.51

The term "accident-prone" was meant for people like Anne Ottenbrite of Whitby, Ontario. Fortunately for Ottenbrite, all of her accidents had been relatively minor. Having previously survived bloody encounters with a plateglass window and a potato processor, on May 21st she dislocated her right kneecap while showing off a new pair of shoes. Unable to take part in the Canadian trials, she was placed on the team anyway. During her brief stay in Los Angeles before the Olympics began, Ottenbrite suffered a whiplash injury to her neck when the van in which she was traveling crashed into the back of another car. Relaxing back at the Olympic Village, she strained a thigh muscle while playing a video game.

Despite all of these mishaps, the 18-year-old Ottenbrite moved ahead of Hiroko Nagasaki after the midway point of the Olympic final and held off the closing rushes of Rapp and Lempereur to win a gold medal. Ottenbrite's victory was a mild surprise, but the real shocker was the performance of 15-year-old Ingrid Lempereur, who bettered her pre-Olympic personal best by 6.36 seconds.

At the Friendship Games on August 20th, Larissa Belokon finished first in 2:29.13 and Sylvia Gerasch second in 2:29.62.

1988 Seoul C: 43, N: 27, D: 9.21. WR: 2:27.27 (Allison Higson)

1. Silke Hörner	GDR	2:26.71	WR
2. Huang Xiaomin	CHN	2:27.49	
3. Antoaneta Frenkeva	BUL	2:28.34	
4. Tania Dangalakova (Bogomilova)	BUL	2:28.43	
5. Yulia Bocharova	SOV/UKR	2:28.54	
6. Ingrid Lempereur	BEL	2:29.42	
7. Allison Higson	CAN	2:29.60	
8. Manuela Dalla Valle	ITA	2:29.86	

Hörner, whose hobby was collecting palm trees in her Leipzig apartment, took the lead from Dangalakova in the third quarter of the race and recaptured the world record she had lost to Higson four months earlier. It was Hörner's third world record at 200 meters.

1992 Barcelona C: 39, N: 28, D: 7.27. WR: 2:25.35 (N. Anita Nall)

1. Kyoko Iwasaki	JPN	2:26.65	OR
2. Lin Li	CHN	2:26.85	
3. N. Anita Nall	USA	2:26.88	
4. Yelena Rudkovskaya	BLR	2:28.47	
5. Guylaine Cloutier	CAN	2:29.88	
6. Nathalie Giguère	CAN	2:30.11	
7. Manuela Dalla Valle	ITA	2:31.21	
8. Alicja Peczak	POL	2:31.76	

On March 2, 1992, Anita Nall, then 15 years old, broke the world record at the United States Olympic trials not once but twice. In the morning she swam 2:25.92 in her qualifying heat and then followed up with a 2:25.35 in the final. Nall won her Olympic heat in 2:27.77, but, much to her surprise, right beside her was 5-foot 1-inch, 99-pound Kyoko Iwasaki in 2:27.78. Six days earlier, on the same day that Nall celebrated her 16th birthday, Iwasaki turned 14 years old. In the final, Nall immediately went into the lead, while Iwasaki lingered in sixth place after 50 meters before moving up to third at the halfway mark, and second with a lap to go. She passed the fading world record holder in the closing meters, as did Lin Li. Iwasaki beat her pre-Olympic personal best by 4.43 seconds while Lin improved hers by 3.94 seconds. Iwasaki is the youngest swimmer ever to win an Olympic gold medal.

100-METER BUTTERFLY

1896–1952 not held

1956 Melbourne C: 12, N: 8, D: 12.5. WR: 1:10.5 (Aartje Voorbij)

1. Shelly Mann	USA	1:11.0	OR
2. Nancy Ramey	USA	1:11.9	
3. Mary Sears	USA	1:14.4	
4. Mária Littomeritzky	HUN	1:14.9	
5. Beverly Bainbridge	AUS	1:15.2	
6. Jutta Langenau	GDR	1:17.4	
7. Elizabeth Whittall	CAN	1:17.9	
8. Sara Barber	CAN	1:18.4	

With world record holder Atie Voorbij absent because of the Dutch boycott, the inaugural women's butterfly event was swept by the Americans. Crippled by polio at the age of six, Shelly Mann began swimming to regain strength in her arms and legs.

1960 Rome C: 25, N: 16, D: 8.30. WR: 1:09.1 (Nancy Ramey)

1. Carolyn Schuler	USA	1:09.5	OR
2. Marianne Heemskerk	HOL	1:10.4	
3. Janice Andrew	AUS	1:12.2	
4. Sheila Watt	GBR	1:13.3	
5. Aartje Voorbij	HOL	1:13.3	
6. Zinaida Belovetskaya	SOV/RUS	1:13.3	
7. Kristina Larsson	SWE	1:13.6	
DNF: Carolyn Wood (USA)			

Fourteen-year old Carolyn Wood had beaten Carolyn Schuler at the U.S. trials. A close second after 70 meters of the Olympic final, Wood swallowed too much water, became confused, and stopped swimming.

1964 Tokyo C: 31, N: 16, D: 10.16 WR (110 yards): 1:05 1 (Ada Kok)

1. Sharon Stouder	USA	1:04.7	WR
2. Ada Kok	HOL	1:05.6	
3. Kathleen Ellis	USA	1:06.0	
4. Ella Pyrhönen	FIN	1:07.3	
5. Donna De Varona	USA	1:08.0	
6. Heike Hustede	GER	1:08.5	
7. Eiko Takahashi	JPN	1:09.1	
8. Mary Stewart	CAN	1:10.0	

Fifteen-year-old Sharon Stouder won 3 gold medals and 1 silver at the Tokyo Games.

1968 Mexico City C: 28, N: 21, D: 10.21. WR: 1:04.5 (Ada Kok)

1. Lynette McClements	AUS	1:05.5
2. Ellie Daniel	USA	1:05.8
3. Susan Shields	USA	1:06.2
4. Ada Kok	HOL	1:06.2
5. Andréa Gyarmati	HUN	1:06.8
6. Heike Hustede	GER	1:06.9
7. Toni Hewitt	USA	1:07.5
8. Helga Lindner	GDR	1:07.6

Lyn McClements was a 17-year-old stenographer from Perth.

1972 Munich C: 30, N: 21, D: 9.1. WR: 1:03.9 (Mayumi Aoki)

1. Mayumi Aoki	JPN	1:03.34	WR
2. Roswitha Beier	GDR	1:03.61	
3. Andréa Gyarmati	HUN	1:03.73	
4. Deena Deardurff	USA	1:03.95	
5. Dana Shrader	USA	1:03.98	
6. Ellie Daniel	USA	1:04.08	
7. Gudrun Beckmann	GER	1:04.15	
8. Noriko Asano	JPN	1:04.25	

Andréa Gyarmati was the daughter of 1952 breaststroke gold medalist Éva Székely and Dezsö Gyarmati, who won three gold medals in water polo. In the semifinals she set a world record of 1:03.80. But in the final, Aoki moved up from seventh place at the midrace turn to recapture the record.

1976 Montreal C: 39, N: 26, D: 7.2. WR: 1:00.13 (Kornelia Ender)

1. Kornelia Ender	GDR	1:00.13	EWR
2. Andrea Pollack	GDR	1:00.98	
3. Wendy Boglioli	USA	1:01.17	
4. Camille Wright	USA	1:01.41	
5. Rosemarie Gabriel (Kother)	GDR	1:01.56	
6. Wendy Quirk	CAN	1:01.75	
7. Lelei Fonoimoana	USA	1:01.95	
8. Tamara Shelofastova	SOV/RUS	1:02.74	

At 7:48 p.m. on July 22, 1976, Kornelia Ender won the 100-meter butterfly final in world record time. At 8:03 she descended from the victory platform and went to the dressing room. At 8:08 she returned to the pool for the final of the 200-meter freestyle. At 8:13 she was racing through the water again, and by 8:15 she had won her second gold medal in 27 minutes.

1980 Moscow C: 24, N: 18, D: 7.24. WR: 59.26 (Mary T. Meagher)

1. Caren Metschuck	GDR	1:00.42
2. Andrea Pollack	GDR	1:00.90
3. Christiane Knacke	GDR	1:01.44
4. Ann Osgerby	GBR	1:02.21
5. Lisa Curry	AUS	1:02.40
6. Agneta Mårtensson	SWE	1:02.61
7. Maria del Milagro Paris	CRC	1:02.89
8. Janet Osgerby	GBR	1:02.90

The British representatives, Ann and Janet Osgerby, were 17-year-old twins from Chorley, Lancashire. Ann was 20 minutes older and 0.69 seconds faster. Missing from the competition due to the anti-Soviet boycott were world record holder Mary T. Meagher and Tracy Caulkins, who clocked 59.41 and 1:00.75, respectively, at the U.S. Outdoor National on August 2.

1984 Los Angeles C: 35, N: 23, D: 8.2. WR: 57.93 (Mary T. Meagher)

1. Mary T. Meagher	USA	59.26
2. Jenna Johnson	USA	1:00.19
3. Karin Seick	GER	1:01.36
4. Annemarie Verstappen	HOL	1:01.56
5. Michelle MacPherson	CAN	1:01.58
6. Janet Tibbits	AUS	1:01.78
7. Cornelia van Bentum	HOL	1:01.94
8. Ina Beyermann	GER	1:02.11

In 1980, 15-year-old Mary T. Meagher of Louisville, Kentucky, was the world record holder in both butterfly events and the favorite to win two gold medals in Moscow until the anti-Soviet boycott forced her to stay home. The following year she lowered her world record by a phenomenal 1.33 seconds. She never approached that time again, but neither did anyone else. In Los Angeles in 1984, Meagher set an Olympic record of 59.05 in the preliminaries and then overcame a fast start by teammate Jenna Johnson to win the first of her three gold medals.

1988 Seoul C: 40, N: 28, D: 9.23. WR: 57.93 (Mary T. Meagher)

1. Kristin Otto	GDR	59.00 OR
2. Birte Weigang	GDR	59.45
3. Qian Hong	CHN	59.52
4. Catherine Plewinski	FRA	59.58
5. Janel Jorgensen	USA	1:00.48
6. Cornelia van Bentum	HOL	1:00.62
7. Mary T. Meagher	USA	1:00.97
8. Wang Xiaohong	CHN	1:01.15

Kristin Otto won her fourth gold medal of the Seoul Games. Birte Weigang is the daughter of Horst Weigang, who won a bronze medal as the goalkeeper for East Germany's 1964 football team.

1992 Barcelona C: 49, N: 34, D: 7.30. WR: 57.93 (Mary T. Meagher)

1. Qian Hong	CHN	58.62 OR
2. Christine Ahmann-Leighton	USA	58.74
3. Catherine Plewinski	FRA	59.01
4. Wang Xiaohong	CHN	59.10
5. Susan O'Neill	AUS	59.69
6. Summer Sanders	USA	59.82
7. Franziska van Almsick	GER	1:00.70
8. Rie Shito	JPN	1:01.16

For nine years after Mary T. Meagher set her world record of 57.93 on August 18, 1981, no one broke the 59-second barrier again, not even Meagher herself. Finally, at the Asian Games in Beijing on September 27, 1990, two Chinese swimmers, Wang Xiaohong and Qian Hong, swam 58.87 and 58.89, respectively. The next sub-59 100-meter butterfly didn't come until the 1992 U.S. Olympic

trials, when Crissy Ahmann-Leighton beat a strong field in 58.61. At the Olympics, Ahmann-Leighton burst into the lead immediately and led Wang and Qian by half a body length at the turn. But it was Qian who had the strongest finish and managed to outtouch Ahmann-Leighton by about eight inches.

200-METER BUTTERFLY

1896-1964 not held

1968 Mexico City C: 21, N: 16, D: 10.24. WR (220 yards): 2:21.0 (Ada Kok)

1. Ada Kok	HOL	2:24.7 OR
2. Helga Lindner	GDR	2:24.8
3. Ellie Daniel	USA	2:25.9
4. Toni Hewitt	USA	2:26.2
5. Heike Hustede	GER	2:27.9
6. Diane Giebel	USA	2:31.7
7. Margaret Auton	GBR	2:33.2
8. Yasuko Fujii	JPN	2:34.3

Six-foot, 183-pound Ada Kok, "The Gentle Giant," had experienced nothing but disappointment in the Olympics. Because of her world records and her general domination of international competitions, she had been expected to win gold medals, but in Tokyo she had to settle for two silver medals in the 100-meter butterfly and the medley relay. Four years later, in Mexico City, Kok was part of the Dutch medley relay team that finished seventh. Then, in the 100-meter butterfly, she finished a disappointing fourth. This left her one last chance for an Olympic victory—the 200-meter butterfly. Her chances seemed slim after her previous defeats, but she recorded the fastest time of the eliminations. In the final she was third at the final turn behind Heike Hustede and Helga Lindner, but Kok's powerful finish gave her a popular and well-deserved victory.

1972 Munich C: 24, N: 17, D: 9.4. WR: 2:16.62 (Karen Moe)

1. Karen Moe	USA	2:15.57 WR
2. Lynn Colella	USA	2:16.34
3. Ellie Daniel	USA	2:16.74
4. Rosemarie Kother	GDR	2:17.11
5. Noriko Asano	JPN	2:19.50
6. Helga Lindner	GDR	2:20.47
7. Gail Neall	AUS	2:21.88
8. Mayumi Aoki	JPN	2:22.84

Karen Moe let Daniel and Kother set the pace for 150 meters and then took the lead after the final turn.

1976 Montreal C: 32, N: 19, D: 7.19. WR: 2:11.22 (Rosemarie Gabriel [Kother])

1. Andrea Pollack	GDR	2:11.41 OR
2. Ulrike Tauber	GDR	2:12.50
3. Rosemarie Gabriel (Kother)	GDR	2:12.86
4. Karen Thornton (Moe)	USA	2:12.90
5. Wendy Quirk	CAN	2:13.68

6. Cheryl Gibson	CAN	2:13.91
7. Tamara Shelofastova	SOV/RUS	2:14.26
8. Natalia Popova	SOV/RUS	2:14.50

1980 Moscow C: 21, N: 14, D: 7.21. WR: 2:07.01 (Mary T. Meagher)

1. Ines Geissler	GDR	2:10.44	OR
2. Sybille Schönrock	GDR	2:10.45	
3. Michelle Ford	AUS	2:11.66	
4. Andrea Pollack	GDR	2:12.13	
5. Dorota Brzozowska	POL	2:14.12	
6. Ann Osgerby	GBR	2:14.83	
7. Agneta Martensson	SWE	2:15.22	
8. Alla Grishchenkova	SOV/RUS	2:15.70	

Geissler led at 50 meters and 100 meters, while Schönrock was first to touch at 150. In the end, the 17-year-old Geissler reached the wall in time to win the closest of victories. However neither woman's time came close to the performance of 15-year-old Mary T. Meagher of Cincinnati, who set a world record of 2:06.37 at the U.S. Outdoor National nine days after the Olympic final.

1984 Los Angeles C: 29, N: 18, D: 8.4. WR: 2:05.96 (Mary T. Meagher)

1. Mary T. Meagher	USA	2:06.90	OR
2. Karen Phillips	AUS	2:10.56	
3. Ina Beyermann	GER	2:11.91	
4. Nancy Hogshead	USA	2:11.98	
5. Samantha Purvis	GBR	2:12.33	
6. Naoko Kume	JPN	2:12.57	
7. Sonja Hausladen	AUT	2:15.38	
8. Cornelia van Bentum	HOL	2:17.39	

Mary T. Meagher led from start to finish and won by seven meters. Her time of 2:06.90 was her fastest since her 1981 world record and gave her the seven fastest times ever. Silver medalist Karen Phillips bettered her pre-Olympic best time by four seconds. First place at the Friendship Games on August 26 went to 1980 Olympic champion Ines Geissler with a time of 2:09.96.

1988 Seoul C: 28, N: 21, D: 9.25. WR: 2:05.96 (Mary T. Meagher)

1. Kathleen Nord	GDR	2:09.51
2. Birte Weigang	GDR	2:09.91
3. Mary T. Meagher	USA	2:10.80
4. Stela Pura	ROM	2:11.28
5. Trina Radke	USA	2:11.55
6. Kiyomi Takahashi	JPN	2:11.62
7. Wang Xiaohong	CHN	2:12.34
8. Cornelia van Bentum	HOL	2:13.17

Mary T. Meagher entered the Olympics as the defending champion, the holder of the 11 fastest times in history and the fastest time of the year (2:09.13 at the U.S. trials). But, like most of the U.S. swimmers in 1988, she was unable to match her trials time and suffered only her third 200-meter butterfly loss in nine years. Twenty-two-year-old Kathleen Nord of Magdeburg overcame team-mate Birte Weigang in the last 50 meters to earn the victory.

1992 Barcelona C: 32, N: 23, D: 7.31. WR: 2:05.96 (Mary T. Meagher)

1. Summer Sanders	USA	2:08.67
2. Wang Xiaohong	CHN	2:09.01
3. Susan O'Neill	AUS	2:09.03
4. Mika Haruna	JPN	2:09.88
5. Rie Shito	JPN	2:10.24
6. Ina "Angie" Wester-Krieg	USA	2:11.46
7. Mette Jacobsen	DEN	2:11.87
8. Ilaria Tocchini	ITA	2:13.78

The defending world champion, 19-year-old Summer Sanders, generally started fast and tried to hold on for the victory. Already in the Barcelona Olympics she had lost both individual medley finals after leading with a lap to go. This time Sanders held back in third place while Susan O'Neill set off at breakneck speed, followed closely by Wang Xiaohong. With one lap left, Sanders was still one-half second behind O'Neill, but the Australian was running out of gas. With each stroke Sanders clawed closer, finally moving ahead in the final meters, while Wang outtouched O'Neill by an inch to take the silver. The race was so fast that the first seven finishers all set personal records.

200-METER INDIVIDUAL MEDLEY

In individual medley races the order of strokes is butterfly, backstroke, breaststroke, and freestyle.

1896–1964 not held

1968 Mexico City C: 39, N: 26, D: 10.20. WR: 2:23.5 (Claudia Kolb)

1. Claudia Kolb	USA	2:24.7	OR
2. Susan Pedersen	USA	2:28.8	
3. Jan Henne	USA	2:31.4	
4. Sabine Steinbach	GDR	2:31.4	
5. Yoshimi Nishigawa	JPN	2:33.7	
6. Marianne Seydel	GDR	2:33.7	
7. Larissa Zakharova	SOV	2:37.0	

DISQ: Shelagh Ratcliffe (GBR)

When she was 14 years old, Claudia Kolb of Santa Clara, California, earned a surprise silver medal in the 200-meter breaststroke. Four years later she overwhelmed her opposition to win both the 200-meter and 400-meter individual medleys.

1972 Munich C: 44, N: 26, D: 8.28. WR: 2:23.5 (Claudia Kolb)

1. Shane Gould	AUS	2:23.07	WR
2. Kornelia Ender	GDR	2:23.59	
3. Lynn Vidali	USA	2:24.06	
4. Jennifer Bartz	USA	2:24.55	
5. Leslie Cliff	CAN	2:24.83	
6. Evelyn Stolze	GDR	2:25.90	

7. Yoshimi Nishigawa	JPN	2:26.35
8. Carolyn Woods	USA	2:27.42

Lynn Vidali led by over a second after 150 meters, but Shane Gould used her freestyle strength to catch her 20 meters later and win the first of her three gold medals. In second place was 13-year-old Kornelia Ender, who won the first of her eight Olympic medals.

1976–1980 not held

1984 Los Angeles C: 27, N: 21, D: 8.3. WR: 2:11.73 (Ute Geweniger)

1. Tracy Caulkins	USA	2:12.64	OR
2. Nancy Hogshead	USA	2:15.17	
3. Michele Pearson	AUS	2:15.92	
4. Lisa Curry	AUS	2:16.75	
5. Christiane Pielke	GER	2:17.82	
6. Manuela Dalla Valle	ITA	2:19.69	
7. Petra Zindler	GER	2:19.86	
8. Katrine Bomstad	NOR	2:20.48	

Tracy Caulkins won the second of her three gold medals. Three weeks later, the Friendship Games competition was won by world record holder Ute Geweniger in 2:11.79. In second place with a time of 2:14.56 was Yelena Dendeberova of the Soviet Union.

1988 Seoul C: 36, N: 24, D: 9.24. WR: 2:11.73 (Ute Geweniger)

1. Daniela Hunger	GDR	2:12.59	OR
2. Yelena Dendeberova	SOV/RUS	2:13.31	
3. Noemi Lung	ROM	2:14.85	
4. Jodie Clatworthy	AUS	2:16.31	
5. Marianne Muis	HOL	2:16.40	
6. Aneta Patrascoiu	ROM	2:16.70	
7. Lin Li	CHN	2:17.42	
8. Whitney Hedgepeth	USA	2:17.99	

Sixteen-year-old Daniela Hunger of Berlin overcame Dendeberova in the final 50 meters.

1992 Barcelona C: 43, N: 31, D: 7.30. WR: 2:11.73 (Ute Geweniger)

1. Lin Li	CHN	2:11.65	WR
2. Summer Sanders	USA	2:11.91	
3. Daniela Hunger	GER	2:13.92	
4. Yelena Dendeberova	RUS	2:15.47	
5. Elli Overton	AUS	2:15.76	
6. Marianne Limpert	CAN	2:17.09	
7. Nancy Sweetnam	CAN	2:17.13	
8. Ewa Synowska	POL	2:18.85	

The final was a terrific duel between Lin Li of Nantung, in Jiangsu Province, and Summer Sanders of Roseville, California. At the 1991 world championships, Lin had come from behind to edge Sanders by .66 seconds. This time the race was even closer. Sanders used her butterfly strength (the next day she won the gold medal in the 200-meter butterfly) to take a lead of .42 seconds after 50 meters. Lin moved ahead on the backstroke lap, but

Sanders regained the lead with the breaststroke. Lin exploited Sanders' freestyle weakness to inch ahead again with 30 meters to go. Sanders made one last challenge in the race to the wall, but Lin held on to win by about 16 inches. Her time of 2:11.65 broke Ute Geweniger's 11-year-old world record.

400-METER INDIVIDUAL MEDLEY

1896–1960 not held

1964 Tokyo C: 22, N: 12, D: 10.17. WR: 5:14.9 (Donna De Varona)

1. Donna De Varona	USA	5:18.7	OR
2. Sharon Finneran	USA	5:24.1	
3. Martha Randall	USA	5:24.2	
4. Veronika Holletz	GDR	5:25.6	
5. Linda McGill	AUS	5:28.4	
6. Elisabeth Heukels	HOL	5:30.3	
7. Anita Lonsbrough	GBR	5:30.5	
8. Márta Egerváry	HUN	5:38.4	

Donna De Varona was a popular and much-photographed winner. She later became a television sports commentator as well as an activist for women in sports.

1968 Mexico City C: 28, N: 19, D: 10.25. WR: 5:04.7 (Claudia Kolb)

1. Claudia Kolb	USA	5:08.5	OR
2. Lynn Vidali	USA	5:22.2	
3. Sabine Steinbach	GDR	5:25.3	
4. Susan Pedersen	USA	5:25.8	
5. Shelagh Ratcliffe	GBR	5:30.5	
6. Marianne Seydel	GDR	5:32.0	
7. Tui Shipston	NZE	5:34.6	
8. Laura Vaca	MEX	5:35.7	

Claudia Kolb won by 20 meters, the most decisive women's swimming victory in 40 years.

1972 Munich C: 38, N: 26, D: 8.31. WR: 5:04.7 (Claudia Kolb)

1. Gail Neall	AUS	5:02.97	WR
2. Leslie Cliff	CAN	5:03.57	
3. Novella Calligaris	ITA	5:03.99	
4. Jennifer Bartz	USA	5:05.56	
5. Evelyn Stolze	GDR	5:06.80	
6. Mary Montgomery	USA	5:09.98	
7. Lynn Vidali	USA	5:13.06	
8. Nina Petrova	SOV/RUS	5:15.68	

Gail Neall, from the Sydney suburb of Gordon, took the lead on the second lap and held it all the way through the backstroke and breaststroke legs. At the beginning of the freestyle, Leslie Cliff made her move and pulled ahead at the final turn. Neall fought back and drew even again with 30 meters to go. The two matched strokes for ten meters. Then Neall pushed ahead to gain the victory and break Claudia Kolb's four-year-old world record. A surprise winner, Neall bettered her personal best by seven seconds.

1976 Montreal C: 20, N: 11, D: 7.24. WR: 4:48.79 (Birgit Treiber)
1. Ulrike Tauber   GDR   4:42.77   WR
2. Cheryl Gibson   CAN   4:48.10
3. Becky Smith   CAN   4:50.48
4. Birgit Treiber   GDR   4:52.40
5. Sabine Kahle   GDR   4:53.50
6. Donnalee Wennerstrom   USA   4:55.34
7. Joann Baker   CAN   5:00.19
8. Monique Rodahl   NZE   5:00.21

Eighteen-year-old Ulrike Tauber of Karl-Marx Stadt bettered the world record by a phenomenal 6.02 seconds.

1980 Moscow C: 16, N: 11, D: 7.26. WR: 4:38.44 (Petra Schneider)
1. Petra Schneider   GDR   4:36.29   WR
2. Sharron Davies   GBR   4:46.83
3. Agnieszka Czopek   POL   4:48.17
4. Grit Slaby   GDR   4:48.54
5. Ulrike Tauber   GDR   4:49.18
6. Sonya Dangalakova   BUL   4:49.25
7. Olga Klevakina   SOV/RUS   4:50.91
8. Magdalena Bialas   POL   4:53.30

Once again the 400-meter individual medley was completely dominated by one swimmer. This time it was an easy win and new world record for 17-year-old Petra Schneider, who had been trained in part by her older teammate Ulrike Tauber. In the United States on July 30, Tracy Caulkins clocked 4:40.61 at the Outdoor National to bolster her position as second fastest female medley swimmer in the world.

1984 Los Angeles C: 18, N: 13, D: 7.29. WR: 4:36.10 (Petra Schneider)
1. Tracy Caulkins   USA   4:39.24
2. Suzanne Landells   AUS   4:48.30
3. Petra Zindler   GER   4:48.57
4. Susan Heon   USA   4:49.41
5. Nathalie Gingras   CAN   4:50.55
6. Donna McGinnis   CAN   4:50.65
7. Gaynor Stanley   GBR   4:52.83
8. Katrine Bomstad   NOR   4:53.28

Since 1978 Tracy Caulkins of Nashville, Tennessee, had set five world records, over 60 U.S. records and had won 48 U.S. national titles, twelve more than any other swimmer. All that was missing from her sterling career was an Olympic championship. That void was filled when she led the 400-meter individual medley from start to finish, winning by almost 15 meters.

1988 Seoul C: 30, N: 22, D: 9.19. WR: 4:36.10 (Petra Schneider)
1. Janet Evans   USA   4:37.76
2. Noemi Lung   ROM   4:39.46
3. Daniela Hunger   GDR   4:39.76
4. Yelena Dendeberova   SOV/RUS   4:40.44

5. Kathleen Nord   GDR   4:41.64
6. Jodie Clatworthy   AUS   4:45.86
7. Lin Li   CHN   4:47.05
8. Donna Procter   AUS   4:47.51

Janet Evans took command on the backstroke leg and won the first of her three gold medals.

1992 Barcelona C: 32, N: 21, D: 7.26. WR: 4:36.10 (Petra Schneider)
1. Krisztina Egerszegi   HUN   4:36.54
2. Lin Li   CHN   4:36.73
3. Summer Sanders   USA   4:37.58
4. Hayley Lewis   AUS   4:43.75
5. Hideko Hiranaka   JPN   4:46.24
6. Daniela Hunger   GER   4:47.57
7. Eri Kimura   JPN   4:47.78
8. Ewa Synowska   POL   4:53.32

Sanders, who later won the 200-meter butterfly, led by a body length after the butterfly leg. Egerszegi, who later won both backstroke golds, sailed past Sanders in the backstroke leg and moved ahead by more than two meters. The breaststroke was the great equalizer. Sanders recaptured the lead while Lin turned the race into a three-woman contest. Sanders, a weak freestyler, couldn't hold on. Egerszegi took the lead for good in the final lap and then held off Lin by a foot. Egerszegi and Lin swam the fastest times since Petra Schneider's 1982 world record.

4 × 100-METER FREESTYLE RELAY

Swimmers who took part in preliminary heats but not in finals are listed in brackets.

1896–1908 not held

1912 Stockholm T: 4, N; 4, D: 7.15.
1. GBR   (Isabella Moore, Jennie Fletcher, Annie   5:52.8   WR
        Speirs, Irene Steer)
2. GER   (Wally Dressel, Louise Otto, Hermine   6:04.6
        Stindt, Margarete Rosenberg)
3. AUT   (Margarete Adler, Klara Milch, Josephine   6:17.0
        Sticker, Berta Zahourek)
4. SWE   (Greta Johansson, Karin Lundgren,   —
        Sonja Johnsson, Vera Thulin)

Australia's two women swimmers, Fanny Durack and Mina Wylie, finished first and second in the individual race. They wanted to compete in the relay and offered to swim two legs each, but their proposal was rejected.

1920 Antwerp T: 3, N: 3, D: 8.29.
1. USA   (Margaret Woodbridge, Frances   5:11.6   WR
        Schroth, Irene Guest, Ethelda Bleibtrey)
2. GBR   (Hilda James, Constance Jeans, Char-   5;40.8
        lotte Radcliffe, Grace McKenzie)
3. SWE   (Aina Berg, Emy Machnow, Karin Nil-   5:43.6
        sson, Jane Gylling)

1924 Paris T: 6, N: 6, D: 7.18.
1. USA	(Gertrude Ederle, Euphrasia Donnelly, Ethel Lackie, Mariechen Wehselau)	4:58.8	WR
2. GBR	(Florence Barker, Grace McKenzie, Irene Vera Tanner, Constance Jeans)	5:17.0	
3. SWE	(Aina Berg, Wivan Pettersson, Gulli Everlund, Hjördis Töpel)	5:35.6	
4. DEN	(Vibeke Möller, Hedevig Rasmussen, Karen Maud Rasmussen, Agnete Olsen)	5:42.4	
5. FRA	(Ernestine Lebrun, Gilberte Mortier, Bibienne Pellegry, Marguerite Protin)	5:43.4	
6. HOL	(Mietje Baron, Alida Bolten, Geertruida Klapwijk, Maria Vierdag)	5:45.8	

1928 Amsterdam T: 7, N: 7, D: 8.9.
1. USA	(Adelaide Lambert, Eleanor Garatti, Albina Osipowich, Martha Norelius, [Josephine McKim, Susan Laird])	4:47.6	WR
2. GBR	(Margaret Cooper, Sarah Stewart, Irene Tanner, Ellen King)	5:02.8	
3. SAF	(Kathleen Russell, Rhoda Rennie, Marie Bedford, Frederica van der Goes)	5:13.4	
4. GER	(Charlotte Lehmann, Reni Erkens-Küpper, Hertha Wunder, Irmintraut Schneider)	5:14.4	
5. FRA	(Bibienne Pellegry, Anne Dupire, Marguerite Ledoux, Claire Horrent, [Georgette Roty])	5.32.0	

DISQ: HOL (Elisabeth Smits, Geertje Baumeister, Maria Vierdag, Maria Braun)

1932 Los Angeles T: 5, N: 5, D: 8.12. WR: 4:47.6 (USA—Lambert, Garatti, Osipowich, Norelius)
1. USA	(Josephine McKim, Helen Johns, Eleanor Saville [Garatti], Helene Madison)	4:38.0	WR
2. HOL	(Maria Vierdag, Maria Oversloot, Cornelia Laddé, Willemijntje den Ouden)	4:47.5	
3. GBR	(Elizabeth Valerie Davies, Helen Varcoe, Margaret Joyce Cooper, Edna Hughes)	4:52.4	
4. CAN	(Irene Pirie, Irene Mullen, Ruth Kerr, Betty Edwards)	5:05.7	
5. JPN	(Kazue Kojima, Hatsuko Morioka, Misao Yokota, Yukie Arata)	5:06.7	

1936 Berlin T: 9, N: 9, D: 8.14. WR: 4:32.8 (HOL—Selbach, Mastenbroek, Wagner, den Ouden)
1. HOL	(Johanna Selbach, Catherina Wagner, Willemijntje den Ouden, Hendrika "Rie" Mastenbroek)	4:36.0	OR
2. GER	(Ruth Halbsguth, Leni Lohmar, Ingeborg Schmitz, Gisela Arendt, [Ursula Pollack])	4:36.8	
3. USA	(Katherine Rawls, Bernice Lapp, Mavis Freeman, Olive McKean, [Elizabeth Ryan])	4:40.2	
4. HUN	(Ilona Ács, Ágnes Biró, Véra Harsányi, Magdolna Lenkei)	4:48.0	
4. CAN	(Mary McConkey, Irene Milton-Pirie, Margaret Stone, Phyllis Dewar)	4:48.0	
6. GBR	(Margaret Jeffery, Zilpha Grant, Edna Hughes, Olive Wadham)	4:51.0	

7. DEN	(Ragnhild Hveger, Bruunstrom, Elvi Svendsen, Eva Arendt)	4:51.4

Germany led for 200 meters before den Ouden gave Holland the lead. The race was still in doubt with 20 meters to go, at which point Mastenbroek sprinted to victory.

1948 London T: 11, N: 11, D: 8.6. WR: 4:27.6 (DEN—Arndt, Kraft, Ove-Peterson, Hveger)
1. USA	(Marie Corridon, Thelma Kalama, Brenda Helser, Ann Curtis)	4:29.2	OR
2. DEN	(Eva Riise, Karen-Margrete Harup, Greta Andersen, Fritze Carstensen, [Elvi Carlsen (Svendsen)])	4:29.6	
3. HOL	(Irma Schuhmacher, Margot Marsman, Marie-Louise Vaessen, Johanna Termeulen)	4:31.6	
4. GBR	(Patricia Nielsen, Margaret Wellington, Lillian Preece, Catherine Gibson)	4:34.7	
5. HUN	(Mária Littomeritzky, Judit Temes, Ilona Novák, Éva Székely)	4:44.8	
6. BRA	(Eleonora Schmitt, Maria Leão da Costa, Talita de Alencar Rodrigues, Piedade Silva Tavares)	4:49.1	
7. FRA	(Josette Arene, Gisele Vallerey, Colette Thomas, Ginette Jany, [Marie Foucher-Cretau])	4:49.8	

DISQ: SWE (Gisela Thidholm, Elisabeth Ahlgren, Marianne Lundquist, Ingegard Fredin)

Ann Curtis swam a spectacular anchor leg to give the United States a come-from-behind victory over Denmark. She was timed in 1:04.4, which unofficially bettered Willy den Ouden's 12-year-old world record for the 100 meters. However, marks set during relays do not qualify for world records unless they are accomplished on the first leg.

1952 Helsinki T: 13, N: 13, D: 8.1. WR: 4:27.2 (HUN—Littomeritzky, Novák, Székely, Szöke)
1. HUN	(Ilona Novák, Judit Temes, Éva Novák, Katalin Szöke, [Mária Littomericzky, Ilona Novák])	4:24.4	WR
2. HOL	(Marie-Louise Linssen [Vaessen], Koosje van Voorn, Johanna Termeulen, Irma Heijting-Schuhmacher)	4:29.0	
3. USA	(Jacqueline La Vine, Marilee Stepan, Joan Alderson, Evelyn Kawamoto)	4:30.1	
4. DEN	(Rita Larsen, Mette Ove-Peterson, Greta Andersen, Ragnhild Andersen-Hveger)	4:36.2	
5. GBR	(Phyllis Linton, Jean Botham, Angela Barnwell, Lillian Preece)	4:37.8	
6. SWE	(Marianne Lundquist, Anita Andersson, Maud Berglund, Ingegärd Fredin)	4:39.0	
7. GER	(Elisabeth Rechlin, Vera Schäferkordt, Kati Jansen, Gisela Jacobs [Arendt])	4:40.3	
8. FRA	(Gaby Tanguy, Maryse Morandini, Ginette Jany, Josette Arene)	4:44.1	

Temes, Novák, and Szöke swam legs of 1:05.8, 1:05.1, and 1:05.7, respectively, each of which was a full second faster than Szöke's time when she won the 100-meter freestyle final four days earlier.

1956 Melbourne T: 10, N: 10, D: 12.6 WR: 4:19.7 (AUS—Crapp, Fraser, Leech, Gibson)

1. AUS (Dawn Fraser, Faith Leech, Sandra Morgan, Lorraine Crapp, [Margeret Gibson]) — 4:17.1 WR
2. USA (Sylvia Ruuska, Shelly Mann, Nancy Simons, Joan Rosazza, [Betty Brey, Nancy Simons, Kathryn Knapp, Marley Shriver]) — 4:19.2
3. SAF (Jeanette Myburgh, Susan Roberts, Natalie Myburgh, Moira Abernathy) — 4:25.7
4. GER Ingrid Künzel, Hertha Hasse, Käthi Jansen, Birgit Klomp) — 4:26.1
5. CAN (Helen Stewart, Gladys Priestley, Sara Barber, Virginia Grant) — 4:28.3
6. SWE (Anita Hellström, Birgitta Wängberg, Anna Larsson, Kate Jobson) — 4:30.0
7. HUN (Mária Littomeritzky, Katalin Szöke, Judit Temes, Valéria Gyenge) — 4:31.1
8. GBR (Frances Hogben, Judith Grinham, Margaret Girvan, Fearne Ewart) — 4:35.8

The Australians got off to a bad start when the starter's gun went off a second time by mistake and lead-off swimmer Dawn Fraser, thinking a false start had been called, stopped swimming. When she realized that the other swimmers had kept going, she caught up quickly and touched off with a two-second lead. The Americans gradually caught up, but Lorraine's Crapp's anchor leg of 1:03.1 sealed the victory.

1960 Rome T: 12, N: 12, D: 9.3. WR (440 yards): 4:16.2 (AUS—Fraser, Colquhoun, Konrads, Crapp)

1. USA (Joan Spillane, Shirley Stobs, Carolyn Wood, S. Christine Von Saltza, [Donna De Varona, Susan Doerr, Sylvia Ruuska, Molly Botkin]) — 4:08.9 WR
2. AUS (Dawn Fraser, Ilsa Konrads, Lorraine Crapp, Alva Colquhoun, [Sandra Morgan, Ruth Everuss]) — 4:11.3
3. GDR& GER (Christel Steffin, Heidi Pechstein, Gisela Weiss, Ursula Brunner) — 4:19.7
4. HUN (Anna Temesvári, Mária Frank, Kátalin Boros, Csilla Dobai-Madarász) — 4:21.2
5. GBR (Natalie Steward, Beryl Noakes, Judy Samuel, Christine Harris) — 4:24.6
6. SWE (Inger Thorngren, Karin Larsson, Kristina Larsson, Birte Segerström) — 4:25.1
7. ITA (Paola Saini, Annamaria Cecchi, Rosanna Contardo, Maria Christina Pacifici, [Daniela Beneck]) — 4:26.8
8. SOV (Irina Liakhovskaya, Ulvi Voog, Galina Sosnova, Marina Shamal) — 4:29.0

In 1956 Lorraine Crapp had been one of Australia's heroines, winning two gold medals and one silver. But in 1960 she had other things on her mind. The night before the Australian team left for Rome she had secretly married Bill Thurlow, one of the doctors associated with the Australian swimmers. Thurlow traveled to Rome on his own and rented an apartment. After the lights were put out at the Olympic Village, Crapp would sneak out and spend the night with her husband. When Australian officials became suspicious of her early morning absences, Crapp admitted her deception. Unfortunately, the officials overreacted. Instead of simply giving her permission to sleep outside the Village as many other married athletes did, they punished her by restricting her movements and keeping watch on her. Demoralized, Crapp swam a lackluster third leg in the freestyle relay, losing a crucial five yards and 2.7 seconds to Carolyn Wood.

1964 Tokyo T: 10, N: 10, D: 10.15. WR: 4:07.6 (USA—Allsup, Stickles, Seidel, Bricker)

1. USA (Sharon Stouder, Donna De Varona, Lillian "Pokey" Watson, Kathleen Ellis, [Jeanne Hallock, Ericka Bricker, Lynne Allsup, Patience Sherman]) — 4:03.8 WR
2. AUS (Robyn Thorn, Janice Murphy, Lynette Bell, Dawn Fraser, [Jan Turner]) — 4:06.9
3. HOL (Paulina van der Wildt, Catharina Beumer, Wilhelmina van Weerdenburg, Erica Terpstra) — 4:12.0
4. HUN (Judit Turóczy, Éva Erdélyi, Katalin Takács, Csilla Dobai-Madarász, [Mária Frank]) — 4:12.1
5. SWE (Ann-Charlott Lilja, Katrin Andersson, Ulla Jäfvert, Ann-Christine Hagberg) — 4:14.0
6. GDR&GER (Martina Grunert, Traudi Beierlein, Rita Schumacher, Heidi Pechstein) — 4:15.0
7. CAN (Mary Stewart, Patricia Thompson, Helen Kennedy, Marion Lay) — 4:15.9
8. ITA (Paola Saini, Maria Christina Pacifici, Mara Sacchi, Daniela Beneck) — 4:17.2

1968 Mexico City T: 15, N: 15, D: 10.26. WR: 4:01.1 (USA, Santa Clara Swim Club—Gustavson, Watson, Carpinelli, Henne)

1. USA (Jane Barkman, Linda Gustavson, Susan Pedersen, Jan Henne) — 4:02.5 OR
2. GDR (Gabriele Wetzko, Roswitha Krause, Uta Schmuck, Martina Grunert, [Gabriele Perthes]) — 4:05.7
3. CAN (Angela Coughlan, Marilyn Corson, Elaine Tanner, Marion Lay) — 4:07.2
4. AUS (Janet Steinbeck, Susan Eddy, Lynette Watson, Lynette Bell, [Julie McDonald]) — 4:08.7
5. HUN (Edit Kovács, Magdolna Patoh, Andréa Gyarmati, Judit Turóczy) — 4:11.0
6. JPN (Shigeko Kawanishi, Yoshimi Nishigawa, Yasuko Fujii, Miwako Kobayashi, [Yumiko Ono]) — 4:13.6

7. GBR   (Shelagh Ratcliffe, Fiona Kellock, Susan   4:18.0
   Williams, Alexandra Jackson)

DISQ: FRA (Marie Kersaudy, Simone Hanner, Daniele Dorleans, Claude Mandonnaud)

1972 Munich T: 16, N: 16, D: 8.30. WR: 3:58.11 (USA—Peyton, Neilson, Barkman, Babashoff)

1. USA   (Sandra Neilson, Jennifer Kemp, Jane   3:55.19   WR
   Barkman, Shirley Babashoff, [Kim
   Peyton, Lynn Skrifvars, Ann Marshall])

2. GDR   (Gabriele Wetzko, Andrea Eife, Elke   3:55.55
   Sehmisch, Kornelia Ender, [Sylvia
   Eichner])

3. GER   (Jutta Weber, Heidemarie Reineck, Gu-   3:57.93
   drun Beckmann, Angela Steinbach)

4. HUN   (Andréa Gyarmati, Judit Turóczy, Edit   4:00.39
   Kovács, Magdolna Patoh)

5. HOL   (Enith Brigitha, Anke Rijnders, Hansje   4:01.49
   Bunschoten, Josien Elzerman)

6. SWE   (Anita Zarnowiecki, Eva Andersson,   4:02.69
   Diana Olsson, Irwi Johansson)

7. CAN   (Wendy Cook, Judy Wright, Mary-Beth   4:03.83
   Rondeau, Leslie Cliff)

8. AUS   (Deborah Palmer, Leanne Francis,   4:04.82
   Sharon Booth, Shane Gould, [Debra
   Cain])

Until August 18, 1972, no women's relay team had broken the four-minute barrier. On that day Neilson, Barkman, Babashoff, and Kim Peyton of the United States recorded a time of 3:58.11. Twelve days later, in the qualifying heats of the Olympics, the East Germans tied that mark. That evening, in the final, the record took another battering. Sandy Neilson took a quarter-second lead over Gabriele Wetzko, and the remaining American swimmers held on with great determination, withstanding a continuous challenge from the East Germans that lasted until the final touch.

1976 Montreal T: 14, N: 14, D: 7.25. WR: 3:48.80 (GDR, Sports Club Dynamo—Krause, Seltman, Gabriel, Pollack)

1. USA   (Kim Peyton, Wendy Boglioli, Jill   3:44.82   WR
   Sterkel, Shirley Babashoff, [Jennifer
   Hooker])

2. GDR   (Kornelia Ender, Petra Priemer, Andrea   3:45.50
   Pollack, Claudia Hempel)

3. CAN   (Gail Amundrud, Barbara Clark, Becky   3:48.81
   Smith, Anne Jardin, [Deborah Clarke])

4. HOL   (Ineke Ran, Linda Faber, Annelies   3:51.67
   Maas, Enith Brigitha)

5. SOV   (Lyubov Kobzova, Irina Vlasova, Ma-   3:52.69
   rina Kliuchnikova, Larissa Tsareva)

6. FRA   (Guylaine Berger, Sylvie Le Noach,   3:56.73
   Caroline Carpentier, Chantal Schertz)

7. SWE   (Pia Martensson, Ylva Persson, Diana   3:57.25
   Olsson, Ida Hansson, [Gunilla Lund-
   berg])

8. GER   (Jutta Weber, Marion Platten, Regina   3:58.33
   Nissen, Beate Jasch, [Gudrun Beck-
   mann])

The freestyle relay was the last women's swimming event of the Montreal Olympics. In the first 12 events, the East Germans had won 11 gold medals, the Soviet Union had won one, and the United States had won none. With 100-meter gold medalist Kornelia Ender swimming the first leg, East Germany took a 1.16-second lead. East Germany's second swimmer was 100-meter silver medalist Petra Priemer. But Wendy Boglioli swam a 55.81 leg to draw the United States 0.35 seconds closer. Jill Sterkel followed with a blistering 55.78, passing Andrea Pollack and giving the United States a lead of 0.40 seconds. Shirley Babashoff's 56.28 assured the United States of a gold medal at last. Babashoff finished her Olympic career with two gold medals, both in the freestyle relay, and six silver medals.

1980 Moscow T: 9, N: 9, D: 7.27. WR: 3:43.43 (USA—Caulkins, Elkins, Sterkel, Woodhead)

1. GDR   (Barbara Krause, Caren Metschuck   3:42.71   WR
   Ines Diers, Sarina Hülsenbeck, [Car-
   mela Schmidt])

2. SWE   (Carina Ljungdahl, Tina Gustafsson,   3:48.93
   Agneta Mårtensson, Agneta Eriksson,
   [Birgitta Jonsson, Helena Peterson])

3. HOL   (Cornelia van Bentum, Wilma van Vel-   3:49.51
   sen, Reggie de Jong, Annelies Maas)

4. GBR   (Sharron Davies, Kaye Lovatt, Jac-   3:51.71
   quelina Willmott, June Croft)

5. AUS   (Lisa Curry, Karen van de Graaf, Rose-   3:54.16
   mary Brown, Michele Pearson)

6. MEX   (Isabel Reuss, Dagmar Erdman, Te-   3:55.41
   resa Rivera, Helen Plaschinski)

7. BUL   (Dobrinka Mincheva, Rumiana Niko-   3:56.34
   lova,   Ani   Kostova,   Sonya
   Dangalakova)

8. SPA   (Natalia Mas, Margarita Armengol,   3:58.73
   Laura Flaque, Gloria Casado)

Although there were only nine teams, two qualifying heats were held to determine which eight teams would advance to the final. In the second heat the Soviet Union was disqualified for an improper changeover, which made it much easier to decide who the finalists would be. The East Germans won easily. If the United States had entered a team they probably would have finished second, based on times from the same period.

1984 Los Angeles T: 12, N: 12, D: 7.31. WR: 3:42.71 (GDR—Krause, Metschuck, Diers, Hülsenbeck)

1. USA   (Jenna Johnson, Carrie Steinseifer, Dara   3:43.43
   Torres, Nancy Hogshead, [Jill Sterkel, Mary
   Wayte])

2. HOL   (Annemarie Verstappen, Elles Voskes, Desi   3:44.40
   Reijers, Cornelia van Bentum, [Wilma van
   Velsen])

3. GER   (Iris Zscherpe, Susanne Schuster, Christiane   3:45.56
   Pielke, Karin Seick)

4. AUS   (Michele Pearson, Angela Russel, Anna   3:47.79
   McVann, Lisa Curry, [Janet Tibbits])

5. CAN   (Pamela Rai, Carol Klimpel, Cheryl McArton,   3:49.50
   Jane Kerr, [Maureen New])

6. GBR (June Croft, Nicola Fibbens, Debra Gore, 3:50.12
Annabelle Cripps)
7. SWE (Maria Kardum, Agneta Eriksson, Petra Hilder, 3:51.24
Karin Furuhed, [Malin Rundgren])
8. FRA (Caroline Amoric, Sophie Kamoun, Veronique 3:52.15
Jardin, Laurence Bensimon)

Three weeks after the Olympics final, the East German Friendship Games team of Kristin Otto, Karen König, Heike Friedrich and Birgit Meineke set a world record of 3:42.41. The Soviet team was second in 3:44.31.

1988 Seoul T: 15, N: 15, D: 9.22. WR: 3:40.57 (GDR—Otto, Stellmach, Schulze, Friedrich)
1. GDR (Kristin Otto, Katrin Meissner, Daniela 3:40.63 OR
Hunger, Manuela Stellmach, [Sabina
Schulze, Heike Friedrich])
2. HOL (Marianne Muis, Mildred Muis, Cornelia 3:43.39
van Bentum, Karin Brienesse, [Diana van
der Plaats])
3. USA (Mary Wayte, Mitzi Kremer, Laura 3:44.25
Walker, Dara Torres, [Paige Zemina, Jill
Sterkel])
4. CHN (Xia Fujie, Yang Wenyi, Lou Yaping, 3:44.69
Zhuang Yong)
5. SOV (Yelena Dendeberova, Svetlana 3:44.99
Issakova, Natalya Trefilova, Svitlana
Kopchykova, [Inna Abramova])
6. CAN (Kathy Bald, Patricia Noall, Andrea Nu- 3:46.75
gent, Jane Kerr, [Kristen Topham, Allison
Higson])
7. GER (Stephanie Ortwig, Marion Aizpors, Chris- 3:46.90
tiane Pielke, Karin Seick, [Katja Ziliox])
8. DEN (Gitta Jensen, Pia Sorensen, Mette Ja- 3:49.25
cobsen, Annette Moldrup Jorgensen)

1992 Barcelona T: 13, N: 13, D: 7.28. WR: 3:40.57 (GDR—Otto, Stellmach, Schulze, Friedrich)
1. USA (Nicole Haislett, Dara Torres, Angelina 3:39.46 WR
Martino, Jennifer Thompson, [Ashley
Tappin, Christine Ahmann-Leighton])
2. CHN (Zhuang Yong, Lu Bin, Yang Wenyi, Le 3:40.12
Jingyi, [Zhao Kun])
3. GER (Franziska van Almsick, Simone Osygus, 3:41.60
Daniela Hunger, Manuela Stellmach,
[Kerstin Kielgass, Annette Hadding])
4. SOV (Natalya Meshcheryakova, Svetlana 3:43.68
Leshukova, Yelena Dendeberova, Ye-
lena Shubina, [Yevgenya Yermakova])
5. HOL (Diana van der Plaats, Mildred Muis, 3:43.74
Marianne Muis, Karin Brienesse, [Inga
de Bruijn])
6. DEN (Gitta Jensen, Mette Jacobsen, Berit 3:47.81
Puggaard, Mette Nielsen, [Annette
Poulsen])
7. SWE (Eva Nyberg, Louise Karlsson, Ellenor 3:48.47
Svensson, Malin Nilsson, [Linda
Olofsson])
8. CAN (Marianne Limpert, Nicole Dryden, An- 3:49.37
drea Nugent, Allison Higson)

Zhuang set an Olympic record of 54.51 on the lead-off leg—in fact, it was the second-fastest time in history. Torres and Martino closed the gap for the United States. By the time Jenny Thompson took off for her anchor leg, she was only a stroke behind the Chinese team. She then swam a sizzling 54.01, the fastest relay leg in history, to win the race and break the six-year-old world record.

4 × 200-METER FREESTYLE RELAY

This event will be held for the first time in 1996.

4 × 100-METER MEDLEY RELAY

In medley relays the order of strokes is backstroke, breaststroke, butterfly, and freestyle.

1896–1956 not held

1960 Rome T: 13, N: 13, D: 9.2. WR: 4:44.6 (USA—Cone, Bancroft, Collins, Von Saltza)
1. USA (Lynn Burke, Patty Kempner, Caro- 4:41.1 WR
lyn Schuler, S. Christine Von
Saltza, [Anne Warner, Carolyn
Wood, Joan Spillane])
2. AUS (Marilyn Wilson, Rosemary 4:45.9
Lassig, Janice Andrew, Dawn Fra-
ser, [Amber Gergay Beckett, Ilsa
Konrads])
3. GDR&GER (Ingrid Schmidt, Ursula Küper, 4:47.6
Bärbel Fuhrmann, Ursel Brunner)
4. HOL (Maria van Velsen, Adelaide den 4:47.6
Haan, Marianne Heemskerk, Erica
Terpstra, [Catharina Lagerberg])
5. GBR (Sylvia Lewis, Anita Lonsbrough, 4:47.6
Sheila Watt, Natalie Steward,
[Jean Oldroyd])
6. HUN (Magdolna Dávid, Klara Bartos- 4:53.7
Killermann, Márta Egerváry, Csilla
Dobai-Madarász)
7. JPN (Satoko Tanaka, Yoshiko 4:56.4
Takamatsu, Shizue Miyabe, Yo-
shiko Sato)
8. SOV (Larissa Viktorova, Lyudmila 4:58.1
Korobova, Zinaida Belovskaya,
Marina Shamal, [Valentina
Poznyak])

U.S. leadoff swimmer Lynn Burke finished her leg in 1:09.0 to break the 100-meter backstroke world record for the fourth time in seven weeks. The race was no contest after that, with the United States winning by seven meters. Burke and Von Saltza were best friends who trained together and lived together in the home of Von Saltza's parents in Saratoga, California. They were both coached by George Haines. They dieted together, cut their hair the same way, and, in Rome, they won gold medals together. Von Saltza went home with three and Burke with two.

1964 Tokyo T: 9, N: 9, D: 10.18. WR: 4:34.6 (USA—Ferguson, Goyette, Ellis, Randall)
1. USA (Cathy Ferguson, Cynthia Goyette, 4:33.9 WR
   Sharon Stouder, Kathleen Ellis, [Nina
   Harmar, Judith Reeder, Susan Pitt, Lillian
   "Pokey" Watson])
2. HOL (Kornelia Winkel, Klena Bimolt, Ada Kok, 4:37.0
   Erica Terpstra, [Aartje Lasterie])
3. SOV (Tatyana Savelyeva, Svetlana Babanina, 4:39.2
   Tetyana Devyatova, Natalya Ustinova)
4. JPN (Satoko Tanaka, Noriko Yamamoto, Eiko 4:42.0
   Takahashi, Michiko Kihara)
5. GBR (Jill Norfolk, Stella Mitchell, Mary Anne 4:45.8
   Cotterill, Elizabeth Long, [Linda
   Ludgrove])
6. CAN (Eileen Weir, Marion Lay, Mary Stewart, 4:49.9
   Helen Kennedy)
DISQ: GDR&GER (Ingrid Schmidt, Bärbel Grimmer, Heike
   Hustede, Martina Grunert), HUN (Mária Balla, Zsuzsa Kovacs,
   Márta Egerváry. Csilla Dobai-Madarász)

Cathy Ferguson gave the United States the lead after the first leg, but Svetlana Babanina, swimming two seconds faster than the official world record, touched first at 200 meters. Sharon Stouder then pulled away by a commanding margin, which Kathy Ellis added to. Stouder finished the Olympics with three gold medals and one silver, Ellis with two gold and two bronze.

1968 Mexico T: 16, N: 16, D: 10.17. WR: 4:28.1 (USA—Hall, Ball, Daniel, Pedersen)
1. USA (Kaye Hall, Catie Ball, Ellie Daniel, Susan 4:28.3 OR
   Pedersen, [Jane Swagerty, Suzy Jones,
   Susan Shields, Jan Henne])
2. AUS (Lynne Watson, Judy Playfair, Lynette 4:30.0
   McClements, Janet Steinbeck, [Lynette
   Bell])
3. GER (Angelika Kraus, Uta Frommater, Heike 4:36.4
   Hustede, Heidemarie Reineck)
4. SOV (Tinatin Lekveishvili, Alla Grebennikova, 4:37.0
   Tetyana Devyatova, Lidiya Hrebets,
   [Larissa Zakharova])
5. GDR (Martina Grunert, Eva Wittke, Helga 4:38.0
   Lindner, Uta Schmuck)
6. GBR (Wendy Burrell, Dorothy Harrison, Marga- 4:38.3
   ret Auton, Alexandra Jackson)
7. HOL (Jacobje Buter, Klena Bimolt, Ada Kok, 4:38.7
   Petronella Bos)
8. HUN (Mária Lantos, Edit Kovács, Andréa 4:42.9
   Gyarmati, Judit Turóczy)

The United States led Australia by 0.7 seconds at 100 meters, 0.3 at 200, and 0.5 at 300 before Susan Pedersen pulled away from Janet Steinbeck for the victory.

1972 Munich T: 16, N: 16, D: 8.30. WR: 4:25.34 (USA—Atwood, Vidali, Daniel, Barkman)
1. USA (Melissa Belote, Catherine Carr, Deena
   Deardurff, Sandra Neilson, [Susan

Atwood, Judith Melick, Dana Shrader, 4:20.75 WR
   Shirley Babashoff])
2. GDR (Christine Herbst, Renate Vogel, Ros- 4:24.91
   witha Beier, Kornelia Ender, [Gabriele
   Wetzko])
3. GER (Silke Pielen, Verena Eberle, Gudrun 4:26.46
   Beckmann, Heidemarie Reineck,
   [Annegret Kober, Edeltraud Koch,
   Jutta Weber])
4. SOV (Tinatin Lekveishvili, Halina Stepanova 4:27.81
   [Prozumenshchykova], Iryna Usty-
   menko, Tatyana Zolotnickaia)
5. HOL (Enith Brigitha, Alie te Riet, Anke 4:29.99
   Rijnders, Hansje Bunschoten, [Frieke
   Buys])
6. JPN (Suzuko Matsumura, Yoko Yamamoto, 4:31.56
   Mayumi Aoki, Yoshimi Nishigawa)
7. CAN (Wendy Cook, Sylvia Dockerill, Marylin 4:31.56
   Corson, Leslie Cliff)
8. SWE (Diana Olsson, Britt-Marie Smedh, Eva 4:32.61
   Wikner, Anita Zarnowiecki)

1976 Montreal T: 17, N: 17, D: 7.18. WR: 4:13.41 (GDR, Sports Club Dynamo—Seltman Nitschke, Pollack, Krause)
1. GDR (Ulrike Richter, Hannelore Anke, An- 4:07.95 WR
   drea Pollack, Kornelia Ender, [Birgit
   Treiber, Carola Nitschke, Rosemarie
   Gabriel])
2. USA (Linda Jezek, Lauri Siering, Camille 4:14.55
   Wright, Shirley Babashoff, [Lelei
   Fonoimoana, Wendy Boglioli])
3. CAN (Wendy Hogg, Robin Corsiglia, Susan 4:15.22
   Sloan, Anne Jardin, [Deborah Clarke])
4. SOV (Nadiya Stavko, Maryna Yurchenya, 4:16.05
   Tamara Shelofastova, Larissa Tsareva)
5. HOL (Diane Edelijn, Wijda Mazereeuw, Jose 4:19.03
   Damen, Enith Brigitha, [Ineke Ran])
6. GBR (Joy Beasley, Margaret Kelly, Susan 4:23.25
   Jenner, Deborah Hill)
7. JPN (Yoshimi Nishigawa, Toshiko Haruoka, 4:23.47
   Yasue Hatsuda, Sachiko Yamazaki)
8. AUS (Michelle Devries, Judith Hudson, 4:25.91
   Linda Hanel, Jenny Tate)

The first women's swimming event to be decided in 1976, the medley relay was won with an awesome display by the East German swimmers. Richter, Anke, Pollack, and Ender each recorded the fastest time for her leg.

1980 Moscow T: 10, N: 10, D: 7.20. WR: 4:07.95 (GDR—Richter, Anke, Pollack, Ender)
1. GDR (Rica Reinisch, Ute Geweniger, Andrea 4:06.67 WR
   Pollack, Caren Metschuck, [Sarina
   Hulsenbeck])
2. GBR (Helen Jameson, Margaret Kelly, Ann 4:12.24
   Osgerby, June Croft)
3. SOV (Yelena Kruglova, Elvira Vasilkova, Alla 4:13.61
   Grishchenkova, Natalya Strunnikova,
   [Irina Aksyonova, Olga Klevakina])

4. SWE (Annika Uvehall, Eva-Marie Håkansson, Agneta Mårtensson, Tina Gustafson) 4:16.91

5. ITA (Laura Foralosso, Sabrina Seminatore, Cinzia Savi-Scarponi, Monica Vallarin) 4:19.05

6. AUS (Lisa Forrest, Lisa Curry, Karen Van De Graaf, Rosemary Brown) 4:19.90

7. ROM (Carmen Bunaciu, Brigitte Press, Mariana Parachiv, Irinel Panulescu) 4:21.27

8. BUL (Sonya Dangalakova, Tania Bogomilova, Ani Moneva, Dobrinka Mincheva) 4:22.38

Rica Reinisch opened with a world-record-equaling backstroke leg and Ute Geweniger followed with 100 meters of breaststroking that bettered the official world record. Pollack and Metschuck recorded the fastest times of their respective legs, and the East Germans were on their way again.

1984 Los Angeles T: 13, N: 13, D: 8.3. WR: 4:05.79 (GDR—Kleber, Geweniger, Geissler, Meineke)

1. USA (Theresa Andrews, Tracy Caulkins, Mary T. Meagher, Nancy Hogshead, [Betsy Mitchell, Susan Rapp, Jenna Johnson, Carrie Steinseifer]) 4:08.34

2. GER (Svenja Schlicht, Ute Hasse, Ina Beyermann, Karin Seick) 4:11.97

3. CAN (Reema Abdo, Anne Ottenbrite, Michelle MacPherson, Pamela Rai) 4:12.98

4. GBR (Beverley Rose, Jean Hill, Nicola Fibbens, June Croft) 4:14.05

5. ITA (Manuela Carosi, Manuela Dalla Valle, Roberta Lanzarotti, Silvia Persi) 4:17.40

6. SWI (Eva Gysling, Patricia Brülhart, Carole Brook, Marie-Thérèse Armentero) 4:19.02

DISQ: JPN (Naomi Sekido, Hiroko Nagasaki, Naoko Kume, Kaori Yanase)

DISQ: SWE (Anna-Karin Eriksson, Eva-Marie Håkansson, Agneta Eriksson, Maria Kardum)

U.S. team members Caulkins, Meagher and Hogshead each won three gold medals in Los Angeles. Their main competition in the medley relay had been expected to come from the Dutch team, which was disqualified for jumping too soon during an exchange in the preliminary round. Three weeks after the Olympic final, the East German Friendship Games team of Ina Kleber, Sylvia Gerasch, Ines Geissler and Birgit Meineke set a world record of 4:03.69. The Soviets were second in 4:08.13.

1988 Seoul T: 18, N: 18, D: 9.24. WR: 4:03.69 (GDR—Kleber, Gerasch, Geissler, Meineke)

1. GDR (Kristin Otto, Silke Hörner, Birte Weigang, Katrin Meissner, [Cornelia Sirch, Manuela Stellmach]) 4:03.74 OR

2. USA (Beth Barr, Tracey McFarlane, Janel Jorgensen, Mary Wayte, [Betsy Mitchell, Mary T. Meagher, Dara Torres]) 4:07.90

3. CAN (Lori Melien, Allison Higson, Jane Kerr, Andrea Nugent, [Keltie Duggan, Patricia Noall]) 4:10.49

4. AUS (Nicole Livingstone, Lara Hooiveld, Fiona Alessandri, Karen Van Wirdum) 4:11.57

5. HOL (Jolanda de Rover, Linda Moes, Cornelia van Bentum, Karin Brienesse) 4:12.19

6. BUL (Bistra Gospodinova, Tania Dangalakova [Bogomilova], Neviana Miteva, Natasha Hristova) 4:12.36

7. GER (Svenja Schlicht, Britta Dahm, Gabi Rehaa, Marion Aizpors) 4:12.89

8. ITA (Lorenza Vigarani, Manuela Dalla Valle, Ilaria Tocchini, Silvia Persi) 4:13.85

1992 Barcelona T: 17, N: 17, D: 7.30. WR: 4:03.69 (GDR—Kleber, Gerasch, Geissler, Meineke)

1. USA (Lea Loveless, N. Anita Nall, Christine Ahmann-Leighton, Jennifer Thompson, [Elizabeth "Janie" Wagstaff, Megan Kleine, Summer Sanders, Nicole Haislett]) 4:02.54 WR

2. GER (Dagmar Hase, Jana Dörries, Franziska van Almsick, Daniela Hunger, [Daniela Brendel, Bettina Ustrowski, Simone Osygus]) 4:05.19

3. SOV (Nina Zhivanevskaya, Yelena Rudkovskaya, Olga Kirichenko, Natalya Meshcheryakova, [Yelena Shubina]) 4:06.44

4. CHN (Lin Li, Lou Xia, Qian Hong, Le Jingyi, [He Cihong]) 4:06.78

5. AUS (Nicole Stevenson [Livingstone], Samantha Riley, Susan O'Neill, Lisa Curry-Kenny, [Joanne Meehan]) 4:07.01

6. CAN (Nicole Dryden, Guylaine Cloutier, Kristin Topham, Andrea Nugent) 4:09.26

7. JPN (Yoko Koikawa, Kyoko Iwasaki, Yoko Kando, Suzu Chiba) 4:09.92

8. HOL (Ellen Elzerman, Kira Bulten, Inge de Bruijn, Marianne Muis) 4:10.87

The team from the United States led from start to finish and broke the eight-year-old world record.

SYNCHRONIZED SWIMMING

Team
Discontinued Events

Synchronized swimming was introduced to the Olympics in 1984 with a solo event and a duet event. Both of these events were dropped after the 1992 Olympics and will be replaced by a team event with eight swimmers on each team. The 1996 team competition will consist of a technical routine, lasting between 2 minutes 40 seconds and 3 minutes, and a free routine, lasting between 4 minutes 45 seconds and 5 minutes 15 seconds. The technical routine accounts for 35 percent of the total score, the free routine for 65 percent. Routines are scored by seven judges on a scale of 0 (failed) to 10.0 (very good). Each judge scores a routine for technical merit and artistic impression. The technical merit score is derived by weighing execution of strokes and figures (40 percent), synchronization within the team and with the music (30 percent), and difficulty of strokes and figures (30 percent). The artistic impression score weighs choreography (60 percent) with music interpretation (20 percent) and manner of presentation (20 percent). The final score for each routine is determined by dropping the highest and lowest score for both technical merit and artistic impression, dividing by five to obtain the average score for the remaining judges, and then multiplying by six for technical merit and four for artistic impression.

Figures range from simple moves like the somersault back tuck to difficult moves such as the Eiffel Tower combined spin. Synchronized swimming has a reputation as a somewhat silly sport, but in fact it is more physically demanding than many other sporting endeavors, such as shooting, dressage, or playing right field in a baseball game.

TEAM

This event will be held for the first time in 1996.

Discontinued Events

SOLO

1984 Los Angeles C: 17, N: 17, D: 8.12.
1.	Tracie Ruiz	USA	198.467
2.	Carolyn Waldo	CAN	195.300

3.	Miwako Motoyoshi	JPN	187.050
4.	Marijke Engelen	HOL	182.632
5.	Gudrun Hänisch	GER	182.017
6.	Caroline Holmyard	GBR	182.000
7.	Muriel Hermine	FRA	180.534
8.	Karin Singer	SWI	178.383

This event, which was added to the Olympic program only two months before the Games began, was won by 21-year-old world champion Tracie Ruiz of Bothell, Washington, whose father was Hawaiian and mother a Norwegian-German mixture. Her Latin surname came from her stepfather.

1988 Seoul C: 46, N: 18, D: 9.30.
1.	Carolyn Waldo	CAN	200.150
2.	Tracie Ruiz-Conforto	USA	197.633
3.	Mikako Kotani	JPN	191.850
4.	Muriel Hermine	FRA	190.100
5.	Karin Singer	SWI	185.600
6.	Nicola Shearn	GBR	181.933
7.	Khristina Falasinidi	SOV/GEO	180.650
8.	Gerlind Scheller	GER	175.983

The rules for 1988 permitted each nation three entrants, but only one swimmer per nation was allowed to advance to the final. Carolyn Waldo of Beaconsfield, Québec, used the compulsory figures to build an insurmountable lead over Ruiz-Conforto, who had defeated Waldo in a pre-Olympic competition in Seoul in June.

1992 Barcelona C: 21, N: 21, D: 8.6.
1.	Kristen Babb-Sprague	USA	191.848
1.	Sylvie Fréchette	CAN	191.717
3.	Fumiko Okuno	JPN	187.056
4.	Olga Sedakova	RUS	185.106
5.	Anne Capron	FRA	182.449
6.	Christina Thalassinidou (Khristina Falasinidi)	GRE	180.244
7.	Kerry Shacklock	GBR	179.839
8.	Marjolijn Both	HOL	179.354

When Tracie Ruiz-Conforto of the United States and Carolyn Waldo of Canada retired following the 1988 Olympics, their places were taken by Kristen Babb-

A thrilling moment in the 1988 solo synchronized swimming competition.

Sprague and Sylvie Fréchette, respectively. Babb-Sprague was forced to begin learning synchronized swimming at the age of three. She entered her first competition when she was six. By the time she won her first United States championship in 1989, when she was 20 years old, she was suffering from extreme pain in her lower back. It turned out that her frontal abdominal muscles were so overdeveloped from a lifetime of synchronized swimming that her oblique stomach muscles were unable to develop. The only cure was to let her muscles atrophy and then rebuild them in a more balanced manner. Babb-Sprague stayed away from the pool for over eight months, but returned to competition in time to win the 1990 United States championship.

While Babb-Sprague was learning her sport in Walnut Creek, California, Sylvie Fréchette was struggling to find pools in which to practice in Montreal. In 1990, the city of Montreal built a pool complex with state-of-the-art

synchro equipment, including underwater cameras and sound system. It was destroyed by fire two weeks after it opened.

In 1991, Fréchette defeated Babb-Sprague at both the world championships and the World Cup, and she went into the Olympics as the favorite. One week before the Barcelona Opening Ceremony, Fréchette returned from a day of training to the condominium she shared with her boyfriend, television sports commentator Sylvain Lake. She found Lake dead, a victim of suicide by carbon monoxide poisoning. She went to Barcelona in shock, but determined to compete.

According to the rules then in force, the competition included a round of figures that counted for 50 percent of the final score. Fréchette, who was strong in figures, hoped to pick up some valuable points to offset the gains that Babb-Sprague was expected to make with her free routine. The figures competition, in which each swimmer performs four required movements, is usually the dullest part of synchronized swimming. But this time, just after Fréchette completed her albatross spin up 180 degrees, something unexpected happened. The exact details depend on whether you believe the Canadian version or the American version.

One thing is certain: One of the five judges, Ana Maria da Silveira of Brazil, gave Fréchette a score of 8.7, then announced that she had made a mistake and tried to change it. She was not allowed to make the change and the score of 8.7 stood. The Canadian team filed a protest. They claimed that da Silveira had intended to give Fréchette a 9.7 rather than an 8.7 but had pushed the wrong button. Noticing her mistake immediately, she tried to change the score, but had trouble with the touch pad. In desperation, she caught the attention of the assistant referee, who was Japanese. Because they had trouble communicating in English, the assistant referee did not understand what da Silveira was trying to tell her. By the time da Silveira was able to alert the referee, Judith McGowan of the United States, the 8.7 had already been displayed to the public as the official score. The rules stated that once a score was made public, it could not be changed.

The Americans conceded that da Silveira had tried to change her score, but challenged her motivation and timing. In figures competition the performers all wear black costumes and a white cap and their names are not announced to the judges until after they have recorded their scores. The Americans theorized that da Silveira had not realized that the woman she was grading was the favorite and had awarded her an 8.7. When she saw Fréchette's name flashed on the scoring screen, and saw that the other judges had given her scores of 9.2, 9.4, 9.5, and 9.6, da Silveira was embarrassed and tried to upgrade the score. McGowan disputed the Canadian claim that da Silveira's intended score was 9.7, stating that it was lower. Indeed, even though the 8.7 was Fréchette's lowest score of the figures competition, a 9.7 would have been the highest score by any judge for any figure by any performer.

A Jury of Appeal voted 11-2 to retain the 8.7. The two dissenting votes came from the Canadian members. The whole controversy would have faded away except for what happened the next day during the free routines. Babb-Sprague came out of the figures with a lead of .251 points. Fréchette then performed an unusually strong free routine and picked up .120 points, leaving her .131 points short of Babb-Sprague, who thus won the gold medal. Had da Silveira's albatross spin score been changed to 9.7, Fréchette would have won by .212 points. Even if da Silveira's revised score had been 9.4, the average of the other judges' scores, Fréchette still would have won by .041 points.

Babb-Sprague was married to professional baseball player Ed Sprague, who happened to play for the Toronto Blue Jays. Kristen flew straight from Barcelona to Toronto to watch Ed play. Whenever Ed came to bat, Canadian fans booed. All Canadian animosity for Ed Sprague dissolved when he helped the Blue Jays win the World Series, but the dispute did not end. Richard Pound, a powerful Canadian member of the executive board of the International Olympic Committee, led the crusade to overturn the official results. With the very existence of synchronized swimming as an Olympic sport on the line, F.I.N.A. capitulated, and in October 1993 they awarded Fréchette a belated gold medal, although Babb-Sprague was allowed to retain hers as well.

DUET

1984 Los Angeles T: 18, N: 18, D: 8.9.
1.	Candy Costie, Tracie Ruiz	USA	195.584
2.	Sharon Hambrook, Kelly Kryczka	CAN	194.234
3.	Saeko Simura, Miwako Motoyoshi	JPN	187.992
4.	Caroline Holmyard, Carolyn Wilson	GBR	184.050
5.	Edith Boss, Karin Singer	SWI	180.109
6.	Catrien Eijken, Marijke Engelen	HOL	179.058

7.	Pascale Besson, Muriel Hermine	FRA	176.709
8.	Claudia Novelo, Pilar Ramirez	MEX	176.409

1988 Seoul T: 15, N: 15, D: 10.1.
1.	Michelle Cameron, Carolyn Waldo	CAN	197.317
2.	Sarah Josephson, Karen Josephson	USA	197.284
3.	Miyako Tanaka, Mikako Kotani	JPN	190.159
4.	Karine Schuler, Anne Capron	FRA	184.792
5.	Edith Boss, Karin Singer	SWI	183.950
6.	Maria Cherniaeva, Tatyana Titova	SOV/RUS	182.667
7.	Nicola Shearn, Lian Goodwin	GBR	179.075
8.	Lourdes Candini, Sonia Cardenas	MEX	176.833

Cameron and Waldo achieved a narrow victory, thanks to a superb performance in the compulsory figures and patriotic judging on the part of Canadian judge Joyce Corner. During the freestyle routine, Corner was the only one of seven judges to give Cameron and Waldo a higher mark than the Josephson twins. Had the scores of the Canadian and American judges been dropped, rather than the highest and lowest scores, the final placings would have been reversed.

1992 Barcelona T: 18, N: 18, D: 8.7.
1.	Karen Josephson, Sarah Josephson	USA	192.175
2.	Penny Vilagos, Vicky Vilagos	CAN	189.394
3.	Fumiko Okuno, Aki Takayama	JPN	186.868
4.	Anna Kozlova, Olga Sedkova	RUS	184.083
5.	Marianne Aeschbacher, Anne Capron	FRA	181.795
6.	Kerry Shacklock, Laila Vakil	GBR	179.366
7.	Marjolijn Both, Tamara Zwart	HOL	179.345
8.	Guan Zewen, Wang Xiaojie	CHN	177.843

Both the Josephsons and the Vilagoses were identical twin sisters. The Josephsons were undefeated since the 1988 Olympics, having won 15 straight meets. The Vilagoses came back after five years away from competition to prepare for the 1992 Olympics. It was the fist time two sets of twins took gold and silver since the Landvoigt and Pimenov twins won the men's coxless pairs rowing at the 1980 Games.

TABLE TENNIS

MEN
Singles
Doubles

WOMEN
Singles
Doubles

Table tennis, also known as ping-pong, is played on a table 9 feet (2.74 meters) long and 5 feet (1.525 meters) wide. The playing surface is 2 feet 6 inches (76 centimeters) above the floor. The table is divided by a net 6 inches (15.25 centimeters) high. The ball, made of celluloid or a similar plastic material, is 1½ inches (38 millimeters) in diameter and weighs .088 ounces (2.5 grams). The racket may be any size, shape, or weight. Rackets are made of wood reinforced with fibrous material and covered with rubber.

Players take turns serving five serves at a time. The rules for a proper serve are quite strict. The server must begin by placing the ball on the open palm of his or her free hand, above the level of the playing surface and behind the end line. The server must toss the ball straight up, without adding spin, at least 6.3 inches (16 centimeters) in the air. As soon as the ball starts falling, the server may hit it. The serve must touch first on the server's side of the table and then pass over the net before touching the receiver's side. For each return after the service, the ball must be hit straight over the net before it touches the table. In doubles matches, the ball must touch first the right half of the server's side and then the right half of the receiver's side. During a rally, players on the same team must alternate hitting the ball. At each change of service in doubles matches, the receiver becomes the server and the server's partner becomes the receiver.

The first player or pair to score 21 points wins the game. However, if the players or pairs are tied at 20, one side must win by 2 points. When the score reaches 20–20, the service changes after each serve instead of after each five serves.

In 1988 and 1992, tournaments began with round-robin pools; however, in 1996, the competitions will use a single-elimination format in which each match is won by the first player or team to win three games.

MEN

SINGLES

1896–1984 not held

1988 Seoul C: 64, N: 35, D: 10.1.

			MATCHES		GAMES	
			W	L	W	L
1.	Yoo Nam-kyu	KOR	11	0	33	3
2.	Kim Ki-taik	KOR	10	1	31	12
3.	Erik Lindh	SWE	10	1	30	12
4.	Tibor Klampár	HUN	8	3	26	17
5.	Jiang Jialiang	CHN	10	1	31	6
6.	Chen Longcan	CHN	8	3	27	12
7.	Jörgen Persson	SWE	8	3	28	14
8.	Jan-Ove Waldner	SWE	8	3	26	13

Final: Yoo—Kim 17–21, 21–19, 21–11, 23–21
3rd Place: Lindh—Klampár 14–21, 21–17, 21–17, 21–16
5th Place: Jiang—Chen 21–12, 21–16, 21–17
7th Place: Persson—Waldner 21–15, 21–16, 21–17

The inaugural men's table tennis tournament was highlighted by the shocking upsets of all five of the top-seeded players, none of whom advanced to the semifinals. In the round of 16, number four ranked Andrzej Grubba of Poland was beaten by the fifth seed, Jörgen Persson, who was in turn eliminated in the quarterfinals by Asian Games champion Yoo Nam-kyu. The quarterfinals also saw the defeat of number two seed Jan-Ove Waldner and number three Chen Longcan, who lost five-game cliffhangers to underdogs Kim Ki-taik and Tibor Klampár. But the biggest stunner was the demise of two-time world champion Jiang Jialiang. Jiang, a national hero of movie-star proportions, was beaten in four games by tenth-ranked Erik Lindh. In the semifinals, Yoo and Kim, responding to a wildly enthusiastic crowd, prevailed in straight games to set up a much-appreciated all-Korean final.

1992 Barcelona C: 64, N: 32, D: 8.6.

			MATCHES		GAMES	
			W	L	W	L
1.	Jan-Ove Waldner	SWE	7	0	18	1
2.	Jean-Philippe Gatien	FRA	6	1	15	9
3.	Kim Taek-soo	KOR	5	1	12	8
3.	Ma Wenge	CHN	5	1	14	4
5.	Ding Yi	AUT	4	1	11	3
5.	Jörgen Persson	SWE	4	1	9	4
5.	Jörg Rosskopf	GER	4	1	10	4
5.	Wang Tao	CHN	4	1	11	4

Final: Waldner—Gatien 21–10, 21–18, 25–23

At his best, such as at the 1989 world championships, Jan-Ove Waldner was unbeatable. But often Waldner played far from his best. At the 1988 Olympics, he was a medal favorite, but finished only eighth. At the 1992 European Championships, only 3½ months before the Olympics, he was also eliminated in the quarterfinals. In Barcelona, however, Waldner played better than he ever had, losing only one game to Jörg Rosskopf and crushing his remaining opponents in straight sets.

DOUBLES

1896–1984 not held

1988 Seoul T: 32, N: 23, D: 9.30.

			MATCHES		GAMES	
			W	L	W	L
1.	CHN	(Chen Longcan, Wei Qingguang)	10	0	20	3
2.	YUG	(Ilija Lupulesku, Zoran Primorać)	8	2	17	8
3.	KOR	(Ahn Jae-hyung, Yoo Nam-kyu)	9	1	18	3
4.	KOR	(Kim Ki-taik, Kim Wan)	7	3	16	7
5.	CHN	(Jiang Jialiang, Xu Zengcai)	9	1	18	5
6.	POL	(Andrzej Grubba, Leszek Kucharski)	7	3	15	7
7.	SWE	(Erik Lindh, Jörgen Persson)	7	3	14	6
8.	SWE	(Mikael Appelgren, Jan-Ove Waldner)	6	4	14	10

Final: Chen/Wei—Lupulesku/Primorać 20–22, 21–8, 21–9
3rd Place: Ahn/Yoo—Kim/Kim 21–13, 21–16
5th Place: Jiang/Xu—Grubba/Kucharski 21–7, 21–12
7th Place: Lindh/Persson—Appelgren/Waldner 21–10, 21–14

The final match was a replay of the 1987 world championship final. The result was also the same, with Chen and Wei defeating Lupulesku and Primorać two games to one.

1992 Barcelona T: 30, N: 23, D: 8.4.

			MATCHES		GAMES	
			W	L	W	L
1.	CHN	(Lu Lin, Wang Tao)	6	0	15	6
2.	GER	(Steffen Fetzner, Jörg Rosskopf)	5	1	14	3
3.	KOR	(Kang Hee-chan, Lee Chul-seung)	3	1	7	6
3.	KOR	(Kim Taek-soo, Yoo Nam-kyu)	3	1	8	3
5.	CHN	(Ma Wenge, Yu Shentong)	3	1	8	4
5.	FRA	(Damien Eloi, Jean-Philippe Gatien)	3	1	7	4
5.	RUS	(Andrei Mazunov, Dmitri Mazunov)	3	1	6	4
5.	YUG	(Slobodan Grujić, Ilija Lupulesku)	3	1	6	4

Final: Lu/Wang—Fetzner/Rosskopf 26–24, 18–21, 21–18, 13–21, 21–14

At 9 a.m. on August 4, two hours before the men's doubles final, Wang Tao and Lu Lin appeared at the Olympic Village bus stop, ready to take the shuttle bus to the Estació del Nord competition site. The bus never came. In a panic, they began jogging to the sports complex, finally hailing a taxi to take them the rest of the way. They arrived just in time for the match and found the stands filled with wildly enthusiastic German fans. In the

first game, Wang and Lu fell behind 15–20 before winning 26–24. In the second game they led 18–12, only to see Fetzner and Rosskopf reel off nine straight points to even the match. The two teams traded games, to make it 2–2. The deciding game was also tied at 10–10, but then Wang and Lu took command and outscored the German pair 11–4 the rest of the way.

WOMEN
SINGLES

1896–1984 not held

1988 Seoul C: 48, N: 28, D: 10.1.

			MATCHES		GAMES	
			W	L	W	L
1.	Chen Jing	CHN	9	0	27	2
2.	Li Huifen	CHN	8	1	26	4
3.	Jiao Zhimin	CHN	8	1	24	9
4.	Marie Hrachová	CZE	6	3	20	12
5.	Flyura Bulatova	SOV/RUS	8	1	24	8
6.	Valentina Popova	SOV/RUS	6	3	18	9
7.	Bettine Vriesekoop	HOL	7	2	21	9
8.	Hong Cha-ok	KOR	5	4	16	15

Final: Chen—Li 21–17, 21–16, 21–23, 15–21, 21–15
3rd Place: Jiao—Hrachová 21–18, 21–19, 21–17
5th Place: Bulatova—Popova 21–16, 21–11, 22–20
7th Place: Vriesekoop—Hong 21–19, 21–16, 25–23

The table tennis world was shocked and somewhat suspicious when Chinese officials announced that their Olympic team would include secondary stars Li Huifen and Chen Jing instead of the number one ranked player in the world, He Zhili, and number three ranked Dai Lili. It turned out that He was being punished for refusing to throw matches to other Chinese players during the 1987 world championship, which she won. She eventually married a Japanese man and moved to Osaka. Chen's coach, Xi Enting, summed up the Olympic prospects of his 21-year-old protégé by saying, "I think there are two possible outcomes: one is that she [Chen] will become famous overnight and the other is that she will yield to the pressure, perform poorly and receive a lasting blow to her confidence."

As it turned out, Chen and Li crushed their opposition. Chen advanced to the final without losing a single game, while Li lost only one. Meanwhile, rumors spread in the Korean press that Li had won her semifinal contest over top seed Jiao Zhimin because Jiao had been ordered to throw the match. Jiao was hounded by the Korean media wherever she went because of interest in her "politically incorrect" romance with South Korean doubles champion Ahn Jae-hyung.

Despite the circus and scandal surrounding the

women's singles tournament, the final was an exciting, hard-fought battle, won three games to two by Chen, who thus escaped "a lasting blow to her confidence."

As for Jiao Zhimin and Ahn Jae-hyung, they did in fact get married and settle in Seoul, where their first child was born three years to the day after the Opening Ceremony of the 1988 Olympics.

1992 Barcelona C: 62, N: 38, D: 8.5.

		MATCHES		GAMES	
		W	L	W	L
1. Deng Yaping	CHN	7	0	18	1
2. Qiao Hong	CHN	6	1	16	5
3. Hyun Jung-hwa	KOR	5	1	12	5
3. Li Bun-hui	PRK	4	1	11	5
5. Chai Po-wa	HKG	4	1	9	4
5. Chen Zihe	CHN	4	1	10	3
5. Emilia Ciosu	ROM	3	1	9	3
5. Yu Sun-bok	PRK	4	1	9	5

Final: Deng—Qiao 21–6, 21–8, 15–21, 23–21

The biggest obstacle in Deng Yaping's career was not her opponents, but her height. When she was 9 years old she won a provincial junior championship but was denied a place on the provincial team because she was too short. In 1988, when she was 15 years old, Deng won the national championship, but was refused a spot on the national team because she was too short. The national coaching staff finally gave in and, in 1989, Deng, still only 16 years old, teamed with Qiao Hong to win the doubles title at the world championships. In 1991, by which time she had topped out at 4 feet 10½ inches, Deng defeated Li Bun-hui of North Korea to win the singles world championship. At the Olympics she obliterated everyone she faced. In the final her opponent was her doubles partner, Qiao Hong. Two days earlier, Deng and Qiao had won the doubles tournament. But with cash awards and other favors at stake, the Deng-Qiao match was a serious affair. Deng won the first two games easily. Then Qiao caught fire, won one game and almost won a second, but Deng won 6 of the last 8 points and prevailed, 23–21.

DOUBLES

1896–1984 not held

1988 Seoul T: 15, N: 15, D: 9.30.

		MATCHES		GAMES	
		W	L	W	L
1. KOR	(Hyun Jung-hwa, Yang Young-ja)	10	0	20	2
2. CHN	(Chen Jing, Jiao Zhimin)	8	1	17	4
3. YUG	(Jasna Fazlić, Gordana Perkucin)	7	3	15	7
4. JPN	(Mika Hoshino, Kiyomi Ishida)	4	5	10	11
5. CZE	(Marie Hrachová, Renata Kasalová)	7	2	14	7
6. SOV	(Flyura Bulatova, Olena Kovtun)	6	4	13	10
7. HOL	(Mirjam Kloppenburg, Bettine Vriesekoop)	5	4	10	11
8. HUN	(Csilla Bátorfi, Edit Urbán)	4	6	11	14

Final: Hyun/Yang—Chen/Jiao 21–19, 16–21, 21–10
3rd Place: Fazlić/Perkucin—Hoshino/Ishida 21–14, 11–21, 21–16
5th Place: Hracová/Kasalová—Bulatova/Kovtun 21–10, 8–21, 21–19
7th Place: Kloppenburg/Vriesekoop—Bátorfi/Urbán 21–18, 21–23, 21–17

Hyun and Yang took an 11–2 lead in the decisive third game of the final, which they went on to win 21–10. Bronze medalists Fazlić and Perkucin were from Bosnia and Serbia, respectively. By 1992 their nation, Yugoslavia, had splintered and they found themselves on different teams. They were allowed to compete as a pair anyway because Fazlić's husband was Serbian, but they were upset in pool play by Hooman (Kloppenburg) and Vriesekoop.

1992 Barcelona T: 31, N: 25, D: 8.3.

		MATCHES		GAMES	
		W	L	W	L
1. CHN	(Deng Yaping, Qiao Hong)	6	0	15	4
2. CHN	(Chen Zihe, Gao Jun)	5	1	13	5
3. PRK	(Li Bun-hui, Yu Sun-bok)	4	1	10	4
3. KOR	(Hong Cha-ok, Hyun Jung-Hwa)	3	1	8	4
5. HKG	(Chai Po-wa, Chan Tan-lui)	3	1	7	3
5. HOL	(Mirjam Hooman [Kloppenburg], Bettine Vriesekoop)	3	1	7	4
5. KOR	(Hong Soon-hwa, Lee Jung-im)	3	1	7	4
5. RUS	(Irina Palina, Yelena Timina)	3	1	6	4

Final: Deng/Qiao—Che/Gao 21–13, 14–21, 21–14, 21–19

The final was delayed for ten minutes because Qiao twisted her ankle just before entering the arena. Two days later, Deng and Qiao faced each other in the singles final.

TENNIS

MEN   **WOMEN**   Discontinued Event
Singles   Singles
Doubles   Doubles

A tennis court is 78 feet (23.77 meters) long and 27 feet (8.23 meters) wide. For doubles play the width is extended 4½ feet (1.37 meters) on each side for a total width of 36 feet (10.97 meters). The court is divided by a net, the height of which is 3 feet (.914 meters) at the center. The lines at the ends of the court are called *base-lines*. On each side of the net, 21 feet (6.4 meters) from it and parallel to it, is drawn a *service line*. A *center service line* is drawn perpendicular to the net, midway between the side lines and extending from the net to the service line. Thus, the forecourt on each side of the net is divided into *service courts*.

A tennis ball must be white or yellow. It must be between 2½ inches (6.35 centimeters) and 2⅝ inches (6.67 centimeters) in diameter and must weigh between 2 ounces (56.7 grams) and 2¹⁄₁₆ ounces (58.5 grams). Tennis balls must meet an official bounce test: when dropped onto concrete from a height of 100 inches (254 centimeters), a ball must bounce between 53 inches (135 centimeters) and 58 inches (147 centimeters).

The frame of a tennis racket may not exceed 32 inches (81.28 centimeters) in length, including the handle, and 12½ inches (31.75 centimeters) in width. The strung surface of the racket may not exceed 15½ (39.37 centimeters) in length and 11½ inches (29.21 centimeters) in width.

In tennis, a point is scored by a player whose opponent is unable to return the ball within the baseline and the sidelines on his or her opponent's side of the court. When a player has no points, the score is called love. When a player wins a point, the score is called 15. When the player scores a second point the score is called 30. A third point is scored 40 and if the player scores a fourth point, he or she wins a game. However, a player is awarded a game only if he has scored two more points than his opponent. If both players have won three points, the score is called deuce. The next point scored by a player is called advantage for that player. If the same player wins the next point, that player wins the game. If the other player wins the next point, the score returns to deuce, and play continues until one player wins two points in a row after the score of deuce. Players alternate service after each game.

The first player to win six games wins a set, except that a player must win by a margin of two games over his opponent. In Olympic tournaments, if both players win six games, a tie-break game is played. The first player to score seven points wins the tie-break, but the player must win by a margin of two points. No tie-break game is played in the third set of a three-set match or the fifth set of a five-set match. Instead, the set continues until one player wins by two games. In 1996, all matches will be won by the first player or pair to win two sets, except in men's finals, which will be run on a best three sets of five basis.

The server must start with both feet behind the base-line, throw the ball in the air, and strike it before it touches the ground. The first service of a game is made from the right side of the court, with subsequent services made from alternating sides thereafter. The ball must pass over the net and hit the ground in the service court diagonally opposite. A service that fails to do so is called a fault. Two faults in a row, known as a double fault, results in a point for the server's opponent. If a served ball hits the net and then lands fairs, it is called a let and is treated as if it never happened.

The rules for doubles matches are the same as those for singles, with some minor differences. The sidelines are wider (see above), although the service court is the same as in singles. Partners alternate serving games. The first player on a team serves an entire game. The next time that it is the team's turn to serve, the other player on the team serves an entire game. The serving pair switches sides after each point, while the players on the receiving team take turns receiving the service.

Olympic tournaments are run on a straight single-elimination basis: one lost match and you are out.

MEN
SINGLES

1896 Athens C: 13, N: 7, D: 4.11.
1. John Boland   GBR/IRL
2. Dionysios Kasdaglis   EGY
3. Momcsilló Topavicza   HUN
3. Konstantinos Paspatis   GRE
5. Aristides Akratopoulos   GRE
5. Evangelis Rallis   GRE
     Final: Boland—Kasdaglis, 6–3, 6–1

Boland was a student at Christ's College, Oxford when he invited a Greek friend, Thrasyvoalos Manaos, to speak at the Oxford Union on the subject of the upcoming Olympic games. During the Easter holidays, Boland traveled to Athens as a spectator, but Manaos, who was by then the secretary of the Organizing Committee, arranged to have Boland entered in the tennis competition. Later in life Boland became a renowned barrister, politician, author, and ardent proponent of both Irish independence and the Irish language.

1900 Paris C: 13, N: 3, D: 7.11.
1. Hugh "Laurie" Doherty   GBR
2. Harold Mahoney   GBR/IRL
3. Reginald Doherty   GBR
3. Arthur Norris   GBR
5. Paul Lecaron   FRA
5. Basil Spalding de Garmendia   USA
    Final: H. Doherty—Mahoney, 6–4, 6–2, 6–3

The Doherty brothers were scheduled to play one another in the semifinals, but refused to do so in a "minor" tournament. Reginald stepped aside and agreed to let his younger brother advance to the final. Between them, Reggie and Laurie won 9 Wimbledon singles championships between 1897 and 1906.

1904 St. Louis C: 27, N: 1, D: 9.3.
1. Beals Wright   USA
2. Robert LeRoy   USA
3. Alonzo Bell   USA
3. Edgar Leonard   USA
5. William Blatherwick (USA), Charles Cresson (USA), John Neely (USA), Semp Russ (USA).
    Final: Wright—LeRoy, 6–4, 6–4

1906 Athens C: 18, N: 6, D: 4.23.
1. Max Decugis   FRA
2. Maurice Germot   FRA
3. Zdenek "Jánsky" Žemla   BOH/CZE
    Final: Decugis—Germot, 6–1, 7–9, 6–1, 6–1

1908 London C: 31, N: 9, D: 7.15.
1. Major Ritchie   GBR
2. Otto Froitzheim   GER
3. Wilberforce Eaves   GBR
4. Ivie Richardson   SAF
5. Charles Brown (CAN), George Caridia (GBR), Charles Dixon (GBR), Maurice Germot (FRA)
    Final: Ritchie—Froitzheim, 7–5, 6–3, 6–4
    3rd Place: Eaves—Richardson, 6–2, 6–2, 6–3

Ritchie was 37 years old when he defeated the 24-year-old Froitzheim.

1908 London C: 7, N: 2, D: 5.14.
Indoor Courts
1. Arthur Gore   GBR
2. George Caridia   GBR

3. Major Ritchie   GBR
4. Wilberforce Eaves   GBR
    Final: Gore—Caridia, 6–3, 7–5, 6–4

Gore played in every Wimbledon tournament that was held between 1888 and 1927. He is the oldest person to win a Wimbledon singles championship (aged 41, in 1909) and the oldest singles finalist (aged 44, in 1912).

1912 Stockholm C: 49, N: 12, D: 7.5.
1. Charles Winslow   SAF
2. Harold Kitson   SAF
3. Oscar Kreuzer   GER
4. Ladislav "Rázný" Žemla   BOH/CZE
5. Louis Heyden (GER), Otto von Müller (GER), Ludwig Salm (AUT), Arthur Zborzil (AUT)
    Final: Winslow—Kitson, 7–5, 4–6, 10–8, 8–6
    3rd Place: Kreuzer—Žemla, 6–2, 3–6, 6–3, 6–1

The level of competition at the 1912 Olympics was somewhat disappointing, due to the fact that the Swedish organizers scheduled the tournament at the same time as the Wimbledon championships.

1912 Stockholm C: 22, N: 6, D: 5.12.
Indoor Courts
1. André Gobert   FRA
2. Charles Dixon   GBR
3. Anthony Wilding   AUS/NZE
4. F. Gordon Lowe   GBR
5. George Caridia   GBR
5. Gunnar Setterwall   SWE
    Final: Gobert—Dixon, 8–6, 6–4, 6–4
    3rd Place: Wilding—Lowe, 4–6, 6–2, 7–5, 6–0

1920 Antwerp C: 41, N: 14, D: 8.23.
1. Louis Raymond   SAF
2. Ichiya Kumagae   JPN
3. Charles Winslow   SAF
4. Oswald Noel Turnbull   GBR
5. Manuel Alonso Areyzaga (SPA), George Dodd (SAF), Gordon Lowe (GBR), Sune Malmström (SWE)
    Final: Raymond—Kumagae, 5–7, 6–4, 7–5, 6–4
    3rd Place: Winslow—Turnbull WO

The second round included one marathon match between Gordon Lowe of Great Britain and A. Zerlendtis of Greece, which lasted for almost six hours over a two-day period. At one point, the ballboys, bored by the prolonged cautious rallying, left the court and went to lunch, forcing Lowe and Zerlindtis to suspend play. Eventually Lowe won, 14–12, 6–8, 5–7, 6–4, 6–4. Lowe was subsequently eliminated in the fourth round after another five-set battle against Winslow. Raymond almost didn't make it into the final, having survived his semifinal match with Turnbull 2–6, 1–6, 6–2, 6–2, 6–1.

1924 Paris C: 82, N: 27, D: 7.20.
1. Vincent Richards   USA
2. Henri Cochet   FRA

3. Umberto Luigi de Morpurgo   ITA
4. Jean Borotra   FRA
5. Toshio Harada (JPN), Samuel Jacob (IND), René Lacoste (FRA), Richard Norris Williams (USA)
   Final: Richards—Cochet, 6–4, 6–4, 5–7, 4–6, 6–2
   3rd Place: de Morpurgo—Borotra, 1–6, 6–1, 8–6, 4–6, 7–5

1928–1984 not held

1988 Seoul C: 64, N: 32, D: 9.30.
1. Miloslav Mečíř   CZE/SLV
2. Timothy Mayotte   USA
3. Stefan Edberg   SWE
3. Bradley Gilbert   USA
5. Paolo Canè (ITA), Martin Jaite (ARG), Michiel Schapers (HOL), Carl-Uwe Steeb (GER)
   Final: Mečíř—Mayotte, 3–6, 6–2, 6–4, 6–2

The critical match of the tournament took place in the semifinals when Wimbledon champion Stefan Edberg faced Slovak Miloslav Mečíř. Edberg, who had won the 1984 Olympic demonstration tournament, had defeated Mečíř in the Wimbledon semifinals in July 4–6, 2–6, 6–4, 6–3, 6–4. But in Seoul it was Mečíř who came from behind to win 3–6, 6–0, 1–6, 6–4, 6–2. Tim Mayotte advanced to the final by losing only one set in five matches, but was no match for Mečíř's hypnotic precision stroking.

1992 Barcelona C: 64, N: 36, D: 8.8.
1. Marc Rosset   SWI
2. Jordi Arresse   SPA
3. Andrei Cherkasov   RUS
3. Goran Ivanišević   CRO
5. Leonardo Lavalle (MEX), Jaime Oncins (BRA), Emilio Sánchez-Vicario (SPA), Fabrice Santoro (FRA)
   Final: Rosset—Arresse, 7–6 (7–2), 6–4, 3–6, 4–6, 8–6

The best professionals in the world showed up for the Olympic tournament. As usual, the top 16 players were seeded so that they wouldn't meet until the later rounds. The organizers needn't have bothered. Of the top 11 seeded players, only one, Goran Ivanišević, made it as far as the quarterfinals. The rest were beaten early by the brutal heat, the slow clay surface, and the patriotic emotions of their unheralded opponents. The first to go was second seed Stefan Edberg of Sweden, who fell in the very first round in straight sets to Russia's Andrei Chesnokov. Tenth seeded Thomas Muster also lost his first match. In the second round, sixth seed Michael Chang of the United States was beaten by Jaime Oncins, seventh seed Guy Forget of France lost in straight sets to Magnus Larsson of Sweden, eighth seed Michael Stich of Germany lost to countryman Carl-Uwe Steeb, ninth seed Wayne Ferreira of South Africa was crushed 6–4, 6–0, 6–2 by Marc Rosset, and eleventh seed Sergei Bruguera of Spain was put away by Holland's third-string player Mark Koevermans.

Tennis fans had barely recovered from these surprises when the third round brought the really big upsets. Fifth seed Boris Becker of Germany lost to Fabrice Santoro,

third seed Pete Sampras of the United States lost in five sets to Andrei Cherkasov, and in the biggest shocker of all, giant killer Marc Rosset sent top seed Jim Courier of the United States packing, 6–4, 6–2, 6–1.

The way seemed clear for Ivanišević, who was proud to be a member of Croatia's first Olympic team at a time when his nation was at war with Yugoslavia. But Ivanišević was worn out after four straight sweltering five-set matches. In the semifinals, he too fell to Rosset—his friend and sometime doubles partner.

And so, rather remarkably, the final was contested by Marc Rosset, who was ranked 44th in the world, and Barcelona-born-and-bred Jordi Arresse, who was ranked 30th. Arresse, Spain's third-string player, had almost been dropped from the team to make way for a hotter player, Carlos Costa, but Costa refused to take Arresse's place. What the final lacked in star quality, it made up for in drama. Rosset took the first two sets, but Arresse, encouraged by an extremely partisan Catalan crowd, won the next two sets. Rosset opened a 4–1 lead in the final set, but Arresse fought back to even the score at 4–4. Both players held their services until it was 7–6 Rosset. Arresse was up 40–15 on his next serve, when, five hours after the match began, Rosset shocked the crowd by winning the next four points and with them the set, the match, and the gold medal. The 21-year-old Rosset had never before made it as far as the quarterfinals of a major tournament.

DOUBLES

1896 Athens T: 6, N: 5, D: 4.11.
1. GBR[IRL] & GER   (John Boland, Fredrich "Fritz" Traun)
2. EGY & GRE   (Dionysios Kasdaglis, Demetrios Petrokokkinos)
3. AUS & GBR   (Edwin Flack, George Robertson)
   Final: Boland/Traun—Kasdaglis/Petrokokkinos, 5–7, 6–4, 6–1

Boland entered the tournament at the last minute, when Traun's partner fell ill. When the Union Jack was run up the pole to honor Boland's half of the victory, he objected vehemently, pointing out that the Irish had a flag of their own. The officials apologized and agreed to have an Irish flag prepared.

At the Closing Ceremony, Britain's George Robertson greatly pleased the crowd by reading an ode which he had written in ancient Greek in Pindaric meter to honor the Olympic Games. Although Robertson admired Greek culture, he had nothing but disdain for the French. Writing after the Games in the *Fortnightly Review,* he blamed the French for "the mismanagement of the international arrangements." He also criticized their athletic development. "Their successes," wrote Robertson, "were confined to bicycling and fencing . . . the former a kind of exercise, by many scarcely admitted to the domain of sport." Robertson blamed the French failures on "a certain impatience and lack of necessary physique."

1900 Paris T: 8, N: 3, D: 7.11.
1. GBR   (Reginald Doherty, Hugh "Laurie" Doherty)
2. USA & FRA   (Basil Spalding de Garmendia, Max Decugis)
3. FRA   (André Prévost, Georges de la Chapelle)
3. GBR [IRL] & GER   (Harold Mahoney, Arthur Norris)
    Final: Doherty/Doherty—de Garmendia/Decugis, 6–1, 6–1, 6–0

The Doherty brothers won the Wimbledon doubles championship a record 8 times between 1897 and 1905.

1904 St. Louis T: 15, N: 2, D: 9.3.
1. USA   (Edgar Leonard, Beals Wright)
2. USA   (Alonzo Bell, Robert LeRoy)
3. USA   (Joseph Wear, Allen West)
3. USA   (Clarence Gamble, Arthur Wear)
5. Charles Cresson, Semp Russ (USA), Ralph McKittrick, Dwight Davis (USA), Hugh McKittrick Jones, Harold Kauffman (USA)
    Final: Leonard/Wright—Bell/LeRoy, 6–4, 6–4, 6–2

1906 Athens T: 7, N: 5, D: 4.25.
1. FRA   (Max Decugis, Maurice Germot)
2. GRE   (Xenophon Kasdaglis, Ioannis Ballis)
3. BOH/CZE   (Zdenek "Jánsky" Žemla, Ladislav "Rázny" Žemla)
4. GRE   (T. Simiriotis, N. Zariphis)
    Final: Decugis/Germot—Kasdaglis/Ballis, 6–4, 6–2, 6–1
    3rd Place: Z. Žemla/L. Žemla—Simiriotis/Zariphis, 6–2, 6–3

1908 London T: 12, N: 7, D: 7.15.
1. GBR   (George Hillyard, Reginald Doherty)
2. GBR/IRL   (Major Ritchie, James Parke)
3. GBR   (Clement Cazalet, Charles Dixon)
    Final: Hillyard/Doherty—Ritchie/Parke, 9–7, 7–5, 9–7

Hillyard and Doherty fended off seven match points in the fourth set of their semifinal contest against Cazelet and Dixon before prevailing 5–7, 2–6, 6–4, 17–15, 6–4.

Hillyard was 44 years old at the time of his Olympic victory.

1908 London T: 5, N: 2, D: 5.14.
Indoor Courts
1. GBR   (Arthur Gore, Herbert Roper Barrett)
2. GBR   (George Simond, George Caridia)
3. SWE   (Gunnar Setterwall, Wollmar Boström)
4. GBR   (Major Ritchie, Lionel Escombe)
    Final: Gore/Barrett—Simond/Caridia, 6–2, 2–6, 6–3, 6–3
    3rd Place: Setterwall/Boström—Ritchie/Escombe, 4–6, 6–3, ;—1–6, 6–0, 6–3

1912 Stockholm T: 21, N: 10, D: 7.4.
1. SAF   (Charles Winslow, Harold Kitson)
2. AUT   (Felix Pipes, Arthur Zborzil)
3. FRA   (Albert Canet, Marc Mény de Marangue)
4. BOH/CZE   (Ladislav "Rázný" Žemla, Jiři Just)
5. Michel Soumarokoff, Aleksandr Alenitzyn (RUS), Charles Wennergren, Carl Olof Nylén (SWE), Robert Spiess, Louis Heyden (GER)
    Final: Winslow/Kitson—Pipes/Zborzil, 4–6, 6–1, 6–2, 6–2
    3rd Place: Canet/Mény—L. Žemla/Just, 13–11, 6–3, 8–6

1912 Stockholm T: 8, N: 3, D: 5.12.
Indoor Courts
1. FRA   (André Gobert, Maurice Germot)
2. SWE   (Gunnar Setterwall, Carl Kempe)
3. GBR   (Charles Dixon, Alfred Ernest Beamish)
4. GBR   (Arthur Gore, Herbert Roper Barrett)
    Final: Gobert/Germot—Setterwall/Kempe, 6–4, 12–14, 6–2, ;—6–4
    3rd Place: Dixon/Beamish—Gore/Barrett, 6–2, 0–6, 10–8, 2–6, 6–3

1920 Antwerp T: 22, N:11, D: 8.24.
1. GBR   (Oswald Noel Turnbull, Maxwell Woosnam)
2. JPN   (Ichiya Kumagae, Seiichiro Kashio)
3. FRA   (Max Decugis, Pierre Albarran)
4. FRA   (François Blanchy, Jacques "Toto" Brugnon)
5. Jack Nielsen, Conrad Langaard (NOR), Brian Norton, Louis Raymond (SAF), George Dodd, Cecil Blackburn (SAF), Mino Balbil DiRobecca, Cesare Colombo (ITA)
    Final: Turnbull/Woosnam—Kamagae/Kashio, 6–2, 5–7, 7–5,;—7–5
    3rd Place: Decugis/Albarran—Blanchy/Brugnon, WO

1924 Paris T: 39, N: 24, D: 7.21.
1. USA   (Vincent Richards, Frank Hunter)
2. FRA   (Jacques "Toto" Brugnon, Henri Cochet)
3. FRA   (Jean Borotra, René Lacoste)
4. SAF   (John Condon, Ivie John Richardson)
5. Henning Müller, Charles Wennergren (SWE), Richard Norris Williams, Watson Washburn (USA), José Alonso Areyzaga, Manuel Alonso Areyzaga (SPA), Subimal Hadi, David Rutnam (IND)
    Final: Richards/Hunter—Brugnon/Cochet, 4–6, 6–2, 6–3, 2–6, 6–3
    3rd Place: Borotra/Lacoste—Condon/Richardson, 6–3, 10–8, 6–3

Richards and Hunter, the reigning champions of Wimbledon, won an arduous five–set semifinal match against Borotra and Lacoste, 6–2, 6–3, 0–6, 5–7, 6–3. They won the final by taking four of the last five games. Brugnon, Cochet, Borotra, and Lacoste, known as the Four Musketeers, won 6 straight Davis Cup titles for France between 1927 and 1932.

1928–1984 not held

1988 Seoul T: 31, N: 31, D: 10.1.
1. USA   (Kenneth Flach, Robert Seguso)
2. SPA   (Emilio Sanchez, Sergio Casal)
3. CZE   (Miloslav Mečíř, Milan Srejber)
3. SWE   (Stefan Edberg, Anders Järryd)
5. Darren Cahill, John Fitzgerald (AUS), Morten Christensen, Michael Tauson (DEN), Guy Forget, Henri Leconte (FRA), Goran Ivaniševćc, Slobodan Živojinović (YUG)
    Final: Flach/Seguso—Sanchez/Casal, 6–3, 6–4, 6–7 (5–7), ;—6–7 (1–7), 9–7

Flach and Seguso led two sets to zero and 5–3 in the third set tie-breaker. But Sanchez and Casal pulled out the next 4 points to take the set, then won another tie-breaker in the fourth set. In the fifth set the Americans led 5–4 with Flach serving. But the gritty Spaniards fought back again, breaking service and moving ahead 6–5. Flach and Seguso fell behind 15–30, but came back to win the game, break Casal's serve, and move up 7–6. Again Sanchez and Casal broke Flach's serve to tie the match. Then Sanchez lost his service and, finally, Seguso served out the game at love and the match was over after 3 hours and 42 minutes.

1992 Barcelona T: 30, N: 30, D: 8.7.
1. GER   (Boris Becker, Michael Stich)
2. SAF   (Wayne Ferreira, Piet Norval)
3. ARG   (Javier Frana, Christian Miniussi)
3. CRO   (Goran Ivanišević, Goran Prpić)
5. Ramesh Krishnan, Leander Paes (IND), George Cosac, Dinu Pescariu (ROM), Sergio Casal, Emilio Sánchez-Vicario (SPA), Jakob Hlasek, Marc Rosset (SWI)
   Final: Becker/Stich—Ferreira/Norval, 7–6, 4–6, 7–6, 6–3

Ferreira and Norval were the first South Africans to stand on the medal platform since South Africa was banned from the Olympics after the 1960 Games. Their victory preceded that of long-distance runner Elana Meyer by less than five hours.

WOMEN
SINGLES

1896 not held

1900 Paris C: 6, N: 4, D: 7.11.
1. Charlotte Cooper   GBR
2. Hélène Prévost   FRA
3. Marion Jones   USA
3. Hedwig Rosenbaum   BOH/CZE
   Final: Cooper—Prévost, 6–1, 6–4

Charlotte "Chattie" Cooper had already won three of her five Wimbledon titles when she traveled to Paris for the Olympics. She was the first female champion of the modern Games.

1904 St. Louis not held

1906 Athens C: 5, N: 1, D: 4.24.
1. Esmee Simiriotou   GRE
2. Sophia Marinou   GRE
3. Euphrosine Paspati   GRE
   Final: Simiriotou—Marinou, 2–6, 6–3, 6–3

1908 London C: 5, N: 1, D: 7.15.
1. Dorothea Lambert Chambers GBR
2. P. Dora Boothby   GBR
3. R. Joan Winch   GBR
   Final: Lambert Chambers—Boothby, 6–1, 7–5

Charlotte Cooper became the first female Olympic champion when she won the tennis tournament in Paris in 1900.

Due to numerous withdrawals, only four matches were contested, and Lambert Chambers won three of them. Boothby advanced to the final without playing a single game. Both Lambert Chambers and 1900 winner Charlotte Cooper were born and raised in Ealing, Middlesex. Between 1903 and 1914 Lambert Chambers won 7 Wimbledon singles titles.

1908 London C: 7, N: 2, D: 5.14.
Indoor Courts
1. Gladys Eastlake-Smith GBR
2. Alice Greene   GBR
3. Märtha Adlerstråhle   SWE
4. Elsa Wallenberg   SWE
   Final: Eastlake-Smith—Greene, 6–2, 4–6, 6–0
   3rd Place: Alderstråhle—Wallenberg, 1–6, 6–3, 6–2

1912 Stockholm C: 8, N: 4, D: 7.4.
1. Marguerite Broquedis   FRA
2. Dora Köring   GER
3. Anna "Molla" Bjurstedt NOR
4. Edit Arnheim   SWE
   Final: Broquedis—Köring, 4–6, 6–3, 6–4
   3rd Place: Bjurstedt—Arnheim, 6–2, 6–2

1912 Stockholm C: 8, N: 3, D: 5.11.
Indoor Courts
1. Edith Hannam   GBR
2. Thora Castenschiold   DEN
3. Mabel Parton   GBR
4. Sigrid Fick   SWE
   Final: Hannam—Castenschiold, 6–4, 6–3
   3rd Place: Parton—Fick, 6–3, 6–3

According to the Official Report of the 1912 Games, in the third-place match, "the difficult screws of [Mrs. Parton] were altogether too much for the Swedish representative."

1920 Antwerp C: 18, N: 7, D: 8.24.
1. Suzanne Lenglen   FRA
2. E. Dorothy Holman   GBR
3. Kathleen "Kitty" McKane   GBR
4. Sigfrid Fick   SWE
5. Elisabeth d'Ayen (FRA), Lily Strömberg (SWE)
   Final: Lenglen—Holman, 6–3, 6–0
   3rd Place: McKane—Fick, 6–2, 6–0

Defending Wimbledon champion Suzanne Lenglen was one of the greatest women tennis players of all time. In the ten sets that it took her to win the Olympic singles title, she lost only four games.

1924 Paris C: 31, N: 14, D: 7.20.
1. Helen Wills   USA
2. Julie "Diddie" Vlasto   FRA
3. Kathleen "Kitty" McKane   GBR
4. Germaine Golding   FRA
5. Elia "Lili" d'Alvarez (SPA), Marion Jessup (USA), Anna "Molla" Bjurstedt-Mallory (NOR), Dorothy Shepherd-Barron (GBR)
   Final: Wills—Vlasto, 6–2, 6–2
   3rd Place: McKane—Golding, 5–7, 6–3, 6–0

In the semifinals McKane won her first set against Vlasto, 6–0, and was leading the second set 3–0 when a disruption occurred which turned the contest around. The match on the center court having just concluded, the Parisian crowd moved over to court number 3 to watch McKane and Vlasto. The umpire, Louis Raymond of South Africa, was calling the score in English and continued to do so, despite increasingly agitated requests from the audience that the score be announced in French. After things settled down, McKane had lost her touch and Vlasto was able to win 13 of the next 16 games to gain a 0–6, 7–5, 6–1 victory. However Vlasto was no match for the 18-year-old sensation Helen Wills, who succeeded Suzanne Lenglen as the queen of tennis.

1928–1984 not held

1988 Seoul C: 48, N: 26, D: 10.1.
1. Stefanie "Steffi" Graf   GER
2. Gabriela Sabatini   ARG
3. Zina Garrison   USA
3. Manuela Maleeva   BUL

5. Rafaella Reggi (ITA), Larissa Savchenko (SOV), Pam Shriver (USA), Natalya Zvereva (SOV/BLR)
   Final: Graf—Sabatini, 6–3, 6–3

In 1984 Steffi Graf, then 15 years old, won the Olympic demonstration tournament despite being its youngest entrant. By 1987 she was ranked number one in the world, and in 1988 she won the Australian Open, the French Open, Wimbledon, and, less than a week before the Olympics, the U.S. Open to become only the fifth player in history to win tennis' Grand Slam. She arrived in Seoul with a 5-month, 35-match winning streak. Her most difficult challenge came in the quarterfinals when she trailed Larissa Savchenko 3–1 in the third set. Graf then won five straight games to close out the match. In the final she faced Gabriela Sabatini, the only player to beat her in 1988. But this time Graf kept Sabatini on the defensive and won in straight sets.

1992 Barcelona C: 64, N: 33, D: 8.7.
1. Jennifer Capriati   USA
2. Stefanie "Steffi" Graf   GER
3. Mary Joe Fernandez   USA
3. Arantxa Sánchez-Vicario   SPA
5. Sabine Applemans (BEL), Anke Huber (GER), Manuela Fragnière-Maleeva (SWI), Conchita Martínez (SPA)
   Final: Capriati—Graf, 3–6, 6–3, 6–4

Three of the four top-ranked players, Monica Seles of Yugoslavia, Gabriela Sabatini of Argentina, and Martina Navratilova of the United States, were declared ineligible for the Olympics because they refused to take part in the Federation Cup. This left an easy road to gold for either defending champion Steffi Graf or local favorite Arantxa Sánchez-Vicario. But it wasn't so easy after all, thanks to 16-year-old prodigy Jennifer Capriati. Capriati turned professional when she was 13 years old. At 14 she became the youngest semifinalist in the history of the French Open and the youngest player to win a match at Wimbledon. At 15 she was the youngest semifinalist in Wimbledon history. She was also making $5 million a year even though she had never made it to a Grand Slam final. By the time the Olympics rolled around, there were rumors that Capriati was burning out from stress. Maybe she was, but not fast enough for Sánchez-Vicario and Graf. In the semifinals Capriati silenced a boisterous Spanish crowd by beating Sánchez-Vicario 6–3, 3–6, 6–1. In the final she faced Graf, who had obliterated her first five opponents in straight sets and who had beaten Capriati the four times they met previously.

The fifth game of the first set lasted 32 points as Graf fought off 9 break points before holding her serve and going on to win the set. Most Graf opponents would have collapsed at that point. Instead, Capriati came back to win the second set and break Graf in the first game of the third set. Graf broke right back in the next game. But after trailing 3–4, Capriati won the last three games to gain the upset victory.

A year later, Capriati did in fact burn out. She dropped out of tennis at the age of 17, was treated at a private psychiatric facility, and in May 1994 she was arrested for possession of marijuana.

DOUBLES

1896–1912 not held

1920 Antwerp T: 9, N: 5, D: 8.24.
1. GBR (Winifred McNair, Kathleen "Kitty" McKane)
2. GBR (W. Geraldine Beamish, E. Dorothy Holman)
3. FRA (Suzanne Lenglen, Elisabeth d'Ayen)
4. BEL (Marie Storms, Fernande Arendt)
5. BEL (Marthe Trasenter-Dupont, Anne Chaudoir)
   Final: McNair/McKane—Beamish/Holman, 8–6, 6–4
   3rd Place: Lenglen/d'Ayen—Storms/Arendt, WO

Kitty McKane withdrew from her singles semifinal in order to conserve her energy for a doubles semi against Lenglen and d'Ayen. It turned out to be a wise decision, as she and 43-year-old Winifred McNair were stretched to the limit to defeat the French pair 2–6, 6–3, 8–6. McKane won a complete set of medals in Antwerp and then added another silver and bronze at the 1924 Olympics. In 1926 McKane and her husband, Leslie Godfree, became the only married couple in history to win the Wimbledon mixed-doubles title.

1924 Paris T: 11, N: 8, D: 7.19.
1. USA (Hazel Wightman, Helen Wills)
2. GBR (Phyllis Covell, Kathleen "Kitty" McKane)
3. GBR (Dorothy Shepherd-Barron, Evelyn Colyer)
4. FRA (Marguerite Billout, Yvonne Bourgeois)
5. SWE (Sigrid Fick, Lily von Essen)
   Final: Wightman/Wills—Covell/McKane, 7–5, 8–6
   3rd Place: Shepherd-Barron/Colyer—Billout/Bourgeois, 6–1,;—6–2

1928–1984 not held

1988 Seoul T: 14, N: 14, D: 9.30.
1. USA (Pam Shriver, Zina Garrison)
2. CZE (Jana Novotná, Helena Suková)
3. AUS (Elizabeth Smylie, Wendy Turnbull)
3. GER (Stefanie "Steffi" Graf, Claudia Kohde-Kilsch)
5. Carling Bassett-Seguso/Jill Hetherington (CAN), Nathalie Tauziat/Isabelle Demongeot (FRA), Etsuko Inoue/Kumiko Okamoto (JPN), Larissa Savchenko/Natalya Zvereva (SOV)
   Final: Shriver/Garrison—Novotná/Suková, 4–6, 6–2, 10–8

With Garrison serving at 9-8 in the final set, she and Shriver lost 5 match points, including two double faults. Finally, on the sixth try, the Americans won when Novotná hit long on a service return.

1992 Barcelona T: 32, N: 32, D: 8.8.
1. USA (Beatriz "Gigi" Fernandez, Mary Joe Fernandez)
2. SPA (Conchita Martínez, Arantxa Sánchez-Vicario)
3. AUS (Rachel McQuillan, Nicole Provis)
3. SOV (Leila Meskhi, Natalya Zvereva)
5. Mercedes Paz/Patricia Tarabini (ARG), Jana Novotná/Andrea Strnadová (CZE), Isabelle Demongeot/Nathalie Tauziat (FRA), Elna Reinach/Mariaan De Swardt (SAF)
   Final: Fernandez/Fernandez—Martínez/Sánchez Vicarío, 7–5, 2–6, 6–2

The final saw 13 service breaks in 28 games. Although Mary Joe and Gigi Fernandez were not related, they did share something besides the same surname: they were both born in the Caribbean. Mary Joe was born in the Dominican Republic to a Cuban mother and a Spanish father. The family moved to the United States when Mary Joe was six months old. Gigi was born in Puerto Rico and settled in the United States when she was 20 years old.

Discontinued Event

MIXED DOUBLES

1900 Paris T: 6, N: 4, D: 7.11.
1. GBR (Charlotte Cooper, Reginald Doherty)
2. FRA&GBR[IRL] (Hélène Prévost, Harold Mahoney)
3. BOH[CZE]&GBR (Hedwig Rosenbaum, Archibald Warden)
3. USA&GBR (Marion Jones, Hugh "Laurie" Doherty)
   Final: Cooper/R. Doherty—Prévost/Mahoney, 6–2, 6–4

1904 St. Louis not held

1906 Athens T: 4, N: 2, D: 4.26.
1. FRA (Marie Decugis, Max Decugis)
2. GRE (Sophia Marinou, Georgios Simiriotis)
3. GRE (Aspasia Matsa, Xenophon Kasdaglis)
   Final: Decugis/Decugis—Marinou/Simiriotis, 6–1, 6–2

1908 London not held

1912 Stockholm T: 6, N: 4, D: 7.5.
1. GER (Dora Köring, Heinrich Schomburgk)
2. SWE (Sigrid Fick, Gunnar Setterwall)
3. FRA (Marguerite Broquedis, Albert Canet)
   Final: Köring/Schomburgk—Fick/Setterwall, 6–4, 6–0

Shortly after the final match began, Mrs. Fick inadvertently smashed her partner in the face rather severely. In the words of the Official Report for 1912: "This little accident seemed to put Setterwall off his game, for his play fell off tremendously. . . ."

1912 Stockholm T: 8, N: 3, D: 5.12.
Indoor Courts
1. GBR (Edith Hannam, Charles Dixon)
2. GBR (F. Helen Aitchison, Herbert Roper Barrett)
3. SWE (Sigrid Fick, Gunnar Setterwall)
4. SWE (Margareta Cederschiöld, Carl Kempe)
   Final: Hannam/Dixon—Aitchison/Barrett, 4–6, 6–3, 6–2
   3rd Place: Fick/Setterwall—Cederschiöld/Kempe WO

1920 Antwerp T: 15, N: 7, D: 8.24.
1. FRA (Suzanne Lenglen, Max Decugis)
2. GBR (Kathleen "Kitty" McKane, Maxwell Woosnam)
3. CZE (Milada Skrbková, Ladislav "Rázný" Žemla)
4. DEN (Amory Folmer-Hansen, Erik Tegner)

5. Anne Chaudoir, Albert Lammens (BEL), Marie Storms, S. Joseph Halot (BEL) .
   Final: Lenglen/Decugis—McKane/Woosnam, 6–4, 6–2
   3rd Place: Skrbková/L. Žemla—Folmer-Hansen/Tegner, 8–6, 6–4

1924 Paris T: 21, N: 14, D: 7.21.
1. USA (Hazel Wightman, Richard Norris Williams)
2. USA (Marion Jessup, Vincent Richards)
3. HOL (Cornelia Bouman, Hendrik Timmer)
4. GBR (Kathleen "Kitty" McKane, John Gilbert)
5. P. Edith Covell, Leslie Godfree (GBR), Sigrid Fick, Henning Müller (SWE), Mary Wallis, Edwin McCrea (IRL)
   Final: Wightman/Williams—Jessup/Richards, 6–2, 6–3
   3rd Place: Bouman/Timmer—McKane/Gilbert, WO

VOLLEYBALL

Men
Women
Beach Volleyball: Men
Beach Volleyball: Women

Volleyball matches are decided on the basis of the best three out of five games. A team wins a game when it scores 15 points, provided the margin is two or more points. If the score is tied at 15, the first team to score 17 points is the winner. Points can only be scored by the serving team. If the defensive team wins a rally, it gains the serve. In the fifth and deciding game, a team may score a point on every play even if the other team is serving.

Each team begins each point with three players near the net and three players in the backcourt. After the serve, all players may leave their positions. A team wins a point when the ball strikes the floor on the opponent's side of the court or when the opposing team hits the ball out of bounds. On each play, a team may touch the ball no more than three times before sending it over the net, although when a player blocks a shot at the net, it does not count as a touch. A player may not touch the ball twice in a row except that a blocker may touch the ball after an attempted block. Rules in force through 1992 prohibited players from touching the ball with parts of their body below the waist. At the 1996 Olympics, players will be allowed to use any part of their bodies, including their feet. Players may not touch the net while hitting the ball, trying to hit the ball, or pretending to try to hit the ball.

Players on a team rotate counter-clockwise after gaining the serve. Each team is permitted six substitute players per game. If a substitute player is later removed from the game, he or she may not return and he or she may only be replaced by the same player for whom he was substituted.

A volleyball court is 18 meters (59 feet) long and 9 meters (29 feet 6 inches) wide. The court is divided by a center line above which is a one-meter (39-inch) net, the top of which is 2.43 meters (7 feet 11½ inches) above the floor for men and 2.24 meters (7 feet 4¼ inches) for women. The net is 9.5 meters (32 feet) long. A volleyball is between 62 and 67 centimeters (25 and 27 inches) in circumference and weighs between 260 and 280 grams (9 and 10 ounces).

MEN

1896–1960 not held

1964 Tokyo T: 10, N: 10, D: 10.23.

		MATCHES		GAMES			
		W	L	W	L	PF	PA
1. SOV	(Ivans Bugajenkovs, Nikolai Burobin, Yuri Chesnokov, Vascha Kacharava, Valery Kalatschikhin, Vitaly Kovalenko, Stanislavs Lugailo, Georgy Mondzolevsky, Yuri Poyarkov, Eduard Sibiryakov, Yuri Venherovsky, Dmitri Voskoboynikov)	8	1	25	5	415	279
2. CZE	(Milan Čuda, Bohumil Golián, Zdenek Humhal, Petr Kop, Josef Labuda, Josef Musil, Karel Paulus, Boris Perušič, Pavel Schenk, Václav Šmidl, Josef Šorm, Ladislav Toman)	8	1	26	10	486	399
3. JPN	(Yutaka Demachi, Tsutomu Koyama, Sadatoshi Sugahara, Naohiro Ikeda, Yasutaka Sato, Toshiaki Kosedo, Tokihiko Higuchi, Masayuki Minami, Takeshi Tokutomi, Teruhisa Moriyama, Yuzo Nakamura, Katsutoshi Nekoda)	7	2	22	12	475	372
4. ROM	(Gheorghe Fieraru, Horatiu Nicolau, Aurel Drăgan, Iuliu Szöcs, William Schreiber, Mihai Grigorovici, Davila Plocon, Nicolae Bărbută, Eduard Derzsi, Mihai Chezan, Constantin Ganciu, Mihai Coste)	6	3	19	15	432	394
5. BUL	(Dimiter Karov, Yvan Gochev, Georgi Konstantinov, Petko Panteleev, Peter Kruchmarov, Simeon Srandev, Lachezar Stoyanov, Boris Gyuderov, Kiril Ivanov, Slav-	5	4	20	16	464	429

	W	L	W	L	PF	PA
cho Slavov, Georgi Spa-sov, Angel Koritarov)						
6. HUN (Béla Czafik, Vilmos Iváncsó, Csaba Lantos, Gábor Bodò, István Molnár, Otto Prouza, Ferenc Tüske, Tibor Flórián, László Gálos, Antal Kangyerka, Mihály Tatár, Ferenc Jánosi)	4	5	18	18	449	474
7. BRA (João Claudio Franca, José Schwart da Costa, Hernando Leao de Oliveira, Newdon Emanuel de Victor, Carlos Albano Feitosa, Marco Antonio Volpi, Carlos Artur Nuzman, José de Oliveira Ramalho, Decio Viotti de Azevedo, Victor Barcellos Borges)	3	6	13	23	410	474
8. HOL (Jacob Korsloot, Jurjaan Kodlen, Johannes Tinkhof, Jan Martinus Oosterbaan, Robert Groenhuijzen, Pieter Swieter, Johan van Wijnen, Jacques de Vink, Dingeman van der Stoep, Jacques Ewalds, Johannes van der Hoek, Franklin Constandse)	2	7	11	24	378	482

The U.S.S.R. was awarded first place on the basis of a better ratio of points for and points against. The Soviets lost to Japan, but won their crucial match against Czechoslovakia, 15–9, 15–8, 5–15, 10–15, 15–7.

1968 Mexico City T: 10, N: 10, D: 10.26.

	MATCHES		GAMES			
	W	L	W	L	PF	PA
1. SOV (Eduard Sibiryakov, Valery Kravchenko, Volodymyr Byelyayev, Yevhen Lapinsky, Oleg Antropov, Vasilijus Matusěvas, Viktor Mykhalchuk, Volodymyr Ivanov, Ivans Bugajenkovs, Georgy Mondzolevsky)	8	1	26	8	464	326
2. JPN (Masayuki Minami, Katsutoshi Nekoda, Mamoru Shiragami, Isao Koizumi, Yasuaki Mitsumori, Jungo Morita, Tadayoshi Yokota, Seiji Oko, Tetsuo Sato, Kenji Shimaoka, Kenji Kimura)	7	2	24	6	430	253
3. CZE (Antonin Procházka, Jiři Svoboda, Lubomir Zaji-	7	2	22	15	454	412

	W	L	W	L	PF	PA
ček, Josef Musil, Josef Smolka, Vladimir Petlak, Petr Kop, František Sokol, Bohumil Golián, Zdenek Groessl, Pavel Schenk, Drahomir Koudelka)						
4. GDR (Horst Peter, Eckhardt Tielscher, Siegfried Schneider, Manfred Heine, Rainer Tscharke, Eckehard Pietzsch, Arnold Schulz, Rudi Schumann, Jürgen Kessel, Walter Toussaint, Jürgen Freiwald, Wolfgang Webner)	6	3	22	12	449	373
5. POL (Stanislaw Zduńczyk, Aleksander Skiba, Jerzy Szymczyk, Edward Skorek, Zbigniew Jasiukiewicz, Tadeusz Siwek, Zdzislaw Ambroziak, Stanislaw Gościniak, Romuald Paszkiewicz, Hubert Wagner, Wojciech Rutkowski, Zbigniew Zarzycki)	6	3	18	11	370	280
6. BUL (Alexander Trenev, Dimiter Zlatanov, Gramen Prinov, Peter Krutschmarov, Alexander Aleksandrov, Zdravko Simeonov, Milio Milev, Dimiter Karov, Kiri Slavov, Dinio Atanasov, Angel Koritarov, Stoyan Stoev)	4	5	16	17	379	385
7. USA (Daniel Patterson, Pedro Velasco, John Henn, Robert May, Larry Rundle, David Bright, Smitty Duke, John Alstrom, Jon Stanley, Thomas Haine,;— Rudy Suwara, Winthrop Davenport)	4	5	15	18	382	414
8. BEL (Jozef Mol, Pul Mesdagh, Fernand Walder, William Bossaerts, Bernard Vailant, Roger Maes, Ronald Vandewal, Hugo Huybrechts, Roger Vandergoten, Benno Saelens, Berto Poosen, Leo Dierckx)	2	7	6	24	239	417

The Soviet team was upset by the United States in their opening contest. Shaken out of their complacency, they went on to win the rest of their matches easily, with only a brief five-set scare from the East Germans. They beat Japan 4–15, 15–13, 15–9, 15–13, in the decisive match.

1972 Munich T: 12, N: 12, D: 9.9.

		MATCHES		GAMES			
		W	L	W	L	PF	PA
1.	JPN	(Kenji Kimura, Yoshihide Fukao, Jungo Morita, Seiji Oko, Tadayoshi Yokota, Katsutoshi Nekoda, Yasuhiro Noguchi, Kenji Shimaoka, Yuzo Nakamura, Tetsuo Nishimoto, Masayuki Minami, Tetsuo Sato)	7	0	21	3	348	192
2.	GDR	(Siegfried Schneider, Arnold Schulz, Wolfgang Webner, Eckehard Pietzsch, Rudi Schumann, Wolfgang Weise, Horst Hagen, Horst Peter, Wolfgang Löwe, Rainer Tscharke, Wolfgang Maibohm, Jürgen Maune)	5	2	16	8	295	256
3.	SOV	(Victor Borsch, Vyacheslav Domani, Vladimir Patkin, Leonid Zaiko, Yuri Starunski, Aleksandr Saprykine, Vladimir Kondra, Efim Chulak, Vladimir Poutiatov, Valery Kravchenko, Yevhen Lapinsky, Yuri Poyarkov)	6	1	19	6	340	296
4.	BUL	(Dimiter Karov, Brunko Iliev, Aleksander Trenev, Ivan Ivanov, Dimiter Zlatanov, Zdravko Simeonov, Tsano Tsanov, Kiril Slavov, Emil Vulchev, Emile Trenev, Luchezar Stoyanov, Ivan Dimitrov)	4	3	15	14	386	347
5.	ROM	(Gabriel Udisteanu, Gyula Bartha, Corneliu Oros, Laurentiu Dumănoiu, William Schreiber, Marian Stamate, Mircea Codoi, Romeo Enescu, Cristian Ion, Stelian Moculescu, Viorel Bălas)	4	3	9	15	300	286
6.	CZE	(Drahomir Koudelka, Vladimir Petlak, Stefan Pipa, Pavel Schenk, Zdenek Groessl, Jaroslav Stanco, Miroslav Nekola, Milan Vapenka, Lubomir Zajićek, Jaroslav Penč, Milan Reznicek, Jaroslav Tomas)	4	3	15	9	321	274
7.	KOR	(Jin Jun-tak, Kim Chung-han, Lee Yong-kwan, Kim Kun-bong, Lee Sun-koo, Choi Jong-ok, Park Kee-won, Kim Kyui-hwan, Chung Dong-kee, Kang Man-soo)						
8.	BRA	(João Jens, Jorge Delano Couto, Antônio Moreno, Luiz Coelho Zech, José Marcelino, Mario Procopio, Paulo de Freitas, Decio Cattaruzzi, Alexandre Celso Kalache)	2	5	12	16	316	373

Note: KOR row values: 3 4 10 13 284 270

Final: JPN—GDR 11–15, 15–2, 15–10, 15–10
3rd Place: SOV—BUL 15–11, 15–8, 15–13
5th Place: ROM—CZE 8–15, 15–7, 15–10, 16–14
7th Place: KOR—BRA 18–16, 15–7, 15–5

1976 Montreal T: 9, N: 9, D: 7.30.

		MATCHES		GAMES			
		W	L	W	L	PF	PA
1.	POL	(Wlodzimierz Stefański, Bronislaw Bebel, Lech Lasko, Edward Skorek, Tomasz Wójtowicz, Wieslaw Gawlowski, Mieczyslaw Rybaczewski, Zbigniew Lubiejewski, Ryszard Bosek, Wlodzimierz Sadalski, Zbigniew Zarzycki, Marek Karbarz)	6	0	18	9	377	293
2.	SOV	(Anatoly Polishuk, Vyacheslav Zaitsev, Efim Chulak, Vladimir Dorohov, Aleksandr Ermilov, Pavels Selivanovs, Oleg Molyboha, Vladimir Kondra, Yuris Starunski, Vladimir Chernyshev, Vladimir Ulanov, Aleksandr Savin, Yuri Chesnokov, Vladimir Patkin)	4	1	14	3	247	162
3.	CUB	(Leonel Marshall Stewart, Victoriano Sarmientos Bios, Ernesto Martínez Hernandez, Victor García Campos, Carlos Salas Pérez, Raul Virches More, Jesús Savigne Savigne, Lorenzo Martínez Cordero, Diego Lapera Sotolougo, Antonio Rodriguez Aguirre, Alfredo Figueredo Ricardo, Jorge Pérez Vento)	4	2	14	7	280	212
4.	JPN	(Takashi Maruyama, Katsutoshi Nekoda, Katsumi Oda, Tetsuo Nishimoto, Yasunori Yasuda, Yoshihide Fukao, Shoi-	2	3	8	8	157	204

chi Yanagimoto, Miki-yasu Tanaka, Tadayoshi Yokota, Seiji Oko, Kenji Shimaoka, Tetsuo Sato)

		W	L	W	L	PF	PA
5. CZE	(Miroslav Nekola, Jaroslav Penč, Stefan Pipa, Vladimir Petlak, Josef Mikunda, Jaroslav Stančo, Vlastimil Lenert, Milan Šlambor, Pavel Rerabek, Josef Vondrka, Drahomir Koudelka, Jaroslav Tomaš)	4	2	14	7	282	234
6. KOR	(Kim Kon-bong, Cho Jas-back, Lee Yong-kwan, Park Ki-won, Chong Moon-kyong, Lee Sun-koo, Lee Choun-pyo, Lee In, Kim Choong-han, Lee Jong-won, Kang Man-soo, Lim Ho-dam)	2	4	10	14	245	295
7. BRA	(Paulo de Freitas, Sergio Danilas, Alexandre Abeid, Eloi Neto, Antônio Mereno, Berhard Rajzman, William da Silva, Alexandre Celso Kalche, José Guimaraes, Jean Luc Rosat, Fernando de Avila, Paulo Petterle)	2	3	8	11	216	228
8. ITA	(Andrea Nannini, Paolo Montorsi, Stefano Sibani, Giorgio Goldoni, Francesco Dall'Olio, Fabrizio Nassi, Rodolfo Giovenzana, Andrea Nencini, Mario Mattioli, Giovanni Lanfranco, Erasmo Salemme, Marco Negri)	0	5	2	15	125	148

Final: POL—SOV 11–15, 15–13, 12–15, 19–17, 15–7
3rd Place: CUB—JPN 15–8, 15–9, 15–8
5th Place: CZE—KOR 15–9, 10–15, 15–2, 15–9
7th Place: BRA—ITA 15–8, 15–6, 15–8

The U.S.S.R. and Poland reached the final match by completely different routes. The Soviet team, whose members averaged 6 feet 4¼ inches, swept through its four preliminary matches without losing a single set. Poland, on the other hand, was extended to five sets in three of their five victories, including a tense 13–15, 10–15, 15–6, 15–9, 20–18 win over Cuba. The Poles, however, were well prepared for such marathons—their daily training regimen required each player to jump 392 times over a four-and-a-half-foot barrier while wearing 20- to 30-pound weights on his legs and body. The turning point in the two-and-a-half-hour final came in the fourth set, with the Soviet Union leading two sets to one and 15–14—one point short of the gold medal. With the contest in the balance, 6-foot 7-inch

Tomasz Wójtowicz smashed a long spike from behind the ten-foot line that saved the day. Eighteen serves later the Poles won the set, 19–17.

1980 Moscow T: 10, N: 10, D: 8.1.

		MATCHES		GAMES			
		W	L	W	L	PF	PA
1. SOV	(Yuri Panchenko, Vyacheslav Zaitsev, Aleksandr Savin, Vladimir Dorokhov, Aleksandr Yermilov, Pavels Selivanovs, Oleg Moliboga, Vladimir Kondra, Vladimir Chernyshev, Fedir Lashchenov, Valery Krivov, Viljar Loor)	6	0	18	2	297	190
2. BUL	(Stoyan Gunchev, Hristo Stoyanov, Dimiter Zlatanov, Dimitar Dimitrov, Petko Petkov, Mitko Todorov, Kaspar Simeonov, Emil Vulchev, Hristo Iliev, Yordan Angelov, Tsano Tsanov, Stefan Dimitrov)	4	2	13	8	263	241
3. ROM	(Corneliu Oros, Laurentiu Dumanoiu, Dan Girleanu, Nicu Stoian, Sorin Macavei, Constantin Sterea, Neculae Vasile Pop, Gunter Enescu, Valter-Korneliu Chifu, Marius Chata-Chitiga)	4	2	13	9	290	230
4. POL	(Robert Malinowski, Maciej Jarosz, Wieslaw Czaja, Lech Lasko, Tomasz Wójtowicz, Wieslaw Gawlowski, Wojciech Drzyzga, Boguslaw Kanicki, Ryszard Bosek, Wlodzimierz Nalazek, Leszek Molenda)	3	3	12	11	303	271
5. BRA	(Joao Granjeiro, Mario Xando Oliveira Neto, Antonio Gueiros, José Montanaro, Antônio Moreno, Renan Dal Zotto, William da Silva, Amauri Ribeiro, Bernardo Rocha Rezende, Jean Luc Rosat, Deraldo Wanderley, Berhard Rajzman)	4	2	13	8	267	214
6. YUG	(Vladimir Bogoevski, Vladimir Trifunović, Alexsandar Tacevski, Ždravko Kuljić, Goran Srbinovski, Ivica Jelić, Boro Jović, Radovan Malević, Mio-	3	3	13	13	310	302

	W	L	W	L	PF	PA
drag Mitić, Ljubomir Travica, Mladen Kasić, Slobodan Lozancić)						
7. CUB (Diego Lapera Sotolongo, Victor García Campos, Luis Oviedo, Ernesto Martínez Hernández, Ricardo Leyva, Jorge Garbey, Raul Vilches More, Carlos Salas Pérez, Antônio Pérez, Leonel Marshall Stewart, Carlos Ruiz, José David)	2	4	11	13	298	280
8. CZE (Igor Prielozny, Pavel Valach, Vlado Sirvon, Jan Repak, Josef Novotny, Jaroslav Smid, Vlastimil Lenert, Nicu Stoian, Jan Cifra, Pavel Rerabek, Josef Pick, Cyril Krejci)	1	5	7	17	253	335

Final: SOV—BUL 15–7, 15–13, 14–16, 15–11
3rd Place: ROM—POL 15–10, 9–15, 15–13, 15–9
5th Place: BRA—YUG 14–16, 15–9, 8–15, 15–10, 15–8
7th Place: CUB—CZE 14–16, 15–7, 15–10, 15–6

The team from Libya had a particularly difficult tournament, losing all five matches and all 15 sets, and scoring only 30 points while giving up 225.

1984 Los Angeles-Long Beach T: 10, N: 10, D: 8.11.

	MATCHES		GAMES			
	W	L	W	L	PF	PA
1. USA (Dusty Dvorak, David Saunders, Stephen Salmons, Paul Sunderland, Rich Duwelius, Stephen Timmons, Craig Buck, Marc Waldie, Chris Marlowe, Aldis Berzins, Pat Powers, Charles "Karch" Kiraly)	5	1	15	4	258	159
2. BRA (Bernardo Rezende, Mário Xando Oliveira Neto, Antônio Ribeiro, José Montanaro, Ruy Campos Nascimento, Ranan Dal Zotto, William Carvalho Silva, Amauri Ribeiro, Marcus Freire, Domingos Lampariello Neto, Berhard Rajzman, Fernando d'Avila)	4	2	13	8	267	214
3. ITA (Marco Negri, Pier Paolo Lucchetta, Gian Carlo Dametto, Franco Bertoli, Francesco Dall'Olio, Piero Rebaudengo, Gio-	4	2	15	7	280	231
vanni Errichiello, Guido De Luigi, Fabio Vullo, Giovanni Lanfranco, Paolo Vecchi, Andrea Lucchetta)						
4. CAN (Glenn Hoag, Terry Danyluk, John Barrett, Dave Jones, Paul Gratton, Al Coulter, Tom Jones, Don Saxton, Randy Wagner, Alex Ketyzynski, Rick Bacon, Garth Pischke)	3	3	10	9	221	212
5. KOR (Lee Jong-kyung, Kang Doo-tae, Chang Yoonchang, Lee Yong-sun, Lee Bum-joo, Yang Jinwung, Moon Yong-kwan,;— Yoo Joong-tak, Kim Ho-chul, No Jin-su, Kang Man-soo, Chung Euy-tak)	5	1	15	8	312	253
6. ARG (Daniel Castellani, Esteban Martínez, Carlos Wagenpfeil, Alejandro Díz, Hugo Conte, Waldo Kantor, Raúl Quiroga, Jon Uriarte, Alcides Cuminetti, Leonardo Wiernes)	2	4	11	13	282	307
7. JPN (Koshi Sobu, Eiji Shimomura, Kazuya Mitake, Eizaburo Mitsuhashi, Hiroaki Okuno, Yasushi Furukawa, Shuji Yamada, Mikiyasu Tanaka, Kimio Sugimoto, Minoru Iwata, Akihiro Iwashima, Shunichi Kawai)	4	2	13	8	271	245
8. CHN (Yan Jianming, Song Jinwei, Yu Juemin, Zhai Jixin, Zhang Yousheng, Yang Liqun, Cao Ping, Shen Keqin, Zuo Yue, Xiao Jinsong, Zhao Duo, Liu Changcheng)	1	5	4	15	200	261

Final: USA—BRA 15–6, 15–6, 15–7
3rd Place: ITA—CAN 15–11, 15–12, 15–8
5th Place: KOR—ARG 15–13, 9–15, 15–9, 15–7
7th Place: JPN—CHN 16–14, 15–9, 15–6

Considering that volleyball was invented in the United States (by William G. Morgan in Holyoke, Massachusetts, in 1895), the U.S. had been remarkably unsuccessful in international competition, qualifying for the Olympics only once since it became an official sport in 1964. However, the long drought ended in 1984. The U.S. team went to Los Angeles with a 24-match winning streak, including four straight victories over the world champion Soviet team, all of which took place in the U.S.S.R. The streak was ended in the fourth match of the tournament when an inspired Brazilian team beat the Americans 15–12, 15–11, 15–2. But five nights later, in the final, the U.S. turned the tables on the Brazilians, overwhelming them in straight sets.

1988 Seoul T: 12, N: 12, D: 10.2.

			MATCHES		GAMES			
			W	L	W	L	PF	PA
1.	USA	(Troy Tanner, David Saunders, Jon Root, Robert Ctvrtlik, R. Douglas Partie, Stephen Timmons, Craig Buck, Scott Fortune, Ricci Luyties, Jeffery Stork, Eric Sato, Charles "Karch" Kiraly)	7	0	21	4	366	211
2.	SOV	(Yuri Panchenko, Andrei Kuznetsov, Vyacheslav Zaitsev, Igor Runov, Vladimir Shkurikhin, Yevgeny Krasilnikov, Raimonds Vilde, Valery Losev, Yuri Sapega, Oleksander Sorokolit, Yaroslav Antonov, Yuri Cherednik)	5	2	18	7	332	282
3.	ARG	(Claudio Zulianello, Daniel Castellani, Esteban Martínez, Alejandro Díz, Daniel Colla, Carlos Weber, Hugo Conte, Waldo Kantor, Raúl Quiroga, Jon Uriarte, Esteban De Palma, Juan Carlos Cuminetti)	4	3	14	12	325	317
4.	BRA	(Mauricio Camargo Lima, Wagner Rocha, Paulo Roese, José Montanaro, Paulo Juroski da Silva, Renan Dal Zotto, William da Silva, Amauri Ribeiro, Antônio Aguiar Gouveia, Domingos Lampariello Neto, Leonidio De Pra Filho, André Falbo Ferreira)	4	3	16	13	374	342
5.	HOL	(Martin Teffer, Pieter-Jan Leeuwerink, Ronald Boudrie, Jan-Marcus Posthuma, Ronald Zoodsma, Ronald Zwerver, Avital Selinger, Edwin Benne, Teunis Buys, Peter Blange, Marco Brouwers, Karl Grabert)	5	2	16	9	314	272
6.	BUL	(Kostadin Mitev, Petyo Draguiev, Borislav Kyossev, Ljubomir Ganev, Ilian Kaziiski, Dimo Tonev, Petko Petkov, Plamen Hristov, Sava Kovachev, Nayden Naydenov, Milcho Milanov, Tzvetan Florov)						
7.	SWE	(Urban Lennartsson, Jannis Kalmazidis, Jan Hedengård Karlsson, Tomas Hoszek, Anders Lundmark, Per-Anders Sääf, Bengt Gustafson, Håakan Björne, Lars Nilsson, Peter Tholse, Patrik Johansson)	3	4	14	16	350	388
8.	FRA	(Philippe Blain, Hervé Mazzon, Eric N'Gapeth, Eric Bouvier, Christophe Meneau, Jean-Marc Jurkovitz, Laurent Tillie, Olivier Rossard, Patrick Duflos, Alain Fabiani, Philippe-Marie Salvan)	3	4	12	13	312	300

Final: USA—SOV 13–15, 15–10, 15–4, 15–8
3rd Place: ARG—BRA 15–10, 15–17, 15–8, 12–15, 15–9
5th Place: HOL—BUL 15–6, 15–8, 15–10
7th Place: SWE—FRA 12–15, 15–5, 8–15, 15–12, 15–12

The U.S. team faced a stiff challenge from Argentina in the preliminary round, losing the first two sets before coming from behind to win the last three, exactly as they had in the 1987 Pan Am Games. In the final, the Americans confronted their number one rivals—and drinking buddies—the team from the U.S.S.R. The two teams had already played nine matches in 1988 with the U.S. winning seven. In the Olympic final, the Americans, all of whom grew up in Southern California, wore down the Soviets in the first two sets, then overwhelmed them in the last two.

The bronze medal match between Argentina and Brazil was an epic struggle that lasted 3 hours and 10 minutes. The starting lineup for the Dutch team, which placed fifth, *averaged* 6 feet 7⅔ inches.

1992 Barcelona T: 12, N: 12, D: 8.9.

			MATCHES		GAMES			
			W	L	W	L	PF	PA
1.	BRA	(Marcelo Teles Negrão, Jorge Souza de Brito, Giovane Farinazzo Gavio, Paulo Juroski Silva, Mauricio Camargo Lima, Janelson Carvalho Santos, Douglas Chiarotti, Antônio Aguiar Gouveia, Talmo Curto de Oliveira, André Falbo Ferreira, Alexandre "Tande"	8	0	24	3	395	263

	W	L	W	L	PF	PA
Ramos Samuel, Amauri Ribeiro)						
2. HOL (Martin Teffer, Henk-Jan Held, Ronald Boudrie, Jan-Marcus Posthuma, Ronald Zwerver, Avital Selinger, Edwin Benne, Peter Blange, Marko Klok, Roelof van der Meulen, Martin van der Horst, Ronald Zoodsma)	4	4	14	14	355	316
3. USA (Robert Ctvrtlik, Stephen Timmons, Scott Fortune, Jeffery Stork, Eric Sato, Carlos Briceno, Nick Becker, Bryan Ivie, Brent Hilliard, Robert Samuelson, R. Douglas Partie)	6	2	20	13	445	400
4. CUB (Freedy Brooks Bongo, Joel Despaigne Charles, Idalbato Valdés Pedro, Lázaro Beltrán Rixo, Félix Millán Casanova, Rodolfo Sánchez Sánchez, Raúl Diago Izquierdo, Abel Sarmientos Bios, Osvaldo Hernández Chembet, Lázaro Marín Ortega, Nicolás Vives Coffigne, Ihosvany Hernández Rivera)	5	3	17	11	356	311
5. ITA (Andrea Gardini, Paolo Tofoli, Roberto Masciarelli, Claudio Marco Galli, Marco Bracci, Lorenzo Bernardi, Luca Cantagalli, Andrea Zorzi, Andrea Lucchetta, Andrea Giani, Fabio Vullo, Michele Pasinato)	6	2	21	8	400	301
6. JPN (Takashi Narita, Katsumi Kawano, Yuichi Nakagaichi, Akihiko Matsuda, Masafumi Oura, Tatsuya Ueta, Masaji Ogino, Katsuyuki Minami, Shigeru Aoyama, Junichi Kuriuzawa, Hideyuki Otake, Masayuki Izumikawa)	3	5	13	20	396	448
7. SOV (Oleg Shatunov, Aleksandr Shadchin, Ruslan Olikhver, Igor Runov, Andrei Kuznetsov, Yevgeny Krasilnikov, Yuri Korovyansky, Dmitri Fomin, Konstantin Ushakov, Yuri Cherednik, Sergei Gorbunov, Pavel Shishkin)	4	4	17	15	399	394
8. SPA (Juan Robles Ania, Venancio Costa Monge, Francisco Sánchez Jover, Jesús Sánchez Jover, José Maroto Díaz, Ángel Alonso Nieto, Benjamín Vicedo Mayor, Héctor López Izquierdo, Francisco Hervas Tiradu, Rafael Pascual Cortés, Ernesto Rodriguez Gómez)	3	5	13	21	396	453

Final: BRA—HOL 15–12, 15–8, 15–5
3rd Place: USA—CUB 12–15, 15–13, 15–7, 15–11
5th Place: ITA—JPN 15–2, 15–7, 15–13
7th Place: SOV—SPA 16–14, 12–15, 15–8, 5–15, 15–12

An unusual incident took place in the opening match between the United States and Japan. The Japanese were leading two games to one and 14–13 in the fourth game, when the umpire, Laert de Souza of Brazil, issued a yellow card to United States middle blocker Bob Samuelson for arguing a call. Because Samuelson had already received a yellow card earlier in the game, he should have been ejected from the match and Japan should have been awarded a point—a point that would have given Japan the victory. But referee Ramis Samedov of Azerbaijan didn't want to end a match on a penalty point and instead waved for play to continue. The Americans fought off match point and went on to win in five games. Japan protested and the next day the International Volleyball Federation control committee voted unanimously to award the victory to Japan. Samuelson suffered from alopecia universalis, a condition that left him bald. As a show of solidarity, the other 11 members of the United States team showed up for their next match with their heads completely shaved. The Americans won their next five matches, but were well beaten by Brazil in the semifinals.

In fact, Brazil raced through the entire tournament without being seriously challenged. The same could not be said of their opponents in the final, the team from the Netherlands. The Dutch placed only fourth in their preliminary pool of six teams, losing to Cuba, Brazil, and the team from the ex–Soviet Union. But in the quarterfinals they stunned tournament favorite Italy, 15–9, 12–15, 8–15, 15–2, 17–16. The Dutch beat the Cubans in straight games in the semifinals, but were outclassed by Brazil in the final.

The Dutch team, which averaged 6 feet 7 inches, would have set the record for the tallest team in Olympic history had not their average been brought down by 5-foot 9-inch Avital Selinger, the coach's son. Ten of their 12 members were at least 2 meters (6 feet 6¾) tall.

WOMEN

1896–1960 not held

1964 Tokyo T: 6, N: 6, D: 10.23.

		MATCHES		GAMES			
		W	L	W	L	PF	PA
1.	JPN (Masae Kasai, Emiko Miyamoto, Kinuko Ta-nida, Yuriko Handa, Yo-shiko Matsumura, Sata Isobe, Katsumi Matsu-mura, Yoko Shinozaki, Setsuko Sasaki, Yuko Fujimoto, Masako Kon-do, Ayano Shibuki)	5	0	15	1	238	93
2.	SOV (Nelli Abramova, Astra Biltauere, Lyudmila Bul-dakova, Lyudmilla Hure-yeva, Valentina Kame-nek, Marita Katusheva, Ninel Lukanina, Valen-tyna Myshak, Tatyana Roshchina, Inna Ryskal, Antonina Ryzchova, Ta-mara Tikhonina)	4	1	12	3	212	97
3.	POL (Krystyna Czajkowska, Maria Golimowska, Krys-tyna Jakubowska, Da-nuta Kordaczuk-Wag-ner, Krystyna Krupa, Jó-zefa Ledwig, Jadwiga Marko, Jadwiga Rutkow-ska, Maria Śliwka, Zofia Szczęśniewska)	3	2	10	6	180	162
4.	ROM (Ana Mocan, Cornelia Lăzeanu, Natalia Todo-rovschi, Doina Ivănescu, Doina Popescu, Sonia Colceru, Lia Vanea, Alex-andrina Chezan, Ileana Enculescu, Elisabeta Go-loşie, Marina Stanca, Doi-na Coste)	2	3	6	9	140	172
5.	USA (Jean Gaertner, Gail O'Rourke, Linda Mur-phy, Lou Galloway, Ver-neda Thomas, Mary Per-ry, Mary Peppler, Nancy Owen, Patricia Bright, Jane Ward, Sharon Pe-terson, Barbara Har-werth)	1	4	3	12	98	213
6.	KOR (Suh Choon-kang, Moon Kyung-sook, Ryoo Choon-ja, Kim Kil-ja, Oh Soon-ok, Chung Jong-uen, Choi Don-hi, Hong Nam-sun, Oh Chung-ja, Yoon Jung-sook, Kwak Ryong-ja, Lee Keun-soo)	0	5	0	15	94	225

The famous 1964 Japanese women's volleyball team in action.

Ten of the 12 members of the Japanese team came from the Nichibo spinning mill in Kaizuku, near Osaka. Their coach, the notorious Hirofumi Daimatsu, was the man-ager of the office supplies procurement department at the mill. Daimatsu was famous for his draconian meth-ods: hitting the young women on the head, kicking them on their hips, insulting them, goading them, making them practice a minimum of six hours a day, seven days a week, 51 weeks a year. He was the first coach to intro-duce the rolling receive, in which a player dives to the ground, hits the ball, rolls over, and returns quickly to her feet.

Japanese sports fans looked forward with great antici-pation to the Olympic volleyball tournament. Their great hopes almost met with disaster when the North Korean team withdrew over a political dispute, leaving the competition one team short of the six required to conduct an official tournament. The Japanese solved the problem by giving the South Korean Olympic Commit-tee team 1,000,000 yen to send a team. The Japanese were never seriously challenged. The only time they lost a set (15–13, to Poland) was because Daimatsu pulled some of his better players when he saw that the Soviet coach was watching. The final Japanese victory over the U.S.S.R. gained an 80 percent audience rating on Japanese television.

After the game, the team captain, 31-year-old Masae Kasai, was invited to the official residence of Japan's prime minister, Eisaku Sato. She confessed to Sato that she wanted to marry, but that her rigorous training schedule had prevented her from meeting any men. Sato promised to help her and subsequently introduced Kasai to Kazuo Nakamura, whom she later married. As for Daimatsu, he quit coaching and joined an advertising agency. In 1968 he was elected to the House of Councilors, the upper house of the Japanese Parliament. He served until 1974 and died of a heart attack in 1978.

1968 Mexico City T: 8, N: 8, D: 10.26.

			MATCHES		GAMES			
			W	L	W	L	PF	PA
1.	SOV	(Lyudmila Buldakova, Lyudmila Mikhailovskaya, Vera Lantratova, Vera Galushka, Tatyana Sarycheva, Tatyana Ponyayeva, Nina Smoleyeva, Inna Ryskal, Galina Leontyeva, Roza Salikhova, Valentina Vinogradova [Kamenek])	7	0	21	3	333	194
2.	JPN	(Setsuko Yoshika, Suzue Takayama, Toyoko Iwahara, Yukiyo Kojima, Sachiko Fukunaka, Kunie Shishikura, Setsuko Inoue, Sumie Oinuma, Keiko Hama)	6	1	19	3	318	147
3.	POL	(Krystyna Czajkowska, Józefa Ledwig, Elżbieta Porzec, Wanda Wiecha, Zofia Szczęśniewska, Krystyna Jakubowska, Lidia Żmuda-Chmielnicka, Barbara Niemczyk, Halina Aszkielowicz, Krystyna Krupa, Jadwiga Marko-Książek, Krystyna Ostromęcka)	5	2	15	11	324	304
4.	PER	(Esperanza Jimenez, Teresa Nuñez, Irma Cordero, Olga Asato, Aida Reyna, Alicia Sanchez, Luisa Fuentes, Ana Maria Ramirez, Norma Velarde)	3	4	12	15	306	327
5.	KOR	(Moon Kyung-sook, Park Kum-sook, Suh Hee-sook, Lee Eun-ok, Hwang Kyu-ok, Lee Hyang-seem, Yang Jin-soo, Kim Young-ja, Kim Oe-sun, An Kyoung-Ja)	3	4	11	14	276	305
6.	CZE	(Pavlina Šteffková, Elena Poláková, Karla Šašková, Jitka Senečká, Vera Strunčová, Vera Hrabáková, Julia Bendeová, Anna Mifková, Irena Tichá, Hana Vlašaková, Eva Siroká, Hilda Mazurová)	3	4	11	15	307	307
7.	MEX	(Isabel Nogueira, Carolina Mendoza, Rogelia Romo, Yolanda Reynoso, Carmen Rodriguez, Gloria Inzua, Alicia Cardenas, Gloria Casales, Patricia Nava, Trinidad Macias, Blanca Garcia, Eloisa Cabada)	1	6	7	18	215	228
8.	USA	(Jane Ward, Nancy Owen, Fanny Hopeau, Barbara Perry, Ninja Jorgensen, Miki McFadden, Sharon Peterson, Patti Bright, Laurie Lewis, Marilyn McReavy, Mary Perry, Kathryn Heck)	0	7	4	21	196	353

The crucial match between the Japanese and the Soviets was won by the U.S.S.R., 15–10, 16–14, 3–15, 15–9. After his team had been booed during its game against Czechoslovakia, the Soviet coach was asked if his players had been affected by the crowd's hostility. He replied, "If my athletes cannot stand such distractions, they are not professionals and should be left home." Reminded that the Olympics were for amateurs only, the embarrassed coach claimed he had been misquoted.

1972 Munich T: 8, N: 8, D: 9.7.

			MATCHES		GAMES			
			W	L	W	L	PF	PA
1.	SOV	(Inna Ryskal, Vera Douiounova [Galushka], Tatyana Tretyakova [Ponyayeva], Nina Smoleyeva, Roza Salikhova, Lyudmila Buldakova, Tatyana Gonobobleva, Lyubov Turina, Galina Leontyeva, Tatyana Sarycheva)	5	0	15	5	270	206
2.	JPN	(Sumie Oinuma, Noriko Yamashita, Seiko Shimakage, Makiko Furukawa, Takako Iida, Katsumi Matsumura, Michiko Shiokawa, Takako Shirai, Mariko Okamoto, Keiko	4	1	14	3	244	131

Hama, Yaeko Yamazaki, Toyoko Iwahara)

		W	L	W	L	PF	PA
3. PRK	(Ri Chun-ok, Kim Myong-suk, Kim Zung-bok, Kang Ok-sun, Kim Yeun-ja, Hwang He-suk, Jang Ok-rim, Paek Myong-suk, Ryom Chun-ja, Kim Su-dae, Jong Ok-jin)	3	2	10	6	211	154
4. KOR	(Kim Young-ja, Lee In-sook, Lee Soon-bok, Jo Hea-chung, Yu Kyung-hwa, Kim Eun-hee, Lee Jung-ja, Yu Jung-hyae, Yoon Young-nae)	2	3	7	9	169	189
5. HUN	(Éva Szalay Sebök, Judit Gerhard Kiss, Emerencia Király Siry, Ilona Buzek Maklári, Judit Hazsik Fekete, Ágnes Torma, Mária Gál, Katalin Schadek Eichler, Judit Blauman Schlégl, Emöke Énekes, Zsuzsanna Török Bokros)	3	2	10	10	256	252
6. CUB	(Mercedes Pérez Hernández, Ana Díaz, Margarita Mayeta, Mercedes Pomares Primelles, Nurys Sebey, Claritza Herrera, Miriam Herrera, Mercedes Roca, Claudina Villaurrutia)	2	3	8	10	181	252
7. CZE	(Irena Svobodova, Ludmila Vinduskova, Jana Semecka, Dorota Jelinkova, Anna Mifkova, Marie Vapenkova, Elena Moskalova, Hilda Mazurova, Maria Malisova, Hana Vlasakova)	1	4	6	12	191	241
8. GER	(Ingrid Lorenz, Annedore Richter, Ursel Westphal, Birgit Pörner, Margret Stender, Annette Ellerbracke, Rike Ruschenburg, Marianne Lepa, Traute Schäfer, Erika Heucke, Regina Pütz)	0	5	0	15	131	228

Final: SOV—JPN 15–11, 4–15, 15–11, 9–15, 15–11
3rd Place: PRK—KOR 15–7, 15–9, 15–9
5th Place: HUN—CUB 13–15, 16–14, 14–16, 15–5, 15–11
7th Place: CZE—GER 15–13, 15–4, 16–14

The final was so closely fought that at one point in the fourth set there were 24 service changes in a row without a single point being scored. During the tournament, a German woman named Ingeborg Schell filed a civil suit against the Japanese coach, Joji Kojima, for using "inhuman methods for making his team fit."

1976 Montreal T: 8, N: 8, D: 7.30.

		MATCHES		GAMES			
		W	L	W	L	PF	PA
1. JPN	(Takako Iida, Mariko Okamoto, Echiko Maeda, Noriko Matsuda, Takako Shirai, Kiyomi Kato, Yuko Arakida, Katsuko Kanesaka, Mariko Yoshida, Shoko Takayanagi, Hiromi Yano, Juri Yokoyama)	5	0	15	0	225	84
2. SOV	(Anna Rostova, Lyudmila Shchetinina, Liliya Osadcha, Natalya Kushnir, Olha Kozakova, Nina Smoleyeva, Lyubov Rudovska, Larissa Bergen, Inna Ryskal, Lyudmila Chernyshova, Zoya Yusova, Nina Muradyan)	4	1	12	7	248	211
3. KOR	(Lee Soon-bok, Yu Jung-hye, Byon Kyung-ja, Lee Soo-nok, Baik Myung-sun, Chang Hee-sook, Ma Kum-ja, Yun Young-nae, Yu Kyung-hwa, Park Mi-kum, Jung Soo-nok, Jo Hea-jung)	3	2	10	11	260	259
4. HUN	(Zsuzsanna Szloboda, Gyöngyi Bardi, Éva Biszku, Zsuzsanna Biszku, Lucia Bánhegyi, Gabriella Feketé Csapó, Ágnes Hubai Gajdos, Judit Blauman Schlégl, Ágnes Torma, Katalin Schadek Eichler, Emerencia Király Siry, Eva Szalay Sebök)	2	3	7	11	192	234
5. CUB	(Mercedes Pérez Hernández, Imilsis Tellez Quesada, Ana Díaz Martínez, Mercedes Pomares Primelles, Lucila Urgelles Savon, Mercedes Roca, Miriam Herrera, Claudina Villaurrutia, Melanea Tartabull, Nelly Barnet Wilson, Ana Maria García Crespo, Evelina Borroto)	3	2	12	9	267	250
6. GDR	(Karla Roffeis, Johanna Strotzer, Cornelia Rickert, Christine Walther, Ingrid Mierzwiak, Helga	1	4	8	14	237	286

	W	L	W	L	PF	PA
Offen, Barbara Czekalla, Jutta Balster, Anke Westendorf, Hannelore Meincke, Monika Meissner, Gudrun Gärtner)						
7. PER (Mercedes Gonzales, Maria Cardenas, Teresa Núñez, Irma Cordero, Ana Cecilia Carrillo, Luisa Merea, Delia Cordova, Silvia Quevedo, Luisa Fuentes, Maria Del Risco, Maria Cervera, Maria Ostolaza)	2	3	9	12	239	250
8. CAN (Carole Bishop, Barbara Dalton, Kathy Girvan, Patty Olson, Regyna Armonas, Anne Ireland, Mary Dempster, Claire Lloyd, Betty Baxter, Connie Lebrun, Debbie Heeps, Audrey Vandervelden)	0	5	6	15	198	292

Final: JPN—SOV 15–7, 15–8, 15–2
3rd Place: KOR—HUN 12–15, 15–12, 15–10, 15–6
5th Place: CUB—GDR 15–12, 15–12, 15–8
7th Place: PER—CAN 15–9, 12–15, 15–4, 15–7

The Japanese team dominated the tournament so completely that only once did an opponent (South Korea) reach double figures in a single game.

1980 Moscow T: 8, N: 8, D: 7.29.

	MATCHES		GAMES			
	W	L	W	L	PF	PA
1. SOV/ RUS (Nadezhda Radzevich, Natalya Razumova, Olga Solovova, Yelena Akhaminova, Yelena Andreyuk, Irina Makagonova, Lyubov Kozyreva, Svetlana Nikishina, Lyudmila Chernyshova, Svetlana Badulina, Lidiya Loginova)	5	0	15	3	254	172
2. GDR (Ute Kostrzewa, Andrea Heim, Annette Schultz, Christine Mummhardt, Heike Lehmann, Barbara Czekalla, Karla Roffeis, Martina Schmidt, Anke Westendorf, Karin Püschel, Brigitte Fetzer, Katharina Bullin)	3	2	11	11	277	271
3. BUL (Tania Dimitrova, Valentina Ilieva, Galina Stancheva, Silva Petrunova, Anka Hristolova, Verka	3	2	12	9	257	225
Borisova, Margarita Gherasimova, Roumiana Kaicheva, Maya Georgieva, Tania Gogova, Tzvetana Bozhurina, Rossitza Dimitrova)						
4. HUN (Julianna Simon Szalonna, Éva Szalay Sebök, Gyöngyi Gerevich [Bardi], Ágnes Balajczá Juhász, Lucia Banhegyi Rado, Gabriella Feketé Csapó, Emöke Szegedi Varghá, Emerencia Király Siry, Ágnes Torma, Erzsébet Vargá Palinkás, Gabriella Lengyel, Bernadett Köszegi)	2	3	10	12	234	279
5. CUB (Mercedes Pérez Hernández, Imilsis Tellez Quesada, Ana Diaz Martínez, Mercedes Pomares Primelles, Mavis Guilarte Fernandez, Erenia Diaz Toca, Maura Alfonso Drake, Josefina Capote Travieso, Nelly Barnet Wilson, Ana Maria García Crespo, Lucila Urgelles Savon)	3	2	10	7	219	166
6. PER (Carmen Pimentel, Gaby Cardenas, Raquel Chumpitaz, Ana Cecilia Carrillo, Maria Del Risco, Cecilia Tait, Silvia Leon, Aurora Heredia, Gina Torrealva, Natalia Malaga)	1	4	7	12	189	257
7. BRA (Denise Porto Mattioli, Ivonette das Neves, Lenice Peluso Oliveira, Regina Vilela Santos, Fernanda Emerick Silva, Paula Rodrigues Mello, Maria Isabel Alencar, Eliana Maria Aleixo, Maria Castanheira, Jacqueline Cruz Silva, Vera Helena Mossa, Rita Cassia Teixeira)	1	4	7	12	210	248
8. ROM (Mariana Ionescu, Gabriela Coman, Dorina Sávoiu, Victoria Georgescu, Ileana Dobroschi, Victoria Banciu, Irina Petculet, Orina Georgescu, Iuliana Enescu, Ioana Liteanu, Corina Crivat, Elena Piron)	2	3	7	13	221	243

Final: SOV—GDR 15–12, 11–15, 15–13, 15–7
3rd Place: BUL—HUN 15–5, 13–15, 6–15, 15–4, 15–8

5th Place: CUB—PER 15–9, 15–7, 12–15, 15–5
7th Place: BRA—ROM 15–8, 15–12, 15–12

1984 Los Angeles-Long Beach T: 8, N: 8, D: 8.7.

			MATCHES		GAMES			
			W	L	W	L	PF	PA
1.	CHN	(Lang Ping, Liang Yan, Zhu Ling, Hou Yuzhu, Yang Xilan, Jiang Ying, Li Yanjun, Yang Xiaojun, Zheng Meizhu, Zhang Rongfang)	4	1	13	3	234	148
2.	USA	(Paula Weishoff, Susan Woodstra, Rita Crockett, Laurie Flachmeier, Carolyn Becker, Flora Hyman, Rose Magers, Julie Vollertsen, Debbie Green, Kimberly Ruddins, Jeanne Beauprey, Linda Chisholm)	4	1	12	6	239	218
3.	JPN	(Yumi Egami, Kimie Morita, Yoko Mitsuya, Miyoko Hirose, Kyoko Ishida, Yoko Kagabu, Norie Hiro, Kayoko Sugiyama, Sachiko Otani, Keiko Miyajima, Emiko Odaka, Kumi Nakada)	4	1	12	5	222	154
4.	PER	(Carmen Pimentel, Rosa Garcia, Isabel Heredia, Gabriela Perez Del Solar, Cecilia Del Risco, Cecilia Tait, Luisa Cervera, Denisse Fajardo, Miriam Gallardo, Gina Torrealva, Natalia Malaga)	2	3	7	11	192	229
5.	KOR	(Lee Eun-kyung, Lee Un-yim, Lee Youngsun, Kim Jeong-sun, Han Kyung-ae, Lee Myung-hee, Kim Ok-soon, Park Mi-hee, Lim Hae-suk)	3	2	12	7	240	194
6.	GER	(Ruth Holzhausen, Gudrun Witte, Beate Bühler, Regina Vossen, Sigrid Terstegge, Andrea Sauvigny, Renate Riek, Marina Staden, Almut Kemperdick, Terry Place-Brandel, Ute Hankers)	2	3	6	9	160	184
7.	BRA	(Vera Leme, Fernanda Da Silva, Monica Da Silva, Maria Salgado, Heloisa Roese, Regina Pereira Uchoa, Jacqueline Silva, Ana Maria Richa, Sandra Lima, Eliani Miranda Da Costa, Luiza	1	4	6	12	212	236
		Pinheiro Machado, Ana Margarida Alvares)						
8.	CAN	(Diane Ratnik, Suzi Smith, Tracy Mills, Joyce Gamborg, Audrey Vandervelden, Monica Hitchcock, Karen Fraser, Rachel Beliveau, Lise Martin, Caroline Cote, Barb Broen, Josee Lebel)	0	5	0	15	88	225

Final: CHN—USA 16–14, 15–3, 15–9
3rd Place: JPN—PER 13–15, 15–4, 15–7, 15–10
5th Place: KOR—GER 15–10, 15–10, 15–2
7th Place: BRA—CAN 15–9, 15–3, 15–8

The Chinese had defeated the U.S. in seven of eight pre-Olympic matches, but when the two teams faced each other for the first time in Los Angeles, in a preliminary match, the more experienced Americans came out on top 15–13, 7–15, 16–14, 15–12. Four nights later they met again to decide the championship. As the Chinese team entered the arena, their star spiker, Lang Ping, noticed a television screen displaying a freeze-frame of the U.S. coach and three of his players wearing gold medals around their necks. Lang stopped, pointed out the image to her teammates and said, "Let's pluck the medals from their necks." The Chinese team then put on a brilliant, almost flawless performance to defeat the U.S. in straight sets.

1988 Seoul T: 8, N: 8, D: 9.29.

			MATCHES		GAMES			
			W	L	W	L	PF	PA
1.	SOV	(Valentina Ogiyenko, Yelena Volkova, Irina Smirnova, Tatyana Sidorenko, Irina Parkhomchuk, Olha Shkurnova, Marina Nikulina, Yelena Ovchinnikova, Olga Krivosheyeva, Marina Kumysh, Tatyana Kravnova, Svetlana Korytova)	4	1	14	5	268	190
2.	PER	(Cenaida Uribe, Rosa García, Gabriela Perez Del Solar, Isabel Heredia, Cecilia Tait, Luisa Cervera, Denisse Fajardo, Alejandra De La Guerra, Gina Torrealva, Natalia Malaga)	4	1	14	9	303	269
3.	CHN	(Li Guojun, Hou Yuzhu, Yang Xilan, Su Huijuan, Jiyang Ying, Cui Yongmei, Yang Xiaojun, Zheng Meizhu, Wu Dan, Li Yueming)	3	2	11	7	217	202

		W	L	W	L	PF	PA
4. JPN	(Yumi Maruyama, Ka-yoko Sugiyama, Reiko Takizawa, Miyako Yama-shita, Akemi Sugiyama, Ichiko Sato, Norie Hiro, Kumi Nakada, Motoko Obayashi, Yukiko Taka-hashi, Sachico Fujita, Noriyuki Muneuchi)	2	3	10	12	256	265
5. GDR	(Steffi Schmidt, Susanne Lahme, Monika Beu, Ar-iane Radfan, Kathrin Langschwager, Maike Arlt, Brit Wiedemann, Ute Steppin, Grit Jen-sen, Dörte Stüdemann, Heike Jensen, Ute Langenau)	3	2	10	9	238	246
6. BRA	(Kerly Santos, Ana Bea-triz Moser, Vera Mossa, Eliani Costa, Ana Maria Richa, Maria Trade, Ana Claudia Ramos, Marcia Cunha, Ana Lucia Barros, Sandra Suruagy, Fernanda Venturini, Si-mone Storm)	1	4	7	14	235	276
7. USA	(Melissa McLinden, An-gela Rock, Elizabeth Masakayan, Kimberly Oden, Kimberly Rud-dins, Caren Kemner, Tammy Webb, Deitre Collins, Laurel Kessel, Prikeba Phipps, Liane Sato, Jayne McHugh)	2	3	9	13	257	263
8. KOR	(Park Mi-hee, Kim Kyung-hee, Kim Kui-soon, Lim Hye-sook, Yoo Young-mi, Nam Soon-ok, Yoon Chung-hye, Park Bok-rye, Kim Yoon-hye, Ji Kyung-hee)	1	4	8	13	224	277

Final: SOV—PER 10–15, 12–15, 15–13, 15–7, 17–15
3rd Place: CHN—JPN 15–13, 15–6, 15–6
5th Place: GDR—BRA 15–9, 15–4, 11–15, 15–11
7th Place: USA—KOR 15–4, 12–15, 13–15, 15–9, 15–8

In 1948 Edwin Vasquez Cam of Peru won a gold medal in free pistol shooting. In the forty years that followed, no Peruvian was able to earn another Olympic title. But in 1988 the Peruvian people caught gold medal fever, pin-ning their hopes on their popular women's volleyball team. The team members were so well known that they were referred to always by their first names: Rosa, Gina, Natalia, Denisse, 6 foot 4½ inch Gabriela, and the media favorite, Cecilia.

With Cuba boycotted out of the Games, Peru's leading rivals were Japan, which had never finished out of the medals; the Soviet Union, which had never placed worse than second; and China, which had won each year's ma-jor tournament from 1981 through 1986 before faltering in 1987. So important was women's volleyball in China that when a new coach had to be chosen, the four leading contenders debated on national television.

In the very first match of the tournament, Japan de-feated the U.S.S.R. in five sets, the final set going to 19–17. Prior to 1988 the Soviets had lost only two of 27 Olympic contests—both to Japan. Three days later, Peru, trailing China 9–14 in the fifth set, scored 7 straight points to win the match. In their next match the Peruvi-ans spotted the U.S. two sets, then came roaring back for another five-set victory. In the first semifinal, the U.S.S.R. obliterated the Chinese 15–0, 15–9, 15–2. The second semi saw Peru take the first two sets from Japan 15–9, 15–6, then lose the next two 6–15, 10–15, before sealing the victory 15–13.

The final took place at 6:30 a.m., Peru time, with al-most the entire nation glued to the nearest television set. The Peruvian women won the first two sets 15–10, 15–12, and led the third 12–6. At this point, with most of the 6500 spectators cheering wildly for Peru, the Soviet coach, Nicolai Karpol, called timeout and made three substitutions. When play resumed, the momentum had shifted. The Soviets outscored the Peruvians 9–1 to win the set. They then took the next set 15–7 and led 6–0 in the fifth set. But Peru would not give in. They fought back to tie the score at 7. The U.S.S.R. moved ahead again, 10–7. Again Peru came from behind to tie. They even took the lead at 15–14. Both sides fought off match points. Finally, the Soviets won 17–15. The Soviet women were so drained, physically and emotionally, that medical personnel had to be rushed onto the court to revive them for the medal ceremony.

Four of the six Soviet starters, as well as coach Karpol, were members of the Uralochka factory team of Sverdlovsk.

1992 Barcelona T: 8, N: 8, D: 8.7.

		MATCHES		GAMES			
		W	L	W	L	PF	PA
1. CUB	(Tania Ortiz Calvo, Marleny Costa Blanco, Mireya Luis Hernández, Lilia Izquierdo Aguirre, Idalmis Gato Moya, Regla Bell McKenzie, Regla Torres Herrera, Norka Latamblet Daudi-not, Mercedes Calderón Martínez, Magaly Carva-jal Rivera)	5	0	15	5	268	238
2. SOV	(Valentina Makovet-skaya [Ogiyenko], Na-talya Morozova, Marina	3	2	12	7	270	194

Pankova [Nikulina], Yelena Batukhtina, Irina Ilchenko [Smirnova], Yevgeniya Artamonova, Yelena Chebukina [Ovchinnikova], Svetlana Korytova)

3.	USA	(Tonya "Teee" Sanders, Yoko Zetterlund, Kimberly Oden, Lori Endicott, Paula Weishoff, Caren Kemner, Tammy Liley, Elaina Oden, Janet Cobbs, Tara Cross-Battle, Liane Sato, Ruth Lawanson)	4	2	16	9	327 280
4.	BRA	(Ana Beatriz Moser, Hilma Caldeira, Ana Alvares, Ana Rodrigues, Cristina Lopes, Leila Barros, Ana Barros, Marcia Cunha, Daniel Chritaro, Fernanda Venturini, Helia Souza)	3	3	11	13	291 299
5.	JPN	(Ichiko Sato, Kumi Nakada, Michiyo Ishikake, Chieko Nakanishi, Motoko Obayashi, Yukiko Takahashi, Ikuyo Namura, Mika Yamauchi, Asako Tajimi, Tomoko Yoshihara, Kiyoko Fukuda, Kazumi Nakamura)	3	2	10	9	253 224
6.	HOL	(Sandra Wiegers, Erna Brinkman, Jacintha Boersma, Vera Koenen, Irena Machovcak, Aafke Hament, Marjolein de Jong, Henriette Weersing, Kirsten Gleis, Helena Crielaard, Alida Moons)	1	4	6	14	215 278
7.	CHN	(Lai Yawen, Li Guojun, Zhou Hong, Ma Fang, Wang Yi, Su Huijuan, Chen Fengqin, Su Liqun, Sun Yue, Wu Dan, Gao Lin, Li Yueming)	1	3	8	9	219 198
8.	SPA	(Virginia Cardona Tapia, Ana Tostado Domingo, Rita Oraa Larrazabal, Inmaculada Torres Cerezo, Laura De La Torre Tur, Marta Gens Barberá, Olga Martín Rubio, Asunción Doménech Dominguez, Inmaculada González Casado, Estela Dom-	0	4	0	12	48 180

inguez Cerviño, Maria del Mar Rey Abad, Carmen Miranda Martínez)

Final: CUB—SOV 16–14, 12–15, 15–12, 15–13
3rd Place: USA—BRA 15–8, 15–6, 15–13
5th Place: JPN—HOL 15–0, 11–15, 15–13, 15–10
7th Place: CHN—SPA 15–1, 15–3, 15–3

The Cuban team was the overwhelming favorite and they did not disappoint. They were, however, hard-pressed by the United States in the semifinals. With the match tied at two games each and the United States leading 9–8 in the deciding game, Cuba scored five straight points and went on to win 15–11. In the final, every game was close right up to the end, but the Cubans were able to score when it counted most, converting the last two points of games one, three and four.

BEACH VOLLEYBALL

The principles of beach volleyball are basically the same as those of normal volleyball, but there are significant differences. To begin with, there are two players on a team, the court is made of sand, and the players wear less clothing. The 1996 tournament will use a double-elimination format leading to semifinals and a final. Preliminary matches will consist of one set played to 15 points. It is not necessary to win by two points. The final match and the third-place match will be the best two out of three sets. The first two sets are won by the first team to score 12 points. If a third and deciding set is required, it must be won by two points, and play can continue beyond 12 until that margin is achieved. As in regular volleyball, in the deciding set a point is scored by whichever team wins a rally rather than only by the serving team. There is no center line on a beach volleyball court and players are not required to keep to a certain position.

MEN

This event will be held for the first time in 1996.

WOMEN

This event will be held for the first time in 1996.

WATER POLO

Water polo is played with seven men on a team including a goalkeeper. Between 1960 and 1980, matches consisted of four five-minute quarters. In 1984 the quarters were extended to seven minutes. Ties are not broken in the preliminary round. In the medal round, if there is a tie after regulation play, play continues with two three-minute overtime periods. If the score is still even, additional three-minute periods are played. Prior to 1996, these overtime periods were played to conclusion; in 1996, matches will end as soon as a goal is scored. A goal is scored when the entire ball passes over the goal line, between the goal posts, and underneath the crossbar. A goal may be scored using any part of the body except a clenched fist. As in basketball, there is a shot clock: each team must take a shot at the goal within 35 seconds of taking possession of the ball. If they fail to do so, the opposing team takes possession.

The field of play in water polo is 30 meters (32 yards 2 feet, 5 inches) from goal line to goal line. The width is 20 meters (21 yards 2 feet 7½ inches). The goal posts are 3 meters (9 feet 10 inches) apart; the underside of the crossbar is 90 centimeters (2 feet 11½ inches) above the surface of the water. The water must be at least 1.8 meters (5 feet 10⅞ inches) deep and preferably 2 meters (6 feet 6¾ inches) deep. The water temperature must be between 25 and 27 degrees centigrade (77 and 80.6 degrees Fahrenheit).

An offside rule is enforced: no offensive player may cross the line two meters in front of the goal unless he is preceded by the ball.

Water polo is a rough sport filled with a variety of fouls and accompanying officials' whistles. *Ordinary* (or common) *fouls* include holding on to the goal posts, holding the entire ball underwater, hitting the ball with a clenched fist (the goalkeeper is exempted within four meters of the goal), touching the ball with both hands at the same time (again the goalkeeper is exempted), impeding the free movement of an opponent who is not holding the ball, pushing an opponent, and wasting time. An ordinary foul is punished by awarding the opposing team a free throw from the point of the foul. If a foul is committed by a defending player within the two-meter area, the free throw is taken from the two-meter line.

Exclusion fouls include interfering with a free throw, intentionally splashing water in an opponent's face, holding an opponent, kicking or striking an opponent, using foul language, showing disrespect for a referee or other official, and committing an act of brutality. Exclusion fouls are punished by the awarding of a free throw and by the exclusion of the guilty player from the match for 20

seconds or until a goal is scored or his own team regains possession.

Penalty fouls include committing a foul within four meters of the goal a player is defending if a referee rules that the foul prevented a probable goal, committing an act of brutality within four meters of the goal, and toppling the goal cage to prevent a probable score. A penalty throw is taken from behind the four-meter line and any player on a team may be chosen to take the shot. At the 1992 Olympics, 83 percent of penalty throws were successful. If a missed penalty throw rebounds off the goal or the goalkeeper, it is considered in play and the match continues.

1896 not held

1900 Paris T: 7, N: 3, D: 8.12.

			W	L	PF	PA
1. GBR	(Osborne Swimming Club, Manchester—Arthur Robertson, Thomas Coe, Eric Robinson, Peter Kemp, George Wilkinson, John Derbyshire, William Lister)		3	0	29	3
2. BEL	(Swimming et Water Polo Club, Brussels—Albert Michant, Fernand Fayaerts, Henri Cohen, Victor de Behr, Oscar Grégoire, Victor Sonnemans, Jean de Backer)		2	1	9	8
3. FRA	(Libellule de Paris—Henri Peslier, Thomas Burgess, Alphonse de Cuyper, Pesloy, Paul Vasseur, Devenot, Louis Laufray)		0	1	1	10
4. FRA	(Pupilles de Neptune de Lille—Louis Martin, Coulon, Fardelle, Favier, Leriche, Charles Treffel, Désiré Merchez)		0	1	1	5

Final GBR 7–2 BEL

A complete record of all the games played in this tournament is not available.

1904 St. Louis T: 3, N: 1, D: 9.6.

			W	L	PF	PA
1. USA	(New York Athletic Club—David Bratton, George Van Cleef, Leo "Budd" Goodwin, Louis Handley, David Hesser, Joseph Ruddy, James Steen)		2	0	11	0
2. USA	(Chicago Athletic Club—Rex Breach, Jerome Steever, Edwin Swatek, Charles Healy, Frank Kehoe, David Hammond, William Tuttle)		0	1	0	6

3. USA (Missouri Athletic Club—John Meyers, Manfred Toeppen, Gwynne Evans, Amadee Reyburn, Fred Schreiner, Agustus Goessling, William Orthwein) — 0 1 0 5

The Missouri team refused to play for second place, so the Chicago team was awarded the silver medal by forfeit. Originally, a German team had also been entered, but when the Germans discovered that what the Americans called "water polo" was actually a strange sport called "softball water polo," they withdrew. The Americans used a deflated ball, and goals only counted if a player held the ball in the opposing goal.

1906 not held

1908 London T: 4, N: 4, D: 7.22.

		W	L	PF	PA
1. GBR	(Charles Smith, George Nevinson, George Cornet, Thomas Thould, George Wilkinson, Paul Radmilovic, Charles Forsyth)	1	0	9	2
2. BEL	(Albert Michant, Herman Meyboom, Victor Boin, Joseph Pletincx, Fernand Feyaerts, Oscar Grégoire, Herman Donners)	2	1	18	14
3. SWE	(Torsten Kumfeldt, Axel Runström, Harald Julin, Pontus Hanson, Gunnar Wennerström, Robert Andersson, Erik Bergvall)	0	1	4	8
4. HOL	(Johan Rühl, Johan Cortlever, Jan Hulswit, Eduard Meijer, Karel Meijer, Pieter Ooms, Bouke Benehga)	0	1	1	8

Final: GBR 9–2 BEL

Paul Radmilovic of the British team eventually took part in five Olympics as a swimmer and water polo player, and also competed in the 1906 Intercalated Games.

1912 Stockholm T: 6, N: 6, D: 7.13.

		W	L	PF	PA
1. GBR	(Charles Smith, George Cornet, Charles Bugbee, Arthur Hill, George Wilkinson, Paul Radmilovic, Isaac Bentham)	3	0	21	8
2. SWE	(Torsten Kumfeldt, Harald Julin, Max Gumpel, Pontus Hanson, Vilhelm Anderson, Robert Andersson, Erik Bergqvist)	3	1	22	11
3. BEL	(Albert Durant, Herman Donners, Victor Boin, Joseph Pletincx, Oscar Grégoire, Herman Meyboom, Félicien Courbet, Jean Hoffman, Pierre Nijs)	3	2	22	21
4. AUT	(Rudolf Buchfelder, Richard Manuel, Walter Schachtitz, Otto Scheff, Josef Wagner, Ernst Kovács, Hermann Buchfelder)	1	3	10	25

		W	L	PF	PA
5. HUN	(Sándor Ádám, László Beleznai, Tibor Fazekas, Jenö Hégner Tóth, Károly Rémi, János Wenk, Imre Zachár)	0	2	9	11
6. FRA	(Gustave Prouvost, Gaston Vanlaere, Georges Rigal, Paul Louis Beulque, Jean Rodier, Jean Thorailler, Henri Decotu, Paul Vasseur)	0	2	3	11

Final: GBR 8–0 AUT

Great Britain's closest call was a 7–5 overtime victory over Belgium.

1920 Antwerp T: 12, N: 12, D: 8.27.

		W	L	PF	PA
1. GBR/IRL	(Charles Smith, Noel Purcell, Christopher Jones, Charles Bugbee, William Dean, Paul Radmilovic, William Peacock)	3	0	19	4
2. BEL	(Albert Durant, Paul Gailly, Pierre Nijs, Joseph Pletincx, Maurice Blitz, René Bauwens, Gérard Blitz, Pierre Dewin)	4	1	27	9
3. SWE	(Theodor Nauman, Pontus Hanson, Max Gumpel, Thorsten Kumfeldt, Vilhelm Anderson, Nils Backlund, Robert Andersson, Erik Andersson, Harald Julin, Erik Bergqvist)	4	1	35	9
4. USA	(Preston Steiger, Sophus Jensen, Michael McDermott, Clement Browne, Herbert Vollmer, Harry Hebner, James Carson, William Vosburgh, G. Albert Taylor, Duke Paoa Kahanamoku, Perry McGillivray, Norman Ross)	2	3	16	19
5. HOL	(Karel Struijs, Carl Kratz, Karel Meijer, Johan Cortlever, Piet Plantenga, Gérard Bohlander, Jan van Silfhout)	1	2	12	11
5. SPA	(Manuel Armanqué Feliu, Balcells, Ramón Berdemás Llunell, José Fontanet Petit, Francisco Gilbert Riera, Luis Gilbert Riera, Enrique Granados Gal, Roisch, Alfonso Tusell Alonso, Antônio Vila-Coro Nadel)	1	2	3	15

Final: GBR 3–2 BEL

The victory of the team from the United Kingdom was not a popular one. After the final match Belgian spectators attacked the British and Irish players, who had to be taken away under the protection of armed guards.

1924 Paris T: 13, N: 13, D: 7.20.

		W	L	PF	PA
1. FRA	(Paul Dujardin, Noël Delberghe, Georges Rigal, Henri Padou, Robert	4	0	16	6

		W	L	PF	PA
	Desmettre, Albert Mayaud, Albert Delborgies)				
2. BEL	(Albert Durant, Joseph Pletincx, Pierre Dewin, Gerard Blitz, Joseph Cludts, Georges Fleurix, Paul Gailly, Jules Thiry, Pierre Vermetten, Joseph de Combe, Maurice Blitz)	4	1	18	10
3. USA	(Frederick Lauer, Oliver Horn, George Mitchell, George Schroth, Herbert Vollmer, P. "Johnny" Weissmuller, Arthur Austin, John Norton, J. Wallace O'Connor)	3	2	13	11
4. SWE	(Theodor Nauman, Gösta Persson, Vilhelm Anderson, Martin Norberg, Erik Andersson, Nils Backlund, Cletus Anderson, Hilmer Wictorin)	3	3	27	12
5. HUN	(István Barta, Tibor Fazekas, Márton Homonnai, Alajos Keserü, Lajos Homonnai, János Wenk, Ferenc Keserü, József Vértesy)	2	2	17	17
6. CZE	(Václav Ankrt, František Franĕk, František Kúrka, Hugo Klempfner, Josef Tomášek, Jiři Reitman, Béla Nemenyi, Jan Hora, František Vacin, Jaroslav Hummelhans)	2	2	11	15
7. HOL	(Gérard Bohlander, Frdereick Bohlander, Willem Bokhoven, Jan den Boer, Jacques Köhler, Karel Struys, Antoine van Senus)	1	2	12	10

Final: FRA 3–0 BEL

The French victory over Belgium came as a great surprise. The Parisian crowd was so excited that, after the playing of the "Marseillaise," they demanded that the Belgian national anthem be played as well. Belgium's loss dropped them into a playoff pool for second place. After defeating Sweden 4–2, they beat the United States, 2–1. However, the Americans lodged a protest, which was allowed. The match was replayed, and the Belgians won again, 2–1.

1928 Amsterdam T: 14, N: 14, D: 8.11.

		W	L	PF	PA
1. GER	(Erich Rademacher, Otto Cordes, Emil Benecke, Fritz Gunst, Joachim Rademacher, Karl Bähre, Max Amann, Johannes Blank)	3	0	18	10
2. HUN	(István Barta, Sándor Ivády, Alajos Keserü, Márton Homonnai, Ferenc Keserü, József Vértesy, Olivér Halassy)	3	1	26	8
3. FRA	(Paul Dujardin, Jules Keignaert, Henri Padou, Emile Bulteel, Achille Tribouillet, Henri Cuvelier, Albert Vandeplancke, Ernest Rogez, Albert Thévenon)	5	1	41	7
4. GBR	(Edward Temme, Paul Radmilovic, Edward Percival Peters, Nicholas Beaman, John "Jack" Budd, Leslie Ablett, Richard Hodgson, John Hat-	2	2	15	21

		W	L	PF	PA
	field, William Quick)				
5. BEL	(J. Brandeleer, René Bouwens, J. Malissart, Gerard Blitz, Pierre Coppieters, Louis van Gheem, Henri de Pauw, F. Visser, A. Mélardy)	1	1	14	6
5. HOL	(Abraham van Olst, Jean van Silfhout, Antoine van Senus, Jacques Köhler, Kees Leenheer, Jan Scholte, Ko Köhler)	1	1	14	6

Final: GER 5–2 HUN

Germany defeated Hungary in overtime after the regulation periods ended in a 2–2 tie.

1932 Los Angeles T: 5, N: 5, D: 8.13.

		W	L	T	PF	PA
1. HUN	(György Bródy, Sándor Ivády, Márton Homonnai, Olivér Halassy, József Vertesy, Janös Németh, Ferenc Keserü, Alajos Keserü, István Barta, Miklós Sárkány)	3	0	0	30	2
2. GER	(Erich Rademacher, Fritz Gunst, Otto Cordes, Emil Benecke, Joachim Rademacher, Heiko Schwartz, Hans Schulze, Hans Eckstein)	2	1	1	23	13
3. USA	(Herbert Wildman, F. Calvert Strong, Charles Finn, C. Harold McAllister, Philip Daubenspeck, Austin Clapp, Wallace O'Connor)	2	1	1	20	12
4. JPN	(Takashige Matsumoto, Akira Fujita, Shuji Doi, Iwao Tokito, Yasutaro Sakagami, Takaji Takebayashi, Tosuke Sawami, Seibei Kimura)	0	3	0	0	37

The team from Brazil, having lost 7–3 to Germany, gave a cheer for their conquerors, climbed out of the pool, and physically attacked the Hungarian referee, Béla Komjadi. They didn't let up until the police arrived. Needless to say, the entire Brazilian team was suspended and their remaining games were forfeited.

1936 Berlin T: 16, N: 16, D: 8.15.

		W	L	T	PF	PA
1. HUN	(György Bródy, Kálmán Hazai, Márton Homonnai, Olivér Halassy, Jenö Brandi, Janös Németh, Mihály Bozsi, György Kutasi, Miklós Sárkány, Sándor Tarics, István Molnár)	8	0	1	57	5
2. GER	(Paul Klingenburg, Bernhard Baier, Gustav Schürger, Fritz Gunst, Josef Hauser, Hans Schneider, Hans Schulze, Fritz Stolze, Heinrich Krug, Alfred Kienzle, Helmuth Schwenn)	8	0	1	56	10

3. BEL (Henri Disy, Joseph de Combe, Henri Stoelen, Fernand Isselé, Albert Castelyns, Gérard Blitz, Pierre Coppieters, Henri de Pauw, Edmond Michiels)   4 3 2 17 17

4. FRA (Georges Delporte, Paul Lambert, Maurice Lefebvre, Henri Padou, Roger Vandecastelle, André Busch, René Joder)   4 5 0 21 37

5. HOL (Johannes van Woerkom, Jean van Oostrom Soede, Rudolf den Hamer, Gerard Regter, Hans Maier, Cornelius van Aelst, Alexander Franken, Herman Veenstra, Jan van Hateren)   3 1 5 23 28

6. AUT (Franz Wenninger, Karl Seitz, Karl Steinbach, Sebastian Ploner, Franz Schönfels, Alfred Lergetporer, Wilhelm Hawlik, Erwin Blasl, Otto Müller, Anton Kunz, Peter Reidl)   5 3 1 31 18

7. SWE (Åke Nauman, Bertil Berg, Tore Ljungqvist, Gösta Persson, Erik Holm, Georg Svensson [Sollermark], Göte Andersson, Tore Lindzén, Runar Sandström)   3 6 0 29 18

8. GBR (Alfred North, David Grogan, William Martin, Robert Mitchell, Leslie Ablett, David McGregor, Ernest Blake)   2 4 3 28 46

Hungary and Germany tied 2–2, but Hungary was awarded first place on the basis of a greater goal differential.

Olivér Halassy played on three Hungarian Olympic water polo teams, despite the fact that one of his legs had been amputated below the knee following a streetcar accident when he was 11. On September 10, 1946, at the age of 37, Halassy was murdered by a Soviet soldier while walking down the street in Budapest.

1948 London T: 18, N: 18, D: 8.7.

		W	L	T	PF	PA
1. ITA	(Pasquale Buonocore, Emilio Bulgarelli, Cesare Rubini, Geminio Ognio, Ermenegildo Arena, Aldo Ghira, Gianfranco Pandolfini, Mario Maioni, Tullio Pandolfini)	8	0	2	47	24
2. HUN	(Endre Györffi, Miklós Holop, Dezsö Gyarmati, Károly Szittya, Oszkár Csuvik, István Szivós, Dezsö Lemhényi, László Jeney, Deszö Fábián, Jenö Brandi)	6	3	1	45	27
3. HOL	(Johannes Rohner, Cornelis Korevaar, Cornelius Braasem, Hans Stam, Albert Ruimschotel, Rudolph van Feggelen, Fritz Smol, Pieter Salomons, Hendrikus Keetelaar)	6	1	3	65	23

4. BEL (Théo-Léo de Smet, Georges Leenheere, Emile d'Hooge, Paul Rigaumont, Fernand Isselé, Willy Simons, Alphonse Martin)   2 2 6 32 25

5. SWE (Rune Öberg, Erik Holm, Rolf Julin, Roland Spángberg, Arne Jutner, Olle Johansson, Åke Julin, Folke Eriksson, Knut Gadd, Olle Ohlsson)   6 3 1 31 14

6. FRA (François Debonnet, Maurice Lefebvre, Robert Le Bras, Marco Diener, Robert Himgi, Roger Dewasch, Jacques Berthe, Raymond Massol, Jacques Viaene, Emile Bermyn, Marcel Spilliaert)   4 2 4 32 24

7. EGY (Ahmed Nessim, Taha El Gamal, Mohamed Khadry, Mohamed Haraga, Dorri El Said, Mohamed Abdel Aziz Khalifa, Samir Gharbo, Mohamed Hemmat)   1 4 5 26 35

8. SPA (Juan Serra Liobet, José Pujol Coma, Carlos Falp Mont, Carlos Marti Arenas, Francisco Castillo Caupana, Augustin Mestres Ribas, Valentin Sabate Mas, Francisco Sabate Figa)   2 8 0 26 33

1952 Helsinki T: 21, N: 21, D: 8.2.

		W	L	T	PF	PA
1. HUN	(László Jeney, György Vízvári, Dezsö Gyarmati, Kálmán Markovits, Antal Bolvári, István Szivós, György Kárpáti, Róbert Antal, Dezsö Fábián, Károly Szittya, Dezsö Lemhényi, István Hasznos, Miklós Martin)	7	0	3	60	21
2. YUG/ CRO	(Zdravko Kovačić, Veljko Bakašun, Ivo Štakula, Ivo Kurtini, Boško Vuksanović, Zdravko Ježic, Lovro Radonjić, Marko Brainović, Vlado Ivković)	7	0	3	46	16
3. ITA	(Raffaello Gambino, Vincenzo Polito, Cesare Rubini, Carlo Peretti, Ermenegildo Arena, Maurizio Mannelli, Renato De Sanzuane, Renato Traiola, Geminio Ognio, Salvatore Gionta, Lucio Ceccarini)	8	2	0	53	29
4. USA	(Harry Bisbey, James Norris, Edward Jaworski, Norman Lake, William Kooistra, Peter Stange, Norman Dornblaser, John Spargo, Robert Hughes, Maroni Burns)	5	6	0	43	41
5. HOL	(Marcus van Gelder, Gerrit Bijsma, Cornelis Korevaar, Cornelius Braasem, Frits Smol, Ru-	7	2	1	45	22

			W	L	T	PF	PA
	dolph van Geggelen, Johannes Cabout)						
6.	BEL	(Théo-Léo de Smet, Alphonse Martin, Joseph Smits, André Laurent, Marcel Heyninck, Roland Sierens, Johan van den Steen, François Maesschalck, Georges Leenheere, Joseph Reynders)	6	3	1	37	35
7.	SOV	(Boris Goikhman, Yevgeny Semenov, Yuri Teplov, Lev Kokorin, Valentin Prokopov, Aleksandr Liferenko, Pyotr Mshvenieradze, Yuri Schlyapin, Vitaly Ushakov)	4	4	2	43	34
8.	SPA	(Leandro Ribera Abad, Ricardo Conde Rosales, José Bazán Vilaldach, Roberto Queralt Alantorn, Antônio Subirana, Augustin Mestres Ribas, José Abellan Pallani, Francisco Castillo Caupano)	3	7	0	33	41

Holland defeated Yugoslavia 3–2 in a game of the semifinal round. However the Yugoslavs protested two decisions of the referee, and the match was ordered replayed. This time Yugoslavia won, 2–1, and advanced to the final round, in which they tied Hungary, 2–2, but lost because of a lower goal differential. One of the Hungarian players was Dezsö Gyarmati, who eventually won medals in five different Olympics (1948–1964.) His wife, Éva Székely, was a breaststroker who won a gold medal in 1952 and a silver in 1956.

1956 Melbourne T: 10, N: 10, D: 12.7.

			W	L	T	PF	PA
1.	HUN	(Ottó Boros, István Hevesi, Dezsö Gyarmati, Kálmán Markovits, Antal Bolvári, Mihály Mayer, György Kárpáti, László Jeney, István Szivós, Tivadar Kanizsa, Ervin Zádor)	7	0	0	32	6
2.	YUG/ CRO	(Zdravko Kovačić, Ivo Cipci, Hrvoje Kačič. Marjan Žurej, Zdravko Ježić, Lovro Radonjič, Tomislav Franjkovič, Vladimir Ivkovič)	6	1	1	28	13
3.	SOV	(Boris Goikhman, Viktor Ageyev, Yuri Schlyapin, Vyacheslav Kurennoi, Pyotr Breus, Pyotr Mshvenieradze, Nodar Gvakharia, Mikhail Ryzhak, Valentin Prokopov, Boris Markarov)	5	3	0	23	20
4.	ITA	(Enzo Cavazzoni, Cesare Rubini, Angelo Marciani, Paolo Pucci, Federico Dennerlein, Giuseppe D'Altrui, Alfonso Buonocore, Cosimo Antonelli, Luigi Mannelli, Maurizio D'Achille)	4	3	0	21	16

			W	L	T	PF	PA
5.	USA	(Robert Horn, William Ross, Robert Frojen, Wallace Wolf, Ronald Severa, James Gaughran, William Kooistra, Kenneth Hahn, Robert Hughes, Sam Kooistra)	2	5	1	18	25
6.	GER	(Karl Neuse, Alfred Obschernikat, Wilfried Bode, Hans-Joachim Schneider, Wilhelm Sturm, Hans-Günther Hilker, Friedhelm Osselmann, Emil Bildstein, Erich Pennekamp, Hans Werner Seher)	1	5	1	18	25
7.	GBR	(Arthur Grady, Gerald Worsell, John "Jack" Jones, Peter Pass, Ronald Turner, Terence Miller, E. Clifford Spooner, John Ferguson, Robert Knights)	3	2	0	25	20
8.	ROM	(Alexandru Marinescu, Zoltan Hospodar, Aurel Zahan, Gavril Nagy, Francisc Simon, Ivan Bordi, Alexandru Szabo, Alexandru Badita, Iosif Deutsch)	3	3	0	30	17

On November 4, 1956, 200,000 Soviet troops invaded Hungary to put down a major revolt against Communist rule. The bitter feelings between the Hungarians and Soviets carried over into the Olympics, which were held less than three weeks later. Hostilities culminated in the water polo match between the two countries on December 6. The game quickly turned into a brawl and was halted by the referee before completion, with Hungary leading 4–0. Hungary was credited with a victory; however the police had to be called in to prevent a riot, as the 5500 spectators wanted to punish the Soviets further. Half of the Hungarian Olympic delegation refused to return to Hungary.

1960 Rome T: 16, N: 16, D: 9.3.

			W	L	T	PF	PA
1.	ITA	(Dante Rossi, Giuseppe D'Altrui, Eraldo Pizzo, Gianni Lonzi, Franco Lavoratori, Rosario Parmegiani, Danio Bardi, Brunello Spinelli, Salvatore Gionta, Amadeo Ambron, Giancarlo Guerrini)	8	0	1	37	15
2.	SOV	(Leri Gogoladze, Givi Chikvanaya, Vyacheslav Kurennoi, Anatoly Kartashov, Yuri Grigorovsky, Pyotr Mshvenieradze, Vladimir Semyonov, Boris Goikhman, Yevgeny Salzyn, Viktor Ageyev, Vladimir Novikov)	6	2	1	35	26
3.	HUN	(Ottó Boros, István Hevesi, Mihály Mayer, Dezsö Gyarmati, Tivadar Kanizsa, Zoltán Dömötör, László Felkai, László Jeney, András Katona, Kálmán Markovits, Péter Rusorán, György	5	2	2	45	22

Kárpáti, János Konrád, András Bodnár)

		W	L	T	PF	PA
4. YUG	(Milan Muškatirovič, Hrvoje Kačić, Zlatko Šimenc, Zdravko Ježić, Marijan Žužej, Ante Nardeli, Mirko Sandič, Božidar Stanišič. Dragoljub Siljak)	7	2	0	31	15
5. ROM	(Mircea Stefănescu, Alexandru Bădiță, Aurel Zahan, Gavrila Blajek, Alexandru Szabo, Anatol Grintescu, Stefan Kroner)	4	3	2	34	26
6. GER	(Hans Hoffmeister, Hans-Joachim Schneider, Hans Schepers, Bernd Strasser, Lajos Nagy, Friedhelm Osselmann, Dieter Seiz, Emil Bildstein, Jürgen Honig)	4	5	0	42	48
7. USA	Robert Horn, Marvin Burns, Ronald Severa, Ronald Crawford, Fred Tisue, Wallace Wolf, Robert Volmer, Gordon Hall, Charles Bittick, Charles McIlroy)	4	5	0	42	48
8. HOL	(Lambertus Kniest, Harry Lamme, Frederik van der Zwan, Harro Ran, Abraham Leenard, Henri Vriend, Alfred van Dorp, Johannes Muller, Hendrik Hermsen)	1	7	1	32	38

1964 Tokyo T: 13, N: 13, D: 10.18.

		W	L	T	PF	PA
1. HUN	(Miklos Ambrus, László Felkai, János Konrád, Zoltán Dömötör, Tivadar Kanizsa, Péter Rusorán, György Kárpáti, Ottó Boros, Mihály Mayer, Dénes Pócsik, András Bodnár, Deszö Gyarmati)	6	0	2	43	17
2. YUG	(Milan Muškatirovič, Ivo Trumbić, Vinko Rosić, Zlatko Šimenc, Bozidar Stanišić, Ante Nardeli, Zoran Janković, Mirko Sandić, Ozren Bonačič, Frane Nonkovič, Karlo Stipanić)	7	0	2	42	16
3. SOV	(Igor Grabovsky, Vladimir Kuznetsov, Boris Grishin, Boris Popov, Nikolai Kalashnikov, Zenon Bortkevich, Nikolai Kuznetsov, Viktor Ageyev, Leonid Osipov, Vladimir Semyonov, Eduard Yegorov)	5	2	1	20	13
4. ITA	(Dante Rossi, Giuseppe D'Altrui, Eraldo Pizzo, Gianni Lonzi, Franco Lavoratori, Rosario Parmegiani, Mario Cevasco, Eugenio Merello, Alberto Spinola, Danio Bardi, Giancarlo Guerrini, Federico Dennerlein)	4	4	0	17	19
5. ROM	(Mircea Ştefănescu, Anatol Grintescu, Alexandru Szabo,	4	3	1	36	28

Ştefan Kroner, Nicolae Firoiu, Gruia Novac, Cornel Mărculescu, Emil Muresan, Aurel Zahan, Iosif Kulineac)

		W	L	T	PF	PA
6. GDR	(Peter Schmidt, Hubert Höhne, Siegfried Ballerstedt, Edgar Thiele, Klaus Schulze, Jürgen Thiel, Klaus Schlenkrich, Heinz Mäder, Dieter Vohs, Jürgen Kluge, Heinz Wittig)	3	5	0	26	26
7. BEL	(Hendrik Hermsen, Abraham Leenards, Willem van Springelen, Gerardus Wormgoor, Alfred van Dorp, Henri Vriend, Nicolaas van der Voet, Willem Vriend, Johan Muller, Jan Bultman, Lambertus Kniest)	2	6	0	28	43
8. HOL	(Bruno de Hesselle, Frank Dosterlinck, Roger de Wilde, Jacques Caufrier, Andre Laurent, Karel de Vis, Jose de Vis, Jose Dumont, Johan van den Steen, Leon Pickers, Joseph Stappers)	4	5	0	37	47

Thirty-seven-year-old Dezsö Gyarmati brought his medal total to three gold, one silver, and one bronze. The Hungarians' narrow victory was the result of a 4–4 tie with Yugoslavia, in which they scored their final goal with only 25 seconds to play. After that they won because of a greater goal differential in the final round. A minor controversy developed when Hungary and Italy complained that the shallow pool (5 feet 10 inches deep) allowed the taller Yugoslav players to stand with their heads above the water.

1968 Mexico City T: 15, N: 15, D: 10.26.

		W	L	T	PF	PA
1. YUG	(Karlo Stipanić, Ivo Trumbić, Ozren Bonačić, Uroš Marović, Ronald Lopatny, Zoran Janković, Miroslav Poljak, Dejan Dabović, Djordje Perišić, Mirko Sandić, Zdravko Hebel)	7	1	1	86	35
2. SOV	(Vadim Gulyayev, Givi Chikvanaya, Boris Grishin, Aleksandr Dolgushin, Oleksei Barkalov, Yuri Grigorovsky, Vladimir Semyonov, Aleksandr Shidlovsky, Vyacheslav Skok, Leonid Osipov, Oleg Bovin)	6	2	0	62	36
3. HUN	Endre Molnár, Mihály Mayer, Istvan Szivós, János Konrád, László Felkai, Ferenc Konrád, Dénes Pócsik, András Bodnár, Zoltán Dömötör, János Steinmetz)	6	2	0	54	26
4. ITA	(Alberto Alberani Samaritani, Eraldo Pizzo, Mario Cevasco, Gianni Lonzi, Enzo Barlocco,	6	2	1	57	38

		W	L	T	PF	PA
	Franco Lavoratori, Gianni De Magistris, Alessandro Ghibellini, Giancarlo Guerrini, Paolo Ferrando, Eugenio Merello)					
5. USA	(Anton Van Dorp, David Ashleigh, Russell Webb, Ronald Crawford, Stanley Cole, Bruce Bradley, L. Dean Willeford, Barry Weitzenberg, Gary Sheerer, John Parker, Steven Barnett)	5	2	1	49	43
6. GDR	(Hans-Georg Fehn, Klaus Schlenkrich, Jürgen Thiel, Siegfried Ballerstedt, Peter Rund, Jürgen Schüler, Jürgen Kluge, Veit Herrmanns, Manfred Herzog, Hans-Ulrich Lange, Peter Schmidt)	6	2	1	78	30
7. HOL	(Feike de Vries, Hans Wouda, Louis Geutjes, Johannes Hoogveld, Alfred van Dorp, Hans Parrell, Nicolaas van der Voet, Ad Moolhuijzen, Bart Bonger, Andreas Hermsen, Evert Kroon)	5	3	1	53	39
8. CUB	(Oscar Periche, Waldimiro Arcos, Miguel Garcia, Rolando Valdes, Ruben Junco, Guillermo Martinez, Ibrahim Rodriguez, Osvaldo García, Roberto Rodriguez, Guillermo Canete, Jesús Perez)	3	4	1	38	51

In the final match, Yugoslavia defeated the U.S.S.R. 13–11 in overtime, despite seven goals by Oleksei Barkalov, including two in the last 35 seconds of regulation. Australia had been accepted as one of the 16 teams to take part in the tournament. However, the Australian Olympic Committee considered it a waste of money to send their team to Mexico City. The players paid their own way, but were not allowed to compete.

1972 Munich T: 16, N: 16, D: 9.4.

		W	L	T	PF	PA
1. SOV	(Vadim Gulyaev, Anatoly Akimov, Aleksandr Dreval, Aleksandr Dolgushin, Vladimir Shmudsky, Aleksandr Kabanov, Oleksei Barkalov, Aleksandr Shidlovsky, Nikolai Melnikov, Leonid Osipov, Vyacheslav Sobchenko)	7	0	2	52	25
2. HUN	(Endre Molnár, András Bodnár, István Görgényi, Zoltán Kásás, Tamás Faragó, László Sárosi, István Szivós, István Magas, Dénes Pócsik, Ferenc Konrád, Tibor Cservenyák)	6	0	3	45	24
3. USA	(James Slatton, Stanley Cole, Russell Webb, Barry Weitzen-	7	1	2	55	41

berg, Gary Sheerer, Bruce Bradley, Peter Asch, James Ferguson, Steven Barnett, John Parker, Eric Lindroth)

		W	L	T	PF	PA
4. GER	(Gerd Olbert, Hermann Haverkamp, Peter Teicher, Kurt Küpper, Günter Wolf, Ingulf Nossek, Ludger Weeke, Kurt Schuhmann, Jürgen Stiefel, Hans Georg Simon, Hans Hoffmeister)	2	2	5	36	31
5. YUG	(Karlo Stipanić, Ratko Rudić, Ozren Bonačić, Uros Marovic, Ronald Lopatny, Zoran Jankovic, Sinisa Belamarić, Dušan Antunović, Djordje Perišić, Mirko Sandić, Milos Marković)	5	4	1	55	48
6. ITA	(Alberto Alberani, Eraldo Pizzo, Roldano Simeoni, Mario Cevasco, Allessandro Ghibellini, Gianni De Magistris, Guglielmo Marsili, Silvio Baracchini, Franco Lavoratori, Sante Marsili, Ferdinando Lignano)	3	4	2	48	42
7. HOL	(Evert Kroon, Hans Wouda, Jan Evert Veer, Hans Hoogveld, Wim Hermsen, Hans Parrel, Ton Schmidt, Mart Bras, Tony Buunk, Gyze Stroboer, Wim van der Schilde)	6	1	2	43	31
8. ROM	(Serban Huber, Bogdan Mihailescu, Gheorghe Zamfirescu, Gruia Novac, Dinu Popescu, Claudiu Rusu, Iosif Kuliniac, Cornel Rusu, Viorel Rus, Radu Lazar, Corneliu Fratila)	5	4	1	62	45

The tournament included a bloody match between Yugoslavia and Cuba, and a contest between Hungary and Italy in which eight players were suspended within one 38-second span.

1976 Montreal T: 12, N: 12, D: 7.27.

		W	L	T	PF	PA
1. HUN	(Endre Molnár, István Szivós Jr., Tamás Faragó, László Sárosi, György Horkai, Gábor Csapó, Attila Sudár, György Kenéz, György Gerendás, Ferenc Konrád, Tibor Cservenyák)	7	0	1	45	32
2. ITA	(Alberto Alberani, Roldano Simeoni, Silvio Baracchini, Sante Marsili, Marcello Del Duca, Gianni De Magistris, Alessandro Ghibellini, Luigi Castagnola, Riccardo De Magistris, Vincenzo D'Angelo, Umberto Panerai)	4	1	3	47	33
3. HOL	(Evert Kroon, Nicolaas Landeweerd, Jan Evert Veer, Hans van Zeeland, Ton Buunk,	5	1	2	32	27

WATER POLO / 719

Piet de Zwarte, Hans Smits, Rik Toonen, Gyze Stroboer, Andy Hoepelman, Alex Boegschoten)

			W	L	T	PF	PA
4.	ROM	Florin Slavei, Corneliu Rusu, Gheorghe Zamfirescu, Adrian Nastasiu, Dinu Popescu, Claudiu Rusu, Ilie Slavei, Liviu Raducanu, Viorel Rus, Adrian Schervan, Doru Spinu)	2	2	4	44	39
5.	YUG	(Milos Marković, Ozren Bonačić, Uros Marović, Predrag Manojlović, Djuro Savinović, Damir Polić, Sinisa Belamarić, Dušan Antunović, Dejan Dabović, Boško Loziča, Zoran Kačić)	1	2	5	46	34
6.	GER	(Günter Kilian, Ludger Weeke, Hans-Georg Simon, Jürgen Stiefel, Roland Freund, Wolfgang Mechler, Martin Jellinghaus, Werner Obschernikat, Horst Kilian, Peter Röhle, Günter Wolf)	2	5	1	24	28
7.	CUB	(Oscar Periche Cordet, Osvaldo Garcia, Ramon Pena, Lazaro Costa, David Rodriguez, Nelson Dominguez Avila, Jorge Rizo Perera, Eugenio Almeneiro, Jesus Perez, Gerardo Rodriguez Peñalver, Oriel Dominguez Avila)	5	1	2	56	31
8.	SOV	(Anatoly Klebanov, Sergei Kotenko, Aleksandr Dreval, Aleksandr Dolgushin, Vitaly Romanchuk, Aleksandr Kabanov, Aleksei Barkalov, Nikolai Melnikov, Nugzar Mshvenieradze, Vladimir Iselidze, Aleksandr Zakharov)	4	2	2	47	28

The Soviet team was so humiliated by their failure to qualify for the final round of six that they tried to withdraw from the losers' round for seventh to 12th places, claiming that five of their players were too ill to compete. After forfeiting one game against Cuba, F.I.N.A. officials convinced them to continue with the tournament.

1980 Moscow T: 12, N: 12, D: 7.29.

			W	L	T	PF	PA
1.	SOV	(Yevgeny Sharonov, Sergei Kotenko, Vladimir Akimov, Yevgeny Grishin, Mait Riisman, Aleksandr Kabanov, Oleksei Barkalov, Erkin Shagayev, Georgy Mshvenieradze, Mikhail Ivanov, Vyacheslav Sobchenko)	8	0	0	58	31
2.	YUG	(Luka Vezilić, Zoran Gopcević, Damir Polić, Ratko Rudić, Zoran Mustur, Zoran Roje, Milivoj Bebić, Slobodan Trifunović,	5	1	2	58	42

Boško Loziča, Predrag Manojlović, Milorad Krivokapić)

			W	L	T	PF	PA
3.	HUN	(Andre Molnár, István Szivós Jr., Attila Sudár, György Gerendás, György Horkai, Gábor Csapó, István Kiss, István Udvardi, László Kuncz, Tamás Faragó, Károly Hauszler)	5	2	1	51	44
4.	SPA	(Manuel Delgado, Gaspar Ventura, Antonio Esteller, Federico Sabria, Manuel Estiarte Ducocastella, Pedro Robert, Jorge Alonso, José Alcázar, Antonio Aguilar, Jorge Carmona, Salvador Franch)	4	4	0	43	42
5.	CUB	(Oscar Periche Cordet, Orlando Cowley del Barrio, Barbaro Diaz Cervantes, Lazaro Costa Mendez, Pedro Rodriguez Rodriguez, Nelson Dominguez Avila, Jorge Rizo Perera, Arturo Ramos Hernandez, Calos Benitez Suarez, Gerardo Rodriguez Peñalver, Oriel Dominguez Avila)	2	3	3	50	49
6.	HOL	(Woulie de Bie, Nicolaas Landeweerd, Jan Evert Veer, Hans van Zeeland, Ton Buunk, Erik Noordergraaf, Stan van Belkum, Adrianus van Mil, Dick Nieuwenhuizen, Jan Jaap Korevaar, Rudolf Misdorp)	2	5	1	42	48
7.	AUS	(Michael Turner, David Neesham, Robert Bryant, Peter Montgomery, Julian Muspratt, Andrew Kerr, Anthony Folson, Charles Turner, Martin Callaghan, Randall Goff, Andrew Steward)	5	2	1	45	39
8.	ITA	(Alberto Alberani, Roldano Simeoni, Alfio Misaggi, Sante Marsili, Massimo Fondelli, Gianni De Magistris, Antonello Steardo, Paolo Ragosa, Romeo Collina, D'Angelo Vincenzo, Umberto Panerai)	4	3	1	40	35

The U.S.S.R. clinched first place with a tension-packed 8–7 victory over Yugoslavia. Between 1928 and 1980, Hungarian water polo teams won medals in twelve consecutive Olympics.

1984 Los Angeles T: 12, N: 12, D: 8.10.

			W	L	T	PF	PA
1.	YUG	(Milorad Krivokapić, Deni Lusić, Zoran Petrović, Bozo Vuletić, Veselin Djuho, Zoran Roje, Milivoj Bebić, Perica Bukić, Goran Sukno, Tomislav Paskvalin, Igor Milanović, Dragan Andrić)	6	0	1	72	44

		W	L	T	PF	PA
2. USA	(Craig Wilson, Kevin Robertson, Gary Figueroa, Peter Campbell, Douglas Burke, Joseph Vargas, Jon Svendsen, John Siman, Andrew McDonald, Terry Schroeder, Jody Campbell, Timothy Shaw)	6	0	1	65	43
3. GER	(Peter Röhle, Thomas Loebb, Frank Otto, Rainer Hoppe, Armando Fernandez, Thomas Huber, Jürgen Schröder, Rainer Osselmann, Hagen Stamm, Roland Freund, Dirk Theismann, Santiago Chalmovsky, Werner Obschernikat)	4	2	1	74	46
4. SPA	(Leandro Ribera, José Morillo, Felix Fernandez, Alberto Canal, Manuel Estiarte Ducocastella, Pedro Robert, Rafael Aguilar, Jorge Signes, Antonio Aguilar, Jorge Carmona, Jordi Sans Juan, Jorge Neira)	3	2	2	73	67
5. AUS	(Michael Turner, Richard Pengelley, Robert Bryant, Peter Montgomery, Russell Sherwell, Andrew Kerr, Raymond Mayers, Charles Turner, Martin Callaghan, Christopher Wybrow, Russell Basser, Julian Muspratt, Glenn Townsend)	2	3	2	58	58
6. HOL	(Woulie de Bie, Nicolaas Landeweerd, Erik Noordegraff, Ed van Es, Ton Buunk, Dick Nieuwenhuizen, Stan van Belkum, Adrianus van Mil, Johan Aantjes, Anton Heiden, Remco Pielstroom, Roald van Noort, Rudolf Misdorp)	2	5	0	45	65
7. ITA	(Roberto Gandolfi, Alfio Misaggi, Andrea Pisano, Antonello Steardo, Mario Fiorillo, Gianni De Magistris, Marco Galli, Marco D'Altrui, Marco Baldineti, Vicenzo D'Angelo, Romeo Collina, Stefano Postiglione, Umberto Panerai)	4	1	2	75	52
8. GRE	(Ioannis Vossos, Spyros Capralos, Sotirios Stathakis, Andreas Gounas, Kiriakos Giannopoulos, Aristidis Kefalogiannis, Anastasios Papanastasiou, Dimitrios Seletopoulos, Antonios Aronis, Markellos Sitarenios, George Mavrotas, Xenofon Moudatsios, Stavros Giannopoulos)	3	2	2	66	65

Trailing 5–2 with less than three minutes remaining in the third quarter of their final match against the U.S., Yugoslavia patiently rallied to tie the game 5–5 with three minutes left in the final period. Tenacious defense allowed the relatively inexperienced Yugoslavians to hold on until the end. The two teams finished with identical records but Yugoslavia won the tournament as a result of a greater goal differential in the medal round.

1988 Seoul T: 12, N: 12, D: 10.1.

		W	L	T	PF	PA
1. YUG	(Aleksandar Šoštar, Deni Lušić, Dubravko Šimenc, Perica Bukić, Veselin Djuho, Dragan Andrić, Mirko Vičević, Igor Gočanin, Mislav Bezmalinović, Tomislav Paškvalin, Igor Milanović, Goran Radjenović, Renco Posinković)	6	1	0	83	55
2. USA	(Craig Wilson, Kevin Robertson, James Bergeson, George Campbell, Douglas Kimball, Craig Klass, Alan Mouchawar, Jeffrey Campbell, Gregory Boyer, Terry Schroeder, Jody Campbell, Christopher Duplanty, Michael Evans)	5	2	0	71	56
3. SOV	(Yevgeny Sharonov, Nurlan Mendygaliev, Yevgeny Grishin, Aleksandr Kolotov, Sergei Naumov, Viktor Berendyuha, Sergei Kotenko, Dmitri Apanasenko, Georgy Mshvenieradze, Mikhail Ivanov, Sergei Markoch, Mykola Smyrnov, Mikhail Giorgadze)	4	2	1	84	51
4. GER	(Peter Röhle, Dirk Jacoby, Frank Otto, Uwe Sterzik, Armando Fernandez, Andreas Ehrl, Ingo Borgmann, Rainer Osselmann, Hagen Stamm, Thomas Huber, Dirk Theismann, René Reimann, Werner Obschernikat)	5	2	0	83	65
5. HUN	(Péter Kuna, Gábor Bujka, Gábor Schmiedt, Zsolt Petőváry, István Pintér, Tibor Keszthelyi, Balázs Vincze, Zoltán Mohi, Tibor Pardi, László Tóth, András Gyöngyösi, Zoltán Kósz, Imre Tóth)	3	2	2	72	57
6. SPA	(Jesús Rollán Prada, Miguel Chillida, Marco Antônio González Junquera, Miguel Perez, Manuel Estiarte Ducocastella, Pere Robert, Jorge Paya, José Antonio Rodriguez, Jordi Sans Juan, Salvador Gómez Aguera, Mariano Moya, Jorge Neira, Pedro García Aguado)	4	2	1	66	55
7. ITA	(Paolo Trapanese, Alfio Misaggi, Andrea Pisano, Antonello Steardo, Alessandro	3	2	2	66	53

Campagna, Paolo Caldarella, Mario Fiorillo, Francesco Porzio, Stefano Postiglione, Riccardo Empestini, Massimiliano Ferretti, Marco D'Altrui, Gianni Averaimo)

		W	L	T	PF	PA
8.	AUS	3	4	0	53	59

(Glenn Townsend, Richard Pengelley, Christopher Harrison, Troy Stockwell, Andrew Wightman, Andrew Kerr, Raymond Mayers, Geoffrey Clark, John Fox, Christopher Wybrow, Simon Asher, Andrew Taylor, Donald Cameron)

Final: YUG 9–7 USA (overtime)
3rd Place: SOV 14–13 GER

Yugoslavia and the United States played each other eight times in the two and a half months before the Olympics; the U.S. won five matches, Yugoslavia three. They met again to open the preliminary round in Seoul. The U.S. won again, this time 7–6 on a goal by Jim Bergeson with 5 seconds to play.

Ten days later, the American and Yugoslavian teams, both of which returned five players from their 1984 Olympic squads, matched up yet again in a replay of the Los Angeles final. In fact, as the championship game developed, there were certain eerie and, for the U.S., unfortunate similarities between the two contests. Just as they had four years earlier, the U.S. team took a 5–2 lead in the third quarter. Then, just as it had four years earlier, the U.S. play became tentative and the Yugoslavians fought back to tie the score 5–5. This time they also took the lead 6–5, although the U.S. scored one more goal to break a 10-minute drought with 2:12 to play. The game ended 6–6.

Following the rather unsatisfactory conclusion of the 1984 Olympics, in which the gold medal was determined by goal differential, the F.I.N.A. decided to change the rules to allow six-minute overtime periods in the medal round. In fact, the 1986 world championship was decided when Yugoslavia's Igor Milanović defeated the U.S.S.R. by scoring a goal with three-tenths of a second remaining in the *fourth* overtime period.

In Seoul no such marathon was needed. Yugoslavia scored three unanswered goals in the first 3:35 of overtime and held on for a 9–7 victory. The Yugoslavian players *averaged* 6 feet 6 inches tall.

1992 Barcelona T: 12, N: 12, D: 8.9.

		W	L	T	PF	PA
1.	ITA	5	0	2	59	50

(Francesco Attolico, Alessandro Bovo, Alessandro Campagna, Paolo Caldarella, Mario Fiorillo, Francesco Porzio, Massimiliano Ferretti, Marco D'Altrui, Ferdinando Gandolfi, Amedeo Pomilio, Giuseppe Porzio, Carlo Silipo, Gianni Averaimo)

		W	L	T	PF	PA
2.	SPA	5	1	1	67	48

(Daniel Ballart Sans, Manuel Estiarte Ducocastella, Pedro García Aguado, Salvador Gómez Aguera, Marco Antonio González, Rubén Michavila Jover, Miguel Oca Gaia, Sergio Pedrerol Cavallé, José Picó Llado, Jesús Rollán Prada, Ricardo Sánchez Alarcón, Jordi Sans Juan, Manuel Silvestre Sánchez)

		W	L	T	PF	PA
3.	SOV	6	1	0	66	45

(Dmitri Apanasenko, Andrei Belofastov, Yevgeny Sharonov, Dmitri Gorshkov, Vladimir Karabutov, Aleksandr Kolotov, Andrei Kovalenko, Nikolai Kozlov, Sergei Markoch, Sergei Naumov, Aleksandr Ogorodnikov, Aleksandr Chigir, Aleksei Vdovin)

		W	L	T	PF	PA
4.	USA	4	2	1	48	38

(Jeffrey Campbell, Christopher Duplanty, Michael Evans, Kirk Everist, Erich Fischer, Charles Harris, Chris Humbert, Douglas Kimbell, Craig Klass, Alex Rousseau, Terry Schroeder, John Vargas, Craig Wilson)

		W	L	T	PF	PA
5.	HUN	4	1	2	69	64

(Péter Kuna, Gábor Schmiedt, Zsolt Petőváry, Balázs Vincze, László Tóth, András Gyöngyösi, Imre Tóth, Tibor Benedek, István Dóczi, Gábor Nemes, Imre Péter, Frank Tóth, Zsolt Varga)

		W	L	T	PF	PA
6.	GER	1	3	3	52	56

(Frank Otto, Uwe Sterzik, Ingo Borgmann, Hagen Stamm, Dirk Theismann, Rene Reimann, Piotr Bukowski, Raúl De la Peña Vega, Jörg Dresel, Torsten Dresel, Carsten Kusch, Reibel Guido, Peter Röhle)

		W	L	T	PF	PA
7.	CUB	2	5	0	66	72

(Juan Barreras Benítez, Norge Blay García, Pablo Cuesta Zulueta, Jorge Del Valle Gutiérrez, Marcelo Derauville De La Cruz, Bárbaro Díaz Cervantes, Lázaro Fernández Bueno, Juan Hernández Olivera, Juan Hernández Silveira, Guillermo Martínez Luis, Iván Pérez Vargas, José Ramos Soler, Ernesto García Piñero)

		W	L	T	PF	PA
8.	AUS	3	2	2	58	53

(Glenn Townsend, Troy Stockwell, Andrew Wightman, Raymond Mayers, Geoffrey Clark, John Fox, Christopher Wybrow, Simon Asher, Daniel Marsden, Gregory McFadden, Guy Newman, Mark Oberman, Paul Oberman)

Final: ITA 9–8 SPA (overtime)
3rd Place: SOV 8–4 USA

In the run-up to the Olympics it was assumed the final would be a showdown between Yugoslavia, the two-time defending Olympic champion, and Spain, seven of whose members were native Barcelonans. Yugoslavia had defeated Spain 8–7 in the final of the 1991 world championships and 11–10 in the final of the 1991 European championships. But two days before the Opening Ceremony of the Barcelona Games, the International Olympic Committee supported United Nations sanctions against Yugoslavia by banning the militarily aggressive nation from the Olympics. Individual athletes from Yugoslavia could compete under the banner of "Independent Olympic Participants," but Yugoslavia was not allowed to take part in team sports, such as water polo.

Surprisingly, it was the team from Italy that provided the challenge to Spain that had been expected to come from Yugoslavia. To say that the Italians and the Spanish were evenly matched is to put it mildly. They first met in pool play and tied 9–9. Four days later they faced each other again in the final.

In the semifinals, Spain had beaten the United States 6–4, while Italy had upset the predominantly Russian team from the ex-Soviet Union 9–8 on a penalty throw by Alessandro Campagna with 2:04 to play. The Yugoslavian team may not have been present at the final, but the Yugoslavian system was very much in evidence: both head coaches, Dragan Matutinović of Spain and Ratko Rudić of Italy, were from Croatia, which had declared its independence from Yugoslavia in June of 1991. Rudić had played for the Yugoslavian Olympic team in 1980 and had coached Yugoslavia to gold medals in 1984 and 1988.

Italy scored first and pulled away to a 4–1 lead late in the second period and a 6–3 lead with two minutes to play in the third period. They were still ahead 7–6 with time running out when Miguel Oca scored for Spain with 34 seconds to play. Two three-minute overtime periods were ordered. There were no scores for the first five minutes, but, with 42 seconds left, Italy's Mario Fiorillo fouled Jordi Sans. Spain's star, four-time Olympian Manuel Estiarte, converted the penalty throw. The predominantly Spanish crowd went wild, but their joy was short-lived. Nine seconds later, Jordi Sans was excluded and Italy capitalized on their one-man advantage when Massimiliano Ferretti evened the score with a backhand shot with 20 seconds on the clock.

During the break before the next overtime period, nerves were raw, and scuffling broke out between the two teams. Back in 1920 a tense tied match between Italy and Spain had ended abruptly during the second overtime period when the Italian team left the pool in a protest against the referee. Seventy-two years later, the Italian team had no intention of repeating the incident. Back into the pool the two teams went. There was no scoring in the third overtime period—or the fourth or the fifth. It appeared that the sixth overtime period would go the same way when Massimiliano Ferretti passed to Ferdinando Gandolfi in the left corner and, with 32 seconds to play, Gandolfi shot the ball past Spanish goalie Jesús Rollán. Spain set up one last play, but Oca's shot with five seconds left hit the crossbar, and the 46-minute marathon was finally over. Ratko Rudić had won his third straight Olympic championship.

WEIGHTLIFTING

Flyweight—54 kg	Light Heavyweight—83 kg
Bantamweight—59 kg	Middle Heavyweight—91 kg
Featherweight—64 kg	First Heavyweight—99 kg
Lightweight—70 kg	Heavyweight—108 kg
Middleweight—76 kg	Super Heavyweight—Unlimited Weight

Each contestant is allowed three attempts at each type of lift. The *snatch* is performed by lifting the bar from the floor to above the head in one movement and holding it there for two seconds. The *clean and jerk,* or *jerk,* is a two-part lift. First the weight is brought up to the clavicle (collarbone) or the chest and then, using the combined strength of arms and legs, it is raised overhead until the arms are vertically extended. The *press,* which was discontinued following the 1972 Olympics, required the lifter to bring the bar to his shoulders, wait two seconds for the judges' approval, and then lift the bar overhead using only the arms. A competitor is allowed 60 seconds from the time his name is called until the beginning of the attempt. If a competitor makes two consecutive attempts, he is allowed two minutes between attempts. When a tie occurs, the man with the lower bodyweight is declared the winner. Until 1992 a lifter who completed a successful lift within 10 kilograms of the world record was allowed a fourth attempt, which did not count as part of the competition, but could count as a world record. In order to distance itself from a period tainted by drug abuse, the International Weightlifting Federation changed all weight categories following the 1992 Olympics, thus wiping out all world records and starting "clean." However, weightlifting remains a sport in crisis. Prior to the 1995 world championships 856 male weightlifters were given doping tests. Incredibly, 62 of them, from 31 different countries, tested positive for steroids. Although such results have led to calls that the sport be banned from the Olympics, the International Weightlifting Federation deserves credit for being the first sports federation to employ testing equipment that can detect traces of steroids up to three months after they have been used rather than the usual three weeks.

FLYWEIGHT
(54 kg—119.05 lbs [1972-1992: 52kg—114.61 lbs)

1896–1968 not held

1972 Munich C: 17, N: 13, D: 8.31. WR: 342.5 kg (Sándor Holczreiter)

		PRESS		SNATCH		JERK		TOTAL KG
1. Zygmunt Smalcerz	POL	112.5	OR	100.0		125.0		337.5
2. Lajos Szücs	HUN	107.5		95.0		127.5		330.0
3. Sándor Holczreiter	HUN	112.5	OR	92.5		122.5		327.5
4. Tetsuhide Sasaki	JPN	105.0		97.5		120.0		322.5
5. Gyi Aung	BUR	95.0		105.0	WR	120.0		320.0
6. Pak Dong-geun	PRK	97.5		90.0		130.0	OR	317.5
7. Chaiya Sukchinda	THA	100.0		92.5		120.0		312.5
8. Ion Hortopan	ROM	97.5		95.0		117.5		310.0

Charlie Depthios of Indonesia took an extra lift at the end of the competition and set a world jerk record of 132.5 kg.

1976 Montreal C: 23, N: 18, D: 7.18. WR: 242.5 kg (Aleksandr Voronin)

		SNATCH		JERK		TOTAL KG	
1. Aleksandr Voronin	SOV/RUS	105.0		137.5	OR	242.5	EWR
2. György Köszegi	HUN	107.5	OR	130.0		237.5	
3. Mohammad Nassiri Seresht	IRN	100.0		135.0		235.0	

			SNATCH	JERK	TOTAL KG
4.	Masatomo Takeuchi	JPN	105.0	127.5	232.5
5.	Francisco Casamayor	CUB	100.0	127.5	227.5
6.	Stefan Leletko	POL	95.0	125.0	220.0
7.	Boleslav Pachol	CZE	95.0	122.5	217.5
8.	Daniel Nuñez Aguiar	CUB	92.5	122.5	215.0

At 4 feet 8¼ inches, Voronin, an electrician from Kerekoo, was the shortest man in the competition. Taking an extra lift after winning the gold medal, he set a world jerk record of 141 kg.

1980 Moscow C: 18, N: 15, D: 7.20. WR: 247.5 kg (Aleksandr Voronin)

			SNATCH		JERK		TOTAL KG	
1.	Kanybek Osmanaliev	SOV/KYR	107.5		137.5	EOR	245.0	OR
2.	Ho Bong-choi	PRK	110.0	OR	135.0		245.0	
3.	Han Gyong-si	PRK	110.0	OR	135.0		245.0	
4.	Béla Oláh	HUN	110.0	OR	135.0		245.0	
5.	Stefan Leletko	POL	105.0		135.0		240.0	
6.	Ferenc Hornyák	HUN	107.5		130.0		237.5	
7.	Francisco Casamayor	CUB	102.5		130.0		232.5	
8.	Adjya Jugdernamjil	MGL	97.5		117.5		215.0	

This unusually close contest was won by Osmaliev as a result of his lower bodyweight. Han and Oláh had registered the same bodyweight, but Han was awarded third place when the two lifters were reweighed *after* the competition and Han was 3½ ounces lighter. Han set a world snatch record of 113 kg on his fourth attempt.

1984 Los Angeles-Westchester C: 20, N: 15, D: 7.29. WR: 262.5 kg (Neno Terziiski)

			SNATCH	JERK	TOTAL KG
1.	Zeng Guoqiang	CHN	105.0	130.0	235.0
2.	Zhou Peishun	CHN	107.5	127.5	235.0
3.	Kazushito Manabe	JPN	102.5	130.0	232.5
4.	Hidemi Miyashita	JPN	107.5	122.5	230.0
5.	Maman Suryaman	INA	102.5	125.0	227.5
6.	Bang Hyo-mun	KOR	100.0	125.0	225.0
7.	José Diaz Lopez	PAN	95.0	125.0	220.0
8.	Levent Erdogan	TUR	95.0	120.0	215.0
DISQ (Drugs): Mahmood Tarha (LEB) 230.0					

No sport was as hard-hit by the 1984 Soviet-bloc boycott as weightlifting. Missing from the competition in the ten weight categories were all ten of the defending world champions, 29 of the 30 medalists at the last world championships, and 94 of the top 100 ranked lifters.

Zeng was awarded first place because he weighed 3½ ounces less than Zhou. Zeng, at 19 years of age, is the youngest weightlifting gold medalist in Olympic history. Tarha, in fourth place, was disqualified because he tested positive for anabolic steroids. At the Friendship Games, held in Varna, Bulgaria, for weightlifters from boycotting nations, the gold medal went to world record holder Neno Terziiski of Bulgaria with a total of 252.5 kg.

1988 Seoul C: 24, N: 18, D: 9.18. WR: 267.5 kg (He Zhuoqiang)

		SNATCH		JERK		TOTAL KG	
1. Sevdalin Marinov	BUL	120.0	WR	150.0	OR	270.0	WR
2. Chun Byung-kwan	KOR	112.5		147.5		260.0	
3. He Zhuoqiang	CHN	112.5		145.0		257.5	
4. Zhang Shoulie	CHN	115.0		142.5		257.5	
5. Jacek Gutowski	POL	112.5		135.0		247.5	
6. Traian Cihărean	ROM	110.0		130.0		240.0	
7. Béla Oláh	HUN	107.5		130.0		237.5	
8. Kazushito Manabe	JPN	105.0		125.0		230.0	

Despite He Zhuoqiang's having set a world record 3 months before the Olympics, Marinov had dominated the division since 1985, when he won the world championship at age 17.

1992 Barcelona C: 17, N: 13, D: 7.27. WR: 272.5 kg (Ivan Ivanov)

		SNATCH	JERK		TOTAL KG
1. Ivan Ivanov	BUL	115.0	150.0	EOR	265.0
2. Lin Qisheng	CHN	115.0	147.5		262.5
3. Traian Cihărean	ROM	112.5	140.0		252.5
4. Ko Kwang-ku	KOR	112.5	140.0		252.5
5. Halil Mutlu	TUR	112.5	135.0		247.5
6. Gil Nam-su	PRK	100.0	135.0		235.0
7. Humberto Feuntes Rodríquez	VEN	100.0	130.0		230.0
8. José Ibáñez Puig	SPA	100.0	127.5		227.5

Ivan Ivanov, one of four Ivan Ivanovs on the 1992 Bulgarian Olympic team, had won the last three world championships.

Albania made its first appearance at the Olympics in 1972. Then the Albanians set a record by boycotting the next four Olympics. In 1992 Albania returned to the Games, after 20 years away. Their first scheduled competitor was Genc Barkici, a flyweight weightlifter who had placed fifth at the European championships three months earlier. Unfortunately, Barkici got his finger caught in a door at the arena the day of the competition and he was forced to withdraw.

BANTAMWEIGHT
(59 kg—130.07 lbs [1948-1992: 56 kg—123 lbs)

1896–1936 not held

1948 London C: 19, N: 14, D: 8.9. WR: 300 kg (Joseph Di Pietro)

		PRESS		SNATCH		JERK		TOTAL KG	
1. Joseph Di Pietro	USA	105.0	OR	90.0		112.5		307.5	WR
2. Julian Creus	GBR	82.5		95.0	OR	120.0		297.5	
3. Richard Tom	USA	87.5		90.0		117.5		295.0	
4. Lee Kyu-hyuk	KOR	77.5		92.5		120.0		290.0	
5. Mahmoud Namjou	IRN	82.5		82.5		122.5	OR	287.5	
6. Marcel Thévenet	FRA	90.0		80.0		110.0		280.0	
7. Rosaire Smith	CAN	82.5		85.0		110.0		277.5	
8. Maurice Crow	NZE	77.5		85.0		110.0		272.5	

The arms of 4-foot 10-inch weightlifter Joe Di Pietro were so short he could barely raise the bar above his head. Yet he was still able to win the 1948 Bantamweight gold medal.

Joe Di Pietro's height was variously reported as 4 feet 8 inches or 4 feet 10 inches. Whichever figure is correct, his arms were so short that he was barely able to raise the bar above his head.

1952 Helsinki C: 19, N: 18, D: 7.25. WR: 317.5 kg (Mahmoud Namjou)

		PRESS	SNATCH		JERK		TOTAL KG	
1. Ivan Udodov	SOV/RUS	90.0	97.5	OR	127.5	OR	315.0	OR
2. Mahmoud Namjou	IRN	90.0	95.0		122.5		307.5	
3. Ali Mirzaii	IRN	95.0	92.5		112.5		300.0	
4. Kim Hae-nam	KOR	80.0	95.0		120.0		295.0	
5. Kamal Mahmoud Mahgoub	EGY	75.0	95.0		122.5		292.5	
6. Pedro Landero	PHI	90.0	87.5		115.0		292.5	
7. Maurice Megennis	GBR	82.5	85.0		112.5		280.0	
8. Lon Mohamed Noor	SIN	77.5	85.0		112.5		275.0	

1956 Melbourne C: 16, N: 13, D: 11.23. WR: 335 kg (Vladimir Stogov)

		PRESS		SNATCH		JERK	TOTAL KG	
1. Charles Vinci	USA	105.0	EOR	105.0	OR	132.5	342.5	WR
2. Vladimir Stogov	SOV/RUS	105.0	EOR	105.0	OR	127.5	337.5	

		PRESS		SNATCH		JERK		TOTAL KG	
3. Mahmoud Namjou	IRN	100.0		102.5		130.0		332.5	
4. Yu In-ho	KOR	90.0		95.0		135.0	OR	320.0	
5. Kim Hae-nam	KOR	85.0		95.0		127.5		307.5	
6. Yoshio Nanbu	JPN	87.5		97.5		120.0		305.0	
7. Reginald Gaffley	SAF	97.5		90.0		117.5		305.0	
8. Yukio Furuyama	JPN	90.0		87.5		125.0		302.5	

As weigh-in time approached, the 4-foot 10-inch Vinci was one and a half pounds overweight. After an hour of running and sweating he was still seven ounces over the limit with 15 minutes to go. Fortunately, a severe last-minute haircut did the trick, and Vinci went on to win the gold medal.

1960 Rome C: 22, N: 18, D: 9.7. WR: 345 kg (Vladimir Stogov)

		PRESS		SNATCH		JERK		TOTAL KG	
1. Charles Vinci	USA	105.0	EOR	107.5	EWR	132.5		345.0	EWR
2. Yoshinobu Miyake	JPN	97.5		105.0		135.0	EOR	337.5	
3. Esmaiil Elmkhan	IRN	97.5		100.0		132.5		330.0	
4. Shigeo Kogure	JPN	90.0		102.5		130.0		322.5	
5. Marian Jankowski	POL	92.5		100.0		130.0		322.5	
6. Imre Földi	HUN	100.0		90.0		130.0		320.0	
7. Yu In-ho	KOR	90.0		95.0		130.0		315.0	
8. Husain Hasan	IRQ	87.5		100.0		125.0		312.5	

1964 Tokyo C: 24, N: 18, D: 10.11. WR: 352.5 kg (Yoshinobu Miyake)

		PRESS		SNATCH		JERK		TOTAL KG	
1. Aleksei Vakhonin	SOV/RUS	110.0		105.0		142.5	OR	357.5	WR
2. Imre Földi	HUN	115.0	OR	102.5		137.5		355.0	
3. Shiro Ichinoseki	JPN	100.0		110.0	OR	137.5		347.5	
4. Henryk Trębicki	POL	105.0		102.5		135.0		342.5	
5. Yang Mu-shin	KOR	97.5		107.5		135.0		340.0	
6. Yukio Furuyama	JPN	105.0		100.0		130.0		335.0	
7. Yu In-ho	KOR	97.5		100.0		137.5		335.0	
8. Martin Dias	GUY	100.0		102.5		132.5		335.0	

Vakhonin, a 4-foot 10¾-inch, 29-year-old coal miner, set a world record in the jerk that was not allowed because he was, by then, overweight. The lift did count as an *Olympic* record, however. The same treatment was given to Ichinoseki's snatch record. Földi, who had sweated down from a featherweight, was handicapped in the snatch because one of his fingers was missing and another was paralyzed. Vakhonin disappeared from international competition prior to the 1968 Olympics after being accused of "conduct unbecoming a Master of Sport."

1968 Mexico City C: 20, N: 19, D: 10.13. WR: 367.5 kg (Gennady Chetin)

		PRESS		SNATCH	JERK		TOTAL KG	
1. Mohammad Nassiri Seresht	IRN	112.5		105.0	150.0	WR	367.5	EWR
2. Imre Földi	HUN	122.5	OR	105.0	140.0		367.5	EWR
3. Henryk Trebicki	POL	115.0		107.5	135.0		357.5	
4. Gennady Chetin	SOV/RUS	110.0		102.5	140.0		352.5	
5. Shiro Ichinoseki	JPN	110.0		107.5	132.5		350.0	
6. Fernando Baez Cruz	PUR	120.0		92.5	132.5		345.0	
7. Atanas Kirov	BUL	105.0		100.0	130.0		335.0	
8. Chaiya Sukchinda	THA	100.0		105.0	125.0		330.0	

Nassiri was awarded first place because his bodyweight was ten ounces less than Földi's.

1972 Munich C: 24, N: 20, D: 8.28. WR: 375 kg (Gennady Chetin)

		PRESS		SNATCH	JERK	TOTAL KG	
1. Imre Földi	HUN	127.5	OR	107.5	142.5	377.5	WR
2. Mohammad Nassiri Seresht	IRN	127.5	OR	100.0	142.5	370.0	
3. Gennady Chetin	SOV/RUS	120.0		107.5	140.0	367.5	
4. Henryk Trebicki	POL	122.5		107.5	135.0	365.0	
5. Atanas Kirov	BUL	117.5		105.0	140.0	362.5	
6. George Vasiliades	AUS	115.0		102.5	137.5	355.0	
7. Hiroshi Ono	JPN	115.0		105.0	135.0	355.0	
8. Georgi Todorov	BUL	110.0		100.0	140.0	350.0	

Tenth-place finisher Koji Miki of Japan set an Olympic snatch record of 112.5 kg and then broke the world record with an extra lift of 114 kg. Polish-born Zeev Friedman, who finished twelfth, was one of the 11 Israelis who were murdered at the Games by Palestinian terrorists.

1976 Montreal C: 24, N: 19, D: 7.19. WR: 260 kg (Atanas Kirov)

		SNATCH		JERK	TOTAL KG	
1. Norair Nurikian	BUL	117.5	OR	145.0	262.5	WR
2. Grzegorz Cziura	POL	115.0		137.5	252.5	
3. Kenkichi Ando	JPN	107.5		142.5	250.0	
4. Leszek Skorupa	POL	112.5		137.5	250.0	
5. Imre Földi	HUN	105.0		140.0	245.0	
6. Bernhard Backfisch	GER	105.0		137.5	242.5	
7. Carlos Lastre	CUB	105.0		135.0	240.0	
8. Fazlollah Dehkhoda	IRN	105.0		135.0	240.0	

Imre Földi became the only weightlifter to take part in five Olympics.

1980 Moscow C: 21, N: 17, D: 7.21. WR: 272.5 kg (Daniel Núñez Aguiar)

		SNATCH		JERK		TOTAL KG	
1. Daniel Nuñez Aguiar	CUB	125.0	WR	150.0		275.0	WR
2. Yurik Sarkisyan	SOV/ARM	112.5		157.5	WR	270.0	
3. Tadeusz Dembończyk	POL	120.0		145.0		265.0	
4. Andreas Letz	GDR	115.0		150.0		265.0	
5. Yang Eui-yong	PRK	112.5		150.0		265.0	
6. Imre Stefanovics	HUN	115.0		145.0		260.0	
7. Gheorghe Maftei	ROM	105.0		142.5		247.5	
8. Pavel Petre	ROM	105.0		140.0		245.0	

Dembończyk was awarded the bronze medal as a result of a post-competition weigh-in.

1984 Los Angeles-Westchester C: 20, N: 18, D: 7.30. WR: 300 kg (Naim Suleymanoğlü)

		SNATCH		JERK	TOTAL KG
1. Wu Shude	CHN	120.0		147.5	267.5
2. Lai Runming	CHN	125.0	EOR	140.0	265.0
3. Masahiro Kotaka	JPN	112.5		140.0	252.5
4. Takashi Ichiba	JPN	110.0		140.0	250.0
5. Kim Chil-bong	KOR	105.0		140.0	245.0

6. Dionisio Muñoz	SPA	110.0	132.5	242.5		
7. Arvo Ojalehto	FIN	105.0	137.5	242.5		
8. Albert Hood	USA	112.5	130.0	242.5		

One of the most popular weightlifters at the Los Angeles Olympics was fourth place finisher Takashi Ichiba, who entertained the audience by performing a back flip *before* each lift.

Few boycotting athletes in 1984 were more missed than world record holder Naim Suleymanoğlu, the 16-year-old boy wonder from Bulgaria. At the Friendship Games in September, Suleymanoğlu defeated Oksen Mirzoyan of the U.S.S.R. 297.5 kg to 295.0 kg. In 1986 Suleymanoğlu, a member of Bulgaria's Turkish minority, defected after a competition in Melbourne, Australia, and moved to Turkey.

1988 Seoul C: 23, N: 17, D: 9.19. WR: 300 kg (Naim Suleymanoğlü)

		SNATCH		JERK		TOTAL KG	
1. Oksen Mirzoyan	SOV/ARM	127.5	OR	165.0	OR	292.5	OR
2. He Yingqiang	CHN	125.0		162.5		287.5	
3. Liu Shoubin	CHN	' 127.5	OR	140.0		267.5	
4. Dirdja Wihardja	INA	112.5		142.5		255.0	
5. Takashi Ichiba	JPN	107.5		145.0		252.5	
6. Kim Kwi-shik	KOR	110.0		142.5		252.5	
7. Joaquin Valle	SPA	112.5		135.0		247.5	
8. Giovanni Scarantino	ITA	110.0		135.0		245.0	

DISQ (Drugs): Mitko Grablev (BUL) 297.5

1992 Barcelona C: 22, N: 17, D: 7.27. WR: 300 kg (Naim Suleymanoğlü)

		SNATCH		JERK	TOTAL KG
1. Chun Byung-kwan	KOR	132.5	OR	155.0	287.5
2. Liu Shoubin	CHN	130.0		147.5	277.5
3. Luo Jianming	CHN	125.0		152.5	277.5
4. Laurent Fombertasse	FRA	112.5		147.5	260.5
5. Katsuhiko Sakuma	JPN	120.0		135.0	255.0
6. Tibor Karczag	HUN	115.0		140.0	255.0
7. Kim Yong-chol	PRK	110.0		145.0	255.0
8. Marek Gorzelniak	POL	115.0		140.0	255.0

Chun did not make his first clean and jerk attempt until all the other lifters had completed theirs.

FEATHERWEIGHT
(64 kg—141.1 lbs [1920-1992: 60 kg—132 lbs)

1896–1912 not held

1920 Antwerp C: 14, N: 11, D: 8.29.

		ONE-HAND SNATCH	ONE-HAND JERK	TWO-HAND JERK	TOTAL KG
1. François de Haes	BEL	60.0	65.0	95.0	220.0
2. Alfred Schmidt	EST	55.0	65.0	90.0	210.0

		ONE-HAND SNATCH	ONE-HAND JERK	TWO-HAND JERK	TOTAL KG
3. Eugène Ryther	SWI	55.0	65.0	90.0	210.0
4. Luigi Gatti	ITA	50.0	55.0	90.0	195.0
5. Ludvik Wágner	CZE	50.0	65.0	80.0	195.0
6. Gustav Eriksson	SWE	47.5	65.0	80.0	192.5
7. Lionel de Haes	BEL	45.0	60.0	85.0	190.0
7. Karl Kõiv	EST	45.0	60.0	85.0	190.0

The rules of 1920 required each lifter to perform the one-hand jerk with whichever arm was not used in the one-arm snatch.

Schmidt was awarded second place after jerking 92.5 kg in a lift-off against Ryther.

1924 Paris C: 21, N: 11, D: 7.21.

		ONE-HAND SNATCH		ONE-HAND JERK		TWO-HAND PRESS	TWO-HAND SNATCH	TWO-HAND JERK		TOTAL KG
1. Pierino Gabetti	ITA	65.0	OR	77.5		72.5	82.5	105.0	OR	402.5
2. Andreas Stadler	AUT	65.0	OR	75.0		65.0	75.0	105.0	OR	385.0
3. Arthur Reinmann	SWI	57.5		70.0		80.0	75.0	100.0		382.5
4. Maurice Martin	FRA	60.0		62.5		75.0	82.5	100.0		380.0
5. Wilhelm Rosinek	AUT	57.5		75.0		67.5	70.0	105.0	OR	375.0
6. Gustav Ernesaks	EST	60.0		80.0	OR	67.5	72.5	92.5		372.5
7. Alfred Baxter	GBR	55.0		65.0		70.0	75.0	105.0	OR	370.0
8. Edgar Juillerat	SWI	55.0		70.0		67.5	75.0	100.0		367.5

Mehmet Djemal Bey of Turkey, who finished 14th, was only 13 years old.

1928 Amsterdam C: 21, N: 13, D: 7.29.

		PRESS		SNATCH		JERK		TOTAL KG	
1. Franz Andrysek	AUT	77.5		90.0	OR	120.0	OR	287.5	OR
2. Pierino Gabetti	ITA	80.0		90.0	OR	112.5		282.5	
3. Hans Wölpert	GER	92.5	WR	82.5		107.5		282.5	
4. Giuseppe Conca	ITA	92.5	WR	80.0		105.0		277.5	
5. Arthur Reinmann	SWI	82.5		82.5		110.0		275.0	
6. Andreas Stadler	AUT	72.5		80.0		115.0		267.5	
7. Henri Baudrand	FRA	77.5		80.0		107.5		265.0	
8. Mehmet Djemal Bey	TUR	85.0		75.0		102.5		262.5	
8. Josef Vacek	CZE	80.0		82.5		100.0		262.5	

1932 Los Angeles C: 6, N: 4, D: 7.31.

		PRESS	SNATCH	JERK	TOTAL KG	
1. Raymond Suvigny	FRA	82.5	87.5	117.5	287.5	EOR
2. Hans Wölpert	GER	85.0	87.5	110.0	282.5	
3. Anthony Terlazzo	USA	82.5	85.0	112.5	280.0	
4. Helmut Schäfer	GER	77.5	77.5	112.5	267.5	
5. Attilio Bescapè	ITA	82.5	77.5	102.5	262.5	
6. Richard Bachtell	USA	70.0	80.0	102.5	252.5	

An eating binge on the way to Los Angeles forced Suvigny to lose ten pounds in one week in order to make the weight limit.

1936 Berlin C: 21, N: 13, D: 8.2. WR: 297.5 kg (Max Walther)

		PRESS		SNATCH		JERK		TOTAL KG	
1. Anthony Terlazzo	USA	92.5	EOR	97.5	OR	122.5		312.5	WR
2. Saleh Mohammed Soliman	EGY	85.0		95.0		125.0	OR	305.0	
3. Ibrahim Hassan Shams	EGY	80.0		95.0		125.0	OR	300.0	
4. Anton Richter	AUT	80.0		97.5	OR	120.0		297.5	
5. Georg Liebsch	GER	92.5	EOR	90.0		107.5		290.0	
6. Attilio Bescapè	ITA	87.5		90.0		110.0		287.5	
7. John Terry	USA	75.0		92.5		120.0		287.5	
8. Max Walther	GER	75.0		90.0		115.0		280.0	

1948 London C: 23, N: 18, D: 8.9. WR: 320 kg (Arvid Anderson)

		PRESS		SNATCH		JERK		TOTAL KG	
1. Mahmoud Fayad	EGY	92.5		105.0	WR	135.0	WR	332.5	WR
2. Rodney Wilkes	TRI	97.5		97.5		122.5		317.5	
3. Jaafar Salmasi	IRN	100.0	OR	97.5		115.0		312.5	
4. Nam Su-il	KOR	92.5		92.5		122.5		307.5	
5. Rodrigo Del Rosario	PHI	97.5		92.5		117.5		307.5	
6. Kotaro Ishikawa	USA	92.5		95.0		120.0		307.5	
7. Johan Runge	DEN	95.0		90.0		120.0		305.0	
8. Max Heral	FRA	85.0		95.0		120.0		300.0	

1952 Helsinki C: 22, N: 21, D: 7.25. WR: 332.5 kg (Mahmoud Fayad)

		PRESS		SNATCH		JERK		TOTAL KG	
1. Rafael Chimishkyan	SOV/GEO	97.5		105.0	EOR	135.0	EOR	337.5	WR
2. Nikolai Saksonov	SOV/RUS	95.0		105.0	EOR	132.5		332.5	
3. Rodney Wilkes	TRI	100.0		100.0		122.5		322.5	
4. Rodrigo Del Rosario	PHI	105.0	OR	92.5		120.0		317.5	
5. Said Khalifa Gouda	EGY	85.0		102.5		125.0		312.5	
6. Chay Weng Yew	SIN	87.5		97.5		127.5		312.5	
7. Balint Nagy	HUN	85.0		97.5		125.0		307.5	
8. Mohsen Tabatabaii	IRN	90.0		97.5		120.0		307.5	

1956 Melbourne C: 21, N: 19, D: 11.23. WR: 350 kg (Rafael Chimishkyan)

		PRESS		SNATCH		JERK		TOTAL KG	
1. Isaac Berger	USA	107.5		107.5	OR	137.5	OR	352.5	WR
2. Yevgeny Minayev	SOV/RUS	115.0	WR	100.0		127.5		342.5	
3. Marian Zieliński	POL	105.0		102.5		127.5		335.0	
4. Rodney Wilkes	TRI	100.0		105.0		125.0		330.0	
5. Hiroyoshi Shiratori	JPN	97.5		100.0		127.5		325.0	
6. Georg Miske	GDR	100.0		95.0		125.0		320.0	
7. Tan Ser Cher	SIN	92.5		92.5		130.0		315.0	
8. Lee Kyung-sob	KOR	90.0		95.0		132.5		312.5	

Ike Berger was the 19-year-old son of a rabbi from Brooklyn.

1960 Rome C: 28, N: 25, D: 9.7. WR: 372.5 kg (Isaac Berger)

		PRESS		SNATCH		JERK		TOTAL KG	
1. Yevgeny Minayev	SOV/RUS	120.0	EWR	110.0	OR	142.5	OR	372.5	EWR
2. Isaac Berger	USA	117.5		105.0		140.0		362.5	
3. Sebastiano Mannironi	ITA	107.5		110.0	OR	135.0		352.5	
4. Kim Hae-nam	KOR	105.0		105.0		135.0		345.0	

		PRESS	SNATCH	JERK	TOTAL KG
5. Yukio Furuyama	JPN	107.5	102.5	135.0	345.0
6. Hosni Abbas	EGY	102.5	95.0	140.0	337.5
7. Tun Kywe	BUR	100.0	100.0	127.5	327.5
8. Alberto Nogar	PHI	97.5	100.0	127.5	325.0

The competition took ten hours and didn't end until four a.m., when Berger twice failed to jerk 152.5 kg. Minayev had lost to Berger six straight times prior to the Olympics. In Rome, he made all nine of his lifts.

1964 Tokyo C: 22, N: 20, D: 10.12. WR: 387.5 kg (Yoshinobu Miyake)

		PRESS		SNATCH		JERK		TOTAL KG	
1. Yoshinobu Miyake	JPN	122.5	OR	122.5	OR	152.5	WR	397.5	WR
2. Isaac Berger	USA	122.5	OR	107.5		152.5	WR	382.5	
3. Mieczyslaw Nowak	POL	112.5		115.0		150.0		377.5	
4. Hiroshi Fukuda	JPN	120.0		115.0		140.0		375.0	
5. Sebastiano Mannironi	ITA	112.5		112.5		145.0		370.0	
6. Kim Hae-nam	KOR	115.0		112.5		140.0		367.5	
7. Rudolf Kozlowski	POL	110.0		107.5		140.0		357.5	
8. Hosni Abbas	EGY	105.0		100.0		137.5		342.5	

Yoshinobu Miyake, who had won the Bantamweight silver medal in 1960, was a 24-year-old lieutenant in the National Self-Defense Force. Only 5 feet tall, he came from a poor family in Miyagi prefecture in northern Japan. His parents sold some pigs to raise the money to see their son compete in the Olympics.

1968 Mexico City C: 28, N: 22, D: 10.14. WR: 397.5 kg (Yoshinobu Miyake)

		PRESS		SNATCH	JERK		TOTAL KG
1. Yoshinobu Miyake	JPN	122.5	EOR	117.5	152.5	EWR	392.5
2. Dito Shanidze	SOV/GEO	120.0		117.5	150.0		387.5
3. Yoshiyuki Miyake	JPN	122.5	EOR	115.0	147.5		385.0
4. Jan Wojnowski	POL	117.5		115.0	150.0		382.5
5. Mieczyslaw Nowak	POL	117.5		110.0	147.5		375.0
6. Nasrollah Dehnavi	IRN	117.5		107.5	140.0		365.0
7. Young Moo-shin	KOR	110.0		115.0	140.0		365.0
8. Manuel Mateos	MEX	120.0		100.0	140.0		360.0

Yoshiyuki Miyake was six years younger than his brother Yoshinobu.

1972 Munich C: 13, N; 11, D: 8.29. WR: 402.5 kg (Dito Shanidze)

		PRESS		SNATCH	JERK		TOTAL KG	
1. Norair Nurikian	BUL	127.5	OR	117.5	157.5	WR	402.5	EWR
2. Dito Shanidze	SOV/GEO	127.5	OR	120.0	152.5		400.0	
3. János Benedek	HUN	125.0		120.0	145.0		390.0	
4. Yoshinobu Miyake	JPN	120.0		120.0	145.0		385.0	
5. Kurt Pittner	AUT	125.0		112.5	145.0		382.5	
6. Rolando Chang	CUB	120.0		115.0	142.5		377.5	
7. Mieczyslaw Nowak	POL	120.0		110.0	145.0		375.0	
8. Peppino Tanti	ITA	120.0		107.5	140.0		367.5	

This division saw the rare appearance of an athlete from Albania. Ymer Pampuri, a circus clown, broke the Olympic record in the press and actually led the competition after the first round due to his lower bodyweight. However, the snatch and the jerk were not practiced in Albania and he could do no better than 12th and tenth in those disciplines. Pampuri wound up in ninth place.

1976 Montreal C: 17, N: 13, D: 7.20. WR: 285 kg (Georgi Todorov)

			SNATCH		JERK		TOTAL KG	
1.	Nikolai Kolesnikov	SOV/RUS	125.0	OR	160.0	OR	285.0	EWR
2.	Georgi Todorov	BUL	122.5		157.5		280.0	
3.	Kazumasa Hirai	JPN	125.0	OR	150.0		275.0	
4.	Takashi Saito	JPN	110.0		152.5		262.5	
5.	Edward Weitz	ISR	110.0		152.5		262.5	
6.	Davoud Maleki	IRN	115.0		145.0		260.0	
7.	Pedro Fuentes	CUB	112.5		145.0		257.5	
8.	Om Jong-guk	PRK	110.0		145.0		255.0	

Kolesnikov set a jerk world record of 161.5 kg on his fourth attempt.

1980 Moscow C: 18, N: 14, D: 7.22. WR: 297.5 kg (Viktor Mazin)

			SNATCH		JERK		TOTAL KG	
1.	Viktor Mazin	SOV/RUS	130.0	OR	160.0	EOR	290.0	OR
2.	Stefan Dimitrov	BUL	127.5		160.0	EOR	287.5	
3.	Marek Seweryn	POL	127.5		155.0		282.5	
4.	Antoni Pawlak	POL	120.0		150.0		275.0	
5.	Julio Loscos	CUB	125.0		150.0		275.0	
6.	František Nedved	CZE	122.5		150.0		272.5	
7.	Victor Perez	CUB	117.5		152.5		270.0	
8.	Gelu Radu	ROM	115.0		150.0		265.0	

1984 Los Angeles-Westchester C: 21, N: 17, D: 7.31. WR: 315 kg (Stefan Topurov)

			SNATCH	JERK	TOTAL KG
1.	Chen Weiqiang	CHN	125.0	157.5	282.5
2.	Gelu Radu	ROM	125.0	155.0	280.0
3.	Tsai Wen-Yee	TAI	125.0	147.5	272.5
4.	Kaoru Wabiko	JPN	120.0	150.0	270.0
5.	Yosuke Muraki	JPN	120.0	147.5	267.5
6.	Lee Myeong-su	KOR	117.5	150.0	267.5
7.	Sorie Enda Nasution	INA	115.0	152.5	267.5
8.	Uolevi Kahelin	FIN	112.5	155.0	267.5

Silver medalist Gelu Radu was the only medalist at the 1983 world championships to take part in the 1984 Olympics. The medal ceremony for this event held a special drama as it marked the first time that the platform was shared by athletes from China and Taiwan. Chen and Tsai shook hands and spoke kindly of each other.

At the Friendship Games in Varna, Bulgaria, in September, Stefan Topurov of Bulgaria broke his own world record with a combined lift of 322.5 kg. He was followed by two Soviet lifters, Yurik Sarkisyan at 315 kg and Anton Kodzhabashev at 295 kg. At the 1983 world championships, Topurov had jerked 180 kg to become the first person in history to lift three times his own bodyweight.

Weightlifters Chen Weiqiang (left) and Tsai Wen-Yee become the first athletes from China and Taiwan to share an Olympic medal platform after taking the gold and bronze medals, respectively, in the 60 kg category in 1984.

1988 Seoul C: 17, N: 14, D: 9.20. WR: 335 kg (Naim Suleymanoğlu)

		SNATCH		JERK		TOTAL KG	
1. Naim Suleymanoğlu	TUR	152.5	WR	190.0	WR	342.5	WR
2. Stefan Topurov	BUL	137.5		175.0		312.5	
3. Ye Huanming	CHN	127.5		160.0		287.5	
4. Min Joon-ki	KOR	125.0		155.0		280.0	
5. Yosuke Muraki	JPN	127.5		150.0		277.5	
6. Giannis Sidriopoulos	GRE	120.0		145.0		265.0	
7. Kazushige Oguri	JPN	117.5		142.5		260.0	
8. Tolentino Murillo	COL	120.0		140.0		260.0	

He was born Naim Suleimanov in the small mountain village of Ptichar in the region of Bulgaria with the highest concentration of ethnic Turks. His father, a zinc miner, was 5 feet tall. His mother, who worked in a hot house, was 4 feet 7½ inches. Naim himself topped out just shy of 5 feet. Short though he may have been, he was also strong. In a nation where weightlifters are heroes, he was quickly discovered by Bulgarian sports officials.

He first competed internationally in a junior championship and, at the age of 14, came within 5½ pounds of breaking the *adult* world record for combined lifts. At 15 he set his first world record and at 16 he became the second lifter to clean and jerk three times his bodyweight. In recognition of his achievements, the Bulgarian government gave Suleimanov his own apartment and a monthly stipend. However, in 1984, at the same time that he was being well treated, the government also began a crackdown on the Turkish minority. In December, Suleimanov returned from a training camp to his parents' hometown of Momchilgrad (they had moved there when he was 3) to discover that a major demonstration by Turks had been violently suppressed by Bulgarian authorities. The anti-Turkish campaign intensified. Mosques were closed, Moslem holidays and burials were banned, and the use of the Turkish language was outlawed, as was the wearing of Turkish clothes. Violators were imprisoned and even executed.

In 1985, Suleimanov attended a ten-day training camp in Melbourne, Australia. There he was approached by Bulgarian defectors of Turkish descent who offered to help him defect. The 18-year-old declined, but told them that if the Bulgarian government changed his name to a non-Islamic one, as they had done to other Turks, he would reconsider. When he returned to Bulgaria his passport was confiscated and he was issued a new one bearing the name Naum Shalamanov. One day he opened up a newspaper and read a faked interview that quoted him as saying that he was proud to retake his "true Bulgarian name." Suleimanov was peppered with letters from Bulgarian Turks who believed the "interview," and accused him of selling his soul.

In December 1986, Suleimanov, by now a two-time world champion, returned to Melbourne for the World Cup competition. When the tournament was over, he joined the rest of the Bulgarian team for a banquet at the Leonda restaurant in the Melbourne suburb of Hawthorn. At one point he excused himself to go to the men's room—and never returned. After hiding out for four days, he presented himself to the Turkish consulate and asked for asylum. He was flown to London where he was met by a private jet belonging to Turkey's prime minister, Turgut Ozal. Upon arrival at the airport in Turkey, Suleimanov kissed the tarmac and became an instant national hero.

Olympic rules state that if an athlete changes nationality, he must wait three years to take part in international competition unless he receives a waiver from the country he has left. The Bulgarian government granted this waiver in 1988 after receiving over $1,000,000 from the Turkish government, as well as an assurance from Suleimanov (who by now had assumed the Turkish equivalent of his original name—Naim Suleymanoğlu) that he would suspend his public criticisms of their policies.

In Seoul, Suleymanoğlu lived up to all expectations. He broke the snatch world record with his second lift, then broke it again with his third. He repeated his double world record in the clean and jerk. His combined total was larger than that of the winner in the lightweight division and his best lifts in both the snatch and jerk were greater than those of Paul Anderson when he won the

The Turkish government paid the Bulgarian government over $1,000,000 to allow Featherweight weightlifter Naim Suleymanoğlu to compete for Turkey in 1988.

heavyweight division in 1956. At that time, Anderson weighed 303 pounds. Suleymanoğlu in 1988 weighed 132.

1992 Barcelona C: 31, N: 25, D: 7.28. WR: 342.5 kg (Naim Suleymanoğlu)

			SNATCH	JERK	TOTAL KG
1.	Naim Suleymanoğlu	TUR	142.5	177.5	320.0
2.	Nikolay Peshalov	BUL	137.5	167.5	305.0
3.	He Yingqiang	CHN	130.0	165.0	295.0
4.	Neno Terziiski	BUL	130.0	165.0	295.0
5.	Leonidis Valerios	GRE	132.5	162.5	295.0
6.	Ro Hyon-il	PRK	127.5	160.0	287.5
7.	Attila Czanka	HUN	127.5	157.5	285.0
8.	Li Jae-son	PRK	130.0	150.0	280.0

When Naim Suleymanoğlu completed his last lift at the 1988 Olympics, he literally kissed the bar good-bye. He was ready to retire. But retirement was easier said than done. When he stepped off the airplane that had carried him from Seoul to the Turkish capital of Ankara, there were an estimated one million people waiting to greet him. Speaking from Kizilay Plaza to a national television audience, he announced, "This is not *my* gold medal! This is the Turkish people's medal!" Suleymanoğlu, Turkey's first gold medalist in 20 years, graduated from being a major hero to being a symbol of his nation. Retirement was out of the question. His story became so widely known around the world that the plight of Bulgaria's Turkish minority became an international issue. The Bulgarian government was forced to allow one-third of the nation's 900,000 Turks to emigrate to Turkey.

Suleymanoğlu defeated Bulgaria's Nikolay Peshalov at the 1989 world championships and then, citing a back injury, he did announce his retirement. At the 1990 world championships, Suleymanoğlu watched Peshalov

win with a total of only 297.5 kilograms. This was too painful for Suleymanoğlu. He reentered training and won back his world title in 1991. Still, it was hard for him to maintain the discipline necessary to stay on top. When he was a teenager, girls had teased him because he was so short. Now he was pursued by numerous women and he fathered a child out of wedlock. The Turkish tabloids followed his every move and photographers surrounded him whenever he appeared in public. At the 1992 European championships, three months before the Olympics, Peshalov tied Suleymanoğlu at 312.5 kilograms and won because of a lower bodyweight. It was Suleymanoğlu's first defeat in 8½ years. It served as a serious wake-up call.

In Barcelona, Suleymanoğlu and Peshalov repeated their European snatch totals of 142.5 kg and 137.5 kg, but the clean-and-jerk was a different story. Peshalov, who had jerked 175 kilograms at the Euros, could do no better than 167.5 at the Olympics. When Peshalov was finished lifting, Suleymanoğlu coolly hoisted 170 kilograms and the contest was over. He made one more successful lift for good measure and then passed his final attempt.

Among the secondary contenders was Marcus Samuel, a man with an unusual story. Samuel was definitely one of the top ten lifters in his weight category, a legitimate qualifier for the Olympics. Unfortunately, Samuel hailed from the Pacific island of Nauru, a nation so small (population: 9000) that it didn't have a national Olympic committee. So Samuel did what he had to do: he acquired citizenship in a "big" country—Western Samoa (population 195,000). In Barcelona, Samuel lifted a total of 275 kilograms and placed a creditable ninth. In 1994, Nauru, thanks to Samuel's accomplishments, was admitted as the 196th—and smallest—nation in the Olympic movement.

LIGHTWEIGHT
(70 kg—154.32 lbs [1920-1992: 67.5 kg—148.75 lbs)

1896–1912 not held

1920 Antwerp C: 12, N: 10, D: 8.29.

			ONE-HAND SNATCH	ONE-HAND JERK	TWO-HAND JERK	TOTAL KG
1.	Alfred Neuland	EST	72.5	75.0	110.0	257.5
2.	Louis Williquet	BEL	60.0	75.0	105.0	240.0
3.	Florimond Rooms	BEL	55.0	70.0	105.0	230.0
4.	Giulio Monti	ITA	55.0	70.0	105.0	230.0
5.	Fernand Arnout	FRA	60.0	60.0	100.0	220.0
5.	Martin Olofsson	SWE	55.0	70.0	95.0	220.0
7.	Vaquette	FRA	55.0	65.0	95.0	215.0
8.	Johny Grun	LUX	52.5	67.5	90.0	210.0
8.	Willem van Nimwegen	HOL	55.0	65.0	90.0	210.0

1924 Paris C: 22, N: 12, D: 7.22.

		ONE-HAND SNATCH	ONE-HAND JERK	TWO-HAND PRESS	TWO-HAND SNATCH	TWO-HAND JERK		TOTAL KG
1. Edmond Décottignies	FRA	70.0	92.5	77.5	85.0	115.0	OR	440.0
2. Anton Zwerina	AUT	75.0 OR	80.0	77.5	82.5	112.5		427.5
3. Bohumil Durdis	CZE	70.0	82.5	72.5	90.0	110.0		425.0
4. Leopold Treffny	AUT	65.0	85.0	77.5	85.0	112.5		425.0
5. Joseph Jaquenoud	SWI	65.0	85.0	77.5	85.0	105.0		417.5
6. Eduard Vanaaseme	EST	65.0	77.5	85.0	80.0	107.5		415.0
7. August Scheffer	HOL	62.5	80.0	80.0	82.5	110.0		415.0
8. Felix Bichsel	SWI	70.0	95.0 WR	65.0	75.0	105.0		410.0

1928 Amsterdam C: 18, N: 12, D: 7.29. WR: 325 kg (Kurt Helbig)

		PRESS	SNATCH	JERK		TOTAL KG
1. Hans Haas	GER	90.0 OR	97.5	135.0	OR	322.5
1. Kurt Helbig	AUT	85.0	102.5 OR	135.0	OR	322.5
3. Fernand Arnout	FRA	85.0	97.5	120.0		302.5
4. Albert Aeschmann	SWI	87.5	90.0	120.0		297.5
5. Willi Reinfrank	GER	85.0	90.0	120.0		295.0
6. Jules Meese	FRA	90.0 OR	87.5	115.0		292.5
7. Anton Hangel	AUT	77.5	90.0	120.0		287.5
8. Gastone Pierini	ITA	90.0 OR	82.5	110.0		282.5

1932 Los Angeles C: 6, N: 4, D: 7.31. WR: 325 kg (Kurt Helbig)

		PRESS	SNATCH	JERK	TOTAL KG
1. René Duverger	FRA	97.5 OR	102.5 EOR	125.0	325.0 EWR
2. Hans Haas	AUT	82.5	100.0	125.0	307.5
3. Gastone Pierini	ITA	92.5	90.0	120.0	302.5
4. Pierino Gabetti	ITA	85.0	95.0	120.0	300.0
5. Arnie Sundberg	USA	77.5	90.0	117.5	285.0
6. Walter Zagurski	USA	82.5	90.0	112.5	285.0

1936 Berlin C: 16, N: 12, D: 8.2. WR: 337.5 kg (Anwar Mohammed Mesbah)

		PRESS	SNATCH	JERK	TOTAL KG	
1. Robert Fein	AUT	105.0 OR	100.0	137.5	342.5	WR
1. Anwar Mohammed Mesbah	EGY	92.5	105.0 OR	145.0 OR	342.5	WR
3. Karl Jansen	GER	95.0	100.0	132.5	327.5	
4. Karl Schwitalle	GER	95.0	100.0	127.5	322.5	
5. John Terpak	USA	97.5	100.0	125.0	322.5	
6. El Sayed Ibrahim Masoud	EGY	90.0	100.0	132.5	322.5	
7. René Duverger	FRA	97.5	95.0	125.0	317.5	
8. Robert Mitchell	USA	85.0	97.5	130.0	312.5	

Originally Mesbah was awarded sole possession of first place because he had weighed three and a half ounces less than Fein at the precompetition weigh-in. The Austrians lodged a protest, which was upheld, and both men received gold medals.

1948 London C: 22, N: 17, D: 8.10. WR: 367.5 kg (Stanley Stanczyk)

		PRESS	SNATCH	JERK	TOTAL KG	
1. Ibrahim Hassan Shams	EGY	97.5	115.0 OR	147.5 OR	360.0	OR
2. Attia Hamouda	EGY	105.0	110.0	145.0	360.0	OR
3. James Halliday	GBR	90.0	110.0	140.0	340.0	

4. John Terpak	USA	102.5		102.5	135.0	340.0	
5. John Stuart	CAN	107.5	OR	100.0	125.0	332.5	
6. Kim Suk-young	KOR	95.0		100.0	135.0	330.0	
7. La See-yun	KOR	90.0		100.0	125.0	330.0	
8. Joseph Pittman	USA	100.0		95.0	127.5	322.5	

Shams won a dramatic confrontation with his teammate Hamouda. After Shams missed a jerk of 145 kg, Hamouda successfully lifted the same weight on his final attempt. This forced Shams, who had set the world jerk record nine years earlier, to add 2.5 kg to the bar if he hoped to tie Hamouda and win as a result of his lower bodyweight. With the audience in complete silence, Shams approached the bar twice and then turned away. The third time, he seized the bar quickly and, in a flash, had it up to his shoulders and over his head for the victory. Shams' 1939 snatch of 116.5 kg stood as a world record until the 1952 Olympics. His 153.5 kg jerk of the same year was still on the books in 1957.

1952 Helsinki C: 24, N: 22, D: 7.26. WR: 367.5 kg (Stanley Stanczyk)

		PRESS	SNATCH		JERK	TOTAL KG	
1. Tamio "Tommy" Kono	USA	105.0	117.5	WR	140.0	362.5	OR
2. Yevgeny Lopatin	SOV/RUS	100.0	107.5		142.5	350.0	

Tommy Kono won three Olympic medals in three different weight categories in 1952, 1956, and 1960. His mental control led one rival to comment, "When Kono looks at me from the wings, he works on me like a python on a rabbit."

		PRESS	SNATCH	JERK	TOTAL KG
3. Verne Barberis	AUS	105.0	105.0	140.0	350.0
4. Kim Chang-hee	KOR	100.0	105.0	140.0	345.0
5. Hassan Ferdows	IRN	102.5	107.5	135.0	345.0
6. Abd El Khadr El Touni	EGY	105.0	107.5	130.0	342.5
7. Johan Runge	DEN	105.0	97.5	127.5	330.0
8. Ging Hwie Thio	INA	105.0	92.5	130.0	327.5

Tommy Kono was a sickly child who suffered from asthma. His parents tried the usual traditional Japanese cures, such as bear kidneys, burned birds, and powdered snakes. "I used to wish with all my might for good health," he said. During World War II he and his family were forced to leave their home in Sacramento, California, and move to the Tule Lake detention camp for Japanese-Americans. It was there that 14-year-old Tommy was introduced to weightlifting. He caught on quickly and began what was to become an amazing career, which included two Olympic gold medals and one silver, and 21 world records set in four different divisions. His ability to move up and down in weight division without losing strength allowed him to fill in wherever the U.S. team needed him; thus each of his three Olympic medals was won in a different category. He accomplished this by following an unusual system of dieting. If he needed to add weight, he would eat six or seven meals a day. If he needed to shed a few pounds, he would restrict himself to "only" three meals a day. In 1954 Kono won the Mr. World contest, and in 1955 and 1957 he was chosen Mr. Universe. He balanced his muscleman image by washing and ironing his own clothes and doing his own cooking and cleaning. Yet another talent of Tommy Kono was his mental control—always an important factor in weightlifting. One of his many victims was Fyodor Bogdanovsky, who always lost to Kono, often performing well below his capabilities. Bogdanovsky once said, "When Kono looks at me from the wings, he works on me like a python on a rabbit."

1956 Melbourne C: 18, N: 17, D: 11.24. WR: 382.5 kg (Nicolai Kostilev)

		PRESS		SNATCH		JERK		TOTAL KG	
1. Ihor Rybak	SOV/UKR	110.0		120.0	OR	150.0	OR	380.0	OR
2. Rafael Khabutdinov	SOV/RUS	125.0	OR	110.0		137.5		372.5	
3. Kim Chang-hee	KOR	107.5		112.5		150.0	OR	370.0	
4. Kenji Onuma	JPN	110.0		110.0		147.5		367.5	
5. Henrik Tamraz	IRN	115.0		105.0		145.0		365.0	
6. Jan Czepulkowski	POL	120.0		105.0		135.0		360.0	
7. Ivan Abadzhiev	BUL	102.5		117.5		137.5		357.5	
8. Nil Tun Maung	BUR	110.0		105.0		137.5		352.5	

1960 Rome C: 33, N: 29, D: 9.8. WR: 390 kg (Viktor Bushuyev)

		PRESS		SNATCH		JERK		TOTAL KG	
1. Viktor Bushuyev	SOV/RUS	125.0	EOR	122.5	OR	150.0		397.5	WR
2. Tan Howe Liang	SIN	115.0		110.0		155.0	OR	380.0	
3. Abdul Wahid Aziz	IRQ	117.5		115.0		147.5		380.0	
4. Marian Zieliński	POL	115.0		110.0		150.0		375.0	
5. Waldemar Baszanowski	POL	105.0		117.5		147.5		380.0	
6. Mihály Huszka	HUN	110.0		107.5		147.5		365.0	
7. Werner Dittrich	GDR	107.5		115.0		140.0		362.5	
7. Zdenek Otáhal	CZE	115.0		107.5		140.0		362.5	

Tan Howe Liang of Singapore and Abdul Wahid Aziz of Iraq are the only athletes from their respective countries to have won an Olympic medal.

1964 Tokyo C: 20, N: 18, D: 10.13. WR: 430 kg (Waldemar Baszanowski)

		PRESS		SNATCH		JERK		TOTAL KG	
1. Waldemar Baszanowski	POL	132.5		135.0	OR	165.0	OR	432.5	WR
2. Vladimir Kaplunov	SOV/RUS	140.0	EWR	127.5		165.0	OR	432.5	WR
3. Marian Zieliński	POL	140.0	EWR	120.0		160.0		420.0	

4. Anthony Garcy	USA	127.5	125.0	160.0	412.5
5. Zdenek Otáhal	CZE	130.0	117.5	152.5	400.0
6. Hiroshi Yamazaki	JPN	120.0	120.0	157.5	397.5
7. Parviz Jalayer	IRN	120.0	120.0	155.0	395.0
8. Alfred Kornprobst	GER	122.5	112.5	150.0	385.0

One of the greatest weightlifters of all time, Waldemar Baszanowski defeated Vladimir Kaplunov because he was ten and a half ounces lighter than his rival. Nine months later, at the European championships in Sofia, Bulgaria, the men tied again, and again Baszanowski was awarded first place as a result of his lower bodyweight.

1968 Mexico City C: 20, N: 17, D: 10.15. WR: 440 kg (Waldemar Baszanowski)

		PRESS	SNATCH		JERK		TOTAL KG	
1. Waldemar Baszanowski	POL	135.0	135.0	EOR	167.5	OR	437.5	OR
2. Parviz Jalayer	IRN	125.0	132.5		165.0		422.5	
3. Marian Zieliński	POL	135.0	125.0		160.0		420.0	
4. Nobuyuki Hatta	JPN	135.0	127.5		155.0		417.5	
5. Won Shin-hee	KOR	127.5	125.0		162.5		415.0	
6. Janós Bagócs	HUN	132.5	122.5		157.5		412.5	
7. Takeo Kimura	JPN	125.0	120.0		160.0		405.0	
8. Kostadin Tilev	BUL	132.5	115.0		150.0		397.5	

1972 Munich C: 22, N: 20, D: 8.30. WR: 450 kg (Waldemar Baszanowski)

		PRESS		SNATCH		JERK		TOTAL KG	
1. Mukharby Kirzhinov	SOV/RUS	147.5		135.0	EOR	177.5	WR	460.0	WR
2. Mladen Kuchev	BUL	157.5	WR	125.0		167.5		450.0	
3. Zbigniew Kaczmarek	POL	145.0		125.0		167.5		437.5	
4. Waldemar Baszanowski	POL	142.5		130.0		162.5		435.0	
5. Nasrollah Dehnavi	IRN	150.0		125.0		160.0		435.0	
6. Jenö Ambrózi	HUN	142.5		120.0		165.0		427.5	
7. Won Shin-hee	KOR	132.5		130.0		165.0		427.5	
8. Masao Kato	JPN	140.0		120.0		165.0		425.0	

1976 Montreal C: 23, N: 19, D: 7.21. WR: 312.5 kg (Mukharbi Kirzhinov)

		SNATCH		JERK	TOTAL KG	
1. Petro Korol	SOV/UKR	135.0	EOR	170.0	305.0	OR
2. Daniel Senet	FRA	135.0	EOR	165.0	300.0	
3. Kazimierz Czarnecki	POL	130.0		165.0	295.0	
4. Gunter Ambrass	GDR	125.0		170.0	295.0	
5. Yatsuo Shimaya	JPN	127.5		165.0	292.5	
6. Roberto Urrutia	CUB	130.0		162.5	292.5	
7. Werner Schraut	GER	127.5		162.5	290.0	
8. Roland Chavigny	FRA	130.0		155.0	285.0	

DISQ (Drugs): Zbigniew Kaczmarek (POL) 307.5

Kaczmarek finished first but was subsequently disqualified after a test revealed that he had taken prohibited drugs.

1980 Moscow C: 20, N: 16, D: 7.23. WR: 337.5 kg (Yanko Russev)

		SNATCH		JERK		TOTAL KG	
1. Yanko Russev	BUL	147.5	OR	195.0	WR	342.5	WR
2. Joachim Kunz	GDR	145.0		190.0		335.0	
3. Mincho Pachov	BUL	142.5		182.5		325.0	
4. Daniel Senet	FRA	147.5	OR	175.0		322.5	
5. Gunter Ambrass	GDR	140.0		180.0		320.0	
6. Zbigniew Kaczmarek	POL	140.0		177.5		317.5	
7. Raul Gonzalez	CUB	145.0		172.5		317.5	
8. Virgel Dociu	ROM	140.0		170.0		310.0	

1984 Los Angeles-Westchester C: 19, N: 17, D: 8.1. WR: 352.5 kg (Andreas Behm)

		SNATCH	JERK	TOTAL KG
1. Yao Jingyuan	CHN	142.5	177.5	320.0
2. Andrei Socaci	ROM	142.5	170.0	312.5
2. Jouni Grönman	FIN	140.0	172.5	312.5
4. Dean Willey	GBR	140.0	170.0	310.0
5. Choji Taira	JPN	132.5	172.5	305.0
6. Yasushige Sasaki	JPN	140.0	162.5	302.5
7. Basil Stellios	AUS	137.5	165.0	302.5
8. Ma Jianping	CHN	130.0	167.5	297.5

First place at the Friendship Games went to 1980 Olympic champion Yanko Russev with a combined total of 337.5 kg. Second was his Bulgarian teammate Alexandr Varbanov at 335 kg.

1988 Seoul C: 29, N: 25, D: 9.21. WR: 355 kg (Mikhail Petrov)

		SNATCH		JERK	TOTAL KG
1. Joachim Kunz	GDR	150.0		190.0	340.0
2. Israil Militosyan	SOV/ARM	155.0	OR	182.5	337.5
3. Li Jinhe	CHN	147.5		177.5	325.0
4. Marek Seweryn	POL	145.0		172.5	317.5
5. Ergun Batmaz	TUR	145.0		172.5	317.5
6. Xiao Minglin	CHN	132.5		172.5	305.0
7. István Kerek	HUN	132.5		170.0	302.5
8. Christos Constandinidis	GRE	137.5		162.5	300.0

DISQ (Drugs): Angel Genchev (BUL) 362.5

Bulgaria entered the 1988 Olympic weightlifting tournament expecting to win four or five gold medals and an equal number of silver medals. At first things appeared to be going well: Sevdalin Marinov won the flyweight division, Mitko Grablev won the bantamweight division, Stefan Topurov took second in the featherweight division, Angel Genchev won the lightweight division, and Borislav Gidikov won the middleweight division. Then disaster struck: Grablev was disqualified when he tested positive for a diuretic used as a masking agent for steroids. Two days later Genchev was disqualified for the same reason. Clearly the Bulgarians had underestimated the sophistication of the Olympic drug-testing equipment. After the announcement of the results of Genchev's drug test, the Bulgarian Weightlifting Federation withdrew the rest of their team from competition.

With Genchev disqualified, the gold medal was awarded to 29-year-old Joachim Kunz, who had not won a major championship in four years.

1992 Barcelona C: 18, N: 16, D: 7.29. WR: 355 kg (Mikhail Petrov)

			SNATCH		JERK	TOTAL KG
1.	Israil Militosyan	ARM	155.0	EOR	182.5	337.5
2.	Yoto Yotov	BUL	150.0		177.5	327.5
3.	Andreas Behm	GER	145.0		175.0	320.0
4.	Abdelmanaane Yahiaoui	ALG	140.0		175.0	315.0
5.	Jouni Grönman	FIN	135.0		170.0	305.0
6.	Eyne Acevedu Tabares	COL	130.0		170.0	300.0
7.	Im Sang-ho	PRK	135.0		165.0	300.0
8.	Timothy McRae	USA	135.0		162.5	297.5

Militosyan's older cousin Vartan won a silver medal in the middleweight division in 1976. Israil himself earned a silver medal in 1988. After beating Yotov at the 1989 world championships, Militosyan lost to Yotov at the European championships of 1990, 1991, and 1992, as well as at the 1991 world championships. When he finally broke this string of second places in Barcelona, he and cousin Vartan, who was also his coach, shared a tearful embrace. Militosyan had dedicated his performance to the memories of his sister, brother, and uncle, who were killed in an earthquake that destroyed his hometown of Gumari three months after the 1988 Olympics.

MIDDLEWEIGHT
(76 kg—167.55 lbs [1920-1992: 75 kg—165 lbs)

1896–1912 not held

1920 Antwerp C: 10, N: 7, D: 8.29.

			ONE-HAND SNATCH	ONE-HAND JERK	TWO-HAND JERK	TOTAL KG
1.	Henri Gance	FRA	65.0	75.0	105.0	245.0
2.	Pietro Bianchi	ITA	60.0	70.0	105.0	235.0
2.	Albert Pettersson	SWE	55.0	75.0	105.0	235.0
4.	Marius Ringelberg	HOL	55.0	65.0	105.0	225.0
5.	Paul Ledran	FRA	55.0	65.0	100.0	220.0
6.	Christian Jensen	DEN	55.0	60.0	100.0	215.0
7.	Marcel Marchand	BEL	55.0	55.0	95.0	205.0
8.	Pieter Belmer	HOL	0.0	65.0	100.0	165.0

Both Bianchi and Pettersson hoisted 107.5 kg in a lift-off, using a two-handed jerk. They then drew lots to determine who would be awarded the silver medal rather than bronze. Bianchi won.

1924 Paris C: 25, N: 13, D: 7.22.

			ONE-HAND SNATCH	ONE-HAND JERK	TWO-HAND PRESS	TWO-HAND SNATCH	TWO-HAND JERK	TOTAL KG
1.	Carlo Galimberti	ITA	77.5	95.0 OR	97.5 WR	95.0	127.5 WR	492.5
2.	Alfred Neuland	EST	82.5 WR	90.0	77.5	90.0	115.0	455.0
3.	Jaan Kikkas	EST	70.0	87.5	80.0	85.0	127.5 WR	450.0

		ONE-HAND SNATCH	ONE-HAND JERK	TWO-HAND PRESS		TWO-HAND SNATCH	TWO-HAND JERK	TOTAL KG
4. Hamed Samy	EGY	72.5	77.5	97.5	WR	85.0	115.0	447.5
5. Albert Aeschmann	SWI	67.5	87.5	82.5		87.5	117.5	442.5
6. Roger François	FRA	72.0	80.0	87.5		87.5	117.5	442.5
7. Rupert Eidler	AUT	65.0	90.0	82.5		85.0	115.0	437.5
8. Pierre Vibert	FRA	72.5	75.0	80.0		85.0	115.0	432.5

1928 Amsterdam C: 23, N: 15, D: 7.29. WR: 320 kg (Carlo Galimberti)

		PRESS		SNATCH		JERK		TOTAL KG	
1. Roger François	FRA	102.5		102.5		130.0		335.0	WR
2. Carlo Galimberti	ITA	105.0	WR	97.5		130.0		332.5	
3. August Scheffer	HOL	97.5		105.0	OR	125.0		327.5	
4. Franz Zinner	GER	87.5		100.0		135.0	OR	322.5	
5. Gaston Le Pût	FRA	92.5		95.0		125.0		312.5	
6. Wilhelm Hofmann	GER	90.0		95.0		120.0		305.0	
7. Houssein Mouktah	EGY	95.0		92.5		120.0		302.5	
8. Jan van Rompey	BEL	92.5		85.0		115.0		292.5	

1932 Los Angeles C: 7, N: 6, D: 7.31. WR: 342.5 kg (Rudolf Ismayr)

		PRESS	SNATCH		JERK		TOTAL KG	
1. Rudolf Ismayr	GER	102.5	110.0	OR	132.5		345.0	WR
2. Carlo Galimberti	ITA	102.5	105.0		132.5		340.0	
3. Karl Hipfinger	AUT	90.0	107.5		140.0	OR	337.5	
4. Roger François	FRA	102.5	102.5		130.0		335.0	
5. Stanley Kratkowski	USA	82.5	102.5		120.0		305.0	
6. Julio Juaneda	ARG	75.0	90.0		120.0		285.0	
7. Sam Termine	USA	87.5	105.0		0.0		192.5	

1936 Berlin C: 16, N: 12, D: 8.5. WR: 385 kg (Khadr Sayed El Touni)

		PRESS		SNATCH		JERK		TOTAL KG	
1. Khadr Sayed El Touni	EGY	117.5	WR	120.0	WR	150.0	OR	387.5	WR
2. Rudolf Ismayr	GER	107.5		102.5		142.5		352.5	

The 1936 Middleweight lifting champion, Khadr Sayed El Touni (center), lifted 15 kilograms more than the Light Heavyweight winner.

			PRESS	SNATCH	JERK	TOTAL KG
3. Adolf Wagner	GER	97.5	112.5	142.5		352.5
4. Anton Hangel	AUT	95.0	110.0	137.5		342.5
5. Stanley Kratkowski	USA	95.0	107.5	135.0		337.5
6. Hans Valla	AUT	102.5	102.5	130.0		335.0
7. Carlo Galimberti	ITA	100.0	102.5	130.0		332.5
8. Pierre Alleene	FRA	90.0	105.0	135.0		330.0

Twenty-one-year-old Khadr Sayed El Touni was one of the sensations of the 1936 Olympics. Not only did he outclass his opponents in the Middleweight division, but he actually lifted 15 kilograms more than the winner of the Light Heavyweight division. El Touni died of electrocution in 1956 while making a home repair.

1948 London C: 24, N: 18, D: 8.10. WR: 405 kg (Stanley Stanczyk)

		PRESS		SNATCH		JERK		TOTAL KG	
1. Frank Spellman	USA	117.5		120.0		152.5		390.0	OR
2. Peter George	USA	105.0		122.5	OR	155.0	OR	382.5	
3. Kim Sung-jip	KOR	122.5	OR	112.5		145.0		380.0	
4. Khadr Sayed El Touni	EGY	120.0		117.5		142.5		380.0	
5. Gérard Gratton	CAN	112.5		107.5		140.0		360.0	
6. Pierre Bouladoux	FRA	102.5		110.0		142.5		355.0	
7. Orlando Garrido Luloaga	CUB	112.5		107.5		135.0		355.0	
8. G. William Watson	GBR	100.0		110.0		140.0		350.0	

Peter George's only chance to win the gold medal was to clean and jerk 165 kg—11 kilograms more than Stanley Stanczyk's world record. After pacing back and forth for twelve tense minutes, the 19-year-old George rubbed his hands with a block of chalk. Suddenly he crushed the chalk to dust and approached the bar. With great deliberation and concentration, he took hold of the weight, prepared his body, and hoisted the bar to his shoulders. The audience burst into applause, but quieted down quickly as George prepared for the second part of the lift. He pushed the bar overhead, but staggered and dropped it and had to settle for second place. Kim Sung-jip was Korea's first Olympic medalist.

1952 Helsinki C: 21, N: 20, D: 7.26. WR: 405 kg (Stanley Stanczyk)

		PRESS		SNATCH		JERK		TOTAL KG	
1. Peter George	USA	115.0		127.5	OR	157.5	OR	400.0	OR
2. Gérard Gratton	CAN	122.5	EOR	112.5		155.0		390.0	
3. Kim Sung-jip	KOR	122.5	EOR	112.5		147.5		382.5	
4. Ismail Ragab	EGY	115.0		117.5		150.0		382.5	
5. Moustafa Laham	LEB	115.0		112.5		142.5		370.0	
6. Åke Hedberg	SWE	102.5		105.0		150.0		357.5	
7. Angel Sposato	ARG	107.5		110.0		140.0		357.5	
8. Jalal Mansouri	IRN	110.0		107.5		140.0		357.5	

1956 Melbourne C: 16, N: 15, D: 11.24. WR: 415 kg (Fyodor Bogdanovsky)

		PRESS		SNATCH		JERK		TOTAL KG	
1. Fyodor Bogdanovsky	SOV/RUS	132.5	OR	122.5		165.0	OR	420.0	WR
2. Peter George	USA	122.5		127.5	EOR	162.5		412.5	

		PRESS	SNATCH	JERK	TOTAL KG
3. Ermanno Pignatti	ITA	117.5	117.5	147.5	302.5
4. Jan Bochenek	POL	120.0	112.5	150.0	382.5
5. Kim Sung-jip	KOR	125.0	110.0	145.0	380.0
6. Krzysztof Beck	POL	122.5	112.5	145.0	380.0
7. Ebrahim Peyravi	IRN	107.5	117.5	147.5	372.5
8. Adrien Gilbert	CAN	112.5	115.0	142.5	370.0

History repeated itself when defending champion Peter George, now a dentist in the U.S. Army, needed a world-record jerk to take first place. He attempted 170 kg, but couldn't make the weight. Nonetheless, his record of one gold and two silver medals is most impressive.

1960 Rome C: 27, N: 20, D: 9.8. WR: 430 kg (Tamio "Tommy" Kono)

		PRESS		SNATCH		JERK		TOTAL KG	
1. Aleksandr Kurynov	SOV/RUS	135.0		132.5	OR	170.0	WR	437.5	WR
2. Tamio "Tommy" Kono	USA	140.0	OR	127.5		160.0		427.5	
3. Gyözö Veres	HUN	130.0		120.0		155.0		405.0	
4. Marcel Paterni	FRA	127.5		120.0		152.5		400.0	
5. Krzysztof Beck	POL	135.0		117.5		147.5		400.0	
6. Mohammad Amitehrani	IRN	117.5		120.0		155.0		392.5	
7. Koh Yung-chang	KOR	115.0		120.0		150.0		385.0	
8. Roland Lortz	GER	115.0		112.5		155.0		382.5	

Tommy Kono, having already won gold medals as a Lightweight in 1952 and as a Light Heavyweight in 1956, decided to compete in the Middleweight division in 1960 because he had heard that Kurynov was "a very tough opponent." He heard right. The 26-year-old Soviet aviation engineer pulled off the victory and topped it with a world-record clean and jerk on his final attempt.

1964 Tokyo C: 19, N: 17, D: 10.14. WR: 445 kg (Viktor Kurentsov)

		PRESS		SNATCH		JERK		TOTAL KG	
1. Hans Zdražila	CZE	130.0		137.5	OR	177.5	WR	445.0	EWR
2. Viktor Kurentsov	SOV/BLR	135.0		130.0		175.0		440.0	
3. Masashi Ouchi	JPN	140.0	EOR	135.0		162.5		437.5	
4. Lee Jong-sup	KOR	130.0		127.5		175.0		432.5	
5. Sadahiro Miwa	JPN	120.0		132.5		170.0		422.5	
6. Mihály Huszka	HUN	135.0		125.0		160.0		420.0	
7. Rolf Maier	FRA	130.0		122.5		165.0		417.5	
8. Veliko Konarov	BUL	130.0		130.0		155.0		415.0	

1968 Mexico City C: 20, N: 17, D: 10.16. WR: 482.5 kg (Viktor Kurentsov)

		PRESS		SNATCH		JERK		TOTAL KG	
1. Viktor Kurentsov	SOV/BLR	152.5	OR	135.0		187.5	WR	475.0	OR
2. Masashi Ouchi	JPN	140.0		140.0	OR	175.0		455.0	
3. Károly Bakos	HUN	137.5		132.5		170.0		440.0	
4. Russell Knipp	USA	147.5		122.5		167.5		437.5	
5. Lee Chun-sik	KOR	140.0		132.5		165.0		437.5	
6. Werner Dittrich	GDR	140.0		130.0		165.0		435.0	
7. Miroslav Kolarik	CZE	140.0		127.5		162.5		430.0	
8. Frederick Lowe	USA	132.5		127.5		170.0		430.0	

In 1964 Kurentsov had entered the Olympics as the holder of the world record. However, in Tokyo he suffered an attack of nervousness and completed only four of his nine lifts. Four years later, at the next Olympics, he was a new man. Between lifts he calmly lay on a bed backstage reading Tolstoi. His winning margin was the largest in the Middleweight division since El Touni's great performance in 1936.

1972 Munich C: 26, N: 22, D: 8.31. WR: 482.5 (Viktor Kurentsov)

		PRESS	SNATCH		JERK	TOTAL KG	
1. Yordan Bikov	BUL	160.0	140.0		185.0	485.0	WR
2. Mohamed Trabulsi	LEB	160.0	140.0		172.5	472.5	
3. Anselmo Silvino	ITA	155.0	140.0		175.0	470.0	
4. Ondrej Hekel	CZE	150.0	142.5	OR	170.0	462.5	
5. Franklin Zielecke	GDR	150.0	140.0		170.0	460.0	
6. Gábor Szarvas	HUN	150.0	135.0		175.0	460.0	
7. András Stark	HUN	152.5	137.5		170.0	460.0	
8. Russell Knipp	USA	160.0	127.5		170.0	457.5	

Vladimir Kanygin of the U.S.S.R. set an Olympic record in the press of 165 kg, but he failed at all three attempts at the snatch and was disqualified.

1976 Montreal C: 17, N: 14, D: 7.22. WR: 345 kg (Yordan Mitkov)

		SNATCH		JERK		TOTAL KG	
1. Yordan Mitkov	BUL	145.0	OR	190.0	OR	335.0	OR
2. Vartan Militosyan	SOV/ARM	145.0	OR	185.0		330.0	
3. Peter Wenzel	GDR	145.0	OR	182.5		327.5	
4. Wolfgang Hübner	GDR	142.5		177.5		320.0	
5. Arvo Ala-Pöntiö	FIN	137.5		177.5		315.0	
6. András Stark	HUN	140.0		175.0		315.0	
7. Ondrej Hekel	CZE	140.0		172.5		312.5	
8. Daniel Zayas	CUB	140.0		170.0		310.0	

DISQ (Drugs): Dragomir Ciorosian (ROM) 320.0

1980 Moscow C: 16, N: 14, D: 7.24. WR: 355 kg (Assen Zlatev)

		SNATCH		JERK		TOTAL KG	
1. Assen Zlatev	BUL	160.0	OR	200.0	OR	360.0	WR
2. Oleksander Pervy	SOV/UKR	157.5		200.0	OR	357.5	
3. Nedelcho Kolev	BUL	157.5		187.5		345.0	
4. Julio Echenique Gonzalez	CUB	145.0		182.5		327.5	
5. Dragomir Ciorosian	ROM	140.0		182.5		322.5	
6. Tapio Kinnunen	FIN	142.5		177.5		320.0	
7. Bertil Sollevi	SWE	137.5		172.5		310.0	
8. Newton Burrowes	GBR	130.0		172.5		302.5	

After the formal competition was over, Zlatev jerked 205.5 kg for a new world record.

1984 Los Angeles-Westchester C: 21, N: 17, D: 8.2. WR: 370.0 kg (Alexandr Varbanov)

		SNATCH	JERK	TOTAL KG
1. Karl-Heinz Radschinsky	GER	150.0	190.0	340.0
2. Jacques Demers	CAN	147.5	187.5	335.0

		SNATCH	JERK	TOTAL KG
3. Dragomir Cioroslan	ROM	147.5	185.0	332.5
4. David Morgan	GBR	145.0	185.0	330.0
5. Li Shunzhu	CHN	147.5	175.0	322.5
6. Mohammed Yaseen Mohammed	IRQ	140.0	180.0	320.0
7. Antonio Pignone	AUS	147.5	170.0	317.5
8. Park Chun-jong	KOR	137.5	175.0	312.5

In 1983 Demers was arrested for smuggling steroid tablets into Canada, although his trial was delayed until after the Olympics. Demers qualified for the Canadian team again in 1988, but was dropped before the Games when he tested positive for steroids despite having injected someone else's clean urine into his bladder. In 1985 Radschinsky was arrested in West Germany for possessing steroids with intent to sell.

At the Friendship Games in September, Zdravko Stoichkov of Bulgaria set a world record of 377.5 kg. In second place was Vladimir Kuznetsov of the U.S.S.R. at 362.5 kg.

1988 Seoul C: 25, N: 20, D: 9.22. WR: 380 kg (Aleksandr Varbanov)

		SNATCH		JERK		TOTAL KG	
1. Borislav Gidikov	BUL	167.5	OR	207.5	OR	375.0	OR
2. Ingo Steinhöfel	GDR	165.0		195.0		360.0	
3. Aleksandr Varbanov	BUL	157.5		200.0		357.5	
4. Cai Yanshu	CHN	157.5		190.0		347.5	
5. Andrei Socaci	ROM	152.5		195.0		347.5	
6. Waldemar Kosiński	POL	152.5		180.0		332.5	
7. Dean Willey	GBR	152.5		180.0		332.5	
8. Roberto "Tony" Urrutia	USA	150.0		177.5		327.5	

DISQ (Drugs): Kalman Csengeri (HUN) 350.0

1992 Barcelona C: 34, N: 27, D: 7.30. WR: 382.5 kg (Aleksandr Varbanov)

		SNATCH	JERK	TOTAL KG
1. Fedor Kassapu	MOL	155.0	202.5	357.5
2. Pablo Lara Rodríguez	CUB	155.0	202.5	357.5
3. Kim Myong-nam	PRK	162.5	190.0	352.5
4. Andrzej Kozlowski	POL	160.0	192.5	352.5
5. Ingo Steinhöfel	GER	155.0	192.5	347.5
6. Raúl Mora Licea	CUB	150.0	195.0	345.0
7. Wlodzimierz Chlebosz	POL	155.0	185.0	340.0
8. Lu Gang	CHN	150.0	185.0	335.0

Fedor Kassapu grew up on a poor collective farm near the small village of Cotovsk. His home had no running water and he developed strength early by carrying water for his family of 12 from a well a quarter of a mile away. He won the gold medal with a full-out effort on his final lift. He tied Lara, but was eight ounces lighter than the Cuban. In May 1995 Kassapu tested positive for the steroid mesterolone and was banned for life.

LIGHT HEAVYWEIGHT

(83 kg—182.98 lbs [1920-1992: 82.5 kg—181.5 lbs)

1896–1912 not held

1920 Antwerp C: 11, N: 9, D: 8.31.

		ONE-HAND SNATCH	ONE-HAND JERK	TWO-HAND JERK	TOTAL KG
1. Ernest Cadine	FRA	70.0	90.0	135.0	295.0
2. Fritz Hünenberger	SWI	75.0	90.0	112.5	277.5
3. Erik Pettersson	SWE	62.5	92.5	112.5	267.5
4. Erik Carlsson	SWE	67.5	75.0	120.0	262.5
5. Maurice Devéne	FRA	65.0	70.0	115.0	250.0
6. Gino Mattiello	ITA	60.0	70.0	105.0	235.0
7. Jan Welter	HOL	65.0	70.0	95.0	230.0
8. Jaroslav Dvořák	CZE	55.0	65.0	107.5	227.5
8. Lionel van de Roye	BEL	57.5	65.0	105.0	227.5

1924 Paris C: 20, N: 12, D: 7.23.

		ONE-HAND SNATCH	ONE-HAND JERK	TWO-HAND PRESS	TWO-HAND SNATCH	TWO-HAND JERK	TOTAL KG
1. Charles Rigoulot	FRA	87.5 OR	92.5	85.0	102.5	135.0 EOR	502.5
2. Fritz Hünenberger	SWI	80.0	107.5 WR	80.0	97.5	125.0	490.0
3. Leopold Friedrich	AUT	75.0	95.0	95.0	95.0	130.0	490.0
4. Karl Freiberger	AUT	75.0	95.0	92.5	95.0	130.0	487.5
5. Carlos Bergara	ARG	80.0	85.0	92.5	97.5	127.5	482.5
6. Mario Giambelli	ITA	77.5	95.0	82.5	95.0	130.0	480.0
7. Anton Schärer	SWI	75.0	85.0	100.0	95.0	120.0	475.0
8. Jaroslav Skobla	CZE	70.0	95.0	92.5	85.0	127.5	470.0

1928 Amsterdam C: 15, N: 10, D: 7.29. WR: 350 kg (Jakob Vogt)

		PRESS	SNATCH	JERK	TOTAL KG
1. El Sayed Mohammed Nosseir	EGY	100.0 EOR	112.5 OR	142.5 WR	355.0 WR
2. Louis Hostin	FRA	100.0 EOR	110.0	142.5 WR	352.5
3. Johannes Verheijen	HOL	95.0	105.0	137.5	337.5
4. Václav Pšenička	CZE	100.0 EOR	105.0	130.0	335.0
4. Jakob Vogt	GER	100.0 EOR	105.0	130.0	335.0
6. Karl Freiberger	AUT	95.0	95.0	132.5	322.5
7. Karl Bierwirth	GER	95.0	95.0	125.0	315.0
7. Pierre Vibert	FRA	95.0	95.0	125.0	315.0
7. Josef Zemann	AUT	75.0	105.0	135.0	315.0

El Sayed Nosseir caused quite a sensation with his prelift ritual of raising his arms and head to the sky and calling out for Allah's assistance. A minor incident occurred during the award ceremony when the band struck up the Austrian national anthem by mistake instead of the French "Marseillaise." There were chuckles throughout the crowd, but the French were not amused.

1932 Los Angeles C: 4, N: 3, D: 7.31. WR: 365 kg (Jakob Vogt)

		PRESS	SNATCH	JERK	TOTAL KG
1. Louis Hostin	FRA	102.5 OR	112.5 EOR	150.0 OR	365.0 EWR
2. Svend Olsen	DEN	102.5 OR	107.5	150.0 OR	360.0

		PRESS	SNATCH	JERK	TOTAL KG
3. Henry Duey	USA	92.5	105.0	132.5	330.0
4. William Good	USA	95.0	97.5	130.0	322.5

Hostin was so confident of victory that he traded jokes with the referee while he was lifting.

1936 Berlin C: 14, N: 9, D: 8.3. WR: 375 kg (Fritz Haller)

		PRESS		SNATCH		JERK		TOTAL KG	
1. Louis Hostin	FRA	110.0	OR	117.5	OR	145.0		372.5	OR
2. Eugen Deutsch	GER	105.0		110.0		150.0	EOR	365.0	
3. Ibrahim Wasif	EGY	100.0		110.0		150.0	EOR	360.0	
4. Helmut Opschruf	GER	97.5		110.0		147.5		355.0	
5. Nicolas Scheitler	LUX	105.0		105.0		140.0		350.0	
6. Fritz Haller	AUT	97.5		110.0		142.5		350.0	
7. William Good	USA	100.0		105.0		145.0		350.0	
8. Mohammed Ahmed Geissa	EGY	95.0		110.0		142.5		347.5	

Eugen Deutsch was originally disqualified for missing all three of his snatch attempts. An hour later the Jury of Appeal validated one of his snatches, giving him the silver medal and causing resentment among many non-German observers. Matters were made worse when, at the medal ceremony, the Turkish flag was raised instead of the French flag and the national anthem of Egypt was played instead of the "Marseillaise."

1948 London C: 16, N: 13, D: 8.11. WR: 425 kg (Grigory Novack)

		PRESS		SNATCH		JERK		TOTAL KG	
1. Stanley Stanczyk	USA	130.0	OR	130.0	OR	157.5	OR	417.5	OR
2. Harold Sakata	USA	110.0		117.5		152.5		380.0	
3. Gösta Magnusson	SWE	110.0		120.0		145.0		375.0	
4. Jean Debuf	FRA	107.5		112.5		150.0		370.0	
5. Osvaldo Forte	ARG	105.0		115.0		147.5		367.5	
6. James Varaleau	CAN	112.5		112.5		140.0		365.0	
7. Juhani Vellamo	FIN	100.0		115.0		140.0		355.0	
8. Rassoul Raiisi	IRN	110.0		110.0		135.0		355.0	

Stanczyk made a great impression on the audience, not only because of his superior lifting, but because of his outstanding sportsmanship. With his third snatch he attempted a new world record of 132.5 kg. He successfully hoisted the weight and the judges signaled a fair lift. However, Stanczyk shook his head and tapped his leg to indicate that his knee had scraped the floor, thus invalidating his lift. Despite this miss, his eventual winning margin of 37.5 kg. was the largest in any division in Olympic history.

Stanley Stanczyk was a well-known figure in weightlifting circles, but the man who really achieved fame was silver medalist Harold Sakata. After completing a successful career as a professional wrestler (using the name Tosh Togo), Sakata became an actor. He eventually reached international stardom in the role of Oddjob in the James Bond film *Goldfinger.*

The 1948 Light Heavyweight silver medalist, Harold Sakata, gained greater fame as the evil Oddjob in the James Bond film Goldfinger.

1952 Helsinki C: 22, N: 19, D: 7.27. WR: 425 kg (Grigory Novack)

		PRESS	SNATCH	JERK		TOTAL KG	
1. Trofim Lomakin	SOV/RUS	125.0	127.5	165.0	OR	417.5	EOR
2. Stanley Stanczyk	USA	127.5	127.5	160.0		415.0	
3. Arkady Vorobyev	SOV/RUS	120.0	127.5	160.0		407.5	
4. Mohammad Hassan Rahnavardi	IRN	120.0	122.5	160.0		402.5	
5. Jean Debuf	FRA	117.5	122.5	160.0		400.0	
6. Issy Bloomberg	SAF	127.5	115.0	150.0		392.5	
7. Osvaldo Forte	ARG	112.5	115.0	155.0		382.5	
8. Clyde Emrich	USA	120.0	115.0	145.0		380.0	

The 1952 Light Heavyweight competition was an excellent three-way contest which unfortunately got caught up in the Cold War. The United States fired the first salvo when they lodged a protest after American Clyde Emrich had a press of 120 kg disallowed. After much fussing and arguing by U.S. officials, Emrich went ahead and made the weight at his next attempt. Then Stanczyk was given credit for a press of 127.5 kg and the Soviets claimed that he had leaned back too far for a legal press. The judges voted 2–1 in Stanczyk's favor. When Vorobyev lost consciousness during his last press attempt, the Americans accused the Russians of drugging their lifters. At the end of the press, Stanczyk led Lomakin by 2.5 kg. Lomakin and Vorobyev both snatched 127.5 kg at their first attempt, while Stanczyk achieved the weight only at his last try. However, both Soviet lifters failed twice at 132.5 kg. So, with only the jerk left, Stanczyk still led Lomakin by 2.5 kg. All three leaders successfully jerked 160 kg. Both Stanczyk and Lomakin missed at 165 kg, but Lomakin had one more attempt left to him. This time he made the weight and moved into first place.

Then came Vorobyev's turn. He decided to go for broke and called for 170 kg—a world record. Vorobyev approached the bar, took hold of it, raised it a couple inches and dropped it again. An argument immediately broke out as to whether his action should be counted as an official attempt. Vorobyev shut out the commotion and prepared himself for another try. When he turned again to the bar, silence returned. He heaved the weight onto his chest and thrust it into the air at arm's length. "Although my muscles strained to the very limit," Vorobyev later wrote, "my heart was singing. I had done it! I had won!" The audience roared with excitement. But then Vorobyev staggered and dropped the bar just as the referee called out, "Release." One judge ruled that it had been a valid lift, but the other two rejected it. Forty minutes of arguing ensued, until finally the results were announced: Lomakin first, Stanczyk second, Vorobyev third.

Vorobyev returned to the dressing room in a deep depression and began slowly to undress. Suddenly his coach burst into the room and told him that he had been awarded one more attempt. But Vorobyev was unprepared. He needed more time to compose himself and warm up, but the officials had already started the clock. Forced to hurry back to the platform, he was unable to handle the weight a second time and fell backward, with the bar pinning him to the floor. The Soviets continued to argue that Vorobyev had been forced to hold his previous lift for more than two seconds, but the results were allowed to stand.

1956 Melbourne C: 10, N: 9, D: 11.26. WR: 435 kg (Tamio "Tommy" Kono)

		PRESS		SNATCH		JERK		TOTAL KG	
1. Tamio "Tommy" Kono	USA	140.0	OR	132.5	OR	175.0	WR	447.5	WR
2. Vasīlijs Stepanovs	SOV/LAT	135.0		130.0		162.5		427.5	
3. James George	USA	120.0		130.0		167.5		417.5	
4. Jalal Mansouri	IRN	132.5		122.5		162.5		417.5	
5. Philip Caira	GBR	127.5		122.5		155.0		405.0	
6. Václav Pšenička	CZE	125.0		120.0		155.0		400.0	
7. Marcel Paterni	FRA	132.5		115.0		147.5		395.0	
8. John Powell	AUS	120.0		117.5		145.0		382.5	

James George used a fourth lift to set a snatch world record of 137.5 kg.

1960 Rome C: 24, N: 21, D: 9.9. WR: 457.5 kg (Rudolf Plukfelder)

		PRESS	SNATCH		JERK		TOTAL KG
1. Ireneusz Paliński	POL	130.0	132.5	EOR	180.0	WR	442.5
2. James George	USA	132.5	132.5	EOR	165.0		430.0
3. Jan Bochenek	POL	130.0	120.0		170.0		420.0

4. Géza Tóth	HUN	125.0	125.0	167.5	417.5	
5. Jouni Kailajärvi	FIN	130.0	125.0	162.5	417.5	
6. Peter Tachev	BUL	130.0	125.0	160.0	415.0	
7. Minoru Kubota	JPN	125.0	120.0	155.0	400.0	
8. Willy Claes	BEL	125.0	112.5	155.0	392.5	

1964 Tokyo C: 24, N: 21, D: 10.16. WR: 477.5 kg (Gyözö Veres)

		PRESS		SNATCH		JERK		TOTAL KG	
1. Rudolf Plukfelder	SOV/UKR	150.0		142.5	OR	182.5		475.0	OR
2. Géza Tóth	HUN	145.0		137.5		185.0	OR	467.5	
3. Gyözö Veres	HUN	155.0	OR	135.0		177.5		467.5	
4. Jerzy Kaczkowski	POL	145.0		135.0		167.5		455.0	
5. Gary Cleveland	USA	152.5		135.0		167.5		455.0	
6. Hyung-woo Lee	KOR	145.0		132.5		175.0		452.5	
7. Kaarlo Kangasniemi	FIN	150.0		135.0		165.0		450.0	
8. Karl Arnold	GDR	140.0		132.5		167.5		435.0	

Thirty-six-year-old Plukfelder is the oldest weightlifter to win an Olympic gold medal.

1968 Mexico City C: 26, N: 22, D: 10.17. WR: 485 kg (Vladimir Byelyayev)

		PRESS		SNATCH		JERK		TOTAL KG	
1. Boris Selitsky	SOV/RUS	150.0		147.5	OR	187.5	OR	485.0	EWR
2. Volodymyr Byelyayev	SOV/UKR	152.5		147.5	OR	185.0		485.0	EWR
3. Norbert Ozimek	POL	150.0		140.0		182.5		472.5	
4. Gyözö Veres	HUN	150.0		140.0		182.5		472.5	
5. Karl Arnold	GDR	155.0	EOR	137.5		175.0		467.5	
6. Hans Zdražila	CZE	135.0		147.5	OR	180.0		462.5	
7. Jouni Kailajärvi	FIN	140.0		130.0		175.0		445.0	
8. Lee Jong-sup	KOR	135.0		130.0		175.0		440.0	

1972 Munich C: 24, N: 21, D: 9.2. WR: 527.5 kg (Valery Shary)

		PRESS		SNATCH		JERK		TOTAL KG	
1. Leif Jenssen	NOR	172.5	OR	150.0	OR	185.0		507.5	OR
2. Norbert Ozimek	POL	165.0		145.0		187.5		497.5	
3. György Horváth	HUN	160.0		142.5		192.5	OR	495.0	
4. Bernhard Radtke	GDR	162.5		145.0		185.0		492.5	
5. Khristos Iakovou	GRE	170.0		137.5		182.5		490.0	
6. Kaarlo Kangasniemi	FIN	150.0		145.0		185.0		480.0	
7. Rolf Milser	GER	165.0		132.5		180.0		477.5	
8. Juhani Avellan	FIN	140.0		145.0		182.5		467.5	

The two Soviet representatives, world champion Boris Pavlov and world record holder Valery Shary, were so intent on beating each other that they started pressing at too high a weight. Both men missed all three attempts and were disqualified. Representing Israel was 28-year-old David Berger, originally of Shaker Heights, Ohio. The next day, Berger was one of the 11 Israelis who were killed by terrorists.

1976 Montreal C: 17, N: 14, D: 7.24. WR: 372.5 kg (Trendafil Stoichev)

		SNATCH		JERK		TOTAL KG	
1. Valery Shary	SOV/BLR	162.5	OR	202.5	OR	365.0	OR
2. Trendafil Stoichev	BUL	162.5	OR	197.5		360.0	

		SNATCH	JERK	TOTAL KG
3. Péter Baczako	HUN	157.5	187.5	345.0
4. Nicolaos Iliadis	GRE	150.0	190.0	340.0
5. Juhani Avellan	FIN	145.0	185.0	330.0
6. Stefan Jacobsson	SWE	147.5	170.0	317.5
7. Sueo Fujishiro	JPN	140.0	175.0	315.0
8. Gerd Kennel	GER	135.0	177.5	312.5

DISQ (Drugs): Blagoi Blagoev (BUL) 362.5

1980 Moscow C: 19, N: 17, D: 7.26. WR: 390 kg (Yurik Vardanyan)

		SNATCH		JERK		TOTAL KG	
1. Yurik Vardanyan	SOV/ARM	177.5	WR	222.5	WR	400.0	WR
2. Blagoi Blagoev	BUL	175.0		197.5		372.5	
3. Dušan Poliačik	CZE	160.0		207.5		367.5	
4. Jan Lisowski	POL	150.0		205.0		355.0	
5. Krassimir Drăndarov	BUL	155.0		200.0		355.0	
6. Pawel Rabczewski	POL	155.0		195.0		350.0	
7. Detlef Blasche	GDR	152.5		192.5		345.0	
8. Juhani Avellan	FIN	150.0		182.5		332.5	

Vardanyan's total would have earned him a gold medal in either of the next two higher weight classes.

1984 Los Angeles-Westchester C: 19, N: 16, D: 8.4. WR: 400 kg (Yurik Vardanyan)

		SNATCH	JERK	TOTAL KG
1. Petre Becheru	ROM	155.0	200.0	355.0
2. Robert Kabbas	AUS	150.0	192.5	342.5
3. Ryoji Isaoka	JPN	150.0	190.0	340.0
4. Newton Burrowes	GBR	147.5	180.0	327.5
5. Ebraheem Elbakh	EGY	145.0	177.5	322.5
6. Lee Kang-seong	KOR	140.0	182.5	322.5
7. Yvan Darsigny	CAN	142.5	180.0	322.5
8. Allister Nalder	NZE	142.5	175.0	317.5

On September 15, at the Friendship Games, Yurik Vardanyan broke his own 4-year-old world record with combined lifts of 405 kg. Second place went to Asen Zlatev of Bulgaria with 380 kg and third to László Király of Hungary with 370 kg.

1988 Seoul C: 22, N: 20, D: 9.24. WR: 405 kg (Yurik Vardanyan)

		SNATCH	JERK	TOTAL KG
1. Israil Arsamakov	SOV/RUS	167.5	210.0	377.5
2. István Messzi	HUN	170.0	200.0	370.0
3. Lee Hyung-kun	KOR	160.0	207.5	367.5
4. David Morgan	GBR	165.0	200.0	365.0
5. Krzysztof Siemion	POL	162.5	195.0	357.5
6. Ryoji Isaoka	JPN	155.0	195.0	350.0
7. Fausto Tosi	ITA	155.0	185.0	340.0
8. Ali Eroğlu	TUR	145.0	185.0	330.0

1992 Barcelona C: 31, N: 26, D: 8.3. WR: 405 kg (Yurik Vardanyan)

		SNATCH	JERK	TOTAL KG
1. Pyrros Dimas	GRE	167.5	202.5	370.0
2. Krzysztof Siemion	POL	165.0	205.0	370.0
— Ibragim Samadov	RUS	167.5	202.5	370.0
4. Chon Chol-ho	PRK	165.0	200.0	365.0
5. Plamen Bratoitchev	BUL	167.5	197.5	365.0
6. Lino Elías Ocaña	CUB	160.0	205.0	365.0
7. Marc Huster	GER	160.0	202.5	362.5
8. José Heredia Ledea	CUB	165.0	197.5	362.5

This was one of the two closest weightlifting contests in Olympic history and also one of the most controversial. In 1991 the Soviet Union collapsed and broke into 15 different independent nations. The International Olympic Committee decided that although the three Baltic nations, Estonia, Latvia, and Lithuania, could organize separate teams for the 1992 Olympics, the remaining 12 ex–Soviet republics would be required to enter a combined squad known as the Unified Team. Unfortunately, in weightlifting the Unified Team was not very unified. The head coach, two-time gold medalist Vassily Alekseyev, was Russian, and he definitely had his prejudices. The overwhelming favorite in the light-heavyweight division was 1990 world champion Altymurat Orazdurdiyev of Turkmenistan. The second entrant from the Unified Team was the 1991 world champion, Ibragim Samadov of Chechnya in Russia. Fifteen minutes before the official weigh-in, Alekseyev informed Orazdurdiyev that he would not be allowed to compete because he would "get in the way" of Samadov. Orazdurdiyev pleaded with Alekseyev and even offered to lose to Samadov and settle for a silver medal. Alekseyev ignored him.

Samadov already felt great pressure. When he received his gold medal at the world championships he didn't smile because he was dissatisfied with his performance. He was that hard on himself. In addition, his family back in Grozny was dependent on the modest income he earned from his weightlifting successes. Now the pressure on Samadov increased enormously.

At the European championships in April, in the absence of Orazdurdiyev, Samadov had won with a total of 370 kilograms. Close behind him were Krzysztof Siemion and Pyrros Dimas at 367.5 kilograms. Dimas was a member of the Greek ethnic minority in Albania and competed for Albania as recently as the 1990 European championships. In February 1991, Dimas and his brother slipped across the border into Greece and were granted Greek citizenship almost immediately.

Although Chon Chol-ho of North Korea was in the gold medal hunt right until his last failed attempt, the real competition was among Samadov, Siemion, and Dimas. With ties decided by lower bodyweight, everyone was aware that Samadov outweighed the other two by five grams (one-sixth of an ounce)—not much, but enough to mean that he needed to lift a higher total than his rivals. Trailing by 2.5 kilograms after the snatch, Siemion pulled even by successfully lifting 205 kilograms after Dimas and Samadov had cleared 202.5 There then followed a series of unsuccessful attempts at 207.5 kilograms. Chon missed twice, Dimas missed twice, Siemion missed once, and Samadov missed once. Everything came down to Samadov's final lift. He cleaned the bar, but couldn't pull off the jerk. A disappointed Samadov placed third because of his higher bodyweight. Since Dimas and Siemion shared the same weight, the gold medal was decided by a new tie-breaking rule: whichever lifter reached his final total first was declared the winner.

In this case it was Dimas, whose 202.5 kg lift preceded Siemion's 205. The Greek contingent in the stands exploded with joy: no Greek had won a weightlifting gold since Dimitris Tophalo triumphed at the Intercalated Games in Athens in 1906.

But the excitement was not over. At the award ceremony, Dimas and Siemion happily received their medals. Not so Samadov. Frustrated with himself and emotionally distraught, Samadov refused to lean forward to allow the bronze medal to be put around his neck. When he finally took it in his hand, he dropped it onto the platform and walked away. I.O.C. officials were outraged at this breach of protocol. They disqualified Samadov, announced that he would not be listed as the bronze-medal winner in the official results, and ordered him to leave the Olympic Village. Samadov came to his senses the next day and apologized, but the I.O.C. refused to reverse its ruling, and the International Weightlifting Federation banned him for life.

Back in Greece after the Olympics, Dimas and the other 1992 Greek gold medalist, hurdler Voula Patoulidou, were treated to a hero's reception. Sixty thousand people packed into the Kallimarmaron Panathenian Stadium that had been used for the 1896 Olympics, while another thirty thousand crowded around outside. Dimas' father, Victor, summed up the mood: "We have almost reached the sky," he said, "on the wings of happiness."

MIDDLE HEAVYWEIGHT
(91 kg—200.62 lbs [1952-1992: 90 kg—198.25 lbs)

1896–1948 not held

1952 Helsinki C: 20, N: 20, D: 7.27. WR: 427.5 kg (Norbert Schemansky)

		PRESS		SNATCH		JERK		TOTAL KG	
1. Norbert Schemansky	USA	127.5		140.0	WR	177.5	WR	445.0	WR
2. Grigory Novak	SOV/RUS	140.0	OR	125.0		145.0		410.0	
3. Lennox Kilgour	TRI	125.0		120.0		157.5		402.5	
4. Mohammed Ibrahim Saleh	EGY	110.0		125.0		162.5		397.5	
5. Firouz Pejhan	IRN	112.5		120.0		155.0		387.5	
6. Kenneth McDonald	AUS	107.5		125.0		152.5		385.0	
7. Francisco Rensonnet	ARG	107.5		112.5		150.0		370.0	
8. Theunis Jonck	SAF	112.5		110.0		145.0		367.5	

The 5-foot 3½-inch, 195-pound Novak was hampered by a leg injury, but it is very doubtful that he could have beaten Detroit's Norbert Schemansky, who upped his own world record by 38½ pounds. Schemansky eventually became the only weightlifter to win four Olympic medals—including a bronze in the Heavyweight division in 1964 at the age of 40.

1956 Melbourne C: 15, N: 14, D: 11.26. WR: 460 kg (Arkady Vorobyov)

		PRESS		SNATCH	JERK		TOTAL KG	
1. Arkady Vorobyov	SOV/RUS	147.5	WR	137.5	177.5	EOR	462.5	WR
2. David Sheppard	USA	140.0		137.5	165.0		442.5	
3. Jean Debuf	FRA	130.0		127.5	167.5		425.0	
4. Mohammad Hassan Rahnavardi	IRN	140.0		127.5	157.5		425.0	
5. Ivan Veselinov	BUL	132.5		120.0	155.0		407.5	
6. Tan Kim Bee	MAL	117.5		122.5	155.0		395.0	
7. Lennox Kilgour	TRI	127.5		117.5	145.0		390.0	
8. Leonard Treganowan	AUS	122.5		117.5	150.0		390.0	

A former deep-sea diver, Vorobyov made up for his disappointment in the controversial 1952 Light Heavyweight competition. He later became a doctor, wrote several textbooks on weightlifting, and served as coach of the Soviet team.

1960 Rome C: 20, N: 17, D: 9.9. WR: 470 kg (Arkady Vorobyov)

		PRESS		SNATCH		JERK		TOTAL KG	
1. Arkady Vorobyov	SOV/RUS	152.5		142.5	OR	177.5	EOR	472.5	WR
2. Trofim Lomakin	SOV/RUS	157.5	WR	130.0		170.0		457.5	
3. Louis Martin	GBR	137.5		137.5		170.0		445.0	
4. John Pulskamp	USA	140.0		125.0		167.5		432.5	
5. François Vincent	FRA	130.0		132.5		160.0		422.5	
6. Vladimir Savov	BUL	110.0		137.5		165.0		412.5	
7. Czeslaw Bialas	POL	130.0		122.5		157.5		410.0	
8. Leonardo Masu	ITA	135.0		117.5		155.0		407.5	

1964 Tokyo C: 19, N: 18, D: 10.17. WR: 480 kg (Louis Martin)

		PRESS		SNATCH		JERK		TOTAL KG	
1. Vladimir Golovanov	SOV/RUS	165.0	OR	142.5	EOR	180.0		487.5	WR
2. Louis Martin	GBR	155.0		140.0		180.0		475.0	
3. Ireneusz Paliński	POL	150.0		135.0		182.5	OR	467.5	
4. William March	USA	155.0		135.0		177.5		467.5	
5. Lazăr Baroga	ROM	145.0		135.0		180.0		460.0	
6. Árpád Nemessányi	HUN	140.0		142.5	EOR	177.5		460.0	
7. Jouni Kailajärvi	FIN	145.0		127.5		180.0		452.5	
8. Peter Tachev	BUL	145.0		130.0		170.0		445.0	

1968 Mexico City C: 29, N: 22, D: 10.18. Wr: 522.5 kg (Kaarlo Kangasniemi)

		PRESS		SNATCH		JERK		TOTAL KG	
1. Kaarlo Kangasniemi	FIN	172.5	OR	157.5	WR	187.5		517.5	OR
2. Jaan Talts	SOV/EST	160.0		150.0		197.5	WR	507.5	
3. Marek Goląb	POL	165.0		145.0		185.0		495.0	
4. Bo Johansson	SWE	165.0		145.0		182.5		492.5	
5. Jaakko Kailajärvi	FIN	145.0		150.0		190.0		485.0	
6. Árpád Nemessányi	HUN	150.0		145.0		187.5		482.5	
7. Philip Grippaldi	USA	155.0		137.5		185.0		477.5	
8. Viteslav Orszag	CZE	157.5		130.0		175.0		462.5	

1972 Munich C: 23, N: 15, D: 9.3. WR: 562.5 kg (David Rigert)

		PRESS	SNATCH	JERK	TOTAL KG	
1. Andon Nikolov	BUL	180.0	155.0	190.0	525.0	OR
2. Atanas Shopov	BUL	180.0	145.0	192.5	517.5	

3. Hans Bettembourg	SWE	182.5	145.0	185.0		512.5	
4. Philip Grippaldi	USA	170.0	140.0	195.0		505.0	
5. Patrick Holbrook	USA	162.5	145.0	197.5	EOR	505.0	
6. Nicolo Ciancio	AUS	170.0	145.0	190.0		505.0	
7. Juan Curbelo	CUB	172.5	140.0	182.5		495.0	
8. Jaakko Kailajärvi	FIN	150.0	150.0	187.5		487.5	

The clear favorite, world record holder David Rigert of Chakhti, set an Olympic record in the press of 187.5 kg. However, he failed at all three of his attempts to snatch 160 kg, despite the fact that he held the world record of 167.5 kg. Rigert was so upset that he literally pulled his hair out and banged his head against a wall. He was finally restrained by his colleagues, but the next day he threw another fit and had to be sent home. Gold-medal-winner Andon Nikolov was a former troublemaker who was introduced to weightlifting in reform school.

1976 Montreal C: 19, N: 16, D: 7.25. WR: 400 kg (David Rigert)

		SNATCH		JERK		TOTAL KG	
1. David Rigert	SOV/KAZ	170.0	OR	212.5	OR	382.5	OR
2. Lee James	USA	165.0		197.5		362.5	
3. Atanas Shopov	BUL	155.0		205.0		360.0	
4. György Rehus	HUN	157.5		192.5		350.0	
5. Peter Petzold	GDR	152.5		192.5		345.0	
6. Alberto Blanco	CUB	152.5		192.5		345.0	
7. Yvon Coussin	FRA	152.5		180.0		332.5	
8. Gudmundur Sigurdsson	ICE	145.0		187.5		332.5	
DISQ (Drugs): Philip Grippaldi (USA) 355.0							

Rigert, the heaviest man to snatch twice his bodyweight, had no reason to lose any hair this time in Montreal, as his excellent lifting gave him a comfortable victory.

1980 Moscow C: 18, N: 16, D: 7.27. WR: 400 kg (David Rigert)

		SNATCH		JERK	TOTAL KG
1. Péter Baczakó	HUN	170.0	EOR	207.5	377.5
2. Rumen Aleksandrov	BUL	170.0	EOR	205.0	375.0
3. Frank Mantek	GDR	165.0		205.0	370.0
4. Dalibor Rehak	CZE	165.0		200.0	365.0
5. Witold Walo	POL	160.0		200.0	360.0
6. Lubomír Sršeň	CZE	160.0		207.5	357.5
7. Vasile Groapă	ROM	160.0		195.0	355.0
8. Nicolaos Iliadis	GRE	150.0		195.0	345.0

David Rigert reverted to his form of eight years earlier when he started snatching at 170 kg, failed at all three attempts, and was eliminated.

1984 Los Angeles-Westchester C: 26, N: 21, D: 8.5. WR: 420 kg (Blagoi Blagoev)

		SNATCH		JERK		TOTAL KG	
1. Nicu Vlad	ROM	172.5	OR	220.0	OR	392.5	OR
2. Dumitru Petre	ROM	165.0		195.0		360.0	
3. David Mercer	GBR	157.5		195.0		352.5	
4. Peter Immesberger	GER	155.0		195.0		350.0	
5. Hwang Woo-won	KOR	152.5		197.5		350.0	

		SNATCH	JERK	TOTAL KG
6. Nikos Iliadis	GRE	155.0	195.0	350.0
7. Henri Junch Hoeg	DEN	152.5	195.0	347.5
8. José Garces	MEX	150.0	192.5	342.5

Handsome Nicu Vlad was known in Romania as "The Apollo of the Barbells." Vlad's total was good enough to win the heavyweight division. At the Friendship Games in Varna on September 16, Viktor Solodov set a world record of 422.5 kg. In second place, at 400 kg., was Blagoi Blagoev, the man whose record Solodov broke.

1988 Seoul C: 29, N: 23, D: 9.25. WR: 422.5 kg (Viktor Solodov)

		SNATCH		JERK		TOTAL KG	
1. Anatoly Khrapaty	SOV/KAZ	187.5	OR	225.0	OR	412.5	OR
2. Nail Mukhamedyarov	SOV/UZB	177.5		222.5		400.0	
3. Slawomir Zawada	POL	180.0		220.0		400.0	
4. Andrzej Piotrowski	POL	165.0		200.0		365.0	
5. Attila Buda	HUN	175.0		185.0		360.0	
6. David Mercer	GBR	157.5		200.0		357.5	
7. Roland Feldhoffer	GER	150.0		200.0		350.0	
8. Keith Boxell	GBR	157.5		192.5		350.0	

1992 Barcelona C: 23, N: 19, D: 8.1. WR: 422.5 kg (Viktor Solodov)

		SNATCH		JERK		TOTAL KG	
1. Kakhi Kakhiachvili	GEO	177.5		235.0	EWR	412.5	EOR
2. Sergei Syrtsov	UZB	190.0	OR	222.5		412.5	EOR
3. Sergiusz Wolczaniecki	POL	172.5		220.0		392.5	
4. Kim Byung-chan	KOR	170.0		210.0		380.0	
5. Ivan Tchakarov	BUL	170.0		207.5		377.5	
6. Emilio Lara Rodríguez	CUB	165.0		210.0		375.0	
7. Peter May	GBR	160.0		195.0		355.0	
8. Harvey Goodman	AUS	157.5		192.5		350.0	

Trailing by 10 kilograms with one attempt remaining, Kakhiachvili called for the world record weight of 235 kilograms. He made it—a remarkable achievement in an era of serious drug testing—and defeated Syrtsov because of his lower bodyweight, a difference of 20 grams (seven-tenths of an ounce).

FIRST HEAVYWEIGHT
(99 kg—218.26 lbs [1980-1992:100 kg—220.25 lbs])

1896–1976 not held

1980 Moscow C: 17, N: 13, D: 7.28. WR: 402.5 kg (David Rigert)

		SNATCH		JERK		TOTAL KG	
1. Ota Zaremba	CZE	180.0	OR	215.0		395.0	OR
2. Igor Nikitin	SOV/RUS	177.5		215.0		392.5	
3. Alberto Blanco Fernandez	CUB	172.5		212.5		385.0	
4. Michael Hennig	GDR	165.0		217.5	OR	382.5	
5. János Sólyomvári	HUN	175.0		205.0		380.0	
6. Manfred Funke	GDR	170.0		207.5		377.5	
7. Anton Baraniak	CZE	165.0		210.0		375.0	
8. László Varga	HUN	172.5		195.0		367.5	

1984 Los Angeles-Westchester C: 16, N: 14, D: 8.6. WR: 440 kg (Yuri Zakharevich)

		SNATCH	JERK		TOTAL KG
1. Rolf Milser	GER	167.5	217.5	EOR	385.0
2. Vasile Groapă	ROM	165.0	217.5	EOR	382.5
3. Pekka Niemi	FIN	160.0	207.5		367.5
4. Kevin Roy	CAN	160.0	197.5		357.5
5. Ken Clark	USA	155.0	197.5		352.5
6. Franz Langthaler	AUT	162.5	187.5		350.0
7. Rich Shanko	USA	155.0	195.0		350.0
8. Jean-Marie Kretz	FRA	150.0	192.5		342.5

International weightlifting competitions are separated into two sessions. In the afternoon the less-distinguished lifters take part in the "B" session and in the evening the leading contenders lift in the "A" session. The top lifter in the 100 kg. division "B" session was 31-year-old Pekka Niemi. Since no "B" lifter had ever won a medal in an international meet, Niemi skipped the evening session and went instead to the Los Angeles Coliseum to watch the track and field events. Niemi was playing with an Electronic Messaging System computer terminal in the press section when a German TV reporter said, "Let's see what you did." Niemi pushed some buttons and on the screen appeared the news that he had finished third. Meanwhile, back at the weightlifting venue at Loyola Marymount University, the medal ceremony was being delayed while officials unsuccessfully searched for Niemi or anyone else from the Finnish delegation. Finally they went ahead with the presentation with the bronze medal platform empty. When Niemi called home to share the good news, he learned that his family had learned of his good fortune on Finnish television before he himself had found out in Los Angeles. The next day Niemi received his medal at a special ceremony, after which he patiently signed 200 autographs.

Six weeks later at the Friendship Games Pavel Kuznetsov of the Soviet Union won first place with a lift total of 427.5 kg. Second was Andor Szanyi of Hungary at 390 kg.

1988 Seoul C: 21, N: 17, D: 9.26. WR: 440 kg (Yuri Zakharevich)

		SNATCH		JERK		TOTAL KG	
1. Pavel Kuznetsov	SOV/RUS	190.0	OR	235.0	OR	425.0	OR
2. Nicu Vlad	ROM	185.0		217.5		402.5	
3. Peter Immesberger	GER	175.0		220.0		395.0	
4. János Bökfi	HUN	180.0		212.5		392.5	
5. Francis Tournefier	FRA	170.0		215.0		385.0	
6. Denis Garon	CAN	160.0		222.5		382.5	
7. Hwang Woo-won	KOR	162.5		220.0		382.5	
8. Franz Langthaler	AUT	172.5		205.0		377.5	
DISQ (Drugs): Andor Szanyi (HUN) 407.5							

1992 Barcelona C: 25, N: 21, D: 8.2. WR: 440 kg (Yuri Zakharevich)

		SNATCH		JERK	TOTAL KG
1. Victor Tregubov	RUS	190.0	EOR	220.0	410.0
2. Timur Taimazov	UKR	185.0		217.5	402.5
3. Waldemar Malak	POL	185.0		215.0	400.0
4. Francis Tournefier	FRA	170.0		217.5	387.5
5. Petar Stefanov	BUL	170.0		210.0	380.0
6. Andrei Danisov	ISR	175.0		202.5	377.5
7. Udo Guse	GER	167.5		210.0	377.5
8. Yoshimitsu Nishimoto	JPN	165.0		207.5	372.5

Bronze medalist Malek was killed in a car accident three months after the Olympics, on November 14. He was 22 years old.

HEAVYWEIGHT
(108 kg—238.1 lbs [1972-1992: 110 kg—242.5 lbs)

1896–1968 not held

1972 Munich C: 26, N: 19, D: 9.22. WR: 590 kg (Valery Yakubovsky)

		PRESS		SNATCH	JERK	TOTAL KG	
1. Jaan Talts	SOV/EST	210.0	OR	165.0	205.0	580.0	OR
2. Aleksandr Kraichev	BUL	197.5		162.5	202.5	562.5	
3. Stefan Grützner	GDR	185.0		162.5	207.5	555.0	
4. Helmut Losch	GDR	190.0		152.5	205.0	547.5	
5. Roberto Vezzani	ITA	192.5		147.5	205.0	545.0	
6. János Hanzlik	HUN	190.0		157.5	195.0	542.5	
7. Kauko Kangasniemi	FIN	175.0		165.0	197.5	537.5	
8. Rainer Dörrzapf	GER	170.0		165.0	187.5	522.5	

1976 Montreal C: 22, N: 18, D: 7.26. WR: 417.5 kg (Valentin Hristov)

		SNATCH		JERK		TOTAL KG
1. Yuri Zaitsev	SOV/RUS	165.0		220.0	OR	385.0
2. Krustiu Semerdzhiev	BUL	170.0	OR	215.0		385.0
3. Tadeusz Rutkowski	POL	167.5		210.0		377.5
4. Pierre Gourrier	FRA	157.5		215.0		372.5
5. Jürgen Ciezki	GDR	162.5		210.0		372.5
6. Javier Gonzalez	CUB	160.0		205.0		365.0
7. Leif Nilsson	SWE	157.5		207.5		365.0
8. Rudolf Strejcek	CZE	162.5		200.0		362.5

DISQ (Drugs): Valentin Hristov (BUL) 400.0, Mark Cameron (USA) 375.0

1980 Moscow C: 13, N: 13, D: 7.29. WR: 420 kg (Leonid Taranenko)

		SNATCH		JERK		TOTAL KG	
1. Leonid Taranenko	SOV/BLR	182.5		240.0	WR	422.5	WR
2. Valentin Hristov	BUL	185.0	OR	220.0		405.0	
3. György Szalai	HUN	172.5		217.5		390.0	
4. Leif Nilsson	SWE	167.5		212.5		380.0	
5. Vinzenz Hortnagl	AUT	170.0		202.5		372.5	
6. Stefan Tasnadi	ROM	165.0		195.0		360.0	
7. Donald Mitchell	AUS	162.5		190.0		352.5	
8. Dimitrios Zarzavatsidis	GRE	155.0		192.5		347.5	

1984 Los Angeles-Westchester C: 15, N: 12, D: 8.7. WR: 440 kg. (Vyacheslav Klokov)

		SNATCH	JERK	TOTAL KG
1. Norberto Oberburger	ITA	175.0	215.0	390.0
2. Stefan Tasnadi	ROM	167.5	212.5	380.0
3. Guy Carlton	USA	167.5	210.0	377.5
4. Frank Seipelt	GER	160.0	207.5	367.5
5. Albert Squires	CAN	165.0	200.0	365.0
6. Richard Eaton	USA	152.5	200.0	352.5
7. Ioannis Gerontas	GRE	152.5	197.5	350.0
8. Olaf Peters	GER	157.5	190.0	347.5

DISQ (Drugs): Göran Pettersson (SWE) 360.0

On September 17, 1980, Olympic champion Leonid Taranenko lifted a world record 442.5 kg. to win at the Friendship Games. Second was Soviet teammate Yuri Zakharevich with 427.5 kg., and third Yanko Georgiev of Bulgaria with 412.5 kg.

1988 Seoul C: 20, N: 15, D: 9.27. WR: 452.5 kg (Yuri Zakharevich)

		SNATCH		JERK		TOTAL KG	
1. Yuri Zakharevich	SOV/RUS	210.0	WR	245.0	WR	455.0	WR
2. József Jacsó	HUN	190.0		237.5		427.5	
3. Ronny Weller	GDR	190.0		235.0		425.0	
4. Michael Schubert	GDR	190.0		235.0		425.0	
5. Aleksandr Popov	SOV/RUS	187.5		232.5		420.0	
6. Norberto Oberburger	ITA	187.5		227.5		415.0	
7. Stanislaw Malysa	POL	180.0		215.0		395.0	
8. Frank Seipelt	GER	170.0		217.5		387.5	

In 1983 Yuri Zakharevich dislocated his left elbow while attempting a snatch world record. Doctors rebuilt his elbow using synthetic tendons. He returned to competition in 1984 and won the next four European championships as well as the next three world championships. In Seoul he broke the snatch world record twice as well as the record for combined total.

1992 Barcelona C: 24, N: 20, D: 8.3. WR: 455.0 kg (Yuri Zakharevich)

		SNATCH	JERK	TOTAL KG
1. Ronny Weller	GER	192.5	240.0	432.5
2. Artur Akoyev	RUS	195.0	235.0	430.0
3. Stefan Botev Khristov	BUL	190.0	227.5	417.5
4. Nicu Vlad	ROM	190.0	215.0	405.0
5. Dariusz Osuch	POL	175.0	222.5	397.5
6. Frank Seipelt	GER	170.0	220.0	390.0
7. Flavio Villavicenia Cabrera	CUB	170.0	217.5	387.5
8. Pavlos Saltsidis	GRE	175.0	210.0	385.0

In December 1989, Ronny Weller was driving down a poorly lit street with his girlfriend when he lost control of his car and crashed into a tree. When he awoke from a coma several days later, he learned that his girlfriend had been killed and he himself had fractured his skull, as well as other parts of his body. His rehabilitation was slow. He finally returned to training in March 1991, and seven months later he finished second to Artur Akoyev at the world championships.

The same month that Weller began training again, Stefan Botev emigrated from Bulgaria to Australia. In May 1992, he was told that he would have to compete for Bulgaria one more time before he could represent Australia. The same thing happened to Nicu Vlad, who left Romania for Australia in January 1991, but was forced to compete for Romania. Vlad, who had intended to compete in the first heavyweight division, was entered in the heavyweight division instead because his Olympic qualifying mark had come during a regional meet at that weight. Giving up over 11½ pounds to all of his main rivals, Vlad finished out of the medals. Weller won the competition by making all six of his lifts.

Mehmed Skender of Bosnia finished 20th and last among those who didn't fail all their lifts, but Skender's preparations were not the same as those of the other lifters. Six weeks before the Olympics, Skender, a telephone repairman, was crouching in a trench, firing a machine gun at the Yugoslav army that was invading his hometown of Zenica, northwest of Sarajevo. Having survived on one meal of rice and macaroni a day, he became ill as soon as he arrived in the Olympic Village and was exposed to meat and rich foods. Before the Games were even over, he rushed back to his family in Zenica.

SUPER HEAVYWEIGHT—UNLIMITED WEIGHT

(Heavyweight 1896-1968)

Historically, the minimum weights for athletes in this category have been:
1920–1948   82.5 kg—181.5 lbs
1952–1968   90 kg—198.25 lbs
1972–1992   110 kg—242.5 lbs

In 1996 the minimum weight will be 108 kilograms (238.1 pounds).

1896 Athens C: 4, N: 3?, D: 4.7.
One-Hand Lift

		KG
1. Launceston Elliot	GBR	71.0
2. Viggo Jensen	DEN	57.2
3. Alexandros Nikolopoulos	GRE	—

Elliot, who lived in India until age 13, was Great Britain's first Olympic champion.

1896 Athens C: 6, N: 5, D: 4.7.
Two-Hand Lift

		KG
1. Viggo Jensen	DEN	111.5
2. Launceston Elliot	GBR	111.5
3. Alexandros Nikolopoulos	GRE	90.0
3. Carl Schuhmann	GER	90.0
3. Momcsilló Topavicza	HUN	90.0
3. Sotirios Versis	GRE	90.0

The first instance of an Olympic judging controversy occurred in the two-handed lift. Jensen and Elliot tied at 111.5 kg, but the Dane was awarded first place as a result of his better style, Elliot having moved one foot while lifting. Jensen was quite a versatile athlete. In addition to

Launceston Elliot, winner of the one-hand lift in 1896.

winning the weightlifting competition, he also finished second in the free pistol, third in the military rifle, and fourth in the rope climb.

1900 Paris not held

1904 St. Louis C: 4, N: 2, D: 9.3.
Two-Hand Lift

		KG
1. Perikles Kakousis	GRE	111.70
2. Oscar Osthoff	USA	84.37
3. Frank Kungler	USA	79.61
4. Oscar Olson	USA	67.81

1904 St. Louis C: 3, N: 1, D: 9.3.
All-Around Dumbbell Contest

1. Oscar Osthoff	USA	48 points
2. Frederick Winters	USA	45 points
3. Frank Kungler	USA	10 points

The all-around dumbbell contest, won by Oscar Osthoff of Milwaukee, consisted of nine different types of lifts as well as an optional section.

1906 Athens C: 12, N: 7, D: 4.27.
One-Hand Lift

		KG
1. Josef Steinbach	AUT	76.55
2. Tullio Camilotti	ITA	73.75
3. Heinrich Schneidereit	GER	70.75
4. Alexandre Maspoli	FRA	70.75
5. Carl Svensson	SWE	65.45
6. Heinrich Rondi	GER	65.45
6. Ioannis Varanakis	GRE	65.45
8. Marcel Dubois	BEL	60.40

A successful lift was not recorded unless the weight was lifted with *each* hand.

1906 Athens C: 10, N: 6, D: 4.27.
Two-Hand Lift

		KG
1. Dimitrios Tofalos	GRE	142.5
2. Josef Steinbach	AUT	136.5
3. Alexandre Maspoli	FRA	129.5
3. Heinrich Rondi	GER	129.5
3. Heinrich Schneidereit	GER	129.5
6. Perikles Kakousis	GRE	121.5
7. Tullio Camilotti	ITA	108.5
7. Stephanos Christopoulos	GRE	108.5
7. Marcel Dubois	BEL	108.5
7. Ioannis Varanakis	GRE	108.5

Josef Steinbach caused a stir when he objected to the rule in the two-hand lift which required that the bar be raised straight to the shoulders before being brought overhead. Steinbach wanted to use the continental style, which allowed him to rest the weight at his waist before moving it to his shoulders. After Tofalos had won the competition and the jury had departed, Steinbach walked back to the bar and, using the forbidden style, lifted it easily over his head. The sportsmanlike Greek crowd, unaware of the rules, thought that Steinbach had been cheated of victory.

Tofalos, the son of a count, had been run over by a wagon as a young boy. His upper arm was crushed and doctors wanted to amputate it, but Tofalos' father wouldn't allow it. Dimitrios recovered the use of his arm even though it was two and a half inches shorter than his uninjured arm. After winning at the Olympics, Tofalos turned professional and eventually went to America, where he entered vaudeville and became a wrestler. In a match against world champion Frank Gotch, Tofalos got caught in one of Gotch's famous toe-holds, but refused to submit. His stubbornness cost him six months in the hospital with a dislocated hip. Tofalos became a U.S. citizen in 1921 and remained a popular figure in professional wrestling and physical culture circles for the rest of his life.

1908–1912 not held

1920 Antwerp C: 6, N: 5, D: 8.31.

		ONE-HAND SNATCH	ONE-HAND JERK	TWO-HAND JERK	TOTAL KG
1. Filippo Bottino	ITA	70.0	75.0	120.0	265.0
2. Joseph Alzin	LUX	65.0	75.0	120.0	260.0
3. Louis Bernot	FRA	65.0	75.0	115.0	255.0
4. Ejnar Jensen	DEN	60.0	75.0	115.0	250.0
5. Richard Brunn	SWE	60.0	80.0	110.0	250.0
6. Joseph Duchâteau	FRA	65.0	72.5	110.0	247.5

1924 Paris C: 19, N: 12, D: 7.24.

		ONE-HAND SNATCH	ONE-HAND JERK		TWO-HAND PRESS	TWO-HAND SNATCH	TWO-HAND JERK		TOTAL KG
1. Giuseppe Tonani	ITA	80.0	95.0		112.5	100.0	130.0		517.5
2. Franz Aigner	AUT	80.0	97.5	OR	112.5	95.0	130.0		515.0
3. Harald Tammer	EST	75.0	95.0		90.0	97.5	140.0	OR	497.5
4. Louis Dannoux	FRA	80.0	95.0		87.5	100.0	135.0		497.5
5. Karlis Leilands	LAT	77.5	87.5		100.0	100.0	132.5		497.5
6. Filippo Bottino	ITA	77.5	85.0		110.0	97.5	125.0		495.0
7. Kaljo-Feliks Raag	EST	80.0	92.5		90.0	97.5	130.0		490.0
8. Claudius Dutrieve	FRA	75.0	82.5		90.0	100.0	120.0		467.5

Places three through five were determined by a two-hand jerk lift-off.

1928 Amsterdam C: 17, N: 11, D: 7.29.

		PRESS		SNATCH		JERK		TOTAL KG	
1. Josef Strassberger	GER	122.5	OR	107.5		142.5		372.5	WR
2. Arnold Luhäär	EST	100.0		110.0	OR	150.0	OR	360.0	
3. Jaroslav Skobla	CZE	100.0		107.5		150.0	OR	357.5	
4. Karlis Leilands	LAT	110.0		105.0		140.0		355.0	
5. Josef Leppelt	AUT	105.0		110.0	OR	140.0		355.0	
5. Rudolf Schilberg	AUT	115.0		105.0		135.0		355.0	
7. Giuseppe Tonani	ITA	117.5		97.5		137.5		352.5	
8. Hermann Volz	GER	97.5		110.0	OR	132.5		340.0	

1932 Los Angeles C: 6, N: 4, D: 7.30. WR: 400 kg (El Sayed Mohammed Nosseir)

		PRESS		SNATCH		JERK		TOTAL KG	
1. Jaroslav Skobla	CZE	112.5		115.0		152.5	OR	380.0	OR
2. Václav Pšenička	CZE	112.5		117.5	OR	147.5		377.5	
3. Josef Strassberger	GER	125.0	OR	110.0		142.5		377.5	
4. Marcel Dumoulin	FRA	95.0		107.5		140.0		342.5	
5. Albert Manger	USA	100.0		92.5		122.5		315.0	
6. Howard Turbyfill	USA	77.5		95.0		132.5		305.0	

Twenty-four years later, Skobla's son Jiři won the bronze medal in the shot put at Melbourne.

1936 Berlin C: 13, N: 9, D: 8.5. WR: 407.5 kg (Václav Pšenička)

		PRESS		SNATCH		JERK		TOTAL KG	
1. Josef Manger	GER	132.5	OR	122.5		155.0		410.0	WR
2. Václav Pšenička	CZE	122.5		125.0		155.0		402.5	
3. Arnold Luhäär	EST	115.0		120.0		165.0	OR	400.0	
4. Ronald Walker	GBR	110.0		127.5	OR	160.0		397.5	
5. Hussein Mokhtar	EGY	112.5		122.5		160.0		395.0	
6. Josef Zemann	AUT	110.0		122.5		155.0		387.5	

		PRESS	SNATCH	JERK	TOTAL KG
7. Paul Wahl	GER	115.0	110.0	150.0	375.0
8. Rudolf Shilberg	AUT	125.0	107.5	140.0	372.5

1948 London C: 16, N: 14, D: 8.11. WR: 455 kg (John Davis)

		PRESS		SNATCH		JERK		TOTAL KG	
1. John Davis	USA	137.5	OR	137.5	OR	177.5	WR	452.5	OR
2. Norbert Schemansky	USA	122.5		132.5		170.0		425.0	
3. Abraham Charité	HOL	127.5		125.0		160.0		412.5	
4. Alfred Knight	GBR	117.5		117.5		155.0		390.0	
5. Hanafi Mustafa	EGY	120.0		115.0		150.0		385.0	
6. Niels Petersen	DEN	115.0		112.5		155.0		382.5	
7. Robert Allart	BEL	122.5		110.0		145.0		377.5	
8. Pieter Taljaard	SAF	117.5		112.5		145.0		375.0	

With his fourth attempt, Davis set a snatch world record of 142.5 kg.

1952 Helsinki C: 13, N: 11, D: 7.27. WR: 482.5 kg (John Davis)

		PRESS		SNATCH		JERK	TOTAL KG	
1. John Davis	USA	150.0	OR	145.0	OR	165.0	460.0	OR
2. James Bradford	USA	140.0		132.5		165.0	437.5	
3. Humberto Selvetti	ARG	150.0	OR	120.0		162.5	432.5	
4. Heinz Schattner	GER	130.0		130.0		162.5	422.5	
5. William David Baillie	CAN	145.0		122.5		152.5	420.0	
6. Norberto Ferreira	ARG	140.0		115.0		155.0	410.0	
7. R. Harold Cleghorn	NZE	130.0		117.5		152.5	400.0	
8. Franz Hölbl	AUT	115.0		117.5		155.0	387.5	

John Davis of Brooklyn was never bested in Olympic competition in either the press, the snatch, or the jerk, and was undefeated in all competitions between 1938 and 1953. An enthusiast singer, he once made a record that sold 71 copies. Fourth-place finisher Schattner was a circus performer. He began his act by hoisting a weightlifting bar attached to two enormous globes. Once they were above his head, the globes opened to reveal his wife and son.

1956 Melbourne C: 9, N: 9, D: 11.26. WR: 519.5 kg (Paul Anderson)

		PRESS		SNATCH		JERK		TOTAL KG	
1. Paul Anderson	USA	167.5		145.0	EOR	187.5	OR	500.0	OR
2. Humberto Selvetti	ARG	175.0	OR	145.0	EOR	180.0		500.0	OR
3. Alberto Pigaiani	ITA	150.0		130.0		172.5		452.5	
4. Firouz Pejhan	IRN	147.5		132.5		170.0		450.0	
5. Eino Mäkinen	FIN	127.5		137.5		167.5		432.5	
6. William David Baillie	CAN	147.5		122.5		162.5		432.5	
7. Franz Hölbl	AUT	142.5		125.0		157.5		425.0	
8. Richard Jones	NZE	125.0		122.5		150.0		397.5	

What had been expected to be an easy victory for Paul Anderson of Toccoa, Georgia, developed instead into a dramatic showdown between Anderson, who had developed a strep throat, and 1952's bronze medalist, Humberto Selvetti of Argentina. Selvetti surprised the audience by taking the lead in the press with a lift of 175 kg, after Anderson had missed twice at 172.5 kg. When it came time for the jerk, Selvetti was still ahead by 7.5 kg. Anderson watched as Selvetti successfully jerked 170 kg and 180 kg before missing at 185. Anderson, deciding to go straight for the victory, called for 187.5 kg for his first attempt. He failed. He tried it a second time, but missed again. Now he was down to one last lift that would determine if he would finish first or last. Straining heroically, Anderson balanced the weight above his head and finished the competition with a weight total of 500 kg, exactly the same as that of Humberto Selvetti. Paul Anderson was a huge man who weighed in at 303¼ pounds (137.9 kg) after losing 60 pounds to get in shape for the Olympics. Ironically though, he won his gold medal because his bodyweight was actually *less* than that of Selvetti, who was a mammoth 316½ pounds (143.5 kg). On June 17, 1957, at an exhibition in Toccoa, Anderson lifted on his back a table carrying 6,270 pounds. Anderson was a devout Christian who operated a home for delinquent and orphaned children until his death on August 15, 1994.

1960 Rome C: 18, N: 15, D: 9.10. WR: 533 kg (Paul Anderson)

		PRESS		SNATCH		JERK		TOTAL KG	
1. Yuri Vlasov	SOV/UKR	180.0	OR	155.0	OR	202.5	WR	537.5	WR
2. James Bradford	USA	180.0	OR	150.0		182.5		512.5	
3. Norbert Schemansky	USA	170.0		150.0		180.0		500.0	
4. Mohamed Mahmoud Ibrahim	EGY	140.0		137.5		177.5		455.0	
5. Eino Mäkinen	FIN	140.0		142.5		172.5		455.0	
6. William David Baillie	CAN	147.5		132.5		170.0		450.0	
7. Alberto Pigaiani	ITA	152.5		127.5		170.0		450.0	
8. Václav Syrovy	CZE	145.0		125.0		172.5		435.0	

Paul Anderson (center), who weighed 303¼ pounds, was awarded first place in 1956 because he weighed less than Humberto Selvetti (left).

Although Vlasov's main opponents were the two veterans Bradford and Schemansky, most of the audience was aware of a third, invisible opponent—Paul Anderson, who had turned professional, but whose world record was still on the books. Vlasov assured himself the gold medal and an Olympic record with his first jerk of 185 kg. He followed with a 195, then stunned the crowd by jerking 202.5 kg and setting two world records (jerk and total lifts) with one lift. After his Olympic victory, Vlasov quit lifting and turned to his great love—writing poetry. But he had trouble selling his work. He was also cast in the role of Pierre Bezukhov in the Soviet epic film *War and Peace*. However, at the last minute director Sergei Bondarchuk took the role for himself. Unable to support himself as a creative artist, Vlasov returned to weightlifting and began preparations for the Tokyo Olympics.

1964 Tokyo C: 21, N: 18, D: 10.18. WR: 580 kg (Yuri Vlasov)

		PRESS		SNATCH		JERK		TOTAL KG	
1. Leonid Zhabotynsky	SOV/UKR	187.5		167.5	OR	217.5	WR	572.5	OR
2. Yuri Vlasov	SOV/UKR	197.5	WR	162.5		210.0		570.0	
3. Norbert Schemansky	USA	180.0		165.0		192.5		537.5	
4. Gary Gubner	USA	175.0		150.0		187.5		512.5	
5. Károly Ecser	HUN	175.0		147.5		185.0		507.5	
6. Mohamed Mahmoud Ibrahim	EGY	162.5		145.0		187.5		495.0	
7. Ivan Veselinov	BUL	165.0		135.0		190.0		490.0	
8. Hwang Ho-dong	KOR	162.5		135.0		185.0		482.5	

Zhabotynsky, a 341-pound Ukrainian, scored a major upset when he came from behind to defeat teammate Yuri Vlasov by breaking Vlasov's world jerk record on his final attempt. A half hour earlier, Zhabotynsky had lulled Vlasov into a false sense of security by going up to him and conceding defeat. When Vlasov realized that he had been made the victim of a dishonest trick, he was furious. "I was choked with tears," he later wrote. "I flung the silver medal through the window. . . . I had always revered the purity, the impartiality of contests of strength. That night, I understood that there is a kind of strength that has nothing to do with justice."

In 1989, Vlasov, by then an outspoken critic of the Soviet sports system, with its emphasis on victory at any cost, was elected to the Council of People's Deputies. On May 30 of that year, he stunned the Communist government when he attacked the K.G.B. in a speech that was broadcast live throughout the nation.

1968 Mexico City C: 17, N: 14, D: 10.19. WR: 590 kg (Leonid Zhabotynsky)

		PRESS		SNATCH		JERK	TOTAL KG	
1. Leonid Zhabotynsky	SOV/UKR	200.0	OR	170.0	OR	202.5	572.5	EOR
2. Serge Reding	BEL	195.0		147.5		212.5	555.0	
3. Joseph Dube	USA	200.0	OR	145.0		210.0	555.0	
4. Manfred Rieger	GDR	175.0		155.0		202.5	532.5	
5. Rudolf Mang	GER	177.5		152.5		195.0	525.0	
6. Mauno Lindroos	FIN	157.5		145.0		192.5	495.0	

7. Kalevi Lahdenranta	FIN	160.0	147.5	185.0	492.5
8. Donald Oliver	NZE	147.5	142.5	200.0	490.0

Zhabotynsky, now up to 359 pounds, reveled in his role of "World's Strongest Man." At the opening ceremony in Mexico City he astonished the crowd by carrying the huge Soviet flag one-handed. In the competition, he was so sure of victory that he passed his last two attempts in the jerk, upsetting the audience, which had hoped to see him try for a world record.

1972 Munich C: 13, N: 11, D: 9.6. WR: 645kg (Vassily Alekseyev)

		PRESS	SNATCH	JERK	TOTAL KG
1. Vassily Alekseyev	SOV/RUS	235.0 OR	175.0 OR	230.0 OR	640.0 OR
2. Rudolf Mang	GER	225.0	170.0	215.0	610.0
3. Gerd Bonk	GDR	200.0	155.0	217.5	572.5
4. Jouko Leppä	FIN	205.0	157.5	210.0	572.5
5. Manfred Rieger	GDR	190.0	162.5	205.0	557.5
6. Petr Pavlasek	CZE	192.5	165.0	200.0	557.5
7. Kalevi Lahdenranta	FIN	190.0	165.0	200.0	555.0
8. Fernando Bernal	CUB	190.0	147.5	207.5	545.0

Vassily Alekseyev, Super Heavyweight weightlifting champion in 1972 and 1976, keeping in shape during the off-season.

Vassily Alekseyev came to international attention on January 24, 1970, when he broke the world record for the press, the jerk, and the three-lift total. On March 18 of the same year, he became the first person to lift a combined total of 600 kg. Six months later, while competing in Columbus, Ohio, he broke the 500-pound barrier for the jerk. Since Alekseyev only operated on the metric system, he was somewhat confused when his successful lift brought him so much attention. At Munich, the 30-year-old champion checked in at 337 pounds. The competition was no competition as Alekseyev racked up a convincing 30 kg winning margin. Married in 1962 to a woman named Olympiada, Alekseyev was spotted in Munich having a breakfast of 26 fried eggs and a steak.

1976 Montreal C: 11, N: 8, D: 7.27. WR: 442.5 kg (Vassily Alekseyev)

		SNATCH		JERK		TOTAL KG
1. Vassily Alekseyev	SOV/RUS	185.0	OR	255.0	WR	440.0
2. Gerd Bonk	GDR	170.0		235.0		405.0
3. Helmut Losch	GDR	165.0		222.5		387.5
4. Jan Nagy	CZE	160.0		227.5		387.5
5. Bruce Wilhelm	USA	172.5		215.0		387.5
6. Gerardo Fernandez	CUB	165.0		200.0		365.0
7. Robert Edmond	AUS	157.5		190.0		347.5
8. Jan-Olof Nolsjo	SWE	152.5		185.0		337.5

DISQ (Drugs): Petř Pavlašek (CZE) 387.5

Once again, Alekseyev, now 34 years old and over 345 pounds, was unchallenged. Between 1970 and 1977 he set 79 world records, a number that is particularly significant when one considers that he allegedly received from the Soviet government a prize of $700 to $1500 every time he broke a world record. He was unbeaten from 1970 until 1978.

1980 Moscow C: 12, N: 8, D: 7.30. WR: 445kg (Vassily Alekseyev)

		SNATCH		JERK	TOTAL KG	
1. Sultan Rakhmanov	SOV/UZB	195.0	OR	245.0	440.0	EOR
2. Jürgen Heuser	GDR	182.5		227.5	410.0	
3. Tadeusz Rutkowski	POL	180.0		227.5	407.5	
4. Rudolf Strejček	CZE	182.5		220.0	402.5	
5. Bohuslav Braum	CZE	180.0		217.5	397.5	
6. Francisco Mendez Polo	CUB	175.0		220.0	395.0	
7. Robert Skolimowski	POL	175.0		210.0	385.0	
8. Talal Najjar	SYR	157.5		205.0	362.5	

Competing for the first time since he was injured during the 1978 world championship, Alekseyev failed three times to snatch 180 kg and was eliminated. Thirty-year-old Sultan Rakhmanov, whose mother was Ukrainian and whose father was an Uzbek, made six perfect lifts to score a decisive victory.

1984 Los Angeles-Westchester C: 9, N: 7, D: 8.8. WR: 465 kg (Aleksandr Gunyashev)

		SNATCH	JERK	TOTAL KG
1. Dean Lukin	AUS	172.5	240.0	412.5
2. Mario Martinez	USA	185.0	225.0	410.0

3. Manfred Nerlinger	GER	177.5	220.0	397.5
4. Ioannis Tsintsaris	GRE	162.5	185.0	347.5
5. Bartholomew Oluoma	NGR	150.0	187.5	337.5
6. Mosad Mosbah	EGY	150.0	180.0	330.0
DISQ (Drugs): Stefan Laggner (AUT) 385.0				

Dean Lukin was a 305-pound millionaire tuna fisherman from Port Lincoln, South Australia.

1988 Seoul C: 17, N: 13, D: 9.29. WR: 472.5 kg (Aleksandr Kurlovich)

		SNATCH		JERK	TOTAL KG	
1. Aleksandr Kurlovich	SOV/ BLR	212.5	OR	250.0	462.5	OR
2. Manfred Nerlinger	GER	190.0		240.0	430.0	
3. Martin Zawieja	GER	182.5		232.5	415.0	
4. Mario Martinez	USA	175.0		232.5	407.5	
5. Petr Hudeček	CZE	175.0		225.0	400.0	
6. Reda El Batoty	EGY	175.0		217.5	392.5	
7. Charles Garzarella	AUS	162.5		207.5	370.0	
8. Paulos Saltsidis	GRE	160.0		207.5	367.5	

In December 1984, Aleksandr Kurlovich was arrested by customs officials in Montreal and charged with importing anabolic steroids with intent to sell. He pleaded guilty and paid a fine of $450. The U.S.S.R. Weightlifting Federation banned him from competition for two years. In 1987 he returned to win the world championship.

Although he failed to make a single successful lift, Jiří Zubrický of Czechoslovakia set a record anyway: at 363½ pounds (164.95 kg), he was the heaviest weightlifter ever to take part in the Olympics.

1992 Barcelona C: 20, N: 16, D: 8.4. WR: 475.0 kg (Leonid Taranenko)

		SNATCH	JERK	TOTAL KG
1. Aleksandr Kurlovich	BLR	205.0	245.0	450.0
2. Leonid Taranenko	BLR	187.5	237.5	425.0
3. Manfred Nerlinger	GER	180.0	232.5	412.5
4. Ernesto Aguero Shell	CUB	182.5	230.0	412.5
5. Mitko Mitev	BUL	180.0	220.0	400.0
6. Jiří Zubrický	CZE	170.0	222.5	392.5
7. Erdinç Aslan	TUR	170.0	220.0	390.0
8. Mario Martinez	USA	170.0	215.0	385.0

Kurlovich made six straight successful lifts to earn his second gold medal. American Mark Henry broke Jiří Zubrický's record as the heaviest weightlifter in history when he weighed in at 366¾ pounds (166.4 kg). He finished in tenth place.

FREESTYLE WRESTLING

Light Flyweight—48 kg	Welterweight—74 kg
Flyweight—52 kg	Middleweight—82 kg
Bantamweight—57 kg	Light Heavyweight—90 kg
Featherweight—62 kg	Heavyweight—100 kg
Lightweight—68 kg	Super Heavyweight—130 kg

International amateur wrestling follows a complicated system of scoring. Beginning in 1984, matches of two three-minute rounds replaced matches of three three-minute rounds. In 1992, contests were reduced to one five-minute round. As a match progresses, contestants score technical points as a result of successful holds, actions, positions of advantage, and near-throws. A match is terminated as a result of a fall or if one wrestler achieves a 10-point lead. A fall is declared when a wrestler holds an opponent so that both of his shoulders are against the mat. If the five-minute mark is reached without a fall or 10-point lead, the wrestler with the most points is declared the winner if he has scored at least three points. Through 1984, in case of a tie, the victory was awarded to the contestant who achieved the highest-scoring move or who scored the last point. In 1988, a three-minute sudden-death overtime period was introduced. An overtime period is also used if neither wrestler has earned three points. If at the end of the overtime period neither of the wrestlers has scored three points, the referee, the judge, and the mat chairman choose the winner by majority vote. Each man is then assigned a certain number of points for the match according to the following chart. Until 1984, scoring was done with negative or "penalty" points rather than positive points.

winner—4   loser—0
  1) victory by fall
  2) technical superiority (ten-point difference), with the loser scoring no technical points
  3) injury
  4) withdrawal
  5) default
  6) disqualification

winner—4   loser—1
  1) victory by technical superiority (ten-point difference), with the loser scoring technical points

winner—3   loser—0
  1) victory by points, with the loser scoring no technical points
  2) victory declared by decision of the officiating team and neither wrestler has scored a technical point

winner—3   loser—1
  1) victory by points, with the loser scoring technical points
  2) victory declared by decision of the officiating team after a tie in which both wrestlers score technical points
  3) victory declared by decision of the officiating team when neither wrestler scores three technical points

Olympic wrestling tournaments have used a variety of formats over the years. According to the system currently in use, wrestlers in each weight category are paired off at random. Winners in this first round advance to table A, losers to table B. Competition continues in both tables. Wrestlers who lose for the first time drop into table B. Wrestlers who lose in table B are eliminated. Classification rounds continue until only two undefeated wrestlers are left in table A. These two wrestlers compete for first and second place. In table B, the classification rounds continue until two wrestlers are left. These two wrestlers compete for third and fourth place. The last two wrestlers to lose in table B compete for fifth and sixth place. Places seven and eight are awarded to the two remaining wrestlers who have gained the most match points.

Wrestling is the only sport with a *maximum* weight limit.

Point Values of Actions and Holds

Par terre position—The defending wrestler begins on his hands and knees; the attacking wrestler begins with both hands on top of his opponent's back.

Danger position—A wrestler is considered to be in the "danger position" when the line of his back or shoulders forms an angle of less than 90 degrees to the mat when he uses the upper part of his body to avoid a fall.

Grand amplitude hold—In the standing position a grand amplitude hold is called when a wrestler causes his opponent to lose all contact with the ground, sweeps him through the air, and brings him down to the mat in a danger position. In the *par terre* position, a grand amplitude hold occurs when a wrestler lifts his opponent from the ground and causes him to land belly-down (3 points) or in a danger position (5 points).

One point to the wrestler who:

(1) brings his opponent to the mat from behind and holds him down with three points of contact (two arms and one knee, or two knees and one arm)

(2) applies a correct hold but does not place his opponent in danger

(3) overcomes, holds, and controls his opponent on the mat by passing behind him

(4) while attacking, has his opponent flee the hold or the mat or whose opponent refuses to start, commits illegal actions or acts of brutality

(5) holds his opponent in a position of danger for five seconds or longer

(6) while in the *par terre* position, after being controlled or brought to the mat, raises himself up to the standing position.

(7) Officials may award 1 extra point when a wrestler uses a hold requiring great technical effort to score a 3- or 5-point lift that causes the attacked wrestler to completely lose contact with the mat.

Two points to the wrestler who:

(1) applies a correct move in the *par terre* position and places his opponent in a position of danger or in a fall position

(2) while attacking, causes his opponent to roll onto his shoulders

(3) while attacking, has an opponent flee the hold by jumping off the mat

(4) while being attacked, is prevented from completing a hold because his opponent uses an illegal hold

(5) while attacked, causes his opponent's shoulder to touch the mat in the course of his opponent's move.

Three points to the wrestler who:

(1) performs a hold in a standing position that brings his opponent into a danger position by direct projection

(2) raises his opponent from the ground and puts him in a danger position

(3) executes a grand amplitude hold that does not place his opponent in a danger position.

Five points to the wrestler who:

(1) performs a grand amplitude hold from the standing position and brings his opponent to a danger position

(2) from the *par terre* position, lifts his opponent off the ground with a grand amplitude move and projects him into a danger position.

LIGHT FLYWEIGHT
(48 kg—106 lbs)

1896–1900 not held

1904 St. Louis C: 4, N: 1, D: 10.15.
(47.6 kg—105 lbs)

		FINAL MATCH	
1. Robert Curry	USA	Fall	2:38
2. John Hein	USA		
3. Gustav Thiefenthaler	USA		

Curry, of New York City, threw Thiefenthaler in 4:05 to qualify for the final.

1906–1968 not held

1972 Munich C: 14, N: 14, D: 8.31.

		ROUND ELIMINATED	PEN. PTS.	FINAL ROUND
1. Roman Dmitriev	SOV/RUS	—	2	4
2. Ognyan Nikolov	BUL	—	5	4
3. Ebrahim Javadi	IRN	—	3.5	4
4. Sefer Baygin	TUR	4	6.5	
5. Ion Arapu	ROM	4	7	
6. Masahiko Umeda	JPN	4	8	
7. Sergio Gonzalez	USA	3	6	
7. Jürgen Möbius	GDR	3	6	

Dmitriev grew up grazing reindeer in Yakutia.

1976 Montreal C: 18, N: 18, D: 7.31.

		ROUND ELIMINATED	PEN. PTS.	FINAL ROUND
1. Hasan Isayev	BUL	—	4	3
2. Roman Dmitriev	SOV/RUS	—	1	5
3. Akira Kudo	JPN	—	0	8
4. Gombo Khishigbaatar	MGL	5	6	
5. Kim Hwa-kyung	KOR	5	6	
6. Li Yong-nam	PRK	5	8	
7. Kuddusi Ozdemir	TUR	4	7	
8. Willi Heckmann	GER	4	8	

Dmitriev actually defeated two-time world champion Isayev, but lost four points as the result of a double disqualification against Kudo.

1980 Moscow C: 14, N: 14, D: 7.29.

		ROUND ELIMINATED	PEN. PTS.	FINAL ROUND
1. Claudio Pollio	ITA	—	5.5	3
2. Jang Se-hong	PRK	—	5	4
3. Sergei Kornilayev	SOV/RUS	—	1	5
4. Jan Falandys	POL	5	6.5	
5. Mahabir Singh	IND	5	9	
6. László Biró	HUN	4	9	
7. Rumen Yordanov	BUL	3	6	
8. Gheorghe Rasovan	ROM	3	7	

Pollio lost to Kornilayev, but won the gold medal anyway after the Soviet wrestler was thrown in the final match by Jang Se-hong, who had been disqualified in his match against Pollio.

1984 Los Angeles-Anaheim C: 7, N: 7, D: 8.9.

		FINAL MATCH	
1. Robert Weaver	USA	Fall	2:58
2. Takashi Irie	JPN		
3. Son Gab-do	KOR	13–7	6:00
4. Gao Wenhe	CHN		
5. Reiner Heugabel	GER	Passivity	5:21
6. Kent Andersson	SWE		
7. Sunil Dutt	IND		

Freestyle Wrestling was hard hit by the Soviet-bloc boycott. Twenty-three of the 30 medalists at the 1983 world championships were from boycotting nations, including nine of the ten gold medal winners. The light flyweight division was so depleted that there were only seven entrants—the smallest wrestling competition since 1932. Bobby Weaver, who had finished second at the 1979 world championships and fifth in 1983, needed a total of only 8 minutes and 26 seconds to dispose of his three opponents.

1988 Seoul C: 19, N: 19, D: 9.29.

			FINAL MATCH	
1. Takashi Kobayashi	JPN		16–4	6:00
2. Ivan Tzonov	BUL			
3. Sergei Karamchakov	SOV/RUS		3–1	6:00
4. Tim Vanni	USA			
5. Reiner Heugabel	GER		Passivity	4:27
6. Ilyas Sukruoğlü	TUR			
7. Volker Anger	GDR		Forfeit	
8. Naser Zeinalnia	IRN			

Two-time defending world champion Li Jae-sik missed the competition because of North Korea's boycott. Lee Sang-ho of South Korea had finished second to Li at the 1987 world championships, but at the Olympics Lee suffered a broken arm in the first minute of his opening match against Takashi Kobayashi. Thereafter, Kobayashi dominated the tournament except for a close call against Ilyas Sukruoğlü. Sukruoğlü led 5–3 with 10 seconds remaining when Kobayashi scored on a 3-point move to win 6–5 and advance to the final.

1992 Barcelona C: 19, N: 19, D: 8.6.

		FINAL MATCH
1. Kim Il	PRK	4–1
2. Kim Jong-shin	KOR	
3. Vugar Orudzhev	BLR	2–1
4. Romică Raşovan	ROM	
5. Tim Vanni	USA	1–0
6. Reiner Heugabel	GER	
7. Aldo Martínez Echavarría	CUB	Injury
8. Tserenbaatar Khosbayar	MGL	

In the final match of the 1991 world championships, Vugar Orudzhev defeated Kim Il 1–0 in overtime. The two met again in the first round at the Olympics. This time Kim won, 9–5. Kim's closest match was a 7–6 victory over Aldo Martínez.

FLYWEIGHT
(52 kg—114 ½ lbs)

1896–1900 not held

1904 St. Louis C: 3, N: 1, D: 10.15.
(52.16 kg–115 lbs)

			FINAL MATCH
1. George Mehnert	USA	Dec.	15:00
2. Gustav Bauer	USA		
3. William Nelson	USA		

1906–1936 not held

1948 London C: 11, N: 11, D: 7.31.

		ROUND ELIMINATED	PEN. PTS.	FINAL ROUND
1. Lennart Viitala	FIN	—	2	2
2. Halit Balamir	TUR	—	4	2
3. Thure Johansson	SWE	—	5	6
4. Rassoul Raiisi	IRN	4	6	
5. Pierre Baudric	FRA	4	7	
6. Kha-Shaba Jadav	IND	3	5	
7. William Jernigan	USA	3	7	

1952 Helsinki C: 16, N: 16, D: 7.23.

		ROUND ELIMINATED	PEN. PTS.	FINAL ROUND
1. Hasan Gemici	TUR	—	4	3
2. Yushu Kitano	JPN	—	4	4
3. Mahmoud Mollaghasemi	IRN	—	3	4
4. Georgy Sayadov	SOV	5	6	
5. Heinrich Weber	GER	4	6	
6. Louis Baise	SAF	4	7	
7. Giordano Degiorgi	ITA	3	5	
7. Robert Peery	USA	3	5	

1956 Melbourne C: 11, N: 11, D: 12.1.

		ROUND ELIMINATED	PEN. PTS.	FINAL ROUND
1. Mirian Tsalkalamanidze	SOV/ GEO	—	5	3
2. Mohammad Ali Khojastépour	IRN	—	3	3
3. Hüseyin Akbaş	TUR	—	2	4
4. Tadashi Asai	JPN	4	7	
5. Richard Delgado	USA	3	6	
5. André Zoete	FRA	3	6	
7. Abdul Aziz	PAK	3	7	
7. Baban Daware	IND	3	7	

Tsalkalamanidze gained the gold medal by throwing Khojastépour after four minutes.

1960 Rome C: 17, N: 17, D: 9.6.

		ROUND ELIMINATED	PEN. PTS.	FINAL ROUND
1. Ahmet Bilek	TUR	—	5	2
2. Masayuki Matsubara	JPN	—	4	4
3. M. Ebrahim Seifpour Saadabadi	IRN	—	3	6
4. Paul Neff	GER	6	9	

5. Elliott Gray Simons	USA	5	8
6. Ali Aliyev	SOV/RUS	5	8
7. Nikola Dimitrov	BUL	4	7
8. André Zoete	FRA	4	8

1964 Tokyo C: 22, N: 22, D: 10.14.

		ROUND ELIMINATED	PEN. PTS.	FINAL ROUND
1. Yoshikatsu Yoshida	JPN	—	2	1
2. Chang Chang-sun	KOR	—	3	3
3. S. Ali Akbar Heidari	IRN	5	6	
4. Ali Aliyev	SOV/RUS	5	7	
4. Cemal Yanilmaz	TUR	5	7	
4. André Zoete	FRA	5	7	
7. Elliott Gray Simons	USA	4	6	
8. Muhammed Niaz	PAK	4	7	

1968 Mexico City C: 23, N: 23, D: 10.20.

		ROUND ELIMINATED	PEN. PTS.	FINAL ROUND
1. Shigeo Nakata	JPN	—	3.5	1
2. Richard Sanders	USA	—	0	4
3. Surenjav Sukhbaatar	MGL	—	5	7
4. Nazar Albaryan	SOV	5	6.5	
5. Vincenzo Grassi	ITA	5	6.5	
6. Sudesh Kumar	IND	5	7.5	
7. Mohammad Ghorbani	IRN	5	8	
7. Paul Neff	GER	5	8	

1972 Munich C: 24, N: 24, D: 8.31.

		ROUND ELIMINATED	PEN. PTS.	FINAL ROUND
1. Kiyomi Kato	JPN	—	1.5	2
2. Arsen Alakhverdiyev	SOV/RUS	—	5.5	5
3. Kim Gwong-hyong	PRK	—	5.5	5
4. Sudesh Sudeshkumar	IND	6	7	
5. Petru Ciarnău	ROM	6	7.5	
6. Gordon Bertie	CAN	5	7.5	
7. Henrik Gál	HUN	4	7	
7. John Kinsella	AUS	4	7	

1976 Montreal C: 19, N: 19, D: 7.31.

		ROUND ELIMINATED	PEN. PTS.	FINAL ROUND
1. Yuji Takada	JPN	—	0	0.5
2. Aleksandr Ivanov	SOV/KAZ	—	1.5	3.5
3. Jeon Hae-sup	KOR	—	2	8
4. Henrik Gál	HUN	5	7	
5. Nermedin Selimov	BUL	5	8.5	
6. Wladyslaw Stecyk	POL	5	9	
7. Li Bong-sun	PRK	4	7	
8. Eloy Abreu	CUB	4	9	

Two-time world champion Yuji Takada of Gunma overwhelmed the field, pinning six of his seven opponents, five of them in less than two minutes. He also outpointed Ivanov 20–11.

1980 Moscow C: 16, N: 16, D: 7.30.

		ROUND ELIMINATED	PEN. PTS.	FINAL ROUND
1. Anatoly Bilohlazov	SOV/UKR	—	1.5	0
2. Wladyslaw Stecyk	POL	—	4	5
3. Nermedin Selimov	BUL	—	4.5	7
4. Lajos Szabó	HUN	6	9	
5. Jang Dok-ryong	PRK	4	6.5	
6. Nanzadying Burgedaa	MGL	4	7	
7. Koce Efremov	YUG	4	8	
8. Hartmut Reich	GDR	3	6.5	

After winning his first two matches on decisions, Anatoly Bilohlazov needed only 4:54 to dispose of his last four opponents. Twenty-four hours and 48 minutes after Bilohlazov won the Flyweight gold medal, his twin brother, Serhei, won the Bantamweight tournament.

1984 Los Angeles-Anaheim C: 17, N: 17, D: 8.10.

		FINAL MATCH	
1. Šaban Trstena	YUG/MAC	Injury	
2. Kim Jong-kyu	KOR		
3. Yuji Takada	JPN	12–0	4:34
4. Ray Takahashi	CAN		
5. Aslan Seyhanli	TUR	14–5	6:00
6. Mahabir Singh	IND		
7. Fritz Niebler	GER		
8. Liang Dejin	CHN		

Kim tore a muscle in his left shoulder during his match with Fritz Niebler of West Germany and was unable to take part in the final. The crucial match for 19-year-old Šaban Trstena of Scopia, Macedonia, was an 8–8 decision over 1976 Olympic champion Yuji Takada.

1988 Seoul C: 31, N: 31, D: 9.30.

		FINAL MATCH	
1. Mitsuru Sato	JPN	13–2	6:00
2. Šaban Trstena	YUG/MAC		
3. Vladimir Toguzov	SOV/RUS	14–1	6:00
4. László Bíró	HUN		
5. Aslan Seyhanli	TUR	5–4	6:00
6. Kim Jong-ho	KOR		
7. Tserenbatar Enebayar	MGL	Injury	
8. Valentin Yordanov	BUL		

Sato threw his first five opponents and then outpointed Kim 15–0 in 4:02 to advance to the final. The favorite had been three-time world champion Valentin Yordanov, who competed under the government-imposed surname Dimitrov. Yordanov won his first three matches, then lost 11–5 to Trstena and 14–1 to Toguzov before withdrawing from the "B" final because of injury.

1992 Barcelona C: 18, N: 18, D: 8.5.

		FINAL MATCH
1. Li Hak-son	PRK	8–1
2. Larry "Zeke" Jones	USA	

		FINAL MATCH
3. Valentin Yordanov	BUL	9–3
4. Kim Sun-hah	KOR	
5. Ahmet Orel	TUR	Injury
6. Mitsuru Sato	JPN	
7. Majid Torkan	IRN	2–1
8. Christopher Woodcroft	CAN	

Li, a relative newcomer who was unknown to most of his opponents, overwhelmed everyone he faced with his speed and aggressiveness. His only close match was a 6–4 victory over Yordanov.

BANTAMWEIGHT
(57 kg—125½ lbs)

1896-1900 not held

1904 St. Louis C: 7, N: 1, D: 10.15.
(56.70 kg—125 lbs)

		FINAL MATCH
1. Isidor "Jack" Niflot	USA	Fall 1:58
2. August Wester	USA	
3. Zenon Strebler	USA	

1906 not held

1908 London C: 13, N: 3, D: 7.20.
(54 kg—119 lbs)

		FINAL MATCH
1. George Mehnert	USA	Fall 11:45; Fall 3:57
2. William Press	GBR	
3. Aubert Côté	CAN	
4. Fitzlloyd Tomkins	GBR	
5. Frank Davis (GBR), Bruce Sansom (GBR), George Saunders (GBR)		

Mehnert, a 26-year-old from Newark, New Jersey, had won the Flyweight championship in St. Louis four years earlier. Côté mortgaged his farm in Québec to pay his way to London. When he returned with a medal, the Canadian Olympic Committee agreed to reimburse him.

1912–1920 not held

1924 Paris C: 12, N: 8, D: 7.14.
(56 kg—123½ lbs)

1. Kustaa Pihlajamäki	FIN
2. Kaarlo Mäkinen	FIN
3. Bryant Hines	USA
4. Gaston Ducayla	FRA

Pihlajamäki won the first of his three Olympic medals (two gold, one silver). His younger brother, Hermanni, also won a gold and a bronze in freestyle wrestling.

1928 Amsterdam C: 8, N: 8, D: 8.1.
(56 kg—123½ lbs)

1. Kaarlo Mäkinen	FIN
2. Edmond Spapen	BEL
3. James Trifunov	CAN
4. Harold Sansum	GBR
5. Robert Hewitt	USA

Sansum was awarded fourth place even though he lost all three of his matches.

1932 Los Angeles C: 8, N: 8, D: 8.3.
(56 kg—123½ lbs)

1. Robert Pearce	USA
2. Ödön Zombori	HUN
3. Aatos Jaskari	FIN
4. Joseph Reid	GBR
5. Georgios Zervinis	GRE
6. Julien Depuichaffray	FRA

1936 Berlin C: 14, N: 14, D: 8.5.
(56 kg—123½ lbs)

		ROUND ELIMINATED	PEN. PTS.	FINAL ROUND
1. Ödön Zombori	HUN	—	4	0
2. Ross Flood	USA	—	2	3
3. Johannes Herbert	GER	5	5	
4. Herman Tuvesson	SWE	5	6	
5. Aatos Jaskari	FIN	4	7	
6. Ahmet Çakiryildiz	TUR	4	7	
7. Marcello Nizzola	ITA	3	5	
8. Cesar Gaudard	SWI	3	6	
8. Auguste Laporte	BEL	3	6	

1948 London C: 15, N: 15, D: 7.31.
(56 kg—123½ lbs)

		ROUND ELIMINATED	PEN. PTS.	FINAL ROUND
1. Nasuh Akar	TUR	—	2	0
2. Gerald Leeman	USA	—	3	3
3. Charles Kouyos	FRA	5	7	
4. Joseph Trimpont	BEL	5	7	
5. Lajos Bencze	HUN	4	5	
5. Raymond Cazaux	GBR	4	5	
5. Sayad Hafez	EGY	4	5	
5. Erik Persson	SWE	4	5	

1952 Helsinki C: 20, N: 20, D: 7.23.

		ROUND ELIMINATED	PEN. PTS.	FINAL ROUND
1. Shohachi Ishii	JPN	—	4	2
2. Rashid Mamedbekov	SOV/AZR	—	3	4
3. Kha-Shaba Jadav	IND	—	4	6
4. Edvin Westerby	SWE	5	7	
5. Cemil Saribacak	TUR	4	5	
6. Lajos Bencze	HUN	4	5	
7. Ferdinand Schmitz	GER	4	6	
8. Eigil Johansen	DEN	3	5	
8. M. Mehdi Yaghoubi	IRN	3	5	

A talented judoka, Ishii was forced to give up judo when U.S. occupation forces banned the sport after World War II. Ishii switched to wrestling and won Japan's first post-war gold medal.

1956 Melbourne C: 14, N: 14, D: 12.1.

		ROUND ELIMI-NATED	PEN. PTS.	FINAL ROUND
1. Mustafa Dağistanli	TUR	—	4	1
2. M. Mehdi Yaghoubi	IRN	—	4	2
3. Mykhalo Shakhov	SOV/UKR	5	6	
4. Lee Sang-kyoon	KOR	5	7	
5. Minoru Iizuka	JPN	4	5	
6. Alfred Kämmerer	GDR	3	5	
7. Din Zahur	PAK	3	6	
8. Adolfo Diaz	ARG	3	7	
8. Tarakeshwar Pandey	IND	3	7	

1960 Rome C: 19, N: 19, D: 9.6.

		ROUND ELIMI-NATED	PEN. PTS.	FINAL ROUND
1. Terrence McCann	USA	—	5	2
2. Nezhdet Zalev	BUL	—	2	4
3. Tadeusz Trojanowski	POL	—	4	6
4. Tadashi Asai	JPN	5	6	
5. Tanuo Jaskari	FIN	5	7	
6. Mykhalo Shakhov	SOV/UKR	5	8	
7. M. Mehdi Yaghoubi	IRN	4	6	
8. Luigi Chinazzo	ITA	4	8	

1964 Tokyo C: 20, N: 20, D: 10.14.

		ROUND ELIMI-NATED	PEN. PTS.	FINAL ROUND
1. Yojiro Uetake	JPN	—	3	2
2. Hüseyin Akbaş	TUR	—	5	4
3. Aydyn Ibragimov	SOV/AZR	—	3	6
4. David Auble	USA	5	6	
5. Choi Young-kil	KOR	5	7	
6. Bishamber Singh	IND	5	8	
7. János Varga	HUN	4	7	
8. Abdollah Khodabande	IRN	3	6	

1968 Mexico City C: 21, N: 21, D: 10.20.

		ROUND ELIMINATED	PEN. PTS.
1. Yojiro Uetake	JPN	—	5.5
2. Donald Behm	USA	7	6.5
3. Abutaleb Talebi Gorgori	IRN	7	7.5
4. Ali Aliyev	SOV/RUS	7	8.5
5. Ivan Shavov	BUL	6	7.5
6. Zbigniew Żedzicki	POL	5	8
7. Bishamber Singh	IND	5	8.5
8. Sukhbaatar Bazaryn	MGL	4	7

1972 Munich C: 28, N: 28, D: 8.31.

		ROUND ELIMINATED	PEN. PTS.	FINAL ROUND
1. Hideaki Yanagida	JPN	—	4	1
2. Richard Sanders	USA	—	4	3
3. László Klinga	HUN	7	8.5	
4. Prem Premnath	IND	7	9	
5. Ivan Shavov	BUL	6	7	
6. Horst Mayer	GDR	6	7.5	
7. Ramezan Kheder	IRN	6	8	
8. Jorge Ramos	CUB	5	6	

Silver medalist Richard Sanders, a bartender from Portland, Oregon, had long hair, a beard, and a mustache, and wore a bead necklace. Seven weeks after the Olympics, Sanders was killed in an automobile accident while touring in Europe. He was 23 years old.

1976 Montreal C: 21, N: 21, D: 7.31.

		ROUND ELIMINATED	PEN. PTS.	FINAL ROUND
1. Vladimir Yumin	SOV/RUS	—	7	2
2. Hans-Dieter Brüchert	GDR	—	3.5	4
3. Masao Arai	JPN	—	4.5	6
4. Miho Dukov	BUL	6	8	
5. Ramezan Kheder	IRN	6	8	
6. Migd Khoilogdorj	MGL	6	8	
7. George Khatziioannidis	GRE	5	8.5	
8. Zbigniew Żedzicki	POL	4	6	

1980 Moscow C: 16, N: 16, D: 7.31.

		ROUND ELIMI-NATED	PEN. PTS.	FINAL ROUND
1. Serhei Bilohlazov	SOV/UKR	—	0	0
2. Li Ho-pyong	PRK	—	6	5
3. Dugarsuren Ouinbold	MGL	—	2	7
4. Ivan Tzochev	BUL	5	7	
5. Aurel Neagu	ROM	4	6	
6. Wieslaw Kończak	POL	4	7	
7. Karim Salman Muhsin	IRQ	4	8	
8. Sándor Németh	HUN	4	9	

Serhei Bilohlazov, the twin brother of Flyweight winner Anatoly Bilohlazov, threw five of his six opponents and defeated Ouinbold by disqualification, after leading in points 15–0. He outpointed his six victims, 58–3.

1984 Los Angeles-Anaheim C: 16, N: 16, D: 8.11.

		FINAL MATCH	
1. Hideaki Tomiyama	JPN	8–3	6:00
2. Barry Davis	USA		
3. Kim Eui-kon	KOR	7–4	6:00
4. Orlando Caceres	PUR		
5. Rohtas Singh	IND	3–2	6:00
6. Zoran Sorov	YUG		
7. Guanbunima	CHN		
8. Ibrahim Akgun	TUR		

With his 85-year-old grandfather in the audience for good luck, and with defending Olympic and world champion Serhei Bihohlazov prevented from competing because of the Soviet-bloc boycott, two-time world champion Hideaki Tomiyama outclassed the field.

1988 Seoul C: 25, N: 25, D: 10.1.

		FINAL MATCH	
1. Serhei Bilohlazov	SOV/UKR	5–1	6:00
2. Askari Mohammadian	IRN		
3. Noh Kyung-sun	KOR	9–8	9:00
4. Ahmet Ak	TUR		
5. Valentin Ivanov	BUL	5–3	6:00
6. Béla Nagy	HUN		
7. Haltma Battul	MGL	3–1	6:00
8. Ryo Kanehama	JPN		

Six-time world champion Serhei Bilohlazov regained his Olympic title without being seriously challenged.

1992 Barcelona C: 18, N: 18, D: 8.7.

		FINAL MATCH
1. Alejandro Puerto Díaz	CUB	5–0
2. Sergei Smal	BLR	
3. Kim Yong-sik	PRK	3–2
4. Remzi Musaoğlu	TUR	
5. Rumen Pavlov	BUL	Fall 0:44
6. Kendall Cross	USA	
7. Jürgen Scheibe	GER	Injury
8. Robert Dawson	CAN	

Puerto shut out five of his opponents and defeated Cross 10–6.

FEATHERWEIGHT
(62 kg—136½ lbs)

1896–1900 not held

1904 St. Louis C: 9, N: 1, D: 10.15.
(61.23 kg—135 lbs)

		FINAL MATCH	
1. Benjamin Bradshaw	USA	Dec	15:00
2. Theodore McLear	USA		
3. Charles Clapper	USA		

1906 not held

1908 London C: 12, N: 2, D: 7.22.
(60.3 kg—132½ lbs)

		FINAL MATCH
1. George Dole	USA	Fall 9:28; Dec 15:00
2. James Slim	GBR	
3. William McKie	GBR	
4. William Tagg	GBR	
5. Arthur Goddard (GBR), James Webster (GBR), James White (GBR)		

Dole, a 5-foot 3½-inch student from Yale, was the only non-British wrestler in the Featherweight division.

1912 not held

1920 Antwerp C: 11, N: 7, D: 8.27.
(60 kg—132 lbs)

		FINAL MATCH
1. Charles Ackerly	USA	Dec
2. Samuel Gerson	USA	
3. Philip Bernard	GBR	
4. Randhir Shinde	IND	

Ackerly, former captain of the Cornell University team, and Gerson, former captain of the University of Pennsylvania team, had each defeated the other once in collegiate competition. Ackerly won the tie-breaker at the A.A.U. championships and then won again across the seas in Antwerp. Thirty-two years later Gerson organized the U.S. Olympians, an alumni association for former members of U.S. Olympic teams.

1924 Paris C: 17, N: 12, D: 7.14.
(61 kg—134½ lbs)
1. Robin Reed	USA
2. Chester Newton	USA
3. Katsutoshi Naito	JPN
4. Sigfrid Hansson	SWE

Reed and Newton were longtime bitter rivals from Portland, Oregon. One of the greatest U.S. wrestlers ever, Reed eventually retired undefeated.

1928 Amsterdam C: 9, N: 9, D: 8.1.
(61 kg—134½ lbs)

		FINAL MATCH
1. Allie Morrison	USA	Injury
2. Kustaa Pihlajamäki	FIN	
3. Hans Minder	SWI	
4. René Rottenfluc	FRA	

1932 Los Angeles C: 10, N: 10, D: 8.3.
(61 kg—134½ lbs)
1. Hermanni Pihlajamäki	FIN
2. Edgar Nemir	USA
3. Einar Karlsson	SWE
4. Joseph Taylor	GBR
5. Ioannis Farmakidis	GRE
6. Jean Chasson	FRA

1936 Berlin C: 15, N: 15, D: 8.4.
(61 kg—134½ lbs)

		ROUND ELIMINATED	PEN. PTS.
1. Kustaa Pihlajamäki	FIN	—	1
2. Francis Millard	USA	6	5
3. Gösta Jönsson	SWE	6	5
4. John Vernon Pettigrew	CAN	5	7
5. Ferenc Tóth	HUN	4	6

6. Mitsuzo Mizutani	JPN	4	7	
7. Marco Gavelli	ITA	3	5	
8. Yasar Erkan (TUR), Nevil Hall (SAF), Norman Morrell (GBR)		3	7	

1948 London C: 17, N: 17, D: 7.31.
(63 kg—139 lbs)

		ROUND ELIMINATED	PEN. PTS.	FINAL ROUND
1. Gazanfer Bilge	TUR	—	0	1
2. Ivar Sjölin	SWE	—	2	3
3. Adolf Müller	SWI	6	5	
4. Paavo Hietala	FIN	5	6	
4. Ferenc Tóth	HUN	5	6	
6. Harold "Hal" Moore	USA	4	5	
7. Antoine Raeymaeckers	BEL	4	6	
8. Abdel Hamid Yacout	EGY	4	7	
8. Arnold Parsons	GBR	4	7	

Bilge was rewarded by the Turkish government with a house and 20,000 liras ($7,142). This made him ineligible for the 1952 Olympics, but he was able to parlay his rewards into a fortune as a bus mogul. In 1963 Bilge was imprisoned after he shot Adil Atan, a business rival who had won a bronze medal as a Light Heavyweight wrestler in 1952.

1952 Helsinki C: 21, N: 21, D: 7.23.
(63 kg—139 lbs)

		ROUND ELIMINATED	PEN. PTS.	FINAL ROUND
1. Bayram Şit	TUR	—	2	1
2. Nasser Givéchi	IRN	—	4	4
3. Josiah Henson	USA	—	5	6
4. Keshav Mangave	IND	5	6	
5. Risaburo Tominaga	JPN	5	7	
6. Rauno Mäkinen	FIN	4	5	
7. Albert Bernard	CAN	4	6	
7. Abdel Essawi	EGY	4	6	

1956 Melbourne C: 13, N: 13, D: 12.1.
(63 kg—139 lbs)

		ROUND ELIMINATED	PEN. PTS.	FINAL ROUND
1. Shozo Sasahara	JPN	—	4	1
2. Joseph Mewis	BEL	—	3	4
3. Erkki Penttilä	FIN	—	4	6
4. Myron Roderick	USA	4	5	
5. Bayram Şit	TUR	4	5	
6. Nasser Givéchi	IRN	4	7	
6. Linar Salimullin	SOV/UKR	4	7	
8. Ram Sarup	IND	3	6	

1960 Rome C: 25, N: 25, D: 9.6.
(63 kg—139 lbs)

		ROUND ELIMINATED	PEN. PTS.	FINAL ROUND
1. Mustafa Dağistanli	TUR	—	4	1
2. Stancho Kolev	BUL	—	3	3
3. Vladimir Rubashvili	SOV/GEO	6	7	

4. Tamiji Sato	JPN	6	7	
5. Joseph Mewis	BEL	5	8	
6. Mohamed Akhtar	PAK	5	9	
7. Abraham Geldenhuys	SAF	4	6	
8. Azohadi Khaden	IRN	4	9	

1964 Tokyo C: 21, N: 21, D: 10.14.
(63 kg—139 lbs)

		ROUND ELIMINATED	PEN. PTS.	FINAL ROUND
1. Osamu Watanabe	JPN	—	2	2
2. Stancho Kolev	BUL	—	5	5
3. Nodar Khokhashvili	SOV/GEO	—	5	5
4. Robert "Bobby" Douglas	USA	5	6	
5. Mohammed Ebrahimi	AFG	5	7	
6. M. Ebrahim Seifpour Saadabadi	IRN	5	8	
7. Rainer Schilling	GER	4	6	
8. Mario Tovar González	MEX	4	7	

Watanabe's 1–0 win over Khokhashvili was his 186th consecutive victory. He didn't give up a single point in any of his six Olympic matches. Kolev was awarded the silver medal because he weighed less than Khokhashvili.

1968 Mexico City C: 23, N: 23, D: 10.20.
(63 kg—139 lbs)

		ROUND ELIMINATED	PEN. PTS.	FINAL ROUND
1. Masaaki Kaneko	JPN	—	1.5	3.5
2. Enyu Todorov	BUL	—	2	4.5
3. S. Shamseddin Seyyedabbasi	IRN	—	2.5	5
4. Nicolaos Karypidis	GRE	5	6.5	
5. Petre Coman	ROM	5	8	
6. Yeikan Tedeyev	SOV/RUS	4	6	
7. Vehbi Akdag	TUR	4	6.5	
7. Ismail Al Karaghouli	IRQ	4	6.5	

1972 Munich C: 26, N: 26, D: 8.31.

		ROUND ELIMINATED	PEN. PTS.	FINAL ROUND
1. Zagalav Abdulbekov	SOV/RUS	—	3.5	2
2. Vehbi Akdag	TUR	—	5.5	5
3. Ivan Krustev	BUL	—	5	5
4. Kiroshi Abe	JPN	6	6	
5. S. Shamseddin Seyyedabbasi	IRN	5	5.5	
6. Petre Coman	ROM	5	6	
7. Joseph Burge House	GUA	5	7	
8. Gerhard Weisenberg	GER	4	8	

1976 Montreal C: 17, N: 17, D: 7.31.

		ROUND ELIMINATED	PEN. PTS.	FINAL ROUND
1. Yang Jung-mo	KOR	—	1	3
2. Zevegin Oidov	MGL	—	3	4
3. Gene Davis	USA	—	8	5
4. Mohsen Farahvashi	IRN	6	10	

		ROUND ELIMINATED	PEN. PTS.	FINAL ROUND
5. Ivan Yankov	BUL	5	8	
6. Sergei Timofeyev	SOV	4	7	
7. Kenkichi Maekawa	JPN	4	8	
8. Helmut Strumpf	GDR	4	9	

Yang Jung-mo was South Korea's first Olympic gold medal winner.

1980 Moscow C: 13, N: 13, D: 7.29.

		ROUND ELIMINATED	PEN. PTS.	FINAL ROUND
1. Magomedgasan Abushev	SOV/RUS	—	2.5	1.5
2. Miho Dukov	BUL	—	5.5	3
3. Georges Khatziioannidis	GRE	—	5	7.5
4. Raul Cascaret Fonseca	CUB	5	6.5	
5. Aurel Suteu	ROM	5	8.5	
6. Ulzibayar Nasanjargal	MGL	4	6	
7. Brian Aspen	GBR	3	6.5	
8. Zoltán Szalontai	HUN	3	7.5	

1984 Los Angeles-Anaheim C: 16, N: 16, D: 8.9.

		FINAL MATCH	
1. Randy Lewis	USA	24–11	4:52
2. Kosei Akaishi	JPN		
3. Lee Jung-keun	KOR	11–6	6:00
4. Cris Brown	AUS		
5. Martin Herbster	GER	11–4	6:00
6. Antonio La Bruna	ITA		
7. Selman Kaygusuz	TUR		
8. Gerard Santoro	FRA		

Randy Lewis of Rapid City, South Dakota, had a much more difficult time getting into the Olympics than he did once he got there. In 1980 Lewis made the U.S. team, but the boycott prevented him from competing. In 1984, at the U.S. Olympic trials, Lewis defeated world championship silver medalist Lee Roy Smith. But Smith filed a protest which was upheld and a re-wrestle was ordered. When Smith emerged victorious, Lewis, supported by U.S. coach Dan Gable, filed a protest of his own. An arbitrator ordered that the final 50 seconds of the original match be re-wrestled. This time Lewis won. The next day, only two days before the Los Angeles opening ceremonies, Lewis defeated Rick Delegatta to finally secure his participation in the Olympics.

Lewis outscored his first four opponents 52–4 to advance to the final, where he overwhelmed Akaishi in the first two minutes of the second period.

1988 Seoul C: 28, N: 28, D: 9.29.

		FINAL MATCH	
1. John Smith	USA	4–0	6:00
2. Stepan Sarkisyan	SOV/ARM		
3. Simeon Shterev	BUL	5–2	6:00
4. Akbar Fallah	IRN		
5. Jörg Helmdach	GER	5–4	6:00
6. Avirmed Enhe	MGL		
7. Giovanni Schillaci	ITA	5–0	6:00
8. Gary Bohay	CAN		

John Smith, the 1987 world champion, qualified for the U.S. Olympic team by twice defeating Randy Lewis, the same man who had prevented John's older brother, Lee Roy, from qualifying in 1984. In Seoul, Smith suffered a fractured nose in his second match with Simeon Shterev. He also wrestled with an abscessed left ear, which had to be drained daily. In the final, Smith demoralized Sarkisyan early in the first round by slipping free of the Armenian's best leghold.

1992 Barcelona C: 21, N: 21, D: 8.7.

		FINAL MATCH	
1. John Smith	USA	6–0	
2. Asgari Mohammadian	IRN		
3. Lazaro Reinoso Martínez	CUB	4–0	
4. Rossen Vassilev	BUL		
5. Gazikhan Azizov	RUS	11–5	
6. Musa Ilhan	AUS		
7. Martin Müller	SWI	Fall	3:39
8. Shin Sang-kew	KOR		

John Smith continued to dominate the 62-kilogram division, winning all three world championships between Olympics, but he almost didn't qualify for the Barcelona Games. At the United States Olympic Wrestle-Off, his 56-match win streak was snapped when he was beaten 4–2 by John Fisher in the first match of a two-out-of-three contest. Smith came back to win the last two matches 3–1 and 6–5. Smith struggled at the Olympics as well. His first two matches were close victories, 3–2 over Ismail Faikoğlu of Turkey and 2–1 over Kim Gwang-chol of North Korea. He even lost one match, 3–1 in overtime, to Lazaro Reinoso. But because Smith had beaten Gazikhan Azizov 17–1 and Azizov had beaten Reinoso, Smith won his pool and made it to the final, where he controlled the contest from the start and earned his second gold medal.

LIGHTWEIGHT
(68 kg—149 ½ lbs)

1896–1900 not held

1904 St. Louis C: 10, N: 1, D: 10.15.
(65.77 kg—145 lbs)

		FINAL MATCH	
1. Otto Roehm	USA	Dec	15:00
2. Rudolph Tesing	USA		
3. Albert Zirkel	USA		

1906 not held

1908 London C: 11, N: 2, D: 7.24.
(66.6 kg—147 lbs)

		FINAL MATCH
1. George de Relwyskow	GBR	Dec 15:00; Dec 15:00
2. William Wood	GBR	
3. Albert Gingell	GBR	
4. George MacKenzie	GBR	

De Relwyskow had already won a silver medal in the Middleweight division when he took first place against the lightweights.

1912 not held

1920 Antwerp C: 11, N: 7, D: 8.27.
(67.5 kg—149 lbs)

		FINAL MATCH
1. Kaarlo "Kalle" Anttila	FIN	Dec
2. Gottfrid Svensson	SWE	
3. Peter Wright	GBR	
4. Auguste Thys	BEL	

1924 Paris C: 16, N: 10, D: 7.14.
(66 kg—145½ lbs)

1. Russell Vis	USA
2. Volmari Vikström	FIN
3. Arvo Haavisto	FIN
4. George Gardner	GBR
5. William Montgomery	CAN
5. Emile Pouvroux	FRA

1928 Amsterdam C: 11, N: 11, D: 8.1.
(66 kg—145½ lbs)

1. Osvald Käpp	EST
2. Charles Pacôme	FRA
3. Eino Leino	FIN
4. Birger Nilsen	NOR
5. Carlo Tesdorf Jörgensen	DEN
6. Clarence Berryman	USA

1932 Los Angeles C: 8, N: 8, D: 8.3.
(66 kg—145½ lbs)

1. Charles Pacôme	FRA
2. Károly Kárpáti	HUN
3. Gustaf Klarén	SWE
4. Melvin Clodfelter	USA
5. Kustaa Pihlajamäki	FIN

In the 1928 final, Pacôme, a law student, had lost a controversial decision to Osvald Käpp. Four years later in Los Angeles, the two met again in the first round. This time Pacôme won on points. Three more victories later, he was awarded the gold medal.

1936 Berlin C: 17, N: 17, D: 8.4.
(66 kg—145½ lbs)

		ROUND ELIMINATED	PEN. PTS.	FINAL ROUND
1. Károly Kárpáti	HUN	—	3	1
2. Wolfgang Ehrl	GER	—	4	2
3. Hermanni Pihlajamäki	FIN	—	4	6

4. Charles Delporte	FRA	5	6
5. Harley De Witt Strong	USA	4	5
6. Paride Romagnoli	ITA	4	7
7. Eiichi Kazama	JPN	4	5
8. Adalbert Toots	EST	4	7

1948 London C: 18, N: 18, D: 7.31.
(67 kg—147½ lbs)

		ROUND ELIMINATED	PEN. PTS.
1. Celal Atik	TUR	—	1
2. Gösta Frändfors	SWE	6	6
3. Hermann Baumann	SWI	6	8
4. Garibaldo Nizzola	ITA	6	10
5. William Koll	USA	4	6
6. Kim Suk-young	KOR	4	7
6. Sulo Leppänen	FIN	4	7
8. László Bakos	HUN	3	5

Atik won five of his six bouts by falls and defeated Leppänen on points.

1952 Helsinki C: 23, N: 23, D: 7.23.
(67 kg—147½ lbs)

		ROUND ELIMINATED	PEN. PTS.	FINAL ROUND
1. Olle Anderberg	SWE	—	1	2
2. Jay Thomas Evans	USA	—	2	4
3. Jahanbakht Towfigh	IRN	—	4	6
4. Armenak Yaltyryan	SOV/UKR	5	7	
5. Risto Talosela	FIN	5	7	
6. Heinrich Nettesheim	GER	4	6	
6. Takeo Shimotori	JPN	4	6	
8. Jan Cools	BEL	4	7	
8. Godfey Pienaar	SAF	4	7	

1956 Melbourne C: 19, N: 19, D: 12.1.
(67 kg—147½ lbs)

		ROUND ELIMINATED	PEN. PTS.
1. Emamali Habibi Goudarzi	IRN	—	4
2. Shigeru Kasahara	JPN	5	6
3. Alimberg Bestayev	SOV/RUS	6	6
4. Gyula Tóth	HUN	5	5
5. Jay Thomas Evans	USA	4	5
5. Garibaldo Nizzola	ITA	4	5
7. Mario Tovar González	MEX	4	7
8. Muhammad Ashraf	PAK	4	7

1960 Rome C: 24, N: 24, D: 9.6.
(67 kg—147½ lbs)

		ROUND ELIMINATED	PEN. PTS.	FINAL ROUND
1. Shelby Wilson	USA	—	5	1
2. Volodymyr Synyavsky	SOV/UKR	—	5	3
3. Enyu Dimov	BUL	6	6	
4. Bong Chang-won	KOR	6	8	
4. Mostafa Tajik	IRN	6	8	

		ROUND ELIMI-NATED	PEN. PTS.	FINAL ROUND
6. Garibaldo Nizzola	ITA	5	7	
7. Martti Peltoniemi	FIN	5	8	
8. Kazuo Abe	JPN	4	8	
8. Raymond Lougheed	CAN	4	8	
8. Hayrullah Sahin	TUR	4	8	

Shelby Wilson of Ponca City, Oklahoma, won the gold medal without registering a single fall.

1964 Tokyo C: 22, N: 22, D: 10.14.
(70 kg—154½ lbs)

		ROUND ELIMI-NATED	PEN. PTS.	FINAL ROUND
1. Enyu Vulchev (Dimov)	BUL	—	5	1
2. Klaus-Jürgen Rost	GER	—	5	3
3. Iwao Horiuchi	JPN	5	6	
4. Mahmut Atalay	TUR	5	6	
5. Abdollah Movahhed Ardabili	IRN	5	7	
6. Zarbeg Beriashvili	SOV/GEO	4	6	
6. Chung Dong-goo	KOR	4	6	
6. Gregory Ruth	USA	4	6	

1968 Mexico City C: 26, N: 26, D: 10.20.
(70 kg—154½ lbs)

		ROUND ELIMI-NATED	PEN. PTS.	FINAL ROUND
1. Abdollah Movahhed Ardabili	IRN	—	4	1
2. Enyu Vulchev (Dimov)	BUL	—	4	3
3. Danzandarja Sereeter	MGL	6	7.5	
4. Wayne Wells	USA	6	8	
5. Zarbeg Beriashvili	SOV/GEO	5	6	
6. Udey Chand	IND	5	6	
7. Iwao Horiuchi	JPN	5	8	
8. Klaus-Jürgen Rost	GER	5	9.5	

1972 Munich C: 25, N: 25, D: 8.31.

		ROUND ELIMI-NATED	PEN. PTS.	FINAL ROUND
1. Danny Gable	USA	—	1.5	2
2. Kikuo Wada	JPN	—	4.5	3
3. Ruslan Ashuraliyev	SOV/RUS	—	4.5	6
4. Tsedendamba Natsagdorj	MGL	5	6	
5. Ali Sahin	TUR	5	6	
6. Udo Schröder	GDR	5	8	
7. Wlodzimierz Cieślak	POL	5	8.5	
8. József Rusznyák	HUN	4	7	

Twenty-three-year-old Dan Gable of Waterloo, Iowa, trained seven hours a day, every day, for three years prior to the Munich Olympics. Between 1963 and 1973 he compiled a record of 299 wins, 6 loses and 3 draws. In 1984 he served as the coach of the U.S. Olympic freestyle wrestling team.

1976 Montreal C: 24, N: 24, D: 7.31.

		ROUND ELIMI-NATED	PEN. PTS.	FINAL ROUND
1. Pavlo Pinigin	SOV/UKR	—	6	3.5
2. Lloyd "Butch" Keaser	USA	—	1	3.5
3. Yasaburo Sugawara	JPN	—	6	5
4. Doncho Zhekov	BUL	6	8.5	
5. José Ramos	CUB	5	7	
6. Tsedendamba Natsagdorj	MGL	5	7	
7. Rami Miron	ISR	5	9	
8. Eberhard Probst	GDR	4	6.5	

Pinigin outpointed Keaser 12–1 in the final match.

1980 Moscow C: 18, N: 18, D: 7.29.

		ROUND ELIMINATED	PEN. PTS.	FINAL ROUND
1. Saipulla Absaidov	SOV/RUS	—	1	1
2. Ivan Yankov	BUL	—	5	4
3. Saban Sejdi	YUG	—	2	7
4. Jagmander Singh	IND	5	6	
5. Eberhard Probst	GDR	5	7.5	
6. Octavian Dusa	ROM	4	7	
7. Ali Hussain Faris	IRQ	4	8	
8. Pekka Rauhala	FIN	4	9.5	

Absaidov outscored his five opponents 59–1, with only Yankov lasting the full nine minutes.

1984 Los Angeles-Anaheim C: 22, N: 22, D: 8.11.

		FINAL MATCH	
1. You In-tak	KOR	5–5	6:00
2. Andrew Rein	USA		
3. Jukka Rauhala	FIN	Injury	3:02
4. Masakazu Kamimura	JPN		
5. Zsigmond Kelevitz	AUS	11–3	6:00
6. Fevzi Seker	TÜR		
7. Erwin Knosp	GER		
8. René Neyer	SWI		

You scored an early 3-point arm throw which eventually gave him the victory. In the second period he suffered a lower back spasm requiring two injury time-outs. He had to be helped onto the victory podium and supported by security personnel during the playing of the Korean national anthem.

1988 Seoul C: 30, N: 30, D: 10.1.

		FINAL MATCH	
1. Arsen Fadzayev	SOV/RUS	6–0	6:00
2. Park Jang-soon	KOR		
3. Nate Carr	USA	5–1	6:00
4. Kosei Akaishi	JPN		
5. David McKay	CAN	4–1	6:00
6. Jukka Rauhala	FIN		
7. Alexander Leipold	GER	14–10	6:00
8. Angel Yasenov	BUL		

Fadzayev, undefeated in international competition and a four-time world champion, overwhelmed each of his six opponents. Park qualified for the final by gaining a controversial 3–2 victory over Carr, which led to the suspension of the officials in charge of the match.

1992 Barcelona C: 21, N: 21, D: 8.5.

			FINAL MATCH
1.	Arsen Fadzayev	RUS	13–1
2.	Valentin Getzov	BUL	
3.	Kosei Akaishi	JPN	4–0
4.	Ali Akbarnejad	IRN	
5.	Fatih Özbaş	TUR	3–1
6.	Ko Young-ho	KOR	
7.	Townsend Saunders	USA	6–3
8.	Christopher Wilson	CAN	

Fadzayev gave up only three points in his five matches.

WELTERWEIGHT
(74 kg—163 lbs)

1896–1900 not held

1904 St. Louis C: 10, N: 1, D: 10.15.
(71.67 kg—158 lbs)

			FINAL MATCH
1.	Charles Erickson	USA	Dec 15:00
2.	William Beckmann	USA	
3.	Jerry Winholtz	USA	

Erickson was a member of the Norwegian Turnverein of Brooklyn.

1906–1920 not held

1924 Paris C: 13, N: 7, D: 7.14.
(72 kg—158½ lbs)
1. Hermann Gehri   SWI
2. Eino Leino   FIN
3. Otto Müller   SWI
4. Guy Lookabough   USA
5. William Johnson   USA

1928 Amsterdam C: 11, N: 11, D: 8.1.
(72 kg—158½ lbs)
1. Arvo Haavisto   FIN
2. Lloyd Appelton   USA
3. Maurice Letchford   CAN
4. Jean Jourlin   FRA
5. T. Harry Morris   AUS

1932 Los Angeles C: 9, N: 9, D: 8.3.
(72 kg—158½ lbs)
1. Jack Van Bebber   USA
2. Daniel MacDonald   CAN
3. Eino Leino   FIN

4. Jean Földeak   GER
5. Gyula Zombori   HUN

1936 Berlin C: 16, N: 16, D: 8.4.
(72 kg—158½ lbs)

			ROUND ELIMINATED	PEN. PTS.	FINAL ROUND
1.	Frank Lewis	USA	—	3	3
2.	Ture Andersson	SWE	—	4	3
3.	Joseph Schleimer	CAN	—	3	6
4.	Jean Jourlin	FRA	5	5	
5.	Willy Angst	SWI	5	7	
6.	Josef Paar	GER	4	5	
7.	Julien Beke	BEL	3	6	
7.	Huseyin Erçetin	TUR	3	6	
7.	John O'Hara	AUS	3	6	

Frank Lewis of Cushing, Oklahoma, was awarded first place even though he was thrown by Andersson in the fourth round. Bronze medalist Joe Schleimer was forced to pay his own way to Berlin. This was not an easy task, considering that he was unemployed. He was able to contribute one-third of his expenses, but the rest came from a fund organized by the Toronto German Club and the local Catholic church.

1948 London C: 16, N: 16, D: 7.31.
(73 kg—161 lbs)

			ROUND ELIMINATED	PEN. PTS.	FINAL ROUND
1.	Yaşar Doğu	TUR	—	0	1
2.	Richard Garrard	AUS	—	2	5
3.	Leland Merrill	USA	—	3	4
4.	Jean-Baptiste Leclerc	FRA	4	6	
5.	Kálmán Sóvári	HUN	4	7	
6.	Frans Westergren	SWE	3	5	
7.	Willy Angst	SWI	3	6	
7.	Harry Peace	CAN	3	6	
7.	Whang Byung-kwan	KOR	3	6	
7.	Abbas Zandi	IRN	3	6	

1952 Helsinki C: 20, N: 20, D: 7.23.
(73 kg—161 lbs)

			ROUND ELIMINATED	PEN. PTS.	FINAL ROUND
1.	William Smith	USA	—	2	4
2.	Per Berlin	SWE	—	3	4
3.	Abdollah Mojtabavi	IRN	—	4	4
4.	Alberto Longarela	ARG	4	5	
5.	Mohamed Hassan Moussa	EGY	4	6	
5.	Ladislav Sekal	CZE	4	6	
5.	Tsuguo Yamazaki	JPN	4	6	
8.	Aleksanteri Keisala	FIN	4	7	

Twenty-three-year-old Bill Smith of Cedar Falls, Iowa, was so surprised by his victory that at the medal ceremony he mounted the third-place stand instead of the winner's pedestal.

1956 Melbourne C: 15, N: 15, D: 12.1.
(73 kg—161 lbs)

		ROUND ELIMI-NATED	PEN. PTS.	FINAL ROUND
1. Mitsuo Ikeda	JPN	—	3	2
2. Ibrahim Zengin	TUR	—	4	3
3. Vakhtang Balavadze	SOV/GEO	—	4	6
4. Per Berlin	SWE	4	5	
4. Nabi Sorouri	IRN	4	5	
4. Coenraad de Villiers	SAF	4	5	
7. Mitjus Petkov	BUL	4	6	
8. Ernest Fischer	USA	3	7	
8. Alfred Tischendorf	GDR	3	7	

1960 Rome C: 23, N: 23, D: 9.6.
(73 kg—161 lbs)

		ROUND ELIMI-NATED	PEN. PTS.	FINAL ROUND
1. Douglas Blubaugh	USA	—	0	1
2. Ismail Ogan	TUR	—	4	4
3. Muhammed Bashir	PAK	—	5	7
4. Gaetano De Vescovi	ITA	5	7	
4. Emamali Habibi Goudarzi	IRN	5	7	
4. Yutaka Kaneko	JPN	5	7	
7. Coenraad de Villiers	SAF	4	7	
8. Åxe Carlsson	SWE	4	8	

Doug Blubaugh of Ponca City, Oklahoma, qualified for the U.S. team by beating his former Oklahoma State teammate Phil Kinyon, after four scoreless draws. In fact, Blubaugh and Kinyon had drawn ten straight matches before Blubaugh finally won a decision. In Rome he tore through the opposition, winning five of his seven bouts by throws and one by default. Only Ogan lasted the full 12 minutes.

1964 Tokyo C: 22, N: 22, D: 10.14.
(78 kg—172 lbs)

		ROUND ELIMI-NATED	PEN. PTS.	FINAL ROUND
1. Ismail Ogan	TUR	—	4	4
2. Guliko Sagaradze	SOV/GEO	—	4	4
3. Mohammad Ali Sanatkaran	IRN	—	4	4
4. Petko Dermendzhiev	BUL	5	8	
5. Yasuo Watanabe	JPN	4	6	
6. Philip Oberlander	CAN	4	6	
7. Muhammad Afzal	PAK	4	7	
8. Madho Singh	IND	4	8	

Ogan was awarded first place because he weighed 2 kg (4.4 lbs) less than Sagaradze. Sanatkaran was relegated to third place because his two draws came in the final round.

1968 Mexico City C: 19, N: 19, D: 10.20.
(78 kg—172 lbs)

		ROUND ELIMI-NATED	PEN. PTS.	FINAL ROUND
1. Mahmut Atalay	TUR	—	4.5	1
2. Daniel Robin	FRA	—	5	3
3. Dagvasuren Purev	MGL	5	6	
4. Ali Mohammad Momeni	IRN	5	6.5	
5. Tatsuo Sasaki	JPN	5	6.5	
6. Yuri Schakmuradov	SOV/AZR	5	8	
7. Stephen Combs	USA	5	8	
7. Angel Sotirov	BUL	5	8	

In 1968, Daniel Robin won silver medals in both the freestyle and Greco-Roman competitions.

1972 Munich C: 25, N: 25, D: 8.31.

		ROUND ELIMINATED	PEN. PTS.	FINAL ROUND
1. Wayne Wells	USA	—	2	2
2. Jan Karlsson	SWE	—	4	4
3. Adolf Seger	GER		5	6
4. Yancho Pavlov	BUL	6	7.5	
5. Mansour Barzegar	IRN	5	7	
5. Wolfgang Nitschke	GDR	5	7	
5. Daniel Robin	FRA	5	7	
8. Miklós Urbanovics	HUN	4	6.5	

Wells was a lawyer from Norman, Oklahoma.

1976 Montreal C: 21, N: 21, D: 7.31.

		ROUND ELIMINATED	PEN. PTS.	FINAL ROUND
1. Jiichiro Date	JPN	—	0	1
2. Mansour Barzegar	IRN	—	2	5
3. Stanley Dziedzic	USA	—	2	6
4. Ruslan Ashuraliyev	SOV/RUS	5	7.5	
5. Marin Pircalabu	ROM	5	9	
6. Fred Hempel	GDR	5	10	
7. Jarmo Overmark	FIN	4	7	
8. Kiro Ristov	YUG	4	8	

Date threw six of his seven opponents and outpointed Dziedzic 10–5.

1980 Moscow C: 18, N: 18, D: 7.30.

		ROUND ELIMINATED	PEN. PTS.	FINAL ROUND
1. Valentin Angelov	BUL	—	2	2
2. Jamtsyin Davajav	MGL	—	6	4
3. Dan Karabin	CZE/SLV	—	7.5	6
4. Anatoly Pinigin	SOV/UKR	6	8.5	
5. Ryszard Ścigalski	POL	5	7	
6. Rajander Singh	IND	4	7	
7. István Fehér	HUN	4	9	
8. Riccardo Niccolini	ITA	4	9	

Angelov earned his gold medal by gaining five victories in one day. The big surprise was his win against Pinigin. Pinigin took Angelov to the mat twice in the first minute, but the Bulgarian came back to register a fall after 1:59.

In the final match Angelov won on points, 6–5, over Davajav.

1984 Los Angeles-Anaheim C: 22, N: 22, D: 8.10.

			FINAL MATCH	
1.	David Schultz	USA	4–1	6:00
2.	Martin Knosp	GER		
3.	Šaban Sejdi	YUG	5–1	6:00
4.	Rajender Singh	IND		
5.	Naomi Higuchi	JPN	7–3	6:00
6.	Han Myung-woo	KOR		
7.	Marc Mongeon	CAN		
8.	Pekka Rauhala	FIN		

The only defending world champion freestyle wrestler to take part in the 1984 Olympics, Dave Schultz won one match by a fall and his other five by a combined score of 42–2. Twenty-four hours after Schultz was awarded his gold medal, his younger brother, Mark, won the middleweight division. Dave retired from competition in 1987 but then began a successful comeback in 1993. He placed fifth at the 1995 world championships, and when the Olympic year of 1996 began he was ranked first in the United States. However, on January 26, he was shot to death by John du Pont, one of the major sponsors of the U.S. freestyle wrestling team.

1988 Seoul C: 30, N: 30, D: 9.30.

			FINAL MATCH	
1.	Kenneth Monday	USA	5–2	6:42
2.	Adlan Varayev	SOV/RUS		
3.	Rakhmad Sukra Sofiyadi	BUL	8–3	6:00
4.	Lodoin Enkhbayer	MGL		
5.	Pekka Rauhala	FIN	Injury	3:00
6.	Ayatollah Vagozari	IRN		
7.	Yoon Kyung-jae	KOR	Injury	
8.	Uwe Westendorf	GDR		

Kenny Monday of Tulsa, Oklahoma, qualified for the final by pinning one opponent and outscoring six others 34–2. For the gold medal, he faced defending world champion Adlan Varayev, who had beaten him in two of their three previous meetings. Neither man scored for over 4 minutes. Then, with 1:45 remaining, Monday took a 1–0 lead with a single-leg pick. Forty-five seconds later Varayev scored with a double-leg takedown to move ahead 2–1. With 17 seconds left, Monday evened the match with a crotch lift reversal. Forty seconds into the sudden death overtime, Monday caught the tiring Varayev in a bodylock, lifted him into the air, and slammed him to the mat for a 3-point takedown. Monday was the first black wrestler to win an Olympic gold medal.

1992 Barcelona C: 18, N: 18, D: 8.6.

			FINAL MATCH	
1.	Park Jang-soon	KOR	1–0	
2.	Kenneth Monday	USA		
3.	Amir Khadem Azghadi	IRN	1–0	6:32
4.	Magomedsalam Gadjiev	RUS		

5.	Krzysztof Walencik	POL	
6.	Gary Holmes	CAN	
7.	János Nagy	HUN	Injury
8.	Lodoin Enkhbayer	MGL	

Park outpointed his pool opponents 25–3; Monday outpointed his 14–0. Both men wrestled cautiously in the final. As the clock ticked down, Monday attacked. Park countered and scored a one-point takedown with 15 seconds left in the match. In the end Monday gave up only that single point in five matches, but he had to settle for second place. Toshihiko Hara of Japan qualified for the match for fifth place, but refused to take part and was disqualified. Walencik and Holmes were awarded their places without a final match.

MIDDLEWEIGHT
(82 kg—181 lbs)

1896–1906 not held

1908 London C: 12, N: 3, D: 7.21.
(73 kg—161 lbs)

			FINAL MATCH
1.	Stanley Bacon	GBR	Dec; Dec
2.	George de Relwyskow	GBR	
3.	Frederick Beck	GBR	
4.	Carl Georg Anderson	SWE	
5.	Edgar Bacon (GBR), Aubrey Coleman (GBR)		

Bacon was 5 feet 3½ inches tall.

1912 not held

1920 Antwerp C: 18, N: 12, D: 8.27.
(75 kg—165½ lbs)

			FINAL MATCH
1.	Eino Leino	FIN	Dec
2.	Väinö Penttala	FIN	
3.	Charles Johnson	USA	
4.	Angus Frantz	USA	
5.	Otto Borgström (SWE), Pierre Derkinderen (BEL), Gudmund Grimstad (NOR), Frits Janssens (BEL)		

1924 Paris C: 14, N: 9, D: 7.14.
(79 kg—174 lbs)

1.	Fritz Hagmann	SWI
2.	Pierre Ollivier	BEL
3.	Viho Pekkala	FIN
4.	Jaako Penttilä	FIN
5.	Robert Christoffersen	DEN
5.	Noel Rhys	GBR

1928 Amsterdam C: 9, N: 9, D: 8.1.
(79 kg—174 lbs)

1.	Ernst Kyburz	SWI
2.	Donald Stockton	CAN
3.	Samuel Rabin	GBR
4.	Ralph Hammond	USA
5.	Andries Praeg	SAF

1932 Los Angeles C: 7, N: 7, D: 8.3.
(79 kg—174 lbs)

1. Ivar Johansson   SWE
2. Kyösti Luukko   FIN
3. József Tunyogi   HUN
4. Robert Hess   USA
5. Sumiyuki Kotani   JPN
6. Emile Poilvé   FRA

This was the first of Johansson's three Olympic gold medals. Four days later he won the Greco-Roman Welterweight division and four *years* later, in Berlin, he was victorious as a Greco-Roman middleweight.

1936 Berlin C: 15, N: 15, D: 8.4.
(79 kg—174 lbs)

		ROUND ELIMINATED	PEN. PTS.	FINAL ROUND
1. Emile Poilvé	FRA	—	1	0
2. Richard Voliva	USA	—	3	3
3. Ahmet Kireçci	TUR	5	6	
4. Ernst Krebs	SWI	5	7	
5. Jaroslav Sysel	CZE	4	6	
6. Kyösti Luukko	FIN	4	7	
7. Ercole Gallegati	ITA	3	5	
8. János Riheczky	HUN	3	5	

Poilvé registered five throws in six matches, as well as a second-round decision over Luukko.

1948 London C: 16, N: 16, D: 7.31.
(79 kg—174 lbs)

		ROUND ELIMINATED	PEN. PTS.	FINAL ROUND
1. Glen Brand	USA	—	2	0
2. Adil Candemir	TUR	—	4	3
3. Erik Lindén	SWE	5	5	
4. Carel Reitz	SAF	4	5	
5. Paavo Sepponen	FIN	4	5	
6. André Brunaud	FRA	4	7	
7. Maurice Vachon	CAN	3	5	
8. Bruce Arthur	AUS	3	6	

Twenty-four-year-old Glen Brand of Clarion, Iowa, was awarded first place after he threw Candemir in the fourth round and then decisioned Lindén in Round 5.

1952 Helsinki C: 17, N: 17, D: 7.23.
(79 kg—174 lbs)

		ROUND ELIMINATED	PEN. PTS.	FINAL ROUND
1. David Tsimakuridze	SOV/ GEO	—	4	2
2. J. P. Gholam Reza Takhti	IRN	—	2	3
3. György Gurics	HUN	—	5	6
4. Gustav Gocke	GER	5	6	
5. Haydar Zafer	TUR	4	5	
6. Leon Genuth	ARG	4	7	
6. Carel Reitz	SAF	4	7	
8. Bengt Lindblad	SWE	3	5	

1956 Melbourne C: 15, N: 15, D: 12.1.
(79 kg—174 lbs)

		ROUND ELIMINATED	PEN. PTS.	FINAL ROUND
1. Nikola Stanchev	BUL	—	4	1
2. Daniel Hodge	USA	—	4	3
3. Georgy Skhirtladze	SOV/GEO	—	4	6
4. Ismet Atli	TUR	5	5	
5. Kazuo Katsuramoto	JPN	4	6	
5. Johann Sterr	GER	4	6	
7. Bengt Lindblad	SWE	3	7	
7. Abbas Zandi	IRN	3	7	

Stanchev was the first Bulgarian to win an Olympic gold medal.

1960 Rome C: 19, N: 19, D: 9.6.
(79 kg—174 lbs)

		ROUND ELIMINATED	PEN. PTS.
1. Hasan Güngör	TUR	—	4
2. Georgy Skhirtladze	SOV/GEO	5	6
3. Hans Yngve Antonsson	SWE	5	6
4. Edward De Witt	USA	5	7
5. Prodan Gardzhev	BUL	4	6
5. Géza Hollósi	HUN	4	6
5. Madho Singh	IND	4	6
8. Takashi Nagai	JPN	4	7

1964 Tokyo C: 16, N: 16, D: 10.14.
(87 kg—192 lbs)

		ROUND ELIMINATED	PEN. PTS.	FINAL ROUND
1. Prodan Gardzhev	BUL	—	5	2
2. Hasan Güngör	TUR	—	5	2
3. Daniel Brand	USA	5	6	
4. Mansour Mehdizadeh	IRN	5	6	
5. Géza Hollósi	HUN	4	6	
5. Tatsuo Sasaki	JPN	4	6	
7. Günther Bauch	GDR	4	9	
7. Faiz Muhammad	PAK	4	9	

Güngör was deprived of a second gold medal because he outweighed Gardzhev by 1 kg (2.2 lbs).

1968 Mexico City C: 22, N: 22, D: 10.20.
(87 kg—192 lbs)

		ROUND ELIMINATED	PEN. PTS.
1. Borys Hurevych	SOV/UKR	—	4.5
2. Jigjid Munkhbat	MGL	7	6.5
3. Prodan Gardzhev	BUL	7	7.5
4. Thomas Peckham	USA	7	8
5. Hüseyin Gürsoy	TUR	6	7
6. Peter Döring	GDR	4	6
7. Ronald Grinstead	GBR	4	8
8. Shigeru Endo	JPN	4	8.5

Hurevych finished the tournament with draws against Munkhbat and Gardzhev. He later served as a model for the sculpture "We Shall Beat Swords into Ploughshares" by Yerhen Vuchetych that stands in front of the United Nations building in New York City.

1972 Munich C: 24, N: 24, D: 8.31.

		ROUND ELIMINATED	PEN. PTS.
1.	Levan Tediashvili SOV/GEO	—	4.5
2.	John Peterson USA	6	6
3.	Vasile Iorga ROM	6	7
4.	Horst Stottmeister GDR	6	7
5.	Tatsuo Sasaki JPN	5	6
6.	Peter Neumair GER	5	7
7.	Kurt Elmgren SWE	4	6
8.	Jan Wypiórczyk POL	4	7

1976 Montreal C: 18, N: 18, D: 7.31.

		ROUND ELIMINATED	PEN. PTS.	FINAL ROUND
1.	John Peterson USA	—	2	0.5
2.	Viktor Novozhilov SOV/RUS	—	5.5	5
3.	Adolf Seger GER	—	6.5	6.5
4.	Mehmet Uzun TUR	6	7.5	
5.	Ismail Abilov BUL	5	7.5	
6.	Henryk Mazur POL	4	6	
7.	István Kovács HUN	4	6	
8.	Masaru Motegi JPN	4	8	

In 1972 John Peterson of Comstock, Wisconsin, won a silver medal, while his brother, Ben, a light heavyweight, won a gold. Four years later in Montreal they reversed medals.

1980 Moscow C: 14, N: 14, D: 7.31.

		ROUND ELIMINATED	PEN. PTS.	FINAL ROUND
1.	Ismail Abilov BUL	—	1	1
2.	Magomedhan Aratsilov SOV/RUS	—	3	3
3.	István Kovács HUN	—	4	8
4.	Henryk Mazur POL	5	8.5	
5.	Abdula Memedi YUG	4	7	
6.	Zevegying Duvchin MGL	4	8	
7.	Gunter Busarello AUT	3	7	
8.	Mohammad Eloulabi SYR	3	7.5	

Abilov outpointed his five opponents 50–5. Only Aratsilov lasted nine minutes, losing a fifth-round 8–4 decision to the 29-year-old Bulgarian champion.

1984 Los Angeles-Anaheim C: 16, N: 16, D: 8.11.

		FINAL MATCH	
1.	Mark Schultz USA	13–0	1:59
2.	Hideyuki Nagashima JPN		
3.	Chris Rinke CAN	5–2	6:00
4.	Reiner Trik GER		
5.	Kim Tae-woo KOR	10–3	6:00
6.	Kenneth Reinsfield NZE		
7.	Iraklis Deskoulidis GRE		
8.	Luciano Ortelli ITA		

With all of the top four 82 kg wrestlers boycotted out of the Olympics, the favorites' role fell to Resit Karabacek of Turkey and Mark Schultz, younger brother of 74 kg champion Dave Schultz. As it happened, Karabacek and Schultz met in the first round. Only 30 seconds into the match Karabacek, who had never before been pinned, was thrown by a single leg counter and the match was over. As Karabacek writhed in agony, having suffered a fractured left elbow, Schultz happily paraded around the mat, showing no interest in his opponent's condition. After escorting Karabacek to the hospital, Turkish officials filed a protest, claiming that Schultz had used an illegal hold. Their protest was upheld and Karabacek, who was unable to continue, was declared the winner by disqualification. However, because the protest was filed more than 30 minutes after the match ended, Schultz was not disqualified from the tournament. An extra judge was assigned to scrutinize the Schultz brothers during the remainder of the competition. Mark Schultz then put together four straight victories to match his brother's gold medal.

1988 Seoul C: 29, N: 29, D: 10.1.

		FINAL MATCH	
1.	Han Myung-woo KOR	4–0	6:00
2.	Necmi Gencalp TUR		
3.	Josef Lohyňa CZE	Passivity	7:54
4.	Aleksandr Tambovtsev SOV/RUS		
5.	Puntsag Suhbat MGL	Injury	
6.	Mark Schultz USA		
7.	Atsushi Ito JPN	5–4	6:29
8.	Hans Gstöttner GDR		

1992 Barcelona C: 19, N: 19, D: 8.7.

		FINAL MATCH	
1.	Kevin Jackson USA	1–0	6:54
2.	Elmadi Zhabrailov RUS		
3.	Rasul Khadem Azghadi IRN	6–0	
4.	Hans Gstöttner GER		
5.	Josef Lohyňa CZE	2–2	10:05
6.	Sebahattin Öztürk TUR		
7.	Nicolae Ghita ROM	4–1	
8.	Francisco Iglesias Serna SPA		

In the final, 1991 world champion Kevin Jackson faced 1989 world champion Elmadi Zhabrailov. They were evenly matched and regulation time ended in a scoreless tie. Forty-six seconds into sudden-death overtime, Zhabrailov secured a deep leg attack. As Jackson scrambled to counterattack, the wrestlers moved out of bounds. The referee, Todor Grudev of Bulgaria, signaled for the action to continue. Zhabrailov's team coach, two-time gold medalist Ivan Yarygin, immediately protested that his man had controlled Jackson and deserved a point, and with it the match and the gold medal. The match was resumed after several minutes and after another minute of fighting, Jackson won with a one-point double-leg takedown. Jackson called out, "Gold medal! Gold medal!" and began celebrating with his supporters. Meanwhile, to say that Zhabrailov was disheartened would be an understatement. He cried and screamed and was inconsolable. When it came time for the medal ceremony, Zhabrailov had to be pushed onto the podium. He accepted his silver medal, but refused to put it around his neck. Although Zhabrailov held nothing against Jackson personally and did not hesitate to congratulate him, the Russian's supporters whipped the crowd into a frenzy and the "Star-Spangled Banner" was drowned out by whistling and booing. The International Wrestling Federation rejected a formal protest on the basis that the official video of the disputed non-point was inconclusive.

LIGHT HEAVYWEIGHT
(90 kg—198 ½ lbs)

1896–1912 not held

1920 Antwerp C: 13, N: 8, D: 8.27.
(80 kg–186½ lbs)

		FINAL MATCH
1. Anders Larsson	SWE	Forfeit
2. Charles Courant	SWI	
3. Walter Maurer	USA	
4. John Redman	USA	

1924 Paris C: 16, N: 10, D: 7.14.
(87 kg—192 lbs)

1. John Spellman	USA
2. Rudolf Svensson	SWE
3. Charles Courant	SWI
4. Carl Westergren	SWE
5. Walter Wilson	GBR
6. George Rumple	CAN

1928 Amsterdam C: 7, N: 7, D: 8.1.
(87 kg—192 lbs)

1. Thure Sjöstedt	SWE
2. Arnold Bögli	SWI
3. Henri Lefèbre	FRA
4. Heywood Edwards	USA
5. Jacques van Assche	BEL

1932 Los Angeles C: 4, N: 4, D: 8.3.
(87 kg—192 lbs)

1. Peter Mehringer	USA
2. Thure Sjöstedt	SWE
3. Eddie Scarf	AUS
4. Henry Madison	CAN

Pete Mehringer of Kinsley, Kansas, first learned how to wrestle from a correspondence course. After the Olympics, he played professional football and worked as a stuntman in Hollywood. His credits included *Knute Rockne, All-American*.

1936 Berlin C: 12, N: 12, D: 8.4.
(87 kg—192 lbs)

		ROUND ELIMINATED	PEN. PTS.	FINAL ROUND
1. Knut Fridell	SWE	—	2	1
2. August Neo	EST	—	5	4
3. Erich Siebert	GER	—	5	6
4. Paul Dätwyler	SWI	4	6	
5. Ray Clemons	USA	4	7	
6. Eddie Scarf	AUS	3	5	
7. Hubert Prokop	CZE	3	7	
8. Ede Virág-Ébner	HUN	3	7	

1948 London C: 15, N: 15, D: 7.31.
(87 kg—192 lbs)

		ROUND ELIMINATED	PEN. PTS.	FINAL ROUND
1. Henry Wittenberg	USA	—	1	2
2. Fritz Stöckli	SWI	—	1	3
3. Bengt Fahlkvist	SWE	—	2	4
4. Muharrem Candaş	TUR	5	7	
4. Fernand Payette	CAN	5	7	
6. Patrick Morton	SAF	3	5	
7. Spyros Deftreraios	GRE	3	6	
7. John Sullivan	GBR	3	6	
7. Oscar Verona	ITA	3	6	

Each of the three matches of the final round was an epic struggle and each was decided by a split decision of the judges. Wittenberg was a 29-year-old New York policeman.

1952 Helsinki C: 13, N: 13, D: 7.23.
(87 kg—192 lbs)

		ROUND ELIMINATED	PEN. PTS.	FINAL ROUND
1. Wiking Palm	SWE	—	4	2
2. Henry Wittenberg	USA	—	4	3
3. Adil Atan	TUR	—	6	5
4. August Englas	SOV/EST	5	7	
5. Abbas Zandi	IRN	4	5	
6. Jacob Theron	SAF	3	5	
7. Max Leichter	GER	3	7	

1956 Melbourne C: 12, N: 12, D: 12.1.
(87 kg—192 lbs)

		ROUND ELIMINATED	PEN. PTS.	FINAL ROUND
1. J. P. Gholam Reza Takhti	IRN	—	0	2
2. Boris Kulayev	SOV/RUS	—	2	4
3. Peter Blair	USA	—	4	6
4. Gerald Martina	IRL	4	6	
5. Adil Atan	TUR	4	7	
5. Kevin Coote	AUS	4	7	
7. Mitsuhiro Ohira	JPN	3	7	
7. Wiking Palm	SWE	3	7	
7. Jacob Theron	SAF	3	7	

1960 Rome C: 19, N: 19, D: 9.6.
(87 kg—192 lbs)

		ROUND ELIMI- NATED	PEN. PTS.	FINAL ROUND
1. İsmet Atli	TUR	—	5	1
2. J. P. Gholam Reza Takhti	IRN	—	0	3
3. Anatoly Albul	SOV/RUS	5	6	
4. Wiking Palm	SWE	5	6	
5. Daniel Brand	USA	5	7	
6. Hermanus van Zyl	SAF	5	9	
7. Singh Sajjan	IND	4	8	
8. Kazuo Abe	JPN	4	9	
8. György Gurics	HUN	4	9	

Takhti pinned his first five opponents before losing on points to Atli. Albul was awarded the bronze medal over Palm on the basis of lower bodyweight.

1964 Tokyo C: 16, N: 16, D: 10.14.
(97 kg—214 lbs)

		ROUND ELIMI- NATED	PEN. PTS.	FINAL ROUND
1. Oleksander Medvid	SOV/UKR	—	3	2
2. Ahmet Ayik	TUR	—	5	4
3. Said Mustafov	BUL	—	5	6
4. J. P. Gholam Reza Takhti	IRN	5	6	
5. Peter Jutzeler	SWI	5	9	
6. Gerald Conine	USA	4	6	
7. Heinz Kiehl	GER	4	7	
8. Imre Vigh	HUN	3	6	

Medvid secured the first of his three gold medals by pinning Mustafov in the final bout after only 39 seconds.

1968 Mexico City C: 16, N: 16, D: 10.20.
(97 kg—214 lbs)

		ROUND ELIMI- NATED	PEN. PTS.	FINAL ROUND
1. Ahmet Ayik	TUR	—	4	2
2. Shota Lomidze	SOV/GEO	—	5	3
3. József Csatári	HUN	—	5	7
4. Said Mustafov	BUL	5	6.5	
5. Khorloo Baianmunkh	MGL	5	8.5	
6. Jess Lewis	USA	4	7	
7. Ryszard Dlugosz	POL	4	7	
8. Gerd Bachmann	GDR	3	6	

1972 Munich C: 23, N: 23, D: 8.31.

		ROUND ELIMINATED	PEN. PTS.	FINAL ROUND
1. Benjamin Peterson	USA	—	4	2
2. Gennady Strakhov	SOV/RUS	—	4	2
3. Károly Bajkó	HUN	6	6.5	
4. Russi Petrov	BUL	6	8.5	
5. Reza Khorrami	IRN	5	7	
5. Barbaro Morgan	CUB	5	7	
7. Günter Spindler	GDR	5	8	
8. Gueclue Mehmet	TUR	4	8	

Ben Peterson, whose brother, John, won a silver medal in the Middleweight division, picked up a surprise gold medal by pinning world champion Russi Petrov after 2:41 of his final bout.

1976 Montreal C: 21, N: 21, D: 7.31.

		ROUND ELIMINATED	PEN. PTS.	FINAL ROUND
1. Levan Tediashvili	SOV/GEO	—	1	2
2. Benjamin Peterson	USA	—	3.5	4
3. Stelica Morcov	ROM	—	7	6
4. Horst Stottmeister	GDR	6	7.5	
5. Terry Paice	CAN	5	7	
6. Pawel Kurczewski	POL	5	8.5	
7. Frank Andersson	SWE	5	8.5	
8. Barbaro Morgan	CUB	4	7.5	

One of the greatest amateur wrestlers of all time, Levan "Teddy" Tediashvili had not lost a match since 1971. At the Munich Olympics he had defeated John Peterson to win the Middleweight division. Four years later Tediashvili moved up to Light Heavyweight and outpointed John's brother, Ben, 11–5 for a second gold medal. Tediashvili, a law student and vineyard worker, was a brash performer who was known to wink at pretty women in the crowd just before pinning his opponents. In 1988, Tediashvili played the part of bandit folk-hero Gogi Kenkeshvili in the film *Khareba and Gogi*.

1980 Moscow C: 15, N: 15, D: 7.29.

		ROUND ELIMI- NATED	PEN. PTS.	FINAL ROUND
1. Sanasar Oganisyan	SOV/RUS	—	2	1.5
2. Uwe Neupert	GDR	—	4.5	4
3. Aleksander Cichoń	POL	—	0.5	6.5
4. Ivan Ginov	BUL	5	7	
5. Dashdorj Tserentogtokh	MGL	5	8.5	
6. Christophe Andanson	FRA	4	7	
7. Ion Ivanov	ROM	4	7.5	
8. Mick Pikos	AUS	4	8	

1984 Los Angeles-Anaheim C: 16, N: 16, D: 8.9.

		FINAL MATCH	
1. Edward Banach	USA	15–3	4:02
2. Akira Ota	JPN		
3. Noel Loban	GBR	5–1	6:00
4. Clark Davis	CAN		
5. Macauley Appah	NGR	Injury	
6. Ismail Temiz	TUR		
7. Majeed Abdul	PAK		
8. Michele Azzola	ITA		

On the way to the final, Ed Banach defeated his first three opponents by a combined score of 37–4, and then threw Majeed Abdul of Pakistan in 48 seconds. Ed was the twin brother of Lou Banach, who won the heavyweight division two nights later.

1988 Seoul C: 28, N: 28, D: 9.29.

		FINAL MATCH	
1. Makharbek Khadartsev	SOV/RUS	16–0	3:27
2. Akira Ota	JPN		
3. Kim Tae-woo	KOR	1–0	6:00
4. Gábor Tóth	HUN		
5. James Scherr	USA	3–1	6:00
6. Rumen Alabakov	BUL		
7. Iraklis Deskoulidis	GRE	4–2	6:00
8. Zeveg Duvchin	MGL		

Two-time world champion Makharbek Khadartsev pinned four of his seven opponents and outpointed two more in less than 3½ minutes. Only Edwin Lins of Austria lasted the full 6 minutes and even he lost 10–1. Khadartsev, like 68-kilogram champion Arsen Fadzayev, grew up in the North Ossetian region of Russia.

1992 Barcelona C: 17, N: 17, D: 8.7.

		FINAL MATCH	
1. Makharbek Khadartsev	RUS	1–0	
2. Kennan Şimşek	TUR		
3. Christopher Campbell	USA	3–1	7:23
4. Puntsag Sukhbat	MGL		
5. Ayub Bani Nosrat	IRN	3–1	7:42
6. Roberto Limonta Vargas	CUB		
7. Marek Garmulewicz	POL	0–0	8:00
8. Renato Lombardo	ITA		

Between Olympic Games, Khadartsev won three more world championships. He was not seriously challenged on his way to the final, outscoring four opponents 27–3. In the final, he scored midway through the bout and stuck to defense until time ran out. In addition to the gold medal, Khadartsev received a special prize. As soon as the match ended, referee Lassi Toivola, officiating the last match of his career, placed his whistle around the winner's neck.

Khadartsev had qualified to be an attorney, although he had yet to practice law. Coincidentally, bronze medalist Chris Campbell was a corporate attorney for an air-conditioning company. Like Khadartsev, Campbell was also a world champion—but Campbell's championship had come back in 1981. In 1980 Campbell made the United States Olympic team, but the U.S. boycott kept him out of the competition. In 1984 he injured his right knee one week before the United States Olympic trials and was forced to withdraw. Discouraged, Campbell retired, but came back five years later. A strict vegetarian and proponent of tai chi ch'uan, Campbell finally earned his Olympic medal at age 37.

HEAVYWEIGHT
(100 kg—220 lbs)

1896–1968 not held

1972 Munich C: 17, N: 17, D: 8.31.

		ROUND ELIMINATED	PEN. PTS.	FINAL ROUND
1. Ivan Yarygin	SOV/RUS	—	0	0
2. Khorloo Baianmunkh	MGL	—	1	5
3. József Csatári	HUN	—	2	7
4. Vasil Todorov	BUL	5	7.5	
5. Enache Panait	ROM	5	9	
6. Ryszard Dlugosz	POL	4	7	
7. Abolfazl Anvari	IRN	4	9	
8. Julio Tamussin	ITA	3	6.5	

In an inspired performance, 23-year-old Ivan Yarygin pinned all seven of his opponents. Only Baianmunkh was able to last more than three minutes with the Soviet strongman. Yarygin spent a total of only 17 minutes and eight seconds on the mat in his seven matches.

1976 Montreal C: 15, N: 15, D: 7.31.

		ROUND ELIMINATED	PEN. PTS.	FINAL ROUND
1. Ivan Yarygin	SOV/RUS	—	2	1.5
2. Russell Hellickson	USA	—	3.5	4
3. Dimo Kostov	BUL	—	4.5	6.5
4. Petr Drozda	CZE	5	8	
5. Khorloo Baianmunkh	MGL	4	5.5	
6. Kazuo Shimizu	JPN	4	8	
7. Hans Stratz	GER	3	7	
8. Daniel Vernik	ARG	3	8	

In 1974 Yarygin was beaten in the European championships by Harald Büttner of East Germany. He was immediately removed from the Soviet team and replaced by veteran Vladimir Gulyutkin, who proceeded to win the 1974 world championship. But at the 1975 world championships, Büttner pinned Gulyutkin in 57 seconds and Yarygin was brought back after a year's absence from international competition. At the 1976 European championships, held in Leningrad three months before the Olympics, Yarygin was back to his old ways, overpowering each of his opponents. In Montreal, Yarygin faced Büttner in the very first round and defeated him 13–5. Yarygin's fifth and final victory was his most difficult, a 19–13 verdict over Russ Hellickson of Oregon, Wisconsin, who had moved up from Light Heavyweight to Heavyweight after losing five straight matches to Levan Tediashvili.

1980 Moscow C: 15, N: 15, D: 7.30.

		ROUND ELIMINATED	PEN. PTS.	FINAL ROUND
1. Illya Mate	SOV/UKR	—	2	1
2. Slavcho Chervenkov	BUL	—	3	3.5
3. Július Strnisko	CZE	—	4	7.5
4. Harald Büttner	GDR	5	6.5	
5. Tomasz Busse	POL	5	7	
6. Vasile Puşcaşu	ROM	4	6	
7. Barbaro Morgan	CUB	3	7.5	
8. Khorloo Baianmunkh	MGL	3	8	

1984 Los Angeles-Anaheim C: 11, N: 11, D: 8.11.

		FINAL MATCH	
1. Louis Banach	USA	Fall	1:01
2. Joseph Atiyeh	SYR		
3. Vasile Puşcaşu	ROM	4–3	6:00
4. Hayri Sezgin	TUR		
5. Tamon Honda	JPN	Injury	
6. Georgios Pikilidis	GRE		
7. Kartar Singh Dhillon	IND		
8. Wayne Brightwell	CAN		

Lou Banach, twin brother of light-heavyweight gold medalist Ed Banach, pinned four of his five opponents, all within two minutes. Only Wayne Brightwell lasted the full six minutes. Joseph Atiyeh, a student at Louisiana State University, was the first representative of Syria ever to win an Olympic medal.

1988 Seoul C: 22, N: 22, D: 9.30.

		FINAL MATCH	
1. Vasile Puşcaşu	ROM	1–0	6:00
2. Leri Khabelov	SOV/GEO		
3. William Scherr	USA	Fall	3:31
4. Uwe Neupert	GDR		
5. Georgi Karaduchev	BUL	Fall	1:32
6. Bold Javhlantugs	MGL		
7. Noel Loban	GBR	Injury	
8. Joe Byung-eun	KOR		

Puşcaşu, competing in his third Olympics at the age of 32, upset two-time world champion Khabelov by engineering a single-leg takedown with 19 seconds left in regulation time.

1992 Barcelona C: 18, N: 18, D: 8.5.

		FINAL MATCH	
1. Leri Khabelov	GEO	2–1	
2. Heiko Balz	GER		
3. Ali Kayali	TUR	2–0	
4. Kim Tae-woo	KOR		
5. Andrzej Radomski	POL	2–0	
6. Subhash Verma	IND		
7. Mark Coleman	USA	2–0	
8. Sándor Kiss	HUN		

Four-time world champion Leri Khabelov qualified for the final by outscoring his first five opponents 24–1. Heiko Balz, the other finalist, didn't give up a single point in his five preliminary matches, while scoring 15 points. Khabelov led 1–0, and then 2–0. Balz picked up a point with a little over a minute remaining, but was unable to score again.

SUPER HEAVYWEIGHT
(Heavyweight 1904—1968)

A maximum weight limit—286 lbs. (130 kg)—was imposed for the first time at the 1988 Olympics.

1896–1900 not held

1904 St. Louis T: 5, N: 1, D: 10.15.

		FINAL MATCH	
1. Bernhuff Hansen	USA	Fall	2:00
2. Frank Kungler	USA		
3. Fred Warmbold	USA		

Hansen, a representative of the Norwegian Turnverein of Brooklyn, needed only 7:30 to pin his three opponents. In 1904 anyone over 158 pounds was considered a heavyweight. Currently, a 158-pound wrestler would compete in the Welterweight division.

1906 not held

1908 London C: 11, N: 3, D: 7.23.

		FINAL MATCH
1. George "Con" O'Kelly	GBR/IRL	Fall 13:27; Fall 3:35
2. Jacob Gundersen	NOR	
3. Edward Barrett	GBR/IRL	
4. Edward Nixson	GBR	
5. Lawrence Bruce	GBR	

Shortly before the Olympic Games, Barrett had defeated O'Kelly for the British Heavyweight championship. But at the Olympics the 221-pound O'Kelly came up against Barrett in the third round and pinned him after 2:14. Gundersen put up a tougher battle, and it took O'Kelly 17:02 to keep him on the mat for the required two falls.

1912 not held

1920 Antwerp C: 8, N: 5, D: 8.27.

		FINAL MATCH
1. Robert Roth	SWI	Dec
2. Nathan Pendleton	USA	
3. Frederick Meyer	USA	
3. Ernst Nilsson	SWE	

1924 Paris C: 12, N: 6, D: 7.14.
1. Harry Steel	USA
2. Henri Wernli	SWI
3. Andrew McDonald	GBR
4. Ernst Nilsson	SWE
5. Johan Richthoff	SWE
6. Edmond Dame	FRA

1928 Amsterdam C: 7, N: 7, D: 8.1.
1. Johan Richthoff	SWE
2. Aukusti Sihvola	FIN
3. Edmond Dame	FRA
4. Edward George	USA
5. Henri Wernli	SWI

Edward "Don" George later became a professional wrestling champion.

1932 Los Angeles C: 3, N: 3, D: 8.3.

		PEN. PTS.
1. Johan Richthoff	SWE	2
2. John Riley	USA	3
3. Nikolaus Hirschl	AUT	6

Richthoff was 34 years old when he successfully defended his Olympic title.

1936 Berlin C: 11, N: 11, D: 8.4.

		ROUND ELIMINATED	PEN. PTS.
1. Kristjan Palusalu	EST	—	2
2. Josef Klapuch	CZE	4	4
3. Hjalmar Nyström	FIN	5	5
4. Nils Åkerlindh	SWE	4	4
5. Robert Herland	FRA	4	6
6. Werner Bürki	SWI	4	7
7. Georg Gehring	GER	3	5
8. George Chiga	CAN	3	6

The 27-year-old Palusalu, one of the quiet heroes of the Berlin Games, achieved a rare double by winning the Heavyweight title in both freestyle and Greco-Roman.

1948 London C: 9, N: 9, D: 7.31.

		ROUND ELIMINATED	PEN. PTS.	FINAL ROUND
1. Gyula Bóbis	HUN	—	2	0
2. Bertil Antonsson	SWE	—	3	2
3. Joseph Armstrong	AUS	—	4	6
4. Sadik Esen	TUR	4	7	
5. Josef Ružička	CZE	3	5	
5. Abolghasem Sakhdari	IRN	3	5	
7. Richard Hutton	USA	3	6	

Bóbis began wrestling as a flyweight and kept moving up in division as he grew, until, at the age of 38, he won the Olympic gold medal as a heavyweight.

1952 Helsinki C: 13, N: 13, D: 7.23.

		ROUND ELIMINATED	PEN. PTS.	FINAL ROUND
1. Arsen Mekokishvili	SOV/RUS	—	2	2
2. Bertil Antonsson	SWE	—	2	3
3. Kenneth Richmond	GBR	—	4	6
4. Irfan Atan	TUR	4	5	
5. William Kerslake	USA	4	6	
6. Taisto Kangasniemi	FIN	4	6	
7. Natale Vecchi	ITA	4	7	
7. Willi Waltner	GER	4	7	

When Ken Richmond entered the ring he was one of the most recognized men in the world, even though no one knew his name. Richmond's muscular body was famous because he was the one who struck the gong at the beginning of J. Arthur Rank films. Richmond almost pinned Mekokishvili in the second minute of their third-round bout, but the 256-pound Georgian broke loose and regained the offensive to win a split decision. The following day Mekokishvili won another split decision from Bertil Antonsson to secure the gold medal.

1956 Melbourne C: 11, N: 11, D: 12.1.

		ROUND ELIMINATED	PEN. PTS.	FINAL ROUND
1. Hamit Kaplan	TUR	—	1	2
2. Yusein Mehmedov	BUL	—	3	3
3. Taisto Kangasniemi	FIN	—	3	6
4. Ray Mitchell	AUS	4	7	
4. Kenneth Richmond	GBR	4	7	
6. Ivan Vykhrystyuk	SOV/UKR	3	5	
7. William Kerslake	USA	3	6	

1960 Rome C: 17, N: 17, D: 9.6.

		ROUND ELIMINATED	PEN. PTS.	FINAL ROUND
1. Wilfried Dietrich	GER	—	1	2
2. Hamit Kaplan	TUR	—	5	4
3. Savkuds Dzarasov	SOV/RUS	—	2	6
4. Pietro Marascalchi	ITA	5	8	
5. Lyutvi Ahmedov	BUL	4	6	
5. János Reznák	HUN	4	6	
7. Bertil Antonsson	SWE	4	7	
8. William Kerslake	USA	4	8	

Dietrich won Greco-Roman silver medals in 1956 and 1960, but his only gold came in freestyle wrestling, after he held defending champion Hamit Kaplan to a draw in the final match.

1964 Tokyo C: 13, N: 13, D: 10.14.

		ROUND ELIMINATED	PEN. PTS.	FINAL ROUND AND 3RD PLACE
1. Oleksander Ivanytsky	SOV/ UKR	—	2	2
2. Lyutvi Ahmedov	BUL	—	3	2
3. Hamit Kaplan	TUR	4	7	2
4. Bohumil Kubat	CZE	4	7	2
5. Denis McNamara	GBR	4	7	8
6. Ştefan Ştîngu	ROM	4	8	
7. Wilfried Dietrich	GER	3	6	
7. Larry Kristoff	USA	3	6	
7. Masanori Saito	JPN	3	6	

Thirty-one-year-old Hamit Kaplan of Amasya, Anatolia, completed his set of Olympic medals by winning the bronze.

1968 Mexico City C: 15, N: 15, D: 10.20.

		ROUND ELIMINATED	PEN. PTS.	FINAL ROUND
1. Oleksander Medvid	SOV/UKR	—	1	1
2. Osman Duraliev	BUL	—	4	3
3. Wilfried Dietrich	GER	—	5	8
4. Ştefan Ştîngu	ROM	5	6	
5. Larry Kristoff	USA	4	6	
6. Abolfazl Anvari	IRN	4	9	
7. Erdeneotchir Elziisaihan	MGL	4	9	
8. Raymond Uytterheaghe	FRA	3	9	

Dietrich won his fifth Olympic medal (one gold, two silver, two bronze) at the age of 35.

1972 Munich C: 13, N: 13, D: 8.31.

		ROUND ELIMI- NATED	PEN. PTS.	FINAL ROUND
1. Oleksander Medvid	SOV/UKR	—	2	1
2. Osman Duraliev	BUL	—	4	3
3. Chris Taylor	USA	5	6	
4. Eskandar Filabi	IRN	5	8.5	
5. Wilfried Dietrich	GER	4	6	
6. Peter Germer	GDR	4	8	
7. Ştefan Ştîngu	ROM	4	8.5	
8. Stanislaw Makowiecki	POL	3	7.5	

The biggest confrontation of the 1972 tournament came in the very first round, when two-time Olympic champion Oleksander Medvid met 6-foot 5-inch, 412-pound Chris Taylor of Dowagiac, Michigan. Medvid had beaten Taylor three times, but this time they fought to a standoff. The 231-pound Ukrainian was awarded a controversial decision when the Turkish referee, Umit Demirag, penalized Taylor for passivity. This evident injustice led to Demirag's dismissal as an Olympic referee, although

Thirty-nine-year-old Wilfried Dietrich (bottom) throwing 412-pound Chris Taylor during the 1972 Super Heavyweight freestyle wrestling tournament.

the judgment against Taylor was allowed to stand. Both Medvid and Taylor won the rest of their bouts. Medvid became the only freestyle wrestler to win gold medals at three different Olympics.

A nasty incident took place in the third-round match between Giyasettin Yilmaz of Turkey and Bulgarian veteran Osman Duraliev. The two men collided in the third minute, and Yilmaz came away with a bleeding nose. Enraged, he refused to go to his corner and was disqualified. Then he went berserk, shouting at the referee, chasing Duraliev, and tearing apart his own dressing room. Yilmaz was finally subdued by 1968 Light Heavyweight gold medalist Ahmet Ayik.

1976 Montreal C: 15, N: 15, D: 7.31.

		ROUND ELIMINATED	PEN. PTS.	FINAL ROUND
1. Soslan Andiyev	SOV/RUS	—	2	1
2. József Balla	HUN	—	7	5
3. Ladislau Simon	ROM	—	6	6
4. Roland Gehrke	GDR	6	8	
5. Nikola Dinev	BUL	5	6	
6. Yorihide Isogai	JPN	4	7	
7. Eskandar Filabi	IRN	4	8	
8. Mamadou Sakho	SEN	4	8.5	

1980 Moscow C: 12, N: 12, D: 7.31.

		ROUND ELIMINATED	PEN. PTS.	FINAL ROUND
1. Soslan Andiyev	SOV/RUS	—	1	1
2. József Balla	HUN	—	5	5
3. Adam Sandurski	POL	—	0	6
4. Roland Gehrke	GDR	4	7	
5. Andrei Ianko	ROM	4	8	
6. Mamadou Sakho	SEN	4	8.5	
7. Petur Ivanov	BUL	3	7	
8. Arturo Diaz	CUB	3	8	

Seven-foot, 297-pound Adam Sandurski demolished his first four opponents in 9:50 but then lost on points, 6–3, to defending champion Soslan Andiyev of Ordzhonikidze, North Ossetia.

1984 Los Angeles-Anaheim C: 8, N: 8, D: 8.10.

		FINAL MATCH	
1. Bruce Baumgartner	USA	10–2	6:00
2. Robert Molle	CAN		
3. Ayhan Taskin	TUR	Fall	1:44
4. Hassan El Hadad	EGY		
5. Mamadou Sakho	SEN	Injury	
6. Vasile Andrei	ROM		
7. Koichi Ishimori	JPN		
8. Panayotis Pikilidis	GRE		

An amiable 264-pounder, Bruce Baumgartner of Haledon, New Jersey, was not seriously challenged in his three matches. Silver medalist Bob Molle barely made it to the Olympics. Ten days before the Opening Ceremony, Molle underwent a two-and-a-half-hour operation for a herniation of the fifth lumbar disc.

In a sport where competitors frequently have to go to great lengths to stay below the weight limit for their division, it is sometimes forgotten that super-heavyweights have to make a minimum weight. Harouna Niang of Mauritania had the unfortunate experience of traveling ten thousand miles to the Olympics and then being disqualified and prevented from competing because he weighed in at only 216 pounds.

1988 Seoul C: 14, N: 14, D: 10.1.

			FINAL MATCH	
1. David Gobezhishvili	SOV/GEO	3–1	6:00
2. Bruce Baumgartner	USA		
3. Andreas Schröder	GDR	Passivity	4:21
4. László Klauz	HUN		
5. Atanas Atanassov	BUL	8–3	6:00
6. Daniel Payne	CAN		
7. Adam Sandurski	POL	7–5	6:00
8. Ralf Bremmer	GER		

David Gobezhishvili was world champion in 1985, but the following year Bruce Baumgartner defeated him three times. Stung by these losses, Soviet wrestling officials removed Gobezhishvili from the national team and replaced him with Aslan Khardartsev, who went on to win the 1987 world championship and the 1988 European championship. However, Gobezhishvili was allowed to represent the U.S.S.R. in the 1988 World Cup, where he defeated Baumgartner. Soviet coach Ivan Yarygin decided to let Gobezhishvili and Khardartsev wrestle without a time limit to determine who would go to the Olympics. Gobezhishvili finally won after almost a half hour. In Seoul, Gobezhishvili, who grew up in the tiny mountain village of Khuruti, in Soviet Georgia, scored his first point against Baumgartner only 17 seconds into the final match. He added two more points in the second period before giving up a single point with 10 seconds left.

1992 Barcelona C: 15, N: 15, D: 8.6.

		FINAL MATCH
1. Bruce Baumgartner	USA	8–0
2. Jeffrey Thue	CAN	
3. David Gobezhishvili	GEO	4–0
4. Mahmut Demir	TUR	
5. Andreas Schröder	GER	Injury
6. Ali Reza Soleimani	IRN	
7. Wang Chunguang	CHN	9–0
8. Park Sung-ha	KOR	

Considered by many to be over the hill after he finished seventh at the 1991 world championships, Bruce Baumgartner came roaring back to regain the Olympic championship. He outscored five of six opponents by a combined total of 35–1 and threw the sixth one in 11 seconds. The critical match was his third-round contest with longtime rival David Gobezhishvili. The two had met 16 times before with Baumgartner leading the series, 10 wins to 6. They were tied 0–0 when, with four seconds left, Baumgartner suddenly dropped Gobezhishvili with what the American described as an "old-fashioned, straight-on, high-level, double-leg takedown."

GRECO-ROMAN WRESTLING

Light Flyweight—48 kg
Flyweight—52 kg
Bantamweight—57 kg
Featherweight—62 kg
Lightweight—68 kg
Welterweight—74 kg

Middleweight—82 kg
Light Heavyweight—90 kg
Heavyweight—100 kg
Super Heavyweight—130 kg
Discontinued Event

In Greco-Roman wrestling the use of the legs for squeezing, pushing, pressing, or lifting an opponent is prohibited, and no holds may be made below the hips. In Greco-Roman, unlike in freestyle, it is necessary to accompany an opponent to the mat during a takedown. The system of scoring is the same as in freestyle wrestling. Despite its name, Greco-Roman wrestling was actually created in nineteenth-century France. It was called Greco-Roman in honor of the ancient cultures that originated modern sports.

LIGHT FLYWEIGHT

(48 kg—106 lbs)

1896–1968 not held

1972 Munich C: 20, N: 20, D: 9.10.

		ROUND ELIMINATED	PEN. PTS.	FINAL ROUND
1. Gheorghe Berceanu	ROM	—	1	1
2. Rahim Aliabadi	IRN	—	5	3
3. Stefan Angelov	BUL	—	3.5	8
4. Raimo Hirvonen	FIN	5	6	
5. Kazuharu Ishida	JPN	5	7	
6. Lorenzo Calafiore	ITA	5	8	
7. Bernd Drechsel	GDR	4	7	
8. Günter Maas	GER	3	6.5	

1976 Montreal C: 15, N: 15, D: 7.24.

		ROUND ELIMINATED	PEN. PTS.	FINAL ROUND
1. Aleksei Shumakov	SOV/RUS	—	0	2
2. Gheorghe Berceanu	ROM	—	2	4
3. Stefan Angelov	BUL	—	3	6
4. Yoshite Moriwaki	JPN	5	8	
5. Dietmar Hinz	GDR	4	6	
6. Mitchell Kawasaki	CAN	4	7	
7. Salin Bora	TUR	4	7	
8. Michael Farina	USA	3	8	
8. Rashid Mohammadzadé	IRN	3	8	

In the final round Shumakov outpointed Angelov 5–4 and Berceanu 10–6.

1980 Moscow C: 10, N: 10, D: 7.22.

		ROUND ELIMINATED	PEN. PTS.	FINAL ROUND
1. Zaksylik Ushkempirov	SOV/KAZ	—	3.5	1.5
2. Constantin Alexandru	ROM	—	6	4
3. Ferenc Seres	HUN	—	7	6.5
4. Pavel Hristov	BUL	5	7.5	
5. Reijo Haaparanta	FIN	4	9	
6. Alfredo Olvera	MEX	3	7.5	
7. Vincenzo Maenza	ITA	2	6.5	
8. Roman Kierpacz	POL	2	7	

1984 Los Angeles-Anaheim C: 12, N: 12, D: 8.1.

		FINAL MATCH	
1. Vincenzo Maenza	ITA	12–0	1:59
2. Markus Scherer	GER		
3. Ikuzo Saito	JPN	7–5	6:00
4. Salih Bora	TUR		
5. Kent Andersson	SWE	10–3	6:00
6. Jun Dae-je	KOR		
7. Li Haisheng	CHN		
8. Lars Ronningen	NOR		

Twenty-two-year-old Vincenzo Maenza of Faenza outscored his four opponents 31–0.

1988 Seoul C: 15, N: 15, D: 9.20.

		FINAL MATCH	
1. Vincenzo Maenza	ITA	3–0	6:00
2. Andrzej Glab	POL		
3. Bratan Tzenov	BUL	Passivity	7:28
4. Magyatdin Allakhverdyev	SOV/AZR		
5. Khaled Alfaraj	SYR	16–6	6:00
6. Markus Scherer	GER		
7. Yang Zhizong	CHN	Injury	
8. Gooun Duk-yong	KOR		

Maenza proved that his 1984 victory over a boycott-depleted field was no fluke by earning an emotional repeat victory in Seoul. He reached the final by defeating Tzenov 4–3 after 42 seconds of sudden death overtime.

1992 Barcelona C: 19, N: 19, D: 7.29.

		FINAL MATCH
1. Oleg Kucherenko	UKR	3–0
2. Vincenzo Maenza	ITA	
3. Wilber Sánchez Amita	CUB	5–0
4. Fuat Yildiz	GER	
5. Iliuţă Dăscălescu	ROM	Forfeit
6. Reza Simkhah Asil	IRN	
7. Lars Rønningen	NOR	Forfeit
8. Pappu Yadav	IND	

Vincenzo Maenza, going for a third straight gold medal, qualified for the final by outpointing his four opponents 54–1. In the final, however, Kucherenko scored three points with a high dive and a gutwrench a mere five seconds after the match began. He spent most of the rest of the bout crawling around the mat while Maenza tried unsuccessfully to turn him.

FLYWEIGHT
(52 kg—114½ lbs)

1896–1936 not held

1948 London C: 13, N: 13, D: 8.6.

		ROUND ELIMINATED	PEN. PTS.	FINAL ROUND
1. Pietro Lombardi	ITA	—	3	1
2. Kenan Olcay	TUR	—	3	3
3. Reino Kangasmaki	FIN	5	6	
4. Malte Möller	SWE	5	6	
5. Gyula Szilágyi	HUN	5	5	
6. Fridtjof Clausen	NOR	4	7	
7. Mohamed Abd El Al	EGY	3	6	
7. Manuel Varela	ARG	3	6	

1952 Helsinki C: 17, N: 17, D: 7.27.

		ROUND ELIMINATED	PEN. PTS.	FINAL ROUND
1. Boris Gurevich	SOV/RUS	—	3	2
2. Ignazio Fabra	ITA	—	3	4
3. Leo Honkala	FIN	—	2	6
4. Heinrich Weber	GER	4	5	
5. Mahmoud Omar Fawzy	EGY	4	6	
5. Bengt Johansson	SWE	4	6	
7. Maurice Mewis	BEL	4	7	
7. Borivoje Vukov	YUG	4	7	

1956 Melbourne C: 11, N: 11, D: 12.6.

		ROUND ELIMINATED	PEN. PTS.	FINAL ROUND
1. Nikolai Solovyov	SOV/RUS	—	4	3
2. Ignazio Fabra	ITA	—	4	4
3. Durum Ali Egribaş	TUR	—	4	4

4. Dumitru Pirvulescu	ROM	4	7
5. István Baranya	HUN	3	5
5. Borivoje Vukov	YUG	3	5
7. Maurice Mewis	BEL	3	6

1960 Rome C: 18, N: 18, D: 8.31.

		ROUND ELIMINATED	PEN. PTS.
1. Dumitru Pirvulescu	ROM	—	5
2. Osman Sayed	EGY	5	6
3. Mohammad Paziraii	IRN	5	6
4. Takashi Hirata	JPN	5	7
5. Ignazio Fabra	ITA	5	8
5. Ivan Kochergin	SOV/RUS	5	8
7. Borivoje Vukov	YUG	4	6
8. Bengt Frandfors	SWE	4	7

1964 Tokyo C: 18, N: 18, D: 10.19.

		ROUND ELIMINATED	PEN. PTS.	FINAL ROUND
1. Tsutomu Hanahara	JPN	—	3	1
2. Angel Kerezov	BUL	—	4	4
3. Dumitru Pirvulescu	ROM	—	2	7
4. Ignazio Fabra	ITA	4	6	
4. Rolf Lacour	GER	4	6	
4. Maurice Mewis	BEL	4	6	
4. J. Richard Wilson	USA	4	6	
8. Burhan Bozkurt	TUR	3	6	
8. Vasilios Ganotis	GRE	3	6	
8. Shin Sang-shik	KOR	3	6	

1968 Mexico City C: 24, N: 24, D: 10.26.

		ROUND ELIMINATED	PEN. PTS.
1. Peter Kirov	BUL	—	5
2. Vladimir Bakulin	SOV/KAZ	6	6
3. Miroslav Zeman	CZE	6	8
4. Imre Alker	HUN	6	8.5
5. Rolf Lacour	GER	5	6
6. Jussi Vesterinen	FIN	5	7.5
7. Enrique Jimenez	MEX	4	6
8. Metin Cikmaz	TUR	4	7
8. Shin Sang-shik	KOR	4	7

1972 Munich C: 22, N: 22, D: 9.10.

		ROUND ELIMINATED	PEN. PTS.	FINAL ROUND
1. Peter Kirov	BUL	—	2	4
2. Koichiro Hirayama	JPN	—	3	5
3. Giuseppe Bognanni	ITA	—	5	7
4. József Doncsecz	HUN	5	8	
4. Jan Michalik	POL	5	8	
4. Miroslav Zeman	CZE	5	8	
7. Vassilios Ganotis	GRE	4	6	
8. Jamsran Munkhotchir	MGL	4	8	

1976 Montreal C: 17, N: 17, D: 7.24.

		ROUND ELIMINATED	PEN. PTS.	FINAL ROUND
1. Vitaly Konstantinov	SOV/RUS	—	3	4
2. Nicu Ginga	ROM	—	5.5	5
3. Koichiro Hirayama	JPN	—	8	5
4. Rolf Krauss	GER	5	8.5	
5. Lajos Rácz	HUN	4	6	
6. Moradali Shirani	IRN	4	7	
7. Antonio Caltabiano	ITA	4	7.5	
8. Baek Seung-hyun	KOR	4	9	

1980 Moscow C: 10, N: 10, D: 7.23.

		ROUND ELIMINATED	PEN. PTS.	FINAL ROUND
1. Vakhtang Blagidze	SOV/GEO	—	1	1
2. Lajos Rácz	HUN	—	4	5
3. Mladen Mladenov	BUL	—	5	6
4. Nicu Ginga	ROM	4	8	
5. Antonín Jelínek	CZE	4	8	
6. Stanislaw Wróblewski	POL	3	7	
7. Taisto Halonen	FIN	2	7	
8. Abdulnasser Eloulabi	SYR	2	8	

Blagidze defeated Rácz, 19–1, in the final match.

1984 Los Angeles-Anaheim C: 12, N: 12, D: 8.2.

		FINAL MATCH	
1. Atsuji Miyahara	JPN	9–4	6:00
2. Daniel Aceves	MEX		
3. Bang Dae-du	KOR	13–1	3:46
4. Hu Richa	CHN		
5. Jon Rønningen	NOR	14–0	2:54
6. Taisto Halonen	FIN		
7. Erol Kemah	TUR		
8. Mihai Cismasu	ROM		

1988 Seoul C: 21, N: 21, D: 9.21.

		FINAL MATCH	
1. Jon Rønningen	NOR	12–7	6:00
2. Atsuji Miyahara	JPN		
3. Lee Jae-suk	KOR	4–3	6:00
4. Aleksandr Ignatenko	SOV/RUS		
5. Roman Kierpacz	POL	Passivity	3:29
6. Tibor Jankovics	CZE		
7. Hristo Fliev	BUL	9–3	6:00
8. Peter Stjernberg	SWE		

1992 Barcelona C: 17, N: 17, D: 7.28.

		FINAL MATCH	
1. Jon Rønningen	NOR	2–1	
2. Alfred Ter-Mkrtychyan	RUS		
3. Min Kyung-kap	KOR	Forfeit	
4. Shawn Sheldon	USA		
5. Bratan Tzenov	BUL	6–1	
6. Valentin Rebegea	ROM		
7. Ismo Kamesaki	FIN	2–1	
8. Senad Rizvanovic	YUG		

Ter-Mkrtychyan was leading 1–0 when Rønningen scored a two-point takedown just as time ran out. Both wrestlers began celebrating. Ter-Mkrtychyan was lifted into the air by his coach at the same time that Norwegian fans were screaming with joy. One side was about to be severely disappointed. After huddling for several seconds, the officials announced that the takedown had occurred before the buzzer and that Rønningen was the victor. Twice Ter-Mkrtychyan collapsed in anguish on his way to the dressing room, while the Norwegians were still dancing in the streets an hour later. Min gained the bronze medal when Sheldon failed to make weight for the final match.

BANTAMWEIGHT
(57 kg—125½ lbs)

1896–1920 not held

1924 Paris C: 25, N: 15, D: 7.10.
(58 kg—128 lbs)
1. Eduard Pütsep   EST
2. Anselm Ahlfors   FIN
3. Väinö Ikonen   FIN
4. Sigfrid Hansson   SWE
5. Adolf Herschmann   AUT
6. Ragnvald Olsen   NOR
7. Armand Magyar   HUN
7. Józef Tasnádi   HUN

1928 Amsterdam C: 19, N: 19, D: 8.5.
(58 kg—128 lbs)
1. Kurt Leucht   GER
2. Jindrich Maudr   CZE
3. Giovanni Gozzi   ITA
4. Oscar Lindelöf   SWE
5. Ödön Zombori   HUN
6. Eduard Pütsep   EST
7. Herman Andersen   DEN
8. Anselm Ahlfors   FIN

1932 Los Angeles C: 7, N: 7, D: 8.7.
(56 kg—123½ lbs)
1. Jakob Brendel   GER
2. Marcello Nizzola   ITA
3. Louis François   FRA
4. Herman Tuvesson   SWE

1936 Berlin C: 18, N: 18, D: 8.9.
(56 kg—123½ lbs)

		ROUND ELIMINATED	PEN. PTS.	FINAL ROUND
1. Márton Lörincz	HUN	—	3	1
2. Egon Svensson	SWE	—	0	3
3. Jakob Brendel	GER	5	5	
4. Väinö Perttunen	FIN	5	5	
5. Iosef Tözer	ROM	5	6	
6. Evald Sikk	EST	4	5	

		ROUND ELIMINATED	PEN. PTS.	FINAL ROUND
7. Robert Voigt	DEN	4	7	
8. Dante Bertoli	ITA	4	7	

1948 London C: 13, N: 13, D: 8.6.

		ROUND ELIMINATED	PEN. PTS.	FINAL ROUND
1. Kurt Pettersén	SWE	—	4	1
2. Ali Mahmoud Hassan	EGY	—	2	3
3. Halil Kaya	TUR	5	6	
4. Taisto Lempinen	FIN	4	5	
5. Elvidio Flamini	ARG	4	6	
6. Lajos Bencze	HUN	3	5	
6. Reidar Maerlie	NOR	3	5	
8. Nikolaos Biris	GRE	3	6	

1952 Helsinki C: 17, N: 17, D: 7.27.

		ROUND ELIMINATED	PEN. PTS.	FINAL ROUND
1. Imre Hódos	HUN	—	4	4
2. Zakaria Chihab	LEB	—	6	4
3. Artem Teryan	SOV/AZR	—	4	4
4. Hubert Persson	SWE	5	7	
5. Reidar Maerlie	NOR	4	5	
6. Ferdinand Schmitz	GER	4	6	
7. Ion Popescu	ROM	4	7	
8. Pietro Lombardi	ITA	3	5	

1956 Melbourne C: 28, N: 28, D: 8.31.

		ROUND ELIMINATED	PEN. PTS.	FINAL ROUND
1. Konstantin Vyrupayev	SOV/RUS	—	4	4
2. Edvin Westerby	SWE	—	1	4
3. Francisc Horvath	ROM	—	4	4
4. Imre Hódos	HUN	4	5	
5. Alfred Kämmerer	GER	4	5	
6. Dinko Petrov	BUL	3	5	
7. Adolfo Díaz	ARG	3	6	

1960 Rome C: 28, N: 28, D: 8.31.

		ROUND ELIMINATED	PEN. PTS.	FINAL ROUND
1. Oleg Karavayev	SOV/BLR	—	2	1
2. Ion Cernea	ROM	—	5	3
3. Dinko Petrov	BUL	5	6	
4. Edvin Westerby	SWE	5	6	
5. Jiři Švec	CZE	5	7	
5. Yasar Yimaz	TUR	5	7	
7. Masamitsu Ichiguchi	JPN	5	8	
7. Bernard Knitter	POL	5	8	

1964 Tokyo C: 18, N: 18, D: 10.19.

		ROUND ELIMINATED	PEN. PTS.
1. Masamitsu Ichiguchi	JPN	—	4
2. Vladlen Trostyansky	SOV/UKR	5	6

		ROUND ELIMINATED	PEN. PTS.	FINAL ROUND
3. Ion Cernea	ROM	5	8	
4. Jiři Švec	CZE	5	8	
5. Karmal Ali	EGY	4	6	
5. Tsviatko Pashkulev	BUL	4	6	
5. Fritz Stange	GER	4	6	
8. Unver Basergil	TUR	4	7	

1968 Mexico City C: 24, N: 24, D: 10.26.

		ROUND ELIMINATED	PEN. PTS.	FINAL ROUND
1. János Varga	HUN	—	6	—
2. Ion Baciu	ROM	6	7.5	4
3. Ivan Kochergin	SOV/RUS	6	7.5	6.5
4. Othon Moschidis	GRE	6	7.5	6.5
5. Koji Sakurama	JPN	5	6.5	
6. Elsayad Ibrahim	EGY	5	9	
6. Kaya Öczan	TUR	5	9	
8. Risto Björlin	FIN	4	6	

1972 Munich C: 30, N: 30, D: 9.10.

		ROUND ELIMINATED	PEN. PTS.	FINAL ROUND
1. Rustem Kazakov	SOV/UZB	—	5	0
2. Hans-Jürgen Veil	GER	—	4	4
3. Risto Björlin	FIN	7	8	
4. János Varga	HUN	7	9	
5. Hristo Traikov	BUL	6	6	
6. Ion Baciu	ROM	5	6	
7. Ikuei Yamamoto	JPN	5	8.5	
8. Józef Lipień	POL	4	8	

World champion Rustem Kazakov pinned local favorite Hans-Jürgen Veil in 2:58 to win the gold medal.

1976 Montreal C: 17, N: 17, D: 7.24.

		ROUND ELIMINATED	PEN. PTS.	FINAL ROUND
1. Pertti Ukkola	FIN	—	4.5	2
2. Ivan Frgić	YUG	—	6	3
3. Farhat Mustafin	SOV/RUS	—	4.5	7
4. Yoshima Suga	JPN	5	8	
5. Mihai Botila	ROM	5	8	
6. Krasimir Stefanov	BUL	4	6	
7. József Doncsecz	HUN	4	7.5	
8. Josef Krysta	CZE	4	8	

Ukkola earned his upset victory by barely outpointing Mustafin and Frgić with scores of 6–5 and 5–4.

1980 Moscow C: 13, N: 13, D: 7.24.

		ROUND ELIMINATED	PEN. PTS.	FINAL ROUND
1. Shamil Serikov	SOV/KAZ	—	1	1
2. Józef Lipień	POL	—	6	7
3. Benni Ljungbeck	SWE	—	5	8
4. Mihai Botila	ROM	5	11.5	
5. Antonino Caltabiano	ITA	4	7	
6. Josef Krysta	CZE	4	7	

7. Gyula Molnár	HUN	4	7
8. Georgi Donev	BUL	3	7

Serikov outpointed Lipień 11–4 in the final match.

1984 Los Angeles-Anaheim C: 16, N: 16, D: 8.3.

		FINAL MATCH	
1. Pasquale Passarelli	GER	8–5	6:00
2. Masaki Eto	JPN		
3. Haralambos Holidis	GRE	2–1	6:00
4. Nicolae Zamfir	ROM		
5. Frank Famiano	USA	Injury	
6. Benni Ljungbeck	SWE		
7. Mehmets Erhat Karadag	TUR		
8. Park Byung-hyo	KOR		

Passarelli, a 27-year-old insurance agent, spent the last 96 seconds of his final match with world champion Eto in a back body arch to avoid being pinned.

1988 Seoul C: 21, N: 21, D: 9.22.

		FINAL MATCH	
1. András Sike	HUN	Injury	3:38
2. Stoyan Balov	BUL		
3. Haralambos Holidis	GRE	6–1	6:00
4. Yang Changling	CHN		
5. Huh Byung-ho	KOR	Fall	1:44
6. Ghazi Salah	IRQ		
7. Aleksandr Chestakov	SOV/BLR	Forfeit	
8. Rifat Yildiz	GER		

Sike was leading 9–0 in the final when Balov retired.

1992 Barcelona C: 19, N: 19, D: 7.30.

		FINAL MATCH	
1. An Han-bong	KOR	6–5	5:36
2. Rifat Yildiz	GER		
3. Sheng Zetian	CHN	5–4	
4. Aleksandr Ignatenko	RUS		
5. William Lara Díaz	CUB	8–1	
6. Marian Sandu	ROM		
7. Keijo Pehkonen	FIN	6–4	
8. Dennis Hall	USA		

Unheralded An Han-bong blasted his first five opponents 41–1. In the final, two-time world champion Rifat Yildiz took a 5–2 lead but ran out of steam as An continued to attack relentlessly.

FEATHERWEIGHT
(62 kg—136½ lbs)

1896–1908 not held

1912 Stockholm C: 38, N: 13, D: 7.12.
(60 kg—132½ lbs)

1. Kaarlo Koskelo	FIN
2. Georg Gerstäcker	GER
3. Otto Lasanen	FIN

4. Kaarlo Leivonen	FIN
5. Erik Öberg	SWE

1920 Antwerp C: 21, N: 12, D: 8.19.
(60 kg—132½ lbs)

1. Oskar Friman	FIN
2. Heikki Kähkönen	FIN
3. Fritiof Svensson	SWE
4. Alexandre Boumans	BEL
5. Aage Tergersen	DEN
6. Josef Beránek	CZE

Friman pinned each of his four opponents within eight minutes.

1924 Paris C: 27, N: 15, D: 7.10.

1. Kaarlo "Kalle" Anttila	FIN
2. Aleksanteri Toivola	FIN
3. Erik Malmberg	SWE
4. Arthur Nord	NOR
5. Fritiof Svensson	SWE
6. Maurice Capron	FRA
6. Ödön Radvány	HUN

Anttila was 36 years old when he won his second Olympic gold medal. In Antwerp in 1920 he had finished first in the freestyle Lightweight division.

1928 Amsterdam C: 20, N: 20, D: 8.5.
(60 kg—132½ lbs)

1. Voldemar Väli	EST
2. Erik Malmberg	SWE
3. Giacomo Quaglia	ITA
4. Károly Kárpáti	HUN
5. Ernst Steinig	GER
6. Aage Meier (DEN), Arakan Saim (TUR), Aleksanteri Toivola (FIN)	

1932 Los Angeles C: 8, N: 8, D: 8.7.
(61 kg—134½ lbs)

1. Giovanni Gozzi	ITA
2. Wolfgang Ehrl	GER
3. Lauri Koskela	FIN
4. Jindřich Maudr	CZE
5. Kiyoshi Kase	JPN

1936 Berlin C: 19, N: 19, D: 8.9.
(61 kg—134½ lbs)

		ROUND ELIMINATED	PEN. PTS.
1. Yaşar Erkan	TUR	—	4
2. Aarne Reini	FIN	7	5
3. Einar Karlsson	SWE	7	5
4. Sebastian Hering	GER	5	5
5. Kristjanis Kundsins	LAT	5	6
6. Valentino Borgia	ITA	4	5
7. Henryk Ślązak	POL	4	6
8. Gyula Móri	HUN	4	6

1948 London C: 17, N: 17, D: 8.6.
(61 kg—134½ lbs)

		ROUND ELIMINATED	PEN. PTS.	FINAL ROUND
1. Mehmet Oktav	TUR	—	3	0
2. Olle Anderberg	SWE	—	3	3
3. Ferenc Tóth	HUN	6	6	
4. Georg Weidner	AUT	5	5	
5. Luigi Campanella	ITA	5	6	
6. Sayed Kandil	EGY	4	7	
6. Egil Solsvik	NOR	4	7	
6. Safi Taha	LEB	4	7	
6. Erkki Talosela	FIN	4	7	

The decisive match took place in the third round, when Oktav threw Anderberg in 2:48.

1952 Helsinki C: 17, N: 17, D: 7.27.
(61 kg—134½ lbs)

		ROUND ELIMINATED	PEN. PTS.	FINAL ROUND
1. Yakiv Punkin	SOV/UKR	—	2	0
2. Imre Polyák	HUN	—	3	4
3. Abdel Rashed	EGY	—	5	6
4. Umberto Trippa	ITA	4	5	
5. Bartholomäus Brötzner	AUT	4	6	
6. Hasan Bozbey	TUR	4	7	
7. Safi Taha	LEB	3	3	
8. Ernest Gondzik	POL	3	5	
8. Erkki Talosela	FIN	3	5	

Punkin finished strongly, pinning Polyák in 1:26 and Rashad in 3:28.

1956 Melbourne C: 10, N: 10, D: 12.6.
(61 kg—134½ lbs)

		ROUND ELIMINATED	PEN. PTS.	FINAL ROUND
1. Rauno Mäkinen	FIN	—	4	4
2. Imre Polyák	HUN	—	3	4
3. Roman Dzneladze	SOV/GEO	—	4	4
4. Müzahir Sille	TUR	4	6	
5. Gunnar Håkansson	SWE	3	5	
6. Umberto Trippa	ITA	3	7	
7. Ion Popescu	ROM	3	7	

Mäkinen was the son of 1928 freestyle Bantamweight winner Kaarlo Mäkinen.

1960 Rome C: 25, N: 25, D: 8.31.
(61 kg—134½ lbs)

		ROUND ELIMINATED	PEN. PTS.	FINAL ROUND
1. Müzahir Sille	TUR	—	5	1
2. Imre Polyák	HUN	—	3	3
3. Konstantin Vyrupayev	SOV/RUS	6	6	
4. Umberto Trippa	ITA	6	6	
5. Mihai Schultz	ROM	6	8	
6. Saiid Ebrahimian	IRN	5	7	

6. Vojtech Toth	CZE	5	7	
8. Lee Allen	USA	4	7	

1964 Tokyo C: 27, N: 27, D: 10.19.
(63 kg—139 lbs)

		ROUND ELIMINATED	PEN. PTS.	FINAL ROUND
1. Imre Polyák	HUN	—	1	2
2. Roman Rurua	SOV/GEO	—	4	2
3. Branislav Martinović	YUG	5	4	
4. Ronald Finley	USA	5	6	
4. Mostafa Mansour	EGY	5	6	
6. Joseph Mewis	BEL	4	6	
6. Rassoul Mirmalek	IRN	4	6	
6. Koji Sakurama	JPN	4	6	

After finishing second three straight times, Polyák finally won an Olympic gold medal.

1968 Mexico City C: 23, N: 23, D: 10.26.
(63 kg—139 lbs)

		ROUND ELIMINATED	PEN. PTS.	FINAL ROUND
1. Roman Rurua	SOV/GEO	—	2	2
2. Hideo Fujimoto	JPN	—	5	2
3. Simeon Popescu	ROM	6	6.5	
4. Dimiter Galinchev	BUL	6	8	
5. Hizir Alakoc	TUR	5	6	
6. Martti Laakso	FIN	4	6	
7. James Hazewinkel	USA	4	8.5	
8. Lothar Schneider	GDR	4	9	

1972 Munich C: 19, N: 19, D: 9.10.

		ROUND ELIMINATED	PEN. PTS.
1. Georgi Markov	BUL	—	3
2. Heinz-Helmut Wehling	GDR	6	6.5
3. Kazimierz Lipień	POL	6	6.5
4. Hideo Fujimoto	JPN	6	7.5
5. Djemal Megrelishvili	SOV/GEO	6	8
6. Ion Păun	ROM	5	7.5
7. Martti Laakso	FIN	5	8
7. Stylianos Mygiakis	GRE	5	8

1976 Montreal C: 17, N: 17, D: 7.24.

		ROUND ELIMINATED	PEN. PTS.	FINAL ROUND
1. Kazimierz Lipień	POL	—	3.5	3.5
2. Nelson Davydyan	SOV/UKR	—	4	4
3. László Réczi	HUN	—	5.5	4.5
4. Teruhiko Miyahara	JPN	7	8	
5. Ion Păun	ROM	6	8	
6. Pekka Hjelt	FIN	4	7	
7. Stylianos Mygiakis	GRE	4	8.5	
8. Stoyan Lazarov	BUL	3	7	

Kazimierz Lipień won the world championship in 1973 and 1974, but in 1975 he lost a controversial decision to Nelson Davydyan. The two met again in the sixth round of the Olympics in Montreal, with Davydyan gaining another controversial victory, 10–6. In that match, Viktor Igumenov, the Soviet coach, was ordered to leave the competition area after he illegally shouted instructions to Davydyan. Igumenov continued to yell orders, but from a greater distance. Lipień salvaged the gold medal anyway by outpointing Réczi 13–4, the nine-point margin reducing Lipień's bad marks for the bout from 1 to 0.5. Lipień's twin brother, Jozef, won a Bantamweight silver medal in 1980. At the 1975 world championships, the Poles were accused of substituting Jozef for Kazimierz in one match. Their accusers should have known better, since Jozef always parted his hair on the left side, while Kazimierz parted his on the right. At the post-tournament press conference in Montreal, Kazimierz, a 27-year-old plumber, advised aspiring wrestlers to abstain from smoking and drinking. "And no women," added bronze medalist László Réczi. But Lipień disagreed. "That is taking sacrifices too far," he said, "women are good to wrestle with, too."

1980 Moscow C: 11, N: 11, D: 7.22.

		ROUND ELIMINATED	PEN. PTS.	FINAL ROUND
1. Stylianos Mygiakis	GRE	—	6	2
2. István Tóth	HUN	—	3	4
3. Boris Kramorenko	SOV/TRM	5	7	
4. Ivan Frgić	YUG	5	7	
5. Panayot Kirov	BUL	4	9	
6. Kazimierz Lipień	POL	3	6	
7. Radwan Karout	SYR	3	8	
8. Michal Vejsada	CZE	3	8	

Mygiakis was the first "Greco" ever to win a Greco-Roman gold medal in the Olympics.

1984 Los Angeles-Anaheim C: 20, N: 20, D: 8.1.

		FINAL MATCH	
1. Kim Weon-kee	KOR	3–3	6:00
2. Kent-Olle Johansson	SWE		
3. Hugo Dietsche	SWI	8–4	6:00
4. Abdurrahim Kuzu	USA		
5. Douglas Yeats	CAN	15–3	4:41
6. Salem Bekhit	EGY		
7. Bernd Gabriel	GER		
8. Seiichi Osanai	JPN		

1988 Seoul C: 17, N: 17, D: 9.20.

		FINAL MATCH	
1. Kamandar Madzhidov	SOV/BLR	6–2	6:00
2. Zhivko Vangelov	BUL		
3. An Dae-hyun	KOR	Passivity	3:15
4. Jenö Bódi	HUN		
5. Peter Behl	GER	5–1	6:00
6. Isaac Anderson	USA		
7. Gilles Jalabert	FRA	Injury	
8. Hugo Dietsche	SWI		

1992 Barcelona C: 21, N: 21, D: 7.30.

		FINAL MATCH
1. M. Akif Pirim	TUR	13–2
2. Sergei Martynov	RUS	
3. Juan Maren Delis	CUB	5–0
4. Wlodzimierz Zawadzki	POL	
5. Jenö Bódi	HUN	Injury
6. Anthony "Buddy" Lee	USA	
7. Stanilsav Grigorov	BUL	Forfeit
8. Hugo Dietsche	SWI	

The final was a rematch of the 1991 world championship at which Martynov won a rough and controversial 2–1 victory over Pirim. This time there was no controversy, as Pirim won handily.

LIGHTWEIGHT
(68 kg—150 lbs)

1896–1904 not held

1906 Athens C: 11, N: 7, D: 5.1.
(75 kg-165½ lbs)

1. Rudolf Watzl	AUT
2. Karl Karlsen	DEN
3. Ferenc Holuban	HUN

1908 London C: 25, N: 10, D: 7.25.
(66.6 kg—147 lbs)

		FINAL MATCH
1. Enrico Porro	ITA	Dec 30:00; Dec 20:00
2. Nikolai Orlov	RUS	
3. Arvid Lindén	FIN	
4. Gunnar Persson	SWE	
5. Gustaf Malmström (SWE), József Maróthy (HUN), Anders Moller (DEN), Ödön Radvány (HUN)		

Porro, a 23-year-old Milanese sailor, was unbeaten in international competition. He was awarded a decision over Orlov after 50 minutes of very little action.

1912 Stockholm C: 48, N: 13, D: 7.13.
(67.5 kg—149 lbs)

1. Eemil Wäre	FIN
2. Gustaf Malmström	SWE
3. Edvin Matiasson	SWE
4. Ödön Radvány	HUN
5. Johan Nilsson	SWE
5. Volmar Vikström	FIN

Wäre pinned all five of his opponents, completing his feat by defeating Malmström after an epic 60-minute struggle.

1920 Antwerp C: 22, N: 12, D: 8.19.
(67.5 kg—149 lbs)

1. Eemil Wäre	FIN
2. Taavi Tamminen	FIN
3. Frithjof Andersen	NOR
4. Frits Janssens	BEL

1924 Paris C: 28, N: 18, D: 7.10.
(67.5 kg—149 lbs)
1. Oskar Friman — FIN
2. Lajos Keresztes — HUN
3. Kalle Westerlund — FIN
4. Albert Kusnets — EST
5. František Kratochvil — CZE
6. Charles Frisenfeldt (DEN), Arne Gaupseth (NOR), Mihály Matura (HUN)

In 1920 Friman won the Featherweight title. Four years later in Paris, at the age of 31, he gained his second gold medal.

1928 Amsterdam C: 19, N: 19, D: 8.5.
(67.5 kg—149 lbs)
1. Lajos Keresztes — HUN
2. Eduard Sperling — GER
3. Edvard Westerlund — FIN
4. Tayare Yalaz — TUR
5. Vladimir Vávra — CZE
6. Walter Massop — HOL
7. Ryszard Błażyca — POL
7. Frits Janssens — BEL

Keresztes turned to wrestling on the advice of a doctor who prescribed the sport as a cure for "prolonged neurosis."

1932 Los Angeles C: 6, N: 6, D: 8.7.
(66 kg—145½ lbs)
1. Erik Malmberg — SWE
2. Abraham Kurland — DEN
3. Eduard Sperling — GER
4. Aarne Reini — FIN

With this victory the 35-year-old Malmberg completed his set of Olympic medals, having previously earned a Featherweight bronze in 1924 and silver in 1928.

1936 Berlin C: 18, N: 18, D: 8.9.
(66 kg—145½ lbs)

		ROUND ELIMINATED	PEN. PTS.	FINAL ROUND
1. Lauri Koskela	FIN	—	2	2
2. Jozef Herda	CZE/SLV	—	3	3
3. Voldemar Väli	EST	—	2	5
4. Herbert Olofsson	SWE	5	5	
5. Alberto Molfino	ITA	4	6	
6. Arild Dahl	NOR	4	7	
7. Zbigniew Szajewski	POL	4	7	
8. Dragomir Borlovan	ROM	3	5	

1948 London C: 17, N: 17, D: 8.6.
(67 kg—147½ lbs)

		ROUND ELIMINATED	PEN. PTS.	3RD PLACE
1. Gustav Freij	SWE	—	2	
2. Aage Eriksen	NOR	5	5	
3. Károly Ferencz	HUN	5	6	1
4. Charif Damage	LEB	5	6	2

5. Johannes Munnikes	HOL	4	6
6. Georgios Petmezas	GRE	4	7
6. Ahmet Senol	TUR	4	7
6. Eino Virtanen	FIN	4	7

1952 Helsinki C: 19, N: 19, D: 7.27.
(67 kg—147½ lbs)

		ROUND ELIMINATED	PEN. PTS.	FINAL ROUND
1. Shazam Safin	SOV/RUS	—	3	1
2. Gustav Freij	SWE	—	3	3
3. Mikuláš Athanasov	CZE/SLV	—	5	6
4. Gyula Tarr	HUN	5	6	
5. Franco Benedetti	ITA	4	7	
5. Dumitru Cuc	ROM	4	7	
5. Kalle Haapasalmi	FIN	4	7	
8. Kamel Hussein	EGY	3	5	
8. Erich Schmidt	SAA/GER	3	5	

1956 Melbourne C: 10, N: 10, D: 12.6.
(67 kg—147½ lbs)

		ROUND ELIMINATED	PEN. PTS.	FINAL ROUND
1. Kyösti Lehtonen	FIN	—	1	1
2. Riza Dogan	TUR	—	6	3
3. Gyula Tóth	HUN	—	2	6
4. Bartholomäus Brötzner	AUT	4	8	
4. Dimiter Yanchev	BUL	4	9	
6. Dumitru Gheorghe	ROM	3	7	

1960 Rome C: 23, N: 23, D: 8.31.
(67 kg—147½ lbs)

		ROUND ELIMINATED	PEN. PTS.	FINAL ROUND
1. Avtandil Koridze	SOV/GEO	—	5	1
2. Branislav Martinović	YUG	—	4	3
3. Gustav Freij	SWE	5	6	
4. Karel Matoušek	CZE	5	6	
— Dimitro Stoyanov (Dimiter Yanchev)	BUL	5	8	
5. Dumitru Gheorghe	ROM	4	7	
5. Ernest Gondzik	POL	4	7	
5. Adil Güngör	TUR	4	7	
5. Mitsuharu Kitamura	JPN	4	7	
5. Kyösti Lehtonen	FIN	4	7	
5. Jacques Pourtau	FRA	4	7	

Charges of "fix" were hurled following a fifth round bout between Koridze and Dimiter Yanchev of Bulgaria, then known as Dimitro Stoyanov. Koridze needed to score a fall to force a final showdown with Martinović. Anything less—a draw or even a points victory—would give the gold medal to the Yugoslav. After 11 minutes of inactivity, with only one minute left before the end of the bout, Koridze spoke a few words to Stoyanov and then threw him to the ground and pinned him. The Yugoslavs immediately lodged a protest. Stoyanov, who had originally been awarded fifth place, was disqualified from the tournament, but Koridze was not punished and went on to defeat Martinovič and to win the gold medal.

1964 Tokyo C: 19, N: 19, D: 10.19.
(70 kg—154½ lbs)

		ROUND ELIMINATED	PEN. PTS.	2ND PLACE
1. Kazim Ayvaz	TUR	—	5	
2. Valeriu Bularcă	ROM	5	6	3
3. David Gvantseladze	SOV/GEO	5	6	4
4. Tokuaki Fujita	JPN	5	6	5
5. Stevan Horvat	YUG	5	7	
6. Eero Tapio	FIN	5	8	
7. Bror Jonsson	SWE	4	6	
8. Ivan Ivanov	BUL	4	7	

1968 Mexico City C: 26, N: 26, D: 10.26.
(70 kg—154½ lbs)

		ROUND ELIMINATED	PEN. PTS.	FINAL ROUND
1. Munji Mumemura	JPN	—	5	3.5
2. Stevan Horvat	YUG	—	5	5
3. Petros Galaktopoulos	GRE	—	5	5.5
4. Klaus Rost	GER	6	8	
5. Eero Tapio	FIN	5	7.5	
6. Werner Holzer	USA	5	8	
6. Gennady Sapunov	SOV/RUS	5	8	
8. Antal Steer	HUN	4	6	

1972 Munich C: 23, N: 23, D: 9.10.

		ROUND ELIMINATED	PEN. PTS.
1. Shamil Khisamutdinov	SOV/RUS	—	2.5
2. Stoyan Apostolov	BUL	6	5
3. Gian-Matteo Ranzi	ITA	6	6
4. Manfred Schöndorfer	GER	6	7.5
5. Takashi Tanoue	JPN	5	6
6. Seyit Hisirli	TUR	4	6
6. Antal Steer	HUN	4	6
8. Sreten Damjanovic	YUG	4	7.5

1976 Munich C: 21, N: 21, D: 7.24.

		ROUND ELIMINATED	PEN. PTS.	FINAL ROUND
1. Suren Nalbandyan	SOV/ARM	—	3	2
2. Ştefan Rusu	ROM	—	3	3
3. Heinz-Helmut Wehling	GDR	—	8	7
4. Lars-Erik Skiöld	SWE	6	9.5	
5. Andrzej Supron	POL	5	8	
6. Manfred Schöndorfer	GER	5	9	
7. Erol Mutlu	TUR	4	6	
8. Markku Yli-Isotalo	FIN	4	7	

The 20-year-old Nalbandyan gained a crucial 5–3 victory over Rusu in the fourth round and then outpointed Supron 7–4 and Wehling 12–9. In 1984, Nalbandyan was sentenced to three years in a labor camp for selling black-market alcohol.

1980 Moscow C: 15, N: 15, D: 7.24.

		ROUND ELIMINATED	PEN. PTS.	FINAL ROUND
1. Ştefan Rusu	ROM	—	4	2
2. Andrzej Supron	POL	—	1	3
3. Lars-Erik Skiöld	SWE	—	1	7
4. Suren Nalbandyan	SOV/ARM	5	8	
5. Buyandelger Bold	MGL	5	9	
6. Ivan Atanassov	BUL	4	8	
7. Reinhard Hartmann	AUT	4	8	
8. Károly Gaál	HUN	3	7	

The cast of characters was almost the same as it was four years earlier. Nalbandyan was the first of the four favorites to be eliminated when he and Rusu were charged with a double disqualification after 7:09 of their fifth-round match. In the final round-robin Rusu outpointed Supron 3–2 and Skiöld 5–1.

1984 Los Angeles-Anaheim C: 14, N: 14, D: 8.3.

		FINAL MATCH	
1. Vlado Lisjak	YUG	Fall	0:57
2. Tapio Sipilä	FIN		
3. James Martinez	USA	Fall	0:25
4. Stefan Negrisan	ROM		
5. Deitmar Streitler	AUT	8–4	6:00
6. Mohamed Mutei Alnakdali	SYR		
7. Shaban Ibrahim	EGY		
8. Sumer Kocak	TUR		

In a major upset, the defending world champion, Tapio Sipilä, was quickly thrown by a late substitute to the Yugoslav team, Vlado Lisjak, a 22-year-old truck driver from the village of Petrinja.

1988 Seoul C: 31, N: 31, D: 9.22.

		FINAL MATCH	
1. Levon Dzhulfalakyan	SOV/ARM	9–3	6:00
2. Kim Sung-moon	KOR		
3. Tapio Sipilä	FIN	7–4	6:00
4. Petrica Carare	ROM		
5. Jerzy Kopański	POL	Passivity	5:07
6. Yasuhiro Okubo	JPN		
7. Morten Brekke	NOR	6–5	6:42
8. Attila Repka	HUN		

Dzhulfalakyan, a 24-year-old Armenian, faced his stiffest challenge from Carare, who forced him into overtime before succumbing.

1992 Barcelona C: 19, N: 19, D: 7.28.

		FINAL MATCH	
1. Attila Repka	HUN	1–0	5:38
2. Islam Duguchiyev	RUS		
3. Rodney Smith	USA	6–3	
4. Cecilio Rodríguez Pérez	CUB		
5. Ghani Yalouz	FRA	Forfeit	
6. Abdollah Chamangoli	IRN		
7. Ryszard Wolny	POL	1–0	
8. Douglas Yeats	CAN		

Repka upset Armenian-born Duguchiyev, the two-time defending world champion, by spinning him over from a bodylock position in sudden-death overtime. The match was halted twice so that Repka's badly swollen hand could be tended.

WELTERWEIGHT

(74 kg—163 lbs)

1896–1928 not held

1932 Los Angeles C: 8, N: 8, D: 8.7.
(72 kg-159 lbs)
1. Ivar Johansson — SWE
2. Väinö Kajander-Kajukorpi — FIN
3. Ercole Gallegati — ITA
4. Osvald Käpp — EST
5. Börge Jensen — DEN

Ivar Johansson, a 29-year-old policeman from Norrköping, put on a remarkable performance from August 1 through August 7. First he won the freestyle Middleweight division with four bouts in three days. Then he spent the next 24 hours fasting and sweating in a sauna so that he could compete as a welterweight in the Greco-Roman competition. Eleven pounds lighter, he won four more matches and earned a second gold medal.

1936 Berlin C: 14, N: 14, D: 8.9.
(72 kg—159 lbs)

		ROUND ELIMINATED	PEN. PTS.	FINAL ROUND
1. Rudolf Svedberg	SWE	—	2	2
2. Fritz Schäfer	GER	—	1	2
3. Eino Virtanen	FIN	—	4	6
4. Eduard Pütsep	EST	5	6	
5. Nurettin Boytorun	TUR	5	7	
5. Silvio Tozzi	ITA	5	7	
7. Jean De Feu	BEL	4	6	
7. Adolf Rieder	SWI	4	6	

1948 London C: 16, N: 16, D: 8.6.
(73 kg—160 lbs)

		ROUND ELIMINATED	PEN. PTS.	FINAL ROUND
1. Gösta Andersson	SWE	—	3	2
2. Miklós Szilvási	HUN	—	3	3
3. Henrik Hansen	DEN	—	4	6
4. René Chesneau	FRA	4	7	
4. Veikko Männikö	FIN	4	7	
4. Josef Schmidt	DEN	4	7	
7. Bjorn Cook	NOR	3	5	
8. Nicolaos Felgen	LUX	3	6	
8. Luigi Rigamonti	ITA	3	6	

1952 Helsinki C: 18, N: 18, D: 7.27.
(73 kg—160 lbs)

		ROUND ELIMINATED	PEN. PTS.	FINAL ROUND
1. Miklós Szilvási	HUN	—	1	1
2. Gösta Andersson	SWE	—	1	4
3. Khalil Taha	LEB	—	5	6
4. Semen Marushkin	SOV	4	6	
5. Marin Belusiça	ROM	3	5	
5. René Chesneau	FRA	3	5	
5. Osvaldo Riva	ITA	3	5	
5. Ahmet Şenol	TUR	3	5	

In 1946, while on duty as a policeman, Miklós Szilvási was accidentally shot in the left leg by a machine gun. His left foot was temporarily paralyzed. Through exercise and willpower, Szilvási regained the use of his foot and represented Hungary at the 1948 Olympics. He finished second, losing a decision to Gösta Andersson in the final match. Four years later the two met again for the championship, and this time Szilvási won a split decision.

1956 Melbourne C: 11, N: 11, D: 12.6.
(73 kg—160 lbs)

		ROUND ELIMINATED	PEN. PTS.	FINAL ROUND
1. Mithat Bayrak	TUR	—	2	2
2. Vladimir Maneyev	SOV/RUS	—	2	4
3. Per Berlin	SWE	—	0	6
4. Veikko Rantanen	FIN	3	5	
5. James Holt	USA	3	6	
5. Siegfried Schäfer	GDR	3	6	
7. Miklós Szilvási	HUN	3	7	
8. Mitiou Petkov	ROM	3	7	

1960 Rome C: 27, N: 27, D: 8.31.
(73 kg—160 lbs)

		ROUND ELIMINATED	PEN. PTS.	FINAL ROUND
1. Mithat Bayrak	TUR	—	5	1
2. Günter Maritschnigg	GER	—	5	5
3. René Schiermeyer	FRA	—	5	6
4. Stevan Horvat	YUG	6	6	
5. Hrigory Hamarnyk	SOV/UKR	6	7	
6. Matti Laakso	FIN	5	7	
7. Antal Rizmayer	HUN	5	8	
8. Hansjörg Hirschbuhl	SWI	4	7	

1964 Tokyo C: 19, N: 19, D: 10.19.
(78 kg—172 lbs)

		ROUND ELIMINATED	PEN. PTS.	FINAL ROUND
1. Anatoly Kolesov	SOV/KAZ	—	7	5
2. Kiril Petkov	BUL	—	7	6
3. Bertil Nyström	SWE	—	7	6
4. Boleslaw Dubicki	POL	—	7	7
5. Antal Rizmayer	HUN	4	6	
5. Ion Tăranu	ROM	4	6	

7. Russell Camilleri	USA	4	7
7. René Schiermeyer	FRA	4	7
7. Asghar Zowghian	IRN	4	7

Five of the last six matches ended in draws, which meant that Kolesov's victory by decision over Dubicki was the tie-breaker.

1968 Mexico City C: 22, N: 22, D: 10.26.
(78 kg—172 lbs)

		ROUND ELIMINATED	PEN. PTS.	FINAL ROUND
1. Rudolf Vesper	GDR	—	4.5	3.5
2. Daniel Robin	FRA	—	5	4
3. Károly Bajkó	HUN	—	5.5	5.5
4. Metodi Zarev	BUL	5	8	
5. Ion Tăranu	ROM	5	9.5	
6. Jan-Ivar Karström	SWE	4	6	
7. Harald Barlie	NOR	4	7	
7. Franz Berger	AUT	4	7	
7. Milovan Nenadic	YUG	4	7	

1972 Munich C: 21, N: 21, D: 9.10.

		ROUND ELIMINATED	PEN. PTS.	FINAL ROUND
1. Vítězslav Mácha	CZE	—	5.5	1
2. Petros Galaktopoulos	GRE	—	3	3
3. Jan Karlsson	SWE	5	6	
4. Ivan Kolev	BUL	5	6.5	
5. Momir Kecman	YUG	5	7.5	
6. Daniel Robin	FRA	5	8	
7. Klaus-Jürgen Pohl	GDR	5	8	
8. Werner Schröter	GER	4	7.5	

Mácha lost his opening bout to Ivan Kolev, but then won five in a row to secure the gold medal. Married to Miss Bohemia of 1971, Mácha was technically a miner, although he actually spent six to seven hours a day training.

1976 Montreal C: 18, N: 18, D: 7.24.

		ROUND ELIMINATED	PEN. PTS.	FINAL ROUND
1. Anatoly Bykov	SOV/RUS	—	1	1
2. Vítězslav Mácha	CZE	—	1.5	3
3. Karlheinz Helbing	GER	—	6	8
4. Mikko Huhtala	FIN	5	7.5	
5. Klaus-Dieter Göpfert	GDR	5	10	
6. Gheorghe Ciobotaru	ROM	4	7	
7. Jan Karlsson	SWE	4	8	
8. Petros Galaktopoulos	GRE	3	7	

Crucial matches took place in the fourth round when Bykov outpointed Ciobotaru 7–6 and Mácha edged Huhtala 4–3. In the fifth round Bykov was awarded a controversial victory by disqualification over Göpfert, with six seconds left and the score tied 5–5. Bykov's final win over Mácha was by a margin of 7–3.

1980 Moscow C: 14, N: 14, D: 7.23.

		ROUND ELIMINATED	PEN. PTS.	FINAL ROUND
1. Ferenc Kocsis	HUN	—	1	2
2. Anatoly Bykov	SOV/RUS	—	4	5
3. Mikko Huhtala	FIN	—	5	7
4. Yanko Shopov	BUL	5	7	
5. Lennart Lundell	SWE	4	6	
6. Vítězslav Mácha	CZE	4	8	
7. Gheorghe Minea	ROM	4	8	
8. Jacques van Lancker	BEL	3	7	

The final bout between Kocsis and Bykov ended with Bykov disqualified for inactivity after 7:21.

1984 Los Angeles-Anaheim C: 17, N: 17, D: 8.2.

		FINAL MATCH	
1. Jouko Salomäki	FIN	5–4	6:00
2. Roger Tallroth	SWE		
3. Ştefan Rusu	ROM	6–1	6:00
4. Kim Young-nam	KOR		
5. Karolj Kasap	YUG	6–3	6:00
6. Martial Mischler	FRA		
7. Christopher Catalfo	USA		
8. Mohamed Hamad	EGY		

Salomäki took a 5–0 lead and held on for the victory. Ştefan Rusu earned a bronze medal to go with the silver and gold he had won in the lightweight division in 1976 and 1980.

1988 Seoul C: 19, N: 19, D: 9.21.

		FINAL MATCH	
1. Kim Young-nam	KOR	2–1	6:00
2. Daulet Turlykhanov	SOV/KAZ		
3. Józef Tracz	POL	2–0	6:00
4. János Takács	HUN		
5. Martial Mischler	FRA	4–1	6:00
6. Borislav Velichkov	BUL		
7. Roger Tallroth	SWE	5–1	6:00
8. Hiromichi Ito	JPN		

Defending Olympic and world champion Jouko Salomäki was quickly eliminated by losing his first two bouts to Tallroth and Mischler. The final pitted Turlykhanov, a Soviet of Korean descent, against Kim, the 28-year-old son of poor farmers in Hampyong in Cholla province. When Kim began wrestling, he practiced on the wooden floor of his high school gymnasium, which was sparsely covered with dried rice stalks because the school could not afford mats. Turlykhanov led 1–0 at the break. But 25 seconds into the second round, Kim rolled his opponent onto his back for a 2-point score, then repelled Turlykhanov's advances for the remainder of the match. Kim was South Korea's first gold-medal winner of the Seoul Olympics. His victory brought great joy to the entire nation and earned him an $800 monthly pension for the rest of his life.

1992 Barcelona C: 21, N: 21, D: 7.29.

		FINAL MATCH
1. Mnatsakan Iskandaryan	ARM	6–3
2. Józef Tracz	POL	
3. Torbjörn Kornbakk	SWE	5–1
4. Nestor Almanza Baro	CUB	
5. Yvon Riemer	FRA	12–0
6. Anton Marchl	AUT	
7. Jaroslav Zeman	CZE	
8. Karlo Kasap	CAN	

Dobri Ivanov of Bulgaria qualified for the seventh-place match, but refused to take part and was disqualified.

MIDDLEWEIGHT

(82 kg—181 lbs)

1896–1904 not held

1906 Athens C: 16, N: 9, D: 5.1.
(85 kg—187½ lbs)
1. Verner Weckman   FIN
2. Rudolf Lindmayer   AUT
3. Robert Behrens   DEN

1908 London C: 21, N: 9, D: 7.25.
(73 kg—161 lbs)

		FINAL MATCH
1. Frithiof Mårtensson	SWE	Dec 20:00; Fall 6:25
2. Mauritz Andersson	SWE	
3. Anders Andersen	DEN	
4. Jóhannes Jósefsson	DEN/ICE	
5. Johannes Belmer (HOL), Johannes Eriksen (DEN), Axel Frank (SWE), Axel Larson (DEN), Marcel Dubois (BEL)		

The final between Mårtensson and Mauritz Andersson was postponed overnight due to a minor injury to Mårtensson. Jósefsson, an Icelandic nationalist forced to compete under the Danish flag, fractured his arm in the semifinals and had to forfeit the match for third place.

1912 Stockholm C: 38, N: 14, D: 7.13.
(75 kg—165½ lbs)
1. Claes Johanson   SWE
2. Martin Klein   RUS/EST
3. Alfred Asikainen   FIN
4. Karl Åberg   FIN
4. August Jokinen   FIN
6. Johannes Sint   HOL

The longest wrestling contest in Olympic history was the semifinal bout between Klein and Asikainen. The two men struggled on for hours under the hot sun, stopping every half hour for a brief refreshment break. Finally, after 11 hours, Klein, an Estonian competing for Czarist Russia, pinned his opponent. However, he was so exhausted by his ordeal that he was unable to take part in the final. Johanson was awarded first place by default.

1920 Antwerp C: 23, N: 12, D: 8.19.
(75 kg—165½ lbs)
1. Carl Westergren   SWE
2. Artur Lindfors   FIN
3. Matti Perttilä   FIN
4. Johannes Eillebrecht HOL

The phenomenal Carl Westergren won the first of his three Olympic gold medals, each in a different division. He pinned Lindfors after 31 minutes 25 seconds.

1924 Paris C: 27, N: 19, D: 7.10.
(75 kg—165½ lbs)
1. Edvard Westerlund   FIN
2. Artur Lindfors   FIN
3. Roman Steinberg   EST
4. Giuseppe Gorletti   ITA
5. Viktor Fischer   AUT
5. Nikola Grbič   YUG
7. Robert Christoffersen DEN
7. Waclaw Okulicz-Kozaryn POL

1928 Amsterdam C: 17, N: 17, D: 8.5.
(75 kg—165½ lbs)
1. Väinö Kokkinen   FIN
2. László Papp   HUN
3. Albert Kusnets   EST
4. Jóhannes Jacobsen   DEN
5. Jean Saenen   BEL
6. František Hála   CZE
7. Enrico Bonassin   ITA
7. Nurettin Boyturun   TUR

Kokkinen, a restaurant owner from Helsinki, pinned all five of his opponents.

1932 Los Angeles C: 4, N: 4, D: 8.7.
(79 kg—174 lbs)
1. Väinö Kokkinen   FIN
2. Jean Földeak   GER
3. Axel Cadier   SWE

1936 Berlin C: 16, N: 16, D: 8.9.
(79 kg—174 lbs)

		ROUND ELIMINATED	PEN. PTS.	FINAL ROUND
1. Ivar Johansson	SWE	—	2	1
2. Ludwig Schweikert	GER	—	3	2
3. József Palotás	HUN	—	4	6
4. Väinö Kokkinen	FIN	5	6	
5. Ibrahim Erabi	EGY	4	6	
6. Ercole Gallegati	ITA	4	6	
7. Francise Cocos	ROM	4	6	
8. Koloman Kis	YUG	3	6	
8. Johans Pointner	AUT	3	6	
8. Josef Pribyl	CZE	3	6	

1948 London C: 13, N: 13, D: 8.6.
(79 kg—174 lbs)

		ROUND ELIMINATED	PEN. PTS.	FINAL ROUND
1. Axel Grönberg	SWE	—	2	1
2. Muhlis Tayfur	TUR	—	4	3
3. Ercole Gallegati	ITA	5	5	
4. Jean-Baptiste Benoy	BEL	5	6	
5. Kaare Larsen	NOR	5	7	
6. Juho Kinnunen	FIN	4	5	
7. Gyula Németi	HUN	4	5	
8. Anton Vogel	AUT	3	6	

1952 Helsinki C: 11, N: 11, D: 7.27.
(79 kg—174 lbs)

		ROUND ELIMINATED	PEN. PTS.	FINAL ROUND
1. Axel Grönberg	SWE	—	4	2
2. Kalervo Rauhala	FIN	—	3	4
3. Nikolai Belov	SOV/RUS	—	3	6
4. Gyula Németi	HUN	4	5	
5. Ali Özdemir	TUR	3	5	
6. Ercole Gallegati	ITA	3	6	
7. Gustav Gocke	GER	3	7	

1956 Melbourne C: 10, N: 10, D: 12.6.
(79 kg—174 lbs)

		ROUND ELIMINATED	PEN. PTS.	FINAL ROUND
1. Givy Kartoziya	SOV/GEO	—	3	2
2. Dimiter Dobrev	BUL	—	4	4
3. Karl-Axel Rune Jansson	SWE	—	5	6
4. Johann Sterr	GER	4	6	
5. György Gurics	HUN	3	5	
6. Viljo Punkari	FIN	3	6	
7. James Peckham	USA	3	7	

1960 Rome C: 24, N: 24, D: 8.31.
(79 kg—174 lbs)

		ROUND ELIMINATED	PEN. PTS.
1. Dimiter Dobrev	BUL	—	4
2. Lothar Metz	GDR	6	6
3. Ion Tăranu	ROM	6	7
4. Kazim Ayvaz	TUR	6	7
5. Boleslaw Dubicki	POL	5	7
5. Nikolai Chuchalov	SOV/RUS	5	7
7. Yacous Romanos	LEB	4	7
8. Russell Camilleri	USA	4	7

1964 Tokyo C: 20, N: 20, D: 10.19.
(87 kg—192 lbs)

		ROUND ELIMINATED	PEN. PTS.	2ND PLACE
1. Branislav Simič	YUG	—	4	
2. Jiři Kormanik	CZE	5	6	1
3. Lothar Metz	GDR	5	6	3

4. Géza Hollósi	HUN	5	7
4. Valentin Olenik	SOV/RUS	5	7
6. Kraliu Bimbalov	BUL	5	8
7. Richard Wayne Baughman	USA	4	7
8. Ismail Selekman	TUR	4	7

Simič, competing in his third Olympics, managed to take first place without having to face either Kormanik or Metz.

1968 Mexico City C: 19, N: 19, D: 10.26.
(87 kg—192 lbs)

		ROUND ELIMINATED	PEN. PTS.
1. Lothar Metz	GDR	—	5
2. Valentin Olenik	SOV/RUS	6	6
3. Branislav Simič	YUG	6	6
4. Nicolae Neguț	ROM	6	8.5
5. Richard Wayne Baughman	USA	5	8
5. Peter Krumov	BUL	5	8
7. Czeslaw Kwinciński	POL	4	7
8. Häkon Overby	NOR	4	7

1972 Munich C: 20, N: 20, D: 9.10.

		ROUND ELIMINATED	PEN. PTS.	FINAL ROUND
1. Csaba Hegedüs	HUN	—	3	2
2. Anatoly Nazarenko	SOV/KAZ	—	4	3
3. Milan Nenadič	YUG/CRO	—	4	7
4. Miroslav Janota	CZE	5	7	
5. Ion Gabor	ROM	5	9	
6. Frank Hartmann	GDR	4	6	
7. Ali Yagmur	TUR	4	7	
8. Kiril Dimitrov	BUL	4	7.5	

Nazarenko, the 1970 world champion, and Hegedüs, the 1971 world champion, met in the very first round, with Hegedüs winning a decision. Neither man lost another bout for the rest of the tournament.

1976 Montreal C: 17, N: 17, D: 7.24.

		ROUND ELIMINATED	PEN. PTS.	FINAL ROUND
1. Momir Petković	YUG	—	4.5	2
2. Vladimir Cheboksarov	SOV/RUS	—	6	4
3. Ivan Kolev	BUL	—	7	6
4. Leif Andersson	SWE	6	8	
5. Miroslav Janota	CZE	5	8	
6. Kazuhiro Takanishi	JPN	5	8.5	
7. Ion Enache	ROM	4	7	
8. Adam Ostrowski	POL	4	7	

The crucial third-round contest between Petković and Cheboksarov ended in a 6–6 tie, but Petković was given the victory after complex tie-breaker rules were invoked.

1980 Moscow C: 12, N: 12, D: 7.24.

		ROUND ELIMI-NATED	PEN. PTS.	FINAL ROUND
1. Gennady Korban	SOV/RUS	—	1	2
2. Jan Dolgowicz	POL	—	7	3
3. Pavel Pavlov	BUL	—	1	7
4. Leif Andersson	SWE	4	8	
5. Detlef Kühn	GDR	3	8	
6. Mihály Toma	HUN	3	8	
7. Mohammad Eloulabi	SYR	3	9	
8. Miroslaw Janota	CZE	2	7	

Korban defeated Dolgowicz, 11–4, and Pavlov, 13–7.

1984 Los Angeles-Anaheim C: 15, N: 15, D: 8.3.

		FINAL MATCH	
1. Ion Draica	ROM	4–3	6:00
2. Dimitrios Thanopoulos	GRE		
3. Sören Claesson	SWE	5–2	6:00
4. Momir Petković	YUG		
5. Jarmo Övermark	FIN	5–3	6:00
6. Mohamed El Ashram	EGY		
7. Louis Santerre	CAN		
8. Kim Sang-kyu	KOR		

1988 Seoul C: 21, N: 21, D: 9.22.

		FINAL MATCH	
1. Mikhail Mamiashvili	SOV/RUS	10–1	6:00
2. Tibor Komáromi	HUN		
3. Kim Sang-kyu	KOR	6–5	6:00

Middleweight Greco-Roman wrestler Mikhail Mamiashvili finds himself in a tight squeeze in his 1988 final match against Tibor Komáromi. Mamiashvili emerged victorious.

4. Stig Arild Kleven	NOR		
5. Goran Kasum	YUG	Passivity	4:26
6. Magnus Fredriksson	SWE		
7. John Morgan	USA	Forfeit	
8. Bogdan Daras	POL		

Mamiashvili had already won three world championships at 74 kilograms when he moved up to challenge 82-kilogram world champion Komáromi in 1988. He defeated the Hungarian at the European championships in May and then again at the Olympics in Seoul. By the time of the next Olympics, Mamiashvili was the head coach of the Greco-Roman team of the ex–Soviet republics, even though he was only 28 years old.

1992 Barcelona C: 20, N: 20, D: 7.30.

		FINAL MATCH
1. Péter Farkas	HUN	6–1
2. Piotr Stepién	POL	
3. Daulet Turlykhanov	KAZ	2–0
4. Magnus Fredriksson	SWE	
5. Timo Niemi	FIN	3–1
6. Goran Kasum	YUG	
7. Thomas Zander	GER	3–1
8. Pavel Frinta	CZE	

LIGHT HEAVYWEIGHT
(90 kg—198 ½ lbs)

1896–1906 not held

1908 London C: 21, N: 9, D: 7.22.
(93 kg—205 lbs)

		FINAL MATCH
1. Verner Weckman	FIN	Lost Fall 4:22; Fall 5:07; Fall 16:10
2. Yrjö Saarela	FIN	
3. Carl Jensen	DEN	
4. Hugó Payr	HUN	
5. Arthur Banbrook (GBR), Marcel Dubois (BEL), Fritz Larsson (SWE), Jacob van Westerop (HOL)		

Weckman, who had won the Middleweight gold medal in 1906, was a 25-year-old engineer. At the award ceremony the Finnish flag was not hoisted. In its place was a sign bearing the word "Finland." Rumors spread that the tyrannical Czarist Russian government had forbidden the use of the Finnish national flag. However, the Finnish colors were raised up the flagpole later in the day.

1912 Stockholm C: 29, N: 11, D: 7.14.
(82.5 kg—182 lbs)

1. —		
2. Anders Ahlgren	SWE	
2. Ivar Böhling	FIN	

Anders Ahlgren and Ivar Böhling wrestled for nine hours in the final of the 1912 Greco-Roman Light Heavyweight division before officials declared a draw.

3. Béla Varga   HUN
4. August Rajala   FIN

Ahlgren fought his way to the final match by pinning six opponents, each within 35 minutes. But in Böhling he met his equal—literally. Ahlgren and Böhling struggled hour after hour without either man giving in, until finally, after nine hours, officials called the contest a draw. The rules of the Olympic competition stated that it was necessary for a first-place winner actually to defeat his adversary, so the officials decided to declare Ahlgren and Böhling co-winners of the second prize.

1920 Antwerp C: 18, N: 11, D: 8.19.
(82 kg—182 lbs)
1. Claes Johanson   SWE
2. Edil Rosenqvist   FIN
3. Johannes Eriksen   DEN
4. Johannes Sint   HOL

1924 Paris C: 22, N: 15, D: 7.10.
(82.5 kg—182 lbs)
1. Carl Westergren   SWE
2. Rudolf Svensson   SWE
3. Onni Pellinen   FIN
4. Ibrahim Moustafa   EGY
5. Emil Weckstén   FIN
6. Rudolf Loos (EST), A. Misset (HOL), Béla Varga (HUN)

Westergren had won the Middleweight title four years earlier in Antwerp.

1928 Amsterdam C: 17, N: 17, D: 8.5.
(82.5 kg—182 lbs)
1. Ibrahim Moustafa   EGY
2. Adolf Rieger   GER
3. Onni Pellinen   FIN
4. Nicolas Appels   BEL
5. Ejnar Hansen   DEN
6. Imre Szalay   HUN

1932 Los Angeles C: 3, N: 3, D: 8.7.
(87 kg—192 lbs)

		PEN. PTS.
1. Rudolf Svensson	SWE	1
2. Onni Pellinen	FIN	3
3. Mario Gruppioni	ITA	6

1936 Berlin C: 13, N: 13, D: 8.9.
(87 kg—192 lbs)

		ROUND ELIMI- NATED	PEN. PTS.	FINAL ROUND
1. Axel Cardier	SWE	—	2	1
2. Edvins Bietags	LAT	—	1	3
3. August Neo	EST	5	5	
4. Werner Seelenbinder	GER	5	6	
5. Umberto Silvestri	ITA	4	6	
6. Olaf Knutsen	NOR	4	6	
7. Franz Foidl	AUT	4	6	
8. Mustafa Avcioglu Cakmak	TUR	3	5	

Seelenbinder was an anti-Nazi hero who was executed in 1944 because of his opposition to Adolf Hitler.

1948 London C: 14, N: 14, D: 8.6.
(87 kg—192 lbs)

		ROUND ELIMI- NATED	PEN. PTS.	FINAL ROUND
1. Karl-Erik Nilsson	SWE	—	2	1
2. Kaelpo Gröndahl	FIN	—	1	3
3. Ibrahim Orabi	EGY	5	6	
4. Gyula Kovács	HUN	4	5	
5. Kenneth Richmond	GBR	4	6	
6. Erling Lauridsen	DEN	4	7	
7. Peter Enzinger	AUT	3	6	
8. Mustafa Avcioglu Cakmak	TUR	3	7	
8. Charles Istaz	BEL	3	7	

An incident of sorts took place in the fifth round, when Nilsson threw Orabi over his head and the referee ruled it a fall. While the Egyptians protested, Orabi stretched out on the mat and refused to move. After 15 minutes Nilsson was called back from the dressing room and ordered to continue the match. Nilsson then scored another fall and the matter was settled.

1952 Helsinki C: 10, N: 10, D: 7.27.
(87 kg—192 lbs)

		ROUND ELIMINATED	PEN. PTS.	FINAL ROUND
1. Kaelpo Gröndahl	FIN	—	2	2
2. Shalva Chikhladze	SOV/RUS	—	4	3
3. Karl-Erik Nilsson	SWE	—	5	6
4. Gyula Kovács	HUN	4	5	
5. Ismet Atli	TUR	3	6	
6. Umberto Silvestri	ITA	3	7	
6. Michel Skaff	LEB	3	7	

The final bout between Gröndahl and Chikhladze was dull and cautious and was won by Gröndahl on a split decision.

1956 Melbourne C: 10, N: 10, D: 12.6.
(87 kg—192 lbs)

		ROUND ELIMINATED	PEN. PTS.	2ND PLACE
1. Valentin Nikolayev	SOV/RUS	—	4	
2. Petko Sirakov	BUL	4	5	1
3. Karl-Erik Nilsson	SWE	4	5	3
4. Robert Steckle	CAN	4	7	
5. Dale Thomas	USA	3	6	
5. Eugen Wiesberger	AUT	3	6	
7. Veikko Lahti	FIN	3	7	
8. Adil Atan	TUR	3	7	

1960 Rome C: 17, N: 17, D: 8.31.
(87 kg—192 lbs)

		ROUND ELIMINATED	PEN. PTS.	FINAL ROUND
1. Tevfik Kiş	TUR	—	6	2
2. Kralyu Bimbalov	BUL	—	6	2
3. Givy Kartoziya	SOV/GEO	6	8	
4. Péter Piti	HUN	6	8	
5. Antero Vanhanen	FIN	5	7	
6. José Panizo Rodriguez	SPA	4	7	
7. Gheorghe Popovici	ROM	4	8	
8. Eugen Wiesberger	AUT	4	8	

Kiş was awarded first place because he weighed less than Bimbalov.

1964 Tokyo C: 18, N: 18, D: 10.19.
(97 kg—214 lbs)

		ROUND ELIMINATED	PEN. PTS.
1. Boyan Radev	BUL	—	2
2. Per Svensson	SWE	5	6
3. Heinz Kiehl	GER	5	6
4. Nicolae Martinescu	ROM	5	8
5. Rostom Abashidze	SOV/GEO	4	6
5. Ferenc Kiss	HUN	4	6
5. Peter Jutzeler	SWI	4	6
8. Eugen Wiesberger	AUT	4	7

Radev breezed through the tournament, aided by the fact that he faced only one wrestler, Martinescu, who finished in the top eight.

1968 Mexico City C: 16, N: 16, D: 10.26.
(97 kg—214 lbs)

		ROUND ELIMINATED	PEN. PTS.	FINAL ROUND
1. Boyan Radev	BUL	—	0.5	2.5
2. Nikolai Yakovenko	SOV/RUS	—	1	3.5
3. Nicolae Martinescu	ROM	—	4	7
4. Per Svensson	SWE	4	6	
5. Tore Hem	NOR	4	8	
6. Peter Jutzeler	SWI	3	6	
6. Cay Malmberg	FIN	3	6	
6. Waclaw Orlowski	POL	3	6	

Radev and Yakovenko tied, but Radev threw Martinescu in 4:58 to win the gold medal.

1972 Munich C: 14, N: 14, D: 9.10.

		ROUND ELIMINATED	PEN. PTS.	FINAL ROUND
1. Valery Rezantsev	SOV/KAZ	—	2	2
2. Josip Čorak	YUG	—	3	5
3. Czeslaw Kwienciński	POL	—	5	5
4. József Percsi	HUN	5	6.5	
5. Håkon Överbye	NOR	5	9	
6. Nicolae Neguţ	ROM	4	8	
7. Kimiichi Tani	JPN	4	9	
8. Günter Kowalewski	GER	3	8	

Rezantsev suffered a first-round draw with Neguţ and then won six straight bouts.

1976 Montreal C: 13, N: 13, D: 7.24.

		ROUND ELIMINATED	PEN. PTS.	FINAL ROUND
1. Valery Rezantsev	SOV/KAZ	—	2	2
2. Stoyan Ivanov	BUL	—	5	5
3. Czeslaw Kwieciński	POL	—	3	7
4. Darko Nisavić	YUG	5	9	
5. Frank Andersson	SWE	4	6	
6. István Séllyei	HUN	4	8	
7. James Johnson	USA	3	8	
7. Sadao Sato	JPN	3	8	

Valery Rezantsev dominated Light Heavyweight Greco-Roman wrestling in the 1970s. He went to Montreal as the defending Olympic champion and the five-time defending world champion. In his final bout he was held to a 6–6 tie by Ivanov, but a tie-breaker gave him the victory anyway.

1980 Moscow C: 15, N: 15, D: 7.22.

		ROUND ELIMINATED	PEN. PTS.	FINAL ROUND
1. Norbert Növényi	HUN	—	1	2
2. Igor Kanygin	SOV/BLR	—	6.5	5
3. Petre Dicu	ROM	—	6	7

4. Frank Andersson	SWE	5	7
5. Thomas Horschel	GDR	4	8
6. José Poll Martinez	CUB	4	8.5
7. Christophe Andanson	FRA	3	6.5
8. Georgios Pozidis	GRE	3	7

Növényi scattered four opponents and then outpointed Kanygin 7–6 and Dicu 4–1.

1984 Los Angeles-Anaheim C: 13, N: 13, D: 8.1.

		FINAL MATCH	
1. Steven Fraser	USA	1–1	6:00
2. Ilie Matei	ROM		
3. Frank Andersson	SWE	5–0	6:00
4. Uwe Sachs	GER		
5. Jean-François Court	FRA	4–2	6:00
6. Georgios Pozidis	GRE		
7. Toni Hannula	FIN		
8. Franz Marx	AUT		

Fraser, a deputy sheriff from Ann Arbor, Michigan, became the first U.S. Greco-Roman wrestler ever to win an Olympic medal. With less than 50 seconds remaining in the final, he trailed Matei 1–0. But then Fraser caught the Romanian in a front headlock. The roar of the crowd seemed to give Fraser an extra injection of strength and he scored a takedown to gain the final point of the match and thus the victory.

1988 Seoul C: 22, N: 22, D: 9.20.

		FINAL MATCH	
1. Atanas Komchev	BUL	4–0	6:00
2. Harri Koskela	FIN		
3. Vladimir Popov	SOV/RUS	Fall	1:36
4. Christer Gulldén	SWE		
5. Andreas Steinbach	GER	Passivity	4:43
6. Franz Pitschmann	AUT		
7. Olaf Koschnitzke	GDR	Forfeit	
8. Georgios Pikilidis	GRE		

1992 Barcelona C: 19, N: 19, D: 7.30.

		FINAL MATCH	
1. Maik Bullmann	GER	5–0	
2. Hakki Başar	TUR		
3. Gogi Koguashvili	GEO	2–0	
4. Mikael Ljungberg	SWE		
5. Hassan Babak	IRN	17–1	3:56
6. Michial Foy	USA		
7. Reynaldo Peña Borroto	CUB	Forfeit	
8. Salvatore Campanella	ITA		

Bullman was the overwhelming favorite, having won the last three world championships. In Barcelona his closest match was a 3–1 victory over Babak. He outscored all five of his opponents by a combined total of 33–1.

HEAVYWEIGHT
(100 kg—220 lbs)

1896—1968 not held

1972 Munich C: 15, N: 15, D: 9.10.

		ROUND ELIMI-NATED	PEN. PTS.	FINAL ROUND
1. Nicolae Martinescu	ROM	—	5.5	0
2. Nikolai Yakovenko	SOV/RUS	—	1	4
3. Ferenc Kiss	HUN	5	6.5	
4. Hristo Ignatov	BUL	5	9	
5. Fredi Albrecht	GDR	4	7	
6. Tore Hem	NOR	4	8	
7. Andrzej Skrzydlewski	POL	4	8.5	
8. Rudolf Luescher	SWI	2	6	

1976 Montreal C: 13, N: 13, D: 7.24.

		ROUND ELIMI-NATED	PEN. PTS.	FINAL ROUND
1. Nikolai Balboshin	SOV/RUS	—	0	0
2. Kamen Goranov	BUL	—	4	5
3. Andrzej Skrzydlewski	POL	—	3	7
4. Brad Rheingans	USA	4	6	
5. Tore Hem	NOR	4	7	
6. Heinz Schäfer	GER	4	8	
7. József Farkas	HUN	3	8	
7. Nicolae Martinescu	ROM	3	8	

Balboshin needed only 16 minutes and 48 seconds to win his five matches.

1980 Moscow C: 9, N: 9, D: 7.23.

		ROUND ELIMI-NATED	PEN. PTS.	FINAL ROUND
1. Georgi Raikov	BUL	—	1	2
2. Roman Bierla	POL	—	1	4
3. Vasile Andrei	ROM	4	7	
4. Refik Memisevic	YUG	4	7	
5. Georgios Pikilidis	GRE	3	8	
6. Oldřich Dvorak	CZE	3	8	
7. Nikolai Balboshin	SOV/RUS	2	4	
8. Svend Erik Studsgaard	DEN	2	8	

Raikov defeated Bierla by disqualification after 7:52. Defending champion Nikolai Balboshin, injured during the second round, was forced to withdraw.

1984 Los Angeles-Anaheim C: 8, N: 8, D: 8.3.

		FINAL MATCH	
1. Vasile Andrei	ROM	12–0	4:16
2. Greg Gibson	USA		
3. Jozef Tertelje	YUG	3–0	6:00
4. Georgios Pikilidis	GRE		
5. Franz Pitschmann	AUT	7–5	6:00
6. Fritz Gerdsmeier	GER		
7. Yoshiro Fujita	JPN		
7. Karl-Johan Gustafsson	SWE		

Andrei defeated each of his four opponents in less than 4½ minutes.

1988 Seoul C: 18, N: 18, D: 9.21.

		FINAL MATCH	
1. Andrzej Wroński	POL	3–1	6:00
2. Gerhard Himmel	GER		
3. Dennis Koslowski	USA	6–0	6:00
4. Ilia Georgiev	BUL		
5. Jožef Tertelje	YUG	Injury	
6. Yoo Young-tai	KOR		
7. Guram Gedekhauri	SOV/GEO	Injury	
8. Tamás Gáspár	HUN		

Andrzej Wroński was one of the most unexpected winners of the Seoul Olympics. Before 1988 he had never placed in the top eight of a major international competition. His most noteworthy accomplishment was finishing *third* in the 1987 Polish championships. Meanwhile, the Olympic field was filled with winners, most notably the defending Olympic champion, Vasile Andrei; the defending world champion, Guram Gedekhauri; the world championship runner-up, Dennis Koslowski; the 1986 world champion, Tamás Gáspár; the 1986 European champion, Jožef Tertelje; and the 1987 European champion, Ilia Georgiev. None of these worthies made it to the final. Gáspár was forced to withdraw after he was injured in his match with Gerhard Himmel, the bronze medalist at the 1988 European championship. The others proceeded to knock each other off. Andrei defeated Gedekhauri, as did Tertelje. Tertelje beat Andrei. Koslowski beat Tertelje. Gedekhauri beat Koslowski. Georgiev lost to both Gáspár and Himmel. Even Wroński lost once when he was pinned by Gedekhauri. In fact, he was the only wrestler at the 1988 Olympics to win a gold medal despite having lost a match.

What Wroński did do was to register three upset victories: 1–0 over Tertelje, 1–0 over Koslowski, and a passivity win over Andrei. In the final he scored all of his points when he lifted Himmel from a prone position and threw him to the mat.

1992 Barcelona C: 16, N: 16, D: 7.28.

		FINAL MATCH	
1. Hector Milián	CUB	2–1	5:25
2. Dennis Koslowski	USA		
3. Sergei Demyashkevich	BLR	1–0	
4. Andrzej Wroński	POL		
5. Andreas Steinbach	GER	4–2	
6. Ion Iremciuc	ROM		
7. Norbert Növényi	HUN	Forfeit	
8. Song Sung-il	KOR		

In the final, Milián scored on a gutwrench at 1:08, then Koslowski tied the score with a front headlock takedown at 3:26. Milián attacked quickly in overtime, got behind Koslowski, and scored with a sudden snapdown at the edge of the mat after only 25 seconds.

SUPER HEAVYWEIGHT
(Heavyweight 1896–1968)

A maximum weight limit—286 lbs. (130 kg)—was imposed for the first time at the 1988 Olympics.

1896 Athens C: 5, N: 4, D: 4.11.

		FINAL MATCH
1. Carl Schuhmann	GER	Fall
2. Georgios Tsitas	GRE	
3. Stephanos Christopoulos	GRE	

All the matches were held outdoors in a sand pit. Although this was technically a Greco-Roman event, legholds were allowed. Schuhmann also won three gold medals in the gymnastics competition and placed fourth in the shot put.

1900–1904 not held

1906 Athens C: 10, N: 6, D: 5.1.
1. Soren Marius Jensen   DEN
2. Henri Baur   AUT
3. Marcel Dubois   BEL

1908 London C: 7, N: 4, D: 7.24.

		FINAL MATCH
1. Richárd Weisz	HUN	Dec 30:00; Dec 30:00
2. Aleksandr Petrov	RUS	
3. Soren Marius Jensen	DEN	
4. Hugó Payr	HUN	

1912 Stockholm C: 18, N: 9, D: 7.14.
1. Yrjö Saarela   FIN
2. Johan Olin   FIN
3. Sören Marius Jensen   DEN
4. Jakob Neser   GER
5. Emil Backenius   FIN
5. Kaarlo "Kalle" Wiljamaa   FIN

The final match between Saarela and Jensen ended when the Dane was overcome by the sun and retired after three hours of wrestling.

1920 Antwerp C: 21, N: 13, D: 8.19.
1. Adolf Lindfors   FIN
2. Poul Hansen   DEN
3. Martti Nieminen   FIN
4. Alexander Weyand   USA

Lindfors pinned Anders Ahlgren of Sweden in the final after 47 minutes 38 seconds. Ahlgren was so worn out from the match that he withdrew from the contest to decide second place.

1924 Paris C: 17, N: 10, D: 7.10.
1. Henri Deglane   FRA
2. Edil Rosenqvist   FIN
3. Rajmund Badó   HUN
4. Emil Larsen   DEN
5. Harry Nilsson (SWE), Janis Polis (LAT), L. Pothier (BEL)

One of the many incidents which plagued the judgeable sports at the Paris Olympics occurred in the second round of the Greco-Roman Heavyweight tournament. Local favorite Henri Deglane, age 22, was pitted against 39-year-old Claes Johanson, who had won the Middleweight title in 1912 and the Light Heavyweight title in 1920. After 20 minutes of fighting, Johanson was declared the winner on points. The French team protested the decision, and the Jury of Appeal ordered the two men to wrestle for six more minutes, after which Deglane was declared the victor. Johanson was so disgusted that he withdrew from the competition. Deglane went on to win four more decisions and the gold medal.

1928 Amsterdam C: 15, N: 15, D: 8.5.
1. Rudolf Svensson — SWE
2. Hjalmar Eemil Nyström — FIN
3. Georg Gehring — GER
4. Eugen Wiesberger — AUT
5. Josef Urban — CZE
6. Rajmund Badó — HUN
7. Mehmed Çoban — TUR
7. Aleardo Donati — ITA

1932 Los Angeles C: 5, N: 5, D: 8.7.
1. Carl Westergren — SWE
2. Josef Urban — CZE
3. Nikolaus Hirschi — AUT
4. Georg Gehring — GER
5. Aleardo Donati — ITA

Westergren, a bus driver from Malmo, compiled an outstanding record at the Olympics. Following in the footsteps of Claes Johanson, he won the Middleweight title in 1920 and the Light Heavyweight title in 1924. In 1928, as a light heavyweight, he was pinned in the first round by Onni Pellinen. However he returned to the Olympics in 1932 as a 36-year-old heavyweight and won a third gold medal.

1936 Berlin C: 12, N: 12, D: 8.9.

		ROUND ELIMINATED	PEN. PTS.	FINAL ROUND
1. Kristjan Palusalu	EST	—	3	1
2. John Nyman	SWE	—	3	3
3. Kurt Hornfischer	GER	5	5	
4. Mehmet Çoban	TUR	4	6	
5. Hjalmar Eemil Nyström	FIN	4	6	
6. Aleardo Donati	ITA	4	7	
7. Joseph Klapuch	CZE	3	6	
8. Alberts Zvejnieks	LAT	3	6	

1948 London C: 9, N: 9, D: 8.6.

		ROUND ELIMINATED	PEN. PTS.	FINAL ROUND
1. Ahmet Kireçci	TUR	—	1	1
2. Tor Nilsson	SWE	—	3	3
3. Guido Fantoni	ITA	—	1	6
4. Taisto Kangasniemi	FIN	3	5	

Carl Westergren won three Greco-Roman wrestling gold medals in three different weight divisions: Middleweight in 1920, Light Heavyweight in 1924, and Heavyweight in 1932 (at the age of 36).

5. József Tarányi	HUN	3	6	
6. Moritz Inderbitzin	SWI	3	7	

Kireçci had received a bronze medal in the freestyle middleweight 12 years earlier in Berlin.

1952 Helsinki C: 10, N: 10, D: 7.27.

		ROUND ELIMINATED	PEN. PTS.	FINAL ROUND
1. Johannes Kotkas	SOV/EST	—	0	0
2. Josef Ružička	CZE	—	3	3

			ROUND ELIMINATED	PEN. PTS.	FINAL ROUND
3.	Tauno Kovanen	FIN	—	6	6
4.	Willi Waltner	GER	4	7	
5.	Alexandru Suli	ROM	3	5	
6.	Bengt Fahlkvist	SWE	3	6	
6.	Antoine Georgoulis	GRE	3	6	
8.	Guido Fantoni	ITA	3	7	

Kotkas, a 37-year-old Estonian from Tartu, pinned his four opponents in an elapsed time of 13 minutes 36 seconds. He had won the European championship in 1938 and was also the Soviet hammer-throw champion in 1943.

1956 Melbourne C: 10, N: 10, D: 12.6.

			ROUND ELIMINATED	PEN. PTS.	FINAL ROUND
1.	Anatoly Parfenov	SOV/RUS	—	4	2
2.	Wilfried Dietrich	GER	—	5	4
3.	Adelmo Bulgarelli	ITA	—	4	6
4.	Hamit Kaplan	TUR	4	6	
5.	Bertíl Antonsson	SWE	4	7	
6.	Taisto Kangasniemi	FIN	3	6	
7.	Yusein Mehmedov	BUL	3	7	
7.	Antoine Georgoulis	GRE	3	7	

Parfenov was one of the least overwhelming Olympic champions ever. He was originally declared the loser in his opening contest with Dietrich. However, a protest by the Soviet team was upheld by the Jury of Appeal. In the second round Parfenov lost to Antonsson. Then he won a forfeit in the third round and received a bye in the fourth round. In the fifth round he gained his only undisputed victory, a decision over Bulgarelli. Fortunately for Parfenov, his two wins were enough to take first place.

1960 Rome C: 12, N: 12, D: 8.31.

			ROUND ELIMINATED	PEN. PTS.	FINAL ROUND
1.	Ivan Bohdan	SOV/UKR	—	4	4
2.	Wilfried Dietrich	GER	—	5	4
3.	Bohumil Kubát	CZE	—	5	4
4.	István Kozma	HUN	4	6	
5.	Lucjan Sosnowski	POL	4	6	
6.	Radoslav Kasabov	BUL	4	8	
7.	Adelmo Bulgarelli	ITA	3	6	
8.	Sten Ragnar Svensson	SWE	3	9	

Dietrich was awarded the silver medal because his bodyweight was less than that of Bohumil "Weeny" Kubát. In fact, it was 88 pounds less than Kubát's. Dietrich weighed 198 pounds, while Kubát weighed 286.

1964 Tokyo C: 11, N: 11, D: 10.19.

			ROUND ELIMINATED	PEN. PTS.	FINAL ROUND
1.	István Kozma	HUN	—	1	2
2.	Anatoly Roshin	SOV/RUS	—	3	2
3.	Wilfried Dietrich	GER	5	7	
4.	Petr Kment	CZE	5	8	
5.	Sten Ragnar Svensson	SWE	4	6	
6.	Robert Pickens	USA	3	7	
7.	Radoslav Kasabov	BUL	3	8	
8.	Tsuneharu Sugiyama	JPN	3	8	

Kozma weighed in at 320 pounds.

1968 Mexico City C: 15, N: 15, D: 10.26.

			ROUND ELIMINATED	PEN. PTS.	FINAL ROUND
1.	István Kozma	HUN	—	2.5	2.5
2.	Anatoly Roshin	SOV/RUS	—	3.5	2.5
3.	Petr Kment	CZE	—	5	8
4.	Sten Ragnar Svensson	SWE	5	7	
5.	Constantin Buşiu	ROM	4	7	
6.	Stefan Petrov	BUL	4	8	
7.	Raymond Uyttterheaeghe	FRA	4	9	
8.	Edward Wojda	POL	4	9.5	

As in 1964, Kozma won the gold medal despite being held to a draw by Roshin. This time the huge Hungarian threw his other four opponents, two of them within 40 seconds. Kment was injured and forced to withdraw from his final two matches against Kozma and Roshin.

1972 Munich C: 13, N: 13, D: 9.10.

			ROUND ELIMINATED	PEN. PTS.	FINAL ROUND
1.	Anatoly Roshin	SOV/RUS	—	2	1
2.	Aleksandr Tomov	BUL	—	3	5
3.	Victor Dolîpschi	ROM	—	4	6
4.	József Csatári	HUN	4	8	
4.	Wilfried Dietrich	GER	4	8	
4.	Istvan Semeredi	YUG	4	8	
7.	Petr Kment	CZE	3	7	

Thirty-eight-year-old Wilfried Dietrich, attempting to win a medal in his fifth consecutive Olympics, was disqualified in his third-round match against Victor Dolîpschi. Dietrich was so upset by the decision that he withdrew from the competition even though he only had four negative points. Forty-year-old Anatoly Roshin was the oldest wrestler ever to win an Olympic medal.

1976 Montreal C: 12, N: 12, D: 7.24.

			ROUND ELIMINATED	PEN. PTS.	FINAL ROUND
1.	Oleksander Kolchynsky	SOV/UKR	—	0	1
2.	Aleksandr Tomov	BUL	—	4	3
3.	Roman Codreanu	ROM	—	2	8

4. Henryk Tomanek	POL	4	8
5. William "Pete" Lee	USA	4	8
6. János Rovnyai	HUN	3	8
7. Einar Gundersen	NOR	3	8
7. Richard Wolff	GER	3	8

Three-time defending world champion Aleksandr Tomov had defeated Kolchynsky six straight times, culminating in the European championships three months before the Olympics. However, in Montreal Tomov was upset in the first round when he was pinned in only 1:14 by 331-pound Pete Lee of Muncie, Indiana. Tomov recovered to win his next three matches and qualify for the final round-robin. In the meantime, Kolchynsky used up only six minutes and 38 seconds in finishing off his first four opponents. He followed this by outpointing Tomov 12–6 in his final bout.

1980 Moscow C: 10, N: 10, D: 7.24.

		ROUND ELIMI-NATED	PEN. PTS.	FINAL ROUND
1. Oleksander Kolchynsky	SOV/UKR	—	0	1
2. Aleksandr Tomov	BUL	—	0	3
3. Hassan Bchara	LEB	—	8	8
4. József Farkas	HUN	4	10	
5. Prvoslav Ilić	YUG	3	8	
6. Roman Codreanu	ROM	3	8	
6. Arturo Diaz Mora	CUB	3	8	
8. Marek Galinski	POL	2	8	

The superiority of Kolchynsky and Tomov was shown by the fact that the other eight wrestlers all reached eight penalty points before the two champions had even received their first bad mark. Kolchynsky, the lightest man in the tournament at 220 pounds, defeated 375-pound Roman Codreanu in 7:50 in his opening bout. Then he disposed of his next four opponents in an elapsed time of 11:27. In the final contest Kolchynsky outpointed Tomov 4–2 to win his second straight gold medal.

1984 Los Angeles-Anaheim C: 8, N: 8, D: 8.2.

		FINAL MATCH	
1. Jeffrey Blatnick	USA	2–0	6:00
2. Refik Memišević	YUG	Passivity	4:16
3. Victor Dolîpschi	ROM		
4. Panagiotis Pikilidis	GRE	7–3	6:00
5. Hassan El Hadad	EGY		
6. Masaya Ando	JPN		
6. Antonio Lapenna	ITA		
DISQ (Drugs): Tomas Johansson (SWE)			

In October of 1982, Jeff Blatnick of Niskayuna, New York, seemed a most unlikely candidate to win a gold medal in the Olympics. To begin with, no U.S. athlete in his sport, Greco-Roman wrestling, had *ever* won an Olympic medal in any division. And, although he had qualified for the 1980 team that was not allowed to go to Moscow, he was no longer considered number one in the nation. And then there was the matter of his health. In May he had noticed small lumps on his neck. In July he

Jeff Blatnick drops to his knees and gives thanks after winning a gold medal in the Super Heavyweight division of the 1984 Greco-Roman wrestling competition. Two years earlier, suffering from cancer, Blatnick had undergone extensive radiation treatment following the removal of his spleen and appendix.

was diagnosed as suffering from Hodgkin's disease, a form of cancer. In August his spleen and appendix were removed and in October he began radiation therapy.

But Jeffrey Blatnick was no quitter. Inspired by the memory of his brother David, who had died in a motorcycle accident in 1977, Blatnick resumed training almost immediately, despite warnings from his doctors. At the 1984 U.S. Olympic trials, he won a controversial two-match victory over 390-pound favorite Pete Lee. Lee was disqualified for slapping in the first match and for inactivity in the second.

Blatnick entered the Olympic tournament as an underdog, but in his first bout he upset gold medal favorite Refik Memišević, when the latter was disqualified for passivity. However, in his second match, Blatnick was defeated 4–3 by Panagiotis Pikilidis. It is unusual for a wrestler to qualify for the final after losing a match, particularly when his preliminary pool consists of only four men. But the next day, Memišević beat Pikilidis and Blatnick found himself one victory away from an Olympic championship. His opponent in the final would be Tomas Johansson, who, at 275 pounds, outweighed Blatnick by over 35 pounds.

Just before he went out to wrestle Johansson, Blatnick saw his parents underneath the stands and approached them.

"It's so close, Jeff, so close," said his father, Carl. "The Swede is big, but you've come too far to let anything stop you now."

Then his mother, Angela, whispered to him, "For David, Jeffrey, for David."

The final match was close and hard-fought. After 4¾ minutes neither wrestler had scored a point, but Blatnick had been cautioned twice, Johansson only once. Then, with only 64 seconds left, Blatnick took Johansson to the mat for a score. With the screams of the crowd getting louder and louder, Blatnick scored again 38 seconds later.

The audience counted down the final seconds and when they reached zero, the arena was filled with emotional celebration. Blatnick fell to his knees, crossed himself, joined his hands in prayer and looked up, far beyond the ceiling. Then, for the first time since his older brother had died seven years earlier, Jeffrey Blatnick cried. And cried and cried and cried. And, judging from the mail he would subsequently receive, all over the world millions of people cried with him. But not all dramatic stories have clean, happy endings. In September of 1985, Blatnick's cancer returned. This time he required 28 sessions of chemotherapy to send it into remission.

As for Johansson, he tested positive for steroids and lost his medal. After serving an 18-month suspension, he won the 1986 world championship, finished third at the 1988 Olympics, and second at the 1992 Olympics.

1988 Seoul C: 16, N: 16, D: 9.22.

		FINAL MATCH	
1. Aleksandr Karelin	SOV/RUS	5-3	6:00
2. Rangel Gerovski	BUL		
3. Tomas Johansson	SWE	Passivity	5:04

4. Hassan El Hadad	EGY		
5. László Klauz	HUN	Passivity	5:00
6. Kazuya Deguchi	JPN		
7. Roman Wroclawski	POL	Forfeit	
8. Duane Koslowski	USA		

Twenty-one-year-old Aleksandr Karelin trailed 3–0 with 30 seconds left in the final, then used a reverse body lift to score a 5–point takedown. Gerovski was the only one of his five opponents to last the full 6 minutes.

1992 Barcelona C: 16, N: 16, D: 7.29.

		FINAL MATCH	
1. Aleksandr Karelin	RUS	Fall	1:33
2. Tomas Johansson	SWE		
3. Ioan Grigoraş	ROM	1–0	
4. László Klauz	HUN		
5. Andrew Borodow	CAN	12–0	
6. Tian Lei	CHN		
7. Juha Ahokas	FIN	1–0	6:27
8. Panagiotis Pikilidis	GRE		

Karelin, undefeated in five years, disposed of his opponents as if they were inanimate objects. Only Ahokas lasted the full five minutes. Karelin needed only 5 minutes 32 seconds to pin the other four. A 6-foot, 3¾-inch, 286-pound giant from Siberia, Karelin weighed 15 pounds at birth. Despite his intimidating presence, he was a soft-spoken student of literature and rhetoric.

Discontinued Event

ALL-AROUND

1906 Athens C: 3, N: 3, D: 5.1.
1. Soren Marius Jensen   DEN
2. Verner Weckman   FIN
3. Rudolf Watzl   AUT

This event brought together the winners of the three weight categories.

YACHTING

MEN	WOMEN	MIXED
Sailboard	Sailboard	Laser
Finn	Europe	Tornado
·470	470	Star
		Soling
		Discontinued Events

Between 1936 and 1988 the medals and places in each yachting class were determined by the combined scores of seven separate races. In 1992 the sailboarders contested ten races and the Soling class adopted a new format: six races followed by match race competition. In 1996 the Soling class will contest ten races followed by match race competition. All other classes will contest eleven races. Since 1968 each yacht has been assessed minus points depending on its order of finish.

1st place: 0	5th place: 10
2nd place: 3	6th place: 11.7
3rd place: 5.7	7th place: 13
4th place: 8	add one point for each subsequent place

At the conclusion of the final race, each yacht is allowed to drop its two worst scores. The remaining minus points are added and the yacht with the lowest total wins. Between 1936 and 1992 each yacht dropped its single worst score.

Ten minutes before the starting gun for a race the yachts are called to the starting line. The intervening minutes are generally devoted to jockeying for position, and penalties are often assessed. During a race the yachts follow a triangular course designated by marks that must be passed on a required side. A yacht is considered to have finished a race when any part of its hull or equipment or crew in a normal position crosses the finish line.

Yachting Terms

Abeam—In a line at a right angle from another yacht's body

Aft—In or near the back or stern part of a yacht

Astern—To the rear of a yacht

Bearing away—Altering course away from the wind until a yacht begins to jibe

Clear astern—A yacht is clear astern of another yacht when its hull and equipment are behind an imaginary line projected abeam from the aftermost point of the other yacht's hull and equipment. The other yacht is *clear ahead.*

Close-hauled—A yacht is close-hauled when sailing by the wind as close as it can lie with advantage in working to windward.

Hull—The body or frame of a yacht, not including its masts, sails, and rigging

Jibing—A yacht begins to jibe at the moment when, with the wind aft, the foot of its mainsail crosses its center line, and completes the jibe when the mainsail has filled on the other tack.

Leeward—The leeward side of a yacht is the one on which it is carrying its mainsail. The opposite side is the *windward* side.

Leeward yacht—When neither of two yachts on the same tack is clear astern, the one on the leeward side of the other is the leeward yacht. The other yacht is the *windward yacht.*

Luffing—Altering course toward the wind

Mark—An object that a yacht must round or pass on a required side

Mast abeam—A windward yacht is mast abeam when its helmsman's line of sight abeam is in front of the leeward yacht's mainmast.

On a tack—A yacht is on a tack except when it is tacking or jibing.

Overlap—Two yachts overlap when neither is clear astern, or when although one is clear astern, an intervening yacht overlaps both of them.

Port—The lefthand side of a yacht, looking forward

Room—The space needed by a yacht to maneuver in a seamanlike manner in the prevailing conditions

Starboard—The righthand side of a yacht, looking forward

Tacking—A yacht is tacking from the moment it is beyond facing directly into the wind until it is borne away to a close-hauled course.

Windward—See leeward.

MEN

SAILBOARD

The 1996 competition will utilize the Mistral, a 12-foot 2-inch long fiberglass windsurfer weighing 34.2 pounds.

1896–1980 not held

1984 Los Angeles-Long Beach C: 38, N: 38, D: 8.8.
Windglider

		PTS.
1. Stephan van den Berg	HOL	27.7
2. Randall Scott Steele	USA	46.0
3. A. Bruce Kendall	NZE	46.4
4. Gildas Guillerot	FRA	52.4
5. Klaus Maran	ITA	54.4
6. Gregory Hyde	AUS	55.7
7. Dirk Meyer	GER	67.2
8. Björn Eybl	AUT	80.0

The inaugural sailboard competition used the Windglider, a board 12 feet 9 inches long and 25½ inches wide which carried 70 square feet of sail.

1988 Seoul-Pusan C: 45, N: 45, D: 9.27.
Lechner Division II

		PTS.
1. A. Bruce Kendall	NZE	35.4
2. Jan Boersma	NLA	42.7
3. Michael Gebhardt	USA	48.0
4. Bart Verschoor	HOL	53.4
5. Robert Nagy	FRA	61.7
6. Francesco Wirz	ITA	63.0
7. Jorge García Velazco	ARG	70.1
8. Carlos Iniesta Mira	SPA	81.7

The Division II board chosen for the competition was a 12-foot-long, round-bottomed sailboard with a 78.6-square-foot sail. The boardsailors faced heavy winds which, on the fifth day, gusted up to 25 knots and stirred up waves of almost 2 meters. In that race, only 19 of the 43 starters completed the course. These conditions should have favored the heavier boardsailors. However, the winner, Bruce Kendall, weighed only 143 pounds. The 24-year-old Kendall did run into problems on land: listening to rock music on a Walkman while skateboarding, he fell off and badly grazed his hand. New Zealand team officials ordered him to stay off his skateboard until after the Olympics.

1992 Barcelona C: 43, N: 43, D: 8.2.
Lechner Division II

		PTS.
1. Franck David	FRA	70.7
2. Michael Gebhardt	USA	71.1
3. Lars Kleppich	AUS	98.7
4. A. Bruce Kendall	NZE	105.7
5. Christoph Sieber	AUT	110.1

6. Asier Fernández de Bobadilla	SPA	117.0
7. Stephan van den Berg	HOL	117.7
8. Amit Insbar	ISR	118.1

Franck David, a 22-year-old from the island of Arz, in Brittany, needed to finish three places ahead of Mike Gebhardt in the tenth and final race to win the gold medal or he had to win the race and have Gebhardt place no better than third. David took an early lead and held it to the end. Gebhardt on the other hand, fell back to seventh place, fought his way up to third, but couldn't catch Bruce Kendall in second place.

Among the more unusual quirks of fate that have decided Olympic championships was one that hit Mike Gebhardt. Prior to the Olympics there had been numerous complaints from boardsailers and other members of the yachting community that the Parc de Mar venue, which was in the harbor of Barcelona, was polluted with garbage and waste that included everything from dead rats to floating refrigerators. Under pressure from the International Yacht Racing Union, Barcelona authorities assigned four garbage vessels to collect the waste daily. Unfortunately for Gebhardt, they didn't get it all. During the last lap of the seventh race, a plastic garbage bag got caught on his board and he was passed by six boardsailers before he could dislodge it. Had Gebhardt been able to stave off even one of those six, he would have won the gold medal.

Trash was not the only danger that boardsailors faced in Barcelona. The day before competition began, Murray McCaig of Canada was bicycling in the Olympic Village when he pulled out to pass a slow-moving bus and was hit by a police car. He came away with a broken leg and was unable to compete.

FINN

The Finn class uses a centerboard dinghy and a one-man crew. It is 4.5 meters (14 feet 9 inches) long and weighs 126 kilograms (278 pounds). The spread of the mainsail is 10.68 square meters (115 square feet). Boats are assigned at random, although since 1976 a helmsman may provide his own sail and mast. The Finn was designed in 1949 by Rickard Sarby of Finland—hence its name. Between 1920 and 1948 other types of centerboard dinghys were used.

1896–1912 not held

1920 Antwerp-Ostende, Amsterdam T: 2, N: 1, D: 9.4.

			PTS.
1. HOL	(Johannes Hin, Franciscus Hin)		4
2. HOL	(Arnoud van der Biesen, Petrus Beukers)		5

The first two races were staged off Ostende, 100 kilometers from Antwerp, on July 7 and 8. The results of the second race were voided because a buoy changed position and a dispute broke out about the course. Because both teams were from the Netherlands, the final two races were rescheduled for September 4—in Holland. Other than the 1956 equestrian events, this was the only time in history that an official event was contested outside the host country.

1924 Paris C: 17, N: 17, D: 7.13.

			PTS.
1.	Léon Huybrechts	BEL	2
2.	Henrik Robert	NOR	7
3.	Hans Dittmar	FIN	8
4.	Santiago Amat Cansino	SPA	8
5.	Johannes Hin	HOL	10
6.	Clarence Hammar	SWE	11
7.	Harold Gordon Fowler	GBR	12
8.	Frederico Guilherme-Burnay	POR	15

The Official Report of 1924 attributes to Huybrechts a sixth sense that allowed him to anticipate changes in wind direction. Second, third, and fourth place were decided by an extra race.

1928 Amsterdam C: 23, N: 20, D: 8.9.

1.	Sven Thorell	SWE
2.	Henrik Robert	NOR
3.	Bertil Broman	FIN
4.	Willem de Vries-Lentsch	HOL
5.	Egon Beyn	GER
6.	Tito Nordio	ITA
7.	Jens Andersen	DEN
8.	Harold Gaydon, Harold Gordon Fowler	GBR

Thorell won four of eight races and also placed second twice.

1932 Los Angeles C: 11, N; 11, D: 8.11.

			PTS.
1.	Jacques Lebrun	FRA	87
2.	Adriaan Maas	HOL	85
3.	Santiago Amat Cansino	SPA	76
4.	Edgar Behr	GER	74
5.	Reginald Dixon	CAN	72
6.	G. Colin Ratsey	GBR	69
7.	Charles Lyon	USA	66
8.	Silvio Treleani	ITA	62

When the official results were announced following the eleventh and final race, Adriaan Maas was declared the winner with 87 points. He was followed by Jacques Lebrun with 79 points. But the decision was not final. After placing fourth in the ninth race, Lebrun had been disqualified and his protest had been rejected by the race judge. Lebrun appealed, and the day after the last race a protest committee reversed the judge's decision. Lebrun's reinstatement added eight points to his total and subtracted two from Maas'. During World War II Lebrun distinguished himself by helping to hide the treasures of the Louvre from the Nazis.

Jacques Lebrun, winner of the 1932 Finn class.

1936 Berlin-Kiel C: 25, N: 25, D: 8.12.

			PTS.
1.	Daniel Kagchelland	HOL	163
2.	Werner Krogmann	GER	150
3.	Peter Scott	GBR	131
4.	Erich Wichmann-Harbeck	CHI	130
5.	Giuseppe Fago	ITA	115
6.	Jacques Lebrun	FRA	109
7.	Tibor Heinrich	HUN	102
8.	Willy Pieper	SWI	99

Bronze medalist Peter Scott was the son of explorer Robert Falcon Scott, who died near the South Pole when Peter was an infant. In 1941 Scott created the camouflage scheme that was eventually used by most of the Allied forces in World War II. After the war, Scott, who had previously been an ardent hunter of geese and ducks, renounced his former ways and became a wild-fowl protection activist. Co-founder of the World Wildlife Fund, he was known as "the patron saint of conservation."

1948 London-Torbay C: 21, N: 21, D: 8.12.

		PTS.
1. Paul Elvström	DEN	5543
2. Ralph Evans	USA	5408
3. Jacobus de Jong	HOL	5204
4. Richard Sarby	SWE	4603
5. Paul McLaughlin	CAN	4535
6. Felix Sienra Castellanos	URU	4079
7. Jean-Jacques Herbulot	FRA	4068
8. Pierre van der Haeghen	BEL	3660

Twenty-year-old Paul Elvström began his Olympic career quietly, failing to finish the first day's race. After five races, the competition appeared to be a tight contest between Evans, McLaughlin, and Sarby. All the others were more than 800 points behind. Elvström was in eighth place. But on the sixth day the young Dane finished first, 23 seconds ahead of Herbulot, and the extra

Paul Elvström won four straight gold medals in the Finn class of the yachting competitions between 1948 and 1960.

301 points that he gained propelled Elvström into third place, 564 points behind Evans. This meant that Evans could clinch the gold medal by finishing third on the final day. However, he landed in fifth place, three minutes away from his goal, while Elvström took first place again, three minutes and seven seconds ahead of de Jong; the 301-point bonus for winning provided the margin of victory in the final standings.

1952 Helsinki C: 28, N: 28, D: 7.28.

		PTS.
1. Paul Elvström	DEN	8209
2. Charles Currey	GBR	5449
3. Richard Sarby	SWE	5051
4. Jacobus de Jong	HOL	5033
5. Wolfgang Erndl	AUT	4273
6. Morits Skaugen	NOR	4073
7. Adelchi Pelaschiar	ITA	4068
8. Paul McLaughlin	CAN	4033

Elvström won three of the first four races and gained so many points that he had earned the gold medal without having to race the last day. He entered anyway and won again. His other placings were a fifth, a third, and a fourth.

1956 Melbourne C: 20, N: 20, D: 12.5.

		PTS.
1. Paul Elvström	DEN	7509
2. André Nelis	BEL	6254
3. John Marvin	USA	5953
4. Jürgen Vogler	GER	4199
5. Richard Sarby	SWE	3990
6. Eric Bongers	SAF	3912
7. Adelchi Pelaschiar	ITA	3409
8. Bruce Kirby	CAN	3213

Elvström finished first in the opening race, fell to eighth and 15th in the next two, and then won each of the last four races.

1960 Rome-Naples C: 35, N: 35, D: 9.7.

		PTS.
1. Paul Elvström	DEN	8171
2. Aleksandr Tšutšelov	SOV/EST	6520
3. André Nelis	BEL	5934
4. Ronald Jenyns	AUS	5758
5. Reinaldo Conrad	BRA	5176
6. Ralph Roberts	NZE	5140
7. Ian Bruce	CAN	5133
8. Kenneth Albury	BAH	5092

Elvström, now 32 years old, chalked up three firsts, one second, and two fifths to clinch his fourth gold medal without having to enter the final race. This time Elvström, who was not in perfect health, declined to start.

1964 Tokyo-Fujisawa C: 33, N: 33, D: 10.21.

		PTS.
1. Wilhelm Kuhweide	GER	7638
2. Peter Barrett	USA	6373

3. Henning Wind	DEN	6190	
4. Peter Mander	NZE	5684	
5. Hubert Raudaschl	AUT	5405	
6. Colin Ryrie	AUS	5273	
7. Joerg Bruder	BRA	4956	
8. Panagiotis Kouligas	GRE	4546	

In 1964 East and West Germany entered a combined team. However, a dispute developed as to which side should be represented in the Finn class. At the last moment the International Yacht Racing Union interceded and authorized the West German helmsman, Willi Kuhweide. Kuhweide sailed well throughout the regatta and won the gold medal by placing second, first, fourth, sixth, fifth, third, and first.

1968 Mexico City-Acapulco C: 36, N: 36, D: 10.21.

		PTS.
1. Valentyn Mankin	SOV/UKR	11.7
2. Hubert Raudaschl	AUT	53.4
3. Fabio Albarelli	ITA	55.1
4. Ronald Jenyns	AUS	67.0
5. Panagiotis Kouligas	GRE	71.0
6. Jan Winquist	FIN	72.0
7. Arne Akerson	SWI	77.0
8. Philippe Soria	FRA	80.0

Mankin had a consistent series, placing third, fifth, first, first, second, second, and first.

1972 Munich-Kiel C: 35, N: 35, D: 9.8.

		PTS.
1. Serge Maury	FRA	58.0
2. Ilias Hatzipavlis	GRE	71.0
3. Viktor Potapov	SOV/RUS	74.7
4. John Bertrand	AUS	76.7
5. Thomas Lundqvist	SWE	81.0
6. Kim Weber	FIN	85.7
7. Hans-Christian Schröder	GDR	91.0
8. György Fináczy	HUN	94.0

1976 Montreal-Kingston C: 28, N: 28, D: 7.27.

		PTS.
1. Jochen Schümann	GDR	35.4
2. Andrei Balashov	SOV/RUS	39.7
3. John Bertrand	AUS	46.4
4. Claudio Biekarck	BRA	54.7
5. Kent Carlson	SWE	66.4
6. Anastassios Boudouris	GRE	77.0
7. David Howlett	GBR	77.7
8. Sanford Riley	CAN	83.0

Schümann and Balashov entered the final race in a tie for first place. Schümann pulled away on the last day and finished 40 seconds ahead of his rival.

John Bertrand made sailing history in 1983 when he broke the 132-year-old U.S. monopoly of the America's Cup with his yacht, *Australia III*.

1980 Moscow-Tallinn C: 21, N: 21, D: 7.29.

		PTS.
1. Esko Rechardt	FIN	36.7
2. Wolfgang Mayrhofer	AUT	46.7
3. Andrei Balashov	SOV/RUS	47.4
4. Claudio Biekarck	BRA	53.0
5. Jochen Schümann	GDR	54.4
6. Kent Carlson	SWE	63.7
7. Ryszard Skarbiński	POL	71.1
8. Mark Neeleman	HOL	76.0

1984 Los Angeles-Long Beach C: 28, N: 28, D: 8.8.

		PTS.
1. Russell Coutts	NZE	34.7
2. John Bertrand	USA	37.0
3. Terry Neilson	CAN	37.7
4. Joaquin Blanco	SPA	60.7
5. Wolfgang Gerz	GER	66.1
6. Chris Pratt	AUS	68.0
7. Michael McIntyre	GBR	70.7
8. Jorge Zarif Neto	BRA	78.7

The decisive moment in the Finn class competition came in the very first race when Bertrand, who finished first, was disqualified for touching Coutt's bow while attempting to port-tack. This provided Coutts with his eventual margin of victory. Coutts was almost disqualified himself at the final weigh-in when his clothing was found to be one pound overweight. However, a third weigh-in, for which Coutts carefully arranged each garment, found him just below the 20 kg maximum.

1988 Seoul-Pusan C: 33, N: 33, D: 9.27.

		PTS.
1. José Luis Doreste Blanco	SPA	38.1
2. Peter Holmberg	VIR	40.4
3. John Cutler	NZE	45.0
4. Stuart Childerley	GBR	50.7
5. Lasse Hjortnaes	DEN	51.0
6. Thomas Schmid	GER	72.1
7. Roy Heiner	HOL	78.4
8. Oleg Khopyorsky	SOV/RUS	81.0

Doreste, whose younger brother, Luis, won a gold medal in the 470 class in 1984, survived a close and bitter contest that wasn't decided until the last race. Doreste, who was disqualified in the fourth race, accused his opponents of trying to win "in the jury room" rather than on the water. Peter Holmberg won the first-ever medal for the U.S. Virgin Islands and would have earned the gold had he not drifted a few feet over the line at the start of the fourth race.

In the fifth race, Lawrence Lemieux of Canada was in second place when he noticed Joseph Chan, the 470 crew from Singapore, struggling in the water 25 yards from his capsized boat. Chan had injured his back and was being swept away by the powerful currents. Lemieux turned around and saved Chan, who was too exhausted to heave himself into the Canadian's boat. The International Olympic Committee gave Lemieux a special award for his act of gallantry. Lemieux, baffled by the attention he received, reminded reporters of what might have happened if he had ignored Chan. "I'm not *that* intense," he said.

1992 Barcelona C: 28, N: 28, D: 8.3.

			PTS.
1.	José van der Ploeg García	SPA	33.4
2.	Brian Ledbetter	USA	54.7
3.	Craig Monk	NZE	64.7
4.	Stuart Childerley	GBR	68.1
5.	Fredrik Lööf	SWE	68.7
6.	Otmar Müller von Blumencron	SWI	70.0
7.	Xavier Rohart	FRA	75.0
8.	Hans Spitzauer	AUT	79.4

Van der Ploeg, a native of Barcelona, secured his victory after six races and didn't take part in the seventh. Hank Lammens of Canada won the second race, but was disqualified because he forgot to pack a life jacket. Without the disqualification he would have placed fourth; instead, he ended up 13th.

470

Designed by French architect André Cornu in 1963, the 470 is a two-person fiberglass craft that is 470 centimeters (15 feet 6 inches) long. Like the Flying Dutchman, it uses a centerboard dinghy and a trapeze. It weighs 120 kilograms (264 pounds). From 1976 through 1984 this event was open to competitors of both sexes. In 1988, the 470 class was divided into two separate competitions, one for men and one for women.

1896–1972 not held

1976 Montreal-Kingston T: 28, N: 28, D: 7.27.

			PTS.
1.	GER	(Frank Hübner, Harro Bode)	42.4
2.	SPA	(Antonio Gorostegui Ceballos, Pedro Millet Soler)	49.7
3.	AUS	(Ian Brown, Ian Ruff)	57.0
4.	SOV/ RUS	(Viktor Potapov, Aleksandr Potapov)	57.0
5.	NZE	(Mark Paterson, Brett Bennett)	59.7
6.	GBR	(Philip Crebbin, Derek Clark)	69.4
7.	SWI	(Jean-Claude Vuithier, Laurent Quellet)	71.7
8.	FRA	(Marc Laurent, Roger Surmin)	79.4

1980 Moscow-Tallinn T: 14, N: 14, D: 7.29.

			PTS.
1.	BRA	(Marcos Rizzo Soares, Eduardo Penido)	36.4
2.	GDR	(Jörn Borowski, Egbert Swensson)	38.7
3.	FIN	(Jouko Lindgren, Georg Tallberg)	39.7
4.	HOL	(Henk Van Gent, Jan Van Den Hondel)	49.4
5.	POL	(Leon Wrobel, Tomasz Stocki)	53.0
6.	SPA	(Gustavo Doreste Blanco, Alfredo Rigau)	54.1
7.	ITA	(Ernesto Treves, Silvio Necchi)	57.7
8.	SWE	(Lars Bengtsson, Stefan Bengtsson)	60.0

Gold medal winners Soares and Penido, wind surfers from Rio de Janeiro, were only 19 and 20 years old, respectively. Had Borowski and Swensson crossed the finish line two seconds sooner in the final race, they would have taken the championship away from the Brazilians. Borowski was the son of Paul Borowski, who won medals in the Dragon class in 1968 and 1972.

1984 Los Angeles-Long Beach T: 28, N: 28, D: 8.8.

			PTS.
1.	SPA	(Luis Doreste Blanco, Roberto Molina Carrasco)	33.7
2.	USA	(Stephan Benjamin, Christopher Steinfeld)	43.0
3.	FRA	(Thierry Peponnet, Luc Pillot)	49.4
4.	GER	(Wolfgang Hunger, Joachim Hunger)	50.1
5.	ITA	(Thomaso Chieffi, Enrico Chieffi)	57.0
6.	FIN	(Peter von Koskull, Johan von Koskull)	67.4
7.	GBR	(Catherine Foster, Peter Newlands)	70.0
8.	ISR	(Shimshon Brokman, Eitan Friedlander)	70.0

The unheralded Spanish duo, born in the Canary Islands and residents of Barcelona, earned their gold medals without having to take part in the final race.

1988 Seoul-Pusan T: 29, N: 29, D: 9.27.

			PTS.
1.	FRA	(Thierry Peponnet, Luc Pillot)	34.7
2.	SOV/EST	(Tõnu Tõniste, Toomas Tõniste)	46.0
3.	USA	(John Shadden, Charlie McKee)	51.0
4.	SPA	(Fernando Leon Boissier, Francisco Sánchez Luna)	55.0
5.	GER	(Wolfgang Hunger, Joachim Hunger)	58.7
6.	NZE	(Peter Evans, Simon Mander)	62.7
7.	ITA	(Sandro Montefusco, Paolo Montefusco)	68.7
8.	CAN	(Nigel Cochrane, Gordon McIlquham)	71.7

The previously unknown Tõniste twins from Estonia won the fourth and fifth races and finished second in the sixth race to take the overall lead. All they had to do to win gold medals was place ahead of Peponnet and Pillot in the final race, which was sailed in near-gale conditions. The Tõnistes were in the lead with less than a lap to go when they suffered a severe capsize and were forced to retire.

1992 Barcelona T: 37, N: 37, D: 8.3.

			PTS.
1.	SPA	(Jordi Calafat Esterlich, Francisco Sánchez Luna)	50.0
2.	USA	(Morgan Reeser, Kevin Burnham)	66.7
3.	EST	(Tõnu Tõniste, Toomas Tõniste)	68.7
4.	FIN	(Petri Leskinen, Mika Aarnikka)	69.7
5.	NOR	(Herman Johannessen, Pål McCarthy)	71.7
6.	GBR	(Paul Brotherton, Andrew Hemmings)	76.4
7.	NZE	(Craig Greenwood, Jon Bilger)	80.4
8.	GER	(Wolfgang Hunger, Rolf Schmidt)	82.4

Calafat and Sánchez won three of the first four races and coasted to victory.

WOMEN
SAILBOARD

1896–1988 not held

1992 Barcelona C: 24, N: 24, D: 8.2.

		PTS.
1. Barbara Kendall	NZE	47.8
2. Zhang Xiaodong	CHN	65.8
3. Dorien de Vries	HOL	68.7
4. Maud Herbert	FRA	78.0
5. Lanee Butler	USA	95.7
6. Penny Way	GBR	99.4
7. Alessandra Sensini	ITA	101.4
8. Jorunn Horgen	NOR	102.7

Barbara Kendall's older brother Bruce won the sailboard gold medal in 1988. Zhang Xiaodong was the first Asian athlete to earn an Olympic yachting medal.

EUROPE

The Europe class is a single-handed dinghy, 11 feet (3.35 meters) long and weighing only 44.9 kilograms (99 pounds). It was designed by Alois Roland of Belgium in 1960.

1896–1988 not held

1992 Barcelona C: 24, N: 24, D: 8.3.

		PTS.
1. Linda Andersen	NOR	48.7
2. Natalia Vía Dufresne Pereña	SPA	57.4
3. Julia Trotman	USA	62.7
4. Jennifer Armstrong	NZE	65.0
5. Dorte Jensen	DEN	65.7
6. Krista Kruuv	EST	67.1
7. Martine van Leeuwen	HOL	67.7
8. Arianna Bogatec	ITA	69.0

Trotman won the first race and placed second in the second race. She was first across the line in the third race, but was disqualified for a premature start. She was still in first place overall after five races, but was disqualified again in the sixth race and had to settle for bronze. Andersen started prematurely once, but also won the third and fourth race.

470

1896–1984 not held

1988 Seoul-Pusan T: 21, N: 21, D: 9.27.

		PTS.
1. USA	(Allison Jolly, Lynne Jewell)	26.7
2. SWE	(Marit Söderström, Birgitta Bengtsson)	40.0
3. SOV/ UKR	(Larysa Moskalenko, Iryna Chunykhovska)	45.4
4. FIN	(Bettina Lemström, Annika Lemström)	47.0
5. GER	(Susanne Meyer, Katrin Adlkofer)	56.4
6. AUS	(Nicola Green, Karyn Davis)	57.0
7. GDR	(Susanne Theel, Silke Preuss)	57.4
8. FRA	(Florence Lebrun, Sophie Berge)	81.7

The first women to take part in Olympic yachting were Frances Clytie Rivett-Carnac of Great Britain, who crewed for her husband in the uncontested 7-meter class in 1908, Dorothy Wright of Great Britain, who crewed for her husband in the 7-meter class in 1920, and Virginie Hériot of France, who won a gold medal in the 8-meter class in 1928. The first woman to skipper an Olympic boat was Britain's Cathy Foster in the 1984 470 class.

Söderström and Jolly had faced each other six times in world championships prior to 1988, with Söderström winning four. However, Jolly's two victories came, significantly, in the Olympic years of 1980 and 1984. In the inaugural women-only competition in Seoul, Jolly and Jewell took two firsts, two seconds, and a third. But because they were disqualified in the fifth race for tacking too close, they needed to finish fourteenth or better in the final race to earn gold medals. Despite the treacherous weather conditions, this did not seem a difficult task. However, in the middle of the race they dropped off a large wave. As a result, the wire connecting the jib to the halyard broke and their jib sail sagged down the jib wire.

"There goes the gold," said Jolly, as they dropped back from fourth place to fifteenth. "We've got to fight!" answered Jewell, who, despite 30 knots of wind and 10-foot waves, spent the next 5 minutes repairing the jib with a small piece of spare twine. With the sail back in place, they managed to finish ninth.

1992 Barcelona T: 17, N: 17, D: 8.3.

		PTS.
1. SPA	(Theresa Zabell Lucas, Patricia Guerra Cabrera)	29.7
2. NZE	(Leslie Egnot, Jan Shearer)	36.7
3. USA	(Jennifer "JJ" Isler, Pamela Healy)	40.7
4. SOV	(Larysa Moskalenko, Alena Pakholchik)	43.0
5. JPN	(Yumiko Shige, Alicia Kinoshita)	53.7
6. FRA	(Florence Lebrun, Odile Barre)	65.7
7. ITA	(Maria Quarra, Anna Maria Barabino)	68.7
8. GER	(Peggy Hardwiger, Christina Pinnow)	71.7

Eight out of 17 boats—almost half the field—were disqualified in the first race for starting prematurely, including all of the eventual medalists. Zabell and Guerra moved into the lead after winning the fourth race, applied more pressure by winning the sixth race, and insured their victory with a seventh place in the final race. Egnot and Shearer moved up from fourth to second by winning the last race, their third win of the regatta. Theresa Zabell was born in Ipswich and maintained dual Spanish and British citizenship.

MIXED

LASER

The Laser was designed in 1969 by Bruce Kirby of the United States. It is 4.24 meters (13 feet 11 inches) long and weighs 59 kilograms (130 pounds). The sail covers 76 square feet.

This event will be held for the first time in 1996.

TORNADO

The Tornado is a two-man catamaran, the fastest of all Olympic classes. The vessel is 6.1 meters (20 feet) long and has a sail area of 235 square feet (21.85 square meters). It was designed in England in 1966.

1896–1972 not held

1976 Montreal-Kingston T: 14, N: 14, D: 7.28.

			PTS.
1.	GBR	(Reginald White, John Osborn)	18.0
2.	USA	(David McFaull, Michael Rothwell)	36.0
3.	GER	(Jörg Spengler, Jörg Schmall)	37.7
4.	AUS	(Brian Lewis, Warren Rock)	44.4
5.	SWE	(Peter Kolni, Jörgen Kolni)	57.4
6.	SWI	(Walter Steiner, Albert Schiess)	63.4
7.	CAN	(Larry Woods, Michael de le Roche)	69.7
8.	ITA	(Franco Pivoli, Cesare Biagi)	71.7

Forty-year-old Reg White and his 30-year-old brother-in-law, John Osborn, won four of the first six races; they were able to sit out the final day.

1980 Moscow-Tallinn T: 11, N: 11, D: 7.29.

			PTS.
1.	BRA	(Alexandre Welter, Lars Sigurd Björkström)	21.4
2.	DEN	(Peter Due, Per Kjergard)	30.4
3.	SWE	(Göran Marström Jörgen Ragnarsson)	33.7
4.	SOV	(Viktor Potapov, Aleksandr Zöbin)	35.1
5.	HOL	(Williem Van Walt Meijer, Govert Brasser)	39.0
6.	FIN	(Pekka Narko, Juha Siira)	47.7
7.	AUT	(Hubert Porkert, Hermann Kupfrier)	67.7
8.	GDR	(Uwe Steingross, Jörg Schramme)	82.0

1984 Los Angeles-Long Beach T: 20, N: 20, D: 8.8.

			PTS.
1.	NZE	(Rex Sellers, Christopher Timms)	14.7
2.	USA	(Randy Smyth, Jay Glaser)	37.0
3.	AUS	(Chris Cairns, John Anderson)	50.4
4.	DEN	(Paul Elvström, Inge Trine Elvström)	51.1
5.	BER	(Alan Burland, Christopher Nash)	53.5
6.	GBR	(Robert White, David Campbell-James)	53.7
7.	BRA	(Lars Grael, Glein Haynes)	74.7
8.	FRA	(Yves Loday, Bernard Pichery)	81.0

This was expected to be a dramatic showdown between Smyth and Cairns. Meanwhile, the sentimental favorite was four-time Finn class Olympic champion Paul Elv-

ström, who came out of retirement to compete with his daughter, Trine. With all the attention focused on these three, Rex Sellers, a 33-year-old lobster fisherman, slipped through for a decisive victory. Sellers and Timms compiled a record of two firsts, three seconds and a third to clinch the gold medal after the sixth race. When asked if he would be back to take part in the final race anyway, Sellers replied, "If we're still standing after tonight's celebration." The New Zealand boat was not at the starting line the next day.

1988 Seoul-Pusan T: 23, N: 23, D: 9.27.

			PTS.
1.	FRA	(Jean-Yves Le Déroff, Nicolas Hénard)	16.0
2.	NZE	(Rex Sellers, Christopher Timms)	35.4
3.	BRA	(Lars Grael, Clinio Freitas)	40.1
4.	AUT	(Norbert Petschel, Christian Claus)	46.0
5.	ITA	(Giorgio Zuccoli, Luca Santella)	60.1
6.	NOR	(Per Arne Nilsen, Carl Johannessen)	67.7
7.	SOV	(Yuri Konovalov, Sergei Kravsov)	70.0
8.	GBR	(Robert White, Jeremy Newman)	70.1

Le Déroff and Hénard, sailing instructors from Brest, took three firsts and two seconds in the first five races, then sailed a cautious fifth to secure the gold medals without having to participate in the final race. In fifteenth place was Paul Elvström of Denmark, competing in his eighth Olympics at the age of 60.

1992 Barcelona T: 22, N: 22, D: 8.2.

			PTS.
1.	FRA	(Yves Loday, Nicolas Hénard)	40.4
2.	USA	(Randy Smyth, Keith Notary)	42.0
3.	AUS	(Mitch Booth, John Forbes)	44.4
4.	NZE	(Rex Sellers, Brian Jones)	51.7
5.	CAN	(David Sweeney, Kevin Smith)	62.7
6.	HOL	(Ron van Teylingen, Paul Manuel)	65.4
7.	AUT	(Andreas Hagara, Roman Hagara)	65.5
8.	BRA	(Lars Schmidt Grael, Clinio Freitas)	69.7

After six races, Smyth and Notary led with 25 points. They were followed by Booth and Forbes with 34.4 and Loday and Hénard with 37.4. The Americans were leading the final race, but light winds made for a slow race. In yachting, at least one boat has to cross the finish line within the time limit (in this case four hours) for the race to count. Smyth and Notary were still ten or fifteen minutes away when the time limit expired. The race was resailed the following day. This time it was won by Sellers and Jones, with Loday and Hénard in second. The American pair needed a ninth place finish to secure the gold medals, but could only manage eleventh. Booth and Forbes also had a shot at gold. They needed to place third, but missed by ten seconds and ended up fifth.

STAR

The Star is a 6.9-meter- (22-foot 8-inch) long shallow keelboat with a 285-square-foot sail. It weighs 676 kilograms (1490 pounds) and has a two-person crew. The Star was designed by Francis Sweisguth of Long Island, New York, in 1910.

1896–1928 not held

1932 Los Angeles T: 7, N: 7, D: 8.12.

			PTS.
1.	USA	(Gilbert Gray, Andrew Libano)	46
2.	GBR	(G. Colin Ratsey, Peter Jaffe)	35
3.	SWE	(Gunnar Asther, Daniel Sundén-Cullberg)	28
4.	CAN	(Henry Wylie, Henry Simmonds)	27
5.	FRA	(Jean-Jacques Herbulot, Jean Peytel)	26
6.	HOL	(Jan Maas, Adriaan Maas)	14
7.	SAF	(Arent Van Soelen, Cecil Goodricke)	7

The *Jupiter*, skippered by 30-year-old Gilbert Gray of New Orleans, won five of the seven races.

1936 Berlin-Kiel T: 12, N: 12, D: 8.10.

			PTS.
1.	GER	(Peter Bischoff, Hans-Joachim Weise)	80
2.	SWE	(Arvid Laurin, Uno Wallentin)	64
3.	HOL	(Willem de Vries-Lentsch, Adriaan Maas)	63
4.	GBR	(Keith Grogno, William Welpy)	56
5.	USA	(William Waterhouse, Woodbridge Metcalf)	51
6.	NOR	(Öivind Christensen, Sigurd Herbern)	44
7.	FRA	(Jean-Jacques Herbulot, Pierre de Montaut)	41
8.	TUR	(Harun Ulman, Behzat Baydar)	38

Bischoff matched Gray's feat of winning five of seven races. The Germans had clinched the gold medals after the sixth race, but raced the next day anyway and won again.

1948 London-Torbay T: 17, N: 17, D: 8.12.

			PTS.
1.	USA	(Hilary Smart, Paul Smart)	5828
2.	CUB	(Carlos De Cárdenas Culmell, Carlos De Cárdenas, Jr.)	4949
3.	HOL	(Adriaan Maas, Edward Stutterheim)	4731
4.	GBR/BAH	(Durward Knowles, Sloan Farrington)	4372
5.	ITA	(Agostino Straulino, Nicolo Rode)	4370
6.	POR	(Joaquim de Mascarenhas Fiúza, Julio de Sousa Leite Gorinho)	4292
7.	AUS	(Alexander Sturrock, Len Fenton)	3828
8.	CAN	(Norman Gooderham, A. Gerald Fairhead)	2635

Paul Smart was a 56-year-old lawyer from New York. His 23-year-old son, Hilary, was a student at Harvard.

1952 Helsinki T: 21, N: 21, D: 7.28.

			PTS.
1.	ITA	(Agostino Straulino, Nicolo Rode)	7635
2.	USA	(John Reid, John Price)	7126
3.	POR	(Joaquim de Mascarenhas Fiúza, Francisco Rebelo de Andrade)	4903
4.	CUB	(Carlos De Cárdenas Culmell, Carlos De Cárdenas, Jr.)	4535

5.	BAH	(Durward Knowles, Sloan Farrington)	4405
6.	FRA	(Edouard Chabert, Jean-Louis Dauris)	3866
7.	SWE	(Bengt Melin, Björn Carlsson)	3785
8.	HOL	(Adriaan Maas, Edward Stutterheim)	3510

The Italians and the Americans engaged in a private battle, winning all seven races and generally leaving the others far behind. Straulino skippered the *Merope* to three firsts and four seconds. The U.S. pair placed first four times and third once, but also finished seventh in the second race and eighth on the final day.

1956 Melbourne T: 12, N: 12, D: 12.5.

			PTS.
1.	USA	(Herbert Williams, Lawrence Low)	5876
2.	ITA	(Agostino Straulino, Nicolo Rode)	5649
3.	BAH	(Durward Knowles, Sloan Farrington)	5223
4.	POR	(Duarte de Almeida Bello, José Bustorff Silva)	3825
5.	FRA	(Philippe Chancerel, Michel Parent)	3126
6.	CUB	(Carlos De Cárdenas Culmell, Jorge De Cárdenas)	2714
7.	GBR	(B. Bruce Banks, Stanley Potter)	2387
8.	SOV/RUS	(Timir Pinegin, Fyodor Shutkov)	1778

Skippered by 48-year-old Sussex-born Herbert Williams of Evanston, Illinois, the *Kathleen* placed first, fifth, second, first, second, second, second.

1960 Rome-Naples T: 26, N: 26, D: 9.7.

			PTS.
1.	SOV/RUS	(Timir Pinegin, Fyodor Shutkov)	7619
2.	POR	(José Quina, Mário Quina)	6665
3.	USA	(William Parks, Robert Halperin)	6269
4.	ITA	(Agostino Straulino, Carlo Rolandi)	6047
5.	SWI	(Hans Bryner, Ulrich Bucher)	5716
6.	BAH	(Durward Knowles, Sloan Farrington)	5282
7.	GER	(Bruno Splieth, Eckart Wagner)	4745
8.	YUG	(Mario Fafangel, Janko Kosmina)	3977

This was the first Soviet victory in Olympic yachting, a sport which had previously been considered the domain of capitalists. Oddly enough, the Soviet craft, the *Tornado,* had been built in Old Greenwich, Connecticut.

1964 Tokyo-Fujisawa T: 17, N: 17, D: 10.21.

			PTS.
1.	BAH	(Durward Knowles, C. Cecil Cooke)	5664
2.	USA	(Richard Stearns, Lynn Williams)	5585
3.	SWE	(Pelle Pettersson, Holger Sundström)	5527
4.	FIN	(Peder Tallberg, Henrik Tallberg)	5402
5.	SOV/RUS	(Timir Pinegin, Fyodor Shutkov)	4305
6.	GER	(Bruno Splieth, Karsten Meyer)	4175
7.	CAN	(David Miller, William West)	3565
8.	POR	(Manuel Duarte, Pinto Fernando)	3330

Forty-six-year-old Durward Knowles was competing in his fifth Olympics. If Stearns and Williams had finished six seconds faster in the last race, they would have won the gold medal.

1968 Mexico City-Acapulco T: 20, N: 20, D: 10.21.

			PTS.
1.	USA	(Lowell North, Peter Barrett)	14.4
2.	NOR	(Peder Lunde, Jr., Per Olav Wiken)	43.7
3.	ITA	(Franco Cavallo, Camilo Gargano)	44.7
4.	DEN	(Paul Elvström, Poul Mik-Meyer)	50.4
5.	BAH	(Durward Knowles, Percival Knowles)	63.4
6.	AUS	(David Forbes, Richard Williamson)	68.7
7.	BRA	(Erik Schmidt, Axel Schmidt)	74.4
8.	SWI	(Edwin Bernet, Rolf Amrein)	75.0

North and Barrett secured first place after six races, but won the seventh race anyway.

1972 Munich-Kiel T: 18, N: 18, D: 9.8.

			PTS.
1.	AUS	(David Forbes, John Anderson)	28.1
2.	SWE	(Pelle Pettersson, Stellan Westerdahl)	44.0
3.	GER	(Wilhelm Kuhweide, Karsten Meyer)	44.4
4.	BRA	(Jorge Bruder, Jan Willem Aten)	52.7
5.	ITA	(Flavio Scala, Mauro Testa)	58.4
6.	POR	(Antonio Correia, Ulrich Anjos)	68.4
7.	GBR	(Stuart Jardine, John Wastall)	68.7
8.	HUN	(András Gosztonyi, György Holovits)	74.0

The Australians were assured of first place after the sixth race. At the same time that John Anderson was winning a gold medal in the Star class, his identical twin brother, Tom, was winning a gold medal in the Dragon class on a different course.

1976 not held

1980 Moscow-Tallinn T: 13, N: 13, D: 7.29.

			PTS.
1.	SOV	(Valentyn Mankin, Aleksandrs Muzičenko)	24.7
2.	AUT	(Hubert Raudaschl, Karl Ferstl)	31.7
3.	ITA	(Giorgio Gorla, Alfio Peraboni)	36.1
4.	SWE	(Peter Sundelin, Håkan Lindström)	44.7
5.	DEN	(Jens Håkon Christensen, Morten Nielsen)	45.7
6.	HOL	(Boudewijn Binkhorst, Jacob Vandenberg)	49.4
7.	SPA	(Antonio Gorostegui Ceballos, José Maria Benavides Accibar)	72.7
8.	GDR	(Wolf-Eberhard Richter, Olaf Engelhardt)	83.7

Forty-one-year-old Valentyn Mankin gained his third gold medal, having won the Finn class in 1968 and the Tempest in 1972. He is the only yachtsman to have earned gold medals in three different classes. He also won a silver in the 1976 Tempest. The Austrians could have won with a fourth-place finish in the last race, but they could do no better than ninth. Most damaging to the Austrians was the third race, in which they were disqualified after finishing first.

1984 Los Angeles-Long Beach T: 19, N: 19, D: 8.8.

			PTS.
1.	USA	(William E. Buchan, Stephen Erickson)	29.7
2.	GER	(Joachim Griese, Michael Marcour)	41.4
3.	ITA	(Giorgio Gorla, Alfio Peraboni)	43.5

4.	SWE	(Kent Carlson, Henrik Eyermann)	43.7
5.	AUT	(Hubert Raudaschl, Karl Ferstl)	53.4
6.	GRE	(Ilias Hatzipavlis, Leonidas Pelekanakis)	67.0
7.	SPA	(Antonio Gorostegui Ceballos, José Luis Doreste Blanco)	74.0
8.	HOL	(Hans Binkhorst, Wilem van Walt Meijer)	76.0

After six races, the gold medal was still up for grabs among the four leaders. Buchan, a 49-year-old building contractor from Seattle, Washington, got off to a poor start and he and Erickson found themselves discussing how to protect third place. But a sudden wind shift, coupled with a mistake by Gorla, who missed a mark and had to go around the buoy again, opened the way for the Americans, who shot through for their third victory of the regatta. As Buchan would later say, "In five minutes we went from nothing to silver to gold. I've been sailing these little suckers for 35 years, and I've never felt the speed I had. I still don't know how I did it." Buchan's son, Carl, won a gold medal in the Flying Dutchman class.

1988 Seoul-Pusan T: 21, N: 21, D: 9.27.

			PTS.
1.	GBR	(Michael McIntyre, P. Bryn Vaile)	45.7
2.	USA	(Mark Reynolds, Hal Haenel)	48.0
3.	BRA	(Torben Grael, Nelson Falcão)	50.0
4.	SWE	(Mats Johansson, Mats Hansson)	56.7
5.	ITA	(Giorgio Gorla, Alfio Peraboni)	63.1
6.	CAN	(D. Ross MacDonald, D. Bruce MacDonald)	63.7
7.	AUS	(Colin Beashel, Gregory Torpy)	66.4
8.	SOV/RUS	(Viktor Solovyov, Aleksandr Zybin)	68.4

McIntyre and Vaile were in fourth place after six races. To earn gold medals they needed to win the final race, with Reynolds and Haenel placing worse than fifth and Grael and Falcão worse than fourth. As it happened, the Brazilians could manage only eighth place; the Americans suffered a broken mast and failed to finish. Meanwhile, McIntyre and Vaile successfully fought off a challenge from the Australian pair to win by 11 seconds. Regarding his upset victory, McIntyre, a car-phone sales manager from West Dean, near Salisbury, said, "In my wildest dreams I thought we could win, but not in any other state of mind."

The skipper of the 19th place Bahamian boat was 1964 Olympic champion Durwood Knowles, who, at age 70, was the third-oldest competitor in any sport in the history of the Olympics. He was also one of only five people to take part in eight Olympics.

1992 Barcelona T: 26, N: 26, D: 8.2.

			PTS.
1.	USA	(Mark Reynolds, Hal Haenel)	31.4
2.	NZE	(Roderick Davies, Donald Cowie)	58.4
3.	CAN	(D. Ross MacDonald, Eric Jespersen)	62.7
4.	HOL	(Mark Neeleman, Jos Schrier)	64.0
5.	SWE	(Hans Wallén, Bobbie Loshe)	65.0
6.	GER	(Hans Vogt, Jörg Fricke)	69.7

7. AUS   (Colin Beashel, David Giles)   71.4
8. GRE   (Iakovos Kiseoglou, Dimitris Boukis)   84.0

Reynolds and Haenel made up for their disappointment of four years earlier by finishing second, first, third, first, third, and eleventh to clinch the victory without having to compete in the final race.

SOLING

The Soling is a three-man keelboat. It is 8.2 meters (26 feet 11 inches) long and weighs 1035 kilograms (2282 pounds). It was designed in 1965 by Jan Herman Linge of Norway.

In 1992 the Soling competition switched to a new format. The six boats that lead the overall standing after six races advance to a round-robin pool in which each crew sails once against every other crew. The top four crews in the pool advance to direct-elimination semifinals. In 1992 the semifinals, the final, and the contest for third place were decided on a best two-out-of-three basis. In 1996 all match races will be best three out of five.

1896–1968 not held

1972 Munich-Kiel T: 26, N: 26, D: 9.8.

			PTS.
1.	USA	(Harry "Buddy" Melges, William Bentsen, William Allen)	8.7
2.	SWE	(Stig Wennerström, Lennart Roslund, Bo Knape, Stefan Krook)	31.7
3.	CAN	(David Miller, John Ekels, Paul Cote)	47.1
4.	FRA	(Jean-Marie le Guillou, Bernard Drubay, Jean-Yves Pellerin)	53.0
5.	GBR	(John Oakeley, Charles Reynolds, Barry Dunning)	54.7
6.	BRA	(Axel Schmidt-Preben, Patrick Matte Mascarenhas, Erik Schmidt-Preben)	64.7
7.	SOV/ RUS	(Timir Pinegin, Valentin Zamotaikin, Rais Galimov)	65.0
8.	POL	(Zygfryd Perlicki, Józef Blaszczyk, Stanislaw Stefański)	75.0

The competition was limited to six races because of bad weather. Paul Elvström, attempting to become the first person in history to win gold medals at five different Olympics, became infuriated and disillusioned by a bumping incident with the French crew, packed up his boat and drove home in a huff after the fifth race, finishing 13th overall. Crown Prince Harald of Norway placed tenth. Less illustrious, but more successful, was helmsman Buddy Melges of Zelda, Wisconsin, who guided his boat to three firsts, a second, a third, and a fourth on his way to the gold medal. In 1992 Melges co-skippered the victorious *America³* in the America's Cup. He is the only skipper to have won both an Olympic championship and the America's Cup.

1976 Montreal-Kingston T: 24, N: 24, D: 7.27.

			PTS.
1.	DEN	(Poul Jensen, Valdemar Bandolowski, Erik Hansen)	46.7
2.	USA	(John Kolius, Walter Glasgow, Richard Hoepfner)	47.4
3.	GDR	(Dieter Below, Michael Zachries, Olaf Engelhard)	47.4
4.	SOV/ RUS	(Boris Budnikov, Valentin Zamotaikin, Nikolai Polyakov)	48.7
5.	HOL	(Geert Bakker, Harald de Vlaming, Pieter Keijzer)	58.0
6.	GER	(Wilhelm Kuhweide, Karsten Meyer, Axel May)	60.7
7.	FRA	(Patrick Haegeli, Patrick Oeuvrard, Bruno Trouble)	64.0
8.	CAN	(Glen Dexter, Alexander "Sandy" Macmillan, Andreas Josenhans)	68.7

The 1976 Soling regatta was so close that the Danish team didn't know they had won until they returned to their berth and saw a large crowd waiting for them. Had they finished seven seconds slower in the final race they would have had to settle for bronze medals instead of gold. Instead, they swept past the French boat before the finish line to place fifth, and the extra 1.7 points provided their margin of victory.

1980 Moscow-Tallinn T: 9, T: 9, D: 7.29.

			PTS.
1.	DEN	(Poul Jensen, Valdemar Bandolowski, Erik Hansen)	23.0
2.	SOV/ RUS	(Boris Budnikov, Aleksandr Budnikov, Nikolai Polyakov)	30.4
3.	GRE	(Anastassios Boudouris, Anastassios Gavrilis, Aristidis Rapanakis)	31.1
4.	GDR	(Dieter Below, Bernd Klenke, Michael Zachries)	37.4
5.	HOL	(Geert Bakker, Steven Bakker, Dick Coster)	45.0
6.	BRA	(Vicente D'Avila Brun, Gastao D'Avila Brun, Roberto Luiz Souza)	47.1
7.	SWI	(Jean-François Corminboeuf, Roger-Claude Guignard, Robert Perret)	71.7
8.	SWE	(Jan Andersson, Göran Andersson, Bertil Larsson)	75.7

The three Danes defended their championship by winning the last two races, with the Soviet boat in second place both times.

1984 Los Angeles-Long Beach T: 22, N: 22, D: 8.8.

			PTS.
1.	USA	(Robert Haines, Edward Trevelyan, Roderick Davis)	33.7
2.	BRA	(Torben Grael, Daniel Adler, Ronaldo Senfft)	43.4
3.	CAN	(Hans Marius Fogh, John Kerr, Steve Calder)	49.7
4.	GBR	(Christopher Law, Edward Leask, Jeremy Richards)	54.7
5.	NOR	(Dag Halfdan Usterud, Stein Lund Halvorsen, Börre Skui)	57.7
6.	GRE	(Anastassios Boudouris, Dimitrios Deligiannis, George Spiridis)	59.2
7.	AUS	(Gary Sheard, Tim Dorning, Dean Gordon)	62.4
8.	GER	(Wilhelm Kuhweide, Axel May, Eckhard Loll)	71.0

The U.S. team won without having to compete in the final race. Bronze medalist Hans Marius Fogh was competing in his sixth Olympics, having won a silver medal in 1960 while representing Denmark in the Flying Dutchman class.

1988 Seoul-Pusan T: 20, N: 20, D: 9.27.

		PTS.
1. GDR	(Jochen Schümann, Thomas Flach, Bernd Jäkel)	11.7
2. USA	(John Kostecki, William Baylis, Robert Billingham)	14.0
3. DEN	(Jesper Bank, Jan Dupont Mathiasen, Steen Secher)	52.7
4. GBR	(Lawrie Smith, Edward Leask, Jeremy Richards)	67.1
5. BRA	(José Paulo Dias, José Augusto Dias, Christoph Bergman)	67.4
6. FRA	(Michel Kermarec, Stanislas Dripaux, Xavier Phelippon)	68.4
7. NZE	(Thomas Dodson, Simon Daubney, Aran Hansen)	74.4
8. SWE	(Lennart Persson, Eje Öberg, Tony Wallin)	77.7

This exciting competition pitted two-time world champion John Kostecki against 1976 Finn gold medalist Jochen Schümann. Earlier in the year, Schümann had defeated Kostecki at the European championships. In Seoul, both men took three firsts and two seconds. Schümann won because his sixth best finish was a third to Kostecki's fourth. In the final race, the East German had to place second. Schümann started poorly, but moved up from ninth place to second by the start of the final leg, then held his position to finish.

1992 Barcelona T: 24, N: 24, D: 8.4.

		FINAL MATCHES
1. DEN	(Jesper Bank, Steen Secher, Jesper Seier)	2–0
2. USA	(Kevin Mahaney, James Brady, Doug Kern)	
3. GBR	(Lawrie Smith, Robert Cruikshank, Simon "Ossie" Stewart)	2–1
4. GER	(Jochen Schümann, Thomas Flach, Bernd Jäkel)	
5. SWE	(Magnus Holmberg, Björn Alm, Johan Barne)	
6. SPA	(Fernando Leon Boissier, Felipe de Borbón, Alfredo Vázquez Jiméner)	
7. CAN	(R. Paul Thomson, R. Stuart Flinn, Philip Gow)	
8. NZE	(Simon Daubney, Russell Coutts, Graham Fleury)	

The American crew led the round-robin pool with four wins and one loss, with the Danes in second place. Both of them won their semifinal match-ups in straight races. In the first race of the final, Bank came from behind to beat Mahaney by less than a boatlength. Just before the start of the second race, Mahaney's boat touched the Danish boat and the Americans were forced to sail a 270-degree penalty turn that left them 26 seconds behind

before they entered the course. Bank did not waste his advantage and the race was never in doubt. One member of the Spanish crew was Prince Felipe, heir to the Spanish throne. His full title was Crown Prince Felipe Juan Pablo Alfonso de Todos los Santos Borbón Schleswig-Borbón Sonderburg Glucksburg.

Discontinued Events

.5–TON CLASS

1900 Paris-Meulan C: 7, N: 1, D: 5.24

			PTS.	TIME
1. Texier		FRA	18	20:40:38
2. Pierre Gervais		FRA	18	20:56:12
3. Henri Monnot		FRA	15	
4. Michel Monnot		FRA	13	
5. G. Semichon		FRA	10	
6. Jean d'Estournelles de Constant		FRA	6	

.5–1 TON CLASS

1900 Paris-Meulan T: 8, N: 3, D: 5.24.

		PTS.	TIME
1. FRA	(E. Michelet, F. Michelet)	17	6:42:01
2. GBR	(Algernon Maudslay, Lorne Currie, John Gretton, Linton Hope)	17	6:44:21
3. FRA	(Jacques Baudrier, Jean Lebret, Marcotte, R. William Martin, Jules Valton)	17	6:49:37
4. FRA	(Jean de Chabannes la Palice)	13	

1–2 TON CLASS

1900 Paris-Meulan T: 5, N: 3, D: 5.24.

		PTS.
1. SWI	(Hermann Alexandre de Pourtalès)	19
2. FRA	(F. Vilamitjana)	17
3. FRA	(Jacques Baudrier)	15

2–3 TON CLASS

1900 Paris-Meulan T: 4, N: 3, D: 5.25.

		PTS.
1. GBR	(William Exshaw)	20
2. FRA	(Susse)	18
3. FRA	(Auguste Donny)	15
4. GER	(Ferdinand Schlatter)	15

Exshaw lived in the Bordeaux region of France, where he was in charge of his family's brandy production business.

3–10 TON CLASS

1900 Paris-Meulan T: 12, N: 3, D: 5.25.

			PTS.
1.	FRA	(Maurice Gufflet)	17
2.	HOL	(Henricus Smulders, Christoff Hooijkaas, Arie van der Velden)	16
3.	FRA	(Gilardoni)	
3.	GBR	(Howard Taylor)	

In this two-race event, Taylor missed the first race because he was delayed at French Customs, but he arrived in time to win the second race.

10–20 TON CLASS

1900 Paris-Le Havre T: 6, N: 2, D: 8.6.

			PTS.
1.	FRA	(Emile Billard, P. Perquer)	29
2.	FRA	(Jean Decazes)	25
3.	GBR	(Edward Hore)	23
4.	FRA	(Cronier)	20
5.	GBR	(S.M. Mellor)	18
6.	FRA	(Jules Valton)	17

20+ TON CLASS

1900 Paris-Le Havre T: ?, N: ?, D: ?.

1.	GBR	(Cecil Quentin)	6:01:06
2.	GBR	(John Calverley)	6:01:26
3.	USA	(Harry Van Bergen)	6:21:32

OPEN CLASS

1900 Paris-Meulan T: ?, N: ?, D: 5.20.

1.	GBR	(Algernon Maudslay, Lorne Currie, John Gretton)	5:56:17
2.	GER	(Martin Wiesner, Heinrich Peters, Ottokar Weise, George Naue, Arthur Bloomfield)	5:58:17
3.	FRA	(E. Michelet, F. Michelet)	6:12:12
4.	FRA	(Emile Sacre)	7:11:08
5.	FRA	(Jean d'Estournelles de Constant)	—

DISQ: Texier (FRA), Louis-Auguste Dormeuil (FRA)

John Gretton is the only person to have won an Olympic championship while serving as a Member of Parliament.

DRAGON

1948 London-Torbay T: 12, N: 12, D: 8.12.

			PTS.
1.	NOR	(Thor Thorvaldsen, Sigve Lie, Håkon Barfod)	4746
2.	SWE	(Folke Bohlin, Hugo Jonsson, Gösta Brodin)	4621
3.	DEN	(William Berntsen, Ole Berntsen, Klaus Baess)	4223
4.	GBR	(William Eric Strain, George Brown, James Wallace)	3943
5.	ITA	(Giuseppe Canessa, Bruno Bianchi, Luigi DeManincor)	3366

6.	FIN	(Rainer Packalen, Niilo Orama, Aatos Hirvisalo)	3057
7.	ARG	(Roberto Sieburger, Jorge Del Rio Sálas, Jorge Sálas Chaves)	2843
8.	HOL	(Cornelis Jonker, Abraham Dudok van Heel, Willem van Duyl)	2508

1952 Helsinki T: 17, N: 17, D: 7.28.

			PTS.
1.	NOR	(Thor Thorvaldsen, Sigve Lie, Håkon Barfod)	6130
2.	SWE	(Per Gedda, Sidney Boldt-Christmas, Erland Almkvist)	5556
3.	GER	(Theodor Thomsen, Erich Natusch, Georg Nowka)	5352
4.	ARG	(Roberto Sieburger, Jorge Del Río Salas, Horacio Campi)	5339
5.	DEN	(Ole Berntsen, William Berntsen, Aage Birch)	4460
6.	HOL	(Willem van Duyl, Abraham Dudok van Heel, Michiel Dudok van Heel)	4041
7.	BRA	(Wolfgang Richter, Peter Mangels, Francisco Felici Italo Osoldi)	2884
8.	POR	(João Tito, Carlos Lourenco, Alberto Graca)	2782

1956 Melbourne T: 16, N: 16, D: 12.5.

			PTS.
1.	SWE	(Folke Bohlin, Bengt Palmquist, Leif Wikström)	5723
2.	DEN	(Ole Berntsen, Cyril Andresen, Christian von Bülow)	5723
3.	GBR	(Graham Mann, Ronald Backus, Jonathan Janson)	4547
4.	ARG	(Jorge Sálas Chavez, Arnoldo Pekelharing, Boris Belada)	4225
5.	AUS	(Graham Drane, Brian Carolan, James Carolane)	3769
6.	ITA	(Sergio Sorrentino, Piero Gorgatto, Adelchi Pelaschiar)	3404
7.	NOR	(Thor Thorvaldsen, Carl Otto Svae, Björn Gulbrandsen)	3253
8.	CAN	(David Howard, Herald Howard, Donald Tytler)	3186

The Swedes came from behind to win the last two races and tie the Danes at 5723 points. Sweden was then awarded first place because they won three races to Denmark's one.

1960 Rome-Naples T: 27, N: 27, D: 9.7.

			PTS.
1.	GRE	(Crown Prince Constantin, Odysseus Eskitzoglou, Georgios Zaimis)	6733
2.	ARG	(Jorge Sálas Chavez, Héctor Calegaris, Jorge Del Río)	5715
3.	ITA	(Antonio Cosentino, Antonio Ciciliano, Giulio De Stefano)	5704
4.	NOR	(Öivind Christensen, Arild Amundsen, Carl Otto Svae)	5403
5.	CAN	(Samuel McDonald, Lynn Watters, Gordon Norton)	5177
6.	DEN	(Aage Birch, Paul Jörgensen, Niels Markussen)	4715
7.	GBR	(Graham Mann, Jonathan Janson, Ian Hannay)	4604
8.	GER	(Hans Ravenborg, Günther Benecke, Peter Rebien)	4329

Twenty-year-old Crown Prince Constantin received the traditional victory dunking by being pushed into the water by his mother, Queen Frederika.

One member of the Philippine crew, which finished twenty-fourth, was Francisco Gonzalez, who gained dubious notoriety four years later when he shot the pilot of a commercial airplane in Northern California, causing the death of forty-four people, including himself. Gonzalez had taken out a $100,000 flight insurance policy before boarding the flight.

1964 Tokyo-Fujisawa T: 23, N: 23, D: 10.21.

			PTS.
1.	DEN	(Ole Berntsen, Christian von Bülow, Ole Poulsen)	5854
2.	GDR	(Peter Ahrendt, Ulrich Mense, Wilfried Lorenz)	5826
3.	USA	(Lowell North, Charles Rogers, Richard Deaver)	5523
4.	GBR	(Edwin Parry, Jeremy Harris, Peter Reade)	5090
5.	BER	(Edmund Cooper, Eugene Simmons, Conrad Soares)	5055
6.	ITA	(Sergio Sorrentino, Sergio Furlan, Annibale Pelaschiar)	4636
7.	BAH	(Godfrey Kelly, Basil Kelly, Robert Eardley)	4294
8.	GRE	(Odysseus Eskitzoglou, Georgios Zaimis, Themistoklis Magoulas)	4188

The East Germans finished 16 seconds short of a gold medal in the final race.

1968 Mexico City-Acapulco T: 23, N: 23, D: 10.21.

			PTS.
1.	USA	(George Friedrichs, Barton Jahncke, Gerald Schreck)	6.0
2.	DEN	(Aage Birch, Poul Höj Jensen, Niels Markussen)	26.4
3.	GDR	(Paul Borowski, Karl-Heinz Thun, Konrad Weichert)	32.7
4.	CAN	(Stephen Tupper, David Miller, Timothy Irwin)	64.1
5.	AUS	(John Cuneo, Thomas Anderson, John Ferguson)	65.0
6.	SWE	(Gunnar Broberg, Lennart Eisner, Sven Hanson)	71.4
7.	GER	(Klaus Oldendorff, Peter Stuicken, Axel May)	74.0
8.	FRA	(Michel Briand, Michel Alexandre, Pierre Blanchard)	81.4

The U.S. crew won four of the seven races and also finished second twice and sixth once.

1972 Munich-Kiel T: 23, N: 23, D: 9.8.

			PTS.
1.	AUS	(John Cuneo, Thomas Anderson, John Shaw)	13.7
2.	GDR	(Paul Borowski, Konrad Weichert, Karl-Heinz Thun)	41.7
3.	USA	(Donald Cohan, Charles Horter, John Marshall)	47.7
4.	GER	(Franz Heilmeier, Richard Kuchler, Konrad Glas)	47.7
5.	NZE	(Ronald Watson, Noel Everett, Fraser Beer)	51.0
6.	SWE	(Jörgen Sundelin, Peter Sundelin, Ulf Sundelin)	67.4
7.	DEN	(Poul Höj Jensen, Frank Höj Jensen, Gunnar Dahlgaard)	68.0
8.	FIN	(Kurt Nyman, Göran Schauman, Aleksander Bielaczyc)	68.7

Skippered by 44-year-old optician John Cuneo, the Australian yacht won the first three races of a competition that was cut short after six races due to inclement weather.

5.5-METER

1952 Helsinki T: 16, N: 16, D: 7.28.

			PTS.
1.	USA	(Britton Chance, Sumner White, Edgar White, Michael Schoettle)	5751
2.	NOR	(Peder Lunde, Sr., Vibeke Lunde, Börre Falkum-Hansen)	5325
3.	SWE	(Folke Wassén, Magnus Wassén, Carl-Erik Ohlson)	4554
4.	POR	(Duarte de Almeida Bello, Fernando Pinto Coelho Bello, Julio Sousa Leite Gorinho)	4450
5.	ARG	(Rodolfo Vollenweider, Tomás Galfrascoli, Ludovico Kempter)	3982
6.	GBR	(Robert Perry, John Dillon, Neil Cochran-Patrick)	3727
7.	SAF	(Leslie Horsfield, Joseph Ellis-Brown, Eric Benningfield)	3338
8.	FIN	(Hans Dittmar, Aarne Castrén, Johan Stadigh)	3292

1956 Melbourne T: 10, N: 10, D: 12.5.

			PTS.
1.	SWE	(Lars Thörn, Hjalmar Karlsson, Sture Stork)	5527
2.	GBR	(Robert Perry, Neil Cochran-Patrick, John Dillon, David Bowker)	4050
3.	AUS	(Alexander Sturrock, Deveraux Mytton, Douglas Buxton)	4022
4.	USA	(Ferdinand Schoettle, Victor Sheronas, John Bryant, Robert Stinson)	3971
5.	NOR	(Peder Lunde, Sr., Odd Harsheim, Halfdan Ditlev-Simonsen, Jr.)	3807
6.	FRA	(Albert Cadot, Jean-Jacques Herbulot, Dominque Perroud)	1779
7.	ITA	(Massimo Oberti, Antonio Carattino, Carlo Spirito, Antonio Cosentino)	1677
8.	SOV	(Konstantin Aleksandrov, Konstantin Melgunov, Lev Alekseyev)	1598

1960 Rome-Naples T: 19, N: 19, D: 9.7.

			PTS.
1.	USA	(George O'Day, James Hunt, David Smith)	6900
2.	DEN	(William Berntsen, Steen Christensen, Sören Hancke)	5678
3.	SWI	(Henri Copponex, Pierre Girard, Manfred Metzger)	5122
4.	ARG	(Roberto Sieburger, Enrique Sieburger, Carlos Sieburger)	4402
5.	SWE	(Bengt Sjösten, Claes Turitz, Göran Witting)	4277
6.	GBR	(Robin Aisher, George Nicholson, John Ruggles)	3807
7.	NOR	(Finn Ferner, Odd Harsheim, Knut Wang)	3765
8.	BAH	(Robert Symonette, Basil Kelly, George Roy Ramsey)	3024

1964 Tokyo-Fujisawa T: 15, N: 15, D: 10.21.

			PTS.
1.	AUS	(William Northram, James Sargeant, Peter O'Donnell)	5981
2.	SWE	(Lars Thörn, Sture Stork, Ernst Arne Karlsson)	5284
3.	USA	(John McNamara, Francis Scully, Joseph Batchelder)	5106
4.	ITA	(Agostino Straulino, Bruno Petronio, Massimo Minervini)	4738
5.	GER	(Fritz Kopperschmidt, Herbert Reich, Eckart Wagner, Uwe Mares)	3057
6.	FIN	(Johann Gullichsen, Karl Peter Frazer, Juhani Salovaara)	3039
7.	CAN	(Samuel McDonald, John Woodward, G. Bernard Skinner)	2955
8.	NOR	(Crown Prince Harald, Eirik Johannessen, Stein Foyen)	2860

Former racing-car driver Bill Northram was a 59-year-old grandfather of five when he skippered the yacht *Barrenjoey* to a gold medal.

1968 Mexico City-Acapulco T: 14, N: 14, D: 10.21.

			PTS.
1.	SWE	(Ulf Sundelin, Jörgen Sundelin, Peter Sundelin)	8.0
2.	SWI	(Louis Noverraz, Bernhard Dunand, Marcel Stern)	32.0
3.	GBR	(Robin Aisher, Adrian Jardine, Paul Anderson)	39.8
4.	GER	(Rudolf Harmstorf, Karl-August Stolze, Harald Stein)	47.4
5.	ITA	(Giuseppe Zucchinetti, Antonio Carattino, Domenico Carattino)	51.1
6.	CAN	(Stanley Leibel, Ernest Weiss, Jack Hasen)	68.0
7.	AUS	(William Solomons, James Hardy, Gilbert Kaufman)	69.4
8.	USA	(Gardner Cox, Stephen Colgate, Stuart Walker)	74.7

The Sundelin brothers, from the small resort town of Ektorp, won five of the seven races, finishing fourth and fifth in the other two. Silver medalist Louis Noverraz was 66 years old.

6-METER

1908 London-Ryde T: 5, N: 4, D: 7.29.
1. GBR (Gilbert Laws, Thomas McMeekin, Charles Crichton)
2. BEL (Léon Huybrechts, Louis Huybrechts, Henri Weewauters)
3. FRA (Henri Arthus, Louis Potheau, Pierre Rabot)
4. GBR (John Leuchars, William Leuchars, Frank Smith)
5. SWE (Karl Sjögren, Birger Gustafsson, Jonas Jonsson)

1912 Stockholm-Nynas T: 6, N: 5, D: 7.22.
1. FRA (Amédée Thubé, Gaston Thubé, Jacques Thubé)
2. DEN (Hans Meulengracht-Madsen, Steen Herschend, Sven Thomsen)
3. SWE (Harald Sandberg, Erik Sandberg, Otto Aust)
4. SWE (Olof Mark, Einar Hagberg, Jonas Jonsson)
5. FIN (Ernst Estlander, Torsten Sandelin, Ragnar Stenbäck)

5. NOR (Edvard Christansen, Hans Ferd. Christiansen, Eigil Kragh Christiansen)

1920 Antwerp T: 2, N: 2, D: 7.9.
1. NOR (Andreas Brecke, Paal Kaasan, Ingolf Röd)
2. BEL (Léon Huybrechts, John Klotz, Charles van den Bussche)

1924 Paris-Le Havre T: 9, N: 9, D: 7.26.

			PTS.
1.	NOR	(Eugen Lunde, Christopher Dahl, Anders Lundgren)	2
2.	DEN	(Wilhelm Vett, Knud Degn, Christian Nielsen)	5
3.	HOL	(Johan Carp, Johannes Guépin, Jan Vreede)	5
4.	SWE	(Nils Rinman, Olle Rinman, Magnus Hellström)	12
5.	BEL	(Léon Huybrechts, John Klotz, Léopold Standaert)	16
5.	FRA	(Georges Herpin, Henri Louit, Pierre Moussié)	16

1928 Amsterdam T: 13, N: 13, D: 8.9.

1.	NOR	(Crown Prince Olav, Johan Anker, Erik Anker, Haakon Bryhn)
2.	DEN	(Niels Otto Möller, Aage Höy-Petersen, Peter Schlütter, Svend Linck)
3.	EST	(Nikolai Veksin, William von Wirén, Eberhard Vogdt, Andreas Fählmann, Georg Fählmann)
4.	HOL	(Hendrik Pluijgers, Carl Huisken, Willem Schouten, Hendrik Fokker)
5.	BEL	(Léon Huybrechts, Arthur Sneyers, Frits Mulder, Ludovic Franck, Willy van Rompaey)
6.	USA	(Herman Whiton, Conway Olmstead, Willets Outerbridge, James Thompson, Frederick Morris)
7.	SWE	(Harry Hansson, Georg Lindahl, Yngve Lindquist, Hakon Reuter)
8.	FRA	—

During World War II, Crown Prince Olav became a symbol of Norwegian resistance to the Nazis. His reign as King Olav V was a popular one and lasted from 1957 until his death in 1991.

1932 Los Angeles T: 3, N: 3, D: 8.12.

			PTS.
1.	SWE	(Tore Holm, Martin Hindorff, Olle Åkerlund, Åke Bergqvist)	18
2.	USA	(Frederick Conant, Robert Carlson, Temple Ashbrook, Charles Smith, Donald Douglas, Emmett Davis)	12
3.	CAN	(Philip Rogers, Gerald Wilson, Gardner Boultbee, Kenneth Glass)	4

The Swedes won all six races.

1936 Berlin-Kiel T: 12, N: 12, D: 8.10.

			PTS.
1.	GBR	(Charles Leaf, Christopher Boardman, Miles Bellville, Russell Harmer, Leonard Martin)	67
2.	NOR	(Magnus Konow, Karsten Konow, Fredrik Meyer, Vadjuv Nyquist, Alf Tveten)	66
3.	SWE	(Sven Salén, Dagmar Salén, Lennart Ekdahl, Martin Hindorff, Torsten Lord)	62

			PTS.
4.	ARG	(Julio Sieburger, Claudio Bincaz, Germán Frers, Edlef Hosmann, Jorge Linck)	52
5.	ITA	(Renato Cosentino, Giuliano Oberti, Massimo Oberti, Giovanni Stampa, Giuseppe Volpi)	50
6.	GER	(Hans Lubinus, Dietrich Christensen, Kurt Frey, Theodor Thomsen, Haimar Wedemeyer)	49
7.	FIN	(Curt Mattson, Yngve Pacius, Ragnar Stenbaeck, Holger Sumelius, Lars-Gunnar Winqvist)	43
8.	HOL	(Johan Carp, Ansco Dokkum, Cornelis Jonker, Herman Looman, Ernst Moltzer)	42

1948 London-Torbay T: 11, N: 11, D: 8.12.

			PTS.
1.	USA	(Herman "Swede" Whiton, Alfred Loomis, James Weekes, James Smith, Michael Mooney)	5472
2.	ARG	(Enrique Sieburger, Emilio Homps, Rufino Rodríguez de le Torre, Rodolfo Rivademar, Julio Sieburger)	5120
3.	SWE	(Tore Holm, Torsten Lord, Martin Hindorff, Karl Ameln, Gösta Salén)	4033
4.	NOR	(Magnus Konow, Anders Evensen, Lars Musaeus, Håkon Solem, Ragnar Hargreaves)	3217
5.	GBR	(James Douglas Hume, James Howden Hume, Brian Hardie, Henry Hardie, Harry Hunter)	2879
6.	BEL	(Ludovic Franck, Emile Hayoit, Willy Huybrechts, Henri van Riel, Willy van Rompaey)	2752
7.	SWI	(Henri Copponex, P. Bonnet, R. Fehlmann, André Firmenich, Emile Lachapelle, Louis Noverraz, Charles Stern, Marcel Stern)	2594
8.	ITA	(Giovanni Reggio, Giorgio Audizio, Renato Costentino, Giuseppe Croce, G. De Luca, Luigi Poggi, Enrico Poggi)	2099

1952 Helsinki T: 11, N: 11, D: 7.28.

			PTS.
1.	USA	(Herman "Swede" Whiton, Eric Ridder, Julian Roosevelt, Everard Endt, John Morgan, Emelyn Whiton)	4870
2.	NOR	(Finn Ferner, Johan Ferner, Erik Heiberg, Carl Mortensen, Tor Arneberg)	4648
3.	FIN	(Ernst Westerlund, Paul Sjöberg, Ragnar Jansson, Adolf Konto, Rolf Turkka)	3944
4.	SWE	(Sven Salén, Martin Hindorff, Torsten Lord, Jacob Lars Lundström, Karl Ameln)	3773
5.	ARG	(Enrique Sieburger, Rufino Rodríguez de la Torre, Werner von Foerster, Horacio Monti, Hércules Morini)	3393
6.	SWI	(Louis Noverraz, André Firmenich, Charles Stern, Marcel Stern, François Chapot)	3020
7.	CAN	(Norman Gooderham, Kenneth Bradfield, William Copeland, William Macintosh, Donald Tytler)	3013
8.	ITA	(Enrico Poggi, Antonio Cosentino, Pietro Reggio, Giusto Spigno, Andrea Ferrari)	2560

Herman Whiton and the *Llanoria* repeated their 1948 triumph, winning the final race by 81 seconds. Finland's bronze-medal-winning yacht, *Ralia,* was the same boat that Sweden had used four years earlier to gain the bronze medal in London. The Swedes had named it *Ali Baba.*

6-METER, 1907 RATING

1920 Antwerp T: 4, N: 2, D: 7.9.

			PTS.
1.	BEL	(Emile Cornellie, Florimond Cornellie, Frédéric-Albert Bruynseels)	5
2.	NOR	(Ejnar Torgersen, Leif Erichsen, Annan Knudsen)	7
3.	NOR	(Henrik Agersborg, Tygve Pedersen, Einar Berntsen)	9
4.	BEL	(Louis Depiére, Raymond Bauwens, Willy Valcke)	9

FLYING DUTCHMAN

The Flying Dutchman class is a centerboard dinghy with a crew of two, one of whom is attached to the boat by a rope and a trapeze. This allows him to lean far outside the craft without falling overboard. The boat is 6.05 meters (19 feet 10 inches) long and weighs 165 kilograms (364 pounds). The Flying Dutchman was designed in 1951 by Conrad Gulcher and U. van Essen of Holland.

1960 Rome-Naples T: 31, N: 31, D: 9.7.

			PTS.
1.	NOR	(Peder Lunde, Jr., Björn Bergvall)	6774
2.	DEN	(Hans Fogh, Ole Erik Petersen)	5991
3.	GER	(Rolf Mulka, Ingo von Bredow, Achim Kadelbach)	5882
4.	ZIM	(David Butler, Christopher Bevan)	5792
5.	HOL	(Gijsbertus Verhagen, Gerardus Lautenschütz)	5452
6.	SOV/RUS	(Aleksandr Shelkovnikov, Viktor Pilchin)	5123
7.	GBR	(William "Slotty" Dawes, James Ramus)	4954
8.	NZE	(Murray Rae, Ronald Watson)	4641

Eighteen-year-old Peder Lunde came from an illustrious sailing family. His grandfather Eugen won a gold medal in the six-meter class in 1924, and his father and mother Peder and Vibeke, won silver medals in the 5.5-meter class in 1952. Young Peder also gained a Star class silver medal in 1968.

1964 Tokyo-Fujisawa T: 21, N: 21, D: 10.21.

			PTS.
1.	NZE	(Helmer Pedersen, Earle Wells)	6255
2.	GBR	(Franklyn Musto, Arthur Morgan)	5556
3.	USA	(Harry Melges, William Bentsen)	5158
4.	DEN	(Ole Erik Petersen, Hans Fogh)	4500
5.	SOV/RUS	(Aleksandr Shelkovnikov, Viktor Pilchin)	4375
6.	HOL	(Gijsbertus Verhagen, Nicolaas de Jong)	4214
7.	FRA	(Marcel-André Buffet, Alain-François Lehoerff)	3864
8.	AUT	(Karl Geiger, Werner Fischer)	3706

Pedersen and Wells got off to a slow start, placing 16th the first day and failing to finish the second race. After that they picked up three firsts, a third, and a fourth.

1968 Mexico City-Acapulco T: 30, N: 30, D: 10.21.

			PTS.
1.	GBR	(Rodney Pattison, Iain Macdonald-Smith)	3.0
2.	GER	(Ullrich Libor, Peter Naumann)	43.7

3.	BRA	(Reinaldo Conrad, Burkhard Cordes)	48.4
4.	AUS	(Carl Ryves, James Sargeant)	49.1
5.	NOR	(Björn Lofteröd, Odd Lofteröd)	52.4
6.	FRA	(Bertrand Cheret, Bruno Trouble)	68.0
7.	CAN	(Roger Green, Stewart Green)	79.0
8.	NZE	(Geoffrey Smale, Ralph Roberts)	84.0

Submarine lieutenant Rod Pattison and solicitor's clerk Iain Macdonald-Smith finished first in the opening race, but were disqualified for interference. Undeterred by what they considered an unjust decision, the two men guided their boat *Superdocious* to five straight victories. Sailing cautiously on the final day, they still placed second to win the competition by a wide margin.

1972 Munich-Kiel T: 29, N: 29, D: 9.8.

			PTS.
1.	GBR	(Rodney Pattisson, Christopher Davies)	22.7
2.	FRA	(Yves Pajot, Marc Pajot)	40.7
3.	GER	(Ullrich, Libor, Peter Naumann)	51.1
4.	BRA	(Reinaldo Conrad, Burkhard Cordes)	62.4
5.	YUG	(Anton Grego, Simo Nikolić)	63.7
6.	SOV	(Vladimir Leontyev, Valery Zubanov)	67.7
7.	DEN	(Hans Fogh, Elrik Brock)	74.4
8.	AUS	(Mark Bethwaite, Timothy Alexander)	75.7

Pattisson and Davies won four of the first six races and didn't bother to start on the final day.

1976 Montreal-Kingston T: 20, N: 20, D: 7.27.

			PTS.
1.	GER	(Jörg Diesch, Eckart Diesch)	34.7
2.	GBR	(Rodney Pattisson, Julian Brooke Houghton)	51.7
3.	BRA	(Reinaldo Conrad, Peter Eicker)	52.1
4.	CAN	(Hans Fogh, Evert Bastet)	57.1
5.	SOV	(Vladimir Leontyev, Valery Zubanov)	59.4
6.	USA	(Norman Freeman, John Mathias)	65.7
7.	SPA	(Alesandro Abascal García, José María Benavides Accibar)	66.0
8.	FRA	(Yves Pajot, Marc Pajot)	72.0

For the third straight time, Rod Pattison was first across the finishing line in the opening race. However, he fell off badly in the last three races, placing 18th, 12th, and 11th. The Diesch brothers were ten points ahead after six races. On the way to the starting line for the final race they discovered that their centerboard was cracked. They returned to shore, obtained permission to replace the board, made the repair, and still arrived on time to compete. They placed fifth, good enough to take the gold medal.

1980 Moscow-Tallinn T: 15, N: 15, D: 7.29.

			PTS.
1.	SPA	(Alesandro Abascal García, Miguel Noguer Castellvi)	19.0
2.	IRL	(David Wilkins, James Wilkinson)	30.0
3.	HUN	(Szabolcs Detre, Zsolt Detre)	45.7
4.	GDR	(Wolfgang Haase, Wolfgang Wenzel)	51.4
5.	SOV	(Vladimir Leontyev, Valery Zubanov)	51.7
6.	DEN	(Jörgen Bojsen Möller, Jacob Bojsen Möller)	54.5

7.	HOL	(Jan Erik Vollebregt, Sjoerd Vollebregt)	54.7
8.	BRA	(Reinaldo Conrad, Manfred Kaufmann)	63.4

Helmsman Alesandro Abascal, a 28-year-old physicist, won without having to take part in the final race. He and medical student Miguel Noguer had three firsts, a second, and two fourths in the first six races.

1984 Los Angeles-Long Beach T: 17, N: 17, D: 8.8.

			PTS.
1.	USA	(Jonathan McKee, William Carl Buchan)	19.7
2.	CAN	(Terry McLaughlin, Evert Bastet)	22.7
3.	GBR	(Jonathan Richards, Peter Allam)	48.7
4.	DEN	(Jörgen Bojsen Möller, Jacob Bojsen Möller)	52.4
5.	GER	(Jörg Diesch, Eckart Diesch)	56.7
6.	BRA	(Alan Adler, Marcus Tenke)	61.7
7.	ITA	(Mario Celon, Claudio Celon)	78.7
8.	ISR	(Yoel Sela, Eldad Amir)	79.4

McLaughlin entered the last race with a three-point lead over McKee, after winning three of the first six races. But the intense jockeying for position found the Canadians over the line at the start, forcing them to go back and re-start. McKee and Buchan, son of Star class winner Bill Buchan, needed to finish two places ahead of McLaughlin and Bastet, which is exactly what they did, placing sixth to the Canadians' eighth.

1988 Seoul-Pusan T: 22, N: 22, D: 9.27.

			PTS.
1.	DEN	(Jörgen Bojsen Möller, Christian Grönborg)	31.4
2.	NOR	(Ole Petter Pollen, Erik Bjorkum)	37.4
3.	CAN	(Frank McLaughlin, John Millen)	48.4
4.	ISR	(Yoel Sela, Eldad Amir)	59.7
5.	NZE	(Murray Jones, Gregory Knowles)	60.0
6.	GBR	(Roger Yeoman, Neal McDonald)	72.7
7.	BRA	(Alan Adler, Marcus Temke)	76.4
8.	GER	(Albert Batzill, Peter Lang)	79.0

The three medal-winning crews trained together in north Jutland, Denmark, an area chosen by Bojsen Möller because the rough ocean conditions were similar to those in Pusan. The Danes clinched first place before the final race.

Sela and Amir almost became Israel's first Olympic medalists. Unfortunately for them, the second race fell on the Jewish high holiday of Yom Kippur. Israeli Olympic officials made it clear that any of their athletes who competed on Yom Kippur would be withdrawn from competition and sent home, a punishment which they did in fact mete out to the Israeli men's 470 crew. Sela and Amir would have won medals had they taken part in the second race and placed higher than eleventh, a result which they bettered in five of their six races.

1992 Barcelona T: 23, N: 23, D: 8.2.

			PTS.
1.	SPA	(Luis Doreste Blanco, Domingo Manrique)	29.7
2.	USA	(Paul Foerster, Stephen Bourdow)	32.7
3.	DEN	(Jörgen Bojsen Möller, Jens Bojsen Möller)	37.7
4.	NZE	(Murray Jones, Gregory Knowles)	68.0
5.	GER	(Albert Batzill, Peter Lang)	70.4

			PTS.
6.	SWE	(Mats Nyberg, Johan Lindell)	78.4
7.	NOR	(Ole Petter Pollen, Knut Frostad)	80.7
8.	SWI	(Jan Eckert, Piet Eckert)	81.7

Foerster and Bourdow won three straight races (the second, third, and fourth), but were still beaten by the more consistent pair of Doreste and Manrique. Doreste had won the 470 class in Los Angeles in 1984.

6.5-METER

1920 Antwerp T: 2, N: 2, D: 7.9.

			PTS.
1.	HOL	(Johan Carp, Petrus Wernink, Bernard Carp)	2
2.	FRA	(Albert Weil, Félix Picon, Robert Monier)	4

TEMPEST

1972 Munich-Kiel T: 21, N: 21, D: 9.8.

			PTS.
1.	SOV/UKR	(Valentyn Mankin, Vitaly Dyrdyra)	28.1
2.	GBR	(Alan Warren, David Hunt)	34.4
3.	USA	(Glen Foster, Peter Dean)	47.7
4.	SWE	(John Albrechtson, Ingvar Hansson)	57.4
5.	HOL	(Bernard Staartjes, Kees Kuppershoek)	58.7
6.	NOR	(Peder Lunde, Jr., Aksel Gresvig)	70.0
7.	BRA	(Mario Buckup, Peter Ficker)	73.7
8.	IRL	(David Wilkins, Sean Whitaker)	74.7

1976 Montreal-Kingston T: 16, N: 16, D: 7.27.

			PTS.
1.	SWE	(John Albrechtson, Ingvar Hansson)	14.0
2.	SOV/UKR	(Valentyn Mankin, Vladyslav Akimenko)	30.4
3.	USA	(Dennis Conner, Conn Findlay)	32.7
4.	GER	(Uwe Mares, Wolf Stadler)	42.1
5.	ITA	(Giuseppe Milone, Roberto Mottola)	55.4
6.	DEN	(Claes Thunbo Christensen, Finn Thunbo Christensen)	62.7
7.	CAN	(Allan Leibel, Lorne Leibel)	65.1
8.	HOL	(Ben Staartjes, Abram Ekels)	78.7

Funeral director Allen Warren and his partner, David Hunt, provided a light touch to the Kingston Regatta. Their six-year-old keelboat, *Gift 'Orse,* was damaged in transit and performed poorly at the Olympics. After the final race, Warren and Hunt took some acetone and a flare and set their boat on fire. "She went lame on us," said Warren, "so we decided the poor, old 'orse should be cremated.""My skipper has style," added Hunt, "but not that much. I tried to persuade him to burn with the ship, but he wouldn't agree."

Bronze medalist Conn Findlay also won two gold medals and one bronze medal in the coxed pair rowing events of 1956–1964. His skipper, Dennis Conner, won the America's Cup in 1980, lost it in 1983, won it back in 1987, and defended it in a catamaran in 1988.

SWALLOW

1948 London-Torbay T: 14, N: 14, D: 8.12.

			PTS.
1.	GBR	(Stewart Morris, David Bond)	5625
2.	POR	(Duarte de Almeida Bello, Fernando Pinto Coelho Bello)	5579
3.	USA	(Lockwood Pirie, Owen Tory)	4352
4.	SWE	(Stig Hedberg, Lars Matton)	3342
5.	DEN	(Johan Rathje, Nolly Petersen)	2935
6.	ITA	(Dario Salata, Achille Roncoroni)	2893
7.	CAN	(John Robertson, Richard Townsend)	2807
8.	NOR	(Övind Christensen, Knut Bengtson)	2768

The Swallow class was the same size as the Star, but with a smaller sail area (200 square feet rather than 285). Morris and Bond came within 15 seconds of losing the gold medal in the final race.

7-METER

1908 London-Ryde T: 1, N: 1, D: 7.29.

1.	GBR	(Charles Rivett-Carnac, S.S. Norman Bingley, Richard Dixon, Frances Clytie Rivett-Carnac)

1912 not held

1920 Antwerp T: 2, N: 2, D: 7.9.

			PTS.
1.	GBR	(Cyril Wright, Dorothy Wright, Robert Coleman, William Maddison)	4
2.	NOR	(Niels Nielsen, Johann Faye, Christian Dick, Sten Abel)	5

8-METER

1908 London-Ryde T: 5, N: 3, D: 7.29.

1.	GBR	(Blair Cochrane, Arthur Wood, Henry Sutton, John Rhodes, Charles Campbell)
2.	SWE	(Carl Hellström, Edmund Thormählen, Eric Wallerius, Erik Sandberg, Harald Wallin)
3.	GBR	(Philip Hunloke, Alfred Hughes, Frederick Hughes, George Ratsey, William Ward)
4.	NOR	(Johan Anker, Einar Hvoslef, Christian Jensen, Magnus Konow, Eilert Falch Lund)
5.	SWE	(John Carlsson, Einar Hagberg, Hjalmar Lönroth, Karl Ljungberg, August Olsson)

1912 Stockholm-Nynas T: 7, N: 4, D: 7.22.

1.	NOR	(Thoralf Glad, Thomas Valentin Aas, Andreas Brecke, Torleiv Corneliussen, Christian Jebe)
2.	SWE	(Bengt Heyman, Emil Henriques, Herbert Westermark, Nils Westermark, Alvar Thiel)
3.	FIN	(Bertil Tallberg, Gunnar Tallberg, Arthur Ahnger, Emil Lindh, Georg Westling)
4.	FIN	(Gustaf Estlander, Curt Andstén, Jarl Andstén, Carl Girsén, Bertil Justén)

5. RUS   (Herman von Adlerberg, Johan Färber, Vladimir Yilevich, Yevgeny Kuhn, Venteslav Kusmichev)

5. SWE   (Fritz Sjöqvist, Johan Sjöqvist, Ragnar Gripe, Theodor Grönfors, Erik Hagström)

1920 Antwerp T: 3, N: 2, D: 7.9.

			PTS.
1.	NOR	(Magnus Konow, Reidar Marthiniussen, Ragnar Vig, Thorleif Christoffersen)	3
2.	NOR	(Jens Salvesen, Lauritz Schmidt, Fin Schiander, Nils Thomas, Ralph Tschudi)	6
3.	BEL	(Albert Grisar, Willy de l'Arbre, Georges Hellebuyck, Léopold Standaert, Henri Weewauters)	9

1924 Paris-Le Havre T: 5, N: 5, D: 7.26.

			PTS.
1.	NOR	(August Ringvold, Sr., Rick Bockelie, Harald Hagen, Ingar Nielsen, August Ringvold, Jr.)	2
2.	GBR	(Edwin Jacob, Thomas Riggs, Walter Riggs, Ernest Roney, Harold Gordon Fowler)	5
3.	FRA	(Louis Bréguet, Pierre Ganthier, Robert Girardet, André Guerrier, Georges Mollard)	5
4.	BEL	(Fernand Carlier, Maurice Passelecq, Emmanuel Pauwels, Victor Vandersleyen, Paul van Halteren)	8
5.	ARG	(Luis Aguirre, César Guerrico, Juan Carlos Milberg, Bernado Milhas, M.R. Uriburu)	—

1928 Amsterdam T: 8, N: 8, D: 8.9.

1. FRA   (Donatien Bouché, André Lesauvage, Jean Lesieur, Virginie Hériot, Charles de la Sabliere, André Derrien)

2. HOL   (Lambertus Doedes, Maarten de Wit, Johannes van Hoolwerff, Gerardus de Vries Lentsch, Hendrik Kersken, Cornelis van Staveren)

3. SWE   (Johan Sandblom, Philip Sandblom, Carl Sandblom, Tore Holm, Clarence Hammar, Wilhelm Törsleff)

4. ITA   (Francesco Giovanelli, Guido Giovanelli, Marcantonio de Beaumont-Bonelli, Carlo Alberto d'Alberti, Edoardo Moscatelli, Mario Bruzzone)

4. NOR   (Jens Salvesen, Magnus Konow, W. Wilhelmsen, Bernhard Lund)

6. USA   (Owen Churchill, Benjamin Weston, Manfred Curry, Frank Hekma, Nicholas Barry Hekma)

7. GBR   (Kenneth Preston, Robert Steele, Joseph Compton, Philip Falle, Ernest Roney, Esmond Roney, Francis Preston)

8. ARG   (Rafael Iglesias, Hugo Tedín Uriburu, Carlos Serante Saavedra, Miguel Bosch, Horacio Seeber)

1932 Los Angeles T: 2, N: 2, D: 8.9.

			PTS.
1.	USA	(Owen Churchill, John Biby, William Cooper, Carl Dorsey, Robert Sutton, Alan Morgan, Pierpont Davis, Alphonse Burnand, Thomas Webster, John Huettner, Richard Moore, Kenneth Carey)	8
2.	CAN	(Ronald Maitland, Ernest Cribb, Harry Jones, Peter Gordon, Hubert Wallace, George Gyles)	4

1936 Berlin-Kiel T: 12, N: 10, D: 8.10.

			PTS.
1.	ITA	(Giovanni Reggio, Bruno Bianchi, Luigi De Manincor, Domenico Mordini, Luigi Poggi, Enrico Poggi)	55
2.	NOR	(Olav Ditlev-Simonsen, John Ditlev-Simonsen, Hans Struknaes, Lauritz Schmidt, Nordahl Wallem, Jacob Tullin Thams)	53
3.	GER	(Hans Howaldt, Alfred Krupp von Bohlen und Halbach, Felix Scheder-Bieschin, Eduard Mohr, Otto Wachs, Fritz Bischoff)	53
4.	SWE	(Marcus Wallenberg, Tore Holm, Wilhelm Moberg, Detlow von Braun, Per Gedda, Bo Westerberg)	51
5.	FIN	(Gunnar Grönblom, Sven Grönblum, Hilding Silander, Oscar Sumelius, Olof Wallin, Walter Kjellberg)	37
6.	GBR	(Kenneth Preston, Francis Preston, Robert Steele, Joseph Compton, John Eddy)	36
7.	ARG	(Rodríguez de la Torre, Mario Ortiz Sauce Aguirre, Hipólito Gil Elizalde, Rafael Iglesias, Guillermo Peralta Rámos)	25
8.	DEN	(Niels Hansen, Hans Tholstrup, Otto Danielsen, Carl Berntsen, Vagn Kastrup, Niels Schibbye)	22

The Germans led after six races, but finished only sixth on the final day. Norway was awarded second place after winning a sail-off against Germany two days later. Jacob Thams of the Norwegian crew had won the ski-jump in the first Winter Olympics at Chamonix in 1924. Alfred Krupp of the German crew was the owner and director of the infamous Krupp armaments works. He was convicted as a war criminal at the Nuremberg trials after World War II.

8-METER, 1907 RATING

1920 Antwerp T: 1, N: 1, D: 7.9.
1. NOR   (August Ringvold, Sr., Thorleif Holbye, Tell Wagle, Kristoffer Olsen, Alf Bruun Jacobsen)

10-METER

1912 Stockholm T: 5, N: 3, D: 7.22.
1. SWE   (Carl Hellström, Erik Wallerius, Harald Wallerius, Humbert Lundén, Herman Nyberg, Harry Rosensvärd, Paul Isberg, Filip Ericsson)

2. FIN   (Harry Wahl, Waldemar Björkstén, Jacob Carl Björnström, Bror Benediktus Brennar, Allan Franck, Erik Lindh, Aarne Pekkalainen)

3. RUS   (Ester Belvselsky, Ernest Brasche, Nikolai Pusnitsky, Aleksandr Rodionov, Yossif Schomaker, Filipp Strauch, Karl Lindblom)

4. SWE   (Björn Bothén, Bo Bothén, Wilhelm Forsberg, Einar Lindén, Karl Lindholm, Erik Waller)

10-METER, 1907 RATING

1920 Antwerp T: 1, N: 1, D: 7.9.
1. NOR (Erik Herseth, Sigurd Holter, Ingar Nielsen, Ole Sörensen, Gunnar Jamvold, Petter Jamvold, Claus Juell)

10-METER 1919 RATING

1920 Antwerp T: 1, N: 1, D: 7.9.
1. NOR (Archer Arentz, Willy Gilbert, Robert Gjertsen, Arne Sejersted, Halfdan Schjött, Trygve Schjött, Otto Falkenberg)

12-METER

1908 London-Firth of Clyde T: 2, N: 1, D: 8.12.
1. GBR (Thomas Glen-Coats, John Downes, John Buchanan, James Bunten, Arthur Downes, David Dunlap, John Mackenzie, Albert Martin, T. Gerald Tait, John Aspin)
2. GBR (Charles MacIver, James Kenion, James Baxter, William Davidson, John Jellico, Thomas Littledale, Charles MacLeod Robertson, John Spence, John Adam, Cecil MacIver)

This was the only event in Olympic history to be staged in Scotland, and in fact it was won in two straight races by a crew of Scotsmen.

1912 Stockholm-Nynas T: 3, N: 3, D: 7.21.
1. NOR (Johan Anker, Alfred Larsen, Nils Bertelsen, Halfdan Hansen, Magnus Konow, Petter Larsen, Eilert Falch Lund, Fritz Staib, Arnfinn Heje, Gustav Thaulow)
2. SWE (Nils Persson, Hugo Clason, Richard Sällström, Nils Lamby, Kurt Gergström, Dick Bergström, Carl Lindqvist, Per Bergman, Sigurd Kander, Folke Johansson)
3. FIN (Ernst Krogius, Max Alfthan, Erik Hartvall, Jarl Hulldén, Sigurd Juslen, Elno Sandelin, John Silén)

12-METER, 1907 RATING

1920 Antwerp T: 1, N: 1, D: 7.9.
1. NOR (Henrik Östervold, Jan Östervold, Ole Östervold, Hans Naess, Lauritz Christiansen, Halvor Mögster, Rasmus Birkeland, Halvor Birkeland, Kristen Östervold)

12-METER, 1919 RATING

1920 Antwerp T: 1, N: 1, D: 7.9.
1. NOR (Johan Friele, Olav Örvig, Arthur Allers, Christen Wiese, Martin Borthen, Egil Reimers, Kaspar Hassel, Thor Örvig, Erik Örvig)

SHARPIE—12 SQUARE METERS

1956 Melbourne T: 13, N: 13, D: 12.5.

		PTS.
1. NZE	(Peter Mander, John Cropp)	6086
2. AUS	(Roland Tasker, John Scott)	6086
3. GBR	(Jasper Blackall, Terence Smith)	4859
4. ITA	(Mario Capio, Emilio Massino)	3928
5. SAF	(John Sully, Alfred Evans)	2917
6. GER	(Rolf Mulka, Ingo von Bredow)	2840
7. SOV	(Boris Iliine, Aleksandr Chumakov)	2479
8. FRA	(Roger Tiriau, Claude Flahault)	2058

Tasker and Scott appeared to have won the final race and the gold medal, but a protest by the French led to their disqualification, leaving the Australians tied in points with New Zealand's Mander and Cropp. The New Zealand pair was awarded first place because they had won three races while the Australians had won only two.

30 SQUARE METERS

1920 Antwerp T: 1, N: 1, D: 7.9.
1. SWE (Gösta Lundqvist, Rolf Steffenburg, Gösta Bengtson, Axel Calvert)

40 SQUARE METERS

1920 Antwerp T: 2, N: 1, D: 7.9.

		PTS.
1. SWE	(Tore Holm, Yngve Holm, Axel Rydin, Georg Tengvall)	4
2. SWE	(Gustav Svensson, Ragnar Svensson, Percy Almstedt, Erik Mellbin)	6

DISCONTINUED SPORTS

Cricket   Polo
Croquet   Rackets
Golf   Roque
Jeu De Paume   Rugby
Lacrosse   Tug of War
Motor Boating

CRICKET

1900 Paris T: 2, N: 2, D: 8.20.
1. GBR   (C.B.K. Beachcroft, John Symes, Frederick Cuming, Montague Toller, Alfred Bowerman, Alfred Powlesland, William Donne, Frederick Christian, George Buckley, Francis Burchell, Harry Corner, Arthur Birkett)
2. FRA   (T.H. Jordan, A.J. Schneidau, R. Horne, Henry Terry, F. Roques, W. Anderson, D. Robinson, W.T. Attrill, W. Browning, A. McEvoy, Philip Tomalin, J. Braid)
Final: GBR 262—104 FRA

Great Britain was represented by the Devon and Somerset Wanderers Cricket Club, France by a team made up mostly of English expatriates.

CROQUET

1900 Paris C: 20, N: 1, D: 7.
Singles—1 Ball

		PTS.
1. Aumoitte	FRA	45
2. Johin	FRA	21

Singles—2 Balls
1. Waydelick   FRA
2. Vignerot   FRA
3. Sautereau   FRA

Doubles
1. FRA (Johin, Aumoitte)

GOLF

1900 Paris-Compiegne C: 12, N: 3, D: 10.2.
Men

		SHOTS
1. Charles Sands	USA	167
2. Walter Rutherford	GBR	168
3. David Robertson	GBR	175
4. Frederick Taylor	USA	182
5. H.E. Daunt	FRA	184
6. George Thorne	GBR	185
7. William Dove	GBR	186
8. Albert Lambert	USA	189

1900 Paris-Compiegne C: 10, N: 2, D: 10.3
Women

		PTS.
1. Margaret Abbott	USA	47
2. Pauline "Polly" Whittier	USA	49
3. Daria Pratt	USA	53
4. Froment-Meurice	FRA	56
5. Ellen Ridgeway	USA	57
6. Fournier-Starlovèze	FRA	58
7. Mary Abbott	USA	65
7. Baronne Fain	FRA	65

Margaret Abbott was the first U.S. woman to win an Olympic gold medal. A 5-foot 11-inch, 22-year-old Chicago socialite, she traveled to Paris in 1899 with her mother, literary editor and novelist Mary Ives Abbott, so that she could study art. Ten women took part in the final nine-hole round of the ladies' golf competition. Abbott later told relatives that she won the tournament "because all the French girls apparently misunderstood the nature of the game scheduled for that day and turned up to play in high heels and tight skirts." Two years later Margaret Abbott, by then a resident of New York City, married political satirist Finley Peter Dunne. She died in 1955, unaware that the tournament she had won was a part of the Olympics.

1904 St. Louis C: 75, N: 2, D: 9.24.
Men

		SHOTS
1. George Lyon	CAN	3 and 2
2. H. Chandler Egan	USA	
3. Burt McKinnie	USA	
4. Francis Newton	USA	
5. Harry Allen (USA), Albert Lambert (USA), Mason Phelps (USA), Daniel Sawyer (USA)		

George Lyon was an eccentric athlete who didn't pick up a golf club until he was 38 years old. Before that he had competed successfully in baseball, tennis, and cricket. Once he even set a Canadian record in the pole vault. Lyon was 46 when he traveled down from Toronto to take part in the Olympics. He caused quite a stir when he played in St. Louis because of his unorthodox swing. He wielded the club more like a cricket bat, provoking some newspapers to criticize his "coal-heaver's swing." On the course he

George Lyon, winner of the 1904 golf event, keeping his ball on the eye.

was an endless source of cheerful energy, singing, telling jokes and even doing handstands. A 36-hole qualifying round reduced the field from 75 to 32. The survivors then engaged in a match play elimination tournament. In the semifinals Lyon defeated Francis Newton, the Pacific Coast champion, on the last of 36 holes. His final match was a surprise victory over the 23-year-old U.S. champion, Chandler Egan. Lyon was awarded a $1500 sterling silver trophy, which he accepted after walking down the path to the ceremony on his hands. In 1908 George Lyon traveled to England to compete in the London Olympics. However, an internal dispute among British golfers caused them to boycott the games, leaving Lyon as the only entrant. Offered the gold medal by default, he refused it. Lyon was still winning championships twenty years later and shot his age for 18 holes from 64 years old until he was 78 years old. He died the following year.

1904 St. Louis T: 3, N: 1, D: 9.17.
Teams

			SHOTS
1.	USA	(Western Golf Association—H. Chandler Egan, Robert Hunter, Kenneth Edwards, Clement Smoot, Walter Egan, Ned Sawyer, Edward "Ned" Cummins, Mason Phelps, Nathaniel Moore, Warren Wood)	1749
2.	USA	(Trans Mississippi Golf Association—Albert Lambert, Stewart Stickney, Bert McKinnie, William Stickney, Ralph McKittrick, Frederick Semple, Francis Newton, Harry Potter, John Cady, John Maxwell)	1770
3.	USA	(United States Golf Association—Douglas Cadwalader, Allan Lard, Jesse Carleton, Simeon Price, Harold Weber, John Rahm, Arthur Hussey, Orus Jones, Harold Fraser, George Oliver)	1839

JEU DE PAUME

Jeu de Paume, also known as "court tennis" or "real tennis," was the forerunner of modern-day tennis.

1908 London C: 11, N: 2, D: 5.28.

			SETS
1.	Jay Gould	USA	6–5, 6–4, 6–4
2.	Eustace Miles	GBR	
3.	Neville Lytton	GBR	6–2, 6–4, 6–4
4.	Arthur Page	GBR	

LACROSSE

1904 St. Louis T: 3, N: 2, D: 7.7.
1. CAN (Shamrock Lacrosse Team, Winnipeg, Manitoba—George Cloutier, George Cattanach, Benjamin Jamieson, Jack Flett, George Bretz, Eli Blanchard, Hilliard Laidlaw, H. Lyle, W. Brennaugh, L.H. Pentland, Sandy Cowan, William Laurie Burns, William Orris)
2. USA (St. Louis Amateur Athletic Association, St. Louis, Missouri—Hunter, Patrick Grogan, George Passmore, William Passmore, Lehman, Hess, J.W. Dowling, A.H. Venn, Sullivan, Murphy, Gibson, Woods, Partridge, Young, Ross)
3. CAN (Mohawk Indians, Brantford, Ontario—Black Hawk, Black Eagle, Almighty Voice, Flat Iron, Spotted Tail, Half Moon, Lightfoot, Snake Eater, Red Jacket, Night Hawk, Rain in Face, Man Afraid Soap)
   Final: Shamrock 6–1 St. Louis
          Shamrock 8–2 St. Louis

1908 London T: 2, N: 2, D: 10.24.
1. CAN (Frank Dixon, George "Doc" Campbell, Angus Dillon, Richard Louis Duckett, George Rennie, Clarence McKerrow, Alexander Turnbull, Henry Hoobin, Ernest Hamilton, John Broderick, Thomas Gorman, Patrick "Paddy' Brennan)
2. GBR (Charles Scott, G. Mason, H.W. Ramsay, E.O. Dutton, J. Parker-Smith, Wilfrid Johnson, Norman Whitley, George Buckland, S.N. Hayes, Gustav Alexander, R.G.W. Martin, Edward Jones)
   Final: CAN 14–10 GBR

Good sportsmanship was the order of the day in the lacrosse competition. When Frank Dixon of Canada broke his stick, R.G.W. Martin of Great Britain offered to withdraw from the game until a new one could be found. The contest was tied at 9–9 when the Canadians scored five straight goals to clinch the victory.

MOTOR BOATING

1908 London C: 14, N: 2, D: 8.28–29.
8-Meter Class, 40 Nautical Miles
1. GBR I. Thomas Thornycroft, Bernard Red- 2:28:26
   wood, John Field-Richard

Under 60-Foot Class, 40 Nautical Miles
1. GBR   I. Thomas Thornycroft, Bernard Red-   2:28:58
wood, John Field-Richard

Forty-four years after his victories at the 1908 Olympics, Thornycroft was selected as an alternate for the 1952 British yachting team. He traveled to Helsinki, but did not compete. He was 70 years old at the time.

Open Class, 40 Nautical Miles
1. FRA   Émile Thubron   2:26:53

POLO

1900 Paris T: 4, N: 4, D: 6.2.
1. GBR&USA   (Foxhunters Hurlingham—Alfred Rawlinson, Frank Mackey, Foxhall Keene, Denis Daly, John Beresford)
2. GBR&USA & SPA   (Wanderers Rugby—Walter McCreery, Frederick Freake, Walter Buckmaster, Jośe de Madre)
3. FRA&GBR   (Bagatelle Paris—Maurice Raoul-Duval, Frederick Gill, Robert Fournier-Sarloveze, Edouard Alphonse de Rothschild)
4. USA&MEX   (Guillermo Hayden Wright, Eustaquio de Escandón y Barrón, Pablo de Escandón y Barrón, Manuel de Escandón y Barrón)
Final: Foxhunters 3–1 Club Rugby

1904-1906 not held

1908 London T: 3, N: 1, D: 6.21.
1. GBR   (Roehampton—Charles Miller, Patteson Nickalls, George Miller, Herbert Wilson)
2. GBR   (Hurlingham—John Wodehouse, Walter Buckmaster, Frederick Freake, Walter Jones)
3. GBR/IRL   (Ireland—Percy O'Reilly, John Hardress Lloyd, John McCann, Auston Rotherham)
Scores: Roehampton 3–1 Hurlingham
Roehampton 8–1 Ireland

1912 not held

1920 Antwerp-Ostende T: 4, N: 4, D: 7.31.

		W	L	PF	PA
1. GBR	(Teignmouth "Timothy" Melvill, Frederick Barrett, John Wodehouse, Vivian Lockett)	2	0	21	14
2. SPA	(Leopoldo Sainz de la Maza y Gutiérrez-Solano, Jacobo Fitz-James Stuart Falcó, Alvaro de Figueroa y Alonso-Martínez, José de Figueroa y Alonso-Martínez, Hernando Fitz-James Stuart y Falcó)	1	1	24	16
3. USA	(Arthur Harris, Terry Allen, John Montgomery, Nelson Margetts)	1	1	14	16

		W	L	PF	PA
4. BEL	(Alfred Grisar, Maurice Lysen, Clément van der Straeten, Gaston Peers de Nieuwburgh)	0	2	6	19
Final: GBR 13–11 SPA

1924 Paris T: 5, N: 5, D: 7.12.

		W	L	PF	PA
1. ARG	(Arturo Kenny, Juan Nelson, Enrique Padilla, Juan Miles, Guillermo Brooke Naylor)	4	0	46	14
2. USA	(Elmer Boeseke, Thomas Hitchcock, Frederick Roe, Rodman Wanamaker)	3	1	43	11
3. GBR	(Frederick Guest, Frederick Barrett, Dennis Bingham, Percival Wise)	2	2	33	24
4. SPA	(Leopoldo Sainz de la Maza y Guttiérrez-Solano, Justo San Miguel y de la Gandara, Luis de Figueroa y Alonso-Martínez, Rafael Henestrosa, Hernando Fitz-James Stuart y Falcó)	1	3	22	42
5. FRA	(Charles de Polignac, Pierre de Jumilhac, Jules Macaire, Hubert de Monbrison, Jean Pastra)	0	4	6	59

The decisive match was the one between Argentina and the United States. Juan Nelson was the hero of the game, scoring a goal in the closing seconds of the seventh and final chukker to give Argentina a surprise 6–5 victory.

1928–1932 not held

1936 Berlin T: 5, N: 5, D: 7.8.

		W	L	T	PF	PA
1. ARG	(Luis Duggan, Roberto Cavanagh, Andrès Gazzotti, Manuel Andrada)	2	0	0	26	5
2. GBR	(Bryan Fowler, William Hinde, David Dawnay, Humphrey Guinness)	1	1	0	13	22
3. MEX	(Juan Garcia Zazueta, Antonio Nava Castillo, Julio Muller Luján, Aberto Ramos Sesma)	1	2	0	32	30
4. HUN	(Tivadar Dienes-Öhm, Imre Szentpály, Dezsö Kovács, István Bethlen, Kálmán Bartalis)	1	1	1	26	30
5. GER	(Heinrich Amsinck, Walter Bartram, Miles Reincke, Arthur Köser)	0	1	1	14	24
Final: ARG 11–0 GBR
3rd Place: MEX 16–2 HUN

Hungary and Germany were so outclassed that they weren't even included in the competition for first or second place. Instead, the tournament was arranged so that they played for the right to play for the bronze medal against the loser among the other three teams. Over 45,000 people watched Argentina's final victory over Great Britain.

RACKETS

1908 London C: 7, N: 1, D: 4.27.
Men's Singles
1. GBR   Evan Noel
2. GBR   Henry Leaf
3. GBR   John Jacob Astor
3. GBR   Henry Brougham
   Final: Noel—Leaf WO

Leaf had to withdraw from the final because he had injured his hand in the doubles competition.

1908 London T: 3, N: 1, D: 4.27.
Men's Doubles
1. GBR   Vane Pennel/John Jacob Astor
2. GBR   Edmund Bury/Cecil Browning
3. GBR   Evan Noel/Henry Leaf
   Final: Pennel/Astor—Bury/Browning, 6–15, 15–7, 16–15, 15–6, 15–7

ROQUE

1904 St. Louis C: 4, N: 1, D: 8.13.

		W	L	PF	PA
1. Charles Jacobus	USA	5	1	187	109
2. Smith Streeter	USA	4	2	156	142
3. Charles Brown	USA	2	4	(109?)	147
4. William Chalfant	USA	1	5	106	160

Roque is a variation of croquet, played on a hard-surfaced court with a raised border that can be used for bank shots. It is unknown how many points Brown scored in his loss to Chalfant.

RUGBY

1900 Paris T: 3, N: 3, D: 10.28.

		W	L	PF	PA
1. FRA	(Alexandre Pharamond, Frantz Reichel, Jean Collas, Constantin Henriquez de Zubiera, Auguste Giroux, André Rischmann, Léon Binoche, A. Albert, Charles Gondouin, Hubert Lefebvre, Emile Sarrade, Wladimir Aitoff, Joseph Olivier, Jean-Guy Gautier, Victor Larchandat, J. Hervé, Albert Roosevelt)	2	0	54	25
2. GER	(Hermann Kreuzer, Arnold Landvoigt, Heinrich Reitz, Jacob Herrmann, Erich Ludwig, Hugo Betting, August Schmierer, Fritz Müller, Adolf Stockhausen, Hans Latscha, Willy Hofmeister, Georg Wenderoth, Eduard Poppe, Richard Ludwig, Albert Arnheim)	0	1	17	27
3. GBR	(H.A. Loveitt, Raymond Whittindale, H.S. Nicol, Claude Whittindale, L.	0	1	8	27

Hood, J. Henry Birtles, J. Cantion, C.P. Deykin, J.G. Wallis, V. Smith, M.L. Logan, F.C. Baylis, M.W. Talbott, Francis Wilson, Arthur Darby)

1908 London T: 2, N: 2, D: 10.19.
1. AUS   (Phillip Carmichael, Charles Russell, Daniel Carroll, John Hickey, Francis Bede-Smith, Christopher McKivatt, Arthur McCabe, Thomas Griffen, John "Jumbo" Barnett, Patrick McCue, Sydney Middleton, Thomas Richards, Malcolm "Mannie" McArthur, Charles McMurtrie, Robert Craig)
2. GBR   (Edward Jackett, J.C. "Barney" Solomon, Bertram Solomon, L.F. Dean, J.T. Jose, Thomas Wedge, James Davey, Richard Jackett, E.J. Jones, Arthur Wilson, Nicholas Tregurtha, A. Lawrey, C.R. Marshall, A. Wilcocks, J. Trevaskis)
   Final: AUS 32–3 GBR

1912 not held

1920 Antwerp T: 2, N: 2, D: 9.5.
1. USA   (Daniel Carroll, Charles Doe, George Fish, James Fitzpatrick, Joseph Hunter, Morris Kirksey, Charles Mehan, William Muldoon, John O'Neil, John Patrick, Cornelius Righter, Rudolph Scholz, Charles Tilden, Heaton Wrenn, Richard "Dink" Templeton)
2. FRA   (André Chilo, Grenet, François Bordes, René Crabos, Edouard Bader, Raoul Thiercelin, Curtet, Jacques Forestier, Maurice Labeyrie, Alfred Eluère, Robert Lavasseur, Adolphe Bousquel, Jean Bruneval, Castex, Pierre Petiteau)
   Final: USA 8–0 FRA

The U.S. team included Morris Kirksey, who also won a silver medal in the 100-meter dash and a gold in the 4 × 100-meter relay, and Dink Templeton, who later became a famous track coach. Another American player was Daniel Carroll, who had been a member of the victorious Australian squad 12 years earlier. He is the only person in any sport to win gold medals while representing different countries.

1924 Paris T: 3, N: 3, D: 5.18.

		W	L	PF	PA
1. USA	(Philip Clark, Norman Cleveland, Hugh Cunningham, Dudley De Groot, Robert Devereaux, George Dixon, Charles Doe, Linn Farrish, Edward Graff, Richard Hyland, Caesar Manelli, John O'Neil, John Patrick, William Rogers, Rudolph Scholz, Colby Slater, Norman Slater, Edward Turkington, Alan Valentine, Alan Williams)	2	0	54	3
2. FRA	(René Araou, Jean Bayard, Louis Beguet, André Béhotéguy, Alexandre Bioussa, Etienne Bonnes, René Bousquet, Aime Cassayet, Clément Dupont, Albert Dupouy, Jean	1	1	61	20

Etchberry, Henri Galau, Gilbert Gerintes, Raoul Got, Adolphe Jauréguy, René Lasserre, Marcel-Frédéric Lubin-Lebrère, Etienne Piquirai, Jean Vaysse)

3. ROM   (Dumitru Armăsel, Eugen Sfetescu,   0 2 3 98
Sorin Mihăilescu, Paul Nedelcovici, Teodor Marian, Mihail Vardala, Soare Sterian, Iosif Nemeş, Atanasie Tănăsescu, Dumitru Volvoreanu, Paul Vidraşcu, Nicolae Mărăscu, Mircea Sfetescu, Gheorghe Bentia, Teodor Florian, Ion Garlesteanu, Gheorge Sfetescu)

Almost 40,000 French spectators watched in horror as their team was thrashed 17–3 by the upstart Americans. After two French players were injured, the U.S. team was booed and hissed for the remainder of the game. Fighting broke out in the stands, and Gideon Nelson, an art student from De Kalb, Illinois, was knocked unconscious after being hit in the face with a walking stick. At the awards ceremony "The Star-Spangled Banner" was drowned out by the booing of the crowd, and the U.S. team had to be escorted from the field under police protection.

TUG OF WAR

In each contest, the first team to pull the other team six feet was declared the winner. If neither team succeeded in so doing in five minutes, the one which had pulled the furthest was given the victory.

1900 Paris T: 2, N: 3, D: 7.16.
1. SWE&DEN (Gustaf Söderström, Karl Staaf, August Nilsson, Eugen Schmidt, Edgar Aabye, Charles Winckler)
2. FRA   (R. Basset, Jean Collas, Charles Gondouin, Joseph Roffo Farrade, Constantin Henriquez de Zubiera)

The U.S. team was unable to take part because three of its six members were engaged in the final of the hammer throw. After the official competition, the American teams took part in a "friendly" tug, which broke up when American spectators rushed forward and joined in. Edgar Aaybe of Denmark was a journalist covering the Games for *Politiken*. He was asked to join the tug of war and ended up on the winning team.

1904 St. Louis T: 6, N: 3, D: 9.1.
1. USA (Milwaukee Athletic Club—Oscar Olson, Sidney Johnson, Henry Seiling, Conrad Magnussen, Pat Flanagan)
2. USA (St. Louis Southwest Turnverein #1—Max Braun, William Seiling, Orin Upshaw, Charles Rose, August Rodenberg)
3. USA (St. Louis Southwest Turnverein #2—Charles Haberkorn, Frank Kungler, Charles Thias, Harry Jacobs, Oscar Friede)

4. USA (New York Athletic Club—Charles Dieges, Samuel Jones, Leon Feuerbach, Charles Chadwick, James Mitchel)
5. GRE (Pan-Hellenic Athletic Club—Nicolaos Georgantas, Perikles Kakousis, Demetrios Demetracopoulos, Anastasios Georgopoulos, Vasileios Metalos)
5. SAF (Boer Team—C. Walker, P. Hillense, J. Schutte, P. Lombard, P. Visser)

1906 Athens T: 4, N: 4, D: 4.30.
1. GER (Heinrich Schneidereit, Heinrich Rondi, Wilhelm Born, Willy Dörr, Karl Kaltenbach, Wilhelm Ritzenhof, Joseph Kramer, Julius Wagner)
2. GRE (Spyros Vellas, Panagiotis Triboulidis, Vasilios Psachos, Georgios Psachos, Konstantinos Lazaris, Spyros Lazaris, Georgios Papachristou, Antonios Tsitas)
3. SWE (Carl Svensson, Anton Gustafsson, Axel Norling, Claes Wersäll, Oswald Holmberg, Erik Granfeit, Gustaf Grönberger, Eric Lemming)
4. AUT (Josef Steinbach, Rudolf Arnold, Henri Baur, Wenzel Goldbach, Rudolf Watzl, Rudolf Lindmayer, Leopold Lahner, Franz Solar)

1908 London T: 5, N: 3, D: 7.18.
1. GBR (City of London Police—William Hirons, Frederick Goodfellow, Edward Barrett, J. James Shephard, Frederick Humphreys, Edwin Mills, Albert Ireton, Frederick Merriman)
2. GBR (Liverpool Police—Patrick Philbin, James Clark, Thomas Butler, Alexander Kidd, George Smith, Thomas Swindlehurst, Daniel McLowry, William Greggan)
3. GBR (K Division Metropolitan Police—Walter Tammas, William Slade, Alexander Munro, Ernest Ebbage, Thomas Homewood, Walter Chaffe, James Woodget, Joseph Dowler)

Surprising as it may seem, the friendly sport of tug of war touched off one of the biggest controversies of the 1908 Games. In the first round, the Liverpool Police pulled the U.S. team over the line in a matter of seconds. The Americans immediately protested that the Liverpudlians had used special illegal boots with steel cleats, spikes, and heels. The British maintained that they were wearing standard, run-of-the-mill police boots, and the protest was disallowed, whereupon the Americans withdrew from the remainder of the competition. After the tournament, the captain of the victorious London City Police team challenged the Americans to a pull in their stockinged feet, but there is no record of such a contest actually taking place.

1912 Stockholm T: 2, N: 2, D: 7.8.
1. SWE (Adolf Bergman, Arvid Andersson, Johan Edman, Erik Fredriksson, Carl Jonsson, Erik Larsson, August Gustafsson, Carl Lindström)
2. GBR (Alexander Munro, J. James Shepherd, John Sewell, Joseph Dowler, Edwin Mills, Frederick Humphreys, Mathias Hynes, Walter Chaffe)

1920 Antwerp T: 5, N: 5, D: 8.18.
1. GBR (George Canning, Frederick Holmes, Edwin Mills, J. James Shepherd, Harold Stiff, John Sewell, Frederick Humphreys, Ernest Thorne)
2. HOL (Wilhelmus Bekkers, Johannes Hangeveld, Sytse Jansma, Hendrikus Janssen, Antonius van Loon, Willem van Loon, Marinus van Rekum, Willem van Rekum)
3. BEL (Edouard Bourguignon, Alphonse Ducatillon, Raymond Maertens, Christin Piek, Henri Pintens, Charles van den Broeck, François van Hoorenbeek, Gustave Wuyts)
   Final: GBR 2—0 HOL

The British team won their two pulls against the Dutch in 28.2 seconds and 13.4 seconds.

Tough pulling in the 1920 tug of war.

SUMMER OLYMPIC RECORDS

These records do not include the Intercalated Games of 1906.

Most Medals
18 Larysa Latynina (SOV/UKR, Gymnastics, 1956–1964)

Most Medals, Men
15 Nikolai Andrianov (SOV/RUS, Gymnastics, 1972–1980)

Most Gold Medals
9 Paavo Nurmi (FIN, Track and Field, 1920–1928)
9 Larysa Latynina (SOV/UKR, Gymnastics, 1956–1964)
9 Mark Spitz (USA, Swimming, 1968–1972)

Most Gold Medals in One Day
4 Vitaly Scherbo (SOV/BLR, Gymnastics, 1992)

Most Silver Medals
6 Mikhail Voronin (SOV/RUS, Gymnastics, 1968–1972)
6 Shirley Babashoff (USA, Swimming, 1972–1976)
6 Aleksandr Dityatin (SOV/RUS, Gymnastics, 1976–1980)
Four of Babashoff's six silver medals were earned behind chemically augmented East German swimmers

Most Bronze Medals
6 Heikki Savolainen (FIN, Gymnastics, 1928–1936, 1952)

Most Bronze Medals, Women
4 Margit Korondi (HUN, Gymnastics, 1952–1956)
4 Sofia Muratova (SOV/RUS, Gymnastics, 1956–1960)
4 Larysa Latynina (SOV/UKR, Gymnastics, 1956–1964)
4 Merlene Ottey (JAM, Track and Field, 1980–1984, 1992)

Most Years Between Medals
28 Tore Holm (SWE, Yachting, 1920–1948)
28 Aladár Gerevich (HUN, Fencing, 1932–1960)

Most Years Between Medals, Women
16 Five different athletes

Most Years Between Gold Medals
28 Aladár Gerevich (HUN, Fencing, 1932–1960)

Most Years Between Gold Medals, Women
12 Seven different athletes

Most Medals in Individual Events
14 Larysa Latynina (SOV/UKR, Gymnastics, 1956–1964)

Most Medals in Individual Events, Men
12 Nikolai Andrianov (SOV/RUS, Gymnastics, 1972–1980)

Most Gold Medals in Individual Events
8 Ray Ewry (USA, Track and Field, 1900–1908)

Most Gold Medals in Individual Events, Women
7 Vera Cáslavská (CZE, Gymnastics, 1964–1968)

Most Consecutive Victories in the Same Event
4 Paul Elvström (DEN, Finn Class Yachting, 1948–1960)
4 Al Oerter (USA, Discus Throw, 1956–1968)

Most Consecutive Victories in the Same Event, Women
3 Larysa Latynina (SOV/UKR, Floor Exercises, 1956–1964)
3 Dawn Fraser (AUS, 100-Meter Freestyle, 1956–1964)

Youngest Medalist
On August 26, 1900, the Dutch coxed pair suddenly needed a replacement coxswain. A French boy was chosen and the Dutch pair rowed to a close victory. The French boy joined in the victory ceremony and had his photograph taken. Then he disappeared. Years of research by numerous historians have failed to turn up a clue as to his name or his actual age. Judging a Parisian boy of 1900 with present-day eyes, he could be anywhere from 7 to 12 years old. If he was really in the upper range, the youngest medalist would be Greek gymnast Dimitrios Loundras, who, at the time that he placed third in the 1896 team parallel bars event, was 10 years 218 days old. Of course, it happened that third place in the 1896 team parallel bars event also meant last place. The youngest known medalist who actually finished ahead of someone else was Luigina Giavotta of Italy, who earned a silver medal in Women's team gymnastics in 1928. She was 11 years 302 days old.

Youngest Medalist in an Individual Event
12 years 24 days Inge Sörensen (DEN, 200-Meter Breaststroke, 1936)

Youngest Medalist in an Individual Event, Men
14 years 11 days Nils Skoglund (DEN, Plain High Diving, 1920)

Youngest Gold Medalist
The French boy who coxed for the Dutch pair in 1900, as mentioned above.

Youngest Gold Medalist, Women
13 years 268 days Marjorie Gestring (USA, Springboard Diving, 1936)

Youngest Gold Medalist in an Individual Event, Men
14 years 309 days Kusuo Kitamura (JPN, 1500-Meter Freestyle, 1932)

Oldest Medalist
72 years 279 days Oscar Swahn (SWE, Team Double-Shot Running Deer Shooting, 1920)

Oldest Medalist and Gold Medalist, Women
53 years 277 days Sybil "Queenie" Newell (GBR, Archery, 1908)

Oldest Medalist in an Individual Event
64 years 256 days Oscar Swahn (SWE, Double-Shot Running Deer Shooting, 1912)

Oldest Medalist and Gold Medalist in an Individual Event, Women
53 years 277 days Sybil "Queenie" Newell (GBR, Archery, 1908)

Oldest Gold Medalist
64 years 257 days Oscar Swahn (SWE, Team Single-Shot Running Deer Shooting, 1912)

Oldest Gold Medalist in an Individual Event
60 years 264 days Oscar Swahn (SWE, Single-Shot Running Deer Shooting, 1908)

Most Olympics Competed In
8 Raimondo d'Inzeo (ITA, Equestrian, 1948–1976)
8 Piero d'Inzeo (ITA, Equestrian, 1948–1976)
8 Paul Elvström (DEN, Yachting, 1948–1960, 1968–1972)
8 Durward Knowles (BAH, Yachting, 1948–1972, 1988)
8 Hurbert Raudaschl (AUT, Yachting, 1964–1992)

Youngest Competitor
See *Youngest Medalist.*

Youngest Competitor, Women
See *Youngest Medalist.*

Oldest Competitor
See *Oldest Medalist.*

Oldest Competitor, Women
70 years 5 days Lorna Johnstone (GBR, Dressage, 1972)

Heaviest Competitor
412 pounds (186.88 kilograms) Chris Taylor (USA, Super Heavyweight Freestyle Wrestling, 1972)

Most Competitors in an Individual Event
163 Men's Cycling Road Race, 1972
In a sense this record could also go to the 185 who took part in the 1952 Men's Gymnastics team event because scores in the team event also applied to the Individual All-Around event.

Most Nations Represented in a Single Event
72 Men's Marathon, 1992

Longest National Win Streak in a Single Event
16 United States, Pole Vault, 1896–1968

Longest Streak in an Event with a Different Nation Winning Each Time
10 Men's Small-Bore Rifle, Prone, 1924–1972

Most Consecutive Boycotts
4 Albania, 1976–1988

First Known Winner in Ancient Olympics
Koroibos (Elis, Stadion [sprint], 776 B.C.)

First Winner in the Ancient Olympics, Women
Kyniska (Sparta, Tethrippon [four-horse chariot race], 396 B.C.

Most Championships, Ancient Olympics
12 Leonidas (Rhodes, Running, 164 B.C.–152 B.C.)

LEADING GOLD-MEDAL NATIONS BY SPORT

This chart includes the Intercalated Games of 1906. Figures for the 1992 Unified Team are included in the totals of the Soviet Union. West Germany is included in the totals for united Germany.

	First		Second	
Track and field, men	United States	250	Finland	47
Track and field, women	United States	36	Soviet Union	34
Archery, men	Belgium	10*	United States	7
Archery, women	South Korea	5	United States	4
Badminton	Indonesia	2		
	South Korea	2		
Baseball	Cuba	1		
Basketball, men	United States	10	Soviet Union	2
Basketball, women	Soviet Union	3	United States	2
Boxing	United States	46	Cuba	19
Canoeing, men	Soviet Union	22	Sweden	11
Canoeing, women	Soviet Union	8	East Germany	6
Cycling	Italy	28	France	27
Diving, men	United States	27	Sweden	4
Diving, women	United States	19	China	5
Equestrian Events	Germany	27	Sweden	17
Fencing, men	France	34	Italy	30
Fencing, women	Hungary	5		
	Germany	5		
	Soviet Union	5		
Football (soccer)	Hungary	3	Great Britain	3
Gymnastics, men	Soviet Union	45	Japan	27
Gymnastics, women	Soviet Union	38	Romania	15
Team handball	Soviet Union	5	Yugoslavia	3
Field hockey	India	8	Pakistan	3
			Great Britain	3
			Soviet Union	7
Judo, men	Japan	16		
Judo, women	France	2		
	Spain	2		
Modern Pentathlon	Sweden	9	Hungary	8
Rowing, men	United States	28	East Germany	20
Rowing, women	East Germany	13	Romania	8
Shooting, men	United States	44	Soviet Union	22
Shooting, women	Soviet Union	4	United States	2
			China	2
Swimming, men	United States	97	Australia	23
Swimming, women	United States	72	East Germany	32
Table tennis	China	5	South Korea	2
Tennis	Great Britain	14	United States	11
Volleyball, men	Soviet Union	3	United States	2
Volleyball, women	Soviet Union	4	Japan	2
Water polo	Hungary	6	Great Britain	4
Weightlifting	Soviet Union	44	United States	15
Wrestling, freestyle	United States	41	Soviet Union	31
Wrestling, Greco-Roman	Soviet Union	37	Finland	19
			Sweden	19
Yachting	United States	16		
	Norway	16		

*Seven of Belgium's gold medals in archery came in 1920, the other three in 1900.

15 EVENTS INCLUDED IN EVERY OLYMPICS

1. 100-meter dash
2. 400-meter run
3. 800-meter run
4. 1500-meter run
5. Marathon
6. 110-meter hurdles
7. High jump
8. Pole vault
9. Long jump
10. Triple jump
11. Shot put
12. Discus throw
13. Individual foil fencing
14. Individual sabre fencing
15. 1500-meter freestyle swimming

Note: The single sculls and the eight-oared shell with coxswain were included in the program for 1896, but were canceled because of bad weather. They have been included every time since then.

OFFICIAL ABBREVIATIONS

Some of the national designations used in this book (see page xxviii) differ from those approved by the International Olympic Committee. Here is a complete list of the 197 nations that are currently recognized by the I.O.C.

AFG	Afghanistan	CRO	Croatia	KAZ	Kazakhstan
AHO	Netherlands Antilles	CUB	Cuba	KEN	Kenya
ALB	Albania	CYP	Cyprus	KGZ	Kyrgyzstan
ALG	Algeria	DEN	Denmark	KOR	South Korea
AND	Andorra	DJI	Djibouti	KSA	Saudi Arabia
ANG	Angola	DMA	Dominica	KUW	Kuwait
ANT	Antigua and Barbuda	DOM	Dominican Republic	LAO	Laos
ARG	Argentina	ECU	Ecuador	LAT	Latvia
ARM	Armenia	EGY	Egypt	LBA	Libya
ARU	Aruba	ESA	El Salvador	LBR	Liberia
ASA	American Samoa	ESP	Spain	LCA	Saint Lucia
AUS	Australia	EST	Estonia	LES	Lesotho
AUT	Austria	ETH	Ethiopia	LIB	Lebanon
AZE	Azerbaijan	FIJ	Fiji	LIE	Liechtenstein
BAH	Bahamas	FIN	Finland	LTU	Lithuania
BAN	Bangladesh	FRA	France	LUX	Luxembourg
BAR	Barbados	GAB	Gabon	MAD	Madagascar
BDI	Burundi	GAM	The Gambia	MAR	Morocco
BEL	Belgium	GBR	Great Britain	MAS	Malaysia
BEN	Benin	GBS	Guinea-Bissau	MAW	Malawi
BER	Bermuda	GEO	Georgia	MDA	Moldova
BHU	Bhutan	GER	Germany	MDV	Maldives
BIH	Bosnia-Herzegovina	GEQ	Equatorial Guinea	MEX	Mexico
BIZ	Belize	GHA	Ghana	MGL	Mongolia
BLR	Belarus	GRE	Greece	MKD	Macedonia
BOL	Bolivia	GRN	Grenada	MLI	Mali
BOT	Botswana	GUA	Guatemala	MLT	Malta
BRA	Brazil	GUI	Guinea	MON	Monaco
BRN	Bahrain	GUM	Guam	MOZ	Mozambique
BRU	Brunei	GUY	Guyana	MRI	Mauritius
BUL	Bulgaria	HAI	Haiti	MTN	Mauritania
BUR	Burkina Faso	HKG	Hong Kong	MYA	Myanmar (Burma)
CAF	Central African Republic	HON	Honduras	NAM	Namibia
CAM	Cambodia	HUN	Hungary	NCA	Nicaragua
CAN	Canada	INA	Indonesia	NED	Netherlands
CAY	Cayman Islands	IND	India	NIG	Niger
CGO	Congo	IRI	Iran	NEP	Nepal
CHA	Chad	IRL	Ireland	NGR	Nigeria
CHI	Chile	IRQ	Iraq	NOR	Norway
CHN	China	ISL	Iceland	NRU	Nauru
CIV	Côte d'Ivoire	ISR	Israel	NZL	New Zealand
CMR	Cameroon	ISV	U.S. Virgin Islands	OMA	Oman
COK	Cook Islands	ITA	Italy	PAK	Pakistan
COL	Colombia	IVB	British Virgin Islands	PAN	Panama
COM	Comoros	JAM	Jamaica	PAR	Paraguay
CPV	Cape Verde	JOR	Jordan	PER	Peru
CRC	Costa Rica	JPN	Japan	PHI	Philippines
				PLE	Palestine
				PNG	Papua–New Guinea
				POL	Poland
				POR	Portugal
				PRK	North Korea

PUR	Puerto Rico
QAT	Qatar
ROM	Romania
RSA	South Africa
RUS	Russia
RWA	Rwanda
SAM	Western Samoa
SEN	Senegal
SEY	Seychelles
SIN	Singapore
SKN	Saint Kitts and Nevis
SLE	Sierra Leone
SLO	Slovenia
SMR	San Marino
SOL	Solomon Islands
SOM	Somalia
SRI	Sri Lanka
STP	Sao Tome and Principe
SUD	Sudan
SUI	Switzerland
SUR	Suriname
SVK	Slovakia
SWE	Sweden
SWZ	Swaziland
SYR	Syria
TAN	Tanzania
TCH	Czech Republic
TGA	Tonga
THA	Thailand
TJK	Tajikistan
TKM	Turkmenistan
TOG	Togo
TPE	Chinese Taipei (Taiwan)
TRI	Trinidad and Tobago
TUN	Tunisia
TUR	Turkey
UAE	United Arab Emirates
UGA	Uganda
UKR	Ukraine
URU	Uruguay
USA	United States of America
UZB	Uzbekistan
VAN	Vanuatu
VEN	Venezuela
VIE	Vietnam
VIN	St. Vincent and the Grenadines
YEM	Yemen
YUG	Yugoslavia
ZAI	Zaire
ZAM	Zambia
ZIM	Zimbabwe